A GUIDE BOOK OF
UNITED STATES COINS
MEGA RED™
4TH EDITION

Washington.

From the Original Portrait Painted by Rembrandt Peale.

George Washington was president of the United States when the
first U.S. Mint was established in Philadelphia, Pennsylvania, in 1792.

THE OFFICIAL RED BOOK®

A GUIDE BOOK OF UNITED STATES COINS

MEGA RED™

4ᵀᴴ EDITION

R.S. YEOMAN

SENIOR EDITOR, Q. DAVID BOWERS

VALUATIONS EDITOR JEFF GARRETT

EDITOR EMERITUS KENNETH BRESSETT

A Fully Illustrated Catalog of Useful Information on Colonial and Federal Coinage, 1616 to Date, With Detailed Photographs to Identify Your Coins and Retail Valuation Charts Indicating How Much They're Worth. Plus Illustrated Grading Instructions With Enlarged Images to Determine Your Coins' Conditions. Insider Tips on Treasures Waiting to be Discovered in Your Pocket Change; Advice on Smart Collecting; and More. Based on the Expertise of More Than 100 Professional Coin Dealers and Researchers. Also Featuring Entertaining Stories, Amazing Essays, and Astounding Facts and Figures About All Manner of Rare and Historical Coins of the United States of America.

A Guide Book of United States Coins™, Deluxe Edition
THE OFFICIAL RED BOOK OF UNITED STATES COINS™

THE OFFICIAL RED BOOK, MEGA RED, and
THE OFFICIAL RED BOOK OF UNITED STATES COINS
are trademarks of Whitman Publishing, LLC.

ISBN: 0794845800
Printed in the United States of America.

© 2018 Whitman Publishing, LLC
1974 Chandlar Drive, Suite D, Pelham, AL 35124

Correspondence concerning this book may be directed to Whitman Publishing, Attn: *Mega Red*, at the address above.

Whitman Publishing, LLC, does not deal in coins; the values shown herein are not offers to buy or sell but are included only as general information. Descriptions of coins are based on the most accurate data available, but could change with further research or discoveries.

Collect all the books in the Bowers Series. *A Guide Book of Morgan Silver Dollars* • *A Guide Book of Double Eagle Gold Coins* • *A Guide Book of United States Type Coins* • *A Guide Book of Modern United States Proof Coin Sets* • *A Guide Book of Shield and Liberty Head Nickels* • *A Guide Book of Flying Eagle and Indian Head Cents* • *A Guide Book of Washington and State Quarters* • *A Guide Book of Buffalo and Jefferson Nickels* • *A Guide Book of Lincoln Cents* • *A Guide Book of United States Commemorative Coins* • *A Guide Book of United States Tokens and Medals* • *A Guide Book of Gold Dollars* • *A Guide Book of Peace Dollars* • *A Guide Book of the Official Red Book of United States Coins* • *A Guide Book of Franklin and Kennedy Half Dollars* • *A Guide Book of Civil War Tokens* • *A Guide Book of Hard Times Tokens* • *A Guide Book of Mercury Dimes, Standing Liberty Quarters, and Liberty Walking Half Dollars* • *A Guide Book of Half Cents and Large Cents* • *A Guide Book of Barber Silver Coins* • *A Guide Book of Liberty Seated Silver Coins* • *A Guide Book of Modern U.S. Dollar Coins* • *A Guide Book of the United States Mint* • *A Guide Book of Gold Eagle Coins.*

For a complete listing of numismatic reference books, supplies, and storage products, visit Whitman Publishing online at www.whitman.com.

If you enjoy U.S. and related coins, join the American Numismatic Association. Visit the ANA online at www.money.org.

WHITMAN™

CONTENTS

CONTENTS

CREDITS AND ACKNOWLEDGMENTS

CONTRIBUTORS TO THE FOURTH MEGA RED

Senior Editor: Q. David Bowers. *Valuations Editor:* Jeff Garrett. *Editor Emeritus:* Kenneth Bressett.
Special Consultants: Philip Bressett, Maxwell Gregory, Robert Rhue, Troy Thoreson, Ben Todd, Jake Walker

The following coin dealers and collectors have contributed pricing information to this edition:

Gary Adkins	Sheridan Downey	John W. Highfill	Joel Rettew Jr.
Mark Albarian	Steve Ellsworth	Brian Hodge	Joel Rettew Sr.
Dominic Albert	Brant Fahnestock	Jesse Iskowitz	Steve Roach
Buddy Alleva	David Fanning	Steve Ivy	Greg Rohan
Richard S. Appel	Gerry Fortin	Joseph Jones	Maurice Rosen
Richard M. August	Pierre Fricke	Donald H. Kagin	Mark Salzberg
Scott A. Barman	John Frost	Bradley S. Karoleff	Gerald R. Scherer Jr.
Mitchell A. Battino	Mike Fuljenz	Jim Koenings	Jeff Shevlin
Lee J. Bellisario	John Gervasoni	George F. Kolbe	Harry E. Schultz
Mark Borckardt	Dennis M. Gillio	Richard A. Lecce	Neil Shafer
Larry Briggs	Ronald J. Gillio	Julian M. Leidman	Roger Siboni
Bill Bugert	Rusty Goe	Denis W. Loring	Rick Snow
H. Robert Campbell	Ira M. Goldberg	Dwight N. Manley	Scott Sparks
Elizabeth Coggan	Lawrence Goldberg	Robert T. McIntire	David M. Sundman
Alan Cohen	Kenneth M. Goldman	Harry Miller	Barry Sunshine
Gary Cohen	Bob Green	Lee S. Minshull	Anthony Terranova
Stephen M. Cohen	J.R. Grellman	Scott P. Mitchell	Rich Uhrich
Steve Contursi	Tom Hallenbeck	Michael C. Moline	Frank Van Valen
Marc Crane	James Halperin	Paul Montgomery	Fred Weinberg
Adam Crum	Ash Harrison	Mike Orlando	David Wnuck
Raymond Czahor	Stephen Hayden	Joseph Parrella	
Charles Davis	Brian Hendelson	Robert M. Paul	

Special credit is due to the following for contributions to the *Guide Book of United States Coins, Deluxe Edition*: Gary Adkins, David W. Akers, John Albanese, David Allison, Jeff Ambio, the American Numismatic Society, Marc Banks, Mitchell Battino, Jack Beymer, Doug Bird, Jon Alan Boka, Mark Borckardt, Q. David Bowers, Kenneth Bressett, Nicholas P. Brown, Roger W. Burdette, David J. Camire, Fonda Chase, Elizabeth Coggan, Greg Cohen, Ray Czahor, John W. Dannreuther, Beth Deisher, Dan Demeo, Cynthia Roden Doty, Richard Doty, Bill Eckberg, Michael Fahey, Bill Fivaz, Pierre Fricke, Jeff Garrett, Ira Goldberg, Lawrence Goldberg, Ken Goldman, J.R. Grellman Jr., Ron Guth, James Halperin, Greg Hannigan, Phil Hinkelman, Daniel W. Holmes Jr., Gwyn Huston, Walter Husak, Tom Hyland, Wayne Imbrogno, Steve Ivy, R.W. Julian, Brad Karoleff, David W. Lange, Julian Leidman, Jon Lerner, Littleton Coin Company, Denis W. Loring, John Lusk, Ron Manley, J.P. Martin, Jim Matthews, Chris Victor-McCawley, Jim McGuigan, Jack McNamara, Harry Miller, Paul Minshull, Scott Mitchell, Charles Moore, Dan Moore, Jim Neiswinter, Eric P. Newman, Numismatic Guaranty Corporation of America (NGC), Joel J. Orosz, John M. Pack, D. Brent Pogue, Michael Printz, Jim Reardon, Tom Reynolds, Harry Salyards, Louis Scuderi, Thomas Serfass, Neil Shafer, Michael Sherrill, Jeff Shevlin, Craig Sholley, the Smithsonian Institution, Rick Snow, Max Spiegel, Lawrence R. Stack, Stack's Bowers

Galleries, David M. Sundman, Barry Sunshine, David Sunshine, James Taylor, Saul Teichman, R. Tettenhorst, Scott Travers, Rich Uhrich, the U.S. Mint, Frank Van Valen, Alan V. Weinberg, Fred Weinberg, Ken and Stephanie Westover, James Wiles, Ray Williams, Doug Winter, David Wnuck, and Winston Zack.

Special credit is due to the following for service and data in the 2018 regular edition of the *Guide Book of United States Coins*: Stewart Blay, Roger W. Burdette, Frank J. Colletti, Columbus–America Discovery Group, Charles Davis, Tom DeLorey, David Fanning, Bill Fivaz, Kevin Flynn, Chuck Furjanic, James C. Gray, Charles Hoskins, R.W. Julian, Richard Kelly, George F. Kolbe, David W. Lange, G.J. Lawson, Andy Lustig, J.P. Martin, Syd Martin, Eric P. Newman, Ken Potter, P. Scott Rubin, Paul Rynearson, Mary Sauvain, Richard J. Schwary, Robert W. Shippee, James Simek, Craig Smith, Jerry Treglia, Mark R. Vitunic, Holland Wallace, Weimar White, John Whitney, Raymond Williams, and John Wright.

Special credit is due to the following for service in past editions: David Akers, John Albanese, Lyman Allen, Jeff Ambio, Michael Aron, Philip E. Benedetti, Richard A. Bagg, Jack Beymer, George Blenker, Walter Breen, John Burns, Jason Carter, Marc Crane, Silvano DiGenova, Ken Duncan, Bob Entlich, John Feigenbaum, George Fitzgerald, Dennis Forgue, Harry Forman, George Fuld, Henry Garrett, William Gay, Harry Gittelson, J.R. Grellman, Ron Guth, John Hamrick, Gene L. Henry, Karl D. Hirtzinger, Michael Hodder, John L. Howes, Robert Jacobs, James J. Jelinski, Larry Johnson, A.M. Kagin, Stanley Kesselman, Jerry Kimmel, Mike Kliman, Paul Koppenhaver, Robert B. Lecce, Ed Leventhal, Stuart Levine, Kevin Lipton, Arnold Margolis, David McCarthy, Chris McCawley, Glenn Miller, Charles Morgan, Richard Nachbar, Casey Noxon, Paul Nugget, John M. Pack, William P. Paul, Thomas Payne, Beth Piper, Doug Plasencia, Andrew Pollock III, John Porter, Mike Ringo, Cherie Schoeps, J.S. Schreiber, Hugh Sconyers, Robert Shaw, Arlie Slabaugh, Thomas Smith, William Spencer, Paul Spiegel, Lawrence R. Stack, Maurice Storck Sr., Charles Surasky, Anthony J. Swiatek, Steve Tanenbaum, Mark Van Winkle, Russell Vaughn, Douglas Winter, and Mark Yaffe.

Special photo credits are due to the following: Al Adams, the American Numismatic Association, Angel Dee's Coins and Collectibles, the Architect of the Capitol (Washington, D.C.), Douglas F. Bird, Karen Bridges, Michael Bugeja, Civil War Token Society, Steve Contursi, Tom Denly, Bill Fivaz, Ira & Larry Goldberg Coins & Collectibles, Colin Gullberg, Isaiah Hageman, Steve Hayden, the estate of Bernard Heller, Heritage Auctions (www.ha.com), Rich Licato, Littleton Coin Co., Tom Mulvaney, Numismatic Guaranty Corporation of America (NGC), PCGS, Doug Plasencia, D. Brent Pogue, Jon Potts, Jim Pruitt, David Reimer, Sarasota Rare Coin Gallery, John Scanlon, Jeff Shevlin, Bob Simpson, Pete Smith, the Smithsonian Institution, Spectrum, Stack's Bowers Galleries, J.T. Stanton, Richard Stinchcomb, Barry Sunshine, Superior Galleries, Steve Tannenbaum, and the United States Mint.

HOW TO USE THIS BOOK

Numismatics, in its purest sense, is the study of items used as money. Today in the United States, as around the world, the term embraces the activities of a diverse community of hobbyists, historians, researchers, museum curators, and others who collect and study coins, tokens, paper money, and similar objects.

Since 1946 the *Guide Book of United States Coins* has served this community as the preeminent annual reference for coin specifications, mintages, values, photographs, and other information important to collectors and students. With more than 23 million copies in print since the first edition, the *Guide Book* (commonly known as the "Red Book") is well established as the most popular reference in numismatics—not to mention one of the best-selling nonfiction books in the history of American publishing. (In 1964 the 18th edition of the Red Book ranked number 5 on the national sales lists, at 1.2 million copies—higher than Dale Carnegie's *How to Win Friends and Influence People* at number 6, and John F. Kennedy's *Profiles in Courage* at number 9.)

Building on this strong foundation, the Deluxe Edition of the *Guide Book of United States Coins* is an expanded and enlarged volume intended to serve not only beginning collectors, but also intermediate to advanced coin collectors, professional coin dealers and auctioneers, researchers, and investors. It features more photographs, detailed higher-grade valuations, additional listings of die varieties and rare early Proof coins, certified-coin population data, auction records, and other resources that provide a wealth of information on every coin type ever made by the U.S. Mint. The Deluxe Edition also expands on the regular edition's coverage of collectible die varieties, with close-up photographs, valuations, and chart notes. It is a handy single-source guide that educates its users in auction and certification trends, retail valuations, and similar aspects of the marketplace.

Like the regular-edition Red Book, the Deluxe Edition includes information on colonial and early American coins and tokens as well as all federal series (copper half cents through gold double eagles). It also covers private and territorial gold pieces; Hard Times tokens; Civil War tokens; Confederate coins; Hawaiian, Puerto Rican, and Philippine coins; Alaskan tokens; misstrikes and errors; numismatic books; Proof and Mint sets; commemorative coins from 1892 to date; silver, gold, and platinum bullion coins; and other topics.

Readers of the *Guide Book of United States Coins, Deluxe Edition,* benefit from the following useful information.

The "Red Book" has become a popular collectible itself, with fans striving to acquire one of each edition dating back to number 1, published in November 1946 with a 1947 cover date. Rare early volumes can be worth $1,000 or more.

R.S. Yeoman, author of the original *Guide Book of United States Coins,* examining press proofs in 1969.

DENOMINATION INTRODUCTIONS

Each coinage denomination is discussed first in an overview of its history, major design types and sub-types, and general collectability by type. (The dollar denomination is divided into silver dollars, trade dollars, and modern dollars.) A second essay gives collectors a more in-depth analysis of specializing in that denomination. *These sections encapsulate decades of numismatic research and market observation, and they should be read in conjunction with the charts, photographs, and other information that follow.*

TYPE-BY-TYPE STUDIES

Within each denomination, each major coin type is laid out in chronological order. As in the regular-edition Red Book, the type's designer and its specifications (weight, composition, diameter, edge treatment, and production facilities) are given. Coinage designs are pictured at actual size except commemorative designs, which are standardized (one Mint State example and one Proof example, when available). Each type section includes summary text on the type's history; aspects of its striking, sharpness, and related characteristics; and its market availability. In-depth grading instructions, with enlarged illustrations, show how to grade each coin type, covering circulation strikes as well as Proofs.

CHARTS

The data charts include these elements:

	Mintage	Cert	Avg	%MS	G-4	VG-8	F-12	VF-20	EF-40	AU-50	MS-60 / PF-60	MS-63 / PF-63	MS-65 / PF-65
1840, Medium Letters (b)	(c)	47	40.0	15%	$140	$190	$275	$450	$800	$1,600	$3,750	$7,750	$23,500
	Auctions: $2,233, MS-62, February 2015; $1,028, AU-58, January 2015; $259, EF-45, May 2015; $188, VF-30, September 2015												
1840, Small Letters, Proof	4–8	7	64.0										$100,000
	Auctions: $30,550, PF-63, November 2013												
1840-O	855,100	130	49.0	27%	$42	$55	$70	$115	$190	$400	$900	$3,500	
	Auctions: $2,350, MS-62, January 2015; $1,410, MS-60, June 2015; $212, EF-45, June 2015; $141, VF-30, June 2015												
1841	310,000	75	54.8	32%	$42	$60	$95	$150	$275	$450	$1,400	$2,800	$9,000
	Auctions: $11,750, MS-65, May 2015; $4,230, MS-64, January 2015; $857, AU-58, June 2015; $364, EF-45, August 2015												
1841, Proof	4–8	6	64.5								$20,000	$45,000	$85,000
	Auctions: $30,550, PF-64, September 2013												

b. The 1840, Medium Letters, half dollars were struck at the New Orleans Mint from a reverse die of the previous style, without mintmark. **c.** Included in circulation-strike 1840, Small Letters, mintage figure. **d.** Included in 1842, Medium Date, mintage figure.

Mintages. Mintage data is compiled from official Mint records whenever possible, and in other cases from more than 70 years of active numismatic research. In instances where the Mint's early records are in question or have been proven faulty, the official numbers are provided and further information is given in chart notes. For some early Proof coins for which no official mintage records exist, an estimated mintage, or the number of coins known in collections, is given. For modern issues (usually those minted within the past five years), the Mint has released production and/or sales numbers that are not yet officially finalized; these are given in italics.

Note that Mint reports are not always reliable for estimating the rarities of coins. In the early years of the Mint, coinage dies of previous years often were used until they became worn or broken. Certain reported quantities, particularly for gold and silver coins, cover the number of pieces struck and make no indication of the quantity that actually reached circulation. Many issues were deposited in the Treasury as backing for paper currency and later were melted without ever being released to the public.

Gold coins struck before August 1, 1834, are rare today because from 1821 onward (and at times before 1821) the gold in the coins was worth more than their face values, so they were struck as bullion and traded at a premium. Many were exported and melted for their precious-metal value.

Mintage figures shown for 1964 through 1966 are for coins bearing those dates. Some of these coins were struck in more than one year and at various mints, both with and without mintmarks. In recent years, mintage figures reported by the Mint have been revised several times and precise amounts remain uncertain.

Mintage figures shown in italics are estimates based on the most accurate information available. Numismatic research is constantly ongoing, and listed figures are sometimes revised, when new information becomes available.

Certified Populations. For each coin of a particular date and mint, a summary is provided of (1) the number of coins certified, (2) the average grade, on the standard 1–70 scale, of those coins graded, and (3) for circulation-strike coins, the percentage certified in Mint State.

These summaries provide the collector and investor with working data useful in comparing coins offered for sale or bid.

Certified population data is provided courtesy of Numismatic Guaranty Corporation of America (NGC), one of the nation's leading professional third-party grading firms.

It should be noted that for most coins, especially rare dates and varieties, the number certified actually represents the quantity of *submissions*, rather than the number of individual coins submitted. For example, a particular 1801 silver dollar that is submitted for certification five times would be counted the same as five individual coins. Such resubmissions can sometimes result in numbers close to or higher than a coin's entire surviving mintage.

Note, too, that the grade number assigned to a "slabbed" (graded and encapsulated) coin does not tell anything about the strength of that particular coin's strike, the quality of its planchet, whether it has been cleaned or dipped, or its overall eye appeal. Such factors are important to a coin's value. Two rare coins of the same date and variety, each with the same amount of surface wear and graded, for example, MS-63, will find different values in the marketplace if one is eye-pleasing and well struck, and the other is dull and poorly struck.

Valuations. Coin values shown in the Deluxe Edition are retail prices compiled from data and market observations provided by active coin dealers, auctioneers, and other qualified observers, under the direction and analysis of Valuations Editor Jeff Garrett and Senior Editor Kenneth Bressett and their consultants. In this guide book, values from under $1 up to several hundred dollars are for "raw" coins—that is, coins that have *not* been graded and encapsulated by a professional third-party grading service. Values near or above $500 reflect typical auction and retail prices seen for professionally certified coins. The valuations of professionally certified coins often are higher than what collectors normally pay for non-certified ("raw") coins. Values of certified coins may vary widely, depending on the grading service.

The coin market is so active in some categories that values can readily change after publication. Values are shown as a guide and are not intended to serve as a price list for any dealer's stock. A dash appearing in a valuations column indicates that coins in that grade exist even though there are no current retail or auction records for them. The dash does not necessarily mean that such coins are exceedingly rare. Italicized numbers indicate unsettled or speculative (estimated) values. A number of listings of rare coins lack valuations or dashes in certain grades, indicating that they are not available, or not believed to exist, in those grades. Proof coins are usually not shown with values in circulated grades.

For wholesale pricing, the *Handbook of United States Coins* (popularly called the Blue Book, and published since 1942), by R.S. Yeoman, contains average prices dealers nationwide will pay for U.S. coins. It is obtainable through most coin dealers, hobby shops, bookstores, and the Internet.

Auction Records. Multiple recent auction records are provided for nearly every coin (some exceptions being coins that are too common to sell individually at auction). Each record indicates:

the price paid for the coin (including any fees)

the grade of the coin

the date (month and year) of the auction

This combination of auction data gives valuable market information for each coin. It also serves as a springboard for further research. Many auction firms have online archives of coins sold, or else their auction catalogs can be studied using the information provided.

Chart notes. Additional information is provided for certain coins in chart notes. Historical background, die-variety diagnostics, notable market conditions, and other specific details are intended to further guide the collector and investor.

Abbreviations. These are some of the abbreviations you'll find in the charts.

%MS—Percentage of coins certified in Mint State

Avg—Average grade (on a 1–70 scale)

BN—Brown; descriptive of the coloration or toning on certain copper coins

Cam—Cameo

Cert—Certified population

DblDie—Doubled Die

DCam—Deep Cameo

DMPL—Deep Mirror Prooflike

D/S—D Over S; a slash between words or letters represents an overdate or overmintmark

Dt—Date

Ex.—Extremely

FB—Full Bands

FBL—Full Bell Lines

FH—Full Head

FS—Full Steps

FT—Full Torch

Horiz—Horizontal

Inv—Inverted

Knbd—Knobbed-Top

Lg—Large

Ltrd—Lettered

Ltrs—Letters

Med—Medium

Mintmk—Mintmark

Obv—Obverse

QuintDie—Quintupled Die

RB—Red and brown; descriptive of the mixture of mint red and brown coloration or toning on a copper coin

RD—Red; descriptive of the mint red color on an untoned copper coin

Rev—Reverse

RPD—Repunched Date

RPM—Repunched Mintmark

Sm—Small

SMS—Special Mint Set

Sq—Square

TransRev—Transitional Reverse

TripDie—Tripled Die

UCam—Ultra Cameo

Var—Variety

COLLECTING U.S. COINS
INVESTING IN RARE COINS

As with the regular edition of the *Guide Book of United States Coins*, those who edit, contribute to, and publish the Deluxe Edition advocate the collecting of coins for pleasure and educational benefits. A secondary consideration is that of investment, the profits of which are usually realized over the long term based on careful purchases. When it comes to investing in rare coins, knowledge is power.

USE COMMON SENSE

The rare-coin market combines some aspects of commodity trading with peculiarities seen more often among markets such as those for fine art, real estate, cut gemstones, and similar investments and collectibles. Armed with knowledge, an investor can have a very rewarding experience buying and selling rare coins. An uneducated investor can just as easily see substantial losses.

The regular edition of the *Guide Book of United States Coins* includes this bit of guidance, which bears repeating here: "The best advice given to anyone considering investing in rare coins is to use common sense." Any collector with common sense would think twice about buying a silver dollar at a flea market for less than its silver value. A common-sense collector who is offered a $1,000 coin from an "unsearched estate," or from a non-specialist who claims to know nothing of its provenance, would refuse it at $500—at least until a diligent examination was possible, and only with an iron-clad return policy and guarantee of authenticity. Profitable investment requires careful selection of qualified dealers (e.g., those professionally credentialed by groups such as the Professional Numismatists Guild [www.pngdealers.com] and the International Association of Professional Numismatists [www.iapn-coins.org]), and educated evaluation of the coins offered for sale.

LEARN ABOUT GRADING

In the past, coin grading was very subjective, and grade descriptions were far from universal. One dealer's "Choice Extremely Fine" might have been another's "About Uncirculated," and adjectives such as *gem* and *brilliant* varied in meaning from collector to collector. Today grading is still a subjective art striving to be an exact science, but progress has been made. The hobby's guidelines have been clearly standardized in systems such as the *Official American Numismatic Association Grading Standards for United States Coins*, and explored further in illustrated books such as *Grading Coins by Photographs: An Action Guide for the Collector and Investor*.

Today there are professional certification services such as NGC, PCGS, ICG, and ANACS that, for a fee, grade and authenticate coins, encapsulating them in sealed "slabs" with their grades noted. These are third-party firms, so called because they are neither buyer nor seller of the coins graded (which guarantees a professional level of impartiality to the process). Professional grading strives to be completely objective, but coins are graded by humans and not computers. This introduces the subjective element of *art* as opposed to *science*. A coin's grade, even if certified by a leading third-party grader (TPG), can be questioned by any collector or dealer—or even by the TPG that graded it, if the coin is resubmitted for a second look. Furthermore, within a given grade a keen observer will find coins that are low-quality, average, and high-quality for that grade. Such factors as luster, color, strength of strike, and overall eye appeal can make, for example, one MS-65 1914 Barber half dollar more visually attractive than another with the same grade. This gives the smart collector the opportunity to "cherrypick," or examine multiple slabbed coins and

The official coin-grading standards of the American Numismatic Association have been codified in book form. This gives every coin collector and dealer a universal "language"—although grading does remain an art as well as a science.

select the highest-quality example for the desired grade. This process builds a better collection than simply accepting a TPG's assigned grades, and is summed up in the guidance of "Buy the coin, not the slab." (Also, note that a coin certified as, for example, MS-64 might have greater eye appeal—and therefore be more desirable to a greater number of collectors—than a less attractive coin graded MS-65.)

Over the years, collectors have observed a trend nicknamed "gradeflation": the reinterpretation, in practice, of the standards applied to a given grade over time. For example, a coin evaluated by a leading TPG in 1994 as MS-63 might be graded today as MS-65 or even MS-66.

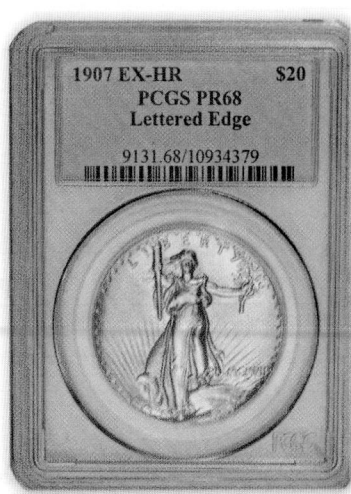

"Slabbed" coins are those that have been professionally graded and encapsulated by a third-party service such as ANACS, NGC, or PCGS.

Learn About What You're Buying

In addition to carefully vetting professional dealers, examining potential purchases for authenticity (see below for more on this topic), and studying the art and science of grading, an investor can profit by *learning* about coins. Each coin type has a cultural history that provides useful collecting/investing knowledge. For example, the Treasury Department often stored Morgan dollars by the thousands (and millions), so a bag of 1,000 Mint State dollars is not unheard of. On the other hand, the purchaser of a seemingly original bank-wrapped roll of 20 Mint State trade dollars would likely be left holding a pound of counterfeit coins.

Similarly, each coin type has a typical strike, surface quality, and related characteristics; knowledge of these features can help reveal fakes and lower-than-average-quality specimens. The investor who knows that a certain coin type is rarely encountered in a certain high grade is more alert to potential opportunities. Conversely, if a type is common in high grades, the savvy investor will pass on an average or below-average coin and wait for a sharper, more attractive example, knowing that time and the marketplace are on his side.

For these reasons, even if you consider yourself more *investor* than *collector*, it is recommended that you read every section of this Deluxe Edition that covers the coin series in which you are interested. The price and data charts provide one level of information, the denomination introductions another, the type summaries and grading guides yet others; combined, they offer a well-rounded education that prices alone cannot provide.

Understand the General Market

Coin values rise when (1) the economic trend is inflationary and speculators turn to tangible assets as a hedge, or when the number of collectors increases, while coin supplies remain stationary or decrease through attrition or melting; (2) dealers replace their stocks of coins only from collectors or other dealers, who expect a profit over what they originally paid; (3) speculators attempt to influence the market through selective buying; or (4) bullion (gold and silver) prices rise.

Coin values decline when (1) changes in collecting habits or economic conditions alter demand for certain coins; (2) speculators sell in large quantities; (3) hoards or large holdings are suddenly released and cannot be quickly absorbed by the normal market; or (4) bullion (gold and silver) prices decline.

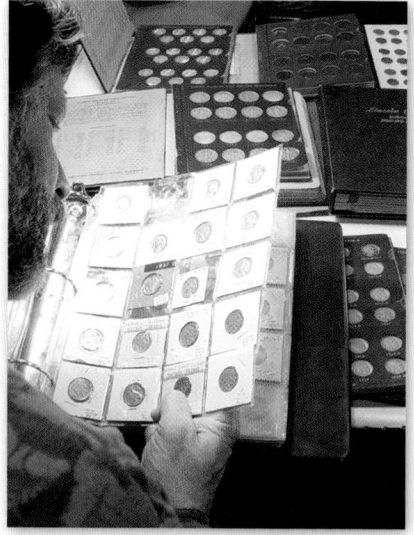

Attending a coin show gives you many opportunities to shop around, examine coins firsthand, talk to experienced collectors and dealers, and learn about the hobby.

Learn From the Experts

A rich numismatic world is available to the investor and collector who seek to learn. News weeklies such as *Coin World* and *Numismatic News* cover the hobby and its markets from many angles, as do a variety of monthly magazines (like *COINage* and *Coins*) and online blogs. Auction sale results, new U.S. Mint products, convention activities, market reports, and other information await the interested reader.

Web sites such as www.Whitman.com/RedBook, www.NumisMaster.com, and www.CoinFacts.com gather and present information from authoritative sources.

Organizations such as the American Numismatic Association (the ANA, online at www.money.org) and the American Numismatic Society (the ANS, at www.numismatics.org), as well as dozens of specialized groups focused on particular coins or series, offer resources and connections to collectors worldwide.

Every major American city and many smaller cities have coin shops where experienced dealers can be consulted for advice and opinions.

Coin shows are another venue for learning from seasoned collectors and investors. The ANA mounts popular shows annually, in different cities. Whitman Coin and Collectibles Expo (WhitmanExpo.com) hosts several shows yearly in Baltimore. Florida United Numismatists (FUN) organizes two shows in the winter and summer each year. All of these shows, and dozens of other local and regional conventions, offer opportunities to talk to other collectors and investors, meet market experts, listen to presentations, and examine hundreds of coins, tokens, and medals.

Books are another means of learning from the hobby's experts. Every collector and investor should have at least a basic numismatic library of standard references. (See the bibliography in the back of this volume.) In addition, nearly every specialty in American coins has one or more books devoted to greater in-depth exploration. Numismatic publishing has experienced a renaissance in recent years, making valuable knowledge more affordable and readily available than ever before. One book essential to the investor's understanding of the rare-coin market is a 672-page volume written by the "dean of American numismatics," Q. David Bowers. The *Expert's Guide to Collecting and Investing in Rare Coins* covers topics such as determining coin prices and values; focusing on rarity; quality and value for the smart buyer; coin-market fads, trends, and cycles; making of the modern market for rare coins; predicting the rare-coin market; techniques of smart buying and bidding; protecting your investment; and more. Robert W. Shippee's *Pleasure and Profit: 100 Lessons for Building and Selling a Collection of Rare Coins* offers first-hand insight from an experienced collector. Beth Deisher's *Cash In Your Coins: Selling the Rare Coins You've Inherited* advises on the selling side of the equation. These are just a few examples of the books awaiting today's collector.

In the long run, coin collectors—even those who seek mainly to profit financially from the hobby—are simply custodians of the relics they collect. Again, the regular edition of the *Guide Book of United States Coins* gives sound advice: "Those who treat rare coins with the consideration and respect they deserve will profit in many ways, not the least of which can be in the form of a sound financial return on one's investments of time and money."

SOME ASPECTS OF COLLECTING

The following topics—mints and mintmarks, checking your coins for authenticity, and coins from treasures and hoards as a key to understanding rarity and value—have proven very popular among collectors.

MINTS AND MINTMARKS

Mintmarks are small letters designating where coins were made. Coins struck at Philadelphia before 1979 (except five-cent pieces of 1942 to 1945) do not have mintmarks. Starting in 1979, a letter P was used on the dollar, and thereafter on all other denominations except the cent. The mintmark position is on the reverse of nearly all coins prior to 1965 (the cent is an exception), and on the obverse after 1967.

C—Charlotte, North Carolina (gold coins only; 1838–1861)

CC—Carson City, Nevada (gold and silver coins only; 1870–1893)

D—Dahlonega, Georgia (gold coins only; 1838–1861)

D—Denver, Colorado (1906 to date)

M—Manila (Philippines; 1920–1941; M not used in early years)

O—New Orleans, Louisiana (gold and silver coins only; 1838–1861; 1879–1909)

P—Philadelphia, Pennsylvania (1793 to date; P not used in early years)

S—San Francisco, California (1854 to date)

W—West Point, New York (1984 to date)

| Charlotte, North Carolina | Carson City, Nevada | Dahlonega, Georgia | Denver, Colorado | Manila, Philippines |

| New Orleans, Louisiana | Philadelphia, Pennsylvania | San Francisco, California | West Point, New York |

Prior to 1996 all dies for U.S. coins were made at the Philadelphia Mint. Some dies are now made at the Denver Mint. Dies for use at other mints are made with the appropriate mintmarks before they are shipped to those mints. Because this was a hand operation prior to 1985, the exact positioning and size of the mintmarks may vary slightly, depending on where and how deeply the punches were impressed. (For an example in this book, see the 1975-D Jefferson nickel.) This also accounts for double-punched and superimposed mintmarks such as the 1938-D, D Over D, and 1938-D, D Over S, Buffalo nickels. Polishing of dies may also alter the apparent size of fine details. Occasionally the mintmark is inadvertently left off a die sent to a branch mint, as was the case with some recent Proof cents, nickels, and dimes. Similarly, some 1982 dimes without mintmarks were made as circulation strikes. The mintmark M was used on coins made in Manila for the Philippines from 1925 through 1941.

Prior to 1900, punches for mintmarks varied greatly in size. This is particularly noticeable in the 1850 to 1880 period, in which the letters range from very small to very large. An attempt to standardize sizes started in 1892 with the Barber series, but exceptions are seen in the 1892-O half dollar and 1905-O dime, both of which have normal and "microscopic" mintmarks. A more or less standard-size, small mintmark was used on all minor coins starting in 1909, and on all dimes, quarters, and halves after the Barber series was replaced in 1916. Slight variations in mintmark size occur through 1945, with notable differences in 1928, when small and large S mintmarks were used.

In recent years a single D or S punch has been used to mark all branch-mint dies. The change to the larger D for Denver coins occurred in 1933. Nickels, dimes, quarter dollars, half dollars, and dollars of 1934 exist with either the old, smaller-size mintmark or the new, larger-size D. All other denominations of 1934 and after are standard. The San Francisco mintmark was changed to a larger size during 1941 and, with the exception of the half dollar, all 1941-S coins are known with either small or large mintmarks. Halves were not changed until 1942, and the 1942-S and 1943-S pieces exist both ways. The

1945-S dime with "microscopic" S is an unexplained use of a punch originally intended for Philippine coins of 1907 through 1920. In 1979, the punches were replaced. Varieties of some 1979 coins appear with either the old- or new-shaped S or D. The S punch was again replaced in 1981 with a punch that yielded a more distinct letter.

The mintmark application technique for Proof coins was changed in 1985, and for circulation-strike production in 1990 and 1991, when the letter was applied directly to the master die rather than being hand punched on each working die. At the same time, all the mintmark letters were made much larger and clearer than those of previous years.

CHECKING YOUR COINS FOR AUTHENTICITY

Coin collectors occasionally encounter counterfeit coins, or coins that have been altered so that they appear to be something other than what they really are. Any coin that does not seem to fit the description of similar pieces listed in this guide book should be looked upon with suspicion. Experienced coin dealers can usually tell quickly whether a coin is genuine, and would never knowingly sell spurious coins to a collector. Rare coins found in circulation or bought from a nonprofessional source should be examined carefully.

The risk of purchasing a spurious coin can be minimized through the use of common sense and an elementary knowledge of the techniques used by counterfeiters. It is well to keep in mind that the more popular a coin is among collectors and the public, the more likely it is that counterfeits and replicas will abound. Until recently, collector coins valued at under $100 were rarely replicated because of the high cost of making such items. The same

These "coins" might appear authentic at first glance, but they're actually modern fakes, made to deceive unwary collectors.

was true of counterfeits made to deceive the public. Few counterfeit coins were made because it was more profitable for the fakers to print paper money. Today, however, counterfeiters in Asia and elsewhere create fakes of a surprising variety of coins, most notably silver dollar types, but also smaller denominations.

The best way to detect counterfeit coins is to compare suspected pieces with others of the same issue. Carefully check size, color, luster, weight, edge devices, and design details. Replicas generally have less detail than their genuine counterparts when studied under magnification. Modern struck counterfeits made to deceive collectors are an exception to this rule. Any questionable gold coin should be referred to an expert for verification.

Cast forgeries are usually poorly made and of incorrect weight. Base metal is often used in place of gold or silver, and the coins are lightweight and often incorrect in color and luster. Deceptive cast pieces have been made using real metal content and modern dental techniques, but these too usually vary in quality and color.

Detection of alterations sometimes involves comparative examination of the suspected areas of a coin (usually mintmarks and date digits) at magnification ranging from 10x to 40x.

Coins of exceptional rarity or value should never be purchased without a written guarantee of authenticity. Professional authentication of rare coins for a fee is available with the services offered by commercial grading services, and by some coin dealers.

Three types of spurious coins you might encounter are replicas, counterfeits, and alterations.

Replicas. Reproductions of famous and historical coins have been distributed for decades by marketing firms and souvenir vendors. These pieces are often tucked away as curios by the original recipients, perhaps in a desk drawer or jewelry box, and later are found by others who believe they have discovered objects of great value. Genuine specimens of extremely rare and/or valuable coins are almost never found in unlikely places.

Most replicas are poorly made, often by the casting method (as opposed to being struck by dies), and are virtually worthless other than as novelties. They can sometimes be identified by a seam that runs around the edge of the piece where the two halves of the casting mold were joined together.

Counterfeits. For many centuries, counterfeiters have produced base-metal forgeries of gold and silver coins to deceive the public in the normal course of trade. These pieces are usually crudely made and easily detected on close examination. Crudely cast counterfeit copies of older coins are the most prevalent. These can usually be detected by the casting bubbles or pimples that can be seen with low-power magnification. Pieces struck from handmade dies are more deceptive, but the engravings do not match those of genuine mint products.

More recently, as coin collecting has gained popularity and rare-coin prices have risen, "numismatic" counterfeits (made not to pass in commerce, but for sale to unsuspecting collectors) have become more common. The majority of these are die-struck counterfeits of gold coins, mass produced overseas since 1950. Forgeries exist of most U.S. gold coins dated between 1870 and 1933, as well as all issues of the gold dollar and three-dollar gold piece. Most of these are very well made, as they were intended to pass the close scrutiny of collectors. Few gold coins of earlier dates have been counterfeited, but false 1799 ten-dollar gold pieces and 1811 five-dollar coins have been made. Gold coins in less than Extremely Fine condition are seldom counterfeited. For more information, including extensive illustrations, consult the *United States Gold Counterfeit Detection Guide*, by Bill Fivaz.

Silver dollars dated 1804, Lafayette commemorative dollars of 1900, several of the low-mintage commemorative half dollars, and 1795 half dimes have been forged in quantity. Minor-coin forgeries made in recent years are the 1909-S V.D.B. Lincoln cent; the 1914-D Lincoln cent; the 1955, Doubled Die Obverse, Lincoln cent; 1877 Indian Head cents; 1856 Flying Eagle cents; and, on a much smaller scale, a variety of dates of half cents and large cents. Nineteenth-century copies of colonial coins are also sometimes encountered (see the *Whitman Encyclopedia of Colonial and Early American Coins*).

Commonly seen modern-day counterfeits produced in China include Bust dollars; Liberty Seated dimes, quarters, halves, and dollars; Morgan dollars; and even American Silver Eagles, all of various dates and mintmarks—some fantastical (for example, Morgan dollars dated in the 1700s).

Alterations. Deceivers occasionally alter coins by the addition, removal, or change of a design feature (such as a mintmark or date digit) or by the polishing, sandblasting, acid etching, toning, or plating of the surface of a genuine piece. Among U.S. gold coins, only the 1927-D double eagle is commonly found with a deceptively added mintmark. On $2.50 and $5 gold coins, 1839 through 1856, New Orleans O mintmarks have been altered to C (for Charlotte, North Carolina) in a few instances.

More than a century ago, fraudsters imitated five-dollar gold pieces by gold-plating 1883 Liberty Head five-cent coins of the type without the word CENTS on the reverse. Other coins commonly created fraudulently through alteration include the 1799 large cent and the 1909-S, 1909-S V.D.B., 1914-D, 1922 "plain," and 1943 "copper" cents. The 1913 Liberty Head nickel has been extensively replicated by the alteration of 1903 and 1912 nickels. Scarce, high-grade Denver and San Francisco Buffalo nickels of the 1920s; 1916-D and 1942, 42 Over 41, dimes; 1918-S, 8 Over 7, quarters; 1932-D and -S quarters; and 1804 silver dollars have all been crafted by the alteration of genuine coins of other dates or mints.

COINS FROM TREASURES AND HOARDS: A KEY TO UNDERSTANDING RARITY AND VALUE

The following discussion of coin treasures and hoards is derived from the writing of Q. David Bowers.

ELEMENTS OF RARITY

In many instances, the mintage of a coin can be a factor in its present-day rarity and value. However, across American numismatics there are many important exceptions, some very dramatic. As an introduction and example, in this book you will find many listings of Morgan silver dollars of 1878 through 1921 for which the mintage figure does not seem to correlate with the coin's price. For example, among such coins the 1901, of which 6,962,000 were made for circulation, is valued at $425,000 in MS-65. In the same series the 1884-CC, of which only 1,136,000 were struck, is listed at $475, or only a tiny fraction of the value of a 1901.

Why the difference? The explanation is that nearly all of the 6,962,000 dollars of 1901 were either placed into circulation at the time and became worn, or were melted generations ago. Very few were saved by collectors, and today MS-65 coins are extreme rarities. On the other hand, of the 1,166,000 1884-CC silver dollars minted, relatively few went into circulation. Vast quantities were sealed in 1,000-coin cloth bags and put into government storage. Generations later, as coin collecting became popular, thousands were paid out by the Treasury Department. Years after that, in the early 1960s, when silver metal rose in value, there was a "run" on long-stored silver dollars, and it was learned in March 1964 that 962,638 1884-CC dollars—84.7% of the original mintage—were still in the hands of the Treasury Department!

With this information, the price disparities become understandable. Even though the 1901 had a high mintage, few were saved, and although worn coins are common, gem MS-65 coins are rarities. In contrast, nearly all of the low-mintage 1884-CC dollars were stored by the government, and today most of them still exist, including some in MS-65 grade.

There are many other situations in which mintages are not particularly relevant to the availability and prices of coins today. Often a special circumstance will lead to certain coins' being saved in especially large quantities, later dramatically affecting the availability and value of such pieces. The following are some of those circumstances.

Excitement of a New Design. In the panorama of American coinage, some new designs have captured the fancy of the public, who saved them in large quantities when they were released. In many other instances new designs were ignored, and coins slipped into circulation unnoticed.

In 1909 great publicity was given to the new Abraham Lincoln portrait to be used on the one-cent piece, replacing the familiar Indian Head motif. On the reverse in tiny letters were the initials, V.D.B., of the coin's designer, Victor David Brenner. The occasion was the 100th anniversary of Lincoln's birth. Coinage commenced at the Philadelphia and San Francisco mints. In total, 27,995,000 1909 V.D.B., cents were struck and 484,000 of the 1909-S V.D.B.

On August 2, 1909, the new cents were released to the public. A mad scramble ensued, and soon banks had to ration the number paid out to any single individual, this being particularly true in the East. (Interest in the West was less intense, and fewer coins were saved there.) A controversy arose as to the V.D.B. initials, and some newspaper notices complained that as Brenner had been paid for his work, there was no point in giving his initials a prominent place on the coins. Never mind that artists' initials had been used on other coins for a long time. As examples, the M initial of George T. Morgan appeared on both the obverse and reverse of silver dollars from 1878 onward; Chief Engraver Charles E. Barber was memorialized by a B on the neck of Miss Liberty on dimes, quarters, and half dollars from 1892 onward; and the recent (1907 onward) double eagles bore the monogram of Augustus Saint-Gaudens prominently on the obverse. In spite of these precedents, the offending V.D.B. initials were removed, and later 1909 and 1909-S cents were made without them.

Word spread that the cents with V.D.B. would be rare, and people saved even more of them. Today, the 1909 V.D.B. cents are readily available in Mint State. The 1909-S V.D.B., of lower mintage and of which far fewer were saved, lists for $1,350 in MS-63.

Other Popular First-Year Coins. Among other United States coins struck since 1792, these first-year-of-issue varieties (a partial list) were saved in large numbers and are especially plentiful today:

- **1837 Liberty Seated, No Stars, half dime.** Several thousand or more were saved, a large number for a half dime of the era. Apparently, their cameo-like appearance made them attractive curiosities at the time, the same being true of the dimes of the same year.

- **1837 Liberty Seated, No Stars, dime.** Somewhat more than a thousand were saved, a large number for a dime of the era.

- **1883 Liberty Head, Without CENTS, nickel.** The U.S. Mint expressed the value of this new design simply as "V," without mention of cents—not particularly unusual, as three-cent pieces of the era were simply denominated as "III." Certain people gold-plated the new nickels and passed them off as five-dollar gold coins of similar diameter. Soon, the Mint added the word CENTS. News accounts were printed that the "mistake" coins without CENTS would be recalled and would become very rare. Americans saved so many that today this variety is the most plentiful in Mint State of any Liberty Head nickel in the entire series from 1883 to 1913.

- **1892 and 1893 World's Columbian Exposition commemorative half dollars.** These, the first U.S. commemorative half dollars, were widely publicized, and hundreds of thousands were saved. Today they are very common in used condition, because quantities were eventually released into circulation as if they were regular half dollars.

- **MCMVII (1907) High-Relief gold twenty-dollar coin.** Although only about 12,000 were minted, at least 6,000 survive today, mostly in Mint State. Released in December 1907, the coin, by famous sculptor Augustus Saint-Gaudens, created a sensation, and soon examples were selling for $30 each. Today, Mint State coins are plentiful, but as the demand for them is extremely strong, choice specimens sell for strong prices. An MS-63 coin lists for $24,000.

- **1913 Buffalo nickel.** These were saved in large quantities, and today there are more Mint State coins of this year in existence than for any other issue of the next 15 years.

Many coins have been saved as special souvenirs. People often notice a new coinage design and will set examples aside from the first year of issue, making high-grade pieces available for later generations of collectors. Pictured: an 1883 No CENTS Liberty Head nickel, a steel 1943 cent, and a 1999 State quarter.

- **1916 Mercury dime.** In 1916, the Mercury dime's first year of issue, Americans saved many of the new coins from the Philadelphia and San Francisco mints. However, for some reason the low-mintage 1916-D was generally overlooked and today is very rare in Mint State.

- **1932 Washington quarter.** At the Philadelphia Mint, 5,504,000 were minted, and it is likely that several hundred thousand were saved, making them plentiful today. The 1932-D quarter was struck to the extent of 436,800, but for some reason was overlooked by the public, with the result that Mint State coins are rare today. On the other hand, of the 408,000 1932-S quarters struck, thousands were saved. Today, Mint State 1932-S quarters are at least 10 to 20 times more readily available than are equivalent examples of the higher-mintage 1932-D.

- **1943 zinc-coated steel cent.** The novel appearance of this coin resulted in many being saved as curiosities.

- **1964 Kennedy half dollar.** The popularity of the assassinated president was such that many of the hundreds of millions of 1964 half dollars were saved as souvenirs both at home and abroad. This was also the last year the 90% silver half dollar was made for circulation (later versions were 40% silver or copper-nickel), which further increased its popularity.

- **1999–2008 State quarters.** From 1999 to 2008, five different quarter dollar designs were produced each year, with motifs honoring the states in the order that they joined the Union. These coins were highly publicized, and hobby companies produced folders, albums, maps, and other holders to store and display them. A Treasury Department study estimated that 98 million Americans saved one or more sets of the coins, starting with the first one issued (Delaware) and continuing to the last (Hawaii).

- **2000 Sacagawea "golden dollar."** These coins, intended to be a popular substitute for paper dollars and to last much longer in circulation, were launched with great fanfare in 2000, and more than just a few were saved by the public. However, the coin did not catch on for general use in commerce. Later issues have been made for sale to collectors, but no quantities have been released for circulation.

COINS FEW PEOPLE NOTICED

In contrast to the examples above, most coins of new designs attracted no particular notice when they were first issued, and were not saved in unusual quantities. In sharp contrast to the highly popular Kennedy half dollar of 1964, its predecessor, the Franklin half dollar (launched in 1948), generated very little interest, and even numismatists generally ignored its debut—perhaps preferring the old Liberty Walking design, which had been a favorite.

Although a long list could be made, here is just a sampling of first-year-of-issue coins that were not noticed in their own time. Few were set aside in like-new condition. Consequently, today they range from scarce to rare in Mint State:

- **1793 half cent and cent.** As popular as these may be today, there is no known instance in which a numismatist or museum in 1793 deliberately saved pieces as souvenirs.

- **1794–1795 Flowing Hair half dimes, half dollars, and silver dollars.** The Flowing Hair coins, highly desired today, seem to have attracted little notice in their time, and again there is no record of any having been deliberately saved.

- **1807 and related Capped Bust coinages.** The Capped Bust and related coins of John Reich, assistant engraver at the Mint, were first used in 1807 on the silver half dollar and gold five-dollar piece, and later on certain other denominations. Today these are extremely popular with collectors, but in their time they were not noticed, and few were saved in Mint State.

- **1840 Liberty Seated dollar.** Examples are very scarce in Mint State today and are virtually unknown in gem preservation.

- **1892 Barber dime, quarter dollar, and half dollar.** In 1892 the new Liberty Head design by Charles E. Barber replaced the long-lived Liberty Seated motif. The new coins received bad press notices. Another factor detracting from public interest was the wide attention focused on the forthcoming commemorative half dollars of the World's Columbian Exposition. Not many of the new Barber coins were saved.

- **1938 Jefferson nickel.** Although the numismatic hobby was dynamic at the time, the new nickel design attracted little notice, and no unusual quantities were saved. The market was still reeling from the burst bubble of the 1935 through 1936 commemorative craze, and there was little incentive to save coins for investment.

THE 1962–1964 TREASURY RELEASE

The Bland-Allison Act of February 28, 1878, was a political boondoggle passed to accommodate silver-mining interests in the West. It mandated that the Treasury Department buy millions of ounces of silver each year and convert it to silver dollars. At the time, the world price of silver bullion was dropping, and there were economic difficulties in the Western mining states. From 1878 to 1904 and again in 1921, silver dollars of the Morgan design were minted under Bland-Allison and subsequent acts, to the extent of 656,989,387 pieces. From 1921 to 1928, and in 1934 and 1935, silver dollars of the Peace design were produced in the amount of 190,577,279 pieces.

Although silver dollars were used in commerce in certain areas of the West, paper currency by and large served the needs of trade and exchange. As these hundreds of millions of newly minted dollars were not needed, most were put up in 1,000-coin canvas bags and stored in Treasury vaults. In 1918, under terms of the Pittman Act, 270,232,722 Morgan dollars were melted. At the time, with World War I in its fifth year, the market for silver was temporarily strong, and there was a call for bullion to ship to India to shore up confidence in Britain's wartime government. No accounting was kept of the dates and mints involved in the destruction. Only the quantities were recorded (this procedure being typical when the Treasury melted old coins). However, hundreds of millions remained. Now and again there was a call for silver dollars for circulation, especially in the West; and in the East and Midwest there was a modest demand for pieces for use as holiday and other gifts; in such instances many were paid out. The example of the high-mintage 1901

Typical silver mining scene, late 1880s.

THE CARSON CITY SILVER DOLLARS
THE LAST OF A LEGACY

The cover to a GSA flyer advertising the Treasury's hoard of Carson City silver dollars for sale.

dollar being rare in Mint State, as most were circulated, is reflective of this. Other coins were stored, such as the low-mintage 1884-CC, of which 84.7% were still in the hands of the Treasury as late as 1964! At this time the Treasury decided to hold back bags that were marked as having Carson City dollars, although in records of storage no account was made of them earlier.

A Carson City Morgan dollar from the Treasury release.

Beginning in a significant way in the 1950s, silver dollars became very popular with numismatists. The rarest of all Morgan silver dollars by 1962 was considered to be the 1903-O. In that year's *Guide Book of United States Coins*, an Uncirculated coin listed for $1,500, the highest price for any variety. Experts estimated that fewer than a dozen Mint State coins existed in all of numismatics. It was presumed that most had been melted in 1918 under the Pittman Act.

Then, in November 1962, during the normal payout of silver dollars as gifts for the holiday season, some long-sealed bags of coins were taken from a Philadelphia Mint vault that had remained under seal since 1929. It was soon found that brilliant 1903-O dollars were among these! A treasure hunt ensued, and hundreds of thousands of these former rarities were found. The rush was on!

From then until March 1964, hundreds of millions of Morgan and Peace dollars were emptied from government and bank storage. At one time a long line of people, some with wheelbarrows, formed outside of the Treasury Building in Washington, D.C., to obtain bags of dollars. Finally only about three million coins remained, mostly the aforementioned Carson City issues, which the Treasury decided to hold back. These were later sold at strong premiums in a series of auctions held by the General Services Administration (GSA). In the meantime, Morgan and Peace dollars became very large and important sections of the coin hobby, as they remain today. However, as can be seen, the combined elements of some coins' having been melted in 1918, others having been placed into circulation generations ago, and still others existing in Mint State from long-stored hoards, results in silver dollar prices that often bear little relation to mintage figures.

OTHER FAMOUS HOARDS

While the great Treasury release of 1962 through 1964 is the most famous of all hoards, quite a few others have attracted interest and attention over the years.

- **The Castine Hoard of Early Silver Coins (discovered in the 1840s).** From November 1840 through April 1841, Captain Stephen Grindle and his son Samuel unearthed many silver coins on their farm on the Bagaduce River about six miles from the harbor of Castine, Maine. The number of pieces found was not recorded, but is believed to have been between 500 and 2,000, buried in 1690 (the latest date observed) or soon afterward. Most pieces were foreign silver coins, but dozens of Massachusetts Pine Tree shillings and related silver coins were found. This hoard stands today as one of the most famous in American history.

- **The Bank of New York Hoard (1856).** Around 1856 a keg containing several thousand 1787 Fugio copper cents was found at the Bank of New York at 44 Wall Street. Each was in Mint State, most with brown toning. For many years these were given out as souvenirs and keepsakes to clients. By 1948, when numismatist Damon G. Douglas examined them, there were 1,641 remaining. Today, many remain at the bank and are appreciated for their history and value.

- **The Nichols Find of Copper Cents (by 1859).** In the annals of American numismatics, one of the most famous hoards is the so-called Nichols Find, consisting of 1796 and 1797 copper cents, Mint State, perhaps about 1,000 in total. These were distributed in the late 1850s by David Nichols. All were absorbed into the hobby community as of 1863, by which time they were worth $3 to $4 each, or less than a thousandth of their present-day value.

- **The Randall Hoard of Copper Cents (1860s).** Sometime soon after the Civil War, a wooden keg filled with as-new copper cents was located, said to have been beneath an old railroad platform in Georgia. Revealed were thousands of coins dated 1816 to 1820, with the 1818 and 1820 being the most numerous. Today, the Randall hoard accounts for most known Mint State examples of these particular dates.

- **The Colonel Cohen Hoard of 1773 Virginia Halfpennies (by the 1870s).** Sometime in the 1870s or earlier, Colonel Mendes I. Cohen, a Baltimore numismatist, obtained a cache of at least 2,200 Uncirculated 1773 Virginia halfpennies. These passed through several hands, and many individual pieces were dispersed along the way. As a result, today they are the only colonial (pre-1776) American coins that can be easily obtained in Mint State.

- **The Exeter Hoard of Massachusetts Silver (1876).** During the excavation of a cellar near the railroad station in Exeter, New Hampshire, a group of 30 to 40 Massachusetts silver shillings was found in the sand, amid the remains of what seemed to be a wooden box. All bore the date 1652 and were of the Pine Tree and Oak Tree types, plus, possibly, a rare Willow Tree shilling.

- **The Economite Treasure (1878).** In 1878 a remarkable hoard of silver coins was found in a subterranean storage area at Economy, Pennsylvania, in a building erected years earlier by the Harmony Society, a utopian work-share community. The March 1881 issue of the *Coin Collector's Journal* gave this inventory: Quarter dollars: 1818 through 1828, 400 pieces. Half dollars: 1794, 150; 1795, 650; 1796, 2; 1797, 1; 1801, 300; 1802, 200; 1803, 300; 1805 Over 04, 25; 1805, 600; 1806, 1,500; 1807, 2,000; 1815, 100. Common half dollars: 1808 through 1836, 111,356. Silver dollars: 1794, 1; 1795, 800; 1796, 125; 1797, 80; 1798 Small Eagle reverse, 30; 1798 Large Eagle reverse, 560; 1799 5 stars facing, 12; 1799, 1,250; 1800, 250; 1801, 1802, and 1803, 600. Foreign silver (French, Spanish, and Spanish-American), total face value: $12,600. Total face value of the hoard: $75,000. Other information indicates that most of the coins had been taken from circulation and showed different degrees of wear.

- **The Hoard of Miser Aaron White (before 1888).** Aaron White, a Connecticut attorney, distrusted paper money and even went so far as to issue his own token with the legend NEVER KEEP A PAPER DOLLAR IN YOUR POCKET TILL TOMORROW. He had a passion for saving coins and accumulated more than 100,000 pieces. After his death the coins were removed to a warehouse. Later, they were placed in the hands of dealer Édouard Frossard, who sold most of them privately and others by auction on July 20, 1888, billing them as "18,000 American and foreign copper coins and tokens selected from the Aaron White hoard." An overall estimate of the White hoard, as it existed before it was given to Frossard, was made by Benjamin P. Wright, and included these: "250 colonial and state copper coins, 60,000 copper large cents (which were mainly 'rusted' and spotted; 5,000 of the nicest ones were picked out and sold for 2¢ each), 60,000 copper-nickel Flying Eagle and Indian cents (apparently most dated 1862 and 1863), 5,000 bronze two-cent pieces, 200 half dollars, 100 silver dollars, 350 gold dollars, and 20,000 to 30,000 foreign copper coins."

- **The Collins Find of 1828 Half Cents (1894).** Circa 1894, Benjamin H. Collins, a Washington, D.C., numismatist, acquired a bag of half cents dated 1828, of the 13-stars variety. Historians believe that about 1,000 coins were involved, all bright Uncirculated. By the early 1950s all but a few hundred had been distributed in the marketplace, and by now it is likely that all have individual owners.

- **The Chapman Hoard of 1806 Half Cents (1906).** About 1906, Philadelphia dealer Henry Chapman acquired a hoard of 1806 half cents. Although no figure was given at the time, it is estimated that a couple hundred or so coins were involved. Most or all had much of their original mint red color, toning to brown, and with light striking at the upper part of the wreath.

- **The Baltimore Find (1934).** One of the most storied hoards in American numismatics is the Baltimore Find, a cache of at least 3,558 gold coins, all dated before 1857. On August 31, 1934, two young boys were playing in the cellar of a rented house at 132 South Eden Street, Baltimore, and found these coins hidden in a wall. Later, more were found in the same location. On May 2, 1935, many of the coins were sold at auction, by which time others had been sold quietly, some unofficially. This hoard included many choice and gem coins dated in the 1850s. Leonard Augsburger's award-winning *Treasure in the Cellar* tells the complete tale.

- **The New Orleans Bank Find (1982).** A few minutes past noon, on October 29, 1982, a bulldozer unearthed a cache of long-hidden silver coins, believed to have been stored in three wooden boxes in the early 1840s. They were mostly Spanish-American issues, but hundreds of United States coins, including 1840-O and 1841-O Liberty Seated quarters, were also found. Men in business suits, ladies in dresses, and others scrambled in the dirt and mud to find treasure. The latest-dated coin found was from 1842. This must have been a secret reserve of some long-forgotten merchant or bank.

- **Wells Fargo Hoard of 1908 $20 (1990s).** In the 1990s, dealer Ron Gillio purchased a hoard of 19,900 examples of the 1908, No Motto, double eagle. For a time these were stored in a Wells Fargo Bank branch, giving the name to the cache. All were Mint State, and many were of choice and gem quality. Offered in the market, these were dispersed over a period of several years.

- **Gold coins from abroad (turn of the 21st century).** In the late 20th and early 21st centuries, some exciting finds of Mint State double eagles were located in foreign banks. Involved were high-grade examples of some Carson City issues in the Liberty Head series and hundreds of scarce-mintmark varieties dated after 1923. As is often the case when hoards are discovered, pieces were filtered into the market without any publicity or an accounting of varieties found.

SUNKEN TREASURE

Throughout American history, tens of thousands of ships have been lost at sea and on inland waters. Only a handful of these vessels were reported as having had significant quantities of coins aboard. In recent decades, numismatists have been front-row center as wrecks from several sidewheel steamers lost in the 1850s and 1860s have yielded rare coins.

The SS *New York* was launched in 1837, carrying passengers between New York City and Charleston, South Carolina. The steamer was carrying $30,000 or more in money when she encountered an unexpected hurricane in the Gulf of Mexico on September 5, 1846. Captain John D. Phillips ordered the anchor dropped, hoping to ride out the storm. The wind and waves increased, however, and for two days those aboard watched as the rigging and other parts of the ship were torn apart. On September 7 the storm prevailed and the *New York* was overwhelmed, sinking into water 60 feet deep. An estimated 17 people—about one third of the passengers and crew—lost their lives. Decades later, in 2006 and 2007, treasure seekers recovered more than 2,000 silver coins and several hundred gold coins from the shipwreck. Most of the silver was heavily etched from exposure to the salt water, but certain of the gold coins were in high grades, including some of the finest known examples of their date and mint.

Eight years after the loss of the *New York*, the SS *Yankee Blade* was off the coast of Santa Barbara, California, steaming at full speed in a heavy fog. Captain Henry T. Randall believed the ship was in deep water far out to sea, and he was trying to establish a speed record—certain to be beneficial in advertising. In fact the steamer was amid the rockbound Channel Islands, and in the fog she smashed onto a rock and got hung up. The date was October 1, 1854. On board was some $152,000 in coins consigned by a banking house, plus other gold, and about 900 passengers and crew. Most of them escaped, but in the ensuing confusion before the *Yankee Blade* sank, between 17 and 50 lost their lives. Over the years most of the coins appear to have been recovered, under circumstances largely unknown. In 1948 the hull was found again and divers visited the wreck. Around 1977 more recoveries were yielded, including 200 to 250 1854-S double eagles. All showed microscopic granularity, possibly from the action of sea-bottom sand, and all had die cracks on the reverse. Little in the way of hard facts has ever reached print.

The wreck and recovery of the SS *Central America* was much better documented. The steamer was lost on September 12, 1857, carrying about $2.6 million in gold treasure, heading from Havana, Cuba, to New York City. A monster hurricane engulfed the ship on the 10th and 11th; Captain William Lewis Herndon enlisted the aid of male passengers to form a bucket brigade to bail water, but their efforts proved futile. The ship was swamped, and the captain ordered the American flag be flown upside-down, a signal of distress. The nearby brig *Marine* approached and nearly all of the *Central America*'s women and children were transferred over, along with some crew members, before the *Central America* was overwhelmed by the waves and went down, with Captain Herndon standing on the paddle box. The steamer ultimately settled 7,200 feet deep, and some 435 lives were lost. The wreck was found in 1987 and over time more than $100 million worth of treasure was brought to the surface. This included more than 5,400 mint-fresh 1857-S double eagles, hundreds of gold ingots (including one weighing 80 pounds), and other coins.

In the 1990s another sidewheel steamer was found: the SS *Brother Jonathan*, lost with few survivors as she attempted to return to safe harbor in Crescent City, California, after hitting stormy weather on her way north to Oregon (January 30, 1865). More than 1,000 gold coins were recovered from the wreck, including many Mint State 1865-S double eagles. Detailed files and photographs recorded every step of the recovery.

In 2003 another 1865 shipwreck was located: that of the SS *Republic*, lost off the coast of Georgia while en route from New York City to New Orleans on October 25, just months after the Civil War ended. The steamer sank in a hurricane along with a reported $400,000 in silver and gold. Recovery efforts brought up 51,000 coins and 14,000 other artifacts (bottles, ceramics, personal items, etc.). The coins included 1,400 double eagles dating from 1838 to 1858, and thousands from the 1850s and 1860s; plus more than 180 different examples of Liberty Seated half dollars, including five 1861-O die combinations attributed to Confederate control of the New Orleans mint. The most valuable single coin was a Mint State 1854-O double eagle, then valued at more than $500,000.

Shipwrecks continue to be found even today, and the hobby community eagerly awaits news of coins and treasure found amidst their watery resting places.

THE STORY OF AMERICAN MONEY

This introduction to U.S. coins is based on the work of the late Dr. Richard G. Doty,
senior curator of numismatics at the Smithsonian Institution.

Much of the early story of American coins focuses on the importation, adaptation, manufacture, and spread of a variety of monetary forms by the European colonizers of America and their descendants. To set the stage, though, we must first render an accounting of earlier peoples—Native Americans—and the monies they created.

Native Americans were more practical than Europeans—their monies were rooted in their immediate experience, in their proximate environment. While Europeans remained wedded to one particular monetary form, coinage, native peoples used what was there and did quite well.

But before we examine any examples in particular, we should realize that, regardless of time or place, any exchange medium must satisfy a number of requirements. If it does so, it will stand as viable money, likely to remain in fashion; if it does not, it will soon be replaced by something else. To be money, objects with *durability* have distinct advantages over their competitors. The aspiring monetary form should be *practical*, either directly or indirectly. It must be *easily quantifiable*. It must be of *moderate scarcity*, rare enough to possess an aura of desirability, plentiful enough so that everyone can see it and have at least a minimal chance of obtaining it. Finally, *beauty*, either for display or for other purposes, gives some potential trading objects an advantage over others (without being an absolute requirement for any of them). With these conditions met, nearly anything, either natural or manufactured, can become money.

Just what media the Native Americans used depended on their location, at least to a degree. Peoples occupying an area rich in fur-bearing animals would probably incorporate pelts into their monetary-exchange practices. But so might adjacent peoples who occupied areas where game was scarce. And while shells might form trading objects for coastal tribes, they might be known and used in the interior as well—at least in areas connected with the seacoast by reasonably easy communication.

THE EARLY AMERICAN "MONEY"

Hides and shells became the foundation of native monetary systems in the lands that would become the United States and Canada. In time, particular types of pelts and particular varieties of shells came to hold a special regard and became units or standards of value. The beaver's skin gained such a role, perhaps because the animal was regarded as sacred by many peoples. Skins of other animals were traded as multiples and fractions of one beaver, and when European commodities came to the tribes, the new goods too were tariffed in terms of so many to one "made" beaver (that is, a properly skinned and tanned pelt).

Elsewhere, shells, clams, and conchs were extremely important, for they were the raw materials behind the most important single type of native currency in all of North America. This was wanpanpiage, wampumpeage, or wampum.

Wampum is an old Algonquian word meaning "a string of white beads." Another term, *suckauhock*, was used for strings fashioned from purple beads, but the earliest European settlers tended to use the shortened term *wampum* indiscriminately, and their practice survives. Wampum consisted of short beads, cut from the shells of clams and conchs, drilled by hand, and strung. This means of trade appears to have originally seen employment when woven into patterned belts, for telling stories and conveying messages. It only gradually came into use as a display of wealth and, finally, as a unit of wealth. We know that it had achieved this final, crucial stage and was an accepted form of money before European settlement, for the explorer Jacques Cartier found it so employed in the mid-1530s. We believe we understand why it achieved popularity as a monetary form: under pre-industrial conditions, wampum was difficult to manufacture. It served as a unit of value because of the work and skill required to make it.

Wampum was popular on the Atlantic seaboard of North America, among both Native Americans and European newcomers. There was a parallel monetary form on the Pacific seaboard, based on the shell of a different sea creature, the dentalium (or tooth shell), but it never captured the attention of the European newcomers in the way that wampum did, and it played little role in post-contact economies.

To the south, other trading objects held sway. In Mexico, copper axe-shaped objects called *siccapili* (in modern Spanish *tajaderas*, "chopping knives") found popularity among Aztecs and their contemporaries—so much so that the earth is still yielding large numbers of them to the plows of modern farmers. Cacao beans were mainstays of the Aztec monetary system, and they illustrate one of the earliest instances of the debasement of a non-coin monetary form: the delicious contents of the cacao bean were sometimes scooped out and substituted with earth, the skin carefully replaced, and the extraction cleverly hidden.

Corn was also used as a trade commodity, and so was gold, either cast into bars or traded in transparent quills so that its purity could be seen by all. Hernán Cortés found tin circulating as money in several of the provinces through which he and his tiny band marched on their way to glory, but his compatriot Francisco Pizarro found much less to the south. The economy of the Inca Empire was paternalistic, socialistic—so planned, in fact, that commercial transactions (and thus the employment of money) were largely unnecessary. But it has been suggested that leaves of the coca plant—the source of a modern, international commodity called cocaine—may have enjoyed a limited monetary function prior to the Spanish conquest.

Elsewhere in the Americas, tribes in what became Venezuela appear to have used strings of shells, a form of money similar to wampum although probably not inspired by it. Some of the Brazilian peoples used arrows; others used stringed beads of snail shells. The latter practice persisted in Mato Grosso, Brazil, well into the 20th century.

The longevity of this particular form of money should alert us to an important fact about "primitive" monetary forms: they did not all obligingly disappear when the first Europeans arrived on American shores. While few of them displayed the persistence seen with the shell money of Mato Grosso (in part because few places in the Americas were as impenetrable as this jungle area in western Brazil), many of them were found as useful by new settlers as old, and they formed essential links between old economies and new.

Indeed, it is difficult to see how the numismatic history of the United States could have been written in the absence of the skins of fur-bearing animals and the shells of creatures of the sea. Along with commodities known to and developed by Native Americans (but not generally used by them for trade) and scant supplies of coinage and other trading objects brought from Europe, furs and shells would form most of the basis of our early money—but not all. A final ingredient was being created to the south, one whose influence would be so persistent and ultimately so potent that it would shape the very way we reckoned and fashioned our symbols of wealth.

Aztec *siccapili* or *tajadera*, an axe-shaped object used as money in Mexico; one was worth 8,000 cacao beans (like those pictured).

THE SPANISH CENTURIES

This final ingredient was the Spanish conquest of most of the Western Hemisphere. It began with Columbus's first voyage in 1492, and in some ways it is still going on, as the spread of Spanish language and culture across today's United States suggests. But it was far more active, and far less peaceful, five centuries ago.

At that time, nothing less than the wholesale exportation of one way of life (and a snuffing-out or radical transmutation of many others) was occurring. We have no idea how many millions died in the process—from new diseases, from new and merciless labor systems—but the event certainly stands as the greatest of all holocausts, the most massive population revolution in all of human history.

While it was running its course, a hybrid society was being created, and in it the Spanish worldview would predominate, first by force, later by tradition. Of course, one of the key elements in the Spanish world was the *coin*—and attached to it was the belief that this small metallic object and wealth were essentially interchangeable, simultaneous concepts. The idea did not originate in Spain, but when Spaniards carried it to the Americas, a number of interesting events took place. All of them stemmed from a central fact: the new lands contained vast quantities of silver and gold.

These metals were, of course, one of the primary reasons Spanish colonization began and was maintained. At first the newcomers were happy merely to appropriate what had been collected by someone else. These metals were sent back to the homeland and were quickly turned into coinage there.

Then, just as they were running through the last of the precious metals they had appropriated, Spain's people soon began finding new, raw sources of American gold and silver. At first this metal was simply refined on the spot and sent in ingot form to Sevilla, where it was turned into coinage and would soon benefit commerce in Spain and eventually all of Europe.

But metal in ingot form would be of no particular use to those who had actually found it. These people, in the Caribbean islands, Mexico, Peru, and Bolivia, were developing expanding consumer economies by the middle years of the 16th century—economies that needed coinage if they were to continue to expand.

And so an obvious though era-defining solution was devised: let the locals make their own coinage, following Spanish forms, denominations, and designs. It was obvious in part because of the primitive minting technology then in force: virtually anybody could make a creditable coin, provided the metal was at hand. But it defined the era because this was the first time anyone had ever done so in the Western Hemisphere. For the first time in human history, the concept and the making of coins spread beyond Europe and Asia, the lands of their birth.

THE EMERGENCE OF A STAPLE

By 1625 no fewer than eight mints had been established in Spanish America. Of them, several didn't last long (those at Santo Domingo, La Plata, Panama, and Cartagena), and two were sporadic (Bogotá and Lima). Two other mints were unqualified successes from the beginning: those of Mexico City, which struck its first coins in 1536, and Potosí, which entered production about four decades later. No final reckoning of the production of these facilities can ever be made, but the combined output of Mexico City and Potosí alone was several billion pieces.

Coins from these mints made their way into the pockets of local burghers, paused there only momentarily, then made their journey to Spain and flowed out of that country almost as soon as they entered it. They paid for wars; they furnished luxuries and even necessities that a local population—enamored of the instant wealth and good life promised by the coins—either could not or would not create at home. Those coins traveled in odd directions and found strange resting places: hordes of them have been discovered along the coast of China, suggesting that the commerce of the 17th century was far more complex than we had previously imagined.

We call these crude coins "cobs," the name perhaps derived from *cabo de barra*, "end of a bar." The name provides a clue to their manufacture. A rough ingot was cast, then crudely sliced into coin-size planchets or blanks. The blanks could be adjusted down to their desired weight by means of a file, after which they were struck by hand. Cobs were struck in both gold and silver, but silver predominated at most mints. Within the coinage of that metal, one denomination in particular came to overshadow all the others. This was the piece of eight, and it would finally become the most successful, longest-lived trade coin in all of human history.

Between its introduction (probably in the 1530s, though possibly somewhat earlier) and its demise, some 400 years would elapse. The piece of eight would be struck at half a dozen mints in Spain, and in more than two dozen mints in Spanish America and the independent successor states. The final examples would appear in 1949, when the failing Nationalist government of Chiang Kai-shek asked the Mexico City mint to strike several million pieces on its behalf as an alternative to its own inflated currency.

The piece of eight's brothers were the Joachimsthaler and its descendants: the Danish daler, the French écu, the British crown, and others, all of which came into being because of a greater abundance of silver during late-medieval and early-modern times. But the piece of eight overshadowed them all because it was able to draw on a larger source of metal than any of its competitors. Its persistence, and that of the other members of the series, surprises us when we least expect it. Consider, for example, that the New York Stock Exchange quoted securities in terms of an eighth of a point until 1997 because the *real*—the eighth of a piece of eight—was the lowest increment allowed on the Wall Street bourse!

Typical "cob" coins of the early 1600s.

INTERLOPERS!

The Spanish conquest did not occur in a vacuum. In Europe, honest amazement over Columbus's success turned quickly to envy, denial, and determined attempts to match it. When the interlopers were done, the map of the Spanish Empire would be greatly altered, and the seeds of a new country would be planted. In time, those seeds would grow into the United States of America.

An unusual Mexican cob, pre-1700. Despite its bizarre shape, the coin was of good Mexican silver, and that was what mattered to those who spent it.

The people who planted those particular seeds were Britons, but they were not the first to dispute Spanish exclusivity in the Americas. The first non-Spaniards to do something about the new transatlantic possibility were Spain's neighbors on the Iberian Peninsula, the Portuguese. Lisbon had been sending explorers down and around the African coast since the mid-1480s; in 1500, one of its captains, Pedro Álvares Cabral, just happened to get blown so far off course that he arrived at a new land altogether, on the far side of the Atlantic. This was named after a rosy-red dyewood found there—Brazil. By the 1530s the Portuguese were making a determined attempt to settle the vast new land that their captain had discovered.

Other Europeans soon entered the fray, first biting off bits of Spanish and Portuguese wealth; they would soon be biting off bits of Spanish and Portuguese *land*, as well. The wealth was appropriated first probably because it involved less of an outlay on the part of national governments. The original Iberian conquests had largely been affairs of private enterprise for public gain; so were many of the early efforts to redistribute the loot.

The first targets of attack were those Spanish vessels carrying home the rich American cargos of silver, gold, and other commodities. By the 1520s these vessels were being attacked and captured, their contents triumphantly carried into French harbors. The Spanish retaliated as best they could, arming their merchantmen and soon creating a convoy system featuring two main arrangements. In the first, vessels brought Spanish (and, increasingly, other European) goods one way, and carried gold, silver, and other American materials the other. In the second, convoys crossed the Pacific, voyaging all the way from Acapulco to the Philippines, carrying pieces of eight to Manila where they were traded for Chinese products, especially spices and silks.

This *flota* system made transport much safer, and it also made matters easier for royal bookkeepers back home because all legal trade was conducted and controlled through a single channel. However, raids on outlying vessels were common, especially when the scourge of hurricanes scattered members of the convoy. Indeed, the weather sent more vessels to the bottom than did Spain's enemies.

There were other ways of capitalizing on Spanish good fortune. A series of increasingly audacious captains, ranging from Hawkins to Drake to Morgan to Anson, conducted raids on Spanish-American cities. These were coastal sites, where rich cargos were gathered prior to shipment to Spain. One could move in quickly, pick up anything of value, and then decamp before the Spanish navy arrived on the scene. To this day, we are impressed by the massive walls of Campeche in Mexico and Cartagena in Colombia—those walls had to be thick if they were to keep out the likes of Sir Francis Drake and company!

Eventually they began doing more than simply raiding: they began wintering over, and what had been targets for looting became places for permanent settlement. As peoples from Scandinavia had with the rich towns on the coasts and rivers of England, Ireland, and France centuries earlier, Britons, French, Danes, Dutchmen, and Swedes began nibbling away at lands that their controllers were unable or unwilling to defend.

The enemies of Spain and Portugal turned up in the strangest places. We most certainly would not expect to see the enterprising Dutch in Brazil. But they were there, nevertheless, occupying the area around Recife for nearly a quarter of a century—and for the record, they were striking the first true Brazilian coins there in 1645, precisely half a century before the Portuguese got around to setting up their first mint at Rio. The French had been in Brazil nearly a hundred years before, but had minted no coins to mark the occasion.

So the islands and bits of the mainland were eaten away. In time, the useful theory of "no peace beyond the line" was proclaimed by Spain and its enemies. It was a way of ensuring that, regardless of peace treaties in Europe, warfare might continue in the Indies as Spain's competitors attempted to take—and Spain attempted to defend and retake—lands and property as the opportunity appeared.

Of course, we are especially interested in the fortunes of one particular group of interlopers, the English. To understand the coins of the United States, we must explore what the English and those who followed managed to do with their particular share of New World treasure.

THE THIRTEEN COLONIES AND THEIR MONIES

British colonization of the future United States began in earnest shortly after 1600. It was carried forward in a number of ways, by diverse peoples, and from a variety of motives. In Virginia, whose first settlement was loyally named *Jamestown* after the reigning British monarch, economic profit was the primary motive. In Massachusetts, a religious motive—the desire to commune with the Deity in a particular, though officially frowned-upon, fashion—led to the Pilgrim settlement at inhospitable Plymouth. A few miles to the north, a second settlement was established some 10 years later, in 1630. Unlike Plymouth, Boston was a going concern from the very beginning, perhaps because its founders were both people of conscience and people of business. Merchants of the town would soon be trading in a number of places where they had no business operating—with interesting effects upon America's money.

The economic and religious motives behind the founding of these colonies and others often were intertwined so completely that neither original colonizers nor subsequent historians could separate them. But this simple fact should not blind us to the complex nature of the fabric of America's early culture. The identity, color, and weave of that fabric would shift over time, as they still do today.

For example, dissenting Protestants were hardly the only sects represented in the new settlements. Maryland, which was first colonized at St. Mary's City in 1634, was meant as a haven for English Catholics. Other non-Anglican peoples came over too: Jews were represented by the 1640s at the latest, while Lutherans would be found here as early as the 1630s.

What's more, the fabric did in fact contain bold colors other than British red, as there was more than one colonizing country along the Eastern seaboard. Swedes penetrated the future Delaware, building Fort Christina (the future Wilmington—loyally named after their current monarch) in 1638, holding power there and along the adjacent rivers until 1655. The Dutch ejected them from that region and nearby settlements in New Jersey in 1655, leaving behind an architectural legacy in the form of the New World's first log cabins.

The Dutch remained the main players in the Middle Colonies, as well as Manhattan Island, until 1664, when Britons swept the Hollanders. Still, those areas long retained a determinedly non-English flavor, including a splendid, distinctly unusual tolerance for non-Christians. The Dutch also left another legacy to those who would follow: they had become accustomed to trading in the Native American monetary medium called wampum, to which they were introducing their English neighbors by the end of the 1620s.

By the mid-1600s, the British and their competitors were moving into new places ranging from Maine to Virginia. Settlers looking for economic opportunity and political liberty were advancing along the Connecticut River by the early and middle 1630s. Other pioneers in search of religious toleration were settling that smallest and quirkiest of British colonies, Rhode Island, just a few years later.

South of Virginia, colonization generally came later. South Carolina was set up as a proprietary colony, an arrangement tending to result in closer ties with the mother country than was usually the case elsewhere. North Carolina, home of the first and failed English colonial experiment at Roanoke in the

1580s, was one of the last places to be settled. The combination of coastal swamps and hostile Native Americans would long act to deter full European colonization of this area, and the European population of North Carolina would long remain modest.

English Catholics, under the protection of King Charles, colonized the region that would become Maryland. Here, they bargain with Native Americans.

That left Pennsylvania and Georgia. Both were "planned" settlements; unlike many other places, these two areas of British colonization were deliberately organized and selected, and they were brought into existence from a mixture of public and private goals. Pennsylvania was intended in part as a home for adherents of another non-Anglican religious sect facing difficulties at home, the Society of Friends (or Quakers). Though the Swedes and Dutch were there first, the pious Quakers had the better of the argument: in 1681, William Penn (to whose father King Charles II of England owed a good deal of money) accepted a royal grant to a vast new domain. This area was named after him—Pennsylvania, or "Penn's Woods."

The motives for founding Georgia were no less laudable. Led by James Oglethorpe, a number of British philanthropists were interested in establishing a haven where debtors might go to get a second chance in life. They shared their aspirations with the British government, which was interested in setting up a buffer zone between its established colonies to the north and Spanish Florida to the south. The goals of both groups coalesced in the founding of Savannah in 1733.

CHALLENGES—AND INNOVATIONS—FOR NEW ENGLAND

By the early years of the 18th century, British colonization had been underway for five generations. What had resulted was not one single, uninterrupted stretch of British red from Maine to Georgia, but a number of nuclei of varying sizes and fortunes, rather like beads on a string—with large spaces between one bead and another.

Despite extensive searching, these colonizers found no gold, no silver, and precious little copper. Indeed, nothing much would be found for more than 200 years. No metal meant no local coins. Combined with two other factors, this metallic dearth would ensure that the monetary development of the future United States could not and would not proceed on a "normal" and preferred path.

The European contribution to the monetary problem was a politico-economic theory of national wealth and power called *mercantilism*. Simply stated, mercantilism viewed a colony and its mother country in a fixed, monopolistic trading relationship, in which almost everything of value found in the ground or grown on the land was sent home. Furthermore, anything needed by the colonists that they could not produce themselves had to be sent from the mother country and paid for in the currency of the mother country. In other words, any coins that the colonies managed to accumulate should be remitted to the metropolis in payment for goods received under the closed economic arrangement.

If we apply the theory of mercantilism to the metal-poor British colonies along the Atlantic coast, logic tells us that the British government would hardly make an effort to export coinage to these shores when it was seeking to extract wealth from them. Furthermore, because trading was legally circumscribed, logic also suggests that the British colonies would remain coin-poor if the British metropolis remained true to the mercantilist idea. And this, of course, it did: hadn't mercantilism enriched the Spanish and the Portuguese?

The American contribution to the monetary crisis was a failure to satisfy the two conditions absolutely necessary for the functioning of a cashless economy: limited trading and a stable population. Had these two conditions been in force, all might have been well—but they weren't.

Almost from the beginning, these British colonies were economic and demographic successes, so that the monetary supply never had a chance of catching up with, much less surpassing, the monetary demand. Far from easily sending coinage back to Britain, people here could have used every spare piece of change that Britain could send. Along with the shortage of native precious metals, this inability of supply to ever meet demand would shape the story of American numismatics for a quarter of a millennium. It was even more important than the influence of mercantilism, as it continued to mold America's money long after the British and their theory had departed its shores.

Faced with perpetual lack and growing need, confronted with the very results of their success, the men and women of New England and the other colonies would replicate, create, try, reject, and redesign every monetary form ever invented anywhere else throughout the entire story of numismatics.

AMERICAN SOLUTIONS TO AMERICAN PROBLEMS

Their first investigations involved barter: if you don't have something, trade something else to get it. While theory tells us that anything can be swapped for anything else, logic tells us that some commodities have a better chance than others of becoming trading goods. The criteria mentioned earlier (durability, utility, scarcity, etc.) held true for the first colonists as they did for the Native Americans who witnessed their arrival.

The Europeans' list of preferred items included shot and powder, which were obviously useful in their new circumstances. It also contained nails, which may seem odd until we stop to think about it. Nails were obviously easily quantifiable, they were durable, they had utility, and they were very scarce in the beginning days of European settlement because they had to be imported from the old country. As such, nails were traded against British currency—a hundred of one size equal to six pence, a hundred of a larger size equal to ten pence, and so forth.

Other trade goods had a more direct connection with the land. In 1612 John Rolfe (who is perhaps better known as the husband of Pocahontas) saved the starving Virginia colony by putting in his first crop of tobacco, which could be traded for necessary supplies. The plant had come to Europe by the beginning of the 1560s, and by the late 1500s and early 1600s it was set to become Europe's latest craze. Consequently, Virginia's first legislature granted tobacco a monetary status in 1619, fixing its value at three shillings per pound for the best grade, half that for the lower grade.

Over the years, though, that high value descended precipitously. Bear in mind two of the primary conditions for the suitability of a commodity as money: it must be kept in short supply, and it must be durable. Tobacco proved to have neither property, as many residents of the Virginia colony soon began growing their own and thereby flooded the market. Also, the product itself was very susceptible to drying out or rotting. That, in turn, led to the development of "tobacco notes"—paper certificates issued against the value of the crop—which hinted at the direction American money would finally take.

Like the cultivation of tobacco, the trapping of wild animals for their pelts was adopted from Native Americans, and this would give colonists another form of commodity money—or rather several forms. While beaver was always the most popular pelt, and was the yardstick against which other pelts (and other goods, ranging from yards of cloth to thread, hats, shirts, and axes) were measured, otter skins were also popular, as were those of foxes and other animals. Furs were more popular in frontier areas than elsewhere, but their usage finally extended from the Atlantic to the Pacific, matching and anticipating the march of European settlement itself.

One more commodity traded in the British colonies was the aforementioned wampum. Among the new arrivals to what would become the United States, the Dutch appear to have taken it up first: they would have obtained it from tribes on Long Island, a major center of wampum production for many years. In 1627 they carried it to Plymouth Colony, from whence it spread across New England and eventually to the South, where it was known as "roanoke."

Wampum was fixed in value to the English penny. It held its relative worth for several decades—but ultimately fell victim to market forces and trickery.

As the incoming colonists happily embraced the medium as another partial solution to their chronic lack of cash, the established tribes began viewing it with increased favor as well, in part because their new neighbors seemed to take it so seriously. The growing popularity of this exchange medium led to two results that we might have anticipated: Wampum was overproduced, and it was adulterated.

When first introduced among European Americans, wampum was tariffed at so many beads to one English penny, in much the same manner as tobacco or nails. These fixed valuations began fraying in the late 1650s, however, as Native Americans—and enterprising Europeans as well—expanded production. Inevitably, wampum's value descended, and the last official use of the medium among Europeans appears to have taken place in the early 1690s. By then other monetary expedients were being pressed into service.

The counterfeiting of wampum, meanwhile, was achieved in Europe by the middle years of the 17th century and was sent to the New World along with other trading goods. A family of immigrants named Campbell began producing ceramic wampum later in the colonial period, and their operation continued until the closing years of the 19th century—which must represent a record of sorts for counterfeit money! Finally, other settlers discovered that the lower-valued white beads could be dyed to look like the more valuable purple variety; native tribes rarely fell for the adulteration, but it did gull the newcomers often enough.

EARLY AMERICAN COINAGE: MASSACHUSETTS

That grown men were playing childish tricks on each other suggests the monetary desperation in which they found themselves. Pelts, nails, tobacco, and wampum of varying plausibility—all would have been gladly cast aside at the sight of a coin. But no metal for such a coin existed. Even if it had, it would have to have been remitted to England, not retained in America. But one spot in the new lands was about to find a way around both limitations. That place was the town of Boston, and what Boston did must not only rank as a benchmark in the story of numismatics, but in that of the human spirit as well.

In 1652 the colonists of Massachusetts Bay began producing crude coins bearing a fancy NE (for "New England") on the obverse and the Roman numerals III, VI, or XII (for three, six, or twelve pence) on the reverse. They received the silver from illegal trade with the sugar islands of the Caribbean. The good people of Boston sent down rum, timber, and grain, and the good people of the Antilles sent back sugar and coins, mostly pieces of eight. These coins should have been sent on to England, but many of them were retained in Massachusetts, especially if they were lightweight or of poor silver quality (and, in fact, the mint at Potosí was then in the midst of a major scandal, corruptible minters having adulterated the silver coinage there).

In order to make the new coins unattractive to Britons and thereby keep them in circulation in the New World, local coiners deliberately made their new coins lightweight (compared to their British counterparts), while still expressing their denominations in British currency. This way, no London merchant would touch the coins (for he would have to go to the trouble of melting them down and selling them as bullion), but a Boston merchant would embrace them, for they would form part of a closed monetary system based on the familiar coins of the mother country.

Boston silversmith John Hull and his partner Robert Saunderson minted these coins between June and October 1652. Minting was stopped when it was realized that the tiny devices were easy targets for the clipper and the forger. The NE coins were soon followed by pieces of a more elaborate design, named after the type of tree occupying the central space on their obverses.

We call the earliest of these tree series "Willow Tree" pieces. They were made in tiny numbers between 1654 and 1660, double- and triple-struck, very rarely showing all of the designs on either side. They were followed by Oak Tree shillings and subdivisions (including a tiny twopence), and the Pine

Tree coins. The Pine Tree shilling is perhaps the most readily available of our early colonial issues; it is also among the most famous of all American coins and will repay a closer look.

On the obverse stands a pine tree. This tree may be an oblique reference to one of New England's few truly valuable exports at the time: timber for masts for the Royal Navy. Around the tree is the name of the colony, rendered as MASATHVSETS, a spelling that supposedly mimicked the sound of the original Native American name for the region. On the reverse, the remainder of the mint name is spelled out, along with the denomination XII, for twelve pence or one shilling, and the date.

It is this date that adds the final element of ingenuity to the Massachusetts silver coinage. With one exception, it is always rendered as 1652 (the exception is the Oak Tree twopence, dated 1662). This was the case for one of two reasons. First, the mint was founded in 1652. However, the second possibility is far more likely: the coins were deliberately and consistently dated 1652 to evade English law.

Under that law, the king enjoyed sole right of coinage. But in 1652, there was no king: Royal Charles's head had been separated from his body some three years earlier, and Cromwell's Commonwealth of England ruled in royalty's place. Surely regicides would scarcely look askance at a Massachusetts coinage.

In 1660 the English monarchy was restored, and there was an even greater reason to retain the old date on the coinage, as an issue dated 1652 could pass for an old coin struck when there was no king. As it turns out, King Charles had more important matters on his mind anyway, and he left the upstart coinage alone for the first two decades of his reign. During those years, the Oak Tree pieces were struck (down to 1667), as well as two issues of Pine Tree coins (between 1667 and 1674, and 1675 and 1682).

From top: Massachusetts Willow Tree shilling, Oak Tree shilling, and Pine Tree shilling.

Hull and Saunderson's contract with the Massachusetts General Court expired in 1682, and there seems to have been no talk about a renewal of the agreement. The tiny mint appears to have been working full bore for the last two years of its existence, as colonial authorities began receiving indications that the Crown was finally about to resume its prerogatives; they accordingly hurried their local coiners along. London did reassert its monopoly over the coinage, and soon enough Sir Edmund Andros was appointed as the new governor of a centralized, dictatorial administration embracing all of New England. Andros had instructions to bring the region to heel; they may have included a forced resumption of barter.

OTHER EARLY AMERICAN COINAGE

While Massachusetts was producing its own coinage, others were coping as best they could. Maryland had coinage produced *for* it; the Catholic noblemen who founded the colony wished to provide convenient money for their co-religionists, and Cecil Calvert, second Lord Baltimore, had been granted the right to coin.

Although none of it is dated, we know that this issue was minted during the winter of 1658–1659, but we have no idea by whom it was struck. It is commonly suggested that these coins were made at the Tower of London, but the members of the series—silver shillings, sixpence, fourpence or "groats," threepence, and a "denarium" or copper penny, of which fewer than ten are known—are well struck and far superior to most British coinage of the period.

The possible connection to the Tower Mint is even less plausible, as Calvert was not convicted of a crime when arrested and questioned in a London court about his coinage. For these reasons and others, Richard Doty, senior curator of numismatics for the Smithsonian Institution, suggested Ireland as a possible site for the Calvert mint: "The fabric of these pieces does not suggest the Tower Mint to me, and a Catholic island would have been a logical and sympathetic place to coin for a Catholic nobleman."

Interestingly, Ireland is linked to a second series circulating in the early colonies, although that link is anything but direct. A Quaker named Mark Newbie (or Newby) led a number of the faithful to settle in the vicinity of the modern city of Camden, New Jersey, and brought with him a cask containing £30 worth of coppers to distribute. These pieces—farthings and halfpennies—are named after him ("Newbie coppers"); they are alternately known as St. Patrick coppers, for that saint adorns their reverses. And that brings us back to Ireland.

The coppers weren't struck there—they had an English origin—but they *were* coined for Irish consumption. They were originally intended to pay Charles I's Catholic troops, who were engaged in fighting Cromwell's people in the Ulster Rebellion. The pieces are believed to have been made in Dublin circa 1663 to 1672, and were finally demonetized by the end of the 1670s. That was when Newbie came across these pieces and gave them a new lease on life.

The St. Patrick coinage's attractive appearance is augmented by a bit of yellow metal (brass, meant to resemble gold), splashed onto the copper during the minting process and positioned so that the king would appear to be receiving a golden crown. This care suggests a limited mintage, a suggestion belied by the known number of die combinations—more than 120 for the farthings alone. They may have been created by Nicholas Briot, using the roller method, but we know far less about these pieces than we would like.

The designs of the so-called St. Patrick coppers were similar for both the farthing- and halfpenny-sized coins. On the halfpenny, the saint is shown blessing the faithful, with the legend ECCE GREX—"Behold the Flock."

The same may be said for a curious issue featuring an elephant on its obverse, intended for British settlement in the Carolinas. We know that much because the reverse of this copper halfpenny token says GOD: PRESERVE: CAROLINA: AND THE: LORDS: PROPRIETORS. It is clearly related to another, much rarer issue with a reference to the northern colonies, whose reverse inscription reads GOD: PRESERVE: NEW: ENGLAND. Both pieces are dated 1694, and both pieces are connected to a third—which is where our mystery begins.

This third token has the arms of London, along with the legend GOD: PRESERVE: LONDON, but no date. Many believe this coin was struck prior to the others, the reverse legend perhaps referring to the plague and Great Fire besetting the English capital in 1665–1666. Others believe that the London token was struck at the same time as the two others, in the mid-1690s, although they are unable to explain the legend.

As for the elephant, it has been suggested the beast was put on the obverse by order of the Royal African Company, which had gotten the copper for the issue from West Africa. Consider, also, that golden guineas from the reign of Charles II and his immediate successors bore a tiny elephant to suggest the origins of the metal they contained.

We know a bit more about one last piece, a fleeting reminder of the attempt by James II to achieve control over the inhabitants of British North America. The issue would be made from tin—a most unstable coining material if used alone, but a sop to the miners of tin-rich Cornwall—and bear an equestrian portrait of the king. They were shipped across the Atlantic, but in the inhospitable climate of the New World, they deteriorated rapidly. Today an unblemished piece is a major rarity. We know why these pieces were made, under whose franchise (Richard Holt's, granted by the king), who designed them (the artist John Croker), and where they were struck (at the Royal Mint, in the Tower of London), but we are somewhat confused as to their denomination. The pieces bear the legend VAL. 24. PART. REAL. (value 1/24-real), suggesting they were to be tied to a Spanish or Spanish-American monetary system rather than a British or British-American one. But this denomination cannot be equated with anything in common use in Spain, Great Britain, or their colonies. Pieces of a similar size were struck at the Tower by James II and circulated as halfpence, and generations of collectors have assumed that these American coins had the same value, regardless of denomination. But it *would* be satisfying to know what James and his coiners had intended.

PAPER MONEY ON THE AMERICAN SCENE

With James's successors, the story of America's money would take an essential new path, one it would follow for the next two centuries. The new monarchs, King William III and Queen Mary, promptly became involved in a war with the French in Canada. This struggle for control of North America would persist through most of the ensuing three-quarters of a century, and it would eventually leave the English victorious, even as the seeds were being planted for their most resounding defeat.

For us, the essential fact is this: English colonists were expected to do their bit for a war effort that was being waged at least partly for their benefit. The first time they were asked to contribute was in 1690, when Massachusetts was asked to pay expenses for a military action by the British against the French in Canada. The request put the colony in a quandary, for there was a scarcity of cash with which to meet it.

Someone in the colonial government hit upon an interesting idea: why not issue official paper certificates to hire the troops and purchase the supplies? This scheme would work because the colony and its citizens knew that they would be reimbursed by the Crown at the end of the war. But because that was the case, the scheme was carried forward another crucial step: because reimbursement had been promised and everyone knew it, and because the paper would therefore circulate as readily as coinage, why not leave it in circulation rather than redeem it at the end of the war, in the process augmenting cash in a cash-strapped economy?

It was done. In 1690 and 1691, two issues with an aggregate face value of £40,000 were printed and circulated. The notes were receivable by the colonial treasurer in payment of taxes at a 5 percent premium, which was another way of ensuring their popularity and use. The paper-money practice soon spread elsewhere, and a new chapter in the global story of numismatics was under way.

The next half-century would see numerous notable developments in paper money, from the public note-issuing bank to engraving, typesetting, and Benjamin Franklin's nature prints.

A SNAPSHOT AT MID-CENTURY: 1750

The year 1750 is a good time to pause for a moment, to review the nature of America's money during the best years of the colonial period. Paper had come to lie at its heart. By that year, 12 of the 13 colonies either had issued paper or were currently doing so, and the 13th, Virginia, would join the parade in 1755. An amazing amount of bartering still occurred as well, and not all of it in the backcountry. However, as this volume is concerned primarily with coins, that is where we will focus.

SUPPLIES FROM THE MOTHERLAND

Great Britain occasionally sent over coins as payment for American participation in its ongoing saga with the French. A large number of halfpennies and farthings arrived on these shores in that very manner in 1749, part of a remittance to Massachusetts for the colony's expedition to capture Cape Breton from the French. Much of the rest of the remittance was made up of silver coin, which likely flowed back to England in short order; but the coppers did stay in America.

The colonists also used coins struck in England but without official British designs. For example, William Wood was contracted by King George I to produce two issues—one for use in Ireland and one for use in the colonies, both of which eventually came to circulate in the latter. The Irish coins featured a seated figure of Hibernia, the American coins a splendid open rose; their common obverse was a right-facing portrait of the king. They were well struck in a handsome alloy invented by Wood, one he called "Bath metal," consisting of three-quarters copper, slightly less than one-quarter zinc, and a tiny amount of silver—though not nearly enough to make the coins struck from it circulate at their stipulated value.

William Wood's Rosa Americana design declared the American Rose to be UTILE DULCI—"Useful and Pleasant." Despite the sweet words, his shortweight coins were a flop.

After the Irish pieces were violently rejected by their intended users out of a combination of outraged nationalism and anger over their short weight, some of the "Hibernia" pieces were later foisted on the colonies, where they met with a somewhat better reception than did Wood's coins specifically struck for American consumption.

Those pieces—issued in twopenny, penny, and halfpenny denominations and known as the "Rosa Americana" coinage—were less than half the weight they theoretically should have been. But more to the point, the Crown had not bothered to consult local assemblies before shipping the coins to New England and New York. Colonials refused to accept them, and the Massachusetts legislature issued emergency parchment money for one penny, twopence, and threepence even *before* Wood's coinage arrived. As a result, the Rosa Americana coinage was never effectively put into circulation in the North (although it did enter commerce in the South somewhat later), and its poor reception persuaded Wood to suspend production early in 1724.

OTHER EXTRANATIONAL ALTERNATIVES

British mints were not the only source of coins used in the British colonies. Regardless of theory and legality, reality found Americans trading all over the world, bringing back foreign coinage as they did so. Provided the coinage was of good gold or silver, it circulated in the colonies by weight, and elaborate tables were prepared and published that enabled businessmen to calculate what a certain coin should weigh and how much it was worth against another.

Thus, pieces from silver French écus to Turkish golden zeri mahbubs were traded. That being said, Americans did come to prefer one issue in particular over others (including anything British): this was the piece of eight. By now, they knew it as the "Mexican dollar" (because most of those coming their way originated at the busy mint at Mexico City) or the "Spanish milled dollar" (because Spain had introduced coining machinery to the Americas by this time, using it to strike the piece of eight). The coins that were struck, and which Americans used, were now indistinguishable from other 18th-century issues, save for one thing: their marvelous, evocative designs.

The obverse of the new piece of eight featured a splendid baroque crowned shield, along with the name and titles of the king of Spain, but it is the reverse that claims our attention. There, the Pillars of Hercules—which had been appearing on Spanish-American coins since the 1530s, a proclamation of the New World origins of the silver they contained—are wrapped by ribbons. It has been suggested that the dollar sign ($) was inspired by the right-hand ribbon.

Here and there, people were beginning to reckon their money in terms of Mexican dollars instead of English sterling. We should not be surprised; the American colonists had been using the piece of eight since the very beginning, and they were now more familiar with it than with several members of the British system, including that nation's closest equivalent, the crown. We know of the change from one system to another by the fact that various colonies begin printing paper

Did the American dollar sign ($) come from the reverse of the Spanish-American piece of eight? Notice the column at the right on this 1732 coin of King Philip V, struck in Mexico City.

money denominated in dollars rather than pounds. Massachusetts led the way in 1750, its notes backed by a deposit of pieces of eight it had recently received. Other colonies would eventually follow, in part because the denomination would soon have a new appeal—that of nationalism.

DOMESTIC EFFORTS

In addition to foreign coins, paper money, and "country pay" or barter, there were several issues of domestic coins: one in Virginia, another in Connecticut, and a third in Pennsylvania. The Virginia issue is known from precisely two examples, brass shilling tokens from the town of Gloucester, dated 1714. We know nothing about the reasons for the issue, beyond the fact that it seems to have been the idea of two local landowners, Christopher Righault and Samuel Dawson.

We know a bit more about the second issue, from Granby, Connecticut. In 1737 an enterprising owner of a copper mine in the region named Samuel Higley issued tokens denominated THE VALUE OF THREE PENCE. When his neighbors complained that his tokens were overvalued, he changed his obverse legend to VALUE ME AS YOU PLEASE, but still retained the III for three pence!

Samuel's brother John took over the mint upon the death of the former, striking undated pieces and a few more dated 1739. We have no idea of the original extent of the Higley issues, but eight obverse dies and five reverses are known. Because most show no signs of breakage, the mint's output could have been fairly extensive. Yet its tokens remain excessively rare today, for Higley's copper was so pure that it was frequently recycled into other uses.

The Pennsylvania issue came about in 1766, a product of the furor over the Stamp Act. James Smithers, a British gunsmith who had just immigrated to Philadelphia, poured all of the frustration felt by the colonials into his "halfpennies" and "farthings," pieces that may have begun as commemorative medalets but which ended up as part of the monetary supply. The portrait on the obverse is of William Pitt the Elder, one of the voices of reason on the British side during the Stamp

This William Pitt halfpenny token refers to the British politician's efforts to have the hated Stamp Act repealed: NO STAMPS.

Act crisis. His more famous son would eventually become prime minister in the 1780s, just in time to deal with an infant United States, created in part by those very policies of coercion that his father had deplored.

Added to these American tokens was an import, one that began with one message and ended with another. In 1760 an Irish buttonmaker named Roche struck halfpenny- and farthing-size copper tokens with the words VOCE POPULI surrounding the head on the obverse, and the word HIBERNIA surrounding a representation of Ireland on the reverse. He probably intended the obverse to remind Dubliners of the deposed Catholic Stuart regime or the virtues of home rule, for the portrait has been identified with the two Jacobite pretenders, while the legend surrounding it is Latin for "By the Voice of the People." But Roche's tokens were eventually shipped to America in large numbers, and colonists there embraced them because their obverse sentiment now seemed an appropriate commemoration of their own struggles against Mad King George.

Regardless of such odds and ends, the primary circulating medium in America was now paper money. Americans had used it to pay for wars on behalf of England; they were about to use it to fight a war *against* England. And when they did so, that previously trustworthy medium would betray their confidence.

THE WAR OF INDEPENDENCE AND ITS AFTERMATH

Of all of the world's wars for national sovereignty, that which created the United States of America is among the most confusing and complex. It has been said that a third of the American people were ardent patriots, another third remained loyal to the mother country, and the final third had no opinion but scrambled to get out of the way of the other two. This observation oversimplifies matters, but there is a grain of truth to it.

The war was generally more popular in New England than it was in the South—but the new nation's greatest general was a Virginian. And the war was fought to free a people. But which one? Certainly not Native Americans. Certainly not African-Americans. And certainly not women—although they might partake of the banquet as guests of their husbands and do the washing-up. Indeed, this was a most confusing war.

We do not even know when the complaining—the perennial practice and right of any colonial people—reached a point that might finally yield a bid for independence. We think it began to accelerate after the final victory against the French in 1763, when Britons and Americans fell to quarreling over the spoils of the war. In this way of thinking, the opening salvo was the Proclamation Act of 1763, wherein King George III drew a line from one end of the Appalachian chain to the other and forbade settlers to cross it. Americans were angered, but the crisis over the Sugar Act in 1764 and the much greater furor over the Stamp Act in 1765—both of which were seen by Britons as revenue-raising measures, and by Americans as intolerable affronts—kept the pot at a boil.

Still, all this doesn't tell us when, or why, the mutual estrangement began. It is obvious this falling-out had deep roots indeed, going back to when the first colonists left one world for another. The earliest settlers found that English habits and customs did not always work in an American setting; they discovered that makeshift, local expedients might actually serve better than orthodox, imported ones, and were branded hayseeds and hicks by their English cousins for doing so.

Through our numismatic examinations, we have already seen the slow process by which transplanted Englishmen were becoming Americans. We have seen it with the Pine Tree shilling, and we have especially seen it with paper money. Give the people who devised such clever monetary schemes a century and a half to evolve in new directions, and there was virtually no chance that they would *not* strike out on their own at one point or another.

But they would still do so with mixed feelings when that time finally came. The estrangement reached its flashpoint in the spring of 1775, when royalist governor Thomas Gage of Massachusetts sent British regulars to Concord to seize military supplies stored there by Americans. Alerted by Paul Revere and William Dawes, Americans assembled on the morning of April 19 on Lexington Green and fired the "shot heard round the world." Not all of their fellow colonists agreed with their stance, nor did all Britons agree with the response of the Redcoats who opposed them. On both sides of the Atlantic, war fever would take some time to build up, clarify, and capture the popular imagination. And it would never monopolize thinking in either place.

FINANCING THE WAR OF INDEPENDENCE

While military aid might in time be forthcoming from Britain's enemies, France and Spain—and golden onzas and silvery écus might come to America along with the soldiers and arms—the insurgents would first have to prove that their unaided cause was a going concern and that they had a chance of defeating England (or were at least capable of holding on until that country gave way). This caution on the part of Britain's former and potential enemies meant that American money would have to pay for an American war, and the form that money would take must be paper, for there was really no other possibility. After all, hadn't that same approach worked during the conflict between the English and the French in Canada?

What Americans failed to realize was that paper money had worked during earlier campaigns because Great Britain had directly or indirectly stood behind the currency being issued. The mother country was scarcely likely to do so in this case unless Americans succeeded in invading, defeating, and occupying it, and extracting such payment by force. Not even the most ardent patriot could have expected this scenario to take place.

Another reason why paper money had worked was that earlier American participation in wars had been limited and short lived. But this conflict would be different: it would go on year after year, and would involve enemy occupation of many of the most productive portions of the upstart nation, including several of its largest cities.

That being said, the revolutionaries did well enough for the first year or two. They had caught the British by surprise and had soon taken most of New England. But they failed in a bid to bring the blessings of liberty to the remainder of British North America, and despite the urgings of Benjamin Franklin and other leaders, Canada would remain in British hands.

Elsewhere, the tide began to move against them. They lost New York City in 1776, General George Washington being defeated at the Battle of Long Island that August. Sir William Howe took the national capital of Philadelphia a year later. A striking American victory at Saratoga in October 1777 would eventually mean a favorable turning for the war, because it would embolden France and Spain to enter the conflict on America's behalf. But it produced little of concrete benefit just yet, and Washington had his hands full simply keeping his army alive through the winter of 1777–1778 at Valley Forge.

America's money reflected all this. In the spring of 1775, the colonies (or "states," as they soon began calling themselves) began the issue of paper currency to pay for their portions of the fighting. So did a new, ad hoc national government, whose modest, temporary powers would eventually be made law under the Articles of Confederation. This central government issued what it called Continental Currency: Benjamin Franklin's old firm (he had taken on a partner named Hall before selling out entirely, and Hall had engaged a partner of his own named Sellers) printed the notes, which were denominated in terms of Spanish milled dollars.

The Continental Congress also had hopes of issuing a coinage, a symbol of its sovereignty, as a bolster to local morale, and as a backing for Continental Currency. When it came time to print the fifth issue of national paper, the dollar note was deliberately omitted, and was replaced with a Continental

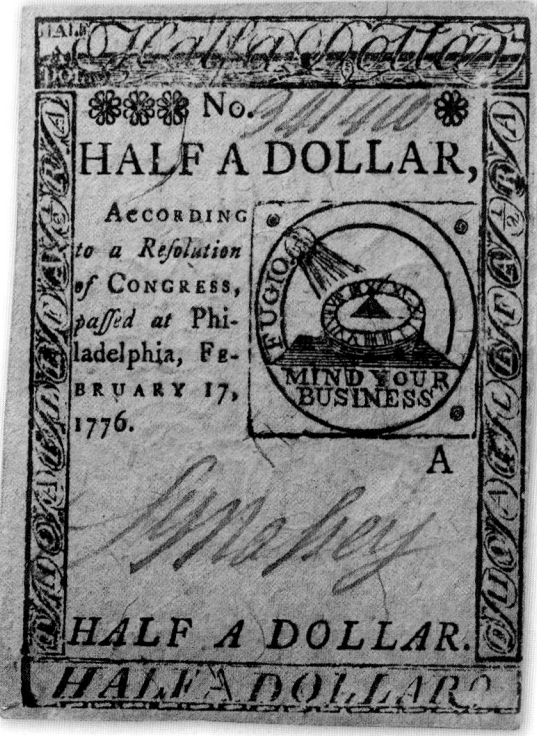

The notes issued by the Continental Congress were denominated in Spanish dollars.

dollar coin, struck from silver provided by the French. Elisha Gallaudet prepared dies for the new issue. He used the motifs—the sundial and the linked rings—from his earlier fractional paper currency.

The national government had no mint at this time, so Gallaudet set up his own facility, either in his hometown of Freehold, New Jersey, or in nearby Philadelphia. He made a few patterns in silver, a few more in brass, and more still in pewter. The latter alloy looked enough like silver to give a good idea of the appearance of the future coinage, but was at the same time soft enough not to damage his dies. Then the project ground to a halt. No French silver was forthcoming, and it soon became impractical to issue a dollar coin in any metal.

Some final observations about Continental Currency may be made. This money was issued from a number of places, reflecting the shifting fortunes of the patriot cause. While the first and last series were from Philadelphia—the original site of the national government—one in 1777 was circulated from Baltimore, while another in 1778 came from York, Pennsylvania—places to which the government had been forced to flee ahead of British troops. The York issue is particularly interesting, because it leads us to a major problem with Continental Currency: it was extensively counterfeited. It was forged by Americans, and there was nothing particularly new about that. But it was also forged by Britons; that *was* new, and contributed to the currency's problems.

THE DECLINE OF AMERICA'S NEW CURRENCY

If we assume that, at the time of the first issue of federal and state paper in the spring of 1775, $1.00 in national or, for example, Maryland-issued paper could purchase one Mexican piece of eight, we see matters as they were for the first 20 months of the war. By the beginning of 1777, Continental Currency was still standing firm, but that of several states was slipping: it then took $1.50 in Maryland notes to purchase that same Mexican dollar.

The autumn of that same year was the crucial point: in October, issues of the states ranged from a ratio of 1.09:1 to 3:1, and the value of Continental Currency had descended as well, down to 1.10:1. This was worrisome, but hardly fatal if it stopped there.

But it did not stop there. By March 1779, even though French and Spanish aid was coming in, state and federal currency alike had slipped to around 10:1 against the piece of eight. By then, the Continental Congress was printing the new, safer, bicolor notes, but it was increasingly unable to persuade anyone to accept them, other than the soldiers who received them as pay. The states had no better luck with their issues, and paper continued to slide. By April 1780, the ratio of Continental Currency to the Spanish dollar was 40:1, and the national government had decided not to issue any more. This was just as well, because by that time, it had circulated nearly a quarter-billion dollars' worth of paper. The states that continued to print money (and most did; what other choice had they?) saw its real value fall to a hundredth, and finally a thousandth, of its stated specie value. By then, they had printed as much money as the federal government, meaning that there was enough paper in circulation to purchase every house, factory, and farm in the new republic several times over—if there were anyone foolish enough to take this currency seriously.

So great was this problem that Congress and the states finally decided to do something about it. By a resolution passed on March 18, 1780, a new issue of paper was authorized, but it was one with a difference. This issue would consist of bills circulated by the states, exchangeable for Continental Currency at 40 to 1, the same value ratio that Continental notes now had against the Mexican dollar. The states of Maryland, Massachusetts, New Hampshire, New Jersey, New York, Pennsylvania, Rhode Island, and Virginia participated in the plan; the other states were either unwilling or unable to do so, or they were still occupied by British troops. In this way, more than $111,000,000 in Continental Currency was removed from circulation; a goodly amount of state paper was also lured in by the same law and destroyed.

In time, much of the remaining federal and state paper of the Revolutionary era was presented and redeemed for federal bonds under the funding plans of Alexander Hamilton and other Federalists. Some of the state issues stayed in circulation for some years, rendering continued (if suspect) service on the local economic scene. Other notes made their way into cupboards and jars, awaiting a redemption that never took place. And a new phrase entered into American English usage: "not worth a Continental," meaning worthless and useless. Americans had been badly mauled by their previously trustworthy exchange medium, and on the national level at least they would not soon forget the experience.

The Americans' war would eventually end, despite the collapse of the medium they had chosen to pay for it. Hoping to reverse the trend symbolized by the surrender of Philadelphia and the loss of the West, Great Britain had struck south, capturing the capitals of Georgia and South Carolina. Troops under Lord Cornwallis then swung north, hoping to roll up the American war effort before France and Spain could make a difference. Eventually, a siege resulted at Yorktown, and when Cornwallis surrendered his forces on October 19, 1781, the war was effectively over—although it would take two years of the canniest American diplomatic efforts to negotiate the peace, with the Treaty of Paris of 1783.

New Coins During a Critical Transition

After Yorktown, Americans were granted an opportunity they had never had before and would never have again. They had defeated an enemy and were therefore free to reject its monetary system as well. Additionally, because their own, makeshift monetary system had buckled, they were enabled and forced to reject it, too. What would they seek to erect in the places of these failed and rejected precursors? Would it work any better?

Americans kept some kinds of paper money, but not all. The states could and did issue such paper (normally expressed in dollar denominations, though not always) because they were sovereign entities. The large amounts of Spanish pieces of eight and French écus that had come in during the final stages of the war enabled states to back some of their notes with promises of specie payment—although this hard money soon left their treasuries and the states continued to print.

Several of the states also espoused a coinage of sorts. The only one to set up its own mint was Massachusetts. It had made a previous attempt to coin back in 1776, as had its neighbor New Hampshire, but the urgent demands of war and a shortage of copper had stopped both projects in the very beginning of the pattern stage. Now Massachusetts made a second, more successful attempt, and its coppers (which contained a generous amount of that metal) made numismatic history: they were the first American coins to bear the denominations CENT and HALF CENT.

The mint that struck the Massachusetts half cents and cents was shut down in early 1789, in compliance with the newly ratified Constitution—and because each coin cost more to produce than its face value.

Other states allowed private mints to produce their coinage, resulting in generally lighter pieces and less artistic imagery. Between late 1785 and early 1789, several firms in Connecticut struck more than 340 varieties of halfpenny-size coppers. New York never got around to formally authorizing coinage, but a number of private mints would create money for it anyway. Their designs sometimes resembled English halfpennies, and sometimes incorporated elements from the state's coat of arms. New Jersey also contracted for its money, and the result was a copious coinage, struck at Rahway Mills, Elizabethtown, Morristown, New York City, and possibly on Staten Island. These coins—dated 1786, 1787, and 1788, but likely struck into 1789 and deliberately back-dated—are also of historical significance, as they were the first circulating American coins to bear the national shield (seen on many later federal issues) and the motto E PLURIBUS UNUM (seen on virtually all later federal issues).

None of the other states circulated its own coinage, although one of them, Virginia, saw the circulation of copper halfpence it had ordered in the final days of the colonial period. Virginia's royal charter of 1609 had given it the right to mint its own coins—the only one of the 13 colonies to enjoy this privilege. It had never set up its own mint due to lack of metal, but its Assembly authorized the Tower Mint to strike a copper coinage for it in May 1773. Some five tons' worth of coins were accordingly prepared and sent across the Atlantic.

By the time they arrived in Virginia, the first acts of the American Revolution were taking place. Thus, most of those Virginia halfpennies that had gotten into trade were soon pulled out, and hoarded for the duration of the war. After Yorktown, however, many did go into trade, where they passed from hand to hand in company with counterfeit and genuine British and Irish halfpence and the sponsored and unsponsored issues of several states—and of an adjacent, independent country: Vermont.

THE UNION GROWS

One of the last areas to be colonized, the Vermont Republic had sided with the Revolution, but it had also become involved in an acrimonious land dispute with its giant neighbor, New York. Until that dispute was settled, it would remain resolutely out of the Union. During that time, the country produced both notes and coins.

Reuben Harmon Jr. was chosen by the Vermont legislature to strike its copper coinage. His diemaker, William Coley of New York, incorporated the idea of the 14th entity into the reverse design of his coppers: here was an all-seeing eye (adapted from a contemporaneous British import, the Nova Constellatio copper), surrounded by 13 stars. The 14th star would be Vermont, and the region's aspirations of becoming a part of the new United States—as soon as those annoying New Yorkers saw matters its way—formed the basis of the reverse legend: STELLA. QUARTA. DECIMA., "The Fourteenth Star."

This reverse was close enough to those on the well-known Nova Constellatio coppers to encourage acceptance, but the landscape obverse Coley chose (or had chosen for him by the lawmakers) met with local resistance. As such, the design was changed, and Harmon and other coiners struck coppers until mid-1789 with a male head on the obverse and a seated female on the reverse.

Thus far, we have been talking mostly about copper coins, and with good reason: the great majority of coinages proposed and circulated during those years *were* copper—in part because of a scarcity of silver and gold. But there was one silver issue that managed to get into circulation, as well as one gold coin.

The circulating issue came from Annapolis, Maryland, and was the product of John Chalmers and Thomas Sparrow, who also engraved Maryland's paper money designs. The most common member of the series was the shilling, whose obverse bears clasped hands, an age-old symbol of amity. Meanwhile the reverse depicts the danger that can follow when friends have a falling-out. Here are two birds squabbling over a worm, oblivious to a serpent ready to attack them at any time. The message is clear enough in the light of current politics: if the states continue to squabble with each other—as they were indeed doing during the period of the Confederation—a greater enemy might destroy them.

Finally, we come to one of the most famous coins in American history, the gold Brasher doubloon. The coin's namesake, Ephraim Brasher of New York, may have struck coppers on a speculative basis. It has been suggested that the Brasher doubloons were patterns for a new copper coinage, struck in gold by way of a *douceur* or bribe to state legislators to secure the contract. If so, the ploy failed, but precisely seven doubloons with one design and an eighth and ninth with another design have survived.

Ephraim Brasher was a New York goldsmith and jeweler. He was also a neighbor and friend of George Washington's. In the late 1780s Brasher struck gold coins about equal in weight to the Spanish doubloon, equivalent to $16. The coins are punched with his initials, EB.

THE RISE OF A NEW CONSTELLATION

In 1783 Robert Morris, superintendent of finance under the Confederation, proposed an ambitious federal coinage. Had it been implemented, it would have meant a completely new direction for American numismatics: it would be fully decimal, with pieces ranging from 5 to 1,000 "units," the latter a silver coin weighing about two-thirds as much as the Mexican dollar. A handful of patterns were struck in Philadelphia, their simple designs featuring an all-seeing eye for the obverse, surrounded by 13 rays and stars, with the legend NOVA CONSTELLATIO, a "New Constellation" in the firmament of nations.

These coins never got beyond the pattern stage because their coiners never secured enough silver for more than a few trial pieces. But they did inspire Morris's assistant, Gouverneur Morris (no relation), to secure another coinage from another source. Gouverneur Morris went to England and partnered with coiner George Wyon to strike undenominated coppers very similar to the ill-fated Philadelphia patterns.

These pieces—dated 1783 and 1785 but apparently struck in 1785 and 1786—found a ready circulation in the United States, for their metal was good and their designs patriotic.

The Nova Constellatio coppers were hardly the only halfpenny-size imports at this time. Thomas Jefferson conceived of a new decimal coinage system based on an old coin, the Spanish or Mexican dollar, to be divided into hundredths. Someone in Congress suggested the name "decad" for the large copper piece that would sit on the bottom rung of the new monetary arrangement.

The name of this coin would eventually be changed to cent, but Thomas Wyon was asked to produce patterns in line with Congress's current idea. What resulted was perhaps the most iconographically loaded coin in early American history—and, ironically, it was struck by an Englishman. On the obverse, the goddess Diana leans against an altar while trampling on a crown. On the altar is a helmet, closely and deliberately resembling a liberty cap. Around her, we see the legend, INIMICA TYRANNIS AMERICANA—"America, Enemy of Tyrants."

There is one more message-bearing copper coin of the period worth mentioning: the "Georgius Triumpho" copper of 1783. The obverse head was probably intended to represent General Washington. The reverse introduces us to the subtleties of the 18th-century mind: a female, presumably representing liberty and independence, is enclosed in a framework with 13 vertical bars, and there are 4 fleurs-de-lis at the corners of the frame. The complete image probably means that American freedom is protected and secured through joint action of the states (the 13 bars), supported on all sides by aid from the French monarchy (the fleurs-de-lis).

Thus, by 1787 the nation's small change was composed of a confusing mixture of state coppers, British and Irish halfpennies, Morris's Nova Constellatio and other British speculative pieces—as well as large numbers of counterfeits manufactured on both sides of the Atlantic. Congress became convinced that a national standard must be issued under its aegis, a full-weight coin of good copper, against which everyone else's issues might be judged.

FLEDGLING ATTEMPTS

Not possessing a mint of its own, Congress had to contract for its money along with everyone else. It picked a Connecticut coiner named James Jarvis to do the work, and it picked the designs—Franklin's old sundial / linked rings concept, seen earlier on fractional notes and the Continental dollar in 1776.

Jarvis had been recommended by his friend Colonel William Duer, to whom he had paid a bribe of $10,000 for the contract. The obliging colonel helped him on his way, giving Jarvis more than 70,000 pounds of federally owned copper with which to begin work. This was a small fraction of what his contract called for, however, and he sailed for Europe in search of more metal.

He failed in his attempt, his somewhat shady reputation making industrialists wary of dealing with him. He finally returned home without his copper.

Meanwhile Jarvis's coining cronies had gotten the federal metal, and they were busily using it to coin lighter-weight Connecticut coppers! To minimize federal suspicion, they did strike some "Fugio" coppers on the federal pattern (their name comes from the obverse legend, the Latin for "I Fly," referring to time on the sundial; they are also known as "Franklin cents"), but fewer than 400,000 pieces were shipped to the treasurer of the United States on May 21, 1788, and Jarvis and his partners fled the country.

Fugio coppers are sometimes called "Franklin cents" because of their legends, attributed to Benjamin Franklin.

Fugio coppers proved unpopular with both the federal government (they were slightly under their legal weight and therefore useless if the federal government were serious about its reform) and with the people (who by this time were unfamiliar with the design). Very few went into circulation, and the government eventually sold what was left of the Fugio coins to a contractor with the unlikely name of Royal Flint.

As it would turn out, Flint was a friend of Colonel Duer's, and so we have come full circle. Flint went bankrupt before he could pay the government and was hauled off to jail. Duer joined him there a few years later; the Fugio story has no heroes.

But it did serve to symbolize what a growing number of people were saying: the government that had sponsored the coins must be strengthened, either reformed or scrapped altogether in favor of a more plausible, dignified, centralized government that would be taken seriously at home and abroad. The current central government could not tax, and it could not keep the peace. It was also incapable of being taken seriously by Europeans, as Britons moved against its newly won territories in the northwest, and Spaniards and others snubbed its diplomats in Europe.

A gathering had been held at Annapolis in September 1786 in the hopes of strengthening the Articles of Confederation. Few states bothered to send delegations, and the meeting broke up without concrete result—except for a promise to hold a second convention in Philadelphia the following spring. Then farmer and Revolutionary War veteran Daniel Shays and his disaffected peers (sinking in debt because they were not paid for their war service) swung into action, terrorizing parts of Massachusetts until dispersed by state militiamen in early 1787.

Shays' Rebellion turned the tide. It sent a shiver of horror through every merchant and creditor in the Republic, for if debtors could revolt in western Massachusetts, they could make trouble anywhere. That spring meeting at Philadelphia would be well attended indeed: out of its deliberations would come a new government, and a new chapter in the story of American numismatics. Most importantly, it would establish for the ages who could make money—and who could not.

"HARD MONEY" AND THE YOUNG REPUBLIC, 1789–1830

The 56 delegates who came to Philadelphia in May 1787 were entrusted with debating and enacting improvements to the Articles of Confederation—most notably, granting the national government the power of direct taxation. The hand of this group of "Federalist" debaters, led by Alexander Hamilton, was first seen in the decision to scrap the old edifice instead of tinkering with it. They wished the new nation to be taken seriously by the other members of the constellation of independent states, and they felt there were no means by which this might be accomplished if the current balance between state and national authority in America were to remain where it was. What's more, the Articles of Confederation, with their weak central control and strong local power (a balance that seemed to be increasingly favoring debtor farmers), were simply bad for business.

Joined to this was a certain snobbery on the part of Alexander Hamilton and many of his fellow delegates. It seemed undeniable that a government of the better sorts of people (or one made up of the rich, the well-born, and the able, in one Federalist's revealing words) was desirable and would be easier to achieve under a new political compact than under the current one. The members of this convention were in basic agreement on what they wanted, and they therefore managed to achieve it in the form of a written document, the Constitution of 1787.

The hands of the propertied delegates were visible throughout the document. States were expressly forbidden to interfere with contracts. The debt of the federal government was expressly recognized, its payment guaranteed. The central government was authorized to put down domestic uprisings. Federal judges were appointed for life, senators would be elected by state legislatures rather than by the people, and the president would receive a relatively long term—four years—and be chosen not by the people, but by an electoral college.

This national conservative trend would continue into the monetary arena. The uncontrolled emission of state and federal paper had threatened ruin to the mercantile classes along the Atlantic seaboard, so when it came time to discuss what sorts of money would be allowed and be created, and by whom, a permanent change was made. The Constitution's framers made their points most explicitly in two clauses of the first section of the new document.

Henceforth, states could not "coin Money; emit Bills of Credit [paper money]; [or] make any Thing but gold and silver Coin a Tender in Payment of Debts" (Article I, Section 10, paragraph 1). From then on, only the national government would have the authority to "coin Money, regulate the Value thereof, and of foreign Coin, and fix the Standard of Weights and Measures" (Article I, Section 8, paragraph 5). The Constitution did not state that the new central government could circulate paper money, and that vagueness was deliberate: Hamilton and his fellow framers were dedicated to the dream of making the United States a "hard money" country (based on specie—gold and silver coins) if this were humanly possible, but they also wanted the escape hatch of federal paper in case of extreme circumstances.

The new basic accord had to be ratified before its shortcomings could become manifest. The delegates to the Constitutional Convention finished their labors on September 8, 1787, sparking more than a year's worth of sincere debate. The tiny state of Delaware was first to swing into position behind the new compact (December 7, 1787) and within a month or so was joined by Pennsylvania, New Jersey, Georgia, and Connecticut. The ninth and crucial state, New Hampshire, ratified the Constitution on June 21, 1788.

Proving that governments can function without unanimity, George Washington was elected the first president by acclamation and got down to business with his new administration in New York City in April 1789, before both North Carolina, in November 1789, and Rhode Island, in May 1790, officially embraced the new system.

The Constitution laid the foundation for the new nation's money.

URGENT MATTERS FOR THE NEW NATION

Among the earliest concerns were finance and money. Alexander Hamilton had persuasively argued that the new government must be a model of fiscal honesty from the outset, and Article VI of the Constitution was sheer genius on the part of the young financier and his adherents. It recognized and assumed the debts of the states and former national government under the Articles of Confederation. This article did *not* specify payment in full—and the amount actually received, in the guise of long-term bonds, was not unduly generous—but the agreement to pay *anything* on notes already widely seen as worthless was a brilliant stroke and shifted loyalty on the part of the business community—which held most of the depreciated paper—away from the local and toward the new national government.

Because Hamilton and his colleagues distrusted paper, and because they were sincerely interested in underscoring the majesty and sovereignty of their new country and creation, they would have to do something about the coinage, and in fairly short order. State issues came to a halt in the spring of 1789, and a copper panic the following July drove both good coins and bad from circulation. A number of public and private groups and merchants took up the slack on the local level, and issues of small-change notes began appearing in commerce that summer. The bills were almost always denominated in pence, although those of the Bank of North America also proclaimed that they were worth one-ninetieth or three-ninetieths of a dollar, an attempt to express their value according to an old system, even as their issuers were moving toward a new.

As for the larger denominations, foreign gold and silver coinage would still be used when available. But the other earlier commercial mainstay was out: the states were no longer able to issue paper money, and the federal power was disinclined to do so. By 1790 there seemed a very real prospect that American business transactions would have to once again be carried on by barter and with Spanish-American currency.

At least the preliminary question of the identity of the American currency unit, and the relation of subordinate and multiple denominations to that unit and to each other, had effectively been answered by the end of the 1780s. In 1792 the law passed: the new American unit would be an old coin, the Spanish-American piece of eight, called by an old name, the dollar, but divided in a new fashion, decimally into dimes and cents.

Americans like to believe that they were the first to devise the concept of a stable, orderly arrangement of monetary denominations based on the number ten, but they were not. The ancient Greeks of Syracuse and other areas had dekadrachms, huge silver pieces equal to ten drachms. And that workhorse of the later Roman Republic and early Roman Empire, the silver denarius, was originally equal to ten copper asses. Neither ancient precursor left an indelible mark on the world's later money, and it would be another millennium and a half before the decimal monetary concept came to stay—this time in Russia, introduced in 1700 by Peter the Great.

That being said, Americans did not base their coinage arrangements on the Russian precedent, nor that of anyone else. On the contrary, the inhabitants of the fledgling United States would see their decimal coinage arrangement adopted around the world—first by Revolutionary France, then by Latin Europe and Latin America, and finally by the erstwhile enemy herself, when British coinage became decimal in 1971.

THE MINT ACT OF 1792

The United States enacted its decimal idea into law with the Mint Act of 1792. Passed on April 2, the law first proclaimed the establishment of a United States mint in the current national capital, Philadelphia, and determined the types of employees for the new facility and their salaries. Second, it established a decimal relationship between the members of the new coinage system and set down what those members would be, what quality and quantity of metal they would contain, and what images they might display.

Finally, the Mint Act guaranteed that the new coining facility would strike gold and silver for the public free of charge—an absolute necessity were the new operation to get the raw materials needed for coinage. What would the new coins be? As we might expect, they would center on the dollar, but the following chart shows all members of the proposed new system.

Metal	Name	Value ($)	Weight	Fineness
Gold	Eagle	10.00	270 grains (17.496 grams)	0.917
Gold	Half eagle	5.00	135 grains (8.748 grams)	0.917
Gold	Quarter eagle	2.50	67.5 grains (4.374 grams)	0.917
Silver	Dollar	1.00	416 grains (26.956 grams)	0.892
Silver	Half dollar	0.50	208 grains (13.478 grams)	0.892
Silver	Quarter dollar	0.25	104 grains (6.739 grams)	0.892
Silver	Disme	0.10	41.6 grains (2.696 grams)	0.892
Silver	Half disme	0.05	20.8 grains (1.348 grams)	0.892
Copper	Cent	0.01	264 grains (17.107 grams)	1.000
Copper	Half cent	0.005	132 grains (8.533 grams)	1.000

A few observations are in order. The word *disme* was shortened rather quickly to *dime*, which was how the word would be pronounced in any case. The copper cents and half cents had their weights reduced before coining began in earnest, as the price of copper had meanwhile risen. And the inclusion of a half cent brings a reminder that this was a hybrid system that treated an old coin in a new way.

That old coin, of course, was the piece of eight, which had always been divided into eight reales. It would continue to circulate beside its new American cousin—indeed it would *need* to continue to do so: it would be decades before there were enough American dollars in circulation to render Spanish-American coins unnecessary. Any American needing change for a real would also need a half cent, since the Spanish-American coin was worth 12-1/2 cents in the new reckoning.

Eight reales, four reales, two reales, and one real, all of the late 1700s.

Similarly, the quarter dollar would find a place in the new system, even though common sense tells us that one-fourth is not really part of a decimal arrangement. But the quarter would equal a coin with which all Americans had long been familiar, the two-real piece. And the quarter eagle ($2.50 gold piece), one suspects, was introduced because it expressed a decimal concept of sorts, equaling ten quarter dollars. In sum, this system was not completely decimal; rather, it contained comfortingly familiar elements in addition to those that were new, which is probably why it became so successful.

The Mint Act of 1792 set down designs for the new coinage in a fairly detailed fashion. Although there was a groundswell of sentiment in favor of depicting the president on the obverses of the new coins, Washington objected, saying it reminded him too much of monarchical practice. And so the Mint Act stipulated that one side of each coin be devoted to "an impression emblematic of liberty," with an inscription to that effect. Gold and silver coins were to incorporate an eagle, the national bird, onto their reverse designs, while reverses for cents and half cents were simply required to express the denomination.

The Mint Act and American coinage were not guaranteed or inevitable. In the years between 1789 and 1792, there was a good deal of talk about outsourcing the coinage to any of several private moneyers in Great Britain, Matthew Boulton's Soho Mint being the leading contender. Congress mulled over the idea of a foreign coiner, but while Boulton sent no samples, another British firm did. This was William and Alexander Walker, who commissioned John G. Hancock Sr. to prepare a handsome series of copper pattern cents as well as rarer pieces without denomination. The national legislature was impressed, but it was finally swayed by the arguments of Thomas Paine and Thomas Jefferson, who believed it simply made no sense to hold American coinage hostage to a European source in dangerous times.

LAYING THE MINT'S FOUNDATION

One of the prime movers in favor of a new coinage was Robert Morris, who had been behind the ill-fated trials of 1783. He found a temporary mint site in the cellar of a coach house belonging to a saw-maker named John Harper, who hired a self-taught diesinker, goldsmith, and silversmith named Peter Getz to cut the dies. Getz made strikings in copper and silver, presumably intended to represent cents and half dollars. Though Congress was not particularly taken with his artistry, Getz's efforts may have nudged Congress in the direction of passing the Mint Act.

Going forward, the government continued to use the coach house for minting purposes. Using dies engraved by Robert Birch, Harper's press struck the first American coin legally authorized by the new government, a half disme with a chubby portrait of Liberty on the obverse, and a scrawny eagle on the reverse. Some 1,500 of these pieces were struck on July 13, 1792.

At this point, the Mint Act was law, but the coining facility it had called into being had not yet opened. It would shortly do so, however: a site at Seventh Street and Sugar Alley was purchased for a trifle more than $4,000; the Republic received the deed on July 18 and the cornerstone was laid July 31. Now the mint proper could be erected.

As the walls were going up, designers and coiners began their work. Between September and December 1792 they experimented with three denominations. Someone contributed an obverse die for a disme companion to Birch's earlier half disme; it was married to a reverse by Birch, and the new chief coiner, Henry Voigt, struck a half dozen or so of the new coins in copper and in silver. Voigt's colleague, Joseph Wright, created a quarter dollar pattern with a charming young head of Liberty obverse and a standing eagle reverse. Two examples

About 1,500 half dismes were struck.

have survived in copper as well as an equal number in "white metal," a soft coining alloy composed mostly of tin.

Chief Coiner Voigt contributed a pattern himself, the "silver center" cent. This represented an attempt to create a coin worth a cent in a size more convenient than one made of pure copper. We do not know precisely how Voigt positioned the plug in the center of the planchet, and the difficulty he encountered appears to have tempted him to strike other patterns from the same dies wherein the silver was either mixed with the copper or was absent altogether. Fewer than 20 pieces of all types are known.

Finally, the man who had designed the half disme struck at one mint designed a cent struck at another. Robert Birch recycled his head from the silver half disme, turned it the other way, and struck a few cent trials in copper and one in white metal. The latter is particularly interesting because of a brief reverse legend, G★W.PT.—for "George Washington President," the final gasp of the movement to honor the nation's chief executive on its coins.

These early pieces are among the most revered members of American numismatics, but with the exception of the Birch half disme, none would have been seen by the average citizen of the day. Still, that citizen was beginning to see the first "real" U.S. coins within a few months. In March 1793, the first issues—copper cents designed by Henry Voigt—began trickling from the new mint. For the obverse, Voigt employed a wild-haired, right-facing head of Liberty design that drew some criticism in the print media of the day. But the real adverse comment was reserved for his reverse, where Voigt reintroduced a design idea that had been in existence since 1776—linked rings, which began as a symbol of national unity but now appeared uncomfortably similar to a chain of slavery.

Mint director David Rittenhouse thus suggested a new design, and cents of this second type were struck through the summer of 1793. They were followed that September by a third attempt, the final contribution of the gifted Joseph Wright. Wright's Liberty borrowed heavily from Augustin Dupré's Libertas Americana medal of 1783, down to the Phrygian cap, an ancient symbol of the newly freed slave, behind her head. That motif, which also appeared on Wright's copper half cents struck between July and September 1793, would be incorporated into the designs of Wright's successors for a century after the engraver's untimely death in late 1793.

All told, the new mint struck 111,512 cents and 35,334 half cents that first year—not bad for a first effort, but scarcely guaranteed to alleviate American monetary difficulties on the lower end of the coin-age scale. The new national coiners expanded their copper output the following year, and the year after that, but their fellow citizens still had recourse to more traditional sources for most of their small change. They kept those small-denomination, local notes in commerce, and they printed even more (sometimes denominated in cents, sometimes in pence). They also imported cent-sized tokens from Great Britain.

TOKEN COINAGE FOR CHANGING TIMES

By the beginning of the 1790s, Britons were experiencing a scarcity of official small change, making that which was suffered by Americans pale in comparison. The last time England had had legal copper money placed into circulation was two decades earlier, but as the country entered the beginning stages of the Industrial Revolution, vast amounts of low-value coinage would be needed to pay the new, salaried workers.

The Royal Mint was reluctant to provide public copper coins, and so private copper would fill in. Their issue began in North Wales in 1787, and by the middle of the next decade hundreds of merchants and firms across England, Scotland, Wales, and Ireland were busily providing the coppers that the Royal Mint would not. By that time, members of the upper and middle classes were beginning to treasure them for their collector interest as well as for their economic utility.

The collector coppers celebrated popular places, called attention to noteworthy historical events, and paid homage to the famous people of the day. It was probably inevitable that American personas and motifs would make their appearance, and while British collectors snapped up the more artistic creations featuring George Washington, the less popular appear to have been sent over to the United States to circulate there beside the new national cents.

The 1790s also saw British presses strike two types of copper tokens specifically intended for circulation among Americans—not simply sent there when rejected at home. The first of these was the Talbot, Allum & Lee cents of 1794–1795, ordered by a merchant house in New York City. These tokens found instant favor as cents—even though they were slightly lighter than the official issue—and the fledgling U.S. Mint found these coppers appealing as well. Needing rolled copper for half-cent planchets in the spring of 1795, Director Rittenhouse bought some 1,076 pounds of the tokens (around 52,000 of them) from William Talbot and recycled them into the national coining process.

The second made-for-America piece was created by Matthew Boulton for Philip Parry Price Myddelton in 1796. Myddelton had come into possession of a huge tract of land in Kentucky, and as part of his efforts to persuade impoverished British farmers and laborers to immigrate to the land, he enlisted Boulton to employ the talented Conrad Heinrich Küchler to design copper tokens for the project. However, these never got beyond the pattern stage, as in 1796 Myddelton was thrown into prison for his ambitious plan—to encourage the departure of British artisans was illegal.

Successes, Challenges, and Innovations

By the time of the Myddelton fiasco, the federal mint had managed to expand its production into metals other than copper. In October 1794, the first silver half dollars were coined, and on the 15th of that month the first representatives of the new American dollar also left the coining press. Of the latter, some 1,758 suitable for circulation were struck on that single day; no more were made until the following year.

Those dollars have much to say about the fledgling Mint and its first products. They were designed by Robert Scot, who would be responsible for most of America's coin designs over the next decade and a half. His dollar's Liberty head and eagle were criticized for their delicacy of execution, but that was hardly his fault: the new mint had no press strong enough to give its dollars a sharp impression, nor would it have until the following year—after which Scot's designs were seen to have improved.

The new dollars would serve as the flagship for American silver coins: any design changes adopted there were usually extended to lower denominations a year or two later. For example, when Scot abandoned his simple eagle for a heraldic one on the dollar, smaller silver coins replicated this substitution as well—as would gold coinage, which was first struck by the Mint in 1795 as eagles and their halves, designed once more by Robert Scot.

By the time the last of the legally mandated denominations—the quarter eagle, which appeared in mid-1796—was being coined, it was becoming apparent that at least a portion of the Mint's production could not be achieved in the ordinary

**The first U.S. silver dollar was of the
Flowing Hair type, designed by Robert Scot.**

way. The difficulty stemmed from two considerations: the low value of cents and half cents, and the time and trouble it took to make them.

Consider for a moment. If you were a Mint director in the late 1790s, and you had a set amount of money to produce during a given term, would you not prefer to meet it by striking eagles rather than cents? Those cents took as much labor to make as did the $10 pieces—more, in fact, because copper was harder to roll and strike than gold. And yet when you were finished, you had a cent instead of an eagle, and you still had virtually all of your coining left to do.

Rolling sheets was not the only problem; as far as anyone knew, the United States was still short of native coining metals. The simple winning of independence had done nothing to alleviate the shortage. Americans had little domestic gold or silver—or copper—which meant that their coiners had to scrounge for it. A 1798 cent exists overstruck on a halfpenny token from Anglesey, North Wales. One wonders whether this was accidental.

SEEKING ASSISTANCE

Of course, there *was* an area blessed with much copper and the technological wherewithal to turn it into blanks: Great Britain. By early 1796 the new U.S. Mint director, Elias Boudinot, was preparing to hold his nose and ask the old enemy for help.

Britain responded. Between 1796 and 1837, Cornish and Welsh copper was made into planchets of two sizes, then sent across the Atlantic to be elaborated into half cents and cents at Philadelphia. While two other firms participated, the favored agency was Boulton, Watt & Company—one more instance of the enterprising Matthew Boulton capitalizing on his ties with America. Boulton's planchets were made from the best copper, of the correct weight, and carefully finished, but they were not always available when needed.

On two occasions, their tardy delivery helped change the course of American numismatic history. The first was in the late 1790s, when Boulton delayed so long in sending copper that the U.S. Mint virtually ceased production in that metal, striking only a few thousand cents in 1799 and no half cents whatsoever between 1797 and 1800. The second occasion took place about 15 years later, but it was scarcely Soho's fault: the United States declared war on Great Britain in the spring of 1812, and the two countries remained hostile for nearly three years. During those years, the Mint struck no half cents and a dwindling number of cents, until it halted production altogether with the last of the 1814-dated coins. Cent coinage resumed in 1816 with the end of the war, and it steadily expanded through the 1820s.

By then, Americans were essentially doing business with only three of the ten denominations stipulated in the Mint Act: cents, half dollars, and half eagles. The cent was becoming essential on the lower end of the monetary scale, especially as the supply of genuine and counterfeit British and Irish halfpennies dwindled through attrition. The half dollar represented a handy amount of money in the United States, and the half eagle was popular because its gold value was conveniently close to other gold coins that Americans were using: the British guinea, the French louis d'or, and the Spanish-American double escudo.

But what about the other seven stars in the American monetary constellation? Several were unpopular and rarely produced because there existed better-known foreign coins that were preferred in trade. Thus, the half dime and dime yielded place to the half real and real, while the quarter dollar was rarely struck because people found it essentially duplicated the Latin American double real.

Other members could not be kept in circulation, most notably the silver dollar. This coin had been overvalued in relation to the piece of eight—it was slightly lighter and composed of slightly less-pure silver—and was thus swapped for pieces of eight in the West Indies, where it passed for par. The gold eagle suffered from similar problems; in 1803, France adopted a new silver-to-gold ratio of 15-1/2 to 1, and it became profitable to ship American gold coins to France for melting.

Seeking to end these evils, in 1804 an irate Boudinot suspended coinage of both eagles and dollars, a suspension that would hold for nearly four decades. The Mint director might have been relieved, for the policy meant that he had two fewer denominations to produce.

And this was a material consideration: the early U.S. Mint was a very inefficient coiner. Its equipment was ancient, made up of the castoffs and hand-me-downs of other countries and other coiners, as well as creaking machinery originally intended for other purposes. Its coiners were not masters of the craft, nor were its designers. The political climate was hostile, to say the least; the Mint regularly came up for review and could have been voted out of existence whenever such examination was made. It indeed came close to being abolished in 1800 and again in 1802; only an 11th-hour decision kept the facility open in the latter instance.

Not until May 19, 1828, would the U.S. Mint be authorized to remain "in force and operation, unless otherwise provided by law." But even by that period, its production had come nowhere close to meeting the demands of the people it attempted to serve.

FOREIGN COINS IN THE UNITED STATES

The same two conditions we saw at the beginning of America's story still held true. The country was metal-poor, and even with materials the Mint had no chance whatsoever of matching the needs of a population which was doubling every two decades. Thus, Americans would do as they had done since the beginning: they would turn to other people's coiners for help.

That being said, the Constitution granted the government the ability to ensure that their new federal creation played a key role in circulation regardless—Article I, Section 8, gave Congress the power to "regulate the Value . . . of foreign Coin." They exercised this power on February 9, 1793, when "an act regulating foreign coins, and for other purposes" was passed. The new law, which went into effect on the following first of July, demonetized all foreign coinage *except* the gold coins of Great Britain, Portugal, France, Spain, and Spanish America, and the silver coins of France and Spain. It also established values at which those coins were to circulate: for example, the Spanish dollar would be worth 100 cents, and its French equivalent 110.

Various successors to the Spanish and Spanish-American piece of eight, such as this Peruvian 8 reales, were widely accepted in U.S. commerce.

The new law was intended as a stopgap. It stipulated that three years from the beginning of American silver and gold coinage, everything foreign except the Spanish and Spanish-American piece of eight would be demonetized. The reality was that the U.S. Mint simply could not make enough domestic coins to replace foreign ones, so Congress climbed down from its lofty but unattainable position of self-sufficiency, renewing the act in 1798, 1802, and 1806. The act was then allowed to expire, but foreign coins were allowed to circulate anyway. By 1816 an act renewing the circulation of foreign gold and silver coins was back on the books, and the provision was renewed periodically until the Act of 1857.

Which foreign coins circulated here? The Spanish and Spanish-American piece of eight led the way in silver, although coins like the Brazilian 960 reis (often a recycled Spanish-American peso, restruck at Bahia or Rio de Janeiro) gave it much competition in the 1810s and 1820s, as did the French five-franc piece, or piastre, in the 1830s.

In gold, British, French, Spanish-American, and Brazilian pieces held sway. The British guinea was important, but the last representatives of this denomination were struck in 1813. Four years later, its successor, the sovereign, emerged as a dominant player in international and intra-American commerce. In terms of sheer popularity, the sovereign would have frequently yielded place to the Spanish and Spanish-American onza or doubloon, particularly in border areas of the Old Southwest.

Aided by recurrent infusions of fresh foreign coinage, the American monetary system limped along. Had Americans had enough coinage of any kind for commercial use, they would have been satisfied; but even with the piece of eight, the sovereign, the gold of Brazil, and the silver of France, they were not receiving all the hard money they needed to keep up with their present and prospective rates of economic development.

What had been true before still held true now: America was a demographic and commercial success, but with an economy that constantly outpaced the orthodox money supply, they replied with an unorthodox one. Just as the Constitution was taking force, just as it was seeking to channel America's money in a particular direction, the prospective users of that money were cutting a path of their own with the paper note from the private bank. Between the years 1790 and 1865, private paper currency would reign.

GOLD!

The era of "rag" money—called "broken-bank notes" by the disrespectful and "obsolete notes" by the serious—lasted from approximately 1782 to 1866, coinciding rather nicely with the antebellum "first American republic." During this period, printers such as Jacob Perkins; Murray, Draper, Fairman & Company; and, later, the American Bank Note Company and National Bank Note Company would combat counterfeiting with ingenious new technologies and create numismatic works of art with their private bank currency. The miracle of 19th-century American growth simply could not have occurred without those paper notes, but the "rag" times would eventually end.

A combination of factors would soon ensure that the paper-money system that had taken three-quarters of a century to construct would only take a few years to demolish. One of these factors was the Civil War (see the following section). But earlier, the inevitability of the private note was challenged by a second, even more surprising event. For the first time in their history, Americans were getting enough precious metal, and enough expertise in coining it, to reduce their age-old dependence on paper.

The big discovery occurred approximately one week after the signing of the Treaty of Guadalupe Hidalgo, which ended the Mexican-American War and granted the United States title to Texas, New Mexico, Arizona, Nevada, Utah, part of Colorado, and California. A Mormon recent arrival to the West named James Marshall observed a glint of bright yellow—gold!—in the tailrace at a sawmill on the American River, near Sacramento. Nothing happened for several weeks because John Augustus Sutter (who owned the mill where the gold was found) did all he could to keep the discovery hidden.

But another Mormon named Sam Brannan wandered by, found out what had happened, and promptly rode back to San Francisco yelling, "Gold! Gold! Gold on the American River!" at the top of his lungs. And, as the saying goes, there went the neighborhood.

Within the next 18 months, some 75,000 gold seekers arrived from the East Coast, Europe, and even Australia. The effects of the California gold rush are almost too enormous to calculate. The discovery upset the old financial ratio between gold and silver, helping to precipitate a monetary instability that would last until both metals were removed from coinage more than 100 years later. It also inflamed tensions between North and South, as it became clear that California was bound to join the Union as a "free" state, therefore aligned with the North in foreign and domestic policy.

Thus, the California gold rush was one of the events leading to the American Civil War—and it would also help to ensure that the North would have the means with which to pursue it. For those interested in the story of America's money, the era has a double significance. First, it brought about a fascinating series of locally made coins, among the most interesting and historic issues in all of American numismatics. Second, the gold rush and related strikes elsewhere would mean that, combined with better coining technology, Americans would for the first time have enough domestic coinage for their monetary needs.

THE SMALLER SOUTHERN STRIKE

These were the great days of private gold coinage. Between 1848 and 1861, makeshift mints were established in California, Utah, Oregon, and Colorado to take advantage of the newly available precious metal, making it useful for local commerce and sending it back East for reworking there. In this, the private Western mints were similar to Spanish-American producers of pieces of eight. In both instances, the idea was to create a useful, feasible coinage *now*; those with artistic sensibilities could improve upon it later. Consequently we should not look for great artwork on these private issues.

Nor should we look for the first of them in California. We should look instead to an isolated area where North Carolina, South Carolina, and Georgia come together. Gold was found in that part of the world shortly before 1800, and, while it sparked nothing quite comparable with the California Gold Rush, there was enough precious metal in those layers and folds of the land to inspire a sizable mining scramble in the late 1820s, the eviction of Native Americans and their replacement by white settlers, and the appearance of private coiners by the early 1830s.

Templeton Reid—a sometime jeweler, gunsmith, watchmaker, and general handyman—was the first, setting up a mint in Milledgeville, Georgia, in 1830 and turning about $1,500 worth of metal into $2.50, $5, and $10 gold pieces. He soon packed up for Gainesville, where he struck a few hundred more coins between August and October 1830, but afterwards he seems to have abandoned coinage for nearly 20 years, relocating to Columbus, Georgia, where he engaged in creating and marketing new and better types of cotton gins.

Reid's coins were simple affairs, featuring his name and the denomination on one side, the origins of the precious metal and (usually) the date on the other. While he was criticized for creating lightweight coins, he made his money from pure gold, and so his coins were worth slightly more than their face value as bullion. This goes far toward explaining their extreme rarity today: most of them were melted down and recoined in Philadelphia.

You may be wondering how Templeton Reid managed to keep from being arrested: after all, if states could not coin money, how could an individual? The answer is that the framers of the Constitution apparently never anticipated that a private citizen would *want* to coin money, assuming instead that federal facilities would provide plentiful coinage for everyone. As we have seen, this did not occur. Private bank notes were one result. Private gold coinage was another.

Reid eventually struck one more coinage, this time shortly after the beginning of the rush to California. Numismatists long assumed that the coiner had followed the lure of metal west, as the coin is a $10 piece designated CALIFORNIA GOLD. But it

When the federal government failed to meet local coinage needs, enterprising Americans struck their own private money. Templeton Reid was one such entrepreneur—a jeweler, gunsmith, and inventor who turned his creativity to coins, including this $10 "Georgia Gold" piece.

now appears more likely that this coin (and a companion $25 piece that was stolen from the U.S. Mint Collection in 1858 and never recovered) was struck in Columbus. The elderly coiner was in no condition to travel and in fact died within a few months of his final foray into private moneying.

Not long after Reid's first issues, a family of German extraction named Bechtler set up shop near Rutherfordton, North Carolina—a few miles southeast of Asheville, a few miles northwest of the South Carolina and Georgia lines, and a local center for the gold trade. The family patriarch, Alt Christoph, soon made himself indispensable as the town's only jeweler and watchmaker. Meanwhile the locals petitioned Congress for a mint to turn their gold nuggets and dust into federal coinage. When they were ignored, they turned to the Bechtlers for help. Thus, the head of the clan was striking quarter and half eagles by July 1831, and by the end of the year, he had created an altogether new American coin: the gold dollar.

In time, the gold region got its mint—or rather two mints, one in Charlotte, North Carolina, and the other in Dahlonega, Georgia. Neither was an unqualified success, but they were enjoying enough trade by the end of the 1830s to persuade Alt Christoph to get out of the private minting business. In 1840 he transferred it to his son August, who moved the mint into the center of town and began striking gold dollars sometime in 1842, minting them in large numbers until his death in July 1846.

This brought a nephew into the trade: Christoph Jr. He continued to coin dollars and $5 pieces until the end of 1849 or the beginning of 1850. By then, the family's gold dollars were facing competition from official coins of the same denomination (first struck in Philadelphia in 1849), and this younger Christoph Bechtler seems to have given up the coining trade to concentrate on the family's earlier profession as a jeweler. Bechtler dollars and other coins continued to circulate alongside ordinary, federal products for many years; most of the surviving examples show evidence of a lengthy life in circulation.

California Gold: A Drama in Three Acts

Numismatist Walter Breen divided California private gold coinage into three main stages. The first began in the winter of 1848–1849 and continued through April 1850. A number of individuals and firms struck $5 and $10 coins at that time, and they created a number of circulating ingots as well. This first stage came to an end after the public learned that several of these issues were debased or contained less than their stated value in gold.

Local authorities then enacted legislation clamping down on private issues, but the laws were not enforceable, and another spate of private issues soon entered commerce. This second stage lasted until March 1851, and it was brought to a close by rumors that the new wave of private issues was also short-weight. No further private coins appeared during the remainder of 1851.

The third and final stage of California private coinage began in January 1852 and continued through 1856. While some new moneyers entered the field and placed their names on issues ranging up to $50, the most interesting event during this stage occurred on the lower end of the scale, as "fractional" gold coins—tariffed at 25¢ and 50¢, plus a related issue of dollars—entered commerce.

In the earliest stage, one of the first firms to strike coins was the Cincinnati Mining & Trading Company, which in 1849 struck a few different coins bearing a distinctive Liberty head with a feather headdress on the obverse and a unique left-facing eagle with a shield on the reverse. Both $5 and $10 coins were made, but their gold content was rumored to be low, and consequently almost all of the firm's products were soon pulled out of circulation and melted down. So were the issues of the Pacific Company, which were also struck in 1849, likely by hand with a sledgehammer.

One of the few firms to make a lasting contribution in this early period was Moffat & Company, which began issuing rectangular ingots in July 1849, graduating to normal coinage later that year. The concern's $5 and $10 gold pieces bore a deliberate similarity to ordinary U.S. gold coins.

The second stage of the California coinage saw the production of excessively rare rectangular ingots at a state assay office, but these soon yielded to orthodox coins: $5, $10, and, for the first time in California, $20 pieces. Two firms stood out here. Baldwin & Company was one, and their $10 gold piece depicting a *vaquero*, or Mexican cowboy, is among the most famous of all private gold issues. Schultz & Company, which set up shop behind the Baldwin mint and struck $5 pieces in 1851, was the other.

The third and final stage lasted for four years, and it saw a new player enter the field: the national government. In the autumn of 1850, a federal assay office of gold was created in San Francisco. It was granted the right to make ingots of refined gold, worth $50 each. A New York watchmaker named Augustus Humbert was appointed to assay the metal, and he, in turn, subcontracted the actual coining of it to Moffat & Company.

Whether or not anyone had so intended, Humbert's octagonal ingots (also called "slugs," or "Californians") entered circulation as ordinary coins—indeed, they were the principal accepted currency in California between 1851 and 1853. By 1852 Humbert was producing $10 as well as $50 ingots, and he added the double-eagle denomination in 1853. Humbert's ingots, with their distinctive eagle-and-shield obverses and engine-turned reverses, were better than anyone else's coins. They led naturally to an even more official coinage, as the assay office closed its doors in late 1853, and four months later a new branch of the U.S. Mint opened in its place.

But even after the establishment of the San Francisco Mint, private coining did not disappear; it persisted for some years. Kellogg & Company alone produced more $20 gold pieces in 1854 than the new federal facility, and those coins filled cashiers' tills in the mid-1850s, as did gigantic round $50 coins struck by two Hungarian veterans of the failed European revolutions of 1848, Count Samuel C. Wass and Agoston P. Molitor. Wass, Molitor & Company produced smaller coins as well, but they achieved immortality with those huge slugs, each of which contained more than a quarter of a troy pound of pure gold.

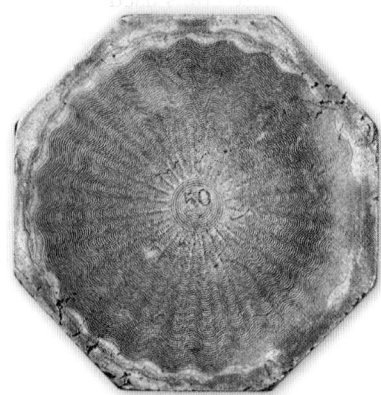

At the other end of the spectrum stood a motley assemblage of jewelers and dentists, people skilled at working with gold in small quantities. They now proceeded to create California "fractional" coins—tiny octagonal and round half dollars and quarters, as well as dollars. Most of the makers are anonymous, and their designs were simple. One thing is certain: coiners of fractional pieces had nothing whatsoever to do with makers of larger-denomination coins; the two groups were entirely separate.

This 1851 $50 gold piece was struck by Moffat & Co. for Augustus Humbert, United States assayer of gold. These heavy coins were called "slugs" because they could knock a man out in a fight— or so the Wild West legend goes.

OTHER REGIONS TAKE THE STAGE

The California gold rush had a ripple effect on the rest of the country. It influenced the tensions between North and South, but it was also responsible for smaller events of numismatic importance in Utah, Oregon, and Colorado. Neither of the first two areas had abundant gold of their own, but both had personal connections with California; many Oregon farmers had abandoned their plows and headed south at the first rumors of the gold strike, and recent migrants from Joseph Smith's peaceable Mormon kingdom near the Great Salt Lake (including the aforementioned Marshall and Brannan) accounted for many of the first prospectors to arrive in the Sacramento Valley.

UTAH: THE LAND OF THE HONEYBEE

Utah was settled in 1847 by followers of Joseph Smith, the martyred prophet of the Latter Day Saints. Led by Brigham Young, the faithful had trekked across the "Great American Desert" in search of a land so remote and so unpromising that other Americans would leave it (and them) alone. Their leader chose a site by the Great Salt Lake, and here the Mormons settled in July 1847.

They had only a limited and brief success in keeping other Americans out of Utah, however. Soon, victory in the Mexican War would grant the United States title to the American West—including the very area where Smith's disciples were building their theocratic state—and the California gold rush would result in thousands of "forty-niners" passing through the region. But the Mormons would stay where they were, and they would soon find that interlopers offered opportunities as well as threats.

Those heading west needed goods of all sorts and were prepared to pay high prices, and Mormon miners and others returning east bore gold, much of which was left behind in Utah. Thus, money could be made, and within a few months of the California strike, authorities in Utah were preparing to make it quite literally; Young enlisted the services of a British convert named John Mobourn Kay to make a distinctive local coinage, and a makeshift mint was in operation by the end of 1848.

The first coins struck were $10 pieces, some 46 of them, produced during the last month of 1848 but dated 1849. Production problems delayed an extension of the coinage until the following September, but from then through 1851, half eagles and quarter eagles were struck in some quantity, and a new denomination also entered American numismatic history: the double eagle, or $20 gold piece.

All of these coins used the same distinctive design, incorporating a three-pointed Phrygian crown—the emblem of the Mormon priesthood—and an abbreviated legend, G.S.L.C.P.G. ("Great Salt Lake City Pure Gold"). However, the gold in the Mormons' coins was *not* pure, and each denomination was only worth about 85 percent of its face value. In consequence, several thousand of the pieces were melted down in San Francisco, victims of the same backlash that was making instant rarities of the Pacific Company's coinage and other suspect issues.

At the end of the 1850s, the Mormon mint tried again, issuing half eagles notable for their incorporation of phonetic alphabet characters and the Mormon name for Utah, *Deseret*. By that time, it had a new source of gold—the region known as Colorado, where the yellow metal had been discovered in 1858. Alfred Cummings, governor of Utah Territory, finally quashed this coinage, but Colorado and its gold would soon write its own chapter in the story of private gold coinage.

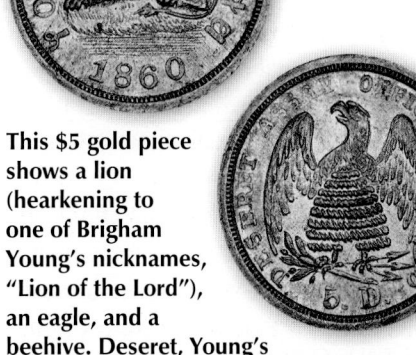

This $5 gold piece shows a lion (hearkening to one of Brigham Young's nicknames, "Lion of the Lord"), an eagle, and a beehive. Deseret, Young's proposed named for the state of Utah, was the word for "honeybee" in the Book of Mormon.

OREGON: THE LAND OF "BEAVER MONEY"

The land of Oregon, occupied jointly by Americans and British for approximately three decades in the early 1800s, became sole property of the United States in 1846 and was formally organized as the Oregon Territory in 1848. Within a year, its citizens would be striking coinage from California gold.

The implements used to create this coinage still exist, housed at the Oregon Historical Society in Portland. Inspecting them makes one thing immediately apparent: the Oregon pioneers struck their eagles and half eagles *by hand*, using a sledgehammer instead of an orthodox coining press. Such a primitive way to coin money worked well enough in this instance for two reasons: Oregonian coiners were only making a few thousand pieces, and they were making them from a soft metal—pure gold from California.

The Oregon coinage was privately struck, but it had nearly begun as an official issue of the territory. Disputes over the value and measuring of gold dust led to a push for a territorial mint, but incoming governor Joseph Lane blocked the bill, arguing that such issues by a territory were illegal under the U.S. Constitution. Lane was on shaky ground; the Constitution indeed forbade coinage by states, but it said nothing about territories. He was the governor, though, and his word prevailed; if there was to be Oregon coinage, it would not be official, but private.

Soon, eight prominent businessmen founded the Oregon Exchange Company to strike those private coins. Their first issue, a $5 gold piece, bears on its obverse a beaver, whose valuable fur had inspired some of the earliest exploration and settlement of the region, and the initials T.O. (for "Territory of Oregon"). The reverse bears the denomination, the amount of gold, and the name of the issuer. Not long after, $10 pieces appeared, following the general designs of the $5 coins.

There was no attempt at assaying or standardization with this "beaver money," but to be on the safe side, the Oregonians made their coins' weights well *above* federal standards: when assayed at Philadelphia, the fives were found to be worth $5.50 and the tens $11. California bankers nevertheless valued them much lower, and they quickly melted down the great majority of the Oregon pieces to make a profit—perhaps 50 coins survive today. Actual coining came to a stop around September 1, 1849. By 1850 gold coins from California were arriving in Oregon in fair numbers, thus ending the monetary emergency that had led to the beaver money.

Colorado: Politics, Pikes Peak, and Parsons

Settlement of Colorado—acquired piecemeal between 1803, with the Louisiana Purchase, and 1848, with Mexico's official cession—began in earnest only after the discovery of gold on the South Platte River in July 1858. That summer brought a scramble comparable to the one in California a decade earlier. In this instance, conditions were even harsher: food was scarce, housing minimal, theft and violence rampant, and law enforcement nonexistent. The nearest secure source of many essential supplies was either Omaha, Nebraska, or St. Joseph, Missouri, and the neighboring Kansas Territory was in the midst of a bloody internal conflict.

Given their conditions, in 1859 Coloradans took the only logical step: they organized their own government, calling the region the "Territory of Jefferson," telling the federal government about it after the fact. By that time, gold dust and nuggets had become the universal media of exchange, and the inconveniences of such a system led to agitation for a local coinage. In 1860 it would be met by a firm calling itself Clark, Gruber & Company.

This concern was already doing business as a bank and assay office, but late in 1859, one of the principals made an arduous trip back East to purchase dies, presses, and the other necessities for a mint. In mid-January 1860, three lots were acquired in Denver City to house the new enterprise, and by early July the mint was ready to strike its first coinage. This was an up-to-date facility, and its output was impressive; between July and October 1860, some $120,000 of quarter eagles, half eagles, eagles, and double eagles was produced. The two lower denominations copied ordinary federal designs (Liberty's head for the obverse, and an eagle with a shield for the reverse), while the $10 and $20 pieces proudly displayed a romantic, if inaccurate, depiction of Pikes Peak on the obverse.

The "Pikes Peak" gold coins of Clark, Gruber & Company show a fanciful view of the famous landmark. The company also made coins with a traditional Liberty-head design.

After a temporary break during a harsh winter, Clark, Gruber & Company replaced Pikes Peak with Liberty on all denominations and struck approximately $240,000 in the next year, followed by $223,000 in 1862. Sadly, only a tiny percentage of these coins have survived, and this mint's days were soon numbered. The federal government never recognized the Jefferson Territory and instead organized the region as the Territory of Colorado in February 1861. Under national control, local enterprises such as private mints would face an uncertain future.

Indeed, the national government forced the sale of the mint in April 1863 on the pretext that the facility would be wanted for a federal facility in Denver. A national branch mint would indeed come into production on the site—but not until 1906. During its first 43 years, the facility would function only as an assay office.

Clark, Gruber & Company was by far the most prolific of the Colorado coiners, but there were two others, located elsewhere in the region. One of these was John J. Conway & Company, which set up shop in August 1861 at Georgia Gulch and made undated quarter eagles, half eagles, and eagles for a brief time. The other coiner was Dr. John D. Parsons, who set up a coining operation at Tarryall Mines, and in 1861 struck a few quarter eagles and half eagles with a most distinctive obverse design—it showed a quartz-reduction mill, used for separating gold from its rocky matrix. The operation came to an abrupt halt when Dr. Parsons ran out of gold, and today no more than half a dozen of his quarter eagles and three of his half eagles are known.

PRIVATE GOLD COINAGE DRAWS TO A CLOSE

The Colorado issues round out the period of private precious-metal coinage in the United States. There would be other strikes of gold and silver, but none of them produced a distinctive coinage. Why did they not? For one, private precious-metal coinage ceased because Congress declared it illegal in 1864. More importantly, though, times had changed.

The American Civil War was approaching its crescendo. The war would bring to a close the supremacy of local power and authority over national. The ending of that old tradition would inevitably have an effect on money; in the new climate, the private, local coin was an anachronism.

At the same time, the underpinnings that could bind the nation's disparate parts were expanding and improving. By 1864 the North was building a transcontinental railroad. Telegraphic communications were expanding as well, fostered by the war effort. What was emerging was the potential for a new, national economy, stretching from one coast to the other. The system would experience growing pains for the remainder of the century, but it would eventually mean that Americans would spend *national* coins when they used metallic money for trade.

And finally, the public coiner—the U.S. Mint—was getting better at the production of money, and was finally able to drive its competitors—the private coiners—from the field. Improvements at the main Philadelphia facility were underway by 1816; a fire at the beginning of the year had destroyed its old wooden millhouse, and Mint director Robert Maskell Patterson used the fire as an opportunity to incorporate a steam engine into the coining process. This engine powered the rolling operation—which at last gave this crucial step the power and precision it required—as well as the planchet-cutter, resulting in an increase in the Mint's productivity.

Mint personnel got better at their craft as well. They were asking Great Britain's Boulton, Watt & Company for technical advice in the mid-1820s, centering on the production of specimen strikes, or Proofs. By 1828 the minters were cautiously experimenting with restraining collars, which kept coins more consistent in shape and quality, and therefore more difficult to counterfeit.

By the end of the 1820s, congressional agitation to close the U.S. Mint had abated, and the institution faced an altogether different problem: space. Thus, the cornerstone for a new mint was laid by 1829, and the facility opened in January 1833. Next on the docket was to upgrade the old machinery; the key player here would be Franklin Peale, employed as all-purpose fact finder by Mint director Samuel Moore.

In this capacity Peale visited the more modern mints in Europe between 1833 and 1835. He investigated the facilities of the British Royal Mint, which used a type of coining press that Boulton had patented in 1790— essentially the traditional screw press, strengthened for connection to a new motive force, the steam engine. Peale also explored the mint in Karlsruhe, in the German grand duchy of Baden. Both there and in Paris he saw a different apparatus, one patented by Diedrich Uhlhorn in 1817 and lately improved upon by M. Thonnelier, which featured a toggle action and was more efficient with the steam power it received. What's more, since it did not coin by means of a screw—the most vulnerable and difficult-to-replace part of the Boulton apparatus—this machine was far more durable.

Peale was sold on the new press, and although he did not purchase one (not being empowered to in any case), he did manage to draw and memorize its essentials. He replicated them once he returned home in mid-1835, and by March 1836, a new press powered by the Mint's steam engine had been built and was striking its first coins. The improvement was clear from the outset: the new machinery could make twice or thrice as many coins as the old methods, and the resulting coins were also much more consistent in strike and finish.

Old ways and new: a half dollar struck in the traditional method (top), and another struck in a new way, by the power of steam (bottom); both were made in 1836.

THE MINT RISES TO PROMINENCE

Meanwhile more coinage metal was discovered. By 1837 a domestic source of copper had been found, breaking the Mint's 40-year dependence on planchets from Boulton, Watt & Company. Soon the Mint would find native suppliers of gold—in North Carolina and Georgia, mentioned earlier—and finally silver.

Just as significantly, Congress passed an Act in 1835 authorizing the establishment of branches of the U.S. Mint at Charlotte, North Carolina; Dahlonega, Georgia; and New Orleans, Louisiana. The first two towns were in convenient proximity to the mines that supplied Reid and the Bechtlers with bullion; and New Orleans was a convenient locale for a supply of precious metal too, in the form of coins from Mexico and elsewhere in Latin America. The Crescent City's economy was booming by the mid-1830s; why not help it along (and bolster local and national pride) by setting up a branch mint there as well?

Thus, by the spring of 1838, the United States had not one official coiner but four, all equipped with steam power and modern coining machinery. While the facilities at Dahlonega and Charlotte never reached expectations and were closed for good at the beginning of the Civil War, the mint in New Orleans was a success from the beginning, coining gold and silver on a regular basis until the outbreak of the conflict, and reopening in 1879 to remain in business for another 30 years.

As we have seen, a Western branch mint was opened in San Francisco in 1854. All the new mints (and the greater productivity of their parent at Philadelphia) led to a momentous decision some three years later, when Congress passed the Coinage Act of 1857, repealing "all former acts authorizing the currency of foreign gold and silver coins, and declaring the same a legal tender in payment for debts." For the first time in their history, the inhabitants of the United States felt confident enough about their own money to prohibit the use of other people's coins. And so all those pieces of eight, sovereigns, louis d'ors, thalers, and onzas assumed their present roles as parts of the nation's numismatic legacy—remembered with thanks, but no longer an active part of an ongoing story.

Ironically, the U.S. Mint would find itself unable to keep its own coins in circulation just four years later, when the quarreling between North and South deepened into a shooting war. In both places, uncertainty drove coinage into hiding and turned the American people back to their traditional expedient, the paper note, just as the potential seemed to have been achieved for banishing it once and for all.

FROM A CIVIL WAR TO A GILDED AGE

The Civil War meant and still means many things to Americans. It has produced feelings that have clarified, deepened, and changed over the past century and a half since the guns fell silent. But for all the complexity, the greatest lesson of the conflict is obvious: Americans would have to pay for the fine words enshrined in the Declaration of Independence with lives lived in a new way. They would have to actually take seriously the stirring phrase about the equality of *all* men.

The tremendously eventful 50 years that followed—called the "Gilded Age" after Mark Twain and Charles Dudley Warner's on-point satirical novel of the era—would see the nation struggle with that idea, all the while undergoing massive expansion and political change. The moniker could not be more apt; was not a *golden* age a period when humankind was at its best, transcending limitations of class, race, sex, and worldview? In reality, this was an age that posed as something solid and worthy, but whose gold plating was thin and easily worn away to reveal the bigotry and brass beneath.

Consider all that occurred between 1865 and 1914. The nation assumed its present borders when Alaska was added in 1867 and Hawaii in 1898, and it gained temporary and sometimes permanent control over other areas, too: the Philippines, Puerto Rico, Guam, the Canal Zone, and Guantánamo Bay. Meanwhile the continental states filled up thanks to increased immigration, improving transportation and communication, and advancing industry. The frontier finally disappeared.

These changes were for the better, or at least neutral, but they inevitably influenced some groups more than others, and caused immense friction and unrest virtually everywhere. Farmers lost their position at the head of the table, and Native Americans got shoved away altogether, locked up on reservations. African Americans saw most of what little they had won taken back in the South with the ending of Reconstruction; those who voyaged north found a scarcely more hospitable reception there. The organized labor movement experienced several sputtering beginnings, and though its days of success lay far distant in the next century, it was becoming increasingly apparent that those who owned the factories and firms owned a good deal more—including major portions of the state and federal governments.

The issue of tariffs and regional grudges caused tension between Democrats and Republicans, but the lasting truth was that the major parties both had an agenda that suited them and the economic elite while generally ignoring the real and worsening problems of the average citizen. As a result, the middle and late portions of the Gilded Age would see two movements for reform, speaking to the needs of the "forgotten man": the Populist and Progressive fronts, the latter of which would make more headway and help eradicate some of the worst social and industrial evils by the end of the period.

At bottom, all of this activity was tending in one direction: the country and its people were becoming ever more interconnected.

CURRENCY DURING THE CIVIL WAR

The Civil War was the defining experience of U.S. history—a true "watershed," to use a word ordinarily reserved by historians for far lesser events. The war split the country's story neatly down the middle;

in four short years the United States became a completely different country. And all this we have been saying about the country's history might be equally applied to its money.

In the four years of the Civil War, America's money would begin in familiar forms, then be constantly altered under pressure, and finally emerge with fundamentally new identities which remain today with minor modifications. Put most simply, the national government would be forced to acquire the same monopolistic powers over bills and notes that it had claimed over coins with the Coinage Act of 1857, as it became clear within six months of its start that the war must be fought and paid for by both sides with the time-honored expedient of paper money.

This money would take different forms, from the familiar private bank note to state notes and federal bills both Union and Confederate. All would be printed in mass quantities, whether by means of engraving, typesetting, or lithography. New media would emerge, including postage currency and bronze Civil War tokens.

Coinage, meanwhile, would be scarce, as gold and silver began disappearing from circulation in both the North and South shortly after the beginning of hostilities (thanks to the hoarding public). The mints at Charlotte, Dahlonega, and New Orleans all closed down in the spring of 1861. But coins would not disappear altogether. With the small number of coins it did produce during the period, the U.S. Mint concentrated on the lower end of the scale: cents bearing the new Indian Head design; a new two-cent piece introduced in 1864 (the first American coin to bear the motto "In God We Trust"); and a second three-cent piece to augment unwanted supplies of the first.

The two-cent coin was one of the shortest-lived series in U.S. coinage, being struck in a ten-year period that ended in 1873.

The three-cent piece takes a bit of explaining. The original version was introduced in 1851, when the postal rate for a first-class letter was lowered to 3¢, and was struck in quantity between then and 1853, first in silver, whose fineness was deliberately low, and later in the fineness current for all other American silver coins, 90 percent. The coiners at the U.S. Mint found their new, tiny coin so unpopular that production was drastically decreased and then ceased altogether in 1873; but early in 1865, they decided to try again—this time with a slightly larger coin struck in copper-nickel. They made a good many of the new pieces that first year, and the coins did in fact perform a modest service on the lower end of the monetary scale, but this version eventually proved as unpopular as the silver examples, and production stopped in 1889.

For what limited success federal coiners enjoyed on the base-metal end of the monetary column, they found even less when they turned to precious metals. Silver coins of the period—which bore Christian Gobrecht's Liberty Seated design, introduced in the late 1830s—were struck in very small number in the early 1860s, and most of them came from the branch mint at San Francisco rather than the parent facility at Philadelphia. In fact, the main U.S. mint virtually closed down at the end of 1861, and only half dollars were produced in a quantity comparable to that of pre-war years.

A similar pattern held for gold coins, most of which bore a rather pedestrian Liberty head with coronet, again designed by Gobrecht. The major exception was the slightly more attractive double eagle, designed by the man responsible for the current cent, the two-cent piece, and both three-cent pieces: James Barton Longacre. Whereas other gold denominations were struck in minuscule quantities after 1861, production of double eagles actually *ascended* through the war.

Virtually all of it, however, was accounted for by the San Francisco Mint, where the large gold coins were quickly struck and shipped east to bolster banking and the war effort. It would take the end of the armed conflict for America's metallic money to truly reemerge; meanwhile Reconstruction and new political ideas were shaping a distinctly new nation.

MONEY IN THE GILDED AGE

The shift from the local to the national, from the particular to the universal, was implicit in the Northern victory of 1865; for the next half century, Americans would have civic calm at home, and thus they had the time and concentration necessary to determine where their new interconnections might lead. Part of the evidence that they were doing so comes from the money they were producing during the Gilded Age.

What do we see when we take a closer look? First, there is a return to coinage with the end of the Civil War. The uncertainty was over: once put in circulation, specie would remain there. Therefore, production of most denominations expanded, at least until the harsh economic times of the middle and later 1870s. The exceptions to this rule were those coins on the lower end of the scale, as issues of cents, two-cent pieces, and three-cent pieces were decreasing by the late 1860s.

On the upper end, the production of gold double eagles continued to rise through the 1870s. The production of these massive capstones increased because there seemed to be an endless supply of gold in the West, and the double eagle was the most efficient way to turn that resource into something useful. The great majority were struck at the San Francisco branch mint, assisted after 1870 by a new federal facility at Carson City, Nevada. This facility was erected primarily in response to the massive Comstock silver strike, but it was also a source of gold coinage until its closing in 1893.

While many of the new double eagles were sent back East, many more stayed near their point of origin—so many, in fact, that Congress had to alleviate the resultant banking nightmare with a new type of paper money, the National Gold Bank Note. Thus, while the national banking system and its notes proliferated throughout the country and homogenized currency, the federal government of the day might indeed respond to local monetary differences and act on behalf of influential interests on the state or regional level. Another example is the story of Western silver and the Morgan dollar.

A QUESTION OF METALS

The United States had long had a "bimetallic" monetary system, one based on two precious metals that were interchangeable with each other at a fixed ratio. This ratio had been established in 1834 at 16:1 (meaning that weight for weight, gold was worth 16 times as much as silver), and the system functioned adequately until the California Gold Rush upset the silver-to-gold ratio in favor of silver coinage. Congress responded to the subsequent melting and exportation of silver by reducing the precious-metal content of the half dollar, quarter, dime, and half dime, a measure that helped get silver coinage back into commerce until the emergency of the Civil War.

Not long before that crisis began, silver had been found near Virginia City, in the Nevada Territory (recently separated from the Utah Territory), and so much of it was shortly being taken from the ground there that the Union soon made Nevada into its own state. The nation's monetary system meanwhile acquired a headache of monumental size and duration, as the 16:1 ratio was again being upset—but this time in favor of gold. Matters worsened still in 1871, when the new German Empire adopted a strict gold standard, exporting nearly two-thirds of its silver stock, and adding more than $200 million of the metal to a market already glutted.

Mine owners and their congressional representatives were vocal in their distress, and the official reply was the Mint Act of February 12, 1873. The act gave with one hand and took away with the other: it put a slightly greater amount of silver in the half dollar, quarter, and dime, and it also created the silver trade dollar, which was intended to compete with the piece of eight in Far Eastern trade; but it halted production of the half dime, three-cent piece, and two-cent piece, and it closed out coinage of the normal silver dollar.

This was the famous "Crime of '73," which would soon become a rallying point for Western silver and Midwestern agrarian interests against the "goldbugs" of the East. Never mind that virtually no silver dollars had been struck during the 1860s and that no one wanted the three million or so that had been struck since 1870; for Western miners, the Mint Act of 1873 was outrage pure and simple, and they spent the next five years fighting to get it repealed. They would see success in 1878 with the passage of the Bland-Allison Act.

The act restored unlimited legal-tender status to silver dollars on the traditional standard, and it committed the U.S. Treasury to purchasing between two and four million dollars' worth of silver bullion each month for production of the new coins. The pieces were to have new designs by George T. Morgan, and his left-facing-portrait head of Liberty and more naturalistic reverse eagle represented a cautious attempt to bring more artistry to American coinage, a movement which gathered force as other denominations were redesigned after 1891. But for now, the dollar's new look was the last thing on most people's minds.

The Morgan silver dollar was struck by the millions starting in 1878.

The reception and significance of the Morgan dollar varied wildly from place to place. The West was partially assuaged, because the region's silver production now had an outlet, and the new dollars were a circulating mainstay there for many years to come. They were also popular in the South, and millions were struck in New Orleans after the reopening of the federal branch mint there in 1879.

THE ISSUE COMES TO A HEAD—AND THEN FADES

As the years went on, other groups grew progressively fonder of the Morgan dollar: medium and small farmers of the Midwest, West, and South, robbed of purchasing power in the 1880s and 1890s by a persistent agricultural depression, began to see the new silver dollars as a possible salvation. If the U.S. Mint coined them in unlimited numbers, then so much money would flood into the economy that the price of farm products would rise, and farmers could thus pay off their debts more easily than before.

But fortunately for the moneyed interests—who had a dislike and distrust of silver and rallied around gold—the Bland-Allison Act had stopped short of giving silver full bimetallic parity with gold at the old 16:1 ratio; it had also offered something less than completely "free" (unlimited) silver coinage. Both of these points would soon become rallying cries for miners and farmers. The Act did, however, allow for a massive coinage of cheap silver at inflated prices, a value-to-denomination ratio that became increasingly unrealistic as yet more silver poured from the mines and mints.

Along with the Morgan dollars, the Bland-Allison Act created a new type of paper currency, the Silver Certificate. This specialized note, originally intended to redeem the new dollars and later extended to the redemption of Legal Tender Notes issued during the Civil War, could not be exchanged for Gold Certificates. Nor would it remotely resemble any other type of federal paper money (the words "silver" and "silver dollars" dominating the designs), so anyone handed a Silver Certificate could immediately spot it and refuse it, demanding payment in a gold-based medium instead. But despite these measures and East Coast opposition, the new currency type gradually assumed a larger role in the national economy, as it was considerably easier to handle than the cumbrous coins it represented.

Today the debate over a gold standard versus a gold-and-silver standard may strike us as academic, but it had real and immediate connotations for those alive during the closing years of the 19th century. When miners and small farmers clamored for "the free and unlimited coinage of silver at the rate of sixteen to one," they were demanding recognition and respect for old ways of life that were now at risk. The fact that they could view endless coinage of a whitish metal with few nonmonetary applications as a panacea suggests that they were not being particularly realistic; but then, the same might be said for the opposition, who viewed the gold standard as sacred and any attempt to add silver as profane.

The issue came to a head in the presidential campaign of 1896, fought out against the backdrop of a miserable, three-year-long depression that had left factory workers unemployed and farmers and miners even worse off than before. Democratic candidate William Jennings Bryan hammered away at the Free Silver idea while Republican William McKinley's adherents spoke for gold coinage and a higher tariff. The latter—called "Big Bill McKinley, Advance Agent of Prosperity"—was elected, and sure enough, prosperity followed.

From this point, the issue of bimetallism faded in importance. When the Republic officially went on a gold standard in March 1900, Bryan and the Democrats railed and ran against it that fall—but no one cared and McKinley was reelected. He had more than prosperity on his side by that time; since he had taken office in March 1897, the United States had acquired an overseas empire. In the broader view of history, the new domains (and the fact that McKinley was reelected in part because of them) represented a historic shift in emphasis on the part of America's people; they were ready to look outward, and what they saw and how they reacted would amend the nature of their numismatic history in some very surprising ways.

New Empire, New Money

Change was in the air by the early 1870s. That the United States was looking abroad for economic gain was suggested by the new trade dollar; why mint such a coin for the Far Eastern trade if you were not interested in that trade yourself? And while the coin may not have lived up to expectations, Chinese merchants accepted it readily enough, until a fall in silver prices in 1876 resulted in millions of the coins recrossing the Pacific.

Another change: Prior to 1857, foreign coins were legal and common in circulation in the United States. By 1876 the Mint was actually beginning to coin for other countries—first for Venezuela, and later for other small nations in the Western Hemisphere, including the Dominican Republic in 1897, El Salvador in 1904, and Costa Rica in 1905. By 1906 it was supplying Mexico (in an interesting case of historical reciprocity), and the Mint would continue to extend its coinage production across Latin America during the first half of the 20th century.

In the 1880s, the U.S. Mint extended its attentions in another overseas direction—to Hawaii. The islands formed an independent kingdom in those days, but American missionaries had been preaching there since 1820, shortly followed by Yankee traders and businessmen. In 1847 an issue of copper keneta (cents) had been prepared for King Kamehameha III by a private mint in Attleboro, Massachusetts, but the issue was poorly received as the monarch's portrait was almost unrecognizable and the reverse denomination was misspelled.

American penetration of the islands increased its pace after 1849. In the early 1880s, King Kalākaua I desired another issue of Hawaiian coinage. His representative, sugar baron Claus Spreckels, approached the U.S. Mint with preliminary designs and a proposal for coining a million dollars' worth of silver into coinage for the island chain. The issue would consist of dala (dollars, on an exact par with the U.S. coin), hapalua (half dollars), hapaha (quarters), and umi keneta (ten-cent pieces)—making it possible to strike the entire issue on planchets left over from regular American coining—all of which were dated 1883.

Of course, Hawaii would eventually be annexed by the United States (1898) and later admitted to the Union, but this Pacific interest was an exception for the period as most of the U.S. Mint's foreign coining adventures were pursued in Spanish America. Two of the nations there for which the United States shortly would coin were Cuba and Panama, and there was a very good reason: the United States had helped create both countries in their modern forms.

In the case of Cuba, it was the Spanish-American War—that is, the U.S. military intervention in the Cuban War of Independence—that sparked the connection. From the time the war was won until 1902, the United States would occupy the island, and from then until 1915 American money would continue to circulate in the newly independent nation. After that, the Philadelphia Mint struck a new, distinctly Cuban coinage until the rise of Fidel Castro.

In the case of Panama, American desire for an interoceanic canal would prompt President Theodore Roosevelt to not only support a Panamanian revolt against controlling Colombia but also to act as midwife to the resultant new country. In this role the United States would strike no fewer than 6 new coins—based on a new coinage unit named for Vasco Núñez de Balboa—ranging from 1/2 to 50 centesimos. Interestingly, however, the mintages of those first issues of 1904 and most succeeding coinages were minuscule, as for the majority of business the country has preferred to use American coinage and American paper currency.

Charles Barber of the U.S. Mint designed this Hawaiian issue featuring King Kalākaua.

Finally, relevant to the topic of American imperialism and its numismatic importance, there was an outcome of the Spanish-American War that was just as important as Cuban independence: the American acquisition of Puerto Rico, Guam, and the Philippine Islands. The first two remain under U.S. control and still use U.S. coinage, and while the third is now independent and uses its own monetary system, the United States did strike coins for the Philippines for some time.

During the Philippines' days as a colony (1899–1935) and a commonwealth (1935–1946), Filipino coins were struck at every current American mint except New Orleans, and starting in 1920 at a new, special facility set up in Manila. The anomalous nature of the islands' status was demonstrated by the designs seen on their coinage: for obverses, a seated Filipino or a standing Filipina, for reverses, an American eagle surmounting an American shield. The coins were created by a local artist named Melecio Figueroa, and they were denominated in centavos and pesos.

A RENAISSANCE IN AMERICAN MONEY

Theodore Roosevelt may be said to be the father of Panamanian numismatics, but numismatists know him far better in an American capacity: more than any other person, he was responsible for an artistic awakening in early 20th-century U.S. coinage. Once reelected in 1904, the energetic leader swung into action.

Roosevelt became involved in numismatics because he was deeply disgusted with the appearance of the American coins then in circulation. The old Gobrecht silver designs had been abandoned in 1891 in favor of new images for the dime, quarter, and half dollar, but these did not represent much of an improvement. Designer Charles E. Barber's Liberty head was acceptable, but his eagle was completely heraldic and appeared outdated even at the time it was introduced.

When it came to minor coinage, James B. Longacre's Indian Princess still graced the cent, more than 40 years after she had first appeared there. A copper-nickel five-cent piece, or "nickel," had been introduced in 1866, but its designs similarly failed to inspire. These included a fancy obverse shield and a reverse numeral by Longacre (used until 1883), and a trite obverse Liberty head and a large reverse "V" by Barber (used thereafter).

The designs of the gold coins annoyed President Roosevelt most of all. Ideas introduced by Gobrecht in 1838 and by Longacre in 1850 were still present on coins ranging from the quarter eagle to the double eagle. Surely, reasoned the president, the nation could do better than *that!*

He knew a gifted sculptor and medalist named Augustus Saint-Gaudens, who had been responsible for an attractive medal in a modern style portraying Christopher Columbus, created in conjunction with the 400th anniversary of the discovery of America. The politician and the artist had maintained contact over the years, and the latter responded magnificently to the former's call for help.

Saint-Gaudens's $10 gold piece featured a simple, left-facing Liberty with a feathered warbonnet (headgear added at the insistence of the president) and a naturalistic eagle inspired by an ancient Egyptian silver coin. His double eagle was still more ambitious, and it is arguably the most beautiful American coin. We see a figure of Liberty on the obverse, striding toward us in the dawn, holding the torch of freedom and the olive branch of peace. On the reverse, we see another eagle, this time soaring above the sun.

Augustus Saint-Gaudens's gold double eagle is considered by many to be the most beautiful U.S. coin ever designed.

Saint-Gaudens would unfortunately die in the summer of 1907, and he never saw the completion of his project. Luckily, though, Barber would succeed in reducing the high relief of his prototypes, making them more practical for striking. This may have robbed the actual coins of a portion of their artistry, but even amended for the worse they were splendid coins.

Roosevelt left office at the beginning of March 1909, also having secured the redesign of the quarter eagle and half eagle before he departed. These coins featured designs somewhat reminiscent of those on Saint-Gaudens's $10 piece, but struck *into* rather than *onto* the planchets, so that the fields of the new coins became their highest points. The innovative treatment engendered criticism (largely because it was assumed it would trap dirt and spread disease), but like the designs by Saint-Gaudens, these by Bela Lyon Pratt would serve on America's gold coinage until the final years of the medium itself.

Roosevelt's successor, William Howard Taft, continued the drive for greater numismatic artistry. A redesigned cent appeared during his first year in office, when Lithuanian immigrant Victor David Brenner created a new design to help the country mark the centenary of the birth of Abraham Lincoln. Slightly amended, Brenner's obverse portrait of "Honest Abe" is still in use; the reverse has changed from the original Wheat Ears, to the Lincoln Memorial (1959), to a set of four different reverses (2009 only, for the 200-year anniversary of Lincoln's birth), to the current Union Shield.

But back to the beginning of the 20th century: numismatic redesign continued after the Democratic Party regained national office in the election of 1912, and the five-cent piece was modified the following year. America's most artistic minor coin resulted: the Indian Head, or Buffalo, nickel showed what a gifted designer (in this case James Earle Fraser) could do with a humble coin in a base metal.

COMMEMORATIVES AND TOKENS

Another event in American numismatics during the Gilded Age was the creation of a coin for celebration rather than for commerce: the commemorative. Its origins in the United States date to 1892. The concept has much deeper roots elsewhere—coinage celebratory of a particular event or personage was known to the ancient Greeks, and was revived here and there in the Renaissance—but commemoratives truly gained popularity in Europe during the 19th century and their attraction eventually extended to the Americas as well.

While some earlier issues (such as the 1848 CAL. quarter eagle) could be considered commemorative coins, collectors begin the American series with a half dollar and quarter issued in conjunction with the World's Columbian Exposition in 1893. Half dollars with a head of Columbus on the obverse and a representation of the *Santa Maria* on the reverse—a collaborative effort between Charles Barber and George Morgan—were produced for sale in 1892 and 1893, while a quarter with Queen Isabella on the obverse and a female figure with a distaff and spindle on the reverse—the work of Barber alone—appeared in 1893. Some 5,000,000 of the half dollars were minted in Philadelphia, along with about 24,000 of the quarters.

From these modest beginnings, a numismatic industry would grow. Barber was responsible for a silver dollar celebrating George Washington and the Marquis de Lafayette dated 1900. The busy designer also tried his hand at a series of tiny commemorative gold dollars made for the Louisiana Purchase Exposition, dated 1903, and the Lewis and Clark Exposition, dated 1904 and 1905.

Meanwhile the career of another American monetary form, the token, was in decline. Like the celebratory coin, the private substitute for the regular coin had roots in the classical world, and we have seen this monetary form during the colonial period and the Civil War. During the Gilded Age, the locus of the token shifted West, as that region was chronically short of small change.

There were silver dollars and gold coins aplenty, but the mints at San Francisco, Carson City, and Denver (which began striking money in 1906) made far fewer small coins than large; they struck no cents until 1908 and no five-cent pieces until 1912. Furthermore, what smaller members of the silver series were struck tended to stay in large Western cities, to the detriment of merchants in small Western towns.

The latter responded as Americans had always addressed a monetary shortage: they obtained and circulated alternative money. Across the region, thousands of types of tokens, struck in brass, copper, zinc, aluminum, and even hard rubber, were called into service to expand the money supply. Because of the federal law of 1864 (which made private coinage illegal), these merchants' tokens generally promised payment in a specific article (a five-cent cigar, for instance) or "in trade," meaning that the customer might use the token as he pleased for the amount indicated on the piece.

These pieces formed a vital part of numismatic Americana during the Gilded Age, but their localism was more apparent than real. A handful of firms in New York and Chicago struck the majority of them. Here as elsewhere, diversity was yielding place to uniformity in the matter of America's money, a trend accelerated in the 20th century.

Tokens struck by merchants were one way to alleviate
the shortage of small-change coins in circulation.

ISOLATION, DEPRESSION, AND
INTERVENTION: AMERICA, 1914–1945

Prior to 1940, a combination of distance, nationalism, and problems and prospects at home kept American attention firmly fixed on domestic affairs rather than foreign ones. This national tendency was never more evident than in the summer of 1914; when citizens of the New World heard that a conflagration had once more erupted in the Old, they heartily congratulated themselves on staying clear of it. They had problems enough at home.

Trusts were everywhere—those faceless octopi that restricted trade, held down wages, and squeezed the "little guy" to death. And along with the oil trust, sugar trust, steel trust, and the like, there was, it appeared, a "money trust." By the time President Woodrow Wilson was inaugurated on March 4, 1913, public opinion was demanding a dismantling of that beast, or at least its containment by the federal government. One way to keep it within bounds might be by exerting a greater federal control over the sinews of the banking system and the paper money employed in its operations. Thus the Federal Reserve Act of 1913 was born, and, in the following year, a new type of currency: the Federal Reserve Note.

The Federal Reserve Act divided the nation into 12 districts, each with a Federal Reserve Bank at its heart. The 12 districts, their cities, and the symbols that each must employ on the notes they issue are as follows:

District	City of Issue	Identification Symbol
1	Boston	1 or A
2	New York City	2 or B
3	Philadelphia	3 or C
4	Cleveland	4 or D
5	Richmond	5 or E
6	Atlanta	6 or F
7	Chicago	7 or G
8	St. Louis	8 or H
9	Minneapolis	9 or I
10	Kansas City, MO	10 or J
11	Dallas	11 or K
12	San Francisco	12 or L

Working in tandem with the Federal Reserve Board in Washington, each of the member banks had the theoretical power and obligation to advise on and act as a watchdog over banking activity within its district.

The Federal Reserve Notes of 1914 and later may have appeared to be local (or at least regional), but they were undeniably products of the national government. All were printed in Washington at the Bureau of Engraving and Printing. Among all the types of federal, state, and local currency issued in America over the past three centuries, this is the only one that has survived to the present.

FROM WORLD WAR I TO THE CRASH

American participation in the Great War (renamed the "First World War" when it became apparent that it would not be the last of its kind) was limited; the Yanks were not there for the first, and worst, of the fighting, and their vision of the conflict was therefore tinged with an aura of romance. This idealism was extremely significant for what happened next: there would be a paradigm shift, from concentration on domestic problems to a crusade to save Europe from itself, "to make the world safe for democracy," in the words of the American leader.

But when U.S. optimism collided with European reality (the Allies' desire to turn their victory in 1918 into a settling of old scores), the outcome was the worst of several possible combinations. Disillusioned, Americans would reject any substantive role in the new, postwar world order. Their disillusionment would extend to matters domestic as well, and the zeal for public reform would be replaced by one for private gain. Thus the Roaring Twenties, a supposedly golden age of unparalleled industrial growth, personal liberation, and new social, economic, and cultural icons: the automobile, the radio, and the flapper.

It was quite an era, but the golden dust of this new age was not scattered equally across the Republic, enriching all of its people. Accustomed to high commodity prices during the war, Midwestern and Southern farmers saw their incomes shrink and their debts rise after the beginning of the 1920s. Factory workers did poorly too, their wages held down by a new, anti-labor stance on the part of public officials. A determined managerial attempt to sell the concepts of the company union and the open shop kept wages depressed as well.

African Americans did still worse. Those who had migrated to the North before and during the war found that they were no more welcome there than they had been in the South. Women did slightly better; at least they now had the vote, and they could exert some influence on the national scene. But all in all, as the 1920s roared on, a disturbing fact became slowly apparent to those who wished to see it: much of the economic boom was based on hot air. All those new buildings, automobiles, radios, and other accessories of the New Era might someday disappear, when everyone's credit, and hence their ability to purchase them, ran out. If that ever happened, matters would become very interesting indeed.

And it happened, of course. In 1928 Herbert Hoover—a former secretary of commerce and one of the architects of the prosperous 1920s—was elected president of the United States. He was inaugurated in March 1929, and some seven months later, the house of cards tumbled down.

A DECLINE IN COINAGE AND PAPER MONEY

The hard times of the Great Depression had a variety of effects on American numismatics. For coinage, the years between 1929 and 1933 saw a decline in production, for those out of work would hardly need an abundance of new coins for their diminishing purchases. In the year of the stock-market crash, no fewer than eight coinage denominations were in current production at the U.S. Mint; the only American denominations not struck that year were dollars and eagles. In 1930 the total was six, and in 1931, four, where it remained in 1932 and 1933. Additionally, two of those four denominations were gold, which was of no earthly value to the average citizen, whose weekly wages were probably less than the value of the smaller denomination (the eagle), if they were being received at all. Only in 1934 did the quantity of denominations struck and coins minted begin rising.

Paper money was still being printed, but currency was now made in a new, smaller model. The types of notes in circulation remained what they had been prior to the crash—Federal Reserve bills, Silver Certificates, Legal Tender Notes, and the rest—but a standardization of design, if not of type, now set in. Of course, the nation's people were far more concerned about the soundness of their currency than the sameness of its designs; worry centered on locally issued National Bank Notes, as banks began failing immediately after the Wall Street crash in the autumn of 1929.

Despite President Hoover's optimism, the number of failures grew. Soon average citizens were taking their savings (if they had any) out of the bank and stuffing them under the mattress, where they could at least keep an eye on them. By late 1932, a crisis was reached; that November, Hoover lost his bid for reelection to Franklin Delano Roosevelt, but the nation would have to wait until the following March (when the new president was inaugurated) for any significant federal intervention.

Meanwhile governors began doing their bit on the state level to stop the hemorrhaging of the banking system by proclaiming "banking holidays," periods during which every bank within their jurisdiction would be forced to close its doors. The first state to take this action was Nevada. The closure was only supposed to last for 12 days, but it was extended indefinitely. By February 1933, other states were following in Nevada's wake, and by the time Hoover finally left the White House and Roosevelt moved in, virtually every bank in the country had shut down or was operating under extreme difficulties.

Once again faced with a shortage of "normal" money, Americans were forced to make money of their own beginning in 1931. In places, these efforts extended until 1939, but the core period coincided with the banking crisis of late 1932 and early 1933. During those few months, Americans gave their money a vitality and variety it had rarely enjoyed before and has never enjoyed since.

They constructed their makeshift money from a variety of materials, including paper, wood (there really were "wooden nickels" during these days), base metal, leather, fish skin, vulcanite, and—in a marvelous instance of history repeating itself—clamshells. A bewildering number of authorities stood behind those issues—large cities, small towns, companies and firms within those cities and towns, and mutual aid associations. This "Depression scrip" appeared in all 48 of the current states, as well as the Alaskan Territory. In short, there was a period of localism in currency fully comparable with that of the 19th century, if of shorter duration.

A citizen of Pismo Beach, California, could reimburse this clamshell for $1 at the Harter Drug Company.

ROOSEVELT AND A NEW DEAL

The incoming Roosevelt administration would take very determined steps to end the banking crisis that had inspired the locally issued scrip. The president proclaimed a national bank holiday on March 6, 1933, that would allow for careful examination of each bank's finances. Solvent banks gradually reopened their doors between the 13th and 15th of March, and those found unsound would stay closed.

This bold stroke, as well as Roosevelt's programs for other aspects of the economy and his self-assured attitude, brought a return of confidence to the nation and a return of normal money to the channels of commerce. It was originally thought that even *more* money in circulation would be necessary, and thus the Federal Reserve *Bank* Note (as opposed to the Federal Reserve Note) was formed as an interim national currency—but normal currency came back into circulation more quickly than anticipated, and the new notes were curtailed later in 1933.

Other types of money were being curtailed as well. Between 1933 and 1935, competing types of national paper currency were eclipsed by the Federal Reserve Note, and the Roosevelt administration concluded that National Banks' right to issue currency should be revoked. Other forms of currency fared scarcely better. The president also demonetized gold coinage (and Gold Certificates, the currency redeemable in gold coin), a policy he and a Democratic Congress would accomplish with successive laws passed in 1933 and 1934.

Under the new philosophy, the printing of the venerable National Bank Note came to a close in 1935; production of Silver Certificates was restricted to lower denominations; and most U.S. currency was made "redeemable in lawful money" rather than spelling out precisely what sort of coin might be received for each note. What Roosevelt and his advisors sought was a plausible currency that was also manageable, manipulable, and capable of expansion in times of depression and of contraction in times of inflation.

They found their solution in the Federal Reserve System with the Federal Reserve Note. Henceforth, this type of currency would reign supreme, and America's paper money would lose most of its individuality and localism. The state-chartered banks of the 1700s and 1800s, and the National Banks that succeeded them and continued the custom of locally issued currency, were history.

AN EXPLOSION OF COMMEMORATIVES

Even as economic and social pressures and prospects (as well as Roosevelt's policies) were increasing "sameness" in American money, the federal government showed itself partial to celebrating the diversity and richness of American history. Beside the state guides produced by the Federal Writers' Workshops in the 1930s and 1940s, it found one of its most lasting expressions on the commemorative coin.

Commemorative coinage came to the United States with the Columbian Exposition celebrations of 1892–1893, and it took root in America by the first years of the new century. Commemoratives were issued from time to time during the 1910s and 1920s. Some of the most notable issues of the period would be the huge round and octagonal $50 pieces produced for the Panama-Pacific Exposition in 1915, as well as the new Peace silver dollar introduced at the end of 1921.

Commemorative coinage continued through the administrations of Harding and Coolidge, ordinarily restricted to a single denomination, the half dollar. Issues of that period tended to focus on events rather than places—battles of the American Revolution, the sesquicentennial of Independence, the centenary of the Monroe Doctrine—but the most successful of them celebrated a place as well as an epoch: the Oregon Trail.

The Oregon Trail half dollar is considered by many to have one of the most artful of U.S. commemorative designs.

The collapse of 1929 brought celebratory coinage to an abrupt end for four years. True, a commemorative was introduced for the bicentennial of George Washington's birth in 1932, but it soon transmogrified into that most pedestrian of 20th-century American circulating coins: the Washington quarter, which is still in production today. The real resumption of commemorative coinage began in 1934, accelerated in 1935, crested in 1936, and continued to enliven America's money through 1939, after which concern with overproduction and possible warfare put a damper on such numismatic enthusiasm.

But while it lasted, what a time it was! A fundamental shift had taken place, and while events would still receive their commemorative due, the real emphasis was now on the places where the events had occurred. Such celebration of local themes was underscored by the employment of local artists to create the designs for the new issues, and while some of the artistic attempts were more successful than others, the overall effect of the multiplicity of commemorative coins was a positive one. American collectors now look back to those days as a golden age of numismatics, even though their parents and grandparents may have thought that the spate of commemoratives was getting out of hand.

FRESH NEW CIRCULATING COINS

The period of the American commemorative coincided with one of the high points of American numismatic artistry on circulating coinage. True, the daring and beautiful designs of Pratt and Saint-Gaudens passed from the scene when gold coinage stopped in 1933, but these were great days indeed for silver and base-metal coinage.

John Flanagan's portrait of George Washington on the quarter dollar may have been a step down, artistically, compared to its dramatic predecessor by Hermon MacNeil. For other circulating denominations during the 1930s, the artistic flowering that Theodore Roosevelt had begun still held sway. Brenner's cent and Fraser's five-cent piece were in everyday use. The dime and half dollar were both redesigned in 1916, and Charles Barber's trite renditions were replaced by magnificent, authentically "patriotic" images by Adolph Alexander Weinman.

As with MacNeil's quarter, Weinman's dime and half dollar were designed just prior to American entry into the First World War, and the themes they incorporated suggested as much. For the dime, a realistic, left-facing head of Liberty imparted a new freshness to American numismatic design, although the wings on the goddess's cap, placed there to symbolize liberty of thought, were mistaken for the attributes of a god and the coin became known as the "Mercury" dime. Weinman's reverse brought an altogether new concept to American coinage: the fasces, emblem of unity, something obviously desired in the face of international danger.

Attractive as was his dime, this artist's half dollar was his greater contribution to U.S. numismatics, and it stands as the most beautiful circulating design ever created for that denomination. On the obverse, we see Liberty wearing an American flag and striding toward the dawn with a bundle of oak and laurel branches in the crook of her left arm; on the reverse is the American eagle, a splendidly naturalistic depiction of the bird.

By the time Weinman's dime and half dollar were replaced in the 1940s, James Earle Fraser's Buffalo nickel had passed from the scene as well, supplanted by Felix Schlag's design honoring Thomas Jefferson. The new coin marked a deepening of the trend away from symbolic representations and toward real people, a move already seen with the Lincoln cent of 1909 and the Washington quarter of 1932. This nickel is still in production today, although it has seen modifications in design over the years, some of them dramatic.

Weinman's Liberty Walking half dollar, like his dime, debuted in 1916 and was part of the U.S. Mint's lineup into the 1940s.

NEW STRUGGLES BRING NEW MONEY

After an uneasy armed truce lasting 21 years, the old adversaries of 1914 squared off once again; war broke out in September 1939, as expansionist Germany attempted one final bluff and found at last that there was a point beyond which the other side (Great Britain and France) would not retreat.

In the beginning, most Americans were quite happy to stay out of the conflict, as they had been in 1914. For the first two-thirds of a year, the war seemed to involve little more than politics, as Hitler absorbed Poland without opposition from his theoretical adversaries. But then came *Blitzkrieg*, as Germany overran Norway, Denmark, the Low Countries, and finally France itself, making the war look very real indeed.

Thus, as the 1940s began, the United States was uncertain. It did not want Germany and its allies to win the war, but getting deeply involved might be the only way to avoid that outcome. Then, as all eyes were on Europe, the event that would tip the scales occurred at a venue Americans regarded as a side-show, if they thought about it at all: on December 7, 1941, Japan attacked the United States at that splendid base the Navy had acquired from the Hawaiian monarchy back in 1887, Pearl Harbor.

Americans would henceforth be as deeply involved in the world conflict as anyone else, declaring war on the Japanese as well as their allies, Hitler's Germany and Mussolini's Italy. U.S. participation in the Second World War lasted some 45 months and left 292,131 dead and 671,801 wounded of the 16,353,659 men and women who served in its armed forces. It would also permanently change America's conduct abroad, as the nation embraced its larger role on the international scene.

But American participation in the Second World War changed even more at home than it did abroad. It planted seeds for future movements, including the empowerment of women and African Americans, groups that played key roles in the war efforts. The conflict was also a hotbed for technological development, resulting in new innovations both good (such as plastics, synthetic fibers centering on nylon, artificial lubricants, and new food products) and controversial (the Bomb).

Of course, the nationwide change also extended to coins and currency. In the case of the former, copper was removed from the cent at the end of 1942. Its alloy was changed to zinc-plated steel in 1943, and melted-down gun-shell casings in 1944, 1945, and 1946. Nickel was deemed a critical war material, too, and so a concoction of copper (56 percent), silver (35 percent), and manganese (9 percent) was introduced in October 1942 and used in the five-cent coin through 1945. More than half a billion coins were made from the threefold alloy, distinguished by their slightly different color and a large mintmark (including a new "P" for Philadelphia) over the dome of Monticello rather than a small one at its right side.

Changes in paper currency occurred more in peripheral areas. The new Hawaiian issues were simply ordinary Silver Certificates upon which a brown seal was substituted for the blue one appropriate to that type of currency. Additionally, the word HAWAII was overprinted twice in small letters on the face and once in gigantic letters on the back. The idea was that the distinctive notes, printed for circulation in Hawaii, could be declared irredeemable if the Japanese occupied the islands and seized the local banks. Notes were also issued for use of American troops in Europe and North Africa; some of this "Allied Military Currency" was denominated in dollars and some was denominated in the currencies of those countries in which U.S. soldiers served, but none was truly American currency.

Meanwhile the U.S. Mint's early activities in providing Latin American countries with coins were expanded dramatically during the war. The Mint continued to supply a number of old customers, and it also created "liberation" issues of several types. For the Philippines (which had had its own mint in Manila since 1920, but which had fallen to Japan early in the war), massive coin issues of the prewar types were prepared in Denver and San Francisco in 1944 and 1945, and placed in Philippine commerce as the islands were liberated by U.S. and local troops.

The U.S. Mint also served as temporary coiner for the Netherlands, supplying its possessions with money of the prewar type when the mother country was unable to do so. Finally, coins were prepared for liberated France and Belgium. Their extreme simplicity of design illustrates the urgency of the times. A two-franc coin was struck in brass for France, while the Mint found a handy way of recycling the unwanted steel-cent planchets of 1943, turning them into the Belgian double francs of 1944.

Thus the coinage and currency of an America at war. For all of the diversity of metals and types, and for all of the interesting experiments, the numismatic expedients of the Second World War left no permanent imprint on the story of the nation's money. When the fighting had ended, reality snapped back into its earlier, prewar mold: normal alloys returned and commemorative issues soon resumed. But an unintended and doleful new coin entered the monetary spectrum as well, and it might serve to symbolize the war and the events that had led up to it.

The coin was a dime, approved late in 1945, introduced early in 1946. The nation's new dime bore the head of the man who had dominated the American war effort and who had died in its pursuit: Franklin Delano Roosevelt. The coin is still in circulation today, linking Americans, many several generations removed from the war, with the man and the events.

COLD WAR AND BEYOND: 1946 TO THE PRESENT

The years since the end of the Second World War have been among the most eventful in American, and indeed human, history. The conflict convinced us that we must look outside our walls, and take larger responsibility for international affairs. Our new relationship meant hot wars in Korea and Vietnam, Kuwait, Afghanistan, and Iraq; a cold war with Russia; and an inability to enjoy the promised fruits of our earlier victory in 1945.

Meanwhile, on a domestic level we have seen several recessions; the longest economic boom in American history; the rise of the suburb and the decline of the central city; multiple cultural and technological revolutions; and a doubling of our population. Changes indeed, changes everywhere, except one place: until very recently, America's money scarcely changed at all.

Throughout history there was a dynamism at work in the coinage and currency of the United States, a dynamism spurred by and reflective of the larger events of the period. Yet here, against a background of some of the greatest alterations ever seen in ways of life, we still use American coinage and paper currency that would be recognizable to the average man and woman of 1946.

What happened? Why did the money become fixed in a single, virtually changeless pattern? And what does this say about larger issues?

The postwar decades of national stress played a major role in the unusual continuity of America's money. When people are constantly bombarded with threats and turmoil, they tend to take what comfort they can in prosaic objects that have "always" been with them in the same reliable form. Coins and paper money can fall into this category.

Between 1989 and 1991, the United States' major perceived foreign threat—the Soviet Union—removed itself from contention, and, for the first time since 1945, a real debate arose and still goes on about the designs on American coinage and paper currency, not only on the part of collectors but on the part of the wider public. Put most simply, America had more important matters on its mind until fairly recently; changes are taking place now that the nation has the leisure to look at its coins and notes with a more critical eye.

Of course, other forces have been at work, too. For example, when it comes to coinage, contemporary minters are mainly concerned with technological considerations; designs are adopted or rejected not primarily because of their looks, but because they will or will not translate well to an easy-to-mass-produce piece of metal. The arrangements that grace American circulating coinage are relatively successful from that standpoint. They are well balanced, obverse to reverse, so that designs on each side come up reasonably well in a single, quick blow of the press. And to the cry of the artist for reform of design comes the response of the minter: if it works, leave it alone. This is one reason for continuity on American coinage.

A new dime in 1946 would honor the fallen president who had rallied the United States throughout the war.

Another is the amount of verbiage that must, either by force of law or by force of tradition, be placed on the coinage. The elements that each coin must bear include the name of the country, a national motto ("E Pluribus Unum"), a second national motto ("In God We Trust"), a *third* national motto ("Liberty"), the denomination, the date, and the place of mintage, symbolized by a mintmark. Once you get all that onto a coin, you have precious little room for anything else, and if a design manages to cram everything in and still proves easy to coin, you will hold onto it very tightly.

AMERICAN MONEY IN STAGNATION

In 1959 the cent was changed in commemoration of Lincoln's 150th birthday and the half-century mark of the Lincoln cent itself. The martyred president continued to form the obverse design. But on the reverse, the "wheat ears" gave way to an attempt to depict the entire Lincoln Memorial—an attempt which found some success from a technological perspective, perhaps less from an artistic one.

Its comrades, the Washington quarter and the Jefferson nickel, seemingly have been in circulation forever. The quarter's basic designs date from 1932, and those of the nickel date from 1938. Both the dime and the half dollar were redesigned shortly after the end of the Second World War. Franklin Delano Roosevelt was placed on the obverse of the dime in 1946. The new dime's design was neat and compact.

In 1947 the last coins using the Weinman designs were struck, replaced by John R. Sinnock's less artistic designs featuring Benjamin Franklin on the obverse and the Liberty Bell on the reverse. In order to comply with the Mint Act of 1792, Sinnock added a tiny eagle to the right of the bell. This odd placement neatly summarizes the somewhat ungainly concept of the entire design, which came to an abrupt end in 1963. The next year saw another new design, this one by Gilroy Roberts and Frank Gasparro, paying homage to the martyred president, John Fitzgerald Kennedy. These designs still appear on half dollars, although the coins themselves are no longer released to banks for general distribution, and rarely appear in circulation.

Another coin that has seen its usage progressively restricted is the metallic dollar. Production for circulation was halted in 1935, and did not resume until 1971, when Frank Gasparro's new dollar appeared featuring a rendition of the *Apollo 11* insignia on the reverse and a left-facing head of President Dwight David Eisenhower on the obverse. The coin was struck only intermittently through 1978.

By that time, the dollar was not circulating except in certain areas of the West, such as the casinos of Las Vegas. In an attempt to increase the coin's convenience and appeal, and to create a more durable dollar than the paper one, the U.S. Mint reduced the coin's size, bringing out a smaller version in the spring of 1979 that replaced Eisenhower with groundbreaking feminist Susan B. Anthony. The Mint made more than 750 million dollars of this version in 1979, but the public was lukewarm about the new entry, and output shrank to less than 100 million in 1980 and less than 14 million in 1981.

The Susan B. Anthony dollar (1979–1999) continued with the reverse design of the earlier Eisenhower dollar.

The Mint then gave up and the coins were put in storage, where most of them still remain. A second release took place in 1999, but it proved no more successful than the first. Of course, no American coin actually contained silver by that point, and virtually none had since the mid-1960s; the United States removed silver from most of its coinage by the Act of July 23, 1965. The value of the precious metal had risen to the point where it eventually was worth the effort to melt down American coins for their silver. Since 1970, when the last of the half dollar's silver was removed, nearly every circulating American coin above five cents has consisted of the same metallic composition, with outer layers of 75 percent copper and 25 percent nickel bonded to cores of pure copper.

But the dime, quarter, and half dollar owed some of their continuing acceptance to their continuity of size and design—plus the fact that they were the *only* dimes, quarters, and halves provided by the government for public use. At the time of the introduction of the Anthony coin, the public already had a paper dollar, as well as a coin of a "real" dollar size: the Eisenhower dollar, which was reassuringly heavy, if not silver.

All of these changes—the elimination of precious metal, the melting of earlier issues, reductions in size (in the case of the dollar), and the freezing of designs—contributed to a curious fact in American numismatics. Fewer and fewer young people became interested in the hobby, for there was less and less to attract them to the coinage of their own country.

Collecting might be said to hinge upon the availability of objects with discernible differences, combined with the attractions of rarity and age. When the oldest coin one is likely to see in circulation is dated 1965; when it looks like every other coin in one's pocket and elsewhere; and when its numbers are counted in the billions, there is little reason to look at pocket change, little reason to collect it, little reason to venture into numismatics.

AN INJECTION OF CREATIVE CHANGE

The commemorative coin served as a partial solution to the dilemma. Three such issues were struck shortly after 1945, celebrating the centenary of the state of Iowa (issues of 1946); paying homage to the educator Booker T. Washington (issues of 1946 through 1951); and granting recognition to Booker T. Washington again, in conjunction with the scientist George Washington Carver (issues of 1951 through 1954). These two individuals were African Americans, and the commemoratives bearing their portraits suggested that members of this race were at least beginning to receive a measure of their due on American coins, anticipating their progress in wider matters.

But there was rather more to the Washington/Carver coin than appeared at first glance. It was promoted by one S.J. Phillips to provide funds "to oppose the spread of communism among Negroes in the interest of National Defense"; the coin appeared at the height of the Cold War, and the government was concerned about subversion in all aspects of society at the time. Phillips was deeply in debt from promoting the earlier half dollar for Booker T. Washington and needed money to pay off creditors and avoid lawsuits. In time, the real purpose of the Washington/Carver coin became common knowledge in Congress, and it cast a pall over the American commemorative lasting for a quarter of a century. Commemorative coinage came to a halt.

In 1975 and 1976, the reverses of the quarter dollar, half dollar, and dollar were redesigned to celebrate the bicentennial of the declaration of American independence. Of the three designs chosen (a Revolutionary War drummer for the quarter, Independence Hall for the half, and the Liberty Bell superimposed on the moon for the dollar), only the quarter design represented a real success; its artist, Jack L. Ahr, took the pains necessary to fit his concept into the circular constraints of a coin. Significantly, all three coins were released into commerce as normal issues, even though special presentation pieces could be purchased if desired.

The commemorative coin had been fully rehabilitated by the early 1980s. In 1982 the 250th anniversary of George Washington's birth was recorded on a new silver half dollar, struck only for collectors and not for circulation. That forecast the future. Since then, a large number of commemoratives have been struck in silver, and there has been a resumption of gold commemorative coinage as well.

It is worth noting that while most of the issues of the 1930s paid homage to places as well as people and events, therefore injecting a note of localism into a national coinage, the issues of the 1980s and later have swung away from localism and toward events, places, and persons of national significance. Their subject matter proclaims as much: the Olympic Games, American immigration, the Korean War, the bicentennial of Congress, the National Baseball Hall of Fame, to name just a few recent topics.

A New Renaissance of American Money

In recent years, nothing less than a renaissance has taken place in America's coinage and currency. Hobbyists have made a determined effort to bring experimentation and localism back to these media and have found congressmen, senators, and numismatic writers sympathetic to the cause. It was slow going at the outset, but the rebirth is well under way.

The State quarters program is a case in point. Writers and hobby representatives such as Kenneth Bressett, Art Kagin, David Ganz, and Harvey Stack were hard at work promoting the idea as early as the beginning of the 1990s, but the first State quarters only came from the presses in 1999. A tremendous amount of pushing, shoving, and dedication had filled the intervening years, but all the effort was worth it; the State quarters did more to increase the ranks of casual and dedicated coin collectors than has any other program, or any other type of coinage, in all American history.

The idea for the program was to gain new collectors and retain old ones by putting coins with obvious differences into circulation. Contests were held in each state to select a unique reverse design, and the coins were issued at a rate of five per year in the same order that the states came into the Union. By doing all this, a sense of *history*, *place*, and *time* was distilled into a small, attractive object that everyone saw and all could afford.

While the quality of the designs varies, each of the coins does what it was intended to do: educate the public; show something of the variety of America; and function as solid, dependable money. The success of the program spawned a similar series of five-cent pieces, coins whose reverses allude to various aspects of the Lewis and Clark expedition while their obverses present us with various portraits of Thomas Jefferson, the president under whose aegis the historic trek took place. The idea was extended to include quarters for the District of Columbia and the five U.S. territories in 2009, followed by a series of National Park quarters starting in 2010. Even the lowly cent was refurbished, in 2009: celebrating Abraham Lincoln's 200th birthday, four new reverse designs were released, each emblematic of a major period in the martyred leader's life. Starting in 2010, the cent has featured a shield design, representing Lincoln's preservation of the Union.

In every case, the goal has been to produce money that everyone can afford to collect from circulation. For those so inclined, the Mint also strikes and sells Proof versions of these coins, along with a sizable run of other commemoratives and bullion coins in precious metals. One of the most successful of these ventures featured James Earle Fraser's designs for the nickel, successfully transferred to silver (in 2001) and gold (in 2006); here, the desire to commemorate merged with the desire to make something that would compete with other countries' bullion coins.

Finally, the past few years have witnessed other attempts at producing a small-sized circulating dollar coin. The first attempt featured Sacagawea on the obverse and a bald eagle in flight on the reverse, the latter standing as perhaps the most beautiful rendition of our national symbol to ever grace a base-metal coin. Struck in an alloy of copper, zinc, manganese, and nickel, this "golden" dollar was introduced in 2000 and was struck until 2008.

And even while acceptance of the first golden dollar coin was in question, the popularity of the State quarters program emboldened the collecting fraternity to request a *second* dollar coin—or rather, a series. These coins (the same size as the first at 26.5 mm, a trifle larger than the quarter) celebrate the administration of every deceased American president from George Washington onward. These coins, which are currently being introduced at the rate of four per year, represent innovation: many of the presidential portraits face the viewer rather than appearing in profile; some mandatory wording (IN GOD WE TRUST and E PLURIBUS UNUM, as well as the actual year of issue) was for a time moved to the

Two new lines of "golden dollars" (the Sacagawea and the Presidential series) are among the U.S. Mint's innovations in recent years.

edge; and a depiction of the Statue of Liberty on the reverse stands in place of the word LIBERTY. Taking the place of the Sacagawea dollar, and running alongside the Presidential dollars, is the series of Native American dollars (2009 to date). These feature an annually changing design that honors the important contributions made by Indian tribes and individual Native Americans to the development and history of the United States.

LOOKING FORWARD

Will any of these new dollars be able to oust that traditional workhorse, the dollar bill? This seems unlikely unless special steps are taken. People are conservative when it comes to what they deem "normal" money, and they are likely to stick with what they know.

What about the survival of the one-cent piece? The 2009 Lincoln commemoratives are about the only pieces of good news for this most humble member of our monetary system. The price of copper rose in the early 1980s, so zinc was substituted for it, but recently the price of zinc has risen too. About the only remaining cheap metallic candidate is aluminum, but public opposition would be expected: we have come to regard aluminum as nearly worthless.

And there's still a larger problem: people simply don't use the cent as they once did. The coin's purchasing power has essentially disappeared. So the previously unmentionable is now being discussed: if we were to do away with the cent, would the Republic survive? Groups have sprung up to defend this hallowed member of the monetary system. Some are composed of traditionalists, who feel the cent must be saved, if only for its symbolic value; others represent the zinc industry, for which the billions of cents struck each year represent a significant profit.

And there is the question of what to do with all those unwanted cents. If we want to save the denomination, how do we get these billions of coins out of dresser drawers and piggy banks and back into trade? The simplest, most elegant solution might involve a permanent halt in production but continuing legality for those coins already struck. Since new cents would not be added to commerce, old ones would come out of hiding, perform at least a part of the role for which they had been created, become worn out, and quietly disappear.

The trials of the dollar and the eclipse of the cent should not cause alarm. At bottom, the American monetary system is always a work in progress. Change is inevitable, and if one world seems to be ending, another is beginning. Here and abroad, money is the product of *people*. And where there are people, there is always movement.

These developments are exciting for the hobbyist, but they are perhaps more important for the historian and student of numismatics: among other things, they proclaim that the exceptional, the unusual, and the local have by no means disappeared from America's media of exchange, and that what appeared at first glance to be a closing door is also an open one, welcoming, beckoning. Who knows where it may lead our people—and our money?

Colonial Issues

FOREIGN COINS IN THE COLONIES

Money had a rich history in America prior to the advent of the United States' national coinage in 1793. When coins tumbled off the presses from the first Philadelphia Mint the country was much more accustomed to coins from other lands. Prior to 1652 there was no local coinage and the only money in circulation was whatever came here from Europe through trade or travel. People were content to use currency, both old and new, whose value was based more on the metal content than on the issuer's reliability. Foreign money in America during the colonial period had become so embedded that it continued to be accepted as legal tender until discontinued by the Coinage Act of February 21, 1857. Coins of this era are so fundamental to American numismatics that every collection should include at least a sampling.

From the very beginning of commerce in America "hard money" was needed for trade with overseas nations. The largest quantity of coinage consisted of English crowns, shillings, and pence, and Spanish and Spanish-American silver pieces of eight, all of which circulated throughout colonial settlements until being sent back to England for critically needed supplies. Additional quantities of coins came from trading furs, lumber, and other exports that provided a limited but much needed supply of hard currency. Of equal importance to commerce were similar coins of other European countries. The large silver Dutch *leeuwendaalder* (Lyon or Lion dollar) and French *écu* saw extensive circulation, as did the Brazilian gold *peças*. Some New York bills of 1709 were even denominated in Lyon dollars. Distinguishing between the relative values of the multitude of different foreign currencies was not a simple task. To facilitate conversions, books and tables showed comparison prices for each currency.

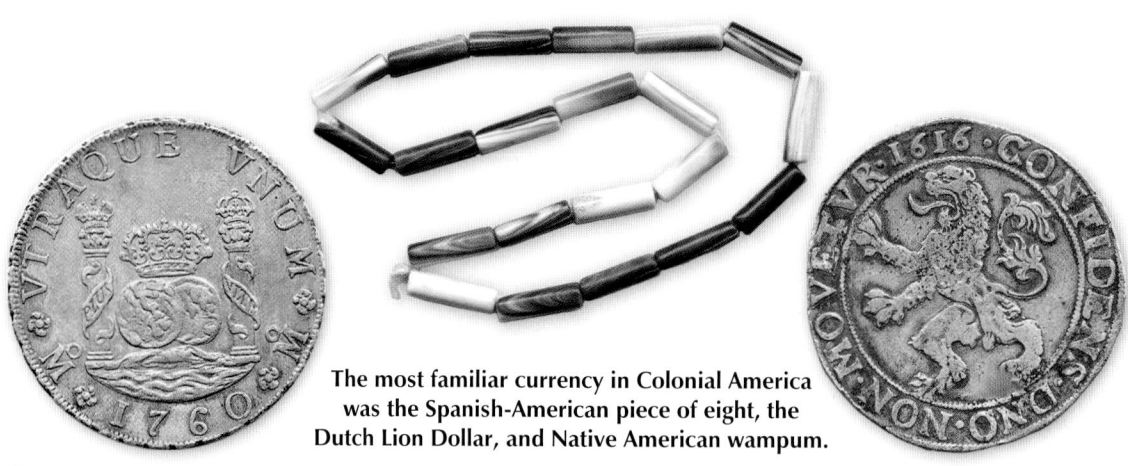

The most familiar currency in Colonial America was the Spanish-American piece of eight, the Dutch Lion Dollar, and Native American wampum.

The popular Spanish-American silver eight reales, Pillar dollar, or piece of eight, which was a radical departure from denominations in terms of English pounds, shillings, and pence, became a model for the American silver dollar, and its fractional parts morphed into the half-dollar and quarter-dollar coins that are now considered decimal fractions of the dollar. The American quarter dollar, which was similar in size and value to the Spanish two-real coin, took on the nickname "two bits"—a moniker that remains today. Similarly, the American one-cent coin has never totally lost its association with the English penny, and is still called that by anyone indifferent to numismatic accuracy.

Coins, tokens, paper money, and promissory notes were not the only media of exchange used during the early formation of the country. Many day-to-day transactions were carried on by barter and credit. Mixed into this financial morass were local trade items such as native wampum, hides, household goods, and tools. Records were kept in the traditional English pounds, shillings, and pence, but debts and taxes were paid in corn, beaver pelts, or money—money being whatever foreign coins were available. The terms "country pay" or "corn" referred to a number of different kinds of grain or even peas. Standard exchange rates were established and country pay was lawfully received at the colonial treasury for taxes.

Beyond these pre-federal considerations are the many kinds of private and state issues of coins and tokens that permeate the colonial period from 1616 to 1776. These are items that catch the attention and imagination of everyone interested in the history and development of early America. Yet, despite their enormous historical importance, forming a basic collection of such items is not nearly as daunting as one might expect.

The coins and tokens described in the next three sections of this book are fundamentally a major-type listing of the metallic money used throughout the pre-federal period. Many collectors use this as a guide to forming a basic set of these pieces. It is not encyclopedic in its scope. Beyond the basic types are numerous sub-varieties of some of the issues, and a wider range of European coins. Some collectors aim for the finest possible condition, while others find great enjoyment in pieces that saw actual circulation and use during the formative days of the country. There are no rules about how or what to collect other than to enjoy owning a genuine piece of early American history.

SPANISH-AMERICAN COINAGE IN THE NEW WORLD

Values shown for these silver coins are for the most common dates and mintmarked pieces of each issue. Similar pieces were struck at Spanish-American mints in Bolivia, Chile, Colombia, Guatemala, Mexico, Panama, Peru, and Santo Domingo.

COB COINAGE – KING PHILIP II (1556–1598) TO KING CHARLES III (1760–1772)

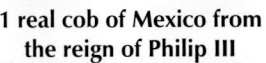

1 real cob of Mexico from the reign of Philip III		1668 2 reales cob struck in Potosi, from the reign of Charles II

	VG	F	VF	EF
Cob Type, 1/2 Real (1556–1773)	$30	$70	$125	$400
Cob Type, 1 Real (1556–1773)	$40	$100	$175	$425
Cob Type, 2 Reales (1556–1773)	$75	$160	$250	$650
Cob Type, 4 Reales (1556–1773)	$110	$250	$300	$800
Cob Type, 8 Reales (1556–1773)	$150	$300	$500	$900

Values are for coins with partial or missing dates. Fully dated coins are valued much higher. Some cobs were also issued beyond these dates and until as late as 1773 in Bolivia.

PILLAR TYPE – KING PHILIP V (1732–1747), KING FERDINAND VI (1747–1760), AND KING CHARLES III (1760–1772)

1734 8 reales Pillar dollar from the reign of Philip V.

1761 2 reales "pistareen" from the reign of Charles III

	VG	F	VF	EF
Pillar Type, 1/2 Real (1732–1772)	$20	$35	$75	$150
Pillar Type, 1 Real (1732–1772)	$30	$50	$80	$175
Pillar Type, 2 Reales (1732–1772)	$40	$65	$120	$300
Pillar Type, 4 Reales (1732–1772)	$150	$375	$675	$900
Pillar Type, 8 Reales (1732–1772)	$120	$200	$450	$675
Spanish 2 Reales "pistareen" (1716–1771)	$20	$35	$60	$120

BUST TYPE – KING CHARLES III (1772–1789), KING CHARLES IV (1789–1808), AND KING FERDINAND VII (1808–1825)

1807 8 reales Bust dollar from the reign of Charles IV.

	VG	F	VF	EF
Bust Type, 1/2 Real (1772–1825)	$10	$15	$35	$100
Bust Type, 1 Real (1772–1825)	$20	$35	$50	$120
Bust Type, 2 Reales (1772–1825)	$25	$50	$75	$180
Bust Type, 4 Reales (1772–1825)	$100	$250	$475	$800
Bust Type, 8 Reales (1772–1825)	$40	$70	$100	$220

The New World began its first coinage in 1536 in Mexico City. By 1732 the first round coins were made and the columnario. or Pillar coinage, became the coin of trade internationally. In 1772 the Bust dollars with the effigy of the king of Spain were placed in circulation. These coins and the Republican style of later Latin American countries circulated legally in the United States until 1857. Parallel issues of Spanish-American gold coins were made during this period. They saw extensive use for international trade and somewhat lesser use in domestic transactions in America. The Spanish silver pistareen was also a popular and convenient coin in circulation.

TYPICAL WORLD COINAGE USED IN COLONIAL AMERICA
NETHERLANDS SILVER COINAGE, 1601–1693

1640 1/2 Leeuwendaalder.

	VG	F	VF	EF
Netherlands, 1/2 Leeuwendaalder (1601–1653)	$60	$120	$225	$450
Netherlands, Leeuwendaalder "Lion Dollar" (1601–1693)	$70	$150	$275	$550

FRENCH SILVER COINAGE OF KING LOUIS XV (1715–1774) AND KING LOUIS XVI (1774–1792)

1791 écu from the reign of Louis XVI.

	VG	F	VF	EF
France, 1/2 Écu (1715–1792)	$25	$80	$150	$325
France, Écu (1715–1792)	$40	$100	$225	$375

See additional listings of French coins authorized for use in North America on pages 111–114.

BRITISH SILVER COINAGE OF KING CHARLES I (1625–1649) TO KING GEORGE III (1760–1820)

1639 6 pence from the reign of Charles I.   1787 shilling from the reign of George III.

	VG	F	VF	EF
England, Threepence (1625–1786)	$15	$25	$60	$90
England, Sixpence (1625–1787)	$20	$35	$80	$100
England, Shilling (1625–1787)	$35	$50	$100	$200
England, Half Crown (1625–1750)	$90	$160	$350	$600
England, Crown (1625–1730)	$200	$450	$800	$1,200

English copper coins and their imitations circulated extensively in early America and are described on pages 127–129.

Other items frequently used as money in early America included cut fractions of various silver coins. These were cut by private individuals. The quarter 8-reales coin was "two bits." Worn and cut portions of coins usually passed for change according to their weight.

BRITISH NEW WORLD ISSUES

SOMMER ISLANDS (BERMUDA)

This coinage, the first struck for the English colonies in the New World, was issued circa 1616. The coins were known as *Hogge Money* or *Hoggies*, from the wild hogs depicted on their obverses.

The Sommer Islands, as Bermuda was known at the time, were under the jurisdiction of the Virginia Company, a joint-stock mercantile venture formed under a British royal patent and headquartered in London. (This venture was actually undertaken by two companies: the Virginia Company of Plymouth, for what is now New England; and the Virginia Company of London, for the American South.)

English government of the islands had started a few years before the coins were issued—by accident! In 1609 Admiral Sir George Somers led a fleet bound from England to the New World, laden with relief supplies for the Virginia settlement of Jamestown. Somers and his ship were separated from the rest of the fleet in a strong storm, and they ran onto the reefs of the Bermuda Islands, some 700 miles from Virginia. (The islands were named for Juan de Bermúdez, who is believed to have stopped there some hundred years earlier.) For ten months Somers and his party were able to live on wild hogs and birds, local plants, and fish, building houses and a church. During this time they also constructed two small ships, in which, in May 1610, most of the shipwrecked colonists continued their interrupted journey to Virginia.

Bermuda became a separate entity of the Virginia Company of London, from November 1612 until June 29, 1615, when "the Governour and Company of the City of London for the Plantacon of the Somer Islands" (often called the Bermuda Company by historians) was officially incorporated under royal charter. This incorporation granted the right of coinage. The coins did not arrive in the islands until May 16, 1616, at the earliest, a year after Bermuda was under its new charter.

The pieces were struck on thin planchets of brass or copper, lightly silvered, in four denominations: shilling, sixpence, threepence, and twopence, each indicated by Roman numerals. A wild hog is the main device and appears on the obverse side of each coin. SOMMER ISLANDS is inscribed (misspelling both the English admiral's name and the corporation's) within beaded circles on the larger denominations. The reverse shows a full-rigged galleon, or carrack, with the flag of St. George on each of four masts. Many examples of these coins show signs of oxidation or pitting.

"In an era when British silver shillings and fractions traded in commerce based on their intrinsic value," writes Q. David Bowers, "the Bermuda pieces were tokens of little value, a fiat currency that circulated in the manner that paper money would later be used worldwide—good as long as both parties had confidence in the value. As might be expected, these coins had little or no trade value other than within the islands, where they were mostly used at the company storehouse, exchanged for supplies" (*Whitman Encyclopedia of Colonial and Early American Coins*).

These coins of Bermuda did not circulate in North America, but they have traditionally been considered part of early "American" coinage. Sylvester S. Crosby, writing in his 1875 masterwork *Early Coins of America*, insisted that the Bermuda coins laid claim to being "the first ever struck for the English colonies in America," this despite the fact that the islands were not a part of the Virginia colony proper. The regular edition of the *Guide Book of United States Coins* has included them in its pre-federal coverage since the first edition, published in 1946.

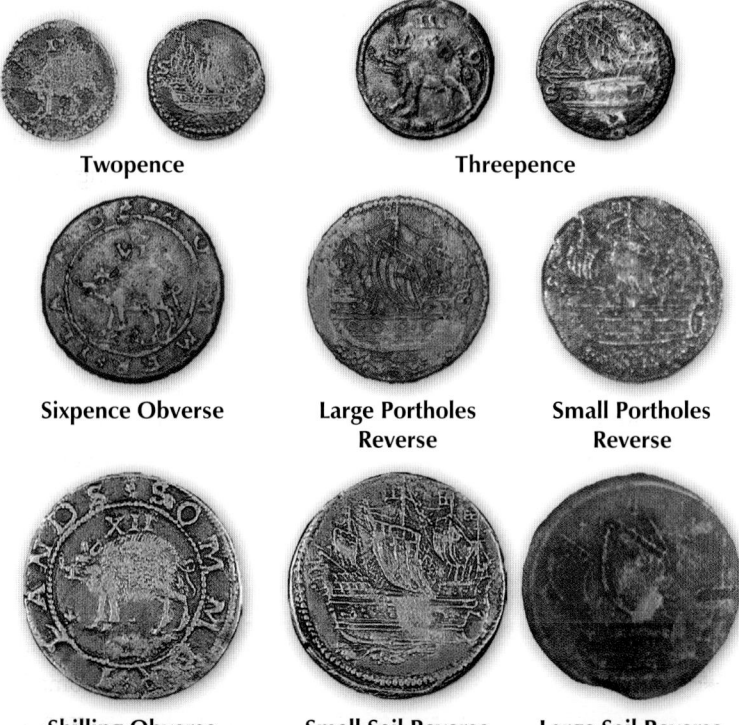

Twopence   Threepence

Sixpence Obverse Large Portholes Small Portholes
        Reverse   Reverse

Shilling Obverse Small Sail Reverse Large Sail Reverse

	AG	G	VG	F	VF	EF
Twopence, Large Star Between Legs	$4,500	$7,000	$11,000	$20,000	$50,000	$75,000
Twopence, Small Star Between Legs	$4,500	$7,000	$11,000	$20,000	$50,000	$75,000
Threepence	—	—	$75,000	$125,000	$175,000	—
Sixpence, Small Portholes	$3,500	$4,500	$7,500	$17,500	$50,000	$70,000
Sixpence, Large Portholes	$3,750	$4,750	$8,000	$20,000	$60,000	$90,000
Shilling, Small Sail	$4,750	$6,500	$11,000	$35,000	$65,000	$95,000
Shilling, Large Sail	$8,000	$15,000	$50,000	$80,000	$110,000	—

MASSACHUSETTS
"NEW ENGLAND" COINAGE (1652)

The earliest authorized medium of exchange in the New England settlements was wampum. The General Court of Massachusetts in 1637 ordered "that wampamege should passe at 6 a penny for any sume under 12 d." Wampum consisted of shells of various colors, ground to the size of kernels of corn. A hole was drilled through each piece so it could be strung on a leather thong for convenience and adornment.

Corn, pelts, and bullets were frequently used in lieu of coins, which were rarely available. Silver and gold coins brought over from England, Holland, and other countries tended to flow back across the Atlantic to purchase needed supplies. The colonists, thus left to their own resources, traded with the friendly Native Americans in kind. In 1661 the law making wampum legal tender was repealed.

Agitation for a standard coinage reached its height in 1651. England, recovering from a civil war between the Puritans and Royalists, ignored the colonists, who took matters into their own hands in 1652.

The Massachusetts General Court in 1652 ordered the first metallic currency—the New England silver threepence, sixpence, and shilling—to be struck in the English Americas (the Spaniards had established a mint in Mexico City in 1535). Silver bullion was procured principally in the form of mixed coinage from the West Indies. The mint was located in Boston, and John Hull was appointed mintmaster; his assistant was Robert Sanderson (or Saunderson). At first, Hull received as compensation one shilling threepence for every 20 shillings coined. This fee was adjusted several times during his term as mintmaster.

The planchets of the New England coins were struck with prepared punches twice (once for the obverse, and once for the reverse). First the letters NE were stamped, and then on the other side the numerical denomination of III, VI, or XII was added.

These are called "NE coins" today.

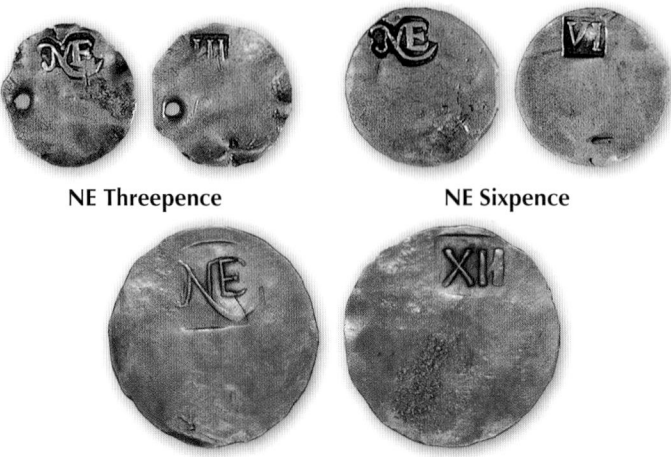

NE Threepence   NE Sixpence

NE Shilling

Early American coins in conditions better than those listed are rare and are consequently valued much higher.

	G	VG	F	VF	EF	AU
NE Threepence (a)				—		
NE Sixpence (b)	$55,000	$90,000	$175,000	$285,000	$400,000	$650,000
NE Shilling	$50,000	$80,000	$125,000	$175,000	$225,000	$300,000

a. Unique. **b.** 8 examples are known.

WILLOW TREE COINAGE (1653–1660)

The simplicity of the designs on the NE coins invited counterfeiting, and clipping or shaving of the edges by charlatans who sought to snip a little bit of metal from a lot of coins and thereby accumulate a pile of silver. Therefore, they were soon replaced by the Willow Tree series.

All of the Willow Tree coins bore the date 1652, when Oliver Cromwell was in power in Britain, after the English civil war and during the Interregnum government. In fact they were minted from 1653 to 1660. The date 1652 may have been used simply because this was the year the coinage was authorized. Output increased over the years, and the coins were plentiful in circulation.

These pieces, like all early American coins, were produced from handmade dies that are often individually distinctive. The tree in the design is known as a "willow" not from any official legislative records, and certainly not from lifelike resemblance to an actual willow tree, but from terminology dating from 1867 in an auction catalog of the Joseph Mickley Collection. To make the coins, a worker likely placed a silver planchet into a rocker press, which forced a curved upper die against a curved or flat bottom die. This would explain the slight elongation and gentle bend of many Willow Tree coins.

NEW ENGLAND is spelled out, instead of being abbreviated, as on the earlier NE coinage.

Among the four classes of Massachusetts silver coins—NE, Willow Tree, Oak Tree, and Pine Tree—the Willow Tree pieces are far and away the rarest today. The die varieties that can be found and identified are of interest to collectors who value each according to individual rarity. Values shown for type coins are for the most frequently seen die variety.

Threepence   Sixpence

Shilling

	G	VG	F	VF	EF
1652 Willow Tree Threepence (a)	—	—	—		
Auctions: $587,500, VF, March 2015					
1652 Willow Tree Sixpence (b)	$20,000	$35,000	$70,000	$160,000	$250,000
Auctions: $253,000, Unc., November 2005					
1652 Willow Tree Shilling	$20,000	$35,000	$60,000	$140,000	$225,000
Auctions: $276,000, EF, November 2005					

a. 3 examples are known. **b.** 14 examples are known.

OAK TREE COINAGE (1660–1667)

The Oak Tree coins of Massachusetts were struck from 1660 to 1667, following the Willow Tree coinage. The 1662-dated twopence of this type was the only coin of the Willow Tree, Oak Tree, and Pine Tree series that did not bear the date 1652. Numismatists are divided on whether the twopence date of 1662 is an error, or a deliberate use of the year that the new denomination was authorized.

The obverse of these coins features a tree traditionally described by numismatists as an oak tree. Although it is deciduous, it does not closely resemble a specific species. On the reverse, NEW ENGLAND is spelled out, surrounding the date and denomination.

In 1660 the Commonwealth of England was dissolved and the British monarchy was restored under King Charles II. At the time, following longstanding tradition and law, the right to produce coins was considered to be a royal sovereign prerogative. Sylvester Crosby in *Early Coins of America* suggested that during the Massachusetts silver coinage period, numerous tributes—including ship masts, 3,000 codfish, and other material items—were sent to the king to placate him and postpone any action on the Massachusetts coinage question. As with many situations involving early American coinage, facts are scarce.

As with other types of Massachusetts silver, a number of die varieties of Oak Tree coinage can be collected and studied. In the marketplace they are seen far more often than are the two earlier types. They are valued according to their individual rarity. Values shown here are for the most frequently seen die varieties.

Twopence

Threepence

Sixpence

Shilling

	G	VG	F	VF	EF	AU	Unc.
1662 Oak Tree Twopence, Small 2	$600	$1,000	$1,800	$3,500	$6,000	$8,500	$13,000
1662 Oak Tree Twopence, Large 2	$600	$1,000	$1,800	$3,500	$6,000	$8,500	$13,000
1652 Oak Tree Threepence, No IN on Obverse	$725	$1,250	$3,000	$6,500	$11,000	$17,000	—
1652 Oak Tree Threepence, IN on Obverse	$725	$1,350	$3,250	$7,000	$13,000	$21,000	$50,000
1652 Oak Tree Sixpence, IN on Reverse	$800	$1,300	$3,200	$7,500	$16,000	$21,000	$40,000
1652 Oak Tree Sixpence, IN on Obverse	$800	$1,300	$3,200	$7,500	$14,000	$19,000	$35,000
1652 Oak Tree Shilling, IN at Left	$750	$1,250	$3,000	$7,000	$10,500	$16,000	$28,000
1652 Oak Tree Shilling, IN at Bottom	$750	$1,250	$3,000	$6,500	$10,000	$14,500	$26,000
1652 Oak Tree Shilling, ANDO	$900	$1,900	$4,000	$8,500	$15,000	$20,000	$34,000
1652 Oak Tree Shilling, Spiny Tree	$750	$1,250	$3,250	$7,000	$12,000	$17,000	$31,000

PINE TREE COINAGE (1667–1682)

The first Pine Tree coins were minted on the same-size planchets as the Oak Tree pieces, in denominations of threepence, sixpence, and shilling. Subsequent issues of the shilling were narrower in diameter and thicker. Large Planchet shillings ranged from 27 to 31 mm in diameter; Small Planchet shillings ranged from 22 to 26 mm in diameter.

The design of the Pine Tree coins borrowed from the flag of the Massachusetts Bay Colony, which featured a pine tree. On the reverse, NEW ENGLAND is spelled out, surrounding the date and a Roman numeral indicating the denomination (III, VI, or XII).

Large quantities of Pine Tree coins were minted. The coinage was abandoned in 1682. A proposal to renew coinage in 1686 was rejected by the General Court of Massachusetts.

As with other types of Massachusetts silver, a number of die varieties of Pine Tree coins are available for collecting and study. In the marketplace, they are valued according to their individual rarity. Values shown here are for the most often seen die varieties.

Threepence

Sixpence

Shilling, Large Planchet (1667–1674)

Shilling, Small Planchet (1675–1682)

	G	VG	F	VF	EF	AU	Unc.
1652 Threepence, Pellets at Trunk	$550	$800	$1,600	$3,200	$6,000	$9,000	$19,000
1652 Threepence, Without Pellets	$550	$800	$1,600	$3,250	$6,000	$9,000	$19,000
1652 Sixpence, Pellets at Trunk	$600	$925	$1,800	$3,600	$6,250	$10,000	$20,000
1652 Sixpence, Without Pellets	$600	$950	$1,900	$3,800	$6,750	$11,000	$21,000
1652 Shilling, Large Planchet (27–31 mm)							
Pellets at Trunk	$700	$1,100	$2,400	$5,000	$9,000	$14,000	$26,000
Without Pellets at Trunk	$700	$1,000	$2,300	$4,750	$8,500	$13,000	$25,000
No H in MASATUSETS	$800	$1,400	$3,000	$7,500	$13,500	$20,000	—
Ligatured NE in Legend	$700	$1,100	$2,400	$5,000	$9,000	$14,000	$26,000
1652 Shilling, Small Planchet (22–26 mm)	$600	$925	$2,200	$4,000	$6,500	$11,000	$25,000

MARYLAND

LORD BALTIMORE COINAGE

Cecil Calvert, the second Lord Baltimore, inherited from his father nearly absolute control over Maryland. Calvert believed he had the right to coin money for the colony, and in 1659 he ordered shillings, sixpences, and groats (four-penny pieces) from the Royal Mint in London and shipped samples to Maryland, to his brother Philip, who was then his secretary for the colony. Calvert's right to strike coins was upheld by Oliver Cromwell's government. The whole issue was small, and while his coins did circulate in Maryland at first, by 1700 they had largely disappeared from commerce.

Calvert's coins bear his portrait on the obverse, with a Latin legend calling him "Lord of Mary's Land." The reverses of the larger denominations bear his family coat of arms and the denomination in Roman numerals. There are several die varieties of each. Some of these coins are found holed and repaired. The copper penny, or denarium, is the rarest denomination, with only nine reported specimens, including some found in recent times by detectorists using electronic devices.

The silver groats (fourpence), sixpence, and shillings were used extensively in commerce, and today most examples show considerable wear. Typical grades include VG, Fine, and VF, often with surface marks or damage. Those graded AU or higher are major rarities. The silver pieces have an engrailed edge.

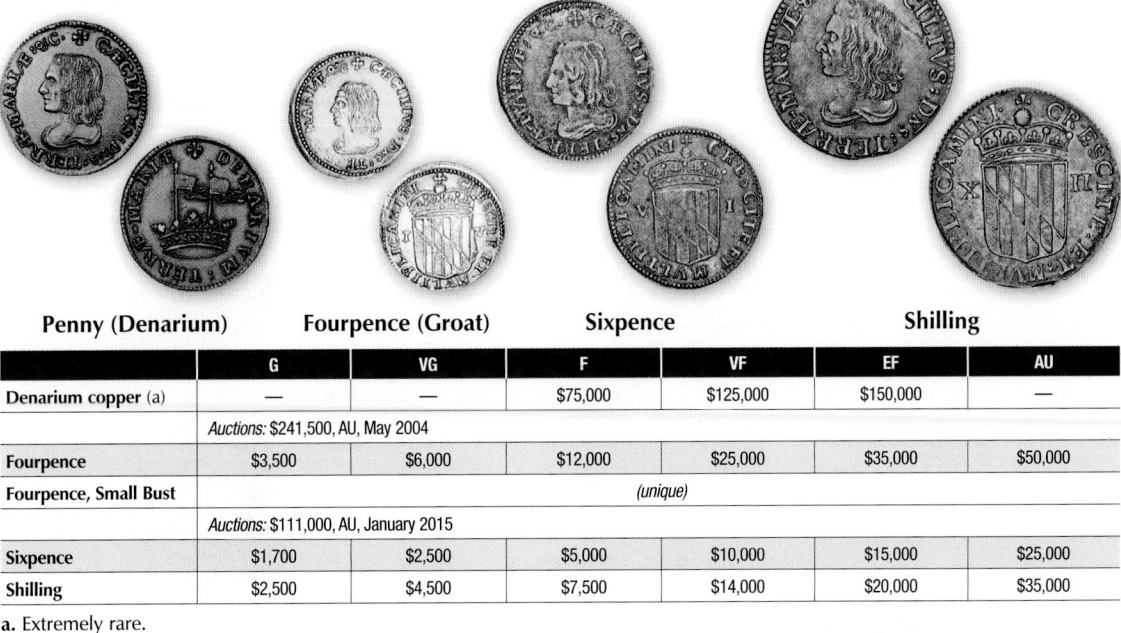

Penny (Denarium)   Fourpence (Groat)   Sixpence   Shilling

	G	VG	F	VF	EF	AU
Denarium copper (a)	—	—	$75,000	$125,000	$150,000	—
	Auctions: $241,500, AU, May 2004					
Fourpence	$3,500	$6,000	$12,000	$25,000	$35,000	$50,000
Fourpence, Small Bust	*(unique)*					
	Auctions: $111,000, AU, January 2015					
Sixpence	$1,700	$2,500	$5,000	$10,000	$15,000	$25,000
Shilling	$2,500	$4,500	$7,500	$14,000	$20,000	$35,000

a. Extremely rare.

NEW JERSEY

ST. PATRICK OR MARK NEWBY COINAGE

Mark Newby was a shopkeeper in Dublin, Ireland, in the 1670s and came to America in November 1681, settling in West Jersey (today's New Jersey). He brought with him a quantity of copper pieces, of two sizes, believed by numismatists to have been struck in Dublin circa 1663 to 1672. These are known as *St. Patrick coppers*. (Alternatively, they may have been struck for circulation in Ireland by Pierre Blondeau to fill an order made by the duke of Ormonde, but this has not been confirmed.) The larger-sized piece, called by collectors a *halfpenny*, bears the arms of the City of Dublin on the shield on the reverse. The smaller-sized piece, called a *farthing*, does not. Although neither bears a denomination, these are designations traditionally assigned by numismatists. Both sizes have reeded edges.

Newby became a member of the legislature of West Jersey, and under his influence the St. Patrick coinage was made legal tender by the General Assembly of New Jersey in May 1682. The legislature did not specify which size piece could circulate, only that the coin was to be worth a halfpenny in trade and that no one would be obliged to accept more than five shillings' worth (120 coins) in one payment. Some numismatists believe the larger-size coin was intended. However, many more farthing-size pieces are known than halfpennies, and numerous coins of the farthing size have been excavated by detectorists in New Jersey, while none of the larger coins have been found this way. Most numismatists believe that the smaller-sized piece was the one authorized as legal tender. Copper coins often circulated in the colonies at twice what they would have been worth in England.

The obverses show King David crowned, kneeling and playing a harp. The legend FLOREAT REX ("May the King Prosper") is separated by a crown. The reverse side of the halfpence shows St. Patrick with a crozier in his left hand and a trefoil in his right, and surrounded by people. At his left side is a shield. The legend is ECCE GREX ("Behold the Flock"). The farthing reverse shows St. Patrick driving away serpents and a dragon as he holds a metropolitan cross in his left hand. The legend reads QUIESCAT PLEBS ("May the People Be at Ease").

The decorative brass insert found on the coinage, usually over the crown on the obverse, was put there to make counterfeiting more difficult. On some pieces this decoration has been removed or does not show. Numerous die variations exist (more than 140 of the smaller coins, and 9 of the larger). The silver strikings, and a unique gold piece, were not authorized as legal tender, although many of the silver coins are heavily worn, suggesting that they were passed many times from hand to hand in commerce, perhaps at the value of a shilling.

St. Patrick "Farthing"   St. Patrick "Halfpenny"

	G	VG	F	VF	EF	AU
St. Patrick "Farthing"	$135	$300	$800	$2,750	$6,000	$14,000
Similar, Halo Around Saint's Head	$750	$1,500	$6,000	$15,000	$40,000	—
Similar, No C in QUIESCAT	$1,000	$4,000	$8,000	$17,000	—	—
St. Patrick "Farthing," Silver	$1,800	$4,500	$9,000	$18,000	$25,000	$35,000
St. Patrick "Farthing," Gold (a)						—
	Auctions: $184,000, AU, January 2005					
St. Patrick "Halfpenny"	$350	$800	$1,000	$2,500	$10,000	$18,000

a. Unique.

COINAGE AUTHORIZED BY BRITISH ROYAL PATENT

AMERICAN PLANTATIONS COINS (1688)

These tokens, struck in nearly pure tin, were the first royally authorized coinage for the British colonies in America. They were made under a franchise granted in August 1688 to Richard Holt, an agent for the owners of several tin mines. Holt proposed that the new issues be made with a Spanish monetary designation to increase their acceptance in the channels of American commerce, where Spanish-American coins were often seen. Thus the tokens are denominated as 1/24 part of a Spanish real.

The obverse shows an equestrian portrait of King James II in armor and flowing garments. The reverse features four heraldic shields (English, Scottish, French, and Irish) connected by chains. The edge is decorated with dots.

Numismatist Eric P. Newman has identified seven different obverse dies and an equal number of reverse dies. Most American Plantation tokens show black oxidation of the tin. Bright, unblemished original specimens are more valuable. (Around 1828 a London coin dealer acquired the original dies and arranged for restrikes to be made for sale. In high grades these pieces are seen more frequently in the marketplace than are originals. They are valuable but worth less than original strikes.)

	G	VG	F	VF	EF	AU	Unc.
(1688) James II Plantation 1/24 Real coinage							
1/24 Part Real	$225	$300	$500	$1,200	$2,000	$4,000	$7,000
1/24 Part Real, ET. HB. REX	$275	$400	$900	$2,000	$3,000	$8,000	$10,000
1/24 Part Real, Sidewise 4 in 24	$425	$1,000	$1,900	$4,500	$6,750	$11,000	$18,000
1/24 Part Real, Arms Transposed	$675	$1,750	$2,900	$7,000	$13,000	$19,000	—
1/24 Part Real, Restrike	$100	$150	$250	$450	$600	$850	$1,700

COINAGE OF WILLIAM WOOD (1722–1733)

William Wood, an English metallurgist, experimented with the production of several pattern coins (of halfpenny, penny, and twopence size) in 1717. In 1722 he was granted royal patents to mint coins for America and Ireland. At the time his productions were largely unpopular as money, but later generations of coin collectors have sought his Rosa Americana coins for their connections to colonial America. The Hibernia coins are similar in some respects; they have no connection with America but are sought as companion pieces.

ROSA AMERICANA COINS (1722–1723, 1733)

On July 12, 1722, William Wood obtained a patent from King George I to make coins for the American colonies. At the time the colonies were facing a serious shortage of circulating coins.

The first pieces Wood struck were undated. Later issues bear the dates 1722, 1723, 1724, and 1733. The Rosa Americana pieces were issued in three denominations—half penny, penny, and twopence—and were intended for America. This type had a fully bloomed rose on the reverse with the words ROSA AMERICANA UTILE DULCI ("American Rose—Useful and Sweet").

The obverse, common to both Rosa Americana and Hibernia pieces, shows the head of George I and the legend GEORGIUS D:G MAG: BRI: FRA: ET. HIB: REX ("George, by the Grace of God, King of Great Britain, France, and Ireland") or abbreviations thereof.

Despite Wood's best efforts, these Rosa Americana coins circulated in the colonies only to a limited extent. They eventually did see use as money, but it was back in England, and likely at values lower than their assigned denominations. (Each was about half the weight of its English counterpart coin.)

The 1733 twopence is a pattern that bears the bust of King George II facing to the left. It was issued by the successors to the original coinage patent, as William Wood had died in 1730.

The coins are made of a brass composition of copper and zinc (sometimes mistakenly referred to as *Bath metal*, an alloy proposed by Wood that would have also included a minute portion of silver). Planchet quality is often rough and porous because the blanks were heated prior to striking. Edges often show file marks.

	VG	F	VF	EF	AU	Unc.
(No date) Twopence, Motto in Ribbon *(illustrated)*	$200	$400	$700	$1,200	$3,000	$5,500
(No date) Twopence, Motto Without Ribbon (a)	—	—	—			

a. 3 examples are known.

	VG	F	VF	EF	AU	Unc.
1722 Halfpenny, VTILE DVLCI	$900	$2,000	$3,500	$6,250	$9,000	
1722 Halfpenny, D.G.REX ROSA AMERI. UTILE DULCI	$150	$200	$400	$850	$1,400	$3,500
1722 Halfpenny, DEI GRATIA REX UTILE DULCI	$150	$200	$400	$800	$1,300	$3,000

	VG	F	VF	EF	AU	Unc.
1722 Penny, GEORGIVS			$12,000	$17,500	$22,500	$30,000
1722 Penny, VTILE DVLCI	$170	$300	$700	$1,100	$2,500	$6,000
1722 Penny, UTILE DULCI	$150	$200	$350	$700	$1,200	$2,750

	VG	F	VF	EF	AU	Unc.
1722 Twopence, Period After REX	$175	$300	$600	$1,200	$2,000	$3,750
1722 Twopence, No Period After REX	$175	$300	$600	$1,200	$2,000	$3,750

	VG	F	VF	EF	AU	Unc.
1723 Halfpenny, Uncrowned Rose	$1,000	$1,800	$3,600	$5,500	$8,500	$12,500
1723 Halfpenny, Crowned Rose	$125	$200	$375	$700	$1,400	$3,000

	VG	F	VF	EF	AU	Unc.
1723 Penny *(illustrated)*	$100	$125	$275	$550	$900	$2,200
1723 Twopence	$150	$250	$350	$800	$1,400	$2,650

	EF	AU	Unc.
1724, 4 Over 3 Penny (pattern), DEI GRATIA	$7,500	$15,000	$20,000
1724, 4 Over 3 Penny (pattern), D GRATIA	$8,750	$20,000	$31,000
(Undated) (1724) Penny, ROSA: SINE: SPINA. (a)	$30,000	$40,000	—

a. 5 examples are known.

1724 Twopence (pattern)	
	Auctions: $25,300, Choice AU, May 2005

1733 Twopence (pattern), Proof

	Auctions: $63,250, Gem PF, May 2005

WOOD'S HIBERNIA COINAGE (1722–1724)

Around the same time that his royal patent was granted to strike the Rosa Americana coins for the American colonies, William Wood received a franchise to produce copper coins for circulation in Ireland. This was ratified on July 22, 1722. The resulting coins, likely struck in Bristol, England, featured a portrait of King George and, on the reverse, a seated figure with a harp and the word HIBERNIA. Their edges are plain. Denominations struck were farthing and halfpenny, with dates of 1722, 1723, and 1724. These Hibernia coins were unpopular in Ireland and faced vocal public criticism, including from satirist Jonathan Swift. "It was asserted that the issues for Ireland were produced without Irish advice or consent, that the arrangements were made in secret and for the private profit of Wood, and that the pieces were seriously underweight" (*Whitman Encyclopedia of Colonial and Early American Coins*). As a result, King George reduced the number of coins allowed by Wood's patent, and the franchise was retired completely in 1725 in exchange for Wood receiving a £24,000 pension over eight years. Some of the unpopular Hibernia coins, meanwhile, may have been sent to the American colonies to circulate as small change. Their popularity with American numismatists stems from the similarity of their obverses to those in the Rosa Americana series.

Numerous varieties exist.

1722, Hibernia Farthing   1722, Hibernia Halfpenny, First Type   1722, Hibernia Halfpenny, Second Type   1723, 3 Over 2, Halfpenny

1724, Hibernia Farthing   1724, Hibernia Halfpenny

	G	VG	F	VF	EF	AU	Unc.
1722 Farthing, D: G: REX	$150	$500	$750	$2,200	$4,000	$8,500	$16,000
1722 Halfpenny, D: G: REX, Rocks at Right (pattern)	—	—	—	$8,000	$12,000	$20,000	$40,000
1722 Halfpenny, First Type, Harp at Left	$50	$80	$125	$250	$500	$800	$1,500
1722 Halfpenny, Second Type, Harp at Right	$45	$70	$100	$200	$450	$750	$1,300
1722 Halfpenny, Second Type, DEII (blunder)	$80	$150	$375	$850	$1,600	$2,100	$3,500
1723 Farthing, D.G.REX	$50	$100	$125	$250	$400	$550	$1,000
1723 Farthing, DEI. GRATIA. REX	$25	$50	$80	$125	$225	$400	$600
1723 Farthing (silver pattern)	$400	$600	$1,000	$2,500	$3,500	$6,000	$9,000
1723 Halfpenny, 3 Over 2 (a)	$40	$60	$125	$350	$500	$900	$1,750
1723 Halfpenny	$25	$45	$75	$125	$250	$375	$700
1723 Halfpenny (silver pattern)			—	—	—	—	—
1724 Farthing	$50	$125	$225	$750	$1,500	$2,000	$4,000
1724 Halfpenny	$45	$100	$150	$350	$650	$1,000	$2,200
1724 Halfpenny, DEI Above Head					—	—	

a. Varieties exist.

VIRGINIA HALFPENNIES (1773–1774)

In 1773 the British Crown authorized coinage of copper halfpennies for the colony of Virginia, not to exceed 25 tons' weight. "This was the first and only colonial coinage authorized and produced in Britain for use in an American colony, thereby giving the Virginia pieces the unique claim of being the only true American colonial coinage" (*Whitman Encyclopedia of Colonial and Early American Coins*). The designs included a laurelled portrait of King George III and the royal coat of arms of the House of Hanover. The coins were struck at the Tower Mint in London. Their edges are plain.

Most Mint State pieces available to collectors today are from a hoard of some 5,000 or more of the halfpennies held by Colonel Mendes I. Cohen of Baltimore, Maryland, in the 1800s. Cohen came from a prominent banking family. His cache was dispersed slowly and carefully from 1875 until 1929, as the coins passed from his estate to his nieces and nephews. Eventually the remaining coins, numbering approximately 2,200, the property of Bertha Cohen, were dispersed in one lot in Baltimore. These pieces gradually filtered out, in groups and individually, into the wider numismatic marketplace.

The Proof patterns that were struck on a large planchet with a wide milled border are often referred to as pennies. The silver pieces dated 1774 are referred to as shillings, but they may have been patterns or trials for a halfpenny or a guinea.

Red Uncirculated pieces without spots are worth considerably more.

	G	VG	F	VF	EF	AU	Unc.
1773 Halfpenny, Period After GEORGIVS	$25	$50	$100	$150	$350	$500	$900
1773 Halfpenny, No Period After GEORGIVS	$35	$75	$140	$200	$400	$600	$1,200

1773, "Penny"   1774, "Shilling"

	PF
1773 "Penny"	$27,000
1774 "Shilling" (a)	$130,000

a. 6 examples are known.

EARLY AMERICAN AND RELATED TOKENS

ELEPHANT TOKENS (CA. 1672–1694)

LONDON ELEPHANT TOKENS

The London Elephant tokens were struck in London circa 1672 to 1694. Although they were undated, two examples are known to have been struck over 1672 British halfpennies. Most were struck in copper, but one was made of brass. Their legend, GOD PRESERVE LONDON, may have been a general plea for divine aid and not a specific reference to the outbreak of plague in 1665 or the great fire of 1666.

These pieces were not struck for the colonies, and they probably did not circulate widely in America, although a few may have been carried there by colonists. They are associated, through a shared obverse die, with the 1694 Carolina and New England Elephant tokens. They have a plain edge but often show the cutting marks from planchet preparation.

	VG	F	VF	EF	AU	Unc.
(1694) Halfpenny, GOD PRESERVE LONDON, Thick Planchet	$350	$600	$900	$1,500	$2,500	$4,200
(1694) Halfpenny, GOD PRESERVE LONDON, Thin Planchet	$550	$1,000	$2,500	$4,000	$6,000	$11,000
Similar, Brass (a)					—	
(1694) Halfpenny, GOD PRESERVE LONDON, Diagonals in Center of Shield	$700	$2,000	$4,500	$8,000	$15,000	$38,000
(1694) Halfpenny, Similar, Sword in Second Quarter of Shield	—	—	$20,000	—	—	—
(1694) Halfpenny, LON DON	$1,100	$2,250	$4,500	$8,500	$15,000	$24,000

a. Unique.

CAROLINA ELEPHANT TOKENS

Although no law is known authorizing coinage for Carolina, two very interesting pieces known as Elephant tokens were made with the date 1694. These copper tokens are of halfpenny denomination. The reverse reads GOD PRESERVE CAROLINA AND THE LORDS PROPRIETERS 1694.

The second and more readily available variety has the last word spelled PROPRIETORS. The correction was made on the original die, for the E shows plainly beneath the O. On the second variety the elephant's tusks nearly touch the milling.

The Carolina pieces were probably struck in England and perhaps intended as advertising to heighten interest in the Carolina Plantation. Another theory suggests they may have been related to or made for the Carolina coffee house in London.

	VG	F	VF	EF	AU	Unc.
1694 PROPRIETERS	$10,000	$30,000	$50,000	$60,000	$80,000	$125,000
1694 PROPRIETORS, O Over E	$6,500	$11,000	$20,000	$40,000	$65,000	$100,000

NEW ENGLAND ELEPHANT TOKENS

Like the Carolina tokens, the New England Elephant tokens are believed to have been struck in England, possibly as promotional pieces to increase interest in the American colonies, or perhaps related to the New England coffee house in London

	VG	F	VF	EF	AU
1694 NEW ENGLAND	$140,000	$160,000	$180,000	$220,000	—

NEW YORKE IN AMERICA TOKENS (1660S OR 1670S)

The New Yorke in America tokens are farthing or halfpenny tokens intended for New York, issued by Francis Lovelace, who was governor from 1668 until 1673. The tokens use the older spelling with a final "e" (YORKE), which predominated before 1710. The obverse shows Cupid pursuing the loveless butterfly-winged Psyche—a rebus on the name Lovelace. The reverse shows a heraldic eagle, identical to the one displayed in fesse, raguly (i.e., on a crenellated bar) on the Lovelace coat of arms. In weight, fabric, and die axis the tokens are similar to certain 1670 farthing tokens of Bristol, England, where they may have been struck. There is no evidence that any of these pieces ever circulated in America. Fewer than two dozen are believed to now exist.

	VG	F	VF	EF
(Undated) Brass or Copper	$10,000	$18,000	$30,000	$60,000
(Undated) Pewter	$10,000	$23,000	$33,000	$72,500

GLOUCESTER TOKENS (1714)

Sylvester S. Crosby, in his book *The Early Coins of America*, stated that these tokens appear to have been intended as a pattern for a shilling—a private coinage by Richard Dawson of Gloucester (county), Virginia. The only specimens known are struck in brass, although the denomination XII indicates that a silver coinage (one shilling) may have been planned. The building depicted on the obverse may represent some public building, possibly the courthouse.

Although neither of the two known examples shows the full legends, combining the pieces shows GLOVCESTER COVRTHOVSE VIRGINIA / RIGHAVLT DAWSON. ANNO.DOM. 1714. This recent discovery has provided a new interpretation of the legends, as a Righault family once owned land near the Gloucester courthouse. A similar, but somewhat smaller, piece possibly dated 1715 exists. The condition of this unique piece is too poor for positive attribution.

	F
1714 Shilling, brass (a)	$120,000

a. 2 examples are known.

HIGLEY OR GRANBY COPPERS (1737–1739)

Dr. Samuel Higley owned a private copper mine near Granby, Connecticut, in an area known for many such operations. Higley was a medical doctor, with a degree from Yale College, who also practiced blacksmithing and experimented in metallurgy. He worked his mine as a private individual, extracting particularly rich copper, smelting it, and shipping much of it to England. He also made his own dies for plain-edged pure-copper "coins" that he issued.

Legend has it that a drink in the local tavern cost three pence, and that Higley paid his bar tabs with his own privately minted coins, denominated as they were with the legend THE VALUE OF THREEPENCE. When his supply of such coppers exceeded the local demand, neighbors complained that they were not worth the denomination stated, and Higley changed the legends to read VALUE ME AS YOU PLEASE and I AM GOOD COPPER (but kept the Roman numeral III on the obverse).

After Samuel Higley's death in May 1737 his older brother John continued his coinage.

The Higley coppers were never officially authorized. There were seven obverse and four reverse dies. All are rare. Electrotypes and cast copies exist.

	AG	G	VG	F	VF
1737 THE VALVE OF THREE PENCE, CONNECTICVT, 3 Hammers	$12,000	$22,500	$42,500	$60,000	$100,000
1737 THE VALVE OF THREE PENCE, I AM GOOD COPPER, 3 Hammers (a)	—	$35,000	$50,000	$80,000	$175,000
1737 VALUE ME AS YOU PLEASE, I AM GOOD COPPER, 3 Hammers	$12,000	$22,500	$42,500	$60,000	$100,000
1737 VALVE • ME • AS • YOU • PLEASE, I • AM • GOOD • COPPER, 3 Hammers (a)			$75,000		
(1737) VALUE • ME • AS • YOU • PLEASE, J • CUT • MY • WAY • THROUGH, Broad Axe	$12,000	$22,500	$42,500	$60,000	$100,000
(1737) THE • WHEELE • GOES • ROUND, Reverse as Above (b)					$376,000
1739 VALUE • ME • AS • YOU • PLEASE, J • CUT • MY • WAY • THROUGH, Broad Axe	$15,000	$25,000	$45,000	$65,000	$125,000

a. This issue has the CONNECTICVT reverse. 3 examples are known. **b.** Unique.

HIBERNIA–VOCE POPULI COINS

These coins, struck in the year 1760, were prepared by Roche, of King Street, Dublin, who was at that time engaged in the manufacture of buttons for the army. Like other Irish tokens, some could have found their way to colonial America and possibly circulated in the colonies with numerous other counterfeit halfpence and "bungtown tokens." There is no evidence to prove that Voce Populi pieces, which bear the legend HIBERNIA (Ireland) on the reverse, ever circulated in North America. Sylvester S. Crosby did not include them in *The Early Coins of America*, 1875. Nor were they covered in Wayte Raymond's *Standard Catalogue of United States Coins* (until Walter Breen revised the section on colonial coins in 1954, after which they were "adopted" by mainstream collectors). Various theories exist regarding the identity of the bust portrait on the obverse, ranging from kings and pretenders to the British throne, to the provost of Dublin College.

There are two distinct issues. Coins from the first, with a "short bust" on the obverse, range in weight from 87 to 120 grains. Those from the second, with a "long bust" on the obverse, range in weight from 129 to 154 grains. Most of the "long bust" varieties have the letter P on the obverse. None of the "short bust" varieties bear the letter P, and, judging from their weight, they may have been contemporary counterfeits.

Farthing, Large Letters

Halfpenny

Halfpenny, VOOE POPULI

Halfpenny, P in Front of Face

	G	VG	F	VF	EF	AU	Unc.
1760 Farthing, Large Letters	$210	$350	$600	$1,250	$2,000	$3,000	$6,500
1760 Farthing, Small Letters			$8,000	$22,000	$60,000	—	—
1760 Halfpenny	$80	$110	$180	$300	$525	$800	$1,250
1760 Halfpenny, VOOE POPULI	$90	$150	$225	$450	$650	$1,100	$3,250
1760 Halfpenny, P Below Bust	$110	$200	$300	$600	$1,000	$1,900	$5,000
1760 Halfpenny, P in Front of Face	$90	$175	$250	$525	$900	$1,600	$4,500

PITT TOKENS (CA. 1769)

William Pitt the Elder, the British statesman who endeared himself to America, is the subject of these brass or copper pieces, probably intended as commemorative medalets. The so-called halfpenny (the larger of the type's two sizes) served as currency during a shortage of regular coinage. The farthing-size tokens are rare.

The reverse legend (THANKS TO THE FRIENDS OF LIBERTY AND TRADE) refers to Pitt's criticism of the Crown's taxation of the American colonies, and his efforts to have the Stamp Act of March 22, 1765, repealed in 1766. The obverse bears a portrait and the legends THE RESTORER OF COMMERCE and NO STAMPS.

"Little is known concerning the circumstances of issue. Robert Vlack suggests that the pieces may have been designed by Paul Revere. Striking may have been accomplished around 1769 by James Smither (or Smithers) of Philadelphia" (*Whitman Encyclopedia of Colonial and Early American Coins*).

Farthing   Halfpenny

	G	VG	F	VF	EF	AU	Unc.
1766 Farthing	$3,500	$6,000	$12,000	$30,000	$42,000	$55,000	
1766 Halfpenny	$300	$500	$750	$1,250	$2,000	$3,000	$8,500
1766 Halfpenny, silvered				$1,800	$4,000	$5,500	$12,000

RHODE ISLAND SHIP MEDALS (CA. 1779)

The circumstances of the issue of these medals (or tokens) are mysterious. They were largely unknown to American coin collectors until 1864, when a specimen was offered in W. Elliot Woodward's sale of the Seavey Collection. It sold for $40—a remarkable price at the time.

The obverse shows the flagship of British admiral Lord Richard Howe at anchor, while the reverse depicts the retreat of American forces from Rhode Island in 1778. The inscriptions show that the coin was meant for a Dutch-speaking audience. The word *vlugtende* ("fleeing") appears on the earlier issues below Howe's flagship—an engraving error. After a limited number of pieces were struck with this word, it was removed on most coins. A wreath was added, eliminating the word *vlugtende*, after which the final coinage took place. It is believed the medal was struck in England circa 1779 or 1780 for the Dutch market, as propaganda to influence Dutch opinion against the American cause. Specimens are known in pinchbeck, copper, and pewter.

Rhode Island Ship Medal (1778–1779)   Legend "vlugtende"   Wreath Below Ship
                                              Below Ship

	VF	EF	AU	Unc.
With "vlugtende" (fleeing) Below Ship, Brass or copper		—		
Wreath Below Ship, Brass or copper	$1,000	$1,750	$2,750	$5,500
Without Wreath Below Ship, Brass or copper	$900	$1,700	$2,500	$5,000
Similar, Pewter	$3,500	$5,500	$8,000	$14,000

JOHN CHALMERS ISSUES (1783)

John Chalmers, a Maryland goldsmith and silversmith, struck a series of silver tokens of his own design in Annapolis in 1783. The dies were by Thomas Sparrow, another silversmith in the town. The shortage of change in circulation and the refusal of the American people to use underweight cut Spanish coins prompted the issuance of these pieces. (Fraudsters would attempt to cut five "quarters" or nine or ten "eighths" out of one Spanish silver dollar, thereby realizing a proportional profit when they were all spent.)

On the Chalmers threepence and shilling obverses, two clasped hands are shown, perhaps symbolizing unity of the several states; the reverse of the threepence has a branch encircled by a wreath. A star within a wreath is on the obverse of the sixpence, with hands clasped upon a cross utilized as the reverse type. On this denomination, the designer's initials TS (for Thomas Sparrow) can be found in the crescents that terminate the horizontal arms of the cross. The reverse of the more common shilling varieties displays two doves competing for a worm underneath a hedge and a snake. The symbolic message is thought to have been against the danger of squabbling with brethren over low-value stakes while a dangerous mutual enemy lurked nearby. The edges of these tokens are crudely reeded. There are only a few known examples of the shilling type with 13 interlinked rings, from which a liberty cap on a pole arises.

Threepence   Sixpence,   Sixpence, Large Date
               Small Date

Shilling, Birds, Short Worm   Shilling, Rings

	VG	F	VF	EF	AU
1783 Threepence	$2,000	$4,000	$8,000	$18,000	$32,500
1783 Sixpence, Small Date	$3,500	$7,500	$19,000	$32,000	$65,000
1783 Sixpence, Large Date	$2,600	$6,000	$15,000	$30,000	$60,000
1783 Shilling, Birds, Long Worm	$1,250	$2,500	$7,000	$12,000	$22,000
1783 Shilling, Birds, Short Worm *(illustrated)*	$1,200	$2,200	$6,500	$10,000	$20,000
1783 Shilling, Rings (a)	*$50,000*	*$100,000*	*$200,000*	—	—

a. 5 examples are known.

FRENCH NEW WORLD ISSUES

None of the coins of the French regime relate specifically to territories that later became part of the United States. They were all general issues for the French colonies of the New World. The coinage of 1670 was authorized by an edict of King Louis XIV dated February 19, 1670, for use in New France,

Acadia, the French settlements in Newfoundland, and the French West Indies. The copper coinage of 1717 to 1722 was authorized by edicts of 1716 and 1721 for use in New France, Louisiana, and the French West Indies.

COINAGE OF 1670

The coinage of 1670 consisted of silver 5 and 15 sols and copper 2 deniers (or "doubles"). A total of 200,000 of the 5 sols and 40,000 of the 15 sols was struck at Paris. Nantes was to have coined the copper, but did not; the reasons for this may never be known, since the archives of the Nantes Mint before 1700 were destroyed. The only known specimen is a pattern struck at Paris. The silver coins were raised in value by a third in 1672 to keep them circulating, but in vain. They rapidly disappeared, and by 1680 none were to be seen. Later they were restored to their original values. This rare issue should not be confused with the common 1670-A 1/12 écu with reverse legend SIT. NOMEN. DOMINI. BENEDICTUM.

The 1670-A double de l'Amerique Françoise was struck at the Paris Mint along with the 5- and 15-sols denominations of the same date. All three were intended to circulate in France's North American colonies. Probably due to an engraving error, very few 1670-A doubles were actually struck. Today, only one is known to survive.

Copper Double   **Silver 5 Sols**

	VG	F	VF	EF	Unc.
1670-A Copper Double (a)			$225,000		
1670-A 5 Sols	$1,000	$2,000	$5,000	$7,500	$21,000
1670-A 15 Sols	$13,000	$32,000	$75,000	$125,000	—

a. Unique.

COINAGE OF 1717–1720

The copper 6 and 12 deniers of 1717 were authorized by an edict of King Louis XV (by order of the six-year-old king's regent, the duke of Orléans) dated December 1716, to be struck at Perpignan (mintmark Q). The order could not be carried out, for the supply of copper was too brassy, and only a few pieces were coined. The issues of 1720, which were struck at multiple mints, are popularly collected for their association with the John Law "Mississippi Bubble" venture.

1720 6 Deniers

1717-Q 12 Deniers

1720 20 Sols

	F	VF	EF
1717-Q 6 Deniers, No Crowned Arms on Reverse (a)			—
1717-Q 12 Deniers, No Crowned Arms on Reverse			$45,000
1720 Liard, Crowned Arms on Reverse, Copper	$350	$500	$900
1720 6 Deniers, Crowned Arms on Reverse, Copper	$550	$900	$1,750
1720 12 Deniers, Crowned Arms on Reverse, Copper	$400	$750	$1,500
1720 20 Sols, Silver	$375	$700	$1,500

a. Extremely rare.

BILLON COINAGE OF 1709–1760

The French colonial coins of 30 deniers were called *mousquetaires* because of the outlined cross on their reverse, evocative of the design on the short coats worn by French musketeers. These coins were produced at Metz and Lyon. The 15 deniers was coined only at Metz. The sou marque and the half sou were coined at almost every French mint, those of Paris being most common. The half sou of 1740 is the only commonly available date. Specimens of the sou marque dated after 1760 were not used in North America. A unique specimen of the 1712-AA 30 deniers is known in the size and weight of the 15-denier coins.

30 Deniers "Mousquetaire"

Sou Marque (24 Deniers)

	VG	F	VF	EF	AU	Unc.
1711–1713-AA 15 Deniers	$150	$300	$500	$1,000	$1,750	$4,000
1709–1713-AA 30 Deniers	$75	$100	$250	$400	$675	$1,500
1709–1713-D 30 Deniers	$75	$100	$250	$400	$675	$1,500
1738–1748 Half Sou Marque, various mints	$60	$100	$200	$350	$575	$1,200
1738–1760 Sou Marque, various mints	$50	$80	$125	$175	$300	$500

COINAGE OF 1721–1722

The copper coinage of 1721 and 1722 was authorized by an edict of King Louis XV dated June 1721. The coins were struck on copper blanks imported from Sweden. Rouen and La Rochelle struck pieces of nine deniers (one sou) in 1721 and 1722. New France received 534,000 pieces, mostly from the mint of La Rochelle, but only 8,180 were put into circulation, as the colonists disliked copper. In 1726 the rest of the issue was sent back to France.

In American coin catalogs of the 1800s, these coins were often called "Louisiana coppers."

	VG	F	VF	EF
1721-B (Rouen)	$500	$1,000	$3,500	$10,000
1721-H (La Rochelle)	$100	$175	$1,000	$2,500
1722-H	$100	$175	$1,000	$2,500
1722-H, 2 Over 1	$175	$275	$1,200	$4,000

FRENCH COLONIES IN GENERAL (1767)

These copper coins were produced for use in the French colonies and only unofficially circulated in Louisiana along with other foreign coins and tokens. Most were counterstamped RF (République Française) for use in the West Indies. The mintmark A signifies the Paris Mint. The edge is decorated with a double row of dots.

	VG	VF	EF	AU
1767 French Colonies, Sou	$120	$250	$700	$1,500
1767 French Colonies, Sou, counterstamped RF	$100	$200	$300	$600

Post-Colonial Issues

The coins explored in this section are classified as "post-colonial" because they came after the colonial period (some during the early months of rebellion; most after the official declaration of independence) but before the first federal Mint was established in Philadelphia in 1792.

Early American coins were produced from hand-engraved dies, which are often individually distinctive. For many types, the great number of die varieties that can be found and identified are of interest to collectors who value each according to its individual rarity. Values shown for type coins in this section are for the most common die variety of each.

SPECULATIVE ISSUES, TOKENS, AND PATTERNS

Nova Constellatio Coppers (1783–1786)

The Nova Constellatio coppers, dated 1783 and 1785 and without denomination, were struck in fairly large quantities in Birmingham, England, and were shipped to New York where they entered circulation. Apparently they resulted from a private coinage venture undertaken by Constable, Rucker & Co., a trading business formed by William Constable, John Rucker, Robert Morris, and Gouverneur Morris as equal partners. The designs and legends were copied from the denominated patterns dated 1783 made in Philadelphia (see page 151). A few additional coppers dated 1786 were made by an inferior diesinker.

"The Nova Constellatio coppers were well received and saw extensive use in commerce, as evidenced by the wear seen on typically specimens today," writes Q. David Bowers in the *Whitman Encyclopedia of Colonial and Early American Coins*. "Later, they were devalued, and many were used as undertypes (planchets) for Connecticut and, to a lesser extent, New Jersey and Vermont coppers."

| 1783, CONSTELLATIO, Pointed Rays, Small U.S. | | 1783, CONSTELLATIO Pointed Rays, Large U.S. | |

	VG	F	VF	EF	AU	Unc.
1783, CONSTELLATIO, Pointed Rays, Small U.S.	$100	$200	$375	$750	$1,300	$3,200
1783, CONSTELLATIO, Pointed Rays, Large U.S.	$100	$225	$650	$1,100	$2,500	$6,750

1783, CONSTELATIO, Blunt Rays

1785, CONSTELATIO, Blunt Rays   **1785, CONSTELLATIO, Pointed Rays**

	VG	F	VF	EF	AU	Unc.
1783, CONSTELATIO, Blunt Rays	$100	$225	$550	$1,000	$1,800	$5,750
1785, CONSTELATIO, Blunt Rays	$100	$225	$550	$1,200	$3,000	$7,200
1785, CONSTELLATIO, Pointed Rays	$100	$200	$375	$750	$1,300	$3,000
1785, Similar, Small, Close Date	$300	$600	$2,500	$4,500	$6,500	$15,000
1786, Similar, Small Date	$4,750	$8,000	$20,000	$30,000		

IMMUNE COLUMBIA PIECES (1785)

These pieces are considered private or unofficial coins. No laws describing them are known. There are several types bearing the seated figure of Justice. These pieces are stylistically related to the Nova Constellatio coppers, with the Immune Columbia motif with liberty cap and scale replacing the LIBERTAS and JUSTITIA design.

1785, Silver, 13 Stars   **1785, Pointed Rays, CONSTELLATIO**

	F	VF	EF
1785, Copper, 13 Stars	$15,000	$27,000	$45,000
1785, Silver, 13 Stars	$25,000	$50,000	$75,000
1785, Pointed Rays, CONSTELLATIO, Extra Star in Reverse Legend, Copper	$15,000	$27,000	$45,000
1785, Pointed Rays, CONSTELLATIO, Gold (a)			—
1785, Blunt Rays, CONSTELLATIO, Copper (b)		$50,000	—

Note: The gold specimen in the National Numismatic Collection (now maintained by the Smithsonian) was acquired in 1843 from collector Matthew A. Stickney in exchange for an 1804 dollar. **a.** Unique. **b.** 2 examples are known.

1785, George III Obverse

	G	VG	F	VF
1785, George III Obverse	$5,500	$8,500	$11,000	$18,000
1785, VERMON AUCTORI Obverse, IMMUNE COLUMBIA	$6,250	$10,000	$15,000	$40,000

1787, IMMUNIS COLUMBIA, Eagle Reverse

	VG	F	VF	EF	AU	Unc.
1787, IMMUNIS COLUMBIA, Eagle Reverse	$600	$1,000	$3,200	$5,000	$7,500	$13,500

Note: Believed to be a prototype for federal coinage; some were coined after 1787.

CONFEDERATIO AND RELATED TOKENS

The Confederatio and associated pieces are believed to be proposed designs for America's early federal coinage. The 1785, Inimica Tyrannis America, variety may owe its design to a sketch by Thomas Jefferson. In all, 12 dies were presumed struck in 13 combinations. No one knows for certain who made these pieces. The combination with a standard reverse die for a 1786 New Jersey copper is especially puzzling. They were all made in small quantities and were circulated. Research is ongoing.

America   Americana   Washington

Immunis   Eagle   Libertas et Justitia

Large Circle   Small Circle   Pattern Shield

The 1786, Immunis Columbia, with scrawny-eagle reverse is a related piece probably made by a different engraver or mint.

	VG	F	VF	EF	AU
1785 Inimica Tyrannis America, Large Circle (a,b)	$40,000	$70,000	$100,000	$175,000	$275,000
1785 Inimica Tyrannis Americana, Small Circle (c,d)	$30,000	$40,000	$50,000	$150,000	$250,000
1785 Inimica Tyrannis Americana, Large Circle, Silver (b,e)		$50,000 (f)			
1785 Gen. Washington, Large Circle (g,h)	$50,000	$75,000	$125,000	$250,000	
1786 Gen. Washington, Eagle (i,j)		$40,000			
(No Date) Gen. Washington, Pattern Shield (k,l)		$75,000	$100,000 (f)		$350,000
1786 Immunis, Pattern Shield (m,n)		$25,000	$50,000	$100,000	$125,000
1786 Immunis, 1785 Large Circle (o,j)	$150,000				$100,000
1786 Eagle, Pattern Shield (p,e)					$200,000
1786 Eagle, 1785 Large Circle (q,j)		$50,000	$85,000		
1785 Libertas et Justitia, 1785 Large Circle (r,e)	$25,000				
1785 Small Circle, 1787 Excelsior Eagle (s,j)		$35,000			
1786 Immunis Columbia, Scrawny Eagle (l)			$50,000	$90,000	

a. America obverse, Large Circle reverse. b. 7 examples are known. c. Americana obverse, Small Circle reverse. d. 9 examples are known. e. 1 example is known. f. Damaged. g. Washington obverse, Large Circle reverse. h. 6 examples are known. i. Washington obverse, Eagle reverse. j. 2 examples are known. k. Washington obverse, Pattern Shield reverse. l. 3 examples are known. m. Immunis obverse, Pattern Shield reverse. n. 17 examples are known. o. Immunis obverse, Large Circle reverse. p. Eagle obverse, Pattern Shield reverse. q. Eagle obverse, Large Circle reverse. r. Libertas et Justitia obverse, Large Circle reverse. s. Small Circle obverse, 1787 Excelsior Eagle reverse. Image of the 1787 Excelsior eagle (facing right) is on page 126.

COINAGE OF THE STATES

New Hampshire (1776)

New Hampshire was the first of the states to consider the subject of coinage following the Declaration of Independence. On March 13, 1776, by which time the colonies were in rebellion but had not yet formally declared their independence, the New Hampshire House of Representatives established a committee to consider the minting of copper coins. The committee recommended such coinage as a way to facilitate small commercial transactions.

William Moulton was empowered to make a limited quantity of coins of pure copper authorized by the State House of Representatives in 1776. Although cast patterns were prepared, it is believed that they were not approved. Little of the proposed coinage was ever actually circulated.

Other purported patterns are of doubtful origin. These include a unique engraved piece and a rare struck piece with large initials WM on the reverse.

	G
1776 New Hampshire Copper	$100,000
Auctions: $172,500, VG-10, March 2012	

MASSACHUSETTS
MASSACHUSETTS UNOFFICIAL COPPERS (1776)

Presumably, in 1776, the year the colonies proclaimed their independence from Britain, three types of Massachusetts coppers were created. Very little is known about their origins or the circumstances of their production. Numismatic historians deduced them to be patterns until recent scholarship cast doubt on their authenticity as coppers of the Revolutionary War era.

The obverse of one of these coppers has a crude pine tree with "1d LM" at its base and the legend MASSACHUSETTS STATE. The reverse has a figure probably intended to represent the Goddess of Liberty, seated on a globe and holding a liberty cap and staff. A dog sits at her feet. The legend LIBERTY AND VIRTUE surrounds the figure, and the date 1776 is situated beneath.

Sylvester S. Crosby, writing in 1875 in *The Early Coins of America*, traced the provenance of this unique copper back to a grocer who sold it to a schoolboy around 1852. The grocer was from "the northerly part" of Boston, and he had "found it many years before while excavating on his premises, in the vicinity of Hull or Charter Street."

	VF
1776 Pine Tree Copper (a)	—

a. Unique, in the Massachusetts Historical Society collection.

A similar piece, probably from the same source as the Pine Tree copper, features a Native American standing with a bow on the obverse, with a worn legend that may read PROVINCE OF MASSA or similar. On the reverse is a seated figure and globe, visible partially visible legend (LIBERTATIS), and the date 1776 at bottom. The only known example was overstruck on a 1747 English halfpenny, and is holed.

	VG
1776 Indian Copper (a)	—

a. Unique.

A third Massachusetts piece is sometimes called the *Janus copper*. On the obverse are three heads, facing left, front, and right, with the legend STATE OF MASSA. 1/2 D. The reverse shows the Goddess of Liberty facing right, resting against a globe. The legend is GODDESS LIBERTY 1776.

	F
1776 Halfpenny, 3 Heads on Obverse (a)	—
Auctions: $44,650, Fine, January 2015; $40,000, Fine, November 1979	

a. Unique.

MASSACHUSETTS AUTHORIZED ISSUES (1787–1788)

An "Act for establishing a mint for the coinage of gold, silver and copper" was passed by the Massachusetts General Court on October 17, 1786. The next year, the council directed that the design of the copper coins should incorporate ". . . the figure of an indian with a bow & arrow & a star on one side, with the word 'Commonwealth,' the reverse a spread eagle with the words—'of Massachusetts A. D. 1787'—" (this wording would be slightly different in the final product).

The coinage of Massachusetts copper cents and half cents in 1787 and 1788 was under the direction of Captain Joshua Witherle of Boston. These were the first coins bearing the denomination *cent* as would be later established by Congress. They were produced in large quantities and are fairly plentiful today. The wear seen on many of the Massachusetts cents and half cents indicates that they enjoyed long circulation in commerce. Many varieties exist, the most valuable being that with arrows in the eagle's right talon.

Most of the dies for these coppers were made by Joseph Callender. Jacob Perkins of Newburyport also engraved some of the 1788 dies.

The mint was abandoned early in 1789, in compliance with the newly ratified U.S. Constitution, and because its production was unprofitable.

1787 Half Cent

1787 Cent, Obverse	Arrows in Right Talon	Arrows in Left Talon

	G	VG	F	VF	EF	AU	Unc.
1787 Half Cent	$100	$125	$225	$500	$750	$1,250	$3,000
1787 Cent, Arrows in Right Talon	$10,000	$16,000	$25,000	$50,000	$75,000	$100,000	$180,000
1787 Cent, Arrows in Left Talon	$100	$110	$200	$600	$1,250	$2,500	$6,000
1787 Cent, "Horned Eagle" (die break)	$110	$135	$235	$650	$1,300	$2,800	$7,000

1788 Half Cent   **1788 Cent, Period After**
MASSACHUSETTS

	G	VG	F	VF	EF	AU	Unc.
1788 Half Cent	$100	$125	$225	$550	$1,000	$1,500	$3,200
1788 Cent, Period After MASSACHUSETTS	$100	$110	$200	$600	$1,250	$2,000	$4,800
1788 Cent, No Period After MASSACHUSETTS	$115	$120	$250	$675	$1,500	$2,800	$6,000

CONNECTICUT (1785–1788)

Authority for establishing a mint near New Haven was granted by the state of Connecticut to Samuel Bishop, Joseph Hopkins, James Hillhouse, and John Goodrich in October 1785. They had petitioned the state's General Assembly for this right, noting the public need—small coins were scarce in circulation and many of those seen were counterfeits. Under the Assembly's grant, the four minters would pay the state's treasury an amount equal to 5 percent of the copper coins they produced. To make a profit, the minters would deduct this royalty, plus their other expenses (including materials, labor, and distribution), from the face value of the coins they struck.

Available records indicate that most of the Connecticut coppers were coined under a subcontract, by Samuel Broome and Jeremiah Platt, former New York merchants. Abel Buell was probably the principal diesinker. Many others were struck by Machin's Mills in Newburgh, New York, and were not authorized by Connecticut. These are as highly prized by collectors as are regular issues.

The Connecticut coppers were often struck crudely and on imperfect planchets. Numerous die varieties exist; over the years, collectors have given many of them distinctive nicknames.

1785 Copper, Bust Facing Left   **1785 Copper, Bust Facing Right**

1785 Copper, African Head

	G	VG	F	VF	EF	AU
1785 Copper, Bust Facing Left	$150	$250	$500	$1,500	$3,600	$8,000
1785 Copper, Bust Facing Right	$35	$60	$125	$475	$1,300	$3,500
1785 Copper, African Head	$70	$120	$400	$1,250	$3,500	$8,000

1786 Copper, ETLIB INDE

1786 Copper, Large Head Facing Right

1786 Copper, Mailed Bust Facing Left

1786 Copper, Draped Bust

1786 Copper, Mailed Bust
Facing Left, Hercules Head

	G	VG	F	VF	EF	AU
1786 Copper, ETLIB INDE	$70	$140	$325	$850	$2,500	$7,000
1786 Copper, Large Head Facing Right	$250	$500	$1,500	$4,600	$10,000	
1786 Copper, Mailed Bust Facing Left	$40	$75	$140	$450	$1,100	$2,800
1786 Copper, Draped Bust	$75	$150	$400	$1,100	$2,750	$6,700
1786 Copper, Mailed Bust Facing Left, Hercules Head	$110	$200	$500	$2,000	$4,750	

1787 Copper, Small Head
Facing Right, ETLIB INDE

1787 Copper, Muttonhead Variety,
Topless Liberty

	G	VG	F	VF	EF	AU
1787 Copper, Small Head Facing Right, ETLIB INDE	$90	$150	$300	$1,600	$4,200	$8,500
1787 Copper, Liberty Seated Facing Right (a)		—				
1787, Mailed Bust Facing Right, INDE ET LIB	$100	$180	$400	$2,200	$5,000	
1787 Copper, Muttonhead	$100	$180	$400	$2,200	$5,000	$9,000

a. 2 examples are known.

1787 Copper, Mailed
Bust Facing Left

1787 Copper,
Laughing Head

1787 Copper,
Reverse

	G	VG	F	VF	EF	AU
1787 Copper, Mailed Bust Facing Left	$40	$65	$120	$400	$1,000	$2,500
1787 Copper, Mailed Bust Facing Left, Laughing Head	$50	$100	$200	$500	$1,100	$2,300

**1787 Copper,
Horned Bust**

	G	VG	F	VF	EF	AU
1787 Copper, Mailed Bust Facing Left, Horned Bust	$40	$65	$120	$375	$750	$1,800
1787 Copper, Mailed Bust Facing Left, Hercules Head *(see 1786 for illustration)*	$400	$800	$2,000	$4,250	$8,000	—
1787 Copper, Mailed Bust Facing Left, Dated 1787 Over 1877	$80	$180	$600	$1,600	$4,750	—
1787 Copper, Mailed Bust Facing Left, 1787 Over 88	$175	$235	$700	$1,800	$5,000	—
1787 Copper, Mailed Bust Facing Left, CONNECT, INDE	$50	$125	$200	$600	$1,500	$3,000
1787 Copper, Mailed Bust Facing Left, CONNECT, INDL	$375	$700	$1,500	$3,200	$7,000	

1787 Copper, Draped Bust Facing Left

	G	VG	F	VF	EF	AU
1787 Copper, Draped Bust Facing Left	$30	$50	$80	$200	$500	$1,000
1787 Copper, Draped Bust Facing Left, AUCIORI	$40	$65	$100	$350	$900	$1,500
1787 Copper, Draped Bust Facing Left, AUCTOPI	$45	$75	$140	$500	$1,200	$2,200
1787 Copper, Draped Bust Facing Left, AUCTOBI	$45	$75	$140	$500	$1,200	$2,000
1787 Copper, Draped Bust Facing Left, CONNFC	$40	$60	$100	$400	$900	$1,500
1787 Copper, Draped Bust Facing Left, CONNLC	$75	$150	$250	$800	$3,000	—
1787 Copper, Draped Bust Facing Left, FNDE	$40	$65	$150	$400	$1,300	$2,400
1787 Copper, Draped Bust Facing Left, ETLIR	$40	$60	$125	$350	$1,000	$1,700
1787 Copper, Draped Bust Facing Left, ETIIB	$40	$60	$125	$350	$1,000	$1,800
1787 Copper, GEORGIVS III Obverse, INDE•ET Reverse	$1,500	$3,250	$3,500	—	—	—

1788 Copper, Mailed Bust Facing Right

	G	VG	F	VF	EF	AU
1788 Copper, Mailed Bust Facing Right	$40	$80	$150	$500	$1,300	$2,500
1788 Copper, GEORGIVS III Obverse *(Reverse as Above)*	$100	$210	$550	$1,550	$3,250	—
1788 Copper, Small Head *(see 1787 for illustration)*	$1,500	$3,750	$4,500	$11,000	$20,000	—

1788 Copper, Mailed Bust Facing Left   **1788 Copper, Draped Bust Facing Left**

	G	VG	F	VF	EF	AU
1788 Copper, Mailed Bust Facing Left	$45	$70	$175	$400	$1,100	$2,200
1788 Copper, Mailed Bust Facing Left, CONNLC	$55	$130	$250	$600	$1,800	$3,200
1788 Copper, Draped Bust Facing Left	$45	$70	$175	$400	$1,100	$2,200
1788 Copper, Draped Bust Facing Left, CONNLC	$85	$200	$450	$1,100	$2,500	$4,000
1788 Copper, Draped Bust Facing Left, INDL ET LIB	$80	$140	$300	$800	$2,000	$3,800

NEW YORK AND RELATED ISSUES (1780S)

No official state coinage for New York is known to have been authorized. However, a number of issues in copper and gold were made relating to the state, by a variety of different issuers.

BRASHER DOUBLOONS (1786–1787)

Among the most famous early American pieces coined before establishment of the U.S. Mint at Philadelphia were those produced by the well-known New York City silversmith, goldsmith, and jeweler Ephraim Brasher, who was a neighbor and friend of George Washington's when that city was the seat of the federal government.

The gold pieces Brasher made weighed about 408 grains and were valued at $15 in New York currency. They were approximately equal to the Spanish doubloon, which was equal to 16 Spanish dollars.

Pieces known as *Lima Style doubloons* were dated 1742, but it is almost certain that they were produced in 1786, and were the first efforts of Brasher to make a circulating coin for regional use. Neither of the two known specimens shows the full legends; but weight, gold content, and hallmark are all identical to those for the 1787-dated Brasher coins. An analogous cast imitation Lima style doubloon dated 1735 bears a hallmark attributed to Standish Barry of Baltimore, Maryland, circa 1787.

The design used on the 1787 Brasher doubloon features an eagle on one side and the arms of New York on the other. In addition to his impressed hallmark, Brasher's name appears in small letters on each of his coins. The unique 1787 gold half doubloon is struck from doubloon dies on an undersized planchet that weighs half as much as the larger coins. It is in the National Numismatic Collection in the Smithsonian Institution.

It is uncertain why Brasher produced these pieces. He may have produced them for his own account, charging a nominal fee to convert metal into coin. He was later commissioned by the government to test and verify other gold coins then in circulation. His hallmark EB was punched on each coin as evidence of his testing and its value. In some cases the foreign coins were weight-adjusted by clipping.

		EF
"1742" (1786) Lima Style gold doubloon (a)		$700,000
	Auctions: $690,000, EF-40, January 2005	

a. 2 examples are known.

		EF
1787 New York gold doubloon, EB on Breast		*$5,000,000*
	Auctions: $2,990,000, EF-45, January 2005	
1787 New York gold doubloon, EB on Wing		*$4,000,000*
	Auctions: $4,582,500, MS-63, January 2014	
1787 New York gold half doubloon (a)		—
Various foreign gold coins with Brasher's EB hallmark		*$5,000–$16,000*

a. Unique, in the Smithsonian Collection.

NEW YORK COPPER COINAGE

Several individuals petitioned the New York Legislature in early 1787 for the right to coin copper for the state, but a coinage was never authorized. Instead, a law was passed to regulate the copper coins already in use. Nevertheless, various unauthorized copper pieces were made privately and issued within the state.

One private mint known as Machin's Mills was organized by Captain Thomas Machin, a distinguished veteran of the Revolutionary War, and situated at the outlet of Orange Pond near Newburgh, New York. Shortly after this mint was formed, on April 18, 1787, it was merged with the Rupert, Vermont, mint operated by Reuben Harmon Jr., who held a coinage grant from the Republic of Vermont. The combined partnership agreed to conduct their business in New York, Vermont, Connecticut, or elsewhere if they could benefit by it (though their only known operation was the one at Newburgh).

The operations at Machin's Mills were conducted in secret and were looked upon with suspicion by the local residents. They minted several varieties of imitation George III halfpence, as well as counterfeit coppers of Connecticut and New Jersey. Only their Vermont coppers had official status.

Mints located in or near New York City were operated by John Bailey and Ephraim Brasher. They had petitioned the legislature on February 12, 1787, for a franchise to coin copper. The extent of their partnership, if any, and details of their operation are unknown. Studies of the state coinage show that they produced primarily the EXCELSIOR and NOVA EBORAC pieces of New York, and possibly the "running fox" New Jersey coppers.

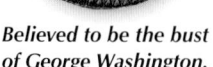

*Believed to be the bust
of George Washington.*

	G	VG	F	VF	EF	AU
1786, NON VI VIRTUTE VICI	$6,000	$10,000	$20,000	$40,000	$67,500	$100,000

**1787 EXCELSIOR Copper,
Large Eagle on Obverse**

**1787 EXCELSIOR Copper,
Eagle on Globe Facing Left**

	G	VG	F	VF	EF
1787 EXCELSIOR Copper, Eagle on Globe Facing Right	$2,750	$4,000	$8,500	$25,000	$60,000
1787 EXCELSIOR Copper, Eagle on Globe Facing Left	$2,750	$3,500	$8,000	$18,000	$40,000
1787 EXCELSIOR Copper, Large Eagle on Obverse, Arrows and Branch Transposed	$4,100	$6,750	$18,000	$35,000	$70,000

1787, George Clinton

1787, Indian and New York Arms

1787, Indian and Eagle on Globe

1787, Indian and George III Reverse

	G	VG	F	VF	EF
1787, George Clinton	$10,000	$20,000	$50,000	$100,000	$250,000
1787, Indian and New York Arms	$10,000	$18,000	$35,000	$50,000	$75,000
1787, Indian and Eagle on Globe	$10,000	$18,000	$30,000	$40,000	$60,000
1787, Indian and George III Reverse (a)	—				

a. 4 examples are known.

BRITISH COPPER COINS AND THEIR IMITATIONS
(INCLUDING MACHIN'S MILLS AND OTHER UNDERWEIGHT COINAGE OF *1786–1789*)

The most common copper coin used for small transactions in early America was the British halfpenny. Wide acceptance and the non–legal-tender status of these copper coins made them a prime choice for unauthorized reproduction by private individuals.

Many such counterfeits were created in America by striking from locally made dies, or by casting or other crude methods. Some were made in England and imported into this country. Pieces dated 1781 and 1785 seem to have been made specifically for this purpose, while others were circulated in both countries.

Genuine regal British halfpence and farthings minted in London and dated 1749 are of special interest to collectors because they were specifically sent to the North American colonies as reimbursement for participation in the expedition against Cape Breton, and circulated extensively throughout New England.

Genuine British halfpenny coppers of both George II (dated 1729–1754) and George III (dated 1770–1775) show finely detailed features within a border of close denticles; the 1 in the date looks like a J. They are boldly struck on good-quality planchets. Their weight is approximately 9.5 grams; their diameter, 29 mm.

British-made lightweight imitation halfpence are generally smaller in diameter and thickness, and weigh less than genuine pieces. Details are crudely engraved or sometimes incomplete. Inscriptions may be misspelled. Planchet quality may be poor.

	G	F	VF	EF	AU
1749, George II British farthing	$20	$40	$75	$175	$250
1749, George II British halfpenny	$25	$50	$100	$200	$300
1770–1775, George III British halfpenny (a)	$15	$20	$50	$100	$250
1770–1775, British imitation halfpenny (a)	$15	$20	$25	$100	$250

a. Values shown are for the most common variety. Rare pieces are sometimes worth significantly more.

During the era of American state coinage, New York diemaker James F. Atlee and/or other coiners minted unauthorized, lightweight, imitation British halfpence. These American-made false coins have the same or similar devices, legends, and, in some cases, dates as genuine regal halfpence, but they contain less copper. Their details are often poorly rendered or missing. Identification of American-made imitations has been confirmed by identifying certain punch marks (such as letters and numerals) and matching them to the distinct punch marks of known engravers.

There are four distinct groups of these halfpence, all linked to the regular state coinage. The first group was probably struck in New York City prior to 1786. The second group was minted in New York City in association with John Bailey and Ephraim Brasher during the first half of 1787. The third group was struck at Machin's Mills during the second half of 1787 and into 1788 or later. A fourth group, made by the Machin's Mills coiners, consists of pieces made from dies that were muled with false dies of the state coinages of Connecticut, Vermont, and New York. Pieces with very crude designs and other dates are believed to have been struck elsewhere in New England.

Georgivs/Britannia
"Machin's Mills" Copper Halfpennies Made in America

Dates used on these pieces were often "evasive," as numismatists describe them today. They include dates not used on genuine pieces and, sometimes, variations in spelling. They are as follows: 1771, 1772, 1774, 1775, and 1776 for the first group; 1747 and 1787 for the second group; and 1776, 1778, 1787, and 1788 for the third group. Pieces generally attributed to James Atlee can be identified by a single outline in the crosses (British Union) of Britannia's shield and large triangular denticles along the coin circumference. The more-valuable American-made pieces are not to be confused with the similar English-made George III counterfeits (some of which have identical dates), or with genuine British half-pence dated 1770 to 1775.

Group I coins dated 1771, 1772, 1774, 1775, and 1776 have distinctive bold designs but lack the fine details of the original coins. Planchets are generally of high quality.

Group II coins dated 1747 and 1787 are generally poorly made. The 1 in the date is not J-shaped, and the denticles are of various sizes. There are no outlines to the stripes in the shield.

Group III coins dated 1776, 1778, 1787, and 1788, struck at Machin's Mills in Newburgh, New York, are similar to coins of Group II, with their triangular-shaped denticles. Most have large dates and berries in the obverse wreath.

	AG	G	VG	F	VF	EF	AU
1747, GEORGIVS II. Group II	$125	$250	$400	$800	$3,500	$8,000	$20,000
1771, GEORGIVS III. Group I	$70	$100	$220	$325	$1,250	$3,000	$6,000
1772, GEORGIVS III. Group I	$80	$150	$250	$500	$1,600	$3,250	$8,000
1772, GEORGIUS III. Group I	$85	$200	$300	$750	$2,300	$4,500	—
1774, GEORGIVS III. Group I	$40	$80	$100	$225	$800	$2,500	$5,000
1774, GEORGIUS III. Group I	$80	$150	$225	$400	$1,750	$3,750	—
1775, GEORGIVS III. Group I	$35	$70	$100	$225	$700	$1,800	$4,750
1776, GEORGIVS III. Group III	$155	$300	$450	$850	$2,500	$7,000	—
1776, GEORCIVS III, Small Date	$1,000	$2,000	$4,500	$9,000	$18,000	$25,000	$35,000
1778, GEORGIVS III. Group III	$40	$70	$125	$275	$750	$2,500	$3,800
1784, GEORGIVS III	$200	$400	$800	$1,500	$3,200	$4,500	$7,500
1787, GEORGIVS III. Group II	$30	$75	$125	$225	$700	$1,400	$3,000
1787, GEORGIVS III. Group III	$30	$75	$125	$225	$700	$1,400	$3,000
1788, GEORGIVS III. Group III	$35	$80	$150	$275	$750	$1,500	$3,500

Note: Values shown are for the most common varieties in each category. Rare pieces can be worth significantly more. Also see related George III combinations under Connecticut, Vermont, and New York.

The muled coins of Group IV are listed separately with the Immune Columbia pieces and with the coins of Connecticut, Vermont, and New York. Other imitation coppers made by unidentified American makers are generally very crude and exceedingly rare. Cast copies of British coins probably circulated along with the imitations without being questioned. Counterfeits of silver Spanish-American coins and Massachusetts tree coins may have also been coined by American minters.

NOVA EBORAC COINAGE FOR NEW YORK

An extensive issue of 1787-dated copper coins appeared, each with a bust on the obverse surrounded by NOVA EBORAC ("New York"). The reverse showed a seated goddess with a sprig in one hand and a liberty cap on a pole in the other hand, with the legend VIRT. ET. LIB. ("Virtue and Liberty") surrounding, and the date 1787 below. The letter punches used on this issue are identical to those used on the Brasher doubloon die. It is likely that John Bailey and Ephraim Brasher operated a minting shop in New York City and produced these and possibly other issues.

1787, NOVA EBORAC, Reverse: Seated Figure Facing Right

1787, NOVA EBORAC, Reverse: Seated Figure Facing Left

1787, NOVA EBORAC, Small Head

1787, NOVA EBORAC, Large Head

	AG	G	F	VF	EF	AU
1787, NOVA EBORAC, Seated Figure Facing Right	$50	$110	$300	$800	$1,500	$3,250
1787, NOVA EBORAC, Seated Figure Facing Left	$50	$100	$250	$700	$1,350	$2,500
1787, NOVA EBORAC, Small Head	$1,700	$4,000	$13,000	$25,000		
1787, NOVA EBORAC, Large Head	$500	$900	$2,000	$5,250	$8,500	

NEW JERSEY (1786–1788)

On June 1, 1786, the New Jersey General Assembly granted to businessman and investor Thomas Goadsby, silversmith and assayer Albion Cox, and minter Walter Mould authority to coin three million coppers weighing six pennyweight and six grains (150 grains total, or 9.72 grams) apiece, to be completed by June 1788, on condition that they deliver to the state treasurer "one Tenth Part of the full Sum they shall strike." These coppers were to pass current at 15 to the shilling. Revolutionary War hero and New Jersey state legislator Matthias Ogden also played a significant financial and political role in the operation.

In an undertaking of this kind, the contractors purchased the metal and assumed all expenses of coining. The difference between these expenses and the total face value of the coins issued represented their profit.

Later, Goadsby and Cox asked authority to coin two-thirds of the total independently of Mould. Their petition was granted November 22, 1786. Mould was known to have produced his coins at Morristown, while Cox and Goadsby operated in Rahway. Coins with a diameter of 30 mm or more are generally considered Morristown products. Coins were also minted in Elizabethtown by Ogden and, without authority, by Machin's Mills.

The obverse shows design elements of the state seal, a horse's head with plow, and the legend NOVA CÆSAREA (New Jersey). The reverse has a United States shield and, for the first time on a coin, the legend E PLURIBUS UNUM (One Composed of Many). More than 140 varieties exist. The majority have the horse's head facing to the right; however, three of the 1788 date show the head facing left. Other variations have a sprig beneath the head, branches below the shield, stars, cinquefoils, a running fox, and other ornaments.

1786, Date Under
Plow Beam

1786, Date Under
Plow, No Coulter

1786 and 1787,
Pattern Shield

	AG	G	F	VF	EF
1786, Date Under Plow Beam			$85,000	$125,000	$200,000
1786, Date Under Plow, No Coulter	$500	$900	$3,000	$7,000	$10,000
1787, Pattern Shield (a)	$400	$700	$1,750	$3,000	$5,000

a. The so-called Pattern Shield reverse was also used on several speculative patterns. See page 117.

1786, Straight
Plow Beam,
Protruding Tongue

1786, Wide Shield

1786, Curved Plow
Beam, Bridle Variety

	AG	G	F	VF	EF	AU
1786, Straight Plow Beam (common varieties)	$25	$55	$175	$500	$850	$1,250
1786, Curved Plow Beam (common varieties)	$25	$55	$175	$500	$875	$1,500
1786, Protruding Tongue	$30	$70	$235	$600	$1,850	$4,500
1786, Wide Shield	$30	$75	$240	$650	$2,000	$5,000
1786, Bridle variety	$30	$75	$240	$650	$2,000	$5,000

1787, PLURIBS Error

1787, Second U Over S
in PLURIBUS

1787, PLURIRUS Error

	AG	G	F	VF	EF	AU
1786, PLUKIBUS error	$30	$75	$250	$450	$1,700	$4,500
1787, PLURIBS error	$40	$125	$500	$1,600	$3,500	$7,500
1787, Second U Over S in PLURIBUS	$40	$160	$470	$1,100	$3,200	$5,000
1787, PLURIRUS error	$40	$160	$470	$1,100	$3,200	$5,500

1787, Sprig
Above Plow

1787, WM
Above Plow

1787, Hidden WM

	AG	G	F	VF	EF	AU
1787, Sprig Above Plow (common varieties)	$25	$65	$220	$650	$1,200	$2,500
1787, No Sprig Above Plow (common varieties)	$25	$65	$220	$550	$900	$1,600
1787, WM Above Plow (a)				—		
1787, Hidden WM in Sprig	$35	$75	$225	$675	$1,800	$3,500

a. Unique.

1787, 1787 Over 1887

1787, Camel Head

1787, Serpent Head

	AG	G	F	VF	EF	AU
1787, 1787 Over 1887	$200	$600	$3,000	$6,000	$15,000	—
1787, Camel Head (snout in high relief)	$30	$60	$200	$650	$900	$1,500
1787, Serpent Head	$35	$85	$400	$1,500	$3,750	$6,000
1787, Goiter Variety	$40	$75	$250	$700	$2,200	$4,500

**1788, Running
Fox Before Legend**

**1788, Indistinct
Coulter**

**1788, Running
Fox After Legend**

1788, Braided Mane

**1788, Horse's
Head Facing Left**

	AG	G	F	VF	EF	AU
1788, Horse's Head Facing Right, several varieties	$25	$60	$175	$550	$900	$1,600
1788, Horse's Head Facing Right, Running Fox Before Legend	$75	$150	$550	$2,000	$4,500	$9,000
1788, Similar, Indistinct Coulter	$150	$650	$2,500	$6,500	$15,000	—
1788, Horse's Head Facing Right, Running Fox After Legend	$9,000	$25,000	$75,000	$100,000	—	
1788, Braided Mane	$50	$300	$1,200	$3,500	$6,000	$12,000
1788, Horse's Head Facing Left	$175	$450	$1,750	$4,750	$12,000	—

REPUBLIC OF VERMONT (1785–1788)

The Republic of Vermont was not formally part of the Union in the 1780s. However, it considered itself American and allied with the original 13 colonies, having declared independence from Britain in January 1777 and having fought in the Revolutionary War. After the war Vermont sought political connection with the United States. Territorial disagreements with New York delayed its entry into the Union, but this was finally accomplished in 1791, when it was admitted as the 14th state. In the meantime, Vermont had already embarked on its own experiments in local coinage.

Reuben Harmon Jr., a storekeeper and entrepreneur of Rupert, Vermont, was granted permission by the Vermont House of Representatives to coin copper pieces for a period of two years beginning July 1, 1785. The well-known Vermont "Landscape" coppers were first produced in that year. The franchise was extended for eight years in 1786.

Harmon's mint was located in the northeast corner of Rupert near a stream known as Millbrook. Colonel William Coley, a New York goldsmith, made the first dies. Some of the late issues were made near Newburgh, New York, by the Machin's Mills coiners.

Most coppers made in Vermont were struck on poor and defective planchets. These included the landscape and Draped Bust Left varieties. Well-struck coins on smooth, full planchets command higher prices. Later pieces made at Machin's Mills are on high-quality planchets but usually have areas of weak striking.

1785, IMMUNE COLUMBIA

1785, VERMONTS	**1785, Reverse**	**1785, VERMONTIS**

1786, VERMONTENSIUM	**1786, Baby Head**

1786, Bust Left	**1786, Reverse**	**1787, Reverse**

	AG	G	VG	F	VF	EF	AU
1785, IMMUNE COLUMBIA	$4,250	$6,250	$10,000	$15,000	$40,000	—	—
1785, VERMONTS	$150	$275	$500	$750	$2,500	$4,500	$9,000
1785, VERMONTIS	$175	$325	$650	$1,400	$4,250	$10,000	$19,500
1786, VERMONTENSIUM	$110	$200	$400	$600	$1,450	$3,550	$7,500
1786, Baby Head	$150	$275	$400	$1,250	$3,000	$9,500	—
1786, Bust Left	$80	$125	$250	$650	$2,400	$4,000	—
1787, Bust Left	$3,000	$4,500	$10,500	$27,000	$42,000	—	

1787, BRITANNIA

	AG	G	VG	F	VF	EF	AU
1787, BRITANNIA (a)	$45	$90	$120	$200	$450	$1,000	$2,200

a. The reverse of this coin is always weak.

1787, 1788, Bust Right (Several Varieties)

	AG	G	VG	F	VF	EF	AU
1787, Bust Right, several varieties	$60	$110	$150	$250	$900	$2,250	$4,000
1788, Bust Right, several varieties	$50	$90	$120	$225	$600	$1,400	$3,250
1788, Backward C in AUCTORI	$3,200	$4,750	$8,000	$17,500	$40,000	$75,000	
1788, *ET LIB* *INDE	$175	$300	$550	$1,250	$4,000	$10,000	—

1788, GEORGIVS III REX / INDE+ ET•LIB+

	AG	G	VG	F	VF	EF	AU
1788, GEORGIVS III REX (a)	$300	$500	$900	$2,200	$4,500	$11,000	

a. This piece should not be confused with the common English halfpence with similar design and reverse legend BRITANNIA.

PRIVATE TOKENS AFTER CONFEDERATION

The formal ratification of the Articles of Confederation—the document signed amongst the original 13 colonies, which established the United States of America as a confederation of sovereign states and served as its first constitution—was accomplished in early 1781. A number of private coinages sprang up after confederation, intended to facilitate local commerce. These were not the products of the federal government, but were tokens issued by businesses and other private concerns.

NORTH AMERICAN TOKENS (DATED 1781)

These tokens were struck in Dublin, Ireland. The obverse shows the seated figure of Hibernia, the personification of Ireland, facing left. The date of issue is believed to have been much later than that shown on the token (1781). Like many Irish tokens, this issue found its way to America in limited quantities and was accepted in commerce near the Canadian border.

	VG	F	VF	EF	AU
1781, Copper or Brass	$60	$100	$200	$650	$1,300

BAR COPPERS (CA. 1785)

The Bar coppers are undated and of uncertain origin. They have 13 parallel and unconnected bars on one side. On the other side is the large roman-letter USA monogram. The design is virtually identical to that used on a Continental Army uniform button.

The significance of the design is clearly defined by its extreme simplicity. The separate 13 states (bars) unite into a single entity as symbolized by the interlocking letters (USA).

These pieces are believed to have first circulated in New York during November 1785, as mentioned in a report in the *New Jersey Gazette* of November 12, 1785. They may have been made in England. Although they are scarce, examples enter the marketplace with regularity, and nearly all are in higher grades.

John Adams Bolen (1826–1907), a numismatist and a master diesinker in Springfield, Massachusetts, struck copies of the Bar copper around 1862. On these copies, the letter A passes under, instead of over, the S. Bolen's intent was not to deceive, and he advertised his copies plainly as reproductions. But his skills were such that W. Elliot Woodward, a leading auctioneer of tokens and medals in the 1860s, vacillated between selling Bolen's copies and describing them as "dangerous counterfeits." Bolen copies of the Bar copper are highly collectible in their own right, but they are less valuable than the originals.

	G	VG	F	VF	EF	AU	Unc.
(Undated) (Circa 1785) Bar Copper	$500	$1,800	$3,000	$6,250	$9,000	$12,500	$21,000

AUCTORI PLEBIS TOKENS (1787)

These tokens are sometimes included with the coins of Connecticut, as they greatly resemble issues of that state. (The obverse features a draped male bust, possibly King George II, wearing laurels and facing left.) They were struck in England by an unknown maker, possibly for use in America.

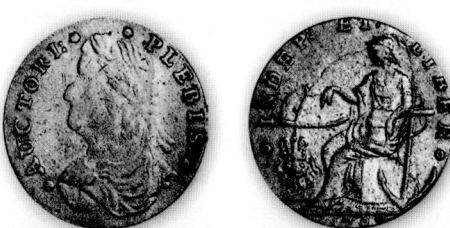

	G	VG	F	VF	EF	AU	Unc.
1787, AUCTORI PLEBIS	$90	$110	$225	$450	$900	$1,600	$7,500

MOTT STORE CARDS (DATED 1789)

These 19th-century store cards have long been included in Early American coin collections because of the date they bear (1789). Most scholars believe these were produced no earlier than 1807 (and possibly in the Hard Times era of the late 1830s) as commemoratives of the founding of the Mott Company, and served as business cards. The firm, operated by Jordan Mott, was located at 240 Water Street, a fashionable section of New York at that time.

The obverse of the token features an eagle with wings spread and an American shield as a breastplate. The eagle holds an olive branch and arrows in its talons. Above is the date 1789, and around the rim is the legend CLOCKS, WATCHES, JEWELRY, SILVERWARE, CHRONOMETERS. The reverse of the token features a regulator clock with the legend MOTT'S N.Y. IMPORTERS, DEALERS, MANUFACTURERS OF GOLD & SILVER WARES.

	VG	F	VF	EF	AU	Unc.
"1789," Mott Token, Thick Planchet	$80	$175	$300	$450	$600	$1,200
"1789," Mott Token, Thin Planchet	$80	$200	$350	$800	$1,500	$2,750
"1789," Mott Token, Entire Edge Engrailed	$80	$300	$450	$1,100	$1,800	$3,500

STANDISH BARRY THREEPENCE (1790)

Standish Barry, of Baltimore, was a watch- and clockmaker, an engraver, and, later, a silversmith. In 1790 he circulated a silver threepence of his own fabrication. The tokens are believed to have been an advertising venture at a time when small change was scarce. The precise date on this piece may indicate that Barry intended to commemorate Independence Day, but there are no records to prove this. The head on the obverse is probably that of James Calhoun, who was active in Baltimore politics in the 1790s. The legend BALTIMORE TOWN JULY 4, 90, appears in the border. An enigmatic gold doubloon is also attributed to Barry (see page 121).

Nearly all examples of the silver threepence show significant wear, suggesting that they circulated for a long time.

	VG	F	VF	EF	AU
1790 Threepence	$10,000	$22,500	$50,000	$80,000	$110,000

ALBANY CHURCH PENNIES (1790)

The First Presbyterian Church of Albany, New York, authorized an issue of 1,000 copper uniface tokens in 1790. These passed at 12 to a shilling. They were used to encourage parishioner donations (at that time, there was a scarcity of small change in circulation). They were also intended to stop contributions of worn and counterfeit coppers (in the words of the church elders' resolution, "in order to add respect to the weekly collections"). Two varieties were made, one with the addition of a large D (the abbreviation for *denarium*, or penny, in the British monetary system) above the word CHURCH. All are rare, with fewer than a dozen of each variety known.

	VG	F	VF	EF
(Undated) (1790) Without D	$10,000	$15,000	$30,000	$50,000
(Undated) (1790) With D Added	$10,000	$15,000	$30,000	$50,000

KENTUCKY TOKENS (CA. 1792–1794)

These tokens were struck in England circa 1792 to 1794. Their obverse legend reads UNANIMITY IS THE STRENGTH OF SOCIETY; the central motif is a hand holding a scroll with the inscription OUR CAUSE IS JUST. The reverse shows a pyramid of 15 starbursts surrounded by rays. Each star in the triangle represents a state, identified by its initial letter. These pieces are usually called *Kentucky cents* or *Kentucky tokens* because the letter K (for Kentucky) happens to be at the top. Some of the edges are plain; others are milled with a diagonal reeding; and some have edge lettering that reads PAYABLE IN LANCASTER LONDON OR BRISTOL, PAYABLE AT BEDWORTH NUNEATON OR HINKLEY, or PAYABLE AT I. FIELDING, etc.

These are not known to have circulated in America. Rather, they were made as produced as collectibles, popular among English numismatists and others at the time. Likely more than 1,000 Kentucky tokens are in the hands of numismatists today.

	VF	EF	AU	Unc.
(1792–1794) Copper, Plain Edge	$185	$275	$450	$850
(1792–1794) Copper, Engrailed Edge	$500	$950	$1,500	$3,000
(1792–1794) Copper, Lettered Edge, PAYABLE AT BEDWORTH, etc.	—	—	—	—
(1792–1794) Copper, Lettered Edge, PAYABLE IN LANCASTER, etc.	$250	$350	$550	$1,200
(1792–1794) Copper, Lettered Edge, PAYABLE AT I. FIELDING, etc.	—	—	—	—

FRANKLIN PRESS TOKENS (1794)

These were English tradesman's tokens of the kind collected by English numismatists in the late 1700s and early 1800s. (As a group, they were popularly called Conder tokens, after James Conder, the man who first cataloged them for collectors.) The Franklin Press tokens did not circulate as money in America, but, being associated with a London shop where Benjamin Franklin once worked, they have long been included in American coin collections.

The obverse features a wood-frame printing press of the style that Benjamin Franklin would have operated by hand as a printer in England in 1725. He had left Philadelphia at the age of 18 to buy printing supplies in London and look for work. Around the central design is the legend SIC ORITOR DOCTRINA SURGETQUE LIBERTAS ("Thus Learning Advances and Liberty Grows"), and below is the date, 1794. The reverse legend reads PAYABLE AT THE FRANKLIN PRESS LONDON.

Most are plain-edged, but rare lettered-edge varieties exist, as well as a unique piece with a diagonally reeded edge.

	VG	VF	EF	AU	Unc.
1794 Franklin Press Token	$100	$250	$350	$550	$900
Similar, Edge Reads AN ASYLUM FOR THE OPPRESS'D OF ALL NATIONS			(unique)		
Similar, Edge Diagonally Reeded			(unique)		

TALBOT, ALLUM & LEE CENTS (1794–1795)

Talbot, Allum & Lee was a firm of importers engaged in the India trade and located at 241 Pearl Street, New York. It placed a large quantity of English-made coppers in circulation during 1794 and 1795.

ONE CENT appears on the 1794 issue, and the legend PAYABLE AT THE STORE OF on the edge. The denomination is not found on the 1795 reverse but the edge legend was changed to read WE PROMISE TO PAY THE BEARER ONE CENT. Rare plain-edged specimens of both dates exist. Exceptional pieces have edges ornamented or with lettering CAMBRIDGE BEDFORD AND HUNTINGDON.X.X.

It is estimated that more than 200,000 of these tokens were minted, though no original records have been located. Varieties and mulings are known; the values shown here are for the most common types.

Many undistributed tokens were sold to the Philadelphia Mint in a time of copper shortage. These were cut down and used by the Mint as planchets for coining 1795 and 1797 half cents.

1794 Cent, With NEW YORK   1795 Cent

	VG	F	VF	EF	AU	Unc.
1794 Cent, With NEW YORK	$65	$80	$225	$350	$550	$1,350
1794 Cent, Without NEW YORK	$500	$850	$2,750	$5,000	$7,500	$16,000
1795 Cent	$60	$80	$200	$300	$400	$800

MYDDELTON TOKENS (1796)

Philip Parry Price Myddelton was an Englishman who bought land in America after the Revolutionary War. He hoped to begin a vibrant farming community along the Ohio River and entice English craftsmen and workers to move there. To this end he contracted the design of a promotional token and had examples made in copper and silver. These tokens were struck at the Soho Mint of Boulton and Watt near Birmingham, England. Although their obverse legend reads BRITISH SETTLEMENT KENTUCKY, and Myddelton planned to order large quantities of the copper version for shipment to the United States, they were never actually issued for circulation in Kentucky. The entrepreneur was arrested in August 1796 and convicted in London for the crime of convincing hundreds of workers to leave England for America. He was jailed in Newgate prison for three and a half years, which ended his Kentucky plans.

The obverse of Myddelton's token shows Hope presenting two "little genii" (his description) to the goddess Liberty. She welcomes them with an open hand. At her feet is a flourishing sapling and a cornucopia representing America's bounty, and she holds a pole with a liberty cap. On the reverse, seated Britannia leans wearily on a downward-pointing spear, looking at the broken scale and fasces—symbols of unity, justice, and liberty—scattered at her feet.

Sylvester S. Crosby, in *The Early Coins of America*, remarked that "In beauty of design and execution, the tokens are unsurpassed by any piece issued for American circulation."

	PF
1796, Proof, Copper	$25,000
1796, Proof, Silver	$32,000

COPPER COMPANY OF UPPER CANADA TOKENS (EARLY 1800S)

These pieces were struck some time in the early 1800s. The obverse is the same as that of the Myddelton token. The new reverse refers to a Canadian firm, the Copper Company of Upper Canada, with the denomination ONE HALF PENNY. These tokens may have been made for numismatic purposes (for sale to collectors), or as part of the coiner's samples. Their maker is unknown. Restrikes were made in England in the 1890s.

	PF
1796, Proof, Copper	$10,000

CASTORLAND MEDALS (1796)

These medals, or "jetons," are dated 1796 and allude to a proposed French settlement known as Castorland. This was to be located on the Black River, in northern New York, not far from the Canadian border. Peter Chassanis of Paris had acquired land that he and others intended to parcel into large farms, with Chassanis heading the settlement's government, two commissaries residing at its seat, Castorville, and four commissaries headquartered in Paris. The medals were to be given as payment ("in recognition of the care which they may bestow upon the common concerns") to the Parisian directors of the colonizing company for their attendance at board meetings.

Some 20 French families, many of them aristocratic refugees from the French Revolution, moved to the settlement between 1796 and 1800. Challenges including sickness, harsh northern New York winters, loss of livestock, and theft of finances proved too much for the company, and Castorland was dissolved in 1814. Many of the surviving settlers moved to more prosperous American communities or returned to Europe.

The obverse of the Castorland medal features a profile portrait of the ancient goddess Sybele, associated with mountains, town and city walls, fertile nature, and wild animals. She wears a *corona muralis* ("walled crown"), laurels, and a draped head covering. The legend reads FRANCO-AMERICANA COLONIA, with CASTORLAND 1796 below. On the reverse the goddess Ceres, patroness of agriculture, stands at a maple with a sap drill while the tree's bounty flows into a waiting bucket. Ceres holds a cornucopia; at her feet are a sickle and a sheaf of wheat. A beaver at the bottom of the reverse further symbolizes Castorland and its resources (*castor* is French for "beaver," an animal crucial to the very profitable North American fur trade in the early 1800s). The legend, in Latin, is SALVE MAGNA PARENS FRUGUM—"Hail, Great Mother of Crops" (from Virgil).

Copy dies of the Castorland medal are still available and have been used at the Paris Mint for restriking throughout the years. Restrikes have a more modern look than originals; their metallic content (in French) is impressed on the edge: ARGENT (silver), CUIVRE (copper), or OR (gold).

	EF	AU	Unc.
1796, Original, Silver (reeded edge, unbroken dies)	$3,000	$4,500	$7,200
1796, Original, Silver (reverse rusted and broken)	$300	$600	$1,500
1796, Original, Bronze (reverse rusted and broken)	$200	$300	$700
(1796) Undated, Restrike, Silver (Paris Mint edge marks)		$30	$70
(1796) Undated, Restrike, Bronze (Paris Mint edge marks)		$20	$40

THEATRE AT NEW YORK TOKENS (CA. 1798)

These penny tokens were issued by Skidmore of London and illustrate the New Theatre (later known as the Park Theatre) in Manhattan, as it appeared circa 1797. The theater was New York City's attempt at a prestigious new level of entertainment, as the famous John Street Theatre (the "Birthplace of American Theater") was suffering from poor management and physical decay in the 1790s. The building's cornerstone was laid on May 5, 1795, and the theater opened on January 29, 1798, with a presentation of entertainments including Shakespeare's *As You Like It*.

The obverse of this copper token features a view of the playhouse building with the legend THE THEATRE AT NEW YORK AMERICA. The reverse shows an allegorical scene of a cornucopia on a dock, with bales, an anchor, and sailing ships. The legend reads MAY COMMERCE FLOURISH. The edge is marked I PROMISE TO PAY ON DEMAND THE BEARER ONE PENNY.

All known examples are struck in copper and have a Proof finish. They were made for collectors, not for use as advertising. Today examples are scarce, with about 20 known.

	EF
	PF
Penny, THE THEATRE AT NEW YORK AMERICA	—
Penny, THE THEATRE AT NEW YORK AMERICA, Proof	$26,000

NEW SPAIN (TEXAS) JOLA TOKENS (1817–1818)

In 1817 the Spanish governor of Texas, Colonel Manuel Pardo, authorized Manuel Barrera to produce 8,000 copper coins known as jolas. These crudely made pieces show the denomination 1/2 [real], the maker's initials and the date on the obverse, and a five-pointed star on the reverse.

The 1817 coins were withdrawn from circulation the following year and replaced by a similar issue of 8,000 pieces. These bear the date 1818 and the initials, JAG, of the maker, José Antonio de la Garza. Several varieties of each issue are known. All are rare.

	F	VF	EF
1817 1/2 Real	$15,000	$25,000	$50,000
1818 1/2 Real, Large or Small Size	$10,000	$25,000	$50,000

NORTH WEST COMPANY TOKENS (1820)

These tokens were probably valued at one beaver skin and struck in Birmingham, England, in 1820 by John Walker & Co. All but two known specimens are holed. Most have been found in Oregon in the region of the Columbia and Umpqua river valleys. They feature a portrait of King George IV on the obverse, with the legend TOKEN and the date 1820. The reverse shows a beaver in the wild, with the legend NORTH WEST COMPANY.

James A. Haxby, in the *Guide Book of Canadian Coins and Tokens*, writes, "The pieces actually issued for circulation were pierced at the top for suspension or stringing. Unholed copper strikes are known with plain or engrailed edge and are very rare. A number of pieces have been found buried in western Canada and as far south as central Oregon."

Holed Brass Token   **Unholed Copper Token**

	AG	G	VG	F	VF
1820, Copper or Brass, holed	$375	$800	$2,250	$4,250	$8,500
1820, Copper, unholed, plain or engrailed edge	—	—	—	—	—

WASHINGTON PIECES

Medals, tokens, and coinage proposals in this interesting series dated from 1783 to 1795 bear the portrait of George Washington. The likenesses in most instances were faithfully reproduced and were designed to honor the first president. Many of these pieces were of English origin and, although dated 1783, probably were made in the 1820s or later.

The legends generally signify a strong unity among the states and the marked display of patriotism that pervaded the new nation during that period. We find among some of these tokens an employment of what were soon to become the nation's official coin devices, namely, the American eagle, the United States shield, and stars. The denomination ONE CENT is used in several instances, while on some of the English pieces HALFPENNY will be found. Several of these pieces were private patterns for proposed coinage contracts.

GEORGIVS TRIUMPHO TOKENS

Although the head shown on these tokens bears a strong resemblance to that on some coins of King George III, many collectors consider the Georgivs Triumpho ("Triumphant George") tokens a commemorative of America's victory in the Revolutionary War.

The reverse side shows the Goddess of Liberty behind a framework of 13 bars and fleurs-de-lis. Holding an olive branch in her right hand and staff of liberty in her left, she is partially encircled by the words VOCE POPOLI ("By the Voice of the People") 1783.

	VG	F	VF	EF	AU	Unc.
1783, GEORGIVS TRIUMPHO	$110	$225	$500	$700	$1,200	$6,000

WASHINGTON PORTRAIT PIECES (1780S TO EARLY 1800S)

Military Bust. "The 1783-dated Washington Military Bust coppers bear a portrait, adapted (with a different perspective on the coin and a wreath added to the head) from a painting by Edward Savage," writes Q. David Bowers in the *Whitman Encyclopedia of Colonial and Early American Coins*. "These seem to have circulated in England as well as America. . . . Many varieties exist, but they are not well known outside of a circle of specialists. Accordingly, the opportunity exists to acquire rare die combinations for little premium over a regular issue."

The reverse features a seated female figure holding an olive branch and a pole topped by a liberty cap. Values shown are for the most common varieties.

1783, Large Military Bust, Point of Bust Close to W

1783, Small Military Bust

	F	VF	EF	AU	Unc.
1783, Large Military Bust	$75	$160	$350	$500	$1,750
1783, Small Military Bust, Plain Edge	$80	$175	$400	$750	$2,500
1783, Small Military Bust, Engrailed Edge	$100	$200	$550	$1,100	$3,000

Draped Bust. Draped Bust coppers dated 1783 depict Washington with the top of a toga draped over his shoulder. One variety includes a button at the folds in front of the toga. Another variety has no button, and has the initial "I" (for Ingram) in the toga, above the right side of the numeral 3 in the date. Both varieties feature a similar reverse design with a female figure seated on a rock, holding an olive branch and a pole surmounted by a liberty cap.

1783, Draped Bust, No Button   **With Button**

	F	VF	EF	AU	Unc.
1783, Draped Bust, No Button *(illustrated)*	$80	$160	$300	$500	$1,600
1783, Draped Bust, With Button (on Drapery at Neck)	$125	$225	$350	$700	$3,200
1783, Draped Bust, Copper Restrike, Plain Edge, Proof	$125	$225	$350	$700	$900
1783, Draped Bust, Copper Restrike, Engrailed Edge, Proof					$750
1783, Draped Bust, Silver Restrike, Engrailed Edge, Proof					$1,800

Unity States. The 1783-dated coppers with the legend UNITY STATES OF AMERICA were likely coined in the early 1800s at the Soho Mint in Birmingham, England. The obverse features a portrait of Washington in a toga and wearing laurels. The reverse is a copy of the wreath design on the copper cent produced by the Philadelphia Mint from 1796 to 1807, with UNITED spelled UNITY, perhaps as a way to evade charges of counterfeiting.

Despite the American denomination of this piece, they likely circulated in England (at the value of a halfpenny), as reflected by examples being found there in quantity in later years. They were imported into the United States as well, for use as a cent, and are mentioned in several counterfeit-detector publications in the 1850s.

1783, Unity States

	VG	VF	EF	AU	Unc.
1783, UNITY STATES	$100	$200	$325	$550	$1,400

Double Head. Although the Washington Double Head cents are undated, some numismatists assign them a date of 1783, given their resemblance to the Military Bust coppers that bear that date (even though those were probably struck years later). They were likely struck in Birmingham, England, by Edward Thomason sometime in the 1820s or later. They were made in England, as evidenced by many having been found there, but long after the Conder token era. They are denominated ONE CENT and, when exported to the United States, circulated along with Hard Times tokens of the 1830s.

Undated
Double-
Head Cent

	F	VF	EF	AU	Unc.
(Undated) Double-Head Cent	$100	$250	$425	$725	$2,400

Ugly Head. The so-called Ugly Head token is a medalet struck in copper and white-metal varieties, possibly satirical, and presumably of American origin. The token's legend reads WASHINGTON THE GREAT D.G. The abbreviation "D.G." on English coins stands for Dei Gratia ("By the Grace of God"), and the portrait appears to be wigless and possibly toothless, leading some numismatists to opine that the token is a satire on George Washington. Bowers notes that the token's date, 1784, has no particular significance in Washington's life. By that year the American Revolution was over and the general had retired his commission as commander-in-chief of the Continental Army. He would not assume the presidency until 1789. The reverse of the token features a design of linked rings with abbreviations for the British colonies, reminiscent of the 1776 Continental dollar.

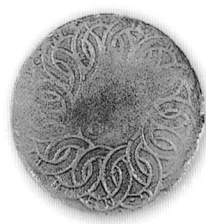

1784,
Ugly
Head

	G
1784, Ugly Head, Copper	$100,000
Auctions: $20,000, Crude Good, December 1983	
1784, Ugly Head, Pewter	*(unique)*

Small and Large Eagle. Small Eagle and Large Eagle one-cent tokens dated 1791 were made in Birmingham, England, sponsored by merchants W. and Alex Walker of that city as proposals for official American coinage. Bowers writes in the *Whitman Encyclopedia of Colonial and Early American Coins* that the Walker firm "shipped a cask filled with these cents, estimated to be about 2,500 Large Eagle and 1,500 Small Eagle coins, to Thomas Ketland & Sons, a Philadelphia contact, to be distributed to legislators. The depiction of Washington was contrary to the president's own desires, who felt that having his image on coins would appear to have the 'stamp of royalty.'"

1791 Cent, Small Eagle Reverse,
Edge Lettered UNITED STATES OF AMERICA

1791 Cent, Large Eagle Reverse

	VG	F	VF	EF	AU	Unc.
1791 Cent, Small Eagle (Date on Reverse)		$475	$650	$800	$1,200	$2,750
1791 Cent, Large Eagle (Date on Obverse)	$150	$350	$550	$750	$1,100	$2,400

Liverpool. The Liverpool Halfpenny tokens were most likely made around 1793. They were intended for circulation as small change in England, although numismatists of the time also sought them for their collections. The obverse shows a uniformed bust of George Washington, as used on the Large Eagle one-cent tokens of 1791. The reverse features a sailing ship and the legend LIVERPOOL HALFPENNY, a design used on various English Conder tokens.

1791 Liverpool Halfpenny

	VG	F	VF	EF	AU	Unc.
1791 Liverpool Halfpenny, Lettered Edge	$750	$1,100	$1,800	$3,000	$5,500	—

1792. An extensive series of 1792-dated Washington pieces was produced in many varieties, bearing no denomination. These apparently were made in England, and were collected by numismatists in addition to circulating as coinage substitutes in America.

1792 Cent, Eagle with 13 Stars Reverse

	VG	F	VF	EF
1792, WASHINGTON PRESIDENT, Eagle With 13 Stars Reverse				
PRESIDENT at Side of Bust, Copper				—
PRESIDENT, Silver			$125,000	—
PRESIDENT, Gold (a)			—	
PRESIDENT Extends Below Bust, Copper (a)				$117,000

a. Unique.

1792, WASHINGTON PRESIDENT   **Legend Reverse**

	VG	F	VF	EF
1792, WASHINGTON PRESIDENT, Legend on Reverse				
Plain Edge, Copper	$2,750	$7,500	$18,000	$50,000
Lettered Edge, Copper	—	—	—	—

(1792) Undated,
**WASHINGTON
BORN VIRGINIA**

	VG	F	VF	EF
(1792) Undated, WASHINGTON BORN VIRGINIA, Eagle With 13 Stars Reverse *(reverse illustrated on previous page)*, **Copper** (a)		—		
(1792) Undated, WASHINGTON BORN VIRGINIA, Legend on Reverse				
Copper	$1,000	$1,800	$3,800	$7,000
Silver	—	—	—	—

a. 3 examples are known.

Peter Getz. Dies engraved by silversmith, mechanic, and inventor Peter Getz of Lancaster, Pennsylvania, are believed to have been made to produce a half dollar and a cent as a proposal to Congress for a private contract coinage before the Philadelphia Mint became a reality. These feature George Washington, in a military bust portrait, and a heraldic eagle.

1792, Small Eagle Reverse **Large Eagle Reverse**

	VG	F	VF	EF	AU	Unc.
1792, Small Eagle, Silver	—	—	—	$300,000		
	Auctions: $241,500, AU, May 2004					
1792, Small Eagle, Copper	$6,000	$12,000	$30,000	$50,000	$75,000	$150,000
	Auctions: $299,000, MS-64 BN, November 2006					
1792, Small Eagle, Ornamented Edge (Circles and Squares), Copper	—	—	—	$175,000		
	Auctions: $207,000, AU, November 2006					
1792, Small Eagle, Ornamented Edge, Silver (a)	—	—	$125,000	$200,000		
	Auctions: $391,000, Gem BU PL, May 2004					
1792, Large Eagle, Silver			—	—		
	Auctions: $34,500, EF, May 2004					

a. 4 examples are known.

Roman Head. The 1792-dated Roman Head cents show Washington in the style of an ancient Roman dignitary. These copper pieces were struck in England for collectors, as opposed to being intended for circulation. Their edge is lettered UNITED STATES OF AMERICA.

1792 Cent, Roman Head

	PF
1792 Cent, Roman Head, Lettered Edge UNITED STATES OF AMERICA, Proof	$90,000

Ship Halfpenny. The 1793 Ship Halfpenny tokens were struck from an overdated (3 Over 2) reverse die. These copper pieces were intended for collectors, but nearly all of them ended up in circulation in England. The more common lettered-edge variety reads PAYABLE IN ANGLESEY LONDON OR LIVERPOOL.

1793 Ship Halfpenny

	VG	F	VF	EF	AU	Unc.
1793 Ship Halfpenny, Lettered Edge	$100	$200	$400	$600	$850	$3,250
1793 Ship Halfpenny, Plain Edge (a)			—	—		

a. Rare.

1795 Copper. Copper tokens dated 1795 were made in large quantities as promotional pieces for the London firm of Clark & Harris, dealers in stoves and fireplace grates. The die work is attributed to Thomas Wyon, and numismatists believe the pieces were struck in Birmingham, England, for circulation in the British Isles (although collectors saved them as well).

The obverse features a right-facing portrait of George Washington in military uniform. Two varieties exist, Small Buttons and Large Buttons (describing the coats on his frock). The legend reads G. WASHINGTON: THE FIRM FRIEND TO PEACE & HUMANITY.

The reverse shows a fireplace with a coal grate, with legends PAYABLE BY CLARK & HARRIS 13. WORMWOOD St. BISHOPSGATE and LONDON 1795.

Most have a diagonally reeded edge, although some are edge-lettered as PAYABLE AT LONDON LIVERPOOL OR BRISTOL.

1795, Large Buttons   **1795, Small Buttons**

	F	VF	EF	AU	Unc.
1795, Large Buttons, Lettered Edge	$180	$350	$700	$1,500	$2,200
1795, Large Buttons, Reeded Edge	$80	$175	$300	$400	$700
1795, Small Buttons, Reeded Edge	$80	$200	$400	$725	$1,750

Liberty and Security. The Liberty and Security halfpenny and penny tokens were made in England in 1795 as collectibles, although the halfpence also circulated widely there as small change. Their designs consist of a portrait of George Washington, identified by name, and a heraldic eagle surmounting a stylized American shield, holding a sprig of olive and several arrows. Some of their edges are plain, and some are lettered with various phrases such as AN ASYLUM FOR THE OPPRESS'D OF ALL NATIONS and BIRMINGHAM REDRUTH & SWANSEA.

Varieties exist in copper and white metal, and with mulings of different reverses.

The common name of this series derives from the reverse legend, LIBERTY AND SECURITY.

1795, Liberty and Security Halfpenny

	F	VF	EF	AU	Unc.
1795 Halfpenny, Plain Edge	$110	$200	$500	$950	$2,650
1795 Halfpenny, LONDON Edge	$100	$210	$525	$750	$2,500
1795 Halfpenny, BIRMINGHAM Edge	$125	$250	$550	$1,100	$2,800
1795 Halfpenny, ASYLUM Edge	$200	$400	$1,100	$2,000	$5,500
1795 Penny, ASYLUM Edge	$2,500	$8,500	$12,500	$18,000	$32,500

(1795) Undated, Liberty and Security Penny, ASYLUM Edge

	F	VF	EF	AU	Unc.
(1795) Undated, Liberty and Security Penny	$275	$450	$650	$1,150	$2,250
Same, Corded Outer Rims	$600	$1,000	$1,800	$2,800	$5,000

North Wales. "The undated North Wales halfpenny issues, believed to have been struck in England in the early 1790s (usually listed as 1795, although this may be two or three years after they were coined), are part of the 'evasion halfpence' series. Accordingly, unlike Conder tokens, they were not created for collectors. None are known to have survived with sharp features and in high grades, as is characteristic of cabinet pieces" (*Whitman Encyclopedia of Colonial and Early American Coins*).

(1795) Undated, NORTH WALES Halfpenny

	G	F	VF	EF	AU
(1795) Undated, NORTH WALES Halfpenny	$90	$200	$500	$1,400	$2,800
(1795) Undated, Lettered Edge	$450	$1,450	$5,000	$8,000	—
(1795) Undated, Two Stars at Each Side of Harp	$2,200	$7,500	$13,500		

Success Tokens. Small and large types exist of these mysterious pieces of unknown date and purpose. Today known as Success tokens, they may have been souvenirs, perhaps struck to commemorate George Washington's second inauguration (March 1793), or 19th-century gaming tokens. They were struck in copper or brass and most likely were made in the mid-1800s. Specimens with original silvering are rare and are valued 20% to 50% higher than others. Varieties exist.

(Undated) SUCCESS Token, Large   (Undated) SUCCESS Token, Small

	F	VF	EF	AU	Unc.
(Undated) SUCCESS Token, Large, Plain or Reeded Edge	$250	$450	$750	$1,400	$2,750
(Undated) SUCCESS Token, Small, Plain or Reeded Edge	$300	$500	$800	$1,600	$3,000

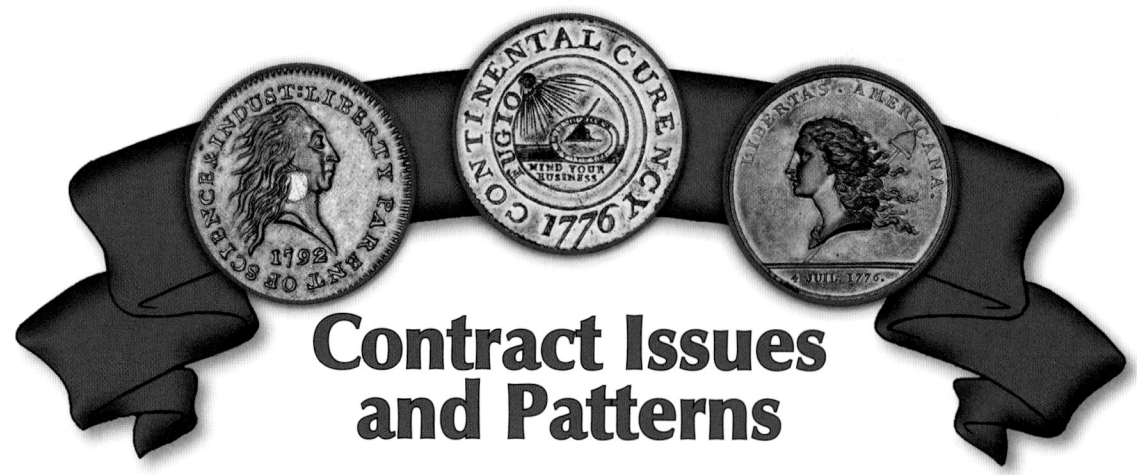

Contract Issues and Patterns

CONTINENTAL CURRENCY (1776)

The Continental Currency dollars (as they are known to numismatists) were made to serve in lieu of a paper dollar, but the exact nature of their monetary role is still unclear. They were the first dollar-sized coins ever attributed to the United States. One obverse die was engraved by someone whose initials were E.G. (thought to be Elisha Gallaudet) and is marked EG FECIT ("EG Made It"). Studies of the coinage show that there may have been two separate emissions made at different mints, one in New York City. The link design on the reverse was suggested by Benjamin Franklin and represents the former colonies.

Varieties result from differences in the spelling of the word CURRENCY and the addition of EG FECIT on the obverse. These coins were struck in pewter, brass, and silver. Pewter pieces served as a dollar, taking the place of a Continental Currency paper note. Brass and silver pieces may have been experimental or patterns. The typical grade encountered for a pewter coin is VF to AU. Examples in original bright Uncirculated condition are worth a strong premium.

Numerous copies and replicas of these coins have been made over the years. Authentication is recommended for all pieces.

			CURRENCY		CURENCY	
	G	F	VF	EF	AU	Unc.
1776 CURENCY, Pewter (a)	$7,750	$12,000	$24,000	$36,000	$50,000	$75,000
1776 CURENCY, Brass (a)	$25,000	$40,000	$75,000	$135,000	$220,000	—
Auctions: $299,000, MS-63, July 2009						
1776 CURENCY, Silver (b)			$1,527,000			
Auctions: $1,410,000, MS-63, May 2014; $1,527,500, MS-62, January 2015; $1,527,500, EF-40, January 2015						
1776 CURRENCY, Pewter	$8,000	$13,000	$25,000	$37,500	$52,500	$80,000
1776 CURRENCY, EG FECIT, Pewter	$8,500	$15,000	$27,000	$40,000	$55,000	$85,000
Auctions: $546,250, MS-67, January 2012						

a. 2 varieties. **b.** 2 examples are known.

	G	F	VF	EF	AU	Unc.
1776 CURRENCY, EG FECIT, Silver (b)		—	—	—	—	$1,500,000
Auctions: $1,410,000, MS-63, May 2014						
1776 CURRENCEY, Pewter	—	—	$65,000		$175,000	—
1776 CURRENCY, Pewter, Ornamented Date (c)				$276,000	$329,000	
Auctions: $276,000, EF-45, July 2009						

b. 2 examples are known. **c.** 3 examples are known.

NOVA CONSTELLATIO PATTERNS (1783)

These Nova Constellatio pieces represent the first official patterns for a coinage of the United States. They were designed by Benjamin Dudley for Gouverneur Morris to carry out his ideas for a decimal coinage system. The 1,000-unit coin is a mark, the 500 a quint. These denominations, together with the small 100-unit piece, were designed to fit in with the many different values for foreign coins that constituted money in America at the time. These pattern pieces represent the first attempt at a decimal ratio, and were the forerunners of our present system of money values. Neither the proposed denominations nor the coins advanced beyond the pattern stage. These unique pieces are all dated 1783. There are two types of the quint. The copper "five" was first brought to the attention of collectors in 1980. Electrotype and cast copies exist.

5 Units

Quint, Plain Obverse

Quint, Legend on Obverse

Quint Reverse

Bit (100 Units)

Mark

1783 (Five) "5," Copper	*(unique)*
1783 (Bit) "100," Silver, Decorated Edge	*(2 known)*
Auctions: $97,500, Unc., November 1979	
1783 (Bit) "100," Silver, Plain Edge	*(unique)*
Auctions: $705,000, AU-55, May 2014	
1783 (Quint) "500," Silver, Plain Obverse	*(unique)*
Auctions: $1,175,000, AU-53, April 2013	
1783 (Quint) "500," Silver, Legend on Obverse	*(unique)*
Auctions: $165,000, Unc., November 1979	
1783 (Mark) "1000," Silver	*(unique)*
Auctions: $190,000, Unc., November 1979	

FUGIO COPPERS (1787)

The first coins issued by authority of the United States for which contract information is known today were the "Fugio" pieces. Entries in the *Journal of Congress* supply interesting information about proceedings relating to this coinage. For example, the entry of Saturday, April 21, 1787, reads as follows: "That the board of treasury be authorized to contract for three hundred tons of copper coin of the federal standard, agreeable to the proposition of Mr. James Jarvis. . . . That it be coined at the expense of the contractor, etc."

On Friday, July 6, 1787, it was "[r]esolved, that the board of treasury direct the contractor for the copper coinage to stamp on one side of each piece the following device, viz: thirteen circles linked together, a small circle in the middle, with the words 'United States,' around it; and in the centre, the words 'We are one'; on the other side of the same piece the following device, viz: a dial with the hours expressed on the face of it; a meridian sun above on one side of which is the word 'Fugio,' [the intended meaning is *time flies*] and on the other the year in figures '1787,' below the dial, the words 'Mind Your Business.'"

The legends have been credited to Benjamin Franklin and are similar in some respects to the 1776 Continental Currency pewter and other coins.

These pieces were coined in New Haven, Connecticut. Most of the copper used in their coinage came from military stores or salvaged metal. The dies were made by Abel Buell of New Haven.

1787, WITH POINTED RAYS

The 1787, With Pointed Rays, was later replaced by the With Club Rays variety.

American Congress Pattern	Cross After Date	Label With Raised Rims

	G	VG	F	VF	EF	AU	Unc.
Obverse Cross After Date, No Cinquefoils							
Reverse Rays and AMERICAN CONGRESS				—	$300,000	$425,000	
Reverse Label with Raised Rims (a)			$14,000	$20,000	$35,000		
Reverse STATES UNITED	$300	$650	$1,200	$3,000	$8,000	$15,000	—
Reverse UNITED STATES	$275	$500	$1,000	$2,500	$5,500	$11,000	—

a. Extremely rare.

Cinquefoil After Date
These types, with pointed rays, have regular obverses punctuated with four cinquefoils (five-leafed ornaments).

	G	VG	F	VF	EF	AU	Unc.
STATES UNITED at Sides of Circle, Cinquefoils on Label	$150	$350	$600	$1,000	$1,500	$2,100	$4,000
STATES UNITED, 1 Over Horizontal 1	$225	$450	$1,000	$4,000	$9,000		
UNITED STATES, 1 Over Horizontal 1	$200	$400	$900	$3,500	$8,000		
UNITED STATES at Sides of Circle	$150	$350	$600	$1,000	$1,750	$2,200	$4,500
STATES UNITED, Label With Raised Rims, Large Letters in WE ARE ONE	$200	$450	$700	$2,200	$4,500	$9,000	$20,000
STATES UNITED, 8-Pointed Star on Label	$200	$400	$600	$1,200	$2,250	$4,250	$9,000
UNITED Above, STATES Below	$850	$1,750	$3,750	$9,000	$12,500	$19,500	—

1787, WITH CLUB RAYS

The 1787, With Club Rays, is differentiated between concave and convex ends.

Rounded Ends **Concave Ends**

	G	VG	F	VF	EF	AU
Club Rays, Rounded Ends	$200	$400	$800	$1,400	$2,600	$5,500
Club Rays, Concave Ends to Rays, FUCIO (C instead of G) (a)	$1,750	$3,750	$8,000	$24,000	$35,000	
Club Rays, Concave Ends, FUGIO, UNITED STATES	$2,200	$5,000	$10,000	$30,000	$40,000	$90,000
Club Rays, Similar, STATES UNITED Reverse	—	—	—	—	—	—

a. Extremely rare.

The so-called New Haven "restrikes" were made for Horatio N. Rust from dies recreated in 1859. These are distinguished by narrow rings on the reverse. At the time the fanciful story was given that teenaged C. Wyllys Betts discovered original dies in 1858 on the site of the Broome & Platt store in New Haven, where the original coins had been made.

New Haven Restrike.
Note narrow rings.

	EF	AU	Unc.
New Haven restrike, Gold (a)		—	—
New Haven restrike, Silver	$3,200	$4,750	$7,500
New Haven restrike, Copper or Brass	$500	$600	$900

a. 2 examples are known.

1792 PROPOSED COINAGE

Some members of the House of Representatives favored a depiction of the president's head on the obverse of each federal coin; others considered the idea an inappropriately monarchical practice. George Washington himself is believed to have expressed disapproval of the use of his portrait on American coins. The majority considered a figure emblematic of Liberty more appropriate, and the Senate finally concurred in this opinion. Robert Birch was an engraver employed to design proposed devices for American coins. He, perhaps together with others, engraved the dies for the disme and half disme. He also cut the dies for the large copper patterns known today as *Birch cents*. Most 1792 half dismes circulated and were considered to be official coinage, rather than patterns; they are summarized here and discussed in more detail under "Half Dismes."

1792 SILVER CENTER CENT

The dies for the 1792 cent with a silver center may have been cut by Henry Voigt. The coins are copper with a silver plug in the center. The idea was to create a coin with an intrinsic or melt-down value of a cent, but of smaller diameter than if it were made entirely of copper. On the obverse is a right-facing portrait of Miss Liberty, the legend LIBERTY PARENT OF SCIENCE & INDUSTRY, and the date 1792.

	F	VF	EF	AU
Cent, Silver Center (a)	$275,000	$450,000	$550,000	$850,000
Auctions: $1,997,500, MS-64, August 2014; $1,410,000, MS-63BN+, May 2014; $705,000, MS-61+, September 2014				
Cent, Without Silver Center (b)	$275,000	$400,000	$500,000	$650,000
Auctions: $603,750, VF-30, January 2008				

a. 14 examples are known, including one unique specimen without plug. **b.** Six or 7 examples are known.

1792 BIRCH CENT

On the large-diameter copper Birch cent, the portrait of Miss Liberty is "bright-eyed and almost smiling," as described in *United States Pattern Coins*. The legend LIBERTY PARENT OF SCIENCE & INDUSTRY surrounds the portrait. BIRCH is lettered on the truncation of her neck, for the engraver. On the reverse is a ribbon-tied wreath with the legend UNITED STATES OF AMERICA and the denomination in fractional terms of a dollar: 1/100. The edge of some examples is lettered TO BE ESTEEMED BE USEFUL (with punctuating stars).

G★W.Pt.

	F	VF	EF
Copper, Lettered Edge, TO BE ESTEEMED * BE USEFUL* (a)	$250,000	$600,000	$700,000
Auctions: $564,000, MS-61, January 2015			
Copper, Plain Edge (b)		$700,000	
Copper, Lettered Edge, TO BE ESTEEMED BE USEFUL * (b)		—	
Auctions: $2,585,000, MS-65H, January 2015			
White Metal, G★W.Pt. (George Washington President) Below Wreath (c)			—

a. Six or seven examples are known. **b.** Two examples are known. **c.** Unique.

1792 HALF DISME

About 1,500 silver half dismes were struck in mid-August 1792 in the shop of John Harper, using equipment ordered for the Philadelphia Mint (the foundation stones of which would be laid on July 31). Nearly all were placed into circulation. In his annual address that autumn, President George Washington noted that these had been so distributed. Their obverse design is a portrait of Miss Liberty similar to the Birch cent's, but facing left. Its legend is abbreviated as LIB. PAR. OF SCIENCE & INDUSTRY. The reverse shows an eagle in flight, with UNI. STATES OF AMERICA around the top, and HALF DISME below.

	Mintage	AG	G	VG	F	VF	EF	AU	Unc.
Silver	1,500	$8,500	$20,000	$27,500	$40,000	$80,000	$110,000	$175,000	$325,000
	Auctions: $1,292,500, SP-67, August 2014								

1792 DISME

The 1792 pattern disme occurs in one silver variety and two copper varieties (plain-edged and the more readily available reeded-edge). The obverse legend is abbreviated as LIBERTY PARENT OF SCIENCE & INDUST., with the date 1792 below Miss Liberty's neck. The reverse features an eagle in flight, different in design from that of the half disme, with UNITED STATES OF AMERICA around the top of the coin and the denomination, DISME, below.

	F	EF	AU	Unc.
Silver (a)	$300,000	$500,000	$1,000,000	
Auctions: $998,750, AU-50, January 2015				
Copper (*illustrated*) (b)	$135,000	$225,000	$450,000	$1,000,000
Auctions: $1,057,500, MS-64, January 2015				

a. 3 examples are known. b. Approximately 15 examples are known.

1792 QUARTER DOLLAR

Joseph Wright, an accomplished artist in the private sector, designed this pattern, thought to have been intended for a quarter dollar. Wright was George Washington's choice for the position of first chief engraver of the Mint, and he later designed the 1793, Liberty Cap, cent in that capacity, but died of yellow fever before being confirmed by Congress. Unique uniface trials of the obverse and reverse also exist.

	EF
1792, Copper *(illustrated)* (a)	$750,000
Auctions: $2,232,500, MS-63, January 2015	
1792, White Metal (b)	$325,000

a. 2 examples are known. **b.** 4 examples are known.

THE LIBERTAS AMERICANA MEDAL (1782)

The Liberty Cap coinage of the fledgling United States was inspired by the famous Libertas Americana medal, whose dies were engraved by Augustin Dupré in Paris in 1782 from a concept and mottoes proposed by Benjamin Franklin. To Franklin (then U.S. minister to France), the infant Hercules symbolized America, strangling two serpents representing the British armies at Saratoga and Yorktown. Minerva, with shield and spear, symbolized France as America's ally, keeping the British Lion at bay. Franklin presented gold examples of the medal to the French king and queen and silver strikings to their ministers, "as a monumental acknowledgment, which may go down to future ages, of the obligations we are under to this nation."

Between 100 and 125 original copper medals exist, and two dozen or more silver; the location of the two gold medals is unknown. Over the years the Paris Mint has issued additional medals that are appreciated and collected at a fraction of the cost for originals.

	PF-50	PF-60	PF-63	PF-65
Libertas Americana medal, Proof, Copper (a)	$8,000	$12,000	$24,000	$50,000
Libertas Americana medal, Proof, Silver (b)	$40,000	$80,000	$120,000	$180,000

a. 100 to 125 examples are known. **b.** At least 24 examples are known.

Half Cents
1793–1857
AN OVERVIEW OF HALF CENTS

Building a type set of the six different major designs in the half cent series can be a challenging and rewarding pursuit. The first design, with Liberty Head facing left with pole and cap, minted only in 1793, is scarce in all grades and will be the most difficult to locate. However, hundreds exist of this American classic, and many are fairly attractive.

The second type, with a *large* Liberty Head facing right with pole and cap, made only in 1794, is scarce with good eye appeal. Most are dark and rough. The next type, the *small* Liberty Head facing right, with pole and cap, is scarce, but enough are on the market that a collector can find a specimen without difficulty.

The Draped Bust half cents, struck from 1800 to 1808, are easily available as a type, including in higher grades. The Classic Head (1809–1836) and Braided Hair (1840–1857) are plentiful as types.

For the earlier half cent types there is ample opportunity for connoisseurship, for quality often varies widely, and every coin is apt to have a different appearance and "personality," even within the same grade.

FOR THE COLLECTOR AND INVESTOR: HALF CENTS AS A SPECIALTY

Collecting half cents by dates and major varieties has been a popular niche specialty for a long time. Some key issues in the series are the 1793; 1796, With Pole to Cap; 1796, Without Pole to Cap, (the most famous of all the rarities); 1802, 2 Over 0, With Reverse of 1800, (a single leaf at each side of the wreath apex, rare but somewhat obscure); 1831; and the Proof-only issues of 1836, 1840 through 1848, Small Date, and 1852.

As there are so many Proof varieties, and each of these is rare as well as expensive, many collectors opt to acquire only the circulation strikes. However, the Proofs are not nearly as expensive as one might think, probably because with so many different dates and varieties needed to complete a Proof collection, the prospect is daunting to many buyers. Proofs of most dates are available in both original and restrike forms. Although this rule is not without exceptions, the original strikings of the 1840–1848 and 1849, Small Date, half cents are usually described as having the Large Berries reverse, while restrikes are of the Small Berries reverse (within the Small Berries issues there are two dies—one with diagonal die striae below RICA, and the other with doubling at the ribbon wreath). Assembling Proofs by reverse varieties is a somewhat esoteric pursuit.

For an exhaustive study of die varieties of circulation strikes and Proofs, *Walter Breen's Encyclopedia of United States Half Cents, 1793–1857*, is definitive. Roger S. Cohen Jr.'s study, *American Half Cents, The "Little Half Sisters,"* gives detailed information on circulation strikes, but omits Proofs.

Die varieties are especially abundant among half cents of the first several types, 1793 to 1808. The year 1804 offers a panorama of dies, some of which have been studied as to die states, referring to the progression of use of a die as it develops wear, cracks, etc. Varieties of 1795 exist with and without the pole to the liberty cap, the Without Pole half cents being the result of a die being relapped (reground to dress the surface), during which process the pole was removed. On the other hand, the 1796, Without Pole, half cent was the result of a die-engraving error—the diecutter forgot to add it. Some half cents of 1795 and 1797 were struck on planchets cut from copper tokens issued by the New York City firm of Talbot, Allum & Lee. Upon close inspection, some of the design details of the tokens can still be seen.

One curious and readily available variety of the 1828 half cent has 12 stars instead of the standard 13. However, in choice Mint State the 12-stars issue becomes a rarity, for, unlike the 13-stars issue, none were ever found in hoards.

The Early American Coppers Club is a special-interest group emphasizing copper half cents and large cents. Its journal, *Penny-Wise*, provides much research, social, and collecting news and information.

LIBERTY CAP, HEAD FACING LEFT (1793)

Designer: *Henry Voigt.* **Weight:** *104 grains (6.74 grams).* **Composition:** *Copper.* **Diameter:** *21.2 to 24.6 mm.* **Edge:** *Lettered TWO HUNDRED FOR A DOLLAR.* **Mint:** *Philadelphia.*

Bowers-Whitman–4,
Cohen-4, Breen-4.

History. Among U.S. coinage, the Liberty Cap, Head Facing Left, design belongs to the small class of one-year-only types. Its design was inspired by Augustin Dupré's Libertas Americana medal. The Liberty Cap dies are often credited to Joseph Wright, who also cut the dies for the related cent, but they were more likely done by Henry Voigt.

Striking and Sharpness. Good-quality copper was used in these half cents, so they are often found light brown and on fairly smooth planchets. Unlike in later types, the borders on both sides are raised beads; certain of these beads can be weak, though this is not the norm. Some varieties are lightly defined at HALF CENT on the reverse, due to a combination of striking and shallow depth of letters in the die. This feature cannot be used in assigning a grade, as in lower grades (up to and including VG-8) these words may be completely missing.

Availability. Most half cents of 1793 are AG-3 to F-12. EF and AU examples are rare, and MS very rare (most being MS–60 to 63). Market grading is often liberal. Early American Coppers Club (EAC) "raw" grades often are lower than those of the certification services.

GRADING STANDARDS

MS-60 to 65 (Mint State). *Obverse:* In the lower ranges, MS–60 and 61, some light abrasions can be seen on the higher areas of the portrait. Luster in the field is incomplete, particularly in the center of the open areas. At the MS-63 level, luster should be complete, with no abrasions evident. In higher levels, the luster is deeper, and some original mint color may be seen. *Reverse:* In the lower ranges some abrasions are seen on the higher

1793; Bowers-Whitman–3, Cohen-3,
Breen-3. Graded MS-60BN.

areas of the leaves. Generally, luster is complete in all ranges, as the open areas are protected by the lettering and wreath. Otherwise, the same comments apply as for the obverse.

Illustrated coin: Well struck and nicely centered on the planchet, this example shows no sign of wear. Its color is a rich orange-brown overall, with a bit of darker gray-brown on the lower-right edge and field of the obverse. The faint roughness on the obverse is a flaw of the original planchet, and is not related to wear.

AU-50, 53, 55, 58 (About Uncirculated). *Obverse:* Friction is seen on the higher parts, particularly on the rounded cheek and on the higher strands of the hair. Friction and scattered marks are in the field, ranging from extensive at AU-50 to minimal at AU-58. Luster may be seen in protected areas, minimal at AU-50, but sometimes extensive on an AU-58 coin. Border beads, if well struck, are separate and boldly defined. *Reverse:* Friction

1793; BW-3, C-3, B-3. Graded AU-58.

is seen on the higher wreath leaves and (not as easy to discern) on the letters. The fields, protected by the designs, show friction, but not as noticeably as on the obverse. At AU–55 and 58 little if any friction is seen. The reverse may have original luster, toned brown, minimal on lower About Uncirculated grades, sometimes extensive at AU-58. Border beads, if well struck, are separate and boldly defined. Grading at the About Uncirculated level is mainly done by viewing the obverse.

Illustrated coin: Two tiny rim bruises can be seen, and some nicks can be seen as well under low magnification, none of which immediately draw the eye. This coin is about as good as can be found in this grade, as many examples of the date are porous.

EF-40, 45 (Extremely Fine). *Obverse:* Wear is seen on the portrait overall, with reduction or elimination of some separation of hair strands on the highest part. The cheek is ever so slightly flat on the highest part. Some leaves will retain some detail, especially where they join the stems. Luster is minimal or non-existent at EF-40 and may survive in traces in protected areas at EF-45. *Reverse:* Wear is seen on the highest wreath and rib-

1793; BW-3, C-3, B-3. Graded EF-45.

bon areas and the letters. Luster is minimal, but likely more noticeable than on the obverse, as the fields are protected by the designs and lettering.

Illustrated coin: The devices are crisp for the grade. Note the glossy golden-tan surfaces and the lack of meaningful contact marks.

VF-20, 30 (Very Fine). *Obverse:* Wear on the portrait has reduced the hair detail to indistinct or flat at the center on a VF-20 coin, with slightly more detail at VF-30. The thin, horizontal (more or less) ribbon near the top of the hair is distinct. The border beads are blended together, with many blurred or missing. No luster is seen. *Reverse:* The leaf details are nearly completely worn away at VF-20, and with slight detail at

1793; BW-3, C-3, B-3. Graded VF-30.

VF-30. The border beads are blended together, with many indistinct. Some berries in the sprays may be worn away, depending on the strike (on strong strikes they can be seen down into Very Good and Good grades). No luster is seen. HALF CENT may be weak, but is fully readable, on certain coins (such as BW-1, C-1, B-1) in which this feature was shallowly cut into the dies.

Illustrated coin: A small planchet crack at 8 o'clock on the obverse rim appears as struck. This planchet crack explains the softness of detail at the borders both in that area at 10 o'clock on the reverse.

F-12, 15 (Fine). *Obverse:* The hair details are mostly worn away, with about one-third visible, mainly at the edges. Border beads are weak or worn away in areas. F-15 shows slightly more detail. *Reverse:* The wreath leaves are worn flat, but their edges are distinct. HALF CENT may be missing on 1793 (Bowers-Whitman–1)—also true of lower grades given below. Border beads are weak or worn away in areas. F-15 shows slightly more detail.

1793; BW-3, C-3, B-3. Graded F-15.

Illustrated coin: Under magnification the surfaces are seen to be lightly porous.

VG-8, 10 (Very Good). *Obverse:* The portrait is well worn, although the eye can be seen, and the hair tips at the right show separation. Border beads are worn away, and the border blends into the field in most if not all of the periphery. LIBERTY and 1793 are bold. VG-10, not an official ANA grading designation, is sometimes applied to especially nice Very Good coins. *Reverse:* The wreath, bow, and lettering are seen in outline

1793; BW-4, C-4, B-4. Graded VG-8.

form, and some leaves and letters may be indistinct in parts. Border beads are worn away, and the border blends into the field in most if not all of the periphery.

Illustrated coin: The scratch from the E of LIBERTY to the base of the cap behind Liberty's head is less evident at the coin's unmagnified size.

G-4, 6 (Good). *Obverse:* The portrait is worn smooth and is seen only in outline form, although the eye position can be discerned. LIBERTY and 1793 are complete, although the date may be weak. *Reverse:* Extensive wear is seen overall. From half to two-thirds of the letters in UNITED STATES OF AMERICA and the fraction numerals are worn away. The reverse shows more evidence of wear than does the obverse,

1793; BW-2, C-2, B-2. Graded G-6.

and is key in assigning this grade. G-6 is often assigned to finer examples in this category.

AG-3 (About Good). *Obverse:* Wear is more extensive than on the preceding. The portrait is visible only in outline. LIBERTY is weak but usually fully discernible. 1793 is weak, and the bottoms of the digits may be worn away. *Reverse:* Parts of the wreath are visible in outline form, and all but a few letters are gone. Grading of AG-3 is usually done by the reverse.

1793; BW-3, C-3, B-3. Graded AG-3.

Fair-2 (Fair). *Obverse:* Worn nearly smooth. Date is partly visible, not necessarily clearly. Head of Miss Liberty is in outline form. Some letters of LIBERTY are discernible. *Reverse:* Worn nearly smooth. Peripheral letters are nearly all gone, with only vestiges remaining. Wreath is in outline form. HALF CENT ranges from readable to missing (the latter on certain die varieties as struck).

1793; BW-2, C-2, B-2. Graded Fair-2.

	Mintage	Cert	Avg	%MS	AG-3	G-4	VG-8	F-12	VF-20	EF-40	AU-50	MS-60BN	MS-63BN
1793	35,334	166	32.4	8%	$2,250	$3,500	$5,500	$9,000	$14,000	$22,500	$27,500	$60,000	$95,000
	Auctions: $176,250, MS-64, February 2016; $47,000, MS-62, November 2016; $1,528, G-4, August 2016												

LIBERTY CAP, HEAD FACING RIGHT (1794–1797)

Designer: *1794—Robert Scot; 1795–1797—Possibly Scot, John Smith Gardner, or other.*
Weight: *1794, thick planchet—6.74 grams; 1795–1797—5.44 grams.* **Composition:** *Copper.*
Diameter: *23.5 mm.* **Edge:** *1794, some of 1795, some of 1797—Lettered TWO HUNDRED*
FOR A DOLLAR; 1795, 1796, most of 1797—Plain; some of 1797—Gripped. **Mint:** *Philadelphia.*

1795, Lettered Edge,
With Pole; BW-1, C-1, B-1.

History. The design of the half cent changed in 1794 to a depiction, by Robert Scot, of Miss Liberty facing right. A smaller-headed portrait was used from 1795 on.

Striking and Sharpness. Half cents of 1794 usually are dark, with rough surfaces, and of low aesthetic quality. Most 1795's are on high-quality planchets, smooth and attractive, this being truer of the later plain-edge type than the early thick-planchet issue. Striking can be weak in areas. Often the denticles are incomplete on one or both sides. Many Small Head coins, particularly of 1795 to 1797, have very little detail on the hair, even in higher grades. Half cents of 1796 vary in quality; higher-grade pieces are usually attractive. Half cents of 1797 are usually seen in low grades and on poor planchets; striking varies widely, but is usually weak in areas. Denticles can be weak or can be prominent in various circulated grades, down to the lowest; on certain varieties of 1795 they are prominent even on well-worn coins. Grades must be assigned carefully, and expertise is recommended—combining knowledge of a given die variety and its relief or sharpness in the die, with observations of actual circulation wear. Grades of certified coins can vary widely in their interpretations.

Availability. As a general type, this issue is scarce, but available. Most are in lower grades, but VF and EF coins appear in the market with regularity.

GRADING STANDARDS

MS-60 to 70 (Mint State). *Obverse:* On MS–60 and 61 coins there are some traces of abrasion on the higher areas of the portrait. Luster in the field is incomplete, particularly in the center of the open areas. At MS-63, luster should be complete, and no abrasion is evident. At higher levels, the luster is deeper, and some original mint color may be seen. At MS-65 there are some scattered contact marks and possibly some traces of finger-

1794; BW-9, C-9, B-9. Graded MS-65.

prints or discoloration, but these should be minimal and not at all distracting. Above MS-65, a coin should approach perfection. *Reverse:* In the lower ranges some abrasions are seen on the higher areas of the leaves. Generally, luster is complete in all ranges, as the open areas are protected by the lettering and wreath. Otherwise, the same comments apply as for the obverse.

Illustrated coin: A spectacular coin of a year seldom seen in Mint State. Both sides have rich, brown surfaces. On the obverse the luster is light, while on the reverse it is not as noticeable. Note that the obverse die is in very high relief and of the Large Head style, while the reverse is in shallower relief.

AU-50, 53, 55, 58 (About Uncirculated). *Obverse:* Friction is seen on the higher parts, particularly the center of the portrait. Friction and scattered marks are in the field, ranging from extensive at AU-50 to minimal at AU-58. To reiterate: knowledge of the die variety is important. For certain shallow-relief dies (such as those of 1797) an About Uncirculated coin may appear to be in a lower grade. Luster may be seen in protected

1794; BW-1a, C-1a, B-1a. Graded AU-50.

areas, minimal at AU-50, but sometimes extensive on an AU-58 coin. *Reverse:* Friction is seen on the higher wreath leaves and (not as easy to discern) on the letters. The fields, protected by the designs, show friction, but not as noticeably as on the obverse. At AU–55 and 58 little if any friction is seen. The reverse may have original luster, toned brown, minimal on lower About Uncirculated grades, sometimes extensive on higher. Grading at the About Uncirculated level is mainly done by viewing the obverse.

Illustrated coin: Note faint ruddy highlights in the protected areas. The devices are boldly impressed. On this variety the 179 in the date was punched low into the die, partly effaced, then repunched in a higher position. On the reverse, a natural planchet fissure, small and as struck, runs from the rim through the M of AMERICA, and a smaller fissure runs from the rim to the E of AMERICA.

EF-40, 45 (Extremely Fine). *Obverse:* Wear is seen on the portrait overall, with some reduction or elimination of the separation of hair strands on the highest part. This varies by die variety, as some are better delineated than others. The cheek shows light wear. Luster is minimal or nonexistent at EF-40, and may survive in traces in protected areas (such as between the letters) at EF-45. *Reverse:* Wear is seen on the highest wreath and ribbon areas and the letters. Luster is minimal, but likely

1795, Pole to Cap, Lettered Edge; BW-1, C-1, B-1. Graded EF-45.

more noticeable than on the obverse, as the fields are protected by the designs and lettering. Sharpness will vary depending on the die variety. Expect certain issues of 1794 and 1797 to be lighter.

Illustrated coin: This coin has bold details and excellent centering.

VF-20, 30 (Very Fine). *Obverse:* Wear on the portrait has reduced the hair detail to indistinct or flat at the center. The border denticles are blended together, with many indistinct. No luster is seen. Again, knowing details of the die variety is important. A VF–20 or 30 1797 is very different in appearance from a 1794, Large Head, in the same grade. *Reverse:* The leaf details are nearly completely worn away at VF-20, with slight

1797; BW-2, C-2. Graded VF-30.

detail at VF-30. The border denticles are blended together, with many indistinct. No luster is seen. The sharpness of details depends on the die variety. Half cents of 1797 require special care in their study.

Illustrated coin: Minor roughness is apparent at the center of both sides, undoubtedly a trace of microporosity from the blank planchet, although the devices are overall bold from a well executed strike.

F-12, 15 (Fine). *Obverse:* The hair details are mostly worn away, with about one-third visible, mainly at the edges. Border denticles are weak or worn away in areas. F-15 shows slightly more detail. *Reverse:* The wreath leaves are worn flat, but their edges are distinct. Border denticles are weak or worn away in areas. F-15 shows slightly more detail.

Illustrated coin: This late-die-state variety has a noticeable die crack in the E of UNITED.

1794, High-Relief Head; BW-7, C-7, B-7. Graded F-15.

VG-8, 10 (Very Good). *Obverse:* The portrait is well worn, although the eye can be seen, and the hair tips at the left show separation. Border denticles are worn away on some issues (not as much for 1795 coins), and the border blends into the field in most if not all of the periphery. LIBERTY and the date are bold. VG-10, not an official ANA grading designation, is sometimes applied to especially nice Very Good coins. *Reverse:* The

1794, High Relief Head; BW-9, C-9, B-9. Graded VG-8.

wreath, bow, and lettering are seen in outline form, and some leaves and letters may be indistinct in parts. Border denticles are worn away, and the border blends into the field in most if not all of the periphery. In certain die varieties and die states, especially of 1797, some letters may be very weak or missing.

Illustrated coin: This coin exhibits roughness in the fields, but the same does not apply to the devices.

G-4, 6 (Good). *Obverse:* The portrait is worn smooth and is seen only in outline form, although the eye position can be discerned. LIBERTY and the date are complete, although the date may be weak. Denticles are gone on some, but not all, die varieties. *Reverse:* Extensive wear is seen overall. From half to two-thirds of the letters in UNITED STATES OF AMERICA, and the fraction numerals, are worn away. Certain shallow-relief dies

1794; BW-2a, C-2a, B-2a. Graded G-4.

may have letters missing. G-6 is often assigned to finer examples in this category.

Illustrated coin: On this coin the surfaces are heavily worn, yet with considerable boldness of detail remaining on the obverse.

AG-3 (About Good). *Obverse:* Wear is more extensive than on the preceding. The portrait is visible only in outline. LIBERTY is weak but usually fully discernible. The date is weak, and the bottoms of the digits may be worn away. *Reverse:* Parts of the wreath are visible in outline form, and all but a few letters are gone. Grading of AG-3 is usually done by the reverse, as the obverse typically appears to be in a slightly higher grade. If split grading were used, more than just a few

1795, Plain Edge, Punctuated Date; BW-5, C-4, B-4. Graded AG-3.

half cents of this type could be designated as G-4 / AG-3 or even G-6 / AG-3.

1794, Normal Head

1794, High-Relief Head

1795, With Pole

1795, No Pole

1795, Punctuated Date

	Mintage	Cert	Avg	%MS	AG-3	G-4	VG-8	F-12	VF-20	EF-40	AU-50	MS-60BN	MS-63BN
1794, All kinds	81,600												
1794, Normal Head		191	33.0	9%	$350	$575	$850	$1,500	$2,250	$5,000	$12,000	$25,000	$55,000
	Auctions: $88,125, MS-63BN, April 2014												
1794, High-Relief Head		15	35.7	7%	$375	$600	$975	$1,650	$3,000	$6,200	$14,500	$27,500	$65,000
	Auctions: $1,586, VF-20, October 2013												
1795, All kinds	139,690												
1795, Lettered Edge, With Pole		59	31.8	12%	$275	$600	$825	$1,350	$2,500	$6,000	$12,000	$17,000	$45,000
	Auctions: $3,525, EF-40, September 2013; $2,820, VF-30, March 2015												
1795, Lettered Edge, Punctuated Date		6	17.0	0%	$300	$675	$875	$1,600	$3,000	$7,000	$13,500	$25,000	$55,000
	Auctions: $12,925, AU-55, August 2013												
1795, Plain Edge, Punctuated Date		7	29.7	14%	$275	$500	$675	$1,250	$2,350	$5,500	$8,500	$14,000	$45,000
	Auctions: $1,501, VF-20, August 2011												
1795, Plain Edge, No Pole (a)		34	28.5	0%	$220	$475	$675	$1,250	$2,000	$4,750	$8,500	$14,000	$25,000
	Auctions: $7,638, AU-55, June 2014												

1796, "Dr. Edwards" Copy		**1797, 1 Above 1**		**1797, Low Head**

	Mintage	Cert	Avg	%MS	AG-3	G-4	VG-8	F-12	VF-20	EF-40	AU-50	MS-60BN	MS-63BN
1796, With Pole (b)	1,390	22	38.6	45%	$10,000	$20,000	$27,500	$37,500	$55,000	$75,000	$95,000	$165,000	
Auctions: $76,375, EF-40, August 2013													
1796, No Pole	(c)	1	62.0	100%	$22,500	$45,000	$65,000	$125,000	$180,000	$250,000	$300,000	$450,000	
Auctions: $891,250, MS-65BN, January 2014; $382, VG-8, September 2013													
1797, All kinds	127,840												
1797, 1 Above 1, Plain Edge		64	25.2	3%	$225	$450	$650	$1,100	$1,800	$4,000	$6,500	$15,000	
Auctions: $7,931, AU, March 2014													
1797, Plain Edge, Low Head		6	11.7	0%	$350	$575	$975	$2,250	$4,500	$14,000	—		
Auctions: $1,495, VG-10, February 2012													
1797, Plain Edge		65	21.8	5%	$275	$450	$750	$1,250	$3,000	$6,000	$8,500	$16,000	
Auctions: $3,055, AU-50, April 2013; $823, F-12, August 2015; $400, VG-8, September 2015; $505, G-6, January 2015													
1797, Lettered Edge		4	14.3	0%	$700	$1,500	$3,000	$7,500	$17,000	$50,000	$75,000		
Auctions: $7,638, VG-10, November 2013; $3,995, VG-10, March 2016													
1797, Gripped Edge		0	n/a		$20,000	$45,000	$75,000	$145,000	—	—	—		
Auctions: $195,500, G-6, September 2011													

a. Many of this date/variety were struck on cut-down cents (coins that had been rejected for circulation by Mint workers), or on planchets cut from English-made Talbot, Allum & Lee tokens (see the *Whitman Encyclopedia of Colonial and Early American Coins*). **b.** The deceptive "Dr. Edwards" struck copy of this coin has a different head and larger letters, as pictured. **c.** Included in 1796, With Pole, mintage figure.

DRAPED BUST (1800–1808)

Designer: *Robert Scot.* **Weight:** *5.44 grams.* **Composition:** *Copper.* **Diameter:** *23.5 mm.* **Edge:** *Plain.* **Mint:** *Philadelphia.*

1804, Crosslet 4, Stems to Wreath; BW-9, C-10, B-9.

History. By the turn of the century the Draped Bust design was already familiar to Americans from its use on cents and silver coins. The motif was introduced to the half cent in 1800, and was used through 1808.

Striking and Sharpness. Striking varies. Weakness is often seen at the center of the obverse and on the wreath leaves on the reverse. Planchet quality is often porous and dark for 1802, 1803, 1807, and 1808 due to the copper stock used.

Availability. As a type, Draped Bust half cents are available in any grade desired, up to and including Mint State, the latter usually dated 1806 (occasionally 1800 and, less often, 1804). The year 1804 includes many different die varieties and die states. Apart from aspects of strike, cherrypicking for planchet quality is essential for 1802, 1803, 1807, and 1808.

GRADING STANDARDS

MS-60 to 70 (Mint State). *Obverse:* In the lower grades, MS–60 and 61, some slight abrasions can be seen on the higher areas of the portrait. Luster in the field is incomplete, particularly in the center of the open areas, which on this type are very extensive. At the MS-63 level, luster should be nearly complete, and no abrasions evident. In higher levels, the luster is complete and deeper and some original mint color may be seen. MS-64

1800; BW-1, C-1, B-1. Graded MS-62.

coins may have some slight discoloration or scattered contact marks. A well-graded MS-65 or higher coin has full, rich luster; no marks visible except under magnification; and a blend of brown toning or nicely mixed (not stained or blotchy) mint color and natural brown toning. *Reverse:* In the lower Mint State ranges some abrasions are seen on the higher areas of the leaves. Generally, luster is complete in all ranges, as the open areas are protected by the lettering and wreath. Sharpness of the leaves can vary by die variety, so check this aspect. Otherwise, the same comments apply as for the obverse.

AU-50, 53, 55, 58 (About Uncirculated). *Obverse:* Friction is seen on the higher parts, particularly the hair of Miss Liberty. Friction and scattered marks are in the field, ranging from extensive at AU-50 to minimal at AU-58. Luster may be seen in protected areas, minimal at AU-50, with more at AU-58. At AU-58 the field may retain some luster, as well. In all instances, the luster is lesser in area and in "depth" than on the reverse of this type.

1800; BW-1, C-1, B-1. Graded AU-58.

Reverse: Friction is evident on the higher wreath leaves and (not as easy to discern) on the letters. Again, the die variety should be checked. The fields, protected by the designs, show friction, but not as noticeably as on the obverse. At AU–55 and 58, little if any friction is seen. The reverse may have original luster, toned brown, minimal on lower About Uncirculated grades, often extensive at AU-58.

   Illustrated coin: The motifs are very boldly rendered, except for partial weakness on the lower obverse and OF on the upper reverse, which is virtually missing due to the late die state.

EF-40, 45 (Extremely Fine). *Obverse:* Wear is seen on the portrait overall, with reduction or elimination of some separation of hair strands on the highest part. The cheek shows light wear. Luster is minimal or non-existent at EF-40, and may survive among the letters of LIBERTY at EF-45. *Reverse:* Wear is seen on the highest wreath and ribbon areas, and the letters. Luster is minimal, but likely more noticeable than on the obverse, as the fields are protected by the designs and lettering.

1800; BW-1, C-1, B-1. Graded EF-40.

VF-20, 30 (Very Fine). *Obverse:* Wear on the portrait has reduced the hair detail to indistinct or flat at the center. The border denticles are blended together, with many indistinct. No luster is seen. *Reverse:* The leaf details are nearly completely worn away at VF-20, and with slight detail at VF-30. The border denticles are blended together, with many indistinct. No luster is seen.

Illustrated coin: Struck from a later die state, the reverse shows a bisecting die crack.

1803; BW-1, C-1, B-1. Graded VF-20.

F-12, 15 (Fine). *Obverse:* The hair details are mostly worn away, with about one-third visible, mainly at the edges. Border denticles are weak or worn away in areas. F-15 shows slightly more detail. *Reverse:* The wreath leaves are worn flat, but their edges are distinct. HALF CENT may be missing on weakly struck varieties (also true of lower grades given below). Border denticles are weak or worn away in areas. F-15 shows slightly more detail.

1804, "Spiked Chin"; BW-5, C-8, B-7. Graded F-15.

Illustrated coin: This is the "Spiked Chin" variety, so called because of a thorn-like projection from the chin. The variety does not affect the grade.

VG-8, 10 (Very Good). *Obverse:* The portrait is well worn, although the eye can be seen, as can hints of hair detail (some at the left shows separation). Curls now appear as mostly solid blobs. Border denticles are worn away on most varieties, and the rim, although usually present, begins to blend into the field. LIBERTY and the date are bold. VG-10, not an official ANA grading designation, is sometimes applied to especially nice Very Good coins. *Reverse:* The wreath, bow, and lettering are seen in outline form, and some leaves and letters may be indistinct in parts. The border may blend into the field on some of the periphery.

1804, Plain 4, Stems to Wreath; BW-12, C-11, B-12. Graded VG-10.

Illustrated coin: This coin is has many scratches, which detract from overall eye appeal.

G-4, 6 (Good). *Obverse:* The portrait is worn smooth and is seen only in outline form, although the eye position can be discerned. LIBERTY and the date are complete, although the date may be weak. The border blends into the field more extensively than on the preceding, but significant areas are still seen. *Reverse:* Extensive wear is seen overall. From one-half to two-thirds of the letters in UNITED STATES OF AMERICA and the fraction numerals are worn away. G-6 is often assigned to finer examples in this category.

1808, 8 Over 7; BW-2, C-2, B-2. Graded G-4.

Illustrated coin: A slightly off-center strike has allowed areas of heavier wear to creep in near the borders. There are many noticeable scratches on the obverse.

AG-3 (About Good). *Obverse:* Wear is more extensive than on the preceding. The portrait is visible only in outline. LIBERTY is weak but usually discernible. The date is weak, and the bottoms of the digits may be worn away, but must be identifiable. *Reverse:* Parts of the wreath are visible in outline form, and all but a few letters are gone.

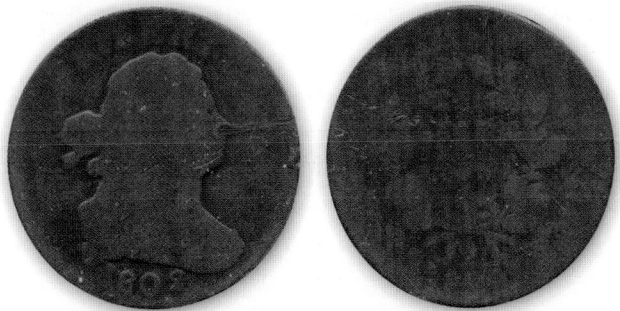

1802, 2 Over 0; BW-2, C-2, B-2. Graded AG-3.

| 1st Reverse (Style of 1800) | 2nd Reverse (Style of 1802) | 1803, Normally Spaced 3 | 1803, Widely Spaced 3 |

| 1804, Plain 4 | 1804, Crosslet 4 |

| Stems to Wreath | Stemless Wreath | 1804, "Spiked Chin" |

	Mintage	Cert	Avg	%MS	AG-3	G-4	VG-8	F-12	VF-20	EF-40	AU-50	MS-60BN	MS-63BN
1800	202,908	222	43.2	29%	$45	$85	$110	$150	$300	$700	$1,000	$2,250	$4,000
Auctions: $282, VF-35, May 2015; $329, VF-25, January 2015; $4,113, VF-20, June 2013													
1802, 2 Over 0, Reverse of 1800	(a)	2	2.0	0%	$10,000	$20,000	$35,000	$55,000	$75,000	$95,000	—		
Auctions: $35,938, VG-8, April 2009; $4,935, AG-0, March 2016													
1802, 2 Over 0, Reverse of 1802	20,266	46	9.2	0%	$375	$750	$1,850	$4,250	$12,500	$25,000	—		
Auctions: $4,406, F-12, February 2013; $940, G-6, June 2015; $940, G-6, March 2016; $940, G-6, August 2016													
1803	(b)	201	30.3	9%	$40	$85	$115	$160	$325	$950	$1,500	$3,250	$7,000
Auctions: $646, VF-35, August 2015; $376, VF-25, June 2015; $235, VF-30, February 2015; $153, VG-8, February 2015													
1803, Widely Spaced 3	92,000	24	32.5	8%	$45	$95	$125	$165	$325	$950	$1,500	$3,500	$7,500
Auctions: $1,840, AU-55, April 2012													
1804, All kinds	1,055,312												
1804, Plain 4, Stems to Wreath		12	30.8	0%	$40	$100	$120	$200	$475	$1,300	$2,200	$4,000	
Auctions: $4,994, AU-58, October 2013; $1,410, EF-45, March 2016; $823, VF-30, August 2015													
1804, Plain 4, Stemless Wreath		215	43.0	16%	$35	$85	$100	$145	$225	$385	$675	$1,300	$2,800
Auctions: $940, AU-58, June 2015; $646, AU-55, October 2015; $588, AU-55, August 2015; $259, AU-50, May 2015													
1804, Crosslet 4, Stemless		57	54.8	46%	$35	$85	$100	$145	$225	$385	$675	$1,300	$2,800
Auctions: $5,141, MS-64BN, September 2013; $376, EF-40, January 2015													
1804, Crosslet 4, Stems		119	44.5	16%	$35	$85	$100	$145	$225	$400	$675	$1,300	$2,800
Auctions: $705, AU-55, March 2015; $470, EF-45, October 2015; $364, EF-40, April 2015; $282, VF-35, August 2015													
1804, "Spiked Chin"		403	42.7	12%	$35	$95	$115	$155	$265	$425	$850	$1,800	$3,600
Auctions: $764, AU-53BN, September 2015; $646, AU-50, February 2015; $423, EF-45, June 2015; $247, EF-40, July 2015													

a. Included in 1800 mintage figure. **b.** Included in 1802, 2 Over 0, Second Reverse, mintage figure.

1805, Medium 5	1805, Small 5	1805, Large 5

1806, Small 6	1806, Large 6	1808, Normal Date	1808, 8 Over 7

	Mintage	Cert	Avg	%MS	AG-3	G-4	VG-8	F-12	VF-20	EF-40	AU-50	MS-60BN	MS-63BN
1805, All kinds	814,464												
1805, Medium 5, Stemless		52	37.8	12%	$35	$85	$100	$145	$225	$400	$750	$1,350	$3,000
Auctions: $4,113, MS-64BN, April 2014; $517, EF-45, January 2015; $447, EF-40, January 2015													
1805, Small 5, Stems		8	13.1	0%	$500	$1,000	$1,650	$4,000	$8,000	$17,000	$50,000		
Auctions: $1,116, VG-8, August 2015; $1,175, G-6, March 2016													
1805, Large 5, Stems		32	33.3	0%	$35	$85	$100	$145	$225	$425	$850	$1,700	$3,750
Auctions: $1,293, AU-55, July 2015; $353, VF-35, June 2015; $223, VF-30, July 2015													
1806, All kinds	356,000												
1806, Small 6, Stems		20	29.7	0%	$90	$235	$425	$750	$1,650	$3,500	$9,000	$12,500	
Auctions: $646, F-15, September 2016; $505, F-12, July 2016; $400, VG-10, March 2016; $188, G-6, August 2016													
1806, Small 6, Stemless		130	45.0	18%	$35	$85	$100	$145	$175	$325	$675	$1,200	$2,900
Auctions: $823, AU-58, January 2015; $564, AU-50, September 2015; $517, AU-50, August 2015; $329, EF-45, February 2015													
1806, Large 6, Stems		91	50.3	43%	$35	$85	$100	$145	$175	$325	$675	$1,200	$2,900
Auctions: $5,581, MS-63RB, June 2014													
1807	476,000	299	35.9	6%	$35	$85	$100	$145	$200	$500	$1,000	$2,000	$3,750
Auctions: $1,175, AU-58, February 2013; $212, VF-20, May 2015													
1808, All kinds	400,000												
1808, Normal Date		148	28.3	1%	$35	$85	$100	$145	$220	$525	$1,300	$2,500	$5,000
Auctions: $823, AU-50, June 2014; $447, EF-45, January 2015; $200, VF-25, June 2015													
1808, 8 Over 7		47	19.8	0%	$80	$150	$350	$750	$2,000	$4,000	$10,000		
Auctions: $2,585, EF-40, April 2013													

CLASSIC HEAD (1809–1836)

Designer: *John Reich.* **Weight:** *5.44 grams.* **Composition:** *Copper.*
Diameter: *23.5 mm.* **Edge:** *Plain.* **Mint:** *Philadelphia.*

Circulation Strike	Proof
1833; BW-1.	*1836; BW-1.*

History. The Classic Head design (by Mint engraver John Reich) made its first appearance on the half cent in 1809, a year after it was adopted for the one-cent coin. A very similar motif of Miss Liberty was used on the quarter eagles and half eagles of the 1830s.

Striking and Sharpness. Coins of 1809 to 1811 usually have areas of light or incomplete striking. Grading coins of the early years requires special care and expertise. Sometimes coins as high as MS appear "blurry" in areas, due to the dies and striking. Those of later years are often found well struck and are easier to grade. Areas to check include the denticles and rims on both sides, the star centers and hair detail on the obverse, and the leaf detail on the reverse.

Availability. As a type this issue is found easily enough, although 1811 is scarce and 1831 and 1836 are notable rarities. MS coins from old hoards exist for certain of the later dates, particularly 1828, 1833, and 1835, but often have spotting, and many seen in the marketplace are cleaned or recolored. Care is advised. Although 1809–1811 half cents are often seen with extensive wear, those of the 1820s and 1830s are not often seen less than VF, as they did not circulate extensively.

GRADING STANDARDS

MS-60 to 70 (Mint State). *Obverse:* In the lower grades, MS–60 and 61, some slight abrasions can be seen on the portrait, most evident on the cheek, as the hair details are complex on this type. Luster in the field is complete or nearly complete. At MS-63, luster should be complete, and no abrasions are evident. In higher levels, the luster is complete and deeper, and some original mint color may be seen. MS-64 coins may have

1810; BW-1, C-1, B-1. Graded MS-64BN.

some slight discoloration or scattered contact marks. A well-graded MS-65 or higher coin has full, rich luster, with no marks visible except under magnification, and has a nice blend of brown toning or nicely mixed (not stained or blotchy) mint color and natural brown toning. Coins dated 1809 to 1811 may exhibit significant weakness of details due to striking (and/or, in the case of most 1811's, porous planchet stock). *Reverse:* In the lower Mint State grades, some abrasions are seen on the higher areas of the leaves. Mint luster is complete in all Mint State grades, as the open areas are protected by the lettering and wreath. Sharpness of the leaves can vary by die variety, so check this aspect. Otherwise, the same comments apply as for the obverse. Coins dated 1809 to 1811 may exhibit significant weakness of details due to striking (and/or, in the case of most 1811's, porous planchet stock).

Illustrated coin: Some surface marks on the coin holder obscure the reverse, but no such marks mar the surface of this sharply struck coin.

AU-50, 53, 55, 58 (About Uncirculated).
Obverse: Friction is seen on the higher parts, particularly the cheek and hair (under magnification) of Miss Liberty. Friction and scattered marks are in the field, ranging from extensive at AU-50 to minimal at AU-58. Luster may be seen in protected areas, minimal at the AU-50 level, with more showing at AU-58. At AU-58 the field may retain some luster as well. *Reverse:* Friction is seen on the

1828, 12 Stars; BW-3, C-2, B-3. Graded AU-58.

higher wreath leaves and (not as easy to discern) on the letters. Again, half cents of 1809 to 1811 require special attention. The fields, protected by the designs, show friction, but not as noticeably as on the obverse. At AU–55 and 58, little if any friction is seen. The reverse may have original luster, toned brown, minimal on lower About Uncirculated grades, often extensive at AU-58.

EF-40, 45 (Extremely Fine). *Obverse:* Wear is seen on the portrait overall, with reduction or elimination of some separation of hair strands. The cheek shows light wear. Luster is minimal or nonexistent at EF-40 but may survive among the letters of LIBERTY at EF-45. *Reverse:* Wear is seen on the highest wreath and ribbon areas and the letters. Luster is minimal, but likely more noticeable than on the obverse, as the fields are protected by the designs and lettering.

1831, Original; BW-1, C-1, B-1. Graded EF-45.

VF-20, 30 (Very Fine). *Obverse:* Wear on the portrait has reduced the hair detail, but much can still be seen (in this respect the present type differs dramatically from earlier types). *Reverse:* The wreath details, except for the edges of the leaves, are worn away at VF-20, and have slightly more detail at VF-30.

    Illustrated coin: This coin is lightly struck at the left-reverse border, despite overall bold striking elsewhere.

1811, Close Date; BW-3, C-3, B-2. Graded VF-30.

F-12, 15 (Fine). *Obverse:* The hair details are fewer than at the preceding level, but many are still present. Stars have flat centers. F-15 shows slightly more detail. *Reverse:* The wreath leaves are worn flat, but their edges are distinct. F-15 shows slightly more detail.

1809, Normal Date. Graded F-15.

VG-8, 10 (Very Good). *Obverse:* The portrait is well worn, although the eye and ear can be seen, as can some hair detail. The border is well defined in most areas. *Reverse:* The wreath, bow, and lettering are seen in outline form, and some leaves and letters may be indistinct in parts. The border is well defined in most areas.

1809, 9 Over Inverted 9; BW-6, C-5, B-5. Graded VG-10.

G-4, 6 (Good). *Obverse:* The portrait is worn smooth and is seen only in outline form. Much of LIBERTY on the headband is readable, but the letters are weak. The stars are bold in outline. Much of the rim can be discerned. *Reverse:* Extensive wear is seen overall. Lettering in UNITED STATES OF AMERICA ranges from weak but complete (although the ANA grading guidelines allow for only half to be readable; the ANA text

1811; BW-1, C-1, B-1. Graded G-6.

illustrates the words in full) to having perhaps a third of the letters missing. HALF CENT is usually bold.

Illustrated coin: While ultimately well-preserved for the grade, this coin is a bit rough in texture, with light pitting and traces of old, inactive surface build up.

AG-3 (About Good). *Obverse:* Wear is more extensive than on the preceding. The portrait is visible only in outline. A few letters of LIBERTY are discernible in the headband. The stars are weak or worn away on their outer edges. The date is light. *Reverse:* The wreath is visible in outline form. Most or even all of UNITED STATES OF AMERICA is worn away. HALF CENT is usually readable.

1811; BW-1, C-1, B-1. Graded AG-3.

PF-60 to 70 (Proof). Proofs were struck of various years in the 1820s and 1830s, with 1831 and 1836 being great rarities (these dates were also restruck at the Mint circa 1859 and later). Some prooflike circulation strikes (especially of the 1833 date) have been certified as Proofs. Except for the years 1831 and 1836, for which Proofs are unequivocal, careful study is advised when contemplating the purchase of a coin described as Proof.

1831, First Restrike; BW-1a, C-PR-2, B-2. Graded PF-66BN.

Blotchy and recolored Proofs are often seen, but hardly ever described as such. Probably fewer than 25 of the Proofs of this type are truly pristine—without one problem or another. *Obverse and Reverse:* Proofs that are extensively hairlined or have dull surfaces, this being characteristic of many issues (1831 and 1836 usually excepted), are graded PF–60 to 62 or 63. This includes artificially toned and recolored coins, a secret that isn't really secret among knowledgeable collectors and dealers, but is rarely described in print. To qualify as PF-65 or higher, hairlines should be microscopic, and there should be no trace of friction. Surfaces should be prooflike or, better, fully mirrored, without dullness.

Illustrated coin: Note the traces of mint red throughout and the blue iridescence of the reverse. The reverse die is severely cracked from the F in OF to the T of UNITED.

1809, Normal Date   **1809, Small 0 Inside 0**   **1809, 9 Over Inverted 9**

1811, Wide Date   **1811, Close Date**   **1828, 13 Stars**   **1828, 12 Stars**

	Mintage	Cert	Avg	%MS	G-4	VG-8	F-12	VF-20	EF-40	AU-50	MS-60BN	MS-63BN	MS-63RB
1809, All kinds	1,154,572												
1809, Normal Date		427	44.0	22%	$55	$75	$100	$115	$150	$300	$850	$1,500	$2,000
Auctions: $588, MS-61BN, June 2015; $823, AU-58, January 2015; $388, AU-55, March 2015; $176, AU-50, January 2015													
1809, Small o Inside 0		16	36.8	0%	$55	$80	$110	$160	$450	$900	$1,400	$5,000	
Auctions: $55, G-4, January 2013													
1809, 9 Over Inverted 9 (a)		238	49.6	18%	$55	$75	$100	$150	$375	$750	$1,300	$2,200	$3,000
Auctions: $1,116, AU-58, June 2015; $423, AU-50, January 2015; $306, EF-45, September 2015; $200, VF-30, May 2015													
1810	215,000	104	40.1	17%	$55	$75	$125	$270	$575	$1,000	$2,000	$3,200	$6,750
Auctions: $2,800, MS-63BN, April 2014; $376, VF-30, May 2015													
1811, All kinds	63,140												
1811, Wide Date		4	27.5	0%	$400	$800	$1,650	$2,750	$6,500	$10,000	$30,000	$75,000	
Auctions: $764, VF-20, December 2015; $494, VF-20, August 2016													
1811, Close Date		7	23.1	0%	$375	$700	$1,600	$2,500	$6,500	$10,000	$30,000	$75,000	
Auctions: $26,450, AU-50, September 2011													
1811, Reverse of 1802, Unofficial Restrike (b)		5	63.8	100%					—	—	$16,000	$20,000	$25,000
Auctions: $23,000, MS-64BN, September 2008													
1825	63,000	296	47.4	22%	$55	$75	$85	$100	$200	$325	$900	$1,800	$3,000
Auctions: $529, MS-61BN, June 2015; $564, AU-55, May 2015; $282, AU-55, January 2015; $259, EF-45, June 2015													
1826	234,000	383	48.2	27%	$55	$75	$85	$100	$150	$300	$600	$1,000	$1,300
Auctions: $999, MS-63BN, August 2015; $764, MS-62BN, September 2015; $306, MS-61BN, May 2015; $165, EF-45, August 2015													
1828, All kinds	606,000												
1828, 13 Stars		139	49.2	37%	$50	$70	$75	$100	$120	$225	$350	$600	$1,000
Auctions: $1,028, MS-64RB, January 2015; $999, MS-64BN, January 2015; $590, MS-63BN, February 2015; $309, MS-62BN, September 2015													
1828, 12 Stars		221	50.3	25%	$50	$70	$85	$120	$250	$425	$1,300	$1,850	$3,500
Auctions: $2,468, MS-63BN, February 2014													
1829	487,000	376	50.6	43%	$50	$70	$75	$100	$140	$220	$400	$700	$1,100
Auctions: $482, MS-63BN, February 2015; $764, MS-61BN, June 2015; $517, AU-58, September 2015; $235, AU-53, September 2015													

a. Traditionally called 9 Over Inverted 9, but recent research shows it not to have an inverted digit. **b.** This coin is extremely rare.

1831, Proof, Restrike   **Reverse of 1831–1836**   **Reverse of 1840–1857**

	Mintage	Cert	Avg	%MS	VG-8	F-12	VF-20	EF-40	AU-50	MS-60BN	MS-63BN	MS-63RB	MS-65RB
											PF-60BN	PF-63BN	PF-65BN
1831, Original (a)		6	52.0	50%					$50,000	$75,000			
Auctions: No auction records available.													
1831, Original, Proof (b)	2,200	5	53.4								$85,000	$125,000	
Auctions: $57,281, PF-60BN, January 2014													
1831, Restrike, Large Berries, Proof (Reverse of 1836)	25–35	9	65.7								$10,000	$15,000	$25,000
Auctions: $47,000, PF-65RB, February 2014													
1831, Restrike, Small Berries, Proof (Reverse of 1840–1857)	10–15	0	n/a								$14,000	$21,500	$40,000
Auctions: $63,250, PF-66BN, July 2009													
1832 (c)	51,000	467	52.0	36%	$65	$80	$90	$125	$200	$325	$475	$875	$4,000
Auctions: $999, MS-64BN, June 2015; $306, MS-62BN, January 2015; $282, MS-61BN, May 2015; $259, AU-58, August 2015													
1832, Proof	10–15	1	64.0								$7,000	$10,000	$17,500
Auctions: $44,063, PF-64BN, January 2014													
1833 (c)	103,000	669	57.2	62%	$65	$80	$90	$125	$200	$325	$450	$750	$3,500
Auctions: $940, MS-64BN, February 2015; $823, MS-64BN, June 2015; $410, MS-63BN, May 2015; $212, AU-58, January 2015													
1833, Proof	25–35	14	64.1								$5,000	$6,000	$10,500
Auctions: $11,163, PF-65BN, March 2013													
1834 (c)	141,000	679	55.1	48%	$65	$80	$90	$125	$200	$300	$450	$750	$3,500
Auctions: $541, MS-64BN, January 2015; $423, MS-63BN, September 2015; $353, MS-62BN, March 2015; $259, AU-58, January 2015													
1834, Proof	25–35	13	64.8								$5,000	$6,000	$11,000
Auctions: $18,800, PF-64RB, August 2013													
1835 (c)	398,000	1,291	54.5	52%	$65	$75	$90	$125	$200	$325	$450	$750	$3,500
Auctions: $823, MS-64BN, August 2015; $646, MS-64, March 2015; $353, MS-63BN, May 2015; $329, MS-62BN, April 2015													
1835, Proof	15–20	2	64.0								$5,000	$6,000	$10,500
Auctions: $11,163, PF-64RB, January 2014													
1836, Original, Proof	140–240	13	63.8								$6,000	$8,000	$12,500
Auctions: $12,925, PF-64BN, April 2013													
1836, Restrike, Proof (Reverse of 1840–1857)	8–15	2	64.5								$9,000	$17,000	$30,000
Auctions: No auction records available.													

a. Circulation strike. **b.** Beware of altered date. **c.** The figures given here are thought to be correct, although Mint records report these quantities for 1833 through 1836 rather than 1832 through 1835.

1837 "HALF CENT" TOKEN

The last circulation-strike half cents of the Classic Head design were minted in 1835, and Proofs of the series were made in 1836 (see next section). No half cents of any format were minted in 1837, 1838, or 1839—it would be 1840 before the denomination started up again, with the Braided Hair type.

To help fill that gap for date-by-date collectors, in the 1930s Wayte Raymond included in his "National" brand of coin albums a slot for a half cent–sized Hard Times token dated 1837. The token had been privately struck in the thousands as a supply of small change in the midst of the country's financial stagnation of the 1830s and early 1840s. It joined several hundred types of larger, cent-sized copper tokens, all privately manufactured and put into circulation by enterprising businesspeople, as substitutes for the federal government's half cents and large cents that were no longer circulating in any quantity.

Raymond's dignifying of the 1837 token brought about a new numismatic tradition. Half-cent collectors began to include the token—despite its not being official federal coinage—in their collections, and today the "Half Cent Worth of Pure Copper" is often found among their treasured coins.

	G-4	VG-8	F-12	VF-20	EF-40	AU-50	MS-60
1837 Token *(not a coin)*	$75	$85	$100	$140	$250	$350	$800

BRAIDED HAIR (1840–1857)

Designer: *Christian Gobrecht.* **Weight:** *5.44 grams.* **Composition:** *Copper.*
Diameter: *23 mm.* **Edge:** *Plain.* **Mint:** *Philadelphia.*

Circulation Strike
1854; BW-1, C-1, B-1.

Proof
1843; BW-1c, C-SR-13, B-3.

History. The Braided Hair half cent debuted in 1840, a year after the same design was introduced on copper cents. There was scant commercial demand for this denomination, so only Proofs were struck from 1840 to 1848 and in 1852. (In 1849–1851 and 1853–1857 both Proofs and circulation strikes were made.) Ultimately the half cent was discontinued by the Act of February 21, 1857. After that point the coins were rapidly withdrawn from circulation, and by 1860 virtually all had disappeared from commerce.

Striking and Sharpness. Many if not most Braided Hair half cents are well struck, and nearly all are on good planchet stock. Check these points for sharpness: the denticles on both sides; the star centers and hair detail on the obverse; and the leaf detail on the reverse.

Availability. Because Braided Hair half cents were not struck for circulation until 1849 and they did not circulate after the 1850s, they never acquired extensive wear. Most coins grade EF-40 and finer. Lower grades are sometimes seen, but are not in demand.

GRADING STANDARDS

MS-60 to 70 (Mint State). *Obverse:* In the lower Mint State grades, MS–60 and 61, some slight abrasion can be seen on the portrait, most evidently on the cheek. Check the tip of the coronet as well. Luster in the field is complete, or nearly so. At MS-63, luster should be complete, and no abrasions evident. At higher levels, the luster is complete and deeper, and some original mint color may be seen. Mint frost on this type is usually

1849, Large Date; BW-3, C-1, B-4. Graded MS-63BN.

deep, sometimes satiny, but hardly ever prooflike. MS-64 coins may have some slight discoloration or scattered contact marks. A well-graded MS-65 or higher coin has full, rich luster; no contact marks visible except under magnification; and a nice blend of brown toning or nicely mixed (not stained or blotchy) mint color and natural brown toning. The late Walter Breen stated that he had never seen an 1853 (common date) half cent with extensive original mint color, but these are plentiful with brown-toned surfaces. *Reverse:* In the lower Mint State grades some abrasions are seen on the higher areas of the leaves. Mint luster is complete in all Mint State grades, as the open areas are protected by the lettering and wreath.

AU-50, 53, 55, 58 (About Uncirculated). *Obverse:* Wear is evident on the cheek, the hair above the forehead, and the tip of the coronet. Friction is evident in the field. At AU-58, luster may be present except in the center of the fields. As the grades go down to AU-50, wear is more evident on the portrait. Wear is seen on the stars, but is not as easy to discern as it is elsewhere. At AU-50 there is either no luster or only traces of luster close

1849, Large Date; BW-3, C-1, B-4. Graded AU-50.

to the letters and devices. *Reverse:* Wear is most evident on the highest areas of the leaves and the ribbon bow. Luster is present in the fields. As the grades go downward from AU-58 to 50, wear increases and luster decreases. At the AU-50 level there is either no luster or traces of luster close to the letters and devices.

Illustrated coin: This coin shows Full Details on both sides, and has eye-pleasing, light-brown surfaces.

EF-40, 45 (Extremely Fine). *Obverse:* Wear is more extensive on the portrait, including the cheek, hair, and coronet. The star centers are worn down slightly. Traces of luster are minimal, if at all existent. *Reverse:* The centers of the leaves are well worn, with detail visible only near the edges of the leaves and nearby, with the higher parts worn flat. Letters show significant wear. Luster, if present, is minimal.

1853; BW-1, C-1, B-1. Graded EF-40.

VF-20, 30 (Very Fine). *Obverse:* Wear is more extensive than at the preceding levels. Some of the strands of hair are fused together. The center radials of the stars are worn nearly completely away. *Reverse:* The leaves show more extensive wear, with details visible at the edges, and only minimally and not on all leaves. The lettering shows smooth, even wear.

The Braided Hair half cent is seldom collected in grades lower than VF-20.

1849, Large Date; BW-3, C-1, B-4. Graded VF-30.

PF-60 to 70 (Proof). For the issues of 1840 to 1848, the 1849, Small Date, and the issues of 1852, only Proofs were made, without related examples for circulation. All were restruck at the Mint. Generally, the quality of these Proofs is very good, with excellent striking of details and nice planchet quality. *Obverse and Reverse:* Superb gems at PF–65 and 66 show hairlines only under high magnification, and at PF–67 none are seen. The

1843, First Restrike; BW-2, C-SR-5, B-2. PF-64RB.

fields are deeply mirrorlike. There is no evidence of friction. At lower levels, hairlines increase, with a profusion at PF–60 to 62 (and also a general dullness of the fields). Typical color for an undipped coin ranges from light or iridescent brown to brown with some traces of mint color. Except for issues in the 1850s, Proofs are nearly always BN or, less often, RB. The rare Proofs of the 1840s are sometimes seen with light wear and can be classified according to the About Uncirculated and Extremely Fine comments above, except in place of "luster" read "Proof surface."

Illustrated coin: Overall this coin's surfaces are smooth, and the dominant sandy-olive patina belies semi reflective tendencies in the fields and gold, apricot and lilac undertones when viewed under direct light.

Large Berries (Original Strike)	Small Berries (Restrike)

	Mintage	Cert	Avg	%MS	VG-8	F-12	VF-20	EF-40	AU-50	MS-60BN	MS-63BN	MS-63RB	MS-65RB
											PF-60BN	PF-63BN	PF-65BN
1840, Original, Proof	*125–150*	11	63.8								$5,350	$6,500	$9,250
	Auctions: $7,475, PF-62BN, August 2006												
1840, Restrike, Proof	*21–25*	8	64.5								$5,350	$6,500	$9,250
	Auctions: $25,850, PF-65RB, June 2014												
1841, Original, Proof	*150–250*	19	64.2								$4,500	$5,500	$8,750
	Auctions: $21,150, PF-65BN, September 2013; $4,700, PF-58, September 2015												
1841, Restrike, Proof	*15–19*	8	64.6								$4,500	$5,500	$8,750
	Auctions: $8,625, PF-66BN, June 2008												

1849, Small Date
(Proof Only)

1849, Large Date

	Mintage	Cert	Avg	%MS	VG-8	F-12	VF-20	EF-40	AU-50	MS-60BN	MS-63BN / PF-60BN	MS-63RB / PF-63BN	MS-65RB / PF-65BN
1842, Original, Proof	120–180	6	63.5								$5,500	$7,000	$10,000
Auctions: $15,275, PF-64BN, February 2014; $12,925, PF-64, January 2015													
1842, Restrike, Proof	35–45	10	64.7								$4,500	$5,500	$8,750
Auctions: $20,700, PF-65RB, April 2010													
1843, Original, Proof	125–200	6	62.7								$4,500	$5,500	$8,750
Auctions: $73,438, PF-65RD, April 2014													
1843, Restrike, Proof	37–44	7	64.7								$4,750	$5,700	$8,750
Auctions: $9,988, PF-64BN, February 2014													
1844, Original, Proof	120–180	9	62.9								$5,000	$6,000	$9,000
Auctions: $4,888, PF-50, May 2008													
1844, Restrike, Proof	21–26	2	65.5								$4,750	$5,750	$8,750
Auctions: $1,777, PF, February 2014													
1845, Original, Proof	110–170	3	65.0								$5,000	$6,000	$9,250
Auctions: $23,500, PF-64BN, April 2013													
1845, Restrike, Proof	20–24	9	64.4								$4,500	$5,400	$9,000
Auctions: $9,200, PF-65BN, October 2011													
1846, Original, Proof	125–200	8	64.0								$5,000	$6,000	$9,000
Auctions: $21,150, PF-64BN, January 2014													
1846, Restrike, Proof	19–24	8	65.0								$4,750	$5,750	$8,750
Auctions: $23,630, PF-66BN, June 2014; $15,275, PF-66BN, October 2015													
1847, Original, Proof	200–300	10	64.4								$5,000	$6,000	$9,250
Auctions: $5,288, PF-63BN, January 2014													
1847, Restrike, Proof	33–44	15	64.7								$4,500	$5,500	$8,500
Auctions: $15,275, PF-66BN, January 2014													
1848, Original, Proof	150–225	3	64.3								$5,500	$6,250	$9,250
Auctions: $10,350, PF-64RB, September 2003													
1848, Restrike, Proof	40–47	12	64.5								$4,500	$5,600	$8,500
Auctions: $6,169, PF-64BN, February 2014													
1849, Large Date	39,864	297	57.6	60%	$60	$70	$90	$150	$240	$500	$700	$900	$2,700
Auctions: $517, MS-63, August 2016; $353, AU-58, June 2016; $176, AU-55, October 2016													
1849, Original, Small Date, Proof	70–90	4	59.0								$4,500	$5,500	$10,000
Auctions: $8,813, PF-64RB, April 2014													
1849, Restrike, Small Date, Proof	30–36	4	64.3								$5,000	$5,750	$9,750
Auctions: $7,344, PF-64BN, January 2014													
1850	39,812	249	57.7	57%	$60	$70	$90	$150	$240	$500	$700	$1,050	$3,000
Auctions: $7,210, MS-65, February 2016; $1,998, MS-64, July 2015; $517, AU-55, March 2016; $447, AU-53, March 2016													
1850, Proof	10–20	9	62.7								$5,000	$7,000	$13,000
Auctions: $17,625, PF-64, May 2015; $5,875, PF-63BN, January 2014													
1851	147,672	829	57.8	60%	$60	$70	$80	$100	$175	$275	$550	$650	$2,000
Auctions: $1,175, MS-64RB, October 2015; $705, MS-64BN, August 2015; $441, MS-64, March 2015; $447, MS-63BN, January 2015													
1851, Proof	10–20	0	n/a								$7,000	$8,000	$20,000
Auctions: No auction records available.													

	Mintage	Cert	Avg	%MS	VG-8	F-12	VF-20	EF-40	AU-50	MS-60BN	MS-63BN PF-60BN	MS-63RB PF-63BN	MS-65RB PF-65BN
1852, Original, Proof	*225–325*	0	n/a										—
Auctions: No auction records available.													
1852, Restrike, Proof	*110–140*	33	64.3								$4,000	$6,000	$9,000
Auctions: $6,463, PF, August 2013													
1853	129,694	1,027	60.4	76%	$60	$70	$80	$100	$175	$275	$550	$650	$1,700
Auctions: $940, MS-65BN, September 2015; $646, MS-64BN, August 2015; $329, MS-63BN, May 2015; $223, MS-61BN, May 2015													
1854	55,358	758	61.0	80%	$60	$70	$80	$100	$165	$275	$550	$650	$1,700
Auctions: $1,410, MS-65BN, August 2015; $541, MS-63RB, June 2015; $230, MS-62BN, September 2015; $161, MS-60, May 2015													
1854, Proof	*10–20*	4	64.3								$3,500	$4,500	$8,000
Auctions: $7,931, PF-65RB, February 2014; $7,344, PF-65RB, January 2015													
1855	56,500	1,066	61.7	85%	$60	$70	$80	$100	$165	$275	$550	$650	$1,600
Auctions: $940, MS-65BN, January 2015; $494, MS-64BN, September 2015; $376, MS-63BN, September 2015													
1855, Proof	*40–60*	19	64.2								$3,500	$4,500	$8,000
Auctions: $5,750, PF-64BN, August 2011													
1856	40,430	404	59.6	71%	$60	$70	$80	$125	$185	$275	$575	$675	$2,000
Auctions: $400, MS-63BN, August 2015; $306, MS-63BN, May 2015; $294, MS-63BN, June 2015; $153, AU-55, May 2015													
1856, Proof	*50–75*	20	64.3								$3,500	$4,500	$8,000
Auctions: $7,050, PF-65BN, January 2015; $8,519, PF, February 2014													
1857	35,180	607	60.4	78%	$75	$95	$125	$180	$260	$400	$650	$750	$2,500
Auctions: $823, MS-64BN, October 2015; $541, MS-63BN, July 2015; $376, MS-62BN, May 2015; $141, AU-50, January 2015													
1857, Proof	*75–100*	37	63.9								$3,500	$4,500	$8,000
Auctions: $14,100, PF-66RB, June 2014; $4,465, PF-64BN, January 2015													

Large Cents
1793–1857

AN OVERVIEW OF LARGE CENTS

Collecting one each of the major types of 1793–1857 copper cents can be a fascinating challenge. Early varieties were struck from hand-engraved dies, often on copper planchets of uncertain quality. It was not until 1836 that steam power was used to run coining presses at the Mint. All earlier issues were made by hand, by two men tugging on the weighted lever arm of a small screw-type press. As might be expected, this resulted in many variations in striking quality.

The first cents of 1793, the Chain varieties, are found with two major differences: AMERI. on the reverse, and the later version with AMERICA spelled out in full. These early issues have been highly desired from the beginning days of the numismatic hobby in America, and remain in the limelight today.

Wreath cents of 1793 occur with the edge displaying a vine and bars motif and also with lettering ONE HUNDRED FOR A DOLLAR. Liberty Cap cents of the 1793–1796 years have lettered edges (ONE HUNDRED FOR A DOLLAR) used in 1793, 1794, and part of 1795, and plain edges for most 1795 coins and all of 1796.

The Draped Bust type commenced partway through 1796 and was continued through 1807. This span includes the notably rare 1799, 9 Over 8, overdate and the 1799 as well as the somewhat rare 1804. Many interesting die varieties occur in this type, particularly with regard to errors on the reverse. The Classic Head cent, designed by John Reich, was introduced in 1808, and was continued through 1814. In 1815 no cents of this date were produced. Then in 1816 the Matron Head commenced, a new motif with a new reverse as well. With modifications this was continued through 1839, in which year the Braided Hair design by Christian Gobrecht made its appearance. Large cents were made continually through January 1857 and then discontinued.

FOR THE COLLECTOR AND INVESTOR: LARGE CENTS AS A SPECIALTY

For the enjoyment of copper cents 1793–1857 it is possible to go far beyond a type set. Today, varieties of the 1793–1814 cents are generally collected by Sheldon numbers (S-1, S-2, etc.), given first in *Early American Cents* and, later, in its revision, *Penny Whimsy*. Building upon this foundation, *Walter Breen's Encyclopedia of Early United States Large Cents, 1793–1814*, gives more information on this date range than available in any other single source.

Among dates and major varieties in the early range of the series, the 1793 issues Chain AMERI., Chain AMERICA, Wreath, and Liberty Cap, the 1799 (far and away the rarest date in the series), and the 1804 are key issues, each a part of an extensive series of more than 300 die varieties through and including 1814.

The most popular way to collect large cents is by basic varieties, mainly dates, overdates, and major varieties. Sometimes, a particular date is selected as a specialty for collecting die varieties by Sheldon numbers.

Generally, grades from Good to VF are popular objectives for the early series from 1793 to 1814, and for some varieties no better coins exist. EF, AU, and Mint State coins are available and are more likely to be sought by collectors of basic dates and major varieties, rather than by specialists seeing long runs of Sheldon numbers. Type-set collectors are also important in the market for high-grade pieces, where sights can be set high as there are fewer varieties to obtain. Accordingly, as a type-set collector one may aspire to own an AU or Mint State cent of the 1796–1807 Draped Bust type. However, for a specialist in die varieties, who wants to acquire more than 100 different specimens from this date range, such high grades might not be feasible to acquire.

Collecting cents of the later dates by basic varieties is an interesting pursuit, and one that is quite attainable in such grades as EF, AU, or even MS-60, most dates after the 1820s being readily available for relatively inexpensive prices. Key issues among 1816–1857 cents include 1823, 3 Over 2; 1823; 1824, 4 Over 2; 1839, 9 Over 6; and a few others. Collecting Braided Hair cents toward the end of the series, 1839 to 1857, is least expensive of all, and most major varieties can be obtained in such grades as MS–60 to 63, with lustrous brown surfaces, for reasonable figures.

FLOWING HAIR, CHAIN REVERSE (1793)

Designer: *Henry Voigt.* **Weight:** *13.48 grams.* **Composition:** *Copper.*
Diameter: *Average 26 to 27 mm.* **Edge:** *Vine and bars design.* **Mint:** *Philadelphia.*

Chain AMERI. Reverse
1793; Bowers-Whitman–1, Sheldon-1, Breen-1.

Chain AMERICA Reverse

Vine-and-Bars Edge

History. The first U.S. cents intended for circulation were struck at the Mint in Philadelphia from February 27 through March 12, 1793. These were of the Flowing Hair design, with a Chain reverse. Several varieties were struck, today these can be attributed by Bowers-Whitman numbers or Sheldon numbers. The first, or Bowers-Whitman–1, Sheldon-1, had AMERICA abbreviated as AMERI. A contemporary account noted that Miss Liberty appeared to be "in a fright," and that the chain motif on the reverse, 15 links intended to symbolize unity of the states in the Union, was an "ill omen" for a land of liberty; accordingly, the design was used for only a short time. The rims on both sides are raised, without denticles or beads.

Striking and Sharpness. The details of Miss Liberty's hair are often indistinct or missing, including on many higher-grade specimens. For all grades and varieties, the reverse is significantly sharper than the obverse. The portrait of Miss Liberty is shallow and is often weak, especially on the BW-1, S-1, variety (which is often missing the date). Note that early copper coins of all kinds may exhibit "tooling" (engraving done outside the Mint in order to simulate details that were worn away or weakly struck to begin with). Also, these old coppers have sometimes been burnished to smooth out areas of porosity. These alterations are considered to be damage, and they significantly decrease a coin's value.

Availability. Demand is higher than supply for all varieties, with fewer than 1,000 or so examples surviving today. Most are in lower grades, from Fair-2 to VG-8. Even heavily worn coins (still identifiable by the chain device) are highly collectible. VF and EF coins are few and far between, and AU and MS are very rare.

GRADING STANDARDS

MS-60 to 70 (Mint State). *Obverse:* In the lower Mint State grades, MS–60 and 61, some slight abrasions can be seen on the higher areas of the portrait. The large open field shows light contact marks and perhaps a few nicks. At MS-63 the luster should be complete, although some very light abrasions or contact marks may be seen on the portrait. At MS-64 or higher—a nearly impossible level for a Chain cent—there is no sign of abrasion anywhere. Mint color is not extensive on any known Mint State coin,

1793; Bowers-Whitman–4, Sheldon-3, Breen-4. Graded MS-66BN.

but traces of red-orange are sometimes seen around the rim and devices on both sides. *Reverse:* In the lower Mint State grades some abrasions are seen on the chain links. There is some abrasion in the field. At MS-63, luster should be unbroken. Some abrasion and minor contact marks may be evident. In still higher grades, luster is deep and there is no sign of abrasion.

Illustrated coin: This coin is sharply struck with full hair detail. It is the Cleneay-Jackman-Ryder specimen mentioned in Sheldon's *Penny Whimsy* as the unrivalled, finest-known example of this variety.

AU-50, 53, 55, 58 (About Uncirculated). *Obverse:* Light wear is seen on the highest areas of the portrait. Some luster is seen in the large open fields at the AU-58 level, less at AU-55, and little if any for AU–53 and 50. Scattered marks are normal and are most evident in the field. At higher levels, some vestiges of luster may be seen among the letters, numerals, and between the hair tips. *Reverse:* Light wear is most evident on the chain, as

1793; BW-4, S-3, B-4. Graded AU-53.

this is the most prominent feature. The letters show wear, but not as extensive. Luster may be seen at the 58 and 55 levels, usually slightly more on the reverse than on the obverse. Generally, the reverse grades higher than the obverse, usually by a step, such as an AU-50 obverse and an AU-53 reverse (such a coin would be listed as the lower of the two, or AU-50).

EF-40, 45 (Extremely Fine). *Obverse:* The center of the portrait is well worn, with the hair visible only in thick strands, although extensive detail remains in the hair tips at the left. No luster is seen. Contact marks are normal in the large expanse of open field, but should be mentioned if they are distracting. *Reverse:* The chain is bold and shows light wear. Other features show wear, as well— more extensive in appearance, as the relief is

1793; BW-4, S-3, B-4. Graded EF-45.

lower. The fields show some friction, but not as much as on the obverse.

VF-20, 30 (Very Fine). *Obverse:* More wear is seen on the portrait, with perhaps half or slightly more of the hair detail showing, mostly near the left edge of the hair. The ear usually is visible (but might not be, depending on the sharpness of strike). The letters in LIBERTY show wear. The rim remains bold (more so than on the reverse). *Reverse:* The chain shows more wear than on the preceding, but is still bold. Other features show more wear and may be weak in areas. The rim may be weak in areas.

1793; BW-5, S-4, B-5. Graded VF-30.

F-12, 15 (Fine). *Obverse:* The hair details are mostly worn away, with about one-third visible, that being on the left. The rim is distinct on most examples. The bottoms of the date digits are weak or possibly worn away. *Reverse:* The chain is bold, as is the lettering within the chain. Lettering around the border shows extensive wear, but is complete. The rim may be flat in areas.

1793; BW-5, S-4, B-5. Graded F-15.

    Illustrated coin: The surface is generally smooth and even under close scrutiny reveals only minor roughness. Note the shallow reverse rim bruise outside the letters AM in AMERICA and some mild encrustation around the letter C in CENT and the nearby chain links.

VG-8, 10 (Very Good). *Obverse:* The portrait is well worn, although Miss Liberty's eye remains bold. Hair detail is gone at the center, but is evident at the left edge of the portrait. LIBERTY is always readable, but may be faded or partly missing on shallow strikes. The date is well worn, with the bottom of the numerals missing (published standards vary on this point, and it used to be the case that a full date was mandatory). *Reverse:* The chain

1793; BW-4, S-3, B-4. Graded VG-10.

remains bold, and the center letters are all readable. Border letters may be weak or incomplete. The rim is smooth in most areas.

    Illustrated coin: The coin is smooth in appearance with the worn areas showing lighter copper, while the fields have trace roughness and the classic black olive texture. Note the planchet flaw right of ONE, which appears as a void in the metal.

G-4, 6 (Good). *Obverse:* The portrait is worn smooth and is seen only in outline form, although the eye position can be discerned. LIBERTY may be weak. The date is weak, but the tops of the numerals can be discerned. *Reverse:* The chain is fully visible in outline form. Central lettering is mostly or completely readable, but light. Peripheral lettering is mostly worn away.

1793; BW-1, S-1, B-1. Graded G-4.

Illustrated coin: Natural obverse planchet flaws, as struck, can be seen both at 12 o'clock on the rim and above and to the left of the date, with other faint fissuring seen on the reverse under low magnification.

AG-3 (About Good). *Obverse:* The portrait is visible as an outline. LIBERTY and the date are mostly or even completely worn away. Contact marks may be extensive. *Reverse:* The chain is fully visible in outline form. Traces of the central letters—or, on better strikes, nearly all of the letters—can be seen. Around the border all letters are worn away.

1793; BW-5, S-4, B-5. Graded AG-3.

	Mintage	Cert	Avg	%MS	AG-3	G-4	VG-8	F-12	VF-20	EF-40	AU-50	MS-60
1793, Chain, All kinds	36,103											
1793, AMERI. in Legend		36	24.0	8%	$5,500	$11,000	$18,500	$28,000	$45,000	$80,000	$175,000	$300,000
	Auctions: $25,850, F-12, August 2016; $18,800, F-12, August 2015; $3,173, Fair-2, March 2015											
1793, AMERICA, Periods		16	22.9	0%	$4,500	$7,750	$15,000	$21,000	$37,500	$60,000	$120,000	$225,000
	Auctions: $22,325, AU-50, September 2013											
1793, AMERICA, No Periods		129	22.0	5%	$4,500	$7,500	$14,000	$19,500	$30,000	$55,000	$100,000	$180,000
	Auctions: $998,750, MS-65BN, January 2013											

FLOWING HAIR, WREATH REVERSE (1793)

Designer: *Henry Voigt.* **Weight:** *13.48 grams.* **Composition:** *Copper.*
Diameter: *26 to 28 mm.* **Edge:** *Vine and bars design, or lettered ONE HUNDRED FOR A DOLLAR followed by either a single or a double leaf.* **Mint:** *Philadelphia.*

1793, Wreath Type, Vine and Bars Edge; BW-11, S-5, B-6.

Vine-and-Bars Edge

Lettered Edge
(ONE HUNDRED FOR A DOLLAR)

History. Between April 9 and July 17, 1793, the U.S. Mint struck and delivered 63,353 large copper cents. Most of these, and perhaps all, were of the Wreath type, although records do not specify when the design types were changed that year. The Wreath cent was named for the new reverse style. Both sides have raised beads at the border, similar to the style used on 1793 half cents.

Striking and Sharpness. These cents usually are fairly well struck, although high-grade pieces often exhibit some weakness on the highest hair tresses and on the leaf details. (On lower-grade pieces these areas are worn, so the point is moot.) Planchet quality varies widely, from smooth, glossy brown to dark and porous. The lettered-edge cents are often seen on defective planchets. Consult Sheldon's *Penny Whimsy (1793–1814)* and photographs to learn the characteristics of certain varieties. The borders have raised beads; on high-grade pieces these are usually very distinct, but they blend together on lower-grade coins and can sometimes be indistinct. The beads are not as prominent as those later used on the 1793 Liberty Cap cents.

Availability. At least several thousand examples exist of the different varieties of the type. Most are in lower grades, from AG-3 to VG-8, although Fine and VF pieces are encountered with regularity. Choice EF, AU, and finer coins see high demand. Some in MS have been billed as "specimen" or "presentation" coins, although this is supposition, as no records exist.

GRADING STANDARDS

MS-60 to 70 (Mint State). *Obverse:* On MS–60 and 61 coins there are some traces of abrasion on the higher areas of the portrait, most particularly the hair. As this area can be lightly struck, careful inspection is needed for evaluation, not as much in Mint State (as other features come into play), but in higher circulated grades. Luster in the field is incomplete at lower Mint State levels, but should be in generous quantity. At MS-63, luster should

1793; BW-12, S-6, B-7. Graded MS-66.

be complete, and no abrasion evident. At higher levels, the luster is deeper, and some original mint color may be seen. At MS-65 there might be some scattered contact marks and possibly bare traces of fingerprints or discoloration. Above MS-65, a coin should approach perfection. A Mint State 1793 Wreath cent is an object of rare beauty. *Reverse:* In the lower Mint State grades some abrasion is seen on the higher areas of the leaves. Generally, luster is complete in all grades, as the open areas are protected by the lettering and wreath. In many ways, the grading guidelines for this type follow those of the 1793 half cent—also with sprays of berries (not seen elsewhere in the series).

Illustrated coin: Remarkably, this coin displays some original Mint orange.

AU-50, 53, 55, 58 (About Uncirculated). *Obverse:* Friction is seen on the highest areas of the hair (which may also be lightly struck) and the cheek. Some scattered marks are normal in the field, ranging from more extensive at AU-50 to minimal at AU-58. *Reverse:* Friction is seen on the higher wreath leaves and (not as easy to discern) on the letters. The fields, protected by the designs (including sprays of berries at the center), show fric-

1793; BW-23, S-11c, B-16c. Graded AU-50.

tion, but not as noticeably as on the obverse. At AU–55 and 58, little if any friction is seen. Border beads, if well struck, are separate and boldly defined.

Illustrated coin: Note the clash marks on the obverse indicative of a late die state. Significant portions of the reverse wreath are clashed in the field from Liberty's nose to the base of the throat, below the bust around the leaf cluster, and between some of the strands of hair at the back of Liberty's head. Additionally, the letters MERICA in the word AMERICA are clashed in the right-obverse field, the letters becoming bolder toward the end of that word.

EF-40, 45 (Extremely Fine). *Obverse:* More extensive wear is seen on the high parts of the hair, creating mostly a solid mass (without detail of strands) of varying width in the area immediately to the left of the face. The cheek shows light wear. Luster is minimal or nonexistent at EF-40, and may survive in traces in protected areas (such as between the letters) at EF-45. *Reverse:* Wear is seen on the highest wreath and ribbon areas, and

1793; BW-17, S-9, B-12. Graded EF-40.

the letters. Luster is minimal, but likely more noticeable than on the obverse, as the fields are protected by the designs and lettering. Some of the beads blend together.

VF-20, 30 (Very Fine). *Obverse:* Wear on the hair is more extensive, and varies depending on the die variety and sharpness of strike. The ANA grading standards suggest that two-thirds of the hair is visible, which in practice can be said to be "more or less." More beads are blended together, but the extent of this blending depends on the striking and variety. Certain parts of the rim are smooth, with beads scarcely visible at all. No

1793; BW-12, S-6, B-7. Graded VF-25.

luster is seen. The date, LIBERTY, and hair ends are bold. *Reverse:* The leaf details are nearly completely worn away at VF-20, with slight detail at VF-30. The border beads are blended together, with many indistinct. Some berries in the sprays are light, but nearly all remain distinct. No luster is seen.

Illustrated coin: The surfaces are a bit rough overall with a few areas also revealing slight verdigris.

F-12, 15 (Fine). *Obverse:* The hair details are mostly worn away, with about one-third visible, mainly at the edges. The ANA grading standards suggest that half of the details are visible, seemingly applying to the total area of the hair. However, the visible part, at the left, also includes intermittent areas of the field. Beads are weak or worn away in areas. F-15 shows slightly more detail. By this grade, scattered light scratches, noticeable contact marks,

1793; BW-17, S-9, B-12. Graded F-12.

and the like are the rule, not the exception. These are not mentioned at all on holders and are often overlooked elsewhere, except in some auction catalogs and price lists. Such marks are implicit for coins in lower grades, and light porosity or granularity is common as well. *Reverse:* The wreath leaves are worn flat, but their edges are distinct. Border beads are weak or worn away in areas. F-15 shows slightly more detail.

Illustrated coin: Despite slight pock-marking on the obverse and scattered rim bruises, this coin features strong definition for an F-12 piece.

VG-8, 10 (Very Good). *Obverse:* The hair is well worn toward the face. Details at the left are mostly blended together in thick strands. The eye, nose, and lips often remain well defined. Border beads are completely gone, or just seen in traces, and part of the rim blends into the field. LIBERTY may be slightly weak. The 1793 date is fully visible, although there may be some lightness. Scattered marks are more common than on

1793; BW-23, S-11c, B-16c. Graded VG-8.

higher grades. *Reverse:* The wreath, bow, and lettering are seen in outline form, and some leaves and letters may be indistinct in parts. Most of the berries remain visible, but weak. Border beads are worn away, and the border blends into the field in most if not all of the periphery.

G-4, 6 (Good). *Obverse:* The hair is worn smooth except for the thick tresses at the left. The eye, nose, and lips show some detail. LIBERTY is weak, with some letters missing. The date is discernible, although partially worn away. The sprig above the date is usually prominent. The border completely blends into the field. *Reverse:* Extensive overall wear. The wreath is seen in outline form, with some areas weak. Usually ONE CENT remains

1793; BW-12, S-6, B-7. Graded G-4.

readable at the center. The border letters and fraction show extensive wear, with some letters very weak or even missing, although most should be discernible. Dark or porous coins may have more details on both sides in an effort to compensate for the roughness. Marks, edge bumps, and so on are normal.

Illustrated coin: Note minor surface roughness. Definition in the major devices is strong for this grade.

AG-3 (About Good). *Obverse:* Wear is more extensive than on the preceding. The eye, nose, and lips may still be discernible, and the sprig above the date can usually be seen. LIBERTY may be very weak or even missing. The date is gone, or just a trace will remain. *Reverse:* Parts of the wreath are visible in outline form. ONE CENT might be readable, but this is not a requirement. Most border letters are gone. If a coin is dark or porous

1793; BW-18, S-8, B-13. Graded AG-3.

it may be graded AG-3 and may be sharper than just described, with the porosity accounting for the lower grade.

Regular Sprig   **Strawberry Leaf**

	Mintage	Cert	Avg	%MS	AG-3	G-4	VG-8	F-12	VF-20	EF-40	AU-50	MS-60BN	MS-63BN
1793, Wreath, All kinds	63,353												
1793, Vine/Bars Edge		201	32.4	13%	$1,250	$3,000	$4,700	$7,000	$13,000	$20,000	$32,500	$55,000	$100,000
	Auctions: $176,250, MS-65BN, June 2015; $44,650, AU-55, August 2015; $8,813, VF-25, October 2016												
1793, Lettered Edge		41	22.6	5%	$1,500	$3,200	$4,750	$7,500	$15,000	$27,500	$36,000	$80,000	$125,000
	Auctions: $18,800, F-15, January 2014; $4,935, F-15, March 2016; $646, VG-8, December 2015												
1793, Strawberry Leaf †	(a)	1	12.0	0%	$275,000	$350,000	$425,000	$950,000					
	Auctions: $381,875, G-4, January 2014												

† Ranked in the *100 Greatest U.S. Coins* (fourth edition). **a.** 4 examples are known.

LIBERTY CAP (1793–1796)

Designer: *1793–1795, thick planchet—Probably Joseph Wright; 1795–1796, thin planchet—John Smith Gardner.* **Weight:** *1793–1795, thick planchet—13.48 grams; 1795–1796, thin planchet—10.89 grams.* **Composition:** *Copper.* **Diameter:** *Average 29 mm.* **Edge:** *1793–1795, thick planchet—Lettered ONE HUNDRED FOR A DOLLAR; 1795–1796, thin planchet—Plain.* **Mint:** *Philadelphia.*

Lettered Edge (1793–1795)

1794, Thick Hair, Close Date, Short Right Stem; BW-80, S-61, B-53.

Reeded Edge (1795)

History. The Liberty Cap design was created in the summer of 1793 by artist and engraver Joseph Wright, who is also believed by some to have designed the 1793 half cent. On the cent, Miss Liberty faces to the right, rather than to the left (as on the half cent). Liberty Cap cents of 1793 have raised beaded borders. Other issues have denticles. Cents of 1794 and some of 1795 are on thick planchets with the edge lettered ONE HUNDRED FOR A DOLLAR, while those made later in 1795, and in 1796, are on thinner planchets and have a plain edge.

Striking and Sharpness. The depth of relief and striking characteristics vary widely, depending on the variety. Points to check are the details of the hair on Miss Liberty, the leaf details on the wreath, and the denticles on both sides. Generally, the earlier, thick-planchet issues are better strikes than are the thin-planchet coins. Plain-edge 1795 cents often have low or shallow rims. To determine the difference between lightness caused by shallow dies and lightness caused by wear, study the characteristics of the die variety involved (see in particular the reverses of 1793, BW-27, S-13, and 1793, BW-28 / BW-29, S-15 / S-12).

Availability. Cents of this type are readily available, although those of 1793 are rare and in great demand, and certain die varieties of the other dates are rare and can command high prices. Typical grades range from AG upward to Fine, VF, and, less often, EF. Attractive AU and MS coins are elusive, and when found are usually dated 1795, the thin planchet variety.

GRADING STANDARDS

MS-60 to 70 (Mint State). *Obverse:* On MS–60 and 61 coins there are some traces of abrasion on the higher areas of the portrait. Luster is incomplete, particularly in the field. At MS-63, luster should be complete, and no abrasion evident. At higher levels, the luster is deeper, and some original mint color may be seen on some examples. At the MS-65 level there may be some scattered contact marks and

1794; BW-12, S-22, B-6. Graded MS-62BN.

possibly some traces of fingerprints or discoloration, but these should be very minimal and not at all distracting. Generally, Liberty Cap cents of 1793 (in particular) and 1794 are harder to find with strong eye appeal than are those of 1795 and 1796. Mint State coins of 1795 often have satiny luster. Above MS-65, a coin should approach perfection, especially if dated 1795 or 1796. Certified Mint State cents can vary in their strictness of interpretation. *Reverse:* In the lower Mint State grades some abrasion is seen on the higher areas of the leaves. Generally, luster is complete in all grades, as the open areas are protected by the lettering and wreath. Often on this type the reverse is shallower than the obverse and has a lower rim.

Illustrated coin: Boldly struck on both the obverse and reverse, with strong hair separation evident on Liberty and some evidence of a central vein on each leaf. Note the small toning speck under the L of LIBERTY.

AU-50, 53, 55, 58 (About Uncirculated). *Obverse:* Very light wear is evident on the highest parts of the hair above and to the left of the ear. Friction is seen on the cheek and the liberty cap. Coins at this level are usually on smooth planchets and have nice eye appeal. Color is very important. Dark and porous coins are relegated to lower grades, even if AU-level sharpness is present. *Reverse:*

1794; BW-98, S-71, B-63. Graded AU-50.

Very light wear is evident on the higher parts of the leaves and the ribbon, and, to a lesser extent, on the lettering. The reverse may have original luster, toned brown, varying from minimal (at lower About Uncirculated grades) to extensive. Grading at the About Uncirculated level is mainly done by viewing the obverse, as many reverses are inherently shallow due to lower-relief dies.

Illustrated coin: Note the rough patch on and below Liberty's cap.

EF-40, 45 (Extremely Fine). *Obverse:* The center of the coin shows wear or a small, flat area, for most dies. Other hair details are strong. Luster is minimal or nonexistent at EF-40, and may survive in traces in protected areas (such as between the letters) at EF-45. *Reverse:* Wear is seen on the highest wreath and ribbon areas and the letters. Luster is minimal, but likely more noticeable than on the

1794; BW-18, S-28, B-10. Graded EF-40.

obverse, as the fields are protected by the designs and lettering. Sharpness varies depending on the die variety but is generally shallower than on the obverse, this being particularly true for many 1795 cents.

VF-20, 30 (Very Fine). *Obverse:* Wear on the portrait has reduced the hair detail to indistinct or flat at the center, and on most varieties the individual strands at the left edge are blended together. One rule does not fit all. The ANA grading standards suggest that 75% of the hair shows, while PCGS suggests 30% to 70% on varieties struck from higher-relief dies, and less than 50% for others. Examples such as this reflect the artistic, rather than sci-

1794, Head of 1794; BW-74, S-57, B-55. Graded VF-30.

entific, nature of grading. *Reverse:* The leaf details are nearly completely worn away at VF-20, and with slight detail at VF-30. Some border letters may be weak, and ditto for the central letters (on later variet-ies of this type). The border denticles are blended together with many indistinct. No luster is seen. The sharpness of details depends on the die variety.

F-12, 15 (Fine). *Obverse:* The hair details are mostly worn away, with about one-third visible, mainly at the lower edges. Border denticles are weak or worn away in areas, depending on the height of the rim when the coin was struck. F-15 shows slightly more detail. *Reverse:* The wreath leaves are worn flat, but their edges are distinct. Border den-ticles are weak or worn away in areas. F-15 shows slightly more detail. At this level and

1794, Head of 1794; BW-98, S-71, B-63. Graded F-15.

lower, planchet darkness and light porosity are common, as are scattered marks.

VG-8, 10 (Very Good). *Obverse:* The hair is more worn than on the preceding, with detail present only in the lower areas. Detail can differ, and widely, depending on the dies. Border denticles are worn away on some issues (not as much for 1793 and 1794 coins), and the border will blend into the field in areas in which the rim was low to begin with, or in areas struck slightly off center. LIBERTY and the date are bold. VG-10 is sometimes applied

1796; BW-1, S-91, B-1. Graded VG-8.

to especially nice Very Good coins. *Reverse:* The wreath, bow, and lettering are seen in outline form, and some leaves and letters may be indistinct in parts. Border denticles are worn away, and the border blends into the field in most if not all of the periphery. In certain die varieties and die states, especially of 1797, some letters may be very weak, or missing.

G-4, 6 (Good). *Obverse:* The portrait is worn smooth and is seen only in outline form, although the eye and nose can be discerned. LIBERTY and the date are complete, although the date may be weak. Denticles are gone on varieties struck with low or shallow rims. *Reverse:* Extensive wear is seen overall. From half to two-thirds of the letters in UNITED STATES OF AMERICA and the fraction numerals are worn away. Certain shallow-relief dies may have letters missing. G-6 is often assigned to finer examples in this category. Darkness, porosity, and marks characterize many coins.

1794, Starred Reverse; BW-59, S-48, B-38. Graded G-4.

Illustrated coin: This coin is an example of the highly sought 1794, Starred Reverse, variety.

AG-3 (About Good). *Obverse:* Wear is more extensive than on the preceding. The portrait is visible only in outline. LIBERTY will typically have some letters worn away. The date is weak, but discernible. *Reverse:* Parts of the wreath are visible in outline form, and all but a few letters are gone. Grading of AG-3 is usually done by the reverse, as the obverse typically appears to be in a slightly higher grade.

1794, Starred Reverse; BW-59, S-48, B-38. Graded AG-3.

Illustrated coin: This coin is closer to G-4 on the obverse, but weak on the reverse, prompting a more conservative grade. While the reverse is worn nearly smooth, almost a third of the stars at the denticles, which mark this cent as a 1794, Starred Reverse, are visible.

Head of 1793 (1793–1794)
Head in high, rounded relief.

Head of 1794 (1794)
Well-defined hair;
hook on lowest curl.

Beaded Border (1793)

Denticle Border
(1794–1796)

	Mintage	Cert	Avg	%MS	AG-3	G-4	VG-8	F-12	VF-20	EF-40	AU-50	MS-60BN	MS-63BN
1793, Liberty Cap	11,056	27	14.0	0%	$3,500	$6,000	$12,000	$17,500	$45,000	$100,000	$200,000		
	Auctions: $21,150, F-12, July 2015; $19,389, VG-10, August 2016; $3,760, VG-8, January 2015; $5,875, AG-3, March 2016												

1794, Normal Reverse

1794, Starred Reverse

Head of 1795 (1794–1796)
Head in low relief;
no hook on lowest curl.

1795, "Jefferson Head"

	Mintage	Cert	Avg	%MS	AG-3	G-4	VG-8	F-12	VF-20	EF-40	AU-50	MS-60BN	MS-63BN
1794, All kinds	918,521												
1794, Head of 1793		21	18.1	14%	$750	$1,500	$3,000	$5,000	$12,000	$25,000	$45,000	$100,000	$200,000
Auctions: $881,250, MS-64BN, January 2013													
1794, Head of 1794		309	32.5	4%	$200	$400	$600	$1,000	$2,100	$4,500	$7,000	$13,000	$27,500
Auctions: $12,925, AU-55, June 2015; $9,988, AU-55, June 2015; $8,813, EF-45, June 2015; $2,468, VF-35, August 2015													
1794, Head in Low Relief		0	n/a		$200	$400	$600	$1,000	$2,100	$4,250	$6,500	$13,000	$25,000
Auctions: No auction records available.													
1794, Exact Head of 1795 (a)		58	33.0	9%	$225	$450	$650	$1,100	$2,300	$5,750	$8,500	$25,000	$45,000
Auctions: $329, VF-20, July 2015; $447, F-15, July 2015; $376, F-12, November 2015													
1794, Starred Reverse †		7	14.0	0%	$13,500	$17,500	$25,000	$50,000	$90,000	$225,000	$700,000		
Auctions: $99,875, VF-25, May 2015; $15,275, AG-3, October 2013													
1794, No Fraction Bar		5	33.0	20%	$240	$500	$850	$1,350	$2,500	$6,500	$15,000	$40,000	$75,000
Auctions: $381,875, MS-64BN, January 2014													
1795, Lettered Edge	37,000	59	28.4	12%	$225	$450	$600	$1,100	$2,350	$5,250	$7,500	$11,000	$25,000
Auctions: $79,313, MS-65BN, April 2013													
1795, Plain Edge	501,500	248	26.6	11%	$175	$350	$500	$850	$1,450	$3,250	$6,000	$8,500	$20,000
Auctions: $21,150, MS-63BN, April 2013; $548, G-6, July 2015													
1795, Reeded Edge	(b)	0	n/a		$125,000	$275,000	$550,000	$900,000					
Auctions: $646,250, VG-10, January 2014													
1795, "Jefferson Head" (c)		1	10.0	0%	$11,000	$22,500	$35,000	$55,000	$125,000	$250,000			
Auctions: $184,000, VF-25, March 2012													
1795, "Jefferson Head," Lettered Edge (c)	(d)	0	n/a			—	$55,000	$90,000	$200,000				
Auctions: No auction records available.													
1796, Liberty Cap	109,825	173	22.4	9%	$250	$450	$750	$1,600	$3,000	$6,500	$12,000	$25,000	$65,000
Auctions: $141,000, MS-64RB, January 2014; $400, AG-3, February 2015; $376, AG-3, May 2015													

† Ranked in the *100 Greatest U.S. Coins* (fourth edition). **a.** The 1794 coin with Head of 1795 has a hooked curl but is in low relief. **b.** 9 examples are known. **c.** The "Jefferson Head" is not a regular Mint issue, but a design struck privately in an attempt to win a federal coinage contract. **d.** 3 examples are known.

DRAPED BUST (1796–1807)

Designer: *Robert Scot.* **Weight:** *10.89 grams.* **Composition:** *Copper.*
Diameter: *Average 29 mm.* **Edge:** *Plain.* **Mint:** *Philadelphia.*

1797, Reverse of 1795, Gripped Edge;
BW-3b, S-121b, B-3b.

History. The Draped Bust cent made its debut in 1796, following a coinage of Liberty Cap cents the same year. The motif, from a drawing by Gilbert Stuart, was first employed on certain silver dollars of 1795. (Its use on half cents did not take place until later, in 1800.) In 1798 Miss Liberty's head was slightly modified in design.

Striking and Sharpness. Most Draped Bust cents were struck on high-quality planchets. (This high planchet quality is less predictable for varieties of 1796, and almost never present for those of 1799 and 1800.) Detail sharpness differs by die variety. Weakness, when present, is usually on the hair behind the forehead, on the leaves in the upper part of the wreath, and among the denticles. However, a weak strike can show up in other areas as well. Many if not most Draped Bust cents are imperfectly centered, with the result that denticles can be bold on one side of a coin and light or even missing on the opposite side; this can occur on obverse as well as reverse. Typically this does not affect value. Certain Draped Bust cents of 1796 have semi-prooflike surfaces. Those of 1799 often have rough or porous surfaces and are found in lower grades.

Availability. As a type, Draped Bust cents are readily available, although the 1799, 9 Over 8, and 1799 are the keys to the series, and the 1804 is elusive. A different scenario evolves when considering engraving errors, repunched dates, and recut letters and numerals; many of these varieties are very difficult to locate. The eye appeal of these rarities usually is below par. Other years are generally available in high grades, VF and finer, well struck (except for some reverse leaves, in instances), on high-quality planchets, and with excellent eye appeal. Dark and porous coins are plentiful among coins graded below VF. True MS coins tend to be MS–60 to 63, when found.

GRADING STANDARDS

MS-60 to 70 (Mint State). *Obverse:* In the lower Mint State grades, MS–60 and 61, some slight abrasion can be seen on the higher areas of the portrait, especially the cheek, and the hair behind the forehead. Luster in the field is incomplete, particularly in the center of the open areas, which on this type are very open, especially at the right. At MS-63, luster should be nearly complete, and no abrasions evident. In higher levels, the lus-

1803, Small Date, Large Fraction;
BW-12, S-258, B-17. Graded MS-63BN.

ter is complete and deeper, and some original mint color should be seen. MS-64 coins may have some slight discoloration or scattered contact marks. A well-graded MS-65 or higher coin will have full, rich luster; no marks visible except under magnification; and a nice blend of brown toning or nicely mixed (not stained or blotchy) mint color and natural brown toning. *Reverse:* In the lower Mint State ranges some abrasions are seen on the higher areas of the leaves. Generally, luster is complete in all Mint State ranges, as the open areas are protected by the lettering and wreath. Sharpness of the leaves can vary by die variety, so check this aspect. Otherwise, the same comments apply as for the obverse.

Illustrated coin: This example is quite attractive despite the scratch on Liberty's bust and another through the D of UNITED. However, the left side of the reverse has toned differently from the rest of the coin's surfaces.

AU-50, 53, 55, 58 (About Uncirculated).
Obverse: Friction is seen on the higher parts, particularly the hair of Miss Liberty and the cheek. Friction and scattered marks are in the field, ranging from more extensive at AU-50 to minimal at AU-58. Luster may be seen in protected areas, minimal at AU-50, more visible at AU-58. At AU-58 the field may retain some luster, as well. In many instances, the luster is smaller in area and lesser in "depth"

1803, Small Date, Large Fraction;
BW-12, S-258, B-17. Graded AU-58.

than on the reverse of this type. Cents of this type can be very beautiful in About Uncirculated. *Reverse:* Friction is seen on the higher wreath leaves and (not as easy to discern) on the letters. Again, the die variety should be checked. The fields, though protected by the designs, show friction, but not as noticeably as on the obverse. At AU–55 and 58, little if any friction is seen. The reverse may have original luster, toned brown, minimal on lower About Uncirculated grades, often extensive at the AU-58 level. General rules for cents follow the half cents of the same type.

Illustrated coin: Note the die crack arcing through the lower-left obverse. This crack was also on the preceding coin, but is more noticeable here.

EF-40, 45 (Extremely Fine). *Obverse:* Wear is seen on the portrait overall, with reduction or elimination of some separation of hair strands on the highest part. By the standards of the Early American Coppers society, if the "spit curl" in front of Liberty's ear is missing, the coin is not EF. The cheek shows more wear than on higher grades, and the drapery covering the bosom is lightly worn on the higher areas. Often weakness in the separa-

1804, Original; BW-1, S-266, B-1. Graded EF-40.

tion of the drapery lines can be attributed to weakness in striking. Luster is minimal or nonexistent at EF-40, and may survive in amongst the letters of LIBERTY at EF-45. *Reverse:* Wear is seen on the highest wreath and ribbon areas, and on the letters. Luster is minimal, but likely more noticeable than on the obverse, as the fields are protected by the designs and lettering. The ANA grading standards state that at EF-45 nearly all of the "ribbing" (veins) in the leaves is visible, and that at EF-40 about 75% is sharp. In practice, striking plays a part as well, and some leaves may be weak even in higher grades.

Illustrated coin: This coin features a few small patches of porosity.

VF-20, 30 (Very Fine). *Obverse:* Wear on the portrait has reduced the hair detail further, especially to the left of the forehead. The rolling curls are solid or flat on their highest areas, as well as by the ribbon behind the hair. The border denticles are blended together, with many indistinct. No luster is seen. *Reverse:* The leaf details are nearly completely worn away at VF-20, and with slight detail at VF-30. The ANA grading

1805; BW-1, S-267, B-1. Graded VF-35.

standards are a bit stricter: 30% remaining at VF-20 and 50% at VF-30. In the marketplace, fewer details can be seen on most certified coins at these levels. The border denticles are blended together with many indistinct. No luster is seen.

F-12, 15 (Fine). *Obverse:* Many hair details are worn away, with perhaps one-half to one-third visible, mainly at the edges and behind the shoulder. Border denticles are weak or worn away in areas. F-15 shows slightly more detail. Porosity and scattered marks become increasingly common at this level and lower. *Reverse:* The wreath leaves are worn flat, but their edges are distinct. Little if anything remains of leaf vein details. Border denticles

1807, 7 Over 6; BW-2, S-273, B-3. Graded F-12.

are weak or worn away in areas. F-15 shows slightly more detail.

Illustrated coin: There are several distracting contact marks on the obverse of this coin. Note the 6 visible under the 7 in the date.

VG-8, 10 (Very Good). *Obverse:* The portrait is well worn, although the eye can be seen, as can hints of hair detail. Some hair at the left shows separation. Curls now appear as mostly solid blobs. Border denticles are worn away on most varieties, and the rim, although usually present, begins to blend into the field. LIBERTY and the date are bold in most areas, with some lightness toward the rim. VG-10 is sometimes applied to espe-

1807, Large Fraction. Graded VG-8.

cially nice Very Good coins. *Reverse:* The wreath, bow, and lettering are seen in outline form, and some leaves and letters may be indistinct in parts. The border may blend into the field on some of the periphery. The strength of the letters is dependent to an extent on the specific die variety.

G-4, 6 (Good). *Obverse:* The portrait is worn smooth and is seen only in outline form, although the eye position can be discerned and some curls can be made out. LIBERTY is readable, but the tops of the letters may fade away. The date is clearly readable, but the lower part of the numerals may be very weak or worn away. The border will blend into the field more extensively than on the preceding, but significant areas will still be seen. *Reverse:*

1799, 9 Over 8; BW-2, S-188, B-2. Graded G-6.

Extensive wear is seen overall. From one-half to two-thirds of the letters in UNITED STATES OF AMERICA and the fraction numerals are worn away. On most varieties, ONE CENT is fairly strong. G-6 is often assigned to finer examples in this category.

Illustrated coin: This coin shows evidence of a past cleaning, but it has retoned.

AG-3 (About Good). *Obverse:* Wear is more extensive than on the preceding. The portrait is visible only in outline. LIBERTY is weak, partially worn away, but usually discernible. The date is weak, and the bottoms of the digits may be worn away, but must be identifiable. *Reverse:* Parts of the wreath are visible in outline form, and all but a few letters are gone. ONE CENT is usually mostly or completely discernible, depending on the variety.

1796, Reverse of 1797; BW-53, S-100, B-24. Graded AG-3.

Illustrated coin: Early American Coppers has graded this same coin at Good.

Reverse of 1794 (1794–1796)
*Note double leaf at top right;
14–16 leaves on left,
16–18 leaves on right.*

Reverse of 1795 (1795–1798)
*Note single leaf at top right;
17–21 leaves on left,
16–20 leaves on right.*

Reverse of 1797 (1796–1807)
*Note double leaf at top right; 16
leaves on left, 19 leaves on right.*

1796, LIHERTY Error

1797, Wreath With Stems

1797, Stemless Wreath

Style 1 Hair
Found on all coins of 1796 and 1797, many 1798 varieties, and 1800, 1800 Over 1798.

Style 2 Hair
Found on coins of 1798–1807. Note the extra curl near shoulders.

1798, 8 Over 7

	Mintage	Cert	Avg	%MS	AG-3	G-4	VG-8	F-12	VF-20	EF-40	AU-50	MS-60BN	MS-63BN
1796, Draped Bust, All kinds	363,375												
1796, Reverse of 1794		36	14.3	0%	$150	$300	$700	$1,150	$2,750	$6,250	$12,500	$18,000	$27,500
Auctions: $11,750, AU-53, January 2014													
1796, Reverse of 1795		23	21.8	4%	$150	$250	$550	$1,100	$2,750	$6,500	$13,000	$19,500	$30,000
Auctions: $20,563, AU-58, January 2014; $764, G-6, October 2015; $646, G-6, October 2015													
1796, Reverse of 1797		25	18.8	12%	$150	$250	$500	$1,100	$2,500	$4,500	$6,750	$9,000	$14,000
Auctions: $28,200, MS-64BN, April 2013													
1796, LIHERTY Error		14	25.0	7%	$250	$500	$1,500	$3,500	$6,000	$14,000	$30,000	$60,000	$85,000
Auctions: $2,350, VF-20, August 2013; $1,704, VG-10, March 2015													
1796, Stemless Reverse	(a)	0	n/a		$25,000								
Auctions: No auction records available.													
1797, All kinds	897,510												
1797, Gripped Edge, 1795-Style Reverse		17	21.5	0%	$115	$175	$350	$650	$1,500	$3,500	$8,000	$26,000	
Auctions: $1,351, VG-8, March 2013													
1797, Plain Edge, 1795-Style Reverse		12	12.7	0%	$125	$200	$375	$750	$1,850	$4,500	$8,500	$26,500	
Auctions: $940, EF-40, June 2014													
1797, 1797 Reverse, With Stems		206	32.4	18%	$80	$175	$300	$500	$1,050	$2,250	$4,000	$6,500	$14,000
Auctions: $41,125, MS-65RB, January 2013; $2,350, EF-45, March 2015; $999, F-15, June 2015; $129, F-12, March 2015													
1797, 1797 Reverse, Stemless		26	23.1	4%	$115	$225	$450	$1,100	$2,500	$7,000	$25,000	$60,000	
Auctions: $1,645, VF-25, January 2014													
1798, All kinds	1,841,745												
1798, 8 Over 7		20	25.7	5%	$150	$250	$550	$1,350	$3,500	$8,000	$16,500		
Auctions: $14,688, AU-58, February 2013													
1798, Reverse of 1796		11	17.1	0%	$100	$200	$600	$750	$2,500	$7,500	$11,000	$20,000	$35,000
Auctions: $3,290, VF-20, September 2013													
1798, Style 1 Hair		90	22.9	1%	$75	$125	$145	$250	$600	$2,200	$5,000	$10,000	$17,750
Auctions: $494, EF-40, June 2015; $494, VF-20, May 2015; $494, F-12, January 2015; $329, F-12, July 2015													
1798, Style 2 Hair		224	29.7	3%	$40	$125	$145	$250	$575	$1,950	$3,500	$8,350	$16,500
Auctions: $823, VF-30, August 2015; $940, VF-25, June 2015; $541, VF-20, January 2015; $376, F-12, January 2015													

a. 3 examples are known.

1799, 9 Over 8   **1799, Normal Date**

1800, 1800 Over 1798   **1800, 80 Over 79**   **1800, Normal Date**

1801, Normal Reverse   **1801, 3 Errors: 1/000,**   **1801, Fraction 1/000**   **1801, 1/100 Over 1/000**
One Stem, and IINITED

	Mintage	Cert	Avg	%MS	AG-3	G-4	VG-8	F-12	VF-20	EF-40	AU-50	MS-60BN	MS-63BN
1799, 9 Over 8	(b)	7	8.7	0%	$2,500	$4,500	$8,500	$16,500	$35,000	$125,000	$275,000	$750,000	
Auctions: $70,500, VF-25, January 2014; $1,293, AG-3, March 2016													
1799, Normal Date	(b)	48	11.4	2%	$1,750	$3,500	$7,000	$13,500	$30,000	$95,000	$225,000	$500,000	
Auctions: $30,550, AU-58, May 2016; $99,875, VF-35, January 2013; $32,900, VF-30, March 2015													
1800, All kinds	2,822,175												
1800, 1800 Over 1798, Style 1 Hair		27	24.9	4%	$45	$75	$135	$285	$1,650	$3,850	$7,000	$10,000	$14,000
Auctions: $2,585, G-6, January 2014													
1800, 80 Over 79, Style 2 Hair		63	22.8	6%	$45	$85	$185	$300	$750	$2,500	$4,000	$8,000	$25,000
Auctions: $19,388, MS-62BN, June 2014													
1800, Normal Date		152	24.1	9%	$40	$85	$125	$250	$750	$2,000	$3,500	$6,500	$14,000
Auctions: $70,500, MS-65BN, January 2013; $1,058, VF-25, June 2015; $705, VF-20, October 2015													
1801, All kinds	1,362,837												
1801, Normal Reverse		150	22.6	5%	$40	$85	$115	$225	$450	$1,250	$3,000	$7,500	$14,500
Auctions: $1,645, EF-40, February 2015; $112, VF-20, July 2015; $494, F-12, August 2015; $282, VG-10, July 2015													
1801, 3 Errors: 1/000, One Stem, and IINITED		24	19.5	8%	$100	$200	$400	$850	$3,000	$7,750	$14,000	$35,000	$115,000
Auctions: $3,525, EF-40, August 2013													
1801, Fraction 1/000		46	21.6	4%	$65	$100	$150	$325	$750	$2,400	$4,500	$12,500	$28,000
Auctions: $4,406, EF-40, January 2014													
1801, 1/100 Over 1/000		10	21.3	10%	$75	$125	$150	$275	$1,000	$2,500	$6,500	$15,000	$27,500
Auctions: $1,528, EF-45, January 2014													

b. Included in 1798, All kinds, mintage figure.

1802, Normal Reverse   **1802, Fraction 1/000**   **1802, Stemless Wreath**

1803, Small Date   **1803, Large Date**

*Note that Small Date varieties have a
blunt 1 in the date, and Large Date varieties
have a pointed 1 and noticeably larger 3.*

1803, Small Fraction   **1803, Large Fraction**   **1803, 1/100 Over 1/000**   **1803, Stemless Wreath**

	Mintage	Cert	Avg	%MS	AG-3	G-4	VG-8	F-12	VF-20	EF-40	AU-50	MS-60BN	MS-63BN
1802, All kinds	3,435,100												
1802, Normal Reverse		470	29.1	3%	$60	$75	$100	$200	$400	$1,000	$2,000	$4,500	$9,500
Auctions: $1,058, AU-50, January 2015; $881, EF-40, January 2015; $705, VF-35, January 2015; $617, VF-30, June 2015													
1802, Fraction 1/000		26	33.7	15%	$65	$115	$175	$300	$650	$1,700	$3,000	$7,250	$15,500
Auctions: $11,163, AU-55, January 2014													
1802, Stemless Wreath		49	29.8	4%	$50	$75	$125	$200	$500	$1,500	$2,750	$6,500	$13,500
Auctions: $2,938, AU-55, October 2013; $646, VF-25, January 2015; $470, VF-25, September 2015; $447, VF-25, August 2015													
1803, All kinds	3,131,691												
1803, Small Date, Small Fraction		177	30.0	6%	$45	$65	$100	$175	$350	$1,100	$1,450	$3,000	$8,500
Auctions: $423, EF-40, November 2015; $646, VF-30, July 2015; $541, VF-30, September 2015; $259, F-12, September 2015													
1803, Small Date, Large Fraction		105	31.1	9%	$45	$65	$100	$200	$350	$1,000	$1,450	$3,000	$8,500
Auctions: $18,800, MS-64BN, January 2014													
1803, Large Date, Small Fraction		3	12.0	0%	$3,500	$7,000	$11,000	$20,000	$35,000	$80,000			
Auctions: $15,275, VF-20, January 2014													
1803, Large Date, Large Fraction		6	45.0	17%	$75	$100	$175	$400	$1,750	$3,500	$8,500		
Auctions: $353, VF-20, August 2013													
1803, 1/100 Over 1/000		18	25.9	6%	$65	$125	$225	$350	$850	$2,450	$4,000	$6,750	$18,000
Auctions: $2,820, EF-45, September 2013													
1803, Stemless Wreath		15	29.7	13%	$50	$100	$135	$250	$800	$2,000	$2,800	$6,000	$17,000
Auctions: $8,225, AU-58, January 2014													

1804, Broken Dies
Bowers-Whitman–1c, Sheldon-266c.

Unofficial 1804 "Restrike"
Bowers-Whitman–3, Breen-1761, Pollock-6050.

Small 1807, 7 Over 6, Blunt 1

Large 1807, 7 Over 6, Pointed 1

1807, Small Fraction

1807, Large Fraction

1807, "Comet" Variety
Note the die break behind Miss Liberty's head.

	Mintage	Cert	Avg	%MS	AG-3	G-4	VG-8	F-12	VF-20	EF-40	AU-50	MS-60BN	MS-63BN
1804 (c)	96,500	98	16.0	1%	$850	$1,200	$2,500	$5,000	$8,500	$20,000	$50,000	$150,000	$650,000
Auctions: $223,250, AU-55, January 2013													
1804, Unofficial Restrike of 1860 (d)		89	61.1	87%						$1,000	$1,100	$1,200	$1,450
Auctions: $489, AU-55, August 2011													
1805	941,116	162	35.5	10%	$45	$75	$100	$225	$500	$1,200	$2,750	$5,250	$16,000
Auctions: $940, VF-35, January 2015; $447, VF-20, February 2015; $376, VF-20, May 2015; $129, VG-10, May 2015													
1806	348,000	93	28.4	9%	$45	$75	$150	$350	$650	$2,000	$3,000	$8,500	$28,000
Auctions: $3,819, AU-50, February 2013													

c. All genuine 1804 cents have a crosslet 4 in the date and a large fraction. The 0 in the date is in line with the O in OF on the reverse. **d.** Discarded Mint dies were used, circa 1860, to create "restrikes" (actually novodels or fantasies) of the scarce 1804 cent for collectors. These combine two unrelated dies: an altered 1803 die was used for the obverse, and a die of the 1820 cent for the reverse. The resulting coins cannot be confused with genuine 1804 cents.

	Mintage	Cert	Avg	%MS	AG-3	G-4	VG-8	F-12	VF-20	EF-40	AU-50	MS-60BN	MS-63BN
1807, All kinds	829,221												
1807, Small 1807, 7 Over 6, Blunt 1		6	15.3	0%	$1,500	$3,000	$4,500	$9,500	$20,000	$45,000	$150,000		
Auctions: $2,585, F-15, January 2014													
1807, Large 1807, 7 Over 6, Pointed 1		85	25.1	8%	$65	$85	$150	$250	$650	$1,500	$3,000	$7,500	$23,500
Auctions: $70,500, MS-65BN, April 2014; $764, VF-25, January 2015													
1807, Small Fraction		7	11.4	0%	$50	$85	$150	$300	$750	$2,500	$4,000	$8,500	$22,500
Auctions: $1,763, AU-50, August 2013													
1807, Large Fraction		31	18.7	0%	$45	$75	$125	$225	$550	$1,250	$2,300	$4,600	$16,500
Auctions: $5,750, AU-58, August 2011; $541, VF-25, October 2015; $364, VF-20, January 2015; $306, F-12, June 2015													
1807, "Comet" Variety		28	31.4	18%	$45	$100	$150	$350	$1,000	$2,850	$4,500	$10,500	$25,500
Auctions: $27,600, MS-61BN, February 2012													

CLASSIC HEAD (1808–1814)

Designer: *John Reich.* **Weight:** *10.89 grams.* **Composition:** *Copper.*
Diameter: *Average 29 mm.* **Edge:** *Plain.* **Mint:** *Philadelphia.*

1808; BW-1, S-277, B-1.

History. The Classic Head design, by U.S. Mint assistant engraver John Reich, debuted in 1808. This cent type was minted through 1814. The quality of the coins' copper was poor during the War of 1812; the hostilities had ended the importation of high-quality planchets from England.

Striking and Sharpness. Striking sharpness varies, but often is poor. The cents of 1809 are notorious for having obverses much weaker than their reverses. Points to look for include sharpness of the denticles (which are often mushy, and in *most* instances inconsistent), star centers (a key area), hair details, and leaf details. Classic Head cents often are dark and porous due to the copper stock used.

Availability. Examples are readily available in grades from well worn to VF and EF, although overall quality often leaves much to be desired. AU and MS coins are elusive. Grading numbers do not mean much, as a connoisseur might prefer a high-quality EF-45 to a poorly struck MS-63. Overall eye appeal of obverse and reverse is often sub-par, a characteristic of this type.

GRADING STANDARDS

MS-60 to 70 (Mint State). *Obverse:* In the lower Mint State grades, MS–60 and 61, some slight abrasions can be seen on the portrait, most evidently on the cheek, as the hair details are complex on this type. Luster in the field is complete or nearly complete; the field is not as open on this type as on the Draped Bust issues. At MS-63, luster should be complete, and no abrasion evident. In higher levels, the luster is complete and deeper, and some orig-

1812, Large Date; BW-1, S-288, B-3. Graded MS-64BN.

inal mint color may be seen. MS-64 coins may have some slight discoloration or scattered contact marks. A well-graded MS-65 or higher coin will have full, rich luster; no marks visible except under magnification; and a nice blend of brown toning or nicely mixed (not stained or blotchy) mint color and natural brown toning. Incomplete striking of some details, especially the obverse stars, is the rule. *Reverse:* In the lower Mint State grades, some abrasion is seen on the higher areas of the leaves. Mint luster is complete in all Mint State grades, as the open areas are protected by the lettering and wreath. Sharpness of the leaves can vary by die variety, so check this aspect. Otherwise, the same comments apply as for the obverse.

Illustrated coin: The central devices are sharply struck and well preserved though obverse stars 1 through 5 are somewhat flat, as is virtually always seen on this type, and the reverse denticles from 8 o'clock to 11 o'clock are soft, which is also typical. This is one of the highest-graded Classic Head cents in existence.

AU-50, 53, 55, 58 (About Uncirculated). *Obverse:* Friction is seen on the higher parts, particularly the cheek. The hair will have friction and light wear, but will not be as obvious. Friction and scattered marks are in the field, ranging from more extensive at AU-50 to minimal at AU-58. Luster may be seen in protected areas, minimal at AU-50, but more visible at AU-58. At AU-58 the open field may retain some luster, as well.

1812, Large Date; BW-2, S-289, B-4. Graded AU-58.

Reverse: Friction is seen on the higher wreath leaves and on the letters. Fields, protected by the designs, show less friction. At the AU–55 and 58 levels little if any friction is seen. The reverse may have original luster, toned brown, minimal on lower About Uncirculated grades, often extensive at AU-58.

EF-40, 45 (Extremely Fine). *Obverse:* Wear is seen on the portrait overall, but most hair detail will still be present. The cheek shows light wear. Luster is minimal or nonexistent at EF-40, and may survive in among the letters of LIBERTY at EF-45. *Reverse:* Wear is seen on the highest wreath and ribbon areas and the letters. Leaf veins are visible except in the highest areas. Luster is minimal, but likely more noticeable than on the obverse, as the fields are protected by the designs and lettering.

1809; BW-1, S-280, B-1. Graded EF-40.

VF-20, 30 (Very Fine). *Obverse:* Wear on the portrait has reduced the hair detail, especially on the area to the right of the cheek and neck, but much can still be seen. *Reverse:* The wreath details, except for the edges of the leaves and certain of the tips (on leaves in lower relief), are worn away at VF-20, and with slightly more detail at VF-30.

1812, Large Date; BW-2, S-289, B-4. Graded VF-25.

F-12, 15 (Fine). *Obverse:* The hair details are fewer than on the preceding, but many are still present. The central hair curl is visible. Stars have flat centers. F-15 shows slightly more detail. The portrait on this type held up well to wear. *Reverse:* The higher areas of wreath leaves are worn flat, but their edges are distinct. F-15 shows slightly more detail.

Illustrated coin: This is a dark and somewhat porous example of what is considered to be the key issue of the Classic Head type.

1809; BW-1, S-280, B-1. Graded F-15.

VG-8, 10 (Very Good). *Obverse:* The portrait is well worn, although the eye and ear can be seen clearly. The hair is mostly blended, but some slight separation can be seen in areas. The border is raised in most or all areas. *Reverse:* The wreath is more worn than on the preceding grade, but there will still be some detail on the leaves. On most coins, ONE CENT is bold. Border letters are light or weak but are fully readable. The border is well defined in most areas.

1808. Graded VG-8.

G-4, 6 (Good). *Obverse:* The portrait is worn smooth and is seen only in outline form. Much or even all of LIBERTY on the headband is readable, but the letters are weak. The stars are weak, only in outline form, and several may be scarcely discernible. *Reverse:* Extensive wear is seen overall. Lettering in UNITED STATES OF AMERICA is weak, but completely discernible. The wreath is in outline, but still fairly bold, and ONE CENT is usually strong.

1808; BW-1, S-277, B-1. Graded G-6.

AG-3 (About Good). *Obverse:* Wear is more extensive than on the preceding. The portrait is visible only in outline. Most letters of LIBERTY are discernible, as this feature is in low relief. The stars are weak or worn away on their outer edges, and the date is light. *Reverse:* The wreath is visible in outline form but remains fairly strong. Most or even all of UNITED STATES OF AMERICA is worn away. ONE CENT is usually easily readable.

1808; BW-2, S-278, B-2. Graded AG-3.

1810, 10 Over 09

1810, Normal Date

1811, Last 1 Over 0

1811, Normal Date

1812, Small Date

1812, Large Date

1814, Plain 4

1814, Crosslet 4

	Mintage	Cert	Avg	%MS	AG-3	G-4	VG-8	F-12	VF-20	EF-40	AU-50	MS-60BN	MS-63BN
1808	1,007,000	114	32.4	14%	$45	$100	$175	$375	$800	$2,500	$4,000	$9,500	$17,500
	Auctions: $25,850, MS-64BN, January 2013; $400, F-12, May 2015; $69, F-12, April 2015												
1809	222,867	66	29.5	8%	$50	$120	$250	$600	$1,500	$4,000	$5,000	$11,500	$25,000
	Auctions: $28,200, MS-63BN, January 2013; $754, F-12, January 2015; $376, G-4, May 2015												
1810, All kinds	1,458,500												
1810, 10 Over 09		50	29.6	10%	$45	$80	$130	$325	$800	$1,700	$2,750	$8,000	$15,000
	Auctions: $10,575, AU-55, April 2013												
1810, Normal Date		136	32.1	13%	$45	$100	$150	$325	$750	$1,600	$2,700	$8,000	$15,000
	Auctions: $32,900, MS-64BN, January 2014; $376, EF-40, January 2015; $1,234, VF-35, January 2015; $940, VF-20, July 2015												
1811, All kinds	218,025												
1811, Last 1 Over 0		27	25.7	11%	$75	$100	$250	$500	$1,750	$5,250	$10,000	$35,000	$60,000
	Auctions: $2,585, VF-25, March 2015; $1,410, VF-20, August 2016; $764, VG-10, August 2015												
1811, Normal Date		79	29.3	14%	$65	$100	$150	$400	$1,000	$2,200	$5,500	$9,500	$20,000
	Auctions: $23,500, MS-64BN, January 2013												
1812, All kinds	1,075,500												
1812, Small Date		35	30.3	6%	$35	$100	$150	$375	$750	$1,600	$2,750	$6,000	$12,000
	Auctions: $44,063, MS-65RB, June 2014; $881, VF-30, August 2015; $94, F-12, March 2015; $153, VG-8, June 2015												
1812, Large Date		32	33.0	9%	$25	$50	$100	$250	$750	$1,600	$2,500	$6,000	$12,000
	Auctions: $3,819, AU-55, January 2014												
1813	418,000	174	37.4	11%	$40	$80	$120	$325	$850	$1,750	$2,800	$6,500	$12,500
	Auctions: $211,500, MS-65BN, January 2013; $940, AU-50, January 2015; $1,880, EF-40, March 2015; $1,116, VF-20, August 2015												
1814, All kinds	357,830												
1814, Plain 4		127	25.1	9%	$25	$80	$130	$325	$750	$1,600	$2,400	$5,000	$12,500
	Auctions: $47,000, MS-65BN, April 2014; $223, VG-10, May 2015; $129, G-6, April 2015; $74, G-4, April 2015												
1814, Crosslet 4		98	28.0	11%	$25	$80	$130	$325	$750	$1,750	$3,000	$5,000	$12,500
	Auctions: $1,028, VF-30, February 2015; $376, VF-20, November 2015; $188, VF-20, May 2015; $259, VG-10, May 2015												

MATRON HEAD (1816–1839)

Designer: *1816–1835, Matron Head—Possibly Robert Scot or John Birch; 1835–1839, Matron Head Modified—Christian Gobrecht.* **Weight:** *10.89 grams.* **Composition:** *Copper.* **Diameter:** *1816–1835, Matron Head—28 to 29 mm; 1835–1839, Matron Head Modified—27.5 mm.* **Edge:** *Plain.* **Mint:** *Philadelphia.*

**Matron Head (1816–1835),
Circulation Strike**
1827; Newcomb-5.

Matron Head, Proof
1831; Newcomb-10.

**Matron Head Modified (1835–1839),
Circulation Strike**
1835; Newcomb-8.

Matron Head Modified, Proof
1837; Newcomb-9.

History. The term *Matron Head* describes cents of 1816 to 1835 (none were struck in 1815). Engraver Christian Gobrecht experimented with various "Matron Head Modified" portraits in the later 1830s.

Striking and Sharpness. Planchet quality is generally very good for Liberty Head cents. Color tends to be lighter on coins of the 1830s than on earlier dates. Striking can vary. Points to check include the obverse stars (in particular), the highest hair details, and the leaves on the reverse. Denticles can range from sharp to weak, and centering is often irregular. The reverse design is essentially the same as that used on the Classic Head of 1808 to 1814, and can be graded the same way. This motif stood up to circulation particularly well.

Availability. As a type, Liberty Head cents are easily available. The scarcest date by far is 1823 (and the related 1823, 3 Over 2, overdate). Cents of 1816 to 1820 (particularly 1818 and 1820) are readily available in MS. Other MS coins are generally scarce, although those of the 1830s are more readily available than those of the teens and 1820s. Circulated examples exist in approximate relationship to their mintages. Planchet quality and striking sharpness vary in all grades.

GRADING STANDARDS

MS-60 to 70 (Mint State). *Obverse:* In the lower Mint State grades, MS–60 and 61, some slight abrasions can be seen on the portrait, most evidently on the cheek, which on this type is very prominent. Higher areas of the hair can be checked, particularly the top and back of Liberty's head, but do not confuse with lightness of strike. Luster in the

1817; N-2. Graded MS-63BN.

field is complete or nearly complete. At MS-63, luster should be complete, and no abrasion is evident.

In higher levels, the luster is complete and deeper, and some original mint color may be seen. MS-64 coins may have some minimal discoloration or scattered contact marks. A well-graded MS-65 or higher coin will have full, rich luster; no marks visible except under magnification; and a nice blend of brown toning or nicely mixed mint color and natural brown toning. Randall Hoard coins of the 1816 to 1820 years usually have much mint red and some black spotting. *Reverse:* In the lower Mint State grades some abrasion is seen on the higher areas of the leaves. Mint luster is complete in all Mint State grades, as the open areas are protected by the lettering and wreath. Sharpness of the leaves can vary by die variety, so check this aspect. Otherwise, the same comments apply as for the obverse.

Illustrated coin: Note the reverse die break running from NI of UNITED to OF A in OF AMERICA.

AU-50, 53, 55, 58 (About Uncirculated).

Obverse: Friction is seen on the higher parts, particularly the cheek. The hair has friction and light wear, usually most notable in the general area above BER of LIBERTY. Friction and scattered marks are in the field, ranging from extensive at AU-50 to minimal at AU-58. Luster may be seen in protected areas, minimal at the AU-50 level, more visible at AU-58. At AU-58 the field may retain some luster as well.

1820, 20 Over 19; N-10. Graded AU-58.

Reverse: Friction is seen on the higher wreath leaves and on the letters. Fields, protected by the designs, show friction. At the AU–55 and 58 levels little if any friction is seen. The reverse may have original luster, toned brown, minimal on lower About Uncirculated grades, often extensive at AU-58.

Illustrated coin: Flecks of darker patination spot both sides, but are particularly evident on the obverse.

EF-40, 45 (Extremely Fine). *Obverse:* Wear

is seen on the portrait overall, but most hair detail is still present, except in higher areas. The cheek shows light wear. Luster is minimal or nonexistent at EF-40, and may survive in among the letters of LIBERTY at EF-45. *Reverse:* Wear is seen on the highest wreath and ribbon areas, and on the letters. Leaf veins are visible except in the highest areas. Luster is minimal, but likely more noticeable

1816. Graded EF-45.

than on the obverse, as the fields are protected by the designs and lettering.

VF-20, 30 (Very Fine). *Obverse:* Wear on

the portrait has reduced the hair detail, especially on the area to the right of the cheek and neck, but much can still be seen. *Reverse:* The wreath details, except for the edges of the leaves and certain of the tips (on leaves in lower relief), are worn away at VF-20, and with slightly more detail at VF-30.

1823; N2. Graded VF-20.

F-12, 15 (Fine). *Obverse:* The hair details are fewer than on the preceding, but still many are present. Wear is extensive above and below the LIBERTY coronet, with the area from the forehead to the coronet worn flat. Stars have flat centers. F-15 shows slightly more detail. *Reverse:* The higher areas of wreath leaves are worn flat, but their edges are distinct. F-15 shows slightly more detail.

1816. Graded F-15.

VG-8, 10 (Very Good). *Obverse:* The portrait is well worn, although the eye and ear can be seen clearly. The hair is mostly blended, but some slight separation can be seen in lower areas. The border is raised in most or all areas. *Reverse:* The wreath is more worn than on the preceding, but still there is some detail on the leaves. On most coins, ONE CENT is bold. Border letters are light or weak but are fully readable. The border is well defined in most areas.

1831, Large Letters; N-9. Graded VG-8.

  Illustrated coin: A die break caused the internal cud which connects stars 3 through 5, and that broken die would have been retired shortly after striking this piece.

G-4, 6 (Good). *Obverse:* The portrait is worn smooth and is seen only in outline form. Much or even all of LIBERTY on the headband is readable, but the letters are weak, and L may be missing. The stars are weak. The rim is usually discernible all around. *Reverse:* Extensive wear is seen overall. Lettering in UNITED STATES OF AMERICA is weak, but completely discernible. The wreath is in outline, but still fairly bold, and ONE CENT

1830; N-9. Graded G-4.

is usually strong. The rim is usually faded into the field in many areas (depending on the die variety).

  Illustrated coin: Note the lovely golden brown and rose surfaces.

AG-3 (About Good). *Obverse:* Wear is more extensive than on the preceding. The portrait is visible only in outline. Most letters of LIBERTY remain discernible in the headband, as this feature is in low relief. The stars are weak or worn away on their outer edges, and the date is light. *Reverse:* The wreath is visible in outline form, but remains fairly strong. Most of UNITED STATES OF AMERICA is worn away. ONE CENT is usually readable, but light.

1818; N-6. Graded AG-3.

PF-60 to 70 (Proof). Proofs were made for cents from 1817 onward. Often, what are called "Proofs" are only partially mirrorlike, and sometimes the striking is casual, e.g., with weakness on certain of the stars. Complicating the situation is the fact that all but one of the same die pairs were also used to make circulation strikes. Many misattributions were made generations ago, some of which have been perpetuated. Except among large-cent

1831, Large Letters; N-9. Graded PF-63BN.

specialists, debate is effectively ended when a certification service seals a coin as a Proof (logic aside). True Proofs with deeply mirrored surfaces are in the small minority. *Obverse and Reverse:* Proofs that are extensively hairlined or have dull surfaces, this being characteristic of many issues (exceptions, when found, are usually dated in the 1830s) are graded PF–60 to 62 or 63. Artificially toned and recolored coins may be graded lower. To qualify as PF-65 or higher, hairlines should be microscopic, and there should be no trace of friction. Surfaces should be prooflike or, better, fully mirrored and without dullness.

Illustrated coin: This coin shows high quality for the grade. The surfaces are a light, reddish brown with areas of deep tan and hints of blue, green, gold and violet as well as considerable faded mint red on the reverse. This is one of two known Proof examples for the year.

| **1817, 13 Stars** | **1817, 15 Stars** |

	Mintage	Cert	Avg	%MS	G-4	VG-8	F-12	VF-20	EF-40	AU-50	MS-60BN / PF-63BN	MS-63BN / PF-64BN	MS-65BN / PF-65BN
1816	2,820,982	332	53.0	55%	$25	$35	$50	$100	$190	$300	$500	$700	$1,800
	Auctions: $823, MS-63BN, October 2015; $259, AU-50, August 2015; $306, EF-45, April 2015; $69, EF-40, October 2015												
1817, All kinds	3,948,400												
1817, 13 Stars		477	51.3	51%	$30	$40	$55	$85	$150	$250	$450	$600	$1,550
	Auctions: $1,293, MS-63BN, January 2015; $1,116, MS-63BN, January 2015; $1,175, MS-62BN, June 2015; $282, MS-60, June 2015												
1817, 15 Stars		45	50.0	24%	$35	$45	$65	$150	$600	$900	$2,800	$3,750	$35,000
	Auctions: $9,400, VF-20, January 2014												
1817, Proof	2–3	1	63.0								$75,000	$100,000	$150,000
	Auctions: $48,300, PF-66, July 2005												
1818	3,167,000	794	57.4	74%	$30	$40	$45	$75	$135	$225	$450	$600	$1,600
	Auctions: $823, MS-64BN, September 2015; $764, MS-63RB, June 2015; $541, MS-62BN, October 2015; $494, MS-62BN, June 2015												

1819, 9 Over 8

1819, Large Date

1819, Small Date

1820, 20 Over 19
Note the 1 under the 2.

1820, Large Date
Note the plain-topped 2.

1820, Small Date
Note the curl-topped 2.

	Mintage	Cert	Avg	%MS	G-4	VG-8	F-12	VF-20	EF-40	AU-50	MS-60BN PF-63BN	MS-63BN PF-64BN	MS-65BN PF-65BN
1819, All kinds	2,671,000												
1819, 9 Over 8		121	50.0	38%	$30	$40	$55	$85	$275	$375	$750	$1,300	$4,000
Auctions: $705, AU-58, October 2015; $259, EF-45, September 2015													
1819, Large Date		257	52.5	54%	$30	$35	$45	$70	$150	$300	$475	$700	$2,000
Auctions: $940, MS-63BN, August 2015; $259, AU-55, May 2015; $202, EF-40, September 2015													
1819, Small Date		102	54.6	60%	$30	$35	$45	$70	$150	$300	$475	$700	$2,000
Auctions: $1,293, MS-63BN, June 2015; $646, AU-58, October 2015; $282, AU-50, August 2015; $212, EF-40, May 2015													
1819, 9 Over 8, Proof	2–3	1	64.0								$30,000	$35,000	$50,000
Auctions: $32,200, PF-64BN, June 2005													
1820, All kinds	4,407,550												
1820, 20 Over 19		44	40.8	27%	$30	$35	$55	$110	$335	$550	$1,000	$1,600	$4,500
Auctions: $764, AU-55, August 2015													
1820, Large Date		113	56.5	70%	$25	$30	$45	$75	$175	$250	$400	$600	$1,250
Auctions: $1,293, MS-63BN, August 2015; $705, MS-63BN, January 2015; $588, MS-63BN, January 2015; $494, MS-60, September 2015													
1820, Small Date		37	51.4	54%	$25	$30	$55	$75	$250	$450	$900	$1,200	$2,800
Auctions: $4,994, MS-64BN, January 2014													
1820, Proof	8–15	3	63.7								$40,000	$50,000	$60,000
Auctions: $46,000, PF-64, November 2008													
1821 (a)	389,000	142	29.9	7%	$45	$55	$135	$375	$1,300	$2,300	$7,750	$11,000	
Auctions: $564, AU-50, January 2015; $494, VF-25, August 2015; $400, VF-20, January 2015; $129, VF-20, May 2015													
1821, Proof	4–6	3	63.0								$35,000	$50,000	$60,000
Auctions: $35,250, PF-62BN, August 2013													
1822	2,072,339	237	43.7	24%	$30	$35	$45	$120	$425	$700	$1,200	$1,800	$4,900
Auctions: $1,058, AU-58, June 2015; $793, AU-58, February 2015; $494, AU-55, January 2015; $517, AU-50, June 2015													
1822, Proof	4–6	1	62.0								$35,000	$50,000	
Auctions: $25,300, PF-63, March 2004													

a. Wide and closely spaced AMER varieties are valued the same.

1823, 3 Over 2

1824, 4 Over 2

Unofficial 1823 "Restrike"
Newcomb-3, Breen-1823, Pollock-6220.

1826, 6 Over 5

**Date Size, Through 1828
(Large, Narrow Date)**

**Date Size, 1828 and
Later (Small, Wide Date)**

	Mintage	Cert	Avg	%MS	G-4	VG-8	F-12	VF-20	EF-40	AU-50	MS-60BN / PF-63BN	MS-63BN / PF-64BN	MS-65BN / PF-65BN
1823, 3 Over 2	(b)	92	23.4	2%	$115	$250	$450	$850	$2,500	$5,000	$15,000	—	
Auctions: $1,645, VF-30, January 2015; $564, F-15, February 2015; $423, F-15, June 2015; $259, VG-10, May 2015													
1823, Normal Date	(b)	53	21.2	4%	$125	$200	$500	$1,250	$3,500	$7,500	$18,500	$30,000	$115,000
Auctions: $3,584, VF-35, January 2014													
1823, Unofficial Restrike (c)		60	63.3	97%				$450	$550	$925	$1,250	$1,500	$1,750
Auctions: $2,350, MS-64BN, December 2013													
1823, Proof	2–3	1	65.0								$55,000	$75,000	
Auctions: No auction records available.													
1823, 3 Over 2, Proof	5–8	3	64.3								$50,000	$60,000	
Auctions: $47,000, PF-64BN, June 2014													
1824, All kinds	1,262,000												
1824, 4 Over 2		44	36.1	11%	$30	$45	$85	$275	$1,500	$2,500	$7,500	$25,000	$35,000
Auctions: $423, VF-25BN, September 2015; $129, VG-10, May 2015; $94, VG-10, June 2015													
1824, Normal Date		136	41.3	16%	$25	$35	$45	$165	$500	$850	$2,400	$4,000	$8,000
Auctions: $564, EF-45, June 2015; $235, EF-40, January 2015; $259, VF-30, September 2015; $235, VF-30, May 2015													
1825	1,461,100	174	43.2	25%	$25	$35	$40	$100	$325	$650	$1,850	$2,750	$7,500
Auctions: $6,463, MS-64BN, January 2014													
1826, All kinds	1,517,425												
1826, 6 Over 5		19	49.7	42%	$30	$50	$100	$275	$975	$1,500	$2,800	$5,500	$20,000
Auctions: $10,575, MS-62BN, January 2014													
1826, Normal Date		274	46.9	33%	$25	$30	$40	$100	$250	$450	$900	$1,500	$3,100
Auctions: $3,290, MS-64, March 2015; $1,234, AU-58, August 2015; $376, AU-53, September 2015; $329, EF-40, June 2015													
1827	2,357,732	243	43.9	27%	$25	$30	$40	$100	$225	$425	$775	$1,400	$3,250
Auctions: $881, AU-58BN, October 2015; $576, AU-55, March 2015; $376, AU-53, May 2015; $259, EF-45, May 2015													
1827, Proof	5–8	2	64.0								$20,000	$25,000	$40,000
Auctions: $20,125, PF-64, March 2004													
1828, All kinds	2,260,624												
1828, Large Narrow Date		79	50.5	30%	$25	$30	$35	$75	$210	$400	$1,250	$1,750	$4,250
Auctions: $3,672, MS-64, March 2015; $881, AU-58, October 2015; $141, VF-30, January 2015													
1828, Small Wide Date		20	49.1	40%	$30	$30	$35	$50	$120	$275	$650	$1,950	$3,500	$20,000
Auctions: $7,638, MS-64BN, February 2013													
1828, Proof	2–3	1	65.0										
Auctions: No auction records available.													

b. Included in 1824, All kinds, mintage figure. **c.** The unofficial 1823 "restrikes" (actually novodels or fantasies) were made at the same time (around 1860) and by the same people as those of 1804. The coins were made from a discarded obverse die of 1823 and an 1813 reverse die—both heavily rusted, producing surface lumps. Most examples have both dies cracked.

Large Letters (1808–1834)
*Note the size and proximity
of individual letters.*

Medium Letters (1829–1837)
*Note the isolation of the
letters, especially of STATES.*

	Mintage	Cert	Avg	%MS	G-4	VG-8	F-12	VF-20	EF-40	AU-50	MS-60BN PF-63BN	MS-63BN PF-64BN	MS-65BN PF-65BN
1829, All kinds	1,414,500												
1829, Large Letters		43	47.4	35%	$25	$30	$35	$85	$200	$385	$650	$1,500	$5,200
Auctions: $646, AU-55, February 2015; $129, VF-25, February 2015													
1829, Medium Letters		16	42.8	19%	$25	$45	$110	$350	$800	$2,500	$6,500	$10,500	$17,000
Auctions: $7,050, AU-58, January 2014													
1829, Proof	2–3	1	64.0								$20,000	$25,000	$40,000
Auctions: $47,000, PF-64RB, January 2014													
1829, Bronzed, Proof	10–15	5	64.6								$18,000	$26,000	$40,000
Auctions: $41,125, PF-65BN, August 2013													
1830, All kinds	1,711,500												
1830, Large Letters		96	47.8	34%	$25	$30	$35	$70	$190	$300	$550	$1,000	$2,700
Auctions: $562, AU-55, August 2015; $646, AU-53, October 2015; $235, EF-40, May 2015; $153, VF-25, May 2015													
1830, Medium Letters		9	30.6	11%	$30	$40	$160	$500	$2,000	$5,000	$14,000	$25,000	$32,000
Auctions: $3,055, EF-40, June 2013													
1830, Proof	2–3	1	64.0								$25,000	$35,000	$150,000
Auctions: $16,500, PF-64, November 1988													
1831, All kinds	3,359,260												
1831, Large Letters		88	52.9	52%	$25	$30	$35	$65	$150	$250	$400	$700	$1,800
Auctions: $212, AU-53, July 2015; $224, AU-50, March 2015													
1831, Medium Letters		43	51.3	42%	$25	$30	$35	$65	$200	$350	$750	$1,600	$2,300
Auctions: $3,290, MS-62BN, January 2014													
1831, Proof	10–20	8	64.1								$14,500	$24,500	$50,000
Auctions: $30,550, PF-65BN, January 2014													
1832, All kinds	2,362,000												
1832, Large Letters		32	54.8	56%	$25	$30	$35	$65	$150	$250	$375	$650	$2,300
Auctions: $3,525, MS-65BN, January 2014; $306, AU-58, June 2015													
1832, Medium Letters		33	57.8	58%	$25	$30	$35	$85	$200	$550	$900	$1,200	$2,900
Auctions: $940, MS-62BN, July 2014													
1832, Proof	2–4	1	64.0								—	—	—
Auctions: No auction records available.													
1833	2,739,000	280	51.5	44%	$25	$30	$35	$65	$150	$250	$375	$750	$2,600
Auctions: $423, AU-58, May 2015; $294, AU-53, May 2015; $223, EF-40, August 2015; $206, EF-40, June 2015													
1833, 3 Over 2, Proof	**(d)**	0	n/a										
Auctions: No auction records available.													

d. The mintage figure is unknown.

1834, Large 8,
Large Stars,
Large Letters
Newcomb-6.

1834, Large 8,
Large Stars,
Medium Letters
Newcomb-5.

1834, Large 8,
Small Stars,
Medium Letters
Newcomb-3.

1834, Small 8,
Large Stars,
Medium Letters
Newcomb-1.

	Mintage	Cert	Avg	%MS	G-4	VG-8	F-12	VF-20	EF-40	AU-50	MS-60BN PF-63BN	MS-63BN PF-64BN	MS-65BN PF-65BN
1834, All kinds	1,855,100												
1834, Large 8, Stars, and Reverse Letters		14	44.4	7%	$25	$35	$75	$200	$550	$1,200	$2,250	$4,000	$8,500
Auctions: $2,820, AU-58, January 2014													
1834, Large 8 and Stars, Medium Letters		6	52.2	33%	$160	$325	$400	$1,000	$3,500	$6,500	$8,500	$12,000	$22,000
Auctions: $58,750, MS-65BN, January 2014; $253, AU-50, June 2015; $165, EF-40, January 2015													
1834, Large 8, Small Stars, Medium Letters		37	46.9	30%	$25	$30	$35	$65	$140	$240	$500	$800	$2,000
Auctions: $1,528, MS-63BN, January 2014													
1834, Small 8, Large Stars, Medium Letters		80	54.0	48%	$25	$30	$35	$65	$140	$240	$350	$625	$1,500
Auctions: $4,994, MS-66BN, January 2014; $823, AU-58, September 2015													
1834, Proof	6–8	4	65.0								$15,000	$21,000	$40,000
Auctions: $52,875, PF-60BN, January 2014													

1835, Large 8,
Large Stars,
Matron Head

1835, Small 8,
Small Stars,
Matron Head

Medium Letters
(1829–1837)

Small Letters
(1837–1839)

1835,
Matron
Head

1835, Head of 1836

1837
Note the plain
hair cords.

1837, Head of 1838
Note the slim bust
and the beaded hair cords.

1839, 1839 Over 1836
Note the closed 9 and
the plain hair cords.

1839, Silly Head
Note the prominent lock
of hair at the forehead.

1839, Booby Head
Note the shoulder tip. Also note the absence of a line under CENT.

	Mintage	Cert	Avg	%MS	G-4	VG-8	F-12	VF-20	EF-40	AU-50	MS-60BN / PF-63BN	MS-63BN / PF-64BN	MS-65BN / PF-65BN
1835, All kinds	3,878,400												
1835, Large 8 and Stars		12	52.8	42%	$25	$30	$35	$75	$225	$400	$750	$1,400	$2,100
Auctions: $16,450, MS-64BN, January 2013													
1835, Small 8 and Stars		49	46.6	29%	$25	$30	$35	$65	$175	$375	$475	$675	$1,750
Auctions: $3,819, MS-63BN, January 2014													
1835, Head of 1836		96	53.6	41%	$25	$30	$35	$55	$125	$250	$350	$550	$1,300
Auctions: $712, MS-62BN, August 2015; $646, AU-58, September 2015; $176, AU-50, October 2015; $106, AU-50, April 2015													
1836	2,111,000	241	51.7	45%	$25	$30	$35	$55	$125	$250	$350	$550	$1,300
Auctions: $881, MS-64BN, January 2015; $447, AU-58, September 2015; $259, AU-55, September 2015; $153, EF-45, August 2015													
1836, Proof	*6–8*	4	64.0								$15,000	$21,000	$40,000
Auctions: $47,000, PF-63RB, June 2014													
1837, All kinds	5,558,300												
1837, Plain Cord, Medium Letters		157	58.5	65%	$25	$30	$35	$55	$125	$250	$350	$550	$1,200
Auctions: $94, VF-35, February 2015													
1837, Plain Cord, Small Letters		27	53.5	48%	$25	$30	$35	$55	$125	$250	$375	$600	$1,500
Auctions: $411, AU-58, February 2014													
1837, Head of 1838		79	58.2	61%	$25	$30	$35	$45	$110	$200	$325	$500	$1,200
Auctions: $1,116, MS-64BN, January 2015; $646, MS-63BN, August 2015; $306, AU-58, August 2015; $235, AU-53, June 2015													
1837, Proof	*8–12*	7	64.0								$30,000		
Auctions: $27,025, PF-63BN, January 2014													
1838	6,370,200	918	54.5	55%	$25	$30	$35	$45	$120	$225	$335	$575	$1,325
Auctions: $1,028, MS-64BN, January 2015; $470, MS-63BN, January 2015; $223, AU-58, August 2015; $223, AU-55, May 2015													
1838, Proof	*10–20*	6	64.3								$14,000	$20,000	$38,000
Auctions: $64,625, PF-64RD, January 2014													
1839, All kinds	3,128,661												
1839, 1839 Over 1836, Plain Cords		59	13.8	0%	$400	$650	$1,450	$3,000	$8,000	$20,000	$65,000	$100,000	$250,000
Auctions: $5,581, VF-35, January 2014; $881, F-12, August 2016; $588, VG-10, September 2016; $529, VG-8, January 2015													
1839, Head of 1838, Beaded Cords		100	53.9	43%	$25	$30	$35	$50	$115	$225	$325	$550	$1,450
Auctions: $1,645, MS-64BN, September 2013; $176, EF-45, February 2015; $141, EF-45, July 2015; $143, VF-35, September 2015													
1839, Silly Head		135	50.9	46%	$25	$30	$35	$75	$200	$400	$850	$1,200	$2,700
Auctions: $12,925, MS-67BN, January 2014; $160, EF-40, July 2015													
1839, Booby Head		230	51.7	48%	$25	$30	$35	$60	$150	$300	$675	$1,100	$2,350
Auctions: $470, AU-53, August 2015; $329, EF-40, May 2015; $141, VF-35, June 2015; $123, VF-25, September 2015													

BRAIDED HAIR (1839–1857)

Designer: *Christian Gobrecht.* **Weight:** *168 grains (10.89 grams).*
Composition: *Copper.* **Diameter:** *27.5 mm.* **Edge:** *Plain.* **Mint:** *Philadelphia.*

Circulation Strike
1845; N-11.

Proof
1852; N-24.

History. Christian Gobrecht's Braided Hair design was introduced in 1839. It loosely followed the design he had created for the 1838 gold eagle. On issues of 1839 through part of 1843, Miss Liberty's portrait is tilted forward, with the left tip of her neck truncation over the 8 of the date. For most issues of 1843 and all later dates her head is larger and aligned in a more vertical position, and the tip of her neck is over the first digit of the date. The reverse lettering was made larger beginning in 1844. The net result is that cents after 1843 are less delicate in appearance than are those of earlier dates. These coins were made in large quantities, except for their final year. They remained in circulation in the United States until the late 1850s, not long enough to be worn down to very low grades. (Some circulated in the eastern part of Canada through the 1860s, accounting for many of the more worn examples seen today.)

Striking and Sharpness. Sharpness can vary. On the obverse, the star centers can be weak, especially for dates in the 1850s, and, less often, there can be lightness on the front of the coronet and the hair. On the reverse the leaves can be light, but most are well struck. The denticles can be mushy and indistinct on either side, this being particularly true of dates in the early and mid-1850s. Flaky or laminated planchets can be a problem, again among coins of the 1850s, in which tiny pieces of metal fall away from the surface, leaving areas in the field that interrupt the luster on MS coins.

Availability. All dates of Braided Hair cents are readily available, with the 1857 somewhat less so (it was minted in January 1857 in low quantity; seemingly not all were released). The delicate-featured issues of 1839 to 1843 are becoming more difficult to find in EF or finer grades without surface problems. Cents dated in the 1850s are usually seen in VF or higher grades. Certain die varieties attributed by Newcomb numbers can be scarce or rare. For issues in the 1850s the differences can be microscopic, thus limiting their numismatic appeal and making them unattributable unless in high grades. Hoards were found of some dates, particularly 1850 to 1856, making MS coins of these years more readily available than would otherwise be the case. MS-64RD or higher coins with *original* color range from scarce to very rare for dates prior to 1850, but those of the 1850s are seen regularly (except for 1857). Coins below VF-20 are not widely collected and, for many issues, are too worn to attribute by die variety.

GRADING STANDARDS

MS-60 to 70 (Mint State). *Obverse:* In the lower Mint State grades, MS–60 and 61, some slight abrasions can be seen on the portrait, most evidently on the cheek. Check the tip of the coronet and the hair above the ear, as well. Luster in the field is complete or nearly so. At MS-63, luster should be complete, and no abrasion evident. If there is weakness on the hair it is due to light striking, not to wear; this also applies for the stars. In

1840, Large Date; N-7. Graded MS-64BN.

higher levels, the luster is complete and deeper, and some original mint color may be seen. Mint frost on this type is usually deep, sometimes satiny, but hardly ever prooflike. MS-64 coins may have some slight discoloration or scattered contact marks. A well-graded MS-65 or higher coin will have full, rich luster; no marks visible except under magnification; and a nice blend of brown toning or nicely mixed (not stained or blotchy) mint color and natural brown toning. MS-64RD or higher coins with original color range from scarce to very rare for dates prior to 1850, but those of the 1850s are seen regularly (except for 1857). *Reverse:* In the lower Mint State grades some abrasion is seen on the higher areas of the leaves. Mint luster is complete in all Mint State ranges, as the open areas are protected by the lettering and wreath. The quality of the luster is the best way to grade both sides of this type.

Illustrated coin: This coin is a light, golden olive with faint tints of pale green in places, with scattered red spotting on both the obverse and reverse. About half of the stars show their centers, but all of the stars are soft.

AU-50, 53, 55, 58 (About Uncirculated). *Obverse:* Wear is evident on the cheek, the hair above the ear, and the tip of the coronet. Friction is evident in the field. At AU-58, luster may be present except in the center of the fields. As the grade goes down to AU-50, wear becomes more evident on the cheek. Wear is seen on the stars, but is not as easy to discern as it is elsewhere and, in any event, many stars are weakly struck. At AU-50 there

1840, Large Date; N-8. Graded AU-58.

will be either no luster or only traces of luster close to the letters and devices. *Reverse:* Wear is most evident on the highest areas of the leaves and the ribbon bow. Luster is present in the fields. As grade goes down from AU–58 to 50, wear increases and luster decreases. At AU-50 there will be either no luster or just traces close to the letters and devices.

EF-40, 45 (Extremely Fine). *Obverse:* Wear is more extensive on the portrait, including the cheek, the hair above the ear, and the coronet. The star centers are worn down slightly (if they were sharply struck to begin with). Traces of luster are minimal, if at all existent. *Reverse:* The centers of the leaves are well worn, with detail visible only near the edges of the leaves and nearby, with the higher parts worn flat. Letters show significant wear. Luster, if present, is minimal.

1842, Large Date; N-6. Graded EF-45.

VF-20, 30 (Very Fine). *Obverse:* Wear is more extensive than on the preceding. Some of the strands of hair are fused together at the top of the head, above the ear, and on the shoulder. The center radials of the stars are nearly completely worn away. *Reverse:* The leaves show more extensive wear. Details are visible at the leaves' edges only minimally and not on all the leaves. The lettering shows smooth, even wear.

1842, Large Date; N-6. Graded VF-30.

F-12, 15 (Fine). *Obverse:* About two-thirds of the hair detail is visible. Extensive wear is seen below the coronet. On the coronet the beginning of the word LIBERTY shows wear, with L sometimes only partially visible. The hair behind the neck is flat. The stars are flat. *Reverse:* The leaves show more wear and are flat except for the lower areas. The ribbon has very little detail.

The Braided Hair large cent is seldom collected in grades lower than F-12.

1839, 9 Over 6; N-1. Graded F-12.

PF-60 to 70 (Proof). Except for the Proof 1841 cent, Proof Braided Hair cents before 1855 range from rare to very rare. Those from 1855 to 1857 are seen with some frequency. Most later Proofs are well struck and of nice quality, but there are exceptions. Most pieces from this era that have been attributed as Proofs really are such, but beware of deeply toned "Proofs" that are actually prooflike, or circulation strikes with polished fields, and

1841, Small Date; N-1. Graded PF-64RB.

recolored. *Obverse and Reverse:* Superb gems PF–65 and 66 show hairlines only under high magnification, and at PF-67 none are seen. The fields usually are deeply mirrorlike on issues after 1843, sometimes less so on earlier dates of this type. Striking should be sharp, including the stars (unlike the situation for many Proofs of the Matron Head type). There is no evidence of friction. In lower grades, hairlines are more numerous, with a profusion of them at the PF–60 to 62 levels, and there is also a general dullness of the fields. Typical color for an undipped coin ranges from light or iridescent brown to brown with some traces of mint color. Except for issues after 1854, Proofs are nearly always BN or, less often, RB. Prooflike pieces are sometimes offered as Proofs. Beware deeply toned "Proofs" and those that do not have full mirrorlike fields.

Illustrated coin: Early Proofs from this period are scarce to extremely rare. This example retains some mint orange in protected areas, as well as exhibiting hints of lilac and electric blue on the obverse.

Small Letters (1839–1843)

Large Letters (1843–1857)

1840, Large Date

1840, Small Date

1840, Small Date
Over Large 18

1842, Small Date

1842, Large Date

	Mintage	Cert	Avg	%MS	G-4	VG-8	F-12	VF-20	EF-40	AU-50	MS-60BN	MS-63BN	MS-65BN
											PF-63BN	PF-64BN	PF-65BN
1839	(a)	84	52.1	49%	$25	$30	$35	$50	$110	$265	$400	$650	$2,250 (b)
	Auctions: $17,625, MS-65RB, January 2014; $1,293, MS-63BN, January 2015; $176, EF-40, May 2015												
1840, All kinds	2,462,700												
1840, Large Date		99	55.7	49%	$25	$30	$35	$40	$85	$200	$300	$500	$1,200
	Auctions: $14,100, MS-64RD, January 2013												
1840, Small Date		50	55.9	50%	$25	$30	$35	$40	$85	$200	$300	$500	$1,200
	Auctions: $541, MS-61BN, August 2015; $259, MS-60, October 2015; $400, AU-58, February 2015												
1840, Small Date Over Large 18		10	43.4	30%	$25	$30	$35	$50	$200	$400	$900	$1,600	$2,350
	Auctions: $16,100, MS-65RB, September 2011												
1840, Proof	15–20	7	64.1								$7,000	$10,500	$20,000
	Auctions: $14,100, PF-63RB, January 2014												
1841, Small Date	1,597,367	158	52.7	46%	$25	$30	$35	$50	$125	$250	$450	$950	$1,650 (c)
	Auctions: $4,113, MS-66BN, June 2014												
1841, Proof	30–50	20	64.3								$6,000	$9,500	$18,500
	Auctions: $21,150, PF-65RB, August 2013												
1842, All kinds	2,383,390												
1842, Small Date		51	52.1	43%	$25	$30	$35	$40	$90	$220	$375	$650	$2,200 (d)
	Auctions: $23,500, MS-64RD, January 2014												
1842, Large Date		145	50.1	42%	$25	$30	$35	$40	$85	$150	$300	$500	$1,800 (c)
	Auctions: $1,175, MS-63BN, August 2015; $881, MS-63BN, June 2015; $259, AU-55, April 2015; $188, AU-55, June 2015												
1842, Proof	10–20	5	64.2								$7,000	$11,000	$20,000
	Auctions: $14,100, PF-64BN, January 2014												

a. Included in 1839, All kinds, mintage figure on page 216. b. Value in MS-65RB is $4,500. c. Value in MS-65RB is $3,000. d. Value in MS-65RB is $4,000.

1844, 44 Over 81

Head of 1840
("Petite Head," 1839–1843)

Head of 1844
("Mature Head," 1843–1857)

1847, 7 Over "Small 7"

1846, Small Date
*Note the squat date
and the closed 6.*

1846, Medium Date
*Note the medium date
height and the ball-top 6.*

1846, Tall Date
*Note the vertically
stretched date and
the open-mouthed 6.*

1851, 51 Over 81
*These are not true
overdates, but are three
of the more spectacular
of several date-punch
blunders of the 1844–
1854 period. The so-called
overdates of 1844 and
1851 each have the date
punched upside down,
then corrected normally.*

1855, Upright 5's

1855, Slanting 5's

1855, Knob on Ear

	Mintage	Cert	Avg	%MS	G-4	VG-8	F-12	VF-20	EF-40	AU-50	MS-60BN PF-63BN	MS-63BN PF-64BN	MS-65BN PF-65BN
1843, All kinds	2,425,342												
1843, Petite Head, Small Letters		176	54.6	58%	$25	$30	$35	$40	$85	$160	$300	$450	$1,750
	Auctions: $1,293, MS-63BN, January 2015; $588, MS-63BN, August 2015; $494, AU-58, August 2015; $376, AU-58, August 2015												
1843, Petite Head, Large Letters		61	53.2	49%	$25	$35	$45	$100	$250	$320	$825	$1,500	$2,300
	Auctions: $4,406, MS-64BN, January 2014												
1843, Mature Head, Large Letters		53	46.7	34%	$25	$30	$35	$45	$150	$275	$550	$900	$2,100
	Auctions: $9,988, MS-64RB, January 2014												
1843, Proof	*10–20*	9	64.4								$7,000	$11,000	$20,000
	Auctions: $25,850, PF-66RB, June 2014												
1844, Normal Date	2,398,752	218	51.7	44%	$25	$30	$35	$40	$85	$160	$300	$500	$1,500
	Auctions: $8,225, MS-65BN, January 2014; $940, MS-62BN, June 2015; $141, AU-53, January 2015												
1844, 44 Over 81	(e)	39	43.7	26%	$35	$40	$60	$120	$250	$550	$1,200	$2,750	$5,500
	Auctions: $1,175, MS-60BN, January 2014; $705, AU-50, September 2016; $212, VF-25, August 2015												
1844, Proof	*10–20*	7	64.6								$13,000	$20,000	$30,000
	Auctions: $55,813, PF-65RD, January 2014; $31,725, PF-64, May 2015												
1845	3,894,804	360	53.5	54%	$25	$30	$35	$40	$75	$135	$225	$375	$1,200
	Auctions: $881, MS-64BN, January 2015; $423, MS-63BN, March 2015; $353, MS-62BN, May 2015; $176, AU-53, January 2015												
1845, Proof	*8–12*	5	63.8								$8,000	$15,000	$25,000
	Auctions: $16,450, PF-64BN, April 2013												

e. Included in 1844, Normal Date, mintage figure.

	Mintage	Cert	Avg	%MS	G-4	VG-8	F-12	VF-20	EF-40	AU-50	MS-60BN	MS-63BN	MS-65BN
											PF-63BN	PF-64BN	PF-65BN
1846, All kinds	4,120,800												
1846, Small Date		310	52.7	55%	$25	$30	$35	$40	$75	$135	$225	$350	$1,200
Auctions: $494, MS-64BN, February 2015; $329, MS-62BN, February 2015; $129, AU-53, February 2015; $119, AU-50, April 2015													
1846, Medium Date		37	56.5	59%	$25	$30	$35	$40	$85	$150	$250	$400	$1,350
Auctions: $705, MS-61BN, March 2013													
1846, Tall Date		65	46.4	38%	$25	$35	$35	$50	$150	$250	$650	$1,000	$2,000
Auctions: $56, VF-30, September 2011													
1846, Proof	8–12	2	66.0								$8,000	$15,000	$25,000
Auctions: $30,550, PF-65BN, June 2014													
1847	6,183,669	779	56.0	59%	$25	$30	$35	$40	$75	$135	$225	$350	$1,250
Auctions: $646, MS-64BN, August 2015; $881, MS-63BN, August 2015; $188, MS-62BN, June 2015; $223, MS-61BN, September 2015													
1847, 7 Over "Small 7"	(f)	38	50.4	42%	$30	$40	$45	$75	$175	$420	$1,000	$1,350	$2,750
Auctions: $9,694, MS-65BN, January 2014													
1847, Proof	8–12	1	64.0								$8,000	$15,000	$25,000
Auctions: $31,050, PF-65RB, February 2011													
1848	6,415,799	817	54.8	54%	$25	$30	$35	$40	$75	$130	$225	$350	$925
Auctions: $1,175, MS-65BN, January 2015; $223, MS-62BN, January 2015; $259, AU-58, January 2015; $129, AU-55, October 2015													
1848, Proof	15–20	10	64.6								$10,000	$15,000	$25,000
Auctions: $14,100, PF-64BN, August 2013													
1849	4,178,500	454	54.6	52%	$25	$30	$35	$40	$85	$150	$250	$450	$1,200
Auctions: $317, MS-62, March 2015; $259, AU-58, October 2015; $353, AU-50, July 2015; $84, EF-40, May 2015													
1849, Proof	6–10	2	64.0								$8,500	$16,000	$25,000
Auctions: $23,500, PF-65RB, August 2013													
1850	4,426,844	1,035	59.1	74%	$25	$30	$35	$40	$65	$125	$180	$230	$650 (g)
Auctions: $1,058, MS-65BN, January 2015; $376, MS-64BN, January 2015; $286, MS-63BN, February 2015; $259, AU-58, June 2015													
1850, Proof	6–10	3	65.0								$10,000	$17,000	$28,000
Auctions: $19,550, PF-64RB, February 2011													
1851, Normal Date	9,889,707	1,495	57.6	65%	$25	$30	$35	$40	$65	$125	$180	$230	$650 (g)
Auctions: $1,058, MS-65BN, August 2015; $411, MS-64BN, May 2015; $306, MS-64BN, October 2015; $100, AU-50, April 2015													
1851, 51 Over 81	(h)	93	57.3	66%	$30	$35	$45	$65	$200	$250	$500	$1,000	$2,400
Auctions: $1,763, MS-65BN, June 2014; $329, AU-55, May 2015													
1852	5,063,094	1,382	59.3	71%	$25	$30	$35	$40	$65	$125	$180	$230	$635 (i)
Auctions: $881, MS-65BN, October 2015; $764, MS-65BN, January 2015; $353, MS-64BN, January 2015; $129, AU-55, February 2015													
1852, Proof	4–6	1	65.0								$10,000	$35,000	$65,000
Auctions: $47,150, PF-64BN, February 2011; $9,528, PF-64, November 2016; $12,925, PF-62, March 2016													
1853	6,641,131	2,191	59.1	70%	$25	$30	$35	$40	$65	$125	$180	$230	$635 (i)
Auctions: $2,115, MS-65RD, January 2015; $588, MS-64RB, January 2015; $235, MS-63BN, January 2015; $212, MS-62BN, June 2015													
1854	4,236,156	1,204	57.5	62%	$25	$30	$35	$40	$65	$125	$180	$230	$650 (g)
Auctions: $360, MS-64BN, October 2015; $282, MS-63BN, May 2015; $212, MS-62BN, January 2015; $141, AU-58, January 2015													
1854, Proof	4–6	5	64.6								$8,500	$10,000	$15,000
Auctions: $28,200, PF-65RB, June 2014													
1855, All kinds	1,574,829												
1855, Upright 5's		424	57.1	59%	$25	$30	$35	$40	$65	$125	$180	$230	$635 (i)
Auctions: $1,116, MS-65RB, January 2015; $400, MS-64BN, June 2015; $282, MS-63BN, July 2015; $200, MS-62BN, January 2015													
1855, Slanting 5's		118	57.6	58%	$25	$30	$35	$45	$65	$130	$200	$275	$1,250 (j)
Auctions: $353, MS-62BN, November 2015; $200, MS-61BN, June 2015; $141, MS-60, January 2015; $153, AU-53, June 2015													
1855, Slanting 5's, Knob on Ear		149	56.0	45%	$30	$35	$45	$55	$110	$225	$360	$525	$2,150
Auctions: $259, AU-50, July 2015; $153, EF-45, September 2015; $100, EF-40, August 2015													
1855, Proof	15–20	10	64.5								$5,500	$7,000	$10,000
Auctions: $8,050, PF-64RB August 2011													

f. Included in 1847 mintage figure. g. Value in MS-65RB is $1,200. h. Included in 1851, Normal Date, mintage figure. i. Value in MS-65RB is $1,150. j. Value in MS-65RB is $2,000.

1856, Upright 5	1856, Slanting 5	1857, Large Date	1857, Small Date

	Mintage	Cert	Avg	%MS	G-4	VG-8	F-12	VF-20	EF-40	AU-50	MS-60BN / PF-63BN	MS-63BN / PF-64BN	MS-65BN / PF-65BN
1856, All kinds	2,690,463												
1856, Upright 5		270	58.2	61%	$25	$30	$35	$40	$65	$130	$200	$270	$675 **(g)**
Auctions: $725, MS-65BN, January 2015; $705, MS-64RB, January 2015; $482, MS-64BN, January 2015; $165, AU-58, September 2015													
1856, Slanting 5		408	56.1	55%	$25	$30	$35	$40	$65	$130	$200	$270	$675 **(g)**
Auctions: $999, MS-66BN, June 2015; $764, MS-65BN, February 2015; $259, MS-63BN, February 2015; $223, MS-62BN, February 2015													
1856, Proof	*40–60*	20	64.7								$5,000	$7,000	$10,000
Auctions: $25,850, PF-66RB, November 2013													
1857, All kinds	333,546												
1857, Large Date		642	56.9	57%	$60	$80	$100	$125	$200	$300	$400	$750	$1,200
Auctions: $823, MS-64BN, January 2015; $558, MS-62, March 2015; $141, AU-50, July 2015; $223, EF-45, October 2015													
1857, Small Date		258	54.5	41%	$65	$85	$110	$135	$200	$310	$500	$850	$1,500
Auctions: $940, MS-64BN, January 2015; $646, MS-63BN, August 2015; $494, MS-62BN, January 2015; $353, AU-55, September 2015													
1857, Large Date, Proof	*100–150*	33	64.5								$5,000	$7,000	$12,500
Auctions: No auction records available.													
1857, Small Date, Proof	*15–20*	8	65.1								$6,000	$8,000	$13,000
Auctions: $52,875, PF-65RD, April 2014													

Note: Numismatic anachronisms dated 1868 were struck in nickel and in copper, featuring the large cent design last used in 1857. These likely were quietly and unofficially sold by Mint employees to collectors. They are classified as Judd-610 and 611 in United States Pattern Coins. **g.** *Value in MS-65RB is $1,200.*

THE PASSING OF THE LARGE CENT AND HALF CENT

By 1857 the U.S. Mint's costs for manufacturing and distributing its half cents and large cents had risen so high that Mint Director James Ross Snowden reported that the copper coins "barely paid expenses." Both denominations had become unpopular, and they rarely circulated outside the nation's larger cities. With this pressure, change was on the horizon. The Treasury Department had recent precedent to tinker with coinage sizes and compositions. For several years in the early 1850s the Mint had issued silver coins of reduced weight, as a way to discourage their melting and export (the coins' silver content had been greater than their face values). On the heels of this coinage reform, new legislation in 1857 replaced the large copper cent with a smaller copper-nickel coin of the same value, and terminated the half cent outright.

The coinage legislation of 1857 brought important benefits to the United States. Under its terms, Spanish coins were redeemed for melting at the Mint and exchanged for the new, small cents. The old-fashioned reckoning of business transactions in Spanish *reales* and *medios*, British shillings, and other currencies was (officially, at least) abandoned, and the American decimal system was popularized. Citizens found the new small cent to be convenient, and it quickly became a favored and useful means of retail trade. Tens of millions would be minted before the decade closed.

The hobby of coin collecting experienced a boom when the large cent and half cent passed away. Casual observers set aside the obsolete coins as mementoes of a time gone by, while more experienced collectors sought to assemble collections composed of one of each date. Over the ensuing decades the study and collecting of these old coppers has become more and more specialized while still attracting hobby newcomers. Their devoted enthusiasts appreciate the coins' historical connections and cultural significance.

Small Cents
1856 to Date
AN OVERVIEW OF SMALL CENTS

On May 25, 1857, the U.S. Mint debuted its new small-diameter Flying Eagle cent. Designed by Chief Engraver James B. Longacre, the obverse featured a flying eagle, copied after Christian Gobrecht's silver dollar of 1836. The reverse showed an agricultural wreath enclosing the denomination. Problems developed with striking the pieces up properly, and in 1859 a new type, the Indian Head cent, was introduced. With several variations this design was continued through 1909. In that year the Lincoln cent with Wheat Ears reverse was introduced. The series was continued for many years, until 1959, when the Memorial Reverse type was introduced, continuing the same Lincoln portrait on the obverse. Then in 2009 four different reverses were introduced to commemorate the 200th anniversary of the birth of Abraham Lincoln. In 2010 a new reverse symbolized President Lincoln's preservation of the Union.

Forming a type set of small cents is done easily enough, although the first two issues, the 1857 and 1858 Flying Eagles, as well as the 1859 Indian Head with laurel wreath reverse, can be expensive in higher grades. Striking quality is a consideration for all small cents from 1857 to the end of the Indian Head series in 1909, but enough exist that finding a needle-sharp piece is simply a matter of time. Lincoln cents are easy enough to find sharply struck, though some varieties are more difficult to find this way than others.

FOR THE COLLECTOR AND INVESTOR: SMALL CENTS AS A SPECIALTY

Flying Eagle and Indian Head cents often are collected together by specialists, who usually aspire to add the pattern 1856 Flying Eagle to the series. Proof Flying Eagle and Indian Head cents form a separate specialty and are widely collected. The Flying Eagle and Indian Cent Collectors Society (www.fly-inclub.org) welcomes aficionados of these series. Its journal, *Longacre's Ledger*, serves as a forum for new discoveries, market information, and the exchange of ideas and research.

One of the foundations of modern American numismatics is the collecting of Lincoln cents, 1909 to date. Collectors have a wide variety of folders, albums, and holders to choose from; these have a tradition dating back to the

This 1857 pattern small cent (J-186) features a proposed head of Liberty, similar to the design that would eventually be used on the nation's nickel three-cent pieces.

1930s, when R.K. Post of Neenah, Wisconsin, launched his "penny boards" (made for him by Whitman Publishing Co., which later acquired the rights), and Wayte Raymond marketed a series of "National" album pages. Today, a search through pocket change might yield coins dating back to 1959, the first year of the Lincoln Memorial reverse, before which date even high-mintage issues are hardly ever seen. A generation ago it was possible to find cents from 1909 onward. However, key issues such as 1909-S V.D.B. (the most famous of all "popular rarities" in the U.S. series), 1914-D, 1924-D, 1926-S, 1931-S, and 1955 Doubled Die Obverse eluded most enthusiasts.

Lincoln cents can be collected casually, or a specialty can be made of them. A dedicated enthusiast may want to secure one each in a grade such as MS-65, also taking care that each is sharply struck. There are quite a few issues, including Denver and San Francisco varieties from about 1916 to the late 1920s, that are plentiful *except* if sharply struck (with full hair detail on the Lincoln portrait, no tiny marks on Lincoln's shoulder, and sharp details and a smooth field on the reverse). Die-variety specialists have dozens of popular doubled dies, overmintmarks, and other varieties to hunt down, using the *Cherrypickers' Guide* as their standard reference. With the Mint's rollout of four new reverse designs in 2009, and another in 2010, the Lincoln cent promises to intrigue another generation of Americans and continue to bring new collectors to the hobby.

FLYING EAGLE (1856–1858)

Designer: *James B. Longacre.* **Weight:** *4.67 grams.* **Composition:** *.880 copper, .120 nickel.*
Diameter: *19 mm.* **Edge:** *Plain.* **Mint:** *Philadelphia.*

Circulation Strike   **Proof**

History. The nation's large copper cents became increasingly expensive to produce, leading the U.S. Mint to experiment with smaller versions during the 1850s. Finally a new design and format were chosen: the Flying Eagle cent, of smaller diameter and 4.67 grams' weight (compared to nearly 11). Many patterns were made of this design in 1856 (for distribution to interested congressmen), and later restrikes (bearing that same date) were extensive, with the result that many numismatists collect the 1856 cent along with the regular series. Distribution of the new 1857 Flying Eagle cents for circulation commenced on May 25 of that year. Problems resulted from striking the design properly, and the motif was discontinued in 1858. Although attempts were made to create a modified, thinner eagle, the unattractive results were scrapped in favor of an entirely new design. The coins remained in circulation until the early 1900s, by which time any found in pocket change were well worn.

Striking and Sharpness. The heavy wreath on the reverse was opposite in the dies (while in the press) from the head and tail of the eagle on the obverse, and, accordingly, many Flying Eagle cents were weakly struck in these areas. Today, this lightness of strike is most visible at each end of the eagle and on the wreath, particularly the higher areas, and on the vertical separation at the middle of the ribbon knot. Striking weakness is most obvious (especially for novice collectors) on the eagle's tail feathers. Many Flying Eagle cents, however, are quite well struck. A first-class Proof should have a fully and deeply mirrored field on both sides, except for those of 1856, which are usually a combination of mirror-like and grainy in character.

Availability. As a type the Flying Eagle cent is easy to find, although some varieties, such as 1856 and 1858, 8 Over 7, range from scarce to rare. Most are seen in worn grades. In MS, many are in the marketplace, although dipping, cleaning, and recoloring (causing staining and spotting) have eliminated the majority from consideration by connoisseurs. Proof Flying Eagle cents dated 1856 are plentiful, surviving from the quantity of perhaps 2,000 to 2,500 or more restruck in 1859 and later. (Today's collectors do not distinguish, price-wise, between the 1856 originals and restrikes dated 1856.) Proofs of 1857 are very rare. Proofs of 1858 are rare, but are significantly more readily available than for 1857. Some prooflike Mint State coins have been called Proofs. Quality is a challenge for Proofs, and problem-free examples are in the minority.

GRADING STANDARDS

Caveat: These grading standards do not take sharpness of strike into account.

MS-60 to 70 (Mint State). *Obverse:* Contact marks, most obvious in the field, are evident at MS-60, diminishing at MS–61, 62, and higher. The eagle, the feathers of which usually hide marks, shows some evidence of contact as well. At Gem MS-65 or finer there is no trace of friction or rubbing. A few tiny nicks or marks may be seen, but none are obvious. At MS-67 and higher levels the coin will approach perfection. A theoretically perfect MS-70 will

1858; Snow-11. Graded MS-64.

have no marks at all evident, even under a strong magnifier. Although in practice this is not always consistent, at MS-66 and higher there should be no staining or other problems, and the coin should have good eye appeal overall. *Reverse:* Check the higher parts of the wreath for slight abrasions at MS–60 to 62. Otherwise, the above guidelines apply.

   Illustrated coin: The surfaces display a healthy satin luster, as well as an iridescent rose and golden-tan patina. The coin is sharply and evenly struck and offers razor-sharp definition.

AU-50, 53, 55, 58 (About Uncirculated). *Obverse:* At AU-50, light wear is seen on the breast of the eagle, the top edge of the closest wing, and, less so, on the head. As both the head and tail tip can be lightly struck, these are not reliable indicators of grade. Luster is present in traces among the letters. At higher About Uncirculated levels the evidence of wear diminishes. An AU-58 coin will have nearly full luster, but friction is seen in the fields, as

1858. Graded AU-53.

are some marks. *Reverse:* At AU-50, light wear is seen on the ribbon bow and the highest areas of the leaves. Some luster is seen (more than on the obverse). Friction is evident, as are some marks, but these will not be as distracting as those on the obverse, as the heavy wreath and lettering are more protective of the reverse field. In higher grades, wear is less, and at AU-58 nearly full luster—or even completely full luster—is seen.

   Illustrated coin: The reverse features a large rim cud.

EF-40, 45 (Extremely Fine). *Obverse:* Wear is more extensive, especially on the eagle's breast and the top of the closest wing. Wear will also show on the other wing in the area below OF. Marks may be more extensive in the field. The wear is slightly greater at EF-40 than at EF-45, although in the marketplace these two grades are not clearly differentiated. *Reverse:* More wear shows on the higher areas of the wreath, but most detail will still be present.

1858, Small Letters. Graded EF-40.

There may be tinges of luster in protected areas, more likely at EF-45 than at EF-40.

VF-20, 30 (Very Fine). *Obverse:* Wear is appreciable, with the breast feathers gone over a larger area and with more wear on the wings. The tail shows significant wear, negating the question as to whether it was well struck originally. Marks are more extensive, although across all grades the durable copper-nickel metal resisted heavy marks and cuts; any such should be separately described. Staining and spotting, not related to grade, is

1858, Small Letters. Graded VF-20.

common. Cherrypicking (examining multiple coins, all slabbed at the same grade level, and selecting the finest of them) at this and lower grades will yield nice coins in any given category. *Reverse:* The wreath is worn flat in the higher and medium–relief areas, although some detail is seen in the lower areas close to the field. ONE / CENT may be slightly weak, depending on the quality of the original strike. Marks are fewer than on the obverse.

F-12, 15 (Fine). *Obverse:* The eagle shows extensive wear, with about half of the feathers gone. Some detail is still seen, especially on the underside of the closest wing, above the breast. *Reverse:* Wear is even more extensive, with the wreath nearing flatness, but still with some detail in the lower areas.

1857. Graded F-12.

VG-8, 10 (Very Good). *Obverse:* On the obverse the eagle is clear in outline form, but only a small number of feathers can be discerned, mostly above the breast. Letters and the date show extensive wear but are complete and clear. *Reverse:* The wreath is now mostly an outline, although some lower-relief features can be differentiated. ONE / CENT may be weak (depending on the strike).

1858, Small Letters. Graded VG-10.

G-4, 6 (Good). *Obverse:* The eagle is nearly completely flat, with just a few feathers, if any, discernible. The rim is worn down, making the outer parts of the letters and the lower part of the date slightly weak, but all are readable. *Reverse:* The wreath is basically in outline form, with hardly any detail. ONE / CENT is weak, usually with CENT weakest. The rim is worn down.

1857. Graded G-4.

AG-3 (About Good). *Obverse:* Wear is extensive, but most of the eagle is visible in outline form. The letters are mostly worn away, with vestiges remaining here and there. The date is partially worn away at the bottom, but is distinct and readable. *Reverse:* The wreath is so worn that it cannot be distinguished from the field in areas, usually toward the top. ONE / CENT is mostly gone, but much of CENT can be discerned (unless the coin was a weak strike to begin with).

1857. Graded AG-3.

PF-60 to 70 (Proof). *Obverse and Reverse:* Gem PF-65 coins have very few hairlines, and these are visible only under a strong magnifying glass. At the PF-67 level or higher there should be no evidence of hairlines or friction at all. PF-60 coins can be dull from repeated dipping and cleaning (remember, hairlines on any Proof were caused by cleaning with an abrasive agent; they had no hairlines when struck). At PF-63 the mirrorlike fields should

1858, Large Letters. Graded PF-65.

be attractive, and hairlines should be minimal, best seen when the coin is held at an angle to the light. No rubbing is seen. PF-64 coins are even nicer.

    Illustrated coin: The fields of this coin are highly reflective for a nickel-alloy Proof cent.

1857, Reverse 25¢ Clash
FS-01-1857-901.

1857, Obverse $20 Clash
FS-01-1857-403.

1858, Large Letters

1858, Small Letters

1858, 8 Over 7
FS-01-1858-301.

	Mintage	Cert	Avg	%MS	G-4	VG-8	F-12	VF-20	EF-40	AU-50	MS-60BN / PF-60	MS-63BN / PF-63BN	MS-65 / PF-65BN
1856 † (a)	*2,000*	0	n/a		$7,000	$7,750	$9,500	$11,000	$13,000	$13,500	$16,000	$20,000	$65,000
Auctions: $32,900, MS-64, April 2013													
1856, Proof	*1,500*	425	58.2								$14,000	$18,500	$27,000
Auctions: $38,188, PF-65, January 2014; $14,100, PF-63, August 2014; $8,813, PF-62, October 2014													
1857	*17,450,000*	3,775	52.1	58%	$30	$40	$50	$60	$150	$215	$380	$950	$3,500
Auctions: $21,150, MS-66, June 2014; $4,113, MS-65, November 2014; $2,468, MS-64+, November 2014; $2,350, MS-64, July 2014													
1857, Obverse 50¢ Clash (b)	(c)	127	33.6	24%					$230	$450	$800	$1,250	
Auctions: $3,525, MS-65, October 2014; $5,816, MS-65, October 2013													
1857, Reverse 25¢ Clash (d)	(c)	40	45.3	35%					$250	$500	$1,000	$2,750	
Auctions: $223, EF-40, July 2014													
1857, Obverse $20 Clash (e)	(c)	21	18.4	0%					$2,500	$6,000	$20,000		
Auctions: $242, F-12, March 2011													
1857, Proof	*100*	35	63.9								$5,000	$8,000	$23,500
Auctions: $34,075, PF-65, October 2014; $8,813, PF-64, October 2014; $34,075, PF, January 2013													
1858, All kinds	24,600,000												
1858, Large Letters		1,692	47.5	47%	$30	$40	$50	$60	$150	$215	$400	$1,000	$3,750
Auctions: $9,988, MS-66, October 2014; $17,625, MS-66, June 2013; $3,290, MS-65, November 2014; $1,645, MS-64, October 2014													
1858, 8 Over 7 (f)		180	52.7	51%	$75	$100	$200	$400	$850	$1,500	$3,650	$11,000	$50,000
Auctions: $74,025, MS-65, October 2014; $764, AU-55, July 2014; $940, AU-50, January 2015													
1858, Small Letters		1,909	46.1	40%	$30	$40	$50	$60	$150	$250	$500	$1,150	$3,750
Auctions: $24,675, MS-66, October 2014; $16,450, MS-66, August 2013; $3,525, MS-65, August 2014; $2,233, MS-64, November 2014													
1858, Large Letters, Proof	*100*	36	64.7								$5,000	$8,000	$23,500
Auctions: $20,563, PF-65, October 2014; $8,225, PF-64, October 2014; $28,200, PF, January 2013													
1858, Small Letters, Proof	*200*	25	64.2								$5,000	$8,000	$23,500
Auctions: $32,900, PF-66, January 2014; $14,100, PF-64, October 2014; $7,638, PF-64, October 2014													

† Ranked in the *100 Greatest U.S. Coins* (fourth edition). **a.** Actually a pattern, but collected along with the regular issue since it shares the same design. See *United States Pattern Coins*, tenth edition. **b.** The obverse die was clashed with the obverse die of a Liberty Seated half dollar. This is most evident through AMERICA. **c.** Included in circulation-strike 1857 mintage figure. **d.** The reverse die was clashed with the reverse die of a Liberty Seated quarter dollar. The outline of the eagle's head is evident above ONE. **e.** The obverse die was clashed with the obverse die of a Liberty Head double eagle. **f.** The flag of the upper-right corner of a 7 can be seen above the second 8 in the date. There is a raised triangular dot in the field above the first 8. Late-die-state specimens are worth considerably less than the values listed, which are for early die states.

INDIAN HEAD (1859–1909)

Variety 1 (Copper-Nickel, Laurel Wreath Reverse, 1859):
Designer: *James B. Longacre.* **Weight:** *4.67 grams.* **Composition:** *.880 copper, .120 nickel.*
Diameter: *19 mm.* **Edge:** *Plain.* **Mint:** *Philadelphia.*

Copper-Nickel,
Laurel Wreath Reverse,
Without Shield (1859)

Copper-Nickel,
Laurel Wreath Reverse,
Without Shield, Proof

Variety 2 (Copper-Nickel, Oak Wreath With Shield, 1860–1864):
Designer: *James B. Longacre.* **Weight:** *4.67 grams.* **Composition:** *.880 copper, .120 nickel.*
Diameter: *19 mm.* **Edge:** *Plain.* **Mint:** *Philadelphia.*

Copper-Nickel,
Oak Wreath Reverse,
With Shield (1860–1864)

Copper-Nickel,
Oak Wreath Reverse,
With Shield, Proof

Variety 3 (Bronze, 1864–1909): **Designer:** *James B. Longacre.*
Weight: *3.11 grams.* **Composition:** *.950 copper, .050 tin and zinc.*
Diameter: *19 mm.* **Edge:** *Plain.* **Mints:** *Philadelphia and San Francisco.*

Bronze, Oak Wreath Reverse,
With Shield (1864–1909)

Bronze, Oak Wreath Reverse,
With Shield, Proof

History. After nearly a dozen varieties of patterns were made in 1858, in 1859 the Indian Head was adopted as the new motif for the cent. Observers of the time noted the incongruity of placing a Native American war bonnet on a bust which was meant to be both female and classically Greek; designer James B. Longacre's earlier use of a feathered tiara on the Indian Head three-dollar gold piece had been viewed as less strange. The reverse of the 1859 coin illustrates an olive (or laurel) wreath. In 1860 this was changed to a wreath of oak and other leaves with a shield at the apex, a design continued through the end of the series in 1909. From 1859 through spring 1864 cents were struck in copper-nickel, the alloy used earlier for Flying Eagle cents. In 1864 a new bronze alloy was adopted.

Indian Head cents remained in circulation through the 1940s, but by the early 1950s were rarely seen. In the 1930s, when Whitman and other coin boards and folders became widely available, collectors picked many key dates out of circulation. The typical grade for the scarce issues of the 1870s was Good or so, and the 1908-S and 1909-S could be found in VF.

Striking and Sharpness. The strike on Indian Head cents can vary widely. On the obverse the points to check include the details at the tips of the feathers and the diamonds on the ribbon. The diamonds *cannot* be used as a grading marker, and the feather tips can be used only if you have familiarity with how sharp the coin was struck to begin with. In general, the reverse is usually sharper, but check the leaf and shield details. On many bronze cents beginning in the 1870s the bottom of the N of ONE and the tops of the EN of CENT are light, as they were in the dies (this is not factored when grading). Check the denticles on both sides. Generally, copper-nickel cents of the early 1860s are candidates for light striking as are later issues in the bronze format, of the 1890s onward.

Availability. In worn grades Indian Head cents are available in proportion to their mintages, in combination with survival rates being higher for the later issues. (The low-mintage 1909-S was saved in larger quantities than the higher-mintage 1877, as an example.) MS coins survive as a matter of chance, with those of 1878 and before being much scarcer than those of 1879 and later, and some of the 1900s being readily available. Many if not most higher-grade MS coins have been dipped or recolored, unless they are a warm orange-red color with traces of natural brown. The search for quality among bronze cents is particularly challenging. Some tiny toning flecks are to be expected on many coins, and as long as they are microscopic they can often be ignored (except in grades on the far side of MS-65). A set of MS-65 coins in RB or RD can be formed quickly, but a collection with *original* color, sharp strike, and excellent eye appeal may take several years.

During the years these coins were in production, collectors who wanted single pieces each year often bought Proofs. In the late 1930s, many 1878–1909 Proof Indian Head cents began to be released from several estate hoards. These had vivid violet and blue iridescent toning from being stored for decades in tissue paper. They are highly sought-after today.

Proofs. Proof Indian Head cents were made of all dates 1859 to 1909. The 1864 bronze variety with a tiny L (for designer James B. Longacre) on the ribbon is a rarity, with only about two dozen known. Generally, Proofs are sharp strikes until the 1890s, when some can be weak. On bronze coins tiny carbon flecks are typical, but should be microscopic. If larger, avoid, and at PF-65 or higher, avoid as well. The majority of Proofs have been dipped, and many bronze pieces have been retoned. Most undipped coins are either rich brown (can be very attractive) or red and brown. The late John J. Pittman spent 50 years trying to find a Gem Proof 1907 Indian Head cent with brilliant original color! Cherrypicking is the order of the day. Extra value can be found in BN and RB, simply because investors won't buy them; instead, they are drawn to RD coins, most of which have been "improved" (dipped and retoned).

Proofs are generally designated BN if the surfaces are mainly brown or iridescent, or have up to perhaps 30% original mint red-orange color (there is little consistency, within the hobby community, in this determination). RB is the designation if the surface is a mixture of red-orange and brown, best if blended together nicely, but often with patches of mint color among brown areas. RD designates a coin with original (in theory) mint-red orange, always blending to slight natural brown toning unless the coin has been dipped. Likely, any RD coin with even a few hairlines has been cleaned (or at least mishandled) at one time; in most such cases, what appears to be mint-red color is not original. Certification services take no notice of this. For this reason, a connoisseur will prefer a gem BN coin with no hairlines to a PF-65 or 66 RD coin with some hairlines. Proof copper-nickel Indian Head cents of 1859 to 1864 need no letter to indicate color, as their hue derives more from the nickel than the copper. As a general rule, these survive in higher grades and with greater eye appeal, as they stayed "brilliant" (the watchword for most collectors until recent decades) and did not need dipping. Moreover, when such pieces were cleaned and acquired hairlines, they tended to be fewer than on a bronze coin, due to the very hard nature of the copper-nickel alloy.

GRADING STANDARDS

Caveat: These grading standards do not take sharpness of strike into account.

MS-60 to 70 (Mint State). *Obverse:* Contact marks, most obvious in the field, are evident at MS-60, diminishing at MS–61, 62, and higher. This abrasion is most noticeable on copper-nickel cents, for it blends in with the background on bronze issues. The cheek of the Indian and the field show some evidence as well. Typical color is BN, occasionally RB at MS–63 and 64, unless dipped to be RD. At gem MS-65 or finer there is no trace of abra-

1860, Pointed Bust. Graded MS-63.

sion. A few tiny nicks or marks may be seen, but none are obvious. At MS-67 and finer the coin will approach perfection. Check "RD" coins for originality. A theoretically perfect MS-70 will have no marks at all, even under a strong magnifier. Although in practice this is not always consistent, at MS-66 and higher there should be no staining or other problems, and the coin should have good eye appeal overall. *Reverse:* Check the high parts of the wreath for abrasion. Otherwise the above comments apply.

Illustrated coin: The surfaces display satin luster and a lovely pinkish-tan patina.

AU-50, 53, 55, 58 (About Uncirculated). *Obverse:* At AU-50, wear is most noticeable on the hair above the ear, on the central portion of the ribbon, on the curl to the right of the ribbon, and near the feather tips, although the last is not a reliable indicator due to striking. Luster is present, but mostly in protected areas. At AU-53 and 55, wear is less. At AU-58 friction is evident, rather than actual wear. Luster, toned brown, is nearly complete at

1861. Graded AU-55.

AU-58, but may be incomplete in the field. *Reverse:* At AU-50, light wear is seen on the ribbon and the higher-relief areas of the leaves, while the lower areas retain their detail. Some luster may be present in protected areas. At AU–53 and 55, wear is less and luster is more extensive. An AU-58 coin will have nearly full luster and show only light friction.

EF-40, 45 (Extremely Fine). *Obverse:* Wear is more extensive, but all of LIBERTY is very clear. Wear is seen on the hair above and below the ear, on the central portion of the ribbon, and on the feather tips. Overall the coin is bold. Scattered marks are normal for this and lower grades, most often seen on the cheek and in the field. *Reverse:* The higher-relief parts of the leaves and ribbon bow show light wear, but details are sharp in lower

1861. Graded EF-45.

areas. Some tiny lines in the vertical stripes in the shield may be blended. Scattered marks may be present, but on all grades they are usually fewer on the reverse than on the obverse.

VF-20, 30 (Very Fine). *Obverse:* Wear is more extensive. LIBERTY shows significant wear on BE, but it is sharp overall. Most hair detail is gone. The feather tips show greater wear (the extent of which will depend on the original strike). The ribbon and hair no longer show separation. *Reverse:* Wear is more extensive than at the preceding level, and many tiny vertical lines are fused together. Detail is still good on lower levels of the leaves.

1870, Shallow N. Graded VF-30.

F-12, 15 (Fine). *Obverse:* Traditionally, the word LIBERTY should be fully readable, but weak on the higher letters of LIB. PCGS suggests this is true, but not if a coin was lightly struck. Full or incomplete, well-struck or lightly struck, no matter what the coin, most buyers still want the word to be discernible. Other areas have correspondingly more wear than on the next-higher grade. *Reverse:* The higher areas of the leaves and the bow show

1870. Graded F-15.

wear. The shield shows greater wear than at the preceding level. Overall, the reverse appears to be less worn than the obverse, this being generally true of all circulated grades.

VG-8, 10 (Very Good). *Obverse:* A total of at least three letters in LIBERTY must be visible. This can be a combination of several partial letters. PCGS does not adhere to this rule and suggests that wear on the feathers is a better indicator. The rim may blend into the field in areas, depending on striking. *Reverse:* Wear is even more extensive. Leaves on the left have hardly any detail, while those on the right may have limited detail. The rim is complete.

1870, Bold N. Graded VG-10.

G-4, 6 (Good). *Obverse:* The coin is worn flat, with the portrait visible mostly in outline form, with only slight indication of feathers. Lettering and date are complete. Part of the rim is usually gone. At G-6, the rim is clearer. *Reverse:* The wreath is nearly flat, although some hints of detail may be seen on the right side. All letters are readable, although the inscription is light at the center (on issues from the 1870s onward). The rim is discern-

1877. Graded G-6.

ible all around, but is light in areas. At G-6 the rim is clearly delineated.

Illustrated coin: The date is actually quite sharp for this grade.

AG-3 (About Good). *Obverse:* Most letters are worn away, as is the rim. The portrait is in outline form. The date is clearly readable, but may be weak or missing at the bottom. *Reverse:* Extensive wear prevails, although the rim will usually be more discernible than on the obverse. Most lettering, or sometimes all, is readable.

1877. Graded AG-3.

PF-60 to 70 (Proof). *Obverse and Reverse:* Gem PF-65 coins will have very few hairlines, and these are visible only under a strong magnifying glass. At any level and color, a Proof with hairlines likely (though not necessarily) has been cleaned. At PF-67 or higher there should be no evidence of hairlines or friction at all. Such a coin is fully original. PF-60 coins can be dull from repeated dipping and cleaning and are often toned iridescent colors. At

1868. Graded PF-64RB.

PF-63 the mirrorlike fields should be attractive, and hairlines should be minimal. These are easiest to see when the coin is held at an angle to the light. No rubbing is seen. PF-64 coins are even nicer.

COPPER-NICKEL COINAGE

1860, Rounded Bust

1860, Pointed Bust

	Mintage	Cert	Avg	%MS	G-4	VG-8	F-12	VF-20	EF-40	AU-50	MS-60BN PF-63BN	MS-63BN PF-64BN	MS-65 PF-65BN
1859	36,400,000	2,191	56.7	62%	$15	$20	$25	$55	$110	$200	$285	$700	$2,800
	Auctions: $23,500, MS-66+, November 2014; $11,750, MS-66, April 2013; $3,966, MS-65, September 2014; $2,233, MS-65, November 2014												
1859, Proof	*800*	189	64.4								$1,500	$2,500	$4,500
	Auctions: $13,513, PF-66Cam, June 2014; $4,700, PF-66, September 2014; $3,173, PF-64, October 2014; $2,585, PF-64, August 2014												
1859, Oak Wreath With Shield, experimental reverse (a)		0	n/a								$1,000		
	Auctions: No auction records available.												
1860, Rounded Bust	20,566,000	1,317	58.6	70%	$10	$15	$20	$35	$70	$110	$185	$250	$1,200
	Auctions: $8,813, MS-66, January 2014; $3,290, MS-66, October 2014; $2,938, MS-66, October 2014; $764, MS-64, December 2014												
1860, Pointed Bust	**(b)**	155	58.6	72%	$20	$25	$30	$50	$100	$165	$300	$575	$3,000
	Auctions: $32,900, MS-67, February 2014; $7,931, MS-66, October 2014; $2,409, MS-65, August 2014; $1,469, MS-64, July 2014												
1860, Rounded Bust, Proof	*1,000*	57	64.8								$900	$1,850	$3,000
	Auctions: $9,989, PF-66, April 2014; $5,875, PF-66, August 2014; $8,813, PF-66, October 2014; $4,137, PF-66, October 2014												

a. 1,000 pieces were made but never released for circulation. **b.** Included in circulation-strike 1860, Rounded Bust, mintage figure.

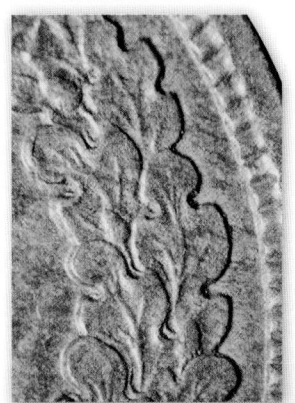

1863, Doubled
Die Reverse
FS-01-1863-801.

	Mintage	Cert	Avg	%MS	G-4	VG-8	F-12	VF-20	EF-40	AU-50	MS-60BN / PF-63BN	MS-63BN / PF-64BN	MS-65 / PF-65BN
1861	10,100,000	1,226	55.8	64%	$25	$35	$45	$60	$110	$175	$225	$400	$1,100
Auctions: $14,100, MS-67, October 2014; $4,113, MS-66, February 2014; $2,820, MS-66, September 2014													
1861, Proof	*1,000*	79	64.2								$1,100	$2,850	$5,500
Auctions: $24,675, PF-66, September 2013; $2,585, PF-64, October 2014; $1,763, PF-64, October 2014													
1862	28,075,000	2,002	60.6	79%	$10	$15	$20	$30	$50	$75	$110	$200	$1,000
Auctions: $15,275, MS-67, February 2013; $11,163, MS-67, October 2014; $8,813, MS-67, November 2014													
1862, Proof	*550*	309	64.7								$850	$1,250	$2,500
Auctions: $11,750, PF-67Cam, September 2014; $2,468, PF-66Cam, November 2014; $4,113, PF-66, June 2014													
1863	49,840,000	2,633	60.6	79%	$10	$15	$20	$30	$50	$75	$110	$200	$1,000
Auctions: $3,055, MS-66, August 2014; $1,998, MS-66, November 2014; $2,820, MS-66, August 2013; $969, MS-65, July 2014													
1863, Doubled Die Reverse (c)	**(d)**	2	62.5	100%					$200	$375	$450	$950	$3,000
Auctions: No auction records available.													
1863, Proof	*460*	142	64.3								$850	$1,250	$2,500
Auctions: $9,988, PF-67Cam, September 2014; $1,998, PF-65Cam, July 2014; $1,058, PF-64Cam, November 2014													
1864, Copper-Nickel	13,740,000	1,601	58.2	72%	$20	$30	$40	$55	$100	$150	$200	$325	$1,300
Auctions: $6,463, MS-66, April 2014; $3,055, MS-66, November 2014; $1,351, MS-65, October 2014; $676, MS-64, July 2014													
1864, Copper-Nickel, Proof	*370*	157	64.3								$850	$1,250	$2,500
Auctions: $8,813, MS-67Cam, September 2014; $12,925, PF-66DCam, July 2014; $1,880, MS-64Cam, August 2014													

c. Strong doubling is evident on the right leaves of the wreath, and, to a lesser degree, on the upper left leaves. **d.** Included in circulation-strike 1863 mintage figure.

BRONZE COINAGE

1864, No L   **1864, With L**

	Mintage	Cert	Avg	%MS	G-4	VG-8	F-12	VF-20	EF-40	AU-50	MS-60BN / PF-63BN	MS-63RB / PF-64RB	MS-65RB / PF-65RD
1864, Bronze, All kinds	39,233,714												
1864, No L		1,376	59.5	82%	$15	$20	$25	$45	$70	$90	$115	$150	$400	$1,000
Auctions: $764, MS-66RB, September 2014; $881, MS-65RD, August 2014; $306, MS-64RB, October 2014; $7,050, VF-30, April 2013													
1864, With L		1,549	51.0	48%	$55	$80	$150	$200	$275	$375	$425	$575	$1,800	$5,000
Auctions: $2,115, MS-65RB, May 2013; $1,469, MS-64RD, November 2014; $1,293, MS-64RB, July 2014; $646, MS-62RB, September 2014													
1864, No L, Proof	*150+*	119	64.6								$500	$1,750	$9,000
Auctions: $17,625, PF-67RB, April 2013; $2,585, PF-65RB, November 2014; $2,129, PF-65RB, October 2014													
1864, With L, Proof	*20+*	5	64.4								$20,000	$50,000	
Auctions: $141,000, PF-65RD, September 2013													

1865, Die Gouge in Headdress
FS-01-1865-1401.

1865, Doubled Die Reverse
FS-01-1865-1801.

1869, 9 Over 9
FS-01-1869-301.

Shallow N

Bold N

	Mintage	Cert	Avg	%MS	G-4	VG-8	F-12	VF-20	EF-40	AU-50	MS-60BN / PF-63BN	MS-63BN / PF-64RB	MS-65RB / PF-65RD	MS-65RD
1865	35,429,286	1,009	60.6	82%	$15	$20	$25	$30	$45	$65	$90	$150	$650	$1,750
Auctions: $1,998, MS-66RB, October 2014; $1,998, MS-65RD, March 2013; $270, MS-64BN, October 2014; $165, MS-64BN, September 2014														
1865, Die Gouge in Headdress (a)	(b)	0	n/a								$500	$750	$1,200	
Auctions: No auction records available.														
1865, Doubled Die Reverse	(b)	10	41.6	40%					$800	$1,100	$2,200	$5,500		
Auctions: $1,175, AU-55, April 2013														
1865, Proof	500+	148	64.2								$375	$800	$7,500	
Auctions: $14,100, PF-65Cam, August 2014; $15,275, PF-66RD, October 2014; $12,925, PF-65RD, June 2014; $3,055, PF-64RD, October 2014														
1866	9,826,500	1,060	54.0	59%	$50	$65	$80	$100	$190	$250	$275	$380	$1,500	$3,000
Auctions: $1,087, MS-66BN, September 2014; $3,290, MS-65RD, June 2014; $499, MS-63RB, August 2014; $212, MS-62BN, October 2014														
1866, Proof	725+	129	64.5								$400	$600	$5,000	
Auctions: $21,150, PF-66Cam, June 2014; $2,820, PF-65Cam, October 2014; $999, PF-65RB, July 2014; $529, PF-64BN, November 2014														
1867	9,821,000	1,043	52.7	58%	$50	$70	$90	$135	$230	$275	$300	$400	$1,600	$5,500
Auctions: $6,463, MS-65RD, February 2014; $1,293, MS-65RB, October 2014; $6,756, MS-65RD, October 2014														
1867, Proof	625+	190	64.4								$400	$600	$5,000	
Auctions: $3,525, PF-66RB, July 2014; $6,463, PF-66RD, March 2014; $705, PF-64RB, August 2014; $306, PF-63BN, October 2014														
1868	10,266,500	1,006	53.2	59%	$40	$50	$70	$125	$170	$220	$250	$360	$925	$2,750
Auctions: $1,880, MS-66RB, September 2014; $29,375, MS-66RD, April 2014; $3,525, MS-65RD, October 2014; $3,055, MS-65RD, August 2014														
1868, Proof	600+	134	64.4								$375	$550	$5,000	
Auctions: $17,625, PF-66RD, June 2014; $6,756, PF-65RD, September 2014; $588, PF-63RB, October 2014														
1869	6,420,000	1,090	45.9	47%	$85	$120	$235	$335	$445	$550	$600	$700	$1,800	$2,750
Auctions: $3,290, MS-66RB, August 2013; $1,763, MS-64RB, October 2014; $499, MS-61BN, November 2014; $1,175, MS-60BN, July 2014														
1869, 9 Over 9	(c)	395	41.5	36%	$125	$225	$450	$575	$725	$825	$975	$1,200	$2,400	
Auctions: $4,113, MS-66, March 2015; $1,645, MS-64RB, November 2014; $3,055, MS-64RD, August 2014; $1,410, MS-63RB, September 2014														
1869, Proof	600+	176	64.4								$380	$650	$3,000	
Auctions: $4,847, PF-66Cam, June 2014; $11,750, PF-66RD, October 2014; $1,528, PF-65RB, October 2014; $558, PF-64RB, November 2014														
1870, Shallow N	5,275,000	6	43.5	17%	$80	$100	$220	$320	$400	$500	$550	$900	$1,600	
Auctions: $1,265, MS-64RB, March 2012														
1870, Bold N	(d)	983	46.9	46%	$55	$75	$200	$280	$375	$450	$500	$850	$1,300	$4,000
Auctions: $23,500, MS-66RD, May 2013; $3,819, MS-65RD, October 2014; $1,880, MS-65RB, November 2014; $705, MS-65BN, July 2014														

Note: Cents dated 1869 and earlier have a shallow N in ONE. Those dated 1870, 1871, or 1872 have either shallow N or bold N, except Proofs of 1872, which were struck only with the bold N, not the shallow N. Those dated 1873 to 1876 all have the bold N. Circulation strikes of 1877 have the shallow N, while Proofs have the bold N. **a.** Currently described as a die gouge in the *Cherrypickers' Guide to Rare Die Varieties*, sixth edition, volume I, the curved "gouge" is a mark from the Janvier reducing lathe. **b.** Included in circulation-strike 1865 mintage figure. **c.** Included in circulation-strike 1869 mintage figure. **d.** Included in circulation-strike 1870, Shallow N, mintage figure.

1870, Doubled Die Reverse	1873, Close 3	1873, Open 3	1873, Doubled LIBERTY
FS-01-1870-801.			FS-01-1873-101.

	Mintage	Cert	Avg	%MS	G-4	VG-8	F-12	VF-20	EF-40	AU-50	MS-60BN / PF-63BN	MS-63RB / PF-64RB	MS-65RB / PF-65RD	MS-65RD
1870, Doubled Die Reverse	(d)	9	62.6	89%					$575	$750	$850	$1,000	$2,500	
Auctions: $1,035, MS-64RB, January 2012														
1870, Shallow N, Proof	1,000+	175	64.3								$425	$525	$1,900	
Auctions: $1,380, PF-65RB, April 2012														
1870, Bold N, Proof	(e)	(f)									$325	$725	$2,500	
Auctions: $3,173, PF-67RB, August 2014; $10,575, PF-66RD, January 2014; $9,988, PF-66RD, July 2014; $1,528, PF-64RD, November 2014														
1871, Shallow N	3,929,500	2	54.0	0%	$130	$180	$325	$450	$575	$650	$775	$1,000	$2,600	
Auctions: $8,225, MS-66, January 2015; $2,585, MS-63RB, February 2013														
1871, Bold N	(g)	1,088	45.8	44%	$70	$85	$250	$350	$475	$525	$550	$800	$2,350	$7,500
Auctions: $44,063, MS-66RD, January 2014; $999, MS-64BN, November 2014; $999, MS-62BN, October 2014														
1871, Shallow N, Proof	960+	199	64.2								$500	$875	$2,350	
Auctions: $7,344, PF-65RD, January 2013														
1871, Bold N, Proof	(h)	(i)									$325	$600	$2,500	
Auctions: $2,350, PF-65RD, June 2014; $499, PF-65BN, October 2014; $294, PF-62BN, November 2014; $282, PF-60BN, November 2014														
1872, Shallow N	4,042,000	5	33.8	0%	$100	$170	$370	$425	$575	$700	$950	$1,250	$4,500	
Auctions: $764, MS-63, March 2016; $881, AU-55, April 2013														
1872, Bold N	(j)	1,292	43.1	37%	$90	$140	$300	$375	$500	$650	$785	$1,150	$4,000	$17,000
Auctions: $28,200, MS-65RD, June 2014; $3,819, MS-65RB, August 2014; $5,581, MS-64RD, October 2014; $588, AU-58BN, July 2014														
1872, Bold N, Proof (k)	950+	226	64.3								$400	$700	$4,300	
Auctions: $7,050, PF-66RD, October 2014; $705, PF-65BN, November 2014; $705, PF-64RB, November 2014; $12,925, PF, October 2013														
1873, All kinds	11,676,500													
1873, Close 3		306	53.6	57%	$25	$35	$65	$125	$185	$235	$410	$550	$2,500	$7,500
Auctions: $6,463, MS-65RD, October 2014; $2,820, MS-65RB, December 2013; $1,293, MS-64RB, October 2014; $793, MS-63RB, July 2014														
1873, Doubled LIBERTY		99	43.2	28%	$200	$350	$825	$1,750	$2,500	$5,250	$7,500	$13,500	$57,500	
Auctions: $15,275, MS-64, March 2015; $9,988, MS-63RB, October 2014; $7,050, MS-63BN, September 2014														
1873, Open 3		576	52.9	52%	$20	$30	$50	$85	$160	$190	$250	$325	$1,275	$6,500
Auctions: $4,406, MS-65RD, April 2014; $3,819, MS-65RD, October 2014; $470, MS-64RB, November 2014; $470, MS-63RB, July 2014														
1873, Close 3, Proof	1,100+	238	64.2								$265	$550	$2,050	
Auctions: $1,293, PF-65RB, April 2013; $589, PF-64RD, October 2014; $470, PF-64RB, October 2014														
1874	14,187,500	966	57.0	66%	$20	$25	$45	$65	$100	$150	$225	$250	$725	$3,500
Auctions: $1,880, MS-65RD, October 2014; $2,820, MS-65RD, April 2013; $1,116, MS-65RB, October 2014; $1,000, MS-64RD, November 2014														
1874, Proof	700	173	64.4								$250	$400	$2,500	
Auctions: $823, PF-66BN, July 2014; $1,175, PF-65RB, June 2013; $617, PF-64RD, October 2014; $470, PF-64RB, July 2014														

Note: Cents dated 1869 and earlier have a shallow N in ONE. Those dated 1870, 1871, or 1872 have either shallow N or bold N, except Proofs of 1872, which were struck only with the bold N, not the shallow N. Those dated 1873 to 1876 all have the bold N. Circulation strikes of 1877 have the shallow N, while Proofs have the bold N. **d.** Included in circulation-strike 1870, Shallow N, mintage figure. **e.** Included in 1870, Shallow N, Proof, mintage figure. **f.** Included in certified population for 1870, Shallow N, Proof. **g.** Included in circulation-strike 1871, Shallow N, mintage figure. **h.** Included in 1871, Shallow N, Proof, mintage figure. **i.** Included in certified population for 1871, Shallow N, Proof. **j.** Included in 1872, Shallow N, mintage figure. **k.** Proofs of 1872 were struck only with the bold N, not the shallow N.

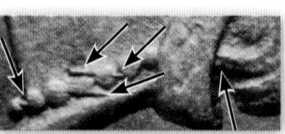

1875, Dot Reverse
FS-01-1875-801.

1880, Doubled Die Obverse, Reverse Clash
FS-01-1880-101.

1882, Misplaced Date
FS-01-1882-401.

	Mintage	Cert	Avg	%MS	G-4	VG-8	F-12	VF-20	EF-40	AU-50	MS-60BN	MS-63BN / PF-63BN	MS-65RB / PF-64RB	MS-65RD / PF-65RD
1875	13,528,000	897	55.9	68%	$20	$35	$60	$75	$120	$160	$235	$260	$900	$3,750
Auctions: $1,763, MS-66RB, July 2014; $5,581, MS-65RD, December 2013; $881, MS-65RB, August 2014; $646, MS-64RB, August 2014														
1875, Dot Reverse (l)	(m)	0	n/a									—		
Auctions: $700, AU-50BN, April 2012														
1875, Proof	700	180	64.2									$250	$500	$5,400
Auctions: $8,813, PF-65RD, June 2014; $306, PF-63RB, October 2014														
1876	7,944,000	880	53.5	59%	$35	$40	$70	$135	$225	$240	$300	$390	$1,000	$3,000
Auctions: $1,998, MS-65RD, October 2014; $1,880, MS-65RD, October 2013; $1,293, MS-65RB, November 2014; $270, MS-62RB, November 2014														
1876, Proof	1,150	215	64.5									$250	$450	$2,250
Auctions: $15,275, PF-66Cam, January 2014; $2,585, PF-66RD, October 2014; $646, PF-64RD, October 2014; $823, PF-64BN, November 2014														
1877 (n)	852,500	3,192	23.2	11%	$900	$1,100	$1,550	$2,000	$2,500	$3,000	$3,800	$4,500	$15,000	$25,000
Auctions: $32,900, MS-65RD, August 2014; $14,100, MS-65RB, January 2014; $14,100, MS-65, August 2016														
1877, Proof	900	266	63.7									$3,000	$4,500	$12,000
Auctions: $9,988, PF-66RD, October 2014; $14,100, PF-66RD, June 2013; $3,525, PF-64RB, October 2014; $3,819, PF-63RB, November 2014														
1878	5,797,500	832	54.7	65%	$35	$45	$60	$110	$200	$275	$325	$380	$950	$2,250
Auctions: $8,813, MS-66RD, September 2014; $1,645, MS-65RD, October 2013; $881, MS-65RB, August 2014; $388, MS-63RB, October 2014														
1878, Proof	2,350	334	64.3									$235	$450	$1,500
Auctions: $7,638, PF-66Cam, June 2014; $1,763, PF-65Cam, August 2014; $1,116, PF-65Cam, November 2014; $588, PF-64RD, October 2014														
1879	16,228,000	877	60.8	83%	$8	$12	$20	$40	$70	$80	$90	$140	$425	$1,250
Auctions: $2,233, MS-65RD, June 2014; $470, MS-65RB, November 2014; $259, MS-64RB, July 2014; $247, MS-63RB, August 2014														
1879, Proof	3,200	384	64.5									$150	$325	$1,200
Auctions: $11,163, PF-67RD, July 2014; $2,115, PF-66Cam, August 2014; $1,645, PF-66RD, October 2014; $217, PF-64BN, November 2014														
1880	38,961,000	754	62.3	90%	$5	$7	$9	$12	$30	$60	$80	$130	$400	$1,150
Auctions: $5,288, MS-66RD, June 2014; $940, MS-65RD, September 2014; $441, MS-65RB, November 2014; $129, MS-64BN, November 2014														
1880, Doubled Die Obverse, Reverse Clash (o)	(p)	8	60.9	75%							$390	$750	$1,500	$2,000
Auctions: $2,070, MS-65BN, June 2009														
1880, Proof	3,955	408	64.4									$150	$325	$1,200
Auctions: $8,813, PF-67RD, June 2014; $969, PF-66RB, August 2014; $705, PF-65RD, July 2014; $646, PF-65RB+, July 2014														

Note: Cents dated 1869 and earlier have a shallow N in ONE. Those dated 1870, 1871, or 1872 have either shallow N or bold N, except Proofs of 1872, which were struck only with the bold N, not the shallow N. Those dated 1873 to 1876 all have the bold N. Circulation strikes of 1877 have the shallow N, while Proofs have the bold N. **l.** In 1875 Mint officials suspected a longtime employee was stealing Indian Head cents. They secretly modified a reverse die by making a small gouge in the N in ONE, and then put the die into production one morning. Later that morning the suspect employee was called aside. He was asked to empty his pockets, revealing 33 of the marked cents. At first he insisted his son gave him this pocket change, but when confronted with the secretly marked die, he admitted his guilt. He tendered his resignation, disgraced, after more than 50 years of service to the Mint. The market value for this variety is not yet reliably established. **m.** Included in circulation-strike 1875 mintage figure. **n.** Beware the numerous counterfeits and altered-date 1877 cents. The latter typically are altered from 1875- or 1879-dated cents. **o.** Doubling is visible on the obverse in higher grades, as a very close spread on LIBERTY. The primary diagnostic, though, is the misaligned die clash evident on the reverse, with obvious reeding running from the upper-right leaf tip, through the E of ONE, and down to the very top of the N of CENT. **p.** Included in circulation-strike 1880 mintage figure.

1886, Variety 1
*The last feather points between
the I and the C in AMERICA.*

1886, Variety 2
*The last feather points between
the C and the A in AMERICA.*

1887, Doubled Die Obverse
FS-01-1887-101.

	Mintage	Cert	Avg	%MS	G-4	VG-8	F-12	VF-20	EF-40	AU-50	MS-60BN	MS-63BN / PF-63BN	MS-65RB / PF-64RB	MS-65RD / PF-65RD
1881	39,208,000	773	62.3	92%	$5	$6	$8	$10	$25	$35	$60	$90	$315	$1,150
Auctions: $1,645, MS-67RB, October 2014; $6,463, MS-66RD, October 2014; $1,528, MS-66RB, August 2014; $1,880, MS-64BN, August 2013														
1881, Proof	3,575	405	64.6									$150	$325	$1,200
Auctions: $2,115, PF-66RB, November 2014; $1,880, PF-66RD, June 2013; $1,234, PF-65Cam, July 2014; $881, PF-65RB, August 2014														
1882	38,578,000	795	62.8	92%	$5	$6	$8	$10	$25	$35	$60	$90	$315	$1,150
Auctions: $294, MS-64RB, July 2014; $247, MS-64RB, October 2014; $3,525, EF-40, April 2013; $66, AU-55BN, October 2014														
1882, Misplaced Date (q)	(r)	4	64.5	100%						$450	$875	$1,700	$6,000	
Auctions: $220, EF-45, February 2007														
1882, Proof	3,100	403	64.6									$150	$325	$1,000
Auctions: $823, PF-66RB, September 2014; $734, PF-66BN, November 2014; $2,703, PF-65RD, January 2014; $323, PF-65BN, July 2014														
1883	45,591,500	784	62.6	91%	$5	$6	$8	$10	$25	$35	$60	$90	$315	$1,150
Auctions: $2,585, MS-66RD, February 2014; $499, MS-65RB, July 2014; $241, MS-65BN, July 2014; $217, MS-64RB, October 2014														
1883, Proof	6,609	584	64.6									$150	$325	$1,200
Auctions: $5,581, PF-67RB, August 2014; $2,938, PF-66RD, March 2013; $646, PF-66BN, November 2014; $441, PF-65RB, November 2014														
1884	23,257,800	728	62.4	90%	$5	$7	$10	$14	$27	$40	$75	$120	$450	$1,350
Auctions: $4,994, MS-66RD, June 2014; $1,645, MS-65RD, September 2014; $257, MS-64RB, August 2014; $368, MS-64RB, November 2014														
1884, Proof	3,942	501	64.8									$150	$325	$1,200
Auctions: $7,050, PF-67Cam, June 2013; $4,113, PF-67RD, September 2014; $1,880, PF-66RD, July 2014; $306, PF-64RB, October 2014														
1885	11,761,594	684	61.8	86%	$8	$9	$15	$30	$65	$80	$110	$200	$650	$1,750
Auctions: $12,925, MS-66RD, April 2013; $1,528, MS-66RB, November 2014; $1,645, MS-65RD, October 2014														
1885, Proof	3,790	466	64.9									$150	$325	$1,200
Auctions: $4,994, PF-68BN, September 2013; $1,528, PF-66RB, July 2014; $2,115, PF-65RD, October 2014; $529, PF-65RB, October 2014														
1886, All kinds	17,650,000													
1886, Variety 1		429	56.5	58%	$6	$8	$20	$50	$140	$175	$200	$250	$975	$5,000
Auctions: $8,813, MS-66RB, June 2013; $1,410, MS-64RD, July 2014; $764, MS-64RB, November 2014; $235, MS-63BN, September 2014														
1886, Variety 2		496	57.6	67%	$7	$12	$25	$75	$175	$220	$325	$500	$2,900	$12,500
Auctions: $9,400, MS-65RD, January 2013; $2,115, MS-65RB, August 2014; $482, MS-60RB, July 2014; $247, AU-58BN, October 2014														
1886, All kinds, Proof	4,290													
1886, Variety 1, Proof		129	64.5									$150	$325	$1,800
Auctions: $3,819, PF-66RD, June 2014; $1,880, PF-66RB, October 2014; $1,763, PF-65RD, October 2014; $558, PF-64RB, August 2014														
1886, Variety 2, Proof		73	64.5									$350	$750	$10,000
Auctions: $1,116, PF-66BN, April 2013; $1,763, PF-64RB+, November 2014; $306, PF-64BN, November 2014; $153, PF-60BN, November 2014														
1887	45,223,523	631	61.9	91%	$3	$4	$5	$8	$18	$28	$55	$80	$575	$1,250
Auctions: $4,700, MS-66RD, November 2014; $8,813, MS-66RD, February 2013; $382, MS-65RB, November 2014; $188, MS-64RB, July 2014														
1887, DblDie Obverse	(s)	27	42.5	19%					$250	$490	$1,000	$2,500	$8,000	
Auctions: $881, MS-62BN, October 2013; $176, VF-25BN, October 2014														
1887, Proof	2,960	327	64.4									$150	$300	$3,500
Auctions: $16,450, PF-66RD, June 2014; $823, PF-66BN, November 2014; $382, PF-64RB, October 2014														

q. The bases of at least four 1s are evident within the beads of the necklace. **r.** Included in circulation-strike 1882 mintage figure.
s. Included in circulation-strike 1887 mintage figure.

1888, Last 8 Over 7
FS-01-1888-301.

1891, Doubled Die Obverse
FS-01-1891-101.

1894, Doubled Date
FS-01-1894-301.

	Mintage	Cert	Avg	%MS	G-4	VG-8	F-12	VF-20	EF-40	AU-50	MS-60BN	MS-63BN / PF-63BN	MS-65RB / PF-64RB	MS-65RD / PF-65RD
1888	37,489,832	771	59.6	85%	$3	$4	$5	$8	$22	$27	$65	$130	$725	$1,500
Auctions: $11,750, MS-66RD, June 2014; $1,704, MS-65RD, July 2014; $1,880, MS-65RD, September 2014; $529, MS-64RD, October 2014
1888, Last 8 Over 7	(t)	12	38.3	17%	$1,250	$1,500	$2,000	$3,500	$7,500	$17,500	$30,000	$50,000		
Auctions: $99,142, MS-66, January 2016; $23,500, AU-58, April 2013
1888, Proof	4,582	281	64.2									$150	$315	$3,500
Auctions: $15,275, PF-66RD, October 2014; $382, PF-64RB, August 2014; $2,585, PF, February 2013; $294, PF-64BN, December 2014
1889	48,866,025	782	62.2	92%	$3	$4	$5	$7	$18	$27	$60	$80	$400	$1,600
Auctions: $13,513, MS-66RD, October 2014; $10,575, MS-66RD, October 2014; $4,113, MS-65RD, April 2014; $1,880, MS-65RD, October 2014
1889, Proof	3,336	282	64.3									$150	$315	$1,750
Auctions: $4,113, PF-66RD, February 2013; $499, PF-65RB, July 2014; $341, PF-64RB, July 2014; $282, PF-64BN, November 2014
1890	57,180,114	729	62.7	93%	$3	$4	$5	$7	$16	$27	$60	$80	$410	$1,000
Auctions: $4,113, MS-66RB, March 2014; $470, MS-64RD, July 2014; $170, MS-64RB, August 2014; $170, MS-63BN, July 2014
1890, Proof	2,740	272	64.1									$150	$315	$1,650
Auctions: $1,058, PF-65RD, October 2014; $1,293, PF-65RD, August 2013; $1,293, PF-64Cam, September 2014; $470, PF-64RD, November 2014
1891	47,070,000	850	62.6	94%	$3	$4	$5	$7	$15	$27	$60	$80	$400	$1,000
Auctions: $9,106, MS-66RD, November 2014; $1,528, MS-65RD, July 2014; $1,293, MS-65RD, August 2014; $135, MS-64RB, August 2014
1891, Doubled Die Obverse	(u)	12	45.9	25%					$250	$450	$775	$1,150		
Auctions: $138, VF-35, December 2011
1891, Proof	2,350	289	64.2									$150	$315	$1,375
Auctions: $18,213, PF-65DCam, July 2014; $911, PF-64Cam, September 2014; $558, PF-64RB, November 2014; $176, PF-62RB, November 2014
1892	37,647,087	755	62.9	94%	$3	$4	$5	$8	$20	$27	$60	$80	$375	$1,000
Auctions: $8,813, MS-66RD, August 2013; $3,055, MS-65RD, October 2014; $1,293, MS-65RD, October 2014; $306, MS-64RD, October 2014
1892, Proof	2,745	305	64.4									$150	$315	$1,200
Auctions: $3,525, PF-67RD, November 2013; $2,585, PF-66Cam, November 2014; $2,233, PF-65RD, October 2014; $1,175, PF-64Cam, July 2014
1893	46,640,000	911	62.9	95%	$3	$4	$5	$8	$20	$27	$60	$80	$320	$850
Auctions: $6,463, MS-67RD, April 2013; $282, MS-64RD, October 2014; $176, MS-64RB, November 2014; $135, MS-63RB, November 2014
1893, Proof	2,195	271	64.2									$150	$315	$1,300
Auctions: $823, PF-65RB, November 2014; $499, PF-64RD, April 2013; $284, PF-64RB, October 2014; $247, PF-63RB, November 2014
1894	16,749,500	851	60.6	84%	$5	$6	$15	$20	$50	$70	$85	$115	$385	$1,000
Auctions: $3,290, MS-66RD, January 2014; $2,585, MS-66RD, October 2014; $2,174, MS-66RD, November 2014; $414, MS-64RD, July 2014
1894, Doubled Date	(v)	99	47.7	55%	$30	$40	$65	$130	$225	$385	$675	$1,200	$4,000	$11,000
Auctions: $5,875, MS-64RD, January 2013; $4,113, MS-64RB, September 2014; $1,116, MS-62, January 2015
1894, Proof	2,632	303	64.1									$150	$315	$1,200
Auctions: $5,581, PF-66RD, September 2013; $1,351, PF-65Cam, November 2014; $558, PF-65RB, November 2014

t. Included in circulation-strike 1888 mintage figure. **u.** Included in circulation-strike 1891 mintage figure. **v.** Included in circulation-strike 1894 mintage figure.

	Mintage	Cert	Avg	%MS	G-4	VG-8	F-12	VF-20	EF-40	AU-50	MS-60BN	MS-63BN	MS-65RB	MS-65RD
												PF-63BN	PF-64RB	PF-65RD
1895	38,341,574	913	62.7	94%	$3	$4	$5	$8	$15	$25	$45	$65	$200	$700
	Auctions: $23,500, MS-67RD, November 2014; $7,050, MS-66RD, January 2014; $1,880, MS-66RD, October 2014; $206, MS-64RB, October 2014													
1895, Proof	2,062	275	64.5									$160	$315	$1,200
	Auctions: $9,988, PF-66Cam, June 2014; $1,880, PF-66RB, November 2014; $823, PF-64RB, November 2014; $260, PF-62RB, November 2014													
1896	39,055,431	688	62.5	94%	$3	$4	$5	$8	$15	$25	$45	$65	$220	$800
	Auctions: $1,528, MS-65RD, July 2014; $259, MS-64RD, July 2014; $182, MS-64RB, August 2014; $59, MS-63BN, October 2014													
1896, Proof	1,862	231	64.3									$150	$300	$1,350
	Auctions: $5,875, PF-65Cam, June 2014; $646, PF-65BN, November 2014; $295, PF-64RB, September 2014; $194, PF-64BN, November 2014													
1897	50,464,392	873	62.5	93%	$3	$4	$5	$8	$15	$25	$45	$65	$200	$800
	Auctions: $31,725, MS-67RD, August 2014; $7,050, MS-66RD, January 2014; $529, MS-64RD, September 2014; $118, MS-64RD, October 2014													
1897, Proof	1,938	263	64.5									$150	$300	$1,200
	Auctions: $6,169, PF-67RD, October 2014; $588, PF-65RB, July 2014; $411, PF-63RB, November 2014; $10,575, PF, January 2013													
1898	49,821,284	937	62.7	93%	$3	$4	$5	$8	$15	$25	$45	$65	$195	$500
	Auctions: $2,820, MS-66RD, April 2013; $368, MS-65RB+, November 2014; $458, MS-64RD+, October 2014; $212, MS-64RD, October 2014													
1898, Proof	1,795	271	64.8									$150	$300	$1,200
	Auctions: $7,931, PF-66Cam, June 2014; $27,025, PF-66RB, August 2014; $2,233, PF-66RD, August 2014; $353, PF-64RB, November 2014													
1899	53,598,000	1,530	63.3	94%	$3	$4	$5	$8	$15	$25	$45	$65	$195	$475
	Auctions: $3,525, MS-66RD, January 2014; $2,233, MS-66RD, September 2014; $1,351, MS-66RD, October 2014; $558, MS-65RD, October 2014													
1899, Proof	2,031	263	64.7									$150	$300	$1,200
	Auctions: $5,875, PF-67RD, June 2014; $764, PF-64Cam, November 2014; $823, PF-66RB, November 2014; $478, PF-65RB, October 2014													
1900	66,831,502	1,041	62.6	93%	$2	$3	$5	$6	$10	$20	$40	$60	$165	$475
	Auctions: $9,988, MS-67RD, December 2013; $2,115, MS-66RD+, July 2014; $1,998, MS-66RD, October 2014; $529, MS-65RD, December 2014													
1900, Proof	2,262	257	64.6									$150	$300	$1,200
	Auctions: $2,350, PF-66RB+, August 2014; $2,115, PF-66RD, October 2014; $5,581, PF-66RD, April 2013; $411, PF-64RD, October 2014													
1901	79,609,158	1,808	63.1	95%	$2	$3	$5	$6	$10	$20	$40	$60	$165	$450
	Auctions: $2,115, MS-67RB, November 2013; $1,293, MS-66RD, August 2014; $588, MS-65RD, August 2014; $194, MS-64RD, July 2014													
1901, Proof	1,985	285	64.8									$150	$300	$1,200
	Auctions: $2,500, PF-67RB, July 2014; $1,528, PF-66RD, October 2014; $999, PF-66RB, August 2014; $4,700, PF, March 2014													
1902	87,374,704	1,730	62.7	94%	$2	$3	$5	$6	$10	$20	$40	$60	$165	$500
	Auctions: $1,998, MS-66RD, July 2014; $2,585, MS-66RD, December 2013; $705, MS-65RD, November 2014; $165, MS-64RD, July 2014													
1902, Proof	2,018	290	64.5									$150	$300	$1,200
	Auctions: $7,344, PF-67RD, June 2014; $823, PF-66RB, November 2014; $1,146, PF-65RD, October 2014; $341, PF-64RB, July 2014													
1903	85,092,703	1,596	62.6	93%	$2	$3	$5	$6	$10	$20	$40	$60	$165	$450
	Auctions: $4,406, MS-67RD, July 2014; $1,998, MS-66RD, October 2014; $1,528, MS-66RD, November 2014; $411, MS-65RD, August 2014													
1903, Proof	1,790	261	64.6									$150	$300	$1,200
	Auctions: $2,820, PF-66RD, October 2014; $1,763, PF-66RB, November 2014; $499, PF-64RD, July 2014 12/29/2014 $10,575, PF, January 2013													
1904	61,326,198	1,365	62.6	93%	$2	$3	$5	$6	$10	$20	$40	$60	$165	$475
	Auctions: $2,585, MS-66RD, June 2014; $441, MS-65RD, November 2014; $183, MS-65RB, July 2014; $59, MS-63RB, November 2014													
1904, Proof	1,817	245	64.2									$150	$300	$1,200
	Auctions: $6,463, PF-67RB, October 2014; $4,994, PF-66Cam, June 2014; $2,585, PF-65Cam, October 2014; $7,931, PF-65RB, July 2014													
1905	80,717,011	1,610	62.8	93%	$2	$3	$5	$6	$10	$20	$40	$60	$165	$500
	Auctions: $19,975, MS-67RD, April 2013; $6,169, MS-66RD+, September 2014; $2,115, MS-66RD, September 2014; $456, MS-65RD, August 2014													
1905, Proof	2,152	258	64.5									$150	$300	$1,200
	Auctions: $411, PF-64RD, October 2014; $529, PF-64RB, November 2014; $8,225, PF, March 2014; $223, PF-63RB, October 2014													
1906	96,020,530	1,851	62.4	91%	$2	$3	$5	$6	$10	$20	$40	$60	$165	$450
	Auctions: $23,500, MS-67RD, June 2014; $2,585, MS-66RD, August 2014; $617, MS-65RD, September 2014; $247, MS-62BN, July 2014													
1906, Proof	1,725	233	64.4									$150	$300	$1,200
	Auctions: $21,150, PF-67Cam, June 2014; $2,820, PF-66RB+, November 2014; $1,704, PF-66RB, November 2014; $2,939, PF-64RB, July 2014													
1907	108,137,143	2,003	62.2	92%	$2	$3	$5	$6	$10	$20	$40	$60	$165	$450
	Auctions: $23,500, MS-67RD, December 2013; $364, MS-65RD, October 2014; $329, MS-65RB, October 2014; $247, MS-64RD, October 2014													
1907, Proof	1,475	216	64.4									$150	$300	$1,250
	Auctions: $4,113, PF-66RD, April 2014; $764, PF-65RD, October 2014; $306, PF-64RB, October 2014; $382, PF-62BN, November 2014													

	Mintage	Cert	Avg	%MS	G-4	VG-8	F-12	VF-20	EF-40	AU-50	MS-60BN	MS-63BN	MS-65RB	MS-65RD
												PF-63BN	PF-64RB	PF-65RD
1908	32,326,367	1,660	63.0	95%	$2	$3	$5	$6	$10	$20	$40	$60	$165	$450
Auctions: $19,975, MS-67RD, February 2013; $3,525, MS-66RD, August 2014; $4,113, MS-66RD+, October 2014; $1,293, MS-65RD, August 2014														
1908, Proof	1,620	292	64.7									$150	$300	$1,200
Auctions: $1,293, PF-66RB, November 2014; $1,175, PF-65RD, January 2014; $382, PF-64RD, October 2014; $2,585, PF-62RB, July 2014														
1908-S	1,115,000	3,284	44.2	33%	$90	$100	$125	$145	$175	$250	$290	$400	$850	$2,000
Auctions: $4,882, MS-66RD, August 2014; $1,763, MS-65RD, October 2014; $3,290, MS-65, March 2015														
1909	14,368,470	2,269	61.9	92%	$12	$15	$17	$20	$25	$30	$45	$65	$175	$475
Auctions: $3,819, MS-67RD, January 2014; $11,163, MS-67RD, August 2014; $4,113, MS-66RD+, September 2014; $3,055, MS-66RD+, November 2014														
1909, Proof	2,175	262	64.6									$150	$300	$1,300
Auctions: $12,925, PF-67RD, June 2014; $1,645, PF-66RD, August 2014; $1,645, PF-64Cam, November 2014; $206, PF-63RB, July 2014														
1909-S	309,000	3,378	39.3	28%	$400	$450	$500	$550	$650	$850	$1,000	$1,200	$2,500	$4,750
Auctions: $9,989, MS-66RD, June 2014; $9,988, MS-66, September 2015; $5,875, MS-65RD, August 2014														

LINCOLN, WHEAT EARS REVERSE (1909–1958)

Variety 1 (Bronze, 1909–1942): **Designer:** *Victor D. Brenner.* **Weight:** *3.11 grams.*
Composition: *.950 copper, .050 tin and zinc.* **Diameter:** *19 mm.*
Edge: *Plain.* **Mints:** *Philadelphia, Denver, and San Francisco.*

Variety 1, Bronze
(1909–1942)

Mintmark location, all varieties 1909 to
date, is on the obverse below the date.

Variety 1, Bronze,
Matte Proof

Variety 2 (Steel, 1943): **Weight:** *2.70 grams.* **Composition:** *Steel, coated with zinc.*
Diameter: *19 mm.* **Edge:** *Plain.* **Mints:** *Philadelphia, Denver, and San Francisco.*

Variety 2, Steel (1943)

Variety 1 Resumed (1944–1958): **Weight:** *3.11 grams.*
Composition: *1944–1946—.950 copper and .050 zinc; 1947–1958—.950 copper and .050 tin and zinc.*
Diameter: *19 mm.* **Edge:** *Plain.* **Mints:** *Philadelphia, Denver, and San Francisco.*

Variety 1 Resumed, Bronze
(1944–1958)

Variety 1 Resumed, Bronze,
Mirror Proof

History. The Lincoln cent debuted in 1909 in honor of the hundredth anniversary of the birth of Abraham Lincoln. Sculptor and engraver Victor David had been chosen to design the new cent because the artistry of Chief Engraver Charles Barber was under heavy criticism at the time. The new cent was released on August 2, 1909, and the earliest coins of the year's issue had Brenner's initials (V.D.B.) on the reverse; this was soon discontinued. (His initials would be restored in 1918, on the obverse, on Lincoln's shoulder.) This was the first U.S. cent to feature the motto IN GOD WE TRUST.

From 1909 to 1942 the coins were struck in bronze. In 1943, during World War II, zinc-coated steel was used for their planchets, as a way to reserve copper for the war effort. The bronze alloy would be resumed in 1944. (Although no bronze cents were officially issued in 1943, a few pieces struck on bronze or silver planchets are known to exist for that year; bronze examples have recently sold for more than $200,000. Such errors presumably occur when an older planchet is mixed in with the normal supply of planchets and goes through the minting process. Through a similar production error, a few 1944 cents were struck on steel planchets. Beware the many regular steel cents of 1943 that were later plated with copper, either as novelties or to deceive collectors; a magnet will reveal their true nature.) In 1944, 1945, and 1946, the Mint used salvaged gun-cartridge cases as its source metal for coining cents. In Mint State, the color of cents of these years can appear slightly different from other bronze Wheat Ears cents.

The Philadelphia, Denver, and San Francisco mints all produced Lincoln Wheat Ears cents, but not in all years. The Wheat Ears reverse design was used from 1909 until the coin's 50th anniversary in 1959, at which time it was replaced with a view of the Lincoln Memorial.

Striking and Sharpness. As a rule, Lincoln cents of 1909 through 1914 are fairly well struck. From 1915 through the end of the 1920s, many are weak, with Denver Mint coins particularly so. Issues of the 1930s onward are mostly well struck. With many different die pairs used over a long period of time, striking quality varies. On the obverse, check for details in Lincoln's hair and beard. Also check the lettering and the inner edge of the rim. Tiny marks on the shoulder of Lincoln indicate a weak strike there; this area cannot be used to determine wear on high-grade coins. (During striking, there was not enough die pressure to fill this, the deepest point of the obverse die; therefore, stray marks on the raw planchet remain evident in this spot.) On the reverse check the wheat stalks, letters, and inner rim. A weak strike will usually manifest itself on the O of ONE (the area directly opposite Lincoln's shoulder). Coins struck from overused or "tired" dies can have grainy or even slightly wavy fields on either side.

Availability. Of the earlier Lincoln Wheat Ears cents, those of 1909 are easily found in MS; later early dates are scarcer, although Philadelphia varieties were made in higher quantities and are more often seen. Beginning in the early 1930s, collectors saved bank-wrapped rolls of Mint State cents in large quantities (starting mainly in 1934, though the low-mintage 1931-S was also hoarded). Dates after this time all are plentiful, although some more so than others, and there are a number of scarce and rare varieties. The collector demand for scarcer Lincoln cents and higher-grade issues is intense, resulting in a strong market. Many Mint State coins before the 1930s have been dipped and recolored, this being particularly true of pieces listed as RD. Others are stained and blotchy.

Proofs. Matte Proof Lincoln cents of a new style were made from 1909 to 1916. These have minutely matte or pebbled surfaces caused by special treatment of the dies. The rims are square and sharp. Such pieces cannot easily be told from certain circulation strikes with similar borders. Certified holders usually list these simply as "Proof," not "Matte Proof." Buy only coins that have been verified by an expert. Most are brown, or brown with tinges of red. Nearly all full "red" coins have been dipped or recolored.

Exceptional specimens dated 1917 are reported to exist, although no records exist to indicate they are true Proofs.

Mirror-finish Proofs were made from 1936 to 1942 and again from 1950 to 1958. Proofs of this era are mostly from dies polished overall (including the portrait), although some later issues have frosted ("cameo") portraits. Quality can be a problem for the 1936 to 1942 issues. Check for carbon spots and recoloring. Proofs of later dates are easy to find.

Generally, Proofs below 63 are unattractive and are not desired by most collectors.

GRADING STANDARDS

Caveat: These grading standards do not take sharpness of strike into account.

MS-60 to 70 (Mint State). *Obverse and Reverse:* At MS-65 and higher, the luster is rich on all areas, except perhaps the shoulder (which may be grainy and show original planchet surface). There is no rubbing, and no contact marks are visible except under magnification. Coins with full or nearly full mint orange-red color can be designated RD; those with full or nearly full brown-toned surfaces can be designated BN; and those with a sub-

1909-S, V.D.B. Graded MS-64RB.

stantial percentage of red-orange and of brown can be called RB. Ideally, MS-65 or finer coins should have good eye appeal, which in the RB category means nicely blended colors, not stained or blotched. Below MS-65, full RD coins become scarce, and at MS–60 to 62 they are virtually non-existent, unless they have been dipped. Copper is a very active metal, and influences that define the grade—such as slight abrasions, contact marks, and so on—also affect the color. The ANA grading standards allow for "dull" and/or "spotted" coins at MS–60 and 61, as well as incomplete luster. In the marketplace, interpretations often vary widely. BN and RB coins at MS–60 and 61 are apt to be more attractive than (dipped) RD coins.

Illustrated coin: The rose-orange color of this cent is better than is usually expected for a coin graded Red Brown. Note some toning streaks on the obverse, lighter than the surrounding surfaces, across Lincoln's forehead and nose.

AU-50, 53, 55, 58 (About Uncirculated). *Obverse:* Slight wear shows on Lincoln's cheekbone to the left of his nose, and also on his beard. At AU–55 or 58 there may be some hints of mint red-orange. Most coins in About Uncirculated are BN, but they are seldom designated by color. *Reverse:* Slight wear is evident on the stalks of wheat to the left and right. Otherwise, the same standards apply as for the obverse.

1920-S. Graded AU-58.

EF-40, 45 (Extremely Fine). *Obverse:* Light wear is seen on Lincoln's portrait, and hair detail is gone on the higher areas, especially above the ear. *Reverse:* Light wear is seen overall, but the parallel lines in the wheat stalks are clearly separated.

1914-D. Graded EF-45.

VF-20, 30 (Very Fine). *Obverse:* Lincoln's portrait is worn all over, with most hair detail gone at the center. Hair separation is seen at the back and the top of the head, but hairs are blended together. The jaw outline is clear. The center of the ear is defined and the bow-tie is clear. The date and lettering is sharp. *Reverse:* More wear is seen, but still the lines in the wheat stalks are separated. Lettering shows wear but is very clear.

1922-D, No D. Graded VF-20.

Illustrated coin: This coin features even wear and few marks.

F-12, 15 (Fine). *Obverse:* More wear is seen overall. Hair definition is less. The center of the ear is partially visible. The jaw outline and bowtie are clear. *Reverse:* Most lines in the wheat stalks are either weak or blended with others, but more than half of the separating lines are clear.

Illustrated coin: Other than one deep contact mark in the cheek, the surfaces are smooth.

1922-D, No D. Graded F-15.

VG-8, 10 (Very Good). *Obverse:* The portrait is more worn, with only slight hair strands visible (thick strands blended). The ear opening is visible. The bowtie and jacket show fewer details. *Reverse:* The lines in the wheat stalks are blended together in flat areas. Perhaps 40% to 50% of the separating lines can be seen. The rim may be weak in areas.

1909-S. Graded VG-10.

G-4, 6 (Good). *Obverse:* The portrait is well worn. Some slight details are seen at the top of the head and the bottom of the coat. LIBERTY is weak. The rim may touch or blend with the tops of the letters forming IN GOD WE TRUST. The date and mintmark (if any) are very clear. *Reverse:* The wheat stalks are flat, with just a few scattered details visible.

1914-D. Graded G-6.

AG-3 (About Good). *Obverse:* Wear is extensive. The portrait is mostly in outline form, with only scattered details visible. LIBERTY is weak and perhaps with some letters missing. IN GOD WE TRUST blends in with the rim, and several letters are very weak or missing. *Reverse:* The rim is worn down to blend with the outside of the wheat stalks in some areas, although some hints of the edge of the stalks can be seen. Lettering is weak, with up to several letters missing.

1913-D. Graded AG-3.

PF-60 to 70 (Matte Proof). *Obverse and Reverse:* At the Matte PF-65 level or higher there are no traces of abrasion or contact marks. Color will range from brown (BN)—the most common—to brown with significant tinges of mint red-orange (RB), or with much mint color (RD). Most RD coins have been dipped. Some tiny flecks are normal on coins certified as PF-65 but should be microscopic or absent above that. Coins in the PF–60 to

1909, V.D.B. Matte Proof. Graded PF-68RD.

63 range are BN or sometimes RB—almost impossible to be RD unless dipped. Lower-grade Proofs usually have poor eye appeal.

Illustrated coin: Most of the red tint is medium orange, but there is a faint pink tint to the upper-left obverse.

PF-60 to 70 (Mirror Proof). *Obverse and Reverse:* PF-65 and higher coins are usually RB (colors should be nicely blended) or RD, the latter with bright red-orange fading slightly to hints of brown. Some tiny flecks are normal on coins certified as PF-65 but should be microscopic or absent above that. PF–60 and 61 coins can be dull, stained, or spotted but still have some original mint color. Coins with fingerprints must be given

1936. Mirror Proof. Graded PF-66RD.

a low numerical grade. Lower-grade Proofs usually have poor eye appeal.

Illustrated coin: The mirrored surfaces are free of blemish.

Designer's initials, V.D.B.
(1909 Reverse Only)

No V.D.B. on Reverse
(1909–1958)

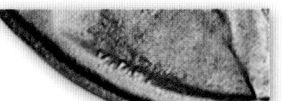

V.D.B. on Shoulder
(Starting 1918)

1909-S, S Over
Horizontal S
FS-01-1909S-1502.

	Mintage	Cert	Avg	%MS	G-4	VG-8	F-12	VF-20	EF-40	AU-50	MS-60BN / PF-63RB	MS-63BN / PF-64RB	MS-65RD / PF-65RD
1909, V.D.B.	27,995,000	12,584	63.4	96%	$15	$16	$17	$18	$19	$20	$25	$30	$165
	Auctions: $881, MS-67RD, July 2014; $823, MS-67RD, September 2014; $1,763, MS-67RD, June 2013; $499, MS-66RD+, August 2014												
1909, V.D.B., Proof (a)	1,194	55	65.0								$9,500	$17,500	
	Auctions: $258,500, PF-67RB+, August 2014; $55,813, PF-66RB, June 2014												
1909-S, V.D.B. † (b)	484,000	8,783	44.1	40%	$600	$625	$675	$725	$950	$1,000	$1,200	$1,350	$4,000
	Auctions: $117,500, MS-67RD, February 2014; $70,500, MS-67, August 2016; $17,625, MS-66RD, August 2014												
1909	72,702,618	2,269	61.9	92%	$4	$5	$6	$7	$8	$12	$17	$20	$160
	Auctions: $1,880, MS-67RD, August 2014; $1,763, MS-67RD, November 2014; $4,406, MS-67RD, April 2013; $670, MS-66RD+, October 2014												
1909, Proof	2,618	262	64.6								$675	$1,150	$2,700
	Auctions: $6,463, PF-66RB+, August 2014; $5,875, PF-66RD, April 2013; $1,782, PF-65RD, August 2014; $1,657, PF-64RD, August 2014												
1909-S	1,825,000	3,484	39.7	37%	$75	$85	$100	$130	$150	$225	$300	$350	$1,000
	Auctions: $10,281, MS-67RD, February 2013; $4,700, MS-66RD, November 2014; $3,760, MS-66, March 2016												
1909-S, S Over Horizontal S	(c)	582	49.9	63%	$95	$100	$120	$150	$200	$275	$325	$370	$1,250
	Auctions: $1,880, MS-66RD, September 2014; $1,880, MS-66, August 2015; $969, MS-65RD, July 2014												
1910	146,801,218	1,269	63.3	95%	$0.35	$0.50	$1	$1.50	$4	$10	$18	$25	$230
	Auctions: $4,406, MS-67RD, June 2014; $3,055, MS-67RD, September 2014; $2,938, MS-67RD, November 2014												
1910, Proof	4,118	244	64.2								$550	$1,100	$2,500
	Auctions: $7,638, PF-67RB, August 2014; $1,764, PF-65RB, July 2014; $470, PF-63RB, August 2014; $3,290, PF, January 2013												
1910-S	6,045,000	1,367	56.1	74%	$17	$20	$22	$25	$45	$80	$100	$120	$650
	Auctions: $15,275, MS-66RD, June 2014; $1,880, MS-66RD, August 2014; $1,998, MS-66RD, October 2014; $206, MS-64RB, November 2014												
1911	101,177,787	691	63.3	96%	$0.45	$0.65	$1.50	$2.50	$6	$11	$21	$50	$400
	Auctions: $7,050, MS-67RD, April 2014; $1,645, MS-66RD, October 2014; $441, MS-65RD, August 2014; $165, MS-64RD, August 2014												
1911, Proof	1,725	206	64.3								$550	$1,050	$3,500
	Auctions: $9,400, PF-66RD, June 2014; $14,688, PF-66RB, August 2014; $853, PF-65BN, October 2014; $705, PF-64RB, August 2014												
1911-D	12,672,000	840	58.4	76%	$6	$7	$10	$20	$50	$75	$95	$125	$1,100
	Auctions: $8,225, MS-66RD, April 2014; $7,050, MS-66RD, October 2014; $6,169, MS-66RD, October 2014; $3,819, MS-65RD, September 2014												
1911-S	4,026,000	1,095	46.8	46%	$35	$45	$55	$60	$75	$110	$185	$235	$2,250
	Auctions: $14,100, MS-66RD, October 2014; $881, MS-65RB, November 2014; $2,820, MS-65RD, August 2013; $505, MS-64RD, October 2014												
1912	68,153,060	679	62.9	94%	$1.25	$1.65	$2.25	$5.50	$13	$25	$35	$50	$475
	Auctions: $18,800, MS-67RD, April 2013; $499, MS-65RD, December 2014; $441, MS-65RD, October 2014; $118, MS-64RD, July 2014												
1912, Proof	2,172	215	64.3								$550	$1,050	$6,000
	Auctions: $3,966, PF-66RB, February 2014; $14,100, PF-66RB+, August 2014; $999, PF-65RB, October 2014; $940, PF-64RB, July 2014												
1912-D	10,411,000	637	56.5	68%	$7	$8	$10	$25	$65	$100	$170	$240	$1,850
	Auctions: $8,238, MS-66RD, September 2014; $1,998, MS-65RD+, November 2014; $7,050, MS-65RD, February 2013; $823, MS-64RD, July 2014												
1912-S	4,431,000	894	48.3	54%	$20	$25	$30	$40	$75	$110	$180	$255	$1,800
	Auctions: $2,820, MS-65RD, October 2014; $4,406, MS-65RD, November 2013; $1,410, MS-64RD, August 2014; $783, MS-64RD, November 2014												

† Ranked in the *100 Greatest U.S. Coins* (fourth edition). *Note:* No early references (pre-1960s), Mint records, or reliable market listings have been found to confirm the existence of true 1917 Proofs. "Examples seen have had nice matte-like surfaces, sometimes on just one side, but have lacked the vital combination of broad, flat rims on both sides and a mirror Proof edge (when viewed edge-on from the side)" (*A Guide Book of Lincoln Cents*). The leading certification services do not recognize Proofs of this year. The editors of this book also do not believe that true Proofs of 1917 exist. **a.** Of the 1,194 coins reported struck, an estimated 400 to 600 were issued. **b.** Many counterfeits exist—some die struck, some made by adding an "S" to a Philadelphia coin. **c.** Included in 1909-S mintage figure.

**1917, Doubled Die
Obverse
FS-01-1917-101.**

	Mintage	Cert	Avg	%MS	G-4	VG-8	F-12	VF-20	EF-40	AU-50	MS-60BN / PF-63RB	MS-63BN / PF-64RB	MS-65RD / PF-65RD
1913	76,532,352	704	62.5	94%	$0.85	$1	$2	$4	$18	$27	$35	$55	$425
Auctions: $19,975, MS-67RD, January 2013; $1,410, MS-66RD, July 2014; $529, MS-65RD, July 2014; $470, MS-65RD, August 2014													
1913, Proof	2,983	319	64.5								$500	$1,050	$2,500
Auctions: $25,850, PF-67RD, January 2014; $8,225, PF-67RB, August 2014; $1,410, PF-65RB, November 2014; $1,058, PF-64RD, October 2014													
1913-D	15,804,000	618	575.8	74%	$3	$3.50	$4.50	$10	$50	$70	$110	$175	$1,650
Auctions: $10,575, MS-66RD, January 2014; $8,225, MS-66RD, October 2014; $881, MS-64RD, August 2014; $705, MS-64RD, September 2014													
1913-S	6,101,000	775	48.9	55%	$10	$15	$20	$30	$60	$100	$175	$225	$3,500
Auctions: $4,406, MS-65RD, June 2014; $676, MS-64RD, July 2014; $388, MS-63RD, September 2014; $823, MS-61BN, October 2014													
1914	75,238,432	730	60.5	86%	$0.75	$1	$2	$6	$20	$40	$55	$70	$500
Auctions: $28,200, MS-67RD, August 2013; $2,585, MS-66RD, November 2014; $499, MS-65RD, July 2014; $270, MS-64RD, September 2014													
1914, Proof	1,365	153	64.7								$550	$1,100	$2,500
Auctions: $3,525, PF-66BN, June 2014; $8,226, PF-66RB+, August 2014; $4,406, PF-66RB, October 2014; $1,410, PF-65RB, July 2014													
1914-D (d)	1,193,000	4,990	24.6	9%	$175	$200	$225	$275	$750	$1,450	$2,000	$3,000	$17,000
Auctions: $28,200, MS-65RD+, October 2014; $18,800, MS-65RD, January 2014; $17,625, MS-65, March 2016													
1914-S	4,137,000	825	42.7	33%	$20	$25	$30	$40	$85	$175	$325	$460	$6,000
Auctions: $5,875, MS-65RD, September 2014; $6,463, MS-65RD, September 2013; $1,528, MS-64RD, July 2014; $793, MS-64BN, October 2014													
1915	29,092,120	606	60.1	84%	$1.75	$2.50	$5	$18	$60	$70	$90	$105	$875
Auctions: $10,575, MS-67RD, September 2014; $3,525, MS-66RD, January 2014; $1,293, MS-66RD, November 2014; $1,116, MS-65RD, August 2014													
1915, Proof	1,150	132	64.7								$600	$1,200	$3,500
Auctions: $4,406, PF-66RB, July 2014; $22,325, PF-66RB+, August 2014; $17,625, PF-65RD, January 2014; $801, PF-64BN, October 2014													
1915-D	22,050,000	941	57.8	79%	$2	$3	$4	$7	$22	$45	$85	$120	$1,100
Auctions: $4,465, MS-66RD, October 2014; $7,638, MS-66RD, June 2013; $1,063, MS-65RD, September 2014; $940, MS-65RD, November 2014													
1915-S	4,833,000	679	46.5	46%	$20	$25	$30	$35	$70	$135	$200	$235	$5,000
Auctions: $23,500, MS-66RD, September 2013; $7,638, MS-65RD, November 2014; $3,055, MS-64RD, October 2014; $852, MS-63RB, July 2014													
1916	131,833,677	871	62.9	96%	$0.30	$0.50	$0.75	$2	$8	$13	$18	$35	$300
Auctions: $2,350, MS-67RD, March 2014; $1,880, MS-67RD, August 2014; $2,820, MS-67RD, October 2014; $505, MS-66RD, July 2014													
1916, Proof	1,050	96	64.7								$1,250	$2,500	$12,000
Auctions: $30,550, PF-66RB+, August 2014; $1,880, PF-64RB, October 2014; $7,931, PF-64RB, June 2014; $4,700, PF-63RB, July 2014													
1916-D	35,956,000	796	60.7	85%	$1	$1.75	$3	$6	$15	$35	$75	$150	$1,500
Auctions: $17,625, MS-66RD, June 2014; $282, MS-65RB, August 2014; $823, MS-64RD+, July 2014; $441, MS-64RD, October 2014													
1916-S	22,510,000	795	58.4	73%	$1.75	$2.25	$3.50	$8	$25	$50	$105	$175	$7,500
Auctions: $911, MS-65RB, July 2014; $7,638, MS-65RD, August 2013; $1,183, MS-64RD, October 2014; $1,410, MS-64RD, November 2014													
1917	196,429,785	780	60.6	90%	$0.30	$0.40	$0.50	$2	$4	$10	$16	$32	$425
Auctions: $823, MS-66RD, September 2014; $1,586, MS-66RD+, November 2014; $2,585, MS-66RD, January 2013; $145, MS-64RD, September 2014													
1917, Doubled Die Obverse	(e)	70	34.1	16%	$85	$145	$225	$450	$1,000	$1,600	$2,750	$5,750	$19,500
Auctions: $499, MS-65RB, October 2014; $329, MS-64RB, July 2014; $705, VF-35, January 2015													
1917-D	55,120,000	670	59.9	81%	$0.80	$1	$1.75	$4.50	$35	$50	$80	$125	$1,650
Auctions: $9,400, MS-65RD, August 2014; $2,350, MS-65RD, August 2013; $1,116, MS-64RD, August 2014; $2,703, MS-64RD, November 2014													
1917-S	32,620,000	469	59.5	81%	$0.50	$0.65	$1	$2.50	$10	$25	$75	$160	$8,500
Auctions: $11,750, MS-67RD, August 2014; $17,625, MS-67RD, November 2014; $881, MS-66RD, November 2014; $4,113, MS-65RD, December 2013													

d. Many counterfeits exist, including crude fakes, sophisticated die-struck forgeries, and altered 1944-D cents (the latter, unlike an authentic 1914-D cent, will have the designer's initials, V.D.B., on the shoulder). **e.** Included in 1917 mintage figure.

1922, No D
FS-01-1922-401.

1922, Weak D

	Mintage	Cert	Avg	%MS	G-4	VG-8	F-12	VF-20	EF-40	AU-50	MS-60BN	MS-63BN	MS-65RD
											PF-63RB	PF-64RB	PF-65RD
1918	288,104,634	630	63.2	95%	$0.20	$0.30	$0.50	$1.50	$3	$8	$16	$27	$350
	Auctions: $423, MS-64BN, September 2014; $200, MS-63RB, August 2014; $74, MS-62BN, November 2014; $14,100, MS, March 2014												
1918-D	47,830,000	502	59.0	75%	$0.75	$1.25	$2.50	$4	$12	$35	$80	$140	$3,500
	Auctions: $25,850, MS-66RD, August 2013; $11,163, MS-65RD, October 2014; $1,528, MS-64RD, November 2014; $764, MS-64RB, August 2014												
1918-S	34,680,000	560	59.7	76%	$0.50	$1	$2	$3	$11	$32	$80	$185	$10,000
	Auctions: $823, MS-67RD, August 2014; $1,058, MS-67RD, October 2014; $499, MS-66RD, August 2014; $3,525, MS-64RD, February 2014												
1919	392,021,000	803	63.1	95%	$0.20	$0.30	$0.40	$1	$3.25	$5	$14	$28	$175
	Auctions: $8,225, MS-68RD, April 2014; $1,058, MS-67RD, October 2014; $499, MS-66RD, August 2014; $182, MS-65RD, September 2014												
1919-D	57,154,000	599	61.4	88%	$0.50	$0.75	$1	$4	$10	$32	$65	$110	$1,500
	Auctions: $1,763, MS-65RD, January 2014; $1,410, MS-65RD, October 2014; $353, MS-64RB, July 2014; $311, MS-64RB, August 2014												
1919-S	139,760,000	668	60.3	82%	$0.20	$0.40	$1	$2	$6	$18	$50	$115	$6,500
	Auctions: $7,638, MS-65RD, April 2014; $482, MS-64RB, July 2014; $259, MS-64RB, November 2014; $123, MS-63BN, December 2014												
1920	310,165,000	730	63.1	95%	$0.20	$0.30	$0.35	$0.50	$2.25	$4	$15	$28	$225
	Auctions: $940, MS-66RD, January 2013; $881, MS-66RD+, September 2014; $705, MS-66RD, September 2014; $200, MS-65RD, November 2014												
1920-D	49,280,000	509	60.4	83%	$1	$2	$3	$6.50	$19	$40	$80	$110	$1,650
	Auctions: $22,325, MS-66RD, June 2014; $283, MS-64RB, November 2014; $182, MS-63RB, October 2014; $45, MS-60BN, November 2014												
1920-S	46,220,000	530	59.3	75%	$0.50	$0.65	$1.50	$2.25	$10	$35	$110	$185	$12,500
	Auctions: $3,173, MS-64RD, October 2014; $2,115, MS-64RD, February 2013; $259, MS-63RB, November 2014; $79, MS-62BN, November 2014												
1921	39,157,000	590	62.6	93%	$0.50	$0.60	$1.30	$2.10	$9	$22	$50	$80	$345
	Auctions: $3,290, MS-66RD, January 2014; $411, MS-65RD, September 2014; $112, MS-64RD, October 2014; $16, MS-60RD, November 2014												
1921-S	15,274,000	707	56.4	62%	$1.50	$2.25	$3.50	$7	$35	$75	$135	$190	$11,500
	Auctions: $1,293, MS-65RB, September 2014; $499, MS-64RB, July 2014; $1,880, MS-64RD, August 2013; $282, MS-63RB, November 2014												
1922-D	7,160,000	1,701	41.2	42%	$20	$21	$25	$27	$40	$75	$110	$165	$1,500
	Auctions: $2,585, MS-65RD, August 2013; $499, MS-64RD, November 2014; $229, MS-63RD, July 2014; $106, MS-62RB, November 2014												
1922, No D (f)	**(g)**	3,280	21.3	2%	$500	$600	$750	$900	$2,000	$4,000	$10,000	$20,000	
	Auctions: $82,250, MS-65BN, April 2013; $20,563, MS-63, February 2015; $3,819, AU-55BN, August 2014												
1922, Weak D (f)	**(g)**	561	16.3	3%	$25	$35	$50	$70	$160	$200	$350	$1,000	
	Auctions: $2,174, MS, April 2014; $376, AU-58BN, October 2014; $329, AU-58BN, October 2014; $153, AU-55BN, October 2014												
1923	74,723,000	592	63.1	97%	$0.35	$0.45	$0.65	$1	$5	$9.50	$15	$30	$350
	Auctions: $4,700, MS-67RD, June 2013; $1,645, MS-66RD+, September 2014; $247, MS-64RD+, July 2014; $84, MS-64RD, November 2014												
1923-S	8,700,000	441	55.7	58%	$5	$7	$8	$12	$40	$90	$220	$390	$17,000
	Auctions: $2,350, MS-65RB, June 2014; $3,055, MS-64RB, October 2014; $823, MS-64RB, November 2014; $353, MS-62RB, August 2014												
1924	75,178,000	411	63.1	95%	$0.20	$0.30	$0.40	$0.85	$5	$10	$24	$50	$375
	Auctions: $16,450, MS-67RD, April 2013; $12,925, MS-67RD, July 2014; $470, MS-65RD, November 2014; $259, MS-64RD, November 2014												
1924-D	2,520,000	1,257	42.6	35%	$40	$45	$50	$60	$125	$175	$300	$350	$12,500
	Auctions: $9,400, MS-65RD, January 2014; $2,820, MS-64RD, November 2014; $1,410, MS-64, March 2016												
1924-S	11,696,000	498	55.5	63%	$2	$2.50	$3.50	$5.50	$20	$75	$125	$225	$20,000
	Auctions: $9,400, MS-64RD, January 2014; $764, MS-64RB, November 2014; $529, MS-63RB, October 2014; $88, MS-60BN, November 2014												

f. 1922 cents with a weak or completely missing mintmark were made from extremely worn dies that originally struck normal 1922-D cents. Three different die pairs were involved; two of them produced "Weak D" coins. One die pair (no. 2, identified by a "strong reverse") is acknowledged as having struck "No D" coins. Weak D cents are worth considerably less. Beware of fraudulently removed mintmark.
g. Included in 1922-D mintage figure.

	Mintage	Cert	Avg	%MS	G-4	VG-8	F-12	VF-20	EF-40	AU-50	MS-60BN	MS-63BN	MS-65RD
											PF-63RB	PF-64RB	PF-65RD
1925	139,949,000	828	64.2	98%	$0.20	$0.25	$0.35	$0.60	$3	$6.50	$10	$20	$135
	Auctions: $1,410, MS-67RD, August 2014; $2,115, MS-67RD, September 2013; $110, MS-65RD, December 2014; $44, MS-64RD, September 2014												
1925-D	22,580,000	639	61.0	86%	$1	$1.30	$2.50	$5	$13	$30	$75	$90	$3,750
	Auctions: $4,113, MS-65RD, January 2014; $764, MS-64RD+, July 2014; $382, MS-64RD, September 2014; $129, MS-63RB, October 2014												
1925-S	26,380,000	502	59.4	77%	$1	$1.50	$2	$4	$12	$30	$90	$200	$18,000
	Auctions: $4,700, MS-65RB, February 2014; $852, MS-64RB, July 2014; $259, MS-63RB, October 2014; $200, MS-62BN, November 2014												
1926	157,088,000	1,038	64.4	99%	$0.20	$0.25	$0.30	$0.50	$2	$4	$8	$18	$75
	Auctions: $1,116, MS-67RD, January 2014; $353, MS-66RD, July 2014; $259, MS-65RD, October 2014; $84, MS-65RD, November 2014												
1926-D	28,020,000	493	59.8	81%	$1.35	$1.75	$3.50	$5.25	$14	$32	$85	$125	$1,750
	Auctions: $4,700, MS-65RD, February 2013; $353, MS-64RB, November 2014; $353, MS-64RB, December 2014; $364, MS-63RB, July 2014												
1926-S	4,550,000	936	53.2	48%	$9	$10	$13	$17	$35	$75	$155	$325	$90,000
	Auctions: $9,988, MS-65RD, October 2013; $1,058, MS-64RD, November 2014; $1,058, MS-63RB, August 2014; $259, MS-62BN, November 2014												
1927	144,440,000	762	63.7	96%	$0.20	$0.25	$0.30	$0.60	$2	$3.50	$10	$20	$125
	Auctions: $7,638, MS-67RD, February 2014; $1,880, MS-67RD, October 2014; $368, MS-66RD, September 2014; $115, MS-65RD, August 2014												
1927-D	27,170,000	584	61.1	85%	$1.25	$1.75	$2.75	$3.75	$7.50	$25	$62	$85	$2,000
	Auctions: $2,233, MS-65RD, January 2014; $617, MS-65RB, July 2014; $159, MS-64RB, September 2014; $212, MS-64RB, December 2014												
1927-S	14,276,000	439	60.1	79%	$1.50	$2	$3	$5	$15	$40	$85	$140	$7,750
	Auctions: $529, MS-64RB, July 2014; $1,763, MS-64RD, June 2013; $535, MS-63RD, November 2014; $86, MS-62BN, November 2014												
1928	134,116,000	845	63.8	97%	$0.20	$0.25	$0.30	$0.60	$2	$3	$9	$13	$120
	Auctions: $1,058, MS-67RD, September 2014; $3,408, MS-67RD, April 2013; $499, MS-66RD, July 2014; $120, MS-65RD, October 2014												
1928-D	31,170,000	532	61.7	86%	$0.75	$1	$1.75	$3	$5.50	$17	$37	$80	$1,000
	Auctions: $7,050, MS-66RD, November 2014; $1,410, MS-65RD, June 2014; $141, MS-64RD, September 2014; $51, MS-63RB, November 2014												
1928-S	17,266,000	345	60.8	84%	$1	$1.60	$2.75	$3.75	$9.50	$30	$75	$100	$4,500
	Auctions: $4,406, MS-65RD, September 2013; $764, MS-64RB, October 2014; $470, MS-64RB, November 2014; $382, MS-63RB, November 2014												
1929	185,262,000	983	64.4	98%	$0.20	$0.25	$0.30	$0.75	$2	$4	$8	$14	$100
	Auctions: $5,581, MS-67RD, April 2014; $1,528, MS-67RD, August 2014; $705, MS-67RD, September 2014; $382, MS-66RD+, August 2014												
1929-D	41,730,000	437	62.6	93%	$0.40	$0.85	$1.25	$2.25	$5.50	$13	$25	$37	$550
	Auctions: $4,113, MS-66RD, January 2014; $2,585, MS-66RD, August 2014; $1,645, MS-66RD, October 2014; $458, MS-65RD, July 2014												
1929-S	50,148,000	699	63.4	96%	$0.50	$0.90	$1.65	$2.35	$5.80	$14	$21	$29	$400
	Auctions: $4,700, MS-66RD, October 2014; $4,113, MS-66RD, March 2013; $411, MS-65RD, October 2014; $65, MS-64RD, October 2014												
1930	157,415,000	3,560	65.3	100%	$0.15	$0.20	$0.25	$0.50	$1.25	$2	$6	$10	$40
	Auctions: $3,525, MS-67RD, February 2014; $823, MS-67RD, August 2014; $108, MS-66RD, October 2014; $40, MS-65RD, October 2014												
1930-D	40,100,000	685	64.1	98%	$0.20	$0.25	$0.30	$0.55	$2.50	$4	$12	$28	$145
	Auctions: $1,645, MS-66RD, June 2014; $441, MS-66RD, October 2014; $142, MS-65RD, August 2014; $141, MS-65RD, September 2014												
1930-S	24,286,000	1,551	64.8	99%	$0.20	$0.25	$0.30	$0.60	$1.75	$6	$10	$12	$90
	Auctions: $6,463, MS-66RD, April 2014; $2,377, MS-66RD, August 2014; $499, MS-66RD, October 2014; $84, MS-65RD, November 2014												
1931	19,396,000	676	64.1	97%	$0.50	$0.75	$1	$1.50	$4	$9	$20	$35	$125
	Auctions: $5,288, MS-67RD, August 2013; $999, MS-66RD, August 2014; $153, MS-65RD, July 2014; $42, MS-64RB, October 2014												
1931-D	4,480,000	794	59.5	70%	$5	$6	$7	$8.50	$13.50	$37	$60	$70	$875
	Auctions: $4,113, MS-66RD, April 2013; $1,528, MS-65RD, August 2014; $270, MS-65RB, October 2014; $165, MS-64RB, July 2014												
1931-S	866,000	4,816	54.8	60%	$60	$75	$85	$100	$125	$150	$175	$195	$550
	Auctions: $2,350, MS-66RD, January 2014; $646, MS-65RD, October 2014; $646, MS-65, August 2015												
1932	9,062,000	737	64.4	97%	$1.50	$1.75	$2	$2.50	$4.50	$12	$20	$28	$100
	Auctions: $259, MS-66RD, November 2014; $940, MS-66RD, September 2013; $95, MS-65RD, October 2014; $34, MS-64RB, October 2014												
1932-D	10,500,000	470	63.7	93%	$1.50	$1.75	$2.50	$2.75	$4.50	$11	$19	$28	$175
	Auctions: $8,519, MS-67RD, November 2013; $206, MS-65RD, August 2014; $56, MS-64RD, September 2014; $49, MS-64RD, October 2014												
1933	14,360,000	706	64.7	98%	$1.50	$1.75	$2.50	$3	$6.25	$13	$20	$30	$115
	Auctions: $2,115, MS-67RD, October 2014; $3,557, MS-67RD, August 2013; $112, MS-65RD, July 2014; $32, MS-64RB, July 2014												
1933-D	6,200,000	1,050	64.3	97%	$3.50	$3.75	$5.50	$7.25	$12	$19	$26	$25	$135
	Auctions: $5,581, MS-67RD, February 2014; $764, MS-67RD, October 2014; $558, MS-66RD+, November 2014; $141, MS-65RD, August 2014												

1934, Doubled Die Obverse
FS-01-1934-101.

1936, Doubled Die Obverse
FS-01-1936-101.

	Mintage	Cert	Avg	%MS	G-4	VG-8	F-12	VF-20	EF-40	AU-50	MS-60BN PF-63RB	MS-63BN PF-64RB	MS-65RD PF-65RD
1934	219,080,000	2,106	65.6	99%	$0.15	$0.18	$0.20	$0.30	$1	$4	$10	$7	$37
	Auctions: $1,058, MS-67RD, September 2014; $1,058, MS-67RD+, November 2014; $764, MS-67RD, December 2013; $33, MS-66RD, November 2014												
1934, Doubled Die Obverse (h)	(i)	4	59.3	75%								$300	
	Auctions: $1,600, MS-64RB, October 2011												
1934-D	28,446,000	929	64.7	98%	$0.20	$0.25	$0.50	$0.75	$2.25	$7.50	$22	$20	$62
	Auctions: $11,163, MS-67RD, April 2014; $229, MS-66RD, July 2014; $123, MS-66RD, October 2014; $223, MS-66RD, December 2014												
1935	245,388,000	1,950	65.6	99%	$0.15	$0.18	$0.20	$0.25	$0.50	$1	$3	$5	$33
	Auctions: $1,293, MS-67RD, March 2014; $106, MS-67RD, October 2014; $92, MS-67RD, November 2014; $106, MS-64RB, November 2014												
1935-D	47,000,000	1,387	65.7	100%	$0.15	$0.18	$0.20	$0.25	$0.50	$2	$5	$6	$39
	Auctions: $823, MS-67RD, February 2014; $153, MS-67RD, August 2014; $141, MS-67RD, October 2014; $588, MS-67RD, November 2014												
1935-S	38,702,000	886	64.8	99%	$0.15	$0.18	$0.25	$0.50	$2	$5	$12	$17	$60
	Auctions: $1,469, MS-67RD, October 2014; $3,055, MS-66RD+, July 2014; $1,175, MS-66RD, October 2014; $106, MS-65RD, December 2014												
1936	309,632,000	2,702	65.4	98%	$0.15	$0.18	$0.25	$0.50	$1.50	$2.60	$5	$2	$30
	Auctions: $705, MS-67RD, February 2014; $353, MS-67RD, July 2014; $2,820, MS-67RD+, September 2014; $306, MS-67RD, October 2014												
1936, Doubled Die Obverse (j)	(k)	52	44.4	29%		$75	$125	$200	$350	$500	$1,500		
	Auctions: $646, MS-62BN, August 2014; $259, AU-50, April 2014; $80, VF-30BN, November 2014; $76, VF-30BN, November 2014												
1936, Proof	5,569	737	64.0								$200	$485	$2,000
	Auctions: $21,150, PF-66Cam, June 2013; $3,525, PF-66RD, October 2014; $2,585, PF-65RD, October 2014; $823, PF-64RD, October 2014												
1936-D	40,620,000	1,749	65.9	100%	$0.15	$0.20	$0.30	$0.50	$1	$2	$4	$2	$21
	Auctions: $646, MS-67RD, August 2013; $411, MS-67RD, October 2014; $145, MS-67RD, October 2014; $79, MS-67RD, December 2014												
1936-S	29,130,000	1,290	65.5	99%	$0.15	$0.25	$0.40	$0.55	$1	$3	$5	$6	$25
	Auctions: $4,259, MS-67RD, February 2014; $2,703, MS-67RD, September 2014; $2,585, MS-67RD, November 2014; $881, MS-66RD+, October 2014												
1937	309,170,000	4,050	66.0	100%	$0.15	$0.20	$0.30	$0.50	$1	$2	$3	$2	$15
	Auctions: $90, MS-67RD, August 2014; $94, MS-67RD, October 2014; $2,233, MS-67RD+, November 2013; $35, MS-66RD, November 2014												
1937, Proof	9,320	878	64.4								$65	$90	$350
	Auctions: $21,150, PF-67Cam, September 2013; $5,288, PF-66Cam, August 2014; $1,763, PF-65Cam, October 2014; $3,643, PF-64RD, July 2014												
1937-D	50,430,000	2,680	66.2	100%	$0.15	$0.20	$0.25	$0.40	$1	$3	$5	$6	$17
	Auctions: $135, MS-67RD, January 2014; $123, MS-67RD, August 2014; $106, MS-67RD, August 2014; $40, MS-66RD, August 2014												
1937-S	34,500,000	1,587	65.9	100%	$0.15	$0.20	$0.30	$0.40	$1	$3	$5	$8	$22
	Auctions: $1,998, MS-67RD, January 2014; $881, MS-67RD+, July 2014; $764, MS-67RD+, July 2014; $55, MS-66RD, July 2014												
1938	156,682,000	2,398	66.0	100%	$0.15	$0.20	$0.30	$0.40	$1	$2	$4	$7	$16
	Auctions: $2,585, MS-67RD+, September 2014; $106, MS-67RD, October 2014; $2,820, MS-67RD, November 2013; $27, MS-66RD, November 2014												
1938, Proof	14,734	1,019	64.5								$60	$80	$200
	Auctions: $2,585, PF-66Cam, January 2014; $1,058, PF-66Cam, September 2014; $1,469, PF-66Cam, November 2014; $881, PF-65Cam, October 2014												
1938-D	20,010,000	2,087	66.1	100%	$0.20	$0.30	$0.50	$0.80	$1.25	$3	$4	$7	$17
	Auctions: $3,055, MS-67RD, January 2014; $3,290, MS-67RD, August 2014; $100, MS-67RD, November 2014; $89, MS-67RD, December 2014												
1938-S	15,180,000	2,604	66.1	100%	$0.40	$0.50	$0.60	$0.75	$1.10	$3	$4	$6	$21
	Auctions: $2,115, MS-67RD+, July 2014; $118, MS-67RD, July 2014; $92, MS-67RD, August 2014; $40, MS-66RD, August 2014												

h. The remains of a secondary 3 and 4 are evident below the primary digits. **i.** Included in 1934 mintage figure. **j.** FS-01-1936-101.
k. Included in circulation-strike 1936 mintage figure.

	Mintage	Cert	Avg	%MS	G-4	VG-8	F-12	VF-20	EF-40	AU-50	MS-60BN PF-63RB	MS-63BN PF-64RB	MS-65RD PF-65RD
1939	316,466,000	3,109	66.0	100%	$0.15	$0.18	$0.20	$0.25	$0.50	$1	$2	$2	$14
Auctions: $108, MS-67RD, August 2014; $106, MS-67RD, October 2014; $705, MS-67RD, June 2013; $38, MS-66RD, December 2014												
1939, Proof	13,520	1,022	64.6								$55	$70	$180
Auctions: $2,820, PF-67RD, January 2014; $1,410, PF-67RD, October 2014; $270, PF-66RD, November 2014; $212, PF-65RD, September 2014												
1939-D	15,160,000	1,770	66.1	100%	$0.50	$0.60	$0.65	$0.85	$1.25	$3	$4	$4	$18
Auctions: $529, MS-67RD, April 2014; $86, MS-67RD, October 2014; $100, MS-67RD, November 2014; $69, MS-67RD, December 2014												
1939-S	52,070,000	3,421	66.0	100%	$0.15	$0.20	$0.30	$0.75	$1	$2.50	$3	$3	$16
Auctions: $1,175, MS-67RD+, July 2014; $1,116, MS-67RD+, August 2014; $3,966, MS-67RD, August 2013; $24, MS-66RD, November 2014												
1940	586,810,000	2,669	66.0	100%	$0.15	$0.18	$0.20	$0.40	$0.60	$1	$2	$2	$14
Auctions: $3,819, MS-67RD, January 2014; $212, MS-67RD, July 2014; $147, MS-67RD, September 2014; $74, MS-65RD, November 2014												
1940, Proof	15,872	1,016	64.5								$45	$60	$170
Auctions: $7,931, PF-67RD, June 2013; $4,700, PF-67RD, August 2014; $6,463, PF-67RD, October 2014; $764, PF-66RD, July 2014												
1940-D	81,390,000	1,520	66.1	100%	$0.15	$0.18	$0.25	$0.60	$0.75	$2	$3	$2	$15
Auctions: $94, MS-67RD, August 2014; $68, MS-67RD, November 2014; $119, MS-67RD, December 2014; $159, MS-67RD, January 2013												
1940-S	112,940,000	2,512	66.0	100%	$0.15	$0.18	$0.20	$0.50	$1	$1.75	$3	$2.25	$15
Auctions: $999, MS-67RD+, November 2014; $100, MS-67RD, November 2014; $79, MS-67RD, December 2014; $306, MS-67RD, June 2013												
1941	887,018,000	3,082	65.9	99%	$0.15	$0.18	$0.20	$0.30	$0.60	$1.50	$2	$1	$14
Auctions: $147, MS-67RD, July 2014; $212, MS-67RD, August 2014; $259, MS-67RD, October 2014; $4,994, MS-65RD, November 2013												
1941, Proof	21,100	1,099	64.4								$40	$55	$165
Auctions: $28,200, PF-67RD, November 2013; $705, PF-66RD, August 2014; $382, PF-66RD, October 2014; $705, PF-64RD, July 2014												
1941-D	128,700,000	1,878	66.4	100%	$0.15	$0.18	$0.20	$0.50	$1	$3	$4	$2	$15
Auctions: $2,115, MS-67RD+, August 2014; $165, MS-67RD, August 2014; $63, MS-67RD, August 2014; $441, MS-67RD, August 2013												
1941-S	92,360,000	2,575	66.1	100%	$0.15	$0.18	$0.30	$0.50	$1	$3	$4	$2	$15
Auctions: $646, MS-67RD, August 2014; $306, MS-67RD, October 2014; $119, MS-67RD, December 2014; $1,880, MS-67RD, November 2013												
1942	657,796,000	2,801	65.8	100%	$0.15	$0.18	$0.20	$0.25	$0.50	$0.75	$1	$1	$14
Auctions: $3,290, MS-67RD+, July 2014; $112, MS-63RB, November 2014; $14,100, AU-58, November 2013; $282, Fair-2BN, November 2014												
1942, Proof	32,600	1,641	64.0								$40	$55	$165
Auctions: $1,880, PF-66Cam, November 2014; $2,115, PF-66Cam, June 2013; $999, PF-65Cam, July 2014; $212, PF-64Cam, November 2014												
1942-D	206,698,000	3,334	66.1	100%	$0.15	$0.18	$0.20	$0.25	$0.50	$0.85	$1	$1	$14
Auctions: $170, MS-67RD, August 2014; $141, MS-67RD, December 2014; $3,055, MS-67RD, November 2013; $20, MS-65RD, November 2014												
1942-S	85,590,000	2,133	65.9	99%	$0.20	$0.25	$0.30	$0.85	$1.25	$5.50	$7	$8	$17
Auctions: $3,290, MS-67RD, February 2014; $2,350, MS-67RD+, September 2014												

	Mintage	Cert	Avg	%MS	F-12	VF-20	EF-40	AU-50	MS-63BN	MS-65	MS-66	MS-67	MS-68
1943, Steel (a)	684,628,670	10,824	66.0	100%	$0.30	$0.35	$0.40	$0.50	$2.50	$8	$35	$175	$1,200
Auctions: $382, MS-67, July 2014; $182, MS-67, November 2014; $1,058, EF-45, September 2014; $1,763, VF-25, October 2014													
1943, Bronze † (a)	**(b)**	8	56.6	25%			$185,000	$225,000					
Auctions: $218,500, AU-58, January 2010													
1943, Silver (a)	**(b)**	0	n/a				$3,500	$5,500					
Auctions: $4,313, AU-58, March 2010													
1943-D	217,660,000	6,834	66.3	100%	$0.35	$0.40	$0.45	$0.75	$3	$10	$35	$225	$1,300
Auctions: $1,175, MS-68, July 2014; $705, MS-68, July 2014; $2,820, MS-68, April 2013; $209, MS-67, October 2014													

† Ranked in the *100 Greatest U.S. Coins* (fourth edition). **a.** Due to a copper shortage in the critical war year 1943, the Treasury used zinc-coated steel for regular-issue cents. A handful were accidentally struck on old bronze and silver planchets, instead of the intended steel planchets. Today about a dozen are known to exist. Numerous regular steel cents have been plated with copper as novelties or with intent to deceive; their true nature is easily revealed with a magnet. **b.** Included in 1943 mintage figure.

**1943-D, Boldly
Doubled
Mintmark**
FS-01-1943D-501.

	Mintage	Cert	Avg	%MS	F-12	VF-20	EF-40	AU-50	MS-63BN	MS-65	MS-66	MS-67	MS-68
1943-D, Boldly Doubled Mintmark (c)	**(d)**	31	64.0	100%	$40	$50	$60	$60	$100	$1,000	$2,500	$7,500	
	Auctions: $1,116, MS-65, December 2013; $411, MS-64, March 2015; $353, MS-63, November 2014												
1943-S	191,550,000	7,368	66.0	100%	$0.40	$0.65	$0.75	$1	$6	$20	$50	$225	$2,000
	Auctions: $306, MS-67, August 2014; $153, MS-67, November 2014; $135, MS-67, December 2014; $165, MS-66, October 2014												

c. FS-01-1943D-501. **d.** Included in 1943-D mintage figure.

   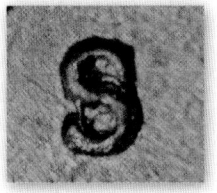

1944-D, D Over S   **1946-S, S Over D**
FS-01-1944D-511.   *FS-01-1946S-511.*

	Mintage	Cert	Avg	%MS	VF-20	EF-40	AU-50	MS-63RB	MS-65RB	MS-65RD	MS-67RD
									PF-65RD	PF-66RD	PF-67RD
1944	1,435,400,000	3,910	65.9	100%	$0.10	$0.20	$0.35	$1	$5	$12	$125
	Auctions: $2,233, MS-67RD+, September 2014; $79, MS-67RD, November 2014; $30,550, AU-58, November 2013										
1944, Steel											
1944-D	430,578,000	3,897	65.6	98%	$0.10	$0.20	$0.35	$0.85	$4	$14	$100
	Auctions: $141, MS-67RD, July 2014; $119, MS-67RD, September 2014; $58, MS-67RD, August 2014; $30,550, AU-53, November 2013										
1944-D, D Over S	**(a)**	102	53.5	51%	$125.00	$175.00	$235.00	$450.00	$700.00	$2,500.00	
	Auctions: $1,116, MS-64RD, January 2014; $470, MS-64RB, September 2014; $517, MS-64, August 2016										
1944-S	282,760,000	5,741	66.0	100%	$0.15	$0.20	$0.35	$0.85	$4	$13	$75
	Auctions: $141, MS-67RD, May 2014; $101, MS-67RD, July 2014; $96, MS-67RD, July 2014										
1945	1,040,515,000	2,871	65.6	100%	$0.10	$0.20	$0.35	$0.85	$2	$8	$200
	Auctions: $764, MS-67RD, November 2014; $41, MS-66RD, August 2014; $36, MS-66RD, August 2014; $3,819, MS-68RD, November 2013										
1945-D	266,268,000	4,188	66.0	100%	$0.10	$0.20	$0.35	$0.85	$2	$9	$125
	Auctions: $2,115, MS-67RD, June 2014; $165, MS-67RD, July 2014; $2,585, MS-67RD, September 2014; $99, MS-67RD, October 2014										
1945-S	181,770,000	4,457	66.3	100%	$0.15	$0.20	$0.35	$0.85	$2	$9	$75
	Auctions: $106, MS-67RD, September 2014; $89, MS-67RD, December 2014; $84, MS-67RD, October 2014; $7,050, AU-58, November 2013										
1946	991,655,000	1,868	65.4	100%	$0.10	$0.20	$0.35	$0.60	$2	$14	$900
	Auctions: $7,168, MS-67RD, January 2014; $2,585, MS-67RD, October 2014; $2,585, MS-67RD, November 2014; $470, MS-66RD+, August 2014										
1946-D	315,690,000	2,487	66.0	100%	$0.10	$0.20	$0.35	$0.60	$2	$10	$200
	Auctions: $2,115, MS-67RD, March 2014; $176, MS-67RD, August 2014; $129, MS-67RD, November 2014; $182, MS-67RD, December 2014										
1946-S	198,100,000	4,900	65.9	100%	$0.15	$0.20	$0.35	$0.60	$2	$10	$200
	Auctions: $470, MS-67RD, July 2014; $470, MS-67RD, December 2014; $940, MS-67RD, September 2013; $20, MS-66RD, November 2014										
1946-S, S Over D	**(b)**	18	61.7	83%	$35	$75	$125	$240		$575	
	Auctions: $541, MS-67, August 2016; $1,998, MS-66RD, June 2014										
1947	190,555,000	1,517	65.5	100%	$0.10	$0.20	$0.40	$1	$3	$12	$1,750
	Auctions: $3,525, MS-67RD, July 2014; $4,113, MS-67RD, April 2013; $294, MS-66RD+, August 2014; $106, MS-66RD, November 2014										
1947-D	194,750,000	2,057	65.8	100%	$0.10	$0.20	$0.40	$0.60	$2	$10	$250
	Auctions: $176, MS-67RD, October 2014; $764, MS-67RD, February 2013										
1947-S	99,000,000	3,132	66.0	100%	$0.20	$0.25	$0.50	$0.85	$2	$12	$200
	Auctions: $1,704, MS-67RD, February 2014; $1,998, MS-67RD+, August 2014; $1,293, MS-67RD+, August 2014; $153, MS-67RD, November 2014										

a. Included in 1944-D mintage figure. **b.** Included in 1946-S mintage figure.

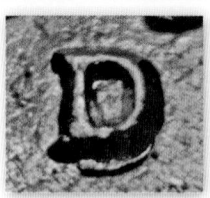

1951-D, D Over S
FS-01-1951D-512.

	Mintage	Cert	Avg	%MS	VF-20	EF-40	AU-50	MS-63RB	MS-65RB	MS-65RD	MS-67RD
									PF-65RD	PF-66RD	PF-67RD
1948	317,570,000	1,448	65.5	100%	$0.10	$0.20	$0.35	$0.85	$2	$15	$2,500
	Auctions: $7,168, MS-67RD, January 2014; $441, MS-66RD+, September 2014; $135, MS-66RD, October 2014; $153, MS-66RD, November 2014										
1948-D	172,637,500	1,791	65.7	100%	$0.10	$0.20	$0.35	$0.60	$2	$11	$650
	Auctions: $353, MS-67RD, October 2014; $259, MS-67RD, November 2014; $188, MS-67RD, November 2014; $999, MS-67RD, August 2013										
1948-S	81,735,000	3,169	66.0	100%	$0.20	$0.30	$0.35	$1	$3	$9	$100
	Auctions: $1,998, MS-67RD+, August 2014; $212, MS-67RD, August 2014; $101, MS-67RD, August 2014; $306, MS-67RD, June 2013										
1949	217,775,000	1,214	65.6	100%	$0.10	$0.20	$0.35	$1	$3	$15	$1,250
	Auctions: $3,055, MS-67RD, July 2014; $247, MS-66RD, October 2014; $159, MS-66RD, October 2014; $4,406, MS, March 2014										
1949-D	153,132,500	1,736	65.6	100%	$0.10	$0.20	$0.35	$1	$3	$14	$500
	Auctions: $1,058, MS-67RD, October 2014; $1,164, MS-67RD, November 2014; $353, MS-67RD, December 2014; $1,763, MS-67RD, June 2013										
1949-S	64,290,000	3,384	66.0	100%	$0.25	$0.30	$0.35	$2	$4	$16	$200
	Auctions: $3,173, MS-67RD, March 2014; $247, MS-67RD, August 2014; $153, MS-67RD, September 2014; $41, MS-66RD, August 2014										
1950	272,635,000	1,384	65.6	100%	$0.10	$0.20	$0.35	$0.85	$2	$18	$600
	Auctions: $1,410, MS-67RD, August 2014; $1,293, MS-67RD, September 2014; $3,055, MS-67RD, August 2013; $96, MS-66RD, August 2014										
1950, Proof	51,386	1,515	65.2						$70	$90	$750
	Auctions: $5,141, PF-67DCam, January 2014; $12,925, PF-66DCam+, September 2014; $482, PF-66Cam, July 2014; $306, PF-65Cam, November 2014										
1950-D	334,950,000	1,993	65.6	99%	$0.10	$0.20	$0.35	$0.60	$2	$17	$650
	Auctions: $353, MS-67RD, November 2014; $282, MS-67RD, December 2014; $212, MS-67RD, December 2014; $15,275, MS-67RD, November 2013										
1950-S	118,505,000	2,000	65.9	100%	$0.15	$0.25	$0.35	$0.85	$2	$13	$400
	Auctions: $9,400, MS-67RD+, September 2014; $588, MS-67RD, October 2014; $529, MS-67RD, December 2014; $1,293, MS-67RD, June 2013										
1951	284,576,000	1,118	65.6	100%	$0.10	$0.25	$0.35	$0.70	$2	$18	$750
	Auctions: $2,291, MS-67RD, July 2014; $5,288, MS-67RD, August 2013; $353, MS-66RD+, August 2014; $411, MS-66RD+, October 2014										
1951, Proof	57,500	1,429	65.6						$65	$85	$225
	Auctions: $1,763, PF-67Cam, April 2013; $376, PF-67RB, September 2014; $206, PF-67RB, November 2014; $90, PF-66RB, September 2014										
1951-D	625,355,000	2,501	65.7	100%	$0.10	$0.12	$0.35	$0.60	$2	$9	$250
	Auctions: $282, MS-67RD, September 2014; $94, MS-67RD, November 2014; $1,410, MS-67RD, June 2013										
1951-D, D Over S	(c)	31	63.6	94%				$100			
	Auctions: $2,350, MS-67RD, April 2014; $82, MS-65RD, August 2014										
1951-S	136,010,000	1,571	65.8	100%	$0.25	$0.30	$0.50	$1	$3	$11	$400
	Auctions: $823, MS-67RD, January 2014; $170, MS-67RD, August 2014; $529, MS-67RD, September 2014; $617, MS-67RD, November 2014										
1952	186,775,000	1,409	65.7	100%	$0.10	$0.15	$0.35	$1	$3	$16	$1,650
	Auctions: $4,994, MS-67RD, April 2014; $2,350, MS-67RD, July 2014; $270, MS-66RD, August 2014; $135, MS-66RD, December 2014										
1952, Proof	81,980	1,522	65.9						$50	$75	$130
	Auctions: $1,528, PF-67Cam, April 2013; $306, PF-66Cam, July 2014; $646, PF-66Cam, October 2014; $646, PF-66RB, September 2014										
1952-D	746,130,000	2,916	65.7	100%	$0.10	$0.15	$0.25	$0.75	$2	$9	$350
	Auctions: $823, MS-67RD, September 2014; $646, MS-67RD, September 2014; $411, MS-67RD, November 2014; $1,058, MS-67RD, December 2013										
1952-S	137,800,004	1,899	66.0	100%	$0.15	$0.20	$0.35	$2	$4	$13	$225
	Auctions: $4,113, MS-67RD+, November 2014; $123, MS-67RD, November 2014; $999, MS-67RD, June 2013										

c. Included in 1951-D mintage figure.

1955, Doubled Die Obverse
FS-01-1955-101.

1955, Doubled Die Obverse, Closeup of Date

1956-D, D Above Shadow D
FS-01-1956D-508.

	Mintage	Cert	Avg	%MS	VF-20	EF-40	AU-50	MS-63RB	MS-65RB / PF-65RD	MS-65RD / PF-66RD	MS-67RD / PF-67RD
1953	256,755,000	1,303	65.5	99%	$0.10	$0.15	$0.20	$0.50	$1	$18	$2,000
	Auctions: $14,100, MS-67RD, January 2014; $8,813, MS-67RD, August 2014; $5,889, MS-67RD, August 2014; $4,700, MS-67RD, October 2014										
1953, Proof	128,800	2,192	66.3						$30	$40	$100
	Auctions: $2,585, PF-67Cam, February 2014; $499, PF-67Cam, July 2014; $1,293, PF-66DCam, October 2014; $223, PF-66Cam, November 2014										
1953-D	700,515,000	2,560	65.7	100%	$0.10	$0.15	$0.20	$0.50	$1	$11	$750
	Auctions: $2,115, MS-67RD, July 2014; $1,998, MS-67RD, November 2014; $3,525, MS-67RD, August 2013; $100, MS-66RD+, October 2014										
1953-S	181,835,000	3,124	66.0	100%	$0.10	$0.15	$0.20	$0.60	$2	$12	$185
	Auctions: $3,055, MS-67RD, March 2014; $306, MS-67RD, July 2014; $153, MS-67RD, November 2014; $69, MS-67RD, December 2014										
1954	71,640,050	1,556	65.4	100%	$0.25	$0.35	$0.45	$0.60	$2	$27	$7,500
	Auctions: $23,500, MS-67RD, March 2014; $1,175, MS-66RD+, July 2014; $1,645, MS-66RD+, August 2014; $881, MS-66RD+, October 2014										
1954, Proof	233,300	2,362	66.4						$20	$30	$60
	Auctions: $2,820, PF-68Cam, April 2013; $115, PF-66Cam, September 2014; $129, PF-66Cam, November 2014; $112, PF-66Cam, November 2014										
1954-D	251,552,500	3,460	65.8	100%	$0.10	$0.12	$0.20	$0.50	$1	$10	$500
	Auctions: $141, MS-67RD, October 2014; $123, MS-67RD, December 2014; $1,293, MS-67RD, June 2013; $36, MS-66RD+, October 2014										
1954-S	96,190,000	7,431	66.0	100%	$0.10	$0.12	$0.20	$0.50	$1	$8	$150
	Auctions: $70, MS-67RD, August 2014; $119, MS-67RD, December 2014; $1,880, MS-67RD, August 2013										
1955	330,958,200	2,216	65.1	97%	$0.10	$0.12	$0.15	$0.35	$1	$19	$800
	Auctions: $1,998, MS-67RD, September 2014; $3,819, MS-67RD, December 2013; $49, MS-66RD, July 2014; $60, MS-66RD, October 2014										
1955, Doubled Die Obverse †	(d)	3,462	58.7	47%	$1,600	$1,750	$2,000	$3,500 (e)	$10,000	$30,000	
	Auctions: $25,850, MS-64RD, January 2014; $4,994, MS-64RB, August 2014; $22,325, MS-64, March 2016										
1955, Proof	378,200	4,470	67.2						$18	$30	$50
	Auctions: $7,638, PF-68DCam, April 2013; $940, PF-67DCam, July 2014; $74, PF-67Cam, September 2014; $135, PF-67Cam, November 2014										
1955-D	563,257,500	4,082	65.6	100%	$0.10	$0.12	$0.15	$0.35	$1	$9	$750
	Auctions: $7,050, MS-67RD, April 2013; $165, MS-66RD+, September 2014; $130, MS-66RD+, October 2014										
1955-S	44,610,000	14,568	66.0	100%	$0.20	$0.30	$0.40	$0.85	$3	$8	$115
	Auctions: $2,115, MS-67RD, February 2014; $470, MS-67RD, July 2014; $270, MS-67RD, August 2014; $170, MS-67RD, October 2014										
1956	420,745,000	2,345	65.7	100%	$0.10	$0.12	$0.15	$0.35	$1	$13	$500
	Auctions: $3,819, MS-67RD, August 2013; $823, MS-67RD, September 2014; $823, MS-67RD, September 2014; $588, MS-67RD, November 2014										
1956, Proof	669,384	4,049	67.3						$10	$25	$30
	Auctions: $7,638, PF-68DCam, June 2013; $705, PF-67DCam, July 2014; $247, PF-66DCam, October 2014; $341, PF-68RD, July 2014										
1956-D	1,098,201,100	4,420	65.6	99%	$0.10	$0.12	$0.15	$0.30	$1	$9	$350
	Auctions: $589, MS-67RD, July 2014; $705, MS-67RD, August 2014; $3,525, MS-67RD+, November 2014; $1,175, MS-67RD, November 2013										
1956-D, D Above Shadow D (f)	(g)	100	63.4	90%	$10	$25	$30	$35		$170	
	Auctions: $1,293, MS-67RD, February 2014										

† Ranked in the *100 Greatest U.S. Coins* (fourth edition). **d.** Included in circulation-strike 1955 mintage figure. **e.** Value in MS-60BN, $2,350; in MS-63BN, $3,500; in MS-65BN, $12,000. Varieties exist with doubling that, while still strong, is weaker than that pictured; these command premiums, but are not nearly as valuable. Note that many counterfeit 1955 Doubled Die cents exist. On authentic pieces, there is a faint die scratch under the left horizontal bar of the T in CENT. **f.** The remains of a totally separated D mintmark are evident in the field below the primary D. **g.** Included in 1956-D mintage figure.

1958, Doubled Die Obverse
FS-01-1958-101.

	Mintage	Cert	Avg	%MS	VF-20	EF-40	AU-50	MS-63RB	MS-65RB / PF-65RD	MS-65RD / PF-66RD	MS-67RD / PF-67RD
1957	282,540,000	2,462	65.7	100%	$0.10	$0.12	$0.15	$0.30	$1	$15	$1,350
Auctions: $515, MS-67RD, September 2014; $470, MS, December 2013											
1957, Proof	1,247,952	5,143	67.3						$10	$25	$30
Auctions: $1,028, PF-68Cam, July 2014; $1,058, PF-68Cam, April 2013; $282, PF-67Cam, November 2014; $84, PF-67Cam, November 2014											
1957-D	1,051,342,000	5,027	65.6	99%	$0.10	$0.12	$0.15	$0.30	$1	$9	$250
Auctions: $705, MS-67RD, August 2014; $558, MS-67RD, October 2014; $2,115, MS-67RD, June 2013											
1958	252,525,000	3,948	65.6	100%	$0.10	$0.12	$0.15	$0.30	$1	$9	$450
Auctions: $194, MS-67RD, August 2014; $881, MS-67RD, October 2014; $1,528, MS-67RD, June 2013											
1958, Doubled Die Obverse (h,i)	(j)	0	n/a					—			
Auctions:											
1958, Proof	875,652	4,738	67.3						$8	$20	$30
Auctions: $1,293, PF-67DCam, June 2013; $1,293, PF-68Cam, July 2014; $74, PF-67Cam, November 2014; $62, PF-67Cam, November 2014											
1958-D	800,953,300	6,665	65.7	100%	$0.10	$0.12	$0.15	$0.30	$1	$8	$150
Auctions: $1,939, MS-67RD, January 2014; $106, MS-67RD, August 2014; $2,585, MS-67RD+, September 2014; $212, MS-67RD, September 2014											

h. 3 examples are known. **i.** No specimens have been reported being found in circulation, Wheat cent bags, Uncirculated rolls, "or other means that would lead to credibility of a true accidental release from the mint" (*Cherrypickers' Guide to Rare Die Varieties*, sixth edition, volume I). **j.** Included in circulation-strike 1958 mintage figure.

LINCOLN, MEMORIAL REVERSE (1959–2008)

Copper Alloy (1959–1982): **Designer:** *Victor D. Brenner (obverse), Frank Gasparro (reverse).*
Weight: *3.11 grams.* **Composition:** *1959–1962—.950 copper, .050 tin and zinc; 1962–1982—.950 copper, .050 zinc.* **Diameter:** *19 mm.* **Edge:** *Plain.* **Mints:** *Philadelphia, Denver, and San Francisco.*

Copper Alloy (1959–1982)   **Copper Alloy, Proof**

Copper-Plated Zinc (1982–2008): **Designer:** *Victor D. Brenner (obverse), Frank Gasparro (reverse).* **Weight:** *2.5 grams.* **Composition:** *copper-plated zinc (core: .992 zinc, .008 copper, with a plating of pure copper; total content .975 zinc, .025 copper).* **Diameter:** *19 mm.* **Edge:** *Plain.* **Mints:** *Philadelphia, Denver, and San Francisco.*

Copper-Plated Zinc (1982–2008)   **Copper-Plated Zinc, Proof**

History. In 1959 a new cent design, by Frank Gasparro, was introduced to mark the 150th anniversary of Abraham Lincoln's birth. Victor Brenner's portrait of Lincoln was maintained on the obverse. The new reverse featured a view of the Lincoln Memorial in Washington, D.C., with Daniel Chester French's massive statue of the president faintly visible within. In 1969 the dies were modified to strengthen the design, and Lincoln's head on the obverse was made slightly smaller. In 1973 the dies were further modified, and the engraver's initials (FG) were enlarged. In 1974 the initials were reduced slightly. During 1982 the dies were modified again and the bust, lettering, and date were made slightly smaller. The Lincoln Memorial reverse was used until 2009, when a switch was made to four new reverse designs honoring the bicentennial of Lincoln's birth. Lincoln Memorial cents were struck for circulation at the Philadelphia, Denver, and San Francisco mints, with the latter in smaller numbers. Partway through 1982 the bronze alloy was discontinued in favor of copper-coated zinc.

Striking and Sharpness. Striking varies and can range from "sloppy" to needle sharp. On the obverse, check Lincoln's hair and beard (although the sharpness of this feature varied in the dies; for more information see *A Guide Book of Lincoln Cents* [Bowers]). Tiny marks on the shoulder of Lincoln indicate a weak strike there. On the reverse the sharpness can vary, including on the tiny statue of Lincoln and the shrubbery. On the reverse there can be light striking on the steps of the Memorial, and at IBU and M of E PLURIBUS UNUM. The quality of the fields can vary, as well. Some early copper-coated zinc cents, particularly of 1982 and 1983, can have planchet blisters or other problems. All Proof Lincoln Memorial cents are of the mirror type, usually with cameo or frosted contrast between the devices and the fields. High quality is common. Special Mint Set (SMS) coins were struck in lieu of Proofs from 1965 to 1967, and in some instances these closely resemble Proofs.

Availability. Coins in this series are plentiful for standard dates and mintmarks. Collectible varieties exist, and are eagerly sought by specialists, who use the *Cherrypickers' Guide to Rare Die Varieties* as their standard reference. Some of the more popular varieties are illustrated and listed herein.

GRADING STANDARDS

Caveat: These grading standards do not take sharpness of strike into account.

MS-60 to 70 (Mint State). *Obverse and Reverse:* At MS-65 and higher, the luster is rich on all areas, except perhaps the shoulder (which may be grainy and show original planchet surface). There is no rubbing, and no contact marks are visible except under magnification. Coins with full or nearly full mint orange-red color can be designated RD; those with full or nearly full brown-toned surfaces can be designated BN; and those with a sub-

1998-D. Graded MS-68.

stantial percentage of red-orange and of brown can be called RB. Ideally, MS-65 or finer coins should have good eye appeal, which in the RB category means nicely blended colors, not stained or blotched. Below MS-65, full RD coins become scarce, and at MS-60 to 62 they are virtually non-existent, unless they have been dipped. Copper is a very active metal, and influences such as slight abrasions, contact marks, and so on that define the grade also affect the color. The ANA grading standards allow for "dull" and/or "spotted" coins at MS–60 and 61, as well as incomplete luster. In the marketplace, interpretations often vary widely. BN and RB coins at MS–60 and 61 are apt to be more attractive than (dipped) RD coins.

AU-50, 53, 55, 58 (About Uncirculated).
Obverse: Same guidelines as for the preceding type except that tinges of original mint-red are sometimes seen on coins that have not been cleaned. *Reverse:* Slight wear is seen on the Lincoln Memorial, particularly on the steps, the columns, and the horizontal architectural elements above.

Illustrated coin: The doubling of the obverse die of this popular variety is easily visible to the naked eye.

1969-S, Double Die Obverse. Graded AU-58.

EF-40, 45 (Extremely Fine). *Obverse:* Light wear is seen on Lincoln's portrait, and hair detail is gone on the higher areas, especially above the ear. *Reverse:* Most detail is gone from the steps of the Lincoln Memorial, and the columns and other higher-relief architectural elements show wear.

The Lincoln cent with Memorial reverse is seldom collected in grades lower than EF-40.

1962-D. Graded EF-40.

PF-60 to 70 (Proof). *Obverse and Reverse:* PF-65 and higher coins are usually RB (colors should be nicely blended) or RD, the latter with bright red-orange fading slightly to hints of brown. Some tiny flecks are normal on coins certified as PF-65 but should be microscopic or absent above that. PF–60 and 61 coins can be dull, stained, or spotted and still have some original mint color. Coins with fingerprints must be given a low numerical grade. Lower-grade Proofs usually have poor eye appeal. Generally, Proofs below PF-64 are not desired by most collectors.

1959. Graded PF-69RD Cameo.

1960, Large Date	1960, Small Date	1960-D, D Over D, Small Over Large Date
		FS-01-1960D-101/501.

	Mintage	Cert	Avg	%MS	MS-63RB	MS-65RD	MS-66RD	MS-67RD
					PF-65RD	PF-67RD	PF-67Cam	PF-68DCam
1959	609,715,000	1,555	65.7	100%	$0.20	$0.30	$37	$550
1959, Proof	1,149,291	4,899	67.4		$3	$22	$55	$865
1959-D	1,279,760,000	1,417	65.8	100%	$0.50	$0.55	$25	$475

1969-S, Doubled Die Obverse
FS-01-1969S-101.

	Mintage	Cert	Avg	%MS	MS-63RB / PF-65RD	MS-65RD / PF-67RD	MS-66RD / PF-67Cam	MS-67RD / PF-68DCam
1960, Large Date (a)	586,405,000	1,955	65.5	100%	$0.20	$0.30	$30	
1960, Small Date (a)	(b)	1,314	35.4	100%	$3	$7	$38	
1960, Large Date, Proof	1,691,602	3,857	67.4		$2	$26	$45	$375
1960, Small Date, Proof	(c)	3,043	67.3		$22	$37	$75	$2,300
1960-D, Large Date (a,d)	1,580,884,000	1,244	65.4	99%	$0.20	$0.30	$30	
1960-D, Small Date (a)	(e)	1,565	65.6	100%	$0.20	$0.30	$30	$1,250
1960, D Over D, Small Over Large Date	(e)	282	64.2	98%	$200	$400	$2,000	
1961	753,345,000	855	65.2	99%	$0.15	$0.30	$50	
1961, Proof	3,028,244	4,359	67.2		$1.50	$23	$40	$375
1961-D	1,753,266,700	1,072	65.4	99%	$0.15	$0.30	$70	$100
1962	606,045,000	1,124	65.5	100%	$0.15	$0.30	$50	
1962, Proof	3,218,019	5,320	67.4		$1.50	$10	$15	$100
1962-D	1,793,148,140	958	65.5	99%	$0.15	$0.30	$75	$250
1963	754,110,000	1,510	65.3	100%	$0.15	$0.30	$60	
1963, Proof	3,075,645	5,539	67.5		$1.50	$10	$14	$55
1963-D	1,774,020,400	667	65.4	100%	$0.15	$0.30	$100	$350
1964	2,648,575,000	842	65.3	100%	$0.15	$0.30	$65	
1964, Proof	3,950,762	9,228	67.8		$1.50	$10	$11	$23
1964-D	3,799,071,500	495	65.4	99%	$0.15	$0.30	$42	
1965	1,497,224,900	495	65.7	100%	$0.20	$0.50	$27	
1965, Special Mint Set	2,360,000	1,705	66.4	100%	$11	$55		
1966	2,188,147,783	347	65.4	99%	$0.20	$0.50	$60	
1966, Special Mint Set	2,261,583	2,255	66.7	100%	$10	$25		
1967	3,048,667,100	334	65.5	100%	$0.20	$0.50	$90	
1967, Special Mint Set	1,863,344	2,415	66.8	100%	$11	$42		
1968	1,707,880,970	406	65.3	100%	$0.25	$0.60	$33	
1968-D	2,886,269,600	810	65.3	100%	$0.15	$0.40	$27	
1968-S	258,270,001	912	65.4	100%	$0.15	$0.40	$29	
1968-S, Proof	3,041,506	1,161	67.2		$1	$12	$16	$50
1969	1,136,910,000	425	65.7	100%	$0.35	$0.70	$55	
1969-D	4,002,832,200	759	65.3	99%	$0.15	$0.30	$28	
1969-S	544,375,000	859	64.4	95%	$0.15	$0.50	$65	
1969-S, Doubled Die Obverse ‡ (f)	(g)	15	58.6	47%	$75,000			
1969-S, Proof	2,934,631	1,280	67.2		$1	$11	$13	$33

‡ Ranked in the *100 Greatest U.S. Modern Coins*. **a.** The alignment of the 1 and 9 in the date can be used for a quick determination of Large versus Small Date. *Large Date:* the top of the 1 is significantly lower than the top of the 9. *Small Date:* the tops of the 1 and 9 are at the same level. **b.** Included in circulation-strike 1960, Large Date, mintage figure. **c.** Included in 1960, Large Date, Proof, mintage figure. **d.** A variety once called 1960-D, Large Date, D Over Horizontal D, has been disproved as such, and is now considered simply a triple-punched D. **e.** Included in 1960-D, Large Date, mintage figure. **f.** Beware of specimens that exhibit only strike doubling, as opposed to a true doubled die; these are worth only face value. See Appendix A of the *Cherrypickers' Guide to Rare Die Varieties*, sixth edition, volume I. **g.** Included in circulation-strike 1969-S mintage figure.

1970-S, Small
Date (High 7)

1970-S, Large Date
(Low 7)

1970-S, Proof, Doubled Die Obverse
FS-01-1970S-101.

1972, Doubled Die Obverse
FS-01-1972-101.

	Mintage	Cert	Avg	%MS	MS-63RB	MS-65RD	MS-66RD	MS-67RD
					PF-65RD	PF-67RD	PF-67Cam	PF-68DCam
1970	1,898,315,000	424	65.6	100%	$0.30	$0.65	$25	$250
1970-D	2,891,438,900	645	65.1	100%	$0.15	$0.30	$70	$900
1970-S, All kinds	690,560,004							
1970-S, Small Date (High 7)		823	64.5	100%	$25	$55	$240	
1970-S, Large Date (Low 7)		1,454	64.8	98%	$0.20	$0.50	$30	$950
1970-S, Doubled Die Obverse		30	63.8	93%				
1970-S, All kinds, Proof	2,632,810							
1970-S, Small Date (High 7), Proof		558	66.6		$40	$65	$150	
1970-S, Large Date (Low 7), Proof		1,180	66.9		$1	$15	$25	$65
1971	1,919,490,000	706	65.4	99%	$0.25	$0.60	$25	
1971, Doubled Die Obverse	(h)	30	63.3	93%		$50		
1971-D	2,911,045,600	306	65.5	100%	$0.20	$0.50	$24	$500
1971-S	525,133,459	434	65.3	97%	$0.20	$0.50	$50	
1971-S, Proof	3,220,733	1,333	67.2		$1	$18	$30	$120
1971-S, Doubled Die Obverse, Proof	(i)	100	66.4		$500	$1,500	$1,750	
1972	2,933,255,000	690	65.2	96%	$0.15	$0.30	$32	
1972, Doubled Die Obverse (j)	(k)	2,375	64.3	98%	$400	$675	$1,150	$4,000
1972-D	2,665,071,400	254	65.2	98%	$0.15	$0.30	$28	
1972-S	376,939,108	313	65.0	98%	$0.25	$0.75	$78	$1,000
1972-S, Proof	3,260,996	818	67.3		$1	$15	$20	$35
1973	3,728,245,000	474	65.6	100%	$0.15	$0.30	$37	$600
1973-D	3,549,576,588	494	65.6	100%	$0.15	$0.30	$37	
1973-S	317,177,295	364	65.4	99%	$0.25	$0.85	$200	
1973-S, Proof	2,760,339	273	67.5		$1	$13	$16	$30
1974	4,232,140,523	396	65.9	100%	$0.15	$0.30	$27	$175
1974-D	4,235,098,000	465	65.6	100%	$0.15	$0.30	$23	$100
1974-S	409,426,660	188	65.2	100%	$0.25	$0.75	$100	$750
1974-S, Proof	2,612,568	328	67.4		$1	$13	$16	$30
1975	5,451,476,142	394	65.8	100%	$0.15	$0.30	$29	$150
1975-D	4,505,275,300	211	65.7	100%	$0.15	$0.30	$28	$350
1975-S, Proof	2,845,450	535	67.2		$3.50	$13	$16	$30
1976	4,674,292,426	269	65.8	100%	$0.15	$0.30	$27	$55
1976-D	4,221,592,455	137	65.4	100%	$0.15	$0.30	$35	$750
1976-S, Proof	4,149,730	811	67.1		$3.20	$13	$16	$30
1977	4,469,930,000	308	66.0	100%	$0.15	$0.30	$55	$130
1977-D	4,194,062,300	437	65.3	100%	$0.15	$0.30	$90	$650
1977-S, Proof	3,251,152	433	68.1		$2.50	$13	$16	$30

h. Included in 1971 mintage figure. i. Included in 1971-S, Proof, mintage figure. j. Several less dramatically doubled varieties exist; these command premiums over the normal coin but are worth considerably less than the variety pictured. Counterfeits of the 1972 doubled die are frequently encountered. k. Included in 1972 mintage figure.

1980, Doubled Die Obverse
FS-01-1980-101.

1982, Large Date   **1982, Small Date**

1983, Doubled Die Reverse
FS-01-1983-801.

1984, Doubled Ear
FS-01-1984-101.

	Mintage	Cert	Avg	%MS	MS-63RB / PF-65RD	MS-65RD / PF-67RD	MS-66RD / PF-67Cam	MS-67RD / PF-68DCam
1978	5,558,605,000	285	65.5	99%	$0.15	$0.30	$80	$625
1978-D	4,280,233,400	242	65.5	100%	$0.15	$0.30	$75	$425
1978-S, Proof	3,127,781	459	67.5		$2.50	$13	$16	$30
1979	6,018,515,000	676	66.5	100%	$0.15	$0.30	$20	$70
1979-D	4,139,357,254	649	65.4	100%	$0.15	$0.30	$60	
1979-S, Type 1, Proof	3,677,175	581	68.3		$5	$11	$13	$17
1979-S, Type 2, Proof	(l)	783	68.1		$6	$17	$20	$30
1980	7,414,705,000	193	65.3	100%	$0.15	$0.30	$27	$125
1980, Doubled Die Obverse	(m)	231	61.7	79%	$225.00	$350.00		
1980-D (n)	5,140,098,660	285	65.3	100%	$0.15	$0.30	$40	$400
1980-S, Proof	3,554,806	889	68.4		$2.50	$10	$11	$15
1981	7,491,750,000	174	65.3	99%	$0.15	$0.30	$35	$125
1981-D	5,373,235,677	206	65.5	99%	$0.15	$0.30	$40	$225
1981-S, Type 1, Proof	4,063,083	1,116	68.3		$3	$10	$11	$15
1981-S, Type 2, Proof	(o)	776	67.9		$15	$28	$38	$55
1982, Large Date	10,712,525,000	150	65.1	100%	$0.20	$0.35	$25	$55
1982, Small Date	(p)	202	65.0	100%	$0.30	$0.50	$45	$125
1982-D, Large Date	6,012,979,368	218	65.4	100%	$0.15	$0.30	$20	$35
1982, Zinc, Large Date	(p)	462	66.3	100%	$0.35	$0.50	$35	$60
1982, Zinc, Small Date	(p)	471	66.5	100%	$0.50	$0.85	$35	
1982-D, Zinc, Large Date	(q)	268	66.4	100%	$0.20	$0.40	$25	$45
1982-D, Zinc, Small Date	(q)	299	66.1	100%	$0.15	$0.30	$15	$275
1982-S, Small Date, Proof	3,857,479	477	68.1		$2.50	$10	$11	$15
1983	7,752,355,000	340	65.6	98%	$0.15	$0.30	$15	$45
1983, Doubled Die Reverse (r)	(s)	973	64.9	98%	$250	$385	$550	$1,200
1983-D	6,467,199,428	292	66.3	100%	$0.15	$0.30	$15	$31
1983-S, Proof	3,279,126	573	68.4		$3	$10	$11	$15
1984	8,151,079,000	234	65.8	99%	$0.15	$0.30	$15	$35
1984, Doubled Ear (t)	(u)	558	65.5	99%	$175	$230	$350	$425
1984-D	5,569,238,906	223	66.1	99%	$0.15	$0.30	$15	$35
1984-S, Proof	3,065,110	506	68.9		$4	$10	$11	$15

l. Included in 1979-S, Type 1, Proof, mintage figure. **m.** Included in 1980 mintage figure. **n.** A variety previously listed in the *Cherrypickers' Guide* as a 1980-D, D Over S, has since been delisted from that catalog. It should command no premium. **o.** Included in 1981-S, Type 1, Proof, mintage figure. **p.** Included in 1982, Large Date, mintage figure. **q.** Included in 1982-D mintage figure. **r.** All reverse lettering is strongly doubled, as are the designer's initials and portions of the Lincoln Memorial. **s.** Included in 1983 mintage figure. **t.** Values are for coins certified as the Doubled Ear variety (FS-101). More than 1,500 certifications exist for all 1984 doubled-die varieties; this number certainly includes FS-101, but it is unknown how many. **u.** Included in 1984 mintage figure.

1992, Normal AM   **1992, Close AM**   **1995, Doubled Die Obverse**
FS-01-1995-101.

	Mintage	Cert	Avg	%MS	MS-63RB / PF-65RD	MS-65RD / PF-67RD	MS-66RD / PF-67Cam	MS-67RD / PF-68DCam
1985	5,648,489,887	566	66.4	100%	$0.15	$0.30	$15	$35
1985-D	5,287,339,926	397	66.8	99%	$0.15	$0.30	$15	$29
1985-S, Proof	3,362,821	558	68.9		$5	$11	$12	$15
1986	4,491,395,493	273	66.6	100%	$0.15	$0.30	$15	$35
1986-D	4,442,866,698	315	66.8	100%	$0.15	$0.30	$15	$35
1986-S, Proof	3,010,497	516	68.9		$7	$11	$12	$15
1987	4,682,466,931	395	66.8	100%	$0.15	$0.30	$15	$29
1987-D	4,879,389,514	535	66.6	100%	$0.15	$0.30	$15	$32
1987-S, Proof	4,227,728	752	68.9		$5	$10	$11	$13
1988	6,092,810,000	220	66.3	99%	$0.15	$0.30	$20	$40
1988-D	5,253,740,443	297	66.6	100%	$0.15	$0.30	$15	$25
1988-S, Proof	3,262,948	468	68.9		$9	$11	$12	$13
1989	7,261,535,000	357	66.5	100%	$0.15	$0.30	$15	$25
1989-D	5,345,467,111	358	66.4	100%	$0.15	$0.30	$15	$31
1989-S, Proof	3,220,194	587	68.9		$9	$11	$12	$13
1990	6,851,765,000	232	66.6	100%	$0.15	$0.30	$19	$36
1990-D	4,922,894,533	309	66.8	100%	$0.15	$0.30	$15	$25
1990-S, Proof	3,299,559	842	69.0		$5	$10	$11	$13
1990, No S, Proof	(v)	76	67.9		$2,750	$4,000	$4,250	$4,500
1991	5,165,940,000	219	66.7	100%	$0.15	$0.30	$14	$25
1991-D	4,158,446,076	358	66.8	100%	$0.15	$0.30	$14	$25
1991-S, Proof	2,867,787	837	69.1		$12	$13	$14	$16
1992	4,648,905,000	531	67.0	100%	$0.15	$0.30	$14	$25
1992, Close AM ‡ (w)	(x)	6	60.5	67%	—	—		
1992-D	4,448,673,300	312	66.7	99%	$0.15	$0.30	$14	$25
1992-D, Close AM ‡ (w)	(y)	19	60.4	68%	—	—		
1992-S, Proof	4,176,560	2,047	69.0		$5	$10	$11	$12
1993	5,684,705,000	268	66.9	100%	$0.15	$0.30	$14	$25
1993-D	6,426,650,571	421	66.9	100%	$0.15	$0.30	$14	$25
1993-S, Proof	3,394,792	1,877	68.9		$9	$10	$11	$12
1994	6,500,850,000	207	66.7	99%	$0.15	$0.30	$14	$25
1994-D	7,131,765,000	283	66.8	99%	$0.15	$0.30	$15	$27
1994-S, Proof	3,269,923	1,612	68.9		$9	$11	$12	$13
1995	6,411,440,000	332	66.6	100%	$0.15	$0.30	$15	$30
1995, Doubled Die Obverse ‡	(z)	18,227	67.2	100%	$35	$50	$90	$220
1995-D	7,128,560,000	289	66.9	99%	$0.15	$0.30	$15	$35
1995-S, Proof	2,797,481	1,686	69.1		$9	$11	$12	$13

‡ Ranked in the *100 Greatest U.S. Modern Coins*. **v.** An estimated 100 to 250 Proofs of 1990 were struck without the S mintmark (apparently from a circulation-strike die, without a mintmark, which had been given a mirror finish). This error escaped the notice of at least 14 people during die preparation and coining. **w.** The reverse hub used for cents from 1974 to 1992 had the AM of AMERICA separated. A new reverse hub with the AM close together was used for all cents in 1993. At least one new reverse die of each type was used for 1992-P and -D cents made for circulation but it is not known if this usage was deliberate or accidental. Proof coinage reverted to the wide-AM design in 1994. In subsequent years a few dies from the circulation-strike hub were used for making Proof coins. **x.** Included in 1992 mintage figure. **y.** Included in 1992-D mintage figure. **z.** Included in 1995 mintage figure.

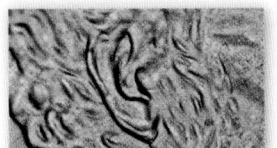

1997, Doubled Ear
FS-01-1997-101.

1999, Normal AM **1999, Wide AM** **1999-S, Proof, Normal AM** **1999-S, Proof, Close AM**

	Mintage	Cert	Avg	%MS	MS-63RB / PF-65RD	MS-65RD / PF-67RD	MS-66RD / PF-67Cam	MS-67RD / PF-68DCam
1996	6,612,465,000	292	66.8	100%	$0.15	$0.30	$12	$18
1996 , Wide AM (w)	(aa)	(bb)			—	—		
1996-D	6,510,795,000	422	66.9	100%	$0.15	$0.30	$12	$18
1996-S, Proof	2,525,265	1,517	69.1		$4.50	$9	$10	$12
1997	4,622,800,000	187	66.5	100%	$0.15	$0.30	$15	$42
1997, Doubled Ear	(cc)	46	65.2	100%	$275	$500		
1997-D	4,576,555,000	240	66.7	100%	$0.15	$0.30	$14	$30
1997-S, Proof	2,796,678	1,442	69.1		$10	$12	$13	$14
1998	5,032,155,000	178	66.3	98%	$0.15	$0.30	$12	$18
1998, Wide AM ‡ (w)	(dd)	298	65.0	97%	$12	$25	$40	$600
1998-D	5,225,353,500	217	66.8	100%	$0.15	$0.30	$17	$57
1998-S, Proof	2,086,507	1,680	69.0		$9	$10	$11	$12
1998-S, Close AM, Proof (cc)	(ff)	73	68.8		$150	$175	$185	$200
1999	5,237,600,000	256	65.6	100%	$0.15	$0.30	$13	$30
1999, Wide AM ‡ (w)	(gg)	182	64.4	95%		$500		$1,500
1999-D	6,360,065,000	260	66.9	100%	$0.15	$0.30	$12	$25
1999-S, Proof	3,347,966	6,121	69.1		$6	$9	$10	$12
1999-S, Close AM, Proof (cc)	(hh)	330	68.4		$80	$100	$125	$150
2000	5,503,200,000	1,046	65.8	100%	$0.15	$0.30	$12	$25
2000, Wide AM (w)	(ii)	939	65.5	100%	$10	$20	$35	$55
2000-D	8,774,220,000	199	66.7	100%	$0.15	$0.30	$12	$25
2000-S, Proof	4,047,993	5,638	69.1		$4	$7	$8	$10
2001	4,959,600,000	104	66.8	100%	$0.15	$0.30	$11	$18
2001-D	5,374,990,000	186	66.9	100%	$0.15	$0.30	$11	$18
2001-S, Proof	3,184,606	4,527	69.1		$4	$7	$8	$10
2002	3,260,800,000	118	67.3	100%	$0.15	$0.30	$11	$16
2002-D	4,028,055,000	140	67.3	100%	$0.15	$0.30	$12	$19
2002-S, Proof	3,211,995	4,804	69.1		$4	$7	$8	$10
2003	3,300,000,000	268	67.0	100%	$0.15	$0.30	$11	$16
2003-D	3,548,000,000	154	66.3	100%	$0.15	$0.30	$10	$15
2003-S, Proof	3,298,439	7,848	69.1		$4	$7	$8	$10

‡ Ranked in the *100 Greatest U.S. Modern Coins*. **w.** The reverse hub used for cents from 1974 to 1992 had the AM of AMERICA separated. A new reverse hub with the AM close together was used for all cents in 1993. At least one new reverse die of each type was used for 1992-P and -D cents made for circulation but it is not known if this usage was deliberate or accidental. Proof coinage reverted to the wide-AM design in 1994. In subsequent years a few dies from the circulation-strike hub were used for making Proof coins. **aa.** Included in 1997 mintage figure. **bb.** Included in 1998 mintage figure. **cc.** Varieties were made in the circulation-strike style, with the A and the M in AMERICA nearly touching each other. On normal Proofs the two letters have a wide space between them. **dd.** Included 1998-S, Proof, mintage figure. **ee.** Included in 1999 mintage figure. **ff.** Included in 1999-S, Proof, mintage figure. **gg.** Included in 2000 mintage figure. **hh.** Included in 1999-S, Proof, mintage figure. **ii.** Included in 2000 mintage figure.

	Mintage	Cert	Avg	%MS	MS-63RB	MS-65RD	MS-66RD	MS-67RD
					PF-65RD	PF-67RD	PF-67Cam	PF-68DCam
2004	3,379,600,000	158	66.8	100%	$0.15	$0.30	$10	$20
2004-D	3,456,400,000	133	66.4	100%	$0.15	$0.30	$10	$18
2004-S, Proof	2,965,422	5,328	69.1		$4	$7	$8	$10
2005	3,935,600,000	2,579	67.3	100%	$0.15	$0.30	$10	$25
2005, Satin Finish	1,160,000	2,393	67.2	100%	$5	$10	$15	$20
2005-D	3,764,450,500	2,494	67.0	100%	$0.15	$0.30	$20	$40
2005-D, Satin Finish	1,160,000	2,271	66.9	100%	$5	$10	$15	$20
2005-S, Proof	3,344,679	10,812	69.1		$4	$7	$8	$10
2006	4,290,000,000	1,442	67.0	100%	$0.15	$0.30	$10	$18
2006, Satin Finish	847,361	1,368	67.1	100%	$5	$10	$15	$20
2006-D	3,944,000,000	1,207	66.7	100%	$0.15	$0.30	$13	$25
2006-D, Satin Finish	847,361	1,079	66.8	100%	$5	$10	$15	$20
2006-S, Proof	3,054,436	5,207	69.2		$4	$7	$8	$10
2007	3,762,400,000	549	66.9	100%	$0.15	$0.30	$16	$30
2007, Satin Finish	895,628	277	66.9	100%	$5	$10	$15	$20
2007-D	3,638,800,000	335	66.1	100%	$0.15	$0.30	$16	$33
2007-D, Satin Finish	895,628	219	66.3	100%	$5	$10	$15	$20
2007-S, Proof	2,577,166	4,655	69.1		$4	$7	$8	$10
2008	2,558,800,000	243	67.3	100%	$0.15	$0.30	$12	$18
2008, Satin Finish	745,464	165	67.8	100%	$5	$10	$15	$20
2008-D	2,849,600,000	229	66.8	100%	$0.15	$0.30	$15	$31
2008-D, Satin Finish	745,464	142	67.3	100%	$5	$10	$15	$20
2008-S, Proof	2,169,561	3,675	69.1		$4	$7	$8	$10

LINCOLN, BICENTENNIAL REVERSES (2009)

Designer: *Victor D. Brenner (obverse); see image captions for reverse designers.*
Weight: *Regular-issue coins—2.5 grams; special coins included in collector sets—3.1 grams.*
Composition: *Regular-issue coins—copper-plated zinc (core: .992 zinc, .008 copper, with a plating of pure copper; total content .975 zinc, .025 copper); special coins included in collector sets—.950 copper, .050 tin and zinc.* **Diameter:** *19 mm.* **Edge:** *Plain.* **Mints:** *Philadelphia, Denver, and San Francisco.*

Circulation Strike

Birth and Early Childhood
Reverse designer: Richard Masters.

Formative Years
Reverse designer: Charles Vickers.

Professional Life
Reverse designer: Joel Iskowitz.

Presidency
Reverse designer: Susan Gamble.

Proof

Birth and Early Childhood, Proof

Formative Years, Proof

Professional Life, Proof

Presidency, Proof

History. The one-cent coins issued during 2009 pay unique tribute to President Abraham Lincoln, commemorating the bicentennial of his birth and the 100th anniversary of the first issuance of the Lincoln cent. Four different reverse designs were issued by the U.S. Mint, each representing a major aspect of Lincoln's life. The obverse retained the traditional profile portrait of previous years.

The reverse designs, released quarterly throughout 2009, are:

- Birth and Early Childhood (designer, Richard Masters; sculptor, Jim Licaretz), depicting a small log cabin like the one in which Lincoln was born in Kentucky.

- Formative Years (designer and sculptor, Charles Vickers), showing a youthful Abe Lincoln taking a break from rail-splitting to read a book, in Indiana.

- Professional Life (designer, Joel Iskowitz; sculptor, Don Everhart), with Lincoln standing in front of the Illinois state capitol in Springfield, symbolic of his pre-presidential career in law and politics.

- Presidency (designer, Susan Gamble; sculptor, Joseph Menna), depicting the partially completed U.S. Capitol dome in Washington, D.C., as it appeared when Lincoln held office.

The coins issued for general circulation were made of the exact same copper-plated composition used in the cent since 1982. Special versions struck for inclusion in collector sets were made of the same alloy as the first Lincoln cents of 1909—95 parts copper and 5 parts tin and zinc—and with a Satin finish.

Several die varieties (both circulation-strike and Proof) exist with minor doubling in the Formative Years reverse. Their values, which vary generally according to the severity of the doubling, are not yet firmly established with an active buy-and-sell market. These and other Lincoln cent die varieties are studied in greater depth in the *Cherrypickers' Guide to Rare Die Varieties*.

Striking and Sharpness. Striking is generally sharp. The quality of the fields can vary. Some 2009 cents, even from original rolls and bags, have surface marks that look like water spots. All Proof Lincoln Bicentennial cents are mirror Proofs, usually with cameo or frosted contrast between the devices and the fields.

Availability. Cents of this year were minted in quantities that, while large, were much smaller than for previous years (in the hundreds of millions, rather than multiple billions), if each of the four designs is considered individually. They are readily available in the numismatic marketplace, and are starting to be seen more frequently in circulation. High-quality Proofs (PF-69 and 70) are common in the secondary market.

GRADING STANDARDS

Caveat: These grading standards do not take sharpness of strike into account.

MS-60 to 70 (Mint State). *Obverse and Reverse:* At MS-65 and higher, luster is rich on all areas; there is no rubbing, and no contact marks are visible except under magnification. Coins with full or nearly full mint orange-red color can be designated RD; those with a substantial percentage of red-orange and of brown can be called RB; and those with full (or nearly full) brown-toned surfaces can be designated BN. Some 2009 cents, even from original rolls and bags, have surface marks that look like water spots.

2009-D, Formative Years. Graded MS-67RD.

The Lincoln Bicentennial cent is seldom collected in grades lower than MS-60.

PF-60 to 70 (Proof). *Obverse and Reverse:* PF-65 and higher coins are RB (with colors nicely blended) or RD, the latter with bright red-orange color sometimes fading to hints of brown. Some tiny flecks are normal on coins certified as PF-65 but should be microscopic or absent above that level. PF–60 and 61 coins can be dull, stained, or spotted and still have some original mint luster. Proof coins with finger-prints are impaired and must be given a lower numerical grade. Lower-grade Proofs usually have poor eye appeal. Generally, Proofs of these types below PF-65 are not desired by most collectors.

**2009-S, Birthplace and Early Childhood.
Graded PF-70RD Deep Cameo.**

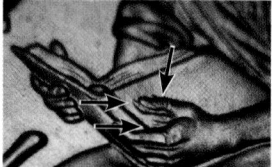

**2009, Formative Years,
Seven Fingers**
FS-01-2009-801.
Other varieties exist.

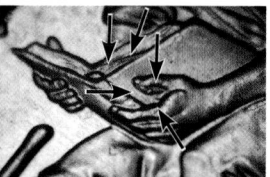

**2009, Formative Years,
Seven Fingers**
FS-01-2009-802.
Other varieties exist.

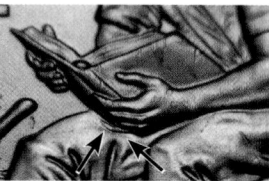

**2009, Formative Years,
Doubled Pinky**
FS-01-2009-805.
Other varieties exist.

**2009, Formative Years,
Skeleton Finger**
FS-01-2009-808.
Other varieties exist.

	Mintage	Cert	Avg	%MS	MS-63RB	MS-65RD	MS-66RD / PF-65RD	MS-67RD / PF-67RD	MS-68RD / PF-67Cam	MS-69RD / PF-68DCam
2009, Birth and Early Childhood	284,400,000	13,953	65.8	100%	$0.15	$0.30	$12	$20		
2009, Birth and Early Childhood, copper, Satin Finish	784,614	1,606	67.7	100%					$15	$45
2009-D, Birth and Early Childhood	350,400,000	4,955	65.9	100%	$0.15	$0.30	$12	$20		
2009-D, Birth and Early Childhood, copper, Satin Finish	784,614	1,690	67.7	100%					$17	$95
2009-S, Birth and Early Childhood, Proof	2,995,615	14,422	69.1				$4	$7	$8	$10
2009, Formative Years (a)	376,000,000	27,034	65.9	100%	$0.15	$0.30	$12	$20		
2009, Formative Years, copper, Satin Finish	784,614	1,504	67.6	100%					$15	$45
2009-D, Formative Years (a)	363,600,000	2,648	65.9	100%	$0.15	$0.30	$12	$20		
2009-D, Formative Years, copper, Satin Finish	784,614	1,542	67.5	100%					$15	$250
2009-S, Formative Years, Proof	2,995,615	14,309	69.1				$4	$7	$8	$10
2009, Professional Life	316,000,000	17,467	66.0	100%	$0.15	$0.30	$12	$20		
2009, Professional Life, copper, Satin Finish	784,614	1,859	67.8	100%					$15	$45
2009-D, Professional Life	336,000,000	1,949	66.0	100%	$0.15	$0.30	$12	$20		
2009-D, Professional Life, copper, Satin Finish	784,614	1,509	67.6	100%					$15	$210
2009-S, Professional Life, Proof	2,995,615	14,366	69.1				$4	$7	$8	$10
2009, Presidency	129,600,000	4,460	65.9	100%	$0.15	$0.30	$12	$20		
2009, Presidency, copper, Satin Finish	784,614	1,507	67.6	100%					$15	$45

a. Several varieties exist with minor die doubling. Their values vary and their market is not yet firmly established.

| | Mintage | Cert | Avg | %MS | MS-63RB | MS-65RD | MS-66RD | MS-67RD | MS-68RD | MS-69RD |
							PF-65RD	PF-67RD	PF-67Cam	PF-68DCam
2009-D, Presidency	198,000,000	1,408	65.9	100%	$0.15	$0.30	$12	$20		
2009-D, Presidency, copper, Satin Finish	784,614	1,632	67.6	100%					$15	$200
2009-S, Presidency, Proof	2,995,615	14,578	69.1				$4	$7	$8	$10

LINCOLN, SHIELD REVERSE (2010 TO DATE)

Designer: *Victor D. Brenner (obverse) and Lyndall Bass (reverse).* **Weight:** *2.5 grams.*
Composition: *Copper-plated zinc (core: .992 zinc, .008 copper,with a plating of pure copper; total content .975 zinc, .025 copper).* **Diameter:** *19 mm.* **Edge:** *Plain.* **Mints:** *Philadelphia, Denver, and San Francisco.*

Circulation Strike

Proof

History. Symbolically capping the life story told by the Lincoln Bicentennial cents of 2009, today's cents feature a reverse design "emblematic of President Lincoln's preservation of the United States as a single and united country." This is the seventh reverse used on the Lincoln type since 1909.

The shield motif was designed by U.S. Mint Artistic Infusion Program Associate Designer Lyndall Bass, and engraved by Mint Sculptor-Engraver Joseph Menna. It was unveiled during the launch ceremony for the fourth and final 2009 Bicentennial cent, held at the Ulysses S. Grant Memorial at the Capitol Building in Washington, D.C., November 12, 2009.

In addition to a new reverse design, the Shield Reverse cents feature a modern update of Victor David Brenner's original portrait for the 1909 Lincoln cent.

Striking and Sharpness. Striking is generally sharp. All Proof Lincoln, Shield Reverse, cents are mirror Proofs, usually with cameo or frosted contrast between the devices and the fields.

Availability. Cents of this design are minted in large quantities. They are readily available in the numismatic marketplace, and have successfully entered circulation through normal distribution channels. High-quality Proofs (PF-69 and 70) are common in the secondary market.

GRADING STANDARDS

Caveat: These grading standards do not take sharpness of strike into account.

MS-60 to 70 (Mint State). *Obverse and Reverse:* At MS-65 and higher, luster is rich on all areas; there is no rubbing, and no contact marks are visible except under magnification. Coins with full or nearly full mint orange-red color can be designated RD; those with a substantial percentage of red-orange and of brown can be called RB; and those with full (or nearly full) brown-toned surfaces can be designated BN. Some 2009 cents, even from original rolls and bags, have surface marks that look like water spots.

2011-D. Graded MS-67RD.

The Lincoln, Shield Reverse, cent is seldom collected in grades lower than MS-60.

PF-60 to 70 (Proof). *Obverse and Reverse:* PF-65 and higher coins are RB (with colors nicely blended) or RD, the latter with bright red-orange color sometimes fading to hints of brown. Some tiny flecks are normal on coins certified as PF-65 but should be microscopic or absent above that level. PF-60 and 61 coins can be dull, stained, or spotted and still have some original mint luster. Proof coins with fingerprints are impaired and must be given a lower numerical grade. Lower-grade Proofs usually have poor eye appeal. Generally, Proofs of this type below PF-65 are not desired by most collectors.

2012-S. Graded PF-70RD Deep Cameo.

	Mintage	Cert	Avg	%MS	MS-63RB	MS-65RD	MS-66RD	MS-67RD
					PF-65RD	PF-67RD	PF-67Cam	PF-68DCam
2010	1,963,630,000	6,853	65.5	100%	$0.15	$0.30	$10	$18
2010, Satin Finish	583,897	275	67.0	100%	$5	$10	$15	$20
2010-D	2,047,200,000	2,332	66.0	100%	$0.15	$0.30	$10	$18
2010-D, Satin Finish	583,897	371	67.6	100%	$5	$10	$15	$20
2010-S, Proof	1,689,364	5,615	69.1		$4	$7	$8	$10
2011	2,402,400,000	478	66.3	100%	$0.15	$0.30	$10	$18
2011-D	2,536,140,000	271	66.8	100%	$0.15	$0.30	$10	$18
2011-S, Proof	1,673,010	6,236	69.1		$5	$7	$8	$10
2012	3,132,000,000	277	67.0	100%	$0.15	$0.30	$10	$18
2012-D	2,883,200,000	171	66.9	100%	$0.15	$0.30	$10	$18
2012-S, Proof	1,239,148	2,092	69.1		$5	$7	$8	$10
2013	3,750,400,000	558	66.3	100%	$0.15	$0.30	$10	$18
2013-D	3,319,600,000	364	66.8	100%	$0.15	$0.30	$10	$18
2013-S, Proof	1,274,505	2,432	69.2		$5	$7	$8	$10
2014	3,990,800,000	592	66.8	100%	$0.15	$0.30	$10	$15
2014-D	4,155,600,000	598	66.7	100%	$0.15	$0.30	$10	$15
2014-S, Proof	1,190,369	3,959	69.3		$5	$7.50	$8	$10
2015	4,691,614,029	0	n/a		$0.15	$0.30	$10	$15
2015-D	4,674,314,029	0	n/a		$0.15	$0.30	$10	$15
2015-S, Proof	1,050,164	0	n/a		$5	$7.50	$8	$10
2016	4,698,296,579	0	n/a		$0.15	$0.30	$10	$15
2016-D	4,420,696,579	0	n/a		$0.15	$0.30	$10	$15
2016-S, Proof	1,011,624	0	n/a		$5	$7.50	$8	$10
2017-P (a)	4,361,491,686				$0.15	$0.30	$10	$15
2017-D	4,273,071,686				$0.15	$0.30	$10	$15
2017-S, Enhanced Unc.						$7.50	$8	$10
2017-S, Proof	926,437				$5	$7.50	$8	$10
2018					$0.15	$0.30	$10	$15
2018-D					$0.15	$0.30	$10	$15
2018-S, Proof					$5	$7.50	$8	$10

a. All 2017-dated cents struck at the Philadelphia Mint bear a P mintmark in honor of the 225th anniversary of U.S. coinage.

Two-Cent Pieces

1864–1873

AN OVERVIEW OF TWO-CENT PIECES

The two-cent piece was introduced in 1864. Made of bronze, it was designed by U.S. Mint chief engraver James B. Longacre, and was the first circulating U.S. coin to bear the motto IN GOD WE TRUST. At the time, coins were scarce in circulation because of the ongoing Civil War and the public's tendency to hoard hard currency, and silver and gold issues were entirely absent. Treasury officials felt that the two-cent piece would prove to be very popular as a companion to the Indian Head cent. However, the introduction of the nickel three-cent piece in 1865 negated much of this advantage, the production of two-cent pieces declined, and by 1873, when the denomination was discontinued, its only coinage consisted of Proofs for collectors.

A full "type set" of the two-cent piece consists of but a single coin. Most available in Mint State are the issues of 1864 and 1865, often seen with original mint orange color fading to natural brown. Proofs are available for all years.

The Coinage Act of 1873 eliminated not only the two-cent piece but also the three-cent silver and half dime.

FOR THE COLLECTOR AND INVESTOR: TWO-CENT PIECES AS A SPECIALTY

Two-cent pieces can be collected by date and variety. A basic display consists of an 1864, Large Motto; 1864, Small Motto (rare); 1873, Close 3; and 1873, Open 3, the latter two being available only in Proof format. Some specialists opt to include just one of the 1873 varieties.

Collectors should select both circulation strikes and Proofs with care, for the number of truly choice *original* (unprocessed, undipped, not retoned) coins is but a small percentage of the whole. As a type, though, the two-cent piece is readily available for collecting.

Several specialized studies of two-cent pieces have been published over a long span of years, the first of significance being "Two-Cent Pieces of the United States," by S.W. Freeman, published in the *Numismatist*, June 1954.

TWO-CENT PIECES (1864–1873)

Designer: *James B. Longacre.* **Weight:** *6.22 grams.*
Composition: *.950 copper, .050 tin and zinc.* **Diameter:** *23 mm.*
Edge: *Plain.* **Mint:** *Philadelphia.*

Circulation Strike   Proof

History. The two-cent piece, struck in bronze like the new Indian Head cents, made its debut under the Mint Act of April 22, 1864. Coins of all kinds were scarce in circulation at the time, due to hoarding. The outcome of the Civil War was uncertain, and Americans desired "hard money." Many millions of two-cent pieces were struck in 1864, after which the mintage declined, due to once-hoarded Indian Head cents becoming available again and to the new nickel three-cent coins being introduced in 1865. Continually decreasing quantities were made through 1872, and only Proofs were struck in the coin's final year, 1873.

Striking and Sharpness. Points to check for sharpness on the obverse include WE in the motto, the leaves, and the horizontal shield lines. On the reverse check the wreath details and the border letters. Check the denticles on both sides. Most coins are quite well struck.

Availability. Most MS coins are dated 1864 or 1865, after which the availability declines sharply, especially for the issue of 1872. Among 1864 coins most seen are of the Large Motto variety. Small Motto coins are elusive. Coins with much or nearly all *original* mint red-orange color are rare for the later years, with most in the marketplace being recolored. The 1864, Small Motto, Proof, is a great rarity, with fewer than two dozen estimated to exist. Coins of 1873 were made only in Proof format, of the Close 3 and Open 3 styles. Proofs of most dates are easily enough acquired. Very few have original color. Do not overlook the many nice brown and red-and-brown pieces on the market (some investors acquire only "red" copper coins, leaving many great values among others). Refer to the comments under Proof Indian Head cents.

GRADING STANDARDS

MS-60 to 70 (Mint State). *Obverse and Reverse:* At MS-65 and higher, the luster is rich on all areas. There is no rubbing, and no contact marks are visible except under magnification. Coins with full or nearly full mint orange-red color can be designated RD (the color on this is often more orange than red), those with full or nearly full brown-toned surfaces can be designated BN, and those with a substantial percentage of red-orange

1864, Large Motto, RPD; Leone-9. Graded MS-66RD.

and of brown can be called RB. Ideally, MS-65 or finer coins should have good eye appeal, which in the RB category means nicely blended colors, not stained or blotched, the latter problem mostly with dipped and irregularly retoned coins. Below MS-65, full RD coins become scarce, although MS-64RD coins can be attractive. These usually have more flecks and tiny spots, while the color remains bright. At MS–60 to 62, RD coins are virtually nonexistent, unless they have been dipped. The ANA standards allow for "dull" and/or "spotted" coins at MS–60 and 61 as well as incomplete luster. As a rule, MS–60 to 63BN coins can be fairly attractive if not spotted or blotched, but those with hints of color usually lack eye appeal.

AU-50, 53, 55, 58 (About Uncirculated). *Obverse:* WE shows light wear, this being the prime place to check. The arrowheads and leaves also show light wear. At AU–50, level wear is more noticeable. At AU–53 and 55, wear is less. At AU-58, friction is evident, rather than actual wear. Luster, toned brown, is nearly complete at AU-58, but may be incomplete in the field. *Reverse:* At AU-50, light wear is seen on the ribbon and the higher-relief areas of the leaves and grains, while the lower areas retain their detail. Some luster may be present in protected areas. At AU–53 and 55, wear is lesser and luster is more extensive. An AU-58 coin will have nearly full luster and show only light friction.

1871. Graded AU-58.

EF-40, 45 (Extremely Fine). *Obverse:* Wear is more extensive. WE shows wear extensively, but still is clear. The leaves lack detail on their highest points. Some scattered marks are normal at this and lower grades. *Reverse:* The higher-relief parts of the leaves and ribbon bow show further wear, as do other areas.

1864, Small Motto. Graded EF-45.

VF-20, 30 (Very Fine). *Obverse:* WE is clear, but not strong. Leaves show more wear, as do all other areas. *Reverse:* Still more wear is seen, but the leaves still are separately defined. The wheat grains are very clear.

1864, Small Motto. Graded VF-20.

F-12, 15 (Fine). *Obverse:* WE is the defining factor and is very weak, but readable, if only barely. Other areas show more wear. The edges of some leaves are gone, blending them into adjacent leaves. *Reverse:* Wear is more extensive. Near the apex of the wreath the edges of some leaves are gone, blending them into adjacent leaves. The grains of wheat are clear, but some are slightly weak.

Illustrated coin: WE is very weak.

1872. Graded F-15.

VG-8, 10 (Very Good). *Obverse:* WE is gone, although the ANA grading standards and *Photograde* suggest "very weak." IN GOD and TRUST are readable, but some areas may be weak. The inner edges of most leaves are gone. *Reverse:* The wear appears to be less extensive than on the obverse. All lettering is bold. A few grains of wheat may be well worn or even missing.

1872. Graded VG-8.

G-4, 6 (Good). *Obverse:* Wear is more extensive, and the leaf bunches are in flat clumps. IN GOD and TRUST are very worn, with a letter or two not visible. *Reverse:* All letters are clear. The wreath is mostly in outline on G-4. On G-6, perhaps half the grains are visible.

1864, Small Motto. Graded G-4.

AG-3 (About Good). *Obverse:* The motto shows only a few letters. The leaves are flat. Only a few horizontal shield stripes can be seen. *Reverse:* The wreath is in outline form. The letters are weak, with 20% to 40% worn away entirely.

1872. Graded AG-3.

PF-60 to 70 (Proof). *Obverse and Reverse:* Gem PF-65 two-cent pieces will have very few hairlines, and these visible only under a strong magnifying glass. At any level and color, a Proof with hairlines has likely been cleaned, a fact usually overlooked. At PF-67 or higher there should be no evidence of hairlines or friction at all. Such a coin is fully original. PF-60 coins can be dull from repeated dipping and cleaning and are often toned iridescent colors or have mottled surfaces. At PF-63, the mirrorlike fields should be attractive, and hairlines should be minimal, most easily seen when the coin is held at an angle to the light. No rubbing is seen. PF-64 coins are even nicer. As a general rule, Proofs of 1873 are of very high quality but, unless dipped or cleaned, are nearly always toned light brown.

1872. Graded PF-64RD.

1864, Small Motto

1864, Large Motto

1865, Plain 5

1865, Fancy 5

	Mintage	Cert	Avg	%MS	G-4	F-12	VF-20	EF-40	AU-50	MS-60BN	MS-63BN PF-63BN	MS-64BN PF-64BN	MS-65RD PF-65RB
1864, Small Motto (a)	(b)	620	51.4	63%	$225	$400	$575	$800	$1,000	$1,500	$1,750	$2,000	$15,000
Auctions: $2,232, MS-65BN, January 2015; $29,375, MS-65, February 2015; $763, EF-45, October 2015													
1864, Large Motto (c)	19,822,500	3,931	60.6	84%	$15	$25	$30	$50	$80	$110	$175	$200	$1,150
Auctions: $1,116, MS-66BN, June 2015; $305, MS-65BN, May 2015; $129, MS-63BN, January 2015; $111, AU-58, October 2015													
1864, Small Motto, Proof † (d)	(e)	8	64.8								$22,500	$27,500	$85,000
Auctions: $105,750, PF-66RD, June 2014													
1864, Large Motto, Proof	100+	129	64.6								$550	$775	$2,750
Auctions: $3,760, PF-66BN, October 2015; $3,642, PF-66BN, January 2015; $3,535, PF-65RB, August 2015; $646, PF-62BN, February 2015													
1865 (f)	13,640,000	2,541	60.2	81%	$15	$25	$30	$50	$80	$110	$175	$200	$1,150
Auctions: $540, MS-65RB, May 2015; $399, MS-65BN, February 2015; $646, MS-64RD, August 2015; $199, MS-64BN, January 2015													
1865, Proof	500+	157	64.7								$450	$550	$1,250
Auctions: $2,820, PF-66RB, October 2015; $3,290, PF-65RB, June 2015; $1,997, PF-65RB, January 2015; $1,178, PF-65BN, January 2015													
1866	3,177,000	539	58.4	74%						$120	$175	$220	$2,000
Auctions: $1,692, MS-65RD, July 2015; $587, MS-64RD, January 2015; $517, MS-64RB, October 2015; $212, MS-64BN, April 2015													
1866, Proof	725+	171	64.7								$450	$550	$1,250
Auctions: $4,700, PF-66RB, July 2015; $1,527, PF-65RB, January 2015; $1,175, PF-65RB, September 2015; $470, PF-64BN, January 2015													

† Ranked in the *100 Greatest U.S. Coins* (fourth edition). **a.** The circulated Small Motto is distinguished by a wider D in GOD, and the first T in TRUST nearly touching the ribbon crease at left. **b.** Included in circulation-strike 1864, Large Motto, mintage figure. **c.** The circulated Large Motto is distinguished by a narrow D in GOD, and a 1 mm gap between the first T in TRUST and the ribbon crease. **d.** 20 to 30 examples are known. **e.** Included in 1864, Large Motto, Proof, mintage figure. **f.** Circulated varieties show the tip of the 5 either plain or fancy (curved).

1867, Doubled Die Obverse
FS-02-1867-101.

1869, Doubled Die Obverse
FS-02-1869-101.

	Mintage	Cert	Avg	%MS	G-4	F-12	VF-20	EF-40	AU-50	MS-60BN / PF-63BN	MS-63BN / PF-64BN	MS-64BN / PF-65RB	MS-65RD / PF-65RB
1867	2,938,750	605	59.0	78%	$20	$30	$35	$50	$80	$130	$190	$235	$3,750
Auctions: $646, MS-64RB, August 2015; $423, MS-64RB, October 2015; $282, MS-64BN, February 2015; $141, MS-61BN, May 2015													
1867, Doubled Die Obverse (g)	(h)	65	44.8	37%	$100	$200	$300	$600	$850	$1,400	$2,500	$3,750	
Auctions: $22,325, MS-65RD, January 2014; $1,175, AU-55, March 2016													
1867, Proof	625+	203	64.7								$450	$550	$1,250
Auctions: $940, PF-65RB, August 2015; $763, PF-65BN, September 2015; $646, PF-64BN, January 2015													
1868	2,803,750	589	59.2	76%	$20	$36	$50	$75	$110	$150	$225	$375	$5,500
Auctions: $1,292, MS-65RB, January 2015; $1,057, MS-65RB, October 2015; $834, MS-64RB, June 2015; $211, MS-63BN, February 2015													
1868, Proof	600+	191	64.8								$450	$550	$1,250
Auctions: $470, PF-64BN, January 2015													
1869	1,546,500	511	58.7	75%	$25	$40	$55	$80	$125	$160	$225	$375	$3,500
Auctions: $2,820, MS-65RD, September 2015; $1,540, MS-65RB, January 2015; $763, MS-65BN, July 2015; $329, MS-64BN, June 2015													
1869, Doubled Die Obverse	(i)	0	n/a							$600	$900	$1,250	
Auctions: No auction records available.													
1869, Proof	600+	237	64.6								$450	$550	$1,300
Auctions: $2,820, PF-66RB, July 2015; $1,527, PF-66RB, October 2015; $1,881, PF-65RD, September 2015; $822, PF-65BN, January 2015													
1870	861,250	407	56.3	71%	$35	$55	$85	$150	$200	$275	$300	$575	$9,500
Auctions: $1,762, MS-65RB, August 2015; $329, MS-63RB, October 2015; $258, MS-62BN, May 2015; $62, EF-40, January 2015													
1870, Proof	1,000+	275	64.5								$450	$600	$1,350
Auctions: $3,290, PF-67BN, July 2015; $1,821, PF-65RD, February 2015; $1,116, PF-65RB, January 2015; $705, PF-65BN, September 2015													
1871	721,250	570	56.8	69%	$40	$85	$110	$165	$225	$300	$375	$800	$7,000
Auctions: $1,292, MS-64RD, January 2015; $1,008, MS-64RB, August 2015; $411, MS-64BN, June 2015; $282, MS-61BN, July 2015													
1871, Proof	960+	277	64.6								$450	$600	$1,375
Auctions: $8,233, PF-66RD, July 2015; $2,115, PF-65RB, August 2015; $1,057, PF-64RB, February 2015; $881, PF-64RB, January 2015													
1872	65,000	335	34.1	26%	$400	$600	$775	$1,100	$1,650	$2,800	$3,600	$3,900	$22,500
Auctions: $3,760, MS-65, March 2016; $2,350, MS-62, October 2016; $999, AU-50, December 2015													
1872, Proof	950+	345	64.5								$900	$950	$1,500
Auctions: $1,762, PF-66RB, June 2015; $1,410, PF-65BN, August 2015; $1,292, PF-65BN, February 2015; $2,820, PF-64BN, June 2015													
1873, Close 3, Proof	400	280	63.9								$3,200	$3,500	$4,500
Auctions: $4,700, PF-66BN, June 2015; $5,141, PF-66, March 2015; $3,535, PF-65RB, October 2015													
1873, Open 3, Proof (Alleged Restrike)	200	130	63.6								$3,000	$3,150	$4,000
Auctions: $11,162, PF-66RB, October 2015; $5,640, PF-66BN, January 2015; $3,966, PF-65, February 2015													

g. This variety is somewhat common in low-end circulated grades, but is considered rare in EF and AU, and very rare in MS.
h. Included in circulation-strike 1867 mintage figure. **i.** Included in circulation-strike 1869 mintage figure.

Three-Cent Pieces
1851–1889

AN OVERVIEW OF THREE-CENT PIECES

SILVER THREE-CENT PIECES

The silver three-cent piece or *trime* is one of the more curious coins in American numismatics. The rising price of silver in 1850 created a situation in which silver coins cost more to produce than their face value. Mintages dropped sharply and older pieces disappeared from circulation. In 1851 a solution was provided by the three-cent piece. Instead of being made with 90% silver content, the fineness was set at 75%. Accordingly, the coins were worth less intrinsically, and there was no advantage in melting them. Large quantities were made through 1853. In that year, the standards for regular silver coins were changed, and other denominations reappeared on the marketplace, making the trime unnecessary. Mintages dropped beginning in 1854, until 1873, when production amounted to just 600 Proofs for collectors.

The term *trime* was first used by the director of the United States Mint, James Ross Snowden, at the time of the coins' production.

Of the three varieties of trimes, Variety 2 (1854–1858) is at once the scarcest and, by far, the most difficult to find with a sharp strike. In fact, not one in fifty Variety 2 coins is needle sharp. Curiously, when such pieces are found they are likely to be dated 1855, the lowest-mintage issue of the type. Trimes of the Variety 1 design (1851–1853) vary widely in striking, but can be found sharp. Variety 3 coins (1859–1873) often are sharp.

Mint State coins are readily found for Variety 1 and are usually in grades from MS–60 to 63 or so, although quite a few gems are around with attractive luster. Sharply struck gems are another matter and require some searching to find. Mint State Variety 2 trimes are all rare, and when seen are apt to be miserably struck and in lower grades. Variety 3 coins are readily found in Mint State, including in MS-65 and higher grades.

Proofs were made of all years, but not in quantity until 1858, when an estimated 210 were struck. For all dates after 1862, high-grade Proofs are much more readily available today than are Mint State coins. Circulated examples are available of all three varieties. While extensively worn coins of Variety 1 are available, most Variety 2 coins are Fine or better and most Variety 3 pieces are VF or better.

FOR THE COLLECTOR AND INVESTOR: SILVER THREE-CENT PIECES AS A SPECIALTY

Trimes cover a fairly long span of years and embrace several design types, but comprise no "impossible" rarities. Accordingly, it is realistic to collect one of each Philadelphia Mint coin from 1851 to 1873 plus the 1851-O. There are two overdates in the series, 1862, 2 Over 1 (which is distinct and occurs only in circulation-strike format) and 1863, 3 Over 2 (only Proofs, and not boldly defined), which some specialists collect and others ignore. A curious variety of 1852 has the first digit of the date over an inverted 2.

Typically, a high-grade set includes Mint State examples of all issues 1851 through 1857 and Proofs after that date. As noted, Variety 2 trimes usually are very poorly struck, save the occasionally encountered sharp 1855. As an example, a specialist in the series who found an 1856 with needle-sharp details, at three times the regular market price, might be well advised to buy it. After 1862, Mint State coins are rare for most dates. The formation of a choice Mint State set 1851 through 1872 plus a Proof 1873 would be a formidable challenge.

A set of circulated coins can be gathered through and including 1862, after which such pieces become very rare. Most later dates will have to be acquired on a catch-as-catch-can basis, perhaps by acquiring impaired Proofs for certain of the years.

NICKEL THREE-CENT PIECES

Nickel three-cent pieces were introduced in 1865 to help fill the need for coins in circulation. At the time, silver and gold issues were hoarded, and were available only at a premium. The nickel three-cent piece joined the Indian Head cent and the new (as of 1864) two-cent piece. The coin proved to be very popular in its time, and millions were struck. In 1866 the nickel five-cent piece was introduced, after which time the demand for the nickel three-cent piece diminished somewhat. However, pieces were made in quantity until 1876. In that year silver coins again returned to circulation, and mintages for the nickel three-cent piece dropped sharply. Only Proofs were made in 1877 and 1878. In later years, mintages ranged from small to modest, except for 1881.

Mint State coins are readily available for the early years, although many if not most have weak striking in areas or are from clashed dies. Pristine, sharp Mint State coins on the market are mostly of later years, in the 1880s, where such pieces are the rule, not the exception.

FOR THE COLLECTOR AND INVESTOR: NICKEL THREE-CENT PIECES AS A SPECIALTY

Nickel three-cent coins are interesting to collect by date sequence from 1865 to 1889. Varieties are provided by the 1873, Close 3, and 1873, Open 3, and the 1887, 7 Over 6, overdate. A set of Mint State coins is considerably more difficult to form than a run of Proofs. A hand-selected set of well-struck coins MS-65 or finer could take several years to complete.

Among Proofs, the rarest year is 1865, probably followed by the "perfect date" (not overdate) 1887. Proofs of the 1860s and early 1870s are scarce in PF-65 with excellent strike and eye appeal. Proofs of the latter decade of coinage are much more readily available and usually are choice.

SILVER THREE-CENT PIECES (TRIMES) (1851–1873)

Variety 1 (1851–1853): **Designer:** *James B. Longacre.* **Weight:** *0.80 gram.*
Composition: *.750 silver, .250 copper.* **Diameter:** *14 mm.*
Edge: *Plain.* **Mints:** *Philadelphia and New Orleans.*

| Variety 1 (1851–1853) | Variety 1, Proof |

Variety 2 (1854–1858): **Designer:** *James B. Longacre.* **Weight:** *0.75 gram.*
Composition: *.900 silver, .100 copper.* **Diameter:** *14 mm.* **Edge:** *Plain.* **Mint:** *Philadelphia.*

| Variety 2 (1854–1858) | Variety 2, Proof |

Variety 3 (1859–1873): **Designer:** *James B. Longacre.* **Weight:** *0.75 gram.*
Composition: *.900 silver, .100 copper.* **Diameter:** *14 mm.* **Edge:** *Plain.* **Mint:** *Philadelphia.*

| Variety 3 (1859–1873) | Variety 3, Proof |

History. In 1850 Americans began hoarding their silver coins, as the flood of gold from California made silver disproportionately valuable. To provide a small coin for commerce, the Mint introduced the silver three-cent piece, or *trime*. These were .750 fine (as opposed to the standard .900 fineness), and contained less than 3¢ of metal, so there was no incentive to hoard or melt them. Three different designs were made, Variety 1 of which was struck from 1851 to 1853. These coins were popular in their time and circulated widely. These are distinguished from the other two designs by having no outline or frame around the obverse star. The Act of February 21, 1853, reduced the amount of silver in other denominations (from the half dime to the half dollar, but not the dollar), which discouraged people from hoarding them. The tiny trime lost the public's favor, and mintages decreased.

In 1854 the design was changed considerably, creating Variety 2, which was made through 1858. The alloy was modified to the standard for other issues and the weight was lightened. A raised border was added to the obverse star plus two line frames around it. On the reverse an olive branch was placed above the III and a bundle of arrows below it. This new motif proved to be very difficult to strike up properly.

In 1859 the design was modified again, creating Variety 3. Demand for the denomination continued to be small, and after 1862 very few were made for circulation, as silver coins were hoarded by the war-weary public and began to trade at a premium. Under the Coinage Act of 1873 the trime was discontinued, and that year only Proofs were struck. Also in that year, nearly the entire production of non-Proof coins of 1863 to 1872 was melted.

Striking and Sharpness. On the Variety 1 obverse the tiny shield at the center of the star often lacks certain details. On the reverse check the details and strength of the III. On both sides check the rims. Needle-sharp coins are in the minority. Sharpness of strike has been nearly completely overlooked in the marketplace.

Trimes of Variety 2 are usually poorly struck, with some or all of these characteristics: obverse lettering weak in places; frames around the star of inconsistent strength or missing in certain areas; shield weak in places; reverse stars irregular and poorly formed; olive branch and arrows weak in areas; weak or irregular rims. Now and then a sharp 1855 is found.

Most Variety 3 trimes are sharply struck. Points to look for include full outlines around the star, full shield on the star, and full leaf details and sharp stars.

Most Proofs are needle sharp and have mirrored surfaces, although some of the late 1860s and early 1870s can have slightly grainy or satiny lustrous surfaces. Striking quality varies. Lint marks and surface problems are not unusual. Careful examination is recommended.

Availability. Circulated examples of the Variety 1 trimes are plentiful. MS coins are often seen, although the 1851-O is scarce in MS and high circulated grades. Most MS coins are lustrous and attractive, especially at 63 and above. Circulated Variety 2 coins are scarce in all grades, particularly so at MS-64 and higher. With a needle-sharp strike, MS-65 and higher are *rarities*. Among Variety 3 trimes, circulated coins of the years 1859 to 1862 are easy to find. All later dates range from scarce to rare in circulation-strike format. MS-63 and better coins 1865 and later are very rare. A few Proofs were made in the early 1850s and are great rarities today. After 1857, production increased to an estimated 210 or so in 1858, through 500 to 700 or so as a yearly average in the 1860s to 1873.

GRADING STANDARDS

MS-60 to 70 (Mint State). *Obverse and Reverse:* At MS-60, some abrasion and very minor contact marks are evident, most noticeably on the obverse star and the C ornament on the reverse. At MS-63, abrasion is hard to detect except under magnification. An MS-65 coin will have no abrasion. Luster should be full and rich (not grainy). Grades above MS-65 are defined by having fewer marks as perfection is approached. Most high-grade Mint State coins are of the Variety 3 design.

1853, Variety 1. Graded MS-66.

AU-50, 53, 55, 58 (About Uncirculated). *Obverse:* Light wear is most obvious on the star arms and shield on Variety 1, and on the points of the frames on Variety 2 and Variety 3. At AU-50, luster is evident, but only on part of the field. At AU-58 luster is nearly complete. *Reverse:* Light wear is seen on the C ornament and III. On Variety 2 and 3, light wear is seen on the leaves and arrows.

Illustrated coin: This is sharply struck, as are most Variety 3 trimes.

1863, Variety 3. Graded AU-50.

EF-40, 45 (Extremely Fine). *Obverse:* More wear is seen, most noticeable on the ridges of the star arms, this in addition to more wear on the frames (Variety 2 and Variety 3). Luster is absent, or seen only in traces. *Reverse:* More wear is seen on the C ornament and III. On Variety 2 and Variety 3 more wear is seen on the leaves and arrows.

1869, Variety 3. Graded EF-45.

VF-20, 30 (Very Fine). *Obverse:* Further wear reduced the relief of the star. On Variety 2 and Variety 3 the frames show further wear and begin to blend together. The center shield shows wear, and its border is indistinct in areas, but its horizontal and vertical stripes are fully delineated (unless the coin was weakly struck). *Reverse:* Still more wear is seen on the C ornament and III. On Variety 2 and Variety 3 the high-relief areas of the

1862, Variety 3. Graded VF-30.

leaves and the feathers of the arrow are partially worn away. Stars are flat at their centers (on sharply struck coins in addition to, as expected, on weak strikes).

F-12, 15 (Fine). *Obverse:* The star is worn so as to have lost most of its relief. On Variety 2 and Variety 3 the frames are mostly blended together. The center shield shows wear, and its border is flat (or else showing only slight separation of its two outlines), but its horizontal and vertical stripes still are delineated (unless the coin was weakly struck). *Reverse:* Still more wear is seen on the C ornament and III. On Variety 2 and Variety 3 the

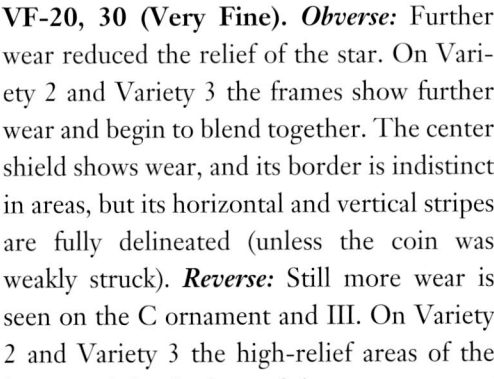

1851, Variety 1. Graded F-12.

high-relief areas of the leaves, and the feathers of the arrow, have slight if any detail. Stars are flat. The designs within the C ornament are missing much detail.

VG-8, 10 (Very Good). *Obverse:* The border is incomplete in places, but all lettering is bold. The horizontal and vertical stripes within the shield begin to blend together, but most remain well delineated. *Reverse:* Still more wear is seen on all areas. The designs within the C ornament have more detail gone.

    Illustrated coin: The obverse of this coin shows VG wear, but if the dent in the star was considered it would grade lower.

1852, Variety 1. Graded VG-10.

G-4, 6 (Good). *Obverse:* The border is worn into the tops of the letters and the bottom of the date. The shield is blended into the star, and only traces of the shield outline remain. In this grade most coins seen are Variety 1. *Reverse:* The border is worn into the outer parts of the stars. Additional wear is seen in all other areas.

1851, Variety 1. Graded G-6.

AG-3 (About Good). *Obverse:* The star is flat. Strong elements of the shield are seen, but the tiny lines are mostly or completely blended together. Lettering and date are weak and partially missing, but the date must be identifiable. In this grade most coins seen are Variety 1. *Reverse:* The border is worn into the stars, with outer elements of the stars now gone. Additional wear is seen in all other areas. The designs within the C ornament are only in outline form.

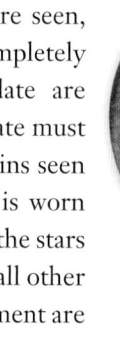

1853, Variety 1. Graded AG-3.

PF-60 to 70 (Proof). *Obverse and Reverse:* Proofs that are extensively cleaned and have many hairlines, or that are dull and grainy, are lower level, such as PF–60 to 62. These are difficult to verify as Proofs. For a trime with medium hairlines and good reflectivity, an assigned grade of PF-64 is indicated, and with relatively few hairlines, gem PF-65. PF-66 should have hairlines so delicate that magnification is needed to see them. Above that, a Proof should be free of such lines.

1857, Variety 2. Graded PF-66.

Illustrated coin: Note the remarkable sharpness of strike, particularly evident on the obverse.

	Mintage	Cert	Avg	%MS	G-4	VG-8	F-12	VF-20	EF-40	AU-50	MS-60	MS-63	MS-65
											PF-63	PF-64	PF-65
1851	5,447,400	1,270	60.9	87%	$30	$45	$50	$65	$80	$165	$200	$275	$675
	Auctions: $3,055, MS-67, July 2015; $2,115, MS-66, June 2015; $1,292, MS-66, September 2015; $446, MS-64, January 2015												
1851, Proof (a)		0	n/a								—		
	Auctions: No auction records available.												
1851-O	720,000	470	58.5	73%	$40	$60	$75	$100	$175	$275	$550	$1,000	$3,000
	Auctions: $11,163, MS-67, July 2014; $12,925, MS-66, December 2013; $793, MS-62, October 2014; $317, AU-55, October 2014												

a. 1 or 2 examples are known.

1852, 1 Over Inverted 2
FS-3S-1852-301.

1853, Repunched Date
FS-3S-1853-301.

1854, Repunched Date
FS-3S-1854-301.

	Mintage	Cert	Avg	%MS	G-4	VG-8	F-12	VF-20	EF-40	AU-50	MS-60 / PF-63	MS-63 / PF-64	MS-65 / PF-65
1852, 1 Over Inverted 2 (b)	(c)	1	61.0	100%					$775	$950	$1,150	$1,425	$1,950
Auctions: No auction records available.													
1852	18,663,500	1,656	57.1	77%	$30	$45	$50	$65	$80	$165	$200	$275	$675
Auctions: $2,643, MS-67, June 2015; $1,057, MS-66, July 2015; $1,028, MS-66, August 2015; $705, MS-65, January 2015													
1852, Proof (d)		0	n/a								—		
Auctions: No auction records available.													
1853	11,400,000	897	53.7	66%	$30	$45	$50	$65	$80	$165	$200	$275	$675
Auctions: $1,233, MS-66, June 2015; $587, MS-65, October 2015; $423, MS-64, January 2015; $152, AU-58, September 2015													
1853, Repunched Date (e)	(f)	0	n/a						$100	$200	$260	$300	$1,000
Auctions: No auction records available.													
1854	671,000	375	59.1	73%	$40	$55	$60	$75	$120	$225	$350	$700	$2,650
Auctions: $3,290, MS-66, June 2015; $2,820, MS-65, January 2015; $646, MS-62, September 2015; $199, AU-53, April 2015													
1854, Repunched Date (g)	(h)	0	n/a						$185	$325	$500	$800	$3,500
Auctions: No auction records available.													
1854, Proof	25–35	8	64.1								$12,000	$17,500	$35,000
Auctions: $32,900, PF-65, January 2015; $41,125, PF-65, June 2014; $14,688, PF-64, October 2014; $6,463, PF-63, August 2015													
1855	139,000	155	54.0	54%	$40	$65	$75	$125	$200	$350	$600	$1,350	$8,000
Auctions: $9,400, MS-66, August 2015; $1,645, MS-64, January 2015; $399, AU-55, April 2015; $305, EF-45, July 2015													
1855, Proof	30–40	24	64.8								$5,000	$8,500	$13,000
Auctions: $21,150, PF-66Cam, October 2014; $8,225, PF-64, October 2014													
1856	1,458,000	352	58.0	69%	$40	$45	$50	$70	$120	$235	$360	$700	$3,000
Auctions: $1,292, MS-64, July 2015; $1,086, MS-64, October 2015; $329, MS-62, May 2015; $352, AU-58, April 2015													
1856, Proof	40–50	30	64.4								$4,300	$6,500	$12,500
Auctions: $22,325, PF-66, August 2016; $19,388, PF-66, February 2015; $9,988, PF-64, October 2015													
1857	1,042,000	356	58.1	76%	$40	$45	$50	$70	$120	$235	$360	$700	$2,500
Auctions: $5,405, MS-66, January 2015; $2,820, MS-65, September 2015; $940, MS-64, October 2015; $646, AU-58, April 2015													
1857, Proof	60–80	37	64.6								$3,750	$5,000	$10,000
Auctions: $15,863, PF-66, June 2014													
1858	1,603,700	643	57.4	67%	$40	$45	$50	$70	$120	$235	$360	$700	$2,500
Auctions: $5,875, MS-67, July 2015; $1,821, MS-65, February 2015; $1,116, MS-64, September 2015; $353, AU-58, April 2015													
1858, Proof	210	106	64.5								$2,750	$4,500	$6,500
Auctions: $12,925, PF-67, August 2015; $6,462, PF-65, October 2015													
1859	364,200	345	60.2	77%	$40	$45	$50	$60	$90	$175	$215	$300	$1,000
Auctions: $1,762, MS-66, January 2015; $1,645, MS-66, September 2015; $881, MS-65, October 2015; $763, MS-65, August 2015													
1859, Proof	800	111	64.1								$750	$1,100	$2,000
Auctions: $4,700, PF-66Cam, August 2015; $2,643, PF-66, June 2015; $1,880, PF-65, January 2015; $1,586, PF-64Cam, February 2015													
1860	286,000	341	58.1	64%	$40	$45	$50	$60	$90	$175	$215	$300	$1,000
Auctions: $434, MS-64, October 2015; $317, MS-63, April 2015; $211, MS-61, May 2015; $166, AU-55, January 2015													
1860, Proof	1,000	79	63.8								$1,000	$1,500	$4,000
Auctions: $4,935, PF-65, August 2015													

b. An inverted 2 is visible beneath the primary 1. "A secondary date punch was obviously punched into the die in an inverted orientation and then corrected after some effacing of the die" (*Cherrypickers' Guide to Rare Die Varieties*, sixth edition, volume I).
c. Included in circulation-strike 1852 mintage figure. **d.** 1 example is known. **e.** Secondary digits are visible to the north of the primary 1 and 8. This repunched date can be detected on lower-grade coins. **f.** Included in 1853 mintage figure. **g.** Secondary digits are visible to the west of the primary digits on the 8 and 5. **h.** Included in circulation-strike 1854 mintage figure.

1862, 2 Over 1
FS-3S-1862-301.

	Mintage	Cert	Avg	%MS	G-4	VG-8	F-12	VF-20	EF-40	AU-50	MS-60 / PF-63	MS-63 / PF-64	MS-65 / PF-65
1861	497,000	863	60.8	77%	$40	$45	$50	$60	$90	$175	$215	$300	$875
	Auctions: $2,938, MS-67, June 2015; $1,410, MS-66, January 2015; $519, MS-64, August 2015; $164, AU-53, May 2015												
1861, Proof	1,000	91	64.1								$750	$1,100	$1,750
	Auctions: $3,055, PF-66, June 2015; $2,351, PF-66, September 2015; $1,175, PF-65, January 2015												
1862, 2 Over 1 (i)	(j)	339	63.4	90%	$40	$45	$50	$60	$95	$190	$240	$350	$1,050
	Auctions: $1,762, MS-66, June 2015; $881, MS-65, August 2015; $540, MS-64, February 2015; $329, AU-58, April 2015												
1862	343,000	1,150	62.5	87%	$40	$45	$50	$60	$90	$175	$215	$285	$875
	Auctions: $2,585, MS-67, September 2015; $1,116, MS-66, June 2015; $734, MS-65, January 2015; $223, AU-58, April 2015												
1862, Proof	550	138	64.0								$750	$1,100	$1,750
	Auctions: $2,127, PF-66, October 2015; $2,115, PF-65, January 2015; $1,527, PF-65, August 2015; $646, PF-63, June 2015												
1863	21,000	81	64.2	96%	$475	$550	$600	$650	$750	$1,000	$1,250	$2,000	$3,500
	Auctions: $7,050, MS-67, January 2015; $5,875, MS-67, October 2015												
1863, So-Called 3 Over 2, Proof	(k)	0	n/a								$2,500	$4,500	$7,500
	Auctions: $8,812, PF-67, January 2015; $12,925, PF-65, July 2015; $5,405, PF-64, October 2015												
1863, Proof	460	139	64.3								$750	$1,100	$1,500
	Auctions: $3,995, PF-66Cam, January 2015; $1,703, PF-65Cam, January 2015												
1864	12,000	92	63.4	92%	$475	$500	$550	$650	$750	$850	$1,200	$1,400	$3,000
	Auctions: $3,760, MS-66, October 2015; $1,116, MS-63, June 2015; $1,880, AU-58, January 2015												
1864, Proof	470	174	64.6								$750	$1,000	$1,500
	Auctions: $2,585, PF-66, August 2015; $3,055, PF-65Cam, January 2015; $1,116, PF-65, July 2015; $1,088, PF-64Cam, August 2015												
1865	8,000	106	62.5	87%	$475	$500	$550	$600	$700	$850	$1,750	$2,350	$4,000
	Auctions: $5,170, MS-67, August 2015; $4,230, MS-66, October 2015; $1,527, MS-64, January 2015; $2,232, MS-63, January 2015												
1865, Proof	500	159	64.4								$750	$1,000	$1,500
	Auctions: $3,642, PF-67, October 2015; $3,995, PF-66, June 2015; $1,645, PF-65, August 2015; $3,290, PF-64, January 2015												
1866	22,000	87	62.9	89%	$450	$500	$525	$625	$800	$950	$1,400	$1,800	$3,750
	Auctions: $11,750, MS-67, October 2015; $8,812, MS-66, October 2015; $998, EF-40, January 2015; $940, EF-40, July 2015												
1866, Proof	725	206	64.2								$750	$1,000	$1,500
	Auctions: $6,462, PF-67, January 2015; $1,762, PF-66, August 2015; $1,292, PF-64, September 2015; $705, PF-63, July 2015												
1867	4,000	46	60.7	83%	$450	$500	$550	$650	$850	$1,200	$1,700	$3,000	$12,500
	Auctions: $14,100, MS-65, October 2015; $4,465, MS-64, August 2015; $3,643, MS-64, September 2015; $1,292, AU-50, July 2015												
1867, Proof	625	263	64.4								$750	$1,000	$1,500
	Auctions: $1,762, PF-66, September 2015; $1,527, PF-65, August 2015; $998, PF-64, January 2015; $822, PF-64, July 2015												

i. A secondary 1 is evident beneath the 2 of the date. "This overdate is believed to be due more to economy (the Mint having used a good die another year) than to error. Circulated examples are about as common as the regular-dated coin" (*Cherrypickers' Guide to Rare Die Varieties*, sixth edition, volume I). **j.** Included in circulation-strike 1862 mintage figure. **k.** Included in 1863, Proof, mintage figure.

	Mintage	Cert	Avg	%MS	F-12	VF-20	EF-40	AU-50	MS-60	MS-63	MS-64	MS-65	MS-66
											PF-63	PF-64	PF-65
1868	3,500	36	60.4	83%	$500	$600	$650	$850	$1,250	$1,500	$2,500	$4,500	$16,000
	Auctions: $21,150, MS-66, October 2015; $28,200, MS-66, May 2015; $5,405, AU-58, July 2015												
1868, Proof	600	269	64.1								$750	$1,000	$1,500
	Auctions: $3,525, PF-66, October 2015; $1,410, PF-66, January 2015; $1,997, PF-65, August 2015; $940, PF-63, September 2015												
1869	4,500	50	62.4	86%	$450	$500	$550	$700	$1,100	$1,200	$1,400	$2,200	$6,750
	Auctions: $9,987, MS-65, October 2015; $4,230, MS-64, October 2015; $1,645, MS-62, August 2015; $940, EF-40, July 2015												
1869, Proof	600	181	64.4								$750	$1,000	$1,500
	Auctions: $7,050, PF-67, August 2015; $1,880, PF-66, January 2015; $1,645, PF-65, October 2015; $423, PF-62, June 2015												
1869, So-Called 9 Over 8, Proof (a)	(b)	0	n/a								$3,000	$5,500	$7,500
	Auctions: $9,987, PF-66, August 2015												
1870	3,000	91	61.7	80%	$450	$500	$550	$650	$750	$950	$1,200	$1,800	$4,500
	Auctions: $7,116, MS-66, October 2015; $470, EF-40, May 2015												
1870, Proof	1,000	245	64.0								$750	$1,000	$1,500
	Auctions: $1,880, PF-66, January 2015; $1,762, PF-65, September 2015; $1,762, PF-64, October 2015; $3,055, PF-63, October 2015												
1871	3,400	149	63.7	91%	$450	$500	$550	$650	$950	$1,050	$1,100	$1,200	$1,950
	Auctions: $3,290, MS-67, June 2015; $1,880, MS-66, February 2015; $1,645, MS-64, January 2015; $1,086, MS-63, November 2015												
1871, Proof	960	221	64.0								$750	$1,000	$1,500
	Auctions: $2,291, PF-66, January 2015; $1,527, PF-65, September 2015; $881, PF-63, July 2015; $646, PF-61, June 2015												
1872	1,000	48	61.5	85%	$600	$750	$850	$1,100	$2,000	$2,250	$2,500	$3,500	$10,000
	Auctions: $14,100, MS-67, August 2015; $54,050, MS-67, February 2015; $4,935, MS-65, October 2015												
1872, Proof	950	233	64.1								$750	$1,000	$1,500
	Auctions: $11,750, PF-67Cam, January 2015; $2,585, PF-66, August 2015; $3,290, PF-65, October 2015; $1,645, PF-65, August 2015												
1873, Close 3, Proof (a)	600	373	64.1								$2,000	$2,500	$3,000
	Auctions: $12,220, PF-67, February 2015; $3,055, PF-66Cam, June 2015												

a. Proof only. b. Included in 1869, Proof, mintage figure.

NICKEL THREE-CENT PIECES (1865–1889)

Designer: *James B. Longacre.* **Weight:** *1.94 grams.* **Composition:** *.750 copper, .250 nickel.* **Diameter:** *17.9 mm.* **Edge:** *Plain.* **Mint:** *Philadelphia.*

Circulation Strike

Proof

History. The copper-nickel three-cent coin debuted in the final year of the Civil War, 1865. The American public was still hoarding silver coins (a situation that would continue until 1876), including the silver three-cent piece. The highest-denomination coin remaining in circulation at the time was the recently introduced two-cent piece. After 1875, when silver coins circulated once again, the three-cent denomination became redundant and mintages dropped. The last pieces were coined in 1889.

Striking and Sharpness. On the obverse check the hair and other portrait details. On the reverse the tiny vertical lines in the Roman numeral III can be weak. Check the denticles on both sides of the coin. Among circulation strikes, clashed dies are common, particularly for the earlier high-mintage years. Generally, coins of the 1860s and 1870s have weakness in one area or another. Many if not most of the 1880s are well struck. Proofs from 1878 onward often have satiny or frosty fields, rather than mirrored surfaces, and resemble circulation strikes.

Availability. Circulated examples of dates from 1865 to the mid-1870s are readily available. MS coins, particularly from the 1860s, are easily found, but often have areas of weakness or lack aesthetic appeal. MS coins of the 1880s are readily found for most dates (except for 1883, 1884, 1885, and 1887), some of them probably sold as Proofs. Many Proofs of the era had slight to extensive mint luster. Proofs were struck of all dates and can be found easily enough in the marketplace. The rarest is the first year of issue, 1865, of which only an estimated 500 or so were made. The vast majority of 1865s have a repunched date. Second rarest (not counting PF-only date of 1877) is the 1887 (perfect date, not the overdate) with a production of about 1,000 coins. Proofs of the years 1865 to 1876 can be difficult to find as true gems, while later Proofs are nearly all gems.

GRADING STANDARDS

MS-60 to 70 (Mint State). *Obverse and Reverse:* Mint luster is complete in the obverse and reverse fields. Lower grades such as MS–60, 61, and 62 can show some evidence of abrasion. This is usually on the area of the hair to the right of the face (on the obverse), and on the highest parts of the wreath (on the reverse). Abrasion can appear as scattered contact marks elsewhere. At MS-63, these marks are few, and on MS-65 they are fewer yet. In grades above MS-65, marks can only be seen under magnification.

1865. Graded MS-61.

AU-50, 53, 55, 58 (About Uncirculated). *Obverse:* Light wear is seen on the portrait, most notably on the upper cheek and on the hair to the right of the face. Mint luster is present in the fields, ranging from partial at AU-50 to nearly complete at AU-58. All details are sharp, unless lightly struck. *Reverse:* Light wear is seen on the top and bottom horizontal edges of the III and the wreath. Luster is partial at AU-50, increasing to nearly full at AU-58. All details are sharp, unless lightly struck.

1881. Graded AU-55.

EF-40, 45 (Extremely Fine). *Obverse:* More wear is seen on the cheek and the hair to the right of the face and neck. The hair to the right of the coronet beads shows light wear. *Reverse:* The wreath still shows most detail on the leaves. Some wear is seen on the vertical lines within III (but striking can also cause weakness). Overall the reverse appears to be very bold.

1889. Graded EF-40.

VF-20, 30 (Very Fine). *Obverse:* Most hair detail is gone, with a continuous flat area to the right of the face and neck, where the higher hair strands have blended together. The hair to the right of the coronet beads shows about half of the strands. *Reverse:* Higher details of the leaves are worn away; the central ridges are seen on some. Wear on the vertical lines in III has caused some to merge, but most are separate.

1880. Graded VF-25.

F-12, 15 (Fine). *Obverse:* Wear is more extensive. The forehead blends into the hair above it. About 10% to 29% of the hair detail to the right of the coronet remains, and much detail is seen lower, at the right edge opposite the ear and neck. Denticles are distinct. *Reverse:* The top (highest-relief) part of most leaves is flat. Many vertical lines in III are fused. Denticles are distinct.

1882. Graded F-15.

VG-8, 10 (Very Good). *Obverse:* Less hair detail shows. Denticles all are clear. *Reverse:* The leaves show more wear. The inner edges of some leaves are worn away, causing leaves to merge. Only about half, or slightly fewer, of the lines in III are discernible.

1865. Graded VG-10.

G-4, 6 (Good). *Obverse:* Most hair details are gone, but some remain at the lower right. The rim is worn smooth in areas, and many denticles are missing. The lettering is weak, but readable. *Reverse:* The leaves mostly are worn flat. Very few lines remain in III. The rim is worn smooth in areas, and many denticles are missing.

1867. Graded G-4.

AG-3 (About Good). *Obverse:* The rim is worn away and into the tops of most of the letters. The date remains bold. *Reverse:* The rim is worn away and into some of the leaves.

1867. Graded AG-3.

PF-60 to 70 (Proof). *Obverse and Reverse:* PF–60, 61, and 62 coins show varying amounts of hairlines in the field, decreasing as the grade increases. Fields may be dull or cloudy on lower-level pieces. At PF-65, hairlines are visible only under magnification and are very light; the cheek of Miss Liberty does not show any friction or "album slide marks." Above PF-65, hairlines become fewer, and in ultra-high grades are nonexistent, this mean-

1878. Graded PF-65.

ing that the coins have never been subject to wiping or abrasive cleaning. At PF-65 or better, expect excellent aesthetic appeal. Blotched, deeply toned, or recolored coins are sometimes seen at Proof levels from PF–60 through 65 or even 66 and should be avoided, but these are less often seen than on contemporary Proof nickel five-cent pieces.

1866, Doubled Die Obverse
FS-3N-1866-101.

	Mintage	Cert	Avg	%MS	G-4	VG-8	VF-20	EF-40	AU-50	MS-60	MS-63 / PF-63	MS-65 / PF-65	MS-66 / PF-66
1865	11,382,000	2,075	59.6	77%	$18	$20	$30	$40	$65	$100	$160	$550	$1,100
Auctions: $1,880, MS-66, January 2015; $399, MS-64, May 2015; $199, MS-61, November 2015; $111, AU-58, June 2015													
1865, Proof	500+	196	64.7								$1,500	$4,250	$6,500
Auctions: $4,583, PF-66, November 2016; $5,288, PF-65, July 2015; $4,113, PF-64, August 2016													
1866	4,801,000	837	60.0	80%	$18	$20	$28	$40	$65	$100	$160	$550	$1,500
Auctions: $7,637, MS-67, August 2015; $1,527, MS-66, June 2015; $111, MS-63, February 2015; $89, MS-62, April 2015													
1866, Doubled Die Obverse (a)	(b)	5	48.4	20%				$150	$250	$350	$450	$1,000	
Auctions: No auction records available.													
1866, Proof	725+	306	64.5								$350	$1,100	$2,000
Auctions: $2,820, PF-66, January 2015; $1,880, PF-66, September 2015; $1,527, PF-65, August 2015; $1,292, PF-65, June 2015													

a. Moderate doubling is visible on AMERICA and on portions of the hair. "The dies clashed midway through the obverse's life. Mid– and late–die-state coins exhibit the clash marks and die cracks as progression occurs. This variety has proven extremely scarce" (*Cherrypickers' Guide to Rare Die Varieties*, sixth edition, volume I). b. Included in circulation-strike 1866 mintage figure.

	Mintage	Cert	Avg	%MS	G-4	VG-8	VF-20	EF-40	AU-50	MS-60	MS-63 / PF-63	MS-65 / PF-65	MS-66 / PF-66
1867	3,915,000	634	59.0	74%	$15	$20	$30	$40	$65	$100	$160	$650	$1,650
Auctions: $238, MS-64, January 2015; $141, MS-63, February 2015; $111, MS-62, May 2015; $79, AU-58, August 2015													
1867, Proof	*625+*	313	64.7								$350	$850	$1,500
Auctions: $9,400, PF-68, July 2015; $1,880, PF-66, January 2015; $1,527, PF-66, September 2015; $763, PF-65, August 2015													
1868	3,252,000	597	59.5	77%	$15	$20	$30	$40	$65	$100	$160	$625	$1,100
Auctions: $881, MS-66, August 2015; $822, MS-65, January 2015; $111, MS-63, February 2015; $117, MS-62, April 2015													
1868, Proof	*600+*	286	64.8								$350	$1,050	$1,450
Auctions: $1,065, PF-66, January 2015; $1,116, PF-65, September 2015; $705, PF-65, August 2015; $446, PF-64, January 2015													
1869	1,604,000	402	60.7	81%	$15	$20	$30	$40	$65	$125	$185	$750	$1,500
Auctions: $1,292, MS-66, August 2015; $141, MS-63, February 2015; $105, MS-62, February 2015; $129, MS-61, November 2015													
1869, Proof	*600+*	376	64.7								$350	$750	$1,150
Auctions: $5,170, PF-67, July 2015; $881, PF-66, January 2015; $1,028, PF-65, October 2015; $705, PF-65, January 2015													
1870	1,335,000	429	60.3	79%	$20	$25	$30	$40	$65	$140	$195	$725	$1,450
Auctions: $223, MS-64, March 2015; $164, MS-63, November 2015; $129, MS-62, May 2015; $84, AU-58, April 2015													
1870, Proof	*1,000+*	354	64.4								$350	$750	$1,150
Auctions: $1,175, PF-66, January 2015; $763, PF-65, September 2015; $329, PF-64, April 2015; $235, MS-61, November 2015													
1871	604,000	238	59.5	80%	$20	$25	$30	$40	$65	$140	$195	$750	$1,500
Auctions: $3,525, MS-67, January 2015; $2,723, MS-66, September 2015; $2,350, MS-66, February 2015; $282, MS-64, May 2015													
1871, Proof	*960+*	366	64.5								$350	$750	$1,150
Auctions: $5,875, PF-67Cam, October 2015; $940, PF-66, February 2015; $763, PF-65, January 2015; $258, PF-63, November 2015													
1872	862,000	198	59.2	75%	$20	$25	$30	$40	$65	$150	$210	$1,200	$2,200
Auctions: $881, MS-66, January 2015; $940, MS-65, October 2015; $211, MS-63, May 2015; $117, MS-62, July 2015													
1872, Proof	*950+*	435	64.5								$350	$750	$1,150
Auctions: $4,700, PF-66, February 2015; $1,600, PF-66, July 2015; $505, PF-65, June 2015; $293, PF-63, November 2015													
1873, Close 3	390,000	109	55.6	65%	$20	$25	$30	$40	$65	$150	$210	$1,350	$2,750
Auctions: $2,232, MS-66, August 2015; $423, MS-64, June 2015; $399, MS-64, October 2015; $237, MS-63, February 2015													
1873, Open 3	783,000	96	53.8	64%	$20	$25	$30	$40	$70	$160	$350	$2,750	$7,500
Auctions: $3,055, MS-65, January 2015; $587, MS-64, June 2015; $223, MS-63, October 2015; $199, MS-63, May 2015													
1873, Close 3, Proof	*1,100+*	449	64.4								$350	$750	$1,250
Auctions: $969, PF-66, August 2015; $734, PF-65, June 2015; $540, PF-65, January 2015; $290, PF-64, November 2015													
1874	790,000	194	57.2	70%	$20	$25	$30	$40	$65	$150	$210	$1,200	$2,000
Auctions: $2,115, MS-66, October 2015; $188, MS-63, August 2015; $176, MS-62, January 2015; $79, AU-58, February 2015													
1874, Proof	*700+*	340	64.6								$350	$750	$1,100
Auctions: $601, PF-66, January 2015; $564, PF-66, October 2015; $587, PF-65, June 2015; $329, PF-64, April 2015													
1875	228,000	230	62.0	89%	$20	$25	$35	$45	$80	$175	$225	$800	$1,500
Auctions: $646, MS-65, August 2015; $329, MS-64, November 2015; $446, AU-58, April 2015; $129, AU-55, May 2015													
1875, Proof	*700+*	252	64.3								$350	$1,000	$1,500
Auctions: $998, PF-65, January 2015; $646, PF-65, June 2015; $470, PF-64, January 2015; $305, PF-64, October 2015													
1876	162,000	131	57.8	72%	$20	$25	$35	$50	$110	$200	$260	$1,600	$2,250
Auctions: $1,880, MS-66, June 2015; $1,292, MS-65, February 2015; $940, MS-64, July 2015; $616, AU-58, May 2015													
1876, Proof	*1,150+*	400	64.5								$350	$700	$1,050
Auctions: $1,057, PF-66, September 2015; $881, PF-66, July 2015; $517, PF-65, January 2015; $540, PF-64, May 2015													
1877, Proof (c)	900	458	64.8								$2,000	$3,750	$4,750
Auctions: $7,344, PF-66, November 2016; $5,875, PF-66, August 2016; $3,525, PF-65, May 2016; $2,820, PF-64, August 2016													
1878, Proof (c)	2,350	693	64.8								$875	$1,000	$1,250
Auctions: $1,527, PF-67, August 2015; $1,410, PF-66, March 2016; $646, PF-63, January 2015; $374, PF-60, May 2015													

c. Proof only.

1887, 7 Over 6, Proof
FS-3N-1887-302.

	Mintage	Cert	Avg	%MS	G-4	VG-8	VF-20	EF-40	AU-50	MS-60	MS-63 / PF-63	MS-65 / PF-65	MS-66 / PF-66
1879	38,000	177	57.1	69%	$60	$70	$90	$125	$175	$300	$400	$850	$1,200
Auctions: $998, MS-66, July 2015; $1,057, MS-65, August 2015; $575, MS-65, January 2015; $258, AU-53, May 2015													
1879, Proof	3,200	953	65.1								$400	$625	$750
Auctions: $2,820, PF-68, January 2015; $998, PF-67, July 2015; $675, PF-66Cam, August 2015; $411, PF-65, May 2015													
1880	21,000	204	58.5	77%	$90	$110	$150	$200	$220	$350	$410	$850	$1,250
Auctions: $705, MS-65, August 2015; $564, MS-64, January 2015; $296, MS-63, October 2015; $211, MS-60, May 2015													
1880, Proof	3,955	981	65.0								$400	$550	$750
Auctions: $540, PF-66, June 2015; $470, PF-66, January 2015; $376, PF-65, November 2015; $298, PF-64, April 2015													
1881	1,077,000	639	58.7	70%	$20	$25	$30	$40	$65	$125	$185	$650	$1,000
Auctions: $493, MS-65, July 2015; $152, MS-63, July 2015; $94, MS-62, August 2015; $89, AU-58, October 2015													
1881, Proof	3,575	1,014	65.2								$375	$550	$750
Auctions: $3,760, PF-68, February 2015; $1,057, PF-67, February 2015; $587, PF-66, January 2015; $282, PF-63, April 2015													
1882	22,200	130	49.1	39%	$125	$135	$200	$225	$275	$450	$600	$1,850	$2,750
Auctions: $587, MS-64, January 2015; $199, VF-30, February 2015; $164, VF-25, October 2015; $164, F-15, July 2015													
1882, Proof	3,100	1,041	65.1								$400	$550	$750
Auctions: $4,230, PF-68, January 2015; $446, PF-65, March 2015; $258, PF-62, August 2015; $199, PF-60, May 2015													
1883	4,000	51	52.7	49%	$275	$325	$450	$550	$850	$1,500	$3,000	$10,000	$15,000
Auctions: $7,638, MS-65, August 2016; $940, AU-50, May 2016; $588, EF-45, September 2016													
1883, Proof	6,609	1,542	64.7								$400	$550	$750
Auctions: $5,287, PF-68, January 2015; $705, PF-66, February 2015; $376, PF-65, November 2015; $235, PF-64, January 2015													
1884	1,700	33	51.3	39%	$550	$800	$1,400	$1,900	$2,750	$3,000	$6,500	$17,500	$22,500
Auctions: $2,115, MS-61, December 2015; $1,998, EF-45, February 2015; $1,880, VF-30, July 2016													
1884, Proof	3,942	1,197	64.8								$400	$550	$750
Auctions: $998, PF-67, October 2015; $734, PF-66, August 2015; $376, PF-65, January 2015; $305, PF-64, February 2015													
1885	1,000	36	57.2	67%	$800	$1,100	$1,750	$2,500	$3,000	$4,500	$6,500	$12,500	$17,500
Auctions: $16,450, MS-66, June 2015; $8,225, MS-65, November 2016; $7,050, MS-64, August 2016; $3,408, AU-55, October 2016													
1885, Proof	3,790	1,005	64.6								$400	$550	$750
Auctions: $646, PF-66, June 2015; $340, PF-64, February 2015; $329, PF-64, January 2015; $258, PF-60, August 2015													
1886, Proof (c)	4,290	1,068	64.7								$400	$625	$800
Auctions: $900, PF-67, January 2015; $505, PF-66, January 2015; $517, PF-65, August 2015; $329, PF-64, February 2015													
1887	5,001	112	55.0	59%	$275	$325	$400	$525	$625	$700	$800	$1,500	$2,250
Auctions: $1,703, MS-66, August 2015; $1,763, MS-66, February 2015; $763, MS-63, July 2015; $705, EF-45, January 2015													
1887, Proof	2,960	353	64.2								$400	$825	$950
Auctions: $1,880, PF-67, June 2015; $540, PF-65, July 2015; $517, PF-65, January 2015; $423, PF-64, May 2015													
1887, 7 Over 6, Proof (d)	(e)	484	64.8								$425	$700	$900
Auctions: $2,585, PF-66, August 2015; $998, PF-66, October 2015; $517, PF-64Cam, January 2015; $376, PF-62, August 2015													
1888	36,501	311	59.1	67%	$50	$65	$75	$90	$150	$300	$400	$750	$1,250
Auctions: $1,527, MS-67, January 2015; $564, MS-65, September 2015; $305, MS-63, May 2015; $446, AU-58, February 2015													
1888, Proof	4,582	1,072	64.8								$400	$550	$750
Auctions: $3,055, PF-68, October 2015; $1,762, PF-67, February 2015; $600, PF-66, January 2015; $446, PF-65, February 2015													
1889	18,125	251	59.1	66%	$80	$100	$135	$220	$250	$350	$450	$800	$1,350
Auctions: $1,645, MS-66, January 2015; $795, MS-66, June 2015; $188, AU-55, May 2015; $176, AU-50, July 2015													
1889, Proof	3,436	1,063	65.0								$400	$550	$750
Auctions: $734, PF-67, January 2015; $646, PF-66, August 2015; $399, PF-65, September 2015; $282, PF-64, January 2015													

c. Proof only. **d.** Strong remnants of the underlying 6 are evident on either side of the lower portion of the 7, with the 1 and both 8's clearly repunched. This Proof overdate is relatively common; note that the regular date can be valued higher than the variety. **e.** Included in 1887, Proof, mintage figure.

Nickel Five-Cent Pieces
1866 to Date

AN OVERVIEW OF NICKEL FIVE-CENT PIECES

Five-cent pieces made of nickel were introduced in 1866, in an era in which the silver half dime as well as other silver denominations were not seen in circulation. More than a dozen designs and their variations have graced the "nickel" in the past 140-plus years.

While Shield nickels of both varieties are slightly scarce in upper Mint State levels, they are within the financial reach of most collectors. Proofs are available of each variety, but the 1866–1867, With Rays, and the 1913 Buffalo, Variety 1, issues are rare.

The quality of strike presents a challenge across the various types of nickel five-cent pieces, most particularly with the 1866–1867, With Rays, for there are fewer possibilities from which to choose. Although 1913–1938 Buffalo, Variety 2, nickels are often poorly struck, there are enough sharp ones that finding a choice example should present no great challenge for the collector.

FOR THE COLLECTOR AND INVESTOR: FIVE-CENT PIECES AS A SPECIALTY

Shield nickels of the 1866–1883 era are often collected by date sequence. A full set includes 1866 and 1867, With Rays, plus 1867 to 1883, Without Rays. In addition, there is the 1879, 9 Over 8, overdate, which is found only in Proof format but is readily available (constituting perhaps a third or so of the Proof mintage of 3,200 for the 1879 year) and the 1883, 3 Over 2 (scarce, and available only as a circulation strike).

Circulation strikes are available of all Shield nickel dates, 1866 to 1883, except 1877 and 1878, which were made only in Proof format. A set of Proofs can be completed except for the 1867, With Rays, which is exceedingly rare in Proof, with an estimated population of fewer than two dozen coins. Most 1878 Proofs are frosty and appear not much different from Mint State, but only Proofs were made this year.

In circulated grades, Shield nickels are available in proportion to their mintage figures. The dates 1879 to 1881 had high Proof mintages (in the context of Proof figures), but low circulation-strike mintages, and thus they are key dates in the latter format. In other words, a gem MS-65 1880 Shield nickel (16,000 coined, but few were saved, as collectors acquired Proofs instead) is exceedingly rare today. In the same year 3,955 Proofs were struck, all were preserved by collectors and dealers, and today the Proof 1880 is one of the most plentiful dates.

Liberty Head nickels of the 1883, Without CENTS (or "No CENTS"), variety are plentiful in Mint State and also in Proof. Later dates With CENTS, through 1912, are generally available in proportion to their mintages. The 1885 and 1886 are considered to be key dates. Proofs are readily collectible, although pristine high-quality examples can be hard to find. The 1912-D and 1912-S are scarce. In 1913 an estimated five Liberty Head nickels were privately made, and today stand as famous rarities.

Among Buffalo nickels, 1913 to 1938, the different dates and mints can be collected easily enough in circulated grades, although certain issues such as 1913-S, Variety 2; 1921-S; and 1926-S are on the scarce side. An overdate, 1918-D, 8 Over 7, is a rarity at all grade levels. Curious varieties are provided by the very rare 1916, Doubled Date; the scarce 1937-D, 3-Legged (the die was heavily polished, resulting in some loss of detail); and the fascinating and readily available 1938-D, D Over S, overmintmark.

In choice or gem Mint State most branch-mint Buffalo nickels, 1914–1927, are fairly scarce, and some are quite rare. Most branch-mint coins of the 1920s are lightly struck in one area or another, with the 1926-D being particularly infamous in this regard. Sharply struck examples of such varieties are worth much more than lightly struck ones, although the grading services take no particular note of such differences. Matte Proofs of dates 1913 to 1916 were struck, and mirror-finish Proofs were made in 1936 and 1937. These exist today in proportion to their mintages.

Jefferson nickels from 1938 to date are readily collectible in Mint State and Proof format. Many otherwise common varieties can be very rare if sharply struck.

Popularized in the 1890s and throughout the beginning of the 1900s, coin-operated machines took cents and other denominations, but the coin of choice was the nickel. Pictured is a postcard for Horn & Hardart restaurants, 1930s, where patrons would serve themselves with such coin-operated devices.

SHIELD (1866–1883)

Designer: *James B. Longacre.* **Weight:** *5 grams.* **Composition:** *.750 copper, .250 nickel.* **Diameter:** *20.5 mm.* **Edge:** *Plain.* **Mint:** *Philadelphia.*

Variety 1, Rays Between Stars (1866–1867)

Variety 1, Rays Between Stars, Proof

Variety 2, Without Rays (1867–1883)

Variety 2, Without Rays, Proof

History. The nickel five-cent piece was introduced in 1866. At the time, silver coins (except the trime) did not circulate in the East or Midwest. The new denomination proved popular, and "nickels" of the Shield variety were made continuously from 1866 to 1883. All 1866 nickels have rays between the stars on the reverse, as do a minority of 1867 issues, after which this feature was dropped. In 1877 and 1878 only Proofs were made, with no circulation strikes. The design, by Chief Engraver James B. Longacre, is somewhat similar to the obverse of the two-cent piece. Some Shield nickels were still seen in circulation in the 1930s, by which time most had been worn nearly smooth.

Striking and Sharpness. Sharpness can be a problem for Shield nickels in the 1860s through 1876, much less so for later years. On the obverse the horizontal shield stripes, vertical stripes, and leaves should be checked. The horizontal stripes in particular can be blended together. On the reverse the star centers can be weak. Check all other areas as well. Die cracks are seen on *most* circulation-strike Shield nickels, and do not affect value. Proof Shield nickels were struck of all dates 1866 to 1883, including two varieties of 1867 (With Rays, a great rarity, and the usually seen Without Rays). Fields range from deeply mirrorlike to somewhat grainy in character to mirror-surface, depending on a given year. Many of 1878, a date struck only in Proof format, have *lustrous* surfaces or prooflike surfaces combined with some luster, resembling a circulation strike. While most Proofs are sharp, some have weakness on the shield on the obverse and/or the star centers on the reverse. Lint marks or tiny recessed marks from scattered debris on the die faces are sometimes encountered, especially on issues of the 1870s, but not factored into the grade in commercial certification unless excessive.

Availability. Circulated coins generally are available in proportion to their mintage quantities (exceptions being the 1873, Open 3, and 1873, Close 3, varieties, which tend to be elusive in all grades despite their relatively high mintage). MS coins are similarly available, except that 1880 is a rarity. Those dated 1882 and 1883 are plentiful.

GRADING STANDARDS

MS-60 to 70 (Mint State). *Obverse and Reverse:* At MS-60 some abrasion and very minor contact marks are evident, most noticeably on high points of the shield on the obverse and the field on the reverse. Sometimes light striking on the shield and stars can be mistaken for light wear, and marks on the numeral 5 on the reverse can be from the original planchet surface not struck up fully. At MS-63 abrasions are hard to detect except

1873, Open 3. Graded MS-66.

under magnification. An MS-65 coin will have no abrasion. Luster should be full and rich (not grainy). Grades above MS-65 are defined by having no marks that can be seen by the naked eye. Higher-grade coins display deeper luster or virtually perfect prooflike surfaces, depending on the dies used.

   Illustrated coin: Note the faint golden toning along the obverse border.

AU-50, 53, 55, 58 (About Uncirculated).
Obverse: Light wear is on the outside edges of the leaves, the frame of the shield, and the horizontal stripes (although the stripes can also be weakly struck). Mint luster is present in the fields, ranging from partial at AU-50 to nearly complete at AU-58. All details are sharp, unless lightly struck. *Reverse:* Light wear is seen on the numeral 5, and friction is seen in the field, identifiable as a change of color (loss of luster).

1867, Rays. Graded AU-58.

Luster is partial at AU-50, increasing to nearly full at AU-58. All details are sharp, unless lightly struck.

EF-40, 45 (Extremely Fine). *Obverse:* Nearly all shield border and leaf detail is visible. Light wear is seen on the shield stripes (but the horizontal stripes can be weakly struck). *Reverse:* More wear is seen on the numeral 5. The radial lines in the stars (if sharply struck to begin with) show slight wear. The field shows more wear.

1867, Rays. Graded EF-40.

VF-20, 30 (Very Fine). *Obverse:* The frame details and leaves show more wear, with much leaf detail gone. The shield stripes show more wear, and some of the vertical lines will begin to blend together. *Reverse:* More wear is seen overall, but some radial detail can still be seen on the stars.

1868. Graded VF-20.

F-12, 15 (Fine). *Obverse:* Most leaves are flat and have little detail, but will remain outlined. The shield frame is mostly flat. Most horizontal lines are blended together, regardless of original strike. Many vertical lines in the stripes are blended together. IN GOD WE TRUST is slightly weak. *Reverse:* All areas are in outline form except for slight traces of the star radials. Lettering is bold.

1867, Without Rays. Graded F-12.

VG-8, 10 (Very Good). *Obverse:* Many leaves are flat and blended with adjacent leaves. The frame is blended and has no details. Only a few horizontal lines may show. Vertical lines in the stripes are mostly blended. IN GOD WE TRUST is weak. *Reverse:* All elements are visible only in outline form. The rim is complete.

1879. Graded VG-10.

G-4, 6 (Good). *Obverse:* The shield and elements are seen in outline form except the vertical stripe separations. IN GOD WE TRUST is weak, and a few letters may be missing. *Reverse:* The rim is mostly if not completely worn away and into the tops of the letters.

   Illustrated coin: Overall this coin is slightly better than G-4, but the 5 in the date is weak, making G-4 an appropriate attribution.

1881. Graded G-4.

AG-3 (About Good). *Obverse:* The rim is worn down and blended with the wreath. Only traces of IN GOD WE TRUST can be seen. The date is fully readable. *Reverse:* The rim is worn down and blended with the letters, some of which may be missing.

1880. Graded AG-3.

PF-60 to 70 (Proof). *Obverse and Reverse:* PF–60, 61, and 62 coins show varying amounts of hairlines in the reverse field in particular, decreasing as the grade increases. Fields may be dull or cloudy on lower-level pieces. At PF-65, hairlines are visible only under magnification and are very light and usually only on the reverse. Above PF-65, hairlines become fewer, and in ultra-high grades are nonexistent, this meaning that the coins have never

1882. Graded PF-66.

been subject to wiping or abrasive cleaning. At PF-65 or better, expect excellent aesthetic appeal.

1866, Repunched Date
Several varieties exist.

	Mintage	Cert	Avg	%MS	G-4	VG-8	F-12	VF-20	EF-40	AU-50	MS-60	MS-63	MS-65
											PF-63	PF-65	PF-66
1866, Rays	14,742,500	1,676	59.9	77%	$30	$45	$50	$100	$160	$240	$300	$425	$1,600
	Auctions: $2,056, MS-65, January 2015; $616, MS-64, February 2015; $176, MS-60, August 2015; $211, AU-58, May 2015												
1866, Repunched Date (a)	(b)	25	49.7	40%	$60	$100	$175	$250	$450	$1,000	$1,500	$3,250	
	Auctions: $12,925, MS-64, August 2014; $8,813, MS-64, October 2014; $1,293, AU-50, March 2013; $1,175, AU-50, August 2014												
1866, Rays, Proof	600+	273	64.7								$1,650	$2,850	$3,500
	Auctions: $2,585, PF-66, September 2015; $3,055, PF-65, January 2015; $1,997, PF-64, January 2015; $1,057, PF-61, October 2015												

a. There are at least five similar, very strong repunched dates for 1866; the values shown are typical for each. b. Included in circulation-strike 1866, Rays, mintage figure.

1873, Close 3	1873, Open 3	1873, Close 3, Doubled-Die Obverse

1873, Close 3, Doubled-Die Obverse

Several varieties exist. Pictured are
FS-05-1873-101 (left) and FS-05-1873-102 (right).

	Mintage	Cert	Avg	%MS	G-4	VG-8	F-12	VF-20	EF-40	AU-50	MS-60	MS-63	MS-65
											PF-63	PF-65	PF-66
1867, Rays	2,019,000	581	58.8	70%	$35	$50	$65	$130	$190	$285	$375	$500	$3,000
	Auctions: $998, MS-64, January 2015; $705, MS-64, October 2015; $517, MS-63, June 2015; $117, EF-40, January 2015												
1867, Rays, Proof †	25+	31	64.5								$25,000	$45,000	$55,000
	Auctions: $64,625, PF-66, January 2015; $25,850, PF-65, August 2015; $34,075, PF-64, August 2015												
1867, No Rays	28,890,500	896	60.2	76%	$25	$30	$35	$50	$65	$110	$140	$225	$800
	Auctions: $1,116, MS-66, October 2015; $705, MS-65, January 2015; $305, MS-64, May 2015; $111, MS-60, February 2015												
1867, No Rays, Proof	600+	259	64.3								$475	$1,850	$3,500
	Auctions: $3,760, PF-66, September 2015; $2,115, PF-66, October 2015; $1,410, PF-65, February 2015; $376, PF-63, January 2015												
1867, No Rays, Pattern Reverse, Proof (c)	(d)	2	65.5	100%							$6,500	$10,000	
	Auctions: $3,760, PF-66, June 2015												
1868	28,817,000	876	60.2	77%	$25	$30	$35	$50	$65	$110	$140	$225	$700
	Auctions: $1,763, MS-66, October 2015; $940, MS-66, August 2016; $764, MS-65, October 2016; $164, MS-63, January 2015.												
1868, Proof	600+	216	64.7								$385	$1,100	$1,750
	Auctions: $1,762, PF-66, September 2015; $1,116, PF-65, June 2015; $822, PF-65, January 2015; $270, PF-63, April 2015												
1869	16,395,000	520	60.2	82%	$25	$30	$35	$50	$65	$110	$140	$225	$750
	Auctions: $587, MS-65, September 2015; $246, MS-64, May 2015; $176, AU-58, January 2015; $56, AU-50, February 2015												
1869, Proof	600+	348	64.6								$385	$700	$1,250
	Auctions: $3,055, PF-67, June 2015; $1,116, PF-66, July 2015; $881, PF-65, January 2015; $646, PF-65, August 2015												
1870	4,806,000	232	58.7	78%	$30	$35	$60	$80	$90	$140	$210	$300	$1,350
	Auctions: $7,638, MS-66, December 2015; $4,465, MS-66, February 2015; $1,292, MS-64, January 2015; $423, MS-64, August 2015												
1870, Proof	1,000+	317	64.3								$385	$700	$1,250
	Auctions: $1,292, PF-66, October 2015; $763, PF-65, January 2015; $646, PF-65, October 2015; $258, PF-63, June 2015												
1871	561,000	102	55.5	68%	$80	$100	$150	$215	$280	$350	$450	$675	$1,950
	Auctions: $4,230, MS-66, August 2016; $3,290, MS-66, August 2016; $3,055, MS-65, January 2015; $2,820, MS-66, October 2016												
1871, Proof	960+	330	64.5								$425	$750	$1,250
	Auctions: $1,527, PF-66, September 2015; $1,410, PF-66, August 2015; $881, PF-65, October 2015; $646, PF-65, January 2015												
1872	6,036,000	272	58.8	72%	$35	$45	$75	$100	$125	$175	$235	$300	$1,350
	Auctions: $3,525, MS-66, August 2016; $3,055, MS-66, May 2015; $1,997, MS-66, January 2015; $1,293, MS-65, October 2016												
1872, Proof	950+	358	64.8								$385	$675	$1,000
	Auctions: $3,055, PF-67, July 2015; $2,585, PF-67, September 2015; $998, PF-66, January 2015; $493, PF-65, January 2015												
1873, Close 3	436,050	63	59.8	75%	$30	$40	$60	$100	$140	$200	$325	$585	$2,000
	Auctions: $1,997, MS-65, August 2015; $822, MS-64, January 2015												
1873, Close 3, Doubled Die Obverse (e)	(f)	15	56.9	60%				$600	$1,000	$2,000	$3,000	$4,000	$10,000
	Auctions: $1,880, MS-64, February 2015												
1873, Open 3	4,113,950	89	59.6	80%	$30	$35	$60	$80	$100	$140	$210	$300	$1,850
	Auctions: $2,115, MS-66, July 2015; $1,880, MS-66, August 2015; $763, MS-64, October 2015; $600, MS-64, May 2015												
1873, Close 3, Proof	1,100+	365	64.5								$385	$675	$1,000
	Auctions: $2,820, PF-67, January 2015; $1,292, PF-66, October 2015; $376, PF-64, February 2015; $258, PF-63, May 2015												

† Ranked in the *100 Greatest U.S. Coins* (fourth edition). **c.** These were made from a pattern (Judd-573) reverse die that is slightly different than the regular Without Rays design. **d.** 21 to 30 examples are known. **e.** There are several varieties of 1873, Close 3, Doubled Die Obverse. The values shown are representative of the more avidly sought varieties; others command smaller premiums. **f.** Included in circulation-strike 1873, Close 3, mintage figure.

 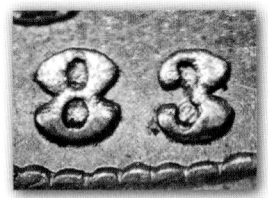

1883, 3 Over 2
Several varieties exist, as well as pieces with a recut 3. Pictured are FS-05-1883-301 (left) and FS-05-1883-305 (right).

	Mintage	Cert	Avg	%MS	G-4	VG-8	F-12	VF-20	EF-40	AU-50	MS-60 PF-63	MS-63 PF-65	MS-65 PF-66
1874	3,538,000	167	60.7	79%	$30	$40	$65	$80	$120	$170	$250	$325	$1,200
Auctions: $5,170, MS-66, October 2015; $2,820, MS-66, August 2015
1874, Proof	700+	304	64.6								$385	$725	$1,100
Auctions: $3,290, PF-67, September 2015; $2,115, PF-66, January 2015; $340, PF-64, May 2015; $258, PF-63, January 2015
1875	2,097,000	161	59.2	79%	$45	$60	$100	$130	$160	$220	$275	$360	$1,250
Auctions: $5,640, MS-66, January 2015; $3,290, MS-66, October 2015; $229, AU-55, May 2015; $188, AU-50, January 2015
1875, Proof	700+	293	64.4								$425	$1,250	$1,850
Auctions: $3,290, PF-67, August 2015; $1,527, PF-66, January 2015; $881, PF-65, July 2015; $517, PF-64, March 2015
1876	2,530,000	259	61.3	86%	$40	$55	$80	$115	$145	$190	$260	$325	$1,000
Auctions: $940, MS-65, June 2015; $376, MS-64, August 2015; $105, AU-55, January 2015; $164, AU-50, January 2015
1876, Proof	1,150+	403	64.6								$385	$750	$1,000
Auctions: $2,350, PF-67, February 2015; $998, PF-66, July 2015; $763, PF-65, August 2015; $376, PF-64, January 2015
1877, Proof (g)	900	423	64.5								$3,400	$4,250	$5,000
Auctions: $9,987, PF-67, September 2015; $6,462, PF-66, July 2015; $4,230, PF-65, June 2015; $3,525, PF-64, January 2015
1878, Proof (g)	2,350	616	64.4								$1,250	$1,650	$2,000
Auctions: $1,880, PF-67, January 2015; $2,232, PF-66, July 2015; $1,233, PF-65, January 2015; $1,265, PF-64, June 2015
1879	25,900	86	56.5	71%	$375	$475	$600	$660	$850	$1,000	$1,250	$1,800	$3,000
Auctions: $10,575, MS-67, July 2015; $5,405, MS-66, August 2016; $4,935, MS-66, March 2016; $2,820, MS-65, July 2015
1879, Proof	3,200	572	64.8								$500	$650	$800
Auctions: $6,462, PF-68, January 2015; $564, PF-65, August 2015; $352, PF-64, May 2015; $282, PF-62, October 2015
1879, 9 Over 8, Proof (h)	(i)	0	n/a								$725	$850	$1,100
Auctions: $2,361, PF-67, June 2015; $646, PF-65, August 2015; $470, PF-64, January 2015; $305, AU-58, November 2015
1880	16,000	38	46.3	24%	$1,500	$2,000	$2,500	$3,000	$6,000	$7,500	$10,000	$20,000	$75,000
Auctions: $117,000, MS-66, January 2015; $8,233, AU-53, August 2016; $5,405, EF-45, March 2016; $3,995, AU-53, October 2015
1880, Proof	3,955	901	64.0								$500	$675	$850
Auctions: $6,462, PF-68, January 2015; $3,995, PF-67, October 2015; $505, PF-65, January 2015; $423, PF-64, May 2015
1881	68,800	160	47.4	49%	$250	$300	$425	$510	$600	$775	$850	$1,000	$2,750
Auctions: $3,173, MS-66, August 2016; $3,055, MS-66, December 2015; $2,350, MS66, October 2015; $822, AU58, January 2015;
1881, Proof	3,575	827	64.9								$500	$675	$850
Auctions: $1,292, PF-67, July 2015; $616, PF-66, October 2015; $493, PF-65, January 2015; $250, PF-62, April 2015
1882	11,472,900	1,065	59.1	81%	$25	$30	$35	$50	$65	$110	$150	$225	$650
Auctions: $3,055, MS-67, July 2016; $734, MS-66, February 2015; $493, MS-65, January 2015; $235, MS-64, October 2015
1882, Proof	3,100	936	65.1								$385	$600	$850
Auctions: $15,275, PF-67, August 2015; $1,116, PF-66, August 2015; $705, PF-66, January 2015; $352, PF-64, May 2015
1883	1,451,500	1,758	61.9	83%	$25	$30	$35	$50	$65	$110	$150	$225	$650
Auctions: $2,938, MS-67, August 2015; $2,820, MS-67, January 2015; $1,057, MS-66, January 2015; $705, MS-66, August 2016
1883, 3 Over 2 (j)	(k)	40	58.3	65%	$250	$325	$650	$950	$1,250	$1,750	$2,100	$2,500	$5,500
Auctions: $7,050, MS-65, January 2015; $1,527, MS-63, January 2015; $1,292, MS-60, June 2015; $1,175, AU-58, January 2015
1883, Proof	5,419	1,139	64.8								$385	$600	$850
Auctions: $6,462, PF-68, January 2015; $470, PF-65, March 2015; $329, PF-64, August 2015; $282, PF-63, October 2015

g. Proof only. **h.** This variety is confirmed only with Proof finish, although Breen mentions two circulation strikes and further mentions that there are "at least two varieties" (*Walter Breen's Complete Encyclopedia of U.S. and Colonial Coins*). In the *Guide Book of Shield and Liberty Head Nickels*, Bowers discusses research and theories from Breen, DeLorey, Spindel, and Julian, noting that the variety's overdate status is "not determined." **i.** Included in 1879, Proof, mintage figure. **j.** Several varieties exist. For more information, see the *Cherrypickers' Guide to Rare Die Varieties*, sixth edition, volume I. "Beware of 1882 Shield nickels with a filled-in, blobby 2, as these are very frequently offered as 1883, 3 Over 2. This is possibly the single most misunderstood coin in all U.S. coinage." (Howard Spindel, communication to Q. David Bowers, quoted in *A Guide Book of Shield and Liberty Head Nickels*.) **k.** Included in circulation-strike 1883 mintage figure.

LIBERTY HEAD (1883–1913)

Designer: *Charles E. Barber.* **Weight:** *5 grams.* **Composition:** *.750 copper, .250 nickel.*
Diameter: *21.2 mm.* **Edge:** *Plain.* **Mints:** *Philadelphia, Denver, and San Francisco.*

Variety 1, Without CENTS (1883)   Variety 1, Without CENTS, Proof

Variety 2, With CENTS (1883–1912)   *Mintmark locations is on the reverse, to the left of CENTS.*   Variety 2, With CENTS, Proof

History. Liberty Head nickels were popular in their time, minted in large quantities most years, and remained in circulation through the 1940s, by which time most were worn down to grades such as AG-3 and G-4. Stray coins could still be found in the early 1950s. Serious numismatic interest in circulated examples began in the 1930s with the popularity of Whitman and other coin boards, folders, and albums. Many of the scarcer dates were picked from circulation at that time. The five known 1913 Liberty Head nickels were not an authorized Mint issue, and were never placed into circulation.

Striking and Sharpness. Many Liberty Head nickels have areas of light striking. On the obverse, this is often seen at the star centers, particularly near the top border. The hair above the forehead can be light as well, and always is thus on 1912-S (the obverse die on this San Francisco issue is slightly bulged). On the reverse, E PLURIBUS UNUM can vary in sharpness of strike. Weakness is often seen at the wreath bow and on the ear of corn to the left (the kernels in the ear can range from indistinct to bold). Even Proofs can be weakly struck in areas. Mint luster can range from minutely pebbly or grainy (but still attractive) to a deep, rich frost. Some later Philadelphia coins show stress marks in the field, particularly the obverse, from the use of "tired" dies. This can be determined only by observation, as "slabbed" grades for MS coins do not indicate the quality of the luster or surfaces. Proof Liberty Head nickels were struck of all dates 1883 to 1912, plus both varieties of 1883 (with and without CENTS). The fields range from deeply mirrorlike to somewhat grainy character to mirror-surface, depending on a given year. While most Proofs are sharp, some have weakness at the star centers and/or the kernels on the ear of corn to the left of the ribbon bow. These weaknesses are overlooked by the certification services. Generally, later issues are more deeply mirrored than are earlier ones. Some years in the 1880s and 1890s can show graininess, a combination of mint luster and mirror quality. Lint marks or tiny recessed marks from scattered debris on the die faces are sometimes encountered, but not factored into third-party–certified grades unless excessive.

Availability. All issues from 1883 to 1912 are readily collectible, although the 1885 (in particular), 1886, and 1912-S are considered to be key dates. Most readily available are well-worn coins in AG-3 and G-4. As a class, VF, EF, and AU pieces are very scarce in relation to demand. MS coins are generally scarce in the 1880s, except for the 1883, Without CENTS, which is plentiful in all grades. MS pieces are less scarce in the 1890s and are easily found for most 20th-century years, save for 1909, 1912-D, and 1912-S, all of which are elusive.

GRADING STANDARDS

MS-60 to 70 (Mint State). *Obverse and Reverse:* Mint luster is complete in the obverse and reverse fields. Lower grades such as MS–60, 61, and 62 can show some evidence of abrasion, usually on the portrait on the obverse and highest parts of the wreath on the reverse, and scattered contact marks elsewhere. At MS-63 these marks are few, and at MS-65 they are fewer yet. In grades above MS-65, marks can only be seen under magnification.

1894. Graded MS-65.

AU-50, 53, 55, 58 (About Uncirculated). *Obverse:* Light wear is seen on the portrait and on the hair under LIB. Mint luster is present in the fields, ranging from partial at AU-50 to nearly complete at AU-58. All details are sharp, unless lightly struck. *Reverse:* Light wear is seen on the V, the other letters, and the wreath. Luster is partial at AU-50, increasing to nearly full at AU-58. All details are sharp, unless lightly struck.

1885. Graded AU-58.

EF-40, 45 (Extremely Fine). *Obverse:* Nearly all hair detail is visible, save for some lightness above the forehead. Stars show radial lines (except for those that may have been lightly struck). Overall bold appearance. *Reverse:* The wreath still shows most detail on the leaves. Denticles are bold inside the rim.

1885. Graded EF-40.

VF-20, 30 (Very Fine). *Obverse:* Letters in LIBERTY are all well defined. Hair detail is seen on the back of the head and some between the ear and the coronet. Denticles are bold. Some stars show radial lines. *Reverse:* Detail is seen in the wreath leaves. Lettering and denticles are bold, although E PLURIBUS UNUM may range from medium-light to bold (depending on the strike).

1888. Graded VF-20.

F-12, 15 (Fine). *Obverse:* All of the letters in LIBERTY are readable, although the I may be quite weak. The detail beginning at the front of hair is visible. Denticles are well defined. *Reverse:* Detail of the leaves begins to fade in the wreath. Denticles are well defined all around the border. E PLURIBUS UNUM has medium definition, and is complete.

1885. Graded F-15.

VG-8, 10 (Very Good). *Obverse:* Three or more letters in LIBERTY can be discerned. This can be a combination of two full letters and two or more partial letters. Some hair detail shows at the back of the head. The rim is well outlined and shows traces of most or even all denticles. *Reverse:* The wreath and lettering are bold, but in outline form. E PLURIBUS UNUM is readable, but may be weak. The rim is complete all around, with traces of most denticles present.

1885. Graded VG-8.

G-4, 6 (Good). *Obverse:* The rim is complete all around. Some denticles show on the inside of the rim. The date, Liberty head, and stars are in outline form. No letters of LIBERTY are visible in the coronet. *Reverse:* V and the wreath are visible in outline form. Most letters are complete, but may be faint. E PLURIBUS UNUM is very weak (this feature can vary, and on some G-4 coins it is better defined). The rim is complete in most areas, but may blend with the field in some parts.

1885. Graded G-6.

AG-3 (About Good). *Obverse:* The head is outlined, with only the ear hole as a detail. The date is well worn; the bottom of the digits can be weak or incomplete. The stars are solid, without detail; some may be incomplete. The rim is indistinct or incomplete in some areas. *Reverse:* Details are nearly all worn away, showing greater effects of wear than does the obverse. V is in outline form. The wreath is in outline form, and may be

1885. Graded AG-3.

indistinct in areas. Lettering ranges from faint to missing, but with some letters readable. The rim is usually worn down into the letters.

PF-60 to 70 (Proof). *Obverse and Reverse:* PF–60, 61, and 62 coins show varying amounts of hairlines in the field, decreasing as the grade increases. Fields may be dull or cloudy on lower-level pieces. At PF-65, hairlines are visible only under magnification and are very light; the cheek of Miss Liberty does not show any abrasion or "album slide marks." Above PF-65, hairlines become fewer, and in ultra-high grades are nonexistent, this meaning that

1883, With CENTS. Graded PF-66 Deep Cameo.

the coins have never been subject to wiping or abrasive cleaning. At PF-65 or better, expect excellent aesthetic appeal. Blotched, deeply toned, or recolored coins can be found at most Proof levels from PF–60 through 65 or even 66, and should be avoided. Watch for artificially toned lower-grade Proofs colored to mask the true nature of the fields.

Illustrated coin: This Proof shows spotting in the fields.

	Mintage	Cert	Avg	%MS	G-4	VG-8	F-12	VF-20	EF-40	AU-50	MS-60 / PF-63	MS-63 / PF-64	MS-65 / PF-65
1883, Without CENTS	5,474,300	7,195	63.3	93%	$7	$8	$9	$11	$15	$18	$35	$50	$225
Auctions: $3,525, MS-67, January 2015; $282, MS-66, June 2015; $164, MS-65, April 2015; $329, MS-64, October 2015													
1883, Without CENTS, Proof	5,219	1,009	64.6								$300	$450	$800
Auctions: $4,935, PF-67, August 2015; $3,055, PF-67, January 2015; $1,057, PF-66, January 2015; $379, PF-64, August 2015													
1883, With CENTS	16,026,200	1,038	61.3	84%	$20	$30	$35	$55	$85	$120	$150	$200	$600
Auctions: $5,875, MS-66, October 2015; $2,115, MS-66, January 2015; $1,292, MS-66, June 2015; $258, MS-64, February 2015													
1883, With CENTS, Proof	6,783	719	64.6								$275	$400	$700
Auctions: $881, PF-64, January 2015; $851, PF-66, September 2015; $822, PF-65, July 2015; $188, PF-63, May 2015													
1884	11,270,000	466	59.2	79%	$20	$30	$35	$55	$85	$130	$190	$300	$1,350
Auctions: $5,875, MS-67, August 2016; $8,225, MS-66, August 2015; $1,997, MS-66, February 2015; $1,351, MS-65, September 2015													
1884, Proof	3,942	785	64.5								$250	$375	$650
Auctions: $3,055, PF-67, June 2015; $763, PF-66, January 2015; $399, PF-65, April 2015; $376, PF-64, May 2015													
1885	1,472,700	839	26.9	26%	$375	$550	$750	$1,000	$1,200	$1,600	$2,000	$3,250	$6,500
Auctions: $14,100, MS-66, January 2015; $11,163, MS-66, August 2016; $5,875, MS-65, March 2016; $7,050, MS-65, August 2015;													
1885, Proof	3,790	812	64.7								$1,150	$1,250	$1,350
Auctions: $2,232, PF-67, January 2015; $1,762, PF-66, June 2015; $1,292, PF-65, October 2015; $1,086, PF-64Cam, August 2015													
1886	3,326,000	767	29.1	28%	$225	$265	$425	$500	$700	$825	$1,200	$2,350	$4,000
Auctions: $13,513, MS-66, August 2016; $3,760, MS-65, September 2016; $3,525, MS-65, October 2016; $763, AU-55, August 2015													
1886, Proof	4,290	801	64.6								$650	$675	$950
Auctions: $2,115, PF-67, January 2015; $969, PF-65, February 2015; $793, PF-65, October 2015; $558, PF-64, May 2015													
1887	15,260,692	474	62.0	88%	$15	$20	$35	$50	$75	$110	$140	$195	$800
Auctions: $8,225, MS-67, December 2015; $7,638, MS-66, May 2015; $5,405, MS-66, January 2015; $1,293, MS-65, September 2016													
1887, Proof	2,960	574	64.3								$250	$345	$550
Auctions: $2,500, PF-67, January 2015; $705, PF-66, June 2015; $211, PF-63, October 2015; $141, PF-62, March 2015													
1888	10,167,901	399	58.2	81%	$30	$40	$60	$120	$175	$220	$275	$340	$1,000
Auctions: $7,050, MS-66, July 2016; $3,055, MS-66, September 2015; $1,763, MS-65, July 2016; $1,293, MS-65, December 2015													
1888, Proof	4,582	786	64.5								$250	$345	$550
Auctions: $3,642, PF-67, February 2015; $525, PF-66, January 2015; $423, PF-65, October 2015; $247, PF-64, May 2015													
1889	15,878,025	573	63.2	95%	$15	$20	$30	$50	$75	$120	$140	$175	$650
Auctions: $1,600, MS-66, January 2015; $705, MS-65, July 2015; $350, MS-64, October 2015; $141, MS-62, April 2015													
1889, Proof	3,336	629	64.6								$250	$345	$550
Auctions: $446, PF-66, January 2015; $493, PF-65, January 2015; $399, PF-65, October 2015; $182, PF-63, July 2015													

1899, Repunched Date,
Early Die State

1899, Repunched Date,
Late Die State

FS-05-1899-301.

	Mintage	Cert	Avg	%MS	G-4	VG-8	F-12	VF-20	EF-40	AU-50	MS-60	MS-63	MS-65
											PF-63	PF-64	PF-65
1890	16,256,532	337	62.0	90%	$10	$20	$25	$40	$65	$110	$160	$200	$950
	Auctions: $16,450, MS-67, October 2015; $9,400, MS-66, May 2015; $3,055, MS-66, October 2016; $705, MS-65, July 2015												
1890, Proof	2,740	474	64.1								$250	$345	$550
	Auctions: $2,467, PF-67, February 2015; $376, PF-65, January 2015; $376, PF-65, October 2015; $282, PF-64, May 2015												
1891	16,832,000	430	62.7	92%	$7	$12	$25	$45	$70	$125	$160	$200	$700
	Auctions: $4,406, MS-66, July 2016; $1,998, MS-66, October 2016; $1,058, MS-65, January 2015; $211, MS-64, October 2015												
1891, Proof	2,350	475	64.4								$250	$345	$550
	Auctions: $2,820, PF-67, February 2015; $705, PF-66, January 2015; $282, PF-64, November 2015; $141, PF-62, May 2015												
1892	11,696,897	461	62.4	92%	$6	$10	$20	$40	$65	$110	$140	$160	$1,000
	Auctions: $3,055, MS-66, January 2015; $1,645, MS-66, August 2015; $1,880, MS-66, July 2015; $822, MS-65, February 2015												
1892, Proof	2,745	514	64.4								$250	$345	$550
	Auctions: $625, PF-66, January 2015; $517, PF-65, October 2015; $282, PF-64, August 2015; $184, PF-63, May 2015												
1893	13,368,000	468	62.9	94%	$6	$10	$20	$40	$65	$110	$140	$160	$750
	Auctions: $1,880, MS-66, January 2015; $1,527, MS-65, February 2015; $1,058, MS-66, July 2016; $176, MS-62, May 2015												
1893, Proof	2,195	465	64.5								$250	$345	$550
	Auctions: $1,292, PF-66, July 2015; $517, PF-65, September 2015; $458, PF-65, January 2015; $434, PF-65, October 2015												
1894	5,410,500	350	58.8	79%	$20	$35	$100	$165	$225	$300	$350	$425	$1,250
	Auctions: $2,526, MS-66, July 2016; $1,410, MS-66, October 2016; $1,527, MS-65, August 2015; $493, MS-64, October 2015												
1894, Proof	2,632	456	64.3								$250	$345	$550
	Auctions: $1,292, PF-67, October 2015; $564, PF-66, January 2015; $540, PF-65, July 2015; $117, PF-60, May 2015												
1895	9,977,822	356	62.2	92%	$6	$8	$22	$45	$70	$115	$140	$200	$1,100
	Auctions: $21,150, MS-67, July 2015; $4,994, MS-65, March 2015; 2,585, MS-65, January 2015; $2,233, MS-65, September 2016												
1895, Proof	2,062	432	64.2								$250	$345	$550
	Auctions: $3,995, PF-67, January 2015; $646, PF-66, August 2015; $399, PF-65, May 2015; $258, PF-64, February 2015												
1896	8,841,058	326	61.6	89%	$9	$18	$35	$65	$90	$150	$190	$265	$1,500
	Auctions: $8,813, MS-66, May 2015; $4,582, MS-66, June 2015; $2,350, MS-66, March 2016; $1,234, MS-65, October 2016												
1896, Proof	1,862	420	64.4								$250	$345	$550
	Auctions: $646, PF-66, October 2015; $587, PF-65, January 2015; $282, PF-64, February 2015; $139, PF-62, May 2015												
1897	20,426,797	465	62.5	93%	$4	$5	$12	$27	$45	$70	$100	$160	$800
	Auctions: $3,525, MS-66, October 2016; $3,055, MS-66, January 2015; $1,057, MS-65, July 2015; $616, MS-64, August 2015												
1897, Proof	1,938	463	64.7								$250	$345	$550
	Auctions: $4,022, PF-68, January 2015; $352, PF-65, November 2015; $176, PF-63, May 2015; $111, PF-60, February 2015												
1898	12,530,292	421	62.7	94%	$4	$5	$12	$27	$45	$75	$150	$185	$600
	Auctions: $2,350, MS-66, March 2015; $1,410, MS-66, August 2016; $763, MS-65, January 2015; $646, MS-65, August 2015												
1898, Proof	1,795	431	64.5								$250	$345	$550
	Auctions: $505, PF-66, January 2015; $364, PF-65, October 2015; $258, PF-64, September 2015; $164, PF-63, May 2015												
1899	26,027,000	749	62.8	94%	$2	$3	$8	$20	$30	$60	$90	$140	$550
	Auctions: $8,813, MS-67, August 2015; $4,230, MS-67, August 2016; $4,230, MS-66, January 2015; $705, MS-66, May 2016												
1899, Repunched Date (a)	**(b)**	0	n/a						$85	$150	$190	$240	$800
	Auctions: No auction records available.												
1899, Proof	2,031	460	64.7								$250	$345	$550
	Auctions: $1,410, PF-67, July 2015; $423, PF-65, January 2015; $258, PF-64, September 2015; $176, PF-63, May 2015												

a. "The loop of a 9, or possibly (but unlikely) an 8, is evident within the lower loop of the second 9. Some specialists believe this to be an 1899/8 overdate. However, we feel it is simply a repunched date, with the secondary 9 far to the south of the primary 9 at the last digit" (*Cherrypickers' Guide to Rare Die Varieties*, sixth edition, volume I). **b.** Included in circulation-strike 1899 mintage figure.

1900, Doubled-Die Reverse
FS-05-1900-801.

	Mintage	Cert	Avg	%MS	G-4	VG-8	F-12	VF-20	EF-40	AU-50	MS-60	MS-63	MS-65
											PF-63	PF-64	PF-65
1900	27,253,733	846	63.1	95%	$2	$3	$8	$15	$30	$65	$90	$140	$500
	Auctions: $7,050, MS-67, January 2015; $4,700, MS-67, August 2016; $1,998, MS-66, July 2016; $117, MS-63, November 2015												
1900, Doubled-Die Reverse (c)	**(d)**	4	61.5	75%					$110	$160	$235	$310	$875
	Auctions: No auction records available.												
1900, Proof	2,262	478	64.8								$250	$345	$550
	Auctions: $5,640, PF-68, January 2015; $675, PF-66, August 2015; $387, PF-65, May 2015; $340, PF-64, March 2015												
1901	26,478,228	767	62.9	96%	$2	$3	$5	$15	$30	$60	$85	$125	$450
	Auctions: $8,812, MS-67, January 2015; $4,700, MS-67, August 2016; $1,399, MS-66, October 2015; $317, MS-65, May 2015												
1901, Proof	1,985	518	64.9								$250	$345	$550
	Auctions: $940, PF-67, January 2015; $587, PF-66, September 2015; $446, PF-65, October 2015; $305, PF-64, January 2015												
1902	31,480,579	765	62.5	93%	$2	$3	$4	$15	$30	$60	$85	$125	$450
	Auctions: $5,405, MS-67, January 2015; $1,645, MS-66, June 2015; $1,058, MS-66, August 2016; $881, MS-66, August 2016												
1902, Proof	2,018	473	64.7								$250	$345	$550
	Auctions: $1,028, PF-67, January 2015; $646, PF-66, June 2015; $399, PF-65, March 2015; $317, PF-64, October 2015												
1903	28,004,935	850	62.9	95%	$2	$3	$4	$15	$30	$60	$85	$125	$450
	Auctions: $4,230, MS-67, October 2016; $3,525, MS-67, November 2016; $1,645, MS-66, January 2015; $423, MS-65, August 2015												
1903, Proof	1,790	543	64.9								$250	$345	$550
	Auctions: $540, PF-66, October 2015; $376, PF-65, September 2015; $293, PF-64, January 2015; $129, PF-61, May 2015												
1904	21,403,167	716	63.1	95%	$2	$3	$4	$15	$30	$60	$85	$125	$450
	Auctions: $1,645, MS-66, June 2015; $999, MS-66, October 2016; $352, MS-65, August 2015; $176, MS-64, February 2015												
1904, Proof	1,817	485	64.3								$250	$345	$550
	Auctions: $998, PF-66, January 2015; $365, PF-65, October 2015; $258, PF-64, April 2015; $179, PF-63, May 2015												
1905	29,825,124	867	62.6	93%	$2	$3	$4	$15	$30	$60	$85	$125	$450
	Auctions: $4,935, MS-67, October 2016; $2,585, MS-66, January 2015; $852, MS-65, March 2015; $517, MS-64, September 2016												
1905, Proof	2,152	461	64.6								$250	$345	$550
	Auctions: $3,525, PF-67, June 2015; $2,585, PF-66, February 2015; $1,410, PF-66, October 2015; $285, PF-64, January 2015												
1906	38,612,000	632	61.6	88%	$2	$3	$4	$15	$30	$60	$85	$125	$550
	Auctions: $5,875, MS-66, January 2015; $423, MS-65, August 2015; $152, MS-64, May 2015; $211, MS-63, February 2015												
1906, Proof	1,725	453	64.6								$250	$345	$550
	Auctions: $3,290, PF-68, August 2015; $1,527, PF-67, October 2015; $1,292, PF-67, January 2015; $587, PF-66, June 2015												
1907	39,213,325	619	61.7	89%	$2	$3	$4	$15	$30	$60	$85	$125	$650
	Auctions: $7,931, MS-66, January 2015; $3,055, MS-66, August 2016; $1,645, MS-66, July 2015; $494, MS-65, October 2016												
1907, Proof	1,475	370	64.7								$250	$345	$550
	Auctions: $2,350, PF-67, February 2015; $616, PF-66, June 2015; $540, PF-66, January 2015; $253, PF-64, September 2015												
1908	22,684,557	568	61.4	90%	$2	$3	$4	$15	$30	$60	$85	$125	$650
	Auctions: $5,288, MS-66, August 2015; $1,293, MS-66, October 2016; $705, MS-65, August 2015; $176, MS-64, October 2015												
1908, Proof	1,620	447	64.6								$250	$345	$550
	Auctions: $8,225, PF-68, October 2015; $2,115, PF-67, January 2015; $763, PF-66, February 2015; $517, PF-65, June 2015												

c. Doubling on this very popular variety is evident on all reverse design elements, including the V, with a stronger spread on the lower quadrant of the reverse. **d.** Included in circulation-strike 1900 mintage figure.

1913, Liberty Head

	Mintage	Cert	Avg	%MS	G-4	VG-8	F-12	VF-20	EF-40	AU-50	MS-60 PF-63	MS-63 PF-64	MS-65 PF-65
1909	11,585,763	417	60.6	85%	$3	$4	$5	$18	$35	$75	$100	$140	$750
Auctions: $4,465, MS-66, October 2015; $2,585, MS-66, August 2016; $793, MS-65, August 2015; $705, MS-65, February 2015													
1909, Proof	4,763	1,342	65.0								$250	$345	$550
Auctions: $1,086, PF-67, October 2015; $493, PF-66, January 2015; $258, PF-64, February 2015; $117, PF-60, April 2015													
1910	30,166,948	657	61.4	87%	$2	$3	$4	$15	$30	$60	$85	$125	$450
Auctions: $3,760, MS-66, January 2015; $211, MS-64, September 2015; $130, MS-63, May 2015; $60, AU-58, June 2015													
1910, Proof	2,405	702	64.9								$250	$345	$550
Auctions: $6,462, PF-68, January 2015; $587, PF-66, June 2015; $399, PF-65, November 2015; $282, PF-64, April 2015													
1911	39,557,639	1,262	62.3	92%	$2	$3	$4	$15	$30	$60	$85	$125	$450
Auctions: $4,230, MS-66, May 2015; $646, MS-66, July 2016; $1,249, MS-65, January 2015; $141, MS-64, October 2015; $99, MS-63, May 2015													
1911, Proof	1,733	585	64.7								$250	$345	$550
Auctions: $600, PF-66, January 2015; $365, PF-65, October 2015; $258, PF-64, June 2015; $170, PF-63, February 2015													
1912	26,234,569	1,107	61.8	91%	$2	$3	$4	$15	$30	$60	$85	$125	$450
Auctions: $5,875, MS-66, January 2015; $446, MS-65, January 2015; $141, MS-64, April 2015; $94, MS-63, September 2015; $74, AU-58, June 2015													
1912, Proof	2,145	583	64.5								$250	$345	$550
Auctions: $2,232, PF-67, January 2015; $910, PF-66, July 2015; $489, PF-65, April 2015; $199, PF-63, October 2015													
1912-D	8,474,000	792	60.1	87%	$3	$4	$10	$40	$85	$175	$300	$400	$1,750
Auctions: $4,230, MS-66, January 2015; $1,703, MS-65, July 2015; $646, MS-64, September 2015; $305, MS-63, May 2015													
1912-S	238,000	1,394	33.6	42%	$145	$155	$200	$450	$850	$1,250	$1,500	$1,800	$3,000
Auctions: $5,170, MS-66, July 2015; $3,525, MS-65, January 2015; $2,585, MS-65, October 2015; $1,997, MS-64, February 2015													
1913 † (e)		0	n/a									$3,500,000	
Auctions: No auction records available.													
1913, Proof † (e)		2	47.5								$4,000,000	$4,250,000	
Auctions: $3,290,000, PF-64, January 2014; $3,172,500, PF-63, April 2013													

† Ranked in the *100 Greatest U.S. Coins* (fourth edition). **e.** An estimated five 1913 Liberty Head nickels (four circulation-strike and one Proof) were struck under irregular circumstances at the Mint. Some researchers consider them all to be Proofs. They were dispersed and are now held in various public and private collections.

INDIAN HEAD OR BUFFALO (1913–1938)

Designer: *James Earle Fraser.* **Weight:** *5 grams.* **Composition:** *.750 copper, .250 nickel.*
Diameter: *21.2 mm.* **Edge:** *Plain.* **Mints:** *Philadelphia, Denver, and San Francisco.*

**Variety 1, FIVE CENTS
on Raised Ground (1913)**

*Mintmark location for all
varieties is on the reverse,
below FIVE CENTS.*

**Variety 1, FIVE CENTS
on Raised Ground, Proof**

**Variety 2, FIVE CENTS
in Recess (1913–1938)**

**Variety 2, FIVE CENTS in Recess,
Matte Proof (1913–1916)**

**Variety 2, FIVE CENTS in
Recess, Satin Proof (1936)**

**Variety 2, FIVE CENTS in Recess,
Mirror Proof (1936–1937)**

History. The Indian Head nickel five-cent piece today is almost universally known as the "Buffalo" nickel, after the American bison on the reverse. The design made its debut in 1913. James Earle Fraser, a sculptor well known in the private sector, was its creator. The obverse features an authentic portrait of a Native American, modeled as a composite from life, with three subjects posing. Unlike any preceding coin made for circulation, the Buffalo nickel had little in the way of open, smooth field surfaces. Instead, most areas on the obverse and reverse were filled with design elements or, especially on the reverse, an irregular background, as on a bas-relief plaque. Soon after the first coins were released, it was thought that the inscription FIVE CENTS, on a high area of the motif, would wear too quickly. The Mint modified the design to lower the ground under the bison, which had been arranged in the form of a mound (on what became known as Variety 1). The flat-ground design is called Variety 2.

Striking and Sharpness. Most circulation-strike Buffalo nickels are poorly struck in one or more areas, and for many Denver and San Francisco issues of the 1920s the striking is very poor. However, enough sharp strikes exist among common dates of the 1930s that one can be found with some patience. Certification services do not reflect the quality of strike on their labels, so examine carefully. The matter of striking sharpness on Buffalo nickels is an exceedingly important aspect for the connoisseur (who might prefer, for example, a sharply struck coin in AU-58 over a fully lustrous MS example with much shallower detail). Points to check on the obverse include the center of the coin, especially the area immediately above the tie on the braid. On the reverse check the fur on the head of the bison, and the fur "line" above the bison's shoulder on its back. On both sides, examine the overall striking of letters and other details.

Availability. Among circulated varieties of standard dates and mintmarks, availability is in proportion to their mintages. Among early issues the 1913-S, Variety 2, is the scarcest. The date wore away more quickly on the Variety 1 coins than on the modified design used from later 1913 through the end of the series. In the 1920s the 1926-S is the hardest to find. Collectors sought Buffalo nickels from circulation until the 1960s, after which most were gone. By that time the dates in the teens were apt to have their dates completely worn away, or be AG-3 or G-4. Among MS nickels, the issues of 1913 were saved in quantity as novelties, although 1913-S, Variety 2, is slightly scarce. Philadelphia Mint issues are readily available through the 1920s, while MS-63 and finer mintmarked issues from 1914 to 1927 can range from scarce to rare. From 1931 to 1938, all dates and mintmarks were saved in roll quantities, and all are plentiful today. Many Buffalo nickels in MS are very rare if with Full Details, this being especially true for mintmarked issues after 1913, into the early 1930s. Sharpness of strike is not noted on certification holders, but a connoisseur would probably rather own a Full Details coin in MS-65 than an MS-66 or higher with a flat strike.

Proofs. Proof Buffalo nickels are of two main styles. Matte Proofs were made from 1913 to 1916 and are rare. These have minutely granular or matte surfaces, are sharply struck with Full Details of the design on both sides, and have edges (as viewed edge-on) that are mirrored, a distinctive figure. These are easily confused with circulation strikes except for the features noted. Certified holders usually list these simply as "Proof," not "Matte Proof." Some early Proofs of 1936 have satiny rather than mirror-like fields. Later Proofs of 1936 and all of 1937 have a mirror surface in the fields. The motifs of the 1936 and 1937 mirror Proofs are lightly polished in the die (not frosty or matte).

GRADING STANDARDS

MS-60 to 70 (Mint State). *Obverse and Reverse:* Mint luster is complete in the obverse and reverse fields, except in areas not fully struck up, in which graininess or marks from the *original planchet surface* can be seen. Lower grades such as MS–60, 61, and 62 can show some evidence of abrasion, usually on the center of the obverse above the braid, and on the reverse at the highest parts of the bison. These two checkpoints are often areas of light

1937-D. Graded MS-67.

striking, so abrasion must be differentiated from original planchet marks. At MS-63 evidences of abrasion are few, and at MS-65 they are fewer yet. In grades above MS-65, a Buffalo nickel should be mark-free.

AU-50, 53, 55, 58 (About Uncirculated). *Obverse:* Light wear is seen on the highest area of the cheek, to the left of the nose, this being the most obvious checkpoint. Light wear is also seen on the highest-relief areas of the hair. Luster is less extensive, and wear more extensive, at AU-50 than at higher grades. An AU-58 coin will have only slight wear and will retain the majority of luster. *Reverse:* Light wear is seen on the shoulder

1925-S. Graded AU-53.

and hip, these being the key checkpoints. Light wear is also seen on the flank of the bison and on the horn and top of the head. Luster is less extensive, and wear more extensive, at AU-50 than at higher grades. An AU-58 coin will have only slight wear and will retain the majority of luster.

EF-40, 45 (Extremely Fine). *Obverse:* More wear is seen on the cheek (in particular) and the rest of the face. The center of the coin above the braid is mostly smooth. Other details are sharp. *Reverse:* More wear is evident. The tip of the horn is well defined on better strikes. The shoulder, flank, and hip show more wear. The tip of the tail may be discernible, but is mostly worn away.

1937-D. Graded EF-40.

VF-20, 30 (Very Fine). *Obverse:* The hair above the braid is mostly flat, but with some details visible. The braid is discernible. The feathers lack most details. On Variety 1 coins the date is light. *Reverse:* Wear is more extensive, with most fur detail on the high area of the shoulder gone, the tip of the tail gone, and the horn flat. Ideally the tip of the horn should show, but in the marketplace many certified coins do not show this. On some coins this is due to a shallow strike.

1937-D, 3-Legged. Graded VF-20.

Illustrated coin: On this highly desirable variety one of the buffalo's forelegs has been polished off of the die, probably as the result of an attempt to remove clash marks.

F-12, 15 (Fine). *Obverse:* Only slight detail remains in the hair above the braid. Some of the braid twists are blended together. LIBERTY is weak, and on some coins the upper part of the letters is faint. The rim still is separate. On all coins, the date shows extensive wear. On Variety 1 coins it is weak. *Reverse:* The horn is half to two-thirds visible. Fur details are gone except on the neck at the highest part of the back.

1918-D. Graded F-12.

VG-8, 10 (Very Good). *Obverse:* Hair details above the braid are further worn, as is the hair at the top of the head. Most braid twists are blended together. The rim is worn down to the tops of the letters in LIBERTY. The date is light on all coins and very weak on those of Variety 1. *Reverse:* The base of the horn is slightly visible. Fur details are worn more, but details can still be seen on the neck and top of the back. The hip and flank beneath are worn flat.

1913-D. Graded VG-8.

G-4, 6 (Good). *Obverse:* Scarcely any hair details are seen at the center, and the braid is flat. The rim and tops of the letters in LIBERTY are blended. The date is weak but readable, with at least the last two numerals showing on earlier issues. *Reverse:* The rim is worn to blend into the tops of some or all letters in UNITED STATES OF AMERICA (except for Variety 1). E PLURIBUS UNUM and FIVE CENTS are full, and the mintmark, if any, is clear. The front part of the bison's head blends into the rim.

1918-D, 8 Over 7. Graded G-4.

AG-3 (About Good). *Obverse:* The head is mostly flat, but the facial features remain clear. LIBERTY is weak and partly missing. The date may be incomplete but must be identifiable. *Reverse:* Further wear is seen. On Variety 1 coins, UNITED STATES OF AMERICA is full and readable. On the Variety 2 the rim is worn further into the letters. The reverse of the Variety 1 nickels is bolder as the overall grade is defined by the date, which wore away more quickly than on the Variety 2.

1913-D, Variety 2. Graded AG-3.

PF-60 to 70 (Matte Proof). *Obverse and Reverse:* Most Matte Proofs are in higher grades. Those with abrasion or contact marks can be graded PF–60 to 62; these are not widely desired. PF-64 can have some abrasion. Tiny flecks are not common, but are sometimes seen. At the Matte PF-65 level or higher there will no traces of abrasion or flecks. Differences between higher-grade Proofs are highly subjective, and one certified at PF-65 can be similar to another at PF-67, and vice-versa.

1915. Graded Matte PF-67.

PF-60 to 70 (Mirror Proof). *Obverse and Reverse:* Most mirror Proofs are in higher grades. PF–60 to 62 coins can have abrasion or minor handling marks, but are usually assigned such grades because of staining or blotches resulting from poor cleaning. PF–63 and 64 can have minor abrasion and staining. Tiny flecks are not common, but are sometimes seen, as are dark stripe lines from the glued seams in the cellophane envelopes used by the Mint. PF-65

1937. Graded Mirror PF-66.

and higher coins should be free of stains, flecks, and abrasion of any kind. Differences between higher-grade Proofs are highly subjective, and one certified PF-65 can be similar to another at PF-67, and vice-versa.

**1913, Variety 1,
3-1/2 Legged**
FS-05-1913-901.

1914, 4 Over 3
FS-05-1914-101.

	Mintage	Cert	Avg	%MS	G-4	VG-8	F-12	VF-20	EF-40	AU-50	MS-60	MS-63	MS-65
											PF-63	PF-64	PF-65
1913, Variety 1	30,992,000	7,987	64.1	96%	$12	$15	$16	$20	$25	$35	$45	$60	$170
	Auctions: $822, MS-67, February 2015; $211, MS-66, March 2015; $129, MS-65, January 2015; $84, MS-64, August 2015												
1913, Variety 1, 3-1/2 Legged (a)	(b)	0	n/a						$400	$500	$750	$1,500	$10,000
	Auctions: $10,350, MS-64, April 2009												
1913, Variety 1, Proof	1,520	310	65.4								$1,600	$2,800	$3,750
	Auctions: $7,637, PF-67, July 2015; $4,230, PF-66, June 2015; $3,760, PF-66, January 2015; $2,115, PF-64, January 2015												
1913-D, Variety 1	5,337,000	2,213	62.6	89%	$15	$20	$25	$35	$45	$60	$75	$80	$300
	Auctions: $1,997, MS-67, June 2015; $329, MS-66, February 2015; $199, MS-65, August 2015; $84, MS-64, January 2015												
1913-S, Variety 1	2,105,000	1,540	60.2	81%	$45	$50	$60	$70	$90	$110	$130	$180	$700
	Auctions: $2,585, MS-66, January 2015; $998, MS-64, August 2015; $164, MS-63, October 2015; $152, MS-62, February 2015												
1913, Variety 2	29,857,186	1,980	62.8	91%	$10	$12	$15	$20	$250	$30	$40	$80	$300
	Auctions: $2,820, MS-67, January 2015; $564, MS-66, October 2015; $493, MS-66, July 2015; $223, MS-65, March 2015												
1913, Variety 2, Proof	1,514	242	65.3								$1,100	$1,300	$2,100
	Auctions: $3,525, PF-67, January 2015; $3,231, PF-66, October 2015; $1,762, PF-66, February 2015; $1,645, PF-65, January 2015												
1913-D, Variety 2	4,156,000	1,262	52.0	55%	$120	$150	$175	$200	$235	$260	$300	$400	$1,100
	Auctions: $1,997, MS-66, January 2015; $310, MS-63, June 2015; $211, AU-58, May 2015; $170, EF-45, February 2015												
1913-S, Variety 2	1,209,000	1,718	47.2	45%	$340	$375	$450	$500	$600	$750	$900	$1,100	$3,250
	Auctions: $3,055, MS-65, January 2015; $1,645, MS-62, February 2015; $727, MS-60, August 2015; $446, AU-58, May 2015												
1914	20,664,463	1,541	58.2	78%	$20	$22	$25	$30	$35	$45	$60	$85	$425
	Auctions: $8,225, MS-67, January 2015; $1,116, MS-66, October 2015; $705, MS-66, September 2016; $246, MS-64, February 2015												
1914, 4 Over 3 (c)	(d)	0	n/a		$200	$250	$325	$525	$1,000	$1,500	$2,800	$6,000	$30,000
	Auctions: $8,338, MS-64, April 2012												
1914, Proof	1,275	419	65.4								$900	$1,300	$2,000
	Auctions: $6,462, PF-67, February 2015; $2,820, PF-66, August 2015; $1,762, PF-66, January 2015; $1,527, PF-65, August 2015												
1914-D	3,912,000	1,234	51.1	54%	$90	$125	$160	$220	$325	$400	$450	$550	$1,300
	Auctions: $587, MS-64, January 2015; $376, MS-63, May 2015; $340, AU-58, February 2015; $211, EF-45, October 2015												
1914-S	3,470,000	1,493	57.2	69%	$26	$38	$45	$65	$90	$160	$200	$425	$2,000
	Auctions: $1,468, MS-65, July 2015; $305, MS-63, March 2015; $235, MS-62, November 2015; $123, AU-58, January 2015												
1915	20,986,220	1,452	62.3	89%	$6	$8	$9	$15	$25	$45	$60	$90	$300
	Auctions: $5,640, MS-67, January 2015; $540, MS-66, February 2015; $940, MS-65, August 2015; $823, MS-66, July 2016												
1915, Proof	1,050	346	65.2								$1,000	$1,350	$1,900
	Auctions: $8,812, PF-67, August 2015; $4,817, PF-67, June 2015; $3,760, PF-67, October 2015; $1,645, PF-66, January 2015												
1915-D	7,569,000	985	57.7	62%	$20	$35	$40	$70	$130	$160	$270	$350	$1,400
	Auctions: $376, MS-64, September 2015; $258, MS-63, January 2015; $236, MS-62, May 2015; $124, AU-58, February 2015												
1915-S	1,505,000	804	48.0	51%	$50	$75	$115	$200	$400	$500	$650	$1,000	$3,000
	Auctions: $3,525, MS-66, October 2015; $3,704, MS-65, August 2015; $1,527, MS-64, June 2015; $1,057, MS-63, January 2015												

a. The reverse die was heavily polished, possibly to remove clash marks, resulting in a die with most of the bison's front leg missing. **b.** Included in circulation-strike 1913, Variety 1, mintage figure. **c.** The straight top bar of the underlying 3 is visible at the top of the 4. The start of the 3's diagonal is seen on the upper right, outside of the 4. On some coins, a hint of the curve of the lower portion of the 3 shows just above the crossbar of the 4. **d.** Included in circulation-strike 1914 mintage figure.

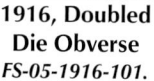

**1916, Doubled
Die Obverse**
FS-05-1916-101.

**1916, Missing
Designer's Initial**
FS-05-1916-401.

**1918, Doubled
Die Reverse**
FS-05-1918-801.

1918-D, 8 Over 7
FS-05-1918D-101.

	Mintage	Cert	Avg	%MS	G-4	VG-8	F-12	VF-20	EF-40	AU-50	MS-60 / PF-63	MS-63 / PF-64	MS-65 / PF-65
1916	63,497,466	2,046	61.8	88%	$6	$7	$8	$10	$15	$25	$50	$85	$300
Auctions: $7,050, MS-67, February 2015; $646, MS-66, August 2016; $235, MS-65, February 2015; $94, MS-64, November 2015													
1916, Doubled Die Obverse (e)	(f)	102	39.2	12%	$3,750	$5,500	$7,750	$11,000	$18,500	$32,000	$60,000	$150,000	
Auctions: $30,550, AU-55, January 2014; $28,200, AU-55, August 2014													
1916, Missing Initial (g)	(f)	0	n/a					$135	$200	$280	$375	$600	
Auctions: $341, AU-55, February 2014													
1916, Proof	600	173	65.4								$1,300	$2,700	$3,750
Auctions: $4,230, PF-66, January 2015; $4,113, PF-66, October 2015; $2,820, PF-64, August 2015; $2,232, PF-64, January 2015													
1916-D	13,333,000	1,216	59.4	73%	$16	$28	$30	$45	$90	$120	$175	$260	$1,350
Auctions: $1,086, MS-65, January 2015; $493, MS-64, February 2015; $235, MS-63, April 2015; $158, MS-62, November 2015													
1916-S	11,860,000	940	58.9	71%	$10	$15	$20	$40	$90	$125	$190	$275	$2,000
Auctions: $3,290, MS-66, January 2015; $2,592, MS-65, February 2015; $1,880, MS-65, October 2015; $188, MS-62, July 2015													
1917	51,424,019	972	61.7	88%	$8	$9	$10	$12	$15	$35	$60	$150	$475
Auctions: $1,763, MS-66, November 2016; $705, MS-66, January 2015; $376, MS-65, August 2015; $176, MS-64, April 2015													
1917-D	9,910,000	906	54.1	59%	$18	$30	$50	$85	$150	$275	$350	$750	$2,000
Auctions: $1,880, MS-65, October 2015; $1,233, MS-64, October 2015; $793, MS-63, January 2015; $329, AU-58, February 2015													
1917-S	4,193,000	749	48.9	48%	$22	$40	$75	$115	$200	$375	$450	$1,200	$3,750
Auctions: $4,230, MS-66, January 2015; $1,527, MS-64, June 2015; $1,028, MS-63, August 2015; $616, MS-62, October 2015													
1918	32,086,314	620	60.5	83%	$6	$7	$8	$15	$35	$50	$125	$325	$1,150
Auctions: $3,055, MS-66, August 2015; $3,055, MS-65, December 2015; $1,645, MS-65, March 2016; $1,292, MS-65, January 2015													
1918, Doubled Die Reverse (h)	(i)	4	43.0	25%	$190	$260	$375	$525	$1,450	$2,300	$3,500	$7,000	
Auctions: $170, VF-20, August 2013													
1918-D, 8 Over 7 † (j)	(k)	792	19.8	6%	$1,000	$1,500	$2,700	$5,500	$8,500	$12,000	$34,000	$57,500	$265,000
Auctions: $1,292, VG-10, March 2015; $940, G-6, January 2015; $822, G-6, July 2015; $763, G-4, January 2015													
1918-D	8,362,000	720	46.8	45%	$22	$40	$65	$135	$225	$350	$450	$1,050	$3,250
Auctions: $5,875, MS-66, January 2015; $2,937, MS-65, July 2015; $575, AU-58, February 2015; $423, AU-58, October 2015													
1918-S	4,882,000	653	53.4	62%	$14	$27	$55	$110	$200	$325	$585	$2,750	$15,000
Auctions: $2,820, MS-63, February 2015; $998, MS-62, January 2015; $399, AU-55, June 2015; $235, EF-45, August 2015													
1919	60,868,000	1,146	62.2	89%	$2.25	$3	$3.50	$8	$15	$35	$55	$125	$450
Auctions: $6,463, MS-67, August 2015; $5,875, MS-67, January 2015; $1,645, MS-66, August 2015; $1,410, MS-65, June 2015													
1919-D	8,006,000	712	47.5	41%	$15	$30	$75	$135	$260	$350	$600	$1,500	$6,000
Auctions: $1,762, MS-64, January 2015; $1,410, MS-63, June 2015; $519, AU-58, October 2015; $305, AU-53, November 2015													
1919-S	7,521,000	778	49.7	44%	$9	$20	$50	$125	$260	$375	$625	$1,800	$10,000
Auctions: $2,585, MS-64, August 2015; $1,292, MS-63, February 2015; $493, AU-58, October 2015; $282, AU-55, January 2015													

† Ranked in the *100 Greatest U.S. Coins* (fourth edition). **e.** The date, chin, throat, feathers, and the tie on the braid are all doubled. "Beware of 1916 nickels with strike doubling on the date offered as this variety. . . . The true doubled die must look like the coin shown here" (*Cherrypickers' Guide to Rare Die Varieties*, sixth edition, volume I). **f.** Included in circulation-strike 1916 mintage figure. **g.** The initial F, for Fraser—normally below the date—is clearly absent. Some dies exist with a partially missing or weak initial; these do not command the premium of the variety with a completely missing initial. **h.** Doubling is most obvious to the north on E PLURIBUS UNUM. Some coins show a die crack from the rim to the bison's rump, just below the tail. **i.** Included in 1918 mintage figure. **j.** "Look for the small die crack immediately above the tie on the braid, leading slightly downward to the Indian's jaw. The beginning of this die break can usually be seen even on lower-grade coins" (*Cherrypickers' Guide to Rare Die Varieties*, sixth edition, volume I). **k.** Included in 1918-D mintage figure.

	Mintage	Cert	Avg	%MS	G-4	VG-8	F-12	VF-20	EF-40	AU-50	MS-60 / PF-63	MS-63 / PF-64	MS-65 / PF-65
1920	63,093,000	883	62.2	90%	$1.50	$2.50	$3	$7	$14	$30	$65	$145	$600
	Auctions: $8,225, MS-67, February 2015; $881, MS-66, November 2016; $764, MS-65, November 2016; $176, MS-64, January 2015												
1920-D	9,418,000	729	51.9	57%	$8	$15	$32	$115	$275	$325	$585	$1,400	$4,250
	Auctions: $3,525, MS-65, January 2015; $1,645, MS-64, June 2015; $881, MS-63, October 2015; $705, MS-62, February 2015												
1920-S	9,689,000	747	53.1	56%	$4.50	$12	$28	$100	$200	$300	$575	$1,850	$15,000
	Auctions: $8,812, MS-65, September 2015; $2,585, MS-64, January 2015; $1,410, MS-63, August 2015; $881, AU-58, February 2015												
1921	10,663,000	763	60.2	81%	$4	$6	$8	$24	$50	$75	$150	$320	$700
	Auctions: $7,050, MS-67, August 2015; $3,995, MS-67, November 2016; $3,055, MS-66, September 2015; $400, MS-64, March 2016;												
1921-S	1,557,000	1,142	32.0	21%	$65	$115	$175	$375	$950	$1,100	$1,600	$2,100	$7,000
	Auctions: $2,585, MS-64, October 2015; $646, AU-50, January 2015; $399, VF-30, August 2015; $199, VF-20, February 2015												
1923	35,715,000	954	62.5	89%	$2	$3	$4	$6	$15	$35	$65	$160	$575
	Auctions: $9,400, MS-67, August 2015; $1,880, MS-66, January 2015; $470, MS-65, April 2015; $176, MS-64, May 2015												
1923-S	6,142,000	1,197	51.1	58%	$8	$10	$30	$135	$300	$400	$600	$900	$6,000
	Auctions: $4,347, MS-65, January 2015; $1,086, MS-64, August 2015; $387, AU-58, May 2015; $282, AU-53, November 2015												
1924	21,620,000	659	62.2	89%	$1.50	$2	$5	$10	$25	$45	$75	$160	$750
	Auctions: $7,050, MS-67, March 2015; $1,645, MS-66, October 2016; $724, MS-65, September 2015; $352, MS-64, March 2015												
1924-D	5,258,000	814	47.8	52%	$8.50	$12	$30	$85	$235	$325	$390	$765	$3,500
	Auctions: $4,465, MS-65, January 2015; $1,880, MS-64, September 2015; $763, AU-58, April 2015; $223, EF-45, July 2015												
1924-S	1,437,000	1,068	28.8	16%	$15	$32	$110	$475	$1,150	$1,700	$2,300	$3,700	$9,500
	Auctions: $5,287, MS-64, July 2015; $1,292, AU-50, June 2015; $470, EF-40, January 2015; $105, F-15, September 2015												
1925	35,565,100	1,004	63.6	95%	$3	$3.50	$4	$8	$15	$35	$45	$100	$350
	Auctions: $7,344, MS-67, August 2015; $4,230, MS-67, June 2015; $2,468, MS-66, August 2016; $352, MS-65, March 2015												
1925-D	4,450,000	789	53.0	65%	$10	$20	$40	$95	$185	$265	$400	$750	$4,000
	Auctions: $940, MS-64, February 2015; $472, MS-62, January 2015; $470, MS-61, July 2015; $352, AU-58, July 2015												
1925-S	6,256,000	878	48.9	48%	$5	$9	$18	$90	$180	$250	$475	$1,850	$20,000
	Auctions: $1,762, MS-64, January 2015; $1,292, MS-63, July 2015; $188, AU-50, May 2015; $135, EF-40, February 2015												
1926	44,693,000	1,455	63.6	96%	$1.25	$1.75	$2.50	$5	$10	$20	$35	$75	$200
	Auctions: $6,463, MS-67, December 2015; $4,465, MS-67, November 2016; $646, MS-66, November 2016; $176, MS-65, October 2016												
1926-D	5,638,000	869	53.7	67%	$10	$18	$28	$110	$185	$300	$350	$500	$3,500
	Auctions: $3,995, MS-65, July 2015; $1,410, MS-64, January 2015; $376, MS-63, April 2015; $258, MS-62, November 2015												
1926-S	970,000	1,791	29.4	11%	$25	$45	$100	$275	$950	$2,650	$4,500	$8,500	$95,000
	Auctions: $11,750, MS-64, January 2015; $2,350, AU-58, February 2015; $1,997, AU-53, June 2015; $705, EF-45, September 2015												
1927	37,981,000	1,069	63.5	95%	$1.25	$1.75	$2.50	$5	$15	$20	$35	$80	$245
	Auctions: $4,935, MS-67, September 2016; $999, MS-66, January 2015; $881, MS-66, December 2015; $164, MS-65, September 2015												
1927, Presentation Strike, Proof (l)	(m)	5	65.0									$30,000	$45,000
	Auctions: $43,125, SP-65, January 2012												
1927-D	5,730,000	778	59.7	83%	$2.50	$6	$10	$35	$80	$135	$180	$310	$6,500
	Auctions: $4,935, MS-65, January 2015; $646, MS-64, October 2015; $376, MS-63, May 2015; $188, AU-58, September 2015												
1927-S	3,430,000	653	54.9	55%	$1.50	$3	$5	$35	$95	$185	$550	$2,000	$12,000
	Auctions: $3,525, MS-64, January 2015; $1,116, MS-62, October 2015; $329, AU-58, August 2015; $282, AU-55, February 2015												
1928	23,411,000	903	63.3	92%	$1.25	$1.75	$2.50	$5	$15	$25	$35	$80	$280
	Auctions: $5,875, MS-67, June 2015; $1,528, MS-66, November 2016; $258, MS-65, October 2015; $258, MS-65, November 2015												
1928-D	6,436,000	1,551	63.1	97%	$1.50	$2.50	$5	$15	$45	$50	$60	$110	$600
	Auctions: $517, MS-65, September 2015; $481, MS-65, August 2015; $129, MS-64, January 2015; $99, MS-63, February 2015												
1928-S	6,936,000	726	60.3	79%	$1.75	$2	$2.50	$11	$26	$110	$260	$550	$2,850
	Auctions: $7,343, MS-65, October 2015; $2,115, MS-65, January 2015; $822, MS-64, August 2015; $458, MS-63, February 2015												

l. Some experts believe that certain 1927 nickels were carefully made circulation strikes; such pieces are sometimes certified as "Examples" or "Presentation Strikes." Professional numismatic opinions vary. See Bowers, *A Guide Book of Buffalo and Jefferson Nickels*. **m.** The mintage figure is unknown.

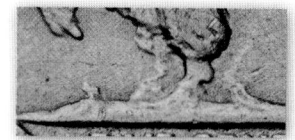

1935, Doubled Die Reverse
FS-05-1935-801.

1936-D, 3-1/2 Legged
FS-05-1936D-901.

	Mintage	Cert	Avg	%MS	G-4	VG-8	F-12	VF-20	EF-40	AU-50	MS-60 / PF-63	MS-63 / PF-64	MS-65 / PF-65
1929	36,446,000	1,221	63.0	94%	$1.25	$1.50	$2.50	$5	$15	$20	$40	$75	$275
Auctions: $8,225, MS-67, September 2016; $5,402, MS-66, January 2015; $212, MS-65, October; $258, MS-64, August 2015													
1929-D	8,370,000	749	62.5	93%	$1.25	$2	$2.50	$7	$32	$45	$60	$130	$1,000
Auctions: $763, MS-65, October 2015; $376, MS-64, February 2015; $282, MS-64, January 2015; $129, MS-63, May 2015													
1929-S	7,754,000	911	62.8	91%	$1.25	$1.50	$2	$4	$12	$25	$55	$80	$375
Auctions: $340, MS-65, January 2015; $329, MS-65, October 2015; $129, MS-64, April 2015; $79, MS-63, May 2015													
1930	22,849,000	1,464	63.2	93%	$1.25	$1.50	$2.50	$4	$11	$20	$35	$75	$220
Auctions: $3,525, MS-67, June 2015; $2,585, MS-67, October 2016; $1,763, MS-66, September 2016; $353, MS-65, October 2016													
1930-S	5,435,000	755	62.5	91%	$1.25	$1.50	$2.50	$4	$15	$35	$65	$120	$385
Auctions: $1,880, MS-66, January 2015; $364, MS-65, February 2015; $188, MS-64, August 2015; $111, MS-63, May 2015													
1931-S	1,200,000	2,079	61.8	89%	$15	$16	$20	$25	$35	$55	$65	$100	$300
Auctions: $616, MS-66, August 2015; $1,057, MS-65, January 2015; $517, MS-65, October 2015; $111, MS-64, May 2015													
1934	20,213,003	1,139	63.4	91%	$1.25	$1.50	$2.50	$4	$10	$18	$50	$65	$300
Auctions: $9,988, MS-67, January 2015; $3,525, MS-67, August 2016; $1,880, MS-66, September 2016; $188, MS-65, August 2016													
1934-D	7,480,000	1,207	63.0	95%	$1.50	$2.50	$4	$9	$20	$45	$80	$125	$550
Auctions: $1,880, MS-66, October 2015; $188, MS-64, August 2015; $152, MS-64, January 2015; $117, MS-63, April 2015													
1935	58,264,000	1,622	63.4	92%	$1	$1.50	$1.75	$2	$5	$10	$22	$45	$120
Auctions: $3,995, MS-67, July 2016; $1,763, MS-67, October 2016; $229, MS-66, March 2015; $164, MS-66, September 2015													
1935, Doubled Die Reverse (n)	(o)	176	30.9	6%	$45	$55	$100	$160	$500	$1,300	$4,000	$6,000	$25,000
Auctions: $329, EF-40, January 2015; $282, VF-35, January 2015; $95, VF-20, July 2015													
1935-D	12,092,000	1,297	63.4	96%	$1	$1.50	$2.50	$6	$18	$42	$75	$85	$400
Auctions: $2,232, MS-67, January 2015; $1,410, MS-66, September 2015; $352, MS-65, March 2015; $89, MS-64, May 2015													
1935-S	10,300,000	1,387	63.6	96%	$1	$1.50	$2	$2.50	$4	$18	$55	$70	$210
Auctions: $2,585, MS-67, January 2015; $305, MS-66, October 2015; $164, MS-65, March 2015; $74, MS-64, May 2015													
1936	118,997,000	3,275	64.1	92%	$1	$1.50	$1.75	$2	$3	$9	$25	$40	$80
Auctions: $646, MS-67, December 2015; $352, MS-67, May 2015; $153, MS-66, August 2016; $339, MS-64, August 2015													
1936, Proof, Both kinds	4,420												
1936, Satin Finish, Proof		632	65.8								$1,050	$1,250	$1,400
Auctions: $6,462, PF-68, July 2015; $2,585, PF-67, June 2015; $1,527, PF-67, October 2015; $1,527, PF-66, January 2015													
1936, Brilliant Finish, Proof		561	65.5								$1,150	$1,500	$1,850
Auctions: $5,875, PF-68, August 2015; $3,290, PF-67, July 2015; $1,762, PF-66, February 2015; $1,762, PF-65, January 2015													
1936-D	24,814,000	2,316	64.0	97%	$1	$1.50	$1.75	$2	$4	$12	$40	$45	$100
Auctions: $1,527, MS-67, January 2015; $123, MS-66, November 2015; $117, MS-66, February 2015; $69, MS-65, April 2015													
1936-D, 3-1/2 Legged (p)	(q)	0	n/a			$600	$1,000	$1,500	$3,500	$4,500	$12,500		
Auctions: $3,290, AU-50, January 2014													
1936-S	14,930,000	1,636	64.4	97%	$1	$1.50	$1.75	$2	$4	$12	$38	$45	$95
Auctions: $822, MS-67, January 2015; $270, MS-66, February 2015; $188, MS-66, November 2015; $94, MS-65, May 2015													

n. Strong doubling is evident on FIVE CENTS, E PLURIBUS UNUM, and the eye, horn, and mane of the bison. This variety (FS-05-1935-801) is extremely rare above VF, and fewer than a dozen are known in MS. Do not mistake it for the more moderately doubled FS-05-1935-803, which commands much lower premiums. **o.** Included in 1935 mintage figure. **p.** The right front leg has been partially polished off the die—similar to the 1937-D, 3-Legged, variety, but not as severe. (This variety is not from the same die as the 1937-D.) Fewer than 40 are known in all grades. Incorrectly listed by Breen as 1936-P. **q.** Included in 1936-D mintage figure.

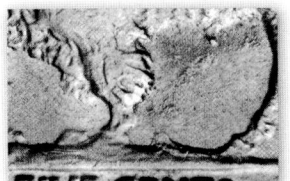

1937-D, 3-Legged
FS-05-1937D-901.

1938-D, D Over S
FS-05-1938D-511.

	Mintage	Cert	Avg	%MS	G-4	VG-8	F-12	VF-20	EF-40	AU-50	MS-60 / PF-63	MS-63 / PF-64	MS-65 / PF-65
1937	79,480,000	7,790	65.2	98%	$1	$1.50	$1.75	$2	$3	$9	$25	$40	$60
	Auctions: $8,225, MS-68, August 2016; $2,820, MS-67, September 2015; $1,059, MS-67, October 2015; $999, MS-67, August 2016												
1937, Proof	5,769	1,601	65.6								$950	$1,050	$1,150
	Auctions: $3,525, PF-68, August 2015; $3,055, PF-67, January 2015; $1,351, PF-66, July 2015; $1,292, PF-65, June 2015												
1937-D	17,826,000	4,256	64.9	97%	$1	$1.50	$1.75	$3	$4	$10	$35	$45	$60
	Auctions: $540, MS-67, January 2015; $423, MS-67, February 2015; $69, MS-66, June 2015; $48, MS-65, March 2015												
1937-D, 3-Legged (r)	(s)	6,415	49.8	27%	$425	$475	$550	$600	$675	$850	$1,850	$4,250	$30,000
	Auctions: $822, AU-55, February 2015; $822, AU-53, August 2015; $646, EF-45, July 2015; $493, F-12, January 2015												
1937-S	5,635,000	3,600	65.0	99%	$1	$1.50	$1.75	$3	$6	$9	$32	$42	$65
	Auctions: $881, MS-67, October 2015; $446, MS-67, January 2015; $62, MS-66, March 2015; $52, MS-64, June 2015												
1938-D	7,020,000	32,054	65.7	100%	$3.50	$4	$4.50	$4.75	$5	$8	$22	$36	$60
	Auctions: $188, MS-67, October 2015; $129, MS-67, January 2015; $50, MS-66, February 2015; $28, MS-65, August 2015												
1938-D, D Over D	(t)	2,620	65.6	100%	$4.50	$6.50	$9	$11	$20	$25	$45	$50	$75
	Auctions: $822, MS-67, October 2015; $564, MS-67, January 2015; $129, MS-66, February 2015; $60, MS-65, June 2015												
1938-D, D Over S (u)	(t)	2,120	65.2	99%	$5.50	$8	$10	$14	$20	$32	$55	$80	$160
	Auctions: $646, MS-67, August 2015; $517, MS-66, November 2015; $188, MS-66, March 2015; $94, MS-65, January 2015												

r. The reverse die was polished heavily, perhaps to remove clash marks, resulting in the shaft of the bison's right front leg missing. Beware altered examples fraudulently passed as genuine. "Look for a line of raised dots from the middle of the bison's belly to the ground as one of the diagnostics on the genuine specimen" (*Cherrypickers' Guide to Rare Die Varieties*, sixth edition, volume I). **s.** Included in 1937-D mintage figure. **t.** Included in 1938-D mintage figure. **u.** There are five different D Over S dies for this date. Varieties other than the one listed here (FS-05-1938D-511) command smaller premiums.

JEFFERSON (1938–2003)

Designer: *Felix Schlag.* **Weight:** *5 grams.* **Composition:** *1938–1942, 1946–2003—.750 copper, .250 nickel; 1942–1945—.560 copper, .350 silver, .090 manganese, with net weight .05626 oz. pure silver.* **Diameter:** *21.2 mm.* **Edge:** *Plain.* **Mints:** *Philadelphia, Denver, and San Francisco.*

Circulation Strike

Mintmark location, 1938–1941 and 1946–1964, is on the reverse, to the right of Monticello.

Mintmark location, 1942–1945, is on the reverse, above Monticello.

Proof

Wartime Silver Alloy (1942–1945)

Mintmark location, 1968–2004, is on the obverse, near the date.

Wartime Silver Alloy, Proof

History. The Jefferson nickel, designed by Felix Schlag in a public competition, made its debut in 1938, and has been a numismatic favorite since. The obverse features a portrait of Thomas Jefferson after the famous bust by Jean Antoine Houdon, and the reverse a front view of Jefferson's home, Monticello.

From partway through 1942 to the end of 1945 a copper-silver-manganese alloy replaced the traditional 75% copper and 25% nickel composition. This was to help save nickel for the war effort. These silver-content coins bear a distinctive P, D, or S mintmark above the dome of Monticello. Starting in 1966, Felix Schlag's initials, FS, were added below the presidential bust. The coinage dies were remodeled to strengthen the design in 1971, 1972, 1977, and 1982. The mintmark position, originally on the reverse to the right of Monticello, was moved to the obverse starting in 1968.

Striking and Sharpness. On the obverse, check for weakness on the portrait, especially in the lower jaw area. On the reverse, most circulation strikes have weak details on the six steps of Monticello, especially under the third pillar from the left, as this section on the reverse was opposite in the dies (in the press) from the high parts of the Jefferson portrait, and metal could not effectively flow in both directions at once. Planchet weight allowance was another cause, the dies being spaced slightly too far apart. Jefferson nickels can be classified as "Full Steps" (FS) if either five or six of Monticello's porch steps (with the top step counting as one) are clear. Notations of 5FS or 6FS can indicate the number of visible steps. It is easier to count the incuse lines than the raised steps. If there are four complete, unbroken lines, the coin qualifies as Full Steps (with five steps); five complete, unbroken lines indicate six full steps. There must be no nicks, cuts, or scratches interrupting the incuse lines. It is difficult to determine a full five-step count on the 1938 and some 1939 issues, as the steps are wavy and ill-defined; a great deal of subjectivity is common for these dates. Even if the steps are mostly or fully defined, check other areas to determine if a coin has Full Details overall. Interestingly, nickels of the 1950s and 1960s are among the most weakly struck. The silver-content coins of the 1940s usually are well struck. Some nickels of the 1950s to 1970s discolored easily, perhaps due to some impurities in the alloy. Proofs were struck from 1938 to 1942, 1950 to 1964, and 1968 to 2003. All have mirror fields. Striking is usually with Full Details, although there are scattered exceptions. Most survivors are in high grade, PF-64 and upward. Most since the 1970s have frosted or cameo contrast on the higher features. Special Mint Set (SMS) coins were struck in lieu of Proofs from 1965 to 1967; these in some instances closely resemble Proofs.

Availability. All basic dates and mintmarks were saved in roll quantities. Scarce issues in MS include 1939-D and 1942-D. The low-mintage 1950-D was a popular speculation in its time, and most of the mintage went into numismatic hands, making MS coins common today. Many different dates and mints are rare if with 5FS or 6FS; consult *A Guide Book of Buffalo and Jefferson Nickels* for details.

GRADING STANDARDS

MS-60 to 70 (Mint State). *Obverse and Reverse:* Mint luster is complete in the obverse and reverse fields, except in areas not fully struck up, in which graininess or marks from the *original planchet surface* can be seen. This may include the jaw, the back of Jefferson's head, and the higher-relief central features of Monticello. The highest parts of the design may have evidence of abrasion and/or contact marks in lower MS grades. Lower grades such

1939. Graded MS-66.

as MS–60, 61, and 62 can show some evidence of abrasion, usually on the same areas that display weak striking. At MS-63, evidences of abrasion are few, and at MS-65 they are fewer yet. In grades above MS-65, a Jefferson nickel should be mark-free.

AU-50, 53, 55, 58 (About Uncirculated). *Obverse:* The cheekbone and the higher points of the hair show light wear, more at AU-50 than at AU-58. Some mint luster will remain on some AU-55 and most AU-58 coins. *Reverse:* The central part of Monticello shows light wear, but is difficult to evaluate as this area often shows weakness of strike. Some mint luster will remain on some AU-55 and most AU-58 coins.

1943-P, 3 Over 2. Graded AU-58.

EF-40, 45 (Extremely Fine). *Obverse:* More wear is evident on the cheekbone. The higher parts of the hair are without detail. *Reverse:* Monticello shows wear overall. The bottom edge of the triangular area above the columns at the center are worn away.

1942-D, D Over Horizontal D. Graded EF-40.

VF-20, 30 (Very Fine). *Obverse:* Most hair detail is lost, except for the back of the head and lower area. The cheekbone is flat and mostly blended into the hair at the right. *Reverse:* Many shallow-relief architectural features are worn away. The windows remain clear and the four columns are distinct.

The Jefferson nickel is seldom collected in grades lower than VF-20.

1945-P, Doubled-Die Reverse. Graded VF-20.

PF-60 to 70 (Proof). *Obverse and Reverse:* Most Proof Jefferson nickels are in higher grades. Those with abrasion or contact marks can be graded PF–60 to 62 or even 63; these are not widely desired by collectors. PF-64 can have some abrasion. Tiny flecks are sometimes seen on coins of 1938 to 1942, as are discolorations (even to the extent of black streaks); these flaws are from cellophane holders. You should avoid such coins. Undipped Proofs of

1975-S. Graded PF-70 Deep Cameo.

the early era often have a slight bluish or yellowish tint. At PF-65 or higher there are no traces of abrasion or flecks. Evaluation of differences between higher-grade Jefferson Proofs is highly subjective; one certified at PF-65 might be similar to another at PF-67, and vice-versa. Striking is typically with full details, although there are scattered exceptions. At PF–69 and 70 there are no traces of abrasion, contact marks, or other flaws.

Five Steps

Six Steps

1939, Doubled
Die Reverse
FS-05-1939-801.

	Mintage	Cert	Avg	%MS	VF-20	EF-40	AU-50	MS-60	MS-63	MS-65	MS-65FS	MS-67
										PF-65	PF-66	PF-67
1938	19,496,000	919	65.5	98%	$0.50	$1	$1.50	$3	$5	$16	$150	$200
	Auctions: $188, MS-66, August 2015; $164, MS-66, May 2015; $141, MS-66, September 2015; $141, MS-66, October 2015											
1938, Proof	19,365	1,254	65.5							$100	$120	$375
	Auctions: $1,997, PF-68, October 2015; $1,057, PF-68, January 2015; $399, PF-67, July 2015; $94, PF-66, August 2015											
1938-D	5,376,000	2,348	66.2	100%	$1.50	$2	$3	$7	$10	$15	$125	$135
	Auctions: $881, MS-67, August 2015; $423, MS-67, January 2015; $141, MS-66, February 2015; $111, MS-66, September 2015											
1938-S	4,105,000	1,160	65.8	99%	$2.50	$3	$3.50	$4.50	$8	$16	$200	$375
	Auctions: $282, MS-67, January 2015; $305, MS-66, February 2015; $258, MS-66, October 2015; $129, MS-65, May 2015											
1939	120,615,000	1,270	65.0	93%	$0.25	$0.50	$1	$2	$2.50	$12	$47	$225
	Auctions: $1,116, MS-67FS, January 2015; $223, MS-66FS, February 2015; $36, MS-66, April 2015; $223, MS-65FS, February 2015											
1939, Doubled Die Reverse (a)	(b)	266	55.0	55%	$80	$110	$150	$200	$375	$1,000	$2,400	$4,000
	Auctions: $89, EF-40, November 2014; $86, EF-40, November 2014; $70, EF-40, November 2014; $7,050, EF-40, August 2013											
1939, Proof	12,535	898	65.4							$120	$170	$450
	Auctions: $2,115, PF-67, January 2015; $447, PF-67, February 2015; $129, PF-66, August 2015; $84, PF-65, October 2015											
1939-D	3,514,000	1,321	65.4	97%	$10	$13	$30	$60	$90	$120	$500	$375
	Auctions: $282, MS-67, January 2015; $129, MS-67, May 2015; $188, MS-66, November 2015; $135, MS-66, January 2015											
1939-S	6,630,000	714	65.0	96%	$2.00	$5	$10	$18	$35	$70	$400	$325
	Auctions: $1,528, MS-67, November 2013; $764, MS-66FS, June 2015; $247, MS-65FS, November 2014; $229, MS-65FS, September 2014											
1940	176,485,000	669	65.8	98%	$0.25	$0.40	$0.75	$1	$1.50	$15	$45	$165
	Auctions: $1,645, MS-67FS, June 2015; $1,320, MS-67FS, July 2015; $969, MS-67FS, August 2016; $153, MS-67, July 2015											
1940, Proof	14,158	902	65.4							$100	$120	$485
	Auctions: $6,463, PF-68, October 2015; $259, PF-67, January 2015; $94, PF-66, May 2015; $79, PF-65, June 2015											
1940-D	43,540,000	1,391	65.9	99%	$0.35	$0.50	$1	$2	$2.50	$15	$45	$85
	Auctions: $229, MS-67FS, November 2013											
1940-S	39,690,000	425	65.5	99%	$0.35	$0.50	$1	$2.25	$3	$12	$70	$250
	Auctions: $5,170, MS-67FS, June 2015; $282, MS-67FS, May 2015; $125, MS-66FS, February 2015; $69, MS-66FS, January 2015											
1941	203,265,000	656	65.8	99%	$0.20	$0.30	$0.50	$0.75	$1.50	$12	$65	$250
	Auctions: $2,010, MS-67FS, December 2015; $1,410, MS-67FS, October 2016; $940, VF-20, October 2014; $705, MS-67FS, September 2016											
1941, Proof	18,720	1,073	65.4							$75	$110	$500
	Auctions: $200, PF-67, April 2015; $112, PF-66, May 2015; $106, PF-66, May 2015; $60, PF-65, August 2015											
1941-D	53,432,000	1,375	66.1	99%	$0.25	$0.40	$1.50	$2.50	$3.50	$12	$45	$80
	Auctions: $1,058, MS-67FS, June 2015; $166, MS-67FS, February 2015; $69, MS-67, February 2015; $54, MS-67, February 2015											
1941-S (c)	43,445,000	296	65.5	98%	$0.30	$0.50	$1.50	$3	$4	$12	$80	$300
	Auctions: $2,585, MS-66FS, April 2014; $282, MS-66FS, November 2014; $259, MS-66FS, January 2015; $106, MS-66FS, August 2015											

a. Very strong doubling is evident to the east of the primary letters, most noticeably on MONTICELLO and FIVE CENTS. Lesser doubling is also visible on UNITED STATES OF AMERICA and the right side of the building. b. Included in circulation-strike 1939 mintage figure. c. Large and small mintmark varieties exist.

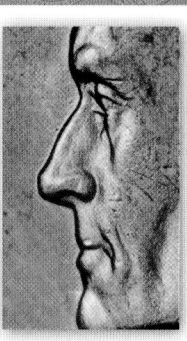

1942-D, D Over Horizontal D	1943-P, 3 Over 2	1943-P, Doubled Die Obverse
FS-05-1942D-501.	FS-05-1943P-101.	The "Doubled Eye" variety. FS-05-1943P-106.

	Mintage	Cert	Avg	%MS	VF-20	EF-40	AU-50	MS-60	MS-63	MS-65 / PF-65	MS-65FS / PF-66	MS-67 / PF-67
1942	49,789,000	682	65.2	99%	$0.30	$0.45	$1.25	$4	$6	$15	$85	$175
	Auctions: $4,700, MS-66FS, July 2015; $2,115, MS-67FS, September 2016; $1,763, MS-66FS, July 2015; $188, MS-66FS, August 2015											
1942, Proof	29,600	1,817	65.7							$90	$100	$180
	Auctions: $1,410, PF-68, January 2015; $423, PF-67, June 2015; $118, PF-66, May 2015; $79, PF-66, January 2015											
1942-D	13,938,000	1,240	65.7	99%	$1	$2	$5	$28	$38	$60	$80	$200
	Auctions: $541, MS-67FS, January 2015; $494, MS-67FS, July 2015; $100, MS-66FS, January 2015; $89, MS-66FS, February 2015											
1942-D, D Over Horizontal D (d)	(e)	82	48.8	30%	$75	$200	$500	$1,500	$3,000	*$9,000*		
	Auctions: $15,275, MS-66, April 2013; $764, AU-58, October 2014; $329, AU-50, August 2014; $44, F-12, September 2014											
1942-P, Silver	57,873,000	4,488	66.3	100%	$2	$2.50	$3.25	$7	$12	$20	$75	$85
	Auctions: $764, MS-67FS, September 2015; $153, MS-67, September 2015; $129, MS-66FS, January 2015											
1942-P, Proof, Silver	27,600	2,783	65.5							$110	$160	$265
	Auctions: $230, PF-67, January 2015; $223, PF-67, January 2015; $100, PF-66, January 2015; $74, PF-64, March 2015											
1942-S	32,900,000	4,267	66.2	100%	$2	$2.50	$3.25	$7	$12	$25	$200	$250
	Auctions: $2,820, MS-67FS, August 2015; $176, MS-66, January 2015; $153, MS-66FS, January 2015; $54, MS-65FS, September 2015											
1943-P, 3 Over 2 (f)	(g)	312	55.2	65%	$50	$100	$165	$225	$260	$700	$1,100	$2,850
	Auctions: $588, MS-66, October 2015; $539, MS-65, January 2015; $376, MS-64, January 2015; $333, MS-63, June 2015											
1943-P	271,165,000	5,222	65.8	98%	$2	$2.50	$3	$5	$8	$20	$40	$65
	Auctions: $881, MS-67FS, June 2015; $646, MS-67FS, January 2015; $118, MS-67, August 2015; $62, MS-66FS, June 2015											
1943-P, Doubled Die Obverse (h)	(g)	129	62.3	82%	$25	$40	$60	$90	$160	$650	$1,000	$1,300
	Auctions: $1,293, MS-66FS, September 2015; $940, MS-66FS, July 2015; $823, MS-66, June 2015; $411, MS-65, October 2015											
1943-D	15,294,000	8,430	66.2	100%	$2	$3.50	$4	$6	$12	$20	$45	$65
	Auctions: $3,760, MS-67FS, August 2015; $1,645, MS-67FS, July 2015; $62, MS-66FS, September 2015; $30, MS-66, September 2015											
1943-S	104,060,000	5,273	66.2	100%	$2	$2.50	$3	$5	$8	$20	$50	$100
	Auctions: $1,645, MS-67FS, February 2015; $517, MS-67FS, January 2015; $94, MS-66FS, January 2015; $69, MS-66FS, June 2015											
1944-P (i)	119,150,000	3,425	66.0	100%	$2	$2.50	$3.25	$7	$12	$30	$80	$150
	Auctions: $259, MS-67, February 2015; $223, MS-67, February 2015; $212, MS-67, February 2015; $106, MS-67, May 2015											
1944-D	32,309,000	5,742	66.3	100%	$2	$2.50	$3	$6	$12	$25	$35	$75
	Auctions: $1,528, MS-67FS, July 2015; $1,410, MS-67FS, January 2015; $100, MS-66FS, January 2015; $79, MS-66FS, April 2015											
1944-S	21,640,000	5,253	66.2	100%	$2	$2.50	$3	$5	$10	$22	$160	$110
	Auctions: $5,170, MS-67FS, July 2015; $2,350, MS-67FS, January 2015; $329, MS-66FS, January 2015; $188, MS-65FS, January 2015											

Note: Genuine examples of some wartime dates were struck in nickel, in error. **d.** The initial D mintmark was punched into the die horizontally, then corrected. "This is the rarest of the major Jefferson nickel varieties in Mint State" (*Cherrypickers' Guide to Rare Die Varieties*, sixth edition, volume I). **e.** Included in 1942-D mintage figure. **f.** "This popular variety was created when the die was first hubbed with a 1942-dated hub, then subsequently hubbed with a 1943-dated hub. The diagonal of the 2 is visible within the lower opening of the 3. Doubling is also visible on LIBERTY and IN GOD WE TRUST. . . . There is at least one 1943-P five-cent piece that has a faint, short die gouge extending upward from the lower ball of the 3; this is often mistaken for the overdate" (*Cherrypickers' Guide to Rare Die Varieties*, sixth edition, volume I). **g.** Included in 1943-P mintage figure. **h.** This variety is nicknamed the "Doubled Eye." Doubling is visible on the date, LIBERTY, the motto, and, most noticeably, Jefferson's eye. **i.** 1944 nickels without mintmarks are counterfeit.

**1945-P, Doubled
Die Reverse**
FS-05-1945P-803.

	Mintage	Cert	Avg	%MS	VF-20	EF-40	AU-50	MS-60	MS-63	MS-65	MS-65FS	MS-67
										PF-65	PF-66	PF-67
1945-P	119,408,100	3,565	65.8	100%	$2	$2.50	$3	$5	$8	$20	$125	$500
Auctions: $9,988, MS-67FS, July 2015; $329, MS-67, October 2015; $223, MS-66FS, January 2015; $58, MS-66, January 2015												
1945-P, DblDie Reverse (j)	(k)	212	64.2	95%	$20	$30	$50	$75	$130	$800	$7,000	
Auctions: $400, MS-65, January 2015; $353, MS-65, February 2015; $212, MS-65, January 2015; $176, MS-64, January 2015												
1945-D	37,158,000	5,922	66.3	100%	$2	$2.50	$3	$5	$8	$20	$40	$100
Auctions: $705, MS-67FS, January 2015; $54, MS-66FS, May 2015; $50, MS-66FS, January 2015; $48, MS-66FS, May 2015												
1945-S	58,939,000	6,087	66.2	100%	$2	$2.50	$3	$5	$8	$20	$200	$200
Auctions: $3,055, MS-67FS, August 2015; $1,116, MS-67FS, January 2015; $1,058, MS-66FS, January 2015												
1946	161,116,000	287	65.0	98%	$0.25	$0.30	$0.35	$0.75	$2.50	$15	$200	
Auctions: $1,763, MS-67, December 2013; $1,528, MS-66FS, August 2016; $1,175, MS-66FS, November 2016; $259, MS-65FS, May 2015												
1946-D	45,292,200	878	65.5	99%	$0.35	$0.40	$0.45	$1	$2.50	$12	$35	$400
Auctions: $2,350, MS-67FS, September 2015; $1,528, MS-67FS, January 2015; $1,175, MS-67FS, October 2015;												
1946-S	13,560,000	761	65.6	99%	$0.40	$0.45	$0.50	$1	$2	$11	$125	$135
Auctions: $353, MS-66FS, December 2014; $306, MS-66FS, July 2015; $223, MS-66FS, October 2014; $529, MS-66FS, April 2014												
1947	95,000,000	414	65.4	99%	$0.25	$0.30	$0.35	$0.75	$1.75	$12	$65	$145
Auctions: $3,760, MS-67FS, January 2015; $564, MS-66FS, July 2015; $153, MS-66FS, February 2015; $150, MS-66FS, January 2015												
1947-D	37,822,000	720	65.7	100%	$0.30	$0.35	$0.40	$0.90	$1.75	$11	$30	$135
Auctions: $940, MS-67FS, October 2015; $79, MS-66FS, January 2015; $74, MS-66FS, May 2015; $69, MS-66FS, November 2015												
1947-S	24,720,000	371	65.2	99%	$0.40	$0.45	$0.50	$1	$1.75	$12	$50	$650
Auctions: $2,056, MS-66FS, June 2014												

Note: Genuine examples of some wartime dates were struck in nickel, in error. **j.** There are several collectible doubled-die reverses for this date. Values are for the variety pictured (FS-05-1945P-801), with a strongly doubled reverse. The doubling spread increases from left to right. **k.** Included in 1945-P mintage figure.

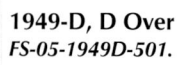

1949-D, D Over S
FS-05-1949D-501.

	Mintage	Cert	Avg	%MS	MS-60	MS-63	MS-65	MS-65FS	MS-66	MS-66FS	MS-67	MS-67FS
										PF-65	PF-66	PF-67
1948	89,348,000	226	65.2	99%	$1	$1.50	$10	$200	$65	$1,250		
Auctions: $1,646, MS-66FS, August 2016; $1,058, MS-66FS, October 2016; $112, MS-65FS, January 2015; $106, MS-65FS, July 2015												
1948-D	44,734,000	602	65.7	100%	$1.60	$4	$10	$30	$45	$85	$150	
Auctions: $588, MS-67FS, January 2015; $112, MS-66FS, November 2015												
1948-S	11,300,000	740	66.0	100%	$1.50	$2.50	$9	$45	$40	$300	$200	
Auctions: $7,050, MS-67FS, January 2015; $4,935, MS-67FS, July 2015; $517, MS-67, January 2015												
1949	60,652,000	273	65.2	99%	$2.50	$9	$12	$1,750	$35			
Auctions: $1,880, MS-65FS, December 2015; $1,553, MS-65FS, February 2010												
1949-D	36,498,000	689	65.4	99%	$1.50	$6	$10	$50	$30	$150	$300	
Auctions: $734, MS-67, January 2015; $411, MS-67, July 2014; $84, MS-67, December 2014												
1949-D, D Over S (a)	(b)	66	63.0	95%	$150	$200	$500	$1,650	$1,000			
Auctions: $564, MS-66, January 2015; $541, MS-66, January 2015; $541, MS-66, July 2015; $494, MS-66, October 2015												
1949-S	9,716,000	334	65.4	99%	$1.75	$5	$10	$200	$55	$850		
Auctions: $15,275, MS-67FS, January 2014; $235, MS-65FS, November 2014; $188, MS-65FS, November 2014												

a. The top serif of the S is visible to the north of the D, with the upper left loop of the S visible to the west of the D. "This variety is quite rare in Mint State and highly sought after. Some may still be found in circulated grades. Some examples have been located in original Mint sets" (*Cherrypickers' Guide to Rare Die Varieties*, sixth edition, volume I). **b.** Included in 1949-D mintage figure.

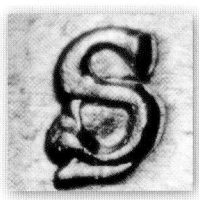

1954-S, S Over D
FS-05-1954S-501.

	Mintage	Cert	Avg	%MS	MS-60	MS-63	MS-65	MS-65FS	MS-66	MS-66FS PF-65	MS-67 PF-66	MS-67FS PF-67
1950	9,796,000	486	65.7	100%	$2	$3.25	$8	$185	$55	$425		
Auctions: $2,820, MS-67, September 2016; $106, MS-65FS, January 2015; $94, MS-65FS, July 2015												
1950, Proof	51,386	1,429	66.1							$75	$85	$125
Auctions: $329, PF-68, October 2015; $188, PF-68, August 2015; $141, PF-66Cam, November 2015; $50, PF-65, July 2015												
1950-D	2,630,030	4,033	65.5	100%	$14	$16	$25	$60	$60	$135	$225	$875
Auctions: $1,293, MS-67FS, August 2015; $250, MS-67, January 2015; $306, MS-66FS, February 2015; $118, MS-66FS, February 2015												
1951	28,552,000	291	65.4	100%	$3	$6.50	$15	$350	$80	$1,000		
Auctions: $1,410, MS-66FS, October 2016; $282, MS-66FS, August 2015; $259, MS-65FS, January 2015; $235, MS-65, August 2015												
1951, Proof	57,500	1,733	66.7							$65	$75	$120
Auctions: $823, PF-68Cam, January 2015; $705, PF-68Cam, October 2015; $129, PF-67Cam, June 2015; $58, PF-67, February 2015												
1951-D	20,460,000	620	65.7	100%	$4	$7	$11	$80	$35	$300	$300	
Auctions: $2,820, MS-66FS, June 2013												
1951-S	7,776,000	475	65.7	100%	$1.50	$2	$12	$200	$45	$1,000		
Auctions: $646, MS-67, August 2015; $194, MS-67, September 2015; $1,293, MS-66FS, January 2015; $881, MS-66FS, January 2015												
1952	63,988,000	257	65.5	100%	$1	$4	$9	$1,000	$175	$2,500	$450	
Auctions: $1,175, MS-67, August 2016; $1,058, MS-67, October 2016; $259, MS-66FS, July 2014; $259, MS-64FS, November 2014												
1952, Proof	81,980	1,768	66.9							$45	$60	$75
Auctions: $176, PF-67Cam, January 2015; $153, PF-67Cam, December 2015; $64, PF-66Cam, December 2015; $26, PF-66, March 2015												
1952-D	30,638,000	413	65.7	100%	$3.50	$6.25	$15	$175	$40	$350	$600	
Auctions: $16,450, MS-67FS, July 2015; $12,338, MS-67FS, January 2015; $329, MS-66FS, August 2015; $112, MS-65FS, January 2015												
1952-S	20,572,000	696	65.6	100%	$1	$1.50	$12	$300	$45	$1,850		
Auctions: $235, MS-65FS, August 2015; $212, MS-65FS, January 2015												
1953	46,644,000	268	65.4	100%	$0.25	$0.75	$8	$2,000	$45	$4,500		
Auctions: $129, PF-67Cam, December 2015; $26, PF-66Cam, August 2015; $54, PF-66, June 2015												
1953, Proof	128,800	2,406	67.1							$45	$50	$65
Auctions: $15,275, PF-68DCam, April 2013; $65, PF-68, September 2014; $135, PF-67Cam, November 2014; $35, PF-67, July 2014												
1953-D	59,878,600	608	65.6	100%	$0.25	$0.75	$9	$225	$45	$850	$450	
Auctions: $129, MS-67, January 2015; $1,880, MS-66FS, July 2015; $135, MS-65FS, August 2015; $141, MS-65, October 2015												
1953-S	19,210,900	488	65.2	100%	$0.75	$1	$10	$5,000	$90			
Auctions: $1,293, MS-64FS, June 2013												
1954	47,684,050	320	65.0	100%	$1	$1.50	$15	$250	$35	$1,250	$225	
Auctions: $999, MS-66FS, November 2014; $259, MS-65FS, January 2015; $207, MS-65FS, February 2010												
1954, Proof	233,300	2,678	67.3							$22	$40	$55
Auctions: $5,875, PF-68DCam, March 2013												
1954-D	117,183,060	272	64.2	98%	$0.60	$1	$30	$700	$125	$2,750	$300	
Auctions: $646, MS-65FS, January 2015; $282, MS-65FS, August 2015; $200, MS-65FS, August 2015; $176, MS-65FS, August 2015												
1954-S	29,384,000	703	64.7	99%	$1.75	$2	$15	$6,000	$125			
Auctions: $1,410, MS-64FS, January 2015; $764, MS-64FS, October 2015												
1954-S, S Over D (c)	(d)	177	63.3	95%	$26	$40	$160	$500	$500			
Auctions: $329, MS-66, January 2015; $159, MS-65, April 2015; $147, MS-65, February 2015; $84, MS-64, April 2015												

c. The overall strength of the strike is the important factor in this overmintmark's value. **d.** Included in 1954-S mintage figure.

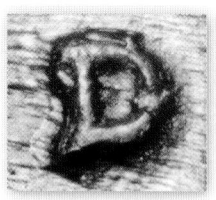

1955-D, D Over S
FS-05-1955D-501.

	Mintage	Cert	Avg	%MS	MS-60	MS-63	MS-65	MS-65FS	MS-66	MS-66FS / PF-65	MS-67 / PF-66	MS-67FS / PF-67
1955	7,888,000	416	65.0	100%	$0.75	$1	$15	$750	$125			
Auctions: $3,643, MS-66FS, September 2016; $382, MS-65FS, April 2014												
1955, Proof	378,200	4,346	67.6							$18	$30	$45
Auctions: $1,175, PF-68DCam, October 2015; $646, PF-68DCam, August 2015; $69, PF-66, July 2015; $54, PF-63, May 2015												
1955-D	74,464,100	414	64.5	98%	$0.50	$0.75	$20	$4,750	$160			
Auctions: $165, MS-66, August 2014; $69, MS-66, November 2015; $999, MS-64FS, February 2013												
1955-D, D Over S (e)	(f)	149	63.9	95%	$36	$57.50	$175	$450	$900			
Auctions: $823, MS-66, August 2015; $165, MS-65, January 2015; $50, MS-63, November 2015												
1956	35,216,000	688	65.4	100%	$0.50	$0.75	$20	$80	$45	$200		$3,000
Auctions: $9,400, MS-67FS, June 2015; $1,293, MS-66FS, December 2015; $588, MS-66FS, June 2014												
1956, Proof	669,384	3,748	67.5							$5	$25	$40
Auctions: $47, PF-69, October 2014; $5,581, PF-68DCam, June 2013												
1956-D	67,222,940	456	65.5	100%	$0.50	$0.75	$20	$675	$40	$2,000	$350	
Auctions: $911, MS-65FS, February 2013												
1957	38,408,000	419	65.0	100%	$0.50	$0.75	$15	$100	$65	$1,650		
Auctions: $441, MS-66FS, April 2014; $400, MS-67, August 2016												
1957, Proof	1,247,952	3,615	67.4							$4	$12	$20
Auctions: $881, PF-68Cam, June 2013												
1957-D	136,828,900	609	65.4	100%	$0.50	$0.70	$15	$175	$35	$1,500		
Auctions: $1,087, MS-66FS, August 2015; $376, MS-66FS, August 2015; $259, MS-66FS, August 2015; $188, MS-66FS, January 2015												
1958	17,088,000	275	64.3	100%	$0.60	$0.80	$12	$1,000	$100			
Auctions: $1,116, MS-66FS, November 2014; $764, MS-65, January 2014; $42, MS-64FS, June 2015												
1958, Proof	875,652	3,402	67.4							$8	$12	$20
Auctions: $7,050, PF-68DCam, April 2013												
1958-D	168,249,120	711	65.4	99%	$0.40	$0.50	$12	$40	$55	$45	$250	$2,500
Auctions: $1,763, MS-67FS, December 2013												
1959	27,248,000	552	65.3	99%	$0.25	$0.50	$10	$65	$85	$575		
Auctions: $764, MS-66FS, August 2016; $617, MS-66FS, September 2016; $165, MS-66FS, August 2015; $165, MS-66FS, August 2015												
1959, Proof	1,149,291	3,403	67.4							$3	$10	$20
Auctions: $7,050, PF-69DCam, April 2013; $1,293, PF-68DCam, September 2014; $494, PF-67DCam, August 2015												
1959-D	160,738,240	460	65.4	99%	$0.25	$0.50	$8	$225	$75	$1,375		
Auctions: $306, MS-66FS, July 2015; $223, MS-66FS, January 2015; $118, MS-65FS, January 2015; $107, MS-65FS, September 2015												
1960	55,416,000	372	65.2	99%	$0.25	$0.50	$8	$2,250	$75			
Auctions: $1,495, MS-65FS, February 2010												
1960, Proof	1,691,602	3,787	67.4							$3	$10	$18
Auctions: $6,463, PF-69DCam, March 2013; $229, PF-69Cam, September 2014												
1960-D	192,582,180	371	65.4	99%	$0.25	$0.50	$10	$2,500	$150		$500	
Auctions: $223, MS-66, February 2013												

e. There are 10 or more different D Over S varieties for 1955. Values shown are for the strongest (FS-05-1955D-501); others command smaller premiums. f. Included in 1955-D mintage figure.

	Mintage	Cert	Avg	%MS	MS-60	MS-63	MS-65	MS-65FS	MS-66	MS-66FS	MS-67	MS-67FS
											PF-65	PF-66	PF-67
1961	73,640,100	365	65.5	100%	$0.25	$0.50	$20	$1,750	$55	$3,000		
	Auctions: $2,530, MS-65FS, February 2010											
1961, Proof	3,028,144	3,944	67.3								$3	$10	$18
	Auctions: $1,763, PF-69DCam, April 2013											
1961-D	229,342,760	309	65.0	100%	$0.25	$0.50	$20	$7,500	$250		$2,000	
	Auctions: $11,163, MS-64FS, February 2013											
1962	97,384,000	364	65.2	99%	$0.25	$0.50	$10	$50	$45	$400	$350	
	Auctions: $21,150, MS-67FS, August 2013											
1962, Proof	3,218,019	4,289	67.3								$3	$10	$18
	Auctions: $823, PF-69DCam, September 2013											
1962-D	280,195,720	202	64.5	98%	$0.25	$0.50	$30		$350			
	Auctions: $89, MS-63FS, November 2014; $118, MS-63FS, June 2013											
1963	175,776,000	619	65.4	100%	$0.25	$0.50	$10	$165	$50	$750	$800	
	Auctions: $1,058, MS-66FS, July 2016; $705, MS-66FS, October 2016; $541, MS-66FS, July 2015; $79, MS-65FS, January 2015											
1963, Proof	3,075,645	4,853	67.4								$3	$10	$18
	Auctions: $329, PF-69UCam, July 2015; $317, PF-69DCam, December 2014; $823, PF-69DCam, September 2013											
1963-D	276,829,460	185	64.0	97%	$0.25	$0.50	$25	$5,250				
	Auctions: $7,475, MS-65FS, February 2010											
1964	1,024,672,000	333	65.2	99%	$0.25	$0.50	$8	$300	$40	$1,450		
	Auctions: $881, MS-66FS, July 2015; $147, MS-65, January 2015; $129, MS-64, August 2015; $62, MS-64, August 2015											
1964, Proof	3,950,762	8,499	68.1								$3	$10	$18
	Auctions: $176, PF-69DCam, January 2015; $112, PF-69DCam, January 2015; $94, PF-69UCam, July 2015											
1964-D	1,787,297,160	411	65.1	99%	$0.25	$0.50	$5	$650	$45	$1,650		
	Auctions: $2,350, MS-66FS, January 2015; $969, MS-66FS, January 2015; $282, MS-65FS, January 2015											
1965	136,131,380	335	65.8	99%	$0.25	$0.50	$5	$60	$50	$250	$5,500	
	Auctions: $165, MS-67, December 2014; $646, MS-66, August 2013											
1965, Special Mint Set ‡	2,360,000	2,439	66.6	100%						$5 (g)	$20	$45
	Auctions: $5,288, PF-67DCam, July 2014; $123, PF-67Cam, September 2014; $79, PF-67Cam, January 2015											
1966	156,208,283	110	65.1	97%		$0.25	$5	$50	$25	$225	$175	
	Auctions: $56, MS-66, July 2014; $322, MS-65DCam, February 2010											
1966, Special Mint Set ‡	2,261,583	2,242	66.8	100%						$5 (h)	$20	$35
	Auctions: $329, PF-67Cam, July 2015; $94, PF-67Cam, January 2015											
1967	107,325,800	289	65.5	99%		$0.25	$5	$50	$25	$235	$185	
	Auctions: $132, MS-66, February 2013											
1967, Special Mint Set ‡	1,863,344	2,651	66.8	100%						$5 (i)	$20	$30
	Auctions: $188, PF-68Cam, August 2015; $823, PF-67DCam, July 2015; $40, PF-67Cam, February 2015											

‡ Ranked in the *100 Greatest U.S. Modern Coins*. **g.** Value in PF-64FS is $10; in PF-65FS, $55. **h.** Value in PF-64FS is $10; in PF-65FS, $65. **i.** Value in PF-64FS is $10; in PF-65FS, $60.

	Mintage	Cert	Avg	%MS	MS-63	MS-64FS	MS-65	MS-65FS	MS-66	MS-66FS	MS-67	MS-67FS
											PF-66	PF-67Cam	PF-69DC
1968-D	91,227,880	629	65.5	100%	$0.25		$4		$35			
	Auctions: No auction records available.											
1968-S	100,396,004	307	65.6	100%	$0.25	$475	$5	$1,250	$35	$2,750	$275	
	Auctions: No auction records available.											
1968-S, Proof	3,041,506	1,413	67.8								$4	$16	$115
	Auctions: $4,406, PF-65, August 2013											
1969-D	202,807,500	442	65.5	100%	$0.25	$10	$4		$115			
	Auctions: $94, MS-66, February 2013											
1969-S	120,165,000	201	65.0	100%	$0.25		$2		$275			
	Auctions: $188, PF-69DCam, January 2015											
1969-S, Proof	2,934,631	1,346	67.8								$4	$10	$400
	Auctions: $282, PF-69DCam, November 2014; $1,116, PF-69DCam, June 2013											

	Mintage	Cert	Avg	%MS	MS-63	MS-64FS	MS-65	MS-65FS	MS-66	MS-66FS	MS-67 / PF-66	MS-67FS / PF-67Cam	MS-67FS / PF-69DC
1970-D	515,485,380	505	64.9	100%	$0.25		$10			$180			
	Auctions: $200, MS-63, August 2013; $200, MS-62, July 2014; $176, MS-62, August 2015												
1970-S	238,832,004	225	64.9	100%	$0.25	$225	$8	$400	$225	$1,500			
	Auctions: $999, MS-66FS, December 2013; $89, MS-64FS, November 2014												
1970-S, Proof	2,632,810	1,317	67.7								$4	$15	$300
	Auctions: $499, PF-69DCam, September 2013; $411, PF-69DCam, September 2014; $376, PF-69DCam, January 2015												

	Mintage	Cert	Avg	%MS	MS-63	MS-64FS	MS-65	MS-65FS	MS-66	MS-66FS	MS-67 / PF-66	MS-67FS / PF-67Cam	MS-69FS / PF-69DC
1971	106,884,000	271	64.8	99%	$0.75	$10	$3	$30	$50	$100			
	Auctions: $127, MS-66FS, February 2010												
1971-D	316,144,800	674	66.0	100%	$0.30	$10	$3	$20	$30	$60		$750	
	Auctions: $646, MS-67FS, August 2013												
1971, No S, Proof ‡ (a)	1,655	101	67.6								$1,100	$1,200	$3,750
	Auctions: $1,704, PF-69Cam, August 2015; $881, PF-68Cam, October 2015; $1,175, PF-67Cam, January 2015; $940, PF-67, January 2015												
1971-S, Proof	3,220,733	1,300	67.7								$8	$20	$600
	Auctions: $1,528, PF-69DCam, June 2013												
1972	202,036,000	123	65.2	99%	$0.25	$10	$3	$40	$60	$300			
	Auctions: $141, MS-66FS, November 2014; $276, MS-66FS, March 2012												
1972-D	351,694,600	165	64.9	99%	$0.25	$10	$3	$40	$75	$350			
	Auctions: $212, MS-63, November 2014; $823, MS-63, August 2013												
1972-S, Proof	3,260,996	1,006	67.6								$8	$20	$120
	Auctions: $58, PF-69DCam, November 2015; $52, PF-69DCam, November 2015; $42, PF-69DCam, October 2015												
1973	384,396,000	221	65.1	100%	$0.25	$10	$3	$30	$45	$150	$110		
	Auctions: $103, MS-66FS, February 2013												
1973-D	261,405,000	252	65.4	100%	$0.25	$10	$3	$25	$30	$60	$90		
	Auctions: $353, MS-65, February 2014												
1973-S, Proof	2,760,339	301	67.8								$7	$15	$30
	Auctions: $44, PF-69DCam, September 2009												
1974	601,752,000	230	64.9	100%	$0.25	$40	$3	$175	$35	$675			
	Auctions: $1,116, MS-66FS, July 2016; $110, MS-65FS, March 2014; $54, MS-65FS, January 2015; $46, MS-65FS, November 2014												
1974-D	277,373,000	155	65.2	99%	$0.25	$15	$3	$40	$45	$110		$1,550	
	Auctions: $34, MS-66FS, November 2014; $200, MS-62, April 2013												
1974-S, Proof	2,612,568	382	67.1								$8	$12	$20
	Auctions: $25, PF-69DCam, March 2008												
1975	181,772,000	221	65.5	100%	$0.50	$20	$3	$50	$55	$250			
	Auctions: $2,820, MS-67FS, January 2015; $129, MS-66FS, August 2015												
1975-D	401,875,300	152	65.3	100%	$0.25	$15	$3	$60	$55	$225			
	Auctions: $176, MS-66FS, August 2015; $153, MS-64FS, August 2015												
1975-S, Proof	2,845,450	533	67.9								$8	$12	$20
	Auctions: $42, PF-68Cam, August 2013												
1976	367,124,000	89	64.7	100%	$0.45	$30	$3	$175	$37	$675		$3,250	
	Auctions: $1,265, MS-66FS, February 2012												
1976-D	563,964,147	215	65.0	100%	$0.45	$10	$3	$30	$40	$250			
	Auctions: $235, MS-65, February 2014; $94, MS-64, July 2014												
1976-S, Proof	4,149,730	808	67.8								$8	$12	$20
	Auctions: $36, PF-70DCam, January 2010												

‡ Ranked in the *100 Greatest U.S. Modern Coins*. **a.** 1971, Proof, nickels without the S mintmark were made in error after an assistant engraver forgot to punch a mintmark into a die. The U.S. Mint estimates that 1,655 such error coins were struck.

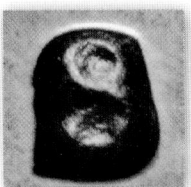
1979-S, Filled S (Type 1), Proof

1979-S, Clear S (Type 2), Proof

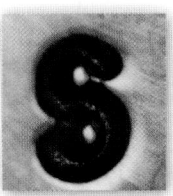
1981-S, Rounded S (Type 1), Proof

1981-S, Flat S (Type 2), Proof

	Mintage	Cert	Avg	%MS	MS-63	MS-64FS	MS-65	MS-65FS	MS-66	MS-66FS	MS-67	MS-67FS	MS-69FS
											PF-66	PF-67Cam	PF-69DC
1977	585,376,000	146	65.3	100%	$0.25	$70	$3	$150	$48	$775			
Auctions: $705, MS-66FS, July 2016; $306, MS-65, September 2015; $881, MS-64, October 2014; $329, MS-63, September 2013													
1977-D	297,313,422	220	64.8	100%	$0.50	$10	$3	$35	$40	$250			
Auctions: $940, MS-68, August 2013													
1977-S, Proof	3,251,152	730	68.3								$7	$12	$20
Auctions: $1,116, PF-70DCam, April 2013													
1978	391,308,000	149	65.2	100%	$0.25	$35	$3	$175	$55	$750			
Auctions: $43, MS-64, July 2014; $259, MS-64, September 2013; $282, MS-63, October 2014													
1978-D	313,092,780	227	64.8	100%	$0.25	$15	$3	$40	$55	$75			
Auctions: $104, MS-66FS, February 2010													
1978-S, Proof	3,127,781	723	68.6								$7	$12	$20
Auctions: $165, PF-70DCam, February 2015; $153, PF-70DCam, February 2015; $129, PF-70DCam, July 2015													
1979	463,188,000	119	65.1	99%	$0.25	$40	$3	$300	$50	$650			
Auctions: $200, MS-63, January 2015; $129, MS-60, September 2015													
1979-D	325,867,672	286	64.8	99%	$0.25	$10	$4	$30	$37	$125			
Auctions: $182, MS-66FS, February 2013													
1979-S, Proof, Both kinds	3,677,175												
1979-S, Type 1, Proof		788	68.6								$7	$12	$22
Auctions: $1,763, PF-70DCam, June 2013													
1979-S, Type 2, Proof		860	68.8								$8	$13	$30
Auctions: $646, PF-70DCam, June 2013													
1980-P	593,004,000	171	65.5	100%	$0.25	$10	$4	$45	$30	$225			
Auctions: $329, MS-64, January 2015; $259, MS-65, January 2015; $240, MS-64, January 2015; $188, MS-60, January 2015													
1980-D	502,323,448	150	65.0	99%	$0.25	$10	$3	$20	$60	$250			
Auctions: $217, MS-66FS, February 2013													
1980-S, Proof	3,554,806	1,009	68.7								$7	$12	$20
Auctions: No auction records available.													
1981-P	657,504,000	195	65.6	99%	$0.25	$100	$3	$500	$50	$1,750			
Auctions: $282, MS-66, January 2015; $223, MS-62, January 2015													
1981-D	364,801,843	177	65.0	100%	$0.25	$10	$3	$30	$35	$150			
Auctions: $206, MS-66FS, June 2014													
1981-S, Proof, Both kinds	4,063,083												
1981-S, Type 1, Proof		1,173	68.6								$7	$12	$20
Auctions: $1,528, PF-70DCam, June 2013													
1981-S, Type 2, Proof		1,015	68.9								$10	$13	$30
Auctions: $3,525, PF-70DCam, April 2013													
1982-P	292,355,000	37	64.6	95%	$5	$12	$10	$50	$35	$275			
Auctions: $881, MS-67, February 2014; $2,350, MS-62, September 2014; $306, MS-62, February 2015													
1982-D	373,726,544	71	65.0	97%	$2	$25	$6	$55	$30	$325			
Auctions: $374, MS-66FS, February 2010													
1982-S, Proof	3,857,479	854	68.8								$8	$12	$20
Auctions: No auction records available.													

	Mintage	Cert	Avg	%MS	MS-63	MS-64FS	MS-65	MS-65FS	MS-66	MS-66FS	MS-67	MS-67FS	MS-69FS
											PF-66	PF-67Cam	PF-69DC
1983-P	561,615,000	41	64.1	93%	$2	$60	$9	$400	$60	$875			
	Auctions: $141, MS-64, January 2015; $64, MS-64, January 2015; $36, MS-64, August 2015												
1983-D	536,726,276	44	64.5	95%	$1.50	$15	$4	$175	$35	$675			
	Auctions: $863, MS-66FS, June 2010; $112, MS-65FS, November 2014												
1983-S, Proof	3,279,126	793	68.8								$8	$12	$20
	Auctions: $1,528, PF-70DCam, June 2013												
1984-P	746,769,000	144	65.4	100%	$1	$10	$3	$25	$40	$75			
	Auctions: $66, MS-66FS, February 2013												
1984-D	517,675,146	136	65.1	99%	$0.25	$10	$3	$30	$65	$135			
	Auctions: $36, MS-65FS, February 2013												
1984-S, Proof	3,065,110	602	68.6								$10	$12	$20
	Auctions: $705, PF-70DCam, June 2013												
1985-P	647,114,962	129	65.5	100%	$0.50	$25	$3	$50	$60	$135			
	Auctions: $89, MS-66FS, November 2014; $70, MS-66FS, November 2014; $259, MS-62, November 2013												
1985-D	459,747,446	114	65.3	100%	$0.50	$10	$3	$40	$45	$125		$1,500	
	Auctions: $196, MS-66FS, June 2010												
1985-S, Proof	3,362,821	635	68.9								$8	$12	$20
	Auctions: $1,528, PF-70DCam, June 2013												
1986-P	536,883,483	139	65.7	100%	$0.50	$10	$3	$50	$35	$175			
	Auctions: $705, MS-66FS, August 2015; $99, MS-66FS, February 2013; $47, MS-66FS, November 2014												
1986-D	361,819,140	114	65.4	100%	$1	$10	$3	$35	$50	$300			
	Auctions: $253, MS-66FS, February 2010												
1986-S, Proof	3,010,497	490	68.9								$9	$13	$20
	Auctions: $3,525, PF-70DCam, April 2013												
1987-P	371,499,481	382	66.0	100%	$0.25	$10	$2.75	$15	$60	$65		$225	
	Auctions: $329, MS-67FS, June 2014												
1987-D	410,590,604	345	65.6	100%	$0.25	$10	$3.50	$20	$30	$125			
	Auctions: $173, MS-67FS, April 2008												
1987-S, Proof	4,227,728	633	68.9								$8	$12	$20
	Auctions: $558, PF-70DCam, June 2013												
1988-P	771,360,000	124	65.8	100%	$0.25	$12	$3	$30	$35	$100			
	Auctions: $329, MS-67, August 2013; $79, MS-64, August 2015; $69, MS-64, July 2014												
1988-D	663,771,652	192	65.3	99%	$0.25	$10.00	$3	$35	$32	$125			
	Auctions: $165, MS-67, June 2014												
1988-S, Proof	3,262,948	572	68.7								$9	$13	$25
	Auctions: $823, PF-70DCam, June 2013												
1989-P	898,812,000	217	65.9	100%	$0.25	$10	$2.75	$20	$25	$35		$650	
	Auctions: $18, AU-50, August 2013												
1989-D	570,842,474	142	65.1	100%	$0.25	$12	$2.75	$40	$35	$180			
	Auctions: $188, MS-66FS, February 2013												
1989-S, Proof	3,220,194	607	69.0								$8	$12	$20
	Auctions: $82, PF-70DCam, May 2013												
1990-P	661,636,000	157	66.0	99%	$0.25	$10	$2.75	$20	$25	$40			
	Auctions: $24, MS-66FS, October 2009												
1990-D	663,938,503	127	65.0	99%	$0.25	$9	$2.75	$30	$45	$200			
	Auctions: $129, MS-67FS, June 2014												
1990-S, Proof	3,299,559	864	69.1								$8	$12	$20
	Auctions: $441, PF-69DCam, June 2014												

	Mintage	Cert	Avg	%MS	MS-63	MS-64FS	MS-65	MS-65FS	MS-66	MS-66FS	MS-67 / PF-66	MS-67FS / PF-67Cam	MS-69FS / PF-69DC
1991-P	614,104,000	96	65.6	100%	$0.30	$10	$2.75	$45	$35	$190			
Auctions: $90, MS-66FS, February 2013													
1991-D	436,496,678	103	65.3	100%	$0.30	$10	$2.75	$25	$35	$160			
Auctions: $76, MS-66FS, February 2013													
1991-S, Proof	2,867,787	773	69.1								$10	$12	$20
Auctions: $64, PF-70DCam, August 2013													
1992-P	399,552,000	144	65.9	100%	$1.50	$10	$3	$20	$28	$50		$1,250	
Auctions: $88, MS-67FS, August 2013													
1992-D	450,565,113	121	65.2	100%	$0.25	$10	$2.75	$30	$40	$160			
Auctions: $72, MS-66FS, February 2013													
1992-S, Proof	4,176,560	1,508	69.1								$8	$12	$20
Auctions: $45, PF-70DCam, May 2013													
1993-P	412,076,000	130	65.8	100%	$0.25	$10	$1	$30	$35	$75			
Auctions: $68, MS-66FS, February 2013													
1993-D	406,084,135	174	65.4	100%	$0.25	$10	$1	$20	$30	$40	$450	$425	
Auctions: $374, MS-67FS, February 2010													
1993-S, Proof	3,394,792	1,549	69.0								$8	$12	$20
Auctions: $47, PF-70DCam, October 2009													
1994-P	722,160,000	162	66.0	100%	$0.25	$10	$2.50	$25	$30	$100	$35		
Auctions: $235, MS-70, January 2015; $881, MS-63, April 2013													
1994-P, Special Uncirculated ‡ (b)	167,703	1,669	68.9	100%	$50	$75	$100	$125	$130	$150	$250	$450	
Auctions: $123, MS-70, November 2014; $66, MS-69FS, March 2013; $40, MS-69, September 2014; $38, MS-69, November 2014													
1994-D	715,762,110	102	64.8	99%	$0.25	$10	$1	$30	$35	$100	$50		
Auctions: $92, MS-66FS, February 2013													
1994-S, Proof	3,269,923	1,394	69.1								$8	$12	$20
Auctions: $33, PF-70DCam, April 2013													
1995-P	774,156,000	187	66.2	100%	$0.25	$20	$1	$40	$20	$90	$25	$250	
Auctions: $499, MS-65, August 2013; $141, MS-63, July 2014													
1995-D	888,112,000	59	65.0	98%	$0.50	$10	$1	$25	$30	$175	$35	$850	
Auctions: $940, MS-67FS, April 2014													
1995-S, Proof	2,797,481	1,355	69.1								$10	$13	$20
Auctions: $79, PF-70DCam, February 2010													
1996-P	829,332,000	195	65.7	100%	$0.25	$18	$1	$20	$25	$30	$35	$350	
Auctions: $129, MS-64, January 2015; $69, MS-64, January 2015													
1996-D	817,736,000	224	65.3	100%	$0.25	$20	$1	$22	$25	$35	$40	$200	
Auctions: $161, MS-67FS, February 2010													
1996-S, Proof	2,525,265	1,391	69.1								$8	$12	$25
Auctions: $56, PF-70DCam, February 2010													
1997-P	470,972,000	79	65.9	100%	$0.50	$10	$2	$45	$25	$175	$50	$350	
Auctions: $306, MS-70FS, July 2015; $118, MS-69FS, February 2015													
1997-P, Special Uncirculated ‡ (b)	25,000	936	69.3	100%	$200	$100	$225	$300	$325	$375	$450	$550	
Auctions: $200, MS-70FS, October 2014; $499, MS-70FS, June 2014; $223, MS-69FS, November 2014; $118, MS-69FS, November 2014													
1997-D	466,640,000	95	65.2	99%	$1	$15	$2	$50	$20	$100	$25	$500	
Auctions: $33, MS-66FS, June 2014													
1997-S, Proof	2,796,678	1,365	69.3								$8	$12	$25
Auctions: $36, PF-70DCam, December 2009													

‡ Ranked in the *100 Greatest U.S. Modern Coins*. **b.** Special "frosted" Uncirculated nickels were included in the 1993, Thomas Jefferson, commemorative dollar packaging (sold in 1994) and in the 1997, Botanic Garden, sets (see related listeing in the "Government Commemorative Sets" section). They resemble Matte Proof coins.

	Mintage	Cert	Avg	%MS	MS-63	MS-64FS	MS-65	MS-65FS	MS-66	MS-66FS	MS-67 / PF-66	MS-67FS / PF-67Cam	MS-69FS / PF-69DC
1998-P	688,272,000	90	65.1	100%	$0.35	$8	$1	$35	$45	$125	$110	$400	
Auctions: $176, MS-65, July 2014; $940, MS-64, August 2014; $42, MS-62, November 2014													
1998-D	635,360,000	96	64.1	97%	$0.35	$10	$1	$100	$60	$450	$150		
Auctions: $66, MS-65FS, November 2014; $90, MS-65FS, June 2014													
1998-S, Proof	2,086,507	1,561	69.3								$8	$12	$25
Auctions: $47, PF-70DCam, November 2009													
1999-P	1,212,000,000	197	65.4	97%	$0.25	$10	$1	$10	$25	$75	$35	$250	
Auctions: $56, MS-65FS, August 2015; $46, MS-64FS, August 2015; $40, MS-65FS, August 2015; $23, MS-63, August 2015													
1999-D	1,066,720,000	172	65.5	99%	$0.25	$8	$1	$15	$30	$300	$50		
Auctions: $106, MS-64, September 2015; $89, MS-64, August 2015													
1999-S, Proof	3,347,966	6,107	69.1								$9	$12	$25
Auctions: $42, PF-70DCam, September 2009													
2000-P	846,240,000	114	65.6	100%	$0.25	$10	$1	$12	$18	$35	$25	$500	
Auctions: $470, MS-67FS, August 2013													
2000-D	1,509,520,000	171	65.9	99%	$0.25	$10	$1	$12	$18	$50	$25	$500	
Auctions: $613, MS-67FS, July 2015; $36, MS-65, August 2015; $56, MS-64FS, August 2015; $56, MS-63, August 2015													
2000-S, Proof	4,047,993	6,463	69.1								$7	$12	$25
Auctions: $17, PF-69DCam, March 2014													
2001-P	675,704,000	87	65.8	99%	$0.25	$8	$1	$10	$12	$20	$25	$40	
Auctions: $50, MS-67FS, June 2013													
2001-D	627,680,000	66	65.6	98%	$0.25	$8	$1	$10	$12	$20	$25	$130	
Auctions: $138, MS-67FS, February 2010													
2001-S, Proof	3,184,606	4,969	69.2								$7	$12	$25
Auctions: $17, PF-69DCam, March 2014													
2002-P	539,280,000	72	65.5	100%	$0.25	$8	$1	$10	$12	$20	$30	$75	
Auctions: $72, MS-67FS, June 2014													
2002-D	691,200,000	57	65.3	95%	$0.25	$8	$1	$10	$12	$90			
Auctions: $74, MS-66FS, February 2013													
2002-S, Proof	3,211,995	5,397	69.1								$7	$12	$25
Auctions: $15, PF-69DCam, February 2013													
2003-P	441,840,000	181	65.7	99%	$0.25	$8	$1	$10	$12	$20	$22	$50	
Auctions: $1,058, MS-68FS, November 2013													
2003-D	383,040,000	129	65.1	100%	$0.25	$8	$1	$15	$12	$80			
Auctions: $86, MS-66FS, February 2013													
2003-S, Proof	3,298,439	9,139	69.2								$7	$12	$25
Auctions: $15, PF-69DCam, March 2014													

WESTWARD JOURNEY (2004–2005)

Designers: *See image captions for designers.* **Weight:** *5 grams.* **Composition:** *.750 copper, .250 nickel.* **Diameter:** *21.2 mm.* **Edge:** *Plain.* **Mints:** *Philadelphia, Denver, and San Francisco.*

| **Westward Journey, Obverse (2004)** *Designer: Felix Schlag.* | **Peace Medal Reverse (2004)** *Designer: Norman E. Nemeth.* | **Keelboat Reverse (2004)** *Designer: Al Maletsky.* | **Westward Journey, Obverse (2005)** *Designer: Joe Fitzgerald.* | **American Bison Reverse (2005)** *Designer: Jamie Franki.* | **Ocean in View Reverse (2005)** *Designer: Joe Fitzgerald.* |

| **Westward Journey, Obverse, Proof** | **Peace Medal Reverse, Proof** | **Keelboat Reverse, Proof** | **Westward Journey, Obverse, Proof** | **American Bison Reverse, Proof** | **Ocean in View Reverse, Proof** |

Mintmark location, 2005, is on the obverse, near the date (2004 location is the same as previous years).

History. In 2004 special designs commemorating the Westward Journey (Lewis and Clark expedition) were introduced. They utilized the previous obverse design paired with two different reverse designs, one representing the Peace Medals given out by Lewis and Clark, the other showing the keelboat that provided much of their transportation. Two new reverse designs were introduced for 2005, showing the American Bison and a representation of Clark's journal entry upon spotting what he thought was the Pacific Ocean (in actuality, they were still approximately 20 miles from the coast). They were paired with a new obverse, a tightly cropped profile of Jefferson facing right.

Striking and Sharpness. On the obverse, check for weakness on the portrait. Proofs were struck for each design. All have mirror fields. Most have frosted or cameo contrast on the higher features.

Availability. All basic dates and mintmarks were saved in roll quantities.

GRADING STANDARDS

MS-60 to 70 (Mint State). *Obverse and Reverse:* Mint luster is complete in the obverse and reverse fields. Check the higher parts of the obverse and reverse for abrasion and contact marks.

The Westward Journey nickels are seldom collected in grades lower than MS-60.

2004-D, Peace Medal. Graded MS-66.

PF-60 to 70 (Proof). *Obverse and Reverse:* Evaluation of differences between higher-grade Jefferson Proofs is highly subjective; one certified at PF-65 might be similar to another at PF-67, and vice-versa. All Proof Westward Journey nickels have mirror fields. Striking is typically with full details, although there are scattered exceptions. Nearly all Westward Journey nickel Proofs are as issued, in PF–69 or 70.

2005-S, Ocean in View. Graded PF-70 Ultra Cameo.

	Mintage	Cert	Avg	%MS	MS-63	MS-65	MS-66	MS-67
						PF-65	PF-67	PF-69DC
2004-P, Peace Medal	361,440,000	2,112	63.7	97%	$0.25	$0.75	$8	$50
	Auctions: $200, MS-67, February 2013							
2004-D, Peace Medal	372,000,000	513	65.6	100%	$0.25	$0.75	$5	$30
	Auctions: $374, MS-68, February 2010							
2004-S, Peace Medal, Proof	2,992,069	11,895	69.2			$8	$12	$25
	Auctions: $15, PF-69DCam, March 2014							
2004-P, Keelboat	366,720,000	269	65.6	100%	$0.25	$0.75	$5	$20
	Auctions: $299, MS-68, February 2010							
2004-D, Keelboat	344,880,000	324	65.9	100%	$0.25	$0.75	$5	$20
	Auctions: No auction records available.							
2004-S, Keelboat, Proof	2,965,422	11,908	69.2			$8	$12	$25
	Auctions: $31, PF-70DCam, November 2013							
2005-P, American Bison	448,320,000	4,275	66.7	100%	$0.35	$1.25	$8	$30
	Auctions: $28, MS-69, January 2010							
2005-P, American Bison, Satin Finish	1,160,000	3,709	67.0	100%	$0.50	$1	$3	$10
	Auctions: No auction records available.							
2005-D, American Bison	487,680,000	4,584	66.1	100%	$0.35	$1.25	$8	$25
	Auctions: $388, MS-66, June 2014; $170, MS-64, November 2014; $26, MS-64, November 2014; $84, MS-64, November 2014							
2005-D, American Bison, Satin Finish	1,160,000	3,219	66.6	100%	$0.50	$1	$3	$10
	Auctions: No auction records available.							
2005-S, American Bison, Proof	3,344,679	19,259	69.2			$10	$14	$30
	Auctions: $34, PF-70DCam, July 2013							
2005-P, Ocean in View	394,080,000	3,286	66.5	100%	$0.25	$0.75	$6	$25
	Auctions: $19, MS-66, February 2010							
2005-P, Ocean in View, Satin Finish	1,160,000	3,040	66.7	100%	$0.50	$1	$3	$10
	Auctions: No auction records available.							
2005-D, Ocean in View	411,120,000	3,481	66.5	100%	$0.25	$0.75	$5	$22
	Auctions: $15, MS-65, August 2009							
2005-D, Ocean in View, Satin Finish	1,160,000	3,248	66.6	100%	$0.50	$1	$3	$10
	Auctions: No auction records available.							
2005-S, Ocean in View, Proof	3,344,679	18,964	69.2			$8	$12	$25
	Auctions: $21, PF-70DCam, November 2013							

JEFFERSON MODIFIED (2006 TO DATE)

Designers: *Jamie Franki (obverse) and Felix Schlag (reverse)*. **Weight:** *5 grams*. **Composition:** *.750 copper, .250 nickel*. **Diameter:** *21.2 mm*. **Edge:** *Plain*. **Mints:** *Philadelphia, Denver, and San Francisco.*

Circulation Strike

Mintmark location, 2006 to date, is on the obverse, below the date.

Proof

History. 2006 saw the return of Felix Schlag's reverse design showing a front view of Jefferson's home, Monticello. It also featured the debut of another new Jefferson portrait on the obverse, this time in three-quarters profile.

Striking and Sharpness. On the obverse, check for weakness on the portrait. Jefferson nickels can be classified as "Full Steps" (FS) if either five or six of Monticello's porch steps (with the top step counting as one) are clear. Notations of 5FS or 6FS can indicate the number of visible steps. It is easier to count the incuse lines than the raised steps. If there are four complete, unbroken lines, the coin qualifies as Full Steps (with five steps); five complete, unbroken lines indicate six full steps. There must be no nicks, cuts, or scratches interrupting the incuse lines. Even if the steps are mostly or fully defined, check other areas to determine if a coin has Full Details overall. Proofs were struck; all have mirror fields. Striking is usually with Full Details, although there are scattered exceptions. Most survivors are in high grade, PF-64 and upward. Most have frosted or cameo contrast on the higher features.

Availability. All basic dates and mintmarks were saved in roll quantities.

GRADING STANDARDS

MS-60 to 70 (Mint State). *Obverse and Reverse:* Mint luster is complete in the obverse and reverse fields. Check the higher parts of the obverse and reverse for abrasion and contact marks.

The Jefferson Modified nickel is seldom collected in grades lower than MS-60.

2011-P. Graded MS-67FS.

PF-60 to 70 (Proof). *Obverse and Reverse:* Evaluation of differences between higher-grade Jefferson Proofs is highly subjective; one certified at PF-65 might be similar to another at PF-67, and vice-versa. All Proof Jefferson Modified nickels have mirror fields. Striking is typically with full details, although there are scattered exceptions. Nearly all Jefferson Modified nickel Proofs are as issued, in PF-69 or 70.

2006-S. Graded PF-70 Deep Cameo.

	Mintage	Cert	Avg	%MS	MS-63	MS-65	MS-65FS	MS-66	MS-66FS	MS-67	MS-67FS / PF-65	MS-68FS / PF-67	MS-69FS / PF-69DC
2006-P, Monticello	693,120,000	281	65.3	100%	$0.25	$0.75	$4	$3	$5	$8	$10	$20	$30
Auctions: $705, MS-67FS, July 2014; $19, MS-64FS, January 2013													
2006-P, Monticello, Satin Finish	847,361	1,233	66.8	100%	$0.50	$1	$2	$3	$5	$10	—	—	—
Auctions: No auction records available.													
2006-D, Monticello	809,280,000	319	65.7	100%	$0.25	$0.75	$5	$4	$6	$9	$22	$30	$50
Auctions: $11, MS-67, July 2008													
2006-D, Monticello, Satin Finish	847,361	1,341	66.9	100%	$0.50	$1	$2	$3	$5	$10	—	—	—
Auctions: No auction records available.													
2006-S, Monticello, Proof	3,054,436	7,347	69.3								$5	$12	$25
Auctions: $32, PF-70DCam, April 2013													
2007-P	571,680,000	46	65.1	100%	$0.25	$0.50	$4	$3	$5	$8	$10	$20	$30
Auctions: $11, MS-68FS, July 2008													
2007-P, Satin Finish	895,628	252	66.3	100%	$0.50	$1	$2	$3	$5	$10	—	—	—
Auctions: No auction records available.													
2007-D	626,160,000	28	64.8	100%	$0.25	$0.50	$5	$4	$6	$9	$22	$30	$50
Auctions: $14, MS-68FS, July 2008													
2007-D, Satin Finish	895,628	217	66.2	100%	$0.50	$1	$2	$3	$5	$10	—	—	—
Auctions: No auction records available.													
2007-S, Proof	2,577,166	5,528	69.3								$4	$12	$30
Auctions: $15, PF-69DCam, May 2013													
2008-P	279,840,000	94	65.5	100%	$0.25	$0.50	$4	$3	$5	$8	$10	$20	$30
Auctions: No auction records available.													
2008-P, Satin Finish	745,464	84	66.9	100%	$0.50	$1	$2	$3	$5	$10	—	—	—
Auctions: No auction records available.													
2008-D	345,600,000	60	64.9	100%	$0.25	$0.50	$5	$4	$6	$9	$22	$30	$50
Auctions: No auction records available.													
2008-D, Satin Finish	745,464	104	67.0	100%	$0.50	$1	$2	$3	$5	$10	—	—	—
Auctions: No auction records available.													
2008-S, Proof	2,169,561	4,113	69.5								$4	$12	$30
Auctions: $56, PF-70DCam, June 2009													
2009-P	39,840,000	209	65.3	100%	$0.30	$0.70	$4	$3	$5	$8	$10	$20	$30
Auctions: No auction records available.													
2009-P, Satin Finish	784,614	191	67.0	100%	$0.50	$1	$2	$3	$5	$10	—	—	—
Auctions: No auction records available.													
2009-D	46,800,000	161	65.1	100%	$0.30	$1	$5	$4	$6	$9	$22	$30	$50
Auctions: No auction records available.													
2009-D, Satin Finish	784,614	196	67.0	100%	$0.50	$1	$2	$3	$5	$10	—	—	—
Auctions: No auction records available.													
2009-S, Proof	2,179,867	6,201	69.3								$4	$12	$30
Auctions: $79, PF-70UCam, November 2009													
2010-P	260,640,000	73	65.8	100%	$0.25	$0.50	$4	$3	$5	$8	$10	$20	$30
Auctions: $15, MS-67FS, June 2013													
2010-P, Satin Finish	583,897	82	66.9	100%	$0.50	$1	$2	$3	$5	$10	—	—	—
Auctions: No auction records available.													
2010-D	229,920,000	109	65.9	100%	$0.25	$0.50	$5	$4	$6	$9	$22	$30	$50
Auctions: No auction records available.													
2010-D, Satin Finish	583,897	96	67.4	100%	$0.50	$1	$2	$3	$5	$10	—	—	—
Auctions: No auction records available.													

	Mintage	Cert	Avg	%MS	MS-63	MS-65	MS-65FS	MS-66	MS-66FS	MS-67	MS-67FS / PF-65	MS-68FS / PF-67	MS-69FS / PF-69DC
2010-S, Proof	1,689,216	4,229	69.3								$4	$12	$30
2011-P	450,000,000	180	66.5	100%	$0.25	$0.50	$4	$3	$5	$8	$10	$20	$30
2011-D	540,240,000	233	66.6	100%	$0.25	$0.50	$5	$4	$6	$9	$22	$30	$50
2011-S, Proof	1,453,276	5,735	69.3								$4	$12	$30
2012-P	464,640,000	113	66.7	100%	$0.25	$0.50	$4	$3	$5	$8	$10	$20	$30
2012-D	558,960,000	114	66.7	100%	$0.25	$0.50	$5	$4	$6	$9	$20	$27	$40
2012-S, Proof	1,237,415	2,205	69.5								$4	$12	$30
2013-P	607,440,000	98	66.4	100%	$0.25	$0.50	$4	$3	$5	$8	$10	$20	$30
2013-D	615,600,000	92	66.6	100%	$0.25	$0.50	$5	$4	$6	$9	$20	$27	$40
2013-S, Proof	802,460	2,287	69.4								$4	$12	$30
2014-P	635,520,000	137	67.0	100%	$0.25	$0.50	$4	$3	$5	$8	$10	$20	$30
2014-D	570,720,000	148	67.1	100%	$0.25	$0.50	$5	$4	$6	$9	$20	$27	$40
2014-S, Proof	665,100	2,760	69.3								$4	$12	$30
2015-P	753,194,029	0	n/a		$0.25	$0.50	$4	$3	$5	$8	$10	$20	$30
2015-D	847,034,029	0	n/a		$0.25	$0.50	$5	$4	$6	$9	$20	$27	$40
2015-S, Proof	1,050,164	0	n/a								$4	$12	$30
2016-P	787,256,579	0	n/a		$0.25	$0.50	$5	$4	$6	$9	$20	$27	$40
2016-D	759,896,579	0	n/a		$0.25	$0.50	$5	$4	$6	$9	$20	$27	$40
2016-S, Proof	1,011,624	0	n/a								$4	$12	$30
2017-P	710,431,686	0	n/a		$0.25	$0.50	$5	$4	$6	$9	$20	$27	$40
2017-D	663,391,686	0	n/a		$0.25	$0.50	$5	$4	$6	$9	$20	$27	$40
2017-S, Enhanced Unc.											$4	$12	$30
2017-S, Proof	926,437	0	n/a								$4	$12	$30
2018-P		0	n/a		$0.25	$0.50	$5	$4	$6	$9	$20	$27	$40
2018-D		0	n/a		$0.25	$0.50	$5	$4	$6	$9	$20	$27	$40
2018-S, Proof		0	n/a								$4	$12	$30

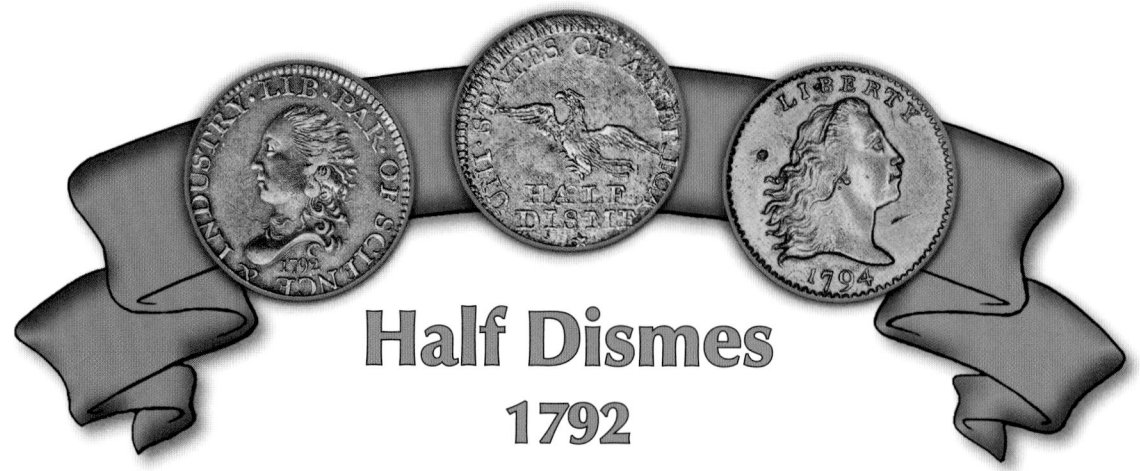

Half Dismes
1792

AN OVERVIEW OF HALF DISMES

Half dimes or five-cent silver coins were provided for in the Mint Act of April 2, 1792. The spelling was stated as *half disme*. The latter word (likely pronounced "dime," as in modern usage, but perhaps in some places as "deem," in the French mode) was used intermittently in government correspondence for years afterward, but on coins dated 1794 and beyond it appeared only as *dime*.

President George Washington, in his fourth annual message to the House of Representatives, November 6, 1792, referred to the half disme:

> In execution of the authority given by the Legislature, measures have been taken for engaging some artists from abroad to aid in the establishment of our Mint; others have been employed at home. Provision has been made of the requisite buildings, and these are now putting into proper condition for the purposes of the establishment.
>
> There has also been a small beginning in the coinage of half-dismes; the want of small coins in circulation calling the first attention to them. The regulation of foreign coins, in correspondence with the principles of our national Coinage, as being essential to their due operation, and to order in our money-concerns, will, I doubt not, be resumed and completed.

The 1792 half dismes are studied in *United States Pattern Coins* (the hobby's standard reference on pattern coins and experimental and trial pieces), and some numismatists have traditionally referred to them as patterns. It is true that they were struck at a private shop in Philadelphia while the official Mint buildings were still in planning. However, several factors point to their status as regular circulating coins. The half disme was authorized as a federal issue by congressional legislation. Its mintage was considerable—some 1,500 or so pieces—and, as noted by President Washington, the coins were meant to alleviate the national need for small change. Furthermore, nearly all surviving examples show signs of extensive wear.

The 1792 half dismes are not commonly collected, simply because they are not common coins; only 200 to 300 are estimated to still exist. However, their rarity, the romance of their connection to the nation's founding, and the mysteries and legends surrounding their creation make them a perennial favorite among numismatists.

The 1792 half disme has often been considered to be a pattern by some numismatists. Nevertheless, the coins entered circulation as currency over the next decade.

HALF DISME (1792)

Designer: *Unknown (possibly Robert Birch).* **Weight:** *1.35 grams.*
Composition: *.8924 silver, .1076 copper.* **Diameter:** *16.5 mm.*
Edge: *Reeded.* **Mint:** *John Harper's shop, Philadelphia.*

**Judd-7, Pollock-7,
Logan-McCloskey–1.**

History. Rumors and legends are par for the course with the 1792 half disme. Martha Washington is sometimes said to have posed for the portrait of Miss Liberty, despite the profile's dissimilarity to life images of the first lady. Longstanding numismatic tradition says that President George Washington had his own silver tableware taken to the mint factory to be melted down, with these little coins being the result. Whether these Washingtonian connections are true or not, other facts are certain: while the Philadelphia Mint was in the planning stage (its cornerstone would be laid on July 31, 1792), dies were being cut for the first federal coinage of that year. The designer may have been Robert Birch, a Mint engraver who created (or helped create) the dies for the half disme, the disme, and other coins. The half dismes were struck in a private facility owned by saw-maker John Harper, in mid-July. It is believed, from Thomas Jefferson's records, that 1,500 were made. Most were placed into circulation. The coin's designs, with a unique head of Miss Liberty and an outstretched eagle, would not be revived when normal production of the half dime denomination started at the Mint's official facilities in 1795.

Striking and Sharpness. These coins usually are fairly well struck, but with some lightness on Miss Liberty's hair above her ear, and on the eagle's breast. Some examples have adjustment marks from the planchet being filed to adjust the weight prior to striking.

Availability. Most of the estimated 200 to 300 surviving coins show extensive wear. Some AU and MS coins exist, several in choice and gem state, perhaps from among the four examples that Mint Director David Rittenhouse is said to have reserved for himself.

GRADING STANDARDS

MS-60 to 70 (Mint State). *Obverse:* No wear is visible. Luster ranges from nearly full at MS-60 to frosty at MS-65 or higher. Toning often masks the surface, so careful inspection is required. *Reverse:* No wear is visible. The field around the eagle is lustrous, ranging from not completely full at MS-60 to deep and frosty at MS-65 and higher.

1792. Graded MS-64.

AU-50, 53, 55, 58 (About Uncirculated).
Obverse: Light wear is seen on the cheek and on the hair (not as easily observable, as certain areas of the hair may be lightly struck). Luster ranges from light and mostly in protected areas at AU-50, to extensive at AU-58. Friction is evident in the field, less so in the higher ranges. *Reverse:* Light wear is seen on the eagle, but is less noticeable on the letters. Luster ranges from light and mostly in protected areas at AU-50, to extensive at AU-58. Friction is evident in the field, less in the higher ranges.

1792. Graded AU-55.

EF-40, 45 (Extremely Fine). *Obverse:* The hair shows medium wear to the right of the face and on the bust end. The fields have no luster. Some luster may be seen among the hair strands and letters. *Reverse:* The eagle shows medium wear on its breast and the right wing, less so on the left wing. HALF DISME shows wear. The fields have no luster. Some luster may be seen among the design elements and letters.

1792. Graded EF-40.

VF-20, 30 (Very Fine). *Obverse:* More wear is seen on the hair, including to the right of the forehead and face, where only a few strands may be seen. The hair tips at the right are well detailed. The bust end is flat on its high area. Letters all show light wear. *Reverse:* The eagle displays significant wear, with its central part flat and most of the detail missing from the right wing. Letters all show light wear.

1792. Graded VF-30.

F-12, 15 (Fine). *Obverse:* The portrait, above the neck, is essentially flat, but details of the eye, the nose, and, to a lesser extent, the lips can be seen. The bust end and neck truncation are flat. Some hair detail can be seen to the right of the neck and behind the head, with individual strands blended into heavy groups. Both obverse and reverse at this grade and lower are apt to show marks, minor digs, and other evidence of handling.

1792. Graded F-12.

Reverse: Wear is more advanced than on a Very Fine coin, with significant reduction of the height of the lettering, and with some letters weak in areas, especially if the rim nearby is flat.

VG-8, 10 (Very Good). *Obverse:* The head has less detail than a Fine coin and is essentially flat except at the neck. Some hair, in thick strands, can be seen. The letters show extensive wear, but are readable. *Reverse:* The eagle is mostly flat, and the letters are well worn, some of them incomplete at the borders. Detail overall is weaker than on the obverse.

1792. Graded VG-10.

G-4, 6 (Good). *Obverse:* There is hardly any detail on the portrait, except that the eye can be seen, as well as some thick hair tips. The date is clear. Around the border the edges of the letters are worn away, and some are weak overall. *Reverse:* The eagle is only in outline form. The letters are very worn, with some missing.

1792. Graded G-6.

AG-3 (About Good). *Obverse:* Extreme wear has reduced the portrait to an even shallower state. Around the border some letters are worn away completely, some partially. The 1792 date can be seen but is weak and may be partly missing. *Reverse:* Traces of the eagle will remain and there are scattered letters and fragments of letters. Most of the coin is worn flat.

Illustrated coin: The scratches on the obverse should be noted.

1792. Graded AG-3.

	Mintage	Cert	Avg	%MS	AG-3	G-4	VG-8	F-12	VF-20	EF-40	AU-50	MS-60	MS-62
1792 †	1,500	41	47.3	39%	$8,500	$20,000	$27,500	$40,000	$80,000	$110,000	$175,000	$250,000	$325,000
	Auctions: $212,750, AU-58, March 2012												

† Ranked in the *100 Greatest U.S. Coins* (fourth edition).

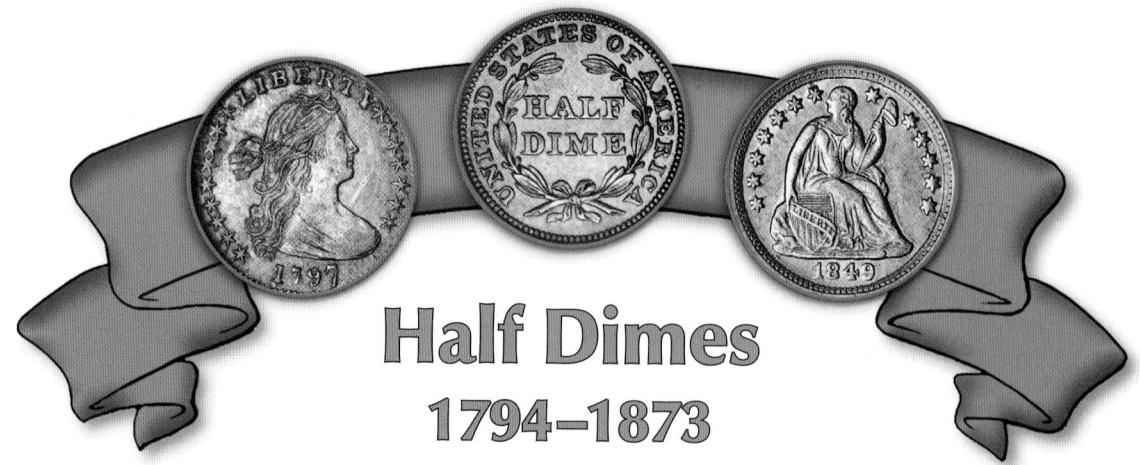

Half Dimes
1794–1873

AN OVERVIEW OF HALF DIMES

The first half dimes, dated 1794 and of the Flowing Hair type, were not actually struck until 1795. In that year additional half dimes with the 1795 date were made. In 1796 and 1797 the short-lived Draped Bust obverse combined with the Small Eagle reverse was used, after which no half dimes were struck until 1801. From that year through 1805, excepting 1804, the Draped Bust obverse was used in combination with the Heraldic Eagle reverse. Then followed a long span of years without any coinage of the denomination. In 1829 the laying of the cornerstone for the second Philadelphia Mint precipitated a new issue, the Capped Bust design, some examples of which were made for the ceremony. Production was resumed for circulation, and half dimes of this motif were made through 1837. In that year the Liberty Seated motif, by Christian Gobrecht, was introduced, to be continued without interruption through 1873, although there were a number of design modifications and changes during that span.

Assembling a set of the different half-dime types is a challenge for the collector. The 1794 and 1795, Flowing Hair, half dimes are fairly scarce at all levels and are quite rare in choice Mint State. Then come the Draped Bust obverse, Small Eagle reverse half dimes of 1796 and 1797. In the late 1960s, researcher Jim Ruddy found that of the various silver types (including the more famous 1796–1797 half dollars), half dimes of this type were the hardest to complete a photographic set of, from the lowest grades to the highest.

Draped Bust obverse, Heraldic Eagle reverse half dimes of the 1800–1805 years are scarce in all grades, more so than generally realized. In Mint State they are very rare, although on occasion some dated 1800 turn up (not often for the others). Finding a *sharply struck* example is next to impossible, and a collector may have to give up on this aspect and settle for one that has some weakness in areas.

Capped Bust half dimes and the several variations of Liberty Seated half dimes will pose no problem at all, and with some small amount of patience a collector will be able to find a sharply struck example in nearly any grade desired.

FOR THE COLLECTOR AND INVESTOR: HALF DIMES AS A SPECIALTY

Collecting half dimes by early die varieties of 1794–1837, and/or by dates and mintmarks (beginning with the 1838-O), has captured the fancy of many numismatists over the years. As these coins are so small it is necessary to have a magnifying glass when studying the series—something the collector of silver dollars and double eagles does not need.

One of the earlier enthusiasts in the field was Philadelphia attorney and numismatist Harold P. Newlin, who in 1883 issued *A Classification of the Early Half Dimes of the United States*. Newlin's two

The new design upon the resumption of the denomination in 1829 was created by Chief Engraver William Kneass. It is thought to have been based upon an earlier design by John Reich.

favorite varieties were the 1792 half disme and the rare 1802, and after reading his enticing prose about the desirability of each, no doubt some collectors in 1883 put both coins on their "must have" lists.

Among early half dimes the rarest and most expensive is the 1802. In 1883 Newlin listed just 16 examples known to him. Although no one has compiled an up-to-date registry, it is likely that fewer than 30 exist. Most are well worn. Other early half dimes range from rare to very rare.

Capped Bust half dimes of the 1829–1837 years are all easily available as dates, but some of the die varieties are very rare. Today, most half dimes on the market are not attributed by varieties, making the search for such things rewarding when a rarity is found for the price of a regular coin.

In 1978 the numismatic world was startled to learn that Chicago dealer Edward Milas had located an 1870-S half dime, a variety not earlier known to exist and not listed in the annual Mint reports. Other than this coin, still unique today, the dates and mints in the Liberty Seated series 1837 to 1873-S are readily collectible by date and mint, with no great rarities. There are several very curious varieties within that span, the most interesting of which may be the 1858, Over Inverted Date. The date was first punched into the die upside down, the error was noted, and then it was corrected.

FLOWING HAIR (1794–1795)

Designer: *Unknown.* **Engraver:** *Robert Scot.*
Weight: *1.35 grams.* **Composition:** *.8924 silver, .1076 copper.*
Diameter: *Approximately 16.5 mm.* **Edge:** *Reeded.* **Mint:** *Philadelphia.*

Logan-McCloskey–8.

History. Half dimes dated 1794 and 1795, of the Flowing Hair type, were all struck in the calendar year 1795, although dies were ready by the end of 1794. The Flowing Hair motif was also used on half dollars and silver dollars of the same years, but not on other denominations.

Striking and Sharpness. Many Flowing Hair half dimes have problems of one sort or another, including adjustment marks (from the planchet being filed down to proper weight) and/or light striking in some areas. On the obverse, check the hair and stars, and on the reverse the breast of the eagle. It may not be possible to find a *needle-sharp* example, but with some extensive searching a fairly decent strike can be obtained. Sharp striking and excellent eye appeal add dramatically to the value.

Availability. Examples appear on the market with frequency, typically in lower circulated grades. Probably 250 to 500 could be classified as MS, most of these dated 1795. Some searching is needed to locate choice examples in any grade. As a rule, half dimes are more readily available than are half dollars and dollars of the same design, and when found are usually more attractive and have fewer problems.

GRADING STANDARDS

MS-60 to 70 (Mint State). *Obverse:* At MS-60 some abrasion and contact marks are evident, most noticeably on the cheek and in the fields. Luster is present, but may be dull or lifeless, and interrupted in patches. At MS-63, contact marks are very few, and abrasion is hard to detect except under magnification. An MS-65 coin has no abrasion, and contact marks are so minute as to require magnification. Luster should be full and rich. Coins

1795; LM-10. Graded MS-63.

graded above MS-65 are more theoretical than actual for this type—but they do exist, and are defined by having fewer marks as perfection is approached. *Reverse:* Comments apply as for the obverse, except that abrasion and contact marks are most noticeable on the eagle at the center. The field area is small and is protected by lettering and the wreath, and in any given grade shows fewer marks than on the obverse.

Illustrated coin: This coin reveals increased olive and blue iridescence under bright light. The central weakness is typical for the striking of this die marriage.

AU-50, 53, 55, 58 (About Uncirculated). *Obverse:* Light wear is seen on the hair area immediately to the left of the face and neck, on the cheek, and on the top of the neck truncation, more so at AU-50 than at AU–53 or 55. An AU-58 coin will have minimal traces of wear. An AU-50 will have luster in protected areas among the stars and letters, with little in the open fields or on the portrait. At AU-58, most luster is present in the fields, but is worn away

1794; LM-3. Graded AU-55.

on the highest parts of the motifs. *Reverse:* Light wear is seen on the eagle's body and right wing. At AU-50, detail is lost in most feathers in this area. However, striking can play a part, and some coins are weak to begin with. Light wear is seen on the wreath and lettering. Luster is the best key to actual wear. This will range from perhaps 20% remaining in protected areas at AU-50 to nearly full mint bloom at AU-58.

Illustrated coin: Liberty's hair displays impressive detail for this grade.

EF-40, 45 (Extremely Fine). *Obverse:* More wear is evident on the portrait, especially on the hair to the left of the face and neck; the cheek; and the tip of the neck truncation. Excellent detail remains in low-relief areas of the hair. The stars show wear, as do the date and letters. Luster, if present at all, is minimal and in protected areas. *Reverse:* The eagle, this being the focal point to check, shows more wear. Observe in combination with a knowl-

1794; LM-2. Graded EF-40.

edge of the die variety, to determine the sharpness of the coin when it was first struck. Some were flat at the center at the time they were made. Additional wear is on the wreath and letters, but many details are present. Some luster may be seen in protected areas, and if present is slightly more abundant than on the obverse.

VF-20, 30 (Very Fine). *Obverse:* The hair is well worn at the VF-20 level, less so at VF-30. The strands are blended so as to be heavy. The cheek shows only slight relief, and the tip of the neck truncation is flat. The stars have more wear, making them appear larger (an optical illusion). *Reverse:* The body of the eagle shows few if any feathers, while the wings have about half of the feathers visible, depending on the strike. The leaves lack

1795; LM-8. Graded VF-30.

detail and are in outline form. Scattered, non-disfiguring marks are normal for this and lower grades. Any major defects should be noted separately.

F-12, 15 (Fine). *Obverse:* Wear is more extensive than on a Very Fine coin, reducing the definition of the thick strands of hair. The cheek has less detail, and the stars appear larger. The rim is distinct and many denticles remain visible. *Reverse:* Wear is more extensive. Now, feather details are reduced, mostly remaining on the right wing. The wreath and lettering are more worn, and the rim is usually weak in areas, although some denticles can be seen.

1794; LM-1. Graded F-12.

Illustrated coin: Two light adjustment marks on the lower left of the portrait date from the time of striking.

VG-8, 10 (Very Good). *Obverse:* The portrait is mostly seen in outline form, with most hair strands gone, although the tips at the lower left are clear. The ear is discernible, as is the eye. The stars appear larger still, again an illusion. The rim is weak in areas. LIBERTY and the date are readable and usually full, although some letters may be weak at their tops. *Reverse:* The eagle is mostly an outline, although some traces of feathers may be seen

1795; LM-9. Graded VG-8.

in the tail and the lower part of the inside of the right wing. The rim is worn, as are the letters, with some weak, but the motto is readable.

G-4, 6 (Good). *Obverse:* Wear is more extensive, and some stars may be missing or only partially visible. The head is an outline, although a few elements of thick hair strands may be seen. The eye is visible only in outline form. The rim is well worn or even missing. LIBERTY is worn, and parts of some letters may be missing, but elements of all are readable. The date is readable, but worn. *Reverse:* The eagle is flat and discernible in outline

1795; LM-8. Graded G-6.

form. The wreath is well worn. Some of the letters may be partly missing. At this level some "averaging" can be done. If the letters are stronger than usual in one area, but some are missing in another area, the coin can still qualify as G-4.

Illustrated coin: There are several adjustment marks on the obverse, but this coin lacks the bisecting obverse die crack typical of later issues struck from this die pair. The reverse die on this coin was rotated 20 degrees out of the normal alignment.

AG-3 (About Good). *Obverse:* Wear is so extensive that the coin is barely identifiable. The head is in outline form, LIBERTY is mostly gone, and the date, while readable, may be partially missing. *Reverse:* The reverse is well worn with parts of the wreath and lettering missing.

1794; LM-4. Graded AG-3.

	Mintage	Cert	Avg	%MS	AG-3	G-4	VG-8	F-12	VF-20	EF-40	AU-50	MS-60
1794	(a)	143	50.5	41%	$850	$1,500	$1,800	$2,850	$4,000	$7,500	$11,000	$17,500
	Auctions: $129,250, MS-65, August 2014; $5,875, EF-45, March 2015; $6,463, EF-40, August 2014; $7,638, F-12, August 2016											
1795	86,416	394	49.3	34%	$550	$1,350	$1,600	$2,000	$3,250	$6,000	$8,000	$11,500
	Auctions: $73,438, MS-66, September 2015; $58,750, MS-65, March 2015; $734, F-12, September 2015; $494, F-12, September 2016											

a. Included in 1795 mintage figure.

DRAPED BUST, SMALL EAGLE REVERSE (1796–1797)

Designer: *Probably Gilbert Stuart.* **Engraver:** *Robert Scot.*
Weight: *1.35 grams.* **Composition:** *.8924 silver, .1076 copper.*
Diameter: *Approximately 16.5 mm.* **Edge:** *Reeded.* **Mint:** *Philadelphia.*

LM-2.

History. Although the Draped Bust obverse design was used on various copper and silver coins circa 1795 to 1808, it was employed in combination with the *Small Eagle* reverse only on silver coins of 1795 to 1798—for the half dime series, only in 1796 and 1797.

Striking and Sharpness. Most 1796–1797 half dimes are weak in at least one area. Points to check for sharpness include the hair of Miss Liberty, the centers of the stars, the bust line, and, on the reverse, the center of the eagle. Check for planchet adjustment marks (these are infrequent). Denticles around the border are usually decent, but may vary in strength from one part of the border to another. Sharp striking and excellent eye appeal add to the value dramatically.

Availability. This type is fairly scarce in *any* grade; in MS-63 and finer, no more than a few dozen examples have been traced. As is advisable for other early silver types, beware of deeply toned or vividly iridescent-toned pieces whose flawed surface characters are obscured by the toning, but which are offered as MS; in truth some of these are barely better than EF.

GRADING STANDARDS

MS-60 to 70 (Mint State). *Obverse:* At MS-60 some abrasion and contact marks are evident, most noticeably on the cheek, on the drapery, and in the right field. Luster is present, but may be dull or lifeless, and interrupted in patches. At MS-63, contact marks are very few, and abrasion is hard to detect except under magnification, although this type is sometimes graded liberally due to its rarity. An MS-65 coin has no abrasion, and contact

1797, 16 Stars; LM-2, Valentine-4. Graded MS-62.

marks are so minute as to require magnification. Luster should be full and rich. Coins graded above MS-65 are more theoretical than actual for this type—but they do exist, and are defined by having fewer marks as perfection is approached. *Reverse:* Comments apply as for the obverse, except that abrasion and marks are most noticeable on the eagle at the center, a situation complicated by the fact that this area was often flatly struck. Grading is best done by the obverse, then verified by the reverse. The field area is small and is protected by lettering and the wreath, and in any given grade shows fewer marks than on the obverse.

Illustrated coin: Note the clash marks in the right obverse field, which are typical for this die variety.

AU-50, 53, 55, 58 (About Uncirculated). *Obverse:* Light wear is seen on the hair area above the ear and extending to left of the forehead, on the ribbon, and on the bosom—more so at AU-50 than at AU–53 or 55. An AU-58 coin has minimal traces of wear. An AU-50 coin has luster in protected areas among the stars and letters, with little in the open fields or on the portrait. At AU-58, most luster is present in the fields, but is worn away on the high-

1796, LIKERTY; LM-1. Graded AU-50.

est parts of the motifs. *Reverse:* Light wear is seen on the eagle's body (keep in mind this area might be lightly struck) and edges of the wings. Light wear is seen on the wreath and lettering. Luster is the best key to actual wear. This ranges from perhaps 20% remaining in protected areas at AU-50 to nearly full mint bloom at AU-58.

Illustrated coin: This is the LIKERTY variety, its fanciful name derived from the top and bottom lines of the B being defective.

EF-40, 45 (Extremely Fine). *Obverse:* More wear is evident on the upper hair area and the ribbon and on the drapery and bosom. Excellent detail will remain in low relief areas of the hair. The stars show wear as will the date and letters. Luster, if present at all, is minimal and in protected areas. *Reverse:* The eagle shows more wear, this being the focal point to check. On most examples, many feathers remain on the interior areas of the wings.

1796, LIKERTY; LM-1. Graded EF-40.

Check the eagle in combination with a knowledge of the die variety to determine the sharpness of the coin when it was first struck. Additional wear is evident on the wreath and letters, but many details are present. Some luster may be seen in protected areas and, if present, is slightly more abundant than on the obverse.

VF-20, 30 (Very Fine). *Obverse:* The higher-relief areas of hair are well worn at VF-20, less so at VF-30. The drapery and bosom show extensive wear. The stars have more wear, making them appear larger (an optical illusion seen on most worn silver coins of this era). *Reverse:* The body of the eagle shows few if any feathers, while the wings have about half of the feathers visible, depending on the strike. The leaves lack most detail

1796, LIKERTY; LM-1. Graded VF-30.

and are in outline form. Scattered, non-disfiguring marks are normal for this and lower grades; any major distractions should be noted separately.

F-12, 15 (Fine). *Obverse:* Wear is more extensive than on a Very Fine coin. Wear is particularly noticeable on the hair, face, and bosom, and the stars appear larger. About half the hair detail remains, most noticeably behind the neck and shoulder. The rim may be partially worn away and may blend into the field. *Reverse:* Wear is more extensive. Feather details are diminished, with fewer than half remaining on the wings. The wreath

1797, 13 Stars; LM-4. Graded F-15.

and lettering are worn further, and the rim is usually weak in areas, although some denticles can be seen.

VG-8, 10 (Very Good). *Obverse:* The portrait is mostly seen in outline form, with most hair strands gone, although there is some definition at the back of the hair and behind the shoulder. The ear is discernible, as is the eye. The stars appear larger still, again an illusion. The rim is weak in areas. LIBERTY and the date are readable and usually full, although some letters may be weak at their tops. *Reverse:* The eagle is mostly an outline,

1796, LIKERTY; LM-1. Graded VG-8.

with parts blending into the field (on lighter strikes). The rim is worn, as are the letters, with some weak, but the motto is readable.

G-4, 6 (Good). *Obverse:* Wear is more extensive, and some stars may be partly missing. The head is an outline. The eye is visible only in outline form. The rim is well worn or even missing in areas. LIBERTY is worn, and parts of some letters may be missing, but elements of all should be readable. The date is readable, but worn. *Reverse:* The eagle is flat and discernible in outline form, and may be blending into the field. The wreath is well

1797, 16 Stars. Graded G-4.

worn. Some of the letters may be partly missing. At this level some "averaging" can be done. If the letters are stronger than usual in one area, but some are missing in another area, the coin can still qualify as G-4.

AG-3 (About Good). *Obverse:* Wear is so extensive that the coin is barely identifiable. The head is in outline form. LIBERTY is mostly gone, as are some of the stars. The date, while readable, may be partially worn away. *Reverse:* The reverse is well worn, with parts of the wreath and lettering missing.

1796, LIKERTY; LM-1. Graded AG-3.

	1796, 6 Over 5		1796, LIKERTY	

	1797, 15 Stars	1797, 16 Stars	1797, 13 Stars

	Mintage	Cert	Avg	%MS	AG-3	G-4	VG-8	F-12	VF-20	EF-40	AU-50	MS-60	MS-63
1796, 6 Over 5	10,230	15	52.2	67%	$700	$1,850	$2,500	$4,000	$5,250	$9,500	$15,000	$25,000	$40,000
Auctions: $31,725, MS-63, August 2013													
1796	(a)	18	50.7	33%	$700	$1,800	$2,200	$3,500	$5,000	$8,750	$13,500	$16,500	$35,000
Auctions: No auction records available.													
1796, LIKERTY (b)	(a)	55	47.1	27%	$700	$1,500	$1,800	$3,450	$4,750	$8,750	$12,500	$16,000	$35,000
Auctions: $17,625, MS-61, September 2013; $1,586, Fair-2, October 2014; $676, Fair-2, October 2014													
1797, 15 Stars	44,527	34	45.1	18%	$700	$1,500	$1,800	$3,450	$4,750	$8,750	$12,500	$16,000	$25,000
Auctions: $70,500, MS-64, June 2014; $7,638, AU-55, October 2014; $7,638, AU-53, March 2015; $494, G-4, September 2015													
1797, 16 Stars	(c)	23	45.3	35%	$700	$1,500	$1,800	$3,450	$4,750	$8,750	$12,500	$16,000	$25,000
Auctions: $54,344, MS-65, June 2014; $734, Fair-2, October 2014; $1,763, Fair-2, August 2014													
1797, 13 Stars	(c)	6	39.2	0%	$750	$2,000	$3,500	$4,500	$6,500	$13,500	$25,000	$40,000	$65,000
Auctions: $25,850, AU-55, February 2013													

a. Included in 1796, 6 Over 5, mintage figure. b. A die imperfection makes the B in LIKERTY somewhat resemble a K. c. Included in 1797, 15 Stars, mintage figure.

DRAPED BUST,
HERALDIC EAGLE REVERSE (1800–1805)

Designer: *Robert Scot.* **Weight:** *1.35 grams.* **Composition:** *.8924 silver, .1076 copper.* **Diameter:** *Approximately 16.5 mm.* **Edge:** *Reeded.* **Mint:** *Philadelphia.*

LM-1.

History. The combination of Draped Bust obverse / Heraldic Eagle reverse was used in the silver half dime series from 1800 to 1805. The obverse style, standardized with 13 stars, is the same as used in 1796 and 1797. During this span the rare 1802 was produced, and none were minted with the date 1804.

Striking and Sharpness. Most 1800–1805 half dimes are lightly struck in one area or another. The obverse stars usually show some weakness. On many coins the central details of Miss Liberty are not sharp. On the reverse the upper right of the shield and the adjacent part of the eagle's wing are often soft, and several or even most stars may be lightly defined (sharp stars show sharply peaked centers); high parts of the clouds are often weak. The area on the reverse opposite the bosom of Miss Liberty may be flat or weak, due to the metal having to flow in both directions when the coins were struck. (The area curving obliquely up and to the right of the eagle's head—exactly mirroring the curvature of the bust on the obverse—is especially prone to weakness of strike.) Denticles are likely to be weak or missing in areas. Many have Mint-caused adjustment marks, from overweight planchets being filed down to proper specifications. In summary, *a sharply struck coin is a goal, not necessarily a reality*. In this series, sharp striking and excellent eye appeal will add to a coin's value dramatically, this being particularly true for all issues from 1801 to 1805.

Availability. This is a challenging type to find with nice eye appeal. Many toned pieces have been recolored to hide flaws or to improve eye appeal. Some are porous or have other problems. The majority of pieces surviving today are dated 1800, and nearly all of the AU or finer coins are of this date.

GRADING STANDARDS

MS-60 to 70 (Mint State). *Obverse:* At MS-60 some abrasion and contact marks are evident, most noticeably on the cheek, on the drapery, and in the right field. Luster is present, but may be dull or lifeless, and interrupted in patches. At MS-63, contact marks are very few, and abrasion is hard to detect except under magnification, although this type is sometimes graded liberally due to its rarity. An MS-65 coin will have no abrasion,

1800; LM-1, V-1. Graded MS-63.

and contact marks are so minute as to require magnification. Luster should be full and rich. Coins graded above MS-65 are more theoretical than actual for this type—but they do exist, and are defined by having fewer marks as perfection is approached. *Reverse:* Comments apply as for the obverse, except that abrasion and contact marks are most noticeable on the eagle's neck, the tips of the wing, and the tail. The field area is complex—with stars above the eagle, the arrows and olive branch, and other features, there is not much open space. Accordingly, marks will not be as noticeable as on the obverse.

AU-50, 53, 55, 58 (About Uncirculated). *Obverse:* Light wear is seen on the hair area above the ear and extending to left of the forehead, on the ribbon, and on the bosom, more so at AU-50 than at AU–53 or 55. An AU-58 coin will have minimal traces of wear. An AU-50 coin will have luster in protected areas among the stars and letters, with little in the open fields or on the portrait. At AU-58, most luster is present in the fields,

1803, Large 8; LM-2. Graded AU-58.

but is worn away on the highest parts of the motifs. *Reverse:* Comments as for Mint State coins, except that the eagle's neck, the tips and top of the wings, the clouds, and the tail show noticeable wear, as do other features. Luster ranges from perhaps 20% remaining in protected areas at AU-50 to nearly full mint bloom at AU-58. Often the reverse of this type retains much more luster than the obverse.

 Illustrated coin: Note the areas of rich, blue toning.

EF-40, 45 (Extremely Fine). *Obverse:* More wear is evident on the upper hair area and the ribbon, and on the drapery and bosom. Excellent detail remains in low-relief areas of the hair. The stars show wear, as do the date and letters. Luster, if present at all, is minimal and only in protected areas. *Reverse:* Wear is greater than on an About Uncirculated coin, overall. The neck lacks feather detail on its highest points. Feathers lose some detail near

1800; LM-1. Graded EF-45.

the edges of the wings, and some areas of the horizontal lines in the shield may be blended together. Some traces of luster may be seen, more so at EF-45 than at EF-40.

   Illustrated coin: The obverse cud break is as struck.

VF-20, 30 (Very Fine). *Obverse:* The higher-relief areas of hair are well worn at VF-20, less so at VF-30. The drapery and bosom show extensive wear. The stars have more wear, making them appear larger (an optical illusion seen on most worn silver coins of this era). *Reverse:* Wear is greater, including on the shield and wing feathers. Star centers are flat. Other areas have lost detail as well.

1800; LM-1. Graded VF-20.

F-12, 15 (Fine). *Obverse:* Wear is more extensive than on a Very Fine coin, particularly noticeable on the hair, face, and bosom, and the stars appear larger. About half the hair detail remains, most noticeably behind the neck and shoulder. The rim may be partially worn away and may blend into the field. *Reverse:* Wear is even more extensive, with the shield and wing feathers being points to observe. The incuse E PLURIBUS UNUM

1801; LM-2. Graded F-15.

may have a few letters worn away. The clouds all seem to be connected. The stars are weak. Parts of the border and lettering may be weak.

VG-8, 10 (Very Good). *Obverse:* The portrait is mostly seen in outline form, with most hair strands gone, although there is some definition at the back of the hair and behind the shoulder. The ear is discernible, as is the eye. The stars appear larger still, again an illusion. The rim is weak in areas. LIBERTY and the date are readable and usually full, although some letters may be weak at their tops. *Reverse:* Half or so of the letters in the motto are worn away. Most feather details are worn away, although separation of some of the lower feathers may be seen. Some stars are faint. The border blends into the field in areas, and some letters are weak.

1800; LM-1. Graded VG-8.

G-4, 6 (Good). *Obverse:* Some stars may be partly missing. The head is an outline. The eye is visible only in outline form. The rim is well worn or even missing in areas. LIBERTY is worn, and parts of some letters may be missing, but elements of all should be readable. The date is readable, but worn. *Reverse:* The upper part of the eagle is flat, and feathers are noticeable only at the lower edge of the wings and do not have detail. The upper part of the shield is flat. Only a few letters of the motto can be seen. The rim is worn extensively, and a few letters may be missing.

1801; LM-2. Graded G-6.

AG-3 (About Good). *Obverse:* Wear is so extensive that the coin is barely identifiable. The head is in outline form. LIBERTY is mostly gone; same for the stars. The date, while readable, may be partially worn away. *Reverse:* Extensive wear is seen overall, with the rim worn away and some areas worn smooth. The eagle can be discerned in outline form, but not necessarily completely. A few stray motto letters may remain.

1800. Graded AG-3.

1800, LIBEKTY

	Mintage	Cert	Avg	%MS	AG-3	G-4	VG-8	F-12	VF-20	EF-40	AU-50	MS-60	MS-63
1800	24,000	162	45.4	23%	$450	$1,100	$1,500	$2,000	$3,000	$6,000	$8,500	$12,500	$20,000
	Auctions: $25,850, MS-64, August 2014; $4,994, AU-50, October 2014; $2,350, EF-40, November 2014; $676, EF-40, October 2015												
1800, LIBEKTY (a)	16,000	44	45.3	30%	$450	$1,200	$1,750	$2,500	$3,250	$6,200	$8,500	$13,000	$22,000
	Auctions: $31,725, MS-64, April 2014; $3,086, VF-25, October 2014; $617, Fair-2, October 2014												

a. A defective die punch gives the R in LIBERTY the appearance of a K.

| | 1803, Large 8 | | | | 1803, Small 8 | | | | | | |

	Mintage	Cert	Avg	%MS	AG-3	G-4	VG-8	F-12	VF-20	EF-40	AU-50	MS-60	MS-63
1801	27,760	28	35.8	18%	$450	$1,500	$2,250	$3,000	$4,000	$6,500	$10,000	$17,500	$27,500
Auctions: $5,581, EF-40, February 2014													
1802 †	3,060	3	50.0	0%	$22,500	$45,000	$65,000	$85,000	$125,000	$250,000	$350,000		
Auctions: $61,688, AU-58, August 2015; $3,290, VF-25, August 2016; $823, VG-8, August 2016; $541, AG-3, September 2015													
1803, Large 8	37,850	10	34.1	20%	$700	$1,100	$1,450	$2,000	$3,000	$6,500	$9,000	$14,000	$25,000
Auctions: $7,050, AU-50, February 2014													
1803, Small 8	(b)	2	58.0	50%	$700	$1,100	$1,500	$2,500	$3,250	$7,000	$10,000	$20,000	$35,000
Auctions: $5,922, EF-35, April 2013; $646, VF-20, November 2016; $999, Fair-2, October 2014													
1805	15,600	30	27.9	3%	$700	$1,100	$1,450	$2,750	$3,500	$9,000	$22,500	$55,000	
Auctions: $1,998, VF-35, August 2015; $823, VF-20, November 2016; $1,058, F-15, February 2015; $646, VG-10, July 2016													

† Ranked in the *100 Greatest U.S. Coins* (fourth edition). **b.** Included in 1803, Large 8, mintage figure.

CAPPED BUST (1829–1837)

Engraver: *William Kneass, after a design by John Reich.* **Weight:** *1.35 grams (changed to 1.34 grams in 1837).*
Composition: *.8924 silver, .1076 copper (changed to .900 silver, .100 copper in 1837).*
Diameter: *Approximately 15.5 mm.* **Edge:** *Reeded.* **Mint:** *Philadelphia.*

Circulation Strike
LM-7.

Proof
LM-4.

History. Half dimes of the Capped Bust design were first struck the morning of July 4, 1829, to be included in the cornerstone time capsule of the new (second) Philadelphia Mint building and, presumably, to have some inexpensive coins on hand for distribution as souvenirs. Engraver John Reich's design was not new; it had been used on half dollars as early as 1807. It was logical to employ it on the new half dime, a coin that had not been made since 1805. The new half dimes proved popular and remained in circulation for many years.

Striking and Sharpness. Striking varies among Capped Bust half dimes, and most show lightness in one area or another. On the obverse, check the hair details to the left of the eye, as well as the star centers. On the reverse, check the eagle's feathers and neck. The motto, which can be a problem on certain other coins of this design (notably half dollars), is usually bold on the half dimes. Denticles range from well defined to somewhat indistinct, and, in general, are sharper on the obverse than on the reverse.

Proofs. Proofs were struck in small quantities, generally as part of silver Proof sets, although perhaps some were made to mark the Mint cornerstone event mentioned above; facts are scarce. True Proofs have fully mirrored fields. Scrutinize deeply toned pieces (deep toning often masks the true nature of a coin, e.g., if it is not a true Proof, or if it has been cleaned or repaired). Some pieces attributed as "Proofs" are not Proofs. This advice applies across the entire Capped Bust silver series.

Availability. Finding an example in any desired grade should not be a challenge. Finding one with Full Details will take more time. Connoisseurship is required at the MS level, given the high value of these coins.

GRADING STANDARDS

MS-60 to 70 (Mint State). *Obverse:* At MS-60 some abrasion and contact marks are evident, most noticeably on the cheek, on the hair below the left part of LIBERTY, and on the area near the drapery clasp. Luster is present, but may be dull or lifeless, and interrupted in patches. At MS-63, contact marks are very few, and abrasion is hard to detect except under magnification. An MS-65 coin has no abrasion, and has contact marks so

1830; LM-3. Graded MS-65.

minute as to require magnification. Luster should be full and rich, usually more so on half dimes than larger coins of the Capped Bust type. Grades above MS-65 are seen now and again, and are defined by having fewer marks as perfection is approached. *Reverse:* Comments apply as for the obverse, except that abrasion and contact marks are most noticeable on the eagle's neck, the top of the wings, the claws, and the flat band that surrounds the incuse motto. The field is mainly protected by design elements and does not show abrasion as much as does the obverse.

AU-50, 53, 55, 58 (About Uncirculated). *Obverse:* Light wear is seen on the cap, the hair below LIBERTY, the hair near the clasp, and the drapery at the bosom. At AU-58, the luster is extensive except in the open area of the field, especially to the right. At AU–50 and 53, luster remains only in protected areas. *Reverse:* Wear is visible on the eagle's neck, the top of the wings, the claws, and the flat band above the eagle. An AU-58 coin will have

1829; LM-4. Graded AU-58.

nearly full luster. At AU–50 and 53, there will still be significant luster, more than on the obverse.

Illustrated coin: Note the rings of toning on the obverse, displaying russet, cobalt, and rosy iridescence.

EF-40, 45 (Extremely Fine). *Obverse:* Wear is most noticeable on the higher areas of the hair. The cap shows more wear, as does the cheek. Stars, usually protected by the rim, still show their centers (unless lightly struck). Luster, if present, is in protected areas among the star points and close to the portrait. *Reverse:* The wings show wear on the higher areas of the feathers, and some details are lost. Feathers in the neck are light. The eagle's claws and the

1837, Small 5 C.; LM-4. Graded EF-40.

leaves show wear. Luster may be present in protected areas, even if there is little or none on the obverse.

VF-20, 30 (Very Fine). *Obverse:* Wear has caused most of the hair to be combined into thick tresses without delicate features. The curl on the neck is flat. Most stars, unless they were weakly struck, retain their interior lines. *Reverse:* Wear is most evident on the eagle's neck, to the left of the shield, and on the leaves and claws. Most feathers in the wing remain distinct.

1834; LM-2. Graded VF-30.

F-12, 15 (Fine). *Obverse:* Wear is more extensive, with much of the hair blended together. The drapery is indistinct at its upper edge. Stars have lost some detail at the centers, but still have relief (are not flat). *Reverse:* Wear is more extensive, now with only about half of the feathers remaining on the wings. Some of the horizontal lines in the shield may be worn away.

1830; LM-6. Graded F-12.

VG-8, 10 (Very Good). *Obverse:* The hair is less distinct, with the area surrounding the face blended into the facial features. LIBERTY is complete, but weak in areas. The stars are nearly flat, although some interior detail can be seen on certain strikings. *Reverse:* Feathers are fewer and mostly appear on the right wing. Other details are weaker. All lettering remains easily visible.

1829. Graded VG-8.

G-4, 6 (Good). *Obverse:* The portrait is mostly in outline, with few interior details discernible. LIBERTY may still be readable or may be partially worn away, depending on the variety. Stars are flat at their centers. *Reverse:* The eagle mostly is in outline form, although some feathers can be seen in the right wing. All letters around the border are clear. E PLURIBUS UNUM may be weak, sometimes with a few letters worn away.

1829; LM-8. Graded G-6.

AG-3 (About Good). *Obverse:* The portrait is an outline, although traces of LIBERTY can still be seen. The rim is worn down, and some stars are weak. The date remains clear. *Reverse:* The reverse shows more wear overall than the obverse, with the rim indistinct in areas and many letters worn away.

1835, Small Date, Large 5 C. Graded AG-3.

PF-60 to 70 (Proof). *Obverse and Reverse:* Proofs that are extensively cleaned and have many hairlines, or that are dull and grainy, are lower level, such as PF–60 to 62. These are not of great interest to specialists unless they are of rare die varieties (such as 1829, LM–1 to 3, described in the image caption). With medium hairlines, an assigned grade of PF-64 may be in order, and with relatively few hairlines, gem PF-65. PF-66 should have

1829; LM-2, V-3. Graded PF-67+.

hairlines so delicate that magnification is needed to see them. Above that, a Proof should be free of such lines. Grading is highly subjective with early Proofs, and eye appeal also is a factor.

Illustrated coin: Stunning in sharpness of strike and attractiveness of toning, this coin is the finest-known Proof of this type.

	Mintage	Cert	Avg	%MS	G-4	VG-8	F-12	VF-20	EF-40	AU-50	MS-60 PF-60	MS-63 PF-63	MS-65 PF-65
1829	1,230,000	735	57.6	63%	$60	$75	$100	$125	$200	$300	$400	$925	$3,000
	Auctions: $881, MS-63, October 2015; $705, MS-63, January 2015; $353, MS-60, June 2015; $329, AU-58, September 2015												
1829, Proof	20–30	8	64.4								$4,500	$10,000	$35,000
	Auctions: $36,719, PF-65Cam, January 2014												
1830	1,240,000	639	57.3	66%	$50	$65	$80	$115	$175	$275	$375	$850	$2,500
	Auctions: $852, MS-63, October 2015; $646, MS-62, February 2015; $400, MS-60, May 2015; $353, AU-58, August 2015												
1830, Proof	10–15	4	64.5								$4,500	$12,500	$37,000
	Auctions: $49,938, PF-66, September 2013; $30,550, PF-64, August 2014												
1831	1,242,700	802	59.6	70%	$50	$65	$80	$115	$175	$250	$375	$850	$2,500
	Auctions: $564, MS-62, June 2015; $376, MS-61, October 2015; $259, MS-60, March 2015; $212, AU-58, January 2015												
1831, Proof	20–30	1	67.0								$4,500	$12,500	$38,000
	Auctions: $73,438, PF-67, January 2014												
1832	965,000	979	58.5	68%	$50	$65	$80	$115	$175	$250	$375	$850	$2,500
	Auctions: $823, MS-63, June 2015; $541, MS-62, January 2015; $376, MS-61, March 2015; $247, AU-55, March 2015												
1832, Proof	5–10	2	64.0								$5,000	$12,500	$40,000
	Auctions: $19,550, PF-64, March 2004												
1833	1,370,000	655	58.3	66%	$50	$65	$80	$115	$175	$250	$375	$850	$2,500
	Auctions: $8,813, MS-67, January 2015; $764, MS-63, January 2015; $470, MS-62, January 2015; $282, MS-60, August 2015												

1834, 3 Over Inverted 3
FS-H10-1834-301.

1835, Large Date

1835, Small Date

Large 5 C.

Small 5 C.

	Mintage	Cert	Avg	%MS	G-4	VG-8	F-12	VF-20	EF-40	AU-50	MS-60	MS-63	MS-65
											PF-60	PF-63	PF-65
1834	1,480,000	637	58.4	65%	$50	$65	$80	$115	$175	$250	$375	$850	$2,500
	Auctions: $6,463, MS-67, September 2015; $646, MS-63, October 2015; $517, MS-62, August 2015; $282, AU-55, June 2015												
1834, 3 Over Inverted 3	(a)	22	54.8	50%	$50	$65	$80	$135	$200	$350	$500	$1,200	$4,000
	Auctions: $25,850, MS-67, May 2015; $5,640, MS-66, August 2016; $1,774, MS-65, February 2015; $376, AU-55, November 2015												
1834, Proof	25–35	14	65.0								$4,500	$10,000	$27,500
	Auctions: $32,900, PF-66, November 2013; $12,925, PF-64, October 2014; $14,100, PF-64, August 2014												
1835, All kinds	2,760,000												
1835, Large Date and 5 C.		52	56.0	60%	$50	$65	$80	$115	$175	$250	$375	$850	$2,500
	Auctions: $376, AU-58, March 2015; $188, AU-50, February 2015; $129, AU-50, July 2015; $89, EF-45, May 2015												
1835, Large Date, Small 5 C.		22	57.9	50%	$50	$65	$80	$115	$175	$250	$375	$850	$2,500
	Auctions: $376, MS-62, September 2015												
1835, Small Date, Large 5 C.		31	55.4	58%	$50	$65	$80	$115	$175	$250	$375	$850	$2,500
	Auctions: $165, MS-60, May 2015												
1835, Small Date and 5 C.		43	55.9	60%	$50	$65	$80	$115	$175	$250	$375	$850	$2,500
	Auctions: $494, MS-62, June 2015; $400, MS-62, June 2015; $400, MS-61, July 2015												
1835, Proof		0	n/a								$5,000	$15,000	
	Auctions: No auction records available.												
1836, Small 5 C.	1,900,000	40	53.8	48%	$50	$65	$80	$115	$175	$250	$375	$850	$2,500
	Auctions: $153, EF-45, May 2015												
1836, Large 5 C.	(b)	26	56.4	65%	$50	$65	$80	$115	$175	$250	$375	$850	$2,500
	Auctions: $423, AU-58, October 2015; $201, AU-55, February 2015; $74, AU-50, February 2015; $129, EF-45, January 2015												
1836, 3 Over Inverted 3	(b)	35	52.9	51%	$55	$75	$100	$135	$200	$350	$675	$1,200	$3,750
	Auctions: $329, AU-58, January 2015												
1836, Proof	5–10	2	65.5								$4,500	$10,000	$35,000
	Auctions: $47,000, PF-66, February 2014												
1837, Small 5 C.	871,000	32	58.4	66%	$65	$85	$100	$185	$300	$500	$975	$2,100	$10,000
	Auctions: $1,880, MS-63, June 2013												
1837, Large 5 C.	(c)	29	51.7	48%	$55	$75	$80	$125	$185	$250	$400	$850	$3,500
	Auctions: $5,288, MS-65, March 2015; $159, AU-50, March 2015; $118, AU-50, June 2015; $129, VF-35, February 2015												
1837, Proof (d)	5–10	10	64.3								$6,500	$10,500	$30,000
	Auctions: No auction records available.												

a. Included in circulation-strike 1834 mintage figure. **b.** Included in 1836, Small 5 C., mintage figure. **c.** Included in 1837, Small 5 C., mintage figure. **d.** The 1837, Proof, coin is untraced.

LIBERTY SEATED (1837–1873)

Variety 1, No Stars on Obverse (1837–1838): **Designer:** *Christian Gobrecht.*
Weight: *1.34 grams.* **Composition:** *.900 silver, .100 copper.*
Diameter: *15.5 mm.* **Edge:** *Reeded.* **Mints:** *Philadelphia and New Orleans.*

**Variety 1, No Stars
on Obverse (1837–1838)**   **Variety 1, No Stars
on Obverse, Proof**

Variety 2, Stars on Obverse (1838–1853): **Designer:** *Christian Gobrecht.*
Weight: *1.34 grams.* **Composition:** *.900 silver, .100 copper.* **Diameter:** *15.5 mm.*
Edge: *Reeded.* **Mints:** *Philadelphia and New Orleans.*

**Variety 2, Stars on
Obverse (1838–1853)**   **Variety 2, Stars
on Obverse, Proof**

Variety 3, Arrows at Date, Reduced Weight (1853–1855):
Designer: *Christian Gobrecht.* **Weight:** *1.24 grams.* **Composition:** *.900 silver, .100 copper.*
Diameter: *15.5 mm.* **Edge:** *Reeded.* **Mints:** *Philadelphia and New Orleans.*

**Variety 3, Arrows at Date,
Reduced Weight (1853–1855)**   **Variety 3, Arrows at Date,
Reduced Weight, Proof**

Variety 2 Resumed, With Weight Standard of Variety 3 (1856–1859):
Designer: *Christian Gobrecht.* **Weight:** *1.24 grams.* **Composition:** *.900 silver, .100 copper.*
Diameter: *15.5 mm.* **Edge:** *Reeded.* **Mints:** *Philadelphia and New Orleans.*

**Variety 2 Resumed, Weight
Standard of Variety 3 (1856–1859)**   **Variety 2 Resumed, Weight
Standard of Variety 3, Proof**

Variety 4, Legend on Obverse (1860–1873): **Designer:** *Christian Gobrecht.*
Weight: *1.24 grams.* **Composition:** *.900 silver, .100 copper.* **Diameter:** *15.5 mm.*
Edge: *Reeded.* **Mints:** *Philadelphia, New Orleans, and San Francisco.*

**Variety 4, Legend on
Obverse (1860–1873)**   *Mintmark location,
1860–1869 and
1872–1873, is on the
reverse, below the bow.*   *Mintmark location,
1870–1872, is on the
reverse, above the bow.*   **Variety 4, Legend
on Obverse, Proof**

History. The Liberty Seated design without obverse stars, known as Variety 1, was used in the half dime and dime series only at the Philadelphia Mint in 1837 and the New Orleans Mint in 1838 (1838-O). The motif, by Christian Gobrecht, follows the obverse inaugurated on the 1836 silver dollar. Miss Liberty has no drapery at her elbow. In 1838 13 obverse stars were added, and in 1840 a restyling (drapery added to the elbow) by Robert Ball Hughes appeared. Arrows were added to the sides of the date starting in 1853, through 1855; these denoted the reduction of weight under the terms of the Act of February 21, 1853. The earlier design resumed in 1856. The reverse design stayed the same during these changes. In 1860 on the half dime the legend UNITED STATES OF AMERICA was moved to the obverse, in place of the stars. The reverse displayed a "cereal wreath" (as it was called in Mint records) enclosing the words HALF DIME.

Striking and Sharpness. For half dimes dated 1837 to 1838, check the highest parts of the Liberty Seated figure (especially the head and horizontal shield stripes) and, on the reverse, the leaves. Check the denticles on both sides. These coins are very attractive, and the starless obverse gives them a cameo-like appearance. For half dimes dated 1838 to 1859, strike quality varies widely. Most from 1838 to 1852 are sharper than later ones, but there are exceptions. (Coins with "mushy" details are especially common among the high-mintage dates of the mid- to late 1850s.) On the obverse, check the star centers, the head and center of Miss Liberty, and the denticles. On the reverse, check the wreath leaves and denticles. Excellent strike and deeply mirrored fields characterized nearly all Proofs. Points to check on coins dated 1860 to 1873 include the head of Miss Liberty on the obverse, the wreath details on the reverse (particularly at the inside upper left, above the H of HALF) and the denticles on both sides. Generally, MS coins have excellent luster, although some struck from relapped dies tend to be prooflike and with many striae. The word LIBERTY is not an infallible guide to grading at lower levels, as on some dies the shield was in lower relief, and the letters wore away less quickly. This guideline should be used in combination with other features. Generally, Proofs are well made, with deeply mirrored fields, although some of the late 1860s and early 1870s can have weak areas. Average quality in the marketplace is higher than for larger Liberty Seated denominations.

Availability. Liberty Seated half dimes are easily available as a type, but with many scarce varieties. The Philadelphia coins are easily available in all grades. The 1838-O is a rarity in true Mint State, often is over-graded, and typically has low eye appeal. Such issues as 1849-O and 1846 are extreme rarities at the true MS level. San Francisco coins, first made in 1863, are rare in MS for the first several years. Grades above MS-65 are seen with regularity, more often than the related No Stars dimes. Quality varies widely, and many MS coins are artificially toned.

Proofs. It is likely that at least several dozen Proofs were made of the 1837 half dime, although perhaps more were made of the related dime. Today, attractive examples exist and are rare. Nearly all designated as Proofs are, indeed, Proofs. If you aspire to acquire one, select an example with deep mirror surfaces. 1858 was the first year Proofs were widely sold to collectors, and an estimated 210 silver sets were distributed. (Proofs were made of earlier dates, but in much smaller numbers.) It is believed that 800 Proofs were struck of 1859, of which slightly more than 400 found buyers. From 1860 to 1873, Proof coins were made in fair quantities each year and are readily available today. The quality of Proofs on the market varies widely, mainly due to cleaning and dipping. Patience and care are needed to find a choice example.

GRADING STANDARDS

MS-60 to 70 (Mint State). *Obverse:* At MS-60 some abrasion and contact marks are evident, most noticeably on the bosom, thighs, and knees. Luster is present, but may be dull or lifeless, and interrupted in patches in the large open field. At MS-63, contact marks are very few, and abrasion is hard to detect except under magnification. An MS-65 coin has no abrasion, and contact marks are so minute as to require magnification. Luster

1844-O, Small O; V-2. Graded MS-64.

should be full and rich, except for Philadelphia (but not San Francisco) half dimes of the early and mid-1860s. Most Mint State coins of 1861 to 1865, Philadelphia issues, will have extensive die striae (from the dies being incompletely finished). Some low-mintage Philadelphia issues may be prooflike (and some may even be mislabeled as Proofs). Clashmarks are common in this era. Half dimes of this type can be very beautiful at this level. *Reverse:* Comments apply as for the obverse except that in lower Mint State grades abrasion and contact marks are most noticeable on the highest parts of the leaves and the ribbon, less so on HALF DIME. The field is mainly protected by design elements and does not show abrasion as much as does the open-field obverse on a given coin.

Illustrated coin: This coin was struck in medallic alignment, as is seen with multiple examples of 1844-O, V-2.

AU-50, 53, 55, 58 (About Uncirculated). *Obverse:* Light wear is seen on the thighs and knees, bosom, and head. At AU-58, the luster is extensive, but incomplete. Friction is seen in the large open field. At AU–50 and 53, luster is less. *Reverse:* Wear is noticeable on the leaves and ribbon. An AU-58 coin has nearly full luster—more so than on the obverse, as the design elements protect the small field areas. At AU–50 and 53, there still is significant luster, more than on the obverse.

1853, Arrows. Graded AU-50.

EF-40, 45 (Extremely Fine). *Obverse:* Further wear is seen on all areas, especially the thighs and knees, bosom, and head. Little or no luster is seen. *Reverse:* Further wear is seen on all areas, most noticeably at the leaves to each side of the wreath apex, and on the ribbon bow knot. Leaves retain details except on the higher areas.

1852-O. Graded EF-40.

VF-20, 30 (Very Fine). *Obverse:* Further wear is seen. Most details of the gown are worn away, except in the lower-relief areas above and to the right of the shield. Hair detail is gone on the higher points. *Reverse:* Wear is more extensive. The highest leaves are flat, particularly the larger leaves at the top of the wreath.

1846. Graded VF-35.

F-12, 15 (Fine). *Obverse:* The seated figure is well worn, but with some detail above and to the right of the shield. LIBERTY on the shield is fully readable, but weak in areas. *Reverse:* Most detail of the leaves is gone. The rim is worn but remains bold, and most if not all denticles are visible.

1844-O; V-6. Graded F-15.

VG-8, 10 (Very Good). *Obverse:* The seated figure is more worn, but some detail can be seen above and to the right of the shield. The shield is discernible. In LIBERTY at least three letters are readable but very weak at VG-8; a few more appear at VG-10. *Reverse:* Further wear has combined the details of most leaves. The rim is complete, but weak in areas. On most coins the reverse appears to be in a slightly higher grade than the obverse.

1846. Graded VG-10.

G-4, 6 (Good). *Obverse:* The seated figure is worn smooth. At G-4 there are no letters in LIBERTY remaining. At G-6, traces of one or two can be seen. *Reverse:* Wear is more extensive. The leaves are all combined and in outline form. The rim is clear but well worn and missing in some areas, causing the outer parts of the peripheral letters to be worn away in some instances. On most coins the reverse appears to be in a slightly higher grade than the obverse.

Illustrated coin: This is a No Stars variety.

1837, Small Date. Graded G-4.

AG-3 (About Good). *Obverse:* The seated figure is mostly visible in outline form, with no detail. The rim is worn away. The date remains clear. *Reverse:* Many if not most letters are worn away, as are parts of the wreath, though this and the interior letters are discernible. The rim can usually be seen, but is weak.

Illustrated coin: This is a No Stars variety.

1837, Small Date. Graded AG-3.

PF-60 to 70 (Proof). *Obverse and Reverse:* Proofs that are extensively cleaned and have many hairlines, or that are dull and grainy, are lower level, such as PF–60 to 62. These are not widely desired, save for the rare (in any grade) date of 1846. Both the half dime and dime Proofs of 1837 were often cleaned, resulting in coins which have lost much of their mirror surface. With medium hairlines and good reflectivity, a grade of PF-64 is

1873. Graded PF-66 Ultra Cameo.

assigned, and with relatively few hairlines, gem PF-65. In various grades hairlines are most easily seen in the obverse field. PF-66 should have hairlines so delicate that magnification is needed to see them. Above that, a Proof should be free of such lines.

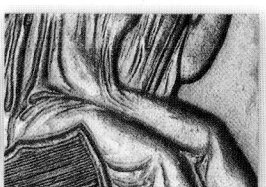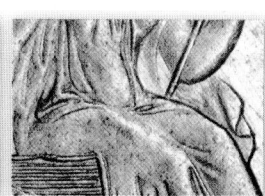

1837, Small Date	1837, Large Date	No Drapery From Elbow	Drapery From Elbow
Note the flat-topped 1.	Note the pointed-top 1.	(1837–1840)	(Starting 1840)

	Mintage	Cert	Avg	%MS	G-4	VG-8	F-12	VF-20	EF-40	AU-50	MS-60 PF-60	MS-63 PF-63	MS-65 PF-65
1837, Small Date	1,405,000	46	58.3	67%	$40	$55	$90	$145	$275	$550	$725	$1,100	$3,200
Auctions: $7,050, MS-67, January 2015; $1,175, MS-64, July 2015; $705, MS-63, January 2015; $793, MS-62, June 2015													
1837, Large Date	(a)	30	61.8	83%	$40	$55	$80	$145	$250	$475	$650	$1,250	$2,950
Auctions: $8,225, MS-67, January 2015; $3,290, MS-66, September 2015; $2,115, MS-65, September 2015; $541, MS-62, January 2015													
1837, Proof	15–20	10	64.3								$6,500	$10,500	$30,000
Auctions: $105,750, PF-67, June 2014													
1838-O, No Stars	70,000	45	46.0	31%	$150	$215	$400	$750	$2,000	$3,000	$5,250	$10,750	$25,550
Auctions: $21,150, MS-65, October 2015; $17,625, MS-64, October 2015; $7,050, MS-62, October 2015; $4,700, MS-62, July 2015													

a. Included in 1837, Small Date, mintage figure.

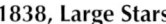

1838, Large Stars

1838, Small Stars

1840-O, No Drapery,
Normal Reverse
*Note four-leaf cluster
next to DIME.*

1840-O, No Drapery,
Transitional Reverse
*Note three-leaf cluster
next to DIME.*

	Mintage	Cert	Avg	%MS	G-4	VG-8	F-12	VF-20	EF-40	AU-50	MS-60	MS-63	MS-65
											PF-60	PF-63	PF-65
1838, No Drapery, Large Stars	2,225,000	726	60.4	75%	$18	$21	$28	$40	$100	$200	$280	$450	$1,900
Auctions: $5,523, MS-67, October 2015; $2,585, MS-66, January 2015; $999, MS-65, January 2015; $705, MS-64, January 2015													
1838, No Drapery, Small Stars	(a)	55	57.8	62%	$22	$40	$70	$150	$225	$400	$625	$1,000	$3,750
Auctions: $3,290, MS-66, October 2015; $2,820, MS-65, October 2015; $423, AU-58, October 2015; $306, AU-55, February 2015													
1838, Proof	4–5	2	64.5								$8,500	$10,500	$45,000
Auctions: $129,250, PF-67, October 2014; $182,125, PF-66, January 2014													
1839, No Drapery	1,069,150	310	60.4	74%	$20	$25	$35	$50	$100	$200	$290	$450	$1,700
Auctions: $5,405, MS-66, October 2015; $1,175, MS-65, February 2015; $400, MS-63, January 2015; $329, MS-60, October 2015													
1839, Proof	5–10	3	64.7								$8,500	$10,500	$35,000
Auctions: $27,600, PF-65Cam, April 2008													
1839-O, No Drapery	1,291,600	81	51.9	42%	$20	$25	$40	$85	$150	$325	$1,000	$2,100	$8,000
Auctions: $16,450, MS-67, May 2015; $7,050, MS-65, October 2015; $1,998, MS-63, January 2015; $1,175, MS-62, August 2015													
1840, No Drapery	1,034,000	301	59.9	73%	$20	$25	$30	$35	$90	$175	$260	$450	$1,450
Auctions: $6,000, MS-67, August 2015; $2,585, MS-66, October 2015; $1,293, MS-65, October 2015; $470, MS-64, January 2015													
1840, No Drapery, Proof	5–10	3	65.7								$8,500	$10,500	$35,000
Auctions: $30,550, PF-64, April 2014													
1840-O, No Drapery	695,000	57	51.5	25%	$40	$70	$100	$160	$220	$475	$1,200	$3,000	$13,000
Auctions: $18,213, MS-66, June 2014; $11,163, MS-65, October 2015; $141, EF-45, July 2014; $80, VF-25, September 2014													
1840-O, No Drapery, Transitional Reverse (b)	100	0	n/a		$300	$500	$675	$800	$1,200	$2,000	$3,500	$12,000	
Auctions: $431, F-15, November 2011													
1840, Drapery	310,085	63	59.3	76%	$35	$50	$70	$140	$210	$360	$460	$825	$2,700
Auctions: $3,995, MS-65, October 2015; $1,763, MS-65, August 2015; $329, AU-55, April 2015													
1840, Drapery, Proof	(c)	0	n/a										
Auctions: No auction records available.													
1840-O, Drapery	240,000	43	46.2	12%	$45	$75	$150	$300	$850	$1,550	$10,000	$22,000	
Auctions: $9,988, AU-58, October 2015; $282, VF-30, September 2015													
1841	1,150,000	184	60.6	80%	$16	$20	$30	$35	$70	$150	$190	$325	$1,100
Auctions: $1,528, MS-66, January 2015; $1,175, MS-65, October 2015; $940, MS-65, October 2015; $141, AU-55, January 2015													
1841, Proof	10–20	4	64.3								$8,500	$12,500	$30,000
Auctions: $28,200, PF-65, October 2014; $46,000, PF-65, January 2008													
1841-O	815,000	57	51.1	28%	$60	$90	$140	$200	$275	$550	$800	$2,500	$6,750
Auctions: $8,225, MS-66, October 2015; $3,173, MS-64, October 2015; $470, AU-55, April 2015													

a. Included in 1838, No Drapery, Large Stars, mintage figure. **b.** "This rare transitional variety exhibits large letters and open or split buds on the reverse die, along with a small O mintmark. The key diagnostic of the variety is three-leaf clusters on either side of the word DIME, while the common reverse has four-leaf clusters" (*Cherrypickers' Guide to Rare Die Varieties*, sixth edition, volume II). **c.** The mintage figure is unknown.

1848, Medium Date	1848, Large Date	1849, So-Called 9 Over 6 FS-H10-1849-302.	1849, 9 Over 8 FS-H10-1849-301.

	Mintage	Cert	Avg	%MS	G-4	VG-8	F-12	VF-20	EF-40	AU-50	MS-60 PF-60	MS-63 PF-63	MS-65 PF-65
1842	815,000	180	59.5	68%	$16	$20	$27	$35	$75	$150	$250	$425	$1,250
Auctions: $3,055, MS-66, May 2015; $1,058, MS-66, October 2015; $652, MS-64, August 2015; $400, MS-63, July 2015													
1842, Proof	*10–20*	5	64.8								$8,000	$10,000	$20,000
Auctions: $12,075, PF-64, January 2010													
1842-O	350,000	37	45.4	22%	$55	$75	$125	$215	$525	$850	$1,275	$2,250	$13,000
Auctions: $18,800, MS-66, May 2015; $13,513, MS-66, October 2015; $1,998, MS-63, October 2015; $1,763, MS-63, October 2015													
1843	815,000	245	58.9	67%	$25	$35	$40	$60	$90	$160	$225	$400	$1,200
Auctions: $1,645, MS-66, October 2015; $676, MS-63, October 2015; $259, MS-62, August 2015; $165, AU-58, April 2015													
1843, 1843 Over 1843, Proof	*10–20*	1	67.0								$8,000	$10,000	$20,000
Auctions: $55,813, PF-67, January 2014													
1844	430,000	168	61.1	84%	$20	$25	$35	$55	$100	$200	$275	$500	$1,400
Auctions: $1,058, MS-66, January 2015; $1,293, MS-65, October 2015; $823, MS-64, October 2015; $423, MS-63, October 2015													
1844, Proof	*15–25*	6	64.5								$8,000	$10,000	$22,500
Auctions: $35,250, PF-67, February 2014; $12,925, PF-64, October 2014													
1844-O	220,000	38	38.0	13%	$80	$130	$275	$550	$1,100	$2,750	$5,000	$10,000	$23,000
Auctions: $7,050, MS-64, October 2015; $1,293, EF-45, January 2015; $317, EF-40, January 2015; $494, VF-30, September 2015													
1845	1,564,000	225	58.6	67%	$16	$20	$27	$35	$60	$145	$225	$365	$1,375
Auctions: $3,995, MS-67, May 2015; $1,175, MS-66, June 2015; $793, MS-64, October 2015; $306, MS-63, March 2015													
1845, Proof	*10–15*	6	65.3								$9,000	$12,500	$25,000
Auctions: $64,625, PF-68, January 2014													
1846	27,000	58	29.5	2%	$850	$1,275	$1,650	$2,500	$4,000	$6,750	$11,000	$28,000	
Auctions: $564, MS-61, September 2016; $1,175, AU-55, March 2016; $999, AU-53, August 2016; $517, EF-45, September 2016													
1846, Proof	*10–20*	8	65.5								$8,000	$10,000	$22,000
Auctions: $35,250, PF-66, June 2014													
1847	1,274,000	221	57.8	67%	$20	$25	$35	$70	$95	$150	$225	$400	$1,000
Auctions: $1,763, MS-66, January 2015; $940, MS-65, January 2015; $447, MS-64, April 2015; $259, MS-63, January 2015													
1847, Proof	*8–12*	3	64.7								$8,000	$10,000	$22,000
Auctions: $38,188, PF-67, October 2014; $36,719, PF-66Cam, April 2014													
1848, Medium Date	668,000	97	57.7	57%	$16	$20	$27	$35	$75	$160	$250	$525	$3,500
Auctions: $3,525, MS-65, May 2015; $1,293, MS-64, June 2015; $447, MS-63, February 2015; $329, AU-58, April 2015													
1848, Large Date	(d)	33	56.9	55%	$35	$50	$80	$150	$190	$300	$625	$2,500	$4,500
Auctions: $14,100, MS-66, May 2015; $1,645, MS-62, September 2015; $470, AU-58, February 2015; $306, AU-53, February 2015													
1848, Proof	*6–8*	2	65.0								$9,000	$12,000	$22,500
Auctions: $63,250, PF-66, July 2008													
1848-O	600,000	78	61.0	82%	$22	$25	$35	$100	$225	$350	$700	$1,400	$2,900
Auctions: $12,338, MS-67, January 2014													
1849, All kinds	1,309,000												
1849, 9 Over 6 (e)		39	56.7	67%	$35	$50	$75	$120	$200	$350	$700	$1,200	$2,100
Auctions: $2,585, MS-65, June 2014; $200, MS-60, September 2014													
1849, 9 Over Widely Placed 6 (f)		23	53.6	43%	$50	$70	$100	$150	$275	$380	$620	$1,400	$2,750
Auctions: $5,405, MS-67, October 2015; $541, MS-62, March 2015; $306, MS-62, April 2015; $270, AU-58, April 2015													

d. Included in 1848, Medium Date, mintage figure. **e.** Fivaz and Stanton contend that this is actually a 9 Over 8 overdate (*Cherrypickers' Guide to Rare Die Varieties*, sixth edition, volume II). **f.** The 4 of the date is at least triple punched, with one secondary 4 south and one east of the primary 4. There is also a secondary numeral east of the lower portion of the 9.

	Mintage	Cert	Avg	%MS	G-4	VG-8	F-12	VF-20	EF-40	AU-50	MS-60	MS-63	MS-65
											PF-60	PF-63	PF-65
1849, Normal Date		157	57.3	56%	$25	$30	$40	$58	$100	$175	$265	$750	$1,450
	Auctions: $4,406, MS-67, June 2014; $270, MS-61, November 2014; $188, AU-58, November 2014												
1849, Proof	8–12	4	65.0								$8,000	$10,000	$22,500
	Auctions: $22,325, PF-65, June 2014												
1849-O	140,000	54	49.6	37%	$45	$60	$120	$220	$575	$1,200	$2,175	$4,000	$8,500
	Auctions: $4,465, MS-64, October 2015; $1,528, MS-61, September 2015; $1,293, AU-53, January 2015; $223, VF-30, February 2015												
1850	955,000	233	61.4	82%	$22	$30	$40	$60	$90	$180	$220	$375	$975
	Auctions: $7,050, MS-67, October 2015; $1,116, MS-66, March 2015; $705, MS-65, July 2015; $494, MS-64, June 2015												
1850, Proof	8–12	4	64.0								$12,000	$20,000	$40,000
	Auctions: $44,650, PF-67, May 2015; $61,688, PF-65, October 2015; $19,975, PF-64, May 2015; $17,626, PF-62, August 2016												
1850-O	690,000	67	55.0	51%	$30	$40	$60	$100	$200	$275	$675	$1,400	$4,000
	Auctions: $11,456, MS-67, January 2015; $7,638, MS-66, October 2015; $1,293, MS-63, October 2015; $212, AU-50, September 2015												
1851	781,000	160	58.8	73%	$18	$22	$28	$40	$75	$140	$190	$325	$1,000
	Auctions: $8,813, MS-67, May 2015; $4,171, MS-67, January 2015; $646, MS-64, October 2015; $235, MS-62, April 2015												
1851-O	860,000	115	56.2	56%	$25	$30	$40	$65	$110	$235	$450	$925	$4,200
	Auctions: $5,170, MS-66, May 2015; $4,465, MS-65, October 2015; $588, MS-62, March 2015; $376, MS-61, February 2015												
1852	1,000,500	181	61.9	83%	$18	$22	$28	$40	$75	$140	$190	$325	$1,050
	Auctions: $1,410, MS-66, October 2015; $705, MS-65, January 2015; $317, MS-63, March 2015; $141, AU-58, September 2015												
1852, Proof	10–15	9	64.2								$8,000	$10,000	$22,500
	Auctions: $30,550, PF-65, January 2014; $19,975, PF-65, June 2015; $14,100, PF-64, October 2014												
1852-O	260,000	55	51.5	40%	$30	$40	$75	$135	$260	$450	$865	$2,000	$7,000
	Auctions: $646, AU-58, August 2015; $353, AU-50, January 2015; $206, AU-50, June 2015; $84, VF-20, June 2015												
1853, No Arrows	135,000	141	59.4	78%	$60	$85	$140	$225	$325	$500	$750	$1,200	$2,300
	Auctions: $2,510, MS-66, July 2015; $1,880, MS-65, September 2015; $1,175, MS-64, January 2015; $940, MS-63, January 2015												
1853-O, No Arrows	160,000	31	34.9	6%	$350	$600	$775	$1,200	$2,400	$3,850	$6,200	$12,500	$29,000
	Auctions: $32,900, MS-65, October 2014; $25,850, MS-65, October 2014; $3,819, AU-55, April 2013; $1,175, VF-25, January 2015												
1853, With Arrows	13,210,020	1,309	56.9	59%	$20	$25	$30	$35	$70	$140	$190	$310	$1,050
	Auctions: $7,638, MS-67, August 2015; $1,880, MS-66, August 2015; $470, MS-64, January 2015; $259, MS-63, January 2015												
1853, With Arrows, Proof (g)	3–5	1	64.0								$20,000	$25,000	
	Auctions: No auction records available.												
1853-O, With Arrows	2,200,000	102	52.5	46%	$25	$30	$40	$65	$100	$240	$350	$1,100	$3,000
	Auctions: $15,275, MS-67, October 2015; $5,405, MS-66, October 2015; $376, MS-61, October 2015; $259, AU-58, September 2015												
1854	5,740,000	645	57.8	67%	$20	$25	$30	$35	$65	$140	$200	$300	$1,100
	Auctions: $7,050, MS-67, October 2015; $1,645, MS-66, June 2015; $1,116, MS-65, January 2015; $494, MS-64, February 2015												
1854, Proof	15–25	10	64.6								$4,000	$7,500	$10,000
	Auctions: $9,694, PF-65, August 2013												
1854-O	1,560,000	103	58.1	64%	$20	$24	$35	$45	$90	$200	$300	$900	$3,200
	Auctions: $15,275, MS-67, October 2015; $4,465, MS-66, October 2015; $1,058, MS-64, October 2015; $999, MS-63, October 2015												
1855	1,750,000	255	60.2	75%	$20	$25	$30	$35	$75	$150	$210	$375	$1,650
	Auctions: $8,813, MS-67, February 2015; $2,585, MS-66, July 2015; $1,293, MS-65, July 2015; $353, MS-63, August 2015												
1855, Proof	15–25	20	65.1								$4,000	$7,500	$11,500
	Auctions: $21,150, PF-66, June 2014; $11,750, PF-65, October 2014; $8,519, PF-65, June 2015												
1855-O	600,000	81	58.6	65%	$20	$25	$35	$85	$200	$380	$700	$1,500	$4,500
	Auctions: $4,230, MS-65, October 2015; $84, VF-35, April 2015												
1856	4,880,000	488	59.3	72%	$18	$22	$25	$35	$60	$115	$185	$275	$900
	Auctions: $1,410, MS-66, October 2015; $846, MS-65, January 2015; $447, MS-63, May 2015; $212, MS-63, January 2015												
1856, Proof	40–60	26	64.8								$2,500	$4,500	$8,000
	Auctions: $8,813, PF-65, October 2015; $4,230, PF-64, October 2015; $4,113, PF-64, July 2015												
1856-O	1,100,000	100	55.8	36%	$18	$22	$25	$55	$110	$240	$450	$900	$1,900
	Auctions: $3,408, MS-66, October 2015; $1,645, MS-65, October 2015; $470, AU-58, April 2015; $235, AU-55, January 2015												

g. This coin is extremely rare.

1858, Repunched High Date
FS-H10-1858-301.

1858, Over Inverted Date
FS-H10-1858-302.

1860, Obverse of 1859, Reverse of 1860
Transitional pattern, with stars (Judd-267).

	Mintage	Cert	Avg	%MS	G-4	VG-8	F-12	VF-20	EF-40	AU-50	MS-60	MS-63	MS-65
											PF-60	PF-63	PF-65
1857	7,280,000	864	59.3	75%	$18	$22	$25	$35	$60	$115	$185	$320	$900
	Auctions: $6,463, MS-68, September 2015; $2,585, MS-67, September 2015; $1,058, MS-66, June 2015; $646, MS-65, January 2015												
1857, Proof	*40–60*	28	65.0								$2,200	$3,000	$5,000
	Auctions: $21,738, PF-67Cam, January 2014; $7,050, PF-66, August 2014; $4,935, PF-66, May 2015												
1857-O	1,380,000	237	57.4	62%	$18	$22	$25	$45	$80	$175	$300	$500	$1,400
	Auctions: $3,525, MS-67, June 2015; $1,293, MS-66, October 2015; $1,058, MS-65, October 2015; $329, MS-62, October 2015												
1858	3,500,000	752	60.3	78%	$18	$22	$25	$35	$60	$125	$170	$320	$900
	Auctions: $2,800, MS-67, January 2015; $999, MS-66, September 2015; $881, MS-65, January 2015; $388, MS-64, March 2015												
1858, Repunched High Date (h)	**(i)**	6	43.2	17%	$25	$40	$60	$100	$150	$250	$475	$850	$2,500
	Auctions: $135, AU-50, November 2014; $65, VF-30, July 2011												
1858, Over Inverted Date (j)	**(i)**	29	54.2	48%	$40	$60	$100	$150	$250	$350	$800	$1,600	$4,500
	Auctions: $7,638, MS-65, February 2014												
1858, Proof	*300*	82	64.1								$750	$1,200	$3,000
	Auctions: $3,055, PF-65Cam, October 2015; $823, PF-62, September 2015												
1858-O	1,660,000	237	59.7	76%	$18	$22	$30	$50	$80	$155	$240	$480	$1,250
	Auctions: $517, MS-64, August 2015; $470, MS-64, October 2015; $435, MS-63, May 2015; $212, MS-61, April 2015												
1859	340,000	246	61.8	83%	$18	$22	$30	$45	$80	$135	$200	$425	$925
	Auctions: $5,640, MS-68, January 2015; $3,290, MS-67, October 2015; $2,585, MS-67, August 2015; $329, MS-63, October 2015												
1859, Proof	*800*	231	64.0								$550	$1,100	$2,500
	Auctions: $5,640, PF-66Cam, September 2015; $3,525, PF-66, October 2015; $2,585, PF-65, October 2015; $1,293, PF-64, March 2015												
1859, Obverse of 1859 (With Stars), Reverse of 1860, Proof (k)	*20*	6	63.5								$20,000	$35,000	$55,000
	Auctions: $34,500, PF-63, August 2010												
1859-O	560,000	127	60.1	73%	$25	$35	$65	$90	$165	$225	$285	$500	$1,750
	Auctions: $4,935, MS-66, October 2015; $881, MS-64, October 2015; $423, MS-63, August 2015; $282, MS-62, October 2015												
1860, Obverse of 1859 (With Stars), Reverse of 1860 (l)	*100*	55	64.4	100%					$2,500	$3,000	$3,750	$6,000	
	Auctions: $5,750, MS-66, February 2012												
1860, Legend on Obverse	798,000	533	62.1	85%	$16	$20	$25	$30	$50	$85	$175	$300	$675
	Auctions: $2,115, MS-67, January 2015; $881, MS-66, January 2015; $705, MS-65, January 2015; $447, MS-64, January 2015												
1860, Proof	1,000	112	64.4								$350	$550	$1,100
	Auctions: $2,115, PF-66Cam, July 2014; $$3,290, PF-66Cam, April 2014; 1,528, PF-65Cam, July 2014												
1860-O	1,060,000	253	59.7	72%	$20	$25	$30	$45	$80	$120	$170	$320	$1,000
	Auctions: $7,050, MS-67, August 2015; $1,116, MS-65, October 2015; $447, MS-64, June 2015; $259, MS-63, October 2015												

h. The date was first punched into the die very high, then corrected and punched into its normal location. The original high-date punch is clearly visible within the upper portions of the primary date. **i.** Included in circulation-strike 1858 mintage figure. **j.** The date was first punched into the die in an inverted orientation, and then corrected. The bases of the secondary digits are evident above the primary digits. **k.** This transitional issue, made surreptitiously at the Mint for a private collector, has the new Liberty Seated die made in the old style of 1859, but with the date of 1860. The reverse is the regular die of 1860, with a cereal wreath. Classified as Judd-267 (*United States Pattern Coins*, tenth edition). **l.** Classified as Judd-232 (*United States Pattern Coins*, tenth edition), this features the obverse design of 1859 and the reverse of 1860.

1861, So-Called 1 Over 0
FS-H10-1861-301.

	Mintage	Cert	Avg	%MS	G-4	VG-8	F-12	VF-20	EF-40	AU-50	MS-60 PF-60	MS-63 PF-63	MS-65 PF-65
1861	3,360,000	663	58.9	69%	$20	$25	$30	$40	$70	$120	$160	$275	$700
Auctions: $2,820, MS-67, October 2015; $1,763, MS-66, August 2015; $617, MS-65, August 2015; $329, MS-64, January 2015													
1861, So-Called 1 Over 0	(m)	0	n/a		$35	$45	$50	$90	$200	$325	$600	$900	$2,000
Auctions: $3,290, MS-66, October 2015; $1,645, MS-65, June 2015; $1,293, MS-64, January 2015; $588, MS-62, February 2015													
1861, Proof	1,000	93	64.4								$350	$550	$1,100
Auctions: $6,169, PF-67, June 2014													
1862	1,492,000	700	61.9	85%	$25	$30	$45	$55	$70	$100	$160	$300	$700
Auctions: $2,115, MS-67, January 2015; $494, MS-65, January 2015; $329, MS-64, January 2015; $259, MS-63, August 2015													
1862, Proof	550	184	64.4								$350	$550	$1,100
Auctions: $3,760, PF-67Cam, June 2015; $1,293, PF-66Cam, October 2015; $960, PF-65, August 2015; $541, PF-63, September 2015													
1863	18,000	120	62.0	88%	$200	$280	$330	$425	$600	$750	$825	$975	$1,800
Auctions: $9,988, MS-68, October 2015; $3,995, MS-67, January 2015; $1,645, MS-66, October 2015; $1,410, MS-66, July 2015													
1863, Proof	460	178	64.1								$350	$550	$1,100
Auctions: $3,760, PF-67, October 2015; $4,700, PF-66Cam, October 2015; $1,293, PF-66, March 2015; $1,175, PF-65, January 2015													
1863-S	100,000	96	59.6	75%	$45	$60	$100	$200	$300	$400	$750	$1,175	$4,000
Auctions: $4,935, MS-66, October 2015; $4,230, MS-65, October 2015; $1,645, MS-64, October 2015; $764, MS-60, June 2015													
1864	48,000	48	58.6	79%	$325	$440	$675	$850	$1,100	$1,200	$1,300	$1,475	$2,800
Auctions: $2,585, MS-65, January 2015; $1,410, MS-64, July 2015; $646, MS-64, January 2015; $541, MS-63, June 2015													
1864, Proof	470	149	64.2								$350	$550	$1,100
Auctions: $4,700, PF-67, August 2014; $4,259, PF-67, June 2014; $1,175, PF-66, September 2015													
1864-S	90,000	59	54.7	53%	$65	$100	$175	$250	$375	$900	$1,200	$2,000	$3,750
Auctions: $4,935, MS-66, October 2015; $2,115, MS-64, October 2015; $224, VF-35, August 2015													
1865	13,000	54	57.5	74%	$400	$475	$550	$750	$900	$1,200	$1,300	$1,650	$2,200
Auctions: $7,638, MS-67, October 2015; $376, G-6, February 2015													
1865, Proof	500	164	64.1								$350	$550	$1,100
Auctions: $1,763, PF-66Cam, July 2015; $1,116, PF-65Cam, August 2015; $764, PF-64Cam, September 2015; $435, PF-63, March 2015													
1865-S	120,000	52	52.6	38%	$50	$80	$125	$200	$350	$600	$950	$2,100	$6,000
Auctions: $881, AU-55, January 2015; $212, EF-40, June 2015													
1866	10,000	62	58.2	79%	$325	$400	$500	$650	$850	$1,000	$1,100	$1,225	$2,500
Auctions: $5,640, MS-67, January 2015; $3,055, MS-66, October 2015; $940, MS-61, October 2015; $999, EF-45, January 2015													
1866, Proof	725	176	64.1								$350	$550	$1,100
Auctions: $19,975, PF-67DCam, January 2015; $2,820, PF-65DCam, January 2015; $580, PF-64, June 2015; $541, PF-63, July 2015													
1866-S	120,000	77	58.1	58%	$45	$60	$90	$150	$225	$300	$500	$950	$4,000
Auctions: $7,638, MS-66, May 2015; $3,760, MS-65, October 2015; $564, MS-61, April 2015; $482, AU-58, April 2015													
1867	8,000	84	60.3	85%	$450	$525	$625	$750	$850	$1,000	$1,200	$1,500	$2,250
Auctions: $2,585, MS-66, October 2015; $8,813, MS-65, October 2015; $1,410, MS-63, September 2015													
1867, Proof	625	226	64.5								$350	$550	$1,100
Auctions: $1,528, PF-66Cam, August 2015; $999, PF-65, January 2015; $823, PF-64Cam, July 2015; $705, PF-64, October 2015													
1867-S	120,000	68	57.2	57%	$30	$40	$60	$90	$250	$325	$575	$1,100	$3,000
Auctions: $3,055, MS-66, February 2015; $2,585, MS-65, August 2015; $881, MS-63, January 2015; $458, AU-58, April 2015													

m. Included in circulation-strike 1861 mintage figure.

1872, Doubled Die Obverse
FS-H10-1872-101.

	Mintage	Cert	Avg	%MS	G-4	VG-8	F-12	VF-20	EF-40	AU-50	MS-60 / PF-60	MS-63 / PF-63	MS-65 / PF-65
1868	88,600	76	60.1	83%	$55	$65	$120	$185	$325	$475	$675	$800	$1,600
	Auctions: $4,230, MS-67, October 2015; $517, AU-58, April 2015												
1868, Proof	600	180	64.1								$350	$550	$1,100
	Auctions: $2,585, PF-66Cam, February 2015; $1,058, PF-65Cam, October 2015; $588, PF-64, September 2015; $376, PF-62, May 2015												
1868-S	280,000	150	61.0	69%	$16	$20	$30	$35	$45	$130	$320	$600	$1,800
	Auctions: $5,170, MS-66, October 2015; $1,410, MS-65, October 2015; $282, MS-62, April 2015; $212, MS-60, January 2015												
1869	208,000	106	62.8	86%	$30	$40	$50	$70	$110	$175	$300	$400	$1,000
	Auctions: $3,760, MS-67, May 2015; $1,880, MS-66, October 2015; $1,058, MS-65, July 2015; $999, MS-65, October 2015												
1869, Proof	600	215	64.3								$350	$550	$1,100
	Auctions: $2,585, PF-67Cam, June 2015; $2,115, PF-67, January 2015; $1,410, PF-66, January 2015; $588, PF-64, January 2015												
1869-S	230,000	81	60.2	78%	$30	$50	$70	$120	$200	$275	$300	$500	$3,500
	Auctions: $4,465, MS-67, May 2015; $3,290, MS-65, October 2015; $306, AU-58, April 2015; $282, AU-55, April 2015												
1870	535,000	301	60.4	78%	$16	$20	$25	$30	$45	$80	$175	$400	$900
	Auctions: $2,820, MS-67, September 2015; $949, MS-66, October 2015; $235, MS-62, February 2015; $129, MS-62, May 2015												
1870, Proof	1,000	182	64.2								$350	$550	$1,100
	Auctions: $1,293, PF-66Cam, October 2015; $764, PF-64Cam, July 2015; $541, PF-63, September 2015; $259, PF-62, May 2015												
1870-S † (n)		1	63.0	100%								$2,000,000	
	Auctions: $661,250, MS-63, July 2004												
1871	1,873,000	494	60.2	73%	$16	$20	$25	$30	$60	$80	$150	$250	$625
	Auctions: $1,410, MS-66, August 2015; $400, MS-64, May 2015; $361, MS-64, July 2015; $62, AU-55, January 2015												
1871, Proof	960	203	64.2								$350	$550	$1,100
	Auctions: $2,468, PF-67Cam, August 2015; $1,175, PF-65Cam, August 2015; $1,293, PF-66, January 2015; $823, PF-64, January 2015												
1871-S	161,000	123	60.7	68%	$18	$22	$32	$65	$80	$180	$250	$500	$1,750
	Auctions: $423, MS-64, January 2015; $235, MS-62, May 2015; $259, MS-61, April 2015; $208, AU-58, April 2015												
1872	2,947,000	427	59.2	72%	$16	$20	$25	$30	$45	$80	$150	$300	$675
	Auctions: $3,760, MS-67, May 2015; $1,469, MS-66, August 2015; $376, MS-64, May 2015; $106, AU-58, April 2015												
1872, DblDie Obv (o)	(p)	8	48.6	0%					$250	$350	$650	$1,500	
	Auctions: $89, EF-45, August 2011												
1872, Proof	950	180	64.2								$350	$550	$1,100
	Auctions: $3,525, PF-67Cam, March 2015; $1,058, PF-65Cam, October 2015; $999, PF-64Cam, October 2015												
1872-S, All kinds	837,000												
1872-S, Mintmark above bow		167	61.6	78%	$20	$25	$30	$45	$50	$80	$150	$300	$750
	Auctions: $2,468, MS-67, May 2015; $764, MS-66, July 2015; $529, MS-65, January 2015; $282, MS-63, April 2015												
1872-S, Mintmark below bow		162	62.0	80%	$20	$25	$30	$45	$55	$120	$160	$300	$675
	Auctions: $2,585, MS-67, January 2015; $1,058, MS-66, September 2015; $353, MS-64, January 2015; $282, MS-63, March 2015												
1873, Close 3 (q)	712,000	151	59.6	73%	$16	$20	$25	$30	$45	$80	$150	$275	$675
	Auctions: $2,820, MS-67, October 2015; $1,528, MS-66, January 2015; $165, MS-62, January 2015; $100, MS-60, May 2015												
1873, Proof	600	245	64.3								$350	$550	$1,100
	Auctions: $1,528, PF-66, March 2015; $1,469, PF-66, June 2015; $1,293, PF-65, January 2015; $580, PF-64, June 2015												
1873-S Close 3 (q)	324,000	263	62.0	84%	$16	$20	$25	$30	$65	$125	$150	$300	$675
	Auctions: $1,175, MS-66, October 2015; $646, MS-65, June 2015; $423, MS-64, August 2015; $376, MS-64, November 2015												

† Ranked in the *100 Greatest U.S. Coins* (fourth edition). **n.** The 1870-S coin is unique. **o.** "Doubling is evident on UNITED STATES OF AMERICA and on most elements of Miss Liberty. AMERICA is the strongest point" (*Cherrypickers' Guide to Rare Die Varieties*, sixth edition, volume II). **p.** Included in circulation-strike 1872 mintage figure. **q.** Close 3 only.

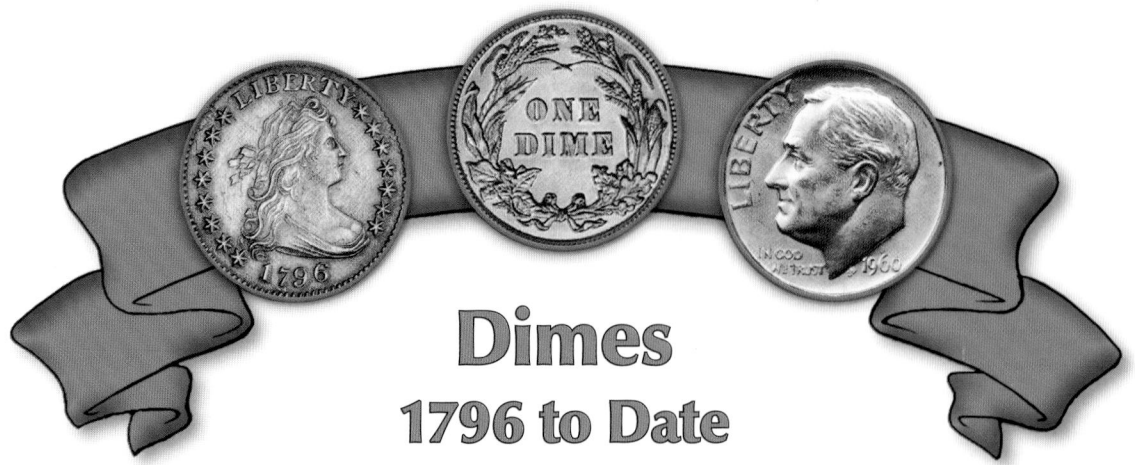

Dimes
1796 to Date

This survey of U.S. dimes is based on the work of Q. David Bowers,
a numismatic professional and author in the field for more than 60 years.

United States dimes are extremely popular among collectors, offering areas of specialization to accommodate almost any budget and level of interest. This chapter covers all U.S. dime types to date in depth. In particular, this edition of *Mega Red* presents the most comprehensive coverage of early dimes—encompassing the Draped Bust and Capped Bust types—ever made in a general-interest book, and has drawn upon many sources, including specialized references, auctions, historical documents, news accounts, and more. These early dimes, especially those of the Capped Bust type, can be very affordable.

The first federal dimes were made at the Philadelphia Mint in 1796 and featured the Draped Bust obverse combined with the Small Eagle reverse. In 1798 the Draped Bust obverse was retained in combination with the new, Heraldic Eagle reverse. The Capped Bust type was introduced in 1809 and continued to 1837, when it was replaced by the Liberty Seated design. With some changes this last style was continued to 1891. The reverse of the Liberty Seated design was the only motif continued into the succeeding Barber series. The Winged Liberty ("Mercury") and Roosevelt dimes followed later in sequence.

A NOTE ABOUT RARITY

Of the several rarity scales that are available to numismatists, this chapter references the standard Sheldon scale (by Dr. William H. Sheldon). The meanings of the rarity abbreviations are as follows:

Rarity	Number Known		Rarity	Number Known
R-1	1,250+		High R-6	13–20
R-2	501–1,250		Low R-7	7–12
R-3	201–500		High R-7	4–6
R-4	76–200		R-8	2 or 3
R-5	31–75		R-9	Unique
Low R-6	21–30			

EARLY DIMES

From the beginning days of wide U.S. numismatic interest in the 1850s up through today, dimes of the Draped Bust and Capped Bust types have always been popular to collect. In the early times this was usually done by date, without reference to the size of numerals or letters.

In 1881 John W. Hazeltine, the leading Philadelphia dealer at the time, published his *Type Table*, which listed die varieties of quarters, half dollars, and dollars but did not include dimes or half dimes.[1] The last had been studied and published in 1883 by Harold P. Newlin. Because of the lack of a reference work, die varieties of dimes were not described or collected widely. There were scattered exceptions, such as John M. Clapp and Frederick C.C. Boyd. In 1945 the Numismatic Gallery (Abe Kosoff and Abner Kreisberg) auctioned Boyd's collection of silver issues, which had been bought outright. As Boyd did not want publicity, the offering was billed as "The World's Greatest Collection." The greatest collection it was not, nor was it even close (it lacked mint-marked coins, for example), but the pieces it did contain were of uniformly high quality. Boyd had studied die varieties of early dimes, and these were listed individually with descriptions. Kosoff later published the dimes separately as the standard reference on the early series. Although the study was far from complete, and details were skimpy, it served a useful purpose.

That changed on September 1, 1984, with the publication of *Early United States Dimes, 1796–1837: A Reference Book of Their Types, Varieties, and Rarity*. The quintet of authors—David Davis, Russell Logan, Allen Lovejoy, John McCloskey, and William Subjack—decided to assign "JR" numbers to the varieties, for John Reich, designer of the later issues. It is often simply called "the JR book," and its numbering system remains in use today.

John Reich Journal

Volume 25 / Issue 2   July 2015

The *John Reich Journal*, publication of the John Reich Collectors Society (JRCS).

In 2015 a work titled *Bust Dime Variety Identification Guide*, by Winston Zack, Louis Scuderi, and Michael Sherrill, with assistance by Barry Sunshine and others, augmented the JR book by providing detailed photographs and technical information. Beyond these standard references, NGC and PCGS give much information on their websites, and much has appeared in auction catalogs and research articles.

The John Reich Collectors Society publishes the *John Reich Journal*, a goldmine of information. Today, a basic library containing the two mentioned books and back issues of the journal can make everyone an expert! In addition, the annual *Guide Book of United States Coins* gives an overview of the more popular varieties and mintages for each year. The information in the present (4th) edition of *Mega Red* includes additional information supplied by Barry Sunshine, a dedicated specialist.

As a general comment, most dimes of the 1796 to 1837 years in the marketplace are in circulated grades, from Almost Good to Very Fine. Most collectors who are John Reich Collectors Society members collect these dimes in either in Good to Fine or Extremely Fine to Almost Uncirculated range. Acquiring the vast majority of die varieties combines being affordable and being an exciting challenge. Also, many an educated early dime collector is able to "cherrypick" rare varieties at the cost of a common-priced example. Aspiring to and collecting Mint State and Proof examples is beyond the patience and budget of most numismatists. Working with a generous budget and over a span of 40 years, D. Brent Pogue formed a cabinet beyond comparison, with Gem being the usual grade. These were auctioned by Stack's Bowers Galleries. The Pogue and Sunshine collections provided numerous images.

Among later dimes, Almost Uncirculated can be a collectible and affordable grade, and Mint State coins appear on the market with some frequency. Proofs are extremely rare, and years can pass between offerings of a given date or variety. There are many differences of opinion and debates between numismatists on the characteristics of a Proof, and the author is not aware of anyone assembling an early Proof dime collection.

DRAPED BUST DIMES (1796–1807)

Small Eagle Reverse: **Designer:** *Probably Gilbert Stuart.* **Engraver:** *Robert Scot.* **Heraldic Eagle Reverse:** **Designer:** *Robert Scot.* **Both Reverse Styles:** **Weight:** *2.70 grams.* **Composition:** *.8924 silver, .1076 copper.* **Diameter:** *approx. 19 mm.* **Edge:** *Reeded.* **Mints:** *All coined at the Philadelphia Mint.*

1796, Small Eagle Reverse (John Reich-1).   1800, Heraldic Eagle Reverse (John Reich-1).

HISTORY AND BACKGROUND

Following the establishment of the Philadelphia Mint in 1792, the issuance of copper, silver, and gold coins was contemplated. While copper half cents and cents were struck at the Mint in 1793, however, silver coins were not produced at the outset, as chief coiner Henry Voigt and assayer Albion Cox were required to post $10,000 personal surety bonds—something neither was capable of doing. By 1794, this requirement was satisfied, and production of half dollars and silver dollars commenced. (Although half dimes dated 1794 exist, pieces with this date were not actually struck until 1795.) The first gold coins were struck in late summer 1795.

The first pieces of the 10-cent denomination were delivered early in 1796—on January 18, to be precise.

The motif of the dimes of 1796 and 1797 is characterized by the Draped Bust of Liberty facing right, with stars to the either side, the word LIBERTY above, and the date below. The Draped Bust is from a design first used on the silver dollar in autumn 1795, and is said generations later by his descendants to have been the work of noted artist Gilbert Stuart (who is probably best remembered today for his painting of George Washington, reproductions of which are a familiar sight in schools across the land). It has been suggested that Philadelphia socialite Anna Willess Willing was the model, but this is unlikely.[2]

This 1914 painting by Edwin Lamasure depicts the Philadelphia Mint as it appeared in the 1790s, when it was producing the first U.S. dimes. These were struck in the coinage building (with flag on cupola); the Mint offices are in the building to the right. The top of the coinage building was destroyed by a fire in 1868, and its actual appearance was unknown when this picture was painted. The cupola added by Lamasure may or may not have topped the original building.

Once the drawings had been approved for the dollar, probably toward the middle of August, they were sent to John Eckstein, who was called by one of his fellow artists a "thorough-going drudge" in his field. Eckstein, who was paid $30 on September 9 for his work, executed a pair of plaster models, not of the whole coin, but just of the Liberty head and reverse eagle/wreath combination. This design was subsequently used on the half dimes, dimes, quarters, and half dollars of 1796.

A 1795 silver dollar, showing the same Draped Bust design, albeit larger, as that used on dimes from 1796 to 1807.

The reverse illustrates a "small" eagle perched on a cloud, enclosed within a wreath and encircled by the inscription UNITED STATES OF AMERICA. The edge is reeded. Interestingly, no mark of denomination appears on early dime issues. It was not until 1809 that a mark of value, "10 C.," was used for the first time.

The Small Eagle motif proved to be ephemeral, and in 1798 it was replaced by the Heraldic Eagle based on the United States coat of arms. In the dime denomination this was used through 1807.

Among early dimes are several interesting varieties. Coins of 1797 are found with 13 or 16 stars on the obverse. The reverse type changed in 1798, and several varieties of early dimes were made with the same reverse dies used to coin gold quarter eagles of similar diameter.

ROBERT SCOT, ENGRAVER

The Philadelphia Mint was authorized under the Coinage Act of April 2, 1792. Machinery was acquired, and a temporary facility was set up in the shop of John Harper, where they awaited the finishing of Mint buildings. This was accomplished in the late summer, after which operations were conducted there. Pattern coins as well as silver half dismes for circulation were made. The engravers included Bob Birch and Henry Voigt. Pattern dismes were also made, these from dies by Voigt. In 1792 Joseph Wright, an engraver of exceptional skill, made patterns. In the summer of 1793 he was hired to be the official engraver at the Mint. Unfortunately, he succumbed to the yellow-fever epidemic of that year and died in September.

Robert Scot, born in the British Isles in 1740, learned the skills of engraving printing plates and metal parts for clocks and other devices in Edinburgh, Scotland. He was also a maker of pocket watches. Scot came to America in 1775. He engraved metal plates for bills of exchange and other items for super-intendent of finance Robert Morris during the Revolutionary War. In 1780 he was appointed engraver for the State of Virginia. He moved to Philadelphia in 1781 and set up a business engraving plates for maps and illustrations. In 1783 he engraved a frontispiece for a Masonic sermon preached by Wm. Smith, D.D., and published by Hall & Sellers. Circa 1788 he engraved plates for Thomas Dobson's edition of *Rees' Encyclopedia*. His name appears in the *Philadelphia Directory* for 1791 as an engraver at 36 Chestnut St., later moving to 2 Carters Alley.

On November 23, 1793, he was appointed engraver at the Mint by director David Rittenhouse. In the ensuing years he engraved coin dies, and was assisted for a time in the mid-1890s by John Gardner (who was not involved with dimes). He kept up his private business, which now included engraving bank notes. This trade passed in 1810 to Murray, Draper, Fairman & Co. in the same city.

Scot engraved the dies for the Draped Bust obverse and Small Eagle and Heraldic Eagle reverses. On occasion, work on medals, punches, and other items was done by outside contractors, including John Reich at the turn of the 19th century. He was later hired as a full-time assistant to Scot in 1807, as Mint director Robert Patterson felt that Scot was not able to do all the work required (see the later Reich biography). It has been popular numismatically to criticize Scot's work, but his coins prove otherwise. He was less active in later years and is said to have been in poor health and with failing eyesight. He remained as Mint engraver as a sinecure until his passing on November 3, 1823.

DRAPED BUST DIMES (1796–1807): GUIDE TO COLLECTING

In the marketplace the average grade for Draped Bust dimes is Good to Fine, with AG-3 being desirable and collectible for the rarities. Very Fine, Extremely Fine, and About Uncirculated coins are more desirable, of course, but even a set of basic *Guide Book* varieties in About Uncirculated grade would cost tens of thousands of dollars. A reasonable alternative is to select grades that are affordable. In general, coins in F-12 to VF-20 can be attractive and desirable if cherrypicked for eye appeal. Sharpness of strike is a different matter entirely. There are some issues for which it is difficult or impossible to find coins with all obverse and reverse features well defined. Dimes of 1807, for example, are usually very weak, especially at the borders, but cherrypicking will get you an above-average example.

The array of JR varieties includes some additional varieties not in the regular *Guide Book*, and collecting them can be a fine challenge. The *John Reich Journal* and the two earlier-mentioned reference books are essential to your enjoyment and success.

The mintage figures given for early dimes are for coins struck during a given calendar year. It was Mint practice from the 1790s into the early 19th century to keep usable dies in service until they became unfit. As a result, the quantity of dimes bearing a given date does not match the precise numbers given for calendar-year mintages. However, the mintages do provide a general guide.

On several occasions, the Mint was closed due to recurring yellow-fever epidemics. The dies were put in storage at the Bank of America. When coinage resumed, the same die pairs were not necessarily used. This and other factors led to interesting variations that can be studied by careful examination of the coins.

DRAPED BUST, SMALL EAGLE REVERSE (1796–1797)

GRADING STANDARDS

MS-60 to 70 (Mint State). *Obverse:* At MS-60, some abrasion and contact marks are evident, most noticeably on the cheek, the drapery, and the right field. Luster is present, but may be dull or lifeless, and interrupted in patches. At MS-63, contact marks are very few, and abrasion is hard to detect except under magnification, although this type is sometimes graded liberally due to its rarity. An MS-65 coin has no abrasion, and contact

1796; JR-3. Graded MS-63.

marks are so minute as to require magnification. Luster should be full and rich. Coins graded above MS-65 are more theoretical than actual for this type—but they do exist, and are defined by having fewer marks as perfection is approached. *Reverse:* Comments apply as for the obverse, except that abrasion and marks are most noticeable on the eagle at the center, a situation complicated by the fact that this area was sometimes lightly struck. The field area is small and is protected by lettering and the wreath, and in any given grade shows fewer marks than on the obverse.

Illustrated coin: This coin is one of only two known with this triangular rim break on the reverse. The dies were likely discarded shortly after the break occurred. Also note the die break from the rim break to the eagle's left wing.

AU-50, 53, 55, 58 (About Uncirculated).
Obverse: Light wear is seen on the hair area above the ear and extending to left of the forehead, on the ribbon, and on the bosom, more so at AU-50 than at AU–53 or 55. An AU-58 coin has minimal traces of wear. An AU-50 coin has luster in protected areas among the stars and letters, with little in the open fields or on the portrait. At AU-58, most luster is present in the fields, but is worn

1796; JR-3. Graded AU-50.

away on the highest parts of the motifs. Generally, grading guidelines for this dime type follow those of the related half dimes. *Reverse:* Light wear is seen on the eagle's body (keep in mind that the higher parts of this area might be lightly struck) and the edges of the wings. Light wear is seen on the wreath and lettering. Luster is the best key to actual wear. This ranges from perhaps 20% remaining in protected areas (at AU-50) to nearly full mint bloom (at AU-58).

EF-40, 45 (Extremely Fine). *Obverse:* More wear is evident on the upper hair area and the ribbon, and on the drapery and bosom. Excellent detail remains in low-relief areas of the hair. The stars show wear as do the date and letters. Luster, if present at all, is minimal and in protected areas. *Reverse:* The eagle shows more wear, this being the focal point to check. Many feathers remain on the interior areas of the wings. Additional wear is

1796; JR-5. Graded EF-45.

on the wreath and letters, but many details are present. Some luster may be seen in protected areas, and if present is slightly more abundant than on the obverse.

Illustrated coin: Note the single adjustment mark running across the eagle's chest. Most examples of this die variety bear similar adjustment marks at varying angles.

VF-20, 30 (Very Fine). *Obverse:* The higher-relief areas of hair are well worn at VF-20, less so at VF-30. The drapery and bosom show extensive wear. The stars have more wear, making them appear larger (an optical illusion seen on most worn silver coins of this era). *Reverse:* The body of the eagle shows few if any feathers, while the wings have about half of the feathers visible, depending on the strike. At VF-30 more than half of the

1796; JR-6. Graded VF-30.

feathers may show. The leaves lack most detail and are in outline form. Scattered, non-disfiguring marks are normal for this and lower grades. Any major defects should be noted separately.

F-12, 15 (Fine). *Obverse:* Wear is more extensive than on a Very Fine coin, particularly noticeable on the hair, face, and bosom, and the stars appear larger. About half the hair detail remains, most noticeably behind the neck and shoulder. The rim may be partially worn away and blend into the field. *Reverse:* Wear is more extensive. Now, feather details are diminished, with fewer than half remaining on the wings. The wreath and lettering

1796; JR-4. Graded F-12.

are worn further, and the rim is usually weak in areas, although some denticles can be seen.

   Illustrated coin: This coin falls at the low end of the Fine range.

VG-8, 10 (Very Good). *Obverse:* The portrait is mostly seen in outline form, with most hair strands gone, although there is some definition at the back of the hair and behind the shoulder. The ear is discernible, as is the eye. The stars appear larger still, again an illusion. The rim is weak in areas. LIBERTY and the date are readable and usually full, although some letters may be weak at their tops. *Reverse:* The eagle is mostly an outline

1796; JR-4. Graded VG-8.

with parts blending into the field (on lighter strikes). The rim is worn, as are the letters, with some weak, but the motto is readable.

G-4, 6 (Good). *Obverse:* Wear is more extensive, and some stars may be partly missing. The head is an outline. The eye is visible only in outline form. The rim is well worn or even missing in areas. LIBERTY is worn, and parts of some letters may be missing, but elements of all should be readable. The date is readable, but worn. *Reverse:* The eagle is flat and discernible in outline form, and may be blending into the field. The wreath is well

1796; JR-6. Graded G-4.

worn. Some of the letters may be partly missing. At this level some "averaging" can be done. If the letters are stronger than usual in one area, but some are missing in another area, the coin can still qualify as G-4.

AG-3 (About Good). *Obverse:* Wear is so extensive that the coin is barely identifiable. The head is in outline form. LIBERTY is mostly gone, same for the stars. The date, while readable, may be partially worn away. *Reverse:* The reverse is well worn with parts of the wreath and lettering missing.

1796; JR-2. Graded AG-3.

1796 Draped Bust Dime, Small Eagle Reverse

1796 • **Circulation-Strike Mintage:** 22,135.

Commentary: As this is the first year of the denomination, there is a surprising number of really great-looking 1796 dimes in existence in all grades. Many of these dimes have very high eye appeal and lovely toning. This makes 1796 a very highly sought-after date with type collectors.

JR-3 to JR-6 share the same obverse die. JR-4, JR-5, and JR-7 share the same reverse die.

JR-1: Rarity-3. *Availability in circulated grades:* 300 to 450 estimated. *Availability in Mint State:* 60 to 75.

Commentary: The JR book states that 40% to 45% of the surviving 1796 dimes are thought to be of the JR-1 variety, and that in Mint State more than half are JR-1 coins. Some early strikes are highly prooflike

JR-1.

and have been called Proofs by some. Late strikes show weakness. Many have a die break to the left of the date. The finest known example, MS-67, sold in June 2014 for $881,250.

	Cert	Avg	% MS	AG-3	G-4	VG-8	F-12	VF-20	EF-40	AU-50	MS-60	MS-63
1796, JR-1	5	34.8	40%	$1,100	$2,500	$3,500	$5,000	$6,500	$10,000	$15,000	$23,000	$35,000

JR-2: R-4. *Availability in circulated grades:* 75 to 150 estimated. *Availability in Mint State:* 5 to 7.

Commentary: This variety is very scarce and constitutes perhaps 10% of the surviving dimes of this date. The finest known is MS-65 and sold for $145,000 in August 2015.

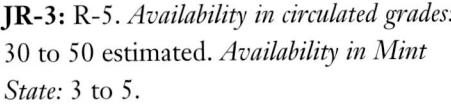

JR-2.

JR-3: R-5. *Availability in circulated grades:* 30 to 50 estimated. *Availability in Mint State:* 3 to 5.

Commentary: This is the second-rarest collectible 1796 variety. The finest known is MS-65.

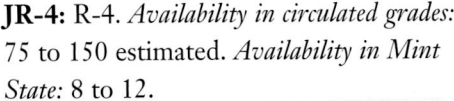

JR-3.

JR-4: R-4. *Availability in circulated grades:* 75 to 150 estimated. *Availability in Mint State:* 8 to 12.

Commentary: The two finest known are thought to be the D. Brent Pogue coin at $235,000 with a long pedigree back to the Malcolm N. Jackson Collection in 1913 and the Ed Price coin from the James A. Stack Collection; each MS-66 or higher.

JR-4.

JR-5: R-5. *Availability in circulated grades:* 25 to 40 estimated. *Availability in Mint State:* 1 or 2.

Commentary: This is the rarest of the collectible varieties among 1796 dimes. The finest known is MS-62. The finest known when the JR book was published was AU-50.

JR-5.

JR-6: R-3. *Availability in circulated grades:* 200 to 300 estimated. *Availability in Mint State:* 10 to 20.

JR-7: R-8. *Availability in circulated grades:* 1.

Commentary: The 1796 dime designated JR-7 is the only unique early dime variety reported by David Quint in his "Bust Dime Census" (JRCS, 2013), another contribution by

JR-6.

one of the leading figures in the hobby. This coin has problems but has the details of the Fair-2 grade. Considering that this is the only one known, the grade might not matter to a specialist!

1797 Draped Bust Dime

1797, 16 Stars • **Circulation-Strike Mintage:** Part of a total mintage of 25,261 for the issue.

JR-1: R-4. *Availability in circulated grades:* 85 to 140 estimated. *Availability in Mint State:* 6 to 9.

Commentary: The finest known of this variety is the D. Brent Pogue coin graded MS-66, which sold for $199,750 in May 2015.

One characteristic of the JR-1 is a die break on the obverse located above the date. As the die was continued to be used it deteriorated; very late die states do not show any date, as that part of the die finally broke off.

The reported mintage of 25,261 for the calendar year 1797 may possibly include as many as 3,864 dimes dated 1796 (delivered February 28, 1797). The 6,380 dimes delivered March 21, if not further

JR-1.

1797, 16 Stars, Late State detail.

1796s, were probably the 16 Stars variety, like the 9,099 of May 26. The 3,958 of June 20 were most like 1797, 13 Stars coins, like the 1,000 of June 30 and the final 960 of August 20, 1797. On August 28 the Mint closed down because of a yellow-fever epidemic, reopening in November. However, no more dimes were coined until July 1798, by which time the Heraldic Eagle dies were ready.

The 16 stars represented the states that made up the Union at the time these coins were struck. Later in the year, the design was changed to 13 stars, representing the original states. This 13-star arrangement continued for many years with very few exceptions. Dimes of 1797, as a date, are significantly more difficult to find in high grades than are those dated 1796. As is the case with quarter dollars, examples of 1796 dimes were saved as souvenirs as the first year of issue. However, 1797 dimes were virtually completely overlooked in this regard.

The reverse die of 1797 JR-1 was also used to strike 1798, 8 Over 7, JR-1.

	Cert	Avg	% MS	AG-3	G-4	VG-8	F-12	VF-20	EF-40	AU-50	MS-60	MS-63
1797, 16 Stars, JR-1	22	38.7	32%	$1,100	$2,500	$3,750	$5,000	$7,000	$12,000	$18,500	$35,000	$65,000

1797, 13 Stars • Circulation-Strike Mintage: Part of a total mintage of 25,261 for the issue.

JR-2: R-4. *Availability in circulated grades:* 75 to 130 estimated. *Availability in Mint State:* 4 to 6.

Commentary: It is believed that JR-2 was minted after the JR-1 as JR-2 has only 13 stars. As the nation grew in number of states, there was no room to add additional stars, so it was decided to return to using 13 stars. Many

JR-2.

examples of JR-2 show advanced pitting over the course of striking. Two top coins are each graded MS-64; one in a private collection and another sold in May 2015 for $176,250.

	Cert	Avg	% MS	AG-3	G-4	VG-8	F-12	VF-20	EF-40	AU-50	MS-60	MS-63
1797, 13 Stars, JR-2	24	26.5	8%	$1,200	$2,800	$4,000	$5,500	$8,000	$13,500	$20,000	$50,000	$80,000

DRAPED BUST, HERALDIC EAGLE REVERSE (1798–1807)

GRADING STANDARDS

MS-60 to 70 (Mint State). *Obverse:* At MS-60 some abrasion and contact marks are evident, most noticeably on the cheek, the drapery at the shoulder, and the right field. Luster is present, but may be dull or lifeless, and interrupted in patches. At MS-63, contact marks are very few, and abrasion is hard to detect except under magnification. An MS-65 coin has no abrasion, and contact marks are so minute as to require magnifica-

1802; JR-4. Graded MS-62.

tion. Luster should be full and rich. Coins graded above MS-65 are more theoretical than actual for this type—but they do exist, and are defined by having fewer marks as perfection is approached. *Reverse:* Comments apply as for the obverse, except that abrasion and marks are most noticeable on the eagle's neck, the tips of the wing, and the tail. The field area is complex, without much open space, given the stars above the eagle, the arrows and olive branch, and other features. Accordingly, marks are not as noticeable as on the obverse.

Illustrated coin: Attractive luster and toning increase the eye appeal and desirability of this coin, despite softer-than-average striking. More than one important 20th-century collector has called this the finest dime of its kind.

AU-50, 53, 55, 58 (About Uncirculated). *Obverse:* Light wear is seen on the hair area above the ear and extending to left of the forehead, on the ribbon, and on the drapery at the shoulder, more so at AU-50 than at AU–53 or 55. An AU-58 coin has minimal traces of wear. An AU-50 coin has luster in protected areas among the stars and letters, with little in the open fields or on the portrait. At AU-58, most luster is present in the fields, but is worn

1800; JR-2. Graded AU-50.

away on the highest parts of the motifs. *Reverse:* Comments as preceding, except that the eagle's neck, the tips and top of the wings, the clouds, and the tail now show noticeable wear, as do other features. As always, a familiarity with a given die variety will help differentiate striking weakness from actual wear. Luster ranges from perhaps 20% remaining in protected areas (at AU-50) to nearly full mint bloom (at AU-58). Often the reverse of this type will retain much more luster than the obverse.

EF-40, 45 (Extremely Fine). *Obverse:* More wear is evident on the upper hair area and the ribbon and on the drapery and bosom. Excellent detail remains in low-relief areas of the hair. The stars show wear, as do the date and letters. Luster, if present at all, is minimal and in protected areas. *Reverse:* The neck lacks feather detail on its highest points. Feathers have lost some detail near the edges of the wings, and some areas of the horizontal lines

1802; JR-2. Graded EF-45.

in the shield may be blended together, particularly at the right (an area that is also susceptible to weak striking). Some traces of luster may be seen, more so at EF-45 than at EF-40.

Illustrated coin: Note the die crack on the reverse from above OF to below the eagle's left foot. There is also some die clashing evident in the field behind the eagle. This reverse was used to coin dimes long after it was damaged.

VF-20, 30 (Very Fine). *Obverse:* The higher-relief areas of hair are well worn at VF-20, less so at VF-30. The drapery and bosom show extensive wear. The stars have more wear, making them appear larger (an optical illusion seen on most worn silver coins of this era). *Reverse:* Wear is greater, including on the shield and wing feathers. Star centers are flat. Other areas have lost detail, as well. E PLURIBUS UNUM is complete (this incuse feature tended to wear away slowly).

1801; JR-1. Graded VF-20.

Illustrated coin: Here is a problem-free example with normal wear for this grade.

F-12, 15 (Fine). *Obverse:* Wear is more extensive than on a Very Fine coin, particularly noticeable on the hair, face, and bosom, and the stars appear larger. About half the hair detail remains, most noticeably behind the neck and shoulder. The rim may be partially worn away and blend into the field. *Reverse:* Wear is even more extensive, with the shield and wing feathers being points to observe. About half of the

1805; JR-2. Graded F-15.

feathers are visible (depending on striking). E PLURIBUS UNUM may have a few letters worn away. The clouds all seem to be connected. The stars are weak. Parts of the border and lettering may be weak.

VG-8, 10 (Very Good). *Obverse:* The portrait is mostly seen in outline form, with most hair strands gone, although there is some definition at the back of the hair and behind the shoulder. The ear may be discernible. The eye is evident. The stars appear larger still, again an illusion. The rim is weak in areas. LIBERTY and the date are readable and usually full, although some letters may be weak at their tops.

1798, 8 Over 7; JR-2. Graded VG-8.

Reverse: Half or so of the letters in the motto are worn away. Most feathers are worn away, although separation of some may be seen. Some stars are faint. The border blends into the field in areas, and some letters are weak. Sharpness can vary widely depending on the die variety. At this level, grading by the obverse first, then checking the reverse, is recommended.

G-4, 6 (Good). *Obverse:* Some stars may be partly missing. The head is an outline. The eye is visible only in outline form. The rim is well worn or even missing in areas. LIBERTY is worn, and parts of some letters may be missing, but elements of all should be readable. The date is readable, but worn. *Reverse:* The upper part of the eagle is flat, and feathers are notice-

1807; JR-1. Graded G-4.

able at the lower edge of the wing. Some scattered feather detail may or may not be seen. The upper part of the shield is flat or nearly so, depending on the variety. Only a few letters of the motto can be seen, although this depends on the variety. The rim is worn extensively, and a few letters may be missing.

AG-3 (About Good). *Obverse:* Wear is very extensive, and some stars and letters are extremely weak or missing entirely. The date is readable. *Reverse:* Extensive wear is seen overall, with the rim worn away and some areas worn smooth. The eagle can be discerned in outline form, but not necessarily completely. A few stray motto letters may remain. Sometimes the obverse can be exceedingly worn (but the

1803; JR-3. Graded AG-3.

date must be readable) and the reverse with more detail, or vice-versa.

1798 Draped Bust Dime

1798, 8 Over 7, 16 Stars • Circulation-Strike Mintage: Part of a total mintage of 27,550 for the issue.

JR-1: R-3. *Availability in circulated grades:* 200 to 300 estimated. *Availability in Mint State:* 12 to 15.

Commentary: The finest known is MS-66. The distinctive reverse die was previously used to strike 1797-dated quarter eagles, for which only a single rare variety is known. The majority of JR-1s have significant die clashing that adds to their numismatic interest. Most are weakly struck on part of the shield. One of the finest examples was sold in the Eric Newman sale in November 2013 for $88,125.

JR-1.

Detail of the overdate.   Detail of the 16 Stars.

	Cert	Avg	% MS	AG-3	G-4	VG-8	F-12	VF-20	EF-40	AU-50	MS-60	MS-63
1798, 8 Over 7, 16 Stars, JR-1	56	50.1	55%	$350	$850	$1,200	$1,500	$2,500	$3,500	$5,000	$8,000	$18,000

1798, 8 Over 7, 13 Stars • Circulation-Strike Mintage: Part of a total mintage of 27,550 for the issue.

JR-2: R-5+. *Availability in circulated grades:* 15 to 25 estimated. *Availability in Mint State:* 4 or 5.

Commentary: This is the rarest variety of the year. Most lack eye appeal. The finest known is MS-63. The D. Brent Pogue coin at that level sold for $199,750.

JR-2.

Detail of the overdate.   Detail of the 13 Stars.

	Cert	Avg	% MS	AG-3	G-4	VG-8	F-12	VF-20	EF-40	AU-50	MS-60	MS-63
1798, 8 Over 7, 13 Stars, JR-2	6	40.7	17%	$350	$1,000	$2,200	$4,250	$7,000	$10,000	$20,000	$55,000	

1798, Small 8 • Circulation-Strike Mintage: Part of a total mintage of 27,550 for the issue.

JR-3: R-5. *Availability in circulated grades:* 30 to 50 estimated. *Availability in Mint State:* 7 to 9.

Commentary: There seems to be no logical reason why the engraver made such a small 8 compared to the size of the 9 and 7 in the date. The reverse is always weakly struck near the stars above the eagle. Most examples have low eye appeal. The D. Brent Pogue Gem sold in May 2015 for $141,000.

JR-3.

	Cert	Avg	% MS	AG-3	G-4	VG-8	F-12	VF-20	EF-40	AU-50	MS-60	MS-63
1798, Small 8, JR-3	4	32.8	25%	$350	$1,000	$2,400	$3,000	$3,500	$5,500	$12,500	$25,000	$40,000

1798, Large 8 • Circulation-Strike Mintage: Part of a total mintage of 27,550 for the issue.

JR-4: R-3. *Availability in circulated grades:* 200 to 300 estimated. *Availability in Mint State:* 14 to 18.

Commentary: The reverse die was first used to strike a 1798 quarter eagle; then this variety was struck, and finally the reverse die was used to strike the 1800 JR-1 dime. Many JR-4s have die cracks on the obverse running from the rim to Liberty's nose and from the chin into the right obverse field. Later die states have additional cracks through the stars and rims. In June 2014, an MS-64 with great eye appeal and many die cracks was sold at auction for $70,500. The finest known is MS-65.

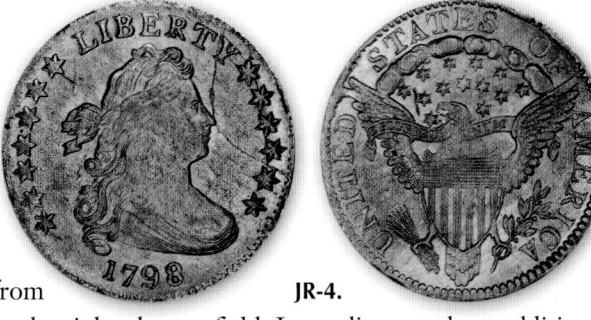

JR-4.

	Cert	Avg	% MS	AG-3	G-4	VG-8	F-12	VF-20	EF-40	AU-50	MS-60	MS-63
1798, Large 8, JR-4	23	47.2	30%	$325	$850	$1,200	$1,500	$2,500	$3,750	$4,500	$8,500	$20,000

1800 Draped Bust Dime

1800 • Circulation-Strike Mintage: 21,760.

JR-1: R-4+. *Availability in circulated grades:* 25 to 35 estimated. *Availability in Mint State:* Probably no more than 3.

Commentary: This is the rarest variety of the year. The JR-1 reverse die was used to strike the 1798 quarter eagle and the 1798 JR-4 dime. The reverse die has narrow A's and a die crack from the rim to the second feather of the eagle's right wing. The finest known is MS-62.

JR-1.

	Cert	Avg	% MS	AG-3	G-4	VG-8	F-12	VF-20	EF-40	AU-50	MS-60	MS-63
1800, JR-1	8	36.5	0%	$325	$850	$1,050	$1,500	$3,000	$4,000	$8,500	$22,500	$42,500

JR-2: R-4+. *Availability in circulated grades:* 30 to 40 estimated. *Availability in Mint State:* 6 to 8 known.

Commentary: The finest known is MS-66. The reverse die was later used to mint 1801 JR-2 dimes.

JR-2.

	Cert	Avg	% MS	AG-3	G-4	VG-8	F-12	VF-20	EF-40	AU-50	MS-60	MS-63
1800, JR-2	13	42.4	23%	$325	$850	$1,050	$1,500	$3,000	$4,000	$8,500	$22,500	$42,500

1801 Draped Bust Dime

1801 • **Circulation-Strike Mintage:** 34,640.

JR-1: R-4. *Availability in circulated grades:* 75 to 125 estimated. *Availability in Mint State:* 4.

Commentary: The key difference between the JR-1 and JR-2 is the size of the first A in STATES, with the JR-1 having a wide A and the JR-2 having a narrow A.

Most 1802 dimes are in low grades and are

JR-1.

weakly struck. Any coin in grading Very Fine or better is rare. Most dimes of this date lack eye appeal. The highest-graded JR-1 is Eugene Gardner's MS-65 coin, which sold for $111,625 in 2014.

	Cert	Avg	% MS	AG-3	G-4	VG-8	F-12	VF-20	EF-40	AU-50	MS-60	MS-63
1801, JR-1	4	20.3	25%	$325	$850	$1,250	$2,000	$3,750	$6,000	$11,000	$30,000	$48,500

JR-2: R-4+. *Availability in circulated grades:* 65 to 100 estimated. *Availability in Mint State:* 3.

Commentary: The JR-2 is very rare. The highest graded example is a Mint State 63.

JR-2.

	Cert	Avg	% MS	AG-3	G-4	VG-8	F-12	VF-20	EF-40	AU-50	MS-60
1801, JR-2	0	n/a		$325	$850	$1,250	$2,000	$3,750	$6,000	$11,000	$30,000

1802 Draped Bust Dime

1802 • **Circulation-Strike Mintage:** 10,975.

JR-1: R-8. *Availability in circulated grades:* 2. *Availability in Mint State:* None known.

Commentary: The first use of the obverse die was on the 1802 quarter eagles. It was later used on the 1803 JR-1 and JR-5 dimes. In 2014, a JR-1 example with Good details that was repaired and whizzed sold for $17,625. The JR-1 can be easily recognized by the position of the E in STATES.

This was considered to be unique when the JR book was published; a second one (Good with problems) was discovered by David W. Lange in 2013.

	Cert	Avg	% MS	AG-3	G-4
1802, JR-1				$18,000	$30,000

JR-2: R-6. *Availability in circulated grades:* 31 to 50 estimated. *Availability in Mint State:* None known.

Commentary: JR-2 is very rare die marriage that is recognized by the reverse die, including the fact that star 2 is far from the O in OF. There are many examples that show die damage around the R in AMERICA. Later die states show

JR-2.

that this die damaged was fixed at the Mint. Later still, the obverse and reverse dies suffered failures, with the obverse shattering along with the reverse.

	Cert	Avg	% MS	AG-3	G-4	VG-8	F-12	VF-20	EF-40	AU-50	MS-62
1802, JR-2	2	58.0	50%	$1,250	$2,000	$2,750	$3,500	$6,500	$13,000	$22,000	$85,000

JR-3: R-6. *Availability in circulated grades:* 20 to 30 estimated. *Availability in Mint State:* 1 known.

Commentary: JR-3 is scarcer than the JR-2 variety. The JR-3 has a wide space between stars 2 and 3, and a die crack runs through CA in AMERICA. The reverse die was first used to strike the 1802 quarter eagle and later the 1803

JR-3.

JR-2 dime. In 2008 an AU-58, then the highest graded example, was sold for $43,125.

	Cert	Avg	% MS	AG-3	G-4	VG-8	F-12	VF-20	EF-40	AU-50	MS-60
1802, JR-3	2	3.0	0%	$1,250	$2,000	$3,000	$4,000	$6,500	$15,000	$35,000	$44,000

JR-4: R-4. *Availability in circulated grades:* 80 to 125 estimated. *Availability in Mint State:* Fewer than 5 known.

Commentary: The JR-4 is the most readily available 1802 dime but is still considered very scarce. The reverse die was used to strike the 1802 quarter eagle and later for the 1804 JR-1 dime and the 1804 quarter eagle. This variety has star 12 pierced by the eagle's beak. The

JR-4.

finest known example is the John J. Pittman, graded MS-62, that sold at auction in May 2015 for $82,250. Another MS-62, the Lovejoy and Bareford example, crossed the block for $138,000 in July 2008.

	Cert	Avg	% MS	AG-3	G-4	VG-8	F-12	VF-20	EF-40	AU-50	MS-60	MS-62
1802, JR-4	7	22.1	14%	$650	$1,500	$2,000	$3,000	$5,000	$10,000	$17,500	$35,000	$75,000

1803 Draped Bust Dime

1803 • Circulation-Strike Mintage: 33,040.

Commentary: According to the JR book, on all dimes of 1803, "This rare dime is probably the most unappreciated of the Draped Bust dime series. At least 10,000 of the dimes reported as minted in 1803 were probably dated 1802, which makes 1803 dimes about as scarce as 1802 dimes."

JR-1: R-6+. *Availability in circulated grades:* Fewer than 10 known. *Availability in Mint State:* None known.

Commentary: On this variety the 3 in the date is tilted to the right. On the reverse the right edge of E in STATES is between clouds 3 and 4. The finest is EF-45. Eye appeal is usually low, so cherrypicking is recommended.

JR-1.

	Cert	Avg	% MS	AG-3	G-4	VG-8	F-12	VF-20	EF-40	AU-50
1803, JR-1	0	n/a		$1,000	$1,500	$2,000	$3,500	$5,500	$19,500	$24,000

JR-2: Low R-6. *Availability in circulated grades:* 20 to 30 estimated. *Availability in Mint State:* None known.

Commentary: The eye appeal is usually low, and some examples of this variety show damage. Many have interesting die cracks at and near the date. The reverse die was used earlier on the 1802 JR-3 dime and the 1802 quarter eagle.

The Louis Eliasberg example graded AU-55 is a very late die state. The finest known is the MS-64 sold in the D. Brent Pogue auction in May 2015 for $211,500.

	Cert	Avg	% MS	AG-3	G-4	VG-8	F-12	VF-20	EF-40	AU-50
1803, JR-2	2	10.0	0%	$1,000	$1,500	$2,500	$4,000	$6,500	$18,500	$24,000

JR-3: R-4. *Availability in circulated grades:* 75 to 100 estimated. *Availability in Mint State:* 2 known.

JR-3.

Detail of the die crack.

	Cert	Avg	% MS	AG-3	G-4	VG-8	F-12	VF-20	EF-40	AU-50	MS-60
1803, JR-3	6	24.7	17%	$350	$900	$1,300	$1,800	$3,200	$6,000	$10,000	$45,000

JR-4: R-5. *Availability in circulated grades:* 30 to 50 estimated. *Availability in Mint State:* 1.

Commentary: Many are damaged or have other problems.

JR-4.

	Cert	Avg	% MS	AG-3	G-4	VG-8	F-12	VF-20	EF-40	AU-50
1803, JR-4	5	18.8	0%	$1,000	$1,500	$2,250	$3,750	$6,250	$17,500	$19,700

JR-5: R-7+. *Availability in circulated grades:* 4 known. *Availability in Mint State:* None known.

Commentary: The finest is Extremely Fine with low eye appeal.

	Cert	Avg	% MS	AG-3	G-4	VG-8	F-12
1803, JR-5	0	n/a		$8,000	$10,000	$14,000	$22,000

1804 Draped Bust Dime

1804, 13 Stars • **Circulation-Strike Mintage:** Part of a total mintage of 8,265 for the issue.

JR-1: R-5. *Availability in circulated grades:* 50 to 60 estimated. *Availability in Mint State:* None.

Commentary: JR-1 dimes are always weakly struck in areas. Most lack eye appeal, so finding an example with excellent eye appeal will take a fair amount of patience. JR-1 and JR-2 used the same obverse die; the key difference between them is the star count on the reverse. The D. Brent Pogue AU-55 example (ex John J. Pittman) sold for $164,500 in May 2015. Another AU-55, this from the James Stack Collection, was sold in April 2009 for $63,250. The reverse of the JR-1 was used to strike the 1802 JR-4 dime and the 1802 quarter eagle.

JR-1.

Detail of the 13 Stars.

	Cert	Avg	% MS	AG-3	G-4	VG-8	F-12	VF-20	EF-40	AU-50
1804, 13 Stars, JR-1	2	55.0	0%	$1,250	$3,000	$5,500	$9,500	$15,000	$30,000	$75,000

1804, 14 Stars • Circulation-Strike Mintage: Part of a total mintage of 8,265 for the issue.

JR-2: R-5. *Availability in circulated grades: 40-50 estimated. Availability in Mint State: 1.*

JR-2.

Commentary: JR-2 is the rarer of the two known 1804 varieties. All show striking weakness in areas. Many lack eye appeal. The star count of 14 was probably an engraving error. This reverse was to produce the 1804 quarter eagle. Later die states are known with die cracks running from star 10 to the nose and from the rim through star 13. There is a single known Mint State example. Grading MS-62, it sold at auction for $367,188 in May 2013. The second finest known is the Louis E. Eliasberg AU-58 coin, which changed hands in May 2015 for $329,000.

Detail of the 14 Stars.

The reverse die of this dime—and several other dimes of the era—was also used to coin gold quarter eagles of like diameter, a very curious situation. Accordingly, it seems logical that there might be a die linkage between half dollars and the similarly sized $10 gold pieces of the Heraldic Eagle reverse style of the same era, but thus far no matching has been found.

	Cert	Avg	% MS	AG-3	G-4	VG-8	F-12	VF-20	EF-40	AU-50	MS-60
1804, 14 Stars, JR-2	10	27.3	10%	$2,000	$5,000	$11,000	$14,500	$25,000	$50,000	$85,000	$330,000

1805 Draped Bust Dime

1805, 4 Berries • Circulation-Strike Mintage: Part of a total mintage of 120,780 for the issue.

JR-2: R-2. *Availability in circulated grades: 1,200 to 1,800 estimated. Availability in Mint State: 25 to 30.*

JR-2.

Commentary: This was the first year that the dime mintage figure crossed the 100,000 mark. Several of the Mint State coins are in the Choice and Gem categories. Many coins in various grades have nice eye appeal, making this a popular date for inclusion in type sets. The different berry counts have made both varieties popular. This variety is readily available in nearly any grade desired, including Mint State. The finest, an MS-67, sold for $188,000 in August 2014.

Detail of the 4 Berries.

	Cert	Avg	% MS	AG-3	G-4	VG-8	F-12	VF-20	EF-40	AU-50	MS-60	MS-63
1805, 4 Berries, JR-2	284	40.0	37%	$250	$600	$950	$1,400	$1,750	$3,000	$3,500	$7,500	$9,000

1805, 5 Berries • **Circulation-Strike Mintage:** Part of a total mintage of 120,780 for the issue.

JR-1.

JR-1: R-4+. *Availability in circulated grades:* 75 to 100 estimated. *Availability in Mint State:* Fewer than 10.

Commentary: This variety is much scarcer than the preceding, although this is not widely known.

Detail of the 5 Berries.

	Cert	Avg	% MS	AG-3	G-4	VG-8	F-12	VF-20	EF-40	AU-50	MS-60	MS-63
1805, 5 Berries, JR-1	43	30.0	19%	$250	$800	$1,200	$2,200	$3,250	$5,000	$8,000	$12,500	$25,000

1807 Draped Bust Dime

1807 • **Circulation-Strike Mintage:** 165,000.

JR-1: R-1. *Availability in circulated grades:* 1,000 to 1,500 estimated. *Availability in Mint State:* 125 to 150.

JR-1.
An exceptionally sharp strike for an 1807.

Commentary: The 1807 dime is the final year using the Draped Bust obverse and the Heraldic Eagle reverse, and only one die marriage exists. Most type collectors select the 1807 because it's relatively common compared to the other Draped Bust dimes. Many Mint state coins exist—more than for any other date of this type. However, most of them are weakly struck at the borders, a factor not reflected in grades given by the certification services. Accordingly, cherrypicking for quality is recommended. There are several known Gems in existence, most with light striking. The highest price realized at auction is the D. Brent Pogue example in May 2015, which sold for $76,375.

The reverse die to coin 1807 dimes was also used for quarter eagles dated 1805, 1806/4, 1806/5, and 1807.

The weakly struck reverse of a typical 1807.

	Cert	Avg	% MS	AG-3	G-4	VG-8	F-12	VF-20	EF-40	AU-50	MS-60	MS-63
1807, JR-1	287	42.3	36%	$250	$550	$850	$1,300	$2,000	$2,750	$3,250	$5,500	$8,500

CAPPED BUST DIMES (1809–1837):

Variety 1, Wide Border (1809–1828)— **Designer:** *John Reich.* **Weight:** *2.70 grams.*
Composition: *.8924 silver, .1076 copper.* **Diameter:** *1809–1827, approx. 19 mm; 1828,
18.5 mm.* **Edge:** *Reeded.* **Mints:** *All coined at the Philadelphia Mint.* **Variety 2, Modified
Design (1828–1837)**—**Designer:** *John Reich.* **Weight:** *1828–1836, 2.70 grams; 1837,
2.69 grams.* **Composition:** *1828–1836, .8924 silver, .1076 copper; 1837, .900 silver,
.100 copper.* **Diameter:** *18.5 mm.* **Edge:** *Reeded.* **Mints:** *All coined at the Philadelphia Mint.*

1836 (JR-2).

HISTORY AND BACKGROUND

In 1807 John Reich, appointed assistant engraver at the Mint this year, redesigned the silver half dollar and the gold half eagle to depict Miss Liberty in a mob cap fitted loosely over her head—a style numismatically known as the Capped Bust design. At the time, production of certain values was intermittent. After 1807 the next dime coinage was in 1809, and the Capped Bust motif was used. For other denominations the Capped Bust made its first appearance on the half dime was made in 1829, the first quarter dollar in 1815, and the first quarter eagle in 1808. After 1804, no silver dollars or gold eagles were made until 1836 and 1838, respectively, by which time new designs by engraver Christian Gobrecht were used.

For the dime series, mintages were intermittent from 1809 to 1825, then continuous from 1827 to 1837. During the same era, Spanish-American silver half-real coins (or *medios*), valued at 12-1/2 cents, were legal tender and were widely used, often interchangeably with federal dimes. A dime had substantial value in its era. In the 1830s a typical day's wage for a laborer was 50 cents. A dime could buy lunch or dinner.

Niles' Weekly Register, July 29, 1837, heralded the end of the Capped Bust design:

New Dime

The *United States Gazette* says: "A friend showed to us on Saturday a ten cent piece of the new coinage; it is smaller in circumference than those formerly emitted; on one side are the words ONE DIME, encircled with a wreath, on the other is a finely cut figure of liberty not the old head and trunk, that once looked so flaring out from our coin—but a neat, tidy female figure, sufficiently dressed, holding in one hand a staff, surmounted with a liberty cap; the other hand sustains a shield, inscribed with the word LIBERTY. The figure is in a sitting posture, and resembles, generally, the representation of Britannia on the English coins."

Capped Bust dimes remained plentiful in general circulation for many years, until the wholesale melting of silver coins during 1850 to early 1853, when the value of silver rose to a point at which coins contained more bullion value than face value.

JOHN REICH, ENGRAVER

John Reich (Johann Matthaus Reich) was born in Fürth, Germany, in 1768, where his father was a prolific medalist said to have been of indifferent talent. Father and son worked together on a number of memorial medals released between the years 1789 and 1800. After working in his father's shop, John emigrated from Hamburg to America aboard the *Anna*, arriving in Philadelphia in August 1800. After a year's indenture to a Philadelphia coppersmith, Reich was "freed" by Henry Voigt, then chief coiner at the Mint.

In the early years Reich did contract work on medals for the Mint and acquitted himself in fine style. Working privately for Joseph Sansom he engraved the dies for several fine medals, including Washington, after Gilbert Stuart; Benjamin Franklin, from the Jean Antoine Houdon bust; the American Beaver medal; a peace medal; and a Tripoli medal presented to Commander Edward Preble in 1806.

In January 1806 this was advertised in Philadelphia:

> A medal in honor of the memory of Washington has been struck at Philadelphia, under the direction of J. Reich, a German artist. The face, a head of General Washington, in his uniform. Inscription, GENERAL WASHINGTON, C.C.A.U.S. (Commander in Chief of the Armies of the United States). Reverse, under the date of the acquisition of Independence, the American eagle, with the thunder-bolt in its claws and the olive branch in its beak, descending upon the section of the globe, on which the United States are delineated by their boundaries.[3]

Another Washington medal, after Stuart's head, is advertised as issued in Philadelphia, October 9, 1806, "In commemoration of the retirement of Washington." The medal is described in *Poulson's Advertiser* as being struck in silver and bearing the following inscriptions:

> Face, A Head of Washington as President. Inscription—G. Washington. Pre. Unit. Sts. Reverse. The ensigns of authority (civil and military) deposited, in laurels, upon the tablet of the United States. Inscription. Commis. Resigned: Presidency Relinquished. 17 97 [*sic*].

The announcement is further made that the dies were executed by "the celebrated Artist John Reich; the likeness from a drawing of Stuart sketched on purpose."

On March 25, 1807, Mint director Robert Patterson wrote to President Thomas Jefferson:

> Our present Engraver. Scot, though indeed a meritorious and faithful officer, is yet so far advanced in life, that he cannot very long be expected to continue his labors. In the event of his sickness or death, the business of the Institution would probably be stopped for some time, since few, if any one could be found qualified to supply his place except Mr. Reich, an artist with whose talents, I presume, you are not unacquainted; and this gentleman not finding business here sufficient for his support, is, I understand, about to remove to Europe. A small salary would, however, retain him in the country, and secure his services to the Mint. And, in truth, the beauty of our coins would be greatly improved by the assistance of his masterly hand.
>
> An assistant engraver [John Gardner] was formerly employed by Mr. Rittenhouse, and by Mr. DeSaussure—and with your approbation, Sir, I would immediately employ Mr. Reich in that capacity. He is willing for the present to accept of the moderate compensation of six hundred dollars per annum; and should this gentleman be employed, perhaps more than his salary would be saved to the public, in which is usually expended on the engraving of dies for medals, but which might then be executed by an artist in their own service, with little or no additional experience.

On April 2, 1807, Patterson wrote to Jefferson again:

> With your approbation I have employed Mr. John Reich as an assistant engraver in the mint at the annual salary of six hundred dollars. He has covenanted to execute any work in the line of his profession, that may be required of him either by the director or chief engraver, whether for the immediate use of the Mint, or for that of the United States, when ordered by any special resolution or act of Congress for that purpose, or by the President, provided that in the execution of any such work, no extraordinary hours of labor or attendance be required without an adequate compensation therefor, so that if any seals should be wanted for the public offices, or dies for the purpose of striking Indian or other medals, they can now be executed in the best stile at the Mint, without any extra expense to the government.

Mr. Reich is now preparing a set of new dies in which some improvements in the devices will be introduced, (adhering, however, strictly to the letter of the law) which it is hoped will meet with public approbation.

The first order of business was to develop new motifs for the coinage. Reich's "Capped Bust" design, as we call it today, was used on the half dollar and half eagle, as noted earlier, followed by its use on the half dime, quarter, and quarter eagle, as also noted.

Reich also created what we call the "Classic Head" design today, featuring Miss Liberty facing to the left, wearing a band inscribed LIBERTY across her head, with hair tresses visible above. This motif was first used on cents of 1808 and continued thereon through 1814. On half cents the Classic Head first appeared in 1809, and it was used on them for a long time afterward, on the intermittent coinage through 1836. In 1834, when chief engraver William A. Kneass made dies for the new Classic Head quarter eagles and half eagles, he swiped Reich's motif of 1808.[4] Kneass was not very original in the things he did, and seemed to be in low gear while at the Mint.

Reich worked at the Mint for the next 10 years, resigning on March 31, 1817, due to failing eyesight or, as some have it, dissatisfaction with his unchanged salary of $600 per year. He traveled westward to Pittsburgh to restore his health and to pursue other interests. He is said by some to have died in Albany, New York, in 1833, although this has been questioned. His name, so important in numismatic circles today, had never been mentioned in an *Annual Report of the Director of the Mint*. (Actually, this was not unusual, and for decades later few other Mint artists were mentioned, either.) In time his coinage became a numismatic specialty, and today the John Reich Collectors Society (JRCS) honors his name. Many of Reich's obverse dies have a small notch in the 13th star, leading to the conclusion that this was his secret sign, called a *privy mark* in numismatic nomenclature, to identify his work.

On the personal side, Reich had a deep interest in music and was well acquainted with the classics. He was one of the founders of the Society of Artists, organized in Philadelphia in 1810, and is entered on the list of Fellows of the Society as "die-sinker at the United States Mint." In 1812 he was one of the first group of Pennsylvania Academicians. The intellectual and social-participation side of Reich has not been well studied.

WILLIAM KNEASS, ENGRAVER

In the chronicles of the Capped Bust design, William Kneass, successor to Scot as engraver, performed a minor role, making or supervising some adjustments to the design, denticles, and coinage.

Kneass was born in Lancaster, Pennsylvania, on September 25, 1780, the son of Christopher and Anna (Feltman) Kneass. In Lancaster on June 23, 1804, he married Mary Turner Honeyman. Later, after her passing, he married Jane Kramer.

It is not known how he learned the art of engraving, but from 1804 and 1805 onward he worked at that trade in Philadelphia, including as a partner in Kneass & Dellaker, and from 1817 to 1820 with James H. Young in Young, Kneass & Co., general engravers. During the War of 1812 he served as a volunteer association in the Field Engineers, a group that built fortifications on the western side of Philadelphia. Later, in 1815, he engraved a plan of this construction based on a drawing by his close friend William Strickland. Kneass named one of his six children after Strickland.

On January 29, 1824, he was appointed as engraver at the Mint, an arrangement facilitated by his friend Adam Eckfeldt, the chief coiner. Biographical notes years later by Patterson DuBois at the Mint included this:

Mr. Kneass is well remembered as an affable, genial "gentleman of the old-school," who had the rare quality of engaging and winning the esteem and affection of children and youth, in whose companionship he found rich delight. Prior to his appointment he had an engraving office on Fourth above Chestnut Street, Philadelphia, which was a well-known rendezvous for the leading wits and men of culture, for which Philadelphia was then eminent.[5]

At the Mint, Kneass did not leave behind a distinguished record of numismatic accomplishments. He is best remembered today for his Classic Head quarter eagle and half eagle of 1834, essentially copies of John Reich's Classic Head design used earlier on the 1808 copper cent. No pattern coins can be definitely attributed to him.

On August 27, 1835, Kneass suffered an incapacitating stroke, after which he did virtually no creative work. Fortunately, Christian Gobrecht was hired at the Mint at this time, under the title of "second" (not assistant) engraver, as the talented and long-admired Gobrecht did not want to be considered lower in position than Kneass. Kneass died on August 27, 1840, after which Gobrecht was given the office. The title of "chief" engraver was not used at this early time.

CAPPED BUST DIMES (1809–1837): GUIDE TO COLLECTING

In the marketplace the average grade for Capped Bust dimes is higher than for the 1796–1807 draped Bust issues. Dates from 1809 through the 1820s are available in Fine to Extremely Fine. Those from the late 1820s through 1837 can be found in Extremely Fine to About Uncirculated for most issues, and Mint State coins, usually in lower levels, are plentiful. Strictly graded MS-65 or finer coins with good eye appeal vary from scarce to rare.

If you design to acquire a single example of the 1809–1837 series for a type set, a year in the 1830s should fit the bill. If you desire specific dates you will have some challenges, with 1822 considered to be a key issue and with 1809 and 1811, 11 Over 09 being scarce. Collecting by JR varieties has been the specialty of many collectors over the years. Absolute completion is not possible. This can be a treasure hunt, as there are many rarities within the series, but as interest in collecting by varieties is not widespread, and as most offerings are not attributed as such, there is the pleasure of buying rarities but paying only common prices. And, there is the distinct possibility of discovering a die or die combination not previously known to scholars. Varieties have been studied in detail only in recent decades, and there is still much to be learned.

As to varieties listed here and in the regular *Guide Book of United States Coins*, the following is an overview.

Coinage was not continuous during this span, and several gaps occur among the earlier years. Interesting varieties include the overdates 1811, 11 Over 09; 1823, 3 Over 2; 1824, 4 Over 2; and 1830, 30 Over 29. The rarity of the latter is hard to determine, for the overdate is very difficult to ascertain on all but the finest specimens, and more examples may exist than is presently believed.

For the year 1828 two notable varieties exist, the Large Date with Curl Base 2, and the Small Date with Square Base 2.

A curious variety occurs among 1814 and 1820 dimes: The same reverse die was used in both of these years to create the so-called STATESOFAMERICA variety, which consists of three words close together without appropriate spacing.

Tradition rears its head in listings of dimes of this era, and thus such varieties as 1823, 3 Over 2, with Small E's or Large E's in the reverse legend; 1829 with Small 10 C., Medium 10 C., or Large 10 C.; and other relatively insignificant date or number sizes occur in catalog listings. Decades ago, when dimes of this span were relatively inexpensive, it was certainly feasible to collect not only by dates but by minute letter differences as well. Today the situation is different, and few people seem to be interested. However, in the regular *Guide Book* these have been "grandfathered" and are still listed, in a nod to tradition. A budding collector of Capped Bust dimes would do well to seek only the dates and overdates, unless he or she plans to devote the coming *years* to acquiring by JR varieties.

Dimes of 1809, the first year of the Capped Bust style, are fairly elusive in all conditions, but in Mint State the issue is very rare. Dimes of 1811 are seen with greater frequency in all grades, with Mint State pieces being elusive, but not to the degree of those dated 1809. All 1811 dimes are 1811, 11 Over 09 overdates. It is not until the third year of dime production of this type, 1814, that issues are less than scarce or rare. The 1814 dimes are readily available in all grades from About Good through Extremely Fine, and even About Uncirculated and Mint State coins appear on the market with some frequency. The 1814 has two different date sizes, with the Small Date variety being much scarcer than the Large Date. The next issue, 1820, is readily available in different grades across the board, although among the 13 individual die varieties known to scholars, some are decidedly rare.

Dimes of 1821, which exist in many die combinations, are available in all grades, although Mint State pieces are apt to be difficult to track down, particularly in view of the demand for them by type-set collectors. The 1821 has two different date sizes—Small and Large—with the Small size being scarcer than the Large size. Dimes of the next year, 1822, are scarce in all grades and constitute one of the most highly desired dates among issues of the 1809–1837 type. Among the population of several hundred known pieces, the majority are in lower grades, although enough Very Fine and Extremely Fine pieces exist that the specialist, with some diligence, can locate one. Mint State coins are a different story and are apt to come to light only when great collections are sold. From time to time this particular date has attracted the fancy of investors and speculators, and a few scattered hoards cross the screen of numismatic history, with a cache of 17 coins in various grades sold by Paramount International Coin Corporation in the 1970s being particularly notable.

Dimes of 1823 are all overdates, 1823, 3 Over 2. Two obverse dies and two reverse dies were combined in the sequence 1-A, 1-B, and 2-B to create a total of three die varieties for the year. The reverse dies are commonly differentiated by having either Small E's in the legend or Large E's.

The 1824 dimes are likewise overdates, in this instance 1824, 4 Over 2. Just one obverse die was used to strike pieces dated this year. Two reverse dies were used; Reverse A is quite common, while Reverse B (distinguished by the 1 in 10 C. having a pointed top as opposed to the common Flat Top 1) is very rare. As noted previously, cherrypicking might get you the rarity for no more than the cost of the common issue.

Of dimes dated 1825, five different die combinations are known, two of which are fairly rare. In 1827, dimes were produced in abundance, with a recorded calendar-year mintage of more than a million pieces, divided into at least 13 known die varieties. As a date, specimens are readily available in all grades, although Mint State pieces are fairly elusive due to the demand on the part of type collectors. Certain die varieties of the year are scarce, however.

Two varieties exist of 1828 dimes: the Large Date (with Curl Base 2) and the Small Date. Years ago it was believed that the Large Date variety was struck in an open collar and was of larger diameter than the Small Date, but measurement of extant specimens reveals that both Large Date and Small Date varieties were produced in a closed collar and are of like diameter. The Small Date variety, however, has denticles that are closely spaced and that are similar to the closely spaced denticles of later issues, while the Large Date has widely spaced denticles similar to the configuration of 1809–1827. Date is not particularly challenging. The Large Date variety is underrated and is a semi-key of the series behind the 1809 and 1811, 11 Over 09.

Dimes of 1829 exist in a number of different varieties, some of which reflect the transition between the old denticle style and the new, with several having old-style reverses with widely spaced denticles. All in all, at least a dozen die varieties have been identified. Examples of the date can be readily found in various grades, although Mint State pieces are elusive. As is true of other dates in this era, a few scattered Proofs were struck for presentation purposes and are exceedingly rare today.

Multiple varieties are known of the 1830 dime, of which two have the 1830, 30 Over 29, overdate. This variety was first showcased by Don Taxay in 1971 in the *Scott* catalog, an effort to create a competitor to the *Guide Book*. At first believed unique, the variety was discovered in duplicate, triplicate, and larger quantities, and now the issue known in two die combinations and is fairly common (although not all show the overdate feature clearly). As a date, 1830 dimes are plentiful and are available in all grades, although higher-condition pieces require some searching to locate. Capped Bust dimes of the dates 1831 through 1837 are readily available in all grades, although those dated 1837 are scarcer than earlier issues.

Another interesting aspect of collecting Capped Bust dimes is finding early dimes with cuds, these being filled-in die breaks, usually near the border, somewhat resembling small blobs of gum. Die cracks developed in the minting process, and when a die further deteriorated, chips of the die sometimes fell away, resulting in these small blobs on the finished coins. Cuds sometimes can be seen in their progress from small to larger.

Capped Bust (1809–1837)

Grading Standards

MS-60 to 70 (Mint State). *Obverse:* The rims are more uniform for the 1828–1837 variety than for the 1809–1828 variety, striking is usually very sharp, and any abrasion occurs evenly on both sides. At MS-60 some abrasion and contact marks are evident, most noticeably on the cheek and on the area near the drapery clasp. Luster is present, but may be dull or lifeless, and interrupted in patches. At MS-63, contact marks are very few, and

1831; JR-5. Graded MS-64.

abrasion is hard to detect except under magnification. An MS-65 coin has no abrasion, and contact marks are so minute as to require magnification. Luster should be full and rich. Grades above MS-65 are seen now and again, and are defined by having fewer marks as perfection is approached. *Reverse:* Comments apply as for the obverse, except that abrasion and contact marks are most noticeable on the eagle's neck, the top of the wings, the claws, and the flat band that surrounds the incuse motto. The field is mainly protected by design elements and does not show abrasion as much as does the obverse.

AU-50, 53, 55, 58 (About Uncirculated). *Obverse:* The rims are more uniform for the 1828–1837 variety than for the 1809–1828 variety, striking is usually very sharp, and any abrasion occurs evenly on both sides. Light wear is seen on the cap, the hair below LIBERTY, the hair near the clasp, and the drapery at the bosom. At AU-58, the luster is extensive except in the open area of the field, especially to the right. At AU–50 and 53, lus-

1814; JR-5. Graded AU-55.

ter remains only in protected areas. As is true of all high grades, sharpness of strike can affect the perception of wear. *Reverse:* Wear is evident on the eagle's neck, the top of the wings, and the claws. An AU-58 has nearly full luster. At AU–50 and 53, there still is significant luster, more than on the obverse.

Illustrated coin: The stars on this coin are weakly struck.

EF-40, 45 (Extremely Fine). *Obverse:* The rims are more uniform for the 1828–1837 variety than for the 1809–1828 variety, striking is usually very sharp, and the wear occurs evenly on both sides. Wear is more extensive, most noticeable on the higher areas of the hair. The cap shows more wear, as does the cheek. Stars still show their centers (unless lightly struck, and *many* are). Luster, if present, is in protected areas among the star points and close to the portrait.

1834, Large 4; JR-1. Graded EF-40.

Reverse: The wings show wear on the higher areas of the feathers (particularly on the right wing), and some details are lost. Feathers in the neck are light. The eagle's claws show wear. Luster may be present in protected areas, even if there is little or none on the obverse.

VF-20, 30 (Very Fine). *Obverse:* The rims are more uniform for the 1828–1837 variety than for the 1809–1828 variety, striking is usually very sharp, and wear occurs evenly on both sides. Wear is more extensive, and most of the hair is combined into thick tresses without delicate features. The curl on the neck is flat. Unless they were weakly struck to begin with, most stars retain their interior lines. *Reverse:* Wear is most evident on the eagle's

1825. Graded VF-30.

neck, to the left of the shield, and on the leaves and claws. Most feathers in the wing remain distinct.

F-12, 15 (Fine). *Obverse:* The rims are more uniform for the 1828–1837 variety than for the 1809–1828 variety, striking is usually very sharp, and wear occurs evenly on both sides. (For both varieties the striking is not as important at this and lower grades.) Wear is more extensive, with much of the hair blended together. The drapery is indistinct along part of its upper edge. Stars have lost detail at the center and some may be flat. The height of obverse rim is important in the amount of wear the coin has received.

1821; JR-7. Graded F-15.

Reverse: Wear is more extensive, now with only about a third to half of the feathers remaining on the wings, more on the wing to the left. Some of the horizontal lines in the shield may be worn away.

VG-8, 10 (Very Good). *Obverse:* The hair is less distinct, with the area surrounding the face blended into the facial features. LIBERTY is complete, but weak in areas. Stars are nearly flat. *Reverse:* Feathers are fewer and mostly visible on the eagle's left wing. Other details are weaker. All lettering remains easily readable, although some letters may be faint.

1822; JR-1. Graded VG-8.

G-4, 6 (Good). *Obverse:* The portrait is mostly in outline, with few interior details discernible. LIBERTY may still be readable or may be partially worn away, depending on the variety (this varies due to the strike characteristics of some die marriages). Stars are flat at their centers. *Reverse:* The eagle is mostly in outline form, although some feathers can be seen in the right wing. All letters around the border are clear on a sharp strike;

1820, Large 0. Graded G-4.

some letters are light or missing on a coin with low rims. E PLURIBUS UNUM may be weak, often with some letters worn away.

Illustrated coin: This is an attractive, problem-free coin at this grade.

AG-3 (About Good). *Obverse:* The portrait is an outline, although traces of LIBERTY can still be seen. The rim is worn down, and some stars are weak. The date remains clear although weak toward the rim. *Reverse:* The reverse shows more wear overall than the obverse, with the rim indistinct in areas and many if not most letters worn away.

1811, 11 Over 09; JR-1. Graded AG-3.

PF-60 to 70 (Proof). *Obverse and Reverse:* Generally, Proof dimes of the 1828–1837 variety are of better quality than the 1809–1828 variety and have Full Details in almost all areas. Proofs of this type can have areas of light striking, such as at the star centers. Proofs that are extensively cleaned and have many hairlines, or that are dull and grainy, are lower level, such as PF–60 to 62. These are not of great interest to specialists unless they

1835; JR-4. Graded PF-65 Cameo.

are of rare die varieties. A PF-64 has fewer hairlines, but they are obvious, perhaps slightly distracting. A Gem PF-65 should have fewer still and full mirrored surfaces (no trace of cloudiness or dullness). PF-66 should have hairlines so delicate that magnification is needed to see them. Above that, a Proof should be free of such lines. Grading is highly subjective with early Proofs, and eye appeal also is a major factor.

Illustrated coin: Note the awkward mix of numerals in the date. Punches of different sizes were used, and the 3 in particular looks clumsy and large in comparison to the 8 and the 5.

1809 Capped Bust Dime

1809 • **Circulation-Strike Mintage:** 51,065.

JR-1. *Availability in circulated grades:* 200 to 300 estimated. *Availability in Mint State:* 15 to 20.

JR-1.

Commentary: The dimes from 1809-dated dies were delivered in five separate groups, three in 1809 and the two on June 6 and December 17, 1810, the last representing continued use of the 1809 die pair. No dimes were struck from 1810-dated dies. The year 1809 is the first of the Capped Bust dime series, with a mintage of 51,065. This new obverse and reverse were designed by John Reich. There is only one known variety struck with the 1809 date, and finding a well-struck 1809 is somewhat of a challenge. Most 1809 dimes have the A in AMERICA filled. With some patience, a collector can locate a nice example from this year, but locating a coin graded About Uncirculated or higher will take some time. Early die states are very scarce.

Years ago it was numismatic tradition that dimes from 1809 through early 1828 were made of a slightly larger diameter than those from late 1828 through 1837, with the former being made without a collar or in an "open collar" and the latter being made in a "closed collar." A detailed explanation in the *Early United States Dimes 1796–1837* book relates that there is no clear delineation between "large-" and "small-" diameter pieces. Diameters gradually reduced from 1827 to 1832, and then they gradually increased again from 1834 to 1837. The open-collar process was used for dimes dated 1809 through 1827, and the closed collar was used for those from 1828 through 1837. In contradiction to what was believed earlier, it is now known that both varieties of 1828—Large Date and Small Date—were struck with closed collars, and both have the same diameter.

	Cert	Avg	% MS	AG-3	G-4	VG-8	F-12	VF-20	EF-40	AU-50	MS-60	MS-63
1809, JR-1	52	36.0	35%	$400	$750	$900	$1,400	$2,250	$3,250	$4,500	$5,500	$8,000

1811, 11 Over 09 Capped Bust Dime

1811, 11 Over 09 • **Circulation-Strike Mintage:** 65,180.

JR-1. *Availability in circulated grades:* 250 to 300 estimated. *Availability in Mint State:* 20 to 25.

JR-1.

Detail of the overdate.

Commentary: All 1811 dimes were minted from an 1809 die. As a result, all 1811 dimes are overdates and are referred to as 1811, 11 Over 09. Even though there were only 65,180 dimes struck in 1811, there are three different die states for this year (see the JR book for these and many other technical details). To those collectors who are not familiar with the different die states, many would think that the coin was damaged. Compared to the 1809, the 1811, 11 Over 09, is slightly more available, but finding a high grade will take a lot of patience.

	Cert	Avg	% MS	AG-3	G-4	VG-8	F-12	VF-20	EF-40	AU-50	MS-60	MS-63
1811, 11 Over 09, JR-1	62	40.2	27%	$50	$200	$350	$800	$1,150	$1,700	$2,200	$4,000	$6,750

1814 Capped Bust Dime

1814, Small Date • Circulation-Strike Mintage: Part of a total mintage of 421,500 for the issue.

JR-1. *Availability in circulated grades:* 750 to 1,000. *Availability in Mint State:* Probably 20 to 20.

Commentary: The 1814 Small Date has only one variety, JR-1. Locating a Mint State or About Uncirculated example will take patience and time. Most are weakly struck in some areas. This variety is considered by many as one of the semi-key dates for this series. Many collectors and dealers misattribute the Small Date as the Large Date. The best way to distinguish the two is the size of the 8 in the date. For the Small Date, the top of the 8 is equal in height to the second 1 in the date. (On the Large Date, the 8 is noticeably taller.) The finest known 1814 Small Date is the Northern Bay / Pogue example that was sold at auction in February 2016 for $94,000.

JR-1.

Detail of the Small Date.

	Cert	Avg	% MS	AG-3	G-4	VG-8	F-12	VF-20	EF-40	AU-50	MS-60	MS-63	MS-65
1814, Small Date, JR-1	35	54.4	57%	$35	$65	$115	$145	$275	$725	$1,200	$2,200	$4,500	$16,000

1814, Large Date • Circulation-Strike Mintage: Part of a total mintage of 421,500 for the issue.

JR-2 to 4. *Availability in circulated grades:* 1,250 to 3,000. *Availability in Mint State:* Probably 150.

Commentary: There are three different die marriages of the Large Date varieties using two obverse and two reverse dies. Each is fairly easy to find, and they range from R-2 to R-3. The best way to differentiate the Large Date from the scarcer Small Date variety is the size of the 8 compared to the second 1 in the date: on the Large Date variety, the 8 is noticeably higher than the second 1 in 1814. (On the Small Date, the 8 and second 1 are of equal height.) On average, most 1814 Large Dates are well struck compared to the other varieties. However, some Large Dates have severe die bulges causing the stars on the right side of the obverse to be completely flat. The JR-2 variety has a period after 10 C. On the JR-3, the second 1 in the date on the obverse is below Liberty's curl, while on JR-4 it is not. There are no premiums for any for the different die marriages.

JR-2.

Detail of the Large Date.

	Cert	Avg	% MS	AG-3	G-4	VG-8	F-12	VF-20	EF-40	AU-50	MS-60	MS-63	MS-65
1814, Large Date	31	48.7	52%	$35	$60	$125	$135	$250	$625	$1,000	$2,000	$4,000	$12,500

1814, STATESOFAMERICA •

Circulation-Strike Mintage: Part of a total mintage of 421,500 for the issue.

JR-5. *Availability in circulated grades:* 100 to 200. *Availability in Mint State:* Probably fewer than 10.

Commentary: The STATESOFAMERICA variety was caused by the lack of spacing on the reverse in the phrase STATES OF AMERICA.

JR-5.

This variety is very scarce and difficult to locate. Many examples are weakly struck, especially on the curls behind the forehead. Most survivors are in circulated grades. In grades Very Fine and higher, locating an example is a challenge. A nice 1814 JR-5 that is attributed as such usually commands a premium. However, most in the marketplace are not so identified. This reverse was also used on 1820 JR-1.

	Cert	Avg	% MS	AG-3	G-4	VG-8	F-12	VF-20	EF-40	AU-50	MS-60	MS-63
1814, STATESOFAMERICA, JR-5	15	40.4	40%	$50	$225	$450	$750	$1,000	$1,650	$2,250	$3,000	$6,250

1820 Capped Bust Dime

An interesting footnote in dime lore relates to Robert Bashlow, a New York City coin dealer who met an unfortunate fate in a hotel fire in Portugal some years ago. During the period from about 1960 to 1965 he made a number of restrikes, mulings, and fantasy pieces of various numismatic issues and, important to the present text, hundreds of strikings from the reverse of an original dime die used at the Philadelphia Mint in 1820, and probably sold as scrap iron a few decades later. The story is told in the *Early United States Dimes 1796–1837* text:

> He took the reverse die to the Kirkwood firm of Edinburgh, Scotland, and had 536 impressions struck in various metals, some with a fantasy obverse and some uniface on larger than normal planchets of varying thicknesses. Upon returning to the states, Bashlow was detained by customs, forced to surrender the die and all of the impressions, and fined $100. Everything was destroyed by Treasury agents, despite pleas from the curator of the Smithsonian Institution to save this historic die. Recently, a uniface specimen on a white metal alloy planchet, weighing 6.6 grams and measuring 26.5 mm in diameter, has surfaced. Reportedly, it was obtained in Scotland from a man who acknowledged seeing a handful of others in that country.

This anecdote doesn't pertain directly to any variety of the 1820 dime—but it illustrates the fascinating history of early dimes, about which much still remains to be discovered.

1820, STATESOFAMERICA • Circulation-Strike Mintage: Part of a total mintage of 942,587 for the issue.

JR-1: R-3. *Availability in circulated grades:* 300 to 450 estimated. *Availability in Mint State:* 15 to 25.

Commentary: This scarce variety has additional popularity from its listing as a separate issue in the *Guide Book of United States Coins.* Most examples show extensive circulation. A coin that is About Uncirculated or finer is a prize.

JR-1.

The reverse die was used on the 1814 JR-5 variety, as here, then recovered for this coinage six years later. The most prominent feature is incorrect spacing of the legend, with STATESOFAMERICA crowded together without additional space between the words. The die state is late, with a bulge through the first four stars. This results in weak details among these stars as well as the reverse lettering opposite.

	Cert	Avg	% MS	AG-3	G-4	VG-8	F-12	VF-20	EF-40	AU-50	MS-60	MS-63
1820, STATESOFAMERICA, JR-1	17	38.2	35%	$90	$150	$300	$450	$700	$1,200	$1,750	$3,000	$5,250

1820, Medium or Small 0 • **Circulation-Strike Mintage:** Part of a total mintage of 942,587 for the issue.

JR-2: R-3. *Availability in circulated grades:* 250 to 350 estimated. *Availability in Mint State:* 10 to 15.

Commentary: The reverse die work on JR-2 is of low expertise, giving rise to the term "Office Boy reverse," borrowed from the descriptor of an amateurish large-cent reverse. The diecutter was an amateur or a drunk (rum was a problem at the Mint) or both. This variety can be found fairly sharply struck. As such it is ideal for a date set.

JR-2.

Detail of the Medium or Small 0.

	Cert	Avg	% MS	AG-3	G-4	VG-8	F-12	VF-20	EF-40	AU-50	MS-60	MS-63	MS-65
1820, Medium or Small 0, JR-2	13	48.8	46%	$30	$65	$115	$150	$225	$650	$1,200	$1,500	$3,500	$15,000

JR-3: R-4. *Availability in circulated grades:* 85 to 175 estimated. *Availability in Mint State:* 5.
Commentary: This is a rarity in any grade above Very Fine.

	Cert	Avg	% MS	AG-3	G-4	VG-8	F-12	VF-20	EF-40	AU-50	MS-60	MS-63	MS-64	MS-65
1820, Medium or Small 0, JR-3	3	31.0	33%	$30	$65	$115	$150	$225	$650	$1,200	$1,500	$3,500	$6,000	$15,000

JR-4: R-4+. *Availability in circulated grades:* 75 to 100 estimated. *Availability in Mint State:* 3.
Commentary: Designated as Small 0 in the JR book. This is one of the key varieties to completing a set of 1820 dimes.

	Cert	Avg	% MS	AG-3	G-4	VG-8	F-12	VF-20	EF-40	AU-50	MS-60	MS-63
1820, Medium or Small 0, JR-4	2	52.5	50%	$35	$75	$135	$200	$325	$850	$1,800	$4,000	$12,500

JR-5: R-4. *Availability in circulated grades:* 100 to 150 estimated. *Availability in Mint State:* Fewer than 15.

Commentary: JR-5 and JR-6 share a common obverse that has a tiny notch out of one of the arms of the star, a characteristic typically attributed to John Reich, who left the Mint in 1817. Likely, this punch was left over from earlier times.

JR-5.

	Cert	Avg	% MS	AG-3	G-4	VG-8	F-12	VF-20	EF-40	AU-50	MS-60	MS-63	MS-64	MS-65
1820, Medium or Small 0, JR-5	5	28.6	20%	$30	$65	$115	$150	$225	$650	$1,200	$1,500	$3,500	$6,000	$15,000

JR-6: R-3. *Availability in circulated grades: 350 to 450 estimated. Availability in Mint State: 2.*

JR-6.

	Cert	Avg	% MS	AG-3	G-4	VG-8	F-12	VF-20	EF-40	AU-50	MS-60	MS-63	MS-64	MS-65
1820, Medium or Small 0, JR-6	7	29.4	14%	$30	$65	$115	$150	$225	$650	$1,200	$1,500	$3,500	$6,000	$15,000

JR-7: R-2. *Availability in circulated grades: 500 to 1,250 estimated. Availability in Mint State: 5 to 10.*

JR-7.

	Cert	Avg	% MS	AG-3	G-4	VG-8	F-12	VF-20	EF-40	AU-50	MS-60	MS-63	MS-64	MS-65
1820, Medium or Small 0, JR-7	10	32.9	20%	$30	$65	$115	$150	$225	$650	$1,200	$1,500	$3,500	$6,000	$15,000

JR-8: R-3. *Availability in circulated grades: 250 to 350 estimated. Availability in Mint State: 5 to 10.*

JR-8.

	Cert	Avg	% MS	AG-3	G-4	VG-8	F-12	VF-20	EF-40	AU-50	MS-60	MS-63	MS-64	MS-65
1820, Medium or Small 0, JR-8	10	36.4	30%	$30	$65	$115	$150	$225	$650	$1,200	$1,500	$3,500	$6,000	$15,000

JR-9: R-4. *Availability in circulated grades: 100 to 200 estimated. Availability in Mint State: 5 to 10.*

	Cert	Avg	% MS	AG-3	G-4	VG-8	F-12	VF-20	EF-40	AU-50	MS-60	MS-63	MS-64	MS-65
1820, Medium or Small 0, JR-9	0	n/a		$30	$65	$115	$150	$225	$650	$1,200	$1,500	$3,500	$6,000	$15,000

JR-10: R-3. *Availability in circulated grades:* 175 to 250 estimated. *Availability in Mint State:* 10 to 15.

JR-10.

	Cert	Avg	% MS	AG-3	G-4	VG-8	F-12	VF-20	EF-40	AU-50	MS-60	MS-63	MS-64	MS-65
1820, Medium or Small 0, JR-10	2	32.5	0%	$30	$65	$115	$150	$225	$650	$1,200	$1,500	$3,500	$6,000	$15,000

1820, Large 0 • Circulation-Strike Mintage: Part of a total mintage of 942,587 for the issue.

JR-11: R-3. *Availability in circulated grades:* 300 to 400 estimated. *Availability in Mint State:* Fewer than 15.

JR-11.

Detail of the Large 0.

	Cert	Avg	% MS	AG-3	G-4	VG-8	F-12	VF-20	EF-40	AU-50	MS-60	MS-62	MS-63	MS-64	MS-65
1820, Large 0, JR-11	10	39.0	10%	$35	$65	$115	$150	$225	$550	$675	$1,400	$2,000	$2,750	$5,000	$12,500

JR-12: R-5+. *Availability in circulated grades:* 50 to 65 estimated. *Availability in Mint State:* None known.

Commentary: Fewer than five are known from Extremely Fine to About Uncirculated.

	Cert	Avg	% MS	AG-3	G-4	VG-8	F-12	VF-20	EF-40	AU-50	MS-60
1820, Large 0, JR-12	3	24.3	0%	$100	$450	$950	$1,200	$3,850	$4,750	$7,500	$12,500

JR-13: R-3. *Availability in circulated grades:* 250 to 300 estimated. *Availability in Mint State:* 25 to 45.

JR-13.

	Cert	Avg	% MS	AG-3	G-4	VG-8	F-12	VF-20	EF-40	AU-50	MS-60	MS-62	MS-63	MS-64	MS-65
1820, Large 0, JR-13	3	20.3	0%	$35	$65	$115	$150	$225	$550	$675	$1,400	$2,000	$2,750	$5,000	$12,500

1821 Capped Bust Dime

1821, Large Date • **Circulation-Strike Mintage:** Part of a total mintage of 1,186,512 for the issue.

Commentary: The 1821 dimes with Large Date range in rarity, as shown below. The values here are for the most plentiful varieties, such as those with R-2 rarities. More than 100 have been certified in Mint State, a figure that no doubt includes duplicate submissions of some coins. JR-6 is the rarity in the series and will bring a strong price if attributed.

	Cert	Avg	% MS	AG-3	G-4	VG-8	F-12	VF-20	EF-40	AU-50	MS-60	MS-63
1821, Large Date	134	32.0	17%	$30	$65	$115	$150	$225	$525	$800	$1,700	$3,250

JR-1: R-2. This is among the several readily available varieties. It common in circulated grades. Expect some softness of strike on the reverse.

JR-2: R-6+, the key to the series. Was R-7 in the JR book in 1984, at which time VF-25 was the finest seen.

JR-3: R-4, reduced from R-6 in the original listing. Most are fairly well struck.

JR-4: R-2. This is a very common variety in circulated grades but, surprisingly, it is quite elusive in Mint State. Some lightness of strike on the eagle's wings is normal.

JR-5: R-3. While common in circulated condition, JR-5 is very elusive in Mint State. Usually seen fairly well struck.

JR-2.

Detail of the Large Date.

JR-6: R-2. This one is available in any grade desired, including into Mint State. Sharp striking is the rule except for the upper area of the eagle's wing to the viewer's left.

JR-6.

JR-7: R-2. This variety is easy enough to find, including into the lower ranges of Mint State. It is usually well struck on the obverse except for the denticles at the top border. The reverse is usually sharp except for some lightness on the eagle.

JR-7.

1821, Small Date • **Circulation-Strike Mintage:** Part of a total mintage of 1,186,512 for the issue.

Commentary: The 1821 dimes with Small Date range in rarity as given below. The following prices are for two most plentiful varieties such as the R-2. JR-10, when attributed, will bring much more.

	Cert	Avg	% MS	AG-3	G-4	VG-8	F-12	VF-20	EF-40	AU-50	MS-60	MS-63
1821, Small Date	79	41.1	39%	$30	$65	$115	$150	$225	$525	$1,000	$1,750	$4,000

JR-8: R-2. This Small Date variety is very easily obtainable in circulated grades. In 1984 the JR book said the finest seen was MS-60. A lot of scouting, plus gradeflation (some About Uncirculated coins of yesteryear are certified as Mint State today), have combined to make Mint State coins collectible, although they are on the scarce side.

JR-9: R-2. This one is slightly scarcer across the board than the preceding variety, but significantly more available in Mint State. It is usually well struck.

JR-9.

Detail of the Small Date.

JR-10: R-4+. Usually well struck, this variety is scarce.

JR-10.

1822 Capped Bust Dime

1822 • **Circulation-Strike Mintage:** 100,000.

JR-1. *Availability in circulated grades:* 200 to 250 estimated. *Availability in Mint State:* 15 to 20.

Commentary: This issue is the key date to the Capped Bust series, and all grades are in strong demand by collectors. There is only one die combination for 1822.

JR-1.

Most of the surviving 1822 dimes are in Very Good and lower levels, and a surprising number are damaged. Locating a nice Fine example with good eye appeal is a challenge, and finding a Very Fine or higher with full denticles is quite difficult. Three Gem Uncirculated examples have been recognized, with the finest of these being in the D. Brent Pogue Collection sale held by Stack's Bowers Galleries. It crossed the block in February 2016 for $129,250.

	Cert	Avg	% MS	AG-3	G-4	VG-8	F-12	VF-20	EF-40	AU-50	MS-60	MS-63	MS-65
1822, JR-1	0	n/a		$1,250	$2,000	$2,750	$3,500	$5,750	$8,000	$11,000	$17,000	$25,000	$70,000

1823, 3 Over 2 Capped Bust Dime

1823, 3 Over 2, Small E's •
Circulation-Strike Mintage: Part of a total mintage of 440,000 for the issue.

JR-1: R-3. *Availability in circulated grades:* 300 to 500 estimated. *Availability in Mint State:* 35 to 40.

Commentary: The 1823, 3 Over 2, Small E's, is generally available in all grades.

One of the four obverse dies used to mint this coin was an 1822 die that was repunched with a 3 over the 2, creating this overdate. The Small E variety is identified by the E in STATES on the reverse: the top of the E in is even with the second S in STATES. Most examples of this variety are well struck except for the eagle's talons, which are generally weakly struck. Examples showing more than 50% of eagle's talon details are quite scarce.

JR-1.

Detail of the Small E. Detail of the overdate.

	Cert	Avg	% MS	AG-3	G-4	VG-8	F-12	VF-20	EF-40	AU-50	MS-60	MS-63	MS-65
1823, 3 Over 2, Small E's, JR-1	9	32.9	22%	$40	$75	$125	$185	$350	$700	$1,000	$1,650	$3,250	$14,000

1823, 3 Over 2, Large E's •
Circulation-Strike Mintage: Part of a total mintage of 440,000 for the issue.

JR-2. *Availability in circulated grades:* 75 to 175 estimated. *Availability in Mint State:* Fewer than 10.

Commentary: The identifying characteristic for the rare JR-2 is star 7 (the highest star on the obverse), which points to the lowest part of Liberty's headband.

This obverse die was used in the minting of the Small E variety.

JR-2.

Detail of the Large E. Detail of the overdate.

	Cert	Avg	% MS	AG-3	G-4	VG-8	F-12	VF-20	EF-40	AU-50	MS-60	MS-63	MS-65
1823, 3 Over 2, Large E's, JR-2	4	25.0	25%	$60	$100	$225	$400	$750	$1,250	$2,000	$3,000	$5,000	$20,000

JR-3: R-2. *Availability in circulated grades:* 600 to 800 estimated. *Availability in Mint State:* 30 to 35.

Commentary: On JR-3, star 7 points to the highest portion of Liberty's headband. The variety is generally available in all grades.

	Cert	Avg	% MS	AG-3	G-4	VG-8	F-12	VF-20	EF-40	AU-50	MS-60	MS-63	MS-65
1823, 3 Over 2, Large E's, JR-3	15	41.8	53%	$40	$75	$125	$185	$350	$700	$1,000	$1,650	$3,250	$15,000

1824, 4 Over 2 Capped Bust Dime

1824, 4 Over 2, Flat Top 1 •

Circulation-Strike Mintage: Part of a total mintage of 510,000 for 1824 and 1825.

JR-1: R-2. *Availability in circulated grades:* 1,250 estimated. *Availability in Mint State:* 30.

Commentary: The Mint produced at least four obverse dies bearing the 1822 date. One of those dies was used to mint the 1822 dimes; two of those dies were repunched to mint the 1823, 3 Over 2, dimes, and the fourth die was used to mint the 1824, 4 Over 2 dimes. Since only one obverse die was used to mint the 1824, 4 Over 2 dime, the two different die marriages result from the Mint's use of a second die for the reverse. The JR-1 variety is generally available to collectors in all grades, including Mint State.

JR-1.

Detail of the Flat Top 1.   Detail of the overdate

	Cert	Avg	% MS	AG-3	G-4	VG-8	F-12	VF-20	EF-40	AU-50	MS-60	MS-63	MS-65
1824, 4 Over 2, Flat Top 1, JR-1	15	18.2	0%	$40	$75	$125	$185	$400	$1,000	$1,500	$2,250	$4,000	$17,500

1824, 4 Over 2, Pointed Top 1 •

Circulation-Strike Mintage: Part of a total mintage of 510,000 for 1824 and 1825.

JR-2: R-5+. *Availability in circulated grades:* 50 estimated. *Availability in Mint State:* None known.

Commentary: The Pointed Top 1 variety is rare and difficult to locate in any grade.

The 1824, 4 Over 2, JR-2 is one of the rarest die marriages of all Capped Bust dimes, and is highly sought by advanced collectors. Of the approximately 50 known examples of the JR-2, none is in Mint State, so finding an Extremely Fine grade example is an achievement. A characteristic of JR-2 is a pointed top

JR-2.

Detail of the Pointed Top 1.   Detail of the overdate.

numeral 1 in the 10 C. denomination on the reverse; this feature is also described as a "curved-top 1" and "perfect serifs at the 1." Contrast this feature to the more common JR-1, on which the 1 in 10 is flat at the top. Collectors like to cherrypick this rare variety, for in the marketplace some are not identified as such.

It is likely that all or most of the 100,000 pieces delivered by the Mint on August 22, 1825, were dated 1824.

	Cert	Avg	% MS	AG-3	G-4	VG-8	F-12	VF-20	EF-40	AU-50
1824, 4 Over 2, Pointed Top 1, JR-2	2	12.0	0%	$250	$325	$750	$1,500	$5,500	$7,500	$8,000

1825 Capped Bust Dime

1825 • Circulation-Strike Mintage: Part of a total mintage of 510,000 for 1824 and 1825.

Commentary: The 1825 dimes have five different die marriages, with three of them (JR-1, 2, and 4) being readily available. The JR-3 and JR-5 combinations are more challenging to locate, and finding one of these in Mint State will take some time—however, their value doesn't carry any premium for scarcity.

The values here are generic values for all 1825 Capped Bust dimes, as in the marketplace there is little difference among them. However, an attributed scarcer variety is likely to sell for slightly more.

	Cert	Avg	% MS	AG-3	G-4	VG-8	F-12	VF-20	EF-40	AU-50	MS-60	MS-63	MS-65
1825	32	31.3	16%	$35	$65	$115	$150	$225	$525	$950	$1,800	$3,500	$15,000

JR-1: R-4. *Availability in circulated grades:* 75 to 175 estimated. *Availability in Mint State:* Probably 10 to 25.

Commentary: Later die states exhibit rim crumbling between stars 3 to 6. The reverse die was earlier used to strike JR-3.

JR-1.

JR-2: R-2. *Availability in circulated grades:* 500 to 750 estimated. *Availability in Mint State:* 40 to 50.

JR-3: R-4. *Availability in circulated grades:* 75 to 175 estimated. *Availability in Mint State:* Probably 10 to 20.

Commentary: Later die states exhibit rim crumbling between stars 3 to 6.

JR-2.

JR-4: R-3. *Availability in circulated grades:* 300 to 500 estimated. *Availability in Mint State:* 25 to 45.

Commentary: Some JR-4 dimes with late die states begin with die cracks through stars 8 to 11, with others creating an obverse cud. There is one known full-obverse-brockage Mint error.

JR-4.

JR-5: R-4. *Availability in circulated grades:* 75 to 175 estimated. *Availability in Mint State:* Probably 10 to 25.

Commentary: This is the toughest die marriage to locate.

JR-5.

1827 Capped Bust Dime

1827, Pointed Top 1 • **Circulation-Strike Mintage:** Part of a total mintage of 1,215,000 for the issue.

JR-1: R-3. *Availability in circulated grades:* 200 to 300 estimated. *Availability in Mint State:* 10 estimated.

Commentary: This first JR variety for 1827, Pointed Top 1 has a repunched 7 in date—a quick identifier. Easy to find in just about any grade desired, examples are well struck on the obverse and, as usual, have some lightness on the reverse.

JR-1.

Detail of repunched 7.

	Cert	Avg	% MS	AG-3	G-4	VG-8	F-12	VF-20	EF-40	AU-50	MS-60	MS-63
1827, Pointed Top 1, JR-1	9	32.0	22%	$35	$75	$135	$185	$275	$525	$850	$1,850	$4,500

JR-3: R-1. *Availability in circulated grades:* 1,250 to 1,500 estimated. *Availability in Mint State:* 5 to 10 estimated.

JR-3.

	Cert	Avg	% MS	AG-3	G-4	VG-8	F-12	VF-20	EF-40	AU-50	MS-60	MS-63	MS-65
1827, Pointed Top 1, JR-3	8	40.1	13%	$25	$65	$115	$165	$250	$525	$700	$1,400	$3,000	$13,500

JR-4: R-2. *Availability in circulated grades:* 600 to 800 estimated. *Availability in Mint State:* 10 to 15.

Commentary: The JR-4 variety is easily enough found in any desired grade. On the obverse some denticles are usually weak.

	Cert	Avg	% MS	AG-3	G-4	VG-8	F-12	VF-20	EF-40	AU-50	MS-60	MS-63	MS-65
1827, Pointed Top 1, JR-4	8	32.9	13%	$25	$65	$115	$165	$250	$525	$700	$1,400	$3,000	$13,500

JR-5: R-3. *Availability in circulated grades:* 300 to 400 estimated. *Availability in Mint State:* 7 to 15.

Commentary: The date is positioned high on JR-5. Examples are usually seen with all design elements well struck, but with some weakness in the denticles.

JR-5.

	Cert	Avg	% MS	AG-3	G-4	VG-8	F-12	VF-20	EF-40	AU-50	MS-60	MS-63	MS-65
1827, Pointed Top 1, JR-5	4	30.3	25%	$25	$65	$115	$165	$250	$525	$700	$1,400	$3,000	$13,500

JR-6: R-2. *Availability in circulated grades:* 800 to 1,000 estimated. *Availability in Mint State:* 15 to 20.

Commentary: This one is common. Examples are usually well struck but with some weakness in the denticles.

JR-6.

	Cert	Avg	% MS	AG-3	G-4	VG-8	F-12	VF-20	EF-40	AU-50	MS-60	MS-63	MS-65
1827, Pointed Top 1, JR-6	14	47.9	36%	$25	$65	$115	$165	$250	$525	$700	$1,400	$3,000	$13,500

JR-7: R-3. *Availability in circulated grades:* 200 to 400 estimated. *Availability in Mint State:* 10.

Commentary: The JR-7 variety is slightly on the scarce side, and most examples are in circulated grades. Striking sharpness is so-so.

JR-7.

	Cert	Avg	% MS	AG-3	G-4	VG-8	F-12	VF-20	EF-40	AU-50	MS-60	MS-63	MS-65
1827, Pointed Top 1, JR-7	5	27.6	0%	$25	$65	$115	$165	$250	$525	$700	$1,400	$3,000	$13,500

JR-8: R-4. *Availability in circulated grades:* 100 to 150 estimated. *Availability in Mint State:* 5 to 7.

Commentary: These are very scarce across the board. Examples are usually well struck except for some obverse denticles.

JR-8.

	Cert	Avg	% MS	AG-3	G-4	VG-8	F-12	VF-20	EF-40	AU-50	MS-60	MS-63	MS-65
1827, Pointed Top 1, JR-8	4	35.0	50%	$25	$65	$115	$165	$250	$525	$700	$1,400	$3,000	$13,500

JR-9: *R-4. Availability in circulated grades:* 100 to 175 estimated. *Availability in Mint State:* 10 to 20.

Commentary: This is one of the tougher varieties of the year. Most examples are well worn, and an Extremely Fine or finer example is a keeper for most specialists. Some lightness of strike is found on both sides.

	Cert	Avg	% MS	AG-3	G-4	VG-8	F-12	VF-20	EF-40	AU-50	MS-60	MS-63	MS-65
1827, Pointed Top 1, JR-9	4	5.0	0%	$25	$65	$115	$165	$250	$525	$700	$1,400	$3,000	$13,500

JR-10: *R-6+. Availability in circulated grades:* 15 to 25 estimated. *Availability in Mint State:* No more than 5 (these were probably struck as presentation pieces).

Commentary: This, the rarest collectible variety of 1827, is usually well struck.

JR-10.

	Cert	Avg	% MS	AG-3	G-4	VG-8	F-12	VF-20	EF-40	AU-50	MS-60	MS-63
1827, Pointed Top 1, JR-10	2	42.5	50%	$4,500	$5,000	$7,500	$8,500	$11,000	$18,500	$20,000	$25,000	$27,500

JR-11: *R-2. Availability in circulated grades:* 600 to 1,000 estimated. *Availability in Mint State:* 10 to 15.

Commentary: Examples of JR-11 are easy to find in just about any desired grade. Sharpness of strike is average.

JR-11.

	Cert	Avg	% MS	AG-3	G-4	VG-8	F-12	VF-20	EF-40	AU-50	MS-60	MS-63	MS-65
1827, Pointed Top 1, JR-11	12	38.2	33%	$25	$65	$115	$165	$250	$525	$700	$1,400	$3,000	$13,500

JR-12: *R-1. Availability in circulated grades:* 1,250 to 1,500 estimated. *Availability in Mint State:* About 20.

Commentary: This is another dime that is among the most plentiful of the decade, and is easy to find in about any grade. Striking sharpness is average.

JR-12.

	Cert	Avg	% MS	AG-3	G-4	VG-8	F-12	VF-20	EF-40	AU-50	MS-60	MS-63	MS-65
1827, Pointed Top 1, JR-12	11	34.6	45%	$25	$65	$115	$165	$250	$525	$700	$1,400	$3,000	$13,500

JR-13: R-3. *Availability in circulated grades:* 250 to 400 estimated. *Availability in Mint State:* 10 estimated.

Commentary: The JR-13 variety is slightly scarce. Most are in circulated grades.

JR-13.

	Cert	Avg	% MS	AG-3	G-4	VG-8	F-12	VF-20	EF-40	AU-50	MS-60	MS-63	MS-65
1827, Pointed Top 1, JR-13	7	28.3	29%	$25	$65	$115	$165	$250	$525	$700	$1,400	$3,000	$13,500

JR-14: R-8. *Availability in circulated grades:* 2 confirmed. *Availability in Mint State:* None.

Commentary: The rarest variety among Capped Bust dimes of the era is JR-14. This variety was not listed in the 1984 book. Specimens are weakly struck.

	Cert	Avg	% MS	VG-8	EF-40
1827, Pointed Top 1, JR-14	0	n/a		$35,000	$45,000

1827, Flat Top 1 • Circulation-Strike Mintage: Part of a total mintage of 1,215,000 for the issue.

JR-2: R-4+. *Availability in circulated grades:* 50 to 55 estimated. *Availability in Mint State:* 1.

Commentary: The 1 in 10 C. is flat across the top, rather than curved. This was a significant rarity as pointed out in the JR book in 1984, when the finest seen was EF-40. Curiously, the book mentioned only the rarity, not the distinctive top of the numeral! The *Guide Book of United States Coins* has had it listed for many years. Most grade Good or Very Good. Examples in Very Fine or better are well across the $1,000 price line. Very Fine and Extremely Fine are the highest grades usually seen.

	Cert	Avg	% MS	G-4	VG-8	F-12	VF-20	EF-40	AU-50
1827, Flat Top 1 in 10 C., JR-2	4	6.8	0%	$225	$375	$900	$1,800	$3,000	$4,500

1828, Large Date, Curl Base 2 Capped Bust Dime

1828, Large Date, Curl Base 2 • Circulation-Strike Mintage: Part of a total mintage of 125,000 for the issue.

JR-2. *Availability in circulated grades:* 200 to 300. *Availability in Mint State:* Fewer than 15.

JR-2.

Commentary: The Large Date, Curl Base 2 variety is generally well struck on the obverse but typically weakly struck on the reverse.

There is very little written and known about this variety, and very few collectors appreciate the rarity of this coin. It is one of the semi-keys of the series, challenging the 1809 and the 1811, 11 Over 09, in difficulty to obtain. This variety is quite scarce and locating a nice example will take some patience. Finding an About Uncirculated is very rare and locating a Mint State is an even greater challenge, and most lack eye appeal.

Detail of the Large Date, Curl Base 2.

The JR-2 variety can be distinguished by the Large Date in comparison to the Small Date variety (JR-1), but another obvious point is that the 2 in the date is curled at its base. The interesting sidebar story to this coin is that the JR-1 was minted with the introduction of a new edge collar designed by William Kneass. After significant deterioration of the Small Date die, the Mint struck the Large Date in a different fashion, with an old-style, wider-denticled, John Reich obverse paired with a new-style Kneass reverse. Even though this coin was struck after the size of the dime width has been reduced, the Large Date is included as a Large Size period.

It is very common that the eagle's head and neck are flatly struck due to reverse die rotation. Later die states show clashing around the 10 on the reverse. In an extremely rare late die state, a retained cud forms from the rim above the motto from the D in UNITED to the second S in STATES. There is an 1828 Large Date brockage Mint error, and it is unique.

The finest known example is the Louis Eliasberg example, which is believed to be Gem and was sold for $40,700 in May 1996. This coin hasn't been auctioned or offered since then. Many great collections didn't have Mint State examples. The famous Norweb and Bareford collections had only About Uncirculateds.

An interesting piece in the October 25, 1828, issue of *Niles' Register* offers this curious comment: "Ten cent pieces. A correspondent of the *Natchez Galaxy* complains of the circulation of ten cent pieces, in Mississippi, as eighths of a dollar. The citizens of that state are said, at their annual visits to the North, to invest considerable sums in these pieces. One individual, it is asserted, carried to Natchez, at one time, five hundred dollars, the profit on which would amount to one hundred and twenty-five dollars."

	Cert	Avg	% MS	AG-3	G-4	VG-8	F-12	VF-20	EF-40	AU-50	MS-60	MS-63	MS-65
1814, Small Date, JR-1	35	54.4	57%	$35	$65	$115	$145	$275	$725	$1,200	$2,200	$4,500	16,000

1828, Small Date, Square Base 2 Capped Bust Dime

1828, Small Date, Square Base 2 •
Circulation-Strike Mintage: Part of a total mintage of 125,000 for the issue.

JR-1. *Availability in circulated grades:* 1,000 to 1,200. *Availability in Mint State:* 30 to 45.

JR-1.

Commentary: Many of these examples show die cracks caused by extensive die deterioration. Finding an 1828 JR-1 will not be difficult, as many are available, but locating a Mint State coin can be a challenge. There are several very rare examples that have highly reflective surfaces and may have been struck as Proofs or presentation pieces.

Detail of the Small Date, Square Base 2.

In 1828, William Kneass introduced a new edge-collar design. The coins minted using this new collar are slightly smaller in size compared to those minted prior to 1828.

The following comment was adapted from the D. Brent Pogue catalog: At the American Numismatic Society Coinage of America conference, two of the five authors of *Early United States Dimes 1796–1837*, Allen F. Lovejoy and William I. Subjack, discussed some technical aspects of the 1828 dimes. One topic was the transition from the large diameter to the small diameter. This was due to the fact that the different types of collars were employed. For JR-1 the Mint used a new style of obverse with narrow denticles in combination with a reverse with old-style denticles.

	Cert	Avg	% MS	AG-3	G-4	VG-8	F-12	VF-20	EF-40	AU-50	MS-60	MS-63	MS-65
1828, Small Date, Square Base 2, JR-1	57	46.8	40%	$35	$65	$100	$175	$250	$475	$750	$1,300	$2,500	$12,000

1829 Capped Bust Dime

1829, Extra Large 10 C. • **Circulation-Strike Mintage:** Part of a total mintage of 770,000 for the issue.

JR-1: R-4+. *Availability in circulated grades:* 50 to 75 estimated. *Availability in Mint State:* Fewer than 5 known.

Commentary: On JR-1, the 10 on the reverse is very large and occupies most of the space below the eagle. This variety, which is usually seen in low grades, is missing in most collections.

	Cert	Avg	% MS	AG-3	G-4	VG-8	F-12	VF-20	EF-40	AU-50	MS-60	MS-63	MS-63
1829, Extra Large 10 C., JR-1	7	39.7	29%	$25	$55	$75	$150	$175	$500	$1,250	$3,000	$6,000	$35,000

1829, Large 10 C. • Circulation-Strike

Mintage: Part of a total mintage of 770,000 for the issue.

JR-2: R-2. *Availability in circulated grades:* 600 to 1,000 estimated. *Availability in Mint State:* 20 to 25.

Commentary: The 10 on the reverse is large, as stated, but not as large as on JR-1. Mint State coins are readily available.

JR-2.

Detail of the Large 10 C.

	Cert	Avg	% MS	AG-3	G-4	VG-8	F-12	VF-20	EF-40	AU-50	MS-60	MS-62	MS-63	MS-64	MS-65
1829, Large 10 C., JR-2	58	36.9	29%	$20	$35	$45	$55	$125	$400	$750	$2,000	$2,800	$4,000	$6,000	$9,000

1829, Small 10 C. • Circulation-Strike Mintage: Part of a total mintage of 770,000 for the issue.

Commentary: The following are generic prices for this variety. The scarcer ones will bring slightly more if attributed.

	Cert	Avg	% MS		G-4	VG-8	F-12	VF-20	EF-40	AU-50	MS-60	MS-62	MS-63	MS-64	MS-65
1829, Small 10 C.	11	46.0	36%		$35	$40	$45	$100	$375	$475	$1,200	$1,750	$2,000	$3,250	$9,000

JR-3: R-4. *Availability in circulated grades:* 150 to 200 estimated. *Availability in Mint State:* 5 to 10.

JR-4: R-2. *Availability in circulated grades:* 750 to 900 estimated. *Availability in Mint State:* 10 to 15.

JR-5: R-4. *Availability in circulated grades:* 100 to 150 estimated. *Availability in Mint State:* 7 to 10.

JR-6: R-3. *Availability in circulated grades:* 250 to 400 estimated. *Availability in Mint State:* 10 to 20.

JR-4.

Detail of the Small 10 C.

JR-7: R-1. *Availability in circulated grades:* 1,500 to 2,000 estimated. *Availability in Mint State:* 15 to 20.

JR-8: R-4. *Availability in circulated grades:* 1,000 to 2,000 estimated. *Availability in Mint State:* 10 to 20.

JR-7.

1829, Small Over Large 10 C. • **Circulation-Strike Mintage:** Part of a total mintage of 770,000 for the issue.

JR-9: R-4. *Availability in circulated grades:* 75 to 125 estimated. *Availability in Mint State:* Fewer than 5 known.

Commentary: Light traces of the undertype can be seen above the final figures.

The JR-9 is very scarce and it is referred to as the Small Over Large denomination. There appears to be doubling at the top of the 1 in the 10 on the reverse. In Mint State they are rare and are sought after by the Capped Bust dime specialists. Most are well struck, so cherrypicking them is somewhat easy.

JR-9.

Detail of the underdate.

	Cert	Avg	% MS	AG-3	G-4	VG-8	F-12	VF-20	EF-40	AU-50	MS-60	MS-62	MS-63	MS-64	MS-65
1829, Small Over Large 10 C., JR-9	6	31.7	33%	$45	$55	$60	$75	$125	$400	$1,000	$2,000	$2,250	$4,250	$9,500	$15,500

1829, Curl Base 2 • **Circulation-Strike Mintage:** Part of a total mintage of 770,000 for the issue.

JR-10: R-5. *Availability in circulated grades:* 35 to 50 estimated. *Availability in Mint State:* None known.

Commentary: The 1829 Curl Base 2 is the rarest die marriage for this date. The highest-graded known examples are Fine and Very Fine. It is easy to identify this variety by viewing the 2 in the date as it is curled, unlike on any other variety. Most are in low grades, and some are damaged.

	Cert	Avg	% MS	AG-3	G-4	VG-8	F-12	VF-20
1829, Curl Base 2, JR-10	8	5.5	0%	$3,000	$5,000	$7,000	$15,000	$25,000

1829, Square Base 2, Medium 10 C. • **Circulation-Strike Mintage:** Part of a total mintage of 770,000 for the issue.

JR-11: R-4. *Availability in circulated grades:* 75 to 125 estimated. *Availability in Mint State:* 10 to 15 known.

JR-11.

	Cert	Avg	% MS	AG-3	G-4	VG-8	F-12	VF-20	EF-40	AU-50	MS-60	MS-62	MS-63	MS-64	MS-65
1829, Square Base 2, Medium 10 C., JR-11	2	42.5	0%	$30	$35	$40	$45	$100	$350	$450	$1,000	$1,400	$2,000	$3,250	$8,500

JR-12: R-3. *Availability in circulated grades:* 75 to 125 estimated. *Availability in Mint State:* 12 to 15 known.

JR-12.

	Cert	Avg	% MS	AG-3	G-4	VG-8	F-12	VF-20	EF-40	AU-50	MS-60	MS-62	MS-63	MS-64	MS-65
1829, Square Base 2, Medium 10 C., JR-12	6	26.5	33%	$45	$55	$60	$75	$125	$400	$1,000	$2,000	$2,250	$4,250	$9,500	$15,500

1830 Capped Bust Dime

1830, 30 Over 29 • **Circulation-Strike Mintage:** Part of a total mintage of 510,000 for the issue.

JR-4: R-2. *Availability in circulated grades:* 1,250 to 1,500 estimated. *Availability in Mint State:* 10.

Commentary: The 1830, 30 Over 29, overdate is a very sought-after coin. The JR-4 and JR-5 varieties share the same obverse die, which was originally dated 1829. The finest known is the Pogue example, which was graded MS-67 with spectacular toning. Most are weakly struck.

This is one of the commonest varieties of the year, but it was not always so. Q. David Bowers describes the situation:

> Unlisted in the *Guide Book of United States Coins*, the 1830/29 made its debut in 1971 in the impressively titled *Scott's Comprehensive Encyclopedia and Catalogue of United States Coins*. Don Taxay was the lead author. John J. Ford Jr., brainchild of the project and fiercely jealous of Whitman's *Guide Book* (Ford owned the rights to the defunct *Standard Catalogue of United States Coins*, which expired in 1958, mainly due to competition from the Red Book), put Walter Breen to work to come up with most of the information. The dime overdate was unpriced, indicating it was a great rarity. I found one, was excited, and sold it for a good price. Then another. Then more. Soon, I and others found it was not rare at all—a poster example of Breen's often-light research. The Scott book never did gain traction. There was a second edition a few years later, after which it disappeared. The 1830/29 dime today is key to a date set of dimes and is easily enough obtained, including in high grades.

	Cert	Avg	% MS	AG-3	G-4	VG-8	F-12	VF-20	EF-40	AU-50	MS-60	MS-63	MS-65
1830, 30 Over 29, JR-4	10	37.1	20%	$25	$45	$55	$100	$140	$400	$650	$1,300	$4,000	$19,000

JR-5: R-5. *Availability in circulated grades:* 35 to 50 estimated. *Availability in Mint State:* Fewer than 5 known.

JR-5.

	Cert	Avg	% MS	AG-3	G-4	VG-8	F-12	VF-20	EF-40	AU-50	MS-60	MS-63	MS-65
1830, 30 Over 29, JR-5	15	46.5	33%	$25	$55	$75	$150	$175	$500	$850	$1,800	$6,000	$30,000

1830, Small 10 C. • Circulation-Strike Mintage: Part of a total mintage of 510,000 for the issue.

JR-2: R-1 (but see below). *Availability in circulated grades:* 1,250 to 1,750 estimated. *Availability in Mint State:* 10 to 20.

Commentary: The Small 10 C. variety of 1830 dime is rated R-1 per conventional wisdom, but specialist Barry Sunshine considers it to be R-4 or close. The finest known is a Gem from the 1997 Eliasberg Collection that crossed the block again in August 2017, this time for $18,800.

JR-2.

	Cert	Avg	% MS	AG-3	G-4	VG-8	F-12	VF-20	EF-40	AU-50	MS-60	MS-62	MS-63	MS-64	MS-65
1830, Small 10 C., JR-2	6	39.2	50%	$20	$40	$50	$85	$125	$375	$650	$1,200	$2,000	$2,500	$4,000	$9,000

1830, Medium 10 C. • Circulation-Strike Mintage: Part of a total mintage of 510,000 for the issue.

Commentary: The following generic prices apply to the R-2 and R-3 varieties. The two R-4s can usually be cherrypicked, but if attributed they will sell for more.

	Cert	Avg	% MS	G-4	VG-8	F-12	VF-20	EF-40	AU-50	MS-60	MS-62	MS-63	MS-64	MS-65
1830, Large 10 C.	37	34.7	22%	$40	$50	$65	$85	$225	$500	$1,200	$2,000	$2,500	$5,000	$12,500

JR-1: R-4+. *Availability in circulated grades:* 50 to 70 estimated. *Availability in Mint State:* None known.

JR-3: R-3. *Availability in circulated grades:* 250 to 400 estimated. *Availability in Mint State:* 10 to 15 estimated.

JR-6: R-2. *Availability in circulated grades:* 500 to 850 estimated. *Availability in Mint State:* 10 to 15.

JR-7: R-4. *Availability in circulated grades:* 125 to 200 estimated. *Availability in Mint State:* 10 to 13 estimated.

JR-3.

JR-8: R-3. *Availability in circulated grades:* 250 to 400 estimated. *Availability in Mint State:* 10 to 15 estimated.

1831 Capped Bust Dime

1831 • **Circulation-Strike Mintage:** 771,350.

Commentary: The 1831 dime varieties are all readily collectible in high grades. The following are generic values for all JR numbers.

	Cert	Avg	% MS	AG-3	G-4	VG-8	F-12	VF-20	EF-40	AU-50	MS-60	MS-63
1831	391	49.8	48%		$35	$40	$50	$80	$250	$450	$1,000	$2,000

JR-1: R-1. This is one of three very common varieties of this year. Some weakness of strike is usual.

JR-1.

JR-2: R-3. These are typically found sharply struck.

JR-2.

JR-3: R-1. The JR-3 is usually sharply struck except for some slight weakness on the eagle.

JR-4: R-2. The obverse is usually lightly struck in some of the central details in high relief. The reverse is usually quite sharp.

JR-3.

JR-5: R-1. The obverse is usually lightly struck in some of the central details in high relief. The reverse is usually quite sharp.

JR-6: R-3. This one is usually sharp on both sides.

JR-5.

1832 Capped Bust Dime

1832 • **Circulation-Strike Mintage:** 522,500.

Commentary: The 1832 dimes are all collectible. Generic prices are given below. If attributed, the R-3 varieties will sell for slightly more, and the single R-4, for a further advance.

	Cert	Avg	% MS	AG-3	G-4	VG-8	F-12	VF-20	EF-40	AU-50	MS-60	MS-63
1832	364	49.5	46%	$15	$35	$40	$50	$80	$250	$450	$1,000	$2,000

JR-1: R-2. All dimes of 1832 have a diameter microscopically smaller than that of the preceding or following dates, due to the reeded collar. The JR-1 variety is usually with weakness at the obverse center.

JR-1.

JR-2: R-2. This variety is well struck overall except for some obverse denticles.

JR-2.

JR-3: R-4. The JR-3 is usually well struck except for some denticles on the reverse.

JR-4: R-3. Some slight weakness is usually seen on both sides.

JR-5: R-2. Some slight weakness is usually seen on both sides.

JR-3.

JR-6: R-3. JR-6 and JR-7 were struck after 1832, as earlier die states are seen on 1833 dimes from this reverse die. Both are usually well struck.

JR-6.

JR-7: R-3. Usually sharply struck.

JR-7.

1833 Capped Bust Dime

1833 • Circulation-Strike Mintage: 485,000.

Commentary: The 1833 dimes present a challenge, as several are quite scarce and demand sharp premiums when classified by JR numbers. For the others these generic prices indicate the ranges.

The second Philadelphia Mint opened this year, replacing the initial facility that had been in use since 1792. The new building continued in use into 1901.

	Cert	Avg	% MS	AG-3	G-4	VG-8	F-12	VF-20	EF-40	AU-50	MS-60	MS-63
1833	448	45.1	39%	$15	$35	$40	$50	$80	$250	$450	$1,000	$2,000

JR-1: R-3. The first JR classification is usually seen sharply struck on the obverse and with weakness on the reverse.

JR-2: R-5. The JR-2 is usually sharp on both the obverse and reverse, except for some reverse denticles.

JR-3: R-6. The finest JR-3 known to the JR compilers in 1984 was About Uncirculated. As with JR-2, examples of JR-3 are usually sharp on both the obverse and reverse, except for some reverse denticles.

JR-2.

JR-4: R-2. The 1 in the date is placed high. The devices are strongly struck but with some denticles usually weak on both sides.

JR-5: R-1. The last 3 in the date is placed high. The variety is listed in the *Guide Book of United States Coins*. It is usually sharp except for some reverse denticles.

JR-5.

Detail of the Last 3 High.

JR-6: R-1. Examples are usually sharp except for some reverse denticles.

JR-7: R-6. This is one of the key varieties among later dimes. It is usually found well struck.

JR-8: R-5. Examples are usually sharp except for some reverse denticles.

JR-6.

JR-9: R-2. These are usually sharply struck.

JR-9.

JR-10: R-3. Like JR-9, these are usually sharply struck.

JR-10.

1834 Capped Bust Dime

1834 • **Circulation-Strike Mintage:** 635,000.

Commentary: The dimes of 1834 are similar to those of recent years—the common mixed with the elusive. Values here are for the more plentiful varieties.

	Cert	Avg	% MS	AG-3	G-4	VG-8	F-12	VF-20	EF-40	AU-50	MS-60	MS-63
1834	444	44.4	39%	$15	$30	$35	$45	$80	$250	$450	$1,000	$2,000

JR-1: R-1. These are usually sharply struck except for some reverse denticles.

JR-1.

JR-2: R-3. Like JR-1, these are usually sharply struck except for some reverse denticles.

JR-3: R-5. Usually sharply struck except for some reverse denticles.

JR-4: R-3. Usually sharply struck except for some reverse denticles.

JR-5: R-1. Some obverse denticles are usually light.

JR-2.

JR-6: R-2. Usually sharply struck except for some reverse denticles.

JR-7: R-4. Usually sharply struck except for some reverse denticles.

1835 Capped Bust Dime

1835 • Circulation-Strike Mintage: 1,410,000.

Commentary: The series of 1835 dimes is fairly extensive, but most varieties are easily enough obtained in high grades. If you are contemplating being a specialist in Capped Bust dimes this year will be a good introduction and training ground.

A note from the JR book: Although the mintage reports indicate that the Mint delivered more Capped Bust dimes in 1835 than in any other year of the Bust dime series, the authors' emission sequence suggests that many of the dimes bearing the date 1835 were struck in 1836 or 1837. (From the 1890s into the first several decades of the 19th century the Mint often kept dies in use until they wore out, often in a later year than dated).

The generic values of this era are continued below.

	Cert	Avg	% MS	AG-3	G-4	VG-8	F-12	VF-20	EF-40	AU-50	MS-60	MS-63
1835	658	46.5	41%	$15	$30	$35	$45	$80	$250	$450	$1,000	$2,000

JR-1: R-1. Examples are usually well struck.

JR-2: R-4. Some slight weakness is usually seen on both sides.

JR-3: R-2. As with JR-2, some slight weakness is usually present on both sides.

JR-4: R-2. These are usually sharply struck.

JR-4.

JR-5: R-1. Examples are usually sharply struck.

JR-6: R-4. Some lightness on the obverse is normal. The reverse is usually quite sharp.

JR-7: R-4. Some slight weakness is on both sides.

JR-8: R-3. These are sharp on the obverse, with some weak denticles on the reverse.

JR-5.

JR-9: R-2. Like JR-8, these are sharp on the obverse and have some weak denticles on the reverse.

JR-9.

1836 Capped Bust Dime

1836 • Circulation-Strike Mintage: 1,190,000.

Commentary: The mintage figure for 1836 dimes is the second-highest recorded in all the Capped Bust dime series, but the survival rate is low compared to its mintage. The JR-1s and JR-2s have a "Fancy 8" in the date, while the JR-3s have a "Block 8." It is interesting that the JR-1s and 2s show in later die states an obverse bisecting die crack.

These were struck with the use of three obverse dies and three reverse dies. There are about fifteen 1836 dimes at the Gem Mint State level.

JR-1: R-3. *Availability in circulated grades:* 300 to 500 estimated. *Availability in Mint State:* 30 to 50.

	Cert	Avg	% MS	AG-3	G-4	VG-8	F-12	VF-20	EF-40	AU-50	MS-60	MS-63	MS-65
1836, JR-1	12	43.7	33%	$15	$30	$35	$40	$80	$250	$450	$1,000	$2,250	$8,000

JR-2: R-2. *Availability in circulated grades:* 500 to 1,250 estimated. *Availability in Mint State:* 40 to 60.

JR-2.

	Cert	Avg	% MS	AG-3	G-4	VG-8	F-12	VF-20	EF-40	AU-50	MS-60	MS-63	MS-65
1836, JR-2	8	25.0	13%	$15	$30	$35	$45	$80	$250	$450	$1,000	$2,250	$8,000

JR-3: R-3. *Availability in circulated grades:* 350 to 500 estimated. *Availability in Mint State:* 30 to 50.

JR-3.

	Cert	Avg	% MS	AG-3	G-4	VG-8	F-12	VF-20	EF-40	AU-50	MS-60	MS-63	MS-65
1836, JR-3	11	48.6	18%	$15	$30	$35	$45	$80	$250	$450	$1,000	$2,250	$8,000

1837 Capped Bust Dime

1837 • **Circulation-Strike Mintage:** 359,500.

JR-1 to JR-4. *Availability in circulated grades:* 1,250 to 2,000. *Availability in Mint State:* 100 to 150.

Commentary: The year 1837 saw the striking of the last of the Capped Bust Dimes. There are four varieties of this issue, and all are generally available. They were struck with the use of two obverse and two reverse dies. As with the 1836 dimes, two styles of the numeral 8 are known—Block 8 (JR-1 to JR-3) and Fancy 8 (JR-4).

The 1837 dimes have many different die cracks of numismatic interest. For example, many of the Fancy 8 variety have an interesting obverse die crack starting at the top and extending down through the 7 in the date.

Steam coinage was introduced at the Mint on March 23, 1836, and at the outset was used to make cents. In 1837 steam presses began making dimes. It is believed that all 1837 Capped Bust dimes were minted prior to the introduction of the Liberty Seated dimes that were delivered on June 30, 1837.

JR-1: R-4. *Availability in circulated grades:* Fewer than 200. *Availability in Mint State:* About 7.

Commentary: This variety is not known with an obverse die crack.

	Cert	Avg	% MS	AG-3	G-4	VG-8	F-12	VF-20	EF-40	AU-50	MS-60	MS-63	MS-65
1837, JR-1	1	62.0	100%	$15	$30	$35	$40	$90	$300	$475	$1,250	$2,500	$8,500

JR-2: R-3.

JR-2.

	Cert	Avg	% MS	AG-3	G-4	VG-8	F-12	VF-20	EF-40	AU-50	MS-60	MS-63	MS-65
1837, JR-2	3	44.7	33%	$15	$30	$35	$45	$80	$250	$450	$1,000	$2,000	$8,000

JR-3: R-2.

	Cert	Avg	% MS	AG-3	G-4	VG-8	F-12	VF-20	EF-40	AU-50	MS-60	MS-63	MS-65
1837, JR-3	11	51.9	55%	$15	$30	$35	$45	$80	$250	$450	$1,000	$2,000	$7,500

JR-4: R-1. This is the most common of the four varieties. It can be attributed by the incomplete top arrow shaft on the reverse.

JR-4.

	Cert	Avg	% MS	AG-3	G-4	VG-8	F-12	VF-20	EF-40	AU-50	MS-60	MS-63	MS-65
1837, JR-4	16	48.0	44%	$15	$30	$35	$45	$80	$250	$450	$1,000	$2,000	$7,500

LIBERTY SEATED DIMES (1837–1891): HISTORY AND BACKGROUND

All Varieties: **Designer:** *Christian Gobrecht.* **Composition:** *.900 silver, .100 copper.* **Diameter:** *17.9 mm.* **Edge:** *Reeded.* ***Variety 1, No Stars on Obverse (1837–1838) and Variety 2, With Stars on Obverse (1838–1853)***—**Weight:** *2.67 grams.* **Mints:** *Philadelphia and New Orleans.* ***Variety 3, Arrows at Date (1853–1855)***—**Weight:** *2.49 grams.* **Mints:** *Philadelphia and New Orleans.* ***Variety 2 Resumed With Weight Standard of Variety 3 (1836–1860)***—**Weight:** *2.49 grams.* **Mints:** *Philadelphia and New Orleans.* ***Variety 4, Legend on Obverse (1860–1873)***—**Weight:** *2.49 grams.* **Mints:** *Philadelphia, New Orleans, and Carson City.* ***Variety 5, Arrows at Date (1873–1873)***— **Weight:** *2.50 grams.* **Mints:** *Philadelphia, New Orleans, and Carson City.*

Variety 1, No Stars on Obverse (1837–1838)

Variety 1, No Stars on Obverse, Proof

Variety 2, Stars on Obverse (1838–1853)

Mintmark location, 1837–1860 (Variety 2), is on the reverse, above the bow.

Variety 2, Stars on Obverse, Proof

Variety 3, Stars on Obverse, Arrows at Date, Reduced Weight (1853–1855)

Variety 3, Stars on Obverse, Arrows at Date, Reduced Weight, Proof

Variety 2 Resumed, Weight Standard of Variety 3 (1856–1860)

Variety 2 Resumed, Weight Standard of Variety 3, Proof

Variety 4, Legend on Obverse (1860–1873)

Mintmark location, 1860 (Variety 4)–1891, is on the reverse, below the bow.

Variety 4, Legend on Obverse, Proof

Variety 5, Legend on Obverse, Arrows at Date, Increased Weight (1873–1874)

Variety 5, Legend on Obverse, Increased Weight, Proof

Variety 4 Resumed, Weight Standard Variety of 5 (1875–1891)

Variety 4 Resumed, Weight Standard Variety of 5, Proof

The Liberty Seated motif by Mint engraver Christian Gobrecht was introduced on dimes in the year 1837, following the coinage of Capped Bust dimes earlier in the year. The issues of 1837 and also of 1838-O (at the New Orleans Mint) featured a plain or starless obverse inspired by the Gobrecht silver dollars of 1836, the first coin on which the design was used. In 1838 stars were added to the obverse of Philadelphia Mint coins, and stars were continued on all dimes through early 1860. In that year the stars were replaced by UNITED STATES OF AMERICA, a style continued through 1891.

The reverse of all Liberty Seated dimes, 1837 to 1891, displayed a wreath, modified in 1860.

Liberty Seated dimes were struck at the Philadelphia Mint continuously from 1837 to 1891; at the New Orleans Mint for most years from 1838 to 1860 and again in 1891; at the San Francisco Mint for most years from 1856 to 1891; and at the Carson City Mint continuously from 1871 to 1878. Mintmarks are on the reverse of the branch-mint issues.

CHRISTIAN GOBRECHT, ENGRAVER

In numismatics today Christian Gobrecht is considered one of the most talented, most accomplished engravers in the history of the Mint. *The Gobrecht Journal*, magazine of the Liberty Seated Collectors Club, bears his name.

The second Philadelphia Mint building, which was opened in 1833, during the era of Capped Bust dimes. It remained in use through the Liberty Seated era and finally closed in 1901, during the era of Charles E. Barber's Liberty Head design.

The New Orleans Mint building (shown in a 1963 photograph). Now a museum, it produced dimes bearing the O mintmark until 1860, and again in 1891.

The building of the storied Carson City Mint (shown in a 1940 photograph), which produced some of the most highly sought-after Liberty Seated dimes.

Gobrecht was born in Hanover, York County, Pennsylvania, on December 23, 1785, the sixth son of John Christopher Gobrecht and Elizabeth (Sands) Gobrecht. Christian demonstrated an early talent for art and mechanics. In his youth he was apprenticed to a clockmaker in Manheim, Pennsylvania; he later moved to Baltimore, where he engraved dials and other ornaments for timepieces and did other engraving work, much of it in association with William H. Freeman, a leading maker of bank-note plates. Still later he became an engraver of type punches for newspapers and documents while continuing to engrave plates for banknotes.

Christian Gobrecht.

Sometime around the year 1811 Gobrecht moved to Philadelphia, where by 1816 he was at work as a bank-note engraver with Murray, Draper, Fairman & Co. In 1817 he devised a medal-ruling machine, which, by means of a pantograph, depicted the contours of a coin or medal as lines on a flat surface, such as a copper engraving plate. The copper or other plate to be ruled was movable, and the item copied remained stationary. At least two versions of this machine were made, the first being able to copy only straight lines and the second with the capability of copying curved as well as straight lines. Not long afterward, others copied certain aspects of his mechanisms, without credit. History has not treated Gobrecht kindly, as his contributions to this device have been largely ignored.

The Gobrecht Journal, magazine of the Liberty Seated Collectors Club.

On May 31, 1818, the artist took as his wife Mary Hamilton Hewes, the daughter of Thomas Hamilton and the widow of Daniel Hewes. The couple had two sons and two daughters. Around 1820 or 1821, Christian Gobrecht invented and manufactured a parlor reed organ operated by keys and bellows, the first example of which was sold to a resident of Lancaster, Pennsylvania. Another example made in 1832 was kept by Gobrecht himself (and at the turn of the 20th century was still owned by his descendants). Intrigued by the automata of Maelzel (whose supposedly mechanical chess player delighted the courts of Europe and was the sensation of its time), Gobrecht created a talking doll and an improvement on the ancient camera lucida device. By 1826 Gobrecht had furnished designs and die models as a private contractor to the Philadelphia Mint.

During the 1820s and early 1830s he executed many commissions for the Mint and private clients, including the seal of St. Peter's Church, the Massachusetts Mechanics Charitable Association award medal (which is encountered with some frequency today), the award medal for the New England Society for the Promotion of Manufactures and the Arts, the Franklin Institute award medal, and a widely admired medal depicting Charles Carroll of Carrollton.

After Robert Scot, engraver at the Mint since 1793, died in 1823, Gobrecht wrote to President James Monroe requesting to be interviewed for the position. Nothing came of this, and William Kneass, an engraver considered to be far less talented by modern historians, was named to the post—a political appointment by presidential prerogative. Mint Director Samuel Moore probably would have chosen Gobrecht, based on his knowledge of the engraver's excellent work.

On February 14, 1825, Moore wrote to Monroe's successor, President John Quincy Adams, "and solicited his permission to introduce, "in the character of assistant engraver, Christian Gobrecht of this city, an artist of great merit." Again, to no avail. Time passed. In 1835 Congress passed an act establishing branch mints at Charlotte, North Carolina; Dahlonega, Georgia; and New Orleans, Louisiana. Many more dies would be needed for this expansion.

In the summer, Mint Director Moore retired and was succeeded by Robert Maskell Patterson, who sought to employ Gobrecht.

The Liberty Seated Design

After production of silver dollars in 1804, coinage of this denomination was suspended. Nearly all had been exported, and the Treasury Department felt that their usefulness for domestic commerce was lost. After the dollar was discontinued the half dollars became the largest silver coins of the realm. They became a familiar sight in commerce and in bank reserves. In 1835, as Director Patterson settled into his office, he advanced the idea of having a new silver dollar made.

On August 1 he wrote to Thomas Sully, one of the most highly regarded artists in Philadelphia:

> In entering upon the execution of my office here I have felt it to be one of the first objects requiring my attention, to endeavor to introduce a change in our coin that may make it a more creditable specimen of taste and art. To accomplish this purpose I look naturally to your valuable aid and accordingly beg that you will execute for the Mint a drawing of what you shall judge a suitable design for the face of the coin.
>
> The only law which governs us in this matter is the following: "Upon the said coins there shall be the following devices and legends, namely: upon one side of said coins there shall be an impression emblematic of liberty, with an inscription of the word Liberty, and the year of the coinage; and upon the reverse of each of the gold and silver coins there shall be the figure or representation of an eagle with this inscription, United States of America, and upon the reverse of each of the copper coins there shall be an inscription which shall impress the denomination of the piece, namely cent or half cent, as the case may require."
>
> For the impression emblematic of liberty you know that our coins have heretofore used a bust. It appears to me that it would be better to introduce an entire figure. When a likeness is to be given as on the European coins the head alone is very properly used in order that the features may be distinctly represented. But, when an emblem only is called for it would seem rather desirable to avoid this individuality in the features. Besides, there is certainly more room for a display of taste and beauty of form when a full figure issued.
>
> The round form of the coin, its small size, and the practical necessity of covering as much of the face as possible seem to require that the figure be in a sitting posture, sitting for example on a rock.
>
> To be distinctly emblematic of liberty I would propose that the figure hold in her right hand the liberty pole surmounted by the pileus, an emblem which is universally understood. I would also suggest that the left hand be made to rest upon the United States shield on which the word Liberty required by law may be inscribed.
>
> For the reverse of the coin I propose an eagle, flying, and rising in its flight amidst a constellation, irregularly disposed, of 24 stars and carrying in its claws a scroll with the words E Pluribus Unum, of many stars our constellation, of many states one union.
>
> As I am desirous that the real American bald eagle should be represented and not, like the heraldic eagle, a mere creature of imagination I have requested Mr. Titian R. Peale to make a design in conformity with the above suggestions and therefore will not trouble you with the reverse of the coin, at least not for the moment.

By 1835 the liberty cap or pileus was a very familiar motif, indeed "universally understood," dating back to at least the era of ancient coinage on which it was featured. Such a cap was presented to slaves when they were given their freedom. In colonial America the liberty cap was widely used to represent freedom from the shackles of British rule. Many towns and cities had liberty poles, tall and with a cap at the top, set up in prominent places. Such were common sights into the early 19th century.

On August 1, 1835, engraver Kneass made a rough sketch of a seated figure with pole and cap, based on his conversation with Director Patterson.

Sketch of Liberty seated made on August 1, 1835, by engraver William Kneass. (Library Company of Philadelphia)

GOBRECHT JOINS THE MINT

On August 27, while full-time employment of Gobrecht was being considered, Kneass suffered a debilitating stroke that made it impossible for him to perform the full work of chief or lead engraver, although the title at that time was simply "engraver." Director Patterson reiterated his predecessor's request for help in the engraving department, and Christian Gobrecht began work at the Mint in September. As noted previously, his title was "second engraver" (not "assistant engraver"). Gobrecht's salary was $1,500 per year.

Drawing of Liberty by Thomas Sully. (Library Company of Philadelphia)

A rendering of Liberty, oil on cardboard. (American Philosophical Society)

On October 5 Patterson wrote to Treasury Secretary Levi Woodbury seeking his approval, along with presidential approval, for creating silver dollars with the Liberty Seated obverse combined with a flying eagle reverse. Once this was received, information relating to the new design was made available to the press.

In November the *Philadelphia Gazette* told of work in progress:

> We learn that a new die for the coins of the United States, is now in a state of preparation, and will be ready for use in the ensuing year. The design was prepared by Sully, and is said to be exceedingly beautiful. It is a full length image of the Goddess of liberty, in a sitting posture, with one hand resting on a shield containing the coat of arms of the United States. On the reverse, will be the American eagle, as at present, without however the shield and coat of arms with which his breast is disfigured, and which somewhat resembles a gridiron, exhibiting the bad taste of broiling a bird with his feathers on. The first coin struck with the new device, will be the dollar, of which there have none been coined for thirty years.[6]

On January 8, 1836, impressions of the obverse design in fusible metal were sent to Secretary Woodbury in Washington for him to show to President Andrew Jackson. On the 12th Woodbury advised Patterson that the president had approved of the design but suggested some modifications. In the same month Gobrecht started work on the reverse eagle (not related to Liberty Seated dimes and thus not discussed in detail here).

Silver dollars, later called Gobrecht dollars by numismatists, were first delivered in December 1836. In 1837 Liberty Seated half dimes and dimes were made with a wreath-motif reverse. These were followed in 1838 by the quarter dollar and in 1839 by the half dollar with the Liberty Seated obverse and a perched eagle on the reverse.

In the meantime Gobrecht worked on other new designs, including the Liberty Head in several forms, culminating with the Braided Hair or Coronet depiction of Miss Liberty used on gold coins beginning 1838–1840 and half cents and large cents starting in 1839 and 1840. He attended to the other duties of the position as well. Christian Gobrecht remained at the Mint until his death in Philadelphia on July 23, 1844.

The Liberty Seated design continued in use for many years, finally ending with the dime, quarter, and half dollar in 1891. Modifications were made by later engravers, including James B. Longacre, who was the engraver from 1844 to 1869, William Barber from 1869 to 1879, and Charles E. Barber beginning in 1880.

OVERVIEW OF LIBERTY SEATED DIMES

Christian Gobrecht's design on the 1837 and 1838-O dimes depicts Liberty seated on a rock, her left hand holding a liberty cap on a pole and her right hand holding a shield inscribed LIBERTY. There is no drapery at her elbow, and there are no stars in the field. The result is a cameo-like appearance of rare beauty. The date is at the bottom border. The obverse design was inspired by the design of the Gobrecht silver dollars of 1836. The reverse consists of an open wreath tied with a ribbon, enclosing ONE / DIME, with UNITED STATES OF AMERICA surrounding.

In 1838 stars were added to the obverse of the Liberty Seated dime. In 1840 drapery was added to Liberty's elbow and an adjustment was made in the alignment of the shield. Through the 1840s and 1850s many different varieties were produced. In 1853 the Liberty Seated design was modified by the addition of tiny arrowheads to the left and right of the date, to signify a decrease in the authorized weight from 41.2 grains to 38.4 grains. These arrows remained in place through 1855, after which they were discontinued, although the reduced weight remained in effect for later years as well, until after February 1873.

In 1860 the obverse was modified by removal of the stars and addition of UNITED STATES OF AMERICA around the border. The reverse was changed as well, now with ONE / DIME in two lines within a cereal wreath. This style was continued through 1891, after which time the Liberty Seated design was replaced by Charles E. Barber's Liberty Head.

LIBERTY SEATED DIME TYPES
1837–1838 • LIBERTY SEATED, VARIETY 1, NO STARS

On the obverse of the coin, Liberty is seated on a rock in three-quarter profile to the right, her head turned back toward the left. Her left arm is raised and bent at the elbow; in her left hand she holds a liberty pole with cap. Her right arm reaches downward, her right hand resting on the corner of a shield inscribed with the word LIBERTY. The shield, placed at the base of the rock, is  tilted sharply to the left. There are no stars on the obverse. On the reverse is a wreath of laurel surrounding the denomination ONE / DIME, all enclosed within the legend UNITED STATES OF AMERICA in small letters (in comparison to the modified reverse of 1840; hence the "Small Letters" style). On the 1838-O, the mintmark is placed within the wreath on the reverse. *Designer:* Christian Gobrecht • *Composition:* .900 silver, .100 copper • *Diameter:* 17.9 mm • *Weight:* 41.25 grains (2.67 grams) • *Edge:* Reeded.

1838–1840 • Liberty Seated, Variety 2, With Stars, No Drapery

The obverse bears the Liberty Seated motif described previously. The shield remains tilted sharply to the left, and there is no extra drapery at Liberty's left elbow. The motif is encircled by 13 stars, which were punched individually into each working die. The reverse is as preceding, and the mintmarks are placed within the wreath. *Designer:* Christian Gobrecht • *Composition:* .900 silver, .100 copper • *Diameter:* 17.9 mm • *Weight:* 41.25 grains (2.67 grams) • *Edge:* Reeded.

1840–1853 • Liberty Seated, Variety 2, With Stars and Drapery

The Liberty Seated obverse has been redesigned slightly, with the most obvious change being the addition of drapery below Liberty's left elbow. The seated figure is slightly smaller, as evidenced by there being larger spaces between the border and the lower left and right of the figure. The liberty cap is smaller and more distant from the border, and Liberty's hand is closer to the cap. The shield has been rotated slightly to the right and is closer to being upright. The drapery to the right of the shield has been redesigned. The stars are now part of the hub, and henceforth there are no variations in their positions.

  The reverse is of the same design, but the wreath is heavier and the letters are larger (hence the "Large Letters" style). Some of the buds in the laurel wreath have split ends, and are widely called "split buds." The mintmarks are placed within the wreath, where they remain through 1860. *Designer:* Christian Gobrecht • *Composition:* .900 silver; .100 copper • *Diameter:* 17.9 mm • *Weight:* 41.2 grains (2.67 grams) • *Edge:* Reeded.

1853–1855 • Liberty Seated, Variety 3, Arrows at Date

The obverse and reverse designs are essentially as preceding. However, thanks to the Coinage Act of February 21, 1853, a new, reduced weight was adopted for the dime; arrows have been added at either side of the date to indicate the new standard. *Designer:* Christian Gobrecht; arrows added by someone on the Mint staff • *Composition:* .900 silver; .100 copper • *Diameter:* 17.9 mm • *Weight:* 38.4 grains (2.49 grams) • *Edge:* Reeded.

1856–1860 • Liberty Seated, Variety 2 Resumed (Weight Standard of Variety 3)

The obverse and reverse designs are as preceding (with new weight standard) but with the arrows removed—the design is the same as that used before 1853. Accordingly, many collectors building type sets ignore this subtype. *Designer:* Christian Gobrecht • *Composition:* .900 silver; .100 copper • *Diameter:* 17.9 mm • *Weight:* 38.4 grains (2.49 grams) • *Edge:* Reeded.

1860–1873 • Liberty Seated, Variety 4, Legend on Obverse

On the obverse, the stars encircling the Liberty Seated motif have been replaced by the legend UNITED STATES OF AMERICA, which has been relocated from the reverse. The seated figure is slightly smaller, as evidenced by wider spacing from the border. The brooch or clasp on Liberty's right shoulder has been modified slightly, and there are some minor changes in details. Brian Greer has divided this into two obverse types:

- **Type I (1860–1861)** shows five vertical lines on the shield above the ribbon inscribed LIBERTY.
- **Type II (1861–1891)** shows six vertical lines on the shield, and Liberty is slightly more slender in appearance.

Type I, 1860–1861:
Five vertical lines on shield.

Type II, 1861–1891:
Six vertical lines on shield.

On the reverse, the laurel wreath has been replaced by a "cereal wreath," as it has been called, composed of oak and maple leaves, wheat, and corn. The larger, fuller wreath fills the space formerly occupied by the legend. The denomination ONE / DIME, in two lines, remains at the center of the wreath. The design was adapted from that used on a pattern half dollar in 1859. Mintmarks are below the bow from 1860 to 1891, with the exception of 1875, when varieties were made with mintmarks above and below the bow.

Brian Greer has divided this into two reverse types:

- On **Type I (1860–1878)**, the left ribbon end is split, and the E in ONE is close to the wreath.
- On **Type II (1876–1891)**, the left ribbon end is pointed, and the E is slightly farther from wreath.

Designer: Christian Gobrecht • *Composition:* .900 silver, .100 copper • *Diameter:* 17.9 mm • *Weight:* 38.4 grains (2.49 grams). As the issues of 1875–1891 are slightly heavier than are coins of this same design minted 1860-1873, the later pieces could be considered as a type or sub-type, but this distinction is generally ignored.

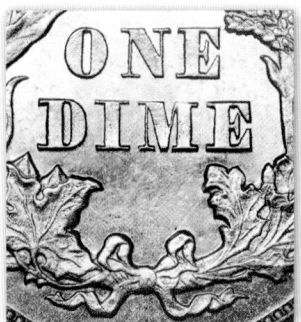

Type I, 1860–1878:
Left ribbon end split, E in ONE close to wreath.

Type II, 1876–1891:
Left ribbon end pointed, E slightly farther from wreath.

1873–1874 • LIBERTY SEATED, VARIETY 5, ARROWS AT DATE

The Liberty Seated obverse motif and legend remain the same as preceding. The reverse changes only slightly. Following the Mint Act of February 12, 1873, the weight of the dime was increased by a very small amount, and arrowheads were added to each side of the date to denote the change. From 1875 to 1891 the arrowheads were discontinued, but the new weight remained the same. *Designer:* Christian Gobrecht • *Composition:* .900 silver, .100 copper • *Diameter:* 17.9 mm. • *Weight:* 38.58 grains (2.50 grams).

1875–1891 • LIBERTY SEATED, VARIETY 4 RESUMED (WEIGHT STANDARD OF VARIETY 5)

The obverse and reverse designs are as preceding, except that the arrows by the date on the reverse have been removed. The weight is unchanged, conforming to the Coinage Act of February 12, 1873. *Designer:* Christian Gobrecht • *Composition:* .900 silver, .100 copper • *Diameter:* 17.9 mm. • *Weight:* 38.58 grains (2.50 grams).

RELEASE AND DISTRIBUTION

Excepting Proofs made for presentation and for collectors, all Liberty Seated dimes were intended for circulation. *Niles' Weekly Register*, July 29, 1837, included this:

New Dime

The *United States Gazette* says: "A friend showed to us on Saturday a ten cent piece of the new coinage; it is smaller in circumference than those formerly emitted; on one side are the words ONE DIME, encircled with a wreath, on the other is a finely cut figure of liberty not the old head and trunk, that once looked so flaring out from our coin—but a neat, tidy female figure, sufficiently dressed, holding in one hand a staff, surmounted with a liberty cap; the other hand sustains a shield, inscribed with the word LIBERTY. The figure is in a sitting posture, and resembles, generally, the representation of Britannia on the English coins.

Liberty Seated dimes were made in quantity in most later years and served in commerce widely, with the result that most became well-worn in time.

The Civil War was declared on April 15, 1861. In the North it was envisioned as an easy win, and President Abraham Lincoln called for men to enlist for 90 days, after which time it surely would be over. That did not happen. The first major clash, the Battle of Bull Run in late July, resulted in a Confederate victory. Union troops scattered and fled. By late 1861 the outcome remained uncertain. In late December, gold coins began to be hoarded—"hard money" offered security. In March 1862 the Treasury Department began issuing Legal Tender Notes. These could be exchanged only for other paper notes and were not redeemable at par in federal silver or gold coins. Fear increased, and by late spring all silver coins were gone from circulation in the East and the Midwest. In the meantime, on the West Coast there were no Legal Tender bills in circulation. The Constitution of the State of California, adopted in 1850, forbade the use of paper money there. Silver coins continued to circulate at par, and any paper money brought into the state was accepted by merchants only at a deep discount.

When the San Francisco Mint began producing dimes in 1856, these went into circulation readily. Similar to the situation with half dimes (first minted in California in 1863), they were very popular with Chinese immigrants, who sent many back to their homeland. Today the average grade of a surviving San Francisco Mint dime of the 1850s or 1860s is much lower than that of one made in Philadelphia.

In the East, dimes continued to be made after the spring of 1862, but they were not seen in commerce. The Mint sold them, but only at a stiff premium, if bought with Legal Tender Notes. Bullion brokers and banks maintained supplies for citizens who wanted to acquire them, again at a premium. It was anticipated that after the Civil War ended, silver coins would reappear in circulation. The public remained suspicious of the solidity of the Treasury Department, and it was not until after April 20, 1876, that silver and paper were on a par, and silver coins, including long-hoarded dimes, were again seen in circulation. The Treasury Department did not anticipate this flood of old coins; to be sure that enough coins were on hand, it had increased mintages sharply from 1875 through 1878. This produced a glut, after which from 1879 through 1881 the mintage of dimes was very small.

Liberty Seated dimes remained in circulation for many years and were a familiar sight into the 1920s. By the end of the 1930s—during which decade coin collecting became very popular—they were gone.

PROOF LIBERTY SEATED DIMES

Proofs were struck at the Philadelphia Mint for all years from 1837 through 1891, although no sets with all copper and silver denominations are known for 1851 and 1853. Some dimes of these years are highly mirrorlike and have been called Proofs, but whether they were intended as such is a matter of debate.

From 1837 to 1858 Proofs were available as single coins and as part of silver sets for face value upon request to the Mint. In the latter year it seems that 210 sets were made, plus single coins. In 1859 the

Mint anticipated a great demand for Proofs and made 800 silver sets, followed by 1,000 each in 1860 and 1861. Proofs of the 1860 and 1861 dimes are far and away the rarest of the decade of the 1860s, as, at the new retail price of $3 per set, many collectors ignored them. It is likely that more than half of the coins were placed into circulation. Among later sets the figures reached lows of 460 and 470 in 1863 and 1864, although most survive today. Ordering Proofs from the Mint involved either paying in silver or gold coins (available only at a premium in the marketplace) or by paying a strong premium in paper money. The Mint would not accept federal paper money at par.

Today, a complete run of Proof dates from 1858 to 1891 can be formed without difficulty. Typical grades are PF-63 and 64. Gems or PF-65 and finer coins are in the minority.

LIBERTY SEATED DIMES (1837–1891): GUIDE TO COLLECTING

Apart from Proof coins, called "Master Coins" in the early days, there was not much interest in Liberty Seated dimes during the years they were issued. Circulation strikes were ignored, including New Orleans and San Francisco branch-mint issues and the later coins of Carson City. The curators of the Mint Cabinet, which was organized in June 1838, had no interest in them. As a result many dimes made in large quantities range from scarce to very rare in Mint State today. Most of the early New Orleans issues range from very rare to nearly impossible to find in Mint State, and for certain Philadelphia dimes before 1853, some, such as 1844 and 1846, are seen more often with Proof finish than in Choice or Gem Mint State.

Liberty Seated dimes were mentioned now and again in the two leading periodicals of the late 19th and early 20th centuries—the *American Journal of Numismatics* and *The Numismatist*. An awakening happened in 1893 with the publication of *Mint Marks, A Treatise on the Coinage of United States Branch Mints*. The author was Augustus G. Heaton, a talented writer, poet, and artist. This engendered an interest in mintmarked coins, but there was no widespread interest in this specialty until the 1909-S V.D.B. Lincoln cent caused a sensation in in August of that year (more information is in the next section, "Barber or Liberty Head Dimes [1892–1916]").

Every now and again articles about mintmarked dimes were published in *The Numismatist*, *Hobbies*, *The Numismatic Scrapbook Magazine*, and elsewhere. As an example, the June 1912 issue of *The Numismatist* included this commentary by Howard R. Newcomb:

Unappreciated Silver Mint Rarities—Dimes

Everyone knows the 1894 San Francisco dime is the rarest in the dime series and one of the greatest rarities of all the United States coins. There are many others that are worth careful consideration in any state of preservation, but that which stands out next in point of rarity is the Carson City dime of 1874. Although the records give 10,817 pieces coined, I have met with less than a half dozen specimens, and all from circulation. 1871-CC, 1872-CC, and 1873-CC, with arrows [the 1873-CC, No Arrows variety was unknown to Newcomb and would not emerge until the American Numismatic Society exhibit two years later, in 1914], follow next, and of these three only the 1871 have I heard of existing in Uncirculated condition. They are all of excessive rarity. I think I am safe in saying that a more recent coin now follows, the 1885-S dime. This piece is more likely to be passed by unnoticed than any other in the series. It recently brought a very low price at auction ($22.10 Uncirculated) if its rarity is taken into consideration with other well-known rarities of the United States series, such as a half cent of 1796.

The 1860-O, 1870-S, 1858-S, 1859-S, and 1856-S are next in the order named; and those possessing these, especially in Uncirculated condition, have some very nice prizes. All the above mentioned pieces, together with a few others not noted, are vastly rarer than the so-called very rare 1860-S dime with stars.

At that time and continuing for years afterward there was no book or guide listing basic varieties of coins by date and mintmark and giving market value. Such was unavailable until 1934, with the publication of *The Standard Catalogue of United States Coins*, followed years later by *A Guide Book of United States Coins* in 1946 (cover date 1947) by Western Publishing Co. (today known as Whitman Publishing).

Interest moved forward, and dramatically, in the 1970s when Kamal Ahwash, a well-known figure at conventions and other gatherings, began extolling the virtues of Liberty Seated coins in general and dimes in particular. In 1977 he self-published the *Encyclopedia of U.S. Liberty Seated Dimes 1837–1891*, essentially a picture book, which enjoyed wide sales and created a lot of attention. This catalyzed the entire Liberty Seated field, resulting in the publication of specialized books in the 1990s by DLRC Press. These included *The Complete Guide to Liberty Seated Dimes*, by Brian Greer, in 1992. In the early 21st century the series "went viral" with Gerry Fortin's *The Definitive Resource for Liberty Seated Dime Variety Collectors*, published only on an Internet site (www.seateddimevarieties.com). In time the numbers assigned by Greer were first supplanted, then largely replaced, by new Fortin numbers that remain in wide use today. In the meantime the Liberty Seated Collectors Club along with their publications, *The Gobrecht Journal* and *E-Gobrecht*, added more interest.

Today the collecting of Liberty Seated dimes is a popular pursuit all across the art and science of numismatics (as the author likes to call it). As several varieties are impossible (or nearly so) to find in Choice Mint State or finer, most enthusiasts content themselves with forming sets in circulated grades, typically from Very Fine upward. With Gerry Fortin's website as a meeting place, there is a lot of interest in die varieties. The offering of many Liberty Seated coins on eBay has also helped the specialty.

BEING A SMART BUYER

First and foremost—and this is true of all Liberty Seated denominations—do not be a slave to grading numbers. There are *two more* factors that can be equally or even more important. Sharpness of strike is very important, and there are many dimes that within a certain certified grade can have a needle-sharp strike or can be weak in areas. Eye appeal is of equal value. Coins can be beautiful to view or they can be dark, stained, or otherwise ugly. Better to have an MS-63 coin that is sharply struck and has good eye appeal than an MS-66 that has lightly struck areas and is not very attractive. Even better, the MS-63 is apt to cost but a fraction of the MS-66!

Cherrypicking Liberty Seated dimes for quality can pay dividends. The grading services pay little or no attention to strike or eye appeal. This provides the opportunity to acquire sharp coins, for varieties for which such exist, without paying any more for them. You can join Gerry Fortin's Internet "club" and report new discoveries. A lot of people have done this. In addition there are many interesting varieties of which the public is not aware—such as repunched and misplaced dates—that often cost no more. The *Cherrypickers' Guide to Rare Die Varieties of United States Coins* describes many such pieces.

For circulated coins, avoid those with nicks or scratches. Proofs are usually quite good, but some have light striking on Liberty's head; quite a few have scattered lint marks from residue on the dies. Eye appeal varies.

AVAILABILITY IN CERTAIN GRADES

The estimates for the numbers existing in various grades are based on conservative grading interpretation. In recent years gradeflation and resubmissions to certification services have increased the numbers of coins listed in PCGS and NGC population reports. In any event, these reports give the number of submissions, not the number of *different* specimens. If the same coin is sent in six times, it appears that six coins have been certified, not just one.

Gradeflation is difficult to analyze. When the author wrote *A Guide Book of Liberty Seated Silver Coins* in 2015, he spent many hours studying the availability of coins in various grades. For dimes the auctions of leading collections such as T. Harrison and John Work Garrett, Louis E. Eliasberg, Eugene Gardner, and others contained many exceptional coins and were duly noted. Beyond that, important dimes were offered in many other sales. The population reports were studied.

Today in 2018, as these words are being written for the fourth edition of *Mega Red*, the true population of dimes has not changed. There have been no important hoards discovered, nor have there been any surprises from long-hidden collections appearing on the market. Stated another way, the availability figures used in 2015 should be able to be used today. They have been re-reviewed, and a few have been changed. The estimates are based on grading interpretations of 2015. Since then, many MS-64 coins have been graded MS-65, and MS-65 coins have been graded MS-66 and MS-67. Perhaps a decade from now, many of today's MS-65 coins will be certified as MS-68. Who knows?

The reason for gradeflation is that it seems to be win-win. The owner of an MS-64 coin is delighted to pay a fee to have it graded MS-65 or MS-66 if the coin increases dramatically in value. It is a win for the grading services as well; it is more profitable to grade the same coin multiple times than to grade it just once.

This brings the subject back to connoisseurship: Use the grade on a holder as a *starting point*. Remember that some MS-64 coins in old holders are of higher quality than MS-65 coins in new holders. Study the sharpness of strike and evaluate eye appeal. There are many MS-63 dimes that under this test are much more desirable than MS-65 dimes with weak striking or ugly surfaces. You are on your own when doing this. It will take time and patience, but your reward will be to build a truly great collection.

Also, while Mint State coins are more desirable than are, say, EF-40 coins, an element of practicality intervenes. Very few collectors aspire to form a set of Mint State and Proof coins, as this would cost hundreds of thousands of dollars, even in low number ranges. The many surveys of the collections of Liberty Seated Collectors Club members show that the vast majority collect circulated coins. Unless you have a very strong bank account, this is the way to go. Coins in Very Fine, Extremely Fine, and About Uncirculated grades are often inexpensive, and the best part of a full set of dates and mintmarks can be acquired. On the other hand, if you also collect modern dollar coins from the 1971 Eisenhower to the latest Native American issue, by all means go for Mint State and Proof.

MARKET NOTES

Today, at the end of the second decade of the 21st century, the market for many federal coins is not as strong as it was several years ago. Many buyers coming into coins hoping to make a quick profit have left. The reduction in prices is seen mostly in Mint State and Proof coins, as circulated coins have been acquired by dedicated numismatists, not investors. The net result is that many Mint State and Proof coins can be purchased from 20% to 30% or less than they would have cost as recently as 2012 and 2013. A slow market often represents a great opportunity to buy.

You have a lot to think about and evaluate. Read and study as much as you can. Go slowly and carefully, and good luck.

LIBERTY SEATED (1837–1891)

GRADING STANDARDS

MS-60 to 70 (Mint State). *Obverse:* At MS-60, some abrasion and contact marks are evident, most noticeably on the bosom and thighs and knees. Luster is present, but may be dull or lifeless, and interrupted in patches in the large open field. At MS-63, contact marks are very few, and abrasion is hard to detect except under magnification. An MS-65 coin has no abrasion, and contact marks are

1876-CC, Variety 1. Graded MS-64.

so minute as to require magnification. Luster should be full and rich, except for Philadelphia (but not San Francisco) dimes of the early and mid-1860s. Most Mint State coins of the 1861 to 1865 years, Philadelphia issues, have extensive die striae (from not completely finishing the die). Some low-mintage Philadelphia issues may be prooflike. Clashmarks are common in this era. This is true of contemporary half dimes as well. Half dimes of this type can be very beautiful at this level. Grades above MS-65 are seen with regularity, more so than for the related No Stars dimes. ***Reverse:*** Comments apply as for the obverse, except that in lower Mint State grades abrasion and contact marks are most noticeable on the highest parts of the leaves and the ribbon, less so on ONE DIME. At MS-65 or higher there are no marks visible to the unaided eye. The field is mainly protected by design elements and does not show abrasion as much as does the open-field obverse on a given coin.

Illustrated coin: Note the blend of pink, lilac, and gold tones.

AU-50, 53, 55, 58 (About Uncirculated).
Obverse: Light wear is seen on the thighs and knees, bosom, and head. At AU-58, the luster is extensive, but incomplete. Friction is seen in the large open field. At AU–50 and 53, luster is less. ***Reverse:*** Wear is evident on the leaves (especially at the top of the wreath) and ribbon. An AU-58 coin has nearly full luster, more so than on the obverse, as the design elements protect the small field areas. At AU–50 and 53, there still is significant luster, more than on the obverse.

1838-O, No Stars; F-101. Graded AU-58.

EF-40, 45 (Extremely Fine). ***Obverse:*** Further wear is seen on all areas, especially the thighs and knees, bosom, and head. Little or no luster is seen. ***Reverse:*** Further wear is seen on all areas, most noticeably at the leaves to each side of the wreath apex and on the ribbon bow knot. Leaves retain details except on the higher areas.

1838-O, No Stars; F-102. Graded EF-45.

VF-20, 30 (Very Fine). ***Obverse:*** Further wear is seen. Most details of the gown are worn away, except in the lower-relief areas above and to the right of the shield. Hair detail is mostly or completely gone. ***Reverse:*** Wear is more extensive. The highest leaves are flat.

1872-CC; F-101. Graded VF-30.

F-12, 15 (Fine). *Obverse:* The seated figure is well worn, with little detail remaining. LIBERTY on the shield is fully readable but weak in areas. On the 1838–1840 subtype Without Drapery, LIBERTY is in higher relief and will wear more quickly; ER may be missing, but other details are at the Fine level. *Reverse:* Most detail of the leaves is gone. The rim is worn but bold, and most if not all denticles are visible.

1874-CC. Graded F-15.

VG-8, 10 (Very Good). *Obverse:* The seated figure is more worn, but some detail can be seen above and to the right of the shield. The shield is discernible. In LIBERTY at least three letters are readable but very weak at VG-8; a few more visible at VG-10. On the 1838–1840 subtype Without Drapery, LIBERTY is in higher relief, and at Very Good only one or two letters may be readable. However, LIBERTY is not an infallible

1843-O; F-101. Graded VG-8.

way to grade this type, as some varieties have the word in low relief on the die, so it wore away slowly. *Reverse:* Further wear has combined the details of most leaves. The rim is complete, but weak in areas. The reverse appears to be in a slightly higher grade than the obverse.

G-4, 6 (Good). *Obverse:* The seated figure is worn smooth. At G-4 there are no letters in LIBERTY remaining on most (but not all) coins. At G-6, traces of one or two can be seen (except on the early No Drapery coins). *Reverse:* Wear is more extensive. The leaves are all combined and in outline form. The rim is well worn and missing in some areas, causing the outer parts of the peripheral letters to be worn away in some instances. On

1873-CC. Graded G-4.

most coins the reverse appears to be in a slightly higher grade than the obverse.

  Illustrated coin: The scratch on the obverse lessens the desirability of this coin.

AG-3 (About Good). *Obverse:* The seated figure is mostly visible in outline form, with no detail. The rim is worn away. The date remains clear. *Reverse:* Many if not most letters are worn away, at least in part. The wreath and interior letters are discernible. The rim is weak.

1874-CC. Graded AG-3.

PF-60 to 70 (Proof). *Obverse and Reverse:* Proofs that are extensively cleaned and have many hairlines, or that are dull and grainy, are lower level, such as PF–60 to 62. These command less attention than more visually appealing pieces, save for the scarce (in any grade) dates of 1844 and 1846, and 1863 through 1867. Both the half dime and dime Proofs of 1837 were often cleaned, resulting in coins that have lost much of their mirror surface. With

1886. Graded PF-67.

medium hairlines and good reflectivity, an assigned grade of PF-64 is indicated, and with relatively few hairlines, Gem PF-65. In various grades hairlines are most easily seen in the obverse field. PF-66 should have hairlines so delicate that magnification is needed to see them. Above that, a Proof should be free of such lines.

1837 Liberty Seated Dime

1837, Large Date, Flat Top 3 •
Circulation-Strike Mintage: Part of a total circulation-strike mintage of 682,500 for the issue.

Commentary: This strike is attributed as Fortin-101. Apparently, the Large Date Liberty Seated dimes were the first produced, as evidenced by the fact that numerous Mint State pieces were saved due to their novelty. For many years these have been in great demand for inclusion in type sets. As a date, specimens are plentiful in most grades. Late dies states show severe cracks and clash marks.

Detail of the Large Date and Flat Top 3.

Availability in circulated grades: The Large Date 1837 strikes are readily available in all grades, the prevalent levels being Very Good through Very Fine. Many were saved as the first year of issue.

Availability in Mint State: Large Date 1837 dimes are the variety most often seen. Brian Greer considered this to be among the four most readily available dimes before 1854. *MS-60 to 62: 500 to 750 estimated to exist; MS-63: 160 to 200; MS-64: 140 to 170; MS-65 or better: 70 to 90.*

	Cert	Avg	%MS	G-4	VG-8	F-12	VF-20	EF-40	AU-50	MS-60	MS-63	MS-64	MS-65	MS-66
1837, Large Date, Flat Top 3	43	49.6	47%	$45	$55	$100	$300	$500	$750	$1,100	$1,800	$4,000	$7,750	$10,000

1837, Large Date, Flat Top 3,
Proof • **Proof Mintage:** Estimated 50+.

Commentary: This die combination (Fortin-101) was also used for circulation strikes. On June 30, 1837, 30 or a few more Proofs were struck for presentation purposes (not for inclusion in silver Proof sets). Apparently, nearly all of these went to non-numismatic recipients, for very few unimpaired specimens exist today. An estimated 35 to 40 are known.

	Cert	Avg	%MS	PF-60	PF-63	PF-65
1837, Large Date, Flat Top 3, Proof	27	64.0		$6,000	$12,000	$32,500

1837, Small Date, Round Top 3 •

Circulation-Strike Mintage: Part of a total circulation-strike mintage of 682,500 for the issue.

Commentary: This variety is designated Fortin-102 to 104.

Availability in circulated grades: The Small Date dimes of 1837 are slightly scarcer than the Large Date dimes but are easily available in all grades, mostly Very Good through Very Fine. *AG-3 to AU-58: 3,000 to 4,000.*

Availability in Mint State: In 1992 Brian Greer considered this to be among the four most readily available dimes before 1854, but this opinion probably would not hold today. Among *Mint State* dimes of this date fewer than 20% are of the Small Date variety.[7] The Eliasberg coin was only AU-55. Very few Mint State coins have been offered in major collections over the years. This relative rarity is not reflected in current market prices. *MS-60 to 62: 120 to 140 estimated to exist; MS-63: 30 to 40; MS-64: 25 to 35; MS-65 or better: 15 to 20.*

Detail of the Small Date and Round Top 3.

	Cert	Avg	%MS	G-4	VG-8	F-12	VF-20	EF-40	AU-50	MS-60	MS-63	MS-64	MS-65	MS-66
1837, Small Date, Round Top 3	38	50.6	45%	$50	$65	$120	$325	$500	$750	$1,200	$2,000	$4,500	$8,500	$15,000

1838-O Liberty Seated Dime, No Stars

1838-O, No Stars • Circulation-Strike Mintage: 406,034+.

Commentary: The 1838-O is designated Fortin-101 (with repunched mintmark) and 102. These are usually fairly well struck. Some examples of the 1838-O show die rust. Some have light striking at the top part of the obverse, and some show significant obverse die erosion since only a single die was employed.

On May 12, the New Orleans Mint superintendent wrote to Mint director Robert M. Patterson: "I have the pleasure of enclosing a specimen of our coinage, a dime, one of the thirty pieces struck on the 8th inst. Mr. [Rufus] Tyler found the press required readjusting and that there was danger of breaking it and only struck a few pieces, ten of which were deposited in the cornerstone of the New American Theatre which was laid the same day, the remainder distributed as mementos of the event."[8]

Based on records in the National Archives, R.W. Julian found that that 367,434 were struck in June and July 1838 and 121,600 additional 1838-O dimes were made in January 1839, suggesting a total mintage far in excess of the 406,034 figure listed above. Notwithstanding this, the 1838-O remains a rarity in high grades today.

In 1893, Augustus G. Heaton described mintmarks on New Orleans coins, as follows: "The O Mint dime coinage has several sizes of the indicative letter which may be classified in three, *large* which is about the height of the letters of the legend 'United States of America' on the coin, the *medium*, about two-thirds, and the *small*, about one-half or rather less." Mintmark sizes on New Orleans issues are found on various dimes of the next quarter century.

Availability in circulated grades: The 1838-O is readily available, but significantly scarcer than the 1837 of the same type. Several thousand exist. The attrition rate of New Orleans dimes was much greater than for Philadelphia.[9]

Availability in Mint State: At the gem level, 1838-O in Mint State is exceedingly rare, and often a span of many years will elapse between offerings. Lower-range Mint State coins are available but scarce. It has been my experience over the years that the majority of the specimens described as Mint State would be more properly described as About Uncirculated. The Eliasberg coin (1996) was MS-64. Brian Greer noted the rumor of the small hoard of Mint State pieces, a grouping of which this author is not aware. *MS-60 to 62: 35 to 45 estimated to exist; MS-63: 17 to 22; MS-64: 14 to 18; MS-65 or better: 7 to 10.*

	Cert	Avg	%MS	G-4	VG-8	F-12	VF-20	EF-40	AU-50	MS-60	MS-63	MS-64	MS-65	MS-66
1838-O, No Stars	180	38.4	17%	$90	$125	$180	$400	$800	$1,200	$3,600	$5,500	$8,500	$20,000	$35,000

1838 Liberty Seated Dime, With Stars

1838, Small Stars • Circulation-Strike

Mintage: Part of a total circulation-strike mintage of 1,992,500 for the issue.

Commentary: It is believed that punches intended for use on the half dime were employed to create the stars on this variety, which is designated Fortin-101. Based on the small sample of seven obverse dies for the Large Stars and one for the Small Stars, the estimated mintage for the Small Stars might be in the 250,000 range. This seems to square with the Small Stars dimes' being readily available today. The stars were individually punched into the working die. The first delivery by the coiner was 30,000 pieces on March 31, 1838. The star size is not known, although some have speculated they were all of the Small Stars style.

Detail of the Small Stars.

Availability in circulated grades: Many exist, mostly in lower grades. Nice Extremely Fine and About Uncirculated coins can be found with some searching.

Availability in Mint State: The Small Stars variety is exceedingly rare in Mint State. *MS-60 to 62: 50 to 75 estimated to exist; MS-63: 25 to 32; MS-64: 15 to 20; MS-65 or better: 12 to 15.*

	Cert	Avg	%MS	G-4	VG-8	F-12	VF-20	EF-40	AU-50	MS-60	MS-63	MS-64	MS-65
1838, Small Stars	79	57.0	63%	$30	$40	$55	$85	$175	$400	$700	$1,350	$2,000	$4,000

1838, Large Stars • Circulation-Strike

Mintage: Part of a total circulation-strike mintage of 1,992,500 for the issue.

Commentary: This dime (Fortin-102 to 114) exists in two well-known varieties, Small Stars and Large Stars, the preceding being by far the rarer.

One variety of the 1838 is known as having "partial drapery," from Liberty's left elbow. In actuality, this is simply a clash mark that appears in the drapery position. *All* 1838 Liberty Seated dimes were designed without drapery (called No Drapery in this book). The stars were individually punched into the working dies.

Eight obverse dies and seven reverse dies in various combinations are known. Three boldly cracked obverse die varieties (Fortin-106, 110a, and 111a) are popular among die-variety collectors.

Detail of the Large Stars.

Availability in circulated grades: The 1838 dime with Large Stars is common in all circulated grades.

Availability in Mint State: Brian Greer considered this to be among the four most widely available dimes before 1854. *MS-60 to 62: 200 to 250 estimated to exist; MS-63: 125 to 150; MS-64: 100 to 125; MS-65 or better: 60 to 80.*

	Cert	Avg	%MS	G-4	VG-8	F-12	VF-20	EF-40	AU-50	MS-60	MS-63	MS-64	MS-65
1838, Large Stars	394	58.0	65%	$25	$30	$35	$48	$150	$300	$425	$850	$1,200	$3,000

1838, Large Stars, Proof • Proof

Mintage: Fewer than 5.

Commentary: The obverse die has stars 1, 5, 8, 9, and 12 repunched. Star 12 was originally punched too low in the die.[10] Eugene Gardner (2014) describes a PF-67 (ex Phil Kaufman) as "likely unique" in Proof format.

	Cert	Avg	%MS	PF-60	PF-63	PF-65
1838, Large Stars, Proof, 1 known	1	67.0				

1838-O Liberty Seated Dime, With Stars

1838-O, Stars • Circulation-Strike Mintage: Unknown, if any; apocryphal.

Commentary: In 1893 in *Mint Marks*, Augustus G. Heaton said: "1838 (of which the mintage is not recorded in the Mint Report) is without stars, with a Large O in the wreath on the reverse, and is rare. There is also a variety with stars and a Small o, which is very rare."

The 1838-O With Stars at present is spectral—unknown to any later researchers—and no further mention of it has been found. Heaton was a careful observer, and his comment indicates that he had either seen one or had received what he considered to be a reliable report of the same.

1839 Liberty Seated Dime

1839 • **Circulation-Strike Mintage:** 1,053,115.

Commentary: The 1839 strike is designated Fortin-101 to 109, with three obverse dies combined with eight reverses. The F-105c "Shattered Obverse" die variety is the most popular Liberty Seated dime variety among advanced variety collectors and is considered scarce, with perhaps a dozen or so known.[11] The mintage figure suggests more varieties remain to be discovered.

Availability in circulated grades: Probably more than 5,000 survive, mostly in lower grades.

Availability in Mint State: Brian Greer considered this to be among the four most widely available dimes before 1854. It is relatively available in Mint State, including high-grade examples, some of which are beyond MS-65. The coins are typically lustrous and frosty. *MS-60 to 62: 120 to 160 estimated to exist; MS-63: 60 to 80; MS-64: 40 to 55; MS-65 or better: 30 to 40.*

	Cert	Avg	%MS	G-4	VG-8	F-12	VF-20	EF-40	AU-50	MS-60	MS-63	MS-64	MS-65
1839	245	59.0	67%	$20	$25	$30	$48	$145	$300	$425	$850	$1,100	$3,000

1839, Proof • **Proof Mintage:** 12 to 15 estimated.

Commentary: Two die pairs, F-105 and 106, were also used for circulation strikes. The Eliasberg PF-63 (1996) had stars 8 and 10 repunched. An estimated 7 to 9 examples are known.

	Cert	Avg	%MS	PF-60	PF-63	PF-65
1839, Proof	3	64.3		$7,000	$10,000	$45,000

1839-O Liberty Seated Dime

1839-O • **Circulation-Strike Mintage:** 1,291,600.

Commentary: Designated Fortin-101 to 110, the 1839-O exists with Small O and Large O varieties, which are not widely collected except by specialists. Brian Greer notes that the Small O is slightly scarcer. It is believed that some proportion of the 1,323,000 calendar-year mintage at New Orleans consisted of 1838-O dimes (see earlier listing).

The coins are usually well struck, but some have slight weakness on the horizontal shield lines.

F-105 with Large O is by far the most widely available in all grades. F-108 is the Huge O reverse variety, struck with a leftover reverse from 1838. This is usually seen in grades from About Good to Very Good and is the rarest of the mintmark sizes.[12]

Availability in circulated grades: Thousands exist, mostly in lower grades.

Availability in Mint State: The 1839-O is fairly scarce, certainly much scarcer than its Philadelphia Mint counterpart, but with patience can be located. Most specimens tend to be at lower Mint State levels. *MS-60 to 62: 25 to 30 estimated to exist; MS-63: 15 to 20; MS-64: 10 to 14; MS-65 or better: 8 to 12.*

	Cert	Avg	%MS	G-4	VG-8	F-12	VF-20	EF-40	AU-50	MS-60	MS-63	MS-64	MS-65
1839-O	90	50.5	41%	$25	$50	$75	$145	$240	$425	$800	$1,950	$3,000	$7,000

1840 Liberty Seated Dime, No Drapery

1840, No Drapery • Circulation-Strike
Mintage: 981,000+.

Commentary: The 1840, designated Fortin-101 to 108, combines eight obverse dies and eight reverse dies. F-103 is the popular "Chin Whiskers" variety.

Availability in circulated grades: This dime is readily available in any grade desired.

Availability in Mint State: The 1840 is fairly scarce, but obtainable, in Mint State grades. *MS-60 to 62: 75 to 100 estimated to exist; MS-63: 35 to 50; MS-64: 25 to 32; MS-65 or better 15 to 20.*

	Cert	Avg	%MS	G-4	VG-8	F-12	VF-20	EF-40	AU-50	MS-60	MS-63	MS-64	MS-65
1840, No Drapery	155	54.1	54%	$20	$25	$30	$48	$150	$300	$425	$850	$1,200	$3,200

1840, No Drapery, Proof • Proof
Mintage: 12 to 15 estimated.

Commentary: Louis E. Eliasberg (1997) PF-63: "Star 2 dramatically repunched. Die lines from denticles over space between OF and A." An estimated 8 to 10 are known.

	Cert	Avg	%MS	PF-60	PF-63	PF-65
1841, No Drapery, Proof	6	64.8				

1840-O Liberty Seated Dime, No Drapery

1840-O, No Drapery • Circulation-Strike Mintage: 1,175,000.

Commentary: Designated Fortin-101 to 111, this issue combines seven obverse dies with eight reverse dies. Striking sharpness varies, but most have some light weakness. Many were struck from severely eroded dies leading to weakness, particularly on the obverse.

Three mintmark sizes are known. There were no 1840-O dies made with drapery.

Availability in circulated grades: The 1840-O is scarce, but no difficulty will be encountered in finding one. Examples are mostly in lower grades, as is true of all dimes of this era. According to Gerry Fortin, "Locating choice examples in Extremely Fine and About Uncirculated will be very challenging as variety collectors have hoarded most that come to market."

Availability in Mint State: This year and mintmark combination is very rare in Mint State, as collecting dimes (and other coins) by mintmark was not followed, to my knowledge, by even a single numismatist in the 1840s, and all specimens slipped casually into circulation. By chance some were saved, but the number surviving is very small. *MS-60 to 62: 8 to 11 estimated to exist; MS-63: 1 or 2; MS-64: 1; MS-65 or better: 1.*

	Cert	Avg	%MS	G-4	VG-8	F-12	VF-20	EF-40	AU-50	MS-60	MS-63	MS-64	MS-65
1840-O, No Drapery	38	39.7	18%	$60	$90	$120	$180	$480	$1,025	$7,200	$14,500	$16,500	$21,500

1840 Liberty Seated Dime, With Drapery

1840, Drapery • **Circulation-Strike**
Mintage: 377,500.

Commentary: This issue (Fortin-101) is often lightly struck on Liberty's head and the corresponding part of the reverse, though well-struck specimens can be found.

In 1840, the seated figure was redesigned slightly, the shield was moved upright from its formerly tilted appearance, and other minor changes were made. On the reverse, the letters are slightly larger. The buds on the laurel wreath have split ends, a style continuing until this style of wreath was replaced by the "cereal" wreath in 1860. Other minor changes were made.

In all grades the 1840 Liberty Seated dime With Drapery is considerably scarcer than its predecessor without. It is believed that the first examples were delivered in December of the year.

Availability in circulated grades: This date is challenging in all circulated grades and substantially more difficult to find than 1840, No Drapery.

Availability in Mint State: The Drapery dime of 1840 is quite rare in Mint State, certainly in the top 15 or 20 percent. Most Mint State pieces tend to be in lower grades. Examples of high-grade coins include Louis E. Eliasberg's (1997) MS-65/66 and Eugene Gardner's (2015) MS-67, MS-64 (2), MS-63, and MS-61. Perusing auctions of notable collections (beyond the purview of this edition of *Mega Red*) is interesting to do. The Internet, especially the Newman Numismatic Portal (https://nnp.wustl.edu), offers a wide opportunity. *MS-60 to 62: 3 to 5 estimated to exist; MS-63: 2 or 3; MS-64: 2 or 3; MS-65 or better: 1 or 2.*

	Cert	Avg	%MS	G-4	VG-8	F-12	VF-20	EF-40	AU-50	MS-60	MS-63	MS-64	MS-65
1840, Drapery	24	43.3	29%	$90	$125	$180	$300	$800	$1,300	$3,000	$12,000	$19,500	$30,000

1841 Liberty Seated Dime, No Drapery

1841, No Drapery, Proof • Proof

Mintage: 2 or more.

Commentary: Two 1841, No Drapery, Proofs (Fortin-101) have been verified; the finer of the two, graded PF-67, sold at auction in 2013 for $305,000. These lack drapery and were made from a die created from a No Drapery hub of a modified style not used anywhere else in the series, per the research of John McCloskey. As such this constitutes a distinctively different and highly important variety.

	Cert	Avg	%MS	PF-60	PF-63	PF-65
1841, No Drapery, Proof	2	60.0			$65,000	

1841 Liberty Seated Dime, With Drapery

1841, Drapery • Circulation-Strike

Mintage: 1,622,500.

Commentary: This issue (Fortin-102 to 110) is usually seen fairly well struck. Some are weak at the head of Liberty and the corresponding part of the reverse (the same can be said of most other dimes of this type).

This issue is readily available in all grades. Eight obverse dies were combined with eight reverse dies. Several obverse dies (F-103, 104, and 105) have bold date repunching.

Availability in circulated grades: The 1841, With Drapery dime is readily available in all grades but more challenging than its New Orleans counterpart.

Availability in Mint State: MS-60 to 62: 70 to 100 estimated to exist; MS-63: 30 to 40; MS-64: 20 to 25; MS-65 or better: 8 to 11.

	Cert	Avg	%MS	G-4	VG-8	F-12	VF-20	EF-40	AU-50	MS-60	MS-63	MS-64	MS-65
1841, Drapery	85	57.6	65%	$20	$25	$30	$35	$60	$140	$425	$775	$1,200	$3,600

1841, Drapery, Proof • Proof Mintage: 1 or more.

Commentary: Only one example has been confirmed, that in Heritage Auction's 2014 sale of the Gardner Collection, PF-63 (and earlier in the 1994 ANA, 1997 Halpern and Warner Collections, 2005 Richmond Collection, and 2008 Kaufman Collection sales).

	Cert	Avg	%MS	PF-60	PF-63	PF-65
1841, Drapery, Proof	1	63.0			$55,000	

1841-O Liberty Seated Dime, With Drapery

1841-O, Drapery • **Circulation-Strike**
Mintage: 2,007,500.

Commentary: This issue (Fortin-101 to 115) is sometimes seen lightly struck at Liberty's head and the corresponding area of the reverse, in common with other dimes of the era, often due to relapping's removal of many details.

The 1841-O dime has drapery at the elbow, as do all Liberty Seated dimes from this point forward. There are two distinctive reverses for this issue. Brian Greer devotes several pages to discussing both of them, calling the earlier the "Closed Bud reverse" and the later or regular style the "Open Bud reverse." This has to do with little slits or lines at the end of the buds on the laurel wreath, which create an "open bud." Elsewhere in numismatics the additions to the wreath are called "berries." In nature the laurel is a flowering plant.

According to Gerry Fortin's website: "There is also an open question as to whether the stated mintage for 1841-O dimes is accurate. Variety 105 with a shattered reverse from use in 1842 and Variety 116 with a reverse die previously known from limited 1842 coinage suggest that 1841 New Orleans dimes could have been struck in 1842 and included in the 1842-O mintage report." Ten obverse dies were combined with 13 reverse dies.

Transitional Reverses with Large O (Fortin-101) and Small O (Fortin-102) mintmark are leftover reverses from 1840. (Regular reverses have Medium O and Small O mintmarks.)

Availability in circulated grades: Thousands exist, but probably less than 1% of the original mintage, a comment appropriate to all New Orleans dimes.

Availability in Mint State: The 1841-O is one of the more readily available Mint State New Orleans dimes of the era, although on an absolute basis it is fairly elusive. The reason for the availability of these is not known. They are not from the October 28, 1982, discovery of buried New Orleans coins, a find consisting mostly of half dollars.[13] *MS-60 to 62: 25 to 32 estimated to exist; MS-63: 12 to 15; MS-64: 6 to 9; MS-65 or better: 3 or 4.*

	Cert	Aug	%MS	G-4	VG-8	F-12	VF-20	EF-40	AU-50	MS-60	MS-63	MS-64	MS-65
1841-O, Drapery	104	42.8	21%	$25	$35	$45	$90	$150	$325	$850	$1,400	$5,400	$9,000

1842 Liberty Seated Dime

1842 • **Circulation-Strike Mintage:**
1,887,500.

Commentary: Designated Fortin-101 to 108, this is one of the more plentiful dimes of the era and is easily obtainable in virtually any circulation-strike grade desired. Die pairings consist of seven obverse and seven reverse dies.

Availability in circulated grades: The 1842 dime is plentiful in all grades, but is not seen as often as its New Orleans Mint counterpart.

Availability in Mint State: MS-60 to 62: 70 to 90 estimated to exist; MS-63: 40 to 50; MS-64: 25 to 30; MS-65 or better: 15 to 20.

	Cert	Avg	%MS	G-4	VG-8	F-12	VF-20	EF-40	AU-50	MS-60	MS-63	MS-64	MS-65
1842	99	52.5	62%	$20	$25	$30	$35	$50	$125	$400	$650	$1,200	$3,000

1842, Proof • Proof Mintage:

9 to 12 estimated.

Commentary: The few 1842 Proofs were struck from two die pairs.[14] About eight or nine are known.

	Cert	Avg	%MS	PF-60	PF-63	PF-65
1842, Proof	4	63.8		$10,000	$15,000	$40,000

1842-O Liberty Seated Dime

1842-O • Circulation-Strike Mintage:
2,020,000.

Commentary: The 1842-O dime (Fortin-101 to 107) is usually not as well struck as the Philadelphia Mint version of the same date. It is typically weak at the "check points" for a dime of this era: Liberty's head and the corresponding part of the wreath on the reverse. It is occasionally seen with poor reverse details due to excessively relapped dies.[15]

This dime is one of those curious pieces in American numismatics which is readily enough available, indeed common, in low grades, but emerges as a major rarity in Mint State. The reason is that the pieces attracted no numismatic interest at the time of issue. Thus, the survival of Mint State coins is strictly a matter of chance. Small O (scarcer) and Medium O mintmarks exist. It has been questioned whether the published mintage figure is accurate. The mintage was struck using four obverse dies and five reverse dies.

Availability in circulated grades: An estimated 4,000 to 8,000—a tiny fraction of the mintage—survive.

Availability in Mint State: The 1842 dime from the New Orleans Mint is very rare in Mint State, and is certainly one of the most elusive varieties in the series. It almost strains credulity that a coin with a mintage on the long side of 2 million would be an ultra-rarity in Mint State. Gerry Fortin reports that known Mint State coins are all of the Medium O style. *MS-60 to 62: 10 to 13 estimated to exist; MS-63: 5 to 7; MS-64: 2 or 3; MS-65 or better: 3 or 4.*

	Cert	Avg	%MS	G-4	VG-8	F-12	VF-20	EF-40	AU-50	MS-60	MS-63	MS-64	MS-65
1842-O	88	41.6	23%	$35	$60	$90	$175	$475	$1,300	$3,500	$6,500	$8,500	$20,000

1843 Liberty Seated Dime

1843 • **Circulation-Strike Mintage:** 1,370,000.

Commentary: Struck using five obverse dies and six reverse dies, the 1843 Liberty Seated dime from the Philadelphia Mint is designated Fortin-101 to 106.

Availability in circulated grades: This issue is easy to find in any desired circulated grade.

Availability in Mint State: Higher-level Mint State pieces are rare, as most in the Mint State category hover in the MS-60 to MS-63 range. *MS-60 to 62: 35 to 45 estimated to exist; MS-63: 18 to 22; MS-64: 12 to 15; MS-65 or better: 4 to 6.*

	Cert	Avg	%MS	G-4	VG-8	F-12	VF-20	EF-40	AU-50	MS-60	MS-63	MS-64	MS-65
1843	80	55.5	51%	$20	$25	$30	$35	$50	$125	$475	$800	$2,100	$4,200

1843, Proof • **Proof Mintage:** 15 to 20 estimated.

Commentary: The Proof of 1843 is Fortin-103; an estimated 10 to 12 are known.

	Cert	Avg	%MS	PF-60	PF-63	PF-65
1843, Proof	10	64.3		$5,000	$10,000	$25,000

1843-O Liberty Seated Dime

1843-O • **Circulation-Strike Mintage:** 150,000.

Commentary: Often lightly struck on the head of Liberty, the 1843-O dimes (Fortin-101) show various differences in the striking of the laurel leaves on the reverse.

The 1843-O is one of the key issues of its era. In About Uncirculated preservation an offering would be truly memorable—in MS-60, extraordinary.

Availability in circulated grades: Fairly scarce in all grades, the 1843-O is particularly elusive Extremely Fine and About Uncirculated. The population is probably only in the mid-hundreds, less than one-half of 1% of the mintage.

Availability in Mint State: These are exceedingly rare in high grade, and only a few exist. A specimen from the Louis Eliasberg sale in 1996 is described thusly: "MS-66. Deeply lustrous and frosty, extraordinarily so. Just a few tiny marks away from absolute perfection. Reverse lightly struck on the wreath, as always on authentic specimens." *MS-60 to 62: 1 estimated to exist; MS-63: 0; MS-64: 0; MS-65 or better: 1.*

	Cert	Avg	%MS	G-4	VG-8	F-12	VF-20	EF-40	AU-50	MS-60	MS-63	MS-64	MS-65
1843-O	51	20.6	0%	$175	$300	$600	$1,350	$3,500	$11,000	$70,000			

1844 Liberty Seated Dime

1844 • Circulation-Strike Mintage: 72,500.

Commentary: The 1844 dime (Fortin-101 and 102), the famous "Orphan Annie" variety, is the best-known Liberty Seated dime of the era, but in high grades a number of the New Orleans pieces are rarer (although a high grade 1844 Philadelphia Mint dime is nothing to be sneezed at). The "Orphan Annie" nickname was first used by Frank C. Ross in the April 1931 issue of *Hobbies Magazine.* Ross held forth in a monthly column into the 1950s and periodically offered suggestions as to the coin's supposed rarity. Ross also enlisted others to hype the 1844 dime, and in October 1935 William Brimelow of Elkhart, Indiana, published an article in *The Numismatist.* The gist was that with a mintage of 72,500 they should be common. Instead, according to Brimelow, they are much rarer than the 1846 with its mintage of 31,200. Were they melted at the Mint? Did some speculator buy most of them? Or? As a result the 1844 is an orphan, so to speak—figuratively all by itself. Today this makes interesting reading, but is considered fanciful. In actuality, the 1846 *is* rarer.[16]

Dimes of this year from the Philadelphia Mint were struck using two obverse dies and two reverse dies.

Availability in circulated grades: This is a well-known scarcity, indeed perhaps the best known among Liberty Seated Dimes of this era, due to its low mintage. However, the interested collector will have no difficulty obtaining one, with the typical grade being Good, Very Good, or Fine. Extremely Fine and About Uncirculated pieces, particularly the latter, are rare. Beginning in 2003 Heritage Auctions offered a hoard of 612 coins in various circulated grades assembled by Terry Brand, a Los Angeles collector, who had accumulated over 900 coins, including more than 450 purchased from Larry Briggs.[17] Most of these were later sold by Heritage Auctions. While Brand was buying, other examples were available in the marketplace.

Availability in Mint State: Mint State 1844 dimes are very rare, more so than realized. Over the years, the author has handled more Proofs than Mint State coins! However, the 1846 is rarer still. *MS-60 to 62: 3 to 5 estimated to exist; MS-63: 4 or 5; MS-64: 2 or 3; MS-65 or better: 3 to 5.*

	Cert	Avg	%MS	G-4	VG-8	F-12	VF-20	EF-40	AU-50	MS-60	MS-63	MS-64	MS-65
1844	111	20.6	8%	$175	$275	$375	$600	$1,100	$1,700	$4,000	$9,500	$15,000	$26,500

1844, Proof • Proof Mintage:

14 to 18 estimated.

Commentary: About 10 to 12 are known of the 1844 Proof (Fortin-101).

	Cert	Avg	%MS	PF-60	PF-63	PF-65
1844, Proof	1	64.0		$17,500	$27,500	$45,000

1845 Liberty Seated Dime

1845 • Circulation-Strike Mintage: 1,755,000.

Commentary: Six obverse dies and nine reverse dies were used to produce the 1845 Liberty Seated dime (Fortin-101 to 110).

Availability in circulated grades: This issue is readily available in all grades.

Availability in Mint State: MS-60 to 62: 120 to 140 estimated to exist; MS-63: 50 to 65; MS-64: 40 to 50; MS-65 or better: 30 to 40.

	Cert	Avg	%MS	G-4	VG-8	F-12	VF-20	EF-40	AU-50	MS-60	MS-63	MS-64	MS-65
1845	154	58.3	68%	$20	$25	$30	$35	$50	$150	$400	$800	$1,250	$3,500

1845, Proof • Proof Mintage:

14 to 16 estimated.

Proofs: On Proofs of 1845 (Fortin-109), the 8 and 4 in the date are heavily double punched, the 5 less so. Artifacts are seen near stars 1 through 6, and 12 through 13. On the reverse, a die line through TE continues to the rim above the S. An estimated 10 to 13 are known.

	Cert	Avg	%MS	PF-60	PF-63	PF-65
1 845, Proof	5	64.8		$7,500	$12,500	$35,000

1845-O Liberty Seated Dime

1845-O • Circulation-Strike Mintage: 230,000.

Commentary: The 1845-O dime is usually fairly well struck, but there are exceptions. This issue is designated Fortin-101.

Availability in circulated grades: These are fairly scarce, though not as scarce as the 1843-O (as

comparison in mintages indicates). They are rare in Extremely Fine condition or finer, and quite rare in About Uncirculated with mint luster.

Availability in Mint State: An Eliasberg specimen was described thusly in 1977: "MS-67. Brilliant, lustrous, and frosty, just about as nice as it was on the day of coining." This example was graded as MS-69 by PCGS when it appeared in the Gardner Collection in 2015; today it stands as the finest. In low ranges of Mint State, examples appear only over a wide span of years, and we would not want to take bets that most such pieces really are Uncirculated. *MS-60 to 62: 1 or 2 estimated to exist; MS-63: 0; MS-64: 0; MS-65 or better: 1.*

	Cert	Avg	%MS	G-4	VG-8	F-12	VF-20	EF-40	AU-50	MS-60	MS-63	MS-64	MS-65
1845-O	49	28.2	4%	$90	$150	$240	$550	$950	$3,000	$12,000	$24,000		

1846 Liberty Seated Dime

1846 • **Circulation-Strike Mintage:** 31,300.

Commentary: Dimes of 1846 are sometimes lightly struck at the head of Liberty, along with the neckline and lower leg. This results in a flat obverse appearance on full Very Fine or Extremely Fine specimens. Struck with two obverse and two reverse dies, the 1846 is designated Fortin-101 and 102.

Availability in circulated grades: Quite scarce in circulated grades, the 1846, when seen, is apt to be Good to Fine. Very Fine pieces are scarcer yet, Extremely Fine examples are rare, and About Uncirculated coins with luster are extremely rare. This is the rarest Philadelphia Mint dime of the era and handily eclipses the more famous 1844 (see that listing for comparison).

Availability in Mint State: The issue is exceedingly rare in high grade; probably just two or three exist. *MS-60 to 62: 1 or 2 estimated to exist; MS-63: 2; MS-64: 0; MS-65 or better: 0.*

	Cert	Avg	%MS	G-4	VG-8	F-12	VF-20	EF-40	AU-50	MS-60	MS-63	MS-64	MS-65
1846	58	21.7	2%	$200	$360	$600	$1,150	$2,500	$8,500	$15,000	$45,000		

1846, Proof • **Proof Mintage:** 15 to 20 estimated.

Commentary: Some minor die flaws and/or repunching are seen at the numbers 46 in the date. Artifacts are present at stars 2 through 6; they are visible (but less so) at star 7 and stars 12 and 13, most being cusp-shaped as on half dimes of this year. From now on, cusps appear with regularity as part of the artifacts mentioned. About 10 to 12 are estimated to be known.

	Cert	Avg	%MS	PF-60	PF-63	PF-65
1846, Proof	7	63.9		$10,000	$15,000	$35,000

1847 Liberty Seated Dime

1847 • **Circulation-Strike Mintage:** 245,000.

Commentary: While the 1847 (Fortin-101 to 104) is not in the class of the 1844 or 1846 Philadelphia Mint dimes, it handily outdistances the 1842, 1843, and 1845 in all grades. One interesting variety, illustrated by Breen and Greer, shows the date numerals overlapping the base of Liberty. Numerals of this date were too large for the space provided, giving a crowded effect.

Availability in circulated grades: These are fairly scarce, as their mintage suggests, but not widely sought after. There are enough to supply the demand, particularly in lower grades.

Availability in Mint State: In Mint State the 1847 is rare, with most examples being in the MS-60 to MS-63 category. Gerry Fortin considers such coins to be unappreciated and undervalued.[18] *MS-60 to 62: 10 to 13 estimated to exist; MS-63: 3 or 4; MS-64: 1 or 2; MS-65 or better: 1.*

	Cert	Avg	%MS	G-4	VG-8	F-12	VF-20	EF-40	AU-50	MS-60	MS-63	MS-64	MS-65
1847	42	48.7	31%	$20	$30	$40	$70	$180	$425	$1,550	$4,000	$6,500	$10,000

1847, Proof • **Proof Mintage:** 12 to 15 estimated.

Commentary: On Proofs (Fortin-104) the date is high and impacts the base. A raised die line is visible under 47 in the date. An estimated 7 to 9 are known.

	Cert	Avg	%MS	PF-60	PF-63	PF-65
1847, Proof	1	66.0		$8,000	$13,000	$35,000

1848 Liberty Seated Dime

1848 • **Circulation-Strike Mintage:** 451,500.

Commentary: The Philadelphia Mint dimes of 1848 (Fortin-101 to 103) are sometimes seen lightly struck at the head and corresponding areas of the reverse. The dates on the various 1848 dimes seem overly large for the space beneath Liberty, giving the numerals a crowded appearance. The issue was struck using three obverse dies and three reverse dies.

Availability in circulated grades: These are fairly plentiful in low grades, although they are not among the commonest issues of the era. Extremely Fine and About Uncirculated coins are slightly scarce.

Availability in Mint State: The 1848 is scarce in Mint State, but on an absolute basis enough are available to satisfy the specialist. As is the norm, most are in the lower Mint State echelons. *MS-60 to 62: 30 to 40 estimated to exist; MS-63: 15 to 20; MS-64: 12 to 15; MS-65 or better: 6 to 8.*[19]

	Cert	Avg	%MS	G-4	VG-8	F-12	VF-20	EF-40	AU-50	MS-60	MS-63	MS-64	MS-65
1848	67	54.9	57%	$20	$25	$32	$50	$85	$180	$725	$975	$2,200	$6,500

1848, Proof • Proof Mintage:

14 to 16 estimated.

Commentary: Proofs of this year show the date high with 18 touching the base. Traces of artifacts are seen at stars 2 through 6. About 10 to 13 are known.

	Cert	Avg	%MS	PF-60	PF-63	PF-65
1848, Proof	9	64.6		$5,000	$10,000	$17,500

1849 Liberty Seated Dime

1849 • **Circulation-Strike Mintage:** 839,000.

Commentary: This issue (Fortin-101 to 107) was struck using five obverse and five reverse dies. It is occasionally seen lightly struck on Liberty's head and the corresponding part of the reverse.

In 1849 the Mint finally gave up on trying to squeeze large date numbers into small spaces, and the date logotype is much smaller than on 1847 and 1848, giving ample surrounding area.

This was the year that the great California Gold Rush began in earnest. By year's end gold was more plentiful in commercial and Mint holdings than ever before in American history. The historic ratio of silver—which had been valued at 15.5 ounces to one ounce of gold—was upset, and in relation silver became more valuable. Starting in a large way in 1850, silver coins from half dimes to dollars were withdrawn from circulation and hoarded or melted. A hundred dollars' worth (face value) of silver coins could be melted for a dollar or two profit. Dimes and other silver coins did not return to general circulation until the summer of 1853 (see the later listing).

Availability in circulated grades: Collectors will find the 1849 dime plentiful in circulated condition.

Availability in Mint State: This issue is rare in Mint State, although enough exist that specialists will not run short. Again, most pieces are in lower levels of Mint State, say MS-60 through MS-63. *MS-60 to 62: 25 to 32 estimated to exist; MS-63: 10 to 13; MS-64: 5 to 7; MS-65 or better: 7 to 9.*[20]

	Cert	Avg	%MS	G-4	VG-8	F-12	VF-20	EF-40	AU-50	MS-60	MS-63	MS-64	MS-65
1849	80	55.0	59%	$20	$25	$30	$40	$75	$180	$375	$900	$1,500	$3,500

1849, Proof • **Proof Mintage:** 10 to 12 estimated.

Commentary: In the 1996 sale of the Eliasberg Collection, an 1849 Proof was described as "9 over 8. An obvious overdate is listed by Breen. Proof only." Today this is known as Fortin-107, "prior 1849/8," presently "Repunched 89." About 6 to 9 are known.

	Cert	Avg	%MS	PF-60	PF-63	PF-65
1849, Proof	2	65.5		$10,000	$12,500	$35,000

1849-O Liberty Seated Dime

1849-O • **Circulation-Strike Mintage:** 300,000.

Commentary: A light strike at the top of the obverse and corresponding part of the reverse is the rule, not the exception, for 1849-O dimes (Fortin-101 to 104).

Four die combinations are known, including the Large O (Fortin-101) and Small O (Fortin-102 to 104) mintmarks, which differ dramatically in appearance. Heaton in 1893 described the 1849-O as "somewhat scarce." Fortin states that the 1849-O is also well known for having been struck with rotated die alignment, the most of any date in the series. Three obverse dies and two reverse dies were used to produce this issue.

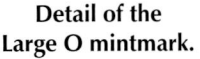

Detail of the Large O mintmark.

Detail of the Small O mintmark.

Availability in circulated grades: This is a well-known semi-key date. Perhaps a couple thousand exist, mostly in worn grades.

Availability in Mint State: In Mint State the 1849-O was once considered to be a nearly impossible rarity. Today a number of them have been certified, but it is still a key to the series. *MS-60 to 62: 7 to 9 estimated to exist; MS-63: 5 to 7; MS-64: 1 or 2; MS-65 or better: 0.* If gradeflation and resubmissions continue, the apparent number of high-grade coins will increase, while in actuality the number of coins does not change. This comment is true across the series.

	Cert	Avg	%MS	G-4	VG-8	F-12	VF-20	EF-40	AU-50	MS-60	MS-63	MS-64	MS-65
1849-O	84	42.3	21%	$25	$35	$75	$150	$375	$950	$2,500	$5,500	$11,000	

1850 Liberty Seated Dime

1850 • **Circulation-Strike Mintage:** 1,931,500.

Commentary: Except in Proof finish, the 1850 dime (Fortin-101 to 112) is readily available in all grades. It was produced with 9 obverse dies and 11 reverse dies.

Availability in circulated grades: This issue is common in circulated condition.

Availability in Mint State: The 1850 is readily available within context of this general era, although it is far scarcer than the common issues of the 1880s. MS-65 or finer coins are challenging to find. *MS-60 to 62: 80 to 100 estimated to exist; MS-63: 30 to 40; MS-64: 20 to 25; MS-65 or better: 8 to 10.*[21]

	Cert	Avg	%MS	G-4	VG-8	F-12	VF-20	EF-40	AU-50	MS-60	MS-63	MS-64	MS-65
1850	149	53.7	55%	$20	$25	$30	$40	$60	$150	$300	$700	$1,500	$4,500

1850, Proof • Proof Mintage:
14 to 16 estimated.

Commentary: In Proof format this was considered to be rarer in the 1950s and 1960s than it is today. Most of the known examples have appeared since then. Still, on an absolute basis it is a first-class rarity, with only about 10 to 12 known.

	Cert	Avg	%MS	PF-60	PF-63	PF-65
1850, Proof	4	64.5		$10,000	$15,000	$35,000

1850-O Liberty Seated Dime

1850-O • Circulation-Strike Mintage:
510,000.

Commentary: New Orleans dimes of 1850 (Fortin-101 to 107) are often seen with Liberty's head lightly struck and with light striking on the corresponding part of the reverse. Three sizes of mintmarks occur and are nicely illustrated in the Greer text and Fortin

website. The Small O has perhaps 30% of the total area of the Large O, and the Medium O is closer to the latter than to the former. PCGS and NGC take no note of mintmark sizes; thus the Large O, which in high grades is rarer than the Small O, would probably cost little if any more to purchase. In *Mint State* the Medium O is the rarest. The mintage was produced with four obverse dies and five reverse dies.

Availability in circulated grades: The issue is somewhat scarce, but hardly rare. Most examples are in low grades.

Availability in Mint State: These are rare in Mint State, although they will prove to be available to the patient collector. Possibly 20 or more are known, some of which are gems (but data may represent resubmissions). *MS-60 to 62: 4 to 6 estimated to exist; MS-63: 6 to 8; MS-64: 5 or 7; MS-65 or better: 4 or 5.*

	Cert	Avg	%MS	G-4	VG-8	F-12	VF-20	EF-40	AU-50	MS-60	MS-63	MS-64	MS-65
1850-O	30	39.2	23%	$25	$60	$90	$120	$300	$900	$1,800	$3,600	$5,400	$8,500

1851 Liberty Seated Dime

1851 • **Circulation-Strike Mintage:** 1,026,500.

Commentary: The 1851 (Fortin-101 to 108) is a readily available date in all grades from well-worn up through lower Mint State levels. Date-placement differences are very slight for this year. Six obverse dies and seven reverse dies were used to produce the 1851 dime.

Availability in circulated grades: The issue is easy to find in circulated condition.

Availability in Mint State: The 1851 is scarce in context of early Liberty Seated Philadelphia Mint dimes, but in absolute terms, this issue is readily available to specialists. Most examples are at lower Mint State levels. *MS-60 to 62: 40 to 50 estimated to exist; MS-63: 15 to 20; MS-64: 10 to 13; MS-65 or better: 6 or 8.*

	Cert	Avg	%MS	G-4	F-12	VF-20	EF-40	AU-50	MS-60	MS-63	MS-64	MS-65
1851	78	53.4	53%	$20	$30	$40	$70	$200	$425	$850	$1,800	$5,000

1851, Proof • **Proof Mintage:** See below.

Commentary: Some coins of 1851 and 1853 have been called Proofs over a long period of years, but it uncertain whether they were actually struck as such or they were from dies polished after relapping or for other reasons. No Proof Sets of this year or of 1853 are known.

1851-O Liberty Seated Dime

1851-O • **Circulation-Strike Mintage:** 400,000.

Commentary: Dimes of this year-date combination are sometimes lightly struck on Liberty's head on the obverse and on the corresponding part of the reverse. Per Fortin, the dies were relapped at some point during usage, leading to weak drapery and overall obverse device details. Designated Fortin-101, this issue was struck with just one die combination.

In keeping with most other New Orleans issues of the era, the 1851-O is very elusive in higher states of preservation, as there was no numismatic interest in coins from this mint at the time of issue. The large mintage suggests that others may exist. These dimes carry a Large O mintmark. Walter Breen lists a Small O mintmark, but this variety has not been confirmed by Gerry Fortin or those who contribute to his website.

Availability in circulated grades: These are fairly scarce in lower circulated grades, as the mintage would tend to indicate. Extremely Fine and, in particular, lustrous About Uncirculated coins are very elusive.

Availability in Mint State: The 1851-O is very rare in higher grades, and in fact is one of the scarcer issues of the series. Many are colorfully toned. *MS-60 to 62: 3 to 5 estimated to exist; MS-63: 1 or 2; MS-64: 1; MS-65 or better: 1.*

	Cert	Avg	%MS	G-4	F-12	VF-20	EF-40	AU-50	MS-60	MS-63	MS-64	MS-65
1851-O	41	47.1	15%	$25	$40	$120	$300	$975	$2,400	$3,750	$6,500	$15,000

1852 Liberty Seated Dime

1852 • **Circulation-Strike Mintage:** 1,535,000.

Commentary: The 1852 dime (Fortin-101 to 118) was produced with 14 obverse dies and 18 reverse dies—a record up to this point in time. F-105b, 110b, and 112b are late die states with partial or retained cud die breaks.

Availability in circulated grades: Circulated dimes of 1852 are common.

Availability in Mint State: This issue is readily available in Mint State. *MS-60 to 62: 150 to 250 estimated to exist; MS-63: 75 to 100; MS-64: 50 to 65; MS-65 or better: 30 to 40.*

	Cert	Avg	%MS	G-4	F-12	VF-20	EF-40	AU-50	MS-60	MS-63	MS-64	MS-65
1852	100	57.3	65%	$20	$30	$40	$60	$125	$300	$650	$1,100	$3,000

1852, Proof • **Proof Mintage:** 9 to 12 estimated.

Commentary: The finest known 1852 Proof (Fortin-113) is an Eliasberg specimen: "Proof-66. No repunching at date, thus not listed by Brian Greer. Minor vestiges of artifacts at stars 2–6. On reverse under magnification diagonal die lines can be seen at the bow." An estimated 7 to 9 are known.

	Cert	Avg	%MS	PF-60	PF-63	PF-65
1852, Proof	8	64.4		$5,000	$10,000	$22,500

1852-O Liberty Seated Dime

1852-O • **Circulation-Strike Mintage:** 430,000.

Commentary: Some lightly struck areas are typical for this issue. Fortin-101 and 102 share the same obverse with high date sloping down to the right, in combination with two reverse dies.

Availability in circulated grades: These are scarce, as the mintage suggests. It was probably the instance that this issue saw more melting than usual due to the high price of silver on the international markets.

Availability in Mint State: The coin is quite scarce in Mint State, particularly at higher levels. *MS-60 to 62: 20 to 25 estimated to exist; MS-63: 10 to 14; MS-64: 7 to 9; MS-65 or better: 2 or 3.*

	Cert	Avg	%MS	G-4	F-12	VF-20	EF-40	AU-50	MS-60	MS-63	MS-64	MS-65
1852-O	57	51.4	49%	$30	$90	$180	$325	$550	$1,800	$3,600	$4,800	$12,500

1853 Liberty Seated Dime, No Arrows

1853, No Arrows • Circulation-Strike
Mintage: 95,000.

Commentary: The 1853, No Arrows, dime is an anomaly, struck to the heavier early (before February 21, 1853) weight standard. Conventional wisdom is that numerous examples of these were melted by the Treasury, and were not released, thereby resulting in effective distribution far lower than the 95,000 mintage. This thought has echoed throughout numismatic writings for many years. Whatever the case may be, this variety is well known as a dime that is scarce in an absolute sense when the entire population is considered, but that in Mint State has survivors more plentiful than logic suggests—indicating a special circumstance of saving as noted above. Fortin-101 and 102 share a common reverse die.

Availability in circulated grades: As noted, these are very scarce in circulated condition. They are usually seen in grades of About Good to Very Good or, interestingly, in higher grades such as Very Fine and Extremely Fine.[22]

Availability in Mint State: Mint State specimens come on the market with some regularity, including at the Gem level. This suggests that a group of high-grade coins may have existed at one time. As is seen, extant Mint State coins are clustered at the top end, an unusual situation. *MS-60 to 62: 10 to 13 estimated to exist; MS-63: 15 to 20; MS-64: 40 to 50; MS-65 or better: 20 to 30.*

	Cert	Avg	%MS	G-4	F-12	VF-20	EF-40	AU-50	MS-60	MS-63	MS-64	MS-65
1853, No Arrows	119	52.6	70%	$110	$300	$475	$650	$800	$950	$1,550	$2,200	$2,500

1853 Liberty Seated Dime, With Arrows

1853, Arrows • Circulation-Strike
Mintage: 12,173,000.

Commentary: The Coinage Act of February 21, 1853, reduced the authorized weight of the dime and other Liberty Seated coins, except the dollar. After this time, newly minted coins yielded no profit by melting, and they remained in circulation in quantity.

On many dies for this new type, the position of the arrowheads varied in relation to the date logotype. Other dies were hubbed, with the date and arrows in the master die. A detailed explanation of this can be found on Gerry Fortin's website, including descriptions of more than two dozen unhubbed varieties.

For unhubbed dies, the issue is designated Fortin-101 to 125, struck with 23 obverse and 25 reverse dies.

Availability in circulated grades: The 1953, With Arrows, dime is extremely common in circulated condition—take your pick of any grade you want! From this year forward the survival ratio of dimes is higher than earlier years (for which many coins were melted).

Availability in Mint State: These are readily available in Mint State, although on an absolute basis they are scarcer than certification service data suggest. The reason for this is that dimes of the With Arrows style have significantly higher value than, for example, more common issues of the late 1880s, and because of this value more have been sent to the certification services. Regardless, specimen examples can easily be obtained in Mint State. *MS-60 to 62: 800 to 1,000 estimated to exist; MS-63: 300 to 400; MS-64: 200 to 250; MS-65 or better: 125 to 150.*

	Cert	Avg	%MS	G-4	F-12	VF-20	EF-40	AU-50	MS-60	MS-63	MS-64	MS-65
1853, Arrows	953	57.3	64%	$20	$25	$30	$50	$150	$325	$675	$950	$1,750

1853, Arrows, Proof • Proof Mintage: See below.

Commentary: See the comments for the 1851 entry. Opinions are divided, and NGC and PCGS each list Proofs in their reports. This raises the old question: Is a coin a Proof if it looks like one? The matter can be argued *ad infinitum.* On the other side of the question, the Mint issued 2,350 Proofs and no circulation strikes of the 1878 Shield nickel, but many of the coins are frosty without a hint of mirror surface. In recent decades many branch-mint coins in particular, but Philadelphia issues as well, that would have been called "proof*like*" years ago are in holders certified as Proof.

	Cert	Avg	%MS	PF-60	PF-63	PF-65
1853, Arrows, Proof	5	64.6		$15,000	$25,000	$65,000

1853-O Liberty Seated Dime, With Arrows

1853-O, Arrows • Circulation-Strike
Mintage: 1,100,000.

Commentary: Dimes of this issue (Fortin-101 to 108) are often lightly struck on the head of Liberty and the corresponding part of the reverse, a condition endemic with most New Orleans issues of this era.

Per Fortin, all 1853-O obverse dies were hubbed from a die containing the date and arrows. Accordingly, there are no date- or arrow-placement variations on 1853 New Orleans dimes. Several obverse dies were poorly hubbed, leading to weak dates. The mintage was produced with four obverse dies and three reverse dies.

Availability in circulated grades: These are common in well-worn grades, with more than enough to go around—although they are not as plentiful as their Philadelphia Mint cousins. About Uncirculated coins are very scarce.

Availability in Mint State: New Orleans Mint dimes of 1853 are quite scarce in Mint State. Logic would dictate that this piece should be about 10 or 11 times scarcer in Mint State than the 1853 Philadelphia version, but in actuality far fewer were saved proportionally, and it is *far* rarer. As the market differential doesn't reflect this, the 1853-O represents an excellent *value* if a Mint State piece can be located. *MS-65 MS-60 to 62: 5 to 8 estimated to exist; MS-63: 2 or 3; MS-64: 2 or 3; MS-65 or better: 1 or 2.*[23]

	Cert	Avg	%MS	G-4	F-12	VF-20	EF-40	AU-50	MS-60	MS-63	MS-64	MS-65
1853-O, Arrows	55	38.6	13%	$25	$85	$125	$300	$650	$2,650	$3,600	$6,500	$10,000

1854 Liberty Seated Dime, With Arrows

1854, Arrows • Circulation-Strike
Mintage: 4,470,000.

Commentary: This is a readily available dime, second only—and a distant second—to the 1853, With Arrows, among issues of this type. The issue is designated Fortin-101 to 112. All dies were hubbed, and there are no positional variations.

The San Francisco Mint opened in 1854, but the first dimes were not struck there until 1856.

Availability in circulated grades: The issue is common in circulated condition.

Availability in Mint State: The 1854, With Arrows, is readily available, but markedly less so than the 1853 of the same type. *MS-60 to 62: 250 to 325 estimated to exist; MS-63: 140 to 160; MS-64: 100 to 125; MS-65 or better: 50 to 80.*

	Cert	Avg	%MS	G-4	F-12	VF-20	EF-40	AU-50	MS-60	MS-63	MS-64	MS-65
1854, Arrows	265	57.0	58%	$20	$25	$30	$50	$175	$325	$675	$950	$1,700

1854, Arrows, Proof • Proof Mintage: 22 to 26 estimated.

Commentary: The finest known 1854, With Arrows, Proof dime (Fortin-111) is the former Eliasberg specimen, described thusly: "Proof-66. Date and arrows high, barely touching base. Tiny die defect at star 6." An estimated 15 to 18 are known.

	Cert	Avg	%MS	PF-60	PF-63	PF-65
1854, Arrows, Proof	9	65.0		$8,000	$15,000	$35,000

1854-O Liberty Seated Dime, With Arrows

1854-O, Arrows • Circulation-Strike
Mintage: 1,770,000.

Commentary: These are sometimes seen lightly struck at Liberty's head and the corresponding part of the reverse. All dies were hubbed, and there are no positional variations. The 1853, With Arrows is designated Fortin-101 to 112.

Availability in circulated grades: These are easy to obtain, mostly in lower grades. However, the number of Extremely Fine and About Uncirculated coins is more than adequate to supply the number of dime specialists.

Availability in Mint State: They are decidedly elusive in Mint State, but not a rarity, and there are enough around that specialists can find one without difficulty. Most are at lower Mint State levels. *MS-60 to 62: 70 to 90 estimated to exist; MS-63: 30 to 40; MS-64: 20 to 25; MS-65 or better: 12 to 15.*

	Cert	Avg	%MS	G-4	F-12	VF-20	EF-40	AU-50	MS-60	MS-63	MS-64	MS-65
1854-O, Arrows	92	56.7	71%	$20	$25	$45	$85	$225	$425	$1,000	$1,500	$4,500

1855 Liberty Seated Dime, With Arrows

1855, Arrows • **Circulation-Strike**
Mintage: 2,075,000.

Commentary: These are usually with areas of light striking. All dies were hubbed, and there are no positional variations. The 1855, With Arrows, is designated Fortin-101 to 108. Several obverse dies are seen with weakly hubbed dates and arrows, especially F-105 and 106.

Availability in circulated grades: The issue is common in circulated condition.

Availability in Mint State: Mint State 1855, With Arrows, dimes are quite scarce in my experience, although certification numbers do not necessarily reflect this. *MS-60 to 62: 100 to 125 estimated to exist; MS-63: 40 to 55; MS-64: 25 to 32; MS-65 or better: 16 to 20.*

	Cert	Avg	%MS	G-4	F-12	VF-20	EF-40	AU-50	MS-60	MS-63	MS-64	MS-65
1855, Arrows	112	58.8	69%	$20	$25	$30	$60	$185	$325	$850	$1,300	$3,000

1855, Arrows, Proof • **Proof Mintage:** 35 to 45 estimated.

Commentary: The Louis E. Eliasberg Collection was home to many excellent Liberty Seated Proof dimes, including an 1855 (Fortin-101) described as follows: "PF-65. Date numerals and arrowheads slightly double-punched in the die. Some raised die finish lines are seen, particularly within the wreath on the reverse, indicating this was a very early striking from new Proof dies. After repeated strikings, die finish lines wear away." About 25 to 30 are known.

	Cert	Avg	%MS	PF-60	PF-63	PF-65
1855, Arrows, Proof	15	64.9		$8,000	$15,000	$35,000

1856 Liberty Seated Dime

1856, Large Date • **Circulation-Strike**
Mintage: 722,500 estimated.

Commentary: These coins are usually well struck, but sometimes with weakness on Liberty's head.

The Large Date (Fortin-101 to 104) is dramatically different from the Small Date, the former having a slanting or italic 5 and very small numerals, the latter having an upright 5 and digits much greater in size—in fact, *oversized* for the space allotted, and at first glance incongruous. The Large Date is from the same logotype punch used to make dies for half cents and $3 pieces.

Detail of the Large Date.

As mentioned in the Small Date commentary, the Large Date version was struck from four obverse dies and four reverse dies. F-103a has a severely relapped obverse die with considerable loss of device details.

Availability in circulated grades: The Large Date dime of 1856 is somewhat scarce, and most are in very low grades.[25]

Availability in Mint State: These are extremely rare in Mint State, and constitute one of the key Philadelphia Mint issues of the series. *MS-60 to 62: 20 to 25 estimated to exist; MS-63: 12 to 15; MS-64: 5 to 8; MS-65 or better: 3 to 5.*

	Cert	Avg	%MS	G-4	F-12	VF-20	EF-40	AU-50	MS-60	MS-63	MS-64	MS-65
1856, Large Date	31	42.3	16%	$40	$90	$120	$180	$300	$600	$2,100	$3,600	$9,500

1856, Small Date • Circulation-Strike

Mintage: 5,057,500 estimated.

Commentary: The 1856, Small Date (Fortin-101 to 123) is sometimes seen with light striking on the top of the obverse and on the corresponding part of the reverse. On some the denticles are flattened or missing.[24]

Small date numerals fit comfortably into the space allotted with room to spare; the same logotype punch was used to make quarter eagle dies. The dime mintage was struck from 21 different obverse dies and 23 reverse dies. For the Large Date (see below) there are four varieties from four obverse and four reverse dies. The total mintage for both varieties is 5,780,000. From this it would seem that 7/8 of the mintage was of the Small Date style and 1/8 of the Large Date, leading to the mintage estimates given here.

Detail of the Small Date.

Availability in circulated grades: The Small Date version is easy to find in any and all grades.

Availability in Mint State: Small Date coins are readily available, often with nice luster. *MS-60 to 62: 150 to 200 estimated to exist; MS-63: 80 to 100; MS-64: 50 to 70; MS-65 or better: 30 to 40.*

	Cert	Avg	%MS	G-4	F-12	VF-20	EF-40	AU-50	MS-60	MS-63	MS-64	MS-65
1856, Small Date	107	48.4	45%	$16	$20	$30	$60	$145	$300	$550	$950	$2,250

1856, Small Date, Proof • Proof

Mintage: 65 to 75.

Commentary: Proofs are designated Fortin-101. Three obverse dentils at about the 4:30 position are flattened. An estimated 45 to 55 are known.

	Cert	Avg	%MS	PF-60	PF-63	PF-65
1856, Small Date, Proof	23	64.6		$2,500	$4,000	$12,000

1856-O Liberty Seated Dime

1856-O, Small Date • Circulation-Strike Mintage: 1,180,000.

Commentary: The Small Date version (Fortin-101 to 109) of the 1856-O issue is often lightly struck at the top of the obverse and the corresponding part of the reverse. It is seen with Medium O (scarce) and the usually seen Large O mintmark sizes. A Small O (Breen-3299) has not been verified. F-104 and 105 have bold repunching on the date and are pursued by variety specialists. Six obverse dies and six reverse dies produced the mintage.

Availability in circulated grades: These are slightly scarce in circulated grades, but certainly are widely enough available that any specialist can find one. They are more rare in Extremely Fine or About Uncirculated grades.

Availability in Mint State: The Small Date coins are quite rare in Mint State, as relatively few were saved at the time of issue. The same is generally true of other New Orleans varieties of the era. *MS-60 to 62: 40 to 55 estimated to exist; MS-63: 18 to 22; MS-64: 10 to 14; MS-65 or better: 4 to 6.*

	Cert	Avg	%MS	G-4	F-12	VF-20	EF-40	AU-50	MS-60	MS-63	MS-64	MS-65
1856-O, Small Date	70	49.0	43%	$20	$60	$90	$150	$360	$800	$1,350	$2,650	$6,000

1856-S Liberty Seated Dime

1856-S, Small Date • Circulation-Strike Mintage: 70,000.

Commentary: The 1856-S (Fortin-101) is important as the first San Francisco Mint coin of this denomination. At the time of issue, not a single numismatist desired to acquire San Francisco Mint pieces (ditto New Orleans coins), as emphasis was on "date only," and a readily available Philadelphia coin would fill the bill.

A large amount of all San Francisco Mint silver coinage was shipped to China, often by merchants and individuals sending to their families back home there.

In *Mint Marks*, Augustus G. Heaton commented in 1893: "The mintmark letter S identifying this series [referring to all years] may also be divided into three sizes: the *large*, being somewhat larger than the letters of the legend, the *medium*, somewhat smaller, and the *small*, about half their height and quite minute." In the same text, Heaton noted that the 1856-S "is rare."

Availability in circulated grades: These first S-Mint dimes are very scarce overall, as their low mintage suggests. Most are in low grades with problems. Extremely Fine coins are in the rare category, and an About Uncirculated piece with luster is of notable numismatic significance.

Availability in Mint State: In higher grades the issue is extremely rare. Just a few exist. As is true for so many rare Liberty Seated coins, grading numbers shift around, making it impossible to be precise about the population. *MS-60 to 62: 3 to 5 estimated to exist; MS-63: 2 or 3; MS-64: 3; MS-65 or better: 4 or 5.*[26]

	Cert	Avg	%MS	G-4	F-12	VF-20	EF-40	AU-50	MS-60	MS-63	MS-64	MS-65
1856-S, Small Date	28	39.3	14%	$240	$650	$1,200	$1,700	$2,400	$7,200	$15,000	$25,000	$45,000

1857 Liberty Seated Dime

1857 • **Circulation-Strike Mintage:** 5,580,000.

Commentary: This date (Fortin-101 to 115) is readily available in all grades. Proofs seem to be a bit scarcer than for 1856, so the mintage may have been a bit less. Fifteen obverse dies and 15 reverse dies were paired in sequence, suggesting that each pair was replaced in one action, rather than individually as they became worn or unserviceable.

Availability in circulated grades: This is one of the commoner dimes of the era.

Availability in Mint State: The 1857 is readily available in higher grades. *MS-60 to 62: 150 to 225 estimated to exist; MS-63: 80 to 100; MS-64: 50 to 65; MS-65 or better: 20 to 30.*

	Cert	Avg	%MS	G-4	F-12	VF-20	EF-40	AU-50	MS-60	MS-63	MS-64	MS-65
1857	342	58.5	70%	$16	$20	$30	$50	$130	$300	$550	$850	$1,950

1857, Proof • **Proof Mintage:** 55 to 65.

Commentary: About 35 to 45 Proofs (Fortin-101) are known.

	Cert	Avg	%MS	PF-60	PF-63	PF-65
1857, Proof	38	64.6		$2,000	$3,750	$5,500

1857-O Liberty Seated Dime

1857-O • **Circulation-Strike Mintage:** 1,540,000.

Commentary: Readily available as a New Orleans Mint issue, this is one of the few New Orleans dimes for which this comment can be made for Mint State examples. Struck from six obverse dies and seven reverse dies, the issue is designated Fortin-101 to 107.

Availability in circulated grades: These are common, in proportion to their mintage—but not as widely available as their Philadelphia Mint counterparts.

Availability in Mint State: In the upper grades the 1857-O is fairly scarce, but enough are around that the specialist will not go unsatisfied. *MS-60 to 62: 110 to 130 estimated to exist; MS-63: 50 to 65; MS-64: 30 to 40; MS-65 or better: 20 to 25.*

	Cert	Avg	%MS	G-4	F-12	VF-20	EF-40	AU-50	MS-60	MS-63	MS-64	MS-65
1857-O	186	58.0	65%	$18	$25	$35	$70	$200	$425	$750	$1,000	$2,150

1858 Liberty Seated Dime

1858 • Circulation-Strike Mintage: 1,540,000.

Commentary: Philadelphia Mint dimes from this year were produced from 10 obverse and 10 reverse dies. They are sometimes seen lightly struck at the top of the obverse and corresponding part of the reverse. Cherrypicking is advised.

Availability in circulated grades: The issue is easy to find in circulated condition.

Availability in Mint State: In Mint State condition the 1858 is readily available, but not common. Most have areas of light striking. *MS-60 to 62: 120 to 140 estimated to exist; MS-63: 55 to 70; MS-64: 35 to 45; MS-65 or better: 20 to 30.*

	Cert	Avg	%MS	G-4	F-12	VF-20	EF-40	AU-50	MS-60	MS-63	MS-64	MS-65
1858	145	57.8	66%	$16	$20	$30	$50	$130	$300	$550	$850	$1,850

1858, Proof • **Proof Mintage:** 300+.

Commentary: Approximately 300 were made for inclusion in silver Proof Sets. Many collectors seeking a run of Proof Liberty Seated dimes start their sets with this year. *PF-60 to 62: 20 to 25 estimated to exist; PF-63: 55 to 65; PF-64: 55 to 65; PF-65 or better: 20 to 25.*

	Cert	Avg	%MS	PF-60	PF-63	PF-65
1858, Proof	79	64.4		$1,000	$2,000	$4,250

1858-O Liberty Seated Dime

1858-O • Circulation-Strike Mintage: 200,000.

Commentary: These are often lightly struck at the top of the obverse and on certain areas of the reverse.

Although 1858-O (Fortin-101) is not recognized as a key date, in Mint State it is a notable rarity, simply because numismatists did not search examples until most had long since disappeared into circulation.

Availability in circulated grades: O-Mint coins of 1858 are scarce in circulated condition, but can be found with searching. They are elusive at the Extremely Fine and About Uncirculated levels.

Availability in Mint State: Above circulated grades, the issue is very rare. *MS-60 to 62: 11 to 15 estimated to exist; MS-63: 5 to 7; MS-64: 4 to 6; MS-65 or better: 4 to 6.*[27]

	Cert	Avg	%MS	G-4	F-12	VF-20	EF-40	AU-50	MS-60	MS-63	MS-64	MS-65
1858-O	52	54.1	38%	$25	$40	$85	$150	$360	$900	$2,000	$4,000	$7,500

1858-S Liberty Seated Dime

1858-S • **Circulation-Strike Mintage:** 60,000.

Commentary: Heaton in 1893 called this issue (now designated Fortin-101 to 103) "rare." Two obverse dies and three reverse dies produced the lot.

Availability in circulated grades: These are notably scarce, and constitute a well-known key date. Most are in low grades and have problems, which is generally true for all San Francisco Liberty Seated coins of this decade. They are rarer still at higher levels such as Extremely Fine and About Uncirculated.

Availability in Mint State: The 1858-S is not only exceedingly rare in Mint State, it is virtually unobtainable except when great specialized collections cross the auction block. *MS-60 to 62: 2 or 3 estimated to exist; MS-63: 1 or 2; MS-64: 1 or 2; MS-65 or better: 2.*

	Cert	Avg	%MS	G-4	F-12	VF-20	EF-40	AU-50	MS-60	MS-63	MS-64	MS-65
1858-S	34	32.4	9%	$150	$325	$775	$1,200	$1,950	$7,200	$17,000	$24,000	

1859 Liberty Seated Dime, With Stars

1859, Stars • **Circulation-Strike Mintage:** 429,200.

Commentary: The 1859 Liberty Seated dime (Fortin-101 to 107) is often seen lightly struck on the head and corresponding part of the reverse. In production, seven obverse dies and seven reverse dies were paired in sequence, the first two only for Proofs.

Availability in circulated grades: The issue is scarce compared to higher-mintage issues of the year, but enough are around that no problem will be experienced in tracking down a decent specimen.

Availability in Mint State: These are easily found with average sharpness, but challenging to find sharply struck. *MS-60 to 62: 200 to 250 estimated to exist; MS-63: 110 to 130; MS-64: 75 to 95; MS-65 or better: 50 to 65.*

	Cert	Avg	%MS	G-4	F-12	VF-20	EF-40	AU-50	MS-60	MS-63	MS-64	MS-65
1859	149	61.6	83%	$20	$22	$32	$60	$140	$300	$650	$850	$2,000

1859, Stars, Regular Issue, Proof •
Proof Mintage: 800.

Commentary: Proof strikes are designated Fortin-101 and 102. It is thought that hundreds of unsold Proofs were placed into circulation. *PF-60 to 62: 130 to 160 estimated to exist; PF-63: 155 to 175; PF-64: 150 to 170; PF-65 or better: 80 to 110.*

	Cert	Avg	%MS	PF-60	PF-63	PF-65
1859, Regular Issue, Proof	208	64.5		$900	$1,250	$2,250

1859, Stars, "Stateless" Issue,
Proof • Proof Mintage: 20–25 estimated.

Commentary: The 1859 issue is a transitional pattern, with stars on the obverse, in keeping with the standard design of the period, but with the reverse displaying a so-called "cereal" wreath enclosing the inscription ONE DIME. Nowhere does the identification UNITED STATES OF AMERICA appear, making this a "stateless" coin. Indeed, the only inscriptions on the issue are the denomination as stated, plus the word LIBERTY emblazoned on the shield. It is listed as Judd-233.

Although this is strictly pattern issue made for the numismatic trade it has been adopted into the regular series thanks to listings in *A Guide Book of United States Coins* and other places. As such, it is highly desired—but it is also very rare, with only about 12 to 14 known.

	Cert	Avg	%MS	PF-60	PF-63	PF-65
1859, "Stateless," Proof	12	64.7		$10,000	$18,500	$25,000

1859-O Liberty Seated Dime, With Stars

1859-O, Stars • Circulation-Strike
Mintage: 480,000.

Commentary: Designated Fortin-101 to 105, the 1859-O was produced with three obverse dies and three reverse dies in various combinations. The Eliasberg gem with Large O mintmark was described thusly: "Seated figure of Liberty from rusted or etched die, giving it a satiny 'Lalique' appearance in contrast with the polished fields. On the reverse there are similar characteristics. The writer conjectures that this die was rusted, but at the New Orleans Mint was given a highly polished finish in order to remove the rust from the fields, thus giving it a beautiful prooflike character. In the process, certain low-relief details were removed."

Availability in circulated grades: Although the issue is common in circulated grades, it is not the most plentiful issue of its era.

Availability in Mint State: They are readily available in relation to the number of specialists desiring Mint State coins, but slightly scarce overall. The mintage of the 1859-O is slightly larger than for its Philadelphia cousin. True to form, New Orleans dimes had a higher proportional attrition rate. *MS-60 to 62: 100 to 130 estimated to exist; MS-63: 40 to 50; MS-64: 25 to 32; MS-65 or better: 20 to 25.*

	Cert	Avg	%MS	G-4	F-12	VF-20	EF-40	AU-50	MS-60	MS-63	MS-64	MS-65
1859-O	126	58.2	69%	$20	$25	$60	$95	$275	$400	$850	$1,150	$2,250

1859-S Liberty Seated Dime, With Stars

1859-S, Stars • Circulation-Strike
Mintage: 60,000.

Commentary: Heaton in 1893 called this issue "rare."[28]

Availability in circulated grades: Below Mint State, the 1859-S is as scarce as its mintage suggests, with a population that is probably in the low hundreds. It is considered to be the rarest San Francisco dime of the decade. Coins in Extremely Fine and About Uncirculated grades are seldom encountered. Brian Greer calls this rare above the Very Fine grade level. Many have surface problems.

Availability in Mint State: These are exceedingly rare at this level. *MS-60 to 62: 1 or 2 estimated to exist; MS-63: 1; MS-64: 0 or 1; MS-65 or better: 1.*

	Cert	Avg	%MS	G-4	F-12	VF-20	EF-40	AU-50	MS-60	MS-63	MS-64	MS-65
1859-S	23	28.0	9%	$180	$475	$1,000	$3,000	$5,400	$18,000	$30,000	$48,000	$90,000

1860-S Liberty Seated Dime, With Stars

1860-S, Stars • Circulation-Strike
Mintage: 140,000.

Commentary: Examples are sometimes seen lightly struck on the top of the obverse and corresponding part of the reverse.

The 1860-S dime (Fortin-101 and 102) has always been a favorite of collectors as it is an anachronism, the With Stars style used 1859 and earlier. By contrast, Philadelphia and New Orleans Mint dimes of this date have the legend UNITED STATES OF AMERICA on the obverse. The mintage was struck from two obverse dies and two reverse dies.

Availability in circulated grades: Circulated coins are quite scarce, but more readily available than the mintage might suggest.

Availability in Mint State: The 1860-S, With Stars is extremely rare in Mint State grades. *MS-60 to 62: 4 to 6 estimated to exist; MS-63: 2 or 3; MS-64: 2 or 3; MS-65 or better: 2 or 3.*

	Cert	Avg	%MS	G-4	F-12	VF-20	EF-40	AU-50	MS-60	MS-63	MS-64	MS-65
1860-S	45	42.9	16%	$60	$150	$300	$480	$950	$2,500	$8,100	$12,500	$42,500

1860 Liberty Seated Dime, With Legend

1860, Legend • Circulation-Strike
Mintage: 606,000.

Commentary: Although the 1860, With Legend dime (Fortin-101 to 113) is usually seen sharply struck, the delicate Type I design was prone to rapid wear and loss of device details. In general, dimes of the 1860–1891 type, when lightly struck, show this on the head of Liberty and, on the reverse, in the wreath detail at the bottom and in the upper left wheat sheaf.

Among dimes of the era, 1860 (as here) and 1860-O have a Type I shield; 1861 comes with both Type I and Type II shields; 1861-S is found with Type I; and 1862 and later with Type II. Thirteen obverse and 13 reverse dies in sequential pairs were used to produce the 1860, With Legend dime.

Availability in circulated grades: These are much scarcer circulated than the mintage suggests, although enough exist in various grades to supply the demand for them.[29]

Availability in Mint State: At higher grade levels, the 1860, With Legend is somewhat scarce—surprisingly so. *MS-60 to 62: 110 to 130 estimated to exist; MS-63: 55 to 70; MS-64: 40 to 50; MS-65 or better: 25 to 35.*

	Cert	Avg	%MS	G-4	F-12	VF-20	EF-40	AU-50	MS-60	MS-63	MS-64	MS-65
1860, Legend	121	62.5	87%	$16	$20	$32	$40	$100	$200	$325	$500	$1,150

1860, Legend, Proof • Proof Mintage: 1,000.

Commentary: Proof strikes are designated Fortin-101. Breen lists a Type II Proof, presently unconfirmed. It seems that many unsold Proofs of this year were placed into circulation, as was also done with Proofs of 1859 and 1861. *PF-60 to 62: 225 to 275 estimated to exist; PF-63: 100 to 135; PF-64: 90 to 120; PF-65 or better: 50 to 70.*

	Cert	Avg	%MS	PF-60	PF-63	PF-65
1860, Legend, Proof	155	64.5		$350	$600	$1,250

1860-O Liberty Seated Dime, With Legend

1860-O, Legend • Circulation-Strike Mintage: 40,000.

Commentary: The New Orleans issue of this year (Fortin-101) displays a Type I shield. The fame of the 1860-O dime, perhaps somewhat undeserved by today's standards, traces its genesis to this comment made by Augustus G. Heaton in 1893: "The 1860-O dime is a very small issue, exceedingly rare, and a great prize." This is the last Liberty Seated dime issue from the New Orleans Mint until 1891.

Availability in circulated grades: These are very elusive, and are decidedly rare in Extremely Fine and About Uncirculated levels. Per Fortin: Most circulated examples will have varying degrees of surface issues, as many were recovered from Civil War sites. The population is in the multiple dozens, most with problems.

Availability in Mint State: The 1860-O is very rare in higher grades, and only a few exist. *MS-60 to 62: 1 or 2 estimated to exist; MS-63: 1; MS-64: 2; MS-65 or better: 1.*

	Cert	Avg	%MS	G-4	F-12	VF-20	EF-40	AU-50	MS-60	MS-63	MS-64	MS-65
1860-O, Legend	47	27.1	6%	$525	$1,500	$2,400	$4,800	$8,500	$18,000	$36,000	$73,500	

1861 Liberty Seated Dime

1861 • **Circulation-Strike Mintage:** 1,883,000.

Commentary: Type I and II shields were placed on circulation strikes in 1861. The Type I is slightly scarcer. Reliable data are not available, as little note has been made of the distinction. Gerry Fortin lists these separately, with Type I designated Fortin-101 to 107, and Type II, Fortin-101 to 113.

Availability in circulated grades: Circulated 1861 dimes are common.

Availability in Mint State: These are plentiful in relation to the demand. *MS-60 to 62: 140 to 170 estimated to exist; MS-63: 70 to 90; MS-64: 45 to 60; MS-65 or better: 30 to 40.*

	Cert	Avg	%MS	G-4	F-12	VF-20	EF-40	AU-50	MS-60	MS-63	MS-64	MS-65
1861	153	58.6	75%	$16	$22	$30	$40	$100	$200	$325	$450	$1,150

1861, Proof • **Proof Mintage:** 1,000.

Commentary: Proof strikes (Fortin-101) have the Type II shield. Some were carelessly made with lint adhering to the dies. On the reverse there is a raised dot on the right upright of the M in DIME. Many unsold Proofs were placed into circulation. Proofs of 1861 are significantly rarer than are those of 1860 with the same official mintage figure. *PF-60 to 62: 190 to 220 estimated to exist; PF-63: 90 to 110; PF-64: 65 to 80; PF-65 or better: 20 to 30.*

	Cert	Avg	%MS	PF-60	PF-63	PF-65
1861, Proof	100	63.9		$350	$650	$1,250

1861-S Liberty Seated Dime

1861-S • **Circulation-Strike Mintage:** 172,500.

Commentary: San Francisco dimes of 1861 (Fortin-101 and 102) are sometimes lightly struck at the top of the obverse and the corresponding part of the reverse. They display the Type I shield, a design subject to rapid wear.

The various San Francisco Mint dates of this era are all prime rarities in Mint State. It seems possible that quantities of these were sent to the Orient; at least, this is true for contemporary half dimes. The mintage was produced from two obverse dies and one reverse die.

Availability in circulated grades: They are fairly scarce, but not a prime rarity, in circulated condition. In About Uncirculated levels the issue is particularly elusive.

Availability in Mint State: In higher grades the 1861-S is very rare; probably fewer than a half dozen are known. *MS-60 to 62: 5 to 7 estimated to exist; MS-63: 1 or 2; MS-64: 1 or 2; MS-65 or better: 2.*

	Cert	Avg	%MS	G-4	F-12	VF-20	EF-40	AU-50	MS-60	MS-63	MS-64	MS-65
1861-S	29	40.9	28%	$150	$425	$650	$900	$1,200	$6,000	$18,000	$30,000	$42,000

1862 Liberty Seated Dime

1862 • **Circulation-Strike Mintage:** 847,000.

Commentary: The 1862 issue (Fortin-101 to 110) is usually seen well struck. Many are prooflike. The Type II shield was in use from this year onward. Ten obverse dies and 10 reverse dies in consecutive pairs produced the mintage.

Availability in circulated grades: Circulated coins are common.

Availability in Mint State: In higher grades the issue is slightly scarce. *MS-60 to 62: 120 to 160 estimated to exist; MS-63: 60 to 80; MS-64: 40 to 55; MS-65 or better: 25 to 35.*

	Cert	Avg	%MS	G-4	F-12	VF-20	EF-40	AU-50	MS-60	MS-63	MS-64	MS-65
1862	184	61.9	89%	$16	$25	$30	$40	$100	$185	$350	$500	$1,150

1862, Proof • **Proof Mintage:** 550.

Commentary: Some were carelessly made with lint adhering to the dies. In PF-65 and finer, they are inexplicably rare. *PF-60 to 62: 190 to 225 estimated to exist; PF-63: 110 to 140; PF-64: 70 to 90; PF-65 or better: 8 to 12.*

	Cert	Avg	%MS	PF-60	PF-63	PF-65
1862, Proof	102	63.7		$350	$650	$1,250

1862-S Liberty Seated Dime

1862-S • **Circulation-Strike Mintage:** 180,750.

Commentary: Designated Fortin-101 and 102, the issue was produced using one obverse die and two reverse dies. Brian Greer mentions a second obverse die, but Gerry Fortin has not seen one and does not list it.

Availability in circulated grades: Circulated coins are quite scarce, but there are enough around to satisfy the population of specialists. Sharp Extremely Fine or lustrous About Uncirculated pieces are rare.

Availability in Mint State: These are very rare; probably fewer than 10 different coins exist, and the author would be hard pressed to personally account for even that many. *MS-60 to 62: 2 or 3 estimated to exist; MS-63: 2 or 3; MS-64: 2 or 3; MS-65 or better: 1.*

	Cert	Avg	%MS	G-4	F-12	VF-20	EF-40	AU-50	MS-60	MS-63	MS-64	MS-65
1862-S	19	36.7	26%	$150	$300	$550	$1,000	$2,400	$4,200	$9,000	$12,000	

1863 Liberty Seated Dime

1863 • **Circulation-Strike Mintage:** 14,000.

Commentary: Philadelphia dimes this year are usually well struck. Die striae (or finish lines) are seen on high-grade coins.

Only one pair of dies was used to strike 1863 dimes, the circulation strikes being coined in March 1863 and Proofs in three batches from March 5 through May 26. Fortin-101 dies were used for Proofs and circulation strikes.

Availability in circulated grades: The issue is very rare in worn grades, existing today in approximate proportion to the mintage. Most are Very Fine to About Uncirculated. This is a highly important and key issue.

Availability in Mint State: Although quite rare at upper grade levels, the 1863 is a bit more plentiful than its lower mintages indicate, due to retention by the Treasury at the time of mintage. Rich Uhrich, a specialist in the series, considers this to be the rarest Philadelphia Mint dime of the 1860s.[30] For this decade Proofs are far more available in the marketplace than are Mint State coins. *MS-60 to 62: 20 to 25 estimated to exist; MS-63: 20 to 25; MS-64: 15 to 20; MS-65 or better: 15 to 20.*

	Cert	Avg	%MS	G-4	F-12	VF-20	EF-40	AU-50	MS-60	MS-63	MS-64	MS-65
1863	42	55.6	81%	$600	$950	$1,000	$1,150	$1,300	$1,500	$2,400	$3,000	$4,000

1863, Proof • **Proof Mintage:** 460.

Commentary: Some 1863 Proofs have obverse die striae (finish lines). The mintage for 1863 was the lowest of the era. *PF-60 to 62: 75 to 90; PF-63: 65 to 85; PF-64: 55 to 67; PF-65 or better: 25 to 32.*

	Cert	Avg	%MS	PF-60	PF-63	PF-65
1863, Proof	158	64.4		$325	$600	$1,250

1863-S Liberty Seated Dime

1863-S • **Circulation-Strike Mintage:** 157,500.

Commentary: The 1863-S (Fortin-101) is typically seen with weak impressions on the head of Liberty, the lower part of her figure, the letters STATES OF AMER in the legend, and the lower part of the reverse. There are some notable exceptions, however.

At the time of issue, the 1863-S dime was placed into circulation on the West Coast and, as with other silver coins of the year (including half dimes), some were shipped to the Orient by Chinese immigrants.

Availability in circulated grades: These are quite scarce, particularly in Extremely Fine or finer.

Availability in Mint State: The issue is very rare in higher grades; probably fewer than a dozen or so exist, and even this estimate may be on the high side. *MS-60 to 62: 4 to 6 estimated to exist; MS-63: 3 or 4; MS-64: 1; MS-65 or better: 1.*

	Cert	Avg	%MS	G-4	F-12	VF-20	EF-40	AU-50	MS-60	MS-63	MS-64	MS-65
1863-S	32	48.8	31%	$120	$300	$480	$900	$1,200	$3,600	$9,500	$12,500	$30,000

1864 Liberty Seated Dime

1864 • **Circulation-Strike Mintage:** 11,000.

Commentary: The 1864 dime, designated Fortin-101 and 102, was produced from two obverse dies and two reverse dies. Both pairs were used for circulation strikes and Proofs.

Availability in circulated grades: In worn grades, the 1864 is a key issue. Most are Very Fine to About Uncirculated.

Availability in Mint State: MS-60 to 62: 10 to 13 estimated to exist; MS-63: 20 to 25; MS-64: 20 to 25; MS-65 or better: 18 to 22.

	Cert	Avg	%MS	G-4	F-12	VF-20	EF-40	AU-50	MS-60	MS-63	MS-64	MS-65
1864	46	56.2	74%	$300	$650	$900	$1,000	$1,150	$1,200	$2,150	$2,750	$5,500

1864, Proof • **Proof Mintage:** 470.

Commentary: *PF-60 to 62: 110 to 130 estimated to exist; PF-63: 100 to 125; PF-64: 75 to 95; PF-65 or better: 40 to 50.*

	Cert	Avg	%MS	PF-60	PF-63	PF-65
1864, Proof	156	64.3		$325	$600	$1,250

1864-S Liberty Seated Dime

1864-S • **Circulation-Strike Mintage:** 230,000.

Commentary: This issue (Fortin-101 to 105) is nearly always lightly struck on the head of Liberty and the corresponding part of the reverse. Locating a fully struck example will take years of searching.[31]

The obverse of one circulation-strike variety is from a deeply basined die, polished to give it a proof-like surface.[32] Three obverse dies and three reverse dies in various combinations produced the mintage.

Availability in circulated grades: Circulated coins are scarce but in sufficient supply that no specialist has ever gone without one.

Availability in Mint State: In upper grades the 1864-S is rare. Many have unsatisfactory surfaces from an aesthetic viewpoint. *MS-60 to 62: 20 to 22 estimated to exist; MS-63: 12 to 15; MS-64: 5 to 7; MS-65 or better: 3 to 5.*

	Cert	Avg	%MS	G-4	F-12	VF-20	EF-40	AU-50	MS-60	MS-63	MS-64	MS-65
1864-S	45	42.0	36%	$120	$240	$360	$800	$1,000	$1,300	$2,000	$7,000	$10,000

1865 Liberty Seated Dime

1865 • **Circulation-Strike Mintage:** 10.000.

Commentary: Designated number 101 and 102 by Gerry Fortin, the 1865 dime was produced with two obverse dies and two reverse dies. Both pairs used for circulation strikes and Proofs.

Availability in circulated grades: Rare in circulated condition, the 1865 is a key issue. Most are Very Fine to About Uncirculated.

Availability in Mint State: These are very scarce. Most are in high grades, and many are somewhat proof-like. *MS-60 to 62: 6 to 9 estimated to exist; MS-63: 8 to 12; MS-64: 12 to 16; MS-65 or better: 10 to 14.*

	Cert	Avg	%MS	G-4	F-12	VF-20	EF-40	AU-50	MS-60	MS-63	MS-64	MS-65
1865	51	56.5	73%	$425	$750	$900	$1,000	$1,150	$1,300	$2,100	$2,500	$3,500

1865, Proof • **Proof Mintage:** 500.

Commentary: A few Proofs have the reverse misaligned 180 degrees. *PF-60 to 62: 60 to 90 estimated to exist; PF-63: 95 to 110; PF-64: 60 to 75; PF-65 or better: 22 to 28.*

	Cert	Avg	%MS	PF-60	PF-63	PF-65
1865, Proof	114	64.1		$350	$650	$1,250

1865-S Liberty Seated Dime

1865-S • **Circulation-Strike Mintage:** 175,000.

Commentary: This issue (Fortin-101 to 105) is nearly always lightly struck on the head of Liberty and the corresponding part of the reverse. Per Gerry Fortin, locating a fully struck example will take years of searching, especially for the F-101 or 102 die pairings.[33] The mintage was struck using three obverse and three reverse dies in various combinations.

Availability in circulated grades: Although these are scarce, they exist in sufficient supply that no specialist has ever been forced to go without one. Many examples in low grades show no mintmark or only faint traces of one, and are sometimes offered as rarer Philadelphia Mint coins.[34]

Availability in Mint State: Higher grades are exceedingly rare. *MS-60 to 62: 5 to 8 estimated; MS-63: 3 to 5; MS-64: 1; MS-65 or better: 1.*

	Cert	Avg	%MS	G-4	F-12	VF-20	EF-40	AU-50	MS-60	MS-63	MS-64	MS-65
1865-S	32	31.8	13%	$120	$360	$725	$1,200	$3,000	$7,200	$19,500	$30,000	$40,000

1866 Liberty Seated Dime

1866 • **Circulation-Strike Mintage:** 8,000.

Commentary: Designated Fortin-101 and 102, the 1866 mintage was produced with two obverse dies and two reverse dies. Both pairs used for circulation strikes and Proofs.

Availability in circulated grades: These are very elusive in circulated condition; most are Very Fine to About Uncirculated. *Proofs* are easier to find than are circulated coins.

Availability in Mint State: The 1866 is quite rare in Mint State. *MS-60 to 62: 15 to 20 estimated to exist; MS-63: 14 to 18; MS-64: 14 to 18; MS-65 or better: 12 to 15.*

	Cert	Avg	%MS	G-4	F-12	VF-20	EF-40	AU-50	MS-60	MS-63	MS-64	MS-65
1866	43	55.7	77%	$725	$1,100	$1,400	$1,600	$1,750	$2,000	$2,500	$2,750	$3,250

1866, Proof • **Proof Mintage:** 725.

Commentary: The base of the 1 in the date is dramatically repunched; the bases of 8 and 7, less so. The coins is usually seen with some lightness on the head, and obverse die-polish lines are visible. *PF-60 to 62: 100 to 125 estimated to exist; PF-63: 150 to 180; PF-64: 75 to 95; PF-65 or better: 45 to 55.*

	Cert	Avg	%MS	PF-60	PF-63	PF-65
1866, Proof	168	64.3		$325	$600	$1,250

1866-S Liberty Seated Dime

1866-S • **Circulation-Strike Mintage:** 135,000.

Commentary: These are usually weak in areas. The mintmark is very light on one reverse die, sometimes causing coins to be mistaken for a Philadelphia issue. Gerry Fortin designates them as numbers 101 to 103. Two obverse and two reverse dies produced the mintage.[35]

Availability in circulated grades: The 1866-S is scarce in worn grades, commensurate with the mintage.

Availability in Mint State: Probably fewer than 20 exist. *MS-60 to 62: 7 to 12 estimated to exist; MS-63: 1 or 2; MS-64: 1 or 2; MS-65 or better: 1 or 2.*[36]

	Cert	Avg	%MS	G-4	F-12	VF-20	EF-40	AU-50	MS-60	MS-63	MS-64	MS-65
1866-S	35	37.9	31%	$120	$240	$425	$625	$1,500	$3,600	$7,200	$9,500	$17,500

1867 Liberty Seated Dime

1867 • **Circulation-Strike Mintage:** 6,000.

Commentary: As a general rule, very few Philadelphia Mint dimes from 1863 through the end of the decade reached circulation. Surviving Mint State coins tend to be in higher grades. Well-worn coins are extremely rare.[37] The 1867 issue (Fortin-101 to 103) was struck with three obverse dies and three reverse dies.

Availability in circulated grades: As the low mintage tends to indicate, these are very scarce. Most are Very Fine to About Uncirculated.

Availability in Mint State: The 1867 is quite rare at this level. Probably somewhere between 50 and 100 exist, mostly in higher grades. *MS-60 to 62: 15 to 20 estimated to exist; MS-63: 10 to 13; MS-64: 25 to 30; MS-65 or better: 25 to 30.*

	Cert	Avg	%MS	G-4	F-12	VF-20	EF-40	AU-50	MS-60	MS-63	MS-64	MS-65
1867	49	60.7	86%	$600	$900	$1,000	$1,100	$1,400	$1,500	$2,100	$3,200	$4,500

1867, Proof • **Proof Mintage:** 625.

Commentary: A few 1867 Proofs (Fortin-101 and 103) have some lightness on the hair and wreath. *PF-60 to 62: 100 to 125 estimated to exist; PF-63: 150 to 180; PF-64: 80 to 95; PF-65 or better: 30 to 40.*

	Cert	Avg	%MS	PF-60	PF-63	PF-65
1867, Proof	132	64.1		$325	$600	$1,250

1867-S Liberty Seated Dime

1867-S • **Circulation-Strike Mintage:** 140,000.

Commentary: San Francisco dimes of 1867 (Fortin-101 and 102, struck with two obverse and two reverse dies) are often seen with light areas on the obverse. The mintmark is small and thin.

Availability in circulated grades: Circulated coins are scarce, in proportion to the mintage.

Availability in Mint State: Above circulated grades the 1867-S is exceedingly rare; probably fewer than 15 exist. *MS-60 to 62: 5 to 7 estimated to exist; MS-63: 3 or 4; MS-64: 3 or 4; MS-65 or better: 1 or 2.*[38]

	Cert	Avg	%MS	G-4	F-12	VF-20	EF-40	AU-50	MS-60	MS-63	MS-64	MS-65
1867-S	30	42.9	33%	$120	$240	$400	$725	$1,550	$1,900	$5,100	$7,200	$10,000

1868 Liberty Seated Dime

1868 • **Circulation-Strike Mintage:** 464,000.

Commentary: Beginning about this time the Engraving Department of the Mint had difficulty with the obverse of the Liberty Seated dime. The first S in STATES occurs in the following styles from now until the end of the series in 1891:

1. Perfect S.
2. Top curve of S is mostly missing (appears as a very thin line). Cited as "broken top to first S."
3. Top curve of S is completely missing; serif is isolated as an "island." Cited as "missing top to first S."
4. Top curve of S is patched with a small "dash." Cited as "dash-patch to top of first S."
5. Top curve of S is patched with a wavy line. Cited as "wavy patch to top of first S."
6. Top curve of S is thin, but nearly complete.

Note that few people collect Liberty Seated dimes by minute die variations; they are mentioned here because their existence is interesting to contemplate.

The 1868 issue (Fortin-101 to 112) was produced by 12 dies in consecutive pairs, an exceptionally high number of dies in relation to the total mintage figure.

Availability in circulated grades: Scarcer than the mintage would suggest, circulated 1868 dimes exist in sufficient quantity to satisfy specialists. In 1993, a group of 500 or so circulated pieces was located in Czechoslovakia. Many were distributed by Heritage.

Availability in Mint State: Again, these are scarcer than their mintage indicates. Probably fewer than 50 Mint State pieces are known, mostly in higher grades. The 1868 is not typically considered to be a rare date in general, but the facts indicate that *in Mint State* it indeed is. Market prices of this and all other low-mintage Philadelphia Mint coins of the era are held down by the ready availability of Proofs. *MS-60 to 62: 10 to 13 estimated to exist; MS-63: 10 to 13; MS-64: 15 to 20; MS-65 or better: 10 to 12.*[39]

	Cert	Avg	%MS	G-4	F-12	VF-20	EF-40	AU-50	MS-60	MS-63	MS-64	MS-65
1868	41	55.2	73%	$18	$30	$40	$65	$150	$300	$850	$1,500	$4,000

1868, Proof • Proof Mintage: 600.

Commentary: Description of the Eliasberg Proof (Fortin-104), adapted: "Some raised die lines are visible on both sides from die preparation; this must have been one of the first impressions from the Proof dies. On obverse top curve of first S in STATES nearly missing. Seated figure somewhat stippled (deliberately to create a cameo effect?); very interesting—actually dramatic under magnification. Concentric arcs are visible at the base of the seated figure, and, especially, at Liberty's neck and bosom, another fascinating characteristic rarely seen elsewhere."[40] Proofs of 1868 are designated Fortin-101 and 104. *PF-60 to 62: 100 to 125 estimated to exist; PF-63: 150 to 180; PF-64: 80 to 95; PF-65 or better: 40 to 55.*

	Cert	Avg	%MS	PF-60	PF-63	PF-65
1868, Proof	156	63.9		$325	$600	$1,250

1868-S Liberty Seated Dime

1868-S • Circulation-Strike Mintage: 260,000.

Commentary: Many 1868-S dimes (Fortin-101) have light striking on the obverse.

It is evident that the number of these were shipped to the Orient, where some had metal carefully shaved from the features of the Liberty Seated figure (a clever way to obtain small amounts of silver without being obvious), and others were made into buttons. Walter Breen referenced a doubled-die reverse, today thought to be the result of strike doubling (die chatter).

Availability in circulated grades: These are scarce, and are traditionally believed to exist in approximate proportion to the mintage. They are very rare at the About Uncirculated level.

Availability in Mint State: The 1868-S is very rare in Mint State, although this is generally overlooked and catalog values do not reflect this. *MS-60 to 62: 12 to 16 estimated to exist; MS-63: 7 to 9; MS-64: 4 to 6; MS-65 or better: 3 or 4.*[41]

	Cert	Avg	%MS	G-4	F-12	VF-20	EF-40	AU-50	MS-60	MS-63	MS-64	MS-65
1868-S	24	48.6	54%	$60	$150	$240	$550	$650	$1,000	$1,500	$2,500	$5,000

1869 Liberty Seated Dime

1869 • Circulation-Strike Mintage: 256,000.

Commentary: For dimes of 1869 (Fortin-101 to 107), the serif or "flag" at the upper left of the 1 in the date is short on most dies, long on Fortin-105 and 106. The mintage was struck by seven obverse and seven reverse dies in consecutive pairs.

Per Gerry Fortin, Long Flag 1 examples come well struck as a rule. Short Flag 1 examples will show weakness at the upper obverse and lower reverse. It was not until the late 20th century and the formation of the Liberty Seated Collectors Club, the publication of a book on Liberty Seated dimes by Kam Ahwash, and the advent of *Walter Breen's Complete Encyclopedia of U.S. and Colonial Coins* (1988) that there was widespread interest in minute die varieties. The later work of Gerry Fortin has been comprehensive to an incredible degree and is the standard for citations, as here.

Availability in circulated grades: Circulated examples are scarce, in proportion to the relatively low mintage. They are quite scarce in Extremely Fine or About Uncirculated.

Availability in Mint State: These are quite rare in Mint State. Fortin states that essentially all Mint State examples were struck with Long Flag 1 dies. The author is aware of only two that were struck with Short Flag 1 die.[42] *MS-60 to 62: 5 to 8 estimated to exist; MS-63: 8 to 12; MS-64: 8 to 12; MS-65 or better: 10 to 15.*

	Cert	Avg	%MS	G-4	F-12	VF-20	EF-40	AU-50	MS-60	MS-63	MS-64	MS-65
1869	30	48.1	50%	$22	$40	$85	$120	$200	$400	$900	$1,750	$3,250

1869, Proof • **Proof Mintage:** 600.

Commentary: Proofs are from Fortin-104, 105, and 106 dies. *PF-60 to 62: 100 to 125 estimated to exist; PF-63: 150 to 180; PF-64: 100 to 130; PF-65 or better: 70 to 90.*

	Cert	Avg	%MS	PF-60	PF-63	PF-65
1869, Proof	178	64.1		$325	$600	$1,250

1869-S Liberty Seated Dime

1869-S • **Circulation-Strike Mintage:** 450,000.

Commentary: This issue (Fortin-101 and 102) is often weak on the head and the corresponding part of the reverse. The coins show two different mintmark styles on the reverse: a small, thin S that typically appears as a blob, and a small, weak S with delicate serifs. Two obverse dies and two reverse dies produced the mintage.

Availability in circulated grades: Circulated coins are scarce, in proportion to the mintage.

Availability in Mint State: Higher-grade 1869-S dimes are quite rare, but generally are more readily available than earlier San Francisco issues. *MS-60 to 62: 24 to 28 estimated to exist; MS-63: 14 to 18; MS-64: 12 to 16; MS-65 or better: 10 to 14.*

	Cert	Avg	%MS	G-4	F-12	VF-20	EF-40	AU-50	MS-60	MS-63	MS-64	MS-65
1869-S	58	59.8	78%	$18	$25	$50	$150	$250	$400	$800	$1,300	$3,000

1870 Liberty Seated Dime

1870 • **Circulation-Strike Mintage:** 470,500.

Commentary: This issue (Fortin-101 to 107) is typically found weakly struck on the head and other features of Liberty, and on the corresponding parts of the reverse. It was produced with the use of obverse dies and seven reverse dies in consecutive pairs.

Availability in circulated grades: The 1870 dime is slightly scarce, and exists in proportion to its mintage.

Availability in Mint State: These are quite scarce in Mint State. *MS-60 to 62: 70 to 90 estimated to exist; MS-63: 30 to 40; MS-64: 16 to 20; MS-65 or better: 10 to 14.*

	Cert	Avg	%MS	G-4	F-12	VF-20	EF-40	AU-50	MS-60	MS-63	MS-64	MS-65
1870	74	60.4	78%	$16	$25	$30	$50	$100	$200	$450	$800	$1,650

1870, Proof • Proof Mintage: 1,000.

Commentary: Proofs of this issue (Fortin-101 and 102) are carelessly made and weak on the obverse. The high mintage of this year does not translate into a proportionally large number of Proofs existing today. Proofs of this year are rarer today than are those of 1869, which has a lower mintage. *PF-60 to 62: 100 to 125 estimated to exist; PF-63: 140 to 170; PF-64: 90 to 120; PF-65 or better: 50 to 65.*

	Cert	Avg	%MS	PF-60	PF-63	PF-65
1870, Proof	159	64.1		$325	$600	$1,250

1870-S Liberty Seated Dime

1870-S • Circulation-Strike Mintage: 50,000.

Commentary: San Francisco dimes of this year (Fortin-101) are often weak at the head of Liberty, and typically weak at IM of DIME.

Although the San Francisco Mint had six pairs of dies on hand for the 1870-S coinage, apparently only one pair was employed, that in November of the year. "A small coinage makes it very rare," noted Augustus G. Heaton in his treatise *Mint Marks* in 1893.

Although 50,000 specimens were struck, it is probably the case that nearly all were exported for use in the China trade (a common fate of San Francisco silver coins in the era before the trade dollar).

Availability in circulated grades: The collector will find these are fairly scarce, as the mintage indicates. They are quite rare in Extremely Fine or better grade, especially if About Uncirculated with luster. Most have rough surfaces.[43]

Availability in Mint State: Walter Breen wrote that in 1977 a hoard of about 15 pieces turned up in England, constituting what probably comprises most of the known pieces. Absent this hoard and, seemingly, at least one other small group of high-grade pieces, the 1870-S would be a major rarity. As it is, probably somewhere around two dozen, more or less, exist. *MS-60 to 62: 7 to 10 estimated to exist; MS-63: 6 to 8; MS-64: 12 to 14; MS-65 or better: 12 to 14.*

	Cert	Avg	%MS	G-4	F-12	VF-20	EF-40	AU-50	MS-60	MS-63	MS-64	MS-65
1870-S	36	36.7	33%	$250	$575	$725	$900	$1,100	$1,800	$2,750	$3,750	$7,500

1871 Liberty Seated Dime

1871 • Circulation-Strike Mintage: 906,750.

Commentary: This issue (Fortin-101 to 114) is often weak at the centers. Fourteen obverse dies and 13 reverse dies were used in production; Fortin-101 and 102 shared a reverse die.

Availability in circulated grades: These are plentiful in circulated condition.

Availability in Mint State: The issue is quite scarce, but not important in the marketplace, as enough Proofs exist to satisfy the demand for the date. *MS-60 to 62: 15 to 20 estimated to exist; MS-63: 20 to 25; MS-64: 20 to 25; MS-65 or better: 9 to 12.*

	Cert	Avg	%MS	G-4	F-12	VF-20	EF-40	AU-50	MS-60	MS-63	MS-64	MS-65
1871	72	58.8	67%	$16	$25	$30	$50	$150	$250	$425	$850	$1,600

1871, Proof • Proof Mintage: 960.

Commentary: Proofs are designated Fortin-101 to 103. *PF-60 to 62: 125 to 160 estimated to exist; PF-63: 130 to 160; PF-64: 90 to 110; PF-65 or better: 40 to 55.*

	Cert	Avg	%MS	PF-60	PF-63	PF-65
1871, Proof	149	64.0		$325	$600	$1,250

1871-CC Liberty Seated Dime

1871-CC • **Circulation-Strike Mintage:** 20,100.

Commentary: This year's Carson City Mint dimes (Fortin-101) are usually seen with slight weakness on the head of Liberty. Note that there are only 89 reeds on the edges of 1871-CC to 1874-CC dimes.

The Carson City Mint opened in 1870, but no dimes were struck there until 1871. It was anticipated that the Mint would see large coinage of gold and silver from the mines of Virginia City, only about 15 miles distant. Instead, political situations and other complications arose, and most precious metal was sent to San Francisco to be coined. As a general rule, Carson City dimes of the first several years are great rarities today.

Availability in circulated grades: These rare coins are highly prized in any state of preservation. The vast majority are quite worn, with Fine and Very Fine being about par. Most have problems of one sort or another, often with a porous or etched surface (this also being characteristic of Carson City dimes of the next two years).[44]

Availability in Mint State: The issue is exceedingly rare in higher grades; just a few exist, including an MS-63 from the 2013 Battle Born Collection and an MS-65 from the 2014 Gardner Collection. *MS-60 to 62: 1 or 2 estimated to exist; MS-63: 1; MS-64: 1; MS-65 or better: 1.*[45]

	Cert	Avg	%MS	G-4	F-12	VF-20	EF-40	AU-50	MS-60	MS-63	MS-64	MS-65
1871-CC	21	34.9	24%	$3,000	$6,000	$8,500	$15,000	$25,000	$50,000	$115,000	$200,000	$300,000

1871-S Liberty Seated Dime

1871-S • Circulation-Strike Mintage: 320,000.

Commentary: This issue (Fortin-101 to 103) is often seen weak at the reverse center. Per Fortin, one variety (F-102) employs a leftover reverse die from 1869 and 1870 with very weak denomination and devices.

Scarce but still quite available in circulated grades, the 1871-S emerges as a rarity in Mint State. In 1893, Heaton wrote that the 1871-S was "abundant." Presumably, generous quantities of worn coins were still found in circulation. The mintage was struck from two obverse dies and two reverse dies.

Availability in circulated grades: These are fairly scarce in circulated condition.

Availability in Mint State: The 1871-S is extremely rare in Mint State; probably fewer than 50 exist. However, catalogs pay scant notice of this due to the relatively high overall mintage, making this one a sleeper. *MS-60 to 62: 16 to 20 estimated to exist; MS-63: 8 to 12; MS-64: 6 to 8; MS-65 or better: 3 to 5.*

	Cert	Avg	%MS	G-4	F-12	VF-20	EF-40	AU-50	MS-60	MS-63	MS-64	MS-65
1871-S	30	54.6	47%	$25	$120	$180	$325	$750	$1,600	$3,600	$5,000	$10,000

1872 Liberty Seated Dime

1872 • Circulation-Strike Mintage: 2,395,500.

Commentary: Circulation-strike 1872 dimes (Fortin-101 to 116) are often lightly struck at the head of Liberty and the corresponding part of the reverse. The issue was produced from 16 obverse dies and 14 reverse dies.

Availability in circulated grades: Circulated coins are common.

Availability in Mint State: Mint State coins are fairly scarce, at least in comparison to issues of the past decade. *MS-60 to 62: 100 to 130 estimated to exist; MS-63: 30 to 40; MS-64: 16 to 20; MS-65 or better: 12 to 15.*

	Cert	Avg	%MS	G-4	F-12	VF-20	EF-40	AU-50	MS-60	MS-63	MS-64	MS-65
1872	80	58.4	70%	$18	$25	$30	$40	$90	$175	$300	$650	$1,100

1872, Doubled Die Reverse •

Circulation-Strike Mintage: Part of the mintage for regular circulation-strike 1872 dimes.

Commentary: The 1872 Doubled Die Reverse (Fortin-105), discovered by Lee Day and attributed as such by Tom DeLorey,[46] is one of the most numismatically significant doubled dies in the entire American series. At the same time, its diagnostics are subtle, and for this reason: In the preparation of a working die for a reverse, the working hub was either lightly impressed into the working die or it was deeply impressed and then mostly ground away. Remaining were just a few traces of the design. The working hub was then rotated 175 degrees and the master die deeply impressed into it. Only slight traces remain of the first impression, most notably a line within the O and a claw-shaped fragment above the right upright of the N

Detail of the
Doubled Reverse.

in DIME; and a curved fragment within the lower part of the interior of the D and the ghost of a leaf to the right of the E in DIME. Scattered other elements can be seen as well. *The Cherrypickers' Guide to Rare Die Varieties* lists this as FS-10-1872-801. This variety is very rare. Larry Briggs has seen only five coins, and probably fewer than 20 are known.[47]

	Cert	Avg	%MS	G-4	F-12	VF-20	EF-40	AU-50	MS-60	MS-63	MS-64	MS-65
1872, Doubled Die Reverse	2	37.5	0%	$100	$350	$550	$850	$1,500	$1,750			

1872, Proof • Proof Mintage: 950.

Commentary: The dies for Proof coins of 1872 (Fortin-103 and 109) were poorly prepared and show many striations. Walter Breen's *Proof Coins Encyclopedia*, p. 143, addresses the indifferent quality of Proof dimes of this era and states, "This sort of carelessness is seen on various denominations during the 1870s; possibly inexperienced employees were on duty making Proofs, possibly there was enough haste and chaos in the Mint that nobody really cared a whistle in a high wind about quality control." *PF-60 to 62: 100 to 125 estimated to exist; PF-63: 150 to 180; PF-64: 100 to 130; PF-65 or better: 50 to 65.*

	Cert	Avg	%MS	PF-60	PF-63	PF-65
1872, Proof	146	63.8		$325	$600	$1,250

1872-CC Liberty Seated Dime

1872-CC • Circulation-Strike Mintage: 35,480.

Commentary: The 1872-CC (Fortin-101), though usually well struck, is sometimes seen with typical weakness at the head of Liberty.

Availability in circulated grades: The issue is rare in circulated condition, but is the most widely available of the 1871-CC to 1874-CC dimes. Most have rough surfaces.[48]

Availability in Mint State: The 1872-CC is exceedingly rare in Mint State. *MS-60 to 62: 0 or 1 estimated to exist; MS-63: 2; MS-64: 0; MS-65: 0.*

	Cert	Avg	%MS	G-4	F-12	VF-20	EF-40	AU-50	MS-60	MS-63	MS-64	MS-65
1872-CC	39	23.8	0%	$1,250	$3,500	$5,500	$10,000	$18,500	$62,500	$200,000	$250,000	

1872-S Liberty Seated Dime

1872-S • Circulation-Strike Mintage: 190,000.

Commentary: Designated Fortin-101, the 1872-S is often lightly struck at the head as well as on certain of the wreath features on the reverse. This is another issue that probably saw shipment in quantity to the Orient, although this is not documented.

Availability in circulated grades: Circulated coins are fairly scarce, as the mintage indicates. However, there are enough to satisfy specialists. For a long time the 1872-S was unappreciated in the marketplace. The turning point may have come from John W. McCloskey's study, "Availability of Liberty Seated Dimes by Grade," in *The Gobrecht Journal*, July 1981. Year after year until his retirement a few years ago McCloskey edited the *The Gobrecht Journal*, creating one of the finest specialized publications in numismatics.

Availability in Mint State: In higher grades the issue is very rare, with probably fewer than two dozen extant. *MS-60 to 62: 7 to 9 estimated to exist; MS-63: 5 to 7; MS-64: 5 to 7; MS-65 or better: 3 to 4.*

	Cert	Avg	%MS	G-4	F-12	VF-20	EF-40	AU-50	MS-60	MS-63	MS-64	MS-65
1872-S	23	50.9	43%	$25	$120	$180	$325	$500	$1,200	$3,500	$7,500	$25,000

1873 Liberty Seated Dime, No Arrows

1873, No Arrows, Close 3 •
Circulation-Strike Mintage: 1,507,400 estimated.

Commentary: Often lightly struck at the central portions of obverse and reverse, this issue (Fortin-101 to 108) is sometimes seen with other areas of weakness as well.

The mintage was produced with eight obverse and eight reverse dies in consecutive pairs. At least one variety was struck after Open 3 coins were made.

Availability in circulated grades: Relatively common in lower circulated grades, the coin is scarcer in higher grades such as Extremely Fine and About Uncirculated.

Detail of the Close 3.

Availability in Mint State: The 1873, No Arrows, Close 3, dime is quite rare in Mint State, but not recognized as such, due the availability of Proofs. *MS-60 to 62: 50 to 70 estimated to exist; MS-63: 25 to 32; MS-64: 15 to 20; MS-65 or better: 12 to 15.*

	Cert	Avg	%MS	G-4	F-12	VF-20	EF-40	AU-50	MS-60	MS-63	MS-64	MS-65
1873, No Arrows, Close 3	45	57.3	62%	$16	$30	$48	$70	$120	$240	$480	$950	$1,500

1873, No Arrows, Close 3, Proof •

Proof Mintage: 600.

Commentary: Proofs are designated Fortin-101. Kamal Ahwash reported a second die, but this has not been confirmed. *PF-60 to 62: 100 to 125 estimated to exist; PF-63: 130 to 160; PF-64: 120 to 150; PF-65 or better: 50 to 65.*

	Cert	Avg	%MS	PF-60	PF-63	PF-65
1873, No Arrows, Close 3, Proof	171	64.3		$325	$600	$1,250

1873, No Arrows, Open 3 •

Circulation-Strike Mintage: 60,000 estimated.

Commentary: The 1873, No Arrows, Open 3, dimes are accorded a separate numbering system (Fortin-101 to 106). Produced with six obverse and four reverse dies, the coins are often lightly struck at the central portions of obverse and reverse.

The Open 3 is rarer than the preceding date style. Mintage figures of 1,507,400 of the Close 3 dimes this year as opposed to 60,000 circulation-strike Open 3 dimes have been estimated by Walter Breen and R.W. Julian, and have been widely accepted in the numismatic literature. However, the generous supply of the Open 3 dimes and the Fortin die data suggest that the mintage was probably at least several hundred thousand.

Detail of the Open 3.

Availability in circulated grades: Scarcer than the preceding, these are elusive in higher grades such as Extremely Fine and About Uncirculated.

Availability in Mint State: In Mint State, as well, the Open 3 coin is rarer than the preceding Close 3. *MS-60 to 62: 20 to 25 estimated to exist; MS-63: 12 to 15; MS-64: 9 to 12; MS-65 or better: 4 or 5.*

	Cert	Avg	%MS	G-4	F-12	VF-20	EF-40	AU-50	MS-60	MS-63	MS-64	MS-65
1873, No Arrows, Open 3	36	46.4	36%	$20	$50	$75	$130	$200	$600	$1,500	$4,500	$15,000

1873-CC Liberty Seated Dime, No Arrows

1873-CC, No Arrows • **Circulation-Strike Mintage:** 12,400.

Commentary: This is one of the most famous of all United States rarities. It was probably saved from the 1873 coins sent to the Assay Commission, although facts on the matter are scarce. It first appeared in Edward Cogan's sale of the John Swan Randall Collection in May 1878.

It was later owned by William H. Woodin, who displayed the coin at the 1914 ANS Exhibit in New York City and consigned it to Wayte Raymond's "Collection of a Prominent American" sale (May 1915), where it realized $170 from New York numismatist Rudolph "Rud" Kohler. Waldo C. Newcomer acquired it in 1915. Charles M. Williams acquired the coin in 1933 from Newcomer via Texas dealer B. Max Mehl. When the coin was consigned to Abe Kosoff's Adolphe Menjou Collection sale on June 15, 1950, it sold for $3,650 to James C. Kelly and Sol Kaplan, who outbid Louis E. Eliasberg Sr. (causing ill feelings on the part of their good customer!). Eliasberg acquired the coin from Kelly and Kaplan for $4,000 on November 7, 1950, while biting his tongue, allowing him to complete his collection of every U.S. coin minted to date. In May 1996 the celebrated dime was lot 1198 in Bowers and Merena Galleries' sale of the Louis E. Eliasberg Collection, where it realized $550,000 from winning bidder Waldo E. "Pat" Bolen Jr. In turn, in Heritage's April 1999 sale of the Waldo E. Bolen, Jr. Collection of 1873-CC Coinage, the coin—now lot 5928—realized $632,500. Purchaser Jay Parrino consigned the coin to sell alongside Bowers and Merena Galleries' sale of Jim Gray's North Carolina Collection (July 2004, lot 2149), where it was acquired for $891,250 by Carson City Mint specialist Rusty Goe. It was sold privately into the Battle Born Collection for an undisclosed sum (PCGS #4661). It was later sold by Stack's Bowers Galleries in August 2012 for $1,840,000.

As the 1873-CC, No Arrows, Liberty Seated dime is a superb satiny gem and shows no evidence of circulation, it seems likely that it was reserved for inspection by the Assay Commission, which met in Philadelphia on Wednesday, February 11, 1874, to review the prior year's gold and silver production from all mints. Parcels of coins from the various mints were opened. Random representative pieces were selected by Assay Commission members and were destructively tested in the Mint laboratory for weight and precious-metal content. Only a few coins reserved for the commission were actually tested; most were later melted or placed into circulation.

An interesting sideline concerning this coin is that in his 1893 study, *Mint Marks*, Augustus, G. Heaton stated that the only 1873-CC dime he knew of was "without the arrowheads." Apparently, he did not know of the 1873-CC *with* arrows! This was an experimental era in American numismatic research; apart from Heaton, relatively little study had been done in the field of mintmarks, and many discoveries were yet to be made. The order of rarities had not yet been sorted out. In fact, among the four issues of the early 1870s known to Heaton—1871-CC; 1872-CC; 1873-CC, No Arrows; and 1874-CC—Heaton considered the 1874 to be "the highest rarity of the four."

Availability in Mint State: Only one is known to exist. It is graded MS-65 (PCGS).

	Cert	Avg	%MS	G-4	F-12	VF-20	EF-40	AU-50	MS-60	MS-63	MS-64	MS-65
1873-CC, No Arrows	0	n/a										$3,000,000

1873 Liberty Seated Dime, With Arrows

1873, Arrows • Circulation-Strike
Mintage: 2,377,700.

Commentary: This issue (Fortin-101 to 124) is often seen with lightness at the head of Liberty and at the upper left of the wreath on the reverse. It was struck with the use of 23 obverse dies and 23 reverse dies. Fortin-111 and 124 have the same obverse die.

Availability in circulated grades: Circulated examples are common.

Availability in Mint State: The issue is fairly plentiful in Mint State, but always in strong demand due to its status as a type coin. *MS-60 to 62: 120 to 150 estimated to exist; MS-63: 65 to 85; MS-64: 45 to 60; MS-65 or better: 25 to 30.*

	Cert	Avg	%MS	G-4	F-12	VF-20	EF-40	AU-50	MS-60	MS-63	MS-64	MS-65
1873, Arrows	192	55.5	58%	$18	$26	$55	$150	$300	$550	$900	$1,650	$4,000

1873, Arrows, Proof • Proof Mintage: 500.

Commentary: *PF-60 to 62: 125 to 160 estimated to exist; PF-63: 130 to 160; PF-64: 90 to 115; PF-65 or better: 40 to 50.*

	Cert	Avg	%MS	PF-60	PF-63	PF-65
1873, Arrows, Proof	104	64.1		$700	$1,000	$3,750

1873, Doubled Die Obverse, Arrows • Circulation-Strike Mintage:

Part of the regular circulation-strike mintage for 1873, With Arrows, dimes.

Commentary: This is the most dramatically obvious doubled die in the Liberty Seated dime series. The doubling is most noticeable in the shield at the upper right, with extra horizontal lines (on a slight slant) and the outline of the right border of the earlier-impressed shield. Gerry Fortin designates it as number 103; *The Cherrypickers' Guide to Rare Die Varieties* lists it as FS-10-1873-2101. Probably fewer than two dozen are known today.

**Detail of the
Doubled Die Obverse**

	Cert	Avg	%MS	G-4	F-12	VF-20	EF-40	AU-50	MS-60	MS-63	MS-64	MS-65
1873, Arrows, Doubled Die Obverse	4	25.3	25%	$475	$1,200	$1,700	$3,300	$6,000	$20,000			

1873-CC Liberty Seated Dime, With Arrows

1873-CC, Arrows • Circulation-Strike
Mintage: 18,791 estimated.

Commentary: Examples are usually well struck. Of all dimes in the Liberty Seated series, the 1873-CC, With Arrows, (Fortin-101) is nearly always seen with a porous or granular surface. The reason for this is not known. Walter Breen says that the issue is "often on porous or rough planchets," implying that before striking, rough planchets were used. This seems unlikely. Dozens exist. Here is a minor numismatic mystery.

Availability in circulated grades: Traditionally this is one of the key issues of the series. Most are well worn, AG-3 to VG-8, and with rough surfaces. Very Fine and better coins are prizes if with nice, problem-free surfaces, but such coins are in the distinct minority. It remains a mystery why so many early Carson City coins, especially dimes, are porous.[49]

Availability in Mint State: In Mint condition the issue is exceedingly rare. *MS-60 to 62: 0 or 1 estimated to exist; MS-63: 0 or 1; MS-64: 0 or 1; MS-65 or better: 2.*

	Cert	Avg	%MS	G-4	F-12	VF-20	EF-40	AU-50	MS-60	MS-63	MS-64	MS-65
1873-CC, Arrows	39	14.9	3%	$3,000	$5,500	$7,500	$14,000	$40,000	$62,500	$125,000	$200,000	$275,000

1873-S Liberty Seated Dime, With Arrows

1873-S, Arrows • Circulation-Strike
Mintage: 455,000.

Commentary: These are often lightly struck on the head and on the upper left of the reverse wreath.

The 1873-S, With Arrows, (Fortin-101 and 102) is a scarce issue—multiples rarer than its Philadelphia Mint counterpart[50]—and is in strong demand due to the arrows feature. Two obverse dies and two reverse dies were used in production.

Availability in circulated grades: This issue is scarce, and examples often have rough surfaces.

Availability in Mint State: This one is fairly rare in Mint State, but specimens appear on the market frequently enough that no advanced specialist need be without one. The population is probably on the order of 50 to 100 pieces. *MS-60 to 62: 15 to 20 estimated to exist; MS-63: 18 to 25; MS-64: 13 to 16; MS-65 or better: 3 or 4.*

	Cert	Avg	%MS	G-4	F-12	VF-20	EF-40	AU-50	MS-60	MS-63	MS-64	MS-65
1873-S, Arrows	61	60.8	87%	$22	$35	$60	$175	$450	$1,000	$2,000	$3,500	$7,500

1874 Liberty Seated Dime, With Arrows

1874, Arrows • Circulation-Strike
Mintage: 2,940,000.

Commentary: The 1874, With Arrows, (Fortin-101 to 115) is sometimes seen lightly struck at the head on the obverse and the upper left of the wreath on the reverse. The arrowheads to the left and right of the date are slanted upward on the 1874, unlike on the 1873. The mintage was produced with 14 obverse dies and 15 reverse dies.

Several 1874 dimes without one or both arrows have been reported (Fortin-106) and are very rare. These were struck from highly polished dies. Experimentation with a combination date and arrows logotype is plausible based on evidence. Normal die preparation required separate date and arrows diesinking.[51] An About Uncirculated example sold for $10,000 on eBay in January 2009.[52]

Availability in circulated grades: Plentiful.

Availability in Mint State: This issue is readily available in Mint State. Even so, it is scarcer than certification-service reports indicate, as a disproportionately high number of these have been submitted for certification due to their relatively high value as type coins. *MS-60 to 62: 150 to 200 estimated to exist; MS-63: 125 to 150; MS-64: 80 to 110; MS-65 or better: 60 to 80.*

	Cert	Avg	%MS	G-4	F-12	VF-20	EF-40	AU-50	MS-60	MS-63	MS-64	MS-65
1874, Arrows	277	56.2	61%	$18	$25	$55	$150	$310	$600	$1,000	$1,400	$4,500

1874, Arrows, Proof • Proof Mintage: 700.

Commentary: Proofs of the 1874, With Arrows, variety are designated Fortin-101. *PF-60 to 62: 150 to 200 estimated to exist; PF-63: 150 to 200; PF-64: 120 to 150; PF-65 or better: 40 to 50.*

	Cert	Avg	%MS	PF-60	PF-63	PF-65
1874, Arrows, Proof	183	63.7		$700	$1,000	$3,750

1874-CC Liberty Seated Dime, With Arrows

1874-CC, Arrows • Circulation-Strike
Mintage: 10,817.

Commentary: As noted in the previous listing, the arrowheads were punched separately into working dies, sometimes causing misalignment as on the 1874-CC.

Without question the 1874-CC (Fortin-101) is one of the most highly prized issues in the entire dime denomination.[53]

Availability in circulated grades: Circulated examples are very scarce, more so than generally realized. Most have rough surfaces. The 1874-CC, With Arrows, handily outdistances its 1873-CC counterpart in terms of rarity.

Availability in Mint State: It is thought that only five exist in Mint State grades, including an MS-62 from the Battle Born Collection and an MS-63 from the Eugene Gardner Collection. *MS-60 to 62: 3 or 4 estimated to exist; MS-63: 1; MS-64: 0; MS-65 or better: 0.*

	Cert	Avg	%MS	G-4	F-12	VF-20	EF-40	AU-50	MS-60	MS-63	MS-64	MS-65
1874-CC, Arrows	12	35.6	17%	$7,500	$14,000	$20,000	$32,500	$55,000	$115,000	$200,000		

1874-S Liberty Seated Dime, With Arrows

1874-S, Arrows • **Circulation-Strike Mintage:** 240,000.

Commentary: The 1874-S, With Arrows, (Fortin-101 and 102) is usually lightly struck at the head of Liberty and the upper left of the reverse, and the mintmark is often a blob. Two obverse dies and two reverse dies produced the mintage.[54]

Availability in circulated grades: The issue is quite scarce in circulated condition.

Availability in Mint State: These are very rare in Mint State, with a population on the order of 25 to 50 pieces. A disproportionately high number of these have been certified due to the fame of the variety and the popularity of the arrows feature. *MS-60 to 62: 15 to 20 estimated to exist; MS-63: 10 to 14; MS-64: 9 to 12; MS-65 or better: 7 to 9.*

	Cert	Avg	%MS	G-4	F-12	VF-20	EF-40	AU-50	MS-60	MS-63	MS-64	MS-65
1874-S, Arrows	48	56.6	67%	$25	$65	$110	$225	$500	$900	$2,000	$3,250	$6,500

1875 Liberty Seated Dime

1875 • **Circulation-Strike Mintage:** 10,350,000.

Commentary: The immense mintage of the 1875 Philadelphia dime was made in anticipation of the resumption of specie (coin) payments the following year, 1876. This happened, and in the next two years a flood of long-hoarded dimes came back onto the market. With new mintages there was a glut of the denomination, which resulted in low mintages for 1879 to 1881, after which time more coins were needed. With 21 obverse dies and 20 reverse dies used to strike more than 10 million coins, the issue claims a wide range of Fortin attribution numbers—from 101 to 124.

Availability in circulated grades: Circulated examples are very common.

Availability in Mint State: This issue is common in uncirculated condition as well. Here begins the era of really common Mint State dimes, a few issues excepted. These issues are much more readily available than population reports suggest, as the vast majority have never been certified. *MS-60 to 62: 350 to 500 estimated to exist; MS-63: 175 to 210; MS-64: 125 to 160; MS-65 or better: 75 to 100.*

	Cert	Avg	%MS	G-4	F-12	VF-20	EF-40	AU-50	MS-60	MS-63	MS-64	MS-65
1875	427	60.6	84%	$15	$20	$25	$35	$80	$150	$250	$400	$700

1875, Proof • **Proof Mintage:** 700.

Commentary: *PF-60 to 62: 125 to 160 estimated to exist; PF-63: 130 to 160; PF-64: 90 to 115; PF-65 or better: 40 to 50.*

	Cert	Avg	%MS	PF-60	PF-63	PF-65
1875, Proof	161	64.4		$300	$600	$1,000

1875-CC Liberty Seated Dime

1875-CC, Mintmark Above Bow •
Circulation-Strike Mintage: Part of a total mintage of 4,645,000 for the issue.

Commentary: This Carson City issue (Fortin-101 to 119) is sometimes lightly struck at Liberty's head and the upper left side of the wreath. The mintage was struck with 13 obverse dies and 18 reverse dies.

Today collectors recognize what may have been the earliest 1875-CC dime variety struck, with mintmark CC widely spaced and with wide reeding (as on Carson City dimes earlier in the decade); the same variety exists with narrow reeding.

The widely spaced CC mintmark with tiny letters was used only on selected dies of the era. The most famous use

Detail of the Mintmark Above Bow

of this style is on the 1873-CC and certain other trade dollars. This situation is numismatic trivia *par excellence.* Those who like minute die varieties can acquire most such pieces for no extra cost by studying offered coins.

In 1893, Heaton wrote, "We have 1875-CC in three varieties: the first has a close CC below the wreath, the second has a close CC within the wreath, and the third has a wide CC within the wreath, the latter two very scarce." Years ago the varieties within the wreath cataloged for less than those below the wreath. Today they are about the same.

For an in-depth study see Gerry Fortin, "An Analysis of Dies for 1875-CC Dimes," *The Gobrecht Journal,* November 2010.

Availability in circulated grades: Circulated 1875-CC dimes with the mintmark above the bow are common in circulated grades.

Availability in Mint State: Mint State examples are common—not as plentiful as certain Philadelphia Mint issues of the late 1880s, but very plentiful in the context of the Carson City series. The finest known

n MS-67 from the Battle Born Collection. *MS-60 to 62: 250 to 325 estimated to exist; MS-63: 160 to
); MS-64: 120 to 150; MS-65 or better: 90 to 120.*

	Cert	Avg	%MS	G-4	F-12	VF-20	EF-40	AU-50	MS-60	MS-63	MS-64	MS-65
5-CC, Mintmark Above Bow	160	51.7	54%	$45	$75	$100	$130	$200	$400	$1,100	$1,600	$3,500

75-CC, Mintmark Below Bow •

rculation-Strike Mintage: Part of a total
ntage of 4,645,000 for the issue.

mmentary: These are sometimes seen
ak at the head of Liberty and on the upper
t of the reverse wreath.

Probably the variety with mintmark below
bow was the second struck. The edge reeding
this is closely spaced as us standard for the era,
like on the Carson City Mint dimes earlier in this decade.
signated Fortin-101 to 104, the mintage was produce
ng three obverse dies and four reverse dies.

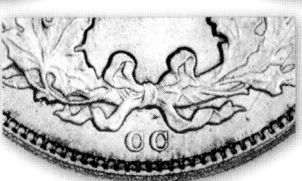

**Detail of the
Mintmark Below Bow.**

ailability in circulated grades: These are scarce in circu-
ed grades.

ailability in Mint State: The 1875-CC, Mintmark Below
w represents the second major variety of this year. It is estimated that of the total Carson City pro-
ction of 4,645,000, fewer than 15 percent were of this variety, making it scarce in comparison to the
le with mintmark within the wreath. However, enough exist across various grades that finding a choice
ample will not be difficult. Even in Mint State they cross the auction block with some frequency.
S-60 to 62: 30 to 40 estimated to exist; MS-63: 20 to 25; MS-64: 25 to 20; MS-65 or better: 12 to 16.

	Cert	Avg	%MS	G-4	F-12	VF-20	EF-40	AU-50	MS-60	MS-63	MS-64	MS-65
75-CC, Mintmark Below Bow	67	54.3	64%	$80	$150	$200	$275	$400	$575	$1,500	$1,950	$4,500

875-S Liberty Seated Dime

875-S, Mintmark Below Bow •

rculation-Strike Mintage: Part of a total
intage of 9,070,000 for the issue.

ommentary: Like so many Liberty Seated
mes, the 1875-S is sometimes seen weakly
ruck on Liberty's head and the upper left
art of the wreath on the reverse. The variety

ith the mintmark placed below the bow is commonly seen struck from fresh obverse dies paired with
eak or eroded reverse dies.[55] Sharp strikes exist but are rare.

Gerry Fortin gives separate numbers to Micro S and Small S varieties:

- Micro S—Fortin-101 to 104 (produced with 3 obverse dies and 4 reverse dies)
- Small S—Fortin-101 to 122 (produced with 18 obverse dies and 20 reverse dies)

vailability in circulated grades: In circulated condition, the 1875-S, Mintmark Below Bow is common.

Availability in Mint State: The variety is somewhat scarcer than expected given the large mintage. *MS-60 to 62: 225 to 275 estimated to exist; MS-63: 130 to 160; MS-64: 50 to 70; MS-65 or better: 8 to 12.*

	Cert	Avg	%MS	G-4	F-12	VF-20	EF-40	AU-50	MS-60	MS-63	MS-64	MS-65
1875-S, Mintmark Below Bow	72	57.0	69%	$15	$20	$25	$40	$95	$175	$285	$475	$1,200

1875-S, Mintmark Above Bow •

Circulation-Strike Mintage: Part of a total mintage of 9,070,000 for the issue.

Commentary: These, too, are often seen lightly struck on the head and on the upper left of the wreath on the reverse, often due to the use of cracked or eroded dies. They bear the so-called "Medium S" mintmark. Designated Fortin-101 to 106, the mintage was struck by two obverse dies and five reverse dies—an unusual ratio.

Availability in circulated grades: The 1875-S with the mintmark above the bow is scarce in circulated grades.

Availability in Mint State: The Mintmark Above Bow variety is rare in Mint State. *MS-60 to 62: 25 to 32 estimated to exist; MS-63: 12 to 15; MS-64: 5 to 7; MS-65 or better: 2 to 4.*[56]

	Cert	Avg	%MS	G-4	F-12	VF-20	EF-40	AU-50	MS-60	MS-63	MS-64	MS-65
1875-S, Mintmark Above Bow				$15	$20	$25	$35	$85	$160	$275	$500	$1,400

1876 Liberty Seated Dime

1876 • **Circulation-Strike Mintage:** 11,460,000.

Commentary: Liberty Seated dimes have two reverse variants (known as types). The Type I reverse, generally used from 1860 through 1877, has two points at the left ribbon end. The newer, Type II reverse, used from 1876 through 1891, has one point on the ribbon end. Both Type I *and* Type II are known for certain issues of 1876 and 1877.

Gerry Fortin gives separate numbers to the two reverse styles:

- Type I Reverse—Fortin-101 to 122 (struck with 22 obverse dies and 21 reverse dies)
- Type II Reverse—Fortin-101 to 105 (struck with 5 obverse and 5 reverse dies in sequence)

Availability in circulated grades: This issue is plentiful in any and all grades.

Availability in Mint State: The 1876 Philadelphia dime is common in Mint State. *MS-60 to 62: 250 to 325 estimated to exist; MS-63: 130 to 160; MS-64: 90 to 120; MS-65 or better: 50 to 70.*

	Cert	Avg	%MS	G-4	F-12	VF-20	EF-40	AU-50	MS-60	MS-63	MS-64	MS-65
1876	353	60.6	84%	$15	$20	$25	$35	$80	$150	$250	$400	$800

1876, Proof • **Proof Mintage:** 1,250.

Commentary: Proof 1876 dimes (Fortin-101 to 103) have the Type I reverse. The large mintage does not translate to the number of coins known today. Many were spent or carelessly handled, perhaps by non-numismatists who bought Proof sets during the centennial year. *PF-60 to 62: 250 to 400 estimated to exist; PF-63: 140 to 170; PF-64: 80 to 110; PF-65 or better: 40 to 50.*

	Cert	Avg	%MS	PF-60	PF-63	PF-65
1876, Proof	161	63.6		$300	$600	$1,000

1876-CC Liberty Seated Dime

1876-CC • **Circulation-Strike Mintage:** 8,270,000.

Commentary: Carson City dimes of 1876 are usually seen well struck. A few—perhaps branch-mint Proofs or presentation strikes—are highly prooflike.[57] Many were struck from corroded or pitted dies, resulting in microscopic bumps on the surface.[58]

The 1876-CC exists with Type I and Type II reverses (see the previous listing), with the Type II being rare. Rare it may be, but dedicated numismatists seeking examples are also few in number, so they can be cherrypicked at the regular price.

Gerry Fortin gives separate numbers to the two reverse styles:

- Type I Reverse—Fortin-101 to 135 (struck using 27 obverse dies and 26 reverse dies)
- Type II Reverse—Fortin-101

Availability in circulated grades: Circulated examples are common, but with the Type II reverse the 1876-CC is very rare and worth much more if sold with proper attribution.

Availability in Mint State: The issue is common in Mint State, although the Type II reverse is very rare within the date. *MS-60 to 62: 200 to 275 estimated to exist; MS-63: 120 to 150; MS-64: 80 to 110; MS-65 or better: 35 to 50.*

	Cert	Avg	%MS	G-4	F-12	VF-20	EF-40	AU-50	MS-60	MS-63	MS-64	MS-65
1876-CC	437	50.7	58%	$30	$50	$65	$85	$125	$350	$675	$1,650	$2,500

VARIETY: *1876-CC, Doubled Die Obverse (FS-10-1876CC-101, 102, 103).* Greer-101A. Fivaz-Stanton list several varieties of doubled obverse dies, with the doubling visible on the peripheral letters and a few other features. Nearly all are struck from heavily oxidized dies, giving the pieces a very granular or porous appearance. The two C's in the reverse mintmark can be level, or the right C can be low or high. A few have a rotated reverse. See next page for images of both the doubling and the different locations of the C.

Doubling on lower folds of gown and lower portion of rock.

Strong spread visible on OF AMERICA.

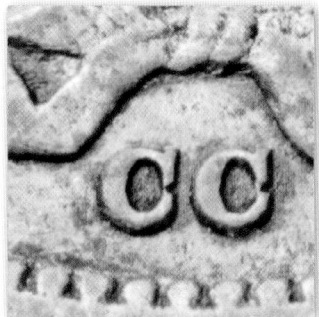

FS-101, with level letters in mintmark.

FS-102, Right C High.

FS-103, Right C Low (rarest).

1876-S Liberty Seated Dime

1876-S • Circulation-Strike Mintage: 10,420,000.

Commentary: The 1876-S (Fortin-101 to 121) is sometimes seen with weak striking at the head of Liberty and on the upper part of the reverse wreath, but is also found well struck. A few are highly prooflike (illustrated).

As with the Philadelphia and the Carson City issues of this date, the 1876-S exists with Type I and Type II reverses. The Type II is the scarcer of the two, but is not in the rarity league with the 1876-CC Type II. A number of date and mintmark varieties exist and are sought by specialists.

Gerry Fortin gives separate numbers to the two reverse styles:

- Type I Reverse—Fortin-101 to 121 (produced with 21 obverse dies and 19 reverse dies)
- Type II Reverse—Fortin-101 to 105 (produced with 4 obverse dies and 3 reverse dies)

Availability in circulated grades: Circulated examples are very common.

Availability in Mint State: The issue is slightly scarce in Mint State grades. *MS-60 to 62: 100 to 130 estimated to exist; MS-63: 40 to 55; MS-64: 25 to 32; MS-65 or better: 15 to 20.*

	Cert	Avg	%MS	G-4	F-12	VF-20	EF-40	AU-50	MS-60	MS-63	MS-64	MS-65
1876-S	101	58.5	74%	$15	$20	$25	$35	$80	$150	$250	$450	$1,750

1877 • Circulation-Strike Mintage:

Part of a total circulation-strike mintage of 7,310,000 for the issue.

Commentary: Gerry Fortin gives separate numbers to the two reverse styles:

- Type I Reverse—Fortin-101 to 109 (produced with 9 obverse dies and 8 reverse dies)
- Type II Reverse—Fortin-101 to 115 (produced with 15 obverse dies and 14 reverse dies)

Availability in circulated grades: Circulated examples are very common.

Availability in Mint State: The 1877 dime is readily available in Mint State. *MS-60 to 62: 400 to 550 estimated to exist; MS-63: 200 to 250; MS-64: 120 to 150; MS-65 or better: 80 to 110.*

	Cert	Avg	%MS	G-4	F-12	VF-20	EF-40	AU-50	MS-60	MS-63	MS-64	MS-65
1877	161	61.0	84%	$15	$20	$25	$35	$80	$150	$250	$450	$850

1877, Proof • Proof Mintage: 510.

Commentary: All 1877 Proofs (Fortin-101) have the Type II reverse. *PF-60 to 62: 80 to 120 estimated to exist; PF-63: 120 to 150; PF-64: 90 to 120; PF-65 or better: 60 to 80.*

	Cert	Avg	%MS	PF-60	PF-63	PF-65
1877, Proof	124	63.9		$300	$600	$1,000

1877-CC Liberty Seated Dime

1877-CC, 7 Over 6 • Circulation-Strike

Mintage: Part of a total circulation-strike mintage of 7,310,000 for the issue.

Commentary: This overdate (Fortin-107 and 108) is *very subtle* and is apt to be overlooked except on the closest examination. This variety can be identified another way: the obverse shield stripes have a long diagonal die scratch through the vertical lines.[59] The second 7 has tiny traces of an earlier 6 in the wide top of the digit. The first overdate was discovered by dealer Rick DeSanctis in Fort Myers, Florida. DeSanctis discovered the overdate in March 2010 while examining a group of previously purchased coins and sent the coin to Gerry Fortin. The find was announced by Paul Gilkes in *Coin World*, April 26, 2010.[60] Searches ensued, another die combination was found, and today the overdate is very collectible.

Detail of the Overdate.

The 1877-CC, 7 Over 6, dime was struck with the use of two obverse dies and two reverse dies. Many are known of each, mostly in circulated grades.

Availability in circulated grades: Extremely Fine and About Uncirculated examples are common. The overdate is not identifiable on well-worn coins.

Availability in Mint State: MS-60 to 62: 50 to 65 estimated to exist; MS-63: 20 to 25; MS-64: 12 to 15; MS-65 or better: 8 to 11.

	Cert	Avg	%MS	G-4	F-12	VF-20	EF-40	AU-50	MS-60	MS-63	MS-64	MS-65
1877-CC, 7 Over 6	0	n/a					$150	$225	$350	$750	$1,100	$2,500

1877-CC • Circulation-Strike Mintage: 7,700,000.

Commentary: Gerry Fortin gives separate numbers to the two reverse styles (also see earlier listing for 1877-CC, 7 Over 6):

- Type I Reverse: Fortin-101 to 110 (struck using 6 obverse dies and 9 reverse dies)
- Type II Reverse: Fortin-101 to 106 and 109 to 121 (13 obverse dies and 14 reverse dies)

Availability in circulated grades: Common in circulated condition, the 1877-CC is very popular—as are all Carson City dimes.

Availability in Mint State: Examples in Mint State are also common. Population data for Carson City issues are higher in proportion to the number known than is such information for high-mintage Philadelphia coins. *MS-60 to 62: 150 to 250 estimated to exist; MS-63: 110 to 130; MS-64: 80 to 100; MS-65 or better: 40 to 60.*

	Cert	Avg	%MS	G-4	F-12	VF-20	EF-40	AU-50	MS-60	MS-63	MS-64	MS-65
1877-CC	467	55.6	71%	$30	$50	$60	$80	$120	$300	$550	$1,100	$2,100

1877-S Liberty Seated Dime

1877-S • Circulation-Strike Mintage: 2,340,000.

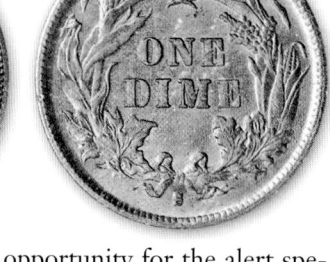

Commentary: Sometimes seen weak at the head of Liberty and the upper part of the reverse.

Examples seen by specialists are all of the "Type II" reverse, although Walter Breen reports that a "Type I" dime has been "reported untraced." Here is a searching opportunity for the alert specialist. Fortin-101 to 115. 10 obverse dies and 11 reverse dies.[61]

Availability in circulated grades: Circulated examples are common on an absolute basis (in proportion to the mintage), but slightly scarcer than certain other issues of the era.

Availability in Mint State: The 1877-S is easy enough to find in Mint State. *MS-60 to 62: 200 to 300 estimated to exist; MS-63: 100 to 130; MS-64: 60 to 80; MS-65 or better: 30 to 40.*

	Cert	Avg	%MS	G-4	F-12	VF-20	EF-40	AU-50	MS-60	MS-63	MS-64	MS-65
1877-S	94	61.4	84%	$15	$20	$25	$35	$80	$150	$300	$650	$1,500

1878 Liberty Seated Dime

1878 • **Circulation-Strike Mintage:** 1,677,200.

Commentary: The mintage dropped this year and would continue to do so, as a large glut of previously hoarded coins entered commerce, and the high mintages of recent years (the Treasury Department thought there would be a scarcity) contributed to a record supply.

This variety exists with Type I and Type II reverses, with most circulation strikes and all Proofs being the latter. Gerry Fortin gives separate numbers to the two reverse styles:

- Type I Reverse: Fortin-101 to 104 (produced by 4 obverse dies and 4 reverse dies in sequence)
- Type II Reverse: Fortin-101 to 110 (produced by 10 obverse dies and 9 reverse dies)

Availability in circulated grades: Circulated examples are common on an absolute basis, but scarcer within the context of the era.

Availability in Mint State: These are somewhat scarce at the Mint State level. *MS-60 to 62: 160 to 190 estimated to exist; MS-63: 90 to 120; MS-64: 50 to 70; MS-65 or better: 35 to 45.*

	Cert	Avg	%MS	G-4	F-12	VF-20	EF-40	AU-50	MS-60	MS-63	MS-64	MS-65
1878	92	61.7	87%	$15	$20	$25	$35	$80	$150	$250	$425	$900

1878, Proof • **Proof Mintage:** 800.

Commentary: All 1878 Proofs (Fortin-101) have the Type II reverse. *PF-60 to 62: 140 to 180 estimated to exist; PF-63: 175 to 210; PF-64: 120 to 150; PF-65 or better: 30 to 40.*

	Cert	Avg	%MS	PF-60	PF-63	PF-65
1878, Proof	165	63.9		$300	$600	$1,000

1878-CC Liberty Seated Dime

1878-CC • **Circulation-Strike Mintage:** 200,000.

Commentary: Carson City dimes of 1878 are usually seen well struck. Per Gerry Fortin, F-101 examples produced with the Type I reverse are seen well struck and often found prooflike. Examples with the Type II reverse were struck with relapped reverse dies, resulting in one to two grade differences between the obverse and reverse. Many Type II dimes will grade fully Fine on obverse and Good with partial mintmark on the reverse.

Heaton called this issue "somewhat scarce" when he wrote of it in 1893 in his treatise *Mint Marks*. Gerry Fortin combines numbers to the two reverse styles:

- Type I Reverse: Fortin-101
- Type II Reverse: Fortin-102 to 104 (1 obverse die and 3 reverse dies)

Availability in circulated grades: These are very scarce in circulated condition, and most are in very low grades. When found with the Type II reverse (see below) the coins have a very unsatisfactory appearance.[62]

Availability in Mint State: Scarce in Mint State, the 1878-CC is still more readily available than the low mintage indicates. Apparently, quite a few were saved. *MS-60 to 62: 50 to 65 estimated to exist; MS-63: 20 to 25; MS-64: 20 to 25; MS-65 or better: 15 to 20.*

	Cert	Avg	%MS	G-4	F-12	VF-20	EF-40	AU-50	MS-60	MS-63	MS-64	MS-65
1878-CC	75	49.8	61%	$150	$275	$400	$500	$725	$1,250	$2,400	$3,500	$5,000

1879 Liberty Seated Dime

1879 • Circulation-Strike Mintage: 14,000.

Commentary: The 1879 (Fortin-101 to 105) is one of the most famous dates among the Liberty Seated dimes, due to its low mintage (Proofs and circulation strikes combined). To an extent, 1880 and 1881 share the limelight for the same reasons.

For many years the 1879 has basked in the glow of publicity as a highly favored date, and this will undoubtedly continue, as there is nothing more magical than a low mintage figure to entice buyers. This is as it should be in this instance. Worn specimens are considerably rarer than either Mint State or Proof examples. Examples are sometimes seen lightly struck on the head of Liberty.

All dimes have Type II reverses from this year forward. The 1879 mintage was produced with five obverse dies and five reverse dies in sequence.

Availability in circulated grades: Very scarce in circulated condition, most 1879s are About Good to Very Fine. Mint State and Proof coins are easier to find for this and the next two years.

Availability in Mint State: At one time this issue was considered to be quite scarce, but certification-service data indicate that it is one of the most plentiful varieties of the era. A hoard of more than 200 of these was once owned by Tatham Stamp and Coin Company of Springfield, Massachusetts, and was bought by the author in the 1950s. These had been kept together since the year of issue. Beginning with the low-mintage silver dimes, quarters, and half dollars of 1879 there was a great numismatic awareness that they might someday become rare, and all from this time forward were saved in appreciable quantities in comparison to the production figures. *MS-60 to 62: 100 to 130 estimated to exist; MS-63: 100 to 130; MS-64: 225 to 350; MS-65 or better: 200 to 300.*

	Cert	Avg	%MS	G-4	F-12	VF-20	EF-40	AU-50	MS-60	MS-63	MS-64	MS-65
1879	207	62.8	92%	$200	$325	$400	$500	$550	$575	$650	$800	$1,100

1879, Proof • **Proof Mintage:** 1,100.

Commentary: Dies for Proofs (Fortin-101 to 104) were also used to make circulation strikes.

In March 1880, the following ad was placed in *Mason's Coin Collectors' Herald.* "1879 Halves, Quarters, and Dimes for sale. U.S. silver half dollars (Uncirculated) $1.10. U.S. silver quarter dollars (Uncirculated) 40 cents. U.S. silver dimes (Uncirculated) 25 cents. Complete set of three pieces, $1.60. Mason & Co. 143 N. Tenth St, Phila., Pa."

Then, in the June 1880 edition of the same paper, came this curious news: "Parties who have been busy the past six months in putting away the Proof sets of 1879, and the Uncirculated fifty, twenty-five and ten cent pieces of the same year, have had but little profit for their pains. Recently one of the corners broke, unexpectedly and Proof sets of 1879 were offered at $5.50, half dollars at 70 cents, quarter dollars at 35 cents, and dimes at 20 cents, while the former prices were respectively $7.00, $1.00, 50, and 30 cents. It is better to get a reasonable profit on scarce coins and sell rather than to be compelled to unload at an unprofitable season."

M.H. Bolender liquidated many coins from the Mason estate. His mail bid sales of May 22, and October 15, 1935, included 145 Proof dimes of 1879. *PF-60 to 62: 180 to 220 estimated to exist; PF-63: 200 to 275; PF-64: 200 to 275; PF-65 or better: 140 to 180.*

	Cert	Avg	%MS	PF-60	PF-63	PF-65
1879, Proof	304	64.2		$300	$600	$1,000

1880 Liberty Seated Dime

1880 • **Circulation-Strike Mintage:** 36,000.

Commentary: Coins in the 1880 issue (Fortin-101 to 103, produced with three obverse and two reverse dies) are sometimes lightly struck on the head of Liberty and the upper left part of the wreath on the reverse.

Availability in circulated grades: Very scarce, as the mintage indicates. Most show extensive wear.

Availability in Mint State: Readily available, as many (but far fewer than for 1879) were sold to collectors at the time of issue. MS-60 to 62: MS-60 to 62: 70 to 90 estimated to exist; MS-63: 90 to 120; MS-64: 120 to 160; MS-65 or better: 100 to 150.

	Cert	Avg	%MS	G-4	F-12	VF-20	EF-40	AU-50	MS-60	MS-63	MS-64	MS-65
1880	150	60.5	83%	$150	$250	$350	$400	$500	$650	$700	$800	$1,250

1880, Proof • **Proof Mintage:** 1,355.

Commentary: Proofs of 1880 are designated Fortin-101 and 102; these dies were also used to coin circulation strikes. The high mintage of this issue is explained by a penchant for coin investment which arose in 1879 and then suddenly faded. At the time, numerous numbers of the public were attracted by gold dollars, $3 pieces, dimes, quarters, half dollars, and trade dollars and sought to buy Proofs primarily. (By 1881, the sentiment had faded considerably.) From *Mason's Coin Collectors' Herald* (June 1880): "Trade dollars of this year are still in demand, in Proof condition, at $2. While Proof sets remain at Mint prices the half dollars, quarters and dimes of this year, for general circulation, have not yet been coined, and we shall probably have a repetition of the speculative excitement which attended the distribution of the halves, quarters and dimes of 1879, in the latter part of the present year."

From the pages of *Mason's Coin & Stamp Collector's Magazine:* (January 1881): "1880 halves, quarters, and dimes. We have the official statement from the Mint that all *bona fide* coin collectors can procure the subsidiary coins as above, by applying to the U. S. Mint this city. All those who fail to procure a set of the 1880 pieces can be supplied at $1.50 per set, postage paid, by writing to this office before the 15th inst. *G.W.M., Baltimore.* Although the report was current, when 1880 sets of halves, quarters and dimes were struck that '100 sets were to be given out and dies destroyed,' we learn that 1,000 sets have been struck at Mint."[63]

Dealer S.K. Harzfeld printed the following in his sale of January 24–25, 1881:

> Lot 1081a: 1880 Half Dollar, Quarter, Dime. Uncirculated: Bright. 3 pieces. The Superintendent of the U.S. Mint, Colonel A.L. Snowden, has authorized me to state that he will furnish on application, to every bona fide collector, two sets of these Uncirculated coins, at face value. As was done in 1879, speculators (not the legitimate coin dealers) tried to secure these coins and to sell them at fancy prices, claiming that only 100 sets were struck. Colonel Snowden, however, stopped at once the sale to these speculators, and had a sufficient number struck ($1,000 worth of each denomination) to supply all bona fide collectors. It is particularly just on my part, to state that Superintendent Snowden shows an earnest effort to suppress the abuses and acts of favoritism I complained of, and to assist the legitimate efforts of legitimate coin sellers. I regret that I cannot say the same of the director of the Mint. Notwithstanding all remonstrances, and the resolution passed by the Numismatic and Antiquarian Society of Philadelphia, the name of whose president—the venerable Eli K. Price—should alone be sufficient to secure respectful consideration on the part of a "public servant," at the hour of writing, the Director has ordered the 150 Goloid Metric Sets, still at the Mint, to be forwarded to Washington, "subject to the order of the Coinage Committee." In other words, we may again have to apply for those sets to some speculator, or some political bummer, or to people who are neither "the wives, the sisters, the cousins, nor the aunts of congressmen." There certainly seems to be room here for the operation of the advocates of Civil Service Reform.

Also see comment under the 1879 listing. *PF-60 to 62: 180 to 220 estimated to exist; PF-63: 200 to 275; PF-64: 200 to 275; PF-65 or better: 150 to 190.*

	Cert	Avg	%MS	PF-60	PF-63	PF-65
1880, Proof	318	64.5		$300	$600	$1,000

1881 Liberty Seated Dime

1881 • **Circulation-Strike Mintage:** 24,000.

Commentary: Some examples from 1881 (Fortin-101 to 103, produced by three obverse and two reverse dies) show lightness in strike at the head of Liberty and the corresponding part of the reverse.

Availability in circulated grades: Circulated coins are scarce, in proportion to the low mintage. Most are in lower grades.

Availability in Mint State: Coins at the Mint State level are somewhat elusive. By 1881 the investment interest in low-mintage pieces wasn't what it had been in 1879 or 1880. *MS-60 to 62: MS-60 to 62: 30 to 40 estimated to exist; MS-63: 60 to 80; MS-64: 50 to 70; MS-65 or better: 25 to 35.*

	Cert	Avg	%MS	G-4	F-12	VF-20	EF-40	AU-50	MS-60	MS-63	MS-64	MS-65
1881	91	55.1	69%	$160	$260	$375	$425	$525	$675	$775	$875	$1,300

1881, Proof • **Proof Mintage:** 975.

Commentary: Designated Fortin-101 to 103, the Proofs of 1881 were struck by three obverse dies and two reverse dies. The first two die pairs were used for circulation strikes as well; F-103 was used only for Proofs. John Dannreuther commented:

> The mintages for the Proofs are 675 and 460 for the first and fourth quarters, which are the F-101 and 102 varieties, used for Mint State and Proof issues, although we don't know which was used for these strikings. There were 50 coins struck in the second quarter, so Gerry [Fortin] and I believe that the F-103 is a Proof-only issue. I discovered this variety while working on my Proof book and neither of us could find a circulation strike. This adds up to 1,185 with 210 either melted, placed into circulation, or sold to dealers, so the net mintage is reported as 975. I doubt they melted these, of course, and the "friends of the Mint" likely obtained them out the back door![64]

PF-60 to 62: 180 to 220 estimated to exist; PF-63: 200 to 250; PF-64: 180 to 230; PF-65 or better: 120 to 130.

	Cert	Avg	%MS	PF-60	PF-63	PF-65
1881, Proof	253	64.6		$300	$600	$1,000

1882 Liberty Seated Dime

1882 • **Circulation-Strike Mintage:** 3,910,000.

Commentary: Philadelphia dimes of 1882 (Fortin-101 to 112) are sometimes lightly struck at the top of the obverse. The mintage was produced with 12 obverse and 12 reverse dies, used in sequence.

Beginning with this year, Philadelphia Mint Liberty Seated dimes are very common. They were saved in large quantities and today are readily available. The June 1882 *Mason's Coin Collectors' Herald* notes the following:

> Forewarned. Forearmed. The year 1882 is creeping on towards the end, and yet there are no U.S. silver half dollars, quarters, or dimes coined for general circulation this year, and it is not likely there will be, and but a few thousand struck off for collectors in December; hence, the reflective collector will perceive the necessity of keeping the matter in mind, else he will pay twice the intrinsic value of the coins in January 1883, when they can be had at par in December, 1882.

Availability in circulated grades: The issue is very common in all grades.

Availability in Mint State: Examples in Mint State are very common. *MS-60 to 62: 1,200 to 1,500 estimated to exist; MS-63: 650 to 800; MS-64: 400 to 550; MS-65 or better: 250 to 325.*

	Cert	Avg	%MS	G-4	F-12	VF-20	EF-40	AU-50	MS-60	MS-63	MS-64	MS-65
1882	390	62.7	92%	$15	$20	$25	$35	$80	$150	$250	$400	$650

1882, Proof • Proof Mintage: 1,100.

Commentary: Some Proofs (Fortin-101) remained unsold by January 1883 and were probably turned over to dealers. *PF-60 to 62: 150 to 200 estimated to exist; PF-63: 230 to 270; PF-64: 190 to 230; PF-65 or better: 180 to 220.*

	Cert	Avg	%MS	PF-60	PF-63	PF-65
1882, Proof	348	64.6		$300	$600	$1,000

1883 Liberty Seated Dime

1883 • Circulation-Strike Mintage: 7,674,673.

Commentary: The more than 7.5 million dimes of 1883 were produced with 21 obverse and 21 reverse dies, used in sequence, and are designated Fortin-101 to 121. They are sometimes seen lightly struck in the upper part of the obverse.

Availability in circulated grades: The issue is very common in all grades, including circulated grades.

Availability in Mint State: Brian Greer considered this to be among the six most common dimes in Mint State. *MS-60 to 62: 1,600 to 2,000 estimated to exist; MS-63: 900 to 1,200; MS-64: 550 to 700; MS-65 or better: 350 to 500.*

	Cert	Avg	%MS	G-4	F-12	VF-20	EF-40	AU-50	MS-60	MS-63	MS-64	MS-65
1883	494	61.2	86%	$15	$20	$25	$35	$80	$150	$250	$400	$650

1883, Proof • Proof Mintage: 1,039.

Commentary: Many Proofs (Fortin-103 and 119) were unsold and were later spent or wholesaled to dealers. *PF-60 to 62: 150 to 200 estimated to exist; PF-63: 225 to 260; PF-64: 180 to 220; PF-65 or better: 150 to 190.*

	Cert	Avg	%MS	PF-60	PF-63	PF-65
1883, Proof	304	64.4		$300	$600	$1,000

1884 Liberty Seated Dime

1884 • **Circulation-Strike Mintage:** 3,365,505.

Commentary: Liberty's head is usually weakly struck on the 1884 dime (Fortin-101 to 111, struck with 11 obverse dies and 10 reverse dies).

Availability in circulated grades: Examples are very common in all grades.

Availability in Mint State: Very common. *MS-60 to 62: 1,200 to 1,500 estimated to exist; MS-63: 650 to 800; MS-64: 350 to 500; MS-65 or better: 200 to 250.*

	Cert	Avg	%MS	G-4	F-12	VF-20	EF-40	AU-50	MS-60	MS-63	MS-64	MS-65
1884	394	62.8	90%	$15	$20	$25	$35	$80	$150	$250	$400	$650

1884, Proof • **Proof Mintage:** 875.

Commentary: Proofs are designated Fortin-101. *PF-60 to 62: 140 to 190 estimated to exist; PF-63: 210 to 250; PF-64: 180 to 220; PF-65 or better: 165 to 195.*

	Cert	Avg	%MS	PF-60	PF-63	PF-65
1884, Proof	312	64.9		$300	$600	$1,000

1884-S Liberty Seated Dime

1884-S • **Circulation-Strike Mintage:** 564,969.

Commentary: This issue (Fortin-101 to 105) is usually well struck but occasionally seen weak at the characteristic points—namely, the top of the head of Liberty and at the top of the reverse. Three obverse dies and three reverse dies, in various combinations, produced the mintage.

The 1884-S has a small S mintmark. This is the first branch-mint dime since 1878, and the first San Francisco Mint dime since 1877. In comparison to the Philadelphia version of the same year, the 1884-S is elusive in all grades.

Availability in circulated grades: In circulated condition, are scarce in proportion to the mintage, and most are extensively worn.

Availability in Mint State: Examples in Mint condition are rare. Most were placed into circulation at the time of issue, during an era in which numismatists were uninterested in mintmarks. *MS-60 to 62: 35 to 45 estimated to exist; MS-63: 15 to 20; MS-64: 12 to 15; MS-65 or better: 3 or 4.*[65]

	Cert	Avg	%MS	G-4	F-12	VF-20	EF-40	AU-50	MS-60	MS-63	MS-64	MS-65
1884-S	61	59.3	72%	$20	$32	$60	$100	$300	$750	$1,100	$1,500	$5,000

1885 Liberty Seated Dime

1885 • **Circulation-Strike Mintage:** 2,532,497.

Commentary: Designated Fortin-101 to 111, the issue was struck with 11 obverse dies and 11 reverse dies in sequence.

Availability in circulated grades: Circulated examples are very common.

Availability in Mint State: The 1885 is common in Mint State. *MS-60 to 62: MS-60 to 62: 1,200 to 1,500 estimated to exist; MS-63: 650 to 800; MS-64: 350 to 500; MS-65 or better: 200 to 250.*

	Cert	Avg	%MS	G-4	F-12	VF-20	EF-40	AU-50	MS-60	MS-63	MS-64	MS-65
1885	359	62.6	91%	$15	$20	$25	$35	$80	$150	$250	$400	$650

1885, Proof • **Proof Mintage:** 930.

Commentary: Proofs are designated Fortin-101. *PF-60 to 62: 140 to 190 estimated to exist; PF-63: 220 to 260; PF-64: 180 to 220; PF-65 or better: 165 to 195.*

	Cert	Avg	%MS	PF-60	PF-63	PF-65
1885, Proof	292	64.8		$300	$600	$1,000

1885-S Liberty Seated Dime

1885-S • **Circulation-Strike Mintage:** 43,690.

Commentary: Augustus G. Heaton stated, "The smallest issue of the whole series makes that piece very rare." At the time, he noted the rarity among San Francisco Liberty Seated dimes in order of descending importance: 1885-S, 1870-S, 1858-S, 1859-S,

and 1856-S. After that, 1866-S, 1860-S, 1867-S, and 1863-S were considered "rather scarce." The 1885-S (Fortin-101) was struck from only one die pair.

Availability in circulated grades: This is a key issue in any grade, and is rare in circulated condition. Lower-grade coins up to F-12 will usually have a reverse that is a full grade less than the obverse.[66] Circulated coins are notorious for having rough surfaces, the cause of which is unknown.[67]

Availability in Mint State: MS-60 to 62: 6 to 9 estimated to exist; MS-63: 1 or 2; MS-64: 1 or 2; MS-65 or better: 1 or 2.[68]

	Cert	Avg	%MS	G-4	F-12	VF-20	EF-40	AU-50	MS-60	MS-63	MS-64	MS-65
1885-S	58	32.5	24%	$450	$850	$1,400	$2,200	$4,000	$5,500	$8,500	$15,000	$27,500

1886 Liberty Seated Dime

1886 • **Circulation-Strike Mintage:** 6,376,684.

Commentary: The Philadelphia dime of 1886 (Fortin-101 to 119) was produced with 19 obverse dies and 19 reverse dies in sequence.

Availability in circulated grades: The issue is very common in all grades.

Availability in Mint State: Brian Greer considered this to be among the six most common dimes in Mint State. *MS-60 to 62: 1,200 to 1,500 estimated to exist; MS-63: 650 to 800; MS-64: 350 to 500; MS-65 or better: 200 to 335.*

	Cert	Avg	%MS	G-4	F-12	VF-20	EF-40	AU-50	MS-60	MS-63	MS-64	MS-65
1886	611	61.9	87%	$15	$20	$25	$35	$80	$150	$250	$400	$650

1886, Proof • **Proof Mintage:** 886.

Commentary: Many Proofs (Fortin-103 and 104) are poorly struck. *PF-60 to 62: 140 to 190 estimated to exist; PF-63: 210 to 250; PF-64: 140 to 180; PF-65 or better: 130 to 145.*

	Cert	Avg	%MS	PF-60	PF-63	PF-65
1886, Proof	286	64.5		$300	$600	$1,000

1886-S Liberty Seated Dime

1886-S • **Circulation-Strike Mintage:** 206,524.

Commentary: The top of the obverse on the 1886-S (Fortin-101 and 102) is often seen lightly struck. The mintage was struck with two obverse dies and two reverse dies; the F-102 die pairing is many times rarer than F-101.

Availability in circulated grades: Examples in circulated condition are scarce, but enough exist that the specialist will not go unsatisfied for very long. Most are in lower grades.

Availability in Mint State: This issue is elusive in Mint State, although traditionally it has not been considered a key issue. *MS-60 to 62: 45 to 65 estimated to exist; MS-63: 30 to 40; MS-64: 20 to 25; MS-65 or better: 20 to 25.*

	Cert	Avg	%MS	G-4	F-12	VF-20	EF-40	AU-50	MS-60	MS-63	MS-64	MS-65
1886-S	54	57.2	74%	$30	$50	$75	$135	$200	$600	$1,000	$2,000	$3,500

1887 Liberty Seated Dime

1887 • **Circulation-Strike Mintage:** 11,283,229.

Commentary: The 1887 issue (Fortin-101 to 117) is sometimes seen lightly struck at the top of the obverse and the upper left of the reverse. Seventeen obverse dies and 17 reverse dies, in sequence, produced the mintage; the pieces were struck at high speed, with little attention as to quality.

Availability in circulated grades: The 1887 is very common in all grades.

Availability in Mint State: Brian Greer considered this to be among the six most common dimes in Mint State. *MS-60 to 62: 1,200 to 1,500 estimated to exist; MS-63: 650 to 800; MS-64: 375 to 500; MS-65 or better: 150 to 200.*

	Cert	Avg	%MS	G-4	F-12	VF-20	EF-40	AU-50	MS-60	MS-63	MS-64	MS-65
1887	588	60.3	83%	$15	$20	$25	$35	$80	$150	$250	$400	$650

1887, Proof • Proof Mintage: 710.

Commentary: Proofs are designated Fortin-101 and 117. *PF-60 to 62: 130 to 180 estimated to exist; PF-63: 200 to 230; PF-64: 120 to 160; PF-65 or better: 75 to 85.*

	Cert	Avg	%MS	PF-60	PF-63	PF-65
1887, Proof	213	64.5		$300	$600	$1,000

1887-S Liberty Seated Dime

1887-S • **Circulation-Strike Mintage:** 4,454,450.

Commentary: Examples of this issue (Fortin-101 to 121) are often lightly struck at the high part of the obverse and the upper left of the wreath on the reverse. It was produced with 19 obverse dies and 18 reverse dies.

Availability in circulated grades: Circulated examples are common.

Availability in Mint State: The issue is likewise common in Mint State. *MS-60 to 62: 200 to 260 estimated to exist; MS-63: 120 to 140; MS-64: 80 to 100; MS-65 or better: 50 to 65.*

	Cert	Avg	%MS	G-4	F-12	VF-20	EF-40	AU-50	MS-60	MS-63	MS-64	MS-65
1887-S	270	59.2	78%	$15	$20	$25	$35	$80	$150	$300	$450	$1,000

1888 Liberty Seated Dime

1888 • **Circulation-Strike Mintage:** 5,495,655.

Commentary: Designated Fortin-101 to 121, the 1888 is often lightly struck at the top of the obverse and corresponding part of the reverse. The mintage was struck by 21 obverse dies and 19 reverse dies.

Availability in circulated grades: These are very common in all grades.

Availability in Mint State: Mint State examples are very common. *MS-60 to 62: 1,200 to 1,500 estimated to exist; MS-63: 650 to 800; MS-64: 350 to 500; MS-65 or better: 200 to 250.*

	Cert	Avg	%MS	G-4	F-12	VF-20	EF-40	AU-50	MS-60	MS-63	MS-64	MS-65
1888	329	60.6	84%	$15	$20	$25	$35	$80	$150	$250	$400	$650

1888 • **Proof Mintage:** 832.

Commentary: Fortin-101 to 103. *PF-60 to 62: 130 to 180 estimated to exist; PF-63: 200 to 230; PF-64: 130 to 170; PF-65 or better: 85 to 105.*

	Cert	Avg	%MS	PF-60	PF-63	PF-65
1888, Proof	211	64.4		$300	$600	$1,000

1888-S Liberty Seated Dime

1888-S • **Circulation-Strike Mintage:** 1,720,000.

Availability in circulated grades: Slightly scarce.

Availability in Mint State: Very scarce in Mint State, although this issue is not usually recognized as such, due to the overall mintage. MS-60 to 62: 50 to 65 estimated to exist; MS-63: 30 to 40; MS-64: 30 to 40; MS-65 or better: 20 to 25.

Commentary: Like dimes from other years and mints, the 1888-S (Fortin-101 to 112; nine obverse and nine reverse dies in various combinations[69]) is often seen with light striking on the high part of the obverse and the corresponding part of the reverse.

The *Report of the Director of the Mint*, 1888, told why the San Francisco Mint struck dimes and quarters during the period indicated:

> Precedence having been given at the mint at Philadelphia to the mandatory coinage of silver dollars, that institution was unable to meet the demand for dimes. The mint at San Francisco was therefore called upon to execute a coinage in dimes, of which $395,284.80 was coined. It was also found that the

stock of quarter dollars held by the sub-treasury at San Francisco was likely to be soon absorbed. The same mint therefore coined during the fiscal year from trade-dollar bullion on hand $192,000 in this denomination of subsidiary coin. This coinage was increased to $250,000 in August 1888.

	Cert	Avg	%MS	G-4	F-12	VF-20	EF-40	AU-50	MS-60	MS-63	MS-64	MS-65
1888-S	71	56.9	63%	$15	$20	$25	$35	$100	$250	$850	$1,150	$3,000

1889 Liberty Seated Dime

1889 • **Circulation-Strike Mintage:** 7,380,000.

Commentary: Examples of the 1889 issue (Fortin-101 to 129) are often lightly struck on the top of the obverse. Twenty-eight obverse dies and 29 reverse dies were used to produce the mintage.

Availability in circulated grades: These are very common in all grades.

Availability in Mint State: The 1889 is very common Mint State. *MS-60 to 62: 1,200 to 1,500 estimated to exist; MS-63: 650 to 800; MS-64: 350 to 500; MS-65 or better: 200 to 250.*

	Cert	Avg	%MS	G-4	F-12	VF-20	EF-40	AU-50	MS-60	MS-63	MS-64	MS-65
1889	365	61.1	85%	$15	$20	$25	$35	$80	$150	$250	$400	$650

1889, Proof • **Proof Mintage:** 711.

Commentary: Proofs are designated Fortin-101 and 102. *PF-60 to 62: 130 to 180 estimated to exist; PF-63: 145 to 190; PF-64: 140 to 180; PF-65 or better: 105 to 130.*

	Cert	Avg	%MS	PF-60	PF-63	PF-65
1889, Proof	176	64.6		$300	$600	$1,000

1889-S Liberty Seated Dime

1889-S • **Circulation-Strike Mintage:** 972,678.

Commentary: Weakness on Liberty's head is the rule for the 1889-S (Fortin-101 to 110), which was produced in Small S (more readily available) and Medium S varieties using seven obverse and seven reverse dies in various combinations.

Availability in circulated grades: Circulated examples are somewhat scarce, but enough exist that specialists can easily find one.

Availability in Mint State: The issue is rare in Mint State. *MS-60 to 62: 40 to 55 estimated to exist; MS-63: 20 to 25; MS-64: 6 to 9; MS-65 or better: 5 to 7.*[70]

	Cert	Avg	%MS	G-4	F-12	VF-20	EF-40	AU-50	MS-60	MS-63	MS-64	MS-65
1889-S	83	60.0	64%	$20	$30	$50	$80	$150	$450	$1,000	$1,250	$3,250

1890 Liberty Seated Dime

1890 • Circulation-Strike Mintage: 9,910,951.

Commentary: Twenty-two obverse dies and 22 reverse dies in sequence produced the 9.9 million 1890 dimes (Fortin-101 to 122).

Availability in circulated grades: These are very common in all grades.

Availability in Mint State: Brian Greer considered this to be among the six most common dimes in Mint State. *MS-60 to 62: 1,400 to 1,700 estimated to exist; MS-63: 800 to 1,100; MS-64: 425 to 575; MS-65 or better: 250 to 325.*

	Cert	Avg	%MS	G-4	F-12	VF-20	EF-40	AU-50	MS-60	MS-63	MS-64	MS-65
1890	581	60.9	84%	$15	$20	$25	$35	$80	$150	$250	$400	$750

VARIETY: *1890, Misplaced Date (FS-10-1890-302).* Fortin-106. The tops of several date numerals are seen in the lower part of Liberty's gown. Discovered by Chris Pilliod.

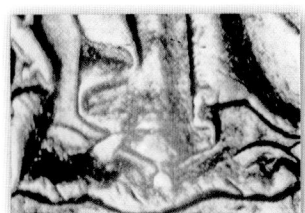

1890, Proof • Proof Mintage: 590.

Commentary: Proof dies (Fortin-101 to 104) were also used to coin circulation strikes. *PF-60 to 62: 130 to 180 estimated to exist; PF-63: 150 to 200; PF-64: 150 to 190; PF-65 or better: 105 to 130.*

	Cert	Avg	%MS	PF-60	PF-63	PF-65
1890, Proof	208	64.4		$300	$600	$1,000

1890-S Liberty Seated Dime

1890-S • Circulation-Strike Mintage: 1,423,076.

Commentary: Thirteen obverse dies and 14 reverse dies produced the mintage of 1890-S (Fortin-101 to 119), which appears in both Small S and Medium S (also called "Large S") varieties. They are sometimes seen lightly struck on the head of Liberty.

Availability in circulated grades: Circulated 1890-S dimes are slightly scarce, despite the high mintage.[71]

Availability in Mint State: In Mint State, examples are scarce but available. *MS-60 to 62: 60 to 80 estimated to exist; MS-63: 30 to 40; MS-64: 20 to 25; MS-65 or better: 16 to 20.*

	Cert	Avg	%MS	G-4	F-12	VF-20	EF-40	AU-50	MS-60	MS-63	MS-64	MS-65
1890-S	116	58.7	77%	$18	$25	$55	$85	$150	$350	$700	$1,000	$1,500

1891 Liberty Seated Dime

1891 • Circulation-Strike Mintage: 15,310,000.

Commentary: Examples of the 1891 (Fortin-101 to 135) are frequently seen with weakness at the top of the obverse and the corresponding part of the reverse.

In July 1891, the *American Journal of Numismatics* had this to say:

> The demand for dimes continues unabated, and most of the recoinage for the present at the U.S. Mint in Philadelphia, will be of that denomination. The coinage of dimes during the last three years has been $3,156,476, or 31,564,762 pieces, the principal part of which was executed at Philadelphia, taxing that mint, with its cramped space, to its utmost capacity. It is proposed to distribute this recoinage between the mints at San Francisco, Philadelphia, and New Orleans.

The mintage was struck with the use of 35 obverse dies and 35 reverse dies in sequence—the longest such run of pairs in the series.

Availability in circulated grades: Circulated examples are extremely common.

Availability in Mint State: Apparently, these are the most common of all Mint State Liberty Seated dimes. *MS-60 to 62: 2,500 to 3,250 estimated to exist; MS-63: 1,200 to 1,500; MS-64: 800 to 1,100; MS-65 or better: 500 to 700.*

	Cert	Avg	%MS	G-4	F-12	VF-20	EF-40	AU-50	MS-60	MS-63	MS-64	MS-65
1891	1,013	61.5	85%	$15	$20	$25	$35	$80	$150	$250	$400	$650

1891, Proof • Proof Mintage: 600.

Commentary: Proofs are designated Fortin-101, 130, and 131. *PF-60 to 62: 120 to 160 estimated to exist; PF-63: 150 to 200; PF-64: 160 to 200; PF-65 or better: 115 to 140.*

	Cert	Avg	%MS	PF-60	PF-63	PF-65
1891, Proof	222	64.8		$300	$600	$1,000

1891-O Liberty Seated Dime

1891-O • **Circulation-Strike Mintage:** Part of a total mintage of 4,540,000 for the issue.

Commentary: Most are well struck with many exhibiting heavy die clashing. The 1891-O date (Fortin-101 to 132) is a playground for shattered dies and die cuds. Excessive striking pressure for a smaller denomination may have been the cause of rapid die failure. Twenty-nine obverse dies and 31 reverse dies were needed to produce the mintage.

The 1891-O dime is desirable as the only New Orleans Mint issue of this denomination after 1860-O, and one of just two of this design type. Enough were preserved that there will be no difficulty in obtaining a specimen in just about any grade desired.

Availability in circulated grades: Circulated examples are common.

Availability in Mint State: The issue is likewise common in Mint State. MS-60 to 62: 160 to 200 estimated to exist; MS-63: 100 to 125; MS-64: 70 to 90; MS-65 or better: 50 to 60.

	Cert	Avg	%MS	G-4	F-12	VF-20	EF-40	AU-50	MS-60	MS-63	MS-64	MS-65
1891-O	226	58.1	80%	$15	$20	$30	$50	$100	$175	$350	$550	$1,500

1891-O, O Over Horizontal O •

Circulation-Strike Mintage: Part of a total mintage of 4,540,000 for the issue.

Commentary: Traces of the earlier O are readily visible at the center. *Cherrypickers' Guide to Rare Die Varieties* lists this as FS-10-1891o-501 (005.6). This is a rare variety.

Detail of the O Over Horizontal O.

	Cert	Avg	%MS	G-4	F-12	VF-20	EF-40	AU-50	MS-60
1891-O, O Over Horizontal O	2	51.5	0%	$60	$120	$150	$225	$1,000	$3,000

1891-S Liberty Seated Dime

1891-S • **Circulation-Strike Mintage:** 3,196,116.

Commentary: The last dime of the Liberty Seated series, the 1891-S (Fortin-101 to 119) is often seen lightly struck on Liberty's head. Both Small S and Medium S varieties exist. The mintage was produced with 12 obverse dies and 14 reverse dies.

Availability in circulated grades: This year-mintmark combination is common in circulated grades.

Availability in Mint State: The 1891-S is very common in Mint State—indeed, it may be the commonest of all Liberty Seated dimes. *MS-60 to 62: 140 to 180 estimated to exist; MS-63: 90 to 120; MS-64: 70 to 90; MS-65 or better: 50 to 60.*

	Cert	Avg	%MS	G-4	F-12	VF-20	EF-40	AU-50	MS-60	MS-63	MS-64	MS-65
1891-S	173	61.6	86%	$15	$20	$25	$35	$80	$175	$300	$450	$850

1891-S, Medium S Over Small S •

Circulation-Strike Mintage: Part of a total mintage of 3,196,116 for the issue.

Commentary: The under-mintmark on this variety is sharp and clear. *Cherrypickers' Guide to Rare Die Varieties* lists this as FS-10-1891s-501 (007).

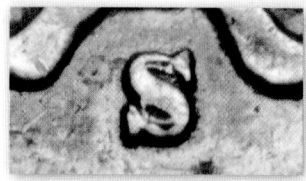

**Detail of the
Medium S Over Small S.**

	Cert	Avg	%MS	G-4	F-12	VF-20	EF-40	AU-50	MS-60
1891S, Medium S Over Small S	4	61.5	75%	$20	$45	$55	$85	$115	$300

BARBER OR LIBERTY HEAD DIMES (1892–1916): HISTORY AND BACKGROUND

Designer: *Charles E. Barber.* **Weight:** *2.50 grams.* **Composition:** *.900 silver, .100 copper (net weight: .07234 oz. pure silver).* **Diameter:** *17.9 mm.* **Edge:** *Reeded.*
Mints: *Philadelphia, Denver, New Orleans, and San Francisco.*

Circulation Strike

Mintmark location is on the reverse, below the bow.

Proof

THE NEW DESIGN

By the late 1890s the Liberty Seated dime, quarter, and half dollar had been a familiar sight for multiple generations. It was time for a change. In *The Annual Report of the Director of the Mint* for 1887, James P. Kimball endorsed the making of new designs. In October 1889 Edward O. Leech became Mint director, succeeding Kimball. Leech invited 10 leading artists to redesign the silver dime, quarter, and half dollar.[72]

Charles E. Barber.

Traditionally, new coinage motifs had originated with the artists and engravers in Philadelphia, not from artists in the private sector. The artists who received the invitation discussed the matter among themselves and then wrote to Leech to state that they would do this only if $100 would be paid for each sketch submitted and $500 for each accepted design. Otherwise a lot of time and effort would be wasted, as only a few designs were to be chosen from the many desired to be submitted.

In the end, the response from the artistic community was not enthusiastic. Submissions came mainly from amateurs, and there is no mention of any from a skilled coin or medal engraver. The designs were reviewed by Henry Mitchell and Augustus Saint-Gaudens, artists in the private sector with the last being especially prominent, and by Charles E. Barber, chief engraver at the Mint. Their report to Leech on June 3:

> Dear Sir:
>
> We would respectfully report that in conformity with your written request we have opened in the presence of the director of the Mint the new designs or models submitted for the silver coins of the United States, under Department circular of April 4, 1891, and have carefully examined the same.
>
> We are of the opinion that none of the designs or models submitted are such a decided improvement upon the present designs of the silver coins of the United States as to be worthy of adoption by the government.
>
> We would respectfully recommend that the services of one or more artists distinguished for work in designing for relief be engaged at a suitable compensation to prepare for the consideration of the Department new designs for the coins of the United States

In July 1891 Director Leech, having accomplished nothing with artists in the private sector, tapped chief engraver Charles E. Barber to prepare coinage designs. The engraver then set about the task, sometimes getting off topic, such as creating a reverse inspired by the Una and the Lion reverse on the 1839 British £5 gold coin, it was said. Barber had a mind of his own and had a higher opinion of his talent than did others in the community of artists. The New York City contingent in particular thought his work on medals was subpar, and it is said that Saint-Gaudens called his art "wretched." However, Barber was indeed in charge of finalizing coin designs that had been accepted by the Treasury, and he resented the input of sculptors in the private sector.

Barber went to work and created an obverse design of Miss Liberty, copied from a French coin. For the reverse of the dime he kept the "cereal wreath" created by James B. Longacre in 1859, with some minor alterations. For the quarter and half dollar, he created a Heraldic Eagle motif. After due discussions and some changes, Leech showed the designs to President Benjamin Harrison, who passed them around among Cabinet members. Harrison suggested some minor changes. Not long afterward the Treasury Department issued this description of the common obverse used on the three denominations:

> On the obverse, Head of Liberty looking to the right; olive wreath around the head and Phrygian cap on the back; on the band or fillet on the front is inscribed "Liberty"; and surrounding the medallion are 13 stars to represent the 13 original states. Directly over the head at the top of the coin is the legend "In God We Trust," and beneath the bust the date.

The commentary concluded with the opinion that the new designs "are a great improvement over those now in use." Thus the "ugly" Liberty Seated motif was scheduled to be replaced. Would there be a dawning of public enthusiasm for the new motifs? It was hoped so. However, this was not to be.

Harper's Weekly, November 21, 1891, included this scathing article by Jno. Gilmore Speed, illustrated by a *rather crude* image of an 1891 pattern supplied by the Treasury Department:

The Design for the New Silver Coins

The mountain has labored and brought forth a mouse.[73] There was much ado last spring about selecting a design for the new silver coins to be made by the mints of the United States. The director of the Mint, Mr. Leech, took a great deal of advice from artists and invited suggestions as to the design to be adopted, and then chose to have the new coins modeled in the department by the engraver of the Mint . . .

He invited a number of sculptors and artists to submit designs, but last spring many of the best men joined in a communication declining to participate in a competition in which even those who were successful would be but poorly paid for the work done. However, this was not the only reason which influenced them in declining. If an American artist had felt that he was doing something to prevent his government from making an artistic blunder he would have been willing to waive the question of compensation; but the other conditions were too hard. The time given in which to make the designs was only six weeks, and this was considered too short a period during which first-class work could be done. In addition, again, these artists were not asked to make designs for the whole coin, but for only one side.

Knowing that the department would probably employ some incompetent artisan to make the other side, artists of standing were indisposed to have their work thus spoiled by part of the coin being good, and the rest atrociously bad. The design adopted shows that this is precisely what would have happened, and the artists who foresaw such a probability were wise in their judgment . . .

Indeed, the difficulties in the way of making a good modern coin are so great that Mr. Augustus Saint-Gaudens did not hesitate to say that in his opinion there were only three or four men in America capable of designing a really admirable coin.

"But," said he, looking at a photograph of the new design made by Mr. Barber, "there are a hundred men who could have done very much better than this. This is inept; this looks like it had been designed by a young lady of sixteen, a miss who had taken only a few lessons in modelling. It is beneath criticism, beneath contempt . . .

Mr. Kenyon Cox, when shown the photographs of the new design, sniffed the air as though it were foul, and said, impatiently, "Every time the government has anything to do in art matters it shows its utter incapacity to deal with such things." When he was asked to express an opinion of the design, he looked at it a moment and said, "It is beneath criticism," and then added, "I think it disgraceful that this great country should have such a coin as this." Mr. Cox was disinclined to say more, for he evidently felt very strongly on the subject, and was too full of disgust at the artistic inferiority of the new design to express himself freely and still preserve his amiable politeness...

Mr. J.S. Hartley, the sculptor, who, when I called at his studio, had just put the finishing touches on his model for the heroic statue of Ericsson to be placed in the Central Park, examined the photographs carefully . . . Of the obverse side, however, with a head of Liberty wearing a Phrygian cap and a laurel wreath, he said that it was evidently the work of an amateur who had mastered very few of the rudiments of modelling. The head he thought unintellectual, and the face even worse, as it suggested that of a disreputable woman just recovering from a prolonged debauch . . .

Several designers were also visited, and to them were the photographs shown. Without exception they pronounced the work to be devoid of merit, and no improvement whatever on the old coins. Such seems to be the universal opinion of the new design of those qualified to judge in such matters. But it has been adopted, and on the 1st of next January the mints will begin stamping the coins with dies made from Mr. Barber's design. And so it will continue until Congress does a good act by repealing a bad law, and enable the government officials to secure the services of men competent to make designs more worthy of the country.

The *American Journal of Numismatics* reviewed the designs in its issue of January 1892 with a mixture of approval with condemnation, in part stating, "There is yet a long distance between them and the ideal National coin. Perhaps that will never be reached."

A MODERN REVIEW

In contrast to comments of years earlier, Cornelius Vermeule, a numismatist and curator at the Museum of Fine Art, Boston, in 1971 praised the Barber design to the skies:

The designs of Barber's coins were more attuned to the times than even he perhaps realized. The plumpish, matronly *gravitas* of Liberty had come to America seven years earlier in the person of Frédéric Bartholdi's giant statue on Bedloe's Island in New York Harbor.[74]

Such sculptures, whether called Liberty or Columbia or The Republic or a personification of intellect, were dominant themes of the Chicago World's Fair, the Columbian Exposition of 1892, termed by Saint-Gaudens "the greatest meeting of artists since the fifteenth century." Chief among these statues was Daniel Chester French's colossal *Republic*, a Pheidian matron holding aloft an eagle on an orb in one hand and a Liberty cap on an emblem in the other. The heavy profile, solemn eyes, thick jaw, and massive neck of the statue are in harmony with what Charles Barber had created for the coinage in the year of the Fair's opening.[75]

Of all American coins long in circulation, no series has stood the wearing demands of modern coinage as well as the half dollar, quarter, dime developed by the chief engraver at Philadelphia. Liberty's cap, incised diadem, and wreath of laurel were designed to echo all the depth and volume of her Olympian countenance. These classical substances are offset, almost literally, by sharply rectangular dentils of the raised rims and by the strength of thirteen six-pointed stars.

On the reverse of the two large coins, an equal constellation of stars has five points and is clustered above the eagle's shaggy, craggy profile. On both sides the simple dignity of motto, legend, and denomination binds the pictorialism into a cohesive tondo. The wealth of irregular surfaces and sharp angles is an almost electrifying aesthetic experience. The wreath of the dime's reverse carries the plasticity of the eagle's feathers into miniature dimensions and entwines the less complicated inscription in forthright fashion. This wreath also exhibits its own freshness and sculptural activity; leaves, berries, and stems are alive with a carefully controlled sense of nature. Even when these coins have been nearly smooth, their outlines suggest the harmony of interior detail in careful planes of relief that make Uncirculated specimens a pleasure to contemplate. The sculptor was unsurpassed in the mechanics of creating a durable design of monumental validity.[76]

It is appropriate at this point to state that criticizing new coin designs had been a tradition for many years. In fact, the first copper cents issued for circulation in 1793 were condemned as being unfit. The Morgan silver dollar design of 1878 received unending criticism. Numismatists feel differently, of course. Today, early copper cents, Morgan silver dollars, and Barber silver coins are collected with a passion.

COINAGE AND CIRCULATION OF BARBER DIMES

Minting of the Barber coins commenced on January 2, 1892. The first delivery to the cashier consisted of $2,000 in dimes, $1,000 in quarters, and $5,000 in half dollars. A shipment of $50 face value was sent that day to Mint director Edward O. Leech in Washington. These were received on the fourth, at which time a set of three was given to President Grover Cleveland and other sets were given to friends.[77]

Production of the dimes, quarters, and half dollars for circulation took place at the three mints then currently in operation—Philadelphia, New Orleans, and San Francisco (see appendix B). The new Denver Mint coined pieces starting in 1906. After 1909 the New Orleans Mint shut down forever. Coinage of all three denominations usually but not always took place at each of the mints in each year. Dimes and quarters of the Barber design were made through 1916, when they were replaced by the Mercury and Standing Liberty designs, respectively. Barber half dollars were made through 1915, followed in 1916 by the Liberty Walking motif.

Far more Barber dimes were minted than of Barber quarters and half dollars combined.

BARBER OR LIBERTY HEAD DIMES (1892–1916): GUIDE TO COLLECTING

Of the three Barber coin denominations the dime is most widely collected today. That has been true for past years as well, dating back to the 1930s when Raymond "National" and other albums were widely sold and made it convenient to store and display coins at the same time. Whitman folders entered the scene, were inexpensive, and did much to boost interest. Even though the Depression pervaded the country, the face value of a dime was not a deterrent. All Barber coins were available in circulation, dating back to 1892, but most were of 20th-century dates. The design of all three denominations is such that with even a modest amount of wear, most of LIBERTY on the obverse disappeared. Amazingly, by 1935 many Barber coins made just 20 years earlier had been worn down to G-4 or even lower.

By the 1930s typical grades for dimes were About Good (AG-3) to Good (G-4) for those dated in the 1890s and Good for those in the early 20th century. Today, for a coin to qualify as VG-8 some letters in LIBERTY must be visible. To merit the Fine-12 designation all letters need to be readable, although those in highest relief can be weak. Exceptions to the rule of well-worn coins were the occasional pieces that had been set aside by choice or chance in the early years. Today we have the situation that perhaps 90% of the coins in collectors' hands are well worn. This is unique to the Barber coin series.

The 1894-S dime, of which just 24 were struck and only 10 can be confirmed today, is non-collectible. As these were not made for general circulation, a collection of "regular issues" can be complete without the 1894-S. On the other hand, if you bought Berkshire Hathaway, Microsoft, or Apple stock at the issue price and still have it, an 1894-S is a "trophy coin" deluxe!

In the grades of AG-3 and G-4, the most elusive issues are those with a combination of low mintage and early dates, these being most of the mintmarked issues of the 1890s plus the 1895 Philadelphia issue. For Mint State coins the same can be said in general, except that for coins having the same mintage range, San Francisco and New Orleans pieces are generally hard to find. More than those from other mints, New Orleans dimes sometimes show weak striking. Remarkably, there is no record of any caches or hoards yielding a significant number of Mint State dimes.

BARBER DIME MINTAGES AS A GUIDE TO RARITY

In descending order, from most common to rarest:

25 million or fewer	1911-D...11,209,000	1912-S....3,420,000	1894......1,330,000
1907.....22,220,000	1897.....10,868,533	1905-O....3,400,000	1910-S....1,240,000
1902.....21,380,000	1908.....10,600,000	1893......3,339,940	1895-S....1,120,000
1906.....19,957,731	1909.....10,240,000	1908-S....3,220,000	1909-S....1,000,000
1913.....19,760,000	**10 million or fewer**	1907-S....3,178,470	**1 million or fewer**
20 million or fewer	1903-O....8,180,000	1906-S....3,136,640	1892-S.....990,710
1899.....19,580,000	1908-D....7,490,000	1899-O....2,650,000	1915-S.....960,000
1903.....19,500,000	1905-S....6,855,199	1906-O....2,610,000	1909-D.....954,000
1912.....19,349,300	1916-S....5,820,000	**2.5 million or fewer**	1894-O.....720,000
1911.....18,870,000	1901-O....5,620,000	1893-S....2,491,401	1895.......690,000
1901.....18,859,665	1915......5,620,000	1909-O....2,287,000	1897-O.....666,000
1916.....18,490,000	1900-S....5,168,270	1898-O....2,130,000	1903-S.....613,300
1900.....17,600,000	1907-O....5,058,000	1914-S....2,100,000	1896-O.....610,000
1914.....17,360,250	**5 million or fewer**	1902-S....2,070,000	1901-S.....593,022
1898.....16,320,000	1902-O....4,500,000	1900-O....2,010,000	1896-S.....575,056
1904.....14,600,357	1907-D....4,080,000	1896......2,000,000	1913-S.....510,000
1905.....14,551,623	1906-D....4,060,000	1899-S....1,867,493	**500,000 or fewer**
1892.....12,120,000	1892-O....3,841,700	1908-O....1,789,000	1895-O.....440,000
1914-D...11,908,000	1911-S....3,520,000	1893-O....1,760,000	**100,000 or fewer**
1912-D...11,760,000	1910-D....3,490,000	1898-S....1,702,507	1894-S.........24
1910.....11,520,000		1897-S....1,342,844	

This gives a good guide to the relative rarity of Barber dimes today. Due to attrition, the dimes of a given mintage in the 1890s are rarer today than those of the 1900s, which in turn are rarer than those of the 1910s. Mint State examples of low-mintage dates and mintmarks of the 1890s are much rarer than those of comparable mintage later in the series. Collecting branch-mint coins did not become popular until after May 1893, when Augustus G. Heaton's *Mint Marks* booklet was published. Even so, widespread interest in mintmarks did not arise until the 1909-S V.D.B. Lincoln cent created a sensation.

PROOF BARBER DIMES

Proof Barber dimes were minted at Philadelphia for every year from 1892 to 1915, but not for the 1916 Barber dime. These were available as part of silver Proof sets. From 1892 to 1904, such sets included the Barber dime, quarter, and half dollar and the Morgan silver dollar. From 1905 to 1915 just the lower three denominations were in the set.

Today, all Proofs are readily collectible. As a general rule the earlier dates are more elusive in grades of PF-65 and better. Availability is also proportional to the mintage figures.

FURTHER COMMENTS

Most Barber dimes are well struck. The points to check for weakness are the word LIBERTY on the obverse and the higher parts of the wreath on the reverse.

For each Barber dime, estimates of availability are given in various grades. These are for *conservatively graded* examples. Due to resubmissions, gradeflation, etc., PCGS and NGC population reports sometimes have higher numbers. Many MS-64 coins of a few years ago are now certified as MS-65.

In the 1980s there was a great flurry of investment interest in many coin series. The result is that prices of coins in higher Mint State and Proof grades increased dramatically. The investors later departed. Now, at the end of the second decade of the 21st century, many high-grade dimes are less expensive than they were years earlier! Today the market is mainly composed of true collectors.

The Barber Coin Collectors Society forms a meeting place for specialists and enthusiasts in coins designed by Charles E. Barber and issues a fine journal. Details can be found on the Internet.

For further reference, *The Complete Guide to Barber Dimes*, by David Lawrence, is an essential reference for the specialist and is recommended as a comprehensive source. Kevin Flynn's *Authoritative Reference on Barber Dimes* features many close-up illustrations of repunched dates and mintmarks and other information.

BARBER DIMES (1892–1916)

GRADING STANDARDS

MS-60 to 70 (Mint State). *Obverse:* At MS-60, some abrasion and contact marks are evident, most noticeably on the cheek and the obverse field to the right. Luster is present, but may be dull or lifeless. Many Barber coins have been cleaned, especially of the earlier dates. At MS-63, contact marks are very few; abrasion still is evident, but less than at lower levels. An MS-65 coin may have minor abrasion on the cheek, but contact marks are so minute as to require magnification. Luster should be full and rich. *Reverse:* Comments apply as for the obverse, except that in lower Mint State grades abrasion and contact marks are most noticeable on the highest parts of the leaves and the ribbon, less so on ONE DIME. At MS-65 or higher, there are no marks visible to the unaided eye. The field is mainly protected by design elements and does not show abrasion as much as does the obverse on a given coin.

Illustrated coin: The striking on this example is razor sharp.

1910. Graded MS-65.

AU-50, 53, 55, 58 (About Uncirculated). *Obverse:* Light wear is seen on the head, especially on the forward hair under LIBERTY. At AU-58, the luster is extensive, but incomplete, especially on the higher parts and in the right field. At AU–50 and 53, luster is less. *Reverse:* Wear is seen on the leaves and ribbon. An AU-58 coin will have nearly full luster, more so than on the obverse, as the design elements protect the small field areas. At AU–50 and 53, there still is significant luster.

1910. Graded AU-53.

EF-40, 45 (Extremely Fine). *Obverse:* Further wear is seen on the head. The hair above the forehead lacks most detail. LIBERTY shows wear but still is strong. *Reverse:* Further wear is seen on all areas, most noticeably at the wreath and ribbon. Leaves retain excellent details except on the higher areas.

1895-O. Graded EF-40.

VF-20, 30 (Very Fine). *Obverse:* The head shows more wear, now with nearly all detail gone in the hair above the forehead. LIBERTY shows wear, but is complete. The leaves on the head all show wear, as does the upper part of the cap. *Reverse:* Wear is more extensive. The details in the highest leaves are weak or missing, but in lower levels the leaf details remain strong.

1914-S. Graded VF-30.

F-12, 15 (Fine). *Obverse:* The head shows extensive wear. LIBERTY, the key place to check, is weak, especially at ER, but is fully readable. The ANA grading standards and *Photograde* adhere to this. PCGS suggests that lightly struck coins "may have letters partially missing." Traditionally, collectors insist on full LIBERTY. *Reverse:* Much detail of the leaves in the higher areas is gone. The rim remains bold.

1901-S. Graded F-12.

Illustrated coin: LIBERTY is readable, but letters ER are light.

VG-8, 10 (Very Good). *Obverse:* A net of three letters in LIBERTY must be readable. Traditionally LI is clear, and after that there is a partial letter or two. *Reverse:* Further wear has made the wreath flat; now only in outline form with only a few traces of details. The rim is complete.

1903-S. Graded VG-10.

G-4, 6 (Good). *Obverse:* The head is in outline form, with the center flat. Most of the rim is there. All letters and the date are full. *Reverse:* The leaves are all combined and in outline form. The rim is weak in areas.

1895-O. Graded G-6.

AG-3 (About Good). *Obverse:* The lettering is readable, but the parts near the border may be worn away. The date is clear. *Reverse:* The wreath and interior letters are partially worn away. The rim is weak.

1895-O. Graded AG-3.

PF-60 to 70 (Proof). *Obverse and Reverse:* Proofs that are extensively cleaned and have many hairlines, or that are dull and grainy, are lower level, such as PF–60 to 62. These are not widely desired, save for the rare (in any grade) year of 1895, and even so most collectors would rather have a lustrous MS-60 than a dull PF-60. With medium hairlines and good reflectivity, an assigned grade of PF-64 is indicated. Tiny horizontal lines on Miss Liberty's cheek, known

1911. Graded PF-67 Deep Cameo.

as *slide marks*, from National and other album slides scuffing the relief of the cheek, are endemic among Barber silver coins. With noticeable marks of this type, the highest grade assignable is PF-64. With relatively few hairlines, a rating of PF-65 can be given. PF-66 should have hairlines so delicate that magnification is needed to see them. Above that, a Proof should be free of any hairlines or other problems.

   Illustrated coin: Proof dimes of 1911 are rare (only 543 minted), but one with a Deep Cameo finish, as displayed by this coin, is *extremely* rare. The coin is fully struck on both sides, and has neither a blemish nor a trace of toning.

1892 Barber Dime

1892 • **Circulation-Strike Mintage:** 12,120,000.

Commentary: As coins of a new design, the Barber dimes of 1892 were occasionally saved by the public, but there was no widespread interest. First, the national economy was in a slump and had been for several years. Second, there had been no excitement about the coin on the part of newspaper writers and editors. In contrast, articles about the 1892 Columbian Exposition commemorative half dollars, the first such in American history, were endless, and public demand for them was strong.

Availability in circulated grades: An estimated 60,000 to 80,000 worn examples exist, mostly AG-3 or G-4.

Availability in Mint State: Thousands of Mint State coins exist as well, including 600 to 750 in MS-65 condition or better. This is the most readily available Mint State variety of the decade.

	Cert	Avg	%MS	G-4	VG-8	F-12	VF-20	EF-40	AU-50	MS-60	MS-63	MS-65
1892	1,388	61.4	84%	$7	$8	$18	$25	$30	$75	$125	$185	$475

1892, Proof • **Proof Mintage:** 1,245.

Availability in Proof format: This is by far the record Proof mintage for the type. Many were sold to the general public, who did not handle them carefully. Gems are rare in proportion to the mintage. *PF-60 to 64: 600 to 800. PF-65 or better: 100 to 120.*

	Cert	Avg	%MS	PF-60	PF-63	PF-65
1892, Proof	296	64.6		$285	$500	$1,000

1892-O Barber Dime

1892-O • **Circulation-Strike Mintage:** 3,841,700.

Availability in circulated grades: Most are AG-3 or G-4. *AG-3 to AU-58: 15,000 to 18,000.*

Availability in Mint State: *MS-60 to 64: 1,000+; MS-65 or better: 75 to 90.*

	Cert	Avg	%MS	G-4	VG-8	F-12	VF-20	EF-40	AU-50	MS-60	MS-63	MS-65
1892-O	252	57.5	71%	$12	$15	$35	$50	$75	$95	$175	$350	$1,250

1892-S Barber Dime

1892-S • Circulation-Strike Mintage: 990,710.

Commentary: A large S mintmark, apparently from the same punch used to create the 1892-S silver dollar, was used throughout the year 1898.

Availability in circulated grades: Most are AG-3 or G-4. David Lawrence stated that this is one of the 12 scarcest Barber dimes in grades G-4 to VG-8, and one of the 11 scarcest Barber dimes in grades F-12 to VF-35. *AG-3 to AU-58: 3,000 to 4,000.*

Availability in Mint State: *MS-60 to MS-64: 150 to 250 (mostly in the lower range); MS-65 or better: 65 to 85.*

	Cert	Avg	%MS	G-4	VG-8	F-12	VF-20	EF-40	AU-50	MS-60	MS-63	MS-65
1892-S	171	44.7	51%	$65	$120	$190	$240	$280	$330	$425	$775	$2,800

1893 Barber Dime

1893 • Circulation-Strike Mintage: 3,339,940.

Commentary: The World's Columbian Exposition opened in Chicago in May and extended into the autumn. Many souvenirs were made by rolling out coins to elongated shape and imprinting them with the exposition name. Most were cents and nickels, but many dimes of various dates were rolled out as well. These are enthusiastically collected today.

The Panic of 1893 affected securities prices and forced the closing of many banks and businesses. It would not be until later in the decade that economic conditions improved.

A Barber dime rolled out as a souvenir.

In the past an 1893, 3 Over 2, was listed in various references, but modern study has revealed it to be a slightly repunched date.

Availability in circulated grades: Most are AG-3 or G-4. *AG-3 to AU-58: 12,000 to 15,000.*

Availability in Mint State: This issue is common in grades from MS-60 to 63, less so in MS-64. As a general rule, but excepting 1894 and 1895, Philadelphia Mint Barber dimes are very easy to find at lower Mint State levels. *MS-65 or better: 200 to 240.*

	Cert	Avg	%MS	G-4	VG-8	F-12	VF-20	EF-40	AU-50	MS-60	MS-63	MS-65
1893	299	58.6	78%	$8	$12	$20	$30	$45	$80	$150	$250	$750

1893, Proof • **Proof Mintage:** 792.

Availability in Proof format: *PF-60 to 64: 280 to 330; PF-65 or better: 65 to 80.*

	Cert	Avg	%MS	PF-60	PF-63	PF-65
1893, Proof	274	65.0		$285	$500	$1,000

1893-O Barber Dime

1893-O • **Circulation-Strike Mintage:** 1,760,000.

Availability in circulated grades: Most are AG-3 or G-4. *AG-3 to AU-58: 5,000 to 6,000.*

Availability in Mint State: *MS-60 to MS-64: 400 to 700; MS-65 or better: 60 to 70.*

	Cert	Avg	%MS	G-4	VG-8	F-12	VF-20	EF-40	AU-50	MS-60	MS-63	MS-65
1893-O	182	48.7	59%	$30	$45	$120	$150	$190	$230	$325	$500	$1,800

1893-S Barber Dime

1893-S • **Circulation-Strike Mintage:** 2,491,401.

Availability in circulated grades: Most are AG-3 or G-4. *AG-3 to AU-58: 7,000 to 9,000.*

Availability in Mint State: There are slightly fewer of these than the higher-mintage 1893-O. San Francisco Barber dimes had a higher attrition rate than did those from other mints. *MS-65 or better: 55 to 65 estimated.*

VARIETY: *1893-S, Repunched Mintmark (FS-10-1893S-501).* A very strong repunched mintmark is visible to the right of the intended mintmark. As a caveat, many of this variety also exhibit strike doubling to the left, but this is a *doubled* mintmark, not tripled. At least several hundred exist in various grades.

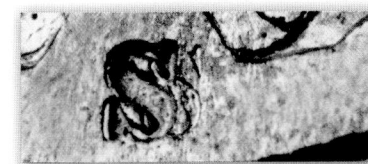

FS-10-1893S-501, Repunched Mintmark

VARIETY: *1893-S, Large S Over Small S.* In *The Numismatic Scrapbook Magazine,* May 1938, Chuck Franzen, a Montana collector, reported owning an 1893-S dime with a large S mintmark struck over a small S. This variety remains otherwise unlocated today. Something to look for!

	Cert	Avg	%MS	G-4	VG-8	F-12	VF-20	EF-40	AU-50	MS-60	MS-63	MS-65
1893-S	155	51.0	58%	$15	$25	$37	$60	$90	$150	$290	$550	$2,500

1894 Barber Dime

1894 • Circulation-Strike Mintage: 1,330,000.

Commentary: One variety has a sharply repunched date, with the original figures being slightly lower than the final ones.

Availability in circulated grades: Most are AG-3 or G-4. *AG-3 to AU-58: 4,000 to 5,000.*

Availability in Mint State: This is a key issue at this level, second in rarity only to the 1895 for Philadelphia Mint issues. *MS-60 to 64: 400 to 600 (mostly at lower levels); MS-65 or better: 80 to 95.*

	Cert	Avg	%MS	G-4	VG-8	F-12	VF-20	EF-40	AU-50	MS-60	MS-63	MS-65
1894	234	48.7	56%	$30	$45	$120	$160	$180	$220	$325	$400	$850

1894, Proof • Proof Mintage: 972.

Availability in Proof format: *Proof-60 to 64: 325 to 400; Proof-65 or better: 100 to 125.*

	Cert	Avg	%MS	PF-60	PF-63	PF-65
1894, Proof	321	64.9		$285	$500	$1,000

1894-O Barber Dime

1894-O • Circulation-Strike Mintage: 720,000.

Commentary: The 1894-O is elusive in all high grades, particularly in Mint State, but as the number of buyers of Barber dimes by date and mint is relatively small, little fame or publicity has been attached to the issue.

Availability in circulated grades: Most are AG-3 to G-4 and were taken out of circulation in the 1930s and 1950s. *AG-3 to AU-58: 2,000 to 2,500.*

Availability in Mint State: At *any* Mint State level an 1894-O is a prize. *MS-60 to 64: Probably fewer than 200; MS-65 or better: 25 to 30.*

	Cert	Avg	%MS	G-4	VG-8	F-12	VF-20	EF-40	AU-50	MS-60	MS-63	MS-65
1894-O	155	25.2	15%	$70	$95	$200	$275	$425	$600	$1,450	$2,300	$11,000

1894-S Barber Dime

1894-S • **Circulation-Strike Mintage:** 24.

Commentary: This is one of America's most famous rarities. The entire mintage of the 1894-S dime consists of just 24 coins struck on June 9, 1894, to balance an account.

None were struck in Proof format, but most high-grade coins are prooflike. Some have been cataloged and certified as Proofs based on their appearance.

A Guide Book of Barber Silver Coins (Atlanta, Georgia, 2015), has an appendix devoted to the 1894-S.

Availability in circulated grades: Two are known, both well worn.

Availability in Mint State: Of the 10 known, all but two are Mint State. *MS-65 or better: 6.*

	Cert	Avg	%MS	PF-60	PF-63	PF-65
1894-S	5	64.2			$1,500,000	$2,000,000

1895 Barber Dime

1895 • **Circulation-Strike Mintage:** 690,000.

Availability in circulated grades: Most are AG-3 or G-4. The low mintage made this a date to look for in the 1930s when many were still in circulation. Very Fine, Extremely Fine, and About Uncirculated coins are very hard to locate. *AG-3 to AU-58: 2,000 to 2,500.*

Availability in Mint State: No more than a few hundred are known in lower Mint State grades. The 1895 is the key date among Philadelphia Mint Barber dimes. *MS-65 or better: 70 to 85.*

	Cert	Avg	%MS	G-4	VG-8	F-12	VF-20	EF-40	AU-50	MS-60	MS-63	MS-65
1895	191	41.2	44%	$80	$160	$325	$475	$550	$625	$725	$800	$2,000

1895, Proof • **Proof Mintage:** 880.

Availability in Proof format: These are sometimes seen with irregular rough areas on the neck. This is the most desired date among Philadelphia Mint Barber dimes, due to the rarity of related Mint State coins. *PF-60 to 64: 400 to 500; PF-65 or better: 95 to 115.*

	Cert	Avg	%MS	PF-60	PF-63	PF-65
1895, Proof	313	64.9		$285	$500	$1,000

1895-O Barber Dime

1895-O • Circulation-Strike Mintage: 440,000.

Commentary: Several minor die variations exist. On some the O mintmark is quite weak from the die having been partially filled with grease or grime.

Availability in circulated grades: Most are AG-3or G-4. Higher-grade coins with partial or full LIBERTY on the obverse are hardly ever seen. *AG-3 to AU-58: 1,000 to 1,200.*

Availability in Mint State: The 1895-O is far and away the rarest Barber dime at the Gem level, except for the 1894-S. Very few Gems have appeared in even the finest collections. *MS-60 to 65: probably fewer than 100; MS-65 or better: about 20.*

	Cert	Avg	%MS	G-4	VG-8	F-12	VF-20	EF-40	AU-50	MS-60	MS-63	MS-65
1895-O	346	16.2	8%	$375	$550	$850	$1,250	$2,400	$3,400	$6,000	$10,000	$30,000

1895-S Barber Dime

1895-S • Circulation-Strike Mintage: 1,120,000.

Commentary: Several varieties exist, the most notable possibly being with the last two date digits being repunched and with the S doubled. However, little premium is attached to this variety despite its rarity.

Availability in circulated grades: Most are AG-3 or G-4; the 1895-S is scarce and desirable in any grade. *AG-3 to AU-58: 3,000 to 3,500.*

Availability in Mint State: *MS-60 to 64: 150 to 250; MS-65 or better: 30 to 35.*

	Cert	Avg	%MS	G-4	VG-8	F-12	VF-20	EF-40	AU-50	MS-60	MS-63	MS-65
1895-S	226	43.5	50%	$42	$60	$135	$190	$240	$310	$500	$850	$3,200

1896 Barber Dime

1896 • Circulation-Strike Mintage: 2,000,000.

Availability in circulated grades: Most are AG-3 or G-4. *AG-3 to AU-58: 7,000 to 9,000.*

Availability in Mint State: More than 1,000 Mint State examples exist. *MS-65 or better: 75 to 95.*

	Cert	Avg	%MS	G-4	VG-8	F-12	VF-20	EF-40	AU-50	MS-60	MS-63	MS-65
1896	149	53.8	70%	$10	$22	$50	$75	$100	$120	$175	$350	$1,000

1896, Proof • Proof Mintage: 762.

Availability in Proof format: *PF-60 to 64: 375 to 525; PF-65 or better: 85 to 100.*

	Cert	Avg	%MS	PF-60	PF-63	PF-65
1896, Proof	253	64.9		$285	$500	$1,000

1896-O Barber Dime

1896-O • Circulation-Strike Mintage: 610,000.

Availability in circulated grades: Most are AG-3 or G-4. A key issue among dimes of this decade, it is very hard to find with partial or full LIBERTY. *AG-3 to AU-58: 3,000 to 3,500.*

Availability in Mint State: The 1896-O is one of the handful of top rarities among Barber dimes in grades MS-60 or higher. It is one of the classic rarities among Gem early Barber dimes. *MS-60 to MS-64: 200 estimated; MS-65 or better: 40 to 50.*

	Cert	Avg	%MS	G-4	VG-8	F-12	VF-20	EF-40	AU-50	MS-60	MS-63	MS-65
1896-O	145	25.5	19%	$80	$160	$290	$350	$450	$650	$900	$2,000	$7,500

1896-S Barber Dime

1896-S • Circulation-Strike Mintage: 575,056.

Availability in circulated grades: Most are AG-3 or G-4. This is one of the key issues in the series—comparable to the 1896-O in many respects. *AG-3 to AU-58: 1,500 to 1,800.*

Availability in Mint State: Probably no more than 200 or so are known in grades MS-60 to 64. *MS-65 or better: 45 to 55.*

	Cert	Avg	%MS	G-4	VG-8	F-12	VF-20	EF-40	AU-50	MS-60	MS-63	MS-65
1896-S	161	33.8	37%	$80	$150	$280	$335	$400	$550	$750	$1,100	$3,000

1897 Barber Dime

1897 • Circulation-Strike Mintage: 10,868,533.

Commentary: Varieties with repunched dates occur but have attracted little attention.

Availability in circulated grades: Most are AG-3 or G-4. *AG-3 to AU-58: 35,000 to 40,000.*

Availability in Mint State: Common in lower Mint State grades. Going forward in the Barber dime series this is also true for later Philadelphia issues. *MS-65 or better: 200 to 240.*

	Cert	Avg	%MS	G-4	VG-8	F-12	VF-20	EF-40	AU-50	MS-60	MS-63	MS-65
1897	472	60.5	83%	$4	$5	$8	$15	$32	$75	$135	$200	$475

1897, Proof • Proof Mintage: 731.

Availability in Proof format: *PF-60 to 64: 400 to 500; PF-65 or better: 95 to 115.*

	Cert	Avg	%MS	PF-60	PF-63	PF-65
1897, Proof	247	64.8		$285	$500	$1,000

1897-O Barber Dime

1897-O • Circulation-Strike Mintage: 666,000.

Availability in circulated grades: Most are AG-3 or G-4. This and the 1897-S are cousins in a way to the 1896-O and S— highly sought-after key issues. *AG-3 to AU-58: 1,800 to 2,200.*

Availability in Mint State: Probably fewer than 500 coins are known in grades from MS-60 to 64. *MS-65 or better: 50 to 60.*

	Cert	Avg	%MS	G-4	VG-8	F-12	VF-20	EF-40	AU-50	MS-60	MS-63	MS-65
1897-O	156	30.4	31%	$65	$115	$280	$375	$475	$600	$900	$1,500	$3,000

1897-S Barber Dime

1897-S • **Circulation-Strike Mintage:** 1,342,844.

Availability in circulated grades: Most are AG-3 or G-4. This is a key issue, joining other branch-mint coins of this and the prior year. *AG-3 to AU-58: 4,000 to 5,000.*

Availability in Mint State: A few hundred exist in MS-60 to MS-64. *MS-65 or better: 65 to 75.*

	Cert	Avg	%MS	G-4	VG-8	F-12	VF-20	EF-40	AU-50	MS-60	MS-63	MS-65
1897-S	119	45.0	44%	$18	$35	$90	$120	$175	$260	$450	$800	$3,000

1898 Barber Dime

1898 • **Circulation-Strike Mintage:** 16,320,000.

Availability in circulated grades: Most are AG-3 or G-4. There are enough around that Extremely Fine and About Uncirculated coins can be easily found. *AG-3 to AU-58: 60,000 to 80,000.*

Availability in Mint State: Examples are common in lower Mint State grades. *MS-65 or better: 300 to 400.*

	Cert	Avg	%MS	G-4	VG-8	F-12	VF-20	EF-40	AU-50	MS-60	MS-63	MS-65
1898	520	59.5	78%	$4	$5	$8	$12	$26	$75	$130	$200	$475

1898, Proof • **Proof Mintage:** 735.

Availability in Proof format: *PF-60 to 64: 475 to 525; PF-65 or better: 80 to 95.*

	Cert	Avg	%MS	PF-60	PF-63	PF-65
1898, Proof	294	65.1		$285	$500	$1,000

1898-O Barber Dime

1898-O • **Circulation-Strike Mintage:** 2,130,000.

Availability in circulated grades: Most are AG-3 or G-4. *AG-3 to AU-58: 6,000 to 8,000.*

Availability in Mint State: Only a few hundred exist in grades MS-60 to MS-64, making it unexpectedly elusive in relation to the mintage. Amazing is the number known in MS-65 or better— only 35 to 40. This is one of the most elusive issues in the series.

	Cert	Avg	%MS	G-4	VG-8	F-12	VF-20	EF-40	AU-50	MS-60	MS-63	MS-65
1898-O	103	47.3	51%	$12	$26	$85	$140	$190	$280	$450	$900	$3,000

1898-S Barber Dime

1898-S • **Circulation-Strike Mintage:** 1,702,507.

Commentary: Some or most of this mintage was shipped to the Philippine Islands after the Spanish-American War ended in the summer of the year. As a result, such dimes were scarce in domestic circulation.

Availability in circulated grades: Most are AG-3 or G-4. *AG-3 to AU-58: 2,000 to 2,500.*

Availability in Mint State: Several hundred lower-level Mint State coins exist. *MS-65 or better: 45 to 55.*

	Cert	Avg	%MS	G-4	VG-8	F-12	VF-20	EF-40	AU-50	MS-60	MS-63	MS-65
1898-S	72	50.7	54%	$8	$15	$32	$45	$80	$150	$375	$1,100	$2,500

1899 Barber Dime

1899 • **Circulation-Strike Mintage:** 19,580,000.

Availability in circulated grades: Most are AG-3 or G-4, but the issue is still easily found in all circulated grades. *AG-3 to AU-58: 100,000 to 125,000.*

Availability in Mint State: Examples are common in lower Mint State grades. *MS-65 or better: 125 to 140.*

	Cert	Avg	%MS	G-4	VG-8	F-12	VF-20	EF-40	AU-50	MS-60	MS-63	MS-65
1899	384	58.7	75%	$4	$5	$8	$12	$25	$75	$130	$200	$475

1899, Proof • Proof Mintage: 846.

Availability in Proof format: *PF-60 to 64: 450 to 600; PF-65 or better: 75 to 90.*

	Cert	Avg	%MS	PF-60	PF-63	PF-65
1899, Proof	240	64.8		$285	$500	$1,000

1899-O Barber Dime

1899-O • **Circulation-Strike Mintage:** 2,650,000.

Commentary: Many of this date and mintmark are weak in areas. Keep your eyes out for a sharp one.

Availability in circulated grades: Most are AG-3 or G-4. *AG-3 to AU-58: 10,000 to 12,000.*

Availability in Mint State: MS-60 to 63 coins are available readily enough. MS-64 examples are scarce, and the coin is inexplicably rare at the Gem level. *MS-65 or better: 45 to 55.*

	Cert	Avg	%MS	G-4	VG-8	F-12	VF-20	EF-40	AU-50	MS-60	MS-63	MS-65
1899-O	128	44.2	44%	$10	$18	$65	$95	$140	$225	$400	$900	$3,750

1899-S Barber Dime

1899-S • **Circulation-Strike Mintage:** 1,867,493.

Commentary: Much of this coinage was shipped to the Philippine Islands for circulation there.

Availability in circulated grades: Most are AG-3 or G-4. *AG-3 to AU-58: 3,500 to 4,000.*

Availability in Mint State: Fewer than 500 coins are estimated to exist in lower Mint State categories. *MS-65 or better: 80 to 95.*

	Cert	Avg	%MS	G-4	VG-8	F-12	VF-20	EF-40	AU-50	MS-60	MS-63	MS-65
1899-S	109	57.0	70%	$9	$16	$32	$35	$45	$110	$300	$650	$2,000

1900 Barber Dime

1900 • **Circulation-Strike Mintage:** 17,600,000.

Availability in circulated grades: Most are G-4. *AG-3 to AU-58: 125,000 to 150,000.*

Availability in Mint State: These are easy to find in lower Mint State grades, this being true of all turn-of-the-20th-century Philadelphia Barber dimes. *MS-65 or better: 90 to 110.*

	Cert	Avg	%MS	G-4	VG-8	F-12	VF-20	EF-40	AU-50	MS-60	MS-63	MS-65
1900	301	59.9	79%	$4	$5	$8	$12	$25	$75	$125	$225	$575

1900, Proof • **Proof Mintage:** 912.

Availability in Proof format: *PF-60 to 64: 350 to 450; PF-65 or better: 65 to 80.*

	Cert	Avg	%MS	PF-60	PF-63	PF-65
1900, Proof	238	64.7		$285	$500	$1,000

1900-O Barber Dime

1900-O • **Circulation-Strike Mintage:** 2,010,000.

Commentary: Some have areas of weakness. Cherrypick for quality.

In his 1988 *Encyclopedia* Walter Breen noted that different mintmarks vary greatly in their position, and that a specimen in the sale of the Gilhousen collection, lot 502, had O leaning crazily to the left. Interest in such variations has been very low, so if you find one it will probably cost little or no premium.

Availability in circulated grades: Most are AG-3 or G-4. Examples in higher circulated grades are elusive. *AG-3 to AU-58: 12,000 to 15,000.*

Availability in Mint State: The 1900-O dime is surprisingly rare in view of its mintage. Survival was more a matter of chance than of numismatic intent. *MS-65 or better: 75 to 90.*

	Cert	Avg	%MS	G-4	VG-8	F-12	VF-20	EF-40	AU-50	MS-60	MS-63	MS-65
1900-O	129	39.8	34%	$18	$38	$110	$160	$220	$360	$650	$1,000	$4,000

1900-S Barber Dime

1900-S • **Circulation-Strike Mintage:** 5,168,270.

Availability in circulated grades: Most are AG-3 or G-4. *AG-3 to AU-58: 40,000 to 50,000.*

Availability in Mint State: These are easy to find in lower Mint State levels. *MS-65 or better: 90 to 110.*

	Cert	Avg	%MS	G-4	VG-8	F-12	VF-20	EF-40	AU-50	MS-60	MS-63	MS-65
1900-S	170	55.9	51%	$5	$6	$12	$20	$30	$75	$175	$325	$1,350

HUB CHANGES IN 1901

If you are interested in minute changes in designs, the following information, not widely known, may be interesting.

In 1901 a new obverse hub die was introduced in the Barber dime series. The differences between the new and the old are very subtle and require magnification to detect. On the old dies, the ribbon touches the left upright of the N in UNITED and a leaf tip is distant from the second S in STATES. On the new, the ribbon is clear of the N and the leaf is very close to the S. This seems to have lowered the relief slightly, almost imperceptibly, with the result that dimes with this obverse did not have the word LIBERTY wear away as quickly, perhaps adding about one to three years to the life of a dime before this happened.

In 1901 a new *reverse* hub die was also introduced in the Barber dime series. The differences between the new and the old are very subtle. On the old the right wreath ribbon is lighter than on the new.

Neither of the two hub changes has ever gained traction with numismatists. As a result, scarcer issues command no special premium.

Detail of Obverse Hub I on an 1892 dime. Note the shape of the leaf tip and its distance from the second S in STATES.

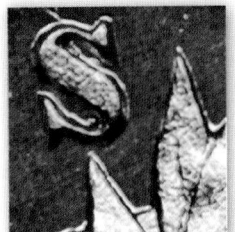

Detail of the same area of Obverse Hub II on a 1911 dime. Note the shape of the leaf tip and its closeness to the second S in STATES.

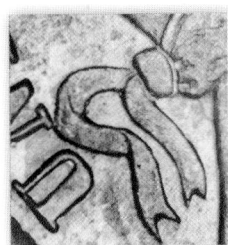

Another detail of Obverse Hub I, this on an 1897 dime. The ribbon touches the left upright of the N in UNITED.

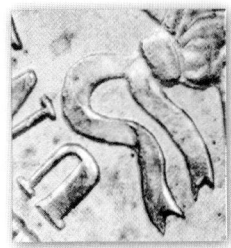

A detail of the same area on Obverse Hub II, this on a 1913 dime. The ribbon is clear of the left upright of the N in UNITED.

Detail of Reverse Hub I on an 1897-O dime. The right wreath ribbon is light.

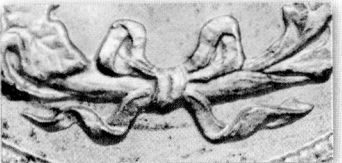

Detail of Hub Reverse Hub II on a 1913 dime. The right wreath ribbon is heavier than on the earlier type.

1901 Barber Dime

1901 • Circulation-Strike Mintage: 18,859,665.

Commentary: All 1901 Philadelphia Mint dimes have Obverse Hub II. For this mint, both I and II reverses were used.

In this year the third Philadelphia Mint opened, replacing the building that had been use since the early 1830s. It was a state-of-the-art facility for most departments.

Availability in circulated grades: Most are G-4. Examples are easy to find in any circulated grade desired. *AG-3 to AU-58: 125,000 to 150,000.*

Availability in Mint State: Common in lower Mint State categories. *MS-65 or better: 150 to 180.*

	Cert	Avg	%MS	G-4	VG-8	F-12	VF-20	EF-40	AU-50	MS-60	MS-63	MS-65
1901	362	59.7	77%	$4	$5	$7	$10	$26	$75	$125	$225	$500

1901, Proof • Proof Mintage: 813.

Availability in Proof format: This year's Proofs of all denominations were made with the portrait features lightly polished in the die, instead of frosted or cameo. This continued through 1904 for most coins. *PF-60 to 64: 350 to 450; PF-65 or better: 65 to 80.*

	Cert	Avg	%MS	PF-60	PF-63	PF-65
1901, Proof	252	64.6		$285	$500	$1,000

1901-O Barber Dime

1901-O • Circulation-Strike Mintage: 5,620,000.

Commentary: Many 1901-O dimes have areas of weakness. Take your time and wait for a sharp one.

The 1901-O has the new hub obverse but the old Reverse Hub I (Reverse Hub II was used beginning with 1902-O).

Availability in circulated grades: Most are G-4. *AG-3 to AU-58: 30,000 to 40,000.*

Availability in Mint State: It is incredible that so few exist, considering the high mintage of this variety. *MS-60 to 64: Probably fewer than 250; MS-65 or better: 45 to 55.*

	Cert	Avg	%MS	G-4	VG-8	F-12	VF-20	EF-40	AU-50	MS-60	MS-63	MS-65
1901-O	130	51.1	46%	$4	$6	$16	$28	$75	$180	$450	$800	$2,200

VARIETY: *1901-O, O Over Horizontal O (FS-10-1901o-501).* This variety shows the O mintmark horizontally punched at the inside top and bottom of the prime O mintmark. This reverse was used with two different obverse dies.[78] These can be found in all grades, but Mint State coins are elusive.

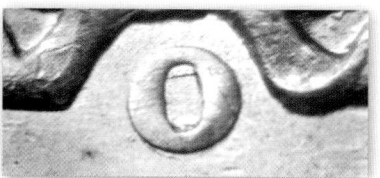

FS-10-1901o-501, Repunched Mintmark.

1901-S Barber Dime

1901-S • Circulation-Strike Mintage: 593,022

Availability in circulated grades: Most are G-4; Fine to About Uncirculated coins are seldom seen. This is a key issue due to its low mintage. *AG-3 to AU-58: 2,500 to 3,000.*

Availability in Mint State: Probably fewer than 200 exist in grades from MS-60 to 64. In any Mint State grade the 1901-S is in demand, perhaps some of this reflecting the aura from the 1901-S quarter rarity. *MS-65 or better: 45 to 55.*

	Cert	Avg	%MS	G-4	VG-8	F-12	VF-20	EF-40	AU-50	MS-60	MS-63	MS-65
1901-S	158	31.2	23%	$80	$150	$350	$450	$550	$675	$1,050	$1,700	$4,250

1902 Barber Dime

1902 • Circulation-Strike Mintage: 21,380,000.

Availability in circulated grades: Most are G-4. Even so, for specialists it is easy enough to find higher-grade coins as desired, as many exist in proportion to the demand for them. *AG-3 to AU-58: 200,000 to 250,000.*

Availability in Mint State: Lower-range Mint State coins are very common due to the huge number produced. Gems are amazingly elusive for a Philadelphia Mint issue with such a huge mintage! A numismatic mystery. *MS-65 or better: 100 to 120.*

	Cert	Avg	%MS	G-4	VG-8	F-12	VF-20	EF-40	AU-50	MS-60	MS-63	MS-65
1902	273	55.2	62%	$4	$5	$6	$8	$25	$75	$125	$225	$525

1902, Proof • **Proof Mintage:** 777.

Availability in Proof format: *PF-60 to 64: 400 to 500; PF-65 or better: 50 to 60.*

	Cert	Avg	%MS	PF-60	PF-63	PF-65
1902, Proof	209	64.2		$285	$500	$1,000

1902-O Barber Dime

1902-O • **Circulation-Strike Mintage:** 4,500,000.

Commentary: These are often weak in areas, but sharp examples can be found. Across the board in other silver denominations, the New Orleans Mint produced many weak coins.

Availability in circulated grades: These are very common when well worn, and most are G-4. They are scarce to rare in any grade in which LIBERTY is readable. *AG-3 to AU-58: 30,000 to 40,000.*

Availability in Mint State: Probably fewer than 200 exist in grades from MS-60 to 64. In Gem Mint State the 1902-O is one of the key issues in the Barber dime series—surprising in view of the multimillion-coin mintage. *MS-65 or better: 25 to 30.*

	Cert	Avg	%MS	G-4	VG-8	F-12	VF-20	EF-40	AU-50	MS-60	MS-63	MS-65
1902-O	124	53.4	54%	$4	$6	$15	$32	$65	$150	$400	$700	$4,000

1902-S Barber Dime

1902-S • **Circulation-Strike Mintage:** 2,070,000.

Commentary: Despite the launch of Augustus G. Heaton's *Mint Marks* treatise in 1893, there was still no widespread interest in collecting branch-mint coins. Hard Times tokens, Civil War tokens, and colonial coins, to cite three examples, were far more popular in 1902 than were silver coins by mintmark varieties. Collectors simply wanted one coin of each date, and Proofs usually sufficed. Even so, interest in silver Proofs declined in this decade.

Availability in circulated grades: Most are G-4. *AG-3 to AU-58: 12,000 to 15,000.*

Availability in Mint State: It is thought that in grades from MS-60 to 64, fewer than 250 exist, making this one of the rarer issues of the era, and yet another numismatic surprise. *MS-65 or better: 45 to 55.*

	Cert	Avg	%MS	G-4	VG-8	F-12	VF-20	EF-40	AU-50	MS-60	MS-63	MS-65
1902-S	97	47.4	49%	$9	$20	$55	$80	$140	$200	$400	$650	$2,750

1903 Barber Dime

1903 • Circulation-Strike Mintage: 19,500,000.

Availability in circulated grades: Most are G-4, but the 1903 is easy to locate in any desired grade. *AG-3 to AU-58: 200,000 to 250,000.*

Availability in Mint State: Examples are readily available in grades from MS-60 to 64, with the population estimated in the high hundreds of coins. *MS-65 or better: 120 to 140.*

	Cert	Avg	%MS	G-4	VG-8	F-12	VF-20	EF-40	AU-50	MS-60	MS-63	MS-65
1903	197	57.0	65%	$4	$5	$6	$8	$25	$75	$125	$225	$800

1903, Proof • Proof Mintage: 755.

Availability in Proof format: *PF-60 to 64: 375 to 475; PF-65 or better: 80 to 95.*

	Cert	Avg	%MS	PF-60	PF-63	PF-65
1903, Proof	217	64.4		$285	$500	$1,000

1903-O Barber Dime

1903-O • Circulation-Strike Mintage: 8,180,000.

Commentary: The 1903-O uses the anachronistic Obverse Hub I in combination with the usual Reverse Hub II of this era.

Availability in circulated grades: Most are G-4. There are enough Fine to About Uncirculated coins to go around to supply numismatic needs. *AG-3 to AU-58: 60,000 to 80,000.*

Availability in Mint State: Probably fewer than 500 coins are known in grades from MS-60 to 64. The rarity at the Gem level of 1903-O is generally reflective of New Orleans dimes with high mintages. Probably no more than a few dozen collectors, if even that many, sought such pieces at the time of issue. When coins were found they were often below the MS-65 grade. *MS-65 or better: 45 to 55.*

	Cert	Avg	%MS	G-4	VG-8	F-12	VF-20	EF-40	AU-50	MS-60	MS-63	MS-65
1903-O	193	53.2	41%	$5	$6	$14	$25	$55	$110	$275	$550	$3,000

1903-S Barber Dime

1903-S • **Circulation-Strike Mintage:** 613,300.

Commentary: Old reverse hubs were used in San Francisco this year. There was no requirement that old hubs needed to be discarded, so they remained in service until they wore out.

Availability in circulated grades: Most are G-4. This is another elusive issue—among the top one dozen scarce varieties in the Barber dime series. *AG-3 to AU-58: 2,000 to 2,500.*

Availability in Mint State: Probably fewer than 250 are known in lower Mint State levels, all being of an elusive nature. *MS-65 or better: 55 to 65.*

	Cert	Avg	%MS	G-4	VG-8	F-12	VF-20	EF-40	AU-50	MS-60	MS-63	MS-65
1903-S	139	29.3	20%	$85	$130	$350	$475	$675	$825	$900	$1,200	$2,250

1904 Barber Dime

1904 • **Circulation-Strike Mintage:** 14,600,357.

Availability in circulated grades: Most are G-4. Similar to the case with other Philadelphia dimes of the era, the 1904 can be found easily in any desired grade. *AG-3 to AU-58: 120,000 to 140,000.*

Availability in Mint State: Lower Mint State grades are quite common, but this is another Barber dime that is surprisingly scarce at upper levels. *MS-65 or better: 150 to 180.*

	Cert	Avg	%MS	G-4	VG-8	F-12	VF-20	EF-40	AU-50	MS-60	MS-63	MS-65
1904	215	57.8	71%	$4	$5	$6	$9	$25	$75	$125	$250	$900

1904, Proof • **Proof Mintage:** 670.

Availability in Proof format: Interest in Proofs continued to wane. A perusal of current issues of *The Numismatist* will dramatically reveal that the action was still in tokens, medals, and early American issues. The Newman Numismatic Portal, free on the Internet (https://nnp.wustl.edu), gives access to all back issues of that and the other leading periodical of the era, the *American Journal of Numismatics*. *PF-60 to 64: 350 to 450; PF-65 or better: 75 to 90.*

	Cert	Avg	%MS	PF-60	PF-63	PF-65
1904, Proof	233	64.2		$285	$500	$1,000

1904-S Barber Dime

1904-S • **Circulation-Strike Mintage:** 800,000.

Availability in circulated grades: Most are G-4. Again, there was hardly any interest in mintmarked dimes at the time, and most passed into circulation. Most survivors were plucked from circulation in the 1930s and 1940s. The average grade of G-4 is higher than that found for dimes of a decade earlier, which spent more time in circulation. *AG-3 to AU-58: 4,000 to 5,000.*

Availability in Mint State: Fewer than 400 coins are known in grades from MS-60 to 64, and they are not often seen in the marketplace. Such pieces are great objects of numismatic desire and are rarer than the mintage would indicate. San Francisco Mint dimes as a class are harder to find, in terms of percentage of their mintages, than are those of Philadelphia and New Orleans. *MS-65 or better: 35 to 40.*

	Cert	Avg	%MS	G-4	VG-8	F-12	VF-20	EF-40	AU-50	MS-60	MS-63	MS-65
1904-S	147	38.1	35%	$45	$75	$160	$235	$325	$475	$800	$1,200	$4,000

1905 Barber Dime

1905 • **Circulation-Strike Mintage:** 14,551,623.

Availability in circulated grades: Easy to find in any grade desired; most are G-4. *AG-3 to AU-58: 100,000 to 125,000.*

Availability in Mint State: Examples are common in lower Mint State ranges. *MS-65 or better: 150 to 175.*

	Cert	Avg	%MS	G-4	VG-8	F-12	VF-20	EF-40	AU-50	MS-60	MS-63	MS-65
1905	222	56.9	65%	$4	$5	$6	$10	$25	$75	$125	$240	$600

1905, Proof • **Proof Mintage:** 727.

Availability in Proof format: *PF-60 to 64: 350 to 450; PF-65 or better: 95 to 115.*

	Cert	Avg	%MS	PF-60	PF-63	PF-65
1905, Proof	214	64.7		$285	$500	$1,000

1905-O Barber Dime

1905-O, Normal O • **Circulation-Strike**
Mintage: 3,400,000.

Commentary: These are often seen with areas of weakness, and patience is required to find a sharp one.

Availability in circulated grades: Most are G-4. *AG-3 to AU-58: 40,000 to 50,000.*

Availability in Mint State: Examples are easy to find in lower Mint State grades. *MS-65 or better: 110 to 120.*

Detail of the Normal O.

	Cert	Avg	%MS	G-4	VG-8	F-12	VF-20	EF-40	AU-50	MS-60	MS-63	MS-65
1905-O	226	48.0	55%	$5	$10	$35	$60	$100	$150	$300	$425	$1,100

1905-O, Micro O • Circulation-Strike

Mintage: Part of the total mintage for the issue.

Commentary: This is one of the most popular issues in the Barber series and is on nearly every want list. Unlike the 1892-O Micro O half dollar, the Micro O dime is readily available in most circulated grades below EF-40. Mint State examples appear now and then. Two different obverse dies were used with this reverse.

  Mehl's Numismatic Monthly, March 1910, included this comment sent by S.E. Young, M.D., of Baywood, Virginia:

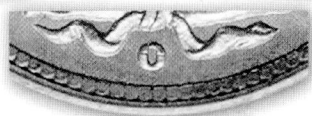

Detail of the Micro O.

Noticing reference to a new mint mark found on 1905 dime from New Orleans Mint set me to looking at mint marks generally. I was to find one dime with the microscopic "O" as described by your correspondent, after looking through all the dimes in two or three post-offices and two banks. This seems to indicate that the 1905 small "O" variety occurs on about one of each 1,000 dimes made at New Orleans since 1900.

  The above seems to overstate the rarity in terms of today's, but the variety is very elusive.

	Cert	Avg	%MS	G-4	VG-8	F-12	VF-20	EF-40	AU-50	MS-60	MS-63	MS-65
1905-O, Micro O	n/a	n/a	n/a	$60	$90	$150	$300	$725	$1,150	$2,700	$5,500	

1905-S Barber Dime

1905-S • **Circulation-Strike Mintage:** 6,855,199.

Commentary: John McCloskey reported that the 1905-S normally is seen with Hub II for the obverse and reverse, but a rare combination with the usual Obverse Hub II and the anachronistic Reverse Hub I exists.

Availability in circulated grades: Most are G-4. *AG-3 to AU-58: 30,000 to 40,000.*

Availability in Mint State: Examples are easy to find in grades from MS-60 to MS-64, a comment that applies to the vast majority of 20th-century Barber dimes. *MS-65 or better: 90 to 110.*

	Cert	Avg	%MS	G-4	VG-8	F-12	VF-20	EF-40	AU-50	MS-60	MS-63	MS-65
1905-S	204	55.9	57%	$4	$6	$9	$20	$40	$95	$250	$325	$950

1906 Barber Dime

1906 • Circulation-Strike Mintage: 19,957,731.

Availability in circulated grades: Most are G-4. Finding a 1906 dime in any grade desired is easy to do. *AG-3 to AU-58: 200,000 to 250,000.*

Availability in Mint State: Examples are common in lower Mint State levels. *MS-65 or better: More than 100.*

	Cert	Avg	%MS	G-4	VG-8	F-12	VF-20	EF-40	AU-50	MS-60	MS-63	MS-65
1906	428	58.3	71%	$4	$5	$6	$10	$25	$75	$125	$200	$475

1906, Proof • Proof Mintage: 675.

Availability in Proof format: *PF-60 to 64: 300 to 400; PF-65 or better: 55 to 65.*

	Cert	Avg	%MS	PF-60	PF-63	PF-65
1906, Proof	187	64.6		$285	$500	$1,000

1906-D Barber Dime

1906-D • Circulation-Strike Mintage: 4,060,000.

Commentary: The 1906-D represents the first year of coinage operation at the new Denver Mint. At 10:59 A.M., Thursday, February 1, 1906, Superintendent F.M. Downer gave a signal, and as part of a public ceremony the first official Denver Mint coins

were struck. On hand was a crowd who heard commentaries and watched the machinery in motion.[79] In the branch mint's first year, silver dimes, quarters, and half dollars were struck, as were gold half eagles, eagles, and double eagles. The same facility, now expanded and with modern equipment, remains in use today.

A number of repunching varieties exist, none of which brings a significant premium.

Availability in circulated grades: Most are G-4. This is a slightly scarcer issue in F-12 or higher grades. *AG-3 to AU-58: 30,000 to 40,000.*

Availability in Mint State: These are easily enough available in lower Mint State range, but are not among the most common. *MS-65 or better: 75 to 90.*

	Cert	Avg	%MS	G-4	VG-8	F-12	VF-20	EF-40	AU-50	MS-60	MS-63	MS-65
1906-D	122	54.3	68%	$4	$5	$8	$15	$35	$80	$175	$350	$1,100

1906-O Barber Dime

1906-O • **Circulation-Strike Mintage:** 2,610,000.

Availability in circulated grades: This issue is elusive in Extremely Fine and About Uncirculated grades; most are G-4. *AG-3 to AU-58: 20,000 to 25,000.*

Availability in Mint State: Probably well over 1,000 exist, up to MS-64. *MS-65 or better: 150 to 180.*

	Cert	Avg	%MS	G-4	VG-8	F-12	VF-20	EF-40	AU-50	MS-60	MS-63	MS-65
1906-O	149	56.9	77%	$6	$14	$45	$75	$110	$130	$200	$300	$950

1906-S Barber Dime

1906-S • **Circulation-Strike Mintage:** 3,136,640.

Commentary: One variety has a triple-punched 6 in the date. Another variety has the S mintmark over an inverted S, as distinguished under magnification.

This was the year of the great San Francisco earthquake and fire. The Mint remained the only building standing in its district and was used for public relief, banking, and other activities.

Availability in circulated grades: Most are G-4. Examples are relatively scarce in F-12 and higher grades. *AG-3 to AU-58: 25,000 to 30,000.*

Availability in Mint State: Although the 1906-S is not among the most common Barber dimes in grades of MS-60 to 64, there are more than enough to supply the demand. *MS-65 or better: 125 to 140.*

	Cert	Avg	%MS	G-4	VG-8	F-12	VF-20	EF-40	AU-50	MS-60	MS-63	MS-65
1906-S	129	57.1	71%	$4	$6	$13	$25	$45	$110	$275	$450	$825

1907 Barber Dime

1907 • **Circulation-Strike Mintage:** 22,220,000.

Commentary: This is the largest circulation-strike mintage in the entire Barber silver series (comprising all three denominations).

Availability in circulated grades: Most are G-4, but the coin is readily available in any grade desired. *AG-3 to AU-58: 125,000 to 150,000.*

Availability in Mint State: Examples are common in lower Mint State grades. *MS-65 or better: 220 to 260.*

	Cert	Avg	%MS	G-4	VG-8	F-12	VF-20	EF-40	AU-50	MS-60	MS-63	MS-65
1907	509	57.0	72%	$4	$5	$6	$10	$25	$75	$125	$225	$475

1907, Proof • Proof Mintage: 575.

Availability in Proof format: At the Gem level this is one of the scarcer Proofs of the denomination. Proofs were ho-hum to most numismatists, who still preferred to collect early federal coins, tokens, medals, colonials, and the like. *PF-60 to 64: 290 to 340; PF-65 or better: 70 to 80.*

	Cert	Avg	%MS	PF-60	PF-63	PF-65
1907, Proof	181	64.7		$285	$500	$1,000

1907-D Barber Dime

1907-D • Circulation-Strike Mintage: 4,080,000.

Availability in circulated grades: Most are G-4. *AG-3 to AU-58: 20,000 to 25,000.*

Availability in Mint State: Scarce in lower Mint State ranges despite a generous mintage, this one is far rarer than the mintage suggests. It is thought by some that three or four barrels of freshly minted coins were lost in a wagon wreck.[80] *MS-65 or better: 45 to 55.*

	Cert	Avg	%MS	G-4	VG-8	F-12	VF-20	EF-40	AU-50	MS-60	MS-63	MS-65
1907-D	88	55.7	68%	$4	$5	$10	$20	$45	$110	$300	$600	$1,300

1907-O Barber Dime

1907-O • Circulation-Strike Mintage: 5,058,000.

Commentary: Most are notoriously weak in areas, including the hair above the forehead. Finding a sharp one will be a challenge.

Availability in circulated grades: The 1907-O is somewhat scarce in Extremely Fine and About Uncirculated grades; most are G-4. *AG-3 to AU-58: 40,000 to 50,000.*

Availability in Mint State: These are easy to find in the lower ranges of Mint State. *MS-65 or better: 90 to 110.*

	Cert	Avg	%MS	G-4	VG-8	F-12	VF-20	EF-40	AU-50	MS-60	MS-63	MS-65
1907-O	172	56.0	72%	$4	$7	$30	$45	$70	$110	$200	$325	$900

1907-S Barber Dime

1907-S • Circulation-Strike Mintage: 3,178,470.

Availability in circulated grades: Most are G-4. These are very common. *AG-3 to AU-58: 25,000 to 30,000.*

Availability in Mint State: The 1907-S is scarce in any Mint State grade. Why it is very rare at the Gem level is a puzzle. Whatever the reason, this is a key among 20th-century Barber dimes. *MS-65 or better: 35 to 40.*

	Cert	Avg	%MS	G-4	VG-8	F-12	VF-20	EF-40	AU-50	MS-60	MS-63	MS-65
1907-S	113	54.4	50%	$4	$6	$15	$27	$75	$150	$400	$700	$1,650

1908 Barber Dime

1908 • Circulation-Strike Mintage: 10,600,000.

Commentary: In this year, die-making at the Philadelphia Mint—where dies for all mints were made—the era of hand-entering four-digit logotypes into production-coinage dies ended. After this there are no variations in date alignments or locations; all are precisely alike. Punching the D and S mintmarks on working dies continued to be done until the late 20th century, so there are variations with mintmark size, position, and orientation among later dies.

In 1908 thousands of counterfeit dimes of this date were circulated from the Boston area.[81] No details as to their quality have been found.

Availability in circulated grades: Most are G-4. Examples are readily available in any desired grade. *AG-3 to AU-58: 80,000 to 100,000.*

Availability in Mint State: These are common in grades from MS-60 to 64. *MS-65 or better: 200 to 240.*

	Cert	Avg	%MS	G-4	VG-8	F-12	VF-20	EF-40	AU-50	MS-60	MS-63	MS-65
1908	358	59.0	78%	$4	$5	$6	$10	$25	$75	$125	$225	$475

1908, Proof • Proof Mintage: 545.

Availability in Proof format: *PF-60 to 64: 280 to 330; PF-65 or better: 50 to 60.*

	Cert	Avg	%MS	PF-60	PF-63	PF-65
1908, Proof	192	64.7		$285	$500	$1,000

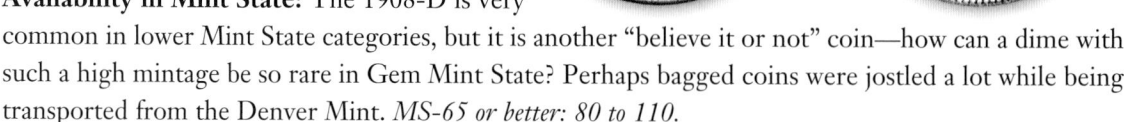

1908-D Barber Dime

1908-D • **Circulation-Strike Mintage:** 7,490,000.

Availability in circulated grades: Most are G-4. The issue is easy enough to find in any desired grade. *AG-3 to AU-58: 60,000 to 80,000.*

Availability in Mint State: The 1908-D is very common in lower Mint State categories, but it is another "believe it or not" coin—how can a dime with such a high mintage be so rare in Gem Mint State? Perhaps bagged coins were jostled a lot while being transported from the Denver Mint. *MS-65 or better: 80 to 110.*

VARIETY: *1908-D, 0 Over 8 (FS-10-1908D-303).* For 1908-D dimes, there are quite a few repunched dates illustrated by Kevin Flynn in his *Authoritative Reference on Barber Dimes.* Most are relatively minor. An unusual one has been selected by Bill Fivaz and J.T. Stanton for inclusion in the *Cherrypickers' Guide to Rare Die Varieties.* On this one, the 0 in 1908 is struck over a previous 8, probably the result of the 1908 logotype's having been punched in too far to the left, then mostly effaced except for the 8 and repunched in the correct position. The center arcs of the earlier 8 show clearly inside the center of the 0. This variety is rare in all grade levels.

FS-10-1908D-303, Repunched Date.

	Cert	Avg	%MS	G-4	VG-8	F-12	VF-20	EF-40	AU-50	MS-60	MS-63	MS-65
1908-D	216	54.6	59%	$4	$5	$6	$10	$30	$75	$130	$300	$750

1908-O Barber Dime

1908-O • **Circulation-Strike Mintage:** 1,789,000.

Commentary: Many are weakly struck in certain areas. Waiting until you find a sharp one costs no more.

Availability in circulated grades: Most are G-4. John Frost commented that, while this issue is not technically scarce as a date, it is a surprisingly tough coin. Often when a collector is building a set, this date is one of the last of the non-keys to be found, especially above Very Good.[82] *AG-3 to AU-58: 12,000 to 15,000.*

Availability in Mint State: The issue is slightly scarce in lower Mint State grades. *MS-65 or better: 100 to 120.*

	Cert	Avg	%MS	G-4	VG-8	F-12	VF-20	EF-40	AU-50	MS-60	MS-63	MS-65
1908-O	129	52.5	64%	$6	$12	$45	$65	$95	$150	$300	$500	$1,000

1908-S Barber Dime

1908-S • **Circulation-Strike Mintage:** 3,220,000.

Availability in circulated grades: Most are G-4. *AG-3 to AU-58: 25,000 to 30,000.*

Availability in Mint State: These are slightly scarce in lower Mint State ranges. *MS-65 or better: 120 to 140.*

	Cert	Avg	%MS	G-4	VG-8	F-12	VF-20	EF-40	AU-50	MS-60	MS-63	MS-65
1908-S	100	54.6	54%	$4	$6	$15	$25	$45	$170	$350	$500	$1,250

1909 Barber Dime

1909 • **Circulation-Strike Mintage:** 10,240,000.

Availability in circulated grades: Most are G-4. Examples are common in higher grades in relation to the number of collectors seeking them. *AG-3 to AU-58: 80,000 to 100,000.*

Availability in Mint State: This one is common in lower Mint State grades. *MS-65 or better: 100 to 120.*

	Cert	Avg	%MS	G-4	VG-8	F-12	VF-20	EF-40	AU-50	MS-60	MS-63	MS-65
1909	328	58.6	78%	$4	$5	$6	$10	$25	$75	$125	$225	$475

1909, **Proof** • **Proof Mintage:** 650.

Availability in Proof format: *PF-60 to 64: 350 to 450; PF-65 or better: 75 to 90.*

	Cert	Avg	%MS	PF-60	PF-63	PF-65
1909, Proof	252	64.6		$285	$500	$1,000

1909-D Barber Dime

1909-D • **Circulation-Strike Mintage:** 954,000.

Availability in circulated grades: Most are G-4. Very scarce in Extremely Fine and About Uncirculated grades, the 1909-D is a key issue in the context of later-date Barber dimes. *AG-3 to AU-58: 4,000 to 5,000.*

Availability in Mint State: These are somewhat scarce in lower Mint State categories. *MS-65 or better: 30 to 40, if indeed that many.*

	Cert	Avg	%MS	G-4	VG-8	F-12	VF-20	EF-40	AU-50	MS-60	MS-63	MS-65
1909-D	121	52.4	59%	$8	$20	$60	$90	$140	$225	$500	$800	$1,700

1909-O Barber Dime

1909-O • Circulation-Strike Mintage: 2,287,000.

Commentary: The typical 1909-O dime is weak in some areas. Sharply struck coins exist but take some searching to find.

This was the last year of New Orleans Mint coinage.

Availability in circulated grades: Most are G-4. *AG-3 to AU-58: 20,000 to 25,000.*

Availability in Mint State: This one is slightly scarce in lower Mint State grades. *MS-65 or better: 80 to 95.*

	Cert	Avg	%MS	G-4	VG-8	F-12	VF-20	EF-40	AU-50	MS-60	MS-63	MS-65
1909-O	122	54.5	66%	$5	$8	$13	$25	$70	$150	$250	$575	$1,400

1909-S Barber Dime

1909-S • Circulation-Strike Mintage: 1,000,000.

Availability in circulated grades: Most are G-4. *AG-3 to AU-58: 8,000 to 10,000.*

Availability in Mint State: Slightly scarce in lower Mint State grades, this is another 20th-century key issue. *MS-65 or better: 55 to 75.*

	Cert	Avg	%MS	G-4	VG-8	F-12	VF-20	EF-40	AU-50	MS-60	MS-63	MS-65
1909-S	108	47.6	59%	$9	$20	$80	$130	$180	$310	$450	$750	$2,200

1910 Barber Dime

1910 • Circulation-Strike Mintage: 11,520,000.

Availability in circulated grades: Most are G-4. *AG-3 to AU-58: 80,000 to 100,000.*

Availability in Mint State: The 1910 issue is easily located in all Mint State grades. *MS-65 or better: 300 to 360.*

	Cert	Avg	%MS	G-4	VG-8	F-12	VF-20	EF-40	AU-50	MS-60	MS-63	MS-65
1910	508	59.6	82%	$4	$5	$6	$10	$24	$75	$125	$225	$475

1910, **Proof** • **Proof Mintage:** 551.

Availability in Proof format: Examples are surprisingly rare at the Gem level. *PF-60 to 64: 300 to 350; PF-65 or better: 50 to 60.*

	Cert	Avg	%MS	PF-60	PF-63	PF-65
1910, Proof	218	64.7		$285	$500	$1,000

1910-D Barber Dime

1910-D • **Circulation-Strike Mintage:** 3,490,000.

Commentary: The 1910-D is often seen with some weakness and dull surfaces. Check the hair above the forehead first.

Availability in circulated grades: Most are G-4. *AG-3 to AU-58: 25,000 to 30,000.*

Availability in Mint State: Lower level Mint State coins are available readily enough. This is another instance of a late-date rarity in Gem Mint State. *MS-65 or better: 60 to 70.*

	Cert	Avg	%MS	G-4	VG-8	F-12	VF-20	EF-40	AU-50	MS-60	MS-63	MS-65
1910-D	98	56.3	68%	$4	$5	$10	$20	$48	$95	$220	$300	$1,200

1910-S Barber Dime

1910-S • **Circulation-Strike Mintage:** 1,240,000.

Commentary: Examples are usually sharp.

Availability in circulated grades: Most are G-4. *AG-3 to AU-58: 10,000 to 12,000.*

Availability in Mint State: The 1910-S is slightly scarce in lower Mint State grades. *MS-65 or better: 100 to 130.*

	Cert	Avg	%MS	G-4	VG-8	F-12	VF-20	EF-40	AU-50	MS-60	MS-63	MS-65
1910-S	81	48.4	48%	$6	$9	$50	$70	$110	$180	$425	$550	$1,900

1911 Barber Dime

1911 • **Circulation-Strike Mintage:** 18,870,000.

Commentary: In this year there was a great scarcity of dimes in circulation in the East and Midwest. To provide metal for coinage the Treasury Department purchased silver bullion in bulk for the first time in two years.[83]

Availability in circulated grades: Most are G-4, but examples are readily available in higher grades. *AG-3 to AU-58: 200,000 to 250,000.*

Availability in Mint State: This one is easily found in lower Mint State grades. *MS-65 or better: 600 to 750.*

	Cert	Avg	%MS	G-4	VG-8	F-12	VF-20	EF-40	AU-50	MS-60	MS-63	MS-65
1911	1,032	59.4	80%	$4	$5	$6	$10	$24	$75	$125	$225	$475

1911, Proof • Proof Mintage: 543.

Availability in Proof format: Proof dimes have a raised ridge, almost like a thin extra leaf, extending from the left ribbon to a denticle. *PF-60 to 64: 290 to 340; PF-65 or better: 65 to 80.*

	Cert	Avg	%MS	PF-60	PF-63	PF-65
1911, Proof	224	64.9		$285	$500	$1,000

1911-D Barber Dime

1911-D • **Circulation-Strike Mintage:** 11,209,000.

Commentary: Most 1911-D dimes are well struck, but there are many exceptions. As always, study the coin carefully. The grade label on a holder tells nothing about sharpness of strike or eye appeal.

Availability in circulated grades: Most are G-4, but the issue is easy to find in all grades. *AG-3 to AU-58: 80,000 to 100,000.*

Availability in Mint State: This is one of the most common Barber silver coins at the Gem level. *MS-65 or better: 600 to 750.*

	Cert	Avg	%MS	G-4	VG-8	F-12	VF-20	EF-40	AU-50	MS-60	MS-63	MS-65
1911-D	282	56.9	71%	$4	$5	$6	$10	$24	$75	$125	$225	$425

1911-S Barber Dime

1911-S • Circulation-Strike Mintage: 3,520,000.

Availability in circulated grades: Most are G-4. *AG-3 to AU-58: 25,000 to 30,000.*

Availability in Mint State: Collectors will find this one easy to locate in any desired Mint State level. *MS-65 or better: 275 to 325.*

	Cert	Avg	%MS	G-4	VG-8	F-12	VF-20	EF-40	AU-50	MS-60	MS-63	MS-65
1911-S	197	59.9	81%	$4	$5	$10	$20	$40	$100	$200	$375	$750

1912 Barber Dime

1912 • Circulation-Strike Mintage: 19,349,300.

Commentary: As a general rule, Philadelphia Mint Barber dimes are well struck. However, among 1912 dimes there are some exceptions, so be aware.

Availability in circulated grades: Most are G-4, but the issue is common in all circulated grades. *AG-3 to AU-58: 200,000 to 250,000.*

Availability in Mint State: Easy to find in lower Mint State ranges, the 1912 is among the commonest issues. *MS-65 or better: 500 to 600.*

	Cert	Avg	%MS	G-4	VG-8	F-12	VF-20	EF-40	AU-50	MS-60	MS-63	MS-65
1912	1,052	59.0	79%	$4	$5	$6	$10	$24	$75	$125	$225	$475

1912, Proof • Proof Mintage: 700.

Availability in Proof format: *PF-60 to 64: 300 to 400; PF-65 or better: 65 to 80.*

	Cert	Avg	%MS	PF-60	PF-63	PF-65
1912, Proof	182	64.4		$285	$500	$1,000

1912-D Barber Dime

1912-D • Circulation-Strike Mintage: 11,760,000.

Commentary: Some 1912-D dimes are sharply struck. Others are not. Take time to find a sharp one.

Availability in circulated grades: This one is easy to find in any grade desired. *AG-3 to AU-58: 80,000 to 100,000.*

Availability in Mint State: Lower Mint State grades are plentiful in the marketplace. *MS-65 or better: 150 to 180.*

	Cert	Avg	%MS	G-4	VG-8	F-12	VF-20	EF-40	AU-50	MS-60	MS-63	MS-65
1912-D	382	53.7	64%	$4	$5	$6	$10	$24	$75	$125	$225	$600

1912-S Barber Dime

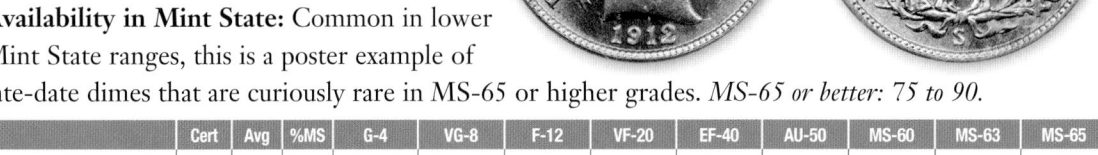

1912-S • Circulation-Strike Mintage: 3,420,000.

Availability in circulated grades: Most are G-4. *AG-3 to AU-58: 30,000 to 40,000.*

Availability in Mint State: Common in lower Mint State ranges, this is a poster example of late-date dimes that are curiously rare in MS-65 or higher grades. *MS-65 or better: 75 to 90.*

	Cert	Avg	%MS	G-4	VG-8	F-12	VF-20	EF-40	AU-50	MS-60	MS-63	MS-65
1912-S	186	58.9	70%	$4	$5	$6	$12	$32	$90	$170	$300	$625

1913 Barber Dime

1913 • Circulation-Strike Mintage: 19,760,000.

Commentary: Dimes of this year from Philadelphia and San Francisco have minor details added in the master die to three of the five leaves directly over the word LIBERTY, in the form of light lines at the centers as shown here.[84]

Availability in circulated grades: Most are G-4. *AG-3 to AU-58: 200,000 to 250,000.*

Availability in Mint State: Examples are very common in lower Mint State ranges. *MS-65 or better: 400 to 480.*

Detail of the reworked leaves.

	Cert	Avg	%MS	G-4	VG-8	F-12	VF-20	EF-40	AU-50	MS-60	MS-63	MS-65
1913	933	56.9	73%	$4	$5	$6	$10	$24	$75	$125	$225	$425

1913, Proof • Proof Mintage: 622.

Availability in Proof format: *PF-60 to 64: 300 to 400; PF-65 or better: 50 to 60.*

	Cert	Avg	%MS	PF-60	PF-63	PF-65
1913, Proof	198	64.1		$285	$500	$1,000

1913-S Barber Dime

1913-S • **Circulation-Strike Mintage:** 510,000.

Commentary: The low mintage has called much attention to this issue over the years. Long ago the author had a bank-wrapped roll of 50 Mint State coins. This is the most widely publicized variety among later Barber dimes.

Availability in circulated grades: Most are G-4. Scarce in Extremely Fine and About Uncirculated grades. *AG-3 to AU-58: 3,000 to 4,000.*

Availability in Mint State: This one is slightly scarce in lower Mint State levels. *MS-65 or better: 120 to 140.*

	Cert	Avg	%MS	G-4	VG-8	F-12	VF-20	EF-40	AU-50	MS-60	MS-63	MS-65
1913-S	252	32.9	35%	$35	$55	$125	$190	$250	$320	$500	$1,100	$2,700

1914 Barber Dime

1914 • **Circulation-Strike Mintage:** 17,360,230.

Availability in circulated grades: Most are G-4. Such coins were common in circulation into the late 1940s. *AG-3 to AU-58: 125,000 to 150,000.*

Availability in Mint State: This one is easy to find in any Mint State level desired, and is one of the most common Barber silver coins at the Gem level. *MS-65 or better: 600 to 750.*

	Cert	Avg	%MS	G-4	VG-8	F-12	VF-20	EF-40	AU-50	MS-60	MS-63	MS-65
1914	942	58.0	79%	$4	$5	$6	$10	$24	$75	$125	$200	$475

1914, **Proof** • **Proof Mintage:** 425.

Availability in Proof format: Only 425 Proofs were minted—the smallest Proof production of any Barber dime. This lack of interest is amazing to contemplate today! *PF-60 to 64: 250 to 300; PF-65 or better: 50 to 60.*

	Cert	Avg	%MS	PF-60	PF-63	PF-65
1914, Proof	165	64.5		$285	$500	$1,000

1914-D Barber Dime

1914-D • **Circulation-Strike Mintage:** 11,908,000.

Commentary: This is the final Denver Mint Barber dime. None were struck there in 1915 or 1916.

Availability in circulated grades: Most are G-4, but examples are easy to find in any grade desired. *AG-3 to AU-58: 180,000 to 100,000.*

Availability in Mint State: The 1914-D is very common in any Mint State grade desired. *MS-65 or better: Over 200.*

	Cert	Avg	%MS	G-4	VG-8	F-12	VF-20	EF-40	AU-50	MS-60	MS-63	MS-65
1914-D	590	54.8	67%	$4	$5	$6	$10	$24	$75	$125	$200	$475

1914-S Barber Dime

1914-S • **Circulation-Strike Mintage:** 2,100,000.

Commentary: Most are sharply struck, but there are exceptions.

Availability in circulated grades: Most are G-4. *AG-3 to AU-58: 15,000 to 18,000.*

Availability in Mint State: This one's easy to find in any desired Mint State level. *MS-65 or better: 110 to 130.*

	Cert	Avg	%MS	G-4	VG-8	F-12	VF-20	EF-40	AU-50	MS-60	MS-63	MS-65
1914-S	179	57.6	76%	$4	$5	$10	$18	$40	$80	$175	$250	$900

1915 Barber Dime

1915 • **Circulation-Strike Mintage:** 5,620,000.

Commentary: The digits on the logotype for this year are somewhat crudely done for an unknown reason—a curiosity.

Most are sharply struck, but there are exceptions.

Availability in circulated grades: Most are G-4, but examples are easy to find in any grade desired. *AG-3 to AU-58: 50,000 to 60,000.*

Availability in Mint State: Examples are common in all Mint State levels. *MS-65 or better: Over 300.*

Detail of the crude date logotype.

	Cert	Avg	%MS	G-4	VG-8	F-12	VF-20	EF-40	AU-50	MS-60	MS-63	MS-65
1915	383	58.0	79%	$4	$5	$6	$10	$24	$75	$125	$225	$425

1915, Proof • **Proof Mintage:** 450.

Availability in Proof format: This is probably the rarest Proof Barber dime at the Gem level. *PF-60 to 64: 275 to 325; PF-65 or better: 30 to 40.*

	Cert	Avg	%MS	PF-60	PF-63	PF-65
1915, Proof	144	64.3		$285	$500	$1,000

1915-S Barber Dime

1915-S • **Circulation-Strike Mintage:** 960,000.

Availability in circulated grades: Most are G-4. *AG-3 to AU-58: 10,000 to 12,000.*

Availability in Mint State: These are slightly scarce in lower Mint State grades. *MS-65 or better: 80 to 95.*

	Cert	Avg	%MS	G-4	VG-8	F-12	VF-20	EF-40	AU-50	MS-60	MS-63	MS-65
1915-S	155	53.8	61%	$7	$12	$35	$50	$70	$140	$275	$400	$1,150

1916 Barber Dime

1916 • Circulation-Strike Mintage: 18,490,000.

Commentary: Many are weakly struck, but sharp examples can be found with diligent searching.

Availability in circulated grades: Most are G-4. *AG-3 to AU-58: 125,000 to 150,000.*

Availability in Mint State: The 1916 dime is easy to find in any desired Mint State grade. *MS-65 or better: 500 to 600.*

	Cert	Avg	%MS	G-4	VG-8	F-12	VF-20	EF-40	AU-50	MS-60	MS-63	MS-65
1916	1,390	58.6	77%	$4	$5	$6	$10	$24	$75	$125	$225	$425

1916-S Barber Dime

1916-S • Circulation-Strike Mintage: 5,820,000.

Commentary: Many are weakly struck in areas, but sharp examples can be found. Again, go beyond the label on a holder and carefully study the coin itself. In today's digital age, this can often be done with sharp Internet images.

Availability in circulated grades: Most are G-4. *AG-3 to AU-58: 55,000 to 55,000.*

Availability in Mint State: The 1916-S is common in various grades from MS-60 to MS-64. *MS-65 or better: 200 to 240.*

	Cert	Avg	%MS	G-4	VG-8	F-12	VF-20	EF-40	AU-50	MS-60	MS-63	MS-65
1916-S	353	59.1	75%	$4	$5	$6	$10	$24	$75	$125	$240	$600

WINGED LIBERTY HEAD OR "MERCURY" DIMES (1916–1945): HISTORY AND BACKGROUND

Designer: *Adolph A. Weinman.* **Weight:** *2.50 grams.* **Composition:** *.900 silver, .100 copper.* **Diameter:** *approx. 17.9 mm.* **Edge:** *Reeded.* **Mints:** *Philadelphia, Denver, and San Francisco.*

Circulation Strike

Mintmark location is on the reverse, at the base of the branch.

Proof

Design Change Wanted

The new coinage of 1916 was the ultimate, the high peak of an evolution that had begun generations earlier. The Mercury dime, as collectors have called it, or the Winged Liberty Head per the Mint's official description, has been a numismatic favorite ever since it made its debut partway into the year 1916, succeeding the Barber dime used since 1892.

As much as collectors love Barber coins today, that was not always the case. By 1914 the New York Numismatic Club, organized in 1908, was one of the most active such organizations in America. At its meeting held on the evening of December 11, 1914, action was taken to encourage the Mint to create new designs. Thomas L. Elder, a member of the executive committee, had severely criticized the existing issues. Members agreed, and William H. Woodin, a long-time collector, was named as chairman.

Elder reinforced his stance in "Some Phases and Needs of American Numismatics," a paper delivered in January to the American Numismatic Society, noting in part:

> I would strongly recommend also that all the numismatic societies interest themselves in a movement to improve the present United States silver coinage of the regular issues. These include the half dollar, quarter, and dime, a type adopted in 1892. The designs may be changed without act of Congress in 1917, when the 25 years of issue shall have elapsed. These coins are almost unparalleled in modern issues for ugliness, and they are in no way indicative of the power and progress of the United States, in fact they should be considered unacceptable to the smallest islands of the seas. In this movement art alliances and sculptor societies should lend their aid and influence.

Dissatisfaction with the current Barber coins was fully realized by the Treasury Department. Mint director Robert W. Woolley met with the Commission of Fine Arts, the body that reviewed designs and made non-binding recommendations, in New York City on December 5 and 6, 1915. By that time artists at the Mint had been working on motifs for about a half year. New designs prepared by chief engraver Charles E. Barber were rejected early in the meeting. It was decided that Adolph A. Weinman and Hermon A. MacNeil be invited to submit motifs. A third sculptor was desired, and Albin Polasek was chosen. On December 27 Woolley met with the three sculptors at the New York Assay Office to discuss the project and determine their interest. The answers were affirmative. Models were to be submitted by April 15, 1916.[85]

Success attended these efforts.

Adolf A. Weinman

THE NEW DIME

A letter from Mint Director Woolley to Weinman, February 28, 1916, gives this information:

> Dear Mr. Weinman:
>
> It gives me pleasure to inform you informally that your models have been accepted for the half dollar and the dime, and that one of the eagles submitted by you is to be used on the reverse of the quarter. In other words, the secretary of the Treasury and I have awarded you tentatively two and one half out of a possible three designs. One of Mr. MacNeil's models has been selected for the obverse of the quarter dollar.
>
> I regret that it will be impossible for me to return your models until Saturday next. I wish to show them to the Fine Arts Commission, and it will be impossible for me to leave Washington before Friday afternoon.
>
> Of course the contents of this letter are to be treated as confidential until such time as the secretary of the Treasury and the director of the Mint decide to make the awards public.
>
> *Respectfully,*
> *[Mint Director Woolley]*

It developed that the Weinman reverse for the quarter was not used, and the model submitted by MacNeil was chosen as the final design.

In July 1916 *The Numismatist* included this:

> On May 30 Secretary [William G.] McAdoo announced the adoption of the new designs for the subsidiary silver coins. They will probably be issued soon after July 1, the beginning of the new fiscal year. The half dollar and dime were designed by Adolph A. Weinman, and the quarter dollar by Hermon A. MacNeil. Several sculptors were commissioned to submit sets of sketch models. From more than 50 models Secretary McAdoo and Mr. Woolley, director of the Mint, selected three sets. Not only will there be a change of design, but each of the three denominations will have a different obverse and reverse. This idea was suggested by Mr. Woolley . . .
>
> The design of the dime is simple. Liberty with a winged cap is shown on the obverse, and on the reverse is a design of a bundle of rods, and a battle-ax, symbolical of unity, "Wherein Lies the Nation's Strength."
>
> Collectors will await with deep interest the appearance of the new coins.

Mercury dimes were released into circulation in October 1916. In December the Treasury Department sent samples of the three coins to the American Numismatic Society, where they were placed on exhibit. On December 2 this announcement was published:

> Washington, D.C. Issuance of the new half dollar coin designed by Adolph A. Weinman, designer of the new dime; and the new quarter designed by Hermon A. MacNeil was deferred today by the Treasury Department until the beginning of 1917. The extraordinary demand for small coins is overtaxing the facilities of the mints, and officials believed calls for the new quarter and half dollar coins would swamp the mints if they are issued at this time.

The new quarters and half dollars were released in January 1917. While the popular press paid much attention to the new dimes, the later-released quarter and half dollar were not as newsworthy as novelties, and fewer articles appeared.

Collectively these three coins spanned the years from to 1916 to 1947, an era that included two world wars, women's suffrage, the recession of the early 1920s (resulting in none of these three denominations' being struck in 1922), the "Roaring Twenties" prosperity, the gloom and doom of the Depression, the beginning and ending of Prohibition, changes during the Roosevelt administration, and the advent of the Atomic Age.

There were vast changes in transportation, communication, science, art, industry, and the American way of life. The world of numismatics changed dramatically as well. In 1916 hardly anyone collected coins by mintmark varieties, there were no standard pricing guides, and albums and folders were far in the future. By the time the last Mercury dime left its coining press in 1945, however, collecting was dynamic.

PATTERN COINS

Several varieties of patterns were made for the Mercury dime, with adjustments to the relief and other refinements applied.[86] Today nearly all of the existing patterns of the 1916 denomination show wear, from light to extensive. One possible explanation is that Secretary of the Treasury McAdoo had a box of these patterns in his home in Virginia. His residence was burgled, the coins stolen, and the thieves, not being aware of their significance, spent them.[87]

Pattern 1916 dime, Judd-1981 as attributed in *United States Pattern Coins* by Dr. J. Hewitt Judd.

Pattern 1916 dime, Judd-1982.

Pattern 1916 dime, Judd-1983.

Pattern 1916 dime, Judd-1984.

The 1916 dime as adopted for circulation, the style used from 1916 to 1945.

In *Renaissance of American Coinage, 1916–1921*, Roger W. Burdette described the portrait on the coin:

> The image on the 1916 dime was derived from two sources:
> The first was a 1912–1913 portrait bust of Elsie Katchel Stevens, wife of lawyer Wallace Stevens. The couple rented an apartment above Weinman's studio, and Stevens and Weinman convinced Elsie to pose for the bust. Elsie had been a sales clerk in a store, and Wallace wanted to boost her status among the other wives at the insurance company where he worked. A portrait by a nationally-known artist was just the thing. By 1916 the Stevenses had moved to Connecticut, so Weinman used the model of Elsie as one source.[88]

Elsie Stevens with baby daughter Holly ca. 1924. (Wallace Stevens Papers, Huntington Library, San Marino, California)

Weinman's *Union Soldiers and Sailors Memorial* in Baltimore and a view of Victory. *(Wikipedia photo by Wehwalt)*

Weinman's depiction of Victory on the Baltimore memorial. *(Wikipedia photo by Wehwalt)*

The second and probably stronger source was Weinman's *Union Soldiers and Sailors Memorial* dedicated on November 6, 1909, in Baltimore. It sits on a high pedestal base making the lowest portions of the figures difficult to see from ground level. When photographs of the dime are compared with the head of Victory from the Memorial the resemblance is unmistakable. On the dime Liberty wears the same breastplate and cap as Victory. Both have hair curls flowing in a similar manner and matching profiles.[89] As the Baltimore monument predates Weinman's meeting the Stevenses, the model obviously is not Elsie.

At present I do not know who the model was, although it was common for most artists to use composite figures in their allegorical works.[90]

What Might Have Been

The reader may already know of the illogical scenario that took place in early August 1909 when the new Lincoln cent design was released. On the reverse were the initials V.D.B., for the designer, Victor David Brenner. The popular press, without researching the matter, printed comments that the V.D.B. initials were an advertisement for Brenner and should be removed, as Brenner had been paid for his work. Writers were seemingly ignorant that current coins already had designers' initials, and on the obverse no less—such as B for Barber on the current silver coins and the prominent monogram ASG on the $20 for designer Augustus Saint-Gaudens.

An Associated Press release, Washington, October 30, stated this:

Monogram of Engraver Appears on Face So Prominently It May Be an Advertisement

Treasury officials are considering whether the initials of the designer of the new dime, put into circulation Monday for the first time, shall be eliminated and coinage suspended temporarily, as was done in the case of the original Lincoln 1 cent piece. On the face of the dime the initials of the artist, A. Weinman, appear prominently in monogram. No law governs the question, but the Treasury Department ordered the letters off under its ruling that no advertisement shall appear upon any coin.

The new dimes were in demand at the Treasury Department Monday, but applicants received only a dollar's worth each. In all $180,000 in the new coins have been minted.

Fortunately and logically, what might have been wasn't!

RELEASE AND DISTRIBUTION OF THE NEW DIME

Minting of the new design began in October 1916, and the first coins were distributed later that month. The release of the dime was described in the December issue of *The Numismatist:*

> The new silver dime was given to the public during the last days of October, and by the time this issue reaches its readers it will be in general circulation. For five months collectors have been anxiously waiting to get a glimpse of what we were told was to be a beautiful coin, and we have not been disappointed.
>
> The opinion of a single man, whether he be artist, sculptor, numismatist, or layman, as to its merits or the beauty of the design, should not weigh heavily. But when a number of men familiar with the coinages of the world from the earliest times all pronounce it a very creditable piece of work and perhaps the most attractive coin this government has ever put in circulation, its popularity with collectors cannot be a matter of doubt.
>
> During the past month *The Numismatist* has received a number of letters from prominent numismatists of the United States, expressing their opinions of the new coin, which we print below. It will be noted that there is not an unfavorable opinion expressed, though there are varying degrees of approval.

COMMENTS AND REVIEWS

The new dime furnished the opportunity for well-known numismatists to make comments, published in *The Numismatist* in December. Edgar H. Adams, the most honored numismatic writer and researcher of the time, wrote from New York City:

> The new dime, in my opinion, is one of the handsomest coins of the denomination that has been issued for regular circulation in this country. There are a few minor features which may be criticized, but the general effect is very commendable. I hope the designs for the new half and quarter dollars will be as satisfactory.

John W. Scott, who had been in the coin trade for many decades and was now retired, said, "The new dime is the best piece of work that the United States Mint has turned out in a century." Farran Zerbe, former president of the American Numismatic Association and in 1915 the distributor of the Panama-Pacific International commemorative coins, stated succinctly, "I am delighted with the new dime." From Philadelphia, Henry Chapman, a coin dealer since 1875, who at the age of 16 went to work in the shop of J.W. Haseltine, wrote, "I think the new dime a very creditable production, and am glad to see such an artistic coin come out from this country."

Wayte Raymond, whose career star was in the ascendancy in New York City, weighed in:

> I think very favorably of the new dimes. The head of Liberty has considerable resemblance to some coins of the Roman Republic and is very artistic. The only criticism I have to make is the fact that the words "In God We Trust" and the date seem to be placed on the die as an afterthought, as there is really no place for them on the obverse.

B. Max Mehl, of Fort Worth, Texas shared this:

> To my mind it did not require very artistic efforts to excel the old issue. The new issue is indeed a welcome addition to our coinage, and one which I think will meet with the approval of thinking numismatists. From a business standpoint I think any new issue is a good thing for the numismatic profession, as it seems to stimulate interest not only among collectors, but among non-collectors, and is the means of bringing out a considerable number of new collectors.

T.L. Comparette, curator of the Mint Collection, shared this:

I am for the most part very favorably impressed with its general appearance. The head is very good, one of the best on our coins. Personally, I should have been glad to see the coin appear with a simpler reverse design.

I should much prefer to see the fasces a simple type, similar to the one on the piece just supplanted, that is, with merely the denomination of the coin within the wreath. Persons inclined toward criticism will find several features justly open to attack, but they are rather in the details of the subject of the types than in the execution of them.

Howland Wood, of the American Numismatic Society in New York City, wrote, "The new dime by Adolph A. Weinman is without doubt the finest example of our new coinage which was begun in 1907 with the advent of the $20 and $10 gold pieces."

Thomas L. Elder, the most important coin dealer in New York City at the time, gave this view:

We have in the new United States dime, designed by Adolph Alexander Weinman, the handsomest American coin. The winged head of Liberty is a real portrait of great beauty and finish. Our American girl in this instance is youthful, refined, and of gentle expression. The addition of wings to the head is taken from ancient art of emblems. The head is not unlike those of Roty and Chaplain shown on so many modern French coins and medals. The obverse lettering is beautifully simple. The spacing of the letters is not a new idea, and was used on a number of dies rejected by the United States. Like the tiny monograms which covered nearly all the ancient Greek coins, Mr. Weinman has added his minute "A.W." joined. The motto "In God We Trust" on the obverse will stop any criticism of religionists.

The reverse is beautiful, but not original. The chief types, a fasces and olive branch joined, are both ancient symbols. The fasces is quoted as "a bundle of rods containing an axe, carried by the lictors before the magistrates of ancient Rome as a symbol of authority." In this case the olive branch partially obstructs our view of the fasces, so that the first glance is puzzling, leaving the reverse not as satisfactory as the obverse. Numismatists will all remember that Anthony Paquet designed some pattern half dollars in 1859 with the figure of Liberty sitting by a shield, holding a fasces in her hand, so this is not a new idea in United States coins. The fasces was a favorite emblem on the later coins of Louis XVI of France, and not a few are seen on other French coins, including those of the Mayence siege. The Roman Republic used it also. The "E Pluribus Unum" on the reverse seems small and hard to read, and the balance of the lettering is badly crowded, but we must admit the artist had no other alternative than to insert it the best way he could. So, after years of waiting and not a little agitation, in which I claim a share, we have here a coin which is second to none we have issued, and it will compare favorably with any in Europe, which is saying much. Let us hope the new quarter and half dollar, soon to appear, will be as creditable.

The same coin prompted an editorial by Frank G. Duffield:

Perhaps one reason why the new dime has made such a hit with numismatists is because the designer has given us innovations on both the obverse and reverse. The female head has been used to typify Liberty on most of our coins, and the conceptions of the designers have varied greatly. The head with the flowing hair on our earliest coins was perhaps the least attractive of all. That on the 1793 Chain cent was a nightmare. Throughout the cent series there was a gradual improvement with the aid of the turban and the coronet. But throughout the entire series of U.S. coins there has been about the head of Liberty an appearance of maturity. It was not youthful. The designer of the new dime has given us a youthful, even girlish head. But the innovation on the obverse consists in adding wings to the head.

This, of course, is not a new type for a coin; it is only new for the United States. The winged head was used almost exclusively on one side of the family or consular coins of the Roman Republic before the Christian era . . .

The girlish Miss Liberty with wings on her cap has already won a place in the numismatist's heart. Of course, dimes are only bits of change in this busy old world, and no one expects to keep them in his pocket for any length of time. They come to us quickly, and go from us even more quickly, without the aid of wings; but this is not an objection to the new coin; those of the old type were equally active in their flights in both directions. The dime has always been a good friend to man, woman and child; it opens many doors to pleasure and amusement. The new one will be fully as good a friend, and a bit of art to admire as well.

The Mercury dime was widely admired by collectors and the public alike and was minted continuously through 1945 with the exceptions of 1922, 1932, and 1933.

WINGED LIBERTY DIMES IN CIRCULATION

Except for the initial interest on the part of the public and collectors alike concerning the new Mercury dime design when it appeared in circulation in late 1916 and early 1917, attention faded. In the absence of albums and folders to display coins and without any pricing or grading guides, numismatic interest in dimes was apathetic at best. Even when low mintage figures were published, as for 1921 and 1921-D, there was no excitement. Because of this the survival of Mint State coins after 1916 was a matter of chance.

When albums became available in the early 1930s, that changed, and dramatically. All of a sudden there was a great demand. By that time the dates from 1916 to the early 1920s in circulation were usually well worn, with Very Fine being a typical grade. Few were Extremely Fine or About Uncirculated, accounting for the rarity of 1916-D, 1921, and 1921-D at those levels. The hunt for Mercury dimes continued nonstop through the mid-1960s, after which silver coins of all denominations became worth more than face value and disappeared from circulation. By that time the early issues, if found, were apt to be About Good or Good.

ASPECTS OF STRIKING

The striking sharpness or lack thereof in this series has not been carefully studied, although David Lange in *The Complete Guide to Mercury Dimes* has published more information than can be found anywhere else.

The sharpness of details is determined by the spacing between the obverse and reverse dies in a coining press. If the dies are positioned closely, all details will be struck sharply, but the dies will wear more quickly. If they are spaced father apart, the features deepest in the dies (creating the highest parts on the coin) will not be struck up and will be flat or weak.

A 1916 dime with the lower obverse rim flatly struck, although the other details are sharp.

On the Mercury dime obverse, flatness can occur mainly on the obverse on the hair covering Liberty's ear, the last digit of the date, and on the rim. Scarcely any numismatic attention has been paid to this.

On the reverse, flatness mostly occurs on the bands across the fasces, especially the middle bands, and on the sticks in the fasces. The bands are composed of two parallel lines with a separation or "split" between. Sometimes the bands are barely split, and other times they have a deep line separating them and the bands are rounded. The latter are far more preferable.

The last digit of the date is weak on this 1920 dime.

Detail of the reverse center of a 1945 dime showing the bands fused together.

Full Bands (FB) on the reverse of a 1942-D, 42 Over 41 dime. The FB feature barely makes the cut. The definition of the bands can vary, and some have a deeper horizontal line and have the bands rounded, unlike here.

Full Bands on the reverse of a 1921-D dime are more boldly separated than on many certified FB coins. Full Bands coins that have the bands rounded are more desirable than those on which the bands are barely split. To determine this, the buyer needs to inspect coins carefully.

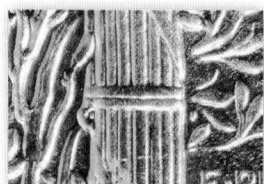

Full Bands on the reverse of a Proof dime. Proofs typically have a deep line separating the bands.

If you are a connoisseur you will want to examine *both sides* carefully and pick a coin that has full details. Doing so takes time and care. Since simplicity is the byword for descriptions in the marketplace, the designation "Full Bands" (FB) provides a quick fix that satisfies the vast majority of coin buyers. This designates a coin in which the two center bands in the faces show a division or recess separating them, but as noted above, further inspection is necessary if you are a connoisseur. Such coins can bring great premiums, never mind that other areas of the coin might be weak! To the author's mind, this system is both illogical and silly. However, the marketplace is the marketplace, and if buyers want FB dimes that are weak in other areas, so be it.

A dramatic example of extraordinary value attached to a dime graded FB is provided by the listing of the 1945 Philadelphia Mint dime in the current issue of the professional edition of *A Guide Book of United States Coins* (i.e., *Mega Red*), the book you are now holding. A regular MS-65 is priced at $28 while one with FB is priced at $10,000!

For a really deluxe specimen of any Mercury dime, find one with FB *plus* sharp striking in other areas as well. This is best done by checking the reverse for FB and then inspecting the obverse. An obverse with full details will cost no more than one with lightness in some areas.

If such a coin is dramatically more expensive, settle for one that is sharp but not quite FB and use the money you save to buy other coins. At least that is what the author would do.

PROOF MERCURY DIMES

Proofs are available for the years from 1936 to 1942, after which production was stopped due to the need to spend more time on the war effort. The mintages increased gradually over this span of years. Today, surviving Proofs exist in proportion to their original mintages.

Proofs were struck from completely polished dies, including the portrait. Certain early issues of 1936 are exceptions and are not from fully polished dies.

WINGED LIBERTY HEAD OR "MERCURY" DIMES (1916–1945)

GRADING STANDARDS

MS-60 to 70 (Mint State). *Obverse:* At MS-60, some abrasion and contact marks are evident on the highest part of the portrait, including the hair immediately to the right of the face and the upper left part of the wing. At MS-63, abrasion is slight at best, less so for MS-64. Album slide marks on the cheek, if present, should not be at any grade above MS-64. An MS-65 coin should display no abrasion or contact marks except under mag-

1928. Graded MS-66, Full Bands.

nification, and MS-66 and higher coins should have none at all. Luster should be full and rich. *Reverse:* Comments apply as for the obverse, except that the highest parts of the fasces, these being the horizontal bands, are the places to check. The field is mainly protected by design elements and does not show contact marks readily.

AU-50, 53, 55, 58 (About Uncirculated). *Obverse:* Light wear is seen on the cheek, the hair immediately to the right of the face, the left edge of the wing, and the upper right of the wing. At AU-58, the luster is extensive, but incomplete, especially on the higher parts and in the field. At AU–50 and 53, luster is less. *Reverse:* Light wear is seen on the higher parts of the fasces. An AU-58 coin has nearly full luster, more so than on the obverse, as the

1942, 42 Over 41. Graded AU-50.

design elements protect the field areas. At AU–50 and 53, there still is significant luster. Generally, the reverse appears to be in a slightly higher grade than the obverse.

EF-40, 45 (Extremely Fine). *Obverse:* Further wear is seen on the head. Many of the hair details are blended together, as are some feather details at the left side of the wing. *Reverse:* The horizontal bands on the fasces may be fused together. The diagonal bands remain in slight relief against the vertical lines (sticks).

1942-D, 42 Over 41; FS-101. Graded EF-45.

VF-20, 30 (Very Fine). *Obverse:* The head shows more wear, now with the forehead and cheek mostly blending into the hair. More feather details are gone. *Reverse:* Wear is more extensive, but the diagonal and horizontal bands on the fasces still are separated from the thin vertical sticks.

1942-D, 42 Over 41; FS-101. Graded VF-20.

F-12, 15 (Fine). *Obverse:* The head shows more wear, the hair has only slight detail, and most of the feathers are gone. In the marketplace a coin in F-12 grade usually has slightly less detail than stated by the ANA grading standards or *Photograde*, from modern interpretations. *Reverse:* Many of the tiny vertical sticks in the fasces are blended together. The bands can be barely discerned and may be worn away at the highest-relief parts.

1916-D. Graded F-12.

VG-8, 10 (Very Good). *Obverse:* Wear is more extensive on the portrait, and only a few feathers are seen on the wing. The outlines between the hair and cap and of the wing are distinct. Lettering is clear, but light in areas. *Reverse:* The rim is complete, or it may be slightly worn away in areas. Only a few traces of the vertical sticks remain in the fasces. Current interpretations in the marketplace are given here and are less strict than those

1921. Graded VG-8.

listed by the ANA grading standards and *Photograde*. Often, earlier issues are graded more liberally than are later dates.

G-4, 6 (Good). *Obverse:* Wear is more extensive, with not all of the outline between the hair and the wing visible. The rim is worn into the edges of the letters and often into the bottom of the last numeral in the date. *Reverse:* The rim is worn away, as are the outer parts of the letters. The fasces is flat or may show a hint of a vertical stick or two. The leaves are thick from wear. The mintmark, if any, is easily seen.

1916-D. Graded G-4.

AG-3 (About Good). *Obverse:* The rim is worn further into the letters. The head is mostly outline all over, except for a few indicates of edges. Folds remain at the top of the cap. The date is clearly visible. *Reverse:* The rim is worn further into the letters. The mintmark, if any, is clear but may be worn away slightly at the bottom. The apparent wear is slightly greater on the reverse than on the obverse.

1916-D. Graded AG-3.

PF-60 to 70 (Proof). *Obverse and Reverse:* Proofs that are extensively cleaned and have many hairlines, or that are dull and grainy, are lower level, such as PF–60 to 62. These are not widely desired, and represent coins that have been mistreated. With medium hairlines and good reflectivity, assigned grades of PF–63 or 64 are appropriate. Tiny horizontal lines on Miss Liberty's cheek, known as *slide marks*, from National and other album slides

1942. Graded PF-67.

scuffing the relief of the cheek, are common; coins with such marks should not be graded higher than PF-64, but sometimes are. With relatively few hairlines and no noticeable slide marks, a rating of PF-65 can be given. PF-66 should have hairlines so delicate that magnification is needed to see them. Above that, a Proof should be free of any hairlines or other problems.

1916 *Winged Liberty Dime*

1916 • Circulation-Strike Mintage: 22,180,080.

Commentary: The first delivery of the new dimes from the Philadelphia Mint arrived in 1916. The large mintage of 22,180,080 coins quickly reached circulation, including to the numismatic community, and inspired many comments such as those quoted earlier.

The Mercury dimes of 1916 were made in higher relief than were later issues. This caused some problems in coin-operated machines. The relief was lowered slightly, most noticeably in the hair curl over Miss Liberty's ear. The front or leading edge of the wing was lowered as well.

Availability and sharpness: 1916 dimes are available in all grades from well-worn to Mint State. Enough were saved in the first year of issue that Mint State coins are easy to find. Most are well struck, resulting in Full Bands coins that sell for a modest premium in comparison to most FB dimes in the rest of the series. The worn coins are those taken out of circulation after the early 1930s, when collecting by dates and mints became popular.

	Cert	Avg	%MS	G-4	VG-8	F-12	VF-20	EF-40	AU-50	MS-60	MS-63	MS-65
1916	2,933	62.3	93%	$4	$5	$7	$8	$15	$25	$35	$48	$150

1916-D Winged Liberty Dime

1916-D • Circulation-Strike Mintage: 264,000.

Commentary: On November 24, 1915, newly installed Mint director F.J.H. von Engelken called a halt to Mercury dime coinage in Denver so that the Mint could fill a huge order for 1916-D Barber quarters, of which 6,540,800 were eventually struck. Regional demand for Mercury dimes was subsequently mostly filled by San Francisco coins.

Four reverse dies were used for the 1916-D coinage. As the first delivery of these coins did not take place until December 29, they did not circulate until early 1917, by which time public interest and newspaper articles about the new design had diminished. Some of these were distributed in Montana.[91] Very few numismatists collected by mintmark varieties. As a result, the survival of Mint State coins is a matter of rare chance. When mintmark collecting did become popular in the 1930s, the 1916-D dime became an object of desire—but by that time, most in circulation were well worn.

Availability and sharpness: The 1916-D dime is the key date and mintmark in the Mercury dime series. Most circulated examples range from About Good to Good, as found in circulation in the 1940s through the mid-1960s. Very Good to Very Fine coins are those mostly found in the 1930s and 1940s. Many Mint State coins exist, and when they are offered at auction there is always excited bidding. The number of buyers for all Mercury dimes is very large, and the market is strong.

Most 1916-D dimes are well struck, and among high-grade issues many have Full Bands, but sell for a significant premium.

	Cert	Avg	%MS	G-4	VG-8	F-12	VF-20	EF-40	AU-50	MS-60	MS-63	MS-65
1916-D	4,584	9.8	5%	$800	$1,500	$2,600	$4,200	$6,000	$8,500	$12,500	$16,000	$25,000

1916-S Winged Liberty Dime

1916-S • Circulation-Strike Mintage: 10,450,000.

Commentary: The first delivery of coins from the San Francisco Mint was on October 24. In time, the generous mintage of 10,450,000 was widely scattered, including many in Rocky Mountain states. The 1916-S dimes were widely distributed from the West Coast to the Midwest, in the last location taking the place of Denver Mint coins that would have been normally used (see the preceding entry). Many were saved by the public. The small S mintmark is very high on most dies.

Availability and sharpness: Most 1916-S dimes are well worn, from Good to Very Fine—pieces taken from circulation starting in the 1930s. These are very common. Mint State coins are easily enough found from pieces saved by the public at the time of issue. Many show light striking at the centers, most evident on the hair covering Liberty's ear and on the fasces on the reverse, on which the vertical sticks can be light, especially in the lower areas. Some have Full Bands, even though there is weakness in the hair and on some sticks. As this is not widely known, if you are seeking an FB coin take your time and find one that has full details overall. It will cost no more.

	Cert	Avg	%MS	G-4	VG-8	F-12	VF-20	EF-40	AU-50	MS-60	MS-63	MS-65
1916-S	1,073	58.3	85%	$4	$6	$9	$12	$20	$25	$42	$65	$215

1917 Winged Liberty Dime

1917 • **Circulation-Strike Mintage:** 55,230,000.

Commentary: Dimes were struck with both the old 1916 hub style in higher relief (David Lange estimates about 12%) and the modified 1917 style. No attention is paid to such differences in the marketplace. America was at war, and large mintages were the rule across all copper, nickel, and silver denominations.

Availability and sharpness: The 1917 dimes are as common as can be in well-worn grades—coins taken from circulation starting in the 1930s. Mint State coins are plentiful by virtue of the large production quantity. Full Bands coins are not rare on an absolute basis, but in higher grades they command a sharp premium.

	Cert	Avg	%MS	G-4	VG-8	F-12	VF-20	EF-40	AU-50	MS-60	MS-63	MS-65
1917	896	62.2	88%	$3	$3.25	$3.50	$6	$8	$12	$30	$60	$170

1917-D Winged Liberty Dime

1917-D • **Circulation-Strike Mintage:** 9,402,000.

Commentary: Most 1917-D dimes are from the 1916 hub (David Lange suggests about 88%). These were widely distributed at the time.

Availability and sharpness: Made in large quantities, 1917-D dimes are common today. Most range from Good to Very Fine. Mint State coins are encountered with frequency. Full Bands coins are in the distinct minority and when seen are usually of the 1917 (or new) hub. Many with FB are weak in other areas (please avoid these!)—another opportunity for cherrypicking. The vast majority of Mercury dime buyers have no clue as to such information.

	Cert	Avg	%MS	G-4	VG-8	F-12	VF-20	EF-40	AU-50	MS-60	MS-63	MS-65
1917-D	604	60.5	79%	$4.50	$6	$11	$22	$45	$95	$145	$350	$1,050

1917-S Winged Liberty Dime

1917-S • **Circulation-Strike Mintage:** 27,330,000.

Commentary: The high mintage is accounted for by the great demand for coins of all denominations during the first year the United States was directly involved in World War I. These were widely distributed at the time of issue.

Availability and sharpness: As is true of other high-mintage Mercury dimes of the era, most survivors are very worn and were taken from circulation after the 1930s. Mint State coins survived as a matter of chance, as there was not a strong numismatic interest in Mercury dimes after the novelty of the 1916 issues passed. Many are well struck. Full Bands coins sell at a premium, but not at high multiples of the regular price.

	Cert	Avg	%MS	G-4	VG-8	F-12	VF-20	EF-40	AU-50	MS-60	MS-63	MS-65
1917-S	636	61.1	82%	$3	$3.25	$4	$7	$12	$30	$60	$180	$500

1918 Winged Liberty Dime

1918 • Circulation-Strike Mintage: 26,680,000.

Commentary: In 1918 the obverse hub was modified slightly. David Lange describes the difference:

> The new obverse hub of 1918 varies only in the details of Liberty's hair and in the contour and detailing of the wing. Liberty's wing follows the contour of her head on both the type of 1916 and the type of 1917, curving away from the viewer and toward the coin's field. On the type of 1918 the wing projects straight backward and remains within a single plane. The tip of each long feather is clearly highlighted by a raised outline not seen on the earlier hubs. The gaps between each of the smaller feathers have been increased to make the feathers more easily distinguished.[92]

These hub differences have not been widely noticed by collectors, but are interesting to contemplate upon close viewing of the coins.

This wartime issue was made in large numbers and widely circulated at the time. For the next several years, until 1921, mintages were generous.

Availability and sharpness: As is true of all other early Mercury dimes with very high mintages, examples are very common today in worn grades. Many Mint State examples exist as well, the last mainly from pieces saved by chance. Full Bands coins sell at a sharp premium, but are not rarities.

	Cert	Avg	%MS	G-4	VG-8	F-12	VF-20	EF-40	AU-50	MS-60	MS-63	MS-65
1918	465	61.9	86%	$3	$4	$6	$12	$25	$40	$70	$125	$425

1918-D Winged Liberty Dime

1918-D • Circulation-Strike Mintage: 22,674,800.

Availability and sharpness: As is true of the others with production quantities over 5,000,000, well-worn coins attract little notice, this being true of all other varieties after 1916-D and before 1921. The 1918-D dimes are mostly lightly struck. Full Bands coins are quite rare and command a dramatic premium.

	Cert	Avg	%MS	G-4	VG-8	F-12	VF-20	EF-40	AU-50	MS-60	MS-63	MS-65
1918-D	549	60.4	83%	$3	$4	$6	$12	$24	$50	$125	$250	$800

1918-S Winged Liberty Dime

1918-S • **Circulation-Strike Mintage:** 19,300,000.

Availability and sharpness: The 1918-S dimes are mostly lightly struck. Full Bands coins are seldom seen and command a high premium. Among FB varieties 1918-S is a true rarity.

	Cert	Avg	%MS	G-4	VG-8	F-12	VF-20	EF-40	AU-50	MS-60	MS-63	MS-65
1918-S	427	61.1	85%	$3	$3.25	$5	$10	$18	$40	$120	$275	$725

1919 Winged Liberty Dime

1919 • **Circulation-Strike Mintage:** 35,740,000.

Availability and sharpness: Examples are plentiful in all grades. Most Mint State coins were saved by chance, as collecting Mercury dimes by date and mint was not popular at the time. Most are well struck. Full Bands coins are easy enough to find but are only a small percentage of the population.

	Cert	Avg	%MS	G-4	VG-8	F-12	VF-20	EF-40	AU-50	MS-60	MS-63	MS-65
1919	535	60.8	85%	$3	$3.25	$4	$6	$10	$30	$45	$150	$375

VARIETY: *1919, Doubled Die Obverse (FS-10-1919-101).* This variety was discovered in February 2015. The discovery coin, graded VF-20, was sold for $3,960 in August 2016. The hunt began. Commentators on the Collectors Universe "U.S. Coin Forum" message board have kept a running tally of known specimens, with 24 reported as of early 2018, the finest being EF-45 (although an AU-50 with environmental damage exists). Prices have varied, sometimes widely, and will probably continue to do so until the variety's rarity and demand factors are better understood, and more transactions take place.

FS-10-1919-101, Doubled Die Obverse.

1919-D Winged Liberty Dime

1919-D • **Circulation-Strike Mintage:** 9,939,000.

Availability and sharpness: Most 1919-D dimes are lightly struck. Mint State coins are elusive in comparison to the demand for them. Full Bands coins are quite rare and command a dramatic premium. Most are not deeply split with rounded bands, so be careful. Also be sure that *other* areas of the coin are sharply struck.

	Cert	Avg	%MS	G-4	VG-8	F-12	VF-20	EF-40	AU-50	MS-60	MS-63	MS-65
1919-D	404	59.9	82%	$4	$7	$12	$24	$35	$75	$200	$450	$1,600

1919-S Winged Liberty Dime

1919-S • Circulation-Strike Mintage: 8,850,000.

Availability and sharpness: Most 1919-S dimes are lightly struck. Similar to the situation for 1919-D, Mint State coins are scarce in proportion to the demand for them. There is no evidence that any were saved in quantity beyond whatever supplies Henry Chapman and John Zug, and to a lesser extent William Pukall, had on hand to accommodate clients wanting current issues. Full Bands coins are quite rare, although not quite as rare as for 1918-S, and command a dramatic premium.

	Cert	Avg	%MS	G-4	VG-8	F-12	VF-20	EF-40	AU-50	MS-60	MS-63	MS-65
1919-S	284	58.6	63%	$3.50	$4	$8	$16	$35	$75	$200	$450	$1,500

1920 Winged Liberty Dime

1920 • Circulation-Strike Mintage: 59,030,000.

Availability and sharpness: The last digit of the date is often weak, as are the rims. Certified holders do not mention such. Cherrypicking is advised, as is true for most Mercury dimes. It costs no more to do this. Dimes with Full Bands are easy enough to find, although they do command a premium.

	Cert	Avg	%MS	G-4	VG-8	F-12	VF-20	EF-40	AU-50	MS-60	MS-63	MS-65
1920	820	63.2	95%	$3	$3.25	$3.50	$5	$8	$15	$35	$75	$260

1920-D Winged Liberty Dime

1920-D • Circulation-Strike Mintage: 19,171,000.

Availability and sharpness: The 0 of the date is often weak due to its closeness to the rim. Cherrypicking is advised. Full Bands coins are rare and command a dramatic premium.

	Cert	Avg	%MS	G-4	VG-8	F-12	VF-20	EF-40	AU-50	MS-60	MS-63	MS-65
1920-D	441	60.9	81%	$3	$3.50	$4.50	$8	$20	$45	$145	$350	$775

1920-S Winged Liberty Dime

1920-S • Circulation-Strike Mintage: 13,820,000.

Availability and sharpness: The last digit of the date is often weak, a characteristic of dimes of this year from all three mints. Full Bands coins are rare and command a dramatic premium. If you seek an FB coin, be sure all other parts are sharply struck. For smart buyers (hopefully including most of the readers of this book!) this point cannot be overemphasized. Besides that element of common sense, finding choice coins takes time—adding to the thrill of the numismatic hunt.

	Cert	Avg	%MS	G-4	VG-8	F-12	VF-20	EF-40	AU-50	MS-60	MS-63	MS-65
1920-S	307	61.0	78%	$3.25	$4.00	$5	$8	$18	$45	$145	$325	$1,450

1921 Winged Liberty Dime

1921 • Circulation-Strike Mintage: 1,230,000.

Commentary: The Philadelphia Mint coins of this year were made in the smallest quantities since the 1916-D. A nationwide financial recession reduced the demand, and no dimes at all were struck in 1922. Following the economic strength after the World War, the economy in 1921 plunged into a slump. Times were tough in 1921 and 1922, resulting in reduced mintages for nearly all coin denominations.

Availability and sharpness: The 1921 dime commands a good premium in all grades from About Good upward. This was a favorite date for collectors to seek in circulation in the 1930s, and duplicate coins, when found, were kept. By the 1950s nearly all had disappeared. The 1916-D, 1921, and 1921-D were the key dates, although the 1931-D and 1931-S were scarce as well.

The date on the 1921 and 1921-D dimes is high and is usually bold on the coins. Most 1921 dimes are well struck, and many have Full Bands. Because of this, the multiplier for the FB price is low in relation to the price for regular coins.

	Cert	Avg	%MS	G-4	VG-8	F-12	VF-20	EF-40	AU-50	MS-60	MS-63	MS-65
1921	1,522	21.4	16%	$45	$75	$125	$250	$575	$850	$1,200	$2,200	$3,500

1921-D Winged Liberty Dime

1921-D • Circulation-Strike Mintage: 1,080,000.

Commentary: For this coinage, 11 obverse dies and 8 reverse dies were made, although it is not certain that all were used. Reverses could be held over for use later. If all obverses were used this indicates a production of about 100,000 coins per die. This is a low figure. For most dates and mints, dies struck 200,000 pieces or more.

Availability and sharpness: Similar to the Philadelphia dimes of this date, the 1921-D coins command a good premium in all grades from About Good upward. This was a favorite date for collectors to look for in circulation in the 1930s, and duplicate coins when found were kept. By the 1950s nearly all had disappeared. Finding one was worthy of an announcement at a coin-club meeting.

The 1921-D dimes are well struck, similar to the Philadelphia coins, and many have Full Bands. Because of this the FB price multiplier is low in relation to the price for regular coins.

	Cert	Avg	%MS	G-4	VG-8	F-12	VF-20	EF-40	AU-50	MS-60	MS-63	MS-65
1921-D	1,611	21.1	16%	$60	$130	$200	$350	$675	$1,250	$1,450	$2,600	$3,500

1923 Winged Liberty Dime

1923 • Circulation-Strike Mintage: 50,130,000.

Commentary: Dimes of this date are common, the start of a string of high-mintage dimes of over two million per year that extended to 1931 (with the exception of 1926-S). Philadelphia Mint coins were made by the tens of millions, as that mint served most of the American population. Denver and San Francisco coins were made in lesser quantities, but still by the millions. Counterfeit "1923-D" dimes were made in the 1920s and circulated widely.

Availability and sharpness: Dimes of 1923 are common in all grades. Full Bands coins are common on an absolute basis but represent only a small fraction of the total population.

	Cert	Avg	%MS	G-4	VG-8	F-12	VF-20	EF-40	AU-50	MS-60	MS-63	MS-65
1923	950	62.8	93%	$3	$3.25	$3.50	$5	$7	$16	$30	$45	$130

1923-S Winged Liberty Dime

1923-S • Circulation-Strike Mintage: 6,440,000.

Availability and sharpness: 1923-S dimes are common in worn grades in proportion to their mintage. Most were saved beginning in the 1930s. Mint State coins are elusive. Full Band dimes are rare; most of them lack rounded bands and can be weak in other areas. Use great care when buying FB pieces, a point that cannot be overemphasized.

	Cert	Avg	%MS	G-4	VG-8	F-12	VF-20	EF-40	AU-50	MS-60	MS-63	MS-65
1923-S	331	59.1	73%	$3	$4	$8	$18	$65	$105	$160	$400	$1,250

1924 Winged Liberty Dime

1924 • Circulation-Strike Mintage: 24,010,000.

Availability and sharpness: Due to the generous mintage, 1924 dimes are common in well-worn grades and easy enough to find in Mint State as well, although these represent only a tiny proportion of survivors. Full Bands coins are readily available but command a premium, as in all cases.

	Cert	Avg	%MS	G-4	VG-8	F-12	VF-20	EF-40	AU-50	MS-60	MS-63	MS-65
1924	550	63.7	95%	$3	$3.25	$4	$6	$15	$30	$45	$100	$210

1924-D Winged Liberty Dime

1924-D • **Circulation-Strike Mintage:** 6,810,000.

Availability and sharpness: Most 1924-D dimes are fairly well struck. Full Bands coins are plentiful in comparison to other branch-mint Mercury dimes of the era.

	Cert	Avg	%MS	G-4	VG-8	F-12	VF-20	EF-40	AU-50	MS-60	MS-63	MS-65
1924-D	452	60.2	82%	$3.50	$4.50	$8	$24	$70	$110	$175	$500	$950

1924-S Winged Liberty Dime

1924-S • **Circulation-Strike Mintage:** 7,120,000.

Availability and sharpness: Although 1924-S is common in lower grades from About Good through Very Good and is readily available in higher circulated grades as well, in Mint State it is one of the rarer issues in the Mercury dime series. Most at that level are in lower ranges, such as MS-60 to 63. With Full Bands this mintmark is very rare.

	Cert	Avg	%MS	G-4	VG-8	F-12	VF-20	EF-40	AU-50	MS-60	MS-63	MS-65
1924-S	354	59.7	76%	$3.50	$4	$6	$10	$60	$110	$200	$525	$1,250

1925 Winged Liberty Dime

1925 • **Circulation-Strike Mintage:** 25,610,000.

Availability and sharpness: Following the trend of Philadelphia Mercury dimes of the decade, the 1925 is very common in worn grades but less so in Mint State; and at any level there is no scarcity. Many if not most are lightly struck in one area or another. Full Bands coins are scarce and can be less than optimal.

	Cert	Avg	%MS	G-4	VG-8	F-12	VF-20	EF-40	AU-50	MS-60	MS-63	MS-65
1925	352	62.6	89%	$3	$3.25	$4	$5	$10	$20	$30	$85	$225

1925-D Winged Liberty Dime

1925-D • Circulation-Strike Mintage: 5,117,000.

Availability and sharpness: The 1925-D dimes are common in lower grades. In Mint State they are somewhat scarce. Many if not most are weakly struck in one area or another, suggesting that care is needed to find quality coins. The same is true for FB coins, which are elusive and often have problems revealed when they are studied carefully.

	Cert	Avg	%MS	G-4	VG-8	F-12	VF-20	EF-40	AU-50	MS-60	MS-63	MS-65
1925-D	312	57.6	65%	$4	$5	$12	$45	$120	$200	$375	$750	$1,700

1925-S Winged Liberty Dime

1925-S • Circulation-Strike Mintage: 5,850,000.

Commentary: This is an ideal example illustrating that a grade on a certified coin can be one thing, but *quality* can be something else entirely. As is true in nearly all federal series, 90% or more of the buyers simply read the labels on holders. The secret for you is that cherrypicking for quality costs no more, although it does take time. Full Bands coins are quite rare and must be checked for quality. The Lange guide is highly recommended for additional information on the series.

Suggestion for grading services: If a coin has Full Bands, so designate it—as you do now. If a coin has FB and a Full Strike everywhere else, call it either FBFS (to preserve the FB designation) or simply FS, which means Full Bands as well as Full Strike. This would probably result in a great shifting of prices. Full Bands dimes would fall dramatically in value if not also Full Strike.

Availability and sharpness: In his *Complete Guide to Mercury Dimes* David W. Lange states: "In the opinion of the author and many others 1925-S holds the record for the most poorly made issue in the series. Both obverse and reverse are plagued by heavy die polishing and erosion and a generally weak strike throughout."

	Cert	Avg	%MS	G-4	VG-8	F-12	VF-20	EF-40	AU-50	MS-60	MS-63	MS-65
1925-S	269	59.8	75%	$3.25	$4	$8	$18	$70	$110	$180	$500	$1,400

1926 Winged Liberty Dime

1926 • Circulation-Strike Mintage: 32,160,000.

Availability and sharpness: By virtue of its large mintage the 1926 is very common in worn grades and is easily found in Mint State. Most are decent strikes. Full Bands coins are plentiful.

	Cert	Avg	%MS	G-4	VG-8	F-12	VF-20	EF-40	AU-50	MS-60	MS-63	MS-65
1926	743	63.1	93%	$3	$3.25	$3.50	$5	$7	$16	$25	$65	$250

1926-D Winged Liberty Dime

1926-D • **Circulation-Strike Mintage:** 6,828,000.

Availability and sharpness: The 1926-D is easily found in circulated grades. Mint State coins are common as well. The Denver Mint spaced the dies too far apart, with the result that most have weakness in some areas. This is a repeated caveat concerning Full Bands coins: they may be weak in other areas.

	Cert	Avg	%MS	G-4	VG-8	F-12	VF-20	EF-40	AU-50	MS-60	MS-63	MS-65
1926-D	466	61.2	85%	$3.25	$4.50	$6	$10	$28	$50	$125	$275	$600

1926-S Winged Liberty Dime

1926-S • **Circulation-Strike Mintage:** 1,520,000.

Commentary: The 1926-S is one of just a few Mercury dimes whose mintage dipped below two million coins.

Availability and sharpness: In worn grades the 1926-S is not scarce, but fewer examples are around than are of other issues of the era. Mint State coins are elusive in comparison to most other varieties and are very rare if MS-65 or better with Full Bands, sharpness in all other areas, and good eye appeal.

	Cert	Avg	%MS	G-4	VG-8	F-12	VF-20	EF-40	AU-50	MS-60	MS-63	MS-65
1926-S	415	43.2	31%	$13	$15	$26	$60	$250	$450	$800	$1,600	$3,250

1927 Winged Liberty Dime

1927 • **Circulation-Strike Mintage:** 28,080,000.

Availability and sharpness: Philadelphia Mint dimes of 1927 are easily available in any grade desired. In the 1950s scattered rolls of this date were sometimes seen.

	Cert	Avg	%MS	G-4	VG-8	F-12	VF-20	EF-40	AU-50	MS-60	MS-63	MS-65
1927	564	62.1	91%	$3	$3.25	$3.50	$5	$7	$15	$30	$60	$150

1927-D Winged Liberty Dime

1927-D • Circulation-Strike Mintage: 4,812,000

Availability and sharpness: The 1927-D dimes are common in worn grades and easily enough found in Mint State. Striking is often irregular, and Full Bands coins, which are rare, and all others need to be examined carefully. In this era the Denver Mint spaced its dies too far apart on many different issues across various denominations, with Buffalo nickels being the most egregious.

	Cert	Avg	%MS	G-4	VG-8	F-12	VF-20	EF-40	AU-50	MS-60	MS-63	MS-65
1927-D	283	58.4	68%	$3.50	$5.50	$8	$25	$80	$100	$200	$400	$1,200

1927-S Winged Liberty Dime

1927-S • Circulation-Strike Mintage: 4,770,000.

Availability and sharpness: The 1927-S is common in well-worn grades. Mint State coins are easy to find and are often fairly well struck except for the central bands on the reverse. Full Bands coins are rare.

	Cert	Avg	%MS	G-4	VG-8	F-12	VF-20	EF-40	AU-50	MS-60	MS-63	MS-65
1927-S	242	59.5	76%	$3.25	$4	$6	$12	$28	$50	$275	$550	$1,400

1928 Winged Liberty Dime

1928 • Circulation-Strike Mintage: 19,480,000.

Availability and sharpness: Dimes of this issue are common in all grades including Mint State. Scattered rolls were in the marketplace in the 1950s. The striking is usually decent. Full Bands coins are in the minority but are still easy enough to find.

	Cert	Avg	%MS	G-4	VG-8	F-12	VF-20	EF-40	AU-50	MS-60	MS-63	MS-65
1928	486	63.6	95%	$3	$3.25	$3.50	$5	$7	$18	$30	$55	$130

1928-D Winged Liberty Dime

1928-D • **Circulation-Strike Mintage:** 4,161,000.

Availability and sharpness: The 1928-D dimes are common in worn grades. In Mint State there are enough to easily satisfy demand. Striking sharpness is often irregular. Full Bands coins are rare, but often have weakness in other areas or have minimal separation of the two central bands.

	Cert	Avg	%MS	G-4	VG-8	F-12	VF-20	EF-40	AU-50	MS-60	MS-63	MS-65
1928-D	293	58.7	76%	$4	$5	$8	$20	$50	$95	$175	$360	$850

1928-S Winged Liberty Dime

1928-S • **Circulation-Strike Mintage:** 7,400,000.

Availability and sharpness: 1928-S dimes are common in any and all grades up through MS-64. In MS-65 they are slightly scarce, and Full Bands coins are elusive. Striking is usually quite good.

	Cert	Avg	%MS	G-4	VG-8	F-12	VF-20	EF-40	AU-50	MS-60	MS-63	MS-65
1928-S	382	62.7	90%	$3	$3.25	$4	$6	$16	$45	$150	$320	$400

VARIETY: *1928-S, Large S Mintmark (FS-10-1928S-501).* Most 1928-S dimes have a small mintmark, as used since 1916. These are common in all grades. Full Bands coins are rare. However, about 20% are larger and heavier, with much of the center filled in. This mintmark was an anomaly and was not used elsewhere in the series. These command a price about twice that of the Small S variety. Full Bands coins are very rare.

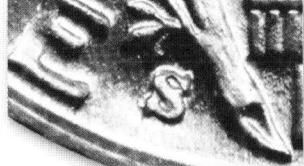

Normal S Mintmark.   **FS-10-1928S-501, Large S Mintmark.**

1929 Winged Liberty Dime

1929 • **Circulation-Strike Mintage:** 25,970,000.

Commentary: This was the peak and final year of the "Roaring Twenties"—a strong economy that saw much new construction, strong prices for stocks and bonds, and more, as epitomized in F. Scott Fitzgerald's novel, *The Great Gatsby.*

Availability and sharpness: Dimes of 1929 were among the coins available for face value plus postage from the Treasury Department in 1932. These are common in all grades. Most are well struck.

	Cert	Avg	%MS	G-4	VG-8	F-12	VF-20	EF-40	AU-50	MS-60	MS-63	MS-65
1929	928	64.0	96%	$3	$3.25	$3.50	$5	$6	$12	$22	$35	$75

1929-D Winged Liberty Dime

1929-D • Circulation-Strike Mintage: 5,034,000.

Availability and sharpness: Like the previous issue, 1929-D dimes were among the coins available for face value plus postage from the Treasury Department in 1932. They are common in all grades. Full Bands coins constitute a small percentage of surviving Mint State pieces but are easy to find.

	Cert	Avg	%MS	G-4	VG-8	F-12	VF-20	EF-40	AU-50	MS-60	MS-63	MS-65
1929-D	1,233	64.2	98%	$3	$3.50	$5	$8	$15	$24	$30	$36	$75

1929-S Winged Liberty Dime

1929-S • Circulation-Strike Mintage: 4,730,000.

Availability and sharpness: As with the Philadelphia and Denver Mint dimes of 1929, the San Francisco dimes this year were among the coins available for face value plus postage from the Treasury Department in 1932. These are common in all grades. Full Bands coins are a small percentage of surviving Mint State pieces.

	Cert	Avg	%MS	G-4	VG-8	F-12	VF-20	EF-40	AU-50	MS-60	MS-63	MS-65
1929-S	414	62.9	91%	$3	$3.25	$3.75	$5	$10	$20	$35	$45	$125

1930 Winged Liberty Dime

1930 • Circulation-Strike Mintage: 6,770,000.

Availability and sharpness: Philadelphia and San Francisco dimes of 1930 were among the coins available for face value plus postage from the Treasury Department in 1932. Examples of those from Philadelphia are common in all grades. Full Bands coins are much scarcer than typical strikes.

	Cert	Avg	%MS	G-4	VG-8	F-12	VF-20	EF-40	AU-50	MS-60	MS-63	MS-65
1930	465	63.2	92%	$3	$3.25	$3.50	$5	$8	$16	$30	$50	$125

1930-S Winged Liberty Dime

1930-S • **Circulation-Strike Mintage:** 1,843,000

Availability and sharpness: Philadelphia and San Francisco dimes of 1930 were among the coins available for face value plus postage from the Treasury Department in 1932. Despite this, Mint State 1930-S coins are elusive in comparison to other dates of the early 1930s, including the lower-mintage 1931 dimes of Denver and San Francisco. Full Bands coins are elusive.

	Cert	Avg	%MS	G-4	VG-8	F-12	VF-20	EF-40	AU-50	MS-60	MS-63	MS-65
1930-S	307	62.1	89%	$3	$4	$5	$7	$15	$45	$80	$150	$210

1931 Winged Liberty Dime

1931 • **Circulation-Strike Mintage:** 3,150,000.

Commentary: The Depression was well underway, not only in America, but in Europe as well. Stocks of dimes in Mint and other Treasury vaults were sufficient enough that no other coinage of this denomination would take place until 1934.

Availability and sharpness: The 1931 dimes were among the coins available for face value plus postage from the Treasury Department in 1932. These are common in all grades today, although Full Bands coins represent only a small percentage of Mint State pieces.

	Cert	Avg	%MS	G-4	VG-8	F-12	VF-20	EF-40	AU-50	MS-60	MS-63	MS-65
1931	487	63.3	93%	$3	$3.10	$4	$6	$10	$22	$35	$70	$150

1931-D Winged Liberty Dime

1931-D • **Circulation-Strike Mintage:** 1,260,000.

Availability and sharpness: The 1931-D dimes were among the coins available for face value plus postage from the Treasury Department in 1932. These seem to have been popular, for rolls were seen with frequency as late as the 1950s. Beginning with the vast expansion of the hobby in 1960 most if not all rolls were broken up. Most are well struck, and Full Bands coins are not hard to find.

	Cert	Avg	%MS	G-4	VG-8	F-12	VF-20	EF-40	AU-50	MS-60	MS-63	MS-65
1931-D	575	61.9	90%	$8	$9	$12	$20	$35	$60	$90	$140	$280

1931-S Winged Liberty Dime

1931-S • Circulation-Strike Mintage: 1,800,000.

Availability and sharpness: The 1931-S dimes were among the coins available for face value plus postage from the Treasury Department in 1932. The same comment as given for 1931-D applies to 1931-S, but somewhat fewer rolls seem to have been purchased.

Full Bands coins are scarce and represent only a small percentage of surviving Mint State pieces.

	Cert	Avg	%MS	G-4	VG-8	F-12	VF-20	EF-40	AU-50	MS-60	MS-63	MS-65
1931-S	430	59.7	82%	$4	$5	$6	$10	$16	$45	$90	$150	$300

1934 Winged Liberty Dime

1934 • Circulation-Strike Mintage: 24,080,000.

Commentary: After a hiatus following 1931, the mintage of dimes was resumed in 1934. It would be continuous through the end of the Mercury dime series in 1945.

From 1934 through 1945 collectors, dealers, and investors set aside large numbers of 50-coin bank-wrapped rolls of Mercury dimes, the only exception being 1934-D (see the next listing). This was the beginning of widespread interest in coins inspired by Wayte Raymond's National albums, which were soon followed by Whitman boards and, later, albums.

Dimes began to be traded in quantity as rolls—without being opened for inspection. No one heard of Full Bands, and there were no different levels of Mint State.

Looking ahead in the marketplace, beginning with the great coin-market boom that started in 1960, most of the earlier-saved rolls of Mercury dimes of the 1930s were broken up and sold as individual coins. This was true of some Mercury dime rolls of the 1940s, but rolls were still traded as such. *The Coin Dealer Newsletter*, launched in California in 1963, gave bid and ask prices for coins, including rolls, and did much to bring large numbers of investors into the market (who did not collect coins in the traditional way, did little reading or studying, and left the market when it crashed in 1965).

Countless millions of worn Mercury dimes of the 1930s and 1940s were melted in the late 1970s during a great run of silver speculation. The metal reached an all-time high of $50.35 per ounce on Comex on January 18, 1980, giving a silver dime the melt-down value of $3.64.

Availability and sharpness: The 4 in 1934 is light. Many coins have Full Bands. Population reports are of very little use in comparing the availability of regular Mint State coins with that of FB coins, as the latter are submitted to the grading services in larger quantities due to their significant value. This point is little understood by investors and casual buyers.

	Cert	Avg	%MS	F-12	VF-20	EF-40	AU-50	MS-60	MS-63	MS-65	MS-65FB	MS-66
1934	1,065	64.4	96%	$2.75	$3	$3.25	$16	$25	$35	$50	$140	$65

1934-D *Winged Liberty Dime*

1934-D • **Circulation-Strike Mintage:** 6,772,000.

Commentary: Large and small mintmarks appear on 1934-D dimes, but in the marketplace not much attention is paid to the differences. The small mintmarks end the style used for many years, and the large mintmarks introduce the size continued through 1945 (except for a variety of 1945-S).

Availability and sharpness: This is the one mintmarked variety of Mercury dimes after 1931 that was not available in roll quantities in the 1950s, although single pieces were common enough. Most are fairly well struck and very attractive. Those with Full Bands are in the minority, however, and command a strong premium.

	Cert	Avg	%MS	F-12	VF-20	EF-40	AU-50	MS-60	MS-63	MS-65	MS-65FB	MS-66
1934-D	729	64.1	95%	$2.75	$3	$8	$33	$50	$60	$85	$325	$230

1935 *Winged Liberty Dime*

1935 • **Circulation-Strike Mintage:** 58,830,000.

Availability and sharpness: The 1935 Mercury dimes are common in all grades. Full Bands coins are in the minority among surviving Mint State pieces but are common on an absolute basis.

	Cert	Avg	%MS	F-12	VF-20	EF-40	AU-50	MS-60	MS-63	MS-65	MS-65FB	MS-66
1935	1,673	65.0	96%	$2.75	$3	$3.25	$7	$10	$15	$35	$75	$60

1935-D *Winged Liberty Dime*

1935-D • **Circulation-Strike Mintage:** 10,477,000.

Availability and sharpness: The 1935-D dimes are common in all grades. Full Bands coins represent a small percentage of Mint State coins and sell at a particularly sharp premium.

	Cert	Avg	%MS	F-12	VF-20	EF-40	AU-50	MS-60	MS-63	MS-65	MS-65FB	MS-66
1935-D	531	63.8	94%	$2.75	$3	$8	$26	$35	$50	$90	$525	$325

1935-S Winged Liberty Dime

1935-S • **Circulation-Strike Mintage:** 15,840,000.

Availability and sharpness: The 1935-S dimes are common in all grades. Full Bands coins are rare in comparison to typical strikes. Cherrypicking is advised as most FB coins are not sharply delineated and the bands can be somewhat flat.

	Cert	Avg	%MS	F-12	VF-20	EF-40	AU-50	MS-60	MS-63	MS-65	MS-65FB	MS-66
1935-S	675	64.6	95%	$2.75	$3	$5	$16	$22	$30	$40	$350	$80

1936 Winged Liberty Dime

1936 • **Circulation-Strike Mintage:** 87,500,000.

Availability and sharpness: Circulation-strike 1936 dimes are common in all grades. Full Bands coins are easy to find, but sell for a premium.

	Cert	Avg	%MS	F-12	VF-20	EF-40	AU-50	MS-60	MS-63	MS-65	MS-65FB	MS-66
1936	2,851	64.9	96%	$2.75	$3	$3.25	$7	$10	$18	$30	$90	$48

1936, Proof • **Proof Mintage:** 4,130.

Commentary: This is the first year that Proofs were made in the Mercury dime series. Production continued in succeeding years through 1942.

Availability: Proofs of 1936 are readily available. Because of the mintage, this is the scarcest Proof date.

	Cert	Avg	%MS	PF-65	PF-66	PF-67
1936, Proof	1,082	65.0		$1,100	$1,250	$2,800

1936-D Winged Liberty Dime

1936-D • **Circulation-Strike Mintage:** 16,132,000.

Availability and sharpness: Denver Mint dimes of 1936 are common in all grades. Most are fairly well struck. The surfaces vary in quality, and deeply frosty coins are in the minority. Full Bands coins are rare in comparison to regular strikes, but enough are around that finding one is easy enough.

	Cert	Avg	%MS	F-12	VF-20	EF-40	AU-50	MS-60	MS-63	MS-65	MS-65FB	MS-66
1936-D	631	64.0	93%	$2.75	$3	$6	$16	$25	$40	$55	$275	$80

1936-S Winged Liberty Dime

1936-S • **Circulation-Strike Mintage:** 9,210,000.

Availability and sharpness: The 1936-S dimes are common in all grades. Most are fairly well struck. Full Bands coins are scarce in comparison to regular strikes, but are common in an absolute sense.

	Cert	Avg	%MS	F-12	VF-20	EF-40	AU-50	MS-60	MS-63	MS-65	MS-65FB	MS-66
1936-S	1,138	65.3	99%	$2.75	$3	$3.25	$13	$23	$30	$38	$95	$55

1937 Winged Liberty Dime

1937 • **Circulation-Strike Mintage:** 56,860,000.

Availability and sharpness: Circulation-strike 1937 dimes are common in all grades. Full Bands coins are easy to find, but sell for a premium.

	Cert	Avg	%MS	F-12	VF-20	EF-40	AU-50	MS-60	MS-63	MS-65	MS-65FB	MS-66
1937	4,368	65.6	99%	$2.75	$3	$3.25	$7	$10	$15	$30	$60	$40

1937, Proof • **Proof Mintage:** 5,756.

Availability: Proofs are readily available. Thanks to the mintage, this is the second-scarcest Proof date.

	Cert	Avg	%MS	PF-65	PF-66	PF-67
1937, Proof	1,271	65.4		$500	$550	$800

1937-D Winged Liberty Dime

1937-D • **Circulation-Strike Mintage:** 14,146,000.

Availability and sharpness: The 1937-D dime is common in all grades. Most are fairly well struck. Full Bands coins are common in an absolute sense.

	Cert	Avg	%MS	F-12	VF-20	EF-40	AU-50	MS-60	MS-63	MS-65	MS-65FB	MS-66
1937-D	1,053	65.2	97%	$2.75	$3	$4	$12	$21	$30	$45	$100	$85

1937-S Winged Liberty Dime

1937-S • Circulation-Strike Mintage: 9,740,000.

Availability and sharpness: The 1937-S dimes are common in all grades. Most are fairly well struck. Full Bands coins are scarce in comparison to regular strikes, but are common in an absolute sense. Many are FB by minimum definition. Cherrypicking is recommended to acquire a really sharp coin.

	Cert	Avg	%MS	F-12	VF-20	EF-40	AU-50	MS-60	MS-63	MS-65	MS-65FB	MS-66
1937-S	2,986	65.3	97%	$2.75	$3	$3.25	$12	$20	$30	$40	$185	$80

1938 Winged Liberty Dime

1938 • Circulation-Strike Mintage: 22,190,000.

Availability and sharpness: Circulation-strike 1938 dimes are common in all grades. Full Bands coins are easy to find, but sell for a premium.

	Cert	Avg	%MS	F-12	VF-20	EF-40	AU-50	MS-60	MS-63	MS-65	MS-65FB	MS-66
1938	1,728	65.5	99%	$2.75	$3	$3.25	$7	$10	$15	$30	$85	$55

1938, Proof • Proof Mintage: 8,728.

Availability: Proofs are readily available. The mintage makes this the third-scarcest Proof date.

	Cert	Avg	%MS	PF-65	PF-66	PF-67
1938, Proof	1,819	65.4		$275	$325	$700

1938-D Winged Liberty Dime

1938-D • Circulation-Strike Mintage: 5,537,000.

Commentary: The 1938-D dime has the lowest mintage of any circulation-strike date and mintmark from 1934 to 1945, inclusive.

Availability and sharpness: Unlike the situation for the slightly higher mintage 1934-D, 1938-D dimes were saved to the extent of hundreds or more rolls and are common in all grades today. Most are fairly well struck. Full Bands coins are common in an absolute sense.

	Cert	Avg	%MS	F-12	VF-20	EF-40	AU-50	MS-60	MS-63	MS-65	MS-65FB	MS-66
1938-D	1,897	65.5	99%	$2.75	$3	$4	$11	$18	$25	$35	$65	$75

1938-S Winged Liberty Dime

1938-S • **Circulation-Strike Mintage:** 8,090,000.

Availability and sharpness: the 1938-S dime is common in all grades. As is true of all regular dates and mint issues of the decade, millions were melted during the silver speculation of the late 1970s. Mint State coins are common and are usually quite attractive. Full Band dimes are much scarcer than regular strikes, but there are enough around that finding one will not be difficult.

	Cert	Avg	%MS	F-12	VF-20	EF-40	AU-50	MS-60	MS-63	MS-65	MS-65FB	MS-66
1938-S	1,046	65.0	97%	$2.75	$3	$3.50	$12	$20	$28	$42	$160	$80

1939 Winged Liberty Dime

1939 • **Circulation-Strike Mintage:** 67,740,000.

Commentary: World War II began in Europe this year with the Nazi invasions of Poland and Czechoslovakia. In America the Depression was ending. The World's Fair held in Flushing Meadows, New York City, was a great success.

Availability and sharpness: Circulation-strike 1939 dimes are common in all grades. Full Bands coins are easy to find but are very scarce in comparison to typical strikes.

	Cert	Avg	%MS	F-12	VF-20	EF-40	AU-50	MS-60	MS-63	MS-65	MS-65FB	MS-66
1939	3,602	65.7	98%	$2.75	$3	$3.25	$6	$8	$12	$26	$180	$40

1939, Proof • **Proof Mintage:** 9,321.

Availability: Proofs are readily available.

	Cert	Avg	%MS	PF-65	PF-66	PF-67
1939, Proof	2,029	65.9		$225	$235	$425

1939-D Winged Liberty Dime

1939-D • **Circulation-Strike Mintage:** 24,394,000.

Availability and sharpness: The 1939-D dimes are common in all grades. Most are sharply struck. This is one variety for which Full Bands coins command only a modest premium.

	Cert	Avg	%MS	F-12	VF-20	EF-40	AU-50	MS-60	MS-63	MS-65	MS-65FB	MS-66
1939-D	3,829	65.6	99%	$2.75	$3	$3.25	$6	$8	$12	$32	$55	$60

1939-S Winged Liberty Dime

1939-S • **Circulation-Strike Mintage:** 10,540,000.

Availability and sharpness: The 1939-S dimes are common in all grades. Full Bands coins represent a small percentage of Mint State coins and sell at a particularly sharp multiplier over a typically struck coin—quite a contrast to the 1939-D.

	Cert	Avg	%MS	F-12	VF-20	EF-40	AU-50	MS-60	MS-63	MS-65	MS-65FB	MS-66
1939-S	869	65.0	96%	$2.75	$3	$4	$13	$23	$30	$42	$725	$110

1940 Winged Liberty Dime

1940 • **Circulation-Strike Mintage:** 65,350,000.

Availability and sharpness: Circulation-strike 1940 dimes are common in all grades. Most are well struck. Full Bands coins are common, but sell at a premium, partly due to the cost of certifying them.

	Cert	Avg	%MS	F-12	VF-20	EF-40	AU-50	MS-60	MS-63	MS-65	MS-65FB	MS-66
1940	3,819	65.6	98%	$2.75	$3	$3.25	$5	$7	$12	$30	$50	$45

1940, Proof • **Proof Mintage:** 11,827.

Availability: Proofs are readily available.

	Cert	Avg	%MS	PF-65	PF-66	PF-67
1940, Proof	2,214	65.6		$180	$200	$375

1940-D Winged Liberty Dime

1940-D • **Circulation-Strike Mintage:** 21,198,000.

Availability and sharpness: The 1940-D dimes are common in all grades. Most are sharply struck with at least partial separation of the central bands. Full Bands coins are common.

	Cert	Avg	%MS	F-12	VF-20	EF-40	AU-50	MS-60	MS-63	MS-65	MS-65FB	MS-66
1940-D	2,649	65.5	99%	$2.75	$3	$3.25	$5	$7	$14	$35	$50	$60

1940-S Winged Liberty Dime

1940-S • **Circulation-Strike Mintage:** 21,560,000.

Availability and sharpness: The 1940-S dimes are common in all grades. Among Mint State coins, those with Full Bands are much scarcer than normal strikes and command a sharp premium.

	Cert	Avg	%MS	F-12	VF-20	EF-40	AU-50	MS-60	MS-63	MS-65	MS-65FB	MS-66
1940-S	2,814	65.5	99%	$2.75	$3	$3.25	$6	$8	$15	$35	$100	$40

1941 Winged Liberty Dime

1941 • **Circulation-Strike Mintage:** 175,090,000.

Commentary: The United States officially entered World War II after the Japanese invasion of Pearl Harbor, Hawaii, on December 7, 1941. Wartime demand soon ramped up dime mintages, which would stay very high through the end of the Mercury series in 1945.

Availability and sharpness: Circulation-strike 1941 dimes are common in all grades. Most are well struck. Full Bands coins are common, but sell at a slight premium, partly due to the cost of certifying them.

	Cert	Avg	%MS	F-12	VF-20	EF-40	AU-50	MS-60	MS-63	MS-65	MS-65FB	MS-66
1941	5,030	65.1	97%	$2.75	$3	$3.25	$5	$7	$12	$30	$50	$45

1941, Proof • Proof Mintage: 16,557.

Availability: Proofs are readily available.

	Cert	Avg	%MS	PF-65	PF-66	PF-67
1941, Proof	2,831	65.5		$175	$200	$325

1941-D Winged Liberty Dime

1941-D • Circulation-Strike Mintage: 45,634,000.

Availability and sharpness: The 1941-D dime is common in all grades. Among Mint State coins, Full Bands are quite common.

	Cert	Avg	%MS	F-12	VF-20	EF-40	AU-50	MS-60	MS-63	MS-65	MS-65FB	MS-66
1941-D	3,806	65.2	98%	$2.75	$3	$3.25	$6	$8	$14	$25	$50	$32

1941-S Winged Liberty Dime

1941-S • Circulation-Strike Mintage: 43,090,000.

Availability and sharpness: The 1941-S dimes are common in all grades. Among Mint State coins, FB dimes are quite common.

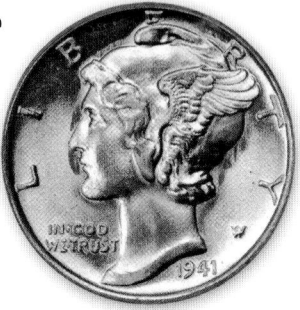

	Cert	Avg	%MS	F-12	VF-20	EF-40	AU-50	MS-60	MS-63	MS-65	MS-65FB	MS-66
1941-S	5,111	65.4	98%	$2.75	$3	$3.25	$5	$7	$12	$30	$50	$38

VARIETY: *1941-S, Large S Mintmark (FS-10-1941S-511).* The vast majority of 1941-S dimes have a small mintmark—the standard size for dimes dating back to 1916. These are readily available in all grades. Full Bands coins are common. Those with Large S are fewer, but the marketplace pays little attention to the difference.

Detail of the Small S Mintmark.

FS-10-1941S-511, Large S Mintmark.

1942, Winged Liberty Dime

1942, 42 Over 41 • Circulation-Strike Mintage: Part of the total mintage for the issue.

Commentary: The 1942, 42 Over 41, overdate was made when a 1941 working die and was overpunched with a 1942 master die. The result was a 1942 date with traces of 1941 under it. Many if not most seem to have been released in New York City and towns and cities north of it. The first published mention was printed in the *Numismatic Scrapbook Magazine*, March 1943:

Detail of the overdate.

> Recently I came across a 1942 dime (I look at every coin I touch) that would pass as brilliant Uncirculated, and on close examination it turned out to be 1942 over 1942. Have you heard or seen anything of this dime or can you tell me where I might get some information about it? Arnold Cohn, Kingston, N.Y.

News spread rapidly, and soon the coins were worth several dollars each. Subway-token sellers in kiosks learned of them and started looking. Several became professional numismatists, including M.L. Kaplan, Herb Tobias, and (less well known) Morris Moscow.

The find caused quite a stir among collectors. Seeking to learn more about the curious coin, Stuart Mosher, editor of *The Numismatist*, wrote to the Mint and received this reply:

> Treasury Department
> Washington 25, D.C.
> June 7, 1946
>
> Dear Mr. Mosher:
>
> Your letter of recent date, addressed to the superintendent of the Mint at Philadelphia, has been referred to this office for attention. You inquired regarding an overdated ten-cent piece and enclosed a photograph thereof.
>
> Since it appears that several like specimens have been found, it may be assumed that they were made from an imperfect die, which under the extreme pressure of war work and lack of experienced personnel, escaped detection.
>
> The dime under consideration, with a date of 1942 over 1941, was not re-punched or re-engraved. In September of each year the engraving of the numerals in the new master die for the following year is started. From this master die a working die hub is drawn. This is retouched if necessary, and then hardened. This hub is used to fabricate all the working (coinage) dies for that year. Therefore, during the months of September, October, November, and December the Engraving Department is working on dies for the current year's coinage and, at the same time, preparing those for the following year. Approximately one thousand dies with new date must be ready by January 1st of each year. During that period when utmost vigilance was required to keep the dies segregated by respective years, a die may have been given one blow with a 1941 hub and then finished with a 1942 hub.
>
> All dies are usually inspected by a number of skilled workmen before they are delivered. Due to the heavy demand for coins the Engraving Department had necessarily streamlined its operations and such an imperfect die apparently escaped attention.
>
> *Very truly yours,*
> *Nellie Tayloe Ross*
> *Director of the Mint*

Availability and sharpness: Editor Stuart Mosher, in reply to a reader's question, commented on the overdate in the September 1947 issue of *The Numismatist*:

> While the 1942 over 1941 dime is not rare at this time, it is difficult to obtain in Uncirculated condition. As far as we know all the pieces in the hands of collectors were found in circulation. When they were discovered an alert employee employed by the New York Independent Subway System was able to locate over 1,000 of them. This same collector reports that they are rarely found in circulation today, and when they are they are badly worn.

Today, examples are easily enough obtained in grades through Extremely Fine and About Uncirculated, but they represent a tiny fraction of the 1942 dimes in existence. Most are fairly well struck. Mint State coins are scarce, and in MS-64 or higher they are rare in comparison to the demand for them. Full Bands coins are in the minority and command a strong premium when found.

	Cert	Avg	%MS	F-12	VF-20	EF-40	AU-50	MS-60	MS-63	MS-65	MS-65FB	MS-66
1942, 42 Over 41	1,831	36.3	6%	$450	$550	$650	$1,000	$2,500	$4,500	$15,000	$45,000	$20,000

1942 • Circulation-Strike Mintage: 205,410,000.

Availability and sharpness: Circulation-strike 1942 dimes are common in all grades, as might be expected from the record mintage—the highest up to this point, although 1944 was even higher. Most are well struck. Full Bands coins are common.

	Cert	Avg	%MS	F-12	VF-20	EF-40	AU-50	MS-60	MS-63	MS-65	MS-65FB	MS-66
1942	6,037	64.9	97%	$2.75	$3	$3.25	$4.50	$6.00	$12.00	$30	$50	$45

1942, Proof • Proof Mintage: 22,329.

Availability: Proofs are readily available. This is the last year they were struck.

	Cert	Avg	%MS	PF-65	PF-66	PF-67
1942, Proof	4,147	65.7		$175	$200	$300

1942-D, Winged Liberty Dime

1942-D, 42 Over 41 • Circulation-Strike Mintage: Part of the total mintage for the issue.

Commentary: Unlike the situation for the Philadelphia Mint overdate, the 1942-D, 42 Over 41, was unknown to collectors until years after the pieces were struck. The motto IN GOD WE TRUST is ever so slightly doubled.

The variety was first listed in the *Guide Book of United States Coins* in the 25th edition, 1972, without pricing; and with pricing, first in the 27th edition, 1974: Fine $150, VF $200. Demand increased dramatically. Several Mint State coins came on the market and brought surprisingly high prices. In August 1981 one with Full Bands sold for a

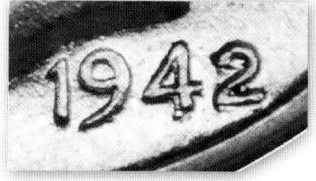

Detail of the overdate.

remarkable $12,000 at the ANA convention auction in New Orleans. In December of the same year another brought $9,000. This was in the era before third-party certification of coins in holders, and in retrospect it is difficult to compare prices, as quality varied. The 1942-D, 42 Over 41, was soon recognized as the most valuable Mercury dime in Mint State.

Availability and sharpness: The 1942-D, 42 Over 41, dimes range from scarce to rare in all grades. After this variety gained notice in the mid-1970s (see the preceding commentary), interest in it became very strong. By that time, Mercury dimes were no longer in circulation. Sorting through accumulations of worn coins yielded hundreds in grades from Very Good to Very Fine or so. Mint State coins survived by chance, and a few were found mixed in with other dimes in bank-wrapped rolls. Such coins always create a lot of attention when sold at auction. Grade for grade they are much rarer than the more-famous 1916-D dimes. Full Bands coins are in the minority and command a strong premium when found.

	Cert	Avg	%MS	F-12	VF-20	EF-40	AU-50	MS-60	MS-63	MS-65	MS-65FB	MS-66
1942-D, 42 Over 41	1,032	33.5	9%	$425	$525	$600	$1,000	$2,500	$4,750	$10,000	$32,000	$12,000

1942-D • Circulation-Strike Mintage: 60,740,000.

Availability and sharpness: The 1942-D dimes are common in all grades. Many were melted in the 1970s. Mint State coins are common, and Full Bands coins are easily found among them.

	Cert	Avg	%MS	F-12	VF-20	EF-40	AU-50	MS-60	MS-63	MS-65	MS-65FB	MS-66
1942-D	4,806	64.5	95%	$2.75	$3	$3.25	$4.50	$6	$12	$28	$48	$45

1942-S Winged Liberty Dime

1942-S • Circulation-Strike Mintage: 49,300,000.

Commentary: All examples seen have a Large S mintmark, although Walter H. Breen stated that 1 in 10 has a Small S mintmark. David W. Lange, who has probably studied Mercury dimes more carefully than anyone else, does not list a Small S variety.

Availability and sharpness: The 1942-S is common in all grades. Among Mint State coins, Full Bands are much scarcer than ordinary strikes.

	Cert	Avg	%MS	F-12	VF-20	EF-40	AU-50	MS-60	MS-63	MS-65	MS-65FB	MS-66
1942-S	2,084	64.9	97%	$2.75	$3	$3.25	$6.00	$8	$20	$30	$150	$50

1943 Winged Liberty Dime

1943 • Circulation-Strike Mintage: 191,710,000.

Commentary: The coin market had been strong since the late 1930s, but beginning in 1943 it expanded widely, and prices of many coins, including dimes, rose dramatically.

Availability and sharpness: As might be expected from the immense mintage, 1943 dimes are easily available in any grade desired. Full Bands coins are common.

	Cert	Avg	%MS	F-12	VF-20	EF-40	AU-50	MS-60	MS-63	MS-65	MS-65FB	MS-66
1943	6,123	65.3	98%	$2.75	$3	$3.25	$4.50	$6	$12	$27	$55	$35

1943-D Winged Liberty Dime

1943-D • Circulation-Strike Mintage: 71,949,000.

Availability and sharpness: The 1943-D dime is very common and easily found in any grade desired. Full Bands coins are plentiful.

	Cert	Avg	%MS	F-12	VF-20	EF-40	AU-50	MS-60	MS-63	MS-65	MS-65FB	MS-66
1943-D	6,459	65.5	99%	$2.75	$3	$3.25	$4.50	$6	$15	$30	$50	$45

1943-S Winged Liberty Dime

1943-S • Circulation-Strike Mintage: 60,400,000.

Availability and sharpness: The 1943-S dimes as a date and mintmark are very common. The S on most has prominent serifs. Most are well struck.

	Cert	Avg	%MS	F-12	VF-20	EF-40	AU-50	MS-60	MS-63	MS-65	MS-65FB	MS-66
1943-S	3,700	65.6	98%	$2.75	$3	$3.25	$5.00	$7	$16	$30	$70	$40

1944 Winged Liberty Dime

1944 • Circulation-Strike Mintage: 231,410,000.

Availability and sharpness: As might be expected from the all-time high mintage figure, 1944 dimes are extremely common. Mint State coins are plentiful. Full Bands coins are easily found as well, but are scarcer than regular strikes and command a multiple premium.

	Cert	Avg	%MS	F-12	VF-20	EF-40	AU-50	MS-60	MS-63	MS-65	MS-65FB	MS-66
1944	7,735	65.3	98%	$2.75	$3	$3.25	$4.50	$6	$12	$25	$80	$45

1944-D Winged Liberty Dime

1944-D • **Circulation-Strike Mintage:** 62,224,000.

Availability and sharpness: The 1944-D dime is very common in all grades. Most are very well struck. Full Bands coins are easy to find.

	Cert	Avg	%MS	F-12	VF-20	EF-40	AU-50	MS-60	MS-63	MS-65	MS-65FB	MS-66
1944-D	8,291	65.7	99%	$2.75	$3	$3.25	$5.00	$7	$15	$30	$50	$48

1944-S Winged Liberty Dime

1944-S • **Circulation-Strike Mintage:** 49,490,000.

Availability and sharpness: San Francisco dimes of 1944 are very common in all grades. Most are very well struck. Full Bands coins are easily to find, but are less often seen than are regular strikes.

	Cert	Avg	%MS	F-12	VF-20	EF-40	AU-50	MS-60	MS-63	MS-65	MS-65FB	MS-66
1944-S	5,925	65.8	99%	$2.75	$3	$3.25	$5.00	$7	$15	$30	$55	$50

1945 Winged Liberty Dime

1945 • **Circulation-Strike Mintage:** 159,130,000.

Availability and sharpness: The 1945 Philadelphia Mint dimes are very common and can be found in any grade desired. Full Bands dimes, a dramatic exception, are extremely rare, and in fact are far rarer than any other FB variety in the series. As such they command an incredible premium (see the introduction to this section).

	Cert	Avg	%MS	F-12	VF-20	EF-40	AU-50	MS-60	MS-63	MS-65	MS-65FB	MS-66
1945	8,706	65.4	99%	$2.75	$3	$3.25	$4.50	$6	$12	$28	$10,000	$45

1945-D Winged Liberty Dime

1945-D • **Circulation-Strike Mintage:** 40,245,000.

Availability and sharpness: Regular die varieties of the 1945-D dime are common in all grades, and Full Bands coins are easily found.

	Cert	Avg	%MS	F-12	VF-20	EF-40	AU-50	MS-60	MS-63	MS-65	MS-65FB	MS-66
1945-D	8,291	65.6	99%	$2.75	$3	$3.25	$4.50	$6	$12	$26	$45	$50

VARIETY: *1945-D, D Over Horizontal D Mintmark (FS-10-1945D-506).* One die has the D mintmark erroneously punched horizontally, and then corrected with a second punching in the correct vertical position. This variety is little known but is far rarer than a regular 1945-D. Examples sell for many multiples of a regular coin.

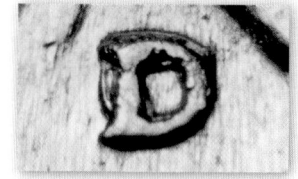

FS-10-1945D-506,
Repunched Mintmark.

1945-S Winged Liberty Dime

1945-S • Circulation-Strike Mintage: 41,920,000.

Availability and sharpness: Regular die varieties of the 1945-D dime are common in all grades. Full Bands coins are in the minority among Mint State coins and sell for several multiples of the prices of regular strikes.

	Cert	Avg	%MS	F-12	VF-20	EF-40	AU-50	MS-60	MS-63	MS-65	MS-65FB	MS-66
1945-S	7,985	65.7	99%	$2.75	$3	$3.25	$4.50	$6	$12	$30	$125	$40

VARIETY: *1945-S, "Micro S" Mintmark (FS-10-1945S-512).* One or more reverse dies had a slightly smaller S mintmark. While hardly microscopic, this variety is known as the "Micro S" and is listed in *A Guide Book of United States Coins.* Accordingly, strong demand has been built for it, and today the variety is widely collected.

Normal S Mintmark.

FS-10-1945S-512,
Micro S Mintmark.

VARIETY: *1945-S, S Over Horizontal S Mintmark (FS-10-1945S-503).* The S mintmark was first punched into the die in a horizontal position and then corrected. Examples sell for many multiples of a regular coin.

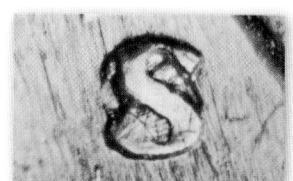

FS-10-1945S-503, S Over
Horizontal S Mintmark.

VARIETY: *1945-S, S Over D Mintmark (FS-10-1945S-511).* This variety has not been confirmed. Traces of a letter, possibly a D, can be seen beneath the S.

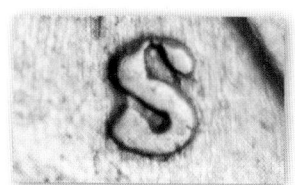

FS-10-1945S-511,
S Over D Mintmark.

ROOSEVELT DIMES (1946 TO DATE): HISTORY AND BACKGROUND

Silver (1946–1964, and some modern Proofs)—**Designer:** *John R. Sinnock.*
Weight: *2.50 grams.* **Composition:** *.900 silver, .100 copper (net weight: .07234 oz. pure silver).*
Diameter: *17.9 mm.* **Edge:** *Reeded.* **Mints:** *Philadelphia, Denver, San Francisco, and West Point.*

Copper-nickel (1965 to date)—**Designer:** *John R. Sinnock.* **Weight:** *2.27 grams.*
Composition: *Outer layers of copper-nickel (.750 copper, .250 nickel) bonded to inner core of pure copper.*
Diameter: *17.9 mm.* **Edge:** *Reeded.* **Mints:** *Philadelphia, Denver, San Francisco, and West Point.*

Silver, Circulation Strike *Mintmark location, 1946–1964, is on the reverse, to the left of the fasces.* **Silver, Proof**

Clad, Circulation Strike *Mintmark location, 1965 to date, is on the obverse, above the date.* **Clad, Proof**

A NEW DIME FOR FDR

In April 1945 President Franklin Delano Roosevelt passed away. He had been in the White House since March 4, 1933, had served three full terms, and was going into his fourth—an unprecedented tenure. His presidency was popular not only for his domestic innovations as chief executive but also for his leadership as commander-in-chief of the American armed forces. His passing was widely mourned. World War II ended in August 1945, by which time Harry S Truman (his middle name was a lone initial), the former vice president, had taken Roosevelt's place.

The Winged Liberty Head or "Mercury" dime had been in circulation since 1916. To honor Roosevelt's memory Congress decided to place his image on the dime. A victim since his teen-age years of Guillain-Barré syndrome, misdiagnosed as infantile paralysis (polio), Roosevelt on January 3, 1938, had established the National Foundation for Infantile Paralysis to combat and, it was hoped, cure the disease. Epidemics of polio often swept areas of America in the summer, forcing the closing of swimming pools and other facilities to prevent transmission of the disease. There were countless thousands of victims, some of whom lived in mechanical "iron lungs" in order to breathe.

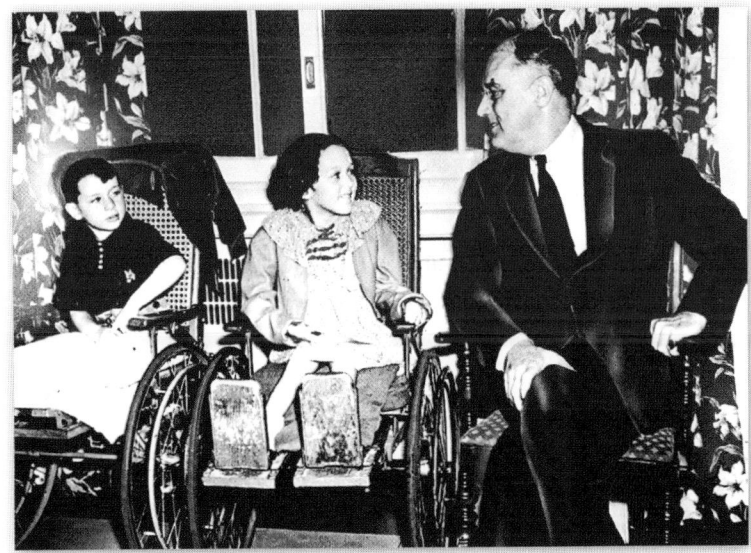

President Roosevelt with polio victims, 1940.

The campaign to raise money became known as the March of Dimes, coined by radio and screen comedian Eddie Cantor as a play on words after the newsreel and radio news series "The March of Time." In its first iteration in early 1938 the effort brought tens of thousands of letters to the White House, each containing one or more dimes, and sometimes other coins or currency, a total of more than $85,000.

In time the campaign raised hundreds of millions of dollars. Years later in 1955 the vaccine developed by Dr. Jonas Salk provided a cure. By that time the foundation had spent $233,000,000 on patient care.

President Roosevelt, the dime, and the search for an end to polio were all combined in the coin that debuted in 1946.

January 25, 1939: Millions of dimes in bags, envelopes, and packages pour into the White House as part of President Franklin Roosevelt's March of Dimes. Barbara Councilor of the White House mail room holds handfuls of the dimes.

FRANKLIN ROOSEVELT'S PLACE IN AMERICAN HISTORY

Franklin Delano Roosevelt, often named in print as FDR, was president of the United States from 1933 to 1945, the longest tenure of any chief executive. Serving under him as vice presidents were John Nance Garner, 1933 to 1941; Henry A. Wallace, 1941 to 1945; and Harry S Truman, 1945.

Roosevelt was born in Hyde Park, New York, on January 30, 1882, the son of James and Sara Delano Roosevelt, members of a prominent family. He was a fifth cousin to Theodore Roosevelt (who from 1901 to 1909 would serve as president). Franklin graduated from Harvard in 1903, and then went to Columbia law school. While there, he married Anna Eleanor Roosevelt, a fifth cousin, over his mother's objections. President Theodore Roosevelt gave the bride away at their March 17, 1905, wedding. The couple would have six children, including one who died in infancy. Eleanor became famous in her own right as a champion of women's rights and other causes. She is remembered as one of the most accomplished First Ladies in history.

Franklin D. Roosevelt around the time of his marriage.

The study of law was boring to Roosevelt, and he dropped out of Columbia in 1907, after having learned enough to pass the New York State bar exam while still a student. He then became affiliated with a prominent law firm, Carter, Ledyard & Milburn, in New York City. Unlike his Republican cousin Theodore, Franklin signed with the Democratic ticket. His handsome appearance, warm personality, and intelligence made him a favorite, and he was encouraged to run for the State Legislature. His bid was successful, and he served from 1911 to 1913, followed by a position as assistant secretary of the Navy, 1913 to 1920. In 1920 he was on the national ticket as vice president, but the Democrats lost to Republican Warren G. Harding.

In August 1921 a worse setback occurred. While swimming in cold water near Campobello Island, New Brunswick, where he had a summer home, he became chilled and sustained cramps. When he tried to stand, his legs would not support him. After some confusion, he was misdiagnosed with poliomyelitis and was confined to a wheelchair. Undaunted, he set about a regimen of exercise and recovery, including bathing

at Warm Springs, a Georgia spa. Recovery was slow and painful and never complete, as he remained wheelchair-bound for the rest of his life.

With remarkable energy and effort Roosevelt resumed his political ambitions. In 1928 he was elected governor of New York, and in 1932 he was the Democratic choice to oppose incumbent Herbert Hoover in the presidential election. By that time the nation was mired in the Great Depression, with bank and business failures and widespread unemployment and distress. While Hoover said that "recovery is just around the corner," there were no signs of that happening.

Roosevelt was always careful to avoid being photographed in his wheelchair. In 1932 most people did not know of his disability, and his physical fitness was not an issue in the election. This was in an era quite different from later times. Personal illnesses, infidelities, and private activities of political figures were not regularly showcased in the news or in gossip columns.

In the November contest Roosevelt won in a landslide with 57 percent of the popular vote, carrying all but six states. Hoover offered to meet with him to share ideas on how to arrest the downward spiral of the economy, but Roosevelt refused, stating that this would just tie his hands. He set about lining up accomplished men for his Cabinet and held meetings individually with them long before he was inaugurated. One of them was William H. Woodin, a long-time numismatic scholar who was named as secretary of the Treasury (but served only briefly, retiring within the year due to a terminal illness).

Roosevelt was sworn into office on March 4, 1933. With a great deal of pre-planning, on March 6 he announced that all banks would be closed, in the so-called Bank Holiday orchestrated by Woodin, so they could be audited regarding their solvency. Those found to be in sound condition were allowed to reopen soon afterward, while banks in questionable condition were closed or forced to merge. On March 12 he had his first radio address, inaugurating a series of popular "fireside chats." A few days later on March 15 the Dow Jones Industrial average went from 53.84 to 62.10, or a gain of 15.34 percent, the highest one-day percentage gain before or since.

Having won the presidency with overwhelming support from the public, Roosevelt immediately set about making vast reforms in other areas as well, including public works and relief, aided by his well-informed Cabinet members. His campaign song, "Happy Days Are Here Again," became a favorite

Roosevelt in 1913.

Posters from political campaigns dating back to the 1910s.

on the airwaves. Roosevelt's first 100 days in office saw unprecedented changes in his "New Deal," as, metaphorically, a poor hand of cards was thrown away and replaced with one that might include some royal and ace cards. For the first time in several years of national economic depression, citizens had hope. In the meantime, Republicans accused the president of anarchy, unconstitutional actions, and other perfidy.

President Franklin D. Roosevelt.

The nation went off the gold standard in on January 30, 1934, taxes were increased, the national budget ran up a huge deficit, and concessions were made to labor interests. Much of this angered businessmen, many of whom said that Roosevelt's New Deal was filled with jokers and for the people was illegal and improper, and needed to be halted.

Year by year, opposition notwithstanding, many of Roosevelt's programs worked, although not without encountering challenges, such as the Dust Bowl in the Midwest in the mid-1930s.

Roosevelt was reelected in 1936, by which time the economy had improved dramatically. This was not to last, and in 1937 a recession set in. January 20 was by then the official inauguration date, replacing the traditional March 4. This reduced the lingering for an ineffective incumbent president who may have lost the November election. On February 5, 1937, President Roosevelt, taking issue with the Supreme Court resisting his innovative (many said radical) government plans to help combat the Depression, proposed increasing the number of justices on the Supreme Court. The idea of "packing" the Court caused outrage and on July 22, 1937, the United States Senate voted down Roosevelt's plan.

A pin for Roosevelt's 1936 presidential reelection campaign. (actual size: 16 mm)

After World War II commenced in Europe in the summer of 1939, Roosevelt worked with British leaders to supply munitions and other goods. This ended the American recession and, truly, happy times were here again in the economy. In 1940 he sought reelection for an unprecedented third term and won. After America entered the conflict in December 1941, Roosevelt worked with the military on strategy, cooperated with allies, and by spring 1945 had come close to victory, by then just entering his fourth term of office. On April 12, 1945, the ailing president died of a cerebral hemorrhage at Warm Springs, Georgia. He was succeeded by his new vice president, Harry S Truman, who had taken office just five weeks earlier and had not yet been briefed on many important matters, including development of the atomic bomb.

Today, historians have mixed views of Roosevelt's presidency, but by any account he was essential in the national recovery from the Great Depression and in America helping win World War II. His place on the 1946 dime was very appropriate.

DESIGN OF THE ROOSEVELT DIME

The plan to honor Roosevelt's memory on the new dime met with wide approval. Chief Engraver John R. Sinnock was tapped to create the designs. The obverse featured a profile portrait of Roosevelt, while the reverse depicted a torch flanked by a branch of olive and a branch of oak. The initials JS, for Sinnock, were placed below the neck truncation.

An International News Service dispatch datelined Philadelphia, January 20, 1946, stated this:

> Distribution of new Roosevelt dimes will start tomorrow. The initial run of two million bright, shiny dimes bearing the image of the late president has already been taken to Washington from the Philadelphia Mint.
>
> Mints in San Francisco and Denver began turning out the new coins yesterday for nationwide release.
>
> Striking of the Roosevelt dime marked the first time in 30 years that the nation's ten-cent piece has been changed. The present Liberty Head dimes, first struck in 1916, will continue in circulation, but no more will be minted.

As to the designer's initials, some wags wondered if Russian dictator Joseph Stalin was being honored. This article in the *Jersey Journal*, Jersey City, New Jersey, December 21, 1946, is typical:

> That "JS" on the front of the new Roosevelt time definitely doesn't mean that Joe Stalin was the designer. But those initials just below the neck of the face of the coin have many false stories that the office of the director over at the Treasury is busy denying one every day.
>
> The real "J.S." is John Sinnock, the chief designer at the Philadelphia Mint. He is designer of the beautiful Purple Heart medal, too.
>
> Many claimed he didn't have the right to put his initials on the coin and that "there is a penitentiary offense for sneaking the J.S. initials on the coin," That isn't true.

Accordingly, on his next coin design, that of the 1948 Franklin half dollar, Sinnock used his full initials, JRS.

Over the course of American coin designs, new issues have usually prompted public commentary, often negative. Although the Roosevelt dime's motif was not highly acclaimed in numismatic circles when it was released, perhaps because its predecessor, the classic "Mercury" dime, was a favorite, the new coins became widely collected.

Engraver John Sinnock's initials on the obverse of the dime.

CHIEF ENGRAVER JOHN R. SINNOCK

John Raymond Sinnock, designer of the Roosevelt dime, was born on July 8, 1888, in Raton, New Mexico. He became interested in art and sculpture and decided to pursue his career in that field. Relocating in the East he studied at the Pennsylvania Museum & School of Industrial Art where he was awarded the Mifflin Scholarship for advanced studies, including in Europe. Later he was an instructor at the Pennsylvania museum for eight years. There he gave day and evening classes in many subjects ranging from sculpture to pottery to costumes. He then became an instructor at the School of Industrial Art at the Western Reserve University in Cleveland, a position he held for ten years.

John R. Sinnock and a model for the new Roosevelt dime.

Sinnock then moved back to Philadelphia and in 1917 joined the Philadelphia Mint staff as an assistant medalist. Among his early work for the Mint was the design of the obverse of the 1918 Illinois Centennial commemorative half dollar. He then resigned, but joined the staff again in 1919. In 1921 when there was a hurry-up call for new dies to make silver dollars (which had last been struck in 1904, and their hubs destroyed in 1910), he made new hubs in imitation of the originals, but with slight differences. His work was sufficiently appreciated that following the death of George T. Morgan he was appointed by President Calvin Coolidge as chief engraver on August 1, 1925, serving for the rest of his life. His designs and engravings included many medals and the Purple Heart award. In addition he did work for local murals and decorations. In 1926 he sculpted the models for the commemorative half dollar and quarter eagle made for the Sesquicentennial International Exposition. In 1932 he made the models for the Washington quarter dollar using designs created by John Flanagan.

Sinnock was a member of several societies including the Philadelphia Sketch Club, the National Sculpture Society, the American Federation of Art, and the American Artists Professional League.

For the October 1941 issue of *The Numismatist* Sinnock contributed an article, "Making Dies at the Philadelphia Mint." *The Numismatic Scrapbook Magazine*, March 1946, told of his work in "John R. Sinnock, Coin Designer," this soon after the release of the Roosevelt dime. Beyond the rather facetious "JS" publicity, it was alleged that his portrait of the president was not original, but had been copied from a bronze bas-relief by sculptress Selma H. Burke. In defense, he said that his portrait was a composite of two studies he did of Roosevelt from life in 1933 and 1934 as well as from photographs he studied.

John R. Sinnock died on May 14, 1947, at the Marine Hospital on Staten Island, New York City, the year before his last coin work, the 1948 Franklin half dollar, was struck for circulation.

THE BURKE DESIGN QUESTION

Artist Selma Burke contended that John Sinnock copied a drawing and sculpture that she created for a bas-relief plaque to decorate the new office building of the Recorder of Deeds in Washington, D.C. President Roosevelt sat for two sketching sessions with Burke. Her plaque was unveiled on September 24, 1945. The Smithsonian's American Art Museum credits Burke's work as the "model" or "inspiration" for the Roosevelt dime, as have some numismatists including Edward C. Rochette, a past president of the American Numismatic Association. Mainstream (non-numismatic) newspaper articles have sometimes identified Burke as the designer of the dime's Roosevelt portrait.

Numismatist Bob Van Ryzin, who interviewed Burke before she passed away in 1995, has said, "I found her to be a very gracious lady, and am convinced she truly believed until her death that she designed the dime."

On the other hand, U.S. Mint curator Dr. Robert Goler, quoted in a January 17, 2018, article in *Atlas Obscura* ("Who Really Designed the American Dime?"), observed that Sinnock began sculpting a presidential-medal portrait of Roosevelt in 1936—Burke's portrait was commissioned in 1943—and that Sinnock "used that particular design of Roosevelt multiple times between then and the president's death in 1945, and it's the same design." As he later would with Burke, the president sat for sketches with Sinnock.

Consensus among numismatic historians today is that Burke was an excellent artist, but that Sinnock was truly the Roosevelt dime's designer. "Ms. Burke had nothing to do with the FDR dime," wrote Roger W. Burdette in *The E-Sylum* (January 28, 2018). "The final

Selma Burke and her portrait of Franklin Roosevelt.

portrait was the outcome of two meetings between Sinnock and sculptor Lee Lawrie, who had been 'deputized' by the Commission of Fine Arts to review the dime designs." Also in *The E-Sylum* (February 4, 2018), medallic-arts expert Dick Johnson wrote, "John Sinnock created his image by making his design of Franklin Roosevelt fit nicely in the circular format, with a more realistic and attractive portrait. The fact of its similarity to Selma Burke's is purely coincidental."

PRODUCTION OF ROOSEVELT DIMES

From its debut until the original alloy was changed after 1964, production took place at the Philadelphia, Denver, and San Francisco mints. In 1955, when it was announced that the San Francisco Mint would cease coinage, perhaps forever, the Lincoln cents and Roosevelt dimes of 1955-S became wildly popular in numismatic circles, and many were saved. (For a time the mint would be known as an assay office; later the San Francisco Mint name was restored.)

In the early 1960s the price of silver rose sharply on international markets. By 1965 a dime, quarter, or half dollar—the denominations then currently made in silver—would have cost more than face value to produce. A new base-metal composition was adopted that year and has been continued in circulating dimes ever since. It consists of outer layers of copper-nickel (75 percent copper and 25 percent nickel) bonded to an inner core of pure copper. The copper is visible by viewing the coin edge-on. The diameter of 17.9 mm was unchanged from earlier times. Clad dimes weigh 2.27 grams each.

Proof dimes were made in the silver series from 1950 through 1964 inclusive and were struck at the Philadelphia Mint. Proof production was resumed in 1968, in copper-nickel alloy, at the San Francisco Mint, with an S mintmark on each coin. In addition to copper-nickel Proofs, Proofs in silver composition have been made at San Francisco since 1992 (and at the West Point Mint in 2015) in limited quantities for collectors. These are sold by the Mint at an additional premium.

Keen-eyed collectors have noted that details such as the size of President Roosevelt's portrait and the lettering of the coin's legends have changed over the years. U.S. Mint chief engraver John Mercanti, in correspondence with Whitman Publishing in July 2017, recalled: "They changed the artwork for currency sometime back in the mid-'70s or early '80s. We changed pennies, nickels, dimes, and quarters. The text was running into the rim in some places because from year to year we never made a new reduction. We would take a die and make a new hub and every year the text would slowly creep to the edge. This is also apparent in older coins. While we fixed the text we redid the portraits a little smaller." Another example: the year-date 2000 required noticeable adjustment of all obverse design elements, with the portrait again reduced in order to fit the date numerals. Similar modifications have been made to the reverse design. Such changes have been made frequently throughout the life of the Roosevelt dime, in the normal course of production. Because they don't alter the major motifs of the design, they are done without fanfare or announcements from the Mint. These modifications are interesting to contemplate, and they shed light on the minting process, but they do not affect market values of the coins.

Hub changes are evident when comparing dimes of consecutive dates, such as these 1999 and 2000 examples.

ROOSEVELT DIMES (1946 TO DATE): GUIDE TO COLLECTING

Dimes have remained a key denomination in circulation and continue to be made in quantity in Philadelphia and Denver.

Today a run of date-and-mintmark circulation-strike varieties contains no rarities, although the 1949, 1949-S, and 1950-S are considered somewhat scarce in the context of the series. A basic full set of circulation-strike Roosevelt dimes in Choice or Gem grades, MS-63 to MS-65, is very affordable and if in an album makes a great display. If you desire to specialize, there are several doubled dies that are scarcer and can be added.

Proof Roosevelt dimes are readily collectible as well, with the earlier dates being scarcer. Some Proofs of the 1950s command an additional premium if the portrait and other relief features have frosty rather than polished surfaces. A full set of regular Proofs is quite affordable. Special Mint Set (SMS) coins were struck in lieu of Proofs from 1965 to 1967 and in some instances closely resemble Proofs. Roosevelt dimes struck for Uncirculated Mint sets from 2005 through 2010 have a special Satin Finish.

Beyond the basics, some Proof dimes of 1968, 1970, 1975, and 1985 were struck in San Francisco with the S mintmark omitted in error. Each of these command a strong premium today. In 1982 the P mintmark was added to Philadelphia Mint dimes for the first time and became standard. Some circulation-strike 1982 dimes were made in Philadelphia without the P mintmark and are scarce today.

Some collectors seek attractively toned examples, their varied hues coming from storage in coin folders, albums, envelopes, or other environments that tarnish the coins' surfaces. As with any such toning, beauty is in the eye of the beholder, and other collectors prefer bright, white surfaces.

Toned Roosevelt dimes.

Roosevelt dimes are popular among registry-set competitors. As of early 2018 NGC has 1,776 registered sets; PCGS has registered 1,416 "major sets" and 558 "specialty sets."

Error collectors seek off-center, double-struck, wrong-planchet, clipped, and other unusual misstruck Roosevelt dimes, and variety collectors look for doubled dies, over-mintmarks, and similar die anomalies. Over-mintmarks in particular are added to many specialized sets.

An off-center Lincoln cent struck on a Roosevelt dime, one of only a handful known.

A 1964-D Roosevelt dime with a clipped planchet.

Numismatist Scott Schechter, writing in *Coin World* ("Roosevelt Dime Reverse Hub Changes Alter Perceptions," June 8, 2015), noted that "Specialists want Roosevelt dimes that are well struck. Specifically, examples showing fully split bands at the top and bottom of the torch on the reverse are most prized. In grading, this attribute is designated as Full Torch (FT) by NGC and Full Bands (FB) by PCGS." This applies to copper-nickel dates as well as silver. Only a tiny percentage of Roosevelt dimes have ever been judged to be FT, and very few numismatists collect them. Accordingly, they can be found by cherrypicking, without paying an additional premium. However, a dime in a certified holder marked *Full Torch* will cost more due to the expense involved in certification, and the perceived rarity (and therefore perceived, by some, value).

Full Torch details.

Regarding reverse details, Schechter wrote:

By the late 1960s, the hub used to make dies for Roosevelt dimes had worn considerably. The dies it created had muted detail, which contributes to the scarcity of well-struck examples. To address this, a new hub was created with crisper detail in 1968. It was used to make dies for Proof coins beginning in mid-1968, and on all circulation-strike dimes from 1971 to 1980.

Called the "Reverse of 1968," a modification to the flame is this reverse design's most distinguishing characteristic. Since the introduction of the Roosevelt dime in 1946, the flame atop the torch had gentle folds. In the 1968 incarnation, lines throughout the reverse were strengthened and two sharp incisions were added to give the flame more definition.

In 2011 it was discovered that 1969, 1970 and 1970-D dimes could be found with both the original Reverse of 1946 and the new Reverse of 1968. For all three issues, the 1968 type is much less common than the 1946 reverse.

Because details are more deeply incised in the new hub, coins with the Reverse of 1968 are more likely to be encountered with fully-split torch bands. Although they are less common overall, right now 1969 dimes with Reverse of 1968 comprise the majority of the full torch examples. This discovery is still very new, but affects a key date in the series.

Roosevelt Dimes, Silver and Clad (1946 to Date)

Grading Standards

MS-60 to 70 (Mint State). *Obverse:* At MS-60, some abrasion and contact marks are evident on the cheek, the hair above the ear, and the neck. At MS-63, abrasion is slight at best, less so for MS-64. An MS-65 coin should display no abrasion or contact marks except under magnification, and MS-66 and higher coins should have none at all. Luster should be full and rich. *Reverse:* Comments apply as for

1955-D. Graded MS-68FB.

the obverse, except that the highest parts of the torch, flame, and leaves are the places to check. On both sides the fields are protected by design elements and do not show contact marks readily.

AU-50, 53, 55, 58 (About Uncirculated). *Obverse:* Light wear is seen on the cheek and higher-relief part of the hair. At AU-58, the luster is extensive, but incomplete, especially on the higher parts and in the field. At AU–50 and 53, luster is less. *Reverse:* Light wear is seen on the higher parts of the torch and leaves. An AU-58 coin has nearly full luster. At AU–50 and 53, there still is significant luster.

1962-D. Graded AU-58.

EF-40, 45 (Extremely Fine). *Obverse:* Further wear is seen on the head. Some details are gone in the hair to the right of the forehead. *Reverse:* Further wear is seen on the torch, but the vertical lines are visible, some just barely. The higher-relief details in the leaves, never strong to begin with, are worn away.

The Roosevelt dime is seldom collected in grades lower than EF-40.

1950-S. Graded EF-40.

PF-60 to 70 (Proof). *Obverse and Reverse:* Proofs that are extensively cleaned and have many hairlines, or that are dull and grainy, are lower level, such as PF–60 to 62. These are not widely desired, and represent coins that have been mistreated. Fortunately, only a few Proof Roosevelt dimes are in this category. With medium hairlines and good reflectivity, assigned grades of PF–63 or 64 are appropriate. PF-65 may have hairlines so delicate that

1983-S, No S. Graded PF-69 Deep Cameo.

magnification is needed to see them. Above that, a Proof should be free of any hairlines or other problems.

Illustrated coin: The S mintmark is missing from this popular variety.

ROOSEVELT DIMES, SILVER (1946–1965)

1946 Roosevelt Dime

1946 • Circulation-Strike Mintage: 255,250,000.

Commentary: In the silver Roosevelt series, the 1964 Philadelphia coinage is one of the most abundant, with only the 1962-D, 1963-D, 1964, and 1964-D coins having higher mintages.

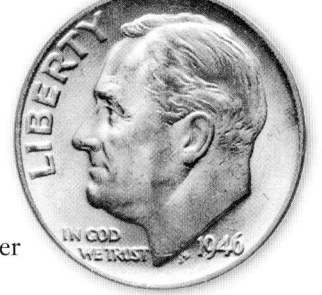

Two obverse hubs were used to produce dies in 1946. In the first, designer John Sinnock's initials were smaller, weaker, and less distinct. In the second they were sharpened and made bolder. Other minor differences involve the strength of Roosevelt's facial details. Collectors do not pay a premium for one hub variety over the other.

Availability and sharpness: The Roosevelt dime was very popular when it debuted, and many of the coins were hoarded by collectors and saved as mementoes by the general public. As a result, the Philadelphia issue, with a mintage in the hundreds of millions, is plentiful in Mint State today. Many have weak details in their strike, and do not have Full Torch (FT) details. Even so, Gems up to MS-66 are common, and even MS-67 examples exist in the hundreds.

	Cert	Avg	%MS	EF-40	MS-63	MS-65	MS-66	MS-67	MS-67FT
1946	1,826	66.0	100%	$2	$4.25	$12	$28	$55	$400

VARIETIES: *1946, Doubled Die Obverse and Reverse (FS-10-1946-103).* The *Cherrypickers' Guide* catalogs six significant die varieties of 1946 Philadelphia issues, all doubled dies, some with visually dramatic doubling. They command premiums generally ranging from $15 to $25 in AU-50 to $60–$200 in MS-65. Many other (minor) repunched mintmarks and doubled dies exist for this date. Most coins in the *Cherrypickers' Guide* can be found for no extra premium by, well, *cherrypicking.* That is what the game is all about. In general, interest in these varieties is not what it was a generation or two ago, but there are still many enthusiastic followers.

FS-10-1946-103, Doubled Die Obverse and Reverse.

1946-D Roosevelt Dime

1946-D • Circulation-Strike Mintage: 61,043,500.

Availability and sharpness: Of the just over 344 million Roosevelt dimes struck in 1946, only a few more than 61 million were minted in Denver. Enough were saved in rolls and kept as souvenirs of the recently deceased President Roosevelt that Mint State examples are common today, in grades up to MS-65, with higher grades obtainable. The strike sharpness for Denver's coins was higher than for Philadelphia and San Francisco this year. Full Torch examples are available.

	Cert	Avg	%MS	EF-40	MS-63	MS-65	MS-66	MS-67	MS-67FT
1946-D	2,279	66.1	100%	$2	$4.25	$14	$30	$50	$150

VARIETIES: *1946-D, Repunched Mintmark (FS-10-1945D-501).* Doubled dies exist for the 1946-D dime, but collectors are more interested in the date's repunched mintmarks. The *Cherrypickers' Guide* lists three examples. Their premiums range from three times the normal price in AU to double (or more) those of the MS-65 and higher grades. Many others exist for the specialist to study.

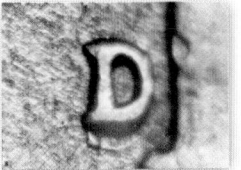

FS-10-1946D-501, Repunched Mintmark.

1946-S Roosevelt Dime

1946-S • Circulation-Strike Mintage: 27,900,000.

Availability and sharpness: San Francisco's dime mintage for 1946 was little over one-tenth that of Philadelphia. Still, from a collector's viewpoint its coins are common, and easily available in grades up through MS-64. Higher grades are less common but still readily obtainable. Strike typically is weak in various parts of the designs, the result of worn or overpolished dies, and few examples measure up to the Full Torch designation.

	Cert	Avg	%MS	EF-40	MS-63	MS-65	MS-66	MS-67	MS-67FT
1946-S	2,805	66.2	100%	$2	$4.50	$20	$32	$75	$175

VARIETIES: *1946-S, Repunched Mintmark (FS-10-1946S-503).* Several repunched mintmarks command premiums; the *Cherrypickers' Guide* lists three different RPMs, each worth $15 in AU-50 and $50 to $55 in MS-65.

**FS-10-1946S-503,
Repunched Mintmark.**

1946-S, San Serif Mintmark (FS-10-1946S-504). Two mintmark varieties are generally recognized for the 1946 San Francisco dimes: Trumpet Tail and the scarcer Knob Tail. Collectors do not usually pay more for one over the other. The *Cherrypickers' Guide* notes a third mintmark style, the extremely rare Sans Serif, which until its discovery was thought to exist only on 1947-S coins.

**FS-10-1946S-504,
San Serif Mintmark.**

1947 Roosevelt Dime

1947 • **Circulation-Strike Mintage:** 121,500,000.

Commentary: Public demand for small-change coins, including dimes, slackened as the United States shifted down from a hectic wartime economy.

Availability and sharpness: Philadelphia's 1947 production of dimes was less than half of its 1946 output. Still, 1947 examples are common and can easily be found in grades up through MS-66. Higher grades are scarcer but obtainable. Strike quality is generally weak, from overused dies, and Full Torch coins are scarce.

	Cert	Avg	%MS	EF-40	MS-63	MS-65	MS-66	MS-67	MS-67FT
1947	1,432	65.6	97%	$2	$6	$12	$24	$75	$250

VARIETY: *1947, Doubled Die Obverse (FS-10-1947-101).* The *Cherrypickers' Guide* lists a single doubled die for this date—a very strongly doubled obverse, worth $30 to $45 in EF to AU, $70 to $140 in low Mint State, and $300 in MS-65.

FS-10-1947-101, Doubled Die Obverse.

1947-D Roosevelt Dime

1947-D • **Circulation-Strike Mintage:** 46,835,000.

Availability and sharpness: The 1947-D Roosevelt dime is readily available in circulated grades, and in Mint State up through MS-65. Higher grades can be found with some searching, but are not as common as in other dates of the era. Denver coins of 1947 are generally stronger in strike than those of Philadelphia and San Francisco. Full Torch examples are accessible for the discerning specialist.

	Cert	Avg	%MS	EF-40	MS-63	MS-65	MS-66	MS-67	MS-67FT
1947-D	1,227	66.2	100%	$2	$6.50	$12	$24	$45	$135

VARIETY: *1947-D, Doubled Die Obverse (FS-10-1947D-101).* Two doubled-die obverse varieties are listed in the *Cherrypickers' Guide*, with doubling strongest on either the date or LIBERTY. These are fairly recent discoveries and have yet to establish firm values.

FS-10-1947D-101, Doubled Die Obverse.

1947-S Roosevelt Dime

1947-S • **Circulation-Strike Mintage:** 34,840,000.

Commentary: More than one style of S mintmark was used for San Francisco's dime production. The Trumpet Tail and Sans Serif varieties are identified. The latter was not used after this year.

Availability and sharpness: 1947-S dimes are easily found in grades up through MS-67. Most are weakly struck from the use of heavily worn dies, and very few have Full Torch details.

	Cert	Avg	%MS	EF-40	MS-63	MS-65	MS-66	MS-67	MS-67FT
1947-S	2,211	66.3	100%	$2	$6	$12	$30	$45	$175

VARIETIES: There are several die varieties for this issue. The *Cherrypickers' Guide* catalogs five—mostly repunched mintmarks, although one doubled-die reverse has also captured the interest of specialists. The RPMs sell for 10 to 15 times the price of a normal 1947-S dime in AU-50 to MS-66 grades. The DDR commands more modest but still impressive premiums of 5 to 10 times the normal price.

FS-1947S-501, Repunched Mintmark. One of the more valuable RPMs for this date.

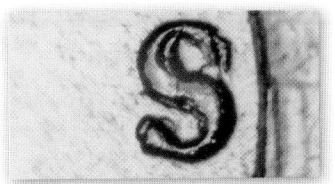

FS-1947S-504, Repunched Mintmark. One of the less valuable, but still popular, RPMs for this date.

FS-1947S-801, Doubled Die Reverse.

1948 Roosevelt Dime

1948 • **Circulation-Strike Mintage:** 74,950,000.

Commentary: Mintage was reduced considerably as the United States entered a recession after World War II. Still, with coin collectors of the era having saved thousands of rolls in Uncirculated condition, today's hobbyists have many Mint State examples to peruse.

Availability and sharpness: Nice 1948 dimes are readily available today in grades up through MS-66. Strike quality was a challenge for the Philadelphia Mint, with production dies used long after they had begun to wear, and many of the resulting coins are found weakly detailed. Well-struck examples with Full Torch details are uncommon.

	Cert	Avg	%MS	EF-40	MS-63	MS-65	MS-66	MS-67	MS-67FT
1948	1,191	66.0	100%	$2	$4.25	$12	$30	$85	$225

VARIETY: *1948, Doubled Die Reverse (FS-10-1948-801).* A doubled-die reverse variety has enjoyed increased popularity since being published in the *Cherrypickers' Guide*. It shows strong doubling on the reverse lettering and the tips of the torch's flame. The DDR sells for $20 in AU-50 and $35 to $45 in lower Mint States grades, up to $150 in MS-66.

FS-10-1948-101, Doubled Die Reverse.

1948-D Roosevelt Dime

1948-D • **Circulation-Strike Mintage:** 52,841,000.

Commentary: By 1948 and beyond there were fewer and fewer die varieties in the Roosevelt dime series, as production standardized and quality control was increased. There is a minor repunched mintmark for the 1948-D—not significant enough to be included in the *Cherrypickers' Guide.*

Availability and sharpness: As with other dates of the era, 1948 saw a higher quality of dime from the Denver Mint than from its sister facility in San Francisco or the main mint in Philadelphia. Mint State 1948-D dimes are easily available in grades up to MS-66. Examples with Full Torch details are easy to find.

	Cert	Avg	%MS	EF-40	MS-63	MS-65	MS-66	MS-67	MS-67FT
1948-D	1,396	66.2	100%	$2	$6	$12	$30	$55	$150

1948-S Roosevelt Dime

1948-S • Circulation-Strike Mintage: 35,520,000.

Availability and sharpness: Hobbyists and coin dealers saved many rolls of 1948-S dimes in their original condition, making the coins readily available today in Mint State grades up through MS-67. Strike quality is generally weaker than for the year's Denver coinage, from San Francisco's over-use of "tired" dies. Coins with Full Torch details are not common.

	Cert	Avg	%MS	EF-40	MS-63	MS-65	MS-66	MS-67	MS-67FT
1948-S	1,689	66.3	100%	$2	$5.50	$12	$32	$55	$150

VARIETY: *1948-S, Repunched Mintmark (FS-10-1948S-501).* There are several repunched mintmarks for the 1948-S dime. The only one listed in the *Cherrypickers' Guide* is described as "one of the more dramatic RPMs for the series," with an underlying S south of the mintmark. It was first cataloged in the popular book's 2012 fifth edition, with its value not yet firmly established.

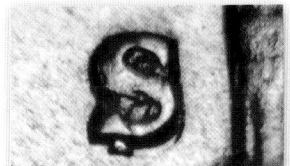

FS-10-1948S-501, Repunched Mintmark.

1949 Roosevelt Dime

1949 • Circulation-Strike Mintage: 30,940,000.

Commentary: The post-war economic recession continued into 1949, reducing the demand for new coins, and the year's production of Roosevelt dimes plunged. Collectors continued to pack away rolls of the coins in Uncirculated condition, so despite the low mintage (second-lowest in the series' Philadelphia production) Mint State examples are easily attainable—for a slight premium.

There are no popular die varieties for Philadelphia's 1949 dime mintage.

Availability and sharpness: Brilliant coins can be readily had in grades up through MS-67. As with other Philadelphia Mint issues of the era, the over-use of worn dies resulted in many weakly struck coins, and few with Full Torch details.

	Cert	Avg	%MS	EF-40	MS-63	MS-65	MS-66	MS-67	MS-67FT
1949	1,316	65.8	99%	$3	$27	$38	$45	$100	$225

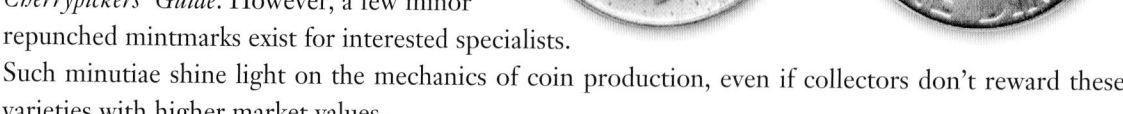

1949-D Roosevelt Dime

1949-D • **Circulation-Strike Mintage:** 26,034,000.

Commentary: No die varieties of 1949-D have reached the levels of popularity and liquidity necessary to be included in the *Cherrypickers' Guide.* However, a few minor repunched mintmarks exist for interested specialists. Such minutiae shine light on the mechanics of coin production, even if collectors don't reward these varieties with higher market values.

Availability and sharpness: Coin collectors in 1949 were more enamored of the year's San Francisco coins (with their mintage about one-half that of the already very low Denver production). Still, they saved enough of the Denver coins in hoarded rolls that Uncirculated examples are easy to acquire today in grades up through MS-67. As with other Denver dimes of the 1940s, their quality was the sharpest of the three mint facilities' output. Coins with Full Torch details are readily available.

	Cert	Avg	%MS	EF-40	MS-63	MS-65	MS-66	MS-67	MS-67FT
1949-D	1,909	66.1	100%	$3	$12	$20	$35	$55	$200

1949-S Roosevelt Dime

1949-S • **Circulation-Strike Mintage:** 13,510,000.

Commentary: The 1949-S is a key in the Roosevelt dime series, with the second-lowest mintage of the silver coinage (behind only the 1955 Philadelphia). Repunched mintmarks are known for the date but generate little interest among most collectors.

Availability and sharpness: Collectors of the era knew that San Francisco's 1949 mintage was low. However, the general poor quality of the coinage didn't allow rolled hoards to be accumulated in high Mint State grades. Today even circulated examples sell for premiums compared to other dates. Lower-end Uncirculated grades are relatively scarce, and higher-end even more so. Full Torch details command significant prices due to the rarity of such quality in this date. Collectors will encounter many examples weakly struck from worn dies before finding the occasional sharply detailed coin.

	Cert	Avg	%MS	EF-40	MS-63	MS-65	MS-66	MS-67	MS-67FT
1949-S	2,453	66.2	99%	$5	$45	$55	$75	$85	$1,250

1950 Roosevelt Dime

1950 • **Circulation-Strike Mintage:** 50,130,114.

Commentary: Dime mintages in 1950 increased as the nation's economy picked up. Coin collectors and dealers continued socking away rolls of each year's new Uncirculated dimes (and other coins). This has given today's generation of collectors many Mint State examples to choose from, not to mention plenty of lower-grade coins that were later plucked from circulation. As is usual with Philadelphia's silver issues, coins struck from tired dies abound, and those with sharp Full Torch details are more scarce, giving specialists something to hunt for.

Availability and sharpness: The 1950 Roosevelt dime of the Philadelphia Mint is readily available in grades up through MS-67, although strike quality is generally unimpressive. The mint was known for pushing its coinage dies close to the point of exhaustion, resulting in many coins with soft, weak details.

	Cert	Avg	%MS	EF-40	MS-63	MS-65	MS-66	MS-67	MS-67FT
1950	1,451	65.9	99%	$3	$13	$16	$35	$125	$250

1950, Proof • **Proof Mintage:** 51,386.

Commentary: The nation's Proof coin production was interrupted in 1942 as the Mint strained to produce enough circulating coins for the booming wartime economy. After the war ended, the recession brought budget constraints that kept the Mint from immediately returning to its Proof coinage. Finally President Harry Truman signed a bill on May 10, 1950, that authorized Proofs to be resumed.

David W. Lange, in *A Guide Book of Modern United States Proof Coin Sets*, wrote: "The coin collecting hobby had experienced marked growth since 1942, and total sales of Proof sets were double those of the last pre-war issue. The popularity of this year's set was undoubtedly increased by the fact that it included the first Proofs made for both the Roosevelt dime and Franklin half dollar."

After the long lapse, the Mint's technicians had to relearn the art of polishing Proof dies and planchets. Many 1950 Proof dimes have a finish more satiny than brilliantly mirrored. Overly polished dies led some Proof coins to lack high-relief details.

A die variety with moderate reverse doubling is known (cataloged in the *Cherrypickers' Guide*); it is of low interest to most collectors and commands only a small premium over normal prices.

Availability: Proof dimes of 1950 are scarce in grades exceeding PF-66. Some have hairlines and/or cloudy surfaces from the packaging of the era (coins placed individually in transparent cellophane envelopes, slightly wider than the coins themselves, stapled together). Some have shallow detail.

	Cert	Avg	%MS	PF-65	PF-66	PF-67
1950, Proof	1,622	66.3		$50	$65	$120

1950-D Roosevelt Dime

1950-D • **Circulation-Strike Mintage:** 46,803,000.

Commentary: The Denver Mint's high production quality continued into the new decade.

Availability and sharpness: With more than 46 million minted, and many saved in roll quantities by collectors and coin dealers, the 1950-D dime is readily available in Mint State today. Coins graded up through MS-66, including those with Full Torch details, are common. Higher-level grades are scarcer but available, at commensurate expense.

	Cert	Avg	%MS	EF-40	MS-63	MS-65	MS-66	MS-67	MS-67FT
1950-D	1,947	66.3	100%	$2	$6	$12	$28	$55	$125

VARIETIES: A variety with a repunched mint-mark—which the *Cherrypickers' Guide* notes "might actually be die damage instead of a variety"—has attracted collector interest among specialists, selling for $400 in MS-63. A doubled-die reverse for the date is also in demand, selling for $40 in EF-40 and up to $550 in MS-66.

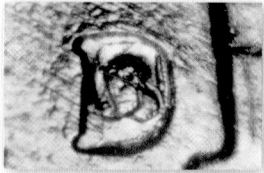

FS-10-1950D-501, **Repunched Mintmark.**

FS-10-1950D-801, **Doubled Die Reverse.**

	Cert	Avg	%MS	EF-40	MS-63	MS-65	MS-66	MS-67	MS-67FT
1950-D, D Over S	0	n/a			$400	$650	$775	$1,050	

1950-S Roosevelt Dime

1950-S • **Circulation-Strike Mintage:** 20,440,000.

Commentary: Although the 1950-S dime doesn't have the lowest mintage in the Roosevelt series, it was low enough to have attracted speculators at the time of its production. Collectors and dealers saved thousands of rolls in Uncirculated condition. As a result, today's enthusiasts have an abundance of nice coins to choose from, though at prices somewhat above the norm.

Availability and sharpness: The 1950-S dime is common in lower Mint State grades; less so in higher, but still readily available. Strike quality was poor for this mintage, a symptom of San Francisco's over-used dies, and coins with Full Torch details are very scarce.

	Cert	Avg	%MS	EF-40	MS-63	MS-65	MS-66	MS-67	MS-67FT
1950-S	1,560	66.1	99%	$5	$38	$55	$75	$85	$300

VARIETY: *1950-S, Repunched Mintmark (FS-10-1950S-501).* The *Cherry-pickers' Guide* catalogs a repunched mintmark for 1950-S that attracts collector demand sufficient to warrant prices of $250 to $750 in MS-63 to 66.

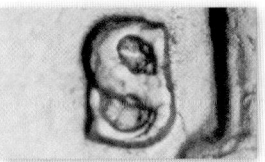

**FS-10-1950S-501,
Repunched Mintmark.**

	Cert	Avg	%MS	EF-40	MS-63	MS-65	MS-66	MS-67	MS-67FT
1950-S, S Over D	0	n/a			$250	$400	$750	$900	$1,675

1951 Roosevelt Dime

1951 • **Circulation-Strike Mintage:** 103,880,102.

Commentary: Beyond the torch on the reverse, other high points to check for strike quality and contact marks include the president's cheek, the hair above his ear, and his neck.

Availability and sharpness: With more than 100 million dimes struck at Philadelphia in 1951, and with speculators and the hobby community saving hundreds of thousands of Uncirculated coins in rolls and bags, today's collectors have many Mint State pieces to examine, in grades up through MS-67. However, Philadelphia's high production came at the expense of quality. Many coins exhibit weak detail from dies rode harder than a nag in the Kentucky Derby. Sharp strikes are scarce. That said, there are examples with Full Torch details to keep specialists happy (at a price, of course).

	Cert	Avg	%MS	EF-40	MS-63	MS-65	MS-66	MS-67	MS-67FT
1951	3,301	66.0	99%	$2	$4.25	$10	$30	$65	$175

1951, Proof • **Proof Mintage:** 57,500.

Commentary: Collector demand for Proof coins was slightly higher in 1951 than in 1950. "The Proofs of 1951, like those of 1950, come in two finishes. While most are fully brilliant, a certain percentage may be found having partially brilliant or somewhat satiny fields" (Lange, *A Guide Book of Modern United States Proof Coin Sets*).

Availability: The 1951 Proof Roosevelt dime is readily available to meet collector demand in grades up through PF-67. Brilliant Proof dimes struck from overly polished dies can lack crisp detail, with elements having been polished away. Cameo Proofs are rare; deep and ultra cameo Proofs are very rare. "Only about 20 percent qualify as cameos, and less than one-half of one percent are deep cameos" (Guth, *PCGS CoinFacts*).

	Cert	Avg	%MS	PF-65	PF-66	PF-67
1951, Proof	1,972	66.7		$50	$65	$100

1951-D Roosevelt Dime

1951-D • **Circulation-Strike Mintage:**
56,529,000.

Commentary: As was usual for the era,
Denver's production quality exceeded that
of Philadelphia and San Francisco this year.

Every year coin collectors and dealers would
accumulate original rolls and mint bags of new
coins, to be traded as commodities as their values
increased. From these deliberately hoarded sources come many of today's Mint State collector coins.

Availability and sharpness: Denver's dimes of 1951 are readily available in Mint State grades up
through MS-67, with a good percentage of coins sharply struck, showing Full Torch details.

	Cert	Avg	%MS	EF-40	MS-63	MS-65	MS-66	MS-67	MS-67FT
1951-D	6,002	66.0	99%	$2	$4	$10	$28	$100	$165

VARIETY: *1951-D, Repunched Mintmark (FS-10-1951D-501).* The 2012
edition of the *Cherrypickers' Guide* included a new listing of a 1951-D repunched
mintmark dime, with an underlying D north of the mintmark, described as
"one of the more dramatic RPMs for the series." Die-variety collectors pay a
premium for this anomaly.

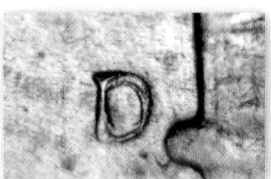

FS-10-1951D-501,
Repunched Mintmark.

1951-S Roosevelt Dime

1951-S • **Circulation-Strike Mintage:**
31,630,000.

Commentary: One challenge for the
discerning Roosevelt dime collector comes
from San Francisco's ongoing overuse of
its coinage dies to the point of exhaustion.
Many of the mint's dimes came off the press
with weak details. While technically Uncirculated,
they can be lacking in elegantly crisp eye appeal.

There are repunched mintmarks known for this date, but none have piqued enough collector interest
to merit inclusion in the *Cherrypickers' Guide*, the hobby's mainstream reference on die varieties.

Availability and sharpness: Collectors and coin dealers continued the longstanding trend of hoarding
rolls of Uncirculated coins, including dimes. As a result there are many 1951-S dimes in Mint State for
today's collectors to cherrypick for high quality. Examples with Full Torch details are scarce.

	Cert	Avg	%MS	EF-40	MS-63	MS-65	MS-66	MS-67	MS-67FT
1951-S	1,691	66.3	100%	$3	$14	$25	$45	$55	$150

1952 Roosevelt Dime

1952 • **Circulation-Strike Mintage:**
99,040,093.

Commentary: As in years past, there was
a popular trend of saving rolls and bags of
Uncirculated coins. Speculators hoped to
cash in when the numismatic value of individual
coins rose in the future. Their foresight has left many
1952 Roosevelt dimes in Mint State for today's collectors.

Strike quality for Philadelphia's 1952 dimes ranged from strong (from new dies) to weak (from over-used dies). Collectors are advised to search until a well-struck example is found.

Availability and sharpness: Mintage reached just under 100 million for Philadelphia's dime output for 1952. Mint State pieces are readily available in grades up through MS-67. Those with Full Torch details are quite rare and command stronger-than-usual premiums.

	Cert	Avg	%MS	EF-40	MS-63	MS-65	MS-66	MS-67	MS-67FT
1952	1,116	65.9	100%	$2	$4.25	$10	$30	$75	$250

1952, Proof • **Proof Mintage:** 81,980.

Commentary: Collector demand for Proof
coins increased by nearly 50 percent in 1952
as the coin-collecting hobby enjoyed a new
boom cycle.

As Proof dies were repeatedly polished
in order to maintain the coins' bright mirror
luster, there would be a loss in detail depth. Thus
some brilliant Proofs have a shallow look. Proofs with a cameo appearance—"frosted" design elements
on polished mirror fields—are scarce to rare.

Availability: Nice-quality Proofs up to PF-68 are readily available for today's collectors. Uniformly brilliant coins are common; some exhibit slightly satiny fields from the polish wearing off their dies.

	Cert	Avg	%MS	PF-65	PF-66	PF-67
1952, Proof	1,717	66.8		$35	$50	$85

1952-D Roosevelt Dime

1952-D • **Circulation-Strike Mintage:**
122,100,000.

Commentary: With a booming economy,
the United States needed more and more
coins to grease the wheels of commerce.
In 1952 that led to a huge increase in dime
output from the Denver Mint—more than
double the mintage of 1951.

Today's collectors are encouraged to search for examples with few bag marks. These are contact marks from coins rubbing against each other in mint sacks. The Denver Mint coinage of the era exhibits these flaws more frequently than their P and S counterparts.

There are several repunched mintmarks for this date, sought by specialists but beyond the interest of most collectors.

Availability and sharpness: This large issue of 1952 dimes is common in Mint State. Those with Full Torch details are proportionally more common than for Philadelphia and San Francisco issues.

	Cert	Avg	%MS	EF-40	MS-63	MS-65	MS-66	MS-67	MS-67FT
1952-D	1,235	66.0	100%	$2	$4.25	$9	$25	$65	$200

1952-S Roosevelt Dime

1952-S • Circulation-Strike Mintage: 44,419,500.

Commentary: Mintage at San Francisco increased dramatically in 1952 in order to help feed the growing American economy and its demand for small change. This was the highest mintage for the San Francisco Mint's Roosevelt dimes.

Availability and sharpness: The 1952-S dime is plentiful at all levels of Mint State up through MS-67, and even well-struck Full Torch examples are easily available, though scarce.

	Cert	Avg	%MS	EF-40	MS-63	MS-65	MS-66	MS-67	MS-67FT
1952-S	1,791	66.3	100%	$3	$8	$12	$35	$50	$250

VARIETY: *1952-S, Repunched Mintmark (FS-10-1952S-501).* There are several repunched mintmarks in this date, one of which is published in the *Cherrypickers' Guide*—a new listing in the fifth edition. It shows an underlying S north of the mintmark. A repunched mintmark would be created when the letter punch used to impress the mintmark into the working die accidentally left two or more offset impressions. The die-making process changed in 1989, when the Mint began placing mintmarks directly on the master dies used to make working dies.

FS-10-1952S-501, Repunched Mintmark.

1953 Roosevelt Dime

1953 • Circulation-Strike Mintage: 53,490,120.

Commentary: The Philadelphia Mint continued to overwork its dies in 1953, striking coins after normal production wore the dies down so much that they made tired-looking dimes. Shallow detail is common even in coins that never saw hand-to-hand circulation. Quality-minded collectors will search for examples that have strong strikes.

Availability and sharpness: The 1953 dime is easily found in Uncirculated grades up through MS-66. In MS-67 it becomes scarcer and commands a slight premium compared to others of the era. Coins with Full Torch details require some searching.

	Cert	Avg	%MS	EF-40	MS-63	MS-65	MS-66	MS-67	MS-67FT
1953	882	65.9	100%	$2	$4	$8	$15	$75	$850

1953, Proof • Proof Mintage: 128,800.

Commentary: Coin collecting continued to grow in popularity in the United States in 1953. Following 1952's increased demand for Proof sets, in 1953 the Mint saw another 50 percent boost in sales. By this time speculators were buying up earlier Proof sets of 1936 to 1942, plus the more recent sets of the early 1950s.

During the 1950s "the Mint took no special effort to preserve the frosty texture that the dies possessed when first placed into the coin press. Some 3,000 to 5,000 Proofs may have been made from each die before it was retired from Proof production, and this frost was quickly worn smooth through repeated striking of coins. Only the first hundred Proofs from each die could be expected to show any frostiness. Perhaps only the first few dozen impressions would result in coins having deep or ultra cameo contrast" (Lange, *A Guide Book of Modern United States Proof Coin Sets*).

Availability: Proof dimes of 1953 are easily found at levels up through PF-68. Increased production led to dies being polished and re-polished, resulting in soft details in many coins. Cameo Proofs of course are in the minority.

	Cert	Avg	%MS	PF-65	PF-66	PF-67
1953, Proof	2,342	66.8		$38	$55	$80

1953-D Roosevelt Dime

1953-D • Circulation-Strike Mintage: 136,433,000.

Commentary: Public demand for coins in commerce boomed with the growing American economy of the early 1950s. The Denver Mint did its part by cranking out dimes in quantities earlier seen only from Philadelphia. Its production quality continued to be higher than that of the other U.S. mints.

Availability and sharpness: Denver dimes of 1953 are easily available in all grades, including Gem Mint State. Well-struck examples with Full Torch details are relatively plentiful for the series.

	Cert	Avg	%MS	EF-40	MS-63	MS-65	MS-66	MS-67	MS-67FT
1953-D	1,213	66.0	100%	$2	$4	$9	$20	$55	$275

VARIETY: *1953-D, Repunched Mintmark (FS-10-1953D-501).* One repunched mintmark die variety shows the first D punched horizontally, with the primary mintmark punched in the correct (vertical) orientation. It sells for five to ten times the price of the normal 1953-D dime in AU-50 to MS-66.

**FS-10-1953D-501,
Repunched Mintmark.**

1953-S Roosevelt Dime

1953-S • Circulation-Strike Mintage: 39,180,000.

Commentary: As was customary in this era, collectors and coin dealers hoarded tens of thousands of Uncirculated dimes by the roll and bagful. San Francisco was always (and still is) a popular mint.

Availability and sharpness: *PCGS CoinFacts* estimates that 1,200,000 1953-S dimes exist in Mint State, including 235,000 in MS-65 or better grades. Gems are plentiful to meet collector demand today. As with other San Francisco silver Roosevelt dimes made for circulation, many suffer from soft details, even in Mint State—a result of being struck from over-used dies.

	Cert	Avg	%MS	EF-40	MS-63	MS-65	MS-66	MS-67	MS-67FT
1953-S	2,862	66.2	100%	$3	$4	$9	$25	$55	$400

VARIETY: *1953-S, Repunched Mintmark (FS-10-1953S-501).* A new die-variety listing was published in the fifth edition (2012) of the *Cherrypickers' Guide:* a 1953-S repunched mintmark with an underlying S north of the mintmark. Specialists pay a premium for this variety.

FS-10-1953S-501, Repunched Mintmark.

1954 Roosevelt Dime

1954 • Circulation-Strike Mintage: 114,010,203.

Commentary: 1954 was another 100 million–plus year for Philadelphia's dime production. Collectors and coin dealers saved many of the coins in Uncirculated rolls and bags, giving today's hobbyists millions of Mint State examples to examine for their collections.

Availability and sharpness: The 1954 dime is easily obtainable in all grades up through MS-66. Finer grades, and coins with sharply struck Full Torch details, are harder to come by, given the Philadelphia Mint's penchant for pushing its coinage dies toward the limits of production. Many 1954 dimes have soft details from being struck by over-worked dies.

	Cert	Avg	%MS	EF-40	MS-63	MS-65	MS-66	MS-67	MS-67FT
1954	1,459	65.8	100%	$2	$4	$8	$20	$55	$425

VARIETY: *1954, Doubled Die Reverse (FS-10-1954-801).* In the 2012 fifth edition of the *Cherrypickers' Guide*, authors Bill Fivaz and J.T. Stanton described a "very exciting variety," a doubled-die reverse with doubling at the bottom of the torch and on the oak stem. Collectors in the know will quietly search for these in dealers' inventories, hoping to find them among the otherwise very common 1954 dimes.

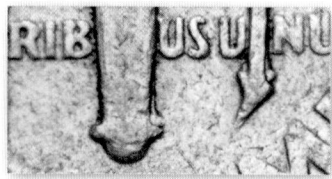

FS-10-1954-801, Doubled Die Reverse.

1954, Proof • **Proof Mintage:** 233,300.

Commentary: The coin-collecting hobby continued to grow in 1954, leading to greater sales of Proof sets. Demand had risen dramatically every year since the post-war Proof program started up again in 1950. Many collectors bought multiple sets—one to keep and the others to sell for a profit later.

The Mint introduced new packaging partway through this year—a "polybag" (polyethylene) material instead of the earlier cellophane envelopes, which tended to split and which could give hairline scratches to pristine Proof coin surfaces. An unfortunate side effect was that the plastic sometimes imparted an unattractive purple-cast toning to some coins. Some such toned Proofs have been cleaned or conserved, with various degrees of success.

Availability: 1954 Proof dimes are easily available in Gem quality up through PF-67. Cameo examples are scarce.

	Cert	Avg	%MS	PF-65	PF-66	PF-67
1954, Proof	2,850	67.0		$18	$25	$30

VARIETY: *1954, Proof, Doubled Die Obverse (FS-10-1954-101).* The *Cherrypickers' Guide* lists a doubled-die obverse variety of the 1954 Proof dime, easily detected by a die chip at the base of the 4. It sells for double to triple the price of a normal Proof.

**FS-10-1954-101,
Doubled Die Obverse.**

1954-D Roosevelt Dime

1954-D • **Circulation-Strike Mintage:** 106,397,000.

Commentary: Denver's production of dimes remained high in 1954, as did the quality of its coinage. Gems are common, and there are more dimes with Full Torch details than seen from Philadelphia and San Francisco.

A repunched mintmark die variety among the 1954-D dimes has failed to generate much interest among mainstream collectors.

Availability and sharpness: The 1954-D dime is easily available in grades up through MS-66 and MS-67, although well-struck Full Torch coins are in the minority.

	Cert	Avg	%MS	EF-40	MS-63	MS-65	MS-66	MS-67	MS-67FT
1954-D	1,432	65.6	97%	$2	$4	$9	$14	$100	$200

1954-S Roosevelt Dime

1954-S • **Circulation-Strike Mintage:** 22,860,000.

Commentary: As usual, the San Francisco Mint overworked its coinage dies in 1954, resulting in many dimes having weak details. Very few exhibit a truly strong strike, leading to high premiums for Full Torch coins to meet the demand of specialists.

Availability and sharpness: Uncirculated 1954-S dimes are easy to find in grades up through MS-67—but Full Strike details are elusive.

	Cert	Avg	%MS	EF-40	MS-63	MS-65	MS-66	MS-67	MS-67FT
1954-S	2,462	66.1	100%	$2	$4	$9	$16	$55	$300

VARIETIES: The *Cherrypickers' Guide* has two die-variety listings for the 1954-S dime. One is a dramatically visible repunched mintmark that sells for five to ten times the price of a regular coin in AU-50 to MS-66. The other is a variety missing designer John Sinnock's initials—likely the result of an overpolished die, and not a deliberate design edit.

FS-10-1954S-501, Repunched Mintmark.

FS-10-1954S-901, Missing Designer's Initials.

1955 Roosevelt Dime

1955 • **Circulation-Strike Mintage:** 12,450,181.

Commentary: With such a low mintage—about one-tenth that of 1954—the 1955 dime might be expected to be a key date and command substantial premiums. However, the coins were saved in such quantities by collectors and dealers that they are readily available today in Mint State. (Moreover, Proofs are easily available to supply the demand for those who want just a single 1955 dime.) "Scarce" is not a relevant descriptor unless you're seeking an MS-67 or finer coin with strong details.

Availability and sharpness: Philadelphia's 1955 dimes are easily available in Mint State up through MS-66, thanks to extensive hoarding. Most have softness in their details from being struck by over-worked dies, but examples with Full Torch details do exist.

	Cert	Avg	%MS	EF-40	MS-63	MS-65	MS-66	MS-67	MS-67FT
1955	2,663	65.9	100%	$2	$4	$8	$16	$75	$1,000

1955, Proof • **Proof Mintage:** 378,200.

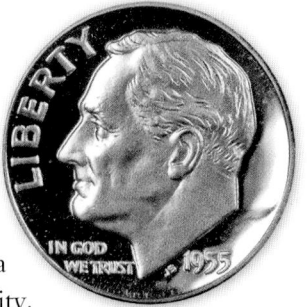

Commentary: Continuing the hobby's 1950s trend, demand was very strong and growing for 1955 Proof sets, with sales rising more than 50 percent over 1954's already record numbers. Many collectors and dealers bought multiple sets, intending to sell their extras for a profit as the hobby enjoyed a boom in popularity.

Proof packaging changed again in 1955: most of the year's Proof coins were individually inserted into polyethylene envelopes, as in 1954; some in the older style of cellophane envelopes; and then, midway through the year, the sets' coins were packaged in a single "pliofilm" envelope and sandwiched between cardstock boards. The improved packaging protected the coins better, resulting in more Gems being available for today's collectors to enjoy.

Availability: 1955 Proof dimes are easily available in levels up through PF-69. Cameo and ultra cameo coins are rare as a percentage of the total mintage, but still accessible and more frequently seen than those of earlier dates.

	Cert	Avg	%MS	PF-65	PF-66	PF-67
1955, Proof	5,209	67.5		$15	$20	$25

1955-D Roosevelt Dime

1955-D • **Circulation-Strike Mintage:** 13,959,000.

Commentary: The coin-collecting hobby was popular in the 1950s, and many collectors and dealers continued to pack away rolls of Uncirculated coins, including the 1955-D dime. Their goal: to trade the coins for a profit when their individual value rose. Collectors today reap the benefit of this practice, as coins that were kept from day-to-day circulation, still in Mint-fresh quality, are now common.

The Denver Mint continued to strike coins of high quality, nicer on average than those of Philadelphia and San Francisco. There is no reason *not* to be discerning and seek well-struck examples.

Availability and sharpness: Common in circulated grades, the 1955-D dime is readily available even in Gem Mint State, up through MS-66. Higher grades, and those Full Torch details, are more scarce, but still fairly easy to find.

	Cert	Avg	%MS	EF-40	MS-63	MS-65	MS-66	MS-67	MS-67FT
1955-D	1,720	65.6	100%	$2	$4	$8	$15	$95	$250

1955-S Roosevelt Dime

1955-S • Circulation-Strike Mintage: 18,510,000.

Commentary: In 1954 the U.S. Mint had analyzed its cost-efficiency in delivering coins for circulation in the Western United States. It determined the best path forward would be to stop coinage at the San Francisco Mint and instead use Denver as the primary supplier for the West. In 1955 San Francisco produced only cents and dimes, and only for three months, before the new plan went into effect. The hobby community was aware of the plan, and coin dealers and collectors—who normally saved rolls of San Francisco coins every year anyway—hoarded huge quantities of the 1955-S cents and dimes. Never having entered circulation, today these are available for hobbyists to examine and add to their collections.

The typical 1955-S dime has soft details, the result of the usual San Francisco practice of this era: strike as many coins as possible from each production die, even after they begin to wear.

Availability and sharpness: The 1955-S dime is readily available in all grades up through MS-67, although, as usual for this mint, higher-grade and sharply struck Full Torch coins are in the minority.

	Cert	Avg	%MS	EF-40	MS-63	MS-65	MS-66	MS-67	MS-67FT
1955-S	3,900	65.9	100%	$2	$4	$8	$15	$55	$1,000

1956 Roosevelt Dime

1956 • Circulation-Strike Mintage: 108,640,000.

Commentary: The Philadelphia Mint continued to overwork its coinage dies, as was usual in this era, resulting in many 1956 dimes being softly detailed. On the consumer end, coin collectors and dealers also continued on their usual path: buying huge quantities of new coins in original rolls and mint bags, and storing them until ready to sell or trade at a profit, as commodities. This practice spared many 1956 dimes from the cruel world of parking meters, candy-vending machines, and the mustard-stained apron pockets of street-cart hot-dog vendors. Today's hobbyists can sort through these Mint State specimens for a well-struck, blemish-free example for their collections.

Availability and sharpness: Philadelphia's 1956 dimes are readily available in grades up through MS-67. Sharp examples with Full Torch details are scarce.

	Cert	Avg	%MS	EF-40	MS-63	MS-65	MS-66	MS-67	MS-67FT
1956	2,331	66.2	100%	$2	$3	$6	$14	$45	$650

1956, Proof • **Proof Mintage:** 669,384.

Commentary: The coin-collecting hobby was buzzing along merrily in 1956, with collectors, dealers, and speculators buying, selling, and trading at a rapid clip. This activity included a record number of Proof sets being sold this year—nearly double the quantity of 1955.

Availability: The Proof dimes of 1956 are easily found in quality up to PF-69, with cameo examples being reasonably common, in context. Ultra cameos are scarce.

	Cert	Avg	%MS	PF-65	PF-66	PF-67
1956, Proof	5,008	67.6		$8	$10	$18

VARIETY: *1956, Proof, Doubled Die Obverse (FS-10-1956-101).* A doubled-die obverse variety is cataloged in the *Cherrypickers' Guide*, with extra thickness in the lettering, date and designer's initials. Mainly of interest to specialists in the series, it sells for three to five times the price of a normal 1956 Proof dime in PF-63 to 66.

FS-10-1956-101,
Doubled Die Obverse.

1956-D Roosevelt Dime

1956-D • **Circulation-Strike Mintage:** 108,015,100.

Commentary: Denver increased its production in 1956 to make up for the 1955 closure of the San Francisco Mint. The large mintage, and collectors' penchant for saving Uncirculated coins in rolls and bags, contributed to the large number of Mint State coins available for today's collectors to peruse. Of course, bagged coins are free to jostle around, and as a result can be found with dings and scratches even though technically considered Uncirculated. Discerning collectors will look for sharp details and clean surfaces.

Availability and sharpness: The 1956-D dime is easily available in circulated grades and Mint State up through MS-65; less common but still accessible in MS-66 and MS-67; and scarce with sharply struck Full Torch details (although more frequently seen than on 1956 Philadelphia dimes).

	Cert	Avg	%MS	EF-40	MS-63	MS-65	MS-66	MS-67	MS-67FT
1956-D	1,117	66.0	100%	$2	$3	$6	$15	$35	$225

1957 Roosevelt Dime

1957 • **Circulation-Strike Mintage:** 160,160,000.

Commentary: The Philadelphia Mint continued its practice of working its dies to the point of exhaustion. Many 1957 dimes, even if Uncirculated, have soft details from being struck by worn-out dies.

The "King of Hobbies" had many enthusiasts who saw each year's new coins as opportunities for profit. They would hoard them by the roll and bag, like squirrels packing away acorns for the winter. Today's collectors can thank that older generation: they were protecting millions of bright new dimes from being dropped into a jukebox for the latest Elvis Presley hit and forever losing their "Uncirculated" status.

Availability and sharpness: The 1957 dime is common due to its large mintage—a "junk silver" coin in circulated grades (available for its silver value), and common in Mint State up through MS-67. Sharply struck coins with Full Torch details, however, are very scarce.

	Cert	Avg	%MS	EF-40	MS-63	MS-65	MS-66	MS-67	MS-67FT
1957	2,342	66.2	100%	$2	$3	$6	$14	$35	$1,500

1957, Proof • Proof Mintage: 1,247,952.

Commentary: 1957 was a banner year for Proof Roosevelt dimes. Collector demand and feverish speculation pushed the Mint's production well past 1 million Proof sets for the first time ever, nearly doubling the already record-high sales from 1956. Lange advises: "The smart shopper will examine 1957 Proof coins carefully for such careless production [soft details from overpolished dies], rather than relying solely on the grade assigned." This is known as *cherrypicking for quality.*

Availability: Proof dimes of 1957 are common at levels up through PF-69. David W. Lange, writing in *A Guide Book of Modern United States Proof Coin Sets*, warns that "Coins struck from severely overpolished and indistinct dies are commonplace for this date." Cameo and ultra cameo coins are unusual, but more easily found than in earlier dates.

	Cert	Avg	%MS	PF-65	PF-66	PF-67
1957, Proof	5,338	67.6		$5	$8	$25

1957-D Roosevelt Dime

1957-D • Circulation-Strike Mintage: 113,354,330.

Commentary: Denver's replacement of dies earlier in their production life, as opposed to Philadelphia's tendency to overwork them until their details were softened—led to a fair quantity of well-struck 1957-D dimes with Full Torch details. With millions of coins to choose from, the savvy collector will look for a strong strike, and also clean, undamaged fields, before making a purchase. Even small coins like the Roosevelt dime can suffer from bagmarked surfaces, caused by random contact with other coins during bagging, distribution, and storage.

Availability and sharpness: The 1957-D is a common Roosevelt dime in grades up through MS-67, with more coins showing well-struck Full Torch details than in previous years—certainly a larger percentage that those of Philadelphia.

	Cert	Avg	%MS	EF-40	MS-63	MS-65	MS-66	MS-67	MS-67FT
1957-D	1,663	66.0	100%	$2	$3	$6	$14	$35	$150

1958 Roosevelt Dime

1958 • **Circulation-Strike Mintage:** 31,910,000.

Commentary: The United States experienced another period of recession in late 1957 and early to mid-1958. Philadelphia's coinage was ordered down in anticipation of lower public demand for small-change coinage.

Collectors, dealers, and speculators continued to salt away quantities of freshly minted coins, including dimes, as was the custom of the day. This activity saved many a Mint State 1958 Roosevelt from the ungentle inner workings of a pay telephone and other abrasive circulation. True, millions would later be destroyed during the 1979–1980 silver boom, when it became obscenely profitable to throw everything into the melting pot, but still hundreds of thousands remain today for collectors to enjoy.

Availability and sharpness: The 1958 dime is easily available in grades up through MS-67, although those with Full Torch details are rare.

	Cert	Avg	%MS	EF-40	MS-63	MS-65	MS-66	MS-67	MS-67FT
1958	2,355	66.2	100%	$2	$3	$7	$15	$25	$1,500

1958, Proof • Proof Mintage: 875,652.

Commentary: The speculative bubble around Proof sets didn't *burst* in 1958, but it certainly deflated. Collectors and others who had bought multiples of the 1957 Proof sets, and later realized the mindboggling mintage tally of more than 1.2 million, came to understand that real demand for all those extra coins didn't exist. Sales of 1958 Proof sets settled down to a more realistic level. The still-healthy quantity of nearly 900,000 translates to many beautiful opportunities for today's coin collectors, 60 years later.

Availability: Gem Proof 1958 dimes are easy to find in levels up through PF-69. Cameo pieces are reasonably available; ultra cameos are scarce.

	Cert	Avg	%MS	PF-65	PF-66	PF-67
1958, Proof	4,593	67.4		$5	$8	$10

1958-D Roosevelt Dime

1958-D • **Circulation-Strike Mintage:** 136,564,600.

Commentary: In 1958 the Treasury Department leaned on the Denver Mint to supply more of the nation's circulating dimes than Philadelphia. Denver's presses reached a new peak of production that year. As was customary in that era, collectors and speculators hoarded rolls and bags of "BU" (Brilliant Uncirculated) coins as they were minted, planning on their numismatic value to go up over time. This resulted in many millions of Mint State coins being available for collectors up to the present day.

The quality of the Denver Mint's coinage continued to be high, superior to that of Philadelphia, as Denver's press operators replaced "tired" dies more frequently.

Availability and sharpness: 1958-D dimes are readily available in grades up through MS-67, and well-struck Full Torch examples are not as elusive as for some years.

	Cert	Avg	%MS	EF-40	MS-63	MS-65	MS-66	MS-67	MS-67FT
1958-D	1,838	66.1	100%	$2	$3	$7	$14	$25	$150

1959 Roosevelt Dime

1959 • Circulation-Strike Mintage: 85,780,000.

Commentary: The so-called Eisenhower Recession of 1958 started to recover by the middle of that year, and in response the Treasury ordered higher production of dimes at the Philadelphia Mint. The hobby trend of saving new coins in roll and bag quantities kept many shiny silver dimes safe from the wear and tear of circulation. Speculators hoped to trade them for a profit as their numismatic value rose. Their foresight led to many Uncirculated 1959 dimes being available to this day.

Availability and sharpness: 1959 dimes are common—valued mainly as bullion in circulated grades, and easily available in Uncirculated grades up through MS-67. Examples with Full Torch details are more frequently seen than those of preceding years.

	Cert	Avg	%MS	EF-40	MS-63	MS-65	MS-66	MS-67	MS-67FT
1959	1,630	65.8	99%	$2	$3	$6	$15	$100	$375

1959, Proof • Proof Mintage: 1,149,291.

Commentary: There were perhaps 250,000 active coin collectors in the United States in the late 1950s, so the sale of more than 1.1 million Proof sets strongly suggests that speculators continued to purchase multiple sets, rather than just one each for their personal collections.

As they had been for several years, the Proof coins of 1959 were packaged in a single pliofilm envelope with sealed pockets for each piece—cent, nickel, dime, quarter, half dollar, and a printed paper token of the Philadelphia Mint.

Availability: 1959 Proof dimes are common up through PF-69 quality, though with cameo examples scarcer than for 1958 and 1957, and ultra cameos very rare.

	Cert	Avg	%MS	PF-65	PF-66	PF-67
1959, Proof	5,090	67.6		$5	$8	$10

1959-D Roosevelt Dime

1959-D • **Circulation-Strike Mintage:** 164,919,790.

Commentary: Denver continued to contribute the majority of dimes for circulation in 1959. The recession of 1958 was over and the Treasury Department ordered greater production of the coins to facilitate commerce. Collectors and speculators continued to hoard Uncirculated coins by the roll and bag, making the 1959-D common today even in high grades.

Availability and sharpness: The 1959-D dime is common in circulated grades and up through MS-67, with Full Torch examples somewhat readily available in the context of the silver series.

	Cert	Avg	%MS	EF-40	MS-63	MS-65	MS-66	MS-67	MS-67FT
1959-D	1,212	66.0	100%	$2	$3	$6	$14	$40	$150

VARIETIES: *Repunched Mintmarks.* The *Cherrypickers' Guide* lists four die varieties of 1959-D dimes, all repunched mintmarks. These sell to specialists for five to ten times the price of normal dimes, in AU-50 to MS-66.

FS-10-1959D-504, Repunched Mintmark, one of the stronger RPMs for this date.

1960 Roosevelt Dime

1960 • **Circulation-Strike Mintage:** 70,390,000.

Commentary: Philadelphia's coinage quality continued to lag behind that of the Denver Mint, although it was improving as dies were replaced more frequently than in the past. Collector and speculator mania for saving rolls and even bags of new coins continued, protecting many Uncirculated 1960 dimes from the *Sturm und Drang* of daily commerce. The hobby was in a boom cycle, with the number of coin collectors doubling or perhaps even tripling this year.

The 1960 dime is common enough to sell as "junk silver" in circulated grades, and not much more in low-end Mint State.

Availability and sharpness: Uncirculated 1960 dimes up through MS-66 are easily found, with MS-67 and finer coins scarcer, especially so with Full Torch details.

	Cert	Avg	%MS	EF-40	MS-63	MS-65	MS-66	MS-67	MS-67FT
1960	1,379	65.8	100%	$2	$3	$6	$14	$65	$375

1960, Proof • Proof Mintage: 1,691,602.

Commentary: David W. Lange, in the *Guide Book of Modern United States Proof Coin Sets*, wrote: "The overall quality of Proof sets improved markedly beginning in 1960. The Mint was less likely to overuse and overpolish the dies, so it is evident that the dies were being replaced more frequently (perhaps this also accounts for the greater number of varieties). Ultra or deep cameo Proofs are still rare, but they become more readily available beginning with 1960."

Some Proof coins of 1960—the Jefferson nickel, Washington quarter, and Franklin half dollar—received "facelifts" in 1960 to improve the sharpness of master hubs and dies that had deteriorated over time. The Roosevelt dime was not included in that cleanup, as the quality of its coinage hubs was still good.

Availability: Beautiful 1960 Proof dimes are easy to find in levels up through PF-69, and with cameo and ultra cameo examples more accessible than those of the 1950s.

	Cert	Avg	%MS	PF-65	PF-66	PF-67
1960, Proof	6,378	67.5		$5	$10	$18

VARIETIES: *1960, Proof, Double-Die Obverse, Early Die State (FS-10-1960-102a).* 1960 was a challenging year for Proof die-making at the Philadelphia Mint. The *Cherrypickers' Guide* catalogs a remarkable seven doubled dies for the year's Roosevelt dimes! Their doubling ranges from moderate to extreme. The most popular of these among specialists will sell for 10 to 20 times the price of a regular Proof—or even more.

FS-10-1960-102a, Doubled Die Obverse, Early Die State.

	Cert	Avg	%MS	PF-65	PF-66	PF-67
1960, Doubled Die Obverse (FS-102a), Proof	0	n/a		$150	$250	

1960-D Roosevelt Dime

1960-D • Circulation-Strike Mintage: 200,160,400.

Commentary: So-called bag marks afflict many Uncirculated 1960-D dimes, from rough contact with other coins during the movement of canvas sacks full of the coins. Well-struck pieces with Full Torch details command the usual high premiums, thanks to the economics of low supply and high specialist demand.

Availability and sharpness: 1960-D dimes are very common in lower Mint State grades up through MS-65, and slightly less common than others of the silver era in MS-66 and 67. Full Torch examples are in the minority, as usual.

	Cert	Avg	%MS	EF-40	MS-63	MS-65	MS-66	MS-67	MS-67FT
1960-D	1,010	65.9	100%	$2	$3	$5	$15	$75	$325

VARIETY: *1960-D, Repunched Mintmark (FS-10-1960D-501).* A repunched mintmark die variety listed in the *Cherrypickers' Guide* brings prices three to five times those of normal 1960-D dimes in AU-50 to MS-66.

**FS-10-1960D-501,
Repunched Mintmark.**

1961 Roosevelt Dime

1961 • **Circulation-Strike Mintage:**
93,730,000.

Commentary: The Treasury Department noticed regional shortages of circulating coins in 1961, and increased the production and distribution of dimes in an attempt to solve the problem. The challenge was actually not on the supply side, but in great quantities of coins being paid into vending machines and not immediately re-entering circulation, as they would have from a shopkeeper's cash register.

Availability and sharpness: Philadelphia's 1961 Roosevelt dimes are common in Uncirculated grades up through MS-67, although the mint's tendency to overwork its production dies led to many coins with soft details. Those with Full Torch sharpness are uncommon. Some coins with semi-prooflike surfaces were struck from Proof dies repurposed for making coins for circulation.

	Cert	Avg	%MS	EF-40	MS-63	MS-65	MS-66	MS-67	MS-67FT
1961	1,256	65.9	100%	$2	$3	$5	$12	$75	$650

1961, Proof • Proof Mintage: 3,028,244.

Commentary: Proof set sales nearly doubled in 1961 because of a discovery the year before—the existence of scarce (and therefore valuable) Small Date cents in some Proof sets of 1960. The excitement over these coins launched even greater interest in the already popular coin-collecting hobby. Thanks to this popularity the 1961 Proof dimes are common today and easy for hobbyists to add to their collections in nearly any quality desired.

Availability: 1961 Proof dimes are easy to find in levels up through PF-69. Cameo and ultra cameo coins are more readily available than for those of the 1950s.

	Cert	Avg	%MS	PF-65	PF-66	PF-67
1961, Proof	6,623	67.4		$5	$8	$12

1961-D Roosevelt Dime

1961-D • **Circulation-Strike Mintage:** 209,146,550.

Commentary: Collectors, coin dealers, and speculators bought and stored these dimes by the roll and bag, hoping for increased value over time and future profits. The coins kept in canvas bags, and moved around in the same as they were traded in bulk, often exhibit tiny contact marks and chatter. These flaws don't keep them from *Uncirculated* status, but in sufficient numbers can preclude a given coin from a high Mint State grade. Discerning collectors seek dimes with not only crisp details but also clean, smooth surfaces unmarred by the travails of coin-on-coin abrasion.

Although the Philadelphia Mint was increasing its quality control in the early 1960s, the Denver Mint continued to produce better-struck coins, on average.

Availability and sharpness: The 1961-D Roosevelt dime is easy to acquire in grades up through MS-66. Full Torch examples are elusive, but less so than those of Philadelphia.

VARIETY: *1961-D, Doubled Die Reverse (FS-10-1961D-801).* One 1961-D doubled-die reverse is listed in the *Cherrypickers' Guide*. Of interest mainly to specialists, it can sell for three to five times the price of a normal dime, in AU-50 to MS-66 grades.

FS-10-1961D-801, **Doubled Die Reverse.**

	Cert	Avg	%MS	EF-40	MS-63	MS-65	MS-66	MS-67	MS-67FT
1961-D	960	65.8	100%	$2	$3	$5	$12	$25	$275

1962 Roosevelt Dime

1962 • **Circulation-Strike Mintage:** 3,218,019.

Commentary: One of the ongoing trends of the hobby in the 1960s was the hoarding of rolls and bags of newly minted coins. This saved many 1962 dimes from circulation, keeping them fresh and shiny for today's collectors. However, those stored in canvas bags and moved in bulk from owner to owner often have tiny marks from shifting and sliding contact with each other. Such flaws, if numerous enough, can detract from an Uncirculated coin's grade.

Proof coin dies that had outlived their usefulness for Proof coinage were pressed into service making circulation-strike coins. From these dies some coins emerged with semi-prooflike surfaces. Collectors take note!

Philadelphia's dime coinage for this year was similar to Denver's in quality—a change from years past, when Denver produced a higher ratio of well-struck coins.

Availability and sharpness: The 1962 dime of Philadelphia is easily available in Uncirculated grades up through MS-66, but slightly less common in higher grades. Well-struck 1962 coins with Full Torch details are more readily available than for the mintages of the 1940s and 1950s.

	Cert	Avg	%MS	EF-40	MS-63	MS-65	MS-66	MS-67	MS-67FT
1962	1,558	65.8	100%	$2	$3	$5	$12	$35	$350

1962, Proof • Proof Mintage: 3,218,019.

Commentary: Proof coins in this era were minted not to actual demand, but according to the quantity the Mint anticipated selling. In other words, if the Mint predicted it would sell 3 million sets of Proof coins, it would produce 3 million sets, and after those 3 million were sold it would start returning customers' checks, uncashed. "Profits" from the sale of Proof sets did not benefit the Mint's operating budget for producing coins for circulation (the bureau's main mission).

Availability: Proof dimes of 1962 are common up through PF-69 quality, with plenty of cameo and ultra cameo examples for specialists and connoisseurs to enjoy.

	Cert	Avg	%MS	PF-65	PF-66	PF-67
1962, Proof	6,387	67.4		$5	$8	$10

1962-D Roosevelt Dime

1962-D • Circulation-Strike Mintage: 334,948,380.

Commentary: As was the mode in this era, Uncirculated 1962-D dimes were hoarded by the thousands in original bank-wrapped rolls and Mint bags. Speculators traded them more like commodities than individual works of numismatic art. It would be up to later collectors to enjoy them as such, picking the well-struck from the shallowly detailed, and the pristine-surfaced from the bagmarked.

Availability and sharpness: Denver's dimes of 1962 are readily found in grades up through MS-66, and those with Full Torch details are sufficient in quantity to satisfy specialist demand.

	Cert	Avg	%MS	EF-40	MS-63	MS-65	MS-66	MS-67	MS-67FT
1962-D	1,142	65.9	99%	$2	$3	$5	$12	$30	$200

VARIETY: *1962-D, Repunched Mintmark (FS-10-1962D-501).* Numismatists Bill Fivaz and J.T. Stanton identify one repunched mintmark variety as being popular and liquid enough to warrant inclusion in the storied *Cherrypickers' Guide*. It commands premiums of 10 to 20 times the price of a normal 1962-D dime, in grades of AU-50 to MS-66.

**FS-10-1962D-501,
Repunched Mintmark.**

1963 Roosevelt Dime

1963 • Circulation-Strike Mintage: 123,650,000.

Commentary: Coin shortages, regional in nature in recent years but nationwide by 1963, compelled the Treasury Department to ramp up the Philadelphia Mint's production to nearly double its 1962 output.

Coin collectors and speculators were long in the habit of saving freshly minted coins in rolls and bags for later sale. When the Treasury announced that it would be discontinuing silver coinage soon, because of the rising cost of the precious metal, this hoarding reached new peaks. Many of today's Mint State 1963 dimes were set aside in this way.

Some 1963 dimes can be found with semi-prooflike surfaces on one or both sides. The Philadelphia Mint's practice was to use its retired Proof dies to strike dimes for circulation, resulting in this effect.

Availability and sharpness: The 1963 Roosevelt dime is common in circulated grades, and also in Mint State up through MS-67. Nicely struck examples with Full Torch details are in good supply.

	Cert	Avg	%MS	EF-40	MS-63	MS-65	MS-66	MS-67	MS-67FT
1963	1,345	65.7	99%	$2	$3	$5	$12	$30	$1,750

VARIETIES: *1963, Doubled Dies.* The *Cherrypickers' Guide* catalogs a doubled-die obverse (popularly called the "Forked Tail" variety) for the 1963 dime. It can be found in Uncirculated Mint Sets. It sells for $11 to $60 in AU-50 to MS-66. A popular doubled-die reverse sells for $15 to $80 or more.

FS-10-1963-101, **Doubled Die Obverse.**

FS-10-1963-805, **Doubled Die Reverse.**

	Cert	Avg	%MS	EF-40	MS-63	MS-65	MS-66	MS-67	MS-67FT
1963, Doubled Die Reverse	0	n/a			$25	$38	$100		

1963, Proof • Proof Mintage: 3,075,645

Availability: Proof 1963 dimes are common in levels up through PF-69, with many cameo and ultra cameo examples available for discerning collectors.

	Cert	Avg	%MS	PF-65	PF-66	PF-67
1963, Proof	8,499	67.5		$5	$8	$10

VARIETIES: *1963-D, Proof, Doubled Die Reverse (FS-10-1963-802).* The *Cherrypickers' Guide* lists four die varieties for the 1963 Proof dime, all doubled-die reverses. The variety with the strongest doubling (pictured here) is worth $70 to $200 or more in PF-63 to PF-66. This one is popular enough among general coin collectors to be included

FS-10-1963-802, **Doubled Die Reverse, Proof.**

in the regular-edition *Red Book*. Others are worth smaller premiums and are of more interest to specialists such as Proof coin collectors, die-variety enthusiasts, and Roosevelt dime fans.

	Cert	Avg		PF-65	PF-66	PF-67
1963, Doubled Die Reverse (FS-802), Proof	0	n/a		$150	$250	

1963-D Roosevelt Dime

1963-D • **Circulation-Strike Mintage:** 421,476,530.

Commentary: Denver's dime production reached a new pinnacle in 1963, with more than 420 million of the silver coins shooting from its presses. The hobbyist and speculator mania for hoarding rolls and even bags of newly minted coins continued in full force this year. This

saved many 1963-D dimes from the abrasion and wear of pocket-change commerce. However, many of those that were stored and moved from place to place in canvas bags exhibit "bag marks"—tiny dings and dents from years of unfettered contact with other coins. Today's collector will look for an example with few such surface flaws.

Availability and sharpness: The 1963-D dime is common in circulated grades and in average Mint State grades up through MS-65. Higher Uncirculated grades are not as common.

	Cert	Avg	%MS	EF-40	MS-63	MS-65	MS-66	MS-67	MS-67FT
1963-D	1,196	65.7	99%	$2	$3	$5	$12	$30	$750

VARIETY: *1963-D, Doubled Die Reverse (FS-10-1963D-801).* The *Cherrypickers' Guide* lists one doubled-die reverse for 1963-D. Most Mint State examples are MS-63 or lower. Values range from $25 in AU-50 to $120 in MS-63 and $275 in MS-66.

FS-10-1963D-801, Doubled Die Reverse.

	Cert	Avg	%MS	EF-40	MS-63	MS-65	MS-66	MS-67	MS-67FT
1963-D, Doubled Die Reverse	0	n/a			$125	$175	$250		

1964 Roosevelt Dime

1964 • **Circulation-Strike Mintage:** 929,360,000.

Commentary: The huge supply of 1964 dimes wasn't minted entirely in 1964. Congress acted on the nationwide coin shortage by passing a bill on July 24. The bill, signed into law by President Lyndon Johnson, would freeze the 1964 date until January

1 of the year following the Treasury Department's indication that the shortage was over. The intent was to stymie coin collectors, whom the Treasury saw as a cause of the coin shortage. While it's true that collectors, dealers, and speculators socked away large quantities of new coins every year, in rolls and bags, in the hopes of selling them later for a profit, there were other, greater forces at work. (Many coins

were sidelined in vending machines instead of quickly re-entering circulation.) The majority (about three-quarters) of Philadelphia's 1964-dated dimes were actually minted in 1965.

Two obverse master dies were used to create working dies for 1964-dated dimes. They vary in the appearance of the numeral 9 in the year date. The first die, with a Pointed 9, is more scarce. The second shows a Blunt 9. Collectors do not pay more for one variety over the other.

Availability and sharpness: The 1964 is one of the most common Roosevelt dimes in absolute terms. The higher grades of Mint State, however, are not quite as common as for other recent dates.

	Cert	Avg	%MS	EF-40	MS-63	MS-65	MS-66	MS-67	MS-67FT
1964	1,865	65.5	99%	$2	$3	$5	$12	$30	$500

VARIETIES: *1964, Doubled Die Reverse (FS-10-1964-801).* The *Cherry-pickers' Guide* lists two doubled-die reverse varieties for the 1964 Philadelphia dimes. The more valuable one (pictured here) sells for close to $200 in MS-65.

FS-10-1964-801,
Doubled-Die Reverse.

1964, Proof • Proof Mintage: 3,950,762.

Commentary: Many collectors seeking a single Roosevelt dime for a type set will choose a 1964 Proof to represent the series, since it is at once readily available in high grades, and inexpensive.

There are two date styles among the 1964 Proof dimes—one with a Pointed 9 and the other with a Blunt 9. Collectors do not differentiate between them, price-wise.

Availability: The 1964 Proof dime is easy to find at levels up through PF-69, including many cameo and ultra cameo coins.

	Cert	Avg	%MS	PF-65	PF-66	PF-67
1964, Proof	15,289	67.8		$5	$8	$10

1964-D Roosevelt Dime

1964-D • **Circulation-Strike Mintage:** 1,357,517,180.

Commentary: With a mintage of more than 1 billion, the 1964-D Roosevelt dime is the highest-production coin in the series. However, as noted in the commentary on Philadelphia's 1964 dimes, not all of Denver's coinage was actually minted in the year 1964. Almost two-thirds of the mintage was produced in 1965 and 1966, with the date frozen at 1964. Congress and the Treasury Department had put too much blame on coin collectors for the nation's coin shortages, and sought to discourage numismatists from hoarding, collecting, and otherwise keeping coins out of circulation by taking away their most distinguishing element—their changing dates.

As with Philadelphia's coinage, two date styles are known, with the numeral 9 either pointed or blunt.

Availability and sharpness: 1964-D Roosevelt dimes are very common in grades up through MS-64, and higher Mint State levels are only slightly scarcer. A good quantity are well-struck with Full Torch details.

	Cert	Avg	%MS	EF-40	MS-63	MS-65	MS-66	MS-67	MS-67FT
1964-D	1,939	65.5	98%	$2	$3	$5	$12	$50	$350

VARIETIES: *1964-D, Doubled Die Reverse (FS-10-1964D-801).* The *Cherrypickers' Guide* lists nine of the most popular die varieties for 1964-D dimes. One of these, a doubled-die reverse, is also popular enough to also be listed in the regular-edition Red Book (and is pictured here). It shows strong doubling on all reverse lettering, the top of the torch flame, and the tips of the leaves. This variety sells for $35 in EF-40, $100 in MS-63, and $160 or more in MS-65.

FS-10-1964D-801, Doubled Die Reverse.

	Cert	Avg	%MS	EF-40	MS-63	MS-65	MS-66	MS-67	MS-67FT
1964-D, Doubled Die Reverse (FS-801)	6	61.5	67%	$35	$100	$160	$235	$400	$750

1964, Special Mint Set, Roosevelt Dime

1964, Special Mint Set • Mintage:
estimated fewer than 50

Commentary: No official documentation exists confirming the creation of Special Mint Sets in 1964. (See the next entry for information on Special Mint Sets of 1965–1967.) A set was first auctioned in 1993, and others have since come to light. The coins may have been minted as a feasibility test for production of Special Mint Sets starting in 1965. Or they may have been produced as a small quantity of unofficial presentation sets of the nation's last 90 percent silver coins (plus the Lincoln cent and Jefferson nickel).

For the 1964 SMS dime, the most common grade of the two dozen or so certification events (not necessarily individual coins) is SP-67. The retail value in that grade is approximately $15,000; note that firm values are difficult to establish because sales are so infrequent.

Availability and sharpness: Estimates as to the number of 1964 Special Mint Sets created range from 15 to 50. The coins are seldom offered for sale or auction. "Each of the five coins in the set . . . had razor-sharp strikes. Rather than the deep, mirror-like surface seen on Proof coins, these coins had a satin sheen, possessing none of the reflectivity seen on Proof coinage. Swirling die polish was evident throughout the coins' fields, indicating that the dies that struck them had received special treatment" (Schechter and Garrett, *100 Greatest U.S. Modern Coins*).

	Cert	Avg	%MS	
1964, SMS			100%	$15,000–$20,000

1965, Special Mint Set, Roosevelt Dime

1965, Special Mint Set • Circulation-Strike Mintage: 2,360,000.

Commentary: In mid-1964 the Treasury Department announced it would no longer offer its traditional annual Proof sets and Uncirculated Mint sets. This decision was spurred by a nationwide shortage of circulating coins—a situation that had led to congressional criticism of the Mint. Director Eva Adams blamed coin collectors for the shortage, and took action to placate Congress. (In addition to curtailing Proof and Mint sets, the Mint removed mintmarks in 1965, 1966, and 1967, in order to discourage collectors from pulling coins from circulation for their collections.) In reality, much of the nationwide shortage was caused by coins languishing in pay-phones and coin-operated vending machines instead of being quickly put back into circulation. As the shortages increased, the general public (not just coin collectors) hoarded coins from the cent to the half dollar.

Instead of its usual packaged coin sets, the Mint issued what it called "Special Mint Sets," in 1965, 1966, and 1967. The 1965 SMS coins were produced starting in the first seven months of 1966, at the San Francisco Assay Office (as the San Francisco Mint, renamed thus in 1958, was then known).

The coins were struck once on unpolished planchets (as opposed to Proof coins, which are struck twice or more on polished planchets).

"As in 1936, and again in 1950, the early deliveries of Special Mint Sets featured coins that were semi-brilliant or satiny. These are highly distinctive, yet they were certainly not equal to Proofs. Later issues dated 1965 featured very brilliant fields, though perhaps not as brilliant as on Proofs. Because the coins were permitted to come into contact with other coins, they suffered numerous tiny marks that further diminished their appeal to collectors" (Lange, *A Guide Book of Modern United States Proof Coin Sets*).

In 1965 Special Mint Sets were packaged in a single pliofilm envelope with sealed pockets for each coin.

Many coin collectors were content to put regular circulation strikes in their folders and albums. The buyers for Special Mint Sets were mostly those had bought Proof coin sets earlier.

Availability and sharpness: These sets, and their individual coins, are common.

	Cert	Avg	%MS	MS-65	MS-66	MS-67
1965, SMS	2,976	67.1	100%	$11	$13	$17

1966, Special Mint Set, Roosevelt Dime

1966, Special Mint Set • Circulation-Strike Mintage: 2,261,583.

Commentary: For general information on Special Mint Sets, see the entry for 1965.

The Special Mint Sets of 1966 brought an innovation to the Mint's packaged collector coins: a rigid, sonically sealed plastic holder. Gone were the individual envelopes and pliofilm of earlier years. Striking of the 1966-dated coins began August 1, 1966, after the Mint had produced enough 1965-dated sets to avoid the latter becoming a rarity.

A few 1966 SMS dimes have somewhat satiny surfaces. Most are almost fully prooflike in brilliance. Overpolished dies caused many 1966 SMS dimes to be struck with missing details.

Availability and sharpness: These sets, and their individual coins, are readily available. Their strike is fairly strong. Overpolished dies often offered prooflike brilliance at the expense of sharp detail.

	Cert	Avg	%MS	MS-65	MS-66	MS-67
1966, SMS	2,559	67.3	100%	$11	$13	$20

1967, Special Mint Set, Roosevelt Dime

1967, Special Mint Set • Circulation-Strike Mintage: 1,863,344.

Commentary: For general information on Special Mint Sets, see the entry for 1965.

All 1967 SMS coins were struck in calendar-year 1967—a departure from the mintages of 1965- and 1966-dated coins. After two years of their production, the San Francisco Assay Office was more adept at creating the coins for the sets, with their quality approaching that of Proof coinage. Brilliant finishes were produced without the dies being overpolished.

Fewer of the 1967 SMS sets were sold than those of 1965 and 1966, through no fault of the coins or their quality. The hobby of coin collecting had suffered a drop in popular interest since its peak in 1964. Also, fewer collectors were willing to buy multiple sets in the hopes of selling their extras for a profit. The Mint's $4.00 issue price, compared to $2.10 for Proof sets last issued in 1964, didn't help matters. Because of lower sales, the 1967 coins have always been the scarcest of the three years.

Availability and sharpness: Complete 1967 Special Mint Sets, and their individual coins, are easily available. Their quality is better than that of their 1965 and 1966 counterparts. Cameo examples are hard to locate; deep and ultra cameo coins are very rare.

	Cert	Avg	%MS	MS-65	MS-66	MS-67
1967, SMS	3,060	67.2	100%	$12	$14	$18

ROOSEVELT DIMES, CLAD AND SILVER (1965 TO DATE)

In the mid-1960s the rising price of silver on international markets reached the point at which, by 1965, it would cost more than face value to strike dimes, quarters, and half dollars in the Mint's traditional .900 fine alloy. Accordingly, in 1965 a new copper-nickel–clad composition was substituted for the circulating dime and quarter, and the fineness of the half dollar lowered to .400.

The new non-silver dimes kept the same John Sinnock designs (Roosevelt portrait, and torch motif) as the 1946–1964 silver issues. Their composition was changed to outer layers of copper-nickel (75 percent copper and 25 percent nickel) bonded to an inner core of pure copper.

Regular copper-nickel coinage has been produced at the Philadelphia and Denver mints. Mintmarks were returned to U.S. coins in 1968 (following a three-year hiatus), and the dime's mintmark at that time was moved to the obverse. The P mintmark was added to Philadelphia Mint dimes for the first time in 1980. By error many 1982 dimes struck in Philadelphia omitted the mintmark, inadvertently creating a scarce variety. The San Francisco Mint has made coins for the numismatic market, and even West Point has struck some special-issue dimes in recent years.

Proof dimes, which had not been made since 1964, were revived in 1968, struck in San Francisco and with an S mintmark. They have been produced continuously since that time. On several occasions the S mintmark was omitted in error from the dies. Examples of these errors are rare, with the 1972 being especially so. The 1975, No S dime was ranked number 1 in *100 Greatest U.S. Modern Coins*, fourth edition.

In addition, starting in 1992 and continuing ever since, Proof silver strikes of 90 percent silver and 10 percent copper—the traditional alloy of yesteryear—have been made at the San Francisco Mint for collectors and sold at a premium. These are packaged in the Mint's annual Silver Proof Sets.

The 1996-W Roosevelt dime, struck at the West Point Mint, was made in the normal copper-nickel composition. This was a commemorative of sorts—not officially part of the Mint's commemorative coin program, but struck to honor the 50th anniversary of the Roosevelt dime. The 1996-W coins were included in the year's Uncirculated Mint Sets—the only coin struck in copper-nickel composition to bear West Point's famous W mintmark.

Other interesting issues came to the fore in 2015 with two dimes minted to celebrate the 75th anniversary of the March of Dimes. A special Philadelphia issue of Reverse Proof dimes was produced with high-relief design elements polished in the dies and fields made frosty. Also that year, for the first time, the West Point Mint produced dimes (in regular Proof format) in silver. These coins were struck for the collectors' market, packaged with the year's March of Dimes commemorative silver dollar, and sold at a premium.

To celebrate the 100th anniversary of the Mercury (or Winged Liberty Head) dime in 2016, at the West Point Mint 2016-W dimes were made in .9999 pure *gold* and sold to collectors. The mintage for this unique dime of an anachronistic design and of a rare metal was limited to 125,000. Should this dime be placed among Roosevelt dimes, as here, or should it be placed after the 1945 Mercury dimes? Opinions have been divided. The regular edition of the *Guide Book of United States Coins* catalogs them chronologically, between the 2015 and 2016 Roosevelt dimes, with a cross-reference in the Mercury dime section.

Collecting one of each date and mintmark of *regular* circulation strikes is affordable and easy to do. Such pieces form an attractive set in an album. The one error variety, 1982 Philadelphia without the P mintmark, is a nice optional addition that costs into the low three figures for a high-grade example. Meanwhile, Proofs in copper-nickel and silver are affordable, and the gold 2015-W is a showpiece. In addition, for specialists there are numerous collectible varieties such as doubled dies.

A GALLERY OF MODERN ROOSEVELT DIMES (1965 TO DATE)

On the following pages are shown images for all the main listings of Roosevelt dimes from 1965 to date, with the exception of the SMS coins, already listed on pages 630 and 631, and the 2016-W Barber Liberty Heat gold issue, listed separately on page 654.

1965   1966

1967

1968

1968-D

1968-S,
Proof

1969

1969-D

1969-S,
Proof

1970

1970-D

1970-S,
Proof

1971

1971-D

1971-S,
Proof

1972

1972-D

1972-S,
Proof

1973

1973-D

1973-S,
Proof

1974

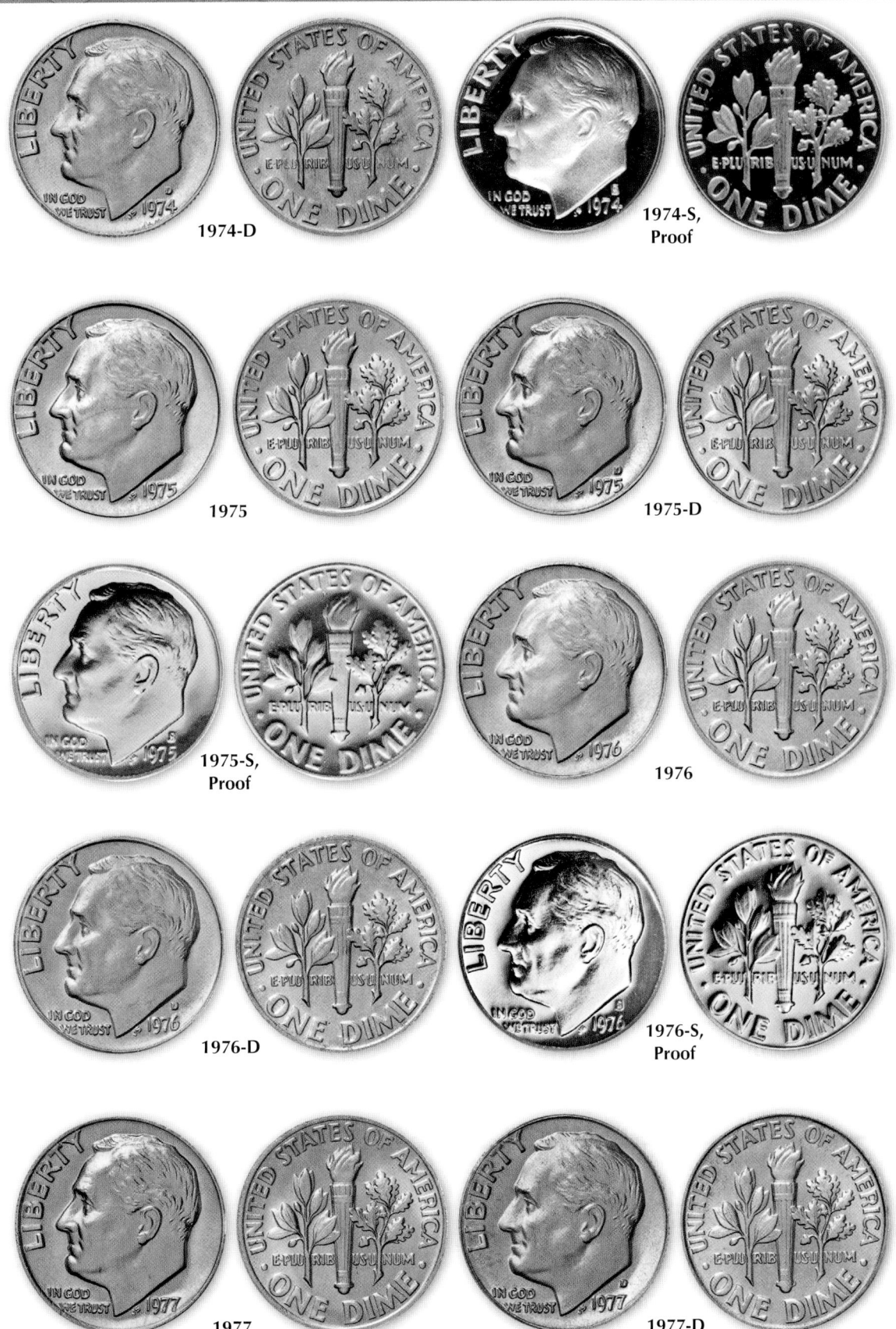

1974-D

1974-S,
Proof

1975

1975-D

1975-S,
Proof

1976

1976-D

1976-S,
Proof

1977

1977-D

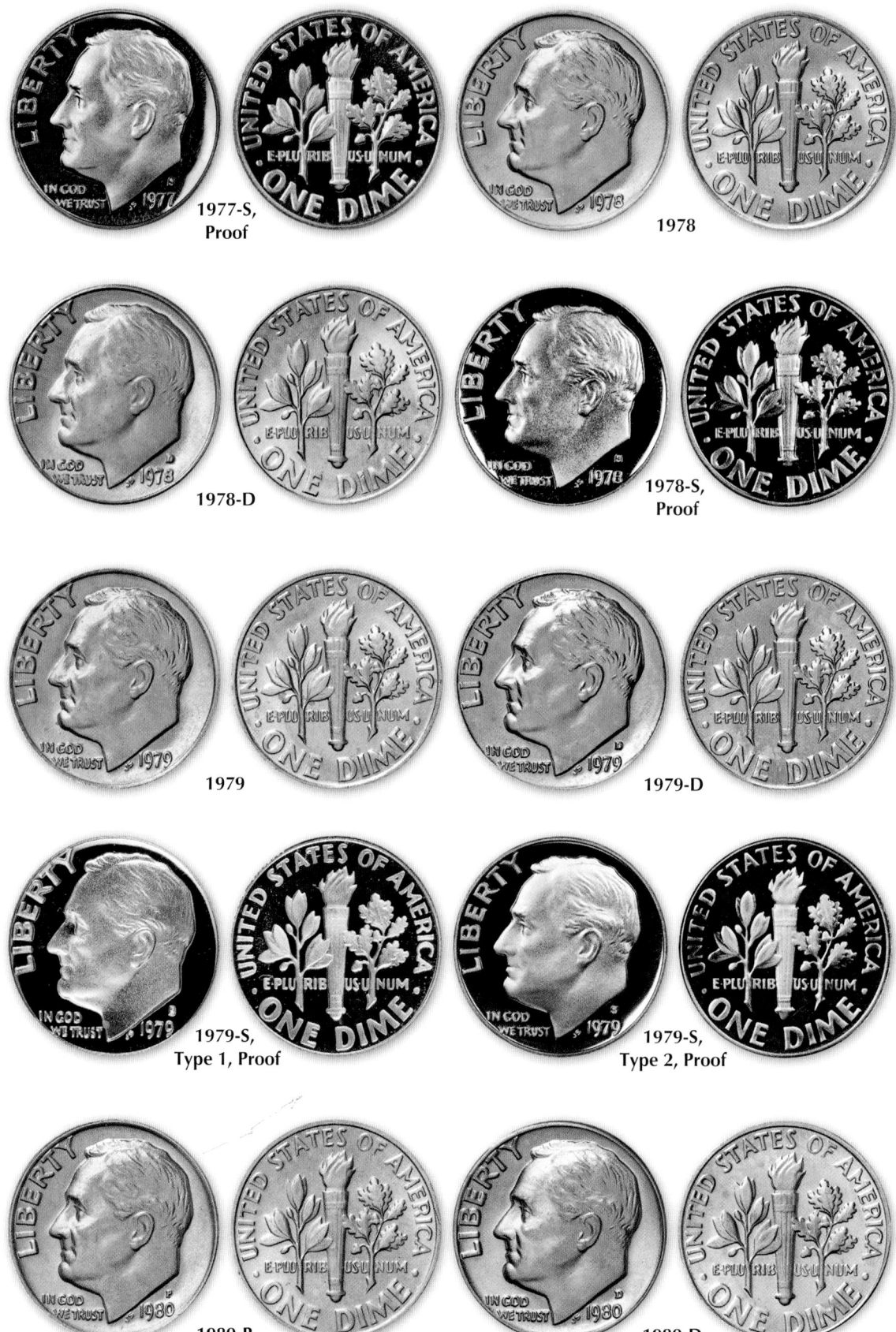

1977-S,
Proof

1978

1978-D

1978-S,
Proof

1979

1979-D

1979-S,
Type 1, Proof

1979-S,
Type 2, Proof

1980-P

1980-D

1980-S, Proof

1981-P

1981-D

1981-S, Type 1, Proof

1981-S, Type 2, Proof

1982-P

1982-D

1982-S, Proof

1983-P

1983-D

1983-S,
Proof

1984-P

1984-D

1984-S,
Proof

1985-P

1985-D

1985-S,
Proof

1986-P

1986-D

1986-S,
Proof

1987-P   1987-D

1987-S,
Proof   1988-P

1988-D   1988-S,
Proof

1989-P   1989-D

1989-S,
Proof   1990-P

1990-D

1990-S,
Proof

1991-P

1991-D

1991-S,
Proof

1992-P

1992-D

1992-S,
Proof

1993-P

1993-D

1993-S, Proof

1994-P

1994-D

1994-S, Proof

1995-P

1995-D

1995-S, Proof

1996-P

1996-D

1996-S, Proof

1996-W

1997-P

1997-D

1997-S,
Proof

1998-P

1998-D

1998-S,
Proof

1999-P

1999-D

1999-S,
Proof

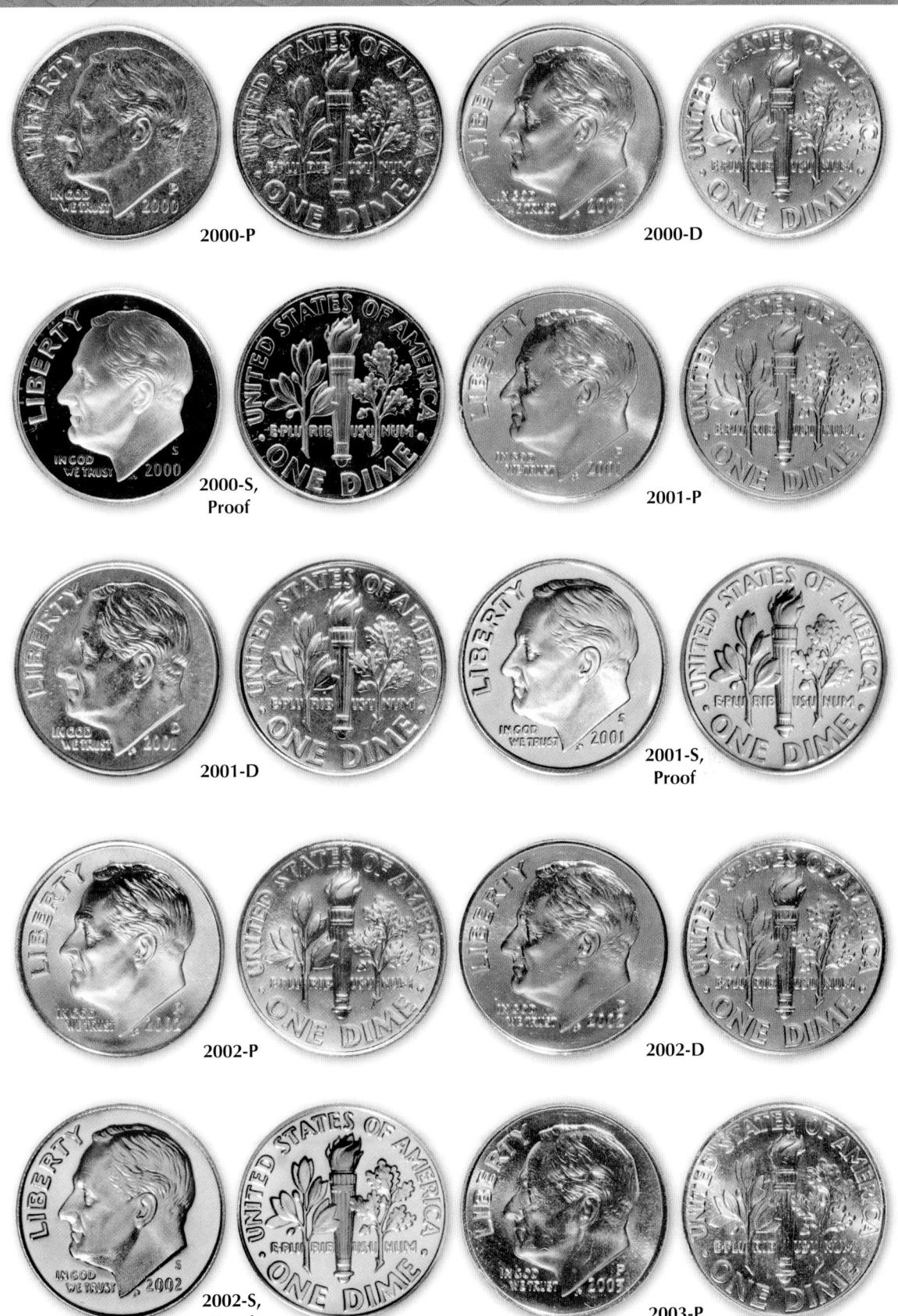

2000-P

2000-D

2000-S, Proof

2001-P

2001-D

2001-S, Proof

2002-P

2002-D

2002-S, Proof

2003-P

2003-D

2003-S,
Proof

2004-P

2004-D

2004-S,
Proof

2005-P

2005-P,
Satin Finish

2005-D

2005-D,
Satin Finish

2005-S,
Proof

2006-P

2006-P, Satin Finish

2006-D

2006-D, Satin Finish

2006-S, Proof

2007-P

2007-P, Satin Finish

2007-D

2007-D, Satin Finish

2007-S, Proof

2008-P

2008-P,
Satin Finish

2008-D

2008-D,
Satin Finish

2008-S,
Proof

2009-P

2009-P,
Satin Finish

2009-D

2009-D,
Satin Finish

2009-S,
Proof

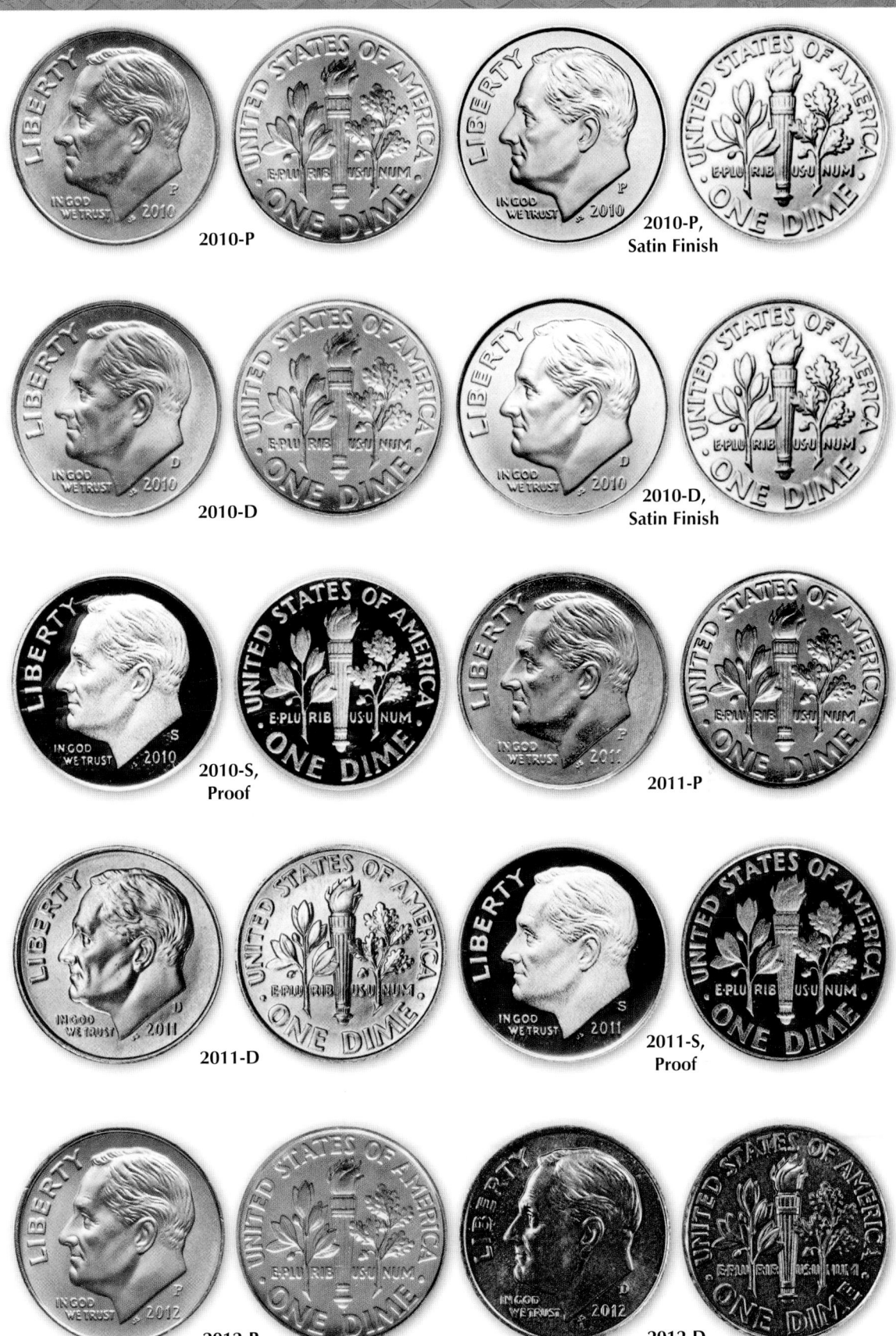

2010-P

2010-P,
Satin Finish

2010-D

2010-D,
Satin Finish

2010-S,
Proof

2011-P

2011-D

2011-S,
Proof

2012-P

2012-D

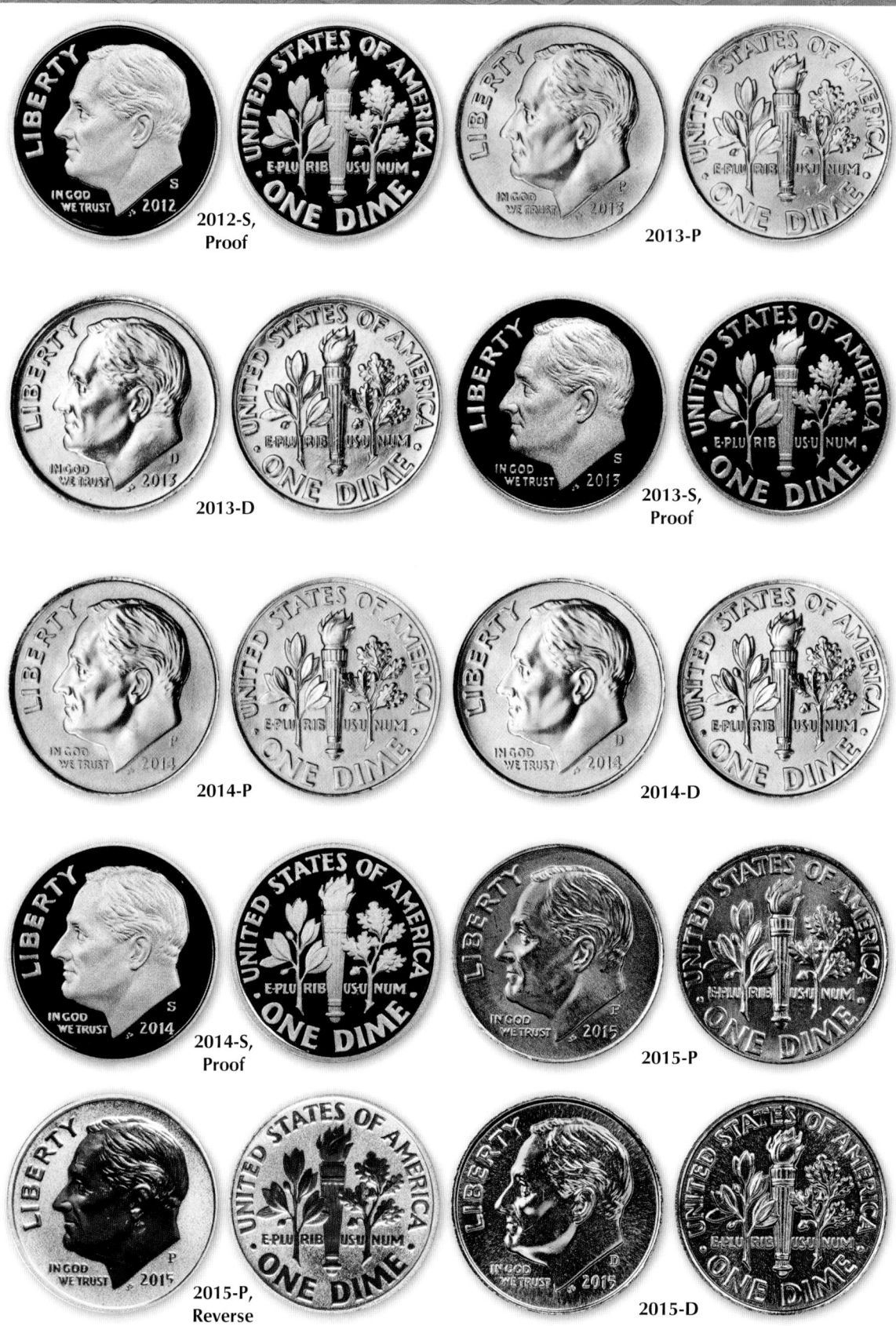

2012-S,
Proof

2013-P

2013-D

2013-S,
Proof

2014-P

2014-D

2014-S,
Proof

2015-P

2015-P,
Reverse
Proof, Silver

2015-D

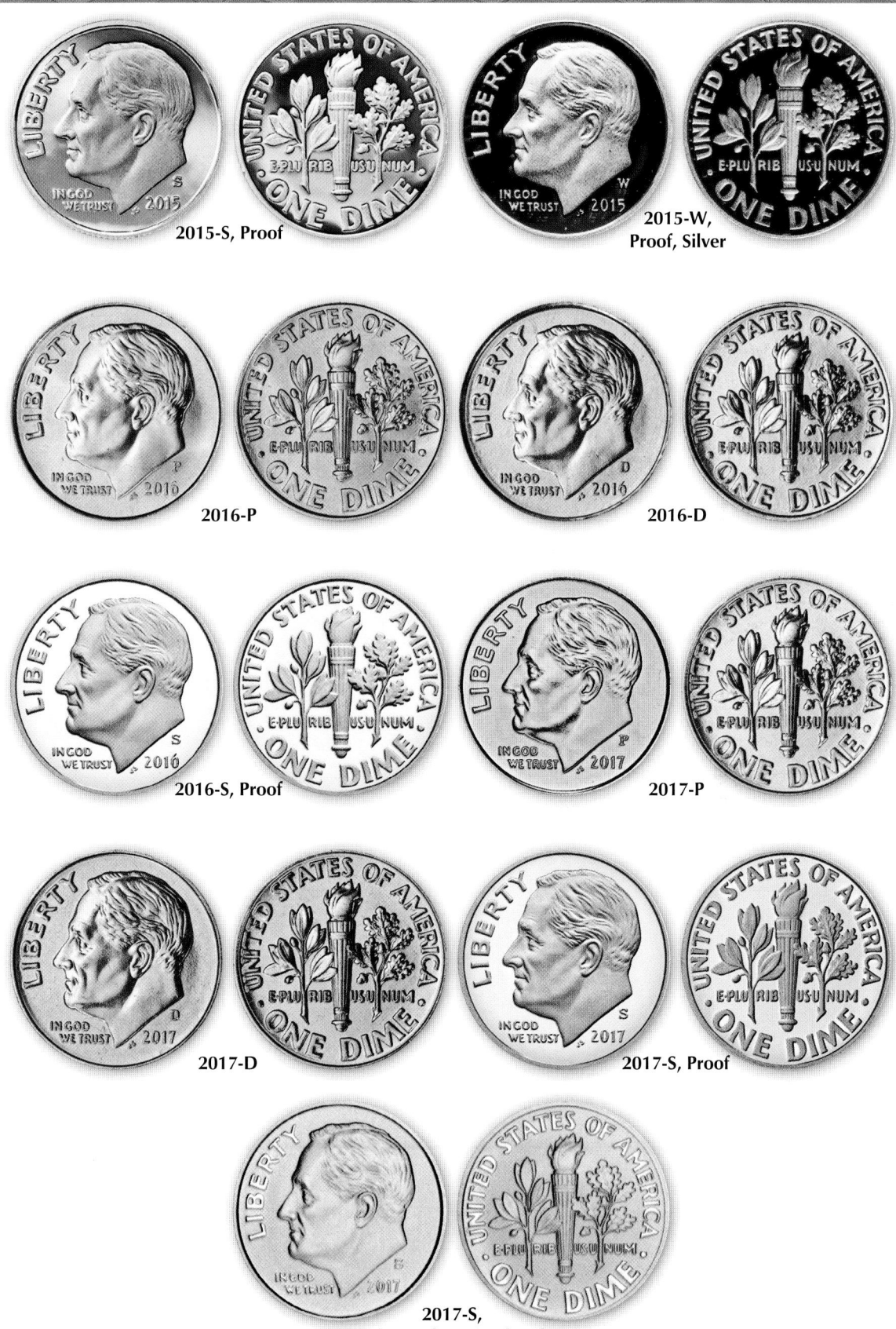

2015-S, Proof

2015-W,
Proof, Silver

2016-P

2016-D

2016-S, Proof

2017-P

2017-D

2017-S, Proof

2017-S,
Enhanced Uncirculated

1967, Doubled Die Obverse
FS-10-1967-101.

1968-S, Doubled Die Obverse, Proof
FS-10-1968S-102.

1968-S, No Mintmark, Proof
FS-10-1968S-501.

1970, Doubled Die Reverse
FS-10-1970-801.

1970-S, No Mintmark, Proof
FS-10-1970S-501.

	Mintage	Cert	Avg	%MS	EF-40	MS-63	MS-65	MS-66	MS-67	MS-67FT
								PF-65	PF-66	PF-67
1965	1,652,140,570	145	65.4	97%			$2	$15	$75	$1,000
1966	1,382,734,540	195	66.2	97%			$2.25	$6	$30	$800
1967	2,244,007,320	210	64.8	87%			$2	$5	$25	$650
1967, Doubled Die Obverse (a)	(b)						$400	$600	$850	
1968	424,470,400	221	65.7	99%			$2	$5	$25	$600
1968-D	480,748,280	777	66.1	100%			$2	$5	$20	$75
1968-S, Proof	3,041,506	1,262	67.9					$2	$4	$6
1968-S, Doubled Die Obverse, Proof (c)	(d)	4	67.0					$350	$500	$750
1968-S, No Mintmark, Proof ‡ (e)	(d)	15	67.7					$12,500	$15,000	$17,500
1969	145,790,000	121	65.0	98%			$3	$6	$30	
1969-D	563,323,870	827	66.0	100%			$2	$6	$25	$750
1969-S, Proof	2,394,631	1,026	68.1					$2	$4	$6
1970	345,570,000	201	64.4	97%			$2	$6	$35	
1970, Doubled Die Reverse (f)	(g)	4	62.3	75%			$300	$650	$1,000	
1970-D	754,942,100	690	65.1	99%			$2	$5	$35	
1970-S, Proof	2,632,810	1,113	67.7					$2	$4	$6
1970-S, No Mintmark, Proof ‡ (e)	(h)	190	67.7					$800	$1,000	$1,100
1971	162,690,000	81	64.9	100%			$2.50	$6	$40	
1971-D	377,914,240	154	65.7	100%			$2.25	$6	$50	$700
1971-S, Proof	3,220,733	1,395	68.1					$2	$4	$6
1972	431,540,000	99	65.1	99%			$2	$6	$60	
1972-D	330,290,000	204	65.7	100%			$2	$6	$40	$800
1972-S, Proof	3,260,996	1,163	68.0					$2	$4	$6
1973	315,670,000	104	65.2	100%			$2	$5	$70	$1,200
1973-D	455,032,426	172	65.4	100%			$2	$6	$50	$500
1973-S, Proof	2,760,339	452	67.7					$2	$4	$6
1974	470,248,000	60	65.0	100%			$2	$5	$25	
1974-D	571,083,000	116	65.5	100%			$2	$5	$25	$1,000
1974-S, Proof	2,612,568	398	67.9					$2	$4	$6

‡ Ranked in the *100 Greatest U.S. Modern Coins*. **a.** This is a very rare doubled die. Its doubling is evident on IN GOD WE TRUST, the date, and the designer's initials. **b.** Included in circulation-strike 1967 mintage figure. **c.** There are several 1968-S, Proof, doubled-die obverse varieties. The one listed here is FS-10-1968S-102 (see the *Cherrypickers' Guide to Rare Die Varieties*, sixth edition, volume II). **d.** Included in 1968-S, Proof, mintage figure. **e.** The S mintmark was inadvertently left off the coinage die; this defect was probably discovered before the end of the die's life. **f.** Doubling on this extremely rare variety is evident on all reverse lettering, especially on UNITED STATES OF AMERICA, with slightly weaker doubling on ONE DIME. **g.** Included in circulation-strike 1970 mintage figure. **h.** Included in 1970-S, Proof, mintage figure.

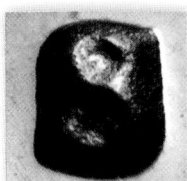

**1979-S, Filled S
(Type 1), Proof**

**1979-S, Clear S
(Type 2), Proof**

**1981-S, Rounded S
(Type 1), Proof**

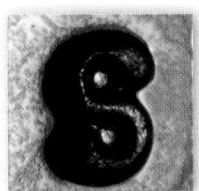

**1981-S, Flat S
(Type 2), Proof**

**1975-S, No Mintmark,
Proof**
FS-10-1975S-501.

**1982, No Mintmark,
Strong Strike**
FS-10-1982-501.

**1982, No Mintmark,
Weak Strike**
FS-10-1982-502.

| | Mintage | Cert | Avg | %MS | EF-40 | MS-63 | MS-65 | MS-66 | MS-67 | MS-67FT |
								PF-65	PF-66	PF-67
1975	585,673,900	125	65.2	98%			$2	$5	$25	$1,000
1975-D	313,705,300	201	66.2	100%			$2	$5	$30	$600
1975-S, Proof	2,845,450	561	68.1					$3	$4	$6
1975-S, No Mintmark, Proof (e)	(i)	0	n/a						$150,000	
1976	568,760,000	139	66.1	100%			$2	$5	$25	$1,200
1976-D	695,222,774	145	65.8	97%			$2	$5	$40	$1,200
1976-S, Proof	4,149,730	887	68.1					$2.75	$4	$6
1977	796,930,000	214	65.8	100%			$2	$5	$25	$1,200
1977-D	376,607,228	124	65.5	100%			$2	$5	$35	$550
1977-S, Proof	3,251,152	847	68.5					$2.50	$4	$6
1978	663,980,000	111	65.6	99%			$2	$5	$27	$300
1978-D	282,847,540	87	65.6	100%			$2	$5	$25	
1978-S, Proof	3,127,781	755	68.9					$2.50	$4	$6
1979	315,440,000	168	65.7	100%			$2	$5	$30	
1979-D	390,921,184	143	65.7	100%			$2	$5	$30	
1979-S, Type 1, Proof	3,677,175	921	69.0					$2.50	$4	$6
1979-S, Type 2, Proof	(j)	1,316	69.2					$5	$6	$8
1980-P	735,170,000	184	65.9	99%			$2	$5	$25	
1980-D	719,354,321	100	65.7	100%			$2	$5	$30	
1980-S, Proof	3,554,806	1,099	68.5					$2.50	$4	$6
1981-P	676,650,000	239	65.9	100%			$2	$5	$40	$70
1981-D	712,284,143	363	66.5	100%			$2	$5	$20	$80
1981-S, Type 1, Proof	4,063,083	1,337	68.9					$2.50	$4	$6
1981-S, Type 2, Proof	(k)	737	69.1					$6	$6	$8
1982, No Mintmark, Strong Strike ‡ (l)	(m)	501	64.3	93%			$200	$300	$550	$1,250
1982, No Mintmark, Weak Strike ‡ (l)	(m)	16	65.1	100%			$65	$100	$250	
1982-P	519,475,000	194	66.2	98%			$7.50	$18	$50	$900
1982-D	542,713,584	132	65.9	98%			$2.50	$6	$25	$600
1982-S, Proof	3,857,479	777	69.0					$2.50	$4	$6

‡ Ranked in the *100 Greatest U.S. Modern Coins*. **e.** The S mintmark was inadvertently left off the coinage die; this defect was probably discovered before the end of the die's life. **h.** Included in 1970-S, Proof, mintage figure. **i.** Included in 1975-S, Proof, mintage figure. **j.** Included in 1979-S, Proof, Type 1, mintage figure. **k.** Included in 1981-S, Proof, Type 1, mintage figure. **l.** The P mintmark was omitted from this working die. There are two versions of this variety: one with a strong strike, and one with a weak strike. The strong strike is far more valuable and in demand than the weak. **m.** Included in 1982-P mintage figure.

	Mintage	Cert	Avg	%MS	EF-40	MS-63	MS-65	MS-66 / PF-65	MS-67 / PF-66	MS-67FT / PF-67
1983-P	647,025,000	119	65.7	97%			$6.50	$15	$30	$250
1983-D	730,129,224	61	65.8	97%			$3.25	8.50	$25	$200
1983-S, Proof	3,279,126	853	69.2					$3	$4	$6
1983-S, No Mintmark, Proof (e) ‡	(n)	158	68.8					$750	$850	$1,000
1984-P	856,669,000	168	66.4	99%			$2	$5	$20	$100
1984-D	704,803,976	122	65.4	100%			$2.25	$5	$20	$150
1984-S, Proof	3,065,110	586	69.1					$2.50	$4	$6
1985-P	705,200,962	131	66.5	100%			$2.25	$5	$25	$150
1985-D	587,979,970	213	66.8	100%			$2.25	$5	$30	$100
1985-S, Proof	3,362,821	647	69.1					$3	$4	$6
1986-P	682,649,693	174	65.9	99%			$2.50	$5	$20	$800
1986-D	473,326,970	189	66.2	99%			$2.50	$5	$20	$700
1986-S, Proof	3,010,497	489	69.1					$4	$5	$7
1987-P	762,709,481	177	66.1	99%			$2	$5	$25	$800
1987-D	653,203,402	175	66.1	99%			$2	$5	$20	$200
1987-S, Proof	4,227,728	636	69.1					$3	$4	$6
1988-P	1,030,550,000	137	65.6	95%			$2	$5	$35	$225
1988-D	962,385,489	153	66.3	99%			$2	$5	$40	$100
1988-S, Proof	3,262,948	457	69.1					$4	$5	$7
1989-P	1,298,400,000	137	66.1	99%			$2	$5	$20	$100
1989-D	896,535,597	194	66.3	99%			$2	$6	$20	$75
1989-S, Proof	3,220,194	472	69.0					$4	$6	$6
1990-P	1,034,340,000	80	66.0	98%			$2	$6	$20	$1,000
1990-D	839,995,824	131	66.3	98%			$2	$4	$25	$2,000
1990-S, Proof	3,299,559	668	69.3					$2.50	$4	$6
1991-P	927,220,000	75	66.3	99%			$2	$4	$20	$100
1991-D	601,241,114	93	66.0	100%			$2	$4	$20	$200
1991-S, Proof	2,867,787	674	69.4					$4	$5	$7
1992-P	593,500,000	90	67.0	100%			$2	$5	$35	$150
1992-D	616,273,932	73	66.2	100%			$2	$4	$30	$175
1992-S, Proof	2,858,981	515	69.5					$3	$4	$6
1992-S, Proof, Silver	1,317,579	1,799	69.3					$6	$7	$8
1993-P	766,180,000	122	66.4	98%			$2	$4	$30	$200
1993-D	750,110,166	102	65.7	99%			$2	$4	$25	$500
1993-S, Proof	2,633,439	536	69.4					$5	$6	$7
1993-S, Proof, Silver	761,353	1,326	69.2					$7	$8	$9
1994-P	1,189,000,000	128	66.4	98%			$2	$4	$25	$200
1994-D	1,303,268,110	70	65.3	99%			$2	$4	$25	$150
1994-S, Proof	2,484,594	465	69.5					$5	$6	$8
1994-S, Proof, Silver	785,329	1,250	69.2					$8	$9	$10
1995-P	1,125,500,000	73	66.8	100%			$2	$4	$30	$300
1995-D	1,274,890,000	90	66.0	98%			$2	$5	$35	$425
1995-S, Proof	2,117,496	440	69.5					$10	$16	$20
1995-S, Proof, Silver	679,985	1,655	69.2					$14	$23	$30
1996-P	1,421,163,000	161	66.7	98%			$2	$4	$25	$45
1996-D	1,400,300,000	195	66.2	99%			$2	$4	$20	$75
1996-W ‡ (o)	1,457,000	0	n/a				$20	$30	$45	$70
1996-S, Proof	1,750,244	463	69.4					$3	$6	$8
1996-S, Proof, Silver	775,021	1,414	69.2					$8	$10	$15

‡ Ranked in the *100 Greatest U.S. Modern Coins*. **e.** The S mintmark was inadvertently left off the coinage die; this defect was probably discovered before the end of the die's life. **n.** Included in 1983-S, Proof, mintage figure. **o.** Issued in Mint sets only, to mark the 50th anniversary of the design.

	Mintage	Cert	Avg	%MS	EF-40	MS-63	MS-65	MS-66 PF-65	MS-67 PF-66	MS-67FT PF-67
1997-P	991,640,000	5,628	66.5	100%			$2	$6	$60	$100
1997-D	979,810,000	78	66.1	99%			$2	$6	$50	$100
1997-S, Proof	2,055,000	382	69.6					$8	$10	$15
1997-S, Proof, Silver	741,678	1,383	69.2					$12	$22	$24
1998-P	1,163,000,000	111	66.5	99%			$2	$3	$18	$100
1998-D	1,172,250,000	104	65.8	99%			$2	$3	$15	$125
1998-S, Proof	2,086,507	357	69.5					$4	$6	$8
1998-S, Proof, Silver	878,792	1,424	69.3					$6	$8	$10
1999-P	2,164,000,000	134	66.7	97%			$2	$3	$15	$30
1999-D	1,397,750,000	122	66.4	99%			$2	$3	$15	$40
1999-S, Proof	2,543,401	2,375	69.2					$4	$6	$8
1999-S, Proof, Silver	804,565	4,223	69.2					$7	$8	$12
2000-P	1,842,500,000	72	65.6	90%			$2	$3	$15	$30
2000-D	1,818,700,000	88	66.4	97%			$2	$3	$15	$30
2000-S, Proof	3,082,572	1,401	69.2					$2.50	$4	$7
2000-S, Proof, Silver	965,421	4,326	69.3					$5	$6	$8
2001-P	1,369,590,000	69	66.5	100%			$2	$3	$12	$30
2001-D	1,412,800,000	88	66.3	95%			$2	$3	$12	$30
2001-S, Proof	2,294,909	1,136	69.4					$2.50	$4	$7
2001-S, Proof, Silver	889,697	3,847	69.4					$5	$6	$8
2002-P	1,187,500,000	46	66.5	98%			$2	$3	$12	$30
2002-D	1,379,500,000	55	66.5	98%			$2	$3	$12	$30
2002-S, Proof	2,319,766	1,593	69.3					$2.50	$4	$7
2002-S, Proof, Silver	892,229	3,583	69.4					$5	$6	$8
2003-P	1,085,500,000	150	66.1	100%			$2	$3	$10	$30
2003-D	986,500,000	107	65.8	100%			$2	$3	$10	$30
2003-S, Proof	2,172,684	3,517	69.3					$2.50	$4	$7
2003-S, Proof, Silver	1,125,755	4,559	69.3					$4.50	$5	$8
2004-P	1,328,000,000	122	66.6	100%			$2	$3	$8	$30
2004-D	1,159,500,000	85	66.5	98%			$2	$3	$8	$35
2004-S, Proof	1,789,488	1,426	69.3					$3	$5	$7
2004-S, Proof, Silver	1,175,934	4,478	69.5					$5	$6	$8
2005-P	1,412,000,000	45	67.0				$2	$3	$8	$65
2005-P, Satin Finish	1,160,000	2,194	67.0	100%	$1	$2	$3	$5	$7	$10
2005-D	1,423,500,000	100	66.0	100%			$2	$3	$8	$70
2005-D, Satin Finish	1,160,000	2,299	66.9	99%	$1	$2	$3	$5	$7	$10
2005-S, Proof	2,275,000	6,095	69.3	100%				$2.50	$4	$7
2005-S, Proof, Silver	1,069,679	5,508	69.5					$5	$6	$8
2006-P	1,381,000,000	119	65.8	99%			$2	$3	$6	$22
2006-P, Satin Finish	847,361	1,188	66.9	100%	$1	$2	$3	$5	$7	$10
2006-D	1,447,000,000	105	66.2	100%			$2	$3	$6	$22
2006-D, Satin Finish	847,361	1,144	66.8	100%	$1	$2	$3	$5	$7	$10
2006-S, Proof	2,000,428	1,984	69.4					$2.50	$4	$7
2006-S, Proof, Silver	1,054,008	3,010	69.5					$5	$6	$8
2007-P	1,047,500,000	27	66.2	100%			$2	$3	$6	$22
2007-P, Satin Finish	895,628	207	66.5	100%	$1	$2	$3	$5	$7	$10
2007-D	1,042,000,000	198	66.2	100%			$2	$3	$6	$22
2007-D, Satin Finish	895,628	233	66.7	100%	$1	$2	$3	$5	$7	$10
2007-S, Proof	1,702,116	1,673	69.6					$2.50	$4	$7
2007-S, Proof, Silver	875,050	3,512	69.6					$5	$6	$8

	Mintage	Cert	Avg	%MS	EF-40	MS-63	MS-65	MS-66 PF-65	MS-67 PF-66	MS-67FT PF-67
2008-P	391,000,000	27	66.0	100%			$2	$3	$5	$22
2008-P, Satin Finish	745,464	93	67.8	100%	$1	$2	$3	$5	$7	$10
2008-D	624,500,000	97	66.2	100%			$2	$3	$5	$22
2008-D, Satin Finish	745,464	132	68.2	100%	$1	$2	$3	$5	$7	$10
2008-S, Proof	1,405,674	1,309	69.7					$2.50	$4	$7
2008-S, Proof, Silver	763,887	3,770	69.8					$5	$6	$8
2009-P	96,500,000	349	65.8	100%			$2	$3	$5	$22
2009-P, Satin Finish	784,614	138	67.6	100%	$1	$2	$3	$5	$7	$10
2009-D	49,500,000	217	66.0	100%			$2	$3	$5	$22
2009-D, Satin Finish	784,614	208	68.4	100%	$1	$2	$3	$5	$7	$10
1999-S, Proof, Silver	804,565	3,361	69.6					$2.50	$4	$7
2009-S, Proof	1,482,502	3,943	69.7					$5	$6	$8
2009-S, Proof, Silver	697,365	129	66.6	100%			$2	$3	$4	$20
2010-P	557,000,000	114	68.1	100%	$1	$2	$3	$5	$7	$10
2010-P, Satin Finish	583,897	112	66.2	100%			$2	$3	$4	$20
2010-D	562,000,000	113	68.4	100%	$1	$2	$3	$5	$7	$10
2010-D, Satin Finish	583,897	1,361	69.5					$2.50	$4	$7
2010-S, Proof	1,103,815	3,786	69.7					$5	$6	$8
2010-S, Proof, Silver	585,401	199	67.3	100%			$2	$3	$4	$20
2011-P	748,000,000	203	67.1	100%			$2	$3	$4	$20
2011-D	754,000,000	2,330	69.5					$2.50	$4	$7
2011-S, Proof	1,098,835	4,732	69.7					$5	$6	$8
2011-S, Proof, Silver	574,175	97	67.0	100%			$2	$3	$4	$20
2012-P	808,000,000	106	66.8	100%			$2	$3	$4	$20
2012-D	868,000,000	1,465	69.5					$2.50	$4	$7
2012-S, Proof	841,972	1,629	69.8					$5	$6	$8
2012-S, Proof, Silver	395,443	86	66.8	100%			$2	$3	$4	$20
2013-P	1,086,500,000	121	67.1	100%			$2	$3	$4	$20
2013-D	1,025,500,000	1,740	69.6					$2.50	$4	$7
2013-S, Proof	802,460	1,875	69.9					$5	$6	$8
2013-S, Proof, Silver	419,719	134	67.3	100%			$2	$3	$4	$20
2014-P	1,125,500,000	188	67.3	100%			$2	$3	$4	$20
2014-D	1,177,000,000	1,565	69.4					$2.50	$4	$7
2014-S, Proof	665,100	3,150	69.8					$5	$6	$8
2014-S, Proof, Silver	393,037	2,878	69.8					$5	$6	$8
2015-P	1,497,824,029	158	67.0	100%			$2	$3	$4	$20
2015-P, Reverse Proof, Silver	74,430	6,521	69.5					$20	$30	$50
2015-D	1,543,814,029	197	67.1	100%			$2	$3	$4	$20
2015-S, Proof	662,854	1,106	69.9					$2.50	$4	$7
2015-S, Proof, Silver	387,310	2,260	69.8					$5	$6	$8
2015-W, Proof, Silver	74,430	6,248	69.5					$15	$25	$40

In 2016 a special .9999 fine gold striking of Adolph A. Weinman's Winged Liberty Head or "Mercury" dime was created to celebrate the 100th anniversary of its introduction. It is smaller than the silver strikings, with a diameter of 16.5 mm and weighing 3.11035 grams. Struck at West Point, it has a reeded edge. Similar strikings were made for the 1916 quarter and half dollar designs.

	Mintage	Cert	Avg	%MS	SP-67	SP-70
2016-W, Mercury Dime Centennial Gold Coin	124,885				$250	$325

Normally scheduled production of clad and silver Roosevelt dimes, in the same standards and specifications as previously, continued in 2016 and beyond, and was not disrupted by the gold Mercury dime.

	Mintage	Cert	Avg	%MS	EF-40	MS-63	MS-65	MS-66	MS-67	MS-67FT
								PF-65	PF-66	PF-67
2016-P	1,517,296,579	99	67.5	100%			$2	$3	$4	$20
2016-D	1,437,296,579	261	67.3	100%			$2	$3	$4	$20
2016-S, Proof	641,775	393	69.8					$2.50	$4	$7
2016-S, Proof, Silver	419,256	2,325	69.9					$5	$6	$8
2017-P	1,437,771,686	134	67.0	100%			$2	$3	$4	$20
2017-D	1,290,771,686	93	66.7	100%			$2	$3	$4	$20
2017-S, Enhanced Unc.								$2.50	$4	$7
2017-S, Proof	592,890	8,378	69.9					$2.50	$4	$7
2017-S, Proof, Silver	382,453	2,897	69.8					$5	$6	$8
2018-P							$2	$3	$4	$20
2018-D							$2	$3	$4	$20
2018-S, Proof								$2.50	$4	$7
2018-S, Proof, Silver								$5	$6	$8

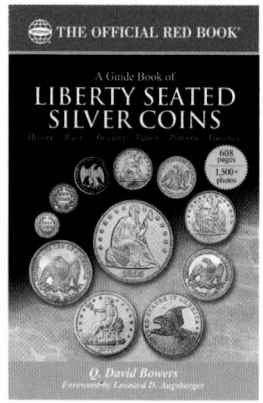
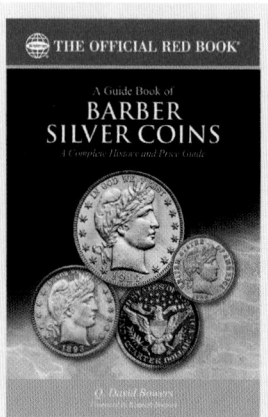
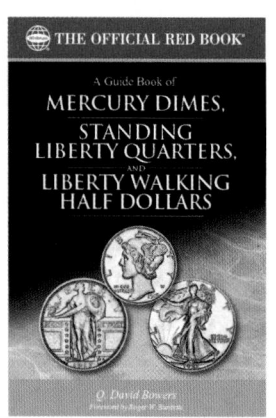

Twenty-Cent Pieces
1875–1878

AN OVERVIEW OF TWENTY-CENT PIECES

The twenty-cent piece, made in silver, proved to be the shortest-lived denomination in American coinage history. The coins were struck in quantity in their first year of issue, 1875, after which it was learned that the public confused them with quarter dollars. Mintages dropped sharply, and in 1877 and 1878 coinage was limited to just Proofs for collectors.

Both sides of the twenty-cent piece were designed by U.S. Mint chief engraver William Barber. The obverse is simply an adaptation of the Liberty Seated motif earlier used on other denominations. The reverse is new and depicts a perched eagle (of the same general appearance as introduced by Barber on the 1873 silver trade dollar).

Only one twenty-cent piece is needed for inclusion in a type set. By far the most readily available in Mint State is the 1875-S, followed by the 1875-CC. These are often somewhat lightly struck on the reverse, particularly near the top of the eagle's wings. The 1875 and 1876 Philadelphia coins are occasionally encountered in Mint State and are usually well struck.

Proofs are readily available for all years, 1875 through 1878.

Senator John P. Jones was involved with the minting of the twenty-cent piece silver coin.

FOR THE COLLECTOR AND INVESTOR: TWENTY-CENT PIECES AS A SPECIALTY

A full date-and-mintmark set of twenty-cent pieces consists of the 1875, 1875-CC, 1875-S, 1876, 1876-CC, 1877, and 1878, the latter two years being available only in Proof format. The great challenge in forming a set is the 1876-CC, of which 10,000 were minted, but, seemingly, all but about two dozen were melted. Those that do survive are typically encountered in Mint State and are widely heralded when they are offered at auction.

LIBERTY SEATED (1875–1878)

Designer: *William Barber.* **Weight:** *5 grams.* **Composition:** *.900 silver, .100 copper.*
Diameter: *22 mm.* **Edge:** *Plain.* **Mints:** *Philadelphia, Carson City, and San Francisco.*

Circulation Strike

Mintmark location
is on the reverse,
below the eagle.

Proof

History. The twenty-cent coin debuted in 1875 as a convenient denomination to make change in the West (at the time silver coins did not circulate in the East or Midwest). The coins sometimes were confused with quarter dollars, given their similar Liberty Seated design on the obverse, and their similar size. The quantity minted dropped considerably in 1876, and in 1877 and 1878 only Proofs were struck. Despite the brief time of their production, these coins were still seen in circulation through the early 1900s, by which time they were often casually used as quarters. Proof coins were made of all years 1875 to 1878.

Striking and Sharpness. Areas of weakness are common. On the obverse, check the head of Miss Liberty and the stars. The word LIBERTY is *raised* on this coin, a curious departure from other Liberty Seated coins of the era, on which it is recessed or incuse (the Gobrecht silver dollars of 1836 and 1839 being exceptions). On the reverse, check the eagle's feathers, especially the top of the wing on the left, but other areas can be weak as well. Some 1875-S coins are highly prooflike. The 1877 and 1878 are Proof-only issues with no related circulation strikes. Most have been cleaned or even lightly polished. Many Proofs in the marketplace have been convincingly retoned to mask problems. Proofs are usually well struck, but more than just a few are somewhat flat on the hair details of Miss Liberty.

Availability. Most often seen is the high-mintage 1875-S, although the 1875 and 1875-CC are encountered with frequency. The 1876 is quite scarce and when seen is usually in high grades and well struck. The 1876-CC is a rarity, and only about two dozen are known, nearly all of which are MS. The eye appeal of MS coins can vary widely. The number of letters in LIBERTY on certain coins graded from VG through VF can vary widely in the marketplace. Proofs most often seen are those of 1875 and 1876. For some unexplained reason, high-quality Proofs of the series' final two years are very hard to find.

GRADING STANDARDS

MS-60 to 70 (Mint State). *Obverse:* At MS-60, some abrasion and contact marks are evident, most noticeably on the bosom and thighs and knees. Luster is present, but may be dull or lifeless. At MS-63, contact marks are very few, and abrasion is hard to detect except under magnification. An MS-65 coin has no abrasion, and contact marks are sufficiently minute as to require magnification. Check the knees of Liberty and the right field.

1875; BF-1. Graded MS-64.

Luster should be full and rich. *Reverse:* Comments apply as for the obverse, except that in lower–Mint State grades abrasion and contact marks are most noticeable on the eagle's breast and the top of the wing to the left. At MS-65 or higher, there are no marks visible to the unaided eye. The field is mainly protected by design elements and does not show abrasion as much as does the obverse on a given coin.

Illustrated coin: Semi-Proof surfaces contrast nicely against the frosted devices of this well-struck piece.

AU-50, 53, 55, 58 (About Uncirculated). *Obverse:* Light wear is seen on the thighs and knees, bosom, and head. At AU-58, the luster is extensive but incomplete, especially in the right field. At AU–50 and 53, luster is less. *Reverse:* Very light wear is evident on the eagle's breast (the prime focal point) and at the top of the wings. An AU-58 coin will have nearly full luster, more so than on the obverse, as the design elements protect the small field areas. At AU–50 and 53, there still are traces of luster.

1875-CC. Graded AU-55.

EF-40, 45 (Extremely Fine). *Obverse:* Further wear is seen on all areas, especially the thighs and knees, bosom, and head. Little or no luster is seen on most coins. From this grade downward, sharpness of strike of the stars and the head does not matter to connoisseurs. *Reverse:* More wear is evident on the eagle's breast and the top of the wings. Some feathers may be blended together, but most details are defined.

1875-S. Graded EF-45.

VF-20, 30 (Very Fine). *Obverse:* Further wear is seen. Most details of the gown are worn away, except in the lower-relief areas above and to the right of the shield. Hair detail is mostly or completely gone. As to whether LIBERTY should be completely readable, this seems to be a matter of debate. On many coins in the marketplace the word is weak or missing one to several letters. ANA grading standards and PCGS require full LIBERTY. *Reverse:* Wear is more extensive, but at least three-quarters of the feathers in the breast and wings are distinct. At VF-30 the head is flat with distinct details; head details are less distinct at VF-20.

1875-S. Graded VF-30.

F-12, 15 (Fine). *Obverse:* The seated figure is well worn, but with some detail above and to the right of the shield. LIBERTY has at least three letters visible (per ANA grading standards). In the marketplace, some have more letters missing. *Reverse:* Wear is extensive, with about half of the feathers flat or blended with others and head details are indistinct except for the eye.

1875-CC. Graded F-15.

VG-8, 10 (Very Good). *Obverse:* The seated figure is more worn, but some detail can be seen above and to the right of the shield. The shield is discernible. In LIBERTY a letter or two may be visible per ANA grading standards. In the marketplace, many have no letters. *Reverse:* Further wear has flattened about half of the feathers. Those remaining are on the inside of the wings. The rim is full and shows many if not most denticles.

1875-S. Graded VG-10.

G-4, 6 (Good). *Obverse:* The seated figure is worn nearly smooth, but with some slight detail above and to the right of the shield. At G-4, there are no letters in LIBERTY remaining. On some at the G-6 level, there may be a trace of letters. *Reverse:* Most feathers in the eagle are gone. The border lettering is weak. The rim is visible partially or completely (depending on the strike).

1875-CC. Graded G-6.

AG-3 (About Good). *Obverse:* The seated figure is mostly visible in outline form, with only a hint of detail. Much of the rim is worn away. The date remains clear. *Reverse:* The border letters are partially worn away. The eagle is mostly in outline form, but with a few details discernible. The rim is weak or missing.

1875-CC. Graded AG-3.

PF-60 to 70 (Proof). *Obverse and Reverse:* Proofs that are extensively cleaned and have many hairlines, or that are dull and grainy, are lower level, such as PF–60 to 62. These are not widely desired. With medium hairlines and good reflectivity, an assigned grade of PF-64 is indicated, and with relatively few hairlines, Gem PF-65. In various grades hairlines are most easily seen in the obverse field. PF-66 should have hairlines so delicate that

1877. Graded PF-61.

magnification is needed to see them. Above that, a Proof should be free of such lines.

   Illustrated coin: Lovely frosted devices are complemented by indigo toning in the peripheries of the fields.

	Mintage	Cert	Avg	%MS	G-4	VG-8	F-12	VF-20	EF-40	AU-50	MS-60	MS-63	MS-65
											PF-60	PF-63	PF-65
1875	38,500	500	53.1	48%	$235	$275	$350	$425	$500	$600	$825	$1,450	$5,000
	Auctions: $1,292, MS-64, August 2015; $940, MS-62, July 2015; $881, MS-61, January 2015; $352, AU-50, February 2015												
1875, Proof	1,200	253	63.6								$1,300	$2,500	$7,500
	Auctions: $7,050, PF-65, August 2015; $4,465, PF-64Cam, July 2015; $3,995, PF-64, January 2015; $2,585, PF-63Cam, October 2015												
1875-CC	133,290	1,002	38.5	30%	$250	$350	$475	$600	$900	$1,300	$1,950	$3,500	$10,000
	Auctions: $7,050, MS-65, August 2015; $2,820, MS-62, January 2015; $2,056, MS-62, September 2015; $1,116, AU-55, June 2015												
1875-S (a)	1,155,000	3,326	48.6	45%	$100	$115	$135	$150	$250	$400	$650	$1,100	$2,350
	Auctions: $52,875, MS-68, August 2015; $6,462, MS-66, June 2015; $2,467, MS-65, March 2015; $540, MS-61, January 2015; $352, AU-53, April 2015												
1875-S, Proof	*10–20*	2	63.0								$15,000	$25,000	$75,000
	Auctions: No auction records available.												
1876	14,750	453	58.1	64%	$235	$275	$350	$400	$500	$600	$900	$1,800	$5,500
	Auctions: $15,275, MS-66, June 2015; $4,700, MS-65, July 2015; $4,465, MS-65, January 2015; $940, AU-58, October 2015												
1876, Proof	1,150	302	63.6								$1,300	$2,500	$7,500
	Auctions: $25,850, PF-68, August 2015; $4,230, PF-64, February 2015; $3,995, PF-64, January 2015; $3,760, PF-63Cam, October 2015												
1876-CC †	10,000	7	64.6	100%						$175,000	$250,000	$375,000	$600,000
	Auctions: $564,000, MS-65, January 2013												
1877, Proof	510	262	63.7								$6,500	$10,000	$17,500
	Auctions: $7,637, PF-65, July 2015; $15,275, PF-64, August 2016; $3,995, PF-62, June 2015; $3,995, PF-62, October 2015												
1878, Proof	600	313	63.6								$4,250	$5,500	$10,000
	Auctions: $28,200, PF-66, August 2016; $4,700, PF-64, March 2015; $3,290, PF-62, September 2016; $1,827, AU-50, September 2015												

† Ranked in the *100 Greatest U.S. Coins* (fourth edition). **a.** There are at least two misplaced-date die varieties of the 1875-S twenty-cent piece. These do not command a premium in the marketplace. A repunched mintmark is likewise common.

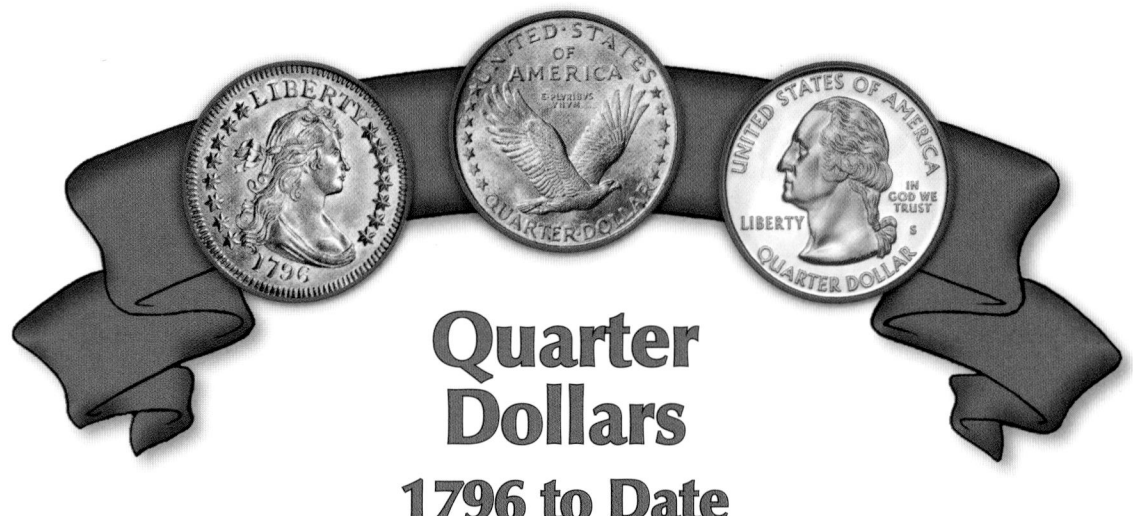

Quarter Dollars
1796 to Date

AN OVERVIEW OF QUARTER DOLLARS

In 1796 the first silver quarters were struck at the Philadelphia Mint. The Draped Bust obverse in combination with the Small Eagle reverse was produced only in this year, after which no pieces of this denomination were produced until 1804. At that time the Draped Bust obverse was continued, but now with the Heraldic Eagle reverse. The coinage proved to be brief and lasted only through 1807, after which no quarters were struck until 1815. The new quarters dated 1815 were of the Capped Bust style, by John Reich. These were produced intermittently through 1838. The Liberty Seated motif, by Christian Gobrecht, made its debut in 1838 and was produced continuously through 1891, with several modifications in design and metallic content over the years. The Liberty Head quarter, today called the Barber quarter after its designer, was introduced in 1892 and minted continuously through 1916. The obverse features the head of Miss Liberty, and the reverse a heraldic eagle. In late 1916 the Standing Liberty by Hermon A. MacNeil became the new design. This was produced through 1930, except for 1922. Some changes to both the obverse and reverse were made partway through 1917.

The Washington quarter dollar was struck in 1932 to observe the 200th anniversary of the birth of our first president. Washington quarters have been struck continuously since then, except for 1933, and with none dated 1975. In 1976 a special Bicentennial motif was introduced. Beginning in 1999 the State quarters were launched, issued at the rate of five per year, covering all 50 states, each coin having its own distinctive design. After this successful and popular program came quarter dollars with motifs celebrating the District of Columbia and U.S. territories. A similar program commemorating national parks started in 2010 and is slated to run through 2021.

While there are no super-rarities among the different *types* of quarter dollars, the first one, the 1796 with Draped Bust obverse and Small Eagle reverse, is hard to find and expensive in all grades. The values are, of course, justified by the great demand for this single-year type.

**Quarter-dollar designers
Hermon A. MacNeil and John Flanagan.**

The collector's greatest challenge in finding a decent strike is in the short-lived 1804–1807 type with the Heraldic Eagle reverse. Sufficient quantities were made that examples from these years are not rarities, but nearly all are weakly struck. Quarters of the 1815–1828 Capped Bust, large planchet, type are available easily enough in worn grades but are scarce to rare in Mint State. Some cherrypicking (close examination for high quality within a given grade) is needed to find a sharp strike.

Respite from the sharp-strike difficulty is at last found with the 1831–1838 type, Capped Bust, small diameter, and without E PLURIBUS UNUM. Most are quite nicely struck. Also, for the first time Mint State coins are generally available with frequency in the marketplace, although those with good eye appeal are in the distinct minority.

The Liberty Seated quarters of the several types made from 1838 to 1891 are generally available in proportion to their mintages, with an allowance for the earlier dates being scarcer than the later ones—as they had a longer time to become worn or lost. Many quarters of earlier dates were melted circa 1850 to 1853, when the price of silver rose on international markets, making such coins worth slightly more than 25 cents in melt-down value.

Barber quarters, 1892–1916, present no difficulty for the collector, except that there is a challenge to find an example with sharp striking overall, including in the telltale area on the reverse at and near the eagle's leg to the right. MS-65 and better Barber quarters are scarcer than generally known (the same can be said for Barber half dollars). Proofs were sold to collectors and saved, and thus they are available in proportion to their mintages, with probably 70% to 80% surviving today.

The Variety 1 Standing Liberty quarter is a rarity if dated 1916, for only 52,000 were struck, and not many were saved. The feasible alternative is the 1917, Variety 1, which is often seen in Mint State, sharply struck, and very beautiful. Standing Liberty quarters of the Variety 2 design, minted from partway through 1917 to 1930, often are weakly struck on the head of Miss Liberty and on the shield rivets, and sometimes other places as well. Diligent searching is needed to locate a nice example.

Washington quarters also present no difficulty for collectors. The State, D.C./Territorial, and America the Beautiful (National Park) reverses are appealing in their diversity and make a fascinating study in themselves.

FOR THE COLLECTOR AND INVESTOR: QUARTER DOLLARS AS A SPECIALTY

The formation of a specialized collection of quarter dollars from 1796 to date, by dates, mints, and major varieties, is a considerable challenge. As a class, quarters are considerably more difficult to acquire than are either dimes or half dollars. Relatively few numismatists have ever concentrated on the entire series.

The 1796 is rare and popular both as a date and a type. The 1804, although elusive in worn grades, is of commanding importance if in AU or Mint State. The 1823, 3 Over 2, is a classic rarity and is nearly always encountered well worn. From the same decade the 1827 is famous. Although Mint records indicate that 4,000 circulation strikes were produced in calendar-year 1827, they were probably struck from 1825-dated or earlier dies, as no unequivocal circulation strike has ever been located. There are, however, a dozen or so Proofs. Originals are distinguished by the 2 (in the 25 C. denomination) having a curved base, while restrikes, also very rare, have a square-base 2.

One of the unsolved mysteries in numismatics involves certain quarter dollars dated 1815 (the die variety known as Browning-1) and 1825, 5 Over 3 (Browning-2), which are often seen counterstamped, above the cap, with either an E or an L. Hundreds exist. As other quarter-dollar die varieties were made during this period, but only these two bear counterstamps, it may be that this was done either at the Mint or elsewhere before they were generally distributed.

Ard W. Browning's 1925 text, *The Early Quarter Dollars of the United States, 1796–1838*, remains the standard reference on the series, together with new information added here and there, including in issues of the *John Reich Journal*, the magazine of the John Reich Collectors Society, and in more recently published books.

The panorama of Liberty Seated quarters from 1838 to 1891 is highlighted by several rarities, notably the 1842, Small Date (known only in Proof format), and the 1873-CC, Without Arrows (of which only five are known, at least three being Mint State). The others are generally available, but some can be almost impossible to find in Mint State, the 1849-O, certain early San Francisco issues, and Carson City coins of the early 1870s being well known in this regard. From the mid-1870s onward Mint State coins are generally available, including choice and gem pieces. Proofs from 1858 onward can be found in proportion to their mintages, with later dates often being seen with higher numerical designations than are earlier ones.

A copy of
Ard W. Browning's
1925 text, *The Early Quarter Dollars of the United States, 1796–1838.*

Barber quarters are collectible by date and mint, although the "big three" rarities, the 1896-S, 1901-S, and 1913-S, are expensive and hard to find.

Standing Liberty quarters, 1916–1930, represent a short-lived series, one easy enough to collect in grades up to MS-63, except for the rare 1918-S, 8 Over 7, overdate. Finding higher-grade coins that are sharply struck is another matter entirely, and over the years few sets of this nature have been assembled.

Washington quarters are all collectible, with no great rarities. However, in relation to the demand for them, certain early issues are elusive, the 1932-D being a well-known example. Modern issues, including the Bicentennial, State, D.C./Territorial, and National Park coins, are at once plentiful, inexpensive, and interesting.

DRAPED BUST, SMALL EAGLE REVERSE (1796)

Designer: *Probably Gilbert Stuart.* **Engraver:** *Robert Scot.*
Weight: *6.74 grams.* **Composition:** *.8924 silver, .1076 copper.*
Diameter: *Approximately 27.5 mm.* **Edge:** *Reeded.* **Mint:** *Philadelphia.*

Browning-2.

History. The Philadelphia Mint coined its first quarter dollar in 1796. Its design followed that of other silver U.S. coins. Only 6,146 were made, followed by a production hiatus until 1804, by which time a new reverse was used. Thus the 1796 was isolated as a single-year type.

Striking and Sharpness. On the obverse, check the hair details and the star centers. Most are well struck. On the reverse, most are well struck except for the head of the eagle, which can be shallow or flat, especially on the Browning-2 variety (there are two known die varieties for this year, Browning-1 being the rarer). Rarely is a Full Details coin encountered. The denticles are unusually bold and serve to frame the motifs. Check for planchet adjustment marks (from overweight planchets being filed down at the Mint to achieve proper weight). A few pieces have carbon streaks, which lower their value. Sharp striking (as on Browning-2) will add to the value. Most MS examples have excellent eye appeal.

Availability. Examples are available in all grades from well worn to superb MS. Nearly all of the latter are highly prooflike, but there are some exceptions. Although hundreds of circulated examples exist, demand for this famous coin exceeds supply in the marketplace, making public offerings a scene of excitement and strong bidding. Hundreds of higher-grade examples also survive, many of them prooflike and attractive. They attract great attention when offered for sale.

GRADING STANDARDS

MS-60 to 70 (Mint State). *Obverse:* At MS-60, some abrasion and contact marks are evident, most noticeably on the cheek, the drapery, and the right field. Luster is present, but may be dull or lifeless, and interrupted in patches. On prooflike coins the contact marks are more prominent. At MS-63, contact marks are very few, and abrasion is hard to detect except under magnification, although this type is sometimes graded liberally due to its

1796; Browning-2. Graded MS-62.

rarity. An MS-65 coin has no abrasion, and contact marks are so minute as to require magnification. Luster should be full and rich. Grades above MS-65 are defined by having fewer marks as perfection is approached. *Reverse:* Comments apply as for the obverse, except that abrasion and contact marks are most noticeable on the eagle at the center, a situation complicated by the fact that this area is typically flatly struck (except on the Browning-2 variety). Grading is best done by the obverse, then verified by the reverse. The field area is small and is protected by lettering and the wreath and in any given grade shows fewer marks than on the obverse.

Illustrated coin: This coin is well struck on the obverse, and the weak striking on the eagle's breast and head is typical of this issue.

AU-50, 53, 55, 58 (About Uncirculated). *Obverse:* Light wear is seen on the hair area above the ear and extending to left of the forehead, on the ribbon, on the drapery at the shoulder, and on the high points of the bust line, more so at AU-50 than at AU–53 or 55. An AU-58 coin has minimal traces of wear. An AU-50 coin has luster in protected areas among the stars and letters, with little in the open fields or on the portrait. At AU-58, most

1796; Browning-2. Graded AU-58.

luster remains in the fields, but is worn away on the highest parts of the motifs. *Reverse:* Light wear is seen on the eagle's body (keep in mind this area is nearly always lightly struck) and the edges of the wings. Light wear is seen on the wreath and lettering. Luster is the best key to actual wear. This ranges from perhaps 20% remaining in protected areas (at AU-50) to nearly full mint bloom (at AU-58).

EF-40, 45 (Extremely Fine). *Obverse:* More wear is evident on the upper hair area and the ribbon, and on the drapery and bosom. Excellent detail remains in low-relief areas of the hair. The stars show wear as do the date and letters. Luster, if present at all, is minimal and in protected areas. *Reverse:* The eagle shows more wear, this being the focal point to check. Most feathers remain on the interior areas of the wings. Additional wear is on

1796; Browning-1. Graded EF-40.

the wreath and letters, but many details are present. Some luster may be seen in protected areas and if present is slightly more abundant than on the obverse.

VF-20, 30 (Very Fine). *Obverse:* The higher-relief areas of hair are well worn at VF-20, less so at VF-30, although much detail remains on the areas below the ear. The drapery and bosom show extensive wear. The stars have more wear, making them appear larger (an optical illusion seen on most worn silver coins of this era). *Reverse:* The body of the eagle shows few if any feathers, while the wings have about half of the feath-

1796; Browning-2. Graded VF-30.

ers visible, mostly on the right wing, depending on the strike. The leaves lack most detail and are in outline form. Scattered, non-disfiguring marks are normal for this and lower grades. Any major defects should be noted separately.

F-12, 15 (Fine). *Obverse:* Wear is more extensive than on a Very Fine coin, particularly noticeable on the hair, face, and bosom. The stars appear larger. About half the hair detail remains, most noticeably behind the neck and shoulder. The denticles remain strong (while on most other silver denominations of this design they become weak at this grade level). *Reverse:* Wear is more extensive. Now feather details are diminished, with

1796; Browning-2. Graded F-12.

fewer than half remaining on the wings. The wreath and lettering are worn further, and the rim is slightly weak in areas, although most denticles can be seen.

VG-8, 10 (Very Good). *Obverse:* The portrait is mostly seen in outline form, with most hair strands gone, although there is some definition at the back of the hair and behind the shoulder. The ear is discernible, as is the eye. The stars appear larger still, again an illusion. The rim is weak in areas. Most denticles are seen, some of them even bold. LIBERTY and the date are readable and usually full, although some letters may be weak

1796; Browning-2. Graded VG-10.

at their tops (the high rim and denticles protect the design more on the quarter dollar than on other silver coins of this type). *Reverse:* The eagle is mostly an outline, with parts blending into the field (on lighter strikes), although some slight feather detail can be seen on the right wing. The rim is worn, as are the letters, with some weak, but the motto is readable. Most denticles remain clear.

G-4, 6 (Good). *Obverse:* Wear is more extensive. The head is an outline. The rim still is present, as are most of the denticles, most well defined. LIBERTY is worn, but complete. The date is bold. *Reverse:* The eagle is flat and discernible in outline form, blending into the field in areas. The wreath is well worn. Some of the letters may be partly missing. Some rim areas and denticles are discernible. At this level some "averaging" can

1796; Browning-1. Graded G-4.

be done. If the letters are stronger than usual in one area, but some are missing in another area, the coin can still qualify as G-4.

AG-3 (About Good). *Obverse:* Wear is so extensive that the coin is barely identifiable. The head is in outline form, LIBERTY is mostly gone, same for the stars, and the date, while readable, may be partially worn away. *Reverse:* The reverse is well worn, with parts of the wreath and lettering missing.

1796; Browning-2. Graded AG-3.

	Mintage	Cert	Avg	%MS	AG-3	G-4	VG-8	F-12	VF-20	EF-40	AU-50	MS-60	MS-63
1796 †	6,146	189	33.8	20%	$7,000	$11,000	$17,000	$25,000	$32,500	$48,500	$62,500	$80,000	$125,000
	Auctions: $105,750, MS-63, August 2016; $25,850, F-15, August 2016												

† Ranked in the *100 Greatest U.S. Coins* (fourth edition).

DRAPED BUST, HERALDIC EAGLE REVERSE (1804–1807)

Designer: *Robert Scot.* **Weight:** *6.74 grams.* **Composition:** *.8924 silver, .1076 copper.*
Diameter: *Approximately 27.5 mm.* **Edge:** *Reeded.* **Mint:** *Philadelphia.*

Browning-1.

History. Early on, the U.S. Mint's production of silver coins in any given year depended on requests made by depositors of silver; they were not made for the Mint's own account. After 1796 no quarters were struck until 1804. When production started up again, the Draped Bust obverse was used, but with the new Heraldic Eagle reverse—similar to that on other silver (and gold) denominations of the time. The Heraldic Eagle design was patterned after the Great Seal of the United States.

Striking and Sharpness. Virtually all examples are lightly struck in one area or another. On the obverse, check the hair details and the star centers. On the reverse, check the shield, stars, feathers, and other design elements. The denticles and rims on both sides often have problems. Quarters of 1807 are usually the lightest struck. Also check for planchet adjustment marks (where an overweight planchet was filed down by a Mint worker to reach acceptable standards). Sharp striking and excellent eye appeal add to a coin's value. This series often is misgraded due to lack of understanding of its strike anomalies.

Availability. All dates are collectible, with 1804 being scarcer than the others and a rarity in MS. Those of 1805, 1806, and 1807 are readily available in the marketplace, usually in circulated grades although MS examples are sometimes seen. Some die varieties are rare. High-grade coins with Full Details are very rare.

GRADING STANDARDS

MS-60 to 70 (Mint State). *Obverse:* At MS-60, some abrasion and contact marks are evident, most noticeably on the cheek, the drapery, and the right field. Luster is present, but may be dull or lifeless, and interrupted in patches. At MS-63, contact marks are very few, and abrasion is hard to detect except under magnification. An MS-65 coin will have no abrasion, and contact marks are so minute as to require magnification. Luster should be

1806; Browning-9. Graded MS-66.

full and rich. Coins graded above MS-65 are more theoretical than actual for this type—but they do exist, and are defined by having fewer marks as perfection is approached. As noted in the introduction, expect weakness in some areas. *Reverse:* Comments apply as for the obverse, except that abrasion and contact marks are most noticeable on the eagle's neck, the tips of the wing, and the tail. The field area is complex, without much open space, given the stars above the eagle, the arrows and olive branch, and other features. Accordingly, marks are not as noticeable as on the obverse.

Illustrated coin: This coin is lightly struck on the right obverse stars and at the center of the reverse. Some planchet adjustment marks are mostly hidden. Some tiny carbon streaks are on the obverse (seemingly typical for Browning-9).

AU-50, 53, 55, 58 (About Uncirculated). *Obverse:* Light wear is seen on the hair area above the ear and extending to left of the forehead, on the ribbon, and on the drapery at the shoulder, more so at AU-50 than at AU–53 or 55. An AU-58 coin has minimal traces of wear. An AU-50 coin has luster in protected areas among the stars and letters, with little in the open fields or on the portrait. At AU-58, most luster is present in the fields, but is worn away on the highest parts of the motifs. *Reverse:* Comments as preceding, except that the eagle's neck, the tips and top of the wings, the clouds, and the tail now show noticeable wear, as do other features. Luster ranges from perhaps 20% remaining in protected areas (at AU-50) to nearly full mint bloom (at AU-58). Often the reverse retains much more luster than the obverse, more so on quarter dollars than on other denominations of this design.

1804; Browning-1. Graded AU-58.

Illustrated coin: Lightly struck on the obverse stars. The reverse has some light areas but is sharp overall. A few planchet adjustment marks are visible. Abundant luster and good eye appeal rank this as an exceptional example of this date, the most difficult of the type to find in high grades.

EF-40, 45 (Extremely Fine). *Obverse:* More wear is evident on the upper hair area and the ribbon, and on the drapery at the shoulder and the bosom. Excellent detail remains in low-relief areas of the hair. The stars show wear, as do the date and letters (note: on most coins of this type the stars are softly struck). Luster, if present at all, is minimal and in protected areas. *Reverse:* Wear is greater than on an About Uncirculated coin, overall. The neck lacks feather detail on its highest points. Feathers have lost some detail near the edges of the wings, and some areas of the horizontal lines in the shield may be blended together. Some traces of luster may be seen, more so at EF-45 than at EF-40.

1804; Browning-1. Graded EF-45.

VF-20, 30 (Very Fine). *Obverse:* The higher-relief areas of hair are well worn at VF-20, less so at VF-30. The drapery and bosom show extensive wear. The stars have more wear, making them appear larger (an optical illusion seen on most worn silver coins of this era). *Reverse:* Wear is greater, including on the shield and wing feathers, although more than half of the feathers are defined. Star centers are flat. Other areas have lost detail as well. Some letters in the motto may be missing, depending on the strike.

1804; Browning-1. Graded VF-30.

F-12, 15 (Fine). *Obverse:* Wear is more extensive than on a Very Fine coin, particularly noticeable on the hair, face, and bosom. The stars appear larger. About half the hair detail remains with the tresses fused so as to appear thick, most noticeably behind the neck and shoulder. The rim may be partially worn away and blend into the field. *Reverse:* Wear is even more extensive, with the shield and wing feathers being points to observe.

1804; Browning-1. Graded F-12.

About half of the feathers can be seen. The incuse E PLURIBUS UNUM may have a few letters worn away. The clouds all seem to be connected. The stars are weak. Parts of the border and lettering may be weak. As with most quarters of this type, peculiarities of striking can account for some weakness.

VG-8, 10 (Very Good). *Obverse:* The portrait is mostly seen in outline form, with most hair strands gone, although there is slight definition at the back of the hair and behind the shoulder. The ear is discernible, as is the eye. The stars appear larger still, again an illusion. The rim is weak in areas. LIBERTY and the date are readable and usually full, although some letters may be weak at their tops. *Reverse:* Wear is more extensive. Half

1804; Browning-1. Graded VG-8.

or so of the letters in the motto are worn away. Most feathers are worn away, although separation of some of the lower feathers may be seen. Some stars are faint. The border blends into the field in areas (depending on striking), and some letters are weak.

G-4, 6 (Good). *Obverse:* Wear is more extensive, and some stars may be partly missing. The head is an outline. The eye is visible only in outline form. The rim is well worn or even missing in areas. LIBERTY is worn, and parts of some letters may be missing, but elements of all should be readable. The date is readable, but worn. *Reverse:* Wear is more extensive. The upper part of the eagle is flat, and feathers are noticeable only at some (but

1804; Browning-1. Graded G-4.

not necessarily all) of the lower edge of the wings, and do not have detail. The shield lacks most of its detail. Only a few letters of the motto can be seen (depending on striking). The rim is worn extensively, and a few letters may be missing.

AG-3 (About Good). *Obverse:* Wear is so extensive that the coin is barely identifiable. The head is in outline form, LIBERTY is mostly gone. Same for the stars. The date, while readable, may be partially worn away. *Reverse:* Extensive wear is seen overall, with the rim worn away and some areas worn smooth. The eagle can be discerned in outline form, but not necessarily completely. A few stray motto letters may remain. Some-times the obverse appears to be more worn than the reverse, or vice-versa.

1804; Browning-1. Graded AG-3.

1806, 6 Over 5

	Mintage	Cert	Avg	%MS	AG-3	G-4	VG-8	F-12	VF-20	EF-40	AU-50	MS-60	MS-63
1804	6,738	128	17.2	4%	$2,500	$4,000	$6,500	$9,500	$12,500	$30,000	$47,000	$95,000	$175,000
Auctions: $6,463, F-15, August 2016; $1,351, Fair-2, January 2015													
1805	121,394	351	23.1	5%	$250	$500	$650	$950	$1,800	$3,750	$5,500	$11,000	$20,000
Auctions: $946, F-15, January 2015; $709, VG-10, June 2015; $564, VG-8, January 2015; $552, VG-8, March 2015													
1806, All kinds	206,124												
1806, 6 Over 5		137	26.4	9%	$300	$575	$700	$1,100	$2,000	$4,250	$6,000	$13,500	$25,000
Auctions: $152,750, MS-66, November 2013; $1,645, EF-40, March 2016; $1,293, VF-20, August 2016; $1,116, VG-10, October 2014													
1806		516	24.1	9%	$225	$500	$650	$950	$1,800	$3,750	$5,500	$11,000	$20,000
Auctions: $1,528, VF-20, March 2015; $764, VF-20, August 2015; $529, VF-20, January 2015; $470, F-12, February 2015													
1807	220,643	278	23.3	12%	$225	$500	$700	$1,000	$1,750	$3,850	$5,500	$11,000	$20,000
Auctions: $764, VG-10, June 2015; $676, VG-10, March 2015; $494, VG-8, July 2015; $424, G-6, June 2015													

CAPPED BUST (1815–1838)

Variety 1, Large Diameter (1815–1828): **Designer:** *John Reich.*
Weight: *6.74 grams.* **Composition:** *.8924 silver, .1076 copper.*
Diameter: *Approximately 27 mm.* **Edge:** *Reeded.* **Mint:** *Philadelphia.*

Variety 1, Large Diameter (1815–1828)
Browning-1.

Variety 1, Large Diameter, Proof
Browning-8.

Variety 2, Reduced Diameter, Motto Removed (1831–1838):
Designer: *William Kneass.* **Weight:** *6.74 grams (changed to 6.68 grams, .900 fine, in 1837).*
Composition: *.8924 silver, .1076 copper.* **Diameter:** *24.3 mm.* **Edge:** *Reeded.* **Mint:** *Philadelphia.*

Variety 2, Reduced Diameter,
Motto Removed (1831–1838)
Browning-1.

Variety 2, Reduced Diameter,
Motto Removed, Proof
Browning-1.

History. The Capped Bust design, by John Reich, was introduced on the half dollar of 1807 but was not used on the quarter until 1815. The difference between the Large Diameter and the Reduced Diameter types resulted from the introduction of the close collar in 1828. Capped Bust, Reduced Diameter, quarter dollars are similar in overall appearance to the preceding type, but with important differences. The diameter is smaller, E PLURIBUS UNUM no longer appears on the reverse, and the denticles are smaller and restyled using a close collar.

Striking and Sharpness. Striking sharpness of Capped Bust, Large Diameter, quarters varies. On the obverse, check the hair of Miss Liberty, the broach clasp (a particular point of observation), and the star centers. On this type the stars are often well defined (in contrast with half dollars of the same design). On the reverse, check the neck of the eagle and its wings, and the letters. The details of the eagle often are superbly defined. Check the scroll or ribbon above the eagle's head for weak or light areas. Examine the denticles on both sides. When weakness occurs it is usually in the center. Proofs were struck for inclusion in sets and for numismatists. Some deeply toned coins, and coins with patches of mint luster, have been described as Proofs but are mostly impostors, some of which have been certified or have "papers" signed by Walter Breen. Be careful! Nearly all coins of the Capped Bust, Reduced Diameter, Motto Removed, variety are very well struck. Check all areas for sharpness. Some quarters of 1833 and 1834 are struck from rusted or otherwise imperfect dies and can be less attractive than coins from undamaged dies. Avoid any Proofs that show patches of mint frost or that are darkly toned.

Availability. Most quarters of the Large Diameter variety range from slightly scarce to rare, with the 1823, 3 Over 2, and the 1827 being famous rarities. Typical coins range from well worn to Fine and VF. AU and MS coins are elusive (and are usually dated before the 1820s), and gems are particularly rare. All authentic Proofs are rarities. Examples of the Reduced Diameter, Motto Removed, variety are readily available of all dates, including many of the first year of issue. Mint frost ranges from satiny (usual) to deeply frosty. Proofs were struck of all dates for inclusion in sets and for sale or trade to numismatists; avoid deeply toned pieces, and seek those with deep and full (not partial) mirror surfaces and good contrast.

GRADING STANDARDS

MS-60 to 70 (Mint State). *Obverse:* At MS-60, some abrasion and contact marks are evident, most noticeably on the cheek, the hair below LIBERTY, and the area near the drapery clasp. Luster is present, but may be dull or lifeless, and interrupted in patches. At MS-63, contact marks are very few, and abrasion is hard to detect except under magnification. An

1831, Large Letters; Browning-5. Graded MS-62.

MS-65 coin has no abrasion, and contact marks are so minute as to require magnification. Luster should be full and rich. Grades above MS-65 are seen now and again and are defined by having fewer marks as perfection is approached. Grading for Reduced Diameter, Motto Removed, examples is similar, except the rims are more uniform, striking is usually very sharp, and the wear occurs evenly on both sides. *Reverse:* Comments apply as for the obverse, except that abrasion and contact marks are most noticeable on the eagle's neck, the top of the wings, the claws, and the flat band that surrounds the incuse motto. The field is mainly protected by design elements and does not show abrasion as much as does the obverse on a given coin.

AU-50, 53, 55, 58 (About Uncirculated). *Obverse:* Light wear is seen on the cap, the hair below LIBERTY, the curl on the neck, the hair near the clasp, and the drapery. At AU-58, the luster is extensive except in the open area of the field, especially to the right. At AU–50 and 53, luster remains only in protected areas. Grading for Reduced Diameter, Motto Removed, examples is similar, except the rims are more uniform, striking is usually

1834; Browning-2. Graded AU-55.

very sharp, and the wear occurs evenly on both sides. *Reverse:* Wear is evident on the eagle's neck, the top of the wings, the claws, and the flat band above the eagle. An AU-58 coin has nearly full luster. At AU–50 and 53, there still is significant luster, more than on the obverse. Generally, light wear is most obvious on the obverse.

EF-40, 45 (Extremely Fine). *Obverse:* Wear is more extensive, most noticeably on the higher areas of the hair. The cap shows more wear, as does the cheek. Most or all stars have some radial lines visible (unless lightly struck, as many are). Luster, if present, is in protected areas among the star points and close to the portrait. Grading for Reduced Diameter, Motto Removed, examples is similar, except the rims are more uniform, striking is

1831, Small Letters; Browning-4. Graded EF-40.

usually very sharp, and the wear occurs evenly on both sides. *Reverse:* The wings show wear on the higher areas of the feathers, and some details are lost. Feathers in the neck are light on some (but not on especially sharp strikes). The eagle's claws and the leaves show wear. Luster may be present in protected areas, even if there is little or none on the obverse.

VF-20, 30 (Very Fine). *Obverse:* Wear is more extensive, and most of the hair is combined into thick tresses without delicate features. The curl on the neck is flat. Details of the drapery are well defined at the lower edge. Unless they were weakly struck, the stars are mostly flat although a few may retain radial lines. Grading for Reduced Diameter, Motto Removed, examples is similar, except the rims are more uniform, striking is usually

1828. Graded VF-20.

very sharp, and the wear occurs evenly on both sides. *Reverse:* Wear is most evident on the eagle's neck, to the left of the shield, and on the leaves and claws. Most feathers in the wing remain distinct, but some show light wear. Overall, the reverse on most quarters at this level shows less wear than the obverse.

F-12, 15 (Fine). *Obverse:* Wear is more extensive, with much of the hair blended together. The drapery is indistinct at its upper edge. The stars are flat. Grading for Reduced Diameter, Motto Removed, examples is similar, except the rims are more uniform, striking is usually very sharp, and the wear occurs evenly on both sides. *Reverse:* Wear is more extensive, now with only about half of the feathers remaining on the wings. The claws on the right are fused at their upper parts.

1815. Graded F-15.

VG-8, 10 (Very Good). *Obverse:* The hair is less distinct, with the area above the face blended into the facial features. LIBERTY is complete, but can be weak in areas. At the left the drapery and bosom are blended together in a flat area. The rim is worn away in areas, and blends into the field. *Reverse:* Feathers are fewer and mostly on the eagle's wing to the left. Other details are weaker. E PLURIBUS UNUM is weak, perhaps with some letters missing. All border lettering remains easily readable.

1828, 25 Over 50 C.; Browning-3. Graded VG-10.

Illustrated coin: Gunmetal toning in the fields contrasts nicely with the lighter devices. The overpunched denomination shows signs of the 50 punched first into the die to the left of both 2 and 5.

G-4, 6 (Good). *Obverse:* The portrait is mostly in outline, with few interior details discernible. LIBERTY may still be readable or may be partially worn away, depending on the variety. Most or all of the border is worn away, and the outer parts of the stars are weak. *Reverse:* The eagle mostly is in outline form, although some feathers can be seen in the wing to the left. All letters around the border are clear. E PLURIBUS UNUM is mostly or completely worn away.

1815; Browning-1. Graded G-4.

AG-3 (About Good). *Obverse:* The portrait is an outline. Most of LIBERTY can still be seen. Stars are weak or missing toward what used to be the rim. The date remains clear, but may be weak at the bottom. *Reverse:* The reverse shows more wear than at G-4, but parts of the rim may remain clear.

1825, 5 Over 4; Browning-3. Graded AG-3.

PF-60 to 70 (Proof). *Obverse and Reverse:* Proofs that are extensively cleaned and have many hairlines, or that are dull and grainy, are lower level, such as PF–60 to 62. While any early Proof coin will attract attention, lower-level examples are not of great interest to specialists unless they are of rare die varieties. With medium hairlines, an assigned grade of PF-64 may be in order and with relatively few, Gem PF-65. PF-66 should have

1833; Browning-1. Graded PF-64 Cameo.

hairlines so delicate that magnification is needed to see them. Above that, a Proof should be free of such lines. Grading is highly subjective with early Proofs, and eye appeal also is a factor.

Illustrated coin: This coin features frosted devices and reflective fields, though the fields are marred by some light scratches.

1818, 8 Over 5	1818, Normal Date

	Mintage	Cert	Avg	%MS	AG-3	G-4	VG-8	F-12	VF-20	EF-40	AU-50	MS-60	MS-63
											PF-60	PF-63	PF-65
1815	89,235	172	43.1	35%	$100	$175	$350	$475	$800	$2,250	$3,500	$5,000	$8,000
	Auctions: $10,575, MS-64, March 2016; $999, VF-30, October 2014; $635, F-15, September 2014; $499, VG-8, September 2014												
1818, 8 Over 5	361,174	108	51.9	57%	$50	$125	$185	$285	$575	$1,600	$2,250	$4,000	$7,250
	Auctions: $176,250, MS-67, November 2013; $270, F-15, July 2014; $259, F-12, October 2014; $88, G-6, July 2014												
1818, Normal Date	(a)	522	39.1	27%	$50	$125	$185	$325	$625	$1,700	$2,350	$4,000	$7,250
	Auctions: $823, VF-35, February 2015; $764, VF-35, January 2015; $674, VF-35, October 2015; $517, VF-35, October 2015												

a. Included in 1818, 8 Over 5, mintage figure.

| 1819, Small 9 | 1819, Large 9 | 1820, Small 0 | 1820, Large 0 |

| 1822, 25 Over 50 C. | 1823, 3 Over 2 | 1824, 4 Over 2 |

| 1825, 5 Over 2 | 1825, 5 Over 4 |

	Mintage	Cert	Avg	%MS	AG-3	G-4	VG-8	F-12	VF-20	EF-40	AU-50 PF-60	MS-60 PF-63	MS-63 PF-65
1819, Small 9	144,000	41	21.0	10%	$50	$125	$185	$285	$575	$1,600	$2,250	$4,250	$8,500
Auctions: $646, EF-45, September 2014; $646, EF-40, June 2015; $353, VF-20, September 2014; $243, VF-20, May 2015
1819, Large 9	(b)	27	35.6	11%	$50	$125	$185	$285	$575	$1,600	$2,450	$5,000	$10,000
Auctions: $23,501, MS-64, November 2013; $764, VF-25, July 2014; $676, VF-25, August 2016; $564, VF-20, August 2016
1820, Small 0	127,444	18	35.8	17%	$50	$125	$185	$285	$575	$1,750	$2,450	$4,000	$6,000
Auctions: $3,055, AU-55, February 2014; $441, VF-20, September 2014; $176, G-6, July 2014; $94, G-6, July 2014
1820, Large 0	(c)	27	39.1	19%	$50	$125	$185	$285	$575	$1,600	$3,750	$6,500	$10,000
Auctions: $41,125, MS-66, November 2013
1820, Proof	6–10	2	65.5									$45,000	$125,000
Auctions: $188,000, PF-66, May 2015; $97,750, PF-64, May 2008
1821	216,851	265	38.6	23%	$50	$125	$185	$285	$575	$1,600	$2,250	$3,500	$7,000
Auctions: $646, VF-30, January 2015; $1,293, VF-25, June 2015; $764, VF-25, July 2015; $112, G-6, November 2014
1821, Proof	6–10	4	65.3									$40,000	$100,000
Auctions: $235,000, PF-67, May 2015; $82,250, PF-65, August 2015; $94,000, PF-65, October 2014; $51,750, PF-64, April 2009
1822	64,080	127	36.3	17%	$150	$225	$350	$600	$1,000	$1,800	$3,000	$7,250	$11,500
Auctions: $25,850, MS-64, November 2013
1822, 25 Over 50 C.	(d)	15	35.3	20%	$2,500	$5,500	$11,000	$17,500	$25,000	$37,500	$45,000	$57,500	$85,000
Auctions: No auction records available.
1822, Proof	6–10	2	65.5									$50,000	$165,000
Auctions: $223,250, PF-65, May 2015; $229,125, PF-65, January 2014
1823, 3 Over 2	17,800	7	42.7	14%	$25,000	$42,500	$55,000	$75,000	$100,000	$125,000	$175,000	$300,000	
Auctions: $17,625, G-4, February 2014
1823, 3 Over 2, Proof	2–4	0	n/a									$175,000	
Auctions: $396,563, PF-64, June 2014
1824, 4 Over 2	168,000	84	25.0	4%	$400	$800	$1,250	$2,000	$3,000	$5,250	$7,500	$25,000	$55,000
Auctions: $35,250, MS-62, June 2014; $1,293, VG-10, January 2015; $999, VG-8, August 2014
1824, 4 Over 2, Proof	2–4	1	63.0									$50,000	
Auctions: No auction records available.
1825, 5 Over 2	(e)	17	34.9	0%	$225	$400	$600	$1,100	$1,350	$4,500	$8,250	$16,000	$27,500
Auctions: $3,290, VF-30, February 2014; $159, G-6, July 2014; $94, G-4, July 2014
1825, 5 Over 4	(e)	158	43.0	22%	$65	$125	$200	$325	$600	$1,500	$2,200	$3,500	$6,500
Auctions: $1,495, EF-45, April 2012
1825, 5 Over 4 Over 3, Proof	6–10	0	n/a									$40,000	
Auctions: $4,313, PF-63, January 2010

b. Included in 1819, Small 9, mintage figure. **c.** Included in circulation-strike 1820, Small 0, mintage figure. **d.** Included in circulation-strike 1822 mintage figure. **e.** Included in circulation-strike 1824, 4 Over 2, mintage figure.

1827, Original, Proof
Curl-Base 2 in 25 C.

1827, Restrike, Proof
Square-Base 2 in 25 C.

1828, 25 Over 50 C.

	Mintage	Cert	Avg	%MS	AG-3	G-4	VG-8	F-12	VF-20	EF-40	AU-50 PF-60	MS-60 PF-63	MS-63 PF-65
1827, 7 Over 3, Original, Proof †	20–30	4	52.5								$125,000	$225,000	$550,000
	Auctions: $411,250, PF-64, June 2014												
1827, 7 Over 3, Restrike, Proof	20–30	10	64.2									$65,000	$115,000
	Auctions: $69,000, PF-66, July 2009												
1828	102,000	180	41.5	26%	$65	$115	$180	$300	$550	$1,500	$2,500	$3,500	$7,500
	Auctions: $764, VF-35, January 2015; $400, VF-25, June 2015; $176, VG-10, May 2015; $106, G-6, August 2015												
1828, 25 Over 50 C.	(f)	21	37.6	19%	$500	$1,000	$1,500	$2,250	$3,500	$7,000	$10,000	$17,500	$85,000
	Auctions: $352,500, MS-67, November 2013; $117,500, MS-63, August 2014												
1828, Proof	8–12	5	64.2								$15,000	$40,000	$100,000
	Auctions: $82,250, PF-65, June 2014												

† Ranked in the *100 Greatest U.S. Coins* (fourth edition). *Note:* Although 4,000 1827 quarters were reported to have been made for circulation, their rarity today (only one worn piece is known, and it could be a circulated Proof) suggests that this quantity was for coins struck in calendar-year 1827 but bearing an earlier date, probably 1825. **f.** Included in circulation-strike 1828 mintage figure.

1831, Small Letters
Browning-2.

1831, Large Letters
Browning-6.

	Mintage	Cert	Avg	%MS	G-4	VG-8	F-12	VF-20	EF-40	AU-50	MS-60 PF-60	MS-63 PF-63	MS-65 PF-65
1831, Small Letters	398,000	69	49.5	23%	$70	$100	$125	$150	$400	$750	$2,000	$4,250	$22,500
	Auctions: $853, AU-50, July 2015; $341, AU-50, July 2015; $382, EF-45, April 2015; $376, EF-45, June 2015												
1831, Large Letters	(a)	47	48.5	28%	$70	$100	$125	$150	$400	$750	$2,400	$4,250	$25,000
	Auctions: $6,463, MS-64, October 2015; $3,525, MS-63, January 2015; $1,175, MS-60, February 2015; $423, EF-45, September 2015												
1831, Large Letters, Proof	20–25	1	65.0								$15,000	$22,500	$75,000
	Auctions: $141,000, PF-66, January 2014; $28,200, PF-63, October 2015												
1832	320,000	192	45.3	27%	$70	$100	$125	$150	$425	$750	$2,000	$4,500	$25,000
	Auctions: $400, EF-45, May 2015; $212, EF-40, May 2015; $259, VF-35, July 2015; $176, VF-30, October 2015												

a. Included in 1831, Small Letters, mintage figure.

1834, O Over F in OF
FS-25-1834-901.

	Mintage	Cert	Avg	%MS	G-4	VG-8	F-12	VF-20	EF-40	AU-50	MS-60 / PF-60	MS-63 / PF-63	MS-65 / PF-65
1833	156,000	197	47.0	27%	$80	$110	$135	$200	$475	$850	$2,150	$4,500	$25,000
	Auctions: $764, AU-50, June 2015; $646, AU-50, March 2015; $353, EF-45, August 2015; $306, VF-35, May 2015												
1833, O Over F in OF (b)	(c)	12	40.6	8%	$85	$120	$165	$235	$500	$900	$2,000	$5,000	$27,500
	Auctions: No auction records available.												
1833, Proof	10–15	4	64.8								$15,000	$25,000	$90,000
	Auctions: $46,000, PF-65Cam, April 2009												
1834	286,000	590	45.1	25%	$70	$100	$125	$150	$400	$750	$2,000	$4,250	$22,500
	Auctions: $28,200, MS-66, January 2015; $8,519, MS-64, January 2015; $6,463, MS-64, August 2015; $4,230, MS-63, October 2015												
1834, O Over F in OF (b)	(d)	60	46.3	17%	$80	$110	$150	$200	$450	$850	$2,000	$5,000	$25,000
	Auctions: $1,116, AU-58, November 2014; $588, AU-50, October 2014												
1834, Proof	20–25	7	64.9								$15,000	$22,500	$75,000
	Auctions: $235,000, PF-66, November 2013												
1835	1,952,000	626	42.5	15%	$70	$100	$125	$150	$400	$750	$2,000	$4,250	$22,500
	Auctions: $611, MS-60, January 2015; $823, AU-55, August 2015; $223, AU-55, July 2015; $764, AU-53, October 2015												
1835, Proof	10–15	5	64.2								$15,000	$35,000	$100,000
	Auctions: $25,850, PF-63, August 2013												
1836	472,000	233	38.5	16%	$70	$100	$125	$150	$400	$750	$2,000	$4,250	$40,000
	Auctions: $940, AU-53, January 2015; $823, AU-53, February 2015; $558, EF-45, November 2014; $329, EF-40, May 2015												
1836, Proof	8–12	2	65.5								$15,000	$25,000	$100,000
	Auctions: $97,750, PF-67, January 2006												
1837	252,400	298	47.5	31%	$70	$100	$125	$150	$400	$750	$2,000	$4,250	$22,500
	Auctions: $646, AU-55, November 2014; $823, AU-50, January 2015; $306, EF-40, November 2014; $200, VF-30, January 2015												
1837, Proof	8–12	2	66.0								$15,000	$25,000	$90,000
	Auctions: $132,250, PF-67, August 2006												
1838	366,000	283	45.3	25%	$70	$100	$125	$150	$400	$750	$2,000	$4,250	$22,550
	Auctions: $82,250, MS-67, September 2015; $646, EF-45, August 2015; $576, EF-45, March 2015; $423, EF-40, August 2015												
1838, Proof	8–12	2	66.0								$25,000	$35,000	$100,000
	Auctions: $48,875, PF-64, July 2011												

b. The OF is re-engraved with the letters connected at the top, and the first A in AMERICA is also re-engraved. Other identifying characteristics: there is no period after the C in the denomination, and the 5 and C are further apart than normal. **c.** Included in circulation-strike 1833 mintage figure. **d.** Included in circulation-strike 1834 mintage figure.

LIBERTY SEATED (1838–1891)

Variety 1, No Motto Above Eagle (1838–1853): **Designer:** *Christian Gobrecht.*
Weight: *6.68 grams.* **Composition:** *.900 silver, .100 copper.* **Diameter:** *24.3 mm.*
Edge: *Reeded.* **Mints:** *Philadelphia and New Orleans.*

Variety 1 (1838–1853)

Mintmark location is on the reverse, below the eagle, for all varieties.

Variety 1, Proof

Variety 2, Arrows at Date, Rays Around Eagle (1853): **Designer:** *Christian Gobrecht.*
Weight: *6.22 grams.* **Composition:** *.900 silver, .100 copper.* **Diameter:** *24.3 mm.*
Edge: *Reeded.* **Mints:** *Philadelphia and New Orleans.*

Variety 2 (1853)   Variety 2, Proof

Variety 3, Arrows at Date, No Rays (1854–1855): **Designer:** *Christian Gobrecht.*
Weight: *6.22 grams.* **Composition:** *.900 silver, .100 copper.* **Diameter:** *24.3 mm.*
Edge: *Reeded.* **Mints:** *Philadelphia, New Orleans, and San Francisco.*

Variety 3 (1854–1855)   Variety 3, Proof

Variety 1 Resumed, With Weight Standard of Variety 2 (1856–1865):
Designer: *Christian Gobrecht.* **Weight:** *6.22 grams.* **Composition:** *.900 silver, .100 copper.*
Diameter: *24.3 mm.* **Edge:** *Reeded.* **Mints:** *Philadelphia, New Orleans, and San Francisco.*

Variety 1 Resumed, Weight
Standard of Variety 2 (1856–1865)   Variety 1 Resumed, Weight
Standard of Variety 2, Proof

Variety 4, Motto Above Eagle (1866–1873): **Designer:** *Christian Gobrecht.*
Weight: *6.22 grams.* **Composition:** *.900 silver, .100 copper.* **Diameter:** *24.3 mm.*
Edge: *Reeded.* **Mints:** *Philadelphia, San Francisco, and Carson City.*

Variety 4 (1866–1873)   Variety 4, Proof

Variety 5, Arrows at Date (1873–1874): **Designer:** *Christian Gobrecht.*
Weight: *6.25 grams.* **Composition:** *.900 silver, .100 copper.* **Diameter:** *24.3 mm.*
Edge: *Reeded.* **Mints:** *Philadelphia, San Francisco, and Carson City.*

Variety 5 (1873–1874)   Variety 5, Proof

Variety 4 Resumed, With Weight Standard of Variety 5 (1875–1891):
Designer: *Christian Gobrecht.* **Weight:** *6.25 grams.* **Composition:** *.900 silver, .100 copper.*
Diameter: *24.3 mm.* **Edge:** *Reeded.* **Mints:** *Philadelphia, New Orleans, and San Francisco.*

Variety 4 Resumed, Weight   Variety 4 Resumed, Weight
Standard of Variety 5 (1875–1891)   Standard of Variety 5, Proof

History. The long-running Liberty Seated design was introduced on the quarter dollar in 1838. Early issues lack drapery at Miss Liberty's elbow and have small lettering on the reverse. Drapery was added in 1840 and continued afterward. In 1853 a reduction in the coin's weight was indicated with the addition of arrows at the date and rays on the reverse (in the field around the eagle). The rays were omitted after 1853, but the arrows were retained through 1855. The motto IN GOD WE TRUST was added to the reverse in 1866. Arrows were placed at the date in the years 1873 and 1874 to denote the change of weight from 6.22 to 6.25 grams. The new weight, without the arrows, continued through 1891.

Striking and Sharpness. On the obverse, check the head of Miss Liberty and the star centers. If these are sharp, then check the central part of the seated figure. On the reverse, check the eagle, particularly the area to the lower left of the shield. Check the denticles on both sides. Generally, the earliest issues are well struck, as are those of the 1880s onward. The word LIBERTY is not an infallible guide to grading at lower levels, as on some dies the shield was in lower relief, and the letters wore away less quickly. This guideline should be used in combination with examining other features. Some Proofs (1858 is an example) have lint marks, and others can have light striking (particularly in the 1870s and 1880s). Avoid "problem" coins and those with deep or artificial (and often colorful) toning.

Availability. Coins of this type are available in proportion to their mintages. MS coins can range from rare to exceedingly rare, as they were mostly ignored by numismatists until the series ended. Quality can vary widely, especially among branch-mint coins. Proofs of the earlier years are very rare. Beginning with 1856, they were made in larger numbers, and from 1859 onward the yearly production was in the multiple hundreds. Proofs of the later era are readily available today; truly choice and gem pieces with no distracting hairlines are in the minority and will require diligent searching.

GRADING STANDARDS

MS-60 to 70 (Mint State). *Obverse:* At MS-60, some abrasion and contact marks are evident, most noticeably on the bosom and thighs and knees. Luster is present, but may be dull or lifeless. At MS-63, contact marks are very few, and abrasion is hard to detect except under magnification. An MS-65 coin has no abrasion, and contact marks are suffi-ciently minute as to require magnification. Check the knees of Liberty and the right

1853, Repunched Date, No Arrows or Rays; FS-301. Graded MS-67.

field. Luster should be full and rich. Most Mint State coins of the 1861 to 1865 years, Philadelphia issues, have extensive die striae (from not completely finishing the die). *Reverse:* Comments apply as for the obverse, except that in lower Mint State grades abrasion and contact marks are most noticeable on the eagle's neck, the claws, and the top of the wings (harder to see there, however). At MS-65 or higher there are no marks visible to the unaided eye. The field is mainly protected by design elements and does not show abrasion as much as does the obverse on a given coin.

Illustrated coin: Note the delicate toning in the fields. In addition to hints of green, rose, and teal there is a good deal of luster as well.

AU-50, 53, 55, 58 (About Uncirculated). *Obverse:* Light wear is seen on the thighs and knees, bosom, and head. At AU-58, the luster is extensive, but incomplete, especially in the right field. At AU–50 and 53, luster is less. *Reverse:* Wear is evident on the eagle's neck, claws, and top of the wings. An AU-58 coin has nearly full luster, more so than on the obverse, as the design elements protect the small field areas. At AU–50 and 53, there still are traces of luster.

1891. Graded AU-53.

EF-40, 45 (Extremely Fine). *Obverse:* Fur-ther wear is seen on all areas, especially the thighs and knees, bosom, and head. Little or no luster is seen on most coins. From this grade downward, sharpness of strike of the stars and the head does not matter to connois-seurs. *Reverse:* Further wear is evident on the eagle's neck, claws, and wings. Some feathers in the right wing may be blended together.

1843. Graded EF-40.

VF-20, 30 (Very Fine). *Obverse:* Further wear is seen. Most details of the gown are worn away, except in the lower-relief areas above and to the right of the shield. Hair detail is mostly or completely gone. *Reverse:* Wear is more extensive, with more feathers blended together, especially in the right wing. The area below the shield shows more wear.

   Illustrated coin: The surfaces of this coin are unusually smooth and problem free for the issue.

1860-S. Graded VF-20.

F-12, 15 (Fine). *Obverse:* The seated figure is well worn, but with some detail above and to the right of the shield. LIBERTY is readable but weak in areas. *Reverse:* Wear is extensive, with about half of the feathers flat or blended with others.

1854-O. Graded F-12.

VG-8, 10 (Very Good). *Obverse:* The seated figure is more worn, but some detail can be seen above and to the right of the shield. The shield is discernible. In LIBERTY at least the equivalent of two or three letters (can be a combination of partial letters) must be readable but can be very weak at VG-8, with a few more visible at VG-10. However, LIBERTY is not an infallible guide to grade this type, as some varieties had the word in low relief on the die, so it wore away slowly. *Reverse:* Further wear has flattened all but a few feathers, and the horizontal lines of the shield are indistinct. The leaves are only in outline form. The rim is visible all around, as are the ends of most denticles.

1872-CC. Graded VG-10.

   Illustrated coin: Note the faint red toning evident in areas of this otherwise pleasingly gray coin.

G-4, 6 (Good). *Obverse:* The seated figure is worn smooth. At G-4 there are no letters in LIBERTY remaining on most (but not all) coins; some coins, especially of the early 1870s, are exceptions. At G-6, traces of one or two can barely be seen. *Reverse:* The designs are only in outline form, although some vertical shield stripes can be seen on some. The rim is worn down, and tops of the border letters are weak or worn away, although the inscription can still be read.

1872-CC. Graded G-6.

AG-3 (About Good). *Obverse:* The seated figure is mostly visible in outline form, with only a hint of detail. Much of the rim is worn away. The date remains clear. *Reverse:* The border letters are partially worn away. The eagle is mostly in outline form, but with a few details discernible. The rim is weak or missing.

1862-S. Graded AG-3.

PF-60 to 70 (Proof). *Obverse and Reverse:* Proofs that are extensively cleaned and have many hairlines, or that are dull and grainy, are lower level, such as PF–60 to 62. These are not widely desired by connoisseurs. With medium hairlines and good reflectivity, an assigned grade of PF-64 is appropriate and with relatively few hairlines, Gem PF-65. In various grades hairlines are most easily seen in the obverse field. PF-66 should have hairlines so delicate that magnification is needed to see them. Above that, a Proof should be free of such lines.

1860. Graded PF-65.

| 1839, No Drapery | 1840-O, Drapery | 1840-O, Drapery, Normal O | 1840-O, Drapery, Large O |

Coins designated Deep Cameo or Ultra Cameo bring a premium of 50% to 100% above listed values.

	Mintage	Cert	Avg	%MS	G-4	VG-8	F-12	VF-20	EF-40	AU-50	MS-60 PF-60	MS-63 PF-63	MS-65 PF-65
1838, No Drapery	466,000	192	52.9	43%	$30	$35	$50	$175	$450	$950	$1,700	$4,000	$35,000
Auctions: $3,055, MS-63, January 2015; $591, AU-53, January 2015; $794, AU-50, January 2015; $364, EF-45, March 2015
1838, Proof	2–3	0	n/a					(extremely rare)					
Auctions: No auction records available.
1839, No Drapery	491,146	146	50.8	26%	$30	$35	$50	$175	$450	$1,050	$1,700	$4,000	$45,000
Auctions: $940, AU-58, June 2015; $1,116, AU-55, September 2015; $823, AU-53, January 2015; $764, AU-53, June 2015
1839, Proof (a)	2–3	1	65.0										$500,000
Auctions: $270,250, PF-65, October 2014; $411,250, PF-65, April 2013
1840-O, No Drapery	382,200	144	46.5	23%	$40	$50	$75	$225	$450	$950	$2,200	$5,500	$35,000
Auctions: $199,750, MS-67, May 2015; $19,975, MS-65, May 2015; $3,533, MS-63, June 2015; $1,410, MS-62, September 2015
1840, Drapery	188,127	43	51.1	30%	$25	$30	$60	$150	$325	$600	$1,650	$4,800	$18,000
Auctions: $17,625, MS-66, May 2015; $16,450, MS-64, October 2015; $423, AU-53, June 2015; $306, AU-53, May 2015
1840, Drapery, Proof	5–8	2	64.5										$75,000
Auctions: $99,889, PF-65, August 2013
1840-O, Drapery	43,000	76	50.8	36%	$36	$50	$90	$150	$300	$600	$1,400	$3,800	$20,000
Auctions: $16,450, MS-65, May 2015; $2,585, MS-63, March 2015; $1,410, MS-62, October 2015; $1,293, AU-58, October 2015
1840-O, Drapery, Large O (b)	(c)	0	n/a							$6,500	$12,000		
Auctions: $3,220, MS-63, December 2010

a. This piece is unique. b. The O mintmark punch is about 25% larger than normal. There are two known reverse dies for this variety, with one showing doubled denticles. c. Included in 1840-O, Drapery, mintage figure.

1842, Small Date
*Philadelphia Small
Date is Proof only.*

1842, Large Date

1842-O, Small Date

1842-O, Large Date

	Mintage	Cert	Avg	%MS	G-4	VG-8	F-12	VF-20	EF-40	AU-50	MS-60 PF-60	MS-63 PF-63	MS-65 PF-65
1841	120,000	59	56.5	59%	$65	$100	$125	$225	$400	$750	$1,200	$2,000	$8,500
Auctions: $28,200, MS-66, May 2015; $8,225, MS-65, October 2015; $6,463, MS-65, October 2015; $1,528, AU-58, August 2015													
1841, Proof	3–5	1	66.0								$65,000	$100,000	$200,000
Auctions: $235,000, PF-66, April 2013; $42,300, PF-61, October 2015; $48,175, PF-61, January 2015													
1841-O	452,000	64	55.3	53%	$35	$45	$55	$125	$280	$360	$850	$1,900	$10,000
Auctions: $1,763, MS-63, August 2015; $646, AU-58, February 2015; $353, AU-53, June 2015; $306, AU-50, June 2015													
1842, Large Date (d)	88,000	44	51.6	32%	$75	$100	$150	$250	$400	$750	$1,600	$4,500	$12,500
Auctions: $1,175, AU-58, August 2015; $423, EF-45, July 2015; $423, EF-40, May 2015; $318, VF-30, January 2015													
1842, Small Date, Proof † (e)	3–5	2	65.0									$60,000	$125,000
Auctions: $164,500, PF-66, January 2015; $282,000, PF-65, October 2014; $258,500, PF-65, August 2013													
1842-O, All kinds	769,000												
1842-O, Small Date		17	22.7	6%	$600	$1,150	$1,600	$3,000	$7,500	$11,000	$27,500	$70,000	
Auctions: $12,925, AU-55, October 2015; $7,638, AU-53, December 2015; $1,763, F-12, August 2015; $940, VG-10, October 2016													
1842-O, Large Date		57	37.2	26%	$35	$45	$55	$125	$275	$600	$1,750	$4,500	
Auctions: $3,290, MS-63, November 2014; $423, MS-60, July 2015; $306, AU-53, November 2014; $141, AU-50, May 2015													
1843	645,600	101	57.5	52%	$25	$30	$35	$75	$200	$400	$675	$1,300	$4,500
Auctions: $4,935, MS-65, May 2015; $483, MS-61, May 2015; $188, AU-55, March 2015; $141, EF-45, May 2015													
1843, Proof	10–15	4	61.0								$12,500	$20,000	$45,000
Auctions: $64,625, PF-66, April 2013													
1843-O	968,000	57	42.7	12%	$35	$75	$150	$350	$1,100	$1,350	$2,450	$4,500	$20,000
Auctions: $19,975, MS-64, May 2015; $7,050, MS-64, May 2015; $3,290, EF-45, October 2015; $1,880, EF-40, February 2015													
1844	421,200	84	55.4	44%	$25	$30	$35	$45	$115	$250	$650	$1,650	$10,000
Auctions: $4,935, MS-64, June 2015; $940, MS-61, June 2015; $306, AU-53, May 2015; $100, AU-50, November 2014													
1844, Proof (f)	3–5	1	66.0										
Auctions: $276,000, PF-66, July 2009													
1844-O	740,000	56	49.0	29%	$35	$45	$55	$90	$200	$425	$1,250	$1,750	$10,000
Auctions: $1,880, MS-63, July 2015; $259, AU-50, July 2015; $141, VF-25, January 2015; $69, VF-20, November 2014													
1845	922,000	123	55.6	46%	$25	$30	$35	$50	$100	$185	$500	$1,250	$6,000
Auctions: $705, MS-62, September 2015; $517, MS-62, February 2015; $494, AU-58, August 2015; $423, AU-58, August 2015													
1845, Proof	6–8	8	64.6									$30,000	$55,000
Auctions: $31,725, PF-65, October 2015; $26,438, PF-64, September 2015; $25,850, PF-64, August 2015													
1846	510,000	79	53.9	38%	$45	$75	$100	$125	$225	$425	$800	$1,850	$12,500
Auctions: $22,325, MS-66, January 2014													
1846, Proof	15–20	11	64.5								$5,000	$10,000	$30,000
Auctions: $25,850, PF-65, April 2013													
1847	734,000	70	53.4	46%	$25	$30	$35	$45	$80	$175	$575	$1,650	$6,500
Auctions: $10,575, MS-65, May 2015; $1,410, MS-63, July 2015; $940, AU-58, May 2015; $705, AU-58, October 2015													
1847, Proof	6–8	4	65.25								$5,000	$10,000	$35,000
Auctions: $17,625, PF-66, October 2015; $28,200, PF-65, November 2013; $14,688, PF-64, July 2014													
1847-O	368,000	42	41.0	12%	$100	$150	$300	$600	$1,000	$2,000	$6,000	$12,500	
Auctions: $8,225, MS-62, October 2015; $4,230, AU-58, August 2015; $1,293, EF-45, June 2015; $376, VF-20, August 2015													

† Ranked in the *100 Greatest U.S. Coins* (fourth edition). **d.** The Large Date was used on the Philadelphia Mint's 1842 coins struck for circulation. **e.** For the Philadelphia Mint's quarters of 1842, the Small Date was used on Proofs only. **f.** 2 examples are known.

1853, Repunched Date, No Arrows or Rays
FS-25-1853-301.

1853, 3 Over 4 (Arrows at Date, Rays Around Eagle)
FS-25-1853-301.

	Mintage	Cert	Avg	%MS	G-4	VG-8	F-12	VF-20	EF-40	AU-50	MS-60	MS-63	MS-65
											PF-60	PF-63	PF-65
1848	146,000	38	47.8	29%	$25	$55	$100	$125	$325	$500	$1,150	$4,750	$12,000
Auctions: $5,170, MS-64, January 2015; $4,230, MS-63, October 2015; $1,116, AU-55, January 2015; $494, EF-45, June 2015													
1848, Proof	5–8	2	65.0								$5,000	$10,000	$30,000
Auctions: $64,625, PF-66, October 2014; $55,813, PF-66, August 2013; $22,325, PF-65, January 2015													
1849	340,000	94	52.7	31%	$25	$30	$40	$75	$125	$275	$900	$1,500	$9,500
Auctions: $11,163, MS-65, August 2015; $8,813, MS-65, May 2015; $8,225, MS-65, August 2015; $1,116, MS-63, January 2015													
1849, Proof	5–8	3	64.3								$5,000	$10,000	$27,500
Auctions: $32,900, PF-65, January 2014													
1849-O	(g)	38	32.1	11%	$1,100	$1,500	$2,000	$3,000	$7,000	$8,500	$17,500	$20,000	
Auctions: $24,675, MS-64, May 2015; $17,625, MS-63, January 2015; $7,050, AU-55, August 2015; $7,050, AU-53, January 2015													
1850	190,800	35	56.1	51%	$25	$50	$65	$95	$250	$600	$1,350	$2,250	$11,000
Auctions: $13,513, MS-65, October 2015; $3,055, MS-64, November 2014; $1,293, MS-60, November 2014; $306, AU-50, June 2015													
1850, Proof	5–8	3	64.0										
Auctions: $258,500, PF-68, August 2013													
1850-O	412,000	66	51.7	38%	$35	$115	$150	$225	$500	$750	$1,600	$4,000	$13,500
Auctions: $9,400, MS-64, October 2015; $3,525, MS-63, August 2015; $447, EF-40, February 2015; $212, VF-35, May 2015													
1851	160,000	41	48.3	29%	$60	$100	$150	$300	$500	$950	$1,350	$2,350	$6,500
Auctions: $4,935, MS-65, October 2015; $646, EF-45, August 2015; $764, EF-40, January 2015; $517, VF-35, August 2015													
1851-O	88,000	38	27.2	8%	$375	$550	$900	$1,000	$2,500	$3,350	$6,700	$32,500	
Auctions: $881, VF-20, June 2015; $823, F-12, August 2015; $764, VG-10, August 2015; $376, G-4, January 2015													
1852	177,060	56	55.6	55%	$65	$100	$135	$250	$500	$650	$1,100	$1,800	$5,500
Auctions: $99,875, MS-68, May 2015; $18,800, MS-66, October 2015; $3,760, MS-65, July 2015; $646, EF-45, August 2015													
1852, Proof	5–8	1	65.0										$75,000
Auctions: $105,750, PF-65, April 2013													
1852-O	96,000	27	30.2	7%	$185	$250	$800	$1,350	$2,250	$5,500	$9,500	$40,000	
Auctions:$17,625, MS-63, November 2016; $21,150, MS-62, May 2015; $18,800, MS-62, October 2015; $2,820, MS-60, October 2016													
1853, Repunched Date, No Arrows or Rays (h)	44,200	44	46.7	45%	$1,250	$2,000	$2,500	$3,250	$4,000	$4,500	$6,000	$7,000	$12,000
Auctions: $32,900, MS-67, June 2015; $19,975, MS-66, October 2015; $9,400, MS-65, October 2015; $3,760, EF-40, June 2015													
1853, Variety 2	15,210,020	1,317	49.3	33%	$25	$30	$35	$45	$175	$350	$1,000	$2,000	$10,000
Auctions: $17,625, MS-65, August 2015; $11,163, MS-65, August 2015; $9,988, MS-65, February 2015; $7,638, MS-65, October 2015													
1853, Variety 2, 3 Over 4 (i)	(j)	52	42.3	21%	$55	$100	$175	$250	$350	$675	$1,850	$4,000	$30,000
Auctions: $9,988, MS-64, October 2014; $617, EF-45, August 2015; $494, EF-45, October 2016; $423, VF-35, September 2015													
1853, Variety 2, Proof	10–15	5	65.2								$30,000	$50,000	$100,000
Auctions: $141,000, PF-66Cam, August 2013; $41,125, PF-64, May 2015; $64,625, PF-64, October 2014													
1853-O, Variety 2	1,332,000	99	45.5	17%	$35	$70	$100	$150	$400	$1,100	$4,250	$10,000	$27,500
Auctions: $17,625, MS-64, October 2015; $1,293, AU-53, August 2015; $1,058, EF-45, February 2015; $494, EF-45, March 2016													

g. Included in 1850-O mintage figure. **h.** The secondary 5 and 3 are evident south of the primary digits. In the past, this variety was erroneously attributed as a 53 Over 2 overdate. This is the only die known for 1853 that lacks the arrows and rays. **i.** In addition to the 3 punched over a 4, there is also evidence of the repunched 8 and 5 (weaker images slightly north and west of the primary digits). The right arrow shaft is also doubled, north of the primary. "On well-worn or late-die-state specimens, the doubling of the arrow shaft may be the only evidence of the overdate. This is the only quarter dollar date known to be punched over the *following* year!" (*Cherrypickers' Guide to Rare Die Varieties*, sixth edition, volume II). **j.** Included in 1853, Variety 2, mintage figure.

   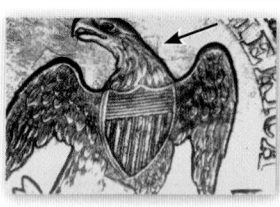

1854-O, Normal O	1854-O, Huge O	1856-S, S Over Small S FS-25-1856S-501.	1857, Clashed Reverse Die FS-25-1857-901.

	Mintage	Cert	Avg	%MS	G-4	VG-8	F-12	VF-20	EF-40	AU-50	MS-60 / PF-60	MS-63 / PF-63	MS-65 / PF-65
1854	12,380,000	689	51.6	35%	$25	$30	$35	$45	$85	$250	$625	$1,200	$6,500
Auctions: $8,225, MS-65, October 2015; $4,230, MS-65, February 2015; $4,230, MS-65, June 2015; $1,998, MS-64, September 2015													
1854, Proof	*20–30*	10	64.2								$8,500	$15,000	$30,000
Auctions: $30,550, PF-66, April 2013													
1854-O, Normal O	1,484,000	100	45.2	33%	$35	$40	$50	$55	$125	$300	$1,100	$1,750	$15,000
Auctions: $23,500, MS-66, October 2015; $15,275, MS-65, January 2015; $14,100, MS-65, October 2015; $247, AU-50, October 2015													
1854-O, Huge O (k)	(l)	60	19.4	0%	$750	$1,350	$1,950	$2,250	$4,500	$7,500			
Auctions: $4,994, EF-45, February 2013; $3,055, VF-30, August 2016; $793, VF-20, March 2015; $423, VG-8, September 2016													
1855	2,857,000	186	53.3	38%	$25	$30	$35	$45	$100	$250	$625	$1,300	$10,000
Auctions: $27,025, MS-67, May 2015; $17,625, MS-66, October 2015; $23,406, MS-65, July 2015; $1,116, MS-63, March 2015													
1855, Proof	*20–30*	10	64.6								$8,500	$15,000	$30,000
Auctions: $28,200, PF-66, October 2014; $21,150, PF-65Cam, April 2013; $8,225, PF-62, October 2015													
1855-O	176,000	33	42.8	30%	$125	$185	$300	$550	$850	$2,000	$3,000	$12,500	
Auctions: $82,250, MS-67, May 2015; $12,925, MS-63, October 2015; $646, VF-25, March 2016; $564, VF-25, October 2016													
1855-S	396,400	33	40.6	15%	$100	$150	$250	$450	$900	$1,200	$2,500	$7,500	$25,000
Auctions: $19,975, MS-65, January 2015; $15,275, MS-64, May 2015; $7,050, MS-63, October 2015; $423, EF-40, May 2015													
1855-S, Proof	*1–2*	1	64.0										
Auctions: $176,250, PF-64, August 2013													
1856	7,264,000	273	52.8	44%	$25	$30	$35	$45	$75	$185	$350	$650	$3,000
Auctions: $3,525, MS-66, January 2015; $3,290, MS-66, July 2015; $5,288, MS-66, October 2015; $3,231, MS-66, June 2015													
1856, Proof	*40–50*	27	64.0								$3,500	$5,500	$13,500
Auctions: $12,959, PF-66, August 2014; $11,750, PF-66, May 2015; $12,925, PF-65, January 2015; $9,400, PF-65, October 2015													
1856-O	968,000	78	46.4	19%	$30	$40	$75	$125	$250	$550	$1,000	$2,000	$12,000
Auctions: $11,163, MS-65, March 2015; $4,230, MS-64, October 2015; $940, AU-58, January 2015; $259, AU-50, September 2015													
1856-S, All kinds	286,000												
1856-S		24	38.3	13%	$250	$325	$600	$800	$1,750	$3,000	$7,500	$13,500	$40,000
Auctions: $9,988, MS-63, October 2016; $11,163, MS-62, August 2016; $441, EF-40, July 2015; $259, EF-40, June 2015													
1856-S, S Over Small S (m)		5	19.0	0%	$500	$750	$1,100	$2,000	$7,000	$12,000			
Auctions: $28,200, AU-58, June 2014													
1857	9,644,000	564	54.7	54%	$25	$30	$35	$45	$75	$185	$350	$600	$2,750
Auctions: $14,100, MS-67, June 2015; $12,925, MS-67, September 2015; $10,575, MS-67, August 2015; $10,575, MS-67, October 2015													
1857, Clashed Rev Die (n)	(o)	5	50.2	40%					$450	$650	$1,000		
Auctions: No auction records available.													
1857, Proof	*40–50*	34	64.0								$3,000	$4,000	$11,000
Auctions: $7,050, PF-66, January 2015; $6,463, PF-66, June 2015; $2,820, PF-63, January 2015; $2,233, PF-62, June 2015													
1857-O	1,180,000	82	49.6	22%	$30	$40	$100	$150	$300	$650	$1,200	$3,000	
Auctions: $7,050, MS-64, October 2015; $2,820, MS-63, October 2015; $2,585, MS-63, October 2015; $1,880, MS-63, August 2015													
1857-S	82,000	44	48.4	20%	$175	$300	$425	$800	$1,150	$1,750	$3,500	$6,000	
Auctions: $11,163, MS-64, October 2015; $8,813, MS-64, October 2015; $940, EF-40, August 2015; $588, VF-30, July 2015													

k. The Huge O mintmark is very large, extremely thick on the left side, and irregular, suggesting that it was punched into the die by hand. **l.** Included in 1854-O mintage figure. **m.** A larger S mintmark was punched over a much smaller S mintmark, the latter probably intended for half-dime production. **n.** The reverse clashed with the reverse die of an 1857 Flying Eagle cent. Images of the cent reverse die are easily visible on either side of the eagle's neck, within the shield, and below the eagle's left wing. **o.** Included in circulation-strike 1857 mintage figure.

	Mintage	Cert	Avg	%MS	G-4	VG-8	F-12	VF-20	EF-40	AU-50	MS-60	MS-63	MS-65
											PF-60	PF-63	PF-65
1858	7,368,000	434	54.2	49%	$25	$30	$35	$45	$75	$185	$350	$600	$2,750
	Auctions: $17,625, MS-67, May 2015; $3,760, MS-66, October 2015; $3,290, MS-66, October 2015; $2,703, MS-65, October 2015												
1858, Proof	300	76	63.6								$1,500	$2,500	$6,500
	Auctions: $28,200, PF-67, September 2015; $9,400, PF-66, October 2014; $7,638, PF-66, October 2015; $4,935, PF-65, February 2015												
1858-O	520,000	44	48.9	14%	$30	$40	$75	$125	$275	$600	$3,250	$10,000	$25,000
	Auctions: $14,100, MS-65, October 2015; $21,150, MS-64, May 2015; $7,638, MS-62, October 2015; $94, EF-45, September 2014												
1858-S	121,000	41	35.6	2%	$250	$400	$600	$1,000	$2,500	$5,000	$22,500		
	Auctions: $35,250, MS-62, May 2015; $28,200, MS-62, October 2015; $8,813, AU-58, October 2015; $1,645, VF-35, August 2015												
1859	1,343,200	146	54.3	44%	$25	$30	$35	$45	$75	$185	$425	$900	$4,500
	Auctions: $3,878, MS-65, January 2015; $3,819, MS-65, January 2015; $3,055, MS-65, September 2015; $1,645, MS-64, August 2015												
1859, Proof	800	154	64.1								$1,000	$1,500	$4,500
	Auctions: $17,625, PF-67, May 2015; $7,638, PF-66, October 2015; $4,583, PF-65Cam, September 2015; $1,998, PF-64Cam, January 2015												
1859-O	260,000	45	51.6	27%	$50	$75	$100	$150	$300	$1,000	$2,500	$6,500	$22,500
	Auctions: $793, AU-55, January 2015; $423, AU-53, August 2015; $329, AU-50, February 2015; $329, AU-50, March 2015												
1859-S	80,000	24	29.0	0%	$375	$575	$850	$1,250	$4,500	$12,000	$50,000		
	Auctions: $9,988, AU-50, October 2015; $6,756, EF-45, January 2015; $940, VF-25, July 2015; $1,028, VG-10, August 2015												
1860	804,400	130	55.6	41%	$25	$30	$35	$65	$100	$185	$500	$850	$5,000
	Auctions: $200, MS-60, May 2015; $130, AU-50, May 2015; $118, EF-40, November 2015; $94, EF-40, August 2015												
1860, Proof	1,000	111	63.9								$700	$1,200	$4,500
	Auctions: $21,150, PF-68, May 2015; $7,050, PF-66, February 2015; $5,875, PF-66, October 2015; $3,525, PF-65, August 2015												
1860-O	388,000	79	53.2	35%	$30	$45	$55	$85	$250	$475	$1,000	$1,750	$12,500
	Auctions: $3,055, MS-64, July 2015; $1,350, MS-63, September 2015; $1,028, MS-62, June 2015; $176, AU-50, October 2015												
1860-S	56,000	22	27.4	0%	$1,000	$1,500	$3,000	$5,000	$9,000	$18,500	$50,000		
	Auctions: $45,825, MS-61, October 2016; $15,275, AU-50, January 2015; $8,225, EF-45, September 2015; $7,638, EF-40, March 2016												
1861	4,853,600	641	57.1	54%	$25	$30	$35	$45	$80	$185	$350	$650	$2,750
	Auctions: $12,925, MS-67, August 2015; $11,750, MS-67, September 2015; $3,760, MS-66, September 2015; $2,350, MS-65, September 2015												
1861, Proof	1,000	104	63.6								$700	$1,200	$4,500
	Auctions: $10,575, PF-67, October 2015; $6,169, PF-66, January 2015; $5,405, PF-66, October 2015; $1,410, PF-64, January 2015												
1861-S	96,000	29	30.5	0%	$600	$900	$1,250	$2,000	$4,500	$12,500	$40,000		
	Auctions: $21,150, AU-58, May 2015; $1,293, VF-20, February 2015; $1,469, F-15, August 2015; $940, F-12, August 2015												
1862	932,000	172	57.0	61%	$25	$30	$35	$50	$85	$185	$350	$650	$2,750
	Auctions: $7,638, MS-67, June 2015; $3,995, MS-66, October 2015; $1,293, MS-64, October 2015; $999, MS-64, October 2015												
1862, Proof	550	134	63.7								$700	$1,200	$4,500
	Auctions: $9,988, PF-67Cam, October 2015; $6,463, PF-66, May 2015; $6,169, PF-66, October 2015; $1,998, PF-64, August 2015												
1862-S	67,000	46	42.3	24%	$175	$300	$450	$600	$1,250	$2,500	$3,500	$7,500	
	Auctions: $6,463, MS-62, October 2015; $3,525, MS-62, January 2015; $2,115, AU-53, July 2015; $447, VF-25, August 2015												
1863	191,600	65	56.1	62%	$40	$50	$75	$130	$275	$425	$650	$1,200	$4,500
	Auctions: $4,935, MS-65, October 2015; $1,586, MS-64, January 2015; $881, MS-62, June 2015; $823, MS-61, June 2015												
1863, Proof	460	156	63.6								$700	$1,200	$4,500
	Auctions: $8,519, PF-67, January 2015; $5,875, PF-66, October 2015; $2,585, PF-64, August 2015; $1,998, PF-64, June 2015												
1864	93,600	62	52.5	56%	$125	$200	$250	$375	$600	$850	$1,250	$2,500	$5,500
	Auctions: $35,250, MS-67, May 2015; $14,100, MS-66, October 2015; $494, AU-50, September 2015; $646, EF-45, August 2015												
1864, Proof	470	187	63.9								$700	$1,200	$4,500
	Auctions: $3,760, PF-65Cam, October 2015; $2,585, PF-64Cam, January 2015; $1,528, PF-64, January 2015; $1,410, PF-63Cam, July 2015												
1864-S	20,000	40	29.5	13%	$875	$1,000	$1,250	$2,000	$4,000	$5,500	$12,000	$22,500	
	Auctions: $28,200, MS-64, October 2015; $3,525, EF-40, August 2015; $1,998, VF-30, March 2016; $1,234, VG-10, August 2015												
1865	58,800	50	47.5	32%	$75	$85	$175	$350	$450	$750	$1,250	$1,850	$10,000
	Auctions: $32,900, MS-67, January 2015; $1,645, MS-62, August 2015; $400, VF-35, April 2015; $153, VF-20, October 2015												
1865, Proof	500	181	63.9								$700	$1,200	$4,500
	Auctions: $23,500, PF-68, May 2015; $12,925, PF-67Cam, October 2015; $5,405, PF-66Cam, October 2015; $8,225, PF-66, September 2015												
1865-S	41,000	43	49.9	42%	$175	$250	$400	$650	$1,100	$1,350	$3,500	$4,500	$17,500
	Auctions: $64,625, MS-66, February 2014; $999, EF-40, October 2014; $764, VF-35, February 2015; $200, G-4, September 2014												

	Mintage	Cert	Avg	%MS	G-4	VG-8	F-12	VF-20	EF-40	AU-50	MS-60 PF-60	MS-63 PF-63	MS-65 PF-65
1866	16,800	45	51.3	62%	$750	$1,000	$1,250	$1,500	$1,650	$1,850	$2,250	$2,750	$8,500
Auctions: $1,410, VF-25, August 2015; $1,175, VF-25, November 2015; $1,058, VF-25, August 2015; $999, VF-20, June 2015													
1866, No Motto, Proof † (p)	1	0	n/a					*(unique)*					
Auctions: No auction records available.													
1866, Proof	725	158	64.0								$500	$850	$2,500
Auctions: $19,975, PF-68, November 2013													
1866-S	28,000	26	29.6	19%	$400	$650	$1,000	$1,500	$1,750	$2,750	$5,000	$10,000	$35,000
Auctions: $25,263, MS-65, October 2014; $5,405, MS-62, December 2015; $1,293, VF-30, September 2014; $1,146, VF-20, December 2015													
1867	20,000	34	43.6	35%	$350	$550	$700	$1,000	$1,500	$1,850	$2,250	$4,500	
Auctions: $9,400, MS-64, October 2015; $6,463, MS-63, October 2015; $3,760, MS-63, October 2015; $1,528, AU-55, October 2015													
1867, Proof	625	169	64.0								$500	$850	$2,250
Auctions: $3,525, PF-66, October 2015; $2,703, PF-64Cam, October 2015; $1,116, PF-64, October 2015; $764, PF-63, September 2015													
1867-S	48,000	19	26.2	11%	$450	$500	$800	$1,250	$2,750	$7,000	$10,500	$15,000	
Auctions: $88,125, MS-67, May 2015; $17,625, MS-64, June 2015; $3,525, EF-45, June 2015; $1,410, VF-25, June 2015													
1868	29,400	32	51.4	53%	$185	$275	$400	$500	$800	$1,100	$1,750	$3,500	$9,000
Auctions: $8,225, MS-65, October 2015; $7,050, MS-65, August 2015; $400, EF-40, May 2015; $354, EF-40, August 2015													
1868, Proof	600	155	63.5								$500	$850	$2,250
Auctions: $4,465, PF-66, January 2015; $3,055, PF-66, October 2015; $2,820, PF-65, January 2015; $2,233, PF-65, September 2015													
1868-S	96,000	42	39.2	24%	$125	$175	$300	$750	$1,100	$2,000	$5,500	$9,500	$20,000
Auctions: $82,250, MS-67, August 2015; $18,800, MS-66, August 2015; $14,100, MS-64, October 2015; $999, EF-40, July 2015													
1869	16,000	27	41.6	41%	$500	$650	$850	$1,000	$1,250	$1,500	$2,250	$4,500	$10,000
Auctions: $1,028, VF-25, August 2015; $646, VF-20, July 2015; $764, F-12, August 2015; $541, G-6, April 2015													
1869, Proof	600	175	63.5								$500	$850	$2,250
Auctions: $18,800, PF-67Cam, November 2013; $4,818, PF-67, October 2015; $3,290, PF-66, October 2015; $445, PF-53, September 2014													
1869-S	76,000	33	36.4	15%	$175	$250	$425	$650	$1,250	$1,650	$4,000	$7,000	$17,500
Auctions: $9,988, MS-64, October 2015; $564, VF-25, July 2015; $400, F-15, August 2015; $447, F-12, February 2015													
1870	86,400	33	50.8	36%	$65	$100	$150	$250	$450	$550	$1,000	$1,750	$5,000
Auctions: $8,813, MS-66, May 2015; $382, EF-45, November 2014; $306, EF-45, April 2015; $212, EF-40, May 2015													
1870, Proof	1,000	163	63.5								$500	$850	$2,250
Auctions: $6,169, PF-67, October 2014; $3,290, PF-66, January 2015; $1,087, PF-64, January 2015; $1,763, PF-63, January 2015													
1870-CC	8,340	25	24.7	0%	$11,000	$13,500	$20,000	$27,500	$45,000	$85,000	$225,000		
Auctions: $188,000, AU-55, May 2015; $70,500, AU-53, January 2014; $35,250, EF-45, August 2015; $10,281, VG-8, August 2015													
1871	118,200	47	51.9	53%	$50	$75	$125	$175	$325	$450	$750	$1,500	$7,000
Auctions: $32,900, MS-67, June 2014; $6,484, MS-65, October 2015; $1,175, MS-63, June 2015; $259, AU-50, May 2015													
1871, Proof	960	148	63.6								$500	$850	$2,250
Auctions: $15,275, PF-68, May 2015; $4,706, PF-67, October 2015; $3,055, PF-66, August 2015; $2,820, PF-66, January 2015													
1871-CC	10,890	14	23.4	7%	$8,000	$12,500	$16,500	$25,000	$37,500	$75,000	$135,000	$150,000	$350,000
Auctions: $352,500, MS-65, June 2014; $79,313, AU-55, October 2015; $14,100, F-12, August 2015; $11,163, VG-8, August 2015													
1871-S	30,900	26	51.7	54%	$900	$1,200	$1,800	$2,250	$3,750	$4,500	$6,750	$10,000	$20,000
Auctions: $17,625, MS-65, October 2015; $4,406, AU-58, March 2015; $2,115, VF-25, August 2015; $2,527, F-12, September 2015													
1872	182,000	60	51.2	42%	$65	$100	$175	$250	$450	$750	$1,350	$2,500	$7,500
Auctions: $6,025, MS-65, August 2015; $2,820, MS-64, February 2015; $2,115, MS-63, August 2015; $541, AU-58, August 2015													
1872, Proof	950	180	64.0								$500	$850	$2,000
Auctions: $6,756, PF-67Cam, October 2015; $2,820, PF-66, June 2015; $2,585, PF-65Cam, March 2015; $1,528, PF-65, January 2015													
1872-CC	22,850	30	19.9	3%	$2,000	$3,000	$4,500	$8,500	$15,000	$20,000	$55,000		
Auctions: $3,567, F-15, August 2015; $1,410, F-12, July 2015; $1,645, G-6, August 2015; $1,087, Fair-2, June 2015													
1872-S	83,000	21	41.4	43%	$1,800	$2,100	$2,500	$3,500	$4,250	$6,500	$9,000	$13,000	$36,000
Auctions: $10,575, MS-63, October 2015; $8,225, AU-55, June 2015; $4,700, F-15, August 2015; $3,995, F-15, August 2015													

† Ranked in the *100 Greatest U.S. Coins* (fourth edition). **p.** The unique 1866, Proof, quarter dollar without motto (as well as the half dollar and dollar of the same design) is not mentioned in the Mint director's report. "Not a pattern, but a muling created at a later date as a numismatic rarity" (*United States Pattern Coins*, tenth edition). Saul Teichman dates its creation to the 1870s. It is classified as Judd-536.

1873, Variety 4, Close 3   **1873, Variety 4, Open 3**

	Mintage	Cert	Avg	%MS	G-4	VG-8	F-12	VF-20	EF-40	AU-50	MS-60	MS-63	MS-65
											PF-60	PF-63	PF-65
1873, Variety 4, Close 3	40,000	15	32.4	20%	$375	$600	$900	$1,300	$3,500	$4,500	$18,000	$35,000	
	Auctions: $9,988, AU-58, April 2014												
1873, Variety 4, Open 3	172,000	38	54.7	58%	$30	$45	$65	$125	$200	$300	$500	$1,100	$5,500
	Auctions: $7,638, MS-66, May 2015; $3,290, MS-64, February 2015; $1,939, MS-64, June 2015; $1,763, MS-63, June 2015												
1873, Variety 4, Proof	600	169	63.6								$500	$850	$2,000
	Auctions: $11,750, PF-67Cam, August 2015; $5,170, PF-67Cam, July 2015; $4,700, PF-66Cam, October 2015; $1,880, PF-65, June 2015												
1873-CC, Variety 4 † (q)	4,000	21	22.0	5%			—	$125,000	$150,000	$200,000	$400,000		
	Auctions: $431,250, MS-63, January 2009; $376,000, MS-63, May 2015												
1873, Variety 5	1,271,200	260	54.6	45%	$25	$30	$40	$60	$225	$425	$850	$1,650	$4,000
	Auctions: $176,250, MS-64, May 2015; $76,375, AU-55, October 2015; $18,800, EF-45, August 2015; $4,465, G-6, July 2015												
1873, Variety 5, Proof	540	149	63.8								$900	$1,350	$5,500
	Auctions: $14,100, PF-67, October 2015; $5,405, PF-66, September 2015; $2,820, PF-64Cam, January 2015; $2,585, PF-64, June 2015												
1873-CC, Variety 5	12,462	3	56.7	67%	$5,000	$9,000	$12,500	$17,000	$25,000	$45,000	$85,000	$125,000	
	Auctions: $176,250, MS-64, May 2015; $76,375, AU-55, October 2015; $4,465, G-6, July 2015; $4,818, G-4, August 2015												
1873-S, Variety 5	156,000	66	49.8	35%	$100	$125	$175	$250	$450	$650	$1,750	$4,500	$17,500
	Auctions: $18,800, MS-65, May 2015; $13,513, MS-65, October 2015; $11,163, MS-65, October 2015; $5,640, MS-64, October 2015												
1874	471,200	104	55.8	51%	$25	$30	$40	$65	$200	$450	$850	$1,350	$3,500
	Auctions: $5,875, MS-66, November 2014; $1,528, MS-63, August 2014; $564, AU-58, May 2015; $89, EF-40, September 2015												
1874, Proof	700	252	64.0								$900	$1,350	$5,500
	Auctions: $17,625, PF-67, May 2015; $7,050, PF-66, October 2015; $2,233, PF-64, February 2015; $1,998, PF-64, March 2015												
1874-S	392,000	156	60.2	77%	$25	$35	$65	$100	$265	$485	$850	$1,350	$3,500
	Auctions: $18,800, MS-67, June 2015; $9,988, MS-67, October 2015; $4,465, MS-66, October 2015; $3,525, MS-65, June 2015												
1875	4,292,800	343	58.2	66%	$25	$30	$35	$45	$65	$160	$275	$550	$1,750
	Auctions: $2,233, MS-66, October 2015; $1,528, MS-65, January 2015; $494, MS-63, September 2015; $376, MS-62, August 2015												
1875, Proof	700	165	63.8								$475	$800	$1,500
	Auctions: $9,988, PF-68Cam, January 2015; $8,225, PF-67Cam, October 2015; $1,800, PF-65Cam, January 2015; $1,116, PF-64Cam, July 2015												
1875-CC	140,000	56	47.9	34%	$175	$300	$600	$750	$1,250	$2,000	$3,750	$7,500	$25,000
	Auctions: $49,350, MS-66, February 2015; $30,550, MS-65, August 2015; $2,064, AU-55, August 2015; $1,311, EF-40, August 2016												
1875-S	680,000	103	55.6	58%	$30	$40	$70	$115	$200	$275	$600	$1,000	$3,500
	Auctions: $6,580, MS-66, January 2015; $3,055, MS-65, October 2014; $68, EF-40, November 2014; $165, VF-35, May 2015												
1876	17,816,000	604	56.7	62%	$25	$30	$35	$45	$65	$160	$275	$550	$1,600
	Auctions: $10,575, MS-67, May 2015; $8,225, MS-67, September 2015; $3,290, MS-66, October 2015; $999, MS-65, October 2015												
1876, Proof	1,150	224	63.8								$475	$800	$1,500
	Auctions: $32,900, PF-68, May 2015; $10,281, PF-68, October 2015; $2,585, PF-66, January 2015; $1,645, PF-65Cam, July 2015												
1876-CC	4,944,000	394	47.4	41%	$50	$85	$125	$150	$200	$300	$600	$1,100	$4,500
	Auctions: $9,400, MS-66, May 2015; $3,672, MS-65, August 2015; $646, MS-63, August 2015; $517, MS-62, September 2015												
1876-S	8,596,000	308	59.4	71%	$25	$30	$35	$45	$65	$160	$275	$550	$1,800
	Auctions: $5,640, MS-66, May 2015; $4,230, MS-66, August 2015; $1,645, MS-65, August 2015; $541, MS-62, March 2015												

† Ranked in the *100 Greatest U.S. Coins* (fourth edition). **q.** 6 examples are known.

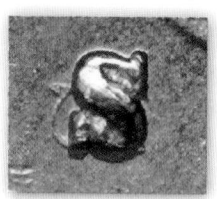

**1877-S, S Over
Horizontal S**
FS-25-1877S-501.

	Mintage	Cert	Avg	%MS	G-4	VG-8	F-12	VF-20	EF-40	AU-50	MS-60	MS-63	MS-65
											PF-60	PF-63	PF-65
1877	10,911,200	429	59.8	75%	$25	$30	$35	$45	$65	$160	$275	$550	$1,300
	Auctions: $3,055, MS-67, July 2015; $2,938, MS-67, September 2015; $2,056, MS-66, September 2015; $940, MS-64, February 2015												
1877, Proof	510	147	63.9								$475	$800	$1,500
	Auctions: $22,325, PF-68Cam, May 2015; $4,700, PF-67, October 2015; $3,055, PF-66Cam, January 2015; $1,528, PF-65, January 2015												
1877-CC (r)	4,192,000	531	54.7	63%	$50	$85	$125	$150	$200	$300	$600	$1,100	$2,250
	Auctions: $15,289, MS-67, July 2015; $5,640, MS-66, October 2015; $3,525, MS-66, July 2015; $1,410, MS-64, July 2015												
1877-S	8,996,000	383	58.6	71%	$25	$30	$35	$45	$65	$160	$275	$550	$1,300
	Auctions: $3,055, MS-67, October 2015; $1,528, MS-66, October 2015; $1,293, MS-65, October 2015; $705, MS-64, October 2015												
1877-S, S Over Horizontal S (s)	(t)	47	58.9	60%	$30	$45	$85	$175	$225	$500	$850	$2,000	$4,000
	Auctions: $23,500, MS-66, June 2014; $1,645, MS-63, July 2014; $217, EF-45, November 2014												
1878	2,260,000	118	56.2	64%	$25	$30	$35	$45	$65	$160	$275	$550	$2,250
	Auctions: $3,055, MS-66, October 2015; $2,585, MS-66, August 2015; $2,233, MS-65, June 2015; $1,763, MS-65, October 2015												
1878, Proof	800	204	63.6								$475	$800	$1,500
	Auctions: $21,150, PF-68, May 2015; $3,525, PF-67, October 2015; $3,525, PF-66Cam, August 2015; $3,760, PF-66, January 2015												
1878-CC	996,000	274	54.7	61%	$55	$75	$85	$125	$200	$375	$1,000	$1,500	$4,000
	Auctions: $823, MS-62, September 2015; $306, AU-50, August 2015; $235, AU-50, October 2015; $282, EF-40, April 2015												
1878-S	140,000	32	52.0	56%	$200	$325	$500	$850	$1,150	$1,500	$2,750	$6,500	$15,000
	Auctions: $14,100, MS-65, January 2015; $1,528, AU-50, June 2015; $882, EF-40, August 2015; $823, VF-30, July 2015												
1879	13,600	216	63.3	92%	$150	$200	$275	$350	$475	$550	$675	$850	$2,100
	Auctions: $23,500, MS-68, May 2015; $4,700, MS-67, May 2015; $1,998, MS-66, September 2015; $1,410, MS-65, January 2015												
1879, Proof	1,100	305	63.9								$475	$800	$1,500
	Auctions: $3,995, PF-67, August 2015; $3,525, PF-67, May 2015; $1,821, PF-66, January 2015; $1,294, PF-65, January 2015												
1880	13,600	134	62.8	88%	$150	$200	$275	$325	$450	$550	$675	$850	$2,250
	Auctions: $4,935, MS-67, October 2015; $3,525, MS-67, October 2015; $2,115, MS-66, July 2015; $1,293, MS-64, March 2015												
1880, Proof	1,355	381	64.3								$475	$800	$1,500
	Auctions: $21,150, PF-68, May 2015; $7,638, PF-68, January 2015; $3,055, PF-67, October 2015; $2,585, PF-66Cam, January 2015												
1881	12,000	104	59.5	82%	$150	$200	$275	$325	$450	$550	$675	$850	$2,100
	Auctions: $4,465, MS-67, October 2015; $2,350, MS-66, October 2015; $494, MS-60, May 2015; $447, VF-20, August 2015												
1881, Proof	975	294	64.3								$475	$800	$1,500
	Auctions: $7,638, PF-68Cam, January 2015; $8,225, PF-68, October 2015; $2,350, PF-66Cam, January 2015; $1,880, PF-66, June 2015												
1882	15,200	78	60.0	82%	$150	$200	$275	$325	$450	$550	$675	$850	$2,100
	Auctions: $19,975, MS-68, September 2015; $14,100, MS-68, May 2015; $646, AU-50, August 2015; $517, EF-45, August 2015												
1882, Proof	1,100	301	64.2								$475	$800	$1,500
	Auctions: $18,800, PF-68Cam, May 2015; $9,400, PF-67DCam, February 2015; $4,465, PF-67, October 2015; $6,463, PF-66DCam, August 2015												
1883	14,400	84	58.7	85%	$150	$200	$275	$325	$450	$550	$675	$850	$2,400
	Auctions: $4,700, MS-66, October 2015; $2,820, MS-66, June 2015; $2,350, MS-65, July 2015; $1,236, MS-64, July 2015												
1883, Proof	1,039	355	64.2								$475	$800	$1,500
	Auctions: $8,225, PF-68, October 2015; $7,638, PF-67, May 2015; $2,350, PF-66Cam, September 2015; $1,645, PF-65, January 2015												

r. The 1877-CC quarter with fine edge-reeding is scarcer than that with normally spaced reeding; in the marketplace, there is no price differential. **s.** This variety, known since the 1950s, was caused by an initial S mintmark being punched into the die horizontally, and then corrected with an upright S mintmark. **t.** Included in 1877-S mintage figure.

	Mintage	Cert	Avg	%MS	G-4	VG-8	F-12	VF-20	EF-40	AU-50	MS-60 / PF-60	MS-63 / PF-63	MS-65 / PF-65
1884	8,000	100	57.4	78%	$210	$250	$325	$360	$480	$550	$675	$850	$2,100
Auctions: $8,519, MS-67, June 2015; $3,290, MS-66, October 2015; $881, AU-53, August 2015; $564, VF-35, August 2015													
1884, Proof	875	282	64.5								$475	$800	$1,500
Auctions: $3,643, PF-67, October 2015; $2,115, PF-66, July 2015; $1,800, PF-66, June 2015; $2,115, PF-65, March 2015													
1885	13,600	83	60.0	77%	$150	$200	$250	$300	$425	$550	$675	$875	$2,400
Auctions: $6,756, MS-67, May 2015; $3,055, MS-66, August 2015; $3,290, MS-65, October 2015; $705, MS-62, October 2015													
1885, Proof	930	267	64.3								$475	$800	$1,500
Auctions: $5,881, PF-67Cam, June 2015; $4,700, PF-67, October 2015; $2,820, PF-67, January 2015; $1,998, PF-66Cam, January 2015													
1886	5,000	42	57.4	76%	$275	$350	$450	$550	$750	$900	$1,000	$1,250	$2,600
Auctions: $6,169, MS-66, August 2015; $2,115, MS-65, October 2015; $1,410, MS-64, June 2015; $1,116, VF-30, August 2015													
1886, Proof	886	293	64.5								$475	$800	$1,500
Auctions: $11,750, PF-68, May 2015; $12,925, PF-67Cam, October 2015; $21,150, PF-67, August 2015; $4,230, PF-66Cam, March 2015													
1887	10,000	101	61.7	85%	$180	$240	$300	$400	$450	$550	$900	$1,150	$2,500
Auctions: $4,935, MS-67, October 2015; $2,585, MS-66, October 2015; $2,295, MS-66, January 2015; $999, MS-62, August 2015													
1887, Proof	710	232	64.4								$475	$800	$1,500
Auctions: $7,638, PF-68, January 2015; $3,760, PF-67, October 2015; $2,350, PF-66Cam, January 2015; $1,880, PF-66, August 2015													
1888	10,001	130	63.2	94%	$180	$240	$300	$400	$450	$550	$700	$900	$1,600
Auctions: $5,640, MS-67, May 2015; $3,760, MS-67, October 2015; $2,350, MS-66, January 2015; $1,351, MS-65, January 2015													
1888, Proof	832	224	64.1								$475	$800	$1,500
Auctions: $3,525, PF-67, January 2015; $3,055, PF-66Cam, August 2015; $1,528, PF-65, January 2015; $282, PF-60, August 2015													
1888-S	1,216,000	148	56.4	67%	$25	$30	$35	$45	$70	$200	$360	$750	$3,000
Auctions: $7,638, MS-66, May 2015; $6,463, MS-66, October 2015; $3,525, MS-65, September 2015; $1,528, MS-64, June 2015													
1889	12,000	177	62.7	89%	$150	$200	$275	$350	$400	$480	$600	$750	$1,950
Auctions: $4,700, MS-67, January 2015; $3,525, MS-66, October 2015; $1,880, MS-65, January 2015; $1,116, MS-64, June 2015													
1889, Proof	711	193	64.5								$475	$800	$1,500
Auctions: $15,275, PF-68, May 2015; $8,519, PF-68, October 2015; $1,880, PF-66, January 2015; $1,645, PF-65Cam, January 2015													
1890	80,000	189	62.4	86%	$120	$150	$180	$240	$275	$325	$480	$900	$1,400
Auctions: $10,589, MS-68, June 2015; $3,995, MS-67, January 2015; $2,233, MS-66, October 2015; $2,350, MS-65, October 2015													
1890, Proof	590	231	64.8								$475	$800	$1,500
Auctions: $4,700, PF-67Cam, September 2015; $3,643, PF-66Cam, January 2015; $1,500, PF-65, June 2015; $1,410, PF-64, August 2015													
1891	3,920,000	671	60.4	76%	$25	$30	$35	$45	$65	$160	$260	$550	$1,800
Auctions: $4,230, MS-67, May 2015; $1,998, MS-65, June 2015; $1,763, MS-66, September 2015; $1,645, MS-66, January 2015													
1891, Proof	600	236	64.6								$475	$800	$1,500
Auctions: $15,275, PF-67, October 2015; $3,760, PF-67, October 2015; $2,820, PF-66, January 2015; $1,528, PF-64Cam, October 2015													
1891-O	68,000	39	40.2	38%	$350	$550	$1,000	$1,350	$2,250	$3,500	$6,500	$12,500	$30,000
Auctions: $28,200, MS-65, May 2015; $22,325, MS-65, January 2015; $14,100, MS-63, August 2015; $852, VG-10, July 2015													
1891-S	2,216,000	198	58.8	71%	$25	$30	$35	$45	$70	$160	$260	$550	$2,000
Auctions: $3,055, MS-66, May 2015; $1,645, MS-65, October 2015; $823, MS-64, October 2015; $564, MS-63, June 2015													

BARBER OR LIBERTY HEAD (1892–1916)

Designer: *Charles E. Barber.* **Weight:** *6.25 grams.*
Composition: *.900 silver, .100 copper (net weight .18084 oz. pure silver).*
Diameter: *24.3 mm.* **Edge:** *Reeded.* **Mints:** *Philadelphia, Denver, New Orleans, and San Francisco.*

Circulation Strike

Mintmark location is on the reverse, below the eagle.

Proof

History. The Liberty Head design was by Charles E. Barber, chief engraver of the U.S. Mint. Barber quarters feature the same obverse motif used on dimes and half dollars of the era, with the designer's initial, B, found at the truncation of the neck of Miss Liberty. The reverse depicts a heraldic eagle holding an olive branch in one talon and arrows in the other, along with a ribbon reading E PLURIBUS UNUM.

Striking and Sharpness. On the obverse, check the hair details and other features. On the reverse, the eagle's leg at the lower right and the arrows can be weak. Also check the upper–right portion of the shield and the nearby wing. Once these coins entered circulation and acquired wear, the word LIBERTY on the headband tended to disappear quickly. Most Proofs are sharply struck, although more than just a few are weak on the eagle's leg at the lower right and on certain parts of the arrows. The Proofs of 1892 to 1901 usually have cameo contrast between the designs and the mirror fields. Later Proofs vary in their contrast.

Availability. Barber quarters in Fine or better grade are scarce. Today, among circulation strikes, 90% or more in existence are G-4 or below. MS coins are available of all dates and mints, but some are very elusive. The 1896-S, 1901-S, and 1913-S are the key dates in all grades. Proofs exist in proportion to their mintages. Choicer examples tend to be of later dates.

Grading Standards

MS-60 to 70 (Mint State). *Obverse:* At MS-60, some abrasion and contact marks are evident, most noticeably on the cheek and the obverse field to the right. Luster is present, but may be dull or lifeless. Many Barber coins have been cleaned, especially of the earlier dates. At MS-63, contact marks are very few. Abrasion still is evident, but less than at lower levels. Indeed, the cheek of Miss Liberty virtually showcases abrasion. An MS-65 coin

1896-S. Graded MS-65.

may have minor abrasion, but contact marks are so minute as to require magnification. Luster should be full and rich. *Reverse:* Comments apply as for the obverse, except that in lower Mint State grades abrasion and contact marks are most noticeable on the head and tail of the eagle and on the tips of the wings. At MS-65 or higher, there are no marks visible to the unaided eye. The field is mainly protected by design elements, and often appears to grade a point or two higher than the obverse.

Illustrated coin: This brilliant coin shows full satin luster.

AU-50, 53, 55, 58 (About Uncirculated). *Obverse:* Light wear is seen on the head, especially on the forward hair under LIBERTY. At AU-58, the luster is extensive but incomplete, especially on the higher parts and in the right field. At AU–50 and 53, luster is less. *Reverse:* Wear is evident on the head and tail of the eagle and on the tips of the wings. At AU–50 and 53, there still is significant luster. An AU-58 coin (as determined by the obverse) can have the reverse appear to be full Mint State.

1911-D. Graded AU-50.

EF-40, 45 (Extremely Fine). *Obverse:* Further wear is seen on the head. The hair above the forehead lacks most detail. LIBERTY shows wear, but still is strong. *Reverse:* Further wear is seen on the head and tail of the eagle and on the tips of the wings, most evident at the left and right extremes of the wings. At this level and below, sharpness of strike on the reverse is not important.

Illustrated coin: Note the subtle lilac and gold toning.

1913-S. Graded EF-40.

VF-20, 30 (Very Fine). *Obverse:* The head shows more wear, now with nearly all detail gone in the hair above the forehead. LIBERTY shows wear, but is complete. The leaves on the head all show wear, as does the upper part of the cap. *Reverse:* Wear is more extensive, particularly noticeable on the outer parts of the wings, the head, the shield, and the tail.

Illustrated coin: The dig and discoloration in Liberty's cheek decrease the appeal of this example.

1896-S. Graded VF-20.

F-12, 15 (Fine). *Obverse:* The head shows extensive wear. LIBERTY, the key place to check, is weak, especially at ER, but is fully readable. The ANA grading standards and *Photograde* adhere to this. PCGS suggests that lightly struck coins "may have letters partially missing." Traditionally, collectors insist on full LIBERTY. *Reverse:* More wear is seen on the reverse in the places as above. E PLURIBUS UNUM is light, with one to several letters worn away.

1913-S. Graded F-15.

VG-8, 10 (Very Good). *Obverse:* A net of three letters in LIBERTY must be readable. Traditionally, LI is clear, and after that there is a partial letter or two. *Reverse:* Further wear has smoothed more than half of the feathers in the wing. The shield is indistinct except for a few traces of interior lines. The motto is partially worn away. The rim is full, and many if not most denticles can be seen.

1914-S. Graded VG-10.

G-4, 6 (Good). *Obverse:* The head is in outline form, with the center flat. Most of the rim is there. All letters and the date are full. *Reverse:* The eagle shows only a few feathers, and only a few scattered letters remain in the motto. The rim may be worn flat in some or all of the area, but the peripheral lettering is clear.

1913-S. Graded G-4.

AG-3 (About Good). *Obverse:* The stars and motto are worn, and the border may be indistinct. Distinctness varies at this level. The date is clear. Grading is usually determined by the reverse. *Reverse:* The rim is gone and the letters are partially worn away. The eagle is mostly flat, perhaps with a few hints of feathers.

1901-S. Graded AG-3.

PF-60 to 70 (Proof). *Obverse and Reverse:* Proofs that are extensively cleaned and have many hairlines, or that are dull and grainy, are lower level, such as PF–60 to 62. These are not widely desired by collectors. With medium hairlines and good reflectivity, an assigned grade of PF-64 is appropriate. Tiny horizontal lines on Miss Liberty's cheek, known as slide marks, from National and other album slides scuffing the relief of the cheek, are endemic on all Barber silver coins. With noticeable marks of this type, the highest grade assignable is PF-64. With relatively few hairlines, a rating of PF-65 can be given. PF-66 should have hairlines so delicate that magnification is needed to see them. Above that, a Proof should be free of any hairlines or other problems.

1913. Graded PF-68 Cameo.

Illustrated coin: Exceptional fields offset the bright devices to high advantage.

1892, Variety 1 Reverse   **1892, Variety 2 Reverse**
Note position of wing tip relative to E in UNITED.

Coins designated Deep Cameo or Ultra Cameo bring a premium of 50% to 100% above listed values.

	Mintage	Cert	Avg	%MS	G-4	VG-8	F-12	VF-20	EF-40	AU-50	MS-60 PF-60	MS-63 PF-63	MS-65 PF-65
1892 (a)	8,236,000	1,742	60.3	72%	$10	$12	$26	$45	$75	$130	$250	$375	$800
Auctions: $9,988, MS-68, January 2015; $2,820, MS-67, July 2015; $1,528, MS-66, August 2015; $1,058, MS-65, August 2015													
1892, Proof	1,245	396	64.7								$385	$700	$1,400
Auctions: $2,820, PF-65DCam, April 2015; $940, PF-64Cam, January 2015; $2,468, PF-64, August 2015; $560, PF-63, September 2015													
1892-O	2,460,000	441	59.2	67%	$15	$20	$45	$60	$95	$160	$275	$400	$1,200
Auctions: $14,100, MS-68, October 2015; $9,106, MS-67, October 2015; $3,055, MS-66, August 2015; $1,645, MS-65, August 2015													
1892-S	964,079	134	48.0	49%	$30	$50	$80	$130	$200	$300	$475	$1,150	$4,000
Auctions: $14,100, MS-66, January 2015; $3,055, MS-65, July 2015; $940, AU-58, June 2016; $447, AU-55, October 2015													
1893	5,444,023	330	57.7	68%	$10	$12	$26	$45	$75	$130	$235	$340	$1,000
Auctions: $1,058, MS-65, January 2015; $470, MS-64, October 2015; $259, MS-61, May 2015; $165, MS-60, May 2015													
1893, Proof	792	299	65.0								$385	$700	$1,400
Auctions: $8,813, PF-68, September 2015; $5,170, PF-67Cam, January 2015; $2,115, PF-66Cam, January 2015; $1,528, PF-65Cam, February 2015													
1893-O	3,396,000	215	56.6	61%	$10	$14	$30	$60	$110	$170	$275	$400	$1,500
Auctions: $8,225, MS-67, October 2015; $2,938, MS-66, February 2015; $1,412, MS-65, January 2015; $517, MS-64, September 2015													
1893-S	1,454,535	103	49.2	57%	$20	$35	$60	$110	$175	$300	$425	$900	$5,000
Auctions: $20,563, MS-67, October 2015; $4,700, MS-66, August 2015; $7,638, MS-65, September 2015; $223, EF-45, May 2015													
1894	3,432,000	188	57.4	71%	$10	$12	$35	$50	$95	$150	$240	$350	$1,050
Auctions: $3,760, MS-66, May 2015; $1,116, MS-65, June 2015; $60, EF-40, May 2015													
1894, Proof	972	338	64.7								$385	$700	$1,400
Auctions: $8,225, PF-68, May 2015; $3,055, PF-67, January 2015; $2,585, PF-66Cam, October 2015; $1,450, PF-65, January 2015													
1894-O	2,852,000	156	54.8	65%	$10	$20	$45	$70	$130	$230	$325	$525	$1,800
Auctions: $11,163, MS-67, May 2015; $9,988, MS-66, October 2015; $1,763, MS-65, January 2015; $259, AU-55, May 2015													
1894-S	2,648,821	209	58.0	72%	$10	$15	$40	$60	$120	$210	$325	$525	$1,800
Auctions: $17,625, MS-67, May 2015; $1,410, MS-65, January 2015; $2,820, MS-64, October 2015; $588, MS-62, August 2015													
1895	4,440,000	237	55.4	68%	$10	$14	$30	$45	$80	$140	$250	$450	$1,250
Auctions: $2,820, MS-66, October 2015; $1,175, MS-65, January 2015; $1,651, MS-64, March 2015; $411, MS-63, May 2015													
1895, Proof	880	274	65.0								$385	$700	$1,400
Auctions: $9,988, PF-68Cam, January 2015; $4,935, PF-67Cam, October 2015; $3,761, PF-66, March 2015; $588, PF-63, July 2015													
1895-O	2,816,000	125	52.1	55%	$12	$20	$50	$70	$140	$230	$400	$900	$2,000
Auctions: $1,528, MS-65, January 2015; $423, AU-58, May 2015; $470, AU-55, February 2015; $69, EF-40, May 2015													
1895-S	1,764,681	121	46.9	46%	$20	$32	$70	$120	$170	$275	$420	$900	$2,500
Auctions: $8,225, MS-68, January 2015; $2,585, MS-64, August 2015; $823, MS-63, August 2015; $705, MS-62, January 2015													
1896	3,874,000	209	56.2	74%	$10	$14	$30	$45	$80	$135	$250	$325	$875
Auctions: $3,760, MS-66, February 2015; $764, MS-65, June 2015; $541, MS-64, October 2015; $165, AU-55, May 2015													
1896, Proof	762	325	65.4								$385	$700	$1,400
Auctions: $8,225, PF-68Cam, February 2015; $4,465, PF-67Cam, January 2015; $1,645, PF-66, January 2015; $1,061, PF-64Cam, January 2015													
1896-O	1,484,000	182	33.2	29%	$55	$85	$200	$320	$550	$800	$1,000	$1,500	$6,000
Auctions: $9,988, MS-66, January 2015; $2,820, MS-64, July 2016; $1,410, MS-63, September 2015; $999, MS-62, August 2015													
1896-S	188,039	482	11.8	7%	$700	$1,500	$2,400	$4,000	$5,250	$7,000	$10,000	$14,500	$42,500
Auctions: $70,500, MS-65, November 2016; $17,038, MS-64, July 2016; $1,998, F-12, February 2015; $1,175, VG-10, September 2015													

a. There are two varieties of the 1892 reverse. Variety 1: the eagle's wing covers only half of the E in UNITED; Variety 2: the eagle's wing covers most of the E. Coins of Variety 1 are somewhat scarcer.

	Mintage	Cert	Avg	%MS	G-4	VG-8	F-12	VF-20	EF-40	AU-50	MS-60	MS-63	MS-65
											PF-60	PF-63	PF-65
1897	8,140,000	298	55.7	67%	$9	$14	$26	$40	$70	$120	$240	$350	$800
Auctions: $5,640, MS-67, May 2015; $2,350, MS-66, September 2015; $329, MS-62, January 2015; $79, EF-45, June 2015													
1897, Proof	731	272	64.8								$385	$700	$1,400
Auctions: $9,988, PF-68Cam, August 2015; $9,988, PF-68, May 2015; $1,410, PF-65Cam, February 2015; $881, PF-64, February 2015													
1897-O	1,414,800	144	33.1	29%	$40	$65	$180	$340	$385	$600	$850	$1,750	$3,000
Auctions: $14,100, MS-67, May 2015; $20,563, MS-66, October 2015; $3,055, MS-65, August 2015; $2,115, MS-64, March 2015													
1897-S	542,229	200	25.6	22%	$120	$150	$300	$550	$825	$1,000	$1,600	$1,800	$6,500
Auctions: $21,150, MS-67, October 2015; $20,563, MS-66, October 2015; $6,463, MS-65, August 2016; $1,998, AU-58, January 2015													
1898	11,100,000	388	52.4	60%	$9	$10	$26	$45	$70	$125	$225	$350	$800
Auctions: $4,700, MS-67, October 2015; $1,763, MS-66, October 2015; $764, MS-65, January 2015; $705, MS-64, August 2015													
1898, Proof	735	319	65.6								$385	$700	$1,400
Auctions: $23,500, PF-69Cam, October 2015; $4,700, PF-67DCam, January 2015; $2,233, PF-66, October 2015; $1,469, PF-65, March 2015													
1898-O	1,868,000	89	45.8	46%	$15	$28	$70	$140	$300	$390	$625	$1,500	$6,000
Auctions: $11,750, MS-66, January 2015; $764, AU-58, January 2015; $329, AU-50, January 2015; $212, EF-45, July 2015													
1898-S	1,020,592	78	51.3	49%	$11	$25	$40	$55	$100	$200	$400	$1,400	$6,500
Auctions: $7,050, MS-65, June 2015; $4,935, MS-64, August 2015; $881, AU-58, January 2015; $541, AU-55, July 2015													
1899	12,624,000	408	50.5	56%	$9	$10	$26	$45	$75	$125	$240	$375	$800
Auctions: $1,293, MS-66, January 2015; $823, MS-65, January 2015; $188, AU-58, September 2015; $165, AU-55, February 2015													
1899, Proof	846	195	64.9								$385	$700	$1,400
Auctions: $5,876, PF-67Cam, July 2015; $1,998, PF-66Cam, August 2015; $494, PF-62, August 2015													
1899-O	2,644,000	108	55.2	58%	$11	$18	$35	$70	$120	$260	$400	$900	$2,750
Auctions: $12,925, MS-67, August 2015; $4,818, MS-66, October 2015; $2,820, MS-65, January 2015; $1,058, MS-64, June 2015													
1899-S	708,000	59	53.3	47%	$27	$40	$95	$110	$140	$270	$425	$1,500	$4,500
Auctions: $9,988, MS-67, June 2015; $940, AU-58, January 2015; $329, AU-55, January 2015; $376, AU-53, May 2015													
1900	10,016,000	308	56.8	71%	$9	$10	$26	$45	$75	$125	$240	$375	$1,200
Auctions: $10,575, MS-67, May 2015; $1,184, MS-65, January 2015; $588, MS-64, July 2015; $317, MS-63, October 2015													
1900, Proof	912	267	64.8								$385	$700	$1,400
Auctions: $7,344, PF-68, May 2015; $3,290, PF-67Cam, October 2015; $2,585, PF-66Cam, January 2015; $1,293, PF-65, January 2015													
1900-O	3,416,000	115	51.1	55%	$12	$26	$65	$110	$150	$310	$525	$750	$3,250
Auctions: $17,626, MS-68, May 2015; $12,925, MS-67, October 2015; $7,050, MS-66, August 2015; $2,350, MS-65, June 2015													
1900-S	1,858,585	132	52.5	31%	$10	$15	$35	$55	$80	$130	$350	$1,000	$3,000
Auctions: $10,575, MS-67, May 2015; $6,169, MS-66, August 2015; $341, MS-61, May 2015; $259, AU-58, January 2015													
1901	8,892,000	342	46.7	54%	$9	$10	$26	$45	$80	$135	$240	$375	$900
Auctions: $2,115, MS-66, October 2015; $940, MS-65, January 2015; $423, MS-64, May 2015; $329, MS-63, May 2015													
1901, Proof	813	255	64.9								$385	$700	$1,400
Auctions: $5,875, PF-68, July 2015; $3,995, PF-67, October 2015; $1,528, PF-66, March 2015; $1,293, PF-65, January 2015													
1901-O	1,612,000	87	31.0	21%	$40	$60	$140	$275	$550	$750	$950	$2,250	$6,750
Auctions: $2,585, MS-63, January 2015; $940, AU-50, July 2015; $705, EF-40, June 2015; $212, F-15, February 2015													
1901-S	72,664	343	8.3	4%	$4,250	$8,000	$12,500	$16,500	$20,000	$30,000	$38,000	$45,000	$75,000
Auctions: $70,500, MS-65, November 2016; $22,325, VF-25, August 2016; $12,925, F-12, July 2016; $7,638, VG-8, January 2015													
1902	12,196,967	330	53.0	56%	$9	$10	$26	$45	$65	$120	$240	$375	$800
Auctions: $7,638, MS-67, May 2015; $2,233, MS-66, October 2015; $999, MS-65, January 2015; $656, MS-64, June 2015													
1902, Proof	777	230	64.3								$385	$700	$1,400
Auctions: $2,820, PF-67, October 2015; $3,055, PF-66, October 2015; $1,410, PF-66, January 2015; $646, PF-63, January 2015													
1902-O	4,748,000	110	49.7	43%	$10	$16	$50	$85	$140	$225	$475	$1,000	$3,000
Auctions: $28,200, MS-68, May 2015; $7,050, MS-66, October 2015; $1,763, MS-64, August 2015; $823, MS-63, July 2015													
1902-S	1,524,612	111	53.1	53%	$14	$22	$55	$90	$160	$240	$500	$700	$3,000
Auctions: $3,995, MS-66, August 2015; $2,233, MS-65, January 2015; $1,410, MS-64, August 2015; $705, MS-63, September 2015													

	Mintage	Cert	Avg	%MS	G-4	VG-8	F-12	VF-20	EF-40	AU-50	MS-60	MS-63	MS-65
											PF-60	PF-63	PF-65
1903	9,759,309	142	53.6	54%	$9	$10	$26	$45	$65	$120	$240	$400	$1,650
	Auctions: $9,400, MS-66, October 2015; $423, MS-64, May 2015; $353, MS-64, November 2015; $94, AU-53, April 2015
1903, Proof	755	286	65.1								$385	$700	$1,400
	Auctions: $5,875, PF-68, May 2015; $3,290, PF-66, August 2015; $823, PF-64, February 2015; $589, PF-62, February 2015
1903-O	3,500,000	101	48.6	40%	$10	$12	$40	$60	$120	$275	$425	$900	$3,500
	Auctions: $32,900, MS-67, May 2015; $3,055, MS-65, October 2015; $176, AU-50, July 2015; $101, EF-45, November 2014
1903-S	1,036,000	85	56.6	71%	$15	$25	$45	$85	$150	$275	$425	$900	$2,000
	Auctions: $19,975, MS-67, May 2015; $4,230, MS-66, October 2015; $1,821, MS-65, September 2015; $1,000, MS-62, May 2015
1904	9,588,143	175	54.2	57%	$9	$10	$26	$45	$70	$120	$240	$375	$1,250
	Auctions: $5,170, MS-66, October 2015; $141, AU-55, August 2015; $125, AU-55, May 2015; $64, EF-40, March 2015
1904, Proof	670	264	64.7								$385	$700	$1,400
	Auctions: $5,405, PF-68, June 2015; $4,230, PF-67, January 2015; $1,528, PF-66, July 2015; $823, PF-64, October 2015
1904-O	2,456,000	143	45.5	39%	$30	$40	$85	$150	$240	$450	$700	$1,000	$4,000
	Auctions: $41,125, MS-67, June 2014
1905	4,967,523	223	46.4	52%	$30	$35	$50	$65	$70	$120	$240	$385	$950
	Auctions: $2,233, MS-66, October 2015; $1,293, MS-66, October 2015; $999, MS-65, July 2015; $353, MS-63, November 2015
1905, Proof	727	248	64.6								$385	$700	$1,400
	Auctions: $3,878, PF-67, January 2015; $3,173, PF-66, September 2015; $1,293, PF-65, February 2015; $881, PF-64, August 2015
1905-O	1,230,000	101	42.2	44%	$40	$60	$120	$220	$260	$350	$475	$1,200	$4,500
	Auctions: $11,750, MS-67, October 2015; $5,170, MS-65, September 2015; $2,585, MS-64, August 2015; $833, MS-62, January 2015
1905-S	1,884,000	121	44.0	40%	$30	$40	$75	$100	$105	$225	$350	$900	$3,500
	Auctions: $3,055, MS-65, August 2015; $1,175, MS-64, September 2015; $646, MS-62, June 2015; $84, VF-30, July 2015
1906	3,655,760	205	58.8	79%	$9	$10	$26	$45	$70	$120	$240	$375	$800
	Auctions: $2,820, MS-66, June 2014
1906, Proof	675	209	64.9								$385	$700	$1,400
	Auctions: $16,450, PF-68, May 2015; $2,233, PF-66, August 2015; $1,410, PF-65, January 2015; $1,351, PF-65, September 2015
1906-D	3,280,000	130	59.0	75%	$9	$10	$30	$50	$70	$145	$250	$425	$1,650
	Auctions: $9,400, MS-67, May 2015; $823, MS-64, January 2015; $235, AU-58, October 2015; $58, EF-40, April 2015
1906-O	2,056,000	139	60.0	77%	$9	$10	$40	$60	$100	$200	$300	$500	$1,350
	Auctions: $11,750, MS-67, October 2015; $5,640, MS-67, May 2015; $2,233, MS-66, October 2015; $1,666, MS-65, September 2015
1907	7,132,000	392	56.4	65%	$9	$10	$26	$40	$65	$120	$240	$375	$800
	Auctions: $6,463, MS-67, October 2015; $1,998, MS-66, October 2015; $705, MS-65, January 2015; $376, MS-64, May 2015
1907, Proof	575	289	65.0								$385	$700	$1,400
	Auctions: $5,170, PF-67Cam, August 2015; $2,115, PF-66, July 2015; $1,293, PF-65Cam, September 2015; $940, PF-64Cam, October 2015
1907-D	2,484,000	112	54.5	66%	$9	$10	$26	$48	$70	$175	$250	$550	$2,500
	Auctions: $1,058, MS-64, July 2015; $999, MS-64, July 2015; $150, AU-53, July 2015; $141, AU-50, May 2015
1907-O	4,560,000	200	55.2	67%	$9	$10	$26	$45	$70	$135	$275	$400	$1,700
	Auctions: $9,988, MS-68, January 2015; $10,575, MS-67, October 2015; $1,293, MS-65, August 2015; $552, MS-64, July 2015
1907-S	1,360,000	74	54.8	72%	$10	$18	$45	$70	$140	$280	$475	$900	$3,250
	Auctions: $6,463, MS-66, September 2015; $5,405, MS-66, October 2015; $3,564, MS-65, August 2015; $223, EF-45, July 2015
1908	4,232,000	243	58.4	72%	$9	$10	$26	$45	$70	$120	$240	$375	$800
	Auctions: $1,116, MS-66, January 2015; $940, MS-65, June 2015; $447, MS-64, January 2015; $329, MS-63, January 2015
1908, Proof	545	189	64.8								$385	$700	$1,400
	Auctions: $5,170, PF-67, October 2015; $1,528, PF-66, February 2015; $1,175, PF-65, June 2015; $823, PF-64, July 2015
1908-D	5,788,000	266	51.7	56%	$9	$10	$26	$45	$70	$120	$240	$375	$800
	Auctions: $2,585, MS-66, October 2015; $1,058, MS-65, August 2015; $306, MS-62, February 2015; $94, AU-50, May 2015
1908-O	6,244,000	254	53.5	68%	$9	$10	$26	$45	$65	$120	$240	$375	$800
	Auctions: $764, MS-65, October 2015; $235, MS-62, January 2015; $176, AU-58, April 2015; $112, AU-53, August 2015
1908-S	784,000	131	46.6	56%	$18	$38	$85	$165	$325	$465	$750	$1,200	$3,500
	Auctions: $7,050, MS-67, October 2015; $2,963, MS-65, January 2015; $1,763, MS-64, January 2015; $1,293, MS-63, September 2015

	Mintage	Cert	Avg	%MS	G-4	VG-8	F-12	VF-20	EF-40	AU-50	MS-60	MS-63	MS-65
											PF-60	PF-63	PF-65
1909	9,268,000	526	55.7	66%	$9	$10	$26	$45	$65	$120	$240	$375	$800
	Auctions: $3,055, MS-66, May 2015; $999, MS-65, January 2015; $494, MS-64, September 2015; $247, MS-62, May 2015												
1909, Proof	650	271	64.8								$385	$700	$1,400
	Auctions: $13,513, PF-68, May 2015; $1,704, PF-66, February 2015; $1,058, PF-64, January 2015; $719, PF-63Cam, June 2015												
1909-D	5,114,000	321	49.5	51%	$9	$10	$26	$45	$85	$150	$240	$375	$800
	Auctions: $9,400, MS-67, May 2015; $1,293, MS-66, October 2015; $2,350, MS-65, October 2015; $705, MS-64, January 2015												
1909-O	712,000	94	35.9	41%	$50	$175	$500	$1,000	$2,250	$3,500	$4,000	$5,000	$7,500
	Auctions: $21,150, MS-67, May 2015; $1,175, VF-35, February 2015; $1,116, VF-25, October 2015; $646, VF-20, December 2015												
1909-S	1,348,000	115	50.0	63%	$9	$10	$35	$55	$90	$185	$285	$725	$1,650
	Auctions: $12,925, MS-67, May 2015; $2,585, MS-66, January 2015; $1,763, MS-65, January 2015; $182, AU-55, September 2015												
1910	2,244,000	201	55.1	73%	$9	$10	$26	$45	$80	$140	$240	$375	$800
	Auctions: $1,528, MS-66, January 2015; $711, MS-65, January 2015; $676, MS-64, August 2015; $176, AU-58, June 2015												
1910, Proof	551	267	65.1								$385	$700	$1,400
	Auctions: $2,703, PF-67Cam, September 2015; $1,998, PF-65Cam, January 2015; $911, PF-64Cam, October 2015; $881, PF-64Cam, October 2015												
1910-D	1,500,000	130	53.3	61%	$10	$11	$45	$70	$125	$240	$350	$800	$1,650
	Auctions: $4,818, MS-67, October 2015; $447, MS-62, February 2015; $376, MS-61, April 2015; $212, AU-55, August 2015												
1911	3,720,000	296	58.5	73%	$9	$10	$26	$45	$70	$125	$240	$375	$800
	Auctions: $3,055, MS-66, August 2015; $764, MS-65, February 2015; $470, MS-64, January 2015; $329, MS-63, October 2015												
1911, Proof	543	236	65.3								$385	$700	$1,400
	Auctions: $7,050, PF-68Cam, February 2015; $3,290, PF-67Cam, October 2015; $2,585, PF-66Cam, October 2015; $1,704, PF-65Cam, October 2015												
1911-D	933,600	119	41.7	41%	$30	$40	$150	$300	$400	$600	$850	$1,200	$4,250
	Auctions: $4,113, MS-65, June 2015; $764, MS-62, January 2015; $705, AU-58, January 2015; $353, EF-45, April 2015												
1911-S	988,000	170	58.7	76%	$9	$10	$55	$85	$165	$280	$375	$775	$1,500
	Auctions: $2,585, MS-66, January 2015; $1,998, MS-66, October 2015; $1,880, MS-65, September 2015; $617, AU-58, January 2015												
1912	4,400,000	447	57.7	76%	$9	$10	$26	$45	$70	$120	$240	$375	$800
	Auctions: $8,225, MS-67, May 2015; $1,410, MS-66, September 2015; $823, MS-65, January 2015; $235, MS-62, February 2015												
1912, Proof	700	213	64.6								$385	$700	$1,400
	Auctions: $19,975, PF-68Cam, May 2015; $3,055, PF-67, February 2015; $2,820, PF-67, March 2015; $1,175, PF-64Cam, September 2015												
1912-S	708,000	107	52.0	64%	$20	$30	$65	$90	$125	$220	$400	$825	$1,750
	Auctions: $11,163, MS-68, May 2015; $5,875, MS-67, June 2015; $1,763, MS-65, January 2015; $1,880, MS-64, August 2015												
1913	484,000	137	45.8	47%	$22	$35	$100	$180	$400	$525	$600	$800	$2,250
	Auctions: $3,055, MS-65, October 2015; $2,585, MS-65, February 2015; $1,998, MS-65, October 2015; $588, AU-58, August 2015												
1913, Proof	613	246	64.5								$385	$700	$1,400
	Auctions: $4,230, PF-67Cam, July 2015; $1,483, PF-66, January 2015; $2,585, PF-65, August 2015; $1,175, PF-64Cam, January 2015												
1913-D	1,450,800	183	54.0	62%	$12	$15	$35	$60	$85	$175	$275	$400	$1,150
	Auctions: $6,756, MS-67, July 2015; $1,704, MS-66, October 2015; $705, MS-64, August 2015; $376, MS-63, May 2015												
1913-S	40,000	505	10.5	9%	$1,650	$2,200	$5,000	$6,500	$7,500	$10,000	$12,700	$18,000	$32,500
	Auctions: $35,250, MS-66, June 2015; $3,995, F-12, July 2015; $2,350, VG-10, September 2016; $1,351, VG-8, September 2016												
1914	6,244,230	678	55.2	66%	$9	$10	$22	$40	$65	$120	$240	$375	$800
	Auctions: $1,763, MS-66, October 2015; $823, MS-65, January 2015; $447, MS-64, June 2015; $329, MS-63, May 2015												
1914, Proof	380	203	64.8								$385	$700	$1,400
	Auctions: $7,050, PF-68, October 2014; $3,525, PF-67, October 2015; $2,938, PF-67, November 2014; $1,763, PF-66, June 2015												
1914-D	3,046,000	350	55.6	69%	$9	$10	$22	$40	$65	$120	$240	$375	$800
	Auctions: $4,700, MS-67, October 2015; $2,938, MS-66, June 2015; $676, MS-65, August 2015; $364, MS-63, August 2015												
1914-S	264,000	425	15.8	12%	$125	$180	$375	$550	$825	$975	$1,400	$1,650	$6,500
	Auctions: $6,463, MS-66, August 2016; $3,290, MS-64, January 2015; $2,468, MS-63, July 2015; $1,880, AU-58, October 2016												

	Mintage	Cert	Avg	%MS	G-4	VG-8	F-12	VF-20	EF-40	AU-50	MS-60	MS-63	MS-65
											PF-60	PF-63	PF-65
1915	3,480,000	497	55.9	72%	$9	$10	$22	$40	$65	$120	$240	$375	$800
	Auctions: $2,350, MS-66, May 2015; $881, MS-65, January 2015; $401, MS-64, August 2015; $376, MS-63, May 2015												
1915, Proof	450	175	64.3								$425	$750	$1,650
	Auctions: $15,275, PF-68, May 2015; $3,055, PF-67, January 2015; $1,234, PF-65, January 2015; $830, PF-64, June 2015												
1915-D	3,694,000	641	57.8	73%	$9	$10	$22	$40	$70	$120	$240	$375	$800
	Auctions: $4,935, MS-67, May 2015; $1,410, MS-66, August 2015; $999, MS-65, January 2015; $388, MS-64, October 2015												
1915-S	704,000	212	50.9	58%	$25	$40	$60	$85	$115	$200	$285	$425	$1,150
	Auctions: $8,225, MS-67, May 2015; $2,820, MS-66, January 2015; $2,468, MS-65, September 2015; $259, MS-62, August 2015												
1916	1,788,000	454	56.8	70%	$9	$10	$22	$40	$70	$120	$240	$375	$800
	Auctions: $3,055, MS-67, October 2015; $1,293, MS-66, August 2015; $940, MS-65, August 2015; $400, MS-64, March 2015												
1916-D	6,540,800	1,539	58.8	75%	$9	$10	$22	$40	$70	$120	$240	$375	$800
	Auctions: $3,525, MS-67, March 2015; $1,528, MS-66, January 2015; $1,058, MS-65, January 2015; $541, MS-64, January 2015												

STANDING LIBERTY (1916–1930)

Variety 1, No Stars Below Eagle (1916–1917): **Designer:** *Hermon A. MacNeil.*
Weight: *6.25 grams.* **Composition:** *.900 silver, .100 copper (net weight .18084 oz. pure silver).*
Diameter: *24.3 mm.* **Edge:** *Reeded.* **Mints:** *Philadelphia, Denver, and San Francisco.*

**Variety 1, No Stars Below Eagle
(1916–1917)**

*Mintmark location is on the
obverse, at the top left of
the date, for both varieties.*

Variety 2, Stars Below Eagle (1917–1930): **Designer:** *Hermon A. MacNeil.*
Weight: *6.25 grams.* **Composition:** *.900 silver, .100 copper (net weight .18084 oz. pure silver).*
Diameter: *24.3 mm.* **Edge:** *Reeded.* **Mints:** *Philadelphia, Denver, and San Francisco.*

**Variety 2, Stars Below Eagle
(1917–1930)**

History. The Standing Liberty quarter dollar, designed by sculptor Hermon A. MacNeil (whose initial, M, is located above and to the right of the date), was greeted with wide acclaimed from its first appearance. All of 1916 and many of 1917 are of the Variety 1 design, with the right breast of Miss Liberty exposed on the obverse and with no stars below the eagle on the reverse. Variety 2 of the Standing Liberty design was introduced in 1917 and continued to the end of the series. Miss Liberty is clothed in a jacket of chainmail armor, and the reverse is slightly redesigned, with stars below the eagle. These changes came at the suggestion of the designer, Hermon A. MacNeil. The Mint also created a 2016 gold Standing Liberty quarter at a smaller dimension. See page 737.

Striking and Sharpness. Many if not most 1916 quarters are somewhat lightly struck on the head and body of Miss Liberty. The 1917, Variety 1, quarters usually are quite well struck. When light striking is found, it is usually on the higher-relief parts of the head, the right knee (not as obvious), and the rivets on the left side of the shield. The 1917 Philadelphia Mint coins are usually sharper than the other varieties of this type. Most coins of the Variety 2 design have areas of light striking. On the obverse these are most notable on the head of Miss Liberty and on the shield, the latter often with the two lower-left rivets weak or missing and with the center emblem on the shield weak. The center of the standing figure can be weak as well, as can the upper-left area at and near the date. After 1924 the date was slightly recessed, eliminating that problem. On the reverse, check the eagle's breast. A misleading term, Full Head (FH), is widely used to describe quarters that have only *partial* head details; such coins often actually have the two lower-left shield rivets poorly struck or not visible at all. Most third-party grading services define these criteria for "Full Head" designation (in order of importance): a full, unbroken hairline from Liberty's brow down to the jawline; all three leaves on the head showing; and a visible ear hole.

Availability. The 1916 quarter is the key to the series. Examples tend to be liberally graded in the real-life marketplace, especially in EF and AU, this in contrast to more careful grading for the less valuable 1917 issues. Circulated coins of 1916 and 1917 often have the date worn partly away, due to the high position of this feature in the design. Among Variety 2 coins, the 1918-S, 8 Over 7, is recognized as the key issue, and the 1919-D, 1921, 1923-S, and 1927-S as quite scarce. MS coins are readily available for most issues, but Full Details coins can be *extreme* rarities. Circulated coins dated from 1917 through 1924 often have the date worn partly away, due to the high position of this feature in the design. On MS coins the luster usually is rich and attractive. No Proof coins of this type were officially issued, but specimen strikings dated 1917 are known to exist.

GRADING STANDARDS

MS-60 to 70 (Mint State). *Obverse:* At MS-60 some abrasion and contact marks are evident on the higher areas, which are also the areas most likely to be weakly struck. This includes the rivets on the shield to the left and the central escutcheon on the shield, the head, and the right leg of Miss Liberty. The luster may not be complete in those areas on weakly struck coins, even those certified above MS-65—the *original planchet surface*

1919. Graded MS-65FH.

may be revealed as it was not smoothed out by striking. Accordingly, grading is best done by evaluating abrasion and mint luster as it is observed. Luster may be dull or lifeless at MS–60 to 62 but should have deep frost at MS-63 or better, particularly in the lower-relief areas. At MS-65 or better, it should be full and rich. *Reverse:* Striking is usually quite good, permitting observation of luster in all areas. Check the eagle's breast and the surface of the right wing. Luster may be dull or lifeless at MS–60 to 62 but should have deep frost at MS-63 or better, particularly in the lower-relief areas. At MS-65 or better, it should be full and rich.

Illustrated coin: See the subtle notes of gold, blue, and pink on this lustrous example.

AU-50, 53, 55, 58 (About Uncirculated).
Obverse: Light wear is seen on the figure of Miss Liberty, especially noticeable around her midriff and right knee. The shield shows wear, as does the highest part of the sash where it crosses Miss Liberty's waist. At AU-58 the luster is extensive, but incomplete on the higher areas, although it should be nearly full in the panels of the parapet to the left and right, and in the upper field. At AU–50 and 53, luster is

1917-S, Variety 1. Graded AU-53.

less. *Reverse:* Wear is most evident on the eagle's breast, the edges of both wings, and the interior area of the right wing. Luster is nearly complete at AU-58, but at AU-50, half or more is gone.

EF-40, 45 (Extremely Fine). *Obverse:* Wear is more extensive, with the higher parts of Miss Liberty now without detail and the front of the right leg flat. The shield is worn. On coins dated from 1917 to 1924 the date shows wear at the top (on those of 1925 to 1930, with the date recessed, the numbers are bold). Little or no luster is seen, except perhaps among the letters. *Reverse:* The eagle shows more wear, with the surface of the right wing being mostly flat. Little or no luster is evident.

1927-S. Graded EF-45.

VF-20, 30 (Very Fine). *Obverse:* Wear is more extensive. The higher-relief areas of Miss Liberty are flat, and the sash crossing her waist is mostly blended into it (some sharply struck pieces being exceptions). The left side of the shield is mostly flat, although its outline can be seen. On quarters dated 1917 to 1924 the top of the date shows more wear. *Reverse:* The eagle shows further wear, with the body blending into the wing above

1919-S. Graded VF-20.

it. Much feather detail is gone from the wing to the left (on quarters dated 1925 to 1930; less so for those dated 1917 to 1924). Most detail is gone from the right wing.

F-12, 15 (Fine). *Obverse:* Miss Liberty is worn nearly flat. Most detail in her gown is gone, except to the left of her leg and below her knee to the right. The stars on the parapet are well worn, with some indistinct. The top of the date is weak. Quarters of the rare 1916 date are slightly weaker than those of 1917 in this and lower grades. On quarters of 1917 to 1924 the top of the date is weak. On those dated 1925 to 1930 the date remains strong.

1917-D. Graded F-12.

Reverse: The eagle shows further wear, this being greater on 1925 to 1930 issues than on the earlier dates.

VG-8, 10 (Very Good). *Obverse:* The obverse is worn further, with fewer details in the skirt, and part of the shield border to the left blended into the standing figure. The date is partially worn away at the top, and quarters from 1917 to 1924 have less detail. Those from 1925 to 1930 retain more detail, and the date is full. *Reverse:* The eagle is worn further, with only about a third of the feathers now discernible, these mostly on the wing to the left.

1921. Graded VG-10.

G-4, 6 (Good). *Obverse:* The wear is more extensive. Most coins have the stars missing, the standing figure flat, and much of the date worn away, although still clearly identifiable. Quarters of 1925 to 1930 show more detail and the date is clear. *Reverse:* The eagle is mostly in outline form, with only a few feather details visible. The rim is worn into the letters, and on quarters of 1916 to 1924, E PLURIBUS UNUM is very faint; it is clear on quarters of later dates.

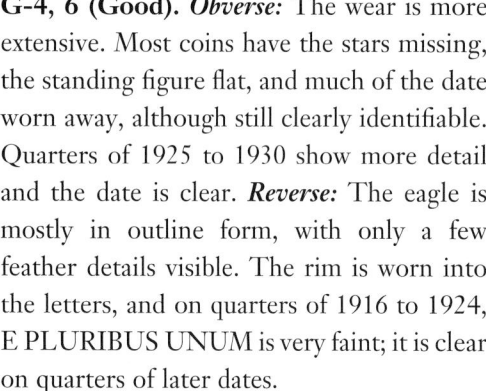

1927-S. Graded G-6.

AG-3 (About Good). *Obverse:* The obverse is worn nearly smooth, and the date is mostly gone. On some coins just one or two digits are seen. Fortunately, those digits are usually on the right, such as a trace of just a 6, which will identify the coin as a 1916. On quarters of 1925 to 1930 the wear is more extensive than for G-4, but most features are discernible and the date is clear. *Reverse:* The eagle is flat, and the border is worn down further.

1921. Graded AG-3.

On quarters of 1916 to 1924, E PLURIBUS UNUM is extremely faint or even missing in areas; it remains readable on quarters of later dates.

Full Head Details, Variety 1
Note the excellently defined cheek, facial features, and wreath.

Full Head Details, Variety 2
Note the full unbroken hairline from brow to neck, all three leaves clearly visible in Liberty's cap, and a visible ear hole.

Pedestal Date
(1917–1924)

Recessed Date
(1925–1930)

1918-S, 8 Over 7
FS-25-1918S-101.

	Mintage	Cert	Avg	%MS	G-4	VG-8	F-12	VF-20	EF-40	AU-50	MS-60	MS-63	MS-65FH
1916 †	52,000	884	44.7	48%	$3,000	$4,500	$6,000	$7,000	$9,000	$11,000	$12,500	$15,000	$35,000
	Auctions: $146,875, MS-67FH, January 2015; $52,875, MS-66FH, January 2015; $35,250, MS-66FH, May 2016; $18,800, MS-64FH, October 2015												
1917, Variety 1	8,740,000	6,791	59.4	78%	$18	$30	$50	$70	$90	$140	$225	$325	$1,000
	Auctions: $4,465, MS-67FH, August 2015; $8,225, MS-66FH, October 2015; $1,821, MS-65FH, January 2015; $646, MS-64FH, February 2015												
1917-D, Variety 1	1,509,200	1,931	59.0	73%	$25	$65	$95	$125	$175	$225	$300	$375	$1,350
	Auctions: $2,585, MS-67, July 2015; $2,585, MS-66FH, August 2015; $3,055, MS-65FH, February 2015; $1,058, MS-64FH, January 2015												
1917-S, Variety 1	1,952,000	1,216	54.1	64%	$30	$75	$115	$150	$200	$275	$350	$425	$2,500
	Auctions: $5,405, MS-66FH, February 2015; $2,703, MS-65FH, June 2015; $705, MS-64FH, June 2015; $364, MS-63, January 2015												
1917, Variety 2	13,880,000	1,571	60.2	77%	$20	$32	$45	$55	$75	$110	$150	$275	$900
	Auctions: $2,585, MS-67, January 2015; $3,525, MS-66FH, February 2015; $1,998, MS-65FH, August 2015; $353, MS-64, October 2015												
1917-D, Variety 2	6,224,400	842	58.4	67%	$30	$45	$65	$90	$110	$150	$225	$300	$1,500
	Auctions: $5,875, MS-66FH, October 2015; $3,995, MS-65FH, August 2015; $1,880, MS-64FH, August 2015; $646, MS-63, August 2015												
1917-S, Variety 2	5,552,000	808	58.8	69%	$35	$50	$75	$105	$125	$165	$235	$325	$2,500
	Auctions: $4,935, MS-66FH, February 2015; $3,525, MS-65FH, August 2015; $1,410, MS-66, October 2015; $400, MS-64, October 2015												
1918	14,240,000	904	60.3	73%	$20	$25	$30	$35	$55	$95	$150	$250	$2,000
	Auctions: $3,525, MS-67, June 2015; $7,638, MS-66FH, August 2015; $1,543, MS-65FH, August 2015; $282, MS-63, November 2015												
1918-D	7,380,000	741	57.7	61%	$22	$30	$60	$75	$120	$150	$200	$360	$3,500
	Auctions: $5,405, MS-66FH, June 2015; $8,813, MS-65FH, February 2015; $646, MS-64, August 2015; $282, MS-62, January 2015												
1918-S	11,072,000	982	55.5	61%	$20	$25	$35	$45	$60	$120	$180	$300	$10,000
	Auctions: $27,025, MS-67FH, August 2015; $22,325, MS-66FH, October 2015; $21,150, MS-65FH, May 2015; $2,350, MS-64FH, February 2015												
1918-S, 8 Over 7 † (a)	(b)	331	40.2	18%	$1,600	$2,200	$3,200	$4,000	$7,000	$9,000	$14,000	$23,000	$250,000
	Auctions: $188,000, MS-64FH, June 2014; $23,500, MS-64, August 2016; $24,675, AU-58FH, July 2014; $17,625, AU-58, January 2015												
1919	11,324,000	1,124	60.3	75%	$25	$35	$50	$65	$80	$105	$150	$210	$1,650
	Auctions: $8,520, MS-67FH, August 2015; $1,058, MS-66, August 2015; $1,939, MS-65FH, August 2015; $1,293, MS-64FH, August 2015												
1919-D	1,944,000	484	46.2	36%	$65	$90	$180	$350	$500	$600	$1,200	$1,800	$45,000
	Auctions: $6,463, MS-66, August 2015; $49,350, MS-65FH, August 2015; $18,800, MS-64FH, August 2015; $2,585, MS-63, June 2015												
1919-S	1,836,000	501	46.8	33%	$65	$90	$150	$300	$500	$600	$1,000	$2,000	$35,000
	Auctions: $6,463, MS-66, August 2015; $24,675, MS-64FH, June 2015; $1,880, MS-63, January 2015; $881, AU-58, October 2015												

† Ranked in the *100 Greatest U.S. Coins* (fourth edition). **a.** This clear overdate was caused by the use of two differently dated hubs when the die was made. "Because of the boldness of the 7, this variety can be confirmed easily in low grades. . . . This variety is extremely rare in high grades. We recommend authentication because alterations do exist. Genuine specimens have a small die chip above the pedestal, just to the left of the lowest star on the right" (*Cherrypickers' Guide to Rare Die Varieties*, sixth edition, volume II). **b.** Included in 1918-S mintage figure.

	Mintage	Cert	Avg	%MS	G-4	VG-8	F-12	VF-20	EF-40	AU-50	MS-60	MS-63	MS-65FH
1920	27,860,000	1,782	60.6	76%	$12	$16	$25	$30	$45	$75	$125	$210	$1,450
	Auctions: $9,400, MS-67, January 2015; $1,528, MS-66, February 2015; $3,290, MS-65FH, August 2015; $470, MS-64FH, October 2015												
1920-D	3,586,400	408	52.9	52%	$50	$60	$80	$120	$165	$235	$400	$1,000	$8,500
	Auctions: $10,575, MS-67, June 2015; $16,450, MS-66FH, October 2015; $4,465, MS-64FH, February 2015; $999, MS-64, March 2015												
1920-S	6,380,000	592	57.5	63%	$20	$25	$35	$50	$70	$150	$275	$700	$20,000
	Auctions: $8,813, MS-66, February 2015; $1,880, MS-65, August 2015; $4,818, MS-64FH, January 2015; $646, MS-63, October 2015												
1921	1,916,000	1,112	43.4	41%	$125	$175	$350	$550	$700	$900	$1,200	$1,900	$7,500
	Auctions: $18,800, MS-66FH, May 2015; $6,463, MS-66, February 2015; $2,820, MS-65, October 2015; $3,055, MS-64FH, January 2015												
1923	9,716,000	1,579	61.2	82%	$12	$18	$25	$35	$45	$80	$150	$200	$2,750
	Auctions: $2,350, MS-67, February 2015; $4,465, MS-65FH, August 2015; $329, MS-64, June 2015; $306, MS-62FH, February 2015												
1923-S	1,360,000	833	47.1	41%	$250	$350	$600	$800	$1,200	$1,700	$2,100	$3,000	$6,500
	Auctions: $18,213, MS-66, September 2016; $4,935, MS-66, August 2015; $5,405, MS-65, November 2016; $3,290, MS-64, January 2015												
1924	10,920,000	1,148	60.5	79%	$12	$16	$22	$32	$45	$80	$150	$225	$1,200
	Auctions: $20,563, MS-68, January 2015; $14,100, MS-67FH, October 2015; $2,820, MS-66FH, June 2015; $470, MS-65, March 2015												
1924-D	3,112,000	1,577	62.1	88%	$40	$45	$70	$100	$150	$180	$225	$350	$3,500
	Auctions: $999, MS-67, September 2015; $18,800, MS-66FH, March 2015; $4,700, MS-65FH, August 2015; $364, MS-64, November 2015												
1924-S	2,860,000	606	58.0	67%	$18	$28	$35	$55	$110	$225	$300	$800	$4,700
	Auctions: $3,760, MS-66, July 2015; $5,875, MS-65FH, March 2015; $1,116, MS-64, September 2015; $1,058, MS-63FH, August 2015												
1925	12,280,000	1,225	61.0	81%	$7.50	$8	$10	$20	$40	$70	$130	$200	$750
	Auctions: $3,055, MS-67, August 2015; $5,405, MS-66FH, May 2015; $1,116, MS-65FH, August 2015; $235, MS-64, July 2015												
1926	11,316,000	1,292	61.4	81%	$7.50	$8	$9	$20	$40	$70	$130	$150	$1,200
	Auctions: $3,760, MS-67, September 2015; $2,585, MS-66FH, October 2015; $353, MS-65, March 2015; $646, MS-64FH, October 2015												
1926-D	1,716,000	2,258	63.0	96%	$7.50	$10	$22	$35	$70	$110	$150	$225	$23,000
	Auctions: $564, MS-66, January 2015; $400, MS-65, December 2015; $447, MS-64, November 2015; $270, MS-63, August 2015												
1926-S	2,700,000	443	54.5	57%	$7.50	$10	$15	$28	$90	$150	$375	$800	$18,000
	Auctions: $4,700, MS-66, August 2015; $17,625, MS-65FH, January 2015; $2,350, MS-65, September 2016; $1,528, MS-64, October 2016												
1927	11,912,000	1,518	60.2	76%	$7.50	$8	$9	$17	$35	$70	$130	$200	$750
	Auctions: $2,820, MS-67, August 2015; $7,050, MS-66FH, August 2015; $447, MS-65, August 2015; $764, MS-64FH, March 2015												
1927-D	976,000	989	59.6	86%	$15	$20	$30	$75	$140	$190	$225	$330	$2,100
	Auctions: $6,463, MS-66FH, June 2015; $793, MS-66, August 2015; $2,585, MS-65FH, August 2015; $353, MS-64, May 2015												
1927-S	396,000	1,237	26.2	12%	$35	$45	$110	$325	$950	$2,000	$4,000	$6,000	$170,000
	Auctions: $11,750, MS-66, August 2016; $9,988, MS-65, September 2016; $28,200, MS-64, November 2016; $6,463, MS-63, August 2016												
1928	6,336,000	990	61.0	80%	$7.50	$8	$9	$17	$35	$65	$120	$175	$1,400
	Auctions: $1,058, MS-67, January 2015; $3,525, MS-66FH, September 2015; $1,410, MS-65FH, August 2015; $306, MS-64, June 2015												
1928-D	1,627,600	1,466	63.0	92%	$7.50	$8	$9	$17	$35	$65	$120	$175	$3,000
	Auctions: $517, MS-66, January 2015; $423, MS-65, March 2015; $353, MS-64, July 2015; $223, MS-63, February 2015												
1928-S (c)	2,644,000	1,460	62.6	89%	$7.50	$8	$9	$22	$40	$70	$120	$190	$1,000
	Auctions: $4,700, MS-67FH, January 2015; $1,410, MS-66, February 2015; $1,293, MS-65FH, October 2015; $400, MS-64, November 2015												
1929	11,140,000	1,896	61.3	80%	$7.50	$8	$9	$17	$35	$65	$120	$175	$700
	Auctions: $1,528, MS-66FH, February 2015; $646, MS-65FH, August 2015; $423, MS-64FH, October 2015; $235, MS-64, April 2015												
1929-D	1,358,000	992	60.6	75%	$7.50	$8	$9	$17	$35	$65	$120	$175	$5,000
	Auctions: $5,405, MS-67, July 2015; $1,116, MS-66, February 2015; $423, MS-65, November 2015; $329, MS-64, October 2015												
1929-S	1,764,000	1,418	61.4	83%	$7.50	$8	$9	$17	$35	$65	$120	$175	$700
	Auctions: $4,935, MS-67FH, February 2015; $1,381, MS-66FH, July 2015; $353, MS-65, October 2015; $235, MS-64, May 2015												
1930	5,632,000	3,589	61.7	79%	$7.50	$8	$9	$17	$35	$65	$120	$175	$675
	Auctions: $2,820, MS-67, February 2015; $1,175, MS-66FH, January 2015; $734, MS-65FH, August 2015; $423, MS-64FH, May 2015												
1930-S	1,556,000	1,089	61.7	84%	$7.50	$8	$9	$17	$35	$65	$120	$175	$700
	Auctions: $2,820, MS-67FH, January 2015; $793, MS-66, January 2015; $494, MS-65, March 2015; $365, MS-64FH, August 2015												

c. Large and small mintmarks exist; their values are the same.

WASHINGTON, EAGLE REVERSE (1932–1998)

Designer: *John Flanagan.* **Weight:** *Silver issue—6.25 grams; clad issue—5.67 grams; silver Proofs—6.25 grams.* **Composition:** *Silver issue—.900 silver, .100 copper (net weight .18084 oz. pure silver); clad issue—outer layers of copper nickel (.750 copper, .250 nickel) bonded to inner core of pure copper; silver Proofs—.900 silver, .100 copper (net weight .18084 oz. pure silver).* **Diameter:** *24.3 mm.* **Edge:** *Reeded.* **Mints:** *Philadelphia, Denver, and San Francisco.*

Circulation Strike   **Proof**

 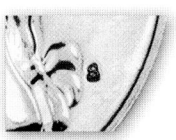

Mintmark location, 1932–1964, is on the reverse, below the eagle.   *Mintmark location, 1965 to date, is on the obverse, to right of the hair ribbon.*

Bicentennial variety: **Designers:** *John Flanagan and Jack L. Ahr.* **Weight:** *Silver issue— 5.75 grams; copper-nickel issue—5.67 grams.* **Composition:** *Silver issue—outer layers of .800 silver, .200 copper bonded to inner core of .209 silver, .791 copper (net weight .0739 oz. pure silver); copper-nickel issue—outer layers of .750 copper, .250 nickel bonded to inner core of pure copper.* **Diameter:** *24.3 mm.* **Edge:** *Reeded.* **Mints:** *Philadelphia, Denver, and San Francisco.*

Bicentennial variety   **Bicentennial variety, Proof**

History. The Washington quarter, designed by New York sculptor John Flanagan, originally was intended to be a commemorative coin, but it ultimately was produced as a regular circulation issue. The obverse is inspired by a famous bust by Jean Antoine Houdon. Flanagan's initials, JF, are at the base of Washington's neck. The reverse features a modernistic eagle perched on a quiver of arrows, with wings unfolding. In October 1973, the Treasury Department announced an open contest for the selection of suitable designs for the Bicentennial reverses of the quarter, half dollar, and dollar, with $5,000 to be awarded to each winner. Twelve semifinalists were chosen, and from these the symbolic entry of Jack L. Ahr was selected for the quarter reverse. It features a military drummer facing left, with a victory torch encircled by 13 stars at the upper left. Except for the dual dating, "1776–1976," the obverse remained unchanged. Pieces with this dual dating were coined during 1975 and 1976. They were struck for general circulation and included in all the U.S. Mint's offerings of Proof and Uncirculated coin sets. (The grading instructions below are for the regular Eagle Reverse variety.)

Striking and Sharpness. The relief of both sides of the Washington quarter issues from 1932 to 1998 is shallow. Accordingly, any lightness of strike is not easily seen. Nearly all are well struck. On all quarters of 1932 and some of 1934, the motto IN GOD WE TRUST is light, as per the design. It was strengthened in 1934.

Availability. The 1932-D and -S are key issues but not rarities. All others are readily available in high grades, but some are scarcer than others. Proof dates available are 1936 to 1942 and 1950 to 1964 (from the Philadelphia Mint) and 1968 to 1998 (from San Francisco). Certain later Proofs are available in clad metal as well as silver strikings. Special Mint Set (SMS) coins were struck in lieu of Proofs from 1965 to 1967; these in some instances closely resemble Proofs. The majority of Proofs made in recent decades are in high levels, PF–66 to 68 or higher.

Note: Values of common-date silver coins have been based on the current bullion price of silver, $17 per ounce, and may vary with the prevailing spot price.

GRADING STANDARDS

MS-60 to 70 (Mint State). *Obverse:* At MS-60, some abrasion and contact marks are evident on the hair above the ear and at the top of the head below the E of LIBERTY. At MS-63, abrasion is slight at best, less so for MS-64. An MS-65 coin should display no abrasion or contact marks except under magnification, and MS-66 and higher coins should have none at all. Luster should be full and rich. *Reverse:* Comments apply as for the obverse, except that the eagle's breast and legs are the places to check. On both sides the fields are protected by design elements and do not show contact marks readily.

1939-D. Graded MS-64.

AU-50, 53, 55, 58 (About Uncirculated). *Obverse:* Light wear is seen on the cheek, the high areas of the hair, and the neck. At AU-58, the luster is extensive but incomplete, especially on the higher parts and in the field. At AU–50 and 53, luster is less. *Reverse:* Light wear is seen on the breast, legs, and upper edges of the wings of the eagle. An AU-58 coin has nearly full luster. At AU–50 and 53, there still is significant luster.

1932-S. Graded AU-55.

EF-40, 45 (Extremely Fine). *Obverse:* Further wear is seen on the head. Higher-relief details are gone in the hair. The higher-relief parts of the neck show wear, most noticeably just above the date. *Reverse:* Further wear is seen on the eagle. Most breast feathers, not strong to begin with, are worn away.

1932-D. Graded EF-40.

VF-20, 30 (Very Fine). *Obverse:* Most hair detail is worn away, except above the curls. The delineation between the temple and the edge of the hair is faint. The curl by the ear is worn flat. Tips of the letters in LIBERTY and the date digits touch the rim in some instances. *Reverse:* More details of the eagle are worn away, and the outlines of the feathers in the wing, while nearly all present, are faint. Tips of the letters touch the rim in

1942-D, Doubled Die Obverse; FS-101. Graded VF-30.

some instances on this and lower grades, but this can vary from coin to coin depending on the strength of the rim.

F-12, 15 (Fine). *Obverse:* Most of the hair is worn flat, with no distinction between the face and the beginning of the hair. There is some detail remaining just above and below the curls. *Reverse:* More feathers are worn away. The end of the branch at the left is worn so as to blend into the wing. The edge of the rim is barely visible and in some areas is worn away. (In this and the Very Good grade, opinions concerning the rim vary in the ANA grading standards and in *Photograde*; PCGS is silent on the matter.)

1932-D. Graded F-12.

VG-8, 10 (Very Good). *Obverse:* Further wear is seen on the head, with most of the upper part of the curls now blending into the hair above. *Reverse:* The rim is worn into the tops of the letters. There is no detail on the leaves. About half of the feathers are outlined, but only faintly.

1932-S. Graded VG-10.

G-4, 6 (Good). *Obverse:* Further wear is seen in all areas. On 1932 and some 1934 coins the IN GOD WE TRUST motto is so worn that some letters are missing. *Reverse:* The rim is worn further into the letters. Fewer details are seen on the eagle's wing. On both sides the coin appears to be "worn flat," with little in relief.

1932-D. Graded G-4.

AG-3 (About Good). *Obverse:* Wear is more extensive, with about half of the letters gone. *Reverse:* Wear is more extensive, with about half of the letters gone. Slight detail remains in the eagle's wings. The mintmark, if any, is very clear.

1942. Graded AG-3.

PF-60 to 70 (Proof). *Obverse and Reverse:* Proofs that are extensively cleaned and have many hairlines, or that are dull and grainy, are lower level, such as PF–60 to 62. These are not widely desired, and represent coins that have been mistreated. Most low-level Proofs are of the 1936 to 1942 dates. With medium hairlines and good reflectivity, assigned grades of PF–63 or 64 are appropriate. PF-66 should have hairlines so delicate that magnification is needed to see them. Above that, a Proof should be free of any hairlines or other problems.

1974-S. Graded PF-70 Deep Cameo.

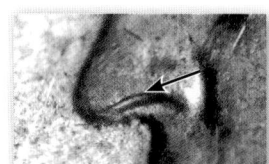
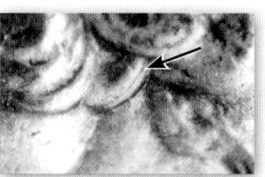

1932, Doubled Die Obverse
FS-25-1932-101.

	Mintage	Cert	Avg	%MS	VG-8	F-12	VF-20	EF-40	AU-50	MS-60	MS-62	MS-63	MS-65
1932	5,404,000	2,020	62.4	86%	$8	$9	$10	$11	$15	$25	$40	$60	$300
	Auctions: $8,813, MS-67, June 2015; $1,763, MS-66, January 2015; $505, MS-65, January 2015; $64, MS-64, February 2015												
1932, DblDie Obv (a)	(b)	23	56.9	30%						$350	$400	$500	$950
	Auctions: $235, MS-62, December 2013												
1932-D	436,800	4,016	39.4	27%	$110	$125	$150	$175	$350	$1,100	$1,200	$1,500	$10,500
	Auctions: $82,250, MS-66, June 2015; $41,125, MS-65, February 2015; $21,738, MS-65, December 2015; $13,513, MS-64, March 2015												
1932-S	408,000	4,928	46.0	38%	$100	$115	$130	$150	$200	$450	$750	$850	$3,300
	Auctions: $2,299, MS-65, January 2015; $1,586, MS-64, January 2015; $617, MS-63, January 2015; $356, AU-58, January 2015												

a. The doubling is evident on the earlobe, the nostril, and the braid of hair. **b.** Included in 1932 mintage figure.

1934, Doubled Die Obverse
FS-25-1934-101.

1934, Light Motto
FS-25-1934-401.

1934, Heavy Motto
FS-25-1934-403.

	Mintage	Cert	Avg	%MS	VG-8	F-12	VF-20	EF-40	AU-50	MS-60	MS-62	MS-63	MS-65
1934, All kinds	31,912,052												
1934, Doubled Die Obverse (c)		199	40.3	28%	$75	$85	$200	$300	$600	$1,000	$1,350	$1,700	$3,650
Auctions: $306, AU-55, May 2015; $329, AU-50, May 2015; $129, F-12, February 2015													
1934, Light Motto (d)		308	63.4	89%	$7.50	$7.75	$8	$10	$24	$60	$80	$135	$275
Auctions: $447, MS-66, August 2015; $259, MS-66, July 2015; $235, MS-65, January 2015; $176, MS-64, January 2015													
1934, Heavy Motto (e)		65	62.3	80%	$7.50	$7.75	$8	$10	$15	$30	$40	$50	$150
Auctions: $470, MS-66, September 2014; $100, MS-65, May 2015; $88, MS-65, August 2014; $118, MS-64, July 2014													
1934-D	3,527,200	1,359	61.1	77%	$7.50	$8	$12	$25	$85	$250	$280	$340	$475
Auctions: $1,058, MS-66, January 2015; $646, MS-65, June 2015; $447, MS-64, July 2015; $165, AU-55, October 2015													
1935	32,484,000	1,980	64.4	94%	$7.50	$7.75	$8	$9	$10	$22	$30	$35	$75
Auctions: $2,820, MS-67, January 2015; $2,115, MS-67, September 2015; $147, MS-66, August 2015; $69, MS-65, June 2015													
1935-D	5,780,000	1,291	61.5	79%	$7.50	$8	$10	$20	$125	$240	$265	$275	$450
Auctions: $517, MS-66, January 2015; $306, MS-64, August 2015; $213, MS-62, August 2015; $141, AU-58, October 2015													
1935-S	5,660,000	1,419	62.6	83%	$7.50	$8	$9	$15	$38	$100	$120	$135	$300
Auctions: $999, MS-67, January 2015; $282, MS-65, May 2015; $141, MS-64, September 2015; $79, MS-62, March 2015													

c. Very strong doubling is visible on the motto, LIBERTY, and the date. **d.** "Notice the considerable weakness in the letters of the motto. In addition, the center point of the W is pointed" (*Cherrypickers' Guide to Rare Die Varieties*, sixth edition, volume II). **e.** The motto has very thick letters, and the central apex of the W is pointed, rising slightly above the other letters.

1937, Doubled Die Obverse
FS-25-1937-101.

	Mintage	Cert	Avg	%MS	EF-40	AU-50	MS-60	MS-63	MS-65 / PF-64	MS-66 / PF-65	MS-67 / PF-67
1936	41,300,000	1,758	64.7	96%	$8	$10	$25	$35	$85	$165	$500
Auctions: $306, MS-67, May 2015; $247, MS-67, October 2015; $89, MS-66, July 2015; $79, MS-65, April 2015											
1936, Proof	3,837	971	64.4						$775	$1,200	$6,500
Auctions: $6,463, PF-67, June 2015; $1,528, PF-66, February 2015; $1,058, PF-65, October 2015; $541, PF-64, January 2015											
1936-D	5,374,000	1,212	60.3	74%	$55	$250	$525	$800	$1,100	$1,250	$4,500
Auctions: $1,528, MS-66, June 2015; $705, MS-64, January 2015; $646, MS-62, February 2015; $429, AU-58, May 2015											
1936-S	3,828,000	1,446	63.7	95%	$15	$50	$120	$140	$250	$450	$1,000
Auctions: $1,528, MS-67, September 2015; $517, MS-66, October 2015; $188, MS-65, February 2015; $106, MS-64, April 2015											
1937	19,696,000	1,143	64.4	96%	$8	$12	$25	$35	$100	$150	$600
Auctions: $6,463, MS-68, June 2015; $881, MS-67, January 2015; $148, MS-66, September 2015; $74, MS-65, August 2015											
1937, Doubled Die Obverse (a)	(b)	48	26.4	10%	$700	$1,500	$2,450	$3,200	$9,000	$16,000	
Auctions: $1,778, MS-63, April 2013; $494, VF-35, July 2015; $188, F-12, November 2014											
1937, Proof	5,542	972	65.1						$325	$450	$900
Auctions: $1,410, PF-67, January 2015; $412, PF-66, November 2015; $306, PF-65, October 2015; $141, PF-62, August 2015											
1937-D	7,189,600	1,205	64.0	95%	$15	$30	$70	$90	$150	$250	$850
Auctions: $1,116, MS-67, August 2015; $235, MS-66, July 2015; $106, MS-65, January 2015; $79, MS-64, July 2015											
1937-S	1,652,000	1,176	63.2	92%	$35	$95	$150	$250	$350	$550	$1,650
Auctions: $705, MS-66, June 2015; $295, MS-65, September 2015; $212, MS-64, May 2015; $200, MS-63, March 2015											

a. Very strong doubling is evident on the motto, LIBERTY, the date, and the end of the braid ribbons. "This variety is considered one of the most important in the series" (*Cherrypickers' Guide to Rare Die Varieties*, sixth edition, volume II). **b.** Included in circulation-strike 1937 mintage figure.

1942-D, Doubled Die Obverse
FS-25-1942D-101.

1942-D, Doubled Die Reverse
FS-25-1942D-801.

	Mintage	Cert	Avg	%MS	EF-40	AU-50	MS-60	MS-63	MS-65	MS-66	MS-67
									PF-64	PF-65	PF-67
1938	9,472,000	1,127	63.5	90%	$15	$45	$95	$110	$225	$250	$700
	Auctions: $734, MS-67, October 2015; $494, MS-67, June 2015; $212, MS-66, July 2015; $141, MS-65, January 2015										
1938, Proof	8,045	1,241	65.0						$160	$200	$1,100
	Auctions: $1,058, PF-67, June 2015; $235, PF-66, October 2015; $153, PF-65, May 2015; $94, PF-63, February 2015										
1938-S	2,832,000	1,419	64.0	96%	$20	$55	$105	$140	$200	$300	$750
	Auctions: $705, MS-67, August 2015; $188, MS-66, January 2015; $155, MS-65, March 2015; $129, MS-64, September 2015										
1939	33,540,000	1,928	65.2	97%	$8	$12	$15	$25	$60	$100	$225
	Auctions: $1,293, MS-68, September 2015; $764, MS-67, June 2015; $64, MS-66, July 2015; $56, MS-65, August 2015										
1939, Proof	8,795	1,241	65.4						$140	$200	$550
	Auctions: $3,055, PF-68, September 2015; $517, PF-67, January 2015; $165, PF-66, July 2015; $112, PF-64, February 2015										
1939-D	7,092,000	1,413	64.6	96%	$11	$20	$40	$50	$100	$160	$450
	Auctions: $494, MS-67, May 2015; $129, MS-66, August 2015; $74, MS-65, January 2015; $36, MS-63, September 2015										
1939-S	2,628,000	1,167	63.7	92%	$20	$60	$95	$135	$275	$300	$850
	Auctions: $764, MS-67, January 2015; $282, MS-66, September 2015; $223, MS-65, February 2015; $100, MS-62, March 2015										
1940	35,704,000	1,442	65.1	97%	$8	$9	$17	$35	$50	$80	$250
	Auctions: $15,275, MS-68, January 2015; $705, MS-67, June 2015; $46, MS-66, May 2015; $28, MS-64, November 2015										
1940, Proof	11,246	1,505	65.4						$95	$120	$500
	Auctions: $1,821, PF-68, June 2015; $541, PF-67, September 2015; $106, PF-66, January 2015; $100, PF-65, February 2015										
1940-D	2,797,600	1,268	64.1	94%	$24	$65	$120	$165	$275	$375	$1,000
	Auctions: $564, MS-67, June 2015; $353, MS-66, January 2015; $147, MS-64, August 2015; $153, MS-63, February 2015										
1940-S	8,244,000	1,234	65.1	97%	$9	$16	$21	$32	$50	$100	$500
	Auctions: $423, MS-67, January 2015; $69, MS-66, April 2015; $50, MS-65, August 2015; $28, MS-64, November 2015										
1941	79,032,000	1,912	65.3	98%	$7.50	$8	$10	$14	$35	$50	$250
	Auctions: $259, MS-67, September 2015; $200, MS-67, January 2015; $38, MS-66, April 2015; $36, MS-65, May 2015										
1941, Proof	15,287	1,840	65.4						$75	$115	$275
	Auctions: $329, PF-67, March 2015; $100, PF-66, November 2015; $79, PF-65, January 2015; $72, PF-64, September 2015										
1941-D	16,714,800	1,405	65.0	98%	$8	$13	$32	$55	$70	$110	$700
	Auctions: $470, MS-67, June 2015; $112, MS-66, January 2015; $94, MS-66, November 2015; $69, MS-63, September 2015										
1941-S	16,080,000	1,236	64.6	95%	$8	$11	$28	$50	$60	$110	$550
	Auctions: $705, MS-67, January 2015; $376, MS-67, October 2015; $106, MS-66, February 2015; $69, MS-65, March 2015										
1942	102,096,000	1,294	64.8	96%	$7.50	$8	$9	$10	$30	$110	$750
	Auctions: $823, MS-67, October 2015; $282, MS-67, January 2015; $141, MS-66, September 2015; $79, MS-66, October 2015										
1942, Proof	21,123	2,274	65.2						$75	$100	$250
	Auctions: $10,575, PF-68, June 2015; $235, PF-67, January 2015; $79, PF-65, May 2015; $56, PF-64, December 2015										
1942-D	17,487,200	1,413	65.2	99%	$8	$10	$17	$20	$40	$150	$400
	Auctions: $223, MS-67, July 2015; $207, MS-67, January 2015; $69, MS-66, January 2015; $58, MS-66, November 2015										
1942-D, DblDie Obv (c)	(d)	58	30.7	7%	$350	$750	$1,800	$3,500	$6,000	$10,500	
	Auctions: $823, MS-64, June 2014; $1,207, AU-55, April 2013; $188, AU-50, August 2014										
1942-D, DblDie Rev (e)	(d)	22	43.8	36%		$385	$500	$700	$1,250	$4,500	
	Auctions: $5,875, MS-66, August 2013										
1942-S	19,384,000	1,355	64.0	93%	$10	$20	$70	$115	$165	$300	$850
	Auctions: $400, MS-67, January 2015; $235, MS-66, April 2015; $118, MS-65, June 2015; $84, MS-64, September 2015										

c. Doubling is evident, with a very strong spread, on LIBERTY, the date, and the motto. d. Included in 1942-D mintage figure.
e. Doubling on this popular variety is most prominent on the eagle's beak, the arrows, and the branch above the mintmark.

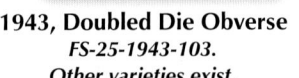

1943, Doubled Die Obverse
FS-25-1943-103.
Other varieties exist.

1943-S, Doubled Die Obverse
FS-25-1943S-101.

	Mintage	Cert	Avg	%MS	EF-40	AU-50	MS-60	MS-63	MS-65	MS-66	MS-67
									PF-64	PF-65	PF-67
1943	99,700,000	2,171	65.0	97%	$7.50	$8	$9	$10	$40	$80	$350
	Auctions: $223, MS-67, September 2015; $165, MS-67, January 2015; $36, MS-66, January 2015										
1943, DblDie Obverse (f)	(g)	10	26.4	10%	$2,500	$3,500	$5,000	$7,500	$12,500	$15,000	
	Auctions: $30, VF-20, March 2012										
1943-D	16,095,600	1,190	65.2	98%	$8	$15	$28	$39	$60	$85	$650
	Auctions: $282, MS-67, August 2015; $217, MS-67, January 2015; $52, MS-66, January 2015; $32, MS-65, February 2015										
1943-S	21,700,000	1,313	65.0	97%	$9	$13	$26	$42	$55	$120	$700
	Auctions: $6,463, MS-68, July 2015; $734, MS-67, January 2015; $89, MS-66, May 2015; $62, MS-66, November 2015										
1943-S, DblDie Obv (h)	(i)	125	44.5	46%	$200	$350	$500	$1,000	$1,800	$4,500	$7,250
	Auctions: $1,293, MS-64, August 2015; $1,528, MS-64, June 2015; $705, MS-64, January 2015; $79, EF-40, August 2015										
1944	104,956,000	2,316	65.4	98%	$7.50	$8	$9	$10	$28	$50	$350
	Auctions: $282, MS-67, October 2015; $165, MS-67, July 2015; $36, MS-66, August 2015										
1944-D	14,600,800	1,997	65.7	99%	$8	$10	$17	$20	$38	$75	$300
	Auctions: $10,575, MS-68, August 2015; $235, MS-67, September 2015; $165, MS-67, January 2015; $50, MS-66, April 2015										
1944-S	12,560,000	1,949	65.7	99%	$8	$10	$14	$20	$32	$60	$250
	Auctions: $317, MS-67, February 2015; $176, MS-67, September 2015; $48, MS-66, August 2015; $129, MS-65, April 2015										
1945	74,372,000	1,732	65.1	99%	$7.50	$8	$9	$10	$38	$95	$550
	Auctions: $16,450, MS-68, January 2015; $2,350, MS-68, October 2015; $329, MS-67, August 2015; $58, MS-66, January 2015										
1945-D	12,341,600	1,246	65.3	99%	$8	$12	$18	$25	$37	$50	$600
	Auctions: $364, MS-67, September 2015; $329, MS-67, May 2015; $42, MS-64, April 2015										
1945-S	17,004,001	1,656	65.4	99%	$7.50	$8	$9	$13	$35	$75	$450
	Auctions: $353, MS-67, October 2015; $236, MS-67, May 2015; $69, MS-66, July 2015; $54, MS-66, May 2015										
1946	53,436,000	1,023	65.2	98%	$7	$8	$9	$10	$38	$85	$900
	Auctions: $353, MS-67, September 2015; $306, MS-67, July 2015; $74, MS-66, January 2015; $20, MS-64, September 2015										
1946-D	9,072,800	2,649	65.6	100%	$7.50	$8	$9	$10	$35	$45	$300
	Auctions: $306, MS-67, November 2015; $165, MS-67, January 2015; $34, MS-65, September 2015										
1946-S	4,204,000	6,082	65.5	100%	$7	$8	$9	$10	$35	$55	$350
	Auctions: $235, MS-67, March 2015; $223, MS-67, November 2015; $58, MS-66, October 2015; $46, MS-66, August 2015										
1947	22,556,000	1,713	65.4	99%	$7.50	$8	$11	$19	$38	$75	$275
	Auctions: $176, MS-67, August 2015; $153, MS-67, October 2015; $56, MS-66, September 2015										
1947-D	15,338,400	2,666	65.7	100%	$7.50	$8	$11	$17	$35	$40	$200
	Auctions: $147, MS-67, December 2015; $84, MS-67, May 2015; $52, MS-66, July 2015; $38, MS-65, April 2015										
1947-S	5,532,000	4,885	65.7	100%	$7	$8	$9	$15	$32	$45	$250
	Auctions: $646, MS-68, September 2015; $165, MS-67, December 2015; $40, MS-66, May 2015; $21, MS-65, July 2015										
1948	35,196,000	2,311	65.4	99%	$7	$8	$9	$10	$31	$45	$185
	Auctions: $135, MS-67, November 2015; $112, MS-67, January 2015; $69, MS-66, May 2015; $52, MS-66, October 2015										
1948-D	16,766,800	1,595	65.3	99%	$7.50	$8	$13	$18	$50	$75	$650
	Auctions: $2,585, MS-67, January 2015; $74, MS-66, February 2015; $52, MS-66, September 2015; $46, MS-65, May 2015										
1948-S	15,960,000	2,709	65.5	99%	$7	$8	$9	$13	$45	$75	$300
	Auctions: $153, MS-67, November 2015; $118, MS-67, January 2015; $129, MS-66, February 2015; $74, MS-66, October 2015										

f. Doubling is very strong on the motto, LIBERTY, and the date. **g.** Included in 1943 mintage figure. **h.** Very strong doubling is visible on the motto, LIBERTY, the designer's initials, and the date. "Values for this variety are generally firm, but do change with market conditions and demand fluctuations" (*Cherrypickers' Guide to Rare Die Varieties*, sixth edition, volume II). **i.** Included in 1943-S mintage figure.

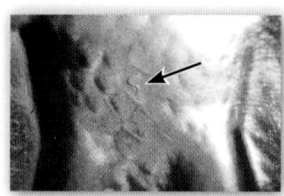

1950-D, D Over S
FS-25-1950D-601.
Other varieties exist.

1950-S, S Over D
FS-25-1950S-601.

1952, Die Damage, Proof
"Superbird" variety.
FS-25-1952-901.

	Mintage	Cert	Avg	%MS	EF-40	AU-50	MS-60	MS-63	MS-65 / PF-64	MS-66 / PF-65	MS-67 / PF-67
1949	9,312,000	1,453	65.1	98%	$10	$14	$35	$47	$70	$100	$350
Auctions: $329, MS-67, August 2015; $282, MS-67, January 2015; $84, MS-66, April 2015; $74, MS-66, October 2015											
1949-D	10,068,400	1,526	65.2	99%	$8	$10	$16	$38	$50	$100	$250
Auctions: $4,700, MS-68, September 2015; $223, MS-67, July 2015; $74, MS-66, January 2015; $74, MS-65, August 2015											
1950	24,920,126	1,390	65.5	99%	$7	$8	$9	$10	$35	$65	$350
Auctions: $529, MS-67, September 2014; $282, MS-67, September 2015; $223, MS-67, January 2015; $52, MS-66, February 2015											
1950, Proof	51,386	1,984	65.9						$60	$65	$150
Auctions: $881, PF-67Cam, January 2015; $106, PF-67, August 2015; $317, PF-66Cam, May 2015; $42, PF-66, August 2015											
1950-D	21,075,600	1,547	64.8	97%	$7	$8	$9	$10	$35	$50	$275
Auctions: $206, MS-67, November 2015; $170, MS-67, May 2015; $56, MS-66, October 2015											
1950-D, D Over S (j)	(k)	130	47.4	27%	$150.00	$225	$325	$550	$3,000	$7,500	
Auctions: $2,585, MS-64, July 2015; $400, MS-62, December 2015; $176, AU-58, June 2015; $100, EF-45, August 2015											
1950-S	10,284,004	1,554	64.6	95%	$7.50	$8	$12	$16	$45	$60	$275
Auctions: $259, MS-67, September 2015; $235, MS-67, January 2015; $106, MS-66, September 2015; $74, MS-66, April 2015											
1950-S, S Over D (l)	(m)	106	53.4	57%	$150	$250	$350	$500	$1,100	$2,000	$5,000
Auctions: $1,880, MS-66, September 2015; $705, MS-65, June 2015; $588, MS-64, February 2015; $306, AU-58, May 2015											
1951	43,448,102	1,566	65.4	99%	$7	$8	$9	$10	$25	$50	$275
Auctions: $450, MS-67, September 2014; $282, MS-67, September 2014; $206, MS-67, November 2015; $176, MS-67, January 2015											
1951, Proof	57,500	1,925	66.0						$55	$65	$125
Auctions: $1,645, PF-68Cam, June 2015; $1,293, PF-68Cam, June 2015; $1,234, PF-68Cam, November 2014; $176, PF-66Cam, February 2015											
1951-D	35,354,800	1,678	65.4	100%	$7	$8	$9	$10	$35	$50	$350
Auctions: $284, MS-67, March 2015; $235, MS-67, July 2015; $76, MS-66, March 2015; $66, MS-66, October 2015											
1951-S	9,048,000	1,645	65.8	100%	$7.50	$8	$10	$15	$40	$75	$165
Auctions: $2,115, MS-68, September 2015; $229, MS-67, February 2015; $176, MS-67, September 2015; $79, MS-66, February 2015											
1952	38,780,093	1,225	65.5	99%	$7.50	$8	$9	$10	$25	$50	$165
Auctions: $494, MS-68, January 2015; $165, MS-67, January 2015; $141, MS-67, December 2015; $42, MS-66, December 2015											
1952, Proof	81,980	1,895	66.3						$40	$45	$100
Auctions: $69, PF-67, August 2015; $46, PF-66, March 2015; $42, PF-66, August 2015; $212, PF-65Cam, May 2015											
1952, Die Damage, Proof (n)	(o)	(p)							$200	$250	
Auctions: $3,525, PF-66DCam, April 2014											
1952-D	49,795,200	1,001	65.2	99%	$7	$8	$9	$10	$40	$75	$1,250
Auctions: $3,878, MS-67, September 2015; $3,055, MS-67, January 2015; $84, MS-66, February 2015; $69, MS-66, October 2015											
1952-S	13,707,800	1,929	65.7	100%	$7.50	$8	$12	$20	$42	$50	$125
Auctions: $4,935, MS-68, October 2015; $153, MS-67, January 2015; $141, MS-67, September 2015; $94, MS-66, October 2015											

j. The upper left curve of the underlying S is visible west and north of the D mintmark. Most Mint State specimens have brilliant surfaces. **k.** Included in 1950-D mintage figure. **l.** Most Mint State specimens have a frosty luster, rather than the brilliant surface seen on most of this year's Mint State D Over S coins. **m.** Included in 1950-S mintage figure. **n.** "There is an unusual S-shaped mark on the breast of the eagle. The cause of this mark is unknown. The nickname for this well-known variety is, suitably, 'Superbird'!" (*Cherrypickers' Guide to Rare Die Varieties*, sixth edition, volume II). **o.** Included in 1952, Proof, mintage figure. **p.** Included in certified population for 1952, Proof.

	Mintage	Cert	Avg	%MS	EF-40	AU-50	MS-60	MS-63	MS-65 / PF-64	MS-66 / PF-65	MS-67 / PF-67
1953	18,536,120	1,031	65.3	99%	$7	$8	$9	$10	$40	$65	$200
	Auctions: $447, MS-67, February 2015; $423, MS-67, January 2015; $52, MS-66, April 2015; $42, MS-66, June 2015										
1953, Proof	128,800	3,453	66.7						$40	$45	$80
	Auctions: $1,293, PF-69Cam, October 2015; $7,638, PF-68DCam, October 2015; $52, PF-67, September 2015; $40, PF-66, August 2015										
1953-D	56,112,400	1,065	65.0	99%	$7	$8	$9	$10	$40	$50	$800
	Auctions: $1,528, MS-67, January 2015; $1,058, MS-67, October 2015; $177, MS-66, October 2015; $54, MS-66, April 2015										
1953-S	14,016,000	2,498	65.6	100%	$7	$8	$9	$10	$30	$50	$175
	Auctions: $235, MS-67, January 2015; $129, MS-67, September 2015; $341, MS-66, February 2015; $62, MS-66, July 2015										
1954	54,412,203	2,182	65.4	99%	$7	$8	$9	$10	$35	$50	$175
	Auctions: $2,820, MS-67+, September 2014; $223, MS-67, October 2014; $200, MS-67, September 2015; $129, MS-67, January 2015										
1954, Proof	233,300	4,065	67.0						$15	$25	$60
	Auctions: $376, PF-69Cam, March 2015; $42, PF-68, August 2015; $411, PF-67DCam, January 2015; $42, PF-66, September 2015										
1954-D	42,305,500	1,322	65.2	100%	$7	$8	$9	$10	$35	$65	$1,000
	Auctions: $2,115, MS-67, January 2015; $705, MS-67, August 2015; $79, MS-66, November 2015; $54, MS-66, April 2015										
1954-S	11,834,722	4,696	65.6	100%	$7	$8	$9	$10	$36	$50	$250
	Auctions: $368, MS-67, November 2014; $200, MS-67, January 2015; $182, MS-67, November 2014; $182, MS-67, March 2015										
1955	18,180,181	2,634	65.3	99%	$7	$8	$9	$10	$30	$60	$450
	Auctions: $353, MS-67, September 2014; $282, MS-67, October 2014; $259, MS-67, June 2015; $212, MS-67, September 2015										
1955, Proof	378,200	5,972	67.4						$15	$25	$50
	Auctions: $1,175, PF-69UCam, January 2015; $764, PF-68UCam, August 2015; $200, PF-67DCam, April 2015										
1955-D	3,182,400	2,902	64.5	100%	$7.50	$8	$9	$10	$60	$100	$1,000
	Auctions: $2,350, MS-66, April 2012										
1956	44,144,000	3,403	65.7	100%	$7	$8	$9	$10	$21	$33	$100
	Auctions: $306, MS-67, May 2015; $129, MS-67, September 2015; $36, MS-65, September 2015; $588, MS-64, October 2014										
1956, Proof	669,384	7,075	67.5						$11	$15	$50
	Auctions: $1,293, PF-69DCam, September 2015; $329, PF-69Cam, August 2015; $89, PF-68UCam, May 2015; $32, PF-68, July 2015										
1956-D	32,334,500	1,062	65.4	100%	$7	$8	$9	$10	$27	$55	$600
	Auctions: $447, MS-67, September 2015; $423, MS-67, January 2015; $48, MS-66, September 2015; $26, MS-66, September 2015										
1957	46,532,000	2,239	65.7	99%	$7	$8	$9	$10	$22	$30	$75
	Auctions: $1,528, MS-68, July 2015; $79, MS-67, January 2015; $69, MS-67, September 2015; $22, MS-66, September 2015										
1957, Proof	1,247,952	6,030	67.3						$11	$15	$45
	Auctions: $188, PF-69Cam, January 2015; $588, PF-68UCam, July 2015; $353, PF-68, May 2015; $200, PF-67DCam, July 2015										
1957-D	77,924,160	1,841	65.5	99%	$7	$8	$9	$10	$25	$50	$200
	Auctions: $1,293, MS-68, September 2015; $259, MS-67, January 2015; $176, MS-67, November 2015; $36, MS-65, February 2015										
1958	6,360,000	4,097	65.8	100%	$7.50	$8	$9	$10	$20	$40	$100
	Auctions: $79, MS-67, February 2015; $69, MS-67, November 2015; $62, MS-67, August 2014; $69, MS-67, November 2014										
1958, Proof	875,652	4,992	67.2						$11	$15	$40
	Auctions: $1,528, PF-68DCam, September 2014; $764, PF-68DCam, November 2014; $235, PF-67DCam, October 2015										
1958-D	78,124,900	2,336	65.6	99%	$7	$8	$9	$10	$25	$45	$200
	Auctions: $353, MS-68, September 2015; $235, MS-67, June 2015; $118, MS-66, November 2015; $30, MS-65, September 2015										
1959	24,384,000	1,773	65.5	100%	$7	$8	$9	$10	$25	$50	$900
	Auctions: $2,585, MS-67, January 2015; $1,763, MS-67, September 2015; $282, MS-66, April 2015; $60, MS-65, August 2015										
1959, Proof	1,149,291	5,512	67.4						$11	$12	$35
	Auctions: $9,400, PF-69DCam, November 2014; $881, PF-68DCam, September 2014; $705, PF-68UCam, November 2015										
1959, Doubled Die Obverse, Proof (q)	(r)	82	66.4						$140	$185	
	Auctions: $150, PF-65, February 2012										
1959-D	62,054,232	1,463	65.1	99%	$7	$8	$9	$10	$25	$60	$1,100
	Auctions: $646, MS-67, August 2015; $470, MS-67, June 2015; $68, MS-66, November 2015; $16, MS-65, November 2014										

q. Dramatic doubling is evident on all obverse lettering, especially IN GOD WE TRUST. There are at least five different doubled-die obverses for this date; the one featured here is FS-25-1959-101. **r.** Included in 1959, Proof, mintage figure.

	Mintage	Cert	Avg	%MS	EF-40	AU-50	MS-60	MS-63	MS-65	MS-66	MS-67
									PF-64	PF-65	PF-67
1960	29,164,000	1,286	65.4	100%	$7	$8	$9	$10	$20	$60	$950
	Auctions: $1,058, MS-67, June 2015; $764, MS-67, September 2015; $100, MS-66, November 2015; $50, MS-66, August 2015										
1960, Proof	1,691,602	5,741	67.1						$10	$11	$30
	Auctions: $2,115, PF-69DCam, September 2014; $999, PF-69DCam, July 2015; $764, PF-69DCam, November 2014; $217, PF-68DCam, November 2014										
1960-D	63,000,324	969	65.1	99%	$7	$8	$9	$10	$20	$55	$1,750
	Auctions: $2,233, MS-67, January 2015; $2,115, MS-67, April 2014; $92, MS-66, September 2014										
1961	37,036,000	1,144	65.2	99%	$7	$8	$9	$10	$15	$55	$1,500
	Auctions: $3,995, MS-67, June 2015; $946, MS-67, June 2015; $940, MS-67, September 2015; $764, MS-67, January 2015										
1961, Proof	3,028,244	7,617	67.3						$10	$11	$30
	Auctions: $1,058, PF-69DCam, June 2015; $881, PF-69DCam, September 2015; $282, PF-69UCam, July 2015; $88, PF-68DCam, November 2014										
1961-D	83,656,928	801	64.9	99%	$7	$8	$9	$10	$15	$110	$3,500
	Auctions: $7,638, MS-67, July 2014; $7,638, MS-67, August 2014; $129, MS-66, November 2015; $112, MS-66, June 2015										
1962	36,156,000	1,420	65.4	99%	$7	$8	$9	$10	$15	$50	$2,000
	Auctions: $881, MS-67, February 2015; $353, MS-67, August 2015; $100, MS-66, August 2015; $52, MS-66, November 2015										
1962, Proof	3,218,019	6,923	67.2						$10	$11	$30
	Auctions: $823, PF-69DCam, June 2015; $447, PF-69UCam, July 2015; $94, PF-68DCam, September 2015										
1962-D	127,554,756	780	64.8	98%	$7	$8	$9	$10	$15	$150	$3,500
	Auctions: $4,759, MS-67, January 2015; $1,293, MS-67, June 2015; $212, MS-66, January 2015; $165, MS-66, June 2015										
1963	74,316,000	2,038	65.3	99%	$7	$8	$9	$10	$15	$50	$900
	Auctions: $1,410, MS-67, February 2015; $940, MS-67, July 2015; $18, MS-66, April 2015; $2,115, MS-62, September 2014										
1963, Proof	3,075,645	8,587	67.4						$10	$11	$30
	Auctions: $223, PF-69DCam, November 2014; $212, PF-69DCam, May 2015; $200, PF-69UCam, July 2015; $22, PF-67DCam, April 2015										
1963-D	135,288,184	850	64.9	98%	$7	$8	$9	$10	$15	$100	$900
	Auctions: $969, MS-67, October 2015; $435, MS-67, June 2015; $74, MS-66, June 2015; $69, MS-66, November 2015										
1964	560,390,585	1,969	64.9	98%	$7	$8	$9	$10	$15	$50	$650
	Auctions: $447, MS-67, January 2015; $353, MS-67, September 2015; $153, MS-66, October 2015										
1964, Proof	3,950,762	11,519	67.8						$10	$11	$30
	Auctions: $329, PF-69DCam, January 2015; $282, PF-69UCam, January 2015; $259, PF-69UCam, July 2015										
1964-D	704,135,528	2,302	64.7	96%	$7	$8	$9	$10	$15	$45	$500
	Auctions: $517, MS-67, June 2015; $447, MS-67, January 2015; $56, MS-66, February 2015										

1966, Doubled Die Reverse
FS-25-1966-801.

	Mintage	Cert	Avg	%MS	MS-63	MS-65	MS-66	MS-67
						PF-65	PF-67Cam	PF-68DC
1965	1,819,717,540	307	64.8	96%	$1	$9	$30	$185
	Auctions: $317, MS-67Cam, August 2015; $141, MS-67Cam, January 2015; $223, MS-67, March 2015; $188, MS-67, January 2015							
1965, Special Mint Set ‡	2,360,000	3,331	66.9			$12	$35	$350
	Auctions: $505, MS-67Cam, January 2014; $588, MS-67Cam, September 2014; $441, MS-67Cam, October 2014							
1966	821,101,500	105	65.0	95%	$1	$7	$25	$125
	Auctions: $376, MS-67, January 2015; $259, MS-67, September 2014; $353, MS-63, January 2015; $212, MS-63, July 2015							
1966, Doubled Die Reverse (a)	(b)	2	58.0	50%	$900	$1,400	$2,250	
	Auctions: $920, EF-45, April 2012							
1966, Special Mint Set ‡	2,261,583	3,171	66.9			$12	$35	$175
	Auctions: $1,293, MS-68Cam, June 2014; $4,113, MS-68Cam, September 2014; $84, MS-67Cam, November 2014							

‡ Ranked in the *100 Greatest U.S. Modern Coins*. **a.** Very strong doubling is visible on all reverse lettering. Note that this is not the 1966 Special Mint Set issue. **b.** Included in circulation-strike 1966 mintage figure.

1968-S, Doubled Die Reverse, Proof
FS-25-1968S-801.

1970-D, Doubled Die Obverse
FS-25-1970D-101.

	Mintage	Cert	Avg	%MS	MS-63 PF-65	MS-65 PF-67Cam	MS-66 PF-68DC	MS-67
1967	1,524,031,848	130	65.7	97%	$1	$6	$35	$150
	Auctions: $118, MS-68, January 2015; $188, MS-67, January 2015; $141, MS-67, November 2015; $95, MS-67, January 2015							
1967, Special Mint Set ‡	1,863,344	3,860	67.0			$12	$50	$350
	Auctions: $212, MS-68Cam, September 2014; $188, MS-68Cam, August 2013							
1968	220,731,500	249	65.8	98%	$1.25	$8	$25	$100
	Auctions: $159, MS-67, July 2014; $141, MS-67, January 2015; $123, MS-67, September 2014; $84, MS-67, July 2015							
1968-D	101,534,000	747	66.0	100%	$1.10	$6	$15	$55
	Auctions: $123, MS-67, March 2013							
1968-S, Proof	3,041,506	1,134	67.4			$5	$15	$150
	Auctions: $194, PF-64, May 2013							
1968-S, Doubled Die Reverse, Proof (c)	(d)	23	66.1			$165		
	Auctions: $196, PF-66, March 2012							
1969	176,212,000	117	64.9	97%	$3	$10	$35	$350
	Auctions: $3,290, MS-67, January 2015; $141, MS-66, January 2015; $135, MS-66, June 2014; $123, MS-66, September 2014							
1969-D	114,372,000	601	65.8	99%	$2.50	$10	$25	$75
	Auctions: $1,998, MS-68, July 2014; $72, MS-67, July 2014; $69, MS-67, April 2015; $200, MS-63, July 2015							
1969-S, Proof	2,934,631	1,508	67.9			$5	$15	$100
	Auctions: $617, PF-69DCam, December 2013							
1970	136,420,000	302	65.3	100%	$1	$10	$40	$100
	Auctions: $153, MS-67, August 2014; $441, MS-67, September 2014; $2,115, MS-67, November 2013; $30, MS-66, July 2014							
1970-D	417,341,364	1,214	65.7	99%	$1	$6	$10	$35
	Auctions: $2,926, MS-68, January 2014; $40, MS-67, December 2015; $182, AU-55, July 2014; $69, EF-45, September 2015							
1970-D, Doubled Die Obverse (e)	(f)	2	59.5	50%	$300	$375	$500	
	Auctions: $2,875, MS-65, January 2012							
1970-S, Proof	2,632,810	1,218	67.9			$5	$15	$125
	Auctions: $705, PF-69DCam, June 2013; $1,175, PF-67Cam, October 2014							
1971	109,284,000	142	64.8	99%	$1	$6	$50	$150
	Auctions: $306, MS-66, August 2015; $212, MS-66, August 2015; $123, MS-66, September 2014; $89, MS-66, August 2015							
1971-D	258,634,428	302	65.9	100%	$1	$6	$20	$100
	Auctions: $4,113, MS-68, September 2013; $86, MS-67, July 2014; $182, MS-67, September 2014; $235, MS-62, October 2015							
1971-S, Proof	3,220,733	1,374	67.8			$5	$15	$300
	Auctions: $1,058, PF-69DCam, December 2013							
1972	215,048,000	246	65.6	100%	$1	$6	$25	$175
	Auctions: $588, MS-67, November 2013							
1972-D	311,067,732	654	66.1	100%	$1	$6	$18	$30
	Auctions: $3,055, MS-68, January 2014; $259, MS-65, October 2014							
1972-S, Proof	3,260,996	997	68.0			$5	$10	$30
	Auctions: $411, PF-65Cam, August 2013							

‡ Ranked in the *100 Greatest U.S. Modern Coins*. **c.** Doubling is evident on all reverse lettering around the rim and the left tips. **d.** Included in 1968-S, Proof, mintage figure. **e.** This extremely rare variety (fewer than a half dozen known) shows very strong doubling on the date, IN GOD WE TRUST, and the ERTY of LIBERTY. **f.** Included in 1970-D mintage figure.

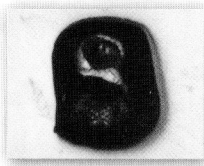

1979-S, Filled S
(Type 1), Proof

1979-S, Clear S
(Type 2), Proof

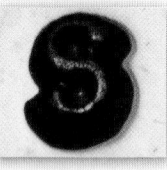

	Mintage	Cert	Avg	%MS	MS-63	MS-65 PF-65	MS-66 PF-67Cam	MS-67 PF-68DC
1973	346,924,000	152	65.3	99%	$1	$6	$25	$175
Auctions: $1,116, MS-67, September 2013								
1973-D	232,977,400	167	65.1	99%	$1	$6	$25	$175
Auctions: $1,410, MS-65, February 2014								
1973-S, Proof	2,760,339	438	68.1			$5	$10	$20
Auctions: $96, PF-67, March 2013								
1974	801,456,000	128	65.1	98%	$1	$6	$25	$175
Auctions: $382, MS-67, November 2013								
1974-D	353,160,300	181	65.4	99%	$1	$7	$25	$75
Auctions: $1,763, MS-64, September 2013								
1974-S, Proof	2,612,568	456	68.1			$5	$10	$20
Auctions: $7,015, PF-70DCam, April 2012								
1776–1976, Copper-Nickel Clad ‡	809,784,016	485	65.5	99%	$1.25	$6	$15	$50
Auctions: $306, MS-62, February 2014								
1776–1976-D, Copper-Nickel Clad	860,118,839	824	65.5	98%	$1.25	$6	$15	$60
Auctions: $66, MS-67, March 2013								
1776–1976-S, Silver Clad	11,000,000	1,195	66.1	100%	$4	$7	$15	$40
Auctions: $129, MS-68, October 2014; $100, MS-68, January 2015; $78, MS-68, August 2014; $64, MS-68, January 2015								
1776–1976-S, Proof, Copper-Nickel Clad	7,059,099	1,776	68.0			$5	$10	$20
Auctions: $253, PF-70DCam, January 2015; $212, PF-70DCam, July 2015; $141, PF-70DCam, November 2015								
1776–1976-S, Proof, Silver Clad	4,000,000	3,373	68.1			$8	$12	$25
Auctions: $376, PF-70DCam, January 2015; $282, PF-70DCam, July 2015; $235, PF-70DCam, October 2015								
1977	468,556,000	142	65.5	99%	$1	$6	$20	$100
Auctions: $123, MS-67, September 2014; $52, MS-66, August 2015; $100, MS-60, September 2015								
1977-D	256,524,978	110	65.0	98%	$1	$6	$25	$125
Auctions: $229, MS-67, September 2014								
1977-S, Proof	3,251,152	872	68.8			$5	$10	$20
Auctions: $70, PF-70DCam, August 2014; $103, PF-70DCam, November 2014; $90, PF-70DCam, May 2013								
1978	521,452,000	175	65.4	99%	$1	$6	$20	$100
Auctions: $165, MS-67, January 2015; $470, MS-65, February 2015; $247, MS-65, August 2015; $259, MS-60, July 2015								
1978-D	287,373,152	164	65.4	99%	$1	$6	$25	$175
Auctions: $26, MS-66, August 2014								
1978-S, Proof	3,127,781	752	68.8			$5	$10	$18
Auctions: $61, PF-70DCam, August 2014; $80, PF-70DCam, May 2013; $12, PF-70DCam, March 2015								
1979	515,708,000	195	65.7	99%	$1	$6	$25	$125
Auctions: $411, MS-66, June 2014; $200, MS-64, February 2015; $176, MS-64, November 2014								
1979-D	489,789,780	159	65.4	99%	$1	$6	$25	$125
Auctions: $441, MS-67, September 2013								
1979-S, Proof, All kinds (g)	3,677,175							
1979-S, Type 1 ("Filled" S), Proof		971	68.8			$5	$10	$18
Auctions: $68, PF-70DCam, August 2014								
1979-S, Type 2 ("Clear" S), Proof		1,048	69.0			$6	$12	$25
Auctions: $529, PF-70DCam, September 2014; $76, PF-70DCam, August 2014; $72, PF-70DCam, September 2014								

‡ Ranked in the *100 Greatest U.S. Modern Coins*. **g.** The mintmark style was changed during 1979 Proof production, creating two distinctly different types. "The Type 2 is the rare variety, and is easily distinguished from the common Type 1. The Type 1 has a very indistinct blob, whereas the Type 2 shows a well-defined S" (*Cherrypickers' Guide to Rare Die Varieties*, sixth edition, volume II).

1981-S, Rounded S
(Type 1), Proof

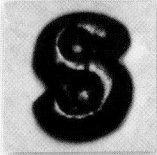 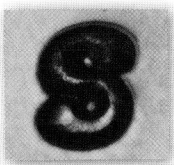

1981-S, Flat S
(Type 2), Proof

	Mintage	Cert	Avg	%MS	MS-63	MS-65	MS-66	MS-67
						PF-65	PF-67Cam	PF-68DC
1980-P	635,832,000	390	65.8	99%	$1	$6	$18	$85
	Auctions: $74, MS-65, November 2015; $56, MS-62, August 2015; $141, AU-58, January 2015							
1980-D	518,327,487	168	65.5	99%	$1	$6	$20	$175
	Auctions: $1,380, MS-67, February 2007							
1980-S, Proof	3,554,806	1,140	68.7			$5	$10	$18
	Auctions: $79, PF-70DCam, May 2013							
1981-P	601,716,000	310	66.0	100%	$1	$6	$15	$100
	Auctions: $176, MS-65, August 2013							
1981-D	575,722,833	327	65.6	99%	$1	$6	$15	$150
	Auctions: $259, MS-67, September 2013							
1981-S, Proof, All kinds (h)	4,063,083							
1981-S, Type 1 ("Rounded" S), Proof		1,393	68.8			$4	$8	$16
	Auctions: $70, PF-70DCam, May 2013							
1981-S, Type 2 ("Flat" S), Proof		917	69.0			$6	$12	$25
	Auctions: $705, PF-70DCam, April 2013							
1982-P	500,931,000	150	65.5	99%	$7	$30	$60	$240
	Auctions: $646, MS-67, January 2015; $282, MS-63, September 2015; $353, AU-50, January 2015							
1982-D	480,042,788	267	65.6	99%	$5	$18	$60	$200
	Auctions: $30, MS-66, March 2013							
1982-S, Proof	3,857,479	935	69.0			$4	$8	$16
	Auctions: $103, PF-70DCam, May 2014; $56, PF-70DCam, September 2014; $47, PF-70DCam, November 2014							
1983-P ‡	673,535,000	859	65.0	98%	$30	$65	$200	$400
	Auctions: $74, MS-66, July 2014; $74, MS-66, September 2014; $423, AU-58, January 2015							
1983-D	617,806,446	106	65.3	100%	$10	$45	$150	$500
	Auctions: $1,058, MS-67, June 2014; $108, MS-66, August 2014; $92, MS-66, September 2014; $84, MS-66, January 2015							
1983-S, Proof	3,279,126	871	68.8			$4	$8	$16
	Auctions: $72, PF-70DCam, September 2014; $90, PF-70DCam, August 2013							
1984-P	676,545,000	173	65.3	97%	$2	$10	$20	$125
	Auctions: $1,058, MS-67, September 2013							
1984-D	546,483,064	91	64.6	98%	$2	$12	$65	$300
	Auctions: $764, MS-67, September 2013							
1984-S, Proof	3,065,110	637	69.0			$4	$8	$16
	Auctions: $80, PF-70DCam, May 2013; $55, PF-70DCam, August 2014; $50, PF-70DCam, August 2015							
1985-P	775,818,962	205	65.5	98%	$2	$15	$25	$100
	Auctions: $764, MS-65, June 2014							
1985-D	519,962,888	212	65.7	99%	$1	$9	$25	$100
	Auctions: $66, MS-66, March 2013							
1985-S, Proof	3,362,821	691	69.0			$4	$8	$16
	Auctions: $86, PF-70DCam, May 2013							

‡ Ranked in the *100 Greatest U.S. Modern Coins*. **h.** The mintmark style was changed during the 1981 Proof production, creating two distinct types. "The Type 2 is the rare variety, and is not easily distinguished from the common Type 1. For most collectors, the easiest difference to discern on the Type 2 is the flatness on the top curve of the S, which is rounded on the Type 1. Additionally, the surface of the Type 2 mintmark is frosted, and the openings in the loops slightly larger" (*Cherrypickers' Guide to Rare Die Varieties*, sixth edition, volume II).

1989-D, Repunched Mintmark
FS-25-1989D-501.

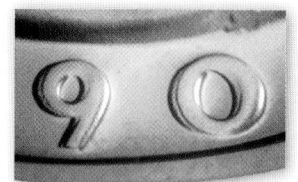

1990-S, Doubled Die Obverse, Proof
FS-25-1990S-101.

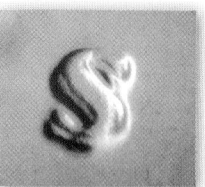

	Mintage	Cert	Avg	%MS	MS-63	MS-65	MS-66	MS-67
						PF-65	PF-67Cam	PF-68DC
1986-P	551,199,333	204	64.8	98%	$2.50	$12	$30	$125
Auctions: $129, MS-64, October 2014; $103, MS-66, September 2014; $100, MS-66, August 2015; $30, MS-66, November 2014								
1986-D	504,298,660	231	65.6	99%	$6	$18	$25	$100
Auctions: $104, MS-66, November 2007								
1986-S, Proof	3,010,497	622	69.1			$4	$8	$16
Auctions: $39, PF-70DCam, August 2013								
1987-P	582,499,481	160	65.2	99%	$1	$9	$40	$200
Auctions: $59, MS-66, December 2007								
1987-D	655,594,696	179	65.6	99%	$1	$6	$20	$150
Auctions: $676, MS-67, January 2015; $66, MS-66, September 2014								
1987-S, Proof	4,227,728	835	69.0			$4	$8	$16
Auctions: No auction records available.								
1988-P	562,052,000	175	65.1	99%	$1.25	$15	$30	$175
Auctions: $66, MS-66, March 2013								
1988-D	596,810,688	154	65.5	100%	$1	$10	$20	$125
Auctions: $66, MS-66, November 2007								
1988-S, Proof	3,262,948	547	69.1			$4	$8	$16
Auctions: $55, PF-70DCam, August 2013								
1989-P	512,868,000	146	65.1	98%	$1	$12	$30	$150
Auctions: $216, MS-66, August 2009								
1989-D	896,535,597	138	65.3	98%	$1	$7	$25	$125
Auctions: $70, MS-66, March 2013								
1989-D, Repunched Mintmark (i)	(j)	0	n/a		$20	$25	$50	
Auctions: No auction records available.								
1989-S, Proof	3,220,194	617	68.9			$4	$8	$16
Auctions: $79, PF-70DCam, January 2010								
1990-P	613,792,000	172	65.9	99%	$1	$10	$20	$100
Auctions: $282, MS-64, June 2014								
1990-D	927,638,181	185	65.8	100%	$1	$10	$20	$125
Auctions: $646, MS-68, April 2014; $52, MS-67, August 2014								
1990-S, Proof	3,299,559	822	69.2			$4	$8	$16
Auctions: $53, PF-68DCam, April 2013								
1990-S, Doubled Die Obverse, Proof ‡ (k)	(l)	5	68.2			$225	$700	
Auctions: $4,888, PF-70DCam, April 2012								
1991-P	570,968,000	136	65.9	99%	$1	$12	$30	$100
Auctions: $90, MS-66, November 2007								
1991-D	630,966,693	94	65.4	100%	$1	$12	$30	$225
Auctions: $66, MS-66, March 2013								
1991-S, Proof	2,867,787	782	69.3			$4	$8	$16
Auctions: $69, PF-70DCam, January 2010								

‡ Ranked in the *100 Greatest U.S. Modern Coins*. **i.** The secondary D mintmark is visible west of the primary D. **j.** Included in 1989-D mintage figure. **k.** Very strong doubling is visible on the date and the mintmark, with slightly less dramatic doubling on IN GOD WE TRUST. **l.** Included in 1990-S, Proof, mintage figure.

	Mintage	Cert	Avg	%MS	MS-63	MS-65	MS-66	MS-67
						PF-65	PF-67Cam	PF-68DC
1992-P	384,764,000	155	65.9	100%	$1.50	$16	$35	$250
Auctions: $242, MS-66, February 2008								
1992-D	389,777,107	132	65.3	98%	$1	$16	$35	$350
Auctions: $1,763, MS-67, November 2013; $47, MS-66, July 2014								
1992-S, Proof	2,858,981	588	69.2			$4	$8	$16
Auctions: $50, PF-70DCam, January 2010								
1992-S, Proof, Silver	1,317,579	1,637	69.2			$9	$12	$22
Auctions: $109, PF-70DCam, January 2010								
1993-P	639,276,000	200	66.1	98%	$1	$7	$20	$85
Auctions: $86, MS-67, August 2014; $306, MS-64, June 2014; $282, MS-64, February 2015								
1993-D	645,476,128	166	65.9	99%	$1	$7	$25	$100
Auctions: $1,298, MS-67, January 2015; $59, MS-67, August 2014; $101, MS-66, September 2014; $36, AU-58, July 2014								
1993-S, Proof	2,633,439	585	69.3			$4	$8	$16
Auctions: $58, PF-70DCam, May 2013								
1993-S, Proof, Silver	761,353	1,256	69.1			$9	$12	$22
Auctions: $70, PF-70DCam, August 2013								
1994-P	825,600,000	136	65.9	100%	$1	$10	$25	$100
Auctions: $70, MS-66, March 2013								
1994-D	880,034,110	118	65.0	96%	$1	$10	$30	$150
Auctions: $123, MS-66, September 2014; $212, MS-64, July 2014								
1994-S, Proof	2,484,594	551	69.3			$4	$8	$16
Auctions: $69, PF-70DCam, January 2010								
1994-S, Proof, Silver	785,329	1,165	69.1			$9	$14	$25
Auctions: $76, PF-70DCam, September 2014; $96, PF-70DCam, May 2013								
1995-P	1,004,336,000	139	66.5	100%	$1.25	$14	$20	$65
Auctions: $129, MS-67, March 2013								
1995-D	1,103,216,000	147	66.1	100%	$1	$13	$20	$75
Auctions: $165, MS-67, September 2014; $38, MS-64, July 2015								
1995-S, Proof	2,117,496	439	69.4			$8	$10	$20
Auctions: $69, PF-70DCam, January 2010								
1995-S, Proof, Silver	679,985	1,318	69.1			$9	$14	$25
Auctions: $68, PF-70DCam, September 2014; $69, PF-70DCam, November 2014; $135, PF-70DCam, May 2013								
1996-P	925,040,000	211	66.5	100%	$1	$10	$18	$30
Auctions: $441, MS-68, March 2013								
1996-D	906,868,000	238	66.2	100%	$1	$10	$18	$30
Auctions: $447, MS-68, March 2013; $165, MS-64, November 2014; $79, MS-63, January 2015								
1996-S, Proof	1,750,244	522	69.3			$5	$8	$18
Auctions: $84, PF-70DCam, January 2010								
1996-S, Proof, Silver	775,021	1,278	69.1			$9	$14	$25
Auctions: $76, PF-70DCam, May 2013								
1997-P	595,740,000	134	66.3	100%	$1	$11	$18	$40
Auctions: $15, MS-60, January 2013								
1997-D	599,680,000	131	66.1	99%	$1	$12	$18	$40
Auctions: $66, MS-67, March 2013								
1997-S, Proof	2,055,000	443	69.5			$5	$8	$18
Auctions: $69, PF-70DCam, January 2010								
1997-S, Proof, Silver	741,678	1,307	69.2			$9	$14	$25
Auctions: $89, PF-70DCam, January 2010								

	Mintage	Cert	Avg	%MS	MS-63	MS-65	MS-66	MS-67
						PF-65	PF-67Cam	PF-68DC
1998-P	896,268,000	164	66.6	99%	$1	$7	$18	$40
	Auctions: $364, MS-68, September 2014; $329, MS-68, June 2014; $306, MS-66, January 2015; $159, MS-64, November 2014							
1998-D	821,000,000	149	65.4	97%	$1	$7	$20	$100
	Auctions: $1,528, MS-67+, January 2015; $364, MS-67, September 2014; $32, MS-66, June 2014; $69, MS-63, August 2015							
1998-S, Proof	2,086,507	488	69.5			$6	$8	$18
	Auctions: $9,988, PF-65, August 2014							
1998-S, Proof, Silver	878,792	1,465	69.2			$9	$12	$22
	Auctions: $70, PF-70DCam, May 2013							

WASHINGTON, STATE, D.C., AND TERRITORIAL (1999–2009)

Designers: *John Flanagan (obverse); see image captions for reverse designers.* **Weight:** *Clad issue—5.67 grams; silver Proofs—6.25 grams.* **Composition:** *Clad issue—Outer layers of copper-nickel (.750 copper, .250 nickel) bonded to inner core of pure copper; silver Proofs— .900 silver, .100 copper (net weight .18084 oz. pure silver).* **Diameter:** *24.3 mm.* **Edge:** *Reeded.* **Mints:** *Clad issue—Philadelphia, Denver, and San Francisco; silver Proofs—San Francisco.*

Circulation Strike

Proof

History. In 1999 the U.S. Mint introduced a new program of State quarters (officially called the United States Mint 50 State Quarters® Program). These were released at the rate of five new reverse designs each year, in combination with a restyled obverse, through 2008. Each design honored the state the coin was issued for, and they were released in public celebrations in the order in which the states joined the Union. The coins became very popular, adding millions of Americans to the ranks of everyday coin collectors, and are still widely collected with enthusiasm. In 2009 the Mint released a similar program of quarter dollars for Washington, D.C., and the five U.S. territories. Circulation strikes were made at the Philadelphia and Denver mints, and special silver-content and Proof issues at San Francisco. Each coin combines a modified obverse depicting George Washington, without a date. The reverses are distinctive and bear the date of issue, the date of statehood (for the State quarters), and other design elements. Each state or district/territory selected its own design.

Some State quarters were accidentally made with "disoriented" dies and are valued higher than ordinary pieces. Normal U.S. coins have dies oriented in coin alignment, such that the reverse appears upside down when the coin is flipped from right to left. Values for the rotated-die quarters vary according to the amount of shifting. The most valuable are those that are shifted 180 degrees, so that both sides appear upright when the coin is turned over (called *medal alignment*).

Striking and Sharpness. State quarters can have light striking on the highest area of the obverse. On the reverse there can be weak areas, depending on the design, seemingly more often seen on Denver Mint coins. Some in the State quarter series were struck through grease, obliterating portions of both the obverse (usually) and reverse designs.

Availability. All modern quarters are readily available in high grades. Typical MS coins are MS–63 and 64 with light abrasion. MS-65 and higher coins are in the minority, but enough exist that finding them is no problem. Around MS-68 many issues are scarce, and higher grades are scarcer yet.

Proofs. State and D.C./Territorial quarter dollar Proofs are made in San Francisco. For certain later issues of Washington quarters as well as State, D.C., and Territorial issues, Proofs are available in copper-nickel–clad metal as well as silver strikings. On some Proofs over-polishing of dies eliminated some details, as on part of the WC (for William Cousins) initials on certain 1999 Delaware pieces.

GRADING STANDARDS

MS-60 to 70 (Mint State). *Obverse:* At MS-60, some abrasion and contact marks are evident on the highest-relief parts of the hair and the cheek. At MS-63, abrasion is slight at best, less so at MS-64. An MS-65 coin should display no abrasion or contact marks except under magnification, and MS-66 and higher coins should have none at all. Luster should be full. *Reverse:* Check the highest-relief areas of the design (these differ from coin to coin). Otherwise, comments are as for the obverse.

2004-D, Wisconsin, Extra Leaf Low. Graded MS-66.

AU-50, 53, 55, 58 (About Uncirculated). *Obverse:* Light wear is seen on the cheek, the high areas of the hair, and the neck. At AU-58, the luster is extensive, but incomplete, especially on the higher parts and in the field. At AU–50 and 53, luster is less. About Uncirculated coins usually lack eye appeal. *Reverse:* Light wear is seen on the higher-relief areas. Otherwise, comments are as for the obverse.

2004-D, Wisconsin, Extra Leaf High. Graded AU-58.

State, D.C., and Territorial quarter dollars are seldom collected in grades lower than AU-50.

PF-60 to 70 (Proof). *Obverse and Reverse:* These coins are so recent, and as only a few have been cleaned, most approach perfection and can be designated PF–68 to 70, the latter only if no contact marks or other problems can be seen under magnification. A cleaned coin with extensive hairlines would not be collectible for most numismatists and would be classified at a lower level such as PF–60 to 63. Those with lighter hairlines qualify for PF–64 or 65.

2008-S, Alaska. Graded PF-70 Ultra Cameo.

1999, Delaware	1999, Pennsylvania	1999, New Jersey	1999, Georgia	1999, Connecticut
Reverse designer:	*Reverse designer:*	*Reverse designer:*	*Reverse designer:*	*Reverse designer:*
William Cousins.	*John Mercanti.*	*Alfred Maletsky.*	*T. James Ferrell.*	*T. James Ferrell.*

	Mintage	Cert	Avg	%MS	AU-50	MS-63	MS-65 / PF-65	MS-66 / PF-66DC	MS-67 / PF-69DC
1999-P, Delaware	373,400,000	1,224	66.0	100%	$0.50	$1.25	$3	$25	$55
1999-D, Delaware	401,424,000	1,358	66.0	100%	$0.50	$1.25	$3	$25	$55
1999-S, Delaware, Proof	3,713,359	6,723	69.2				$7	$8	$20
1999-S, Delaware, Proof, Silver	804,565	12,897	69.0				$30	$35	$50
1999-P, Pennsylvania	349,000,000	1,112	66.1	100%	$0.50	$1.25	$3	$25	$55
1999-D, Pennsylvania	358,332,000	993	65.9	100%	$0.50	$1.25	$3	$25	$55
1999-S, Pennsylvania, Proof	3,713,359	6,492	69.2				$7	$8	$20
1999-S, Pennsylvania, Proof, Silver	804,565	12,326	69.1				$30	$35	$50
1999-P, New Jersey	363,200,000	1,063	66.1	100%	$0.50	$1.25	$3	$25	$55
1999-D, New Jersey	299,028,000	1,196	66.0	100%	$0.50	$1.25	$3	$25	$55
1999-S, New Jersey, Proof	3,713,359	6,489	69.2				$7	$8	$20
1999-S, New Jersey, Proof, Silver	804,565	12,418	69.1				$30	$35	$50
1999-P, Georgia	451,188,000	1,173	65.7	99%	$0.50	$1.25	$3	$25	$55
1999-D, Georgia	488,744,000	1,172	65.8	99%	$0.50	$1.25	$3	$25	$55
1999-S, Georgia, Proof	3,713,359	6,525	69.2				$7	$8	$20
1999-S, Georgia, Proof, Silver	804,565	12,523	69.1				$30	$35	$50
1999-P, Connecticut	688,744,000	1,348	65.6	99%	$0.50	$1.25	$3	$25	$55
1999-D, Connecticut	657,880,000	2,280	65.4	100%	$0.50	$1.25	$3	$25	$55
1999-S, Connecticut, Proof	3,713,359	6,561	69.3				$7	$8	$20
1999-S, Connecticut, Proof, Silver	804,565	12,338	69.1				$30	$35	$50

2000, Massachusetts	2000, Maryland	2000, South Carolina	2000, New Hampshire	2000, Virginia
Reverse designer:	*Reverse designer:*	*Reverse designer:*	*Reverse designer:*	*Reverse designer:*
Thomas D. Rogers Sr.	*Thomas D. Rogers Sr.*	*Thomas D. Rogers Sr.*	*William Cousins.*	*Edgar Z. Steever.*

	Mintage	Cert	Avg	%MS	AU-50	MS-63	MS-65 / PF-65	MS-66 / PF-66DC	MS-67 / PF-69DC
2000-P, Massachusetts	628,600,000	914	66.2	100%	$0.35	$1	$2	$15	$40
2000-D, Massachusetts	535,184,000	661	66.1	100%	$0.35	$1	$2	$15	$40
2000-S, Massachusetts, Proof	4,020,172	4,628	69.2				$3	$4	$15
2000-S, Massachusetts, Proof, Silver	965,421	9,695	69.2				$8	$10	$20
2000-P, Maryland	678,200,000	631	65.9	99%	$0.35	$1	$2	$15	$40
2000-D, Maryland	556,532,000	641	66.0	100%	$0.35	$1	$2	$15	$40
2000-S, Maryland, Proof	4,020,172	4,530	69.2				$3	$4	$15
2000-S, Maryland, Proof, Silver	965,421	9,825	69.2				$8	$10	$20

	Mintage	Cert	Avg	%MS	AU-50	MS-63	MS-65 / PF-65	MS-66 / PF-66DC	MS-67 / PF-69DC
2000-P, South Carolina	742,576,000	605	66.1	100%	$0.35	$1	$2	$15	$40
2000-D, South Carolina	566,208,000	748	66.3	100%	$0.35	$1	$2	$15	$40
2000-S, South Carolina, Proof	4,020,172	4,583	69.2				$3	$4	$15
2000-S, South Carolina, Proof, Silver	965,421	9,489	69.2				$8	$10	$20
2000-P, New Hampshire	673,040,000	560	65.6	99%	$0.35	$1	$2	$15	$40
2000-D, New Hampshire	495,976,000	582	66.0	100%	$0.35	$1	$2	$15	$40
2000-S, New Hampshire, Proof	4,020,172	4,589	69.2				$3	$4	$15
2000-S, New Hampshire, Proof, Silver	965,421	9,479	69.1				$8	$10	$20
2000-P, Virginia	943,000,000	675	66.1	100%	$0.35	$1	$2	$15	$40
2000-D, Virginia	651,616,000	593	66.1	99%	$0.35	$1	$2	$15	$40
2000-S, Virginia, Proof	4,020,172	4,573	69.2				$3	$4	$15
2000-S, Virginia, Proof, Silver	965,421	9,622	69.2				$8	$10	$20

2001, New York
Reverse designer: Alfred Maletsky.

2001, North Carolina
Reverse designer: John Mercanti.

2001, Rhode Island
Reverse designer: Thomas D. Rogers Sr.

2001, Vermont
Reverse designer: T. James Ferrell.

2001, Kentucky
Reverse designer: T. James Ferrell.

	Mintage	Cert	Avg	%MS	AU-50	MS-63	MS-65 / PF-65	MS-66 / PF-66DC	MS-67 / PF-69DC
2001-P, New York	655,400,000	397	66.1	100%	$0.35	$1	$2	$15	$40
2001-D, New York	619,640,000	467	66.2	100%	$0.35	$1	$2	$15	$40
2001-S, New York, Proof	3,094,140	3,670	69.2				$3	$8	$15
2001-S, New York, Proof, Silver	889,697	7,862	69.2				$10	$15	$20
2001-P, North Carolina	627,600,000	386	66.3	100%	$0.35	$1	$2	$15	$40
2001-D, North Carolina	427,876,000	415	66.3	100%	$0.35	$1	$2	$15	$40
2001-S, North Carolina, Proof	3,094,140	3,760	69.2				$3	$8	$15
2001-S, North Carolina, Proof, Silver	889,697	7,794	69.2				$10	$15	$20
2001-P, Rhode Island	423,000,000	316	66.0	100%	$0.35	$1	$2	$15	$40
2001-D, Rhode Island	447,100,000	370	66.0	100%	$0.35	$1	$2	$15	$40
2001-S, Rhode Island, Proof	3,094,140	3,360	69.2				$3	$8	$15
2001-S, Rhode Island, Proof, Silver	889,697	7,870	69.2				$10	$15	$20
2001-P, Vermont	423,400,000	1,882	65.7	100%	$0.35	$1	$2	$15	$40
2001-D, Vermont	459,404,000	383	66.3	100%	$0.35	$1	$2	$15	$40
2001-S, Vermont, Proof	3,094,140	3,533	69.3				$3	$8	$15
2001-S, Vermont, Proof, Silver	889,697	7,922	69.3				$10	$15	$20
2001-P, Kentucky	353,000,000	392	66.3	100%	$0.35	$1.25	$1.50	$16	$40
2001-D, Kentucky	370,564,000	305	66.1	100%	$0.35	$1.25	$1.50	$16	$40
2001-S, Kentucky, Proof	3,094,140	3,395	69.3				$3	$8	$15
2001-S, Kentucky, Proof, Silver	889,697	7,818	69.2				$10	$15	$20

2002, Tennessee
Reverse designer: Donna Weaver.

2002, Ohio
Reverse designer: Donna Weaver.

2002, Louisiana
Reverse designer: John Mercanti.

2002, Indiana
Reverse designer: Donna Weaver.

2002, Mississippi
Reverse designer: Donna Weaver.

	Mintage	Cert	Avg	%MS	AU-50	MS-63	MS-65 / PF-65	MS-66 / PF-66DC	MS-67 / PF-69DC
2002-P, Tennessee	361,600,000	312	66.5	100%	$0.75	$1.75	$3	$18	$40
2002-D, Tennessee	286,468,000	313	66.4	100%	$0.75	$1.75	$3	$18	$40
2002-S, Tennessee, Proof	3,084,245	2,946	69.2				$3	$5	$15
2002-S, Tennessee, Proof, Silver	892,229	7,583	69.2				$8	$10	$20
2002-P, Ohio	217,200,000	349	66.7	100%	$0.35	$1	$1.25	$10	$30
2002-D, Ohio	414,832,000	292	66.2	100%	$0.35	$1	$1.25	$10	$30
2002-S, Ohio, Proof	3,084,245	2,933	69.3				$3	$5	$15
2002-S, Ohio, Proof, Silver	892,229	7,677	69.2				$8	$10	$20
2002-P, Louisiana	362,000,000	267	66.7	100%	$0.35	$1	$1.25	$10	$30
2002-D, Louisiana	402,204,000	223	66.3	100%	$0.35	$1	$1.25	$10	$30
2002-S, Louisiana, Proof	3,084,245	2,941	69.2				$3	$5	$15
2002-S, Louisiana, Proof, Silver	892,229	7,394	69.2				$8	$10	$20
2002-P, Indiana	362,600,000	313	66.5	99%	$0.35	$1	$1.25	$10	$30
2002-D, Indiana	327,200,000	249	66.3	100%	$0.35	$1	$1.25	$10	$30
2002-S, Indiana, Proof	3,084,245	2,965	69.2				$3	$5	$15
2002-S, Indiana, Proof, Silver	892,229	7,511	69.2				$8	$10	$20
2002-P, Mississippi	290,000,000	284	66.3	100%	$0.35	$1	$1.25	$10	$30
2002-D, Mississippi	289,600,000	232	66.4	100%	$0.35	$1	$1.25	$10	$30
2002-S, Mississippi, Proof	3,084,245	3,001	69.3				$3	$5	$15
2002-S, Mississippi, Proof, Silver	892,229	7,775	69.2				$8	$10	$20

2003, Illinois
Reverse designer: Donna Weaver.

2003, Alabama
Reverse designer: Norman E. Nemeth.

2003, Maine
Reverse designer: Donna Weaver.

2003, Missouri
Reverse designer: Alfred Maletsky.

2003, Arkansas
Reverse designer: John Mercanti.

	Mintage	Cert	Avg	%MS	AU-50	MS-63	MS-65 / PF-65	MS-66 / PF-66DC	MS-67 / PF-69DC
2003-P, Illinois	225,800,000	258	65.9	100%	$0.50	$1.50	$2	$12	$32
2003-D, Illinois	237,400,000	2,074	65.2	100%	$0.50	$1.50	$2	$12	$32
2003-S, Illinois, Proof	3,408,516	5,613	69.3				$3	$5	$15
2003-S, Illinois, Proof, Silver	1,125,755	8,403	69.2				$8	$9	$20
2003-P, Alabama	225,000,000	281	65.7	100%	$0.35	$1	$1.25	$10	$30
2003-D, Alabama	232,400,000	2,076	65.1	100%	$0.35	$1	$1.25	$10	$30
2003-S, Alabama, Proof	3,408,516	5,699	69.3				$3	$5	$15
2003-S, Alabama, Proof, Silver	1,125,755	8,396	69.2				$8	$9	$20

	Mintage	Cert	Avg	%MS	AU-50	MS-63	MS-65 / PF-65	MS-66 / PF-66DC	MS-67 / PF-69DC
2003-P, Maine	217,400,000	250	65.8	100%	$0.35	$1	$1.25	$10	$30
2003-D, Maine	231,400,000	2,076	65.2	100%	$0.35	$1	$1.25	$10	$30
2003-S, Maine, Proof	3,408,516	5,565	69.2				$3	$5	$15
2003-S, Maine, Proof, Silver	1,125,755	8,285	69.2				$8	$9	$20
2003-P, Missouri	225,000,000	266	65.9	99%	$0.35	$1	$1.25	$10	$30
2003-D, Missouri	228,200,000	2,087	65.2	100%	$0.35	$1	$1.25	$10	$30
2003-S, Missouri, Proof	3,408,516	5,756	69.3				$3	$5	$15
2003-S, Missouri, Proof, Silver	1,125,755	8,387	69.2				$8	$9	$20
2003-P, Arkansas	228,000,000	240	65.8	100%	$0.35	$1	$1.25	$10	$30
2003-D, Arkansas	229,800,000	2,113	65.2	100%	$0.40	$1	$1.25	$10	$30
2003-S, Arkansas, Proof	3,408,516	5,704	69.3				$3	$5	$15
2003-S, Arkansas, Proof, Silver	1,125,755	8,425	69.2				$8	$9	$20

2004, Michigan
Reverse designer: Donna Weaver.

2004, Florida
Reverse designer: T. James Ferrell.

2004, Texas
Reverse designer: Norman E. Nemeth.

2004, Iowa
Reverse designer: John Mercanti.

2004, Wisconsin
Reverse designer: Alfred Maletsky.

2004-D, Wisconsin, Normal Reverse

2004-D, Wisconsin, Extra Leaf High
FS-25-2004D-WI-5901.

2004-D, Wisconsin, Extra Leaf Low
FS-25-2004D-WI-5902.

	Mintage	Cert	Avg	%MS	AU-50	MS-63	MS-65 / PF-65	MS-66 / PF-66DC	MS-67 / PF-69DC
2004-P, Michigan	233,800,000	2,359	65.2	100%	$0.35	$0.75	$1	$10	$30
2004-D, Michigan	225,800,000	403	67.3	100%	$0.35	$0.75	$1	$10	$30
2004-S, Michigan, Proof	2,740,684	3,860	69.3				$3	$5	$15
2004-S, Michigan, Proof, Silver	1,769,786	9,815	69.3				$8	$10	$20
2004-P, Florida	240,200,000	2,351	65.2	100%	$0.35	$0.75	$1	$10	$30
2004-D, Florida	241,600,000	306	66.9	100%	$0.35	$0.75	$1	$10	$30
2004-S, Florida, Proof	2,740,684	3,786	69.3				$3	$5	$15
2004-S, Florida, Proof, Silver	1,769,786	9,635	69.2				$8	$10	$20
2004-P, Texas	278,800,000	2,387	65.2	100%	$0.35	$0.75	$1	$10	$30
2004-D, Texas	263,000,000	327	66.9	100%	$0.35	$0.75	$1	$10	$30
2004-S, Texas, Proof	2,740,684	3,902	69.3				$3	$5	$15
2004-S, Texas, Proof, Silver	1,769,786	10,043	69.3				$8	$10	$20
2004-P, Iowa	213,800,000	2,320	65.1	100%	$0.35	$0.75	$1	$10	$30
2004-D, Iowa	251,400,000	288	66.9	100%	$0.35	$0.75	$1	$10	$30
2004-S, Iowa, Proof	2,740,684	3,941	69.4				$3	$5	$15
2004-S, Iowa, Proof, Silver	1,769,786	9,919	69.3				$8	$10	$20

| | Mintage | Cert | Avg | %MS | AU-50 | MS-63 | MS-65 | MS-66 | MS-67 |
							PF-65	PF-66DC	PF-69DC
2004-P, Wisconsin	226,400,000	2,553	65.2	100%	$0.35	$0.75	$1	$10	$30
2004-D, Wisconsin	226,800,000	2,795	65.7	100%	$0.35	$0.75	$1	$10	$30
2004-D, Wisconsin, Extra Leaf High ‡ (a)	(b)	4,757	64.8	96%	$75	$150	$200	$300	$500
2004-D, Wisconsin, Extra Leaf Low ‡ (a)	(b)	6,412	64.9	97%	$50	$130	$165	$275	$450
2004-S, Wisconsin, Proof	2,740,684	3,930	69.3				$3	$5	$15
2004-S, Wisconsin, Proof, Silver	1,769,786	10,049	69.3				$8	$10	$20

‡ Ranked in the *100 Greatest U.S. Modern Coins*. **a.** Some 2004-D, Wisconsin, quarters show one of two different die flaws on the reverse, in the shape of an extra leaf on the corn. **b.** Included in 2004-D, Wisconsin, mintage figure.

2005, California	2005, Minnesota	2005, Oregon	2005, Kansas	2005, West Virginia
Reverse designer: Don Everhart.	Reverse designer: Charles Vickers.	Reverse designer: Donna Weaver.	Reverse designer: Norman E. Nemeth.	Reverse designer: John Mercanti.

| | Mintage | Cert | Avg | %MS | AU-50 | MS-63 | MS-65 | MS-66 | MS-67 |
							PF-65	PF-66DC	PF-69DC
2005-P, California	257,200,000	460	65.9	100%	$0.30	$0.75	$1.10	$10	$30
2005-P, California, Satin Finish	1,160,000	2,839	67.0	100%	$1	$2	$3	$5	$12
2005-D, California	263,200,000	289	66.2	99%	$0.30	$0.75	$1.10	$10	$30
2005-D, California, Satin Finish	1,160,000	2,519	66.9	100%	$1	$2	$3	$5	$12
2005-S, California, Proof	3,262,960	8,595	69.3				$3	$4.50	$15
2005-S, California, Proof, Silver	1,678,649	10,884	69.4				$8	$10	$20
2005-P, Minnesota	239,600,000	364	65.1	98%	$0.30	$0.75	$1	$10	$30
2005-P, Minnesota, Satin Finish	1,160,000	2,959	67.2	100%	$1	$2	$3	$5	$12
2005-D, Minnesota	248,400,000	184	66.1	99%	$0.30	$0.75	$1	$10	$30
2005-D, Minnesota, Satin Finish	1,160,000	2,737	67.1	100%	$1	$2	$3	$5	$12
2005-S, Minnesota, Proof	3,262,960	8,560	69.3				$3	$4.50	$15
2005-S, Minnesota, Proof, Silver	1,678,649	10,634	69.4				$8	$10	$20
2005-P, Oregon	316,200,000	256	65.2	100%	$0.30	$0.75	$1	$10	$30
2005-P, Oregon, Satin Finish	1,160,000	3,007	67.2	100%	$1	$2	$3	$5	$12
2005-D, Oregon	404,000,000	142	66.2	100%	$0.30	$0.75	$1	$10	$30
2005-D, Oregon, Satin Finish	1,160,000	2,736	67.1	100%	$1	$2	$3	$5	$12
2005-S, Oregon, Proof	3,262,960	8,522	69.3				$3	$4.50	$15
2005-S, Oregon, Proof, Silver	1,678,649	10,627	69.4				$8	$10	$20
2005-P, Kansas	263,400,000	333	65.0	98%	$0.30	$0.75	$1	$10	$30
2005-P, Kansas, Satin Finish	1,160,000	2,556	66.8	100%	$1	$2	$3	$5	$12
2005-D, Kansas	300,000,000	229	66.3	100%	$0.30	$0.75	$1	$10	$30
2005-D, Kansas, Satin Finish	1,160,000	2,645	67.0	100%	$1	$2	$3	$5	$12
2005-S, Kansas, Proof	3,262,960	8,577	69.3				$3	$4.50	$15
2005-S, Kansas, Proof, Silver	1,678,649	10,748	69.3				$8	$10	$20
2005-P, West Virginia	365,400,000	300	65.3	100%	$0.30	$0.75	$1	$10	$30
2005-P, West Virginia, Satin Finish	1,160,000	2,831	67.0	100%	$1	$2	$3	$5	$12
2005-D, West Virginia	356,200,000	185	66.2	99%	$0.30	$0.75	$1	$10	$30
2005-D, West Virginia, Satin Finish	1,160,000	2,431	66.9	100%	$1	$2	$3	$5	$12
2005-S, West Virginia, Proof	3,262,960	8,588	69.3				$3	$4.50	$15
2005-S, West Virginia, Proof, Silver	1,678,649	10,755	69.4				$8	$10	$20

2006, Nevada	**2006, Nebraska**	**2006, Colorado**	**2006, North Dakota**	**2006, South Dakota**
Reverse designer: Don Everhart.	*Reverse designer: Charles Vickers.*	*Reverse designer: Norman E. Nemeth.*	*Reverse designer: Donna Weaver.*	*Reverse designer: John Mercanti.*

	Mintage	Cert	Avg	%MS	AU-50	MS-63	MS-65 / PF-65	MS-66 / PF-66DC	MS-67 / PF-69DC
2006-P, Nevada	277,000,000	275	66.1	100%	$0.30	$0.75	$1	$10	$30
2006-P, Nevada, Satin Finish	847,361	1,055	66.6	100%	$1	$2	$3	$5	$12
2006-D, Nevada	312,800,000	358	66.5	100%	$0.30	$0.75	$1	$10	$30
2006-D, Nevada, Satin Finish	847,361	1,279	66.9	100%	$1	$2	$3	$5	$12
2006-S, Nevada, Proof	2,882,428	5,953	69.4				$3	$4.50	$15
2006-S, Nevada, Proof, Silver	1,585,008	9,576	69.5				$8	$9	$20
2006-P, Nebraska	318,000,000	142	66.0	100%	$0.30	$0.75	$1	$10	$30
2006-P, Nebraska, Satin Finish	847,361	1,340	67.0	100%	$1	$2	$3	$5	$12
2006-D, Nebraska	273,000,000	264	66.5	100%	$0.30	$0.75	$1	$10	$30
2006-D, Nebraska, Satin Finish	847,361	1,593	67.2	100%	$1	$2	$3	$5	$12
2006-S, Nebraska, Proof	2,882,428	5,954	69.4				$3	$4.50	$15
2006-S, Nebraska, Proof, Silver	1,585,008	9,466	69.5				$8	$9	$20
2006-P, Colorado	274,800,000	256	66.2	100%	$0.30	$0.75	$1	$10	$30
2006-P, Colorado, Satin Finish	847,361	1,188	66.8	100%	$1	$2	$3	$5	$12
2006-D, Colorado	294,200,000	424	66.4	100%	$0.30	$0.75	$1	$10	$30
2006-D, Colorado, Satin Finish	847,361	1,509	67.2	100%	$1	$2	$3	$5	$12
2006-S, Colorado, Proof	2,882,428	5,941	69.4				$3	$4.50	$15
2006-S, Colorado, Proof, Silver	1,585,008	9,562	69.5				$8	$9	$20
2006-P, North Dakota	305,800,000	182	65.8	99%	$0.30	$0.75	$1	$10	$30
2006-P, North Dakota, Satin Finish	847,361	1,141	66.8	100%	$1	$2	$3	$5	$12
2006-D, North Dakota	359,000,000	271	66.2	100%	$0.30	$0.75	$1	$10	$30
2006-D, North Dakota, Satin Finish	847,361	1,542	67.1	100%	$1	$2	$3	$5	$12
2006-S, North Dakota, Proof	2,882,428	5,952	69.4				$3	$4.50	$15
2006-S, North Dakota, Proof, Silver	1,585,008	9,559	69.5				$8	$9	$20
2006-P, South Dakota	245,000,000	166	66.0	100%	$0.30	$0.75	$1	$10	$30
2006-P, South Dakota, Satin Finish	847,361	1,319	66.9	100%	$1	$2	$3	$5	$12
2006-D, South Dakota	265,800,000	188	66.2	99%	$0.30	$0.75	$1	$10	$30
2006-D, South Dakota, Satin Finish	847,361	1,550	67.1	100%	$1	$2	$3	$5	$12
2006-S, South Dakota, Proof	2,882,428	5,960	69.5				$3	$4.50	$15
2006-S, South Dakota, Proof, Silver	1,585,008	9,555	69.5				$8	$9	$20

2007, Montana	**2007, Washington**	**2007, Idaho**	**2007, Wyoming**	**2007, Utah**
Reverse designer: Don Everhart.	*Reverse designer: Charles Vickers.*	*Reverse designer: Don Everhart.*	*Reverse designer: Norman E. Nemeth.*	*Reverse designer: Joseph Menna.*

	Mintage	Cert	Avg	%MS	AU-50	MS-63	MS-65 / PF-65	MS-66 / PF-66DC	MS-67 / PF-69DC
2007-P, Montana	257,000,000	114	66.1	100%	$0.30	$0.75	$1	$10	$30

	Mintage	Cert	Avg	%MS	AU-50	MS-63	MS-65 / PF-65	MS-66 / PF-66DC	MS-67 / PF-69DC
2007-P, Montana, Satin Finish	895,628	325	66.5	100%	$1	$2	$3	$5	$12
2007-D, Montana	256,240,000	159	65.9	99%	$0.30	$0.75	$1	$10	$30
2007-D, Montana, Satin Finish	895,628	322	66.5	100%	$1	$2	$3	$5	$12
2007-S, Montana, Proof	2,374,778	3,429	69.5				$3	$4.50	$15
2007-S, Montana, Proof, Silver	1,313,481	7,972	69.4				$8	$9	$20
2007-P, Washington	265,200,000	143	66.1	100%	$0.30	$0.75	$1	$10	$30
2007-P, Washington, Satin Finish	895,628	309	66.4	100%	$1	$2	$3	$5	$12
2007-D, Washington	280,000,000	150	66.0	99%	$0.30	$0.75	$1	$10	$30
2007-D, Washington, Satin Finish	895,628	340	66.7	100%	$1	$2	$3	$5	$12
2007-S, Washington, Proof	2,374,778	3,217	69.5				$3	$4.50	$15
2007-S, Washington, Proof, Silver	1,313,481	7,928	69.4				$8	$9	$20
2007-P, Idaho	294,600,000	76	65.8	100%	$0.30	$0.75	$1	$10	$30
2007-P, Idaho, Satin Finish	895,628	348	66.6	100%	$1	$2	$3	$5	$12
2007-D, Idaho	286,800,000	118	66.2	100%	$0.30	$0.75	$1	$10	$30
2007-D, Idaho, Satin Finish	895,628	328	66.5	100%	$1	$2	$3	$5	$12
2007-S, Idaho, Proof	2,374,778	3,234	69.5				$3	$4.50	$15
2007-S, Idaho, Proof, Silver	1,313,481	7,980	69.4				$8	$9	$20
2007-P, Wyoming	243,600,000	73	65.2	100%	$0.30	$0.75	$1	$10	$30
2007-P, Wyoming, Satin Finish	895,628	288	66.1	100%	$1	$2	$3	$5	$12
2007-D, Wyoming	320,800,000	134	65.9	99%	$0.30	$0.75	$1	$10	$30
2007-D, Wyoming, Satin Finish	895,628	331	66.4	100%	$1	$2	$3	$5	$12
2007-S, Wyoming, Proof	2,374,778	3,158	69.4				$3	$4.50	$15
2007-S, Wyoming, Proof, Silver	1,313,481	7,841	69.3				$8	$9	$20
2007-P, Utah	255,000,000	128	65.6	100%	$0.30	$0.75	$1	$10	$30
2007-P, Utah, Satin Finish	895,628	304	66.3	100%	$1	$2	$3	$5	$12
2007-D, Utah	253,200,000	192	66.2	100%	$0.30	$0.75	$1	$10	$30
2007-D, Utah, Satin Finish	895,628	329	66.6	100%	$1	$2	$3	$5	$12
2007-S, Utah, Proof	2,374,778	3,178	69.5				$3	$4.50	$15
2007-S, Utah, Proof, Silver	1,313,481	7,985	69.4				$8	$9	$20

2008, Oklahoma
Reverse designer: Phebe Hemphill.

2008, New Mexico
Reverse designer: Don Everhart.

2008, Arizona
Reverse designer: Joseph Menna.

2008, Alaska
Reverse designer: Charles Vickers.

2008, Hawaii
Reverse designer: Don Everhart.

	Mintage	Cert	Avg	%MS	AU-50	MS-63	MS-65 / PF-65	MS-66 / PF-66DC	MS-67 / PF-69DC
2008-P, Oklahoma	222,000,000	68	65.7	99%	$0.30	$0.75	$1	$10	$30
2008-P, Oklahoma, Satin Finish	745,464	129	67.3	100%	$1	$2	$3	$5	$12
2008-D, Oklahoma	194,600,000	102	66.2	100%	$0.30	$0.75	$1	$10	$30
2008-D, Oklahoma, Satin Finish	745,464	107	67.2	100%	$1	$2	$3	$5	$12
2008-S, Oklahoma, Proof	2,078,112	3,511	69.5				$3	$5	$18
2008-S, Oklahoma, Proof, Silver	1,192,908	8,375	69.5				$8	$10	$22
2008-P, New Mexico	244,200,000	85	65.4	100%	$0.30	$0.75	$1	$10	$30
2008-P, New Mexico, Satin Finish	745,464	107	67.1	100%	$1	$2	$3	$5	$12
2008-D, New Mexico	244,400,000	123	66.3	100%	$0.30	$0.75	$1	$10	$30
2008-D, New Mexico, Satin Finish	745,464	81	67.0	100%	$1	$2	$3	$5	$12

	Mintage	Cert	Avg	%MS	AU-50	MS-63	MS-65 PF-65	MS-66 PF-66DC	MS-67 PF-69DC
2008-S, New Mexico, Proof	2,078,112	3,574	69.4				$3	$5	$18
2008-S, New Mexico, Proof, Silver	1,192,908	8,236	69.5				$8	$10	$22
2008-P, Arizona	244,600,000	126	65.8	100%	$0.30	$0.75	$1	$10	$30
2008-P, Arizona, Satin Finish	745,464	126	67.3	100%	$1	$2	$3	$5	$12
2008-D, Arizona	265,000,000	48	65.9	98%	$0.30	$0.75	$1	$10	$30
2008-D, Arizona, Satin Finish	745,464	92	67.4	100%	$1	$2	$3	$5	$12
2008-S, Arizona, Proof	2,078,112	3,659	69.6				$3	$5	$18
2008-S, Arizona, Proof, Silver	1,192,908	8,607	69.5				$8	$10	$22
2008-P, Alaska	251,800,000	66	65.6	100%	$0.30	$0.75	$1	$10	$30
2008-P, Alaska, Satin Finish	745,464	122	67.2	100%	$1	$2	$3	$5	$12
2008-D, Alaska	254,000,000	67	65.9	100%	$0.30	$0.75	$1	$10	$30
2008-D, Alaska, Satin Finish	745,464	90	66.9	100%	$1	$2	$3	$5	$12
2008-S, Alaska, Proof	2,078,112	3,493	69.5				$3	$5	$18
2008-S, Alaska, Proof, Silver	1,192,908	8,534	69.5				$8	$10	$22
2008-P, Hawaii	254,000,000	138	65.4	100%	$0.30	$0.75	$1	$10	$30
2008-P, Hawaii, Satin Finish	745,464	127	67.2	100%	$1	$2	$3	$5	$12
2008-D, Hawaii	263,600,000	66	65.7	100%	$0.30	$0.75	$1	$10	$30
2008-D, Hawaii, Satin Finish	745,464	101	67.0	100%	$1	$2	$3	$5	$12
2008-S, Hawaii, Proof	2,078,112	3,516	69.4				$3	$10	$25
2008-S, Hawaii, Proof, Silver	1,192,908	8,547	69.4				$8	$10	$22

2009, District of Columbia
Reverse designer: Don Everhart.

2009, Puerto Rico
Reverse designer: Joseph Menna.

2009, Guam
Reverse designer: Jim Licaretz.

2009, American Samoa
Reverse designer: Charles Vickers.

2009, U.S. Virgin Islands
Reverse designer: Joseph Menna.

2009, Northern Mariana Islands
Reverse designer: Phebe Hemphill.

	Mintage	Cert	Avg	%MS	AU-50	MS-63	MS-65 PF-65	MS-66 PF-66DC	MS-67 PF-69DC
2009-P, District of Columbia	83,600,000	89	66.1	100%	$0.50	$1	$1.50	$10	$30
2009-P, District of Columbia, Satin Finish	784,614	247	67.6	100%	$1	$2	$3	$5	$12
2009-D, District of Columbia	88,800,000	121	66.3	100%	$0.50	$1	$1.50	$10	$30
2009-D, District of Columbia, Satin Finish	784,614	254	67.9	100%	$1	$2	$3	$5	$12
2009-S, District of Columbia, Proof	2,113,478	4,150	69.6				$3	$4.50	$15
2009-S, District of Columbia, Proof, Silver	996,548	6,508	69.7				$8	$9	$20
2009-P, Puerto Rico	53,200,000	95	65.9	100%	$0.50	$1	$1.50	$10	$30
2009-P, Puerto Rico, Satin Finish	784,614	180	67.5	100%	$1	$2	$3	$5	$12
2009-D, Puerto Rico	86,000,000	82	66.6	100%	$0.50	$1	$1.50	$10	$30
2009-D, Puerto Rico, Satin Finish	784,614	234	67.8	100%	$1	$2	$3	$5	$12
2009-S, Puerto Rico, Proof	2,113,478	4,134	69.6				$3	$4.50	$15
2009-S, Puerto Rico, Proof, Silver	996,548	6,685	69.7				$8	$9	$20

	Mintage	Cert	Avg	%MS	AU-50	MS-63	MS-65 PF-65	MS-66 PF-66DC	MS-67 PF-69DC
2009-P, Guam	45,000,000	48	66.1	100%	$0.50	$1	$1.50	$10	$30
2009-P, Guam, Satin Finish	784,614	227	67.3	100%	$1	$2	$3	$5	$12
2009-D, Guam	42,600,000	67	66.6	100%	$0.50	$1	$1.50	$10	$30
2009-D, Guam, Satin Finish	784,614	215	67.5	100%	$1	$2	$3	$5	$12
2009-S, Guam, Proof	2,113,478	4,036	69.6				$3	$4.50	$15
2009-S, Guam, Proof, Silver	996,548	6,448	69.7				$8	$9	$20
2009-P, American Samoa	42,600,000	106	66.5	100%	$0.50	$1	$1.50	$10	$30
2009-P, American Samoa, Satin Finish	784,614	293	67.8	100%	$1	$2	$3	$5	$12
2009-D, American Samoa	39,600,000	135	67.0	100%	$0.50	$1	$1.50	$10	$30
2009-D, American Samoa, Satin Finish	784,614	338	68.2	100%	$1	$2	$3	$5	$12
2009-S, American Samoa, Proof	2,113,478	4,202	69.6				$3	$4.50	$15
2009-S, American Samoa, Proof, Silver	996,548	6,590	69.7				$8	$9	$20
2009-P, U.S. Virgin Islands	41,000,000	125	66.6	100%	$0.75	$1	$1.50	$12	$32
2009-P, U.S. Virgin Islands, Satin Finish	784,614	286	67.2	100%	$1	$2	$3	$5	$12
2009-D, U.S. Virgin Islands	41,000,000	118	66.6	100%	$0.75	$1	$1.50	$12	$32
2009-D, U.S. Virgin Islands, Satin Finish	784,614	315	67.8	100%	$1	$2	$3	$5	$12
2009-S, U.S. Virgin Islands, Proof	2,113,478	4,176	69.6				$3	$4.50	$15
2009-S, U.S. Virgin Islands, Proof, Silver	996,548	6,562	69.7				$8	$9	$20
2009-P, Northern Mariana Islands	35,200,000	120	66.7	100%	$0.50	$1	$1.50	$10	$30
2009-P, Northern Mariana Islands, Satin Finish	784,614	296	67.8	100%	$1	$2	$3	$5	$12
2009-D, Northern Mariana Islands	37,600,000	123	66.7	100%	$0.50	$1	$1.50	$10	$30
2009-D, Northern Mariana Islands, Satin Finish	784,614	286	67.7	100%	$1	$2	$3	$5	$12
2009-S, Northern Mariana Islands, Proof	2,113,478	4,177	69.6				$3	$4.50	$15
2009-S, Northern Mariana Islands, Proof, Silver	996,548	6,550	69.7			.	$8	$9	$20

WASHINGTON, AMERICA THE BEAUTIFUL™ (2010 TO DATE)

Designers: *John Flanagan (obverse); see image captions for reverse designers.* **Weight:** *Clad issue—5.67 grams; silver Proofs—6.25 grams.* **Composition:** *Clad issue—Outer layers of copper-nickel (.750 copper, .250 nickel) bonded to inner core of pure copper; silver Proofs—.900 silver, .100 copper (net weight .18084 oz. pure silver).* **Diameter:** *24.3 mm.* **Edge:** *Reeded.* **Mints:** *Clad issue—Philadelphia, Denver, and San Francisco; silver Proofs—San Francisco.*

Circulation Strike

Proof

History. In 2010 the U.S. Mint introduced a new program of quarters honoring national parks and historic sites in each state, the District of Columbia, and the five U.S. territories. It will run through 2021. These are released at the rate of five new reverse designs each year, in combination with the obverse found on the State and D.C./Territorial quarters of previous years. Circulation strikes are made at the Philadelphia and Denver mints, and special silver-content and Proof issues at San Francisco. Each coin combines a modified obverse depicting George Washington, without a date. The reverses are distinctive and bear the date of issue and a special design showcasing a national park in the state, district, or territory. The official title of the series is the America the Beautiful™ Quarters Program; popularly, they are known as National Park quarters.

In 2012, the U.S. Mint introduced a new innovation in the National Park quarters program. For the first time since the 1950s, the San Francisco Mint is being used to produce quarters in a non-Proof format. These Uncirculated coins are made in limited quantities for collectors. They can be purchased directly from the Mint for a premium above their face value, as opposed to being released into circulation like normal quarters. Unlike the Uncirculated S-mintmark Bicentennial quarters dated 1976, which were 40% silver and sold only in sets, the S-mintmark National Park quarters are of normal copper-nickel–clad composition and are sold in bags of 100 and rolls of 40 coins. Thus the 2012-S coins are considered the first circulation-strike quarters made at San Francisco since 1954. The S-mintmark coins have been made of each National Park design from 2012 to date.

Striking and Sharpness. These quarters can have light striking on the highest area of the obverse. On the reverse there can be weak areas, depending on the design, seemingly more often seen on Denver Mint coins.

Availability. All modern quarters are readily available in high grades. Typical MS coins are MS–63 and 64 with light abrasion. MS-65 and higher coins are in the minority, but enough exist that finding them is no problem. Around MS-68 many issues are scarce, and higher grades are scarcer yet. The S-mintmark coins are proportionally scarce compared to Philadelphia and Denver issues, and are not seen in circulation. They are available for direct purchase from the U.S. Mint in their year of issue, and from the secondary market after that.

Proofs. National Park quarter dollar Proofs are made in San Francisco. For certain later issues, Proofs are available in clad metal as well as silver strikings. On some Proofs over-polishing of dies has eliminated some details.

GRADING STANDARDS

MS-60 to 70 (Mint State). *Obverse:* At MS-60, some abrasion and contact marks are evident on the highest-relief parts of the hair and the cheek. At MS-63, abrasion is slight at best, less so at MS-64. An MS-65 coin should display no abrasion or contact marks except under magnification, and MS-66 and higher coins should have none at all. Luster should be full. *Reverse:* Check the highest-relief areas of the design (these differ from coin to coin). Otherwise, comments are as for the obverse.

2010-D, Hot Springs (AR). Graded MS-68.

PF-60 to 70 (Proof). *Obverse and Reverse:* These coins are so recent, and as only a few have been cleaned, most approach perfection and can be designated PF–68 to 70, the latter only if no contact marks or other problems can be seen under magnification. A cleaned coin with extensive hairlines would not be collectible for most numismatists and would be classified at a lower level such as PF–60 to 63. Those with lighter hairlines qualify for PF–64 or 65.

2010-S, Grand Canyon (AZ). Graded PF-69 Ultra Cameo.

2010, Hot Springs National Park (AR)
Reverse designer: Don Everhart.

2010, Yellowstone National Park (WY)
Reverse designer: Don Everhart.

2010, Yosemite National Park (CA)
Reverse designer: Joseph Menna.

2010, Grand Canyon National Park (AZ)
Reverse designer: Phebe Hemphill.

2010, Mt. Hood National Forest (OR)
Reverse designer: Phebe Hemphill.

	Mintage	Cert	Avg	%MS	AU-50	MS-63	MS-65 / PF-65	MS-66 / PF-66DC	MS-67 / PF-69DC
2010-P, Hot Springs National Park (AR)	35,600,000	711	66.1	100%	$0.45	$0.50	$1	$10	$30
2010-P, Hot Springs National Park (AR), Satin Finish	583,897	366	67.5	100%	$1	$2	$3	$5	$12
2010-D, Hot Springs National Park (AR)	34,000,000	1,547	65.6	100%	$0.45	$0.50	$1	$10	$30
2010-D, Hot Springs National Park (AR), Satin Finish	583,897	417	67.5	100%	$1	$2	$3	$5	$12
2010-S, Hot Springs National Park (AR), Proof	1,402,889	4,044	69.5				$3	$4.50	$15
2010-S, Hot Springs, National Park (AR), Proof, Silver	859,417	11,246	69.6				$8	$9	$20
2010-P, Yellowstone National Park (WY)	33,600,000	446	66.1	100%	$0.45	$0.50	$1	$10	$30
2010-P, Yellowstone National Park (WY), Satin Finish	583,897	345	67.4	100%	$1	$2	$3	$5	$12
2010-D, Yellowstone National Park (WY)	34,800,000	764	65.8	100%	$0.45	$0.50	$1	$10	$30
2010-D, Yellowstone National Park (WY), Satin Finish	583,897	360	67.4	100%	$1	$2	$3	$5	$12
2010-S, Yellowstone National Park (WY), Proof	1,404,259	4,083	69.5				$3	$4.50	$15
2010-S, Yellowstone National Park (WY), Proof, Silver	859,417	11,256	69.7				$8	$9	$20
2010-P, Yosemite National Park (CA)	35,200,000	288	66.1	100%	$0.50	$0.75	$1.25	$12	$30
2010-P, Yosemite National Park (CA), Satin Finish	583,897	372	67.3	100%	$1	$2	$3	$5	$12
2010-D, Yosemite National Park (CA)	34,800,000	617	66.0	100%	$0.50	$0.75	$1.25	$12	$30
2010-D, Yosemite National Park (CA), Satin Finish	583,897	397	67.4	100%	$1	$2	$3	$5	$12
2010-S, Yosemite National Park (CA), Proof	1,401,522	4,009	69.5				$3	$4.50	$15
2010-S, Yosemite National Park (CA), Proof, Silver	859,417	11,155	69.6				$8	$9	$20
2010-P, Grand Canyon National Park (AZ)	34,800,000	374	66.3	100%	$0.45	$0.50	$1	$10	$30
2010-P, Grand Canyon National Park (AZ), Satin Finish	583,897	386	67.5	100%	$1	$2	$3	$5	$12
2010-D, Grand Canyon National Park (AZ)	35,400,000	630	66.1	100%	$0.45	$0.50	$1	$10	$30
2010-D, Grand Canyon National Park (AZ), Satin Finish	583,897	433	67.7	100%	$1	$2	$3	$5	$12
2010-S, Grand Canyon National Park (AZ), Proof	1,401,462	3,995	69.5				$3	$4.50	$15
2010-S, Grand Canyon National Park (AZ), Proof, Silver	859,417	11,173	69.6				$8	$9	$20
2010-P, Mt. Hood National Forest (OR)	34,400,000	215	66.1	100%	$0.45	$0.50	$1	$10	$30
2010-P, Mt. Hood National Forest (OR), Satin Finish	583,897	338	67.3	100%	$1	$2	$3	$5	$12
2010-D, Mt. Hood National Forest (OR)	34,400,000	415	65.6	100%	$0.45	$0.50	$1	$10	$30
2010-D, Mt. Hood National Forest (OR), Satin Finish	583,897	433	67.5	100%	$1	$2	$3	$5	$12
2010-S, Mt. Hood National Forest (OR), Proof	1,398,106	4,010	69.4				$3	$4.50	$15
2010-S, Mt. Hood National Forest (OR), Proof, Silver	859,417	11,350	69.6				$8	$9	$20

2011, Gettysburg National Military Park (PA)
Reverse designer: Joel Iskowitz.

2011, Glacier National Park (MT)
Reverse designer: Barbara Fox.

2011, Olympic National Park (WA)
Reverse designer: Susan Gamble.

2011, Vicksburg National Military Park (MS)
Reverse designer: Thomas Cleveland.

2011, Chickasaw National Recreation Area (OK)
Reverse designer: Donna Weaver.

	Mintage	Cert	Avg	%MS	AU-50	MS-63	MS-65 / PF-65	MS-66 / PF-66DC	MS-67 / PF-69DC
2011-P, Gettysburg National Military Park (PA)	30,800,000	756	66.3	100%	$0.50	$0.75	$1.25	$12	$30
2011-D, Gettysburg National Military Park (PA)	30,400,000	303	66.5	100%	$0.50	$0.75	$1.25	$12	$30
2011-S, Gettysburg National Military Park (PA), Proof	1,273,068	2,756	69.5				$3	$4.50	$15
2011-S, Gettysburg National Military Park (PA), Proof, Silver	722,076	5,993	69.7				$8	$9	$20
2011-P, Glacier National Park (MT)	30,400,000	292	67.1	100%	$0.45	$0.50	$1	$10	$30
2011-D, Glacier National Park (MT)	31,200,000	457	65.9	100%	$0.45	$0.50	$1	$10	$30
2011-S, Glacier National Park (MT), Proof	1,269,422	2,754	69.6				$3	$4.50	$15
2011-S, Glacier National Park (MT), Proof, Silver	722,076	6,150	69.7				$8	$9	$20
2011-P, Olympic National Park (WA)	30,400,000	308	67.1	100%	$0.45	$0.50	$1	$10	$30
2011-D, Olympic National Park (WA)	30,600,000	556	66.2	100%	$0.45	$0.50	$1	$10	$30
2011-S, Olympic National Park (WA), Proof	1,268,231	2,768	69.6				$3	$4.50	$15
2011-S, Olympic National Park (WA), Proof, Silver	722,076	5,973	69.7				$8	$9	$20
2011-P, Vicksburg National Military Park (MS)	30,800,000	280	66.8	100%	$0.45	$0.50	$1	$10	$30
2011-D, Vicksburg National Military Park (MS)	33,400,000	475	66.3	100%	$0.45	$0.50	$1	$10	$30
2011-S, Vicksburg National Military Park (MS), Proof	1,268,623	2,761	69.5				$3	$4.50	$15
2011-S, Vicksburg National Military Park (MS), Proof, Silver	722,076	6,015	69.7				$8	$9	$20
2011-P, Chickasaw National Recreation Area (OK)	73,800,000	324	67.2	100%	$0.45	$0.50	$1	$10	$30
2011-D, Chickasaw National Recreation Area (OK)	69,400,000	430	66.2	100%	$0.45	$0.50	$1	$10	$30
2011-S, Chickasaw National Recreation Area (OK), Proof	1,266,825	2,749	69.5				$3	$4.50	$15
2011-S, Chickasaw National Recreation Area (OK), Proof, Silver	722,076	5,931	69.6				$8	$9	$20

2012, El Yunque National Forest (PR)
Reverse designer: Gary Whitley.

2012, Chaco Culture National Historical Park (NM)
Reverse designer: Donna Weaver.

2012, Acadia National Park (ME)
Reverse designer: Barbara Fox.

2012, Hawai'i Volcanoes National Park (HI)
Reverse designer: Charles L. Vickers.

2012, Denali National Park and Preserve (AK)
Reverse designer: Susan Gamble.

	Mintage	Cert	Avg	%MS	AU-50	MS-63	MS-65 / PF-65	MS-66 / PF-66DC	MS-67 / PF-69DC
2012-P, El Yunque National Forest (PR)	25,800,000	562	66.1	100%	$0.45	$0.50	$1	$10	$30
2012-D, El Yunque National Forest (PR)	25,000,000	252	66.8	100%	$0.45	$0.50	$1	$10	$30
2012-S, El Yunque National Forest (PR) (a)	1,680,140	610	66.4	100%		$1	$2	$12	$35
2012-S, El Yunque National Forest (PR), Proof	1,012,094	2,022	69.3				$3	$4.50	$15
2012-S, El Yunque National Forest (PR), Proof, Silver	608,060	4,954	69.7				$8	$9	$20
2012-P, Chaco Culture National Historical Park (NM)	22,000,000	146	67.2	100%	$0.45	$0.50	$1	$10	$30
2012-D, Chaco Culture National Historical Park (NM)	22,000,000	355	66.2	100%	$0.45	$0.50	$1	$10	$30
2012-S, Chaco Culture National Historical Park (NM) (a)	1,389,020	375	66.5	100%		$1	$2	$12	$35
2012-S, Chaco Culture National Historical Park (NM), Proof	961,464	2,011	69.3				$3	$4.50	$15
2012-S, Chaco Culture National Historical Park (NM), Proof, Silver	608,060	4,703	69.7				$8	$9	$20
2012-P, Acadia National Park (ME)	24,800,000	343	65.6	100%	$0.45	$0.50	$1	$10	$30
2012-D, Acadia National Park (ME)	21,606,000	114	66.7	100%	$0.45	$0.50	$1	$10	$30
2012-S, Acadia National Park (ME) (a)	1,409,120	453	66.3	100%		$1	$2	$12	$35
2012-S, Acadia National Park (ME), Proof	962,038	2,015	69.3				$3	$4.50	$15
2012-S, Acadia National Park (ME), Proof, Silver	608,060	4,873	69.7				$8	$9	$20

a. Not issued for circulation. From 2012 to date, the San Francisco Mint has made relatively small quantities of Uncirculated S-mintmark quarters of each design in the National Park series. These can be purchased by collectors directly from the U.S. Mint, in bags of 100 or rolls of 40 coins, for a premium above face value.

	Mintage	Cert	Avg	%MS	AU-50	MS-63	MS-65 PF-65	MS-66 PF-66DC	MS-67 PF-69DC
2012-P, Hawai'i Volcanoes National Park (HI)	46,200,000	133	67.1	100%	$0.45	$0.50	$1	$10	$30
2012-D, Hawai'i Volcanoes National Park (HI)	78,600,000	406	66.1	100%	$0.45	$0.50	$1	$10	$30
2012-S, Hawai'i Volcanoes National Park (HI) (a)	1,409,120	406	66.4	100%	$0.45	$0.50	$1	$12	$35
2012-S, Hawai'i Volcanoes National Park (HI), Proof	962,447	2,017	69.3				$3	$4.50	$15
2012-S, Hawai'i Volcanoes National Park (HI), Proof, Silver	608,060	5,014	69.7				$8	$9	$20
2012-P, Denali National Park and Preserve (AK)	135,400,000	152	67.0	100%	$0.40	$0.50	$1	$10	$30
2012-D, Denali National Park and Preserve (AK)	166,600,000	439	66.2	100%	$0.40	$0.50	$1	$10	$30
2012-S, Denali National Park and Preserve (AK) (a)	1,409,220	532	66.2	100%		$1	$2	$12	$35
2012-S, Denali National Park and Preserve (AK), Proof	959,602	2,019	69.3				$3	$4.50	$15
2012-S, Denali National Park and Preserve (AK), Proof, Silver	608,060	4,900	69.7				$8	$9	$20

a. Not issued for circulation. From 2012 to date, the San Francisco Mint has made Uncirculated S-mintmark quarters of each design in the National Park series. These can be purchased by collectors directly from the U.S. Mint, in bags of 100 or rolls of 40 coins, for a premium above face value.

2013, White Mountain National Forest (NH) *Reverse designer: Phebe Hemphill.*	2013, Perry's Victory and International Peace Memorial (OH) *Reverse designer: Don Everhart.*	2013, Great Basin National Park (NV) *Reverse designer: Ronald D. Sanders.*	2013, Fort McHenry National Monument and Historic Shrine (MD) *Reverse designer: Joseph Menna.*	2013, Mount Rushmore National Memorial (SD) *Reverse designer: Joseph Menna.*

	Mintage	Cert	Avg	%MS	AU-50	MS-63	MS-65 PF-65	MS-66 PF-66DC	MS-67 PF-69DC
2013-P, White Mountain National Forest (NH)	68,800,000	538	66.5	100%	$0.45	$0.50	$1	$10	$30
2013-D, White Mountain National Forest (NH)	107,600,000	295	67.1	100%	$0.45	$0.50	$1	$10	$30
2013-S, White Mountain National Forest (NH) (a)	1,606,900	350	66.4	100%		$1	$2	$12	$35
2013-S, White Mountain National Forest (NH), Proof	989,803	1,868	69.5				$3	$4.50	$15
2013-S, White Mountain National Forest (NH), Proof, Silver	467,691	4,976	69.7				$8	$9	$20
2013-P, Perry's Victory and Int'l Peace Memorial (OH)	107,800,000	464	66.5	100%	$0.45	$0.50	$1	$10	$30
2013-D, Perry's Victory and Int'l Peace Memorial (OH)	131,600,000	264	67.2	100%	$0.45	$0.50	$1	$10	$30
2013-S, Perry's Victory and Int'l Peace Memorial (OH) (a)	1,425,860	260	66.4	100%		$1	$2	$12	$35
2013-S, Perry's Victory and Int'l Peace Memorial (OH), Proof	947,815	1,841	69.5				$3	$4.50	$15
2013-S, Perry's Victory and Int'l Peace Memorial (OH), Proof, Silver	467,691	4,859	69.7				$8	$9	$20
2013-P, Great Basin National Park (NV)	122,400,000	215	66.9	100%	$0.45	$0.50	$1	$10	$30
2013-D, Great Basin National Park (NV)	141,400,000	442	66.5	100%	$0.45	$0.50	$1	$10	$30
2013-S, Great Basin National Park (NV) (a)	1,316,500	296	66.9	100%		$1	$2	$12	$35
2013-S, Great Basin National Park (NV), Proof	945,777	1,841	69.5				$3	$4.50	$15
2013-S, Great Basin National Park (NV), Proof, Silver	467,691	5,031	69.7				$8	$9	$20
2013-P, Ft. McHenry Nat'l Monument / Historic Shrine (MD)	120,000,000	486	66.5	100%	$0.45	$0.50	$1	$10	$30
2013-D, Ft. McHenry Nat'l Monument / Historic Shrine (MD)	151,400,000	299	67.2	100%	$0.45	$0.50	$1	$10	$30
2013-S, Ft. McHenry Nat'l Monument / Historic Shrine (MD) (a)	1,313,680	498	67.1	100%		$1	$2	$12	$35
2013-S, Ft. McHenry Nat'l Monument / Historic Shrine (MD), Proof	946,380	1,839	69.5				$3	$4.50	$15
2013-S, Ft. McHenry National Monument / Historic Shrine (MD), Proof, Silver	467,691	4,989	69.7				$8	$9	$20

a. Not issued for circulation. From 2012 to date, the San Francisco Mint has made Uncirculated S-mintmark quarters of each design in the National Park series. These can be purchased by collectors directly from the U.S. Mint, in bags of 100 or rolls of 40 coins, for a premium above face value.

	Mintage	Cert	Avg	%MS	AU-50	MS-63	MS-65	MS-66	MS-67
							PF-65	PF-66DC	PF-69DC
2013-P, Mount Rushmore National Memorial (SD)	231,800,000	191	66.9	100%	$0.45	$0.50	$1	$10	$30
2013-D, Mount Rushmore National Memorial (SD)	272,400,000	438	66.3	100%	$0.45	$0.50	$1	$10	$30
2013-S, Mount Rushmore National Memorial (SD) (a)	1,373,260	445	66.9	100%		$1	$2	$12	$35
2013-S, Mount Rushmore National Memorial (SD), Proof	958,853	1,840	69.5				$3	$4.50	$15
2013-S, Mount Rushmore National Memorial (SD), Proof, Silver	467,691	4,999	69.7				$8	$9	$20

a. Not issued for circulation. From 2012 to date, the San Francisco Mint has made Uncirculated S-mintmark quarters of each design in the National Park series. These can be purchased by collectors directly from the U.S. Mint, in bags of 100 or rolls of 40 coins, for a premium above face value.

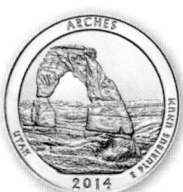

2014, Great Smoky Mountains National Park (TN)
Reverse designer: Chris Costello.

2014, Shenandoah National Park (VA)
Reverse designer: Phebe Hemphill.

2014, Arches National Park (UT)
Reverse designer: Donna Weaver.

2014, Great Sand Dunes National Park (CO)
Reverse designer: Don Everhart.

2014, Everglades National Park (FL)
Reverse designer: Joel Iskowitz.

	Mintage	Cert	Avg	%MS	AU-50	MS-63	MS-65	MS-66	MS-67
							PF-65	PF-66DC	PF-69DC
2014-P, Great Smoky Mountains National Park (TN)	73,200,000	413	66.6	100%	$0.45	$0.50	$1	$10	$30
2014-D, Great Smoky Mountains National Park (TN)	99,400,000	259	67.4	100%	$0.45	$0.50	$1	$10	$30
2014-S, Great Smoky Mountains National Park (TN) (a)	1,360,780	485	66.7	100%		$1	$2	$12	$35
2014-S, Great Smoky Mountains National Park (TN), Proof	881,896	2,081	69.5				$3	$4.50	$15
2014-S, Great Smoky Mountains National Park (TN), Proof, Silver	472,107	4,286	69.7				$8	$9	$20
2014-P, Shenandoah National Park (VA)	112,800,000	413	66.4	100%	$0.45	$0.50	$1	$10	$30
2014-D, Shenandoah National Park (VA)	197,800,000	236	67.4	100%	$0.45	$0.50	$1	$10	$30
2014-S, Shenandoah National Park (VA) (a)	1,260,700	695	66.9	100%		$1	$2	$12	$35
2014-S, Shenandoah National Park (VA), Proof	846,441	2,075	69.5				$3	$4.50	$15
2014-S, Shenandoah National Park (VA), Proof, Silver	472,107	4,291	69.7				$8	$9	$20
2014-P, Arches National Park (UT)	214,200,000	252	67.3	100%	$0.45	$0.50	$1	$10	$30
2014-D, Arches National Park (UT)	251,400,000	295	67.4	100%	$0.45	$0.50	$1	$10	$30
2014-S, Arches National Park (UT) (a)	1,226,220	575	66.8	100%		$1	$2	$12	$35
2014-S, Arches National Park (UT), Proof	844,775	2,078	69.4				$3	$4.50	$15
2014-S, Arches National Park (UT), Proof, Silver	472,107	4,418	69.7				$8	$9	$20
2014-P, Great Sand Dunes National Park (CO)	159,600,000	186	67.4	100%	$0.45	$0.50	$1	$10	$30
2014-D, Great Sand Dunes National Park (CO)	171,800,000	224	67.6	100%	$0.45	$0.50	$1	$10	$30
2014-S, Great Sand Dunes National Park (CO) (a)	1,170,500	822	67.1	100%		$1	$2	$12	$35
2014-S, Great Sand Dunes National Park (CO), Proof	843,238	2,074	69.5				$3	$4.50	$15
2014-S, Great Sand Dunes National Park (CO), Proof, Silver	472,107	4,284	69.7				$8	$9	$20
2014-P, Everglades National Park (FL)	157,601,200	198	67.3	100%	$0.45	$0.50	$1	$10	$30
2014-D, Everglades National Park (FL)	142,400,000	286	67.6	100%	$0.45	$0.50	$1	$10	$30
2014-S, Everglades National Park (FL) (a)	1,173,720	0	n/a			$1	$2	$12	$35
2014-S, Everglades National Park (FL), Proof	856,139	2,076	69.5				$3	$4.50	$15
2014-S, Everglades National Park (FL), Proof, Silver	472,107	4,283	69.7				$8	$9	$20

a. Not issued for circulation. From 2012 to date, the San Francisco Mint has made Uncirculated S-mintmark quarters of each design in the National Park series. These can be purchased by collectors directly from the U.S. Mint, in bags of 100 or rolls of 40 coins, for a premium above face value.

2015, Homestead National Monument of America (NE)
Reverse designer: Ronald D. Sanders.

2015, Kisatchie National Forest (LA)
Reverse designer: Susan Gamble.

2015, Blue Ridge Parkway (NC)
Reverse designer: Frank Morris.

2015, Bombay Hook National Wildlife Refuge (DE)
Reverse designer: Joel Iskowitz.

2015, Saratoga National Historical Park (NY)
Reverse designer: Barbara Fox.

	Mintage	Cert	Avg	%MS	AU-50	MS-63	MS-65	MS-66	MS-67
							PF-65	PF-66DC	PF-69DC
2015-P, Homestead National Monument of America (NE)	214,780,456	2,383	64.8	100%	$0.50	$0.75	$1	$10	$30
2015-D, Homestead National Monument of America (NE)	248,980,456	129	66.8	100%	$0.50	$0.75	$1	$10	$30
2015-S, Homestead National Monument of America (NE) (a)	1,135,460	1,022	67.0	100%		$2	$3	$12	$35
2015-S, Homestead National Monument of America (NE), Proof	778,319	1,666	69.6				$3	$4.50	$15
2015-S, Homestead National Monument of America (NE), Proof, Silver	490,621	3,892	69.5				$8	$9	$20
2015-P, Kisatchie National Forest (LA)	397,579,544	228	67.3	100%	$0.50	$0.75	$1	$10	$30
2015-D, Kisatchie National Forest (LA)	379,979,544	178	67.0	100%	$0.50	$0.75	$1	$10	$30
2015-S, Kisatchie National Forest (LA) (a)	1,099,380	596	67.0	100%		$2	$3	$12	$35
2015-S, Kisatchie National Forest (LA), Proof	777,407	1,600	69.6				$3	$4.50	$15
2015-S, Kisatchie National Forest (LA), Proof, Silver	490,621	3,911	69.5				$8	$9	$20
2015-P, Blue Ridge Parkway (NC)	326,947,055	132	66.8	100%	$0.50	$0.75	$1	$10	$30
2015-D, Blue Ridge Parkway (NC)	506,529,955	165	66.9	100%	$0.50	$0.75	$1	$10	$30
2015-S, Blue Ridge Parkway (NC) (a)	1,096,620	356	66.5	100%		$2	$3	$12	$35
2015-S, Blue Ridge Parkway (NC), Proof	779,338	1,599	69.6				$3	$4.50	$15
2015-S, Blue Ridge Parkway (NC), Proof, Silver	490,621	3,884	69.5				$8	$9	$20
2015-P, Bombay Hook National Wildlife Refuge (DE)	275,377,747	189	67.1	100%	$0.50	$0.75	$1	$10	$30
2015-D, Bombay Hook National Wildlife Refuge (DE)	206,777,747	239	67.2	100%	$0.50	$0.75	$1	$10	$30
2015-S, Bombay Hook National Wildlife Refuge (DE) (a)	923,960	270	66.7	100%		$2	$3	$12	$35
2015-S, Bombay Hook National Wildlife Refuge (DE), Proof	775,610	1,603	69.5				$3	$4.50	$15
2015-S, Bombay Hook National Wildlife Refuge (DE), Proof, Silver	490,621	3,908	69.5				$8	$9	$20
2015-P, Saratoga National Historical Park (NY)	223,379,266	130	67.0	100%	$0.50	$0.75	$1	$10	$30
2015-D, Saratoga National Historical Park (NY)	216,179,266	179	67.0	100%	$0.50	$0.75	$1	$10	$30
2015-S, Saratoga National Historical Park (NY) (a)	888,380	276	66.9	100%		$2	$3	$12	$35
2015-S, Saratoga National Historical Park (NY), Proof	777,129	1,604	69.5				$3	$4.50	$15
2015-S, Saratoga National Historical Park (NY), Proof, Silver	490,621	3,892	69.5				$8	$9	$20

a. Not issued for circulation. From 2012 to date, the San Francisco Mint has made Uncirculated S-mintmark quarters of each design in the National Park series. These can be purchased by collectors directly from the U.S. Mint, in bags of 100 or rolls of 40 coins, for a premium above face value.

In 2016 a special .9999 fine gold striking of Hermon A. MacNeil's Standing Liberty quarter was created to celebrate the 100th anniversary of its introduction. It is smaller than the silver strikings, with a diameter of 22 mm and weighing 7.776 grams. Struck at West Point, it has a reeded edge. Similar strikings were made for the 1916 dime and half dollar designs.

	Mintage	Cert	Avg	%MS	SP-67	SP-70
2016-W, Standing Liberty Centennial Gold Coin	91,752				$475	$600

Normally scheduled production of clad and silver America the Beautiful quarters, in the same standards and specifications as previously, continued in 2016 and beyond, and was not disrupted by the gold Standing Liberty quarter.

  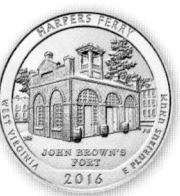  

2016, Shawnee National Forest (IL)
Reverse designer: Justin Kunz.

2016, Cumberland Gap National Historic Park (KY)
Reverse designer: Barbara Fox.

2016, Harpers Ferry National Historical Park (WV)
Reverse designer: Thomas Hipschen.

2016, Theodore Roosevelt National Park (ND)
Reverse designer: Joel Iskowitz.

2016, Fort Moultrie at Fort Sumter National Monument (SC)
Reverse designer: Richard Scott.

	Mintage	Cert	Avg	%MS	AU-50	MS-63	MS-65 / PF-65	MS-66 / PF-66DC	MS-67 / PF-69DC
2016-P, Shawnee National Forest (IL)	157,075,976	216	67.0	100%	$0.50	$0.75	$1	$10	$30
2016-D, Shawnee National Forest (IL)	153,087,436	244	66.9	100%	$0.50	$0.75	$1	$10	$30
2016-S, Shawnee National Forest (IL) (a)	883,200	241	66.8	100%		$2	$3	$12	$35
2016-S, Shawnee National Forest (IL), Proof	731,529	1,134	69.7				$3	$4.50	$15
2016-S, Shawnee National Forest (IL), Proof, Silver	514,905	3,965	69.7				$8	$9	$20
2016-P, Cumberland Gap National Historical Park (KY)	216,674,939	260	67.1	100%	$0.50	$0.75	$1	$10	$30
2016-D, Cumberland Gap National Historical Park (KY)	224,468,139	349	67.3	100%	$0.50	$0.75	$1	$10	$30
2016-S, Cumberland Gap National Historical Park (KY) (a)	1,021,160	259	66.6	100%		$2	$3	$12	$35
2016-S, Cumberland Gap National Historical Park (KY), Proof	701,325	1,131	69.7				$3	$4.50	$15
2016-S, Cumberland Gap National Historical Park (KY), Proof, Silver	514,905	3,984	69.7				$8	$9	$20
2016-P, Harpers Ferry National Historical Park (WV)	435,902,470	191	66.7	100%	$0.50	$0.75	$1	$10	$30
2016-D, Harpers Ferry National Historical Park (WV)	425,267,270	209	67.0	100%	$0.50	$0.75	$1	$10	$30
2016-S, Harpers Ferry National Historical Park (WV) (a)	1,035,880	269	66.7	100%		$2	$3	$12	$35
2016-S, Harpers Ferry National Historical Park (WV), Proof	700,636	1,142	69.7				$3	$4.50	$15
2016-S, Harpers Ferry National Historical Park (WV), Proof, Silver	514,905	4,023	69.7				$8	$9	$20
2016-P, Theodore Roosevelt National Park (ND)	232,893,034	202	66.9	100%	$0.50	$0.75	$1	$10	$30
2016-D, Theodore Roosevelt National Park (ND)	224,477,934	231	66.9	100%	$0.50	$0.75	$1	$10	$30
2016-S, Theodore Roosevelt National Park (ND) (a)	1,057,060	1	66.0	100%		$2	$3	$12	$35
2016-S, Theodore Roosevelt National Park (ND), Proof	702,220	1,130	69.7				$3	$4.50	$15
2016-S, Theodore Roosevelt National Park (ND), Proof, Silver	514,905	3,967	69.7				$8	$9	$20

a. Not issued for circulation. From 2012 to date, the San Francisco Mint has made Uncirculated S-mintmark quarters of each design in the National Park series. These can be purchased by collectors directly from the U.S. Mint, in bags of 100 or rolls of 40 coins, for a premium above face value.

| | Mintage | Cert | Avg | %MS | AU-50 | MS-63 | MS-65 | MS-66 | MS-67 |
							PF-65	PF-66DC	PF-69DC
2016-P, Fort Moultrie (Fort Sumter National Monument) (SC)	155,623,080	225	67.0	100%	$0.50	$0.75	$1	$10	$30
2016-D, Fort Moultrie (Fort Sumter National Monument) (SC)	143,415,780	260	67.1	100%	$0.50	$0.75	$1	$10	$30
2016-S, Fort Moultrie (Fort Sumter National Monument) (SC) (a)	966,300	1	67.0	100%		$2	$3	$12	$35
2016-S, Fort Moultrie (Fort Sumter National Monument) (SC), Proof	716,470	1,128	69.7				$3	$4.50	$15
2016-S, Fort Moultrie (Fort Sumter National Monument) (SC), Proof, Silver	514,905	4,061	69.7				$8	$9	$20

a. Not issued for circulation. From 2012 to date, the San Francisco Mint has made Uncirculated S-mintmark quarters of each design in the National Park series. These can be purchased by collectors directly from the U.S. Mint, in bags of 100 or rolls of 40 coins, for a premium above face value.

2017, Effigy Mounds National Monument (IA) Reverse designer: Richard Masters. | **2017, Frederick Douglass National Historic Site (DC)** Reverse designer: Thomas Hipschen. | **2017, Ozark National Scenic Riverways (MO)** Reverse designer: Ronald D. Sanders. | **2017, Ellis Island (Statue of Liberty National Monument) (NJ)** Reverse designer: Barbara Fox. | **2017, George Rogers Clark National Historical Park (IN)** Reverse designer: Frank Morris.

| | Mintage | Cert | Avg | %MS | AU-50 | MS-63 | MS-65 | MS-66 | MS-67 |
							PF-65	PF-66DC	PF-69DC
2017-P, Effigy Mounds National Monument (IA)					$0.50	$0.75	$1	$10	$30
2017-D, Effigy Mounds National Monument (IA)					$0.50	$0.75	$1	$10	$30
2017-S, Effigy Mounds National Monument (IA) (a)						$2	$3	$12	$35
2017-S, Effigy Mounds National Monument (IA), Enhanced Uncirculated							$3	$4.50	$15
2017-S, Effigy Mounds National Monument (IA), Proof							$3	$4.50	$15
2017-S, Effigy Mounds National Monument (IA), Proof, Silver							$8	$9	$20
2017-P, Frederick Douglass National Historic Site (DC)					$0.50	$0.75	$1	$10	$30
2017-D, Frederick Douglass National Historic Site (DC)					$0.50	$0.75	$1	$10	$30
2017-S, Frederick Douglass National Historic Site (DC) (a)						$2	$3	$12	$35
2017-S, Frederick Douglass National Historic Site (DC), Enhanced Uncirculated							$3	$4.50	$15
2017-S, Frederick Douglass National Historic Site (DC), Proof							$3	$4.50	$15
2017-S, Frederick Douglass National Historic Site (DC), Proof, Silver							$8	$9	$20
2017-P, Ozark National Scenic Riverways (MO)					$0.50	$0.75	$1	$10	$30
2017-D, Ozark National Scenic Riverways (MO)					$0.50	$0.75	$1	$10	$30
2017-S, Ozark National Scenic Riverways (MO) (a)						$2	$3	$12	$35
2017-S, Ozark National Scenic Riverways (MO), Enhanced Uncirculated							$3	$4.50	$15
2017-S, Ozark National Scenic Riverways (MO), Proof							$3	$4.50	$15
2017-S, Ozark National Scenic Riverways (MO), Proof, Silver							$8	$9	$20

a. Not issued for circulation. From 2012 to date, the San Francisco Mint has made Uncirculated S-mintmark quarters of each design in the National Park series. These can be purchased by collectors directly from the U.S. Mint, in bags of 100 or rolls of 40 coins, for a premium above face value.

	Mintage	Cert	Avg	%MS	AU-50	MS-63	MS-65	MS-66	MS-67
							PF-65	PF-66DC	PF-69DC
2017-P, Ellis Island (Statue of Liberty National Monument) (NJ)					$0.50	$0.75	$1	$10	$30
2017-D, Ellis Island (Statue of Liberty National Monument) (NJ)					$0.50	$0.75	$1	$10	$30
2017-S, Ellis Island (Statue of Liberty National Monument) (NJ) (a)						$2	$3	$12	$35
2017-S, Ellis Island (Statue of Liberty National Monument) (NJ), Enhanced Uncirculated							$3	$4.50	$15
2017-S, Ellis Island (Statue of Liberty National Monument) (NJ), Proof							$3	$4.50	$15
2017-S, Ellis Island (Statue of Liberty National Monument) (NJ), Proof, Silver							$8	$9	$20
2017-P, George Rogers Clark National Historical Park (IN)					$0.50	$0.75	$1	$10	$30
2017-D, George Rogers Clark National Historical Park (IN)					$0.50	$0.75	$1	$10	$30
2017-S, George Rogers Clark National Historical Park (IN) (a)						$2	$3	$12	$35
2017-S, George Rogers Clark National Historical Park (IN), Enhanced Uncirculated							$3	$4.50	$15
2017-S, George Rogers Clark National Historical Park (IN), Proof							$3	$4.50	$15
2017-S, George Rogers Clark National Historical Park (IN), Proof, Silver							$8	$9	$20

a. Not issued for circulation. From 2012 to date, the San Francisco Mint has made Uncirculated S-mintmark quarters of each design in the National Park series. These can be purchased by collectors directly from the U.S. Mint, in bags of 100 or rolls of 40 coins, for a premium above face value.

| **2018, Pictured Rocks National Lakeshore (MI)** *Reverse designer: Paul C. Balan.* | **2018, Apostle Islands National Lakeshore (WI)** *Reverse designer: Richard Masters.* | **2018, Voyageurs National Park (MN)** *Reverse designer: Patricia Lucas-Morris.* | **2018, Cumberland Island National Seashore (GA)** *Reverse designer: Donna Weaver.* | **2018, Block Island National Wildlife Refuge (RI)** *Reverse designer: Chris Costello.* |

	Mintage	Cert	Avg	%MS	AU-50	MS-63	MS-65	MS-66	MS-67
							PF-65	PF-66DC	PF-69DC
2018-P, Pictured Rocks National Lakeshore (MI)	157,075,976	216	67.0	100%	$0.50	$0.75	$1	$10	$30
2018-D, Pictured Rocks National Lakeshore (MI)	153,087,436	244	66.9	100%	$0.50	$0.75	$1	$10	$30
2018-S, Pictured Rocks National Lakeshore (MI) (a)	883,200	241	66.8	100%		$2	$3	$12	$35
2018-S, Pictured Rocks National Lakeshore (MI), Proof	731,529	1,134	69.7				$3	$4.50	$15
2018-S, Pictured Rocks National Lakeshore (MI), Proof, Silver	514,905	3,965	69.7				$8	$9	$20
2018-P, Apostle Islands National Lakeshore (WI)	216,674,939	260	67.1	100%	$0.50	$0.75	$1	$10	$30
2018-D, Apostle Islands National Lakeshore (WI)	224,468,139	349	67.3	100%	$0.50	$0.75	$1	$10	$30
2018-S, Apostle Islands National Lakeshore (WI) (a)	1,021,160	259	66.6	100%		$2	$3	$12	$35
2018-S, Apostle Islands National Lakeshore (WI), Proof	701,325	1,131	69.7				$3	$4.50	$15

a. Not issued for circulation. From 2012 to date, the San Francisco Mint has made Uncirculated S-mintmark quarters of each design in the National Park series. These can be purchased by collectors directly from the U.S. Mint, in bags of 100 or rolls of 40 coins, for a premium above face value.

	Mintage	Cert	Avg	%MS	AU-50	MS-63	MS-65	MS-66	MS-67
							PF-65	PF-66DC	PF-69DC
2018-S, Apostle Islands National Lakeshore (WI), Proof, Silver	155,623,080	225	67.0	100%	$0.50	$0.75	$1	$10	$30
2018-P, Voyageurs National Park (MN)	143,415,780	260	67.1	100%	$0.50	$0.75	$1	$10	$30
2018-D, Voyageurs National Park (MN)	966,300	1	67.0	100%		$2	$3	$12	$35
2018-S, Voyageurs National Park (MN) (a)	716,470	1,128	69.7				$3	$4.50	$15
2018-S, Voyageurs National Park (MN), Proof	514,905	4,061	69.7				$8	$9	$20
2018-S, Voyageurs National Park (MN), Proof, Silver	514,905	4,061	69.7				$8	$9	$20
2018-P, Cumberland Island National Seashore (GA)	514,905	4,061	69.7				$8	$9	$20
2018-D, Cumberland Island National Seashore (GA)	514,905	4,061	69.7				$8	$9	$20
2018-S, Cumberland Island National Seashore (GA) (a)	514,905	4,061	69.7				$8	$9	$20
2018-S, Cumberland Island National Seashore (GA), Proof	514,905	4,061	69.7				$8	$9	$20
2018-S, Cumberland Island National Seashore (GA), Proof, Silver	514,905	4,061	69.7				$8	$9	$20
2018-P, Block Island National Wildlife Refuge (RI)	514,905	4,061	69.7				$8	$9	$20
2018-D, Block Island National Wildlife Refuge (RI)	514,905	4,061	69.7				$8	$9	$20
2018-S, Block Island National Wildlife Refuge (RI) (a)	514,905	4,061	69.7				$8	$9	$20
2018-S, Block Island National Wildlife Refuge (RI), Proof	514,905	4,061	69.7				$8	$9	$20
2018-S, Block Island National Wildlife Refuge (RI), Proof, Silver	514,905	4,061	69.7				$8	$9	$20

a. Not issued for circulation. From 2012 to date, the San Francisco Mint has made Uncirculated S-mintmark quarters of each design in the National Park series. These can be purchased by collectors directly from the U.S. Mint, in bags of 100 or rolls of 40 coins, for a premium above face value.

Half Dollars
1794 to Date
AN OVERVIEW OF HALF DOLLARS

Many hobbyists consider a collection of half dollars to be one of the most satisfying in the American series. The panorama of designs is extensive, ranging from the early Flowing Hair issues of 1794 and 1795 down to classic 20th-century motifs and the presidential portrait of the present day. The large size of half dollar coins makes them convenient to view and easy to enjoy.

Among the types, the 1794–1795 Flowing Hair half dollar is readily available in circulated grades and rare in Mint State, but at any level is hard to find well struck and without adjustment marks (evidence of where a Mint worker filed an overweight planchet down to proper weight). Most on the market are dated 1795. Careful selection for quality is advised.

The next type, dated 1796–1797 with a Draped Bust obverse and Small Eagle reverse, is the scarcest in the American silver series excepting the 1839 Gobrecht dollar. (However, the latter is available in Proof restrike form, yielding choice and gem examples, so it can be considered in a different category from the circulation-strike 1796–1797 half dollar type.) It might not be possible to be particular, but, finances permitting, a collector should take some time and endeavor to find an example that is sharply struck on both sides. Needle-sharp striking is more of a theory than a practicality, and some compromise in this regard may be necessary.

Half dollars of the 1801–1807 type, with the obverse as preceding but now with the Heraldic Eagle reverse, are plentiful enough in worn grades but somewhat scarce in Mint State. Striking is seldom needle-sharp and ranges from average to very poor. However, there are enough coins in the marketplace that collectors can afford to take their time and seek a sharp strike.

Capped Bust half dollars with a lettered edge, 1807–1836, abound in just about any grade desired. Again, striking is a consideration, and some searching is needed for a high-quality strike. Generally, those in the late 1820s and the 1830s are better struck than are those of earlier dates, the earlier coins being scarcer and more expensive in any event.

The short-lived type of 1836–1837, Capped Bust with a reeded edge and with the denomination spelled as 50 CENTS, is available easily enough through the high-mintage 1837, but most have problems with the quality of striking. Then comes the 1838–1839 type of the same obverse style, its reverse modified with a slightly different eagle and with the denomination as HALF DOL. Generally these are fairly well struck.

Liberty Seated half dollars of the several styles within the series, 1839–1891, admit of no great rarities for the type collector, save for the 1839, No Drapery, in levels of MS-63 and finer. However, among the earlier types in particular, sharply struck pieces are in the minority. Curiously, the most readily available Mint State Liberty Seated half dollars also are the lowest-mintage issues, the dates 1879 and later, as these were recognized as desirable at the time of issue and were widely saved.

Barber half dollars were not popular in their time, and while Proofs exist in proportion to their production figures, few circulation-strike coins were saved by collectors and Mint State examples are quite scarce today. In fact, as a type, a Barber half dollar dated 1900 or later in Mint State is the scarcest of all silver issues of that century. Well-struck MS-63 and better Barber half dollars, with the upper-right corner of the shield and the leg at lower right showing full details, are significantly scarcer than generally realized.

Liberty Walking half dollars, minted from 1916 to 1947, are plentiful in all grades. Again, some attention should be made to striking sharpness, which makes the search become more intense. Fortunately there are countless thousands of MS-63 and finer coins of the 1940s on the market, giving collectors a wide choice. Then come Franklin half dollars, made only from 1948 to 1963, with representative coins easy enough to acquire in about any grade desired. Kennedy half dollars exist in several varieties, all of which are available without any problem. Among these and other modern coins care needs to be taken for value received versus price paid. Modern issues in, for example, MS–65 and 66, selected for quality, are for many collectors preferable to MS–69 or 70 coins offered at a much higher price.

The release of the Franklin half dollar was announced to the coin-collecting world on the front page of the *Numismatist*, June 1948.

FOR THE COLLECTOR AND INVESTOR: HALF DOLLARS AS A SPECIALTY

Many collectors over the years have pursued half dollars by date, mint, and variety. Except for the series of copper cents, half dollars are the most generally available coins over a nearly continuous span, making them possible to collect for reasonable cost. Also, enough die varieties exist that this can form another focus of interest and importance.

In general, the half dollars of the early era form a concentration in themselves. Die varieties can be attributed by Overton numbers, as listed by Al C. Overton in his immensely popular *Early Half Dollar Die Varieties 1794–1836*. Glenn R. Peterson's book, *The Ultimate Guide to Attributing Bust Half Dollars*, is also useful in this regard. The John Reich Collectors Society (www.jrcs.org) publishes the *John Reich Journal* and serves as a forum for the exchange of information, updates, news about die varieties, and the like.

Among rarities in the early years, the 1796 and 1797 half dollars with the Draped Bust obverse and Small Eagle reverse are perhaps the most famous, needed for variety collections as well as one example for a type set. Variety enthusiasts aspire to get two of 1796—one with 15 stars on the obverse and the other with 16 stars—plus the 1797.

Draped Bust half dollars from 1801 through 1807 have a number of rare die varieties (as listed by Overton), but the basic varieties are easy enough to find. The 1805, 5 Over 4, overdate is particularly popular, as there was no "perfect date" 1804, and this is the closest collectors can come to it.

A vast and interesting field in early American numismatics is that of the Capped Bust half dollar, 1807–1836, with a lettered edge. Several hundred different die combinations exist, and many collectors are active in their pursuit, using the Overton book as a road map. All the major varieties are readily collectible except the 1817, 7 Over 4, overdate, of which only about a half dozen exist. The 1815, 5 Over 2, is considered the key issue among the specific dates (rather than varieties of dates). The majority of these survive in VF grade, not often lower and not often higher either—an interesting situation. During the 1820s vast quantities of these were transferred among banks, not wearing down from as much hand-to-hand circulation as they might have otherwise. While many if not most of the varieties listed herein can be obtained in Mint State, most collectors opt for VF or EF, these grades showing the necessary details but also permitting a budget to be stretched to include more varieties, rather than just a few high-grade pieces. Choice and gem examples can be found here and there, and are most plentiful among the later dates.

Among the Capped Bust half dollars of reduced size, 1836–1837, the 1836 is a key date, with fewer than 5,000 believed to have been minted. The next type, 1838 and 1839, Capped Bust, reeded edge, with a modified eagle on the reverse, includes the famous 1838-O rarity, of which only 20 are said to have been struck (per a note published in 1894 in the catalog of the Friesner Collection). These have a prooflike surface. Interestingly, they were not struck until 1839. In the same year, 1839-O half dollars were also struck, to the extensive quantity of 178,976 pieces; they are unusual as the mintmark is on the obverse, an odd placement for the era.

Within the series of Liberty Seated half dollars, collectors generally seek the varieties listed herein, although certain dedicated specialists will consult the *Complete Guide to Liberty Seated Half Dollars*, by Randy Wiley and Bill Bugert—a volume that delineates many interesting features, including the number of different reeds on the edges of certain coins.

Among Liberty Seated half dollars there is just one "impossible" rarity, that being the 1853-O coin without arrows at the date. Only three exist, and each shows extensive wear. At the San Francisco Mint, half dollars were first struck in 1855, and at the Carson City Mint in 1870. Generally, large quantities were minted of most dates and mintmark varieties of Liberty Seated half dollars, making them readily obtainable today. Except for the later dates, 1879 to 1891, Mint State pieces are generally scarce, gems especially so. Many specialists in half dollars belong to the Liberty Seated Collectors Club (LSCC, at www.lsccweb.org) and receive its magazine, *The Gobrecht Journal*.

Proof Liberty Seated halves can be collected by date sequence from 1858 onward. Survivors exist in proportion to their mintage quantities. Generally those before the mid-1870s often are found cleaned or hairlined, and more care is needed in selecting choice examples than is necessary for the later dates.

Barber half dollars were made continuously from 1892 through 1915, in such quantities that today there are no great rarities in the series. However, a number of issues are quite scarce, even in well-worn grades, and in MS-63 and better many are difficult to find. These coins had little honor in the era in which they were issued, and few numismatists saved them. Proofs were made each year from 1892 to 1915 and today can be obtained in proportion to their mintages. However, those of 1914 and 1915 are hard to find with choice, original surfaces—decades ago a collector hoarded these two dates and polished the ones in his possession.

Liberty Walking half dollars are popular to collect by date and mint. Scarce varieties include the 1917-S with obverse mintmark, the three issues of 1921, and the low mintage 1938-D, although the latter is not inordinately expensive. Mint State pieces are most readily available for 1916 and 1917, and then especially so in the 1930s and 1940s. Striking quality can be a problem, particularly for issues of the mid-1920s and also the later dates. For example, with a needle-sharp strike the 1923-S is an extreme rarity. Among later coins the 1940-S and 1941-S often are weakly struck.

Franklin half dollars minted from 1948 through 1963 have been very popular in recent decades. The complete series of dates and mintmarks is short and contains no scarce or rare pieces in higher grades such as MS–63 and 64. However, if you consider the element of sharp striking, usually defined as Full Bell Lines (FBL) on the reverse, certain otherwise common dates become elusive. Proofs of most years can also be readily collected.

Kennedy half dollars are easily enough collected, and so many have been made by this time that nearly 200 date-and-mintmark combinations extend from 1964 to present, including a gold version that marks the design's 50th anniversary. The wise collector will select coins that have a meeting point between a high grade such as MS–65 or 66 (or equivalent Proofs) and a reasonable price.

FLOWING HAIR (1794–1795)

Designer: *Robert Scot.* **Weight:** *13.48 grams.*
Composition: *.8924 silver, .1076 copper.* **Diameter:** *Approximately 32.5 mm.*
Edge: *FIFTY CENTS OR HALF A DOLLAR with decorations between the words.* **Mint:** *Philadelphia.*

Overton-104

History. The Flowing Hair design inaugurated the half-dollar denomination. They were immediately popular, as was evident in 1795, when many depositors of silver at the Philadelphia Mint asked for half dollars in return. The same motif was used on half dimes and silver dollars of the same years. Early half dollars have been extensively collected by die varieties, of which many exist for most dates. Valuations given below are in each case for the most readily available variety; scarcer ones, as listed by Overton, generally command higher prices.

Striking and Sharpness. Many have problems of one sort or another, including adjustment marks from the planchet being filed down to proper weight and mushy denticles. On the obverse, check the hair details and the stars. On the reverse, check the breast of the eagle in particular. As with other silver coins of this design, it may not be possible to find a *needle-sharp* example, but with some extensive searching a fairly decent strike can be obtained. Sharp striking and excellent eye appeal add to the value dramatically. However, very few 1794 and 1795 halves are uniformly sharp on both sides.

Availability. Probably 3,500 to 6,000 circulated Flowing Hair half dollars exist. Most are dated 1795, the 1794 being considered a rare date (though not among the great U.S. coin rarities). Typical grades are Good to Fine. EF and AU grades are elusive in regard to the total population. Probably 100 or so could be graded MS (nearly all of them 1795). Unlike half dollars of the 1796–1797 type, none of these are known to have been made with prooflike surfaces.

GRADING STANDARDS

MS-60 to 70 (Mint State). *Obverse:* At MS-60, some abrasion and contact marks are evident, most noticeably on the cheek and in the fields. This denomination, heavier than the half dime of the same design, was more susceptible to contact and other outside influences. A typical half dollar certified at MS–60 or 61 today might well have been designated as About Uncirculated a generation ago. Luster is present, but may be dull or lifeless, and

1795; Overton-110a. Graded MS-63.

interrupted in patches, perhaps as much from old cleaning as from contact the coin may have received. At MS-63, contact marks are very few, and abrasion is present, but not as noticeable. An MS-65 coin has no abrasion, and contact marks are very few. Luster should be full and rich. Higher grades are seldom seen in this type, but are defined in theory by having fewer marks as perfection is approached. ***Reverse:*** Comments apply as for the obverse, except that abrasion and contact marks are most noticeable on the eagle at the center. This area is often lightly struck, so in all grades do not mistake weak striking for actual wear. Knowledge of specific die varieties is helpful in this regard. The field area is small and is protected by lettering and the wreath, and in any given grade shows fewer marks than on the obverse.

Illustrated coin: This is a well-struck example with superb eye appeal.

AU-50, 53, 55, 58 (About Uncirculated).
Obverse: Light wear is seen on the hair area immediately to the left of the face and above the forehead, on the cheek, and, to a lesser extent, on the top of the neck truncation, more so at AU-50 than at AU–53 or 55. An AU-58 coin has minimal traces of wear. An AU-50 coin has luster in protected areas among the stars and letters, with little in the open fields or on the portrait. At AU-58,

1795; O-116. Graded AU-55.

much luster is present in the fields but is worn away on the highest parts of the motifs. ***Reverse:*** Light wear is seen on the eagle's body and the upper part of both wings. On well-struck pieces the details of the wing features are excellent. At AU-50, detail is lost in some feathers in this area. However, striking can play a part, as some coins were weakly struck to begin with. Light wear is seen on the wreath and lettering, but is harder to discern. Luster is the best key to actual wear. This will range from perhaps 20% remaining in protected areas (at AU-50) to nearly full mint bloom (at AU-58), although among certified coins the amounts of luster can vary widely.

Illustrated coin: Significant luster remains in protected areas on this attractive early half dollar.

EF-40, 45 (Extremely Fine). *Obverse:* More wear is evident on the portrait, especially on the hair to the left of and above the forehead, and in the back below the LI of LIBERTY. The tip of the neck truncation shows flatness, and the cheek is worn. Excellent detail remains in low-relief areas of the hair. The stars show wear, as do the date and letters. Luster, if present at all, is minimal and in protected areas. ***Reverse:*** The eagle shows more

1794; O-101. Graded EF-40.

wear on the body and on the tops of the wings. Interior wing detail is good on most coins (depending on the variety and the striking), and the tail feathers can be discerned. Additional wear is on the wreath and letters, but many details are present. Some luster may be seen in protected areas and if present is slightly more abundant than on the obverse.

Illustrated coin: Note some lightness of the stars at the right and at the reverse center, as struck. The scrape on the reverse below the ribbon knot was mentioned by the cataloger in an auction offering.

VF-20, 30 (Very Fine). *Obverse:* The hair is well worn at VF-20, less so at VF-30, and is most noticeable in the upper part of the head, the area above the level of the eye, and extending to the back. The strands are blended as to be heavy. The cheek shows only slight relief, and the tip of the neck truncation is flat. The stars have more wear, making them appear larger (an optical illusion). Scattered marks are common on half dollars at this level

1795; O-109. Graded VF-20.

and below, and should be mentioned if particularly serious. *Reverse:* The body of the eagle shows few if any feathers, while the wings have perhaps a quarter or a third of the feathers visible depending on the strike, with sharper strikes having up to half visible (as PCGS suggests). *Photograde* and the ANA grading standards suggest half of the feathers on all, which may be the case on coins that were well struck to begin with. The leaves lack detail and are in outline form. Scattered, non-disfiguring marks are normal for this and lower grades. Any major defects should be noted separately.

   Illustrated coin: On this variety in this grade, the denticles are especially prominent on each side. Such aspects vary from coin to coin.

F-12, 15 (Fine). *Obverse:* Wear is more extensive than on the preceding, with less hair visible. The ear position can be seen, as can the eye. The cheek is nearly flat, and the stars appear larger. The rim is distinct and most denticles remain visible. *Reverse:* Wear is more extensive. Now, feather details are fewer, mostly remaining on the wing to the left. The wreath and lettering are more worn, and the rim is usually weak in areas, although most denticles can be seen.

1795; O-107. Graded F-12.

VG-8, 10 (Very Good). *Obverse:* The portrait is mostly seen in outline form, with most hair strands gone save for an area centered behind the neck. The hair tips at the lower left are clear. The eye location is barely discernible. The stars appear larger still and often quite bold, again an illusion. The rim is weak in areas. LIBERTY and the date are readable and usually full, although some letters may be weak at their tops. *Reverse:* The

1795; O-109. Graded VG-8.

eagle is mostly an outline, although traces of the separation between the body and the right wing can sometimes be seen. The rim is worn, as are the letters, with some weak, but the motto is readable. On many coins the rim remains fairly prominent.

   Illustrated coin: Note a spot, a tiny edge bruise, and some adjustment marks. A cataloger mentioned that "the top of the obverse is slightly soft due to axial misalignment"—a technical note. On any half dollar of this era, knowledge of the varieties and peculiarities of striking is useful.

G-4, 6 (Good). *Obverse:* Wear is more extensive, and some stars may be missing or only partially visible. The head is an outline, although a few elements of thick hair strands may be seen. The rim is well worn or even missing. LIBERTY is worn, and parts of some letters may be missing, but elements of all should be readable. The date is readable, but worn. *Reverse:* The eagle is flat and discernible in outline form. The wreath is well

1794; O-106. Graded G-6.

worn. Some of the letters may be partly missing. At this level some "averaging" can be done. If the letters are stronger than usual in one area, but some are missing in another area, the coin can still qualify as G-4. Often on this type in lower grades the reverse is more detailed than the obverse.

AG-3 (About Good). *Obverse:* Wear is very extensive. The head is in outline form (perhaps partly blended into the field). LIBERTY is mostly gone. The date, while readable, may be partially worn away. Some stars are missing. *Reverse:* The reverse is well worn, with parts of the wreath and lettering very weak or even missing. The details that remain and those that do not is often dependent on the particular die variety.

1795; O-116. Graded AG-3.

| 1795, Normal Date | 1795, Recut Date | 1795, Two Leaves Under Each Wing | 1795, Three Leaves Under Each Wing |

	Mintage	Cert	Avg	%MS	AG-3	G-4	VG-8	F-12	VF-20	EF-40	AU-50	AU-55	MS-60
1794	23,464	339	21.8	2%	$2,500	$4,500	$7,000	$12,000	$23,000	$40,000	$65,000	$105,000	$225,000
	Auctions: $152,750, MS-61, June 2014; $19,975, VF-30, March 2016; $18,800, VF-30, August 2014; $12,925, VF-20, August 2014												
1795, All kinds (a)	299,680												
1795, Normal Date		1,106	24.0	5%	$650	$1,100	$1,500	$2,750	$3,900	$11,000	$17,500	$21,000	$45,000
	Auctions: $129,250, MS-62, November 2013; $1,998, F-12, March 2015; $881, G-6, September 2015; $705, AG-3, June 2015												
1795, Recut Date		25	22.8	0%	$650	$1,150	$1,550	$2,750	$4,250	$11,000	$20,500	$25,000	$45,000
	Auctions: $1,651, F-12, March 2014; $1,645, VG-8, September 2014												
1795, 3 Leaves Under Each Wing		15	25.0	0%	$1,100	$2,350	$3,250	$4,600	$8,500	$20,000	$40,000	$42,000	$65,000
	Auctions: $8,519, VF, March 2014												

a. Varieties of 1795 are known with the final S in STATES over a D; with the A in STATES over an E; and with the Y in LIBERTY over a star. All are scarce. Some 1794 and 1795 half dollars were weight-adjusted by insertion of a silver plug in the center of the blank planchet before the coin was struck.

DRAPED BUST, SMALL EAGLE REVERSE (1796–1797)

Designer: *Robert Scot.* **Weight:** *13.48 grams.*
Composition: *.8924 silver, .1076 copper.* **Diameter:** *Approximately 32.5 mm.*
Edge: *FIFTY CENTS OR HALF A DOLLAR with decorations between words.* **Mint:** *Philadelphia.*

O-101a.

History. Robert Scot's Draped Bust design is similar to that used on the half dime, dime, quarter, and silver dollar of this era. In 1796 and 1797 there was little demand for half dollars and the combined mintage for the two years was therefore low. Among design types of U.S. silver coins made in circulation-strike format this is the Holy Grail—a classic rarity, with no common date in the series.

Striking and Sharpness. On the obverse, check the hair details and the stars. On the reverse, first check the breast of the eagle, but examine other areas as well. Also check the denticles on both sides. Look especially for coins that do not have significant adjustment marks (from an overweight planchet being filed down to correct specifications). Coins of this denomination are on average better struck than are half dimes, dimes, quarters (which have reverse problems), and dollars in the Draped Bust suite.

Availability. Examples are rare in any grade—survivors likely number only in the hundreds of coins. MS examples are particularly rare, and when seen are nearly always dated 1796. Some of these have partially prooflike surfaces. Any half dollar of this type has strong market demand.

GRADING STANDARDS

MS-60 to 70 (Mint State). *Obverse:* At MS-60, some abrasion and contact marks are evident, most noticeably on the cheek, the drapery at the shoulder, and the right field. Also check the hair to the left of the forehead. Luster is present, but may be dull or lifeless, and interrupted in patches. At MS-63, contact marks are few, and abrasion is hard to detect, although this type is sometimes graded liberally due to its rarity. An MS-65 coin has

1797; O-101a. Graded MS-66.

no abrasion, and contact marks are so minute as to require magnification. Luster should be full and rich. Coins graded above MS-65 are more theoretical than actual for this type, although some notable pieces have crossed the auction block. These are defined by having fewer marks as perfection is approached. *Reverse:* Comments apply as for the obverse, except that abrasion and contact marks are most noticeable on the eagle at the center, a situation that should be evaluated by considering the original striking (which can be quite sharp, but with many exceptions). The field area is small and is protected by lettering and the wreath, and in any given grade shows fewer marks than on the obverse.

Illustrated coin: This superb gem has prooflike surfaces.

AU-50, 53, 55, 58 (About Uncirculated). *Obverse:* Light wear is seen on the hair area above the ear and extending to the left of the forehead, on the ribbon, and on the drapery at the shoulder, more so at AU-50 than at AU–53 or 55. An AU-58 coin has minimal traces of wear. An AU-50 coin has luster in protected areas among the stars and letters, with little in the open fields or on the portrait. At AU-58, most luster is present in the fields, but is worn

1797; O-101a. Graded AU-50.

away on the highest parts of the motifs. *Reverse:* Light wear is seen on the eagle's body and the edges of the wings. Light wear is seen on the wreath and lettering. Luster is the best key to actual wear. This ranges from perhaps 20% remaining in protected areas (at AU-50) to nearly full mint bloom (at AU-58).

EF-40, 45 (Extremely Fine). *Obverse:* More wear is evident on the upper hair area, particularly to the left of the forehead and also below the LI of LIBERTY, in the ribbon, and on the drapery and bosom. Excellent detail remains in low-relief areas of the hair. The stars show wear as do the date and letters. Luster, if present at all, is minimal and in protected areas. *Reverse:* The eagle shows more wear, this being the focal point to

1796, 15 Stars; O-101. Graded EF-40.

check. Many feathers remain on the interior areas of the wings. Additional wear is on the wreath and letters, but many details are present. Some luster may be seen in protected areas and if present is slightly more abundant than on the obverse.

VF-20, 30 (Very Fine). *Obverse:* The higher-relief areas of hair are well worn at VF-20, less so at VF-30. The drapery and bosom show extensive wear. The stars have more wear. *Reverse:* The body of the eagle shows few if any feathers, while the wings have about half or more of the feathers visible, depending on the strike. The leaves lack most detail and are outlined. Scattered, non-disfiguring marks are normal for this and

1796, 16 Stars; O-103. Graded VF-20.

lower grades; major defects should be noted separately.

F-12, 15 (Fine). *Obverse:* Wear is more extensive than on a Very Fine coin, particularly noticeable on the hair, face, and bosom. The stars appear larger (an optical illusion). About half the hair detail remains, most noticeably behind the neck and shoulder. The rim may be partially worn away and blend into the field, but on many coins it remains intact. *Reverse:* Wear is more extensive. Now, feather details are diminished,

1797; O-101a. Graded F-15.

with fewer than half remaining on the wings. The wreath and lettering are worn further, and the rim is usually weak in areas, but most denticles can be seen.

VG-8, 10 (Very Good). *Obverse:* The portrait is mostly seen in outline form, with most hair strands gone, although there is some definition at the back of the hair and behind the shoulder. The ear is barely discernible and the eye is fairly distinct. The stars appear larger still, again an illusion. The rim is weak in areas, but shows most denticles. LIBERTY and the date are readable and usually full, although some letters may be weak at their

1796, 16 Stars; O-102. Graded VG-10.

tops. *Reverse:* The eagle is mostly an outline, with parts blending into the field (on lighter strikes). The rim is worn, as are the letters, with some weak, but the motto is readable.

G-4, 6 (Good). *Obverse:* Wear is more extensive, and some stars may be partly missing. The head is an outline. The eye is visible only in outline form. The rim is well worn or even missing in areas, but many denticles remain. LIBERTY is worn. The letters and date are weak but fully readable. *Reverse:* The eagle is flat and discernible in outline form, and may be blending into the field. The wreath is well worn. Some of the letters may

1797. Graded G-4.

be partly missing. At this level some "averaging" can be done. If the letters are stronger than usual in one area, but some are missing in another area, the coin can still qualify as G-4.

AG-3 (About Good). *Obverse:* Wear is so extensive that the coin is barely identifiable. The head is in outline form. LIBERTY is mostly gone; same for the stars. The date, while readable, may be partially worn away. *Reverse:* The reverse is well worn, with parts of the wreath and lettering missing. On most coins the reverse shows more wear than the obverse.

1797. Graded AG-3.

1796, 15 Stars

1796, 16 Stars

	Mintage	Cert	Avg	%MS	AG-3	G-4	VG-8	F-12	VF-20	EF-40	AU-50	AU-58	MS-60
1796, 15 Stars †	(a)	20	40.6	35%	$23,000	$35,000	$42,500	$52,000	$75,000	$115,000	$165,000	$235,000	$290,000
Auctions: No auction records available.													
1796, 16 Stars †	(a)	14	34.2	29%	$23,000	$36,500	$43,500	$56,000	$71,000	$110,000	$170,000	$250,000	$300,000
Auctions: $470,000, MS-63, November 2013													
1797, 15 Stars †	3,918	55	27.8	7%	$23,000	$37,500	$45,000	$57,500	$75,000	$110,000	$165,000	$225,000	$300,000
Auctions: $17,625, MS-64, August 2015; $8,225, AU-53, November 2015; $4,406, EF-40, August 2015; $329, VF-20, September 2016													

† Ranked in the *100 Greatest U.S. Coins* (fourth edition). **a.** Included in 1797, 15 Stars, mintage figure.

DRAPED BUST, HERALDIC EAGLE REVERSE (1801–1807)

Designer: *Robert Scot.* **Weight:** *13.48 grams.*
Composition: *.8924 silver, .1076 copper.* **Diameter:** *Approximately 32.5 mm.*
Edge: *FIFTY CENTS OR HALF A DOLLAR with decorations between words.* **Mint:** *Philadelphia.*

O-101.

History. The half dollar's Draped Bust, Heraldic Eagle design is similar to that of other silver coins of the era. While dies were prepared for the 1804 half dollar, none were minted in that year, despite Mint reports that state otherwise.

Striking and Sharpness. Most have light striking in one area or another. On the obverse, check the hair details and, in particular, the star centers. On the reverse, check the stars above the eagle, the clouds, the details of the shield, and the eagle's wings. Check the denticles on both sides. Adjustment marks are sometimes seen, from overweight planchets being filed down to correct weight, but not as often as on earlier half dollar types. Typically, the earlier years are better struck; many of 1806 and nearly all of 1807 are poorly struck. Sharp striking and excellent eye appeal add to the value dramatically, this being particularly true for those of 1805 to 1807, which are often weak (particularly 1807).

Availability. Earlier years are scarce in the marketplace, beginning with the elusive 1801 and including the 1802, after which they are more readily available. Some die varieties are scarce. Most MS coins are dated 1806 and 1807, but all are scarce. Finding sharply struck high-grade coins is almost impossible, a goal more than a reality.

GRADING STANDARDS

MS-60 to 70 (Mint State). *Obverse:* At MS-60, some abrasion and contact marks are evident, most noticeably on the cheek, the drapery at the shoulder, and the right field. Luster is present, but may be dull or lifeless, and interrupted in patches. At MS-63, contact marks are very few, and abrasion is hard to detect except under magnification. An MS-65 coin has no abrasion, and contact marks are so minute as to require magnifica-

1803, Large 3; O-101. Graded MS-63.

tion. Luster should be full and rich. Coins grading above MS-65 are more theoretical than actual for this type—but they do exist, and are defined by having fewer marks as perfection is approached. Later years usually have areas of flat striking. *Reverse:* Comments apply as for the obverse, except that abrasion and contact marks are most noticeable on the eagle's neck, the tips of the wing, and the tail. The field area is complex, without much open space, given the stars above the eagle, the arrows and olive branch, and other features. Accordingly, marks are not as noticeable as on the obverse.

Illustrated coin: This is an extraordinary strike with superb eye appeal. A connoisseur might prefer this coin to an MS-65 example with flat striking.

AU-50, 53, 55, 58 (About Uncirculated). *Obverse:* Light wear is seen on the hair area above the ear and extending to left of the forehead, on the ribbon, and on the bosom, more so at AU-50 than at AU–53 or 55. An AU-58 coin has minimal traces of wear. An AU-50 coin has luster in protected areas among the stars and letters, with little in the open fields or on the portrait. At AU-58, most luster is present in the fields, but is worn

1806, Pointed 6, No Stem; O-109. Graded AU-50.

away on the highest parts of the motifs. *Reverse:* Comments as preceding, except that the eagle's neck, the tips and top of the wings, the clouds, and the tail now show noticeable wear, as do other features. Luster ranges from perhaps 20% remaining in protected areas (at AU-50) to nearly full mint bloom (at AU-58). Often the reverse of this type retains much more luster than the obverse.

Illustrated coin: This example has gray and lilac toning.

EF-40, 45 (Extremely Fine). *Obverse:* More wear is evident on the upper hair area and the ribbon, and on the drapery and bosom. Excellent detail remains in low-relief areas of the hair. The stars show wear, as do the date and letters. Luster, if present at all, is minimal and in protected areas. *Reverse:* Wear is greater than on an About Uncirculated coin, overall. The neck lacks feather detail on its highest points. Feathers have lost some detail

1807; O-105. Graded EF-40.

near the edges of the wings, and some areas of the horizontal lines in the shield may be blended together. Some traces of luster may be seen, more so at EF-45 than at EF-40.

Illustrated coin: Light striking at the obverse center is normal for this die variety.

VF-20, 30 (Very Fine). *Obverse:* The higher-relief areas of hair are well worn at VF-20, less so at VF-30. The drapery on the shoulder and the bosom show extensive wear. The stars have more wear, making them appear larger (an optical illusion seen on most worn silver coins of this era). *Reverse:* Wear is greater, including on the shield and wing feathers. Half to two-thirds of the feathers are visible. Star centers are flat. Other areas have lost detail as well.

1806, 6 Over Inverted 9; O-111a. Graded VF-30.

Illustrated coin: Note the cud break on the reverse rim over the E in UNITED.

F-12, 15 (Fine). *Obverse:* Wear is more extensive than on a Very Fine coin, particularly noticeable on the hair, face, and bosom. The stars appear larger. About half the hair detail remains, most noticeably behind the neck and shoulder, but the fine hair is now combined into thicker tresses. The rim may be partially worn away and blend into the field. *Reverse:* Wear is even more extensive, with the shield and wing feathers being

1805; O-109. Graded F-15.

points to observe. The incuse E PLURIBUS UNUM may have half or more of the letters worn away (depending on striking). The clouds all appear connected. The stars are weak. Parts of the border and lettering may be weak.

VG-8, 10 (Very Good). *Obverse:* The portrait is mostly seen in outline form, with most hair strands gone, although there is some definition at the back of the hair and behind the shoulder. The ear is discernible as is the eye. The stars appear larger still, again an illusion. The rim is weak in areas. LIBERTY and the date are readable and usually full, although some letters may be weak at their tops. *Reverse:* Wear is more extensive. Half

1805, 5 Over 4; O-103. Graded VG-8.

or more of the letters in the motto are worn away. Most feathers are worn away, although separation of some of the lower feathers may be seen. Some stars are faint (depending on the strike). The border blends into the field in areas and some letters are weak.

G-4, 6 (Good). *Obverse:* Wear is more extensive, and some stars may be partly missing. The head is mostly an outline, although some hair strand outlines may be visible on some strikings. The rim is well worn or even missing in areas. LIBERTY is worn, and parts of some letters may be missing, but elements should be readable. The date is readable, but worn. *Reverse:* Wear is more extensive. The upper part of the eagle is flat. Feathers are

1805; O-111. Graded G-4.

noticeable only at the lower edge of the wings, and do not have detail. The upper part of the shield is flat or mostly so (depending on the strike). Only a few letters of the motto can be seen. The rim is worn extensively, and a few letters may be missing.

AG-3 (About Good). *Obverse:* Wear is so extensive that the coin is barely identifiable. The head is in outline form. LIBERTY is mostly gone; same for the stars. The date, while readable, may be partially worn away. *Reverse:* Extensive wear is seen overall, with the rim worn away and some areas worn smooth. The eagle can be discerned in outline form, but not necessarily completely. A few stray motto letters may remain.

1801. Graded AG-3.

	Mintage	Cert	Avg	%MS	G-4	VG-8	F-12	VF-20	EF-40	AU-50	AU-55	MS-60	MS-63
1801	30,289	144	28.1	2%	$875	$1,350	$2,400	$3,500	$6,000	$15,000	$25,000	$75,000	$160,000
	Auctions: $329,000, MS-64, November 2013; $4,700, EF-40, March 2015; $576, G-4, October 2014; $517, AG-3, July 2015												
1802	29,890	101	31.2	0%	$1,000	$1,500	$2,650	$3,500	$7,500	$17,000	$26,500	$60,000	
	Auctions: $70,500, AU-58, August 2013; $3,173, VF-20, August 2014; $2,115, F-15, August 2014												

1803, Small 3

1803, Large 3

1805, 5 Over 4

1805, Normal Date

1806, 6 Over 5

1806, 6 Over Inverted 6

1806, Stem Not
Through Claw

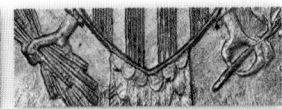
1806, Stem Through Claw

1806, Knobbed-Top 6, Large Stars
With traces of overdate.

1806, Knobbed-Top 6, Small Stars

	Mintage	Cert	Avg	%MS	G-4	VG-8	F-12	VF-20	EF-40	AU-50	AU-55	MS-60	MS-63
1803, All kinds	188,234												
1803, Small 3		43	37.2	2%	$350	$475	$650	$1,000	$2,750	$5,500	$9,500	$25,000	$115,000
Auctions: $49,938, MS-62, June 2014													
1803, Large 3		125	32.1	4%	$275	$425	$500	$900	$2,000	$5,000	$7,000	$22,500	$65,000
Auctions: $1,763, EF-40, March 2015; $881, VF-30, June 2015; $752, VF-25, March 2015; $552, VF-20, March 2015													
1805, All kinds	211,722												
1805, 5 Over 4		118	33.2	2%	$400	$800	$1,000	$1,650	$3,500	$7,500	$12,750	$35,000	$85,000
Auctions: $3,055, EF-40, March 2016; $2,233, VF-30, August 2015; $999, F-12, June 2015; $9,106, VG-8, March 2015													
1805, Normal Date		418	32.4	2%	$260	$350	$475	$850	$2,250	$5,000	$6,500	$22,500	$35,000
Auctions: $4,406, AU-50, March 2015; $2,350, EF-45, May 2015; $1,528, VF-25, September 2015; $617, F-15, August 2015													
1806, All kinds	839,576												
1806, 6 Over 5		210	32.6	3%	$300	$400	$600	$900	$2,350	$5,000	$6,500	$13,500	$45,000
Auctions: $21,150, MS-61, November 2013; $881, VF-30, September 2014; $794, VF-25, January 2015; $764, VF-20, July 2014													
1806, 6 Over Inverted 6		71	26.7	1%	$350	$500	$925	$1,500	$3,500	$8,500	$12,500	$27,500	$50,000
Auctions: $28,200, MS-61, November 2013; $999, F-12, September 2014; $940, F-12, August 2014; $999, Fair-2, August 2014													
1806, Knobbed 6, Large Stars (Traces of Overdate)		37	29.5	0%	$225	$275	$400	$700	$2,000	$5,000	$7,000		
Auctions: $2,364, EF-40, August 2013													
1806, Knobbed 6, Small Stars		41	30.7	0%	$250	$325	$500	$700	$2,000	$5,000	$7,000	$12,000	$35,000
Auctions: $2,350, EF-45, January 2014; $435, F-15, July 2014													
1806, Knobbed 6, Stem Not Through Claw		0	n/a		$60,000	$65,000	$70,000	$85,000	$125,000				
Auctions: $126,500, EF-40, January 2009													
1806, Pointed 6, Stem Through Claw		285	32.8	6%	$225	$275	$400	$700	$1,750	$4,500	$5,750	$9,500	$20,000
Auctions: $35,250, MS-64, November 2013; $7,638, AU-53, August 2014; $447, F-12, October 2015; $327, VG-10, February 2015													
1806, Pointed 6, Stem Through Claw, E Over A in STATES		8	21.3	0%	$400	$900	$1,600	$3,200	$7,500	$20,000			
Auctions: $4,465, VF-20, January 2015													
1806, Pointed 6, Stem Not Through Claw		113	36.1	6%	$225	$275	$400	$700	$2,000	$4,500	$5,750	$9,500	$20,000
Auctions: $12,925, MS-62, November 2013; $3,840, AU-55, August 2014; $1,293, EF-40, January 2015; $881, VF-30, July 2015													
1807	301,076	1,154	33.5	7%	$225	$275	$400	$700	$1,850	$4,750	$5,500	$9,500	$20,000
Auctions: $1,528, EF-40, March 2015; $588, VF-20, February 2015; $400, F-12, August 2015; $306, VG-10, May 2015													

CAPPED BUST, LETTERED EDGE (1807–1836)

Designer: *John Reich.* **Weight:** *13.48 grams.*
Composition: *.8924 silver, .1076 copper.* **Diameter:** *Approximately 32.5 mm.*
Edge: *1807–1814—FIFTY CENTS OR HALF A DOLLAR;*
1814–1831—star added between DOLLAR and FIFTY;
1832–1836—vertical lines added between words. **Mint:** *Philadelphia.*

First Style (1807–1808)
O-104.

Remodeled Portrait and Eagle
(1809–1836)
O-109.

Remodeled Portrait and Eagle, Proof
O-103.

History. The Capped Bust design was created by Mint assistant engraver John Reich; the motif was widely used, in several variations, on much of the era's coinage. Reich was the first artist to consistently include the denomination in his designs for U.S. gold and silver coins. The half dollar, minted continuously from 1807 to 1836, except 1816, was the largest silver coin of the realm at the time (silver dollars had not been struck since 1804).

Striking and Sharpness. On the obverse, check the hair and broach details. The stars are often flatly struck on Capped Bust half dollars, much more so than on other denominations. On the reverse, check the motto band and the eagle's head, and the wing to the left, as well as other areas (the neck feathers, often lightly struck on other denominations of Capped Bust silver, are usually fairly sharp on half dollars). The E PLURIBUS UNUM band is often weak in the area left of its center; this does not normally occur on other Capped Bust silver coins. Inspect the denticles on both sides. Generally, later dates are better struck than are earlier ones. Many half dollars have semi-prooflike surfaces, or patches of mirror-like character interspersed with luster. Others can have nearly full prooflike surfaces, with patches of luster being in the minority (and often in the left obverse field); some of these have been mischaracterized as "Proofs." Some issues from the early 1830s have little digs or "bite marks" on the portrait, possibly from some sort of a gadget used to eject them from the press. Unlike the Capped Bust half dime, dime, and quarter dollar, the half dollar is particularly subject to very wide variations in striking quality.

True Proofs have deeply mirrored surfaces. Impostors are often seen, with deeply toned surfaces or with patches of mint luster. This situation is more prevalent with half dollars than with any other Capped Bust denomination. Proceed slowly, and be careful. There are some crushed-lettered-edge ("CLE")

Proofs of the 1833 to 1835 era that are especially beautiful and are more deeply mirrorlike than original issues. Some of these are restrikes (not necessarily an important consideration, but worth mentioning), believed to have been made at the Mint beginning in the spring of 1859.

Availability. Examples of most dates and overdates are easily found in just about any grade desired, from Fine and VF to MS. (As the largest silver coin struck between 1803 and 1836, these half dollars spent much of their time in bags, transferred from bank to bank, rather than wearing down in circulation.) The later years are the most readily available and are also seen in higher average grades. Many die varieties range from scarce to rare. Proofs were made in limited numbers for presentation purposes and for distribution to numismatists.

GRADING STANDARDS

MS-60 to 70 (Mint State). *Obverse:* At MS-60, some abrasion and contact marks are evident, most noticeably on the cheek, the hair below the left part of LIBERTY, the cap, and the front part of the bosom and drapery. These areas also coincide with the highest parts of the coin and are thus susceptible to lightness of strike. Complicating matters is that when an area is lightly struck, and the planchet is not forced into the deepest parts

1827, Square Base 2; O-104. Graded MS-60.

of the die, the *original planchet surface* (which may exhibit scuffing and nicks) is visible. A lightly struck coin can have virtually perfect luster in the fields, deep and rich, and yet appear to be "worn" on the higher parts, due to the lightness of strike. This is a very sophisticated concept and is hard to quantify. In practice, the original planchet surface will usually be considered as wear on the finished coin, which of course is not true. Such grades as high About Uncirculated and low Mint State levels are often assigned to pieces that, if well struck, would be MS–64 and 65. As a matter of practicality, but not of logic, you will need to do the same. If a coin has original planchet abrasions, but otherwise is a Gem, those abrasions must be taken into consideration. Apart from this, on well-struck coins in lower Mint State grades, luster is present, but may be dull or lifeless, and interrupted in patches. At MS-63, on a well-struck coin, contact marks are very few, and abrasion is hard to detect except under magnification. A well-struck MS-65 coin has no abrasion, and contact marks are so minute as to require magnification. Luster should be full and rich. Grades above MS-65 are seen now and again and are defined by having fewer marks as perfection is approached. *Reverse:* Comments apply as for the obverse, except that nearly all coins with weak striking on the obverse (so as to reveal original planchet surface) do not show such original surface on the reverse, except perhaps on the motto ribbon. Accordingly, market grading is usually by the obverse only, even if the reverse seems to be in much better preservation. On well-struck coins, abrasion and contact marks are most noticeable on the eagle's head, the top of the wings, the claws, and the flat band that surrounds the incuse motto. The field is mainly protected by design elements and does not show abrasion as much as does the obverse on a given coin.

Illustrated coin: This is an exceptional coin at the low Mint State level.

AU-50, 53, 55, 58 (About Uncirculated). *Obverse:* Light wear is seen on the cheek, the hair below the left part of LIBERTY, the cap, and the front part of the bosom and drapery. Some of this apparent "wear" may be related to the original planchet surface (as noted under Mint State, above), but at the About Uncirculated level the distinction is less important. On a well-struck coin, at AU-58 the luster is extensive except in the open area of the field, espe-

1820, Curl Base 2, Small Date; O-103. Graded AU-55.

cially to the right. At AU–50 and 53, luster remains only in protected areas. *Reverse:* Wear is evident on the eagle's head, the top of the wings, the claws, and the flat band above the eagle. An AU-58 coin has nearly full luster. At AU–50 and 53, there still is significant luster, more than on the obverse.

Illustrated coin: An attractive coin by any measure, this has light toning and ample areas of original luster.

EF-40, 45 (Extremely Fine). *Obverse:* Wear is more extensive, most noticeably on the higher areas of the hair. The cap shows more wear, as does the cheek. Luster, if present, is in protected areas among the star points and close to the portrait. *Reverse:* The wings show wear on the higher areas of the feathers, and some details are lost. The top of the head and the beak are flat. The eagle's claws and the leaves show wear. Luster may be present in protected areas, even if there is little or none on the obverse.

1810; O-110. Graded EF-45.

Illustrated coin: This coin probably was lightly cleaned years ago so as to give a light silver color, which added some hairlines, but now it has halo toning around the borders that adds attractiveness.

VF-20, 30 (Very Fine). *Obverse:* Wear is more extensive, and most of the hair is combined into thick tresses without delicate features. The curl on the neck is flat. The cap shows significant wear at its top, and the left part of the drapery and bosom is nearly flat. Stars are flat at their centers (even if sharply struck to begin with). *Reverse:* Wear is most evident on the eagle's head, the tops of the wings, and the leaves and claws. Nearly all feathers in the wing remain distinct.

1815, 5 Over 2; O-101. Graded VF-30.

Illustrated coin: The areas of wear appear exaggerated due to the light toning, a feature often observed on half dollars of this date but not as often among other years.

F-12, 15 (Fine). *Obverse:* Wear is more extensive, with much of the hair blended together. The drapery is indistinct on most of its upper edge. The stars are flat at their centers. LIBERTY remains bold. *Reverse:* Wear is more extensive, now with only about half of the feathers remaining on the wings, more on the right wing. The head shows the eye, nostril, and beak but no details. The claws show more wear. Other features are worn as well, but not as noticeable as the key points mentioned.

1827, Square Base 2; O-122. Graded F-12.

VG-8, 10 (Very Good). *Obverse:* The hair is less distinct, with the forehead blended into the hair above. LIBERTY is complete, but may be slightly weak in areas. The stars are flat. The rim is distinct, with most if not all denticles visible. *Reverse:* Feathers are fewer and mostly on the right wing, although sharp strikes can show detail in both wings. Other details are weaker. All lettering remains easily readable.

1831; O-120. Graded VG-8.

Illustrated coin: This coin was cleaned and partially retoned. It is sharply struck on the reverse.

G-4, 6 (Good). *Obverse:* The portrait is mostly in outline, with few interior details discernible. LIBERTY may still be readable or may be partially worn away, depending on the variety. The rim is weak, but distinct in most areas. *Reverse:* The eagle is mostly in outline form, although some feathers can be seen in the right wing. All letters around the border are clear. E PLURIBUS UNUM may be weak. Overall, a typical coin has the reverse in a slightly higher grade than the obverse.

1808. Graded G-4.

AG-3 (About Good). *Obverse:* The portrait is an outline, although some of LIBERTY can still be seen. The rim is worn down, and some stars are blended into it. The date remains clear, but is weak at the bottom (on most but not all). *Reverse:* At this level the reverse shows more wear overall than the obverse, with the rim indistinct in areas and many letters worn away. This is an interesting turnabout from the situation of most G-4 coins.

1824. Graded AG-3.

PF-60 to 70 (Proof). *Obverse and Reverse:* Proofs of this type have confused experts for a long time (as have large copper cents of the same era). Proofs that were extensively cleaned and therefore have many hairlines, or that are dull and grainy, are lower level, such as PF–60 to 62. While any early Proof half dollar will generate interest among collectors, lower levels are not of great interest to specialists unless they are of rare die varieties. With medium

1836; O-108. Graded PF-64 Cameo.

hairlines, an assigned grade of PF-64 may be in order and with relatively few, Gem PF-65. PF-66 should have hairlines so delicate that magnification is needed to see them. Above that, a Proof should be free of such lines. Grading is highly subjective with early Proofs, with eye appeal being a major factor.

1807, Small Stars

1807, Large Stars

1807, Large Stars,
50 Over 20

1807, "Bearded" Liberty

1808, 8 Over 7

	Mintage	Cert	Avg	%MS	G-4	F-12	VF-20	EF-40	AU-50	AU-55	MS-60 PF-63	MS-63 PF-64	MS-65 PF-65
1807, All kinds	750,500												
1807, Small Stars		35	35.7	6%	$225	$650	$1,000	$2,400	$5,500	$6,500	$20,000	$35,000	$75,000
	Auctions: $28,200, MS-61, January 2014; $999, EF-40, August 2014; $1,058, VF-30, March 2016; $823, VF-25, January 2015												
1807, Large Stars		37	38.5	8%	$175	$500	$750	$2,000	$3,500	$6,000	$15,000	$32,500	$150,000
	Auctions: $152,750, MS-65, November 2013; $646, VF-25, September 2016												
1807, Large Stars, 50 Over 20		146	39.3	6%	$185	$450	$700	$1,400	$2,700	$3,750	$5,750	$11,000	$125,000
	Auctions: $1,293, EF-45, January 2015; $940, VF-35, February 2015; $764, VF-35, January 2015; $282, VG-10, February 2015												
1807, "Bearded" Liberty (a)		34	29.6	0%	$700	$2,000	$3,500	$6,500	$12,500	$20,000		—	
	Auctions: $5,405, EF-45, February 2015; $4,700, VF-30, March 2015												
1808, All kinds	1,368,600												
1808, 8 Over 7		202	41.3	10%	$100	$185	$350	$650	$1,500	$2,250	$4,500	$10,000	$25,000
	Auctions: $21,150, MS-65, November 2013; $676, EF-45, January 2015; $705, EF-40, July 2014; $388, VF-35, October 2014												
1808		606	41.1	14%	$75	$150	$250	$450	$1,150	$1,850	$3,250	$6,000	$19,000
	Auctions: $1,175, AU-50, August 2015; $705, EF-45, March 2015; $259, VF-20, April 2015; $212, F-15, March 2015												

a. Also called the Bearded Goddess variety; a die crack gives the illusion of long whiskers growing from Miss Liberty's chin.

1809, xxxx Edge	**1809, ||||| Edge**
Experimental edge has "xxxx" between the words.	*Experimental edge has "|||||" between the words.*

1811, (18.11), 11 Over 10	**1811, Small 8**	**1811, Large 8**
The date is "punctuated" with a period.		

1812, 2 Over 1, Small 8	**1812, 2 Over 1, Large 8**	**1812, Two Leaves Below Wing**	**1812, Single Leaf Below Wing**

	Mintage	Cert	Avg	%MS	G-4	F-12	VF-20	EF-40	AU-50	AU-55	MS-60 / PF-63	MS-63 / PF-64	MS-65 / PF-65
1809, All kinds	1,405,810												
1809, Normal Edge		638	42.9	14%	$100	$175	$250	$500	$900	$1,500	$3,000	$8,500	$22,500
Auctions: $764, AU-55, February 2015; $494, EF-40, April 2015; $353, VF-35, August 2015; $165, F-15, January 2015													
1809, xxxx Edge		58	36.3	3%	$150	$250	$425	$1,100	$1,750	$4,000	$8,500	$15,000	
Auctions: $1,645, AU-50, April 2014; $411, VF-25, July 2014													
1809, IIIII Edge		134	39.1	9%	$100	$150	$250	$650	$1,200	$2,500	$4,750	$12,500	$35,000
Auctions: $38,188, MS-66, April 2014													
1810	1,276,276	721	42.8	13%	$75	$135	$200	$400	$800	$1,400	$2,750	$6,500	$20,000
Auctions: $646, AU-53, January 2015; $505, AU-50, June 2015; $447, EF-40, June 2015; $282, VF-35, October 2015													
1811, All kinds	1,203,644												
1811, (18.11), 11 Over 10		122	42.6	11%	$100	$250	$400	$650	$1,400	$2,750	$5,500	$10,000	
Auctions: $9,988, MS-63, February 2016; $6,463, AU-58, January 2014; $423, VF-35, August 2015; $494, VF-30, June 2015													
1811, Small 8		225	44.3	16%	$75	$135	$200	$385	$800	$1,200	$2,500	$4,000	$17,000
Auctions: $999, AU-55, January 2015; $1,175, AU-53, February 2015; $494, VF-35, March 2015; $188, VF-20, June 2015													
1811, Large 8		63	46.2	3%	$75	$125	$170	$325	$800	$1,500	$3,000	$5,000	$17,250
Auctions: $1,880, AU-58, January 2015; $329, EF-45, June 2015; $494, EF-40, October 2015; $282, VF-35, March 2015													
1812, All kinds	1,628,059												
1812, 2 Over 1, Small 8		124	43.0	18%	$115	$200	$300	$650	$1,200	$2,000	$3,500	$8,500	$25,000
Auctions: $1,293, AU-55, July 2014; $306, VF-30, March 2015; $248, VF-25, October 2015; $182, F-15, October 2015													
1812, 2 Over 1, Large 8		17	36.0	0%	$2,000	$5,500	$10,000	$13,000	$24,000	$30,000			
Auctions: $14,100, AU-58, August 2013; $8,225, VF-30, August 2014													
1812		1024	46.7	25%	$75	$135	$175	$450	$750	$1,100	$2,200	$4,000	$15,000
Auctions: $44,063, MS-65, November 2013; $441, AU-50, October 2014; $470, EF-45, August 2014; $324, EF-40, October 2014													
1812, Single Leaf Below Wing		2	31.5	0%	$750	$1,300	$2,400	$3,750	$7,000	$12,000	$17,000	$30,000	
Auctions: No auction records available.													

1813, 50 C. Over UNI.

1814, 4 Over 3

1814, E Over A in STATES

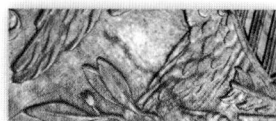

1814, Two Leaves
Below Wing

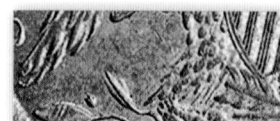

1814, Single Leaf
Below Wing

1815, 5 Over 2

1817, 7 Over 3

1817, 7 Over 4

1817, Dated 181.7
*The date is "punctuated"
with a period between
the second 1 and the 7.*

1817, Two Leaves
Below Wing

1817, Single Leaf
Below Wing

	Mintage	Cert	Avg	%MS	G-4	F-12	VF-20	EF-40	AU-50	AU-55	MS-60 / PF-63	MS-63 / PF-64	MS-65 / PF-65
1813, All kinds	1,241,903												
1813		676	45.0	17%	$75	$115	$160	$400	$750	$1,250	$2,500	$4,500	$16,000
Auctions: $881, AU-53, September 2015; $423, EF-45, January 2015; $353, EF-40, May 2015; $212, VF-30, October 2015													
1813, 50 C. Over UNI		76	47.9	21%	$115	$250	$400	$800	$1,400	$2,100	$3,500	$6,000	
Auctions: $24,675, MS-64, June 2014													
1814, All kinds	1,039,075												
1814, 4 Over 3		109	41.4	12%	$135	$250	$400	$800	$2,000	$2,650	$4,500	$8,500	$35,000
Auctions: $1,175, EF-45, June 2015; $823, EF-40, September 2015; $353, VF-35, March 2015; $482, VF-25, February 2015													
1814, E Over A in STATES		30	40.4	7%	$135	$300	$500	$1,500	$3,500	$6,500	$8,500	$12,500	
Auctions: $4,700, AU-55, January 2014; $505, VF-35, July 2014													
1814		609	47.5	23%	$85	$150	$225	$600	$800	$1,300	$2,250	$4,500	$14,000
Auctions: $22,325, MS-65, November 2013; $3,290, MS-62, August 2014; $705, AU-50, October 2014; $382, EF-45, September 2014													
1814, Single Leaf Below Wing		25	34.3	0%	$85	$150	$225	$550	$1,750	$2,250	$3,200	$6,000	
Auctions: $3,408, AU-50, August 2014; $705, EF-40, November 2013; $159, VF-20, October 2014													
1815, 5 Over 2	47,150	253	43.1	11%	$1,450	$3,250	$4,500	$5,500	$10,000	$13,000	$18,500	$50,000	
Auctions: $117,500, MS-64, November 2013; $7,931, EF-45, August 2016; $5,581, EF-40, March 2015													
1817, All kinds	1,215,567												
1817, 7 Over 3		158	40.0	14%	$165	$450	$650	$1,250	$3,000	$4,750	$8,500	$14,500	$42,500
Auctions: $28,200, MS-64, November 2013; $823, AU-50, January 2015; $541, F-15, October 2015; $499, F-15, July 2014													
1817, 7 Over 4 † (b)		1	35.0	0%	$65,000	$150,000	$200,000	$275,000	$375,000				
Auctions: $184,000, VF-20, August 2010													
1817, Dated 181.7		32	44.1	9%	$100	$200	$300	$650	$1,750	$2,500	$3,500	$7,500	$22,000
Auctions: $3,055, AU-58, August 2013; $529, VF-30, July 2014													
1817		580	43.1	14%	$100	$145	$200	$400	$750	$1,100	$2,500	$4,000	$15,500
Auctions: $508, AU-53, January 2015; $541, AU-50, June 2015; $325, EF-45, May 2015; $153, F-12, August 2015													
1817, Single Leaf Below Wing		13	38.6	8%	$100	$150	$200	$475	$1,000	$1,650	$2,750	$4,500	
Auctions: $3,055, AU-55, April 2013													

† Ranked in the *100 Greatest U.S. Coins* (fourth edition). **b.** 8 examples are known.

| 1818, First 8 Small, Second 8 Over 7 | 1818, First 8 Large, Second 8 Over 7 | 1819, Small 9 Over 8 | 1819, Large 9 Over 8 |

| 1820, 20 Over 19, Square Base 2 | 1820, 20 Over 19, Curl Base 2 | 1820, Curl Base, No Knob 2, Small Date | 1820, Square Base, Knob 2, Large Date |

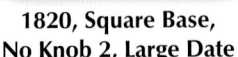

1820, Square Base, No Knob 2, Large Date

1820, Broken Serifs on E's
Compare with normal serifs on 1834, Large Letters, reverse.

	Mintage	Cert	Avg	%MS	G-4	F-12	VF-20	EF-40	AU-50	AU-55	MS-60 / PF-63	MS-63 / PF-64	MS-65 / PF-65
1818, All kinds	1,960,322												
1818, 8 Over 7, Small 8		59	45.6	12%	$90	$145	$250	$500	$1,350	$1,900	$2,900	$8,500	$20,000
Auctions: $881, AU-53, August 2014; $499, EF-40, September 2014; $270, VF-35, March 2015; $165, F-15, October 2015													
1818, 8 Over 7, Large 8		77	43.2	9%	$90	$145	$225	$475	$1,250	$1,800	$3,250	$7,000	$25,000
Auctions: $1,645, AU-55, January 2015; $999, AU-50, September 2014; $764, EF-40, August 2014; $212, VF-25, October 2015													
1818		743	46.6	16%	$70	$100	$155	$300	$600	$1,250	$2,200	$4,250	$13,500
Auctions: $2,174, MS-62, May 2015; $1,528, AU-55, January 2015; $353, EF-45, January 2015; $235, EF-40, May 2015													
1818, Proof	3–5	4	65.5								$50,000	$65,000	$80,000
Auctions: $100,625, PF-65, April 2011													
1819, All kinds	2,208,000												
1819, Small 9 Over 8		63	39.5	3%	$75	$120	$200	$375	$825	$1,350	$2,250	$5,500	$20,000
Auctions: $588, AU-50, July 2015; $353, EF-45, May 2015; $235, VF-35, May 2015; $141, VF-20, May 2015													
1819, Large 9 Over 8		148	45.5	8%	$75	$120	$175	$350	$750	$1,400	$4,000	$7,500	$25,000
Auctions: $734, AU-53, October 2014; $1,763, AU-50, September 2015; $329, EF-40, January 2015; $206, Fair-2, October 2014													
1819		543	44.0	17%	$75	$100	$150	$325	$650	$1,150	$2,000	$4,500	$20,000
Auctions: $823, AU-55, February 2015; $646, AU-53, July 2015; $259, EF-40, May 2015; $400, VF-35, October 2015													
1820, All kinds	751,122												
1820, 20 Over 19, Square 2		49	40.7	12%	$100	$150	$250	$650	$1,250	$2,000	$2,650	$8,500	$35,000
Auctions: $15,863, MS-63, January 2014; $3,819, AU-58, August 2014; $382, VF-30, July 2014													
1820, 20 Over 19, Curl Base 2		63	42.8	3%	$100	$150	$250	$600	$1,100	$2,250	$3,250	$10,000	$35,000
Auctions: $8,225, MS-63, January 2014; $1,028, AU-50, January 2015; $940, AU-50, March 2015; $470, VF-35, May 2015													
1820, Curl Base 2, Small Dt		36	50.4	14%	$100	$200	$275	$500	$1,000	$1,750	$4,500	$10,500	$25,000
Auctions: $823, AU-50, January 2015; $705, AU-53, January 2015; $376, VF-35, March 2015; $165, F-12, August 2015													
1820, Sq Base Knob 2, Lg Dt		61	49.3	11%	$100	$175	$250	$500	$950	$1,600	$3,250	$6,000	$20,000
Auctions: $18,800, MS-64, January 2014; $517, MS-60, August 2015; $1,880, AU-55, October 2014; $411, EF-40, March 2015													
1820, Sq Base No Knob 2, Large Date		62	47.1	11%	$100	$175	$250	$500	$850	$1,600	$3,250	$6,500	$20,000
Auctions: $61,688, MS-65, June 2014; $1,293, AU-53, March 2015; $259, AU-50, August 2015; $1,058, EF-45, July 2014													
1820, Broken Serifs on E's		10	40.4	20%	$500	$1,250	$3,250	$6,500	$10,000	$13,500	$25,000		
Auctions: $4,888, VF-35, December 2011													
1820, Proof	3–5	1	63.0								$50,000	$65,000	$80,000
Auctions: No auction records available.													

1822, So-Called 2 Over 1

1823, Normal Date   1823, Broken 3   1823, Patched 3   1823, Ugly 3

1824, Normal Date   1824, 4 Over 1   **1824, 4 Over Various Dates** *Probably 4 Over 2 Over 0.*   **1824, 4 Over 4** *4 Over 4 varieties are easily mistaken for the scarcer 4 Over 1. Note the distance between the 2's and 4's in each.*

	Mintage	Cert	Avg	%MS	G-4	F-12	VF-20	EF-40	AU-50	AU-55	MS-60 / PF-63	MS-63 / PF-64	MS-65 / PF-65
1821	1,305,797	699	46.4	17%	$70	$100	$145	$275	$650	$850	$1,650	$3,250	$15,000
Auctions: $447, AU-50, May 2015; $282, EF-45, March 2015; $306, EF-40, August 2015; $84, VG-10, February 2015													
1821, Proof	3–5	3	64.0								$50,000	$65,000	$80,000
Auctions: No auction records available.													
1822, All kinds	1,559,573												
1822		765	48.1	25%	$70	$100	$155	$300	$500	$800	$1,350	$2,850	$14,000
Auctions: $823, AU-55, February 2015; $282, EF-40, April 2015; $153, VF-35, May 2015; $94, F-15, February 2015													
1822, So-Called 2 Over 1		108	48.8	22%	$100	$140	$225	$600	$1,100	$1,650	$2,500	$5,500	$20,000
Auctions: $1,410, MS-60, November 2013; $1,645, EF-45, September 2014; $306, VF-30, October 2014													
1822, Proof	3–5	1	64.0								$50,000	$65,000	$100,000
Auctions: $55,813, PF-64, June 2014													
1823, All kinds	1,694,200												
1823, Broken 3		50	40.7	16%	$120	$225	$400	$750	$2,250	$3,000	$5,500	$11,000	$40,000
Auctions: $23,500, MS-64, November 2013													
1823, Patched 3		52	48.8	31%	$100	$150	$275	$700	$1,600	$2,250	$4,250	$6,500	$22,500
Auctions: $4,113, MS-63, March 2015; $1,410, AU-50, January 2015; $353, EF-45, February 2015; $165, VF-25, May 2015													
1823, Ugly 3		25	46.6	16%	$100	$150	$250	$650	$2,250	$3,500	$5,500	$10,000	$30,000
Auctions: $4,113, AU-55, January 2014													
1823, Normal		931	47.3	21%	$70	$100	$130	$250	$500	$800	$1,250	$2,850	$12,500
Auctions: $94,000, MS-67, November 2013; $3,290, MS-64, August 2014; $2,115, MS-62, August 2014; $1,410, MS-62, August 2014													
1823, Proof	3–5	1	63.0								$50,000	$65,000	$80,000
Auctions: $80,500, PF-63, April 2011													
1824, All kinds	3,504,954												
1824, 4 Over Various Dates		70	43.4	10%	$70	$145	$175	$350	$1,250	$1,750	$3,250	$5,500	$15,000
Auctions: $11,163, MS-64, June 2014; $1,116, AU-53, August 2015; $306, VF-25, February 2015; $129, F-15, September 2015													
1824, 4 Over 1		95	49.4	35%	$75	$115	$175	$350	$750	$1,200	$2,250	$6,500	$20,000
Auctions: $799, AU-53, September 2014; $529, AU-53, September 2014; $517, AU-50, January 2015; $353, EF-40, October 2015													
1824, 4 Over 4 (c)		156	47.9	19%	$75	$110	$140	$210	$700	$1,200	$1,500	$2,950	$12,000
Auctions: $558, AU-50, August 2014; $558, AU-50, July 2014; $458, AU-50, January 2015; $235, VF-30, October 2015													
1824, Normal		1,168	47.0	22%	$75	$100	$115	$175	$500	$850	$1,150	$2,000	$14,000
Auctions: $10,575, MS-65, January 2015; $2,820, MS-63, March 2015; $223, EF-45, March 2015; $94, F-15, August 2015													

c. 2 varieties.

1827, 7 Over 6

1827, Square Base 2

1827, Curl Base 2

1828, Curl Base, No Knob 2

1828, Curl Base, Knob 2

1828, Square Base 2, Large 8's

1828, Square Base 2, Small 8's

1828, Large Letters

1828, Small Letters

	Mintage	Cert	Avg	%MS	G-4	F-12	VF-20	EF-40	AU-50	AU-55	MS-60 / PF-63	MS-63 / PF-64	MS-65 / PF-65
1825	2,943,166	1,299	50.6	26%	$75	$100	$115	$175	$425	$500	$1,150	$2,250	$12,000
Auctions: $541, AU-58, January 2015; $176, EF-45, March 2015; $188, EF-40, March 2015; $112, VF-30, July 2015													
1825, Proof	3–5	1	66.0								$50,000	$65,000	$80,000
Auctions: $32,200, PF-62, May 2008													
1826	4,004,180	1,937	50.8	26%	$75	$100	$115	$175	$350	$525	$1,150	$2,000	$9,500
Auctions: $1,058, MS-61, January 2015; $881, AU-55, September 2015; $182, EF-40, March 2015; $89, VF-30, January 2015													
1826, Proof	3–5	1	65.0								$50,000	$65,000	$80,000
Auctions: $76,375, PF-65, September 2013													
1827, All kinds	5,493,400												
1827, 7 Over 6		180	50.7	23%	$100	$150	$200	$450	$1,000	$1,500	$2,350	$4,250	$15,000
Auctions: $18,800, MS-65, November 2013; $764, AU-55, October 2014													
1827, Square Base 2		704	49.0	17%	$75	$100	$115	$175	$400	$525	$1,200	$2,500	$10,000
Auctions: $764, MS-60, June 2015; $494, AU-55, January 2015; $329, AU-50, May 2015; $165, EF-40, July 2015													
1827, Curl Base 2		56	49.7	11%	$75	$100	$130	$300	$550	$850	$1,500	$3,250	$17,500
Auctions: $8,813, MS-64, January 2014													
1827, Proof	5–8	3	64.7								$50,000	$65,000	$80,000
Auctions: $21,150, PF-62, September 2013													
1828, All kinds	3,075,200												
1828, Curl Base No Knob 2		82	51.0	17%	$70	$100	$130	$200	$450	$650	$1,350	$2,250	$10,000
Auctions: $5,875, MS-65, March 2015; $940, AU-58, June 2015; $764, AU-55, October 2015; $247, EF-45, April 2015													
1828, Curl Base Knob 2		37	52.5	24%	$70	$115	$150	$250	$700	$950	$2,000	$4,500	$12,000
Auctions: $19,975, MS-65, April 2013; $382, AU-58, July 2014; $259, EF-45, May 2015													
1828, Square Base 2, Large 8's		53	49.2	11%	$70	$95	$115	$165	$350	$550	$1,150	$2,000	$11,000
Auctions: $32,900, MS-66, November 2013; $306, AU-50, October 2014; $112, EF-45, October 2014													
1828, Square Base 2, Small 8's, Large Letters		310	49.6	17%	$65	$90	$115	$165	$350	$550	$1,150	$2,000	$9,000
Auctions: $329, AU-50, October 2015; $223, EF-45, January 2015; $192, VF-35, May 2015; $188, VF-30, October 2015													
1828, Square Base 2, Small 8's and Letters		26	49.5	4%	$75	$105	$150	$250	$600	$750	$1,500	$3,000	$11,000
Auctions: $30,550, MS-65, April 2014; $411, AU-50, July 2014													

1829, 9 Over 7

1830, Small 0

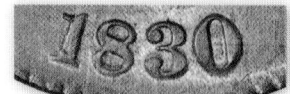
1830, Large 0

1830, Large Letters

Experimental Edge of 1830
Raised segment lines angled to the right.

Experimental Edge of 1830–1831
Raised segment lines angled to the left.

Edge Adopted for Coinage, 1830–1836
Straight vertical lines.

1832, Large Letters Reverse
O-101a. Note the prominent die crack.

	Mintage	Cert	Avg	%MS	G-4	F-12	VF-20	EF-40	AU-50	AU-55	MS-60	MS-63	MS-65
											PF-63	PF-64	PF-65
1829, All kinds	3,712,156												
1829, 9 Over 7		231	51.3	24%	$70	$120	$165	$350	$750	$1,000	$1,500	$3,500	$22,500
	Auctions: $2,115, MS-61, January 2015; $558, AU-53, September 2014; $353, EF-45, July 2014; $141, VF-25, October 2015												
1829		1108	48.1	22%	$60	$80	$110	$180	$400	$500	$1,150	$2,000	$10,000
	Auctions: $16,450, MS-66, March 2015; $1,058, AU-55, January 2015; $306, AU-50, June 2015; $153, EF-45, March 2015												
1829, Large Letters		30	54.4	27%	$65	$90	$120	$200	$400	$550	$1,200	$2,500	$10,500
	Auctions: $194, AU-50, September 2013												
1829, Proof	*6–9*	5	64.2								$50,000	$65,000	$80,000
	Auctions: $102,813, PF-64, January 2014												
1830, All kinds	4,764,800												
1830, Small 0		551	47.7	13%	$65	$90	$120	$180	$375	$550	$1,100	$2,100	$10,000
	Auctions: $1,410, MS-61, January 2015; $589, AU-58, August 2015; $217, EF-45, July 2015; $100, VF-25, September 2015												
1830, Large 0		143	50.7	16%	$65	$90	$120	$180	$375	$550	$1,000	$2,100	$10,000
	Auctions: $41,125, MS-66, November 2013; $588, AU-58, July 2014; $482, AU-55, July 2014; $353, AU-53, July 2014												
1830, Large Letters		12	33.3	8%	$1,400	$2,950	$3,800	$4,800	$9,000	$14,000	$17,500	$22,000	
	Auctions: $2,990, VF-35, October 2011												
1830, Proof	*3–5*	2	64.5								$50,000	$65,000	$80,000
	Auctions: $41,400, PF-64, January 2005												
1831	5,873,660	1,961	51.3	25%	$65	$90	$110	$180	$375	$500	$1,100	$2,000	$10,000
	Auctions: $922, MS-61, January 2015; $541, AU-58, August 2015; $306, AU-53, October 2015; $153, EF-40, February 2015												
1831, Proof	*3–5*	2	64.5								$50,000	$65,000	$80,000
	Auctions: $79,313, PF-65, April 2013												
1832, All kinds	4,797,000												
1832		1,802	50.8	23%	$65	$90	$110	$180	$375	$500	$1,100	$2,000	$10,000
	Auctions: $999, MS-62, January 2015; $764, AU-58, January 2015; $212, EF-45, March 2015; $112, VF-35, October 2015												
1832, Large Letters		79	50.6	14%	$65	$90	$110	$180	$375	$500	$1,100	$2,000	$10,000
	Auctions: $4,406, MS-64, November 2013; $364, AU-55, July 2014; $382, AU-50, August 2014												
1832, Proof	*6–9*	3	64.7								$50,000	$65,000	$80,000
	Auctions: $29,900, PF-63, January 2008												

1834, Large Date

1834, Small Date

1834, Large Letters

1834, Small Letters

1836, Over 1336

	Mintage	Cert	Avg	%MS	G-4	F-12	VF-20	EF-40	AU-50	AU-55	MS-60	MS-63	MS-65
											PF-63	PF-64	PF-65
1833	5,206,000	1,762	50.8	22%	$65	$90	$110	$180	$375	$500	$1,100	$2,000	$10,000
Auctions: $353, AU-55, February 2015; $317, AU-53, August 2015; $270, AU-50, May 2015; $188, EF-45, April 2015													
1833, Proof	*1–2*	4	63.8										
Auctions: No auction records available.													
1833, Crushed Lettered Edge, Proof	*3–5*	2	64.5								$40,000	$65,000	$95,000
Auctions: No auction records available.													
1834, All kinds	6,412,004												
1834, Large Date and Letters		144	50.3	18%	$60	$80	$110	$180	$375	$500	$1,100	$2,000	$9,000
Auctions: $564, AU-58, January 2015; $135, EF-45, May 2015; $159, EF-40, July 2015; $153, VF-35, February 2015													
1834, Large Date, Small Letters		220	50.6	18%	$60	$80	$110	$180	$375	$500	$1,100	$2,000	$9,000
Auctions: $823, AU-58, January 2015; $447, AU-55, August 2015; $376, AU-53, June 2015; $200, EF-45, April 2015													
1834, Small Date, Stars, Letters		429	49.1	13%	$60	$80	$110	$180	$375	$500	$1,100	$2,000	$9,000
Auctions: $764, AU-58, February 2015; $350, AU-55, May 2015; $120, EF-40, January 2015; $94, VF-35, September 2015													
1834, Proof	*8–12*	7	64.6								$40,000	$65,000	$95,000
Auctions: $23,710, PF-63, November 2013													
1834, Crushed Lettered Edge, Proof	*3–5*	1	55.0								$40,000	$65,000	$95,000
Auctions: No auction records available.													
1835	5,352,006	1092	49.1	20%	$60	$80	$110	$180	$375	$500	$1,100	$2,000	$9,000
Auctions: $881, AU-58, August 2015; $350, AU-55, February 2015; $212, EF-45, August 2015; $141, VF-35, October 2015													
1835, Proof	*5–8*	2	63.0								$40,000	$65,000	$95,000
Auctions: $43,125, PF-64, August 2007													
1835, Crushed Lettered Edge, Proof	*3–5*	2	65.0								$40,000	$65,000	$95,000
Auctions: No auction records available.													
1836, All kinds	6,545,000												
1836		1,603	48.6	20%	$60	$80	$110	$180	$375	$500	$1,100	$2,000	$9,000
Auctions: $823, AU-58, August 2015; $282, AU-50, January 2015; $100, VF-30, August 2015; $94, VF-25, October 2015													
1836, 1836 Over 1336		65	48.7	12%	$80	$100	$130	$225	$475	$700	$1,200	$2,500	$10,000
Auctions: $2,703, MS-64, August 2014; $499, AU-53, July 2014; $270, AU-50, March 2015; $194, VF-35, December 2014													
1836, 50 Over 00		50	50.7	20%	$125	$200	$350	$500	$925	$1,500	$2,500	$5,000	$30,000
Auctions: $1,645, AU-55, February 2013													
1836, Beaded Border on Reverse (d)		44	43.9	16%	$85	$120	$140	$250	$525	$675	$1,300	$2,400	$9,500
Auctions: $494, AU-53, May 2015; $212, EF-45, February 2015; $153, VF-35, September 2015 $112, EF-40, November 2014													
1836, Lettered Edge, Proof	*8–12*	5	64.4								$40,000	$65,000	$95,000
Auctions: $96,938, PF-66, November 2013													
1836, 50 Over 00, Proof	*3–5*	2	64.5								$50,000	$80,000	$115,000
Auctions: $81,937, PF-65, October 2006													

d. The same beaded-border reverse die was used for Proofs of 1833, 1834, and 1835 with the crushed edge lettering; all are very rare.

CAPPED BUST, REEDED EDGE (1836–1839)

Designer: *Christian Gobrecht.* **Weight:** *13.36 grams.* **Composition:** *.900 silver, .100 copper.*
Diameter: *30 mm.* **Edge:** *Reeded.* **Mint:** *Philadelphia.*

Reverse 50 CENTS (1836–1837)   Reverse 50 CENTS, Proof

Reverse HALF DOL. (1838–1839)

Mintmark
location is
on the obverse,
above the date.

Reverse HALF DOL., Proof

History. This half dollar type features a slight restyling of John Reich's Capped Bust design, modified by Christian Gobrecht. It is of smaller diameter than the preceding type, and made with a reeded edge. The reverse is of two variations: the 1836–1837, with 50 CENTS; and the 1838–1839, with HALF DOL.

Striking and Sharpness. The key points for observation are the stars on the obverse. On the reverse, check the border letters and the details of the eagle. The 1839-O nearly always shows die cracks, often extensive (these have no effect on desirability or market value).

Availability. The 1836 is rare. The 1838-O is a famous rarity, and the 1839-O is scarce. The others are easily available in nearly any grade desired, with 1837 being the most common. Proofs are occasionally encountered of the year 1836 and are quite rare. Authentic Proofs of 1837 exist but for all practical purposes are unobtainable. Most 1838-O (a rarity) and a few 1839-O coins have been called branch-mint Proofs.

GRADING STANDARDS

MS-60 to 70 (Mint State). *Obverse and Reverse:* Grading guidelines are the same as for the 1807–1836 type, except on this type the rims are more uniform. On the 1836–1837 dates the reverse rim is generally lower than the obverse, causing the reverse to wear slightly more quickly. On the 1838–1839 type (with slightly different lettering) the wear occurs evenly on both sides, and light striking showing areas of the original planchet on the obverse does not occur here.

1837. Graded MS-62.

Illustrated coin: This example displays light gray toning with a sprinkling of gold over fully lustrous surfaces.

AU-50, 53, 55, 58 (About Uncirculated). *Obverse and Reverse:* Grading guidelines are the same as for the 1807–1836 type, except on this type the rims are more uniform. On the 1836–1837 dates the reverse rim is generally lower than the obverse, causing the reverse to wear slightly more quickly. On the 1838–1839 type (with slightly different lettering) the wear occurs evenly on both sides.

1836. Graded AU-53.

EF-40, 45 (Extremely Fine). *Obverse and Reverse:* Grading guidelines are the same as for the 1807–1836 type, except on this type the rims are more uniform. On the 1836–1837 dates the reverse rim is generally lower than the obverse, causing the reverse to wear slightly more quickly. On the 1838–1839 type (with slightly different lettering) the wear occurs evenly on both sides.

1836. Graded EF-40.

VF-20, 30 (Very Fine). *Obverse and Reverse:* Grading guidelines are the same as for the 1807–1836 type, except on this type the rims are more uniform. On the 1836–1837 dates the reverse rim is generally lower than the obverse, causing the reverse to wear slightly more quickly. On the 1838–1839 type (with slightly different lettering) the wear occurs evenly on both sides.

1836. Graded VF-20.

F-12, 15 (Fine). *Obverse and Reverse:* Grading guidelines are the same as for the 1807–1836 type, except on this type the rims are more uniform. On the 1836–1837 dates the reverse rim is generally lower than the obverse, causing the reverse to wear slightly more quickly. On the 1838–1839 type (with slightly different lettering) the wear occurs evenly on both sides.

1839-O. Graded F-15.

VG-8, 10 (Very Good). *Obverse and Reverse:* Grading guidelines are the same as for the 1807–1836 type, except on this type the rims are more uniform. On the 1836–1837 dates the reverse rim is generally lower than the obverse, causing the reverse to wear slightly more quickly. On the 1838–1839 type (with slightly different lettering) the wear occurs evenly on both sides.

1836. Graded VG-10.

G-4, 6 (Good). *Obverse and Reverse:* Grading guidelines are the same as for the 1807–1836 type, except on this type the rims are more uniform. On the 1836–1837 dates the reverse rim is generally lower than the obverse, causing the reverse to wear slightly more quickly. On the 1838–1839 type (with slightly different lettering) the wear occurs evenly on both sides.

1838. Graded G-4.

AG-3 (About Good). *Obverse and Reverse:* Grading guidelines are the same as for the 1807–1836 type, except on this type the rims are more uniform. On the 1836–1837 dates the reverse rim is generally lower than the obverse, causing the reverse to wear slightly more quickly. On the 1838–1839 type (with slightly different lettering) the wear occurs evenly on both sides.

1836. Graded AG-3.

PF-60 to 70 (Proof). *Obverse and Reverse:* Proofs in grades of PF–60 to 62 show extensive hairlines and cloudiness. At PF-63, hairlines are obvious, but the mirrored fields are attractive. PF–64 and 65 coins have fewer hairlines, but they still are obvious when the coin is slowly turned while held at an angle to the light. PF-66 coins require a magnifier to discern hairlines, and higher grades should have no hairlines.

1836. Graded PF-64 Cameo.

1839, Regular Letters Reverse   **1839, Small Letters Reverse**

	Mintage	Cert	Avg	%MS	G-4	F-12	VF-20	EF-40	AU-50	AU-55	MS-60	MS-63	MS-65
											PF-60	PF-63	PF-65
1836	*1,200+*	210	48.3	17%	$1,000	$1,750	$2,150	$3,500	$5,000	$6,000	$9,500	$20,000	$65,000
Auctions: $38,188, MS-64, October 2014; $423, AU-58, September 2015; $4,113, AU-53, March 2015; $3,290, EF-45, March 2015													
1836, Reeded Edge, Proof	*10–15*	10	63.7								$45,000	$65,000	$90,000
Auctions: $32,900, PF-63, April 2013													
1837	3,629,820	1,523	53.3	34%	$70	$105	$125	$225	$475	$625	$1,200	$2,750	$17,500
Auctions: $11,456, MS-64, March 2015; $1,645, MS-62, January 2015; $425, AU-55, June 2015; $247, EF-45, August 2015													
1837, Proof	*4–6*	2	63.5								$50,000	$75,000	$100,000
Auctions: $32,200, PF-62, July 2008													
1838	3,546,000	1,139	52.3	27%	$70	$105	$125	$225	$475	$675	$1,200	$2,750	$18,000
Auctions: $17,625, MS-66, May 2015; $1,645, MS-62, January 2015; $588, AU-55, January 2015; $235, EF-45, June 2015													
1838, Proof	*3–5*	0	n/a								$50,000	$75,000	$100,000
Auctions: $129,250, PF-64, April 2014													
1838-O, Proof † (a)	20	4	59.0								$750,000	$950,000	
Auctions: $193,875, PF-65, March 2015; $646,250, PF-64, May 2015; $293,750, PF-50, August 2015													
1839	1,392,976	525	50.7	24%	$75	$115	$150	$275	$500	$750	$1,400	$3,100	$30,000
Auctions: $5,288, MS-64, March 2015; $470, AU-55, January 2015; $259, EF-45, June 2015; $235, EF-40, June 2015													
1839, Small Letters Reverse (b)		2	52.5	0%	$40,000	$55,000	$60,000	$65,000					
Auctions: $50,025, AU-50, January 2010													
1839, Reeded Edge, Proof (c)	n/a	0	n/a								—		
Auctions: No auction records available.													
1839-O	116,000	276	46.9	18%	$425	$950	$1,200	$2,000	$2,500	$3,500	$6,500	$12,500	$42,500
Auctions: $52,875, MS-65, July 2015; $1,528, VF-25, June 2015; $2,585, EF-40, August 2016; $1,293, F-12, August 2016													
1839-O, Proof	*5–10*	4	62.8								$150,000	$200,000	$250,000
Auctions: $92,000, PF-63, March 2012													

† Ranked in the *100 Greatest U.S. Coins* (fourth edition). **a.** The 1838-O, Proof, was the first branch-mint half dollar, though it was not mentioned in the Mint director's report. The New Orleans chief coiner stated that only 20 were struck. **b.** Extremely rare. **c.** Unverified.

LIBERTY SEATED (1839–1891)

Variety 1, No Motto Above Eagle (1839–1853): **Designer:** *Christian Gobrecht.*
Weight: *13.36 grams.* **Composition:** *.900 silver, .100 copper.* **Diameter:** *30.6 mm.*
Edge: *Reeded.* **Mints:** *Philadelphia and New Orleans.*

Mintmark
location is
on the reverse,
below the eagle,
for all varieties.

Variety 1 (1839–1853)   Variety 1, Proof

Variety 2, Arrows at Date, Rays Around Eagle (1853): **Designer:** *Christian Gobrecht.*
Weight: *12.44 grams.* **Composition:** *.900 silver, .100 copper.* **Diameter:** *30.6 mm.*
Edge: *Reeded.* **Mints:** *Philadelphia and New Orleans.*

Variety 2 (1853)   Variety 2, Proof

Variety 3, Arrows at Date, No Rays (1854–1855): **Designer:** *Christian Gobrecht.*
Weight: *12.44 grams.* **Composition:** *.900 silver, .100 copper.* **Diameter:** *30.6 mm.*
Edge: *Reeded.* **Mints:** *Philadelphia, New Orleans, and San Francisco.*

Variety 3 (1854–1855)   Variety 3, Proof

Variety 1 Resumed, With Weight Standard of Variety 2 (1856–1866):
Designer: *Christian Gobrecht.* **Weight:** *12.44 grams.* **Composition:** *.900 silver, .100 copper.*
Diameter: *30.6 mm.* **Edge:** *Reeded.* **Mints:** *Philadelphia, New Orleans, and San Francisco.*

Variety 1 Resumed, Weight Standard   Variety 1 Resumed, Weight Standard
of Variety 2 (1856–1866)   of Variety 2, Proof

Variety 4, Motto Above Eagle (1866–1873): **Designer:** *Christian Gobrecht.*
Weight: *12.44 grams.* **Composition:** *.900 silver, .100 copper.* **Diameter:** *30.6 mm.*
Edge: *Reeded.* **Mints:** *Philadelphia, San Francisco, and Carson City.*

Variety 4 (1866–1873)

Variety 4, Proof

Variety 5, Arrows at Date (1873–1874): **Designer:** *Christian Gobrecht.*
Weight: *12.50 grams.* **Composition:** *.900 silver, .100 copper.* **Diameter:** *30.6 mm.*
Edge: *Reeded.* **Mints:** *Philadelphia, San Francisco, and Carson City.*

Variety 5 (1873–1874)

Variety 5, Proof

Variety 4 Resumed, With Weight Standard of Variety 5 (1875–1891): **Designer:** *Christian Gobrecht.*
Weight: *12.50 grams.* **Composition:** *.900 silver, .100 copper.* **Diameter:** *30.6 mm.*
Edge: *Reeded.* **Mints:** *Philadelphia, San Francisco, and Carson City.*

**Variety 4 Resumed, Weight Standard
of Variety 5 (1875–1891)**

**Variety 4 Resumed, Weight Standard
of Variety 5, Proof**

History. Half dollars of the Liberty Seated type were struck every year from 1839 to 1891. The designs varied slightly over the years, but with the basic obverse and reverse motifs remaining the same (e.g., from 1842 to 1853 the coins bore a modified reverse with large letters in the legend, and in 1846 the date size was enlarged). Large quantities were made until 1879, at which time there was a glut of silver coins in commerce. After that mintages were reduced.

The earliest Liberty Seated half dollars, dated 1839, lacked drapery at Miss Liberty's elbow. In that year Robert Ball Hughes modified Christian Gobrecht's design by adding drapery, a feature that continued for the rest of the series.

Striking and Sharpness. On the obverse, first check the head of Miss Liberty and the star centers. On coins of the Arrows at Date variety, especially 1855, the word LIBERTY tends to wear faster compared to earlier and later varieties. On the reverse, check the eagle at the lower left. Afterward, check all other features. Generally, the higher-mintage issues are the least well struck, and many New Orleans Mint coins can be lightly struck, particularly those of the 1850s. The luster on MS coins usually is very attractive. Resurfaced dies often are prooflike, some with the drapery polished away (as with 1877-S, in particular). Above and beyond issues of strike, the Small Letters coins of 1839 to 1842 have narrower, lower rims that afforded less protection to the central devices of the reverse. In contrast, the No Motto, Large Letters, coins have wider, higher rims that tend to better protect the central devices. Many pre–Civil War dates, particularly of the 1840s, show evidence of extensive die polishing in the fields (especially evident in the open expanses of the obverse). From grades of EF downward, sharpness of strike of the stars and the head does not matter to connoisseurs. Quality is often lacking, with lint marks seen on some issues of the late 1850s and early 1860s. Light striking is occasionally seen on the star centers and the head of Miss Liberty; connoisseurs avoid coins with this detraction, but most buyers will not be aware. Slide marks (usually seen on the right knee) from coin albums can be a problem, more so on Liberty Seated halves than on lower denominations of this design.

Availability. Collecting these coins is a popular pursuit with many enthusiasts. Examples of the higher-mintage dates are readily available, with earlier years being much scarcer than later ones. Most often seen among MS coins are issues from the mid-1870s onward. Circulated coins from well worn through AU can be found of most dates and mintmarks; these are avidly sought. Proofs were made in most years, with production beginning in a particularly significant way in 1858, when an estimated 210 silver sets were sold. Today, Proofs from 1858 through 1891 are readily available.

GRADING STANDARDS

MS-60 to 70 (Mint State). *Obverse:* At MS-60, some abrasion and contact marks are evident, most noticeably on the bosom and thighs and knees. Luster is present, but may be dull or lifeless. At MS-63, contact marks are very few, and abrasion is hard to detect except under magnification. An MS-65 coin has no abrasion, and contact marks are sufficiently minute as to require magnification. Check the knees of Liberty and the right field. Luster

1856-O. Graded MS-63.

should be full and rich. Most Mint State coins of the 1861 to 1865 years, Philadelphia issues, have extensive die striae (from dies not being completely finished); note that these are *raised* (whereas cleaning hairlines are incuse). *Reverse:* Comments as preceding, except that in lower Mint State grades abrasion and contact marks are most noticeable on the eagle's head, neck, and claws, and the top of the wings (harder to see there, however). At MS-65 or higher there are no marks visible to the unaided eye. The field is mainly protected by design elements and does not show abrasion as much as does the obverse on a given coin.

AU-50, 53, 55, 58 (About Uncirculated). *Obverse:* Light wear is seen on the thighs and knees, bosom, and head. At AU-58, the luster is extensive, but incomplete, especially in the right field. At AU–50 and 53, luster is less. *Reverse:* Wear is evident on the eagle's neck, the claws, and the top of the wings. An AU-58 coin has nearly full luster, more so than on the obverse, as the design elements protect the small field areas. At AU–50 and 53, there still are traces of luster.

1841-O. Graded AU-55.

Illustrated coin: Gray toning is evident on this coin. The reverse is lightly struck, a characteristic that should not be mistaken for wear.

EF-40, 45 (Extremely Fine). *Obverse:* Further wear is seen on all areas, especially the thighs and knees, bosom, and head. Little or no luster is seen on most coins. From this grade downward, sharpness of strike of stars and the head does not matter to connoisseurs. *Reverse:* Further wear is evident on the eagle's neck, claws, and wings.

1839, No Drapery From Elbow. Graded EF-40.

VF-20, 30 (Very Fine). *Obverse:* Further wear is seen. Most details of the gown are worn away, except in the lower-relief areas above and to the right of the shield. Hair detail is mostly or completely gone. *Reverse:* Wear is more extensive, with some of the feathers blended together.

1839, No Drapery From Elbow. Graded VF-20.

F-12, 15 (Fine). *Obverse:* The seated figure is well worn, but with some detail above and to the right of the shield. LIBERTY is readable but weak in areas, perhaps with a letter missing (a slightly looser interpretation than the demand for full LIBERTY a generation ago). *Reverse:* Wear is extensive, with about a third to half of the feathers flat or blended with others.

1842-O, Small Date. Graded F-12.

VG-8, 10 (Very Good). *Obverse:* The seated figure is more worn, but some detail can be seen above and to the right of the shield. The shield is discernible, but the upper-right section may be flat and blended into the seated figure. In LIBERTY at least the equivalent of two or three letters (can be a combination of partial letters) must be readable, possibly very weak at VG-8, with a few more visible at VG-10. In the marketplace and among certified coins, parts of

1873-CC, Arrows at Date. Graded VG-8.

two letters seem to be allowed. Per PCGS, "localized weakness may obscure some letters." LIBERTY is *not* an infallible guide: some varieties have the word in low relief on the die, so it wore away slowly. *Reverse:* Further wear has flattened all but a few feathers, and many if not most horizontal lines of the shield are indistinct. The leaves are only in outline form. The rim is visible all around, as are the ends of most denticles.

G-4, 6 (Good). *Obverse:* The seated figure is worn nearly smooth. At G-4 there are no letters in LIBERTY remaining on most (but not all) coins; some coins, especially of the early 1870s, are exceptions. At G-6, traces of one or two can barely be seen and more details can be seen in the figure. *Reverse:* The eagle shows only a few details of the shield and feathers. The rim is worn down, and the tops of the border letters are weak or worn away, although the inscription can still be read.

1873, No Arrows, Open 3. Graded G-6.

AG-3 (About Good). *Obverse:* The seated figure is visible in outline form. Much or all of the rim is worn away. The date remains clear. *Reverse:* The border letters are partially worn away. The eagle is mostly in outline form, but with a few details discernible. The rim is weak or missing.

1873, No Arrows, Open 3. Graded AG-3.

PF-60 to 70 (Proof). *Obverse and Reverse:* Proofs that are extensively cleaned and have many hairlines, or that are dull and grainy, are lower level, such as PF–60 to 62. These are not widely desired, save for the low mintage (in circulation-strike format) years from 1879 to 1891. With medium hairlines and good reflectivity, an assigned grade of PF-64 is appropriate, and with relatively few hairlines, Gem PF-65. In various grades hairlines are most easily seen in the obverse field. PF-66 should have hairlines so delicate that magnification is needed to see them. Above that, a Proof should be free of such lines.

1889. Graded PF-65.

No Drapery From Elbow (1839)		Drapery From Elbow (Starting 1839)

	Mintage	Cert	Avg	%MS	G-4	VG-8	F-12	VF-20	EF-40	AU-50	MS-60 / PF-60	MS-63 / PF-63	MS-65 / PF-65
1839, No Drapery From Elbow	(a)	172	46.6	15%	$45	$145	$400	$650	$1,400	$2,000	$6,500	$27,500	$150,000
Auctions: $2,180, EF-40, January 2015; $881, VF-30, June 2015; $705, VF-25, August 2015; $595, VF-20, February 2015													
1839, No Drapery, Proof	4–6	6	63.2								$100,000	$135,000	$250,000
Auctions: $223,250, PF-64, November 2013													
1839, Drapery From Elbow	1,972,400	170	51.1	32%	$45	$75	$85	$125	$250	$500	$1,300	$2,300	$17,500
Auctions: $4,230, MS-64, January 2015; $541, AU-55, January 2015; $564, AU-53, January 2015; $541, AU-50, May 2015													
1839, Drapery, Proof	1–2	1	64.0									$95,000	$200,000
Auctions: $184,000, PF-64, April 2008													
1840, Small Letters	1,435,008	236	51.2	26%	$50	$65	$75	$150	$300	$425	$800	$1,400	$7,500
Auctions: $5,640, MS-65, October 2015; $329, AU-50, February 2015													

a. Included in circulation-strike 1839, Drapery From Elbow, mintage figure.

Small Letters in Legend (1839–1841)   **1840 (Only), Medium Letters, Large Eagle**   **Large Letters in Legend (1842–1853)**

1842, Small Date   **1842, Medium Date**

	Mintage	Cert	Avg	%MS	G-4	VG-8	F-12	VF-20	EF-40	AU-50	MS-60 / PF-60	MS-63 / PF-63	MS-65 / PF-65
1840, Medium Letters (b)	(c)	50	41.9	18%	$180	$250	$450	$650	$1,100	$2,000	$4,000	$8,750	$45,000
Auctions: $2,233, MS-62, February 2015; $1,028, AU-58, January 2015; $259, EF-45, May 2015; $188, VF-30, September 2015													
1840, Small Letters, Proof	4–8	7	64.0										$65,000
Auctions: $49,350, PF-65, May 2015; $30,550, PF-63, November 2013													
1840-O	855,100	130	48.0	25%	$42	$60	$100	$165	$300	$500	$1,650	$4,500	
Auctions: $2,350, MS-62, January 2015; $1,410, MS-60, June 2015; $212, EF-45, June 2015; $141, VF-30, June 2015													
1841	310,000	77	54.9	32%	$42	$80	$95	$200	$350	$650	$1,400	$2,800	$9,000
Auctions: $11,750, MS-65, May 2015; $4,230, MS-64, January 2015; $857, AU-58, June 2015; $364, EF-45, August 2015													
1841, Proof	4–8	6	64.5								$20,000	$25,000	$45,000
Auctions: $30,550, PF-64, September 2013													
1841-O	401,000	116	51.1	25%	$42	$70	$115	$175	$300	$650	$1,250	$3,500	$12,000
Auctions: $27,025, MS-66, May 2015; $447, AU-53, July 2015; $259, EF-45, May 2015; $153, VF-30, July 2015													
1842, Sm Date, Sm Letters	(d)	0	n/a		$15,000	$20,000	$25,000	$30,000	$35,000	$40,000			
Auctions: $99,875, MS-64, June 2014													
1842, Medium Date	2,012,764	137	49.4	15%	$42	$60	$75	$140	$225	$400	$975	$2,000	$7,000
Auctions: $2,585, MS-64, October 2015; $353, MS-60, August 2015; $360, AU-58, May 2015; $129, EF-40, September 2015													
1842, Sm Date, Lg Letters	(d)	56	51.7	27%	$42	$60	$90	$180	$225	$500	$1,300	$3,300	$23,000
Auctions: $21,150, MS-65, April 2014; $2,585, MS-63, January 2015; $306, EF-45, May 2015; $176, VF-25, August 2015													
1842, Sm Date, Lg Ltrs, Proof	4–8	5	64.2								$15,000	$25,000	$45,000
Auctions: $44,063, PF-66, June 2014													
1842-O, Sm Date, Sm Letters	203,000	36	36.1	6%	$575	$1,000	$1,400	$2,250	$4,000	$8,000	$16,500	$32,500	
Auctions: $35,250, MS-62, January 2014; ; $3,760, EF-40, January 2015; $764, VG-10, November 2014; $823, VG-8, September 2014													
1842-O, Med Date, Lg Letters	754,000	64	47.8	20%	$42	$60	$80	$100	$250	$600	$1,800	$4,500	$20,000
Auctions: $19,975, MS-65, January 2015; $517, AU-50, July 2015; $282, EF-45, July 2015; $212, VF-35, January 2015													
1843	3,844,000	235	50.6	28%	$42	$55	$65	$100	$180	$300	$900	$1,800	$7,750
Auctions: $4,935, MS-65, January 2015; $201, AU-50, January 2015; $212, EF-45, August 2015; $89, VF-25, March 2015													
1843, Proof	4–8	3	63.7								$15,000	$27,500	$60,000
Auctions: $70,500, PF-65Cam, August 2013; $44,063, PF-64, October 2014													
1843-O	2,268,000	112	50.6	38%	$60	$70	$80	$100	$165	$450	$1,400	$3,250	$25,000
Auctions: $3,290, MS-63, January 2015; $764, AU-58, August 2015; $646, AU-55, June 2015; $223, EF-40, January 2015													

b. The 1840, Medium Letters, half dollars were struck at the New Orleans Mint from a reverse die of the previous style, without mintmark. **c.** Included in circulation-strike 1840, Small Letters, mintage figure. **d.** Included in 1842, Medium Date, mintage figure.

1846, Medium Date

1844-O, Doubled Date
FS-50-1844o-301.

1846, Tall Date

1846-O, Medium Date

1846-O, Tall Date

1847, 7 Over 6
FS-50-1847-301.

	Mintage	Cert	Avg	%MS	G-4	VG-8	F-12	VF-20	EF-40	AU-50	MS-60 PF-60	MS-63 PF-63	MS-65 PF-65
1844	1,766,000	149	53.4	33%	$42	$55	$70	$115	$180	$325	$700	$1,700	$8,750
Auctions: $12,338, MS-65, May 2015; $223, AU-50, August 2015; $129, EF-45, May 2015; $247, EF-40, February 2015												
1844, Proof	3–6	1	62.0										$75,000
Auctions: $149,500, PF-66Cam, January 2008; $31,725, PF-64, May 2015												
1844-O	2,005,000	111	46.3	31%	$42	$55	$70	$115	$250	$475	$1,350	$3,000	$13,500
Auctions: $10,575, MS-64, May 2015; $764, AU-58, January 2015; $295, AU-50, October 2015; $376, EF-45, October 2015												
1844-O, Doubled Date (e)	(f)	20	41.2	5%	$500	$800	$1,100	$1,600	$2,750	$6,000	$8,500		
Auctions: $6,463, AU-55, February 2013; $115, VG-8, July 2014; $235, Fair-2, October 2014												
1845	589,000	56	49.8	21%	$55	$70	$80	$135	$240	$400	$1,000	$3,500	
Auctions: $3,055, MS-64, January 2015; $447, AU-55, June 2015; $536, AU-53, January 2015; $235, VF-30, January 2015												
1845, Proof	3–6	3	65.0								$15,000	$30,000	$65,000
Auctions: $57,500, PF-64, May 2008												
1845-O	2,094,000	120	45.9	22%	$42	$70	$85	$120	$200	$360	$850	$3,000	$9,000
Auctions: $329, AU-50, November 2015; $259, AU-50, November 2015; $353, EF-45, May 2015; $223, EF-40, August 2015												
1845-O, No Drapery (g)	(h)	19	49.3	21%	$100	$125	$150	$180	$480	$800	$1,400	$4,500	
Auctions: $6,463, MS-64, June 2014												
1846, All kinds	2,210,000												
1846, Medium Date		79	50.9	27%	$42	$60	$75	$85	$180	$480	$1,000	$1,550	$12,000
Auctions: $1,293, MS-63, January 2015; $705, AU-58, June 2015; $223, AU-50, May 2015; $165, EF-40, August 2015												
1846, Tall Date		107	52.8	27%	$100	$120	$180	$275	$360	$500	$1,300	$2,750	
Auctions: $881, AU-58, September 2015; $588, AU-53, October 2015; $423, AU-53, May 2015; $317, EF-45, April 2015												
1846, 6 Over Horizontal 6 (i)		37	47.9	16%	$225	$300	$500	$1,000	$1,650	$2,500	$4,750	$10,000	$20,000
Auctions: $7,050, MS-62, June 2014												
1846, Med Letters, Proof	15–20	11	63.5								$11,000	$21,000	$50,000
Auctions: $28,200, PF-64, October 2014; $23,500, PF-63, January 2014; $14,100, PF-63, March 2015												
1846-O, Medium Date	2,304,000	101	43.1	19%	$42	$60	$100	$150	$275	$425	$1,500	$3,600	$20,000
Auctions: $2,820, MS-62, January 2015; $588, AU-55, January 2015; $376, AU-53, July 2015; $153, VF-35, March 2015												
1846-O, Tall Date	(j)	28	37.3	7%	$250	$375	$550	$1,000	$1,800	$2,500	$9,500	$15,000	
Auctions: $1,528, EF-45, January 2015; $881, VF-30, June 2015; $306, F-15, June 2015; $360, VG-10, January 2015												
1847, 7 Over 6 (k)	(l)	4	46.8	25%	$1,500	$2,250	$3,250	$4,250	$10,000	$13,500	$27,500		
Auctions: $17,038, AU-55, May 2015; $5,875, AU-50, August 2014; $8,225, VF-35, August 2014; $5,640, VF-35, January 2015												
1847	1,156,000	114	51.8	23%	$42	$60	$85	$110	$220	$250	$600	$1,650	$7,000
Auctions: $8,813, MS-65, May 2015; $1,410, MS-63, February 2015; $235, AU-53, May 2015; $165, EF-40, October 2015												
1847, Proof	15–20	10	63.5								$10,000	$20,000	$45,000
Auctions: $12,338, PF-63, August 2013												
1847-O	2,584,000	97	49.6	30%	$50	$65	$75	$100	$210	$450	$1,000	$2,750	$15,000
Auctions: $30,550, MS-66, May 2015; $1,880, MS-62, January 2015; $378, AU-53, February 2015; $176, EF-40, October 2015												

e. This rare variety shows all four numerals protruding from the rock above the primary date. **f.** Included in 1844-O mintage figure. **g.** The drapery is missing because of excessive polishing of the die. **h.** Included in 1845-O mintage figure. **i.** This variety can be detected in low grades. **j.** Included in 1846-O, Medium Date, mintage figure. **k.** Remains of an underlying 6 are visible below and between the primary 4 and 7. "The overdate might not be evident on later die states" (*Cherrypickers' Guide to Rare Die Varieties,* sixth edition, volume II). **l.** Included in circulation-strike 1847 mintage figure.

	Mintage	Cert	Avg	%MS	G-4	VG-8	F-12	VF-20	EF-40	AU-50	MS-60	MS-63	MS-65
											PF-60	PF-63	PF-65
1848	580,000	69	54.2	45%	$45	$65	$120	$200	$325	$650	$1,200	$2,500	$14,000
	Auctions: $7,638, MS-64, January 2015; $617, AU-55, March 2015; $341, EF-45, August 2015; $235, VF-35, May 2015												
1848, Proof	4–8	2	66.0								$10,000	$20,000	$45,000
	Auctions: $34,075, PF-64, June 2014												
1848-O	3,180,000	109	48.3	22%	$42	$50	$70	$120	$250	$500	$1,200	$2,200	$24,500
	Auctions: $940, AU-58, January 2015; $999, AU-55, June 2015; $306, EF-45, July 2015; $141, VF-35, August 2015												
1849	1,252,000	104	56.1	38%	$45	$75	$80	$115	$200	$400	$1,000	$2,250	$13,500
	Auctions: $10,575, MS-65, January 2015; $517, AU-58, June 2015; $400, AU-53, August 2015; $294, EF-45, March 2015												
1849, Proof	4–8	4	65.0								$10,000	$20,000	$45,000
	Auctions: $70,500, PF-66, January 2014; $38,188, PF-66, October 2014; $18,800, PF-63, October 2015												
1849-O	2,310,000	81	48.9	26%	$45	$65	$80	$120	$350	$850	$1,600	$2,700	$17,000
	Auctions: $793, AU-55, January 2015; $564, AU-53, January 2015; $153, VF-35, January 2015; $129, VF-30, August 2015												
1850	227,000	89	54.0	34%	$275	$375	$450	$575	$850	$1,250	$2,000	$4,000	$19,500
	Auctions: $117,500, MS-67, May 2015; $15,275, MS-65, November 2013; $764, EF-40, August 2015; $447, Fair-2, October 2014												
1850, Proof	4–8	4	63.8								$13,000	$27,500	$60,000
	Auctions: $20,125, PF-64, July 2009												
1850-O	2,456,000	90	52.9	40%	$42	$55	$65	$95	$200	$425	$800	$1,500	$15,000
	Auctions: $28,200, MS-66, May 2015; $329, AU-50, May 2015; $259, EF-40, November 2015; $165, VF-35, August 2015												
1851	200,750	49	58.2	61%	$750	$850	$1,000	$1,250	$1,600	$1,750	$3,500	$5,000	$12,500
	Auctions: $49,938, MS-66, June 2014; $2,820, AU-58, January 2015; $1,645, EF-45, September 2014; $881, Fair-2, October 2014												
1851-O	402,000	58	53.0	45%	$42	$100	$150	$200	$400	$850	$1,400	$3,000	$10,000
	Auctions: $999, AU-55, January 2015; $940, AU-53, September 2015; $588, EF-45, November 2015; $376, VF-35, August 2015												
1852	77,130	74	56.4	53%	$350	$500	$600	$850	$1,150	$1,450	$2,250	$3,250	$11,000
	Auctions: $12,338, MS-66, October 2014; $3,525, MS-62, January 2015; $2,115, AU-58, January 2015; $1,410, AU-53, July 2014												
1852, Proof	3–6	3	62.7									$35,000	$55,000
	Auctions: $74,750, PF-65, July 2008												
1852-O	144,000	42	45.4	12%	$275	$450	$600	$800	$1,100	$1,800	$3,500	$10,000	$35,000
	Auctions: $1,116, EF-40, June 2015; $940, VF-20, February 2015; $823, F-15, July 2015; $764, F-15, September 2015												
1852-O, Proof	2–3	1	62.0									$37,500	
	Auctions: $24,150, PF-62, May 2001												
1853-O, Variety 1 † (m)		1	40.0	0%	$200,000	$275,000	$350,000	$500,000					
	Auctions: $368,000, VF-35, October 2006; $199,750, VG-8, August 2015												
1853, Variety 2	3,532,708	1,148	49.9	24%	$50	$75	$100	$140	$300	$600	$1,500	$3,500	$22,000
	Auctions: $73,438, MS-66, January 2015; $28,200, MS-66, May 2015; $282, EF-45, October 2015; $165, VF-35, August 2015												
1853, Variety 2, Proof	5–10	4	65.0									$50,000	$150,000
	Auctions: $117,500, PF-65, October 2014; $184,000, PF-65, January 2012; $94,000, PF-64, October 2014												
1853-O, Variety 2	1,328,000	218	43.6	15%	$50	$75	$95	$140	$350	$750	$2,750	$5,500	$40,000
	Auctions: $12,338, MS-64, January 2015; $1,058, AU-55, August 2015; $259, EF-40, January 2015; $176, VF-25, June 2015												
1854	2,982,000	503	52.3	27%	$42	$50	$65	$85	$155	$375	$625	$1,500	$8,750
	Auctions: $1,645, MS-63, February 2015; $282, AU-55, June 2015; $153, EF-40, January 2015; $79, VF-30, January 2015												
1854, Proof	15–20	14	64.8								$8,500	$13,500	$30,000
	Auctions: $70,500, PF-67, November 2013												
1854-O	5,240,000	761	50.5	30%	$42	$50	$65	$85	$155	$350	$650	$1,500	$7,500
	Auctions: $5,405, MS-65, January 2015; $470, MS-61, September 2015; $494, AU-58, August 2015; $94, VF-35, January 2015												

† Ranked in the *100 Greatest U.S. Coins* (fourth edition). **m.** 4 examples are known.

1855, 1855 Over 854
FS-50-1855-301.

	Mintage	Cert	Avg	%MS	G-4	VG-8	F-12	VF-20	EF-40	AU-50	MS-60	MS-63	MS-65
											PF-60	PF-63	PF-65
1855, All kinds	759,500												
1855, 1855 Over 1854		54	48.0	28%	$75	$90	$175	$360	$500	$1,200	$2,250	$3,600	$11,500
Auctions: $353, AU-50, November 2014; $588, EF-45, January 2015; $423, EF-45, July 2015; $411, VF-35, December 2014													
1855, Normal Date		152	54.3	38%	$42	$50	$65	$85	$155	$400	$800	$1,750	$12,500
Auctions: $881, AU-58, June 2015; $329, AU-53, January 2015; $176, EF-45, January 2015; $118, VF-35, August 2015													
1855, 55 Over 54, Proof	1–2	0	n/a								$10,000	$22,000	$60,000
Auctions: $30,550, PF-64, June 2014													
1855, Proof	15–20	8	64.5								$7,500	$12,500	$35,000
Auctions: $41,125, PF-66Cam, June 2014													
1855-O	3,688,000	532	52.2	29%	$42	$50	$65	$85	$155	$350	$650	$1,500	$9,500
Auctions: $705, MS-62, September 2015; $423, AU-58, May 2015; $172, EF-45, March 2015; $100, VF-35, May 2015													
1855-S	129,950	54	33.5	6%	$450	$1,000	$1,350	$1,750	$3,500	$7,600	$35,000	$50,000	
Auctions: $41,125, MS-61, October 2014; $14,688, AU-55, January 2015; $8,225, AU-53, July 2014; $423, G-4, October 2015													
1855-S, Proof	2–3	1	65.0									$150,000	
Auctions: $276,000, PF-65, August 2011													
1856	938,000	124	52.7	33%	$42	$60	$65	$85	$130	$240	$600	$1,200	$5,750
Auctions: $16,450, MS-66, May 2015; $376, AU-58, November 2015; $188, AU-50, March 2015; $176, EF-45, March 2015													
1856, Proof	20–30	20	64.3								$4,000	$6,500	$23,000
Auctions: $17,625, PF-65, October 2014; $17,625, PF-65, November 2013													
1856-O	2,658,000	270	52.6	39%	$42	$60	$75	$100	$135	$240	$500	$1,100	$6,000
Auctions: $4,818, MS-65, January 2015; $470, MS-61, September 2015; $282, AU-53, May 2015; $141, EF-45, July 2015													
1856-S	211,000	35	42.5	11%	$95	$150	$240	$450	$1,100	$2,100	$5,000	$13,000	
Auctions: $12,925, MS-63, May 2015; $3,055, AU-58, January 2015; $881, VF-35, August 2015; $499, VF-35, October 2014													
1857	1,988,000	243	52.5	33%	$42	$50	$75	$85	$125	$250	$450	$1,100	$4,800
Auctions: $3,525, MS-65, January 2015; $764, MS-63, September 2015; $400, AU-58, July 2015; $282, AU-55, August 2015													
1857, Proof	30–50	37	63.8								$3,000	$4,500	$23,000
Auctions: $23,500, PF-66, June 2013													
1857-O	818,000	79	48.3	11%	$42	$55	$75	$90	$150	$275	$1,350	$3,500	$12,000
Auctions: $517, AU-58, June 2015; $259, AU-53, May 2015; $212, EF-45, August 2015; $182, EF-40, June 2015													
1857-S	158,000	35	44.9	14%	$150	$180	$250	$425	$1,400	$2,000	$3,600	$10,000	$35,000
Auctions: $61,688, MS-66, June 2014; $400, EF-40, August 2014; $176, VG-8, October 2014													
1858	4,225,700	608	52.4	30%	$42	$50	$75	$85	$125	$240	$450	$1,100	$5,000
Auctions: $1,058, MS-63, January 2015; $423, AU-58, August 2015; $259, AU-55, October 2015; $147, EF-45, February 2015													
1858, Proof	300+	56	63.7								$1,400	$2,250	$6,500
Auctions: $7,050, PF-65, February 2015; $6,756, PF-65, January 2015; $6,463, PF-64, October 2015; $1,821, PF-63, October 2015													
1858-O	7,294,000	507	47.0	19%	$42	$60	$65	$85	$130	$240	$475	$1,200	$8,500
Auctions: $411, MS-61, June 2015; $470, AU-58, January 2015; $141, EF-45, September 2015; $123, EF-40, March 2015													
1858-S	476,000	68	47.9	19%	$55	$80	$120	$200	$350	$675	$1,700	$4,000	$13,500
Auctions: $505, AU-53, March 2015; $423, AU-50, August 2015; $400, EF-45, November 2015; $235, VF-30, February 2015													

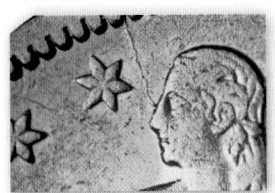

1861-O, Cracked Obverse Die
FS-50-1861o-401.

	Mintage	Cert	Avg	%MS	G-4	VG-8	F-12	VF-20	EF-40	AU-50	MS-60	MS-63	MS-65
											PF-60	PF-63	PF-65
1859	747,200	192	53.9	33%	$42	$60	$65	$85	$150	$300	$500	$1,100	$5,250
	Auctions: $18,213, MS-67, May 2015; $1,293, MS-61, January 2015; $329, AU-55, October 2015; $153, EF-40, August 2015												
1859, Proof	800	147	63.5								$1,150	$1,600	$5,500
	Auctions: $12,925, PF-67, October 2015; $7,050, PF-66, January 2015; $4,004, PF-65, September 2015; $4,700, PF-64, August 2015												
1859-O	2,834,000	249	47.4	20%	$42	$65	$75	$95	$150	$300	$650	$1,800	$7,500
	Auctions: $9,988, MS-66, May 2015; $541, MS-62, September 2015; $376, AU-55, February 2015; $141, EF-40, September 2015												
1859-S	566,000	70	55.9	51%	$45	$55	$70	$170	$270	$600	$1,300	$3,000	$8,500
	Auctions: $47,000, MS-68, May 2015; $646, AU-55, February 2015; $329, EF-40, May 2015; $306, EF-40, August 2015												
1860	302,700	81	55.5	42%	$42	$55	$70	$85	$150	$325	$650	$1,100	$5,000
	Auctions: $940, MS-62, January 2015; $423, AU-55, October 2015; $400, AU-55, May 2015; $247, EF-45, March 2015												
1860, Proof	1,000	131	63.9								$750	$1,600	$5,000
	Auctions: $29,375, PF-67, May 2015; $2,585, PF-64, January 2015; $1,998, PF-63, July 2015; $1,410, PF-63, June 2015												
1860-O	1,290,000	256	52.2	37%	$45	$60	$70	$100	$175	$300	$650	$1,300	$5,000
	Auctions: $940, MS-63, January 2015; $306, AU-55, May 2015; $235, AU-50, May 2015; $206, EF-45, August 2015												
1860-S	472,000	73	52.0	34%	$50	$70	$115	$150	$275	$500	$1,400	$3,750	$15,000
	Auctions: $1,116, AU-58, July 2015; $646, AU-55, October 2014; $165, AU-50, November 2014; $282, EF-40, April 2015												
1861	2,887,400	482	55.5	46%	$50	$60	$75	$90	$140	$300	$575	$1,200	$5,000
	Auctions: $10,575, MS-66, January 2015; $306, AU-53, May 2015; $165, EF-45, February 2015; $112, VF-35, October 2015												
1861, Proof	1,000	102	63.6								$750	$1,600	$5,000
	Auctions: $1,351, PF-63, September 2015; $823, PF-61, July 2014; $764, PF-60, January 2015												
1861-O (n)	2,532,633	315	50.0	37%	$70	$90	$120	$180	$300	$900	$1,500	$2,800	$6,500
	Auctions: $2,820, MS-64, January 2015; $1,528, AU-53, June 2015; $259, EF-45, March 2015; $212, F-15, October 2015												
1861-O, Cracked Obv (o)	**(p)**	99	49.5	30%	$360	$550	$775	$1,450	$3,000	$4,500	$14,000		
	Auctions: $16,450, MS-62, October 2014; $11,750, AU-58, September 2013; $4,700, EF-40, August 2014; $3,525, EF-40, August 2014												
1861-S	939,500	119	43.3	16%	$55	$65	$95	$120	$400	$700	$1,200	$2,700	$20,000
	Auctions: $3,760, MS-64, January 2015; $588, AU-55, June 2015; $259, EF-40, September 2015; $112, VF-20, August 2015												
1862	253,000	78	54.2	58%	$70	$100	$140	$180	$350	$550	$850	$1,500	$6,000
	Auctions: $18,800, MS-66, May 2015; $881, MS-62, July 2015; $282, EF-45, August 2015; $259, EF-40, February 2015												
1862, Proof	550	199	63.6								$750	$1,600	$5,000
	Auctions: $9,988, PF-65Cam, February 2015; $4,935, PF-65, February 2015; $4,230, PF-65, October 2015; $4,113, PF-65, March 2015												
1862-S	1,352,000	129	52.7	38%	$55	$75	$85	$90	$240	$400	$1,100	$2,700	$25,000
	Auctions: $42,300, MS-66, May 2015; $1,058, MS-61, February 2015; $793, AU-55, January 2015; $223, EF-40, August 2015												
1863	503,200	95	55.6	55%	$45	$70	$95	$150	$250	$475	$800	$1,350	$7,500
	Auctions: $24,675, MS-67, January 2015; $212, AU-50, February 2015; $329, EF-45, February 2015; $270, VF-30, December 2014												
1863, Proof	460	135	63.5								$750	$1,600	$5,000
	Auctions: $7,638, PF-66, October 2015; $4,700, PF-65, February 2015; $2,468, PF-64, March 2015; $2,233, PF-64, January 2015												
1863-S	916,000	72	40.9	19%	$45	$70	$95	$140	$275	$550	$1,300	$2,500	$12,000
	Auctions: $3,408, MS-64, January 2015; $588, AU-55, January 2015; $165, EF-40, September 2015; $84, VF-20, October 2015												

n. The 1861-O mintage includes 330,000 half dollars struck by the United States government; 1,240,000 struck for the State of Louisiana after it seceded from the Union; and 962,633 struck after Louisiana joined the Confederate States of America. All of these coins were made from federal dies, rendering it impossible to distinguish one from another with but one exception. **o.** In 1861, the New Orleans Mint used a federal obverse die and a Confederate reverse die to strike a handful of Confederate half dollars. That particular obverse die was also paired with a regular federal reverse die to strike some 1861-O half dollars, which today are popular among collectors, especially in higher grades. Their identifying feature is a die crack running from the denticles to the right of the sixth star down to Miss Liberty's nose (and to her shoulder below her jaw). **p.** Included in 1861-O mintage figure.

	Mintage	Cert	Avg	%MS	G-4	VG-8	F-12	VF-20	EF-40	AU-50	MS-60	MS-63	MS-65
											PF-60	PF-63	PF-65
1864	379,100	97	56.6	60%	$45	$65	$120	$300	$450	$800	$1,300	$1,800	$7,500
	Auctions: $999, MS-62, July 2015; $646, AU-53, August 2015; $376, AU-50, September 2015; $306, EF-40, February 2015												
1864, Proof	470	155	63.7								$750	$1,600	$5,000
	Auctions: $2,233, PF-64, September 2015; $1,175, PF-62, June 2015; $940, PF-62, September 2015; $676, PF-60, October 2015												
1864-S	658,000	68	43.7	18%	$70	$110	$150	$250	$450	$750	$1,800	$4,250	$15,000
	Auctions: $4,700, MS-63, February 2015; $940, AU-55, January 2015; $247, VF-30, August 2015; $235, VF-25, May 2015												
1865	511,400	78	52.3	45%	$70	$95	$120	$150	$350	$700	$1,400	$2,100	$5,500
	Auctions: $32,900, MS-67, May 2015; $3,290, MS-64, February 2015; $764, AU-53, June 2015; $282, EF-40, August 2015												
1865, Proof	500	201	64.0								$750	$1,600	$5,000
	Auctions: $7,050, PF-66, July 2015; $4,465, PF-65Cam, June 2015; $4,700, PF-65, January 2015; $2,115, PF-64, October 2015												
1865-S	675,000	68	43.7	18%	$75	$115	$150	$225	$400	$650	$2,000	$3,500	$50,000
	Auctions: $42,300, MS-65, May 2015; $705, AU-53, June 2015; $282, EF-40, May 2015; $247, VF-35, August 2015												
1866-S, Variety 1	60,000	70	28.4	13%	$450	$600	$875	$1,250	$2,300	$3,000	$9,500	$20,000	$70,000
	Auctions: $164,500, MS-67, November 2013; $2,585, EF-45, August 2014; $1,410, VF-35, July 2014; $676, F-12, July 2014												
1866, Variety 4	744,900	110	51.1	47%	$60	$75	$90	$115	$190	$250	$700	$2,100	$5,850
	Auctions: $5,170, MS-66, January 2015; $282, AU-53, May 2015; $200, EF-45, May 2015; $118, VF-25, August 2015												
1866, Variety 4, Proof	725	117	63.7								$700	$1,500	$3,200
	Auctions: $3,643, PF-66, January 2015; $3,525, PF-66, July 2015; $2,115, PF-64Cam, November 2014; $1,116, PF-63, October 2015												
1866, No Motto, Proof † (q)	1	1	62.0								$750		$3,200
	Auctions: No auction records available.												
1866-S, Variety 4	994,000	78	44.9	24%	$45	$60	$70	$110	$220	$360	$700	$2,250	$12,000
	Auctions: $881, AU-55, January 2015; $259, EF-45, May 2015; $223, EF-40, August 2015; $176, VF-30, January 2015												
1867	449,300	61	50.2	38%	$42	$50	$110	$190	$290	$500	$800	$1,600	$5,000
	Auctions: $999, AU-58, January 2015; $235, EF-45, May 2015; $329, EF-40, May 2015; $259, VF-35, July 2015												
1867, Proof	625	168	64.0								$700	$1,500	$3,200
	Auctions: $8,225, PF-66Cam, October 2015; $3,995, PF-65Cam, February 2015; $3,290, PF-64Cam, January 2015; $793, PF-62, July 2015												
1867-S	1,196,000	98	48.9	26%	$42	$50	$85	$120	$180	$650	$1,250	$3,000	$12,500
	Auctions: $1,116, AU-58, January 2015; $306, AU-53, January 2015; $176, EF-45, October 2015; $188, VF-30, June 2015												
1868	417,600	51	49.6	33%	$50	$60	$90	$175	$275	$525	$800	$2,000	$7,000
	Auctions: $9,988, MS-65, May 2015; $1,175, MS-63, January 2015; $494, AU-55, July 2015; $259, VF-30, May 2015												
1868, Proof	600	161	63.8								$700	$1,500	$3,200
	Auctions: $4,230, PF-66, February 2015; $2,585, PF-65, August 2015; $823, PF-62, July 2015; $564, PF-61, March 2015												
1868-S	1,160,000	81	48.8	15%	$45	$50	$65	$120	$240	$375	$1,000	$2,100	$12,500
	Auctions: $17,625, MS-66, May 2015; $564, AU-55, January 2015; $353, AU-53, November 2015; $349, AU-53, March 2015												
1869	795,300	138	53.8	33%	$42	$60	$70	$95	$160	$325	$800	$1,600	$10,000
	Auctions: $1,293, MS-62, June 2015; $376, AU-55, October 2015; $200, EF-45, May 2015; $200, EF-40, May 2015												
1869, Proof	600	154	63.6								$700	$1,500	$3,200
	Auctions: $7,638, PF-67, May 2015; $6,169, PF-67, September 2015; $1,410, PF-64, January 2015; $1,293, PF-64, February 2015												
1869-S	656,000	61	47.9	34%	$42	$60	$70	$140	$250	$475	$1,000	$2,600	$7,500
	Auctions: $259, AU-50, November 2015; $189, AU-50, August 2015; $141, EF-40, May 2015; $94, EF-40, February 2015												
1870	633,900	82	50.4	33%	$42	$60	$70	$100	$190	$300	$725	$1,500	$8,000
	Auctions: $1,058, MS-62, January 2015; $376, AU-53, November 2015; $212, EF-40, August 2015; $165, VF-30, January 2015												
1870, Proof	1,000	131	63.2								$700	$1,350	$3,400
	Auctions: $1,645, PF-64, March 2015; $1,528, PF-64, May 2015; $1,175, PF-63, September 2015; $1,058, PF-63, January 2015												
1870-CC	54,617	65	27.0	6%	$1,750	$2,750	$4,750	$6,500	$12,000	$32,000	$85,000	—	
	Auctions: $28,200, AU-50, August 2016; $17,625, EF-45, January 2015; $11,750, EF-45, January 2015; $7,050, VF-30, January 2015												
1870-S	1,004,000	50	45.1	18%	$70	$100	$120	$180	$475	$750	$2,300	$4,000	$32,000
	Auctions: $1,293, AU-55, January 2015; $376, EF-45, January 2015; $306, EF-40, May 2015; $176, VF-25, February 2015												

† Ranked in the *100 Greatest U.S. Coins* (fourth edition). **q.** Classified as Judd-538 (*United States Pattern Coins*, tenth edition). This fantasy piece was deliberately struck for pharmacist and coin collector Robert Coulton Davis, likely around 1869 or in the early 1870s, along with the No Motto Proof quarter and dollar of the same date.

1873, Close 3   **1873, Open 3**

	Mintage	Cert	Avg	%MS	G-4	VG-8	F-12	VF-20	EF-40	AU-50	MS-60 PF-60	MS-63 PF-63	MS-65 PF-65
1871	1,203,600	163	52.9	37%	$45	$50	$65	$85	$130	$260	$650	$1,150	$4,750
Auctions: $3,525, MS-64, May 2015; $223, AU-50, March 2015; $176, EF-45, October 2015; $91, VF-30, March 2015													
1871, Proof	960	167	63.3								$700	$1,300	$3,400
Auctions: $4,230, PF-66, January 2015; $2,703, PF-65, January 2015; $1,410, PF-64, June 2015; $1,058, PF-63, January 2015													
1871-CC	153,950	55	28.4	5%	$525	$750	$1,250	$1,750	$3,250	$6,000	$30,000	$55,000	
Auctions: $76,375, MS-64, May 2015; $3,055, EF-45, January 2015; $1,998, VF-30, January 2015; $259, AG-3, November 2015													
1871-S	2,178,000	127	47.1	20%	$45	$65	$85	$100	$150	$375	$950	$1,850	$8,000
Auctions: $2,611, MS-64, May 2015; $294, AU-53, July 2015; $165, EF-45, November 2015; $112, EF-40, August 2015													
1872	880,600	86	50.1	28%	$45	$55	$75	$85	$120	$285	$800	$1,400	$5,500
Auctions: $1,528, MS-62, February 2015; $329, AU-55, August 2015; $223, AU-50, May 2015; $153, AU-50, January 2015													
1872, Proof	950	160	63.6								$700	$1,300	$2,800
Auctions: $5,523, PF-65Cam, June 2015; $4,935, PF-65Cam, January 2015; $4,465, PF-65Cam, February 2015													
1872-CC	257,000	107	27.7	1%	$300	$600	$800	$1,250	$2,500	$5,000	$25,000	$70,000	
Auctions: $4,230, AU-53, January 2015; $2,115, EF-45, August 2016; $447, F-12, October 2015; $282, VG-8, May 2015													
1872-S	580,000	50	47.8	28%	$45	$65	$100	$180	$300	$575	$1,100	$3,000	$13,500
Auctions: $2,820, MS-63, February 2015; $1,028, AU-55, June 2015; $353, EF-45, April 2015; $306, VF-30, May 2015													
1873, Close 3, Variety 4	587,000	81	48.6	23%	$45	$55	$80	$110	$175	$300	$750	$1,500	$6,000
Auctions: $1,410, AU-58, July 2015; $212, AU-53, May 2015; $176, EF-45, July 2015; $94, EF-40, May 2015													
1873, Open 3, Variety 4	214,200	14	31.2	0%	$3,250	$4,500	$5,500	$6,750	$8,000	$13,500	$50,000	$95,000	
Auctions: $55,813, MS-61, October 2014; $21,150, AU-58, January 2015; $4,230, VG-8, January 2015; $3,290, VG-8, August 2014													
1873, Variety 4, Proof	600	179	63.8								$700	$1,300	$2,800
Auctions: $8,813, PF-66, June 2015; $3,290, PF-65, February 2015; $1,410, PF-64, September 2015; $618, PF-61, June 2015													
1873-CC, Variety 4	122,500	51	32.4	14%	$375	$800	$1,250	$2,250	$4,250	$6,500	$12,000	$32,500	$80,000
Auctions: $5,053, AU-50, January 2015; $423, G-6, August 2015; $306, G-6, October 2015; $206, AG-3, November 2015													
1873-S, Variety 4 (r)	5,000	0	n/a										
Auctions: No auction records available.													
1873, Variety 5	1,815,200	301	50.5	36%	$45	$50	$80	$100	$250	$475	$950	$1,800	$15,000
Auctions: $1,293, AU-58, January 2015; $259, EF-45, November 2015; $159, VF-35, August 2015; $107, VF-25, February 2015													
1873, Variety 5, Proof	800	142	63.7								$1,000	$2,200	$9,000
Auctions: $12,925, PF-66, September 2014; $6,463, PF-65, March 2015; $2,174, PF-63, June 2015; $1,763, PF-63, January 2015													
1873-CC, Variety 5	214,560	112	36.4	13%	$250	$500	$850	$1,150	$2,250	$3,750	$10,000	$20,000	$50,000
Auctions: $2,497, EF-45, January 2015; $764, VF-20, June 2015; $376, VG-10, October 2015; $176, AG-3, November 2015													
1873-S, Variety 5	228,000	47	46.4	19%	$55	$120	$180	$250	$500	$750	$2,500	$8,000	$35,000
Auctions: $705, AU-50, May 2015; $364, AU-50, November 2015; $208, EF-40, October 2015; $165, VF-20, May 2015													
1874	2,359,600	372	52.9	41%	$45	$50	$70	$100	$250	$450	$950	$1,875	$15,000
Auctions: $25,850, MS-66, May 2015; $200, MS-60, October 2015; $364, AU-53, June 2015; $259, EF-45, August 2015													
1874, Proof	700	203	63.3								$1,000	$2,200	$9,000
Auctions: $11,750, PF-66, January 2015; $6,169, PF-65, June 2015; $4,465, PF-64Cam, June 2015; $1,469, PF-62, August 2015													
1874-CC	59,000	70	32.9	16%	$1,250	$1,750	$2,250	$3,500	$6,000	$9,000	$15,000	$30,000	$95,000
Auctions: $94,000, MS-65, May 2015; $44,650, MS-64, January 2015; $1,293, VG-10, October 2014; $1,410, VG-8, September 2014													
1874-S	394,000	54	51.5	44%	$100	$180	$225	$250	$375	$700	$1,700	$3,000	$25,000
Auctions: $15,275, MS-65, January 2015; $4,406, MS-64, March 2015; $1,116, AU-55, June 2015; $282, VF-35, August 2015													

r. The 1873-S, No Arrows, half dollar is unknown in any collection.

1877, 7 Over 6
FS-50-1877-301.

	Mintage	Cert	Avg	%MS	G-4	VG-8	F-12	VF-20	EF-40	AU-50	MS-60 PF-60	MS-63 PF-63	MS-65 PF-65
1875	6,026,800	386	53.9	49%	$40	$50	$65	$80	$125	$225	$475	$800	$3,000
Auctions: $1,410, MS-64, January 2015; $1,116, MS-63, August 2015; $376, AU-58, April 2015; $129, EF-45, March 2015												
1875, Proof	700	136	63.7								$600	$1,150	$2,700
Auctions: $12,925, PF-67, May 2015; $4,465, PF-66, February 2015; $3,055, PF-65Cam, January 2015; $810, PF-62, March 2015												
1875-CC	1,008,000	161	45.0	37%	$75	$125	$225	$325	$550	$1,000	$1,500	$2,850	$8,500
Auctions: $881, AU-55, July 2015; $999, AU-53, January 2015; $881, AU-50, January 2015; $353, VF-30, May 2015												
1875-S	3,200,000	269	57.9	68%	$40	$45	$65	$80	$120	$215	$475	$800	$3,000
Auctions: $2,820, MS-65, January 2015; $646, MS-63, August 2015; $329, AU-55, November 2015; $165, EF-45, August 2015												
1876	8,418,000	436	52.9	45%	$40	$45	$65	$80	$120	$215	$475	$800	$3,800
Auctions: $3,055, MS-65, March 2015; $588, MS-62, February 2015; $176, AU-53, January 2015; $94, VF-35, January 2015												
1876, Proof	1,150	212	63.5								$600	$1,150	$2,700
Auctions: $3,055, PF-65Cam, February 2015; $1,410, PF-64, November 2014; $1,116, PF-62Cam, August 2014; $646, PF-61, September 2014												
1876-CC	1,956,000	214	47.8	41%	$100	$125	$135	$175	$350	$650	$1,100	$1,800	$5,500
Auctions: $1,528, AU-58, January 2015; $212, VF-35, August 2015; $212, VF-25, February 2015; $69, VG-10, March 2015												
1876-S	4,528,000	216	53.2	49%	$40	$45	$65	$80	$120	$225	$450	$800	$3,600
Auctions: $3,173, MS-65, January 2015; $212, AU-55, July 2015; $176, AU-50, May 2015; $118, EF-45, June 2015												
1877	8,304,000	368	52.9	51%	$40	$60	$70	$80	$120	$225	$450	$800	$3,200
Auctions: $6,463, MS-67, May 2015; $376, AU-58, July 2015; $200, EF-45, November 2015; $71, EF-40, March 2015												
1877, 7 Over 6 (s)	(t)	0	n/a			$275	$450	$625	$1,200	$2,200	$3,750	$12,000	
Auctions: $3,335, MS-62, August 2009												
1877, Proof	510	171	63.4								$600	$1,150	$2,700
Auctions: $11,750, PF-66Cam, February 2015; $3,290, PF-66, October 2015; $1,528, PF-64, January 2015; $881, PF-62, March 2015												
1877-CC	1,420,000	241	52.3	61%	$100	$125	$135	$200	$350	$450	$1,150	$2,250	$5,000
Auctions: $7,931, MS-66, May 2015; $960, AU-58, January 2015; $212, VF-20, May 2015; $100, VG-10, June 2015												
1877-S	5,356,000	528	55.5	55%	$40	$45	$65	$80	$100	$225	$475	$800	$3,000
Auctions: $19,975, MS-67, May 2015; $353, AU-58, March 2015; $206, AU-50, January 2015; $153, EF-45, August 2015												
1878	1,377,600	109	53.4	48%	$45	$90	$120	$135	$150	$240	$425	$1,100	$5,200
Auctions: $705, MS-62, January 2015; $259, AU-50, November 2015; $119, VF-35, June 2015; $84, F-12, May 2015												
1878, Proof	800	226	64.1								$600	$1,150	$2,700
Auctions: $35,250, PF-68, May 2015; $4,935, PF-66Cam, October 2015; $1,998, PF-64, January 2015; $969, PF-63, January 2015												
1878-CC	62,000	49	27.2	16%	$1,200	$1,500	$2,500	$3,000	$4,000	$5,500	$12,000	$24,000	$50,000
Auctions: $64,625, MS-65, June 2014; $1,763, VG-10, September 2014; $881, G-4, November 2014												
1878-S	12,000	13	37.3	46%	$30,000	$40,000	$45,000	$55,000	$67,500	$70,000	$100,000	$150,000	$250,000
Auctions: $199,750, MS-64, June 2014; $58,750, AU-50, August 2014												
1879	4,800	253	60.6	82%	$275	$315	$425	$550	$750	$900	$1,050	$1,300	$3,250
Auctions: $2,938, MS-65, January 2015; $940, AU-55, June 2015; $881, AU-53, June 2015; $705, EF-40, January 2015												
1879, Proof	1,100	319	63.7								$600	$1,150	$2,700
Auctions: $8,225, PF-67Cam, February 2015; $2,468, PF-65, March 2015; $1,410, PF-64, January 2015; $911, PF-62, March 2015												
1880	8,400	104	59.0	77%	$265	$315	$425	$550	$750	$900	$1,050	$1,500	$4,000
Auctions: $8,225, MS-67, May 2015; $4,230, MS-66, January 2015; $1,293, AU-58, June 2015; $1,087, AU-55, June 2015												
1880, Proof	1,355	385	63.8								$600	$1,150	$2,700
Auctions: $7,050, PF-66Cam, August 2015; $2,938, PF-66, January 2015; $1,645, PF-64, July 2015												

s. The top portion of a 6 is visible on the upper surface of the last 7. **t.** Included in circulation-strike 1877 mintage figure.

	Mintage	Cert	Avg	%MS	G-4	VG-8	F-12	VF-20	EF-40	AU-50	MS-60 PF-60	MS-63 PF-63	MS-65 PF-65
1881	10,000	106	55.9	74%	$265	$315	$425	$550	$750	$900	$1,050	$1,500	$4,000
	Auctions: $9,400, MS-67, June 2014												
1881, Proof	975	335	63.9								$600	$1,150	$2,700
	Auctions: $9,400, PF-68, May 2015; $6,698, PF-67, July 2014; $2,820, PF-65Cam, July 2014; $2,938, PF-65, September 2014												
1882	4,400	77	58.0	74%	$280	$315	$425	$550	$750	$900	$1,050	$1,600	$4,750
	Auctions: $4,700, MS-65, January 2015; $2,291, MS-64, January 2015; $646, VF-25, October 2015; $470, VG-8, October 2015												
1882, Proof	1,100	318	64.0								$600	$1,150	$2,700
	Auctions: $15,275, PF-67Cam, November 2013; $6,463, PF-66DCam, August 2014; $6,169, PF-65DCam, August 2014; $1,763, PF-63DCam, August 2015												
1883	8,000	92	54.9	66%	$280	$310	$425	$550	$750	$900	$1,050	$1,500	$4,250
	Auctions: $5,640, MS-66, May 2015; $1,116, MS-61, June 2015; $911, AU-58, June 2015; $306, AG-3, October 2015												
1883, Proof	1,039	333	64.0								$600	$1,150	$2,700
	Auctions: $11,163, PF-67Cam, October 2014; $7,638, PF-67Cam, November 2014; $1,998, PF-64Cam, March 2015; $1,528, PF-63Cam, June 2015												
1884	4,400	98	60.6	87%	$350	$400	$450	$550	$775	$925	$1,100	$1,500	$4,500
	Auctions: $21,150, MS-67, January 2015; $15,275, MS-67, June 2014; $1,234, EF-45, July 2015; $517, VG-10, October 2015												
1884, Proof	875	223	63.9								$600	$1,150	$2,700
	Auctions: $7,931, PF-67, May 2015; $2,233, PF-65, September 2015; $1,528, PF-64, August 2015; $764, PF-61, January 2015												
1885	5,200	77	55.8	69%	$325	$375	$425	$550	$750	$900	$1,050	$1,500	$4,250
	Auctions: $4,230, MS-66, January 2015; $1,998, MS-63, January 2015; $1,058, AU-55, February 2015; $1,410, EF-45, January 2015												
1885, Proof	930	301	64.1								$600	$1,150	$2,700
	Auctions: $5,758, PF-67, September 2015; $2,585, PF-65Cam, September 2015; $1,351, PF-63Cam, March 2015; $823, PF-61, July 2015												
1886	5,000	91	56.9	77%	$400	$475	$575	$600	$800	$900	$1,100	$1,500	$4,250
	Auctions: $25,850, MS-67, May 2015; $617, AU-50, June 2015; $646, VG-10, August 2015; $517, VG-8, October 2015												
1886, Proof	886	248	63.9								$600	$1,150	$2,700
	Auctions: $11,163, PF-67Cam, August 2015; $3,290, PF-66, June 2015; $2,585, PF-65, January 2015; $1,116, PF-62, June 2015												
1887	5,000	115	57.4	73%	$450	$500	$600	$700	$800	$950	$1,100	$1,400	$4,250
	Auctions: $24,675, MS-67, June 2014; $1,116, AU-50, August 2014; $734, EF-40, October 2014												
1887, Proof	710	186	64.2								$600	$1,150	$2,700
	Auctions: $29,375, PF-68DCam, November 2013												
1888	12,001	127	56.3	69%	$275	$300	$450	$550	$700	$750	$1,000	$1,350	$4,000
	Auctions: $8,813, MS-67, January 2015; $4,230, MS-66, January 2015; $852, AU-50, March 2015; $447, VG-10, October 2015												
1888, Proof	832	219	63.8								$600	$1,150	$2,700
	Auctions: $8,225, PF-67, July 2015; $3,760, PF-66, February 2015; $2,820, PF-65, October 2015; $2,350, PF-64Cam, January 2015												
1889	12,000	112	55.4	68%	$250	$300	$450	$550	$700	$750	$1,000	$1,250	$4,000
	Auctions: $8,225, MS-66, May 2015; $2,115, MS-64, January 2015; $823, AU-55, June 2015; $588, VF-25, October 2015												
1889, Proof	711	195	63.8								$600	$1,150	$2,700
	Auctions: $2,820, PF-66, August 2015; $2,115, PF-65, March 2015; $2,233, PF-64, January 2015; $1,175, PF-63, June 2015												
1890	12,000	105	57.1	76%	$250	$300	$450	$550	$700	$750	$1,000	$1,150	$4,000
	Auctions: $676, MS-60, February 2015; $705, AU-50, September 2015; $676, AU-50, June 2015; $411, VG-8, October 2015												
1890, Proof	590	209	64.4								$600	$1,150	$2,700
	Auctions: $9,988, PF-67Cam, May 2015; $2,585, PF-65, January 2015; $1,645, PF-64Cam, February 2015; $823, PF-62Cam, January 2015												
1891	200,000	176	56.5	68%	$55	$75	$135	$150	$225	$240	$450	$1,200	$3,800
	Auctions: $423, AU-55, November 2015; $541, AU-53, May 2015; $141, VF-35, August 2015; $125, VF-30, October 2015												
1891, Proof	600	194	64.2								$600	$1,150	$2,700
	Auctions: $5,405, PF-67, January 2015; $4,230, PF-66, February 2015; $1,410, PF-64, January 2015; $1,175, PF-63, June 2015												

BARBER OR LIBERTY HEAD (1892–1915)

Designer: *Charles E. Barber.* **Weight:** *12.50 grams.* **Composition:** *.900 silver, .100 copper.*
Diameter: *30.6 mm.* **Edge:** *Reeded.* **Mints:** *Philadelphia, Denver, New Orleans, and San Francisco.*

Circulation Strike

Mintmark location is on the reverse, below the eagle.

Proof

History. Charles E. Barber, chief engraver of the U.S. Mint, crafted the eponymous "Barber" or Liberty Head half dollars along with similarly designed dimes and quarters of the same era. His initial, B, is at the truncation of Miss Liberty's neck. Production of the coins was continuous from 1892 to 1915, stopping a year before the dime and quarter of the same design.

Striking and Sharpness. On the obverse, check Miss Liberty's hair details and other features. On the reverse, the eagle's leg at the lower right and the arrows often are weak, and there can be weakness at the upper right of the shield and the nearby wing area. At EF and below, sharpness of strike on the reverse is not important. Most Proofs are sharply struck, although many are weak on the eagle's leg at the lower right and on certain parts of the arrows and/or the upper-right area of the shield and the nearby wing. The Proofs of 1892 to 1901 usually have cameo contrast between the designs and the mirror fields. Those of 1914 and 1915 are often with extensive hairlines or other problems.

Availability. Most examples seen in the marketplace are well worn. There are no rarities in the Barber half dollar series, although some are scarcer than others. Coins that are Fine or better are much scarcer—in particular the San Francisco Mint issues of 1901, 1904, and 1907. MS coins are available of all dates and mints, but some are very elusive. Proofs exist in proportion to their mintages. Choicer examples tend to be of later dates, similar to other Barber coins.

GRADING STANDARDS

MS-60 to 70 (Mint State). *Obverse:* At MS-60, some abrasion and contact marks are evident, most noticeably on the cheek and the obverse field to the right. Luster is present, but may be dull or lifeless. Many Barber coins have been cleaned, especially of the earlier dates. At MS-63, contact marks are very few; abrasion still is evident but less than at lower levels. Indeed, the cheek of Miss Liberty virtually showcases abrasion. This is even more evident on a half dollar than on lower denominations. An

1909. Graded MS-62.

MS-65 coin may have minor abrasion, but contact marks are so minute as to require magnification. Luster should be full and rich. *Reverse:* Comments apply as for the obverse, except that in lower Mint State grades abrasion and contact marks are most noticeable on the head and tail of the eagle and on the tips of the wings. At MS-65 or higher there are no marks visible to the unaided eye. The field is mainly protected by design elements, so the reverse often appears to grade a point or two higher than the obverse.

Illustrated coin: On this example, mottled light-brown toning appears over lustrous surfaces.

AU-50, 53, 55, 58 (About Uncirculated). *Obverse:* Light wear is seen on the head, especially on the forward hair under LIBERTY. At AU-58, the luster is extensive but incomplete, especially on the higher parts and in the right field. At AU–50 and 53, luster is less. *Reverse:* Wear is seen on the head and tail of the eagle and on the tips of the wings. At AU–50 and 53, there still is significant luster. An AU-58 coin (as determined by the obverse) can have the reverse appear to be full Mint State.

1915-D. Graded AU-53.

Illustrated coin: Areas of original Mint luster can be seen on this coin, more so on the reverse than on the obverse.

EF-40, 45 (Extremely Fine). *Obverse:* Further wear is seen on the head. The hair above the forehead lacks most detail. LIBERTY shows wear but still is strong. *Reverse:* Further wear is seen on the head and tail of the eagle and on the tips of the wings, most evident at the left and right extremes of the wings At this level and below, sharpness of strike on the reverse is not important.

1908. Graded EF-45.

VF-20, 30 (Very Fine). *Obverse:* The head shows more wear, now with nearly all detail gone in the hair above the forehead. LIBERTY shows wear, but is complete. The leaves on the head all show wear, as does the upper part of the cap. *Reverse:* Wear is more extensive, particularly noticeable on the outer parts of the wings, the head, the shield, and the tail.

Illustrated coin: This coin is seemingly lightly cleaned.

1897-S. Graded VF-30.

F-12, 15 (Fine). *Obverse:* The head shows extensive wear. LIBERTY, the key place to check, is weak, especially at ER, but is fully readable. The ANA grading standards and *Photograde* adhere to this. PCGS suggests that lightly struck coins "may have letters partially missing." Traditionally, collectors insist on full LIBERTY. *Reverse:* More wear is seen on the reverse, in the places as above. E PLURIBUS UNUM is light, with one to several letters worn away.

1909-O. Graded F-12.

VG-8, 10 (Very Good). *Obverse:* A net of three letters in LIBERTY must be readable. Traditionally LI is clear, and after that there is a partial letter or two. *Reverse:* Further wear has smoothed more than half of the feathers in the wing. The shield is indistinct except for a few traces of interior lines. The motto is partially worn away. The rim is full, and many if not most denticles can be seen.

1915-S. Graded VG-8.

G-4, 6 (Good). *Obverse:* The head is in outline form, with the center flat. Most of the rim is there and all letters and the date are full. *Reverse:* The eagle shows only a few feathers, and only a few scattered letters remain in the motto. The rim may be worn flat in some or all of the area, but the peripheral lettering is clear.

Illustrated coin: On this coin the obverse is perhaps G-6 and the reverse AG-3. The grade might be averaged as G-4.

1892-O. Graded G-4.

AG-3 (About Good). *Obverse:* The stars and motto are worn, and the border may be indistinct. Distinctness varies at this level. The date is clear. Grading is usually determined by the reverse. *Reverse:* The rim is gone and the letters are partially worn away. The eagle is mostly flat, perhaps with a few hints of feathers. Usually, the obverse appears to be in a slightly higher grade than the reverse.

1896-S. Graded AG-3.

PF-60 to 70 (Proof). *Obverse and Reverse:* Proofs that are extensively cleaned and have many hairlines, or that are dull and grainy, are lower level, such as PF–60 to 62; these are not widely desired. With medium hairlines and good reflectivity, an assigned grade of PF-64 is appropriate. Tiny horizontal lines on Miss Liberty's cheek, known as slide marks, from National and other album slides scuffing the relief of the cheek, are endemic on all Barber

1914. Graded PF-61.

silver coins. With noticeable marks of this type, the highest grade assignable is PF-64. With relatively few hairlines, a rating of PF-65 can be given. PF-66 should have hairlines so delicate that magnification is needed to see them. Above that, a Proof should be free of any hairlines or other problems.

Illustrated coin: This is an attractive coin at the relatively low PF-61 grade.

1892-O, Normal O   **1892-O, Micro O**
FS-50-1892o-501.

	Mintage	Cert	Avg	%MS	G-4	VG-8	F-12	VF-20	EF-40	AU-50	MS-60 PF-60	MS-63 PF-63	MS-65 PF-65
1892	934,000	999	58.7	73%	$27	$35	$70	$135	$210	$350	$600	$925	$2,000
Auctions: $39,950, MS-68, October 2015; $1,116, MS-64, January 2015; $353, AU-55, May 2015; $247, EF-45, September 2015													
1892, Proof	1,245	371	64.4								$525	$1,100	$1,400
Auctions: $7,639, PF-68, January 2015; $9,400, PF-67UCam, October 2015; $4,700, PF-66, January 2015; $2,585, PF-64DCam, August 2015													
1892-O	390,000	432	34.7	34%	$300	$475	$600	$675	$700	$850	$1,100	$1,850	$3,250
Auctions: $47,000, MS-68, August 2015; $588, AU-55, October 2015; $725, AU-53, January 2015; $200, G-4, February 2015													
1892-O, Micro O (a)	(b)	13	27.5	31%	$3,500	$7,500	$10,000	$12,500	$15,000	$20,000	$32,500	$45,000	$85,000
Auctions: $36,014, MS-63, June 2014; $3,055, G-4, March 2016; $3,055, AG-3, September 2016													
1892-S	1,029,028	326	27.5	22%	$275	$340	$400	$550	$750	$925	$1,200	$2,250	$5,500
Auctions: $30,550, MS-67, October 2015; $646, EF-40, January 2015; $259, VG-8, June 2015; $188, G-6, November 2015													
1893	1,826,000	291	54.1	53%	$25	$30	$80	$160	$210	$400	$600	$1,000	$3,000
Auctions: $28,200, MS-67, August 2015; $1,058, MS-64, October 2015; $212, EF-40, September 2015; $306, VF-35, January 2015													
1893, Proof	792	280	64.4								$525	$1,100	$1,400
Auctions: $18,800, PF-68Cam, August 2015; $4,530, PF-67, February 2015; $1,265, PF-63Cam, June 2015; $564, PF-61, September 2015													
1893-O	1,389,000	219	49.7	58%	$40	$75	$135	$250	$350	$500	$900	$1,250	$8,500
Auctions: $18,800, MS-66, July 2015; $1,880, MS-64, March 2015; $505, MS-60, September 2015; $588, AU-53, July 2015													
1893-S	740,000	262	21.9	18%	$150	$210	$550	$800	$1,200	$1,600	$2,250	$4,000	$17,000
Auctions: $12,925, MS-65, February 2015; $1,763, AU-58, August 2015; $388, F-12, October 2015; $212, VG-10, February 2015													
1894	1,148,000	237	46.2	51%	$30	$50	$115	$200	$300	$375	$600	$1,100	$2,500
Auctions: $17,625, MS-67, October 2015; $306, AU-55, May 2015; $223, EF-40, May 2015; $188, VF-30, January 2015													
1894, Proof	972	313	64.2								$525	$1,100	$1,400
Auctions: $4,406, PF-67, June 2015; $4,113, PF-66, May 2015; $1,293, PF-64, July 2015; $3,055, PF-63, January 2015													
1894-O	2,138,000	200	48.6	56%	$25	$35	$90	$170	$300	$375	$600	$1,150	$5,000
Auctions: $14,100, MS-66, August 2015; $999, AU-58, June 2015; $194, VF-20, August 2015; $106, F-15, January 2015													
1894-S	4,048,690	235	45.3	46%	$22	$25	$70	$140	$215	$400	$650	$1,400	$6,500
Auctions: $8,813, MS-66, May 2015; $1,175, MS-63, June 2015; $329, AU-50, September 2015; $212, VF-25, June 2015													
1895	1,834,338	212	48.8	53%	$18	$25	$70	$140	$210	$400	$600	$900	$2,650
Auctions: $5,170, MS-66, October 2015; $1,058, MS-64, January 2015; $517, AU-55, October 2015; $306, AU-50, May 2015													
1895, Proof	880	354	64.5								$525	$1,100	$1,400
Auctions: $3,819, PF-67, March 2015; $3,290, PF-66, June 2015; $2,100, PF-65, November 2014; $1,755, PF-65, October 2015													
1895-O	1,766,000	166	37.9	36%	$40	$60	$130	$180	$260	$385	$750	$1,450	$5,000
Auctions: $25,850, MS-67, October 2015; $541, AU-50, July 2015; $176, EF-45, January 2015; $79, VG-10, February 2015													
1895-S	1,108,086	179	49.8	61%	$30	$65	$140	$250	$300	$385	$625	$1,250	$5,000
Auctions: $11,163, MS-66, August 2015; $794, AU-55, July 2015; $355, VF-30, January 2015; $94, F-12, May 2015													
1896	950,000	138	49.6	53%	$35	$45	$90	$160	$240	$365	$600	$1,000	$3,600
Auctions: $25,850, MS-67, October 2015; $1,293, MS-64, September 2015; $852, MS-63, January 2015; $176, VF-25, January 2015													
1896, Proof	762	265	64.4								$525	$1,100	$1,400
Auctions: $7,050, PF-67Cam, October 2015; $1,880, PF-64, August 2015; $940, PF-63, February 2015; $881, PF-62, June 2015													
1896-O	924,000	124	25.6	15%	$50	$70	$210	$500	$2,200	$3,300	$6,000	$10,500	$24,000
Auctions: $88,125, MS-67, August 2015; $3,525, AU-55, July 2016; $3,525, AU-55, October 2015; $646, VF-30, January 2015													
1896-S	1,140,948	191	24.5	23%	$115	$165	$240	$425	$959	$1,450	$2,500	$3,750	$8,000
Auctions: $23,500, MS-66, May 2015; $1,528, EF-45, September 2015; $881, VF-35, October 2015; $212, VG-8, February 2015													

a. This variety "was created when an O mintmark punch for quarters was used in place of the regular, larger mintmark intended for use on half dollar dies. . . . Many examples show strong strike doubling on reverse" (*Cherrypickers' Guide to Rare Die Varieties*, sixth edition, volume II). **b.** Included in 1892-O mintage figure.

	Mintage	Cert	Avg	%MS	G-4	VG-8	F-12	VF-20	EF-40	AU-50	MS-60 / PF-60	MS-63 / PF-63	MS-65 / PF-65
1897	2,480,000	251	51.9	52%	$20	$22	$45	$95	$200	$375	$600	$950	$3,250
	Auctions: $19,388, MS-67, August 2015; $212, EF-45, January 2015; $141, VF-30, May 2015; $52, F-15, September 2015													
1897, Proof	731	328	64.8								$525	$1,100	$1,400
	Auctions: $61,688, PF-69UCam, August 2015; $18,800, PF-68DCam, January 2015; $5,875, PF-67Cam, October 2015; $4,465, PF-65Cam, January 2015													
1897-O	632,000	299	15.9	10%	$160	$230	$500	$750	$1,050	$1,300	$2,000	$4,000	$8,000
	Auctions: $25,850, MS-67, October 2015; $8,813, MS-66, October 2016; $940, VF-25, January 2015; $259, VG-10, August 2015													
1897-S	933,900	256	21.4	18%	$150	$220	$350	$550	$900	$1,450	$2,750	$3,750	$6,750
	Auctions: $35,250, MS-67, May 2015; $4,230, AU-58, August 2015; $282, F-12, November 2015; $176, VG-8, May 2015													
1898	2,956,000	252	48.5	46%	$18	$20	$45	$95	$200	$375	$600	$900	$3,000
	Auctions: $37,600, MS-67, October 2015; $5,170, MS-66, January 2015; $482, AU-58, June 2015; $353, AU-53, January 2015													
1898, Proof	735	268	64.9								$525	$1,100	$1,400
	Auctions: $15,275, PF-68Cam, January 2015; $12,925, PF-67Cam, August 2015; $2,938, PF-66Cam, September 2015; $1,528, PF-64Cam, January 2015													
1898-O	874,000	135	32.5	27%	$38	$90	$240	$400	$540	$775	$1,500	$2,600	$6,500
	Auctions: $22,325, MS-67, October 2015; $2,233, AU-50, January 2015; $553, VF-30, July 2015; $212, F-12, August 2015													
1898-S	2,358,550	145	40.2	25%	$30	$48	$90	$185	$340	$500	$1,500	$3,600	$8,000
	Auctions: $4,700, MS-64, January 2015; $3,564, MS-64, September 2015; $823, AU-55, August 2015; $247, VF-30, January 2015													
1899	5,538,000	388	47.9	43%	$18	$20	$45	$95	$200	$375	$600	$1,000	$2,250
	Auctions: $19,975, MS-67, August 2015; $400, AU-58, April 2015; $376, AU-55, September 2015; $112, VF-30, February 2015													
1899, Proof	846	212	64.4								$525	$1,100	$1,400
	Auctions: $11,163, PF-68, August 2015; $3,290, PF-66Cam, October 2015; $1,234, PF-64Cam, March 2015; $646, PF-62, July 2015													
1899-O	1,724,000	139	40.4	40%	$25	$35	$80	$165	$275	$400	$700	$1,600	$4,500
	Auctions: $11,750, MS-66, May 2015; $3,760, MS-65, August 2015; $2,820, AU-58, January 2015; $141, VF-30, November 2015													
1899-S	1,686,411	136	46.7	37%	$25	$40	$90	$175	$300	$400	$850	$2,000	$4,500
	Auctions: $17,625, MS-67, August 2015; $764, AU-58, January 2015; $259, EF-45, June 2015; $141, VF-25, November 2015													
1900	4,762,000	377	51.7	52%	$17	$19	$45	$95	$200	$375	$600	$850	$2,250
	Auctions: $19,975, MS-67, October 2015; $4,700, MS-66, May 2015; $376, AU-58, August 2015; $147, VF-35, December 2015													
1900, Proof	912	296	64.6								$525	$1,100	$1,400
	Auctions: $10,869, PF-68Cam, October 2015; $7,638, PF-67Cam, August 2015; $2,115, PF-65, February 2015; $940, PF-63, January 2015													
1900-O	2,744,000	112	38.5	29%	$18	$25	$60	$170	$325	$550	$1,200	$3,400	$10,000
	Auctions: $37,600, MS-67, May 2015; $30,550, MS-66, August 2015; $5,170, MS-64, January 2015; $376, AU-50, May 2015													
1900-S	2,560,322	131	44.6	26%	$17	$19	$45	$100	$210	$375	$650	$2,400	$10,000
	Auctions: $22,325, MS-67, May 2015; $14,100, MS-66, October 2015; $470, AU-58, January 2015; $353, AU-53, February 2015													
1901	4,268,000	346	50.2	42%	$17	$18	$45	$95	$200	$375	$550	$850	$2,350
	Auctions: $17,625, MS-67, August 2015; $376, AU-58, January 2015; $165, VF-30, October 2015; $123, VF-25, April 2015													
1901, Proof	813	267	64.5								$525	$1,100	$1,400
	Auctions: $32,900, PF-69Cam, August 2015; $9,106, PF-68, September 2015; $1,175, PF-64, January 2015; $881, PF-63, March 2015													
1901-O	1,124,000	87	42.2	43%	$17	$26	$80	$230	$1,100	$1,500	$2,400	$4,000	$13,500
	Auctions: $6,169, MS-64, August 2015; $1,528, AU-55, September 2015; $470, VF-35, July 2015; $317, VF-20, August 2015													
1901-S	847,044	108	24.1	16%	$32	$55	$165	$400	$1,250	$1,600	$3,500	$6,500	$12,000
	Auctions: $11,750, MS-65, August 2015; $9,694, MS-65, October 2016; $2,703, AU-55, September 2015													
1902	4,922,000	308	48.7	42%	$17	$18	$45	$95	$200	$375	$550	$900	$2,250
	Auctions: $14,100, MS-67, October 2015; $517, MS-62, February 2015; $541, AU-58, February 2015; $84, VF-25, January 2015													
1902, Proof	777	238	64.1								$525	$1,100	$1,400
	Auctions: $4,113, PF-67, March 2015; $4,230, PF-66Cam, February 2015; $2,233, PF-65, January 2015; $1,293, PF-64, January 2015													
1902-O	2,526,000	142	43.7	37%	$17	$20	$55	$105	$220	$400	$900	$2,500	$7,500
	Auctions: $16,450, MS-67, August 2015; $1,763, MS-63, October 2015; $1,528, AU-58, June 2015; $129, VF-30, April 2015													
1902-S	1,460,670	83	42.9	42%	$19	$28	$65	$150	$250	$400	$900	$2,400	$4,250
	Auctions: $28,200, MS-67+, August 2015; $10,575, MS-66, October 2015; $5,170, MS-65, August 2015; $5,170, MS-64, October 2015													

	Mintage	Cert	Avg	%MS	G-4	VG-8	F-12	VF-20	EF-40	AU-50	MS-60 PF-60	MS-63 PF-63	MS-65 PF-65
1903	2,278,000	124	48.3	45%	$17	$18	$45	$95	$200	$375	$550	$1,500	$7,200
	Auctions: $12,925, MS-66, May 2015; $4,230, MS-65, June 2015; $588, AU-58, June 2015; $165, VF-30, January 2015												
1903, Proof	755	256	64.5								$525	$1,100	$1,400
	Auctions: $12,925, PF-68, May 2015; $4,348, PF-66Cam, January 2015; $2,938, PF-66, June 2015; $1,382, PF-64, February 2015												
1903-O	2,100,000	186	50.4	53%	$17	$18	$55	$125	$210	$400	$800	$1,700	$4,500
	Auctions: $9,988, MS-66, May 2015; $4,230, MS-65, August 2015; $646, AU-55, January 2015; $353, EF-45, January 2015												
1903-S	1,920,772	121	44.6	50%	$17	$19	$60	$130	$230	$450	$950	$1,700	$3,500
	Auctions: $17,625, MS-67, May 2015; $1,763, AU-58, July 2015; $308, EF-40, January 2015; $153, VF-25, February 2015												
1904	2,992,000	212	48.5	43%	$17	$18	$35	$85	$200	$375	$600	$1,000	$4,000
	Auctions: $4,465, MS-66, August 2015; $250, AU-55, May 2015; $259, EF-45, May 2015; $89, VF-25, January 2015												
1904, Proof	670	262	64.3								$525	$1,100	$1,400
	Auctions: $12,925, PF-68, October 2015; $3,878, PF-67, October 2015; $2,820, PF-66, July 2015; $2,291, PF-65, January 2015												
1904-O	1,117,600	95	39.5	24%	$22	$35	$95	$235	$400	$800	$1,700	$3,750	$10,750
	Auctions: $12,925, MS-66, October 2015; $2,233, MS-60, June 2015; $705, AU-55, June 2015; $881, EF-45, January 2015												
1904-S	553,038	212	20.4	9%	$48	$150	$350	$850	$3,750	$7,000	$12,000	$20,000	$39,000
	Auctions: $91,063, MS-67, August 2015; $28,200, MS-64, March 2016; $3,055, EF-45, July 2015; $2,820, VF-35, January 2015												
1905	662,000	128	45.9	45%	$25	$29	$85	$185	$265	$425	$700	$1,600	$4,800
	Auctions: $16,450, MS-67, October 2015; $4,583, MS-65, January 2015; $823, AU-58, July 2015; $223, EF-45, February 2015												
1905, Proof	727	212	64.1								$525	$1,100	$1,400
	Auctions: $9,106, PF-68, August 2015; $2,585, PF-66, October 2015; $2,350, PF-65, March 2015; $1,645, PF-64, January 2015												
1905-O	505,000	133	46.9	61%	$30	$45	$125	$225	$350	$525	$850	$1,750	$4,500
	Auctions: $56,400, MS-68, January 2015; $8,813, MS-67, October 2015; $2,233, AU-58, June 2015; $118, F-12, January 2015												
1905-S	2,494,000	134	39.7	36%	$16	$19	$53	$140	$240	$400	$700	$1,600	$7,500
	Auctions: $14,100, MS-67, August 2015; $1,410, AU-58, August 2015; $259, EF-45, April 2015; $179, VF-30, May 2015												
1906	2,638,000	375	50.9	53%	$16	$17	$45	$95	$200	$375	$550	$950	$2,100
	Auctions: $15,275, MS-67, August 2015; $2,703, MS-65, March 2015; $329, AU-53, January 2015; $188, EF-45, May 2015												
1906, Proof	675	257	64.5								$525	$1,100	$1,400
	Auctions: $10,869, PF-68, May 2015; $4,230, PF-67, October 2015; $2,938, PF-66, July 2015; $2,176, PF-65, January 2015												
1906-D	4,028,000	306	46.9	44%	$16	$17	$45	$95	$200	$375	$550	$950	$2,600
	Auctions: $47,000, MS-67, May 2015; $423, AU-58, June 2015; $223, EF-45, August 2015; $118, VF-30, February 2015												
1906-O	2,446,000	139	39.1	31%	$16	$19	$42	$95	$200	$400	$900	$1,400	$5,500
	Auctions: $18,800, MS-67, May 2015; $7,050, MS-66, October 2015; $282, EF-45, September 2015; $94, F-15, June 2015												
1906-S	1,740,154	131	48.4	48%	$16	$19	$53	$115	$210	$375	$625	$1,400	$3,000
	Auctions: $15,275, MS-67, May 2015; $940, MS-62, February 2015; $1,058, AU-55, January 2015; $212, VF-25, January 2015												
1907	2,598,000	323	52.9	60%	$16	$17	$45	$95	$200	$375	$550	$950	$2,100
	Auctions: $3,995, MS-66, January 2015; $881, MS-63, October 2015; $282, AU-53, May 2015; $165, VF-35, February 2015												
1907, Proof	575	191	64.2								$525	$1,100	$1,400
	Auctions: $18,800, PF-68, June 2014												
1907-D	3,856,000	355	47.8	46%	$16	$17	$45	$95	$200	$375	$550	$950	$2,100
	Auctions: $3,055, MS-66, October 2015; $1,116, MS-63, August 2015; $353, AU-53, April 2015; $112, VF-30, May 2015												
1907-O	3,946,600	301	48.4	53%	$16	$17	$45	$95	$200	$375	$550	$950	$2,100
	Auctions: $16,450, MS-67, August 2015; $306, AU-50, January 2015; $153, EF-40, August 2015; $212, VF-35, May 2015												
1907-S	1,250,000	99	36.1	31%	$18	$30	$85	$185	$425	$725	$2,500	$6,000	$11,000
	Auctions: $17,625, MS-67, October 2015; $2,585, AU-53, January 2015; $450, VF-35, May 2015; $165, F-15, May 2015												
1908	1,354,000	203	51.0	58%	$16	$17	$45	$95	$200	$375	$550	$950	$2,100
	Auctions: $12,925, MS-67, August 2015; $2,233, MS-65, June 2015; $1,058, MS-64, March 2015; $911, MS-63, January 2015												
1908, Proof	545	178	64.3								$525	$1,100	$1,400
	Auctions: $7,050, PF-68, October 2015; $2,115, PF-65, June 2015; $823, PF-63, September 2015; $764, PF-62, June 2015												
1908-D	3,280,000	391	45.4	41%	$16	$17	$45	$95	$200	$375	$550	$950	$2,300
	Auctions: $22,325, MS-68, October 2015; $2,350, MS-65, March 2015; $306, AU-55, January 2015; $176, EF-45, September 2015												
1908-O	5,360,000	307	45.0	46%	$16	$17	$45	$95	$200	$375	$550	$950	$2,100
	Auctions: $15,275, MS-67, August 2015; $793, MS-63, June 2015; $646, AU-58, January 2015; $646, AU-53, May 2015												
1908-S	1,644,828	110	35.6	36%	$16	$25	$75	$160	$400	$600	$1,100	$2,750	$8,500
	Auctions: $7,050, MS-66, August 2015; $3,819, MS-65, March 2015; $3,055, MS-64, January 2015; $2,585, AU-58, August 2015												

1909-S, Inverted Mintmark
FS-50-1909S-501.

1911-S, Repunched Mintmark
FS-50-1911S-501.

	Mintage	Cert	Avg	%MS	G-4	VG-8	F-12	VF-20	EF-40	AU-50	MS-60	MS-63	MS-65
											PF-60	PF-63	PF-65
1909	2,368,000	501	47.4	50%	$16	$17	$45	$95	$200	$375	$550	$950	$2,100
	Auctions: $3,760, MS-66, May 2015; $447, AU-55, February 2015; $306, AU-53, October 2015; $165, EF-40, January 2015												
1909, Proof	650	287	64.5								$525	$1,100	$1,400
	Auctions: $11,163, PF-68Cam, May 2015; $1,880, PF-64, January 2015; $940, PF-63, October 2015; $881, PF-62, June 2015												
1909-O	925,400	157	35.6	36%	$18	$22	$65	$175	$375	$650	$1,100	$1,650	$4,500
	Auctions: $$16,450, MS-66, May 2015; $2,820, MS-64, September 2015; $705, AU-50, July 2015; $106, F-15, August 2015												
1909-S	1,764,000	165	33.9	29%	$16	$17	$45	$110	$250	$475	$750	$1,300	$3,500
	Auctions: $17,625, MS-67, May 2015; $3,525, MS-65, January 2015; $329, EF-45, January 2015; $259, EF-40, February 2015												
1909-S, Inverted Mintmark (c)	**(d)**	0	n/a							$425	$675	$1,550	
	Auctions: $11,750, MS-67, October 2015; $4,406, MS-66, November 2014; $141, VF-35, June 2015; $206, VF-30, August 2014												
1910	418,000	168	46.6	50%	$20	$30	$95	$175	$320	$410	$600	$1,100	$3,200
	Auctions: $8,225, MS-66, August 2015; $646, MS-61, September 2015; $764, AU-58, October 2015; $188, VF-25, May 2015												
1910, Proof	551	256	64.5								$525	$1,100	$1,400
	Auctions: $15,275, PF-68, October 2015; $5,875, PF-67Cam, January 2015; $1,175, PF-64, August 2015												
1910-S	1,948,000	149	35.4	30%	$18	$20	$35	$95	$200	$375	$700	$2,000	$4,000
	Auctions: $15,275, MS-67, October 2015; $376, AU-50, January 2015; $147, VF-35, October 2015; $141, VF-30, May 2015												
1911	1,406,000	346	52.4	59%	$16	$17	$45	$95	$200	$375	$550	$950	$2,100
	Auctions: $4,702, MS-66, August 2015; $494, MS-62, January 2015; $306, AU-55, January 2015; $129, VF-30, January 2015												
1911, Proof	543	240	64.5								$525	$1,100	$1,400
	Auctions: $16,450, PF-67, October 2015; $1,175, PF-64, October 2015; $588, PF-62, September 2015; $541, PF-61, June 2015												
1911-D	695,080	154	51.3	58%	$16	$17	$45	$95	$200	$375	$550	$950	$2,100
	Auctions: $15,275, MS-67, October 2015; $2,115, MS-65, September 2015; $1,704, MS-64, June 2015; $1,177, MS-64, July 2015												
1911-S	1,272,000	125	34.9	28%	$18	$20	$40	$120	$240	$425	$700	$1,500	$4,000
	Auctions: $42,300, MS-67, August 2015; $3,532, MS-65, August 2015; $118, VF-30, April 2015; $106, VF-25, February 2015												
1911-S, Repunched Mintmark (e)	**(f)**	0	n/a							$475	$750	$1,600	$5,400
	Auctions: $4,888, MS-65, December 2009												
1912	1,550,000	403	50.8	55%	$16	$17	$45	$95	$200	$375	$550	$950	$2,100
	Auctions: $15,275, MS-66, May 2015; $2,233, MS-65, January 2015; $1,116, MS-64, January 2015; $423, AU-58, September 2015												
1912, Proof	700	193	64.0								$525	$1,100	$1,400
	Auctions: $8,813, PF-68, May 2015; $4,465, PF-67, January 2015; $1,763, PF-65, October 2015; $881, PF-63, June 2015												
1912-D	2,300,800	607	49.3	52%	$16	$17	$45	$95	$200	$375	$550	$950	$2,100
	Auctions: $4,700, MS-66, October 2015; $353, AU-58, February 2015; $176, EF-40, May 2015; $94, VF-20, July 2015												
1912-S	1,370,000	239	40.6	44%	$16	$18	$45	$100	$200	$425	$600	$1,000	$3,250
	Auctions: $12,338, MS-67, August 2015; $376, AU-50, October 2015; $200, EF-40, January 2015; $129, VF-25, January 2015												
1913	188,000	468	17.4	11%	$75	$90	$210	$425	$800	$1,200	$1,750	$2,100	$4,000
	Auctions: $8,225, MS-66, October 2015; $494, VF-20, June 2015; $79, VG-8, February 2015; $59, G-6, August 2015												
1913, Proof	627	199	64.0								$600	$1,100	$1,500
	Auctions: $3,055, PF-66, October 2015; $1,293, PF-64, August 2015; $940, PF-63, June 2015; $541, PF-62, June 2015												
1913-D	534,000	281	51.9	51%	$16	$17	$45	$95	$200	$375	$550	$950	$3,700
	Auctions: $7,050, MS-66, August 2015; $282, AU-55, July 2015; $353, AU-53, April 2015; $306, EF-40, November 2015												
1913-S	604,000	163	41.6	48%	$16	$25	$55	$120	$275	$400	$800	$1,700	$4,000
	Auctions: $21,150, MS-67, October 2015; $12,925, MS-66, September 2015; $1,763, MS-64, January 2015												

c. The S mintmark was punched into the die upside-down (with the top slightly wider than the base). d. Included in 1909-S mintage figure. e. The lower serif of the underlying mintmark is visible protruding from the primary serif. f. Included in 1911-S mintage figure.

	Mintage	Cert	Avg	%MS	G-4	VG-8	F-12	VF-20	EF-40	AU-50	MS-60 / PF-60	MS-63 / PF-63	MS-65 / PF-65
1914	124,230	533	20.0	17%	$125	$140	$325	$550	$1,000	$1,150	$1,500	$2,100	$7,000
	Auctions: $9,988, MS-65, January 2015; $2,585, AU-58, September 2015; $294, F-15, May 2015; $129, VG-8, February 2015												
1914, Proof	380	174	64.4								$650	$1,200	$1,700
	Auctions: $5,875, PF-67, October 2015; $4,700, PF-66, June 2015; $2,056, PF-64, October 2015; $423, PF-58, June 2015												
1914-S	992,000	193	40.3	41%	$16	$20	$40	$100	$200	$400	$600	$1,150	$3,500
	Auctions: $22,325, MS-66, February 2015; $235, EF-40, January 2015; $118, VF-25, May 2015; $79, F-15, March 2015												
1915	138,000	572	15.7	7%	$85	$135	$285	$375	$650	$1,000	$1,400	$2,250	$5,750
	Auctions: $11,750, MS-66, August 2015; $6,463, MS-66, October 2016; $4,230, MS-65, July 2016												
1915, Proof	450	175	64.5								$700	$1,200	$1,800
	Auctions: $15,275, PF-68, May 2015; $2,703, PF-66, January 2015; $3,290, PF-65, October 2015; $1,528, PF-64, August 2015												
1915-D	1,170,400	685	52.0	56%	$16	$17	$45	$95	$200	$375	$550	$850	$2,000
	Auctions: $4,465, MS-66, July 2015; $188, AU-50, February 2015; $188, EF-45, October 2015; $165, EF-40, May 2015												
1915-S	1,604,000	529	48.0	53%	$16	$17	$45	$95	$200	$375	$550	$850	$2,000
	Auctions: $8,225, MS-67, August 2015; $588, AU-58, October 2015; $112, VF-25, May 2015; $52, F-12, February 2015												

LIBERTY WALKING (1916–1947)

Designer: *Adolph A. Weinman.* **Weight:** *12.50 grams.*
Composition: *.900 silver, .100 copper (net weight .36169 oz. pure silver).*
Diameter: *30.6 mm.* **Edge:** *Reeded.* **Mints:** *Philadelphia, Denver, and San Francisco.*

Circulation Strike   Proof

Mintmark location, 1916–1917, is on the obverse, below the motto.   *Mintmark location, 1917–1947, is on the reverse, below the branch.*

History. The Liberty Walking half dollar was designed by Adolph A. Weinman, the sculptor who also created the Mercury or Winged Liberty Head dime. His monogram appears under the tips of the eagle's wing feathers. Mintage was intermittent from 1916 to 1947, with none struck in 1922, 1924, 1925, 1926, 1930, 1931, and 1932. On the 1916 coins and some of the 1917 coins, the mintmark is located on the obverse, below IN GOD WE TRUST. Other coins of 1917, and those through 1947, have the mintmark on the reverse, under the pine branch. The Mint also created a 2016 gold Liberty Walking half dollar at a smaller dimension. See page 819.

Striking and Sharpness. Most circulation-strike Liberty Walking half dollars are lightly struck. In this respect they are similar to Standing Liberty quarters of the same era. On the obverse, the key points to check are Miss Liberty's left hand, the higher parts and lines in the skirt, and her head; after that, check all other areas. *Very few* coins are sharply struck in these areas, and for some issues sharp strikes might not exist at all. On the reverse, check the breast of the eagle.

Proofs were made beginning in 1936 and continuing through 1942. The entire die was polished (including the figure of Miss Liberty and the eagle), generating coins of low contrast. Proofs are usually fairly well struck. Most Proofs of 1941 are from over-polished dies, with the AW monogram of the designer no longer present. Striking sharpness can vary. Seek coins with full head and left-hand details.

Availability. All dates and mintmarks are readily collectible, although some, such as 1917-S (obverse mintmark), 1919-D, the three issues of 1921, and 1938-D, are scarce. Earlier years are often seen with extensive wear. MS coins are most often seen of the three issues of 1916, the 1917, and those of 1933 to 1947. Collectors saved the issues of the 1940s in large quantities, making the coins common today. As noted, coins with Full Details can range from scarce to extremely rare for certain dates. Half dollars dated 1928-D are counterfeit.

Note: Values of common-date silver coins have been based on the current bullion price of silver, $17 per ounce, and may vary with the prevailing spot price.

GRADING STANDARDS

MS-60 to 70 (Mint State). *Obverse:* At MS-60, some abrasion and contact marks are evident on the higher areas, which are also the areas most likely to be weakly struck. This includes Miss Liberty's left arm, her hand, and the areas of the skirt covering her left leg. The luster may not be complete in those areas on weakly struck coins (even those certified above MS-65)—the *original planchet surface* may be revealed, as it was not smoothed out by strik-

1917. Graded MS-65.

ing. Accordingly, grading is best done by evaluating abrasion as it is observed *in the right field*, plus evaluating the mint luster. Luster may be dull or lifeless at MS–60 to 62, but should have deep frost at MS-63 or better, particularly in the lower-relief areas. At MS-65 or better, it should be full and rich. Sometimes, to compensate for flat striking, certified coins with virtually flawless luster in the fields, evocative of an MS–65 or 66 grade, are called MS–63 or a lower grade. Such coins would seem to offer a lot of value for the money, if the variety is one that is not found with Full Details (1923-S is one of many examples). *Reverse:* Striking is usually better, permitting observation of luster in all areas except the eagle's body, which may be lightly struck. Luster may be dull or lifeless at MS–60 to 62, but should have deep frost at MS-63 or better, particularly in the lower-relief areas. At MS-65 or better, it should be full and rich.

Illustrated coin: This is a lustrous gem example.

AU-50, 53, 55, 58 (About Uncirculated). *Obverse:* Light wear is seen on the higher-relief areas of Miss Liberty, the vertical area from her head down to the date. At AU-58, the luster in the field is extensive, but is interrupted by friction and light wear. At AU–50 and 53, luster is less. *Reverse:* Wear is most evident on the eagle's breast immediately under the neck feathers, the left leg, and the top of the left wing. Luster is nearly complete at AU-58, but at AU-50 half or more is gone.

1921. Graded AU-50.

EF-40, 45 (Extremely Fine). *Obverse:* Wear is more extensive, with the higher parts of Miss Liberty now without detail, and with no skirt lines visible directly over her left leg. Little or no luster is seen. *Reverse:* The eagle shows more wear overall, with the highest parts of the body and left leg worn flat.

1919. Graded EF-40.

VF-20, 30 (Very Fine). *Obverse:* Wear is more extensive, and Miss Liberty is worn mostly flat in the line from her head to her left foot. Her skirt is worn, but most lines are seen, except over the leg and to the left and right. The lower part of her cape (to the left of her waist) is worn. *Reverse:* The eagle is worn smooth from the head to the left leg, and the right leg is flat at the top. Most feathers in the wings are delineated, but weak.

1921-S. Graded VF-20.

F-12, 15 (Fine). *Obverse:* Wear is more extensive, now with only a few light lines visible in the skirt. The rays of the sun are weak below the cape, and may be worn away at their tips. *Reverse:* Wear is more extensive, with most details now gone on the eagle's right leg. Delineation of the feathers is less, and most in the upper area and right edge of the left wing are blended together.

1918-S. Graded F-12.

VG-8, 10 (Very Good). *Obverse:* Wear is slightly more extensive, but the rim still is defined all around. The tops of the date numerals are worn and blend slightly into the ground above. *Reverse:* Wear is more extensive. On the left wing only a few feathers are delineated, and on the shoulder of the right wing most detail is gone. Detail in the pine branch is lost and it appears as a clump.

1921-D. Graded VG-8.

G-4, 6 (Good). *Obverse:* Miss Liberty is worn flat, with her head, neck, and arms all blended together. Folds can be seen at the bottom of the skirt, and nearly all gown lines are visible. The rim is worn done into the tops of some of the letters. *Reverse:* All areas show more wear. The rim is worn down into the tops of some of the letters, particularly at the top border.

1917-S, Obverse Mintmark. Graded G-4.

AG-3 (About Good). *Obverse:* Wear is more extensive. The sun's rays are nearly all gone, the motto is very light and sometimes incomplete, and the rim is worn down into more of the letters. *Reverse:* Wear is more extensive, with the eagle essentially worn flat. The rim is worn down into more of the letters.

1918. Graded AG-3.

PF-60 to 70 (Proof). *Obverse and Reverse:* Proofs that are extensively cleaned and have many hairlines, or that are dull and grainy, are lower level, such as PF–60 to 62. These are not widely desired, and represent coins that have been mistreated. With medium hairlines and good reflectivity, assigned grades of PF–63 or 64 are appropriate. Tiny horizontal lines on Miss Liberty's leg, known as slide marks, from National and other album

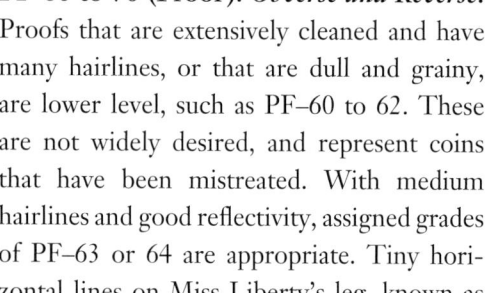

1939. Graded PF-65.

slides scuffing the relief of the cheek, are common; coins with such marks should not be graded higher than PF-64, but sometimes are. With relatively few hairlines and no noticeable slide marks, a rating of PF-65 can be given. PF-66 should have hairlines so delicate that magnification is needed to see them. Above that, a Proof should be free of any hairlines or other problems.

Illustrated coin: This example is a brilliant gem Proof.

	Mintage	Cert	Avg	%MS	G-4	VG-8	F-12	VF-20	EF-40	AU-50	MS-60 PF-64	MS-63 PF-65	MS-65 PF-67
1916	608,000	1,563	52.6	68%	$50	$55	$90	$160	$250	$265	$450	$650	$2,600
	Auctions: $35,250, MS-67, August 2015; $588, MS-61, August 2015; $329, AU-55, May 2015; $118, F-15, February 2015												
1916-D, Obverse Mintmark	1,014,400	1,785	51.4	63%	$50	$60	$85	$135	$215	$240	$450	$725	$2,600
	Auctions: $4,935, MS-66, August 2015; $400, AU-58, October 2015; $200, EF-45, February 2015; $141, VF-25, February 2015												
1916-S, Obverse Mintmark	508,000	1,076	34.3	39%	$120	$140	$275	$435	$650	$800	$1,600	$2,100	$6,500
	Auctions: $9,988, MS-65, June 2015; $1,821, AU-58, August 2015; $411, VF-25, January 2015; $160, VG-10, December 2015												

	Mintage	Cert	Avg	%MS	G-4	VG-8	F-12	VF-20	EF-40	AU-50	MS-60	MS-63	MS-65
											PF-64	PF-65	PF-67
1917	12,292,000	2,263	61.7	83%	$18	$19	$20	$21	$40	$70	$150	$210	$1,100
	Auctions: $2,233, MS-66, June 2015; $353, MS-64, August 2015; $118, MS-61, April 2015; $94, AU-58, February 2015												
1917-D, Obverse Mintmark	765,400	989	53.2	59%	$25	$35	$80	$150	$240	$325	$800	$1,150	$7,500
	Auctions: $32,900, MS-66, August 2015; $5,640, MS-65, September 2015; $705, AU-58, February 2015; $282, EF-45, April 2015												
1917-S, Obverse Mintmark	952,000	556	43.8	42%	$18	$19	$45	$145	$280	$515	$1,200	$2,200	$16,000
	Auctions: $152,750, MS-67, August 2015; $21,150, MS-65, August 2015; $376, VF-35, February 2015; $112, F-12, January 2015												
1917-D, Reverse Mintmark	1,940,000	603	53.7	49%	$27	$50	$140	$375	$750	$1,300	$3,250	$5,500	$26,000
	Auctions: $28,200, MS-66, August 2015; $1,410, AU-58, February 2015; $470, AU-53, November 2015; $141, VF-30, June 2015												
1917-S, Reverse Mintmark	5,554,000	874	57.7	67%	$18	$19	$20	$35	$70	$170	$700	$1,800	$12,500
	Auctions: $37,600, MS-66, August 2015; $10,869, MS-65, January 2015; $541, AU-58, October 2015; $212, EF-45, February 2015												
1918	6,634,000	795	58.3	67%	$18	$19	$20	$65	$155	$265	$625	$1,250	$4,500
	Auctions: $32,900, MS-66, August 2015; $4,230, MS-65, June 2015; $306, AU-55, May 2015; $84, VF-35, August 2015												
1918-D	3,853,040	764	54.3	58%	$18	$19	$38	$100	$250	$475	$1,500	$3,500	$30,000
	Auctions: $99,875, MS-66, August 2015; $35,250, MS-65, August 2015; $84, VF-30, January 2015; $40, F-15, September 2015												
1918-S	10,282,000	907	57.0	64%	$18	$19	$20	$35	$80	$200	$600	$2,150	$18,500
	Auctions: $18,800, MS-65, August 2015; $4,700, MS-64, March 2015; $376, AU-55, May 2015; $123, EF-45, January 2015												
1919	962,000	571	43.0	41%	$25	$32	$78	$265	$515	$950	$2,350	$3,500	$7,500
	Auctions: $54,050, MS-67, August 2015; $32,900, MS-66, May 2015; $4,113, MS-64, January 2015; $1,116, AU-53, October 2015												
1919-D	1,165,000	603	40.6	37%	$26	$40	$115	$345	$825	$1,900	$4,750	$13,000	$225,000
	Auctions: $32,900, MS-64, August 2016; $30,550, MS-64, August 2015; $5,170, MS-62, November 2016; $1,939, AU-50, July 2015												
1919-S	1,552,000	498	39.7	28%	$20	$30	$85	$275	$815	$1,600	$4,000	$8,750	$27,500
	Auctions: $44,650, MS-66, August 2016; $42,300, MS-66, August 2015; $11,750, MS-64, January 2015; $2,233, AU-50, June 2015												
1920	6,372,000	854	59.7	75%	$18	$19	$20	$45	$80	$160	$425	$700	$4,200
	Auctions: $7,050, MS-66, January 2015; $564, MS-63, August 2015; $329, AU-58, April 2015; $123, EF-45, August 2015												
1920-D	1,551,000	359	44.1	44%	$18	$20	$75	$250	$450	$925	$3,000	$4,500	$17,500
	Auctions: $54,050, MS-66, August 2015; $2,585, AU-58, June 2015; $823, EF-45, June 2015; $235, VF-25, March 2015												
1920-S	4,624,000	517	52.0	52%	$18	$18.50	$23	$90	$230	$600	$1,200	$3,000	$15,000
	Auctions: $58,750, MS-66, August 2015; $999, AU-58, January 2015; $376, EF-45, August 2015; $141, VF-35, April 2015												
1921	246,000	1,356	18.6	14%	$135	$200	$325	$775	$2,000	$2,900	$6,000	$7,500	$22,500
	Auctions: $54,050, MS-66, August 2015; $10,575, MS-64, January 2015; $1,410, VF-35, August 2015; $176, VG-8, January 2015												
1921-D	208,000	1,602	16.5	11%	$200	$350	$550	$850	$2,850	$5,500	$9,250	$14,000	$42,500
	Auctions: $94,000, MS-66, August 2015; $37,600, MS-65, August 2016; $3,290, EF-40, March 2015; $1,175, VF-20, January 2015												
1921-S	548,000	1,233	19.7	9%	$48	$80	$250	$800	$4,500	$8,000	$20,000	$32,000	$110,000
	Auctions: $117,500, MS-65, August 2015; $70,500, MS-64, August 2016; $8,813, AU-53, March 2015; $3,055, EF-40, January 2015												
1923-S	2,178,000	451	49.8	50%	$13	$15	$30	$110	$365	$1,400	$2,750	$4,250	$16,000
	Auctions: $25,850, MS-66, August 2015; $2,233, MS-62, September 2015; $1,645, AU-55, February 2015; $376, EF-40, September 2015												
1927-S	2,392,000	620	56.9	70%	$13	$15	$18	$50	$160	$450	$1,200	$2,050	$11,000
	Auctions: $44,650, MS-66, August 2015; $969, AU-55, August 2015; $707, AU-53, June 2015; $259, EF-45, October 2015												
1928-S (a,b)	1,940,000	498	54.7	62%	$13	$15	$19	$75	$180	$500	$1,250	$3,000	$9,500
	Auctions: $25,850, MS-66, August 2015; $8,813, MS-65, September 2015; $1,410, AU-58, June 2015; $940, AU-55, January 2015												
1929-D	1,001,200	893	57.8	60%	$12	$15	$18	$30	$100	$190	$450	$800	$3,000
	Auctions: $5,405, MS-66, May 2015; $646, MS-63, August 2015; $282, AU-55, January 2015; $118, EF-45, August 2015												
1929-S	1,902,000	800	57.6	67%	$12	$15	$18	$35	$115	$230	$500	$1,200	$3,500
	Auctions: $3,290, MS-66, January 2015; $1,293, MS-64, October 2015; $400, AU-58, September 2015; $106, EF-45, May 2015												
1933-S	1,786,000	996	57.3	56%	$12	$15	$18	$20	$60	$240	$750	$1,500	$3,250
	Auctions: $25,850, MS-67, June 2015; $1,410, MS-63, September 2015; $705, AU-58, January 2015; $282, AU-55, May 2015												
1934	6,964,000	2,542	63.4	90%	$9	$10	$11	$16	$19	$26	$75	$100	$375
	Auctions: $5,405, MS-67, August 2015; $118, MS-64, October 2015; $94, MS-63, August 2015; $79, MS-61, March 2015												
1934-D (a)	2,361,000	1,393	62.6	88%	$9	$10	$11	$16	$35	$85	$140	$250	$1,200
	Auctions: $3,819, MS-66, August 2015; $306, MS-64, June 2015; $223, MS-63, September 2015; $141, AU-50, October 2015												
1934-S	3,652,000	895	60.5	70%	$9	$10	$11	$16	$30	$90	$365	$750	$3,000
	Auctions: $30,550, MS-67, August 2015; $2,585, MS-65, July 2015; $1,001, MS-64, January 2015; $79, AU-53, January 2015												

a. Large and small mintmark varieties exist. **b.** Half dollars dated 1928-D are counterfeit.

1936, Doubled Die Obverse
FS-50-1936-101.

	Mintage	Cert	Avg	%MS	G-4	VG-8	F-12	VF-20	EF-40	AU-50	MS-60	MS-63	MS-65
											PF-64	PF-65	PF-67
1935	9,162,000	2,544	63.5	92%	$9	$10	$11	$16	$19	$25	$40	$70	$275
Auctions: $11,750, MS-68, October 2015; $4,935, MS-67, August 2015; $200, MS-65, August 2015; $89, MS-64, February 2015													
1935-D	3,003,800	1,022	62.4	87%	$9	$10	$11	$16	$30	$65	$140	$300	$1,750
Auctions: $8,225, MS-66, May 2015; $1,821, MS-65, August 2015; $259, MS-62, January 2015; $100, MS-60, November 2015													
1935-S	3,854,000	877	61.9	84%	$9	$10	$11	$16	$26	$95	$275	$465	$2,350
Auctions: $5,640, MS-66, January 2015; $1,293, MS-64, October 2015; $564, MS-63, August 2015; $259, AU-58, March 2015													
1936	12,614,000	3,574	63.9	94%	$9	$10	$11	$16	$18	$25	$45	$75	$210
Auctions: $1,528, MS-67, June 2015; $306, MS-66, September 2015; $212, MS-65, January 2015; $89, MS-64, August 2015													
1936, DblDie Obv (c)	**(d)**	0	n/a		$500	$600							
Auctions: $235, MS-65, January 2015; $940, MS-65, December 2013													
1936, Proof	3,901	1,346	64.8								$2,400	$3,200	$9,000
Auctions: $14,689, PF-67, June 2015; $4,348, PF-66, July 2015; $2,820, PF-65, January 2015; $2,820, PF-64, October 2016													
1936-D	4,252,400	1,748	63.5	94%	$9	$10	$11	$16	$20	$50	$85	$120	$400
Auctions: $4,935, MS-67, August 2015; $2,585, MS-66, February 2015; $212, MS-64, September 2015; $79, MS-63, June 2015													
1936-S	3,884,000	1,312	63.4	94%	$9	$10	$11	$16	$22	$60	$130	$200	$650
Auctions: $19,975, MS-67, August 2015; $881, MS-65, January 2015; $329, MS-64, May 2015; $217, MS-63, September 2015													
1937	9,522,000	3,234	63.8	93%	$9	$10	$11	$16	$18	$25	$40	$70	$150
Auctions: $1,528, MS-67, June 2015; $270, MS-66, July 2015; $259, MS-65, January 2015; $84, MS-64, August 2015													
1937, Proof	5,728	1,538	65.2								$650	$850	$1,600
Auctions: $5,640, PF-68, January 2015; $2,115, PF-67, August 2015; $564, PF-64, January 2015; $470, PF-63, October 2015													
1937-D	1,676,000	1,189	63.0	88%	$9	$10	$11	$18	$32	$100	$215	$265	$700
Auctions: $5,170, MS-67, August 2015; $482, MS-65, October 2015; $235, MS-63, January 2015; $153, AU-58, January 2015													
1937-S	2,090,000	1,270	63.6	94%	$9	$10	$11	$16	$25	$60	$165	$210	$625
Auctions: $8,813, MS-67, August 2015; $353, MS-65, October 2015; $247, MS-64, February 2015; $129, MS-62, July 2015													
1938	4,110,000	2,301	63.4	92%	$9	$10	$11	$18	$20	$45	$70	$160	$300
Auctions: $2,585, MS-67, January 2015; $212, MS-65, September 2015; $123, MS-63, May 2015; $46, AU-55, May 2015													
1938, Proof	8,152	1,834	65.4								$500	$675	$1,100
Auctions: $14,100, PF-68, January 2015; $764, PF-66, August 2015; $734, PF-65, June 2015; $430, PF-64, October 2015													
1938-D	491,600	2,949	41.6	39%	$55	$65	$90	$100	$160	$225	$475	$650	$1,200
Auctions: $5,640, MS-67, June 2015; $1,410, MS-65, July 2015; $400, AU-58, February 2015; $176, EF-45, January 2015													
1939	6,812,000	3,705	64.3	94%	$9	$10	$11	$16	$18	$26	$40	$65	$155
Auctions: $8,225, MS-68, August 2015; $194, MS-66, September 2015; $118, MS-65, January 2015; $84, MS-64, September 2015													
1939, Proof	8,808	2,008	65.6								$450	$600	$900
Auctions: $4,935, PF-68, August 2015; $570, PF-66, March 2015; $646, PF-65, February 2015; $388, PF-64, July 2015													
1939-D	4,267,800	2,944	64.2	96%	$9	$10	$11	$16	$18	$25	$43	$75	$145
Auctions: $4,700, MS-67, January 2015; $270, MS-66, October 2015; $165, MS-65, August 2015; $94, MS-64, February 2015													
1939-S	2,552,000	1,975	64.4	96%	$9	$10	$11	$16	$26	$70	$150	$180	$240
Auctions: $12,925, MS-68, September 2015; $564, MS-66, October 2015; $153, MS-64, April 2015; $74, AU-58, June 2015													
1940	9,156,000	4,152	64.2	95%	$9	$10	$11	$16	$18	$22	$35	$55	$120
Auctions: $7,050, MS-68, August 2015; $294, MS-66, January 2015; $89, MS-65, September 2015; $94, MS-64, April 2015													
1940, Proof	11,279	2,322	65.5								$450	$500	$825
Auctions: $3,290, PF-68, January 2015; $517, PF-66, June 2015; $423, PF-65, October 2015; $376, PF-64, February 2015													
1940-S	4,550,000	3,089	63.8	97%	$9	$10	$11	$16	$18	$35	$45	$80	$280
Auctions: $27,025, MS-67, June 2015; $823, MS-66, October 2015; $235, MS-65, August 2015; $112, MS-64, February 2015													

c. No examples have yet been discovered grading better than Fine. "Extremely strong doubling is evident on the date. Less doubling is evident on IN GOD WE TRUST, the skirt, and some other elements" (*Cherrypickers' Guide to Rare Die Varieties*, sixth edition, volume II). Several varieties exist; this one is FS-50-1936-101. d. Included in circulation-strike 1936 mintage figure.

1945, Missing Designer's Initials
FS-50-1945-901.

	Mintage	Cert	Avg	%MS	G-4	VG-8	F-12	VF-20	EF-40	AU-50	MS-60 PF-64	MS-63 PF-65	MS-65 PF-67
1941	24,192,000	11,273	64.2	94%	$9	$10	$11	$16	$18	$22	$35	$55	$100
	Auctions: $2,938, MS-68, January 2015; $588, MS-67, August 2015; $79, MS-65, February 2015; $46, MS-64, October 2015												
1941, Proof (e)	15,412	2,596	65.3								$450	$500	$800
	Auctions: $7,050, PF-68, August 2015; $646, PF-67, October 2015; $400, PF-65, September 2015; $400, PF-64, February 2015												
1941-D	11,248,400	5,982	64.3	96%	$9	$10	$11	$16	$18	$22	$38	$65	$125
	Auctions: $881, MS-67, January 2015; $176, MS-66, November 2015; $118, MS-65, July 2015; $67, MS-64, May 2015												
1941-S	8,098,000	5,875	63.2	91%	$9	$10	$11	$16	$18	$26	$75	$120	$600
	Auctions: $35,250, MS-67, August 2015; $1,293, MS-66, January 2015; $141, MS-64, April 2015; $64, MS-61, June 2015												
1942	47,818,000	16,804	63.9	93%	$9	$10	$11	$16	$18	$22	$40	$60	$100
	Auctions: $3,290, MS-67+, February 2015; $129, MS-66, July 2015; $84, MS-65, August 2015; $46, MS-64, October 2015												
1942, Proof	21,120	4,374	65.6								$450	$500	$800
	Auctions: $4,465, PF-68, June 2015; $1,528, PF-67+, August 2015; $400, PF-65, October 2015; $470, PF-64, January 2015												
1942-D	10,973,800	4,349	64.3	96%	$9	$10	$11	$16	$18	$20	$40	$80	$200
	Auctions: $834, MS-67, June 2015; $212, MS-66, January 2015; $165, MS-65, October 2015; $84, MS-64, February 2015												
1942-S (a)	12,708,000	4,584	63.7	96%	$9	$10	$11	$16	$18	$22	$40	$80	$330
	Auctions: $1,116, MS-66, February 2015; $306, MS-65, January 2015; $94, MS-64, November 2015; $118, MS-63, February 2015												
1943	53,190,000	17,109	63.9	93%	$9	$10	$11	$16	$18	$20	$35	$50	$100
	Auctions: $21,150, MS-68, August 2015; $1,293, MS-67+, January 2015; $74, MS-64+, April 2015; $40, MS-63, February 2015												
1943-D	11,346,000	5,189	64.6	96%	$9	$10	$11	$16	$18	$24	$48	$75	$190
	Auctions: $4,935, MS-68, June 2015; $646, MS-67, February 2015; $94, MS-64, August 2015; $40, MS-62, October 2015												
1943-S	13,450,000	5,258	64.0	97%	$9	$10	$11	$16	$18	$25	$42	$60	$240
	Auctions: $6,463, MS-67, August 2015; $4,465, MS-66+, February 2015; $200, MS-65, August 2015; $69, MS-64, May 2015												
1944	28,206,000	9,975	63.8	94%	$9	$10	$11	$16	$18	$20	$35	$50	$105
	Auctions: $3,525, MS-67, August 2015; $76, MS-65, March 2015; $56, MS-64, October 2015; $32, MS-60, March 2015												
1944-D	9,769,000	6,228	64.6	97%	$9	$10	$11	$16	$18	$20	$40	$60	$105
	Auctions: $1,528, MS-67+, September 2015; $183, MS-66, January 2015; $118, MS-65, March 2015; $89, MS-64, February 2015												
1944-S	8,904,000	6,200	63.9	98%	$9	$10	$11	$16	$18	$24	$40	$63	$325
	Auctions: $3,290, MS-66+, June 2015; $376, MS-65, July 2015; $84, MS-64, February 2015; $44, MS-62, October 2015												
1945	31,502,000	13,832	63.9	95%	$9	$10	$11	$16	$18	$20	$35	$50	$100
	Auctions: $1,645, MS-67, July 2015; $89, MS-65, October 2015; $94, MS-64, August 2015; $44, MS-63, February 2015												
1945, Missing Initials	(f)	28	55.8	64%						$100	$150	$250	
	Auctions: $705, MS-64, January 2014												
1945-D	9,966,800	9,046	64.8	98%	$9	$10	$11	$17.50	$18	$20	$35	$60	$120
	Auctions: $14,100, MS-68, August 2015; $4,465, MS-67+, August 2015; $94, MS-65, May 2015; $64, MS-64, February 2015												
1945-S	10,156,000	7,582	64.3	98%	$9	$10	$11	$17.50	$18	$24	$38	$55	$120
	Auctions: $6,463, MS-67, January 2015; $212, MS-66, August 2015; $106, MS-65, April 2015; $74, MS-64, February 2015												

a. Large and small mintmark varieties exist. **e.** The variety without the designer's initials was created by the over-polishing of dies.
f. Included in 1945 mintage figure.

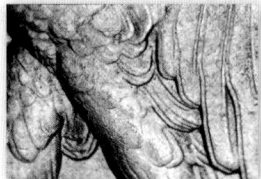 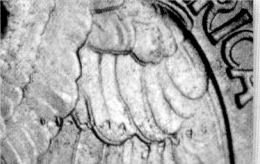  

1946, Doubled Die Reverse
FS-50-1946-801.

	Mintage	Cert	Avg	%MS	G-4	VG-8	F-12	VF-20	EF-40	AU-50	MS-60 / PF-64	MS-63 / PF-65	MS-65 / PF-67
1946	12,118,000	7,064	63.9	96%	$9	$10	$11	$17.50	$18	$20	$37	$50	$120
Auctions: $3,525, MS-67, August 2015; $176, MS-66, April 2015; $112, MS-65, April 2015; $94, MS-64, September 2015													
1946, DblDie Rev (g)	(h)	186	52.0	40%	$20	$24	$28	$40	$65	$125	$275	$550	$2,500
Auctions: $2,233, MS-64, January 2015; $188, AU-58, April 2015; $84, EF-45, August 2015; $79, F-15, April 2015													
1946-D	2,151,000	13,296	64.8	100%	$9	$10	$11	$17.50	$22	$32	$47	$60	$105
Auctions: $3,760, MS-67, August 2015; $141, MS-66, January 2015; $60, MS-64, October 2015; $42, MS-62, October 2015													
1946-S	3,724,000	8,727	64.7	99%	$9	$10	$11	$17.50	$18	$25	$43	$58	$100
Auctions: $8,225, MS-67, October 2015; $217, MS-66, February 2015; $100, MS-65, July 2015; $89, MS-64, May 2015													
1947	4,094,000	7,657	64.3	98%	$9	$10	$11	$17.50	$18	$25	$48	$60	$110
Auctions: $9,400, MS-67, February 2015; $188, MS-66, November 2015; $123, MS-65, July 2015; $64, MS-64, October 2015													
1947-D	3,900,600	8,537	64.6	99%	$9	$10	$11	$17.50	$18	$30	$45	$60	$105
Auctions: $5,640, MS-67, August 2015; $182, MS-66, April 2015; $129, MS-65, September 2015; $69, MS-64, July 2015													

g. Very strong doubling is visible on E PLURIBUS UNUM, the eagle's wing feathers and left wing, and the branch. **h.** Included in 1946 mintage figure.

FRANKLIN (1948–1963)

Designer: *John R. Sinnock.* **Weight:** *12.50 grams.*
Composition: *.900 silver, .100 copper (net weight .36169 oz. pure silver).*
Diameter: *30.6 mm.* **Edge:** *Reeded.* **Mints:** *Philadelphia, Denver, and San Francisco.*

Circulation Strike   Mintmark location is on the reverse, above the beam.   **Proof**

History. U.S. Mint chief engraver John R. Sinnock developed a motif for a silver half dime in 1942; it was proposed but never adopted for regular coinage. In 1948, the year after Sinnock died, his Franklin half dollar was introduced, its design an adaptation of his earlier half dime motif. The Liberty Bell is similar to that used by Sinnock on the 1926 Sesquicentennial commemorative half dollar modeled from a sketch by John Frederick Lewis. The designs were finished by Sinnock's successor, chief engraver Gilroy Roberts. The coin-collecting community paid little attention to the Franklin half dollar at the time, but today the coins are widely collected.

Striking and Sharpness. Given the indistinct details of the obverse, sharpness of strike usually is ignored. On the reverse, if the bottom lines of the Liberty Bell are complete the coin may be designated as Full Bell Lines (FBL). Virtually all Proofs are well struck.

Availability. All dates and mintmarks are easily available in grades from VF upward. Lower-level MS coins can be unattractive due to contact marks and abrasion, particularly noticeable on the obverse.

High-quality gems are generally inexpensive, although varieties that are rare with FBL can be costly amid much competition in the marketplace. Most collectors seek MS coins. Grades below EF are not widely desired. Proofs were made from 1950 to 1963 and are available today in proportion to their mintages. Those with cameo-frosted devices are in the minority and often sell for strong premiums.

Note: Values of common-date silver coins have been based on the current bullion price of silver, $17 per ounce, and may vary with the prevailing spot price.

GRADING STANDARDS

MS-60 to 70 (Mint State). *Obverse:* At MS-60, some abrasion and contact marks are evident on the cheek, on the hair left of the ear, and the neck. At MS-63, abrasion is slight at best, less so for MS-64. An MS-65 coin should display no abrasion or contact marks except under magnification, and MS-66 and higher coins should have none at all. Luster should be full and rich. As details are shallow on this design, the amount and "depth" of luster is important to grading.

1951-S. Graded MS-65.

Reverse: General comments apply as for the obverse. The points to check are the bell harness, the words PASS AND STOW on the upper area of the Liberty Bell, and the bottom of the bell.

Illustrated coin: Satiny brilliance is seen on the obverse of this coin, light golden toning on the reverse.

AU-50, 53, 55, 58 (About Uncirculated). *Obverse:* At AU-50, medium wear is evident on the portrait, and most of the luster in the field is gone. At AU-53, wear is less and luster is more extensive. AU–55 and 58 coins show much luster. Wear is noticeable on the portrait and, to a lesser extent, in the field. *Reverse:* At AU-50, medium wear is evident on most of the Liberty Bell, and most of the luster in the field is gone. At AU-53, wear is

1949-D. Graded AU-50.

slightly less. AU–55 and 58 coins show much luster. Light wear is seen on the higher areas of the bell.

EF-40, 45 (Extremely Fine). *Obverse:* Wear is more extensive, and some hair detail (never strong to begin with) is lost. There is no luster. *Reverse:* Wear is seen overall. The inscription on the bell is weak, and the highest parts of the bottom horizontal lines are worn away. There is no luster.

The Franklin half dollar is seldom collected in grades lower than EF-40.

1955. Graded EF-40.

PF-60 to 70 (Proof). *Obverse and Reverse:* Proofs that are extensively cleaned and have many hairlines, or that are dull and grainy, are lower level, such as PF–60 to 62. These are not widely desired, and represent coins that have been mistreated. Fortunately, only a few Proof Franklin half dollars are in this category. With medium hairlines and good reflectivity, assigned grades of PF–63 or 64 are appropriate. PF-66 should have hairlines so delicate that magnification is needed to see them. Above that, a Proof should be free of any hairlines or other problems.

1950. Graded PF-65 Cameo.

Full Bell Lines

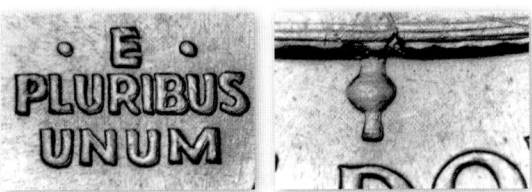

1948, Doubled Die Reverse
FS-50-1948-801.

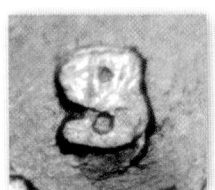

1949-S, Repunched Mintmark
FS-50-1949S-501.

	Mintage	Cert	Avg	%MS	VF-20	EF-40	MS-60	MS-63	MS-64	MS-65	MS-65FBL PF-64	MS-66 PF-65	MS-66FBL PF-65DC
1948	3,006,814	4,368	64.1	97%	$9	$11	$20	$27	$35	$80	$140	$300	$400
Auctions: $3,760, MS-67FBL, September 2015; $1,410, MS-66FBL+, June 2015; $84, MS-65FBL, August 2015; $46, MS-64FBL, August 2015													
1948, Doubled Die Reverse (a)	(b)	33	63.8	100%				$75	$125	$200	$300	$550	
Auctions: No auction records available.													
1948-D	4,028,600	4,100	64.0	98%	$9	$11	$20	$24	$30	$115	$185	$500	$550
Auctions: $19,975, MS-67FBL, January 2015; $12,925, MS-67FBL, July 2015; $135, MS-65FBL, February 2015; $74, MS-64, January 2015													
1949	5,614,000	2,875	63.1	89%	$12	$18	$40	$70	$75	$120	$155	$325	$425
Auctions: $1,469, MS-66FBL+, September 2015; $212, MS-65FBL, November 2015; $188, MS-65FBL, July 2015; $62, MS-64FBL, January 2015													
1949-D	4,120,600	2,952	63.3	95%	$12	$18	$45	$75	$90	$500	$750	$1,250	$1,750
Auctions: $1,116, MS-66, July 2016; $1,058, MS-66, August 2016; $1,058, MS-66, September 2016; $5,640, MS-66, October 2016													
1949-S	3,744,000	3,360	63.9	95%	$12	$20	$65	$95	$115	$140	$500	$275	$525
Auctions: $6,463, MS-67FBL, June 2015; $259, MS-66, September 2015; $200, MS-65FBL, May 2015; $74, MS-64, January 2015													
1949-S, Doubled Mintmark (c)	(d)	9	60.7	67%				$120	$170	$280	$350	$575	
Auctions: $223, MS-65, January 2014													
1950	7,742,123	2,486	63.6	93%	$9	$11	$30	$35	$55	$110	$190	$300	$550
Auctions: $18,213, MS-67FBL, August 2015; $1,528, MS-66FBL, January 2015; $259, MS-65, February 2015; $56, MS-64FBL, November 2015													
1950, Proof	51,386	3,513	64.8								$425	$575	$15,000
Auctions: $4,230, PF-67, January 2015; $7,638, PF-66Cam, October 2015; $1,645, PF-65Cam, July 2015; $376, PF-64, June 2015													
1950-D	8,031,600	2,578	63.4	95%	$9	$11	$26	$40	$70	$250	$375	$900	$1,350
Auctions: $2,585, MS-66FBL, January 2015; $1,058, MS-66FBL, June 2015; $235, MS-65FBL, May 2015; $46, MS-64FBL, August 2015													

a. Doubling is visible on E PLURIBUS UNUM, UNITED, HALF DOLLAR, the dots, and the Liberty Bell's clapper. "There are several similar, yet lesser, DDRs for this date" (*Cherrypickers' Guide to Rare Die Varieties*, sixth edition, volume II). The variety listed and pictured is FS-50-1948-801. **b.** Included in 1948 mintage figure. **c.** The secondary mintmark is visible south of the primary. CONECA lists two other repunched mintmarks for this date; the one illustrated and listed here is FS-50-1949S-501. **d.** Included in 1949-S mintage figure.

1951-S, Doubled Die Reverse
FS-50-1951S-801.

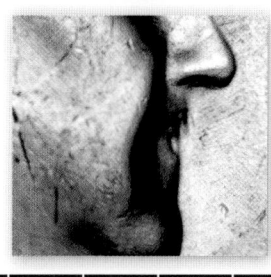

**1955, Clashed
Obverse Die
"Bugs Bunny"
variety**
FS-50-1955-401.

	Mintage	Cert	Avg	%MS	VF-20	EF-40	MS-60	MS-63	MS-64	MS-65	MS-65FBL PF-64	MS-66 PF-65	MS-66FBL PF-65DC
1951	16,802,102	2,719	63.9	95%	$9	$11	$14	$24	$35	$70	$235	$250	$525
	Auctions: $1,410, MS-66FBL, July 2015; $200, MS-66, July 2015; $235, MS-65FBL, September 2015; $44, MS-65, January 2015												
1951, Proof	57,500	3,563	64.9								$320	$400	$3,000
	Auctions: $4,465, PF-68, June 2015; $3,290, PF-67Cam, February 2015; $494, PF-65Cam, July 2015; $259, PF-64, March 2015												
1951-D	9,475,200	2,117	63.6	96%	$9	$11	$30	$45	$70	$150	$250	$650	$850
	Auctions: $764, MS-66FBL, January 2015; $141, MS-65FBL, July 2015; $84, MS-64FBL, April 2015; $28, MS-63FBL, July 2015												
1951-S	13,696,000	2,801	64.1	97%	$9	$11	$25	$35	$50	$70	$400	$200	$1,100
	Auctions: $1,645, MS-67, October 2015; $588, MS-66FBL, July 2015; $176, MS-64FBL, January 2015; $46, MS-63, May 2015												
1951-S, DblDie Rev (e)	(f)	9	64.4	100%				$80	$110	$275	$725	$900	
	Auctions: $188, MS-65, January 2014												
1952	21,192,093	2,753	64.0	96%	$9	$11	$14	$23	$32	$70	$125	$225	$350
	Auctions: $4,935, MS-67FBL, July 2015; $200, MS-66FBL, February 2015; $94, MS-65FBL, February 2015; $48, MS-64FBL, November 2015												
1952, Proof	81,980	4,114	65.3								$180	$225	$4,500
	Auctions: $3,821, PF-67Cam, August 2015; $8,813, PF-66DCam, June 2015; $260, PF-66, October 2015; $118, PF-64, January 2015												
1952-D	25,395,600	2,580	63.8	97%	$9	$11	$14	$23	$32	$125	$180	$600	$750
	Auctions: $564, MS-66FBL, January 2015; $176, MS-65FBL, September 2015; $129, MS-65FBL, February 2015; $40, MS-64FBL, February 2015												
1952-S	5,526,000	2,634	64.5	99%	$12	$17	$50	$70	$80	$100	$750	$225	$2,000
	Auctions: $21,150, MS-67FBL, February 2015; $1,645, MS-67, January 2015; $129, MS-66, July 2015; $423, MS-64FBL, January 2015												
1953	2,668,120	2,264	64.0	98%	$9	$10	$14	$27	$40	$100	$635	$450	$1,500
	Auctions: $2,233, MS-66FBL, January 2015; $306, MS-66, March 2015; $646, MS-65FBL, October 2015; $129, MS-64FBL, May 2015												
1953, Proof	128,800	5,535	65.6								$125	$190	$1,400
	Auctions: $4,230, PF-68Cam, August 2015; $2,585, PF-66DCam, January 2015; $165, PF-66, February 2015; $84, PF-64, May 2015												
1953-D	20,900,400	3,341	63.9	98%	$9	$10	$14	$23	$38	$110	$175	$550	$725
	Auctions: $494, MS-66FBL, February 2015; $112, MS-65FBL, February 2015; $74, MS-65, May 2015; $56, MS-64FBL, October 2015												
1953-S	4,148,000	5,297	64.8	100%	$9	$10	$25	$35	$48	$70	$25,500	$350	$35,000
	Auctions: $2,233, MS-67, January 2015; $447, MS-66, June 2015; $21,150, MS-65FBL, September 2015; $100, MS-65, September 2015												
1954	13,188,202	4,393	64.2	99%	$9	$10	$14	$20	$30	$70	$120	$300	$600
	Auctions: $1,880, MS-66FBL, July 2015; $823, MS-66FBL, October 2015; $153, MS-65FBL, January 2015; $38, MS-64FBL, July 2015												
1954, Proof	233,300	7,574	66.3								$65	$85	$425
	Auctions: $14,100, PF-68DCam, October 2015; $270, PF-67, May 2015; $129, PF-66Cam, May 2015; $34, PF-64, August 2015												
1954-D	25,445,580	5,361	64.1	99%	$9	$10	$14	$24	$28	$90	$140	$375	$800
	Auctions: $588, MS-66FBL, June 2015; $353, MS-66, February 2015; $89, MS-65FBL, January 2015; $54, MS-65, May 2015												
1954-S	4,993,400	8,322	64.7	100%	$12	$14	$16	$24	$35	$50	$250	$240	$1,050
	Auctions: $1,763, MS-67, July 2015; $194, MS-66, November 2015; $188, MS-65FBL, September 2015; $56, MS-64FBL, February 2015												
1955	2,498,181	7,767	64.1	99%	$18	$22	$25	$30	$40	$55	$115	$150	$425
	Auctions: $1,763, MS-66FBL, January 2015; $52, MS-65, September 2015; $38, MS-64FBL, April 2015; $40, MS-63FBL, April 2015												
1955, Clashed Obverse Die (g)	(h)	673	62.7	100%				$48	$65	$130	$350	$265	$700
	Auctions: $423, MS-66FBL, February 2013; $129, MS-64FBL, September 2014; $76, MS-64FBL, September 2014												
1955, Proof	378,200	12,490	66.9								$65	$75	$425
	Auctions: $4,700, PF-68DCam, October 2015; $212, PF-68, January 2015; $165, PF-67Cam, March 2015; $141, PF-66, August 2015												

e. Doubling is evident on the eagle's tail feathers and left wing, as well as on E PLURIBUS UNUM. This variety is FS-50-1951S-801.
f. Included in 1951-S mintage figure. **g.** This variety, popularly known as the "Bugs Bunny," has evidence of clash marks that appear as two buckteeth on Benjamin Franklin. **h.** Included in circulation-strike 1955 mintage figure.

1957, Tripled Die Reverse, Proof
FS-50-1957-801.

1959, Doubled Die Reverse
FS-50-1959-801.

	Mintage	Cert	Avg	%MS	VF-20	EF-40	MS-60	MS-63	MS-64	MS-65	MS-65FBL / PF-64	MS-66 / PF-65	MS-66FBL / PF-65DC
1956	4,032,000	9,997	64.3	100%	$9	$10	$14	$25	$28	$42	$100	$80	$275
Auctions: $353, MS-67, January 2015; $176, MS-66FBL, September 2015; $106, MS-66, July 2015; $60, MS-65FBL, December 2015													
1956, Proof	669,384	4,612	67.1								$35	$45	$100
Auctions: $2,820, PF-69DCam, September 2015; $329, PF-69, February 2015; $118, PF-68, February 2015; $376, PF-67, July 2015													
1957	5,114,000	4,753	64.7	100%	$9	$10	$14	$19	$25	$40	$125	$85	$225
Auctions: $$1,763, MS-67FBL, October 2015; $329, MS-67, January 2015; $94, MS-66FBL, October 2015; $48, MS-66, October 2015													
1957, Proof	1,247,952	18,370	67.0								$25	$28	$250
Auctions: $2,585, PF-69Cam, September 2015; $112, PF-68, June 2015; $90, PF-67, July 2015; $84, PF-66Cam, February 2015													
1957, Tripled Die Reverse, Proof (i)	(j)	7	66.4								$75	$90	$800
Auctions: No auction records available.													
1957-D	19,966,850	5,288	64.4	99%	$9	$10	$14	$19	$23	$40	$75	$85	$375
Auctions: $3,055, MS-67FBL, October 2015; $764, MS-67, October 2015; $212, MS-66FBL, February 2015; $123, MS-65, August 2015													
1958	4,042,000	6,558	64.6	99%	$9	$10	$14	$19	$24	$45	$125	$80	$350
Auctions: $4,700, MS-67FBL, January 2015; $400, MS-67, February 2015; $353, MS-67, September 2015; $44, MS-66, April 2015													
1958, Proof	875,652	13,547	66.8								$18	$25	$675
Auctions: $705, PF-69Cam, July 2015; $2,115, PF-67UCam, July 2015; $153, PF-67Cam, March 2015; $20, PF-63, September 2015													
1958-D	23,962,412	6,508	64.5	99%	$9	$10	$14	$18	$19	$45	$70	$75	$475
Auctions: $1,175, MS-67FBL, October 2015; $588, MS-67, January 2015; $153, MS-66FBL, February 2015; $20, MS-64, May 2015													
1959	6,200,000	4,894	64.3	99%	$9	$10	$14	$18	$20	$70	$225	$800	$1,750
Auctions: $1,763, MS-66FBL, January 2015; $154, MS-65FBL, May 2015; $84, MS-65, November 2015; $46, MS-64, May 2015													
1959, Doubled Die Reverse (k)	(l)	60	64.0	98%			$85	$90	$120	$450	$1,125		
Auctions: $1,528, MS-66, October 2016; $431, MS-65FBL, March 2011													
1959, Proof	1,149,291	15,291	66.8								$18	$22	$2,000
Auctions: $1,529, PF-68Cam, January 2015; $423, PF-67Cam, February 2015; $341, PF-67Cam, March 2015; $235, PF-66Cam, October 2015													
1959-D	13,053,750	4,874	64.3	99%	$9	$10	$14	$18	$22	$90	$140	$775	$1,050
Auctions: $1,528, MS-66FBL, August 2015; $470, MS-66, January 2015; $118, MS-65FBL, February 2015; $89, MS-65FBL, September 2015													
1960	6,024,000	4,563	64.2	100%	$9	$10	$14	$18	$19	$100	$225	$550	$1,500
Auctions: $1,293, MS-66FBL, January 2015; $1,058, MS-66FBL, September 2015; $176, MS-65FBL, February 2015; $153, MS-65FBL, November 2014													
1960, Proof	1,691,602	17,161	66.8								$18	$22	$100
Auctions: $646, PF-69, January 2015; $1,369, PF-68UCam, July 2015; $176, PF-68Cam, March 2015; $46, PF-66, August 2015													
1960, Doubled Die Obverse, Proof (m)	(n)	72	66.2								$80	$95	$400
Auctions: $160, PF-67, May 2012													
1960-D	18,215,812	3,908	64.0	99%	$9	$10	$14	$18	$28	$200	$450	$650	$1,500
Auctions: $1,645, MS-66FBL, February 2015; $331, MS-65FBL, August 2015; $112, MS-65, July 2015; $28, MS-64FBL, January 2015													

i. A closely tripled image is evident on E PLURIBUS UNUM, portions of UNITED STATES OF AMERICA, and HALF DOLLAR.
j. Included in 1957, Proof, mintage figure. k. Strong doubling is evident on the eagle; doubling is also visible on E PLURIBUS UNUM, UNITED, and portions of the Liberty Bell. l. Included in circulation-strike 1959 mintage figure. m. Doubling is visible on LIBERTY, TRUST, and the date. n. Included in 1960, Proof, mintage figure.

1961, Doubled Die Reverse, Proof
FS-50-1961-801.

	Mintage	Cert	Avg	%MS	VF-20	EF-40	MS-60	MS-63	MS-64	MS-65	MS-65FBL	MS-66	MS-66FBL
											PF-64	PF-65	PF-65DC
1961	8,290,000	4,713	64.2	99%	$9	$10	$14	$18	$25	$75	$900	$600	$5,000
	Auctions: $8,225, MS-66FBL, July 2015; $881, MS-66, September 2015; $40, MS-65, July 2015; $84, MS-64FBL, May 2015												
1961, Proof	3,028,244	22,375	66.8								$18	$22	$125
	Auctions: $1,880, PF-68DCam, January 2015; $306, PF-68Cam, January 2015; $129, PF-68, July 2015; $84, PF-67Cam, May 2015												
1961, Doubled Die Reverse, Proof (o)	(p)	90	65.6								$2,200	$2,900	
	Auctions: $4,935, PF-67, August 2015; $5,405, PF-67, July 2016; $2,350, PF-65, June 2014; $1,880, PF-64, July 2014												
1961-D	20,276,442	3,652	64.0	99%	$9	$10	$14	$18	$25	$110	$450	$600	$3,000
	Auctions: $3,302, MS-66FBL, February 2015; $1,175, MS-66, January 2015; $423, MS-65FBL, January 2015; $79, MS-65, October 2015												
1962	9,714,000	3,957	64.1	99%	$9	$10	$14	$18	$25	$90	$1,750	$750	$11,000
	Auctions: $7,638, MS-66FBL, October 2015; $1,645, MS-65FBL, January 2015; $200, MS-64FBL, February 2015; $36, MS-63FBL, July 2015												
1962, Proof	3,218,019	28,342	66.7								$18	$22	$60
	Auctions: $153, PF-68Cam, July 2015; $212, PF-67UCam, April 2015; $26, PF-67, September 2015; $56, PF-66Cam, April 2015												
1962, Doubled Die Obverse, Proof (q)	(r)	0	n/a								$25	$30	$150
	Auctions: No auction records available.												
1962-D	35,473,281	4,426	64.0	99%	$9	$10	$14	$18	$25	$120	$450	$1,000	$4,500
	Auctions: $4,230, MS-66FBL, January 2015; $60, MS-65, March 2015; $22, MS-64, October 2015; $38, MS-63FBL, March 2015												
1963	22,164,000	12,017	64.3	99%	$9	$10	$14	$18	$19	$40	$1,150	$750	$15,000
	Auctions: $$17,625, MS-66FBL, October 2015; $1,880, MS-65FBL, January 2015; $1,116, MS-65FBL, October 2015; $330, MS-64FBL, January 2015												
1963, Proof	3,075,645	27,551	66.9								$18	$22	$52
	Auctions: $364, PF-69, February 2015; $1,998, PF-68DCam, September 2015; $118, PF-68Cam, January 2015; $129, PF-67Cam, June 2015												
1963-D	67,069,292	9,338	64.1	98%	$9	$10	$14	$18	$19	$45	$175	$350	$1,050
	Auctions: $1,175, MS-66FBL, July 2015; $282, MS-65FBL, September 2015; $153, MS-65FBL, March 2015; $36, MS-64FBL, April 2015												

o. Other reverse doubled dies exist for this date. The variety pictured and listed here (FS-50-1961-801) is by far the most dramatic. Very strong doubling is evident on the reverse lettering. **p.** Included in 1961, Proof, mintage figure. **q.** Doubling is visible on the 62 of the date and on WE TRUST. **r.** Included in 1962, Proof, mintage figure.

KENNEDY (1964 TO DATE)

Designers: *Gilroy Roberts and Frank Gasparro.* **Weight:** *1964, modern silver Proofs, and 2014 silver—12.50 grams; 1965–1970—11.50 grams; 1971 to date—11.34 grams.* **Composition:** *1964 and modern silver Proofs—.900 silver, .100 copper (net weight .36169 oz. pure silver); 1965–1970—outer layers of .800 silver and .200 copper bonded to inner core of .209 silver, .791 copper (net weight .1479 oz. pure silver); 1971 to date—outer layers of copper-nickel (.750 copper, .250 nickel) bonded to inner core of pure copper; 2014 gold—.9999 gold (net weight .75 oz. pure gold).* **Diameter:** *30.6 mm.* **Edge:** *Reeded.* **Mints:** *Philadelphia, Denver, and San Francisco.*

Circulation Strike   Proof

Mintmark location, 1964, is on the reverse, below the claw holding the branch.

Mintmark location, 1968 to date, is on the obverse, above the date.

Bicentennial variety: **Designers:** *Gilroy Roberts and Seth Huntington.* **Weight:** *Silver clad—11.50 grams; copper-nickel clad—11.34 grams.* **Composition:** *Silver clad—outer layers of .800 silver, .200 copper bonded to inner core of .209 silver, .791 copper (net weight .14792 oz. pure silver); copper-nickel clad—outer layers of copper-nickel (.750 copper, .250 nickel) bonded to inner core of pure copper.* **Diameter:** *30.6 mm.* **Edge:** *Reeded.* **Mints:** *Philadelphia, Denver, and San Francisco.*

Bicentennial variety   Bicentennial variety, Proof

50th Anniversary varieties: **Designers:** *Gilroy Roberts and Frank Gasparro.*
Weight: *Gold—23.33 grams; silver Proofs and Unc.—12.50 grams; copper-nickel clad—11.34 grams.* **Composition:** *Gold—.9999 gold (net weight .75 oz. pure gold); silver—.900 silver, .100 copper (net weight .36169 oz. pure silver); copper-nickel clad—outer layers of copper-nickel (.750 copper, .250 nickel) bonded to inner core of pure copper.* **Diameter:** *30.6 mm.*
Edge: *Reeded.* **Mints:** *Philadelphia, Denver, San Francisco, and West Point.*

50th Anniversary variety, gold

50th Anniversary variety, Uncirculated

50th Anniversary variety, Enhanced Uncirculated

50th Anniversary variety, Proof

50th Anniversary variety, Reverse Proof

History. Kennedy half dollars, minted from 1964 to date, were struck in 90% silver the first year, then with 40% silver content through 1970, and in later years in copper-nickel (except for special silver issues made for collectors and a gold issue in 2014). The obverse, by Chief Engraver Gilroy Roberts, features a portrait of President John F. Kennedy, while the reverse, by Frank Gasparro, displays a modern version of a heraldic eagle.

The 1976 Bicentennial coin shows Philadelphia's Independence Hall, a design by Seth G. Huntington. The obverse was unchanged except for the dual dating 1776–1976. The Bicentennial half dollars were struck during 1975 and 1976 and were used for general circulation as well as being included in Proof and Uncirculated sets for 1975 and 1976.

The year 2014 brought several special issues to mark the 50th year of the Kennedy half dollar: a .9999 fine gold version containing three-quarters of an ounce of pure gold; a Proof in silver; a Reverse Proof in silver; an Enhanced Uncirculated in silver; and an Uncirculated in silver. These coins are dual-dated 1964–2014 on the obverse. They were offered for sale by the U.S. Mint in a number of packages and options.

Striking and Sharpness. Nearly all are well struck. Check the highest points of the hair on the obverse and the highest details on the reverse.

Availability. All issues are common in high circulated grades as well as MS and Proof.

Proofs and Special Mint Set Coins. Proofs of 1964 were struck at the Philadelphia Mint. Those from 1968 to date have been made in San Francisco. All are easily obtained. Most from the 1970s to date have cameo contrast. Special Mint Set (SMS) coins were struck in lieu of Proofs from 1965 to 1967; in some instances, these closely resemble Proofs. Silver Proofs have been struck in recent years, for Silver Proof sets and for the 2014 50th Anniversary issue (which also includes a Reverse Proof). In 1998, a special Matte Proof silver Kennedy half dollar was struck for inclusion in the Robert F. Kennedy commemorative coin set.

Note: Values of common-date silver coins have been based on the current bullion price of silver, $17 per ounce, and may vary with the prevailing spot price.

GRADING STANDARDS

MS-60 to 70 (Mint State). *Obverse:* At MS-60, some abrasion and contact marks are evident on the cheek, and on the hair to the right of the forehead and temple. At MS-63, abrasion is slight at most, and less so for MS-64. An MS-65 coin should display no abrasion or contact marks except under magnification, and MS-66 and higher coins should have none at all. Luster should be full and rich. *Reverse:* Comments apply as for the

1964-D. Graded MS-66.

obverse, except that the highest parts of the eagle at the center are the key places to check.

AU-50, 53, 55, 58 (About Uncirculated). *Obverse:* Light wear is seen on the cheek and higher-relief area of the hair below the part, high above the ear. At AU-58, the luster is extensive but incomplete, especially on the higher parts and in the field. At AU–50 and 53, luster is less. *Reverse:* Light wear is seen on the higher parts of the eagle. At AU–50 and 53 there still is significant luster.

1964. Graded AU-55.

EF-40, 45 (Extremely Fine). *Obverse:* Further wear is seen on the head. More details are gone on the higher parts of the hair. *Reverse:* Further wear is seen on the eagle in particular, but also on other areas in high relief (including the leaves, arrowheads, and clouds).

The Kennedy half dollar is seldom collected in grades lower than EF-40.

1964. Graded EF-45.

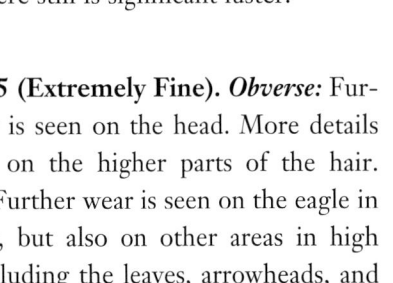

PF-60 to 70 (Proof). *Obverse and Reverse:* Proofs that are extensively cleaned and have many hairlines, or that are dull and grainy, are lower level, such as PF–60 to 62. There are not many of these in the marketplace. With medium hairlines and good reflectivity, assigned grades of PF–63 or 64 are appropriate. With relatively few hairlines a rating of PF-65 can be given. PF-66 should have hairlines so delicate that magnification is needed to see them. Above that, a Proof should be free of any hairlines or other problems.

1964. Graded PF-66.

1964, Doubled Die Obverse
FS-50-1964-102.

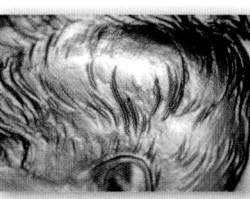

1964, Heavily Accented Hair, Proof
FS-50-1964-401.

1964-D, Doubled Die Obverse
FS-50-1964D-101.

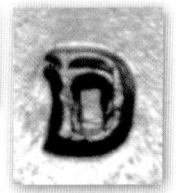

1964-D, Repunched Mintmark
FS-50-1964D-502.

| | Mintage | Cert | Avg | %MS | MS-60 | MS-63 | MS-65 | MS-66 | MS-67 |
							PF-65	PF-67Cam	PF-68DC
1964	273,304,004	9,389	64.5	99%	$11	$12	$20	$75	$750
Auctions: $1,234, MS-67, October 2015; $118, MS-66, January 2015; $34, MS-65, April 2015; $37, MS-64, April 2015									
1964, Doubled Die Obverse (a)	(b)	15	64.5	100%		$35	$65	$250	
Auctions: $69, MS-65, June 2015; $52, MS-64, August 2015; $34, MS-64, August 2015									
1964, Proof	3,950,762	31,246	67.5				$20	$60	$400
Auctions: $4,700, PF-70, August 2015; $4,230, PF-69DCam, August 2015; $364, PF-68DCam, January 2015									
1964, Heavily Accented Hair, Proof ‡ (c)	(d)	11,367	66.5				$45	$375	$10,000
Auctions: $1,645, PF-69, June 2015; $212, PF-67, April 2015; $89, PF-65, September 2015; $40, PF-63, October 2015									
1964-D	156,205,446	5,138	64.4	99%	$11	$12	$20	$150	$950
Auctions: $2,291, MS-67, February 2015; $1,880, MS-67, January 2015; $69, MS-65, January 2015; $60, MS-65, August 2015									
1964-D, Doubled Die Obverse (e)	(f)	32	61.9	69%		$45	$125	$300	
Auctions: $60, MS-66, November 2011; $89, MS-65, June 2015; $36, MS-64, August 2015									
1964-D, Repunched Mintmark (g)	(f)	26	63.4	92%		$45	$150	$800	
Auctions: $130, AU-55, June 2010									

‡ Ranked in the *100 Greatest U.S. Modern Coins.* **a.** There are several doubled-die obverses for the 1964 Kennedy half dollar. The one pictured and listed is FS-50-1964-102. **b.** Included in circulation-strike 1964 mintage figure. **c.** This variety "is identifiable by the enhanced hairline in the central area of the hair, just below the part. However, the easiest way to identify the variety is the weak or broken lower left serif of the I (in LIBERTY)" (*Cherrypickers' Guide to Rare Die Varieties*, sixth edition, volume II). **d.** Included in 1964, Proof, mintage figure. **e.** Doubling on this variety is evident on the date, IN GOD WE TRUST, the designer's initials, and the LI and TY of LIBERTY. "This is a very popular variety. It is extremely rare above MS-65" (*Cherrypickers' Guide to Rare Die Varieties*, sixth edition, volume II). There are other doubled-die obverses for 1964-D. The one pictured and listed is FS-50-1964D-101. **f.** Included in 1964-D mintage figure. **g.** There are several repunched mintmarks for 1964-D. The one listed is FS-50-1964D-502.

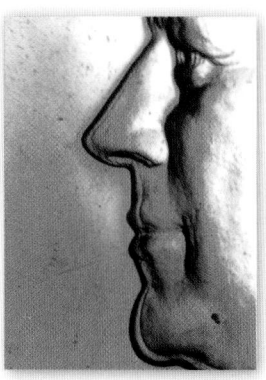
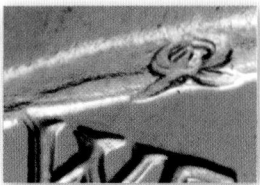
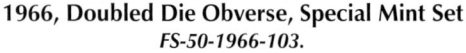
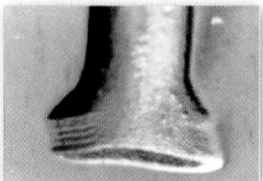

1966, Doubled Die Obverse, Special Mint Set
FS-50-1966-103.

1967, Quintupled Die Obverse, Special Mint Set
FS-50-1967-101.

	Mintage	Cert	Avg	%MS	MS-63	MS-65	MS-66	MS-67
					PF-65	PF-67Cam	PF-68DC	
1965	65,879,366	1,406	64.7	99%	$6	$17	$150	$1,500
Auctions: $470, MS-67, January 2015; $282, MS-67, October 2015; $259, MS-66, July 2015								
1965, Special Mint Set ‡	2,360,000	11,583	66.6			$9	$400	
Auctions: $999, MS-67, September 2016; $2,350, MS-66, October 2015; $823, MS-65, July 2015								
1966	108,984,932	1,386	64.7	98%	$6	$25	$325	$5,000
Auctions: No auction records available.								
1966, Special Mint Set ‡	2,261,583	12,871	66.8			$9	$100	
Auctions: $376, MS-68, September 2015; $1,410, MS-67, October 2015; $94, MS-67, July 2015								
1966, Special Mint Set, Doubled Die Obverse (a)	**(b)**	197	66.7			$65	$250	
Auctions: $176, MS-67, October 2015; $153, MS-67, September 2015; $940, MS-67, August 2016								
1967	295,046,978	1,476	64.5	96%	$6	$22	$150	$1,750
Auctions: $17,625, MS-68, August 2015; $3,525, MS-67, October 2015; $100, MS-67, October 2015								
1967, Special Mint Set ‡	1,863,344	11,949	66.7			$9	$90	
Auctions: $200, PF-68, September 2014; $734, PF-67DCam, November 2014								
1967, Special Mint Set, Quintupled Die Obverse (c)	**(d)**	32	66.4			$135	$600	
Auctions: $19,975, MS-69, August 2016; $176, MS-68, March 2016; $705, MS-67, July 2016								
1968-D	246,951,930	2,702	64.8	99%	$6	$20	$50	$1,000
Auctions: $1,763, MS-67, January 2015; $1,293, MS-67, October 2015; $46, MS-66, April 2015								
1968-S, Proof	3,041,506	7,305	67.7			$8	$22	$50
Auctions: $10,575, PF-70DCam, August 2015; $329, PF-69DCam, August 2015								
1969-D	129,881,800	1,903	64.6	99%	$6	$30	$250	$1,600
Auctions: $1,116, MS-66, March 2016; $30,550, MS-65, August 2016; $823, MS-63, December 2015								
1969-S, Proof	2,934,631	10,568	67.9			$8	$23	$45
Auctions: $224, PF-69DCam, January 2014								
1970-D ‡	2,150,000	4,523	64.3	100%	$20	$42	$215	$775
Auctions: $622, MS-66, November 2016; $235, MS-66, September 2015; $74, MS-65, October 2015								
1970-S, Proof	2,632,810	9,407	67.9			$15	$30	$50
Auctions: $306, PF-69DCam, January 2015; $282, PF-69DCam, January 2015								
1971	155,164,000	220	64.3	95%	$3	$15	$45	$200
Auctions: $170, MS-66, May 2014								
1971-D	302,097,424	981	65.1	96%	$3	$10	$22	$70
Auctions: $235, MS-67, January 2015; $112, MS-67, March 2015; $100, MS-66, July 2015								
1971-S, Proof	3,220,733	5,483	67.8			$4	$20	$100
Auctions: $1,821, PF-67, July 2013								

‡ Ranked in the *100 Greatest U.S. Modern Coins*. **a.** There are several doubled-die obverse varieties of the 1966, Special Mint Set, half dollar. The one listed is FS-50-1966-103, with strong doubling evident on the profile, IN GOD WE TRUST, the eye, the hair, and the designer's initials. **b.** Included in 1966, Special Mint Set, mintage figure. **c.** "A prominent quintupled (at least) spread is evident on RTY of LIBERTY, with strong multiple images on all obverse lettering and portions of the hair" (*Cherrypickers' Guide to Rare Die Varieties*, sixth edition, volume II). **d.** Included in 1967, Special Mint Set, mintage figure.

**1972, Doubled Die
Obverse**
FS-50-1972-101.

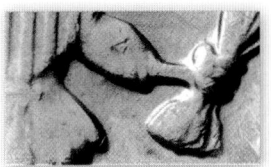

**1972-D, Missing
Designer's Initials**
FS-50-1972D-901.

	Mintage	Cert	Avg	%MS	MS-63	MS-65	MS-66	MS-67
						PF-65	PF-67Cam	PF-68DC
1972	153,180,000	341	64.9	96%	$3	$15	$50	$290
Auctions: $36, MS-66, July 2014								
1972, Doubled Die Obverse (e)	(f)	2	58.0	0%	$140	$165	$225	$450
Auctions: $90, AU-50, March 2011								
1972-D	141,890,000	573	65.2	98%	$3	$10	$23	$100
Auctions: $153, MS-67, November 2015; $94, MS-67, October 2015; $17, MS-66, July 2015								
1972-D, Missing Designer's Initials	(g)	5	58.2	20%	$50	$75	$150	$250
Auctions: $380, EF-45, October 2009								
1972-S, Proof	3,260,996	4,189	68.0			$4	$16	$25
Auctions: $92, PF-69DCam, June 2014								
1973	64,964,000	240	64.7	97%	$3	$15	$45	$155
Auctions: $282, MS-67, August 2014; $153, MS-67, October 2015; $38, MS-66, October 2015								
1973-D	83,171,400	410	65.1	98%	$3	$11	$20	$170
Auctions: $329, MS-67, July 2014; $206, MS-67, October 2015								
1973-S, Proof	2,760,339	825	68.2			$3	$16	$25
Auctions: $2,350, PF-70DCam, December 2011								
1974	201,596,000	203	64.3	96%	$3	$20	$35	$145
Auctions: $3,290, MS-67, October 2015; $2,350, MS-67, August 2014; $37, MS-66, March 2008								
1974-D	79,066,300	307	64.7	94%	$3	$15	$35	$175
Auctions: $382, MS-67, August 2014; $259, MS-67, October 2015; $65, MS-65, June 2014								
1974-D, Doubled Die Obverse ‡ (h)	(i)	434	63.8	95%	$40	$100	$200	$450
Auctions: $411, MS-66, July 2014; $135, MS-65, July 2014; $28, MS-63, October 2014								
1974-S, Proof	2,612,568	872	68.1			$4	$9	$18
Auctions: $4,406, PF-70DCam, March 2014								
1776–1976, Copper-Nickel Clad ‡	234,308,000	457	64.2	95%	$3	$15	$50	$125
Auctions: $1,998, MS-67, August 2014; $2,350, MS-62, February 2014								
1776–1976-D, Copper-Nickel Clad	287,565,248	854	64.9	98%	$3	$15	$25	$375
Auctions: $1,116, MS-67, October 2015; $79, MS-65, August 2015; $999, AU-58, August 2015								
1776–1976-S, Silver Clad	11,000,000	1,403	66.0	100%	$8	$10	$15	$30
Auctions: $217, MS-68, July 2014; $188, MS-68, October 2015; $153, MS-68, September 2015; $141, MS-68, May 2015								
1776–1976-S, Proof, Copper-Nickel Clad	7,059,099	1,976	67.8			$4	$13	$18
Auctions: $3,290, PF-70DCam, January 2015; $2,585, PF-70DCam, July 2015; $2,233, PF-70DCam, August 2015								
1776–1976-S, Proof, Silver Clad (j)	4,000,000	3,545	68.2			$12	$15	$25
Auctions: $881, PF-70DCam, January 2015; $881, PF-70DCam, July 2015; $750, PF-70DCam, August 2015								
1977	43,598,000	386	65.3	99%	$3	$12	$28	$120
Auctions: $1,116, MS-67, November 2014; $764, MS-67, June 2014; $259, MS-67, August 2014								
1977-D	31,449,106	191	65.1	98%	$3	$15	$22	$85
Auctions: $176, MS-67, August 2014; $153, MS-67, October 2015; $21, MS-66, August 2007								
1977-S, Proof	3,251,152	1,338	68.7			$4	$9	$15
Auctions: $141, PF-70DCam, February 2015; $129, PF-70DCam, March 2015; $106, PF-70DCam, August 2015								

‡ Ranked in the *100 Greatest U.S. Modern Coins*. **e.** Doubling is strongly evident on IN GOD WE TRUST and on the date. This variety is very rare above MS-65. **f.** Included in 1972 mintage figure. **g.** Included in 1972-D mintage figure. **h.** Strong doubling is visible on IN GOD WE TRUST, the date, and LIBERTY. **i.** Included in 1974-D mintage figure. **j.** Mintage figures for 1976-S silver coins are approximate. Many were melted in 1982.

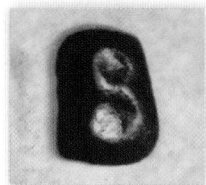

1979-S, Filled S (Type 1), Proof | **1979-S, Clear S (Type 2), Proof** | **1981-S, Rounded S (Type 1), Proof** | **1981-S, Flat S (Type 2), Proof**

	Mintage	Cert	Avg	%MS	MS-63 / PF-65	MS-65 / PF-67Cam	MS-66 / PF-67Cam	MS-67 / PF-68DC
1978	14,350,000	262	65.2	99%	$3	$12	$20	$150
	Auctions: $411, MS-67, August 2014; $212, MS-67, October 2015; $19, MS-66, July 2008							
1978-D	13,765,799	225	65.1	100%	$3	$10	$23	$150
	Auctions: $881, MS-67, August 2014; $18, MS-66, September 2008							
1978-S, Proof	3,127,781	1,487	68.8			$3	$12	$18
	Auctions: $106, PF-70DCam, February 2015; $89, PF-70DCam, June 2015; $84, PF-70DCam, October 2015; $74, PF-70DCam, May 2015							
1979	68,312,000	339	65.2	98%	$3	$10	$25	$150
	Auctions: $423, MS-67, July 2014; $306, MS-67, October 2015; $188, MS-64, September 2015; $764, AU-58, July 2015							
1979-D	15,815,422	299	65.2	100%	$3	$12	$25	$160
	Auctions: $823, MS-67, October 2015; $764, MS-67, August 2014; $11, MS-66, September 2008							
1979-S, Proof, All kinds (k)	3,677,175							
1979-S, Type 1, Proof		2,115	68.9			$3	$11	$14
	Auctions: $200, PF-70DCam, April 2012							
1979-S, Type 2, Proof		1,703	69.0			$25	$27	$30
	Auctions: $588, PF-70DCam, February 2013							
1980-P	44,134,000	368	65.5	99%	$3	$10	$17	$35
	Auctions: $129, MS-67, July 2014; $129, MS-67, October 2015; $42, MS-67, October 2015							
1980-D	33,456,449	192	64.8	98%	$3	$15	$55	$175
	Auctions: $4,935, MS-68, October 2015; $212, MS-67, October 2015; $138, MS-66, September 2008; $65, MS-66, October 2015							
1980-S, Proof	3,554,806	2,089	68.8			$3	$12	$15
	Auctions: $135, PF-70DCam, July 2015; $106, PF-70DCam, November 2015; $100, PF-70DCam, October 2015; $60							
1981-P	29,544,000	339	65.3	99%	$3	$12	$25	$260
	Auctions: No auction records available.							
1981-D	27,839,533	134	64.2	99%	$3	$18	$40	$350
	Auctions: $1,880, MS-67, August 2014; $50, MS-66, June 2014							
1981-S, Proof, All kinds (l)	4,063,083							
1981-S, Type 1, Proof		2,458	68.8			$3	$12	$15
	Auctions: $259, PF-70DCam, June 2013							
1981-S, Type 2, Proof		1,157	68.9			$25	$29	$33
	Auctions: $2,585, PF-70DCam, November 2013							
1982-P	10,819,000	212	64.8	98%	$7	$23	$70	$425
	Auctions: $153, MS-66, October 2015; $74, MS-65, October 2015; $69, MS-65, August 2015; $42, MS-64, October 2015							
1982-D	13,140,102	297	65.3	99%	$7	$18	$40	$325
	Auctions: $3,290, MS-67, November 2013; $999, MS-67, August 2014; $823, MS-67, October 2015; $141, MS-66, October 2015							
1982-S, Proof	3,857,479	1,517	69.0			$4	$12	$15
	Auctions: $529, PF-70DCam, June 2013							

k. The mintmark style of 1979-S, Proof, coins was changed during production, resulting in two distinct types. The scarcer, well-defined Type 2 is easily distinguished from the more common blob-like Type 1. **l.** The mintmark style of the 1981-S, Proof, coins was changed during production, creating two different types. The scarcer Type 2 is not easily distinguished from the common Type 1. Type 2 is flat on the top curve of the S, compared to Type 1, which has a more rounded top. The surface of Type 2 is frosted, and the openings in the loops are slightly larger.

**1988-S, Doubled Die
Obverse, Proof**
FS-50-1988S-101.

	Mintage	Cert	Avg	%MS	MS-63	MS-65	MS-66	MS-67
						PF-65	PF-67Cam	PF-68DC
1983-P	34,139,000	358	65.2	98%	$8	$22	$45	$200
	Auctions: $147, MS-65, April 2014							
1983-D	32,472,244	211	64.9	98%	$7	$15	$30	$330
	Auctions: $1,645, MS-67, August 2014; $646, MS-67, October 2015; $13, MS-66, October 2008							
1983-S, Proof	3,279,126	1,487	69.0			$4	$12	$15
	Auctions: $115, PF-70DCam, August 2013							
1984-P	26,029,000	225	65.5	99%	$3	$12	$38	$250
	Auctions: $1,116, MS-67, August 2014; $940, MS-67, October 2015; $98, MS-66, September 2008							
1984-D	26,262,158	211	65.1	100%	$3	$17	$40	$350
	Auctions: $3,290, MS-67, October 2015; $2,820, MS-67, August 2014; $11, MS-66, September 2008							
1984-S, Proof	3,065,110	1,086	69.0			$4	$12	$15
	Auctions: $382, PF-70DCam, June 2013							
1985-P	18,706,962	271	65.9	100%	$5	$15	$25	$90
	Auctions: $123, MS-67, July 2014; $62, MS-67, October 2015							
1985-D	19,814,034	378	66.1	100%	$5	$12	$15	$45
	Auctions: $159, MS-67, July 2014; $112, MS-67, October 2015							
1985-S, Proof	3,362,821	1,286	69.0			$4	$12	$15
	Auctions: $135, PF-70DCam, November 2015; $106, PF-70DCam, August 2013							
1986-P	13,107,633	297	66.0	100%	$6	$13	$28	$70
	Auctions: $282, MS-67, July 2014; $118, MS-67, October 2015; $112, MS-67, August 2015							
1986-D	15,336,145	396	66.1	100%	$5	$11	$20	$45
	Auctions: $57, MS-67, July 2014							
1986-S, Proof	3,010,497	976	69.0			$4	$12	$15
	Auctions: $106, PF-70DCam, October 2015; $94, PF-70DCam, March 2015; $94, PF-70DCam, July 2015							
1987-P ‡ (m)	2,890,758	464	65.6	100%	$5	$15	$30	$100
	Auctions: $4,113, MS-68, October 2015; $3,290, MS-68, August 2014; $223, MS-67, October 2015							
1987-D ‡ (m)	2,890,758	618	66.0	100%	$5	$12	$23	$50
	Auctions: $3,055, MS-68, October 2015; $2,585, MS-68, August 2014; $21, MS-67, October 2008							
1987-S, Proof	4,227,728	1,586	69.1			$4	$12	$15
	Auctions: $96, PF-70DCam, August 2013							
1988-P	13,626,000	223	65.8	100%	$5	$15	$28	$90
	Auctions: $282, MS-67, July 2014; $153, MS-67, October 2015							
1988-D	12,000,096	357	66.2	100%	$4	$12	$25	$40
	Auctions: $57, MS-67, July 2014							
1988-S, Proof	3,262,948	1,139	69.1			$4	$12	$15
	Auctions: $113, PF-70DCam, May 2013							
1988-S, Doubled Die Obverse, Proof (n)	(o)	12	68.8			$110	$160	
	Auctions: $260, PF-68UCam, February 2011							

‡ Ranked in the *100 Greatest U.S. Modern Coins*. **m.** Not issued for circulation; included with Mint and Souvenir sets. **n.** Clear doubling is visible on IN GOD WE TRUST, the date, and the mintmark. Some doubling is also evident on LIBERTY and the mintmark. **o.** Included in 1988-S, Proof, mintage figure.

	Mintage	Cert	Avg	%MS	MS-63	MS-65	MS-66	MS-67
						PF-65	PF-67Cam	PF-68DC
1989-P	24,542,000	277	65.7	99%	$4	$15	$23	$90
	Auctions: $282, MS-67, October 2015; $259, MS-67, July 2014							
1989-D	23,000,216	347	66.0	100%	$3	$11	$18	$60
	Auctions: $129, MS-67, July 2014; $74, MS-67, October 2015							
1989-S, Proof	3,220,194	1,049	69.0			$5	$12	$20
	Auctions: $123, PF-70DCam, May 2013							
1990-P	22,278,000	196	65.8	100%	$3	$11	$22	$150
	Auctions: $259, MS-67, October 2015; $200, MS-66, November 2015; $153, MS-66, November 2015; $106, MS-65, November 2014							
1990-D	20,096,242	236	65.6	100%	$3	$16	$32	$200
	Auctions: $31, MS-66, October 2008							
1990-S, Proof	3,299,559	1,204	69.1			$5	$12	$18
	Auctions: $82, PF-70DCam, May 2013							
1991-P	14,874,000	236	66.0	100%	$4	$12	$25	$200
	Auctions: $217, MS-67, July 2014; $165, MS-67, October 2015							
1991-D	15,054,678	260	65.8	100%	$4	$15	$30	$300
	Auctions: $920, MS-67, September 2008; $329, MS-67, August 2014; $294, MS-67, October 2015							
1991-S, Proof	2,867,787	1,104	69.3			$10	$14	$20
	Auctions: $68, PF-70DCam, July 2013							
1992-P	17,628,000	211	65.9	100%	$3	$11	$22	$25
	Auctions: $2,350, MS-68, August 2014; $11, MS-67, October 2008							
1992-D	17,000,106	156	66.1	100%	$3	$10	$18	$30
	Auctions: $147, MS-67, August 2014; $30, MS-67, August 2014; $46, MS-67, July 2014							
1992-S, Proof	2,858,981	706	69.2			$5	$14	$20
	Auctions: $35, PF-70DCam, May 2013							
1992-S, Proof, Silver	1,317,579	2,363	69.1			$17	$20	$25
	Auctions: $92, PF-70DCam, July 2013							
1993-P	15,510,000	348	66.4	99%	$3	$11	$20	$40
	Auctions: $58, MS-67, July 2014							
1993-D	15,000,006	619	66.0	100%	$3	$10	$22	$60
	Auctions: $2,585, MS-68, August 2014; $11, MS-66, October 2008							
1993-S, Proof	2,633,439	766	69.3			$8	$17	$23
	Auctions: $31, PF-70DCam, May 2013							
1993-S, Proof, Silver	761,353	1,796	69.1			$27	$30	$37
	Auctions: $99, PF-70DCam, May 2014							
1994-P	23,718,000	431	65.8	100%	$3	$10	$20	$55
	Auctions: $2,115, MS-68, August 2014; $10, MS-66, October 2008							
1994-D	23,828,110	205	65.8	100%	$3	$10	$20	$75
	Auctions: $364, MS-67, July 2014; $141, MS-67, October 2015							
1994-S, Proof	2,484,594	728	69.3			$8	$17	$23
	Auctions: $45, PF-70DCam, May 2013							
1994-S, Proof, Silver	785,329	1,711	69.1			$26	$33	$35
	Auctions: $206, PF-70DCam, February 2013							
1995-P	26,496,000	251	66.1	99%	$3	$10	$17	$40
	Auctions: $55, MS-67, July 2014							
1995-D	26,288,000	308	66.2	100%	$3	$10	$20	$50
	Auctions: $2,585, MS-68, August 2014; $13, MS-67, October 2008							
1995-S, Proof	2,117,496	674	69.3			$16	$20	$25
	Auctions: $66, PF-70DCam, August 2013							
1995-S, Proof, Silver ‡	679,985	2,039	69.1			$38	$40	$45
	Auctions: $135, PF-70DCam, May 2014							

‡ Ranked in the *100 Greatest U.S. Modern Coins.*

	Mintage	Cert	Avg	%MS	MS-63	MS-65	MS-66	MS-67
						PF-65	PF-67Cam	PF-68DC
1996-P	24,442,000	354	66.2	99%	$3	$10	$17	$35
	Auctions: $247, MS-68, July 2014; $165, MS-68, October 2015							
1996-D	24,744,000	348	66.0	99%	$3	$10	$17	$35
	Auctions: $1,293, MS-68, August 2014; $999, MS-68, January 2015; $11, MS-67, October 2008							
1996-S, Proof	1,750,244	666	69.2			$10	$15	$22
	Auctions: $66, PF-70DCam, August 2013							
1996-S, Proof, Silver	775,021	1,685	69.1			$30	$35	$40
	Auctions: $135, PF-70DCam, August 2013							
1997-P	20,882,000	174	66.2	99%	$3	$12	$30	$80
	Auctions: $60, MS-67, July 2014							
1997-D	19,876,000	281	65.9	100%	$3	$13	$30	$90
	Auctions: $646, MS-68, June 2013; $123, MS-67, July 2014; $79, MS-67, October 2015							
1997-S, Proof	2,055,000	575	69.3			$12	$20	$25
	Auctions: $76, PF-70DCam, August 2013							
1997-S, Proof, Silver	741,678	1,779	69.2			$30	$40	$50
	Auctions: $96, PF-70DCam, August 2013							
1998-P	15,646,000	220	66.3	100%	$3	$15	$35	$70
	Auctions: $76, MS-67, July 2014							
1998-D	15,064,000	210	65.8	100%	$3	$11	$20	$70
	Auctions: $62, MS-67, July 2014							
1998-S, Proof	2,086,507	685	69.4			$10	$17	$23
	Auctions: $56, PF-70DCam, August 2013							
1998-S, Proof, Silver	878,792	2,008	69.3			$18	$25	$35
	Auctions: $88, PF-70DCam, August 2013							
1998-S, Matte Finish Proof, Silver ‡ (p)	*62,000*	2,249	69.2			$125		
	Auctions: $113, PF-69, November 2014; $170, PF-69, March 2015; $165, PF-69, March 2015							
1999-P	8,900,000	243	66.4	100%	$3	$10	$20	$30
	Auctions: $2,115, MS-69, June 2013; $823, MS-68, August 2014							
1999-D	10,682,000	247	66.2	100%	$3	$10	$16	$23
	Auctions: $1,998, MS-68, August 2014; $10, MS-66, October 2008							
1999-S, Proof	2,543,401	3,436	69.3			$13	$16	$20
	Auctions: $90, PF-70DCam, May 2013							
1999-S, Proof, Silver	804,565	5,731	69.1			$25	$30	$32
	Auctions: $147, PF-70DCam, August 2013							
2000-P	22,600,000	134	66.0	100%	$3	$10	$17	$35
	Auctions: $764, MS-68, August 2014; $48, MS-67, October 2008							
2000-D	19,466,000	229	66.0	100%	$3	$10	$20	$40
	Auctions: $123, MS-67, July 2014; $94, MS-67, October 2015							
2000-S, Proof	3,082,483	2,712	69.3			$5	$12	$16
	Auctions: $58, PF-70DCam, May 2013							
2000-S, Proof, Silver	965,421	6,556	69.2			$14	$18	$20
	Auctions: $78, PF-70DCam, May 2013							
2001-P	21,200,000	407	65.5	100%	$3	$8	$15	$28
	Auctions: $176, MS-68, September 2015; $60, MS-68, October 2015							
2001-D	19,504,000	451	65.8	100%	$3	$8	$13	$28
	Auctions: $247, MS-68, July 2014; $153, MS-68, October 2015							
2001-S, Proof	2,294,909	2,061	69.3			$6	$10	$13
	Auctions: $76, PF-70DCam, May 2013							
2001-S, Proof, Silver	889,697	4,931	69.2			$15	$21	$23
	Auctions: $90, PF-70DCam, May 2013							

‡ Ranked in the *100 Greatest U.S. Modern Coins*. **p.** Minted for inclusion in the Robert F. Kennedy commemorative set (along with an RFK commemorative dollar).

	Mintage	Cert	Avg	%MS	MS-63 / PF-65	MS-65 / PF-67Cam	MS-66 / PF-68DC	MS-67
2002-P (q)	3,100,000	225	65.6	100%	$3	$8	$15	$30
Auctions: $182, MS-68, June 2014; $135, MS-68, January 2015; $129, MS-68, October 2015; $118, MS-68, July 2014								
2002-D (q)	2,500,000	240	65.8	100%	$3	$9	$20	$40
Auctions: $2,115, MS-69, June 2013								
2002-S, Proof	2,319,766	2,103	69.2			$5	$13	$16
Auctions: $60, PF-70DCam, May 2013								
2002-S, Proof, Silver	892,229	5,089	69.3			$14	$18	$20
Auctions: $61, PF-70DCam, May 2013								
2003-P (q)	2,500,000	279	65.8	100%	$3	$9	$20	$30
Auctions: $59, MS-67, July 2014								
2003-D (q)	2,500,000	262	65.8	100%	$3	$8	$16	$25
Auctions: $51, MS-67, July 2014								
2003-S, Proof	2,172,684	4,126	69.2			$5	$12	$16
Auctions: $62, PF-70DCam, August 2015; $35, PF-70DCam, May 2013								
2003-S, Proof, Silver	1,125,755	6,033	69.2			$14	$18	$20
Auctions: $76, PF-70DCam, November 2014; $82, PF-70DCam, May 2014								
2004-P (q)	2,900,000	254	66.2	100%	$3	$8	$17	$30
Auctions: $100, MS-67, October 2015; $86, MS-67, July 2014								
2004-D (q)	2,900,000	404	66.3	100%	$3	$8	$16	$25
Auctions: $423, MS-68, July 2014; $235, MS-68, October 2015								
2004-S, Proof	1,789,488	1,883	69.2			$13	$17	$24
Auctions: $66, PF-70DCam, August 2013								
2004-S, Proof, Silver	1,175,934	5,879	69.2			$20	$22	$23
Auctions: $69, PF-70DCam, January 2013								
2005-P (q)	3,800,000	232	66.0	100%	$4	$18	$25	$75
Auctions: $470, MS-67, October 2015; $42, MS-66, July 2014								
2005-P, Satin Finish (q)	1,160,000	2,518	67.0	100%	$2	$5	$8	$15
Auctions: No auction records available.								
2005-D (q)	3,500,000	265	66.3	100%	$4	$15	$23	$40
Auctions: $1,116, MS-68, August 2014; $11, MS-66, October 2008								
2005-D, Satin Finish (q)	1,160,000	2,189	66.7	100%	$2	$5	$8	$15
Auctions: No auction records available.								
2005-S, Proof	2,275,000	7,128	69.2			$5	$12	$16
Auctions: $66, PF-70DCam, August 2013								
2005-S, Proof, Silver	1,069,679	7,291	69.3			$12	$18	$20
Auctions: $74, PF-70DCam, January 2013								
2006-P (q)	2,400,000	204	66.7	100%	$2	$9	$22	$26
Auctions: $42, MS-69, January 2009; $764, MS-68, August 2014; $376, MS-68, October 2015								
2006-P, Satin Finish (q)	847,361	1,371	66.8	100%	$2	$5	$8	$15
Auctions: No auction records available.								
2006-D (q)	2,000,000	197	66.3	100%	$2	$7	$15	$28
Auctions: $82, MS-67, July 2014; $60, MS-67, October 2015								
2006-D, Satin Finish (q)	847,361	1,363	66.8	100%	$2	$5	$8	$15
Auctions: No auction records available.								
2006-S, Proof	2,000,428	2,780	69.3			$5	$12	$16
Auctions: $46, PF-70DCam, August 2013								
2006-S, Proof, Silver	1,054,008	4,165	69.4			$12	$18	$20
Auctions: $76, PF-70DCam, August 2013								
2007-P (q)	2,400,000	173	66.5	100%	$2	$6	$11	$17
Auctions: $270, MS-68, July 2014; $100, MS-68, October 2015								

q. Not issued for circulation. Sold directly to the public in rolls and small bags.

	Mintage	Cert	Avg	%MS	MS-63 / PF-65	MS-65 / PF-67Cam	MS-66 / PF-67Cam	MS-67 / PF-68DC
2007-P, Satin Finish (q)	895,628	360	66.8	100%	$2	$5	$8	$15
Auctions: No auction records available.								
2007-D (q)	2,400,000	137	66.1	100%	$2	$6	$15	$30
Auctions: $15, MS-69, January 2009								
2007-D, Satin Finish (q)	895,628	382	66.9	100%	$2	$5	$8	$15
Auctions: No auction records available.								
2007-S, Proof	1,702,116	2,849	69.3			$5	$12	$16
Auctions: $64, PF-70DCam, January 2013								
2007-S, Proof, Silver	875,050	3,719	69.4			$14	$19	$22
Auctions: $86, PF-70DCam, August 2013								
2008-P (q)	1,700,000	213	66.3	100%	$2	$8	$20	$40
Auctions: $1,410, MS-68, August 2014; $12, SP-67, April 2012								
2008-P, Satin Finish (q)	745,464	100	67.1	100%	$2	$5	$8	$15
Auctions: No auction records available.								
2008-D (q)	1,700,000	104	65.8	100%	$2	$8	$20	$45
Auctions: $24, MS-66, June 2011								
2008-D, Satin Finish (q)	745,464	77	67.0	100%	$2	$5	$8	$15
Auctions: No auction records available.								
2008-S, Proof	1,405,674	1,793	69.3			$5	$12	$16
Auctions: $71, PF-70DCam, November 2013								
2008-S, Proof, Silver	763,887	3,781	69.4			$14	$20	$23
Auctions: $66, PF-70DCam, August 2013								
2009-P (q)	1,900,000	191	66.2	100%	$2	$6	$12	$25
Auctions: $1,998, MS-68, August 2014; $6, MS-66, November 2011								
2009-P, Satin Finish (q)	784,614	236	67.1	100%	$2	$5	$8	$15
Auctions: No auction records available.								
2009-D (q)	1,900,000	148	66.2	100%	$2	$6	$12	$30
Auctions: $27, MS-66, February 2012								
2009-D, Satin Finish (q)	784,614	272	67.5	100%	$2	$5	$8	$15
Auctions: No auction records available.								
2009-S, Proof	1,482,502	3,626	69.3			$5	$12	$16
Auctions: $31, PF-70DCam, May 2013								
2009-S, Proof, Silver	697,365	4,592	69.3			$14	$18	$20
Auctions: $41, PF-70DCam, May 2013								
2010-P (q)	1,800,000	256	66.6	100%	$2	$6	$12	$25
Auctions: $23, MS-67, July 2014								
2010-P, Satin Finish (q)	583,897	244	67.1	100%	$2	$5	$8	$15
Auctions: No auction records available.								
2010-D (q)	1,700,000	174	66.3	100%	$2	$6	$12	$30
Auctions: $3,995, MS-68, August 2015; $101, MS-67, July 2014; $48, MS-67, October 2015								
2010-D, Satin Finish (q)	583,897	330	67.6	100%	$2	$5	$8	$15
Auctions: No auction records available.								
2010-S, Proof	1,103,815	1,294	69.3			$5	$12	$16
Auctions: $48, PF-70DCam, August 2013								
2010-S, Proof, Silver	585,401	4,205	69.6			$14	$18	$20
Auctions: $48, PF-70DCam, May 2013								
2011-P (q)	1,750,000	465	66.7	100%	$2	$6	$12	$25
Auctions: $229, MS-68, July 2014; $176, MS-68, October 2015								
2011-D (q)	1,700,000	401	66.5	100%	$2	$6	$12	$25
Auctions: $1,116, MS-68, August 2014; $1,058, MS-68, August 2014; $33, MS-67, January 2012								

q. Not issued for circulation. Sold directly to the public in rolls and small bags.

	Mintage	Cert	Avg	%MS	MS-63	MS-65 PF-65	MS-66 PF-67Cam	MS-67 PF-68DC
2011-S, Proof	1,098,835	2,318	69.4			$5	$12	$16
Auctions: $21, PF-70UCam, March 2012								
2011-S, Proof, Silver	574,175	4,990	69.7			$14	$18	$20
Auctions: $39, PF-70DCam, August 2014; $36, PF-70DCam, April 2012								
2012-P (q)	1,800,000	247	66.8	100%	$2	$6	$12	$25
Auctions: No auction records available.								
2012-D (q)	1,700,000	285	66.7	100%	$2	$6	$12	$25
Auctions: No auction records available.								
2012-S, Proof	843,705	1,895	69.3			$5	$12	$16
Auctions: $51, PF-70DCam, May 2013								
2012-S, Proof, Silver	445,612	2,067	69.6			$14	$18	$20
Auctions: No auction records available.								
2013-P (q)	5,000,000	298	66.8	100%	$2	$6	$12	$25
Auctions: No auction records available.								
2013-D (q)	4,600,000	326	66.9	100%	$2	$6	$12	$25
Auctions: No auction records available.								
2013-S, Proof	*854,785*	1,906	69.3			$5	$12	$16
Auctions: No auction records available.								
2013-S, Proof, Silver	467,691	2,232	69.6			$14	$18	$20
Auctions: No auction records available.								
2014-P (q)	2,500,000	415	66.7	100%	$2	$4	$10	$20
Auctions: No auction records available.								
2014-P, High Relief (r)		9,781	67.0	100%				
2014-P, Proof, Silver (s)	*219,173*	16,127	69.6			$15	$30	$35
Auctions: No auction records available.								
2014-D (q)	*2,100,000*	646	67.2	100%	$2	$4	$10	$20
Auctions: No auction records available.								
2014-D, High Relief (r)		9,331	66.9	100%				
2014-D, Silver (s)	*219,173*	16,031	69.7	100%	$10	$15	$20	$23
Auctions: No auction records available.								
2014-S, Enhanced Uncirculated, Silver (s)	*219,173*	16,978	69.8	100%	$10	$15	$20	$25
Auctions: No auction records available.								
2014-S, Proof	*767,977*	2,567	69.3			$15	$20	$19
Auctions: No auction records available.								
2014-S, Proof, Silver	472,107	5,185	69.5			$15	$20	$23
Auctions: No auction records available.								
2014-W, Reverse Proof, Silver (s)	*219,173*	16,491	69.7			$20	$25	$35
Auctions: No auction records available.								
2014-W, 50th Anniversary, Proof, Gold (t)	73,772	10,132	69.7			$850	$900	$1,100
Auctions: No auction records available.								

q. Not issued for circulation. Sold directly to the public in rolls and small bags. **r.** To celebrate the 50th anniversary of the Kennedy half dollar, in 2014 the U.S. Mint issued an Uncirculated two-coin set featuring a Kennedy half dollar from Philadelphia and one from Denver. **s.** Featured in the 2014 half dollar silver-coin collection released by the U.S. Mint to commemorate the 50th anniversary of the Kennedy half dollar. **t.** First gold half dollar offered by the U.S. Mint. It commemorates the 50th anniversary of the first release of the Kennedy half dollar in 1964. Dual-dated 1964–2014.

	Mintage	Cert	Avg	%MS	MS-63	MS-65	MS-66	MS-67
					PF-65	PF-67Cam	PF-68DC
2015-P (q)	3,990,229	416	66.3	100%	$2	$6	$12	$25
	Auctions: No auction records available.							
2015-D (q)	3,182,749	521	66.4	100%	$2	$6	$12	$25
	Auctions: No auction records available.							
2015-S, Proof	662,854	2,917	69.4			$5	$12	$16
	Auctions: No auction records available.							
2015-S, Proof, Silver	387,310	3,034	69.5			$14	$18	$20
	Auctions: No auction records available.							

q. Not issued for circulation. Sold directly to the public in rolls and small bags.

In 2016 a special .9999 fine gold striking of Adolf A. Weinman's Liberty Walking half dollar was created to celebrate the 100th anniversary of its introduction. It is smaller than the silver strikings, with a diameter of 27 mm and weighing 15.552 grams. Struck at West Point, it has a reeded edge. Similar strikings were made for the 1916 dime and quarter designs.

	Mintage	Cert	Avg	%MS	SP-67	SP-70
2016-W, Liberty Walking Centennial Gold Coin	65,512				$875	$1,100

Normally scheduled production of clad and silver Kennedy half dollars, in the same standards and specifications as previously, continued in 2016 and beyond, and was not disrupted by the gold Liberty Walking half dollar.

	Mintage	Cert	Avg	%MS	MS-63	MS-65	MS-66	MS-67
					PF-65	PF-67Cam	PF-68DC
2016-P (q)	3,535,879	64	67.0	100%	$2	$6	$12	$25
2016-D (q)	2,866,439	0	n/a		$2	$6	$12	$25
2016-S, Proof	641,775	891	69.5			$5	$12	$16
2016-S, Proof, Silver	419,256	2,580	69.6			$14	$18	$20
2017-P (q)	2,902,686				$2	$6	$12	$25
2017-D (q)	3,594,046				$2	$6	$12	$25
2017-S, Enhanced Unc.						$5	$12	$16
2017-S, Proof	592,890					$5	$12	$16
2017-S, Proof, Silver	382,453					$14	$18	$20
2018-P (q)								
2018-D (q)								
2018-S, Proof								
2018-S, Proof, Silver								

q. Not issued for circulation. Sold directly to the public in rolls and small bags.

Silver Dollars
1794–1935

AN OVERVIEW OF SILVER DOLLARS

The silver dollar was authorized by Congress on April 2, 1792, and first coined in 1794. This denomination includes some of the most popular series in American numismatics.

The first coin of the denomination, the Flowing Hair dollar, is easy enough to obtain (given the proper budget) in grades from VF through low Mint State. Striking usually ranges from poor to barely acceptable, and adjustment marks (from an overweight planchet being filed down to correct weight) are often seen. Accordingly, careful examination is needed to find a good example.

The silver dollar with the Draped Bust obverse in combination with the Small Eagle reverse was made from 1795 through 1798, with most examples being dated 1796 or 1797. Today both the 1796 and 1797 exist in about the same numbers. Although mintage figures refer to the quantities produced in the given calendar year, these do not necessarily refer to the dates on the coins themselves, as Mint workers would use coinage dies into the next calendar year. Silver dollars of this type are fairly scarce. Sharpness of strike presents a challenge to the collector, and usually there are weaknesses in details, particularly on the reverse eagle.

The 1798 to 1804 type features a Draped Bust obverse and Heraldic Eagle reverse. Many such coins exist, mostly in grades from VF through lower Mint State levels. Striking can be indifferent, but the population of surviving coins is such that collectors have more to choose from, and can select for quality.

The Gobrecht silver dollars of 1836 (starless obverse, stars on reverse, plain edge) and 1839 (stars on obverse, starless reverse, reeded edge) present a special challenge in the formation of a type set. For quite a few years these were considered by numismatists to be *patterns*, and thus anyone forming a type set of regular-issue U.S. coins did not have to notice them. However, in recent decades, research by R.W. Julian (in particular), Walter Breen, and others, has revealed that the vast majority of 1836 and 1839 silver dollars originally produced were put into circulation at face value. Accordingly, they were coins of the realm at the time, were spent as currency, and are deserving of a place among regular coinage types.

The 1836 Gobrecht dollar is easy enough to find in today's marketplace, although expensive. The original production amounted to 1,600 coins, to which an unknown number of restrikes can be added. The main problem arises with the 1839, made only to the extent of 300 pieces. Those that exist today nearly always have abundant signs of circulation. This is the rarest of all major U.S. coin design types, even outclassing the 1796–1797 half dollar and the 1808 quarter eagle.

In 1840 the regular Liberty Seated dollar made its appearance, with the reverse depicting a perched eagle holding an olive branch and arrows. This style was continued through 1873, with minor modifications over the years; for example, in 1866 the motto IN GOD WE TRUST was added to the reverse.

Generally, Liberty Seated dollars can be easily enough found in circulated grades from VF up, as well as low Mint State levels. MS-63 and higher pieces are in the minority, particularly of the 1840–1865 type.

Morgan silver dollars, made by the hundreds of millions from 1878 through 1921, are easily found, with the 1881-S being at once the most common of all varieties existing today in gem condition and also usually seen with sharp strike and nice appearance.

Peace silver dollars of 1921 through 1935 exist in large quantities. Some collectors select the first year of issue, 1921, as a separate type, as the design is in high relief. The 1921 is plentiful in Mint State, but rarely is found sharply struck at the obverse and reverse center. Later Peace dollars with shallow relief abound in MS-63 and finer grades, although strike quality can be a problem.

The Peace dollar was the last of the United States' circulating .900 fine silver dollars. One final type of dollar coin was produced in the large 38.1 mm format—the Eisenhower dollar, often colloquially called a "silver dollar" even though its regular issues were made of copper and nickel. Since the Eisenhower dollar, U.S. coins of this denomination have been produced in smaller diameters and in base metals. These modern dollars are explored in detail in the next chapter. The U.S. Mint has also produced various *commemorative* silver dollars from 1900 to date, and the one-ounce American Silver Eagle bullion coin has a denomination of one dollar. These coins are covered in the Commemoratives and Bullion sections, respectively.

FOR THE COLLECTOR AND INVESTOR: SILVER DOLLARS AS A SPECIALTY

Generally, silver dollars of the 1794–1803 years are collected by dates and major types.

Although the 1794, of which an estimated 135 or so exist today, is famous and expensive, other varieties are eminently affordable in such grades as VF and EF. Beyond the listings herein there is a rich panorama of die varieties, most extensively delineated in the 1993 two-volume study *Silver Dollars and Trade Dollars of the United States: A Complete Encyclopedia*. This built upon earlier works, including J.W. Haseltine's *Type Table of United States Dollars, Half Dollars and Quarter Dollars*, and, especially, the long-term standard work by M.H. Bolender, *The United States Early Silver Dollars from 1794 to 1803*. In many instances among early dollars the number of aficionados desiring a particularly rare die combination may be even smaller than the population of coins available—with the result that not much premium has to be paid.

The 1804 silver dollar is a study in itself. None were actually produced in the year 1804. Several were made in 1834 as presentation pieces for foreign dignitaries, and even later examples were made for private collectors. Only a handful exist of this classic rarity, the "King of American Coins."

After 1803 it is a long jump to 1836, when silver dollars (of the Gobrecht design) were again struck for circulation. In 1839 more Gobrecht dollars were struck, with the design modified. In addition to the listings in this book are a number of other die combinations, edge and metal varieties, etc., including pieces of the year 1838, most of which are pattern restrikes (studied in *United States Pattern Coins*). These are avidly desired and collected.

Forming a specialized collection of Liberty Seated dollars from 1840 through 1873 has been a pursuit of many collectors over the years. Generally, the Philadelphia Mint dates are available without difficulty, although the 1851 and 1852 are typically acquired as Proof restrikes—originals of both years being prohibitively rare. Most difficult to find in higher grades are coins of the branch mints, including the famous 1870-S, of which only 10 are known to exist and for which no mintage quantity figure was ever listed in official reports. Branch-mint pieces, starting with the 1846-O, were placed into circulation and used extensively. Beginning in 1870, dollars of this type were struck at Carson City; these also are seen with evidence of circulation. The only exceptions to this are certain dollars of 1859-O and 1860-O which turned up in very "baggy" Mint State preservation (showing contact marks from other coins) among Treasury hoards, to the extent of several thousand pieces of both dates combined.

Morgan silver dollars from 1878 through 1921 are one of the most active and popular series in American numismatics. Approximately 100 different major varieties can be collected, although certain unusual varieties (not basic dates and mintmarks) can be dropped from a collection or added as desired. The vast majority of Morgan dollars can be found in Mint State. When these coins were first minted there was little need for them in circulation, and hundreds of millions of coins piled up in Treasury and other vaults. Although many were melted in 1918, enough remained that untold millions exist today in the hands of the public.

Varieties such as the 1881-S are common and are normally seen in high grades with sharp strike, but others with high mintages, the 1886-O and 1896-O being examples, are quite rare in MS-63 and finer, and when seen usually have rather poor eye appeal. Accordingly, quite a bit of discernment is recommended for the savvy collector.

Peace silver dollars, minted from 1921 to 1935, include the High Relief style of 1921, and the shallow-relief motif of 1922 to 1935. A basic set of 24 different dates and mintmarks is easily enough obtained, including in Mint State. The most elusive is the 1934-S.

Anthony de Francisci, designer of the Peace dollar, used his wife Teresa (ranked in the *100 Greatest Women on Coins*) as the model for his Miss Liberty.

FLOWING HAIR (1794–1795)

Engraver: *Robert Scot.* **Weight:** *26.96 grams.* **Composition:** *.900 silver, .100 copper (net weight 0.78011 oz. pure silver).* **Diameter:** *Approximately 39–40 mm.* **Edge:** *HUNDRED CENTS ONE DOLLAR OR UNIT with decorations between words.* **Mint:** *Philadelphia.*

Bowers-Borckardt–24, Bolender-13.

History. The first U.S. silver dollars were of the Flowing Hair design. In 1794 only 1,758 were released for circulation (slightly fewer than were struck), and the next year nearly 100 times that amount. These coins were popular in their time and circulated for decades afterward. Many were used in international trade, particularly in the Caribbean.

Striking and Sharpness. On the obverse, check the hair details. It is essential to check the die variety, as certain varieties were struck with very little detail at the center. Accordingly, high-grade examples can appear to be well worn on the hair. Check the star centers, as well. On the reverse, check the breast and wings of the eagle. All 1794 dollars are lightly struck at the lower left of the obverse (often at portions of the date) and to a lesser extent the corresponding part of the reverse. Many coins of both dates have planchet adjustment marks (from overweight blanks being filed down to proper weight before striking), often heavy and sometimes even disfiguring; these are not noted by the certification services. Expect weakness in some areas on dollars of this type; a coin with Full Details on both sides is virtually unheard of. Sharp striking and excellent eye appeal add to the value dramatically. These coins are very difficult to find problem-free, even in MS.

Availability. The 1794 is rare in all grades, with an estimated 125 to 135 known, including a handful in MS. The 1795 is easily available, with an estimated 4,000 to 7,500 still existing, although some die varieties range from scarce to rare. Many if not most have been dipped at one time or another, and many have been retoned, often satisfactorily. The existence of *any* luster is an exception between EF-40 and AU-58. MS coins are quite scarce (perhaps 150 to 250 existing, most dated 1795), especially at MS-63 or above.

Varieties listed herein are those most significant to collectors, but numerous minor variations may be found because each of the early dies was made individually. (Values of varieties not listed in this guide depend on collector interest and demand.) Blanks were weighed before the dollars were struck and overweight pieces were filed to remove excess silver. Coins with old adjustment marks from this filing process may be worth less than the values shown here. Some Flowing Hair dollars were weight-adjusted through insertion of a small (8 mm) silver plug in the center of the blank planchet before the coin was struck.

GRADING STANDARDS

MS-60 to 70 (Mint State). *Obverse:* At MS-60, some abrasion and contact marks are evident, most noticeably on the cheek and in the fields. Luster is present, but may be dull or lifeless, and interrupted in patches. At MS-63, contact marks are very few, and abrasion is light and not obvious. An MS-65 coin has little or, better yet, no abrasion, and contact marks are minute. Luster should be full

**1794; BB-1, Bolender-1. Graded MS-64.
Fully brilliant and highly lustrous.**

and rich. Coins graded above MS-65 are more theoretical than actual for this type—but they do exist, and are defined by having fewer marks as perfection is approached. *Reverse:* Comments apply as for the obverse, except that abrasion and contact marks are most noticeable on the eagle at the center, although most dollars of this type are lightly struck in the higher points of that area. The field area is small and is protected by lettering and the wreath and in any given grade shows fewer marks than on the obverse.

Illustrated coin: Like all 1794 dollars, this coin is weak at the left obverse and the corresponding part of the reverse. Planchet flaws are seen at stars 3 and 5. The center obverse is very well struck.

AU-50, 53, 55, 58 (About Uncirculated). *Obverse:* Light wear is seen on the hair area immediately to the left of the face and neck (except for those flatly struck there), on the cheek, and on the top of the neck truncation, more so at AU-50 than at AU–53 or 55. An AU-58 coin has minimal traces of wear. An AU-50 coin has luster in protected areas among the stars and letters, with little luster in the open fields or the portrait. Some certified coins have

1795, Two Leaves; BB-21, Bolender-1. Graded AU-58.

virtually no luster, but are considered high quality in other aspects. At AU-58, most luster is partially present in the fields. On any high-grade dollar, luster is often a better key to grading than is the appearance of wear. *Reverse:* Light wear is seen on the eagle's body and the upper edges of the wings. At AU-50, detail is lost for some of the feathers in this area. However, some coins are weak to begin with. Light wear is seen on the wreath and lettering. Again, luster is the best key to actual wear. This ranges from perhaps 20% remaining in protected areas (at AU-50) to two-thirds or more (at AU-58). Generally, the reverse has more luster than the obverse.

Illustrated coin: This coin shows above-average striking sharpness on the obverse.

EF-40, 45 (Extremely Fine). *Obverse:* More wear is evident on the portrait, especially on the hair to the left of the face and neck (again, remember that some varieties were struck with flatness in this area), the cheek, and the tip of the neck truncation. Excellent detail remains in low-relief areas of the hair. The stars show wear, as do the date and letters. Luster, if present at all, is minimal and in protected areas. *Reverse:* The eagle shows more

1795, Three Leaves; BB-26, Bolender-12a. Graded EF-40.

wear, this being the focal point to check. Most or nearly all detail is well defined. These aspects should be reviewed in combination with knowledge of the die variety, to determine the sharpness of the coin when it was first struck. Most silver dollars of this type were flat at the highest area of the center at the time they were made, as this was opposite the highest point of the hair in the press when the coins were struck. Additional wear is on the wreath and letters, but many details are present. Some luster may be seen in protected areas, and if present is slightly more abundant than on the obverse.

Illustrated coin: On the obverse, a massive die crack extends upward through the 7 of the date.

VF-20, 30 (Very Fine). *Obverse:* The hair is well worn at VF-20, less so at VF-30. On well-struck varieties the weakness is in the area left of the temple and cheek. The strands are blended as to be heavy. The cheek shows only slight relief. The stars have more wear, making them appear larger (an optical illusion). *Reverse:* The body of the eagle shows few if any feathers, while the wings have a third to half of the feathers visible, depending on the strike. The leaves

1795, Two Leaves; BB-21, Bolender-1. Graded VF-20.

lack most detail, but veins can be seen on a few. Scattered, non-disfiguring marks are normal for this and lower grades. Any major defects should be noted separately.

Illustrated coin: Light rim bumps should be noted. This coin features attractive medium toning.

F-12, 15 (Fine). *Obverse:* Wear is more extensive than on the preceding, reducing the definition of the thick strands of hair. The cheek has less detail, but the eye is usually well defined. On most coins, the stars appear larger. The rim is distinct in most areas, and many denticles remain visible. *Reverse:* Wear is more extensive. Now, feather details are fewer, mostly remaining on the wing to the left and at the extreme tip of the wing on the

1795, Three Leaves; BB-27, Bolender-5. Graded F-12.

right. As always, the die variety in question can have an influence on this. The wreath and lettering are worn further. The rim is usually complete, with most denticles visible.

Illustrated coin: This variety is flatly struck on the head, and examples in higher grades show no detail at the center. Note the smooth, even wear with some marks.

VG-8, 10 (Very Good). *Obverse:* The portrait is mostly seen in outline form, with most hair strands gone, although some are visible left of the neck, and the tips at the lower left are clear. The eye is distinct. The stars appear larger still, again an illusion. LIBERTY and the date are readable and usually full, although some letters may be weak at their tops. The rim is usually complete, and many denticles can be seen. *Reverse:* The eagle is mostly an

1795, Two Leaves; BB-11, Bolender-3. Graded VG-10.

outline, although some traces of feathers may be seen in the tail and the lower part of the inside of the right wing. The rim is worn, as are the letters, with some weak, but the motto is readable.

Illustrated coin: This coin shows some microscopic granularity overall. It is an interesting variety with a silver plug inserted at the center of the planchet prior to minting, to slightly increase the weight; this feature can barely be seen in outline form.

G-4, 6 (Good). *Obverse:* Wear is more extensive. LIBERTY and the stars are all there, but weak. The head is an outline, although the eye can still be seen. The rim is well worn or even missing. LIBERTY is worn, and parts of some letters may be missing, but elements of all should be readable. The date is readable, but worn. *Reverse:* The eagle is flat and discernible in outline form. The wreath is well worn. Some of the letters may be partly miss-

1795, Two Leaves; BB-11, Bolender-1. Graded G-6.

ing. At this level some "averaging" can be done. If the letters are stronger than usual in one area, but some are missing in another area, the coin can still qualify as G-4.

Illustrated coin: This is an attractive example with smooth, even wear and a few defects.

AG-3 (About Good). *Obverse:* Wear is extensive, but some stars and letters can usually be discerned. The head is in outline form. The date, while readable, may be partially worn away. *Reverse:* The reverse is well worn, with parts of the wreath and lettering missing.

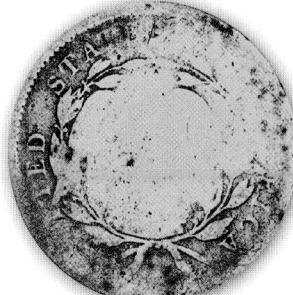

1795, Three Leaves. Graded AG-3.

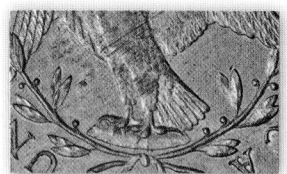

1795, Two Leaves Beneath Each Wing

1795, Three Leaves Beneath Each Wing

1795, Silver Plug
BB-15, Bolender-7.

	Mintage	Cert	Avg	%MS	AG-3	G-4	VG-8	F-12	VF-20	EF-40	AU-50	MS-60	MS-63
1794 †	1,758	35	36.9	17%	$37,500	$65,000	$100,000	$135,000	$165,000	$300,000	$525,000	$1,000,000	$1,600,000
Auctions: $305,500, EF-40, January 2014; $223,250, VF-35, August 2014													
1794, Silver Plug (a)	(b)	1	66.0	100%									
Auctions: No auction records available.													
1795, All kinds	160,295												
1795, Two Leaves		192	31.8	6%	$1,100	$2,250	$2,750	$4,350	$6,000	$13,500	$20,000	$70,000	$175,000
Auctions: $25,850, AU-55, August 2013; $9,400, EF-40, November 2015; $4,994, VF-35, August 2014; $5,993, VF-30, August 2014													
1795, Three Leaves		178	34.8	3%	$1,100	$2,250	$2,500	$4,100	$5,500	$12,000	$19,500	$65,000	$160,000
Auctions: $31,725, AU-55, July 2015; $11,750, AU-50, August 2015; $14,100, EF-40, March 2016 $3,819, F-15, March 2015													
1795, Silver Plug		34	33.1	6%	$1,500	$2,800	$4,750	$8,500	$16,000	$27,500	$45,000	$150,000	
Auctions: $99,875, AU-55, August 2013; $10,575, VG-10, August 2016													

† Ranked in the *100 Greatest U.S. Coins* (fourth edition). **a.** This unique piece, graded SP-66, shows evidence of planchet adjustment marks, as well as traces of a silver plug that was added to bring the coin's weight up to specification. **b.** Included in 1794 mintage figure.

DRAPED BUST, SMALL EAGLE REVERSE (1795–1798)

Designer: *Robert Scot.* **Weight:** *26.96 grams.* **Composition:** *.8924 silver, .1076 copper (net weight .77352 oz. pure silver).* **Diameter:** *Approximately 39–40 mm.* **Edge:** *HUNDRED CENTS ONE DOLLAR OR UNIT with decorations between words.* **Mint:** *Philadelphia.*

BB-51, Bolender-14.

History. The Draped Bust silver dollar with the Small Eagle reverse, inaugurated in 1795, brought the first appearance of this popular obverse portrait—a depiction of Miss Liberty that later was used on other silver denominations as well as copper half cents and cents. The motif was continued into 1798. Production of the Draped Bust silver dollars started at the end of the year on a new mint press that was first used for striking Flowing Hair dollars that summer. Draped Bust dollars circulated widely, especially outside the United States, and in the Caribbean in particular.

Striking and Sharpness. On the obverse, check the highest areas of the hair, the bust line, and the centers of the stars. On the reverse, check the feathers on the eagle's breast and wings. Examine the denticles. Planchet adjustment marks (from the filing down of overweight blanks) are common and should be avoided. Studying die varieties can be helpful for accurate grading. For example, the Small Letters reverse, a long-lived die design used from 1795 to 1798, has shallow relief and is usually seen with a low rim, with the result that its grade is lower than that of the obverse. On some reverse dies the eagle has very little detail. Fairly sharp striking (not necessarily Full Details) and excellent eye appeal add to the value dramatically.

Availability. These silver dollars are readily available as a type, although certain varieties range from scarce to very rare. MS coins are elusive and when seen are usually of the 1795 date, sometimes with prooflike surfaces. Most coins have been dipped and/or retoned, some successfully. These coins acquired marks more readily than did smaller denominations, and such are to be expected (but should be noted along with the grade, if distracting). Careful buying is needed to obtain coins with good eye appeal. Many AU examples are deeply toned and recolored.

The Smithsonian's National Numismatic Collection includes a unique Specimen 1794 dollar, plugged, and a unique Specimen 1797 10 Stars Left, 6 Stars Right, dollar.

GRADING STANDARDS

MS-60 to 70 (Mint State). *Obverse:* At MS-60, some abrasion and contact marks are evident, most noticeably on the cheek, the drapery at the shoulder, and the right field. Luster is present, but may be dull or lifeless, and interrupted in patches. At MS-63, contact marks are few, and abrasion is harder to detect. Many coins listed as Mint State are deeply toned, making it impossible to evaluate abrasion and even light wear; these are best avoided completely. An MS-65 coin has

1796, Small Date, Large Letters; BB-61, Bolender-2. Graded MS-60.

no abrasion, and contact marks are so minute as to require magnification. Luster should be full and rich. Coins grading above MS-65 are more theoretical than actual for this type—but they do exist, and are defined by having fewer marks as perfection is approached. *Reverse:* Comments apply as for the obverse, except that abrasion and contact marks are most noticeable on the eagle at the center, a situation complicated by the fact that this area was often flatly struck, not only on the famous Small Letters dies used from 1795 to 1798, but on some others as well. Grading is best done by the obverse, then verified by the reverse. In the Mint State category the amount of luster is usually a good key to grading. The field area is small and is protected by lettering and the wreath, and in any given grade shows fewer marks than on the obverse.

Illustrated coin: Note the tiny dig near Miss Liberty's ear. This coin is fairly well struck overall, but with some lightness on the eagle's body and leg on the right. It has excellent eye appeal.

AU-50, 53, 55, 58 (About Uncirculated). *Obverse:* Light wear is seen on the hair area above the ear and extending to left of the forehead, on the ribbon, and on the drapery at the shoulder, more so at AU-50 than at AU-53 or 55. An AU-58 coin has minimal traces of wear. An AU-50 coin has luster in protected areas among the stars and letters, with little in the open fields or on the portrait. At AU-58, most luster is present in the fields, but is worn away on the highest parts of the motifs. At this level

1797, Stars 9x7, Large Letters; BB-73, Bolender-1. Graded AU-50.

there are many deeply toned and recolored coins, necessitating caution when buying. *Reverse:* Light wear is seen on the eagle's body (keep in mind this area might be lightly struck) and edges of the wings. Light wear is seen on the wreath and lettering. Luster is the best key to actual wear. This ranges from perhaps 20% remaining in protected areas (at AU-50) to nearly full mint bloom (at AU-58).

Illustrated coin: This coin has some lightness of strike, but is better than average. It has some dings and marks, but these are not immediately obvious; without them, the coin might grade higher. This illustrates the many variables on these large, heavy coins. No single rule fits all.

EF-40, 45 (Extremely Fine). *Obverse:* More wear is evident on the upper hair area and the ribbon, and on the drapery and bosom. Excellent detail remains in low-relief areas of the hair. The stars show wear, as do the date and letters. Luster, if present at all, is minimal and in protected areas. For any and all dollars of this type, knowledge of die variety characteristics is essential to grading. Once again, one rule does not fit all. *Reverse:* The eagle, this being the focal point to check, shows more wear. On most strikings, the majority of feathers remain on the interior areas of the wings. Additional wear is on the wreath and letters, but many details are present. Some luster may be seen in protected areas and if present is slightly more abundant than on the obverse.

1796, Small Date, Large Letters; BB-61, Bolender-4. Graded EF-40.

Illustrated coin: Some marks are on the neck and a small pit is above the eagle's beak.

VF-20, 30 (Very Fine). *Obverse:* The higher-relief areas of hair are well worn at VF-20, less so at VF-30. The drapery and bosom show extensive wear, usually resulting in loss of most detail below the neck. The stars have more wear, making them appear larger. *Reverse:* The body of the eagle shows few if any feathers, while the wings have about half of the feathers visible, depending on the strike. The leaves lack most detail and are in outline form. Scattered, non-disfiguring marks are normal for this and lower grades. Any major defects should be noted separately.

1797, Stars 9x7, Small Letters; BB-72, Bolender-2. Graded VF-20.

Illustrated coin: This is the particularly famous Small Letters die (one of three Small Letters dies used for this type) first used in 1795 and last used in 1798. Used on 1795 BB-51, later 1796 BB-62, BB-63, and BB-66 now relapped, 1797 BB-72, and 1798 BB-81. The rims are low, and the eagle is in low relief. For coins struck from this particular reverse die, grading must be done by the obverse only.

F-12, 15 (Fine). *Obverse:* Wear is more extensive than on a Very Fine coin, particularly noticeable on the hair, face, and bosom. The stars appear larger. About half the hair detail remains, most noticeably behind the neck and shoulder. The rim shows wear but is complete or nearly so, with most denticles visible. *Reverse:* Wear is more extensive. Now, feather details are diminished, with relatively few remaining on the wings. The wreath and lettering are worn further, and the rim is usually weak in areas, although most denticles can be seen.

1796, Large Date, Small Letters; BB-65, Bolender-5. Graded F-12.

Illustrated coin: This is not the long-lived Small Letters die discussed above; this Small Letters die was used only in 1796. It is distinguished by a piece out of the die at the lower right of the reverse.

VG-8, 10 (Very Good). *Obverse:* The portrait is worn further, with much detail lost in the area above the level of the ear, although the curl over the forehead is delineated. There is some definition at the back of the hair and behind the shoulder, with the hair now combined to form thick strands. The ear is discernible, as is the eye. The stars appear larger still, again an illusion. The rim is weak in areas. LIBERTY and the date are readable and usually full. The rim is worn away in

1796, Small Date, Large Letters;
BB-61, Bolender-4. Graded VG-10.

areas, although many denticles can still be discerned. *Reverse:* The eagle is mostly an outline, with parts blending into the field (on lighter strikes). The rim is worn, as are the letters, with some weak, but the motto is readable.

Illustrated coin: Note the vertical scratches on the cheek.

G-4, 6 (Good). *Obverse:* Wear is more extensive, and some stars may be partly missing. The head is an outline. The eye is visible only in outline form. The rim is well worn or even missing in areas. LIBERTY is worn, and parts of some letters may be missing, but elements of all should be readable. The date is readable, but worn. Usually the date is rather bold. *Reverse:* The eagle is flat and discernible in outline form, and may be blending into the field. The wreath is well worn. Some

1797, Stars 9x7, Large Letters;
BB-73, Bolender-1. Graded G-4.

of the letters may be partly missing (for some shallow-relief dies with low rims). At this level some "averaging" can be done. If the letters are stronger than usual in one area, but some are missing in another area, the coin can still qualify as G-4. This general rule is applicable to most other series as well.

Illustrated coin: This is a well-circulated coin with several edge bumps.

AG-3 (About Good). *Obverse:* Wear is very extensive, but most letters and stars should be discernible. The head is in outline form. The date, while readable, may be partially worn away. *Reverse:* The reverse is well worn, with parts of the wreath and lettering missing. At this level, the reverse usually gives much less information than does the obverse.

1796, Large Date, Small Letters;
BB-65, Bolender-5a. Graded AG-3.

1795, Off-Center Bust

1795, Centered Bust

1796, Small Date

1796, Large Date

Small Letters

Large Letters

1797, 10 Stars Left, 6 Right

1797, 9 Stars Left, 7 Right

1798, 15 Stars on Obverse

1798, 13 Stars on Obverse

	Mintage	Cert	Avg	%MS	AG-3	G-4	VG-8	F-12	VF-20	EF-40	AU-50	MS-60	MS-63
1795, All kinds	42,738												
1795, Off-Center Bust		99	38.2	7%	$960	$1,450	$2,150	$3,500	$5,100	$9,500	$14,500	$60,000	$150,000
		Auctions: $763,750, MS-66, May 2016; $30,550, AU-58, February 2015; $12,925, EF-45, August 2014; $1,528, G-4, July 2015											
1795, Centered Bust		36	38.4	14%	$960	$1,450	$2,150	$3,500	$5,100	$9,500	$15,500	$55,000	$150,000
		Auctions: $12,925, AU-55, March 2016; $17,625, AU-50, March 2013; $13,513, AU-50, February 2015; $7,638, EF-45, August 2014											
1796, All kinds	79,920												
1796, Small Date, Small Letters (a)		24	40.5	4%	$825	$1,550	$2,100	$3,800	$5,500	$9,500	$14,000	$62,500	$150,000
		Auctions: $1,175,000, MS-65, April 2013; $4,406, VF-30, August 2014; $3,290, F-12, October 2014											
1796, Small Date, Large Letters		49	36.8	2%	$825	$1,550	$2,100	$3,800	$5,500	$9,500	$14,000	$75,000	$200,000
		Auctions: $352,500, MS-63, November 2013; $10,575, AU-53, August 2016; $14,100, AU-50, November 2015; $7,638, EF-45, August 2014											
1796, Large Date, Small Letters		52	33.1	6%	$825	$1,550	$2,100	$3,400	$5,250	$9,500	$14,000	$62,500	$160,000
		Auctions: $12,338, AU-50, August 2014; $13,513, AU-50, August 2013; $9,988, AU-50, February 2016; $6,463, EF-45, August 2016											
1797, All kinds	7,776												
1797, 10 Stars Left, 6 Right		117	38.2	7%	$850	$1,550	$2,000	$3,000	$5,000	$9,000	$13,750	$62,000	$125,000
		Auctions: $440,625, MS-64, November 2013; $182,267, MS-64, July 2015; $5,170, VF-30, March 2016; $4,406, VF-25, August 2014											
1797, 9 Stars Left, 7 Right, Large Letters		84	35.5	5%	$850	$1,550	$2,000	$3,100	$6,000	$9,500	$13,500	$63,000	$135,000
		Auctions: $381,875, MS-64, November 2013; $5,288, VF-30, August 2014; $2,820, F-12, August 2014											
1797, 9 Stars Left, 7 Right, Small Letters		33	32.8	3%	$1,200	$1,800	$2,750	$3,900	$8,200	$15,000	$32,500	$110,000	
		Auctions: $164,500, MS-62, November 2013; $7,638, VF-20, August 2014; $1,763, G-4, March 2015											
1798, All kinds (b)	327,536												
1798, 15 Stars on Obverse		33	37.8	6%	$1,100	$1,750	$2,650	$3,800	$8,000	$14,500	$24,500	$84,000	$155,000
		Auctions: $258,500, MS-63, November 2013; $7,050, VF-35, August 2015; $6,169, VF-35, August 2014; $9,988, VF-25, August 2014											
1798, 13 Stars on Obverse		31	38.5	6%	$1,000	$1,700	$2,100	$3,500	$7,750	$13,000	$20,000	$150,000	
		Auctions: $37,600, AU-58, August 2015; $9,988, EF-40, August 2016; $9,106, EF-40, August 2014; $3,525, VF-25, March 2016											

a. 3 varieties. b. The Mint struck 327,536 silver dollars in 1798, but did not record how many of each type (Small Eagle reverse and Heraldic Eagle reverse).

DRAPED BUST, HERALDIC EAGLE REVERSE (1798–1804)

Designer: *Robert Scot.* **Weight:** *26.96 grams.* **Composition:** *.8924 silver, .1076 copper (net weight .77352 oz. pure silver).* **Diameter:** *Approximately 39–40 mm.* **Edge:** *HUNDRED CENTS ONE DOLLAR OR UNIT with decorations between words.* **Mint:** *Philadelphia.*

Circulation Strike
BB-241, Bolender-6.

Proof (Restrike)
BB-302.

History. The design of the silver dollar closely follows that of other silver coins of the era. The two earliest reverse dies of 1798 have five vertical lines in the stripes in the shield. All dollar dies thereafter have four vertical lines. Production of the Draped Bust dollar continued through early 1804, but in that year the coins were struck from earlier-dated dies.

1804 silver dollars were first struck in 1834 from 1804-dated dies prepared at that time. (As a class these can be called *novodels*, rather than *restrikes*, as no originals were ever made in 1804.) The 1804 dollars were produced in Proof format. Later, probably circa 1859, a new reverse die was made up and combined with the earlier 1804 obverse (made in 1834). Those coins made in 1834 and around that time are today known as Class I dollars, whereas those made with a different reverse, beginning in 1859 and continuing perhaps through the 1870s, are known as Class III. An intermediate variety, from the Class III die combination but with a plain instead of lettered edge, is in the Smithsonian Institution's National Numismatic Collection and is known as Class II. All varieties combined comprise 15 different specimens. The 1804 dollar has been called the "King of American Coins" for well over a century and has achieved great fame. Interested numismatists are directed to *The Fantastic 1804 Dollar, Tribute Edition* (2009).

Striking and Sharpness. Very few of these coins have Full Details. On the obverse, check the highest points of the hair, the details of the drapery, and the centers of the stars. On the reverse, check the shield, the eagle, the stars above the eagle, and the clouds. Examine the denticles on both sides. Planchet adjustment marks are often seen, from overweight blanks being filed down to proper specifications, but they usually are lighter than on the earlier silver dollar types. The relief of the dies and the height of the rims can vary, affecting sharpness. Sharp striking and excellent eye appeal add to the value dramatically. Top-grade MS coins, when found, usually are dated 1800.

Availability. This is the most readily available type among the early silver dollars. Most often seen are the dates 1798 and 1799. Many varieties are available in any grade desired, although MS–63 and 65 coins are elusive. Other die varieties are rare at any level. As with other early dollars, connoisseurship is needed to acquire high-quality coins. These silver dollars usually have problems. To evaluate one for the market it is necessary to grade it, determine its quality of striking, and examine the characteristics of its surface. Nearly all have been dipped or cleaned.

Proofs. There were no Proofs coined in the era this type was issued. Years later, in 1834, the U.S. Mint made up new dies with the 1804 date and struck an unknown number of Proofs, perhaps a dozen or so, for inclusion in presentation Proof sets for foreign dignitaries. Today these are called Class I 1804 dollars. Eight examples are known, one of which shows circulation. The finest by far is the Sultan of Muscat coin, which approaches perfection. Circa 1858 or 1859 the Mint prepared a new obverse die dated 1804 and struck an unknown number of examples for private sale to collectors and dealers—the Class III dollars. No records were kept. These were artificially worn to give them the appearance of original dollars struck in 1804.

Sometime between circa 1858 and the 1870s, the Mint prepared new obverse dies dated 1801, 1802, and 1803, and struck Proof dollars for secret sale to the numismatic market. Many if not most were distributed through J.W. Haseltine, a Philadelphia dealer who had close connections with Mint officials. Today these are known as "Proof restrikes." All are rare, the 1801 being particularly so.

Class I 1804 dollars typically show hairlines and light abrasion. Grading is usually very liberal, in view of the fame of this rarity (not that this is logical). Circulated examples of Class I and Class III 1804 dollars have been graded using prefixes such as EF and AU. Proof restrikes of 1801 to 1803 generally survive in much higher grades, PF–64 or finer.

GRADING STANDARDS

MS-60 to 70 (Mint State). *Obverse:* At MS-60, some abrasion and contact marks are evident, most noticeably on the cheek, the drapery, and the right field. Luster is present, but may be dull or lifeless, and interrupted in patches. At MS-63, contact marks are very few, and abrasion is hard to detect except under magnification. Knowledge of the die variety is desirable, but on balance the portraits on this type are usually quite well struck. An MS-65 coin has no abrasion, and contact marks are so minute as to require magnification.

1798, 10 Arrows; BB-108, Bolender-13. Graded MS-63.

Luster should be full and rich. Coins grading above MS-65 are more theoretical than actual for this type—but they do exist and are defined by having fewer marks as perfection is approached. *Reverse:* Comments apply as for the obverse, except that abrasion and contact marks are most noticeable on the eagle's neck, the tips of the wing, and the tail. The field area is complex, without much open space, given the stars above the eagle, the arrows and olive branch, and other features. Accordingly, marks will not be as noticeable as on the obverse.

Illustrated coin: This coin is well struck, essentially problem free, and with superb eye appeal.

AU-50, 53, 55, 58 (About Uncirculated). *Obverse:* Light wear is seen on the hair area above the ear and extending to left of the forehead, on the ribbon, and on the drapery and bosom, more so at AU-50 than AU-53 or 55. An AU-58 coin has minimal traces of wear. An AU-50 coin has luster in protected areas among the stars and letters, with little in the open fields or on the portrait. At AU-58, much luster is present in the fields, but is worn away on the highest parts of the

1799, Irregular Date, 13-Star Reverse; BB-152, Bolender-15. Graded AU-50.

motifs. *Reverse:* Comments as preceding, except that the eagle's neck, the tips and top of the wings, the clouds, and the tail now show noticeable wear, as do other features. Luster ranges from perhaps 20% remaining in protected areas (at AU-50) to nearly full mint bloom (at AU-58). Sometimes the reverse of this type retains much more luster than the obverse, this being dependent on the height of the rim and the depth of the strike (particularly at the center).

Illustrated coin: This is an attractive and problem-free coin.

EF-40, 45 (Extremely Fine). *Obverse:* More wear is evident on the upper hair area and the ribbon, and on the drapery and bosom. The shoulder is a key spot to check for wear. Excellent detail remains in low-relief areas of the hair. The stars show wear, as do the date and letters. Luster, if present at all, is minimal and in protected areas. *Reverse:* Wear is greater than on an AU coin, overall. The neck has lost its feather detail on the highest points. Feathers have lost some detail near the edges of the wings. Some traces of luster may be seen, more so at EF-45 than at EF-40.

1802, Narrow Normal Date;
BB-241, Bolender-6. Graded EF-45.

Illustrated coin: This is an attractive example retaining some mint luster. It has above-average striking sharpness.

VF-20, 30 (Very Fine). *Obverse:* The higher-relief areas of hair are well worn at VF-20, less so at VF-30. The drapery at the shoulder and the bosom show extensive wear. The stars have more wear, making them appear larger (an optical illusion seen on most worn silver coins of this era). *Reverse:* Wear is greater, including on the shield and the wing feathers. Most of the feathers on the wings are clear. The star centers are flat. Other areas have lost detail as well.

1799; BB-157, Bolender-5. Graded VF-20.

Illustrated coin: Some scratches appear on the portrait. This coin was cleaned long ago and now is retoned. It is a typical early dollar at this grade.

F-12, 15 (Fine). *Obverse:* Wear is more extensive than on a Very Fine coin, particularly on the hair, face, and bosom. The stars appear larger. About half the hair detail remains, most noticeably behind the neck and shoulder. The rim may be partially worn away and blend into the field. *Reverse:* Wear is even more extensive, with the shield and wing feathers being points to observe. Half or slightly more of the feathers will remain clear. The incuse E PLURIBUS UNUM

1798, Pointed 9, Close Date;
BB-122, Bolender-14. Graded F-12.

may have a few letters worn away. The clouds all seem to be connected except on varieties in which they are spaced apart. The stars are weak. Parts of the border and lettering may be weak.

Illustrated coin: This coin was cleaned long ago. Cleaning and retoning is common on dollars of this era, but often is not noted by the grading services.

VG-8, 10 (Very Good). *Obverse:* The portrait is mostly seen in outline form, with most hair strands gone, although there is some definition at the back of the hair and behind the shoulder. The ear is discernible, as is the eye. The stars appear larger still, again an illusion. The rim is weak in areas. LIBERTY and the date are readable and usually full, although some letters may be weak at their tops. *Reverse:* Wear is more extensive. Half

1799. Graded VG-8.

or more of the letters in the motto are worn away. Most feathers are worn away, although separation of some of the lower feathers may be seen at the edges of the wings. Some stars are faint or missing. The border blends into the field in areas and some letters are weak. As always, a particular die variety can vary in areas of weakness.

G-4, 6 (Good). *Obverse:* Wear is more extensive, and some stars may be partly missing. The head is an outline. The eye is visible only in outline form. The rim is well worn or even missing in areas. LIBERTY is worn, and parts of some letters may be missing, but elements of all should be readable. The date is readable, but worn. *Reverse:* Wear is more extensive. The upper part of the eagle is flat. The feathers are noticeable only at the lower

1799; BB-169, Bolender-21. Graded G-4.

edge of the wings, sometimes incompletely, and do not have detail. The upper part of the shield is mostly flat. Only a few letters of the motto can be seen, if any at all. The rim is worn extensively, and the letters are well worn, but the inscription should be readable.

    Illustrated coin: This coin has some marks, but is respectable for the grade.

AG-3 (About Good). *Obverse:* Wear is so extensive that the coin is barely identifiable. The head is in outline form. LIBERTY is mostly gone; same for the stars. The date, while readable, may be partially worn away. *Reverse:* Extensive wear is seen overall, with the rim worn away and some areas worn smooth. The eagle can be discerned in outline form, but not necessarily completely. A few stray motto letters may remain.

1799. Graded AG-3.

PF-60 to 70 (Proof). *Obverse and Reverse:* For lower Proof levels, extensive abrasion is seen in the fields, or even evidence of circulation (the Mickley example of the 1804 Class I, earlier graded as AU-50, was certified as PF-62 by a leading certification service in 2008). Numbers assigned by grading services have been erratic. No rules are known, and grading has not been consistent.

1804, Class I. Proof.

1798, Knob 9

1798, Pointed 9

1798, Pointed 9, Close Date

1798, Pointed 9, Wide Date

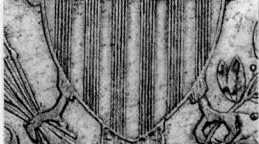

Five Vertical Lines in Shield's Stripes

Four Vertical Lines in Shield's Stripes

1798, Pointed 9, 10 Arrows

1798, Pointed 9, 4 Berries

1799, 99 Over 98, 15-Star Reverse

1799, 99 Over 98, 13-Star Reverse

1799, Irregular Date, 15-Star Reverse

1799, Irregular Date, 13-Star Reverse

1799, Irregular Date

1799, Normal Date

1800, Very Wide Date, Low 8

1800, "Dotted Date"

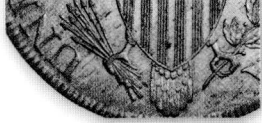

1800, Only 12 Arrows

1800, AMERICAI

1799, 8 Stars Left, 5 Stars Right

	Mintage	Cert	Avg	%MS	G-4	VG-8	F-12	VF-20	EF-40	AU-50	MS-60 / PF-63	MS-63 / PF-64	MS-65 / PF-65
1798, Knob 9, 5 Vertical Lines	(a)	3	35.0	0%	$850	$1,050	$1,450	$2,600	$4,250	$7,500	$22,000	$70,000	—
Auctions: $10,063, AU-50, September 2011													
1798, Knob 9, 4 Vertical Lines	(a)	8	50.9	25%	$850	$1,050	$1,450	$2,600	$4,250	$7,500	—		
Auctions: $9,775, AU-50, September 2011													
1798, Knob 9, 10 Arrows	(a)	8	34.4	0%	$850	$1,050	$1,450	$2,600	$4,250	$7,500	—		
Auctions: $7,175, AU-53, September 2013													
1798, Pointed 9, Close Date	(a)	150	37.6	3%	$850	$1,050	$1,450	$2,600	$4,250	$7,500	$22,000	$70,000	$155,000
Auctions: $5,302, AU-50, October 2014; $4,348, EF-45, July 2015; $3,290, EF-40, March 2015; $940, VG-10, January 2015													
1798, Pointed 9, Wide Date	(a)	163	36.0	6%	$850	$1,050	$1,450	$2,600	$4,250	$7,500	$22,000	$70,000	$155,000
Auctions: $3,290, EF-45, October 2015; $3,525, EF-40, August 2015; $2,115, VF-30, June 2015; $911, VF-20, September 2015													
1798, Pointed 9, 5 Vertical Lines	(a)	53	37.2	2%	$850	$1,050	$1,450	$2,600	$4,250	$7,500	$25,000	—	—
Auctions: $8,225, AU-53, September 2013													
1798, Pointed 9, 10 Arrows	(a)	56	32.2	4%	$900	$1,100	$1,750	$3,100	$4,900	$9,250	$23,500	$80,000	—
Auctions: $13,513, AU-53, August 2016; $4,700, EF-45, September 2016; $1,880, VF-25, July 2016													
1798, Pointed 9, 4 Berries	(a)	36	29.0	0%	$900	$1,050	$1,650	$2,800	$4,700	$8,500	$21,500	$67,500	$155,000
Auctions: $4,465, AU-53, September 2015; $3,290, EF-40, September 2015; $2,233, VF-30, January 2015													
1799, All kinds	423,515												
1799, 99 Over 98, 15-Star Reverse (b)		47	43.8	17%	$960	$1,250	$1,800	$2,850	$5,200	$8,700	$23,000	$57,000	—
Auctions: $88,125, MS-64, October 2015; $29,375, MS-62, August 2014; $4,406, EF-45, September 2014; $3,055, EF-40, March 2016													
1799, 99 Over 98, 13-Star Reverse		34	36.4	6%	$950	$1,150	$1,750	$2,700	$4,700	$8,500	$22,400	$56,500	—
Auctions: $852, F-12, November 2014; $646, AG-3, July 2015													
1799, Irregular Date, 15-Star Reverse		14	32.2	0%	$950	$1,050	$1,550	$2,550	$4,700	$8,500	$23,000	—	—
Auctions: $3,055, VF-35, September 2013													
1799, Irregular Date, 13-Star Reverse		28	37.3	7%	$950	$1,050	$1,550	$2,550	$4,700	$8,250	$22,000	$56,500	$185,000
Auctions: $99,875, MS-64, August 2013; $2,409, VF-30, October 2014													
1799, Normal Date		1,977	35.5	4%	$900	$1,050	$1,550	$2,550	$4,700	$8,250	$22,400	$56,500	$185,000
Auctions: $5,875, AU-53, March 2015; $1,998, VF-25, May 2015; $1,998, VF-20, November 2015; $1,645, F-15, August 2015													
1799, 8 Stars Left, 5 Right		36	38.7	6%	$1,000	$1,250	$1,900	$3,100	$5,750	$13,500	$32,500	$92,500	—
Auctions: $5,640, EF-45, May 2016; $3,290, EF-45, August 2016; $4,113, EF-40, February 2015; $646, VG-8, November 2014													
1800, All kinds	220,920												
1800, Very Wide Date, Low 8		19	39.1	0%	$900	$1,050	$1,600	$2,350	$4,500	$8,500	$24,500	$60,000	—
Auctions: $11,750, AU-53, January 2014; $8,813, AU-53, August 2014; $2,233, VF-30, March 2015; $1,763, F-15, August 2014													
1800, "Dotted Date" (c)		34	39.2	12%	$900	$1,050	$1,650	$2,500	$5,200	$8,500	$24,500	$59,000	$185,000
Auctions: $11,750, AU-55, August 2014; $9,988, AU-53, August 2013; $2,350, VF-30, October 2014; $999, VF-20, January 2015													
1800, Only 12 Arrows		31	40.5	13%	$900	$1,050	$1,600	$2,400	$4,600	$8,500	$24,500	$60,000	—
Auctions: $6,463, AU-50, September 2013; $2,938, EF-40, March 2015; $1,880, VF-25, August 2014													
1800, Normal Dies		843	36.6	2%	$900	$1,050	$1,600	$2,400	$4,600	$8,500	$24,000	$55,000	$185,000
Auctions: $17,625, AU-58, August 2014; $12,925, AU-55, August 2014; $2,233, VF-30, November 2015; $494, VG-8, July 2015													
1800, AMERICAI (d)		41	38.5	10%	$900	$1,050	$1,600	$2,400	$4,600	$8,000	$26,500	—	—
Auctions: $223,250, MS-65, November 2013													

Note: The two earliest reverse dies of 1798 have five vertical lines in the stripes in the shield. All dollar dies thereafter have four vertical lines. **a.** The Mint struck 327,536 silver dollars in 1798, but did not record how many of each type (Small Eagle reverse and Heraldic Eagle reverse). **b.** The engraver of the reverse die accidentally engraved 15 stars, instead of the 13 needed to represent the original Colonies. He attempted to cover the two extra stars under the leftmost and rightmost clouds, but their points stick out slightly. **c.** The "dotted" date is the result of die breaks. **d.** A reverse-die flaw resulted in what appears to be a sans-serif letter I after AMERICA. "Perhaps from a punch or from a stray piece of metal during the die making process" (Bowers, *Silver Dollars & Trade Dollars of the United States*).

1802, 2 Over 1,
Narrow Date

1802, 2 Over 1,
Wide Date

1802, Narrow
Normal Date

1802, Wide Normal Date

1803, Small 3

1803, Large 3

	Mintage	Cert	Avg	%MS	G-4	VG-8	F-12	VF-20	EF-40	AU-50	MS-60 / PF-63	MS-63 / PF-64	MS-65 / PF-65
1801	54,454	304	37.7	5%	$900	$1,050	$1,600	$2,400	$4,900	$8,350	$29,500	$82,500	$235,000
	Auctions: $329,000, MS-65, November 2013; $3,525, EF-40, October 2014; $764, VG-8, January 2015												
1801, Restrike, Proof † (e)	*2 known*	1	66.0								$850,000	$1,000,000	—
	Auctions: No auction records available.												
1802, All kinds	41,650												
1802, 2 Over 1, Narrow Date		22	37.8	9%	$950	$1,100	$1,800	$2,500	$5,000	$9,100	$30,000	$65,000	—
	Auctions: $11,750, AU-58, February 2013; $2,115, VF-30, January 2015; $2,820, VF-20, October 2014												
1802, 2 Over 1, Wide Date		35	34.2	6%	$1,000	$1,150	$1,900	$2,600	$5,250	$9,500	$32,000	$70,000	—
	Auctions: $6,463, AU-53, January 2015; $4,465, EF-40, February 2015; $2,820, VF-25, January 2015; $2,585, VF-25, October 2015												
1802, Narrow Normal Date		57	41.5	16%	$950	$1,100	$1,700	$2,400	$4,900	$8,000	$23,500	$65,000	$240,000
	Auctions: $54,050, MS-63, January 2015; $25,850, MS-61, May 2015; $12,925, AU-55, June 2015; $2,350, VF-25, January 2015												
1802, Wide Normal Date		8	40.4	0%	$1,000	$1,050	$1,850	$2,650	$5,000	$9,500	$36,000	$72,500	$300,000
	Auctions: $10,869, AU-55, August 2013; $2,350, VF-35, August 2015; $3,525, VF-30, January 2015												
1802, Restrike, Proof † (e)	*4 known*	3	64.0								$400,000	$600,000	$1,000,000
	Auctions: $920,000, PF-65Cam, April 2008												
1803, All kinds	85,634												
1803, Small 3		69	37.7	7%	$1,000	$1,050	$1,800	$2,650	$5,000	$9,000	$27,000	$70,000	—
	Auctions: $117,500, MS-63, November 2013; $2,585, VF-35, October 2014; $2,350, VF-30, August 2014; $999, F-12, July 2014												
1803, Large 3		72	38.0	4%	$1,000	$1,050	$1,800	$2,650	$5,000	$9,000	$27,000	$70,000	—
	Auctions: $6,463, EF-45, August 2014; $2,174, VF-20, March 2015; $1,410, VF-20, August 2015; $646, VF-20, August 2015												
1803, Restrike, Proof † (e)	*3 known*	7	65.6								$400,000	$600,000	$1,000,000
	Auctions: $851,875, PF-66, January 2013												

† Ranked in the *100 Greatest U.S. Coins* (fourth edition). **e.** "The Proof silver dollars of 1801, 1802, and 1803 are all extremely rare, valuable, and desirable, although none of them were made anywhere near the dates on the coins, nor do they share any die characteristics with any real silver dollars made from 1801 to 1803" (*100 Greatest U.S. Coins*, fourth edition).

1804 Dollar, Proof

1804, First Reverse, Proof

1804, Second Reverse, Proof

Note the position of the words STATES OF in relation to the clouds.

	Mintage	Cert	Avg	%MS	G-4	VG-8	F-12	VF-20	EF-40	AU-50	MS-60	MS-63	MS-65
											PF-63	PF-64	PF-65
1804, First Reverse, Class I, Proof (f)	8 known	6	50.0								$4,000,000	$4,500,000	$6,000,000
Auctions: $3,877,500, PF-62, August 2013													
1804, Second Reverse, Restrike, Class III, Proof (f)	6 known	4	59.3										
Auctions: $2,300,000, PF-58, April 2009; $1,880,000, PF-55, August 2014													
1804, Second Reverse, Restrike, Plain Edge, Class II, Proof (f,g)	1	0	n/a										
Auctions: No auction records available.													
1804, Electrotype of Unique Plain-Edge Specimen (f,h)	4	0	n/a										
Auctions: No auction records available.													

f. The 1804 dollars as a group are ranked among the *100 Greatest U.S. Coins.* g. The plain-edge restrike is in the Smithsonian's National Numismatic Collection. h. These electrotypes were made by the U.S. Mint.

GOBRECHT (1836–1839)

No Stars on Obverse, Stars on Reverse (1836):

Designer: *Christian Gobrecht.* **Weight:** *26.96 grams.*
Composition: *.8924 silver, .1076 copper (net weight .77352 oz. pure silver).*
Diameter: *39–40 mm.* **Edge:** *Plain.*

No Stars on Obverse, Stars on Reverse

Stars on Obverse, No Stars on Reverse (1838–1839): **Designer:** *Christian Gobrecht.*
Weight: *26.73 grams.* **Composition:** *.900 silver, .100 copper*
(net weight .77345 oz. pure silver). **Diameter:** *39–40 mm.* **Edge:** *Reeded.*

Stars on Obverse, No Stars on Reverse

History. Suspension of silver dollar coinage was lifted in 1831, but it was not until 1835 that steps were taken to resume their production. Late that year, Mint Director R.M. Patterson had engraver Christian Gobrecht prepare a pair of dies based on motifs by Thomas Sully and Titian Peale. The first obverse die, dated 1836, bore the seated figure of Miss Liberty with the inscription C. GOBRECHT F. ("F." for the Latin word *Fecit*, or "made it") in the field above the date. On the reverse die was a large eagle flying left, surrounded by 26 stars and the legend UNITED STATES OF AMERICA • ONE DOLLAR •. It is unknown whether coins were struck from these dies at that time. A new obverse die with Gobrecht's name on the base of Liberty was prepared, and in December 1836, a thousand plain-edged pieces were struck for circulation. These coins weighed 416 grains, the standard enacted in 1792.

The feeder mechanism that was used, apparently designed for coins of half dollar size or smaller, damaged the reverse die's rim. Attempts were made to solve the problem by rotating the reverse die at various times during the striking run, but this only extended the damage to both sides of the rim. The original 1836 issue is thus known in multiple die alignments:

Die Alignment I—head of Liberty opposite DO in DOLLAR; eagle flying upward.

Die Alignment II—head of Liberty opposite ES in STATES; eagle flying upward.

Die Alignment III—head of Liberty opposite N of ONE; eagle flying level.

Die Alignment IV—head of Liberty opposite F in OF; eagle flying level.

Original 1836 die orientation using
either "coin" or "medal" turn.

Die alignment of original issues
dated 1838 and 1839.

Restrikes were made from the late 1850s through the early 1870s. They were struck using the original obverse die and a different reverse die with cracks through NITED STATES O and OLLA, and in Die Alignment III.

In January 1837, the standard weight for the dollar was lowered to 412-1/2 grains, and on January 8, 1837, Benjamin Franklin Peale wrote an internal memorandum to Mint Director Patterson noting, among other things, that the new dollar had received much criticism for looking too medallic, rather than like a coin. Peale felt this was due to the "smooth" edge and suggested striking with a segmented, lettered-edge collar like one he had seen in France. In March 1837, the dies of 1836 were used to strike 600 pieces (whether with plain or reeded edge is unknown). According to reports, the results were unsatisfactory and the coins were destroyed—although a single example, with a reeded edge, is known. It is unclear whether it was part of the March striking, from an earlier 1837 striking caused by the Peale memo, or struck at some later period.

Pattern pieces were struck in 1838 using modified dies with Gobrecht's name removed from the base, 13 stars added to the obverse, and the 26 stars removed from the reverse. These were struck in alignment IV using a reeded-edge collar. In 1839, 300 pieces were struck for circulation, also in alignment IV. Both of these were restruck in alignment III and possibly alignment IV in the late 1850s through early 1870s.

Striking and Sharpness. Striking is usually very good. Check the details on Miss Liberty's head and the higher parts of the eagle. Note that the word LIBERTY is raised.

Availability. 1836 Gobrecht dollars are available in grades from so-called Very Fine upward (the coins were struck as Proofs, and worn examples are properly designated as PF-30, PF-40, and so on; however, sometimes they are found graded as Fine, VF, and EF for levels below PF-50). Most in the marketplace range from PF–50 to 62. Most have contact marks. Truly pristine PF-65 and better examples are very elusive. The demand for these coins is intense. For the 1839, circulated grades typically are PF-50 or higher, often with damage. Pristine Proofs are available, but virtually all are restrikes.

GRADING STANDARDS

PF-60 to 70 (Proof). *Obverse and Reverse:* Many Proofs have been extensively cleaned and have many hairlines and dull fields. This is more applicable to 1836 than to 1839. Grades are PF–60 to 61 or 62. With medium hairlines and good reflectivity, an assigned grade of PF-64 is appropriate, and with relatively few hairlines, Gem PF-65. In various grades hairlines are most easily seen in the obverse field. PF-66 should have hairlines so

1839. Graded PF-65.

delicate that magnification is needed to see them. Above that, a Proof should be free of such lines.

Illustrated coin: This is a restrike made at the Mint in or after spring 1859.

PF-50, 53, 55, 58 (Proof). *Obverse:* Light wear is seen on the thighs and knees, bosom, and head. At PF-58, the Proof surface is extensive, but the open fields show abrasion. At PF-50 and 53, most if not all mirror surface is gone and there are scattered marks. *Reverse:* Wear is most evident on the eagle's breast and the top of the wings. Mirror surface ranges from perhaps 60% complete (at PF-58) to none (at PF-50).

1836. Graded PF-58.

Illustrated coin: This original 1836 Gobrecht dollar, of which 1,000 were coined in 1836, is nicely toned and has excellent eye appeal.

PF-40 to 45 (Proof). *Obverse:* Further wear is seen on all areas, especially the thighs and knees, bosom, and head. The center of LIBERTY, which is in relief, is weak. Most at this level and lower are the 1836 issues. *Reverse:* Further wear is evident on the eagle, including the back edge of the closest wing, the top of the farthest wing, and the tail.

1836. Graded PF-45.

PF-20, 25, 30, 35 (Proof). *Obverse:* Further wear is seen. Many details of the gown are worn away, but the lower-relief areas above and to the right of the shield remain well defined. Hair detail is mostly or completely gone. LIBERTY is weak at the center. *Reverse:* Even more wear is evident on the eagle, with only about 60% of the feathers visible.

1836. Graded PF-20.

	Cert	Avg	%MS	PF-20	PF-40	PF-50	PF-60	PF-62	PF-63	PF-64	PF-65
1836. C. GOBRECHT F. on base. Judd-60. Plain edge, no stars on obverse, stars in field on reverse. Die alignment I, ↑↓. Circulation issue. 1,000 struck (a)	209	55.7		$12,500	$15,000	$18,000	$25,000	$27,000	$40,000	$75,000	$125,000
Auctions: $82,250, PF-64, May 2016											
1836. As above. Plain edge. Judd-60. Die alignment II, ↑↑, and die alignment IV, ↑↑. Circulation issue struck in 1837. 600 struck (a)	(b)			$13,000	$16,000	$21,000	$25,000	$30,000	$45,000	$75,000	$125,000
Auctions: $12,338, PF-50, October 2016; $9,988, PF-50, June 2015											

a. Originals. Although these are listed in Judd as patterns, they are considered circulation strikes. b. Included in 1836, C. GOBRECHT F. on base, certified population.

	Cert	Avg	%MS	PF-20	PF-40	PF-50	PF-60	PF-62	PF-63	PF-64	PF-65
1838. Obverse stars added around border, reeded edge. Judd-84. Designer's name removed. Reverse, eagle flying in plain field. Die alignment IV, ↑↑.	28	62.3					$55,000	$65,000	$75,000	$85,000	$150,000
Auctions: $83,375, PF-64, July 2008											
1839. As above. Reeded edge. Judd-104. Die alignment IV, ↑↑. Circulation issue. 300 struck	47	62.6		$15,000	$17,500	$22,500	$29,000	$38,500	$55,000	$80,000	$150,000
Auctions: $18,975, PF-45, November 2011											

Restrike

	Cert	Avg	%MS	PF-20	PF-40	PF-50	PF-60	PF-62	PF-63	PF-64	PF-65
1836. Name below base; eagle in starry field; plain edge. Judd-58. Die alignment III, ↑↓, and die alignment IV, ↑↑. (a)	12 (b)	64.0		$17,500	$30,000	$70,000	$75,000	$80,000	$85,000	$100,000	$125,000
Auctions: $34,500, PF-63, April 2012											
1836. Name on base; plain edge. Judd-60. Die alignment III, ↑↓. (a,c)	(d)			$15,000	$20,000	$23,500	$26,000	$35,000	$45,000	$55,000	$90,000
Auctions: $18,975, PF-61, September 2010											
1836. C. GOBRECHT F. on base. Judd-61. Reeded edge. No stars on obverse, stars in field on reverse. Die alignment IV, ↑↑. (a)	0	n/a		*(extremely rare)*							
Auctions: $195,000, PF-63, May 2003											
1838. Designer's name removed; reeded edge. Judd-84. Die alignment III, ↑↓, and die alignment IV, ↑↑. (a)	(d)			$25,000	$30,000	$35,000	$47,500	$62,500	$75,000	$85,000	$125,000
Auctions: $83,375, PF-64, March 2012											
1839. Designer's name removed; eagle in plain field; reeded edge. Judd-104. Die alignment III, ↑↓, and die alignment IV, ↑↑. (a)	(d)			$20,000	$25,000	$37,500	$42,500	$50,000	$60,000	$70,000	$100,000
Auctions: $51,750, PF-64, April 2012											

Note: Restrikes were produced from the late 1850s to the 1870s, and are not official Mint issues. They were all oriented in either die alignment III (coin turn) or die alignment IV (medal turn), with the eagle flying level. Almost all were struck from a cracked reverse die. For detailed analysis of these pieces, consult *United States Pattern Coins*, tenth edition. **a.** Restrikes. Listed in Judd as patterns. **b.** Many originals were certified as restrikes in years past. This figure includes some of these originals. **c.** 30 to 40 are known. **d.** Included in figure for first listing with this Judd number, as the grading services do not consistently distinguish between originals and restrikes.

LIBERTY SEATED (1840–1873)

No Motto (1840–1865): **Designer:** *Christian Gobrecht.* **Weight:** *26.73 grams.*
Composition: *.900 silver, .100 copper (net weight .77344 oz. pure silver).*
Diameter: *38.1 mm.* **Edge:** *Reeded.* **Mints:** *Philadelphia, New Orleans, and San Francisco.*

Mintmark location
is on the reverse,
below the eagle,
for all varieties.

No Motto
(1840–1865)

No Motto, Proof

With Motto IN GOD WE TRUST (1866–1873): **Designer:** *Christian Gobrecht.*
Weight: *26.73 grams.* **Composition:** *.900 silver, .100 copper (net weight .77344 oz. pure silver).*
Diameter: *38.1 mm.* **Edge:** *Reeded.* **Mints:** *Philadelphia, Carson City, and San Francisco.*

With Motto
IN GOD
WE TRUST
(1866–1873)

With Motto
IN GOD
WE TRUST,
Proof

History. The Liberty Seated dollar was minted every year from 1840 to 1873, with an obverse design modified from that of the 1839 Gobrecht dollar. On the reverse, the flying eagle of the Gobrecht dollar was replaced with a perched eagle similar to that of contemporary quarter and half dollars. The dollars, minted in modest numbers, circulated in the United States through 1850. In that year the rising value of silver on the international markets brought the cost of minting each coin to more than $1. Production continued for the international, rather than domestic, market, through 1873, when the trade dollar took the Liberty Seated dollar's place.

Striking and Sharpness. On the obverse, check the head of Miss Liberty and the centers of the stars. On the reverse, check the feathers of the eagle. The denticles usually are sharp. Dollars of 1857 usually are weakly struck, but have semi-prooflike surfaces. The word LIBERTY is in a high-relief area on the coin, with the result that it wore away quickly. Therefore this feature cannot be used as the only guide to grading an obverse. From EF downward, strike sharpness in the stars and the head does not matter to connoisseurs. Proof coins were made for all dates. All of 1851 and 1853 are restrikes, as are most of 1852. In 1858 only Proofs were struck, to the extent of an estimated 210 pieces, with no related circulation strikes. Most early dates were restruck at the Mint, augmenting the supply of originals. Nearly all Proofs are very well struck.

Availability. All issues from 1840 to 1850 are available in proportion to their mintages. Those of 1851 to the late 1860s are either scarce or rare in circulated grades, and in MS they range from rare to extremely rare, despite generous mintages in some instances. The later-date coins were shipped to China and later melted. Coins of the 1870s are more readily available, although some are scarce to rare. Today, Proofs from 1858 to 1873 are readily available, but high-quality examples with superb eye appeal are in the minority. Most Proofs prior to 1860 survive only in grades below PF-65 if strict grading is applied.

GRADING STANDARDS

MS-60 to 70 (Mint State). *Obverse:* At MS-60, some abrasion and contact marks are evident, most noticeably on the bosom and thighs and knees. Luster is present, but may be dull or lifeless. At MS-63, contact marks are very few, and abrasion is minimal. An MS-65 coin has no abrasion in the fields (but may have a hint on the knees), and contact marks are trivial. Check the knees of Liberty and the right field. Luster should be full and

1864. Graded MS-65.

rich on later issues, not necessarily so for dates in the 1840s. Most Mint State coins of the 1861 to 1865 years, Philadelphia issues, have extensive die striae (from not completely finishing the die). *Reverse:* Comments apply as for the obverse, except that in lower Mint State grades, abrasion and marks are most noticeable on the eagle's head, the neck, the claws, and the top of the wings (harder to see there, however). At MS-65 or higher, there are no marks visible to the unaided eye. The field is mainly protected by design elements and does not show abrasion as much as does the obverse on a given coin.

Illustrated coin: The fields show striations from incomplete polishing of the dies, but this does not affect the grade.

AU-50, 53, 55, 58 (About Uncirculated). *Obverse:* Light wear is seen on the thighs and knees, bosom, and head. At AU-58, the luster is extensive but incomplete, especially in the right field. At AU–50 and 53, luster is less. *Reverse:* Wear is visible on the eagle's neck, the claws, and the top of the wings. An AU-58 coin has nearly full luster. At AU–50 and 53, there still are traces of luster.

Illustrated coin: This is an attractive example with much of the original luster.

1842. Graded AU-58.

EF-40, 45 (Extremely Fine). *Obverse:* Further wear is seen on all areas, especially the thighs and knees, bosom, and head. Little or no luster is seen on most coins. From this grade downward, strike sharpness in the stars and the head does not matter to connoisseurs. *Reverse:* Further wear is evident on the eagle's neck, claws, and the wings, although on well-struck coins nearly all details are sharp.

1846. Graded EF-40.

VF-20, 30 (Very Fine). *Obverse:* Further wear is seen. Many details of the gown are worn away, but the lower-relief areas above and to the right of the shield remain well defined. Hair detail is mostly or completely gone. The word LIBERTY is weak at BE (PCGS allows BER to be missing "on some coins"). *Reverse:* Wear is more extensive, with some feathers blended together, especially on the neck for a typical coin. Detail remains quite good overall.

1854. Graded VF-20.

F-12, 15 (Fine). *Obverse:* The seated figure is well worn, but with some detail above and to the right of the shield. BER in LIBERTY is visible only in part or missing entirely. *Reverse:* Wear is extensive, with about a third to half of the feathers flat or blended with others.

    Illustrated coin: The reverse is stronger than the obverse on this coin.

1872-CC. Graded F-12.

VG-8, 10 (Very Good). *Obverse:* The seated figure is more worn, but some detail can be seen above and to the right of the shield. The shield is discernible, but the upper-right section may be flat and blended into the seated figure. In LIBERTY two or three letters, or a combination totaling that, are readable. *Reverse.* Further wear has flattened half or slightly more of the feathers (depending on the strike). The rim is visible all around, as are the ends of the denticles. A Very Good Liberty Seated dollar usually has more detail overall than a lower-denomination coin of the same design.

1871-CC. Graded VG-8.

G-4, 6 (Good). *Obverse:* The seated figure is worn nearly smooth. The stars and date are complete, but may be weak toward the periphery. *Reverse:* The eagle shows only a few details of the shield and feathers. The rim is worn down. The tops of the border letters are weak or worn away, although the inscription can still be read.

1850-O. Graded G-6.

AG-3 (About Good). *Obverse:* The seated figure is visible in outline form. Much or all of the rim is worn away. The stars are weak and some may be missing. The date remains clear. *Reverse:* The border letters are partially worn away. The eagle is mostly in outline form, but with a few details discernible. The rim is weak or missing.

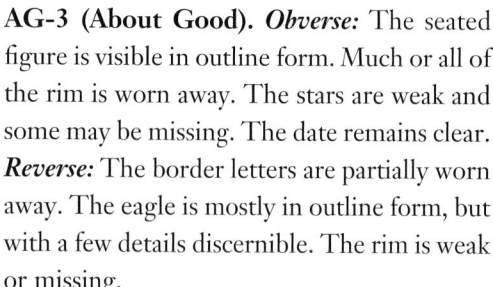

1872. Graded AG-3.

PF-60 to 70 (Proof). *Obverse and Reverse:* Proofs that are extensively cleaned and have many hairlines, or that are dull and grainy, are lower level, such as PF–60 to 62. These are not widely desired, except for use as fillers for the dates (most circulation-strike dollars are rare after 1849 and before 1870). The rarities of 1851, 1852, and 1858 are in demand no matter what the grade. With medium hairlines and good reflectivity, an assigned

1861. Graded PF-63.

grade of PF-64 is appropriate, and with relatively few hairlines, gem PF-65. In various grades hairlines are most easily seen in the obverse field. PF-66 should have hairlines so delicate that magnification is needed to see them. Above that, a Proof should be free of such lines.

    Illustrated coin: The frosty cameo motifs on this example contrast with the deeply mirrored fields.

**1851, Original,
High Date**

**1851, Restrike,
Proof**
Date is centered.

1852, Original

**1852, Restrike,
Proof**

	Mintage	Cert	Avg	%MS	VG-8	F-12	VF-20	EF-40	AU-50	MS-60 / PF-60	MS-63 / PF-63	MS-65 / PF-65
1840	61,005	268	49.4	20%	$450	$500	$575	$850	$1,500	$5,500	$14,500	—
Auctions: $12,925, MS-63, October 2015; $1,240, EF-45, January 2015; $705, VF-35, August 2015; $517, VF-25, January 2015												
1840, Proof	*40–60*	27	63.3							$12,500	$22,500	$75,000
Auctions: $85,188, PF-64Cam, April 2013												
1841	173,000	272	49.9	18%	$450	$500	$575	$700	$1,050	$2,750	$8,000	$90,000
Auctions: $2,820, MS-62, January 2015; $1,528, AU-58, January 2015; $541, EF-45, August 2015; $400, VF-35, February 2015												
1841, Proof	*10–15*	4	63.0							$30,000	$70,000	$250,000
Auctions: $94,000, PF-64, October 2014; $141,000, PF-64, April 2013												
1842	184,618	623	48.6	14%	$450	$500	$575	$600	$950	$2,400	$5,000	$90,000
Auctions: $19,975, MS-64, September 2016; $11,163, MS-64, May 2015; $7,344, MS-64, July 2016; $1,528, AU-58, June 2015												
1842, Proof	*10–15*	8	63.3							$15,000	$35,000	$80,000
Auctions: $57,281, PF-65, August 2013												
1843	165,100	514	48.0	11%	$450	$500	$575	$600	$950	$2,400	$7,000	$100,000
Auctions: $3,055, MS-62, June 2015; $940, AU-55, August 2015; $517, EF-45, January 2015; $411, F-15, June 2015												
1843, Proof	*10–15*	8	63.4							$15,000	$30,000	$110,000
Auctions: $52,875, PF-64, August 2013												
1844	20,000	161	51.0	13%	$450	$500	$575	$800	$1,250	$5,000	$14,000	$100,000
Auctions: $3,055, AU-58, January 2015; $940, AU-50, July 2015; $541, VF-30, January 2015; $541, VF-25, March 2015												
1844, Proof	*10–15*	8	63.9							$12,500	$30,000	$110,000
Auctions: $70,500, PF-65, April 2013; $44,063, PF-64, October 2014												
1845	24,500	188	50.0	11%	$450	$500	$575	$800	$1,500	$9,000	$25,000	$150,000
Auctions: $31,725, MS-63, May 2015; $5,170, MS-61, June 2015; $2,350, AU-58, January 2015; $676, VF-30, January 2015												
1845, Proof	*10–15*	10	63.8							$12,500	$30,000	$75,000
Auctions: $141,000, PF-67, August 2013												

	Mintage	Cert	Avg	%MS	VG-8	F-12	VF-20	EF-40	AU-50	MS-60 PF-60	MS-63 PF-63	MS-65 PF-65
1846	110,600	513	50.1	16%	$450	$500	$575	$650	$1,000	$2,500	$5,500	$90,000
	Auctions: $6,463, MS-64, October 2015; $2,585, MS-61, January 2015; $1,175, AU-55, June 2015; $570, EF-40, July 2015											
1846, Proof	10–15	14	62.9							$12,500	$30,000	$105,000
	Auctions: $94,000, PF-66, April 2013											
1846-O	59,000	179	46.7	11%	$450	$500	$575	$800	$1,400	$7,250	$17,000	$100,000
	Auctions: $70,501, MS-64, January 2015; $4,230, MS-60, January 2015; $881, EF-40, January 2015; $505, VF-20, March 2015											
1847	140,750	526	50.5	16%	$450	$500	$575	$600	$850	$2,700	$5,500	$90,000
	Auctions: $5,875, MS-64, October 2015; $4,700, MS-63, October 2015; $2,115, AU-58, August 2015; $793, EF-45, October 2015											
1847, Proof	10–15	16	63.9							$12,500	$22,000	$60,000
	Auctions: $35,250, PF-65, October 2014; $41,125, PF-65, April 2013											
1848	15,000	98	49.0	10%	$450	$650	$750	$1,100	$1,500	$4,750	$13,000	$90,000
	Auctions: $47,000, MS-64, May 2015; $5,993, MS-61, September 2014; $2,350, AU-55, January 2015; $646, EF-40, January 2015											
1848, Proof	10–15	10	64.2							$12,500	$30,000	$75,000
	Auctions: $117,500, PF-67, August 2013											
1849	62,600	304	53.3	25%	$450	$500	$575	$700	$1,000	$2,600	$6,750	$90,000
	Auctions: $2,585, MS-62, June 2015; $1,763, AU-58, January 2015; $588, EF-40, August 2015; $400, VF-35, March 2015											
1849, Proof	10–15	9	63.9							$13,500	$34,000	$75,000
	Auctions: $129,250, PF-67, April 2013											
1850	7,500	116	54.9	34%	$550	$750	$1,100	$1,800	$2,500	$6,500	$14,000	$90,000
	Auctions: $7,638, MS-61, July 2015; $3,995, MS-60, January 2015; $4,230, AU-58, February 2015; $2,996, AU-53, February 2015											
1850, Proof	20–30	15	63.8							$12,500	$25,000	$50,000
	Auctions: $51,406, PF-66, August 2013; $19,975, PF-64, October 2014											
1850-O	40,000	145	43.1	10%	$450	$500	$750	$1,450	$3,200	$11,500	$25,000	$120,000
	Auctions: $3,055, AU-50, July 2015; $2,350, EF-45, January 2015; $823, VF-30, January 2015; $646, F-15, October 2015											
1851, Original, High Date † (a)	1,300	26	61.1	73%	$10,000	$12,500	$13,500	$20,000	$27,500	$35,000	$65,000	$140,000
	Auctions: $70,500, MS-64, January 2015; $42,300, MS-63, May 2015; $28,200, AU-58, September 2015											
1851, Restrike, Proof (a)	35–50	18	62.9							$20,000	$30,000	$75,000
	Auctions: $99,875, PF-65Cam, April 2014											
1852, Original † (a)	1,100	19	59.8	68%	$5,500	$10,000	$13,500	$17,500	$27,500	$40,000	$60,000	$140,000
	Auctions: $70,500, MS-63, January 2015; $34,075, AU-58, June 2014; $23,500, AU-50, September 2014											
1852, Original, Proof (a)	20–30	3	64.3							$27,500	$43,500	$75,000
	Auctions: $57,500, PF-65Cam, January 2009											
1852, Restrike, Proof (a)	20–30	17	63.6							$17,500	$30,000	$70,000
	Auctions: $70,500, PF-65, June 2014											
1853	46,110	148	57.9	55%	$350	$450	$650	$1,100	$1,300	$3,200	$7,250	$85,000
	Auctions: $12,925, MS-64, August 2016; $11,163, MS-64, March 2016; $2,350, AU-58, February 2015											
1853, Restrike, Proof (b)	15–20	6	63.7							$20,000	$37,000	$110,000
	Auctions: $152,750, PF-66Cam, August 2013; $105,750, PF-66, October 2014; $16,318, PF-58, October 2015											
1854	33,140	46	55.6	43%	$1,500	$2,500	$3,000	$4,150	$5,500	$9,000	$13,000	$95,000
	Auctions: $21,738, MS-64, May 2015; $6,169, AU-58, January 2015; $5,053, EF-45, June 2015; $4,465, VF-35, August 2015											
1854, Proof	40–60	16	63.7							$12,500	$16,500	$45,000
	Auctions: $49,938, PF-66, April 2013; $21,150, PF-64, May 2015; $15,275, PF-62, August 2014											
1855	26,000	57	53.9	32%	$1,250	$2,000	$3,000	$4,500	$5,250	$8,000	$30,000	—
	Auctions: $7,050, AU-58, October 2015; $4,700, AU-50, January 2015; $4,465, AU-50, August 2015; $5,640, EF-45, August 2015											
1855, Proof	40–60	21	64.0							$12,500	$16,000	$40,000
	Auctions: $45,531, PF-66, August 2013											

† Ranked in the *100 Greatest U.S. Coins* (fourth edition). **a.** Silver dollars of 1851 are found in two formats: originals struck for circulation and Proof restrikes made years later. Silver dollars of 1852 are found in these formats and also as original Proofs. "As part of [Mint Director] James Ross Snowden's restriking activities in 1859, Proof examples of certain rare silver dollars of earlier dates were made, including the 1851 and 1852. For the 1851 dollar, the original die (with four-date digit logotype slanting slightly upward and the date close to the base of Liberty) probably could not be located in 1859. In any event, a different die, not originally used in 1851, with the date horizontal and centered, was employed. Whether this die was created new in 1859 and given an 1851 date, or whether it was made in 1851 and not used at that time, is not known" (*United States Pattern Coins*, tenth edition). **b.** Made at the Mint from postdated dies circa 1862.

	Mintage	Cert	Avg	%MS	VG-8	F-12	VF-20	EF-40	AU-50	MS-60	MS-63	MS-65
										PF-60	PF-63	PF-65
1856	63,500	54	52.4	28%	$425	$525	$750	$1,600	$3,500	$5,000	$15,000	$85,000
	Auctions: $4,230, AU-58, January 2015; $3,290, EF-45, January 2015; $1,763, VF-20, June 2015; $1,234, F-15, October 2015											
1856, Proof	*40–60*	38	63.7							$5,500	$13,000	$30,000
	Auctions: $30,550, PF-65, October 2014; $27,025, PF-65, April 2013; $23,500, PF-65, May 2015; $13,513, PF-64, January 2015											
1857	94,000	89	58.9	71%	$425	$525	$750	$1,550	$1,900	$3,250	$9,500	$85,000
	Auctions: $76,375, MS-66, May 2015; $10,575, MS-64, October 2015; $5,405, AU-58, January 2015; $2,233, EF-45, January 2015											
1857, Proof	*50–70*	28	64.0							$7,000	$13,500	$30,000
	Auctions: No auction records available.											
1858, Proof (c)	300	72	62.4							$10,000	$14,000	$35,000
	Auctions: $11,456, PF-63, October 2014; $11,163, PF-63, September 2015; $14,100, PF-62, August 2015; $9,400, PF-61, January 2015											
1859	255,700	79	55.5	44%	$400	$425	$525	$750	$1,225	$2,500	$6,000	$85,000
	Auctions: $8,813, MS-64, January 2015; $5,170, MS-63, July 2015; $3,290, MS-61, June 2015; $1,880, AU-55, February 2015											
1859, Proof	800	154	63.9							$2,400	$4,750	$12,000
	Auctions: $5,640, PF-64, January 2015; $5,405, PF-64, June 2015; $3,258, PF-62, January 2015; $2,088, PF-60, January 2015											
1859-O	360,000	652	52.7	47%	$400	$425	$450	$600	$850	$2,050	$5,000	$65,000
	Auctions: $2,820, MS-62, February 2015; $764, AU-53, September 2015; $329, VF-25, February 2015; $259, F-15, September 2015											
1859-S	20,000	144	46.4	17%	$500	$550	$850	$1,700	$3,350	$13,000	$29,000	
	Auctions: $30,550, MS-63, August 2016; $17,625, MS-63, September 2015; $10,575, MS-62, October 2015; $9,400, MS-62, March 2016											
1860	217,600	120	56.8	53%	$425	$450	$525	$650	$850	$2,100	$5,000	$75,000
	Auctions: $6,463, MS-64, August 2015; $1,175, AU-53, July 2015; $823, AU-50, January 2015; $564, EF-40, January 2015											
1860, Proof	1,330	149	63.7							$2,400	$4,750	$12,000
	Auctions: $64,625, PF-67, April 2013; $24,675, PF-66, May 2015; $22,325, PF-66, October 2015; $4,230, PF-63, July 2015											
1860-O	515,000	924	53.7	51%	$400	$425	$450	$600	$785	$1,900	$3,750	$60,000
	Auctions: $6,169, MS-64, January 2015; $853, AU-55, June 2015; $541, EF-45, January 2015; $494, EF-40, June 2015											
1861	77,500	76	55.7	59%	$775	$1,100	$1,500	$2,500	$3,000	$3,750	$5,850	$65,000
	Auctions: $50,525, MS-65, May 2015; $8,225, MS-64, November 2014; $2,585, MS-60, June 2015; $3,055, EF-45, January 2015											
1861, Proof	1,000	99	63.4							$2,400	$4,750	$12,000
	Auctions: $4,994, PF-63Cam+, September 2014; $76,375, PF-66, June 2014											
1862	11,540	89	55.6	64%	$700	$1,100	$1,600	$2,750	$3,750	$6,750	$9,000	$65,000
	Auctions: $31,725, MS-64, June 2014; $12,925, MS-64, November 2014; $5,405, AU-53, January 2015; $3,525, EF-40, November 2014											
1862, Proof	550	168	63.3							$2,400	$4,750	$11,500
	Auctions: $38,775, PF-67, January 2015; $35,250, PF-67, August 2015; $6,169, PF-64, January 2015; $2,820, PF-62, January 2015											
1863	27,200	81	55.0	59%	$800	$1,100	$1,750	$1,850	$2,000	$3,575	$7,000	$50,000
	Auctions: $9,988, MS-64, August 2015; $8,813, MS-64, January 2015; $3,055, AU-53, July 2015; $1,763, EF-40, January 2015											
1863, Proof	460	141	63.6							$2,400	$4,750	$11,500
	Auctions: $129,250, PF-69, April 2013; $18,800, PF-66, May 2015; $9,988, PF-65, August 2014; $3,760, PF-63, January 2015											
1864	30,700	89	48.4	26%	$475	$550	$700	$1,000	$1,600	$3,575	$7,500	$60,000
	Auctions: $47,000, MS-65, May 2015; $1,058, AU-50, January 2015; $1,998, EF-45, October 2015; $1,528, EF-45, March 2015											
1864, Proof	470	160	63.5							$2,400	$4,750	$11,500
	Auctions: $52,875, PF-68, April 2013											
1865 (d)	46,500	77	51.3	32%	$425	$450	$650	$1,600	$2,100	$3,000	$7,500	$80,000
	Auctions: $5,405, MS-61, October 2015; $3,408, AU-55, January 2015; $1,116, AU-50, January 2015; $1,763, EF-40, February 2015											
1865, Proof	500	190	63.9							$2,400	$4,750	$11,500
	Auctions: $19,975, PF-66, August 2015; $10,575, PF-65, June 2015; $4,600, PF-63Cam, August 2015; $3,995, PF-63, July 2015											

c. Proof only. **d.** There is a common doubled-die reverse variety for 1865, which does not command a premium in today's market. "Doubling is evident only on the U of UNITED. . . . This is probably the most common variety for this date" (*Cherrypickers' Guide to Rare Die Varieties*, sixth edition, volume II).

1869, Repunched Date
FS-S1-1869-302.
Other varieties exist.

	Mintage	Cert	Avg	%MS	VG-8	F-12	VF-20	EF-40	AU-50	MS-60 PF-60	MS-63 PF-63	MS-65 PF-65
1866	48,900	113	52.0	35%	$425	$450	$575	$850	$1,100	$2,300	$5,500	$65,000
Auctions: $4,230, MS-63, January 2015; $2,291, MS-61, January 2015; $1,293, AU-50, August 2015; $823, EF-45, January 2015
1866, Proof	725	229	63.5							$2,100	$3,800	$11,500
Auctions: $19,975, PF-66Cam, October 2015; $17,625, PF-66Cam, May 2015; $6,463, PF-64, October 2015; $3,525, PF-62Cam, June 2015
1866, No Motto, Proof † (e)	*2 known*	2	64.0								—	
Auctions: No auction records available.
1867	46,900	72	49.4	35%	$425	$450	$575	$850	$1,050	$2,200	$5,300	$70,000
Auctions: $$11,163, MS-64, June 2015; $8,813, MS-64, October 2015; $881, AU-50, February 2015; $881, EF-40, January 2015
1867, Proof	625	217	63.4							$2,100	$3,900	$11,500
Auctions: $56,400, PF-65, May 2015; $47,588, PF-65, October 2015; $5,405, PF-64Cam, January 2015; $2,938, PF-63, June 2015
1868	162,100	115	48.0	17%	$425	$450	$500	$800	$1,150	$2,400	$7,000	$65,000
Auctions: $705, AU-50, January 2015; $764, EF-45, September 2015; $764, EF-40, January 2015; $423, EF-40, September 2015
1868, Proof	600	209	63.7							$2,100	$3,800	$11,500
Auctions: $3,290, PF-63, September 2015; $2,291, PF-62, August 2015; $2,115, PF-62, January 2015; $1,763, PF-61, October 2014
1869	423,700	135	50.1	33%	$425	$450	$500	$750	$1,050	$2,300	$5,250	$65,000
Auctions: $3,995, MS-63, September 2015; $4,230, MS-62, January 2015; $494, VF-30, June 2015; $423, VF-25, May 2015
1869, Repunched Date (f)	(g)	0	n/a						$1,100	$2,750	$7,000	
Auctions: $4,406, MS-62, October 2014
1869, Proof	600	207	63.5							$2,100	$3,800	$11,500
Auctions: $9,988, PF-64DCam, October 2014; $6,463, PF-64Cam, October 2014; $5,875, PF-64Cam, November 2014
1870	415,000	244	48.7	26%	$425	$450	$525	$600	$950	$2,100	$4,750	$55,000
Auctions: $56,400, MS-65+, May 2015; $1,175, AU-55, March 2015; $470, VF-35, January 2015; $400, VF-25, August 2015
1870, Proof	1,000	212	63.3							$2,100	$3,800	$11,500
Auctions: $17,625, PF-66Cam, September 2015; $9,106, PF-65, October 2015; $5,405, PF-64Cam, August 2015; $3,055, PF-63, July 2015
1870-CC	11,758	223	40.9	8%	$950	$1,400	$2,500	$4,500	$5,500	$25,000	$40,000	—
Auctions: $19,975, AU-58+, August 2015; $10,575, AU-55, July 2016; $9,988, AU-55, November 2016; $6,463, AU-50, January 2015
1870-S †	(h)	4	47.0	0%	$200,000	$250,000	$400,000	$525,000	$800,000	$1,750,000	—	
Auctions: $763,750, EF-40, January 2014
1871	1,073,800	805	45.3	20%	$425	$450	$525	$600	$1,050	$2,100	$4,650	$50,000
Auctions: $50,525, MS-65, January 2015; $705, AU-50, March 2015; $470, EF-45, June 2015; $306, VF-20, December 2015
1871, Proof	960	203	62.9							$2,100	$3,800	$11,500
Auctions: $21,150, PF-66, January 2015; $15,863, PF-66, October 2015; $4,700, PF-64, September 2015; $1,998, PF-61, October 2015
1871-CC	1,376	45	41.7	9%	$3,500	$6,000	$7,500	$13,500	$22,500	$75,000	$175,000	—
Auctions: $5,640, AU-50, January 2015; $11,163, VF-35, January 2015; $4,935, VF-25, January 2015; $3,760, F-12, January 2015

† Ranked in the *100 Greatest U.S. Coins* (fourth edition). **e.** The 1866, No Motto, dollar is classified as Judd-540 (*United States Pattern Coins*). Two examples of this fantasy piece are known; at least one was deliberately struck for pharmacist and coin collector Robert Coulton Davis, likely around 1869 or in the early 1870s, along with the No Motto Proof quarter and half dollar of the same date. The three-coin set is on display at the American Numismatic Association's Edward C. Rochette Money Museum in Colorado Springs. "A second 1866 'No Motto' silver dollar resurfaced in the 1970s before entering a private Midwestern collection in the early 1980s. After not meeting its auction reserve price in September 2003, the coin was sold privately for nearly a million dollars some time later" (*100 Greatest U.S. Coins*, fourth edition). **f.** There are several repunched dates known for 1869. The one listed is FS-S1-1869-302. The top flag of a secondary 1 is evident midway between the primary 1 and the 8. **g.** Included in circulation-strike 1869 mintage figure. **h.** The Mint shows no record of 1870-S dollars being struck, but about a dozen are known to exist. The 1870-S silver dollars may have been struck as mementos of the laying of the cornerstone of the San Francisco Mint (May 25, 1870).

	Mintage	Cert	Avg	%MS	VG-8	F-12	VF-20	EF-40	AU-50	MS-60 / PF-60	MS-63 / PF-63	MS-65 / PF-65
1872	1,105,500	593	43.6	16%	$425	$450	$525	$600	$950	$2,050	$4,700	$50,000
	Auctions: $14,100, MS-64, August 2015; $940, AU-53, January 2015; $329, F-15, August 2015; $176, G-4, February 2015											
1872, Proof	950	178	63.1							$2,100	$3,800	$11,500
	Auctions: $9,988, PF-65, August 2015; $8,813, PF-65, March 2015; $7,638, PF-64, May 2015; $1,410, PF-60, January 2015											
1872-CC	3,150	88	41.1	16%	$3,000	$4,000	$4,500	$6,500	$10,000	$28,000	$100,000	$300,000
	Auctions: $28,200, MS-62, October 2015; $11,750, AU-53, February 2015; $5,640, EF-45, August 2015; $2,468, VG-10, February 2015											
1872-S	9,000	112	42.9	11%	$500	$675	$950	$1,975	$3,500	$12,000	$37,500	
	Auctions: $7,050, MS-61, October 2015; $6,463, AU-58, January 2015; $1,528, EF-40, October 2015; $1,410, VF-35, January 2015											
1873	293,000	184	52.0	39%	$475	$500	$550	$600	$975	$2,100	$4,850	$60,000
	Auctions: $58,750, MS-65, May 2015; $11,750, MS-64+, January 2015; $881, EF-45, October 2015; $646, VF-35, February 2015											
1873, Proof	600	185	63.3							$2,100	$3,800	$11,500
	Auctions: $16,450, PF-65Cam+, August 2014; $9,988, PF-65, June 2015; $16,450, PF-64, August 2015; $940, PF-60, January 2015											
1873-CC	2,300	26	43.5	15%	$9,500	$13,500	$22,500	$32,500	$45,000	$115,000	$190,000	$500,000
	Auctions: $105,750, MS-61, May 2015; $56,400, AU-55, August 2015; $35,250, EF-45, November 2014; $11,163, EF-40, January 2015											
1873-S (i)	700	0	n/a									
	Auctions: No auction records available.											

i. The 1873-S is unknown in any collection, public or private, despite Mint records indicating that 700 were struck. None have ever been seen.

MORGAN (1878–1921)

Designer: *George T. Morgan.* **Weight:** *26.73 grams.* **Composition:** *.900 silver, .100 copper (net weight .77344 oz. pure silver).* **Diameter:** *38.1 mm.*
Edge: *Reeded.* **Mints:** *Philadelphia, New Orleans, Carson City, Denver, and San Francisco.*

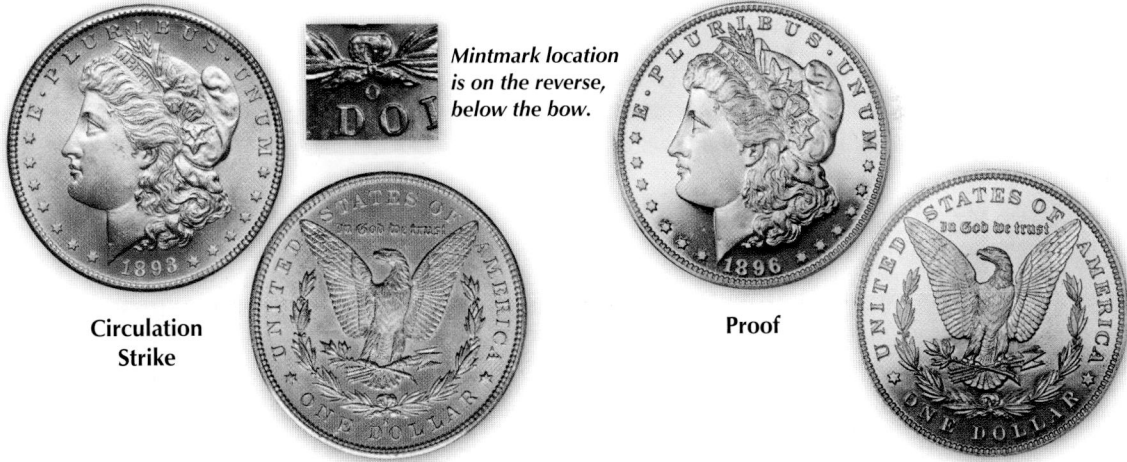

Mintmark location is on the reverse, below the bow.

Circulation Strike

Proof

History. The Morgan dollar, named for English-born designer George T. Morgan, was struck every year from 1878 to 1904, and again in 1921. The coin's production benefited Western silver interests by creating an artificial federal demand for the metal, whose market value had dropped sharply by 1878. Hundreds of millions of the coins, stored in cloth bags of 1,000 each, piled up in government vaults. In the 1900s some were melted, but immense quantities were bought by collectors and investors; today they are the most widely collected of all coins of their era.

Striking and Sharpness. On coins of 1878 to 1900, check the hair above Miss Liberty's ear and, on the reverse, the breast feathers of the eagle. These are weak on many issues, particularly those of the New Orleans Mint. From 1900 to 1904 a new reverse hub was used, and breast feathers, while discernible, are not as sharp. In 1921 new dies were made in lower relief, with certain areas indistinct. Many Morgan dollars have partially or fully prooflike surfaces. These are designated as Prooflike (PL), Deep Prooflike (DPL), or Deep Mirror Prooflike (DMPL). Certification practices can be erratic, and some DMPL-certified coins are not fully mirrored. All prooflike coins tend to emphasize contact marks, with the result that lower MS levels can be unattractive. *A Guide Book of Morgan Silver Dollars* (Bowers) and other references furnish information as to which dates and mintmarks are easily found with Full Details and which usually are weak, as well as the availability of the various levels of prooflike surface.

Proofs were struck from 1878 to 1904, with those of 1878 to 1901 generally having cameo contrast, and 1902 to 1904 having the portrait lightly polished in the die. Some are lightly struck; check the hair above Liberty's ear (in particular), and the eagle's breast feathers. In 1921 many so-called Zerbe Proofs (named thus after numismatic entrepreneur Farran Zerbe), with many microscopic die-finish lines, were made. A very few deeply mirrored 1921 coins were made, called Chapman Proofs (after coin dealer Henry Chapman, who started marketing them shortly after their production). Some Zerbe Proofs have been miscertified as Chapman Proofs.

Availability. All dates and mints of Morgan dollars are available in grades from well worn to MS. Some issues such as certain Carson City coins are rare if worn and common in MS. Other issues such as the 1901 Philadelphia coins are common if worn and are rarities at MS-65. The 1889-CC and 1893-S, and the Proof 1895, are considered to be the key issues. Varieties listed herein are some of those most significant to collectors. Numerous other variations exist, studied in the *Cherrypickers' Guide to Rare Die Varieties* and other specialized texts. Values shown herein are for the most common pieces. Values of varieties not listed in this guide depend on collector interest and demand.

Note: Values of common-date silver coins have been based on the current bullion price of silver, $17 per ounce, and may vary with the prevailing spot price.

GRADING STANDARDS

MS-60 to 70 (Mint State). *Obverse:* At MS-60, some abrasion and contact marks are evident, most noticeably on the cheek and on the hair above the ear. The left field also shows such marks. Luster is present, but may be dull or lifeless. At MS-63, contact marks are extensive but not distracting. Abrasion still is evident, but less than at lower levels. Indeed, the cheek of Miss Liberty showcases abrasion. An MS-65 coin may have minor abrasion, but

1895-O. Graded MS-61.

contact marks are so minute as to require magnification. Luster should be full and rich. Coins with proof-like surfaces such as PL, DPL, and DMPL display abrasion and contact marks much more noticeably than coins with frosty surfaces; in grades below MS-64 many are unattractive. With today's loose and sometimes contradictory interpretations, many at MS-64 appear to have extensive marks as well. *Reverse:* Comments apply as for the obverse, except that in lower Mint State grades abrasion and contact marks are most noticeable on the eagle's breast. At MS-65 or higher there are no marks visible to the unaided eye. The field is mainly protected by design elements, so the reverse often appears to grade a point or two higher than the obverse. A Morgan dollar can have an MS-63 obverse and an MS-65 reverse, as was indeed the nomenclature used prior to the single-number system. A careful cataloger may want to describe each side separately for a particularly valuable or rare Morgan dollar. An example with an MS-63 obverse and an MS-65 reverse should have an overall grade of MS-63, as the obverse is traditionally given prominence.

Illustrated coin: This is a lustrous and attractive example.

AU-50, 53, 55, 58 (About Uncirculated).
Obverse: Light wear is seen on the cheek and, to a lesser extent, on the hair below the coronet. Generally, the hair details mask friction and wear and it is not as easy to notice as on the cheek and in the fields. At AU-58, the luster is extensive, but incomplete, especially on the higher parts and in the left field. At AU–50 and 53, luster is less, but still is present. PL, DPL, and DMPL coins are not widely desired at these levels, as the marks are too distracting. *Reverse:* Wear is evident on the head, breast, wing tips, and, to a lesser extent, in the field. An AU-58 coin (as determined by the obverse) can have a reverse that appears to be full Mint State. (Incidentally, this is also true of Barber quarter dollars and half dollars.)

1889-CC. Graded AU-58.

Illustrated coin: This is a lustrous example of the rarest Carson City Morgan dollar. As is typical of AU-58 dollars of this design, the reverse appears to be full Mint State, as the field is protected by the design elements.

EF-40, 45 (Extremely Fine). *Obverse:* Further wear is seen on the cheek in particular. The hair near the forehead and temple has flatness in areas, most noticeable above the ear. Some luster can be seen in protected areas on many coins, but is not needed to define the EF-40 and 45 grades. *Reverse:* Further wear is seen on the breast of the eagle (most noticeably), the wing tips, and the leaves.

1879-CC. Graded EF-40.

VF-20, 30 (Very Fine). *Obverse:* The head shows more wear, now with most of the detail gone in the areas adjacent to the forehead and temple. The lower area has most hair fused into large strands. *Reverse:* Wear is more extensive on the breast and on the feathers in the upper area of the wings, especially the right wing, and on the legs. The high area of the leaves has no detail.

1889-CC. Graded VF-20.

F-12, 15 (Fine). *Obverse:* The head shows more wear, with most hair detail gone, and with a large flat area above the ear. Less detail is seen in the lower curls. *Reverse:* More wear is seen on the reverse, with the eagle's breast and legs flat and about a third of the feather detail gone, mostly near the tops of the wings.

1893-S. Graded F-15.

VG-8, 10 (Very Good). *Obverse:* More hair details are gone, especially from the area from the top of the head down to the ear. The details of the lower part of the cap are gone. The rim is weak in areas, and some denticles are worn away. *Reverse:* Further wear has smoothed more than half of the feathers in the wing. The leaves are flat except for the lowest areas. The rim is weak in areas.

1892-CC. Graded VG-8.

G-4, 6 (Good). *Obverse:* The head is in outline form, with most details gone. LIBERTY still is readable. The eye position and lips are discernible. Most of the rim is worn away. *Reverse:* The eagle shows some feathers near the bottom of the wings, but nearly all others are gone. The leaves are seen in outline form. The rim is mostly worn away. Some letters have details toward the border worn away.

The Morgan dollar is seldom collected in grades lower than G-4.

Illustrated coin: Here is a well-worn example of this key issue.

1893-S. Graded G-4.

PF-60 to 70 (Proof). *Obverse and Reverse:* Dull, grainy Proofs, or extensively cleaned ones with many hairlines, are lower level (PF–60 to 62). Only the 1895 is desirable at such low grades. Those with medium hairlines and good reflectivity may grade at about PF-64, and with relatively few hairlines, Gem PF-65. Hairlines are most easily seen in the obverse field. Horizontal slide marks on Miss Liberty's cheek, caused by clear slides on

1898. Graded PF-64.

some coin albums, are common. PF-66 may have hairlines so delicate that magnification is needed to see them. Above that, a Proof should be free of such lines, including slide marks.

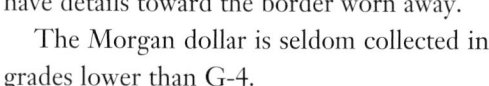

First Reverse
Eight tail feathers.

Second Reverse
Parallel top arrow feather,
concave breast.

Third Reverse
Slanted top arrow feather,
convex breast.

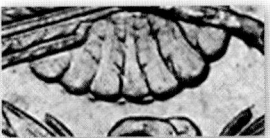

1878, Doubled
Tail Feathers
FS-S1-1878-032.

1878, 8 Feathers,
Obverse Die Gouge
The "Wild Eye" variety.
VAM-14.11. FS-S1-1878-014.11.

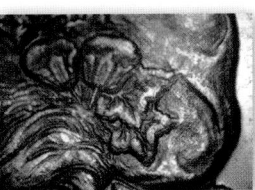

1878, 7 Over 8 Tail Feathers, Tripled Leaves
VAM-44. FS-S1-1878-044.

	Mintage	Cert	Avg	%MS	VF-20	EF-40	AU-50	MS-60	MS-63	MS-64	MS-64DMPL	MS-65	MS-65DMPL
											PF-60	PF-63	PF-65
1878, 8 Feathers	*749,500*	12,415	62.0	94%	$85	$100	$120	$200	$285	$475	$4,000	$1,250	$21,000
	Auctions: $1,586, MS-65, January 2015; $212, MS-62, May 2015; $125, AU-55, February 2015; $89, EF-45, May 2015												
1878, 8 Feathers, Obverse Die Gouge (a)	(b)	7	60.4	71%				$8,000	$13,000	$24,000			
	Auctions: $16,100, MS-62, August 2011												
1878, 7 Feathers, All kinds	*9,759,300*												
1878, 7 Over 8, Clear Doubled Feathers	(c)	2,480	61.5	91%	$50	$55	$75	$200	$275	$500	$5,200	$1,600	$16,000
	Auctions: $1,410, MS-64, January 2015; $223, MS-63, August 2015; $188, MS-62, June 2015; $52, EF-45, February 2015												
1878, 7 Over 8, Tripled Leaves (d)	(c)	22	50.8	23%			$5,900	$12,000	$23,000				
	Auctions: $820, MS-65, September 2015; $206, MS-64, January 2015; $106, MS-62, June 2015; $62, AU-58, February 2015												
1878, 7 Feathers, 2nd Reverse (e)	(c)	15,210	62.3	95%	$45	$48	$60	$90	$150	$250	$2,200	$900	$11,000
	Auctions: $3,760, MS-66, January 2015; $176, MS-63, June 2015; $84, MS-61, February 2015; $62, AU-55, April 2015												
1878, 7 Feathers, 3rd Reverse (e)	(c)	5,474	61.5	90%	$45	$48	$50	$110	$250	$450	$5,500	$1,750	$23,000
	Auctions: $11,163, MS-66, August 2015												

a. Two spikes protrude from the front of Liberty's eye. "Fewer than a dozen specimens are known of this Top 100 variety and any sale is a landmark event" (*Cherrypickers' Guide to Rare Die Varieties*, sixth edition, volume II). **b.** Included in circulation-strike 1878, 8 Feathers, mintage figure. **c.** Included in circulation-strike 1878, 7 Feathers, mintage figure. **d.** Called the "King of VAMs" (Van Allen / Mallis varieties), this variety shows three to five weak tail feathers under the seven primary feathers. On the obverse, tripling is evident on the cotton bolls and the leaves, and doubling on LIBERTY. Values are fluid for this popular variety. **e.** The Second Reverse is sometimes known as "Concave Breast" or "Reverse of 1878." The Third Reverse is sometimes known as "Round Breast" or "Reverse of 1879."

1880, 80 Over 79
VAM-6. FS-S1-1880-006.

	Mintage	Cert	Avg	%MS	VF-20	EF-40	AU-50	MS-60	MS-63	MS-64	MS-64DMPL / PF-60	MS-65 / PF-63	MS-65DMPL / PF-65
1878, 8 Feathers, Proof	500	135	64.2								$1,500	$3,500	$11,500
Auctions: $70,500, PF-67, January 2015; $11,163, PF-65Cam, January 2015; $14,100, PF-64Cam+, August 2015; $5,053, PF-64, August 2015													
1878, 7 Feathers, 2nd Reverse, Proof	250	100	63.6								$2,750	$3,750	$12,500
Auctions: $8,225, PF-63, March 2015; $6,463, PF-63, August 2015; $4,700, PF-63, October 2014; $6,463, PF-62, September 2014													
1878, 7 Feathers, 3rd Reverse, Proof (e)	(f)	5	62.4								$16,500	$85,000	$200,000
Auctions: $155,250, PF-64, November 2004													
1878-CC	2,212,000	26,131	60.4	88%	$120	$140	$180	$400	$475	$575	$2,800	$1,650	$10,000
Auctions: $17,625, MS-66, August 2016; $14,100, MS-66, November 2016; $12,925, MS-66, October 2016; $6,463, MS-66, January 2015													
1878-S	9,774,000	46,773	63.1	98%	$45	$47	$48	$65	$100	$120	$2,000	$300	$10,000
Auctions: $8,225, MS-67, January 2015; $306, MS-65, November 2015; $79, MS-63, May 2015; $2,703, EF-45, February 2015													
1879	14,806,000	12,467	62.6	94%	$35	$37	$40	$55	$90	$155	$2,100	$650	$15,000
Auctions: $2,468, MS-66, January 2015; $617, MS-65, November 2015; $141, MS-64, February 2015; $118, MS-60, August 2015													
1879, Proof	1,100	322	64.2								$1,300	$3,200	$5,500
Auctions: $14,100, PF-67Cam, August 2015; $4,583, PF-64Cam, January 2015; $2,585, PF-63, January 2015; $1,763, PF-62, August 2015													
1879-CC, CC Over CC	756,000	2,101	48.1	51%	$290	$770	$1,700	$4,200	$6,750	$10,000	$40,000	$42,500	$60,000
Auctions: $4,700, MS-62, March 2015; $1,058, EF-45, January 2015; $541, VF-35, September 2015; $176, VG-10, February 2015													
1879-CC, Clear CC	(g)	3,672	48.3	58%	$290	$750	$2,200	$4,500	$8,000	$11,000	$23,500	$22,500	$47,500
Auctions: $21,150, MS-65, September 2015; $9,694, MS-64, January 2015; $705, EF-40, July 2015; $481, VF-35, July 2015													
1879-O	2,887,000	9,058	61.3	84%	$40	$42	$47	$90	$250	$600	$4,250	$2,750	$22,000
Auctions: $17,625, MS-66, August 2015; $3,525, MS-65, January 2015; $112, MS-61, May 2015; $56, AU-55, March 2015													
1879-O, Proof (h)	4–8	5	64.4										$275,000
Auctions: $176,250, PF-64, August 2013													
1879-S, 2nd Reverse	9,110,000	2,418	60.3	80%	$40	$45	$70	$190	$600	$1,500	$8,000	$4,250	$21,000
Auctions: $3,290, MS-65, January 2015; $1,704, MS-64, January 2015; $84, AU-55, August 2015; $200, AU-53, May 2015													
1879-S, 3rd Reverse	(i)	104,060	64.2	100%	$32	$35	$39	$55	$65	$80	$500	$170	$1,300
Auctions: $5,758, MS-68, June 2015; $1,351, MS-67, January 2015; $112, MS-64, September 2015; $282, MS-63, November 2015													
1880	12,600,000	14,112	62.7	96%	$35	$37	$39	$50	$75	$145	$1,150	$625	$6,000
Auctions: $4,230, MS-66, June 2015; $588, MS-65, October 2015; $141, MS-64, July 2015; $194, AU-53, February 2015													
1880, 80 Over 79 (j)	(k)	1	45.0	0%	$35	$37	$48	$150	$600	$2,500		$3,000	
Auctions: $764, AU-58, January 2015; $200, AU-55, February 2015; $176, AU-53, November 2014; $153, AU-50, January 2015													
1880, Proof	1,355	428	64.8								$1,300	$3,000	$5,500
Auctions: $10,575, PF-67Cam, August 2015; $9,988, PF-66Cam+, June 2015; $6,169, PF-65, August 2015; $2,585, PF-62, March 2015													

e. The Second Reverse is sometimes known as "Concave Breast" or "Reverse of 1878." The Third Reverse is sometimes known as "Round Breast" or "Reverse of 1879." **f.** Included in 1878, 7 Feathers, Proof, mintage figure. **g.** Included in 1879-CC, CC Over CC, mintage figure. **h.** Some numismatists classify these as Deep Mirror Prooflike circulation strikes, rather than as Proofs. **i.** Included in 1879-S, 2nd Reverse, mintage figure. **j.** Several die varieties exist; values shown are for the most common. **k.** Included in circulation-strike 1880 mintage figure.

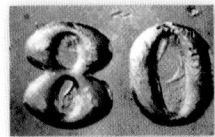
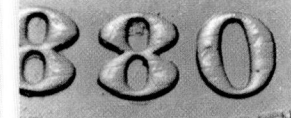

1880-CC, 80 Over 79
VAM-4. FS-S1-1880CC-004.

1880-CC, 8 Over High 7
VAM-5. FS-S1-1880CC-005.

1880-CC, 8 Over Low 7
VAM-6. FS-S1-1880CC-006.

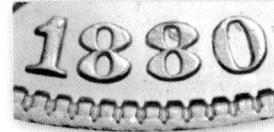

1880-O, 80 Over 79
VAM-4. FS-S1-1880o-004.

1880-O, Die Gouge
The "Hangnail" variety.
VAM-49. FS-S1-1880o-049.

	Mintage	Cert	Avg	%MS	VF-20	EF-40	AU-50	MS-60	MS-63	MS-64	MS-64DMPL / PF-60	MS-65 / PF-63	MS-65DMPL / PF-65
1880-CC, All kinds	591,000												
1880-CC, 80 Over 79, 2nd Reverse (l)		1,323	62.8	99%	$220	$285	$350	$500	$650	$1,150	$5,000	$2,500	$20,000
Auctions: $8,225, MS-66, March 2015; $1,058, MS-64, January 2015; $734, MS-63, March 2015; $129, G-4, January 2015													
1880-CC, 8 Over 7, 2nd Reverse		328	63.4	100%	$210	$285	$325	$550	$600	$1,000	$5,000	$1,850	$20,000
Auctions: $1,998, MS-64, August 2015; $881, MS-64, July 2015; $588, MS-62, August 2015; $235, VG-10, August 2015													
1880-CC, 8 Over High 7, 3rd Reverse (m)		588	63.5	100%	$210	$275	$325	$500	$575	$700	$2,450	$1,000	$9,000
Auctions: $852, MS-64+, March 2015; $588, MS-64, January 2015; $541, MS-63, September 2015; $529, MS-63, December 2015													
1880-CC, 8 Over Low 7, 3rd Reverse (n)		475	63.5	100%	$270	$365	$475	$600	$750	$850	$2,700	$1,000	$9,000
Auctions: $1,763, MS-65, March 2015; $905, MS-64, September 2015; $764, MS-64, June 2015; $494, MS-63, August 2015													
1880-CC, 3rd Reverse		0	n/a		$210	$275	$325	$500	$575	$700	$2,450	$1,000	$9,000
Auctions: $18,800, MS-67, January 2015; $259, EF-45, February 2015; $200, VF-25, September 2015; $112, G-6, July 2015													
1880-O, All kinds	5,305,000												
1880-O, 80 Over 79 (o)		248	59.5	66%	$35	$37	$43	$90	$375	$1,550	$7,250	$15,000	$62,500
Auctions: $353, MS-63, January 2015; $341, MS-63, September 2015; $353, AU-58, January 2015; $165, AU-58, March 2015													
1880-O		10,302	60.5	75%	$35	$37	$48	$150	$600	$2,500	$8,000		
Auctions: $14,100, MS-65, January 2015; $329, MS-63, November 2015; $64, AU-58, August 2015; $48, AU-55, February 2015													
1880-O, Die Gouge (p)		214	56.0	36%	$200	$450	$900	$2,000	—				
Auctions: $15,275, MS-65, January 2015; $94, AU-58, March 2015; $74, AU-58, January 2015; $69, AU-58, February 2015													
1880-S, All kinds	8,900,000												
1880-S, 80 Over 79		814	63.9	99%	$35	$40	$46	$55	$75	$125	$450	$275	$1,500
Auctions: $435, MS-66, January 2015; $188, MS-65, October 2015; $112, MS-64, April 2015; $94, MS-64, February 2015													
1880-S, 0 Over 9		937	64.0	100%	$35	$40	$46	$63	$75	$125	$450	$275	$1,500
Auctions: $1,058, MS-66+, January 2015; $176, MS-65, April 2015; $129, MS-64, May 2015; $89, MS-63, September 2015													
1880-S		153,690	64.2	100%	$32	$37	$39	$50	$60	$80	$450	$135	$1,000
Auctions: $12,925, MS-68, February 2015; $3,525, MS-65, January 2015; $282, MS-64, November 2015; $182, MS-63, May 2015													

l. The top crossbar and diagonal stem of an underlying 79 are clearly seen within the 8. Extensive polishing marks are visible within the 0. **m.** An almost complete 7 is visible inside the last 8 of the date. The top edge of the 7 touches the top inside of the 8. **n.** A complete 7 is visible inside the last 8 of the date. The crossbar of the underlying 7 can be seen in the top loop and the diagonal of the 7 is visible in the lower loop. **o.** The crossbar of the underlying 7 is visible within the upper loop of the second 8. The 1 and the first 8 are slightly doubled to the right. **p.** On the reverse of the "Hangnail" variety, a die gouge runs from the bottom of the arrow feather, across the feathers, and out the eagle's rightmost tail feather. On the obverse, the top-left part of the second 8 has a spike.

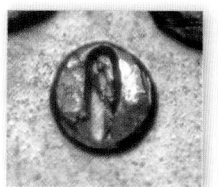
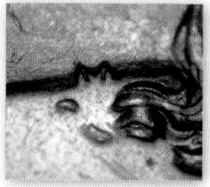

1881-O, Repunched Mintmark
VAM-5. FS-S1-1881o-005.

1882-O, O Over S
VAM-4. FS-S1-1882o-004.

	Mintage	Cert	Avg	%MS	VF-20	EF-40	AU-50	MS-60	MS-63	MS-64	MS-64DMPL	MS-65	MS-65DMPL
											PF-60	PF-63	PF-65
1881	9,163,000	11,333	63.1	98%	$35	$37	$42	$53	$75	$170	$1,375	$600	$19,500
	Auctions: $2,350, MS-66, August 2015; $588, MS-65, June 2015; $118, MS-64, October 2015; $79, MS-63, January 2015												
1881, Proof	984	265	64.2								$1,300	$3,000	$5,500
	Auctions: $5,581, PF-65Cam, July 2014; $8,813, PF-67, August 2014; $14,100, PF-67, October 2014; $2,468, PF-63, January 2015												
1881-CC	296,000	22,036	63.2	98%	$400	$425	$440	$500	$575	$625	$1,200	$900	$3,000
	Auctions: $7,050, MS-67+, October 2015; $517, MS-64, January 2015; $470, MS-61, April 2015; $306, VF-20, March 2015												
1881-O	5,708,000	17,947	62.6	95%	$35	$37	$39	$50	$70	$185	$900	$1,150	$18,000
	Auctions: $10,575, MS-66, June 2015; $3,290, MS-65+, August 2015; $129, MS-64, July 2015; $48, AU-58, June 2015												
1881-O, Repunched Mintmark (q)	(r)	84	61.8	99%				$80	$110	$225	—	$1,450	$1,500
	Auctions: $218, MS-64, March 2012												
1881-O, Doubled Die Obverse (s)	(r)	32	56.7	25%			$175	$400	—	—			
	Auctions: $150, AU-50, September 2011												
1881-S	12,760,000	252,423	64.1	100%	$32	$37	$39	$50	$60	$80	$475	$135	$1,000
	Auctions: $5,405, MS-68+, January 2015; $129, MS-65, September 2015; $74, MS-64+, May 2015; $188, MS-63, November 2015												
1882	11,100,000	20,122	63.2	98%	$35	$37	$39	$50	$65	$120	$1,000	$425	$6,500
	Auctions: $3,173, MS-66+, August 2015; $112, MS-64+, March 2015; $61, MS-63, June 2015; $294, AU-58, January 2015												
1882, Proof	1,100	358	64.4								$1,300	$3,000	$5,500
	Auctions: $14,688, PF-67Cam, October 2015; $9,400, PF-66DCam, August 2015; $4,935, PF-65, January 2015; $4,465, PF-64, January 2015												
1882-CC	1,133,000	41,072	63.2	99%	$110	$120	$145	$210	$235	$275	$625	$525	$1,900
	Auctions: $6,463, MS-67, January 2015; $129, AU-53, May 2015; $112, EF-40, June 2015; $84, VG-8, February 2015												
1882-O	6,090,000	18,312	62.8	96%	$35	$37	$42	$50	$80	$135	$1,300	$850	$5,200
	Auctions: $4,583, MS-66, July 2015; $84, MS-64, February 2015; $56, MS-62, February 2015; $54, AU-55, July 2015												
1882-O, O Over S (t)	(u)	4,034	56.6	41%	$50	$70	$120	$235	$750	$2,000	$8,500	$50,000	$62,500
	Auctions: $1,528, MS-64, March 2016; $911, MS-63, March 2015; $376, MS-62, July 2015; $94, AU-58, January 2015; $42, VF-35, April 2015												
1882-S	9,250,000	80,981	64.2	100%	$32	$37	$39	$50	$65	$80	$950	$135	$3,800
	Auctions: $4,465, MS-68, October 2015; $1,058, MS-67, July 2015; $176, MS-65, August 2015; $84, MS-64, January 2015												
1883	12,290,000	23,890	63.6	99%	$35	$37	$39	$50	$70	$100	$450	$175	$1,600
	Auctions: $5,875, MS-67+, October 2015; $188, MS-65, May 2015; $89, MS-64, January 2015; $60, MS-63, August 2015												
1883, Proof	1,039	296	64.1								$1,300	$3,000	$5,500
	Auctions: $16,450, PF-67, January 2015; $8,225, PF-66Cam, January 2015; $2,468, PF-63, June 2015; $1,410, PF-61, September 2015												
1883-CC	1,204,000	54,155	63.5	99%	$110	$120	$145	$210	$225	$265	$525	$475	$1,300
	Auctions: $3,760, MS-67, January 2015; $4,230, MS-66+, January 2015; $423, MS-65, November 2015; $229, MS-61, July 2015												
1883-O	8,725,000	131,979	63.4	100%	$32	$37	$39	$50	$60	$80	$500	$140	$1,450
	Auctions: $2,585, MS-67, January 2015; $129, MS-65, October 2015; $74, MS-64, August 2015; $79, MS-62, February 2015												
1883-O, Proof (v)	4–8	2	64.0										$200,000
	Auctions: $270,250, PF-67Cam, April 2013												
1883-S	6,250,000	5,646	55.4	33%	$35	$53	$140	$750	$2,350	$5,250	$75,000	$32,500	$125,000
	Auctions: $17,625, MS-65, September 2015; $1,351, MS-61, June 2015; $341, AU-58, January 2015; $50, EF-45, May 2015												

q. A diagonal image, the remains of one or two additional O mintmark punches, is visible within the primary O. **r.** Included in 1881-O mintage figure. **s.** Clear doubling is evident on the back outside of Liberty's ear **t.** Several varieties exist. **u.** Included in 1882-O mintage figure. **v.** "A numismatic tradition exists, dating back well over a century, that 12 full Proofs were struck of the 1883-O Morgan dollar. And, they may have been, although the differentiation between a cameo DMPL and a 'branch mint Proof' would be difficult to explain" (*A Guide Book of Morgan Silver Dollars*, fifth edition).

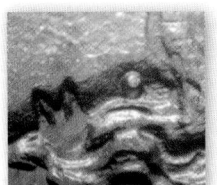 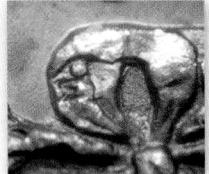

1884, Large Dot
VAM-3. FS-S1-1884-003.

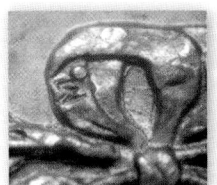 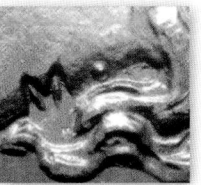

1884, Small Dot
VAM-4. FS-S1-1884-004.

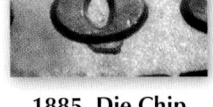

1885, Die Chip
VAM-8. FS-S1-1885-008.

1886, Repunched Date
VAM-20. FS-S1-1886-020.

	Mintage	Cert	Avg	%MS	VF-20	EF-40	AU-50	MS-60	MS-63	MS-64	MS-64DMPL	MS-65	MS-65DMPL
											PF-60	PF-63	PF-65
1884, All kinds	14,070,000												
1884		18,410	63.3	98%	$35	$37	$39	$50	$70	$100	$850	$300	$5,000
Auctions: $25,850, MS-68, January 2015; $1,880, MS-66, October 2015; $94, MS-64, February 2015; $64, MS-63, July 2015													
1884, Large Dot (w)		98	55.2	44%			$55	$85	$225	—			
Auctions: $80, MS-62, May 2014; $74, AU-55, September 2014													
1884, Small Dot (w)		245	61.9	91%			$65	$90	$325	—			
Auctions: $182, MS-63, September 2014; $153, MS-63, February 2015; $141, MS-63, September 2014; $123, MS-63, July 2015													
1884, Proof	875	210	64.4								$1,300	$3,000	$5,500
Auctions: $8,813, PF-66Cam, July 2015; $4,259, PF-65, March 2015; $4,406, PF-64Cam, March 2015; $3,760, PF-63Cam, January 2015													
1884-CC	1,136,000	62,237	63.6	100%	$140	$150	$160	$210	$225	$265	$550	$475	$1,300
Auctions: $5,170, MS-67, June 2015; $423, MS-65, November 2015; $306, MS-64, February 2015; $223, MS-62, March 2015													
1884-O	9,730,000	212,636	63.5	100%	$32	$37	$39	$50	$60	$80	$450	$135	$1,000
Auctions: $2,585, MS-67, January 2015; $188, MS-65, June 2015; $74, MS-64, September 2015; $188, MS-63, February 2015													
1884-S	3,200,000	7,919	52.4	5%	$40	$60	$290	$7,200	$35,000	$125,000	$135,000	$235,000	$275,000
Auctions: $123,375, MS-64, January 2015; $41,125, MS-63, November 2016; $22,325, MS-62, August 2015; $17,625, MS-62, March 2016													
1885	17,787,000	79,158	63.7	99%	$32	$37	$39	$50	$60	$75	$450	$135	$1,000
Auctions: $2,174, MS-67, October 2015; $147, MS-65, August 2015; $764, MS-64, October 2015; $329, MS-63, November 2015													
1885, Die Chip (x)	(y)	14	62.4	93%			$70	$95	$525	—			
Auctions: No auction records available.													
1885, Proof	930	249	64.3								$1,300	$3,000	$5,500
Auctions: $9,400, PF-66Cam, June 2015; $7,050, PF-65, July 2015; $4,935, PF-64Cam, August 2015; $2,938, PF-63, July 2015													
1885-CC	228,000	21,866	63.5	99%	$550	$570	$590	$700	$800	$875	$1,300	$1,100	$2,400
Auctions: $14,100, MS-67, October 2015; $2,468, MS-66+, January 2015; $676, MS-62, July 2015; $423, F-12, February 2015													
1885-O	9,185,000	207,615	63.7	100%	$32	$37	$39	$50	$60	$75	$450	$135	$1,000
Auctions: $37,600, MS-68, January 2015; $329, MS-66, November 2015; $118, MS-64, November 2015; $74, MS-63, February 2015													
1885-S	1,497,000	6,578	60.8	82%	$50	$63	$110	$250	$300	$675	$5,000	$1,650	$45,000
Auctions: $4,700, MS-66, June 2015; $1,645, MS-65, May 2015; $212, MS-60, April 2015; $79, AU-50, January 2015													
1886	19,963,000	135,282	63.8	100%	$32	$37	$39	$50	$60	$75	$475	$135	$1,300
Auctions: $4,465, MS-68, June 2015; $1,293, MS-67, August 2015; $176, MS-65, November 2015; $62, MS-64, May 2015													
1886, RPD (z)	(aa)	10	60.1	70%			$2,250	$3,500	$5,500	—			
Auctions: $3,819, MS-64, September 2013													
1886, Proof	886	240	64.1								$1,300	$3,000	$5,500
Auctions: $8,813, PF-67, October 2014; $5,875, PF-66, October 2014; $5,405, PF-66, January 2015; $1,939, PF-62, July 2015													

w. A raised dot, either Large or Small, is visible after the designer's initial and on the reverse ribbon. "These dots varieties are thought to have been used as some sort of identifier" (*Cherrypickers' Guide to Rare Die Varieties*, sixth edition, volume II). **x.** A large, raised die chip is evident below the second 8. **y.** Included in circulation-strike 1885 mintage figure. **z.** Repunching is especially evident in the base of the 1, and the lower loop of the 6. **aa.** Included in circulation-strike 1886 mintage figure.

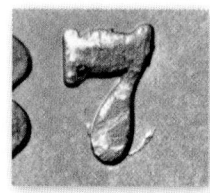

1887, 7 Over 6
VAM-2.
FS-S1-1887-002.

1887-O, 7 Over 6
VAM-3. FS-S1-1887o-003.

1888-O, Obverse Die Break
The "Scarface" variety.
VAM-1B. FS-S1-1888o-001b.

1888-O, Doubled Die Obverse
The "Hot Lips" variety.
VAM-4. FS-S1-1888o-004.

	Mintage	Cert	Avg	%MS	VF-20	EF-40	AU-50	MS-60	MS-63	MS-64	MS-64DMPL	MS-65	MS-65DMPL
											PF-60	PF-63	PF-65
1886-O	10,710,000	6,092	55.7	29%	$39	$45	$75	$900	$3,250	$11,000	$70,000	$165,000	$300,000
	Auctions: $12,338, MS-64, January 2015; $1,293, MS-61, June 2015; $317, AU-58, July 2015; $282, AU-50, April 2015												
1886-O, Clashed Die (bb)	(cc)	11	51.5	0%				$225	$950	$5,500	—		
	Auctions: $282, AU-58, July 2015; $176, AU-55, August 2015; $89, AU-50, January 2015; $31, EF-45, March 2015												
1886-S	750,000	4,763	59.9	74%	$78	$105	$150	$350	$475	$800	$8,500	$2,000	$27,000
	Auctions: $5,875, MS-66, August 2015; $423, MS-63, May 2015; $188, AU-58, March 2015; $90, EF-45, January 2015												
1887, 7 Over 6	(dd)	1,035	62.5	94%	$48	$70	$165	$400	$475	$750	$4,750	$1,800	$26,000
	Auctions: $764, MS-64, August 2015; $400, MS-63, January 2015; $376, MS-62, December 2015; $353, MS-61, January 2015												
1887	20,290,000	195,124	63.7	100%	$32	$37	$39	$50	$60	$75	$450	$135	$1,000
	Auctions: $1,087, MS-67, August 2015; $2,585, MS-66, January 2015; $69, MS-63, February 2015; $40, AU-58, September 2015												
1887, Proof	710	223	64.3								$1,300	$3,000	$5,500
	Auctions: $17,038, PF-67, May 2015; $3,055, PF-64, October 2015; $3,408, PF-63, January 2015; $823, PF-60, January 2015												
1887-O, 7 Over 6	(ee)	567	60.6	83%	$48	$65	$175	$450	$1,750	$4,800		$27,000	
	Auctions: $5,581, MS-64, January 2014; $1,586, MS-63, January 2015; $705, MS-60, October 2014; $447, MS-60, January 2015												
1887-O	11,550,000	10,051	62.2	94%	$35	$42	$55	$70	$125	$375	$1,700	$2,250	$13,500
	Auctions: $2,585, MS-65, January 2015; $306, MS-64, August 2015; $129, MS-63, October 2015; $94, MS-62, March 2015												
1887-S	1,771,000	7,084	61.2	81%	$40	$45	$50	$135	$275	$600	$7,000	$1,800	$27,500
	Auctions: $4,465, MS-66, August 2015; $3,525, MS-65+, September 2015; $176, MS-62, September 2015; $79, AU-58, February 2015												
1888	19,183,000	48,563	63.6	99%	$35	$37	$39	$50	$60	$75	$450	$225	$2,400
	Auctions: $4,935, MS-67, July 2015; $376, MS-66, October 2015; $166, MS-65, August 2015; $96, MS-64+, January 2015												
1888, Proof	833	194	63.9								$1,300	$3,000	$5,500
	Auctions: $24,675, PF-66Cam, April 2013; $5,288, PF-65, October 2015												
1888-O	12,150,000	25,562	63.1	99%	$35	$37	$39	$50	$70	$110	$500	$475	$4,500
	Auctions: $4,583, MS-66, January 2015; $94, MS-64, September 2015; $69, MS-63, November 2015; $517, AU-58, January 2015												
1888-O, Obverse Die Break (ff)	(gg)	68	62.0	99%				$2,250	$4,750	$8,500			
	Auctions: $14,688, MS-64, December 2013												
1888-O, Doubled Die Obverse (hh)	(gg)	883	32.0	1%	$145	$290	$900	$20,000	$30,000	—			
	Auctions: $6,169, MS-66, January 2015; $764, MS-64, August 2015; $235, AU-58, December 2015; $141, EF-45, March 2015												
1888-S	657,000	5,362	58.6	70%	$175	$185	$205	$315	$475	$800	$2,850	$3,000	$15,500
	Auctions: $6,169, MS-66, January 2015; $764, MS-64, August 2015; $235, AU-58, December 2015; $141, EF-45, March 2015												

bb. Clashing of the E of LIBERTY is evident between the eagle's tail feathers and the bow on the wreath **cc.** Included in 1886-O mintage figure. **dd.** Included in circulation-strike 1887 mintage figure. **ee.** Included in 1887-O mintage figure. **ff.** A major die break runs from the rim between E and P, through the field, and all the way across Liberty's face and neck. This variety is nicknamed "Scarface." **gg.** Included in 1888-O mintage figure. **hh.** Doubling is visible on the lips (especially), nose, eye, chin, entire profile, and part of the hair. This variety is nicknamed "Hot Lips."

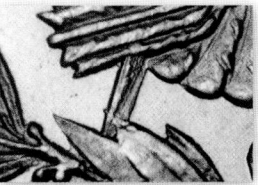

1889, Die Break	**1889-O, Clashed Die**	**1890-CC, Die Gouge**	**1890-O, Die Gouges**
The "Bar Wing" variety.	*VAM-1A. FS-S1-1889o-001a.*	*The "Tailbar" variety.*	*The "Comet" variety.*
VAM-22. FS-S1-1889-022.		*VAM-4. FS-S1-1890CC-004.*	*VAM-10. FS-S1-1890o-010.*

	Mintage	Cert	Avg	%MS	VF-20	EF-40	AU-50	MS-60	MS-63	MS-64	MS-64DMPL / PF-60	MS-65 / PF-63	MS-65DMPL / PF-65
1889	21,726,000	48,862	63.1	98%	$35	$37	$39	$50	$65	$80	$700	$250	$3,600
Auctions: $5,004, MS-66+, January 2015; $235, MS-65, September 2015; $84, MS-64, February 2015; $64, MS-63, July 2015													
1889, Die Break (ii)	(jj)	304	59.6	67%				$80	$150	$275	$300	$2,500	
Auctions: $182, MS-63, September 2014; $106, MS-62, February 2015; $89, MS-62, September 2014; $84, MS-61, September 2014													
1889, Proof	811	192	64.2								$1,300	$3,000	$5,500
Auctions: $12,925, PF-66Cam, August 2015; $3,290, PF-64Cam, January 2015; $3,055, PF-64, January 2015; $3,290, PF-63, January 2015													
1889-CC	350,000	4,854	32.4	11%	$1,150	$2,750	$7,500	$25,000	$47,500	$75,000	$85,000	$325,000	$350,000
Auctions: $16,450, MS-61, January 2015; $7,344, AU-53, February 2015; $705, VG-10, June 2015; $376, AG-3, August 2015													
1889-O	11,875,000	4,795	60.1	82%	$35	$37	$55	$185	$375	$900	$6,500	$3,750	$17,500
Auctions: $8,813, MS-65+, January 2015; $646, MS-64, July 2015; $200, MS-61, October 2015; $64, AU-55, January 2015													
1889-O, Clashed Die (kk)	(ll)	42	37.9	2%				$975	$2,000	—	—		
Auctions: $4,465, MS-61, August 2015; $940, AU-58, August 2015; $740, AU-55, January 2015; $217, VF-35, March 2015													
1889-S	700,000	6,637	60.8	77%	$60	$75	$105	$275	$350	$625	$5,500	$1,650	$37,500
Auctions: $3,055, MS-66, August 2015; $223, MS-61, March 2015; $135, AU-58, January 2015; $94, AU-53, December 2015													
1890	16,802,000	18,431	62.8	97%	$35	$37	$43	$53	$85	$150	$2,500	$1,200	$20,000
Auctions: $2,820, MS-65+, June 2015; $194, MS-64+, March 2015; $141, MS-64, January 2015; $74, MS-63, August 2015													
1890, Proof	590	230	64.8								$1,300	$3,000	$5,500
Auctions: $88,125, PF-69DCam, April 2013; $12,925, PF-66Cam, July 2014; $4,259, PF-64Cam, November 2014													
1890-CC	2,309,041	8,403	55.2	73%	$110	$140	$190	$500	$875	$1,450	$2,800	$3,600	$13,750
Auctions: $70,500, MS-64, August 2016; $58,750, MS-63, August 2016; $36,425, MS-62, September 2016; $25,850, MS-61, February 2016													
1890-CC, Die Gouge (mm)	(nn)	454	46.4	47%				$650	$1,150	$2,950	—		
Auctions: $3,760, MS-63, January 2015; $911, AU-55, January 2015; $470, EF-45, January 2015; $223, F-12, November 2015													
1890-O	10,701,000	9,759	62.4	96%	$35	$37	$49	$75	$95	$300	$1,500	$1,600	$9,250
Auctions: $2,585, MS-65, June 2015; $376, MS-64+, July 2015; $94, MS-63, December 2015; $79, MS-62, January 2015													
1890-O, Die Gouges (oo)	(pp)	63	61.0	84%				$65	$90	$250	—		$2,000
Auctions: $2,233, MS-65, February 2015; $1,410, MS-64+, July 2015; $306, MS-64, September 2015; $188, MS-63, January 2015													
1890-S	8,230,373	10,150	62.2	91%	$35	$37	$45	$70	$100	$300	$3,200	$1,000	$9,250
Auctions: $4,230, MS-66+, January 2015; $1,087, MS-65, September 2015; $329, MS-64+, August 2015; $84, MS-62, February 2015													

ii. A die break is visible on the top of the eagle's right wing. This variety is nicknamed the "Bar Wing." Different obverse die pairings exist. jj. Included in circulation-strike 1889 mintage figure. kk. The E of LIBERTY is visible in the field below the eagle's tail feathers and slightly left of the bow. This variety is extremely rare in Mint State, and unknown above MS-61. ll. Included in 1889-O mintage figure. mm. A heavy die gouge extends from between the eagle's first tail feather and the lowest arrow feather to the leaves in the wreath below. "This is an extremely popular and highly marketable variety, especially in Mint State" (*Cherrypickers' Guide to Rare Die Varieties*, sixth edition, volume II). This variety is nicknamed the "Tailbar." nn. Included in 1890-CC mintage figure. oo. Die gouges are evident to the right of the date. This variety is nicknamed the "Comet." pp. Included in 1890-O mintage figure.

1891-O, Clashed Die
VAM-1A. FS-S1-1891o-001a.

1891-O, Pitted Reverse Die
VAM-1B. FS-S1-1891o-001b.

	Mintage	Cert	Avg	%MS	VF-20	EF-40	AU-50	MS-60	MS-63	MS-64	MS-64DMPL / PF-60	MS-65 / PF-63	MS-65DMPL / PF-65
1891	8,693,556	7,594	61.6	91%	$35	$40	$45	$75	$200	$650	$6,900	$3,500	$23,000
	Auctions: $12,925, MS-65+, October 2015; $564, MS-64, July 2015; $89, MS-62, December 2015; $50, AU-58, January 2015
1891, Proof	650	224	64.4								$1,300	$3,000	$5,500
	Auctions: $4,583, PF-65, October 2015; $3,525, PF-64Cam, January 2015; $3,408, PF-64Cam, January 2015; $2,938, PF-63, August 2015
1891-CC	1,618,000	11,458	59.5	84%	$110	$140	$190	$450	$750	$1,200	$4,500	$4,250	$32,000
	Auctions: $4,935, MS-65, August 2015; $881, MS-63, January 2015; $282, AU-58, December 2015; $206, EF-45, March 2015
1891-O	7,954,529	4,830	61.1	89%	$35	$40	$55	$200	$375	$750	$7,250	$5,500	$36,500
	Auctions: $8,225, MS-65, June 2015; $517, MS-64, September 2015; $235, MS-62, January 2015; $79, AU-58, February 2015
1891-O, Clashed Die (qq)	(rr)	156	36.4	1%			$235	$400	$1,350	—			
	Auctions: $517, AU-53, January 2015; $153, AU-50, June 2015; $79, AU-50, November 2014; $48, F-12, November 2014
1891-O, Pitted Reverse Die (ss)	(rr)	10	51.2	0%			$370		—	—			
	Auctions: $4,700, MS-65, June 2014; $3,055, MS-65, October 2014; $3,290, MS-65, November 2014; $2,585, MS-64, October 2014
1891-S	5,296,000	6,797	62.3	91%	$35	$40	$45	$70	$150	$325	$3,200	$1,250	$20,000
	Auctions: $5,640, MS-66, June 2015; $1,234, MS-65, September 2015; $118, MS-63, December 2015; $46, AU-58, May 2015
1892	1,036,000	4,833	59.9	72%	$43	$53	$90	$300	$500	$1,100	$3,200	$3,500	$18,000
	Auctions: $4,230, MS-65+, January 2015; $1,704, MS-64, August 2015; $84, AU-53, December 2015; $46, VF-35, May 2015
1892, Proof	1,245	367	64.3								$1,300	$3,000	$5,500
	Auctions: $14,100, PF-67, January 2015; $6,169, PF-65Cam, October 2015; $3,878, PF-64, August 2015; $2,350, PF-63, September 2015
1892-CC	1,352,000	6,122	54.8	71%	$285	$450	$690	$1,500	$2,250	$3,200	$9,000	$6,750	$36,000
	Auctions: $22,913, MS-66, August 2015; $7,638, MS-65, September 2015; $588, AU-53, February 2015; $458, EF-45, December 2015
1892-O	2,744,000	5,367	60.6	83%	$40	$48	$70	$290	$400	$850	$20,000	$4,500	$50,000
	Auctions: $3,525, MS-65, January 2015; $1,763, MS-64+, August 2015; $306, MS-62, September 2015; $259, MS-61, March 2015
1892-S	1,200,000	4,012	40.3	1%	$140	$300	$1,650	$40,000	$65,000	$115,000	$145,000	$185,000	$250,000
	Auctions: $82,250, MS-62, August 2016; $39,950, MS-61, November 2016; $21,150, AU-58, November 2016; $20,563, AU-58, August 2015
1893	378,000	5,043	51.5	44%	$225	$275	$400	$725	$1,050	$2,300	$32,500	$5,000	$67,500
	Auctions: $10,313, MS-65+, June 2015; $350, AU-55, December 2015; $235, EF-45, January 2015; $147, VG-10, February 2015
1893, Proof	792	249	64.0								$1,300	$3,000	$5,500
	Auctions: $35,250, PF-68, May 2015; $3,995, PF-64, October 2015; $1,763, PF-62, January 2015; $911, PF-58, February 2015
1893-CC	677,000	4,286	39.9	41%	$625	$1,500	$2,400	$5,000	$8,250	$16,000	$46,000	$80,000	$85,000
	Auctions: $25,850, MS-64+, July 2015; $5,170, MS-62, August 2015; $2,350, AU-50, January 2015; $705, VF-30, February 2015
1893-CC, Proof (tt)	4–8	10	63.8										$200,000
	Auctions: $149,500, PF-65, August 2011
1893-O	300,000	3,493	41.4	20%	$325	$475	$775	$3,400	$7,250	$17,000	$100,000	$185,000	$275,000
	Auctions: $11,163, MS-64, March 2015; $5,170, MS-62, January 2015; $1,351, AU-55, February 2015; $235, VF-20, June 2015
1893-S † (uu,vv)	100,000	2,992	20.5	1%	$5,200	$8,500	$20,000	$120,000	$225,000	$350,000	$400,000	$650,000	$750,000
	Auctions: $282,000, MS-63, July 2015; $88,125, MS-61, November 2016; $25,850, AU-55, January 2015; $23,500, AU-53, August 2016

qq. The evidence of a clashed die is visible below the eagle's tail feathers and slightly left of the bow, where the E in LIBERTY has been transferred from the obverse die. **rr.** Included in 1891-O mintage figure. **ss.** Pitting on the reverse is visible around the ONE and on the bottom of the wreath above and between ONE and DOLLAR. This variety is rare in circulated grades, and unknown in Mint State. **tt.** Some numismatists classify these as Deep Mirror Prooflike circulation strikes, rather than as Proofs. **uu.** "All 1893-S Morgan dollars were struck from a single die pairing. Genuine 1893-S silver dollars display a diagonal die scratch in the top of the T in LIBERTY. This diagnostic can be seen even on very low-grade examples" (*100 Greatest U.S. Coins*, fourth edition). **vv.** Beware of altered or otherwise fraudulent mintmarks.

1899-O, Micro O
*VAM-4, 5, 6, 31, and
32. FS-S1-1899o-501.*

	Mintage	Cert	Avg	%MS	VF-20	EF-40	AU-50	MS-60	MS-63	MS-64	MS-64DMPL / PF-60	MS-65 / PF-63	MS-65DMPL / PF-65
1894 (vv)	110,000	3,687	46.3	26%	$875	$1,000	$1,250	$3,400	$4,750	$9,000	$60,000	$40,000	$90,000
Auctions: $28,200, MS-65, January 2015; $881, VF-35, July 2015; $823, F-15, February 2015; $541, G-6, October 2015													
1894, Proof	972	349	64.1								$2,500	$3,500	$6,500
Auctions: $44,063, PF-67Cam, April 2013; $14,100, PF-66Cam, October 2014													
1894-O	1,723,000	5,060	50.6	21%	$60	$115	$260	$1,300	$4,750	$10,000	$29,000	$60,000	$65,000
Auctions: $19,388, MS-64+, June 2015; $2,104, MS-62, July 2015; $212, AU-55, February 2015; $56, VF-30, May 2015													
1894-S	1,260,000	3,427	55.4	63%	$95	$150	$450	$825	$1,100	$2,250	$22,000	$6,500	$35,000
Auctions: $18,800, MS-66, March 2015; $8,225, MS-65, August 2015; $411, AU-55, February 2015; $212, EF-45, April 2015													
1895, Proof † (ww)	880	374	62.1								$45,000	$50,000	$75,000
Auctions: $58,750, PF-65Cam, January 2015; $58,750, PF-64Cam, November 2014; $42,300, PF-63Cam, January 2015													
1895-O	450,000	5,737	39.2	3%	$350	$550	$1,100	$17,500	$50,000	$80,000	$140,000	$200,000	$240,000
Auctions: $79,313, MS-64, January 2015; $24,675, MS-62, July 2015; $16,450, MS-61, November 2016; $852, AU-50, February 2015; $353													
1895-O, Proof (tt)	2–3	5	64.0		*(extremely rare)*								
Auctions: $528,750, PF-66, June 2013													
1895-S	400,000	2,982	36.1	26%	$675	$1,000	$1,600	$4,200	$6,000	$11,000	$19,500	$22,500	$40,000
Auctions: $11,750, MS-64+, January 2015; $3,055, AU-58, August 2015; $1,087, EF-45, October 2015; $400, F-12, December 2015													
1896	9,976,000	56,047	63.5	99%	$35	$37	$39	$50	$60	$85	$450	$165	$1,200
Auctions: $3,055, MS-67, January 2015; $764, MS-66+, July 2015; $80, MS-64, March 2015; $94, MS-63, October 2015													
1896, Proof	762	281	64.9								$1,300	$3,000	$5,500
Auctions: $39,950, PF-68DCam, February 2015; $19,975, PF-68, October 2014; $3,672, PF-63DCam, November 2014; $1,528, PF-60, July 2014													
1896-O	4,900,000	6,544	54.4	20%	$39	$43	$160	$1,500	$7,750	$37,500	$60,000	$165,000	$200,000
Auctions: $17,038, MS-63, August 2015; $1,500, MS-61, June 2015; $176, AU-55, January 2015; $58, EF-45, October 2015													
1896-S	5,000,000	1,760	48.3	41%	$70	$220	$775	$2,100	$3,650	$5,500	$57,500	$17,500	$100,000
Auctions: $15,275, MS-65, July 2015; $9,106, MS-64, June 2015; $1,293, AU-55, January 2015; $200, EF-40, December 2015													
1897	2,822,000	17,954	63.3	98%	$35	$37	$39	$50	$65	$85	$500	$250	$3,700
Auctions: $6,463, MS-67, July 2015; $1,533, MS-66+, January 2015; $235, MS-65, October 2015; $79, MS-64, December 2015													
1897, Proof	731	217	64.4								$1,300	$3,000	$5,500
Auctions: $7,050, PF-66, June 2015; $4,935, PF-65, February 2015; $2,056, PF-62, September 2014; $881, PF-60, November 2014													
1897-O	4,004,000	6,579	55.4	23%	$35	$41	$100	$1,050	$4,500	$16,000	$37,500	$65,000	$75,000
Auctions: $9,988, MS-64, October 2015; $4,700, MS-63, August 2015; $1,182, MS-61, July 2015; $259, AU-58, December 2015													
1897-S	5,825,000	8,512	62.8	93%	$35	$37	$45	$85	$125	$185	$1,100	$550	$3,000
Auctions: $5,170, MS-67, August 2015; $1,293, MS-66, January 2015; $306, MS-64, October 2015; $46, AU-58, September 2015													
1898	5,884,000	22,920	63.5	98%	$35	$37	$39	$50	$60	$75	$450	$200	$1,300
Auctions: $5,170, MS-67, January 2015; $206, MS-65, November 2015; $84, MS-64, August 2015; $142, MS-63, May 2015													
1898, Proof	735	254	64.7								$1,300	$3,000	$5,500
Auctions: $25,850, PF-68Cam, January 2015; $21,150, PF-68, May 2015; $9,400, PF-65DCam, January 2015; $3,055, PF-63, August 2015													
1898-O	4,440,000	73,216	63.9	100%	$35	$37	$39	$50	$60	$75	$450	$135	$1,025
Auctions: $2,820, MS-67, June 2015; $470, MS-66+, August 2015; $129, MS-65, August 2015; $84, MS-64, January 2015													
1898-S	4,102,000	3,473	59.5	67%	$40	$50	$100	$275	$450	$600	$3,250	$1,550	$13,750
Auctions: $15,275, MS-66+, August 2015; $764, MS-64, January 2015; $282, MS-61, September 2015; $129, AU-58, March 2015													

† Ranked in the *100 Greatest U.S. Coins* (fourth edition). **tt.** Some numismatists classify these as Deep Mirror Prooflike circulation strikes, rather than as Proofs. **vv.** Beware of altered or otherwise fraudulent mintmarks. **ww.** Mint records indicate that 12,000 1895 Morgan dollars were struck for circulation; however, none have ever been seen. In order to complete their collections, date-by-date collectors are forced to acquire one of the 880 Proofs struck that year, causing much competition for this, "The King of the Morgan Dollars."

**1900-O, Obverse
Die Crack**
VAM-29A. FS-S1-1900o-029a.

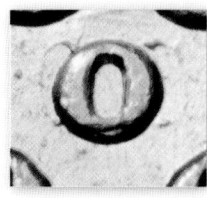

1900-O, O Over CC
Various VAMs.
FS-S1-1900o-501.

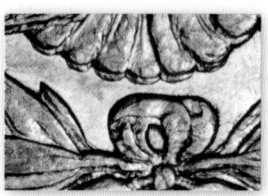

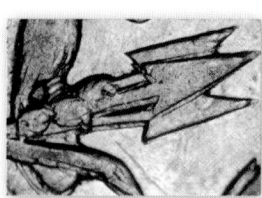

1901, Doubled Die Reverse
The "Shifted Eagle" variety. VAM-3. FS-S1-1901-003.

	Mintage	Cert	Avg	%MS	VF-20	EF-40	AU-50	MS-60	MS-63	MS-64	MS-64DMPL	MS-65	MS-65DMPL
											PF-60	PF-63	PF-65
1899	330,000	10,468	61.3	87%	$180	$200	$225	$260	$275	$375	$1,200	$875	$2,300
	Auctions: $4,465, MS-66, August 2015; $259, MS-63, October 2015; $141, AU-53, December 2015; $165, EF-45, March 2015												
1899, Proof	846	226	64.2								$1,300	$3,000	$5,500
	Auctions: $22,325, PF-68, June 2015; $9,988, PF-67, June 2015; $2,820, PF-63, January 2015; $1,410, PF-61, July 2015												
1899-O	12,290,000	58,451	63.7	100%	$35	$37	$39	$50	$60	$80	$500	$135	$1,650
	Auctions: $4,230, MS-67, August 2015; $940, MS-66+, January 2015; $282, MS-66, September 2015; $79, MS-64, November 2015												
1899-O, Micro O (xx)	(yy)	614	37.1	3%		$140	$375	$1,000	—				
	Auctions: $306, AU-55, September 2015; $200, AU-53, October 2015; $69, AU-50, January 2015; $84, EF-45, January 2015												
1899-S	2,562,000	3,112	60.1	74%	$48	$65	$140	$380	$525	$800	$3,800	$2,000	$23,000
	Auctions: $37,600, MS-67, August 2015; $3,995, MS-66, January 2015; $411, MS-61, August 2015; $121, AU-55, February 2015												
1900	8,830,000	33,625	63.6	98%	$35	$37	$39	$50	$60	$75	$9,000	$145	$40,000
	Auctions: $8,225, MS-67, February 2015; $3,290, MS-66+, February 2015; $223, MS-65, October 2015; $63, MS-63, June 2015												
1900, Proof	912	275	64.3								$1,300	$3,000	$5,500
	Auctions: $8,813, PF-67, January 2015; $7,050, PF-65Cam, August 2015; $5,170, PF-65, January 2015; $2,174, PF-62, March 2015												
1900-O	12,590,000	44,969	63.7	99%	$35	$37	$39	$50	$60	$75	$1,100	$145	$5,750
	Auctions: $2,585, MS-67, January 2015; $1,175, MS-66+, September 2015; $135, MS-65, June 2015; $94, MS-63, November 2015												
1900-O, Obverse Die Crack (zz)	(aaa)	71	29.2	6%			$700		—	—			
	Auctions: $306, AU-58, January 2015; $153, EF-40, October 2014; $112, VF-30, February 2015; $94, VF-25, July 2015												
1900-O, O Over CC (bbb)	(aaa)	3,301	59.3	81%	$65	$105	$170	$325	$725	$900	$8,500	$2,100	$19,000
	Auctions: $1,293, MS-64, January 2015; $447, MS-62, December 2015; $235, AU-58, June 2015; $153, EF-40, February 2015												
1900-S	3,540,000	4,160	60.7	75%	$40	$48	$90	$300	$375	$600	$19,000	$1,450	$35,000
	Auctions: $2,233, MS-65+, January 2015; $306, MS-62, June 2015; $129, AU-58, March 2015; $50, EF-45, September 2015												
1901 (ccc)	6,962,000	4,907	53.8	14%	$50	$115	$280	$3,500	$15,000	$50,000	$70,000	$425,000	
	Auctions: $1,880, MS-62, August 2016; $1,058, AU-58, October 2016												
1901, Doubled Die Reverse (ddd)	(eee)	112	40.8	2%	$350	$1,100	$1,900	$4,500	—				
	Auctions: $41,125, MS-62, August 2013												
1901, Proof	813	278	63.8								$1,600	$3,000	$5,500
	Auctions: $28,200, PF-68, May 2015; $12,925, PF-67, August 2015; $7,050, PF-65Cam, June 2015; $2,820, PF-62Cam, July 2015												
1901-O	13,320,000	38,645	63.6	100%	$35	$37	$39	$50	$60	$75	$1,200	$150	$8,500
	Auctions: $19,975, MS-67, March 2015; $4,465, MS-66+, January 2015; $223, MS-65, August 2015; $94, MS-64, June 2015												
1901-S	2,284,000	2,694	58.7	69%	$45	$65	$200	$550	$800	$1,250	$21,000	$2,250	$30,000
	Auctions: $42,300, MS-67, February 2015; $9,400, MS-66, August 2015; $282, AU-58, September 2015; $42, EF-40, January 2015												

xx. The O mintmark is smaller than normal; its punch was probably intended for a Barber half dollar. Five different dies are known, all scarce. **yy.** Included in 1899-O mintage figure. **zz.** A die break is visible from the rim through the date to just below the lower point of the bust. This variety is very rare in Mint State. **aaa.** Included in 1900-O mintage figure. **bbb.** An O mintmark was punched into the die over a previously punched CC mintmark. There are at least seven different dies involved; the one pictured is VAM-9. **ccc.** Beware of a fraudulently removed mintmark intended to make a less valuable 1901-O or 1901-S appear to be a 1901 dollar. **ddd.** Doubling is visible on the eagle's tail feathers, and also on IN GOD WE TRUST, as well as on the arrows, wreath, and bow. This variety is nicknamed the "Shifted Eagle." It is very rare in Mint State. **eee.** Included in circulation-strike 1901 mintage figure.

**1903-S,
Small S
Mintmark**
*VAM-2.
FS-S1-1903S-002.*

	Mintage	Cert	Avg	%MS	VF-20	EF-40	AU-50	MS-60	MS-63	MS-64	MS-64DMPL / PF-60	MS-65 / PF-63	MS-65DMPL / PF-65
1902	7,994,000	6,168	63.1	95%	$35	$37	$45	$55	$125	$165	$13,000	$400	$20,000
	Auctions: $5,405, MS-67, June 2015; $1,645, MS-66, September 2015; $129, MS-64, August 2015; $106, MS-63, January 2015												
1902, Proof	777	238	64.3								$1,300	$3,000	$5,500
	Auctions: $9,400, PF-67, January 2015; $11,750, PF-66, August 2015; $5,053, PF-65, February 2015; $2,820, PF-63, January 2015												
1902-O	8,636,000	70,628	63.6	100%	$35	$37	$45	$55	$60	$75	$2,800	$155	$13,500
	Auctions: $15,275, MS-67, February 2015; $3,055, MS-66+, June 2015; $200, MS-65+, September 2015; $89, MS-64, May 2015												
1902-S	1,530,000	3,605	57.3	69%	$140	$190	$275	$380	$625	$825	$8,000	$2,000	$14,000
	Auctions: $6,463, MS-66, August 2015; $646, MS-63, June 2015; $259, AU-58, December 2015; $79, F-12, January 2015												
1903	4,652,000	13,030	63.4	95%	$50	$55	$65	$78	$85	$115	$7,500	$250	$22,500
	Auctions: $3,526, MS-67, August 2015; $1,293, MS-66+, October 2015; $223, MS-65, February 2015; $89, MS-64, December 2015												
1903, Proof	755	264	64.2								$1,300	$3,000	$5,500
	Auctions: $3,995, PF-64, January 2015; $3,819, PF-64, March 2015; $3,055, PF-63, August 2015; $1,998, PF-62, January 2015												
1903-O	4,450,000	8,131	63.0	98%	$340	$350	$365	$415	$450	$500	$1,800	$675	$6,400
	Auctions: $3,760, MS-67, January 2015; $2,585, MS-66+, June 2015; $823, MS-65, September 2015; $376, MS-64, December 2015												
1903-S	1,241,000	2,569	33.7	11%	$205	$350	$1,600	$5,000	$7,000	$8,500	$15,000	$11,000	$38,000
	Auctions: $7,638, MS-64, January 2015; $6,770, MS-63, January 2015; $2,115, AU-55, October 2015; $188, VF-35, November 2015												
1903-S, Small S (fff)	(ggg)	144	23.5	1%			$6,400		—	—			
	Auctions: $588, VF-30, January 2015; $329, VF-20, January 2015; $112, VG-10, May 2015; $94, G-4, February 2015												
1904	2,788,000	4,753	61.8	89%	$40	$47	$55	$100	$250	$500	$42,500	$1,850	$60,000
	Auctions: $9,988, MS-66, August 2015; $2,233, MS-65, September 2015; $376, MS-64, January 2015; $79, AU-58, October 2015												
1904, Proof	650	291	63.9								$1,300	$3,000	$5,500
	Auctions: $22,325, PF-68, May 2015; $7,638, PF-66, March 2015; $3,995, PF-64+, February 2015; $2,820, PF-64, January 2015												
1904-O	3,720,000	137,541	63.7	100%	$35	$37	$39	$50	$60	$75	$450	$135	$1,150
	Auctions: $4,465, MS-67, January 2015; $400, MS-66, September 2015; $153, MS-65, July 2015; $74, MS-64+, February 2015												
1904-S	2,304,000	2,198	46.0	30%	$80	$200	$500	$2,600	$4,800	$5,750	$13,000	$10,000	$22,000
	Auctions: $16,450, MS-66, June 2015; $4,935, MS-64, August 2015; $2,350, AU-58, January 2015; $200, EF-45, December 2015												
1921	44,690,000	114,656	63.4	99%	$32	$34	$35	$40	$45	$50	$7,750	$135	$11,500
	Auctions: $3,055, MS-66+, January 2015; $182, MS-65, May 2015; $100, MS-64, September 2015; $129, MS-62, August 2015												
1921, Zerbe Proof (hhh)	150–250	75	64.0								$4,000	$5,500	$12,000
	Auctions: $29,375, PF-66, August 2015; $11,163, PF-65, June 2015; $11,163, PF-64, January 2015; $9,401, SP-63, August 2015												
1921, Chapman Proof (iii)	25–40	1	66.0								$20,000	$35,000	$75,000
	Auctions: $61,688, PF-65, April 2013												
1921-D	20,345,000	17,318	62.9	94%	$32	$34	$35	$50	$65	$115	$7,500	$325	$12,000
	Auctions: $3,760, MS-66, August 2015; $259, MS-65, August 2015; $112, MS-64, December 2015; $100, AU-53, January 2015												
1921-S	21,695,000	13,805	62.7	95%	$32	$34	$35	$50	$75	$135	$12,000	$800	$30,000
	Auctions: $3,819, MS-66, January 2015; $852, MS-65, February 2015; $84, MS-64, May 2015; $69, MS-63, October 2015												
1921-S, Zerbe Proof (hhh)	1–2	0	n/a										$140,000
	Auctions: $117,500, PF-65, August 2013												

fff. The S mintmark is smaller than normal, possibly intended to be punched into a Barber half dollar die. **ggg.** Included in 1903-S mintage figure. **hhh.** "Pieces called Zerbe Proofs are simply circulation strikes with a semi-prooflike character, not as nice as on the earlier-noted [mirrorlike] prooflike pieces, struck from dies that were slightly polished, but that retained countless minute striae and preparation lines. In the view of the writer [Bowers], Zerbe Proofs have no basis in numismatic fact or history, although opinions differ on the subject. It seems highly unlikely that these were produced as Proofs for collectors. If indeed they were furnished to Farran Zerbe, a leading numismatic entrepreneur of the era, it is likely that they were simply regular production pieces. Zerbe had a fine collection and certainly knew what a brilliant Proof should look like, and he never would have accepted such pieces as mirror Proofs" (*A Guide Book of Morgan Silver Dollars*, fifth edition). **iii.** Breen stated that 12 Chapman Proofs were minted (*Walter Breen's Encyclopedia of U.S. and Colonial Proof Coins, 1792–1977*); Bowers estimates fewer than 30 (*A Guide Book of Morgan Silver Dollars*, fifth edition). These are sometimes called *Chapman Proofs* because Philadelphia coin dealer Henry Chapman advertised them for sale within a few months of their production.

PEACE (1921–1935)

Designer: *Anthony de Francisci.* **Weight:** *26.73 grams.*
Composition: *.900 silver, .100 copper (net weight .77344 oz. pure silver).*
Diameter: *38.1 mm.* **Edge:** *Reeded.* **Mints:** *Philadelphia, Denver, and San Francisco.*

Mintmark location is on the reverse, to the left of the tail feathers.

Circulation Strike

Proof

History. In 1921, following the melting of more than 270 million silver dollars as legislated by the Pittman Act of 1918, the U.S. Treasury struck millions more silver dollars of the Morgan type while a new Peace dollar was in development. Sculptor and medalist Anthony de Francisci created the Peace design, originally intended as a commemorative of the end of the hostilities of the Great War. The obverse features a flowing-haired Miss Liberty wearing a spiked tiara, and the reverse an eagle perched before the rising sun. The designer's monogram is located in the field of the coin under the neck of Miss Liberty. Coins of 1921 were struck in high relief; this caused weakness at the centers, so the design was changed to low relief in 1922. The dollars were struck until 1928, then again in 1934 and 1935. Legislation dated August 3, 1964, authorized the coinage of 45 million silver dollars, and 316,076 dollars of the Peace design dated 1964 were struck at the Denver Mint in 1965. Plans for completing this coinage were subsequently abandoned and all of these coins were melted. None were preserved or released for circulation; details are found in *A Guide Book of Peace Dollars* (Burdette).

Striking and Sharpness. Peace dollars of 1921 are always lightly struck at the center of the obverse, with hair detail not showing in an area. The size of this flat spot can vary. For this and other Peace dollars, check the hair detail at the center and, on the reverse, the feathers on the eagle. Many coins are struck from overly used dies, giving a grainy appearance to the fields, particularly the obverse. On many Peace dollars tiny white "milk spots" are seen, left over from when they were struck; these are not as desirable in the marketplace as unspotted coins.

Availability. All dates and mintmarks are readily available. Although some are well worn, they are generally collected in EF and finer grades. MS coins are available for each, with the 1934-S considered to be the key date. San Francisco issues of the 1920s, except for 1926-S, are often heavily bagmarked from coming into contact with other coins during shipment, storage, and other handling. The appearance of luster varies from issue to issue and can be deeply frosty, or—in the instance of Philadelphia Mint coins of 1928, 1934, and 1935—satiny or "creamy."

Proofs. Some Sandblast Proofs were made in 1921 and a limited issue in 1922 in high relief. These are rare today. Seemingly, a few Satin Proofs were also made in 1921. Sandblast Proofs of 1922 have a peculiar whitish surface in most instances, sometimes interrupted by small dark flecks or spots. There are a number of impostors among certified "Proofs."

Note: Values of common-date silver coins have been based on the current bullion price of silver, $17 per ounce, and may vary with the prevailing spot price.

GRADING STANDARDS

MS-60 to 70 (Mint State). *Obverse:* At MS-60, some abrasion and contact marks are evident, most noticeably on the cheek and on the hair to the right of the face and forehead. Luster is present, but may be dull or lifeless. At MS-63, contact marks are extensive but not distracting. Abrasion still is evident, but less than at lower levels. MS-64 coins are slightly finer. Some Peace dollars have whitish "milk spots" in the field; while these are

1921. Graded MS-64.

not caused by handling, but seem to have been from liquid at the mint or in storage, coins with these spots are rarely graded higher than MS–63 or 64. An MS-65 coin may have minor abrasion, but contact marks are so minute as to require magnification. Luster should be full and rich on earlier issues, and either frosty or satiny on later issues, depending on the date and mint. *Reverse:* At MS-60 some abrasion and contact marks are evident, most noticeably on the eagle's shoulder and nearby. Otherwise, comments apply as for the obverse.

Illustrated coin: Note the scattered marks that are practically definitive of the grade. The high relief of this particular year results in light striking at the center; this is normal and not to be mistaken for wear.

AU-50, 53, 55, 58 (About Uncirculated). *Obverse:* Light wear is seen on the cheek and the highest-relief areas of the hair. The neck truncation edge also shows wear. At AU-58, the luster is extensive, but incomplete. At AU–50 and 53, luster is less but still present. *Reverse:* Wear is evident on the eagle's shoulder and back. Otherwise, comments apply as for the obverse.

1934-S. Graded AU-53.

Illustrated coin: This coin shows medium and somewhat mottled toning. Luster is still seen in protected areas.

EF-40, 45 (Extremely Fine). *Obverse:* Further wear is seen on the highest-relief areas of the hair, with many strands now blended together. Some luster can usually be seen in protected areas on many coins, but is not needed to define the EF–40 and 45 grades. *Reverse:* Further wear is seen on the eagle, and the upper 60% of the feathers have most detail gone, except for the delineation of the edges of rows of feathers. PEACE shows light wear.

1928. Graded EF-40.

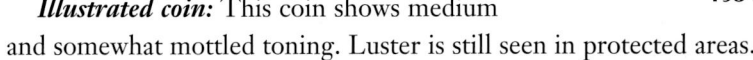

VF-20, 30 (Very Fine). *Obverse:* More wear shows on the hair, with more tiny strands now blended into heavy strands. *Reverse:* Further wear has resulted in very little feather detail except on the neck and tail. The rock shows wear. PEACE is slightly weak.

1934-D. Graded VF-30.

F-12, 15 (Fine). *Obverse:* Most of the hair is worn flat, with thick strands blended together, interrupted by fewer divisions than on higher grades. The rim is full. *Reverse:* Fewer feather details show. Most of the eagle, except for the tail feathers and some traces of feathers at the neck, is in outline only. The rays between the left side of the eagle and PEACE are weak and some details are worn away.

The Peace dollar is seldom collected in grades lower than F-12.

1921. Graded F-12.

PF-60 to 70 (Proof). *Obverse and Reverse:* Proofs of both types usually display very few handling marks or defects. To qualify as Satin PF-65 or Sandblast PF-65 or finer, contact marks must be microscopic.

1921. Satin Finish Proof.

1921, Line Through L
VAM-3. FS-S1-1921-003.

| | Mintage | Cert | Avg | %MS | VF-20 | EF-40 | AU-50 | MS-60 | MS-62 | MS-63 | MS-64 | MS-65 | MS-66 |
											PF-60	PF-63	PF-65
1921, High Relief	1,006,473	15,071	59.0	75%	$110	$135	$150	$275	$375	$450	$850	$1,900	$6,000
	Auctions: $70,500, MS-67, August 2015; $5,875, MS-66, August 2016; $4,700, MS-66, January 2015; $2,820, MS-66, November 2016												
1921, High Relief, Line Through L (a)	(b)	57	60.7	79%			$225	$315	$400	$500	$900	$2,400	
	Auctions: $940, MS-63, June 2013												
1921, Satin Finish Proof	10–20	17	63.6								$15,000	$30,000	$75,000
	Auctions: $32,200, PF-64, July 2009												
1921, Sandblast Finish Proof	5–8	3	64.0										$85,000
	Auctions: $99,875, PF-66, January 2014; $129,250, PF-64, August 2014												

a. A ray runs through the first L in DOLLAR, instead of behind it. b. Included in 1921, High Relief, mintage figure.

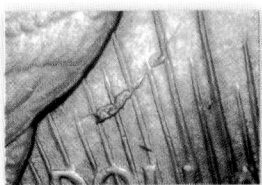

1922, Die Break in Field
VAM-1F. FS-S1-1922-001f.

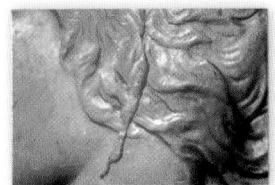

1922, Die Break at Ear
The "Ear Ring" variety.
VAM-2A. FS-S1-1922-002a.

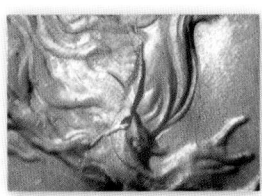

1922, Die Break in Hair
The 1922 "Extra Hair" variety.
VAM-2C. FS-S1-1922-002c.

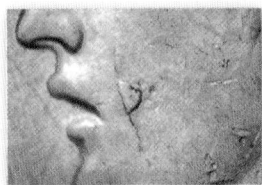

1922, Die Break on Cheek
The "Scar Cheek" variety.
VAM-5A. FS-S1-1922-005a.

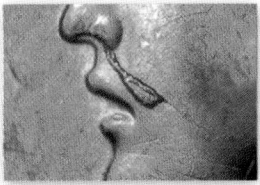

1922, Die Break at Nose
The "Moustache" variety.
VAM-12A. FS-S1-1922-012a.

	Mintage	Cert	Avg	%MS	VF-20	EF-40	AU-50	MS-60	MS-62	MS-63	MS-64 / PF-60	MS-65 / PF-63	MS-66 / PF-65
1922, High Relief (c)	35,401	0	n/a				—						
Auctions: No auction records available.													
1922, Normal Relief	51,737,000	195	63.5	99%	$25	$27	$28	$30	$32	$36	$40	$125	$450
Auctions: $11,163, MS-67, August 2015; $1,175, MS-66, March 2015; $176, MS-65, February 2015; $188, MS-64, October 2015													
1922, Die Break in Field (d)	(e)	60	56.0	32%				$400	$800	$1,750	$2,500		
Auctions: $1,528, MS-64, December 2013; $646, MS-63, July 2016; $153, MS-61, July 2015; $58, AU-55, September 2014													
1922, Die Break at Ear (f)	(e)	64	58.5	52%				$290	$650	$1,400	$2,300		
Auctions: $306, MS-64, July 2016; $1,293, MS-63, December 2013													
1922, Die Break in Hair (g)	(e)	231	57.2	52%				$90	$180	$300	$385		
Auctions: $153, MS-64, February 2015; $76, MS-62, March 2015; $74, MS-62, October 2014; $69, MS-61, September 2014													
1922, Die Break on Cheek (h)	(e)	37	59.6	68%				$190	$400	$550			
Auctions: $259, MS-63, February 2015; $165, MS-63, February 2015; $165, MS-61, February 2015; $200, AU-58, September 2014													
1922, Die Break at Nose (i)	(e)	148	58.4	45%				$90	$200	$325	$500	$975	
Auctions: $223, MS-62, January 2015; $212, MS-62, March 2015; $129, AU-58, February 2015; $112, AU-58, September 2015													
1922, High Relief, Sandblast Finish Proof	10–15	11	65.0										$200,000
Auctions: $329,000, PF-67, January 2014													
1922, Low Relief, Sandblast Finish Proof	3–6	2	65.0										—
Auctions: $35,200, PF-65, November 1988													
1922, Low Relief, Satin Finish Proof	3–6	1	63.0										$150,000
Auctions: $44,850, PF-60, November 2009													
1922-D	15,063,000	7,380	63.0	94%	$28	$30	$33	$50	$55	$85	$150	$600	$1,900
Auctions: $39,950, MS-67, August 2015; $7,050, MS-66+, February 2015; $734, MS-65+, October 2015; $153, MS-64, January 2015													
1922-S	17,475,000	6,180	62.2	92%	$28	$30	$33	$50	$60	$95	$270	$1,500	$30,000
Auctions: $8,813, MS-66, January 2015; $4,230, MS-65+, August 2015; $259, MS-64, February 2015; $36, AU-58, September 2015													

c. 1 example is known. **d.** A die break is visible in the field above DOLLAR. "This variety has turned out to be much rarer than previously thought, and is very scarce in grades above EF" (*Cherrypickers' Guide to Rare Die Varieties*, sixth edition, volume II). **e.** Included in 1922, Normal Relief, mintage figure. **f.** A major die break near Liberty's ear, dangling down to her neck, gives this variety its nickname, the "Ear Ring." Several die states are known. **g.** An irregular line of raised metal runs along the back of Liberty's hair. This is called the "Extra Hair" variety. Several die states are known. **h.** Liberty's cheek has a raised, almost triangular chunk of metal along a vertical die break. Also, the reverse is lightly tripled. This variety, called the "Scarface," is very scarce in Mint State. **i.** A die break is visible running from Liberty's nose along the top of her mouth. This is known as the "Moustache" variety.

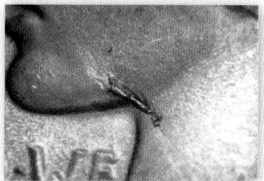

1923, Die Break at Jaw
The "Whisker Jaw" variety.
VAM-1A. FS-S1-1923-001a.

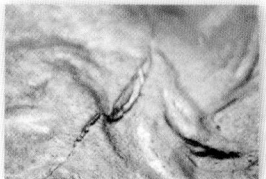

1923, Die Break in Hair
The 1923 "Extra Hair"
variety. VAM-1B.
FS-S1-1923-001b.

1923, Die Break on
O in DOLLAR
The "Tail on O" variety.
VAM-1C. FS-S1-1923-001c.

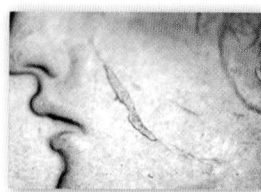

1923, Die Break on Cheek
The "Whisker Cheek" variety.
VAM-1D. FS-S1-1923-001d.

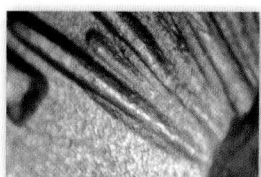

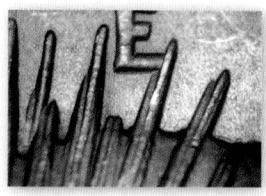

1923, Doubled Die Obverse
The "Double Tiara" variety. VAM-2. FS-S1-1923-002.

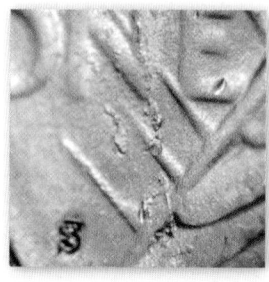

1923-S, Pitted Reverse
VAM-1C. FS-S1-1923S-001c.

1924, Die Break on Wing
The "Broken Wing" variety.
VAM-5A. FS-S1-1924-005a.

	Mintage	Cert	Avg	%MS	VF-20	EF-40	AU-50	MS-60	MS-62	MS-63	MS-64	MS-65	MS-66
											PF-60	PF-63	PF-65
1923	30,800,000	286,626	63.7	100%	$25	$27	$28	$30	$32	$36	$40	$125	$475
	Auctions: $4,465, MS-67, January 2015; $940, MS-66+, February 2015; $64, MS-64, May 2015; $40, MS-62, July 2015												
1923, Die Break at Jaw (j)	(k)	207	61.6	82%			$80	$125	$175	$265	$550		$1,250
	Auctions: $282, MS-65, February 2015; $141, MS-64, March 2015; $129, MS-64, January 2015; $76, MS-62, March 2015												
1923, Die Break in Hair (l)	(k)	80	61.7	88%			$125	$200	$300	$400	$600		
	Auctions: $400, MS-65, February 2015; $59, MS-64, September 2014; $115, MS-63, August 2014; $84, MS-63, September 2014												
1923, Die Break on O (m)	(k)	68	58.8	72%			$275	$650	$1,150	$1,800			
	Auctions: $2,468, MS-65, April 2014; $423, MS-64, July 2016												
1923, Die Break on Cheek (n)	(k)	103	60.3	67%			$165	$250	$350	$475	$875		
	Auctions: $206, MS-64, March 2015; $235, MS-63, February 2015; $165, MS-62, August 2015; $200, AU-55, June 2015												
1923, DblDie Obverse (o)	(k)	68	61.8	81%			$58	$75	$100	$160	$375		
	Auctions: $329, MS-65, February 2015; $129, MS-62, January 2015; $74, MS-62, July 2015; $129, AU-58, February 2015												
1923-D	6,811,000	3,620	62.1	89%	$28	$30	$40	$70	$90	$160	$375	$1,000	$4,000
	Auctions: $17,625, MS-66+, August 2015; $282, MS-64, September 2015; $123, MS-63, October 2015; $46, AU-55, January 2015												
1923-S	19,020,000	6,814	62.0	91%	$28	$30	$36	$55	$70	$90	$400	$3,000	$30,000
	Auctions: $4,230, MS-65, January 2015; $705, MS-64, February 2015; $112, MS-63, June 2015; $38, AU-58, November 2015												
1923-S, Pitted Reverse (p)	(q)	35	58.2	54%			$125	$250	—	$450	$975		
	Auctions: $282, MS-63, December 2013												
1924	11,811,000	46,403	63.8	99%	$25	$28	$30	$32	$35	$40	$50	$125	$600
	Auctions: $12,925, MS-67, August 2015; $1,293, MS-66+, January 2015; $217, MS-65, September 2015; $94, MS-64+, November 2015												
1924, Die Break on Wing (r)	(s)	52	61.3	79%			$130	$200	$375	$475			
	Auctions: $2,233, MS-67, January 2015; $423, MS-64, January 2015; $282, MS-63, February 2015; $106, MS-62, August 2014												
1924-S	1,728,000	4,350	60.4	72%	$28	$40	$60	$220	$325	$475	$1,200	$6,500	$43,500
	Auctions: $11,163, MS-65, June 2015; $9,400, MS-65, August 2015; $4,230, MS-64+, January 2015; $2,233, MS-64, July 2016												

j. A die break bridges Liberty's cheek and jaw. This is the "Whisker Jaw" variety. **k.** Included in 1923 mintage figure. **l.** A significant die break runs diagonally across the strands of Liberty's hair; die breaks may also be visible toward the back of her hair. This variety is nicknamed the 1923 "Extra Hair." **m.** A die break trails from the O of DOLLAR. This variety, called the "Tail on O," is very rare in any grade. **n.** A die break runs down Liberty's cheek toward the junction of the chin and neck. This is the "Whisker Cheek" variety. **o.** Doubling is most evident in the wide spread on the rays of Liberty's tiara, especially those under the BER of LIBERTY. This is the "Double Tiara" variety. **p.** "Pitting runs from the eagle's back tail-feathers, just to the right of the mintmark, upward to the N in ONE. . . . This is the most important Pitted Reverse variety in the Peace dollar series" (*Cherrypickers' Guide to Rare Die Varieties,* sixth edition, volume II). **q.** Included in 1923-S mintage figure. **r.** A dramatic die break runs down and across the entire width of the eagle's back. This is the "Broken Wing" variety. **s.** Included in 1924 mintage figure.

1925, Missing Ray
VAM-5. FS-S1-1925-005.

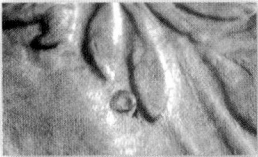

1926-S, Reverse Dot
The "Extra Berry" variety.
VAM-4. FS-S1-1926S-004.

1934-D, Doubled Die Obverse, Small D
VAM-4. FS-S1-1934D-004.

	Mintage	Cert	Avg	%MS	VF-20	EF-40	AU-50	MS-60	MS-62	MS-63	MS-64 / PF-60	MS-65 / PF-63	MS-66 / PF-65
1925	10,198,000	51,997	63.9	99%	$25	$28	$30	$32	$35	$40	$50	$125	$525
	Auctions: $5,405, MS-67, January 2015; $1,528, MS-66, June 2015; $123, MS-65+, March 2015; $74, MS-64, February 2015												
1925, Missing Ray (t)	(u)	96	62.8	92%			$65	$85	$100	$145	$250	$400	
	Auctions: $129, MS-64, December 2013; $200, MS-63, February 2015; $59, MS-62, September 2014; $47, MS-62, September 2014												
1925-S	1,610,000	5,936	61.8	86%	$28	$32	$45	$100	$180	$280	$850	$25,000	—
	Auctions: $30,550, MS-65; $24,675, MS-65, January 2015; $12,925, MS-65, September 2016; $3,055, MS-64, January 2015												
1926	1,939,000	9,565	63.2	97%	$28	$32	$37	$52	$100	$110	$140	$500	$1,750
	Auctions: $3,760, MS-66, August 2015; $376, MS-65, September 2015; $106, MS-64, June 2015; $94, AU-58, January 2015												
1926-D	2,348,700	3,746	62.2	86%	$28	$32	$44	$85	$140	$230	$410	$1,000	$2,500
	Auctions: $47,000, MS-67, August 2015; $3,760, MS-66, August 2015; $1,528, MS-65, January 2015; $153, MS-63, May 2015												
1926-S	6,980,000	6,220	62.3	89%	$28	$32	$38	$60	$75	$120	$275	$900	$3,500
	Auctions: $6,463, MS-66, August 2015; $1,058, MS-65, September 2015; $206, MS-64, November 2015; $84, MS-63, January 2015												
1926-S, Reverse Dot (v)	(w)	46	57.0	54%			$55	$90	$140	$200	$360		
	Auctions: $165, MS-64, September 2014; $223, MS-63, February 2015; $129, MS-63, September 2015; $61, AU-58, November 2014												
1927	848,000	6,122	62.0	88%	$39	$42	$50	$85	$120	$200	$625	$1,750	$20,000
	Auctions: $23,500, MS-66, September 2015; $3,290, MS-65, January 2015; $79, MS-61, December 2015; $54, AU-58, March 2015												
1927-D	1,268,900	3,570	60.8	77%	$39	$45	$75	$180	$250	$400	$1,050	$3,500	$25,000
	Auctions: $9,988, MS-65+, January 2015; $793, MS-64, August 2015; $79, AU-55, March 2015; $74, AU-53, September 2015												
1927-S	866,000	4,076	61.0	80%	$39	$45	$75	$200	$265	$575	$1,200	$8,500	$45,000
	Auctions: $8,225, MS-65, January 2015; $4,700, MS-65, March 2016; $1,763, MS-64, June 2015; $470, MS-63+, October 2015												
1928	360,649	7,972	58.8	66%	$275	$320	$340	$475	$600	$750	$1,150	$3,750	$25,000
	Auctions: $39,950, MS-66, August 2015; $7,050, MS-65, January 2015; $400, AU-58, May 2015; $235, EF-40, February 2015												
1928-S	1,632,000	5,547	60.5	75%	$39	$48	$65	$250	$300	$450	$1,100	$16,500	—
	Auctions: $42,300, MS-65+, August 2015; $2,585, MS-64+, February 2015; $470, MS-63, November 2015; $94, AU-55, May 2015												
1934	954,057	5,649	62.3	88%	$44	$45	$50	$115	$170	$225	$375	$675	$2,250
	Auctions: $11,750, MS-66+, January 2015; $1,175, MS-65, September 2015; $494, MS-64, May 2015; $69, AU-58, December 2015												
1934-D (x)	1,569,500	5,256	60.8	77%	$44	$45	$50	$150	$250	$375	$550	$1,250	$3,500
	Auctions: $10,575, MS-66, August 2015; $1,880, MS-64+, June 2015; $306, MS-63, November 2015; $64, AU-58, February 2015												
1934-D, DblDie Obv, Sm D (y)	(z)	67	56.1	49%	$115	$185	$375	$750	$900	$1,650			
	Auctions: $999, MS-63, January 2015; $306, MS-62, September 2015; $364, AU-58, January 2015; $353, AU-55, February 2015												
1934-S	1,011,000	3,923	50.1	33%	$80	$175	$500	$2,500	$3,200	$4,500	$7,000	$9,000	$27,500
	Auctions: $32,900, MS-66, August 2015; $9,988, MS-65+, January 2015; $6,463, MS-64, February 2015; $118, EF-40, October 2015												
1935	1,576,000	7,302	62.6	90%	$44	$45	$50	$85	$90	$125	$275	$750	$2,250
	Auctions: $9,988, MS-66+, June 2015; $517, MS-65, October 2015; $129, MS-63, February 2015; $94, MS-62, July 2015												
1935-S (aa)	1,964,000	3,651	60.9	79%	$44	$50	$88	$275	$325	$500	$650	$1,250	$3,000
	Auctions: $16,450, MS-66+, August 2015; $881, MS-64, February 2015; $400, MS-63, May 2015; $153, AU-58, September 2015												
1964-D (bb)	316,076	0	n/a	*(none known to exist)*									
	Auctions: No auction records available.												

t. This variety is the result of a reverse die polished with too much gusto. The partially effaced remains of bold clash marks are evident, but the topmost internal ray is missing. **u.** Included in 1925 mintage figure. **v.** A raised circular dot of metal is visible to the left of the bottom olive leaf. This is nicknamed the "Extra Berry" variety. **w.** Included in 1926-S mintage figure. **x.** Varieties exist with small and large mintmarks. **y.** The obverse shows strong doubling on most letters of IN GOD WE TRUST, the rays on the right, and especially on Liberty's profile. The mintmark is a small D, shaped much like that of the 1920s-era D punches. **z.** Included in 1934-D mintage figure. **aa.** Varieties exist with either three or four rays below ONE. They are valued equally in the marketplace. **bb.** The entire mintage of 1964-D Peace dollars was melted by government order. Deceptive reproductions exist.

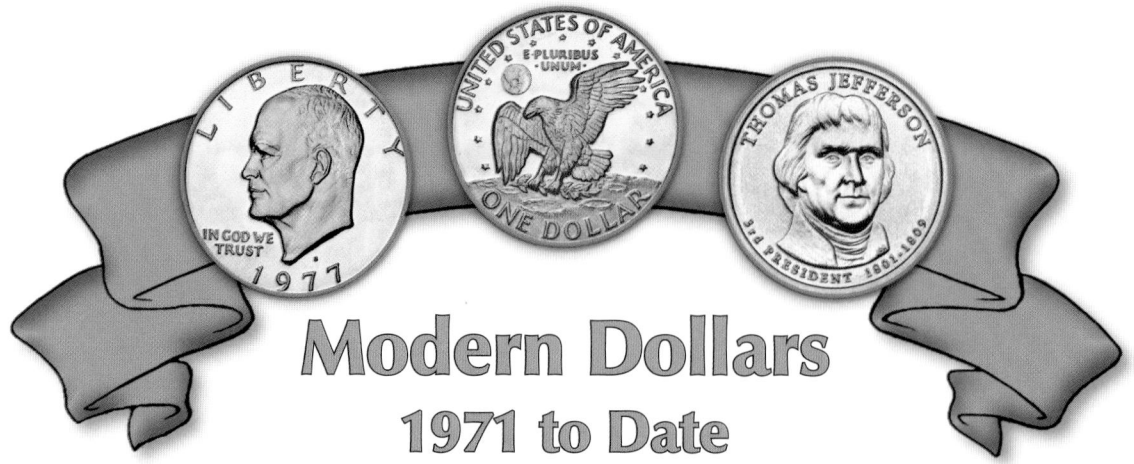

Modern Dollars
1971 to Date

AN OVERVIEW OF MODERN DOLLARS

After the last Peace dollars rolled off the presses at the San Francisco and Philadelphia mints in 1935, there was a long lapse in silver dollar coinage until 1965. In that year the Denver Mint struck Peace dollars dated 1964—the start of production of 45 million coins authorized by legislation of August 3, 1964. This coinage ultimately was stopped after 316,076 of the new Peace dollars were made; they were held back from being released into circulation and melted. It would be another six years before the United States had a new dollar coin, and it would not be silver.

Production of the next dollar started in 1971. The coin was the size of the 20th century's earlier silver dollars, but made in copper-nickel for circulation (and, in much smaller quantities, in .400 fine silver for collectors). Its motifs honor the late President Dwight D. Eisenhower, and the Apollo 11 spaceflight that had landed the first men on the Moon in 1969.

Silver dollars had long since disappeared from circulation, but there was demand for dollar coins in Las Vegas, Reno, and other centers of legalized gambling. Casinos otherwise had to depend on gaming chips and tokens.

The Eisenhower dollar was minted from 1971 to 1978, with those made in 1975 and 1976 being dual-dated 1776–1976 for the national bicentennial. In 1979 the "Ike" dollar was replaced by a smaller-format coin, the Susan B. Anthony dollar, honoring the famous women's-rights leader. Its reverse design shows an eagle landing on the Moon, similar to that of its predecessor (this design had in turn been based on the official insignia of the Apollo 11 mission). The Anthony dollar was struck in 1979, 1980, and 1981; then, in 1999 an additional final mintage of more than 40 million coins was produced to meet the needs of the vending-machine industry until distribution of the next year's new-design dollars could begin.

Presidential golden dollars cover the span from the 1st president of the United States, George Washington, to the 40th president, Ronald Reagan.

The year 2000 marked the debut of the first of several types of "golden" dollars, so called for the lustrous color of their manganese-brass surfaces. First came the Sacagawea dollar, minted from 2000 to 2008, with its conceptualized portrait of the young Shoshone Native American interpreter and guide who assisted the Lewis and Clark expedition of the early 1800s. A series of Native American dollars, each celebrating a different aspect of Native culture and historical importance, which began in 2009 and is ongoing today, is an offshoot of the Sacagawea dollar. And, since 2007, the golden-dollar format has been the canvas for a series of presidential portrait dollars honoring the nation's chief executives.

FOR THE COLLECTOR AND INVESTOR: MODERN DOLLARS AS A SPECIALTY

Eisenhower dollars, Susan B. Anthony dollars, and the golden dollars of various types are all easily found in today's marketplace. Dealers often have an abundance on hand of every date, mint, and most varieties. Banks sometimes have small quantities of Eisenhower or Anthony dollars. The current series are available directly from the U.S. Mint in collector formats and in rolls and bags of circulation strikes.

Eisenhower dollars are easily obtained in choice Mint State, although some of the coins made for circulation, especially of the earlier years, tend to be blemished with contact marks from jostling other coins during minting, transportation, and storage. Gems can be elusive. The Mint issued many options for collectors, including Proofs and .400 fine silver issues. Specialists look for die varieties including modified features, doubled dies, changes in depth of relief in the design, and other popular anomalies and variations that increase the challenge of building an extensive collection in what is otherwise a fairly short coinage series. Some Denver Mint dollars of 1974 and 1977 are also known to be struck in error, in silver clad composition rather than the intended copper-nickel.

Anthony dollars, too, are easy to assemble into a complete, high-grade collection of dates and mints. Specialists can focus on both varieties of 1979-P (Narrow Rim and Wide Rim), and varieties of S mintmark styles among the Proofs. Even these are common enough to easily acquire. Those seeking a harder challenge can search for the elusive 1980-S, Repunched Mintmark, Proof.

The Sacagawea dollar series includes several uncommon varieties that make an otherwise easy-to-collect type more challenging. The 2000-P coins include popular die varieties as detailed herein. Later dates were struck in smaller quantities and not issued for circulation, but still are readily available in high grades in the numismatic marketplace.

Native American dollars of 2009 to date are readily available in high grades.

The Presidential dollar series includes some error varieties with plain edges, instead of the normal lettered edge. These can be added to a date-and-mintmark collection for reasonable premiums. Otherwise the entire series is readily collectible from the secondary market and, for the current year of issue, in quantity directly from the U.S. Mint.

EISENHOWER (1971–1978)

Designer: *Frank Gasparro.* **Weight:** *Silver issue—24.59 grams; copper-nickel issue—22.68 grams.*
Composition: *Silver issue—40% silver, 60% copper, consisting of outer layers of .800 silver,
.200 copper bonded to inner core of .209 silver, .791 copper (net weight .3161 oz. pure silver);
copper-nickel issue—outer layers of .750 copper, .250 nickel bonded to inner core of pure copper.*
Diameter: *38.1 mm.* **Edge:** *Reeded.* **Mints:** *Philadelphia, Denver, and San Francisco.*

Circulation
Strike

Proof

Mintmark location is
on the obverse, between
the bust and the date.

Bicentennial variety: **Designers:** *Frank Gasparro and Dennis R. Williams.*
Weight: *Silver issue—24.59 grams; copper-nickel issue—22.68 grams.*
Composition: *Silver issue—outer layers of .800 silver, .200 copper bonded
to inner core of .209 silver, .791 copper (net weight .3161 oz. pure silver);
copper-nickel issue—outer layers of .750 copper, .250 nickel bonded to inner core of pure copper.*
Diameter: *38.1 mm.* **Edge:** *Reeded.* **Mints:** *Philadelphia, Denver, and San Francisco.*

Bicentennial
variety

Bicentennial
variety, Proof

History. Honoring both President Dwight D. Eisenhower and the first landing of man on the Moon, this coin is the work of Chief Engraver Frank Gasparro, whose initials are on the truncation of the president's neck and below the eagle. The reverse is an adaptation of the official Apollo 11 insignia. Collectors' coins were struck in 40% silver composition and sold by the Mint at a premium, and the circulation issue (for years a staple of the casino trade) was made in copper-nickel.

The dies for the Eisenhower dollar were modified several times by changing the relief, strengthening the design, and making Earth (above the eagle) more clearly defined.

Low-relief (Variety 1) dies, with a flattened Earth and three islands off the coast of Florida, were used for all copper-nickel issues of 1971, Uncirculated silver coins of 1971, and most copper-nickel coins of 1972.

High-relief (Variety 2) dies, with a round Earth and weak or indistinct islands, were used for all Proofs of 1971, all silver issues of 1972, and the reverse of some exceptional and scarce Philadelphia copper-nickel coins of 1972.

Improved high-relief reverse dies (Variety 3) were used for late-1972 Philadelphia copper-nickel coins and for all subsequent issues. Modified high-relief dies were also used on all issues beginning in 1973.

A few 1974-D and 1977-D dollars were made, in error, in silver clad composition.

A special reverse design was selected for the nation's Bicentennial. Nearly a thousand entries were submitted after the Treasury announced an open competition in October 1973. After the field was narrowed down to 12 semifinalists, the judges chose a rendition of the Liberty Bell superimposed on the Moon to appear on the dollar coins. The obverse remained unchanged except for the dual date 1776–1976, which appeared on all dollars made during 1975 and 1976. These dual-dated coins were included in the various offerings of Proof and Uncirculated coins made by the Mint. They were also struck for general circulation. The lettering was slightly modified early in 1975 to produce a more attractive design.

Striking and Sharpness. Striking generally is very good. For circulation strikes, on the obverse check the high parts of the portrait, and on the reverse, the details of the eagle. Nearly all Proofs are well struck and of high quality.

Availability. MS coins are common in the marketplace, although several early varieties are elusive at MS-65 or higher grades. Lower grades are not widely collected. Proofs were made of the various issues (both copper-nickel clad and silver clad from 1971 to 1976; copper-nickel only in 1977 and 1978). All are readily available in the marketplace today.

Note: Values of common-date silver coins have been based on the current bullion price of silver, $17 per ounce, and may vary with the prevailing spot price.

GRADING STANDARDS

MS-60 to 70 (Mint State). *Obverse:* At MS-60, some abrasion and contact marks are evident, most noticeably on the cheek, jaw, and temple. Luster is present, but may be dull or lifeless. At MS-63, contact marks are extensive but not distracting. Abrasion still is evident, but less than at lower levels. MS-64 coins are slightly finer. An MS-65 coin may have minor abrasion, but contact marks are so minute as to require magnification. Luster

1971-S. Graded MS-65.

should be full and rich. *Reverse:* At MS-60, some abrasion and contact marks are evident, most noticeably on the eagle's breast, head, and talons. Otherwise, the same comments apply as for the obverse.

AU-50, 53, 55, 58 (About Uncirculated). *Obverse:* Light wear is seen on the higher-relief areas of the portrait. At AU-58, the luster is extensive, but incomplete. At AU–50 and 53, luster is less but still present. *Reverse:* Further wear is evident on the eagle, particularly the head, breast, talons, and tops of the wings. Otherwise, the same comments apply as for the obverse.

The Eisenhower dollar is seldom collected in grades lower than AU-50.

1972. Graded AU-50.

PF-60 to 70 (Proof). *Obverse and Reverse:* Proofs that are extensively cleaned and have many hairlines, or that are dull and grainy, are lower level, such as PF–60 to 62. There are not many of these in the marketplace. With medium hairlines and good reflectivity, assigned grades of PF–63 or 64 are appropriate. With relatively few hairlines a rating of PF-65 can be given. PF-66 may have hairlines so delicate that magnification is needed

1776–1976-S, Bicentennial. Graded PF-68.

to see them. Above that, a Proof should be free of any hairlines or other problems.

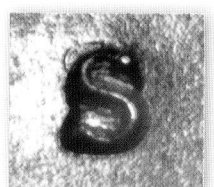

1971-S, Silver Clad, Repunched Mintmark

1971-S, Silver Clad, Polished Die
The "Peg Leg R" variety.

1971-S, Silver Clad, Doubled Die Obverse, Proof

1972-S, Silver Clad, Doubled Die Obverse, Proof

1973-S, Silver Clad, Doubled Die Obverse, Proof

	Mintage	Cert	Avg	%MS	EF-40 / PF-65	MS-63 / PF-67Cam	MS-65 / PF-67Cam	MS-66 / PF-68DC
1971, Copper-Nickel Clad, Reverse A ‡ (a)	47,799,000	1,537	64.0	97%	$2.25	$6	$120	$750
1971-D, Copper-Nickel Clad, Variety 1, Reverse A	68,587,424	2,842	64.7	97%	$3.50	$5	$100	$250
1971-D, Copper-Nickel Clad, Variety 2, Reverse B	(b)	0	n/a		$2	$5	$50	$130
1971-S, Silver Clad, Reverse A	6,868,530	4,099	65.2	100%		$13	$20	$60
1971-S, Silver Clad, Repunched Mintmark (c,d)	(e)	17	64.9	100%			$225	$350
1971-S, Silver Clad, Polished Die (f)	(e)	0	n/a				$125	$250
1971-S, Silver Clad, Proof, Reverse A	4,265,234	5,214	68.1			$14	$15	$25
1971-S, Silver Clad, Doubled Die Obverse, Proof (g,h)	(i)	42	67.6			$90	$150	
1972, Copper-Nickel Clad, All kinds	75,890,000							
1972, Copper-Nickel Clad, Variety 1, Reverse A (j)		1,284	63.9	98%	$2	$5	$140	$2,500
1972, Copper-Nickel Clad, Variety 2, Reverse D ‡ (k)		540	62.3	87%	$7	$80	$1,300	$8,500
1972, Copper-Nickel Clad, Variety 3, Reverse E (l)		1,006	64.2	98%	$2.50	$5	$125	$750
1972-D, Copper-Nickel Clad, Reverse A	92,548,511	1,692	64.5	97%	$2	$5	$30	$150
1972-S, Silver Clad	2,193,056	4,598	66.5	100%		$13	$15	$20
1972-S, Silver Clad, Proof	1,811,631	3,793	68.2			$14	$15	$25
1972-S, Silver Clad, Doubled Die Obverse, Proof (g)	(n)	21	67.9					—
1973, Copper-Nickel Clad ‡ (o)	2,000,056	1,087	64.5	100%		$13	$65	$500
1973-D, Copper-Nickel Clad ‡ (p)	2,000,000	1,061	64.5	100%		$13	$50	$250
1973-S, Copper-Nickel Clad (q)	(r)	0	n/a					
1973-S, Silver Clad	1,883,140	3,105	66.3	100%		$14	$18	$35
1973-S, Copper-Nickel Clad, Proof	2,760,339	1,207	68.1			$14	$16	$30
1973-S, Silver Clad, Proof	1,013,646	3,281	68.1			$35	$37	$50
1973-S, Silver Clad, DblDie Obv, Proof (m)	(k)	8	68.0					—

‡ Ranked in the *100 Greatest U.S. Modern Coins*. Only issued in Mint sets. **a.** Auction: $823, MS-66, August 2015. **b.** Included in 1971-D, Copper-Nickel Clad, Variety 1, mintage figure. **c.** A secondary S is visible protruding northwest of the primary S. "This is one of fewer than a half dozen RPMs known for the entire series" (*Cherrypickers' Guide to Rare Die Varieties*, sixth edition, volume II). **d.** Auction: $253, MS-66, July 2011. **e.** Included in circulation-strike 1971-S, Silver Clad, mintage figure. **f.** The left leg of the R in LIBERTY was overpolished. This is popularly known as the "Peg Leg R" variety. **g.** Strong doubling is visible on IN GOD WE TRUST, the date, and LIBER of LIBERTY. There are at least two doubled-die obverses for this date (valued similarly); the one listed is FS-S1-1971S-103. "This obverse is also paired with a minor doubled-die reverse" (*Cherrypickers' Guide to Rare Die Varieties*, sixth edition, volume II). **h.** Auction: $2,585, PF-69Cam, January 2016. **i.** Included in 1971-S, Proof, Silver Clad, mintage figure. **j.** Auction: $1,528, MS-66, August 2015. **k.** Auction: $329, MS-64+, May 2015. **l.** Auction: $2,820, MS-66, January 2015. **m.** A medium spread of doubling is evident on IN GOD WE TRUST, LIBERTY, and slightly on the date. **n.** Included in 1972-S, Proof, Silver Clad, mintage figure. **o.** Auction: $940, MS-66, January 2015. **p.** Auction: $12,925, MS-67, June 2013. **q.** Two reported to exist. **r.** Included in 1973-D, Copper-Nickel Clad, mintage figure. **s.** Included in 1973-S, Proof, Silver Clad, mintage figure.

	Mintage	Cert	Avg	%MS	EF-40 / PF-65	MS-63 / PF-67Cam	MS-65 / PF-68DC	MS-66
1974, Copper-Nickel Clad	27,366,000	1,288	64.5	99%	$2	$6	$60	$550
1974-D, Copper-Nickel Clad	45,517,000	7,717	65.0	100%	$2	$6	$38	$130
1974-S, Silver Clad	1,900,156	4,067	66.5	100%		$13	$20	$25
1974-S, Copper-Nickel Clad, Proof	2,612,568	1,017	68.0			$7	$10	$20
1974-S, Silver Clad, Proof	1,306,579	3,707	68.3			$15	$16	$30
1776–1976, Copper-Nickel Clad, Variety 1 (t)	4,019,000	889	64.2	100%	$2	$8	$160	$1,500
1776–1976, Copper-Nickel Clad, Variety 2	113,318,000	3,111	64.8	99%	$2	$5	$30	$125
1776–1976-D, Copper-Nickel Clad, Variety 1	21,048,710	1,967	64.8	99%	$2	$5	$50	$185
1776–1976-D, Copper-Nickel Clad, Variety 2	82,179,564	5,546	65.0	100%	$2	$5	$28	$60
1776–1976-S, Copper-Nickel Clad, Variety 1, Proof ‡ (u)	2,845,450	1,282	67.9			$12	$15	$30
1776–1976-S, Copper-Nickel Clad, Variety 2, Proof	4,149,730	1,731	68.1			$8	$12	$30
1776–1976, Silver Clad, Variety 2		0	n/a					
1776–1976, Silver Clad, Variety 2, Proof		0	n/a			—		
1776–1976-S, Silver Clad, Variety 1	11,000,000	2,904	66.2	100%		$17	$20	$30
1776–1976-S, Silver Clad, Variety 1, Proof	4,000,000	4,281	68.1			$19	$20	$35
1977, Copper-Nickel Clad	12,596,000	2,502	65.0	100%	$2	$6	$35	$135
1977-D, Copper-Nickel Clad	32,983,006	15,438	65.1	100%	$2	$6	$35	$170
1977-S, Copper-Nickel Clad, Proof	3,251,152	1,790	68.4			$5	$7	$15
1978, Copper-Nickel Clad	25,702,000	1,066	64.8	99%	$2	$6	$45	$160
1978-D, Copper-Nickel Clad	33,012,890	4,968	65.0	100%	$2	$6	$40	$125
1978-S, Copper-Nickel Clad, Proof	3,127,781	1,891	68.5			$5	$7	$15

‡ Ranked in the *100 Greatest U.S. Modern Coins*. Only issued in Mint sets. **t.** Auction: $129, MS-65, January 2015. **u.** Auction: $2,820, PF-70DCam, October 2015.

SUSAN B. ANTHONY (1979–1999)

Designer: *Frank Gasparro.* **Weight:** *8.1 grams.*
Composition: *Outer layers of copper-nickel (.750 copper, .250 nickel) bonded to inner core of pure copper.* **Diameter:** *26.5 mm.*
Edge: *Reeded.* **Mints:** *Philadelphia, Denver, and San Francisco.*

Circulation Strike

Mintmark location is on the obverse, above the left tip of the bust.

Proof

History. The Susan B. Anthony dollar was designed by Frank Gasparro, chief engraver of the U.S. Mint, following a congressional mandate. It features a portrait of the famous suffragette, along with an eagle-and-Moon motif reduced from the coin's larger predecessor, the Eisenhower dollar. Legislators hoped that these so-called mini-dollars would be an efficient substitute for paper dollars, which wear much more quickly in circulation. A large mintage in 1979 was followed by smaller quantities in 1980 and 1981, and then a hiatus of almost 20 years. The coins were not popular in circulation, with some members of the public complaining that they were too easily confused with the similarly sized quarter dollar. A final coinage of Anthony dollars was struck in 1999—a stopgap measure to ensure the Treasury's supply of dollar coins before the Sacagawea dollar was launched in 2000.

Striking and Sharpness. Most are well struck, but check the highest areas of both sides.

Availability. Susan B. Anthony dollars are readily available in MS, although those of 1981 are less common than those of 1979 and 1980. Circulated coins are not widely sought by collectors. Proofs were made of all issues and are readily available today.

GRADING STANDARDS

MS-60 to 70 (Mint State). *Obverse:* At MS-60, some abrasion and contact marks are evident, most noticeably on the cheek and upper center of the hair. Luster is present, but may be dull or lifeless. At MS-63, contact marks are extensive but not distracting. Abrasion still is evident, but less than at lower levels. MS-64 coins are slightly finer. An MS-65 coin may have minor abrasion, but contact marks are so minute as to require magnification. Lus-

1980-D. Graded MS-65.

ter should be full and rich. *Reverse:* At MS-60, some abrasion and contact marks are evident, most noticeably on the eagle's breast, head, and talons. Otherwise, the same comments apply as for the obverse.

AU-50, 53, 55, 58 (About Uncirculated). *Obverse:* Light wear is seen on the higher-relief areas of the portrait. At AU-58, the luster is extensive but incomplete. At AU–50 and 53, luster is less but still present. *Reverse:* Further wear is evident on the eagle, particularly the head, breast, talons, and tops of the wings. Otherwise, the same comments apply as for the obverse.

1979-D. Graded AU-50.

The Susan B. Anthony dollar is seldom collected in grades lower than AU-50.

PF-60 to 70 (Proof). *Obverse and Reverse:* Proofs that are extensively cleaned and have many hairlines, or that are dull and grainy, are lower level, such as PF–60 to 62. This comment is more theoretical than practical, as nearly all Proofs have been well kept. With medium hairlines and good reflectivity, assigned grades of PF–63 or 64 are appropriate. With relatively few hairlines a rating of PF-65

1979-S, Type 2. Graded PF-70 Deep Cameo.

can be given. PF-66 may have hairlines so delicate that magnification is needed to see them. Above that, all the way to PF-70, a Proof should be free of any hairlines or other problems under strong magnification.

1979-P, Narrow Rim
The "Far Date" variety.

1979-P, Wide Rim
The "Near Date" variety.

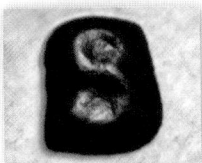
1979-S, Filled S (Type 1), Proof

1979-S, Clear S (Type 2), Proof

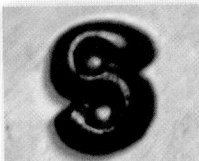
1981-S, Rounded S (Type 1), Proof

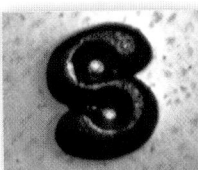
1981-S, Flat S (Type 2), Proof

1980-S, Repunched Mintmark, Proof
FS-C1-1980S-501

	Mintage	Cert	Avg	%MS	MS-63	MS-64	MS-65	MS-66
							PF-65	PF-68DC
1979-P, Narrow Rim (a)	360,222,000	784	64.9	98%	$6	$8	$10	$20
1979-P, Wide Rim ‡ (a,b)	(c)	1,509	64.7	96%	$38	$45	$55	$135
1979-D	288,015,744	1,017	65.3	99%	$7	$10	$12	$25
1979-S	109,576,000	844	65.3	99%	$6	$8	$10	$20
1979-S, Type 1, Proof (d)	3,677,175	4,127	68.9				$7	$10
1979-S, Type 2, Proof ‡ (d,e)	(f)	2,941	68.9				$50	$60
1980-P	27,610,000	1,224	65.8	100%	$5	$8	$10	$15
1980-D	41,628,708	1,091	65.6	100%	$5	$8	$10	$15
1980-S	20,422,000	1,142	65.2	100%	$10	$12	$15	$25
1980-S, Proof	3,554,806	3,904	68.9				$6	$10
1980-S, RPM, Proof (g)		0	n/a				—	—
1981-P (h)	3,000,000	879	65.6	100%	$12	$15	$20	$55
1981-D (h)	3,250,000	1,046	65.7	100%	$10	$12	$15	$25
1981-S ‡ (h)	3,492,000	670	64.6	100%	$20	$25	$35	$250
1981-S, Type 1, Proof	4,063,083	4,660	68.9				$6	$10
1981-S, Type 2, Proof ‡ (i)	(j)	2,692	68.7				$120	$140
1999-P (k)	29,592,000	736	66.2	100%	$3	$5	$10	$15
1999-D (k)	11,776,000	941	66.5	100%	$3	$5	$10	$15
1999-P, Proof (l)	750,000	5,283	69.3				$22	$28

‡ Ranked in the *100 Greatest U.S. Modern Coins*. **a.** The obverse design was modified in 1979 to widen the border rim. Late issues of 1979-P and subsequent issues have the wide rim. The 1979-P Wide Rim dollar is nicknamed the "Near Date" because the numerals are closer to the rim. **b.** Auction: $259, MS-67, January 2015. **c.** Included in 1979-P, Narrow Rim, mintage figure. **d.** The S mintmark punch was changed in 1979 to create a clearer mintmark. **e.** Auction: $188, PF-70DCam, June 2015. **f.** Included in 1979-S, Variety 1, Proof, mintage figure. **g.** "The remnants of a previously punched S appear left of the primary S. . . . Very few specimens of this variety have surfaced to date" (*Cherrypickers' Guide to Rare Die Varieties*, sixth edition, volume II). **h.** 1981-P, -D, and -S dollars were issued only in Mint Sets. **i.** Auction: $764, PF-70DCam, February 2015. **j.** Included in 1981-S, Variety 1, Proof, mintage figure. **k.** Dies for the 1999 dollars were further modified to strengthen details on the reverse. **l.** The mintage reflects the total for the Proof coins dated 1999, which were sold through 2003.

SACAGAWEA (2000–2008)

Designers: *Glenna Goodacre (obverse), Thomas D. Rogers Sr. (reverse).*
Weight: *8.1 grams.* **Composition:** *Pure copper core with outer layers of manganese brass (.770 copper, .120 zinc, .070 manganese, and .040 nickel).*
Diameter: *26.5 mm.* **Edge:** *Plain.* **Mints:** *Philadelphia, Denver, and San Francisco; 22-karat gold experimental specimens dated 2000-W were struck at West Point in 1999.*

Circulation Strike

Mintmark location is on the obverse, below the date.

Proof

History. The Sacagawea dollar was launched in 2000, with a distinctive golden color and a plain edge to distinguish it from other denominations or coins of similar size. (One complaint leveled against the Susan B. Anthony dollar was that it too closely resembled the quarter dollar; both were silvery, with reeded edges, and with only about two millimeters' difference in diameter.) The new coinage alloy and the change in appearance were mandated by the United States Dollar Coin Act of 1997. The core of the coin is pure copper, and the golden outer layer is of manganese brass. The obverse shows a modern artist's conception of Sacagawea, the Shoshone Indian who assisted the Lewis and Clark expedition, and her infant son, Jean Baptiste. (No known contemporary portraits of them exist.) The reverse shows an eagle in flight.

In 1999, about a dozen Sacagawea dollars were struck in 22-karat gold at the West Point Mint, as experimental or presentation pieces. These featured a prototype reverse design with boldly detailed tail feathers on the eagle. The following year, a small number of early circulation strikes from the Philadelphia Mint also featured that same prototype design. These are popularly called "Cheerio" dollars, as the coins were packaged as a promotion in boxes of Cheerios cereal (their unusual nature was not recognized at the time). Today collectors seek them as rare and desirable varieties.

In addition to the regular Uncirculated or Mint State coins produced in large quantities, smaller numbers of Satin Finish dollars were made of the 2005 to 2008 years, Philadelphia and Denver mints. Sold at an additional premium, most of these exist today in grades of MS-67 and upward and are designated SP (Specimen) or SMS (Special Mint Set) by the commercial grading services.

Several distinct finishes can be identified on the Sacagawea dollars as a result of the Mint's attempts to adjust the dies, blanks, strikes, or finishing to produce coins with minimal spotting and better surface color. One group of 5,000 pieces, dated 2000 and with a special finish, was presented to sculptor Glenna Goodacre in payment for the obverse design. These have since entered the numismatic market and command a significant premium.

Another peculiarity in the Sacagawea series is a numismatic mule (a coin made from mismatched dies)—the combination of an undated State quarter obverse and a Sacagawea dollar reverse. Examples of this error are extremely rare.

Striking and Sharpness. Most are very well struck. Weakness sometimes is evident on the higher design points. Special issues are uniformly sharply struck.

Availability. These coins are common in high grades, and are usually collected in MS and Proof.

Grading Standards

MS-60 to 70 (Mint State). *Obverse:* At MS-60, some abrasion and contact marks are evident, most noticeably on the cheekbone and the drapery near the baby's head. Luster is present, but may be dull or lifeless. At MS-63, contact marks are extensive but not distracting. Abrasion still is evident, but less than at lower levels. MS-64 coins are slightly finer. An MS-65 coin may have minor abrasion, but contact marks are so minute as to require magnification. Luster should be full and rich. *Reverse:* At MS-60, some abrasion and contact marks are evident, most noticeably on the eagle's breast. Otherwise, the same comments apply as for the obverse.

2006-D. Graded MS-65.

AU-50, 53, 55, 58 (About Uncirculated). *Obverse:* Light wear is seen on cheekbone, drapery, and elsewhere. At AU-58, the luster is extensive, but incomplete. At AU–50 and 53, luster is less but still present. *Reverse:* Further wear is evident on the eagle. Otherwise, the same comments apply as for the obverse.

The Sacagawea dollar is seldom collected in grades lower than AU-50.

2000-P. Graded AU-55.

PF-60 to 70 (Proof). *Obverse and Reverse:* Proofs that are extensively cleaned and have many hairlines, or that are dull and grainy, are lower level, such as PF–60 to 62. This comment is more theoretical than practical, as nearly all Proofs have been well kept. With medium hairlines and good reflectivity, assigned grades of PF–63 or 64 are appropriate. With relatively few hairlines a rating of PF-65 can be given. PF-66 may have hair-

2002-S. Graded PF-69.

lines so delicate that magnification is needed to see them. Above that, all the way to PF-70, a Proof should be free of any hairlines or other problems under strong magnification.

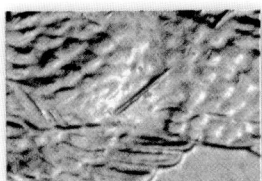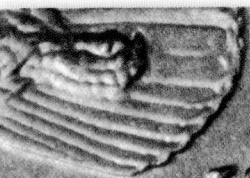

| 2000-P, Reverse Die Aberrations *The "Speared Eagle" variety.* | 2000-P, Normal Feathers | 2000-P, Boldly Detailed Tail Feathers |

	Mintage	Cert	Avg	%MS	MS-64	MS-65 / PF-65	MS-66 / PF-69DC
2000-P	767,140,000	5,787	66.7	100%	$2.50	$5	$12
2000-P, Reverse Die Aberrations (a,b)	(c)	74	67.4	100%		$700	$1,250
2000-P, Boldly Detailed Tail Feathers ‡ (d,e)	5,500	2	64.0	100%	$500	$550	$650
2000-P, Goodacre Presentation Finish ‡ (f,g)	5,000	85	66.1	100%		$3,500	$5,500
2000-D	518,916,000	7,517	66.4	100%	$4	$8	$15
2000-S, Proof	4,047,904	15,844	69.1			$6	$15
2001-P	62,468,000	682	67.1	100%	$2	$4	$6
2001-D	70,939,500	401	65.9	100%	$2	$4	$6
2001-S, Proof	3,183,740	11,255	69.2			$6	$20

‡ Ranked in the *100 Greatest U.S. Modern Coins*. **a.** Two spike-like die aberrations appear through the breast of the eagle. This variety is nicknamed the "Speared Eagle." **b.** Auction: $2,012, MS-67, January 2012. **c.** Included in 2000-P mintage figure. **d.** The feathers of the eagle are finely enhanced. This is nicknamed the "Cheerios" variety, as the coins were included as a promotion in boxes of Cheerios cereal. **e.** Auction: $8,195, MS-67, September 2008. **f.** A group of 5,000 coins, dated 2000 and with a special finish, were presented to sculptor Glenna Goodacre in payment for the obverse design. **g.** Auction: $541, MS-68, June 2015.

	Mintage	Cert	Avg	%MS	MS-64	MS-65 PF-65	MS-66 PF-69DC
2002-P (h)	3,865,610	393	67.1	100%	$2	$4	$10
2002-D (h)	3,732,000	363	66.3	100%	$2	$4	$8
2002-S, Proof	3,211,995	9,298	69.2			$6	$15
2003-P (h)	3,080,000	689	66.7	100%	$3	$5	$8
2003-D (h)	3,080,000	605	66.1	100%	$3	$5	$8
2003-S, Proof	3,298,439	12,608	69.2			$6	$15
2004-P (h)	2,660,000	578	66.8	100%	$2	$4	$8
2004-D (h)	2,660,000	703	66.6	100%	$2	$4	$8
2004-S, Proof	2,965,422	12,090	69.2			$6	$15
2005-P (h)	2,520,000	351	66.3	100%	$7	$10	$20
2005-P, Satin Finish (h)	1,160,000	4,012	67.0	100%	$3	$5	$12
2005-D (h)	2,520,000	594	66.1	100%	$7	$10	$20
2005-D, Satin Finish (h)	1,160,000	3,707	66.6	100%	$3	$5	$12
2005-S, Proof	3,344,679	17,543	69.2			$6	$15
2006-P (h)	4,900,000	378	66.1	100%	$2	$4	$8
2006-P, Satin Finish (h)	847,631	1,560	66.9	100%	$3	$5	$12
2006-D (h)	2,800,000	580	65.9	100%	$2	$4	$8
2006-D, Satin Finish (h)	847,631	1,503	66.9	100%	$3	$5	$12
2006-S, Proof	3,054,436	8,553	69.3			$6	$15
2007-P (h)	3,640,000	569	66.7	100%	$3	$5	$8
2007-P, Satin Finish (h)	895,628	569	67.0	100%	$3	$5	$12
2007-D (h)	3,920,000	882	66.5	100%	$3	$5	$8
2007-D, Satin Finish (h)	895,628	621	66.9	100%	$3	$5	$12
2007-S, Proof	2,577,166	8,763	69.2			$6	$15
2008-P (h)	1,820,000	242	66.4	100%	$3	$5	$8
2008-P, Satin Finish (h)	745,464	284	67.1	100%	$3	$5	$12
2008-D (h)	1,820,000	678	66.8	100%	$3	$5	$8
2008-D, Satin Finish (h)	745,464	363	67.3	100%	$3	$5	$12
2008-S, Proof	2,169,561	6,342	69.2			$6	$15

h. Not issued for circulation.

NATIVE AMERICAN (2009 TO DATE)

Designers: *Glenna Goodacre (obverse); see image captions for reverse designers.*
Weight: *8.1 grams.* **Composition:** *Pure copper core with outer layers of manganese brass (.770 copper, .120 zinc, .070 manganese, and .040 nickel).*
Diameter: *26.5 mm.* **Edge:** *Lettered.* **Mints:** *Philadelphia, Denver, and San Francisco.*

Circulation Strike

Mintmark location is on the rim.

Proof

History. Since 2009, the reverse of the golden dollar has featured an annually changing design that memorializes Native Americans and, in the words of the authorizing legislation, "the important contributions made by Indian tribes and individual Native Americans to the development [and history] of the United States." The coins are marked (incuse) on their edges with the year of minting, the mintmark, and the legend E PLURIBUS UNUM. The Native American $1 Coin Act also specified that at least 20% of the total mintage of dollar coins in any given year (including Presidential dollars) will be Native American dollars. Production of all dollar coins minted after 2011 has been limited to numismatic sales (Proofs and other collector formats, and circulation strikes in rolls and bags available directly from the U.S. Mint); none are issued for circulation, as they have proven unpopular in commerce.

The obverse of the Native American dollar coin is a modified version of the Sacagawea dollar, featuring that coin's central portraits (of Sacagawea and Jean Baptiste), and the legends LIBERTY and IN GOD WE TRUST. The date and mintmark, as noted above, are on the coin's edge. Each new reverse design is chosen by the secretary of the Treasury following consultation with the Senate Committee on Indian Affairs, the Congressional Native American Caucus of the House of Representatives, the Commission of Fine Arts, and the National Congress of American Indians. Design proposals are also reviewed by the Citizens Coinage Advisory Committee.

In addition to the regular Uncirculated or Mint State coins produced in large quantities, smaller numbers of Satin Finish dollars were made of the 2009-P, 2009-D, 2010-P, and 2010-D issues. Sold at an additional premium, most of these exist today in grades of MS-67 and upward and are designated SP (Specimen) or SMS (Special Mint Set) by the commercial grading services. 50,000 2014-D coins were made with Enhanced Uncirculated finish and were sold at an extra premium. Most of these grade MS–68 to 70. In 2015 at the West Point Mint 90,000 2015-W dollars were struck with Enhanced Uncirculated finish. These are unique up to this time as the only collectible West Point dollars in any of the three "golden dollar" series (Sacagawea, Native American, and Presidential). Nearly all are in grades MS–68 to 70.

Some error coins have been discovered without edge lettering.

Striking and Sharpness. Most examples are very well struck. Check the higher points of the design. Special issues are uniformly sharply struck.

Availability. Native American dollars are common in high grades, and are usually collected in MS and Proof. Distribution for public circulation has been slow despite Mint efforts such as the $1 Coin Direct Ship program (intended "to make $1 coins readily available to the public, at no additional cost [including shipping], so they can be easily introduced into circulation—particularly by using them for retail transactions, vending, and mass transit"). Proofs have been made each year and are readily available.

GRADING STANDARDS

MS-60 to 70 (Mint State). *Obverse:* At MS-60, some abrasion and contact marks are evident, most noticeably on the cheekbone and the drapery near the baby's head. Luster is present, but may be dull or lifeless. At MS-63, contact marks are extensive but not distracting. Abrasion still is evident, but less than at lower levels. MS-64 coins are slightly finer. An MS-65 coin may have minor abrasion, but contact marks are so minute as to require magnification. Luster should be full and rich. *Reverse:* At MS-60, some abrasion and contact marks are evident, most noticeably on the eagle's breast. Otherwise, the same comments apply as for the obverse.

2009-P, Three Sisters. Graded MS-68.

Native American dollars are seldom collected in grades lower than MS-60.

PF-60 to 70 (Proof). *Obverse and Reverse:* Proofs that are extensively cleaned and have many hairlines, or that are dull and grainy, are lower level, such as PF–60 to 62. This comment is more theoretical than practical, as nearly all Proofs have been well kept. With medium hairlines and good reflectivity, assigned grades of PF–63 or 64 are appropriate. With relatively few hairlines a rating of PF-65 can be given. PF-66 may have hairlines so delicate that magnification is needed to see them. Above that, all the way to PF-70, a Proof should be free of any hairlines or other problems under strong magnification.

2009-S, Three Sisters. Graded PF-70 Deep Cameo.

Three Sisters (2009)
Reverse designer: Norman E. Nemeth.

Great Law of Peace (2010)
Reverse designer: Thomas Cleveland.

Wampanoag Treaty (2011)
Reverse designer: Richard Masters.

Trade Routes in the 17th Century (2012)
Reverse designer: Thomas Cleveland.

Treaty With the Delawares (2013)
Reverse designer: Susan Gamble.

Native Hospitality (2014)
Reverse designer: Chris Costello.

Mohawk Ironworkers (2015)
Reverse designer: Ronald D. Sanders.

Code Talkers (2016)
Reverse designer: Thomas D. Rogers Sr.

Sequoyah (2017)
Reverse designer: Chris Costello.

Jim Thorpe (2018)
Reverse designer: Michael Gaudioso.

	Mintage	Cert	Avg	%MS	MS-64	MS-65	MS-66
						PF-65	PF-69DC
2009-P, Three Sisters	39,200,000	344	66.1	100%	$3	$5	$8
2009-P, Three Sisters, Satin Finish	784,614	587	67.3	100%	$3	$5	$12
2009-D, Three Sisters	35,700,000	268	65.4	100%	$3	$5	$8
2009-D, Three Sisters, Satin Finish	784,614	441	67.2	100%	$3	$5	$12
2009-S, Three Sisters, Proof	2,179,867	9,860	69.2			$8	$15
2010-P, Great Law	32,060,000	463	66.0	100%	$3	$5	$8
2010-P, Great Law, Satin Finish	583,897	301	67.4	100%	$3	$5	$12
2010-D, Great Law	48,720,000	365	65.8	100%	$3	$5	$8
2010-D, Great Law, Satin Finish	583,897	375	67.5	100%	$3	$5	$12
2010-S, Great Law, Proof	1,689,216	6,209	69.2			$8	$15
2011-P, Wampanoag Treaty	29,400,000	371	66.7	100%	$3	$5	$8
2011-D, Wampanoag Treaty	48,160,000	416	67.0	100%	$3	$5	$8
2011-S, Wampanoag Treaty, Proof	1,673,010	7,764	69.2			$8	$15
2012-P, Trade Routes	2,800,000	224	67.2	100%	$3	$5	$8
2012-D, Trade Routes	3,080,000	1,333	67.3	100%	$3	$5	$8
2012-S, Trade Routes, Proof	1,189,445	4,635	69.3			$15	$20

| | Mintage | Cert | Avg | %MS | MS-64 | MS-65 | MS-66 |
						PF-65	PF-69DC
2013-P, Treaty With the Delawares	1,820,000	327	67.0	100%	$3	$5	$8
2013-D, Treaty With the Delawares	1,820,000	1,266	67.1	100%	$3	$5	$8
2013-S, Treaty With the Delawares, Proof	1,222,180	4,198	69.5			$8	$15
2014-P, Native Hospitality	3,080,000	206	67.0	100%	$3	$6	$9
2014-D, Native Hospitality	2,800,000	535	67.2	100%	$3	$6	$9
2014-D, Native Hospitality, Enhanced Unc.	50,000	5,184	68.9	100%	$8	$10	$15
2014-S, Native Hospitality, Proof	1,144,154	6,363	69.3			$8	$15
2015-P, Mohawk Ironworkers	2,800,000	181	66.6	100%	$3	$5	$6
2015-D, Mohawk Ironworkers	2,240,000	1,513	66.9	100%	$3	$5	$6
2015-S, Mohawk Ironworkers, Proof	1,050,394	5,743	69.4			$8	$15
2015-W, Mohawk Ironworkers, Enhanced Unc.					$15	$20	$30
2016-P, Code Talkers	2,800,000	14	65.4	100%	$3	$5	$6
2016-D, Code Talkers	2,100,000	22	66.5	100%	$3	$5	$6
2016-S, Code Talkers, Enhanced Uncirculated					$15	$20	$30
2016-S, Code Talkers, Proof	931,866	2,689	69.5			$8	$15
2017-P, Sequoyah					$3	$5	$6
2017-D, Sequoyah					$3	$5	$6
2017-S, Sequoyah, Proof						$8	$15
2018-P, Jim Thorpe					$3	$5	$6
2018-D, Jim Thorpe					$3	$5	$6
2018-S, Jim Thorpe, Proof						$8	$15

PRESIDENTIAL (2007–2016)

Designers: *Various (obverse); Don Everhart (reverse).* **Weight:** *8.1 grams.*
Composition: *Pure copper core with outer layers of manganese brass (.770 copper, .120 zinc, .070 manganese, and .040 nickel).* **Diameter:** *26.5 mm.* **Edge:** *Lettered.* **Mints:** *Philadelphia, Denver, and San Francisco.*

Obverse Style, 2007–2008, Circulation Strike
No motto on obverse.

Obverse Style, 2009–2016, Circulation Strike
Motto beneath portrait.

Common Reverse, Circulation Strike

Proof

Date, Mintmark, and Mottos Incused on Edge
IN GOD WE TRUST moved to obverse in 2009.

History. Presidential dollars debuted in 2007 and are scheduled for issue at the rate of four designs per year through 2015, with the program's two final coins issued in 2016. The series starts with George Washington and continues in order of office. Living presidents are ineligible, so the program is slated to end with Gerald Ford. Each coin has a common reverse showing the Statue of Liberty. The series began with the date, mintmark, and mottos IN GOD WE TRUST and E PLURIBUS UNUM incused on the edge of the coins; in 2009 IN GOD WE TRUST was moved from the edge to the obverse after some public criticism of the "Godless dollars."

In December 2011, Secretary of the Treasury Timothy Geithner directed that the U.S. Mint suspend minting and issuing circulating Presidential dollars. "Regular circulating demand for the coins will be met through the Federal Reserve Bank's existing inventory of circulating coins minted prior to 2012," the Mint announced. Collector formats, however, have continued to be issued.

In addition to the regular Uncirculated or Mint State coins produced in large quantities, smaller numbers of Satin Finish dollars were made of the 2007 to 2010 years, Philadelphia and Denver Mints. Sold at an additional premium, most of these exist today in grades of MS-67 and upward and are designated SP (Specimen) or SMS (Special Mint Set) by the commercial grading services. Catching collectors, dealers, and others by surprise, the Coin and Chronicles sets of Presidential dollars were introduced in 2015. A small number of additional (to the regular Uncirculated) coins were made with Reverse Proof finish and sold at a sharp premium as part of Coin and Chronicles sets, which also included a brochure and a medal. Most collectors desired only the dollar. The Eisenhower and Truman sets, the first offered, sold out quickly, leaving many Mint clients disappointed. Letters of protest filled the columns of Coin World and Numismatic News when the only option to secure them seemed to be paying double or triple issue price on eBay and other venues. These were carefully produced, and nearly all grade MS–68 to 70. "First strike" and other notations on holders add little or nothing to the resale value of these or other modern coins.

Some Presidential dollars were inadvertently struck with the edge lettering missing. A 2009-D, John Tyler, variety has the wrong date, 2010, on the edge.

Striking and Sharpness. These usually are well struck, but check the higher-relief parts of each side. Special issues are uniformly sharp.

Availability. Presidential dollars are very common in MS. Most have from a few too many bagmarks, with true MS-65 and better coins in the minority.

GRADING STANDARDS

MS-60 to 70 (Mint State). *Obverse:* At MS-60, some abrasion and contact marks are evident, most noticeably on the highest-relief areas of the portrait, the exact location varying with the president depicted. Luster is present, but may be dull or lifeless. At MS-63, contact marks are extensive but not distracting. Abrasion still is evident, but less than at lower levels. MS-64 coins are slightly finer. An MS-65 coin may have minor abrasion, but contact marks

2007-P, Washington. Graded MS-68.

are so minute as to require magnification. Luster should be full and rich. *Reverse:* At MS-60, some abrasion and contact marks are evident, most noticeably on the cheek and arm. Otherwise, the same comments apply as for the obverse.

AU-50, 53, 55, 58 (About Uncirculated).
Obverse: Light wear is seen on the portrait, most prominently on the higher-relief areas. At AU-58, the luster is extensive, but incomplete. At AU–50 and 53, luster is less, but still is present. *Reverse:* Further wear is evident on statue. Otherwise, the same comments apply as for the obverse.

Presidential dollars are seldom collected in grades lower than AU-50.

2007-P, Madison. Graded AU-53.

PF-60 to 70 (Proof). *Obverse and Reverse:* Proofs that are extensively cleaned and have many hairlines, or that are dull and grainy, are lower level, such as PF–60 to 62. This comment is more theoretical than practical, as nearly all Proofs have been well kept. With medium hairlines and good reflectivity, assigned grades of PF–63 or 64 are appropriate. With relatively few hairlines a rating of PF-65 can be given. PF-66 may have hairlines so del-

2007-S, Madison. Graded PF-65.

icate that magnification is needed to see them. Above that, all the way to PF-70, a Proof should be free of any hairlines or other problems under strong magnification.

| 2007, Washington | 2007, J. Adams | 2007, Jefferson | 2007, Madison |

	Mintage	Cert	Avg	%MS	MS-64	MS-65 PF-65	MS-66 PF-69DC
2007-P, Washington	176,680,000	17,800	65.0	100%	$2	$3	$6
2007-P, Washington, Satin Finish	895,628	761	66.3	100%	$3	$5	$12
2007-P, Washington, Plain Edge ‡ (a,b)	(c)	43,472	64.7	100%	$30	$40	$65
2007-D, Washington	163,680,000	14,557	65.1	100%	$1.50	$3	$6
2007-D, Washington, Satin Finish	895,628	929	66.9	100%	$3	$5	$12
2007-S, Washington, Proof	3,965,989	45,159	69.2			$4	$15
2007-P, J. Adams	112,420,000	20,141	64.6	100%	$1.50	$3	$6
2007-P, J. Adams, Satin Finish	895,628	827	66.4	100%	$3	$5	$12
2007-D, J. Adams	112,140,000	5,851	65.0	100%	$1.50	$3	$6
2007-D, J. Adams, Satin Finish	895,628	911	67.0	100%	$3	$5	$12
2007-S, J. Adams, Proof	3,965,989	44,915	69.2			$4	$15
2007-P, Jefferson	100,800,000	4,988	65.3	100%	$1.50	$3	$6
2007-P, Jefferson, Satin Finish	895,628	894	66.5	100%	$3	$5	$12
2007-D, Jefferson	102,810,000	5,651	65.3	100%	$1.50	$3	$6
2007-D, Jefferson, Satin Finish	895,628	921	66.9	100%	$3	$5	$12
2007-S, Jefferson, Proof	3,965,989	45,007	69.2			$4	$15
2007-P, Madison	84,560,000	2,678	65.4	100%	$1.50	$3	$6
2007-P, Madison, Satin Finish	895,628	868	66.6	100%	$3	$5	$12
2007-D, Madison	87,780,000	3,015	65.4	100%	$1.50	$3	$6
2007-D, Madison, Satin Finish	87,780,000	883	66.9	100%	$3	$5	$12
2007-S, Madison, Proof	3,965,989	45,269	69.2			$4	$15

‡ Ranked in the *100 Greatest U.S. Modern Coins*. **a.** Some circulation-strike Washington dollars are known without the normal edge lettering (date, mintmark, IN GOD WE TRUST, and E PLURIBUS UNUM). **b.** Auction: $235, MS-67, September 2015. **c.** Included in 2007-P, Washington, mintage figure.

2008, Monroe

2008, J.Q. Adams

2008, Jackson

2008, Van Buren

	Mintage	Cert	Avg	%MS	MS-64	MS-65	MS-66
						PF-65	PF-69DC
2008-P, Monroe	64,260,000	2,269	65.6	100%	$1.50	$3	$6
2008-P, Monroe, Satin Finish	745,464	400	67.0	100%	$3	$5	$12
2008-D, Monroe	60,230,000	1,799	65.3	100%	$1.50	$3	$6
2008-D, Monroe, Satin Finish	745,464	421	67.1	100%	$3	$5	$12
2008-S, Monroe, Proof	3,083,940	24,174	69.2			$4	$15
2008-P, J.Q. Adams	57,540,000	2,607	65.9	100%	$1.50	$3	$6
2008-P, J.Q. Adams, Satin Finish	745,464	418	66.9	100%	$3	$5	$12
2008-D, J.Q. Adams	57,720,000	2,057	65.7	100%	$1.50	$3	$6
2008-D, J.Q. Adams, Satin Finish	745,464	426	67.2	100%	$3	$5	$12
2008-S, J.Q. Adams, Proof	3,083,940	24,180	69.3			$4	$15
2008-P, Jackson	61,180,000	3,044	65.7	100%	$1.50	$3	$6
2008-P, Jackson, Satin Finish	745,464	387	67.1	100%	$3	$5	$12
2008-D, Jackson	61,070,000	1,932	65.2	100%	$1.50	$3	$6
2008-D, Jackson, Satin Finish	745,464	420	67.3	100%	$3	$5	$12
2008-S, Jackson, Proof	3,083,940	24,151	69.2			$4	$15
2008-P, Van Buren	51,520,000	1,405	65.8	100%	$1.50	$3	$6
2008-P, Van Buren, Satin Finish	745,464	393	66.8	100%	$3	$5	$12
2008-D, Van Buren	50,960,000	933	65.2	100%	$1.50	$3	$6
2008-D, Van Buren, Satin Finish	745,464	389	67.0	100%	$3	$5	$12
2008-S, Van Buren, Proof	3,083,940	24,214	69.3			$4	$15

2009, W.H. Harrison

2009, Tyler

2009, Polk

2009, Taylor

	Mintage	Cert	Avg	%MS	MS-64	MS-65	MS-66
						PF-65	PF-69DC
2009-P, W.H. Harrison	43,260,000	1,122	65.5	100%	$1.50	$3	$6
2009-P, W.H. Harrison, Satin Finish	784,614	494	67.3	100%	$3	$5	$12
2009-D, W.H. Harrison	55,160,000	1,154	65.2	100%	$1.50	$3	$6
2009-D, W.H. Harrison, Satin Finish	784,614	461	67.5	100%	$3	$5	$12
2009-S, W.H. Harrison, Proof	2,809,452	17,982	69.2			$4	$15
2009-P, Tyler	43,540,000	1,020	65.3	100%	$1.50	$3	$6
2009-P, Tyler, Satin Finish	784,614	340	67.1	100%	$3	$5	$12
2009-D, Tyler	43,540,000	1002	65.2	100%	$1.50	$3	$6
2009-D, Tyler, Satin Finish	784,614	283	67.0	100%	$3	$5	$12
2009-D, Tyler, 2010 Edge	(d)	10	66.0	100%	—	—	—
2009-S, Tyler, Proof	2,809,452	17,950	69.2			$4	$15

d. Included in 2009-D, Tyler, mintage figure.

| | Mintage | Cert | Avg | %MS | MS-64 | MS-65 | MS-66 |
						PF-65	PF-69DC
2009-P, Polk	46,620,000	1,035	66.0	100%	$1.50	$3	$6
2009-P, Polk, Satin Finish	784,614	408	67.3	100%	$3	$5	$12
2009-D, Polk	41,720,000	770	65.4	100%	$1.50	$3	$6
2009-D, Polk, Satin Finish	784,614	377	67.3	100%	$3	$5	$12
2009-S, Polk, Proof	2,809,452	17,957	69.2			$4	$15
2009-P, Taylor	41,580,000	781	65.7	100%	$1.50	$3	$6
2009-P, Taylor, Satin Finish	784,614	481	67.6	100%	$3	$5	$12
2009-D, Taylor	36,680,000	784	65.6	100%	$1.50	$3	$6
2009-D, Taylor, Satin Finish	784,614	424	67.4	100%	$3	$5	$12
2009-S, Taylor, Proof	2,809,452	18,115	69.3			$4	$15

| **2010, Fillmore** | **2010, Pierce** | **2010, Buchanan** | **2010, Lincoln** |

| | Mintage | Cert | Avg | %MS | MS-64 | MS-65 | MS-66 |
						PF-65	PF-69DC
2010-P, Fillmore	37,520,000	862	65.6	100%	$1.50	$3	$6
2010-P, Fillmore, Satin Finish	583,897	418	67.3	100%	$3	$5	$12
2010-D, Fillmore	36,960,000	603	65.2	100%	$1.50	$3	$6
2010-D, Fillmore, Satin Finish	583,897	567	67.5	100%	$3	$5	$12
2010-S, Fillmore, Proof	2,224,827	15,324	69.2			$5	$15
2010-P, Pierce	38,220,000	760	65.6	100%	$1.50	$3	$6
2010-P, Pierce, Satin Finish	583,897	434	67.4	100%	$3	$5	$12
2010-D, Pierce	38,360,000	692	65.5	100%	$1.50	$3	$6
2010-D, Pierce, Satin Finish	583,897	583	67.6	100%	$3	$5	$12
2010-S, Pierce, Proof	2,224,827	15,274	69.2			$5	$15
2010-P, Buchanan	36,820,000	355	65.6	100%	$1.50	$3	$6
2010-P, Buchanan, Satin Finish	583,897	433	67.2	100%	$3	$5	$12
2010-D, Buchanan	36,540,000	496	65.3	100%	$1.50	$3	$6
2010-D, Buchanan, Satin Finish	583,897	562	67.5	100%	$3	$5	$12
2010-S, Buchanan, Proof	2,224,827	15,347	69.2			$5	$15
2010-P, Lincoln	49,000,000	724	65.5	100%	$1.50	$3	$6
2010-P, Lincoln, Satin Finish	583,897	681	67.1	100%	$3	$5	$12
2010-D, Lincoln	48,020,000	376	65.2	100%	$1.50	$3	$6
2010-D, Lincoln, Satin Finish	583,897	922	67.4	100%	$3	$5	$12
2010-S, Lincoln, Proof	2,224,827	16,054	69.2			$5	$15

| **2011, A. Johnson** | **2011, Grant** | **2011, Hayes** | **2011, Garfield** |

	Mintage	Cert	Avg	%MS	MS-64	MS-65 PF-65	MS-66 PF-69DC
2011-P, A. Johnson	35,560,000	390	66.7	100%	$1.50	$3	$6
2011-D, A. Johnson	37,100,000	374	67.0	100%	$1.50	$3	$6
2011-S, A. Johnson, Proof	1,972,863	8,118	69.2			$8	$15
2011-P, Grant	38,080,000	427	66.8	100%	$1.50	$3	$6
2011-D, Grant	37,940,000	394	67.0	100%	$1.50	$3	$6
2011-S, Grant, Proof	1,972,863	8,180	69.2			$8	$15
2011-P, Hayes	37,660,000	388	66.5	100%	$1.50	$3	$6
2011-D, Hayes	36,820,000	395	67.1	100%	$1.50	$3	$6
2011-S, Hayes, Proof	1,972,863	8,259	69.3			$8	$15
2011-P, Garfield	37,100,000	339	66.4	100%	$1.50	$3	$6
2011-D, Garfield	37,100,000	348	67.0	100%	$2	$3	$6
2011-S, Garfield, Proof	1,972,863	8,251	69.2			$8	$15

2012, Arthur	2012, Cleveland, First Term	2012, B. Harrison	2012, Cleveland, Second Term

	Mintage	Cert	Avg	%MS	MS-64	MS-65 PF-65	MS-66 PF-69DC
2012-P, Arthur (e)	6,020,000	709	66.8	100%	$2	$3	$6
2012-D, Arthur (e)	4,060,000	282	67.1	100%	$2	$3	$6
2012-S, Arthur, Proof	1,438,743	5,123	69.3			$12	$20
2012-P, Cleveland, First Term (e)	5,460,000	739	66.7	100%	$2	$3	$6
2012-D, Cleveland, First Term (e)	4,060,000	252	66.9	100%	$2	$3	$6
2012-S, Cleveland, First Term, Proof	1,438,743	5,147	69.3			$12	$20
2012-P, B. Harrison (e)	5,640,001	727	66.6	100%	$2	$3	$6
2012-D, B. Harrison (e)	4,200,000	252	67.1	100%	$2	$3	$6
2012-S, B. Harrison, Proof	1,438,743	5,118	69.3			$12	$20
2012-P, Cleveland, Second Term (e)	10,680,000	693	66.6	100%	$2	$3	$6
2012-D, Cleveland, Second Term (e)	3,920,000	259	67.1	100%	$2	$3	$6
2012-S, Cleveland, Second Term, Proof	1,438,743	5,084	69.3			$12	$20

e. Not issued for circulation.

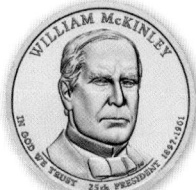   

2013, McKinley	2013, T. Roosevelt	2013, Taft	2013, Wilson

	Mintage	Cert	Avg	%MS	MS-64	MS-65 PF-65	MS-66 PF-69DC
2013-P, McKinley (e)	4,760,000	746	67.1	100%	$2	$3	$6
2013-D, McKinley (e)	3,365,100	155	67.0	100%	$2	$3	$6
2013-S, McKinley, Proof	1,488,798	4,953	69.5			$6	$16

e. Not issued for circulation.

	Mintage	Cert	Avg	%MS	MS-64	MS-65	MS-66
						PF-65	PF-69DC
2013-P, T. Roosevelt (e)	5,310,700	1,009	67.1	100%	$2	$3	$6
2013-D, T. Roosevelt (e)	3,920,000	292	66.6	100%	$2	$3	$6
2013-S, T. Roosevelt, Proof	1,503,943	4,990	69.5			$6	$16
2013-P, Taft (e)	4,760,000	877	67.1	100%	$2	$3	$6
2013-D, Taft (e)	3,360,000	212	67.0	100%	$2	$3	$6
2013-S, Taft, Proof	1,488,798	4,903	69.5			$6	$16
2013-P, Wilson (e)	4,620,000	950	67.4	100%	$2	$3	$6
2013-D, Wilson (e)	3,360,000	197	67.2	100%	$2	$3	$6
2013-S, Wilson, Proof	1,488,798	4,899	69.5			$6	$16

e. Not issued for circulation.

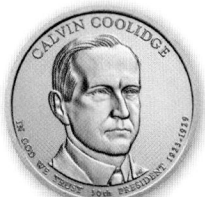

| 2014, Harding | 2014, Coolidge | 2014, Hoover | 2014, F.D. Roosevelt |

	Mintage	Cert	Avg	%MS	MS-64	MS-65	MS-66
						PF-65	PF-69DC
2014-P, Harding (e)	6,160,000	264	66.8	100%	$2	$3	$6
2014-D, Harding (e)	3,780,000	221	67.0	100%	$2	$3	$6
2014-S, Harding, Proof	1,373,569	4,188	69.5			$7	$16
2014-P, Coolidge (e)	4,480,000	308	67.2	100%	$2	$3	$6
2014-D, Coolidge (e)	3,780,000	192	67.2	100%	$2	$3	$6
2014-S, Coolidge, Proof	1,373,569	4,208	69.5			$7	$16
2014-P, Hoover (e)	4,480,000	251	67.0	100%	$2	$3	$6
2014-D, Hoover (e)	3,780,000	201	67.1	100%	$2	$3	$6
2014-S, Hoover, Proof	1,373,569	4,190	69.4			$7	$16
2014-P, F.D. Roosevelt (e)	4,760,000	296	67.1	100%	$2	$3	$6
2014-D, F.D. Roosevelt (e)	3,920,000	163	67.2	100%	$2	$3	$6
2014-S, F.D. Roosevelt, Proof	1,392,619	4,214	69.5			$7	$16

e. Not issued for circulation.

| 2015, Truman | 2015, Eisenhower | 2015, Kennedy | 2015, L.B. Johnson |

	Mintage	Cert	Avg	%MS	MS-64	MS-65	MS-66
						PF-65	PF-69DC
2015-P, Truman (e)	7,431,677	1,058	66.9	100%	$2	$3	$5
2015-P, Truman, Reverse Proof	16,812	1,471	69.0			$175	$225
2015-D, Truman (e)	5,231,090	173	67.1	100%	$2	$3	$5
2015-S, Truman, Proof	1,272,462	5,286	69.4			$6	$15

e. Not issued for circulation.

	Mintage	Cert	Avg	%MS	MS-64	MS-65	MS-66
						PF-65	PF-69DC
2015-P, Eisenhower (e)	7,265,242	974	66.8	100%	$2	$3	$5
2015-P, Eisenhower, Reverse Proof	16,744	1,179	68.9			$150	$200
2015-D, Eisenhower (e)	5,572,123	161	67.0	100%	$2	$3	$5
2015-S, Eisenhower, Proof	1,272,462	5,295	69.4			$6	$15
2015-P, Kennedy (e)	9,904,779	1,389	66.7	100%	$2	$3	$5
2015-P, Kennedy, Reverse Proof	49,051	2,757	69.0			$80	$125
2015-D, Kennedy (e)	8,599,310	230	67.2	100%	$2	$3	$5
2015-S, Kennedy, Proof	1,272,462	5,404	69.4			$6	$15
2015-P, L.B. Johnson (e)	7,944,164	987	66.8	100%	$2	$3	$5
2015-P, L.B. Johnson, Reverse Proof	23,905	1,385	68.8			$75	$90
2015-D, L.B. Johnson (e)	4,292,408	169	66.9	100%	$2	$3	$5
2015-S, L.B. Johnson, Proof	1,272,462	5,289	69.4			$6	$15

e. Not issued for circulation.

2016, Nixon   **2016, Ford**   **2016, Reagan**

	Mintage	Cert	Avg	%MS	MS-64	MS-65	MS-66
						PF-65	PF-69DC
2016-P, Richard M. Nixon (e)	8,602,433	146	66.7	100%	$2	$3	$5
2016-D, Richard M. Nixon (e)	7,138,903	304	67.0	100%	$2	$3	$5
2016-S, Richard M. Nixon, Proof	1,196,592	4,910	69.5			$6	$15
2016-P, Gerald Ford (e)	8,452,486	124	66.5	100%	$2	$3	$5
2016-D, Gerald Ford (e)	7,712,584	302	66.8	100%	$2	$3	$5
2016-S, Gerald Ford, Proof	1,196,592	4,904	69.5			$6	$15
2016-P, Ronald Reagan (e)	10,902,054	155	66.7	100%	$2	$3	$5
2016-D, Ronald Reagan (e)	9,288,601	302	67.0	100%	$2	$3	$5
2016-S, Ronald Reagan, Proof	1,196,592	4,910	69.5			$6	$15
2016-P, Ronald Reagan, Reverse Proof	47,448	1,142	69.1			$75	$90

e. Not issued for circulation.

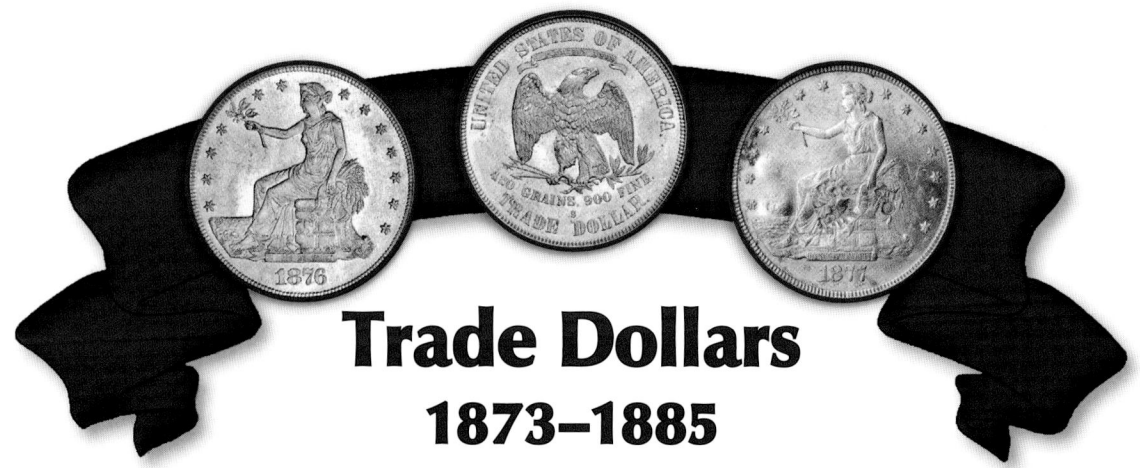

Trade Dollars
1873–1885

AN OVERVIEW OF TRADE DOLLARS

A new denomination, the silver trade dollar, was authorized by the Coinage Act of 1873. This provided that a coin weighing 420 grains, of .900 fine silver, be struck for use in the export trade. By comparison, contemporary Liberty Seated silver dollars weighed 412.5 grains. Produced in quantity from 1873 through 1878, the trade dollars were a great success, particularly in China, where merchants preferred silver to gold and would not accept paper money of any kind. Coinage would have continued except for passage of the Bland-Allison Act of February 28, 1878, which authorized the government to buy millions of ounces of silver each year and resume the production of standard silver dollars (which had not been minted since 1873). The trade dollar was discontinued forthwith; however, Proof impressions were made for numismatists through 1883, plus a small quantity of Proofs distributed privately in 1884 and 1885, coins of these last two issues being great rarities today.

Choosing a trade dollar for a type set is easy enough to do, the choices being a circulation strike, which requires some connoisseurship, or a Proof, most of which are sharply struck and attractive. Enough exist in both formats that collectors will easily find a nice example, except that MS-65 and better pieces are elusive.

FOR THE COLLECTOR AND INVESTOR: TRADE DOLLARS AS A SPECIALTY

There are two great rarities among trade dollars: the Proof-only 1884, of which just ten are known, and the Proof-only 1885, of which only five are known. Neither was produced openly, and examples were sold for the private profit of Mint officials, going to John W. Haseltine, a Philadelphia dealer who was a favored outlet for such things. The existence of these coins was not generally known to numismatists until 1907–1908, when examples began to appear on the market. As to the mintage figures, the numbers five and ten have no official origin, but are said to represent the number once held by Haseltine. Relatively few numismatists have been able to afford examples of these two dates.

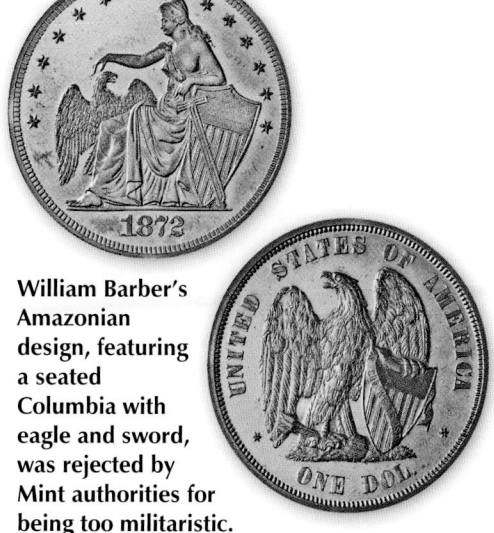

William Barber's Amazonian design, featuring a seated Columbia with eagle and sword, was rejected by Mint authorities for being too militaristic.

Beyond the above, a complete collection of trade dollars of the 1873 to 1883 years can be formed with some effort. Proofs were made of each year during this span, and after 1878 *only* Proofs were made, at the Philadelphia Mint, with no branch-mint issues. Proofs had greater appeal than Mint State circulation strikes to collectors of an earlier era, and more were saved, with the result that Proofs of the otherwise common dates 1873 to 1877 are much harder to find today, especially in choice condition.

Circulation strikes were regularly minted from 1873 through 1878, with production greatest at the San Francisco and Carson City mints, these being closest to eastern Asia, where the coins were used in commerce. Some trade dollars (but not many) went into domestic circulation (they were legal tender until that status was repealed on July 22, 1876). Later, after 1876, they traded widely in the United States but were valued by their silver content, not their face value. In 1878 the 412.5-grain Morgan dollar was worth $1.00 in circulation, while the heavier 420-grain trade dollar was worth only its melt-down value of about $0.90.

Very few of the circulating issues were saved by numismatists, with the result today that assembling a collection in choice or gem Mint State can be a great challenge. The key issue is the 1878-CC, with the lowest mintage by far in the series—scarce in any and all grades. As trade dollars became numismatically popular in the United States, thousands were repatriated from China, often bearing Chinese characters called *chopmarks*, which were applied by bankers and merchants. More often than not the imported coins had been harshly cleaned in China, as the owners thought shiny coins were more desirable. However, many choice and undamaged pieces were imported as well. The pieces with chopmarks are collectible in their own right in view of their historical significance.

Collectors are warned that many modern counterfeit trade dollars lurk in the marketplace.

TRADE DOLLAR (1873–1885)

Designer: *William Barber.* **Weight:** *27.22 grams.*
Composition: *.900 silver, .100 copper (net weight .7874 oz. pure silver).*
Diameter: *38.1 mm.* **Edge:** *Reeded.* **Mints:** *Philadelphia, Carson City, and San Francisco.*

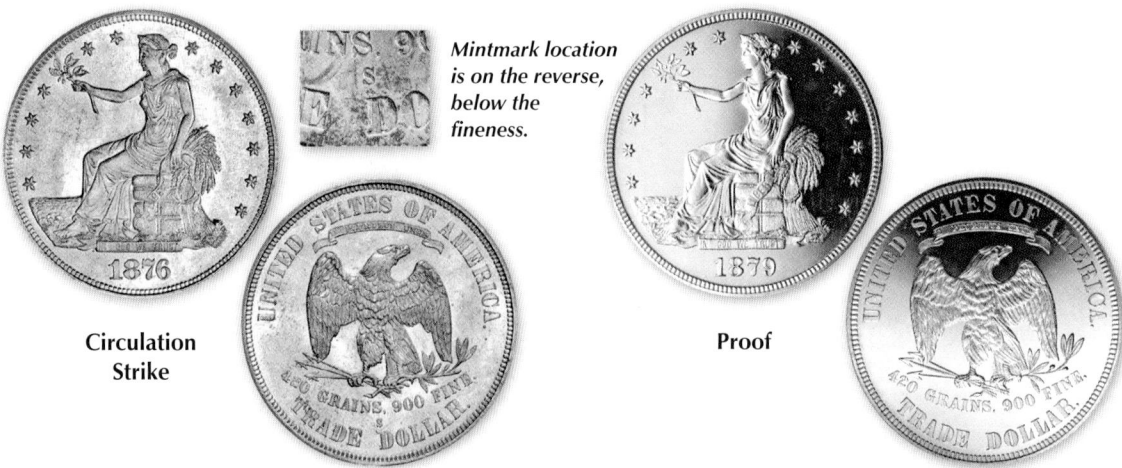

Mintmark location is on the reverse, below the fineness.

Circulation Strike

Proof

History. Trade dollars were minted under the Coinage Act of 1873. Containing 420 grains of .900 fine silver, they were heavier than the Liberty Seated dollar (of 412.5 grains). They were made for use in the China export trade and proved to be a great success. Some circulated at par in the United States, until they were demonetized by the Act of July 22, 1876, after which they circulated at their silver value, which was slightly lower than their face value. The Bland-Allison Act of 1878 provided for the new "Morgan" silver dollar, and trade dollars were discontinued, although Proofs continued to be made through 1885. Modifications to the trade dollar design are distinguished as follows.

Reverse 1: With a berry under the eagle's left talon; the lowest arrowhead ends over the 0 in 420. (Used on all coins from all mints in 1873 and 1874, and occasionally in 1875 and 1876.)

Reverse 2: Without an extra berry under the talon; the lowest arrowhead ends over the 2 in 420. (Used occasionally at all mints from 1875 through 1876, and on all coins from all mints 1877 through 1885.)

Obverse 1: The ends of the scroll point to the left; the extended hand has only three fingers. (Used on coins at all mints, 1873 through 1876.)

Obverse 2: The ends of the scroll point downward; the extended hand has four fingers. (Used in combination with Reverse 2 on one variety of 1876-S, and on all coins at all mints from 1877 through 1885.)

Striking and Sharpness. Weakness is often seen. On the obverse, check Miss Liberty's head and the star centers first. On the reverse, check the feathers on the eagle, particularly on the legs. Luster can range from dull to deeply frosty. In EF and lower grades, strike sharpness on the stars and the head does not matter to connoisseurs. Some Proofs are lightly struck on the head and the stars on the obverse and the leg feathers of the eagle on the reverse.

Availability. The 1878-CC is a rarity. Other dates and mintmarks are readily collected in grades from EF to MS. Lower grades are not often seen, for these coins did not circulate for a long time. Many used in China have counterstamps, called *chopmarks*, which are of interest to collectors. On an MS-63 or better coin a chopmark will decrease its value, but on EF and AU coins specialists eagerly seek them. MS coins are mostly in the lower ranges, often with unsatisfactory surfaces. True gems are very scarce. Proofs for collectors were made from 1873 to 1883 in quantity to supply the demand. In addition, a few were secretly made in 1884 and 1885. Most survivors are of high quality today, although gems of the 1873 to 1877 years are much harder to find than are those of 1878 to 1883.

Note: In recent years a flood of modern counterfeit trade dollars, many coming from China, has deluged the market.

Grading Standards

MS-60 to 70 (Mint State). *Obverse:* At MS-60, some abrasion and contact marks are evident, most noticeably on the left breast, left arm, and left knee. Luster is present, but may be dull or lifeless. Many of these coins are light in color or even brilliant, having been repatriated from China, and have been cleaned to remove sediment and discoloration. At MS-63, contact marks are very few, and abrasion is minimal. An MS-65 coin has

1875-S, Reverse 1. Graded MS-61.

no abrasion in the fields (but may have a hint on the higher parts of the seated figure), and contact marks are trivial. Luster should be full and rich. *Reverse:* Comments apply as for the obverse, except that in lower Mint State grades abrasion and contact marks are most noticeable on the eagle's head, the claws, and the top of the wings. At MS-65 or higher there are no marks visible to the unaided eye. The field is mainly protected by design elements and does not show abrasion as much as does the obverse on a given coin.

Illustrated coin: Some friction in the fields is seen, but much of the original luster remains.

AU-50, 53, 55, 58 (About Uncirculated). *Obverse:* Light wear is seen on the knees, bosom, and head. At AU-58, the luster is extensive but incomplete. At AU–50 and 53, luster is less. *Reverse:* Wear is visible on the eagle's head, the claws, and the top of the wings. An AU-58 coin will have nearly full luster. At AU–50 and 53, there still are traces of luster.

1876, Reverse 2. Graded AU-53.

Illustrated coin: This example shows light, even wear. Most of the luster is gone, except in protected areas, but it has excellent eye appeal for the grade.

EF-40, 45 (Extremely Fine). *Obverse:* Further wear is seen on all areas, especially the head, the left breast, the left arm, the left leg, and the bale on which Miss Liberty is seated. Little or no luster is seen on most coins. From this grade downward, strike sharpness on the stars and the head does not matter to connoisseurs. *Reverse:* Further wear is evident on the eagle's head, legs, claws, and wings, although on well-struck coins nearly all feather details on the wings are sharp.

1876-CC, Reverse 1. Graded EF-40.

VF-20, 30 (Very Fine). *Obverse:* Further wear is seen on the seated figure, although more than half the details of her dress are visible. Details of the wheat sheaf are mostly intact. IN GOD WE TRUST and LIBERTY are clear. *Reverse:* Wear is more extensive; some feathers are blended together, with two-thirds or more still visible.

1877-S. Graded VF-30.

F-12, 15 (Fine). *Obverse:* The seated figure is further worn, with fewer details of the dress visible. Most details in the wheat sheaf are clear. Both mottos are readable, but some letters may be weak. *Reverse:* Wear is extensive, with about half to nearly two-thirds of the feathers flat or blended with others. The eagle's left leg is mostly flat. Wear is seen on the raised E PLURIBUS UNUM, and one or two letters may be missing.

1873-CC. Graded F-12.

The trade dollar is seldom collected in grades lower than F-12.

PF-60 to 70 (Proof). *Obverse and Reverse:* Proofs that are extensively cleaned and have many hairlines, or that are dull and grainy, are lower level, such as PF–60 to 62. These are not widely desired. With medium hairlines and good reflectivity, an assigned grade of PF-64 is appropriate, and with relatively few hairlines, gem PF-65. In various grades hairlines are most easily seen in the obverse field. PF-66 may have hairlines so delicate

1882. Graded PF-62.

that magnification is needed to see them. Above that, a Proof should be free of such lines.

Illustrated coin: This coin has medium-gray toning overall.

Chopmarked Trade Dollar

Examples of chopmarks.

	Mintage	Cert	Avg	%MS	VG-8	F-12	VF-20	EF-40	AU-50	MS-60	MS-63 / PF-60	MS-64 / PF-63	MS-65 / PF-65
1873	396,900	183	57.5	65%	$165	$185	$225	$325	$650	$1,100	$3,000	$4,000	$9,000
	Auctions: $3,760, MS-64, August 2015; $3,668, MS-64, January 2015; $646, AU-55, September 2015; $588, AU-50, March 2015												
1873, Proof	600	159	63.1								$1,500	$3,000	$7,000
	Auctions: $8,225, PF-65, March 2015; $3,055, PF-64, September 2015; $3,055, PF-63Cam, June 2015; $2,720, PF-62Cam, July 2015												
1873-CC	124,500	131	52.9	27%	$350	$700	$950	$1,500	$3,000	$9,500	$25,000	$45,000	$110,000
	Auctions: $11,763, MS-62, October 2016; $5,288, AU-58, August 2015; $3,290, AU-58, February 2015; $3,290, AU-55, February 2015; $2,233, EF-45												
1873-S	703,000	109	59.6	71%	$175	$200	$300	$450	$675	$1,600	$3,800	$5,000	$17,000
	Auctions: $3,995, MS-63, July 2015; $2,820, MS-63, June 2015; $646, AU-55, March 2015; $165, VF-30, September 2015												

  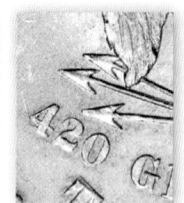 

Reverse 1	**Reverse 2**
Arrowheads end over 0; *berry under eagle's left talon.*	*Arrowheads end over 2;* *no berry under talon.*

Obverse 1	**Obverse 2**
Hand has three fingers; *scroll points left.*	*Hand has four fingers;* *scroll points downward.*

1875-S, S Over CC
FS-T1-1875S-501.

	Mintage	Cert	Avg	%MS	VG-8	F-12	VF-20	EF-40	AU-50	MS-60	MS-63	MS-64	MS-65
											PF-60	PF-63	PF-65
1874	987,100	146	57.6	62%	$165	$185	$225	$300	$425	$1,200	$2,400	$3,900	$13,000
	Auctions: $9,400, MS-65, August 2015; $2,350, MS-63, January 2015; $823, AU-58, September 2015; $400, EF-45, October 2015												
1874, Proof	700	206	63.2								$1,500	$3,000	$6,500
	Auctions: $8,813, PF-66, January 2015; $11,456, PF-65Cam, October 2015; $3,878, PF-64Cam, August 2015; $2,468, PF-62, October 2015												
1874-CC	1,373,200	238	57.8	62%	$280	$400	$475	$650	$1,100	$3,000	$7,250	$15,000	$35,000
	Auctions: $17,038, MS-64, August 2016; $14,100, MS-64, October 2015; $12,925, MS-64, August 2015; $7,050, MS-63, August 2015												
1874-S	2,549,000	321	59.6	68%	$165	$185	$200	$300	$325	$875	$1,900	$3,000	$12,000
	Auctions: $1,645, MS-63, July 2015; $1,129, MS-62, September 2015; $911, MS-61, July 2015; $376, AU-53, July 2015												
1875	218,200	106	58.0	70%	$240	$375	$525	$750	$1,250	$2,700	$5,250	$7,500	$21,000
	Auctions: $1,175, AU-53, September 2015; $541, AU-50, June 2015; $353, EF-40, April 2015; $1,763, VF-30, January 2015												
1875, Reverse 2	(a)	1	64.0	100%	$240	$375	$525	$750	$1,250	$2,600	$4,650	$9,000	$21,000
	Auctions: $4,888, MS-64, April 2012												
1875, Proof	700	228	63.3								$1,500	$3,000	$6,500
	Auctions: $28,200, PF-66, May 2015; $7,638, PF-65, August 2015; $3,290, PF-64Cam, June 2015; $2,233, PF-62, July 2015												
1875-CC, All kinds	1,573,700												
1875-CC		325	55.0	48%	$275	$375	$475	$575	$850	$2,500	$6,000	$11,500	$35,000
	Auctions: $8,813, MS-64, August 2016; $823, MS-60, June 2015; $969, AU-53, December 2015; $646, EF-40, June 2015; $376, VF-25												
1875-CC, Reverse 2	0	n/a			$275	$375	$475	$650	$925	$2,500	$5,500	$10,500	$33,500
	Auctions: $1,610, AU-58, January 2012												
1875-S, All kinds	4,487,000												
1875-S		973	60.1	76%	$165	$185	$225	$300	$350	$875	$1,650	$2,900	$9,000
	Auctions: $1,058, MS-62, August 2015; $881, MS-61, September 2015; $447, AU-58, April 2015; $282, EF-45, December 2015												
1875-S, Reverse 2		5	61.4	80%	$165	$185	$200	$325	$400	$1,175	$2,350	$3,400	$11,000
	Auctions: $69,000, MS-67, January 2012												
1875-S, S Over CC (b)		57	58.6	49%	$265	$400	$525	$1,000	$1,700	$5,000	$13,000	$22,500	$40,000
	Auctions: $24,675, MS-64, May 2015; $11,750, MS-64, March 2016; $4,113, MS-61, January 2015; $2,585, AU-58, October 2015												

a. Included in circulation-strike 1875 mintage figure. **b.** A weak C from the underlying CC mintmark is visible to the right of the S mintmark.

1876-CC, Doubled Die Reverse
FS-T1-1876CC-801.

1876-S, Doubled Die Obverse
FS-T1-1876S-101.

	Mintage	Cert	Avg	%MS	VG-8	F-12	VF-20	EF-40	AU-50	MS-60	MS-63	MS-64	MS-65
											PF-60	PF-63	PF-65
1876	455,000	465	59.2	75%	$165	$185	$200	$300	$335	$1,050	$2,400	$3,200	$12,000
	Auctions: $400, MS-60, May 2015; $494, AU-55, August 2015; $212, AU-50, February 2015; $212, EF-45, June 2015												
1876, Obverse 2, Reverse 2 (c)	(d)	0	n/a							—			
	Auctions: No auction records available.												
1876, Reverse 2	(d)	0	n/a		$165	$185	$225	$300	$335	$900	$2,000	$3,200	$11,000
	Auctions: $2,760, MS-64, April 2012												
1876, Proof	1,150	283	62.8								$1,500	$3,000	$6,500
	Auctions: $15,275, PF-66Cam, October 2015; $3,760, PF-64Cam, June 2015; $2,703, PF-63, January 2015; $1,410, PF-60, February 2015												
1876-CC, All kinds	509,000												
1876-CC		138	54.5	38%	$350	$450	$575	$775	$2,000	$6,250	$27,000	$37,500	$100,000
	Auctions: $2,820, AU-58, February 2015; $2,585, AU-55, February 2015; $1,528, AU-53, March 2016; $646, AU-50, September 2014; $1,293												
1876-CC, Reverse 1		1	53.0	0%	$325	$450	$600	$875	$2,350	$7,250	$29,500	$40,000	$115,000
	Auctions: $3,220, MS-60, February 2006												
1876-CC, Doubled Die Reverse (e)		33	54.9	27%	$500	$650	$1,150	$1,550	$2,100	$10,000	—		
	Auctions: $2,350, MS-60, February 2014; $1,087, AU-50, June 2015; $382, AU-50, September 2014												
1876-S, All kinds	5,227,000												
1876-S		883	57.0	56%	$165	$185	$200	$300	$350	$900	$1,700	$3,000	$11,000
	Auctions: $1,175, MS-62, January 2015; $705, AU-58, May 2015; $400, AU-55, October 2015; $200, EF-40, October 2015												
1876-S, Doubled Die Obverse (f)		0	n/a					$1,400	$1,750	$2,200			
	Auctions: No auction records available.												
1876-S, Reverse 2		3	57.0	0%	$165	$185	$200	$300	$350	$900	$1,700	$3,000	$11,000
	Auctions: $1,506, MS-63, September 2011												
1876-S, Obverse 2, Reverse 2		1	58.0	0%	$165	$200	$300	$500	$850	$1,500	$2,650	$3,700	$13,500
	Auctions: $1,495, MS-60 CAC, August 2011												

c. Extremely rare. **d.** Included in circulation-strike 1876 mintage figure. **e.** Doubling is visible on the branches on the right, the eagle's talons, the right wing tip, and the eagle's beak; and is very strong on E PLURIBUS UNUM. Weaker doubling is seen on UNITED STATES OF AMERICA. "Considered by most to be the strongest reverse doubled die in the series, this variety is one of the highlights of the trade dollar varieties and is thought to be extremely rare in grades above AU" (*Cherrypickers' Guide to Rare Die Varieties*, sixth edition, volume II). **f.** Doubling is visible on Liberty's hand, chin, and left foot, and on the olive branch. "This DDO is easily the rarest doubled die in the series, and is considered extremely rare in grades above AU. Most known examples are cleaned. The variety is known as the king of the trade dollar varieties" (*Cherrypickers' Guide to Rare Die Varieties*, sixth edition, volume II).

1877, Doubled Die Obverse
FS-T1-1877-101.

1877-S, Repunched Date
FS-T1-1877S-301.

1877-S, Doubled Die Reverse
FS-T1-1877S-801.

1877-S, Doubled Die Reverse
FS-T1-1877S-802.

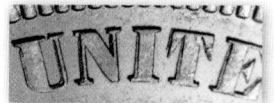 

1878-S, Doubled Die Reverse
FS-T1-1878S-801.

	Mintage	Cert	Avg	%MS	VG-8	F-12	VF-20	EF-40	AU-50	MS-60 / PF-60	MS-63 / PF-63	MS-64 / PF-64	MS-65 / PF-65
1877	3,039,200	654	51.6	44%	$165	$200	$225	$325	$350	$950	$2,100	$3,400	$9,500
Auctions: $16,450, MS-65, October2015; $12,925, MS-65, October 2015; $1,528, MS-63, January 2015; $1,058, MS-62, March 2016; $999													
1877, DblDie Obv (g)	(h)	2	60.0	50%				$300	$400	$1,250			
Auctions: No auction records available.													
1877, Proof	510	202	63.5							$1,650	$3,500		$7,000
Auctions: $3,055, PF-64, March 2015; $3,290, PF-63Cam, June 2015; $1,528, PF-60, January 2015; $1,293, PF-60, June 2015													
1877-CC	534,000	135	54.6	53%	$285	$425	$550	$725	$1,000	$4,000	$12,500	$28,500	$65,000
Auctions: $25,850, MS-64, August 2015; $14,100, MS-64, March 2015; $7,638, MS-63, August 2016; $7,638, MS-63, February 2015													
1877-S	9,519,000	1,543	54.7	50%	$165	$185	$200	$300	$325	$1,000	$2,050	$3,100	$9,000
Auctions: $6,463, MS-65, January 2015; $1,351, MS-63, October 2015; $212, EF-45, March 2015; $136, VF-30, June 2015													
1877-S, Repunched Date (i)	(j)	0	n/a					$550	$800	$1,600			
Auctions: $250, EF-45, May 2010													
1877-S, DblDie Rev (k)	(j)	2	55.5	0%				$300	$425	$1,300			
Auctions: No auction records available.													
1877-S, DblDie Rev (l)	(j)	6	52.7	50%				$300	$400	$1,200			
Auctions: $1,323, MS-62, April 2011													
1878	0	n/a						$1,500					
Auctions: No auction records available.													
1878, Proof	900	340	63.7							$1,500	$3,000		$6,500
Auctions: $12,338, PF-66, May 2015; $6,463, PF-65Cam, August 2015; $8,813, PF-64DCam, September 2015; $2,820, PF-63Cam, August 2015													
1878-CC (m)	97,000	90	47.7	29%	$700	$1,175	$1,675	$3,750	$5,000	$13,500	$35,000	$75,000	$130,000
Auctions: $18,800, MS-62, May 2015; $12,338, MS-61, February 2015; $11,163, AU-58, August 2015; $10,575, AU-58, June 2015													
1878-S	4,162,000	1118	51.8	40%	$165	$185	$200	$300	$350	$900	$1,700	$3,250	$9,000
Auctions: $28,200, MS-66, May 2015; $2,703, MS-64, August 2015; $329, AU-55, January 2015; $200, EF-40, October 2015													
1878-S, DblDie Rev (n)	(o)	14	53.6	36%				$450	$550	$1,300			
Auctions: $1,000, MS-62, August 2011													

g. Doubling on this rare variety is evident on the wheat stalks, LIBERTY, IN GOD WE TRUST, and stars 11, 12, and 13. **h.** Included in circulation-strike 1877 mintage figure. **i.** A secondary 7 protrudes prominently south from the last 7. **j.** Included in 1877-S mintage figure. **k.** Doubling is visible on E PLURIBUS UNUM, the ribbon, and UNITED STATES OF AMERICA. There are at least two different doubled-die reverses for 1877-S; this one is FS-T1-1877S-801. "Considered a highlight of the trade dollar varieties" (*Cherrypickers' Guide to Rare Die Varieties*, sixth edition, volume II). **l.** Minor doubling is visible on nearly all reverse lettering, especially on 420 GRAINS. This reverse doubled die is more common than the preceding; it is listed as FS-T1-1877S-802. **m.** On July 19, 1878, a quantity of 44,148 trade dollars was melted by the Mint. Many of these may have been 1878-CC. **n.** Strong doubling is visible on the entire lower left of the reverse, on the arrow points and shafts, and on 420 GRAINS; slight doubling is evident on the motto. Rare in AU and higher grades. There are at least two doubled-die reverses for this date; the one listed is FS-T1-1878S-801. **o.** Included in 1878-S mintage figure.

	Mintage	Cert	Avg	%MS	VG-8	F-12	VF-20	EF-40	AU-50	MS-60	MS-63	MS-64	MS-65
											PF-60	PF-63	PF-65
1879, Proof	1,541	554	63.7								$1,500	$3,000	$6,500
	Auctions: $15,863, PF-67Cam, January 2015; $8,813, PF-66Cam, September 2015; $5,053, PF-65+, September 2015; $1,763, PF-62, January 2015												
1880, Proof	1,987	700	63.5								$1,500	$3,000	$6,500
	Auctions: $15,275, PF-67, August 2015; $11,750, PF-66UCam, January 2015; $3,408, PF-64Cam, January 2015; $2,585, PF-63, January 2015												
1881, Proof	960	419	63.7								$1,500	$3,000	$6,500
	Auctions: $$8,225, PF-66, May 2015; $4,818, PF-65, October 2015; $4,700, PF-64Cam+, September 2015; $1,763, PF-62, January 2015												
1882, Proof	1,097	517	63.9								$1,500	$3,000	$6,500
	Auctions: $19,975, PF-66DCam, August 2015; $5,405, PF-65, August 2015; $3,760, PF-64Cam, October 2015; $3,055, PF-63Cam, August 2015												
1883, Proof	979	493	63.7								$1,500	$3,000	$6,500
	Auctions: $14,100, PF-66Cam, August 2015; $7,638, PF-65, August 2015; $4,935, PF-64Cam, June 2015; $2,374, PF-63, January 2015												
1884, Proof † (p)	10	6	63.7									$650,000	$1,100,000
	Auctions: $998,750, PF-65, January 2014												
1885, Proof † (p)	5	2	62.0									$2,000,000	$3,500,000
	Auctions: $1,006,250, PF-62, November 2004												

† Ranked in the *100 Greatest U.S. Coins* (fourth edition). **p.** Trade dollars of 1884 and 1885 were unknown to the numismatic community until 1907 and 1908. None are listed in the Mint director's report, and numismatists believe that they are not a part of the regular Mint issue but were produced secretly for private sale to collectors.

Gold Dollars
1849–1889

AN OVERVIEW OF GOLD DOLLARS

Coinage of the gold dollar was authorized by the Act of March 3, 1849, after the start of the California Gold Rush.

Although a case could be made for designating the Small Head, Open Wreath, gold dollar as a separate type, it is not generally collected as such. Instead, pieces dated from 1849 through 1854 (whether Open Wreath or Close Wreath) are collectively designated as Type 1. Examples today are readily available in all grades, although truly choice and gem Mint State pieces are in the minority.

In contrast, the Type 2 design, produced at the Philadelphia Mint in part of 1854, and at the Philadelphia, Charlotte, Dahlonega, and New Orleans mints in 1855, and only at the San Francisco Mint in 1856, is a great challenge. Examples are scarcer in all grades than are those of types 1 and 3. Choice and gem coins are especially rare. Striking is a great problem, and while some sharp pieces exist, probably 80% or more have areas of weakness, typically at the 85 (center two digits) of the date, but also often on the headdress and elsewhere. Further, the borders are sometimes imperfect.

Type 3 gold dollars, made from 1856 through 1889, are easier to acquire in nearly any grade desired, including choice and gem Mint State. Most are well struck and in Mint State have excellent eye appeal. Among Type 3 gold dollars the dates from 1879 through 1889 inclusive are most often seen, as these were widely saved by coin dealers and collectors at the time and did not circulate to any appreciable extent. Gold dollar coins also were popular as Christmas gifts in the late 1800s. Some of these have very low mintage figures, making them very appealing to today's collectors.

North Carolina Representative James Iver McKay was among the proponents for the introduction of a gold dollar coin. He introduced a bill to authorize the denomination into the House of Representatives on February 20, 1849.

FOR THE COLLECTOR AND INVESTOR: GOLD DOLLARS AS A SPECIALTY

Forming a specialized collection of gold dollars is a fascinating pursuit, one that has drawn the attention of many numismatists over the years. A complete run of date-and-mintmark issues from 1849 through 1889 includes no impossible rarities, although the 1875, with just 20 Proofs and 400 circulation strikes made, is the key date and can challenge collectors. While the dollars of 1879 through 1889 often have remarkably low mintages, they were saved in quantity, and certain of these dates are easily obtainable (although not necessarily inexpensive).

The branch-mint gold dollars of the early years present a special challenge. Among the Charlotte Mint varieties the 1849 comes with an Open Wreath (of which just five are presently known, with a rumor of a sixth) and with a Close Wreath, the latter being scarce but available. Later Charlotte gold dollars, extending through 1859, range from scarce to rare. The 1857-C is notorious for its poor striking.

Gold dollars were struck at the Dahlonega Mint from 1849 through 1861. In the latter year the facility was under the control of the Confederate States of America, and thus the 1861-D gold dollars, rare in any event, are even more desirable as true Confederate coins. The New Orleans Mint also produced gold dollars, which in general are better struck than those of the Charlotte and Dahlonega mints. From 1854 intermittently to 1860, and then in 1870, gold dollars were struck in San Francisco. These Western issues are usually sharply defined and range from scarce to rare. In particular, choice and gem Mint State pieces are elusive.

LIBERTY HEAD (1849–1854)

Designer: *James B. Longacre.* **Weight:** *1.672 grams.*
Composition: *.900 gold, .100 copper (net weight .04837 oz. pure gold).*
Diameter: *13 mm.* **Edge:** *Reeded.* **Mints:** *Philadelphia, Charlotte, Dahlonega, New Orleans, and San Francisco.*

Open Wreath Reverse   Close Wreath Reverse   Proof   Mintmark location is on the reverse, below the wreath.

History. U.S. Mint chief engraver James Barton Longacre designed the nation's gold dollars. This first type measured 13 mm in diameter, which proved to be inconvenient, and the two later types were enlarged to 15 mm.

Striking and Sharpness. As a rule, Type 1 gold dollars struck in Philadelphia are sharper than those of the Charlotte and Dahlonega mints. On the obverse, check the highest areas of the hair below the coronet. On the reverse, check the wreath and the central two figures in the date. On both sides check the denticles, which can be mushy or indistinct (particularly on Charlotte and Dahlonega coins, which often have planchet roughness as well).

Availability. All dates and mintmarks are readily collectible, save for the 1849-C, Open Wreath, variety. MS coins often are found for the Philadelphia issues but can be elusive for the branch mints. Charlotte and Dahlonega coins often have striking problems. The few gold dollars of this type that are less than VF in grade usually are damaged or have problems. Although a few Proofs were coined in the early years, they are for all practical purposes unobtainable. Only about a dozen are known.

GRADING STANDARDS

MS-60 to 70 (Mint State). *Obverse:* At MS–60 to 62, there is abrasion on the hair below the coronet (an area that can be weakly struck as well) and on the cheeks. Marks may be seen. At MS-63, there may be slight abrasion. Luster is irregular. At MS-64, abrasion is less. Luster is rich on most coins, less so on Charlotte and Dahlonega varieties. At MS-65 and above, luster is deep and frosty. At MS-66 and higher, no marks at all are visible

1854, Close Wreath. Graded MS-62.

without magnification. *Reverse:* On MS–60 to 62 coins, there is abrasion on the 1, the highest parts of the leaves, and the ribbon. Otherwise, the same comments apply as for the obverse.

Illustrated coin: Some friction is visible on the portrait and in the fields.

AU-50, 53, 55, 58 (About Uncirculated). *Obverse:* Light wear on the hair below the coronet and the cheek is very noticeable at AU-50, and progressively less at higher levels to AU-58. Luster is minimal at AU-50 and scattered and incomplete at AU-58. Some tiny nicks and contact marks are to be expected and should be mentioned if they are distracting. *Reverse:* Light wear on the 1, the wreath, and the ribbon characterize an AU-50 coin,

1853-D. Graded AU-58.

progressively less at higher levels to AU-58. Otherwise, the same comments apply as for the obverse.

Illustrated coin: Much of the luster remains, especially in protected areas.

EF-40, 45 (Extremely Fine). *Obverse:* Medium wear is seen on the hair below the coronet, extending to near the bun, and on the curls below. Detail is partially gone on the hair to the right of the coronet. Luster is gone on most coins. *Reverse:* Light wear is seen overall, and the highest parts of the leaves are flat. Luster is gone.

1849-C, Close Wreath. Graded EF-45.

VF-20, 30 (Very Fine). *Obverse:* Most hair detail is gone, except in the lower-relief areas and on the lower curls. Star centers are flat. *Reverse:* The wreath and other areas show more wear. Most detail is gone on the higher-relief leaves.

This gold dollar is seldom collected in grades lower than VF-20.

1851-D. Graded VF-25.

PF-60 to 70 (Proof). *Obverse and Reverse:* PF–60 to 62 coins have extensive hairlines and may have nicks and contact marks. At PF-63, hairlines are prominent, but the mirror surface is very reflective. PF-64 coins have fewer hairlines. At PF-65, hairlines should be minimal and mostly seen only under magnification. One cannot be "choosy" with Proofs of this type, as only a few exist.

1849, Open Wreath. Proof.

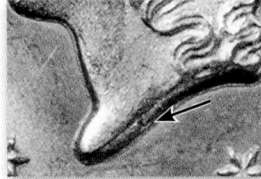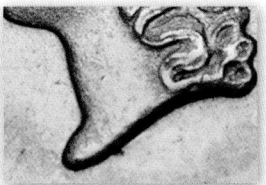

1849, With L • 1849, No L

	Mintage	Cert	Avg	%MS	VF-20	EF-40	AU-50	AU-55	AU-58	MS-60	MS-63	MS-64	MS-65 PF-60
1849, Open Wreath, So-Called Small Head, With L (a)	688,567	963	60.9	74%	$225	$250	$275	$300	$325	$350	$1,500	$2,100	$4,250
Auctions: $1,763, MS-64, June 2015; $705, MS-62, January 2015; $188, AU-58, January 2015; $235, AU-50, July 2015													
1849, Open Wreath, So-Called Small Head, No L (a)	(b)	390	62.2	86%	$225	$275	$300	$325	$400	$775	$1,650	$2,100	$4,750
Auctions: $4,935, MS-65, July 2015; $1,293, MS-63, January 2015; $881, MS-61, February 2015; $823, MS-60, October 2015													
1849, Open Wreath, So-Called Large Head (a)	(b)	0	n/a		$225	$250	$275	$275	$325	$350	$1,250	$1,900	$4,250
Auctions: $3,760, MS-65, January 2015; $1,495, MS-64, April 2012													
1849, Close Wreath	(b)	482	61.6	80%	$215	$250	$275	$295	$325	$650	$1,500	$1,950	$5,500
Auctions: $25,850, MS-66, August 2015; $705, MS-62, August 2015; $376, AU-58, August 2015; $329, AU-50, March 2015													
1849, Open Wreath, So-Called Small Head, No L, Proof (c)	unknown	3	62.7		*(extremely rare)*								
Auctions: No auction records available.													
1849-C, Open Wreath (d)	(b)	2	32.5	0%	$200,000	$225,000	$250,000	$300,000	$365,000	$450,000	$650,000		
Auctions: $3,220, AU-58, April 2012													
1849-C, Close Wreath	11,634	101	55.9	33%	$1,300	$1,850	$2,500	$4,000	$5,750	$9,000	$17,500	$45,000	
Auctions: $49,350, MS-64, August 2015; $10,281, MS-62, September 2013; $1,058, AU-50, January 2015; $2,820, EF-45, July 2014													
1849-D, Open Wreath	21,588	0	n/a		$1,500	$2,100	$2,600	$3,250	$3,750	$5,500	$11,500	$22,500	$55,000
Auctions: $22,325, MS-64, April 2013; $4,465, MS-62, January 2015; $3,760, MS-61, January 2015; $2,585, AU-55, September 2014													
1849-O, Open Wreath	215,000	0	n/a		$245	$325	$400	$485	$600	$1,000	$3,500	$7,000	$12,500
Auctions: $11,750, MS-65, March 2015; $999, MS-61, September 2015; $423, AU-58, June 2015; $259, EF-45, November 2015													

a. It is now well known that the so-called Small Head and Large Head coins are from the same punch. **b.** Included in 1849, Open Wreath, So-Called Small Head, With L, mintage figure. **c.** 2 to 3 examples are known. **d.** This coin is extremely rare.

	Mintage	Cert	Avg	%MS	VF-20	EF-40	AU-50	AU-55	AU-58	MS-60	MS-63	MS-64	MS-65
													PF-60
1850	481,953	542	59.9	67%	$215	$250	$265	$285	$300	$425	$850	$1,350	$4,000
	Auctions: $32,900, MS-67, August 2015; $2,585, MS-64, October 2015; $447, MS-61, June 2015; $235, AU-55, January 2015												
1850, Proof (e)	*unknown*	0	n/a										$100,000
	Auctions: No auction records available.												
1850-C	6,966	80	54.6	25%	$1,450	$1,850	$2,500	$4,000	$4,750	$8,000	$23,500		
	Auctions: $24,675, MS-63, February 2015; $19,975, MS-63, January 2014; $17,625, MS-63, November 2014; $11,163, MS-61, September 2016												
1850-D	8,382	97	54.6	25%	$1,500	$2,150	$3,250	$5,000	$7,000	$10,500	$25,000	$37,500	
	Auctions: $3,290, AU-55, January 2015; $3,204, AU-50, July 2014												
1850-O	14,000	197	58.2	43%	$300	$500	$950	$1,150	$1,850	$3,000	$6,500	$13,500	
	Auctions: $2,532, MS-61, April 2012												
1851	3,317,671	4,468	61.1	80%	$185	$195	$215	$235	$275	$325	$550	$800	$2,500
	Auctions: $3,995, MS-66, July 2015; $329, MS-61, January 2015; $229, AU-55, April 2015; $1,528, EF-45, September 2015												
1851-C	41,267	398	57.2	34%	$1,350	$1,650	$2,000	$2,250	$2,550	$3,200	$6,250	$13,500	$25,000
	Auctions: $5,376, MS-63, January 2015; $3,525, MS-62, June 2015; $2,468, AU-58, March 2015; $2,056, AU-55, January 2015												
1851-D	9,882	139	58.0	41%	$1,500	$1,800	$2,500	$3,000	$3,650	$5,000	$14,500	$22,500	$45,000
	Auctions: $14,688, MS-64, October 2014; $7,638, MS-62, February 2015; $4,113, AU-58, October 2014; $2,233, AU-50, March 2015												
1851-O	290,000	900	58.5	46%	$225	$265	$325	$425	$450	$800	$2,000	$4,000	$9,500
	Auctions: $12,925, MS-65, August 2015; $764, MS-61, January 2015; $270, AU-55, November 2015; $194, EF-45, January 2015												
1852	2,045,351	4,023	61.2	80%	$185	$195	$215	$235	$275	$325	$550	$800	$2,500
	Auctions: $4,700, MS-66, July 2015; $470, MS-63, August 2015; $259, AU-58, May 2015; $235, AU-55, August 2015												
1852-C	9,434	150	57.2	41%	$1,500	$1,850	$2,250	$2,750	$3,000	$4,250	$10,500	$16,500	$30,000
	Auctions: $15,863, MS-64, February 2013; $2,128, AU-55, October 2014; $2,585, AU-53, July 2014; $1,880, EF-40, July 2015												
1852-D	6,360	107	56.4	26%	$1,500	$2,250	$2,750	$3,750	$5,000	$8,500	$30,000		
	Auctions: $4,230, AU-58, February 2015; $4,994, AU-55, July 2014; $4,230, EF-45, January 2015												
1852-O	140,000	475	56.9	33%	$225	$265	$400	$600	$750	$1,300	$4,200	$12,500	$35,000
	Auctions: $37,600, MS-65, August 2015; $2,497, MS-63, January 2015; $541, AU-58, January 2015; $237, AU-53, June 2015												
1853	4,076,051	10,644	61.2	81%	$185	$195	$215	$235	$275	$325	$550	$800	$2,500
	Auctions: $20,575, MS-67, August 2015; $881, MS-64, February 2015; $353, MS-61, August 2015; $235, AU-55, November 2015												
1853-C	11,515	130	57.0	37%	$1,350	$1,600	$2,100	$2,600	$3,500	$4,750	$13,000	$22,000	$40,000
	Auctions: $14,100, MS-64, January 2014; $4,406, MS-62, August 2014; $9,988, MS-62, October 2014; $1,593, EF-40, July 2014												
1853-D	6,583	132	57.7	30%	$1,500	$2,000	$2,500	$4,250	$5,500	$8,500	$22,000	$32,500	$50,000
	Auctions: $17,038, MS-63, June 2015; $8,225, MS-62, June 2015; $6,933, MS-61, January 2015; $3,055, AU-55, October 2014												
1853-O	290,000	1,285	59.5	57%	$225	$255	$335	$425	$450	$800	$1,900	$2,750	$8,000
	Auctions: $23,500, MS-66, August 2015; $1,058, MS-62, January 2015; $259, AU-55, June 2015; $212, AU-50, February 2015												
1854	855,502	3,749	61.5	86%	$185	$195	$215	$235	$275	$325	$550	$800	$2,500
	Auctions: $19,975, MS-67, August 2015; $5,170, MS-66, August 2015; $376, MS-62, November 2015; $282, AU-55, October 2015												
1854, Proof	*unknown*	0	n/a		*(unique, in the Bass Foundation Collection)*								
	Auctions: No auction records available.												
1854-D	2,935	75	56.1	33%	$2,000	$2,500	$5,250	$6,500	$7,750	$11,000	$30,000	$65,000	
	Auctions: $7,638, MS-61, October 2015; $6,465, AU-58, July 2015; $5,640, AU-58, January 2015; $4,465, EF-45, September 2016												
1854-S	14,632	148	58.5	39%	$450	$650	$1,000	$1,350	$1,850	$2,500	$6,500	$14,500	$35,000
	Auctions: $56,400, MS-65, August 2015; $2,820, MS-62, January 2015; $1,528, AU-58, January 2015; $1,058, AU-53, February 2015												

e. 2 examples are known.

INDIAN PRINCESS HEAD, SMALL HEAD (1854–1856)

Designer: *James B. Longacre.* **Weight:** *1.672 grams.*
Composition: *.900 gold, .100 copper (net weight .04837 oz. pure gold).* **Diameter:** *15 mm.*
Edge: *Reeded.* **Mints:** *Philadelphia, Charlotte, Dahlonega, New Orleans, San Francisco.*

Circulation Strike

Mintmark location
is on the reverse,
below the wreath.

Proof

History. The Type 2 gold dollar, with the diameter increased from 13 mm to 15 mm, was first made in 1854. The headdress is decorated with *ostrich* plumes, which would not have been used in any genuine Native American headgear. The design proved difficult to strike, leading to its modification in 1856.

Striking and Sharpness. On the obverse, check the highest area of the hair below the coronet and the tips of the feathers. Check the letters. On the reverse, check the ribbon bow knot and in particular the two central digits of the dates. Examine the digits on both sides. Nearly all have problems. This type is often softly struck in the centers, with weak hair detail and the numerals 85 in the date sometimes faint—this should not be confused with wear. The 1855-C and 1855-D coins are often poorly struck and on rough planchets.

Availability. All Type 2 gold dollars are collectible, but the Charlotte and Dahlonega coins are rare. With patience, Full Details coins are available of 1854, 1855, and 1856-S, but virtually impossible to find for the branch-mint issues of 1855. The few gold dollars of this type that are less than VF in grade usually are damaged or have problems. Proofs exist of the 1854 and 1855 issues, but were made in very small quantities.

GRADING STANDARDS

MS-60 to 70 (Mint State). *Obverse:* At MS–60 to 62, there is abrasion on the hair below the band lettered LIBERTY (an area that can be weakly struck as well), on the tips of the feather plumes, and throughout the field. Contact marks may also be seen. At MS-63, there should be only slight abrasions. Luster is irregular. At MS-64, abrasions and marks are less. Luster is rich on most coins, less so on Charlotte and Dahlonega issues. At

1854. Graded MS-61.

MS-65 and above, luster is deep and frosty, with no marks at all visible without magnification at MS-66 and higher. *Reverse:* At MS–60 to 62, there may be abrasions on the 1, on the highest parts of the leaves, on the ribbon knot, and in the field. Otherwise, the same comments apply as for the obverse.

Illustrated coin: Some loss of luster is evident in the fields, but strong luster remains among the letters and in other protected areas. Good eye appeal is elusive for this type.

AU-50, 53, 55, 58 (About Uncirculated).
Obverse: Light wear on the hair below the coronet, the cheek, and the tips of the feather plumes is very noticeable at AU-50, progressively less at higher levels to AU-58. Luster is minimal at AU-50 and scattered and incomplete at AU-58. Some tiny nicks and contact marks are to be expected and should be mentioned if they are distracting. *Reverse:* Light wear on the 1, the wreath, and the ribbon

1855. Graded AU-55.

knot characterize an AU-50 coin, progressively less at higher levels to AU-58. Otherwise, the same comments apply as for the obverse.

Illustrated coin: This coin was lightly struck at the center. Clash marks appear on both sides, most prominent within the wreath on the reverse.

EF-40, 45 (Extremely Fine). *Obverse:* Medium wear is seen on the hair below the coronet and on the feather plume tips. Detail is partially gone on the hair, although the usual light striking may make this moot. Luster is gone on most coins. *Reverse:* Light wear is seen overall, and the highest parts of the leaves are flat. Luster is gone on most coins.

Illustrated coin: This coin was lightly struck at the centers, but overall has extraordinary quality.

1855-C. Graded EF-40.

VF-20, 30 (Very Fine). *Obverse:* Most hair detail is gone, except at the back of the lower curls. The feather plume ends are flat. *Reverse:* The wreath and other areas show more wear. Most detail is gone on the higher-relief leaves.

This gold dollar is seldom collected in grades lower than VF-20.

Illustrated coin: This coin is well worn, but has an exceptionally bold date, indicating that it must have been a very sharp strike.

1854. Graded VF-25.

PF-60 to 70 (Proof). *Obverse and Reverse:* PF–60 to 62 coins have extensive hairlines and may have nicks and contact marks. At PF-63, hairlines are prominent, but the mirror surface is very reflective. PF-64 coins have fewer hairlines. At PF-65, hairlines should be minimal and mostly seen only under magnification. There should be no nicks or marks. PF-66 and higher coins have no marks or hairlines visible to the unaided eye.

1854. Graded PF-66.

1854, Doubled Die Obverse
FS-G1-1854-1101.

	Mintage	Cert	Avg	%MS	VF-20	EF-40	AU-50	AU-55	MS-60	MS-62	MS-63 / PF-63	MS-64 / PF-64	MS-65 / PF-65
1854	783,943	5,861	57.3	28%	$325	$425	$500	$625	$1,250	$2,250	$5,750	$8,500	$27,500
Auctions: $51,700, MS-66, August 2015; $1,880, MS-62, January 2015; $402, AU-53, October 2015; $329, EF-40, August 2015													
1854, Doubled Die Obverse (a)	(b)	14	56.1	7%					$2,500	$5,500	$7,500	$12,500	
Auctions: $3,738, MS-62, December 2011													
1854, Proof	4 known	5	64.6								$200,000	$300,000	$425,000
Auctions: $218,500, PF-64DCam, March 2009													
1855	758,269	5,409	57.2	29%	$325	$425	$500	$625	$1,250	$2,250	$5,750	$8,500	$27,500
Auctions: $54,050, MS-66, August 2015; $4,230, MS-63, January 2015; $640, AU-58, February 2015; $529, EF-40, April 2015													
1855, Proof	unknown	6	64.8								$165,000	$225,000	$325,000
Auctions: $397,800, PF, September 2013													
1855-C	9,803	187	51.3	9%	$2,350	$4,500	$6,500	$10,000	$25,000	$35,000			
Auctions: $24,675, MS-61, January 2015; $7,638, AU-55, June 2015; $5,611, AU-50, June 2015; $4,230, EF-40, June 2015													
1855-D	1,811	43	53.5	12%	$10,000	$15,000	$25,000	$30,000	$55,000	$70,000	$100,000	$165,000	
Auctions: $164,500, MS-64, August 2015; $28,200, AU-55, September 2016; $8,225, AU-50, July 2015; $52,875, EF-45, July 2014													
1855-O	55,000	499	54.8	14%	$775	$1,250	$1,850	$2,850	$8,000	$15,000	$30,000	$45,000	
Auctions: $3,525, AU-58, June 2015; $2,585, AU-55, January 2015; $1,998, AU-50, July 2015; $705, VF-25, January 2015													
1856-S	24,600	213	54.7	15%	$850	$1,500	$2,250	$3,500	$7,500	$15,000	$25,000	$45,000	
Auctions: $52,875, MS-64, February 2013; $5,640, AU-58, January 2015; $3,290, AU-58, January 2015; $282, VF-20, August 2015													

a. Check for strong doubling on UNITED STATES OF AMERICA, the beads in the headdress, the feathers, and portions of LIBERTY.
b. Included in circulation-strike 1854 mintage figure.

INDIAN PRINCESS HEAD, LARGE HEAD (1856–1889)

Designer: *James B. Longacre.* **Weight:** *1.672 grams.*
Composition: *.900 gold, .100 copper (net weight .04837 oz. pure gold).* **Diameter:** *15 mm.*
Edge: *Reeded.* **Mints:** *Philadelphia, Charlotte, Dahlonega, and San Francisco.*

Circulation Strike **Proof**

History. The design of the Indian Princess Head was modified in 1856. The new Type 3 portrait is larger and in shallower relief. After this change, most (but not all) gold dollars were struck with strong detail. Gold dollars of this type did not circulate extensively after 1861, except in the West. As they did not see heavy use, today most pieces are EF or better. MS coins are readily available, particularly of the dates 1879 through 1889 (during those years the coins were popular among investors and speculators, and many were saved). These gold dollars were very popular with jewelers, who would purchase them at a price of $1.50 for use in a variety of ornaments.

Striking and Sharpness. These dollars usually are well struck, but many exceptions exist. Charlotte and Dahlonega coins are usually weak in areas and can have planchet problems. On all coins, check the hair details on the obverse. The word LIBERTY may be only partially present or missing completely, as the dies were made this way for some issues, particularly in the 1870s; this does not affect their desirability. On the reverse, check the ribbon knot and the two central date numerals. Check the denticles on both sides. Copper stains are sometimes seen on issues of the 1880s due to incomplete mixing of the alloy. Many coins of the 1860s onward have highly prooflike surfaces.

Availability. All Type 3 gold dollars are collectible, but many issues are scarce. Most MS-65 or finer coins are dated from 1879 to 1889. The few gold dollars of this type that are less than VF usually are damaged or have problems. Proofs were made of all years. Most range from rare to very rare, some dates in the 1880s being exceptions. Some later dates have high Proof mintages, but likely many of these coins were sold to the jewelry trade (as the Mint was reluctant to release circulation strikes to this market sector). Such coins were incorporated into jewelry and no longer exist as collectible coins.

GRADING STANDARDS

MS-60 to 70 (Mint State). *Obverse:* At MS–60 to 62, there is abrasion on the hair below the band lettered LIBERTY (an area that can be weakly struck as well), on the tips of the feather plumes, and throughout the field. Contact marks may also be seen. At MS-63, there should be only slight abrasions. Luster is irregular. At MS-64, abrasions and marks are less. Luster is rich on most coins, less so on Charlotte and Dahlonega issues. At

1878. Graded MS-67.

MS-65 and above, luster is deep and frosty, with no marks at all visible without magnification at MS-66 and higher. *Reverse:* At MS–60 to 62, there may be abrasions on the 1, on the highest parts of the leaves, on the ribbon knot, and in the field. Otherwise, the same comments apply as for the obverse.

Illustrated coin: This exceptionally high-grade coin has superb eye appeal.

AU-50, 53, 55, 58 (About Uncirculated). *Obverse:* Light wear on the hair below the coronet, the cheek, and the tips of the feather plumes is very noticeable at AU-50, progressively less at higher levels to AU-58. Luster is minimal at AU-50 and scattered and incomplete at AU-58. Some tiny nicks and contact marks are to be expected and should be mentioned if they are distracting. *Reverse:* Light wear on the 1, the wreath, and the ribbon knot

1857-C. Graded AU-58.

knot characterize an AU-50 coin, progressively less at higher levels to AU-58. Otherwise, the same comments apply as for the obverse.

Illustrated coin: The obverse field is slightly bulged. This coin is lightly struck at the center, unusual for most Type 3 gold dollars, but sometimes seen on Charlotte and Dahlonega varieties. Among 1857-C gold dollars this coin is exceptional. Most have poor striking and/or planchet problems.

EF-40, 45 (Extremely Fine). *Obverse:* Medium wear is seen on the hair below the coronet and on the feather plume tips. Detail is partially gone on the hair, although the usual light striking may make this moot. Luster is gone on most coins. *Reverse:* Light wear is seen overall, and the highest parts of the leaves are flat. Luster is gone on most coins.

1859-S. Graded EF-40.

VF-20, 30 (Very Fine). *Obverse:* Most hair detail is gone, except at the back of the lower curls. The feather plume ends are flat. *Reverse:* The wreath and other areas show more wear. Most detail is gone on the higher-relief leaves.

This gold dollar is seldom collected in grades lower than VF-20.

Illustrated coin: This coin is lightly struck at the center obverse, as well as at the U and IC in the border lettering. It is lightly struck at the center of the reverse.

1859-D. Graded VF-20.

PF-60 to 70 (Proof). *Obverse and Reverse:* PF-60 to 62 coins have extensive hairlines and may have nicks and contact marks. At PF-63, hairlines are prominent, but the mirror surface is very reflective. PF-64 coins have fewer hairlines. At PF-65, hairlines should be minimal and mostly seen only under magnification. There should be no nicks or marks. PF-66 and higher coins have no marks or hairlines visible to the unaided eye.

1884. Graded PF-68.

Illustrated coin: This splendid cameo Proof is one of the finest graded.

	Mintage	Cert	Avg	%MS	VF-20	EF-40	AU-50	AU-55	MS-60	MS-62	MS-63 PF-63	MS-64 PF-64	MS-65 PF-65
1856, All kinds	1,762,936												
1856, Upright 5		338	58.9	49%	$275	$300	$375	$450	$650	$850	$1,500	$2,100	$9,500
	Auctions: $16,450, MS-66, July 2015; $1,998, MS-64, September 2015; $447, MS-61, September 2015; $259, AU-55, September 2015												
1856, Slant 5		1,508	59.2	53%	$245	$250	$265	$285	$575	$650	$900	$1,100	$2,500
	Auctions: $42,300, MS-68, August 2015; $400, MS-62, January 2015; $306, AU-58, June 2015; $212, AU-50, November 2015												
1856, Slant 5, Proof	*unknown*	5	66.0								$30,000	$35,000	$65,000
	Auctions: $30,550, PF, January 2013												
1856-D	1,460	35	55.3	14%	$5,000	$8,000	$9,000	$12,000	$27,500	$45,000	$80,000		
	Auctions: $15,275, AU-58, September 2016; $11,750, AU-58, September 2013; $8,225, AU-50, September 2016; $7,050, EF-45, July 2014												

1862, Doubled Die Obverse
FS-G1-1862-101.

	Mintage	Cert	Avg	%MS	VF-20	EF-40	AU-50	AU-55	MS-60	MS-62	MS-63 / PF-63	MS-64 / PF-64	MS-65 / PF-65
1857	774,789	1,321	60.0	63%	$245	$250	$265	$285	$575	$650	$800	$1,200	$2,850
	Auctions: $51,700, MS-68, August 2015; $823, MS-64, October 2015; $353, MS-61, September 2015; $329, AU-50, October 2015												
1857, Proof	unknown	6	64.8								$20,000	$24,000	$45,000
	Auctions: $16,100, PF-63Cam, June 2008												
1857-C	13,280	144	53.6	8%	$1,350	$1,750	$3,250	$5,000	$11,000	$16,500			
	Auctions: $8,813, MS-61, January 2015; $3,290, AU-55, March 2015; $3,102, AU-55, January 2015; $3,055, EF-45, January 2015												
1857-D	3,533	95	55.3	17%	$1,500	$2,400	$3,750	$5,000	$10,500	$17,500			
	Auctions: $5,581, AU-58, April 2013; $3,525, AU-53, October 2014; $2,238, EF-45, July 2014												
1857-S	10,000	114	54.1	15%	$450	$750	$1,250	$2,000	$5,750	$8,500	$20,000	$35,000	
	Auctions: $3,995, MS-61, January 2015; $3,775, MS-61, June 2015; $2,350, AU-55, July 2014; $999, AU-53, January 2015												
1858	117,995	251	60.1	61%	$245	$250	$265	$285	$475	$650	$950	$1,400	$4,750
	Auctions: $51,700, MS-68, August 2015; $1,410, MS-63, September 2015; $282, AU-55, July 2015; $235, AU-53, January 2015												
1858, Proof	unknown	15	64.7								$13,500	$15,000	$30,000
	Auctions: $32,900, PF-66Cam+, November 2014; $79,313, PF, March 2014												
1858-D	3,477	113	55.5	28%	$1,500	$2,250	$3,750	$4,750	$8,500	$12,500	$21,500	$37,500	$60,000
	Auctions: $7,638, MS-61, December 2013; $4,230, AU-58, February 2015; $1,439, AU-50, September 2014; $1,998, EF-45, July 2014												
1858-S	10,000	101	54.3	12%	$425	$750	$1,300	$1,750	$5,500	$9,000	$15,000	$25,000	$40,000
	Auctions: $25,850, MS-64, August 2015; $7,050, MS-62, June 2015; $4,348, MS-61, August 2015; $852, AU-50, January 2015												
1859	168,244	420	60.6	71%	$245	$250	$255	$285	$400	$450	$800	$1,100	$2,500
	Auctions: $37,600, MS-68, August 2015; $1,998, MS-65, August 2015; $376, MS-61, August 2015; $282, AU-58, January 2015												
1859, Proof	80	13	64.8								$10,000	$12,000	$20,000
	Auctions: $22,325, PF-64, August 2013												
1859-C	5,235	83	57.0	28%	$2,000	$2,750	$3,750	$5,000	$7,000	$13,500	$25,000		
	Auctions: $15,275, MS-63, June 2015; $5,640, AU-58, June 2015; $4,465, AU-55, July 2015; $2,585, AU-50, August 2015												
1859-D	4,952	115	57.1	28%	$1,600	$2,250	$3,250	$4,750	$8,750	$12,500	$22,500	$32,500	$55,000
	Auctions: $11,750, MS-62, June 2013; $3,290, AU-55, July 2014; $3,055, AU-53, February 2015; $911, AU-50, November 2014												
1859-S	15,000	154	52.2	10%	$300	$575	$1,250	$1,900	$5,000	$8,000	$14,500	$24,000	
	Auctions: $6,169, MS-62, February 2013; $3,760, MS-61, January 2015; $1,469, AU-58, June 2015; $306, EF-40, September 2015												
1860	36,514	168	61.2	81%	$245	$250	$275	$300	$525	$675	$1,250	$2,250	$7,500
	Auctions: $10,869, MS-65, August 2015; $881, MS-63, September 2015; $646, MS-61, August 2015; $329, AU-55, February 2015												
1860, Proof	154	18	64.7								$8,000	$10,000	$17,500
	Auctions: $27,600, PF-66, January 2012												
1860-D	1,566	64	54.9	20%	$3,750	$6,500	$10,000	$11,500	$20,000	$27,500	$50,000	$65,000	
	Auctions: $42,300, MS-64, February 2013; $11,750, AU-50, June 2015; $6,463, EF-40, July 2014												
1860-S	13,000	149	56.2	26%	$350	$500	$775	$1,100	$2,650	$4,000	$6,000	$11,000	$30,000
	Auctions: $31,725, MS-65, August 2015; $1,998, MS-61, January 2015; $1,116, AU-55, January 2015; $317, AU-50, October 2015												
1861	527,150	1,478	61.3	83%	$245	$250	$265	$285	$575	$675	$750	$1,400	$2,500
	Auctions: $32,900, MS-67, August 2015; $2,585, MS-65, September 2015; $494, MS-61, January 2015; $212, EF-45, January 2015												
1861, Proof	349	15	64.7								$8,000	$11,000	$17,500
	Auctions: $17,625, PF-65Cam, October 2014												
1861-D	1,250	27	58.1	37%	$25,000	$30,000	$40,000	$57,500	$75,000	$85,000	$120,000	$145,000	$185,000
	Auctions: $111,625, MS-63, June 2013; $70,500, MS-61, January 2015; $30,550, EF-45, July 2014												
1862	1,361,355	3,087	61.7	88%	$245	$250	$265	$285	$485	$525	$750	$875	$2,000
	Auctions: $25,850, MS-67, August 2015; $4,230, MS-66, August 2015; $353, MS-61, April 2015; $223, AU-55, January 2015												
1862, DblDie Obv (a)	(b)	18	61.6	83%	$750	$1,500	$2,000	$2,500	$4,000	$4,750	$5,750		
	Auctions: $675, MS-62, February 2011; $447, AU-50, April 2015												

a. Doubling, visible on the entire obverse, is most evident on the tops of the hair curls and the feathers. **b.** Included in circulation-strike 1862 mintage figure.

	Mintage	Cert	Avg	%MS	VF-20	EF-40	AU-50	AU-55	MS-60	MS-62	MS-63 / PF-63	MS-64 / PF-64	MS-65 / PF-65
1862, Proof	35	19	64.9								$8,000	$11,000	$17,000
	Auctions: $7,475, PF-63UCam, April 2008												
1863	6,200	35	61.5	74%	$1,350	$2,000	$3,250	$4,500	$6,000	$7,500	$10,000	$13,500	$22,500
	Auctions: $193,875, MS-68, August 2015; $10,575, MS-64, October 2014; $8,813, MS-63, April 2013; $5,434, AU-55, July 2014												
1863, Proof	50	18	65.2								$10,000	$15,000	$22,500
	Auctions: $58,750, PF, February 2013												
1864	5,900	70	61.3	79%	$650	$850	$1,250	$1,350	$1,750	$2,500	$4,000	$6,500	$8,750
	Auctions: $70,500, MS-68, August 2015; $705, MS-60, October 2014; $1,293, AU-55, July 2014; $235, AU-50, March 2015												
1864, Proof	50	13	64.2								$10,000	$15,000	$22,500
	Auctions: $32,200, PF-66UCam, October 2011												
1865	3,700	36	62.2	83%	$750	$1,000	$1,100	$1,350	$2,000	$2,750	$4,750	$5,750	$11,500
	Auctions: $15,275, MS-66, August 2015; $12,925, MS-65, July 2015; $3,055, MS-61, October 2014; $1,116, EF-45, July 2014												
1865, Proof	25	13	65.2								$10,000	$15,000	$22,500
	Auctions: $25,300, PF-65, August 2011												
1866	7,100	76	62.4	84%	$450	$600	$700	$800	$1,250	$1,550	$2,500	$3,500	$5,750
	Auctions: $23,500, MS-67, August 2015; $4,700, MS-66, January 2015; $1,175, MS-62, January 2015; $646, AU-55, January 2015												
1866, Proof	30	19	65.4								$10,000	$15,000	$22,500
	Auctions: $27,600, PF-67UCam, August 2007												
1867	5,200	77	61.5	71%	$450	$625	$750	$850	$1,200	$1,500	$2,000	$2,750	$6,500
	Auctions: $9,400, MS-66, August 2015; $1,763, MS-63, January 2015; $1,058, MS-61, January 2015; $823, MS-60, February 2015												
1867, Proof	50	13	63.5								$10,000	$15,000	$22,500
	Auctions: $19,975, PF-66Cam, August 2014												
1868	10,500	127	60.9	76%	$450	$600	$700	$800	$1,000	$1,500	$2,000	$2,750	$6,500
	Auctions: $35,250, MS-68, August 2015; $5,940, MS-66, June 2015; $881, MS-61, October 2015; $329, MS-60, May 2015												
1868, Proof	25	9	64.4								$10,000	$15,000	$22,500
	Auctions: $29,900, PF-66UCam+, August 2011												
1869	5,900	89	61.6	82%	$450	$600	$700	$800	$1,150	$1,600	$2,250	$2,750	$5,500
	Auctions: $42,300, MS-68, August 2015; $2,115, MS-64, January 2015; $1,293, MS-62, September 2015; $940, AU-58, January 2015												
1869, Proof	25	10	64.0								$10,000	$15,000	$22,500
	Auctions: $19,975, PF-65Cam, April 2014												
1870	6,300	113	61.6	77%	$450	$600	$700	$800	$1,000	$1,500	$2,000	$2,750	$4,500
	Auctions: $18,800, MS-67, August 2015; $1,410, MS-63, January 2015; $676, MS-61, July 2015; $588, AU-58, September 2015												
1870, Proof	35	9	62.6								$10,000	$15,000	$22,500
	Auctions: $17,625, PF-64, January 2014												
1870-S	3,000	56	60.0	61%	$700	$875	$1,250	$1,750	$2,750	$4,000	$8,000	$12,500	$32,500
	Auctions: $35,250, MS-68, August 2015; $3,878, MS-62, January 2015; $3,525, AU-58, September 2015; $1,293, AU-50, January 2015												
1871	3,900	123	62.2	89%	$350	$450	$575	$675	$900	$1,100	$1,600	$2,250	$4,250
	Auctions: $35,250, MS-68, August 2015; $823, MS-61, October 2014; $412, MS-60, September 2014; $852, AU-58, July 2014												
1871, Proof	30	4	66.3								$10,000	$15,000	$22,500
	Auctions: $27,600, PF-65DCam, November 2011												
1872	3,500	69	60.6	72%	$350	$425	$575	$700	$1,000	$1,250	$2,250	$3,000	$5,000
	Auctions: $14,100, MS-67, August 2015; $1,528, MS-63, October 2015; $764, AU-58, January 2015; $517, AU-55, June 2015												
1872, Proof	30	15	64.2								$10,000	$15,000	$22,500
	Auctions: $4,888, PF-61, March 2011												
1873, Close 3	1,800	115	60.4	70%	$425	$750	$1,100	$1,150	$1,700	$2,500	$4,000	$7,500	$15,000
	Auctions: $1,529, MS-62, August 2015; $1,293, MS-61, April 2015; $1,183, MS-61, September 2015; $832, AU-58, June 2015												
1873, Open 3	123,300	2,258	61.8	91%	$245	$250	$265	$285	$350	$450	$575	$800	$1,500
	Auctions: $35,250, MS-68, August 2015; $1,410, MS-64, January 2015; $541, MS-63, August 2015; $353, MS-60, June 2015												
1873, Close 3, Proof	25	6	63.0								$15,000	$22,500	$35,000
	Auctions: $30,550, PF-65, August 2014												
1874	198,800	3999	62.2	93%	$245	$250	$265	$285	$350	$450	$575	$800	$1,350
	Auctions: $10,575, MS-68, October 2015; $940, MS-65, January 2015; $341, MS-61, June 2015; $259, AU-53, June 2015												

	Mintage	Cert	Avg	%MS	VF-20	EF-40	AU-50	AU-55	MS-60	MS-62	MS-63	MS-64	MS-65
											PF-63	PF-64	PF-65
1874, Proof	20	7	64.4								$12,000	$15,000	$25,000
	Auctions: $12,650, PF-64UC+, August 2010												
1875	400	30	61.5	83%	$3,500	$5,000	$6,000	$6,500	$10,000	$12,000	$16,000	$25,000	$40,000
	Auctions: $76,375, MS-66, August 2015; $22,325, MS-64, April 2013; $2,820, MS-60, October 2014; $5,875, AU-53, July 2014												
1875, Proof	20	11	64.1								$18,500	$30,000	$45,000
	Auctions: $55,813, PF-66DCam, November 2013												
1876	3,200	145	61.5	79%	$325	$375	$500	$600	$750	$1,000	$1,350	$1,500	$4,000
	Auctions: $28,200, MS-67, October 2015; $940, MS-62, July 2014; $588, AU-55, September 2014; $646, AU-50, October 2014												
1876, Proof	45	17	64.7								$7,000	$11,000	$15,000
	Auctions: $34,075, PF-66DCam, June 2013; $16,450, PF-65DCam, September 2014												
1877	3,900	178	62.1	83%	$300	$375	$525	$600	$800	$1,000	$1,400	$1,550	$3,500
	Auctions: $12,338, MS-67, August 2015; $541, AU-58, June 2015; $423, AU-55, August 2015; $329, AU-55, January 2015												
1877, Proof	20	16	64.8								$8,000	$11,000	$15,000
	Auctions: $7,638, PF, February 2014												
1878	3,000	153	61.8	88%	$300	$350	$400	$500	$775	$900	$1,200	$1,450	$3,250
	Auctions: $32,900, MS-67, August 2015; $2,849, MS-65, August 2015; $1,175, MS-62, October 2014; $764, MS-61, July 2014												
1878, Proof	20	13	64.3								$7,500	$11,000	$15,000
	Auctions: $19,550, PF-65DCam, January 2012												
1879	3,000	204	63.3	92%	$265	$300	$325	$350	$650	$800	$1,150	$1,300	$2,750
	Auctions: $5,640, MS-67, July 2015; $4,113, MS-66, August 2015; $1,175, MS-64, January 2015; $270, AU-55, January 2015												
1879, Proof	30	9	64.3								$6,500	$10,500	$15,000
	Auctions: $8,225, PF, August 2013												
1880	1,600	293	65.4	99%	$265	$300	$325	$350	$575	$700	$900	$1,050	$2,350
	Auctions: $8,813, MS-68, January 2015; $7,050, MS-68, June 2015; $2,849, MS-67, August 2015; $2,585, MS-66, January 2015												
1880, Proof	36	29	64.4								$5,500	$10,500	$12,000
	Auctions: $18,800, PF-65DCam, February 2013												
1881	7,620	383	64.7	97%	$250	$285	$325	$350	$575	$700	$900	$1,050	$1,800
	Auctions: $12,925, MS-68, August 2015; $2,644, MS-67, October 2015; $1,645, MS-66, October 2015; $517, MS-63, March 2015												
1881, Proof	87	28	64.7								$5,000	$8,500	$12,500
	Auctions: $2,820, PF-60, September 2014; $19,975, PF, March 2014												
1882	5,000	217	64.2	96%	$250	$285	$325	$350	$575	$700	$900	$1,050	$1,500
	Auctions: $16,450, MS-68, August 2015; $1,998, MS-66, September 2015; $1,645, MS-66, August 2015; $646, MS-62, July 2014												
1882, Proof	125	35	65.3								$5,000	$8,500	$11,500
	Auctions: $20,563, PF-67UCam, January 2015; $8,813, PF-64DCam, November 2014; $15,275, PF, August 2013												
1883	10,800	491	64.1	97%	$250	$285	$325	$350	$575	$700	$900	$1,050	$1,500
	Auctions: $18,800, MS-68, August 2015; $4,230, MS-67, September 2015; $3,055, MS-64, January 2015; $564, MS-62, January 2015												
1883, Proof	207	47	65.0								$5,000	$8,000	$11,500
	Auctions: $9,400, PF-65Cam, February 2013												
1884	5,230	229	63.4	97%	$250	$285	$325	$350	$575	$700	$900	$1,050	$1,500
	Auctions: $8,225, MS-68, July 2015; $3,995, MS-67, June 2015; $705, MS-64, January 2015; $588, MS-62, June 2015												
1884, Proof	1,006	62	65.3								$5,000	$7,000	$10,500
	Auctions: $29,250, PF, September 2013												
1885	11,156	455	63.7	96%	$250	$285	$325	$350	$575	$700	$900	$1,050	$1,500
	Auctions: $7,638, MS-68, June 2015; $1,763, MS-66, June 2015; $1,175, MS-65, October 2015; $235, AU-55, January 2015												
1885, Proof	1,105	110	64.9								$5,000	$7,000	$10,500
	Auctions: $16,450, PF-66, August 2015; $9,400, PF-65Cam, July 2014; $28,200, PF, August 2013												
1886	5,000	318	63.1	97%	$250	$285	$325	$350	$575	$700	$900	$1,050	$1,500
	Auctions: $4,113, MS-67, January 2015; $1,645, MS-65, February 2015; $470, MS-61, July 2015; $282, AU-50, January 2015												
1886, Proof	1,016	72	64.4								$5,000	$7,000	$10,500
	Auctions: $18,800, PF-67Cam, August 2014; $13,513, PF-67Cam, January 2015; $14,100, PF-66Cam, January 2015; $12,925, PF-66Cam, November 2014												

	Mintage	Cert	Avg	%MS	VF-20	EF-40	AU-50	AU-55	MS-60	MS-62	MS-63	MS-64	MS-65
											PF-63	PF-64	PF-65
1887	7,500	484	63.8	99%	$250	$285	$300	$315	$575	$675	$900	$1,050	$1,500
	Auctions: $35,250, MS-68, August 2015; $1,645, MS-66, October 2015; $494, MS-63, January 2015; $306, MS-60, November 2015												
1887, Proof	1,043	63	64.7								$5,000	$7,000	$10,500
	Auctions: $10,575, PF-65DCam, September 2013; $10,288, PF-65Cam+, October 2014; $4,700, PF-64Cam, January 2015												
1888	15,501	738	63.7	97%	$250	$285	$300	$315	$575	$600	$650	$800	$1,200
	Auctions: $15,275, MS-68, August 2015; $2,961, MS-67, July 2015; $1,645, MS-66, January 2015; $881, MS-64, February 2015												
1888, Proof	1,079	94	64.5								$5,000	$7,000	$10,500
	Auctions: $18,800, PF-66DCam, April 2013												
1889	28,950	2,009	64.2	98%	$250	$285	$300	$315	$575	$600	$650	$800	$1,200
	Auctions: $8,225, MS-68, August 2015; $3,055, MS-67, July 2015; $764, MS-64, January 2015; $400, MS-62, October 2015												
1889, Proof	1,779	35	64.2								$5,000	$7,000	$10,500
	Auctions: $12,925, PF-66Cam, April 2013												

Gold Quarter Eagles ($2.50) 1796–1929

AN OVERVIEW OF GOLD QUARTER EAGLES

The quarter eagle, denominated at one-fourth of an eagle, or $2.50, was authorized by the Act of April 2, 1792. Early types in the series range from rare to very rare. The first, the 1796 without stars on the obverse, Heraldic Eagle motif on the reverse, is a classic, one of the most desired of all pieces needed for a type set, and accordingly expensive. Most examples are in such grades as EF and AU.

Quarter eagles with stars on the obverse and with the Heraldic Eagle reverse were produced from 1796 intermittently through 1807. Today they exist in modest numbers, particularly in grades such as EF and AU, but on an absolute basis are fairly rare.

The standalone 1808 Draped Bust type, by John Reich, of which only 2,710 were minted, is the rarest single type coin in the entire American copper, nickel, silver, and gold series, possibly excepting the 1839 Gobrecht dollar (in a different category, as Proof restrikes were made). Examples of the 1808 can be found in various grades from VF through AU, and only rarely higher.

The next style of quarter eagle, from 1821 through 1827, is scarce, but when seen is usually in grades such as EF, AU, or even the low levels of Mint State. The same can be said for the modified quarter eagle of 1829 through early 1834.

Finally, with the advent of the Classic Head in late 1834, continuing through 1839, quarter eagles become more readily available. Examples can be found in nearly any grade from VF into the lower levels of Mint State. Then come the Liberty Head quarter eagles, minted continuously from 1840 through 1907, in sufficient numbers and for such a long time that it is not difficult to obtain an example to illustrate the type, with choice and gem Mint State coins being plentiful for the dates of the early 20th century.

The last quarter eagles are of the Indian Head type, minted from 1908 through 1929. These pieces are plentiful today, but grading can be difficult, as they were struck in sunken relief and the highest part on the coin is the field (this area was immediately subject to contact marks and wear). Although many opportunities exist in the marketplace, a collector should approach a purchase with care, seeking an example that has frosty, lustrous fields.

FOR THE COLLECTOR AND INVESTOR: GOLD QUARTER EAGLES AS A SPECIALTY

Collecting quarter eagles by dates, mintmarks, and major varieties is a very appealing pursuit. Although many are scarce and rare—this description applies to any variety from 1796 through early 1834—none are truly impossible to obtain. Among the Classic Head issues of 1834–1839, branch-mint coins are especially scarce in higher grades.

Liberty Head quarter eagles, produced continuously from 1840 through 1907, include a number of key issues, such as the famous 1854-S (usually seen in well-circulated grades), the Proof-only 1863 (of which only 30 were struck), and a number of elusive mintmarks. Of particular interest is the 1848 coin with CAL. counterstamped on the reverse, signifying that the coin was made from gold bullion brought to the Philadelphia Mint in a special shipment from California.

CAPPED BUST TO RIGHT (1796–1807)

Designer: *Robert Scot.* **Weight:** *4.37 grams.* **Composition:** *.9167 gold, .0833 silver and copper.* **Diameter:** *Approximately 20 mm.* **Edge:** *Reeded.* **Mint:** *Philadelphia.*

No Stars on Obverse (1796)
Bass-Dannreuther–2.

Stars on Obverse (1796–1807)
Bass-Dannreuther–3.

History. The first quarter eagles were struck intermittently during the late 1790s and early 1800s, with consistently small mintages. The earliest issues of 1796 lack obverse stars. They likely circulated domestically, rather than being exported in international trade.

Striking and Sharpness. Most have light striking in one area or another. On the obverse, check the hair details and the stars. On the reverse, check the shield, stars, and clouds. Examine the denticles on both sides. Planchet adjustment marks (from a coin's overweight planchet being filed down to correct specifications) are seen on many coins and are not noted by the certification services. On high-grade coins the luster usually is very attractive. Certain reverse dies of this type were also used to make dimes of the era, which were almost exactly the same diameter.

Availability. Most Capped Bust to Right quarter eagles in the marketplace are EF or AU. MS coins are elusive; when seen, they usually are of later dates.

GRADING STANDARDS

MS-60 to 70 (Mint State). *Obverse:* At MS-60, some abrasion and contact marks are evident, most noticeably on the hair to the left of Miss Liberty's forehead and on the higher-relief areas of the cap. On the No Stars quarter eagles, there is some abrasion in the field—more so than the With Stars coins, on which the field is more protected. Luster is present, but may be dull or lifeless, and

1802, 2 Over 1. Graded MS-61.

interrupted in patches. At MS-63, contact marks are few, and abrasion is very light. An MS-65 coin will have hardly any abrasion, and contact marks are so minute as to require magnification. Luster should be full and rich. Coins grading above MS-65 exist more in theory than in reality for this type—but they do exist, and are defined by having fewer marks as perfection is approached. *Reverse:* Comments apply as for the obverse, except that abrasion and contact marks are most noticeable on the upper part of the eagle and the clouds. The field area is complex; there is not much open space, with stars above the eagle, the arrows and olive branch, and other features. Accordingly, marks are not as noticeable as on the obverse.

Illustrated coin: Some friction appears on the higher areas of this example, but the fields retain nearly full luster, and the coin overall has nice eye appeal.

AU-50, 53, 55, 58 (About Uncirculated). *Obverse:* Light wear is seen on the cheek, the hair immediately to the left of the face, and the cap, more so at AU-50 than at AU–53 or 55. An AU-58 coin has minimal traces of wear. An AU-50 coin has luster in protected areas among the stars and letters, with little in the open fields or on the portrait. At AU-58 most luster is present in the fields, but is worn away on the highest parts of the motifs. The

1796, No Stars; BD-2. Graded AU-58.

1796 No Stars type has less luster in any given grade. *Reverse:* Comments as for Mint State, except that the eagle's neck, the tips and top of the wings, the clouds, and the tail now show noticeable wear, as do other features. Luster ranges from perhaps 40% remaining in protected areas at AU-50 to nearly full mint bloom at AU-58. Often the reverse of this type retains much more luster than does the obverse.

EF-40, 45 (Extremely Fine). *Obverse:* Wear is evident all over the portrait, with some loss of detail in the hair to the left of Miss Liberty's face. Excellent detail remains in low-relief areas of the hair, such as the front curl and the back of the head. The stars show wear, as do the date and letters. Luster, if present at all, is minimal and in protected areas. *Reverse:* Wear is greater than at the About Uncirculated level. The neck lacks feather detail on its

1802; BD-1. Graded EF-45.

highest points. Feathers have lost some detail near the edges of the wings, and some areas of the horizontal lines in the shield may be blended together. Some traces of luster may be seen, more so at EF-45 than at EF-40. Overall, the reverse appears to be in a slightly higher grade than the obverse.

VF-20, 30 (Very Fine). *Obverse:* The higher-relief areas of hair are well worn at VF-20, less so at VF-30. The stars are flat at their centers. *Reverse:* Wear is greater, including on the shield and wing feathers. The star centers are flat. Other areas have lost detail as well. E PLURIBUS UNUM is easy to read.

The Capped Bust to Right quarter eagle is seldom collected in grades lower than VF-20.

1796, With Stars; BD-3. Graded VF-30.

	Mintage	Cert	Avg	%MS	F-12	VF-20	EF-40	AU-50	AU-55	AU-58	MS-60	MS-63	MS-64
1796, No Stars on Obverse	963	34	57.3	35%	$55,000	$75,000	$95,000	$125,000	$165,000	$200,000	$250,000	$750,000	$1,000,000 (a)
	Auctions: $352,500, MS-61, October 2015; $123,375, AU-58, February 2016; $82,250, EF-40, October 2015; $94,000, VF-30, December 2013												
1796, Stars on Obverse	432	25	58.3	48%	$45,000	$65,000	$75,000	$100,000	$130,000	$165,000	$200,000	$500,000	$650,000
	Auctions: $111,625, AU-58, February 2016; $102,813, AU-58, March 2014; $223,250, AU-58, November 2014												
1797	427	16	49.5	13%	$16,500	$25,000	$40,000	$65,000	$125,000	$165,000	$185,000	$350,000	$500,000
	Auctions: $105,750, AU-53, April 2013												

a. Value in MS-65 is $2,000,000.

| 1798, Close Date | 1798, Wide Date | 1804, 13-Star Reverse | 1804, 14-Star Reverse |

	Mintage	Cert	Avg	%MS	F-12	VF-20	EF-40	AU-50	AU-55	AU-58	MS-60	MS-63	MS-64
1798, All kinds	1,094												
1798, Close Date		20	57.1	30%				$30,000	$43,500	$55,000	$75,000	$135,000	
	Auctions: $18,800, AU-50, August 2014												
1798, Wide Date	(b)							$30,000	$43,500	$55,000	$75,000	$135,000	
	Auctions: $70,500, AU-58, November 2014; $44,063, AU-50, June 2014												
1802	3,035	73	56.6	34%	$6,000	$8,000	$14,500	$17,500	$20,000	$23,500	$32,500	$75,000	$200,000
	Auctions: $20,563, AU-58, August 2014; $21,150, AU-58, March 2013; $16,450, AU-50, August 2014; $15,275, EF-45, August 2014												
1804, 13-Star Reverse	(c)	3	50.0	0%	$75,000	$100,000	$150,000	$200,000	$300,000	$500,000			
	Auctions: $322,000, AU-58, July 2009												
1804, 14-Star Reverse	3,327	61	52.8	18%	$6,500	$9,500	$15,000	$18,000	$21,000	$25,000	$35,000	$150,000	
	Auctions: $44,063, MS-62, April 2014; $70,501, MS-62, November 2014; $21,738, AU-58, November 2014; $19,975, AU-55, August 2014												
1805	1,781	53	54.9	30%	$5,750	$8,500	$14,000	$18,000	$21,000	$23,500	$32,500	$135,000	
	Auctions: $32,900, MS-60, March 2015; $20,563, AU-58, August 2014; $23,500, AU-55, November 2014; $14,100, AU-53, October 2014												
1806, 6 Over 4, 8 Stars Left, 5 Right	1,136	26	53.6	35%	$5,750	$9,000	$14,000	$18,000	$22,500	$27,500	$35,000	$150,000	
	Auctions: $30,550, MS-61, June 2014; $22,325, AU-58, August 2014; $21,150, AU-58, August 2014; $20,563, AU-58, October 2014												
1806, 6 Over 5, 7 Stars Left, 6 Right	480	14	57.5	50%	$12,000	$15,000	$20,000	$40,000	$57,500	$67,500	$95,000	$300,000	
	Auctions: $67,563, AU-About Uncirculated, February 2014												
1807	6,812	118	55.7	35%	$5,750	$8,500	$13,250	$17,000	$20,000	$23,500	$32,500	$85,000	$200,000
	Auctions: $44,063, MS-62, March 2014; $24,675, AU-58, March 2015; $17,625, AU-55, August 2014; $11,750, AU-50, November 2014												

b. Included in certified population for 1798, Close Date. c. Included in 1804, 14-Star Reverse, mintage figure.

DRAPED BUST TO LEFT, LARGE SIZE (1808)

Designer: *John Reich.* **Weight:** *4.37 grams.* **Composition:** *.9167 gold, .0833 silver and copper.* **Diameter:** *Approximately 20 mm.* **Edge:** *Reeded.*

History. John Reich's Draped Bust was an adaptation of the design introduced in 1807 on the half dollar. On the quarter eagle it was used for a single year only, with fewer than 3,000 coins struck, making it the rarest of the major gold coin types (indeed, the rarest of any U.S. coin type).

Striking and Sharpness. All examples are lightly struck on one area or another, particularly the stars and rims. The rims are low and sometimes missing or nearly so (on the obverse), causing quarter eagles of this type to wear more quickly than otherwise might be the case. Sharpness of strike is overlooked by most buyers.

Availability. Examples are rare in any grade. Typical grades are EF and AU. Lower grades are seldom seen, as the coins did not circulate to any great extent. Gold coins of this era were not seen in circulation after 1821, so they did not get a chance to acquire significant wear.

GRADING STANDARDS

MS-60 to 70 (Mint State). *Obverse:* At MS-60, some abrasion and contact marks are seen on the cheek, on the hair below the LIBERTY inscription, and on the highest-relief folds of the cap. Luster is present, but may be dull or lifeless, and interrupted in patches. At MS-63, contact marks are few, and abrasion is very light. Abrasion is even less at MS-64. (Discussion of such high grades in these early coins starts to enter the realm of

1808; BD-1. Graded MS-63.

theory.) Quarter eagles of this type are almost, but not quite, non-existent in a combination of high grade and nice eye appeal. *Reverse:* Comments apply as for the obverse, except that abrasion is most noticeable on the eagle's neck and highest area of the wings.

    Illustrated coin: Superbly struck, this coin is a "poster example" with few peers.

AU-50, 53, 55, 58 (About Uncirculated). *Obverse:* Light wear is seen on the cheek and higher-relief areas of the hair and cap. Friction and scattered marks are in the field, ranging from extensive at AU-50 to minimal at AU-58. The low rim affords little protection to the field of this coin, but the stars in relief help. Luster may be seen in protected areas, minimal at AU-50, but less so at AU-58. At AU-58 the field retains some lus-

1808. Graded AU-50.

ter as well. *Reverse:* Comments are as for a Mint State coin, except that the eagle's neck, the top of the wings, the leaves, and the arrowheads now show noticeable wear, as do other features. Luster ranges from perhaps 40% remaining in protected areas at AU-50 to nearly full mint bloom at AU-58. Often the reverse of this type retains much more luster than does the obverse, as on this type the motto, eagle, and lettering protect the surrounding flat areas.

    Illustrated coin: Note some lightness of strike.

EF-40, 45 (Extremely Fine). *Obverse:* More wear is seen on the portrait, the hair, the cap, and the drapery near the clasp. Luster is likely to be absent on the obverse due to the low rim. *Reverse:* Wear is more extensive on the eagle, including the top of the wings, the head, the top of the shield, and the claws. Some traces of luster may be seen in protected areas, more so at EF-45 than at EF-40.

1808. Graded EF-40.

VF-20, 30 (Very Fine). *Obverse:* Wear on the portrait has reduced the hair detail, especially to the right of the face and the top of the head, but much can still be seen. *Reverse:* Wear on the eagle is greater, and details of feathers near the shield and near the top of the wings are weak or missing. All other features show wear, but most are fairly sharp. Generally, Draped Bust gold coins at this grade level lack eye appeal.

1808. Graded VF-20.

The Draped Bust to Left, Large Size, quarter eagle is seldom collected in grades lower than VF-20.

Illustrated coin: This is a nice, problem-free example of a lower but very desirable grade for this rare issue.

	Mintage	Cert	Avg	%MS	F-12	VF-20	EF-40	AU-50	AU-55	AU-58	MS-60	MS-62	MS-63	MS-64
1808	2,710	44	54.4	32%	$32,500	$45,000	$60,000	$90,000	$105,000	$120,000	$175,000	$275,000	$450,000	$750,000
	Auctions: $223,250, MS-61, March 2016; $126,900, MS-60, January 2013; $80,781, AU-55, August 2014													

CAPPED HEAD TO LEFT (1821–1834)

Designer: *John Reich.* **Weight:** *4.37 grams.* **Composition:** *.9167 gold, .0833 silver and copper.*
Diameter: *1821–1827—18.5 mm; 1829–1834—approximately 18.2 mm.*
Edge: *Reeded.* **Mint:** *Philadelphia.*

Large Diameter, Circulation Strike
BD-1.

Large Diameter, Proof

Small Diameter, Circulation Strike
BD-1.

Small Diameter, Proof

History. Capped Head to Left quarter eagles dated 1821 through 1827 have a larger diameter and larger letters, dates, and stars than those of 1829 to 1834. The same grading standards apply to both. Gold coins of this type did not circulate in commerce, because their face value was lower than their bullion value. Many legislators, who had the option to draw their pay in specie (silver and gold coinage), took advantage of this fact to sell their salaries at a premium for paper money. Most wear was due to use as pocket pieces, or from minor handling.

Striking and Sharpness. Most Capped Head to Left quarter eagles are well struck. On the obverse, check the hair details (which on the Large Diameter style can be light in areas) and the stars. On the reverse, check the eagle. On both sides inspect the denticles. Fields are often semi-prooflike on higher grades.

Availability. All Capped Head to Left quarter eagles are rare. Grades typically range from EF to MS, with choice examples in the latter category being scarce, and gems being very rare. Proof coins were made on a limited basis for presentation and for sale to numismatists. All Proof examples are exceedingly rare today, and are usually encountered only when great collections are dispersed.

GRADING STANDARDS

MS-60 to 70 (Mint State). *Obverse:* At MS-60, some abrasion and contact marks are seen on the cheek, on the hair below the LIBERTY inscription, and on the highest-relief folds of the cap. Luster is present, but may be dull or lifeless, and interrupted in patches. At MS-63, contact marks are few, and abrasion is very light. Abrasion is even less at MS-64. (Discussion of such high grades in these early coins starts to enter the realm of theory.) Quarter eagles of this type are almost, but not quite, non-existent in a combination of high grade and nice eye appeal. *Reverse:* Comments apply as for the obverse, except that abrasion is most noticeable on the eagle's neck and highest area of the wings.

1827, BD-1. Graded MS-65.

Illustrated coin: This is a well-struck lustrous gem.

AU-50, 53, 55, 58 (About Uncirculated). *Obverse:* Light wear is seen on the cheek and higher-relief areas of the hair and cap. Friction and scattered marks are in the field, ranging from extensive at AU-50 to minimal at AU-58. The low rim affords little protection to the field of this coin, but the stars in relief help. Luster may be seen in protected areas, minimal at AU-50, but less so at AU-58. At AU-58 the field retains some luster as well.

1833; BD-1. Graded AU-53.

Reverse: Comments are as for a Mint State coin, except that the eagle's neck, the top of the wings, the leaves, and the arrowheads now show noticeable wear, as do other features. Luster ranges from perhaps 40% remaining in protected areas at AU-50 to nearly full mint bloom at AU-58. Often the reverse of this type retains much more luster than does the obverse, as on this type the motto, eagle, and lettering protect the surrounding flat areas.

EF-40, 45 (Extremely Fine). *Obverse:* More wear is seen on the portrait, the hair, the cap, and the drapery near the clasp. Luster is likely to be absent on the obverse due to the low rim. *Reverse:* Wear is more extensive on the eagle, including the top of the wings, the head, the top of the shield, and the claws. Some traces of luster may be seen in protected areas, more so at EF-45 than at EF-40.

1821; BD-1. Graded EF-40.

The Capped Head to Left quarter eagle is seldom collected in grades lower than EF-40.

PF-60 to 70 (Proof). *Obverse and Reverse:*
PF–60 to 62 coins have extensive hairlines and may have nicks and contact marks. At PF-63, hairlines are prominent, but the mirror surface is very reflective. PF-64 coins have fewer hairlines. At PF-65, hairlines should be minimal and mostly seen only under magnification. There should be no nicks or marks. PF-66 and higher coins should have no marks or hairlines visible to the unaided eye.

1824, 4 Over 1. Proof.

	Mintage	Cert	Avg	%MS	F-12	VF-20	EF-40	AU-50	AU-55	AU-58	MS-60	MS-63 / PF-63	MS-65 / PF-64
1821	6,448	20	57.4	40%	$6,750	$9,000	$13,500	$16,000	$17,500	$23,500	$35,000	$85,000	
	Auctions: $44,063, MS-62, March 2014												
1821, Proof	3–5	3	64.7									$275,000	$450,000
	Auctions: $241,500, PF-64Cam, January 2007												
1824, 4 Over 1	2,600	29	56.7	38%	$6,750	$9,500	$14,000	$16,500	$18,750	$25,000	$35,000	$80,000	
	Auctions: $18,800, AU-58, August 2013												
1824, 4 Over 1, Proof	3–5	0	n/a		*(unique, in the Smithsonian's National Numismatic Collection)*								
	Auctions: No auction records available.												
1825	4,434	50	58.8	56%	$6,750	$8,000	$13,000	$15,500	$17,500	$23,500	$32,500	$65,000	
	Auctions: $141,000, MS-65, November 2014; $105,750, MS-64, March 2014; $38,188, MS-62, July 2014; $32,900, MS-61, August 2014												
1825, Proof (a)	unknown	0	n/a										
	Auctions: No auction records available.												
1826, 6 Over 6	760	8	55.4	0%	$10,000	$12,500	$17,000	$25,000	$32,500	$40,000	$62,500		
	Auctions: $44,063, AU-58, August 2014; $27,025, AU-55, November 2014; $45,531, AU-55, September 2013												
1826, 6 Over 5, Proof (b)	unknown	0	n/a										
	Auctions: No auction records available.												
1827	2,800	25	58.4	60%	$6,500	$9,500	$13,100	$17,500	$19,500	$32,500	$35,000	$65,000	
	Auctions: $58,750, MS-63, September 2014; $21,150, AU-58, August 2014; $28,200, AU-55, February 2013												
1827, Proof (c)	unknown	0	n/a										
	Auctions: No auction records available.												
1829	3,403	44	60.0	64%	$6,000	$7,500	$9,500	$13,000	$17,000	$18,500	$22,500	$35,000	$100,000
	Auctions: $41,125, MS-63, June 2013; $12,925, AU-55, August 2014												
1829, Proof	2–4	0	n/a		*(extremely rare; 2–3 known)*								
	Auctions: No auction records available.												
1830	4,540	46	60.1	52%	$6,000	$7,500	$9,500	$13,000	$17,000	$18,500	$22,500	$35,000	$85,000
	Auctions: $29,375, MS-63, November 2013; $24,675, MS-62, November 2014; $22,913, MS-62, November 2014												
1830, Proof (d)	unknown	0	n/a										
	Auctions: No auction records available.												
1831	4,520	61	60.2	66%	$6,000	$7,500	$9,500	$13,000	$17,000	$18,500	$22,500	$35,000	$85,000
	Auctions: $28,200, MS-63, September 2014; $18,800, AU-58, February 2013; $15,863, AU-58, August 2014												
1831, Proof	6–10	2	64.5									$100,000	$150,000
	Auctions: $30,550, PF-60, September 2013												
1832	4,400	40	57.5	43%	$6,000	$7,500	$9,500	$13,000	$17,000	$18,500	$22,500	$37,500	$95,000
	Auctions: $21,150, MS-61, March 2014; $22,913, MS-61, August 2014; $15,275, AU-58, August 2014; $12,338, AU-55, August 2014												
1832, Proof	2–4	0	n/a		*(unique, in the Bass Foundation Collection)*								
	Auctions: No auction records available.												

a. The 1825 quarter eagle might not exist in Proof; see the *Encyclopedia of U.S. Gold Coins, 1795–1933*. **b.** Proofs have been reported, but none have been authenticated. **c.** Proof 1827 quarter eagles almost certainly were made, but none are known to exist. **d.** Examples identified as Proofs are extremely rare, many are impaired, and none have been certified.

	Mintage	Cert	Avg	%MS	F-12	VF-20	EF-40	AU-50	AU-55	AU-58	MS-60	MS-63	MS-65
												PF-63	PF-64
1833	4,160	45	59.2	53%	$6,000	$7,500	$9,500	$13,000	$17,000	$18,500	$22,500	$35,000	$95,000
	Auctions: $41,125, MS-63, August 2013; $15,275, AU-58, August 2014												
1833, Proof	2–4	0	n/a		(extremely rare; 3–4 known)								
	Auctions: No auction records available.												
1834, With Motto	4,000	8	54.4	13%	$20,000	$27,500	$55,000	$85,000	$115,000	$135,000	$185,000	$275,000	
	Auctions: $19,975, AU-50, November 2014												
1834, With Motto, Proof	4–8	0	n/a		(extremely rare; 3–5 known)								
	Auctions: No auction records available.												

CLASSIC HEAD, NO MOTTO ON REVERSE (1834–1839)

Designer: *William Kneass.* **Weight:** *4.18 grams.*
Composition: *.8992 gold, .1008 silver and copper (changed to .900 gold in 1837).*
Diameter: *18.2 mm.* **Edge:** *Reeded.* **Mints:** *Philadelphia, Charlotte, Dahlonega, and New Orleans.*

Circulation Strike
Breen-6143.

**Mintmark location
is on the obverse,
above the date.**

Proof

History. Gold quarter eagles had not circulated at face value in the United States since 1821, as the price of bullion necessitated more than $2.50 worth of gold to produce a single coin. Accordingly, they traded at their bullion value. The Act of June 28, 1834, provided lower weights for gold coins, after which the issues (of new designs to differentiate them from the old) circulated effectively. The Classic Head design by William Kneass is an adaptation of the head created by John Reich for the cent of 1808. The reverse illustrates a perched eagle. The motto E PLURIBUS UNUM, seen on earlier gold coins, no longer is present. These coins circulated widely until mid-1861 (for this reason, many show extensive wear). After that, they were hoarded by the public because of financial uncertainty during the Civil War.

Striking and Sharpness. Weakness is often seen on the higher areas of the hair curls. Also check the star centers. On the reverse, check the rims. The denticles usually are well struck.

Availability. Most coins range from VF to AU or lower ranges of MS. Most MS coins are of the first three years. MS-63 to 65 examples are rare. Good eye appeal can be elusive. Proofs were made in small quantities, and today probably only a couple dozen or so survive, most bearing the 1834 date.

GRADING STANDARDS

MS-60 to 70 (Mint State). *Obverse:* At MS-60, some abrasion and contact marks are seen on the portrait, most noticeably on the cheek, as the hair details are complex on this type. Luster is present, but may be dull or lifeless, and interrupted in patches. Many low-level Mint State coins have grainy surfaces. At MS-63, contact marks are few, and abrasion is very light. Abrasion is even less at MS-64. An MS-65 coin has hardly any abrasion, and contact marks are minute. Luster should be full and rich and is often more intense on the

1834. Graded MS-65.

obverse. Grades above MS-65 are defined by having fewer marks as perfection is approached. *Reverse:* Comments apply as for the obverse, except that abrasion is most noticeable on the eagle's neck and the highest area of the wings.

Illustrated coin: This coin is especially well struck.

AU-50, 53, 55, 58 (About Uncirculated).
Obverse: Friction is seen on the higher parts, particularly the cheek and hair (under magnification) of Miss Liberty. Friction and scattered marks are in the field, ranging from extensive at AU-50 to minimal at AU-58. Luster may be seen in protected areas, minimal at AU-50 but more visible at AU-58. On an AU-58 coin the field retains some luster as well. *Reverse:* Comments as for Mint State,

1837. Graded AU-55.

except that the eagle's neck, the top of the wings, the leaves, and the arrowheads now show noticeable wear, as do other features. Luster ranges from perhaps 40% remaining in protected areas at AU-50 to nearly full mint bloom at AU-58. Often the reverse of this type retains much more luster than does the obverse.

Illustrated coin: The coin has light wear overall, but traces of luster can be seen here and there.

EF-40, 45 (Extremely Fine). *Obverse:* Wear is seen on the portrait overall, with reduction or elimination of some separation of hair strands, especially in the area close to the face. The cheek shows light wear. Luster is minimal or nonexistent at EF-40, and may survive in among the letters of LIBERTY at EF-45. *Reverse:* Wear is greater than on an About Uncirculated coin. On most (but not all) coins the eagle's neck lacks some feather

1834. Graded EF-40.

detail on its highest points. Feathers have lost some detail near the edges and tips of the wings. Some areas of the horizontal lines in the shield may be blended together. Some traces of luster may be seen, more so at EF-45 than at EF-40.

Illustrated coin: This coin is well struck.

VF-20, 30 (Very Fine). *Obverse:* Wear on the portrait has reduced the hair detail, especially to the right of the face and the top of the head, but much can still be seen. *Reverse:* Wear is greater, including on the shield and wing feathers. Generally, Classic Head gold at this grade level lacks eye appeal.

The Classic Head quarter eagle is seldom collected in grades lower than VF-20.

Illustrated coin: This coin was lightly

1836. Graded VF-30.

cleaned. It is lightly struck at the centers, although at this grade level that is not important.

PF-60 to 70 (Proof). *Obverse and Reverse:*
PF–60 to 62 coins have extensive hairlines and may have nicks and contact marks. At PF-63, hairlines are prominent, but the mirror surface is very reflective. PF-64 coins have fewer hairlines. At PF-65, hairlines should be minimal and mostly seen only under magnification. There should be no nicks or marks. PF-66 and higher coins should have no marks or hairlines visible to the unaided eye.

1836. Graded PF-65 Cameo.

1836, Script 8   1836, Block 8

	Mintage	Cert	Avg	%MS	F-12	VF-20	EF-40	AU-50	AU-55	AU-58	MS-60 / PF-60	MS-63 / PF-63	MS-65 / PF-65
1834, No Motto	112,234	1,017	56.2	31%	$365	$600	$800	$1,250	$1,650	$2,100	$3,500	$10,000	$50,000
Auctions: $3,525, MS-61, February 2015; $1,645, AU-58, June 2015; $1,293, AU-50, June 2015; $794, EF-40, January 2015												
1834, No Motto, Proof	*15–25*	6	64.3								$35,000	$100,000	$275,000
Auctions: $138,000, PF-64Cam, January 2011												
1835	131,402	318	54.1	29%	$365	$600	$800	$1,250	$1,650	$2,100	$3,600	$10,500	$50,000
Auctions: $7,050, MS-63, January 2015; $1,770, AU-58, August 2015; $1,528, AU-55, June 2015; $1,116, AU-53, July 2015												
1835, Proof	*5–8*	1	65.0								$35,000	$100,000	$300,000
Auctions: No auction records available.												
1836, All kinds	547,986												
1836, Script 8 (a)		529	51.4	20%	$365	$600	$800	$1,250	$1,650	$2,100	$3,500	$10,000	$42,500
Auctions: $7,638, MS-63, September 2015; $3,055, MS-61, October 2015; $1,424, AU-50, June 2015; $423, VF-30, January 2015												
1836, Block 8		488	50.1	16%	$365	$600	$800	$1,250	$1,650	$2,100	$3,500	$10,000	$42,500
Auctions: $9,400, MS-64, January 2015; $3,290, MS-61, September 2015; $999, AU-50, October 2015; $764, EF-45, January 2015												
1836, Proof	*5–8*	7	65.0								$35,000	$115,000	$300,000
Auctions: $195,500, PF-64Cam, April 2012												
1837	45,080	265	52.2	17%	$385	$625	$1,200	$2,000	$2,500	$3,500	$5,250	$13,500	$55,000
Auctions: $11,750, MS-63, January 2014; $2,585, MS-60, August 2014; $3,055, AU-58, November 2014; $1,528, AU-50, October 2014												
1837, Proof (b)	*3–5*	2	64.5								$32,500	$125,000	$350,000
Auctions: No auction records available.												
1838	47,030	295	53.3	22%	$385	$625	$1,000	$1,500	$1,750	$2,600	$4,250	$11,500	$47,500
Auctions: $2,468, AU-58, August 2015; $1,469, AU-55, August 2015; $1,058, AU-50, January 2015; $541, VF-35, January 2015												
1838, Proof	*2–4*	0	n/a		*(unique, in the Bass Foundation Collection)*								
Auctions: No auction records available.												
1838-C	7,880	65	55.2	17%	$2,500	$4,500	$7,500	$10,000	$12,500	$17,500	$26,500	$50,000	
Auctions: $8,225, AU-53, October 2016; $3,055, AU-50, June 2015; $6,463, EF-45, August 2016; $6,756, EF-40, January 2015												

Note: So-called 9 Over 8 varieties for Philadelphia, Charlotte, and Denver mints were made from defective punches. **a.** Also known as the "Head of 1835." **b.** Two Proofs of 1837 are known; one is in the Smithsonian's National Numismatic Collection. A third example has been rumored, but its existence is not verified.

	Mintage	Cert	Avg	%MS	F-12	VF-20	EF-40	AU-50	AU-55	AU-58	MS-60	MS-63	MS-65
											PF-60	PF-63	PF-65
1839	27,021	91	52.5	15%	$650	$950	$1,650	$2,750	$3,500	$6,000	$9,500	$30,000	
	Auctions: $28,200, MS-61, August 2013; $4,700, AU-58, January 2015; $3,701, AU-58, January 2015; $1,116, AU-50, June 2015												
1839, Proof (c)	4–6	1	62.0		*(extremely rare)*								
	Auctions: $136,679, PF-62, August 2006												
1839-C	18,140	216	52.6	8%	$1,750	$3,500	$5,500	$8,500	$10,000	$15,000	$25,000	$65,000	
	Auctions: $44,063, MS-62, September 2015; $21,150, MS-61, August 2016; $7,403, MS-60, January 2015; $7,050, AU-55, June 2015												
1839-D	13,674	117	48.4	10%	$2,500	$4,500	$6,750	$8,500	$13,500	$20,000	$30,000	$55,000	
	Auctions: $105,750, MS-64, January 2013; $19,975, AU-58, November 2014; $18,800, AU-58, August 2015; $9,988, AU-55, July 2015												
1839-O	17,781	320	52.8	19%	$950	$1,500	$2,500	$4,000	$6,500	$7,500	$10,000	$30,000	
	Auctions: $32,900, MS-64, September 2015; $11,163, AU-58, August 2015; $3,995, AU-53, July 2015; $2,350, EF-45, August 2015												

c. Three Proofs of 1839 are reported to exist; only two are presently accounted for.

LIBERTY HEAD (1840–1907)

Designer: *Christian Gobrecht.* **Weight:** *4.18 grams.*
Composition: *.900 gold, .100 copper (net weight .12094 oz. pure gold).* **Diameter:** *18 mm.*
Edge: *Reeded.* **Mints:** *Philadelphia, Charlotte, Dahlonega, New Orleans, and San Francisco.*

Circulation Strike

Mintmark location is on the reverse, above the denomination.

Proof

History. The Liberty Head quarter eagle debuted in 1840 and was a workhorse of American commerce for decades, being minted until 1907. Christian Gobrecht's design closely follows those used on half eagles and eagles of the same era.

In 1848, about 230 ounces of gold were sent to Secretary of War William L. Marcy by Colonel R.B. Mason, military governor of California. The gold was turned over to the Philadelphia Mint and made into quarter eagles. The distinguishing mark CAL. was punched above the eagle on the reverse of these coins, while they were in the die. Several pieces with prooflike surfaces are known.

A modified reverse design (with smaller letters and arrowheads) was used on Philadelphia quarter eagles from 1859 through 1907, and on San Francisco issues of 1877, 1878, and 1879. A few Philadelphia Mint pieces were made in 1859, 1860, and 1861 with the old Large Letters reverse design.

Striking and Sharpness. On the obverse, check the highest points of the hair, and the star centers. On the reverse, check the eagle's neck, and the area to the lower left of the shield and the lower part of the eagle. Examine the denticles on both sides. Branch-mint coins struck before the Civil War often are lightly struck in areas and have weak denticles. Often, a certified EF coin from the Dahlonega or Charlotte mint will not appear any sharper than a VF coin from Philadelphia. There are exceptions, and some C and D coins are sharp. The careful study of photographs is useful in acquainting you with the peculiarities of a given date or mint. Most quarter eagles from the 1880s to 1907 are sharp in all areas. Tiny copper staining spots (from improperly mixed alloy) can be a problem. Cameo contrast is the rule for Proofs prior to 1902, when the portrait was polished in the die (a few years later cameo-contrast coins were again made).

Availability. Early dates and mintmarks are generally scarce to rare in MS and very rare in MS–63 to 65 or finer, with only a few exceptions. Coins of Charlotte and Dahlonega (all of which are especially avidly collected) are usually EF or AU, or overgraded low MS. Rarities for the type include 1841, 1854-S, and 1875. Coins of the 1860s onward generally are seen with sharper striking and in higher average grades. Typically, San Francisco quarter eagles are in lower average grades than are those from the Philadelphia Mint, as Philadelphia coins did not circulate at par in the East and Midwest from late December 1861 until December 1878, and thus did not acquire as much wear. MS coins are readily available for the early-1900s years, and usually have outstanding eye appeal. Proofs exist relative to their original mintages; all prior to the 1890s are rare.

Note: Values of common-date gold coins have been based on the current bullion price of gold, $1,300 per ounce, and may vary with the prevailing spot price.

Grading Standards

MS-60 to 70 (Mint State). *Obverse:* At MS-60, some abrasion and contact marks are evident, most noticeably on the hair to the right of Miss Liberty's forehead, and on the jaw. Luster is present, but may be dull or lifeless, and interrupted in patches. At MS-63, contact marks are few, and abrasion is very light. An MS-65 coin has hardly any abrasion, and contact marks are so minute as to require magnification. Luster should be full and rich.

1859-S. Graded MS-65.

Grades above MS-65 are usually found late in the series and are defined by having fewer marks as perfection is approached. *Reverse:* Comments apply as for the obverse, except that abrasion and contact marks are most noticeable on the eagle's neck and to the lower left of the shield.

Illustrated coin: Sharply struck, bright, and with abundant luster and great eye appeal, this is a "just right" coin for the connoisseur.

AU-50, 53, 55, 58 (About Uncirculated). *Obverse:* Light wear is seen on the face, the hair to the right of the face, and the highest area of the hair bun, more so at AU-50 than at AU–53 or 55. An AU-58 coin has minimal traces of wear. An AU-50 coin has luster in protected areas among the stars and letters, with little in the open fields or on the portrait. At AU-58, most luster is present in the fields, but is worn away on the highest parts

1855-D. Graded AU-55.

of the motifs. *Reverse:* Comments apply as for the preceding, except that the eagle shows wear in all of the higher areas, as well as the leaves and arrowheads. Luster ranges from perhaps 40% remaining in protected areas at AU-50 to nearly full mint bloom at AU-58. Often the reverse of this type retains more luster than the obverse.

Illustrated coin: The example has the bold rims often seen on Dahlonega Mint coins of this denomination.

EF-40, 45 (Extremely Fine). *Obverse:* Wear is evident on all high areas of the portrait, including the hair to the right of the forehead, the tip of the coronet, and the hair bun. The stars show light wear at their centers. Luster, if present at all, is minimal and in protected areas such as between the star points. *Reverse:* Wear is greater than on an AU coin. The eagle's neck is nearly smooth, much detail is lost on the right wing, and there is flatness at

1860-C. Graded EF-40.

the lower left of the shield, and on the leaves and arrowheads. Traces of luster may be seen, more so at EF-45 than at EF-40. Overall, the reverse appears to be in a slightly higher grade than the obverse.

Illustrated coin: This is an attractive coin with medium wear.

VF-20, 30 (Very Fine). *Obverse:* The higher-relief areas of hair are worn flat at VF-20, less so at VF-30. The hair to the right of the coronet is merged into heavy strands. The stars are flat at their centers. *Reverse:* Much of the eagle is flat, with less than 50% of the feather detail remaining. The vertical shield stripes, being deeply recessed, remain bold.

The Liberty Head quarter eagle is seldom collected in grades lower than VF-20.

1843-O, Small Date, Crosslet 4. Graded VF-20.

PF-60 to 70 (Proof). *Obverse and Reverse:* PF–60 to 62 coins have extensive hairlines and may have nicks and contact marks. At PF-63, hairlines are prominent, but the mirror surface is very reflective. PF-64 coins have fewer hairlines; PF-65, minimal hairlines mostly seen only under magnification, and no nicks or marks. PF-66 and higher coins should have no marks or hairlines visible to the unaided eye.

1895. Graded PF-66.

Illustrated coin: This is an exceptional gem in rich yellow-orange gold.

	Mintage	Cert	Avg	%MS	VF-20	EF-40	AU-50	AU-55	AU-58	MS-60	MS-62	MS-63
												PF-63
1840	18,859	103	50.1	12%	$850	$1,100	$2,400	$3,000	$4,250	$6,500	$8,000	$11,500 (a)
Auctions: $2,468, AU-58, April 2013; $1,777, AU-53, October 2014; $564, AU-50, July 2015; $999, VF-30, June 2015												
1840, Proof	3–6	0	n/a		*(extremely rare; 3 known)*							
Auctions: No auction records available.												
1840-C	12,822	152	52.2	10%	$1,850	$3,250	$4,250	$6,250	$7,500	$10,000	$16,500	$24,000
Auctions: $3,525, AU-58, March 2015; $1,087, AU-50, February 2015; $2,115, EF-45, October 2014; $1,645, VF-25, June 2015												
1840-D	3,532	44	48.8	7%	$3,500	$8,500	$12,000	$18,000	$25,000	$35,000	$75,000	
Auctions: $28,200, MS-60, August 2016; $11,163, AU-55, November 2016												
1840-O	33,580	111	51.4	13%	$500	$1,000	$2,000	$3,250	$5,000	$9,000	$14,000	$25,000
Auctions: $14,100, MS-62, April 2014; $7,344, MS-61, October 2014; $4,113, AU-58, July 2015; $270, VF-20, August 2014												

a. Value in MS-64 is $22,500.

1843-C, Small Date, Crosslet 4	1843-C, Large Date, Plain 4	1843-O, Small Date, Crosslet 4	1843-O, Large Date, Plain 4

	Mintage	Cert	Avg	%MS	VF-20	EF-40	AU-50	AU-55	AU-58	MS-60	MS-62	MS-63 PF-63
1841 (b)	*unknown*	0	n/a		$75,000	$100,000	$125,000	$140,000	$160,000	$225,000		
	Auctions: $149,500, PF-55, April 2012											
1841, Proof	*15–20*	5	57.0									$250,000
	Auctions: $149,500, PF-55, April 2012											
1841-C	10,281	104	51.5	6%	$1,500	$2,250	$4,250	$6,000	$8,500	$15,000	$25,000	
	Auctions: $28,200, MS-62, March 2014; $5,875, AU-58, November 2014; $3,055, AU-50, June 2015; $2,468, EF-45, January 2015											
1841-D	4,164	55	46.9	5%	$2,500	$4,500	$9,000	$12,000	$15,000	$25,000	$40,000	$55,000
	Auctions: $23,500, MS-60, August 2015; $10,575, AU-55, September 2016; $8,225, AU-55, October 2015; $7,638, AU-55, April 2013											
1842	2,823	22	49.9	5%	$1,200	$3,000	$6,000	$8,000	$10,000	$17,500	$35,000	
	Auctions: $15,275, MS-60, January 2014; $7,931, AU-55, August 2015; $7,050, AU-55, July 2014; $3,819, EF-40, November 2014											
1842, Proof	*2–3*	0	n/a		*(unique, in the Smithsonian's National Numismatic Collection)*							
	Auctions: No auction records available.											
1842-C	6,729	59	47.5	5%	$2,000	$3,250	$6,750	$9,250	$10,500	$22,500	$37,500	
	Auctions: $8,813, AU-55, September 2014; $5,581, AU, February 2014; $3,760, EF-45, January 2015; $1,645, VF-20, January 2015											
1842-D	4,643	69	48.6	6%	$2,500	$5,000	$8,500	$10,500	$17,500	$32,500	$55,000	
	Auctions: $25,850, AU-58, August 2015; $15,275, AU-58, August 2015; $13,513, AU-58, September 2015; $9,400, AU-55, June 2015											
1842-O	19,800	151	48.9	9%	$525	$1,400	$2,250	$4,000	$6,500	$8,500	$12,500	$25,000
	Auctions: $7,638, MS-61, August 2015; $3,760, AU-58, October 2015; $1,293, EF-45, September 2015; $259, F-12, November 2015											
1843	100,546	197	54.3	11%	$350	$450	$700	$900	$1,250	$2,500	$4,000	$6,500
	Auctions: $3,231, MS-62, January 2015; $764, AU-58, January 2015; $470, AU-53, July 2015; $376, AU-50, January 2015											
1843, Proof	*4–8*	3	64.3		*(extremely rare; 5–6 known)*							
	Auctions: No auction records available.											
1843-C, Small Date, Crosslet 4	2,988	53	51.9	9%	$2,500	$5,250	$7,500	$10,000	$12,500	$22,500	$35,000	
	Auctions: $4,406, MS-63, August 2014; $499, MS-60, July 2014; $646, AU-55, July 2014; $441, AU-55, October 2014											
1843-C, Large Date, Plain 4	23,076	204	48.2	9%	$1,500	$2,000	$3,000	$4,250	$5,500	$8,000	$12,500	$18,500
	Auctions: $4,230, AU-58, August 2015; $3,525, AU-53, January 2015; $2,115, EF-45, January 2015; $764, VF-20, January 2015											
1843-D, Small Date, Crosslet 4	36,209	273	50.0	8%	$1,750	$2,250	$3,250	$4,500	$5,500	$6,500	$15,000	$25,000
	Auctions: $4,406, MS-63, August 2014; $499, MS-60, July 2014; $646, AU-55, July 2014; $441, AU-55, October 2014											
1843-O, Small Date, Crosslet 4	288,002	527	53.0	16%	$350	$375	$475	$750	$1,000	$1,750	$3,000	$6,500
	Auctions: $4,465, MS-63, June 2015; $764, AU-58, September 2015; $317, AU-50, October 2015; $259, F-15, August 2015											
1843-O, Large Date, Plain 4	76,000	132	53.8	14%	$400	$600	$1,750	$2,750	$4,000	$6,250	$13,000	$20,000
	Auctions: $15,275, MS-62, February 2014; $5,875, MS-61, June 2015; $3,525, AU-55, August 2015											
1844	6,784	52	51.6	10%	$450	$750	$2,000	$3,000	$4,250	$8,500	$13,500	
	Auctions: $15,275, MS-61, January 2014											
1844, Proof	*3–6*	1	66.0		*(extremely rare; 4–5 known)*							
	Auctions: No auction records available.											
1844-C	11,622	119	48.7	11%	$1,500	$2,500	$5,500	$6,500	$8,500	$14,000	$22,500	$40,000
	Auctions: $14,100, MS-61, January 2014; $6,756, AU-58, July 2015; $2,350, AU-50, August 2014; $3,055, VF-30, June 2015											
1844-D	17,332	159	52.2	13%	$1,650	$2,500	$3,250	$4,000	$5,250	$7,500	$12,500	$22,500
	Auctions: $17,038, MS-63, April 2014; $1,645, AU-50, January 2015; $2,585, EF-45, August 2014											

b. Values are for circulated Proofs; existence of circulation strikes is unclear.

	Mintage	Cert	Avg	%MS	VF-20	EF-40	AU-50	AU-55	AU-58	MS-60	MS-62	MS-63 PF-63
1845	91,051	252	55.3	27%	$375	$400	$500	$600	$675	$1,250	$2,250	$4,750 (c)
	Auctions: $18,800, MS-65, January 2014; $14,100, MS-65, October 2014; $1,410, MS-61, March 2015; $235, AU-50, May 2015											
1845, Proof	*4–8*	2	67.0		*(extremely rare; 4–5 known)*							
	Auctions: No auction records available.											
1845-D	19,460	161	51.3	6%	$1,650	$2,350	$3,250	$4,250	$6,000	$10,000	$22,500	$40,000
	Auctions: $35,250, MS-63, January 2014											
1845-O	4,000	59	50.3	2%	$1,300	$2,500	$6,500	$8,500	$11,500	$22,500	$30,000	$50,000
	Auctions: $5,875, AU-50, January 2014											
1846	21,598	134	55.6	19%	$360	$550	$900	$1,100	$2,250	$5,000	$15,000	$20,000
	Auctions: $3,760, MS-61, August 2015; $1,293, AU-58, July 2015; $734, AU-53, October 2015; $646, AU-50, January 2015											
1846, Proof	*4–8*	1	64.0		*(extremely rare; 4–5 known)*							
	Auctions: $106,375, PF-64Cam, January 2011											
1846-C	4,808	66	50.7	9%	$1,700	$2,750	$6,000	$8,500	$11,500	$16,000	$20,000	$35,000
	Auctions: $15,275, MS-62, April 2014											
1846-D	19,303	171	51.5	9%	$1,750	$2,500	$3,250	$4,500	$6,250	$9,000	$13,500	$28,500
	Auctions: $7,638, MS-61, June 2013; $1,528, AU-50, August 2014; $3,055, EF-45, February 2015; $3,408, EF-40, July 2015											
1846-D, D Over D	(d)	4	52.0	0%		$2,750	$3,750	$5,500	$7,500	$15,000		
	Auctions: $5,175, AU-55, November 2011											
1846-O	62,000	287	51.1	8%	$400	$525	$1,200	$2,000	$3,500	$5,500	$10,000	$18,500
	Auctions: $4,700, MS-61, February 2013; $423, AU-50, August 2015; $552, EF-45, June 2015; $400, EF-40, June 2015											
1847	29,814	125	55.0	19%	$375	$450	$800	$1,200	$1,650	$3,000	$4,500	$8,000
	Auctions: $3,055, MS-61, November 2014; $1,175, AU-58, June 2013											
1847, Proof	*2–3*	0	n/a		*(unique, in the Smithsonian's National Numismatic Collection)*							
	Auctions: No auction records available.											
1847-C	23,226	248	52.4	14%	$1,500	$2,350	$3,000	$3,500	$4,500	$5,750	$8,000	$15,000
	Auctions: $3,525, AU-58, August 2015; $2,820, AU-50, July 2015; $2,364, AU-50, September 2015; $1,821, AU-50, January 2015											
1847-D	15,784	165	52.6	13%	$1,650	$2,500	$3,250	$5,000	$5,500	$8,750	$13,500	$24,000
	Auctions: $9,404, MS, February 2014; $2,820, AU-53, August 2014; $2,350, AU-50, January 2015											
1847-O	124,000	326	50.0	10%	$350	$425	$1,000	$1,750	$2,750	$4,000	$10,000	$16,000
	Auctions: $1,645, AU-55, January 2015; $764, AU-53, February 2015; $376, EF-40, May 2015; $259, VF-20, January 2015											

c. Value in MS-64 is $8,500. **d.** Included in 1846-D mintage figure.

1848, CAL. Above Eagle

	Mintage	Cert	Avg	%MS	VF-20	EF-40	AU-50	AU-55	MS-60	MS-62	MS-63 PF-60	MS-64 PF-63	MS-65 PF-65
1848	6,500	59	54.6	27%	$550	$950	$2,000	$3,000	$5,500	$8,500	$15,000	$25,000	
	Auctions: $5,640, AU-55, September 2015; $2,585, AU-50, February 2014; $823, AU-50, July 2014												
1848, CAL. Above Eagle	1,389	44	56.8	43%	$35,000	$45,000	$52,500	$55,000	$80,000	$115,000	$125,000	$150,000	$200,000
	Auctions: $55,813, AU-58, October 2015; $32,900, VF-25, September 2016												
1848, Proof	*3–6*	0	n/a		*(extremely rare; 3–4 known)*								
	Auctions: $96,600, PF-64, January 2008												
1848-C	16,788	158	50.4	9%	$1,500	$2,500	$3,500	$4,500	$11,500	$20,000	$32,500		
	Auctions: $15,275, MS-62, March 2014												
1848-D	13,771	150	53.6	13%	$1,500	$2,650	$3,750	$4,250	$8,000	$13,500	$28,000		
	Auctions: $25,850, MS-63, April 2014												

	Mintage	Cert	Avg	%MS	VF-20	EF-40	AU-50	AU-55	MS-60	MS-62	MS-63 / PF-60	MS-64 / PF-63	MS-65 / PF-65
1849	23,294	136	55.1	16%	$450	$650	$950	$1,250	$2,500	$3,750	$7,500	$14,000	
	Auctions: $3,525, MS-62, March 2014; $3,055, MS-62, January 2015; $999, AU-55, July 2014; $764, AU-55, October 2015												
1849-C	10,220	100	50.6	8%	$1,500	$2,500	$4,500	$8,000	$15,000	$40,000	$65,000		
	Auctions: $15,275, MS-62, August 2015; $15,275, MS-61, January 2014; $12,338, MS-60, September 2016; $6,463, AU-58, November 2016; $4,700												
1849-D	10,945	141	52.9	8%	$2,000	$2,750	$3,750	$5,500	$14,500	$23,500	—		
	Auctions: $4,348, AU-55, September 2016; $2,820, AU-50, November 2016; $2,468, EF-40, August 2016												
1850	252,923	470	56.3	24%	$360	$375	$400	$500	$1,050	$2,000	$3,500	$7,500	
	Auctions: $940, MS-61, January 2015; $423, AU-58, September 2015; $376, AU-53, May 2015; $259, EF-40, July 2015												
1850, Proof	2–4	0	n/a		*(extremely rare; 1–2 known)*								
	Auctions: $41,250, PF-62, June 1995												
1850-C	9,148	140	51.1	14%	$1,500	$2,500	$3,500	$5,000	$11,000	$20,000	$32,500		
	Auctions: $8,879, MS-61, August 2014; $8,813, MS-61, October 2014; $12,925, MS-60, March 2014; $881, EF-40, January 2015												
1850-D	12,148	136	52.4	9%	$1,600	$2,750	$3,750	$5,500	$12,500	$25,000	$47,500		
	Auctions: $23,500, MS-62, April 2014; $18,800, MS-62, March 2016; $10,575, MS-61, January 2015; $5,434, AU-55, August 2015												
1850-O	84,000	333	50.8	3%	$400	$575	$1,250	$1,500	$4,000	$7,000	$15,000		
	Auctions: $1,645, AU-58, March 2015; $1,410, AU-58, June 2015; $764, EF-45, August 2015; $447, EF-45, February 2015												
1851	1,372,748	854	58.9	54%	$325	$350	$375	$400	$550	$750	$1,100	$2,000	$5,500
	Auctions: $9,400, MS-66, February 2015; $376, MS-61, October 2015; $400, AU-58, March 2015; $266, AU-53, May 2015												
1851-C	14,923	112	50.8	14%	$1,500	$2,450	$3,750	$5,000	$8,500	$15,000	$32,500		
	Auctions: $5,640, MS-61, September 2015; $3,290, AU-53, January 2015; $2,820, AU-53, January 2015; $2,115, EF-40, July 2015												
1851-D	11,264	85	51.3	6%	$1,650	$2,500	$4,000	$5,500	$10,500	$15,000	$32,500	$50,000	
	Auctions: $7,638, AU-58, December 2013; $2,115, AU-50, September 2014												
1851-O	148,000	448	53.4	9%	$400	$475	$950	$1,500	$4,500	$7,500	$11,500	$23,500	
	Auctions: $3,539, MS-61, February 2015; $2,143, AU-58, January 2015; $823, AU-55, October 2015; $646, AU-50, January 2015												
1852	1,159,681	1,047	59.7	59%	$325	$350	$375	$400	$550	$850	$1,100	$2,250	$5,500
	Auctions: $4,818, MS-65, June 2015; $1,998, MS-64, February 2015; $588, MS-62, June 2015; $329, AU-58, July 2015												
1852-C	9,772	94	52.5	9%	$1,500	$2,500	$4,000	$5,750	$12,500	$22,500	$32,500		
	Auctions: $6,463, AU-58, August 2015; $4,465, AU-55, July 2015; $3,525, AU-53, October 2015; $4,935, AU-50, February 2015												
1852-D	4,078	54	53.5	9%	$1,850	$3,250	$6,000	$8,000	$15,750	$30,000	$42,500	$65,000	
	Auctions: $8,813, AU-53, August 2013												
1852-O	140,000	518	52.7	6%	$400	$450	$950	$1,500	$4,500	$8,000	$11,000		
	Auctions: $4,465, MS-61, August 2015; $1,410, AU-58, July 2015; $764, AU-55, January 2015; $617, AU-53, July 2015												
1853	1,404,668	1,502	59.7	58%	$300	$325	$350	$365	$550	$600	$1,000	$1,500	$5,000
	Auctions: $9,988, MS-66, June 2015; $676, MS-62, March 2015; $306, AU-58, June 2015; $247, AU-50, January 2015												
1853-D	3,178	49	52.6	14%	$2,000	$3,500	$5,000	$6,000	$13,500	$30,000	$45,000		
	Auctions: $25,850, MS-62, January 2014; $12,338, MS-61, October 2014; $13,513, MS-61, November 2014; $4,113, AU-50, July 2014												
1854	596,258	720	59.1	50%	$300	$325	$350	$365	$550	$750	$1,250	$2,500	$6,000
	Auctions: $4,230, MS-65, January 2015; $470, MS-61, January 2015; $294, AU-55, August 2015; $376, AU-50, February 2015												
1854, Proof	2–4	0	n/a		*(unique, in the Bass Foundation Collection)*								
	Auctions: No auction records available.												
1854-C	7,295	108	54.1	19%	$1,500	$2,600	$5,000	$6,500	$12,000	$22,500	$37,500		
	Auctions: $9,988, MS-61, June 2013; $4,994, AU-58, August 2014; $4,230, AU-53, August 2015; $3,525, EF-45, January 2015												
1854-D	1,760	23	48.9	17%	$3,500	$7,500	$10,000	$12,500	$27,500	$40,000	$70,000		
	Auctions: $5,405, EF-40, November 2016; $2,938, VF-30, September 2016												
1854-O	153,000	519	53.6	8%	$385	$400	$575	$800	$1,500	$4,500	$9,000	$15,000	
	Auctions: $2,585, MS-61, February 2015; $435, MS-60, September 2015; $329, AU-53, January 2015; $329, EF-45, October 2015												
1854-S	246	6	35.3	0%	$275,000	$400,000	$450,000	$500,000					
	Auctions: $282,000, EF-35, October 2013												

Old Reverse (Pre-1859)   **New Reverse**

	Mintage	Cert	Avg	%MS	VF-20	EF-40	AU-50	AU-55	MS-60	MS-62	MS-63 / PF-60	MS-64 / PF-63	MS-65 / PF-65
1855	235,480	401	59.4	54%	$300	$325	$350	$365	$550	$1,100	$1,600	$3,250	$7,000
Auctions: $2,585, MS-64, October 2015; $764, MS-62, July 2015; $447, MS-61, July 2015; $329, AU-58, April 2015													
1855-C	3,677	71	54.6	23%	$2,250	$4,000	$6,000	$10,000	$20,000	$27,500	$42,500		
Auctions: $23,500, MS-62, January 2014													
1855-D	1,123	25	53.5	12%	$4,500	$8,000	$13,500	$20,000	$50,000				
Auctions: $25,850, AU-55, July 2014; $8,225, EF-45, March 2015													
1856	384,240	628	59.4	54%	$300	$325	$350	$365	$450	$850	$1,250	$3,000	$5,500
Auctions: $3,995, MS-65, July 2015; $1,234, MS-63, July 2015; $376, AU-58, March 2015; $282, AU-53, May 2015													
1856, Proof	6–8	0	n/a								$35,000	$55,000	$145,000
Auctions: No auction records available.													
1856-C	7,913	95	52.5	17%	$1,650	$2,750	$4,000	$6,000	$11,500	$20,000	$25,000		
Auctions: $6,463, AU-58, April 2013; $4,465, AU-58, August 2015; $4,230, AU-55, August 2015; $1,410, AU-50, October 2014													
1856-D	874	17	52.7	24%	$10,000	$15,000	$30,000	$37,500	$75,000				
Auctions: $55,813, AU-58, March 2014													
1856-O	21,100	145	53.5	10%	$385	$700	$1,500	$2,100	$10,000	$35,000			
Auctions: $7,050, MS-61, August 2013													
1856-S	72,120	206	51.6	14%	$385	$450	$850	$1,250	$5,000	$8,000	$12,000	$15,000	$27,500
Auctions: $2,585, AU-58, September 2015; $1,821, AU-58, September 2015; $1,410, AU-58, June 2015; $1,058, AU-50, January 2015													
1857	214,130	465	59.5	55%	$300	$325	$350	$365	$450	$850	$1,250	$2,500	$6,500
Auctions: $5,904, MS-65, July 2015; $423, MS-61, January 2015; $282, MS-60, November 2015; $282, AU-55, May 2015													
1857, Proof	6–8	0	n/a								$35,000	$57,500	$125,000
Auctions: No auction records available.													
1857-D	2,364	61	56.5	28%	$1,750	$2,800	$4,000	$5,500	$12,000	$22,000	$30,000		
Auctions: $18,800, MS-62, April 2014; $4,935, AU-55, June 2015; $1,586, AU-50, January 2015; $1,528, AU-50, July 2014													
1857-O	34,000	270	55.1	19%	$385	$400	$1,250	$1,850	$4,250	$7,500	$13,000	$22,500	
Auctions: $6,463, MS-62, April 2014; $4,113, MS-61, November 2014; $1,998, AU-58, January 2015; $823, AU-53, January 2015													
1857-S	69,200	184	51.7	11%	$385	$475	$1,200	$2,000	$5,500	$7,500	$13,500	$25,000	
Auctions: $5,875, MS-61, June 2015; $1,775, AU-58, July 2015; $1,293, AU-55, January 2015; $317, VF-35, July 2014													
1858	47,377	192	58.2	36%	$375	$390	$450	$500	$1,100	$1,850	$3,000	$6,000	$13,500
Auctions: $999, MS-61, January 2015; $564, AU-58, October 2015; $376, AU-55, February 2015; $353, AU-53, May 2015													
1858, Proof	6–8	3	65.3								$25,000	$45,000	$115,000
Auctions: $82,250, PF, March 2014													
1858-C	9,056	140	54.7	28%	$1,500	$2,250	$3,500	$4,250	$8,000	$14,000	$25,000		
Auctions: $11,163, MS-62, January 2014; $4,113, AU-58, November 2014; $3,525, AU-58, November 2014													
1859, Old Reverse	39,364	130	57.8	34%	$375	$500	$850	$1,000	$2,000	$3,500	$6,000	$10,000	
Auctions: $1,102, AU, February 2014; $456, AU-50, November 2014; $411, EF-40, August 2014													
1859, New Reverse	(a)	50	57.9	18%	$360	$370	$500	$650	$1,200	$1,750	$3,000	$7,250	$11,000
Auctions: $3,290, MS-63, October 2014; $3,055, MS-63, August 2015; $1,998, MS-62, November 2014; $2,879, MS, January 2014													
1859, Proof (b)	80	2	63								$15,000	$30,000	$75,000
Auctions: $80,500, PF-66, July 2005													

a. Included in circulation-strike 1859, Old Reverse, mintage figure. **b.** Nearly all 1859 Proofs are of the Old Reverse style.

1862, 2 Over 1	1873, Close 3	1873, Open 3

	Mintage	Cert	Avg	%MS	VF-20	EF-40	AU-50	AU-55	MS-60	MS-62	MS-63	MS-64	MS-65
											PF-60	PF-63	PF-65
1859-D	2,244	93	55.0	15%	$2,200	$3,250	$4,750	$6,500	$17,500	$40,000			
	Auctions: $44,063, MS-62, August 2015; $24,675, MS-62, August 2015; $13,513, MS-60, September 2015; $14,100, AU-58, September 2016												
1859-S	15,200	97	49.5	9%	$475	$950	$2,000	$2,750	$5,500	$9,000	$16,000		
	Auctions: $4,994, MS-61, April 2014; $4,847, MS-61, August 2014; $3,290, AU-58, October 2014; $2,585, AU-58, July 2014												
1860, Old Reverse	22,563	33	56.2	33%	$1,250	$2,000	$2,750	$4,000	$5,000	$6,000	$10,000		
	Auctions: $6,463, MS-62, April 2013												
1860, New Reverse	(c)	53	58.5	43%	$350	$370	$450	$600	$1,100	$1,750	$2,750	$7,500	$13,500
	Auctions: $1,763, MS-60, August 2013												
1860, Proof (d)	112	9	63.8								$14,000	$22,500	$40,000
	Auctions: $11,550, PF-64Cam, October 1993												
1860-C	7,469	113	51.6	10%	$1,850	$2,500	$3,500	$6,000	$15,000	$22,000	$32,500		
	Auctions: $25,850, MS-63, January 2014; $14,100, MS-61, June 2015; $12,925, MS-61, August 2015; $8,813, AU-58, September 2015												
1860-S	35,600	122	47.2	8%	$425	$675	$1,150	$1,750	$3,500	$7,000	$15,000		
	Auctions: $6,756, MS-62, August 2013; $317, EF-40, November 2014												
1861, Old Reverse	1,283,788	131	58.2	37%	$525	$1,000	$1,500	$1,850	$3,750	$6,500	$10,000		
	Auctions: $11,163, MS-64, October 2015; $8,225, MS-63, August 2016; $3,760, MS-61, September 2016; $2,849, MS-61, July 2016												
1861, New Reverse	(e)	1,472	59.5	56%	$300	$325	$350	$365	$650	$1,000	$1,750	$3,000	$4,500
	Auctions: $9,400, MS-66, January 2015; $646, MS-61, July 2015; $353, AU-55, September 2015; $329, AU-50, September 2015												
1861, Proof (f)	90	3	65.3								$12,000	$20,000	$40,000
	Auctions: $44,850, PF-65DCam, September 2005												
1861-S	24,000	94	46.6	7%	$500	$825	$3,000	$4,750	$7,250	$20,000			
	Auctions: $5,875, AU-58, April 2013												
1862, 2 Over 1	(g)	55	54.5	15%	$1,000	$1,850	$3,000	$4,750	$8,000	$15,000	$35,000		
	Auctions: $9,400, MS-61, January 2014; $558, AU-50, July 2014												
1862	98,508	196	56.3	30%	$400	$600	$1,000	$2,000	$4,750	$6,500	$11,000	$18,500	
	Auctions: $8,225, MS-63, August 2015; $4,700, MS-62, October 2015; $2,381, AU-58, January 2015; $1,116, AU-50, January 2015												
1862, Proof	35	11	64.7								$12,000	$20,000	$40,000
	Auctions: $46,000, PF-65UCam, February 2007												
1862-S	8,000	134	46.7	8%	$1,500	$2,000	$3,750	$5,000	$16,000	$24,000	$35,000		
	Auctions: $23,500, MS-62, January 2014												
1863, Proof (h)	30	7	64.4								$50,000	$75,000	$125,000
	Auctions: $45,531, PF-58, April 2014												
1863-S	10,800	76	46.1	9%	$700	$1,500	$4,500	$6,500	$15,000	$20,000	$30,000		
	Auctions: $3,290, EF-45, March 2013												
1864	2,824	8	53.4	25%	$6,500	$13,500	$25,000	$47,500	$75,000				
	Auctions: $48,469, AU-55, March 2014												
1864, Proof	50	15	64.7								$12,000	$25,000	$55,000
	Auctions: $30,550, PF-64Cam, April 2014												
1865	1,520	17	53.5	0%	$4,500	$8,500	$20,000	$27,500	$40,000	$45,000	$60,000		
	Auctions: $15,891, AU-55, June 2013; $16,450, AU-50, November 2016; $11,163, EF-45, August 2015; $4,113, VF-20, November 2014												
1865, Proof	25	13	63.9								$13,500	$20,000	$55,000
	Auctions: $48,875, PF-65UCam, January 2012												
1865-S	23,376	97	45.0	4%	$750	$1,250	$2,000	$2,500	$4,500	$10,000	$15,000		
	Auctions: $1,998, AU-53, March 2014												

c. Included in 1860, Old Reverse, mintage figure. **d.** All known 1860 Proofs are of the New Reverse style. **e.** Included in 1861, Old Reverse, mintage figure. **f.** All 1861 Proofs were struck in the New Reverse style. **g.** Included in circulation-strike 1862 mintage figure. **h.** Proof only.

	Mintage	Cert	Avg	%MS	VF-20	EF-40	AU-50	AU-55	MS-60	MS-62	MS-63 / PF-60	MS-64 / PF-63	MS-65 / PF-65
1866	3,080	37	51.5	16%	$1,150	$3,000	$5,250	$7,500	$12,500	$20,000	$25,000	$35,000	
Auctions: $7,050, AU-58, February 2013													
1866, Proof	30	14	64.0								$10,000	$17,500	$45,000
Auctions: $23,500, PF-64Cam, April 2014													
1866-S	38,960	195	47.1	5%	$450	$750	$1,500	$2,500	$7,500	$12,500	$25,000		
Auctions: $7,050, MS-61, August 2015; $1,880, AU-58, July 2015; $470, EF-45, January 2015; $376, VF-25, January 2015													
1867	3,200	37	54.9	27%	$350	$650	$1,350	$1,700	$4,500	$6,500	$12,000	$13,500	$35,000
Auctions: $1,544, AU-55, July 2014; $1,645, AU-55, May 2013													
1867, Proof	50	11	64.1								$10,000	$16,000	$35,000
Auctions: $35,250, PF-65DCam, October 2015; $18,800, PF-64DCam, October 2014; $99,875, PF, August 2013													
1867-S	28,000	167	47.1	6%	$350	$650	$1,250	$1,600	$3,850	$5,000	$12,000	$15,000	
Auctions: $1,163, AU-50, September 2015; $940, EF-45, August 2015; $541, EF-45, January 2015; $306, VF-30, November 2015													
1868	3,600	145	56.9	23%	$325	$425	$700	$800	$2,250	$4,500	$7,500	$15,000	
Auctions: $3,290, MS-61, August 2014; $1,998, MS-61, November 2014; $1,880, AU-58, July 2015; $881, AU-58, February 2015													
1868, Proof	25	5	63.4								$9,500	$16,500	$45,000
Auctions: $43,700, PF-65Cam, January 2009													
1868-S	34,000	248	51.8	7%	$325	$425	$950	$1,400	$4,000	$6,000	$10,000	$16,000	
Auctions: $2,820, AU-58, August 2015; $999, AU-55, January 2015; $529, AU-50, July 2015; $447, EF-45, June 2015													
1869	4,320	143	56.7	23%	$325	$425	$700	$1,150	$2,750	$5,000	$10,000	$20,000	
Auctions: $19,975, MS-64, August 2014; $1,058, AU-58, January 2015; $881, AU-55, July 2015; $940, AU-50, June 2015													
1869, Proof	25	17	64.1								$8,500	$15,000	$40,000
Auctions: $12,650, PF-63, October 2011													
1869-S	29,500	224	51.6	8%	$325	$475	$700	$1,350	$3,500	$5,500	$9,250	$13,000	
Auctions: $3,525, MS-62, October 2015; $1,645, AU-58, January 2015; $1,528, AU-58, August 2015; $1,528, AU-58, June 2015													
1870	4,520	91	56.8	20%	$325	$400	$750	$1,250	$3,250	$5,000	$8,000		
Auctions: $4,994, MS-61, January 2014; $3,525, MS-61, January 2015; $3,760, MS-60, August 2015; $1,645, AU-58, August 2015													
1870, Proof	35	5	63.8								$8,500	$15,000	$40,000
Auctions: $70,500, PF-66DCam, January 2014													
1870-S	16,000	142	51.0	9%	$325	$400	$900	$1,500	$4,000	$8,500	$12,500	$20,000	
Auctions: $8,225, MS-62, January 2014; $1,528, AU-58, July 2014; $1,645, AU-50, October 2015; $447, AU-50, September 2015													
1871	5,320	118	56.3	24%	$325	$400	$750	$1,000	$2,000	$2,750	$4,000	$8,000	
Auctions: $999, AU-58, July 2015; $705, AU-55, October 2015; $646, AU-55, July 2015; $306, AU-50, January 2015													
1871, Proof	30	9	64.4								$8,500	$15,000	$40,000
Auctions: $19,975, PF-64DCam, August 2014													
1871-S	22,000	203	52.5	11%	$325	$400	$550	$1,000	$2,000	$3,000	$4,350	$9,000	$17,500
Auctions: $1,087, AU-55, August 2015; $517, AU-53, June 2015; $423, AU-53, February 2015; $282, VF-30, November 2015													
1872	3,000	65	56.0	15%	$400	$700	$1,100	$2,000	$4,350	$9,000	$15,000	$25,000	
Auctions: $2,596, AU-58, March 2014													
1872, Proof	30	9	64.8								$8,500	$15,000	$37,500
Auctions: $34,075, PF-65Cam, March 2013													
1872-S	18,000	189	50.6	8%	$325	$400	$950	$1,250	$4,000	$6,000	$10,500	$13,500	
Auctions: $3,594, MS-61, April 2012													
1873, Close 3	55,200	601	59.9	62%	$325	$375	$400	$425	$500	$650	$1,250	$1,750	$4,500
Auctions: $3,525, MS-65, June 2015; $1,763, MS-64, June 2015; $1,293, MS-64, September 2015; $705, MS-63, July 2015													
1873, Open 3	122,800	518	60.7	74%	$300	$350	$375	$385	$500	$600	$800	$1,250	$4,250
Auctions: $11,750, MS-66, July 2015; $1,116, MS-64, October 2015; $400, MS-62, August 2015; $329, AU-58, July 2015													
1873, Close 3, Proof	25	11	62.7								$8,500	$15,000	$40,000
Auctions: $23,500, PF-63Cam, August 2014; $19,388, PF, August 2013													
1873-S	27,000	254	50.0	7%	$325	$400	$975	$1,000	$2,000	$4,000	$6,500	$13,500	
Auctions: $11,750, MS-64, August 2015; $3,525, MS-62, October 2015; $620, AU-55, February 2015; $447, EF-45, May 2015													

	Mintage	Cert	Avg	%MS	VF-20	EF-40	AU-50	AU-55	MS-60	MS-62	MS-63 / PF-60	MS-64 / PF-63	MS-65 / PF-65
1874	3,920	113	56.9	26%	$325	$375	$650	$1,050	$2,000	$4,000	$6,000	$9,500	$25,000
Auctions: $3,525, MS-62, August 2013													
1874, Proof	20	11	64.4								$8,500	$17,500	$50,000
Auctions: $38,188, PF-64DCam, August 2014													
1875	400	25	57.1	20%	$5,500	$7,500	$12,500	$15,000	$27,500	$32,500	$45,000		
Auctions: $25,850, MS-61, January 2015; $25,850, MS-61, August 2013; $28,200, MS-60, October 2016; $15,275, AU-58, October 2014													
1875, Proof	20	10	63.6								$25,000	$50,000	$115,000
Auctions: $94,000, PF, October 2013													
1875-S	11,600	184	54.0	16%	$325	$375	$650	$1,100	$3,500	$5,000	$7,250	$12,000	
Auctions: $5,581, MS-63, October 2014; $1,087, AU-58, July 2015; $999, AU-58, June 2015; $676, AU-53, August 2014													
1876	4,176	133	53.9	14%	$350	$600	$950	$1,750	$3,250	$5,500	$7,500	$12,000	
Auctions: $5,581, MS-62, March 2014; $3,055, MS-61, September 2015; $2,350, MS-60, October 2015; $823, AU-53, October 2015													
1876, Proof	45	16	64.4								$7,500	$15,000	$35,000
Auctions: $39,950, PF, January 2013													
1876-S	5,000	140	54.1	16%	$325	$525	$950	$1,350	$3,000	$4,000	$8,500		
Auctions: $8,225, MS-63, January 2014; $2,820, MS-61, August 2014; $1,880, AU-58, November 2015; $734, AU-53, June 2015													
1877	1,632	108	56.7	31%	$400	$750	$1,000	$1,500	$3,000	$4,500	$8,500	$15,000	
Auctions: $4,406, MS-62, April 2014; $3,055, MS-61, August 2014; $1,763, AU-58, June 2015; $884, AU-50, March 2015													
1877, Proof	20	6	64.0								$7,500	$15,000	$35,000
Auctions: $8,050, PF-55, November 2011													
1877-S	35,400	405	58.7	45%	$325	$350	$375	$400	$650	$1,250	$2,350	$4,000	$10,000
Auctions: $376, AU-58, June 2015; $259, AU-58, January 2015; $282, AU-53, May 2015; $329, AU-50, May 2015													
1878	286,240	2,402	60.8	74%	$300	$325	$350	$375	$450	$500	$700	$1,000	$2,000
Auctions: $12,925, MS-67, July 2015; $999, MS-64, August 2015; $541, MS-62, February 2015; $329, AU-58, June 2015													
1878, Proof	20	11	64.4								$7,500	$15,000	$35,000
Auctions: $50,313, PF-65DCam, April 2012													
1878-S	178,000	734	59.2	52%	$300	$365	$375	$385	$500	$850	$1,500	$3,500	$12,000
Auctions: $12,925, MS-66, January 2015; $423, MS-61, June 2015; $353, AU-58, October 2015; $353, AU-53, September 2015													
1879	88,960	965	60.7	73%	$300	$365	$375	$425	$525	$550	$800	$1,000	$3,000
Auctions: $7,638, MS-66, September 2015; $940, MS-64, January 2015; $423, MS-61, October 2015; $282, AU-58, May 2015													
1879, Proof	30	8	65.0								$7,500	$13,000	$32,500
Auctions: $40,250, PF-67Cam, January 2011													
1879-S	43,500	224	54.2	9%	$300	$365	$550	$850	$1,750	$3,500	$4,500	$17,500	
Auctions: $423, MS-60, January 2015; $400, MS-60, February 2015; $617, AU-58, July 2015; $259, EF-45, January 2015													
1880	2,960	145	58.7	46%	$375	$425	$650	$800	$1,500	$2,000	$3,750	$6,000	$12,500
Auctions: $2,820, MS-62, October 2013; $1,410, MS-61, February 2015; $1,410, AU-58, November 2014; $999, AU-58, January 2015													
1880, Proof	36	15	63.4								$6,500	$12,500	$27,500
Auctions: $3,244, PF-55, January 2011													
1881	640	74	56.7	27%	$2,000	$3,000	$5,000	$6,000	$10,000	$15,000	$20,000	$25,000	
Auctions: $12,925, MS-61, November 2016; $11,750, MS-61, August 2016; $7,931, MS-60, June 2013; $5,875, AU-58, August 2014													
1881, Proof	51	22	64.1								$6,500	$13,500	$27,500
Auctions: $34,075, PF-65DCam, August 2013; $14,100, PF-64DCam, July 2014													
1882	4,000	166	59.6	52%	$375	$425	$575	$700	$1,250	$2,000	$2,750	$4,500	$10,000
Auctions: $9,400, MS-66, November 2014; $1,058, AU-58, July 2015; $282, AU-50, July 2015; $259, AU-50, July 2015													
1882, Proof	67	13	65.3								$4,500	$9,500	$25,000
Auctions: $9,487, PF-64, May 2006													
1883	1,920	61	58.1	33%	$1,000	$2,000	$2,750	$4,500	$5,500	$6,000	$7,500	$10,000	$15,000
Auctions: $4,994, MS-61, June 2014													
1883, Proof	82	22	64.8								$4,500	$9,500	$25,000
Auctions: $28,200, PF, March 2014													

1891, Doubled Die Reverse
FS-G2.5-1891-801.

	Mintage	Cert	Avg	%MS	VF-20	EF-40	AU-50	AU-55	MS-60	MS-62	MS-63	MS-64	MS-65
											PF-60	PF-63	PF-65
1884	1,950	120	60.0	63%	$375	$500	$800	$1,000	$2,000	$2,500	$3,500	$6,500	$20,000
	Auctions: $18,800, MS-65, June 2015; $2,468, MS-62, June 2014; $1,645, MS-61, June 2015; $1,058, AU-58, August 2014												
1884, Proof	73	25	64.0								$4,500	$9,500	$25,000
	Auctions: $82,250, PF, August 2013												
1885	800	50	58.4	44%	$1,100	$2,000	$2,750	$3,250	$5,500	$7,000	$10,000	$15,000	$25,000
	Auctions: $13,513, MS-63, March 2014; $1,423, AU-50, July 2014												
1885, Proof	87	22	64.2								$5,000	$9,000	$27,500
	Auctions: $56,160, PF, September 2013												
1886	4,000	146	59.5	53%	$375	$400	$550	$600	$1,250	$2,000	$3,500	$7,000	$12,000
	Auctions: $1,528, MS-62, July 2014; $823, AU-58, September 2015; $823, AU-58, July 2015; $518, AU-53, June 2015												
1886, Proof	88	32	64.3								$4,500	$9,500	$25,000
	Auctions: $40,538, PF, August 2013												
1887	6,160	210	60.0	66%	$375	$400	$450	$500	$800	$1,250	$1,500	$4,000	$15,000
	Auctions: $15,275, MS-65, August 2015; $881, MS-62, February 2015; $764, AU-58, January 2015; $329, AU-50, October 2015												
1887, Proof	122	25	64.0								$4,500	$9,500	$25,000
	Auctions: $58,750, PF, August 2013												
1888	16,001	465	61.9	88%	$325	$365	$375	$385	$450	$650	$900	$1,850	$4,500
	Auctions: $8,225, MS-66, August 2015; $1,234, MS-64, January 2015; $541, MS-62, January 2015; $376, MS-61, August 2015												
1888, Proof	97	30	64.5								$4,500	$8,500	$25,000
	Auctions: $25,850, PF-65Cam, February 2013; $6,463, PF-63, November 2014; $5,288, PF-62, August 2014												
1889	17,600	404	61.5	87%	$325	$365	$375	$385	$450	$650	$950	$1,650	$5,500
	Auctions: $6,463, MS-65, July 2014; $441, MS-61, August 2014; $341, AU-58, October 2014; $329, AU-58, July 2015												
1889, Proof	48	17	64.9								$4,500	$8,500	$25,000
	Auctions: $31,792, PF-65DCam, August 2014												
1890	8,720	233	60.8	69%	$325	$375	$385	$400	$650	$800	$1,500	$3,000	$9,000
	Auctions: $9,400, MS-65, July 2015; $940, MS-62, August 2015; $646, AU-58, May 2015; $400, AU-55, June 2015												
1890, Proof	93	52	64.6								$4,500	$8,500	$20,000
	Auctions: $19,388, PF-65DCam, June 2014; $29,458, PF-65, October 2014												
1891	10,960	321	60.9	75%	$350	$385	$400	$425	$550	$700	$1,450	$1,850	$6,000
	Auctions: $2,233, MS-64, November 2014; $1,645, MS-64, June 2015; $447, MS-61, February 2015; $411, AU-58, May 2015												
1891, Doubled Die Reverse	(i)	0	n/a					$500	$850	$1,500	$2,500	$3,000	$5,500
	Auctions: $823, MS-63, November 2014												
1891, Proof	80	26	65.5								$4,500	$8,000	$20,000
	Auctions: $30,550, PF, April 2013												
1892	2,440	137	61.2	81%	$350	$400	$475	$525	$900	$1,100	$2,250	$4,000	$8,000
	Auctions: $21,150, MS-67, November 2013; $8,527, MS-66, August 2014; $7,931, MS-66, November 2014; $1,998, MS-63, October 2014												
1892, Proof	105	30	64.5								$4,500	$8,000	$20,000
	Auctions: $111,625, PF, February 2013												
1893	30,000	908	62.3	91%	$325	$350	$375	$385	$550	$800	$1,250	$1,350	$1,750
	Auctions: $7,050, MS-67, January 2015; $3,290, MS-66, January 2015; $494, MS-62, April 2015; $259, MS-60, January 2015												
1893, Proof	106	38	65.1								$4,500	$7,500	$20,000
	Auctions: $21,150, PF-66DCam, September 2014; $44,063, PF, August 2013												

i. Included in circulation-strike 1891 mintage figure.

	Mintage	Cert	Avg	%MS	VF-20	EF-40	AU-50	AU-55	MS-60	MS-62	MS-63 / PF-60	MS-64 / PF-63	MS-65 / PF-65
1894	4,000	243	61.9	86%	$360	$365	$375	$475	$750	$900	$1,350	$1,750	$5,500
Auctions: $3,525, MS-65, January 2015; $1,410, MS-62, July 2015; $833, MS-61, January 2015; $823, MS-61, August 2015
1894, Proof	122	66	64.5								$4,500	$7,500	$20,000
Auctions: $21,150, PF-66DCam, September 2014; $44,063, PF, August 2013
1895	6,000	266	62.4	92%	$360	$365	$375	$385	$575	$725	$1,100	$1,650	$3,750
Auctions: $8,519, MS-66, March 2013
1895, Proof	119	72	65.0								$4,500	$7,500	$20,000
Auctions: $23,500, PF-66DCam, January 2014; $28,200, PF-66DCam, August 2014; $9,400, PF-64DCam, January 2015
1896	19,070	716	62.6	94%	$300	$325	$375	$385	$500	$600	$800	$1,000	$2,000
Auctions: $7,344, MS-67, March 2014; $1,998, MS-65, September 2014; $940, MS-64, March 2015; $306, AU-58, July 2015
1896, Proof	132	66	64.7								$4,500	$7,500	$20,000
Auctions: $3,819, PF-62, March 2015; $3,055, PF-62, November 2014; $21,150, PF, October 2013
1897	29,768	1,055	62.8	95%	$300	$325	$375	$385	$500	$525	$700	$900	$1,750
Auctions: $7,638, MS-67, January 2015; $3,055, MS-66, July 2015; $881, MS-64, October 2015; $447, MS-62, January 2015
1897, Proof	136	84	64.8								$4,500	$7,500	$20,000
Auctions: $27,025, PF, March 2014
1898	24,000	791	63.2	97%	$300	$315	$325	$350	$475	$525	$675	$800	$1,500
Auctions: $7,638, MS-67, January 2015; $2,879, MS-66, August 2015; $364, MS-61, September 2015; $294, MS-60, April 2015
1898, Proof	165	115	64.3								$4,500	$7,500	$20,000
Auctions: $25,850, PF-66DCam, September 2014; $25,850, PF-66DCam, September 2014; $5,941, PF-64Cam, June 2015
1899	27,200	817	62.8	97%	$275	$300	$325	$350	$425	$475	$575	$625	$1,500
Auctions: $2,585, MS-66, June 2015; $1,998, MS-65, July 2015; $1,414, MS-65, June 2015; $969, MS-64, June 2015
1899, Proof	150	137	64.4								$4,500	$7,500	$20,000
Auctions: $36,425, PF, August 2013
1900	67,000	2,029	63.0	96%	$275	$285	$300	$325	$400	$425	$475	$575	$900
Auctions: $3,290, MS-67, June 2015; $940, MS-65, January 2015; $705, MS-64, October 2015; $541, MS-62, July 2015
1900, Proof	205	193	64.0								$4,500	$7,500	$17,500
Auctions: $56,400, PF-68DCam+, October 2015; $37,600, PF-68UCam, June 2015; $64,625, PF-68DCam, November 2014
1901	91,100	2,364	62.9	96%	$275	$285	$300	$325	$400	$425	$475	$575	$900
Auctions: $4,700, MS-67, August 2014; $1,351, MS-65, January 2015; $541, MS-63, January 2015; $447, MS-62, January 2015
1901, Proof	223	136	64.3								$4,500	$7,500	$17,500
Auctions: $28,200, PF-67DCam, October 2014; $16,450, PF-66Cam+, June 2015; $11,750, PF-64Cam, September 2014
1902	133,540	3,451	63.0	97%	$275	$285	$300	$325	$400	$425	$475	$575	$900
Auctions: $5,405, MS-67, January 2015; $646, MS-64, August 2015; $329, MS-61, April 2015; $282, MS-60, January 2015
1902, Proof	193	104	64.0								$4,500	$7,500	$17,500
Auctions: $5,640, PF-64, June 2015; $3,290, PF-62, June 2015; $2,585, PF-61, January 2015; $1,528, PF-50, August 2015
1903	201,060	6,151	63.1	97%	$275	$285	$300	$325	$400	$425	$475	$575	$900
Auctions: $9,400, MS-68, January 2015; $2,350, MS-67, January 2015; $376, MS-62, February 2015; $235, MS-60, June 2015
1903, Proof	197	123	63.0								$4,500	$7,500	$17,500
Auctions: $12,925, PF-65, January 2015; $7,050, PF-64, August 2014; $3,173, PF-62, November 2014; $3,055, PF-62, March 2015
1904	160,790	4,664	63.0	96%	$275	$285	$300	$325	$400	$425	$475	$575	$900
Auctions: $28,200, MS-68, January 2013; $3,290, MS-67, July 2015; $2,585, MS-67, November 2014; $1,351, MS-66, November 2014
1904, Proof	170	114	64.1								$4,500	$7,500	$17,500
Auctions: $4,700, PF-63, January 2015; $1,293, MS-66, October 2015; $270, MS-60, January 2015; $259, AU-55, January 2015
1905 (j)	217,800	6,509	63.1	96%	$275	$285	$300	$325	$400	$425	$475	$575	$900
Auctions: $3,995, MS-67, August 2015; $1,528, MS-66, August 2015; $329, MS-62, July 2015; $282, AU-58, February 2015
1905, Proof	144	122	63.6								$4,500	$7,500	$17,500
Auctions: $8,225, PF-64, October 2014; $6,463, PF-64, July 2015; $6,463, PF-64, February 2015; $1,058, PF, March 2015

j. Pieces dated 1905-S are counterfeit.

	Mintage	Cert	Avg	%MS	VF-20	EF-40	AU-50	AU-55	MS-60	MS-62	MS-63 PF-60	MS-64 PF-63	MS-65 PF-65
1906	176,330	5,489	63.0	97%	$275	$285	$300	$325	$400	$425	$475	$575	$900
	Auctions: $21,150, MS-68, October 2015; $1,528, MS-66, January 2015; $353, MS-61, June 2015; $306, AU-58, June 2015												
1906, Proof	160	136	64.5								$4,500	$7,500	$17,500
	Auctions: $7,638, PF-64Cam, August 2014; $8,225, PF-64Cam, September 2014; $44,063, PF, August 2013												
1907	336,294	9,201	63.1	97%	$275	$285	$300	$325	$400	$425	$475	$575	$900
	Auctions: $12,925, MS-68, January 2015; $1,351, MS-66, June 2015; $494, MS-62, January 2015; $282, MS-60, June 2015												
1907, Proof	154	113	64.7								$4,500	$7,500	$17,500
	Auctions: $32,900, PF-68, April 2013; $21,738, PF-65+, January 2015; $4,700, PF-63Cam, September 2014												

INDIAN HEAD (1908–1929)

Designer: *Bela Lyon Pratt.* **Weight:** *4.18 grams.*
Composition: *.900 gold, .100 copper (net weight .12094 oz. pure gold).*
Diameter: *18 mm.* **Edge:** *Reeded.* **Mints:** *Philadelphia and Denver.*

Circulation Strike   **Mintmark is on the reverse, to the left of arrows.**   **Sandblast Finish Proof**   **Satin Finish Proof**

History. The Indian Head design—used on both the quarter eagle and the half eagle—is unusual in that the lettering and motifs are in sunken relief. (The design sometimes is erroneously described as incuse.) The designer, sculptor Bela Lyon Pratt, was chosen by President Theodore Roosevelt after Augustus Saint-Gaudens died before beginning his own design. Pratt modeled the head on Chief Hollow Horn Bear of the Lakota. The "standing eagle" reverse design was based on the reverse of Saint-Gaudens's Indian Head $10 gold coin of 1907; Pratt was a pupil of the famous sculptor.

Some Americans worried that the sunken designs of the Indian Head quarter eagle would accumulate dirt and germs—an unfounded fear. As the smallest gold denomination of the era, these coins were popular for use as souvenirs and gifts, but they did not circulate as money except in the West.

Striking and Sharpness. The striking quality of Indian Head quarter eagles varies. On many early issues the rims are flat, while on others, including most of the 1920s, they are slightly raised. Some have traces of a wire rim, usually on the reverse. Look for weakness on the high parts of the Indian's bonnet (particularly the garland of flowers) and in the feather details in the headdress. On the reverse, check the feathers on the highest area of the wing, the top of the shoulder. On some issues of the 1911-D, the D mintmark can be weak.

Availability. This design was not popular with collectors, and they saved relatively few of the coins. However, many coins were given as gifts and preserved in high quality. The survival of MS-63 and better coins is a matter of chance, especially for the issues dated from 1909 to 1915. The only scarce issue is 1911-D. Luster can range from deeply frosty to grainy. As the fields are the highest areas of the coin, luster diminished quickly as examples were circulated or jostled with others in bags. The Indian Head quarter eagle is one of the most challenging series for professional graders, and opinions can vary widely.

Proofs. Sandblast (also called Matte) Proofs were made in 1908 and 1911 to 1915, while Satin (also called Roman Finish) Proofs were made in 1909 and 1910. The Sandblast issues are usually somewhat dull, while the Satin Proofs are usually of a light-yellow gold. In their time the Proofs of both styles, made for all gold series, were not popular with numismatists. Today, they are in strong demand. As a class these are significantly more readily available than half eagles of the same date and style of finish.

Most are in grades from PF-63 upward. At lower levels coins can show light contact marks. Some microscopic bright flecks may have been caused by the sandblasting process and, although they do not represent handling, usually result in a coin being assigned a slightly lower grade.

Note: Values of common-date gold coins have been based on the current bullion price of gold, $1,300 per ounce, and may vary with the prevailing spot price.

GRADING STANDARDS

MS-60 to 70 (Mint State). *Obverse:* On MS–60 to 62 coins there is abrasion in the field, this representing the highest part of the coin. Abrasion is also evident on the headdress. Marks and, occasionally, a microscopic pin scratch may be seen. At MS-63, there may be some abrasion and some tiny marks. Luster is irregular. At MS-64, abrasion is less. Luster is rich. At MS-65 and above, luster is deep and frosty. No marks at all are visible

1911-D. Graded MS-64.

without magnification at MS-66 and higher. *Reverse:* At MS–60 to 62, there is abrasion in the field, this representing the highest part of the coin. Abrasion is also evident on the eagle's wing. Otherwise, the same comments apply as for the obverse.

Illustrated coin: This lustrous example has excellent eye appeal.

AU-50, 53, 55, 58 (About Uncirculated). *Obverse:* Friction on the cheek is very noticeable at AU-50, progressively less at higher levels to AU-58. The headdress shows light wear, most evident on the ribbon above the forehead and on the garland. Luster is minimal at AU-50 and scattered and incomplete at AU-58. Nicks and contact marks are to be expected. *Reverse:* Friction on the wing and neck is very noticeable at AU-50, increasingly

1911-D. Graded AU-55.

less at higher levels to AU-58. Otherwise, the same comments apply as for the obverse.

Illustrated coin: Much of the original luster remains in the incuse areas but not in the fields, which are the highest points on this design.

EF-40, 45 (Extremely Fine). *Obverse:* Light wear characterizes the portrait and headdress. Luster is gone. Marks and tiny scratches are to be expected, but not distracting. *Reverse:* Light wear is most evident on the eagle's head and wing, although other areas are lightly worn as well. Luster is gone. Marks and tiny scratches are to be expected, but not distracting.

1911-D. Graded EF-40.

VF-20, 30 (Very Fine). *Obverse:* Many details of the ribbon above the forehead and the garland are worn away. Many feather vanes are blended together. The field is dull and has contact marks. *Reverse:* The neck and the upper part of the wing show extensive wear, other areas less so. The field is dull and has contact marks.

The Indian Head quarter eagle is seldom collected in grades lower than VF-20.

1912. Graded VF-20.

PF-60 to 70 (Proof). *Obverse and Reverse:* At PF–60 to 63, there is light abrasion and some contact marks; the lower the grade, the higher the quantity. On Sandblast Proofs these show up as visually unappealing bright spots. At PF-64 and higher levels, marks are fewer, with magnification needed to see any at PF-65. At PF-66, there should be none at all.

Illustrated coin: This is a Sandblast Proof of exceptionally high quality.

1913, Sandblast Finish. Graded PF-66.

	Mintage	Cert	Avg	%MS	VF-20	EF-40	AU-50	MS-60	MS-62	MS-63 PF-60	MS-64 PF-63	MS-65 PF-65
1908	564,821	9,673	61.5	84%	$300	$325	$350	$400	$550	$700	$1,200	$2,500
Auctions: $7,931, MS-66, August 2015; $1,645, MS-64, July 2015; $353, MS-61, February 2015; $235, AU-50, August 2015												
1908, Sandblast Finish Proof	236	136	65.2							$4,500	$10,000	$25,000
Auctions: $49,938, PF-68, April 2014; $70,500, PF-67, January 2015; $38,188, PF-66, August 2014; $5,170, PF-58, February 2015												
1909	441,760	7,604	61.2	79%	$300	$325	$350	$400	$600	$1,050	$1,750	$4,000
Auctions: $11,750, MS-66, October 2015; $2,115, MS-64, January 2015; $317, MS-60, August 2015; $282, AU-58, January 2015												
1909, Satin Finish Proof	139	49	64.3							$4,000	$11,000	$35,000
Auctions: $57,500, PF-67, January 2011												
1910	492,000	8,777	61.4	85%	$300	$325	$350	$400	$500	$900	$1,300	$3,000
Auctions: $2,938, MS-65, August 2015; $1,293, MS-64, June 2015; $376, MS-62, July 2015; $282, AU-58, March 2015												
1910, Satin Finish Proof	682	106	65.1							$4,000	$11,000	$27,500
Auctions: $64,625, PF-67, January 2015; $23,500, PF-65, July 2015; $27,600, PF-64+, September 2011												
1910, Sandblast Finish Proof (a)	*unknown*	0	n/a				*(unique)*					
Auctions: $47,000, PF-66, August 2014												
1911	704,000	13,164	61.2	81%	$300	$325	$350	$400	$500	$700	$1,000	$3,250
Auctions: $3,525, MS-65, January 2015; $470, MS-62, June 2015; $423, AU-58, March 2015; $306, AU-55, June 2015												
1911, Sandblast Finish Proof	191	98	65.8							$4,500	$10,000	$25,000
Auctions: $27,025, PF-66, January 2014												
1911-D (b)	55,680	5,015	59.8	57%	$2,750	$4,000	$4,750	$7,750	$10,000	$13,500	$20,000	$50,000
Auctions: $52,875, MS-65, August 2015; $37,600, MS-65, February 2016; $3,525, MS-65, January 2015; $25,850, MS-64, October 2016												
1911-D, Weak D	(c)	219	54.0	3%	$1,000	$1,500	$2,500	$4,000				
Auctions: $2,645, AU-55, April 2012												

a. The sole known example is part of a complete 1910 Sandblast Finish Proof gold set. Other examples may exist, but have not yet been confirmed. **b.** Beware of counterfeit and altered pieces. **c.** Included in 1911-D mintage figure.

	Mintage	Cert	Avg	%MS	VF-20	EF-40	AU-50	MS-60	MS-62	MS-63 / PF-60	MS-64 / PF-63	MS-65 / PF-65
1912	616,000	9,309	60.7	74%	$325	$350	$375	$400	$550	$1,250	$2,250	$12,500
	Auctions: $14,100, MS-65, October 2015; $2,350, MS-64, September 2015; $400, MS-61, July 2015; $282, AU-55, February 2015											
1912, Sandblast Finish Proof	197	48	65.6							$4,500	$10,000	$30,000
	Auctions: $35,250, PF-66, October 2014; $41,125, PF-66, September 2013											
1913	722,000	12,688	61.1	80%	$325	$350	$375	$400	$525	$625	$1,000	$3,500
	Auctions: $3,290, MS-65, January 2015; $499, MS-62, February 2015; $264, AU-58, February 2015; $259, AU-50, February 2015											
1913, Sandblast Finish Proof	165	56	65.9							$4,500	$11,500	$35,000
	Auctions: $31,050, PF-67, January 2012											
1914	240,000	7,893	60.7	74%	$350	$375	$450	$550	$1,100	$2,000	$4,500	$15,000
	Auctions: $24,675, MS-65, January 2015; $23,500, MS-65, December 2015; $18,800, MS-65, August 2016; $16,450, MS-65, August 2015											
1914, Sandblast Finish Proof	117	77	65.2							$4,500	$10,000	$27,500
	Auctions: $12,650, PF-64, April 2012											
1914-D	448,000	10,893	61.1	79%	$325	$350	$375	$450	$550	$1,250	$2,000	$12,500
	Auctions: $15,275, MS-65, August 2015; $2,233, MS-64, June 2015; $376, MS-61, September 2015; $282, AU-55, November 2015											
1915	606,000	12,062	61.3	82%	$300	$325	$350	$400	$500	$600	$1,250	$3,000
	Auctions: $25,850, MS-66, October 2015; $1,058, MS-64, January 2015; $376, AU-58, March 2015; $259, AU-50, June 2015											
1915, Sandblast Finish Proof	100	43	65.2							$6,000	$12,500	$35,000
	Auctions: $41,688, PF-66, January 2012											
1925-D	578,000	20,999	62.3	93%	$300	$325	$350	$400	$475	$500	$800	$1,500
	Auctions: $6,500, MS-66, January 2015; $881, MS-64, January 2015; $329, MS-61, June 2015; $376, AU-58, March 2015											
1926	446,000	18,950	62.3	95%	$300	$325	$350	$400	$475	$500	$800	$1,500
	Auctions: $5,875, MS-66, January 2015; $705, MS-64, January 2015; $329, MS-61, January 2015; $259, MS-60, June 2015											
1927	388,000	15,518	62.3	95%	$300	$325	$350	$400	$475	$500	$800	$1,500
	Auctions: $14,688, MS-66, October 2015; $447, MS-63, November 2015; $306, MS-61, March 2015; $311, AU-58, July 2015											
1928	416,000	16,856	62.4	97%	$300	$325	$350	$400	$475	$500	$800	$1,500
	Auctions: $8,225, MS-66, September 2015; $764, MS-64, July 2015; $376, MS-62, March 2015; $247, AU-50, March 2015											
1929	532,000	20,603	62.4	98%	$300	$325	$350	$400	$475	$500	$800	$3,000
	Auctions: $7,638, MS-65, October 2015; $764, MS-64, August 2015; $376, MS-62, August 2015; $353, MS-60, October 2015											

Three-Dollar Gold Pieces
1854–1889

AN OVERVIEW OF THREE-DOLLAR GOLD PIECES

The three-dollar gold coin denomination was conceived in 1853 and first produced for circulation in 1854. Although there were high hopes for it at the outset, and mintages were generous, the value was redundant given the $2.50 quarter eagle then in circulation. Mintages declined, and although pieces were struck each year through 1889, very few actually circulated after the 1850s.

Although many different three-dollar dates are available at reasonable prices, most numismatists opt to acquire either a circulated or Mint State 1854 (significant as the first year of issue; also, in this year the word DOLLARS is in smaller letters than on later issues) or a Mint State coin from the low-mintage era of 1879–1889. Similar to the situation for gold dollars, although the mintages of these later pieces were low, they were popularly saved at the time, and many more have survived in high quality than might otherwise be the case.

Some numismatists have observed that $3 gold pieces might have been commonly used to purchase sheets of 100 3¢ stamps.

FOR THE COLLECTOR AND INVESTOR:
THREE-DOLLAR GOLD PIECES AS A SPECIALTY

Collecting three-dollar pieces by date and mint would at first seem to be daunting, but it is less challenging than expected, outside of a handful of pieces. The 1870-S is unique (in the Harry W. Bass Jr. Collection on loan to the American Numismatic Association), the 1875 and 1876 were made only in Proof format to the extent of 20 and 45 pieces respectively, and the 1873 is quite rare. Beyond that, examples of coins in grades such as EF and AU (including some varieties with very low mintages) can be purchased for reasonable prices.

Choice examples can be elusive, this being particularly true of branch-mint issues of the 1854–1860 years. Generally, Mint State Philadelphia pieces are rare after 1855, but then come on the market with frequency for 1861 and later, with dates in the 1860s being scarcer than later issues. Coins of the years 1878 and 1879 were made in larger quantities, with the 1878 in particular being easy to find today, although examples usually are quite bag-marked. The low-mintage three-dollar pieces of 1879 through 1889 were popular at the time of issue, many were saved, and today Mint State pieces exist to a greater extent than would otherwise be the case.

INDIAN PRINCESS HEAD (1854–1889)

Designer: *James B. Longacre.* **Weight:** *5.015 grams.*
Composition: *.900 gold, .100 copper (net weight .14512 oz. pure gold).* **Diameter:** *20.5 mm.*
Edge: *Reeded.* **Mints:** *Philadelphia, Dahlonega, New Orleans, and San Francisco.*

Circulation Strike

Mintmark location is on the reverse, below the wreath.

Proof

History. The three-dollar gold coin was designed by U.S. Mint chief engraver James B. Longacre, and first struck in 1854. The quarter eagle and half eagle had already been in use for a long time, and the reason for the creation of this odd new denomination is uncertain, although some numismatists note it could have been used to buy a sheet of current 3¢ postage stamps or a group of 100 silver trimes. After a large initial mintage in 1854, the coins were struck in smaller annual quantities. These coins were more popular on the West Coast, but, even in that region, use of this denomination dropped off sharply by the 1870s.

Striking and Sharpness. Points to observe on the obverse include the tips of the feathers in the head-dress, and the hair details below the band inscribed LIBERTY. Focal points on the reverse are the wreath details (especially the vertical division in the ribbon knot), and the two central date numerals. Many of the later issues—particularly those of the early 1880s—are prooflike.

Availability. In circulated grades the issues of 1854 to 1860 survive in approximate proportion to their mintages. MS coins are plentiful for the first-year Philadelphia issue, 1854, but are scarce to rare for other years and for all branch-mint issues. For the 1860s and 1870s most are in grades such as EF, AU, and low MS, except for 1874 and in particular 1878, easily found in MS. Dates from 1879 to 1889 have a higher survival ratio and are mostly in MS, often at MS-65.

Proofs. Proofs were struck of all years. All prior to the 1880s are very rare today, with issues of the 1850s being exceedingly so. Coins of 1875 and 1876 were made only in Proof format, with no related circulation strikes. Most often seen in the marketplace are the higher-mintage Proofs of the 1880s. Some have patches of graininess or hints of non-Proof surface on the obverse, or an aura or "ghosting" near the portrait, an artifact of striking.

GRADING STANDARDS

MS-60 to 70 (Mint State). *Obverse:* On MS–60 to 62 coins there is abrasion on the hair below the band lettered LIBERTY (an area that can be weakly struck as well) and on tips of the feather plumes. At MS-63, there may be slight abrasion. Luster can be irregular. At MS-64, abrasion is less. Luster is rich on most coins, less so on the 1854-D (which is often overgraded). At MS-65 and above,

1879. Graded MS-64.

luster is deep and frosty, with no marks at all visible without magnification at MS-66 and higher. *Reverse:* On MS–60 to 62 coins there is abrasion on the 1, the highest parts of the leaves, and the ribbon knot. Otherwise, the same comments apply as for the obverse.

Illustrated coin: Satiny luster and partial mirror surfaces yield excellent eye appeal.

AU-50, 53, 55, 58 (About Uncirculated).
Obverse: Light wear on the hair below the coronet, the cheek, and the tips of the feather plumes is very noticeable at AU-50, increasingly less at higher levels to AU-58. Luster is minimal at AU-50 and scattered and incomplete at AU-58. Some tiny nicks and contact marks are to be expected and should be mentioned if they are distracting. *Reverse:* Light wear on the 1, the wreath, and the ribbon knot characterize an AU-50 coin, increasingly less at higher levels to AU-58. Otherwise, the same comments apply as for the obverse.

1854. Graded AU-55.

Illustrated coin: Most of the original luster is gone, but perhaps 15% remains in the protected areas.

EF-40, 45 (Extremely Fine). *Obverse:* Medium wear is seen on the hair below the coronet and on the feather plume tips. Detail is partially gone on the hair. Luster is gone on most coins. *Reverse:* Light wear is seen overall, and the highest parts of the leaves are flat, but detail remains elsewhere. Luster is gone on most coins.

Illustrated coin: Note the mushy denticles (as seen on all but one specimen of this, the only Dahlonega variety in the series).

1854-D. Graded EF-40.

VF-20, 30 (Very Fine). *Obverse:* Most hair detail is gone, except at the back of the lower curls. The feather plume ends are flat. *Reverse:* The wreath and other areas show more wear. Most detail is gone on the higher-relief leaves.

Three-dollar gold pieces are seldom collected in grades lower than VF-20.

1874. Graded VF-20.

PF-60 to 70 (Proof). *Obverse and Reverse:* PF-60 to 62 coins have extensive hairlines and may have nicks and contact marks. At PF-63, hairlines are prominent, but the mirror surface is very reflective. PF-64 coins have fewer hairlines. At PF-65, hairlines should be minimal and mostly seen only under magnification. There should be no nicks or marks. PF-66 and higher coins should have no marks or hairlines visible to the unaided eye.

1876. Graded PF-61.

Illustrated coin: Extensive friction is visible in the fields, but the mirror surface can be seen in protected areas. This is still a desirable example of a date of which only 45 were minted.

	Mintage	Cert	Avg	%MS	VF-20	EF-40	AU-50	AU-55	MS-60	MS-62	MS-63	MS-65
										PF-60	PF-63	PF-65
1854	138,618	4,101	55.4	22%	$850	$1,000	$1,100	$1,250	$2,250	$2,750	$4,250	$12,500
	Auctions: $17,050, MS-66, January 2015; $1,293, AU-58, January 2015; $999, EF-45, January 2015; $447, VF-20, May 2015											
1854, Proof	*15–20*	7	62.0							$35,000	$80,000	$175,000
	Auctions: $164,500, PF-64Cam, November 2013; $30,550, PF-61, January 2015											
1854-D	1,120	99	51.1	9%	$20,000	$27,500	$45,000	$50,000	$100,000	$200,000		
	Auctions: $188,000, MS-62, February 2016; $39,950, AU-53, September 2016; $52,875, EF-35, March 2013											
1854-O	24,000	844	49.4	3%	$2,000	$3,250	$4,000	$8,500	$40,000	$75,000	$110,000	
	Auctions: $76,375, MS-62; $58,750, MS-62, March 2016; $23,500, AU-58, March 2016; $12,338, AU-55, September 2016; $8,225, AU-55, July 2015											
1855	50,555	1,262	54.2	19%	$950	$1,050	$1,150	$1,250	$2,250	$3,500	$5,500	$30,000
	Auctions: $5,170, MS-63, July 2015; $1,645, AU-58, October 2015; $794, EF-40, January 2015; $541, VF-20, June 2015											
1855, Proof	*4–8*	0	n/a							$35,000	$75,000	$200,000
	Auctions: $75,900, PF-64Cam, November 2003											
1855-S	6,600	163	42.5	2%	$1,650	$3,000	$7,000	$12,000	$32,500	$55,000	$100,000	
	Auctions: $55,225, MS-62, February 2016; $17,625, AU-58, November 2013; $2,820, EF-45, August 2015; $1,763, EF-40, March 2015											
1855-S, Proof	*unknown*	1	64.0									
	Auctions: $1,322,500, PF-64Cam, August 2011											
1856	26,010	781	55.0	19%	$850	$1,000	$1,150	$1,300	$3,000	$4,250	$7,500	$35,000
	Auctions: $1,645, AU-58, August 2015; $999, AU-50, June 2015; $823, EF-45, October 2015; $494, VG-10, September 2015											
1856, Proof	*8–10*	2	63.5							$19,500	$45,000	$125,000
	Auctions: $28,750, PF-62Cam, March 2011											
1856-S (a)	34,500	549	45.5	5%	$1,000	$1,500	$2,750	$4,000	$12,000	$18,500	$30,000	
	Auctions: $2,115, AU-55, October 2015; $1,116, AU-50, July 2015; $1,175, EF-40, July 2015; $552, VF-20, July 2015											
1857	20,891	639	54.8	18%	$850	$1,200	$1,350	$1,500	$3,500	$4,500	$8,500	$35,000
	Auctions: $14,100, MS-64, August 2015; $7,050, MS-63, June 2015; $1,175, AU-50, June 2015; $617, EF-40, October 2015											
1857, Proof	*8–12*	1	64.0							$17,500	$30,000	$125,000
	Auctions: No auction records available.											
1857-S	14,000	198	43.3	2%	$1,450	$2,500	$5,500	$9,000	$21,500	$45,000	$60,000	$100,000
	Auctions: $12,925, AU-58, November 2014; $6,463, AU-55, April 2013; $2,115, EF-45, January 2015; $999, VF-25, October 2015											
1858	2,133	107	52.6	8%	$1,300	$2,250	$3,750	$5,500	$12,000	$15,000	$22,500	
	Auctions: $7,931, AU-58, August 2013											
1858, Proof	*8–12*	4	65.0							$15,000	$30,000	$95,000
	Auctions: $85,188, PF-65Cam, April 2013; $94,000, PF-65, October 2014; $91,063, PF-65, January 2015											
1859	15,558	588	55.5	21%	$900	$1,250	$1,350	$1,750	$3,250	$4,500	$7,500	$25,000
	Auctions: $38,188, MS-66, June 2013; $10,575, MS-64, July 2014; $9,988, MS-64, August 2014; $9,400, MS-64, September 2014											
1859, Proof	80	9	64.3							$8,500	$20,000	$60,000
	Auctions: $59,925, PF-65DCam, April 2014											
1860	7,036	326	55.4	22%	$950	$1,300	$1,800	$1,950	$3,500	$6,500	$7,500	$30,000
	Auctions: $5,875, MS-63, January 2015; $1,645, MS-60, October 2015; $1,763, AU-53, January 2015; $940, AU-50, June 2015											
1860, Proof	119	14	64.6							$8,000	$16,000	$55,000
	Auctions: $88,125, PF-67Cam, September 2014; $67,563, PF-66Cam, August 2013											
1860-S	7,000	148	42.4	3%	$1,300	$2,750	$7,000	$11,500	$25,000	$50,000	—	
	Auctions: $25,850, MS-61, February 2016; $21,150, AU-58, August 2015; $2,938, EF-45, March 2016; $999, F-15, October 2015											
1861	5,959	270	55.0	23%	$1,500	$2,500	$3,500	$4,500	$7,000	$11,000	$12,500	$35,000
	Auctions: $17,625, MS-64, September 2015; $6,169, AU-58, January 2015; $2,115, AU-50, August 2014; $2,585, VF-35, September 2015											
1861, Proof	113	5	64.8							$8,000	$16,000	$55,000
	Auctions: $37,375, PF-64Cam, January 2011											
1862	5,750	206	54.9	22%	$1,500	$2,500	$4,250	$4,750	$7,000	$11,000	$13,500	$40,000
	Auctions: $6,463, AU-58, August 2015; $4,230, AU-53, October 2015; $1,293, AU-50, January 2015; $423, VG-8, July 2015											
1862, Proof	35	9	64.9							$8,000	$16,000	$55,000
	Auctions: $74,750, PF-66UCam, August 2009											

a. Collectors recognize three mintmark sizes: Large (very rare); Medium (common), and Small (rare).

	Mintage	Cert	Avg	%MS	VF-20	EF-40	AU-50	AU-55	MS-60	MS-62 / PF-60	MS-63 / PF-63	MS-65 / PF-65
1863	5,000	244	55.7	25%	$1,500	$2,500	$4,000	$4,500	$8,000	$12,500	$15,000	$35,000
	Auctions: $61,700, MS-67, July 2015; $28,200, MS-66, August 2015; $8,225, MS-61, June 2015; $3,055, AU-50, October 2015											
1863, Proof	39	10	63.4							$8,000	$16,000	$50,000
	Auctions: $80,500, PF-66UCam, March 2011											
1864	2,630	157	56.2	28%	$1,650	$3,000	$4,750	$6,000	$8,000	$13,000	$15,000	$45,000
	Auctions: $5,584, AU-58, June 2015; $4,935, AU-55, January 2015; $3,560, EF-45, October 2015; $588, VF-20, July 2015											
1864, Proof	50	18	62.8							$8,000	$16,000	$50,000
	Auctions: $48,875, PF-64DCam, April 2012											
1865	1,140	71	56.2	35%	$2,500	$4,500	$7,500	$9,500	$15,000	$23,500	$30,000	$55,000
	Auctions: $70,500, MS-66, January 2014; $3,290, VF-25, November 2014											
1865, Proof	25	8	63.8							$8,500	$20,000	$50,000
	Auctions: $46,000, PF-64Cam, March 2006											
1865, Proof Restrike (b)	5	0	n/a		*(extremely rare)*							
	Auctions: No auction records available.											
1866	4,000	171	55.8	25%	$1,150	$1,350	$2,250	$2,500	$4,500	$7,500	$10,000	$35,000
	Auctions: $12,925, MS-64, June 2015; $7,638, MS-63, November 2014; $2,115, AU-55, October 2015; $1,116, AU-50, August 2015											
1866, Proof	30	9	63.7							$8,000	$16,500	$50,000
	Auctions: $46,000, PF-64DCam, April 2011											
1867	2,600	128	56.5	23%	$1,300	$1,500	$2,500	$3,250	$5,500	$11,000	$15,000	$35,000
	Auctions: $141,000, MS-67, January 2014											
1867, Proof	50	10	62.8							$8,000	$16,500	$50,000
	Auctions: $19,388, PF-63DCam, October 2014; $52,875, PF-66Cam, August 2014; $64,625, PF-66Cam, August 2013											
1868 (c)	4,850	366	56.8	26%	$1,150	$1,350	$2,000	$2,500	$4,250	$6,000	$10,000	$30,000
	Auctions: $6,463, MS-63, January 2015; $3,290, AU-55, September 2015; $940, AU-50, August 2015; $823, VF-20, October 2015											
1868, Proof	25	9	64.3							$8,000	$16,500	$50,000
	Auctions: $57,500, PF-65Cam, January 2011											
1869 (c)	2,500	178	54.6	17%	$1,150	$1,400	$2,200	$2,800	$4,750	$9,000	$13,500	$45,000
	Auctions: $9,988, MS-63, August 2014; $3,525, MS-61, January 2015; $2,350, AU-55, March 2015; $1,763, AU-53, October 2015											
1869, Proof	25	4	64.5							$8,000	$16,500	$50,000
	Auctions: $57,500, PF-65UCam, February 2009											
1870	3,500	280	54.3	12%	$1,150	$1,550	$2,500	$2,750	$4,500	$10,000	$15,000	
	Auctions: $51,700, MS-65, January 2015; $2,820, AU-58, June 2015; $1,293, AU-50, January 2015; $823, EF-40, July 2015											
1870, Proof	35	10	62.9							$8,000	$16,500	$50,000
	Auctions: $55,813, PF-64Cam, January 2014											
1870-S (d)	0	n/a			*(unique, in the Bass Foundation Collection)*							
	Auctions: $687,500, EF-40, October 1982											
1871	1,300	190	56.6	22%	$1,150	$1,650	$2,250	$3,000	$4,750	$9,000	$12,750	$35,000
	Auctions: $9,400, MS-63, November 2014; $6,463, MS-62, October 2014; $3,055, AU-58, October 2015; $1,880, AU-53, September 2015											
1871, Proof	30	5	62.2							$8,000	$16,500	$55,000
	Auctions: $19,550, PF-63Cam, September 2007											
1872	2,000	201	56.5	24%	$1,150	$1,650	$2,250	$3,000	$4,750	$8,500	$12,500	
	Auctions: $7,638, MS-62, August 2014; $7,050, MS-62, November 2014; $4,700, MS-62, February 2015; $3,290, AU-58, January 2015											
1872, Proof	30	22	62.8							$8,000	$16,500	$47,500
	Auctions: $9,400, MS-62, November 2013; $7,638, AU-58, July 2014; $5,581, AU-58, November 2014; $2,115, AU-50, August 2014											

b. Sometime around 1873, the Mint restruck a small number of 1865 three-dollar pieces using an obverse die of 1872 and a newly created reverse with the date slanting up to the right (previously listed in *United States Pattern Coins* as Judd-440). Two examples are known in gold. Versions were also made in copper (Judd-441) for interested collectors. **c.** Varieties showing traces of possible overdating include 1868, 8 Over 7; 1869, 9 Over 8; and 1878, 8 Over 7. **d.** A second example of the 1870-S is rumored to exist in the cornerstone of the San Francisco Mint, but the precise location of the cornerstone has long been unknown.

	Mintage	Cert	Avg	%MS	VF-20	EF-40	AU-50	AU-55	MS-60	MS-62 / PF-60	MS-63 / PF-63	MS-65 / PF-65
1873, Close 3	(e)	51	56.4	20%	$5,500	$9,500	$13,500	$18,500	$30,000	$40,000	$55,000	
	Auctions: $51,700, MS-64, February 2016; $24,675, MS-61, May 2015											
1873, Open 3 (Original), Proof (f)	25	6	64.0							$25,000	$32,500	$70,000
	Auctions: $212,750, PF-65DCam, September 2008; $164,500, PF-65, February 2016											
1873, Close 3, Proof	(g)	0	n/a							$25,000	$37,500	$75,000
	Auctions: $37,375, PF-61, January 2011											
1874	41,800	2,929	56.5	28%	$850	$1,000	$1,050	$1,150	$2,150	$2,750	$4,000	$13,500
	Auctions: $14,100, MS-66, October 2015; $1,998, MS-61, June 2015; $705, AU-50, July 2015; $564, F-15, September 2015											
1874, Proof	20	9	64.3							$12,500	$28,000	$60,000
	Auctions: $54,625, PF-65Cam, January 2012											
1875, Proof (h)	20	8	62.8							$95,000	$165,000	$275,000
	Auctions: $329,000, PF-65, February 2016; $164,500, PF-64, January 2015											
1876, Proof (h)	45	28	63.9							$25,000	$50,000	$85,000
	Auctions: $76,375, PF-65Cam, June 2013											
1877	1,468	36	56.9	25%	$4,500	$7,500	$12,500	$15,000	$30,000	$35,000	$50,000	
	Auctions: $70,500, MS-64, February 2016; $22,325, MS-61, August 2013; $18,800, AU-58, September 2015; $17,625, AU-58, July 2015											
1877, Proof	20	14	63.1							$12,500	$30,000	$55,000
	Auctions: $64,400, PF-65DCam, November 2011											
1878 (c)	82,304	5,388	59.3	57%	$850	$1,000	$1,050	$1,150	$2,150	$2,750	$4,000	$9,500
	Auctions: $23,500, MS-66, January 2015; $999, AU-55, February 2015; $646, EF-40, September 2015; $423, AG-3, February 2015											
1878, Proof	20	8	63.8							$12,500	$27,500	$55,000
	Auctions: $877, PF, June 2014											
1879	3,000	408	60.8	67%	$1,000	$1,300	$2,000	$2,750	$3,750	$5,500	$7,000	$13,500
	Auctions: $19,975, MS-66, February 2015; $4,935, MS-64, July 2015; $2,233, AU-58, October 2015; $881, AU-50, September 2015											
1879, Proof	30	12	64.7							$10,000	$17,000	$42,500
	Auctions: $14,375, PF-63Cam, October 2011											
1880	1,000	122	62.2	89%	$1,450	$2,000	$3,500	$3,750	$5,000	$7,000	$9,000	$20,000
	Auctions: $16,450, MS-65, January 2015; $5,875, MS-62, June 2015; $3,995, MS-62, October 2015; $2,820, MS-60, October 2015											
1880, Proof	36	16	64.0							$10,000	$17,000	$42,500
	Auctions: $51,113, PF, August 2013											
1881	500	105	57.7	40%	$3,000	$5,000	$8,000	$9,500	$12,000	$15,000	$22,500	$50,000
	Auctions: $35,250, MS-64, September 2014; $14,100, MS-62, February 2015; $6,463, AU-55, January 2015; $3,290, EF-40, January 2015											
1881, Proof	54	27	64.1							$10,000	$17,000	$42,500
	Auctions: $32,200, PF-64Cam, January 2011											
1882	1,500	266	59.0	55%	$1,250	$1,750	$2,500	$3,000	$4,000	$6,750	$10,000	$25,000
	Auctions: $22,325, MS-65, August 2015; $3,643, MS-61, August 2015; $2,950, AU-58, September 2015; $705, AU-50, June 2015											
1882, Proof	76	33	63.2							$7,500	$13,500	$35,000
	Auctions: $38,188, PF-65DCam, September 2014; $28,200, PF-64DCam, March 2014											
1883	900	136	58.6	57%	$1,500	$2,500	$3,000	$3,500	$4,500	$6,500	$8,500	$25,000
	Auctions: $21,150, MS-65, June 2015; $3,760, MS-61, February 2015; $4,465, MS-60, July 2015; $2,820, AU-53, January 2015											
1883, Proof	89	39	64.3							$7,500	$13,500	$35,000
	Auctions: $70,500, PF-66Cam+, November 2014; $38,188, PF-65Cam, April 2013											
1884	1,000	52	60.3	67%	$1,750	$2,500	$3,500	$4,000	$5,500	$7,500	$10,000	$25,000
	Auctions: $7,931, MS-62, August 2013											
1884, Proof	106	40	64.0							$7,500	$13,500	$35,000
	Auctions: $30,550, PF-65DCam, September 2014; $23,500, PF-64DCam, August 2013											

c. Varieties showing traces of possible overdating include 1868, 8 Over 7; 1869, 9 Over 8; and 1878, 8 Over 7. e. The mintage figure for the 1873, Close 3, coins is unknown. Research suggests that only Proofs may have been struck (none for circulation), and those perhaps as late as 1879. f. Mint records report 25 Proof coins (with no reference to the style, Open or Close, of the number 3 in the date). The actual mintage may be as high as 100 to 1,000 coins. g. Included in 1873, Open 3 (Original), Proof, mintage figure. h. Proof only.

	Mintage	Cert	Avg	%MS	VF-20	EF-40	AU-50	AU-55	MS-60	MS-62	MS-63	MS-65
										PF-60	PF-63	PF-65
1885	800	154	59.5	56%	$1,650	$2,500	$3,750	$4,500	$6,000	$9,000	$13,500	$27,500
Auctions: $27,025, MS-65, January 2015; $7,638, MS-62+, August 2014; $4,700, AU-58, January 2015; $3,995, AU-58, October 2015												
1885, Proof	110	54	63.5							$7,500	$13,500	$35,000
Auctions: $10,281, PF-63, November 2014; $8,813, PF-62, October 2014; $76,050, PF, September 2013												
1886	1,000	163	58.0	44%	$1,500	$1,950	$2,750	$3,750	$5,000	$7,500	$13,500	$40,000
Auctions: $11,163, MS-63, January 2015; $4,465, MS-61, September 2015; $2,233, MS-60, August 2015; $1,293, AU-50, January 2015												
1886, Proof	142	72	64.1							$7,500	$13,500	$35,000
Auctions: $38,188, PF-65DCam, April 2013												
1887	6,000	220	60.5	67%	$1,000	$1,350	$2,000	$2,250	$3,000	$4,250	$5,500	$14,500
Auctions: $11,750, MS-65, August 2015; $3,995, MS-63, January 2015; $1,410, AU-53, October 2015; $953, AU-50, September 2015												
1887, Proof	160	70	63.8							$7,500	$13,500	$35,000
Auctions: $64,625, PF-67Cam, August 2013												
1888	5,000	516	60.8	72%	$950	$1,250	$1,750	$1,850	$3,000	$4,250	$4,500	$11,500
Auctions: $7,638, MS-65, October 2015; $4,935, MS-64, January 2015; $3,599, MS-63, January 2015; $3,055, MS-61, October 2015												
1888, Proof	291	97	64.1							$7,500	$12,500	$32,500
Auctions: $38,188, PF-66Cam, November 2013; $15,863, PF-64Cam+, November 2014; $9,988, PF-63Cam, October 2015												
1889	2,300	317	60.6	68%	$850	$1,150	$1,450	$1,650	$3,000	$4,250	$4,500	$11,500
Auctions: $15,275, MS-65, February 2015; $5,170, MS-63, January 2015; $3,760, MS-60, October 2015; $2,350, AU-58, October 2015												
1889, Proof	129	51	63.7							$7,500	$12,500	$35,000
Auctions: $25,850, PF-65Cam, January 2014; $7,050, PF-62, November 2014												

Four-Dollar Gold Pieces
1879–1880

AN OVERVIEW OF FOUR-DOLLAR GOLD PIECES

The four-dollar pattern gold coin, or Stella, is not widely collected, simply because of its rarity. For type-set purposes some numismatists opt to acquire a single example of the only issue readily available, Charles Barber's 1879 Flowing Hair, although these are expensive. However, the Coiled Hair style is a different type, much rarer, and a collector with the means might acquire an example of that design as well.

FOR THE COLLECTOR AND INVESTOR: FOUR-DOLLAR GOLD PIECES AS A SPECIALTY

Over the past century perhaps two dozen numismatists have put together complete sets of one of each gold striking of the 1879 and 1880 Flowing Hair and Coiled Hair Stella, this being made possible by collections being dispersed and sold to others, as it is unlikely that even as many as 20 complete sets could exist at one time.

John A. Kasson, a former Iowa congressman, originally proposed the four-dollar gold piece, or "Stella."

STELLA, FLOWING HAIR AND COILED HAIR (1879–1880)

Designers: *Charles E. Barber (Flowing Hair, and common reverse); George T. Morgan (Coiled Hair).*
Weight: *7.0 grams.* **Composition:** *Approximately .857 gold, .042 silver, .100 copper.*
Diameter: *22 mm.* **Edge:** *Reeded.* **Mint:** *Philadelphia.*

Flowing Hair   Coiled Hair

History. The four-dollar gold Stellas of 1879 and 1880 are Proof-only patterns, not regular issues. However, as they have been listed in popular references for decades, collectors have adopted them into the regular gold series. The obverse inscription notes the coins' metallic content in proportions of gold, silver, and copper in the metric system, intended to facilitate their use in foreign countries, where the value could be quickly determined. The Stella was proposed by John A. Kasson (formerly a U.S. representative from Iowa and chairman of the House Committee on Coinage, Weights, and Measures; in 1879 serving as envoy extraordinary and minister plenipotentiary to Austria-Hungary). It is believed that Charles E. Barber designed the Flowing Hair type (as well as the reverse common to both types), and George T. Morgan designed the Coiled Hair. Those dated 1879 were struck for congressional examination; popular testimony of the era suggests that the Flowing Hair Stella became a favorite gift for congressmen's lovers in the Washington demimonde. The only issue produced in quantity was the 1879, Flowing Hair. The others were made in secret and sold privately by Mint officers and employees. The Coiled Hair Stella was not generally known to the numismatic community until they were illustrated in *The Numismatist* in the early 20th century. Stellas are cataloged by their Judd numbers, assigned in the standard reference, *United States Pattern Coins.*

Striking and Sharpness. On nearly all examples the high parts of the hair are flat, often with striations. The other areas of the coin are typically well struck. Tiny planchet irregularities are common.

Availability. The 1879 Flowing Hair is often available on the market—usually in PF–61 to 64, although higher-condition examples come on the market with regularity (as do lightly handled and impaired coins). The 1880 Flowing Hair is typically found in PF–63 or higher. Both years of Coiled Hair Stellas are great rarities; typical grades are PF–63 to 65, with a flat strike on the head and with some tiny planchet flaws.

GRADING STANDARDS

PF-60 to 70 (Proof). *Obverse and Reverse:* PF–60 to 62 coins have extensive hairlines and may have nicks and contact marks. At PF-63, hairlines are prominent, but the mirror surface is very reflective. PF-64 coins have fewer hairlines. At PF-65, hairlines should be minimal and mostly seen only under magnification. There should be no nicks or marks. PF-66 and higher coins should have no marks or hairlines visible to the unaided eye.

1879, Flowing Hair; J-1657. Graded PF-62.

Illustrated coin: A nick above the head and some light friction define the grade, but the coin has nice eye appeal overall.

PF-60 to 70 (Proof). *Obverse and Reverse:* PF–60 to 62 coins have extensive hairlines and may have nicks and contact marks. At PF-63, hairlines are prominent, but the mirror surface is very reflective. PF-64 coins have fewer hairlines. At PF-65, hairlines should be minimal and mostly seen only under magnification. There should be no nicks or marks. PF-66 and higher coins should have no marks or hairlines visible to the unaided eye.

1879, Coiled Hair; J-1660. Graded PF-65.

	Mintage	Cert	Avg	%MS	PF-40	PF-50	PF-60	PF-63	PF-64	PF-65	PF-66	PF-67
1879, Flowing Hair, Proof	425+	233	63.8		$85,000	$95,000	$115,000	$150,000	$175,000	$210,000	$250,000	$350,000
Auctions: $305,500, MS-67, August 2016; $205,625, MS-65, August 2015; $199,750, MS-65, August 2015; $182,125, PF-65, November 2014												
1879, Coiled Hair, Proof	12–15 known	13	65.1				$275,000	$450,000	$500,000	$800,000	$1,100,000	$1,250,000
Auctions: $1,041,300, PF, September 2013												
1880, Flowing Hair, Proof	17–20 known	20	64.9				$175,000	$325,000	$350,000	$450,000	$550,000	$750,000
Auctions: $417,125, MS-65, June 2015; $352,500, MS-65, August 2016; $959,400, PF, September 2013												
1880, Coiled Hair, Proof	8–10 known	12	64.9				$600,000	$775,000	$875,000	$1,250,000	$1,750,000	$2,000,000
Auctions: $2,574,000, PF, September 2013; $1,116,250, PF-65, June 2015												

Note: Many individual high-value rare coins are submitted for certification and grading multiple times over the years, which can inflate the number of certifications above the number of coins actually minted.

Gold Half Eagles ($5)
1795–1929

AN OVERVIEW OF GOLD HALF EAGLES

The half eagle was the first gold coin actually struck for the United States. The five-dollar gold piece was authorized by the Act of April 2, 1792, and the first batch was minted in 1795.

Forming a type set of half eagles is a daunting but achievable challenge—if a collector has the finances and some determination. Examples of the first type, with Capped Bust to Right (conical cap obverse), and with an eagle on a palm branch on the reverse, regularly come up on the market, usually of the date 1795. Typical grades range from EF to lower Mint State levels. Such pieces are scarce, and the demand for them is strong. The next type, the Heraldic Eagle motif, first struck in 1798, but also known from a 1795-dated die used later, was produced through 1807, and is easily enough obtained today. Again, typical grades range from EF to Mint State. MS-63 and better coins are available, but are in the distinct minority.

The short-lived Capped Bust to Left style, 1807–1812, can be found in similar grades, although such pieces did not circulate as extensively, and AU and Mint State levels are the rule, with VF pieces being unusual. Then follows the era of rarities. The Capped Head to Left, stars surrounding head, large diameter, 1813–1829 style is available largely courtesy of the first date of issue, 1813. This is the only date seen with some frequency. When available, examples tend to be choice. The later stretch of this series includes some formidable rarities, among which are the famous 1815 and the even rarer 1822, along with a whole string of other seldom-seen varieties in the 1820s. The same style, but of reduced diameter, 1829–1834, also is rare; examples of the 1830s turn up with some regularity, but these often lack eye appeal. For some reason, half eagles of the early 1830s are often heavily marked and abraded, which is not true at all for coins of the 1820s.

William Woodin, secretary of the Treasury under Franklin D. Roosevelt, built upon the findings of J. Colvin Randall in his research of half eagle die varieties.

Classic Head half eagles, capless and without the motto E PLURIBUS UNUM, first minted in August 1834, are easily enough obtained. Those seen in today's marketplace are usually of the first several dates, and less frequently of 1837 or 1838.

Grades range from VF upward, reflecting their extensive use in circulation. Mint State coins can be found on occasion and are scarce. Choice and gem pieces are rare.

With just a few exceptions, Liberty Head half eagles of the 1839–1866 type without the motto IN GOD WE TRUST are very plentiful in worn grades, including certain of the higher-mintage issues from the popular Charlotte and Dahlonega mints (permitting interesting varieties to be added to a type set). Mint State coins are scarce, and when seen are usually in lower levels such as MS–60 and 62. Gems of any date are rare. Then follow the Liberty Head pieces with the motto IN GOD WE TRUST on the reverse, 1866 through 1908; the earlier years are mostly encountered in worn grades, the later ones are easy enough to find in Mint State. Proofs were made of all Liberty Head half eagle dates, and today they are generally collectible from about 1860 onward.

With two exceptions (1909-O and 1929), the Indian Head half eagles of 1908 to 1929 are common enough in worn grades as well as low Mint State levels, but true gems, accurately graded and with lustrous, frosty surfaces, are quite rare. The field is the highest area of the coin and thus is quite susceptible to scuffs and marks. Probably the most readily available dates in higher grades are 1908 and 1909, with the 1909-D being plentiful due to a hoard that came on the market a generation ago.

FOR THE COLLECTOR AND INVESTOR: GOLD HALF EAGLES AS A SPECIALTY

While in the annals of American numismatics dozens of old-time numismatists collected half eagles by date (or, less often, by date *and* mint), today rarities are so widely scattered and are so expensive that few collectors can rise to the challenge.

Early half eagles can be collected by dates and basic varieties, and also by die varieties. The year 1795 in particular is rich in the latter, and years ago several scholars described such varieties, beginning with J. Colvin Randall in the 1870s, continuing to William H. Woodin in the early 1900s, then Edgar H. Adams, Thomas Ollive Mabbott, and Walter Breen. In more recent times Robert Miller, Harry W. Bass Jr., John Dannreuther, and others have added their research to the literature.

Among early half eagles there are two unique varieties: the 1797 with a 16-star obverse, and the 1797 with a 15-star obverse, both with the Heraldic Eagle reverse, likely struck in 1798. Of the later 1822, just three are known, two of which are in the National Numismatic Collection at the Smithsonian Institution. Of all early half eagles the 1815 was far and away the most famous during the 19th century. (In the 1880s a publication on the Mint Collection stated that the two highlights there were the 1815 half eagle and the unique 1849 double eagle.) At the time the rarer 1822 was not recognized for its elusive nature. Today an estimated 11 examples of the 1815 half eagles exist, mostly in higher circulated grades, including those in museums. There are only two known of the 1825, 5 Over 4, overdate, but it is not at all famous, probably because it is an overdate variety, not a single date on its own. Half eagles of 1826 through 1829 all are rare, with the 1829 being particularly well known. The latter date includes early pieces with regular diameter and later ones with the diameter reduced. Generally, all half eagles from 1815 through 1834 are scarce, some of them particularly so.

Classic Head half eagles of 1834 to 1838 include the scarce 1838-C and 1838-D, the first of the Charlotte and Dahlonega mints respectively; none are prohibitively rare. Generally, the higher-grade pieces are found toward the beginning of the Classic Head series, especially bearing the date 1834.

Liberty Head half eagles are readily available of most dates and mints from 1839 to 1908, save for the one great rarity, the 1854-S, of which just three are known (one is in the Smithsonian). There is a vast panorama of Charlotte and Dahlonega issues through 1861, most of which were made in fairly large quantities, as this was the highest denomination ever struck at each of these mints (larger-capacity presses were not on hand). Accordingly, they are highly collectible today. Some varieties are scarce, but none are completely out of reach. Typical grades range from VF to EF and AU, occasionally Mint State, though not often MS-63 or higher.

Among San Francisco half eagles most of the early issues are scarce, as such pieces circulated extensively and there was no thought to saving numismatic examples. However, there are not many specialists in the field, and for some varieties it can be said that collectors are harder to find than are the coins themselves, yielding the opportunity to purchase truly rare pieces for significantly less than would otherwise be the case. Carson City half eagles were minted beginning in 1870 and continuing intermittently through 1893. Most of the early issues range from scarce to rare, the 1870-CC being particularly well known in this regard. Proofs of the Liberty Head type are generally collectible from the 1860s onward, with most on the market being of the higher-mintage issues of the 1890s and 1900s.

Among Indian Head half eagles, 1908 to 1929, the 1909-O is the rarest of the early coins, and when seen is usually worn. A choice or gem Mint State 1909-O is an incredible rarity. However, enough worn 1909-O half eagles exist, including many brought from overseas hoards in recent decades, that a piece in VF or so grade presents no problem. Half eagles of 1929, of which just 662,000 were minted, were mostly melted, it seems. A couple hundred or so exist today, nearly all of which are Mint State, but nicked and with bagmarks, MS–60 to 62 or 63. Truly high-quality gems are exceedingly rare.

CAPPED BUST TO RIGHT, SMALL EAGLE REVERSE (1795–1798)

Designer: *Robert Scot.* **Weight:** *8.75 grams.*
Composition: *.9167 gold, .0833 silver and copper.*
Diameter: *Approximately 25 mm.* **Edge:** *Reeded.* **Mint:** *Philadelphia.*

Bass-Dannreuther–6.

History. Half eagles of this style, the first federal gold coins, were introduced in July 1795. The obverse features Miss Liberty wearing a conical cap, a design generally called Capped Bust to Right. The reverse depicts a "small" eagle perched on a palm branch. The same motif was used on contemporary $10 gold coins. No Proofs or presentation strikes were made of this type.

Striking and Sharpness. On the obverse, check the star centers and the hair details. On the reverse, check the feathers of the eagle, particularly on the breast. Examine the denticles on both sides. Adjustment marks (from Mint workers filing down overweight planchets to acceptable standards) often are visible, but are not explicitly noted by the grading services.

Availability. Typical grades range from EF to AU and low MS. MS-63 and better coins are rare; when seen, they usually are of the 1795 date (of which many different die varieties exist). Certain varieties are rare, most famously the 1798 with Small Eagle reverse.

GRADING STANDARDS

MS-60 to 70 (Mint State). *Obverse:* At MS-60, some abrasion and contact marks are evident, most noticeably on the hair to the left of Miss Liberty's forehead and on the higher-relief areas of the cap. Luster is present, but may be dull or lifeless, and interrupted in patches. At MS-63, contact marks are few, and abrasion is very light. An MS-65 coin has hardly any abrasion, and contact marks are so minute as to require magnifica-

1795, S Over D in STATES; BD-6. Graded MS-63.

tion. Luster should be full and rich. Grades above MS-65 for this type are more often theoretical than actual—but they do exist and are defined by having fewer marks as perfection is approached. *Reverse:* Comments apply as for the obverse, except that abrasion and contact marks are most noticeable on the breast and head of the eagle. The field area is mainly protected by the eagle, branch, and lettering.

Illustrated coin: This is the error die with the second S over an erroneous D in STATES (which originally read as STATED).

AU-50, 53, 55, 58 (About Uncirculated). *Obverse:* Light wear is seen on the cheek, the hair immediately to the left of the face, and the cap, more at AU-50 than at AU–53 or 55. An AU-58 coin has minimal traces of wear. An AU-50 coin has luster in protected areas among the stars and letters, with little in the open fields or on the portrait. At AU-58, most luster is present in the fields but is worn away on the highest parts of the motifs.

1795; BD-7. Graded AU-58.

Reverse: Comments as preceding, except that the eagle shows light wear on the breast and head in particular, but also at the tip of the wing on the left and elsewhere. Luster ranges from perhaps 40% remaining in protected areas (at AU-50) to nearly full mint bloom (at AU-58).

EF-40, 45 (Extremely Fine). *Obverse:* Wear is evident all over the portrait, with some loss of detail in the hair to the left of Miss Liberty's face. Excellent detail remains in low-relief areas of the hair, such as the front curl and at the back of her head. The stars show wear, as do the date and letters. Luster, if present at all, is minimal and in protected areas. *Reverse:* Wear is greater than on an About Uncirculated coin. The breast, neck, and legs of the

1795; BD-4. Graded EF-40.

eagle lack nearly all feather detail. More wear is seen on the edges of the wing. Some traces of luster may be seen, more so at EF-45 than at EF-40.

VF-20, 30 (Very Fine). *Obverse:* The higher-relief areas of hair are well worn at VF-20, less so at VF-30. The stars are flat at their centers. *Reverse:* Wear is greater, the eagle is flat in most areas, and about 40% to 60% of the wing feathers can be seen.

The Capped Bust to Right half eagle with Small Eagle reverse is seldom collected in grades lower than VF-20.

Illustrated coin: While exhibiting typical wear for a VF-20 coin, this specimen also shows rim damage from having been mounted as jewelry at some point in time.

1795. Graded VF-20.

1796, 6 Over 5

1797, 15-Star Obverse

1797, 16-Star Obverse

	Mintage	Cert	Avg	%MS	F-12	VF-20	EF-40	AU-50	AU-55	MS-60	MS-62	MS-63	MS-64
1795	8,707	224	55.1	29%	$21,500	$25,000	$32,500	$40,000	$47,500	$75,000	$100,000	$165,000	$300,000 (a)
Auctions: $587,500, MS-66H, January 2015; $64,625, MS-61, February 2013; $64,625, AU-58, August 2014; $52,875, AU-58, August 2014													
1795, S Over D in STATES (b)	(c)	0	n/a					$42,000	$50,000	$77,500			
Auctions: $345,000, MS-65PL, July 2009													
1796, 6 Over 5	6,196	37	56.6	43%	$20,000	$25,000	$40,000	$60,000	$75,000	$110,000	$150,000	$225,000	$350,000
Auctions: $67,563, AU-58, February 2014; $45,531, AU-55, October 2014; $52,875, AU-53, August 2014													
1797, All kinds	3,609												
1797, 15-Star Obverse		4	56.5	25%	$27,000	$45,000	$65,000	$125,000	$155,000	$275,000			
Auctions: $235,000, AU-58, August 2015: $152,750, AU-53, January 2014													
1797, 16-Star Obverse		6	56.7	17%	$25,000	$40,000	$55,000	$87,500	$145,000	$275,000			
Auctions: $411,250, MS-61, August 2013													
1798, Small Eagle (d)	*unknown*	2	50.0	0%		$500,000	$650,000	$850,000	$1,250,000				
Auctions: $1,175,000, AU-55, September 2015													

a. Value in MS-65 is $525,000. **b.** The final S in STATES is punched over an erroneous D. **c.** Included in 1795, Small Eagle, mintage figure. **d.** The reverse of the 1798, Small Eagle, was from a 1795 die. The obverse has an arched die crack or flaw beneath the date. 7 examples are known, and the finest is an AU-55 from the collection of King Farouk of Egypt.

CAPPED BUST TO RIGHT, HERALDIC EAGLE REVERSE (1795–1807)

Designer: *Robert Scot.* **Weight:** *8.75 grams.*
Composition: *.9167 gold, .0833 silver and copper.*
Diameter: *Approximately 25 mm.* **Edge:** *Reeded.* **Mint:** *Philadelphia.*

BD-15.

History. For this type, the obverse design is the same as that of the preceding. The reverse features a heraldic eagle, as used on other silver and gold coins of the era. Some half eagles of the Heraldic Eagle Reverse design are dated 1795, but these were actually struck in 1798, from a leftover obverse coinage die. The *Encyclopedia of U.S. Gold Coins, 1795–1933* notes that "No Proofs were made, but one 1795 half eagle with a Heraldic Eagle reverse has been certified as a Specimen."

Striking and Sharpness. On the obverse, check the star centers and the hair details. On the reverse, check the upper part of the shield, the lower part of the eagle's neck, the eagle's wing, the stars above the eagle, and the clouds. Inspect the denticles on both sides. Adjustment marks (from overweight planchets being filed down to correct standards by Mint workers) can be an aesthetic problem and are not explicitly identified by the grading services.

Availability. Although there are many rare die varieties, as a type this half eagle is plentiful. Typical grades are EF to lower MS. MS-63 and higher coins are seen with some frequency and usually are dated from 1802 to 1807. Sharply struck coins without adjustment marks are in the minority.

GRADING STANDARDS

MS-60 to 70 (Mint State). *Obverse:* At MS-60, some abrasion and contact marks are evident, most noticeably on the hair to the left of Miss Liberty's forehead and on the higher-relief areas of the cap. Luster is present, but may be dull or lifeless, and interrupted in patches. At MS-63, contact marks are few, and abrasion is very light. An MS-65 coin has hardly any abrasion, and contact marks are so minute as to require magnifica-

1802, 2 Over 1. Graded MS-62.

tion. Luster should be full and rich. Grades above MS-65 are not often seen but are defined by having fewer marks as perfection is approached. *Reverse:* Comments apply as for the obverse, except that abrasion and contact marks are most noticeable on the upper part of the eagle and the clouds. The field area is complex, with not much open space, given the stars above the eagle, the arrows and olive branch, and other features. Accordingly, marks are not as noticeable as on the obverse.

Illustrated coin: This is an attractive coin with rich luster. Some friction is visible on the higher points and in the obverse field.

AU-50, 53, 55, 58 (About Uncirculated). *Obverse:* Light wear is seen on the cheek, the hair immediately to the left of the face, and the cap, more at AU-50 than at AU–53 or 55. An AU-58 coin has minimal traces of wear. An AU-50 coin has luster in protected areas among the stars and letters, with little in the open fields or on the portrait. At AU-58, most luster is present in the fields, but is worn away on the highest parts of the motifs.

1804. Graded AU-58.

Reverse: Comments as preceding, except that the eagle's neck, the tips and top of the wings, the clouds, and the tail now show noticeable wear, as do other features. Luster ranges from perhaps 40% remaining in protected areas (at AU-50) to nearly full mint bloom (at AU-58). Often the reverse of this type retains much more luster than the obverse.

   Illustrated coin: An abrasion in the left obverse field keeps this otherwise lustrous and attractive coin below the Mint State level.

EF-40, 45 (Extremely Fine). *Obverse:* Wear is evident all over the portrait, with some loss of detail in the hair to the left of Miss Liberty's face. Excellent detail remains in low-relief areas of the hair, such as the front curl and at the back of her head. The stars show wear, as do the date and letters. Luster, if present at all, is minimal and in protected areas. *Reverse:* Wear is greater than on an About Uncirculated coin. The neck lacks feather detail on its

1804, Small 8 Over Large 8; BD-7. Graded EF-45.

highest points. Feathers have lost some detail near the edges of the wings, and some areas of the horizontal lines in the shield may be blended together. Some traces of luster may be seen, more so at EF-45 than at EF-40. Overall, the reverse appears to be in a slightly higher grade than the obverse.

VF-20, 30 (Very Fine). *Obverse:* The higher-relief areas of hair are well worn at VF-20, less so at VF-30. The stars are flat at their centers. *Reverse:* Wear is greater, including on the shield and wing feathers. The star centers are flat. Other areas have lost detail as well. E PLURIBUS UNUM may be light or worn away in areas.

   The Capped Bust to Right half eagle with Heraldic Eagle reverse is seldom collected in grades lower than VF-20.

1798, Large 8, 13-Star Reverse; BD-4. Graded VF-20.

1797, 16-Star Obverse   1797, 15-Star Obverse

1797, 7 Over 5   1798, Small 8   1798, Large 8

1798, 13-Star Reverse   1798, 14-Star Reverse   1799, Small Reverse Stars   1799, Large Reverse Stars

	Mintage	Cert	Avg	%MS	F-12	VF-20	EF-40	AU-50	AU-55	MS-60	MS-62	MS-63	MS-64
1795	(a)	19	60.2	68%	$20,000	$25,000	$35,000	$60,000	$75,000	$100,000	$150,000	$200,000	$300,000
Auctions: No auction records available.													
1797, 7 Over 5	(a)	4	58.8	50%	$22,500	$35,000	$45,000	$75,000	$115,000	$200,000			
Auctions: $126,500, AU-58, September 2005													
1797, 16-Star Obverse	(a)	0	n/a		*(unique, in Smithsonian's National Numismatic Collection)*								
Auctions: No auction records available.													
1797, 15-Star Obverse	(a)	0	n/a		*(unique, in Smithsonian's National Numismatic Collection)*								
Auctions: No auction records available.													
1798, All kinds	24,867												
1798, Small 8		24	56.3	25%	$6,000	$8,000	$12,500	$18,500	$22,000	$32,500	$50,000	$77,500	
Auctions: $18,800, AU-53, April 2014													
1798, Large 8, 13-Star Reverse		185	59.3	57%	$5,000	$6,000	$10,000	$17,000	$21,000	$30,000	$40,000	$60,000	
Auctions: $21,150, AU-55, August 2014; $19,975, AU-55, November 2014; $16,450, AU-53, August 2014; $12,925, AU-50, January 2014													
1798, Large 8, 14-Star Reverse		185	59.3	57%	$5,500	$7,000	$15,000	$25,000	$35,000	$100,000			
Auctions: $32,900, AU-55, August 2014; $25,850, AU-55, October 2014; $25,850, AU, February 2014													
1799, All kinds	7,451												
1799, Small Reverse Stars		10	59.7	50%	$5,000	$7,000	$10,000	$14,000	$18,000	$27,500	$37,500	$65,000	$100,000
Auctions: $47,000, MS-62, February 2013; $19,975, AU-58, August 2014; $13,513, AU-55, September 2014; $4,711, EF-40, August 2014													
1799, Large Reverse Stars		17	58.1	59%	$5,000	$7,000	$10,000	$14,000	$18,000	$27,500	$37,500	$65,000	$100,000
Auctions: $70,500, MS-63, January 2014; $16,450, AU-55, August 2014; $11,750, AU-53, August 2014													

a. The 1795 and 1797 Heraldic Eagle half eagles are thought to have been struck in 1798 and are included in that year's mintage figure of 24,867.

1800, Pointed 1

1800, Blunt 1

1800, 8 Arrows

1800, 9 Arrows

1802, 2 Over 1
FS-G5-1802/1-301.

1803, 3 Over 2

1804, Small 8

**1804, Small 8
Over Large 8**

**1806, Pointed-Top 6,
Stars 8 and 5**

**Closeup of
Pointed-Top 6**

**1806, Round-Top 6,
Stars 7 and 6**

**Closeup of
Round-Top 6**

	Mintage	Cert	Avg	%MS	F-12	VF-20	EF-40	AU-50	AU-55	MS-60	MS-62	MS-63	MS-64
1800	37,628	258	56.7	40%	$4,500	$5,500	$7,750	$11,000	$12,500	$17,500	$22,500	$40,000	$85,000
Auctions: $16,100, MS-62, April 2012; $11,750, AU-55, January 2015													
1800, Pointed 1 (b)	(c)	0	n/a					$21,000	$24,000	$28,000			
Auctions: $25,850, MS-63, November 2014; $21,150, MS-62, November 2013; $12,338, MS-61, October 2014													
1800, 9 Arrows (d)	(c)	0	n/a					$17,500	$21,500				
Auctions: No auction records available.													
1802, 2 Over 1	53,176	274	57.5	39%	$4,000	$5,000	$7,000	$10,000	$12,000	$16,000	$18,500	$35,000	$57,500 (e)
Auctions: $58,750, MS-64, January 2014; $16,450, MS-62, October 2014; $11,750, AU-58, September 2014; $5,141, AU, March 2015													
1803, 3 Over 2	33,506	320	57.4	44%	$4,000	$5,000	$7,000	$10,000	$12,500	$19,500	$25,000	$42,500	$80,000 (f)
Auctions: $12,925, MS-62, October 2014; $14,100, MS-62, November 2014; $20,563, MS-62, October 2013; $10,575, AU-58, August 2014													
1804, All kinds	30,475												
1804, Small 8		36	60.2	67%	$4,000	$5,000	$7,000	$10,000	$11,500	$16,500	$22,000	$32,500	$60,000
Auctions: $18,800, MS-62, January 2014; $10,575, AU-58, August 2014; $12,925, AU-55, August 2014; $5,875, AU-50, August 2014													
1804, Small 8 Over Large 8 (g)		64	59.4	56%	$4,000	$5,000	$7,000	$10,500	$12,500	$19,500	$25,000	$42,500	$75,000
Auctions: $32,900, MS-63, January 2014; $8,813, AU-53, August 2014; $8,813, AU-53, November 2014; $5,581, AU-50, September 2014													
1805	33,183	185	59.3	57%	$4,500	$5,500	$7,750	$11,000	$12,500	$16,000	$21,000	$35,000	$60,000 (h)
Auctions: $15,275, MS-62, August 2014; $14,688, MS-61, November 2014; $16,450, MS, February 2014; $12,925, AU-58, November 2014													
1806, Pointed-Top 6	9,676	75	57.4	51%	$4,000	$5,000	$7,000	$10,000	$12,000	$16,500	$20,000	$36,500	$60,000 (h)
Auctions: $15,275, MS-61, August 2014; $15,275, MS-60, August 2014; $12,925, MS-60, February 2016; $4,406, AU, March 2015													
1806, Rounded-Top 6	54,417	182	58.5	53%	$4,000	$5,000	$7,000	$10,000	$11,500	$15,500	$19,000	$32,500	$50,000 (h)
Auctions: $111,625, MS-65, March 2013; $48,469, MS-64, August 2014; $19,388, MS-62, August 2014; $18,213, MS-62, October 2014													

b. 4 to 6 examples are known. **c.** Included in 1800 mintage figure. **d.** 18 to 25 examples are known. **e.** Value in MS-65 is $135,000.
f. Value in MS-65 is $125,000. **g.** Created when the engraver mistakenly used an 8 punch intended for $10 gold coins, then corrected the error by overpunching with a much smaller 8. **h.** Value in MS-65 is $120,000.

**1807, Small
Reverse Stars**

**1807, Large
Reverse Stars**

	Mintage	Cert	Avg	%MS	F-12	VF-20	EF-40	AU-50	AU-55	MS-60	MS-62	MS-63	MS-64
1807, All kinds	32,488												
1807, Small Reverse Stars		0	n/a		$5,000	$6,500	$8,000	$10,000	$11,500	$15,500	$18,000	$32,500	$50,000
Auctions: $44,563, MS-64, January 2012													
1807, Large Reverse Stars		0	n/a		$5,000	$6,500	$8,000	$10,000	$11,500	$15,500	$18,000	$32,500	$50,000
Auctions: $21,850, MS-63, January 2012; $1,880, F-12, October 2015													

DRAPED BUST TO LEFT (1807–1812)

Designer: *John Reich.* **Weight:** *8.75 grams.*
Composition: *.9167 gold, .0833 silver and copper.*
Diameter: *Approximately 25 mm.* **Edge:** *Reeded.* **Mint:** *Philadelphia.*

BD-8.

History. This half eagle motif, designed by John Reich and stylistically related to his Capped Bust half dollar of 1807, was used for several years in the early 1800s. Quantities minted were high, and the coins saw wide circulation. No Proof examples were made of this type.

Striking and Sharpness. The striking usually is quite good and is significantly better than on earlier half eagle types. Adjustment marks (from overweight planchets being filed down to acceptable weight) are seen only occasionally. On the obverse, check the star centers and the hair details. On the reverse, check the eagle, particularity at the shield and the lower left. Examine the denticles on both sides.

Availability. After 1821 gold coins of this standard no longer circulated, as their bullion value exceeded their face value. Accordingly, they never sustained extensive wear, and nearly all examples are in EF or higher grades (coins used as pocket pieces or incorporated into jewelry are exceptions). As a type this issue is readily available in grades up to MS-63, although MS–64 and 65 coins are seen on occasion. Most have excellent eye appeal.

GRADING STANDARDS

MS-60 to 70 (Mint State). *Obverse:* At MS-60, some abrasion and contact marks are seen on the cheek, the hair below the LIBERTY inscription, and the highest-relief folds of the cap. Luster is present, but may be dull or lifeless, and interrupted in patches. At MS-63, contact marks are few, and abrasion is very light. At MS-64, abrasion is even less. An MS-65 coin has hardly any abrasion, and contact marks are minute. Luster should be

1808. Graded MS-60.

full and rich and is often more intense on the obverse. Grades above MS-65 are defined by having fewer marks as perfection is approached. *Reverse:* Comments apply as for the obverse, except that abrasion is most noticeable on the eagle's neck and the highest area of the wings.

Illustrated coin: This attractive Draped Bust to Left half eagle has nice luster.

AU-50, 53, 55, 58 (About Uncirculated). *Obverse:* Light wear is seen on the cheek and the higher-relief areas of the hair and cap. Friction and scattered marks are in the field, ranging from extensive at AU-50 to minimal at AU-58. Luster may be seen in protected areas, minimal at AU-50 but more evident at AU-58. On an AU-58 coin the field retains some luster as well. *Reverse:* Comments as preceding, except that the eagle's neck, the

1811, Tall 5. Graded AU-58.

top of the wings, the leaves, and the arrowheads now show noticeable wear, as do other features. Luster ranges from perhaps 40% remaining in protected areas (at AU-50) to nearly full mint bloom (at AU-58). Often the reverse of this type retains much more luster than the obverse, as the motto, eagle, and lettering protect the surrounding flat areas.

Illustrated coin: This lustrous example is well struck.

EF-40, 45 (Extremely Fine). *Obverse:* More wear is seen on the portrait, the hair, the cap, and the drapery near the clasp. Luster is minimal or nonexistent at EF-40, and may be slight at EF-45. *Reverse:* Wear is more extensive on the eagle, including the top of the wings, the head, the top of the shield, and the claws. Some traces of luster may be seen, more so at EF-45 than at EF-40.

1807; BD-8. Graded EF-40.

VF-20, 30 (Very Fine). *Obverse:* Wear on the portrait has reduced the hair detail, especially to the right of the face and the top of the head, but much can still be seen. *Reverse:* Wear on the eagle is greater, and details of feathers near the shield and near the top of the wings are weak or missing. All other features show wear, but most are fairly sharp. Generally, Draped Bust gold coins at this grade level lack eye appeal.

1807; BD-8. Graded VF-20.

The Draped Bust to Left half eagle is seldom collected in grades lower than VF-20.

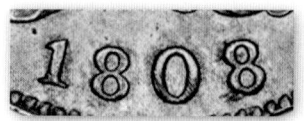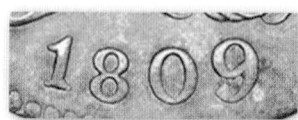

| 1808, 8 Over 7 | 1808, Normal Date | 1809, 9 Over 8 |

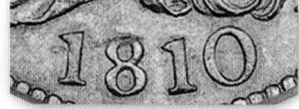

| 1810, Small Date | 1810, Large Date |

| Small 5 | Large 5 | Tall 5 |

	Mintage	Cert	Avg	%MS	F-12	VF-20	EF-40	AU-50	AU-55	MS-60	MS-62	MS-63	MS-64
1807	51,605	248	58.6	52%	$3,250	$4,750	$5,750	$8,250	$9,750	$14,000	$16,500	$26,000	$38,500 (a)
Auctions: $76,375, MS-65, April 2013; $19,975, MS-63, October 2014; $11,750, MS-62, August 2014; $12,338, MS-62, November 2014													
1808, All kinds	55,578												
1808, 8 Over 7		48	58.6	56%	$3,250	$5,000	$6,500	$9,000	$11,500	$18,500	$25,000	$35,000	$65,000
Auctions: $24,675, MS-62, August 2014; $19,388, MS-61, June 2014; $6,463, EF-45, November 2015													
1808		181	58.1	52%	$3,000	$4,500	$5,500	$8,000	$9,500	$13,500	$15,500	$28,500	$35,500 (b)
Auctions: $25,850, MS-63, March 2013; $12,925, MS-60, October 2014; $4,113, MS, March 2015; $7,638, AU-58, November 2014													
1809, 9 Over 8	33,875	184	58.6	55%	$3,000	$4,500	$5,500	$9,250	$10,500	$14,000	$16,500	$27,500	$52,500
Auctions: $51,406, MS-64, January 2014; $11,750, MS-61, August 2014; $8,001, AU-53, August 2014													
1810, All kinds	100,287												
1810, Small Date, Small 5		6	54.8	33%	$20,000	$40,000	$55,000	$75,000	$80,000	$100,000	$125,000		
Auctions: $19,388, 88, November 2015: $18,800, AU-50, January 2014													
1810, Small Date, Tall 5		80	57.6	51%	$3,000	$4,500	$5,500	$8,000	$9,500	$14,000	$16,000	$29,000	$55,000
Auctions: $58,750, MS-64, August 2016; $12,925, MS-62, January 2014; $12,925, MS-62, August 2014; $12,925, AU-58, September 2014													
1810, Large Date, Small 5		83	57.7	53%	$30,000	$55,000	$75,000	$110,000	$130,000	$200,000			
Auctions: No auction records available.													
1810, Large Date, Large 5		258	59.2	63%	$3,000	$4,500	$5,500	$8,000	$9,500	$13,000	$14,500	$26,000	$40,000 (c)
Auctions: $32,900, MS-64, January 2014; $11,750, MS-62, November 2014; $8,813, AU-58, August 2014; $9,988, AU-55, March 2015													

a. Value in MS-65 is $100,000. **b.** Value in MS-65 is $127,500. **c.** Value in MS-65 is $100,000.

	Mintage	Cert	Avg	%MS	F-12	VF-20	EF-40	AU-50	AU-55	MS-60	MS-62	MS-63	MS-64
1811, All kinds	99,581												
1811, Small 5		27	55.7	44%	$3,000	$4,500	$5,500	$8,000	$9,500	$13,000	$14,500	$26,000	$40,000 (c)
	Auctions: $64,625, MS-64, August 2013; $10,575, MS-61, July 2014; $4,994, MS-60, October 2014; $3,836, AU-50, September 2014												
1811, Tall 5		45	60.1	62%	$3,000	$4,500	$5,500	$8,000	$9,500	$13,000	$14,500	$26,000	$40,000 (c)
	Auctions: $76,375, MS-65, August 2013; $9,400, AU-58, August 2014; $1,880, EF-40, July 2014; $3,055, EF-40, September 2014												
1812	58,087	222	59.0	64%	$3,000	$4,500	$5,500	$8,000	$9,500	$13,000	$14,500	$26,000	$40,000
	Auctions: $30,550, MS-64, November 2014; $61,688, MS-64, August 2013; $4,465, MS-60, August 2015												

c. Value in MS-65 is $100,000.

CAPPED HEAD TO LEFT (1813–1834)

Designer: *John Reich (design modified by William Kneass in 1829).*
Weight: *8.75 grams.* **Composition:** *.9167 gold, .0833 silver and copper.*
Diameter: *25 mm (reduced to 23.8 mm in 1829).* **Edge:** *Reeded.* **Mint:** *Philadelphia.*

Circulation Strike
BD-1.

Proof
BD-3.

History. Half eagles of the Capped Head to Left design are divided into issues of 1813 to 1829 (with a larger diameter), and issues of 1829 to 1834 (with a smaller diameter, and smaller letters, dates, and stars). Those dated 1813 to 1815 are in bold relief and sometimes collected as a separate variety.

Striking and Sharpness. On the obverse, check the star centers and the hair details (these details are usually less distinct on the 1829–1834 smaller-diameter coins). On the reverse, check the eagle. Most examples are well struck. Adjustment marks (from overweight planchets being filed down to acceptable specifications at the mint) are not often encountered. Proof coins were struck on a limited basis for inclusion in sets and for numismatists. Over the years some prooflike Mint State pieces have been classified as Proofs.

Availability. The 1813 and 1814, 4 Over 3, are seen with some frequency and constitute the main supply available for assembling type sets. Other dates range from very rare to extremely rare, with the 1822 topping the list (just three are known, two of which are in the Smithsonian Institution). As gold coins did not circulate after 1821, issues of 1813 to 1820 are usually seen in high-level AU or in MS, and those of the 1820s in MS. The half eagles of the early 1830s are exceptions; these usually show light wear and are much rarer in high-level MS. All Proofs are exceedingly rare.

GRADING STANDARDS

MS-60 to 70 (Mint State). *Obverse:* At MS-60, some abrasion and contact marks are seen on the cheek, the hair below the LIBERTY inscription, and the highest-relief folds of the cap. Luster is present, but may be dull or lifeless, and interrupted in patches. At MS-63, contact marks are few, and abrasion is very light. At MS-64, abrasion is even less. An MS-65 coin has hardly any abrasion, and

1832, 13 Obverse Stars; BD-1. Graded MS-63.

contact marks are minute. Luster should be full and rich and is often more intense on the obverse. Grades above MS-65 are defined by having fewer marks as perfection is approached. *Reverse:* Comments apply as for the obverse, except that abrasion is most noticeable on the eagle's neck and the highest area of the wings.

AU-50, 53, 55, 58 (About Uncirculated). *Obverse:* Light wear is seen on the cheek and the higher-relief areas of the hair and cap. Friction and scattered marks are in the field, ranging from extensive at AU-50 to minimal at AU-58. Luster may be seen in protected areas, minimal at AU-50 but more evident at AU-58. On an AU-58 coin the field retains some luster as well. *Reverse:* Comments as preceding, except that the eagle's neck, the

1813; BD-1. Graded AU-50.

top of the wings, the leaves, and the arrowheads now show noticeable wear, as do other features. Luster ranges from perhaps 40% remaining in protected areas (at AU-50) to nearly full mint bloom (at AU-58). Often the reverse of this type retains much more luster than the obverse, as the motto, eagle, and lettering protect the surrounding flat areas.

EF-40, 45 (Extremely Fine). *Obverse:* More wear is seen on the portrait, the hair, the cap, and the drapery near the clasp. Luster is minimal or nonexistent at EF-40, and may be slight at EF-45. *Reverse:* Wear is more extensive on the eagle, including the top of the wings, the head, the top of the shield, and the claws. Some traces of luster may be seen, more so at EF-45 than at EF-40.

The Capped Head half eagle is seldom collected in grades lower than EF-40.

1813; BD-1. Graded EF-45.

PF-60 to 70 (Proof). *Obverse and Reverse:* PF–60 to 62 coins have extensive hairlines and may have nicks and contact marks. At PF-63, hairlines are prominent, but the mirror surface is very reflective. PF-64 coins have fewer hairlines. At PF-65, hairlines should be minimal and mostly seen only under magnification. There should be no nicks or marks. PF-66 and higher coins should have no marks or hairlines visible to the unaided eye.

1829, Small Date, Reduced Diameter; BD-2. Proof.

1820, Curved-Base 2	1820, Square-Base 2	1820, Small Letters	1820, Large Letters

	Mintage	Cert	Avg	%MS	F-12	VF-20	EF-40	AU-50	AU-55	MS-60	MS-62	MS-63	MS-64
											PF-63	PF-64	PF-65
1813	95,428	281	58.7	56%	$4,750	$5,750	$7,000	$10,000	$11,000	$15,000	$17,500	$28,500	$40,000 (a)
Auctions: $49,350, MS-64, January 2013; $15,863, MS-62, August 2014; $6,463, MS-60, September 2014; $9,400, AU-55, October 2014													
1814, 4 Over 3	15,454	62	59.8	66%	$5,500	$7,000	$9,000	$12,000	$13,000	$20,000	$27,500	$40,000	$60,000
Auctions: $14,688, AU-58, January 2014; $11,764, AU-55, November 2014													
1815 (b)	635	4	57.8	50%			$200,000	$275,000	$325,000	$400,000	$500,000	$600,000	
Auctions: $822,500, MS-65, February 2016; $460,000, MS-64, January 2009													
1818, All kinds	48,588												
1818		38	59.5	61%	$5,000	$6,000	$7,500	$15,500	$18,500	$25,000	$30,000	$47,000	$75,000 (c)
Auctions: $38,188, MS-62, November 2014; $19,388, MS-62, November 2014; $15,863, AU-50, September 2013													
1818, STATESOF one word		41	60.3	71%	$5,500	$7,000	$9,000	$14,000	$17,000	$22,500	$30,000	$50,000	$77,500
Auctions: $23,500, MS-62, January 2014; $4,994, AU-50, September 2014													
1818, I Over O		6	62.5	100%	$5,000	$6,500	$8,000	$11,000	$15,000	$30,000	$35,000	$70,000	$75,000 (d)
Auctions: $135,125, MS-65, January 2014													
1819, All kinds	51,723												
1819		3	51.7	33%			$65,000	$80,000	$95,000	$150,000	$200,000		
Auctions: $38,188, AU-50, August 2014													
1819, I Over O		7	55.6	29%			$50,000	$65,000	$80,000	$125,000	$180,000	$225,000	
Auctions: $67,563, AU-55, January 2014													
1820, All kinds	263,806												
1820, Curved-Base 2, Small Letters		1	62.0	100%	$5,250	$7,000	$11,000	$14,000	$20,000	$27,500	$32,500	$65,000	$170,000
Auctions: $172,500, MS-64, January 2012													
1820, Curved-Base 2, Large Letters		1	64.0	100%	$5,000	$6,750	$8,500	$12,500	$17,500	$25,000	$27,500	$37,500	$75,000
Auctions: $19,975, MS-60, January 2014; $11,750, MS-60, September 2014													
1820, Square-Base 2		5	62.2	100%	$5,500	$7,000	$11,000	$16,000	$20,000	$27,500	$32,500	$47,500	$65,000
Auctions: $31,725, MS-63, January 2014													
1820, Square-Base 2, Proof (e)	2–3	1	64.0		*(unique, in the Bass Foundation Collection)*								
Auctions: No auction records available.													
1821	34,641	5	57.0	60%	$25,000	$35,000	$60,000	$100,000	$150,000	$215,000	$265,000	$400,000	
Auctions: $540,000, MS-63+, January 2015; $141,000, AU-55, January 2014													
1821, Proof (f)	3–5	0	n/a		*(extremely rare)*								
Auctions: No auction records available.													
1822 (g)	17,796	2	45.0	0%					$8,000,000				
Auctions: No auction records available.													
1822, Proof (h)	unknown	0	n/a		*(extremely rare)*								
Auctions: No auction records available.													

a. Value in MS-65 is $95,000. **b.** 11 examples are known. **c.** Value in MS-65 is $135,000. **d.** Value in MS-65 is $140,000. **e.** Some experts have questioned the Proof status of this unique piece; the surface of the coin is reflective, but it is not as convincing as other true Proofs of the type. Prior claims that as many as four Proofs exist of this date have not been substantiated. **f.** 2 examples are known. One is in the Harry W. Bass Jr. Foundation Collection, and another is in the Smithsonian's National Numismatic Collection. **g.** 3 examples are known. **h.** 3 examples are known, though the Proof status of these pieces has been questioned.

1825, 5 Over Partial 4

1825, 5 Over 4

1828, 8 Over 7

1829, Large Date
BD-1.

1829, Small Date
BD-2.

	Mintage	Cert	Avg	%MS	F-12	VF-20	EF-40	AU-50	AU-55	MS-60	MS-62	MS-63	MS-64
											PF-63	PF-64	PF-65
1823	14,485	25	56.8	44%	$8,500	$10,000	$15,000	$20,000	$25,000	$35,000	$40,000	$55,000	$75,000
	Auctions: $82,250, MS-64, January 2014; $29,375, MS-62, August 2014												
1823, Proof (i)	unknown	0	n/a										
	Auctions: No auction records available.												
1824	17,340	16	60.4	63%	$14,000	$20,000	$30,000	$37,500	$50,000	$75,000	$95,000	$130,000	$150,000 (j)
	Auctions: $199,750, MS-65, January 2014												
1824, Proof (k)	unknown	0	n/a										
	Auctions: No auction records available.												
1825, 5 Over Partial 4 (l)	29,060	7	61.4	86%	$14,000	$20,000	$30,000	$37,500	$47,500	$75,000	$100,000	$130,000	$150,000
	Auctions: $99,875, MS-61, January 2014												
1825, 5 Over 4 (m)	(n)	2	56.5	50%			$550,000	$750,000					
	Auctions: $940,000, MS-64, May 2016: $690,000, AU-50, July 2008												
1825, 5 Over Partial 4, Proof (o)	1–2	0	n/a		*(unique, in the Smithsonian's National Numismatic Collection)*								
	Auctions: No auction records available.												
1826	18,069	6	63.8	100%	$10,000	$15,000	$20,000	$30,000	$40,000	$70,000	$80,000	$115,000	
	Auctions: $546,000, MS-66, January 2015; $763,750, MS-66, January 2014												
1826, Proof	2–4	0	n/a		*(unique, in the Smithsonian's National Numismatic Collection)*								
	Auctions: No auction records available.												
1827	24,913	14	62.9	93%	$20,000	$25,000	$30,000	$40,000	$50,000	$65,000	$75,000	$125,000	$150,000
	Auctions: $141,000, MS-64, January 2014												
1827, Proof (p)	unknown	0	n/a										
	Auctions: No auction records available.												
1828, 8 Over 7 (q)	(r)	3	63.3	100%				$100,000	$175,000	$300,000	$400,000	$500,000	$750,000
	Auctions: $632,500, MS-64, January 2012												
1828	28,029	3	60.7	67%		$50,000	$70,000	$90,000	$125,000	$200,000	$225,000	$325,000	$450,000
	Auctions: $499,375, MS-64, April 2013												
1828, Proof	1–2	0	n/a		*(unique, in the Smithsonian's National Numismatic Collection)*								
	Auctions: No auction records available.												
1829, Large Date	57,442	2	66.0	100%			—	—		$225,000	$300,000	$425,000	$600,000
	Auctions: $763,750, MS-66+, May 2016												
1829, Large Date, Proof	2–4	0	n/a								$1,400,000		
	Auctions: $1,380,000, PF-64, January 2012												

i. The only auction references for a Proof 1823 half eagle are from 1885 and 1962. Neither coin (assuming they are not the same specimen) has been examined by today's standards to confirm its Proof status. **j.** Value in MS-65 is $275,000. **k.** No 1824 Proof half eagles are known to exist, despite previous claims that the Smithsonian's Mint collection specimen (actually an MS-62 circulation strike) is a Proof. **l.** Sometimes called 1825, 5 Over 1. **m.** 2 examples are known. **n.** Included in circulation-strike 1825, 5 Over Partial 4, mintage figure. **o.** The Smithsonian's example is a PF-67 with a mirrored obverse and frosty reverse. A second example, reported to have resided in King Farouk's collection, has not been confirmed. **p.** Two purported 1827 Proofs have been revealed to be circulation strikes: the Smithsonian's example is an MS-64, and the Bass example is prooflike. **q.** 5 examples are known. **r.** Included in circulation-strike 1828 mintage figure.

Small 5 D.

Large 5 D.

1832, Curved-Base 2, 12-Star Obverse

1832, Square-Base 2, 13-Star Obverse

1833, Large Date

1833, Small Date

1834, Plain 4

1834, Crosslet 4

	Mintage	Cert	Avg	%MS	F-12	VF-20	EF-40	AU-50	AU-55	MS-60 / PF-63	MS-62 / PF-64	MS-63 / PF-65
1829, Sm Dt, Reduced Diameter	(a)	2	61.5	100%	$60,000	$90,000	$150,000	$200,000	$250,000	$375,000	$450,000	$500,000
Auctions: $881,250, MS-65+, May 2016; $431,250, MS-61, January 2012												
1829, Small Date, Proof (b)	2–4	0	n/a		*(extremely rare)*							
Auctions: $881,250, MS-65, May 2016												
1830, Small or Large 5 D. (c)	126,351	21	60.0	71%	$20,000	$27,500	$40,000	$45,000	$52,500	$75,000	$85,000	$100,000
Auctions: $73,438, MS-63, January 2014; $47,000, AU-58, August 2014; $41,125, AU-58, October 2014												
1830, Proof (d)	2–4	2	63.5		*(extremely rare)*							
Auctions: No auction records available.												
1831, Small or Large 5 D. (e)	140,594	11	60.6	64%	$20,000	$27,500	$40,000	$45,000	$52,500	$75,000	$85,000	$100,000
Auctions: $82,250, MS-61, January 2014												
1832, Curved-Base 2, 12 Stars (f)	(g)	2	60.5	50%	$300,000	$350,000	$450,000	$500,000				
Auctions: $822,500, MS-63, May 2016												
1832, Square-Base 2, 13 Stars	157,487	12	61.8	75%	$20,000	$27,500	$40,000	$45,000	$55,000	$95,000	$110,000	$140,000 (h)
Auctions: $176,250, MS-65, January 2014												
1832, Square-Base 2, 13 Stars, Proof	2–3	0	n/a		*(extremely rare)*							
Auctions: No auction records available.												
1833, Large Date	196,630	2	63.0	100%	$20,000	$27,500	$40,000	$45,000	$52,500	$75,000	$80,000	$100,000 (i)
Auctions: $29,375, AU-50, April 2014												
1833, Small Date (j)	(k)	1	61.0	100%	$20,000	$27,500	$40,000	$45,000	$52,500	$70,000	$100,000	$125,000 (l)
Auctions: $126,500, MS-63 PQ, May 2006												
1833, Proof (m)	4–6	4	61.3		*(extremely rare)*							
Auctions: $977,500, PF-67, January 2005												
1834, All kinds	50,141											
1834, Plain 4		17	58.3	53%	$20,000	$27,500	$40,000	$45,000	$52,500	$75,000	$80,000	$100,000
Auctions: $143,750, MS-65, August 2011												
1834, Crosslet 4		9	57.6	56%	$21,500	$30,000	$40,000	$47,500	$57,000	$85,000	$110,000	$140,000
Auctions: $49,350, MS-63, May 2016: $45,531, AU-55, January 2014												

a. Included in circulation-strike 1829, Large Date, mintage figure (see chart on page 970). **b.** 2 examples are known. One is in the Harry W. Bass Jr. Foundation Collection, and another of equal quality (PF-66) is in the Smithsonian's National Numismatic Collection. **c.** The 1830, Small 5 D. is slightly rarer than the Large 5 D. Certified population reports are unclear, and auction-lot catalogers typically do not differentiate between the two varieties. **d.** 2 examples are known. One is in the Byron Reed collection at the Durham Museum, Omaha, Nebraska. **e.** The 1831, Small 5 D. is estimated to be three to four times rarer than the Large 5 D. Both are extremely rare. **f.** 5 examples are known. **g.** Included in circulation-strike 1832, Square-Base 2, 13 Stars, mintage figure. **h.** Value in MS-64 is $140,000. **i.** Value in MS-64 is $150,000. **j.** The 1833 Small Date is slightly scarcer than the Large Date. **k.** Included in 1833, Large Date, mintage figure. **l.** Value in MS-64 is $175,000. **m.** 4 or 5 examples are known.

CLASSIC HEAD, NO MOTTO ON REVERSE (1834–1838)

Designer: *William Kneass.* **Weight:** *8.36 grams.*
Composition: *(1834–1836) .8992 gold, .1008 silver and copper; (1837–1838) .900 gold.*
Diameter: *22.5 mm.* **Edge:** *Reeded.* **Mints:** *Philadelphia, Charlotte, and Dahlonega.*

| **Circulation Strike** | **Mintmark location is on the** | **Proof** |
| McCloskey-2. | obverse, above the date. | McCloskey-5. |

History. U.S. Mint chief engraver William Kneass based the half eagle's Classic Head design on John Reich's cent of 1808. Minted under the Act of June 28, 1834, the coins' reduced size and weight encouraged circulation over melting or export, and they served American commerce until hoarding became extensive during the Civil War. Accordingly, many show considerable wear.

Striking and Sharpness. On the obverse, weakness is often seen on the higher areas of the hair curls. Also check the star centers. On the reverse, check the rims. The denticles are usually well struck.

Availability. Most coins range from VF to AU or lower grades of MS. Most MS coins are dated 1834. MS-63 and better examples are rare. Good eye appeal can be elusive. Proofs of the Classic Head type were made in small quantities, and today probably only a couple dozen or so survive, most bearing the 1834 date.

GRADING STANDARDS

1834, Plain 4. Graded MS-65.

MS-60 to 70 (Mint State). *Obverse:* At MS-60, some abrasion and contact marks are seen on the portrait, most noticeably on the cheek, as the hair details are complex on this type. Luster is present, but may be dull or lifeless, and interrupted in patches. Many low-level Mint State coins have grainy surfaces. At MS-63, contact marks are few, and abrasion is very light. Abrasion is even less at MS-64. An MS-65 coin will have hardly any abrasion, and contact marks are minute. Luster should be full and rich and is often more intense on the obverse. Grades above MS-65 are defined by having fewer marks as perfection is approached. *Reverse:* Comments apply as for the obverse, except that abrasion is most noticeable in the field, on the eagle's neck, and on the highest area of the wings. Most Mint State coins in the marketplace are graded liberally, with slight abrasion on both sides of MS-65 coins.

Illustrated coin: This well-struck coin has some light abrasion, most evident in the reverse field.

AU-50, 53, 55, 58 (About Uncirculated). *Obverse:* Friction is seen on the higher parts, particularly the cheek and the hair (under magnification) of Miss Liberty. Friction and scattered marks are in the field, ranging from extensive at AU-50 to minimal at AU-58. Luster may be seen in protected areas, minimal at AU-50, more evident at AU-58. On an AU-58 coin the field retains some luster as well. *Reverse:* Comments as preceding, except

1834, Crosslet 4. Graded AU-50.

that the eagle's neck, the top of the wings, the leaves, and the arrowheads now show noticeable wear, as do other features. Luster ranges from perhaps 40% remaining in protected areas (at AU-50) to nearly full mint bloom (at AU-58). Often the reverse of this type retains much more luster than the obverse.

EF-40, 45 (Extremely Fine). *Obverse:* Wear is seen on the portrait overall, with reduction or elimination of some separation of hair strands, especially in the area close to the face. The cheek shows light wear. Luster is minimal or nonexistent at EF-40, and may survive in among the letters of LIBERTY at EF-45. *Reverse:* Wear is greater than on an About Uncirculated coin. On most (but not all) coins the neck lacks some feather detail

1837, Script 8. Graded EF-40.

on its highest points. Feathers have lost some detail near the edges and tips of the wings, and some areas of the horizontal lines in the shield may be blended together. Some traces of luster may be seen, more so at EF-45 than at EF-40.

VF-20, 30 (Very Fine). *Obverse:* Wear on the portrait has reduced the hair detail, especially to the right of the face and the top of the head, but much can still be seen. *Reverse:* Wear is greater, including on the shield and the wing feathers. Generally, Classic Head gold at this grade level lacks eye appeal.

The Classic Head half eagle is seldom collected in grades lower than VF-20.

1835, Block 8. Graded VF-30.

PF-60 to 70 (Proof). *Obverse and Reverse:* PF–60 to 62 coins have extensive hairlines and may have nicks and contact marks. At PF-63, hairlines are prominent, but the mirror surface is very reflective. PF-64 coins have fewer hairlines. At PF-65, hairlines should be minimal and mostly seen only under magnification. There should be no nicks or marks. PF-66 and higher coins should have no marks or hairlines visible to the unaided eye.

1834, Plain 4. Graded PF-65.

1834, Plain 4   1834, Crosslet 4

	Mintage	Cert	Avg	%MS	VF-20	EF-40	AU-50	AU-55	MS-60	MS-62 PF-63	MS-63 PF-64	MS-64 PF-65
1834, Plain 4 (a)	657,460	2,166	51.2	13%	$625	$850	$1,350	$1,750	$4,500	$6,500	$11,500	$22,500
Auctions: $4,230, MS-61, February 2015; $1,704, AU-55, September 2015; $824, EF-45, July 2015; $447, VF-20, May 2015
1834, Crosslet 4	(b)	87	46.1	10%	$2,250	$4,000	$6,000	$9,500	$23,500	$27,500	$55,000	$100,000
Auctions: $14,688, MS-61, January 2015; $6,463, AU-55, January 2015; $5,581, AU-50, January 2015; $3,995, EF-45, September 2015
1834, Plain 4, Proof	8–12	4	63.3							$85,000	$135,000	$200,000
Auctions: $109,250, PF-63Cam, January 2011
1835 (a)	371,534	716	51.2	13%	$625	$825	$1,350	$1,800	$4,500	$6,500	$11,000	$25,000
Auctions: $9,988, MS-63, September 2015; $2,115, AU-58, September 2015; $1,058, AU-53, August 2015; $517, F-12, November 2015
1835, Proof (c)	4–6	1	68.0							$100,000	$150,000	$250,000
Auctions: $690,000, PF-67, January 2005
1836 (a)	553,147	1,215	50.0	12%	$625	$825	$1,450	$1,900	$4,500	$6,500	$11,000	$25,000
Auctions: $3,353, MS-61, January 2015; $1,175, AU-55, October 2015; $631, EF-40, March 2015; $588, VF-30, August 2015
1836, Proof (d)	4–6	2	67.0		*(extremely rare)*							
Auctions: No auction records available.
1837 (a)	207,121	448	50.7	12%	$625	$850	$1,550	$2,100	$5,500	$8,500	$18,500	$35,000
Auctions: $21,738, MS-63, October 2013; $3,525, MS-61, October 2015; $1,763, AU-55, August 2014; $999, EF-45, January 2015
1837, Proof	4–6	0	n/a		*(unique, in the Smithsonian's National Numismatic Collection)*							
Auctions: No auction records available.
1838	286,588	689	51.8	13%	$675	$850	$1,500	$2,050	$4,500	$8,500	$12,500	$35,000
Auctions: $2,233, AU-58, August 2015; $1,645, AU-55, January 2015; $940, EF-45, June 2015; $447, EF-40, January 2015
1838, Proof	2–3	1	65.0		*(unique, in the Bass Foundation Collection)*							
Auctions: No auction records available.
1838-C	17,179	106	44.5	4%	$6,500	$10,000	$15,000	$25,000	$75,000	$115,000	$250,000	
Auctions: $235,000, MS-63, May 2016; $8,813, EF-45, September 2016; $10,575, EF-40, August 2013; $5,405, EF-40, June 2015
1838-D	20,583	134	49.5	8%	$7,000	$8,500	$12,500	$18,500	$35,000	$50,000	$85,000	
Auctions: $94,000, MS-63, May 2016; $21,150, MS-60, January 2014; $21,150, AU-58, October 2016; $21,738, AU-55, August 2014

a. Varieties have either a script 8 or block-style 8 in the date. (See illustrations of similar quarter eagles on page 928.) b. Included in circulation-strike, 1838, Plain 4, mintage figure. c. 3 or 4 examples are known. d. 3 or 4 examples are known.

LIBERTY HEAD (1839–1908)

Designer: *Christian Gobrecht.* **Weight:** *8.359 grams.*
Composition: *.900 gold, .100 copper (net weight .24187 oz. pure gold).*
Diameter: *(1839–1840) 22.5 mm; (1840–1908) 21.6 mm.* **Edge:** *Reeded.*
Mints: *Philadelphia, Charlotte, Dahlonega, Denver, New Orleans, San Francisco, and Carson City.*

Large Diameter, Without Motto, Circulation Strike (1839–1840)
McCloskey–1-A.

Mintmark location, 1839, is on the obverse, above the date.

Large Diameter, Without Motto, Proof

Reduced Diameter, Without Motto, Circulation Strike (1840–1865)

Mintmark location, 1840–1908, is on the reverse, below the eagle.

Reduced Diameter, Without Motto, Proof

  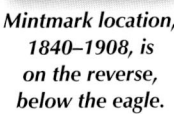  

With Motto, Circulation Strike (1866–1908)

With Motto, Proof

History. Christian Gobrecht's Liberty Head half eagle design was introduced in 1839. The mintmark (for branch-mint coins) in that year was located on the obverse; for all later issues it was relocated to the reverse. The motto IN GOD WE TRUST was added to the reverse in 1866.

Striking and Sharpness. On the obverse, check the highest points of the hair and the star centers; the reverse, the eagle's neck, the area to the lower left of the shield, and the lower part of the eagle. Generally, the eagle on the $5 coins is better struck than on quarter eagles. Examine the denticles on both sides. Branch-mint coins struck before the Civil War are often lightly struck in areas. San Francisco half eagles are in lower average grades than are those from the Philadelphia Mint, as Philadelphia coins did not circulate at par in the East and Midwest from late December 1861 until December 1878, thus acquiring less wear. Most late 19th- and early 20th-century coins are sharp in all areas; for these issues, tiny copper staining spots (from improperly mixed coinage alloy) can be a problem. Cameo contrast is the rule for Proofs prior to 1902. Beginning that year the portrait was polished in the die, although a few years later cameo-contrast coins were again made.

Availability. Early dates and mintmarks are typically scarce to rare in MS, very rare in MS–63 to 65. Charlotte and Dahlonega coins are usually EF or AU, or overgraded as low MS, as seen with quarter eagles. The 1854-S and several varieties in the 1860s and 1870s are rare. Coins from 1880 onward are seen in higher than average grades. Proof coins exist in relation to their original mintages; issues prior to the 1890s are rare.

Note: Values of common-date gold coins have been based on the current bullion price of gold, $1,300 per ounce, and may vary with the prevailing spot price.

GRADING STANDARDS

MS-60 to 70 (Mint State). *Obverse:* At MS-60, some abrasion and contact marks are evident, most noticeably on the hair to the right of Miss Liberty's forehead and on the jaw. Luster is present, but may be dull or lifeless, and interrupted in patches. At MS-63, contact marks are few, and abrasion is very light. An MS-65 coin has only slight abrasion, and contact marks are so minute as to require

1848-C. Graded MS-63.

magnification. Luster should be full and rich. Grades above MS-65 are defined by having fewer marks as perfection is approached. *Reverse:* Comments apply as for the obverse, except that abrasion and contact marks are most noticeable on the eagle's neck and to the lower left of the shield.

 Illustrated coin: Friction is seen in the obverse fields amid luster; on the reverse, luster is nearly complete.

AU-50, 53, 55, 58 (About Uncirculated). *Obverse:* Light wear is seen on the face, the hair to the right of the face, and the highest area of the hair bun, more so at AU-50 than at AU–53 or 55. An AU-58 coin has minimal traces of wear. An AU-50 coin has luster in protected areas among the stars and letters, with little in the open fields or on the portrait. At AU-58, most luster is present in the fields, but is worn away on the highest parts

1840. Graded AU-55.

of the motifs. Striking must be taken into consideration, for a lightly struck coin can be About Uncirculated, but be weak in the central areas. *Reverse:* Comments as preceding, except that the eagle shows wear in all of the higher areas, as well as the leaves and arrowheads. From 1866 to 1908 the motto IN GOD WE TRUST helped protect the field, with the result that luster is more extensive on this side in comparison to the obverse. Luster ranges from perhaps 50% remaining in protected areas (at AU-50) to nearly full mint bloom (at AU-58).

EF-40, 45 (Extremely Fine). *Obverse:* Wear is evident on all high areas of the portrait, including the hair to the right of the forehead, the tip of the coronet, the back of the head, and the hair bun. The stars show light wear at their centers (unless protected by a high rim). Luster, if present at all, is minimal and in protected areas such as between the star points. *Reverse:* Wear is greater than on an About Uncirculated coin, and flatness is

1844. Graded EF-40.

seen on the feather ends, the leaves, and elsewhere. Some traces of luster may be seen, more so at EF-45 than at EF-40. Overall, the reverse appears to be in a slightly higher grade than the obverse on coins from 1866 to 1908 (With Motto).

 Illustrated coin: This coin is well struck on both sides.

VF-20, 30 (Very Fine). *Obverse:* The higher-relief areas of hair are worn flat at VF-20, less so at VF-30. The hair to the right of the coronet is merged into heavy strands. The stars are flat at their centers. *Reverse:* Feather detail is mostly worn away on the neck and legs, less so on the wings. The vertical shield stripes, being deeply recessed, remain bold.

The Liberty Head half eagle is seldom collected in grades lower than VF-20.

PF-60 to 70 (Proof). *Obverse and Reverse:* PF–60 to 62 coins have extensive hairlines and may have nicks and contact marks. At PF-63, hairlines are prominent, but the mirror surface is very reflective. PF-64 coins have fewer hairlines. At PF-65, hairlines should be minimal and mostly seen only under magnification. There should be no nicks or marks. PF-66 and higher coins should have no marks or hairlines visible to the unaided eye.

1858-C. Graded VF-20.

1872. Graded PF-55.

	Mintage	Cert	Avg	%MS	VF-20	EF-40	AU-50	AU-55	MS-60	MS-63	MS-64	MS-65
										PF-63	PF-64	PF-65
1839	118,143	238	51.3	14%	$600	$1,000	$1,800	$2,500	$6,500	$27,500	$50,000	
	Auctions: $11,764, MS-62, January 2015; $3,760, AU-58, August 2015; $1,528, AU-55, January 2015; $1,410, AU-50, September 2015											
1839, Proof (a)	2–3	1	61.0		*(extremely rare)*							
	Auctions: $184,000, PF-61, January 2010											
1839-C	17,205	85	49.0	16%	$2,500	$4,750	$9,500	$13,500	$24,500	$65,000		
	Auctions: $111,625, MS-64, May 2016; $42,300, MS-63, March 2016: $23,500, MS-61, January 2014; $16,450, MS-60, January 2015											
1839-D	18,939	114	46.0	5%	$3,000	$5,000	$8,500	$16,000	$30,000			
	Auctions: $9,400, AU-53, September 2013; $4,700, AU-50, July 2015; $4,700, EF-45, February 2015; $2,350, EF-40, November 2014											
1840 (b)	137,382	331	51.2	8%	$550	$625	$1,000	$1,600	$3,250	$9,000	$25,000	
	Auctions: $2,585, AU-58, October 2015; $2,115, AU-58, June 2015; $999, AU-53, January 2015; $646, EF-45, January 2015											
1840, Proof	2–3	0	n/a		*(unique, in the Smithsonian's National Numismatic Collection)*							
	Auctions: No auction records available.											
1840-C	18,992	93	48.0	11%	$2,000	$3,500	$5,500	$6,500	$18,500	$55,000	$85,000	
	Auctions: $28,200, MS-62, January 2014; $5,581, AU-55, February 2015; $4,700, AU-50, August 2015; $1,645, VF-20, August 2014											
1840-D	22,896	72	50.7	19%	$2,250	$3,500	$5,750	$7,250	$14,000	$45,000		
	Auctions: $14,100, MS-61, December 2013; $881, F-12, August 2014											
1840-O (b)	40,120	156	51.4	11%	$600	$1,150	$2,250	$2,500	$9,500	$37,500		
	Auctions: $5,405, AU-58, June 2015; $2,350, AU-55, October 2015; $1,763, AU-55, January 2015; $764, AU-50, January 2015											
1841	15,833	69	52.9	26%	$550	$950	$1,600	$1,850	$4,500	$12,000	$18,500	$37,500
	Auctions: $1,763, AU-55, December 2013											
1841, Proof (c)	2–3	1	63.0		*(extremely rare)*							
	Auctions: No auction records available.											
1841-C	21,467	92	48.7	9%	$1,850	$2,500	$4,500	$5,750	$15,000	$40,000	$65,000	
	Auctions: $5,581, AU-58, January 2014; $4,230, AU-55, September 2015; $1,939, EF-40, January 2015; $1,705, VF-35, August 2014											

a. 2 or 3 examples are known. **b.** Scarce varieties of the 1840 coins have the fine edge-reeding and wide rims of the 1839 issues. This is referred to as the broad-mill variety. **c.** 2 examples are known. One is in the Smithsonian's National Numismatic Collection; the other is ex Eliasberg Collection.

Small Letters	Large Letters	Small Date	Large Date

	Mintage	Cert	Avg	%MS	VF-20	EF-40	AU-50	AU-55	MS-60 MS-63 MS-64 MS-65

| | Mintage | Cert | Avg | %MS | VF-20 | EF-40 | AU-50 | AU-55 | MS-60 | MS-63 | MS-64 | MS-65 |
										PF-63	PF-64	PF-65
1841-D	27,492	101	49.6	22%	$2,250	$3,000	$4,500	$5,000	$12,500	$22,000	$45,000	
Auctions: $9,988, MS-61, January 2014; $8,578, MS-60, August 2014												
1841-O (d)	50	0	n/a									
Auctions: No auction records available.												
1842, All kinds	27,578											
1842, Small Letters		25	53.4	16%	$650	$1,000	$2,500	$4,000	$11,000	$22,000	$32,500	$60,000
Auctions: $15,275, MS-62, January 2014												
1842, Large Letters		21	48.6	0%	$725	$1,600	$3,750	$5,500	$12,500	$25,000		
Auctions: $4,113, AU-55, April 2014; $4,700, AU-55, August 2014												
1842, Small Letters, Proof (e)	4–6	1	64.0		(extremely rare)							
Auctions: $172,500, PF-64CamH, January 2009												
1842-C, All kinds	27,432											
1842-C, Small Date		25	51.6	20%	$9,000	$17,500	$25,000	$32,500	$75,000	$125,000		
Auctions: $111,625, MS-63, January 2015; $49,938, AU-58, July 2014; $20,563, AU-53, January 2015; $16,450, EF-45, August 2016												
1842-C, Large Date		103	50.7	14%	$2,000	$2,550	$3,750	$5,000	$12,500	$30,000	$45,000	
Auctions: $25,850, MS-63, September 2013; $11,750, MS-61, November 2014												
1842-D, All kinds	59,608											
1842-D, Small Date		158	46.1	5%	$2,000	$2,600	$3,750	$5,000	$12,500	$30,000		
Auctions: $16,450, MS-62, April 2014; $3,995, AU-55, October 2015; $2,350, EF-45, July 2014; $764, F-12, January 2015												
1842-D, Large Date		25	44.7	8%	$3,000	$5,500	$11,000	$18,500	$42,500			
Auctions: $7,050, MS-60, January 2014												
1842-O	16,400	49	45.1	4%	$2,500	$4,000	$9,500	$13,500	$22,500	$45,000		
Auctions: $7,638, AU-53, January 2014; $734, VF-20, January 2015; $646, VF-20, August 2014; $823, F-12, January 2015												
1843	611,205	559	53.5	14%	$500	$525	$575	$600	$1,400	$9,500	$17,500	$37,500
Auctions: $1,410, MS-61, January 2015; $1,175, MS-60, September 2015; $535, AU-55, January 2015; $447, EF-45, September 2015												
1843, Proof (f)	4–8	4	64.0		(extremely rare)							
Auctions: $34,500, PF-58, August 2009												
1843-C	44,277	159	44.9	9%	$1,800	$2,500	$3,750	$4,500	$9,500	$25,000	$55,000	
Auctions: $8,813, MS-61, October 2015; $3,084, AU-53, February 2015; $2,838, AU-50, November 2014; $2,233, EF-45, January 2015												
1843-D	98,452	233	46.3	9%	$2,000	$2,500	$3,500	$4,250	$10,000	$20,000	$50,000	
Auctions: $19,975, MS-63, April 2013; $4,406, MS-60, November 2014; $5,434, AU-58, September 2014; $1,998, AU-50, August 2015												
1843-D, Proof (g)	unknown	1	65.0									—
Auctions: No auction records available.												
1843-O, Small Letters	19,075	73	46.9	8%	$850	$1,650	$2,500	$4,500	$17,500	$35,000	$50,000	$65,000
Auctions: $5,940, AU-58, January 2015; $2,585, AU-50, October 2014; $3,760, EF-45, September 2015; $1,116, EF-40, November 2014												
1843-O, Large Letters	82,000	111	49.8	19%	$650	$1,250	$2,000	$3,500	$10,000	$25,000	$35,000	
Auctions: $19,975, MS-62, January 2014; $5,875, AU-58, March 2015; $5,170, AU-58, July 2015; $797, EF-40, August 2014												

d. Official Mint records report 8,350 coins struck at the New Orleans Mint in 1841. However, most—if not all—were actually dated 1840. No 1841-O half eagle has ever appeared on the market. **e.** Of the examples known today, one is in the Smithsonian's National Numismatic Collection, and another is ex Pittman Collection. **f.** 4 or 5 examples are known. **g.** One non-circulation example of the 1843-D half eagle, probably a presentation strike of some sort, has been certified by NGC as a Specimen (rated Specimen-65).

**1846-D, High
Second D Over D**

	Mintage	Cert	Avg	%MS	VF-20	EF-40	AU-50	AU-55	MS-60	MS-63 / PF-63	MS-64 / PF-64	MS-65 / PF-65
1844	340,330	338	53.1	12%	$500	$525	$575	$625	$1,950	$9,500	$18,000	$55,000
	Auctions: $3,525, MS-62, October 2015; $564, AU-53, June 2015; $494, AU-50, January 2015; $388, VF-30, September 2015											
1844, Proof (h)	*3–5*	1	64.0		*(extremely rare)*							
	Auctions: No auction records available.											
1844-C	23,631	88	45.7	7%	$2,250	$3,250	$4,750	$7,000	$13,500	$30,000		
	Auctions: $4,230, AU-55, January 2015; $3,290, AU-55, January 2015; $2,957, VF-35, March 2015; $999, G-6, October 2015											
1844-D	88,982	249	46.4	8%	$2,000	$2,750	$3,750	$4,500	$8,500	$25,000	$40,000	
	Auctions: $7,638, MS-61, June 2015; $6,000, MS-60, January 2015; $5,405, EF-40, July 2015; $1,763, VF-35, September 2015											
1844-O	364,600	674	50.3	9%	$550	$600	$825	$1,200	$4,000	$12,500	$25,000	$45,000
	Auctions: $1,880, AU-58, June 2015; $646, EF-45, July 2015; $494, EF-45, September 2015; $400, EF-40, October 2015											
1844-O, Proof (i)	*1*	0	n/a		*(unique)*							
	Auctions: No auction records available.											
1845	417,099	382	53.7	13%	$500	$550	$600	$650	$2,000	$8,000	$16,000	
	Auctions: $12,925, MS-64, July 2015; $1,235, AU-58, July 2015; $447, AU-53, January 2015; $470, EF-45, July 2015											
1845, Proof (j)	*5–8*	3	64.7		*(extremely rare)*							
	Auctions: $149,500, PF-66UCam, August 2004											
1845-D	90,629	284	49.7	8%	$2,000	$2,650	$3,500	$4,500	$9,000	$22,500	$37,500	$85,000
	Auctions: $7,050, MS-61, June 2015; $4,230, AU-58, January 2015; $2,056, EF-45, January 2015; $1,058, VG-8, October 2015											
1845-O	41,000	141	50.8	13%	$750	$1,200	$2,500	$4,500	$10,000	$27,500		
	Auctions: $6,463, AU-58, December 2013											
1846, All kinds	395,942											
1846, Large Date		214	53.2	12%	$450	$500	$650	$700	$2,000	$13,000	$18,500	
	Auctions: $16,450, MS-63, January 2015; $11,456, MS-63, September 2015; $1,058, MS-60, September 2015; $400, EF-45, June 2015											
1846, Small Date		92	54.1	15%	$475	$600	$800	$1,000	$3,500	$13,500	$20,000	
	Auctions: $3,055, MS-61, October 2015; $2,585, MS-60, January 2015; $1,528, AU-58, July 2014; $388, EF-40, July 2014											
1846, Proof (k)	*6–10*	1	64.0		*(extremely rare)*							
	Auctions: $161,000, PF-64Cam, January 2011											
1846-C	12,995	69	48.9	10%	$2,000	$3,500	$4,750	$6,500	$15,000	$57,500	$80,000	
	Auctions: $12,925, MS-60, October 2015; $10,575, MS-60, January 2014											
1846-D, All kinds	80,294											
1846-D (l)		129	47.6	3%	$2,150	$2,750	$3,750	$4,750	$12,000			
	Auctions: $3,055, AU-53, August 2014; $5,640, AU-50, July 2015; $2,350, EF-45, September 2015; $1,058, EF-40, August 2014											
1846-D, High Second D Over D		127	49.6	6%	$2,000	$2,500	$4,000	$5,000	$11,000	$25,000		
	Auctions: $21,150, MS-63, January 2014; $2,115, EF-45, August 2014; $2,115, EF-40, January 2015; $1,763, VF-25, January 2015											
1846-O	58,000	147	49.4	5%	$675	$1,000	$3,000	$4,500	$11,000	$25,000		
	Auctions: $9,400, MS-61, January 2014; $4,230, AU-55, October 2015; $1,528, EF-45, July 2015; $881, EF-40, July 2014											

h. 2 examples are known. One is in the Smithsonian's National Numismatic Collection; the other is ex Pittman Collection. **i.** This unique coin first sold in 1890; pedigree is ex Seavy, Parmelee, Woodin, Newcomer, Farouk, Kosoff; current location unknown. **j.** 4 or 5 examples are known. **k.** 4 or 5 examples are known. Of the 20 or so Proof sets made in 1846, experts believe only 4 or 5 contained the year's gold coinage. **l.** The 1846-D half eagle with a normal mintmark actually is rarer than the variety with a boldly repunched D Over D mintmark.

| 1847, Top of Extra 7 Very Low at Border FS-G5-1847-301. | 1848-D, D Over D | 1850-C, Normal C | 1850-C, Weak C |

	Mintage	Cert	Avg	%MS	VF-20	EF-40	AU-50	AU-55	MS-60	MS-63	MS-64	MS-65
										PF-63	PF-64	PF-65
1847, All kinds	915,981											
1847		775	54.4	18%	$450	$550	$600	$625	$1,650	$6,000	$12,500	
Auctions: $2,820, MS-62, June 2015; $940, AU-58, September 2015; $517, AU-53, September 2015; $388, EF-45, January 2015												
1847, Top of Extra 7 Very Low at Border		164	55.1	16%	$525	$575	$675	$1,100	$2,150	$8,500	$13,000	
Auctions: $3,173, MS-62, October 2013; $1,998, MS-61, November 2014; $705, AU-53, October 2015												
1847, Proof	2–3	0	n/a		*(unique, in the Smithsonian's National Numismatic Collection)*							
Auctions: No auction records available.												
1847-C	84,151	258	46.2	6%	$2,000	$2,350	$3,500	$4,500	$9,500	$27,500	$37,500	$75,000
Auctions: $4,406, AU-58, April 2014; $3,525, AU-55, October 2015; $2,350, EF-45, July 2014; $1,763, EF-40, August 2014												
1847-D	64,405	156	48.4	10%	$2,000	$2,500	$3,500	$5,000	$8,500	$16,500		
Auctions: $3,995, AU-55, October 2015; $3,995, AU-55, January 2015; $4,261, AU-50, January 2015; $2,056, EF-45, January 2015												
1847-O	12,000	45	44.3	4%	$3,000	$7,500	$11,500	$13,500	$27,000			
Auctions: $14,100, AU-53, January 2014; $11,163, AU-53, January 2015; $4,113, AU-50, August 2014												
1848	260,775	338	53.4	11%	$450	$525	$600	$700	$1,750	$9,500	$25,000	
Auctions: $1,058, MS-60, April 2013; $705, AU-58, August 2015; $564, AU-53, September 2015; $515, EF-45, July 2014												
1848, Proof (m)	6–10	0	n/a		*(extremely rare)*							
Auctions: No auction records available.												
1848-C	64,472	188	46.3	4%	$2,000	$2,500	$3,500	$5,500	$15,000	$40,000	$65,000	
Auctions: $3,055, AU-53, January 2015; $2,115, AU-50, June 2015; $1,880, AU-50, June 2015; $1,586, VF-30, January 2015												
1848-D	47,465	117	48.5	5%	$1,850	$2,750	$3,500	$5,500	$12,500	$25,000	$65,000	
Auctions: $5,640, AU-58, February 2015; $4,113, AU-55, April 2014; $2,241, EF-45, August 2014; $2,115, EF-40, July 2014												
1848-D, D Over D	(n)	0	n/a				$9,000	$20,000				
Auctions: $29,900, MS-62, May 2008												
1849	133,070	210	52.9	14%	$450	$525	$675	$825	$2,750	$10,000	$15,000	
Auctions: $2,585, MS-61, August 2014; $5,288, MS-61, April 2013; $911, AU-55, August 2014; $705, AU-53, November 2014												
1849-C	64,823	223	50.0	10%	$2,000	$2,500	$3,250	$4,750	$8,500	$23,500	$40,000	
Auctions: $4,230, AU-55, September 2015; $2,585, AU-53, February 2015; $1,645, AU-50, February 2015; $2,233, EF-45, August 2015												
1849-D	39,036	141	49.1	4%	$2,000	$2,750	$3,500	$4,500	$11,500	$35,000		
Auctions: $5,288, AU-58, April 2013; $2,233, AU-50, September 2015; $2,585, EF-45, August 2014												
1850	64,491	142	49.9	4%	$450	$525	$975	$1,250	$3,000	$12,500	$32,000	$75,000
Auctions: $1,293, AU-58, October 2014; $1,028, AU-55, April 2014; $705, AU-50, October 2015; $499, EF-40, August 2014												
1850-C	63,591	165	48.0	12%	$2,000	$2,350	$3,250	$4,250	$9,000	$18,500	$40,000	
Auctions: $8,813, MS-61, February 2013; $3,995, AU-50, January 2015; $2,056, AU-50, August 2015; $1,763, VF-35, August 2015												
1850-C, Weak C (o)	(p)	45	49.7	9%	$1,200	$1,500	$2,000	$2,500	$4,500			
Auctions: $3,819, MS-61, August 2014; $1,293, EF-45, July 2014; $1,116, EF-45, October 2015; $1,058, VF-35, January 2015												
1850-D	43,984	135	48.6	3%	$2,000	$2,750	$3,750	$5,000	$22,500			
Auctions: $5,640, AU-58, October 2015; $5,170, AU-53, February 2015; $1,293, AU-50, August 2015; $2,115, EF-45, August 2014												

m. 2 examples are known. One is in the Smithsonian's National Numismatic Collection; the other is ex Pittman Collection. **n.** Included in 1848-D mintage figure **o.** Several branch-mint half eagles of the early 1850s can exhibit weak (sometimes very weak or almost invisible) mintmarks; such coins generally trade at deep discounts. **p.** Included in 1850-C mintage figure.

1851-D, Normal D **1851-D, Weak D** **1854, Doubled Die Obverse**
FS-G5-1854-101.

1854-C, Normal C **1854-C, Weak C** **1854-D, Normal D** **1854-D, Weak D**

	Mintage	Cert	Avg	%MS	VF-20	EF-40	AU-50	AU-55	MS-60	MS-63	MS-64	MS-65
										PF-63	PF-64	PF-65
1851	377,505	414	54.6	15%	$450	$525	$575	$650	$2,500	$8,500	$22,500	
	Auctions: $2,820, MS-61, February 2015; $705, AU-55, June 2015; $447, AU-53, February 2015; $353, EF-40, July 2015											
1851-C	49,176	141	48.5	11%	$2,000	$2,500	$3,500	$4,500	$11,000	$37,500	$55,000	
	Auctions: $30,550, MS-63, April 2013; $3,760, AU-55, January 2015; $2,820, AU-53, February 2015; $2,468, AU-50, September 2016											
1851-D	62,710	118	49.5	7%	$2,000	$2,500	$3,750	$5,500	$12,000	$25,000	$45,000	
	Auctions: $16,450, MS-62, January 2014											
1851-D, Weak D (o)	(q)	10	56.9	40%	$1,200	$1,500	$2,000	$2,500				
	Auctions: $2,185, AU-50, July 2009											
1851-O	41,000	134	47.1	1%	$850	$1,500	$3,750	$5,750	$12,000	$25,000	$60,000	
	Auctions: $11,163, MS-61, October 2014; $6,463, AU-58, June 2013; $3,055, AU-50, July 2014; $447, EF-40, January 2015											
1852	573,901	737	54.8	15%	$450	$500	$575	$600	$1,500	$6,500	$12,500	$27,500
	Auctions: $9,400, MS-64, January 2015; $3,055, MS-62, August 2015; $646, AU-55, October 2015; $477, AU-55, May 2015											
1852-C	72,574	244	49.5	16%	$2,000	$2,500	$3,500	$4,250	$6,500	$20,000	$27,500	
	Auctions: $28,200, MS-64, August 2013; $9,694, MS-62, January 2015; $2,585, MS-60, November 2014; $2,468, EF-45, January 2015											
1852-D	91,584	271	48.8	8%	$2,000	$2,600	$3,700	$5,000	$9,500	$25,000		
	Auctions: $3,290, AU-55, June 2015; $3,290, AU-53, August 2015; $2,233, EF-45, June 2015; $1,645, VF-25, January 2015											
1853	305,770	558	54.4	15%	$450	$500	$575	$600	$1,500	$5,750	$16,000	$60,000
	Auctions: $15,863, MS-64, October 2015; $2,115, MS-62, March 2015; $1,528, MS-61, June 2015; $423, EF-40, January 2015											
1853-C	65,571	164	48.9	12%	$2,000	$2,500	$3,500	$4,250	$6,750	$21,500	$55,000	
	Auctions: $8,225, MS-62, January 2015; $1,998, MS-60, January 2015; $4,406, AU-58, August 2014; $852, VF-20, February 2015											
1853-D	89,678	343	51.1	12%	$2,000	$2,400	$3,400	$4,500	$6,750	$15,000	$55,000	
	Auctions: $13,513, MS-63, October 2015; $6,463, MS-61, January 2015; $3,290, AU-55, June 2015; $2,233, EF-45, October 2015											
1854	160,675	348	54.6	16%	$450	$500	$575	$850	$2,000	$8,500	$15,000	
	Auctions: $764, AU-58, August 2015; $530, AU-55, June 2015; $470, AU-50, June 2015; $423, AU-50, April 2015											
1854, Doubled Die Obverse	(r)	34	53.9	9%				$1,350	$2,500			
	Auctions: $1,998, AU-55, October 2014											
1854, Proof (s)	*unknown*	0	n/a									
	Auctions: No auction records available.											
1854-C	39,283	102	48.8	8%	$2,000	$2,500	$4,000	$5,000	$12,000	$37,500		
	Auctions: $35,250, MS-63, April 2014; $3,819, AU-50, March 2015; $1,998, AU-50, January 2015; $2,115, EF-40, January 2015											
1854-C, Weak C (o)	(t)	41	49.8	15%	$1,200	$1,500	$1,750	$2,500	$6,500	$12,000		
	Auctions: $12,338, MS-63, January 2014; $4,584, MS-60, September 2014											
1854-D	56,413	222	53.3	22%	$2,000	$2,500	$3,750	$4,500	$8,000	$23,500	$42,500	$75,000
	Auctions: $8,813, MS-62, June 2013; $3,825, AU-55, March 2015; $3,055, EF-45, January 2015; $940, VF-30, January 2015											
1854-D, Weak D (o)	(u)	15	50.9	7%	$1,200	$1,500	$1,750	$2,500	$4,500			
	Auctions: $5,581, MS-61, September 2014; $1,998, AU-55, April 2014											

o. Several branch-mint half eagles of the early 1850s can exhibit weak (sometimes very weak or almost invisible) mintmarks; such coins generally trade at deep discounts. **q.** Included in 1851-D mintage figure. **r.** Included in circulation-strike 1854 mintage figure **s.** According to Walter Breen, a complete 1854 Proof set was presented to dignitaries of the sovereign German city of Bremen who visited the Philadelphia Mint. The set resided in Bremen until it disappeared almost 100 years later, during World War II. **t.** Included in 1854-C mintage figure. **u.** Included in 1854-D mintage figure.

	Mintage	Cert	Avg	%MS	VF-20	EF-40	AU-50	AU-55	MS-60	MS-63 PF-63	MS-64 PF-64	MS-65 PF-65
1854-O	46,000	180	51.0	6%	$550	$800	$1,350	$2,250	$6,500	$22,500		
	Auctions: $2,585, AU-58, October 2015; $1,234, AU-53, June 2015; $764, EF-40, January 2015; $494, VF-30, January 2015											
1854-S (v)	268	1	58.0	0%			—	$5,000,000	—			
	Auctions: No auction records available.											
1855	117,098	261	53.8	12%	$450	$500	$575	$600	$1,650	$7,500	$16,500	
	Auctions: $2,115, MS-61, October 2015; $588, AU-58, October 2015; $470, AU-53, August 2014; $388, AU-53, November 2014											
1855-C	39,788	144	50.1	10%	$2,250	$2,500	$3,750	$4,500	$12,000	$42,500	$65,000	
	Auctions: $11,163, MS-61, August 2016: $9,694, MS-61, April 2013; $7,638, AU-58, January 2015; $1,763, AU-50, January 2015											
1855-D	22,432	79	50.9	9%	$2,000	$2,750	$3,600	$5,000	$13,500	$35,000		
	Auctions: $15,275, MS-61, January 2014; $3,819, MS-60, August 2014; $2,820, EF-45, July 2014; $5,640, VF-30, July 2015											
1855-O	11,100	55	49.5	4%	$1,250	$2,750	$4,500	$6,000	$20,000			
	Auctions: $8,225, AU-58, January 2015; $4,700, AU-50, September 2014; $3,290, AU-50, November 2014; $3,525, EF-40, January 2015											
1855-S	61,000	109	48.4	3%	$700	$1,250	$2,250	$4,000	$12,500			
	Auctions: $3,055, AU-58, September 2015; $2,115, AU-53, July 2014; $940, AU-50, August 2014; $1,351, EF-45, July 2014											
1856	197,990	403	54.0	11%	$450	$500	$550	$575	$2,000	$8,000	$17,000	$50,000
	Auctions: $6,182, MS-63, October 2015; $2,115, MS-61, September 2015; $470, AU-55, August 2015; $317, AU-50, June 2015											
1856-C	28,457	139	51.2	9%	$2,000	$2,500	$3,750	$6,000	$12,500	$45,000		
	Auctions: $17,625, MS-62, January 2014; $3,055, AU-50, September 2015; $2,820, AU-50, February 2015; $1,351, AU-50, January 2015											
1856-D	19,786	106	49.6	12%	$2,000	$2,500	$3,750	$5,750	$8,500	$27,500	$50,000	
	Auctions: $12,925, MS-62, January 2014; $3,878, AU-53, August 2015; $3,878, AU-53, January 2015; $1,880, VF-25, July 2014											
1856-O	10,000	48	49.5	10%	$1,000	$1,850	$4,250	$6,500	$12,500			
	Auctions: $10,575, MS-60, April 2014											
1856-S	105,100	155	47.9	4%	$575	$700	$1,250	$2,000	$7,500	$25,000	$37,500	
	Auctions: $4,700, AU-58, January 2014; $1,763, AU-55, January 2015; $1,116, AU-55, November 2014; $951, AU-53, July 2014											
1857	98,188	303	55.3	14%	$450	$475	$525	$575	$1,850	$5,500	$15,000	
	Auctions: $5,170, MS-63, January 2015; $1,528, MS-61, January 2015; $1,293, MS-61, September 2015; $705, AU-58, October 2015											
1857, Proof (w)	3–6	1	65.0				*(extremely rare)*					
	Auctions: $230,000, PF-65Cam, January 2007											
1857-C	31,360	171	53.0	16%	$2,000	$2,500	$3,500	$4,750	$7,500	$27,500		
	Auctions: $22,325, MS-63, January 2014; $8,813, MS-61, August 2015; $6,756, AU-55, July 2015; $2,115, EF-45, July 2014											
1857-D	17,046	100	52.1	14%	$2,000	$2,600	$3,750	$5,000	$10,000	$37,500		
	Auctions: $9,988, MS-61, January 2014; $5,581, AU-58, October 2014; $5,405, AU-58, January 2015; $1,586, VF-25, August 2014											
1857-O	13,000	82	48.8	4%	$1,000	$1,700	$3,750	$5,500	$13,500	$45,000		
	Auctions: $41,125, MS-63, April 2014; $3,672, AU-53, October 2014											
1857-S	87,000	123	47.3	4%	$600	$800	$1,250	$2,500	$10,500	$20,000		
	Auctions: $2,820, AU-58, September 2015; $2,350, AU-58, September 2015; $881, AU-55, August 2014; $1,528, AU-55, September 2014											
1858	15,136	80	53.6	19%	$550	$575	$750	$1,250	$3,000	$8,000	$12,500	$35,000
	Auctions: $14,100, MS-64, June 2015; $4,935, MS-62, August 2015; $1,410, AU-55, August 2014; $881, EF-40, August 2015											
1858, Proof (x)	4–6	5	65.6							$75,000	$100,000	$150,000
	Auctions: $195,500, PF-66UCamH, March 2006											
1858-C	38,856	191	51.5	13%	$2,000	$2,500	$3,750	$4,500	$9,000	$30,000		
	Auctions: $9,400, MS-61, August 2013; $3,055, AU-55, August 2014; $2,585, EF-40, January 2015; $1,175, EF-40, August 2015											
1858-D	15,362	121	51.4	8%	$2,000	$2,500	$3,750	$4,750	$10,500	$32,500	$45,000	
	Auctions: $17,625, MS-61, June 2013; $9,988, MS-61, February 2015; $7,638, MS-61, August 2014; $3,525, AU-55, June 2015											
1858-S	18,600	55	47.0	0%	$1,500	$3,000	$5,750	$9,000	$27,500			
	Auctions: $7,050, AU-55, March 2014											

v. 3 examples are known. **w.** 2 examples are known. **x.** 4 or 5 examples are known today. One resides in the Smithsonian's National Numismatic Collection, another in the collection of the American Numismatic Society. In recent decades the collections of Eliasberg, Trompeter, and Bass have included examples.

	Mintage	Cert	Avg	%MS	VF-20	EF-40	AU-50	AU-55	MS-60	MS-63 / PF-63	MS-64 / PF-64	MS-65 / PF-65
1859	16,734	98	50.6	8%	$550	$750	$1,500	$1,750	$6,000	$18,000		
	Auctions: $17,625, MS-63 Prooflike, June 2014; $21,150, MS-62, April 2015; $2,585, AU-58, August 2015; $2,115, AU-55, October 2015											
1859, Proof	80	5	63.8							$45,000	$75,000	$125,000
	Auctions: $158,625, PF-66UCam, August 2015											
1859-C	31,847	157	50.7	9%	$2,000	$2,500	$3,500	$4,750	$10,500	$32,500		
	Auctions: $8,225, MS-61, January 2014; $4,113, AU-55, August 2014; $1,645, AU-50, July 2014; $1,469, VF-25, August 2014											
1859-D	10,366	104	51.9	13%	$2,000	$2,750	$3,750	$5,000	$10,000	$35,000		
	Auctions: $19,975, MS-62, January 2014; $2,938, MS-60, July 2014; $7,050, AU-58, June 2015; $2,115, AU-50, January 2015											
1859-S	13,220	31	47.5	3%	$1,500	$3,500	$4,750	$6,500	$25,000			
	Auctions: $8,695, AU-58, October 2013; $6,463, AU-53, August 2014; $4,230, EF-45, October 2015											
1860	19,763	120	52.8	6%	$600	$1,000	$1,500	$2,000	$3,500	$17,500	$25,000	
	Auctions: $4,700, AU-58, January 2014; $2,233, AU-58, August 2014; $646, AU-50, July 2014											
1860, Proof	62	5	64.6							$37,500	$65,000	$100,000
	Auctions: $103,500, PF-66CamH, January 2012											
1860-C	14,813	119	53.2	18%	$2,000	$2,750	$4,000	$6,250	$11,000	$27,500	$50,000	
	Auctions: $20,124, MS-63, April 2013; $4,113, AU-50, August 2014; $3,525, AU-50, June 2015; $2,585, EF-40, October 2014											
1860-D	14,635	133	51.3	13%	$2,250	$3,500	$4,500	$6,500	$12,500	$40,000	$65,000	
	Auctions: $14,100, MS-62, March 2014; $5,405, AU-58, June 2015; $3,760, AU-53, February 2015; $3,760, EF-45, September 2015											
1860-S	21,200	57	45.7	2%	$2,000	$3,500	$6,500	$9,500	$27,500			
	Auctions: $19,975, AU-58, April 2014; $4,994, AU-53, October 2014; $2,585, EF-45, September 2014											
1861	688,084	1,813	55.5	16%	$450	$475	$525	$575	$1,750	$6,000	$10,500	$30,000
	Auctions: $32,900, MS-65, January 2015; $2,820, MS-62, January 2015; $1,528, AU-55, January 2015; $376, EF-40, June 2015											
1861, Proof	66	2	65.0							$35,000	$60,000	$100,000
	Auctions: $117,500, PF-66Cam, August 2015											
1861-C	6,879	78	51.3	9%	$6,000	$8,500	$12,500	$15,000	$30,000	$85,000		
	Auctions: $25,850, MS-61, January 2014; $6,463, AU-50, January 2015; $3,290, AU-50, August 2014; $9,694, EF-45, January 2015											
1861-D	1,597	36	53.5	11%	$20,000	$30,000	$45,000	$55,000	$85,000	$175,000		
	Auctions: $99,875, MS-62, January 2014; $42,314, AU-53, August 2016; $42,300, AU-50, September 2016											
1861-S	18,000	45	43.3	0%	$3,250	$6,500	$8,500	$12,000				
	Auctions: $11,163, AU-53, March 2014; $9,988, AU-53, January 2015; $8,813, AU-53, January 2015; $4,259, VF-35, August 2014											
1862	4,430	36	51.7	3%	$2,500	$4,250	$7,000	$10,000	$30,000			
	Auctions: $14,702, AU-58, August 2014; $17,625, AU-55, April 2013											
1862, Proof	35	8	64.5							$35,000	$60,000	$100,000
	Auctions: $92,000, PF-65UCam, August 2011											
1862-S	9,500	42	40.8	5%	$4,000	$8,000	$10,500	$15,000	$40,000			
	Auctions: $15,275, AU-53, March 2014; $4,406, VF-25, August 2014											
1863	2,442	18	53.1	11%	$3,500	$8,500	$18,500	$25,000	$55,000			
	Auctions: $35,250, AU-58, September 2016; $32,900, AU-58, August 2016: $30,550, AU-58, January 2014; $15,275, AU-50, March 2016											
1863, Proof	30	3	65.3							$35,000	$60,000	$100,000
	Auctions: $69,000, PF-64DCam, November 2005											
1863-S	17,000	50	41.4	0%	$3,000	$4,500	$12,500	$17,500	$35,000			
	Auctions: $16,450, AU-55, March 2014											
1864	4,170	53	50.9	8%	$3,000	$4,500	$8,500	$11,000	$20,000			
	Auctions: $12,925, AU-55, January 2014; $10,575, AU-55, June 2015; $10,281, AU-55, October 2015											
1864, Proof	50	18	64.6							$35,000	$60,000	$100,000
	Auctions: $103,500, PF-65UCam, October 2011											
1864-S	3,888	9	39.3	0%	$12,500	$35,000	$55,000	$60,000				
	Auctions: $79,313, EF-45, March 2014											

	Mintage	Cert	Avg	%MS	VF-20	EF-40	AU-50	AU-55	MS-60	MS-63	MS-64	MS-65
										PF-63	PF-64	PF-65
1865	1,270	24	53.5	17%	$6,000	$12,000	$20,000	$22,500	$35,000			
	Auctions: $17,626, AU-55, August 2014; $18,800, AU-53, January 2014; $17,625, AU-53, August 2015											
1865, Proof	25	13	64.5							$35,000	$60,000	$100,000
	Auctions: $86,250, PF-65UCam, April 2012											
1865-S	27,612	87	43.4	6%	$2,750	$4,500	$6,500	$7,500	$13,500	$35,000	$60,000	
	Auctions: $8,813, AU-55, March 2014; $5,875, EF-45, August 2014											
1866-S, No Motto	9,000	53	37.8	0%	$2,250	$5,000	$8,500	$11,000	$30,000			
	Auctions: $14,688, AU-58, March 2014; $14,100, AU-58, January 2015; $5,581, AU-50, August 2014; $2,350, VF-20, August 2014											
1866, Motto Above Eagle	6,700	42	53.9	14%	$1,000	$2,000	$3,000	$4,250	$11,500	$40,000		
	Auctions: $34,075, MS-63, February 2013; $12,338, MS-61, January 2015; $3,290, AU-55, August 2014; $3,055, EF-40, September 2015											
1866, Motto Above Eagle, Proof	30	6	61.8							$25,000	$35,000	$65,000
	Auctions: $80,500, PF-66UCamH, August 2010											
1866-S, Motto Above Eagle	34,920	47	38.0	2%	$1,150	$2,500	$7,000	$10,000	$25,000			
	Auctions: $4,994, AU-50, June 2013; $2,585, EF-45, August 2014; $1,469, VF-30, October 2014											
1867	6,870	55	49.6	2%	$850	$1,500	$3,000	$4,000	$10,000			
	Auctions: $16,450, MS-61, September 2014; $8,813, MS-60, January 2014; $881, AU-50, August 2014											
1867, Proof	50	4	63.3							$25,000	$35,000	$60,000
	Auctions: $21,150, PF-63Cam, August 2014											
1867-S	29,000	81	39.2	0%	$1,100	$2,000	$5,500	$8,500				
	Auctions: $1,351, EF-40, January 2015; $1,293, VF-30, October 2015; $1,058, VF-20, June 2015; $458, F-12, January 2015											
1868	5,700	51	51.2	4%	$600	$1,000	$2,500	$4,750	$10,000			
	Auctions: $16,450, MS-61, April 2013; $5,405, AU-58, October 2015; $4,935, AU-55, July 2015; $2,233, AU-50, August 2014											
1868, Proof	25	3	64.7							$25,000	$35,000	$60,000
	Auctions: $69,000, PF-64DCam, June 2008											
1868-S	52,000	111	43.7	5%	$525	$1,250	$2,750	$4,250	$20,000			
	Auctions: $18,213, MS-61, June 2015; $23,500, MS-60, March 2014; $1,645, AU-53, October 2014; $1,827, AU-50, July 2014											
1869	1,760	38	52.3	8%	$1,000	$2,500	$5,000	$7,500	$15,000	$27,000	$37,500	
	Auctions: $9,400, AU-55, April 2014; $4,700, AU-53, February 2015; $4,700, EF-45, September 2016; $2,267, EF-40, August 2014											
1869, Proof	25	6	64.0							$25,000	$35,000	$60,000
	Auctions: $69,000, PF-65Cam, April 2012											
1869-S	31,000	121	41.9	3%	$575	$1,500	$3,000	$5,500	$18,000			
	Auctions: $17,625, MS-61, July 2014; $2,233, AU-50, September 2015; $1,998, EF-45, August 2014											
1870	4,000	45	48.8	2%	$900	$2,000	$3,750	$4,750	$15,000			
	Auctions: $7,640, AU-58, September 2014; $8,225, AU-55, January 2014; $2,180, VF-30, October 2015; $1,410, VF-30, October 2014											
1870, Proof	35	1	66.0							$25,000	$35,000	$75,000
	Auctions: $82,250, PF-64, January 2014											
1870-CC	7,675	44	33.5	2%	$22,500	$30,000	$42,500	$60,000	$110,000			
	Auctions: $47,000, AU-53, January 2014											
1870-S	17,000	97	39.6	0%	$1,000	$2,250	$5,500	$8,500	$25,000			
	Auctions: $12,925, AU-58, August 2014; $1,763, AU-50, September 2015; $2,115, EF-40, July 2014; $1,116, VF-25, August 2014											
1871	3,200	48	53.3	8%	$750	$1,500	$2,500	$4,500	$10,000			
	Auctions: $15,275, MS-61, September 2013; $3,525, AU-55, August 2014; $2,820, AU-53, August 2014											
1871, Proof	30	7	61.4							$25,000	$35,000	$60,000
	Auctions: $73,438, PF-66Cam, August 2015; $70,500, PF-65Cam, September 2014											
1871-CC	20,770	89	37.2	2%	$3,500	$6,500	$12,000	$20,000	$55,000	$75,000		
	Auctions: $48,469, MS-61, April 2013; $2,115, EF-40, July 2014; $5,288, EF-40, September 2014; $3,173, VF-30, August 2014											
1871-S	25,000	104	45.5	2%	$525	$1,000	$2,500	$4,000	$12,500			
	Auctions: $35,250, MS-63, August 2014; $25,850, MS-61, March 2014; $2,364, AU-50, August 2015; $2,585, VF-25, August 2014											

1873, Close 3   1873, Open 3

	Mintage	Cert	Avg	%MS	VF-20	EF-40	AU-50	AU-55	MS-60	MS-63 / PF-63	MS-64 / PF-64	MS-65 / PF-65
1872	1,660	26	54.3	15%	$1,000	$1,500	$3,000	$4,500	$10,500	$17,500	$22,500	
	Auctions: $5,434, AU-58, April 2014											
1872, Proof	30	6	62.5							$22,500	$35,000	$60,000
	Auctions: $7,188, PF-55, March 2012											
1872-CC	16,980	70	34.7	0%	$3,250	$6,750	$13,500	$23,500				
	Auctions: $28,200, AU-58, March 2014; $11,764, AU-50, August 2014; $1,175, F-12, November 2014											
1872-S	36,400	114	42.5	2%	$600	$1,000	$2,500	$3,750	$12,000			
	Auctions: $3,055, AU-55, October 2014; $2,233, AU-50, August 2015; $1,998, AU-50, February 2015; $1,880, AU-50, October 2015											
1873, Close 3	112,480	306	55.7	24%	$350	$375	$475	$550	$1,000	$4,500	$7,500	$20,000
	Auctions: $5,875, MS-64, December 2013; $3,055, MS-63, July 2015; $852, MS-61, September 2014; $470, AU-58, August 2014											
1873, Open 3	112,505	338	55.8	25%	$350	$375	$450	$500	$700	$3,500	$6,500	$15,000
	Auctions: $5,875, MS-64, September 2013; $2,703, MS-63, May 2015; $363, AU-58, August 2015; $317, EF-40, October 2014											
1873, Close 3, Proof	25	9	64.4							$22,500	$35,000	$60,000
	Auctions: $24,675, PF-63Cam, August 2014; $12,338, PF-58, January 2014											
1873-CC	7,416	35	33.1	3%	$7,500	$15,000	$25,000	$35,000	$75,000	$180,000		
	Auctions: $11,750, AU-50, August 2014; $21,150, AU-50, January 2013; $14,688, EF-45, September 2016; $5,581, F-12, August 2014											
1873-S	31,000	109	42.2	1%	$600	$1,100	$2,250	$4,500	$18,500			
	Auctions: $2,233, AU-55, August 2014; $3,173, AU-53, January 2014; $823, VF-35, January 2015; $376, VF-20, November 2015											
1874	3,488	57	49.9	7%	$800	$1,350	$2,250	$3,000	$10,000	$22,500		
	Auctions: $4,700, AU-58, January 2014; $3,290, AU-55, August 2014											
1874, Proof	20	3	66.0							$27,500	$40,000	$65,000
	Auctions: $54,625, PF-65CamH, August 2011											
1874-CC	21,198	131	38.4	1%	$2,750	$4,500	$10,000	$17,000	$35,000			
	Auctions: $21,738, AU-58, August 2014; $14,100, AU-55, August 2015; $4,348, VF-35, February 2015; $734, F, March 2015											
1874-S	16,000	88	41.8	0%	$800	$1,500	$3,000	$4,500				
	Auctions: $3,760, AU-55, August 2015; $2,820, AU-55, January 2015; $2,820, AU-53, September 2015; $1,645, EF-45, October 2015											
1875	200	2	50.0	0%	$85,000	$100,000	$150,000	$225,000				
	Auctions: $211,500, AU-55, April 2014											
1875, Proof (y)	20	6	61.2							$150,000	$175,000	$250,000
	Auctions: $176,250, PF-65Cam, January 2014											
1875-CC	11,828	88	37.5	0%	$3,750	$6,500	$14,500	$22,500	$45,000	$115,000		
	Auctions: $17,625, AU-58, January 2014											
1875-S	9,000	67	42.3	3%	$1,000	$2,500	$4,000	$8,000	$18,500			
	Auctions: $8,813, AU-58, August 2014; $3,819, AU-55, August 2014; $2,585, AU-50, August 2014; $3,055, AU-50, August 2013											
1876	1,432	25	55.6	16%	$1,750	$4,500	$5,500	$7,500	$14,000	$25,000	$30,000	$40,000
	Auctions: $19,975, MS-63, March 2013											
1876, Proof	45	18	64.0							$20,000	$25,000	$47,500
	Auctions: $48,469, PF-65Cam, February 2013											
1876-CC	6,887	75	38.8	1%	$4,500	$8,000	$13,500	$17,500	$40,000			
	Auctions: $21,150, AU-58, March 2014; $4,113, VF-25, July 2014											
1876-S	4,000	23	39.3	4%	$3,000	$5,000	$10,000	$12,500	$30,000			
	Auctions: $18,800, AU-58, March 2014											

y. The mintages of only 200 circulation strikes and 20 Proofs for the year 1875 combine to make the Proof a high-demand coin; hence its strong market value.

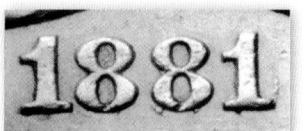
1881, Final 1 Over 0
FS-G5-1881-301.

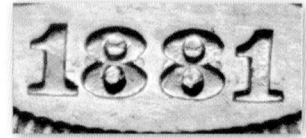
1881, Recut 1881 Over 1881
FS-G5-1881-303.

	Mintage	Cert	Avg	%MS	VF-20	EF-40	AU-50	AU-55	MS-60	MS-63 / PF-63	MS-64 / PF-64	MS-65 / PF-65
1877	1,132	47	54.5	23%	$2,000	$3,500	$5,000	$6,000	$12,500			
Auctions: $7,638, AU-58, April 2014; $1,645, AU-50, June 2015; $1,469, AU-50, August 2015; $3,525, EF-45, July 2014												
1877, Proof	20	3	65.0							$22,500	$32,500	$57,500
Auctions: $51,750, PF-63, June 2005												
1877-CC	8,680	99	39.8	0%	$3,000	$5,500	$12,000	$16,500	$50,000			
Auctions: $14,688, AU-55, November 2014; $11,163, AU-53, July 2014; $8,871, AU-50, January 2015; $3,760, AU-50, August 2015												
1877-S	26,700	125	44.9	1%	$500	$600	$1,500	$3,000	$8,500	$18,500	$30,000	
Auctions: $1,645, AU-55, February 2015; $1,293, AU-53, August 2014; $1,175, EF-45, August 2014; $411, EF-40, June 2015												
1878	131,720	410	58.8	52%	$350	$365	$375	$385	$575	$1,750	$4,000	$8,500
Auctions: $8,813, MS-65, January 2015; $8,225, MS-65, September 2015; $3,525, MS-64, August 2014; $400, AU-58, March 2015												
1878, Proof	20	8	64.1							$22,500	$32,500	$57,500
Auctions: $31,725, PF-63DCam, June 2014												
1878-CC	9,054	53	45.3	4%	$5,500	$11,000	$17,500	$32,000	$75,000			
Auctions: $47,000, AU-58, March 2014; $7,344, VF-25, September 2016												
1878-S	144,700	496	56.2	23%	$350	$365	$375	$385	$650	$4,000	$7,000	
Auctions: $423, AU-58, August 2015; $400, AU-55, March 2015; $323, AU-50, September 2015; $341, EF-45, August 2015												
1879	301,920	705	59.2	56%	$350	$365	$375	$385	$450	$1,500	$3,600	$8,500
Auctions: $6,463, MS-65, September 2014; $4,406, MS-64, September 2014; $2,115, MS-64, March 2015; $458, MS-60, February 2015												
1879, Proof	30	6	64.2							$22,500	$30,000	$55,000
Auctions: $63,250, PF-65Cam, April 2012												
1879-CC	17,281	160	44.1	4%	$1,750	$2,750	$4,000	$7,500	$25,000			
Auctions: $21,150, MS-60, March 2014; $8,813, AU-58, August 2014; $1,116, VG-8, June 2015; $764, G-6, July 2014												
1879-S	426,200	733	57.1	26%	$350	$365	$375	$385	$600	$1,750	$6,000	$25,000
Auctions: $1,058, MS-63, January 2015; $541, MS-61, February 2015; $376, AU-58, January 2015; $282, AU-50, July 2015												
1880	3,166,400	3,043	59.8	73%	$350	$365	$375	$385	$450	$650	$1,000	$2,500
Auctions: $10,575, MS-66, October 2015; $4,348, MS-65, August 2015; $705, MS-63, July 2015; $376, EF-40, February 2015												
1880, Proof	36	8	65.5							$17,500	$30,000	$52,500
Auctions: $72,702, PF-67Cam, August 2006												
1880-CC	51,017	318	46.1	4%	$1,250	$1,500	$2,000	$4,500	$12,500	$45,000		
Auctions: $14,100, MS-61, September 2016: $11,750, MS-61, January 2014; $705, VF-20, January 2015; $1,058, F-15, January 2015												
1880-S	1,348,900	2,282	61.0	84%	$350	$365	$375	$385	$450	$650	$1,100	$8,500
Auctions: $1,410, MS-64, January 2015; $940, MS-64, January 2015; $400, MS-62, January 2015; $329, AU-55, February 2015												
1881, Final 1 Over 0 (z)	(aa)	110	58.3	52%	$475	$500	$550	$675	$1,350	$3,000	$8,000	
Auctions: $2,233, MS-63, January 2014; $646, AU-55, August 2014; $499, EF-40, July 2014												
1881, Recut 1881 Over 1881	(aa)	0	n/a					$535	$625	$1,325		
Auctions: $705, MS-63, August 2014; $1,528, MS-62, April 2014												
1881	5,708,760	17,235	61.5	92%	$350	$365	$375	$385	$450	$600	$950	$2,250
Auctions: $1,058, MS-64, June 2015; $435, MS-62, March 2015; $423, MS-61, July 2015; $329, AU-55, July 2015												
1881, Proof	42	10	65.8							$16,500	$25,000	$40,000
Auctions: $37,375, PF-65Cam, January 2011												
1881-CC	13,886	84	45.3	8%	$1,750	$3,500	$7,000	$10,500	$25,000	$55,000		
Auctions: $32,900, MS-62, May 2013; $11,750, AU-58, September 2016; $3,055, EF-40, August 2014; $1,763, VF-30, July 2014												
1881-S	969,000	1,960	61.3	89%	$350	$365	$375	$385	$450	$650	$1,250	$4,000
Auctions: $1,058, MS-64, January 2015; $969, MS-64, February 2015; $687, MS-63, January 2015; $494, MS-62, January 2015												

z. The last digit of the date is repunched over the remnants of a zero; this is easily visible with the naked eye, making the 1 Over 0 a popular variety. **aa.** Included in circulation-strike 1881 mintage figure.

	Mintage	Cert	Avg	%MS	VF-20	EF-40	AU-50	AU-55	MS-60	MS-63 / PF-63	MS-64 / PF-64	MS-65 / PF-65
1882	2,514,520	7,857	61.5	91%	$350	$365	$375	$385	$450	$650	$1,000	$3,500
Auctions: $2,468, MS-65, May 2015; $999, MS-64, August 2015; $588, MS-63, August 2015; $454, MS-62, February 2015											
1882, Proof	48	12	64.3							$15,500	$25,000	$40,000
Auctions: $9,085, PF-63Cam, February 2010											
1882-CC	82,817	568	50.9	5%	$1,000	$1,500	$2,000	$4,000	$11,500	$35,000		
Auctions: $18,800, MS-62, February 2015; $1,175, AU-50, February 2015; $1,116, AU-50, January 2015; $734, EF-40, February 2015											
1882-S	969,000	2,434	61.6	92%	$350	$365	$375	$385	$500	$600	$1,000	$2,250
Auctions: $3,408, MS-65, January 2015; $999, MS-64, January 2015; $823, MS-64, January 2015; $447, MS-62, January 2015											
1883	233,400	485	60.3	71%	$350	$365	$375	$385	$500	$1,500	$2,250	$12,500
Auctions: $17,625, MS-67, February 2013; $1,410, MS-64, September 2015; $1,116, MS-63, June 2015; $411, AU-58, August 2014											
1883, Proof	61	8	64.1							$15,500	$25,000	$40,000
Auctions: $5,288, PF-55, September 2014											
1883-CC	12,598	126	49.9	6%	$2,000	$3,000	$4,500	$6,750	$18,500	$50,000		
Auctions: $18,213, MS-61, August 2014; $7,638, AU-58, August 2015; $5,875, AU-55, January 2015; $3,305, AU-50, September 2016											
1883-S	83,200	257	58.4	55%	$350	$365	$375	$385	$750	$1,775	$7,000	
Auctions: $7,050, MS-64, August 2013; $706, MS-61, July 2015; $382, AU-58, January 2015; $1,058, AU-53, August 2014											
1884	191,030	462	59.1	58%	$350	$365	$375	$385	$550	$1,650	$3,000	$9,000
Auctions: $2,468, MS-64, February 2013; $881, MS-62, July 2015; $588, MS-62, November 2015; $588, MS-61, August 2015											
1884, Proof	48	7	64.4							$15,500	$25,000	$40,000
Auctions: $39,100, PF-66UCam, November 2010											
1884-CC	16,402	177	49.3	3%	$1,100	$1,500	$4,500	$6,500	$20,000			
Auctions: $8,225, AU-58, January 2014; $8,519, AU-58, October 2014; $4,994, AU-55, August 2014											
1884-S	177,000	460	59.8	68%	$350	$365	$375	$385	$450	$1,150	$2,300	$9,000
Auctions: $999, MS-63, August 2015; $940, MS-63, June 2015; $588, MS-62, October 2015; $541, MS-62, August 2015											
1885	601,440	1,402	61.2	84%	$350	$365	$375	$385	$450	$600	$1,250	$4,500
Auctions: $1,528, MS-64, July 2015; $676, MS-63, July 2015; $517, MS-62, May 2015; $400, AU-53, February 2015											
1885, Proof	66	19	64.6							$15,500	$25,000	$40,000
Auctions: $70,500, PF-67UCam, August 2015; $56,400, PF-66UCam, January 2015; $31,725, PF-65DCam, August 2014											
1885-S	1,211,500	4,444	61.9	94%	$350	$365	$375	$385	$450	$600	$900	$2,000
Auctions: $5,170, MS-66, January 2015; $705, MS-63, August 2015; $458, MS-61, January 2015; $376, AU-55, July 2015											
1886	388,360	724	60.2	70%	$350	$365	$375	$385	$450	$650	$2,250	$5,500
Auctions: $5,288, MS-65, June 2013; $573, MS-63, August 2014; $499, MS-61, July 2014											
1886, Proof	72	10	64.2							$15,500	$25,000	$40,000
Auctions: $57,281, PF, March 2014											
1886-S	3,268,000	8,625	61.4	93%	$350	$365	$375	$385	$450	$550	$900	$2,000
Auctions: $2,350, MS-65, January 2015; $823, MS-64, October 2015; $458, MS-62, January 2015; $400, MS-60, October 2015											
1887, Proof (bb)	87	18	62.9							$65,000	$80,000	$115,000
Auctions: $54,050, PF, August 2013											
1887-S	1,912,000	3,473	61.1	91%	$350	$365	$375	$385	$450	$600	$1,200	$4,000
Auctions: $1,410, MS-64, January 2015; $940, MS-64, July 2015; $881, MS-64, July 2015; $470, MS-62, June 2015											
1888	18,201	169	59.8	68%	$350	$365	$375	$385	$650	$1,750	$3,000	$12,500
Auctions: $1,775, MS-63, January 2014; $764, MS-61, January 2015; $588, MS-60, August 2014											
1888, Proof	95	18	64.7							$13,500	$20,000	$32,500
Auctions: $34,500, PF-65DCam, October 2008											
1888-S	293,900	347	55.0	22%	$350	$365	$375	$450	$1,000	$3,000		
Auctions: $2,350, MS-64, August 2013; $1,116, MS-63, October 2014; $470, AU-53, July 2014; $368, EF-40, August 2014											
1889	7,520	158	58.1	42%	$500	$600	$700	$950	$1,400	$4,500	$6,000	
Auctions: $4,406, MS-63, June 2014; $1,763, MS-62, September 2015; $1,058, AU-55, July 2015; $1,175, AU-53, August 2014											
1889, Proof	45	13	64.3							$14,000	$22,500	$35,000
Auctions: $29,900, PF-65Cam, January 2011											

bb. Proof only.

	Mintage	Cert	Avg	%MS	VF-20	EF-40	AU-50	AU-55	MS-60	MS-63 / PF-63	MS-64 / PF-64	MS-65 / PF-65
1890	4,240	75	55.6	28%	$550	$675	$850	$1,250	$2,250	$6,000	$10,000	$15,000
	Auctions: $5,581, MS-62, June 2014; $1,000, AU-55, July 2014; $823, AU-50, August 2014											
1890, Proof	88	31	64.7							$14,000	$22,500	$35,000
	Auctions: $24,675, PF-64DCam, January 2014											
1890-CC	53,800	628	57.2	47%	$800	$950	$1,100	$1,300	$2,250	$8,500	$15,000	$45,000
	Auctions: $11,750, MS-64, June 2015; $9,400, MS-63, October 2015; $5,640, MS-63, March 2016; $2,820, MS-62, June 2015											
1891	61,360	384	60.5	78%	$350	$365	$375	$385	$500	$1,250	$3,250	$12,000
	Auctions: $4,700, MS-64, February 2013; $499, MS-61, August 2014; $400, AU-58, August 2015; $353, AU-53, September 2015											
1891, Proof	53	14	65.0							$13,500	$20,000	$32,500
	Auctions: $19,550, PF-64DCam, January 2010											
1891-CC	208,000	2,111	57.9	52%	$875	$950	$1,150	$1,350	$2,250	$5,000	$7,500	$32,500
	Auctions: $5,875, MS-64, January 2015; $1,175, AU-58, June 2015; $823, EF-45, July 2015; $764, VF-30, October 2015											
1892	753,480	2,118	61.5	92%	$350	$365	$375	$385	$450	$600	$1,100	$2,000
	Auctions: $3,760, MS-66, July 2015; $2,585, MS-65, September 2015; $823, MS-63, January 2015; $329, AU-50, September 2015											
1892, Proof	92	16	64.5							$13,500	$18,000	$32,500
	Auctions: $6,325, PF-62Cam, December 2011											
1892-CC	82,968	764	53.8	20%	$750	$850	$1,100	$1,250	$2,500	$9,000	$20,000	$40,000
	Auctions: $2,511, MS-61, February 2015; $1,058, AU-55, January 2015; $881, EF-45, January 2015; $541, VG-8, January 2015											
1892-O	10,000	40	57.5	40%	$1,750	$2,250	$2,500	$3,500	$5,500	$18,500		
	Auctions: $8,225, MS-62, December 2013; $3,290, AU-58, July 2014; $3,290, AU-58, August 2014											
1892-S	298,400	452	57.8	45%	$350	$365	$375	$385	$450	$1,800	$4,250	$7,500
	Auctions: $4,230, MS-64, January 2015; $2,350, MS-63, April 2013; $823, MS-62, August 2015; $400, MS-60, October 2015											
1893	1,528,120	8,415	62.0	97%	$350	$365	$375	$385	$450	$575	$800	$2,250
	Auctions: $4,230, MS-66, June 2015; $3,995, MS-66, January 2015; $940, MS-64, September 2015; $852, MS-64, January 2015											
1893, Proof	77	19	64.7							$13,500	$18,000	$32,500
	Auctions: $70,500, PF, August 2013											
1893-CC	60,000	684	55.7	26%	$950	$1,100	$1,300	$1,800	$3,000	$10,000	$20,000	$30,000
	Auctions: $24,675, MS-64, August 2015; $2,115, AU-58, June 2015; $1,410, AU-53, July 2015; $969, EF-40, February 2015											
1893-O	110,000	453	58.8	50%	$400	$450	$500	$550	$1,000	$5,000	$9,500	
	Auctions: $7,638, MS-64, January 2014; $1,880, MS-62, July 2015; $541, MS-60, August 2015; $529, AU-58, August 2014											
1893-S	224,000	1,074	61.0	84%	$350	$365	$375	$385	$450	$600	$1,750	$8,500
	Auctions: $1,645, MS-64, October 2015; $999, MS-64, July 2015; $482, MS-62, October 2015; $447, MS-61, October 2015											
1894	957,880	3,624	61.8	96%	$350	$365	$375	$385	$450	$600	$900	$3,300
	Auctions: $3,760, MS-65, January 2015; $1,058, MS-64, June 2015; $458, MS-62, August 2015; $329, MS-60, July 2015											
1894, Proof	75	25	64.1							$13,500	$18,500	$32,500
	Auctions: $58,750, PF-67DCam, October 2014; $37,600, PF-66UCam, August 2015; $29,375, PF-64UCam, August 2015											
1894-O	16,600	329	57.6	34%	$425	$450	$550	$800	$2,000	$8,500		
	Auctions: $3,525, MS-62, June 2014; $1,888, MS-61, July 2014; $1,175, AU-58, September 2015; $823, AU-55, November 2014											
1894-S	55,900	232	53.3	13%	$400	$425	$450	$650	$2,500	$9,000	$16,000	
	Auctions: $3,819, MS-62, March 2015; $2,938, MS-62, July 2015; $2,350, MS-60, February 2015; $881, AU-58, August 2014											
1895	1,345,855	8,387	61.8	95%	$350	$365	$375	$385	$425	$600	$800	$2,000
	Auctions: $19,975, MS-67, January 2015; $7,931, MS-66, February 2015; $564, MS-63, July 2015; $423, MS-61, May 2015											
1895, Proof	81	24	64.8							$12,500	$18,000	$30,000
	Auctions: $6,233, PF-60, February 2014											
1895-S	112,000	317	53.4	8%	$375	$425	$450	$650	$1,500	$5,000	$8,000	$20,000
	Auctions: $2,350, MS-62, September 2015; $1,645, MS-61, September 2015; $1,586, MS-61, June 2015; $447, AU-53, October 2015											
1896	58,960	508	61.8	93%	$350	$365	$375	$385	$425	$600	$1,500	$7,500
	Auctions: $1,410, MS-64, August 2015; $1,293, MS-64, June 2015; $1,293, MS-64, January 2015; $382, AU-55, August 2014											
1896, Proof	103	25	65.0							$12,500	$18,000	$30,000
	Auctions: $35,250, PF-65DCam, September 2014											
1896-S	155,400	391	54.5	19%	$350	$365	$375	$385	$1,100	$5,500	$8,500	$20,000
	Auctions: $7,064, MS-64, January 2015; $4,230, MS-63, July 2015; $3,525, MS-63, August 2015; $2,233, MS-62, January 2015											

1901-S, Final 1 Over 0
FS-G5-1901S-301.

	Mintage	Cert	Avg	%MS	VF-20	EF-40	AU-50	AU-55	MS-60	MS-63 PF-63	MS-64 PF-64	MS-65 PF-65
1897	867,800	4,328	61.6	92%	$350	$365	$375	$385	$425	$600	$800	$2,000
	Auctions: $8,225, MS-66, January 2015; $1,175, MS-64, August 2015; $505, MS-62, July 2015; $388, AU-58, July 2015											
1897, Proof	83	24	64.5							$12,500	$18,000	$30,000
	Auctions: $9,988, PF-63, June 2014											
1897-S	354,000	425	56.1	26%	$350	$365	$375	$385	$800	$4,500	$7,000	
	Auctions: $15,275, MS-66, March 2015; $1,645, MS-62, July 2014; $499, MS-61, August 2014; $388, AU-58, November 2015											
1898	633,420	2,532	61.6	93%	$350	$365	$375	$385	$425	$600	$1,500	$3,500
	Auctions: $8,225, MS-66, June 2015; $3,643, MS-65, June 2015; $1,028, MS-64, June 2015; $447, MS-62, August 2015											
1898, Proof	75	38	64.7							$12,500	$18,000	$30,000
	Auctions: $105,750, PF-67UCam, August 2015; $29,375, PF-65DCam, September 2014; $18,800, PF-64DCam+, August 2015											
1898-S	1,397,400	701	59.2	67%	$350	$365	$375	$385	$450	$1,100	$2,750	$8,000
	Auctions: $70,500, MS-68, June 2015; $5,434, MS-65, June 2014; $7,050, MS-65, October 2014; $4,406, MS-64, August 2014											
1899	1,710,630	13,285	62.5	98%	$350	$365	$375	$385	$425	$600	$800	$2,000
	Auctions: $2,938, MS-66, June 2015; $2,585, MS-65, January 2015; $447, MS-62, January 2015; $388, AU-55, June 2015											
1899, Proof	99	30	64.5							$12,500	$18,000	$30,000
	Auctions: $134,550, PF, September 2013											
1899-S	1,545,000	987	59.5	70%	$350	$365	$375	$385	$450	$1,000	$1,750	$7,500
	Auctions: $1,410, MS-64, January 2015; $764, MS-63, January 2015; $734, MS-62, August 2015; $447, MS-62, March 2015											
1900	1,405,500	16,718	62.1	96%	$350	$365	$375	$385	$425	$575	$800	$2,000
	Auctions: $5,875, MS-66, January 2015; $2,820, MS-65, September 2015; $423, MS-62, July 2015; $329, MS-60, July 2015											
1900, Proof	230	64	64.2							$12,500	$18,000	$30,000
	Auctions: $35,250, PF-65DCam, September 2013											
1900-S	329,000	525	60.2	70%	$350	$365	$375	$385	$450	$850	$900	$9,500
	Auctions: $1,293, MS-64, March 2013; $940, MS-64, January 2015; $705, MS-63, August 2014; $529, MS-62, August 2014											
1901	615,900	5,491	61.9	93%	$350	$365	$375	$385	$425	$575	$750	$2,000
	Auctions: $16,450, MS-67, January 2015; $881, MS-64, July 2015; $823, MS-64, June 2015; $423, MS-62, May 2015											
1901, Proof	140	44	64.2							$12,500	$18,000	$30,000
	Auctions: $28,200, PF-65DCam, August 2014											
1901-S, All kinds	3,648,000											
1901-S, Final 1 Over 0		372	60.5	69%	$350	$365	$475	$500	$550	$1,250	$1,750	$3,750
	Auctions: $1,645, MS-64, January 2015; $1,116, MS-63, August 2014; $470, MS-62, October 2014; $401, AU-55, March 2015											
1901-S		7,540	62.0	92%	$350	$365	$375	$385	$425	$575	$750	$2,000
	Auctions: $2,585, MS-66, January 2015; $999, MS-64, June 2015; $705, MS-64, June 2015; $564, MS-63, August 2015											
1902	172,400	1,528	61.8	94%	$350	$365	$375	$385	$425	$575	$750	$2,000
	Auctions: $18,800, MS-67, October 2015; $2,820, MS-65, August 2015; $646, MS-63, June 2015; $535, MS-63, August 2015											
1902, Proof	162	28	63.3							$12,500	$18,000	$30,000
	Auctions: $12,925, PF-64, April 2013											
1902-S	939,000	2,665	62.1	92%	$350	$365	$375	$385	$425	$575	$750	$2,000
	Auctions: $23,500, MS-67, January 2014; $1,998, MS-65, January 2015; $588, MS-63, July 2015; $436, MS-62, March 2015											
1903	226,870	1,898	61.6	92%	$350	$365	$375	$385	$425	$575	$750	$2,000
	Auctions: $3,290, MS-66, July 2014; $3,819, MS-65, February 2014; $2,820, MS-65, September 2015; $423, MS-62, August 2015											
1903, Proof	154	55	63.9							$12,500	$18,000	$30,000
	Auctions: $32,900, PF-65, October 2014; $30,550, PF-65, August 2015; $66,975, PF, March 2014											
1903-S	1,855,000	4,442	62.0	92%	$350	$365	$375	$385	$425	$575	$750	$2,000
	Auctions: $2,585, MS-66, June 2015; $1,763, MS-65, January 2015; $764, MS-64, February 2015; $881, MS-63, September 2015											

	Mintage	Cert	Avg	%MS	VF-20	EF-40	AU-50	AU-55	MS-60	MS-63 / PF-63	MS-64 / PF-64	MS-65 / PF-65
1904	392,000	4,119	62.0	95%	$350	$365	$375	$385	$425	$575	$750	$2,000
Auctions: $5,170, MS-66, August 2015; $2,128, MS-65, July 2015; $482, MS-63, October 2015; $353, AU-58, June 2015											
1904, Proof	136	58	64.0							$12,500	$18,000	$30,000
Auctions: $31,725, PF-66Cam, June 2013											
1904-S	97,000	279	57.4	35%	$350	$365	$400	$450	$800	$3,000	$5,000	$8,500
Auctions: $4,113, MS-64, April 2013; $2,056, MS-63, January 2015; $423, AU-58, August 2015; $470, AU-55, October 2015											
1905	302,200	2,832	61.9	94%	$350	$365	$375	$385	$425	$575	$750	$2,000
Auctions: $2,350, MS-65, July 2015; $1,880, MS-65, February 2015; $999, MS-64, January 2015; $793, MS-64, June 2015											
1905, Proof	108	33	62.9							$12,500	$18,000	$30,000
Auctions: $23,000, PF-65Cam, October 2010											
1905-S	880,700	947	57.4	32%	$350	$365	$400	$475	$650	$1,500	$3,000	$8,000
Auctions: $764, MS-62, July 2015; $411, MS-61, March 2015; $347, AU-58, April 2015; $341, AU-53, March 2015											
1906	348,735	2,928	61.8	93%	$350	$365	$375	$385	$425	$575	$750	$2,000
Auctions: $7,050, MS-66, January 2015; $1,293, MS-64, September 2015; $517, MS-61, June 2015; $447, AU-55, January 2015											
1906, Proof	85	57	63.8							$12,500	$18,000	$30,000
Auctions: $64,625, PF-66Cam, August 2013											
1906-D	320,000	2,748	62.1	94%	$350	$365	$375	$385	$425	$575	$750	$2,000
Auctions: $4,935, MS-66, January 2015; $940, MS-64, August 2015; $823, MS-64, August 2015; $423, MS-60, February 2015											
1906-S	598,000	695	60.0	71%	$350	$365	$400	$450	$500	$1,000	$1,650	$4,500
Auctions: $793, MS-63, January 2015; $646, MS-63, February 2015; $470, MS-62, January 2015; $517, MS-61, June 2015											
1907	626,100	9,264	62.2	96%	$350	$365	$375	$385	$425	$575	$750	$2,000
Auctions: $7,638, MS-67, June 2015; $4,230, MS-66, August 2015; $1,175, MS-64, August 2015; $1,058, MS-64, August 2015											
1907, Proof	92	43	64.0							$12,500	$18,000	$30,000
Auctions: $24,675, PF-65Cam, April 2014											
1907-D	888,000	4,620	62.0	94%	$350	$365	$375	$385	$425	$575	$750	$2,000
Auctions: $1,704, MS-65, February 2015; $1,410, MS-64, September 2015; $423, MS-62, February 2015; $396, MS-61, July 2015											
1908	421,874	6,524	62.4	96%	$350	$365	$375	$385	$425	$575	$750	$2,000
Auctions: $4,465, MS-66, January 2015; $2,585, MS-65, August 2015; $999, MS-64, January 2015; $617, MS-63, January 2015											

INDIAN HEAD (1908–1929)

Designer: *Bela Lyon Pratt.* **Weight:** *8.359 grams.*
Composition: *.900 gold, .100 copper (net weight .24187 oz. pure gold).* **Diameter:** *21.6 mm.*
Edge: *Reeded.* **Mints:** *Philadelphia, Denver, New Orleans, and San Francisco.*

Circulation Strike   **Sandblast Finish Proof**   **Satin Finish Proof**

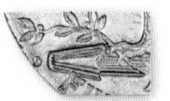

*Mintmark location
is on the reverse, to
the left of the arrows.*

History. The Indian Head half eagle made its first appearance in 1908; it was minted continuously through 1916, and again in 1929. Its design elements are in sunken relief (sometimes imprecisely called "incuse"), like those of the similar quarter eagle; the mintmark is raised. On most examples the rims are flat, while on others they are slightly raised. These coins saw limited circulation in the West, and were rarely encountered elsewhere.

Striking and Sharpness. Striking quality of Indian Head half eagles varies. Look for weakness on the high parts of the Indian's bonnet and in the feather details in the headdress. On the reverse, check the feathers on the highest area of the wing.

Proofs. Sandblast (also called Matte) Proofs were made in 1908 and from 1911 to 1915, while Satin (also called Roman Finish) Proofs were made in 1909 and 1910. At lower levels, these coins can show light contact marks. Some microscopic bright flecks may be caused by the sandblasting process and, although they do not represent handling, usually result in a coin being assigned a slightly lower grade.

Availability. Indian Head half eagles were not popular with numismatists of the time, who saved very few. Rare issues include the 1909-O, which usually is seen with evidence of circulation (often extensive) and the 1929, most of which are in MS. Luster can range from deeply frosty to grainy. Because the fields are the highest areas of the coin, luster diminished quickly as the coins were circulated or jostled with others in bags. When Proof examples are seen, they are usually in higher Proof grades, PF-64 and above. As a class these half eagles are rarer than quarter eagles of the same date and style of finish.

Note: Values of common-date gold coins have been based on the current bullion price of gold, $1,300 per ounce, and may vary with the prevailing spot price.

GRADING STANDARDS

MS-60 to 70 (Mint State). *Obverse:* At MS–60 to 62, there is abrasion in the field, this representing the highest part of the coin. Abrasion is also evident on the headdress. Marks and, occasionally, a microscopic pin scratch may be seen. At MS-63, there may be some abrasion and some tiny marks. Luster is irregular. At MS-64, abrasion is less. Luster is rich. At MS-65 and above, luster is deep and frosty, with no marks at all visible with-

1911-D. Graded MS-62.

out magnification at MS-66 and higher. *Reverse:* At MS–60 to 62 there is abrasion in the field, this representing the highest part of the coin. Abrasion is also evident on the eagle's wing. Otherwise, the same comments apply as for the obverse.

　Illustrated coin: This example is lustrous and attractive. Most of the luster in the fields (the highest-relief area of this unusual design) is still intact.

AU-50, 53, 55, 58 (About Uncirculated). *Obverse:* Friction on the cheek is very notice-able at AU-50, increasingly less at higher lev-els to AU-58. The headdress shows light wear, most evident on the ribbon above the forehead and on the garland. Luster is mini-mal at AU-50 and scattered and incomplete at AU-58. Nicks and contact marks are to be expected. *Reverse:* Friction on the wing and neck is very noticeable at AU-50, increasingly

1911. Graded AU-50.

less noticeable at higher levels to AU-58. Otherwise, the same comments apply as for the obverse.

EF-40, 45 (Extremely Fine). *Obverse:* Light wear will characterize the portrait and head-dress. Luster is gone. Marks and tiny scratches are to be expected, but not distracting. *Reverse:* Light wear is most evident on the eagle's head and wing, although other areas are lightly worn as well. Luster is gone. Marks and tiny scratches are to be expected, but not distracting.

1909-O. Graded EF-40.

VF-20, 30 (Very Fine). *Obverse:* Many details of the garland and of the ribbon above the forehead are worn away. Many feather vanes are blended together. The field is dull and has contact marks. *Reverse:* The neck and the upper part of the wing show extensive wear, other areas less so. The field is dull and has contact marks.

The Indian Head half eagle is seldom collected in grades lower than VF-20.

1909. Graded VF-25.

Illustrated coin: Some bumps are seen on the top obverse rim and should be mentioned in a description.

PF-60 to 70 (Proof). *Obverse and Reverse:* At PF–60 to 63, there is light abrasion and some contact marks (the lower the grade, the higher the quantity). On Sandblast Proofs these show up as visually unappealing bright spots. At PF-64 and higher levels, marks are fewer, with magnification needed to see any at PF-65. At PF-66, there should be none at all.

Illustrated coin: This is a particularly nice example.

1911, Sandblast Finish. Graded PF-67.

	Mintage	Cert	Avg	%MS	VF-20	EF-40	AU-50	AU-55	AU-58	MS-60	MS-62	MS-63	MS-65
											PF-63	PF-64	PF-65
1908	577,845	7,651	61.4	85%	$400	$420	$440	$460	$475	$500	$650	$1,250	$8,000
	Auctions: $51,700, MS-67, January 2015; $911, MS-62, August 2015; $558, AU-58, February 2015; $376, AU-55, March 2015												
1908, Sandblast Finish Proof	167	86	65.2								$15,000	$25,000	$45,000
	Auctions: $152,750, PF, August 2013												
1908-D	148,000	2,796	62.3	94%	$400	$420	$440	$460	$475	$650	$800	$1,250	$25,000
	Auctions: $3,290, MS-64, September 2015; $1,351, MS-63, June 2015; $705, MS-61, August 2015; $470, AU-58, July 2015												
1908-S	82,000	539	57.7	42%	$575	$700	$1,000	$1,350	$1,750	$2,750	$5,500	$9,000	$17,500
	Auctions: $47,000, MS-67, August 2014; $17,625, MS-65, January 2015; $7,344, MS-63, January 2015; $1,175, AU-55, July 2015												

	Mintage	Cert	Avg	%MS	VF-20	EF-40	AU-50	AU-55	AU-58	MS-60	MS-62 / PF-63	MS-63 / PF-64	MS-65 / PF-65
1909	627,060	6,960	61.0	83%	$400	$420	$440	$460	$475	$525	$650	$1,250	$8,000
Auctions: $7,638, MS-65, February 2015; $2,115, MS-64, October 2015; $676, MS-62, October 2015; $764, MS-61, July 2015													
1909, Satin Finish Proof	78	36	65.3								$17,500	$30,000	$50,000
Auctions: $82,250, PF-67, August 2014; $55,813, PF-66, August 2014; $99,875, PF-66, February 2013													
1909, Sandblast Finish Proof (a)	*unknown*	1	67.0										
Auctions: No auction records available.													
1909-D	3,423,560	32,146	61.5	87%	$400	$420	$440	$460	$475	$525	$650	$1,250	$8,000
Auctions: $2,350, MS-64, March 2015; $764, MS-62, June 2015; $552, MS-61, September 2015; $353, EF-40, April 2015													
1909-O (b)	34,200	984	55.5	14%	$4,750	$7,500	$11,000	$16,500	$25,000	$40,000	$65,000	$85,000	$400,000
Auctions: $56,400, MS-62, December 2015: $35,250, MS-61, August 2015; $32,900, MS-61, March 2016													
1909-S	297,200	711	56.7	29%	$425	$450	$475	$550	$725	$2,250	$5,500	$10,000	$50,000
Auctions: $5,640, MS-62, January 2015; $3,410, MS-61, January 2015; $529, AU-55, March 2015; $400, EF-40, February 2015													
1910	604,000	7,071	60.9	80%	$400	$420	$440	$460	$475	$525	$650	$1,250	$8,000
Auctions: $17,625, MS-65, August 2015; $1,998, MS-64, February 2015; $999, MS-63, October 2015; $447, MS-60, May 2015													
1910, Satin Finish Proof	250	48	65.3								$17,500	$25,000	$45,000
Auctions: $146,250, PF, September 2013													
1910, Sandblast Finish Proof (c)	*unknown*	0	n/a										
Auctions: No auction records available.													
1910-D	193,600	1,189	60.4	75%	$400	$420	$440	$460	$475	$525	$1,200	$2,500	$26,000
Auctions: $7,050, MS-64, January 2015; $1,029, MS-62, January 2015; $617, MS-61, June 2015; $400, AU-55, May 2015													
1910-S	770,200	1,532	57.0	27%	$425	$450	$475	$500	$800	$1,500	$3,500	$9,500	$75,000
Auctions: $3,290, MS-62, March 2015; $2,056, MS-61, January 2015; $676, AU-58, August 2015; $517, AU-55, August 2015													
1911	915,000	10,914	60.7	77%	$400	$420	$440	$460	$475	$525	$650	$1,250	$8,000
Auctions: $8,225, MS-65, January 2015; $1,880, MS-64, January 2015; $529, MS-61, September 2015													
1911, Sandblast Finish Proof	139	54	65.7								$15,000	$25,000	$45,000
Auctions: $99,875, PF-67, April 2013													
1911-D	72,500	1,434	55.9	16%	$750	$1,000	$1,750	$3,000	$4,500	$8,500	$20,000	$37,500	$225,000
Auctions: $36,425, MS-63, December 2015: $12,925, MS-62, August 2015; $8,813, MS-61, January 2015													
1911-S	1,416,000	2,757	57.2	36%	$425	$450	$475	$500	$600	$900	$2,000	$4,500	$42,500
Auctions: $12,925, MS-64, January 2015; $1,175, MS-61, July 2015; $494, AU-55, June 2015; $376, EF-45, March 2015													
1912	790,000	10,394	60.9	81%	$400	$420	$440	$460	$475	$525	$650	$1,250	$8,000
Auctions: $7,050, MS-65, January 2015; $2,820, MS-64, June 2015; $447, MS-61, October 2015; $482, AU-58, July 2015													
1912, Sandblast Finish Proof	144	38	66.4								$15,000	$25,000	$45,000
Auctions: $58,750, PF-66, September 2013													
1912-S	392,000	1,544	56.1	17%	$425	$450	$475	$600	$900	$1,850	$5,500	$15,000	$175,000
Auctions: $5,405, MS-62, August 2015; $2,820, MS-61, October 2015; $1,293, AU-58, August 2015; $449, AU-53, March 2015													
1913	915,901	11,984	60.9	82%	$400	$420	$440	$460	$475	$525	$650	$1,250	$8,000
Auctions: $2,585, MS-64, March 2015; $1,058, MS-63, October 2015; $764, MS-61, June 2015; $423, AU-58, July 2015													
1913, Sandblast Finish Proof	99	25	66.2								$15,000	$25,000	$45,000
Auctions: $51,750, PF-67, July 2011													
1913-S	408,000	1,881	56.4	23%	$525	$575	$625	$800	$875	$2,500	$6,000	$15,000	$120,000
Auctions: $4,600, MS-62, January 2015; $823, AU-58, July 2015; $470, AU-53, February 2015; $340, EF-40, February 2015													
1914	247,000	2,842	60.8	77%	$400	$420	$440	$460	$475	$525	$800	$1,750	$12,500
Auctions: $9,400, MS-65, January 2015; $5,170, MS-64, August 2015; $1,028, MS-62, June 2015; $541, MS-61, March 2015													
1914, Sandblast Finish Proof	125	33	65.8								$15,000	$25,000	$45,000
Auctions: $93,600, PF, September 2013													
1914-D	247,000	2,618	60.5	72%	$400	$420	$440	$460	$475	$600	$900	$2,250	$2,000
Auctions: $3,760, MS-64, October 2015; $1,880, MS-63, July 2015; $1,058, MS-61, February 2015; $470, AU-58, February 2015													
1914-S	263,000	1,500	57.8	35%	$425	$450	$475	$525	$850	$1,750	$4,500	$8,000	$125,000
Auctions: $16,450, MS-63, August 2015; $2,115, AU-58, September 2015; $470, AU-53, May 2015; $382, VF-35, June 2015													

a. This unique coin is certified by NGC as PF-67. **b.** Beware spurious "O" mintmark. **c.** This unique coin is part of the unique complete 1910 Sandblast Finish Proof gold set.

	Mintage	Cert	Avg	%MS	VF-20	EF-40	AU-50	AU-55	AU-58	MS-60	MS-62	MS-63	MS-65
											PF-63	PF-64	PF-65
1915 (d)	588,000	6,448	60.8	76%	$400	$420	$440	$460	$475	$525	$650	$1,250	$8,000
	Auctions: $9,988, MS-65, August 2015; $3,760, MS-64, September 2015; $764, MS-62, August 2015; $646, MS-61, June 2015												
1915, Sandblast Finish Proof	75	22	65.2								$17,500	$25,000	$55,000
	Auctions: $47,000, PF-66, June 2014												
1915-S	164,000	1,319	56.3	21%	$425	$450	$500	$700	$1,250	$2,500	$7,500	$12,500	$125,000
	Auctions: $5,640, MS-62, January 2015; $3,525, MS-61, January 2015; $1,116, AU-58, October 2015; $364, AU-50, March 2015												
1916-S	240,000	2,069	58.9	48%	$450	$485	$525	$625	$850	$1,250	$2,500	$5,000	$32,500
	Auctions: $41,126, MS-65, August 2015; $1,410, MS-61, October 2015; $400, AU-55, March 2015; $376, AU-50, October 2015												
1929	662,000	220	62.4	91%	$18,500	$20,000	$23,500	$25,000	$30,000	$35,000	$40,000	$50,000	$115,000
	Auctions: $54,050, MS-64, January 2015; $51,700, MS-64, January 2015; $47,000, MS-64, September 2016; $37,600, MS-62, August 2015												

d. Pieces dated 1915-D are counterfeit.

Gold Eagles ($10)
1795–1933

AN OVERVIEW OF GOLD EAGLES

The ten-dollar gold coin, or *eagle*, was first produced in 1795. Coinage authority for the denomination, including its weight and fineness, had been specified by the Act of April 2, 1792.

The Capped Bust to Right with Small Eagle reverse is the rarest of the early ten-dollar coin types. However, when seen they tend to be in higher grades such as EF, AU, or low levels of Mint State. The Heraldic Eagle reverse issues from 1797 through 1804 are much more readily available and in slightly higher average grade.

The Liberty Head eagles without the motto IN GOD WE TRUST, minted from 1838 through 1865, are elusive in any Mint State grade, although VF and EF pieces are plentiful, and there are enough AU coins to easily satisfy collector demands. Some collectors have considered the 1838 and 1839, 9 Over 8, with the head of Miss Liberty tilted forward in relation to the date, to be a separate type. Eagles with IN GOD WE TRUST on the reverse, produced from 1866 to 1907, are plentiful in high grades, including choice and gem Mint State. Some of these were repatriated from overseas bank vaults beginning in the second half of the 20th century.

The Saint-Gaudens eagles of 1907, of the style with periods between and flanking the words E PLURIBUS UNUM, exist in the Wire Rim and Rounded Rim varieties. These can be collected as a distinct type, or not. Most readily available is the Wire Rim style, of which somewhat more than 400 are likely to exist today, nearly all in Mint State, often choice or gem. These coins were made as regular issues but soon became numismatic delicacies for Treasury officials to distribute as they saw fit. Some were to have gone to museums, but in reality most were secretly filtered out through favored coin dealers. Then comes the 1907–1908 style, without periods, easily available in EF, AU, and lower Mint State levels, although gems are elusive.

The final eagle type, the 1908–1933 style with IN GOD WE TRUST on the reverse, is readily obtained in grades from EF through MS-63. Higher-grade pieces are elusive, and

This pattern eagle of 1878, struck in copper and designated J-1580, was designed by George Morgan and strongly resembles the silver dollar design that bears his name.

when seen are often dated 1932, a year in which 4,463,000 were struck—more than any other coin in the history of the denomination.

FOR THE COLLECTOR AND INVESTOR: GOLD EAGLES AS A SPECIALTY

Collecting ten-dollar gold coins by die varieties is unusual, as the series includes so many scarce and rare coins. However, unlike other denominations, none is in the "impossible" category, and with some patience a full set of significant varieties, as listed in this book, can be obtained.

The early issues with a Small Eagle reverse, minted from 1795 through 1797, and those with the Heraldic Eagle reverse of 1797 through 1804, can be collected and studied by die varieties, with *United States Ten Dollar Gold Eagles 1795–1804*, by Anthony Teraskza, being one useful guide. *Early U.S. Gold Coin Varieties: A Study of Die States, 1795–1834*, by John W. Dannreuther and Harry W. Bass Jr., offers an abundance of information and enlarged photographs for study. In addition to the regular issues, a few 1804 restrike ten-dollar pieces exist from 1804-dated dies newly created in 1834.

Liberty Head eagles from 1838 through 1866 (without the motto IN GOD WE TRUST) comprise many scarce dates and mintmarks. Years ago the 1858, of which only 2,521 were minted, was highly acclaimed as a landmark issue, but since then the publicity has faded. In any event, although certain date-and-mintmark varieties are rare, the number of numismatists collecting them by date sequence is very small, and thus opportunities exist to acquire very elusive pieces at a much smaller proportionate premium than would be possible in, say, the gold dollar series. No full set of Mint State early eagles has ever been formed; probably none ever will be. EF and AU are typically the grades of choice, with Mint State pieces added when available.

Later Liberty Head eagles of the 1866–1907 style (with the motto IN GOD WE TRUST) include some low-mintage issues, but again these are not impossible to collect. The most famous is the 1875 Philadelphia coin, of which just 100 circulation strikes were made. Although smaller numbers exist for Proof-only mintages, in terms of those made for commerce the 1875 sets a record. The low-mintage 1879-O (1,500 made) and 1883-O (800) also have attracted much attention. Again, these pieces, while rare, are available to the specialist, as there is not a great deal of competition.

Among Indian Head eagles the 1907, With Periods, Wire Rim, is famous, popular, and rare. Examples come on the market with regularity but are expensive due to the demand they attract. The Rounded Rim style is much rarer and when seen is usually in choice Mint State.

The regular without-periods 1907 and 1908 eagles are easy enough to obtain in Mint State, although gems are elusive. The varieties from 1908 through 1916 include no great rarities, although some are scarcer than others. Not many such pieces were saved at the time they were issued, and, accordingly, gems are elusive. However, grades such as AU and low Mint State will present no problem. Among later eagles, the 1920-S, 1930-S, and 1933 are rarities. In particular the 1920-S is difficult to find in choice and gem Mint State. The 1933 eagle is usually found in Mint State, but is expensive due to the publicity given to it. Readily available at reasonable prices are the 1926 and 1932.

CAPPED BUST TO RIGHT, SMALL EAGLE REVERSE (1795–1797)

Designer: *Robert Scot.* **Weight:** *17.50 grams.*
Composition: *.9167 gold, .0833 silver and copper.*
Diameter: *Approximately 33 mm.* **Edge:** *Reeded.* **Mint:** *Philadelphia.*

Bass-Dannreuther–1.

History. Eagles of this style, the first in the denomination, debuted in the autumn of 1795. The obverse features Miss Liberty dressed in a conical cap. The reverse shows a "small" eagle perched on a palm branch and holding a laurel in his beak. The same motif was used on contemporary gold half eagles.

Striking and Sharpness. On the obverse, check the star centers and the hair details. On the reverse, check the feathers of the eagle. In particular, the breast feathers often are weakly struck. Examine the denticles on both sides. Adjustment marks (from a Mint worker filing an overweight planchet down to the correct weight) often are visible, but are not noted by the grading services.

Availability. Typical grades range from EF to AU and low MS. MS-63 and higher coins are rare; when seen, they usually are of the 1795 or 1796 dates. Certain varieties are rare. While no Proofs of this type were made, certain eagles of 1796 have prooflike surfaces and are particularly attractive if in high grades.

GRADING STANDARDS

MS-60 to 70 (Mint State). *Obverse:* At MS-60, some abrasion and contact marks are evident, most noticeably on the hair to the left of Miss Liberty's forehead and on the higher-relief areas of the cap. Luster is present, but may be dull or lifeless, and interrupted in patches. At MS-63, contact marks are few, and abrasion is very light. An MS-65 coin has hardly any abrasion, and contact marks are so minute as to require magnifica-

1795, 13 Leaves; BD-5. Graded MS-63.

tion. Luster should be full and rich. On prooflike coins in any Mint State grade, abrasion and surface marks are much more noticeable. Coins above MS-65 exist more in theory than in reality for this type—but they do exist, and are defined by having fewer marks as perfection is approached. *Reverse:* Comments apply as for the obverse, except that abrasion and contact marks are most noticeable on the breast and head of the eagle. The field area is mainly protected by the eagle, branch, and lettering.

AU-50, 53, 55, 58 (About Uncirculated). *Obverse:* Light wear is seen on the cheek, the hair immediately to the left of the face, and the cap, more so at AU-50 than at AU–53 or 55. An AU-58 coin has minimal traces of wear. An AU-50 coin has luster in protected areas among the stars and letters, with little in the open fields or on the portrait. At AU-58, most luster is present in the fields, but is worn away on the highest parts of the motifs.

1796. Graded AU-58.

Reverse: Comments as preceding, except that the eagle shows light wear on the breast and head in particular, but also at the tip of the wing on the left and elsewhere. Luster ranges from perhaps 40% remaining in protected areas (at AU-50) to nearly full mint bloom (at AU-58).

   Illustrated coin: This example shows light wear overall, with hints of original luster in protected areas.

EF-40, 45 (Extremely Fine). *Obverse:* Wear is evident all over the portrait, with some loss of detail in the hair to the left of Miss Liberty's face. Excellent detail remains in low-relief areas of the hair, such as the front curl and at the back of her head. The stars show wear, as do the date and letters. Luster, if present at all, is minimal and in protected areas. *Reverse:* Wear is greater than on an About Uncirculated coin. The breast, neck, and legs of the

1795, 9 Leaves; BD-3. Graded EF-45.

eagle lack nearly all feather detail. More wear is seen on the edges of the wing. Some traces of luster may be seen, more so at EF-45 than at EF-40.

VF-20, 30 (Very Fine). *Obverse:* The higher-relief areas of hair are well worn at VF-20, less so at VF-30. The stars are flat at their centers. *Reverse:* Wear is greater, the eagle is flat in most areas, and about 40% to 60% of the wing feathers can be seen.

   The Capped Bust to Right eagle coin with Small Eagle reverse is seldom collected in grades lower than VF-20.

1795, 13 Leaves; BD-2. Graded VF-30.

 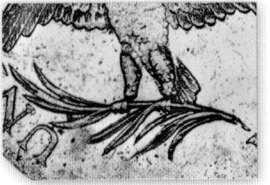

1795, 13 Leaves	1795, 9 Leaves

	Mintage	Cert	Avg	%MS	F-12	VF-20	EF-40	AU-50	AU-55	MS-60	MS-62	MS-63
1795, 13 Leaves Below Eagle	5,583	53	55.2	26%	$27,500	$35,000	$50,000	$55,000	$72,500	$105,000	$150,000	$300,000 **(a)**
Auctions: $152,750, MS-62, November 2014; $64,625, AU-55, August 2016; $49,938, EF-45, August 2014												
1795, 9 Leaves Below Eagle †	**(b)**	15	56.9	20%	$75,000	$85,000	$95,000	$135,000	$175,000	$250,000	$350,000	$500,000
Auctions: $146,875, EF-45, August 2014; $47,000, EF-40, January 2014												
1796	4,146	67	56.7	25%	$32,500	$37,500	$55,000	$60,000	$75,000	$125,000	$225,000	$425,000
Auctions: $164,500, MS-62, April 2014; $82,250, AU-55, August 2014												
1797, Small Eagle	3,615	28	55.1	32%	$40,000	$55,000	$80,000	$115,000	$130,000	$225,000	$375,000	$500,000
Auctions: $164,500, AU-58, August 2014; $91,063, EF-45, August 2016; $47,000, EF-40, August 2014												

† Ranked in the *100 Greatest U.S. Coins* (fourth edition). **a.** Value in MS-64 is $475,000. **b.** Included in 1795, 13 Leaves Below Eagle, mintage figure.

CAPPED BUST TO RIGHT, HERALDIC EAGLE REVERSE (1797–1804)

Designer: *Robert Scot.* **Weight:** *17.50 grams.*
Composition: *.9167 gold, .0833 silver and copper.*
Diameter: *Approximately 33 mm.* **Edge:** *Reeded.* **Mint:** *Philadelphia.*

Circulation Strike	Proof
BD-2.	

History. Gold eagles of this type combine the previous obverse style with the Heraldic Eagle—a modification of the Great Seal of the United States—as used on other silver and gold coins of the era. Regarding the Proofs dated 1804: There were no Proofs coined in the era in which this type was issued, and all eagle and silver dollar production was suspended by President Thomas Jefferson in 1804. Years later, in 1834, the Mint made up new dies with the 1804 date (this time featuring a Plain 4 rather than a Crosslet 4) and struck a number of Proofs (the quantity unknown today, but perhaps a dozen or so) for inclusion in presentation Proof sets for foreign dignitaries.

Striking and Sharpness. On the obverse, check the star centers and the hair details. On the reverse, check the upper part of the shield, the lower part of the eagle's neck, the eagle's wing, the stars above the eagle, and the clouds. Inspect the denticles on both sides. Adjustment marks (from where an overweight planchet was filed down to correct specifications) can be problematic; these are not identified by the grading services.

Availability. Mintages of this type were erratic. Eagles of 1797 appear in the market with some regularity, while those of 1798 are rare. Usually seen are the issues of 1799 through 1803. Typical grades range from EF to lower MS. MS-62 and higher coins are seen with some frequency and usually are dated 1799 and later. The 1804 circulation strike is rare in true MS. Sharply struck coins without planchet adjustment marks are in the minority. Only a handful of the aforementioned 1804 Proofs survive today.

GRADING STANDARDS

MS-60 to 70 (Mint State). *Obverse:* At MS-60, some abrasion and contact marks are evident, most noticeably on the hair to the left of Miss Liberty's forehead and on the higher-relief areas of the cap. Luster is present, but may be dull or lifeless, and interrupted in patches. At MS-63, contact marks are few, and abrasion is very light. An MS-65 coin has even less abrasion (most observable in the right field), and contact marks are so

1799, Large Stars; BD-10. Graded MS-65.

minute as to require magnification. Luster should be full and rich. Coins graded above MS-65 are more theoretical than actual for this type—but they do exist, and are defined by having fewer marks as perfection is approached. Large-size eagles are usually graded with slightly less strictness than the lower gold denominations of this type. *Reverse:* Comments apply as for the obverse, except that abrasion and contact marks are most noticeable on the upper part of the eagle and the clouds. The field area is complex, without much open space, given the stars above the eagle, the arrows and olive branch, and other features. Accordingly, marks are not as noticeable as on the obverse.

Illustrated coin: This coin has an exceptionally sharp strike overall, but with some lightness on the eagle's dexter (viewer's left) talon. Note some trivial abrasion in the right obverse field.

AU-50, 53, 55, 58 (About Uncirculated). *Obverse:* Light wear is seen on the cheek, the hair immediately to the left of the face, and the cap, more so at AU-50 than at AU–53 or 55. An AU-58 coin has minimal traces of wear. An AU-50 coin has luster in protected areas among the stars and letters, with little in the open fields or on the portrait. At AU-58, most luster is present in the fields, but is worn away on the highest parts of the

1799, Small Stars; BD-7. Graded AU-50.

motifs. *Reverse:* Comments as preceding, except that the eagle's neck, the tips and top of the wings, the clouds, and the tail now show noticeable wear, as do other features. Luster ranges from perhaps 40% remaining in protected areas (at AU-50) to nearly full mint bloom (at AU-58). Often the reverse of this type retains much more luster than the obverse.

Illustrated coin: Note some lightness of strike at the center of the obverse. Significant luster remains.

EF-40, 45 (Extremely Fine). *Obverse:* Wear is evident all over the portrait, with some loss of detail in the hair to the left of Miss Liberty's face. Excellent detail remains in low-relief areas of the hair, such as the front curl and at the back of her head. The stars show wear as do the date and letters. Luster, if present at all, is minimal and in protected areas. *Reverse:* Wear is greater than on the preceding. The neck lacks some feather detail on its highest points. Feathers have lost some detail near the edges of the wings, and some areas of the horizontal lines in the shield may be blended together. Some traces of luster may be seen, more so at EF-45 than at EF-40. Overall, the reverse appears to be in a slightly higher grade than the obverse.

1801; BD-2. Graded EF-45.

VF-20, 30 (Very Fine). *Obverse:* The higher-relief areas of hair are well worn at VF-20, less so at VF-30. *Reverse:* Wear is greater, including on the shield and wing feathers. The star centers are flat. Other areas have lost detail as well. E PLURIBUS UNUM may be faint in areas, but is usually sharp.

The Capped Bust to Right eagle coin with Heraldic Eagle reverse is seldom collected in grades lower than VF-20.

1799, Small Stars; BD-7. Graded VF-30.

PF-60 to 70 (Proof). *Obverse and Reverse:* PF–60 to 62 coins have extensive hairlines and may have nicks and contact marks. At PF-63, hairlines are prominent, but the mirror surface is very reflective. PF-64 coins have fewer hairlines. At PF-65, hairlines should be minimal and mostly seen only under magnification. There should be no nicks or marks.

1804, Plain 4; BD-2. Proof.

1798, 8 Over 7, 9 Stars Left, 4 Right	1798, 8 Over 7, 7 Stars Left, 6 Right	1799, Small Obverse Stars	1799, Large Obverse Stars

1803, Small Reverse Stars	1803, Large Reverse Stars

	Mintage	Cert	Avg	%MS	F-12	VF-20	EF-40	AU-50	AU-55	MS-60	MS-62 / PF-63	MS-63 / PF-64	MS-64 / PF-65
1797	10,940	162	55.7	30%	$12,500	$15,000	$20,000	$32,500	$40,000	$55,000	$95,000	$150,000	$225,000
Auctions: $117,500, MS-63, April 2014; $44,063, MS-61, November 2014; $41,125, AU-58, August 2014; $34,075, AU-58, August 2014												
1798, 8 Over 7, 9 Stars Left, 4 Stars Right †	900	28	56.7	32%	$22,500	$27,500	$40,000	$55,000	$70,000	$125,000	$215,000	$300,000	
Auctions: $176,250, MS-62, April 2014; $76,375, AU-55, August 2016												
1798, 8 Over 7, 7 Stars Left, 6 Stars Right †	842	4	52.5	25%	$45,000	$60,000	$95,000	$175,000	$225,000	$400,000	$650,000		
Auctions: $352,500, AU-58, August 2016; $161,000, AU-55, January 2005; $176,250, AU-50, August 2014												
1799, Small Obverse Stars	37,449	34	57.6	44%	$9,500	$12,500	$16,000	$20,000	$23,500	$32,500	$42,500	$67,500	$135,000
Auctions: $9,988, AU-58, September 2014; $25,850, AU-58, August 2014; $24,675, AU-55, January 2014; $15,275, AU-50, August 2014												
1799, Large Obverse Stars	(a)	31	58.9	58%	$9,500	$12,500	$16,000	$20,000	$23,500	$32,500	$42,500	$67,500	$115,000
Auctions: $32,900, MS-62, October 2014; $19,975, AU-58, August 2014; $16,450, AU-53, November 2014; $9,400, AU, March 2015												
1800	5,999	107	57.3	41%	$9,500	$13,000	$16,500	$21,500	$24,500	$35,000	$52,500	$85,000	$160,000
Auctions: $117,500, MS-64, January 2014; $32,900, MS-61, August 2014; $15,275, AU-50, August 2014; $7,638, AU-50, July 2014												
1801	44,344	412	58.6	52%	$9,500	$11,000	$15,000	$18,500	$21,000	$30,000	$40,000	$65,000	$125,000
Auctions: $88,125, MS-64, March 2013; $48,763, MS-63, August 2014; $45,535, MS-63, August 2014; $29,375, MS-61, October 2014												
1803, Small Reverse Stars	15,017	22	57.1	45%	$10,000	$12,000	$16,000	$21,500	$23,500	$37,500	$50,000	$65,000	$135,000
Auctions: $28,200, MS-61, January 2014; $15,875, AU-55, November 2014; $17,625, AU-55, August 2014; $13,513, AU-55, August 2014												
1803, Large Reverse Stars (b)	(c)	9	58.2	44%	$10,000	$12,000	$16,000	$21,500	$23,500	$37,500	$50,000	$65,000	$135,000
Auctions: $99,875, MS-64, January 2014; $42,594, MS-62, August 2014; $24,675, AU-53, August 2014												
1804, Crosslet 4	3,757	53	58.8	49%	$20,000	$25,000	$37,500	$50,000	$65,000	$85,000	$100,000	$175,000	
Auctions: $73,438, MS-61, January 2014; $64,625, MS-60, August 2014; $58,750, AU-58, August 2014												
1804, Plain 4, Proof † (d)	5–8	2	65.0								$4,000,000	$4,500,000	$5,000,000
Auctions: $73,438, MS-61, January 2014												

† Ranked in the *100 Greatest U.S. Coins* (fourth edition). **a.** Included in 1799, Small Obverse Stars, mintage figure. **b.** A variety without the tiny 14th star in the cloud is very rare; 6 or 7 examples are known. It does not command a significant premium. **c.** Included in 1803, Small Reverse Stars, mintage figure. **d.** These coins were minted in 1834 (from newly created dies with the date 1804) for presentation sets for foreign dignitaries. 3 or four 4 are known today.

LIBERTY HEAD (1838–1907)

Designer: *Christian Gobrecht.* **Weight:** *16.718 grams.*
Composition: *.900 gold, .100 copper (net weight: .48375 oz. pure gold).* **Diameter:** *27 mm.*
Edge: *Reeded.* **Mints:** *Philadelphia, Carson City, Denver, New Orleans, and San Francisco.*

No Motto Above Eagle (1838–1866)

No Motto Above Eagle, Proof

Motto Above Eagle (1866–1907)

Motto Above Eagle, Proof

History. Production of the gold eagle, suspended after 1804, started up again in 1838 with the Liberty Head design. The coin's weight and diameter was reduced from the specifications of the earlier type. For the first time in the denomination's history, its value, TEN D., was shown. Midway through 1839 the style was modified slightly, including in the letters (made smaller) and in the tilt of Miss Liberty's portrait. In 1866 the motto IN GOD WE TRUST was placed on a banner above the eagle's head.

Striking and Sharpness. On the obverse, check the highest points of the hair and the star centers. On the reverse, check the eagle's neck, and the area to the lower left of the shield and the lower part of the eagle. Examine the denticles on both sides. Branch-mint coins issued before the Civil War often are lightly struck in areas, and some Carson City coins of the early 1870s can have areas of lightness. Most late 19th-century and early 20th-century coins are sharp in all areas. Tiny copper staining spots (from improperly mixed alloy) can be a problem for those issues. Cameo contrast is the rule for Proofs prior to 1902. Beginning that year the portrait was polished in the die, imparting a mirror finish across the entire design, although a few years later cameo-contrast coins were again made.

Availability. Early dates and mintmarks are generally scarce to rare in MS and very rare in MS-63 and better grades, with only a few exceptions. These were workhorse coins in commerce; VF and EF grades are the rule for dates through the 1870s, and for some dates the finest known grade can be AU. In MS, Liberty Head eagles as a type are rarer than either quarter eagles or half eagles of the same design. Indeed, the majority of Mint State examples were only discovered in recent decades, resting in European banks, and some varieties are not known to exist at this level. Eagles of the 1880s onward generally are seen in higher average grades. Proof coins exist in relation to their original mintages, with all issues prior to the 1890s being very rare.

Note: Values of common-date gold coins have been based on the current bullion price of gold, $1,300 per ounce, and may vary with the prevailing spot price.

GRADING STANDARDS

MS-60 to 70 (Mint State). *Obverse:* At MS-60, some abrasion and contact marks are evident, most noticeably on the hair to the right of Miss Liberty's forehead and on the jaw. Luster is present, but may be dull or lifeless, and interrupted in patches. At MS-63, contact marks are few, and abrasion is very light. An MS-65 coin has hardly any abrasion, and contact marks are so minute as to require magnification. Luster should be full and rich.

1880. Graded MS-63.

For most dates, coins graded above MS-65 exist more in theory than in actuality—but they do exist, and are defined by having fewer marks as perfection is approached. *Reverse:* Comments apply as for the obverse, except that abrasion and contact marks are most noticeable on the eagle's neck and to the lower left of the shield.

Illustrated coin: This coin is brilliant and lustrous with scattered marks in the field, as is typical for this grade.

AU-50, 53, 55, 58 (About Uncirculated). *Obverse:* Light wear is seen on the face, the hair to the right of the face, and the highest area of the hair bun, more so at AU-50 than at AU–53 or 55. An AU-58 coin has minimal traces of wear. An AU-50 coin has luster in protected areas among the stars and letters, with little in the open fields or on the portrait. At AU-58 most luster is present in the fields, but is worn away on the highest parts

1839, Large Letters, 9 Over 8. Graded AU-53.

of the motifs. *Reverse:* Comments as preceding, except that the eagle shows wear in all of the higher areas, as well as the leaves and arrowheads. Luster ranges from perhaps 40% remaining in protected areas (at AU-50) to nearly full mint bloom (at AU-58). Often the reverse of this type retains more luster than the obverse.

EF-40, 45 (Extremely Fine). *Obverse:* Wear is evident on all high areas of the portrait, including the hair to the right of the forehead, the tip of the coronet, and the hair bun. The stars show light wear at their centers. Luster, if present at all, is minimal and in protected areas such as between the star points. *Reverse:* Wear is greater than on an About Uncirculated coin. On the $10 coins (in contrast to the $2.50 and $5 of the same design), most of the details on

1868. Graded EF-40.

the eagle are sharp. There is flatness on the leaves and arrowheads. Some traces of luster may be seen, more so at EF-45 than at EF-40.

Illustrated coin: Note the many contact marks on both sides.

VF-20, 30 (Very Fine). *Obverse:* The higher-relief areas of hair are worn flat at VF-20, less so at VF-30. The hair to the right of the coronet is merged into heavy strands. The stars are flat at their centers. *Reverse:* The eagle is worn further, with most neck feathers gone and with the feathers in the wing having flat tips. The branch leaves have little or no detail. The vertical shield stripes, being deeply recessed, remain bold.

1838. Graded VF-25.

The Liberty Head eagle is seldom collected in grades lower than VF-20.

PF-60 to 70 (Proof). *Obverse and Reverse:* PF–60 to 62 coins have extensive hairlines and may have nicks and contact marks. At PF-63, hairlines are prominent, but the mirror surface is very reflective. PF-64 coins have fewer hairlines. At PF-65, hairlines should be minimal and mostly seen only under magnification. There should be no nicks or marks. PF-66 and higher coins should have no marks or hairlines visible to the unaided eye.

1862. Graded PF-65.

Illustrated coin: This is a museum-quality gem, with cameo-contrast motifs and mirror fields.

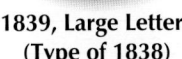

1839, Large Letters
(Type of 1838)

1839, Small Letters
(Type of 1840)

	Mintage	Cert	Avg	%MS	VF-20	EF-40	AU-50	AU-55	AU-58	MS-60	MS-63	MS-65
										PF-63	PF-64	PF-65
1838	7,200	59	48.1	3%	$4,250	$10,000	$20,000	$30,000	$65,000	$80,000	$125,000	
Auctions: $105,750, MS-63, May 2016; $64,625, AU-58, August 2016: $41,125, AU-58, August 2014; $7,638, EF-40, August 2015												
1838, Proof † (a)	4–6	1	65.0		*(extremely rare)*							
Auctions: $500,000, ChPF, May 1998												
1839, Large Letters (b)	25,801	163	50.5	10%	$2,000	$4,500	$6,500	$11,500	$15,000	$32,500	$85,000	$350,000
Auctions: $10,575, AU-58, September 2015; $9,694, AU-55, August 2015; $9,400, AU-55, August 2016; $4,759, AU-50, August 2015												
1839, Small Letters	12,447	39	46.9	3%	$3,500	$9,500	$13,500	$20,000	$27,500	$45,000	$135,000	
Auctions: $47,000, AU-58, February 2014; $9,988, AU-50, September 2015; $3,995, 35, September 2016												
1839, Large Letters, Proof (c)	4–6	1	67.0		*(extremely rare)*							
Auctions: $1,610,000, PF-67UCam, January 2007												

† Ranked in the *100 Greatest U.S. Coins* (fourth edition). **a.** 3 examples are known. **b.** The Large Letters style is also known as the "Type of 1838," because of the distinct style of the 1838 Liberty Head motif. The Small Letters style (or "Type of 1840") was used on subsequent issues. **c.** 3 examples are known.

1842, Small Date   **1842, Large Date**

	Mintage	Cert	Avg	%MS	VF-20	EF-40	AU-50	AU-55	AU-58	MS-60	MS-63	MS-65
										PF-63	PF-64	PF-65
1840	47,338	177	49.3	3%	$1,000	$1,100	$1,550	$2,750	$5,500	$9,500		
	Auctions: $35,250, MS-62, August 2014; $15,275, MS-61, June 2015; $1,528, AU-53, June 2015; $1,645, EF-40, September 2015											
1840, Proof (d)	1–2	0	n/a		*(unique, in the Smithsonian's National Numismatic Collection)*							
	Auctions: No auction records available.											
1841	63,131	207	49.9	7%	$1,000	$1,050	$1,350	$2,500	$4,500	$8,000		
	Auctions: $9,400, MS-61, February 2014; $4,230, AU-58, August 2015; $1,645, AU-55, February 2015; $1,116, AU-53, June 2015											
1841, Proof (e)	4–6	1	61.0		*(extremely rare)*							
	Auctions: No auction records available.											
1841-O	2,500	45	44.3	0%	$4,500	$12,500	$22,500	$25,000	$32,500			
	Auctions: $25,850, AU-53, January 2014; $21,150, AU-50, September 2016; $14,688, AU-50, October 2014; $9,988, VF-25, August 2016											
1842, Small Date	18,623	97	51.4	6%	$1,000	$1,150	$1,750	$3,000	$5,000	$12,500	$40,000	
	Auctions: $12,925, MS-61, June 2015; $2,115, AU-55, January 2015; $1,175, AU-50, February 2015; $940, AU-50, January 2015											
1842, Large Date	62,884	118	51.7	4%	$1,000	$1,050	$1,650	$2,500	$5,000	$15,000	$35,000	$125,000
	Auctions: $2,233, MS-60, January 2014											
1842, Small Date, Proof (f)	2	0	n/a		*(extremely rare)*							
	Auctions: No auction records available.											
1842-O	27,400	263	48.2	2%	$1,250	$1,650	$3,250	$7,500	$14,500	$35,000	$95,000	
	Auctions: $8,825, AU-55, March 2014; $4,230, AU-53, August 2015; $2,115, AU-50, July 2016; $999, AU-50, July 2015											
1843	75,462	200	49.6	3%	$1,000	$1,150	$1,850	$3,850	$7,500	$14,500		
	Auctions: $3,055, AU-55, October 2015; $1,763, AU-50, August 2015; $1,058, EF-40, January 2015; $1,011, VF-30, March 2015											
1843, Doubled Die	(g)	0	n/a									
	Auctions: No auction records available.											
1843, Proof (h)	6–8	3	62.7		*(extremely rare)*							
	Auctions: No auction records available.											
1843-O	175,162	426	49.6	2%	$1,050	$1,200	$1,800	$3,250	$5,500	$12,000		
	Auctions: $7,050, AU-58, February 2015; $2,585, AU-53, July 2015; $1,175, AU-50, January 2015; $1,058, VF-35, January 2015											
1844	6,361	40	49.4	5%	$2,000	$4,000	$5,500	$7,500	$15,000	$20,000	$75,000	
	Auctions: $24,170, AU-55, January 2014											
1844, Proof (i)	6–8	1	63.0		*(extremely rare)*							
	Auctions: No auction records available.											
1844-O	118,700	380	50.9	5%	$1,050	$1,100	$1,850	$4,500	$8,500	$15,000		
	Auctions: $7,931, AU-58, June 2013; $2,585, AU-53, July 2015; $2,585, AU-53, March 2015; $1,293, EF-45, November 2014											
1844-O, Proof †	1	1	65.0									
	Auctions: No auction records available.											
1845	26,153	114	48.8	3%	$1,000	$1,100	$2,350	$3,250	$6,000	$15,000		
	Auctions: $4,994, AU-55, April 2013											
1845, Proof (j)	6–8	1	65.0		*(extremely rare)*							
	Auctions: $120,750, PF-64, August 1999											
1845-O	47,500	230	49.7	5%	$1,050	$1,500	$3,000	$7,500	$10,000	$15,000	$50,000	
	Auctions: $2,820, AU-53, November 2014; $881, AU-50, October 2014; $3,819, AU, March 2014; $764, EF-40, January 2015											

† Ranked in the *100 Greatest U.S. Coins* (fourth edition). **d.** While there is only one known example known of this coin, it is possible that other 1840 Proof eagles were made, given that duplicates are known of the quarter eagle and half eagle denominations. **e.** 3 examples are known. **f.** 2 examples are known. **g.** Included in circulation-strike 1843 mintage figure. **h.** 5 examples are known. **i.** 3 or 4 examples are known. **j.** 4 or 5 examples are known.

1846-O, 6 Over 5

1850, Large Date

1850, Small Date

	Mintage	Cert	Avg	%MS	VF-20	EF-40	AU-50	AU-55	AU-58	MS-60 / PF-63	MS-63 / PF-64	MS-65 / PF-65
1846	20,095	90	47.6	4%	$1,150	$1,350	$4,000	$6,500	$10,000	$20,000		
	Auctions: $4,994, AU-55, September 2014; $4,406, AU-55, September 2014; $8,225, AU-55, January 2014; $3,760, AU-50, June 2015											
1846, Proof (k)	6–8	1	64.0		*(extremely rare)*							
	Auctions: $161,000, PF-64Cam, January 2011											
1846-O, All kinds	81,780											
1846-O		149	45.9	1%	$1,200	$1,850	$3,500	$6,000	$8,500	$13,500		
	Auctions: $2,820, AU-50, January 2014											
1846-O, 6 Over 5		13	55.3	8%	$1,300	$2,250	$4,000	$7,500	$15,000	$35,000		
	Auctions: $3,525, AU-50, January 2014											
1847	862,258	1,340	52.3	5%	$850	$950	$1,000	$1,100	$1,650	$3,500	$21,500	
	Auctions: $894, AU-55, June 2015; $823, AU-53, February 2015; $764, AU-50, January 2015; $881, EF-40, July 2015											
1847, Proof	1–2	0	n/a		*(unique, in the Smithsonian's National Numismatic Collection)*							
	Auctions: No auction records available.											
1847-O	571,500	1,068	50.2	2%	$950	$1,050	$1,150	$1,600	$2,500	$6,000	$30,000	
	Auctions: $2,056, AU-58, August 2015; $1,528, AU-55, October 2015; $1,058, AU-50, July 2015; $881, VF-30, January 2015											
1848	145,484	403	51.8	7%	$850	$950	$1,000	$1,350	$1,750	$4,500	$23,500	
	Auctions: $64,625, MS-64, October 2014; $3,760, MS-60, June 2015; $940, AU-53, June 2015; $881, EF-45, January 2015											
1848, Proof (l)	3–5	1	64.0		*(extremely rare)*							
	Auctions: No auction records available.											
1848-O	35,850	182	49.0	4%	$1,100	$3,250	$4,000	$6,500	$11,000	$15,000	$35,000	$95,000
	Auctions: $51,700, MS-64, January 2015; $2,820, MS-60, October 2014; $3,525, AU-50, September 2015; $2,820, AU-50, June 2015											
1849	653,618	1,191	50.7	4%	$850	$1,100	$1,300	$1,500	$1,850	$3,750	$15,000	
	Auctions: $4,467, MS-61, June 2015; $999, AU-55, August 2015; $1,058, EF-45, August 2015; $676, VF-25, October 2015											
1849, Recut 1849 Over 849	(m)	39	49.8	8%				$4,000	$6,000			
	Auctions: $978, EF-40, May 2011											
1849-O	23,900	105	47.8	2%	$1,750	$3,500	$5,500	$9,500	$13,500	$25,000		
	Auctions: $5,875, AU-53, October 2013											
1850, All kinds	291,451											
1850, Large Date		526	50.8	4%	$900	$1,000	$1,100	$1,250	$1,850	$4,500	$20,000	
	Auctions: $3,525, MS-60, September 2015; $1,116, AU-55, February 2015; $1,058, AU-53, August 2015; $940, AU-50, October 2015											
1850, Small Date		145	49.6	5%	$950	$1,200	$1,850	$2,750	$4,500	$8,000	$30,000	
	Auctions: $10,575, MS-61, August 2015; $1,528, AU-53, October 2015; $1,058, EF-45, July 2015; $999, EF-40, February 2015											
1850-O	57,500	208	47.6	1%	$1,350	$2,000	$3,500	$5,500	$8,500	$20,000		
	Auctions: $6,169, AU-58, November 2014; $3,967, AU-55, March 2015; $1,293, VF-35, January 2015; $1,293, VF-30, September 2015											
1851	176,328	344	52.3	6%	$850	$1,000	$1,100	$1,250	$1,850	$4,250	$30,000	
	Auctions: $852, AU-50, September 2014; $881, AU-50, August 2014; $3,819, MS-61, September 2013; $734, VF-30, October 2014											
1851-O	263,000	993	50.9	2%	$1,000	$1,200	$1,750	$2,750	$4,000	$8,000	$35,000	
	Auctions: $18,800, MS-61, January 2015; $2,820, AU-55, January 2015; $1,293, EF-45, August 2015; $705, VF-20, January 2015											
1852	263,106	744	53.0	6%	$850	$1,000	$1,050	$1,250	$1,650	$4,250		
	Auctions: $3,995, MS-61, July 2015; $1,146, AU-55, July 2015; $940, AU-50, July 2015; $823, VF-35, February 2015											
1852-O	18,000	101	49.7	2%	$1,650	$2,500	$6,000	$10,000	$22,500	$45,000		
	Auctions: $7,638, AU-55, August 2015; $3,290, AU-53, November 2014; $18,800, AU, February 2014; $12,925, AU-50, November 2016											

k. 4 examples are known. **l.** 2 examples are known. **m.** Included in circulation-strike 1849 mintage figure.

1853, 3 Over 2	1854-O, Large Date	1854-O, Small Date

	Mintage	Cert	Avg	%MS	VF-20	EF-40	AU-50	AU-55	AU-58	MS-60 / PF-63	MS-63 / PF-64	MS-65 / PF-65
1853, All kinds	201,253											
1853, 3 Over 2		164	52.3	2%	$1,150	$1,500	$2,000	$3,250	$6,500			
Auctions: $14,688, MS-61, June 2015; $11,779, MS-60, August 2015; $5,875, AU-58, October 2014; $2,350, AU-55, June 2015												
1853		778	53.8	6%	$850	$900	$1,050	$1,150	$1,650	$4,000	$17,000	
Auctions: $34,075, MS-64, October 2014; $3,819, MS-61, November 2014; $999, AU-55, January 2015; $793, AU-53, January 2015												
1853-O	51,000	260	51.1	3%	$1,200	$1,600	$2,250	$4,500	$9,500	$15,000		
Auctions: $16,450, MS-61, November 2014; $9,400, MS-60, June 2015; $6,463, AU-58, October 2014; $881, AU-50, January 2015												
1853-O, Proof (n)	1	1	61.0									
Auctions: No auction records available.												
1854	54,250	296	52.7	4%	$900	$1,050	$1,250	$1,650	$2,750	$6,500	$27,500	
Auctions: $2,350, AU-58, September 2015; $2,115, AU-58, August 2015; $1,410, AU-55, June 2015; $1,293, AU-55, May 2015												
1854, Proof (o)	unknown	1	55.0									
Auctions: No auction records available.												
1854-O, Large Date (p)	52,500	161	53.7	9%	$1,150	$1,350	$2,000	$3,250	$6,000	$10,500		
Auctions: $10,869, MS-60, August 2013; $1,998, AU-53, November 2014; $2,585, EF-40, September 2015												
1854-O, Small Date (q)	(r)	116	53.1	1%	$1,150	$1,500	$2,250	$3,500	$4,750	$10,500		
Auctions: $1,821, AU-55, August 2013												
1854-S	123,826	498	50.4	2%	$1,000	$1,200	$2,000	$3,250	$6,500	$12,500		
Auctions: $4,935, AU-58, June 2015; $3,290, AU-55, June 2015; $1,998, AU-53, January 2015; $1,293, AU-50, August 2015												
1855	121,701	629	54.3	11%	$900	$1,100	$1,350	$1,500	$2,000	$4,750	$17,500	
Auctions: $7,115, MS-62, September 2015; $2,233, AU-58, August 2015; $1,058, AU-53, August 2015; $881, EF-45, January 2015												
1855, Proof (s)	unknown	0	n/a									
Auctions: No auction records available.												
1855-O	18,000	110	49.3	0%	$1,250	$3,500	$6,000	$10,000	$18,500	$27,500		
Auctions: $17,625, AU-58, January 2014												
1855-S	9,000	32	49.1	0%	$2,250	$3,500	$6,500	$10,000	$20,000			
Auctions: $17,625, AU-58, March 2014												
1856	60,490	344	53.9	11%	$900	$1,000	$1,150	$1,250	$1,500	$4,000	$15,000	
Auctions: $3,995, MS-61, January 2015; $2,242, AU-58, January 2015; $881, AU-53, February 2015; $793, EF-45, February 2015												
1856, Proof (s)	unknown	0	n/a									
Auctions: No auction records available.												
1856-O	14,500	114	50.0	4%	$1,350	$2,500	$4,500	$7,000	$12,500	$25,000		
Auctions: $10,869, AU-58, September 2016: $4,406, AU-55, January 2014; $4,700, AU-53, August 2016												
1856-S	68,000	279	50.3	1%	$900	$1,150	$1,500	$2,500	$4,500	$11,500	$27,500	
Auctions: $9,988, MS-61, April 2014; $3,290, AU-58, November 2014; $1,763, AU-55, October 2015; $1,116, AU-53, June 2015												

n. The 1853-O Proof listed here is not a Proof from a technical standpoint. This unique coin has in the past been called a presentation piece and a branch-mint Proof. "Although the piece does not have the same convincing texture as the 1844-O Proof eagle, it is clearly different from the regular-issue eagles found for the year and mint" (*Encyclopedia of U.S. Gold Coins, 1795–1933*, second edition). **o.** According to Walter Breen, in July 1854 a set of Proof coins was given by the United States to representatives of the sovereign German city of Bremen. Various Proof 1854 gold dollars, quarter eagles, and three-dollar gold pieces have come to light, along with a single gold eagle. **p.** The Large Date variety was made in error, when the diesinker used a date punch for a silver dollar on the much smaller ten-dollar die. **q.** The Small Date variety is scarce in AU. Only 3 or 4 MS examples are known, none finer than MS-60. **r.** Included in 1854-O, Large Date, mintage figure. **s.** No Proof 1855 or 1856 eagles have been confirmed, but Wayte Raymond claimed to have seen one of each some time prior to 1949.

	Mintage	Cert	Avg	%MS	VF-20	EF-40	AU-50	AU-55	AU-58	MS-60 PF-63	MS-63 PF-64	MS-65 PF-65
1857	16,606	128	52.0	6%	$900	$1,000	$1,650	$3,500	$5,500	$12,000		
	Auctions: $4,406, AU-58, April 2014; $1,293, EF-45, September 2014											
1857, Proof	2–3	1	66.0									
	Auctions: No auction records available.											
1857-O	5,500	60	51.7	0%	$2,000	$3,500	$6,000	$11,500	$25,000			
	Auctions: $22,325, AU-58, August 2014; $8,225, AU-55, February 2014											
1857-S	26,000	71	47.5	3%	$1,350	$1,850	$2,500	$4,500	$7,000	$11,000	$27,500	
	Auctions: $8,225, AU-58, July 2014; $5,875, AU-55, January 2015; $3,378, EF-45, August 2014; $4,465, EF-40, September 2015											
1858 (t)	2,521	34	49.3	9%	$6,000	$7,500	$12,500	$17,500	$25,000	$40,000		
	Auctions: $15,275, AU-53, February 2014											
1858, Proof (u)	4–6	2	64.0		*(extremely rare)*							
	Auctions: No auction records available.											
1858-O	20,000	193	51.4	4%	$1,250	$1,600	$2,750	$3,750	$5,500	$9,000	$32,500	
	Auctions: $6,463, AU-58, January 2015; $2,585, AU-55, January 2015; $1,293, AU-50, October 2015; $1,645, EF-45, January 2015											
1858-S	11,800	51	51.2	0%	$1,800	$3,000	$5,500	$12,000	$20,000			
	Auctions: $15,275, AU-58, April 2013; $3,055, EF-45, November 2014; $2,820, EF-40, October 2015; $2,115, EF-40, November 2014											
1859	16,013	162	50.9	6%	$1,000	$1,250	$1,500	$2,250	$4,000	$9,000	$40,000	
	Auctions: $41,125, MS-62, November 2014; $47,000, MS-62, April 2014; $1,175, EF-45, July 2015; $734, VF-20, January 2015											
1859, Proof	80	5	63.6							$75,000	$150,000	$200,000
	Auctions: No auction records available.											
1859-O	2,300	22	50.7	5%	$5,000	$10,000	$25,000	$30,000	$45,000			
	Auctions: $28,200, AU-50, December 2013											
1859-S	7,000	37	43.6	3%	$3,000	$5,500	$20,000	$22,500	$27,500	$50,000		
	Auctions: $14,100, AU-53, October 2014; $3,525, AU-50, June 2015; $6,463, EF-45, October 2015; $3,290, EF-40, August 2014											
1860	15,055	146	51.9	8%	$900	$1,100	$1,750	$2,500	$3,000	$7,500	$25,000	
	Auctions: $70,500, MS-64, February 2013; $14,100, MS-62, June 2015; $1,645, AU-50, September 2014; $1,293, EF-45, January 2015											
1860, Proof	50	5	63.6							$50,000	$100,000	$135,000
	Auctions: $142,175, PF-64DCam, April 2014											
1860-O	11,100	126	51.4	6%	$1,450	$2,500	$4,000	$6,000	$8,000	$17,500		
	Auctions: $8,814, AU-About Uncirculated, March 2014											
1860-S	5,000	21	48.0	10%	$3,000	$5,500	$13,000	$20,000	$35,000	$50,000		
	Auctions: $28,200, AU-55, March 2014; $25,850, AU-55, May 2016; $9,400, VF-35, August 2016; $7,050, VF-30, September 2016											
1861	113,164	751	54.9	13%	$925	$1,050	$1,500	$2,500	$4,000	$6,500	$20,000	
	Auctions: $8,225, MS-62, August 2015; $7,652, MS-62, January 2015; $4,113, AU-58, July 2014; $940, AU-50, January 2015											
1861, Proof	69	6	64.2							$45,000	$85,000	$125,000
	Auctions: $129,250, PF-64Cam, March 2013											
1861-S	15,500	74	49.9	1%	$4,000	$8,500	$12,500	$17,500	$25,000	$47,500		
	Auctions: $25,850, AU-58, March 2014; $9,400, AU-53, August 2015; $7,638, AU-53, September 2014; $6,463, EF-40, June 2015											
1862	10,960	88	51.4	13%	$1,000	$2,250	$5,000	$6,500	$10,000	$18,500	$37,500	
	Auctions: $18,800, MS-61, October 2015; $7,050, AU-55, January 2015; $6,169, AU-53, July 2015; $4,935, AU-50, September 2015											
1862, Proof	35	5	64.4							$42,500	$85,000	$125,000
	Auctions: $152,750, PF-65DCam, August 2013											
1862-S	12,500	46	45.8	0%	$2,500	$4,000	$10,000	$12,500	$20,000	$100,000		
	Auctions: $21,150, AU-58, October 2014; $5,581, EF-35, February 2014											
1863	1,218	16	52.0	19%	$9,000	$16,000	$30,000	$40,000	$55,000	$75,000		
	Auctions: $49,938, AU-53, January 2014; $42,300, EF-45, September 2016; $35,250, EF-45, August 2016											
1863, Proof	30	12	64.2							$42,500	$85,000	$125,000
	Auctions: $299,000, PF-65DCam, August 2011											
1863-S	10,000	32	46.0	3%	$5,500	$13,000	$25,000	$32,500	$37,500	$45,000		
	Auctions: $32,900, AU-53, February 2014; $12,925, AU-50, October 2015; $15,275, EF-45, October 2014; $5,875, F-12, November 2014											

t. Beware of fraudulently removed mintmark. **u.** 4 or 5 examples are known.

1865-S, 865
Over Inverted 186

	Mintage	Cert	Avg	%MS	VF-20	EF-40	AU-50	AU-55	AU-58	MS-60	MS-63	MS-65
										PF-63	PF-64	PF-65
1864	3,530	24	50.0	17%	$4,500	$10,000	$20,000	$27,500	$32,500	$42,500		
Auctions: $41,125, AU-55, October 2014; $28,200, AU-55, January 2014												
1864, Proof	50	17	63.8							$42,500	$85,000	$125,000
Auctions: $138,000, PF-64UCam, October 2011												
1864-S	2,500	7	42.9	0%	$35,000	$75,000	$135,000	$165,000				
Auctions: $146,875, AU-53, March 2014												
1865	3,980	31	50.5	6%	$5,000	$9,000	$15,000	$20,000	$27,500	$47,500	$90,000	
Auctions: $15,275, AU-53, October 2014; $18,800, AU-53, January 2014; $13,513, AU-50, October 2014; $12,925, AU-50, August 2015												
1865, Proof	25	13	64.1							$42,500	$85,000	$125,000
Auctions: $528,750, PF, August 2013												
1865-S, All kinds	16,700											
1865-S		32	40.2	3%	$7,500	$12,500	$17,500	$25,000	$32,500	$55,000		
Auctions: $5,170, VF-25, September 2016; $4,230, VF-20, September 2016: $6,756, F-12, February 2013												
1865-S, 865 Over Inverted 186		39	43.2	3%	$7,500	$15,000	$21,000	$27,500	$35,000	$45,000		
Auctions: $20,563, AU-55, January 2015; $27,025, AU-53, March 2014; $9,400, EF-45, October 2015; $1,880, VG-8, August 2014												
1866-S, No Motto	8,500	33	47.1	3%	$3,000	$4,000	$12,000	$20,000	$27,500	$55,000		
Auctions: $14,950, EF-45, August 2011												
1866, With Motto	3,750	46	49.5	13%	$1,500	$2,750	$5,000	$10,000	$25,000	$45,000		
Auctions: $32,900, MS-61, January 2015; $14,100, AU-55, September 2013; $4,054, AU-50, August 2015; $1,763, EF-40, January 2015												
1866, Proof	30	8	64.1							$35,000	$55,000	$85,000
Auctions: $66,125, PF-64UCam+H, January 2012												
1866-S, With Motto	11,500	40	49.0	0%	$2,500	$4,000	$7,250	$10,000	$17,500			
Auctions: $15,275, AU-58, March 2014; $9,988, AU-55, August 2014; $4,230, EF-45, July 2015; $4,230, VF-35, January 2015												
1867	3,090	61	49.3	3%	$2,000	$3,000	$5,500	$11,500	$22,500	$35,000		
Auctions: $30,550, AU-58, August 2013												
1867, Proof	50	4	64.8							$35,000	$55,000	$85,000
Auctions: $64,625, PF-65Cam, August 2014; $64,625, PF-64Cam+, February 2015; $54,344, PF-64Cam, October 2014												
1867-S	9,000	37	47.5	0%	$3,250	$6,000	$9,000	$13,500	$25,000			
Auctions: $12,925, AU-55, July 2016;$9,988, AU-53, June 2013; $6,463, AU-50, September 2016												
1868	10,630	158	50.9	5%	$850	$1,250	$1,850	$3,500	$6,000	$17,500		
Auctions: $5,875, AU-58, February 2015; $4,700, AU-58, July 2015; $1,645, AU-50, January 2015; $2,350, EF-45, September 2015												
1868, Proof	25	4	64.8							$35,000	$55,000	$85,000
Auctions: $24,150, PF-62Cam, June 2005												
1868-S	13,500	71	48.3	0%	$1,250	$2,250	$4,000	$10,000	$17,500			
Auctions: $5,875, AU-58, August 2014; $4,700, AU-55, July 2015; $1,469, AU-50, August 2015; $2,115, EF-40, August 2014												
1869	1,830	39	50.6	8%	$1,500	$3,500	$5,500	$11,500	$15,000	$30,000		
Auctions: $14,100, AU-58, August 2013												
1869, Proof	25	8	63.8							$35,000	$55,000	$80,000
Auctions: $161,000, PF-67UCam+H, February 2012												
1869-S	6,430	37	47.2	3%	$2,200	$3,500	$5,500	$11,000	$18,500	$27,500		
Auctions: $16,450, AU-58, January 2015; $11,163, AU-55, August 2015; $7,638, AU-55, January 2015; $1,528, EF-40, October 2015												

	Mintage	Cert	Avg	%MS	VF-20	EF-40	AU-50	AU-55	AU-58	MS-60 / PF-63	MS-63 / PF-64	MS-65 / PF-65
1870	3,990	68	49.0	1%	$1,100	$1,650	$3,000	$7,500	$15,000	$25,000		
Auctions: $10,575, AU-55, January 2014												
1870, Proof	35	4	64.5							$35,000	$55,000	$80,000
Auctions: $97,750, PF-65UCam, January 2010												
1870-CC	5,908	33	41.7	0%	$35,000	$55,000	$80,000	$145,000				
Auctions: $135,125, AU-55, March 2014; $36,719, VF-35, August 2014; $28,200, VG-10, August 2015												
1870-S	8,000	60	42.0	0%	$1,500	$3,500	$5,500	$11,000	$15,000	$27,500		
Auctions: $12,925, AU-58, March 2014												
1871	1,790	49	50.7	0%	$1,400	$2,400	$4,500	$8,500	$15,000	$22,500		
Auctions: $15,275, AU-58, September 2013; $9,400, AU-55, March 2015; $4,583, AU-50, July 2015; $3,290, EF-40, August 2014												
1871, Proof	30	5	63.2							$35,000	$55,000	$80,000
Auctions: $76,375, PF-64DCam, August 2013												
1871-CC	8,085	71	46.1	3%	$5,500	$15,000	$20,000	$27,000	$40,000	$75,000		
Auctions: $35,250, AU-58, October 2014; $14,100, AU-53, January 2015; $5,170, AU-50, June 2015; $19,975, EF-45, August 2016												
1871-S	16,500	84	42.8	0%	$1,450	$2,000	$4,500	$7,000	$12,500			
Auctions: $10,281, AU-58, March 2014; $2,115, AU-50, July 2014; $1,116, AU-58, October 2015; $2,231, EF-45, February 2015												
1872	1,620	21	51.0	5%	$2,150	$4,000	$9,000	$11,000	$15,000	$30,000		
Auctions: $38,188, AU-58, August 2014; $16,450, AU-55, August 2015; $16,450, AU-55, February 2015; $6,169, EF-45, July 2015												
1872, Proof	30	7	64.7							$35,000	$55,000	$80,000
Auctions: $48,875, PF-64DCam, June 2012												
1872-CC	4,600	53	43.2	0%	$8,500	$15,000	$27,500	$42,500	$62,500			
Auctions: $47,000, AU, February 2014; $9,988, EF-40, August 2014												
1872-S	17,300	140	47.3	1%	$975	$1,500	$2,000	$4,250	$8,500	$17,500		
Auctions: $8,225, AU-58, October 2014; $7,050, AU-58, March 2014; $5,640, AU-58, January 2015; $1,645, EF-45, July 2015												
1873	800	21	50.0	0%	$10,000	$20,000	$35,000	$47,500	$65,000	$75,000		
Auctions: $64,625, AU-58, May 2016; $55,813, AU-55, January 2014; $30,550, AU-53, September 2016; $21,738, AU-53, January 2015												
1873, Proof	25	9	63.7							$37,500	$65,000	$85,000
Auctions: $74,750, PF-65Cam+, February 2012												
1873-CC	4,543	38	41.0	0%	$12,500	$20,000	$45,000	$75,000	$100,000			
Auctions: $58,750, AU-53, March 2014; $44,650, AU-50, August 2016												
1873-S	12,000	83	42.8	0%	$1,000	$2,250	$4,250	$7,000	$13,500	$27,500		
Auctions: $4,700, AU-53, March 2013												
1874	53,140	347	56.1	21%	$750	$850	$900	$925	$1,000	$1,500	$7,500	$40,000
Auctions: $1,410, MS-61, September 2014; $1,058, AU-58, August 2015; $940, AU-58, September 2015; $999, AU-50, October 2014												
1874, Proof	20	1	62.0							$35,000	$65,000	$85,000
Auctions: $29,500, PF-64Cam, September 2006												
1874-CC	16,767	151	41.6	1%	$3,250	$6,000	$12,500	$20,000	$40,000	$65,000	$200,000	
Auctions: $30,550, AU-58, May 2013; $3,643, VF-35, June 2015; $2,585, F-15, January 2015; $1,410, VG-8, February 2015												
1874-S	10,000	96	42.3	0%	$1,500	$2,250	$5,000	$8,000	$16,000			
Auctions: $12,338, AU-58, July 2014; $2,644, EF-45, August 2014; $940, VF-20, February 2015												
1875	100	7	45.4	0%	$125,000	$165,000	$225,000	$375,000				
Auctions: $211,500, AU-50, February 2014												
1875, Proof	20	4	64.5							$155,000	$200,000	$275,000
Auctions: $164,500, PF-50, January 2014												
1875-CC	7,715	69	38.2	3%	$6,000	$10,000	$17,500	$35,000	$75,000	$100,000	$175,000	
Auctions: $8,225, EF-45, February 2014												

	Mintage	Cert	Avg	%MS	VF-20	EF-40	AU-50	AU-55	AU-58	MS-60	MS-63	MS-65
										PF-63	PF-64	PF-65
1876	687	20	51.1	5%	$5,000	$10,000	$22,500	$35,000	$50,000	$75,000		
	Auctions: $70,500, AU-58, January 2015; $28,200, AU-55, June 2015; $22,325, AU-53, August 2015; $18,800, AU-53, July 2014											
1876, Proof	45	14	63.7							$32,500	$45,000	$75,000
	Auctions: $100,625, PF-65Cam, April 2011											
1876-CC	4,696	95	41.7	0%	$5,500	$13,500	$20,000	$35,000	$55,000			
	Auctions: $14,100, AU-50, October 2013											
1876-S	5,000	48	45.0	0%	$1,275	$1,800	$5,500	$9,500	$20,000			
	Auctions: $22,325, AU-55, October 2013											
1877	797	30	54.0	0%	$4,000	$6,500	$10,000	$13,500	$17,500	$45,000		
	Auctions: $64,625, MS-61, March 2015; $11,163, AU-55, July 2014; $11,163, AU-55, January 2014; $3,290, EF-40, February 2015											
1877, Proof	20	3	64.7							$35,000	$45,000	$75,000
	Auctions: $39,100, PF-64Cam, April 2002											
1877-CC	3,332	42	40.0	0%	$8,500	$12,500	$25,000	$35,000	$55,000			
	Auctions: $10,575, EF-45, April 2014											
1877-S	17,000	167	46.7	2%	$850	$1,250	$1,800	$4,500	$11,000	$30,000		
	Auctions: $3,290, AU-55, September 2015; $881, AU-50, September 2015; $1,116, EF-45, September 2015; $1,116, EF-45, June 2015											
1878	73,780	361	57.9	43%	$675	$685	$700	$750	$850	$1,000	$5,500	
	Auctions: $1,410, MS-62, July 2015; $881, MS-61, September 2015; $852, MS-61, September 2015; $823, MS-61, January 2015											
1878, Proof	20	4	63.8							$27,500	$45,000	$75,000
	Auctions: $25,300, PF-63, August 2011											
1878-CC	3,244	38	46.4	3%	$7,500	$15,000	$25,000	$45,000	$75,000	$125,000		
	Auctions: $64,625, AU-55, September 2016: $28,200, AU-55, March 2014; $19,388, AU-50, August 2016											
1878-S	26,100	221	47.8	2%	$850	$950	$1,350	$2,000	$3,500	$11,500	$25,000	
	Auctions: $2,938, AU-58, October 2015; $1,410, AU-55, February 2015; $1,293, AU-50, October 2015; $646, EF-40, September 2014											
1879	384,740	928	58.8	53%	$675	$685	$700	$775	$850	$900	$3,000	
	Auctions: $2,585, MS-63, July 2015; $940, MS-61, August 2015; $711, MS-60, October 2015; $646, AU-58, January 2015											
1879, Proof	30	6	63.2							$25,000	$37,500	$65,000
	Auctions: $52,875, PF-65Cam, February 2013											
1879-CC	1,762	37	42.6	3%	$17,500	$25,000	$40,000	$55,000	$75,000			
	Auctions: $41,125, AU-50, March 2014											
1879-O	1,500	48	49.4	4%	$10,000	$17,500	$25,000	$35,000	$55,000	$75,000		
	Auctions: $88,125, MS-61, June 2014; $23,500, EF-45, August 2016; $14,688, VF-30, September 2016											
1879-S	224,000	466	56.9	25%	$675	$685	$700	$800	$850	$1,150	$6,000	
	Auctions: $1,410, MS-62, January 2015; $881, MS-60, June 2015; $999, AU-58, August 2015; $705, AU-55, October 2015											
1880	1,644,840	2,153	59.9	81%	$675	$685	$725	$800	$825	$950	$1,500	
	Auctions: $19,975, MS-65, August 2013; $764, MS-61, June 2015; $705, VF-35, February 2015; $646, AG-3, January 2015											
1880, Proof	36	5	64.2							$22,500	$35,000	$60,000
	Auctions: $32,200, PF-64, October 1999											
1880-CC	11,190	187	50.6	6%	$2,000	$2,750	$4,000	$6,500	$10,000	$22,500		
	Auctions: $2,761, AU-53, August 2013; $1,175, EF-40, July 2014											
1880-O	9,200	186	51.9	5%	$1,500	$2,500	$4,250	$5,500	$10,500	$20,000		
	Auctions: $3,760, AU-55, August 2015; $4,230, AU-50, September 2015; $2,233, AU-50, August 2015; $4,113, EF-40, June 2014											
1880-S	506,250	1,036	60.2	78%	$675	$685	$725	$775	$825	$900	$2,000	
	Auctions: $4,465, MS-64, October 2015; $1,293, MS-63, July 2015; $1,175, MS-62, August 2015; $764, MS-61, September 2015											
1881	3,877,220	12,760	60.9	94%	$675	$685	$725	$775	$800	$850	$1,000	$15,000
	Auctions: $2,115, MS-64, February 2015; $999, MS-63, January 2015; $705, MS-62, October 2014; $676, MS-61, January 2015											
1881, Proof	40	5	65.2							$22,500	$32,500	$55,000
	Auctions: $56,063, PF-65, October 2011											
1881-CC	24,015	344	52.3	13%	$1,750	$2,500	$3,500	$4,500	$5,000	$8,500		
	Auctions: $12,925, MS-62, April 2013; $4,113, AU-58, January 2015; $1,116, AU-50, July 2014; $1,763, EF-40, January 2015											
1881-O	8,350	177	52.1	7%	$1,150	$1,500	$3,000	$5,000	$7,000	$13,500		
	Auctions: $12,338, MS-60, January 2014											
1881-S	970,000	2,556	60.7	91%	$675	$685	$700	$750	$800	$850	$1,500	
	Auctions: $2,585, MS-63, January 2015; $1,763, MS-63, October 2015; $764, MS-62, January 2015; $734, MS-62, June 2015											

	Mintage	Cert	Avg	%MS	VF-20	EF-40	AU-50	AU-55	AU-58	MS-60 / PF-63	MS-63 / PF-64	MS-65 / PF-65
1882	2,324,440	13,788	61.2	96%	$675	$685	$700	$750	$800	$850	$1,000	
Auctions: $1,175, MS-63, August 2015; $823, MS-62, August 2015; $881, MS-61, June 2015; $777, MS-61, September 2015												
1882, Proof	40	9	64.2							$20,000	$32,500	$55,000
Auctions: $43,125, PF-65Cam, October 2009												
1882-CC	6,764	144	52.4	2%	$2,000	$3,500	$5,500	$11,500	$22,500	$35,000		
Auctions: $25,850, MS-60, July 2014; $7,344, AU-55, February 2015; $4,935, EF-45, July 2015; $1,645, EF-40, January 2015												
1882-O	10,820	195	52.5	10%	$1,150	$1,500	$2,250	$4,500	$7,500	$10,000	$45,000	
Auctions: $30,550, MS-62, January 2014; $2,389, AU-53, September 2014; $1,410, VF-35, September 2015												
1882-S	132,000	343	60.6	86%	$675	$685	$700	$750	$800	$850	$2,500	
Auctions: $1,880, MS-63, January 2015; $1,293, MS-62, October 2015; $1,234, MS-62, August 2015; $1,087, MS-62, October 2015												
1883	208,700	1,431	61.2	95%	$675	$685	$700	$750	$800	$850	$1,350	
Auctions: $3,995, MS-64, January 2015; $1,880, MS-63, October 2015; $1,293, MS-63, August 2015; $881, MS-62, July 2015												
1883, Proof	40	9	64.3							$20,000	$32,500	$55,000
Auctions: $8,813, PF-60, July 2014												
1883-CC	12,000	344	49.3	4%	$1,650	$2,500	$4,500	$8,500	$18,500	$37,500		
Auctions: $41,125, MS-61, October 2014; $3,055, AU-50, October 2015; $2,820, EF-40, June 2015; $1,586, VF-20, January 2015												
1883-O	800	20	51.2	5%	$12,500	$27,500	$42,500	$65,000	$85,000	$125,000		
Auctions: $82,250, AU-58, August 2014; $70,500, AU-58, January 2015; $70,500, AU-55, February 2014; $47,000, AU-50, October 2014												
1883-S	38,000	138	56.0	40%	$675	$685	$700	$750	$800	$1,150	$8,500	
Auctions: $11,163, MS-63, February 2013; $2,056, MS-62, January 2015; $1,293, MS-61, August 2015; $823, AU-58, November 2014												
1884	76,860	354	58.3	44%	$675	$685	$700	$750	$800	$950	$4,250	
Auctions: $846, MS-61, July 2014; $823, AU-55, February 2014												
1884, Proof	45	7	64.6							$20,000	$32,500	$55,000
Auctions: $37,375, PF-64DCam, March 2012												
1884-CC	9,925	174	50.7	6%	$1,750	$3,000	$5,500	$7,500	$13,500	$17,500	$65,000	
Auctions: $17,625, AU-58, September 2016: $17,625, AU-58, February 2014; $9,988, AU-58, August 2016; $3,760, AU-55, August 2015												
1884-S	124,250	538	59.4	67%	$675	$685	$700	$750	$800	$850	$4,500	
Auctions: $4,994, MS-63, July 2014; $1,175, MS-62, September 2015; $1,116, MS-62, September 2015; $1,175, MS-61, October 2015												
1885	253,462	655	60.5	84%	$675	$685	$700	$750	$800	$850	$2,000	$20,000
Auctions: $1,880, MS-63, October 2013; $1,528, MS-63, November 2014; $1,410, MS-63, July 2015; $823, MS-60, August 2014												
1885, Proof	65	12	63.5							$20,000	$32,500	$52,500
Auctions: $57,500, PF-66UCam, January 2012												
1885-S	228,000	849	60.8	87%	$675	$685	$700	$750	$800	$850	$1,150	
Auctions: $5,875, MS-64, August 2014; $4,406, MS-63, August 2013; $705, MS-62, October 2014; $881, MS-62, July 2014												
1886	236,100	639	59.3	64%	$675	$685	$700	$750	$800	$850	$2,000	
Auctions: $1,998, MS-63, June 2015; $764, MS-61, October 2015; $823, AU-58, June 2015; $564, VF-30, October 2015												
1886, Proof	60	18	62.7							$18,500	$32,500	$52,500
Auctions: $39,656, PF-64DCam, April 2014												
1886-S	826,000	3,054	61.3	95%	$675	$685	$700	$750	$800	$850	$1,000	
Auctions: $1,116, MS-63, January 2015; $999, MS-63, January 2015; $969, MS-63, May 2015; $852, MS-63, July 2015												
1887	53,600	280	57.8	43%	$675	$685	$700	$750	$800	$1,000	$4,500	
Auctions: $4,465, MS-63, June 2015; $1,351, MS-62, February 2015; $881, MS-61, January 2015; $999, AU-58, August 2015												
1887, Proof	80	17	63.9							$18,500	$32,500	$52,500
Auctions: $64,625, PF-65DCam, April 2014												
1887-S	817,000	1,526	60.9	90%	$675	$685	$700	$750	$800	$850	$1,500	
Auctions: $3,819, MS-64, January 2015; $1,293, MS-63, January 2015; $1,234, MS-63, February 2015; $1,116, MS-63, January 2015												
1888	132,921	472	58.8	57%	$675	$685	$700	$750	$800	$850	$3,000	
Auctions: $2,820, MS-63, January 2015; $1,175, MS-62, February 2015; $1,028, MS-62, August 2015; $940, MS-61, September 2015												
1888, Proof	75	12	64.1							$18,500	$32,500	$52,500
Auctions: $17,250, PF-63DCam, February 2009												
1888-O	21,335	643	60.2	80%	$725	$800	$850	$1,000	$1,100	$1,250	$6,000	
Auctions: $21,150, MS-64, August 2013; $999, MS-62, October 2014; $1,293, MS-61, July 2014; $734, MS-60, January 2015												
1888-S	648,700	1,930	60.8	90%	$675	$685	$700	$750	$800	$850	$1,200	
Auctions: $1,763, MS-63, August 2015; $1,528, MS-63, July 2015; $881, MS-62, January 2015; $764, AU-58, January 2015												

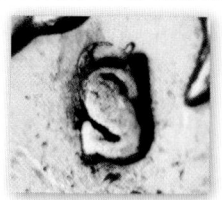

1889-S, Repunched Mintmark
FS-G10-1889S-501.

	Mintage	Cert	Avg	%MS	VF-20	EF-40	AU-50	AU-55	AU-58	MS-60	MS-63	MS-65
										PF-63	PF-64	PF-65
1889	4,440	114	58.7	54%	$875	$925	$950	$1,350	$2,500	$3,500	$10,000	
	Auctions: $4,935, MS-62, June 2015; $3,995, MS-61, August 2015; $1,998, AU-58, June 2015; $1,528, AU-50, January 2015											
1889, Proof	45	4	64.3							$18,000	$32,500	$52,500
	Auctions: $23,500, PF-64Cam, August 2014; $4,994, PF-60, April 2013											
1889-S	425,400	1,284	60.8	89%	$675	$685	$700	$750	$800	$850	$1,250	
	Auctions: $999, MS-63, January 2015; $764, MS-62, February 2015; $823, MS-61, July 2015; $676, AU-55, June 2015											
1889-S, Repunched Mintmark	(v)	1	45.0	0%				$900	$975	$1,025	$1,850	
	Auctions: $1,035, MS-63, August 2006											
1890	57,980	443	59.0	63%	$675	$685	$700	$750	$800	$900	$3,500	$15,000
	Auctions: $2,820, MS-63, July 2014; $1,058, MS-62, November 2014; $1,116, MS-62, September 2014; $764, MS-60, October 2015											
1890, Proof	63	23	63.8							$16,500	$25,000	$47,500
	Auctions: $29,900, PF-64UCam, January 2012											
1890-CC	17,500	379	57.0	40%	$1,250	$1,550	$2,250	$2,750	$3,750	$4,500	$22,500	
	Auctions: $15,863, MS-63, August 2016; $9,400, MS-62, August 2016: $7,050, MS-62, August 2015; $4,935, MS-61, June 2015											
1891	91,820	720	61.2	95%	$675	$685	$700	$750	$800	$900	$2,500	
	Auctions: $7,344, MS-64, November 2013; $1,998, MS-63, August 2014; $1,410, MS-62, July 2014; $716, MS-62, October 2015											
1891, Proof	48	20	64.2							$16,500	$25,000	$47,500
	Auctions: $54,625, PF-65Cam, February 2012											
1891-CC	103,732	2,411	58.4	57%	$125	$1,450	$1,650	$2,250	$2,650	$2,850	$8,500	
	Auctions: $14,688, MS-64, June 2015; $2,115, MS-61, July 2015; $1,763, AU-55, August 2015; $1,410, AU-50, August 2015											
1892	797,480	8,644	61.4	98%	$675	$685	$700	$750	$800	$850	$1,000	$7,500
	Auctions: $6,756, MS-65, October 2013; $1,028, MS-63, July 2014; $652, MS-62, October 2014; $852, MS-62, August 2014											
1892, Proof	72	12	63.7							$16,500	$25,000	$47,500
	Auctions: $4,406, PF-55, January 2014											
1892-CC	40,000	487	52.4	7%	$1,250	$1,500	$2,000	$2,750	$3,500	$5,500	$30,000	
	Auctions: $1,763, AU-53, August 2014; $1,528, EF-45, February 2015; $823, EF-40, October 2015; $1,528, VF-35, January 2015											
1892-O	28,688	712	60.2	79%	$725	$800	$850	$900	$1,000	$1,250	$8,000	
	Auctions: $1,998, MS-62, August 2015; $1,763, MS-62, September 2015; $1,410, MS-60, July 2015; $764, AU-55, January 2015											
1892-S	115,500	315	59.1	65%	$675	$685	$700	$750	$950	$1,050	$2,000	
	Auctions: $940, MS-62, July 2015; $852, MS-62, January 2015; $764, MS-61, January 2015; $764, AU-58, January 2015											
1893	1,840,840	35,775	61.8	99%	$675	$685	$700	$750	$800	$850	$950	$6,500
	Auctions: $1,645, MS-64, August 2015; $1,528, MS-63, July 2015; $734, MS-62, August 2015; $705, MS-61, June 2015											
1893, Proof	55	16	63.2							$16,500	$25,000	$47,500
	Auctions: $30,550, PF-64DCam, August 2014; $58,750, PF, March 2014											
1893-CC	14,000	243	52.2	6%	$1,650	$2,000	$3,500	$5,500	$9,500	$17,500		
	Auctions: $18,800, MS-61, January 2014; $6,463, AU-58, July 2015; $4,465, AU-55, September 2015; $4,465, AU-55, July 2015											
1893-O	17,000	448	59.7	70%	$725	$800	$850	$975	$1,000	$1,250	$5,000	
	Auctions: $4,465, MS-63, June 2015; $1,293, MS-61, September 2014; $4,406, AU-58, September 2013; $823, AU-53, January 2015											
1893-S	141,350	633	60.2	79%	$675	$685	$700	$750	$800	$850	$2,000	
	Auctions: $999, MS-62, July 2015; $940, MS-62, July 2015; $881, MS-62, February 2015; $823, MS-62, March 2015											

v. Included in 1889-S mintage figure.

	Mintage	Cert	Avg	%MS	VF-20	EF-40	AU-50	AU-55	AU-58	MS-60 / PF-63	MS-63 / PF-64	MS-65 / PF-65
1894	2,470,735	37,487	61.7	99%	$675	$685	$700	$750	$800	$850	$1,000	$7,500
Auctions: $5,942, MS-65, October 2015; $1,528, MS-64, October 2015; $705, MS-62, June 2015; $650, MS-60, January 2015												
1894, Proof	43	11	64.1							$16,500	$25,000	$47,500
Auctions: $105,750, PF-65, January 2014												
1894-O	107,500	900	57.4	35%	$725	$800	$850	$975	$1,000	$1,200	$5,500	
Auctions: $1,410, MS-61, July 2015; $940, AU-58, August 2015; $823, AU-53, June 2015; $705, AU-50, January 2015												
1894-S	25,000	160	53.6	13%	$750	$775	$950	$1,100	$1,800	$3,500		
Auctions: $9,988, MS-61, March 2014; $1,058, AU-55, September 2014; $1,293, AU-50, September 2015												
1895	567,770	11,493	61.7	99%	$675	$685	$700	$750	$800	$850	$1,000	$11,000
Auctions: $9,400, MS-65, June 2015; $1,410, MS-64, January 2015; $1,058, MS-63, November 2015; $764, AU-58, June 2015												
1895, Proof	56	18	63.8							$16,000	$25,000	$47,500
Auctions: $51,750, PF-65UCam, January 2012												
1895-O	98,000	721	58.8	49%	$725	$775	$850	$975	$1,000	$1,200	$6,000	
Auctions: $9,400, MS-63, February 2013; $940, AU-55, July 2015; $764, AU-55, January 2015; $705, EF-45, January 2015												
1895-S	49,000	226	52.6	9%	$850	$925	$975	$1,000	$1,150	$2,000	$8,000	
Auctions: $5,875, MS-62, October 2014; $4,700, MS-62, November 2014; $966, AU-55, May 2015; $846, AU-55, September 2014												
1896	76,270	1,454	61.7	98%	$675	$685	$700	$750	$800	$850	$1,200	$12,000
Auctions: $1,293, MS-63, July 2015; $911, MS-63, May 2015; $881, MS-62, July 2015; $823, MS-62, October 2015												
1896, Proof	78	18	64.1							$16,000	$25,000	$47,500
Auctions: $89,125, PF-66DCam, April 2012; $70,500, PF-66, September 2014												
1896-S	123,750	468	54.1	14%	$725	$750	$775	$850	$900	$1,750	$8,000	
Auctions: $2,233, MS-62, January 2015; $823, AU-55, September 2015; $617, AU-50, October 2015; $705, EF-45, June 2015												
1897	1,000,090	10,028	61.6	97%	$675	$685	$700	$750	$800	$850	$1,000	$5,500
Auctions: $5,875, MS-65, August 2015; $2,233, MS-64, September 2015; $1,528, MS-64, October 2015; $764, MS-62, February 2015												
1897, Proof	69	12	64.3							$16,000	$25,000	$47,500
Auctions: $19,975, PF, August 2013												
1897-O	42,500	394	58.7	47%	$725	$750	$775	$900	$1,000	$1,350	$6,500	$27,500
Auctions: $6,169, MS-63, March 2013; $2,350, MS-62, June 2015; $1,880, AU-58, July 2014; $999, AU-55, January 2015												
1897-S	234,750	362	57.2	35%	$675	$685	$700	$750	$800	$850	$5,500	$25,000
Auctions: $1,058, MS-62, February 2015; $823, MS-61, July 2015; $823, MS-60, October 2015; $734, AU-55, September 2015												
1898	812,130	4,160	61.3	94%	$675	$685	$700	$750	$800	$850	$1,000	$6,500
Auctions: $5,599, MS-65, August 2015; $2,056, MS-64, August 2015; $1,293, MS-63, February 2015; $999, MS-63, January 2015												
1898, Proof	67	27	65.2							$16,000	$25,000	$47,500
Auctions: $58,750, PF-66DCam, September 2014; $85,188, PF-66DCam, April 2013												
1898-S	473,600	458	60.2	85%	$675	$685	$700	$750	$800	$850	$2,000	$15,000
Auctions: $3,290, MS-63, January 2014; $1,116, MS-62, October 2015; $870, MS-61, July 2014; $764, MS-61, October 2015												
1899	1,262,219	21,409	62.1	98%	$675	$685	$700	$750	$800	$850	$950	$2,750
Auctions: $25,850, MS-67, June 2015; $17,625, MS-66, January 2015; $1,175, MS-63, September 2015; $764, MS-62, October 2015												
1899, Proof	86	37	64.4							$15,000	$25,000	$45,000
Auctions: $76,375, PF-67DCam, September 2014; $56,400, PF, March 2014												
1899-O	37,047	231	59.1	48%	$750	$775	$800	$950	$1,000	$1,350	$7,500	
Auctions: $7,638, MS-63, October 2015; $2,115, MS-62, July 2015; $1,763, MS-62, January 2015; $940, AU-55, July 2014												
1899-S	841,000	699	60.1	79%	$675	$685	$700	$750	$800	$850	$2,000	$15,000
Auctions: $3,525, MS-64, January 2015; $1,293, MS-63, May 2015; $1,028, MS-63, July 2015; $764, EF-40, July 2015												
1900	293,840	6,671	62.1	99%	$675	$685	$700	$750	$800	$825	$950	$3,500
Auctions: $3,643, MS-65, January 2015; $2,500, MS-65, January 2015; $1,351, MS-64, July 2015; $940, MS-63, August 2014												
1900, Proof	120	49	64.4							$15,000	$25,000	$45,000
Auctions: $1,880, PF, February 2014												
1900-S	81,000	187	58.0	39%	$675	$685	$700	$750	$800	$1,000	$5,500	$20,000
Auctions: $6,169, MS-63, September 2013; $658, AU-58, November 2014; $705, AU-58, July 2014												

	Mintage	Cert	Avg	%MS	VF-20	EF-40	AU-50	AU-55	AU-58	MS-60	MS-63	MS-65
										PF-63	PF-64	PF-65
1901	1,718,740	24,650	62.3	98%	$675	$685	$700	$750	$800	$825	$950	$2,750
	Auctions: $7,931, MS-66, October 2015; $3,200, MS-65, January 2015; $999, MS-63, January 2015; $940, MS-62, June 2015
1901, Proof	85	49	63.8							$15,000	$25,000	$45,000
	Auctions: $48,875, PF-66Cam, January 2012
1901-O	72,041	444	60.0	68%	$750	$775	$800	$925	$975	$1,150	$3,250	$15,000
	Auctions: $6,169, MS-64, June 2014
1901-S	2,812,750	18,193	62.9	99%	$675	$685	$700	$750	$800	$825	$950	$2,750
	Auctions: $19,975, MS-67, January 2015; $3,290, MS-65, August 2015; $1,146, MS-64, March 2015; $1,251, MS-63, August 2015
1902	82,400	726	61.2	90%	$675	$685	$700	$750	$800	$850	$1,500	$9,000
	Auctions: $1,528, MS-63, June 2015; $1,293, MS-63, September 2015; $1,645, MS-62, August 2015; $712, AU-58, February 2015
1902, Proof	113	27	63.7							$15,000	$25,000	$45,000
	Auctions: $61,688, PF-67, February 2013
1902-S	469,500	2,908	62.8	99%	$675	$685	$700	$750	$800	$825	$950	$2,750
	Auctions: $8,519, MS-66, February 2014; $1,058, MS-63, September 2014; $1,058, MS-63, August 2014
1903	125,830	1,039	61.3	91%	$675	$685	$700	$750	$800	$850	$950	$7,000
	Auctions: $1,116, MS-64, October 2014; $6,463, MS-65, January 2014; $1,058, MS-63, October 2014; $1,058, MS-63, August 2014
1903, Proof	96	43	64.4							$15,000	$25,000	$45,000
	Auctions: $39,950, PF, October 2013
1903-O	112,771	1,196	60.2	72%	$725	$750	$800	$925	$1,000	$1,200	$2,500	$17,500
	Auctions: $1,645, MS-62, September 2016: $1,175, MS-62, January 2015; $999, MS-61, January 2015; $940, AU-58, September 2015
1903-S	538,000	993	62.3	92%	$675	$685	$700	$750	$800	$850	$1,000	$2,750
	Auctions: $9,106, MS-66, September 2015; $4,935, MS-66, July 2015; $4,935, MS-65, January 2015; $2,350, MS-64, June 2015
1904	161,930	1,188	61.3	92%	$675	$685	$700	$750	$800	$850	$1,500	$8,500
	Auctions: $1,763, MS-64, October 2015; $1,293, MS-64, July 2015; $999, MS-63, June 2015; $999, MS-63, April 2015
1904, Proof	108	35	63.3							$15,000	$25,000	$45,000
	Auctions: $64,625, PF-66Cam, June 2013
1904-O	108,950	678	60.1	69%	$725	$750	$800	$925	$1,000	$1,200	$3,000	$20,000
	Auctions: $19,975, MS-65, January 2015; $1,410, MS-62, July 2015; $734, AU-58, January 2015; $764, AU-55, February 2015
1905	200,992	2,307	61.7	94%	$675	$685	$700	$750	$800	$850	$1,200	$5,500
	Auctions: $24,675, MS-67, September 2015; $1,880, MS-64, June 2015; $1,880, MS-64, February 2015; $1,528, MS-64, June 2015
1905, Proof	86	35	63.6							$15,000	$25,000	$45,000
	Auctions: $76,050, PF, September 2013
1905-S	369,250	592	57.0	27%	$675	$685	$700	$750	$800	$850	$3,500	$30,000
	Auctions: $1,645, MS-62, July 2015; $940, MS-61, July 2015; $705, AU-58, January 2015; $617, AU-55, October 2015
1906	165,420	1,560	61.2	91%	$675	$685	$700	$750	$800	$850	$1,250	$8,000
	Auctions: $1,998, MS-64, July 2015; $1,058, MS-63, July 2015; $1,058, MS-63, December 2014; $652, MS-61, October 2014
1906, Proof	77	35	64.2							$15,000	$25,000	$45,000
	Auctions: $41,125, PF, February 2013
1906-D	981,000	3,918	61.4	91%	$675	$685	$700	$750	$800	$850	$1,000	$6,500
	Auctions: $2,938, MS-64, June 2015; $1,058, MS-63, August 2015; $881, MS-62, September 2015; $764, MS-61, January 2015
1906-O	86,895	358	60.3	68%	$725	$750	$800	$925	$1,000	$1,100	$4,750	$20,000
	Auctions: $21,150, MS-65, October 2014; $5,875, MS-64, August 2014; $1,645, MS-62, January 2015; $1,175, MS-62, October 2014
1906-S	457,000	582	58.1	45%	$675	$685	$700	$750	$800	$850	$2,500	$16,500
	Auctions: $12,925, MS-64, February 2015; $1,998, MS-63, January 2015; $1,880, MS-63, January 2015; $1,528, MS-63, June 2015
1907	1,203,899	24,710	62.0	98%	$675	$685	$700	$750	$800	$850	$950	$2,750
	Auctions: $3,525, MS-65, October 2015; $1,645, MS-64, October 2015; $764, MS-62, June 2015; $913, MS-61, July 2015
1907, Proof	74	56	64.0							$15,000	$25,000	$45,000
	Auctions: $54,050, PF-65Cam, January 2015; $33,638, PF-65Cam, March 2012; $29,375, PF-64Cam, August 2014
1907-D	1,030,000	557	61.4	89%	$675	$685	$700	$750	$800	$850	$1,650	$13,500
	Auctions: $2,585, MS-64, August 2015; $2,233, MS-64, January 2015; $1,821, MS-63, November 2014; $823, MS-61, August 2014
1907-S	210,500	374	58.9	55%	$675	$685	$700	$750	$800	$850	$3,500	$20,000
	Auctions: $1,880, MS-62, September 2015; $969, MS-62, August 2015; $881, MS-61, January 2015; $823, MS-61, February 2015

INDIAN HEAD (1907–1933)

Designer: *Augustus Saint-Gaudens.* **Weight:** *16.718 grams.*
Composition: *.900 gold, .100 copper (net weight: .48375 oz. pure gold).*
Diameter: *27 mm.* **Edge:** *1907–1911—46 raised stars; 1912–1933—48 raised stars.*
Mints: *Philadelphia, Denver, and San Francisco.*

No Motto (1907–1908)

Mintmark location, 1908-D (No Motto), is on the reverse, at the tip of the branch.

Mintmark location, 1908 (With Motto)–1930, is on the reverse, to the left of the arrows.

With Motto (1908–1933)

With Motto, Sandblast Finish Proof   **With Motto, Satin Finish Proof**

History. The Indian Head eagle, designed by sculptor Augustus Saint-Gaudens and championed by President Theodore Roosevelt, was struck from 1907 to 1916, and again in intermittent issues through the 1920s and early 1930s. Saint-Gaudens's original design proved impractical to strike and thus was modified slightly by Charles Barber before any large quantities were produced. Not long after (in July 1908), the motto IN GOD WE TRUST was added to the reverse, where it remained to the end of the series. These coins were widely used until 1918, in circulation in the American West and for export.

Striking and Sharpness. On the obverse, check the hair details and the vanes in the feathers. On the reverse, check the shoulder of the eagle. As well-struck coins are available for all varieties, avoid those that are weakly struck. Some examples may exhibit a pink-green color or rust-red "copper spots." Luster varies, but is often deeply frosty. On other coins, particularly from 1910 to 1916, it may be grainy.

Proofs. Sandblast (also called Matte) Proofs were made each year from 1907 through 1915. These have dull surfaces, much like fine-grained sandpaper. Satin (also called Roman Finish) Proofs were made in 1908, 1909, and 1910; they have satiny surfaces and are bright yellow.

Availability. Key rarities in this series are the rolled (or round) rim and wire rim 1907 coins, and the 1920-S, 1930-S, and 1933. Others are generally more readily available. MS-63 and higher coins are generally scarce to rare for the mintmarked issues. The Indian Head eagle is a very popular series. Most such coins in collectors' hands were exported in their time, then brought back to America after World War II. All of the Proofs are rare today.

Note: Values of common-date gold coins have been based on the current bullion price of gold, $1,300 per ounce, and may vary with the prevailing spot price.

GRADING STANDARDS

MS-60 to 70 (Mint State). *Obverse:* At MS-60, some abrasion and contact marks are evident, most noticeably on the hair to the left of Miss Liberty's forehead and in the left field. Luster is present, but may be dull or lifeless, and interrupted in patches. At MS-63, contact marks are few, and abrasion is very light. An MS-65 coin has hardly any abrasion, and contact marks are minute. Luster should be full and rich. Grades above MS-65 are defined by

1907. Graded MS-62.

having fewer marks as perfection is approached. *Reverse:* Comments apply as for the obverse, except that abrasion and contact marks are most noticeable on the front of the left wing and in the left field.

Illustrated coin: This is a brilliant and lustrous example.

AU-50, 53, 55, 58 (About Uncirculated). *Obverse:* Light wear is seen on the cheek, the hair to the right of the face, and the head-dress, more so at AU-50 coin than at AU–53 or 55. An AU-58 coin has minimal traces of wear. An AU-50 coin has luster in protected areas among the stars and in the small field area to the right. At AU-58, most luster is present in the fields but is worn away on the highest parts of the Indian. *Reverse:* Com-

1908-D. Graded AU-58.

ments as preceding, except that the eagle's left wing, left leg, neck, and leg show light wear. Luster ranges from perhaps 40% (at AU-50) to nearly full mint bloom (at AU-58).

Illustrated coin: With nearly full original luster, this coin has remarkable eye appeal.

EF-40, 45 (Extremely Fine). *Obverse:* More wear is evident on the hair to the right of the face, and the feather vanes lack some details, although most are present. Luster, if present at all, is minimal. *Reverse:* Wear is greater than on the preceding. The front edge of the left wing is worn and blends into the top of the left leg. Some traces of luster may be seen, more so at EF-45 than at EF-40.

1907. Graded EF-40.

VF-20, 30 (Very Fine). *Obverse:* The Indian's forehead blends into the hair to the right. Feather-vane detail is gone except in the lower areas. *Reverse:* Wear is greater on the eagle, with only a few details remaining on the back of the left wing and the tail.

The Indian Head eagle is seldom collected in grades lower than VF-20.

1908-S. Graded VF-25.

PF-60 to 70 (Proof). *Obverse and Reverse:* At PF–60 to 63, there is light abrasion and some contact marks (the lower the grade, the higher the quantity). On Sandblast Proofs these show up as visually unappealing bright spots. At PF-64 and higher levels, marks are fewer, with magnification needed to see any at PF-65. At PF-66, there should be none at all.

1915. Sandblast Finish. Graded PF-65.

No Periods	Periods

	Mintage	Cert	Avg	%MS	VF-20	EF-40	AU-50	AU-55	MS-60	MS-62 / PF-63	MS-63 / PF-64	MS-65 / PF-65
1907, Wire Rim, Periods	500	175	63.5	93%		$25,000	$27,500	$29,500	$35,000	$37,500	$45,000	$75,000
	Auctions: $82,250, MS-65, August 2016: $67,563, MS-65, October 2015; $58,750, MS-65, August 2015; $56,400, MS-65, May 2016											
1907, Rounded Rim, Periods Before and After •E•PLURIBUS•UNUM• † (a)	50	30	62.7	83%		$60,000	$65,000	$70,000	$85,000	$100,000	$165,000	$300,000
	Auctions: $470,000, MS-67, August 2013											
1907, No Periods	239,406	7,719	61.6	85%	$750	$800	$850	$900	$1,250	$1,850	$2,500	$7,000
	Auctions: $35,250, MS-67, August 2015; $5,170, MS-64, June 2015; $1,293, AU-58, January 2015; $999, AU-50, February 2015											
1907, Wire Rim, Periods, Plain Edge, Proof (b)	*unknown*	0	n/a									
	Auctions: $359,375, PF-62, August 2010											
1907, Rounded Rim, Periods, Satin Finish Proof	*unknown*	0	n/a			*(extremely rare)*						
	Auctions: $2,185,000, PF-67, January 2011											
1907, Sandblast Finish Proof (c)	*unknown*	0	n/a			*(extremely rare)*						
	Auctions: No auction records available.											

† Ranked in the *100 Greatest U.S. Coins* (fourth edition). **a.** All but 50 of the 31,500 coins were melted at the mint. **b.** According to the *Encyclopedia of U.S. Gold Coins, 1795–1933,* the only confirmed example may be from the Captain North set of 1907 and 1908 gold coins sold by Stack's in the 1970s. **c.** 2 or 3 examples are known.

	Mintage	Cert	Avg	%MS	VF-20	EF-40	AU-50	AU-55	MS-60	MS-62 PF-63	MS-63 PF-64	MS-65 PF-65
1908, No Motto	33,500	813	61.0	78%	$800	$850	$875	$925	$1,500	$3,000	$5,500	$15,000
	Auctions: $19,975, MS-66, October 2015; $7,050, MS-64, January 2015; $3,055, MS-62, October 2015; $1,763, AU-58, June 2015											
1908-D, No Motto	210,000	1,020	59.5	55%	$750	$825	$850	$875	$1,500	$3,000	$6,500	$35,000
	Auctions: $13,513, MS-64, January 2015; $2,233, MS-61, February 2015; $1,234, AU-58, August 2015; $734, EF-45, October 2015											
1908, With Motto	341,370	4,734	60.8	80%	$700	$725	$750	$775	$1,000	$1,150	$1,450	$5,500
	Auctions: $32,900, MS-66, October 2015; $1,998, MS-63, March 2015; $1,058, AU-58, August 2015; $764, EF-45, February 2015											
1908, With Motto, Sandblast Finish Proof	116	53	65.2							$20,000	$32,500	$55,000
	Auctions: $69,000, PF-66, January 2012; $79,313, PF-65, August 2014; $61,688, PF-65, January 2015											
1908, With Motto, Satin Finish Proof (d)	(e)	1	64.0					*(extremely rare)*				
	Auctions: No auction records available.											
1908-D, With Motto	836,500	824	59.0	55%	$800	$850	$925	$975	$1,250	$2,500	$3,000	$30,000
	Auctions: $5,640, MS-63, January 2015; $3,525, MS-62, October 2015; $1,293, MS-61, January 2015; $999, AU-58, August 2015											
1908-S	59,850	811	54.7	20%	$700	$725	$750	$775	$1,500	$3,000	$4,500	$17,500
	Auctions: $35,251, MS-66, October 2015; $14,100, MS-64, March 2015; $4,113, AU-58, September 2015; $999, EF-45, February 2015											
1909	184,789	2,225	60.6	74%	$700	$725	$750	$775	$850	$900	$1,200	$6,500
	Auctions: $5,640, MS-64, June 2015; $3,290, MS-63, January 2015; $1,058, MS-62, March 2015; $940, MS-61, June 2015											
1909, Satin Finish Proof	74	0	n/a							$20,000	$35,000	$75,000
	Auctions: $48,875, PF-65, July 2011											
1909, Sandblast Finish Proof (f)	(g)	0	n/a					*(extremely rare)*				
	Auctions: No auction records available.											
1909-D	121,540	1,065	59.4	57%	$800	$850	$925	$975	$1,250	$2,500	$3,000	$30,000
	Auctions: $4,113, MS-63, January 2015; $2,115, MS-62, March 2015; $999, AU-58, August 2015; $940, AU-55, August 2015											
1909-S	292,350	873	57.3	34%	$700	$725	$750	$775	$1,500	$3,000	$4,500	$17,500
	Auctions: $7,638, MS-64, October 2015; $1,880, MS-61, September 2015; $1,116, AU-58, June 2015; $800, AU-53, August 2015											
1910	318,500	6,605	61.6	89%	$700	$725	$750	$775	$850	$900	$1,200	$6,500
	Auctions: $17,625, MS-66, January 2015; $1,645, MS-64, January 2015; $940, MS-61, September 2015; $676, MS-60, October 2015											
1910, Satin Finish Proof	204	27	65.4							$20,000	$35,000	$75,000
	Auctions: $80,500, PF-67, January 2012											
1910, Sandblast Finish Proof (h)	(i)	1	66.0									
	Auctions: No auction records available.											
1910-D	2,356,640	13,069	61.6	90%	$700	$725	$750	$775	$850	$900	$1,000	$6,500
	Auctions: $13,513, MS-66, October 2015; $1,998, MS-64, January 2015; $837, MS-60, June 2015; $705, AU-58, October 2015											
1910-S	811,000	1,902	57.0	31%	$700	$725	$750	$775	$1,000	$2,250	$6,500	$45,000
	Auctions: $12,925, MS-64, January 2015; $1,645, MS-61, August 2015; $1,410, AU-58, January 2015; $823, AU-58, August 2015											
1911	505,500	10,468	61.5	87%	$700	$725	$750	$775	$850	$950	$1,050	$6,000
	Auctions: $30,550, MS-67, August 2015; $9,988, MS-66, September 2015; $1,293, MS-63, February 2015; $705, AU-55, August 2015											
1911, Sandblast Finish Proof	95	24	66.3							$20,000	$32,500	$60,000
	Auctions: $152,750, PF-67, November 2013; $76,375, PF-66, August 2015; $74,025, PF-66, October 2014											
1911-D	30,100	941	54.9	17%	$1,250	$1,500	$2,200	$3,500	$12,500	$15,000	$30,000	$250,000
	Auctions: $23,500, MS-63, October 2015; $22,325, MS-63, August 2016; $30,550, MS-62, January 2015; $6,169, AU-58, January 2015											
1911-S	51,000	383	56.8	28%	$800	$850	$925	$975	$3,000	$6,500	$11,000	$25,000
	Auctions: $24,793, MS-65, October 2015; $3,525, MS-61, October 2015; $2,820, AU-58, September 2015; $1,645, AU-50, February 2015											

d. 3 or 4 examples are known. **e.** Included in 1908, With Motto, Matte Proof, mintage figure. **f.** 2 or 3 examples are known. **g.** Included in 1909, Satin Finish Proof, mintage figure. **h.** The only example known is part of the unique complete 1910 Matte Proof gold set. **i.** Included in 1910, Satin Finish Proof, mintage figure.

	Mintage	Cert	Avg	%MS	VF-20	EF-40	AU-50	AU-55	MS-60	MS-62 / PF-63	MS-63 / PF-64	MS-65 / PF-65
1912	405,000	7,142	61.3	86%	$700	$725	$750	$775	$875	$1,000	$1,100	$8,000
Auctions: $54,050, MS-67, January 2015; $3,290, MS-64, January 2015; $881, MS-61, September 2015; $705, AU-55, August 2015												
1912, Sandblast Finish Proof	83	21	65.6							$20,000	$32,500	$60,000
Auctions: $99,875, PF, March 2014												
1912-S	300,000	1,192	57.2	27%	$725	$750	$775	$825	$1,250	$2,500	$6,000	$35,000
Auctions: $12,402, MS-64, October 2015; $1,116, AU-58, August 2015; $734, AU-50, February 2015; $705, EF-45, January 2015												
1913	442,000	6,312	61.1	83%	$700	$725	$750	$775	$875	$1,000	$1,250	$6,500
Auctions: $14,100, MS-66, January 2015; $3,408, MS-64, February 2015; $881, MS-62, June 2015; $705, AU-58, July 2015												
1913, Sandblast Finish Proof	71	25	65.4							$20,000	$32,500	$60,000
Auctions: $63,250, PF-66, January 2012												
1913-S	66,000	974	55.0	13%	$1,000	$1,100	$1,200	$2,250	$7,500	$12,500	$25,000	$150,000
Auctions: $22,325, MS-63, January 2015; $4,243, AU-58, February 2015; $1,528, AU-53, June 2015; $852, EF-40, January 2015												
1914	151,000	2,346	61.1	82%	$700	$725	$750	$775	$875	$975	$1,650	$8,500
Auctions: $10,869, MS-65, October 2015; $2,832, MS-64, January 2015; $1,998, MS-63, January 2015; $881, MS-62, May 2015												
1914, Sandblast Finish Proof	50	32	65.7							$20,000	$32,500	$60,000
Auctions: $96,938, PF, October 2013												
1914-D	343,500	2,898	60.7	75%	$700	$725	$750	$775	$875	$1,000	$1,500	$12,500
Auctions: $9,988, MS-65, October 2015; $1,998, MS-63, January 2015; $887, MS-61, June 2015; $764, AU-55, October 2015												
1914-S	208,000	1,095	58.3	40%	$700	$725	$750	$825	$2,000	$3,250	$5,500	$30,000
Auctions: $16,450, MS-64, October 2015; $1,645, AU-58, January 2015; $705, AU-53, August 2015; $709, EF-45, August 2015												
1915	351,000	4,544	61.1	80%	$700	$725	$750	$775	$900	$975	$1,650	$6,500
Auctions: $6,463, MS-65, January 2015; $2,350, MS-63, January 2015; $823, MS-60, September 2015; $823, AU-58, September 2015												
1915, Sandblast Finish Proof	75	17	65.7							$22,500	$32,500	$70,000
Auctions: $94,000, PF, August 2013												
1915-S	59,000	430	57.3	26%	$900	$1,000	$1,050	$1,750	$5,500	$12,500	$20,000	$65,000
Auctions: $19,975, MS-62, September 2015; $6,611, MS-61, August 2015; $3,408, AU-58, January 2015; $1,058, AU-50, January 2015												
1916-S	138,500	927	59.0	49%	$950	$985	$1,000	$1,100	$1,500	$2,750	$6,500	$25,000
Auctions: $7,050, MS-63, August 2015; $1,763, MS-61, October 2015; $1,528, AU-58, August 2015; $764, AU-50, September 2015												
1920-S	126,500	53	59.5	55%	$20,000	$25,000	$32,500	$40,000	$60,000	$75,000	$105,000	$225,000
Auctions: $70,500, MS-62, September 2015; $70,500, MS-61, June 2015; $64,625, MS-61, October 2015; $47,000, AU-58, January 2015												
1926	1,014,000	41,128	62.5	99%	$700	$725	$750	$775	$875	$900	$950	$2,750
Auctions: $7,638, MS-66, October 2015; $1,469, MS-64, October 2015; $823, MS-61, June 2015; $646, MS-60, July 2015												
1930-S	96,000	63	63.6	95%	$20,000	$22,500	$25,000	$30,000	$40,000	$45,000	$55,000	$100,000
Auctions: $85,188, MS-65, September 2014; $70,500, MS-64, March 2014; $17,625, MS-60, January 2015												
1932	4,463,000	60,919	62.9	100%	$700	$725	$750	$775	$875	$900	$950	$2,750
Auctions: $10,869, MS-66, January 2015; $2,482, MS-65, March 2015; $1,528, MS-63, August 2015; $793, MS-60, July 2015												
1933 † (j)	312,500	11	64.4	100%						$300,000	$325,000	$400,000	$750,000
Auctions: $587,500, MS-65, June 2015: $367,188, MS-64, August 2013												

† Ranked in the *100 Greatest U.S. Coins* (fourth edition). **j.** Nearly all were melted at the mint.

Gold Double Eagles ($20)
1850–1933

AN OVERVIEW OF GOLD DOUBLE EAGLES

Congress authorized the double eagle, or twenty-dollar coin—the largest denomination of all regular U.S. coinage issues—by the Act of March 3, 1849, in response to the huge amounts of gold coming from California.

Double eagles are at once large and impressive to own. Many gold collectors form a type set of the six major double eagle designs (with the 1861 Paquet added as a sub-type if desired). Thanks to overseas hoards repatriated since the 1950s, finding choice and gem Mint State examples is no problem at all for the later types.

The first double eagle type, the Liberty Head of 1850 to 1866 without the motto IN GOD WE TRUST, is generally available in grades from VF up. Mint State pieces were elusive prior to the 1990s, but the market supply was augmented by more than 5,000 pieces—including some gems—found in the discovery of the long-lost treasure ship SS *Central America*. The SS *Brother Jonathan*, lost at sea in 1865, was recovered in the 1990s and yielded hundreds of Mint State 1865-S double eagles, along with some dated 1864 and a few earlier. The wreck of the SS *Republic*, lost in 1865 while on a voyage from New York City to New Orleans and salvaged in 2003, also yielded some very attractive Mint State double eagles of this first Liberty Head type.

The Liberty Head type from 1866 through 1876, with the motto IN GOD WE TRUST above the eagle and with the denomination expressed as TWENTY D., is the rarest in MS-63 and higher grades. Many EF and AU coins have been repatriated from overseas holdings, as have quite a few in such grades as MS–60 through 62. However, true gems are hardly ever seen.

Liberty Head double eagles of the 1877–1907 type with the IN GOD WE TRUST motto and with the denomination spelled out as TWENTY DOLLARS are exceedingly plentiful in just about any grade desired, with gems being readily available of certain issues of the early 20th century. While it is easy to obtain a gem of a common date, some collectors of type coins have opted to acquire a coin of special historical interest, such as a Carson City issue.

The famous Saint-Gaudens MCMVII High Relief double eagle of 1907 was saved in quantity by the general public as well as by numismatists, and today it is likely that at least 5,000 to 6,000 exist, representing about half of the mintage. Most of these are in varying degrees of Mint State, with quite a few graded as MS–64 and 65. Those in lower grades such as VF and EF often were used for jewelry or were polished, or have other problems. This particular design is a great favorite with collectors, and although the coins are not rarities, they are hardly inexpensive.

The so-called Arabic Numerals 1907–1908 Saint-Gaudens design is available in nearly any grade desired, with MS-60 through MS-63 or MS-64 pieces being plentiful and inexpensive. Double eagles of the final type, 1908–1933, are abundant in any grade desired, with choice and gem coins being plentiful.

FOR THE COLLECTOR AND INVESTOR: GOLD DOUBLE EAGLES AS A SPECIALTY

Collecting double eagles by date and mint is more popular than one might think. Offhand, one might assume that these high denominations, laden with a number of rare dates, would attract few enthusiasts. However, over a long period of years more collectors have specialized in double eagles than have specialized in five-dollar or ten-dollar pieces.

Two particularly notable collections of double eagles by date and mint, from the earliest times to the latest, were formed by Louis E. Eliasberg of Baltimore, and Jeff Browning of Dallas. Both have been dispersed across the auction block. The first was cataloged by Bowers and Ruddy in 1982, and the second was offered by Stack's and Sotheby's in 2001. In addition, dozens of other collections over the years have had large numbers of double eagles, some specializing in the Liberty Head types of 1850–1907, others only with the Saint-Gaudens types from 1907 onward, and others addressing the entire range.

Among rarities in the double eagle series are the 1854-O and 1856-O, each known only to the extent of a few dozen pieces; the 1861 Philadelphia Mint coins with Paquet reverse (two known); the Proof-only issues of 1883, 1884, and 1887; several other low-mintage varieties of this era; the famous Carson City issue of 1870-CC; and various issues from 1920 onward, including 1920-S, 1921, mintmarked coins after 1923, and all dates after 1928. Punctuating these rarities is a number of readily available pieces, including the very common Philadelphia issues from 1922 through 1928 inclusive.

LIBERTY HEAD (1849–1907)

Designer: *James B. Longacre.* **Weight:** *33.436 grams.*
Composition: *.900 gold, .100 copper (net weight: .96750 oz. pure gold).* **Diameter** *34 mm.*
Edge: *Reeded.* **Mints:** *Philadelphia, Carson City, Denver, New Orleans, and San Francisco.*

No Motto (1849–1866)   No Motto, Proof

**Mintmark location is on
the reverse, below the eagle.**

With Motto (1866–1907)   With Motto, Proof

History. The twenty-dollar denomination was introduced to circulation in 1850 (after a unique pattern, which currently resides in the Smithsonian's National Numismatic Collection, was minted in 1849). The large new coin was ideal for converting the flood of California gold rush bullion into federal legal tender. U.S. Mint chief engraver James B. Longacre designed the coin. A different reverse, designed by Anthony Paquet with taller letters than Longacre's design, was tested in 1861 but ultimately not used past that date. In 1866 the motto IN GOD WE TRUST was added to the reverse. In 1877 the denomination on the reverse, formerly given as TWENTY D., was changed to TWENTY DOLLARS. The double eagle denomination proved to be very popular, especially for export. By 1933, more than 75 percent of the American gold used to strike coins from the 1850s onward had been used to make double eagles. Oddly, some of the coins of 1850 to 1858 appear to have the word LIBERTY misspelled as LLBERTY.

Striking and Sharpness. On the obverse, check the star centers and the hair details. As made, the hair details are less distinct on many coins of 1859 (when a slight modification was made) through the 1890s, and knowledge of this is important. Later issues usually have exquisite detail. The reverse usually is well struck, but check the eagle and other features. The denticles are sharp on nearly all coins, but should be checked. Proofs were made in all years from 1858 to 1907, and a few were made before then. Proofs of 1902 onward, particularly 1903, have the portrait polished in the die, imparting a mirror finish across the design, and lack the cameo contrast of earlier dates.

Availability. Basic dates and mintmarks are available in proportion to their mintages. Key issues include the 1854-O, 1856-O, 1861 Paquet Reverse, 1861-S Paquet Reverse, 1866 No Motto, 1870-CC, 1879-O, and several Philadelphia Mint dates of the 1880s The vast majority of others are readily collectible. Among early coins, MS examples from about 1854 to 1857 are available, most notably the 1857-S and certain varieties of the 1860s. Most varieties of the 1880s onward, and particularly of the 1890s and 1900s, are easily available in MS, due to the repatriation of millions of coins that had been exported overseas. Proofs dated through the 1870s are all very rare today; those of the 1880s are less so; and those of the 1890s and 1900s are scarce. Many Proofs have been mishandled. Dates that are Proof-only (and those that are very rare in circulation-strike form) are in demand even if impaired. These include 1883, 1884, 1885, 1886, and 1887.

Note: Values of common-date gold coins have been based on the current bullion price of gold, $1,300 per ounce, and may vary with the prevailing spot price.

GRADING STANDARDS

MS-60 to 70 (Mint State). *Obverse:* At MS-60, some abrasion and contact marks are evident, most noticeably on the hair to the right of Miss Liberty's forehead and on the cheek. Luster is present, but may be dull or lifeless, and interrupted in patches. At MS-63, contact marks are few, and abrasion is light. An MS-65 coin has little abrasion, and contact marks are minute. Luster should be full and rich. Grades above MS-65 are defined by

1876-S. Graded MS-64.

having fewer marks as perfection is approached. *Reverse:* Comments apply as for the obverse, except that abrasion and contact marks are most noticeable on eagle's neck, wingtips, and tail.

AU-50, 53, 55, 58 (About Uncirculated). *Obverse:* Light wear is seen on the face, the hair to the right of the face, and the highest area of the hair behind the coronet, more so at AU-50 than at AU–53 or 55. An AU-58 coin has minimal traces of wear. An AU-50 coin has luster in protected areas among the stars and letters, with little in the open fields or on the portrait. At AU-58 most luster is present in the fields, but is worn away on the highest parts of the motifs. *Reverse:* Comments as preceding, except that the eagle and ornaments show wear in all of the higher areas. Luster ranges from perhaps 40% remaining in protected areas (at AU-50) to nearly full mint bloom (at AU-58). Often the reverse of this type retains more luster than the obverse.

1856-S. Graded AU-53.

Illustrated coin: Much of the original luster still remains at this grade level, especially on the reverse.

EF-40, 45 (Extremely Fine). *Obverse:* Wear is evident on all high areas of the portrait, including the hair to the right of the forehead, the tip of the coronet, and hair behind the coronet. The curl to the right of the neck is flat on its highest-relief area. Luster, if present at all, is minimal and in protected areas such as between the star points. *Reverse:* Wear is greater than on an About Uncirculated coin. The eagle's neck and wingtips show wear, as do the ornaments and rays. Some traces of luster may be seen, more so at EF-45 than at EF-40. Overall, the reverse appears to be in a slightly higher grade than the obverse.

1855-S. Graded EF-45.

VF-20, 30 (Very Fine). *Obverse:* The higher-relief areas of hair are worn flat at VF-20, less so at VF-30. The hair to the right of the coronet is merged into heavy strands and is flat at the back, as is part of the bow. The curl to the right of the neck is flat. *Reverse:* The eagle shows further wear on the head, the tops of the wings, and the tail. The ornament has flat spots.

The Liberty Head double eagle is seldom collected in grades lower than VF-20.

1857-S. Graded VF-20.

Illustrated coin: Note the small test cut or mark on the top rim.

PF-60 to 70 (Proof). *Obverse and Reverse:* PF–60 to 62 coins have extensive hairlines and may have nicks and contact marks. At PF-63, hairlines are prominent, but the mirror surface is very reflective. PF-64 coins have fewer hairlines. At PF-65, hairlines should be relatively few. These large and heavy coins reveal hairlines more readily than do the lower denominations, mostly seen only under magnification. PF-66 and higher coins should have no marks or hairlines visible to the unaided eye.

1903. Graded PF-64.

Illustrated coin: A beautiful Proof, this is just a few hairlines away from a higher level.

Value TWENTY D.
(1849–1876)

Value TWENTY DOLLARS
(1877–1907)

1853, So-called 3 Over 2
Note rust under LIBERTY.
FS-G20-1853-301.

	Mintage	Cert	Avg	%MS	VF-20	EF-40	AU-50	AU-55	MS-60	MS-62	MS-63	MS-65
										PF-63	PF-64	PF-65
1849, Proof (a)	1	0	n/a		(unique; in the Smithsonian's National Numismatic Collection)							
	Auctions: No auction records available.											
1850	1,170,261	1,514	50.3	5%	$2,500	$3,500	$5,500	$8,000	$16,500	$40,000	$60,000	$200,000
	Auctions: $42,300, MS-62, August 2015; $7,344, AU-55, August 2015; $4,465, AU-50, June 2015; $2,585, EF-40, January 2015											
1850, Proof (b)	1–2	0	n/a									
	Auctions: No auction records available.											
1850-O	141,000	331	47.2	2%	$5,500	$8,000	$15,000	$24,500	$75,000			
	Auctions: $58,750, MS-61, January 2015; $21,150, AU-55, January 2015; $9,400, EF-45, August 2015; $4,465, VF-25, August 2015											
1851	2,087,155	1,161	51.4	7%	$2,000	$2,250	$2,750	$3,250	$6,500	$14,500	$30,000	
	Auctions: $14,100, MS-62, July 2015; $5,170, AU-55, August 2015; $1,645, EF-40, January 2015; $1,772, VF-35, June 2015											
1851-O	315,000	738	49.6	3%	$2,750	$5,000	$7,500	$12,500	$28,500	$65,000	$125,000	
	Auctions: $13,513, AU-58, August 2015; $7,638, AU-53, October 2015; $6,463, AU-50, January 2015; $4,818, EF-45, October 2015											
1852	2,053,026	1,912	51.6	6%	$2,000	$2,250	$2,750	$3,750	$6,500	$14,500	$22,500	
	Auctions: $10,600, MS-62, October 2015; $3,819, AU-58, March 2015; $1,704, AU-50, January 2015; $1,998, EF-40, January 2015											
1852-O	190,000	584	51.3	4%	$2,500	$4,500	$7,500	$13,500	$37,500	$55,000	$95,000	
	Auctions: $27,061, AU-58, August 2015; $5,640, AU-50, September 2015; $3,408, EF-40, July 2015; $2,291, VF-20, August 2015											
1853, All kinds	1,261,326											
1853, So-called 3 Over 2 (c)		210	52.5	3%	$3,000	$4,000	$7,500	$12,500	$42,500	$55,000		
	Auctions: $28,200, AU-58, August 2014; $28,200, AU-58, October 2014: $17,625, AU-58, April 2014											
1853		1,307	52.5	5%	$2,000	$2,250	$2,750	$3,250	$6,500	$16,500	$30,000	
	Auctions: $7,638, MS-61, February 2015; $6,169, AU-58, January 2015; $2,848, AU-53, January 2015; $1,880, EF-40, August 2015											
1853-O	71,000	228	49.6	3%	$3,000	$6,500	$12,500	$17,500	$37,500			
	Auctions: $14,100, AU-55, August 2015; $11,750, AU-55, January 2015; $10,575, AU-50, January 2015; $7,638, EF-45, August 2015											

a. An unknown quantity of Proof 1849 double eagles was struck as patterns; all but two were melted. One (current location unknown) was sent to Treasury secretary W.M. Meredith; the other was placed in the Mint collection in Philadelphia, and transferred with that collection to the Smithsonian in 1923. **b.** Although no examples currently are known, it is likely that a small number of Proof 1850 double eagles were struck. For the years 1851 to 1857, no Proofs are known. **c.** Although overlaid photographs indicate this is not a true overdate, what appear to be remnants of a numeral are visible beneath the 3 in the date. This variety also shows a rust spot underneath the R of LIBERTY.

1854, Small Date   1854, Large Date

	Mintage	Cert	Avg	%MS	VF-20	EF-40	AU-50	AU-55	MS-60	MS-62 / PF-63	MS-63 / PF-64	MS-65 / PF-65
1854, All kinds	757,899											
1854, Small Date		635	52.3	4%	$2,000	$2,250	$2,850	$3,750	$9,500	$18,000	$35,000	
Auctions: $11,163, MS-61, January 2015; $4,714, AU-55, January 2015; $2,233, EF-45, October 2015; $1,645, VF-30, August 2015											
1854, Large Date		127	52.9	8%	$3,500	$4,250	$10,000	$16,000	$37,500	$50,000	$65,000	
Auctions: $55,813, MS-61, August 2014; $19,975, AU-58, October 2014; $9,988, AU-53, September 2015; $9,400, AU-50, August 2015											
1854-O † (d)	3,250	16	53.1	0%	$145,000	$225,000	$375,000	$425,000	—			
Auctions: $440,625, AU-55, April 2014; $340,750, AU-55, August 2015; $329,000, AU-50, August 2014											
1854-S	141,468	218	52.5	23%	$3,000	$4,250	$10,500	$16,000	$30,000	$37,500	$50,000	$90,000
Auctions: $16,450, AU-55, August 2015; $16,450, AU-55, September 2016; $21,738, AU-53, February 2015; $14,688, AU-53, July 2015											
1854-S, Proof † (e)	*unknown*	0	n/a		*(unique; in the Smithsonian's National Numismatic Collection)*							
Auctions: No auction records available.											
1855	364,666	402	53.0	5%	$2,000	$2,350	$3,000	$4,500	$12,000	$23,500	$65,000	
Auctions: $5,170, AU-58, September 2015; $3,878, AU-55, February 2015; $2,820, AU-53, August 2015; $2,350, AU-50, January 2015											
1855-O	8,000	47	50.5	9%	$13,500	$35,000	$50,000	$67,500	$125,000			
Auctions: $141,000, MS-61, January 2014; $70,500, AU-58, August 2015; $58,750, AU-55, August 2014; $28,200, AU-50, October 2014											
1855-S	879,675	1,097	51.6	3%	$2,000	$2,150	$2,500	$3,750	$8,000	$13,750	$25,000	
Auctions: $11,163, MS-61, July 2015; $3,819, AU-58, March 2015; $1,704, EF-40, June 2015; $1,528, VF-20, August 2015											
1856	329,878	367	52.5	6%	$2,150	$2,250	$3,250	$4,500	$11,000	$17,500	$35,000	
Auctions: $7,050, AU-58, October 2015; $4,465, AU-55, June 2015; $3,290, AU-53, January 2015; $3,995, AU-50, August 2015											
1856-O † (f)	2,250	9	51.3	0%	$145,000	$250,000	$375,000	$425,000				
Auctions: $340,750, AU-55, August 2015; $425,938, AU-53, August 2014; $164,500, AU-50, August 2014; $381,875, EF-45, January 2014											
1856-O, Proof (g)	*unknown*	1	63.0									
Auctions: $1,437,500, SP-63, May 2009											
1856-S	1189750	1,249	51.5	4%	$2,000	$2,350	$2,750	$3,500	$6,500	$12,500	$16,500	$45,000
Auctions: $7,344, MS-61, June 2015; $4,935, AU-58, September 2015; $5,170, AU-53, January 2015; $2,115, EF-40, September 2015											
1857	439,375	521	53.4	10%	$2,000	$2,500	$2,750	$3,500	$7,500	$14,500	$40,000	
Auctions: $5,875, MS-60, January 2015; $3,760, AU-58, January 2015; $2,350, AU-53, September 2015; $2,585, EF-45, January 2015											
1857-O	30,000	149	52.4	6%	$4,750	$9,500	$15,000	$25,000	$52,500	$125,000	$250,000	
Auctions: $21,150, AU-53, August 2015; $11,163, AU-50, January 2015; $7,050, EF-40, October 2015; $2,585, VF-20, September 2015											
1857-S † (h)	970,500	1,499	54.6	27%	$2,000	$2,250	$2,500	$3,250	$5,500	$7,000	$9,000	$14,500
Auctions: $15,863, MS-65, September 2015; $5,405, AU-58, August 2015; $2,233, AU-53, July 2015; $2,233, EF-40, January 2015											
1858	211,714	461	52.4	7%	$2,150	$2,500	$3,500	$4,500	$9,000	$30,000	$45,000	
Auctions: $19,975, MS-62, January 2015; $4,935, AU-58, October 2015; $2,820, AU-53, October 2015; $3,055, EF-45, August 2015											
1858, Proof (i)	*unknown*	0	n/a		*(extremely rare)*							
Auctions: No auction records available.											
1858-O	35,250	145	51.4	6%	$5,000	$9,500	$20,000	$32,500	$60,000	$75,000		
Auctions: $164,500, MS-63, January 2015; AU-58, August 2015; $9,988, AU-50, August 2015; $7,050, AU-50, January 2015											
1858-S	846,710	1,107	51.1	2%	$2,000	$2,250	$3,000	$3,750	$10,000	$15,000	$45,000	
Auctions: $8,225, MS-60, October 2015; $7,638, AU-58, January 2015; $2,879, AU-53, June 2015; $1,528, EF-40, January 2015											

† Ranked in the *100 Greatest U.S. Coins* (fourth edition). **d.** Probably fewer than 35 exist, most in VF and EF. **e.** This unique coin, perhaps more accurately described as a presentation strike than a Proof, was sent to the Mint collection in Philadelphia by San Francisco Mint superintendent Lewis A. Birdsall. It may have been the first coin struck for the year, set aside to recognize the opening of the San Francisco Mint. **f.** Probably fewer than 25 exist, most in VF and EF. **g.** This prooflike presentation strike is unique. **h.** The treasure of the shipwrecked SS *Central America* included thousands of 1857-S double eagles in high grades. Different size mintmark varieties exist; the Large S variety is rarest. **i.** 3 or 4 examples are known.

1861-S, Normal Reverse

1861-S, Paquet Reverse
Note taller letters.

	Mintage	Cert	Avg	%MS	VF-20	EF-40	AU-50	AU-55	MS-60	MS-62 PF-63	MS-63 PF-64	MS-65 PF-65
1859	43,597	131	51.6	5%	$3,250	$6,500	$12,500	$15,000	$32,000	$47,500		
	Auctions: $17,625, AU-55, August 2015; $12,925, AU-50, August 2015; $3,290, AU-50, August 2014; $7,050, EF-40, October 2015											
1859, Proof (j)	80	6	62.7							$225,000	$400,000	$500,000
	Auctions: $210,600, PF, June 2014											
1859-O	9,100	60	50.5	2%	$9,500	$25,000	$50,000	$65,000	$125,000			
	Auctions: $28,200, MS-60, August 2014: $105,750, AU-58, September 2016; $76,375, AU-58, August 2014											
1859-S	636,445	842	50.9	3%	$2,000	$2,250	$2,800	$4,500	$13,500	$30,000	$57,500	
	Auctions: $9,400, AU-58, August 2015; $3,995, AU-55, July 2015; $2,820, AU-53, October 2015; $2,585, EF-45, September 2015											
1860	577,611	975	53.9	11%	$2,000	$2,150	$2,500	$3,000	$6,500	$12,000	$22,500	
	Auctions: $10,575, MS-61, August 2015; $3,301, AU-58, January 2015; $2,644, AU-55, June 2015; $2,585, AU-53, January 2015											
1860, Proof (k)	59	9	64.3							$125,000	$250,000	$400,000
	Auctions: $367,188, PF-66Cam, August 2014											
1860-O	6,600	60	51.4	3%	$12,500	$35,000	$55,000	$67,500				
	Auctions: $64,625, AU-58, August 2015; $55,813, AU-53, August 2014; $30,550, EF-40, January 2015											
1860-S	544,950	767	51.4	3%	$2,000	$2,250	$2,750	$4,000	$10,000	$20,000	$35,000	
	Auctions: $7,050, AU-58, January 2015; $3,673, AU-55, January 2015; $3,760, AU-53, August 2015; $1,528, VF-20, February 2015											
1861	2,976,387	3,462	54.3	16%	$2,000	$2,150	$2,500	$3,250	$6,500	$10,000	$18,500	$57,500
	Auctions: $8,813, MS-62, July 2015; $4,465, AU-58, February 2015; $1,998, AU-50, July 2015; $2,115, EF-40, January 2015											
1861, Proof (l)	66	2	64.0							$125,000	$250,000	$375,000
	Auctions: $44,850, PF-65DCam, September 2005											
1861-O	17,741	108	48.1	5%	$15,000	$35,000	$55,000	$67,500	$150,000			
	Auctions: $51,406, AU-50, March 2015; $44,650, AU-50, August 2015; $16,450, AU, March 2015; $11,163, AU-50, January 2015											
1861-S	768,000	857	50.8	3%	$2,000	$2,250	$3,250	$5,000	$16,000	$32,500	$47,500	
	Auctions: $3,525, MS-60, October 2015; $4,935, AU-58, January 2015; $2,350, AU-50, July 2015; $2,115, EF-45, August 2015											
1861, Paquet Rev (Tall Ltrs) † (m)	*unknown*	1	67.0	100%					$2,000,000			
	Auctions: $1,645,000, MS-61, August 2014											
1861-S, Paquet Rev (Tall Ltrs) † (n)	19,250	76	48.6	0%	$55,000	$75,000	$90,000	$115,000	$275,000			
	Auctions: $223,250, AU-58, April 2014; $164,500, AU-58, August 2015; $152,750, AU-58, August 2015; $105,750, 0, August 2016											
1862	92,098	100	52.0	15%	$4,500	$11,000	$15,000	$20,000	$40,000	$55,000	$70,000	
	Auctions: $70,500, MS-62, August 2014; $49,938, MS-62, August 2014; $28,200, AU-58, August 2015											
1862, Proof (o)	35	6	64.2							$125,000	$250,000	$375,000
	Auctions: $381,875, PF-65Cam, April 2014											
1862-S	854,173	1,105	51.2	4%	$2,000	$2,500	$3,500	$5,000	$13,500	$30,000	$50,000	
	Auctions: $9,400, AU-58, January 2015; $3,995, AU-55, October 2015; $2,470, AU-50, August 2015; $2,585, EF-45, February 2015											

† Ranked in the *100 Greatest U.S. Coins* (fourth edition). **j.** 7 or 8 examples are known. **k.** Fewer than 10 examples are known. **l.** 5 or 6 examples are known. **m.** Once thought to be a pattern; now known to have been intended for circulation. 2 examples are known. **n.** Approximately 100 examples are known, most in VF and EF. **o.** Approximately 12 examples are known.

	Mintage	Cert	Avg	%MS	VF-20	EF-40	AU-50	AU-55	MS-60	MS-62	MS-63	MS-65
										PF-63	PF-64	PF-65
1863	142,760	204	52.8	12%	$3,000	$5,500	$11,000	$15,000	$32,500	$55,000	$85,000	
Auctions: $85,188, MS-63, January 2015; $21,150, AU-58, September 2015; $20,563, AU-58, January 2015; $17,625, AU-55, August 2015												
1863, Proof (p)	30	8	64.3							$125,000	$250,000	$375,000
Auctions: $381,875, PF-66Cam, August 2014; $345,150, PF, September 2013												
1863-S	966,570	1,456	51.6	9%	$2,150	$2,500	$3,000	$4,000	$10,000	$21,000	$35,000	
Auctions: $5,405, AU-58, August 2015; $4,230, AU-55, August 2015; $2,115, EF-45, August 2015; $1,880, VF-30, January 2015												
1864	204,235	307	52.5	9%	$3,000	$5,500	$9,000	$11,000	$25,000	$47,500	$75,000	
Auctions: $282,000, MS-65, April 2014; $8,813, AU-53, August 2015; $4,230, EF-40, August 2015; $3,760, EF-40, January 2015												
1864, Proof (q)	50	10	64.4							$125,000	$250,000	$375,000
Auctions: $199,750, PF-64Cam, April 2014												
1864-S	793,660	1,017	51.4	12%	$2,000	$2,250	$2,750	$3,500	$11,000	$20,000	$45,000	$110,000
Auctions: $19,975, MS-62, August 2015; $4,935, AU-53, February 2015; $1,998, EF-45, August 2015; $1,763, VF-35, July 2015												
1865	351,175	791	56.9	42%	$2,250	$2,750	$3,000	$3,750	$7,500	$14,500	$22,500	$57,500
Auctions: $45,825, MS-65, October 2015; $3,290, AU-55, March 2015; $2,350, AU-50, January 2015; $2,115, EF-45, August 2015												
1865, Proof (r)	25	7	64.9							$125,000	$250,000	$375,000
Auctions: $440,625, PF-66DCam, April 2014												
1865-S	1,042,500	1,415	53.8	33%	$2,000	$2,150	$2,750	$3,500	$7,000	$11,000	$13,500	$30,000
Auctions: $25,850, MS-65, September 2015; $10,588, MS-62, August 2015; $2,233, AU-53, January 2015; $2,350, EF-45, August 2015												
1866-S, No Motto	120,000	160	47.7	4%	$10,000	$22,500	$37,500	$65,000	$155,000	$250,000		
Auctions: $30,550, AU-50, October 2015; $28,200, AU-50, July 2015; $35,250, EF-45, August 2015; $8,225, VF-20, October 2015												

p. Approximately 12 examples are known. **q.** 12 to 15 examples are known. **r.** Fewer than 10 examples are known.

**1866, With Motto,
Doubled Die Reverse**
FS-G20-1866-801.

	Mintage	Cert	Avg	%MS	VF-20	EF-40	AU-50	AU-55	MS-60	MS-62	MS-63	MS-64
										PF-63	PF-64	PF-65
1866, With Motto	698,745	595	53.5	9%	$1,600	$1,850	$2,500	$5,000	$12,000	$32,500	$65,000	
Auctions: $25,850, MS-61, January 2015; $9,400, AU-58, August 2015; $3,995, AU-55, January 2015; $3,055, AU-50, September 2015												
1866, With Motto, Doubled Die Reverse	(a)	0	n/a				$4,000	$6,000				
Auctions: $12,650, MS-61, August 2010												
1866, With Motto, Proof (b)	30	7	64.6							$57,500	$125,000	$225,000
Auctions: $126,500, PF-64, May 2007												
1866-S, With Motto	842,250	795	49.7	3%	$1,950	$2,250	$4,000	$8,000	$20,000	$45,000		
Auctions: $15,275, AU-58, August 2015; $9,400, AU-55, February 2015; $3,760, AU-50, January 2015; $2,820, EF-40, August 2015												
1867	251,015	391	56.9	41%	$1,600	$1,700	$1,800	$3,750	$7,750	$16,500	$32,500	
Auctions: $258,500, MS-66, November 2014; $9,400, MS-61, August 2015; $7,638, MS-61, August 2015; $6,492, AU-58, August 2015												
1867, Proof (c)	50	5	65.0							$57,500	$125,000	$225,000
Auctions: $129,250, PF-64DCam, January 2015; $129,250, PF-64DCam, August 2014; $38,188, PF-61Cam, August 2014												
1867-S	920,750	1,196	50.9	3%	$1,500	$1,700	$2,250	$4,500	$14,000	$32,500		
Auctions: $17,038, MS-61, January 2015; $8,225, AU-58, July 2015; $2,115, AU-53, January 2015; $1,763, EF-45, August 2015												

a. Included in circulation-strike 1866 mintage figure. **b.** Approximately 15 examples are known. **c.** 10 to 12 examples are known.

Open 3   Close 3

	Mintage	Cert	Avg	%MS	VF-20	EF-40	AU-50	AU-55	MS-60	MS-62 / PF-63	MS-63 / PF-64	MS-64 / PF-65
1868	98,575	198	51.8	5%	$2,000	$2,500	$4,000	$7,000	$22,500	$47,500	$75,000	
Auctions: $44,063, MS-62, August 2014; $18,800, AU-58, August 2015; $8,813, AU-53, June 2015; $4,113, EF-45, August 2014												
1868, Proof (d)	25	7	64.3							$65,000	$125,000	$225,000
Auctions: $149,500, PF-64DCam Plus, August 2011												
1868-S	837,500	1,477	51.8	3%	$1,500	$1,650	$1,800	$3,250	$11,000	$32,500		
Auctions: $16,450, MS-61, January 2015; $7,050, AU-58, January 2015; $1,645, AU-50, February 2015; $1,410, EF-45, January 2015												
1869	175,130	347	53.0	3%	$1,500	$1,650	$1,800	$4,000	$10,000	$20,000	$37,500	
Auctions: $108,688, MS-64, January 2014; $9,988, MS-60, January 2015; $2,115, AU-53, February 2015; $3,290, AU-50, August 2015												
1869, Proof (e)	25	7	65.0							$65,000	$125,000	$225,000
Auctions: $106,375, PF-64DCam, February 2009												
1869-S	686,750	1,442	52.3	5%	$1,500	$1,750	$1,850	$3,000	$10,000	$25,000	$42,500	
Auctions: $37,600, MS-62, August 2015; $7,638, AU-58, June 2015; $2,705, AU-55, February 2015; $1,880, AU-53, July 2015												
1870	155,150	270	54.0	15%	$1,500	$1,650	$2,500	$5,500	$16,000	$30,000	$50,000	
Auctions: $22,325, MS-61, June 2015; $14,688, MS-60, June 2015; $7,638, AU-58, August 2015; $6,463, AU-55, August 2015												
1870, Proof (f)	35	5	65.2							$65,000	$125,000	$225,000
Auctions: $503,100, PF, September 2013												
1870-CC † (g)	3,789	33	40.5	0%	$225,000	$250,000	$350,000	$475,000				
Auctions: $411,250, AU-53, March 2014; $58,815, EF-40, August 2014; $188,000, VF-30, October 2014; $182,125, VF-30, August 2015												
1870-S	982,000	1,463	52.3	5%	$1,500	$1,650	$1,750	$2,500	$7,000	$22,500	$55,000	
Auctions: $10,869, MS-61, September 2015; $2,000, AU-55, January 2015; $1,528, AU-50, January 2015; $1,410, EF-40, September 2015												
1871	80,120	277	53.4	5%	$1,650	$1,750	$2,500	$4,500	$8,500	$25,000	$45,000	
Auctions: $4,935, AU-58, January 2015; $4,848, AU-55, August 2015; $2,585, AU-50, September 2015; $2,820, EF-45, July 2015												
1871, Proof (h)	30	6	63.8							$65,000	$125,000	$225,000
Auctions: $26,450, PF-62Cam, August 2004												
1871-CC	17,387	175	48.8	3%	$25,000	$37,500	$55,000	$70,000	$125,000			
Auctions: $111,625, MS-60, August 2015; $64,625, AU-55, October 2016; $56,400, AU-53, January 2015; $30,550, AU-50, September 2015												
1871-S	928,000	1,796	54.2	11%	$1,500	$1,600	$1,750	$2,250	$4,500	$10,000	$22,500	
Auctions: $10,575, MS-62, August 2015; $6,463, MS-61, March 2016; $3,525, MS-60, March 2016; $2,471, AU-58, July 2015												
1872	251,850	725	55.2	12%	$1,500	$1,600	$1,750	$2,200	$5,500	$15,000	$25,000	
Auctions: $28,200, MS-63, January 2015; $2,820, AU-58, October 2015; $2,291, AU-53, January 2015; $1,528, EF-40, October 2015												
1872, Proof (i)	30	4	63.5							$65,000	$125,000	$225,000
Auctions: $135,125, PF-64, October 2014												
1872-CC	26,900	418	49.4	3%	$5,500	$9,500	$15,500	$22,500	$75,000			
Auctions: $94,000, MS-61, August 2015; $54,050, AU-58, January 2015; $13,513, AU-50, August 2015; $7,050, EF-40, January 2015												
1872-S	780,000	1,655	54.3	10%	$1,500	$1,600	$1,750	$1,850	$4,250	$13,500	$30,000	
Auctions: $25,850, MS-63, February 2015; $4,700, MS-61, March 2015; $1,880, AU-55, August 2015; $1,645, EF-45, August 2015												
1873, Close 3	1,709,800	400	54.5	12%	$1,500	$1,600	$1,750	$2,000	$4,500	$14,000		
Auctions: $3,525, MS-60, July 2015; $2,115, AU-55, January 2015; $1,880, AU-55, August 2015; $1,586, AU-55, October 2015												
1873, Open 3	(j)	8,330	58.6	52%	$1,500	$1,550	$1,600	$1,650	$1,850	$2,500	$7,500	
Auctions: $6,463, MS-63, January 2015; $1,645, AU-58, August 2015; $1,322, AU-53, September 2015; $1,234, EF-45, May 2015												
1873, Close 3, Proof (k)	25	7	63.9							$65,000	$125,000	$225,000
Auctions: $230,000, PF-65UCam, April 2011												

† Ranked in the *100 Greatest U.S. Coins* (fourth edition). **d.** Approximately 12 examples are known. **e.** Approximately 12 examples are known. **f.** Approximately 12 examples are known. **g.** An estimated 35 to 50 examples are believed to exist; most are in VF with extensive abrasions. **h.** Fewer than 10 examples are known. **i.** Fewer than 12 examples are known. **j.** Included in circulation-strike 1873, Close 3, mintage figure. **k.** 10 to 12 examples are known.

	Mintage	Cert	Avg	%MS	VF-20	EF-40	AU-50	AU-55	MS-60	MS-62 / PF-63	MS-63 / PF-64	MS-64 / PF-65
1873-CC, Close 3	22,410	396	52.1	5%	$5,000	$8,000	$17,500	$25,000	$55,000	$95,000	$150,000	
Auctions: $25,850, AU-55, August 2015; $18,800, AU-55, January 2015; $15,863, AU-53, August 2015; $7,050, EF-40, October 2015												
1873-S, Close 3	1,040,600	1,791	54.8	14%	$1,500	$1,600	$1,675	$1,750	$2,650	$9,500	$27,500	
Auctions: $7,638, MS-61, August 2015; $2,115, AU-58, February 2015; $1,410, AU-53, October 2015; $1,528, EF-45, September 2015												
1873-S, Open 3	(l)	894	54.4	11%	$1,500	$1,725	$1,775	$2,750	$9,500			
Auctions: $14,100, MS-61, September 2015; $4,230, AU-58, August 2015; $1,528, AU-53, June 2015; $1,293, EF-45, September 2015												
1874	366,780	1,156	57.0	27%	$1,500	$1,550	$1,600	$1,650	$3,000	$13,000	$20,000	
Auctions: $39,950, MS-64, August 2015; $3,760, MS-60, January 2015; $2,585, AU-55, August 2015; $1,351, AU-50, January 2015												
1874, Proof (m)	20	5	63.6							$75,000	$135,000	$275,000
Auctions: $218,500, PF-64UCamH, January 2012												
1874-CC	115,085	1,337	49.0	1%	$3,500	$4,500	$6,500	$10,000	$27,500	$60,000		
Auctions: $21,150, AU-58, August 2015; $5,640, AU-53, October 2015; $3,760, EF-45, July 2015; $2,350, VF-30, January 2015												
1874-S	1,214,000	3,644	56.0	19%	$1,500	$1,550	$1,600	$1,700	$2,500	$5,500	$28,500	
Auctions: $7,050, MS-62, June 2015; $1,998, MS-60, January 2015; $1,645, AU-55, February 2015; $1,293, EF-45, January 2015												
1875	295,720	1,555	59.2	58%	$1,500	$1,550	$1,600	$1,700	$2,250	$3,000	$10,000	
Auctions: $8,225, MS-63, September 2015; $2,585, MS-60, August 2015; $1,528, AU-58, January 2015; $1,351, AU-55, January 2015												
1875, Proof (n)	20	5	63.8							$100,000	$150,000	$275,000
Auctions: $94,300, PF-63Cam, August 2009												
1875-CC	111,151	1,719	53.4	28%	$3,500	$4,000	$4,500	$6,000	$12,500	$22,500	$37,500	
Auctions: $28,200, MS-63, January 2015; $7,344, AU-58, July 2015; $2,585, AU-50, January 2015; $2,820, EF-45, March 2015												
1875-S	1,230,000	4,442	56.8	27%	$1,500	$1,550	$1,600	$1,700	$2,150	$4,000	$12,500	
Auctions: $16,450, MS-63, July 2015; $1,645, AU-58, August 2015; $1,410, AU-53, October 2015; $1,293, VF-35, January 2015												
1876	583,860	2,775	57.9	38%	$1,500	$1,550	$1,600	$1,700	$2,000	$4,000	$10,000	
Auctions: $3,995, MS-62, January 2015; $1,410, AU-55, September 2015; $1,351, AU-53, January 2015; $1,528, EF-40, September 2015												
1876, Proof (o)	45	13	63.8							$55,000	$75,000	$135,000
Auctions: $152,750, PF-64DCam, February 2013												
1876-CC	138,441	2,048	52.2	12%	$3,000	$4,000	$5,500	$6,000	$12,500	$25,000	$35,000	
Auctions: $12,925, MS-60, October 2015; $8,813, AU-58, August 2015; $3,995, AU-50, October 2015; $2,585, VF-20, August 2015												
1876-S	1,597,000	7,018	57.0	31%	$1,500	$1,550	$1,600	$1,700	$2,000	$3,000	$8,500	
Auctions: $42,300, MS-64, August 2015; $2,291, MS-61, August 2015; $1,528, AU-55, September 2015; $1,528, AU-50, October 2015												

l. Included in 1873-S, Close 3, mintage figure. **m.** Fewer than 10 examples are known. **n.** 10 to 12 examples are known.
o. Approximately 15 examples are known.

	Mintage	Cert	Avg	%MS	VF-20	EF-40	AU-50	AU-55	MS-60	MS-62 / PF-63	MS-63 / PF-64	MS-65 / PF-65
1877	397,650	1,044	59.3	66%	$1,400	$1,450	$1,550	$1,600	$2,100	$4,500	$17,500	
Auctions: $3,995, MS-62, January 2015; $3,055, MS-61, August 2015; $2,000, MS-61, January 2015; $1,880, MS-61, July 2015												
1877, Proof (a)	20	8	63.5							$40,000	$75,000	$135,000
Auctions: $21,150, PF-58, February 2013												
1877-CC	42,565	865	49.1	3%	$3,000	$4,000	$7,000	$12,500	$30,000	$65,000		
Auctions: $24,675, AU-58, September 2015; $9,400, AU-55, August 2015; $4,700, AU-50, August 2015; $3,525, EF-40, January 2015												
1877-S	1,735,000	2,287	58.9	60%	$1,400	$1,425	$1,475	$1,500	$1,850	$5,000	$19,000	$45,000
Auctions: $5,170, MS-62, February 2015; $1,998, MS-61, December 2015; $1,528, MS-60, February 2015; $1,645, AU-58, August 2015												
1878	543,625	1,618	59.8	70%	$1,400	$1,425	$1,475	$1,500	$1,750	$3,750	$15,000	
Auctions: $9,400, MS-63, September 2015; $1,998, MS-61, July 2015; $1,645, AU-58, August 2015; $1,645, AU-55, August 2015												
1878, Proof (b)	20	8	64.5							$40,000	$65,000	$135,000
Auctions: $69,000, PF-64Cam, April 2011												
1878-CC	13,180	338	46.9	2%	$5,500	$10,000	$14,500	$25,000	$47,500	$75,000		
Auctions: $19,975, AU-55, August 2015; $9,400, EF-45, August 2015; $7,638, EF-40, July 2015; $6,169, VF-35, January 2015												
1878-S	1,739,000	1,592	58.1	56%	$1,400	$1,425	$1,475	$1,500	$1,750	$5,500	$20,000	
Auctions: $6,169, MS-62, September 2015; $1,763, MS-60, August 2015; $1,763, AU-58, July 2015; $1,351, AU-55, January 2015												

a. 10 to 12 examples are known. b. Fewer than 10 examples are known.

	Mintage	Cert	Avg	%MS	VF-20	EF-40	AU-50	AU-55	MS-60	MS-62	MS-63	MS-65
										PF-63	PF-64	PF-65
1879	207,600	611	58.3	45%	$1,400	$1,425	$1,475	$1,500	$2,150	$6,500	$17,500	
	Auctions: $3,290, MS-61, September 2015; $2,585, MS-61, February 2015; $2,350, MS-60, August 2015; $2,115, AU-58, September 2015											
1879, Proof (c)	30	4	64.0							$40,000	$65,000	$135,000
	Auctions: $57,500, PF-64, July 2009											
1879-CC	10,708	321	49.9	3%	$6,750	$12,000	$22,500	$28,500	$60,000	$85,000		
	Auctions: $28,200, AU-55, July 2015; $4,230, AU-50, August 2015; $11,899, EF-45, January 2015; $3,055, EF-40, October 2015											
1879-O	2,325	82	49.4	11%	$25,000	$45,000	$50,000	$65,000	$135,000	$175,000	$200,000	
	Auctions: $135,125, MS-60, January 2014; $70,500, AU-58, August 2015; $35,250, AU-50, August 2014; $37,600, VF-25, September 2016											
1879-S	1,223,800	1,335	57.4	30%	$1,400	$1,425	$1,475	$1,500	$2,250	$16,500	$40,000	
	Auctions: $4,714, MS-61, January 2015; $2,585, AU-58, July 2015; $1,316, AU-55, January 2015; $1,539, AU-53, August 2015											
1880	51,420	393	55.3	15%	$1,475	$1,500	$1,575	$1,750	$8,500	$25,000	$35,000	
	Auctions: $15,275, MS-61, August 2015; $3,525, AU-58, February 2015; $3,760, AU-55, August 2015; $2,820, AU-53, September 2015											
1880, Proof (d)	36	4	64.3							$40,000	$65,000	$135,000
	Auctions: $217,375, PF-65DCam, August 2014; $235,000, PF, March 2014											
1880-S	836,000	922	58.0	39%	$1,375	$1,425	$1,475	$1,500	$1,800	$8,500	$22,500	
	Auctions: $5,405, MS-62, January 2015; $4,700, MS-61, August 2015; $1,645, AU-58, June 2015; $1,645, AU-53, August 2015											
1881	2,199	31	53.7	16%	$17,500	$27,500	$45,000	$60,000	$125,000			
	Auctions: $141,000, MS-61, August 2015; $141,000, MS-61, January 2015; $82,290, AU-58, September 2016; $56,400, AU-58, August 2015											
1881, Proof (e)	61	7	63.7							$40,000	$75,000	$135,000
	Auctions: $172,500, PF-65Cam, January 2011											
1881-S	727,000	776	58.5	53%	$1,375	$1,385	$1,400	$1,425	$1,850	$6,500	$22,500	
	Auctions: $10,575, MS-62, January 2015; $1,998, MS-61, February 2015; $2,233, AU-58, August 2015; $3,055, AU-55, September 2015											
1882	571	14	54.5	7%	$27,500	$50,000	$85,000	$100,000	$135,000	$175,000	$225,000	
	Auctions: $94,000, AU-58, January 2014; $129,250, AU-55, August 2014											
1882, Proof (f)	59	6	63.7							$40,000	$75,000	$125,000
	Auctions: $161,000, PF-64Cam, January 2011											
1882-CC	39,140	962	53.2	6%	$3,000	$4,000	$5,000	$7,500	$15,000	$35,000	$100,000	
	Auctions: $12,925, AU-58, July 2015; $7,050, AU-55, January 2015; $5,288, AU-53, September 2015; $3,055, EF-45, February 2015											
1882-S	1,125,000	1,446	59.0	61%	$1,375	$1,385	$1,400	$1,425	$1,750	$4,500	$16,500	
	Auctions: $12,925, MS-63, June 2015; $3,995, MS-62, September 2015; $1,528, MS-60, July 2015; $1,552, AU-58, October 2015											
1883, Proof (g)	92	11	64.1							$115,000	$150,000	$250,000
	Auctions: $282,000, PF-65DCam, January 2014; $158,625, PF-64DCam, August 2014											
1883-CC	59,962	1,279	52.5	8%	$3,000	$3,500	$5,250	$7,500	$13,500	$27,500	$40,000	
	Auctions: $19,975, MS-61, January 2015; $11,750, AU-58, June 2015; $5,875, AU-53, August 2015; $2,820, EF-45, February 2015											
1883-S	1,189,000	2,202	59.7	72%	$1,375	$1,385	$1,400	$1,425	$1,750	$2,250	$6,500	
	Auctions: $14,100, MS-64, June 2015; $1,528, MS-61, March 2015; $1,469, AU-55, January 2015; $1,293, EF-45, January 2015											
1884, Proof (h)	71	10	63.1							$110,000	$150,000	$250,000
	Auctions: $246,750, PF-65DCam, January 2015; $235,000, PF-65DCam, August 2014; $246,750, PF-66Cam, April 2014											
1884-CC	81,139	1,698	54.1	18%	$2,750	$3,500	$5,000	$7,000	$12,000	$27,000	$45,000	
	Auctions: $28,200, MS-62, June 2015; $5,244, AU-55, August 2015; $3,290, EF-40, July 2015; $3,525, VG-10, August 2015											
1884-S	916,000	2,622	60.5	82%	$1,375	$1,385	$1,400	$1,425	$1,900	$2,500	$6,500	$45,000
	Auctions: $3,761, MS-63, January 2015; $1,998, MS-61, August 2015; $1,396, MS-60, January 2015; $1,351, AU-58, January 2015											
1885	751	53	55.8	28%	$22,500	$30,000	$45,000	$65,000	$85,000	$105,000	$135,000	
	Auctions: $82,250, MS-62, October 2014; $14,100, MS-60, November 2014; $58,750, AU-58, January 2014											
1885, Proof (i)	77	11	64.1							$40,000	$85,000	$120,000
	Auctions: $35,250, PF-61DCam, September 2014											
1885-CC	9,450	296	50.8	6%	$6,500	$12,000	$16,500	$22,500	$42,500	$65,000	$125,000	
	Auctions: $61,688, MS-62, March 2015; $37,600, MS-61, January 2015; $23,500, AU-55, August 2015; $3,055, AU-50, June 2015											
1885-S	683,500	2,278	60.8	86%	$1,375	$1,385	$1,400	$1,425	$1,800	$2,250	$4,000	
	Auctions: $3,995, MS-63, January 2015; $1,998, MS-62, August 2015; $1,998, MS-61, August 2015; $1,528, AU-58, August 2015											

c. 10 to 12 examples are known. **d.** 10 to 12 examples are known. **e.** Fewer than 20 examples are known. **f.** 12 to 15 examples are known. **g.** Proof only. Approximately 20 examples are known. **h.** Proof only. Approximately 20 examples are known. **i.** 15 to 20 examples are known.

1888, Doubled Die Reverse
FS-G20-1888-801.

	Mintage	Cert	Avg	%MS	VF-20	EF-40	AU-50	AU-55	MS-60	MS-62	MS-63	MS-65
										PF-63	PF-64	PF-65
1886	1,000	28	54.9	7%	$40,000	$75,000	$85,000	$100,000	$135,000	$145,000	$165,000	
	Auctions: $129,250, MS-60, January 2014; $111,625, AU-58, August 2014; $76,375, AU-53, August 2015; $73,438, EF-45, August 2015											
1886, Proof (j)	106	18	64.4							$42,500	$75,000	$115,000
	Auctions: $19,975, PF-60, January 2014											
1887, Proof (k)	121	10	65.1							$67,500	$85,000	$125,000
	Auctions: $258,500, PF-66, January 2014; $123,375, PF-65Cam, August 2014; $117,500, PF-65Cam, August 2015											
1887-S	283,000	927	60.0	73%	$1,375	$1,385	$1,400	$1,425	$1,800	$5,000	$12,500	
	Auctions: $9,694, MS-63, January 2015; $4,935, MS-62, January 2015; $4,700, MS-62, August 2015; $2,585, MS-61, October 2015											
1888	226,161	1,086	60.1	73%	$1,375	$1,385	$1,400	$1,425	$2,250	$3,500	$12,000	$30,000
	Auctions: $4,465, MS-62, June 2015; $2,115, MS-61, September 2015; $1,763, MS-60, August 2015; $1,469, AU-55, January 2015											
1888, Doubled Die Reverse	(l)	21	60.0	76%					$3,000	$3,750		
	Auctions: $3,819, MS-62, April 2013											
1888, Proof (m)	105	20	64.3							$30,000	$45,000	$85,000
	Auctions: $126,500, PF-65DCam, April 2012											
1888-S	859,600	2,592	60.7	84%	$1,375	$1,385	$1,400	$1,425	$1,750	$2,250	$4,250	
	Auctions: $5,640, MS-63, August 2015; $2,291, MS-62, February 2015; $1,998, MS-61, August 2015; $1,557, AU-58, August 2015											
1889	44,070	533	60.5	82%	$1,375	$1,385	$1,400	$1,425	$2,150	$4,250	$15,000	
	Auctions: $5,405, MS-62, August 2015; $2,585, MS-61, February 2015; $1,880, AU-55, August 2015; $1,645, AU-50, September 2015											
1889, Proof (n)	41	10	63.5							$30,000	$45,000	$85,000
	Auctions: $352,500, PF-65, January 2014											
1889-CC	30,945	858	52.5	8%	$3,500	$4,000	$6,500	$8,500	$14,000	$30,000	$45,000	
	Auctions: $16,450, MS-61, January 2015; $14,688, MS-60, June 2015; $7,638, AU-55, August 2015; $5,699, AU-53, August 2015											
1889-S	774,700	1,974	60.6	83%	$1,375	$1,385	$1,400	$1,425	$1,850	$2,500	$3,750	
	Auctions: $21,150, MS-65, January 2015; $2,115, MS-62, July 2015; $1,998, MS-61, September 2015; $1,410, AU-50, January 2015											
1890	75,940	649	60.6	81%	$1,375	$1,385	$1,400	$1,425	$1,750	$3,250	$10,000	$35,000
	Auctions: $7,931, MS-63, January 2015; $2,820, MS-62, October 2015; $2,115, AU-58, August 2015; $2,115, AU-50, September 2015											
1890, Proof (o)	55	13	65.2							$30,000	$45,000	$85,000
	Auctions: $92,000, PF-65UCam, August 2011											
1890-CC	91,209	2,214	52.9	9%	$3,000	$4,000	$5,000	$7,000	$14,500	$25,000	$45,000	
	Auctions: $25,850, MS-62, June 2015; $10,575, AU-58, August 2015; $5,875, AU-50, February 2015; $3,055, EF-40, October 2015											
1890-S	802,750	1,791	60.0	73%	$1,375	$1,385	$1,400	$1,425	$1,600	$2,000	$5,000	
	Auctions: $21,150, MS-65, January 2015; $3,995, MS-63, June 2015; $2,056, MS-62, June 2015; $1,586, MS-61, September 2015											
1891	1,390	41	55.3	12%	$15,000	$22,500	$40,000	$50,000	$85,000	$102,500		
	Auctions: $82,250, MS-61, January 2014; $52,889, AU-58, November 2016; $52,875, AU-58, August 2014											
1891, Proof (p)	52	27	63.7							$30,000	$45,000	$85,000
	Auctions: $655,200, PF, September 2013											
1891-CC	5,000	253	54.0	15%	$8,500	$15,000	$22,000	$27,500	$45,000	$65,000	$90,000	
	Auctions: $41,125, MS-61, March 2015; $38,775, MS-60, January 2015; $28,200, AU-55, October 2016; $23,500, AU-55, July 2015											
1891-S	1,288,125	5,553	61.1	91%	$1,375	$1,385	$1,400	$1,425	$1,600	$1,650	$2,750	
	Auctions: $4,935, MS-64, July 2015; $2,468, MS-63, January 2015; $1,998, MS-62, July 2015; $1,880, MS-62, August 2015											

j. 20 to 25 examples are known. **k.** Proof only. More than 30 examples are known. **l.** Included in circulation-strike 1888 mintage figure. **m.** 20 to 30 examples are known. **n.** 10 to 12 examples are known. **o.** Approximately 15 examples are known. **p.** 20 to 25 examples are known.

	Mintage	Cert	Avg	%MS	VF-20	EF-40	AU-50	AU-55	MS-60	MS-62 / PF-63	MS-63 / PF-64	MS-65 / PF-65
1892	4,430	117	56.2	32%	$4,500	$6,500	$10,000	$13,500	$22,500	$35,000	$45,000	$85,000
Auctions: $32,900, MS-62, August 2015; $23,500, MS-61, March 2016; $5,640, MS-60, July 2015; $11,788, AU-55, August 2014												
1892, Proof (q)	93	15	64.3							$30,000	$45,000	$85,000
Auctions: $188,000, PF-66DCam, January 2014												
1892-CC	27,265	826	54.3	22%	$2,850	$4,000	$5,000	$8,500	$16,500	$35,000	$45,000	
Auctions: $35,250, MS-63, August 2015; $28,200, MS-62, February 2016; $9,988, AU-58, July 2015; $4,465, AU-53, July 2015												
1892-S	930,150	4,477	61.1	91%	$1,375	$1,385	$1,400	$1,425	$1,525	$1,650	$2,500	$22,500
Auctions: $17,625, MS-65, January 2015; $8,225, MS-64, August 2015; $1,592, MS-62, August 2015; $1,351, AU-55, January 2015												
1893	344,280	5,966	61.6	98%	$1,375	$1,385	$1,400	$1,425	$1,525	$1,575	$2,500	
Auctions: $3,643, MS-63, February 2015; $2,826, MS-63, October 2015; $1,998, MS-62, August 2015; $1,410, MS-60, October 2015												
1893, Proof (r)	59	5	63.4							$30,000	$45,000	$85,000
Auctions: $15,525, PF-60Cam, August 2011												
1893-CC	18,402	748	57.7	50%	$3,500	$4,500	$6,500	$8,500	$15,000	$25,000	$50,000	
Auctions: $19,975, MS-62, August 2015; $17,625, MS-62, July 2015: $28,200, MS-61, September 2016; $14,688, MS-61, June 2015												
1893-S	996,175	5,267	61.1	92%	$1,450	$1,475	$1,485	$1,500	$1,650	$1,675	$3,250	
Auctions: $3,290, MS-63, February 2015; $2,820, MS-63, January 2015; $1,763, MS-62, August 2015; $1,645, MS-62, July 2015												
1894	1,368,940	15,435	61.4	97%	$1,375	$1,385	$1,400	$1,425	$1,525	$1,575	$2,000	$25,000
Auctions: $22,325, MS-65, January 2015; $4,700, MS-64, February 2015; $1,645, MS-62, September 2015; $1,351, AU-55, January 2015												
1894, Proof (s)	50	13	63.8							$30,000	$45,000	$85,000
Auctions: $54,625, PF-64Cam, January 2005												
1894-S	1,048,550	5,673	61.2	93%	$1,375	$1,385	$1,400	$1,425	$1,525	$1,575	$2,750	$23,000
Auctions: $4,935, MS-64, January 2015; $2,585, MS-63, February 2015; $1,763, MS-62, August 2015; $1,351, MS-61, January 2015												
1895	1,114,605	22,087	61.7	98%	$1,375	$1,385	$1,400	$1,425	$1,525	$1,575	$2,100	$20,000
Auctions: $3,055, MS-64, January 2015; $1,880, MS-63, August 2015; $1,528, MS-62, August 2015; $1,293, AU-58, February 2015												
1895, Proof	51	11	64.2							$30,000	$45,000	$85,000
Auctions: $82,250, PF-65Cam, September 2014												
1895-S	1,143,500	7,363	61.3	94%	$1,375	$1,385	$1,400	$1,425	$1,525	$1,650	$2,250	$12,500
Auctions: $9,583, MS-65, January 2015; $3,878, MS-64, February 2015; $1,763, MS-62, October 2015; $1,293, MS-60, June 2015												
1896	792,535	10,297	61.7	97%	$1,375	$1,385	$1,400	$1,425	$1,525	$1,575	$2,000	$18,000
Auctions: $3,290, MS-64, September 2015; $2,056, MS-63, January 2015; $1,763, MS-62, July 2015; $1,704, MS-62, September 2015												
1896, Proof (t)	128	38	64.0							$30,000	$45,000	$85,000
Auctions: $97,750, PF-65DCam, April 2012												
1896-S	1,403,925	9,274	61.3	94%	$1,375	$1,385	$1,400	$1,425	$1,525	$1,575	$2,250	$25,000
Auctions: $3,055, MS-63, January 2015; $2,468, MS-63, February 2015; $1,645, MS-62, September 2015; $1,528, MS-61, January 2015												
1897	1,383,175	18,096	61.7	98%	$1,375	$1,385	$1,400	$1,425	$1,525	$1,575	$2,000	$20,000
Auctions: $2,585, MS-64, January 2015; $2,115, MS-63, August 2015; $1,763, MS-62, September 2015; $1,351, MS-61, January 2015												
1897, Proof (u)	86	23	64.1							$30,000	$45,000	$85,000
Auctions: $73,438, PF-64Cam, August 2014; $30,550, PF-62Cam, April 2013												
1897-S	1,470,250	12,894	61.6	95%	$1,375	$1,385	$1,400	$1,425	$1,525	$1,650	$2,250	$18,000
Auctions: $16,450, MS-65, January 2015; $3,643, MS-64, June 2015; $1,763, MS-62, August 2015; $1,351, MS-61, January 2015												
1898	170,395	1,728	61.2	89%	$1,375	$1,385	$1,400	$1,425	$2,000	$2,250	$3,500	
Auctions: $4,818, MS-63, October 2015; $2,585, MS-62, August 2015; $1,410, MS-61, January 2015; $1,410, AU-58, January 2015												
1898, Proof (v)	75	35	64.2							$30,000	$45,000	$85,000
Auctions: $52,875, PF-64DCam, September 2014; $117,500, PF-65Cam, April 2013												
1898-S	2,575,175	22,750	61.7	96%	$1,375	$1,385	$1,400	$1,425	$1,525	$1,575	$2,000	$8,500
Auctions: $9,400, MS-65, June 2015; $1,645, MS-62, September 2015; $1,351, AU-58, January 2015; $1,351, AU-55, January 2015												

q. Approximately 25 examples are known. **r.** 15 to 20 examples are known. **s.** 15 to 20 examples are known. **t.** 45 to 50 examples are known. **u.** 20 to 25 examples are known. **v.** 35 to 40 examples are known.

	Mintage	Cert	Avg	%MS	VF-20	EF-40	AU-50	AU-55	MS-60	MS-62 / PF-63	MS-63 / PF-64	MS-65 / PF-65
1899	1,669,300	24,341	62.0	98%	$1,375	$1,385	$1,400	$1,425	$1,525	$1,575	$1,750	$8,500
	Auctions: $7,638, MS-65, September 2015; $4,113, MS-64, June 2015; $1,410, MS-61, October 2015; $1,528, AU-58, August 2015											
1899, Proof (w)	84	29	64.2							$30,000	$45,000	$85,000
	Auctions: $76,375, PF, March 2014											
1899-S	2,010,300	9,282	61.3	91%	$1,375	$1,385	$1,400	$1,425	$1,525	$1,575	$2,500	$20,000
	Auctions: $2,291, MS-63, September 2015; $1,939, MS-63, February 2015; $1,763, MS-62, August 2015; $1,645, MS-62, August 2015											
1900	1,874,460	53,270	62.4	99%	$1,375	$1,385	$1,400	$1,425	$1,525	$1,575	$1,650	$5,500
	Auctions: $7,344, MS-65, August 2015; $2,820, MS-64, August 2015; $1,821, MS-62, June 2015; $1,293, MS-60, July 2015											
1900, Proof (x)	124	30	64.6							$30,000	$45,000	$85,000
	Auctions: $88,125, PF, March 2014											
1900-S	2,459,500	7,801	61.1	93%	$1,375	$1,385	$1,400	$1,425	$1,525	$1,575	$2,250	$22,500
	Auctions: $3,055, MS-63, August 2015; $1,763, MS-62, August 2015; $1,422, MS-60, August 2015; $1,410, AU-58, October 2015											
1901	111,430	5,438	62.9	99%	$1,375	$1,385	$1,400	$1,425	$1,525	$1,575	$1,750	$3,000
	Auctions: $3,290, MS-65, January 2015; $2,115, MS-64, August 2015; $1,880, MS-63, February 2015; $1,645, MS-62, August 2015											
1901, Proof (y)	96	41	62.9							$30,000	$45,000	$85,000
	Auctions: $68,150, PF, February 2013											
1901-S	1,596,000	3,119	61.1	93%	$1,375	$1,385	$1,400	$1,425	$1,525	$1,575	$3,750	$22,500
	Auctions: $3,525, MS-63, February 2015; $2,938, MS-63, September 2015; $2,115, MS-62, August 2015; $2,350, MS-61, August 2015											
1902	31,140	511	59.9	67%	$1,375	$1,385	$1,400	$1,425	$2,500	$6,000	$10,000	
	Auctions: $4,700, MS-62, July 2015; $3,995, MS-61, August 2015; $2,350, MS-61, January 2015; $2,820, AU-58, August 2015											
1902, Proof (z)	114	29	63.1							$30,000	$45,000	$85,000
	Auctions: $9,400, PF-50, January 2014											
1902-S	1,753,625	4,507	61.0	93%	$1,375	$1,385	$1,400	$1,425	$1,525	$1,575	$3,250	$30,000
	Auctions: $28,200, MS-65, October 2015; $3,525, MS-63, January 2015; $1,410, MS-60, January 2015; $1,351, AU-58, June 2015											
1903	287,270	12,579	62.9	100%	$1,375	$1,385	$1,400	$1,425	$1,525	$1,575	$1,650	$3,000
	Auctions: $3,290, MS-65, January 2015; $2,585, MS-64, August 2015; $1,645, MS-63, August 2015; $1,410, MS-61, January 2015											
1903, Proof (aa)	158	38	62.9							$30,000	$45,000	$85,000
	Auctions: $63,450, PF, March 2014											
1903-S	954,000	6,473	61.8	98%	$1,375	$1,385	$1,400	$1,425	$1,525	$1,575	$2,250	$14,500
	Auctions: $3,290, MS-64, September 2015; $2,174, MS-63, June 2015; $1,481, MS-62, August 2015; $1,422, AU-55, August 2015											
1904	6,256,699	225,037	62.6	99%	$1,375	$1,385	$1,400	$1,425	$1,525	$1,575	$1,650	$2,750
	Auctions: $5,875, MS-66, October 2015; $4,818, MS-65, March 2015; $1,528, MS-62, August 2015; $1,351, MS-60, June 2015											
1904, Proof (bb)	98	41	63.7							$30,000	$45,000	$85,000
	Auctions: $146,875, PF-67Cam, August 2013											
1904-S	5,134,175	24,431	62.4	98%	$1,375	$1,385	$1,400	$1,425	$1,525	$1,575	$1,650	$2,750
	Auctions: $4,465, MS-65, January 2015; $2,350, MS-64, January 2015; $1,645, MS-62, August 2015; $1,293, AU-58, January 2015											
1905	58,919	799	59.3	59%	$1,375	$1,385	$1,400	$1,425	$2,500	$6,500	$15,000	$85,000
	Auctions: $6,463, MS-62, August 2015; $5,405, MS-62, July 2015; $1,763, AU-58, June 2015; $1,763, AU-53, August 2015											
1905, Proof (cc)	92	26	62.8							$30,000	$45,000	$85,000
	Auctions: $10,005, PF-58, January 2012											
1905-S	1,813,000	2,324	61.1	89%	$1,375	$1,385	$1,400	$1,425	$1,525	$1,575	$3,500	$20,000
	Auctions: $4,935, MS-64, July 2015; $3,525, MS-63, January 2015; $2,468, MS-62, August 2015; $1,645, MS-61, September 2015											

w. Fewer than 30 examples are known. **x.** Approximately 50 examples are known. **y.** 40 to 50 examples are known. **z.** Fewer than 50 examples are known. **aa.** 40 to 50 examples are known. **bb.** Approximately 50 examples are known. **cc.** 30 to 40 examples are known.

	Mintage	Cert	Avg	%MS	VF-20	EF-40	AU-50	AU-55	MS-60	MS-62 / PF-63	MS-63 / PF-64	MS-65 / PF-65
1906	69,596	691	60.4	75%	$1,400	$1,475	$1,500	$1,600	$1,800	$5,000	$8,500	$32,500
	Auctions: $14,361, MS-64, August 2015; $4,230, MS-62, August 2015; $3,760, MS-61, August 2015; $3,055, AU-58, August 2015											
1906, Proof (dd)	94	45	63.4							$30,000	$45,000	$85,000
	Auctions: $85,188, PF, August 2013											
1906-D	620,250	1,870	61.8	96%	$1,375	$1,385	$1,400	$1,425	$1,525	$1,575	$4,000	$20,000
	Auctions: $10,575, MS-64, August 2015; $3,525, MS-63, January 2015; $3,760, MS-62, August 2015; $1,410, MS-61, January 2015											
1906-D, Proof (ee)	6	0	n/a		*(extremely rare)*							
	Auctions: No auction records available.											
1906-S	2,065,750	4,555	61.5	95%	$1,375	$1,385	$1,400	$1,425	$1,525	$1,575	$2,250	$25,000
	Auctions: $25,850, MS-65, January 2015; $4,935, MS-64, October 2015; $1,645, MS-62, August 2015; $1,645, EF-45, August 2015											
1907	1,451,786	32,059	61.9	99%	$1,375	$1,385	$1,400	$1,425	$1,525	$1,575	$1,650	$7,500
	Auctions: $2,820, MS-64, July 2015; $1,471, MS-62, August 2015; $1,351, MS-60, January 2015; $1,351, AU-55, January 2015											
1907, Proof (ff)	78	49	63.6							$30,000	$45,000	$85,000
	Auctions: $40,250, PF-64Cam, January 2012											
1907-D	842,250	2,295	62.4	96%	$1,375	$1,385	$1,400	$1,425	$1,525	$1,575	$3,500	$8,500
	Auctions: $8,813, MS-65, March 2015; $4,230, MS-64, January 2015; $1,998, MS-62, September 2015; $1,528, MS-61, January 2015											
1907-D, Proof (gg)	*unknown*	1	62.0									
	Auctions: $71,875, PF-62, January 2004											
1907-S	2,165,800	3,487	61.8	95%	$1,375	$1,385	$1,400	$1,425	$1,525	$1,575	$3,000	$22,500
	Auctions: $17,625, MS-65, June 2015; $5,875, MS-64, March 2015; $2,820, MS-63, August 2015; $1,410, MS-61, January 2015											

dd. 45 to 50 examples are known. **ee.** Six 1906-D presentation strikes were made to commemorate the first coinage of double eagles at the Denver Mint. The coins were well documented at the time; however, at present only two are accounted for. **ff.** 25 to 50 examples are known. **gg.** Believed to have once been part of the collection of King Farouk of Egypt; cleaned.

SAINT-GAUDENS, HIGH RELIEF AND ULTRA HIGH RELIEF, MCMVII (1907)

Designer: *Augustus Saint-Gaudens.* **Weight:** *33.436 grams.*
Composition: *.900 gold, .100 copper (net weight: .96750 oz. pure gold).*
Diameter *34 mm.* **Edge:** *E PLURIBUS UNUM with words divided by stars*
(one specimen of the high-relief variety with plain edge is known). **Mint:** *Philadelphia.*

Circulation Strike   Proof, Ultra High Relief Pattern

History. Created by famous artist Augustus Saint-Gaudens under a commission arranged by President Theodore Roosevelt, this double eagle was first made (in pattern form) with ultra high relief, sculptural in its effect, on both sides and the date in Roman numerals. The story of its production is well known and has been described in several books, notably *Renaissance of American Coinage, 1905–1908* (Burdette) and *Striking Change: The Great Artistic Collaboration of Theodore Roosevelt and August Saint-Gaudens* (Moran). After the Ultra High Relief patterns of 1907, a modified High Relief version was developed to facilitate production. Each coin required three blows of the press to strike up properly. Most featured a flat rim (now known as the Flat Rim variety), but planchet metal would occasionally be squeezed up between the collar and the die, resulting in the Wire Rim variety; this can exist around part of or the entire circumference of the coin. The coins were made on a medal press in December 1907 and January 1908, to the extent of fewer than 13,000 pieces. In the meantime, production was under way for low-relief coins, easier to mint in quantities sufficient for commerce—these dated 1907 rather than MCMVII. Today the MCMVII double eagle is a favorite among collectors, and when surveys are taken of beautiful and popular designs (as in *100 Greatest U.S. Coins*, by Garrett and Guth), it always ranks near the top.

Striking and Sharpness. The striking usually is good. Check the left knee of Miss Liberty, which sometimes shows lightness of strike and, most often, shows flatness or wear (sometimes concealed by postmint etching or clever tooling). Check the Capitol at the lower left. On the reverse, check the high points at the top of the eagle. The surface on all is a delicate matte texture, grainy rather than deeply frosty. Under examination the fields show myriad tiny raised curlicues and other die-finish marks. There is no record of any MCMVII double eagles being made as *Proofs*, nor is there any early numismatic record of any being sold as Proofs. Walter Breen in the 1960s made up some guidelines for Proofs, which some graders have adopted. Some homemade "Proofs" have been made by pickling or sandblasting the surface of regular coins—*caveat emptor.*

Availability. Half or more of the original mintage still exist today, as many were saved, and these grade mostly from AU-50 to MS-62. Circulated examples often have been cleaned, polished, or used in jewelry. Higher-grade coins are seen with some frequency, up to MS-65. Overgrading is common.

GRADING STANDARDS

MS-60 to 70 (Mint State). *Obverse:* At MS-60, some abrasion and contact marks are seen on Liberty's chest. The left knee is flat on lower Mint State coins and all circulated coins. Scattered marks and abrasion are in the field. Satiny luster is present, but may be dull or lifeless, and interrupted in patches. Many coins at this level have been cleaned. At MS-63, contact marks are fewer, and abrasion is light, but the knee still has a flat spot. An MS-65 coin

MCMVII (1907), High Relief. Graded MS-63.

has little abrasion and few marks. Grades above MS-65 are defined by having fewer marks as perfection is approached. *Reverse:* Comments apply as for the obverse, except that abrasion and contact marks are most noticeable on the side of the eagle's body and the top of the left wing.

Illustrated coin: This is a splendid choice striking.

AU-50, 53, 55, 58 (About Uncirculated). *Obverse:* Light wear is seen on the chest, the left leg, and the field, more so at AU-50 than at AU-53 or 55. An AU-58 coin has fewer traces of wear. An AU-50 coin has satiny luster in protected areas among the rays, with little in the open field above. At AU-58, most luster is present. *Reverse:* Comments as preceding, except that the side of the eagle below the front of the wing, the top of the wing, and the field

MCMVII (1907), High Relief. Graded AU-55.

show light wear. Satiny luster ranges from perhaps 40% (at AU-50) to nearly full mint bloom (at AU-58).

EF-40, 45 (Extremely Fine). *Obverse:* Wear is seen on all the higher-relief areas of the standing figure and on the rock at the lower right. Luster is minimal, if present at all. Eye appeal is apt to be lacking. Nearly all Extremely Fine coins have been cleaned. *Reverse:* The eagle shows more wear overall, especially at the bottom and on the tops of the wings.

MCMVII (1907), High Relief. Graded EF-45.

VF-20, 30 (Very Fine). *Obverse:* Most details of the standing figure are flat, her face is incomplete, and the tips of the rays are weak. Eye appeal is usually poor. As these coins did not circulate to any extent, a Very Fine coin was likely carried as a pocket piece. *Reverse:* Wear is greater overall, but most evident on the eagle. Detail is good at the center of the left wing, but worn away in most other areas of the bird.

MCMVII (1907), High Relief. Graded VF-30.

The MCMVII (1907) High Relief double eagle is seldom collected in grades lower than VF-20.

	Mintage	Cert	Avg	%MS	VF-20	EF-40	AU-50	AU-55	MS-60 PF-63	MS-62 PF-64	MS-63 PF-65	MS-65 PF-67
1907, High Relief, MCMVII, Wire Rim † (a)	12,367	1,370	62.2	90%	$9,000	$11,000	$12,000	$13,000	$15,000	$18,500	$24,000	$45,000
Auctions: $71,675, MS-66, October 2015; $44,650, MS-65, November 2016; $18,800, AU-55, August 2015; $11,163, AU-55, October 2016												
1907, High Relief, MCMVII, Flat Rim †	(b)	570	62.4	86%	$9,000	$11,000	$12,000	$13,500	$15,000	$20,000	$24,000	$47,500
Auctions: $117,500, MS-67, January 2015; $70,500, MS-66, August 2016; $16,450, AU-58, September 2015												
1907, High Relief, MCMVII, Wire or Flat Rim, Proof	unknown	0	n/a						$30,000	$42,500	$75,000	
Auctions: $32,900, PF-64, February 2013												
1907, Ultra High Relief, Plain Edge, Proof	(c)	0	n/a									
Auctions: No auction records available.												
1907, Ultra High Relief, Inverted Edge, Proof	(c)	0	n/a									
Auctions: No auction records available.												
1907, Ultra High Relief, Lettered Edge, Proof †	16–22	3	67.3								$2,250,000	$2,500,000
Auctions: $2,115,000, PF-68, January 2015; $1,840,000, PF-68, January 2007												

† Ranked in the *100 Greatest U.S. Coins* (fourth edition). **a.** The Wire Rim and Flat Rim varieties were the result of different collars used in the minting process. The Flat Rim is considered slightly scarcer, but this has not led to large value differentials, as both varieties are very popular among collectors. **b.** Included in 1907, High Relief, MCMVII, Wire Rim, mintage figure. **c.** Included in 1907, Ultra High Relief, Lettered Edge, Proof, mintage figure.

SAINT-GAUDENS, FLAT RELIEF, ARABIC NUMERALS (1907–1933)

Designer: *Augustus Saint-Gaudens.* **Weight:** *33.436 grams.*
Composition: *.900 gold, .100 copper (net weight: .96750 oz. pure gold).*
Diameter: *34 mm.* **Edge:** *E PLURIBUS UNUM with words divided by stars.*
Mints: *Philadelphia, Denver, and San Francisco.*

No Motto (1907–1908)

Mintmark location is on
the obverse, above the date.

With Motto (1908–1933)

With Motto, Proof

History. In autumn 1907 U.S. Mint chief engraver Charles E. Barber modified Augustus Saint-Gaudens's design by lowering its relief and substituting Arabic (not Roman) numerals. Coins of this type were struck in large quantities from 1907 to 1916 and again from 1920 to 1933. In July 1908 the motto IN GOD WE TRUST was added to the reverse. Coins dated 1907 to 1911 have 46 stars on the obverse; coins of 1912 to 1933 have 48 stars. Sandblast (also called Matte) Proofs were made in 1908 and from 1911 to 1915; Satin (also called Roman Finish) Proofs were made in 1909 and 1910.

The vast majority of these coins were exported. Since World War II millions have been repatriated, supplying most of those in numismatic hands today.

Striking and Sharpness. The details are often light on the obverse. Check the bosom of Miss Liberty, the covering of which tends to be weak on 1907 and, especially, 1908 No Motto coins. Check the Capitol building and its immediate area at the lower left. The reverse usually is well struck, but check the feathers on the eagle and the top of the wings. The Matte Proofs have dull surfaces, much like fine-grained sandpaper, while the Satin Proofs have satiny surfaces and are bright yellow.

Availability. Most dates and mintmarks range from very common to slightly scarce, punctuated with scarce to very rare issues such as 1908-S, 1920-S, 1921, mintmarked coins from 1924 to 1927, and all issues of 1929 to 1933. From their initial mintages, most of the double eagles of the 1920s were returned to the Mint and melted in the 1930s. Some, however, were unofficially saved by Treasury employees. Estimates of the quantities saved range from a few dozen to several hundred thousand, depending on the date; this explains the high values for coins that, judged only by their initial mintages, should otherwise be more common. Probably a million or more MS coins exist of certain dates, most notably 1908 No Motto, 1924, 1925, 1926, and 1928 (especially common). Quality varies, as many have contact marks.

Philadelphia Mint coins from 1922 onward usually are seen with excellent eye appeal. Common varieties are not usually collected in grades below MS. All of the Proofs are rare today.

Note: Values of common-date gold coins have been based on the current bullion price of gold, $1,300 per ounce, and may vary with the prevailing spot price.

GRADING STANDARDS

MS-60 to 70 (Mint State). *Obverse:* At MS-60, some abrasion and contact marks are seen on Liberty's chest and left knee, and scattered marks and abrasion are in the field. Luster is present, but may be dull or lifeless, and interrupted in patches. At MS-63, contact marks are fewer, and abrasion is light. An MS-65 coin has little abrasion and few marks, although quality among certified coins can vary. On a conservatively graded coin the lus-

1924. Graded MS-65.

ter should be full and rich. Grades above MS-65 are defined by having fewer marks as perfection is approached. Generally, Mint State coins of 1922 onward are choicer and more attractive than the earlier issues. *Reverse:* Comments apply as for the obverse, except that abrasion and contact marks are most noticeable on the eagle's left wing.

AU-50, 53, 55, 58 (About Uncirculated). *Obverse:* Light wear is seen on the chest, the left knee, the midriff, and across the field, more so at AU-50 than at AU–53 or 55. An AU-58 coin has minimal traces of wear. An AU-50 coin has luster in protected areas among the rays, with little in the open field above. At AU-58, most luster is present. *Reverse:* Comments as preceding, except that the side of the eagle below the front of the wing, the top of

1909, 9 Over 8. Graded AU-50.

the wing, and the field show light wear. Luster ranges from perhaps 40% (at AU-50) to nearly full mint bloom (at AU-58).

EF-40, 45 (Extremely Fine). *Obverse:* Wear is seen on all the higher-relief areas of the standing figure and on the rock at the lower right. Luster is minimal, if present at all. Eye appeal is apt to be lacking. *Reverse:* The eagle shows more wear overall, especially at the bottom and on the tops of the wings.

1908-S. Graded EF-40.

VF-20, 30 (Very Fine). *Obverse:* Most details of the standing figure are flat, her face is incomplete, and the tips of the rays are weak. Eye appeal is usually poor. *Reverse:* Wear is greater overall, but most evident on the eagle. Detail is good at the center of the left wing, but worn away in most other areas of the bird.

The Saint-Gaudens double eagle is seldom collected in grades lower than VF-20.

1914. Graded VF-20.

PF-60 to 70 (Proof). *Obverse and Reverse:* At PF–60 to 63, there is light abrasion and some contact marks (the lower the grade, the higher the quantity). On Sandblast Proofs these show up as visually unappealing bright spots. At PF-64 and higher levels, marks are fewer, with magnification needed to see any at PF-65. At PF-66, there should be none at all.

1909, Satin Finish. Graded PF-66.

	Mintage	Cert	Avg	%MS	VF-20	EF-40	AU-50	AU-55	MS-60	MS-62 / PF-63	MS-63 / PF-64	MS-65 / PF-65
1907, Arabic Numerals	361,667	10,226	62.7	97%	$1,400	$1,450	$1,475	$1,500	$1,850	$1,875	$2,000	$3,750
	Auctions: $5,170, MS-66, January 2015; $4,113, MS-65, January 2015; $2,585, MS-64, August 2015; $1,645, MS-62, February 2015											
1907, Proof (a)	*unknown*	0	n/a					*(extremely rare)*				
	Auctions: $70,500, MS-64, January 2015; $47,000, MS-64, August 2015											
1908, No Motto	4,271,551	139,212	63.3	100%	$1,250	$1,275	$1,300	$1,325	$1,400	$1,425	$1,450	$1,750
	Auctions: $6,463, MS-67, June 2015; $4,700, MS-66, February 2015; $1,763, MS-63, September 2015; $1,469, MS-61, September 2015											
1908-D, No Motto	663,750	4,360	62.4	97%	$1,250	$1,275	$1,300	$1,325	$1,600	$1,700	$1,750	$7,500
	Auctions: $9,400, MS-65, August 2015; $2,820, MS-64, August 2015; $1,586, MS-63, February 2015; $1,528, MS-62, September 2015											
1908, With Motto	156,258	2,105	62.0	95%	$1,400	$1,550	$1,650	$1,750	$1,875	$1,900	$2,250	$13,500
	Auctions: $5,170, MS-64, January 2015; $2,233, MS-63, March 2015; $1,645, MS-62, October 2015; $1,645, MS-60, July 2015											
1908, With Motto, Sandblast Finish Proof	101	77	65.3							$30,000	$50,000	$75,000
	Auctions: $57,500, PF-66+, June 2012											
1908, With Motto, Satin Finish Proof (b)	*unknown*	0	n/a					*(extremely rare)*				
	Auctions: $152,750, PF, August 2013											
1908-D, With Motto	349,500	2,237	62.5	93%	$1,250	$1,275	$1,300	$1,325	$1,400	$1,425	$2,000	$4,500
	Auctions: $21,150, MS-66, June 2015; $7,050, MS-65, January 2015; $3,525, MS-64, October 2015; $1,880, MS-62, July 2015											
1908-S, With Motto	22,000	518	56.1	33%	$2,500	$3,750	$6,000	$7,000	$11,500	$15,000	$22,500	$50,000
	Auctions: $21,150, MS-63, August 2015; $4,935, AU-53, July 2015; $3,878, EF-45, February 2015; $3,055, VF-35, August 2015											

a. 2 or 3 examples are known. **b.** 3 or 4 examples are known.

1909, 9 Over 8

	Mintage	Cert	Avg	%MS	VF-20	EF-40	AU-50	AU-55	MS-60	MS-62 PF-63	MS-63 PF-64	MS-65 PF-65
1909, All kinds	161,282											
1909, 9 Over 8 (c)		1,676	59.2	56%	$1,250	$1,275	$1,300	$1,325	$1,550	$1,850	$2,750	$37,500
Auctions: $14,153, MS-64, July 2015; $4,700, MS-63, January 2015; $1,880, AU-58, September 2015; $1,645, AU-50, August 2015												
1909		1,375	60.7	76%	$1,500	$1,550	$1,600	$1,650	$2,000	$3,000	$4,500	$40,000
Auctions: $35,250, MS-65, June 2015; $1,586, MS-61, April 2015; $1,469, AU-58, January 2015; $1,593, AU-53, July 2015												
1909, Satin Finish Proof	67	31	65.4							$32,500	$50,000	$85,000
Auctions: $184,860, PF, September 2013												
1909-D	52,500	507	59.7	60%	$1,600	$1,700	$1,750	$1,950	$3,250	$4,000	$6,000	$32,500
Auctions: $11,750, MS-64, July 2015; $5,640, MS-63, February 2015; $2,820, AU-58, September 2015; $1,528, AU-50, July 2015												
1909-S	2,774,925	5,776	62.6	96%	$1,250	$1,275	$1,300	$1,325	$1,400	$1,425	$1,650	$4,500
Auctions: $22,913, MS-66, July 2015; $2,938, MS-64, January 2015; $1,763, MS-63, June 2015; $1,645, MS-62, January 2015												
1910	482,000	8,352	62.3	98%	$1,250	$1,275	$1,300	$1,325	$1,400	$1,425	$1,650	$7,000
Auctions: $6,463, MS-65, September 2015; $3,055, MS-64, January 2015; $1,704, MS-63, August 2015; $1,704, MS-62, January 2015												
1910, Satin Finish Proof	167	0	n/a							$32,500	$50,000	$85,000
Auctions: $76,375, PF-65, August 2014; $56,063, PF-65, June 2012												
1910, Sandblast Finish Proof (d)	*unknown*	37	65.6					*(unique)*				
Auctions: No auction records available.												
1910-D	429,000	6,916	62.9	97%	$1,250	$1,275	$1,300	$1,325	$1,400	$1,425	$1,600	$2,750
Auctions: $9,400, MS-66, January 2015; $2,350, MS-65, July 2015; $1,763, MS-64, October 2015; $1,469, MS-62, September 2015												
1910-S	2,128,250	4,440	61.7	90%	$1,250	$1,275	$1,300	$1,325	$1,400	$1,425	$1,700	$6,500
Auctions: $88,125, MS-67, January 2015; $3,760, MS-64, January 2015; $1,998, MS-63, August 2015; $1,528, MS-62, October 2015												
1911	197,250	2,778	61.9	90%	$1,250	$1,275	$1,300	$1,325	$1,500	$1,600	$2,500	$15,000
Auctions: $17,038, MS-66, January 2015; $4,935, MS-64, June 2015; $1,763, MS-62, August 2015; $1,528, EF-45, September 2015												
1911, Sandblast Finish Proof	100	45	66.1							$30,000	$45,000	$80,000
Auctions: $157,950, PF, September 2013												
1911-D	846,500	12,034	63.4	98%	$1,250	$1,275	$1,300	$1,325	$1,400	$1,425	$1,600	$2,450
Auctions: $3,760, MS-66, January 2015; $2,644, MS-64, August 2015; $1,586, MS-63, July 2015; $1,469, MS-62, September 2015												
1911-S	775,750	5,417	62.8	97%	$1,250	$1,275	$1,300	$1,325	$1,400	$1,425	$1,650	$4,250
Auctions: $11,221, MS-66, October 2015; $5,758, MS-65, January 2015; $1,880, MS-63, February 2015; $1,469, MS-62, September 2015												
1912	149,750	2,463	61.5	88%	$1,250	$1,275	$1,300	$1,325	$1,500	$1,600	$2,250	$23,500
Auctions: $19,975, MS-65, September 2015; $5,640, MS-64, January 2015; $1,528, MS-61, February 2015; $1,469, AU-58, January 2015												
1912, Sandblast Finish Proof	74	54	66.0							$30,000	$45,000	$80,000
Auctions: $211,500, PF-67, August 2013												
1913	168,780	2,707	61.4	89%	$1,250	$1,275	$1,300	$1,325	$1,550	$1,800	$2,500	$55,000
Auctions: $11,750, MS-64, January 2015; $1,763, MS-62, July 2015; $1,645, MS-61, October 2015; $1,410, AU-58, January 2015												
1913, Sandblast Finish Proof	50	31	65.5							$30,000	$45,000	$80,000
Auctions: $79,313, PF, August 2013												
1913-D	393,500	3,990	62.5	95%	$1,250	$1,275	$1,300	$1,325	$1,450	$1,600	$1,750	$5,500
Auctions: $22,325, MS-66, February 2015; $6,463, MS-65, August 2015; $2,585, MS-64, October 2015; $2,350, MS-63, September 2015												
1913-S	34,000	1,153	61.6	86%	$1,750	$1,850	$2,000	$2,100	$2,350	$3,000	$4,500	$30,000
Auctions: $9,400, MS-64, January 2015; $3,055, MS-62, January 2015; $2,233, MS-61, July 2015; $2,585, AU-58, September 2015												

c. This is one of the few Saint-Gaudens double eagle die varieties that commands a premium over the regular coin. d. Part of the unique complete 1910 Sandblast Finish Proof gold set.

1922, Doubled Die Reverse

	Mintage	Cert	Avg	%MS	VF-20	EF-40	AU-50	AU-55	MS-60	MS-62	MS-63	MS-65
										PF-63	PF-64	PF-65
1914	95,250	1,754	62.0	91%	$1,300	$1,325	$1,350	$1,375	$1,500	$1,600	$2,750	$18,500
	Auctions: $7,638, MS-64, January 2015; $7,050, MS-64, January 2015; $2,585, MS-63, August 2015; $2,115, MS-62, July 2015											
1914, Sandblast Finish Proof	70	28	65.5							$30,000	$45,000	$80,000
	Auctions: $60,375, PF-66, June 2012											
1914-D	453,000	6,833	63.0	97%	$1,250	$1,275	$1,300	$1,325	$1,400	$1,425	$1,650	$2,750
	Auctions: $3,055, MS-65, August 2015; $2,140, MS-64, September 2015; $1,788, MS-64, January 2015; $1,645, MS-63, October 2015											
1914-S	1,498,000	21,779	63.1	99%	$1,250	$1,275	$1,300	$1,325	$1,400	$1,425	$1,600	$2,500
	Auctions: $4,583, MS-66, December 2015; $1,763, MS-64, September 2015; $1,410, MS-61, September 2015; $1,293, MS-60, June 2015											
1915	152,000	2,255	61.8	89%	$1,250	$1,275	$1,300	$1,325	$1,500	$1,650	$2,000	$18,500
	Auctions: $5,170, MS-64, January 2015; $3,055, MS-63, September 2015; $1,586, MS-61, July 2015; $1,410, AU-55, January 2015											
1915, Sandblast Finish Proof	50	41	64.8							$32,500	$50,000	$100,000
	Auctions: $63,250, PF-66, August 2011											
1915-S	567,500	16,062	63.3	99%	$1,250	$1,275	$1,300	$1,325	$1,400	$1,425	$1,600	$2,250
	Auctions: $4,700, MS-66, June 2015; $1,528, MS-64, October 2015; $1,528, MS-63, June 2015; $1,410, MS-62, September 2015											
1916-S	796,000	4,284	63.4	97%	$1,250	$1,275	$1,300	$1,325	$1,400	$1,425	$1,800	$3,000
	Auctions: $4,935, MS-66, January 2015; $2,233, MS-64, January 2015; $1,763, MS-63, September 2015; $1,469, AU-58, January 2015											
1920	228,250	6,913	62.1	99%	$1,250	$1,275	$1,300	$1,325	$1,400	$1,425	$1,700	$55,000
	Auctions: $5,170, MS-64, January 2015; $4,348, MS-64, August 2015; $2,233, MS-63, January 2015; $1,528, MS-62, September 2015											
1920-S	558,000	74	60.8	73%	$16,500	$20,000	$25,000	$32,500	$50,000	$67,500	$85,000	$275,000
	Auctions: $517,000, MS-65, November 2016; $99,875, MS-64, January 2015; $70,500, MS-63, January 2015; $44,650, AU-58, May 2016											
1921	528,500	70	59.1	57%	$25,000	$37,500	$55,000	$65,000	$100,000	$125,000	$225,000	$600,000
	Auctions$199,750, MS-63, August 2016; $164,500, MS-63, January 2014; $105,750, MS-62, August 2014; $94,000, MS-62, January 2015											
1921, Proof † (e)	*unknown*	1	64.0				*(extremely rare)*					
	Auctions: $1,495,000, PF-64+, 2006; $203,500, PF, 2000											
1922	1,375,500	55,035	62.6	100%	$1,250	$1,275	$1,300	$1,325	$1,400	$1,425	$1,650	$3,750
	Auctions: $11,750, MS-66, August 2015; $3,290, MS-65, January 2015; $2,585, MS-64, August 2015; $1,351, MS-61, September 2015											
1922, DblDie Rev	(f)	4	63.3	100%			$2,000	$2,200	$2,500	$2,750	$3,500	
	Auctions: $2,115, MS-64, December 2013											
1922-S	2,658,000	916	62.6	97%	$1,850	$1,900	$2,000	$2,150	$2,650	$3,000	$5,000	$40,000
	Auctions: $9,988, MS-64, July 2015; $3,408, MS-63, January 2015; $3,290, MS-62, January 2015; $3,290, MS-61, July 2015											
1923	566,000	30,609	62.5	100%	$1,250	$1,275	$1,300	$1,325	$1,400	$1,425	$1,500	$4,000
	Auctions: $3,760, MS-65, January 2015; $2,350, MS-64, August 2015; $2,115, MS-64, June 2015; $1,528, MS-63, July 2015											
1923-D	1,702,250	5,981	64.3	100%	$1,250	$1,275	$1,300	$1,325	$1,400	$1,425	$1,500	$2,150
	Auctions: $11,750, MS-67, February 2015; $2,585, MS-66, October 2015; $2,350, MS-65, February 2015; $1,469, MS-62, March 2015											
1924	4,323,500	313,684	63.4	100%	$1,250	$1,275	$1,300	$1,325	$1,400	$1,425	$1,450	$1,750
	Auctions: $6,463, MS-67, January 2015; $3,760, MS-66, June 2015; $1,528, MS-62, October 2015; $1,293, MS-60, February 2015											
1924-D	3,049,500	450	62.0	89%	$2,200	$2,500	$2,650	$3,250	$4,250	$5,500	$8,500	$70,000
	Auctions: $12,925, MS-64, August 2015; $3,290, MS-60, July 2015; $1,998, AU-53, August 2015; $1,763, AU-50, January 2015											
1924-S	2,927,500	478	62.5	93%	$2,200	$2,500	$2,650	$3,250	$4,500	$6,000	$9,500	$65,000
	Auctions: $16,450, MS-64, January 2015; $9,106, MS-63, January 2015; $3,173, MS-60, January 2015; $2,233, MS-60, January 2015											

† Ranked in the *100 Greatest U.S. Coins* (fourth edition). **e.** Prior to the first public auction of a 1921 presentation-strike double eagle (a lightly cleaned specimen) in summer 2000, this variety was unknown to the numismatic community at large. That example reportedly was struck in 1921 to celebrate the birth of Joseph Baker, nephew of U.S. Mint director Raymond T. Baker. In 2006 a second example (this one with original, uncleaned surfaces) was discovered and subsequently auctioned. **f.** Included in 1922 mintage figure.

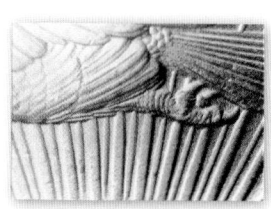

1925, Doubled Die Reverse   **1933 Saint-Gaudens Double Eagle**

	Mintage	Cert	Avg	%MS	VF-20	EF-40	AU-50	AU-55	MS-60	MS-62	MS-63	MS-65
										PF-63	PF-64	PF-65
1925	2,831,750	54,298	63.2	100%	$1,250	$1,275	$1,300	$1,325	$1,400	$1,425	$1,450	$1,750
	Auctions: $4,230, MS-66, August 2015; $1,528, MS-64, June 2015; $1,293, MS-62, June 2015; $1,421, MS-60, October 2015											
1925, Doubled Die Reverse (g)	(h)	20	63.9	100%			$2,000	$2,500	$2,750	$3,000	$3,500	
	Auctions: $3,055, MS-65, December 2013											
1925-D	2,938,500	308	62.6	98%	$2,600	$3,200	$3,750	$4,250	$5,500	$7,500	$10,000	$75,000
	Auctions: $64,625, MS-65, June 2015; $12,925, MS-64, August 2014; $7,638, MS-62, June 2015; $4,465, MS-61, August 2015											
1925-S	3,776,500	422	59.3	57%	$2,250	$3,000	$4,000	$5,500	$9,500	$12,000	$15,500	$100,000
	Auctions: $11,456, MS-63, August 2015; $8,225, MS-61, January 2015; $5,170, AU-58, January 2015; $5,405, AU-55, August 2015											
1926	816,750	23,575	63.6	100%	$1,250	$1,275	$1,300	$1,325	$1,400	$1,425	$1,450	$1,750
	Auctions: $1,821, MS-65, August 2015; $1,645, MS-64, June 2015; $1,528, MS-64, October 2015; $1,469, MS-63, March 2015											
1926-D	481,000	103	61.2	88%	$8,000	$11,000	$12,500	$13,500	$14,500	$20,000	$25,000	$150,000
	Auctions: $47,000, MS-64, March 2014; $22,325, MS-63, June 2015; $14,100, MS-62, September 2015; $11,163, AU-58, September 2015											
1926-S	2,041,500	678	63.1	97%	$2,150	$2,450	$2,750	$2,950	$3,500	$4,000	$5,500	$25,000
	Auctions: $18,277, MS-65, October 2015; $8,226, MS-64, June 2015; $5,170, MS-63, February 2015; $2,115, MS-60, January 2015											
1927	2,946,750	143,922	63.5	100%	$1,250	$1,275	$1,300	$1,325	$1,400	$1,425	$1,450	$1,750
	Auctions: $3,525, MS-66, September 2015; $2,585, MS-65, June 2015; $1,351, MS-61, September 2015; $1,410, MS-60, October 2015											
1927-D †	180,000	5	64.0	80%			$500,000	$550,000	$750,000	$850,000	$1,300,000	$1,750,000
	Auctions: $1,997,500, MS-66, January 2014											
1927-S	3,107,000	121	61.3	75%			$14,000	$16,000	$26,000	$37,500	$45,000	$110,000
	Auctions: $105,750, MS-65, March 2014; $42,300, MS-63, August 2016; $25,850, MS-62, June 2015; $17,625, AU-55, January 2015											
1928	8,816,000	49,431	63.3	100%	$1,250	$1,275	$1,300	$1,325	$1,400	$1,425	$1,450	$1,750
	Auctions: $18,800, MS-67, August 2015; $4,818, MS-66, September 2015; $1,998, MS-64, June 2015; $1,379, MS-60, August 2015											
1929	1,779,750	126	63.1	96%			$13,500	$15,500	$20,000	$30,000	$35,000	$75,000
	Auctions: $57,281, MS-65, August 2014; $37,600, MS-64, January 2015; $32,900, MS-63, September 2015; $15,863, MS-60, August 2014											
1930-S	74,000	21	64.1	100%			$42,000	$45,000	$65,000	$75,000	$90,000	$175,000
	Auctions: $176,382, MS-65, March 2014; $164,500, MS-65, September 2014; $146,875, MS-64, November 2016; $164,500, MS-63, August 2014											
1931	2,938,250	34	64.3	100%			$22,500	$25,000	$35,000	$50,000	$65,000	$100,000
	Auctions: $105,751, MS-65, September 2014; $105,750, MS-65, August 2016; $76,375, MS-65, March 2014; $64,625, MS-64, August 2014											
1931-D	106,500	42	63.3	98%			$22,500	$25,000	$35,000	$50,000	$65,000	$100,000
	Auctions: $129,250, MS-65, September 2014; $99,875, MS-64, January 2014; $94,000, MS-64, November 2016; $64,625, MS-62, August 2014											
1932	1,101,750	70	63.9	100%			$22,500	$25,000	$35,000	$50,000	$65,000	$100,000
	Auctions: $108,688, MS-66, March 2014; $99,875, MS-66, August 2014; $94,000, MS-64, August 2014											
1933 † (i)	445,500	0	n/a		*(extremely rare)*							
	Auctions: $7,590,000, Gem BU, July 2002											

† Ranked in the *100 Greatest U.S. Coins* (fourth edition). **g.** Doubling is evident on the eagle's feathers, the rays, and IN GOD WE TRUST. **h.** Included in 1925 mintage figure. **i.** All but a few 1933 double eagles were to have been melted at the mint. Today 13 examples are known to have survived. Only one, said to have previously been in the collection of King Farouk of Egypt, has ever been sold at auction. The federal government has ruled that others are illegal to own privately.

U.S. Commemoratives
1892–1954 and 1982 to Date

AN OVERVIEW OF CLASSIC COMMEMORATIVES

Commemorative coins have been popular since the time of ancient Greece and Rome. In the beginning they recorded and honored important events and passed along the news of the day. Today commemorative coins, which are highly esteemed by collectors, have been issued by many modern nations—none of which has surpassed the United States when it comes to these impressive mementoes.

The unique position occupied by commemoratives in the United States coinage is largely due to the fact that, with few exceptions, all commemorative coins have real historical significance. The progress and advance of people in the New World are presented in an interesting and instructive manner on our commemorative coins. Such a record of history artistically presented on U.S. gold, silver, and other memorial issues appeals strongly to the collector who favors the romantic, storytelling side of numismatics. It is the historical features of our commemoratives, in fact, that create interest among many people who would otherwise have little interest in coins, and would not otherwise consider themselves collectors.

Proposed coin programs are considered by two congressional committees: the Senate Committee on Banking, Housing, and Urban Affairs; and the House Financial Services Committee. Once a program is approved by Congress, the independent Citizens Coinage Advisory Committee (ccac.gov) and the U.S. Commission of Fine Arts (cfa.gov) advise the secretary of the Treasury on its coin designs.

These special coins are usually issued either to commemorate events or to help pay for monuments, programs, or celebrations that commemorate historical persons, places, or things. Pre-1982 commemorative coins were offered in most instances by a commission in charge of the event to be commemorated and sold at a premium over face value.

Commemorative coins are popularly collected either by major types or in sets with mintmark varieties. The pieces covered in this section of the *Guide Book of United States Coins, Deluxe Edition*, are those of the "classic" era of U.S. commemoratives, 1892 to 1954. All commemoratives are of the standard weight and fineness of their regular-issue 20th-century gold and silver counterparts, and all are legal tender.

A note about mintages and distribution numbers: Unless otherwise stated, the coinage figures given in each "Distribution" column represent the total released mintage: the total mintage (including assay coins), minus the quantity of unsold coins. In many cases, larger quantities were minted but not all were sold. Unsold coins usually were returned to the mint and melted, although sometimes quantities were placed in circulation at face value. A limited number of Proof strikings or presentation pieces were made for some of the classic commemorative issues.

A note about price performance: It has mostly been in recent decades that the general public has learned about commemorative coins. They have long been popular with coin collectors who enjoy the artistry and history associated with them, as well as the profit to be made from owning these rare pieces. Very few of them ever reached circulation because they were all originally sold above face value, and because they are all so rare. Most of the early issues were of the half dollar denomination, often made in quantities of fewer than 20,000 pieces. This is minuscule when compared to the regular half dollar coins that are made by the millions each year, and still rarely seen in circulation.

At the beginning of 1988, prices of classic commemoratives in MS-65 condition had risen so high that most collectors had to content themselves with pieces in lower grades. Investors continued to apply pressure to the high-quality pieces, driving prices even higher, while the collector community went after coins in grades from AU to MS-63. For several months the pressure from both influences caused prices to rise very rapidly (for all issues and grades) without even taking the price-adjustment breather that usually goes along with such activity.

By 1990, prices dropped to the point that several of the commemoratives began to look like bargains once again. Many of the MS-65 pieces held firm at price levels above the $3,000 mark, but others were still available at under $500 even for coins of similar mintage. Coins in MS–63 or 64 were priced at but a fraction of the MS-65 prices, which would seem to make them reasonably priced because the demand for these pieces is universal, and not keyed simply to grade, rarity, or speculator pressure.

Historically, the entire series of commemorative coins has frequently undergone a roller-coaster cycle of price adjustments. These cycles have usually been of short duration, lasting from months to years, with prices always recovering and eventually exceeding previous levels.

See pages 1098 and 1099 for discussion of modern commemorative coins of 1982 to date, page 1195 for pricing of government commemorative sets, and page 1502 for an alphabetical cross-reference list of all commemoratives.

WORLD'S COLUMBIAN EXPOSITION HALF DOLLAR (1892–1893)

Designers: *Charles E. Barber (obverse), George T. Morgan (reverse).* **Weight:** *12.50 grams.*
Composition: *.900 silver, .100 copper (net weight .3617 oz. pure silver).*
Diameter: *30.6 mm.* **Edge:** *Reeded.* **Mint:** *Philadelphia.*

The first U.S. commemorative coin was the Columbian half dollar sold at the World's Columbian Exposition—also known as the Chicago World's Fair—during 1893. The event celebrated the 400th anniversary of Christopher Columbus's arrival in the New World. A great many of the coins remained unsold and a substantial quantity was later released for circulation at face value or melted.

Designs. *Obverse:* Charles Barber's conception of Christopher Columbus, derived from a plaster model by Olin Levi Warner, taken from the explorer's portrait on an 1892 Spanish medal. The medal's portrait was inspired by a statue by Jeronimo Suñel, which itself was from an imagined likeness by Charles Legrand. *Reverse:* A sailing ship atop two globes representing the Old World and the New World. The vessel is from a plaster model by Olin Levi Warner, taken from a model made in Spain of Columbus's flagship, the *Santa Maria.*

Mintage and Melting Data. *Maximum authorized*—5,000,000 (both years combined). *Number minted*—1892: 950,000 (including an unknown number of assay coins; approximately 100 Proofs were struck as well); 1893: 4,052,105 (including 2,105 assay coins). *Number melted*—1893: 2,501,700. *Net distribution*—1892: 950,000; 1893: 1,550,405.

Original Cost and Issuer. Sale price $1. Issued by the Exposition.

Key to Collecting. Both dates are common in all grades through MS-65, and are often available in MS-66 and higher. The typical high-grade coin is lustrous and frosty; some have attractive, original light-blue or iridescent toning. Well-worn examples are very common, as the Treasury Department eventually released large quantities into circulation at face value. Striking usually is good. Some coins can be weak at the center—on the higher areas of the portrait and, on the reverse, in the details of the ship's sails. Most have contact marks from handling and distribution. High-grade 1892 coins typically are better struck than those of 1893. Approximately 100 brilliant Proofs were struck for each date; they vary widely in quality and eye appeal.

First Points of Wear. *Obverse:* The eyebrow, the cheek, and the hair at the back of the forehead. (The hair area sometimes is flatly struck.) *Reverse:* The top of the rear sail, and the right side of the Eastern Hemisphere.

	Distribution	Cert	Avg	%MS	AU-50	MS-60	MS-62	MS-63	MS-64	MS-65	MS-66
									PF-63	PF-64	PF-65
1892	950,000	5,661	63.2	95%	$25	$30	$45	$70	$100	$275	$700
	Auctions: $2,350, MS-67, August 2016; $1,410, MS-66, September 2016										
1892, Proof	100	38	64.0						$5,750	$7,000	$13,000
	Auctions: $8,225, PF-65, November 2013										
1893	1,550,405	6,101	62.3	88%	$25	$30	$45	$70	$100	$275	$700
	Auctions: $8,229, MS-67, June 2015; $1,293, MS-66, July 2015; $400, MS-65, January 2015; $118, MS-64, August 2015										
1893, Proof	3–5	1	63.0								
	Auctions: $15,275, PF-66, January 2014; $5,830, PF-64, September 1993										

Note: Various repunched dates exist for both dates; these command little or no premium in the marketplace. For more information, see the *Cherrypickers' Guide to Rare Die Varieties*, sixth edition, volume II.

WORLD'S COLUMBIAN EXPOSITION ISABELLA QUARTER (1893)

Designer: *Charles E. Barber.* **Weight:** *6.25 grams.* **Composition:** *.900 silver, .100 copper (net weight .18084 oz. pure silver).* **Diameter:** *24.3 mm.* **Edge:** *Reeded.* **Mint:** *Philadelphia.*

In 1893 the Board of Lady Managers of the World's Columbian Exposition (also known as the Chicago World's Fair) petitioned for a souvenir quarter dollar. Authority was granted March 3, 1893, for the coin, which is known as the *Isabella quarter*.

Designs. *Obverse:* Crowned profile portrait of Spain's Queen Isabella, who sponsored Christopher Columbus's voyages to the New World. *Reverse:* A lady kneeling with a distaff and spindle, symbolic of the industry of American women.

Mintage and Melting Data. Authorized on March 3, 1893. *Maximum authorized*—40,000. *Number minted*—40,023 (including 23 assay coins). *Number melted*—15,809. *Net distribution*—24,214.

Original Cost and Issuer. Sale price $1. Issued by the Board of Lady Managers, World's Columbian Exposition.

Key to Collecting. Most examples in the marketplace are in Mint State, including many choice and gem pieces. Most are well struck and show full details, with richly lustrous fields. Connoisseurs avoid darkly toned, stained, and recolored coins. Many lower-grade Mint State examples have marks on Isabella's cheek and on the higher parts of the reverse design. The left obverse field often has marks made from contact with other coins during minting, storage, and distribution. The certification services have classified some coins with mirrored fields as Proofs, although no official records exist for the production of such.

First Points of Wear. *Obverse:* Isabella's cheekbone, and the center of the lower part of the crown. *Reverse:* The strand of wool at the lower-left thigh.

	Distribution	Cert	Avg	%MS	AU-50	MS-60	MS-62	MS-63	MS-64 / PF-63	MS-65 / PF-64	MS-66 / PF-65
1893	24,214	3,771	62.4	88%	$325	$385	$475	$625	$925	$2,150	$3,750
	Auctions: $17,625, MS-67, January 2015; $329, AU-58, February 2015; $306, EF-40, July 2015; $235, VF-30, February 2015										
1893, Proof	*100–105*	46	63.8						$4,750	$7,750	$13,000
	Auctions: $6,463, PF-64, July 2015; $5,640, PF-64, June 2015; $5,288, PF-64, October 2014										

LAFAYETTE DOLLAR (1900)

Designer: *Charles E. Barber.* **Weight:** *26.73 grams.* **Composition:** *.900 silver, .100 copper (net weight .7736 oz. pure silver).* **Diameter:** *38.1 mm.* **Edge:** *Reeded.* **Mint:** *Philadelphia.*

This issue—which was the first commemorative coin of one-dollar denomination, as well as the first authorized U.S. coin to bear a portrait of a U.S. president—commemorated the erection of a statue of Marquis de Lafayette in Paris in connection with the 1900 Paris Exposition (Exposition Universelle).

Designs. *Obverse:* Conjoined portraits of the marquis de Lafayette and George Washington. *Reverse:* Side view of the equestrian statue erected by the youth of the United States in honor of Lafayette. This view was based on an early model of the statue; the final version that was erected in Paris is slightly different.

Mintage and Melting Data. Authorized on March 3, 1899. *Maximum authorized—50,000. Number minted—50,026 (including 26 assay coins). Number melted—14,000. Net distribution—36,026.*

Original Cost and Issuer. Sale price $2. Issued by the Lafayette Memorial Commission through the American Trust & Savings Bank of Chicago.

Key to Collecting. Most surviving examples show evidence of circulation or other mishandling. The typical grade is AU. In Mint State, most are MS–60 to 63, and many are dull or unattractive, having been dipped or cleaned multiple times. Many have marks and dings. Properly graded MS-64 coins are very scarce, and MS-65 or higher gems are very rare, especially if with good eye appeal. Several die varieties exist and are collected by specialists.

Varieties. *Obverse varieties:* (1) Small point on the bust of Washington. The tip of Lafayette's bust is over the top of the L in DOLLAR. The AT in STATES is cut high. (2) The left foot of the final A in AMERICA is recut, and the A in STATES is high. The second S in STATES is repunched (this is diagnostic). (3) The AT in STATES is recut and the final S is low. The letter F in OF and in LAFAYETTE is broken from the lower tip of the crossbar and to the right base extension, and AMERICA is spaced A ME RI C A. The period after OF is close to the A of AMERICA. The tip of Lafayette's vest falls to the right of the top of the first L in DOLLAR. (4) The C in AMERICA is repunched at the inside top (this is diagnostic). The CA in AMERICA is spaced differently from the obverses previously described. *Reverse varieties:* (A) There are 14 long leaves and a long stem. The tip of the lowest leaf is over the 1 in 1900. (B) There are 14 shorter leaves and a short stem. The tip of the lowest leaf is over the space between the 1 and 9 in 1900. (C) There are 14 medium leaves and a short, bent stem. The tip of the lowest leaf is over the 9 in 1900. (D) There are 15 long leaves and a short, bent stem. The tip of the lowest leaf is over the 9 in 1900. (E) The tip of the lowest leaf is over the space to the left of the 1 in 1900.

First Points of Wear. *Obverse:* Washington's cheekbone, and Lafayette's lower hair curl. *Reverse:* The fringe of Lafayette's epaulet, and the horse's blinder and left rear leg bone.

	Distribution	Cert	Avg	%MS	AU-50	MS-60	MS-62	MS-63	MS-64	MS-65	MS-66
1900	36,026	2,580	61.9	87%	$485	$875	$1,200	$1,650	$2,750	$6,750	$15,000
	Auctions: $73,438, MS-67, January 2015; $564, AU-58, January 2015; $376, EF-40, November 2015; $329, VF-30, July 2015										

LOUISIANA PURCHASE EXPOSITION JEFFERSON GOLD DOLLAR (1903)

Designer: *Charles E. Barber (assisted by George T. Morgan).* **Weight:** *1.672 grams.*
Composition: *.900 gold, .100 copper (net weight .04837 oz. pure gold).*
Diameter: *15 mm.* **Edge:** *Reeded.* **Mint:** *Philadelphia.*

The first commemorative U.S. gold coins were authorized for the Louisiana Purchase Exposition, held in St. Louis in 1904. The event commemorated the 100th anniversary of the United States' purchase of the Louisiana Territory from France, an acquisition overseen by President Thomas Jefferson.

Designs. *Obverse:* Bewigged profile portrait of Thomas Jefferson, inspired by an early-1800s medal by John Reich, after Jean-Antoine Houdon's bust. *Reverse:* Inscription and branch.

Mintage and Melting Data. Authorized on June 28, 1902. *Maximum authorized*—250,000 (both types combined). *Number minted*—250,258 (125,000 of each type; including 258 assay coins comprising both types). *Number melted*—215,250 (total for both types; no account was kept of the portraits; 250 assay coins were melted). *Net distribution*—35,000 (estimated at 17,500 of each type).

Original Cost and Issuer. Sale price $3. Issued by the Louisiana Purchase Exposition Company, St. Louis, Missouri (sales through Farran Zerbe). Some were sold as mounted in spoons, brooches, and stick pins; 100 certified Proofs of each design were made, mounted in an opening in a rectangular piece of imprinted cardboard.

Key to Collecting. Market demand is strong, from collectors and investors alike, as most surviving examples are in choice or gem Mint State, with strong eye appeal. Most specimens are very lustrous and frosty. An occasional coin is prooflike. Avoid any with copper stains (from improper mixing of the gold/copper alloy). Proofs enter the market rarely and garner much publicity.

First Points of Wear. *Obverse:* Portrait's cheekbone and sideburn. *Reverse:* Date and denomination.

	Distribution	Cert	Avg	%MS	AU-50	MS-60	MS-62	MS-63	MS-64	MS-65	MS-66
									PF-63	PF-64	PF-65
1903	17,500	2,262	63.9	94%	$550	$625	$700	$825	$925	$1,300	$1,675
	Auctions: $5,993, MS-67, July 2015; $1,293, MS-64, July 2015; $470, AU-58, January 2015; $329, AU-50, January 2015										
1903, Proof (a)	100	31	64.9								
	Auctions: $37,375, PF-67UCamH, January 2012										

a. The first 100 Jefferson gold dollars were struck in brilliant Proof format. True Proofs exhibit deeply mirrored fields and are sharply struck. Many also have frosted devices, giving them a cameo appearance. "Although many of the coins seen today have been certified and lack original packaging, they were originally housed in cardboard holders certifying each coin as having been one of the first 100 impressions from the dies. The original holders are quite interesting, with the coin covered by a small piece of wax paper and a piece of string sealed by dark red wax. The coins are difficult to see behind the wax paper, and the author has seen holders with a circulation-strike example substituted for the Proof piece. Caution should be used when purchasing an example of this extreme rarity" (*Encyclopedia of U.S. Gold Coins, 1795–1933*, second edition).

LOUISIANA PURCHASE EXPOSITION MCKINLEY GOLD DOLLAR (1903)

Designer: *Charles E. Barber (assisted by George T. Morgan).* **Weight:** *1.672 grams.*
Composition: *.900 gold, .100 copper (net weight .04837 oz. pure gold).*
Diameter: *15 mm.* **Edge:** *Reeded.* **Mint:** *Philadelphia.*

President William McKinley—who had been assassinated while in office two years before the Louisiana Purchase Exposition—was remembered on a gold dollar issued alongside the aforementioned coin featuring Thomas Jefferson. Like Jefferson, McKinley oversaw expansion of U.S. territory, with the acquisition of Puerto Rico, Guam, and the Philippines, as well as the annexation of Hawaii.

Designs. *Obverse:* Bareheaded profile portrait of William McKinley, derived from his presidential medal (designed, like this coin, by Charles Barber). *Reverse:* Inscriptions and branch.

Mintage and Melting Data. Authorized on June 28, 1902. *Maximum authorized*—250,000 (both types combined). *Number minted*—250,258 (125,000 of each type; including 258 assay coins comprising both types). *Number melted*—215,250 (total for both types; no account was kept of the portraits; 250 assay coins were melted). *Net distribution*—35,000 (estimated at 17,500 of each type).

Original Cost and Issuer. Sale price $3. Issued by the Louisiana Purchase Exposition Company, St. Louis, Missouri (sales through Farran Zerbe). Some were sold as mounted in spoons, brooches, and stick pins; 100 certified Proofs of each design were made, mounted in an opening in a rectangular piece of imprinted cardboard.

Key to Collecting. Market demand is strong, from collectors and investors alike, as most surviving examples are in choice or gem Mint State, with strong eye appeal. Most specimens are very lustrous and frosty. An occasional coin is prooflike. Avoid any with copper stains (from improper mixing of the gold/copper alloy). Proofs enter the market rarely and garner much publicity.

First Points of Wear. *Obverse:* Portrait's cheekbone and sideburn. *Reverse:* Date and denomination.

	Distribution	Cert	Avg	%MS	AU-50	MS-60	MS-62	MS-63	MS-64	MS-65	MS-66
									PF-63	PF-64	PF-65
1903	17,500	2,143	63.9	96%	$550	$600	$625	$700	$850	$1,275	$1,700
	Auctions: $8,813, MS-68, January 2015; $1,763, MS-66, January 2015; $517, MS-63, January 2015; $376, AU-58, August 2015										
1903, Proof (a)	100	27	64.3								
	Auctions: $14,950, PF-65Cam, April 2012										

a. Like the Jefferson issue, the first 100 McKinley gold dollars were struck as Proofs, and packaged as such. "Prooflike circulation strikes are quite common for the issue, and true Proofs can be distinguished by deeply mirrored surfaces and cameo devices. Certification is highly recommended" (*Encyclopedia of U.S. Gold Coins, 1795–1933*, second edition).

LEWIS AND CLARK EXPOSITION GOLD DOLLAR (1904–1905)

Designer: *Charles E. Barber.* **Weight:** *1.672 grams.* **Composition:** *.900 gold, .100 copper (net weight .04837 oz. pure gold).* **Diameter:** *15 mm.* **Edge:** *Reeded.* **Mint:** *Philadelphia.*

A souvenir issue of gold dollars was struck to mark the Lewis and Clark Centennial Exposition, held in Portland, Oregon, in 1905. The sale of these coins financed the erection of a bronze memorial of the Shoshone Indian guide Sacagawea, who assisted in the famous expedition.

Designs. *Obverse:* Bareheaded profile portrait of Meriwether Lewis. *Reverse:* Bareheaded profile portrait of William Clark. These portraits were inspired by works of Charles Willson Peale.

Mintage and Melting Data. Authorized on April 13, 1904. *Maximum authorized*—250,000 (both years combined). *Number minted*—1904: 25,028 (including 28 assay coins); 1905: 35,041 (including 41 assay coins). *Number melted*—1904: 15,003; 1905: 25,000. *Net distribution*—1904: 10,025; 1905: 10,041.

Original Cost and Issuer. Sales price $2 (some at $2.50); many were probably discounted further. Issued by the Lewis and Clark Centennial and American Pacific Exposition and Oriental Fair Company, Portland, Oregon (sales through Farran Zerbe and others).

Key to Collecting. Most surviving examples show evidence of handling. Some exhibit die problems (a rough raised area of irregularity at the denticles). Most range from AU–50 to 58, with an occasional MS–60 to 63. MS-64 coins are scarce, and MS-65 rare. Pristine examples are very rare. Most MS coins have areas of prooflike finish; some are deeply lustrous and frosty. The 1905-dated issue is noticeably scarcer than the 1904.

First Points of Wear. *Obverse:* Lewis's temple. *Reverse:* Clark's temple.

	Distribution	Cert	Avg	%MS	AU-50	MS-60	MS-62	MS-63	MS-64	MS-65	MS-66
									PF-63	PF-64	PF-65
1904	10,025	1,263	63.4	95%	$900	$1,050	$1,125	$1,200	$2,150	$4,650	$7,250
	Auctions: $15,275, MS-67, January 2015; $6,580, MS-66, January 2015; $734, MS-61, February 2015; $400, AU-50, May 2015										
1904, Proof	2–3	2	63.5								
	Auctions: $30,550, PF-64, August 2015										
1905	10,041	1,250	62.8	92%	$950	$1,350	$1,385	$1,425	$2,875	$8,150	$12,500
	Auctions: $35,250, MS-67, January 2015; $19,388, MS-66, January 2015; $1,880, MS-63, January 2015; $705, MS-60, June 2015										

PANAMA-PACIFIC INTERNATIONAL EXPOSITION HALF DOLLAR (1915)

Designers: *Charles E. Barber (obverse), George T. Morgan (assisting Barber on reverse).*
Weight: *12.50 grams.* **Composition:** *.900 silver, .100 copper (net weight .3617 oz. pure silver).*
Diameter: *30.6 mm.* **Edge:** *Reeded.* **Mint:** *San Francisco.*

The Panama-Pacific International Exposition held in San Francisco in 1915 celebrated the opening of the Panama Canal, as well as the revival of the Bay Area following the 1906 earthquake and fire. Five commemorative coins in four different denominations, including a half dollar, were issued in conjunction with the event.

Designs. *Obverse:* Columbia scattering flowers, alongside a child holding a cornucopia, representing the bounty of the American West; the Golden Gate in the background. *Reverse:* A spread-winged eagle perched on a shield, with branches of oak and olive.

Mintage and Melting Data. Authorized by the Act of January 16, 1915. *Maximum authorized*—200,000. *Number minted*—60,030 (including 30 assay coins). *Number melted*—32,896 (including the 30 assay coins; 29,876 were melted on September 7, 1916 and the balance on October 30, 1916). *Net distribution*—27,134.

Original Cost and Issuer. Sale price $1. Issued by the Coin and Medal Department (Farran Zerbe), Panama-Pacific International Exposition, San Francisco, California (combination offers included a set of four coins, including the buyer's choice of one $50, in a leather case, for $100; and a set of five coins in a copper frame for $200).

Key to Collecting. The half dollar does not have the typical deep mint frost associated with earlier silver issues. Most are satiny in appearance with the high parts in particular having a microscopically grainy finish. Many pieces have an inner line around the perimeter near the rim, a die characteristic. On the reverse of all known coins, the eagle's breast feathers are indistinct, which sometimes gives MS coins the appearance of having light wear. Most surviving coins grade from AU-50 to MS-63.

First Points of Wear. *Obverse:* Columbia's left shoulder. *Reverse:* The eagle's breast.

	Distribution	Cert	Avg	%MS	AU-50	MS-60	MS-62	MS-63	MS-64	MS-65	MS-66
1915-S	27,134	2,718	63.3	93%	$375	$525	$650	$750	$925	$1,325	$2,500
	Auctions: $13,513, MS-67, August 2015; $646, MS-61, October 2015; $247, AU-50, July 2015; $165, VF-25, February 2015										

PANAMA-PACIFIC INTERNATIONAL EXPOSITION GOLD DOLLAR (1915)

Designer: *Charles Keck.* **Weight:** *1.672 grams.* **Composition:** *.900 gold, .100 copper (net weight .04837 oz. pure gold).* **Diameter:** *15 mm.* **Edge:** *Reeded.* **Mint:** *San Francisco.*

Coin dealer and entrepreneur Farran Zerbe conceived of a program of five different commemorative coins across four denominations (including the gold dollar) in conjunction with the Panama-Pacific International Exposition in 1915. The event was held in what eventually constituted a miniature city, whose sculptures and impressive architecture were intended to remind one of Rome or some other distant and romantic place, but which at night was more apt to resemble Coney Island.

Designs. *Obverse:* Capped profile portrait of a Panama Canal laborer. *Reverse:* Two dolphins, symbolizing the Atlantic and Pacific oceans, and legends.

Mintage and Melting Data. Authorized by the Act of January 16, 1915. *Maximum authorized*—25,000. *Number minted*—25,034 (including 34 assay coins). *Number melted*—10,034 (including the 34 assay coins; melted at the San Francisco Mint on October 30, 1916). *Net distribution*—15,000.

Original Cost and Issuer. Sale price $2 (and a few at $2.25). Issued by the Coin and Medal Department (Farran Zerbe), Panama-Pacific International Exposition, San Francisco, California (combination offers included, among others, a set of four coins, with the buyer's choice of one fifty-dollar coin, in a leather case, for $100; and a set of five coins in a copper frame for $200).

Key to Collecting. Most examples are in Mint State. Many exhibit deep mint frost. Friction is common, especially on the obverse.

First Points of Wear. *Obverse:* The peak of the laborer's cap. *Reverse:* The heads of the dolphins, and the denomination.

	Distribution	Cert	Avg	%MS	AU-50	MS-60	MS-62	MS-63	MS-64	MS-65	MS-66
1915-S	15,000	3,767	63.6	94%	$525	$585	$615	$675	$825	$1,300	$1,775

Auctions: $3,538, MS-67, January 2015; $1,733, MS-64, August 2015; $441, AU-55, April 2015; $329, EF-40, April 2015

PANAMA-PACIFIC INTERNATIONAL EXPOSITION QUARTER EAGLE (1915)

Designer: *Charles E. Barber (obverse), George T. Morgan (reverse).* **Weight:** *4.18 grams.*
Composition: *.900 gold, .100 copper (net weight .12094 oz. pure gold).*
Diameter: *18 mm.* **Edge:** *Reeded.* **Mint:** *San Francisco.*

The 1915 Panama-Pacific International Exposition—a name chosen to reflect the recently completed Panama Canal, as well as Pacific Ocean commerce—was planned to be the ultimate world's fair. Foreign countries, domestic manufacturers, artists, concessionaires, and others were invited to the 10-month event, which drew an estimated 19 million visitors. This quarter eagle was among the five coins issued to commemorate the celebration.

Designs. *Obverse:* Columbia seated on a hippocampus, holding a caduceus, symbolic of Medicine's triumph over yellow fever in Panama during the canal's construction. *Reverse:* An eagle, standing on a plaque inscribed E PLURIBUS UNUM, with raised wings.

Mintage and Melting Data. Authorized by the Act of January 16, 1915. *Maximum authorized*—10,000. *Number minted*—10,017 (including 17 assay coins). *Number melted*—3,268 (including the 17 assay coins; melted at the San Francisco Mint on October 30, 1916). *Net distribution*—6,749.

Original Cost and Issuer. Sale price $4. Issued by the Coin and Medal Department (Farran Zerbe), Panama-Pacific International Exposition, San Francisco, California (combination offers included, among others, a set of four coins, with the buyer's choice of one fifty-dollar coin, in a leather case, for $100; and a set of five coins in a copper frame for $200).

Key to Collecting. Most grade from AU-55 to MS-63. MS-64 coins are elusive, and MS-65 rare. Most MS pieces show a satiny, sometimes grainy luster.

First Points of Wear. *Obverse:* Columbia's head, breast, and knee. *Reverse:* The torch band and the eagle's leg.

	Distribution	Cert	Avg	%MS	AU-50	MS-60	MS-62	MS-63	MS-64	MS-65	MS-66
									PF-63	PF-64	PF-65
1915-S	6,749	1,987	64.5	96%	$1,550	$2,150	$2,850	$3,950	$4,750	$5,250	$6,000
	Auctions: $12,925, MS-67, January 2015; $6,463, MS-66, February 2015; $5,405, MS-64, January 2015; $2,233, AU-50, August 2015										
1915-S, Proof (a)	*unique*	0	n/a								
	Auctions: No auction records available.										

a. This unique Satin Finish Proof resides in the National Numismatic Collection of the Smithsonian Institution.

PANAMA-PACIFIC INTERNATIONAL EXPOSITION
FIFTY-DOLLAR GOLD PIECE (1915)

Designer: *Robert Aitken.* **Weight:** *83.59 grams.* **Composition:** *.900 gold, .100 copper (net weight 2.4186 oz. pure gold).* **Diameter:** *43 mm (round), 44.9 mm (octagonal, measured point to point).* **Edge:** *Reeded.* **Mint:** *San Francisco.*

Both round and octagonal $50 gold pieces were struck as part of the series commemorating the Panama-Pacific International Exposition in 1915. These coins, along with the half dollars in the same series, were the first U.S. commemoratives to feature the motto IN GOD WE TRUST.

Designs. Round: *Obverse:* Helmeted profile portrait of Minerva, with shield and armor. *Reverse:* An owl, symbolic of wisdom, vigilant on a pine branch, with pinecones. Octagonal: *Obverse and reverse:* Same as the round coin, but with dolphins in the eight angled exergues on obverse and reverse.

Mintage and Melting Data. Authorized by the Act of January 16, 1915. Round: *Maximum authorized*—Round: 1,500; Octagonal:

1,500. *Number minted* (including 10 assay coins)—Round: 1,510 (including 10 assay coins); Octagonal: 1,509 (including 9 assay coins). *Number melted*—Round: 1,027; Octagonal: 864. *Net distribution*—Round: 483; Octagonal: 645.

Original Cost and Issuer. Round and octagonal: Sale price, each, $100. Coin and Medal Department (Farran Zerbe), Panama-Pacific International Exposition, San Francisco, California. Combination offers included a set of four coins (buyer's choice of one fifty-dollar coin) in a leather case for $100, and a set of five coins in a copper frame for $200, this issued after the Exposition closed.

Key to Collecting. Because such small quantities were issued, these hefty gold commemoratives today are rare in any grade. The round coins trade hands slightly less frequently than the octagonal. Typical grades are MS–63 or 64 for coins kept in an original box or frame over the years, or AU-58 to MS-63 if removed. Coins that have been cleaned or lightly polished exhibit a multitude of tiny hairlines; such pieces are avoided by connoisseurs.

First Points of Wear. *Obverse:* Minerva's cheek. *Reverse:* The owl's upper breast.

	Distribution	Cert	Avg	%MS	AU-50	MS-60	MS-62	MS-63	MS-64	MS-65	MS-66
1915-S, Round	483	414	63.4	95%	$55,000	$75,000	$80,000	$90,000	$120,000	$195,000	$240,000
	Auctions: $176,250, MS-65, August 2015; $79,313, MS-63, January 2015; $64,625, MS-61, July 2015; $51,700, MS-60, January 2015										
1915-S, Octagonal	645	458	63.1	95%	$55,000	$71,500	$77,500	$85,000	$110,000	$195,000	$245,000
	Auctions: $258,500, MS-67, January 2015; $123,375, MS-65, August 2015; $70,500, MS-62, September 2015; $55,225, AU-55, September 2015										

McKinley Memorial Gold Dollar (1916–1917)

Designers: *Charles E. Barber (obverse) and George T. Morgan (reverse).* **Weight:** *1.672 grams.*
Composition: *.900 gold, .100 copper (net weight .04837 oz. pure gold).*
Diameter: *15 mm.* **Edge:** *Reeded.* **Mint:** *Philadelphia.*

The sale of the William McKinley dollars aided in paying for a memorial building at Niles, Ohio, the martyred president's birthplace.

Designs. *Obverse:* Bareheaded profile portrait of William McKinley. *Reverse:* Artist's rendition of the proposed McKinley Birthplace Memorial intended to be erected in Niles, Ohio.

Mintage and Melting Data. Authorized on February 23, 1916. *Maximum authorized*—100,000 (both years combined). *Number minted*—1916: 20,026 (including 26 assay coins); 1917: 10,014 (including 14 assay coins). *Number melted*—1916: 5,000 (estimated); 1917: 5,000 (estimated). *Net distribution*—1916: 15,000 (estimated); 1917: 5,000 (estimated).

Original Cost and Issuer. Sale price $3. Issued by the National McKinley Birthplace Memorial Association, Youngstown, Ohio.

Key to Collecting. The obverse of the 1916 issue often displays friction while its reverse can appear as choice Mint State. Prooflike fields are common. Some are highly prooflike on both sides. The 1917 issue is much harder to find than the 1916; examples usually are in higher grades with rich luster on both sides, and often exhibit a pale yellow color.

First Points of Wear. *Obverse:* McKinley's temple area, and the hair above his ear. *Reverse:* The pillar above the second 1 in the date; and the bottom of the flagpole.

	Distribution	Cert	Avg	%MS	AU-50	MS-60	MS-62	MS-63	MS-64 / PF-63	MS-65 / PF-64	MS-66 / PF-65
1916	*15,000*	2,602	63.7	96%	$485	$535	$550	$575	$685	$1,200	$1,625
	Auctions: $4,465, MS-67, August 2015; $1,528, MS-66, July 2015; $376, MS-61, January 2015; $447, AU-58, October 2015										
1916, Proof	*3–6*	1	63.0								
	Auctions: $37,375, PF-63, January 2012										
1917	*5,000*	1,516	63.6	94%	$550	$650	$700	$825	$950	$1,600	$2,000
	Auctions: $7,344, MS-67, January 2015; $2,585, MS-66, July 2015; $541, MS-62, October 2015; $306, MS-60, May 2015										

ILLINOIS CENTENNIAL HALF DOLLAR (1918)

Designers: *George T. Morgan (obverse) and John R. Sinnock (reverse).* **Weight:** *12.50 grams.*
Composition: *.900 silver, .100 copper (net weight .3617 oz. pure silver).*
Diameter: *30.6 mm.* **Edge:** *Reeded.* **Mint:** *Philadelphia.*

This coin was authorized to commemorate the 100th anniversary of the admission of Illinois into the Union, and was the first souvenir piece for such an event. The head of Abraham Lincoln on the obverse was based on that of a statue of the celebrated president by Andrew O'Connor in Springfield, Illinois.

Designs. *Obverse:* Bareheaded, beardless profile portrait of Abraham Lincoln, facing right. *Reverse:* A fierce eagle atop a crag, clutching a shield and carrying a banner; from the Illinois state seal.

Mintage Data. Authorized on June 1, 1918. *Maximum authorized*—100,000. *Number minted*—100,000 (plus 58 assay coins).

Original Cost and Issuer. Sale price $1. Issued by the Illinois Centennial Commission, through various outlets.

Key to Collecting. Examples were struck with deep, frosty finishes, giving Mint State pieces an unusually attractive appearance. The obverse typically shows contact marks or friction on Lincoln's cheek and on other high parts of his portrait. The field typically shows contact marks. The reverse usually grades from one to three points higher than the obverse, due to the protective nature of its complicated design. Most examples are lustrous and frosty, although a few are seen with partially prooflike fields.

First Points of Wear. *Obverse:* The hair above Lincoln's ear. *Reverse:* The eagle's breast. (Note that the breast was sometimes flatly struck; look for differences in texture or color of the metal.)

	Distribution	Cert	Avg	%MS	AU-50	MS-60	MS-62	MS-63	MS-64	MS-65	MS-66
1918	100,058	4,323	63.9	98%	$130	$150	$160	$170	$225	$325	$685
	Auctions: $5,640, MS-67, January 2015; $823, MS-66, January 2015; $212, MS-64, February 2015; $84, AU-55, February 2015										

MAINE CENTENNIAL HALF DOLLAR (1920)

Designer: *Anthony de Francisci.* **Weight:** *12.50 grams.* **Composition:** *.900 silver, .100 copper (net weight .3617 oz. pure silver).* **Diameter:** *30.6 mm.* **Edge:** *Reeded.* **Mint:** *Philadelphia.*

Congress authorized the Maine Centennial half dollar on May 10, 1920, to be sold at the centennial celebration at Portland. They were received too late for this event and were sold by the state treasurer for many years.

Designs. *Obverse:* Arms of the state of Maine, with the Latin word DIRIGO ("I Direct"). *Reverse:* The centennial inscription enclosed by a wreath.

Mintage Data. Authorized on May 10, 1920. *Maximum authorized*—100,000. *Number minted*—50,028 (including 28 assay coins).

Original Cost and Issuer. Sale price $1. Issued by the Maine Centennial Commission.

Key to Collecting. Relatively few Maine half dollars were sold to the hobby community; the majority of coins distributed saw careless handling by the general public. Most examples show friction or handling marks on the center of the shield on the obverse. The fields were not completely finished in the dies and always show tiny raised lines or die-finishing marks; at first glance these may appear to be hairlines or scratches, but they have no effect on the grade. Appealing examples in higher Mint State levels are much more elusive than the high mintage might suggest.

First Points of Wear. *Obverse:* The left hand of the scythe holder; the right hand of the anchor holder. (Note that the moose and the pine tree are weakly struck.) *Reverse:* The bow knot.

	Distribution	Cert	Avg	%MS	AU-50	MS-60	MS-62	MS-63	MS-64	MS-65	MS-66
1920	50,028	2,940	64.1	98%	$125	$150	$155	$160	$200	$400	$550
	Auctions: $10,575, MS-68, January 2015; $3,290, MS-67, September 2015; $200, MS-64, January 2015; $74, EF-40, September 2015										

PILGRIM TERCENTENARY HALF DOLLAR (1920–1921)

Designer: *Cyrus E. Dallin.* **Weight:** *12.50 grams.* **Composition:** *.900 silver, .100 copper (net weight .3617 oz. pure silver).* **Diameter:** *30.6 mm.* **Edge:** *Reeded.* **Mint:** *Philadelphia.*

To commemorate the landing of the Pilgrims at Plymouth, Massachusetts, in 1620, Congress authorized a special half dollar on May 12, 1920. The first issue had no date on the obverse. The coins struck in 1921 show that date in addition to 1620–1920.

Designs. *Obverse:* Artist's conception of a partial standing portrait of Governor William Bradford holding a book. *Reverse:* The *Mayflower* in full sail.

Mintage and Melting Data. Authorized on May 12, 1920. *Maximum authorized*—300,000 (both years combined). *Number minted*—1920: 200,112 (including 112 assay coins); 1921: 100,053 (including 53 assay coins). *Number melted*—1920: 48,000; 1921: 80,000. *Net distribution*—1920: 152,112; 1921: 20,053.

Original Cost and Issuer. Sale price $1. Issued by the Pilgrim Tercentenary Commission.

Key to Collecting. The 1920 issue is common, and the 1921 slightly scarce. Coins grading MS-64 and higher usually have excellent eye appeal, though many exceptions exist. Most coins have scattered contact marks, particularly on the obverse. Nearly all 1921 coins are this way. Many coins (particularly coins which are early impressions from the dies) show tiny raised lines in the obverse field, representing die finish marks; these are not to be confused with hairlines or other evidences of friction (which are recessed).

First Points of Wear. *Obverse:* Cheekbone, hair over ear, and the high areas of Governor Bradford's hat. *Reverse:* The ship's rigging and stern, the crow's nest, and the rim.

	Distribution	Cert	Avg	%MS	AU-50	MS-60	MS-62	MS-63	MS-64	MS-65	MS-66
1920	152,112	4,843	63.8	97%	$80	$90	$95	$100	$125	$225	$525
	Auctions: $6,756, MS-67, September 2015; $543, MS-66, October 2015; $153, MS-64, September 2015; $80, MS-62, September 2015										
1921, With Added Date	20,053	2,107	64.2	99%	$165	$180	$185	$195	$215	$275	$675
	Auctions: $5,876, MS-67, January 2015; $1,880, MS-66, July 2015; $447, MS-64, February 2015; $141, AU-58, March 2015										

MISSOURI CENTENNIAL HALF DOLLAR (1921)

Designer: *Robert Aitken.* **Weight:** *12.50 grams.* **Composition:** *.900 silver, .100 copper (net weight .3617 oz. pure silver).* **Diameter:** *30.6 mm.* **Edge:** *Reeded.* **Mint:** *Philadelphia.*

The 100th anniversary of the admission of Missouri to the Union was celebrated in the city of Sedalia during August 1921. To mark the occasion, Congress authorized the coinage of a fifty-cent piece.

Designs. *Obverse:* Coonskin-capped profile portrait of a frontiersman. One variety has 2★4 in the field; the other is plain. *Reverse:* Standing figures of a frontiersman and an Indian looking westward, against a starry field; SEDALIA (the location of the Missouri centennial exposition) incused below.

Mintage and Melting Data. Authorized on March 4, 1921. *Maximum authorized*—250,000 (both varieties combined). *Number minted*—50,028 (both varieties combined; including 28 assay coins). *Number melted*—29,600. *Net distribution*—20,428 (estimated; 9,400 for 1921 2★4 and 11,400 for 1921 Plain).

Original Cost and Issuer. Sale price $1. Issued by the Missouri Centennial Committee, through the Sedalia Trust Company.

Key to Collecting. Most grade from AU-55 to MS-63; have friction and contact marks on the higher areas of the design; and are lightly struck at the center of the portrait of Boone on the obverse, and at the torsos of the two figures on the reverse. MS-65 and higher coins with sharply struck centers are rarities.

First Points of Wear. *Obverse:* The hair in back of the ear. *Reverse:* The frontiersman's arm and shoulder.

	Distribution	Cert	Avg	%MS	AU-50	MS-60	MS-62	MS-63	MS-64	MS-65	MS-66
									PF-63	PF-64	PF-65
1921, "2★4" in Field	9,400	1,640	63.7	98%	$625	$700	$850	$975	$1,100	$1,725	$7,250
	Auctions: $6,169, MS-66, January 2015; $2,291, MS-65, August 2015; $705, MS-62, September 2015; $646, AU-58, September 2015										
1921, "2★4" in Field, Matte Proof	1–2	0	n/a								
	Auctions: No auction records available.										
1921, Plain	11,400	1,987	63.2	95%	$400	$550	$650	$775	$900	$2,250	$6,650
	Auctions: $5,640, MS-66, September 2015; $2,468, MS-65, January 2015; $353, AU-58, January 2015; $259, AU-50, November 2015										

ALABAMA CENTENNIAL HALF DOLLAR (1921)

Designer: *Laura Gardin Fraser.* **Weight:** *12.50 grams.* **Composition:** *.900 silver, .100 copper (net weight .3617 oz. pure silver).* **Diameter:** *30.6 mm.* **Edge:** *Reeded.* **Mint:** *Philadelphia.*

The Alabama half dollars were authorized in 1920 and struck until 1921 for the statehood centennial, which was celebrated in 1919. The coins were offered first during President Warren Harding's visit to Birmingham, October 26, 1921. T.E. Kilby's likeness on the obverse was first instance of a living person's portrait on a United States coin.

Designs. *Obverse:* Conjoined bareheaded profile portraits of William Wyatt Bibb, the first governor of Alabama, and Thomas Kilby, governor at the time of the centennial. *Reverse:* A dynamic eagle perched on a shield, clutching arrows and holding a banner; from the Alabama state seal.

Mintage and Melting Data. Authorized on May 10, 1920. *Maximum authorized*—100,000. *Number minted*—70,044 (including 44 assay coins). *Number melted*—5,000. *Net distribution*—2X2: estimated as 30,000; Plain: estimated as 35,000.

Original Cost and Issuer. Sale price $1. Issued by the Alabama Centennial Commission.

Key to Collecting. Most of these coins were sold to citizens of Alabama, and of those, few were acquired by numismatists. Many are in circulated grades (typical being EF or AU), with most surviving pieces grading MS-63 or less. Those grading MS-65 or finer are rare. Nearly all show friction or contact marks on Governor Kilby's cheek on the obverse, and many are flatly struck on the eagle's left leg and talons on the reverse. These coins were produced carelessly, and many lack sharpness and luster (sharply struck examples are very rare). Nicks and marks from the original planchets are often found on the areas of light striking. The eagle's upper leg is often lightly struck, particularly on the plain variety. The 2X2 coins usually are better struck than the plain variety.

First Points of Wear. *Obverse:* Kirby's forehead and the area to the left of his earlobe. *Reverse:* The eagle's lower neck and the top of its wings.

	Distribution	Cert	Avg	%MS	AU-50	MS-60	MS-62	MS-63	MS-64	MS-65	MS-66
1921, "2X2" in Field	*6,006*	1,706	63.4	95%	$285	$350	$375	$450	$550	$1,350	$2,650
	Auctions: $11,750, MS-67, August 2015; $3,525, MS-66, July 2015; $411, MS-63, September 2015; $188, AU-50, February 2015										
1921, Plain	*16,014*	2,029	62.7	90%	$160	$225	$300	$425	$460	$1,175	$1,850
	Auctions: $19,975, MS-67, January 2015; $5,405, MS-66, January 2015; $235, MS-62, March 2015; $141, AU-58, August 2015										

GRANT MEMORIAL HALF DOLLAR (1922)

Designer: *Laura Gardin Fraser.* **Weight:** *12.50 grams.* **Composition:** *.900 silver, .100 copper (net weight .3617 oz. pure silver).* **Diameter:** *30.6 mm.* **Edge:** *Reeded.* **Mint:** *Philadelphia.*

This half dollar (along with the Grant Memorial gold dollar) was struck during 1922 as a centenary souvenir of Ulysses S. Grant's birth. The Ulysses S. Grant Centenary Memorial Association originally planned celebrations in Clermont County, Ohio; the construction of community buildings in Georgetown and Bethel; and the laying of a five-mile highway from New Richmond to Point Pleasant in addition to the coins, but the buildings and highway never came to fruition.

Designs. *Obverse:* Bareheaded profile portrait of Ulysses S. Grant in a military coat. One variety has a star above GRANT. *Reverse:* View of the house Grant was born in (Point Pleasant, Ohio), amidst a wooded setting.

Mintage Data. Authorized on February 2, 1922. *Number minted*—With Star: 5,016 (including 16 assay coins); No Star: 5,000. *Net distribution*—10,016 (both varieties combined).

Original Cost and Issuer. Sale price $3 for either variety. Issued by the U.S. Grant Centenary Memorial Commission (mail orders were serviced by Hugh L. Nichols, chairman, Batavia, Ohio).

Key to Collecting. Almost all known specimens are MS–63 to 65 or better. MS–66 and 67 examples are easy to find. Some lower-grade coins show friction on Grant's cheek and hair. Some specimens have dull surfaces; these are avoided by connoisseurs.

First Points of Wear. *Obverse:* Grant's cheekbone and hair. *Reverse:* The leaves of the tree under the U in TRUST.

	Distribution	Cert	Avg	%MS	AU-50	MS-60	MS-62	MS-63	MS-64	MS-65	MS-66
1922, Star in Obverse Field	4,256	1,306	63.6	97%	$900	$1,200	$1,450	$1,675	$2,675	$5,750	$9,750
	Auctions: $37,600, MS-67, January 2015; $12,926, MS-66, July 2015; $764, AU-53, August 2015; $646, EF-40, August 2015										
1922, No Star in Obverse Field	67,405	3,614	63.7	97%	$110	$120	$135	$150	$250	$550	$1,000
	Auctions: $3,760, MS-67, September 2015; $2,115, MS-66, August 2015; $165, MS-61, February 2015; $60, AU-58, February 2015										

GRANT MEMORIAL GOLD DOLLAR (1922)

Designer: *Laura Gardin Fraser.* **Weight:** *1.672 grams.* **Composition:** *.900 gold, .100 copper (net weight .04837 oz. pure gold).* **Diameter:** *15 mm.* **Edge:** *Reeded.* **Mint:** *Philadelphia.*

The Ulysses S. Grant Centenary Memorial Association, incorporated in 1921, marked the 100th birth anniversary of the Civil War general and U.S. president with this gold dollar (as well as a commemorative half dollar).

Designs. *Obverse:* Bareheaded profile portrait of Ulysses S. Grant in a military coat. One variety has a star above GRANT. *Reverse:* View of the house Grant was born in (Point Pleasant, Ohio), amidst a wooded setting.

Mintage Data. Authorized on February 2, 1922. *Number minted*—With Star: 5,016 (including 16 assay coins); No Star: 5,000. *Net distribution*—10,016 (both varieties combined).

Original Cost and Issuer. Sale price $3 for either type. Issued by the U.S. Grant Centenary Memorial Commission (mail orders were serviced by Hugh L. Nichols, chairman, Batavia, Ohio).

Key to Collecting. Almost all known specimens are MS–63 to 65 or better. MS–66 and 67 examples are easy to find. Some lower-grade coins show friction on Grant's cheek and hair. Some specimens have dull surfaces; these are avoided by connoisseurs.

First Points of Wear. *Obverse:* Grant's cheekbone and hair. *Reverse:* The leaves of the tree under the U in TRUST.

	Distribution	Cert	Avg	%MS	AU-50	MS-60	MS-62	MS-63	MS-64	MS-65	MS-66
1922, With Star	5,016	1,307	64.8	99%	$1,500	$1,525	$1,575	$1,750	$1,800	$2,100	$2,250
	Auctions: $12,925, MS-68, January 2015; $6,463, MS-67, June 2015; $1,410, MS-64, October 2015; $646, AU-50, May 2015										
1922, No Star	5,016	1,228	64.4	97%	$1,200	$1,325	$1,400	$1,450	$1,650	$2,100	$2,500
	Auctions: $3,760, MS-67, August 2015; $3,055, MS-66, July 2015; $1,586, MS-64, February 2015; $764, MS-60, October 2015										

MONROE DOCTRINE CENTENNIAL HALF DOLLAR (1923)

Designer: *Chester Beach.* **Weight:** *12.50 grams.* **Composition:** *.900 silver, .100 copper (net weight .3617 oz. pure silver).* **Diameter:** *30.6 mm.* **Edge:** *Reeded.* **Mint:** *San Francisco.*

The California film industry promoted this issue in conjunction with a motion-picture exposition held in June 1923. The coin purportedly commemorated the 100th anniversary of the Monroe Doctrine, which warned that European countries that interfered with countries in the Western Hemisphere or established new colonies there would be met with disapproval or worse from the U.S. government.

Designs. *Obverse:* Conjoined bareheaded profile portraits of presidents James Monroe and John Quincy Adams. *Reverse:* Stylized depiction of the continents of North and South America as female figures in the outlines of the two land masses.

Mintage Data. Authorized on January 24, 1923. *Maximum authorized*—300,000. *Number minted*—274,077 (including 77 assay coins). *Net distribution*—274,077.

Original Cost and Issuer. Sale price $1. Issued by the Los Angeles Clearing House, representing backers of the First Annual American Historical Revue and Motion Picture Industry Exposition.

Key to Collecting. Most examples show friction or wear. MS coins are common. Evaluating the numerical grade of MS–60 to 63 coins is difficult because of the design's weak definition. Low-magnification inspection usually shows nicks and graininess at the highest point of the obverse center; these flaws are from the original planchets. Many examples of this coin have been doctored and artificially toned in attempts to earn higher grades upon certification; these are avoided by connoisseurs.

First Points of Wear. *Obverse:* Adams's cheekbone. *Reverse:* The upper figure, underneath the CT in DOCTRINE.

	Distribution	Cert	Avg	%MS	AU-50	MS-60	MS-62	MS-63	MS-64	MS-65	MS-66
1923-S	274,077	3,675	63.1	96%	$50	$80	$100	$120	$225	$975	$2,750
	Auctions: $11,163, MS-67, August 2015; $5,640, MS-66, January 2015; $1,645, MS-65, January 2015; $84, MS-62, July 2015										

HUGUENOT-WALLOON TERCENTENARY HALF DOLLAR (1924)

Designer: *George T. Morgan (with model modifications by James Earle Fraser).*
Weight: *12.50 grams.* **Composition:** *.900 silver, .100 copper (net weight .3617 oz. pure silver).*
Diameter: *30.6 mm.* **Edge:** *Reeded.* **Mint:** *Philadelphia.*

Settling of the Huguenots and Walloons in the New World was the occasion commemorated by this issue. New Netherland, now New York, was founded in 1624 by this group of Dutch colonists. Interestingly, the persons represented on the obverse were not directly concerned with the occasion; both Admiral Gaspard de Coligny and Prince William the Silent were dead long before the settlement.

Designs. *Obverse:* Hat-clad profile portraits representing Admiral Gaspard de Coligny and Prince William the Silent, first stadtholder of the Netherlands. *Reverse:* The ship *Nieuw Nederland* in full sail.

Mintage Data. Authorized on February 26, 1923. *Maximum authorized*—300,000. *Number minted*—142,080 (including 80 assay coins). *Net distribution*—142,080.

Original Cost and Issuer. Sale price $1. Issued by the Huguenot-Walloon New Netherland Commission, Inc., and designated outlets.

Key to Collecting. This coin is readily available on the market, with most examples in MS–60 to 63. Those grading MS–64 and 65 are also found quite often; MS-66 coins are scarcer. Relatively few worn pieces exist. Friction and contact marks are sometimes seen on the cheek of Admiral Coligny on the obverse, and on the masts and ship's rigging on the reverse. Many coins have been cleaned or repeatedly dipped. Connoisseurs avoid deeply toned or stained coins, even those certified with high numerical grades. MS coins usually have satiny (rather than deeply lustrous or frosty) surfaces, and may have a gray appearance. High in the reverse field of most coins is a "bright" spot interrupting the luster, from a touch of polish in the die.

First Points of Wear. *Obverse:* Coligny's cheekbone. *Reverse:* The rim near the F in FOUNDING and over the RY in TERCENTENARY; the lower part of the highest sail; the center of the ship's stern.

	Distribution	Cert	Avg	%MS	AU-50	MS-60	MS-62	MS-63	MS-64	MS-65	MS-66
1924	142,080	3,330	64.2	98%	$125	$130	$140	$160	$175	$240	$650
	Auctions: $15,275, MS-68, August 2015; $6,756, MS-67, September 2015; $100, MS-60, January 2015; $89, AU-58, January 2015										

LEXINGTON-CONCORD SESQUICENTENNIAL HALF DOLLAR (1925)

Designer: *Chester Beach.* **Weight:** *12.50 grams.* **Composition:** *.900 silver, .100 copper (net weight .3617 oz. pure silver).* **Diameter:** *30.6 mm.* **Edge:** *Reeded.* **Mint:** *Philadelphia.*

The Battle of Lexington and Concord—fought in 1775 just one day after Paul Revere's famous ride—is commemorated on this coin. Sculptor James Earle Fraser of the Commission of Fine Arts approved Beach's designs, but protested that the local committees had made a poor choice of subject matter.

Designs. *Obverse:* A view of *The Concord Minute Man of 1775* statue, by Daniel Chester French, located in Concord, Massachusetts. *Reverse:* Lexington's Old Belfry, whose tolling bell roused the Minute Men to action in 1775.

Mintage and Melting Data. Authorized on January 14, 1925. *Maximum authorized*—300,000. *Number minted*—162,099 (including 99 assay coins). *Number melted*—86. *Net distribution*—162,013.

Original Cost and Issuer. Sale price $1. Issued by the U.S. Lexington-Concord Sesquicentennial Commission, through local banks.

Key to Collecting. Examples are easily found in all grades, with most being in high AU or low MS grades, although eye appeal can vary widely. MS-65 coins are scarce in comparison to those in MS–60 through 64. Some specimens are deeply frosty and lustrous, whereas others have partially prooflike fields.

First Points of Wear. *Obverse:* The thighs of the Minuteman. *Reverse:* The top edge of the belfry.

	Distribution	Cert	Avg	%MS	AU-50	MS-60	MS-62	MS-63	MS-64	MS-65	MS-66
1925	162,013	4,173	63.6	97%	$75	$85	$90	$100	$135	$375	$750
	Auctions: $6,463, MS-67, July 2015; $1,645, MS-66, January 2015; $106, MS-63, June 2015; $69, AU-58, October 2015										

STONE MOUNTAIN MEMORIAL HALF DOLLAR (1925)

Designer: *Gutzon Borglum.* **Weight:** *12.50 grams.* **Composition:** *.900 silver, .100 copper (net weight .3617 oz. pure silver).* **Diameter:** *30.6 mm.* **Edge:** *Reeded.* **Mint:** *Philadelphia.*

The first of these half dollars were struck at Philadelphia on January 21, 1925, Confederate general Stonewall Jackson's birthday. Funds received from the sale of this large issue were devoted to the expense of carving figures of Confederate leaders and soldiers on Stone Mountain in Georgia. The coin's designer, Gutzon Borglum, was the original sculptor for that project, but left due to differences with the Stone Mountain Confederate Monumental Association. Augustus Lukeman took over in his stead, and the carving was completed and dedicated in 1970; Borglum would meanwhile go on to create the presidents' heads at Mount Rushmore.

Designs. *Obverse:* Equestrian portraits of Civil War generals Robert E. Lee and Thomas "Stonewall" Jackson. *Reverse:* An eagle perched on a cliff with wings in mid-spread.

Mintage and Melting Data. *Maximum authorized*—5,000,000. *Number minted*—2,314,709 (including 4,709 assay coins). *Number melted*—1,000,000. *Net distribution*—1,314,709.

Original Cost and Issuer. Sale price $1. Issued by the Stone Mountain Confederate Monumental Association through many outlets, including promotions involving pieces counterstamped with abbreviations for Southern states.

Key to Collecting. This is the most plentiful commemorative from the 1920s. Examples are easily found in grades ranging from lightly worn through gem Mint State (many with outstanding eye appeal). Circulated coins are also found, as well as those that were counterstamped for special fundraising sales. The typical coin has very lustrous and frosty surfaces, although the reverse field may be somewhat satiny.

First Points of Wear. *Obverse:* Lee's elbow and leg. *Reverse:* The eagle's breast.

	Distribution	Cert	Avg	%MS	AU-50	MS-60	MS-62	MS-63	MS-64	MS-65	MS-66
1925	1,314,709	8,572	63.9	96%	$55	$65	$70	$80	$135	$185	$350
	Auctions: $3,055, MS-67, January 2015; $564, MS-66, August 2015; $182, MS-64, March 2015; $50, AU-58, September 2015										

CALIFORNIA DIAMOND JUBILEE HALF DOLLAR (1925)

Designer: *Jo Mora.* **Weight:** *12.50 grams.* **Composition:** *.900 silver, .100 copper (net weight .3617 oz. pure silver).* **Diameter:** *30.6 mm.* **Edge:** *Reeded.* **Mint:** *San Francisco.*

The celebration for which these coins were struck marked the 75th anniversary of the admission of California into the Union. Notably, James Earle Fraser of the Commission of Fine Arts criticized Jo Mora's designs at the time. Art historian Cornelius Vermeule, however, called the coin "one of America's greatest works of numismatic art" in his book *Numismatic Art in America*.

Designs. *Obverse:* A rustic miner, squatting to pan for gold. *Reverse:* A grizzly bear, as taken from the California state flag.

Mintage and Melting Data. Authorized on February 24, 1925, part of the act also providing for the 1925 Fort Vancouver and 1927 Vermont half dollars. *Maximum authorized—300,000. Number minted—150,200 (including 200 assay coins). Number melted—63,606. Net distribution—86,594.*

Original Cost and Issuer. Sale price $1. Issued by the San Francisco Citizens' Committee through the San Francisco Clearing House Association and the Los Angeles Clearing House.

Key to Collecting. This coin's design is such that even a small amount of handling produces friction on the shoulder and high parts of the bear, in particular. As a result, most grade in the AU-55 to MS-62 range, and higher-level MS examples are rare. This issue exists in two finishes: frosty/lustrous, and the rarer "chrome-like" or prooflike. The frosty-finish pieces display some lack of die definition of the details. The prooflike pieces have heavily brushed and highly polished dies. Many specimens certified in high grades are toned, sometimes deeply, which can mask evidence of friction. Coins with no traces of friction are rarities.

First Points of Wear. *Obverse:* The folds of the miner's shirt sleeve. *Reverse:* The shoulder of the bear.

	Distribution	Cert	Avg	%MS	AU-50	MS-60	MS-62	MS-63	MS-64	MS-65	MS-66
									PF-63	PF-64	PF-65
1925-S	86,594	4,248	63.9	96%	$185	$200	$205	$210	$375	$450	$875
	Auctions: $12,925, MS-68, January 2015; $4,465, MS-67, September 2015; $165, MS-62, October 2015; $129, AU-55, March 2015										
1925-S, Matte Proof	*1–2*	1	65.0								
	Auctions: No auction records available.										

FORT VANCOUVER CENTENNIAL HALF DOLLAR (1925)

Designer: *Laura Gardin Fraser.* **Weight:** *12.50 grams.* **Composition:** *.900 silver, .100 copper (net weight .3617 oz. pure silver).* **Diameter:** *30.6 mm.* **Edge:** *Reeded.* **Mint:** *San Francisco.*

The sale of these half dollars at $1 each helped to finance the pageant staged for the celebration of the 100th anniversary of the construction of Fort Vancouver. As part of the publicity, pilot Oakley G. Kelly made a round-trip flight from Vancouver to San Francisco and back again to pick up and deliver the entire issue—which weighed 1,462 pounds.

Designs. *Obverse:* Bareheaded profile portrait of Dr. John McLoughlin, who built Fort Vancouver (Washington) on the Columbia River in 1825. *Reverse:* A pioneer in buckskin with a musket in his hands, with Fort Vancouver in the background.

Mintage and Melting Data. Authorized on February 24, 1925. *Maximum authorized*—300,000. *Number minted* (including 28 assay coins)—50,028. *Number melted*—35,034. *Net distribution*—14,994.

Original Cost and Issuer. Sale price $1. The Fort Vancouver Centennial Corporation, Vancouver, Washington.

Key to Collecting. This coin's design is such that even a small amount of handling produced friction on the higher spots. As a result, higher-level MS examples are rare.

First Points of Wear. *Obverse:* McLoughlin's temple area. *Reverse:* The pioneer's right knee.

	Distribution	Cert	Avg	%MS	AU-50	MS-60	MS-62	MS-63	MS-64	MS-65	MS-66
									PF-63	PF-64	PF-65
1925	14,994	2,274	64.0	96%	$300	$340	$350	$375	$450	$625	$975
	Auctions: $4,772, MS-67, September 2015; $2,115, MS-66, September 2015; $212, AU-53, March 2015; $129, EF-40, September 2015										
1925, Matte Proof	2–3	0	n/a								
	Auctions: $188,000, PF-66, April 2015										

SESQUICENTENNIAL OF AMERICAN INDEPENDENCE HALF DOLLAR (1926)

Designer: *John R. Sinnock.* **Weight:** *12.50 grams.* **Composition:** *.900 silver, .100 copper (net weight .3617 oz. pure silver).* **Diameter:** *30.6 mm.* **Edge:** *Reeded.* **Mint:** *Philadelphia.*

The 150th anniversary of the signing of the Declaration of Independence was the occasion for an international fair held in Philadelphia in 1926. To help raise funds for financing the fair, special issues of half dollars (as well as quarter eagles, below) were authorized by Congress. The use of Calvin Coolidge's likeness marked the first time a portrait of a president appeared on a coin struck during his own lifetime.

Designs. *Obverse:* Conjoined profile portraits of bewigged George Washington and bareheaded Calvin Coolidge. *Reverse:* The Liberty Bell.

Mintage and Melting Data. Authorized on March 23, 1925. *Maximum authorized*—1,000,000. *Number minted*—1,000,528 (including 528 assay coins). *Number melted*—859,408. *Net distribution*—141,120.

Original Cost and Issuer. Sale price $1. Issued by the National Sesquicentennial Exhibition Association.

Key to Collecting. Accurate grading can be problematic for this coin. Many examples certified at high grades have mottled or deeply toned surfaces that obfuscate examination, and others have been recolored. Most have graininess—marks from the original planchet—on the highest part of the portrait.

First Points of Wear. *Obverse:* Washington's cheekbone. *Reverse:* The area below the lower inscription on the Liberty Bell.

	Distribution	Cert	Avg	%MS	AU-50	MS-60	MS-62	MS-63	MS-64	MS-65	MS-66
1926	141,120	4,465	63.1	96%	$75	$90	$100	$130	$225	$2,000	$8,000
	Auctions: $5,288, MS-66, July 2015; $1,880, MS-65, January 2015; $112, MS-62, February 2015; $84, AU-55, July 2015										

SESQUICENTENNIAL OF AMERICAN INDEPENDENCE QUARTER EAGLE (1926)

Designer: *John R. Sinnock.* **Weight:** *4.18 grams.* **Composition:** *.900 gold, .100 copper (net weight .12094 oz. pure gold).* **Diameter:** *18 mm.* **Edge:** *Reeded.* **Mint:** *Philadelphia.*

This quarter eagle, along with a related half dollar, was sold to finance the National Sesquicentennial Exposition in Philadelphia (which marked the 150th anniversary of the signing of the Declaration of Independence). Note that though the issuer was known as the National Sesquicentennial *Exhibition* Association, the event was primarily billed with *Exposition* in its name.

Designs. *Obverse:* Miss Liberty standing, holding in one hand a scroll representing the Declaration of Independence and in the other, the Torch of Freedom. *Reverse:* A front view of Independence Hall in Philadelphia.

Mintage and Melting Data. Authorized on March 23, 1925. *Maximum authorized—200,000. Number minted—200,226 (including 226 assay coins). Number melted—154,207. Net distribution—46,019.*

Original Cost and Issuer. Sale price $4. National Sesquicentennial Exhibition Association.

Key to Collecting. Nearly all examples show evidence of handling and contact from careless production at the Mint, and from later indifference by their buyers. Most coins range from AU-55 to MS-62 in grade, and have scattered marks in the fields. MS-65 examples are rare. Well-struck coins are seldom seen. Some pieces show copper stains; connoisseurs avoid these.

First Points of Wear. *Obverse:* The bottom of the scroll held by Liberty. *Reverse:* The area below the top of the tower; and the central portion above the roof.

	Distribution	Cert	Avg	%MS	AU-50	MS-60	MS-62	MS-63	MS-64	MS-65	MS-66
									PF-63	PF-64	PF-65
1926	46,019	7,544	63.0	93%	$410	$465	$525	$625	$875	$2,350	$6,750
	Auctions: $25,850, MS-67, January 2015; $6,463, MS-66, January 2015; $494, MS-62, January 2015; $282, AU-55, September 2015										
1926, Matte Proof (a)	*unique*	1	65.0								
	Auctions: No auction records available.										

a. "The coin is unique and displays a matte surface similar to the Proof gold coins of 1908 to 1915. The coin was reportedly from the estate of the designer, John R. Sinnock, who is best known for his Roosevelt dime and Franklin half dollar designs. The piece was in the possession of coin dealer David Bullowa in the 1950s. Another example is rumored by Breen, but the whereabouts or existence of the coin is unknown" (*Encyclopedia of U.S. Gold Coins, 1795–1933*, second edition).

OREGON TRAIL MEMORIAL HALF DOLLAR (1926–1939)

Designers: *James Earle Fraser and Laura Gardin Fraser.* **Weight:** *12.50 grams.*
Composition: *.900 silver, .100 copper (net weight .3617 oz. pure silver).*
Diameter: *30.6 mm.* **Edge:** *Reeded.* **Mints:** *Philadelphia, San Francisco, and Denver.*

These coins—the longest-running series of commemoratives—were struck in commemoration of the Oregon Trail and in memory of the pioneers, many of whom lie buried along the famous 2,000-mile highway of history. This was the first commemorative to be struck at more than one Mint facility, and also the first commemorative to be struck at the Denver Mint.

Designs. *Obverse:* A pioneer family in a Conestoga wagon, heading west into the sunset. *Reverse:* A standing Indian with a bow, arm outstretched, and a map of the United States in the background.

Mintage and Melting Data. *Maximum authorized*—6,000,000 (for the entire series from 1926 onward). *Number minted*—1926: 48,030 (including 30 assay coins); 1926-S: 100,055 (including 55 assay coins); 1928: 50,028 (including 28 assay coins); 1933-D: 5,250 (including an unrecorded number of assay coins); 1934-D: 7,006 (including 6 assay coins); 1936: 10,006 (including 6 assay coins); 1936-S: 5,006 (including 6 assay coins); 1937-D: 12,008 (including 8 assay coins); 1938-P: 6,006 (including 6 assay coins); 1938-D: 6,005 (including 5 assay coins); 1938-S: 6,006 (including 6 assay coins). *Number melted*—1926: 75 (defective coins); 1926-S: 17,000; 1928: 44,000; 1933-D: 242 (probably defective coins). *Net distribution*—1926: 47,955; 1926-S: 83,055; 1928: 6,028; 1933-D: 5,008; 1934-D: 7,006; 1936: 10,006; 1936-S: 5,006; 1937-D: 12,008; 1938-P: 6,006; 1938-D: 6,005; 1938-S: 6,006.

Original Cost and Issuer. Sale price $1; later raised. Issued by the Oregon Trail Memorial Association, Inc.; some sold through Scott Stamp & Coin Co., Inc., and some sold through Whitman Centennial, Inc., Walla Walla, Washington. From 1937 onward, distributed solely by the Oregon Trail Memorial Association, Inc.

Key to Collecting. Although most of the later issues have low mintages, they are not rare in the marketplace, because the majority were originally sold to coin collectors and dealers. As a result, most surviving coins are in MS. The quality of the surface finish varies, with earlier issues tending to be frosty and lustrous and later issues (particularly those dated 1938 and 1939) having somewhat grainy or satiny fields. Grading requires care. Look for friction or contact marks on the high points of the Indian and the Conestoga wagon, but, more importantly, check both surfaces carefully for scattered cuts and marks. All three mints had difficulty in striking up the rims properly, causing many rejections. Those deemed acceptable and shipped out usually had full rims, but it is best to check when buying.

First Points of Wear. *Obverse:* The hip of the ox, and high points of the wagon (note that the top rear of the wagon was weakly struck in some years). *Reverse:* The Indian's left thumb and fingers (note that some pieces show flatness on the thumb and first finger, due to a weak strike).

	Distribution	Cert	Avg	%MS	AU-50	MS-60	MS-62	MS-63	MS-64 PF-63	MS-65 PF-64	MS-66 PF-65
1926	47,955	2,188	64.4	98%	$135	$160	$170	$190	$210	$250	$325
	Auctions: $999, MS-67, June 2015; $412, MS-66, November 2015; $235, MS-63, May 2015; $112, MS-61, February 2015										
1926, Matte Proof	1–2	1	65.0								
	Auctions: No auction records available.										
1926-S	83,055	3,048	64.6	97%	$135	$160	$170	$190	$210	$260	$350
	Auctions: $14,100, MS-68, January 2015; $1,998, MS-67, January 2015; $247, MS-65, June 2015; $129, MS-60, May 2015										
1928 (same as 1926)	6,028	1,311	65.3	100%	$160	$180	$185	$200	$240	$300	$435
	Auctions: $1,410, MS-67, September 2015; $400, MS-66, September 2015; $306, MS-65, February 2015; $223, MS-64, January 2015										
1933-D	5,008	1,037	65.0	100%	$350	$365	$375	$390	$400	$450	$575
	Auctions: $1,880, MS-67, June 2015; $564, MS-66, January 2015; $329, MS-65, August 2015; $329, MS-64, May 2015										
1934-D	7,006	1,337	64.8	100%	$190	$200	$205	$210	$215	$300	$450
	Auctions: $1,175, MS-67, September 2015; $376, MS-66, August 2015; $212, MS-65, August 2015; $188, MS-63, October 2015										
1936	10,006	1,606	65.3	100%	$160	$180	$190	$200	$220	$260	$280
	Auctions: $11,163, MS-68, September 2015; $1,293, MS-67, July 2015; $341, MS-66, February 2015; $200, MS-64, February 2015										
1936-S	5,006	1,138	65.5	100%	$170	$180	$190	$200	$225	$260	$335
	Auctions: $1,763, MS-68, November 2014; $10,575, MS-68, January 2013; $670, MS-67+, October 2014; $425, MS-67, November 2014										
1937-D	12,008	2,356	65.9	100%	$165	$180	$185	$195	$225	$250	$315
	Auctions: $4,935, MS-68, January 2015; $1,116, MS-67, September 2015; $353, MS-66, February 2015; $200, MS-64, February 2015										
1938 (same as 1926)	6,006	1,250	65.4	100%	$180	$190	$195	$200	$225	$265	$360
	Auctions: $1,410, MS-67, January 2015; $306, MS-66, June 2015; $259, MS-65, February 2015; $153, MS-63, May 2015										
1938-D	6,005	1,427	65.8	100%	$180	$190	$195	$200	$225	$275	$340
	Auctions: $5,405, MS-68, January 2015; $764, MS-67, August 2015; $306, MS-66, October 2015; $129, MS-63, May 2015										
1938-S	6,006	1,286	65.5	100%	$180	$190	$195	$200	$225	$300	$340
	Auctions: $6,933, MS-68, March 2015; $1,293, MS-67, January 2015; $306, MS-66, January 2015; $182, MS-64, September 2015										
Set of 1938 P-D-S					$550	$575	$585	$600	$675	$850	$1,050
	Auctions: $2,070, MS-67/67/67, February 2012; $617, MS-64/64/64, March 2015										
1939	3,004	769	65.5	100%	$450	$480	$500	$515	$535	$600	$650
	Auctions: $2,350, MS-67, January 2015; $823, MS-66, January 2015; $564, MS-65, January 2015; $494, MS-64, October 2015										
1939-D	3,004	796	65.8	100%	$450	$480	$500	$515	$535	$575	$600
	Auctions: $9,400, MS-68, January 2015; $1,880, MS-67, January 2015; $541, MS-65, January 2015; $353, AU-50, September 2015										
1939-S	3,005	788	65.5	100%	$450	$480	$500	$515	$535	$600	$650
	Auctions: $4,230, MS-68, January 2015; $1,410, MS-67, August 2015; $881, MS-66, January 2015; $588, MS-64, October 2015										
Set of 1939 P-D-S					$1,350	$1,450	$1,500	$1,550	$1,625	$1,800	$1,900
	Auctions: $5,175, MS-67/67/67, January 2012; $1,528, MS-65/65/65, March 2015										

VERMONT SESQUICENTENNIAL HALF DOLLAR (1927)

Designer: *Charles Keck.* **Weight:** *12.50 grams.* **Composition:** *.900 silver, .100 copper (net weight .3617 oz. pure silver).* **Diameter:** *30.6 mm.* **Edge:** *Reeded.* **Mint:** *Philadelphia.*

This souvenir issue commemorates the 150th anniversary of the Battle of Bennington and the independence of Vermont. Authorized in 1925, it was not coined until 1927. The Vermont Sesquicentennial Commission intended that funds derived would benefit the study of history.

Designs. *Obverse:* Profile portrait of a bewigged Ira Allen. *Reverse:* A catamount walking left.

Mintage and Melting Data. Authorized by the Act of February 24, 1925. *Maximum authorized*—40,000. *Number minted*—40,034 (including 34 assay coins). *Number melted*—11,892. *Net distribution*—28,142.

Original Cost and Issuer. Sale price $1. Issued by the Vermont Sesquicentennial Commission (Bennington Battle Monument and Historical Association).

Key to Collecting. The Vermont half dollar was struck with the highest relief of any commemorative issue to that date. Despite the depth of the work in the dies, nearly all of the coins were struck up properly and show excellent detail. Unfortunately, the height of the obverse portrait encourages evidence of contact at the central points, and nearly all coins show some friction on Allen's cheek. Most are in grades of MS–62 to 64 and are deeply lustrous and frosty. Cleaned examples are often seen—and are avoided by connoisseurs.

First Points of Wear. *Obverse:* Allen's cheek, and the hair above his ear and in the temple area. *Reverse:* The catamount's upper shoulder.

	Distribution	Cert	Avg	%MS	AU-50	MS-60	MS-62	MS-63	MS-64	MS-65	MS-66
1927	28,142	3,120	63.9	97%	$250	$265	$270	$275	$325	$460	$750

Auctions: $3,290, MS-67, August 2015; $1,293, MS-66, January 2015; $282, MS-64, February 2015; $176, AU-53, January 2015

HAWAIIAN SESQUICENTENNIAL HALF DOLLAR (1928)

Designer: *Juliette M. Fraser.* **Weight:** *12.50 grams.* **Composition:** *.900 silver, .100 copper (net weight .3617 oz. pure silver).* **Diameter:** *30.6 mm.* **Edge:** *Reeded.* **Mint:** *Philadelphia.*

This issue was struck to commemorate the 150th anniversary of the arrival on the Hawaiian Islands of Captain James Cook in 1778. The coin's $2 price was the highest ever for a commemorative half dollar up to that point.

Designs. *Obverse:* Portrait of Captain James Cook. *Reverse:* A Hawaiian chieftain standing with arm outstretched and holding a spear.

Mintage Data. Authorized on March 7, 1928. *Maximum authorized*—10,000. *Number minted*—10,008 (including 8 assay coins and 50 Sandblast Proofs). *Net distribution*—10,008.

Original Cost and Issuer. Sale price $2. Issued by the Captain Cook Sesquicentennial Commission, through the Bank of Hawaii, Ltd.

Key to Collecting. This is the scarcest of classic U.S. commemorative coins. It is elusive in all grades, and highly prized. Most are AU-55 to MS-62 or slightly finer; those grading MS-65 or above are especially difficult to find. Most examples show contact or friction on the higher design areas. Some coins have a somewhat satiny surface, whereas others are lustrous and frosty. Many undipped pieces have a yellowish tint. Beware of coins which have been repeatedly dipped or cleaned. Problem-free examples are rarer even than the low mintage would suggest. Fake "Sandblast Proofs" exist; these are coins dipped in acid.

First Points of Wear. *Obverse:* Cook's cheekbone. *Reverse:* The chieftain's legs; his fingers and the hand holding the spear.

	Distribution	Cert	Avg	%MS	AU-50	MS-60	MS-62	MS-63	MS-64	MS-65	MS-66
									PF-63	PF-64	PF-65
1928	10,008	1,694	63.7	98%	$1,800	$2,100	$2,200	$2,475	$2,875	$3,750	$6,350
	Auctions: $17,625, MS-67, August 2015; $9,988, MS-66, January 2015; $4,230, MS-65, January 2015; $1,410, MS-60, June 2015										
1928, Proof (a)	*50*	27	64.1						$20,000	$30,000	$50,000
	Auctions: $25,300, PF-64, August 2004; $33,350, PF-64, January 2012; $21,850, PF-64, February 2000; $13,225, PF-63, January 2004										

a. Sandblast Proof presentation pieces. "Of the production figure, 50 were Sandblast Proofs, made by a special process which imparted a dull, grainy finish to the pieces, similar to that used on certain Mint medals of the era as well as on gold Proof coins circa 1908–1915" (*Guide Book of United States Commemorative Coins*).

MARYLAND TERCENTENARY HALF DOLLAR (1934)

Designer: *Hans Schuler*. **Weight:** *12.50 grams*. **Composition:** *.900 silver, .100 copper (net weight .3617 oz. pure silver)*. **Diameter:** *30.6 mm*. **Edge:** *Reeded*. **Mint:** *Philadelphia*.

The 300th anniversary of the founding of the Maryland Colony by Cecil Calvert (known as Lord Baltimore) was the occasion for this special coin. The profits from the sale of this issue were used to finance the celebration in Baltimore during 1934. John Work Garrett, distinguished American diplomat and well-known numismatist, was among the citizens of Maryland who endorsed the commemorative half dollar proposal on behalf of the Maryland Tercentenary Commission of Baltimore.

Designs. *Obverse:* Three-quarter portrait of Cecil Calvert, Lord Baltimore. *Reverse:* The state seal and motto of Maryland.

Mintage Data. Authorized on May 9, 1934. *Maximum authorized—25,000. Number minted—25,015* (including 15 assay coins). *Net distribution—25,015.*

Original Cost and Issuer. Sale price $1. Issued by the Maryland Tercentenary Commission, through various outlets.

Key to Collecting. The coin's field has an unusual "rippled" appearance, similar to a sculptured plaque, so nicks and other marks that would be visible on a coin with flat fields are not as readily noticed. Most examples grade MS–62 to 64. Finer pieces, strictly graded, are elusive. This issue was not handled with care at the time of mintage and distribution, and nearly all show scattered contact marks. Some exist struck from a reverse die broken from the right side of the shield to a point opposite the upper right of the 4 in the date 1634.

First Points of Wear. *Obverse:* Lord Baltimore's nose (the nose usually appears flatly struck; also check the reverse for wear). *Reverse:* The top of the coronet on top of the shield, and the tops of the draperies.

	Distribution	Cert	Avg	%MS	AU-50	MS-60	MS-62	MS-63	MS-64	MS-65	MS-66
									PF-63	PF-64	PF-65
1934	25,015	3,466	64.7	100%	$130	$140	$150	$165	$175	$210	$325
	Auctions: $2,115, MS-67, January 2015; $447, MS-66, August 2015; $212, MS-65, January 2015; $119, MS-60, February 2015										
1934, Matte Proof	*2–4*	2	63.0								
	Auctions: $109,250, PF-64, March 2012										

TEXAS INDEPENDENCE CENTENNIAL HALF DOLLAR (1934–1938)

Designer: *Pompeo Coppini.* **Weight:** *12.50 grams.*
Composition: *.900 silver, .100 copper (net weight .3617 oz. pure silver).*
Diameter: *30.6 mm.* **Edge:** *Reeded.* **Mints:** *Philadelphia, Denver, and San Francisco.*

This issue commemorated the independence of Texas in 1836. Proceeds from the sale of the coin were intended to finance the Centennial Exposition, which was eventually held in Dallas. Sales were lower than expected, but the event was still held and attracted about 7 million visitors.

Designs. *Obverse:* A perched eagle with a large five-pointed star in the background. *Reverse:* The goddess Victory kneeling, with medallions and portraits of General Sam Houston and Stephen Austin, founders of the republic and state of Texas, along with other Texan icons.

Mintage and Melting Data. Authorized on June 15, 1933. *Maximum authorized*—1,500,000 (for the entire series 1934 onward). 1934: *Number minted*—1934: 205,113 (including 113 assay coins); 1935-P: 10,008 (including 8 assay coins); 1935-D: 10,007 (including 7 assay coins); 1935-S: 10,008 (including 8 assay coins); 1936-P: 10,008 (including 8 assay coins); 1936-D: 10,007 (including 7 assay coins); 1936-S: 10,008 (including 8 assay coins); 1937-P: 8,005 (including 5 assay coins); 1937-D: 8,006 (including 6 assay coins); 1937-S: 8,007 (including 7 assay coins); 1938-P: 5,005 (including 5 assay coins); 1938-D: 5,005 (including 5 assay coins); 1938-S: 5,006 (including 6 assay coins). *Number melted*—1934: 143,650; 1935-P: 12 (probably defective coins); 1936-P: 12 (probably defective coins); 1937-P: 1,434; 1937-D: 1,401; 1937-S: 1,370; 1938-P: 1,225; 1938-D: 1,230; 1938-S: 1,192. *Net distribution*—1934: 61,463; 1935-P: 9,996; 1935-D: 10,007; 1935-S: 10,008; 1936-P: 9,996; 1936-D: 10,007; 1936-S: 10,008; 1937-P: 6,571; 1937-D: 6,605; 1937-S: 6,637; 1938-P: 3,780; 1938-D: 3,775; 1938-S: 3,814.

Original Cost and Issuer. Sale price $1; later raised. Issued by the American Legion Texas Centennial Committee, Austin, Texas, from 1934 through 1936; issued by the Texas Memorial Museum Centennial Coin Campaign in 1937 and 1938.

Key to Collecting. The typical example grades MS–64 or 65. Early issues are very lustrous and frosty; those produced toward the end of the series are more satiny.

First Points of Wear. *Obverse:* The eagle's upper breast and upper leg. *Reverse:* The forehead and knee of Victory.

	Distribution	Cert	Avg	%MS	AU-50	MS-60	MS-62	MS-63	MS-64	MS-65	MS-66
1934	61,463	2,537	64.5	98%	$130	$140	$145	$150	$165	$175	$300
Auctions: $1,293, MS-67, July 2015; $306, MS-66, January 2015; $129, MS-64, September 2015; $100, MS-60, June 2015											
1935 (same as 1934)	9,996	1,590	65.6	100%	$130	$140	$145	$150	$160	$175	$290
Auctions: $3,525, MS-68, January 2015; $1,998, MS-67, August 2015; $188, MS-65, September 2015; $106, MS-60, May 2015											
1935-D	10,007	1,607	65.5	100%	$130	$140	$145	$150	$160	$175	$290
Auctions: $3,290, MS-68, September 2015; $1,410, MS-67, June 2015; $235, MS-66, May 2015; $153, MS-60, May 2015											
1935-S	10,008	1,356	65.2	100%	$130	$140	$145	$150	$160	$175	$290
Auctions: $705, MS-67, January 2015; $259, MS-66, May 2015; $212, MS-65, August 2015; $129, MS-63, October 2015											
Set of 1935 P-D-S					$400	$425	$450	$465	$500	$600	$1,075
Auctions: $940, MS-67/67/67, March 2015; $871, MS-66/66/66, December 2011; $470, MS-65/65/65, April 2015											

	Distribution	Cert	Avg	%MS	AU-50	MS-60	MS-62	MS-63	MS-64	MS-65	MS-66
1936 (same as 1934)	8,911	1,453	65.4	100%	$145	$150	$155	$165	$180	$225	$290
	Auctions: $14,100, MS-68, July 2015; $823, MS-67, June 2015; $382, MS-66, January 2015; $141, MS-64, January 2015									
1936-D	9,039	1,650	65.7	100%	$145	$150	$160	$180	$190	$240	$300
	Auctions: $2,820, MS-68, July 2015; $705, MS-67, August 2015; $329, MS-66, March 2015; $123, MS-64, May 2015									
1936-S	9,055	1,349	65.3	100%	$145	$150	$160	$180	$190	$240	$275
	Auctions: $1,058, MS-67, October 2015; $282, MS-66, September 2015; $176, MS-65, September 2015; $123, MS-64, March 2015									
Set of 1936 P-D-S					$435	$450	$475	$525	$575	$725	$875
	Auctions: $863, MS-66/66/66, December 2011; $705, MS-65/65/65, March 2015									
1937 (same as 1934)	6,571	1,184	65.2	100%	$140	$150	$160	$165	$175	$200	$300
	Auctions: $12,925, MS-68, August 2015; $2,585, MS-67, August 2015; $200, MS-65, April 2015; $147, MS-63, October 2015									
1937-D	6,605	1,238	65.4	100%	$140	$150	$160	$165	$175	$200	$300
	Auctions: $3,760, MS-68, January 2015; $1,175, MS-67, September 2015; $129, MS-62, October 2015; $89, MS-60, January 2015									
1937-S	6,637	1,250	65.3	100%	$140	$150	$160	$165	$175	$200	$300
	Auctions: $1,880, MS-67, February 2015; $329, MS-66, February 2015; $259, MS-66, September 2015; $200, MS-65, October 2015									
Set of 1937 P-D-S					$610	$650	$700	$775	$865	$1,000	$1,500
	Auctions: $625, MS-66/66/66, April 2012; $617, MS-66/66/66, March 2015; $541, MS-65/65/65, September 2015									
1938 (same as 1934)	3,780	847	65.1	100%	$300	$325	$335	$375	$415	$500	$750
	Auctions: $1,645, MS-67, January 2015; $823, MS-66, January 2015; $400, MS-65, July 2015; $176, MS-63, October 2015									
1938-D	3,775	887	65.4	100%	$300	$325	$335	$375	$415	$500	$750
	Auctions: $1,880, MS-67, August 2015; $447, MS-66, January 2015; $447, MS-66, January 2015; $294, MS-64, October 2015									
1938-S	3,814	881	65.3	100%	$300	$325	$335	$375	$385	$485	$850
	Auctions: $2,233, MS-67, January 2015; $646, MS-66, January 2015; $329, MS-65, October 2015; $176, MS-63, October 2015									
Set of 1938 P-D-S					$900	$975	$1,025	$1,125	$1,200	$1,475	$2,150
	Auctions: $604, MS-64/65/64, June 2012									

DANIEL BOONE BICENTENNIAL HALF DOLLAR (1934–1938)

Designer: *Augustus Lukeman.* **Weight:** *12.50 grams.*
Composition: *.900 silver, .100 copper (net weight .3617 oz. pure silver).*
Diameter: *30.6 mm.* **Edge:** *Reeded.* **Mints:** *Philadelphia, Denver, and San Francisco.*

This coin type, which was minted for five years, was first struck in 1934 to commemorate the 200th anniversary of the birth of Daniel Boone, famous frontiersman, trapper, and explorer. Coinage covered several years, similar to the schedule for the Texas issues; 1934 coins are the only examples with true bicentennial status.

Designs. *Obverse:* Artist's conception of Daniel Boone in a profile portrait. *Reverse:* Standing figures of Boone and Blackfish, war chief of the Chillicothe band of the Shawnee tribe. (In 1935 the date 1934 was added to the reverse design.)

Mintage and Melting Data. Authorized on May 26, 1934 and, with "1934" added to modify the design, on August 26, 1935. *Maximum authorized*—600,000 (for the entire series from 1934 onward). *Number minted*—1934: 10,007 (including 7 assay coins); 1935-P: 10,010 (including 10 assay coins); 1935-D: 5,005 (including 5 assay coins); 1935-S: 5,005 (including 5 assay coins); 1935-P, "Small 1934": 10,008 (including 8 assay coins); 1935-D, "Small 1934": 2,003; 1935-S, "Small 1934": 2,004; 1936-P: 12,012 (including 12 assay coins); 1936-D: 5,005 (including 5 assay coins); 1936-S: 5,006 (including 6 assay coins); 1937-P: 15,010 (including 10 assay coins); 1937-D: 7,506 (including 6 assay coins); 1937-S: 5,006 (including 6 assay coins); 1938-P: 5,005 (including 5 assay coins); 1938-D: 5,005 (including 5 assay coins); 1938-S: 5,006 (including 6 assay coins). *Number melted*—1937-P: 5,200; 1937-D: 5,000; 1937-S: 2,500; 1938-P: 2,905; 1938-D: 2,905; 1938-S: 2,906. *Net distribution*—1934: 10,007; 1935-P: 10,010; 1935-D: 5,005; 1935-S: 5,005; 1935-P, "Small 1934": 10,008 (including 8 assay coins); 1935-D, "Small 1934": 2,003; 1935-S, "Small 1934": 2,004; 1936-P: 12,012; 1936-D: 5,005; 1936-S: 5,006; 1937-P: 9,810; 1937-D: 2,506; 1937-S: 2,506; 1938-P: 2,100; 1938-D: 2,100; 1938-S: 2,100.

Original Cost and Issuer. Sale prices varied by mintmark, from a low of $1.10 per 1935-P coin to a high of $5.15 per 1937-S coin. Issued by Daniel Boone Bicentennial Commission (and its division, the Pioneer National Monument Association), Phoenix Hotel, Lexington, Kentucky (C. Frank Dunn, "sole distributor").

Key to Collecting. Most collectors desire just a single coin to represent the type, but there are enough specialists who want one of each date and mintmark to ensure a ready market whenever the scarcer sets come up for sale. Most surviving coins are in MS, with MS–64 to 66 pieces readily available for most issues. Early issues in the series are characterized by deep frosty mint luster, whereas issues toward the end of the run, particularly 1937 and 1938, often are seen with a satin finish and relatively little luster (because of the methods of die preparation and striking). The 1937-S is very often seen with prooflike surfaces, and the 1938-S occasionally so. In general, the Boone commemoratives were handled carefully at the time of minting and distribution, but scattered contact marks are often visible.

First Points of Wear. *Obverse:* The hair behind Boone's ear. *Reverse:* The left shoulder of the Indian.

	Distribution	Cert	Avg	%MS	AU-50	MS-60	MS-62	MS-63	MS-64	MS-65	MS-66
1934	10,007	1,050	64.8	100%	$130	$135	$140	$150	$160	$225	$275
Auctions: $1,528, MS-67, January 2015; $569, MS-66, January 2015; $165, MS-65, September 2015; $94, MS-60, January 2015											
1935	10,010	1,201	64.7	100%	$130	$135	$140	$150	$175	$200	$250
Auctions: $1,175, MS-67, January 2015; $200, MS-66, January 2015; $176, MS-65, January 2015; $94, MS-62, February 2015											
1935-D	5,005	676	64.6	100%	$130	$135	$140	$150	$200	$225	$350
Auctions: $2,115, MS-67, January 2015; $201, MS-65, October 2015; $175, MS-65, March 2015; $153, MS-64, January 2015											
1935-S	5,005	848	65.0	100%	$130	$135	$140	$150	$175	$200	$275
Auctions: $1,116, MS-67, October 2015; $376, MS-66, January 2015; $176, MS-65, February 2015; $106, MS-60, July 2015											
Set of 1935 P-D-S					$405	$420	$450	$450		$625	$875
Auctions: $380, MS-64/64/64, December 2011											
1935, With Small 1934	10,008	1,319	64.9	100%	$130	$140	$145	$150	$160	$180	$290
Auctions: $1,528, MS-67, July 2015; $282, MS-66, January 2015; $188, MS-65, April 2015; $106, MS-60, May 2015											
1935-D, Same type	2,003	505	65.2	100%	$250	$265	$275	$325	$425	$775	$875
Auctions: $6,463, MS-68, January 2015; $881, MS-66, January 2015; $646, MS-65, January 2015; $306, MS-64, January 2015											
1935-S, Same type	2,004	492	64.8	100%	$250	$265	$275	$325	$425	$650	$875
Auctions: $4,230, MS-67, January 2015; $1,528, MS-66, September 2015; $541, MS-65, January 2015; $248, MS-64, April 2015											
Set of 1935 P-D-S, With Added Date					$650	$675	$700	$800	$1,025	$1,625	$2,050
Auctions: $925, MS-65/63/64, May 2012											
1936	12,012	1,507	64.8	100%	$130	$135	$140	$150	$170	$215	$325
Auctions: $7,050, MS-68, October 2015; $940, MS-67, January 2015; $306, MS-66, January 2015; $100, MS-63, February 2015											
1936-D	5,005	850	65.0	100%	$130	$135	$140	$150	$170	$215	$275
Auctions: $1,293, MS-67, June 2015; $235, MS-66, September 2015; $188, MS-65, July 2015; $100, MS-63, February 2015											
1936-S	5,006	895	65.1	100%	$130	$135	$140	$150	$170	$215	$275
Auctions: $11,163, MS-68, January 2015; $705, MS-67, August 2015; $353, MS-66, September 2015; $102, MS-63, August 2015											
Set of 1936 P-D-S					$400	$415	$425	$450	$525	$650	$875
Auctions: $920, MS-66/66/66 Plus, November 2011											

	Distribution	Cert	Avg	%MS	AU-50	MS-60	MS-62	MS-63	MS-64	MS-65	MS-66
1937	9,810	1,391	64.9	100%	$130	$135	$140	$150	$170	$215	$360
Auctions: $2,585, MS-67, October 2015; $376, MS-66, March 2015; $200, MS-65, February 2015; $100, MS-60, September 2015											
1937-D	2,506	556	64.9	100%	$130	$135	$140	$150	$170	$215	$335
Auctions: $1,528, MS-67, October 2015; $376, MS-66, April 2015; $294, MS-65, January 2015; $212, MS-64, January 2015											
1937-S	2,506	677	65.0	100%	$130	$135	$140	$150	$170	$215	$275
Auctions: $1,645, MS-67, January 2015; $470, MS-66, May 2015; $353, MS-65, January 2015; $118, MS-63, August 2015											
Set of 1937 P-D-S					$400	$410	$425	$450	$525	$650	$1,000
Auctions: $564, MS-66/65/64, November 2011											
1938	2,100	462	64.8	100%	$220	$230	$240	$250	$275	$450	$600
Auctions: $2,585, MS-67, July 2015; $946, MS-66, January 2015; $306, MS-65, September 2015; $236, MS-63, February 2015											
1938-D	2,100	490	65.1	100%	$220	$230	$240	$250	$275	$425	$650
Auctions: $7,050, MS-67, January 2015; $823, MS-66, January 2015; $423, MS-65, February 2015; $259, MS-63, February 2015											
1938-S	2,100	492	64.9	100%	$220	$230	$240	$250	$275	$425	$600
Auctions: $1,410, MS-67, August 2015; $1,087, MS-66, January 2015; $235, MS-63, July 2015; $188, AU-50, November 2015											
Set of 1938 P-D-S					$675	$700	$725	$750	$825	$1,300	$1,850
Auctions: $4,312, MS-66/66/65, September 2011											

CONNECTICUT TERCENTENARY HALF DOLLAR (1935)

Designer: *Henry Kreis.* **Weight:** *12.50 grams.* **Composition:** *.900 silver, .100 copper (net weight .3617 oz. pure silver).* **Diameter:** *30.6 mm.* **Edge:** *Reeded.* **Mint:** *Philadelphia.*

In commemoration of the 300th anniversary of the founding of the colony of Connecticut, a souvenir half dollar was struck. According to legend, the Royal Charter of the colony was secreted in the Charter Tree (seen on the coin's reverse) during the reign of King James II, who wished to revoke it. The charter was produced after the king's overthrow in 1688, and the colony continued under its protection.

Designs. *Obverse:* A modernistic eagle, standing. *Reverse:* The Charter Oak.

Mintage Data. Authorized on June 21, 1934. *Maximum authorized—25,000. Number minted—25,018* (including 18 assay coins). *Net distribution—25,018.*

Original Cost and Issuer. Sale price $1. Issued by the Connecticut Tercentenary Commission.

Key to Collecting. Most examples survive in upper AU and lower MS grades. Higher-grade coins such as MS-65 are elusive. Friction and/or marks are often obvious on the broad expanse of wing on the obverse, and, in particular, at the ground or baseline of the oak tree on the reverse. Examples that are otherwise lustrous, frosty, and very attractive, often have friction on the wing.

First Points of Wear. *Obverse:* The top of the eagle's wing. *Reverse:* The ground above ON and TI in CONNECTICUT.

	Distribution	Cert	Avg	%MS	AU-50	MS-60	MS-62	MS-63	MS-64 / PF-63	MS-65 / PF-64	MS-66 / PF-65
1935	25,018	3,503	64.5	99%	$215	$220	$225	$235	$250	$415	$550
Auctions: $2,350, MS-67, January 2015; $823, MS-66, October 2015; $376, MS-65, January 2015; $188, MS-60, July 2015											
1935, Matte Proof	*1–2*	1	65.0								
Auctions: No auction records available.											

ARKANSAS CENTENNIAL HALF DOLLAR (1935–1939)

Designer: *Edward E. Burr.* **Weight:** *12.50 grams.*
Composition: *.900 silver, .100 copper (net weight .3617 oz. pure silver).*
Diameter: *30.6 mm.* **Edge:** *Reeded.* **Mints:** *Philadelphia, Denver, and San Francisco.*

This souvenir issue marked the 100th anniversary of the admission of Arkansas into the Union. The 1936 through 1939 issues were the same as those of 1935 except for the dates. The coin's four-year lifespan was intended to maximize profits, and sluggish sales contributed to the crash of the commemorative market and subsequent suspension of commemorative coinage in 1939.

Designs. *Obverse:* An eagle with outstretched wings, stars, and other elements of the Arkansas state seal. *Reverse:* Portraits of a Liberty in a Phrygian cap and an Indian chief of 1836.

Mintage and Melting Data. Authorized on May 14, 1934. *Maximum authorized*—500,000 (for the entire series from 1935 onward). *Number minted* (including 5, 5, and 6 assay coins)—1935-P: 13,012 (including 5 assay coins); 1935-D: 5,505 (including 5 assay coins); 1935-S: 5,506 (including 6 assay coins); 1936-P: 10,010 (including 10 assay coins); 1936-D: 10,010 (including 10 assay coins); 1936-S: 10,012 (including 12 assay coins); 1937-P: 5,505 (including 5 assay coins); 1937-D: 5,505 (including 5 assay coins); 1937-S: 5,506 (including 6 assay coins); 1938-P: 6,006 (including 6 assay coins); 1938-D: 6,005 (including 5 assay coins); 1938-S: 6,006 (including 6 assay coins); 1939-P: 2,140 (including 4 assay coins); 1939-D: 2,104 (including 4 assay coins); 1939-S: 2,105 (including 5 assay coins). *Number melted*—1936-P: 350; 1936-D: 350; 1936-S: 350; 1938-P: 2,850; 1938-D: 2,850; 1938-S: 2,850. *Net distribution*—1935-P: 13,012; 1935-D: 5,505; 1935-S: 5,506; 1936-P: 9,660; 1936-D: 9,660; 1936-S: 9,662; 1937-P: 5,505; 1937-D: 5,505; 1937-S: 5,506; 1938-P: 3,156; 1938-D: 3,155; 1938-S: 3,156; 1939-P: 2,104; 1939-D: 2,104; 1939-S: 2,105.

Original Cost and Issuer. Sale prices varied by mintmark, from a low of $1 per coin to $12 for a set of three. Issued by the Arkansas Centennial Commission in 1935, 1936, 1938, and 1939 (note that dealer B. Max Mehl bought quantities and retailed them at higher prices in 1935). Issued by Stack's of New York City in 1937.

Key to Collecting. The coin sets were produced with a satiny, almost "greasy" finish; even freshly minted coins appeared as if they had been dipped or repeatedly cleaned. Issues of 1937 to 1939 are usually more satisfactory but still are not deeply lustrous. The prominence of the girl's portrait on the center of the obverse renders that part of the coin prone to receiving bagmarks, scuffs, and other evidence of handling. As a result, relatively few pieces have great eye appeal. The obverse area where the ribbon crosses the eagle's breast is often very weak. Some examples are lightly struck on the eagle just behind its head.

First Points of Wear. *Obverse:* The eagle's head and the top of the left wing. *Reverse:* The band of the girl's cap, behind her eye.

	Distribution	Cert	Avg	%MS	AU-50	MS-60	MS-62	MS-63	MS-64	MS-65	MS-66
									PF-63	PF-64	PF-65
1935	13,012	1,167	64.4	100%	$90	$95	$105	$110	$120	$150	$425
Auctions: $1,116, MS-67, September 2014; $1,528, MS-67 Plus, July 2014; $400, MS-66, December 2014; $558, MS-66, October 2014											
1935-D	5,505	849	64.7	100%	$90	$95	$105	$110	$120	$150	$425
Auctions: $1,880, MS-67, January 2015; $400, MS-66, August 2015; $153, MS-65, January 2015; $100, MS-64, September 2015											
1935-S	5,506	857	64.6	100%	$90	$95	$105	$110	$120	$225	$550
Auctions: $1,939, MS-67, January 2015; $705, MS-66, September 2015; $100, MS-64, January 2015; $74, MS-62, February 2015											
Set of 1935 P-D-S					$270	$300	$315	$330	$360	$525	$1,400
Auctions: $322, MS-64/64/64 Plus, April 2012											
1936	9,660	1,011	64.3	100%	$90	$95	$105	$110	$120	$170	$550
Auctions: $1,998, MS-67, September 2015; $1,116, MS-66, July 2015; $120, MS-64, September 2015; $79, MS-60, August 2015											
1936-D	9,660	970	64.5	100%	$90	$95	$105	$110	$120	$175	$575
Auctions: $2,585, MS-67, January 2015; $353, MS-66, January 2015; $259, MS-65, July 2015; $100, MS-63, January 2015											
1936-S	9,662	990	64.4	100%	$90	$95	$105	$110	$120	$225	$775
Auctions: $1,528, MS-67, January 2015; $282, MS-66, September 2015; $153, MS-65, September 2015; $94, MS-63, October 2015											
Set of 1936 P-D-S					$270	$285	$315	$330	$360	$475	$1,900
Auctions: $300, MS-64/64/65, December 2011											
1937	5,505	749	64.3	100%	$110	$115	$120	$125	$130	$175	$485
Auctions: $2,585, MS-67, June 2015; $541, MS-66, January 2015; $129, MS-64, January 2015; $118, MS-63, August 2015											
1937-D	5,505	797	64.5	100%	$110	$115	$120	$125	$130	$165	$550
Auctions: $2,233, MS-67, January 2015; $494, MS-66, January 2015; $165, MS-64, September 2015; $79, MS-63, April 2015											
1937-S	5,506	654	64.2	100%	$110	$115	$120	$125	$130	$365	$825
Auctions: $999, MS-66, September 2015; $940, MS-66, September 2015; $200, MS-65, May 2015; $79, MS-63, January 2015											
Set of 1937 P-D-S					$330	$345	$360	$375	$400	$725	$1,875
Auctions: $600, MS-65/65/65, January 2012											
1938	3,156	535	64.4	100%	$135	$140	$150	$175	$215	$425	$1,075
Auctions: $3,290, MS-67, August 2015; $705, MS-66, January 2015; $306, MS-65, February 2015; $106, MS-63, April 2015											
1938-D	3,155	562	64.4	100%	$135	$145	$145	$150	$215	$275	$775
Auctions: $3,055, MS-67, January 2015; $881, MS-66, January 2015; $259, MS-64, June 2015; $123, MS-63, February 2015											
1938-S	3,156	510	64.3	100%	$140	$145	$150	$160	$215	$365	$950
Auctions: $1,058, MS-66, July 2015; $999, MS-66, September 2015; $282, MS-65, January 2015; $153, MS-64, April 2015											
Set of 1938 P-D-S					$415	$435	$450	$500	$650	$1,075	$2,800
Auctions: $2,900, MS-66/66/66, April 2012; $411, MS-63/63/63, October 2015											
Set of 1938 P-D-S, Matte Proof	1–2										
Auctions: No auction records available.											
1939	2,104	439	64.2	100%	$230	$240	$250	$265	$300	$850	$3,250
Auctions: $1,880, MS-66, June 2015; $1,763, MS-66, July 2015; $610, MS-65, January 2015; $306, MS-64, September 2015											
1939-D	2,104	464	64.4	100%	$230	$240	$250	$265	$300	$775	$1,150
Auctions: $3,995, MS-67, August 2015; $1,146, MS-66, January 2015; $470, MS-65, January 2015; $270, MS-63, March 2015											
1939-S	2,105	502	64.5	100%	$240	$240	$250	$265	$300	$875	$1,325
Auctions: $3,760, MS-67, August 2015; $1,939, MS-66, January 2015; $764, MS-65, January 2015; $294, MS-64, April 2015											
Set of 1939 P-D-S					$700	$725	$750	$800	$900	$2,500	$5,750
Auctions: $1,610, MS-65/65/65, February 2012											

ARKANSAS CENTENNIAL—ROBINSON HALF DOLLAR (1936)

Designers: *Henry Kreis (obverse) and Edward E. Burr (reverse).* **Weight:** *12.50 grams (net weight .3617 oz. pure silver).* **Composition:** *.900 silver, .100 copper.* **Diameter:** *30.6 mm.* **Edge:** *Reeded.* **Mints:** *Philadelphia, Denver, San Francisco.*

A new reverse design for the Arkansas Centennial coin (see preceding coin) was authorized by the Act of June 26, 1936. Senator Joseph T. Robinson was still living at the time his portrait was used. Note that though it is normally true that portraits appear on the obverse of coins, the side bearing Robinson's likeness is indeed technically the reverse of this coin.

Designs. *Obverse:* An eagle with outstretched wings, stars, and other elements of the Arkansas state seal. *Reverse:* Bareheaded profile portrait of Senator Joseph T. Robinson.

Mintage Data. Authorized on June 26, 1936. *Maximum authorized—*50,000 (minimum 25,000). *Number minted—*25,265 (including 15 assay coins). *Net distribution—*25,265.

Original Cost and Issuer. Sale price $1.85. Issued by Stack's of New York City.

Key to Collecting. Most known coins are in MS, as most or all were originally sold to collectors and coin dealers. Examples are plentiful in the marketplace, usually grading MS–62 to 64. The coins were not handled with care during production, so many have contact marks on Robinson's portrait and elsewhere. Some examples are lightly struck on the eagle, just behind the head.

First Points of Wear. *Obverse:* The eagle's head and the top of the left wing. *Reverse:* Robinson's cheekbone.

	Distribution	Cert	Avg	%MS	AU-50	MS-60	MS-62	MS-63	MS-64	MS-65	MS-66
1936	25,265	2,738	64.3	100%	$105	$120	$125	$135	$160	$215	$375
	Auctions: $3,290, MS-67, August 2015; $617, MS-66, January 2015; $212, MS-65, February 2015; $112, MS-63, January 2015										

HUDSON, NEW YORK, SESQUICENTENNIAL HALF DOLLAR (1935)

Designer: *Chester Beach.* **Weight:** *12.50 grams.* **Composition:** *.900 silver, .100 copper (net weight .3617 oz. pure silver).* **Diameter:** *30.6 mm.* **Edge:** *Reeded.* **Mint:** *Philadelphia.*

This souvenir half dollar marked the 150th anniversary of the founding of Hudson, New York, which was named after the explorer Henry Hudson. The area was actually settled in 1662, but not given its permanent name and formally incorporated until 1785. The distribution of these coins was widely criticized, as certain dealers were allowed to purchase large quantities at $1 or less and then resold them at dramatically inflated prices.

Designs. *Obverse:* The ship *Half Moon*, captained by Henry Hudson, in full sail. *Reverse:* The ocean god Neptune seated backward on a whale (derived from the seal of the city of Hudson); in the background, a mermaid blowing a shell.

Mintage Data. Approved May 2, 1935. *Maximum authorized*—10,000. *Number minted*—10,008 (including 8 assay coins). *Net distribution*—10,008.

Original Cost and Issuer. Sale price $1. Issued by the Hudson Sesquicentennial Committee, through the First National Bank & Trust Company of Hudson.

Key to Collecting. Examples are readily available in the marketplace. Note that deep or artificial toning, which can make close inspection impossible, has led some certified coins to certified grades that are higher than they should be. True gems are very rare. These coins were struck at high speed and with little care to preserve their quality; by the time they were originally distributed most pieces showed nicks, contact marks, and other evidence of handling. Most are lustrous and frosty (except on the central devices), and grade in the lower MS levels. MS–62 to 64 are typical. Carefully graded MS-65 coins are scarce, and anything higher is very rare.

First Points of Wear. *Obverse:* The center of the lower middle sail. *Reverse:* The motto on the ribbon, and the figure of Neptune (both of which may also be lightly struck).

	Distribution	Cert	Avg	%MS	AU-50	MS-60	MS-62	MS-63	MS-64	MS-65	MS-66
1935	10,008	1,995	64.1	98%	$700	$725	$765	$825	$900	$1,150	$1,500
	Auctions: $8,519, MS-67, July 2015; $2,350, MS-66, September 2015; $1,087, MS-65, September 2015; $588, MS-60, January 2015										

CALIFORNIA PACIFIC INTERNATIONAL EXPOSITION HALF DOLLAR (1935–1936)

Designer: *Robert Aitken.* **Weight:** *12.50 grams.* **Composition:** *.900 silver, .100 copper (net weight .3617 oz. pure silver).* **Diameter:** *30.6 mm.* **Edge:** *Reeded.* **Mints:** *San Francisco and Denver.*

Congress approved the coinage of souvenir half dollars for the California Pacific International Exposition on May 3, 1935. The event—held in San Diego's Balboa Park—was attended by only 4 million people, and interest in the coin was not particularly strong.

Designs. *Obverse:* Minerva seated, holding a spear and shield, with a grizzly bear to her right (from California's state seal). *Reverse:* The Chapel of St. Francis and the California Tower, at the California Pacific International Exposition in San Diego.

Mintage and Melting Data. Originally authorized on May 3, 1935; 1936-D issues authorized on May 6, 1936 (for recoinage of melted 1935-S issues). *Maximum authorized*—1935-S: 250,000; 1936-D: 180,000. *Number minted*—1935-S: 250,132 (including 132 assay coins); 1936-D: 180,092 (including 92 assay coins). *Number melted*—1935-S: 180,000; 1936-D: 150,000. *Net distribution*—1935-S: 70,132; 1936-D: 30,092.

Original Cost and Issuer. Sale prices $1 (1935-S; increased to $3 in 1937; dropped to $2 in 1938) and $1.50 (1936-D; increased to $3 in 1937; reduced to $1 in 1938). Issued by the California Pacific International Exposition Company.

Key to Collecting. Both the 1935-S and 1936-D issues were coined with deeply frosty and lustrous surfaces. The eye appeal usually is excellent. The design made these coins susceptible to bagmarks, and most survivors, even in higher MS grades, show evidence of handling. Minerva, in particular, usually displays some graininess or contact marks, even on coins given high numerical grades. Most coins are deeply lustrous and frosty. On the 1935 San Francisco coins the S mintmark usually is flat, and on the Denver coins the California Tower is often lightly struck at the top.

First Points of Wear. *Obverse:* The bosom and knees of Minerva. *Reverse:* The top right edge of the tower. (The 1936-D was flatly struck in this area; examine the texture of the surface to determine if actual wear exists.)

	Distribution	Cert	Avg	%MS	AU-50	MS-60	MS-62	MS-63	MS-64	MS-65	MS-66
1935-S	70,132	4,742	64.9	100%	$100	$105	$110	$115	$120	$135	$160
	Auctions: $2,115, MS-67, September 2015; $223, MS-66, September 2015; $153, MS-65, August 2015; $106, MS-60, February 2015										
1936-D	30,092	2,764	64.9	100%	$100	$105	$110	$115	$120	$140	$225
	Auctions: $1,528, MS-67, January 2015; $188, MS-66, September 2015; $176, MS-65, February 2015; $106, MS-64, September 2015										

OLD SPANISH TRAIL HALF DOLLAR (1935)

Designer: *L.W. Hoffecker.* **Weight:** *12.50 grams.* **Composition:** *.900 silver, .100 copper (net weight .3617 oz. pure silver).* **Diameter:** *30.6 mm.* **Edge:** *Reeded.* **Mint:** *Philadelphia.*

This coin commemorated the 400th anniversary of the overland trek of the Alvar Nuñez Cabeza de Vaca Expedition through the Gulf states in 1535. The coin's designer and distributor, L.W. Hoffecker, is known to have had his hands in many of this era's commemoratives (and the exploitative practices surrounding them).

Designs. *Obverse:* The head of a steer, inspired by the explorer's last name: Cabeza de Vaca translates to "head of cow." *Reverse:* A map of the Southeastern states and a yucca tree.

Mintage Data. Authorized on June 5, 1935. *Maximum authorized*—10,000. *Number minted*—10,008.

Original Cost and Issuer. Sale price $2. Issued by L.W. Hoffecker, trading as the El Paso Museum Coin Committee.

Key to Collecting. These coins were handled with care during their production and shipping—still, most show scattered contact marks. The typical grade is MS-65 and higher. The fields are usually somewhat satiny and gray, not deeply lustrous and frosty.

First Points of Wear. *Obverse:* The top of the cow's head. *Reverse:* The lettering at the top.

	Distribution	Cert	Avg	%MS	AU-50	MS-60	MS-62	MS-63	MS-64	MS-65	MS-66
1935	10,008	1,878	65.0	100%	$1,050	$1,100	$1,125	$1,150	$1,225	$1,275	$1,450
	Auctions: $2,468, MS-67, September 2015; $1,763, MS-66, January 2015; $1,410, MS-65, January 2015; $764, MS-60, June 2015										

PROVIDENCE, RHODE ISLAND, TERCENTENARY HALF DOLLAR (1936)

Designers: *Arthur G. Carey and John H. Benson.* **Weight:** *12.50 grams.*
Composition: *.900 silver, .100 copper (net weight .3617 oz. pure silver).*
Diameter: *30.6 mm.* **Edge:** *Reeded.* **Mints:** *Philadelphia, Denver, and San Francisco.*

The 300th anniversary of Roger Williams's founding of Providence was the occasion for this special half dollar in 1936. Interestingly, no mention of Providence is to be found on the coin. The distribution of this coin, like that of many other commemoratives of the 1930s, was wrapped in controversy—phony news releases reported that the coin was sold out when it was indeed not, and certain dealers procured large amounts at low prices only to resell for tidy profits.

Designs. *Obverse:* Roger Williams, the founder of Rhode Island, being welcomed by an Indian. *Reverse:* Elements from the Rhode Island state seal, including the anchor of Hope and a shield.

Mintage Data. Authorized on May 2, 1935. *Maximum authorized*—50,000. *Number minted*—1936-P: 20,013 (including 13 assay coins); 1936-D: 15,010 (including 10 assay coins); 1936-S: 15,011 (including 11 assay coins). *Net distribution*—1936-P: 20,013; 1936-D: 15,010; 1936-S: 15,011.

Original Cost and Issuer. Sale price $1. Issued by the Rhode Island and Providence Plantations Tercentenary Committee, Inc.

Key to Collecting. These coins are readily available singly and in sets, with typical grades being MS–63 to 65. Contact marks are common. Higher-level coins, such as MS–66 and 67, are not hard to find, but are elusive in comparison to the lesser-condition pieces. The 1936 (in particular) and 1936-S are sometimes found with prooflike surfaces. Most specimens have a combination of satiny/frosty surface. Many are light gray in color.

First Points of Wear. *Obverse:* The prow of the canoe, and the Indian's right shoulder. *Reverse:* The center of the anchor, and surrounding areas.

	Distribution	Cert	Avg	%MS	AU-50	MS-60	MS-62	MS-63	MS-64	MS-65	MS-66
1936	20,013	2,413	64.7	100%	$95	$105	$110	$120	$130	$150	$185
Auctions: $823, MS-67, July 2015; $165, MS-66, August 2015; $212, MS-65, May 2015; $79, MS-60, February 2015											
1936-D	15,010	1,787	64.7	100%	$95	$105	$110	$120	$130	$150	$185
Auctions: $969, MS-67, November 2015; $435, MS-66, January 2015; $176, MS-65, August 2015; $100, MS-64, May 2015											
1936-S	15,011	1,526	64.6	100%	$95	$105	$110	$120	$150	$185	$300
Auctions: $2,820, MS-67, January 2015; $470, MS-66, November 2015; $112, MS-64, May 2015; $69, EF-45, September 2015											
Set of 1936 P-D-S					$300	$325	$345	$360	$410	$500	$675
Auctions: $2,185, MS-66/66/66, January 2012											

CLEVELAND CENTENNIAL / GREAT LAKES EXPOSITION HALF DOLLAR (1936)

Designer: *Brenda Putnam.* **Weight:** *12.50 grams.* **Composition:** *.900 silver, .100 copper (net weight .3617 oz. pure silver).* **Diameter:** *30.6 mm.* **Edge:** *Reeded.* **Mint:** *Philadelphia.*

A special coinage of fifty-cent pieces was authorized in commemoration of the centennial celebration of Cleveland, Ohio, on the occasion of the Great Lakes Exposition held there in 1936. Numismatic entrepreneur Thomas G. Melish was behind the coins' production and distribution—though he served as the Cleveland Centennial Commemorative Coin Association's treasurer while based in Cincinnati.

Designs. *Obverse:* Bewigged profile portrait of Moses Cleaveland. *Reverse:* A map of the Great Lakes region with nine stars marking various cities, and a compass point at the city of Cleveland.

Mintage Data. Authorized on May 5, 1936. *Maximum authorized*—50,000 (minimum 25,000). *Number minted*—50,030 (including 30 assay coins). *Net distribution*—50,030.

Original Cost and Issuer. Sale prices: one coin for $1.65; two for $1.60 each; three for $1.58 each; five for $1.56 each; ten for $1.55 each; twenty for $1.54 each; fifty for $1.53 each; one hundred for $1.52 each. Issued by the Cleveland Centennial Commemorative Coin Association (Thomas G. Melish, Cincinnati).

Key to Collecting. The Cleveland half dollar is the most readily available issue from 1936—a bumper-crop year for U.S. commemoratives. Nearly all coins are in Mint State, typically from MS–63 to 65, and most are very lustrous and frosty. This issue was not handled with care at the Mint, and scattered contact marks are typically found on both obverse and reverse.

First Points of Wear. *Obverse:* The hair behind Cleaveland's ear. *Reverse:* The top of the compass, and the land (non-lake) areas of the map.

	Distribution	Cert	Avg	%MS	AU-50	MS-60	MS-62	MS-63	MS-64	MS-65	MS-66
1936	50,030	4,882	64.6	100%	$100	$110	$120	$130	$135	$160	$240
	Auctions: $3,995, MS-68, June 2015; $1,293, MS-67, September 2015; $247, MS-66, November 2015; $65, MS-62, March 2015										

WISCONSIN TERRITORIAL CENTENNIAL HALF DOLLAR (1936)

Designer: *David Parsons.* **Weight:** *12.50 grams.* **Composition:** *.900 silver, .100 copper (net weight .3617 oz. pure silver).* **Diameter:** *30.6 mm.* **Edge:** *Reeded.* **Mint:** *Philadelphia.*

The 100th anniversary of the Wisconsin territorial government was the occasion for this issue. Benjamin Hawkins, a New York artist, made changes to the original designs by University of Wisconsin student David Parsons so that the piece conformed to technical requirements.

Designs. *Obverse:* A badger on a log, from the state emblem; and arrows representing the Black Hawk War of the 1830s. *Reverse:* A miner's arm holding a pickaxe over a mound of lead ore, derived from Wisconsin's territorial seal.

Mintage Data. Authorized on May 15, 1936. *Minimum authorized*—25,000 (unlimited maximum). *Number minted*—25,015 (including 15 assay coins). *Net distribution*—25,015.

Original Cost and Issuer. Sale price $1.50 plus 7¢ postage for the first coin, 2¢ postage for each additional coin (later sold for $1.25 each in lots of 10 coins, and still later sold for $3 per coin). Issued by the Wisconsin Centennial Coin Committee (also known as the Coinage Committee of the Wisconsin Centennial Commission). Unsold remainders were distributed, into the 1950s, by the State Historical Society.

Key to Collecting. Examples are readily available in the marketplace. Most grade MS–62 to 64—although higher grades are not rare—and are very lustrous and frosty, except for the higher areas of the design (which often have a slightly polished appearance).

First Points of Wear. *Obverse:* The flank and shoulder of the badger. *Reverse:* The miner's hand.

	Distribution	Cert	Avg	%MS	AU-50	MS-60	MS-62	MS-63	MS-64	MS-65	MS-66
1936	25,015	3,843	65.3	100%	$175	$180	$185	$195	$210	$240	$275
	Auctions: $3,055, MS-68, January 2015; $881, MS-67, January 2015; $235, MS-65, August 2015; $129, MS-60, November 2015										

CINCINNATI MUSIC CENTER HALF DOLLAR (1936)

Designer: *Constance Ortmayer.* **Weight:** *12.50 grams.*
Composition: *.900 silver, .100 copper (net weight .3617 oz. pure silver).*
Diameter: *30.6 mm.* **Edge:** *Reeded.* **Mints:** *Philadelphia, Denver, and San Francisco.*

Although the head of Stephen Foster, "America's Troubadour," dominates the obverse of this special issue, the anniversary celebrated bears little to no relation to him. Foster did live in Cincinnati for a time, but never worked in music while there. The coins were supposedly struck to commemorate the 50th anniversary in 1936 of Cincinnati as a center of music, but the issue was really a personal project of numismatist Thomas G. Melish.

Designs. *Obverse:* Bareheaded profile portrait of Stephen Foster, "America's Troubadour." *Reverse:* A woman playing a lyre, personifying Music.

Mintage Data. Authorized on March 31, 1936. *Maximum authorized*—15,000. *Number minted*—1936-P: 5,005 (including 5 assay coins); 1936-D: 5,005 (including 5 assay coins); 1936-S: 5,006 (including 6 assay coins). *Net distribution*—1936-P: 5,005; 1936-D: 5,005; 1936-S: 5,006.

Original Cost and Issuer. Sale price $7.75 per set of three (actually $7.50 plus 25¢ for the display container with cellophane slide front). Issued by the Cincinnati Musical Center Commemorative Coin Association, Ohio (Thomas G. Melish).

Key to Collecting. Nearly all sets of these coins were bought by collectors and investors, thus most still exist in Mint State, primarily MS–63 to 65. Conservatively graded MS-65 and finer pieces are rare. Most coins were carelessly handled at the mints, and nearly all show scattered contact marks. This issue has a somewhat satiny or "greasy" surface, instead of fields with deep luster and frost. Denver Mint coins are typically found in slightly higher grades than their Philadelphia and San Francisco Mint companions.

First Points of Wear. *Obverse:* The hair at Foster's temple. *Reverse:* The left breast, and the skirt, of the female figure.

	Distribution	Cert	Avg	%MS	AU-50	MS-60	MS-62	MS-63	MS-64	MS-65	MS-66
1936	5,005	882	64.4	100%	$285	$300	$325	$360	$385	$450	$650
	Auctions: $4,700, MS-67, January 2015; $2,115, MS-66, January 2015; $423, MS-65, September 2015; $329, MS-64, January 2015										
1936-D	5,005	1,230	64.9	100%	$285	$300	$325	$360	$385	$450	$650
	Auctions: $3,290, MS-67, September 2015; $940, MS-66, January 2015; $705, MS-65, January 2015; $188, MS-60, November 2015										
1936-S	5,006	890	64.1	100%	$285	$300	$325	$360	$385	$475	$875
	Auctions: $3,055, MS-66, January 2015; $470, MS-65, January 2015; $329, MS-64, January 2015; $306, MS-63, January 2015										
Set of 1935 P-D-S					$875	$900	$975	$1,100	$1,125	$1,375	$2,600
	Auctions: $4,198, MS-66/66/66, February 2012										

LONG ISLAND TERCENTENARY HALF DOLLAR (1936)

Designer: *Howard K. Weinman.* **Weight:** *12.50 grams.* **Composition:** *.900 silver, .100 copper (net weight .3617 oz. pure silver).* **Diameter:** *30.6 mm.* **Edge:** *Reeded.* **Mint:** *Philadelphia.*

This souvenir issue was authorized to commemorate the 300th anniversary of the first white settlement on Long Island, which was made at Jamaica Bay by Dutch colonists. This was the first issue for which a date was specified (1936) irrespective of the year minted or issued, as a safeguard against extending the coinage over a period of years. This measure proved effective in preventing many of the profiteering problems that arose with other commemorative issues of the era.

Designs. *Obverse:* Conjoined profile portraits of a Dutch settler and an Algonquin Indian. *Reverse:* A Dutch vessel with full-blown sails.

Mintage and Melting Data. Authorized on April 13, 1936. *Maximum authorized*—100,000. *Number minted*—100,053 (including 53 assay coins). *Number melted*—18,227. *Net distribution*—81,826.

Original Cost and Issuer. Sale price $1. Issued by the Long Island Tercentenary Committee, through various banks and other outlets.

Key to Collecting. These are among the most plentiful survivors from the commemorative issues of the 1930s, and examples grading MS–64 to 66 are readily obtainable. The coins were minted and handled carelessly, and at the time of distribution most showed nicks, bagmarks, and other evidence of contact; these grade from AU-50 to MS-60. Most coins have, as struck, a satiny or slightly "greasy" luster and are not deeply frosty.

First Points of Wear. *Obverse:* The hair and the cheekbone of the Dutch settler. *Reverse:* The center of the lower middle sail.

	Distribution	Cert	Avg	%MS	AU-50	MS-60	MS-62	MS-63	MS-64	MS-65	MS-66
1936	81,826	4,562	64.2	99%	$85	$95	$100	$110	$115	$195	$450
	Auctions: $9,988, MS-67, September 2015; $1,293, MS-66, January 2015; $129, MS-64, February 2015; $52, EF-40, July 2015										

YORK COUNTY, MAINE, TERCENTENARY HALF DOLLAR (1936)

Designer: *Walter H. Rich.* **Weight:** *12.50 grams.* **Composition:** *.900 silver, .100 copper (net weight .3617 oz. pure silver).* **Diameter:** *30.6 mm.* **Edge:** *Reeded.* **Mint:** *Philadelphia.*

A souvenir half dollar was authorized by Congress upon the 300th anniversary of the founding of York County, Maine. While the commemorated event was considered somewhat obscure, the proposing and distributing group—the York County Tercentenary Commemorative Coin Commission, led by ardent numismatist Walter P. Nichols—was lauded for its diligence and proper handling of the release.

Designs. *Obverse:* Brown's Garrison, on the Saco River (site of the original settlement in York County in 1636). *Reverse:* An adaptation of the seal of York County.

Mintage Data. *Maximum authorized*—30,000. *Number minted*—25,015 (including 15 assay coins).

Original Cost and Issuer. Sale price $1.50 ($1.65 postpaid by mail to out-of-state buyers). Issued by the York County Tercentenary Commemorative Coin Commission, York National Bank, Saco, Maine.

Key to Collecting. This issue was well handled at the Mint and in distribution, so most examples are in higher grades and are relatively free of marks. On the reverse, the top of the shield is a key point. Some coins have been brushed and have a myriad of fine hairlines; these can be detected by examining the coin at various angles to the light. MS–64 and 65 coins are readily found in the marketplace.

First Points of Wear. *Obverse:* The mounted sentry near the corner of the fort; the stockade; and the rim of the coin. *Reverse:* The pine tree in the shield; the top-right area of the shield; and the rim.

	Distribution	Cert	Avg	%MS	AU-50	MS-60	MS-62	MS-63	MS-64	MS-65	MS-66
1936	25,015	3,467	65.4	100%	$160	$165	$170	$180	$195	$215	$260
	Auctions: $1,763, MS-68, August 2015; $881, MS-67, September 2015; $259, MS-66, January 2015; $121, MS-60, January 2015										

BRIDGEPORT, CONNECTICUT, CENTENNIAL HALF DOLLAR (1936)

Designer: *Henry Kreis.* **Weight:** *12.50 grams.* **Composition:** *.900 silver, .100 copper (net weight .3617 oz. pure silver).* **Diameter:** *30.6 mm.* **Edge:** *Reeded.* **Mint:** *Philadelphia.*

In commemoration of the 100th anniversary of the incorporation of the city of Bridgeport, a special fifty-cent piece was authorized on May 15, 1936. The city—actually originally founded in 1639—served as an important center in the 17th and 18th centuries.

Designs. *Obverse:* Bareheaded profile portrait of P.T. Barnum, Bridgeport's most famous citizen. *Reverse:* An art deco eagle, standing.

Mintage Data. Authorized on May 15, 1936. *Minimum authorized*—25,000 (unlimited maximum). *Number minted*—25,015 (including 15 assay coins). *Net distribution*—25,015.

Original Cost and Issuer. Sale price $2. Issued by Bridgeport Centennial, Inc., through the First National Bank and Trust Co. and other banks.

Key to Collecting. These coins are readily available in the marketplace. Most grade from MS–62 to 64. Many have been cleaned or lightly polished, but pristine MS-65 pieces are readily available. Obvious friction rub and/or marks are often seen. Some coins were struck from dies with lightly polished fields and have a prooflike or partially prooflike appearance in those areas.

First Points of Wear. *Obverse:* Barnum's cheek. *Reverse:* The eagle's wing.

	Distribution	Cert	Avg	%MS	AU-50	MS-60	MS-62	MS-63	MS-64	MS-65	MS-66
1936	25,015	3,128	64.6	100%	$120	$125	$130	$135	$145	$180	$300
	Auctions: $1,880, MS-67, September 2015; $353, MS-66, February 2015; $235, MS-65, August 2015; $106, MS-60, May 2015										

LYNCHBURG, VIRGINIA, SESQUICENTENNIAL HALF DOLLAR (1936)

Designer: *Charles Keck.* **Weight:** *12.50 grams.* **Composition:** *.900 silver, .100 copper (net weight .3617 oz. pure silver).* **Diameter:** *30.6 mm.* **Edge:** *Reeded.* **Mint:** *Philadelphia.*

The issuance of a charter to the city of Lynchburg in 1786 was commemorated in 1936 by a special coinage of half dollars. Interestingly, Lynchburg native Senator Carter Glass objected to the use of portraits of living persons on coins, but was featured on the issue anyway. It was considered that a portrait of John Lynch—for whom the city was named— would be used, but no such likeness existed.

Designs. *Obverse:* Bareheaded profile portrait of Senator Carter Glass, a native of Lynchburg and former secretary of the Treasury. *Reverse:* A figure of Miss Liberty standing before the old Lynchburg courthouse.

Mintage Data. Authorized on May 28, 1936. *Maximum authorized*—20,000. *Number minted*—20,013 (including 13 assay coins). *Net distribution*—20,013.

Original Cost and Issuer. Sale price $1. Issued by the Lynchburg Sesqui-Centennial Association.

Key to Collecting. Most of these half dollars are in higher grades; MS–65 and 66 examples are readily available in the marketplace. Some show graininess (from striking) on the high areas of the obverse portrait and on the bosom and skirt of Miss Liberty, or show evidences of handling or contact in the same areas. Surfaces are often somewhat satiny, instead of deeply lustrous and frosty. Often the reverse field is semi-prooflike. This issue must have been handled with particular care at the Mint.

First Points of Wear. *Obverse:* The hair above Glass's ear. *Reverse:* The hair of Miss Liberty, the folds of her gown, and her bosom.

	Distribution	Cert	Avg	%MS	AU-50	MS-60	MS-62	MS-63	MS-64	MS-65	MS-66
1936	20,013	2,620	64.8	100%	$225	$230	$235	$240	$260	$300	$365
	Auctions: $2,820, MS-67, January 2015; $294, MS-66, June 2015; $170, MS-63, October 2015; $118, AU-58, August 2015										

ELGIN, ILLINOIS, CENTENNIAL HALF DOLLAR (1936)

Designer: *Trygve Rovelstad.* **Weight:** *12.50 grams.* **Composition:** *.900 silver, .100 copper (net weight .3617 oz. pure silver).* **Diameter:** *30.6 mm.* **Edge:** *Reeded.* **Mint:** *Philadelphia.*

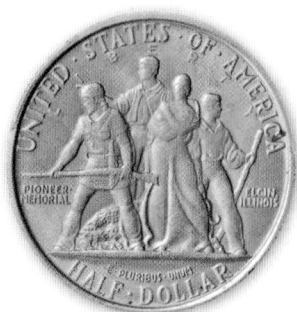

The 100th anniversary of the founding of Elgin, Illinois, was marked by a special issue of half dollars in 1936. The year 1673 (seen on the obverse) bears no relation to the event but refers to the year in which Louis Joliet and Jacques Marquette entered Illinois Territory.

Designs. *Obverse:* The fur-capped profile of a bearded pioneer (a close-up view of the statue depicted on the reverse). *Reverse:* The Pioneer Memorial statuary group, whose creation was financed by the sale of these coins.

Mintage and Melting Data. Authorized on June 16, 1936. *Maximum authorized*—25,000. *Number minted*—25,015 (including 15 assay coins). *Number melted*—5,000. *Net distribution*—20,015.

Original Cost and Issuer. Sale price $1.50. Issued by the Elgin Centennial Monumental Committee, El Paso, Texas (L.W. Hoffecker in charge), through banks in and near Elgin, including the First National Bank of Elgin, the Elgin National Bank, and the Union National Bank.

Key to Collecting. Elgin half dollars are fairly plentiful in today's marketplace. They seem to have been handled with particular care at the time of minting, as most have fewer bagmarks than many other commemoratives of the same era. Typical coins grade MS–64 to 66. The surfaces often have a matte-like appearance (seemingly a combination of a lustrous circulation strike and a Matte Proof) quite different from other commemorative issues of 1936. Some coins are fairly frosty. On many a bright spot is evident on the reverse below the A of AMERICA, the result of an inadvertent polishing on a small area of the die. Chief Engraver John Sinnock made a few Matte Proofs, perhaps as many as 10, by pickling coins in acid at the Mint.

First Points of Wear. *Obverse:* The cheek of the pioneer. *Reverse:* The rifleman's left shoulder. (Note that a lack of detailed facial features is the result of striking, not wear, and that the infant is always weakly struck.)

	Distribution	Cert	Avg	%MS	AU-50	MS-60	MS-62	MS-63	MS-64	MS-65	MS-66
1936	20,015	3,337	65.0	100%	$180	$195	$200	$210	$215	$235	$265

Auctions: $3,995, MS-68, January 2015; $1,880, MS-67, September 2015; $200, MS-65, April 2015; $165, MS-60, February 2015

ALBANY, NEW YORK, CHARTER HALF DOLLAR (1936)

Designer: *Gertrude K. Lathrop.* **Weight:** *12.50 grams.* **Composition:** *.900 silver, .100 copper (net weight .3617 oz. pure silver).* **Diameter:** *30.6 mm.* **Edge:** *Reeded.* **Mint:** *Philadelphia.*

The 250th anniversary of the granting of a charter to the city of Albany—an event of strictly local significance—was the occasion for this commemorative half dollar. Amusingly, designer Gertrude K. Lathrop kept a live beaver in her studio (courtesy of the state Conservation Department) during her work.

Designs. *Obverse:* A plump beaver gnawing on a maple branch—fauna and flora evocative of Albany and New York State, respectively. *Reverse:* A scene with Albany's first mayor, Peter Schuyler, and his secretary, Robert Livingston, accepting the city's charter in 1686 from Governor Thomas Dongan of New York.

Mintage and Melting Data. Authorized on June 16, 1936. *Maximum authorized*—25,000. *Number minted*—25,013 (including 13 assay coins). *Number melted*—7,342. *Net distribution*—17,671.

Original Cost and Issuer. Sale price $1. Issued by the Albany Dongan Charter Coin Committee.

Key to Collecting. This issue was fairly carefully handled during production and distribution, and most examples are relatively free of marks in the fields. Most specimens are lustrous and frosty, although the frost has satiny aspects. Albany half dollars are readily available on the market. The typical example grades from MS–63 to 65 and has at least minor friction and marks.

First Points of Wear. *Obverse:* The hip of the beaver (nearly all coins show at least minor evidence of contact here). *Reverse:* The sleeve of Dongan (the figure at left).

	Distribution	Cert	Avg	%MS	AU-50	MS-60	MS-62	MS-63	MS-64	MS-65	MS-66
1936	17,671	2,961	64.8	100%	$220	$230	$235	$240	$250	$285	$425
	Auctions: $1,293, MS-67, September 2015; $470, MS-66, February 2015; $282, MS-65, June 2015; $176, MS-60, September 2015										

SAN FRANCISCO–OAKLAND BAY BRIDGE OPENING HALF DOLLAR (1936)

Designer: *Jacques Schnier.* **Weight:** *12.50 grams.* **Composition:** *.900 silver, .100 copper (net weight .3617 oz. pure silver).* **Diameter:** *30.6 mm.* **Edge:** *Reeded.* **Mint:** *San Francisco.*

The opening of the San Francisco Bay Bridge was the occasion for a special souvenir fifty-cent piece. The bear depicted on the obverse was a composite of animals in local zoos.

Designs. *Obverse:* A stylized grizzly bear standing on all fours and facing the viewer. *Reverse:* A fading-to-the-horizon view of the San Francisco–Oakland Bay Bridge and part of San Francisco.

Mintage and Melting Data. Authorized on June 26, 1936. *Maximum authorized*—200,000. *Number minted*—100,055 (including 55 assay coins). *Number melted*—28,631. *Net distribution*—71,424.

Original Cost and Issuer. Sale price $1.50. Issued by the Coin Committee of the San Francisco–Oakland Bay Bridge Celebration.

Key to Collecting. These coins are readily available in today's marketplace, with most grading MS–62 to 64, typically with contact marks on the grizzly bear. The reverse design, being complex with many protective devices, normally appears free of marks, unless viewed at an angle under a strong light. The grade of the reverse for a given coin often is a point or two higher than that of the obverse. The fields of this coin often have a "greasy" appearance, rather than being deeply lustrous and frosty.

First Points of Wear. *Obverse:* The bear's body, in particular the left shoulder. *Reverse:* The clouds.

	Distribution	Cert	Avg	%MS	AU-50	MS-60	MS-62	MS-63	MS-64	MS-65	MS-66
1936-S	71,424	3,757	64.6	99%	$145	$150	$160	$175	$185	$215	$340
	Auctions: $1,763, MS-67, January 2015; $764, MS-66, September 2015; $153, MS-64, January 2015; $129, AU-58, January 2015										

COLUMBIA, SOUTH CAROLINA, SESQUICENTENNIAL HALF DOLLAR (1936)

Designer: *A. Wolfe Davidson.* **Weight:** *12.50 grams.*
Composition: *.900 silver, .100 copper (net weight .3617 oz. pure silver).*
Diameter: *30.6 mm.* **Edge:** *Reeded.* **Mints:** *Philadelphia, Denver, and San Francisco.*

Souvenir half dollars were authorized to help finance the extensive celebrations marking the sesquicentennial of the founding of Columbia, South Carolina, in 1786. The pieces had not been minted by the time of the actual celebrations, which took place in late March 1936, and only reached collectors (which the Columbia Sesqui-Centennial Commission expressed desire to sell to instead of to dealers) in December.

Designs. *Obverse:* Justice, with sword and scales, standing before the state capitol of 1786 and the capitol of 1936. *Reverse:* A palmetto tree, the state emblem, with stars encircling.

Mintage Data. Authorized on March 18, 1936. *Maximum authorized*—25,000. *Number minted*—1936-P: 9,007; 1936-D: 8,009; 1936-S: 8,007. *Net distribution*—1936-P: 9,007; 1936-D: 8,009; 1936-S: 8,007.

Original Cost and Issuer. Sale price $6.45 per set of three (single coins $2.15 each). Issued by the Columbia Sesqui-Centennial Commission.

Key to Collecting. These coins were widely distributed at the time of issue, and examples are readily obtainable today. Most grade from MS–63 to 65. They were treated carefully in their minting and distribution, so most coins exhibit lustrous surfaces with very few handling marks. Nearly all, however, show friction on the bosom of Justice and, to a lesser extent, on the high areas of the palmetto-tree foliage on the reverse.

First Points of Wear. *Obverse:* The right breast of Justice. *Reverse:* The top of the palmetto tree.

	Distribution	Cert	Avg	%MS	AU-50	MS-60	MS-62	MS-63	MS-64	MS-65	MS-66
1936	9,007	1,564	65.2	100%	$180	$215	$220	$225	$230	$245	$300
	Auctions: $2,585, MS-68, June 2015; $705, MS-67, May 2015; $235, MS-64, July 2015; $376, MS-62, October 2015										
1936-D	8,009	1,602	65.6	100%	$180	$215	$220	$225	$230	$245	$300
	Auctions: $705, MS-67, June 2015; $294, MS-66, February 2015; $212, MS-65, August 2015; $194, MS-63, July 2015										
1936-S	8,007	1,547	65.4	100%	$180	$215	$220	$225	$230	$245	$300
	Auctions: $7,638, MS-68, August 2015; $999, MS-67, September 2015; $306, MS-66, January 2015; $165, MS-63, October 2015										
Set of 1936 P-D-S					$540	$650	$660	$675	$700	$750	$900
	Auctions: $690, MS-65/66/65, February 2012										

DELAWARE TERCENTENARY HALF DOLLAR (1936)

Designer: *Carl L. Schmitz.* **Weight:** *12.50 grams.* **Composition:** *.900 silver, .100 copper (net weight .3617 oz. pure silver).* **Diameter:** *30.6 mm.* **Edge:** *Reeded.* **Mint:** *Philadelphia.*

The 300th anniversary of the landing of the Swedes in Delaware was the occasion for a souvenir issue of half dollars—as well as a two-krona coin issued in Sweden. The colonists landed on the spot that is now Wilmington and established a church, which is the oldest Protestant church in the United States still used for worship. Carl L. Schmitz's designs were chosen through a competition. These coins were authorized in 1936 and struck in 1937, but not released until 1938, as the Swedes' arrival was actually in 1638.

Designs. *Obverse:* Old Swedes Church. *Reverse:* The ship *Kalmar Nyckel.*

Mintage and Melting Data. Authorized on May 15, 1936. *Minimum authorized*—25,000 (unlimited maximum). *Number minted*—25,015 (including 15 assay coins). *Number melted*—4,022. *Net distribution*—20,993.

Original Cost and Issuer. Sale price $1.75. Issued by the Delaware Swedish Tercentenary Commission, through the Equitable Trust Company of Wilmington.

Key to Collecting. Most examples in today's marketplace grade MS–64 or 65, though they typically exhibit numerous original planchet nicks and marks. Most coins are very lustrous and frosty.

First Points of Wear. *Obverse:* The roof above the church entrance. (Note that the triangular section at the top of the entrance is weakly struck, giving an appearance of wear.) *Reverse:* The center of the lower middle sail (also often shows graininess and nicks from the original planchet).

	Distribution	Cert	Avg	%MS	AU-50	MS-60	MS-62	MS-63	MS-64	MS-65	MS-66
1936	20,993	2,984	64.7	100%	$220	$230	$235	$240	$250	$285	$375

Auctions: $881, MS-67, January 2015; $541, MS-66, October 2015; $188, MS-63, September 2015; $176, MS-60, August 2015

BATTLE OF GETTYSBURG ANNIVERSARY HALF DOLLAR (1936)

Designer: *Frank Vittor.* **weight:** *12.50 grams.* **Composition:** *.900 silver, .100 copper (net weight .3617 oz. pure silver).* **Diameter:** *30.6 mm.* **Edge:** *Reeded.* **Mint:** *Philadelphia.*

On June 16, 1936, Congress authorized a coinage of fifty-cent pieces in commemoration of the 75th anniversary of the 1863 Battle of Gettysburg. Similar to the previously mentioned Delaware Tercentenary coins, the coins were authorized two years before the event commemorated, and were minted a year early as well (in 1937). Paul L. Roy, secretary of the Pennsylvania State Commission, desired for the pieces to be struck at multiple mints—so as to sell more expensive sets of three coins, rather than just Philadelphia issues—but no coins were struck in Denver or San Francisco in the end.

Designs. *Obverse:* Uniformed profile portraits of a Union soldier and a Confederate soldier. *Reverse:* Union and Confederate shields separated by a fasces.

Mintage and Melting Data. Authorized on June 16, 1936. *Maximum authorized—50,000. Number minted—50,028 (including 28 assay coins). Number melted—23,100. Net distribution—26,928.*

Original Cost and Issuer. Sale price $1.65. Issued by the Pennsylvania State Commission, Hotel Gettysburg, Gettysburg. The price was later raised to $2.65 for coins offered by the American Legion, Department of Pennsylvania.

Key to Collecting. Examples are fairly plentiful in the marketplace. The typical coin grades from MS–63 to 65, is deeply frosty and lustrous, and shows scattered contact marks, which are most evident on the cheeks of the soldiers on the obverse and, on the reverse, on the two shields (particularly at the top of the Union shield on the left side of the coin).

First Points of Wear. *Obverse:* The cheekbones of each soldier. *Reverse:* The three ribbons on the fasces, and the top of the Union shield.

	Distribution	Cert	Avg	%MS	AU-50	MS-60	MS-62	MS-63	MS-64	MS-65	MS-66
1936	26,928	3,377	64.4	99%	$460	$475	$480	$490	$600	$800	$1,375

Auctions: $2,703, MS-67, January 2015; $1,763, MS-66, July 2015; $541, MS-64, September 2015; $423, AU-55, September 2015

Norfolk, Virginia, Bicentennial Half Dollar (1936)

Designers: *William M. and Marjorie E. Simpson.* **Weight:** *12.50 grams.*
Composition: *.900 silver, .100 copper (net weight .3617 oz. pure silver).*
Diameter: *30.6 mm.* **Edge:** *Reeded.* **Mint:** *Philadelphia.*

To provide funds for the celebration of Norfolk's anniversary of its growth from a township in 1682 to a royal borough in 1736, Congress first passed a law for the striking of medals. The proponents, however, being dissatisfied, finally succeeded in winning authority for half dollars commemorating the 300th anniversary of the original Norfolk land grant and the 200th anniversary of the establishment of the borough. In a strange twist, none of the five dates on these coins actually reflects the year of the coins' actual striking (1937).

Designs. *Obverse:* The seal of the city of Norfolk, Virginia, with a three-masted ship at center. *Reverse:* The city's royal mace, presented by Lieutenant Governor Robert Dinwiddie in 1753.

Mintage and Melting Data. Authorized on June 28, 1937. *Maximum authorized—25,000. Number minted—25,013 (including 13 assay coins). Number melted—8,077. Net distribution—16,936.*

Original Cost and Issuer. Sale price $1.50 locally ($1.65 by mail for the first coin, $1.55 for each additional). Issued by the Norfolk Advertising Board, Norfolk Association of Commerce.

Key to Collecting. Examples are fairly plentiful in today's marketplace, with most in high MS grades. The cluttered nature of the design had a positive effect: all of the lettering served to protect the fields and devices from nicks and marks, with the result that MS–65 and 66 coins are plentiful.

First Points of Wear. *Obverse:* The sails of the ship, especially the lower rear sail. *Reverse:* The area below the crown on the royal mace.

	Distribution	Cert	Avg	%MS	AU-50	MS-60	MS-62	MS-63	MS-64	MS-65	MS-66
1936	16,936	2,802	65.9	100%	$310	$320	$325	$340	$350	$360	$380

Auctions: $1,175, MS-68, September 2015; $482, MS-67, August 2015; $388, MS-66, May 2015; $306, MS-64, August 2015

ROANOKE ISLAND, NORTH CAROLINA, 350TH ANNIVERSARY HALF DOLLAR (1937)

Designer: *William M. Simpson.* **Weight:** *12.50 grams.* **Composition:** *.900 silver, .100 copper (net weight .3617 oz. pure silver).* **Diameter:** *30.6 mm.* **Edge:** *Reeded.* **Mint:** *Philadelphia.*

A celebration was held in Old Fort Raleigh in 1937 to commemorate the 350th anniversary of Sir Walter Raleigh's "Lost Colony" and the birth of Virginia Dare, the first white child born in British North America. Interestingly, Raleigh himself never actually visited America, but only sent ships of colonists who eventually founded a city in his name.

Designs. *Obverse:* Profile portrait of Sir Walter Raleigh in plumed hat and fancy collar. *Reverse:* Ellinor Dare and her baby, Virginia, the first white child born in the Americas to English parents.

Mintage and Melting Data. *Minimum authorized*—25,000 (unlimited maximum). *Number minted*—50,030 (including 30 assay coins). *Number melted*—21,000. *Net distribution*—29,030.

Original Cost and Issuer. Sale price $1.65. Issued by the Roanoke Colony Memorial Association of Manteo.

Key to Collecting. Most of these coins were handled with care during their minting, and today are in high grades. MS-65 pieces are plentiful. Most coins are lustrous and frosty. Partially prooflike pieces are occasionally seen (sometimes offered as "presentation pieces" or "prooflike presentation pieces").

First Points of Wear. *Obverse:* Raleigh's cheek and the brim of his hat. *Reverse:* The head of Ellinor Dare.

	Distribution	Cert	Avg	%MS	AU-50	MS-60	MS-62	MS-63	MS-64	MS-65	MS-66
1937	29,030	3,936	65.1	100%	$180	$185	$190	$200	$215	$240	$260

Auctions: $5,170, MS-68, October 2015; $940, MS-67, August 2015; $188, MS-64, September 2015; $112, AU-50, November 2015

BATTLE OF ANTIETAM ANNIVERSARY HALF DOLLAR (1937)

Designer: *William M. Simpson.* **Weight:** *12.50 grams.* **Composition:** *.900 silver, .100 copper (net weight .3617 oz. pure silver).* **Diameter:** *30.6 mm.* **Edge:** *Reeded.* **Mint:** *Philadelphia.*

A souvenir half dollar was struck in 1937 to commemorate the 75th anniversary of the famous Civil War battle to thwart Robert E. Lee's invasion of Maryland. The Battle of Antietam, which took place on September 17, 1862, was one of the bloodiest single-day battles of the war, with more than 23,000 men killed, wounded, or missing.

Designs. *Obverse:* Uniformed profile portraits of generals Robert E. Lee and George B. McClellan, opponent commanders during the Battle of Antietam. *Reverse:* Burnside Bridge, an important tactical objective of the battle.

Mintage and Melting Data. Authorized on June 24, 1937. *Maximum authorized*—50,000. *Number minted*—50,028 (including 28 assay coins). *Number melted*—32,000. *Net distribution*—18,028.

Original Cost and Issuer. Sale price $1.65. Issued by the Washington County Historical Society, Hagerstown, Maryland.

Key to Collecting. Antietam half dollars were handled with care during production. More often seen are scattered small marks, particularly on the upper part of the obverse. Most examples are very lustrous and frosty. MS-65 and finer coins are plentiful in the marketplace.

First Points of Wear. *Obverse:* Lee's cheekbone. *Reverse:* The leaves of the trees; the bridge; and the rim of the coin.

	Distribution	Cert	Avg	%MS	AU-50	MS-60	MS-62	MS-63	MS-64	MS-65	MS-66
1937	18,028	2,718	65.1	100%	$575	$600	$615	$625	$635	$650	$725
	Auctions: $4,935, MS-68, January 2015; $1,411, MS-67, February 2015; $705, MS-65, September 2015; $447, AU-50, January 2015										

NEW ROCHELLE, NEW YORK, 250TH ANNIVERSARY HALF DOLLAR (1938)

Designer: *Gertrude K. Lathrop.* **Weight:** *12.50 grams.* **Composition:** *.900 silver, .100 copper (net weight .3617 oz. pure silver).* **Diameter:** *30.6 mm.* **Edge:** *Reeded.* **Mint:** *Philadelphia.*

To observe the founding of New Rochelle in 1688 by French Huguenots, a special half dollar was issued in 1938. The title to the land that the Huguenots purchased from John Pell provided that a fattened calf be given away every year on June 20; this is represented the obverse of the coin.

Designs. *Obverse:* John Pell, who sold the French Huguenots the land for New Rochelle, and a fatted calf, an annual provision of the sale. *Reverse:* A fleur-de-lis, adapted from the seal of the city.

Mintage and Melting Data. Authorized on May 5, 1936. *Maximum authorized—25,000. Number minted—25,015 (including 15 assay coins). Number melted—9,749. Net distribution—15,266.*

Original Cost and Issuer. Sale price $2. Issued by the New Rochelle Commemorative Coin Committee, through the First National Bank of New Rochelle, New Rochelle, New York.

Key to Collecting. These half dollars received better-than-average care and handling during the minting and distribution process. The typical coin grades MS-64 or higher. Some examples show very light handling marks, but most are relatively problem-free. Some show areas of graininess or light striking on the high spots of the calf on the obverse, and on the highest area of the iris on the reverse. The majority of pieces have lustrous, frosty surfaces, and a few are prooflike (the latter are sometimes offered as "presentation pieces"). A total of 50 Specimen strikings were given to important people in New Rochelle, as well as to the Coinage Committee and some members of the Westchester County Coin Club.

First Points of Wear. *Obverse:* The hip of the calf. *Reverse:* The bulbous part of the fleur-de-lis. (Note that on the central petal the midrib is flatly struck.)

	Distribution	Cert	Avg	%MS	AU-50	MS-60	MS-62	MS-63	MS-64	MS-65	MS-66
									PF-63	PF-64	PF-65
1938	15,266	2,570	65.0	100%	$310	$320	$330	$350	$360	$385	$425
	Auctions: $1,410, MS-67, July 2015; $494, MS-66, September 2015; $400, MS-65, January 2015; $317, MS-64, January 2015										
1938, Proof	*1–2*	2	61.0								
	Auctions: No auction records available.										

IOWA CENTENNIAL HALF DOLLAR (1946)

Designer: *Adam Pietz.* **Weight:** *12.50 grams.* **Composition:** *.900 silver, .100 copper (net weight .3617 oz. pure silver).* **Diameter:** *30.6 mm.* **Edge:** *Reeded.* **Mint:** *Philadelphia.*

This half dollar, commemorating the 100th anniversary of Iowa's statehood, was sold first to the residents of Iowa and only a small remainder to others. Numismatists of the time, having largely forgotten the deceptions and hucksterism of the 1930s (and also seen the values of previously issued commemoratives rebound from a low point in 1941), were excited to see the first commemorative coin struck in some years. Nearly all of the issue was disposed of quickly, except for 500 that were held back to be distributed in 1996, and another 500 slated for 2046.

Designs. *Obverse:* The Old Stone Capitol building at Iowa City. *Reverse:* An eagle with wings spreading, adapted from the Iowa state seal.

Mintage Data. Authorized on August 7, 1946. *Maximum authorized*—100,000. *Number minted*—100,057 (including 57 assay coins).

Original Cost and Issuer. Sale price $2.50 to in-state buyers, $3 to those out of state. Issued by the Iowa Centennial Committee, Des Moines, Iowa.

Key to Collecting. Most coins are in varying degrees of Mint State, and are lustrous and frosty. MS–63 to 66 are typical grades. The nature of the design, without open field areas, is such that a slight amount of friction and contact is usually not noticeable.

First Points of Wear. *Obverse:* The clouds above the Capitol, and the shafts of the building near the upper-left and upper-right windows. *Reverse:* The back of the eagle's head and neck. (Note that the head sometimes is flatly struck.)

	Distribution	Cert	Avg	%MS	AU-50	MS-60	MS-62	MS-63	MS-64	MS-65	MS-66
1946	100,057	5,987	65.5	100%	$90	$95	$100	$105	$110	$130	$150
	Auctions: $4,700, MS-68, January 2015; $270, MS-67, August 2015; $212, MS-66, October 2015; $84, MS-63, August 2015										

BOOKER T. WASHINGTON MEMORIAL HALF DOLLAR (1946–1951)

Designer: *Isaac S. Hathaway.* **Weight:** *12.50 grams.*
Composition: *.900 silver, .100 copper (net weight .3617 oz. pure silver).*
Diameter: *30.6 mm.* **Edge:** *Reeded.* **Mints:** *Philadelphia, Denver, and San Francisco.*

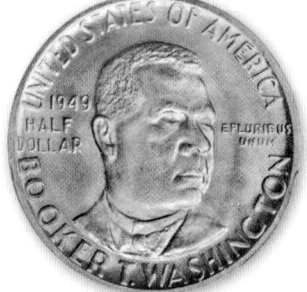 

This commemorative coin was issued to perpetuate the ideals and teachings of African-American educator and presidential advisor Booker T. Washington and to construct memorials to his memory. Issued from all mints, it received wide distribution from the start. Unfortunately, the provision that the coins could be minted over several years led to many of the same problems seen with the Arkansas, Boone, Oregon Trail, and Texas pieces from the prior decade.

Designs. *Obverse:* Bareheaded three-quarters profile portrait of Booker T. Washington. *Reverse:* The Hall of Fame at New York University and a slave cabin.

Mintage Data. Authorized on August 7, 1946. *Maximum authorized*—5,000,000 (for the entire series 1946 onward). *Number minted*—1946-P: 1,000,546 (including 546 assay coins); 1946-D: 200,113 (including 113 assay coins); 1946-S: 500,279 (including 279 assay coins); 1947-P: 100,017 (including 17 assay coins); 1947-D: 100,017 (including 17 assay coins); 1947-S: 100,017 (including 17 assay coins); 1948-P: 20,005 (including 5 assay coins); 1948-D: 20,005 (including 5 assay coins); 1948-S: 20,005 (including 5 assay coins); 1949-P: 12,004 (including 4 assay coins); 1949-D: 12,004 (including 4 assay coins); 1949-S: 12,004 (including 4 assay coins); 1950-P: 12,004 (including 4 assay coins); 1950-D: 12,004 (including 4 assay coins); 1950-S: 512,091 (including 91 assay coins); 1951-P: 510,082 (including 82 assay coins); 1951-D: 12,004 (including 4 assay coins); 1951-S: 12,004 (including 4 assay coins). *Net distribution*—1946-P: 700,546 (estimated); 1946-D: 50,000 (estimated); 1946-S: 500,279 (estimated); 1947-P: 6,000 (estimated); 1947-D: 6,000 (estimated); 1947-S: 6,000 (estimated); 1948-P: 8,005; 1948-D: 8,005; 1948-S: 8,005; 1949-P: 6,004; 1949-D: 6,004; 1949-S: 6,004; 1950-P: 6,004; 1950-D: 6,004; 1950-S: 62,091 (estimated); 1951-P: 210,082 (estimated); 1951-D: 7,004; 1951-S: 7,004.

Original Cost and Issuer. Original sale price $1 per coin for Philadelphia and San Francisco, $1.50 for Denver, plus 10¢ postage per coin. In 1946, issued by the Booker T. Washington Birthplace Memorial Commission, Inc., Rocky Mount, Virginia (Dr. S.J. Phillips in charge); Stack's of New York City; and Bebee Stamp & Coin Company (a.k.a. Bebee's). For later issues, costs and distributors varied.

Key to Collecting. Of all commemorative half dollar issues produced up to this point, the Booker T. Washington half dollars were made with the least amount of care during the coining process at the mints. At the time of release, nearly all were poorly struck on the obverse and were marked with abrasions and nicks. Many have graininess and marks on Washington's cheek, from the original planchet surface that did not strike up fully. Many coins grade from MS–60 to (liberally graded) 65. Some have natural or artificial toning that masks the true condition and facilitates gem certification. Prooflike coins are sometimes seen, including for 1947-S (in particular), 1948-S, 1949, and 1951-S. These are not at all mirror-like, but still have surfaces different from the normal mint frost.

First Points of Wear. *Obverse:* Washington's cheekbone. *Reverse:* The center lettering (FROM SLAVE CABIN TO HALL OF FAME, etc.).

	Distribution	Cert	Avg	%MS	AU-50	MS-60	MS-62	MS-63	MS-64	MS-65	MS-66
1946	700,546	2,887	64.6	99%	$18	$20	$21	$25	$35	$60	$125
Auctions: $1,293, MS-67, January 2015; $705, MS-67, March 2015; $141, MS-66, June 2015; $60, MS-65, March 2015											
1946-D	50,000	1,679	64.8	100%	$18	$20	$22	$25	$30	$60	$170
Auctions: $5,405, MS-68, July 2015; $1,410, MS-67, August 2015; $286, MS-66, October 2015; $32, MS-64, April 2015											
1946-S	500,279	2,432	64.9	99%	$18	$20	$22	$25	$30	$60	$115
Auctions: $4,113, MS-68, March 2015; $1,645, MS-67, August 2015; $123, MS-66, March 2015; $259, MS-64, November 2015											
Set of 1946 P-D-S					$55	$60	$70	$75	$100	$180	$425
Auctions: $110, MS-65/65/65, May 2012											
1947	6,000	881	64.9	100%	$18	$25	$40	$55	$60	$75	$300
Auctions: $3,525, MS-67, July 2015; $400, MS-66, January 2015; $259, MS-66, February 2015; $54, MS-65, January 2015											
1947-D	6,000	691	65.0	100%	$18	$30	$40	$55	$60	$85	$350
Auctions: $1,645, MS-67, June 2015; $494, MS-66, January 2015; $329, MS-66, August 2015; $84, MS-65, September 2015											
1947-S	6,000	904	65.1	100%	$18	$30	$40	$55	$60	$85	$160
Auctions: $2,585, MS-67, January 2015; $176, MS-66, November 2015; $64, MS-65, April 2015; $69, MS-64, January 2015											
Set of 1947 P-D-S					$55	$85	$120	$165	$180	$250	$825
Auctions: $196, MS-65/65/65, January 2012											

	Distribution	Cert	Avg	%MS	AU-50	MS-60	MS-62	MS-63	MS-64	MS-65	MS-66
1948	8,005	807	65.2	100%	$18	$25	$50	$65	$75	$80	$195
Auctions: $999, MS-67, June 2015; $282, MS-66, September 2015; $235, MS-66, February 2015; $79, MS-65, February 2015											
1948-D	8,005	820	65.2	100%	$25	$30	$45	$60	$70	$85	$180
Auctions: $1,028, MS-67, February 2015; $176, MS-66, November 2015; $94, MS-65, January 2015; $36, MS-64, April 2015											
1948-S	8,005	955	65.4	100%	$25	$30	$45	$60	$70	$90	$180
Auctions: $1,293, MS-67, February 2015; $212, MS-66, February 2015; $70, MS-65, February 2015; $38, MS-64, April 2015											
Set of 1948 P-D-S					$70	$85	$150	$185	$215	$260	$525
Auctions: $220, MS-66/65/65, June 2012											
1949	6,004	826	65.2	100%	$18	$20	$21	$25	$35	$100	$200
Auctions: $2,233, MS-67, January 2015; $400, MS-66, February 2015; $141, MS-65, April 2015; $84, MS-64, January 2015											
1949-D	6,004	778	65.2	100%	$18	$20	$21	$25	$35	$100	$175
Auctions: $1,058, MS-67, October 2015; $165, MS-66, April 2015; $112, MS-65, April 2015; $74, MS-64, January 2015											
1949-S	6,004	843	65.5	100%	$18	$20	$21	$25	$35	$100	$175
Auctions: $940, MS-67, October 2015; $212, MS-66, September 2015; $188, MS-65, September 2015; $79, MS-64, February 2015											
Set of 1949 P-D-S					$54	$60	$63	$75	$105	$300	$525
Auctions: $320, MS-65/66/66, May 2012											
1950	6,004	637	65.2	100%	$20	$20	$21	$25	$35	$60	$200
Auctions: $541, MS-67, October 2015; $300, MS-66, May 2015; $200, MS-66, October 2015; $74, MS-65, May 2015											
1950-D	6,004	615	65.1	100%	$20	$20	$21	$25	$35	$60	$175
Auctions: $1,763, MS-67, February 2015; $282, MS-66, August 2015; $212, MS-66, September 2015; $84, MS-65, January 2015											
1950-S	62,091	1,282	65.2	100%	$20	$20	$21	$25	$35	$60	$125
Auctions: $940, MS-67, January 2015; $764, MS-67, August 2015; $141, MS-66, August 2015; $34, MS-65, April 2015											
Set of 1950 P-D-S					$60	$60	$65	$75	$135	$185	$500
Auctions: $725, MS-66/66/66, April 2012											
1951	210,082	1,310	64.6	100%	$18	$25	$30	$40	$50	$50	$135
Auctions: $1,528, MS-67, June 2015; $376, MS-66, January 2015; $147, MS-65, March 2015; $40, MS-64, April 2015											
1951-D	7,004	673	65.3	100%	$25	$40	$50	$60	$75	$100	$150
Auctions: $764, MS-67, January 2015; $259, MS-66, September 2015; $141, MS-65, January 2015; $56, MS-63, April 2015											
1951-S	7,004	768	65.5	100%	$22	$30	$40	$60	$75	$100	$150
Auctions: $764, MS-67, September 2015; $646, MS-67, September 2015; $170, MS-66, July 2015; $165, MS-66, November 2015											
Set of 1951 P-D-S					$65	$95	$120	$160	$200	$250	$450
Auctions: $475, MS-66/66/66, May 2012; $153, MS-66/66/66, March 2015											

CARVER / WASHINGTON COMMEMORATIVE HALF DOLLAR (1951–1954)

Designer: *Isaac S. Hathaway.* **Weight:** *12.50 grams.*
Composition: *.900 silver, .100 copper (net weight .3617 oz. pure silver).*
Diameter: *30.6 mm.* **Edge:** *Reeded.* **Mints:** *Philadelphia, Denver, and San Francisco.*

Designed by Isaac Scott Hathaway, this coin portrays the conjoined busts of two prominent black Americans. Booker T. Washington was a lecturer, educator, and principal of Tuskegee Institute. He urged training to advance independence and efficiency for his race. George Washington Carver was an agricultural chemist who worked to improve the economy of the American South. He spent part of his life

teaching crop improvement and new uses for soybeans, peanuts, sweet potatoes, and cotton waste. Controversy erupted when it came to light that money obtained from the sale of these commemoratives was to be used "to oppose the spread of communism among Negroes in the interest of national defense."

Designs. *Obverse:* Conjoined bareheaded profile portraits of George Washington Carver and Booker T. Washington. *Reverse:* A map of the United States, with legends.

Mintage Data. Signed into law by President Harry S Truman on September 21, 1951. *Maximum authorized*—3,415,631 (total for all issues 1951 onward; consisting of 1,581,631 undistributed Booker T. Washington coins which could be converted into Carver-Washington coins, plus the unused 1,834,000 earlier authorization for Booker T. Washington coins). The following include author's estimates: 1951-P-D-S: *Number minted* (including 18, 4, and 4 assay coins)—110,018; 10,004; 10,004. *Net distribution*—20,018 (estimated); 10,004 (estimated); 10,004 (estimated). 1952-P-D-S: *Number minted* (including 292, 6, and 6 assay coins)—2,006,292; 8,006; 8,006. *Net distribution*—1,106,292 (estimated); 8,006 (estimated); 8,006 (estimated). 1953-P-D-S: *Number minted* (including 3, 3, and 20 assay coins)—8,003; 8,003; 108,020. *Net distribution*—8,003 (estimated); 8,003 (estimated); 88,020 (estimated). 1954-P-D-S: *Number minted* (including 6, 6, and 24 assay coins)—12,006; 12,006; 122,024. *Net distribution*—12,006 (estimated); 12,006 (estimated); 42,024 (estimated).

Original Cost and Issuer. 1951-P-D-S: $10 per set. 1952-P-D-S: $10 per set; many Philadelphia coins were sold at or near face value through banks. 1953-P-D-S: $10 per set; some 1953-S coins were distributed at or near face value (Bebee's prices $9 until January 15, 1952, $10 after that date). 1954-P-D-S: Official sale price: $10 per set; some 1954-S coins were paid out at face value (Bebee's prices for sets $9 until January 20, 1954, $12 after that date). Issued mainly by the Carver-Washington Coin Commission acting for the Booker T. Washington Birthplace Memorial Foundation (Booker Washington Birthplace, Virginia) and the George Washington Carver National Monument Foundation (Diamond, Missouri). Also, for some issues, these dealers: Stack's, Bebee Stamp & Coin Company, Sol Kaplan, and R. Green.

Key to Collecting. Nearly all coins of this issue were handled casually at the mints and also during the distribution process. Most were not fully struck up, with the result that under magnification many tiny nicks and marks can be seen on the higher parts, originating from planchet marks that were not obliterated during the striking process. Many MS examples are available on the market.

First Points of Wear. *Obverse:* Carver's cheekbone. (Note that some pieces were struck poorly in this area; check the reverse also for wear.) *Reverse:* The lettering U.S.A. on the map.

	Distribution	Cert	Avg	%MS	AU-50	MS-60	MS-62	MS-63	MS-64	MS-65	MS-66
1951	20,018	1,032	64.1	100%	$18	$20	$21	$25	$60	$180	$600
Auctions: $940, MS-66, August 2015; $705, MS-66, January 2015; $141, MS-65, August 2015; $36, MS-64, April 2015											
1951-D	10,004	669	64.7	100%	$22	$25	$30	$40	$45	$80	$360
Auctions: $376, MS-66, February 2015; $89, MS-65, January 2015; $84, MS-65, January 2015; $79, MS-65, August 2015											
1951-S	10,004	834	65.1	100%	$22	$25	$30	$45	$55	$85	$180
Auctions: $1,763, MS-67, August 2015; $400, MS-66, August 2015; $275, MS-66, November 2015; $112, MS-65, August 2015											
Set of 1951 P-D-S					$65	$70	$85	$110	$160	$350	$1,150
Auctions: $140, MS-64/64/64, June 2012											
1952	1,106,292	4,015	64.2	98%	$18	$25	$26	$27	$30	$60	$200
Auctions: $2,820, MS-67, January 2015; $1,880, MS-67, August 2015; $306, MS-66, September 2015; $26, MS-60, August 2015											
1952-D	8,006	520	64.5	100%	$24	$30	$35	$45	$70	$135	$600
Auctions: $764, MS-66, January 2015; $517, MS-66, September 2015; $106, MS-65, August 2015; $30, MS-64, April 2015											
1952-S	8,006	686	65.1	100%	$24	$30	$35	$40	$50	$90	$210
Auctions: $3,200, MS-67, January 2015; $282, MS-66, September 2015; $84, MS-65, August 2015; $50, MS-64, August 2015											
Set of 1952 P-D-S					$70	$85	$100	$115	$150	$285	$1,025
Auctions: $230, MS-65/65/65, March 2012											

	Distribution	Cert	Avg	%MS	AU-50	MS-60	MS-62	MS-63	MS-64	MS-65	MS-66
1953	8,003	602	64.7	100%	$22	$30	$35	$40	$50	$95	$450
	Auctions: $259, MS-66, January 2015; $94, MS-65, September 2015; $89, MS-65, October 2015; $36, MS-64, May 2015										
1953-D	8,003	486	64.4	100%	$18	$40	$45	$50	$55	$110	$725
	Auctions: $376, MS-65, July 2015; $84, MS-65, May 2015; $48, MS-64, August 2015; $30, MS-64, August 2015										
1953-S	88,020	1,316	64.8	100%	$22	$25	$28	$30	$45	$60	$300
	Auctions: $3,290, MS-67, August 2015; $3,055, MS-67, March 2015; $282, MS-66, October 2015; $170, MS-65, May 2015										
Set of 1953 P-D-S					$65	$95	$110	$120	$150	$270	$1,500
	Auctions: $300, MS-66/65/65, May 2012										
1954	12,006	818	64.6	100%	$20	$25	$27	$30	$40	$60	$450
	Auctions: $282, MS-66, November 2015; $94, MS-65, July 2015; $79, MS-65, February 2015; $46, MS-64, April 2015										
1954-D	12,006	714	64.4	100%	$25	$30	$35	$40	$45	$85	$550
	Auctions: $676, MS-66, February 2015; $423, MS-66, August 2015; $100, MS-65, August 2015; $82, MS-65, January 2015										
1954-S	42,024	1,190	64.6	100%	$20	$25	$27	$30	$40	$60	$350
	Auctions: $1,998, MS-67, June 2015; $306, MS-66, August 2015; $84, MS-65, August 2015; $34, MS-64, August 2015										
Set of 1954 P-D-S					$65	$80	$90	$100	$125	$210	$1,350
	Auctions: $316, MS-65/65/65, March 2012										

AN OVERVIEW OF MODERN COMMEMORATIVES

No commemorative coins were made by the U.S. Mint from 1955 through 1981. As the years went by, the numismatic community missed having new commemoratives to collect, and many endorsements for events and subjects worthy of the honor were made through letters to congressmen and other officials, which were often reprinted in pages of *The Numismatist*, the *Numismatic Scrapbook Magazine*, *Numismatic News*, and *Coin World*.

Finally, in 1982, the Treasury Department issued the first commemorative coin since 1954—a silver half dollar celebrating the 250th anniversary of the birth of George Washington. This time around, distribution was placed in the hands of the Bureau of the Mint (today called the U.S. Mint) rather than with a commission or private individuals. The profits accrued to the Treasury Department and the U.S. government. The issue was well received in the numismatic community, with more than seven million of the half dollars sold nationwide.

Then came the 1983 and 1984 Los Angeles Olympiad coins, minted in the subject years for the Los Angeles Olympiad held in 1984. These comprised a diverse and somewhat experimental series, with dollars of two different designs and, for the first time, a commemorative ten-dollar gold coin. Sales were satisfactory, and the supply easily met the demand from collectors and investors.

The concept of a surcharge, or built-in fee, was introduced, with a certain amount per coin going to a congressionally designated beneficiary—in the instance of the Olympic coins, the Los Angeles Olympic Organizing Committee. These and related surcharges became controversial with collectors, some of whom resented making involuntary donations when they bought coins. Today the practice continues, though without as much controversy. Surcharges are the spark that has ignited most commemorative programs, as potential recipients of the earmarked profits launch intense lobbying campaigns in Congress.

In 1986 the 100th anniversary of the completion of the Statue of Liberty was commemorated by the issuance of a copper-nickel–clad half dollar (first of its kind in the commemorative series), a silver dollar, and a five-dollar gold coin, with varied motifs, each depicting on the obverse the Statue of Liberty or an element therefrom. Unprecedented millions of coins were sold.

Then followed a lull in commemorative purchases, although the Mint continued to issue coins celebrating more Olympic Games, various national anniversaries, and significant people, places, events, and other subjects. Some years saw four or five or more individual commemorative programs. Some were well received by the hobby community, but sales of most fell far short of projections. In certain cases these low sales would eventually prove beneficial for collectors who placed orders from the Mint. An example is the 1995 five-dollar commemorative honoring baseball star and Civil Rights hero Jackie Robinson. Only 5,174 Uncirculated pieces were sold, creating a modern rarity.

Most modern commemorative coins have seen only modest secondary-market appreciation, if any. Beyond their retail values, however, the coins will always have significant historical, cultural, and sentimental value. The 2001 American Buffalo silver dollar created a sensation with its bold design harkening back to the classic Buffalo nickel of 1913 to 1938; the issue sold out quickly and soon was commanding high premiums in the collector market. It remains popular and valuable today. In 2014, the National Baseball Hall of Fame commemoratives (a three-coin suite in copper-nickel, silver, and gold) captured mainstream-media headlines and national TV news coverage. Other modern commemoratives have honored American inventors and explorers, branches of the U.S. military, Boy Scouts and Girl Scouts, the Civil Rights Act of 1964, and other important themes, continuing a tradition of special coinage dating back to 1892 and giving today's collectors a broad spectrum of issues to study and cherish.

See page 1195 for pricing of government commemorative sets and page 1502 for an alphabetical cross-reference list of all commemoratives.

George Washington 250th Anniversary of Birth Half Dollar (1982)

Designer: *Elizabeth Jones.* **Weight:** *12.50 grams.*
Composition: *.900 silver, .100 copper (net weight .3617 oz. pure silver).*
Diameter: *30.6 mm.* **Edge:** *Reeded.* **Mints:** *Denver (Uncirculated) and San Francisco (Proof).*

This coin, the first commemorative half dollar issued since 1954, celebrated the 250th anniversary of the birth of George Washington. It was also the first 90% silver coin produced by the U.S. Mint since 1964.

Designs. *Obverse:* George Washington on horseback. *Reverse:* Mount Vernon.

Mintage Data. Authorized by Public Law 97-014, signed by President Ronald Reagan on December 23, 1981. *Maximum authorized*—10,000,000. *Number minted*—1982-D: 478,716; 1982-S: 868,326. *Net distribution*—1982-D: 2,210,458 Uncirculated; 1982-S: 4,894,044 Proof.

Original Cost. Sale prices originally $8.50 (Uncirculated) and $10.50 (Proof), later raised to $10 and $12, respectively.

Key to Collecting. Today, Uncirculated 1982-D and Proof 1982-S Washington half dollars are plentiful on the market and are readily available in as-issued condition. They are popular and highly regarded as part of the modern commemorative series.

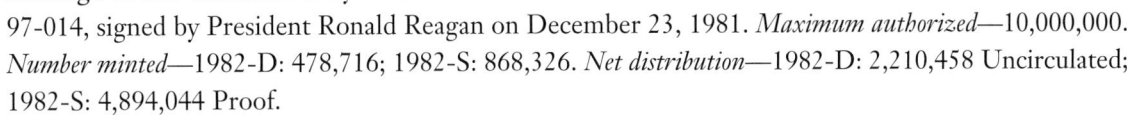

	Distribution	Cert	Avg	%MS	MS-67
					PF-67
1982-D	2,210,458	4,491	66.9	100%	$12
	Auctions: $123, MS-69, June 2014				
1982-S, Proof	4,894,044	10,403	69.0		$10
	Auctions: $110, PF-70, June 2014; $106, PF-70, September 2015; $106, PF-70, November 2014; $74, PF-70UCam, June 2015				

LOS ANGELES OLYMPIAD DISCUS THROWER SILVER DOLLAR (1983)

Designer: *Elizabeth Jones.* **Weight:** *26.73 grams.* **Composition:** *.900 silver, .100 copper (net weight .7736 oz. pure silver).* **Diameter:** *38.1 mm.* **Edge:** *Reeded.*
Mints: *Philadelphia and Denver (Uncirculated), San Francisco (Uncirculated and Proof).*

Three distinctive coins were issued to commemorate the 1984 Los Angeles Summer Olympic Games. The 1983 Discus Thrower dollar was the first commemorative silver dollar since the 1900 Lafayette issue.

Designs. *Obverse:* Representation of the traditional Greek discus thrower inspired by the ancient work of the sculptor Myron. *Reverse:* The head and upper body of an American eagle.

Mintage Data. Authorized by Public Law 97-220, signed by President Ronald Reagan on July 22, 1982. *Maximum authorized*—50,000,000 totally for 1983 and 1984. *Number minted*—1983-P: 294,543 Uncirculated; 1983-D: 174,014 Uncirculated; 1983-S: 174,014 Uncirculated and 1,577,025 Proof.

Original Cost. Sale prices $28 (Uncirculated) and $24.95 (Proof, ordered in advance); Proof raised later to $29, and still later to $32. Part of the $10 surcharge per coin went to the U.S. Olympic Committee and the Los Angeles Olympic Organizing Committee.

Key to Collecting. These pieces in both Uncirculated and Proof format can be found today for prices near their issue cost. The vast quantities issued (never mind that 52 million were not sold) made them common. Nearly all surviving coins are in superb gem preservation. Today the aftermarket is supported by coin collectors, not by Olympic sports enthusiasts.

	Distribution	Cert	Avg	%MS	MS-67
					PF-67
1983-P	294,543	2,375	69.0	100%	$30
	Auctions: $499, MS-70, September 2014				
1983-D	174,014	1,747	69.0	100%	$30
	Auctions: $7,638, MS-70, April 2013				
1983-S	174,014	1,824	69.0	100%	$30
	Auctions: $8,813, MS-70, April 2013				
1983-S, Proof	1,577,025	5,014	69.0		$30
	Auctions: $1,175, PF-70DCam, April 2014				

LOS ANGELES OLYMPIAD OLYMPIC COLISEUM SILVER DOLLAR (1984)

Designer: *John Mercanti.* **Weight:** *26.73 grams.* **Composition:** *.900 silver, .100 copper (net weight .7736 oz. pure silver).* **Diameter:** *38.1 mm.* **Edge:** *Reeded.*
Mints: *Philadelphia and Denver (Uncirculated), San Francisco (Uncirculated and Proof).*

This coin became a reality at the insistence of the Los Angeles Olympic Organizing Committee. The semi-nude figures on the obverse created some controversy.

Designs. *Obverse:* Robert Graham's headless torso sculptures at the entrance of the Los Angeles Memorial Coliseum. *Reverse:* Perched eagle looking back over its left wing.

Mintage Data. Authorized by Public Law 97-220, signed by President Ronald Reagan on July 22, 1982. *Maximum authorized*—50,000,000 totally for 1983 and 1984. *Number minted*—1984-P: 217,954 Uncirculated; 1984-D: 116,675 Uncirculated; 1984-S: 116,675 Uncirculated and 1,801,210 Proof.

Original Cost. Sales prices $28 (Uncirculated) and $32 (Proof); Proof later raised to $35. Part of the $10 surcharge per coin went to the U.S. Olympic Committee and the Los Angeles Olympic Organizing Committee.

Key to Collecting. These pieces in both Uncirculated and Proof format can be found today for close to what they cost at the time of issue. The vast quantities issued (never mind that 52 million were not sold) made them common. Nearly all surviving coins are in superb gem preservation. Today, the after-market is supported by coin collectors, not by Olympic sports enthusiasts.

	Distribution	Cert	Avg	%MS	MS-67 PF-67
1984-P	217,954	1,742	69.0	100%	$30
Auctions: $705, MS-70, September 2013; $456, MS-70, September 2014; $447, MS-70, August 2015					
1984-D	116,675	1,246	68.9	100%	$32
Auctions: $4,994, MS-70, April 2013					
1984-S	116,675	1,263	68.9	100%	$32
Auctions: $9,400, MS-70, April 2013					
1984-S, Proof	1,801,210	4,323	68.9		$30
Auctions: $411, PF-70DCam, September 2014; $558, PF-70DCam, April 2013					

LOS ANGELES OLYMPIAD $10 GOLD COIN (1984)

Designer: *John Mercanti.* **Weight:** *16.718 grams.* **Composition:** *.900 gold, .100 copper (net weight .4837 oz. pure gold).* **Diameter:** *27 mm.* **Edge:** *Reeded.*
Mints: *Philadelphia, Denver, and San Francisco (Proof); West Point (Uncirculated and Proof).*

This ten-dollar coin was the first commemorative to be struck in gold since the 1926 Sesquicentennial $2.50 gold pieces. Mint engraver John Mercanti based the obverse design on a sketch by James Peed of the Bureau of the Mint's Washington office.

Designs. *Obverse:* Two runners holding aloft the Olympic torch. *Reverse:* Adaptation of the Great Seal of the United States.

Mintage Data. Authorized by Public Law 97-220, signed by President Ronald Reagan on July 22, 1982. *Maximum authorized*—2,000,000. *Number minted*—1984-P: 33,309 Proof; 1984-D: 34,533 Proof; 1984-S: 48,551 Proof; 1984-W: 75,886 Uncirculated and 381,085 Proof.

Original Cost. Sales prices $339 (Uncirculated) and $353 (Proof). Part of the $35 surcharge per coin went to the U.S. Olympic Committee and the Los Angeles Olympic Organizing Committee.

Key to Collecting. These coins are necessarily expensive due to their gold content, but are still quite reasonable. Nearly all surviving coins are in superb gem preservation. Today, the aftermarket is supported by coin collectors, not by Olympic sports enthusiasts.

	Distribution	Cert	Avg	%MS	MS-67
					PF-67
1984-W	75,886	1,649	69.3	100%	$750
	Auctions: $764, MS-70, September 2014; $893, MS-70, April 2013; $611, MS-69, October 2014				
1984-P, Proof	33,309	1,876	69.0		$700
	Auctions: $1,763, PF-70DCam, April 2013; $823, PF-70DCam, September 2014; $624, PF-69DCam, October 2014; $588, PF-69, June 2015				
1984-D, Proof	34,533	1,961	69.1		$700
	Auctions: $1,116, PF-70DCam, April 2013; $617, PF-69DCam, October 2014; $611, PF-69DCam, October 2014; $564, PF-69, June 2015				
1984-S, Proof	48,551	1,844	69.2		$700
	Auctions: $823, PF-70DCam, April 2013; $618, PF-69DCam, October 2014; $588, PF-69, June 2015				
1984-W, Proof	381,085	5,894	69.1		$700
	Auctions: $646, PF-70UCam, January 2015; $646, PF-70UCam, July 2015; $646, PF-70UCam, July 2015; $588, PF-69, June 2015				

STATUE OF LIBERTY CENTENNIAL HALF DOLLAR (1986)

Designer: *Edgar Z. Steever IV (obverse), Sherl Winter (reverse).* **Weight:** *11.34 grams.*
Composition: *.9167 copper, .0833 nickel.* **Diameter:** *30.61 mm.*
Edge: *Reeded.* **Mints:** *Denver (Uncirculated) and San Francisco (Proof).*

The 100th anniversary of the dedication of the Statue of Liberty in New York City harbor in 1886 furnished the occasion for the issuance of three different commemorative coins in 1986. The clad half dollar was the first U.S. commemorative issued in copper-nickel format.

Designs. *Obverse:* Ship of immigrants steaming into New York harbor, with the Statue of Liberty greeting them in the foreground and the New York skyline in the distance. *Reverse:* Scene of an immigrant family with their belongings on the threshold of America.

Mintage Data. Authorized by the Act of July 9, 1985. *Maximum authorized*—25,000,000. *Number minted*—1986-D: 928,008 Uncirculated; 1986-S: 6,925,627 Proof.

Original Cost. Sale prices $5 (Uncirculated, pre-order) and $6.50 (Proof, pre-order); Uncirculated later raised to $6, and Proof later raised to $7.50.

Key to Collecting. So many 1986 Statue of Liberty half dollars were issued that the aftermarket affords the possibility of purchasing the coins not much above the original offering price. Nearly all are superb gems.

	Distribution	Cert	Avg	%MS	MS-67
					PF-67
1986-D	928,008	2,858	69.0	100%	$5
Auctions: $411, MS-70, April 2013					
1986-S, Proof	6,925,627	11,727	69.0		$5
Auctions: $84, PF-69DCam, January 2015; $129, PF-67, October 2015					

STATUE OF LIBERTY CENTENNIAL SILVER DOLLAR (1986)

Designer: *John Mercanti.* **Weight:** *26.73 grams.* **Composition:** *.900 silver, .100 copper (net weight .7736 oz. pure silver).* **Diameter:** *38.1 mm.* **Edge:** *Reeded.*
Mints: *Philadelphia (Uncirculated) and San Francisco (Proof).*

These coins, which are also known as Ellis Island silver dollars, feature an excerpt from Emma Lazarus's poem, *The New Colossus.*

Designs. *Obverse:* Statue of Liberty in the foreground, with the Ellis Island immigration center behind her. *Reverse:* Liberty's torch, along with the words GIVE ME YOUR TIRED, YOUR POOR, YOUR HUDDLED MASSES YEARNING TO BREATHE FREE.

Mintage Data. Authorized by the Act of July 9, 1985. *Maximum authorized*—10,000,000. *Number minted*—1986-P: 723,635 Uncirculated; 1986-S: 6,414,638 Proof.

Original Cost. Sale prices $20.50 (Uncirculated, pre-order) and $22.50 (Proof, pre-order); Uncirculated later raised to $22, and Proof later raised to $24.

Key to Collecting. Nearly all coins of this issue are superb gems.

	Distribution	Cert	Avg	%MS	MS-67
					PF-67
1986-P	723,635	4,000	69.0	100%	$25
Auctions: $170, MS-70, January 2013; $27, MS-69, August 2014					
1986-S, Proof	6,414,638	12,650	69.0		$25
Auctions: $141, PF-70DCam, April 2014; $106, PF-70DCam, April 2013; $70, PF-69DCam, August 2014; $188, PF-69DCam, November 2014					

STATUE OF LIBERTY CENTENNIAL $5 GOLD COIN (1986)

Designer: *Elizabeth Jones.* **Weight:** *8.359 grams.* **Composition:** *.900 gold, .100 copper (net weight .242 oz. pure gold).* **Diameter:** *21.6 mm.* **Edge:** *Reeded.* **Mint:** *West Point.*

The designs on these five-dollar gold coins created a sensation in the numismatic community and were widely discussed, and the coin received Krause Publications' Coin of the Year Award. The entire authorization of a half million coins was spoken for—the only complete sellout of any commemorative coin of the 1980s.

Designs. *Obverse:* Face and crown of the Statue of Liberty. *Reverse:* American eagle in flight.

Mintage Data. Authorized by the Act of July 9, 1985. *Maximum authorized—500,000. Number minted—95,248 Uncirculated and 404,013 Proof.*

Original Cost. Sale prices $160 (Uncirculated, pre-order) and $170 (Proof, pre-order); Uncirculated later raised to $165, and Proof later raised to $175.

Key to Collecting. So many 1986 Statue of Liberty commemoratives were issued that the aftermarket affords the possibility of purchasing the coins at prices near bullion value. Nearly all coins of this issue are superb gems.

	Distribution	Cert	Avg	%MS	MS-67 PF-67
1986-W	95,248	3,869	69.5	100%	$400
	Auctions: $353, MS-70, August 2014; $329, MS-70, September 2014; $329, MS-70, November 2014; $441, MS-70, February 2013				
1986-W, Proof	404,013	10,817	69.3		$325
	Auctions: $306, PF-70, September 2015; $306, MS-70, April 2015; $282, PF-70, October 2015; $329, PF-69DCam, October 2014				

CONSTITUTION BICENTENNIAL SILVER DOLLAR (1987)

Designer: *Patricia Lewis Verani.* **Weight:** *26.73 grams.*
Composition: *.900 silver, .100 copper (net weight .7736 oz. pure silver).*
Diameter: *38.1 mm.* **Edge:** *Reeded.* **Mints:** *Philadelphia (Uncirculated) and San Francisco (Proof).*

In connection with the 200th anniversary of the U.S. Constitution, observed in 1987, Congress held a competition to design both a silver dollar and a five-dollar gold coin.

Designs. *Obverse:* Quill pen, a sheaf of parchment, and the words WE THE PEOPLE. *Reverse:* Cross-section of Americans from various periods representing various lifestyles.

Mintage Data. Authorized by Public Law 99-582, signed by President Ronald Reagan on October 29, 1986. *Maximum authorized*—1,000,000. *Number minted*—1987-P: 451,629 Uncirculated; 1987-S: 2,747,116 Proof.

Original Cost. Sale prices $22.50 (Uncirculated, pre-issue) and $24 (Proof, pre-issue); Uncirculated later raised to $26, and Proof later raised to $28. A $7 surcharge per coin went toward reducing the national debt.

Key to Collecting. Today, these coins remain inexpensive. Nearly all are superb gems.

	Distribution	Cert	Avg	%MS	MS-67
					PF-67
1987-P	451,629	3,463	69.1	100%	$25
Auctions: $90, MS-70, January 2013					
1987-S, Proof	2,747,116	5,874	68.9		$25
Auctions: $115, PF-70DCam, April 2013					

CONSTITUTION BICENTENNIAL $5 GOLD COIN (1987)

Designer: *Marcel Jovine.* **Weight:** *8.359 grams.* **Composition:** *.900 gold, .100 copper (net weight .242 oz. pure gold).* **Diameter:** *21.6 mm.* **Edge:** *Reeded.* **Mint:** *West Point.*

A modernistic design by Marcel Jovine was selected for the five-dollar gold coin honoring the bicentennial of the U.S. Constitution.

Designs. *Obverse:* Stylized eagle holding a massive quill pen. *Reverse:* Large quill pen with nine stars to the left (symbolizing the first colonies to ratify the Constitution) and four to the right (representing the remaining original states).

Mintage Data. Authorized by Public Law 99-582, signed by President Ronald Reagan on October 29, 1986. *Maximum authorized*—1,000,000. *Number minted*—214,225 Uncirculated and 651,659 Proof.

Original Cost. Sale prices $195 (Uncirculated, pre-issue) and $200 (Proof, pre-issue); Uncirculated later raised to $215, and Proof later raised to $225.

Key to Collecting. Nearly all coins of this issue are superb gems.

	Distribution	Cert	Avg	%MS	MS-67
					PF-67
1987-W	214,225	7,505	69.7	100%	$400
Auctions: $353, MS-70, August 2015; $317, MS-70, August 2015; $306, MS-70, August 2015; $300, MS-70, September 2015					
1987-W, Proof	651,659	16,511	69.5		$325
Auctions: $376, PF-70UCam, September 2015; $353, PF-70UCam, January 2015; $329, PF-70UCam, October 2015					

SEOUL OLYMPIAD SILVER DOLLAR (1988)

Designer: *Patricia Lewis Verani (obverse), Sherl Winter (reverse).* **Weight:** *26.73 grams.*
Composition: *.900 silver, .100 copper (net weight .7736 oz. pure silver).*
Diameter: *38.1 mm.* **Edge:** *Reeded.* **Mints:** *Denver (Uncirculated) and San Francisco (Proof).*

The holding of the 1988 Summer Olympic Games in Seoul, Republic of South Korea, furnished the opportunity for the issuance of this silver dollar (as well as a five-dollar gold coin; see next entry).

Designs. *Obverse:* One hand holding an Olympic torch as another hand holds another torch to ignite it. *Reverse:* Olympic rings surrounded by a wreath.

Mintage Data. Authorized by Public Law 100-141, signed by President Ronald Reagan on October 28, 1987. *Maximum authorized*—10,000,000. *Number minted*—1988-D: 191,368 Uncirculated; 1988-S: 1,359,366 Proof.

Original Cost. Sale prices $22 (Uncirculated, pre-issue) and $23 (Proof, pre-issue); Uncirculated later raised to $27, and Proof later raised to $29. The surcharge of $7 per coin went to the U.S. Olympic Committee.

Key to Collecting. These coins are inexpensive. The numismatic market, representing actual buyers and sellers, is not extensive enough to maintain large premiums over the price of hundreds of thousands of coins purchased by the non-numismatic public and then later sold when their novelty passed. Nearly all coins are superb gems.

	Distribution	Cert	Avg	%MS	MS-67
					PF-67
1988-D	191,368	2,099	69.0	100%	$25
Auctions: $247, MS-70, September 2014					
1988-S, Proof	1,359,366	4,762	68.9		$25
Auctions: $135, PF-70DCam, September 2014; $141, PF-70DCam, April 2013					

SEOUL OLYMPIAD $5 GOLD COIN (1988)

Designer: *Elizabeth Jones (obverse), Marcel Jovine (reverse).* **Weight:** *8.359 grams.*
Composition: *.900 gold, .100 copper (net weight .242 oz. pure gold).*
Diameter: *21.6 mm.* **Edge:** *Reeded.* **Mint:** *West Point.*

Elizabeth Jones's five-dollar obverse design is considered by many to be the high point of commemorative coinage art of the late 20th century. Some observers suggested that, because the event was not held in the United States, the Seoul Olympics were not an appropriate subject for American coinage; regardless, the gold coin was praised to the skies.

Designs. *Obverse:* Nike, goddess of Victory, wearing a crown of olive leaves. *Reverse:* Stylized Olympic flame.

Mintage Data. Authorized by Public Law 100-141, signed by President Ronald Reagan on October 28, 1987. *Maximum authorized*—1,000,000. *Number minted*—62,913 Uncirculated and 281,465 Proof.

Original Cost. Sale prices $200 (Uncirculated, pre-issue) and $205 (Proof, pre-issue); Uncirculated later raised to $225, and Proof later raised to $235. The surcharge of $35 per coin went to the U.S. Olympic Committee.

Key to Collecting. Examples are readily available today.

	Distribution	Cert	Avg	%MS	MS-67
					PF-67
1988-W	62,913	2,366	69.5	100%	$375
	Auctions: $306, MS-69, August 2014; $423, MS-69, March 2013				
1988-W, Proof	281,465	9,653	69.4		$325
	Auctions: $447, PF-70UCam, March 2015; $376, PF-70UCam, March 2015; $353, PF-70UCam, October 2015; $317, PF-70UCam, April 2015				

CONGRESS BICENTENNIAL HALF DOLLAR (1989)

Designer: *Patricia Lewis Verani (obverse), William Woodward (reverse).*
Weight: *11.34 grams.* **Composition:** *.9167 copper, .0833 nickel.* **Diameter:** *30.61 mm.*
Edge: *Reeded.* **Mints:** *Denver (Uncirculated) and San Francisco (Proof).*

The 200th anniversary of the operation of Congress under the U.S. Constitution was observed in 1989, and a suite of commemorative coins was authorized to observe the bicentennial, among them this copper-nickel half dollar.

Designs. *Obverse:* The head of the *Freedom* statue (erected on top of the Capitol dome in 1863) is shown at the center, with inscriptions around, including LIBERTY in oversize letters at the bottom border. *Reverse:* A distant front view of the Capital is shown, with arcs of stars above and below, with appropriate lettering.

Mintage Data. Authorized by Public Law 100-673, signed by President Ronald Reagan on November 17, 1988. The coins were to be dated 1989 and could be minted through June 30, 1990. *Maximum authorized*—4,000,000. *Number minted*—1989-D: 163,753 Uncirculated; 1989-S: 767,897 Proof.

Original Cost. Sale prices $5 (Uncirculated, pre-issue) and $7 (Proof, pre-issue); Uncirculated later raised to $6, and Proof later raised to $8. The surcharge of $1 per coin went to the Capitol Preservation Fund.

Key to Collecting. Not popular with numismatists in 1989, these coins still languish in the marketplace. Exceptions are coins certified in ultra-high grades. The Uncirculated 1989-D half dollar exists with a misaligned reverse, oriented in the same direction as the obverse, instead of the usual 180 degree separation. These are rare and valuable, but are not widely known. Likely, some remain undiscovered in buyers' hands.

	Distribution	Cert	Avg	%MS	MS-67
					PF-67
1989-D	163,753	1,154	69.0	100%	$10
	Auctions: $4,113, MS-70, April 2013				
1989-S, Proof	767,897	2,737	69.0		$10
	Auctions: $382, PF-70, September 2014				

CONGRESS BICENTENNIAL SILVER DOLLAR (1989)

Designer: *William Woodward.* **Weight:** *26.73 grams.*
Composition: *.900 silver, .100 copper (net weight .7736 oz. pure silver).*
Diameter: *38.1 mm.* **Edge:** *Reeded.* **Mints:** *Denver (Uncirculated) and San Francisco (Proof).*

To inaugurate the Congress Bicentennial coins, four coining presses weighing seven tons each were brought from the Philadelphia Mint to the east front of the Capitol building, where in a special ceremony on June 14, 1989, the first silver dollars and five-dollar gold coins were struck (but no half dollars).

Designs. *Obverse:* The statue of *Freedom* full length, with a cloud and rays of glory behind. Lettering around the border. *Reverse:* The mace of the House of Representatives, which is in the House Chamber when that body is in session.

Mintage Data. Authorized by Public Law 100-673, signed by President Ronald Reagan on November 17, 1988. The coins were to be dated 1989 and could be minted through June 30, 1990. *Maximum authorized*—3,000,000. *Number minted*—1989-D: 135,203 Uncirculated; 1989-S: 762,198 Proof.

Original Cost. Sale prices $23 (Uncirculated, pre-issue) and $25 (Proof, pre-issue): Uncirculated later raised to $26, and Proof later raised to $29. Surcharge of $7 per coin went to the Capitol Preservation Fund.

Key to Collecting. Not popular with numismatists in 1989, these coins today can be found for prices close to bullion value. Exceptions are coins certified in ultra-high grades.

	Distribution	Cert	Avg	%MS	MS-67
					PF-67
1989-D	135,203	2,465	69.0	100%	$28
	Auctions: $646, MS-70, September 2014; $940, MS-70, April 2013				
1989-S, Proof	762,198	3,756	68.9		$30
	Auctions: $457, PF-70DCam, May 2013; $42, PF-69DCam, July 2014; $106, PF-69DCam, November 2014; $940, PF-70, March 2013				

CONGRESS BICENTENNIAL $5 GOLD COIN (1989)

Designer: *John Mercanti.* **Weight:** *8.359 grams.* **Composition:** *.900 gold, .100 copper (net weight .242 oz. pure gold).* **Diameter:** *21.6 mm.* **Edge:** *Reeded.* **Mint:** *West Point.*

To diversify the motifs of the three Congress Bicentennial commemorative coins, 11 artists from the private sector were invited to submit designs, as were members of the Mint's Engraving Department staff. The designs for this five-dollar gold coin were praised in the *Annual Report of the Director of the Mint*, 1989, which stated that the obverse displayed "a spectacular rendition of the Capitol dome," while the reverse "center[ed] around a dramatic portrait of the majestic eagle atop the canopy overlooking the Old Senate Chamber."

Designs. *Obverse:* The dome of the Capitol is shown, with lettering around. *Reverse:* The eagle in the old Senate chamber is depicted, with lettering surrounding.

Mintage Data. Authorized by Public Law 100-673, signed by President Ronald Reagan on November 17, 1988. The coins were to be dated 1989 and could be minted through June 30, 1990. *Maximum authorized*—1,000,000. *Number minted*—46,899 Uncirculated and 164,690 Proof.

Original Cost. Sale prices $185 (Uncirculated, pre-issue) and $195 (Proof, pre-issue); Uncirculated later raised to $200, and Proof later raised to $215. Surcharge of $35 per coin went to the Capitol Preservation Fund.

Key to Collecting. Not popular with numismatists in 1989, these coins today can be purchased in the secondary marketplace for prices close to their bullion value. Exceptions are coins certified in ultra-high grades.

	Distribution	Cert	Avg	%MS	MS-67
					PF-67
1989-W	46,899	2,249	69.5	100%	$375
	Auctions: $646, MS-70, September 2014; $376, MS-70, May 2015; $400, MS-69, April 2013				
1989-W, Proof	164,690	5,521	69.4		$325
	Auctions: $341, PF-70UCam, October 2015; $341, PF-70, July 2015; $323, PF-70DCam, April 2015; $306, PF-70DCam, January 2015				

EISENHOWER CENTENNIAL SILVER DOLLAR (1990)

Designer: *John Mercanti (obverse), Marcel Jovine (reverse).* **Weight:** *26.73 grams.*
Composition: *.900 silver, .100 copper (net weight .7736 oz. pure silver).* **Diameter:** *38.1 mm.*
Edge: *Reeded.* **Mints:** *West Point (Uncirculated) and Philadelphia (Proof).*

Five outside artists as well as the artists on the Mint Engraving Department staff were invited to submit designs for this silver dollar. In August 1989, secretary of the Treasury Nicholas F. Brady made the final selections.

This is the only U.S. coin to feature two portraits of the same person on the same side. The reverse shows Eisenhower's retirement residence, identified as EISENHOWER HOME.

Designs. *Obverse:* Profile of President Eisenhower facing right, superimposed over his own left-facing profile as a five-star general. *Reverse:* Eisenhower retirement home at Gettysburg, a national historic site.

Mintage Data. Authorized by Public Law 100-467, signed by President Ronald Reagan on October 3, 1988. *Maximum authorized*—4,000,000. *Number minted*—1990-W: 241,669 Uncirculated; 1990-P: 1,144,461 Proof.

Original Cost. Sale prices $23 (Uncirculated, pre-issue) and $25 (Proof, pre-issue; Uncirculated later raised to $26, and Proof later raised to $29. Surcharge of $7 per coin went to reduce public debt.

Key to Collecting. Eisenhower Centennial dollars are appreciated as a fine addition to the commemorative series. Examples are plentiful and inexpensive in the marketplace. Nearly all are superb gems.

	Distribution	Cert	Avg	%MS	MS-67
					PF-67
1990-W	241,669	2,174	69.1	100%	$35
	Auctions: $206, MS-70, March 2013				
1990-P, Proof	1,144,461	4,180	69.0		$30
	Auctions: $135, PF-70DCam, September 2014; $201, PF-70DCam, March 2013; $42, PF-69DCam, July 2014; $165, PF-68DCam, March 2015				

KOREAN WAR MEMORIAL SILVER DOLLAR (1991)

Designer: *John Mercanti (obverse), James Ferrell (reverse).* **Weight:** *26.73 grams.*
Composition: *.900 silver, .100 copper (net weight .7736 oz. pure silver).*
Diameter: *38.1 mm.* **Edge:** *Reeded.* **Mints:** *Denver (Uncirculated) and Philadelphia (Proof).*

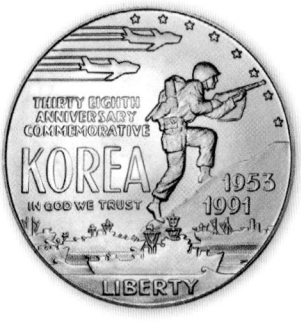 

In the annals of commemoratives, one of the more curious entries is the 1991 silver dollar observing the 38th anniversary of the end of the Korean War, struck to honor those who served there. The 38th anniversary was chosen—rather than the 50th or some other typical anniversary—because, during that war, the 38th degree of latitude on the map defined the division between North and South Korea.

Buyers reacted favorably to the coin, and more than 800,000 were produced.

Designs. *Obverse:* Two F-86 Sabrejet fighter aircraft flying to the right, a helmeted soldier carrying a backpack climbing a hill, and the inscriptions: THIRTY EIGHTH / ANNIVERSARY / COMMEMORATIVE / KOREA / IN GOD WE TRUST / 1953 / 1991. At the bottom of the coin are five Navy ships above the word LIBERTY. *Reverse:* Outline map of North and South Korea, divided. An eagle's head (representing the United States) is depicted to the right. Near the bottom is the symbol of Korea.

Mintage Data. Authorized by Public Law 101-495 of October 31, 1990. *Maximum authorized*—1,000,000. *Number minted*—1991-D: 213,049 Uncirculated; 1991-P: 618,488 Proof.

Original Cost. Sale prices $23 (Uncirculated, pre-issue) and $28 (Proof, pre-issue); Uncirculated later raised to $26, and Proof later raised to $31. A surcharge of $7 went to fund the Korean War Veterans Memorial.

Key to Collecting. Gem Uncirculated and Proof coins are readily available in the marketplace.

	Distribution	Cert	Avg	%MS	MS-67 PF-67
1991-D	213,049	2,346	69.1	100%	$35
	Auctions: $76, MS-70, July 2014; $106, MS-70, January 2013; $69, MS-70, May 2015				
1991-P, Proof	618,488	3,023	68.9		$35
	Auctions: $382, PF-70DCam, September 2014; $505, PF-70DCam, March 2013				

MOUNT RUSHMORE GOLDEN ANNIVERSARY HALF DOLLAR (1991)

Designer: *Marcel Jovine (obverse), T. James Ferrell (reverse).* **Weight:** *11.34 grams.*
Composition: *.9167 copper, .0833 nickel.* **Diameter:** *30.61 mm.* **Edge:** *Reeded.*
Mints: *Denver (Uncirculated) and San Francisco (Proof).*

This half dollar was part of a trio of coins struck to mark the Mount Rushmore National Memorial's 50th anniversary. Surcharges from their sale were divided between the Treasury Department and the Mount Rushmore National Memorial Society of Black Hills, North Dakota, with money going toward restoration work on the landmark.

Designs. *Obverse:* View of Mount Rushmore with rays of the sun behind. *Reverse:* An American bison with the words GOLDEN ANNIVERSARY.

Mintage Data. Authorized by the Mount Rushmore National Memorial Coin Act (Public Law 101-332, July 16, 1990). *Maximum authorized*—2,500,000. *Number minted*—1991-D: 172,754 Uncirculated; 1991-S: 753,257 Proof.

Original Cost. Sale prices $6 (Uncirculated) and $8.50 (Proof); Uncirculated later raised to $7, and Proof later raised to $9.50. Fifty percent of the surcharge of $1 per coin went to the Mount Rushmore National Memorial Society of Black Hills; the balance went to the U.S. Treasury.

Key to Collecting. Examples are easily available today. The coins were carefully struck, with the result that nearly all are superb gems.

	Distribution	Cert	Avg	%MS	MS-67
					PF-67
1991-D	172,754	1,708	69.1	100%	$15
	Auctions: $306, MS-70, September 2014; $823, MS-70, March 2013				
1991-S, Proof	753,257	3,190	69.1		$12
	Auctions: No auction records available.				

MOUNT RUSHMORE GOLDEN ANNIVERSARY SILVER DOLLAR (1991)

Designer: *Marika Somogyi (obverse), Frank Gasparro (reverse).* **Weight:** *26.73 grams.*
Composition: *.900 silver, .100 copper (net weight .7736 oz. pure silver).* **Diameter:** *38.1 mm.*
Edge: *Reeded.* **Mints:** *Philadelphia (Uncirculated) and San Francisco (Proof).*

The Mount Rushmore silver dollar displays the traditional portraits of presidents George Washington, Thomas Jefferson, Theodore Roosevelt, and Abraham Lincoln as sculpted on the mountain by Gutzon Borglum. The reverse was by former chief sculptor-engraver of the U.S. Mint Frank Gasparro.

Designs. *Obverse:* View of Mount Rushmore with an olive wreath prominently below. *Reverse:* The Great Seal of the United States, surrounded by a sunburst, above an outline map of the continental part of the United States inscribed SHRINE OF / DEMOCRACY.

Mintage Data. Authorized by the Mount Rushmore National Memorial Coin Act (Public Law 101-332, July 16, 1990). *Maximum authorized*—2,500,000. *Number minted*—1991-P: 133,139 Uncirculated; 1991-S: 738,419 Proof.

Original Cost. Sale prices $23 (Uncirculated, pre-issue) and $28 (Proof, pre-issue); Uncirculated later raised to $28, and Proof later raised to $31. Fifty percent of the surcharge of $7 per coin went to the Mount Rushmore National Memorial Society of Black Hills; the balance went to the U.S. Treasury.

Key to Collecting. Examples are easily available today. The coins were carefully struck, with the result that nearly all are superb gems.

	Distribution	Cert	Avg	%MS	MS-67
					PF-67
1991-P	133,139	1,849	69.3	100%	$40
	Auctions: $80, MS-70, July 2014; $92, MS-70, January 2013				
1991-S, Proof	738,419	3,793	69.0		$35
	Auctions: $194, PF-70DCam, September 2014; $176, PF-70DCam, June 2013; $174, PF-70DCam, February 2013; $53, PF-69DCam, July 2014				

MOUNT RUSHMORE GOLDEN ANNIVERSARY $5 GOLD COIN (1991)

Designer: *John Mercanti (obverse), William Lamb (reverse).* **Weight:** *8.359 grams.*
Composition: *.900 gold, .100 copper (net weight .242 oz. pure gold).*
Diameter: *21.6 mm.* **Edge:** *Reeded.* **Mint:** *West Point.*

The reverse of the five-dollar Mount Rushmore coin consisted solely of lettering, with no emblems or motifs, the first such instance in the history of U.S. commemorative coins.

Designs. *Obverse:* An American eagle flying above the monument with LIBERTY and date in the field. *Reverse:* MOUNT RUSHMORE NATIONAL MEMORIAL in script type.

Mintage Data. Authorized by the Mount Rushmore National Memorial Coin Act (Public Law 101-332, July 16, 1990). *Maximum authorized—* 500,000. *Number minted—*31,959 Uncirculated and 111,991 Proof.

Original Cost. Sale prices $185 (Uncirculated, pre-issue) and $195 (Proof, pre-issue); Uncirculated later raised to $210, and Proof later raised to $225. Fifty percent of the surcharge of $35 per coin went to the Mount Rushmore National Memorial Society of Black Hills; the balance went to the U.S. Treasury.

Key to Collecting. Examples are easily available today. The coins were carefully struck, with the result that nearly all are superb gems.

	Distribution	Cert	Avg	%MS	MS-67 / PF-67
1991-W	31,959	1,623	69.6	100%	$375
	Auctions: $653, MS-70, September 2014; $573, MS-70, November 2014; $353, MS-70, May 2015; $353, MS-70, April 2015				
1991-W, Proof	111,991	4,098	69.4		$325
	Auctions: $456, PF-70DCam, February 2013; $423, PF-70DCam, May 2015; $306, PF-69DCam, October 2014				

UNITED SERVICE ORGANIZATIONS SILVER DOLLAR (1991)

Designer: *Robert Lamb (obverse), John Mercanti (reverse).* **Weight:** *26.73 grams.*
Composition: *.900 silver, .100 copper (net weight .7736 oz. pure silver).*
Diameter: *38.1 mm.* **Edge:** *Reeded.* **Mints:** *Denver (Uncirculated) and San Francisco (Proof).*

The United Service Organizations is a congressionally chartered nonprofit group that provides services, programs, and live entertainment to U.S. military troops and their families. The 50th anniversary of the USO was commemorated with this silver dollar in 1991.

Designs. *Obverse:* Consists entirely of lettering, except for a banner upon which appears USO. Inscriptions include IN GOD WE TRUST, 50th ANNIVERSARY (in script), USO (on a banner, as noted; with three stars to each side), and LIBERTY 1991. *Reverse:* Illustrates an eagle, facing right, with a ribbon inscribed USO in its beak, perched atop a world globe. An arc of 11 stars is in the space below the globe. The legends include FIFTY YEARS / SERVICE (on the left side of the coin), TO SERVICE / PEOPLE (on the right side of the coin).

Mintage Data. Authorized by Public Law 101-404, October 2, 1990. *Maximum authorized*—1,000,000. *Number minted*—1991-D: 124,958 Uncirculated; 1991-S: 321,275 Proof.

Original Cost. Sale prices $23 (Uncirculated, pre-issue) and $28 (Proof, pre-issue); Uncirculated later raised to $26, and Proof later raised to $31. Fifty percent of the surcharge of $7 per coin went to the USO; the balance went toward reducing the national debt.

Key to Collecting. Mintages were low compared to other recent commemorative silver dollars. Today these coins can be purchased for slightly more than their bullion value.

	Distribution	Cert	Avg	%MS	MS-67 PF-67
1991-D	124,958	2,106	69.1	100%	$35
	Auctions: $92, MS-70, March 2013; $86, MS-70, July 2014; $66, MS-70, May 2015				
1991-S, Proof	321,275	2,293	69.0		$30
	Auctions: $881, PF-70DCam, September 2014; $235, PF-70DCam, September 2014; $382, PF-70DCam, April 2013				

CHRISTOPHER COLUMBUS QUINCENTENARY HALF DOLLAR (1992)

Designer: *T. James Ferrell.* **Weight:** *11.34 grams.* **Composition:** *.9167 copper, .0833 nickel.* **Diameter:** *30.61 mm.* **Edge:** *Reeded.* **Mints:** *Denver (Uncirculated) and San Francisco (Proof).*

The 500th anniversary of Christopher Columbus's first trip to the new world was observed in 1992 by a suite of commemoratives, including this clad half dollar. The numismatic tradition fit in nicely with the World's Columbian Exposition coins of a century earlier—the first commemorative half dollars issued in 1892 and 1893.

Designs. *Obverse:* A full-length figure of Columbus walking ashore, with a rowboat and the flagship *Santa Maria* in the background. *Reverse:* The reverse shows Columbus's three ships—the *Nina*, *Pinta*, and *Santa Maria*.

Mintage Data. Authorized by Public Law 102-281, signed by President George H.W. Bush on May 13, 1992. *Maximum authorized*—6,000,000. *Number minted*—1992-D: 135,702 Uncirculated; 1992-S: 390,154 Proof.

Original Cost. Sale prices $6.50 (Uncirculated, pre-issue) and $8.50 (Proof, pre-issue); Uncirculated later raised to $7.50, and Proof later raised to $9.50. A surcharge of $1 per coin went to the Christopher Columbus Quincentenary Coins and Fellowship Foundation.

Key to Collecting. Examples in the marketplace remain reasonably priced. Nearly all are superb gems.

	Distribution	Cert	Avg	%MS	MS-67 PF-67
1992-D	135,702	956	69.2	100%	$10
	Auctions: $86, MS-70, April 2013				
1992-S, Proof	390,154	2,569	69.1		$10
	Auctions: No auction records available.				

CHRISTOPHER COLUMBUS QUINCENTENARY SILVER DOLLAR (1992)

Designer: *John Mercanti (obverse), Thomas D. Rogers Sr. (reverse).* **Weight:** *26.73 grams.*
Composition: *.900 silver, .100 copper (net weight .7736 oz. pure silver).*
Diameter: *38.1 mm.* **Edge:** *Reeded.* **Mints:** *Denver (Uncirculated) and Philadelphia (Proof).*

Representative Frank Annunzio, a Democrat from Illinois who was prominent in coin legislation for some time, introduced the bill that led to these commemoratives. Interestingly, on the approved sketch for this silver dollar's obverse design, Columbus was depicted holding a telescope—but after it was pointed out that such instrument had not been invented yet in 1492, it was changed to a scroll on the final coin.

Designs. *Obverse:* Columbus standing, holding a flag in his right hand, with a scroll in his left hand, and with a globe on a stand. Three ships are shown in the distance, in a panel at the top border. *Reverse:* A split image is shown, depicting exploration in 1492 at the left, with half of a sailing vessel, and in 1992 at the right, with most of a space shuttle shown in a vertical position, with the earth in the distance.

Mintage Data. Authorized by Public Law 102-281, signed by President George H.W. Bush on May 13, 1992. *Maximum authorized*—4,000,000. *Number minted*—1992-D: 106,949 Uncirculated; 1992-P: 385,241 Proof.

Original Cost. Sale prices $23 (Uncirculated, pre-issue) and $27 (Proof, pre-issue); Uncirculated later raised to $28, and Proof later raised to $31. A surcharge of $7 per coin went to the Christopher Columbus Quincentenary Coins and Fellowship Foundation.

Key to Collecting. Examples in the marketplace remain reasonably priced. Nearly all are superb gems.

	Distribution	Cert	Avg	%MS	MS-67
					PF-67
1992-D	106,949	1,761	69.2	100%	$40
	Auctions: $135, MS-70, March 2013; $86, MS-70, July 2014; $62, MS-70, September 2015				
1992-P, Proof	385,241	2,722	69.0		$35
	Auctions: $441, PF-70DCam, September 2014; $418, PF-70DCam, June 2013; $96, PF-70DCam, April 2013				

CHRISTOPHER COLUMBUS QUINCENTENARY $5 GOLD COIN (1992)

Designer: *T. James Ferrell (obverse), Thomas D. Rogers Sr. (reverse).* **Weight:** *8.359 grams.*
Composition: *.900 gold, .100 copper (net weight .242 oz. pure gold).*
Diameter: *21.6 mm.* **Edge:** *Reeded.* **Mint:** *West Point.*

No portrait from the life of Christopher Columbus is known to exist, so the five-dollar gold commemorative features T. James Ferrell's artistic imagining of the explorer's profile.

Designs. *Obverse:* The artist's conception of Columbus's face is shown gazing to the left toward an outline map of the New World. *Reverse:* The crest of the Admiral of the Ocean Sea and a chart dated 1492 are depicted.

Mintage Data. Authorized by Public Law 102-281, signed by President George H.W. Bush on May 13, 1992. *Maximum authorized—1,000,000. Number minted—*24,329 Uncirculated and 79,730 Proof.

Original Cost. Sale prices $180 (Uncirculated, pre-issue) and $190 (Proof, pre-issue); Uncirculated later raised to $210, and Proof later raised to $225. A surcharge of $35 per coin went to the Christopher Columbus Quincentenary Coins and Fellowship Foundation.

Key to Collecting. Examples in the marketplace remain reasonably priced. Nearly all are superb gems.

	Distribution	Cert	Avg	%MS	MS-67
					PF-67
1992-W	24,329	1,330	69.6	100%	$375
Auctions: $447, MS-70, June 2014; $646, MS-70, September 2014; $317, MS-69, August 2014; $306, MS-69, August 2014					
1992-W, Proof	79,730	2,837	69.5		$325
Auctions: $353, PF-70DCam, May 2015; $329, PF-70DCam, May 2015; $435, PF-69DCam, April 2013; $306, PF-69DCam, August 2014					

XXV OLYMPIC GAMES HALF DOLLAR (1992)

Designer: *William Cousins (obverse), Steven M. Bieda (reverse).*
Weight: *11.34 grams.* **Composition:** *.9167 copper, .0833 nickel.* **Diameter:** *30.61 mm.*
Edge: *Reeded.* **Mints:** *Philadelphia (Uncirculated) and San Francisco (Proof).*

In 1992 the XXV Winter Olympic Games were held in Albertville and Savoie, France, while the Summer Games took place in Barcelona, Spain. Although the events did not take place in the United States, the rationale for a commemorative coin issue was, in part, to raise money to train American athletes. The same line of reasoning had been used for the coins made in connection with the 1988 Olympic Games held in Seoul, South Korea.

Designs. *Obverse:* A pony-tailed female gymnast doing the stretch against a background of stars and stripes. *Reverse:* The Olympic torch and an olive branch, with CITIUS / ALTIUS / FORTIUS nearby in three lines, Latin for "faster, higher, stronger."

Mintage Data. Authorized by the 1992 Olympic Commemorative Coin Act, Public Law 101-406, signed by President George H.W. Bush on October 3, 1990. *Maximum authorized—6,000,000. Number minted—*1992-P: 161,607 Uncirculated; 1992-S: 519,645 Proof.

Original Cost. Sale prices $6 (Uncirculated, pre-issue) and $8.50 (Proof, pre-issue); Uncirculated later raised to $7.50, and Proof later raised to $9.50. The surcharge of $1 per coin went to the U.S. Olympic Committee.

Key to Collecting. Examples are easily available today. Nearly all are gems.

	Distribution	Cert	Avg	%MS	MS-67
					PF-67
1992-P	161,607	1,111	69.3	100%	$10
Auctions: $59, MS-70, January 2013					
1992-S, Proof	519,645	2,547	69.2		$10
Auctions: No auction records available.					

XXV Olympic Games Silver Dollar (1992)

Designer: *John R. Deecken (obverse), Marcel Jovine (reverse).* **Weight:** *26.73 grams.*
Composition: *.900 silver, .100 copper (net weight .7736 oz. pure silver).* **Diameter:** *38.1 mm.*
Edge: *Lettered (Uncirculated), reeded (Proof).* **Mints:** *Denver (Uncirculated) and San Francisco (Proof).*

The image on this coin's obverse fit closely that of Fleer's card showing popular baseball player Nolan Ryan, of the Texas Rangers, but the designer denied there was any connection when queried on the subject by the Treasury Department. The Denver Mint Uncirculated dollars have XXV OLYMPIAD incuse four times around the edge, alternately inverted, on a reeded background; these are the first lettered-edge U.S. coins since the 1933 double eagle.

Designs. *Obverse:* A pitcher is shown about to throw a ball to a batter. *Reverse:* A shield, intertwined Olympic rings, and olive branches make up the main design.

Mintage Data. Authorized by the 1992 Olympic Commemorative Coin Act, Public Law 101-406, signed by President George H.W. Bush on October 3, 1990. *Maximum authorized*—4,000,000. *Number minted*—1992-D: 187,552 Uncirculated; 1992-S: 504,505 Proof.

Original Cost. Sale prices $24 (Uncirculated, pre-issue) and $28 (Proof, pre-issue); Uncirculated later raised to $28, and Proof later raised to $32. The surcharge of $1 per coin went to the U.S. Olympic Committee.

Key to Collecting. Examples are easily available today. Nearly all are gems.

	Distribution	Cert	Avg	%MS	MS-67 / PF-67
1992-D	187,552	3,696	69.0	100%	$38
	Auctions: $247, MS-70, April 2013				
1992-S, Proof	504,505	2,927	69.0		$35
	Auctions: $588, PF-70DCam, September 2013; $84, PF-70, February 2013; $30, PF-69UCam, January 2015				

XXV Olympic Games $5 Gold Coin (1992)

Designer: *James Sharpe (obverse), James Peed (reverse).* **Weight:** *8.359 grams.*
Composition: *.900 gold, .100 copper (net weight .242 oz. pure gold).*
Diameter: *21.6 mm.* **Edge:** *Reeded.* **Mint:** *West Point.*

The five-dollar entry in the XXV commemorative coin program features a dynamic sprinter against a backdrop of the U.S. flag. Sales were relatively low compared to other recent gold commemoratives.

Designs. *Obverse:* A sprinter running forward with a vertical U.S. flag in the background. *Reverse:* A heraldic eagle with five Olympic rings and USA above.

Mintage Data. Authorized by the 1992 Olympic Commemorative Coin Act, Public Law 101-406, signed by President George H.W. Bush on October 3, 1990. *Maximum authorized—500,000. Number minted—*27,732 Uncirculated and 77,313 Proof.

Original Cost. Sale prices $185 (Uncirculated, pre-issue) and $195 (Proof, pre-issue); Uncirculated later raised to $215, and Proof later raised to $230. The surcharge of $35 per coin went to the U.S. Olympic Committee.

Key to Collecting. Examples are easily available today. Nearly all are gems.

	Distribution	Cert	Avg	%MS	MS-67 PF-67
1992-W	27,732	1,569	69.7	100%	$375
	Auctions: $376, MS-70, May 2015; $364, MS-70, May 2015; $350, MS-70, April 2015; $329, MS-70, June 2015				
1992-W, Proof	77,313	3,117	69.5		$325
	Auctions: $423, PF-70UCam, March 2015; $364, PF-70UCam, April 2015; $358, PF-70UCam, March 2015; $333, PF-70UCam, May 2015				

WHITE HOUSE 200TH ANNIVERSARY SILVER DOLLAR (1992)

Designer: *Edgar Z. Steever IV (obverse), Chester Y. Martin (reverse).* **Weight:** *26.73 grams.*
Composition: *.900 silver, .100 copper (net weight .7736 oz. pure silver).*
Diameter: *38.1 mm.* **Edge:** *Reeded.* **Mints:** *Denver (Uncirculated) and West Point (Proof).*

This coin is one of few depicting Washington buildings that sold out its full authorized limit. Foliage, two trees, and a fountain were in the original sketch, but were removed at the suggestion of the Fine Arts Commission, yielding a clean and crisp design.

Designs. *Obverse:* The north portico of the White House is shown in a plan view, without shrubbery or background. *Reverse:* James Hoban, architect of the first White House, in a half-length portrait with the original entrance door.

Mintage Data. Authorized by Public Law 102-281, signed by President George H.W. Bush on May 13, 1992. *Maximum authorized—500,000. Number minted—*1992-D: 123,803 Uncirculated; 1992-W: 375,851 Proof.

Original Cost. Sale prices (pre-issue only) $23 (Uncirculated) and $28 (Proof). The surcharge of $10 per coin went towards the preservation of public rooms within the White House.

Key to Collecting. The White House dollar has remained popular ever since its issuance. Examples are readily available today and are nearly always found in superb gem preservation, as issued.

	Distribution	Cert	Avg	%MS	MS-67 PF-67
1992-D	123,803	2,030	69.2	100%	$28
	Auctions: $108, MS-70, January 2013				
1992-W, Proof	375,851	2,904	69.0		$35
	Auctions: $194, PF-70DCam, April 2013				

BILL OF RIGHTS HALF DOLLAR (1993)

Designer: *T. James Ferrell (obverse), Dean McMullen (reverse).* **Weight:** *12.5 grams.*
Composition: *.900 silver, .100 copper.* **Diameter:** *30.6 mm.* **Edge:** *Reeded.*
Mints: *West Point (Uncirculated) and San Francisco (Proof).*

This silver half dollar, as well as the silver dollar and five-dollar gold coin issued alongside it, honored James Madison and the Bill of Rights, added to the Constitution in 1789 and intended to give basic rights and freedoms to all Americans. These were the first half dollars to be composed of 90% silver since the George Washington 250th Anniversary of Birth coins in 1982.

Designs. *Obverse:* James Madison seated at a desk, penning the Bill of Rights. Montpelier, Madison's Virginia home, is shown in the distance. *Reverse:* A hand holds a flaming torch, with inscriptions to each side.

Mintage Data. Authorized by Public Law 101-281, part of the White House Commemorative Coin Act, on May 13, 1992. *Maximum authorized*—1,000,000. *Number minted*—1993-W: 193,346 Uncirculated; 1993-S: 586,315 Proof.

Original Cost. Sale prices $9.75 (Uncirculated, pre-issue) and $12.50 (Proof, pre-issue); Uncirculated later increased in $11.50, and Proof later increased to $13.50. The surcharge went to the James Madison Memorial Scholarship Trust Fund.

Key to Collecting. Following the pattern of other commemoratives of the early 1990s, these coins are readily available on the market, typically in superb gem preservation.

	Distribution	Cert	Avg	%MS	MS-67 PF-67
1993-W	193,346	1,186	69.2	100%	$20
	Auctions: $82, MS-70, April 2013				
1993-S, Proof	586,315	2,761	69.0		$15
	Auctions: $441, PF-70DCam, April 2013; $382, PF-70DCam, April 2013				

BILL OF RIGHTS SILVER DOLLAR (1993)

Designer: *William Krawczewicz (obverse), Dean McMullen (reverse).* **Weight:** *26.73 grams.*
Composition: *.900 silver, .100 copper (net weight .7736 oz. pure silver).*
Diameter: *38.1 mm.* **Edge:** *Reeded.* **Mints:** *Denver (Uncirculated) and San Francisco (Proof).*

On June 1, 1992, U.S. Treasurer Catalina Vasquez Villalpando announced a nationwide competition seeking designs for the James Madison / Bill of Rights Commemorative Coin Program, with all entries to be received by August 31. Secretary of the Treasury Nicholas F. Brady selected his favorite motifs from 815 submissions, which were then sent to the Commission of Fine Arts for review. Many changes were suggested, including simplifying the appearance of Madison's residence, Montpelier.

Designs. *Obverse:* Portrait of James Madison facing right and slightly forward. *Reverse:* Montpelier.

Mintage Data. Authorized by Public Law 101-281, part of the White House Commemorative Coin Act, on May 13, 1992. *Maximum authorized*—900,000. *Number minted*—1993-D: 98,383 Uncirculated; 1993-S: 534,001 Proof.

Original Cost. Sale prices $22 (Uncirculated, pre-issue) and $25 (Proof, pre-issue); Uncirculated later raised to $27, and Proof later raised to $29. The surcharge went to the James Madison Memorial Scholarship Trust Fund.

Key to Collecting. Following the pattern of other commemoratives of the early 1990s, these coins are readily available on the market, typically in superb gem preservation.

	Distribution	Cert	Avg	%MS	MS-67 / PF-67
1993-D	98,383	1,411	69.1	100%	$40
	Auctions: $182, MS-70, January 2013				
1993-S, Proof	534,001	2,421	68.9		$35
	Auctions: No auction records available.				

BILL OF RIGHTS $5 GOLD COIN (1993)

Designer: *Scott R. Blazek (obverse), Joseph D. Peña (reverse).* **Weight:** *8.359 grams.*
Composition: *.900 gold, .100 copper (net weight .242 oz. pure gold).*
Diameter: *21.6 mm.* **Edge:** *Reeded.* **Mint:** *West Point.*

The coin project that resulted in this five-dollar gold coin (and the related half dollar and silver dollar) was encouraged by the Madison Foundation.

Designs. *Obverse:* Portrait of Madison, waist up, reading the Bill of Rights. *Reverse:* Quotation by Madison with an eagle above and small torch and laurel branch at the border below.

Mintage Data. Authorized by Public Law 101-281, part of the White House Commemorative Coin Act, on May 13, 1992. *Maximum authorized*—300,000. *Number minted*—23,266 Uncirculated and 78,651 Proof.

Original Cost. Sale prices $175 (Uncirculated, pre-issue) and $185 (Proof, pre-issue); Uncirculated later raised to $205, and Proof later raised to $220. The surcharge of $10 per coin went to the James Madison Memorial Scholarship Trust Fund.

Key to Collecting. Following the pattern of other commemoratives of the early 1990s, these coins are readily available on the market, typically in superb gem preservation.

	Distribution	Cert	Avg	%MS	MS-67 / PF-67
1993-W	23,266	1,344	69.6	100%	$375
	Auctions: $329, MS-70, August 2014; $652, MS-70, September 2014; $400, MS-69, March 2013				
1993-W, Proof	78,651	3,272	69.4		$325
	Auctions: $306, PF-70DCam, November 2014; $435, PF-70DCam, March 2013; $317, PF-69DCam, August 2014; $329, PF-69DCam, October 2014				

50TH ANNIVERSARY OF WORLD WAR II HALF DOLLAR (1991–1995)

Designer: *George Klauba (obverse), Bill J. Leftwich (reverse).* **Weight:** *11.34 grams.*
Composition: *.9167 copper, .0833 nickel.* **Diameter:** *30.61 mm.* **Edge:** *Reeded.* **Mint:** *Philadelphia.*

These half dollars and the other World War II 50th-anniversary coins were issued in 1993 and dated 1991–1995. Despite the importance of the war commemorated, the coins met with a lukewarm response by purchasers.

Designs. *Obverse:* The heads of a soldier, sailor, and airman are shown superimposed on a V (for victory), with a B-17 bomber flying overhead. *Reverse:* An American Marine is shown in action during the takeover of a Japanese-held island in the South Pacific. A carrier-based fighter plane flies overhead.

Mintage Data. Authorized by Public Law 102-414, signed by President William J. Clinton on October 14, 1992. *Maximum authorized*—2,000,000. *Number minted*—197,072 Uncirculated and 317,396 Proof.

Original Cost. Sale prices $8 (Uncirculated, pre-issue) and $9 (Proof, pre-issue); Uncirculated later raised to $9, and Proof later raised to $10. The surcharge of $2 per coin was split between the American Battle Monuments Commission (to aid in the construction of the World War II Monument in the nation's capital) and the Battle of Normandy Foundation (to assist in the erection of a monument in France).

Key to Collecting. Examples are easily enough found in the marketplace today and are nearly always of superb gem quality.

	Distribution	Cert	Avg	%MS	MS-67
					PF-67
1991–1995 (1993-P)	197,072	1,232	69.1	100%	$15
	Auctions: $165, MS-70Cam, September 2014; $529, MS-70Cam, April 2013; $153, MS-70, June 2013				
1991–1995 (1993-P), Proof	317,396	2,090	69.0		$15
	Auctions: No auction records available.				

50TH ANNIVERSARY OF WORLD WAR II SILVER DOLLAR (1991–1995)

Designer: *Thomas D. Rogers Sr.* **Weight:** *26.73 grams.*
Composition: *.900 silver, .100 copper (net weight .7736 oz. pure silver).*
Diameter: *38.1 mm.* **Edge:** *Reeded.* **Mints:** *Denver (Uncirculated) and West Point (Proof).*

 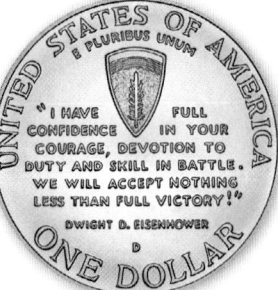

The designs for these silver dollars and the related half dollars and five-dollar gold coins were the result of a competition. The works of five artists were selected (only one of them, Thomas D. Rogers Sr., being from the Mint staff). It was mandated that the dollar use the Battle of Normandy as a theme.

Designs. *Obverse:* An American soldier is shown as he runs ashore on the beach in Normandy during the D-Day invasion on June 6, 1944, which launched from England to liberate France. *Reverse:* The reverse illustrates the shoulder patch used on a uniform of Dwight D. Eisenhower's Supreme Headquarters Allied Expeditionary Force, with a quotation from Eisenhower.

Mintage Data. Authorized by Public Law 102-414, signed by President William J. Clinton on October 14, 1992. *Maximum authorized*—1,000,000. *Number minted*—1993-D: 107,240 Uncirculated; 1993-W: 342,041 Proof.

Original Cost. Sale prices $23 (Uncirculated, pre-issue) and $27 (Proof, pre-issue); Uncirculated later raised to $28, and Proof later raised to $31. The surcharge of $2 per coin was split between the American Battle Monuments Commission (to aid in the construction of the World War II Monument in the nation's capital) and the Battle of Normandy Foundation (to assist in the erection of a monument in France).

Key to Collecting. Examples are easily enough found in the marketplace today and are nearly always of superb gem quality.

	Distribution	Cert	Avg	%MS	MS-67 PF-67
1991–1995 (1993-D)	107,240	1,996	69.3	100%	$45
	Auctions: $118, MS-70, January 2013; $86, MS-70, July 2014; $74, MS-70, August 2015; $74, MS-70, May 2015				
1991–1995 (1993-W), Proof	342,041	3,201	69.0		$45
	Auctions: $206, PF-70DCam, September 2014				

50TH ANNIVERSARY OF WORLD WAR II $5 GOLD COIN (1991–1995)

Designer: *Charles J. Madsen (obverse), Edward Southworth Fisher (reverse).*
Weight: *8.359 grams.* **Composition:** *.900 gold, .100 copper (net weight .242 oz. pure gold).*
Diameter: *21.6 mm.* **Edge:** *Reeded.* **Mint:** *West Point.*

The approval of the American Legion, Veterans of Foreign Wars of the United States, American Veterans of World War, Korea and Vietnam (AMVETS), and the Disabled American Veterans, was required for the designs of all three 50th Anniversary of World War II commemoratives. The five-dollar coin was mandated to reflect the Allied victory in the war.

Designs. *Obverse:* An American soldier holds his rifle and raises his arm to indicate victory. *Reverse:* A large V (for victory) is at the center, with three dots and a dash over it, the Morse code for that letter. Branches are to each side.

Mintage Data. Authorized by Public Law 102-414, signed by President William J. Clinton on October 14, 1992. *Maximum authorized*—300,000. *Number minted*—23,672 Uncirculated and 67,026 Proof.

Original Cost. Sale prices $170 (Uncirculated, pre-issue) and $185 (Proof, pre-issue); Uncirculated later raised to $185, and Proof later raised to $220. The surcharge of $35 per coin was split between the American Battle Monuments Commission (to aid in the construction of the World War II Monument in the nation's capital) and the Battle of Normandy Foundation (to assist in the erection of a monument in France).

Key to Collecting. Examples are easily enough found in the marketplace today and are nearly always of superb gem quality.

	Distribution	Cert	Avg	%MS	MS-67
					PF-67
1991–1995 (1993-W)	23,672	1,421	69.6	100%	$400
	Auctions: $646, MS-70, September 2014; $411, MS-70, April 2013; $353, MS-69, August 2014				
1991–1995 (1993-W), Proof	67,026	2,540	69.3		$400
	Auctions: $458, PF-70DCam, April 2013; $382, PF-70DCam, April 2013; $333, PF-69DCam, August 2014				

THOMAS JEFFERSON SILVER DOLLAR (1993)

Designer: *T. James Ferrell.* **Weight:** *26.73 grams.*
Composition: *.900 silver, .100 copper (net weight .7736 oz. pure silver).*
Diameter: *38.1 mm.* **Edge:** *Reeded.* **Mints:** *Philadelphia (Uncirculated) and San Francisco (Proof).*

The 250th anniversary in 1993 of the birth of Thomas Jefferson in 1743 furnished the occasion for a commemorative silver dollar. The obverse portrait was based on an 1805 painting by Gilbert Stuart.

Designs. *Obverse:* Profile bust of President Thomas Jefferson. *Reverse:* Monticello, Jefferson's home.

Mintage Data. Authorized under Public Law 103-186, signed by President William J. Clinton on December 14, 1993. *Maximum authorized*—600,000. *Number minted*—1993-P: 266,927 Uncirculated; 1993-S: 332,891 Proof.

Original Cost. Sale prices $27 (Uncirculated, pre-issue) and $31 (Proof, pre-issue); Uncirculated later raised to $32, and Proof later raised to $35. The surcharge of $10 per coin went to the Jefferson Endowment Fund.

Key to Collecting. Although the Jefferson dollar was a popular sellout in its time, examples are easily found in the numismatic marketplace and are nearly always of superb gem quality. Most in demand, from the enthusiasm of five-cent piece collectors, are the special sets issued with the frosty Uncirculated 1994-P Jefferson nickel.

	Distribution	Cert	Avg	%MS	MS-67
					PF-67
1993-P	266,927	3,064	69.2	100%	$30
	Auctions: $86, MS-70, January 2013				
1993-S, Proof	332,891	2,637	69.0		$20
	Auctions: $400, PF-70DCam, March 2013				

U.S. CAPITOL BICENTENNIAL SILVER DOLLAR (1994)

Designer: *William Cousins (obverse), John Mercanti (reverse).* **Weight:** *26.73 grams.*
Composition: *.900 silver, .100 copper (net weight .7736 oz. pure silver).*
Diameter: *38.1 mm.* **Edge:** *Reeded.* **Mints:** *Denver (Uncirculated) and San Francisco (Proof).*

These silver dollars commemorated the 200th anniversary of the U.S. Capitol in Washington, D.C. Although the Federal City, as it was called, was laid out in the 1790s, it was not until 1800 that the federal government relocated there from Philadelphia. In honor of the recently deceased first president, the name was changed to Washington City, or, in popular use, Washington. The Capitol building design represented the work of several architects and artists, among them Benjamin Latrobe, Charles Bulfinch, and Constantino Brumidi.

Designs. *Obverse:* Dome of the Capitol with stars surrounding the *Freedom* statue. *Reverse:* Shield with four American flags, branches, and surmounted by an eagle, a motif based on the center area of a stained-glass window near the House and Senate grand staircases (produced by J. & G. Gibson, of Philadelphia, in 1859 and 1860).

Mintage Data. Authorized by Public Law 103-186, signed by President William J. Clinton on December 14, 1993. *Maximum authorized*—500,000. *Number minted*—1994-D: 68,332 Uncirculated; 1994-S: 279,579 Proof.

Original Cost. Sale prices $32 (Uncirculated, pre-issue) and $36 (Proof, pre-issue; Uncirculated later raised to $37, and Proof later raised to $40. The surcharge of $15 per coin went to the United States Capitol Preservation Commission. A Mint announcement noted that this was to go "for the construction of the Capitol Visitor Center" (itself the subject of a 2001 commemorative dollar).

Key to Collecting. Superb gem Mint State and Proof coins are easily available.

	Distribution	Cert	Avg	%MS	MS-67 / PF-67
1994-D	68,332	1,570	69.4	100%	$40
Auctions: $101, MS-70, January 2013; $100, MS-70, August 2015; $80, MS-70, July 2014					
1994-S, Proof	279,579	1,850	69.0		$35
Auctions: $294, PF-70DCam, April 2013; $270, PF-70DCam, September 2014; $217, PF-70DCam, August 2014					

U.S. Prisoner of War Memorial Silver Dollar (1994)

Designer: *Tom Nielsen (obverse), Edgar Z. Steever IV (reverse).* **Weight:** *26.73 grams.*
Composition: *.900 silver, .100 copper (net weight .7736 oz. pure silver).*
Diameter: *38.1 mm.* **Edge:** *Reeded.* **Mints:** *West Point (Uncirculated) and Philadelphia (Proof).*

The proposed National Prisoner of War Museum set the stage for the issuance of a silver dollar observing the tribulations of prisoners held by foreign military powers. The obverse designer, Nielsen, was a decorated former prisoner of war employed by the Bureau of Veterans Affairs.

Designs. *Obverse:* An eagle with a chain on one leg flies through a circle of barbed wire, representing flight to freedom. *Reverse:* Plan view, with landscaping, of the proposed National Prisoner of War Museum.

Mintage Data. Authorized by Public Law 103-186, signed by President William J. Clinton on December 14, 1993. *Maximum authorized*—500,000. *Number minted*—1994-W: 54,893 Uncirculated; 1994-P: 224,449 Proof.

Original Cost. Sale prices $27 (Uncirculated, pre-issue) and $31 (Proof, pre-issue); Uncirculated later raised to $32, and Proof later raised to $35. The surcharge of $10 per coin went toward the construction of the museum.

Key to Collecting. The 1994-W dollar is in special demand due to its relatively low mintage. Both varieties are seen with frequency in the marketplace and are nearly always superb gems.

	Distribution	Cert	Avg	%MS	MS-67
					PF-67
1994-W	54,893	1,909	69.4	100%	$80
	Auctions: $129, MS-70, January 2014; $100, MS-70, February 2015; $94, MS-70, January 2015; $87, MS-70, May 2015				
1994-P, Proof	224,449	2,439	68.9		$45
	Auctions: $1,116, PF-70DCam, September 2014; $999, PF-70DCam, September 2014; $1,763, PF-70DCam, January 2013				

Women in Military Service Memorial Silver Dollar (1994)

Designer: *T. James Ferrell.* **Weight:** *26.73 grams.*
Composition: *.900 silver, .100 copper (net weight .7736 oz. pure silver).*
Diameter: *38.1 mm.* **Edge:** *Reeded.* **Mints:** *West Point (Uncirculated) and Philadelphia (Proof).*

These coins were issued to honor women in the military and help fund the Women in Military Service for America Memorial at the ceremonial entrance to Arlington National Cemetery (which became a reality and opened in October 1997 on a 4.2-acre site).

Designs. *Obverse:* Servicewomen from the Army, Marine Corps, Navy, Air Force, and

Coast Guard, with the names of these branches around the border. *Reverse:* A diagonal view of the front of the proposed the Women in Military Service for America Memorial.

Mintage Data. Authorized by Public Law 103-186, signed by President William J. Clinton on December 14, 1993. *Maximum authorized*—500,000. *Number minted*—1994-W: 69,860 Uncirculated; 1994-P: 241,278 Proof.

Original Cost. Sale prices $27 (Uncirculated, pre-issue) and $31 (Proof, pre-issue); Uncirculated later raised to $32, and Proof later raised to $35. The surcharge of $10 per coin went towards the construction of the memorial.

Key to Collecting. Mirroring the situation for other commemoratives of the era, these are easily enough found on the market and are usually in superb gem grades.

	Distribution	Cert	Avg	%MS	MS-67
					PF-67
1994-W	69,860	3,281	69.3	100%	$35
Auctions: $72, MS-70, April 2013					
1994-P, Proof	241,278	2,211	68.9		$40
Auctions: $646, PF-70DCam, April 2013					

VIETNAM VETERANS MEMORIAL SILVER DOLLAR (1994)

Designer: *John Mercanti (obverse), Thomas D. Rogers Sr. (reverse).* **Weight:** *26.73 grams.*
Composition: *.900 silver, .100 copper (net weight .7736 oz. pure silver).*
Diameter: *38.1 mm.* **Edge:** *Reeded.* **Mints:** *West Point (Uncirculated) and Philadelphia (Proof).*

In Washington, D.C., the Vietnam Veterans Memorial, often called the Memorial Wall, has been one of the city's prime attractions since it was dedicated in 1984.

Designs. *Obverse:* A hand touching the Wall. In the distance to the right is the Washington Monument. *Reverse:* Three military medals and ribbons surrounded with lettering.

Mintage Data. Authorized by Public Law 103-186, signed by President William J. Clinton on December 14, 1993. *Maximum authorized*—500,000. *Number minted*—1994-W: 57,290 Uncirculated; 1994-P: 227,671 Proof.

Original Cost. Sale prices $27 (Uncirculated) and $31 (Proof); Uncirculated later raised to $32, and Proof later raised to $35. The surcharge of $10 per coin went towards the construction of a visitor's center near the Memorial.

Key to Collecting. Gem specimens are easily available. The aftermarket price for this dollar is stronger than for most others of the early 1990s.

	Distribution	Cert	Avg	%MS	MS-67
					PF-67
1994-W	57,290	1,780	69.3	100%	$80
Auctions: $141, MS-70, January 2013; $103, MS-70, July 2014; $84, MS-70, May 2015					
1994-P, Proof	227,671	3,033	68.9		$65
Auctions: $2,115, PF-70DCam, April 2013; $793, PF-70DCam, August 2015; $770, PF-70DCam, September 2014					

WORLD CUP TOURNAMENT HALF DOLLAR (1994)

Designer: *Richard T. LaRoche (obverse), Dean McMullen (reverse).* **Weight:** *11.34 grams.*
Composition: *.9167 copper, .0833 nickel.* **Diameter:** *30.61 mm.* **Edge:** *Reeded.*
Mints: *Denver (Uncirculated) and Philadelphia (Proof).*

The United States' hosting of the XV FIFA World Cup playoff—the culmination of soccer games among 141 nations—was commemorated with this copper-nickel half dollar, as well as a silver dollar and a five-dollar gold coin.

Designs. *Obverse:* A soccer player in action, on the run with a ball near his feet. *Reverse:* The World Cup USA logo at the center, flanked by branches.

Mintage Data. Authorized by Public Law 102-281, signed by President George H.W. Bush on May 13, 1992. *Maximum authorized*—5,000,000. *Number minted*—1994-D: 168,208 Uncirculated; 1994-P: 609,354 Proof.

Original Cost. Sale prices $8.75 (Uncirculated, pre-issue) and $9.75 (Proof, pre-issue); Uncirculated later raised to $9.50, and Proof later raised to $10.50. The surcharge of $1 per coin went to the World Cup Organizing Committee.

Key to Collecting. The World Cup coins are reasonably priced in the secondary market. Nearly all are superb gems.

	Distribution	Cert	Avg	%MS	MS-67 PF-67
1994-D	168,208	936	69.1	100%	$10
	Auctions: $212, MS-70, September 2014				
1994-P, Proof	609,354	2,882	69.0		$10
	Auctions: $411, PF-70, September 2014; $558, PF-70, April 2013				

WORLD CUP TOURNAMENT SILVER DOLLAR (1994)

Designer: *Dean McMullen.* **Weight:** *26.73 grams.*
Composition: *.900 silver, .100 copper (net weight .7736 oz. pure silver).*
Diameter: *38.1 mm.* **Edge:** *Reeded.* **Mints:** *Denver (Uncirculated) and San Francisco (Proof).*

In terms of mintage goals, this program was one of the greatest failures in the history of American commemorative coinage. The U.S. Mint stated it lost $3.5 million in the effort, noting that there simply were too many commemorative programs in progress, each with excessive mintage expectations. The only winner in the World Cup scenario seemed to be the recipient of the surcharge.

Designs. *Obverse:* Two competing soccer players converge on a soccer ball in play. *Reverse:* The World Cup USA logo at the center, flanked by branches.

Mintage Data. Authorized by Public Law 102-281, signed by President George H.W. Bush on May 13, 1992. *Maximum authorized*—5,000,000. *Number minted*—1994-D: 81,524 Uncirculated; 1994-S: 577,090 Proof.

Original Cost. Sale prices $23 (Uncirculated, pre-issue) and $27 (Proof, pre-issue); Uncirculated later raised to $28, and Proof later raised to $31. The surcharge of $7 per coin went to the World Cup Organizing Committee.

Key to Collecting. The World Cup coins are reasonably priced in the secondary market. Nearly all are superb gems.

	Distribution	Cert	Avg	%MS	MS-67 PF-67
1994-D	81,524	1,329	69.0	100%	$45
	Auctions: $329, MS-70, September 2014; $764, MS-70, April 2013				
1994-S, Proof	577,090	2,645	69.0		$35
	Auctions: $170, PF-70DCam, September 2014; $294, PF-70DCam, April 2013				

WORLD CUP TOURNAMENT $5 GOLD COIN (1994)

Designer: *William J. Krawczewicz (obverse), Dean McMullen (reverse).* **Weight:** *8.359 grams.*
Composition: *.900 gold, .100 copper (net weight .242 oz. pure gold).*
Diameter: *21.6 mm.* **Edge:** *Reeded.* **Mint:** *West Point.*

The U.S. Mint's many recent commemoratives had caused buyer fatigue by the time the World Cup Tournament coins came out. Collectors blamed the Mint for creating coins that few people wanted. The complaints should have gone to Congress instead. Faced with so many coins to produce, often with very short deadlines, the Mint simply had no time to call for designs to be submitted from leading artists.

Designs. *Obverse:* The World Cup trophy. *Reverse:* The World Cup USA logo at the center, flanked by branches.

Mintage Data. Authorized by Public Law 102-281, signed by President George H.W. Bush on May 13, 1992. *Maximum authorized*—750,000. *Number minted*—22,447 Uncirculated and 89,614 Proof.

Original Cost. Sale prices $170 (Uncirculated, pre-issue) and $185 (Proof, pre-issue); Uncirculated later raised to $200, and Proof later raised to $220. The surcharge of $35 per coin went to the World Cup Organizing Committee.

Key to Collecting. The World Cup coins are reasonably priced in the secondary market. Nearly all are superb gems.

	Distribution	Cert	Avg	%MS	MS-67 PF-67
1994-W	22,447	1,079	69.5	100%	$400
	Auctions: $382, MS-70, September 2014; $382, MS-70, November 2014; $448, MS-70, April 2013; $306, MS-69, November 2014				
1994-W, Proof	89,614	2,179	69.3		$400
	Auctions: $470, PF-70DCam, June 2013; $295, PF-69DCam, October 2014; $306, PF-68DCam, February 2015				

XXVI OLYMPIAD BASKETBALL HALF DOLLAR (1995)

Designer: *Clint Hansen (obverse), T. James Ferrell (reverse).* **Weight:** *11.34 grams.*
Composition: *.9167 copper, .0833 nickel.* **Diameter:** *30.61 mm.* **Edge:** *Reeded.* **Mint:** *San Francisco.*

Men's basketball has been an Olympic sport since the 1936 Summer Games in Berlin. The 1996 U.S. team, also known as "Dream Team III," won the gold medal at the Summer Games in Atlanta.

Designs. *Obverse:* Three basketball players. *Reverse:* Symbol of the Atlanta Committee for the Olympic Games superimposed over the Atlantic Ocean as viewed from space.

Mintage Data. Authorized by Public Law 102-390, signed by President George H.W. Bush on October 6, 1992. *Maximum authorized*—2,000,000. *Number minted*—171,001 Uncirculated and 169,655 Proof.

Original Cost. Sale prices $10.50 (Uncirculated, pre-issue) and $11.50 (Proof, pre-issue); Uncirculated later raised to $11.50, and Proof later raised to $12.50. The surcharge per coin went to the Atlanta Olympic Committee.

Key to Collecting. Enough 1995 and 1996 Olympics coins are on the aftermarket that finding designs of choice, or forming a set, will be no problem. The obverse designs are varied, and in total the collection is an excellent representation of this quadrennial worldwide competition.

	Distribution	Cert	Avg	%MS	MS-67
					PF-67
1995-S	171,001	1,436	69.3	100%	$20
	Auctions: $118, MS-70, July 2014; $76, MS-70, July 2013				
1995-S, Proof	169,655	2,014	69.1		$15
	Auctions: No auction records available.				

XXVI OLYMPIAD BASEBALL HALF DOLLAR (1995)

Designer: *Edgar Z. Steever IV (obverse), T. James Ferrell (reverse).* **Weight:** *11.34 grams.*
Composition: *.9167 copper, .0833 nickel.* **Diameter:** *30.61 mm.* **Edge:** *Reeded.* **Mint:** *San Francisco.*

Baseball was an official Olympic sport at each Summer Games between 1992 and 2008, but was voted out of the 2012 London Olympics and will remain off the docket until at least 2024 following a 2013 International Olympic Committee vote. The team representing Cuba took home the gold medal at the 1996 Atlanta Olympics.

Designs. *Obverse:* Batter at the plate with catcher and umpire. *Reverse:* Symbol of the Atlanta Committee for the Olympic Games superimposed over the Atlantic Ocean as viewed from space.

Mintage Data. Authorized by Public Law 102-390, signed by President George H.W. Bush on October 6, 1992. *Maximum authorized*—2,000,000. *Number minted*—164,605 Uncirculated and 118,087 Proof.

Original Cost. Sale prices $10.50 (Uncirculated, pre-issue) and $11.50 (Proof, pre-issue); Uncirculated later raised to $11.50, and Proof later raised to $12.50. The surcharge per coin went to the Atlanta Olympic Committee.

Key to Collecting. Enough 1995 and 1996 Olympics coins are on the aftermarket that finding designs of choice, or forming a set, will be no problem. The obverse designs are varied, and in total the collection is an excellent representation of this quadrennial worldwide competition.

	Distribution	Cert	Avg	%MS	MS-67
					PF-67
1995-S	164,605	1,098	69.3	100%	$20
Auctions: $130, MS-70, April 2013					
1995-S, Proof	118,087	1,593	69.1		$20
Auctions: $329, PF-70DCam, September 2014; $200, PF-70DCam, September 2014					

XXVI OLYMPIAD GYMNASTICS SILVER DOLLAR (1995)

Designer: *James C. Sharpe (obverse), William Krawczewicz (reverse).* **Weight:** *26.73 grams.*
Composition: *.900 silver, .100 copper (net weight .7736 oz. pure silver).*
Diameter: *38.1 mm.* **Edge:** *Reeded.* **Mints:** *Denver (Uncirculated) and Philadelphia (Proof).*

The men's gymnastics competition has been held at each Olympic Summer Games since the birth of the modern Olympic movement in 1896. Russia won the gold medal in the team all-around event at the 1996 Games in Atlanta.

Designs. *Obverse:* Men's gymnastics. *Reverse:* Clasped hands of two athletes with torch above.

Mintage Data. Authorized by Public Law 102-390, signed by President George H.W. Bush on October 6, 1992. *Maximum authorized*—750,000. *Number minted*—1995-D: 42,497 Uncirculated; 1995-P: 182,676 Proof.

Original Cost. Sale prices $27.95 (Uncirculated, pre-issue) and $30.95 (Proof, pre-issue); Uncirculated later raised to $31.95, and Proof later raised to $34.95. The surcharge per coin went to the Atlanta Olympic Committee.

Key to Collecting. Enough 1995 and 1996 Olympics coins are on the aftermarket that finding designs of choice, or forming a set, will be no problem. The obverse designs are varied, and in total the collection is an excellent representation of this quadrennial worldwide competition.

	Distribution	Cert	Avg	%MS	MS-67
					PF-67
1995-D	42,497	1,531	69.2	100%	$50
Auctions: $90, MS-70, April 2013					
1995-P, Proof	182,676	2,117	69.0		$35
Auctions: No auction records available.					

XXVI OLYMPIAD TRACK AND FIELD SILVER DOLLAR (1995)

Designer: *John Mercanti (obverse), William Krawczewicz (reverse).* **Weight:** *26.73 grams.*
Composition: *.900 silver, .100 copper (net weight .7736 oz. pure silver).*
Diameter: *38.1 mm.* **Edge:** *Reeded.* **Mints:** *Denver (Uncirculated) and Philadelphia (Proof).*

Track and field—grouped with road running and racewalking in the overarching "athletics" category—has been a part of the Olympics from the birth of the modern Games and traces its roots to the ancient Greek Olympics. At the 1996 Summer Games in Atlanta, the United States took home 13 gold medals between its men's and women's track and field teams, easily the most of any nation.

Designs. *Obverse:* Men competing in track and field. *Reverse:* Clasped hands of two athletes with torch above.

Mintage Data. Authorized by Public Law 102-390, signed by President George H.W. Bush on October 6, 1992. *Maximum authorized*—750,000. *Number minted*—1995-D: 24,976 Uncirculated; 1995-P: 136,935 Proof.

Original Cost. Sale prices $27.95 (Uncirculated, pre-issue) and $30.95 (Proof, pre-issue); Uncirculated later raised to $31.95, and Proof later raised to $34.95. The surcharge per coin went to the Atlanta Olympic Committee.

Key to Collecting. Enough 1995 and 1996 Olympics coins are on the aftermarket that finding designs of choice, or forming a set, will be no problem. The obverse designs are varied, and in total the collection is an excellent representation of this quadrennial worldwide competition.

	Distribution	Cert	Avg	%MS	MS-67
					PF-67
1995-D	24,976	826	69.3	100%	$75
	Auctions: $159, MS-70, July 2014				
1995-P, Proof	136,935	1,479	69.0		$35
	Auctions: $411, PF-70DCam, September 2014				

XXVI OLYMPIAD CYCLING SILVER DOLLAR (1995)

Designer: *John Mercanti (obverse), William Krawczewicz (reverse).* **Weight:** *26.73 grams.*
Composition: *.900 silver, .100 copper (net weight .7736 oz. pure silver).*
Diameter: *38.1 mm.* **Edge:** *Reeded.* **Mints:** *Denver (Uncirculated) and Philadelphia (Proof).*

Part of the Summer Games from the inception of the modern Olympic movement in 1896, cycling has been expanded over the years to include more track races, mountain biking, and BMX racing. France dominated the podium at the 1996 Olympics in Atlanta, taking home the most gold medals (five) and total medals (nine).

Designs. *Obverse:* Men cycling. *Reverse:* Clasped hands of two athletes with torch above.

Mintage Data. Authorized by Public Law 102-390, signed by President George H.W. Bush on October 6, 1992. *Maximum authorized*—750,000. *Number minted*—1995-D: 19,662 Uncirculated; 1995-P: 118,795 Proof.

Original Cost. Sale prices $27.95 (Uncirculated, pre-issue) and $30.95 (Proof, pre-issue); Uncirculated later raised to $31.95, and Proof later raised to $34.95. The surcharge per coin went to the Atlanta Olympic Committee.

Key to Collecting. Enough 1995 and 1996 Olympics coins are on the aftermarket that finding designs of choice, or forming a set, will be no problem. The obverse designs are varied, and in total the collection is an excellent representation of this quadrennial worldwide competition.

	Distribution	Cert	Avg	%MS	MS-67
					PF-67
1995-D	19,662	913	69.3	100%	$140
	Auctions: $206, MS-70, July 2014; $200, MS-70, April 2013; $112, MS-69, November 2014				
1995-P, Proof	118,795	1,469	69.0		$40
	Auctions: $707, PF-70DCam, September 2014				

PARALYMPICS BLIND RUNNER SILVER DOLLAR (1995)

Designer: *James C. Sharpe (obverse), William Krawczewicz (reverse).* **Weight:** *26.73 grams.*
Composition: *.900 silver, .100 copper (net weight .7736 oz. pure silver).*
Diameter: *38.1 mm.* **Edge:** *Reeded.* **Mints:** *Denver (Uncirculated) and Philadelphia (Proof).*

Track and field events (under the umbrella of "athletics") have been a part of the Summer Paralympic Games since 1960. Spanish athletes took home a number of medals in the track events for visually impaired athletes at the 1996 Summer Paralympic Games, including the gold in two of the men's 100-meter dash events (Júlio Requena in the T-10 race, and Juan António Prieto in the T-11 race) and both of the women's 100-meter dash events (Purificación Santamarta in the T-10 race, and Beatríz Mendoza in the T-11 race).

Designs. *Obverse:* Blind runner tethered to a seeing companion in a race. *Reverse:* Clasped hands of two athletes with torch above.

Mintage Data. Authorized by Public Law 102-390, signed by President George H.W. Bush on October 6, 1992. *Maximum authorized*—750,000. *Number minted*—1995-D: 28,649 Uncirculated; 1995-P: 138,337 Proof.

Original Cost. Sale prices $27.95 (Uncirculated, pre-issue) and $30.95 (Proof, pre-issue); Uncirculated later raised to $31.95, and Proof later raised to $34.95. The surcharge per coin went to the Atlanta Olympic Committee.

Key to Collecting. Enough 1995 and 1996 Olympics coins are on the aftermarket that finding designs of choice, or forming a set, will be no problem. The obverse designs are varied, and in total the collection is an excellent representation of this quadrennial worldwide competition.

	Distribution	Cert	Avg	%MS	MS-67
					PF-67
1995-D	28,649	1,294	69.3	100%	$35
	Auctions: No auction records available.				
1995-P, Proof	138,337	1,630	69.0		$40
	Auctions: No auction records available.				

XXVI Olympiad Torch Runner $5 Gold Coin (1995)

Designer: *Frank Gasparro.* **Weight:** *8.359 grams.*
Composition: *.900 gold, .100 copper (net weight .242 oz. pure gold).*
Diameter: *21.6 mm.* **Edge:** *Reeded.* **Mint:** *West Point.*

Whereas the concept of the Olympic flame dates from the concept of the ancient Games of ancient Greece, the torch relay has only been a tradition since 1936, when Carl Diem introduced the concept for the Berlin Summer Games. The 1996 Olympic torch relay spanned 112 days, approximately 18,030 miles, and 13,267 torch bearers before ending in Atlanta on July 19, 1996.

Designs. *Obverse:* Olympic runner carrying a torch. *Reverse:* Bald eagle with a banner in its beak with the Olympic Centennial dates 1896–1996.

Mintage Data. Authorized by Public Law 102-390, signed by President George H.W. Bush on October 6, 1992. *Maximum authorized*—175,000. *Number minted*—14,675 Uncirculated and 57,442 Proof.

Original Cost. Sale prices $229 (Uncirculated, pre-issue) and $239 (Proof, pre-issue); Uncirculated later raised to $249, and Proof later raised to $259. The surcharge per coin went to the Atlanta Olympic Committee.

Key to Collecting. Enough 1995 and 1996 Olympics coins are on the aftermarket that finding designs of choice, or forming a set, will be no problem. The obverse designs are varied, and in total the collection is an excellent representation of this quadrennial worldwide competition.

	Distribution	Cert	Avg	%MS	MS-67
					PF-67
1995-W	14,675	1,017	69.7	100%	$575
	Auctions: $646, MS-70, February 2015; $447, MS-70, May 2015; $423, MS-70, May 2015; $353, MS-69, January 2015				
1995-W, Proof	57,442	1,841	69.3		$325
	Auctions: No auction records available.				

XXVI OLYMPIAD STADIUM $5 GOLD COIN (1995)

Designer: *Marcel Jovine (obverse), Frank Gasparro (reverse).* **Weight:** *8.359 grams.*
Composition: *.900 gold, .100 copper (net weight .242 oz. pure gold).*
Diameter: *21.6 mm.* **Edge:** *Reeded.* **Mint:** *West Point.*

Centennial Olympic Stadium was constructed in Atlanta for the 1996 Summer Games. The 85,000-seat venue hosted the track and field events, as well as the closing ceremony, and then was reconstructed into Turner Field, home of Major League Baseball's Atlanta Braves for two decades.

Designs. *Obverse:* Aerial view of the Olympic Stadium from a distance to the side. *Reverse:* Same as described for the Olympic Torch Runner $5 gold coin.

Mintage Data. Authorized by Public Law 102-390, signed by President George H.W. Bush on October 6, 1992. *Maximum authorized*—175,000. *Number minted*—10,579 Uncirculated and 43,124 Proof.

Original Cost. Sale prices $229 (Uncirculated, pre-issue) and $239 (Proof, pre-issue); Uncirculated later raised to $249, and Proof later raised to $259. The surcharge per coin went to the Atlanta Olympic Committee.

Key to Collecting. Enough 1995 and 1996 Olympics coins are on the aftermarket that finding designs of choice, or forming a set, will be no problem. The obverse designs are varied, and in total the collection is an excellent representation of this quadrennial worldwide competition.

	Distribution	Cert	Avg	%MS	MS-67 / PF-67
1995-W	10,579	968	69.6	100%	$1,100
	Auctions: $823, MS-70, February 2015; $764, MS-70, January 2015; $823, MS-69, February 2015; $646, MS-69, February 2015				
1995-W, Proof	43,124	1,834	69.4		$325
	Auctions: $499, PF-70DCam, June 2014; $470, PF-70DCam, June 2014				

XXVI OLYMPIAD SWIMMING HALF DOLLAR (1996)

Designer: *William Krawczewicz (obverse), Malcolm Farley (reverse).* **Weight:** *11.34 grams.*
Composition: *.9167 copper, .0833 nickel.* **Diameter:** *30.61 mm.* **Edge:** *Reeded.* **Mint:** *San Francisco.*

Swimming—an Olympic sport since the modern Games began in 1896—was dominated by U.S. athletes at the 1996 Summer Games in Atlanta. Americans took home a total of 26 medals (more than double the 12 each of Russia and Germany, which come next on the list), and swept all six relay events across the men's and women's competitions.

Designs. *Obverse:* Male swimmer. *Reverse:* Symbols of the Olympic games, including flame, torch, rings, Greek column, and 100 (the latter to observe the 100th anniversary of the modern Olympic games inaugurated with the 1896 Games in Athens).

Mintage Data. Authorized by Public Law 102-390, signed by President George H.W. Bush on October 6, 1992. *Maximum authorized*—3,000,000. *Number minted*—49,533 Uncirculated and 114,315 Proof.

Original Cost. Sale prices $10.50 (Uncirculated, pre-issue) and $11.50 (Proof, pre-issue); Uncirculated later raised to $11.50, and Proof later raised to $12.50. The surcharge per coin went to the Atlanta Olympic Committee.

Key to Collecting. Enough 1995 and 1996 Olympics coins are on the aftermarket that finding designs of choice, or forming a set, will be no problem. The obverse designs are varied, and in total the collection is an excellent representation of this quadrennial worldwide competition.

	Distribution	Cert	Avg	%MS	MS-67
					PF-67
1996-S	49,533	852	69.1	100%	$125
	Auctions: $499, MS-70, September 2013				
1996-S, Proof	114,315	984	69.1		$30
	Auctions: No auction records available.				

XXVI Olympiad Soccer Half Dollar (1996)

Designer: *Clint Hansen (obverse), Malcolm Farley (reverse).* **Weight:** *11.34 grams.*
Composition: *.9167 copper, .0833 nickel.* **Diameter:** *30.61 mm.* **Edge:** *Reeded.* **Mint:** *San Francisco.*

Women's soccer debuted as an Olympic sport at the 1996 Summer Games in Atlanta. The host nation's team—featuring such names as Mia Hamm, Brandi Chastain, and Briana Scurry—was victorious in the gold medal game.

Designs. *Obverse:* Women playing soccer. *Reverse:* Symbols of the Olympic games, including flame, torch, rings, Greek column, and 100.

Mintage Data. Authorized by Public Law 102-390, signed by President George H.W. Bush on October 6, 1992. *Maximum authorized*—3,000,000. *Number minted*—52,836 Uncirculated and 112,412 Proof.

Original Cost. Sale prices $10.50 (Uncirculated, pre-issue) and $11.50 (Proof, pre-issue); Uncirculated later raised to $11.50, and Proof later raised to $12.50. The surcharge per coin went to the Atlanta Olympic Committee.

Key to Collecting. Enough 1995 and 1996 Olympics coins are on the aftermarket that finding designs of choice, or forming a set, will be no problem. The obverse designs are varied, and in total the collection is an excellent representation of this quadrennial worldwide competition.

	Distribution	Cert	Avg	%MS	MS-67
					PF-67
1996-S	52,836	622	69.3	100%	$110
	Auctions: $147, MS-70, July 2014; $170, MS-70, August 2013				
1996-S, Proof	112,412	961	69.0		$75
	Auctions: $294, PF-70DCam, September 2014				

XXVI Olympiad Tennis Silver Dollar (1996)

Designer: *James C. Sharpe (obverse), Thomas D. Rogers Sr. (reverse).* **Weight:** *26.73 grams.*
Composition: *.900 silver, .100 copper (net weight .7736 oz. pure silver).*
Diameter: *38.1 mm.* **Edge:** *Reeded.* **Mints:** *Denver (Uncirculated) and Philadelphia (Proof).*

Women's tennis was first a part of the Olympics in 1900, and singles competition was regularly held for the Summer Games between 1908 and 1924. Subsequent disputes between the International Lawn Tennis Federation and the International Olympic Committee led to both men's and women's tennis being removed from the Games for more than 60 years, but the sport returned permanently in 1988. U.S. athletes took both the women's singles gold medal (Lindsay Davenport) and women's doubles gold medal (Gigi Fernandez and Mary Joe Fernandez) at the 1996 Games in Atlanta.

Designs. *Obverse:* Woman playing tennis. *Reverse:* Atlanta Committee for the Olympic Games logo with torch and flame.

Mintage Data. Authorized by Public Law 102-390, signed by President George H.W. Bush on October 6, 1992. *Maximum authorized*—1,000,000. *Number minted*—1996-D: 15,983 Uncirculated; 1996-P: 92,016 Proof.

Original Cost. Sale prices $27.95 (Uncirculated, pre-issue) and $30.95 (Proof, pre-issue); Uncirculated later raised to $31.95, and Proof later raised to $34.95. The surcharge per coin went to the Atlanta Olympic Committee.

Key to Collecting. Enough 1995 and 1996 Olympics coins are on the aftermarket that finding designs of choice, or forming a set, will be no problem. The obverse designs are varied, and in total the collection is an excellent representation of this quadrennial worldwide competition.

	Distribution	Cert	Avg	%MS	MS-67 / PF-67
1996-D	15,983	779	69.1	100%	$225
	Auctions: $206, MS-70, September 2014; $482, MS-70, April 2013; $170, MS-69, July 2014; $170, MS-69, November 2014				
1996-P, Proof	92,016	1,314	68.9		$75
	Auctions: $355, PF-69DCam, November 2014				

XXVI Olympiad Rowing Silver Dollar (1996)

Designer: *Bart Forbes (obverse), Thomas D. Rogers Sr. (reverse).* **Weight:** *26.73 grams.*
Composition: *.900 silver, .100 copper (net weight .7736 oz. pure silver).*
Diameter: *38.1 mm.* **Edge:** *Reeded.* **Mints:** *Denver (Uncirculated) and Philadelphia (Proof).*

Rowing has been an official Olympic sport from the first modern Games in 1896, though coincidentally the competition was cancelled for that event due to weather concerns. At the 1996 Summer Olympics in Atlanta, Australia won the most medals (six, two gold).

Designs. *Obverse:* Men rowing. *Reverse:* Atlanta Committee for the Olympic Games logo with torch and flame.

Mintage Data. Authorized by Public Law 102-390, signed by President George H.W. Bush on October 6, 1992. *Maximum authorized*—1,000,000. *Number minted*—1996-D: 16,258 Uncirculated; 1996-P: 151,890 Proof.

Original Cost. Sale prices $27.95 (Uncirculated, pre-issue) and $30.95 (Proof, pre-issue); Uncirculated later raised to $31.95, and Proof later raised to $34.95. The surcharge per coin went to the Atlanta Olympic Committee.

Key to Collecting. Enough 1995 and 1996 Olympics coins are on the aftermarket that finding designs of choice, or forming a set, will be no problem. The obverse designs are varied, and in total the collection is an excellent representation of this quadrennial worldwide competition.

	Distribution	Cert	Avg	%MS	MS-67
					PF-67
1996-D	16,258	728	69.2	100%	$225
Auctions: $382, MS-70, April 2013; $153, MS-69, November 2014; $147, MS-69, November 2014					
1996-P, Proof	151,890	1,294	68.9		$70
Auctions: $6,169, PF-70DCam, September 2014					

XXVI Olympiad High Jump Silver Dollar (1996)

Designer: *Calvin Massey (obverse), Thomas D. Rogers Sr. (reverse).* **Weight:** *26.73 grams.*
Composition: *.900 silver, .100 copper (net weight .7736 oz. pure silver).*
Diameter: *38.1 mm.* **Edge:** *Reeded.* **Mints:** *Denver (Uncirculated) and Philadelphia (Proof).*

High jump has been one of the Olympic track and field program's events since the inaugural modern Games in 1896. At the 1996 Atlanta Olympics, the United States' Charles Austin won the gold medal in the men's competition with a height cleared of 2.39 meters.

Designs. *Obverse:* Athlete doing the "Fosbury Flop" maneuver. *Reverse:* Atlanta Committee for the Olympic Games logo with torch and flame.

Mintage Data. Authorized by Public Law 102-390, signed by President George H.W. Bush on October 6, 1992. *Maximum authorized*—1,000,000. *Number minted*—1996-D: 15,697 Uncirculated; 1996-P: 124,502 Proof.

Original Cost. Sale prices $27.95 (Uncirculated, pre-issue) and $30.95 (Proof, pre-issue); Uncirculated later raised to $31.95, and Proof later raised to $34.95. The surcharge per coin went to the Atlanta Olympic Committee.

Key to Collecting. Enough 1995 and 1996 Olympics coins are on the aftermarket that finding designs of choice, or forming a set, will be no problem. The obverse designs are varied, and in total the collection is an excellent representation of this quadrennial worldwide competition.

	Distribution	Cert	Avg	%MS	MS-67
					PF-67
1996-D	15,697	723	69.1	100%	$250
	Auctions: $441, MS-70, April 2013; $147, MS-69, July 2014; $165, MS-69, November 2014				
1996-P, Proof	124,502	1,352	68.9		$45
	Auctions: No auction records available.				

PARALYMPICS WHEELCHAIR SILVER DOLLAR (1996)

Designer: *James C. Sharpe (obverse), Thomas D. Rogers Sr. (reverse).* **Weight:** *26.73 grams.*
Composition: *.900 silver, .100 copper (net weight .7736 oz. pure silver).*
Diameter: *38.1 mm.* **Edge:** *Reeded.* **Mints:** *Denver (Uncirculated) and Philadelphia (Proof).*

Wheelchair racing events have comprised part of the Paralympic track and field program since 1960. Several countries were represented on the podium, though the United States' Shawn Meredith (gold medals in the T-51 400-meter and 800-meter), France's Claude Issorat (gold medals in the T-53 200-meter and 800-meter), and Switzerland's Heinz Frei (gold medals in the T52-53 1,500-meter and 10,000-meter) had particularly strong showings.

Designs. *Obverse:* Athlete in a racing wheelchair competing in a track and field competition. *Reverse:* Atlanta Committee for the Olympic Games logo with torch and flame.

Mintage Data. Authorized by Public Law 102-390, signed by President George H.W. Bush on October 6, 1992. *Maximum authorized*—1,000,000. *Number minted*—1996-D: 14,497 Uncirculated; 1996-P: 84,280 Proof.

Original Cost. Sale prices $27.95 (Uncirculated, pre-issue) and $30.95 (Proof, pre-issue); Uncirculated later raised to $31.95, and Proof later raised to $34.95. The surcharge per coin went to the Atlanta Olympic Committee.

Key to Collecting. Enough 1995 and 1996 Olympics coins are on the aftermarket that finding designs of choice, or forming a set, will be no problem. The obverse designs are varied, and in total the collection is an excellent representation of this quadrennial worldwide competition.

	Distribution	Cert	Avg	%MS	MS-67
					PF-67
1996-D	14,497	1,294	69.3	100%	$240
	Auctions: $499, MS-70, April 2013; $223, MS-70, June 2015; $153, MS-69, November 2014; $129, MS-69, November 2014				
1996-P, Proof	84,280	1,630	69.0		$70
	Auctions: No auction records available.				

XXVI OLYMPIAD FLAG BEARER $5 GOLD COIN (1996)

Designer: *Patricia Lewis Verani (obverse), William Krawczewicz (reverse).*
Weight: *8.359 grams.* **Composition:** *.900 gold, .100 copper (net weight .242 oz. pure gold).*
Diameter: *21.6 mm.* **Edge:** *Reeded.* **Mint:** *West Point.*

For the opening and closing ceremonies of each Olympic Games, each participating nation selects two flagbearers from among its athletes to lead its delegation in the Parade of Nations (opening) and Parade of Flags (closing). Wrestler Bruce Baumgartner served as the United States's flagbearer for the opening ceremony of the 1996 Summer Games, and show jumper Michael Matz was awarded the honor for the closing ceremony.

Designs. *Obverse:* Athlete with a flag followed by a crowd. *Reverse:* Atlanta Committee for the Olympic Games logo within laurel leaves.

Mintage Data. Authorized by Public Law 102-390, signed by President George H.W. Bush on October 6, 1992. *Maximum authorized*—300,000. *Number minted*—9,174 Uncirculated and 32,886 Proof.

Original Cost. Sale prices $229 (Uncirculated, pre-issue) and $239 (Proof, pre-issue); Uncirculated later raised to $249, and Proof later raised to $259. The surcharge per coin went to the Atlanta Olympic Committee.

Key to Collecting. Enough 1995 and 1996 Olympics coins are on the aftermarket that finding designs of choice, or forming a set, will be no problem. The obverse designs are varied, and in total the collection is an excellent representation of this quadrennial worldwide competition.

	Distribution	Cert	Avg	%MS	MS-67
					PF-67
1996-W	9,174	720	69.5	100%	$550
	Auctions: $881, MS-70, October 2015; $881, MS-70, February 2015; $494, MS-69, January 2015; $329, MS-69, September 2015				
1996-W, Proof	32,886	1,313	69.3		$325
	Auctions: No auction records available.				

XXVI Olympiad Cauldron $5 Gold Coin (1996)

Designer: *Frank Gasparro (obverse), William Krawczewicz (reverse).*
Weight: *8.359 grams.* **Composition:** *.900 gold, .100 copper (net weight .242 oz. pure gold).*
Diameter: *21.6 mm.* **Edge:** *Reeded.* **Mint:** *West Point.*

The tradition of maintaining an Olympic flame hearkens to the ancient Greek Olympics, during which a fire was kept burning to represent the theft of fire from Zeus by Prometheus. The concept became part of the modern Games in 1928 and now serves as the culmination of the Olympic torch relay. At the 1996 Summer Games in Atlanta, boxing legend and American icon Muhammad Ali (himself a gold medalist at the 1960 Olympics) was the final torch bearer and lit the cauldron.

Designs. *Obverse:* Lighting of the Olympic flame. *Reverse:* Atlanta Committee for the Olympic Games logo within laurel leaves.

Mintage Data. Authorized by Public Law 102-390, signed by President George H.W. Bush on October 6, 1992. *Maximum authorized*—300,000. *Number minted*—9,210 Uncirculated and 38,555 Proof.

Original Cost. Sale prices $229 (Uncirculated, pre-issue) and $239 (Proof, pre-issue); Uncirculated later raised to $249, and Proof later raised to $259. The surcharge per coin went to the Atlanta Olympic Committee.

Key to Collecting. Enough 1995 and 1996 Olympics coins are on the aftermarket that finding designs of choice, or forming a set, will be no problem. The obverse designs are varied, and in total the collection is an excellent representation of this quadrennial worldwide competition.

	Distribution	Cert	Avg	%MS	MS-67 / PF-67
1996-W	9,210	807	69.4	100%	$1,150
	Auctions: $1,116, MS-70, February 2015; $940, MS-70, October 2015; $823, MS-69, January 2015; $705, MS-69, November 2014				
1996-W, Proof	38,555	2,208	69.3		$325
	Auctions: $505, PF-70UCam, March 2015; $423, PF-70UCam, March 2015; $353, PF-70UCam, May 2015				

Civil War Battlefield Preservation Half Dollar (1995)

Designer: *Don Troiani (obverse), T. James Ferrell (reverse).* **Weight:** *11.34 grams.*
Composition: *.9167 copper, .0833 nickel.* **Diameter:** *30.61 mm.* **Edge:** *Reeded.* **Mint:** *San Francisco.*

Preserving battlefields associated with the Civil War (1861–1865) formed the topic for a suite of three commemorative coins, including this copper-nickel half dollar.

Designs. *Obverse:* Drummer standing. *Reverse:* Cannon overlooking battlefield with inscription above.

Mintage Data. Authorized by Public Law 102-379. *Maximum authorized*—2,000,000. *Number minted*—119,520 Uncirculated and 330,002 Proof.

Original Cost. Sale prices $9.50 (Uncirculated, pre-issue) and $10.75 (Proof, pre-issue); Uncirculated later raised to $10.25, and Proof later raised to $11.75. The surcharge of $2 per coin went to the Civil War Trust for the preservation of historically significant battlefields.

Key to Collecting. This coin, as well as those two issued alongside it, are readily available in the marketplace today. Most are superb gems.

	Distribution	Cert	Avg	%MS	MS-67
					PF-67
1995-S	119,520	992	69.3	100%	$40
	Auctions: $206, MS-70, May 2014; $153, MS-70, July 2014; $112, MS-70, June 2015				
1995-S, Proof	330,002	1,828	69.0		$30
	Auctions: $188, PF-68DCam, November 2014				

CIVIL WAR BATTLEFIELD PRESERVATION SILVER DOLLAR (1995)

Designer: *Don Troiani (obverse), John Mercanti (reverse).* **Weight:** *26.73 grams.*
Composition: *.900 silver, .100 copper (net weight .7736 oz. pure silver).*
Diameter: *38.1 mm.* **Edge:** *Reeded.* **Mints:** *Philadelphia (Uncirculated) and San Francisco (Proof).*

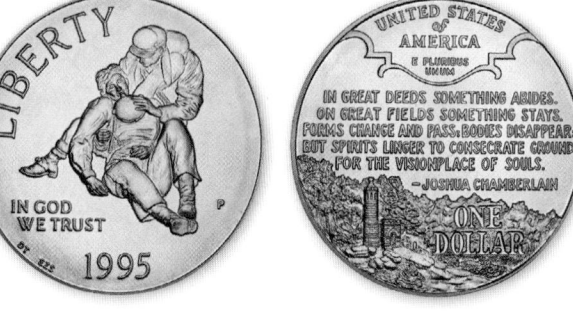

Civil War history attracts millions of followers, and books on the subject are always very popular. While total sales of the Civil War Battlefield Preservation silver dollar didn't approach the million coins authorized, sales of the Proof version were stronger than those of many recent silver dollars.

Designs. *Obverse:* Soldier offering canteen to a wounded comrade. *Reverse:* Gettysburg landscape with a quotation from Joshua Chamberlain, hero in that battle.

Mintage Data. Authorized by Public Law 102-379. *Maximum authorized*—1,000,000. *Number minted*—1995-P: 45,866 Uncirculated; 1995-S: 437,114 Proof.

Original Cost. Sale prices $27 (Uncirculated, pre-issue) and $30 (Proof, pre-issue); Uncirculated later raised to $30, and Proof later raised to $34. The surcharge of $7 per coin went to the Civil War Trust for the preservation of historically significant battlefields.

Key to Collecting. This coin, as well as those two issued alongside it, are readily available in the marketplace today. Most are superb gems.

	Distribution	Cert	Avg	%MS	MS-67
					PF-67
1995-P	45,866	1,259	69.1	100%	$65
	Auctions: $247, MS-70, April 2013				
1995-S, Proof	437,114	3,135	69.0		$45
	Auctions: $435, PF-70DCam, March 2013; $306, PF-70DCam, April 2013				

CIVIL WAR BATTLEFIELD PRESERVATION $5 GOLD COIN (1995)

Designer: *Don Troiani (obverse), Alfred F. Maletsky (reverse).* **Weight:** *8.359 grams.*
Composition: *.900 gold, .100 copper.* **Diameter:** *21.6 mm.* **Edge:** *Reeded.* **Mint:** *West Point.*

Troiani, the designer of this coin's obverse as well as those of the other two Civil War Battlefield Preservation commemoratives, is an artist in the private sector well known for his depictions of battle scenes.

Designs. *Obverse:* Bugler on horseback sounding a call. *Reverse:* Eagle perched on a shield.

Mintage Data. Authorized by Public Law 102-379. *Maximum authorized*—300,000. *Number minted*—12,735 Uncirculated and 55,246 Proof.

Original Cost. Sale prices $180 (Uncirculated, pre-issue) and $195 (Proof, pre-issue); Uncirculated later raised to $190, and Proof later raised to $225. The surcharge of $35 per coin went to the Civil War Trust for the preservation of historically significant battlefields.

Key to Collecting. This coin, as well as those two issued alongside it, are readily available in the marketplace today. Most are superb gems.

	Distribution	Cert	Avg	%MS	MS-67
					PF-67
1995-W	12,735	820	69.7	100%	$450
	Auctions: $517, MS-70, January 2015; $494, MS-70, April 2015; $482, MS-70, January 2015; $329, MS-69, August 2015				
1995-W, Proof	55,246	1,945	69.3		$400
	Auctions: $482, PF-70DCam, July 2015; $306, PF-69UCam, October 2015; $329, PF-69DCam, October 2015; $306, PF-69DCam, August 2015				

SPECIAL OLYMPICS WORLD GAMES SILVER DOLLAR (1995)

Designer: *T. James Ferrell from a portrait by Jamie Wyeth (obverse), Thomas D. Rogers Sr. (reverse).*
Weight: *26.73 grams.* **Composition:** *.900 silver, .100 copper (net weight .7736 oz. pure silver).*
Diameter: *38.1 mm.* **Edge:** *Reeded.* **Mints:** *West Point (Uncirculated) and Philadelphia (Proof).*

This silver dollar's subject, Eunice Kennedy Shriver, was not only the first living female on U.S. coinage, but also the sister of former president John F. Kennedy and the aunt of Joseph F. Kennedy II, the House representative who sponsored the bill that created the coin. She is credited on the silver dollar as the founder of the Special Olympics.

Designs. *Obverse:* Portrait of Eunice Shriver.
Reverse: Representation of a Special Olympics medal, a rose, and a quotation by Shriver.

Mintage Data. Authorized by Public Law 103-328, signed by President William J. Clinton on September 29, 1994. *Maximum authorized*—800,000. *Number minted*—1995-W: 89,301 Uncirculated; 1995-P: 351,764 Proof.

Original Cost. Sale prices $30 (Uncirculated, pre-issue) and $33 (Proof, pre-issue); Uncirculated later raised to $32, and Proof later raised to $37. The surcharge of $10 per coin went to the Special Olympics to support the 1995 World Summer Games.

Key to Collecting. These coins are plentiful in the marketplace. Most are superb gems.

	Distribution	Cert	Avg	%MS	MS-67
					PF-67
1995-W	89,301	965	69.2	100%	$40
	Auctions: $135, MS-70, April 2013				
1995-P, Proof	351,764	1,499	69.0		$35
	Auctions: $360, PF-70DCam, March 2013				

NATIONAL COMMUNITY SERVICE SILVER DOLLAR (1996)

Designer: *Thomas D. Rogers Sr. from a medal by Augustus Saint-Gaudens (obverse), William C. Cousins (reverse).* **Weight:** *26.73 grams.* **Composition:** *.900 silver, .100 copper (net weight .7736 oz. pure silver).* **Diameter:** *38.1 mm.* **Edge:** *Reeded.* **Mint:** *San Francisco.*

In 1996 the National Community Service dollar was sponsored by Representative Joseph D. Kennedy of Massachusetts, who also sponsored the Special Olympics World Games dollar.

Designs. *Obverse:* Standing figure of Liberty. *Reverse:* SERVICE FOR AMERICA in three lines, with a wreath around, and other lettering at the border.

Mintage Data. Authorized by Public Law 103-328, signed by President William J. Clinton on September 29, 1994. *Maximum authorized*—500,000. *Number minted*—23,500 Uncirculated and 101,543 Proof.

Original Cost. Sale prices $30 (Uncirculated, pre-issue) and $33 (Proof, pre-issue); Uncirculated later raised to $32, and Proof later raised to $37. The surcharge of $10 per coin went to the National Community Service Trust.

Key to Collecting. Uncirculated examples are scarce by virtue of their low mintage, but demand is scarce as well, with the result that they can be purchased easily enough. Both formats are usually seen in superb gem preservation.

	Distribution	Cert	Avg	%MS	MS-67
					PF-67
1996-S	23,500	1,094	69.3	100%	$125
	Auctions: $153, MS-70, August 2014; $129, MS-70, June 2015; $88, MS-69, July 2014; $86, MS-69, November 2014				
1996-S, Proof	101,543	2,012	69.1		$35
	Auctions: $195, PF-70DCam, April 2013				

SMITHSONIAN INSTITUTION 150TH ANNIVERSARY SILVER DOLLAR (1996)

Designer: *Thomas D. Rogers Sr. (obverse), John Mercanti (reverse).* **Weight:** *26.73 grams.*
Composition: *.900 silver, .100 copper (net weight .7736 oz. pure silver).* **Diameter:** *38.1 mm.*
Edge: *Reeded.* **Mints:** *Denver (Uncirculated) and Philadelphia (Proof).*

This silver dollar, as well as a five-dollar gold coin, marked the 150th anniversary of Congress establishing the Smithsonian Institution in Washington, D.C., on August 10, 1846. Named for James Smithson—an English scientist whose will funded the entity—the institution quickly became America's national museum.

Designs. *Obverse:* The "Castle" building on the Mall in Washington, the original home of the Smithsonian Institution. Branches to each side. *Reverse:* Goddess of Knowledge sitting on top of a globe. In her left hand she holds a torch, in the right a scroll inscribed ART / HISTORY / SCIENCE. In the field to the right in several lines is FOR THE INCREASE AND DIFFUSION OF KNOWLEDGE.

Mintage Data. Authorized by Public Law 104-96, signed by President William J. Clinton on January 10, 1996. *Maximum authorized—650,000. Number minted—1996-D: 31,320 Uncirculated; 1996-P: 129,152 Proof.*

Original Cost. Sale prices $30 (Uncirculated, pre-issue) and $33 (Proof, pre-issue); Uncirculated later raised to $32, and Proof later raised to $37. The surcharge of $10 per coin went to the Smithsonian Board of Regents.

Key to Collecting. This silver dollar and the five-dollar gold coin issued alongside it have risen in value considerably since their release. Today examples can be found readily in the marketplace and are nearly always superb gems.

	Distribution	Cert	Avg	%MS	MS-67
					PF-67
1996-D	31,320	1,085	69.4	100%	$75
	Auctions: $119, MS-70, July 2014; $100, MS-70, February 2015; $89, MS-70, February 2015; $65, MS-69, October 2014				
1996-P, Proof	129,152	1,856	69.0		$40
	Auctions: $447, PF-70DCam, March 2013				

SMITHSONIAN INSTITUTION 150TH ANNIVERSARY $5 GOLD COIN (1996)

Designer: *Alfred F. Maletsky (obverse), T. James Ferrell (reverse).* **Weight:** *8.359 grams.*
Composition: *.900 gold, .100 copper (net weight .242 oz. pure gold).*
Diameter: *21.6 mm.* **Edge:** *Reeded.* **Mint:** *West Point.*

The U.S. Mint offered the two 1996 Smithsonian commemorative coins via several new options, including the 50,000-set Young Collectors Edition and incorporated in jewelry items.

Designs. *Obverse:* Bust of James Smithson facing left. *Reverse:* Sunburst with SMITHSONIAN below.

Mintage Data. Authorized by Public Law 104-96, signed by President William J. Clinton on January 10, 1996. *Maximum authorized*—100,000. *Number minted*—9,068 Uncirculated and 21,772 Proof.

Original Cost. Sale prices $180 (Uncirculated, pre-issue) and $195 (Proof, pre-issue); Uncirculated later raised to $205, and Proof later raised to $225. The surcharge of $10 per coin went to the Smithsonian Board of Regents.

Key to Collecting. Both Smithsonian Institution 150th Anniversary coins have risen in value considerably since their release. Today examples can be found readily in the marketplace and are nearly always superb gems.

	Distribution	Cert	Avg	%MS	MS-67
					PF-67
1996-W	9,068	855	69.4	100%	$400
	Auctions: $646, MS-70, September 2014; $541, MS-70, January 2015; $447, MS-70, April 2015; $382, MS-69, August 2014				
1996-W, Proof	21,772	1,303	69.2		$325
	Auctions: $706, PF-70DCam, April 2013; $588, PF-70DCam, September 2014; $529, PF-70DCam, September 2014				

U.S. BOTANIC GARDEN SILVER DOLLAR (1997)

Designer: *Edgar Z. Steever IV (obverse), William C. Cousins (reverse).* **Weight:** *26.73 grams.*
Composition: *Silver .900, copper .100 (net weight .7736 oz. pure silver).*
Diameter: *38.1 mm.* **Edge:** *Reeded.* **Mint:** *Philadelphia.*

These coins were purportedly struck to celebrate the 175th anniversary of the United States Botanic Garden (which would have been 1995), but they were dated on one side as 1997. The authorizing legislation that created the coins specified that the French façade of the U.S. Botanic Garden be shown on the obverse and a rose on the reverse.

Designs. *Obverse:* Façade of the United States
Botanic Garden in plan view without landscaping. *Reverse:* A rose at the center with a garland of roses above. The inscription below includes the anniversary dates 1820–1995. Note that some listings designate the rose side as the obverse.

Mintage Data. Authorized by Public Law 103-328, signed by President William J. Clinton on September 29, 1994. *Maximum authorized*—500,000. *Number minted*—58,505 Uncirculated and 189,671 Proof.

Original Cost. Sale prices $30 (Uncirculated, pre-issue) and $33 (Proof, pre-issue); Uncirculated later raised to $33, and Proof later raised to $37. The surcharge of $10 per coin went to the National Fund for the Botanic Garden.

Key to Collecting. These coins are readily available on the market today. Nearly all are superb gems. Ironically, the most popular related item is the Mint package containing the 1997-P special-finish Jefferson nickel, the demand coming from collectors of five-cent pieces! Only 25,000 sets were sold. This is *déjà vu* of the 1993 Jefferson dollar offer.

	Distribution	Cert	Avg	%MS	MS-67 PF-67
1997-P	58,505	1,567	69.1	100%	$30
Auctions: $159, MS-70, July 2014; $170, MS-70, April 2013					
1997-P, Proof	189,671	1,515	69.0		$45
Auctions: $441, PF-70DCam, April 2013; $306, PF-70UCam, February 2015; $306, PF-70DCam, September 2014					

NATIONAL LAW ENFORCEMENT OFFICERS MEMORIAL SILVER DOLLAR (1997)

Designer: *Alfred F. Maletsky (obverse from a photograph by Larry Ruggieri).* **Weight:** *26.73 grams.*
Composition: *.900 silver, .100 copper (net weight .7736 oz. pure silver).*
Diameter: *38.1 mm.* **Edge:** *Reeded.* **Mint:** *Philadelphia.*

The National Law Enforcement Officers Memorial at Judiciary Square in Washington, D.C., dedicated on October 15, 1991, was the subject of this commemorative. The monument honors more than 14,000 men and women who gave their lives in the line of duty.

Designs. *Obverse:* United States Park Police officers Robert Chelsey and Kelcy Stefansson making a rubbing of a fellow officer's name.
Reverse: Shield with a rose across it, evocative of the sacrifices made by officers.

Mintage Data. Authorized by Public Law 104-329, signed by President William J. Clinton on October 20, 1996. *Maximum authorized*—500,000. *Number minted*—28,575 Uncirculated and 110,428 Proof.

Original Cost. Sale prices $30 (Uncirculated, pre-issue) and $33 (Proof, pre-issue); Uncirculated later raised to $32, and Proof later raised to $37.

Key to Collecting. Once the distribution figures were published, the missed opportunity was realized—collectors saw that these coins would be a modern rarity. The market price rose to a sharp premium, where it remains today. Nearly all coins approach perfection in quality.

	Distribution	Cert	Avg	%MS	MS-67 PF-67
1997-P	28,575	832	69.3	100%	$125
Auctions: $259, MS-70, May 2013; $206, MS-70, August 2014; $84, MS-69, February 2015					
1997-P, Proof	110,428	1,616	69.0		$65
Auctions: $353, PF-70DCam, April 2013; $243, PF-70DCam, September 2014; $60, PF-69DCam, January 2015					

JACKIE ROBINSON SILVER DOLLAR (1997)

Designer: *Alfred F. Maletsky (obverse), T. James Ferrell (reverse).* **Weight:** *26.73 grams.*
Composition: *.900 silver, .100 copper (net weight .7736 oz. pure silver).*
Diameter: *38.1 mm.* **Edge:** *Reeded.* **Mint:** *San Francisco.*

This silver dollar and a concurrently issued five-dollar gold coin commemorated the 50th anniversary of the first acceptance of a black player in a major league baseball game, Jack ("Jackie") Robinson being the hero. The watershed event took place at Ebbets Field on April 15, 1947.

Designs. *Obverse:* Robinson in game action stealing home plate, evocative of a 1955 World Series play in a contest between the New York Yankees and the Brooklyn Dodgers. *Reverse:* 50th anniversary logotype of the Jackie Robinson Foundation (a motif worn by all Major League Baseball players in the 1997 season) surrounded with lettering of two baseball accomplishments.

Mintage Data. Authorized on October 20, 1996, by Public Law 104-329, part of the United States Commemorative Coin Act of 1996, with a provision tied to Public Law 104-328 (for the Botanic Garden dollar). Coins could be minted for a full year beginning July 1, 1997. *Maximum authorized—200,000. Number minted—30,180 Uncirculated and 110,002 Proof.*

Original Cost. Sale prices $30 (Uncirculated, pre-issue) and $33 (Proof, pre-issue); Uncirculated later raised to $32, and Proof later raised to $37. The surcharge of $10 per coin went to the Jackie Robinson Foundation.

Key to Collecting. Although the Jackie Robinson coins were losers in the sales figures of the U.S. Mint, the small quantities issued made both coins winners in the return-on-investment sweepstakes. Today, each of these can be found without a problem, and nearly all are in superb gem preservation.

	Distribution	Cert	Avg	%MS	MS-67 PF-67
1997-S	30,180	1,192	69.1	100%	$90
	Auctions: $411, MS-70, October 2014; $682, MS-70, January 2013				
1997-S, Proof	110,002	2,129	69.0		$65
	Auctions: $999, PF-70DCam, September 2014; $646, PF-70DCam, September 2013				

JACKIE ROBINSON $5 GOLD COIN (1997)

Designer: *William C. Cousins (obverse), James Peed (reverse).* **Weight:** *8.359 grams.*
Composition: *.900 gold, .100 copper (net weight .242 oz. pure gold).*
Diameter: *21.6 mm.* **Edge:** *Reeded.* **Mint:** *West Point.*

The U.S. Mint's marketing of the Jackie Robinson coins was innovative, as it had been in recent times. One promotion featured a reproduction of a rare baseball trading card, with the distinction of being the first such card ever issued by the U.S. government. But no matter how important Robinson's legacy was, buyers voted with their pocketbooks, and sales were low—making the Uncirculated gold coin a modern rarity.

Designs. *Obverse:* Portrait of Robinson in his later years as a civil-rights and political activist. *Reverse:* Detail of the seam on a baseball, Robinson's 1919–1972 life dates, and the inscription "Life of Courage."

Mintage Data. Authorized on October 20, 1996, by Public Law 104-329, part of the United States Commemorative Coin Act of 1996, with a provision tied to Public Law 104-328 (for the Botanic Garden dollar). Coins could be minted for a full year beginning July 1, 1997. *Maximum authorized*—100,000. *Number minted*—5,174 Uncirculated and 24,072 Proof.

Original Cost. Sale prices $180 (Uncirculated, pre-issue) and $195 (Proof, pre-issue); Uncirculated later raised to $205, and Proof later raised to $225. The surcharge of $35 per coin went to the Jackie Robinson Foundation.

Key to Collecting. The Jackie Robinson five-dollar gold coin takes top honors as the key issue among modern commemoratives. Especially rare and valuable is the Uncirculated version.

	Distribution	Cert	Avg	%MS	MS-67
					PF-67
1997-W	5,174	841	69.3	100%	$1,600
	Auctions: $3,290, MS-70, February 2015; $3,055, MS-70, June 2015; $1,763, MS-69, February 2015; $1,645, MS-69, February 2015				
1997-W, Proof	24,072	1,524	69.3		$550
	Auctions: $376, PF-69DCam, April 2015; $376, PF-69DCam, January 2015; $367, PF-69UCam, February 2015				

FRANKLIN D. ROOSEVELT $5 GOLD COIN (1997)

Designer: *T. James Ferrell (obverse), James Peed (reverse).* **Weight:** *8.359 grams.*
Composition: *.900 gold, .100 copper (net weight .242 oz. pure gold).*
Diameter: *21.6 mm.* **Edge:** *Reeded.* **Mint:** *West Point.*

Considering that newly inaugurated President Franklin D. Roosevelt suspended the mintage and paying out of U.S. gold coins in 1933, it was ironic that he should later have a gold coin commemorating his life. The year 1997 does not seem to have been a special anniversary date of any kind, as it was 115 years after his birth, 64 years after his inauguration, and 52 years after his death.

Designs. *Obverse:* Upper torso and head of Roosevelt facing right, based on one of the president's favorite photographs, taken when he was reviewing the U.S. Navy fleet in San Francisco Bay. *Reverse:* Presidential seal displayed at Roosevelt's 1933 inaugural.

Mintage Data. Authorized by Public Law 104-329, signed by President William J. Clinton on October 20, 1996. *Maximum authorized*—100,000. *Number minted*—11,894 Uncirculated and 29,474 Proof.

Original Cost. Sale prices $180 (Uncirculated, pre-issue) and $195 (Proof, pre-issue); Uncirculated later raised to $205, and Proof later raised to $225. A portion of the surcharge of $35 per coin went to the Franklin Delano Roosevelt Memorial Commission.

Key to Collecting. Since the mintages for both Uncirculated and Proof formats were low, their values rose substantially on the aftermarket. Examples are easily available today and are nearly always in superb gem preservation.

	Distribution	Cert	Avg	%MS	MS-67
					PF-67
1997-W	11,894	873	69.5	100%	$475
	Auctions: $705, MS-70, August 2014; $611, MS-70, August 2014; $541, MS-70, April 2015; $535, MS-70, April 2015				
1997-W, Proof	29,474	1,763	69.3		$325
	Auctions: $447, PF-69DCam, March 2013				

BLACK REVOLUTIONARY WAR PATRIOTS SILVER DOLLAR (1998)

Designer: *John Mercanti (obverse), Ed Dwight (reverse).* **Weight:** *26.73 grams.*
Composition: *.900 silver, .100 copper (net weight .7736 oz. pure silver).*
Diameter: *38.1 mm.* **Edge:** *Reeded.* **Mint:** *San Francisco.*

This coin commemorates black Revolutionary War patriots and the 275th anniversary of the birth of Crispus Attucks, the first patriot killed in the infamous Boston Massacre in 1770 (an event predating the Revolutionary War, one among many incidents that inflamed the pro-independence passions of Americans).

Designs. *Obverse:* U.S. Mint engraver John Mercanti's conception of Crispus Attucks. *Reverse:* A black patriot family, a detail from the proposed Black Patriots Memorial.

Mintage Data. Authorized by Public Law 104-329, signed by President William J. Clinton on October 20, 1996. *Maximum authorized*—500,000. *Number minted*—37,210 Uncirculated and 75,070 Proof.

Original Cost. Sale prices $30 (Uncirculated, pre-issue) and $33 (Proof, pre-issue); Uncirculated later raised to $32, and Proof later raised to $37. A portion of the surcharge of $10 per coin went to the Black Revolutionary War Patriots Foundation to fund the construction of the Black Patriots Memorial in Washington, D.C.

Key to Collecting. These coins became highly desirable when the low mintage figures were published. Examples remain valuable today, and deservedly so. Nearly all are superb gems.

	Distribution	Cert	Avg	%MS	MS-67
					PF-67
1998-S	37,210	1,265	69.2	100%	$90
	Auctions: $176, MS-70, April 2013				
1998-S, Proof	75,070	1,458	69.0		$60
	Auctions: $353, PF-70DCam, April 2013				

ROBERT F. KENNEDY SILVER DOLLAR (1998)

Designer: *Thomas D. Rogers Sr.* **Weight:** *26.73 grams.*
Composition: *.900 silver, .100 copper (net weight .7736 oz. pure silver).*
Diameter: *38.1 mm.* **Edge:** *Reeded.* **Mint:** *San Francisco.*

These coins marked the 30th anniversary of the death of Robert F. Kennedy, attorney general of the United States appointed by his brother, President John F. Kennedy.

Designs. *Obverse:* Portrait of Robert F. Kennedy. *Reverse:* Eagle perched on a shield with JUSTICE above, Senate seal to lower left.

Mintage Data. Authorized by Public Law 103-328, signed by President William J. Clinton on September 29, 1994. *Maximum authorized*—500,000. *Number minted*—106,422 Uncirculated and 99,020 Proof.

Original Cost. Sale prices $30 (Uncirculated, pre-issue) and $33 (Proof, pre-issue); Uncirculated later raised to $32, and Proof later raised to $37. A portion of the surcharge of $10 per coin went to the Robert F. Kennedy Memorial.

Key to Collecting. Upon their publication the mintage figures were viewed as being attractively low from a numismatic viewpoint. Examples are easily found today and are usually superb gems.

	Distribution	Cert	Avg	%MS	MS-67
					PF-67
1998-S	106,422	3,057	69.3	100%	$40
	Auctions: $70, MS-70, July 2014; $129, MS-70, April 2013				
1998-S, Proof	99,020	1,511	69.0		$75
	Auctions: $282, PF-70DCam, September 2014; $270, PF-70DCam, September 2014				

DOLLEY MADISON SILVER DOLLAR (1999)

Designer: *Tiffany & Co.* **Weight:** *26.73 grams.*
Composition: *.900 silver, .100 copper (net weight .7736 oz. pure silver).*
Diameter: *38.1 mm.* **Edge:** *Reeded.* **Mint:** *Philadelphia.*

If the myth that Martha Washington was the subject for the 1792 silver half disme is discarded, Dolley Madison, wife of President James Madison, became the first of the first ladies to be depicted on a legal-tender U.S. coin with this silver dollar. The designs by Tiffany & Co. were modeled by T. James Ferrell (obverse) and Thomas D. Rogers Sr. (reverse). Note the T&Co. logo in a flower petal on the obverse and at the base of the trees to the right on the reverse.

Designs. *Obverse:* Portrait of Dolley Madison as depicted near the ice house (in the style of classic pergola) on the grounds of the family estate, Montpelier. A bouquet of cape jasmines is to the left. *Reverse:* Angular view of the front of Montpelier, complete with landscaping.

Mintage Data. Authorized by Public Law 104-329, signed by President William J. Clinton on October 20, 1996. *Maximum authorized*—500,000. *Number minted*—89,104 Uncirculated and 224,403 Proof.

Original Cost. Sale prices $30 (Uncirculated, pre-issue) and $33 (Proof, pre-issue); Uncirculated later raised to $32, and Proof later raised to $37. A portion of the surcharge of $10 per coin went to the National Trust for Historic Preservation.

Key to Collecting. The Dolley Madison dollars have been popular with collectors ever since they were first sold. Examples can be obtained with little effort and are usually superb gems.

	Distribution	Cert	Avg	%MS	MS-67 PF-67
1999-P	89,104	2,187	69.4	100%	$35
	Auctions: $90, MS-70, April 2013				
1999-P, Proof	224,403	2,629	69.1		$35
	Auctions: $106, PF-70DCam, April 2013				

GEORGE WASHINGTON DEATH BICENTENNIAL $5 GOLD COIN (1999)

Designer: *Laura Garden Fraser.* **Weight:** *8.359 grams.*
Composition: *.900 gold, .100 copper (net weight .242 oz. pure gold).*
Diameter: *21.6 mm.* **Edge:** *Reeded.* **Mint:** *West Point.*

The 200th anniversary of George Washington's death was commemorated with this coin. In 1932 Laura Garden Fraser's proposed Washington portrait for the quarter dollar had been rejected in favor of the portrait design by John Flanagan, but it was resurrected for this commemorative gold coin.

Designs. *Obverse:* A portrait of Washington inspired by the bust modeled in 1785 for French sculptor Jean Antoine Houdon. *Reverse:* A perched eagle with feathers widely separated at left and right.

Mintage Data. Authorized on October 20, 1996, by Public Law 104-329, part of the United States Commemorative Coin Act of 1996. *Maximum authorized*—100,000 pieces (both formats combined). *Number minted*—22,511 Uncirculated and 41,693 Proof.

Original Cost. Sale prices $180 (Uncirculated, pre-issue) and $195 (Proof, pre-issue); Uncirculated later raised to $195, and Proof later raised to $225. A portion of the surcharge went to the Mount Vernon Ladies' Association, which cares for Washington's home today.

Key to Collecting. This coin is readily available in any high grade desired.

	Distribution	Cert	Avg	%MS	MS-67 PF-67
1999-W	22,511	1,494	69.5	100%	$325
	Auctions: $423, MS-70, April 2015; $423, MS-70, April 2015; $400, MS-70, April 2015; $353, MS-70, April 2015				
1999-W, Proof	41,693	2,101	69.4		$325
	Auctions: $705, PF-70DCam, March 2013; $400, PF-70UCam, April 2015; $382, PF-69DCam, July 2014				

YELLOWSTONE NATIONAL PARK SILVER DOLLAR (1999)

Designer: *Edgar Z. Steever IV (obverse), William C. Cousins (reverse).* **Weight:** *26.73 grams.*
Composition: *.900 silver, .100 copper (net weight .7736 oz. pure silver).*
Diameter: *38.1 mm.* **Edge:** *Reeded.* **Mint:** *Philadelphia.*

This coin commemorated the 125th anniversary of the establishment of Yellowstone National Park. Technically, it came out and was dated two years later than it should have, as the park was founded in 1872 (and therefore the 125th anniversary would have been in 1997, not 1999).

Designs. *Obverse:* An unidentified geyser (not the famed Old Faithful, for the terrain is different) is shown in action. YELLOWSTONE is above, with other inscriptions to the left center and below, as illustrated. *Reverse:* A bison is shown, facing left. In the background is a mountain range with sun and resplendent rays (an adaptation of the seal of the Department of the Interior).

Mintage Data. Authorized on October 20, 1996, by Public Law 104-329, part of the United States Commemorative Coin Act of 1996. The catch-all legislation authorized seven commemoratives to be issued from 1997 to 1999. *Maximum authorized*—500,000 (both formats combined). *Number minted*—82,563 Uncirculated and 187,595 Proof.

Original Cost. Sale prices $30 (Uncirculated, pre-issue) and $33 (Proof, pre-issue); Uncirculated later raised to $32, and Proof later raised to $37.

Key to Collecting. Easily obtainable in the numismatic marketplace, nearly always in high grades. Investors are attracted to coins certified as MS-70 or PF-70, but few can tell the difference between these and coins at the 69 level. Only a tiny fraction of the mintage has ever been certified.

	Distribution	Cert	Avg	%MS	MS-67 / PF-67
1999-P	82,563	1,872	69.3	100%	$55
Auctions: No auction records available.					
1999-P, Proof	187,595	2,203	69.0		$50
Auctions: $282, PF-70UCam, July 2015					

LIBRARY OF CONGRESS BICENTENNIAL SILVER DOLLAR (2000)

Designer: *Thomas D. Rogers Sr. (obverse), John Mercanti (reverse).* **Weight:** *26.73 grams.*
Composition: *.900 silver, .100 copper (net weight .7736 oz. pure silver).*
Diameter: *38.1 mm.* **Edge:** *Reeded.* **Mint:** *Philadelphia.*

The Library of Congress, located across the street from the U.S. Capitol in Washington, celebrated its 200th anniversary on April 24, 2000; these silver dollars and a ten-dollar bimetallic coin were issued to honor the milestone.

Designs. *Obverse:* An open book, with its spine resting on a closed book, with the torch of the Library of Congress dome behind. *Reverse:* The dome part of the Library of Congress.

Mintage Data. Authorized by Public Law 105-268, signed by President William J. Clinton on October 19, 1996. *Maximum authorized*—500,000. *Number minted*—53,264 Uncirculated and 198,503 Proof.

Original Cost. Sale prices $25 (Uncirculated, pre-issue) and $28 (Proof, pre-issue); Uncirculated later raised to $27, and Proof later raised to $32. A portion of the surcharges went to the Library of Congress Trust Fund Board.

Key to Collecting. The Library of Congress silver dollar (as well as the ten-dollar bimetallic coin issued alongside it) is readily available in the marketplace today, nearly always of the superb gem quality, as issued.

	Distribution	Cert	Avg	%MS	MS-67 PF-67
2000-P	53,264	1,616	69.4	100%	$30
	Auctions: $108, MS-70, April 2013; $76, MS-70, July 2014; $74, MS-70, October 2015				
2000-P, Proof	198,503	1,973	69.0		$30
	Auctions: $188, PF-70DCam, September 2014; $635, PF-70DCam, April 2013				

LIBRARY OF CONGRESS BICENTENNIAL $10 BIMETALLIC COIN (2000)

Designer: *John Mercanti (obverse), Thomas D. Rogers Sr. (reverse).*
Weight: *16.259 grams.* **Composition:** *.480 gold, .480 platinum, .040 alloy.*
Diameter: *27 mm.* **Edge:** *Reeded.* **Mint:** *West Point.*

This coin was the U.S. Mint's first gold/platinum bimetallic coin. The Library of Congress—the original location of which was burned by the British, but which was resurrected using Thomas Jefferson's personal book collection—is today a repository that includes 18 million books and more than 100 million other items, including periodicals, films, prints, photographs, and recordings.

Designs. *Obverse:* The torch of the Library of Congress dome. *Reverse:* An eagle surrounded by a wreath.

Mintage Data. Authorized by Public Law 105-268, signed by President William J. Clinton on October 19, 1996. *Maximum authorized*—200,000. *Number minted*—7,261 Uncirculated and 27,445 Proof.

Original Cost. Sale prices $380 (Uncirculated, pre-issue) and $395 (Proof, pre-issue); Uncirculated later raised to $405, and Proof later raised to $425. A portion of the surcharges went to the Library of Congress Trust Fund Board.

Key to Collecting. The Library of Congress ten-dollar bimetallic coin (as well as the silver dollar issued alongside it) is readily available in the marketplace today, nearly always of the superb gem quality as issued.

	Distribution	Cert	Avg	%MS	MS-67 PF-67
2000-W	7,261	1,420	69.7	100%	$1,400
	Auctions: $2,115, MS-70, June 2015; $1,998, MS-70, August 2015; $1,293, MS-69, October 2015; $1,175, MS-69, June 2015				
2000-W, Proof	27,445	3,176	69.2		$1,100
	Auctions: $2,115, PF-70DCam, September 2015; $1,763, PF-70UCam, October 2015; $823, PF-69UCam, October 2015				

Leif Ericson Millennium Silver Dollar (2000)

Designer: *John Mercanti (obverse), T. James Ferrell (reverse).* **Weight:** *26.73 grams.*
Composition: *.900 silver, .100 copper (net weight .7736 oz. pure silver).*
Diameter: *38.1 mm.* **Edge:** *Reeded.* **Mint:** *Philadelphia.*

This silver dollar was issued in cooperation with a foreign government, the Republic of Iceland, which also sponsored its own coin, struck at the Philadelphia Mint (but with no mintmark), a silver 1,000 krónur. Both commemorated the millennium of the year 1000, the approximate departure date of Leif Ericson and his crew from Iceland to the New World.

Designs. *Obverse:* Portrait of Leif Ericson, an artist's conception, as no actual image survives—based on the image used on the Iceland 1 krónur coin. The helmeted head of the explorer is shown facing right. *Reverse:* A Viking long ship with high prow under full sail, FOUNDER OF THE NEW WORLD above, other inscriptions below.

Mintage Data. Authorized under Public Law 106-126. *Maximum authorized*—500,000. *Number minted*—28,150 Uncirculated and 144,748 Proof.

Original Cost. Sale prices $30 (Uncirculated, pre-issue) and $33 (Proof, pre-issue); Uncirculated later raised to $32, and Proof later raised to $37. The surcharge of $10 per coin went to the Leifur Eiriksson Foundation for funding student exchanges between the United States and Iceland.

Key to Collecting. These coins are readily available in the marketplace today.

	Distribution	Cert	Avg	%MS	MS-67 PF-67
2000-P	28,150	1,307	69.4	100%	$75
	Auctions: $223, MS-70, June 2015; $212, MS-70, January 2013; $176, MS-70, July 2014				
2000-P, Proof	144,748	2,212	69.0		$60
	Auctions: $999, PF-70DCam, September 2014; $999, PF-70DCam, April 2013				

American Buffalo Silver Dollar (2001)

Designer: *James Earle Fraser.* **Weight:** *26.73 grams.*
Composition: *.900 silver, .100 copper (net weight .7736 oz. pure silver).*
Diameter: *38.1 mm.* **Edge:** *Reeded.* **Mints:** *Denver (Uncirculated) and Philadelphia (Proof).*

James Earle Fraser's design, originally used on nickels from 1913 to 1938, was modified slightly by Mint engravers for this silver dollar. Commonly called the "American Buffalo Commemorative," the coin debuted at the groundbreaking for the Smithsonian Institution's National Museum of the American Indian and was very well received.

Designs. *Obverse:* Portrait of a Native American facing right. *Reverse:* An American bison standing, facing left.

Mintage Data. Authorized by Public Law 106-375, October 27, 2000. *Maximum authorized*—500,000. *Number minted*—2001-D: 227,131 Uncirculated; 2001-P: 272,869 Proof.

Original Cost. Sale prices (pre-issue only) $30 (Uncirculated) and $33 (Proof). The surcharge of $10 per coin went to the National Museum of the American Indian.

Key to Collecting. Both the Uncirculated and Proof of the 2001 American Buffalo were carefully produced to high standards of quality. Nearly all examples today grade at high levels, including MS-70 and PF-70, these ultra-grades commanding a sharp premium for investors. Coins grading 68 or 69 often have little or any real difference in quality and would seem to be the best buys.

	Distribution	Cert	Avg	%MS	MS-67
					PF-67
2001-D	227,131	14,874	69.1	100%	$175
Auctions: $259, MS-70, February 2015; $235, MS-70, July 2015; $259, MS-69, June 2015; $165, MS-69, January 2015					
2001-P, Proof	272,869	15,783	69.1		$175
Auctions: $376, PF-70DCam, February 2015; $353, PF-70DCam, January 2015; $153, PF-69DCam, June 2015; $141, PF-69DCam, June 2015					

U.S. CAPITOL VISITOR CENTER HALF DOLLAR (2001)

Designer: *Dean McMullen (obverse), Alex Shagin and Marcel Jovine (reverse).* **Weight:** *11.34 grams.* **Composition:** *.9167 copper, .0833 nickel.* **Diameter:** *30.61 mm.* **Edge:** *Reeded.* **Mint:** *Philadelphia.*

In 1991 Congress voted on a Visitor Center to be established near the U.S. Capitol building. This copper-nickel half dollar, as well as a silver dollar and a ten-dollar gold coin, were decided upon to provide the funds through sale surcharges. The center and the coins did not become a reality until more than a decade later, though.

Designs. *Obverse:* The north wing of the original U.S. Capitol (burned by the British in 1814) is shown superimposed on a plan view of the present building. *Reverse:* Within a circle of 16 stars are inscriptions referring to the first meeting of the Senate and House.

Mintage Data. Authorized by Public Law 106-126, signed by President William J. Clinton on December 6, 1999. *Maximum authorized*—750,000. *Number minted*—99,157 Uncirculated and 77,962 Proof.

Original Cost. Sale prices $7.75 (Uncirculated, pre-issue) and $10.75 (Proof, pre-issue); Uncirculated later raised to $8.50, and Proof later raised to $11.50. The $3 surcharge per coin went towards the construction of the Visitor Center.

Key to Collecting. Today, this half dollar is readily available on the market, nearly always in the same gem quality as issued.

	Distribution	Cert	Avg	%MS	MS-67
					PF-67
2001-P	99,157	3,427	69.5	100%	$20
Auctions: $153, MS-70, August 2013					
2001-P, Proof	77,962	1,359	69.0		$16
Auctions: No auction records available.					

U.S. Capitol Visitor Center Silver Dollar (2001)

Designer: *Marika Somogyi (obverse)*, *John Mercanti (reverse)*. **Weight:** *26.73 grams.*
Composition: *.900 silver, .100 copper (net weight .7736 oz. pure silver).*
Diameter: *38.1 mm.* **Edge:** *Reeded.* **Mint:** *Philadelphia.*

The U.S. Capitol Visitor Center, as first proposed, was to offer free exhibits and films, and it was believed that the center would eliminate lengthy waits to view the Capitol proper. However, presumably many would still want to visit the Capitol itself, and no further plan to eliminate waiting time was presented. After the September 11, 2001, terrorist attack on the World Trade Center in New York City and the Pentagon in the District of Columbia, security at the Capitol was heightened—and the concept of the Visitor Center became even more important.

Designs. *Obverse:* The original Capitol is shown with the date 1800, and a much smaller later Capitol, with the date 2001—a variation on the same theme as used on the half dollar. *Reverse:* An eagle reminiscent of Mint engraver John Mercanti's reverse for the 1986 silver bullion "Eagle" dollar. In the present incarnation, the national bird wears a ribbon lettered U.S. CAPITOL VISITOR CENTER.

Mintage Data. Authorized by Public Law 106-126, signed by President William J. Clinton on December 6, 1999. *Maximum authorized*—500,000. *Number minted*—35,380 Uncirculated and 143,793 Proof.

Original Cost. Sale prices $27 (Uncirculated, pre-issue) and $29 (Proof, pre-issue); Uncirculated later raised to $29, and Proof later raised to $33. The $10 surcharge per coin went towards the construction of the Visitor Center.

Key to Collecting. Today, this silver dollar is readily available on the market, nearly always in the same gem quality as issued.

	Distribution	Cert	Avg	%MS	MS-67 / PF-67
2001-P	35,380	1,811	69.3	100%	$40
	Auctions: $129, MS-70, April 2013				
2001-P, Proof	143,793	2,203	69.0		$60
	Auctions: $294, PF-70DCam, February 2014; $4,113, PF-70DCam, April 2013				

U.S. Capitol Visitor Center $5 Gold Coin (2001)

Designer: *Elizabeth Jones.* **Weight:** *8.359 grams.* **Composition:** *.900 gold, .100 copper (net weight .242 oz. pure gold).* **Diameter:** *21.6 mm.* **Edge:** *Reeded.* **Mint:** *West Point.*

If there was a potential highlight for what proved to be yet another underperforming commemorative issue—with sales far below projections—it was that Elizabeth Jones, former chief engraver at the Mint, was tapped to do the obverse of the $5 gold coin in the Capitol Visitor Center series. The result might not be a showcase for her remarkable talent, given the nature of the subject, but it rounds out the suite of three commemorative coins with detailed architectural motifs.

Designs. *Obverse:* Section of a Corinthian column. *Reverse:* The 1800 Capitol (interestingly, with slightly different architectural details and proportions than seen on the other coins).

Mintage Data. Authorized by Public Law 106-126, signed by President William J. Clinton on December 6, 1999. *Maximum authorized*—100,000. *Number minted*—6,761 Uncirculated and 27,652 Proof.

Original Cost. Sale prices $175 (Uncirculated, pre-issue) and $177 (Proof, pre-issue); Uncirculated later raised to $200, and Proof later raised to $207. The $35 surcharge per coin went towards the construction of the Visitor Center.

Key to Collecting. Of all the Capitol Visitor Center commemoratives, the Uncirculated five-dollar gold coin is least often seen. After the distribution figure of only 6,761 was released for that coin, buyers clamored to acquire them, and the price rose sharply. Today, it still sells at one of the greatest premiums of any modern commemorative.

	Distribution	Cert	Avg	%MS	MS-67
					PF-67
2001-W	6,761	2,055	69.5	100%	$1,100
	Auctions: $1,087, MS-70, July 2014; $1,058, MS-70, August 2014; $881, MS-70, January 2015; $764, MS-70, June 2015				
2001-W, Proof	27,652	1,883	69.4		$325
	Auctions: No auction records available.				

SALT LAKE CITY OLYMPIC WINTER GAMES SILVER DOLLAR (2002)

Designer: *John Mercanti (obverse), Donna Weaver (reverse).* **Weight:** *26.73 grams.*
Composition: *.900 silver, .100 copper (net weight .7736 oz. pure silver).*
Diameter: *38.1 mm.* **Edge:** *Reeded.* **Mint:** *Denver (Uncirculated) and Philadelphia (Proof).*

In February 2002, Salt Lake City, Utah, was the focal point for the XIX Olympic Winter Games, a quadrennial event. Congress authorized both this silver dollar and a five-dollar gold coin to commemorate the competition.

Designs. *Obverse:* A stylized geometric figure representing an ice crystal. Five interlocked Olympic rings and inscriptions complete the picture, including XIX OLYMPIC WINTER GAMES. *Reverse:* The skyline of Salt Lake City is shown with exaggerated dimensions, with the rugged Wasatch Mountains in the distance. XIX OLYMPIC GAMES is repeated on the reverse.

Mintage Data. Authorized by Public Law 106-435, the Salt Lake Olympic Winter Games Commemorative Coin Act, signed by President William J. Clinton on November 6, 2000. *Maximum authorized*—400,000. *Number minted*—2002-D: 40,257 Uncirculated; 2002-P: 166,864 Proof.

Original Cost. Sale prices $30 (Uncirculated, pre-issue) and $33 (Proof, pre-issue); Uncirculated were later raised to $32, and Proof were later raised to $37. The surcharge of $10 per coin went to the Salt Lake Organizing Committee for the Olympic Winter Games of 2002 and the United States Olympic Committee.

Key to Collecting. As might be expected, coins encapsulated as MS-70 and PF-70 sell for strong prices to investors and Registry Set compilers. Most collectors are nicely satisfied with 68 and 69 grades, or the normal issue quality, since the coins are little different in actual appearance.

	Distribution	Cert	Avg	%MS	MS-67
					PF-67
2002-D	40,257	1,567	69.5	100%	$45
	Auctions: $94, MS-70, January 2013				
2002-P, Proof	166,864	2,175	69.1		$40
	Auctions: $217, PF-70DCam, April 2013				

SALT LAKE CITY OLYMPIC WINTER GAMES $5 GOLD COIN (2002)

Designer: *Donna Weaver.* **Weight:** *8.359 grams.*
Composition: *.900 gold, .100 copper (net weight .242 oz. pure gold).*
Diameter: *21.6 mm.* **Edge:** *Reeded.* **Mint:** *West Point.*

The design of the 2002 Olympic Winter Games commemoratives attracted little favorable notice outside of advertising publicity, and, once again, sales were low—all the more surprising, for Olympic coins often attract international buyers.

Designs. *Obverse:* An ice crystal dominates, superimposed over a geometric creation representing "Rhythm of the Land," but not identified. Also appearing are the date and SALT LAKE. *Reverse:* The outline of the Olympic cauldron is shown, with geometric sails above representing flames.

Mintage Data. Authorized by Public Law 106-435, the Salt Lake Olympic Winter Games Commemorative Coin Act, signed by President William J. Clinton on November 6, 2000. *Maximum authorized—* 80,000. *Number minted—*10,585 Uncirculated and 32,877 Proof.

Original Cost. Sale prices $180 (Uncirculated, pre-issue) and $195 (Proof, pre-issue); Uncirculated were later raised to $205, and Proof were later raised to $225. The surcharge of $10 per coin went to the Salt Lake Organizing Committee for the Olympic Winter Games of 2002 and the United States Olympic Committee.

Key to Collecting. Although the mintage of the Uncirculated $5 in particular was quite low, there was not much interest in the immediate aftermarket. Coins graded MS-70 and PF-70 sell for strong prices to investors and Registry Set compilers.

	Distribution	Cert	Avg	%MS	MS-67
					PF-67
2002-W	10,585	1,197	69.5	100%	$325
	Auctions: $499, MS-70, August 2013; $397, MS-70, September 2014; $353, MS-70, April 2015				
2002-W, Proof	32,877	1,231	69.5		$325
	Auctions: $400, PF-70UCam, May 2015; $376, PF-70UCam, April 2015; $108, PF-70DCam, April 2013; $33, PF-69DCam, August 2014				

WEST POINT (U.S. MILITARY ACADEMY) BICENTENNIAL SILVER DOLLAR (2002)

Designer: *T. James Ferrell (obverse), John Mercanti (reverse).* **Weight:** *26.73 grams.*
Composition: *.900 silver, .100 copper (net weight .7736 oz. pure silver).*
Diameter: *38.1 mm.* **Edge:** *Reeded.* **Mint:** *West Point.*

The 200th anniversary of the U.S. Military Academy at West Point, New York, was celebrated with this coin. The Cadet Chapel is shown on the obverse of the dollar.

Designs. *Obverse:* A fine depiction of the Academy color guard in a parade, with Washington Hall and the Cadet Chapel in the distance—and minimum intrusion of lettering—projects this to the forefront of commemorative designs of the era. *Reverse:* The West Point Bicentennial logotype is shown, an adaptation of the Academy seal, showing at the center an ancient Greek helmet with a sword and shield.

Mintage Data. Authorized several years earlier by Public Law 103-328, signed by President William J. Clinton on September 29, 1994. *Maximum authorized*—500,000. *Number minted*—103,201 Uncirculated and 288,293 Proof.

Original Cost. Sale prices $30 (Uncirculated, pre-issue) and $32 (Proof, pre-issue); Uncirculated later raised to $32, and Proof later raised to $37. The surcharge of $10 per coin went to the Association of Graduates.

Key to Collecting. The scenario is familiar: enough coins were struck to satisfy all comers during the period of issue, with the result that there was no unsatisfied demand. Coins certified at the MS-70 level appeal to a special group of buyers and command strong premiums.

	Distribution	Cert	Avg	%MS	MS-67
					PF-67
2002-W	103,201	4,472	69.5	100%	$35
	Auctions: No auction records available.				
2002-W, Proof	288,293	5,565	69.3		$35
	Auctions: No auction records available.				

FIRST FLIGHT CENTENNIAL HALF DOLLAR (2003)

Designer: *John Mercanti (obverse), Norman E. Nemeth (reverse).* **Weight:** *11.34 grams.*
Composition: *.9167 copper, .0833 nickel.* **Diameter:** *30.61 mm.* **Edge:** *Reeded.* **Mint:** *Philadelphia.*

To celebrate the 100th anniversary of powered aircraft flight by Orville and Wilbur Wright in 1903, Congress authorized a set of 2003-dated commemoratives, including this copper-nickel half dollar.

Designs. *Obverse:* Wright Monument at Kill Devil Hill on the North Carolina seashore. *Reverse:* Wright Flyer biplane in flight.

Mintage Data. Authorized by Public Law 105-124, as an amendment and tag-on to the 50 States Commemorative Coin Program Act (which authorized the State quarters), signed by President William J. Clinton on December 1, 1997. *Maximum authorized*—750,000. *Number minted*—57,122 Uncirculated and 109,710 Proof.

Original Cost. Sale prices $9.75 (Uncirculated, pre-issue) and $12.50 (Proof, pre-issue); Uncirculated later raised to $10.75, and Proof later raised to $13.50. The surcharge of $1 per coin went to the First Flight Centennial Foundation, a private nonprofit group founded in 1995.

Key to Collecting. Values fell after sales concluded. In time, they recovered. Today, all the coins in this set sell for a premium. Superb gems are easily enough found.

	Distribution	Cert	Avg	%MS	MS-67 PF-67
2003-P	57,122	2,186	69.5	100%	$15
	Auctions: $50, MS-70, April 2013				
2003-P, Proof	109,710	2,093	69.1		$17
	Auctions: No auction records available.				

First Flight Centennial Silver Dollar (2003)

Designer: *T. James Ferrell (obverse), Norman E. Nemeth (reverse).* **Weight:** *26.73 grams.* **Composition:** *.900 silver, .100 copper (net weight .7736 oz. pure silver).* **Diameter:** *38.1 mm.* **Edge:** *Reeded.* **Mint:** *Philadelphia.*

The release of this coin and the two other First Flight Centennial commemoratives with it marked the third straight year that a coin featuring the Wrights' plane was featured on a U.S. coin. In 2001, the North Carolina State quarter had portrayed the Wright Flyer, and the Ohio State quarter did the same in 2002 (though an astronaut was also incorporated).

Designs. *Obverse:* Conjoined portraits of Orville and Wilbur Wright. *Reverse:* The Wright brothers' plane in flight.

Mintage Data. Authorized by Public Law 105-124, as an amendment and tag-on to the 50 States Commemorative Coin Program Act (which authorized the State quarters), signed by President William J. Clinton on December 1, 1997. *Maximum authorized*—500,000. *Number minted*—53,533 Uncirculated and 190,240 Proof.

Original Cost. Sale prices $31 (Uncirculated, pre-issue) and $33 (Proof, pre-issue); Uncirculated later raised to $33, and Proof later raised to $37. The surcharge of $1 per coin went to the First Flight Centennial Foundation, a private nonprofit group founded in 1995.

Key to Collecting. Values fell after sales concluded, but they did recover in time. Today, all the coins in this program sell for a premium. Superb gems are easily enough found.

	Distribution	Cert	Avg	%MS	MS-67 PF-67
2003-P	53,533	3,154	69.4	100%	$45
	Auctions: $94, MS-70, May 2013				
2003-P, Proof	190,240	3,133	69.0		$45
	Auctions: $423, PF-70DCam, March 2013; $141, PF-70DCam, April 2013				

FIRST FLIGHT CENTENNIAL $10 GOLD COIN (2003)

Designer: *Donna Weaver (obverse), Norman E. Nemeth (reverse).* **Weight:** *16.718 grams.*
Composition: *.900 gold, .100 copper (net weight .4837 oz. pure gold).*
Diameter: *27 mm.* **Edge:** *Reeded.* **Mint:** *West Point.*

None of the First Flight Centennial commemoratives sold particularly well. The redundancy of the motifs undoubtedly contributed to this: each had the same reverse motif of the Wright brothers' plane, and the two largest denominations each pictured the Wright brothers.

Designs. *Obverse:* Portraits of Orville and Wilbur Wright. *Reverse:* Wright Brothers' plane in flight with an eagle overhead.

Mintage Data. Authorized by Public Law 105-124, as an amendment and tag-on to the 50 States Commemorative Coin Program Act (which authorized the State quarters), signed by President William J. Clinton on December 1, 1997. *Maximum authorized*—100,000. *Number minted*—10,009 Uncirculated and 21,676 Proof.

Original Cost. Sale prices $340 (Uncirculated, pre-issue) and $350 (Proof, pre-issue); Uncirculated later raised to $365, and Proof later raised to $375. The surcharge of $1 per coin went to the First Flight Centennial Foundation, a private nonprofit group founded in 1995.

Key to Collecting. Values fell after sales concluded, but they did recover in time. Today, all the coins in this commemorative program sell for a premium. Superb gems are easily enough found.

	Distribution	Cert	Avg	%MS	MS-67 PF-67
2003-W	10,009	1,914	69.8	100%	$900
	Auctions: $823, MS-70, July 2015; $793, MS-70, January 2015; $617, MS-69, July 2015; $588, MS-69, June 2015				
2003-W, Proof	21,676	1,626	69.3		$700
	Auctions: $823, PF-70DCam, July 2014; $1,293, PF-70DCam, April 2013				

THOMAS ALVA EDISON SILVER DOLLAR (2004)

Designer: *Donna Weaver (obverse), John Mercanti (reverse).* **Weight:** *26.73 grams.*
Composition: *.900 silver, .100 copper (net weight .7736 oz. pure silver).*
Diameter: *38.1 mm.* **Edge:** *Reeded.* **Mint:** *Philadelphia.*

The 125th anniversary of the October 21, 1879, demonstration by Thomas Edison of his first successful electric light bulb was the event commemorated with this silver dollar. Despite sales falling far short of the authorized amount, the Edison dollar was well received by collectors. Interestingly, several proposals had earlier been made for commemoratives to be issued in 1997 to observe the 150th anniversary of Edison's February 11, 1847, birth in Milan, Ohio.

Designs. *Obverse:* Waist-up portrait of Edison holding a light bulb in his right hand. *Reverse:* Light bulb of the 1879 style mounted on a base, with arcs surrounding.

Mintage Data. Authorized by Public Law 105-331, signed by President William J. Clinton on December 6, 1999. *Maximum authorized*—500,000. *Number minted*—92,510 Uncirculated and 211,055 Proof.

Original Cost. Sale prices $31 (Uncirculated, pre-issue) and $33 (Proof, pre-issue); Uncirculated later raised to $33, and Proof later raised to $37. The surcharge of $10 per coin was to be divided evenly among the Port Huron (Michigan) Museum of Arts and History, the Edison Birthplace Association, the National Park Service, the Edison Plaza Museum, the Edison Winter Home and Museum, the Edison Institute, the Edison Memorial Tower, and the Hall of Electrical History.

Key to Collecting. Examples are plentiful. Nearly all are superb gems. As was the situation for many other U.S. Mint issues of the period, promoters who had coins encased in certified holders marked MS-70 or PF-70 were able to persuade, or at least imply, to investors (but not to seasoned collectors) that coins of such quality were rarities, and obtained strong prices for them. Smart buyers simply purchased examples remaining in original Mint holders, of which many were just as nice as the "70" coins.

	Distribution	Cert	Avg	%MS	MS-67
					PF-67
2004-P	92,510	2,807	69.3	100%	$35
Auctions: $90, MS-70, April 2013					
2004-P, Proof	211,055	3,402	69.1		$35
Auctions: $78, PF-70DCam, July 2014; $141, PF-70DCam, March 2013					

LEWIS AND CLARK BICENTENNIAL SILVER DOLLAR (2004)

Designer: *Donna Weaver.* **Weight:** *26.73 grams.*
Composition: *.900 silver, .100 copper (net weight .7736 oz. pure silver).*
Diameter: *38.1 mm.* **Edge:** *Reeded.* **Mint:** *Philadelphia.*

This was one of the most successful commemorative programs, despite the fact that many events across the nation celebrating the bicentennial were flops. Note that the Lewis and Clark Expedition had previously been commemorated with gold dollars dated 1903 for the Louisiana Purchase Exposition (St. Louis World's Fair held in 1904) and those of 1904 and 1905 for the Lewis and Clark Exposition (Portland, Oregon, 1905).

Designs. *Obverse:* Meriwether Lewis and William Clark standing with a river and foliage in the distance as a separate motif. Lewis holds the barrel end of his rifle in one hand and a journal in the other and is looking at Clark, who is gazing to the distance in the opposite direction. *Reverse:* Copy of the reverse of the Jefferson Indian Peace medal designed by John Reich and presented to Indians on the expedition (the identical motif was also revived for use on one variety of the 2004 Jefferson nickel). Feathers are to the left and right, and 17 stars are above.

Mintage Data. Authorized by Public Law 106-136, signed by President William J. Clinton on December 6, 1999. *Maximum authorized*—500,000. *Number minted*—142,015 Uncirculated and 351,989 Proof.

Original Cost. Sale prices $33 (Uncirculated, pre-issue) and $35 (Proof, pre-issue); Uncirculated later raised to $35, and Proof later raised to $39. Two-thirds of the surcharge of $10 per coin went to the National Council of the Lewis and Clark Bicentennial, while one-third went to the National Park Service for the bicentennial celebration.

Key to Collecting. Superb gem coins are readily available.

	Distribution	Cert	Avg	%MS	MS-67 PF-67
2004-P	142,015	4,128	69.4	100%	$35
	Auctions: $90, MS-70, April 2013				
2004-P, Proof	351,989	5,721	69.1		$35
	Auctions: $88, PF-70DCam, February 2013				

MARINE CORPS 230TH ANNIVERSARY SILVER DOLLAR (2005)

Designer: *Norman E. Nemeth (obverse), Charles L. Vickers (reverse).* **Weight:** *26.73 grams.*
Composition: *.900 silver, .100 copper (net weight .7736 oz. pure silver).*
Diameter: *38.1 mm.* **Edge:** *Reeded.* **Mint:** *Philadelphia.*

The widespread appreciation of the heritage of the Marine Corps plus the fame of the obverse design taken from Joe Rosenthal's photograph of the flag-raising at Iwo Jima, propelled this coin to remarkable success. For the first time in recent memory, pandemonium reigned in the coin market, as prices rose, buyers clamored to find all they could, and most dealers were sold out. Within a year, interest turned to other things, and the prices dropped, but not down to the issue levels.

Designs. *Obverse:* Marines raising the Stars and Stripes over Iwo Jima as shown on the famous photograph by Joe Rosenthal. *Reverse:* Eagle, globe, and anchor emblem of the Marine Corps.

Mintage Data. Authorized under Public Law 108-291, signed by President George W. Bush on August 6, 2004. *Maximum authorized*—500,000, later increased to 600,000. *Number minted*—49,671 Uncirculated and 548,810 Proof.

Original Cost. Sale prices $33 (Uncirculated, pre-issue) and $35 (Proof, pre-issue); Uncirculated later raised to $35, and Proof later raised to $39. The surcharge of $10 per coin went toward the construction of the Marine Corps Heritage Center at the base in Quantico, Virginia.

Key to Collecting. Superb gem coins are readily available.

	Distribution	Cert	Avg	%MS	MS-67 PF-67
2005-P	49,671	12,110	69.6	100%	$50
	Auctions: $89, MS-70, January 2015; $76, MS-70, July 2014; $62, MS-70, August 2014				
2005-P, Proof	548,810	14,272	69.2		$50
	Auctions: $165, PF-70DCam, November 2013				

CHIEF JUSTICE JOHN MARSHALL SILVER DOLLAR (2005)

Designer: *John Mercanti (obverse), Donna Weaver (reverse).* **Weight:** *26.73 grams.*
Composition: *.900 silver, .100 copper (net weight .7736 oz. pure silver).*
Diameter: *38.1 mm.* **Edge:** *Reeded.* **Mint:** *Philadelphia.*

Chief Justice John Marshall, who served 34 years in that post in the U.S. Supreme Court, was the subject for this commemorative dollar. Mint engravers submitted designs for the coin, with six depictions of Marshall inspired by a painting by Saint-Mèmin, ten from an oil painting by Rembrandt Peale, and three from a statue by William W. Story. It was John Mercanti's interpretation of the Saint-Mèmin work that was selected.

Designs. *Obverse:* Portrait of Marshall, adapted from a painting made in March 1808 by Charles-Balthazar-Julien Fevret de Saint-Mèmin, of France. *Reverse:* The old Supreme Court Chamber within the Capitol.

Mintage Data. Authorized by Public Law 108-290, signed by President George W. Bush on August 9, 2004. *Maximum authorized*—400,000. *Number minted*—67,096 Uncirculated and 196,753 Proof.

Original Cost. Sale prices $33 (Uncirculated, pre-issue) and $35 (Proof, pre-issue); Uncirculated later raised to $35, and Proof later raised to $39. The surcharge of $10 per coin went to the Supreme Court Historical Society.

Key to Collecting. Superb gem coins are available in the marketplace.

	Distribution	Cert	Avg	%MS	MS-67
					PF-67
2005-P	67,096	2,353	69.6	100%	$45
Auctions: $106, MS-70, January 2013					
2005-P, Proof	196,753	3,259	69.3		$35
Auctions: $86, PF-70DCam, July 2014; $92, PF-70DCam, March 2013					

BENJAMIN FRANKLIN TERCENTENARY SCIENTIST SILVER DOLLAR (2006)

Designer: *Norman E. Nemeth (obverse), Charles L. Vickers (reverse).* **Weight:** *26.73 grams.*
Composition: *.900 silver, .100 copper (net weight .7736 oz. pure silver).*
Diameter: *38.1 mm.* **Edge:** *Reeded.* **Mint:** *Philadelphia.*

Two silver dollars were issued to commemorate the 300th anniversary of Benjamin Franklin's birth. This version celebrated Franklin's scientific accomplishments, which included discoveries in fields from electricity to oceanography to demographics.

Designs. *Obverse:* Franklin standing with a kite on a string, evocative of his experiments with lightning in June 1752. *Reverse:* Franklin's political cartoon, featuring a snake cut apart, titled "Join, or Die," reflecting the sentiment that the colonies should unite during the French and Indian War (and which had nothing to do with perceived offenses by the British, at this early time). This appeared in Franklin's *Pennsylvania Gazette* on May 9, 1754.

Mintage Data. Authorized by Public Law 104-463, the Benjamin Franklin Tercentenary Act, and signed by President George W. Bush on December 21, 2004. *Maximum authorized*—250,000. *Number minted*—58,000 Uncirculated, 142,000 Proof.

Original Cost. Sale prices $33 (Uncirculated, pre-issue) and $35 (Proof, pre-issue); Uncirculated later raised to $35, and Proof later raised to $39. The surcharge of $10 per coin went to the Franklin Institute.

Key to Collecting. Superb gems are easily found in the marketplace.

	Distribution	Cert	Avg	%MS	MS-67 PF-67
2006-P	58,000	7,643	69.7	100%	$35
Auctions: $76, MS-70, January 2013					
2006-P, Proof	142,000	9,868	69.4		$45
Auctions: No auction records available.					

BENJAMIN FRANKLIN TERCENTENARY
FOUNDING FATHER SILVER DOLLAR (2006)

Designer: *Don Everhart (obverse), Donna Weaver (reverse).* **Weight:** *26.73 grams.*
Composition: *.900 silver, .100 copper (net weight .7736 oz. pure silver).*
Diameter: *38.1 mm.* **Edge:** *Reeded.* **Mint:** *Philadelphia.*

The bill authorizing the issue of this silver dollar and its counterpart (see previous coin) took note of many of his accomplishments, stating he was "the only Founding Father to sign all of our Nation's organizational documents," who printed "official currency for the colonies of Pennsylvania, Delaware, New Jersey and Maryland," and helped design the Great Seal of the United States.

Designs. *Obverse:* Head and shoulders portrait of Franklin facing forward slightly to the viewer's right, with his signature reproduced below. *Reverse:* Copy of a 1776 Continental dollar within a frame of modern lettering. The mottoes on this coin were suggested by Franklin.

Mintage Data. Authorized by Public Law 104-463, the Benjamin Franklin Tercentenary Act, and signed by President George W. Bush on December 21, 2004. *Maximum authorized*—250,000. *Number minted*—58,000 Uncirculated, 142,000 Proof.

Original Cost. Sale prices $33 (Uncirculated, pre-issue) and $35 (Proof, pre-issue); Uncirculated later raised to $35, and Proof later raised to $39. The surcharge of $10 per coin went to the Franklin Institute.

Key to Collecting. Superb gems are easily found in the marketplace.

	Distribution	Cert	Avg	%MS	MS-67 PF-67
2006-P	58,000	8,232	69.8	100%	$35
Auctions: $90, MS-70, April 2013					
2006-P, Proof	142,000	10,164	69.7		$35
Auctions: $96, PF-70DCam, January 2013; $103, PF-70DCam, April 2013					

SAN FRANCISCO OLD MINT CENTENNIAL SILVER DOLLAR (2006)

Designer: *Sherl J. Winter (obverse), Joseph Menna after George T. Morgan (reverse).*
Weight: *26.73 grams.* **Composition:** *.900 silver, .100 copper (net weight .7736 oz. pure silver).*
Diameter: *38.1 mm.* **Edge:** *Reeded.* **Mint:** *San Francisco.*

This coin and the five-dollar gold coin issued alongside it celebrated the 100th anniversary of the second San Francisco Mint surviving the 1906 Bay Area earthquake and fire.

Designs. *Obverse:* The Second San Francisco Mint as viewed from off the left front corner. *Reverse:* Copy of the reverse of a standard Morgan silver dollar of the era 1878–1921, said to have been taken from a 1904-S.

Mintage Data. Authorized by Public Law 109-230, the San Francisco Old Mint Commemorative Act, signed by President George W. Bush in June 2006. *Maximum authorized—500,000. Number minted—* 67,100 Uncirculated and 160,870 Proof.

Original Cost. Sale prices $33 (Uncirculated, pre-issue) and $35 (Proof, pre-issue); Uncirculated later raised to $35, and Proof later raised to $39. The surcharge of $10 per coin went to the "San Francisco Museum and Historical Society for rehabilitating the Historic Old Mint as a city museum and an American Coin and Gold Rush Museum."

Key to Collecting. Superb gems are easily found in the marketplace.

	Distribution	Cert	Avg	%MS	MS-67
					PF-67
2006-S	67,100	4,570	69.6	100%	$45
	Auctions: $94, MS-70, January 2013				
2006-S, Proof	160,870	8,491	69.2		$35
	Auctions: No auction records available.				

SAN FRANCISCO OLD MINT CENTENNIAL $5 GOLD COIN (2006)

Designer: *Charles L. Vickers (obverse), Don Everhart after Christian Gobrecht (reverse).*
Weight: *8.359 grams.* **Composition:** *.900 gold, .100 copper (net weight .242 oz. pure gold).*
Diameter: *21.6 mm.* **Edge:** *Reeded.* **Mint:** *San Francisco.*

The designs of this coin and the corresponding silver dollar both had obverses showing the same subject (albeit from a different view), and reverses being copies of old coinage designs.

Designs. *Obverse:* Front view of the portico of the Second San Francisco Mint, with a portion of the building to each side. Modeled after an 1869 construction drawing by Supervising Architect A.B. Mullet. *Reverse:* Copy of the reverse of the Liberty Head half eagle with motto IN GOD WE TRUST, as regularly used from 1866 to 1907.

Mintage Data. Authorized by Public Law 109-230, the San Francisco Old Mint Commemorative Act, signed by President George W. Bush in June 2006. *Maximum authorized*—100,000. *Number minted*—17,500 Uncirculated and 44,174 Proof.

Original Cost. Sale prices $220 (Uncirculated, pre-issue) and $230 (Proof, pre-issue); Uncirculated later raised to $245, and Proof later raised to $255. The surcharge of $35 per coin went to the "San Francisco Museum and Historical Society for rehabilitating the Historic Old Mint as a city museum and an American Coin and Gold Rush Museum."

Key to Collecting. Superb gems are easily found in the marketplace.

	Distribution	Cert	Avg	%MS	MS-67
					PF-67
2006-S	17,500	2,786	69.7	100%	$325
Auctions: $329, MS-70, October 2014; $294, MS-70, July 2015; $306, MS-69, July 2015; $282, MS-69, October 2015					
2006-S, Proof	44,174	3,882	69.5		$325
Auctions: $376, PF-70UCam, February 2015; $353, PF-70UCam, July 2015; $341, PF-70UCam, February 2015					

JAMESTOWN 400TH ANNIVERSARY SILVER DOLLAR (2007)

Designer: *Donna Weaver (obverse), Susan Gamble (reverse).* **Weight:** *26.73 grams.*
Composition: *.900 silver, .100 copper (net weight .7736 oz. pure silver).*
Diameter: *38.1 mm.* **Edge:** *Reeded.* **Mint:** *Philadelphia.*

Note that Jamestown was also honored on the 2000 Virginia State quarter.

Designs. *Obverse:* Captain John Smith is shown with an Indian man and woman. *Reverse:* Three sailing ships are shown, elements already seen from the 2000 State quarter, but differently arranged.

Mintage Data. Authorized by Public Law 108-289, the Jamestown 400th Anniversary Commemorative Coin Act, signed by President George W. Bush on August 6, 2004. *Maximum authorized*—500,000. *Number minted*—81,034 Uncirculated and 260,363 Proof.

Original Cost. Sale prices $33 (Uncirculated, pre-issue) and $35 (Proof, pre-issue); Uncirculated later raised to $35, and Proof later raised to $39. The surcharge of $20 per coin went to fund the public observance of the anniversary.

Key to Collecting. Superb gem coins are readily available.

	Distribution	Cert	Avg	%MS	MS-67
					PF-67
2007-P	81,034	7,671	69.6	100%	$40
Auctions: $90, MS-70, April 2013					
2007-P, Proof	260,363	10,829	69.5		$35
Auctions: $100, PF-70DCam, April 2013					

JAMESTOWN 400TH ANNIVERSARY $5 GOLD COIN (2007)

Designer: *John Mercanti (obverse), Susan Gamble (reverse).* **Weight:** *8.359 grams.*
Composition: *.900 gold, .100 copper (net weight .242 oz. pure gold).*
Diameter: *21.6 mm.* **Edge:** *Reeded.* **Mint:** *West Point.*

Susan Gamble, who designed the reverse of both this coin and the silver dollar issued alongside it, was a participant in the Mint's Artistic Infusion Program, which was created to bring artists in from the private sector to upgrade the quality of coin designs.

Designs. *Obverse:* Captain John Smith is shown with Indian chief Powhatan, who holds a bag of corn. *Reverse:* Ruins of the old church at Jamestown.

Mintage Data. Authorized by Public Law 108-289, the Jamestown 400th Anniversary Commemorative Coin Act, signed by President George W. Bush on August 6, 2004. *Maximum authorized—100,000. Number minted—18,623* Uncirculated and 47,123 Proof.

Original Cost. Sale prices $33 (Uncirculated, pre-issue) and $35 (Proof, pre-issue); Uncirculated later raised to $35, and Proof later raised to $39. The surcharge of $35 per coin went to fund the public observance of the anniversary.

Key to Collecting. Superb gem coins are readily available.

	Distribution	Cert	Avg	%MS	MS-67 / PF-67
2007-W	18,623	3,225	69.8	100%	$325
	Auctions: $353, MS-70, April 2015; $329, MS-70, November 2014; $306, MS-70, July 2015; $294, MS-70, July 2015				
2007-W, Proof	47,123	4,152	69.6		$325
	Auctions: $341, PF-70DCam, July 2014; $317, PF-70DCam, August 2014; $306, PF-70UCam, July 2015				

LITTLE ROCK CENTRAL HIGH SCHOOL DESEGREGATION SILVER DOLLAR (2007)

Designer: *Richard Masters (obverse), Don Everhart (reverse).* **Weight:** *26.73 grams.*
Composition: *.900 silver, .100 copper (net weight .7736 oz. pure silver).*
Diameter: *38.1 mm.* **Edge:** *Reeded.* **Mint:** *Philadelphia.*

This coin commemorated the 50th anniversary of the desegregation of Little Rock Central High School, which was the result of the landmark U.S. Supreme Court case *Brown v. the Board of Education.*

Designs. *Obverse:* The feet of the "Little Rock Nine" students are shown, escorted by a soldier. *Reverse:* Little Rock Central High School as it appeared in 1957.

Mintage Data. Authorized by Public Law 109-146, the Little Rock Central High School Desegregation 50th Anniversary Commemorative Coin Act, signed by President George W. Bush on December 22, 2005. *Maximum authorized*—500,000. *Number minted*—66,093 Uncirculated and 124,678 Proof.

Original Cost. Sale prices $33 (Uncirculated, pre-issue) and $35 (Proof, pre-issue); Uncirculated later raised to $35, and Proof later raised to $39. The surcharge of $10 per coin went toward improvements at the Little Rock Central High School National Historic Site.

Key to Collecting. Superb gem coins are readily available.

	Distribution	Cert	Avg	%MS	MS-67 PF-67
2007-P	66,093	2,652	69.7	100%	$35
	Auctions: $79, MS-70, October 2014; $90, MS-70, April 2013				
2007-P, Proof	124,678	3,058	69.5		$35
	Auctions: $80, PF-70DCam, July 2014; $113, PF-70DCam, April 2013				

BALD EAGLE RECOVERY AND NATIONAL EMBLEM HALF DOLLAR (2008)

Designer: *Susan Gamble (obverse), Donna Weaver (reverse).* **Weight:** *11.34 grams.*
Composition: *.9167 copper, .0833 nickel.* **Diameter:** *30.61 mm.* **Edge:** *Reeded.* **Mint:** *San Francisco.*

This copper-nickel half dollar, as well as the silver dollar and five-dollar gold coin issued alongside it, was issued to commemorate the recovery of the bald eagle species, the 35th anniversary of the Endangered Species Act of 1973, and the removal of the bald eagle from the Endangered Species List.

Designs. *Obverse:* Two eaglets and an egg in a bald eagle nest. *Reverse:* "Challenger," a non-releasable bald eagle in the care of the American Eagle Foundation and the first of his species to be trained to free-fly into major sporting events during the National Anthem.

Mintage Data. Authorized by Public Law 108-486, the Bald Eagle Commemorative Coin Act, signed by President George W. Bush on December 23, 2004. *Maximum authorized*—750,000. *Number minted*—120,180 Uncirculated and 220,577 Proof.

Original Cost. Sale prices $7.95 (Uncirculated, pre-issue) and $9.95 (Proof, pre-issue); Uncirculated later raised to $8.95, and Proof later raised to $10.95. The surcharge of $3 per coin went to the American Eagle Foundation of Tennessee for the purposes of continuing its work to save and protect bald eagles nationally.

Key to Collecting. Superb gem coins are readily available.

	Distribution	Cert	Avg	%MS	MS-67 PF-67
2008-S	120,180	6,797	69.8	100%	$15
	Auctions: $30, MS-70, April 2013				
2008-S, Proof	220,577	8,831	69.7		$16
	Auctions: No auction records available.				

BALD EAGLE RECOVERY AND NATIONAL EMBLEM SILVER DOLLAR (2008)

Designer: *Joel Iskowitz (obverse), Jim Licaretz (reverse).* **Weight:** *26.73 grams.*
Composition: *.900 silver, .100 copper (net weight .7736 oz. pure silver).*
Diameter: *38.1 mm.* **Edge:** *Reeded.* **Mint:** *Philadelphia.*

The bald eagle, selected in 1782 by the Second Continental Congress as the national emblem of the United States, was common at the time of the nation's establishment. Through the years, however, poaching, habitat destruction, pesticides, and food-source contamination reduced the number of nesting pairs from approximately 100,000 to just more than 400 in the early 1960s. Fortunately, conservationists have saved the species in the past five decades.

Designs. *Obverse:* Bald eagle in flight, mountains in background. *Reverse:* The Great Seal of the United States used from 1782 to 1841.

Mintage Data. Authorized by Public Law 108-486, the Bald Eagle Commemorative Coin Act, signed by President George W. Bush on December 23, 2004. *Maximum authorized—500,000. Number minted—*119,204 Uncirculated and 294,601 Proof.

Original Cost. Sale prices $35.95 (Uncirculated, pre-issue) and $39.95 (Proof, pre-issue); Uncirculated later raised to $37.95, and Proof later raised to $43.95. The surcharge of $10 per coin went to the American Eagle Foundation of Tennessee for the purposes of continuing its work to save and protect bald eagles nationally.

Key to Collecting. Superb gem coins are readily available.

	Distribution	Cert	Avg	%MS	MS-67 / PF-67
2008-P	119,204	9,088	69.7	100%	$30
Auctions: $90, MS-70, April 2013					
2008-P, Proof	294,601	13,566	69.3		$35
Auctions: $92, PF-70DCam, July 2014; $89, PF-70UCam, July 2015; $79, PF-70DCam, July 2014					

BALD EAGLE RECOVERY AND NATIONAL EMBLEM $5 GOLD COIN (2008)

Designer: *Susan Gamble (obverse), Don Everhart (reverse).* **Weight:** *8.359 grams.*
Composition: *.900 gold, .100 copper (net weight .242 oz. pure gold).*
Diameter: *21.6 grams.* **Edge:** *Reeded.* **Mint:** *West Point.*

Government entities, private organizations, and citizens were all part of the bald eagle's recovery from near-extinction in the middle of the 1900s. Bans on certain pesticides, protections granted under the Endangered Species Act of 1973, and captive-breeding and nest-watch programs have been crucial and have led to the removal of the national emblem from the Endangered Species List.

Designs. *Obverse:* Two bald eagles perched on a branch. *Reverse:* The current Great Seal of the United States.

Mintage Data. Authorized by Public Law 108-486, the Bald Eagle Commemorative Coin Act, signed by President George W. Bush on December 23, 2004. *Maximum authorized*—100,000. *Number minted*—15,009 Uncirculated and 59,269 Proof.

Original Cost. Sale prices $284.95 (Uncirculated, pre-issue) and $294.95 (Proof, pre-issue); Uncirculated later raised to $309.95, and Proof later raised to $319.95. The surcharge of $35 per coin went to the American Eagle Foundation of Tennessee for the purposes of continuing its work to save and protect bald eagles nationally.

Key to Collecting. Superb gem coins are readily available.

	Distribution	Cert	Avg	%MS	MS-67 PF-67
2008-W	15,009	1,067	69.9	100%	$325
	Auctions: $458, MS-70, January 2013				
2008-W, Proof	59,269	1,830	69.8		$325
	Auctions: $442, PF-70DCam, March 2014; $427, PF-70DCam, September 2014; $306, PF-70UCam, July 2015				

ABRAHAM LINCOLN BICENTENNIAL SILVER DOLLAR (2009)

Designer: *Justin Kunz (obverse), Phebe Hemphill (reverse).* **Weight:** *26.73 grams.*
Composition: *.900 silver, .100 copper (net weight .7736 oz. pure silver).*
Diameter: *38.1 mm.* **Edge:** *Reeded.* **Mint:** *Philadelphia.*

These coins, issued to mark the 200th anniversary of President Abraham Lincoln's birth, were extremely popular with collectors. The 450,000 pieces allocated to individual coin sales sold out after a month. Note that this anniversary was also commemorated with the release of four different reverse designs for the 2009 Lincoln cents.

Designs. *Obverse:* A portrait of Abraham Lincoln in three-quarter view. *Reverse:* The final 43 words of President Lincoln's Gettysburg Address, surrounded by a laurel wreath.

Mintage Data. Authorized Public Law 109-285, the Abraham Lincoln Commemorative Coin Act, signed by President George W. Bush on September 27, 2006. *Maximum authorized*—500,000. *Number minted*—125,000 Uncirculated and 325,000 Proof.

Original Cost. Sale prices $31.95 (Uncirculated, pre-issue) and $37.95 (Proof, pre-issue); Uncirculated later raised to $33.95, and Proof later raised to $41.95. The surcharge of $10 per coin went to the Abraham Lincoln Bicentennial Commission.

Key to Collecting. Superb gem coins are readily available.

	Distribution	Cert	Avg	%MS	MS-67 PF-67
2009-P	125,000	10,129	69.8	100%	$35
	Auctions: $96, MS-70, February 2014; $60, MS-70, June 2015; $56, MS-70, July 2014				
2009-P, Proof	325,000	18,239	69.4		$35
	Auctions: $353, PF-70DCam, November 2014; $90, PF-70DCam, August 2014; $74, PF-70DCam, June 2015				

LOUIS BRAILLE BICENTENNIAL SILVER DOLLAR (2009)

Designer: *Joel Iskowitz (obverse), Phebe Hemphill (reverse).* **Weight:** *26.73 grams.*
Composition: *.900 silver, .100 copper (net weight .7736 oz. pure silver).*
Diameter: *38.1 mm.* **Edge:** *Reeded.* **Mint:** *Philadelphia.*

The 200th anniversary of the birth of Louis Braille—the inventor of the eponymous system which is used by the blind to read and write—furnished the occasion for this commemorative. Fittingly, this was the first U.S. coin to feature readable Braille.

Designs. *Obverse:* A forward-facing portrait of Louis Braille. *Reverse:* The word Braille (in Braille code, abbreviated Brl) above a child reading a book in Braille.

Mintage Data. Authorized by Public Law 109-247, the Louis Braille Bicentennial–Braille Literacy Commemorative Coin Act, signed by President George W. Bush on July 27, 2006. *Maximum authorized*—400,000. *Number minted*—82,639 Uncirculated and 135,235 Proof.

Original Cost. Sale prices $31.95 (Uncirculated, pre-issue) and $37.95 (Proof, pre-issue); Uncirculated later raised to $33.95, and Proof later raised to $41.95. The surcharge of $10 per coin went to the National Federation of the Blind.

Key to Collecting. Superb gem coins are readily available.

	Distribution	Cert	Avg	%MS	MS-67 / PF-67
2009-P	82,639	3,438	69.4	100%	$30
	Auctions: $90, MS-70, April 2013				
2009-P, Proof	135,235	4,432	69.1		$30
	Auctions: $94, PF-70DCam, July 2014; $94, PF-70DCam, April 2013				

AMERICAN VETERANS DISABLED FOR LIFE SILVER DOLLAR (2010)

Designer: *Don Everhart.* **Weight:** *26.73 grams.*
Composition: *.900 silver, .100 copper (net weight .7736 oz. pure silver).*
Diameter: *38.1 mm.* **Edge:** *Reeded.* **Mint:** *West Point.*

This coin honored those members of the U.S. Armed Forces who have made extraordinary personal sacrifices in defense of the country.

Designs. *Obverse:* The legs and boots of three veterans, one of whom is using a pair of crutches. *Reverse:* The words "Take This Moment to Honor Our Disabled Defenders of Freedom," surrounded by a laurel wreath with a forget-me-not (widely known as a symbol for those who fought and became disabled in World War I) at its base.

Mintage Data. Authorized by Public Law 110-277, the American Veterans Disabled for Life Commemorative Coin Act, signed by President George W. Bush on July 17, 2008. *Maximum authorized*—350,000. *Number minted*—78,301 Uncirculated and 202,770 Proof.

Original Cost. Sale prices $33.95 (Uncirculated, pre-issue) and $39.95 (Proof, pre-issue); Uncirculated later raised to $35.95, and Proof later raised to $43.95. The surcharge of $10 per coin went to the Disabled Veterans' LIFE Memorial Foundation for the purpose of constructing the American Veterans' Disabled for Life Memorial in Washington, D.C.

Key to Collecting. Superb gem coins are readily available.

	Distribution	Cert	Avg	%MS	MS-67 / PF-67
2010-W	78,301	3,994	69.8	100%	$35
Auctions: $70, MS-70, May 2013					
2010-W, Proof	202,770	5,088	69.7		$30
Auctions: $78, PF-70DCam, May 2013; $42, PF-70DCam, September 2014					

BOY SCOUTS OF AMERICA CENTENNIAL SILVER DOLLAR (2010)

Designer: *Donna Weaver (obverse), Jim Licaretz from the universal logo of the Boy Scouts of America (reverse).* **Weight:** *26.73 grams.* **Composition:** *.900 silver, .100 copper (net weight .7736 oz. pure silver).* **Diameter:** *38.1 mm.* **Edge:** *Reeded.* **Mint:** *Philadelphia.*

The 100th anniversary of the establishment of the Boy Scouts of America was celebrated with this silver dollar. The design was somewhat controversial due to its inclusion of a female but was specifically requested by the organization itself so as to portray the evolution of the Boy Scouts over time to include all American youth.

Designs. *Obverse:* A Cub Scout, a female member of the Venturer Program, and a Boy Scout saluting. *Reverse:* The universal logo of the Boy Scouts of America, featuring an eagle bearing a shield on a fleur-de-lis.

Mintage Data. Authorized by Public Law 110-363, the Boy Scouts of America Centennial Commemorative Coin Act, signed by President George W. Bush on October 8, 2008. *Maximum authorized—350,000. Number minted—105,020 Uncirculated and 244,693 Proof.*

Original Cost. Sale prices $33.95 (Uncirculated, pre-issue) and $39.95 (Proof, pre-issue); Uncirculated later raised to $35.95, and Proof later raised to $43.95. The surcharge of $10 per coin went to the National Boy Scouts of America Foundation; the funds were then meant to be made available to local councils in the form of grants for the extension of Scouting in hard-to-serve areas.

Key to Collecting. Superb gem coins are readily available.

	Distribution	Cert	Avg	%MS	MS-67 / PF-67
2010-P	105,020	7,292	69.8	100%	$30
Auctions: $82, MS-70, March 2013					
2010-P, Proof	244,963	8,166	69.4		$35
Auctions: $82, PF-70DCam, March 2013					

U.S. ARMY HALF DOLLAR (2011)

Designer: *Donna Weaver (obverse), Thomas Cleveland (reverse).* **Weight:** *11.34 grams.*
Composition: *.9167 copper, .0833 nickel.* **Diameter:** *30.61 mm.*
Edge: *Reeded.* **Mints:** *Denver (Uncirculated) and San Francisco (Proof).*

This copper-nickel half dollar was one of three commemoratives released in honor of the U.S. Army in 2011, by which time the entity had already defended the nation for 236 years. The reverse design was praised by the Citizens Coinage Advisory Committee (CCAC) and the Commission of Fine Arts.

Designs. *Obverse:* Three scenes split in a "storyboard" fashion (from left to right): a soldier surveying; two servicemen laying a flood wall; the Redstone Army rocket at takeoff. *Reverse:* A Continental with a musket, with 13 stars (representing the first states) in an arc above.

Mintage Data. Authorized by Public Law 110-450, the United States Army Commemorative Coin Act of 2008, signed by President George W. Bush on December 1, 2008. *Maximum authorized*—750,000. *Number minted*—2011-D: 39,442 Uncirculated; 2011-S: 68,332 Proof.

Original Cost. Sale prices $15.95 (Uncirculated, pre-issue) and $17.95 (Proof, pre-issue); Uncirculated later raised to $19.95, and Proof raised to $21.95. The surcharge of $5 went toward the yet-to-be-constructed National Museum of the United States Army.

Key to Collecting. Superb gem coins are readily available.

	Distribution	Cert	Avg	%MS	MS-67
					PF-67
2011-D	39,442	2,557	69.0	100%	$70
	Auctions: No auction records available.				
2011-S, Proof	68,332	2,459	69.5		$35
	Auctions: No auction records available.				

U.S. ARMY SILVER DOLLAR (2011)

Designer: *Richard Masters (obverse), Susan Gamble (reverse).* **Weight:** *26.73 grams.*
Composition: *.900 silver, .100 copper (net weight .7736 oz. pure silver).* **Diameter:** *38.1 mm.*
Edge: *Reeded.* **Mints:** *San Francisco (Uncirculated) and Philadelphia (Proof).*

The act authorizing this silver dollar (as well as the related copper-nickel half dollar and five-dollar gold coin) called for the coins to be "emblematic of the traditions, history, and heritage of the U.S. Army and its role in American society from the Colonial period to today."

Designs. *Obverse:* A male and female soldier back-to-back in front of a globe. *Reverse:* The Great Seal of the United States (which appears on Army uniforms) inside a ring that bears the seven core values of the Army (Loyalty, Duty, Respect, Selfless Service, Honor, Integrity, and Personal Courage).

Mintage Data. Authorized by Public Law 110-450, the United States Army Commemorative Coin Act of 2008, signed by President George W. Bush on December 1, 2008. *Maximum authorized*—500,000. *Number minted*—2011-S: 43,512 Uncirculated; 2011-P: 119,829 Proof.

Original Cost. Sale prices $49.95 (Uncirculated, pre-issue) and $54.95 (Proof, pre-issue); Uncirculated later raised to $54.95, and Proof later raised to $59.95. The surcharge of $10 per coin went toward the yet-to-be-constructed National Museum of the United States Army.

Key to Collecting. Superb gem coins are readily available.

	Distribution	Cert	Avg	%MS	MS-67 PF-67
2011-S	43,512	2,364	69.7	100%	$50
	Auctions: No auction records available.				
2011-P, Proof	119,829	3,869	69.5		$45
	Auctions: $80, PF-70DCam, April 2013				

U.S. ARMY $5 GOLD COIN (2011)

Designer: *Joel Iskowitz (obverse), Joseph Menna from the U.S. Army emblem (reverse).*
Weight: *8.359 grams.* **Composition:** *.900 gold, .100 copper (net weight .242 oz. pure gold).*
Diameter: *21.6 mm.* **Edge:** *Reeded.* **Mints:** *Philadelphia (Uncirculated) and West Point (Proof).*

By depicting soldiers from five distinct eras in U.S. history, the obverse of this five-dollar gold coin symbolizes the "continuity of strength and readiness" of the Army.

Designs. *Obverse:* Five U.S. Army soldiers representing various eras (from left to right): Revolutionary War, Civil War, modern era, World War II, and World War I. *Reverse:* The U.S. Army emblem, which features various items representative of home life and war time and the phrase "This We'll Defend" on a banner.

Mintage Data. Authorized by Public Law 110-450, the United States Army Commemorative Coin Act of 2008, signed by President George W. Bush on December 1, 2008. *Maximum authorized*—100,000. *Number minted*—2011-P: 8,052 Uncirculated; 2011-W: 17,148 Proof.

Original Cost. Sale prices $439.95 (Uncirculated, pre-issue) and $449.95 (Proof, pre-issue); Uncirculated later raised to $444.95, and Proof later raised to $454.95. The surcharge of $35 per coin went toward the yet-to-be-constructed National Museum of the United States Army.

Key to Collecting. Superb gem coins are readily available.

	Distribution	Cert	Avg	%MS	MS-67 PF-67
2011-P	8,052	442	69.9	100%	$425
	Auctions: $560, MS-70, September 2013				
2011-W, Proof	17,148	566	69.7		$425
	Auctions: $353, PF-69DCam, May 2014				

MEDAL OF HONOR SILVER DOLLAR (2011)

Designer: *Jim Licaretz (obverse), Richard Masters (reverse).* **Weight:** *26.73 grams.*
Composition: *.900 silver, .100 copper (net weight .7736 oz. pure silver).*
Diameter: *38.1 mm.* **Edge:** *Reeded.* **Mints:** *San Francisco (Uncirculated) and Philadelphia (Proof).*

The 150th anniversary of the creation of the Medal of Honor—the highest award for valor in action in the U.S. Armed Forces—was the impetus for this commemorative silver dollar, as well as a five-dollar gold coin.

Designs. *Obverse:* From left to right, the Medals of Honor of the Army, Navy, and Air Force. *Reverse:* An infantry soldier carrying a wounded soldier to safety on his back.

Mintage Data. Authorized by Public Law 111-91, the Medal of Honor Commemorative Coin Act of 2009, signed by President Barack Obama on November 6, 2009. *Maximum authorized*—500,000. *Number minted*—2011-S: 44,752 Uncirculated; 2011-P: 112,833 Proof.

Original Cost. Sale prices $49.95 (Uncirculated, pre-issue) and $54.95 (Proof, pre-issue); Uncirculated later raised to $54.95, and Proof later raised to $59.95. The surcharge of $10 per coin went to the Congressional Medal of Honor Foundation to help finance its educational, scholarship, and outreach programs.

Key to Collecting. Superb gem coins are readily available.

	Distribution	Cert	Avg	%MS	MS-67 / PF-67
2011-S	44,752	2,842	69.6	100%	$50
	Auctions: $100, MS-70, April 2013				
2011-P, Proof	112,833	2,221	69.3		$45
	Auctions: $123, PF-70DCam, March 2013				

MEDAL OF HONOR $5 GOLD COIN (2011)

Designer: *Joseph Menna (obverse), Joel Iskowitz (reverse).* **Weight:** *8.359 grams.*
Composition: *.900 gold, .100 copper (net weight .242 oz. pure gold).* **Diameter:** *21.6 mm.*
Edge: *Reeded.* **Mints:** *Philadelphia (Uncirculated) and West Point (Proof).*

This coin and the silver dollar issued alongside it were created in recognition of the Medal of Honor, the Navy's greatest personal award, first authorized by Congress in 1861. Though counterparts are now given in the Army and Air Force as well, fewer than 3,500 Medals of Honor have ever been awarded to date.

Designs. *Obverse:* The original Medal of Honor, the Navy's highest individual decoration. *Reverse:* Minerva, holding a shield and the U.S. flag on a staff, in front of munitions and a Civil War–era cannon.

Mintage Data. Authorized by Public Law 111-91, the Medal of Honor Commemorative Coin Act of 2009, signed by President Barack Obama on November 6, 2009. *Maximum authorized*—100,000. *Number minted*—2011-P: 8,233 Uncirculated; 2011-W: 17,999 Proof.

Original Cost. Sale prices $439.95 (Uncirculated, pre-issue) and $449.95 (Proof, pre issue); Uncirculated later raised to $444.95, and Proof later raised to $454.95. The surcharge of $35 per coin went to the Congressional Medal of Honor Foundation to help finance its educational, scholarship, and outreach programs.

Key to Collecting. Superb gem coins are readily available.

	Distribution	Cert	Avg	%MS	MS-67
					PF-67
2011-P	8,233	491	69.8	100%	$550
Auctions: $470, MS-70, November 2014; $470, MS-70, August 2014; $400, MS-70, January 2015; $400, MS-69, January 2015					
2011-W, Proof	17,999	523	69.6		$425
Auctions: $646, PF-70DCam, February 2015; $646, PF-70DCam, November 2014; $558, PF-70DCam, July 2014					

INFANTRY SOLDIER SILVER DOLLAR (2012)

Designer: *Joel Iskowitz (obverse), Ronald D. Sanders (reverse).* **Weight:** *26.73 grams.*
Composition: *.900 silver, .100 copper (net weight .7736 oz. pure silver).*
Diameter: *38.1 mm.* **Edge:** *Reeded.* **Mint:** *West Point.*

This coin recognizes the long history and crucial role of the U.S. Army Infantry. The infantry has accounted for more than half of all the Medals of Honor awarded, despite being just one of many branches of the Army.

Designs. *Obverse:* An infantry soldier advancing and motioning for others to follow. *Reverse:* The infantry insignia of two crossed rifles.

Mintage Data. Authorized by Public Law 110-357, the National Infantry Museum and Soldier Center Commemorative Coin Act, signed by President George W. Bush on October 8, 2008. *Maximum authorized*—350,000. *Number minted*—44,352 Uncirculated and 161,218 Proof.

Original Cost. Sale prices $44.95 (Uncirculated, pre-issue) and $49.95 (Proof, pre-issue); Uncirculated later raised to $49.95, and Proof later raised to $54.95. The surcharge of $10 per coin went to an endowment to support the maintenance of the National Infantry Museum and Solider Center in Columbus, Georgia.

Key to Collecting. Superb gem coins are readily available.

	Distribution	Cert	Avg	%MS	MS-67
					PF-67
2012-W	44,348	2,004	69.8	100%	$45
Auctions: $69, MS-70, April 2013					
2012-W, Proof	161,151	2,923	69.2		$50
Auctions: $74, PF-70DCam, April 2013					

STAR-SPANGLED BANNER SILVER DOLLAR (2012)

Designer: *Joel Iskowitz (obverse), William C. Burgard II (reverse).* **Weight:** *26.73 grams.*
Composition: *.900 silver, .100 copper (net weight .7736 oz. pure silver).*
Diameter: *38.1 mm.* **Edge:** *Reeded.* **Mint:** *Philadelphia.*

The 200th anniversary of the War of 1812—particularly the Battle of Baltimore, which is recounted in the U.S. National Anthem—was commemorated with this silver dollar, as well as a five-dollar gold coin issued alongside it.

Designs. *Obverse:* Miss Liberty waving the 15-star version of the U.S. flag with Fort McHenry in the background. *Reverse:* A waving modern U.S. flag.

Mintage Data. Authorized by Public Law 111-232, the Star-Spangled Banner Commemorative Coin Act, signed by President Barack Obama on August 16, 2010. *Maximum authorized*—500,000. *Number minted*—41,686 Uncirculated and 169,065 Proof.

Original Cost. Sale prices $44.95 (Uncirculated, pre-issue) and $49.95 (Proof, pre-issue); Uncirculated later raised to $49.95, and Proof later raised to $54.95. The surcharge of $10 per coin went to the Maryland War of 1812 Bicentennial Commission for the purpose of supporting bicentennial activities, educational outreach activities, and preservation and improvement activities pertaining to the sites and structures relating to the War of 1812.

Key to Collecting. Superb gem coins are readily available.

	Distribution	Cert	Avg	%MS	MS-67 / PF-67
2012-P	41,686	2,057	69.8	100%	$50
	Auctions: $100, MS-70, April 2013; $94, MS-70, October 2014				
2012-P, Proof	169,065	3,212	69.4		$50
	Auctions: $94, PF-70DCam, April 2013; $153, PF-69DCam, November 2014				

STAR-SPANGLED BANNER $5 GOLD COIN (2012)

Designer: *Donna Weaver (obverse), Richard Masters (reverse).* **Weight:** *8.359 grams.*
Composition: *.900 gold, .100 copper (net weight .242 oz. pure gold).*
Diameter: *21.6 mm.* **Edge:** *Reeded.* **Mint:** *West Point.*

The reverse of this commemorative coin features the first five words of the Star-Spangled Banner in the handwriting of Francis Scott Key, the man who penned it. On September 7, 1814, Key visited the British fleet in the Chesapeake Bay to secure the release of his friend Dr. William Beanes. Key secured Beanes's release, but the two were held by the British during the bombardment of Fort McHenry. It was on the morning of September 14, 1814, that the shelling stopped and Key saw through the smoke the massive American flag, flying above the U.S. fort, that would inspire his song.

Designs. *Obverse:* A naval battle, with a U.S. ship in the foreground and a British vessel in the background. *Reverse:* The words "O say can you see" over an arrangement of 13 stripes and 15 stars, representing the U.S. flag.

Mintage Data. Authorized by Public Law 111-232, the Star-Spangled Banner Commemorative Coin Act, signed by President Barack Obama on August 16, 2010. *Maximum authorized*—100,000. *Number minted*—7,027 Uncirculated and 18,313 Proof.

Original Cost. Sale prices $519.30 (Uncirculated, pre-issue) and $529.30 (Proof, pre-issue); both prices later increased by a base of $5 plus the change in gold market value. The surcharge of $35 per coin went to the Maryland War of 1812 Bicentennial Commission for the purpose of supporting bicentennial activities, educational outreach activities, and preservation and improvement activities pertaining to the sites and structures relating to the War of 1812.

Key to Collecting. Superb gem coins are readily available.

	Distribution	Cert	Avg	%MS	MS-67
					PF-67
2012-W	7,027	645	69.9	100%	$500
Auctions: $618, MS-70, September 2013					
2012-W, Proof	18,313	497	69.8		$400
Auctions: $470, PF-70DCam, April 2014					

GIRL SCOUTS OF THE U.S.A. CENTENNIAL SILVER DOLLAR (2013)

Designer: *Barbara Fox (obverse), Chris Costello (reverse).* **Weight:** *26.73 grams.*
Composition: *.900 silver, .100 copper (net weight .7736 oz. pure silver).*
Diameter: *38.1 mm.* **Edge:** *Reeded.* **Mint:** *West Point.*

This commemorative silver dollar was issued as part of the celebration of the Girl Scouts of the United States of America's 100th anniversary of establishment. The Citizens Coinage Advisory Committee was particularly enthusiastic about this beautiful design.

Designs. *Obverse:* Three Girl Scouts of varying ages and ethnicities. The three girls are meant to reflect the organization's diversity. *Reverse:* The iconic Girl Scouts trefoil symbol.

Mintage Data. Authorized by Public Law 111-86, the 2013 Girl Scouts of the USA Centennial Commemorative Coin Program, signed by President Barack Obama on October 29, 2009. *Maximum authorized*—350,000. *Number minted*—31,714 Uncirculated and 86,353 Proof.

Original Cost. Sale prices $50.95 (Uncirculated, pre-issue) and $54.95 (Proof, pre-issue); Uncirculated later raised to $55.95, and Proof later raised to $59.95. The surcharge of $10 per coin went to the Girl Scouts of the United States of America.

Key to Collecting. Superb gem coins are readily available.

	Distribution	Cert	Avg	%MS	MS-67
					PF-67
2013-W	37,462	1,010	69.9	100%	$45
Auctions: No auction records available.					
2013-W, Proof	86,355	1,756	69.3		$55
Auctions: No auction records available.					

5-Star Generals Half Dollar (2013)

Designer: *Phebe Hemphill.* **Weight:** *11.34 grams.* **Composition:** *.9167 copper, .0833 nickel.*
Diameter: *30.61 mm.* **Edge:** *Reeded.* **Mints:** *Denver (Uncirculated) and San Francisco (Proof).*

The 5-star generals of the U.S. Army—as well as the institution that they each graduated from, the U.S. Army Command and General Staff College—were commemorated with this half dollar, as well as a silver dollar and five-dollar gold coin issued as part of the program.

Designs. *Obverse:* Side-by-side portraits of General Henry "Hap" Arnold and General Omar N. Bradley, 5-star insignia at center. *Reverse:* Heraldic crest of Fort Leavenworth, home of the U.S. Army Command and General Staff College.

Mintage Data. Authorized by Public Law 111-262, the 5-Star Generals Commemorative Coin Act, signed by President Barack Obama on October 8, 2010. *Maximum authorized—750,000. Number minted—2013-D:* 38,191 Uncirculated; 2013-P: 47,337 Proof.

Original Cost. Sale prices $16.95 (Uncirculated, pre-issue) and $17.95 (Proof, pre-issue); Uncirculated later raised to $20.95, and Proof later raised to $21.95. The surcharge of $5 per coin went to the Command and General Staff College Foundation.

Key to Collecting. Superb gem coins are readily available.

	Distribution	Cert	Avg	%MS	MS-67
					PF-67
2013-D	38,095	1,057	69.0	100%	$40
Auctions: No auction records available.					
2013-S, Proof	47,326	2,296	69.4		$30
Auctions: No auction records available.					

5-Star Generals Silver Dollar (2013)

Designer: *Richard Masters (obverse), Barbara Fox (reverse).* **Weight:** *26.73 grams.*
Composition: *.900 silver, .100 copper (net weight .7736 oz. pure silver).*
Diameter: *38.1 mm.* **Edge:** *Reeded.* **Mints:** *West Point (Uncirculated) and Philadelphia (Proof).*

Each of the 5-star generals was given one appearance across this series of three commemoratives. Note that Dwight Eisenhower, who is featured on this silver dollar along with George C. Marshall, had previously appeared on another commemorative silver dollar that marked the centennial of his birth in 1990.

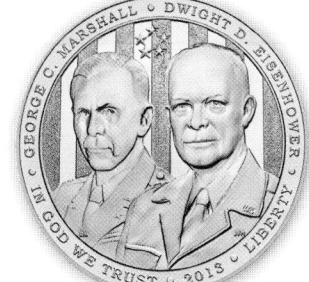

Designs. *Obverse:* Side-by-side portraits of General George C. Marshall and General Dwight D. Eisenhower against a striped background, 5-star insignia at top center. *Reverse:* The Leavenworth Lamp, a symbol of the Command and General Staff College.

Mintage Data. Authorized by Public Law 111-262, the 5-Star Generals Commemorative Coin Act, signed by President Barack Obama on October 8, 2010. *Maximum authorized*—500,000. *Number minted*—2013-W: 34,639 Uncirculated; 2013-P: 69,290 Proof.

Original Cost. Sale prices $50.95 (Uncirculated, pre-issue) and $54.95 (Proof, pre-issue); Uncirculated later raised to $55.95, and Proof later raised to $59.95. The surcharge of $10 per coin went to the Command and General Staff College Foundation.

Key to Collecting. Superb gem coins are readily available.

	Distribution	Cert	Avg	%MS	MS-67 PF-67
2013-W	34,638	1,665	69.9	100%	$90
	Auctions: No auction records available.				
2013-P, Proof	69,283	2,669	69.7		$70
	Auctions: No auction records available.				

5-STAR GENERALS $5 GOLD COIN (2013)

Designer: *Ronald D. Sanders (obverse), Barbara Fox (reverse).* **Weight:** *8.359 grams.*
Composition: *.900 gold, .100 copper (net weight .242 oz. pure gold).*
Diameter: *21.6 mm.* **Edge:** *Reeded.* **Mints:** *Philadelphia (Uncirculated) and West Point (Proof).*

The Leavenworth Lamp, seen on the reverse of this coin as well as that of the silver dollar in this series, is a symbol of the Command and General Staff College. The institution celebrated its 132nd anniversary in the year these coins were released.

Designs. *Obverse:* A portrait of General Douglas MacArthur and the 5-star insignia to the right. *Reverse:* The Leavenworth Lamp, a symbol of the Command and General Staff College.

Mintage Data. Authorized by Public Law 111-262, the 5-Star Generals Commemorative Coin Act, signed by President Barack Obama on October 8, 2010. *Maximum authorized*—100,000. *Number minted*—2013-P: 5,674 Uncirculated; 2013-W: 15,949 Proof.

Original Cost. Sale prices $480.50 (Uncirculated, pre-issue) and $485.50 (Proof, pre-issue); both prices later increased by a base of $5 plus the change in gold market value. The surcharge of $35 per coin went to the Command and General Staff College Foundation.

Key to Collecting. Superb gem coins are readily available.

	Distribution	Cert	Avg	%MS	MS-67 PF-67
2013-P	5,667	518	69.9	100%	$1,000
	Auctions: No auction records available.				
2013-W, Proof	15,844	565	69.8		$500
	Auctions: $499, PF-70DCam, September 2014				

NATIONAL BASEBALL HALL OF FAME HALF DOLLAR (2014)

Designer: *Cassie McFarland (obverse), Don Everhart (reverse).* **Weight:** *11.34 grams.*
Composition: *.9167 copper, .0833 nickel.* **Diameter:** *30.61 mm.* **Edge:** *Reeded.*
Mints: *Denver (Uncirculated) and San Francisco (Proof).*

This half dollar and the silver dollar and five-dollar gold coin issued alongside it were the first "curved" coins to be produced by the U.S. Mint—that is, the obverse is concave, and the reverse is convex. The three commemorated the 75th anniversary of the National Baseball Hall of Fame in Cooperstown, New York.

Designs. *Obverse:* A baseball glove, concave.
Reverse: A baseball, convex.

Mintage Data. Authorized by Public Law 112-152, the National Baseball Hall of Fame Commemorative Coin Act, signed by President Barack Obama on August 3, 2012. *Maximum authorized*—750,000. *Number minted*—2014-D: 147,934 Uncirculated; 2014-S: 258,643.

Original Cost. Sale prices $18.95 (Uncirculated, pre-issue) and $19.95 (Proof, pre-issue); Uncirculated later raised to $22.95, and Proof later raised to $23.95. The surcharge of $5 per coin went to the National Baseball Hall of Fame.

Key to Collecting. Superb gem coins are readily available.

	Distribution	Cert	Avg	%MS	MS-67 / PF-67
2014-D	*142,405*	9,868	69.5	100%	$40
	Auctions: No auction records available.				
2014-S, Proof	*249,049*	35,164	69.6		$30
	Auctions: No auction records available.				

NATIONAL BASEBALL HALL OF FAME SILVER DOLLAR (2014)

Designer: *Cassie McFarland (obverse), Don Everhart (reverse).* **Weight:** *26.73 grams.*
Composition: *.900 silver, .100 copper (net weight .7736 oz. pure silver).*
Diameter: *38.1 mm.* **Edge:** *Reeded.* **Mint:** *Philadelphia.*

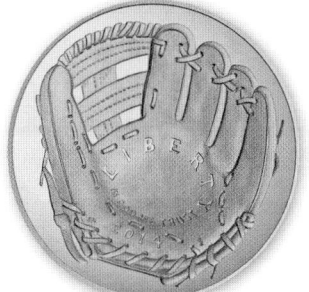 

Coins shaped like this silver dollar (as well as the corresponding half dollar and five-dollar gold coin) had previously been minted by Monnaie de Paris in commemoration of the 2009 International Year of Astronomy. The National Baseball Hall of Fame coins were the first curved issues for the U.S. Mint.

Designs. *Obverse:* A baseball glove, concave.
Reverse: A baseball, convex.

Mintage Data. Authorized by Public Law 112-152, the National Baseball Hall of Fame Commemorative Coin Act, signed by President Barack Obama on August 3, 2012. *Maximum authorized*—400,000. *Number minted*—137,909 Uncirculated and 268,076 Proof.

Original Cost. Sale prices $47.95 (Uncirculated, pre-issue) and $51.95 (Proof, pre-issue); Uncirculated later raised to $52.95, and Proof later raised to $56.95. The surcharge of $10 per coin went to the National Baseball Hall of Fame.

Key to Collecting. Superb gem coins are readily available.

	Distribution	Cert	Avg	%MS	MS-67 / PF-67
2014-P	131,910	19,896	69.7	100%	$75
	Auctions: No auction records available.				
2014-P, Proof	267,847	4,332	69.9		$75
	Auctions: No auction records available.				

NATIONAL BASEBALL HALL OF FAME $5 GOLD COIN (2014)

Designer: *Cassie McFarland (obverse), Don Everhart (reverse).* **Weight:** *8.359 grams.*
Composition: *.900 gold, .100 copper (net weight .242 oz. pure gold).*
Diameter: *21.6 mm.* **Edge:** *Reeded.* **Mint:** *West Point.*

The common obverse design for these coins was selected through a national competition, and the Department of the Treasury chose California artist Cassie McFarland's submission after input from the National Baseball Hall of Fame, the U.S. Commission of Fine Arts, and the Citizens Coinage Advisory Committee.

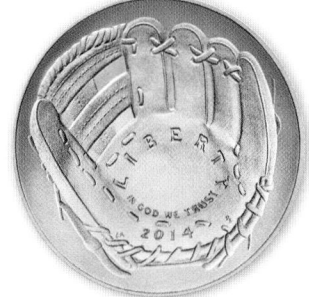

Designs. *Obverse:* A baseball glove, concave.
Reverse: A baseball, convex.

Mintage Data. Authorized by Public Law 112-152, the National Baseball Hall of Fame Commemorative Coin Act, signed by President Barack Obama on August 3, 2012. *Maximum authorized*—50,000. *Number minted*—18,000 Uncirculated and 32,495 Proof.

Original Cost. Sale prices $431.90 (Uncirculated, pre-issue) and $436.90 (Proof, pre-issue); Uncirculated later raised to $436.90, and Proof later raised to $441.90. The surcharge of $35 per coin went to the National Baseball Hall of Fame.

Key to Collecting. Superb gem coins are readily available.

	Distribution	Cert	Avg	%MS	MS-67 / PF-67
2014-W	17,674	2,282	69.9	100%	$850
	Auctions: No auction records available.				
2014-W, Proof	32,428	4,539	69.9		$800
	Auctions: No auction records available.				

CIVIL RIGHTS ACT OF 1964 SILVER DOLLAR (2014)

Designer: *Justin Kunz (obverse), Donna Weaver (reverse).* **Weight:** *26.73 grams.*
Composition: *.900 silver, .100 copper (net weight .7736 oz. pure silver).*
Diameter: *38.1 mm.* **Edge:** *Reeded.* **Mint:** *Philadelphia.*

This silver dollar commemorated the 50th anniversary of the Civil Rights Act of 1964, which greatly expanded American civil rights protections; outlawed racial segregation in public places and places of public accommodation; and funded federal programs.

Designs. *Obverse:* Three people holding hands at a Civil Rights march; man on left holding sign that reads WE SHALL OVERCOME.
Reverse: Three intertwined flames representing freedom of education, freedom to vote, and freedom to control one's own destiny. Inspired by a quote by Dr. Martin Luther King Jr.

Mintage Data. Authorized by Public Law 110-451, the Civil Rights Act of 1964 Commemorative Coin Act, signed by President George W. Bush on December 2, 2008. *Maximum authorized—350,000. Number minted—24,720* Uncirculated and 61,992 Proof.

Original Cost. Sale prices $44.95 (Uncirculated, pre-issue) and $49.95 (Proof, pre-issue); Uncirculated later raised to $49.95, and Proof later raised to $54.95. The surcharge of $10 per coin went to the United Negro College Fund, which has provided scholarships and internships for minority students for the past 70 years.

Key to Collecting. Superb gem coins are readily available.

	Distribution	Cert	Avg	%MS	MS-67
					PF-67
2014-P	24,720	830	69.6	100%	$80
	Auctions: No auction records available.				
2014-P, Proof	61,992	935	69.4		$70
	Auctions: No auction records available.				

U.S. MARSHALS SERVICE 225TH ANNIVERSARY HALF DOLLAR (2015)

Designer: *Joel Iskowitz (obverse), Susan Gamble (reverse).* **Weight:** *11.34 grams.*
Composition: *.9167 copper, .0833 nickel.* **Diameter:** *30.61 mm.*
Edge: *Reeded.* **Mints:** *Denver (Uncirculated) and San Francisco (Proof).*

The 225th anniversary of the establishment of the U.S. Marshals Service was commemorated with the release of a series including this half dollar as well as a silver dollar and five-dollar gold coin. The actual anniversary—September 24, 2014—was marked with a celebration in Washington, D.C., and the issuance of 35 special preview sets to employees of the Service.

Designs. *Obverse:* An Old West marshal and his horse at left, and a modern marshal in tactical gear at right. *Reverse:* Lady Justice holding scales and the U.S. Marshals Service star and standing over a copy of the Constitution, a stack of books, handcuffs, and a whiskey jug, each representing areas of responsibility of the Service in the past or present.

Mintage Data. Authorized by Public Law 112-104, the United States Marshals Service 225th Anniversary Commemorative Coin Act, signed into law by President Barack Obama on April 2, 2012. *Maximum authorized—750,000. Number minted—2015-D: 29,400 Uncirculated; 2015-S: 60,763 Proof (as of press time).*

Original Cost. Sale prices $13.95 (Uncirculated, pre-issue) and $14.95 (Proof, pre-issue); Uncirculated later raised to $17.95, and Proof later raised to $18.95. The surcharge of $3 per coin went to the U.S. Marshals Museum.

Key to Collecting. Superb gem coins are readily available.

	Distribution	Cert	Avg	%MS	MS-67
					PF-67
2015-D	30,231	1,462	69.2	100%	$20
	Auctions: No auction records available.				
2015-S, Proof	76,549	2,029	69.2		$20
	Auctions: No auction records available.				

U.S. MARSHALS SERVICE 225TH ANNIVERSARY SILVER DOLLAR (2015)

Designer: *Richard Masters (obverse), Frank Morris (reverse).* **Weight:** *26.73 grams.*
Composition: *.900 silver, .100 copper (net weight .7736 oz. pure silver).*
Diameter: *38.1 mm.* **Edge:** *Reeded.* **Mint:** *Philadelphia.*

The first federal law-enforcement officers of the United States, the U.S. Marshals were created under section 27 of the Act of Congress entitled "Chapter XX—An Act to Establish the Judicial Courts of the United States." The original 13 men to serve were confirmed on September 26, 1789.

Designs. *Obverse:* U.S. marshals riding on horseback under the U.S. Marshals Service star. *Reverse:* A U.S. marshal of the frontier era holding a "wanted" poster.

Mintage Data. Authorized by Public Law 112-104, the United States Marshals Service 225th Anniversary Commemorative Coin Act, signed into law by President Barack Obama on April 2, 2012. *Maximum authorized—500,000. Number minted—37,588 Uncirculated and 107,847 Proof (as of press time).*

Original Cost. Sale prices $43.95 (Uncirculated, pre-issue) and $46.95 (Proof, pre-issue): Uncirculated later raised to $48.95, and Proof later raised to $51.95. The surcharge of $10 went to the U.S. Marshals Museum.

Key to Collecting. Superb gem coins are readily available.

	Distribution	Cert	Avg	%MS	MS-67
					PF-67
2015-P	38,149	2,531	69.7	100%	$50
	Auctions: No auction records available.				
2015-P, Proof	124,329	3,738	69.1		$50
	Auctions: No auction records available.				

U.S. MARSHALS SERVICE 225TH ANNIVERSARY $5 GOLD COIN (2015)

Designer: *Donna Weaver (obverse), Paul C. Balan (reverse).* **Weight:** *8.359 grams.*
Composition: *.900 gold, .100 copper (net weight .242 oz. pure gold).*
Diameter: *21.6 mm.* **Edge:** *Reeded.* **Mint:** *West Point.*

The U.S. Marshals officially became the U.S. Marshals Service in 1969 by order of the Department of Justice. The Service achieved Bureau status in 1974 and today is the primary agency for fugitive operations, as well as protection of officers of the court and court buildings.

Designs. *Obverse:* The U.S. Marshals Service star superimposed on a mountain range. *Reverse:* An eagle, shield on chest, holding a banner and draped flag.

Mintage Data. Authorized by Public Law 112-104, the United States Marshals Service 225th Anniversary Commemorative Coin Act, signed into law by President Barack Obama on April 2, 2012. *Maximum authorized*—100,000. *Number minted*—6,592 Uncirculated and 9,671 Proof (as of press time)

Original Cost. Sale prices $395.45 (Uncirculated, pre-issue) and $400.45 (Proof, pre-issue): Uncirculated later raised to $400.45, and Proof later raised to $405.45. The surcharge of $35 per coin went to the U.S. Marshals Museum.

Key to Collecting. Superb gem coins are readily available.

	Distribution	Cert	Avg	%MS	MS-67 / PF-67
2015-W	6,743	588	69.9	100%	$400
	Auctions: No auction records available.				
2015-W, Proof	24,959	948	69.8		$400
	Auctions: No auction records available.				

MARCH OF DIMES 75TH ANNIVERSARY SILVER DOLLAR (2015)

Designer: *Paul C. Balan (obverse), Don Everhart (reverse).* **Weight:** *26.73 grams.*
Composition: *.900 silver, .100 copper (net weight .7736 oz. pure silver).*
Diameter: *38.1 mm.* **Edge:** *Reeded.* **Mints:** *Philadelphia (Uncirculated) and West Point (Proof).*

Inspired by his own struggle with polio, President Franklin Delano Roosevelt created the National Foundation for Infantile Paralysis, now known as the March of Dimes, on January 3, 1938. This coin celebrated the organization's 75th anniversary (despite coming out after the actual date of said event) and recognized its accomplishments, which included the funding of research which resulted in Dr. Jonas Salk and Dr. Albert Sabin's polio vaccines.

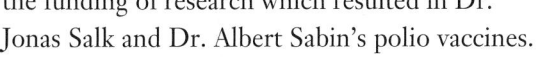

Designs. *Obverse:* A profile view of President Franklin Delano Roosevelt and Dr. Jonas Salk. *Reverse:* A sleeping baby cradled in its parent's hand.

Mintage Data. Authorized by Public Law 112-209, the March of Dimes Commemorative Coin Act of 2012, signed into law by President Barack Obama on December 18, 2012. *Maximum authorized*—500,000. *Number minted*—2015-D: 24,387 Uncirculated; 2015-W: 56,718 Proof (as of press time)

Original Cost. Sale prices $43.95 (Uncirculated, pre-issue) and $46.95 (Proof, pre-issue): Uncirculated later raised to $48.95, and Proof later raised to $51.95. The surcharge of $10 per coin went to the March of Dimes to help finance research, education, and services aimed at improving the health of women, infants, and children.

Key to Collecting. Superb gem coins are readily available.

	Distribution	Cert	Avg	%MS	MS-67 PF-67
2015-P	24,742	1,135	69.8	100%	$50
	Auctions: No auction records available.				
2015-W, Proof	32,030	6,713	69.6		$50
	Auctions: No auction records available.				

Mark Twain Silver Dollar (2016)

Designer: *Chris Costello (obverse), Patricia Lucas-Morris (reverse).* **Weight:** *26.73 grams.*
Composition: *.900 silver, .100 copper (net weight .7736 oz. pure silver).*
Diameter: *38.1 mm.* **Edge:** *Reeded.* **Mint:** *Philadelphia.*

Samuel Langhorne Clemens—better known by his pen name, Mark Twain—is among the most celebrated authors in U.S. history. His *Adventures of Huckleberry Finn*, originally published in 1885, is often referred to as "The Great American Novel."

Designs. *Obverse:* A portrait of Mark Twain holding a pipe, with the smoke forming a silhouette of Huck Finn and Jim on their raft. *Reverse:* Depictions of several characters from Mark Twain's works, including the knight and horse from *A Connecticut Yankee in King Arthur's Court*, the frog from *The Celebrated Jumping Frog of Calaveras County*, and Huck and Jim from *Adventures of Huckleberry Finn.*

Mintage Data. Authorized by Public Law 112-201, the Mark Twain Commemorative Coin Act, signed into law by President Barack Obama on December 4, 2012. *Maximum authorized*—350,000. *Number minted*—To be determined.

Original Cost. Sale prices $44.95 (Uncirculated, pre-issue) and $45.95 (Proof, pre-issue). Uncirculated later raised to $49.95, and Proof later raised to $50.95. The surcharge of $10 per coin is to be distributed evenly between the Mark Twain House & Museum in Hartford, Conn.; the University of California, Berkeley, for the benefit of the Mark Twain Project at the Bancroft Library; Elmira College in New York; and the Mark Twain Boyhood Home and Museum in Hannibal, Missouri.

Key to Collecting. Superb gem coins are readily available.

	Distribution	Cert	Avg	%MS	MS-67 / PF-67
2016-P	26,281	2,452	69.8	100%	45
Auctions: No auction records available.					
2016-P, Proof	78,536	2,678	69.8	100%	45
Auctions: No auction records available.					

MARK TWAIN $5 GOLD COIN (2016)

Designer: *Benjamin Sowers (obverse), Ronald D. Sanders (reverse).* **Weight:** *8.359 grams.*
Composition: *.900 gold, .100 copper (net weight .242 oz. pure gold).*
Diameter: *21.6 mm.* **Edge:** *Reeded.* **Mint:** *West Point.*

The designs for the Mark Twain commemorative coins were unveiled two days before the 180th anniversary of his birth, November 30, 2015. Interestingly, Twain was born shortly after a visit by Halley's Comet, and he later predicted that he would "go out with it," too. He passed away two days after the comet returned.

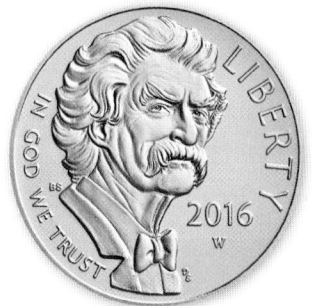 

Designs. *Obverse:* A portrait of Mark Twain.
Reverse: A steamboat on the Mississippi River.

Mintage Data. Authorized by Public Law 112-201, the Mark Twain Commemorative Coin Act, signed into law by President Barack Obama on December 4, 2012. *Maximum authorized*—100,000. *Number minted*—To be determined.

Original Cost. Sale prices $359 (Uncirculated, pre-issue) and $364 (Proof, pre-issue). Uncirculated later raised to $364, and Proof later raised to $369. The surcharge of $35 per coin is to be distributed evenly between the Mark Twain House & Museum in Hartford, Conn.; the University of California, Berkeley, for the benefit of the Mark Twain Project at the Bancroft Library; Elmira College in New York; and the Mark Twain Boyhood Home and Museum in Hannibal, Missouri.

Key to Collecting. Superb gem coins are readily available.

	Distribution	Cert	Avg	%MS	MS-67 / PF-67
2016-W	5,695	395	70.0	100%	$370
Auctions: No auction records available.					
2016-W, Proof	13,266	501	69.8	100%	$376
Auctions: No auction records available.					

NATIONAL PARK SERVICE 100TH ANNIVERSARY HALF DOLLAR (2016)

Designer: *Barbara Fox (obverse), Thomas Hipschen (reverse).* **Weight:** *11.34 grams.*
Composition: *.9167 copper, .0833 nickel.* **Diameter:** *30.61 mm.*
Edge: *Reeded.* **Mints:** *Denver (Uncirculated) and San Francisco (Proof).*

The National Park Service was created through the National Park Service Organic Act, signed into law by President Woodrow Wilson on August 25, 1916. Today the agency employs approximately 20,000 people and operates on a budget of nearly $3 billion.

Designs. *Obverse:* A hiker taking in a mountain landscape above a child observing a frog. *Reverse:* The National Park Service logo.

Mintage Data. Authorized by Public Law 113-291, signed into law by President Barack Obama on December 19, 2014. *Maximum authorized*—750,000. *Number minted*—To be determined.

Original Cost. Sale prices $20.95 (Uncirculated, pre-issue) and $21.95 (Proof, pre-issue). Uncirculated later raised to $24.95, and Proof later raised to $25.95. The surcharge of $5 per coin is assigned to the National Park Foundation.

Key to Collecting. Superb gem coins are readily available.

	Distribution	Cert	Avg	%MS	MS-67 PF-67
2016-D	21,019	465	69.4	100%	$21
	Auctions: No auction records available.				
2016-S, Proof	54,844	653	69.6	100%	$22
	Auctions: No auction records available.				

NATIONAL PARK SERVICE 100TH ANNIVERSARY SILVER DOLLAR (2016)

Designer: *Joseph Menna (obverse), Chris Costello (reverse).* **Weight:** *26.73 grams.*
Composition: *.900 silver, .100 copper (net weight .7736 oz. pure silver).*
Diameter: *38.1 mm.* **Edge:** *Reeded.* **Mint:** *Philadelphia.*

The United States' National Parks range from Alaska's Gates of the Arctic National Park—an expanse of pristine wilderness devoid of any actual park facilities—to American Samoa National Park, which features coral reefs, rainforests, and volcanic mountains.

Designs. *Obverse:* Yellowstone National Park's Old Faithful geyser with a bison in the foreground. *Reverse:* A Latina Folklórico dancer and the National Park Service logo.

Mintage Data. Authorized by Public Law 113-291, signed into law by President Barack Obama on December 19, 2014. *Maximum authorized*—500,000. *Number minted*—To be determined.

Original Cost. Sale prices $44.95 (Uncirculated, pre-issue) and $45.95 (Proof, pre-issue). Uncirculated later raised to $49.95, and Proof later raised to $50.95. The surcharge of $10 per coin is assigned to the National Park Foundation.

Key to Collecting. Superb gem coins are readily available.

	Distribution	Cert	Avg	%MS	MS-67 PF-67
2016-P	20,994	756	69.7	100%	$50
	Auctions: No auction records available.				
2016-P, Proof	77,309	1,148	69.4	100%	$51
	Auctions: No auction records available.				

National Park Service 100th Anniversary $5 Gold Coin (2016)

Designer: *Don Everhart.* **Weight:** *8.359 grams.* **Composition:** *.900 gold, .100 copper (net weight .242 oz. pure gold).* **Diameter:** *21.6 mm.* **Edge:** *Reeded.* **Mint:** *West Point.*

The National Park Service acts as the steward of 409 official "units," which includes the 59 National Parks as well as the country's National Monuments, National Preserves, National Historic Sites, and more.

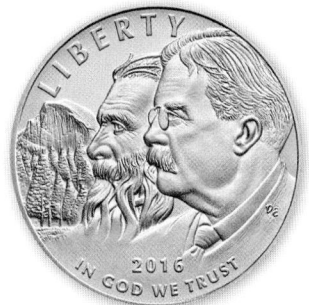 

Designs. *Obverse:* Profiles of John Muir and Theodore Roosevelt with Yosemite National Park's Half Dome in the background. *Reverse:* The National Park Service logo.

Mintage Data. Authorized by Public Law 113-291, signed into law by President Barack Obama on December 19, 2014. *Maximum authorized*—100,000. *Number minted*—To be determined.

Original Cost. Sale prices to be determined. The surcharge of $35 per coin is assigned to the National Park Foundation.

Key to Collecting. Superb gem coins are readily available.

	Distribution	Cert	Avg	%MS	MS-67 PF-67
2016-W	5,150	275	70.0	100%	$375
	Auctions: No auction records available.				
2016-W, Proof	19,506	536	69.8	100%	$370
	Auctions: No auction records available.				

LIONS CLUB INTERNATIONAL CENTURY OF SERVICE SILVER DOLLAR (2017)

Designer: *Joel Iskowitz (obverse), Patricia Lucas-Morris (reverse).* **Weight:** *26.73 grams.*
Composition: *.900 silver, .100 copper (net weight .7736 oz. pure silver).*
Diameter: *38.1 mm.* **Edge:** *Reeded.* **Mints:** *Philadelphia.*

In 1917, Melvin Jones founded the Lions Clubs International as a service club organization with the simple guiding principle of "We Serve." The organization empowers its volunteers to serve their communities, meet humanitarian needs, encourage peace, and promote international understanding. Services participated in include community, environmental, youth, health programs, and disaster relief work.

Designs. *Obverse:* The portrait of founder Melvin Jones is paired with the Lions Clubs International logo. *Reverse:* A male and female lion with a lion cub superimposed over a globe.

Mintage Data. Authorized by Public Law 112-181, the Lions Clubs International Century of Service Commemorative Coin Act, signed into law by President Barack Obama on October 5, 2012 to commemorate the organization's centennial in 2017. *Maximum authorized—400,000. Number minted—*To be determined.

Original Cost. Sale prices $46.95 (Uncirculated, pre-issue) and $47.95 (Proof, pre-issue): Uncirculated later raised to $51.95, and Proof later raised to $52.95. The surcharge of $10 per coin was paid to the Lions Clubs International Foundation to further its programs for the blind and visually impaired, invest in adaptive technologies for the disabled, and invest in youth and those affected by major disaster.

Key to Collecting. Superb gem coins are readily available.

	Distribution	Cert	Avg	%MS	MS-67
					PF-67
2017-P	17,250				$50
	Auctions: No auction records available.				
2017-P, Proof	68,525				$51
	Auctions: No auction records available.				

BOYS TOWN CENTENNIAL HALF DOLLAR (2017)

Designer: *Chris Costello.* **Weight:** *11.34 grams.* **Composition:** *.9167 copper, .0833 nickel.*
Diameter: *30.61 mm.* **Edge:** *Reeded.* **Mints:** *San Francisco and Denver.*

Through its Boys Town National Hotline, Boys Town National Research Hospital, and other community services, Boys Town provides treatment for the behavioral, emotional, and physical problems of children and families in 11 regions across the country. Boys Town programs impact the lives of more than two million children and families each year.

Designs. *Obverse:* Two brothers from 1917 walk toward Father Flanagan's Boys Home and a pylon erected at the facility in the 1940s, symbolizing what the home would grow into. *Reverse:* A present-day Boys Town neighborhood of homes overlooked by the profiles of Boys Town graduates.

Mintage Data. Authorized by Public Law 114-30, the Boys Town Centennial Commemorative Coin Program Act of 2015, signed into law by President Barack Obama on July 6, 2015. *Maximum authorized—* 300,000. *Number minted—*To be determined.

Original Cost. Sale prices to be determined. The surcharge of $5 per coin went to Boys Town to carry out its cause of caring for and assisting children and families in underserved communities across America.

Key to Collecting. Superb gem coins are readily available.

	Distribution	Cert	Avg	%MS	MS-67
					PF-67
2017-S	15,549				$21
	Auctions: No auction records available.				
2017-D, Proof	23,213				$22
	Auctions: No auction records available.				

Boys Town Centennial Silver Dollar (2017)

Designer: *Emily Damstra.* **Weight:** *26.73 grams.* **Composition:** *.900 silver, .100 copper (net weight .7736 oz. pure silver).* **Diameter:** *38.1 mm.* **Edge:** *Reeded.* **Mints:** *Philadelphia.*

Father Edward Flanagan, a young parish priest, founded Boys Town on the maxim: "Every child could be a productive citizen if given love, a home, an education, and a trade." From the beginning boys of all races and religions were welcomed, and eventually the institution grew to support girls and families as well.

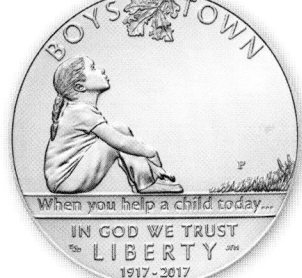 

Designs. *Obverse:* A young girl sitting under a tree alone, looking up plaintively. *Reverse:* A family holding hands and playing under the same tree with the same girl.

Mintage Data. Authorized by Public Law 114-30, the Boys Town Centennial Commemorative Coin Program Act of 2015, signed into law by President Barack Obama on July 6, 2015. *Maximum authorized—* 350,000. *Number minted—*To be determined.

Original Cost. Sale prices to be determined. The surcharge of $10 per coin went to Boys Town to carry out its cause of caring for and assisting children and families in underserved communities across America.

Key to Collecting. Superb gem coins are readily available.

	Distribution	Cert	Avg	%MS	MS-67
					PF-67
2017-P	12,256				$50
	Auctions: No auction records available.				
2017-P, Proof	31,644				$51
	Auctions: No auction records available.				

BOYS TOWN CENTENNIAL $5 GOLD COIN (2017)

Designer: *Donna Weaver.* **Weight:** *8.359 grams.* **Composition:** *.900 gold, .060 silver, .040 copper (net weight .242 oz. pure gold).* **Diameter:** *21.6 mm.* **Edge:** *Reeded.* **Mint:** *West Point.*

Father Flanagan's Home for Boys, or "Boys Town" as it became known, was founded in rented a boarding house with $90 he had borrowed. It has grown exponentially since its founding in 1917. Today it is one of the largest non-profit organizations in the country, dedicated to serving at-risk children and families of all backgrounds and religions.

Designs. *Obverse:* A portrait of Father Flanagan. *Reverse:* An outstretched hand holding a sprouting acorn.

Mintage Data. Authorized by Public Law 114-30, the Boys Town Centennial Commemorative Coin Program Act of 2015, signed into law by President Barack Obama on July 6, 2015. *Maximum authorized—* 50,000. *Number minted—* To be determined.

Original Cost. Sale prices to be determined. The surcharge of $35 per coin went to Boys Town to carry out its cause of caring for and assisting children and families in underserved communities across America.

Key to Collecting. Superb gem coins are readily available.

	Distribution	Cert	Avg	%MS	MS-67
					PF-67
2017-W	2,947				2,947
	Auctions: No auction records available.				
2017-W, Proof	7,370				$370
	Auctions: No auction records available.				

WORLD WAR I CENTENNIAL SILVER DOLLAR (2018)

Designer: *LeRoy Transfield (obverse and reverse).* **Weight:** *26.73 grams.*
Composition: *.900 silver, .100 copper (net weight .7736 oz. pure silver).*
Diameter: *38.1 mm.* **Edge:** *Reeded.* **Mint:** *Philadelphia.*

This silver dollar commemorates the centennial of America's involvement in World War I (April 1917 to November 1918) and honors the more than four million men and women from the United States who served during the war. In support of the coin program, the Mint created special companion silver medals honoring each of the five branches of the U.S. Armed Forces that were active during the war. Each set included a Proof silver dollar and a Proof medal.

Designs. *Obverse:* "Soldier's Charge" depicts a doughboy gripping a rifle, with twines of barbed wire in the lower right. *Reverse:* "Poppies in the Wire" features abstract poppies—symbols of war remembrance—mixed in with barbed wire continued from the obverse.

Mintage Data. Authorized by Public Law 113-212, the World War I American Veterans Centennial Commemorative Coin Act, and signed by President Barack Obama on December 16, 2014. *Maximum authorized*—350,000 total. *Number minted*—15,979 Uncirculated, 39,956 individual Proofs, 62,660 Proofs in coin-and-medal sets (mintages as of February 2018; not final).

Original Cost. Sale prices $48.95 (Uncirculated, introductory) and $51.95 (Proof, introductory); later raised to $53.95 and $56.95. A surcharge of $10 went to the United States Foundation for the Commemoration of the World Wars, a non-profit organization that supports the U.S. World War I Centennial Commission in public outreach and education about American involvement in the war. The surcharge is expected to be used to help create a new National World War I Memorial at Pershing Park, a block from the White House.

The coin and medal sets were limited to 100,000 units across all five options; their issue price was $99.95.

Key to Collecting. Superb gems are easily found in the marketplace.

	Distribution	Cert	Avg	%MS	MS-67 / PF-67
2018-P					$50
Auctions: No auction records available.					
2018-P, Proof					$51
Auctions: No auction records available.					

BREAST CANCER AWARENESS HALF DOLLAR (2018)

Designer: *Emily Damstra.* **Weight:** *11.34 grams.* **Composition:** *.9167 copper, .0833 nickel.* **Diameter:** *30.61 mm.* **Edge:** *Reeded.* **Mints:** *Denver and San Francisco.*

This suite of three coins commemorates the role of awareness and education in funding cancer research to improve outcomes and save lives. All three coins share the same designs.

Designs. *Obverse:* A butterfly flies above two women. The older woman has her hands on her chest and a relieved expression on her face. The younger, with a scarf on her head, holds one hand over her chest and the other raised in a fist as if she is ready to fight. *Reverse:* A tiger swallowtail butterfly in flight, symbolic of hope.

Mintage Data. Authorized by Public Law 114-148, the Breast Cancer Awareness Commemorative Coin Act, and signed by President Barack Obama on April 29, 2016. *Maximum authorized*—750,000 total. *Number minted*—To be determined.

Original Cost. Sale prices to be determined. A surcharges of $5 is assigned to the Breast Cancer Research Foundation.

	Distribution	Cert	Avg	%MS	MS-67 / PF-67
2018-D					$21
Auctions: No auction records available.					
2018-S, Proof					$22
Auctions: No auction records available.					

BREAST CANCER AWARENESS SILVER DOLLAR (2018)

Designer: *Emily Damstra.* **Weight:** *26.73 grams.* **Composition:** *.900 silver, .100 copper (net weight .7736 oz. pure silver).* **Diameter:** *38.1 mm.* **Edge:** *Reeded.* **Mint:** *Philadelphia.*

This suite of three coins commemorates the role of awareness and education in funding cancer research to improve outcomes and save lives. All three coins share the same designs.

Designs. *Obverse:* A butterfly flies above two women. The older woman has her hands on her chest and a relieved expression on her face. The younger, with a scarf on her head, holds one hand over her chest and the other raised in a fist as if she is ready to fight. *Reverse:* A tiger swallowtail butterfly in flight, symbolic of hope.

Mintage Data. Authorized by Public Law 114-148, the Breast Cancer Awareness Commemorative Coin Act, and signed by President Barack Obama on April 29, 2016. *Maximum authorized*—400,000 total. *Number minted*—To be determined.

Original Cost. Sale prices to be determined. A surcharges of $10 is assigned to the Breast Cancer Research Foundation.

	Distribution	Cert	Avg	%MS	MS-67
					PF-67
2018-P					$50
Auctions: No auction records available.					
2017-, Proof					$51
Auctions: No auction records available.					

BREAST CANCER AWARENESS $5 GOLD COIN (2017)

Designer: *Emily Damstra.* **Weight:** *8.359 grams.* **Composition:** *.900 gold, .060 silver, .040 copper (net weight .242 oz. pure gold).* **Diameter:** *21.6 mm.* **Edge:** *Reeded.* **Mint:** *West Point.*

This suite of three coins commemorates the role of awareness and education in funding cancer research to improve outcomes and save lives. The $5 gold coin, with slightly more copper and zinc than the standard alloy, has a pink hue, symbolizing breast cancer awareness. All three coins share the same designs.

Designs. *Obverse:* A butterfly flies above two women. The older woman has her hands on her chest and a relieved expression on her face. The younger, with a scarf on her head, holds one hand over her chest and the other raised in a fist as if she is ready to fight. *Reverse:* A tiger swallowtail butterfly in flight, symbolic of hope.

Mintage Data. Authorized by Public Law 114-148, the Breast Cancer Awareness Commemorative Coin Act, and signed by President Barack Obama on April 29, 2016. *Maximum authorized*—50,000 total. *Number minted*—To be determined.

Original Cost. Sale prices to be determined. A surcharges of $35 is assigned to the Breast Cancer Research Foundation.

	Distribution	Cert	Avg	%MS	MS-67	
					PF-67	
2018-W	2,947				2,947	
2018-W, Proof	7,370				$370	

GOVERNMENT COMMEMORATIVE SETS

	Value
(1983–1984) LOS ANGELES OLYMPIAD	
1983 and 1984 Proof silver dollars	$65
1983 and 1984 6-coin set. One each of 1983 and 1984 silver dollars, both Proof and Uncirculated gold $10 (a)	$1,550
1983 3-piece collector set. 1983 P, D, and S Uncirculated silver dollars	$90
1984 3-piece collector set. 1984 P, D, and S Uncirculated silver dollars	$90
1983 and 1984 gold and silver Uncirculated set. One each of 1983 and 1984 Uncirculated silver dollars and one 1984 Uncirculated gold $10	$800
1983 and 1984 gold and silver Proof set. One each of 1983 and 1984 Proof silver dollars and one 1984 Proof gold $10	$800
(1986) STATUE OF LIBERTY	
2-coin set. Proof silver dollar and clad half dollar	$25
3-coin set. Proof silver dollar, clad half dollar, and gold $5	$400
2-coin set. Uncirculated silver dollar and clad half dollar	$35
2-coin set. Uncirculated and Proof gold $5	$750
3-coin set. Uncirculated silver dollar, clad half dollar, and gold $5	$400
6-coin set. One each of Proof and Uncirculated half dollar, silver dollar, and gold $5 (a)	$800
(1987) CONSTITUTION	
2-coin set. Uncirculated silver dollar and gold $5	$425
2-coin set. Proof silver dollar and gold $5	$410
4-coin set. One each of Proof and Uncirculated silver dollar and gold $5 (a)	$800
(1988) SEOUL OLYMPIAD	
2-coin set. Uncirculated silver dollar and gold $5	$400
2-coin set. Proof silver dollar and gold $5	$410
4-coin set. One each of Proof and Uncirculated silver dollar and gold $5 (a)	$800
(1989) CONGRESS	
2-coin set. Proof clad half dollar and silver dollar	$35
3-coin set. Proof clad half dollar, silver dollar, and gold $5	$400
2-coin set. Uncirculated clad half dollar and silver dollar	$35
3-coin set. Uncirculated clad half dollar, silver dollar, and gold $5	$400
6-coin set. One each of Proof and Uncirculated clad half dollar, silver dollar, and gold $5 (a)	$850
(1991) MOUNT RUSHMORE	
2-coin set. Uncirculated clad half dollar and silver dollar	$50
2-coin set. Proof clad half dollar and silver dollar	$45
3-coin set. Uncirculated clad half dollar, silver dollar, and gold $5	$425
3-coin set. Proof half dollar, silver dollar, and gold $5	$400
6-coin set. One each of Proof and Uncirculated clad half dollar, silver dollar, and gold $5 (a)	$900
(1992) XXV OLYMPIAD	
2-coin set. Uncirculated clad half dollar and silver dollar	$50
2-coin set. Proof clad half dollar and silver dollar	$40
3-coin set. Uncirculated clad half dollar, silver dollar, and gold $5	$425
3-coin set. Proof half dollar, silver dollar, and gold $5	$400
6-coin set. One each of Proof and Uncirculated clad half dollar, silver dollar, and gold $5 (a)	$900

a. Packaged in cherrywood box.

	Value
(1992) CHRISTOPHER COLUMBUS	
2-coin set. Uncirculated clad half dollar and silver dollar	$50
2-coin set. Proof clad half dollar and silver dollar	$45
3-coin set. Uncirculated clad half dollar, silver dollar, and gold $5	$425
3-coin set. Proof half dollar, silver dollar, and gold $5	$400
6-coin set. One each of Proof and Uncirculated clad half dollar, silver dollar, and gold $5 (a)	$900
(1993) BILL OF RIGHTS	
2-coin set. Uncirculated silver half dollar and silver dollar	$60
2-coin set. Proof silver half dollar and silver dollar	$50
3-coin set. Uncirculated silver half dollar, silver dollar, and gold $5	$450
3-coin set. Proof half dollar, silver dollar, and gold $5	$400
6-coin set. One each of Proof and Uncirculated silver half dollar, silver dollar, and gold $5 (a)	$900
"Young Collector" set. Silver half dollar	$35
Educational set. Silver half dollar and James Madison medal	$35
Proof silver half dollar and 25-cent stamp	$20
(1993) WORLD WAR II	
2-coin set. Uncirculated clad half dollar and silver dollar	$60
2-coin set. Proof clad half dollar and silver dollar	$45
3-coin set. Uncirculated clad half dollar, silver dollar, and gold $5	$425
3-coin set. Proof clad half dollar, silver dollar, and gold $5	$400
6-coin set. One each of Proof and Uncirculated clad half dollar, silver dollar, and gold $5 (a)	$900
"Young Collector" set. Clad half dollar	$30
Victory Medal set. Uncirculated clad half dollar and reproduction medal	$40
(1993) THOMAS JEFFERSON	
"Coinage and Currency" set (issued in 1994). Silver dollar, "frosted" Uncirculated Jefferson nickel, and $2 note	$110
(1994) WORLD CUP SOCCER	
2-coin set. Uncirculated clad half dollar and silver dollar	$50
2-coin set. Proof clad half dollar and silver dollar	$45
3-coin set. Uncirculated clad half dollar, silver dollar, and gold $5	$425
3-coin set. Proof clad half dollar, silver dollar, and gold $5	$400
6-coin set. One each of Proof and Uncirculated clad half dollar, silver dollar, and gold $5 (a)	$900
"Young Collector" set. Uncirculated clad half dollar	$20
"Special Edition" set. Proof clad half dollar and silver dollar	$50
(1994) U.S. VETERANS	
3-coin set. Uncirculated POW, Vietnam, and Women in Military Service silver dollars	$200
3-coin set. Proof POW, Vietnam, and Women in Military Service silver dollars	$150
(1995) SPECIAL OLYMPICS	
2-coin set. Proof Special Olympics silver dollar, 1995-S Kennedy half dollar	$150
(1995) CIVIL WAR BATTLEFIELD PRESERVATION	
2-coin set. Uncirculated clad half dollar and silver dollar	$100
2-coin set. Proof clad half dollar and silver dollar	$90
3-coin set. Uncirculated clad half dollar, silver dollar, and gold $5	$650
3-coin set. Proof clad half dollar, silver dollar, and gold $5	$500
6-coin set. One each of Proof and Uncirculated clad half dollar, silver dollar, and gold $5 (a)	$1,150
"Young Collector" set. Uncirculated clad half dollar	$50
2-coin "Union" set. Clad half dollar and silver dollar	$125
3-coin "Union" set. Clad half dollar, silver dollar, and gold $5	$550

a. Packaged in cherrywood box.

	Value
(1995–1996) CENTENNIAL OLYMPIC GAMES	
4-coin set #1. Uncirculated clad half dollar (Basketball), silver dollars (Gymnastics, Paralympics), gold $5 (Torch Bearer)	$800
4-coin set #2. Proof clad half dollar (Basketball), silver dollars (Gymnastics, Paralympics), gold $5 (Torch Bearer)	$600
4-coin set #3. Proof half dollar (Baseball), dollars (Cyclist, Track Runner), gold $5 (Olympic Stadium)	$600
2-coin set #1: Proof silver dollars (Gymnastics, Paralympics)	$80
"Young Collector" set. Uncirculated Basketball clad half dollar	$35
"Young Collector" set. Uncirculated Baseball clad half dollar	$35
"Young Collector" set. Uncirculated Swimming clad half dollar	$200
"Young Collector" set. Uncirculated Soccer clad half dollar	$175
1995–1996 16-coin Uncirculated set. One each of all Uncirculated coins (a)	$7,500
1995–1996 16-coin Proof set. One each of all Proof coins (a)	$1,800
1995–1996 8-coin Proof silver dollars set	$400
1995–1996 32-coin set. One each of all Uncirculated and Proof coins (a)	$7,000
(1996) NATIONAL COMMUNITY SERVICE	
Proof silver dollar and Saint-Gaudens stamp	$100
(1996) SMITHSONIAN INSTITUTION 150TH ANNIVERSARY	
2-coin set. Proof silver dollar and gold $5	$400
4-coin set. One each of Proof and Uncirculated silver dollar and gold $5 (a)	$950
"Young Collector" set. Proof silver dollar	$100
(1997) U.S. BOTANIC GARDEN	
"Coinage and Currency" set. Uncirculated silver dollar, "frosted" Uncirculated Jefferson nickel, and $1 note	$250
(1997) JACKIE ROBINSON	
2-coin set. Proof silver dollar and gold $5	$600
4-coin set. One each of Proof and Uncirculated silver dollar and gold $5 (a)	$2,000
3-piece "Legacy" set. Baseball card, pin, and gold $5 (a)	$750
(1997) FRANKLIN D. ROOSEVELT	
2-coin set. One each of Proof and Uncirculated gold $5	$900
(1997) NATIONAL LAW ENFORCEMENT OFFICERS MEMORIAL	
Insignia set. Silver dollar, lapel pin, and patch	$200
(1998) ROBERT F. KENNEDY	
2-coin set. RFK silver dollar and JFK silver half dollar	$200
2-coin set. Proof and Uncirculated RFK silver dollars	$110
(1998) BLACK REVOLUTIONARY WAR PATRIOTS	
2-coin set. Proof and Uncirculated silver dollars	$150
"Young Collector" set. Uncirculated silver dollar	$150
Black Revolutionary War Patriots set. Silver dollar and four stamps	$150
(1999) DOLLEY MADISON	
2-coin set. Proof and Uncirculated silver dollars	$75
(1999) GEORGE WASHINGTON DEATH	
2-coin set. One each of Proof and Uncirculated gold $5	$800
(1999) YELLOWSTONE NATIONAL PARK	
2-coin set. One each of Proof and Uncirculated silver dollars	$100
(2000) LEIF ERICSON MILLENNIUM	
2-coin set. Proof silver dollar and Icelandic 1,000 kronur	$100
(2000) MILLENNIUM COIN AND CURRENCY SET	
3-piece set. Uncirculated 2000 Sacagawea dollar; Uncirculated 2000 Silver Eagle; George Washington $1 note, series 1999	$100
(2001) AMERICAN BUFFALO	
2-coin set. One each of Proof and Uncirculated silver dollars	$350
"Coinage and Currency" set. Uncirculated American Buffalo silver dollar, face reprint of 1899 $5 Indian Chief Silver Certificate, 1987 Chief Red Cloud 10¢ stamp, 2001 Bison 21¢ stamp	$200

a. Packaged in cherrywood box.

	Value
(2001) U.S. CAPITOL VISITOR CENTER	
3-coin set. Proof clad half dollar, silver dollar, and gold $5	$400
(2002) SALT LAKE OLYMPIC GAMES	
2-coin set. Proof silver dollar and gold $5	$400
4-coin set. One each of Proof and Uncirculated silver dollar and gold $5	$900
(2003) FIRST FLIGHT CENTENNIAL	
3-coin set. Proof clad half dollar, silver dollar, and gold $10	$1,125
(2003) LEGACIES OF FREEDOM	
Uncirculated 2003 $1 American Eagle silver bullion coin and an Uncirculated 2002 £2 Silver Britannia coin	$75
(2004) THOMAS A. EDISON	
Edison set. Uncirculated silver dollar and light bulb	$75
(2004) LEWIS AND CLARK	
Coin and Pouch set. Proof silver dollar and beaded pouch	$200
"Coinage and Currency" set. Uncirculated silver dollar, Sacagawea golden dollar, two 2005 nickels, replica 1901 $10 Bison note, silver-plated Peace Medal replica, three stamps, two booklets	$100
(2004) WESTWARD JOURNEY NICKEL SERIES	
Westward Journey Nickel Series™ Coin and Medal set. Proof Sacagawea golden dollar, two 2004 Proof nickels, silver-plated Peace Medal replica	$60
(2005) WESTWARD JOURNEY NICKEL SERIES	
Westward Journey Nickel Series™ Coin and Medal set. Proof Sacagawea golden dollar, two 2005 Proof nickels, silver-plated Peace Medal replica	$40
(2005) CHIEF JUSTICE JOHN MARSHALL	
"Coin and Chronicles" set. Uncirculated silver dollar, booklet, BEP intaglio portrait	$65
(2005) AMERICAN LEGACY	
American Legacy Collection. Proof Marine Corps silver dollar, Proof John Marshall silver dollar, 11-piece Proof set	$100
(2005) MARINE CORPS 230TH ANNIVERSARY	
Marine Corps Uncirculated silver dollar and stamp set	$100
(2006) BENJAMIN FRANKLIN	
"Coin and Chronicles" set. Uncirculated "Scientist" silver dollar, four stamps, *Poor Richard's Almanack* replica, intaglio print	$75
(2006) AMERICAN LEGACY	
American Legacy Collection. Proof 2006-P Benjamin Franklin, Founding Father silver dollar; Proof 2006-S San Francisco Old Mint silver dollar; Proof cent, nickel, dime, quarter, half dollar, and dollar	$90
(2007) AMERICAN LEGACY	
American Legacy Collection. 16 Proof coins for 2007: five state quarters; four Presidential dollars; Jamestown and Little Rock Central High School Desegregation silver dollars; Proof cent, nickel, dime, half dollar, and dollar	$140
(2007) LITTLE ROCK CENTRAL HIGH SCHOOL DESEGREGATION	
Little Rock Coin and Medal set. Uncirculated 2007-P silver dollar, bronze medal	$175
(2008) BALD EAGLE	
3-piece set. Proof clad half dollar, silver dollar, and gold $5	$400
Bald Eagle Coin and Medal Set. Uncirculated silver dollar, bronze medal	$70
"Young Collector" set. Uncirculated clad half dollar	$18
(2008) AMERICAN LEGACY	
American Legacy Collection. 15 Proof coins for 2008: cent, nickel, dime, half dollar, and dollar; five state quarters; four Presidential dollars; Bald Eagle silver dollar	$150
(2009) LOUIS BRAILLE	
Uncirculated silver dollar in tri-folded package	$50
(2009) ABRAHAM LINCOLN COIN AND CHRONICLES	
Four Proof 2009-S cents and Abraham Lincoln Proof silver dollar	$150
(2012) STAR-SPANGLED BANNER	
2-coin set. Proof silver dollar and gold $5	$450
(2013) 5-STAR GENERALS	
3-coin set. Proof clad half dollar, silver dollar, and gold $5	$600
Profile Collection. Uncirculated half dollar and silver dollar, replica of 1962 General MacArthur Congressional gold medal	$80

	Value
(2013) THEODORE ROOSEVELT COIN AND CHRONICLES	
Theodore Roosevelt Proof Presidential dollar, silver Presidential medal, National Wildlife Refuge System Centennial bronze medal, and Roosevelt print	$60
(2013) GIRL SCOUTS OF THE U.S.A.	
"Young Collector" set. Uncirculated silver dollar	$60
(2014) FRANKLIN D. ROOSEVELT COIN AND CHRONICLES	
Franklin D. Roosevelt Proof dime and Presidential dollar, bronze Presidential medal, silver Presidential medal, four stamps, information booklet	$60
(2014) NATIONAL BASEBALL HALL OF FAME	
"Young Collector" set. Uncirculated silver dollar	$50
(2014) AMERICAN $1 COIN AND CURRENCY SET	
2014-D Native American—Native Hospitality Enhanced Uncirculated dollar and $1 Federal Reserve Note	$30
(2015) HARRY S. TRUMAN COIN AND CHRONICLES	
Harry S. Truman Reverse Proof Presidential dollar, silver Presidential medal, one stamp, information booklet	$300
(2015) DWIGHT D. EISENHOWER COIN AND CHRONICLES	
Dwight D. Eisenhower Reverse Proof Presidential dollar, silver Presidential medal, one stamp, information booklet	$150
(2015) JOHN F. KENNEDY COIN AND CHRONICLES	
John F. Kennedy Reverse Proof Presidential dollar, silver Presidential medal, one stamp, information booklet	$100
(2015) LYNDON B. JOHNSON COIN AND CHRONICLES	
Lyndon B. Johnson Reverse Proof Presidential dollar, silver Presidential medal, one stamp, information booklet	$100
(2015) MARCH OF DIMES SPECIAL SILVER SET	
Proof dime and March of Dimes silver dollar, Reverse Proof dime	$80
(2015) AMERICAN $1 COIN AND CURRENCY SET	
2015-W Native American—Mohawk Ironworkers Enhanced Uncirculated dollar and $1 Federal Reserve Note	$25
(2016) NATIONAL PARK SERVICE 100TH ANNIVERSARY	
3-piece set. Proof clad half dollar, silver dollar, and gold $5	$550
(2016) RONALD REAGAN COIN AND CHRONICLES	
Ronald Reagan Reverse Proof Presidential dollar, 2016-W American Eagle silver Proof dollar, Ronald and Nancy Reagan bronze medal, engraved Ronald Reagan Presidential portrait, information booklet	$125
(2016) AMERICAN $1 COIN AND CURRENCY SET	
2016-W Native American—Code Talkers Enhanced Uncirculated dollar and $1 Federal Reserve Note	$25
(2017) BOYS TOWN CENTENNIAL	
3-piece set. Proof clad half dollar, silver dollar, and gold $5	$460
(2018) BREAST CANCER AWARENESS COIN AND STAMP SET	
Breast Cancer Awareness commemorative Proof half dollar and Proof silver Breast Cancer Awareness stamp	$100
(2018) WORLD WAR I CENTENNIAL SILVER DOLLAR AND AIR SERVICE MEDAL SET	
World War I Centennial commemorative Proof silver dollar and Proof silver Air Service medal	$100
(2018) WORLD WAR I CENTENNIAL SILVER DOLLAR AND ARMY MEDAL SET	
World War I Centennial commemorative Proof silver dollar and Proof silver Army medal	$100
(2018) WORLD WAR I CENTENNIAL SILVER DOLLAR AND COAST GUARD MEDAL SET	
World War I Centennial commemorative Proof silver dollar and Proof silver Coast Guard medal	$100
(2018) WORLD WAR I CENTENNIAL SILVER DOLLAR AND MARINE CORPS MEDAL SET	
World War I Centennial commemorative Proof silver dollar and Proof silver Marine Corps medal	$100
(2018) WORLD WAR I CENTENNIAL SILVER DOLLAR AND NAVY MEDAL SET	
World War I Centennial commemorative Proof silver dollar and Proof silver Navy medal	$100

Proof and Mint Sets
1936 to Date
AN OVERVIEW OF PROOF AND MINT SETS
PROOF COINS AND SETS

A Proof is a specimen coin struck for presentation, souvenir, exhibition, or numismatic purposes. Before 1968, Proofs were made only at the Philadelphia Mint, except in a few rare instances in which presentation pieces were struck at branch mints. Today Proofs are made at the San Francisco and West Point mints.

The term *Proof* refers not to the condition of a coin, but to its method of manufacture. Regular-production coins (struck for circulation) in Mint State have coruscating, frosty luster; soft details; and minor imperfections. A Proof coin can usually be distinguished by its sharpness of detail, high wire edge, and extremely brilliant, mirrorlike surface. All Proofs are originally sold by the Mint at a premium.

Very few Proof coins were made prior to 1856. Because of their rarity and infrequent sales, they are not all listed in the regular edition of the *Guide Book of United States Coins*. However, here, in the *Deluxe Edition*, you will find them listed individually within their respective denominations.

Frosted Proofs were issued prior to 1936 and starting again in the late 1970s. These have a brilliant, mirrorlike field with contrasting dull or frosted design.

Matte Proofs have a granular, "sandblast" surface instead of the mirror finish. Matte Proof cents, nickels, and gold coins were issued from 1908 to 1916; a few 1921 and 1922 silver dollars and a 1998-S half dollar were also struck in this manner.

Brilliant Proofs have been issued from 1936 to date. These have a uniformly brilliant, mirrorlike surface and sharp, high-relief details.

Reverse Proofs were first struck for bullion coins in 2006, and regularly denominated, silver-struck coins have also been made with this finish since 2014. As their name implies, the devices, not the field, have a brilliant, mirrorlike finish, while the field has a matte finish.

"Prooflike" coins are occasionally seen. These are examples struck from dies that were lightly polished, often inadvertently during the removal of lines, contact marks, and other marks in the fields. In other instances, such as with certain New Orleans gold coins of the 1850s, the dies were polished in the machine shop of the mint. They are not true Proofs, but may have most of the characteristics of a Proof coin and generally command a premium. Collectors should beware of coins that have been buffed to look like Proofs; magnification will reveal polishing lines and loss of detail.

After a lapse of some 20 years, Proof coins were struck at the Philadelphia Mint from 1936 to 1942, inclusive. During these years the Mint offered Proof coins to collectors for individual sale, rather than in officially packaged sets, as such.

In 1942, when the composition of the five-cent piece was changed from copper-nickel to copper-silver-manganese, there were two Proof types of this denomination available to collectors.

The striking of all Proof coins was temporarily suspended from 1943 through 1949, and again from 1965 through 1967; during the latter period, Special Mint Sets were struck (see page 1202). Proof sets were resumed in 1968.

Sets from 1936 through 1972 included the cent, nickel, dime, quarter, and half dollar; from 1973 through 1981 the dollar was also included, and again from 2000 on. Regular Proof sets issued from 1982 to 1998 contain the cent through the half dollar. Specially packaged Prestige sets containing commemorative coins were sold from 1983 through 1997 at an additional premium. From 1999 to 2009, sets contain five different Statehood or Territorial quarters, and from 2010 to 2021, different National Parks quarters. In 1999 Proof dollars were sold separately. Four-piece Presidential dollar sets have been issued since 2007.

As part of a memorial John F. Kennedy half dollar set released in 2014, Reverse Proofs struck in silver at West Point were introduced. The Philadelphia mint first struck Reverse Proofs in 2015, also in silver, for inclusion in the March of Dimes commemorative set. Additionally, Coin and Chronicles sets of 2015 include Philadelphia-struck Reverse Proofs of the Presidential dollars of the year.

With the recent State and Territorial quarters programs, as well as the ongoing National Park quarters and Presidential dollars programs, the U.S. Mint has offered Proof sets featuring each of the designs issued for a particular year.

From time to time the Mint issues special Proof sets. One recent example is the four-piece 2009-S Lincoln Bicentennial set, which included each of the special cent designs issued that year, but coined in 95% copper (the Lincoln cent's original 1909 alloy).

Collectors are encouraged to consult David W. Lange's *Guide Book of Modern United States Proof Coin Sets* for detailed coverage and illustrations of Proof sets from 1936 to date.

HOW MODERN PROOF COINS ARE MADE

Selected dies are inspected for perfection and are highly polished and cleaned. They are again wiped clean or polished after every 15 to 25 impressions and are replaced frequently to avoid imperfections from wear. Coinage blanks for Proof coins are polished and cleaned to ensure high quality in striking. They are then hand fed into the coinage press one at a time, each blank receiving two or more blows from the dies to bring up sharp, high-relief details. The coinage operation is done at slow speed with extra pressure. Finished Proofs are individually inspected and are handled with gloves or tongs. They also receive a final inspection by packers before being sonically sealed in special plastic cases.

MINT SETS

Official Uncirculated Mint sets are specially packaged by the government for sale to collectors. They contain Uncirculated examples of each year's coins for every denomination issued from each mint. Before 2005, the coins were the same as those normally intended for circulation and were not minted with any special consideration for quality. From 2005 to 2010, however, Mint sets were made with a satin finish rather than the traditional Uncirculated luster. As in the past, coins struck only as Proofs are not included.

Uncirculated Mint sets sold by the Treasury from 1947 through 1958 contained two examples of each regular-issue coin. These were packaged in cardboard holders that did not protect the coins from tarnish. Nicely preserved early sets generally command a 10 to 20% premium above average values. Since 1959, sets have been sealed in protective plastic envelopes.

Privately assembled Mint sets, and Souvenir sets produced for sale at the Philadelphia or Denver mints for special occasions, are valued according to the individual pieces they contain. Only the official, government-packaged full sets are included in the following list. No Mint Sets were produced in 1950, 1982, or 1983, though Souvenir sets were sold in the latter two years (see the final section of this overview).

From time to time the Mint issues special Mint sets. One recent example is the 1996-P-D Mint set, which also included a 1996-W dime (released only in those sets).

SPECIAL MINT SETS

In mid-1964 the Treasury department announced that the Mint would not offer Proof sets or Mint sets the following year. This was prompted by a nationwide shortage of circulating coins, which was wrongly blamed on coin collectors.

In 1966 the San Francisco Assay Office began striking coins dated 1965, for inclusion in so-called United States Special Mint Sets. These were issued in pliofilm packaging similar to that of recent Proof sets. The coins in early 1965 Special Mint Sets are semi-brilliant or satiny (distinctive, but not equal in quality to Proofs); the coins in later 1965 sets feature very brilliant fields (but again not reaching Proof brilliance).

The San Francisco Assay Office started striking 1966-dated coins in August of that year, and its Special Mint Sets were packaged in rigid, sonically sealed plastic holders. The coins were struck once on unpolished planchets, unlike Proof coins (which are struck at least twice on polished planchets). Also unlike Proofs, the SMS coins were allowed to come into contact with each other during their production, which accounts for minor contact marks and abrasions. To achieve a brilliant finish, Mint technicians overpolished the coinage dies. The result was a tradeoff: most of the coins have prooflike brilliance, but many are missing polished-off design details, such as Frank Gasparro's initials on the half dollar.

All 1967-dated coinage was struck in that calendar year. Nearly all SMS coins of 1967 have fully brilliant, prooflike finishes. This brilliance was achieved without overpolishing the dies, resulting in coins that approach the quality of true Proofs. Sales of the 1967 sets were lackluster, however. The popularity of coin collecting had dropped from its peak in 1964. Also, collectors and speculators did not anticipate much secondary-market profit from the sets, which had an issue price of $4.00, compared to $2.10 for a 1964 Proof set. As a result, fewer collectors bought multiples of the 1967 sets, and today they are generally worth more than those of 1965 and 1966.

Similar SMS coins dated 1964 exist as single pieces and in sets. Like the 1965 through 1967 SMS coins, they have a semi-brilliant or satiny finish but are not equal in quality to Proofs. They are referred to as SP (Special Strike) coins and command much higher prices than their regular SMS counterparts.

SOUVENIR SETS

Uncirculated Souvenir sets were packaged and sold in gift shops at the Philadelphia and Denver mints in 1982 and 1983 in place of the "official Mint sets," which were not made in those years. A bronze Mint medal is packaged with each set. Similar sets were also made in other years.

1936 Proof Set
Liberty Walking half dollar, Washington quarter dollar, Mercury or Winged Liberty dime, Buffalo nickel, and Lincoln cent with Wheat Ears reverse.

1938 Proof Set
Buffalo nickel replaced with the new Jefferson nickel.

1950 Proof Set
*There was a seven-year hiatus (1943–1949) before Proof sets were issued again after
World War II. By 1950 the Liberty Walking half dollar had been replaced by the Franklin half
dollar (introduced 1948), and the Mercury dime by the Roosevelt dime (introduced 1946).*

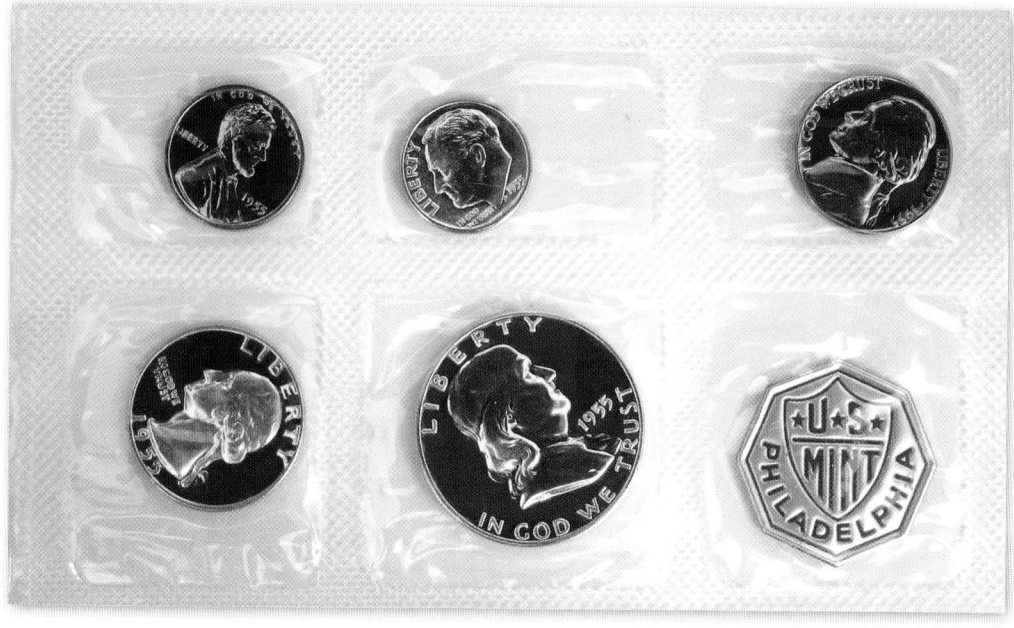

1955 Proof Set
*Issued in traditional individual envelopes, or in the new pliofilm package
(pictured), with a Philadelphia Mint embossed paper seal with a metallic finish.*

MODERN PROOF SETS (1936 TO DATE)

	Mintage	Issue Price	Face Value	Current Value
1936	3,837	$1.89	$0.91	$6,500
1937	5,542	$1.89	$0.91	$2,850
1938	8,045	$1.89	$0.91	$1,200
1939	8,795	$1.89	$0.91	$1,150
1940	11,246	$1.89	$0.91	$975
1941	15,287	$1.89	$0.91	$875
1942, Both nickels	21,120	$1.89	$0.96	$1,000
1942, One nickel	(a)	$1.89	$0.91	$875

a. Included in 1942, Both nickels, mintage figure.

	Mintage	Issue Price	Face Value	Current Value
1950	51,386	$2.10	$0.91	$575
1951	57,500	$2.10	$0.91	$575
1952	81,980	$2.10	$0.91	$240
1953	128,800	$2.10	$0.91	$225
1954	233,300	$2.10	$0.91	$145
1955, Box pack	378,200	$2.10	$0.91	$125
1955, Flat pack	(b)	$2.10	$0.91	$165
1956	669,384	$2.10	$0.91	$80
1957	1,247,952	$2.10	$0.91	$37
1958	875,652	$2.10	$0.91	$36
1959	1,149,291	$2.10	$0.91	$34
1960, With Large Date cent	1,691,602	$2.10	$0.91	$37
1960, With Small Date cent	(c)	$2.10	$0.91	$40
1961	3,028,244	$2.10	$0.91	$30
1962	3,218,019	$2.10	$0.91	$30
1963	3,075,645	$2.10	$0.91	$30
1964	3,950,762	$2.10	$0.91	$30
1968-S	3,041,506	$5	$0.91	$8
1968-S, With No S dime	(d)	$5	$0.91	$15,000
1969-S	2,934,631	$5	$0.91	$8
1970-S	2,632,810	$5	$0.91	$12
1970-S, With Small Date cent	(e)	$5	$0.91	$90
1970-S, With No S dime *(estimated mintage: 2,200)*	(e)	$5	$0.91	$950
1971-S	3,220,733	$5	$0.91	$4
1971-S, With No S nickel *(estimated mintage: 1,655)*	(f)	$5	$0.91	$1,250
1972-S	3,260,996	$5	$0.91	$5
1973-S	2,760,339	$7	$1.91	$9
1974-S	2,612,568	$7	$1.91	$11
1975-S, With 1976 quarter, half, and dollar	2,845,450	$7	$1.91	$10
1975-S, With No S dime	(g)	$7	$1.91	$250,000
1976-S	4,149,730	$7	$1.91	$8
1976-S, Silver clad, 3-piece set	3,998,621	$15	$1.75	$25
1977-S	3,251,152	$9	$1.91	$8
1978-S	3,127,781	$9	$1.91	$8
1979-S, Type 1	3,677,175	$9	$1.91	$8
1979-S, Type 2	(h)	$9	$1.91	$55
1980-S	3,554,806	$10	$1.91	$5
1981-S, Type 1	4,063,083	$11	$1.91	$6
1981-S, Type 2 (all six coins in set)	(i)	$11	$1.91	$275
1982-S	3,857,479	$11	$0.91	$5
1983-S	3,138,765	$11	$0.91	$5
1983-S, With No S dime	(j)	$11	$0.91	$750
1983-S, Prestige set (Olympic dollar)	140,361	$59	$1.91	$50
1984-S	2,748,430	$11	$0.91	$5
1904-S, Prestige set (Olympic dollar)	316,680	$59	$1.91	$30
1985-S	3,362,821	$11	$0.91	$4
1986-S	2,411,180	$11	$0.91	$7
1986-S, Prestige set (Statue of Liberty half, dollar)	599,317	$48.50	$2.41	$25

b. Included in 1955, Box pack, mintage figure. **c.** Included in 1960, With Large Date cent, mintage figure. **d.** Included in 1968-S mintage figure. **e.** Included in 1970-S mintage figure. **f.** Included in 1971-S mintage figure. **g.** Included in 1975-S, With 1976 quarter, half, and dollar, mintage figure. **h.** Included in 1979-S, Type 1, mintage figure. **i.** Included in 1981-S, Type 1, mintage figure. **j.** Included in 1983-S mintage figure.

	Mintage	Issue Price	Face Value	Current Value
1987-S	3,792,233	$11	$0.91	$5
1987-S, Prestige set (Constitution dollar)	435,495	$45	$1.91	$25
1988-S	3,031,287	$11	$0.91	$6
1988-S, Prestige set (Olympic dollar)	231,661	$45	$1.91	$35
1989-S	3,009,107	$11	$0.91	$5
1989-S, Prestige set (Congressional half, dollar)	211,807	$45	$2.41	$35
1990-S	2,793,433	$11	$0.91	$6
1990-S, With No S cent	3,555	$11	$0.91	$4,250
1990-S, With No S cent (Prestige set)	(k)	$45	$1.91	$4,750
1990-S, Prestige set (Eisenhower dollar)	506,126	$45	$1.91	$30
1991-S	2,610,833	$11	$0.91	$5
1991-S, Prestige set (Mt. Rushmore half, dollar)	256,954	$59	$2.41	$40
1992-S	2,675,618	$11	$0.91	$5
1992-S, Prestige set (Olympic half, dollar)	183,293	$56	$2.41	$50
1992-S, Silver	1,009,586	$11	$0.91	$20
1992-S, Silver Premier set	308,055	$37	$0.91	$25
1993-S	2,409,394	$12.50	$0.91	$6
1993-S, Prestige set (Bill of Rights half, dollar)	224,045	$57	$2.41	$45
1993-S, Silver	570,213	$21	$0.91	$30
1993-S, Silver Premier set	191,140	$37.50	$0.91	$40
1994-S	2,308,701	$12.50	$0.91	$5
1994-S, Prestige set (World Cup half, dollar)	175,893	$57	$2.41	$40
1994-S, Silver	636,009	$21	$0.91	$30
1994-S, Silver Premier set	149,320	$37.50	$0.91	$40
1995-S	2,010,384	$12.50	$0.91	$12
1995-S, Prestige set (Civil War half, dollar)	107,112	$57	$2.41	$100
1995-S, Silver	549,878	$21	$0.91	$65
1995-S, Silver Premier set	130,107	$37.50	$0.91	$65
1996-S	1,695,244	$12.50	$0.91	$8
1996-S, Prestige set (Olympic half, dollar)	55,000	$57	$2.41	$375
1996-S, Silver	623,655	$21	$0.91	$30
1996-S, Silver Premier set	151,366	$37.50	$0.91	$35
1997-S	1,975,000	$12.50	$0.91	$9
1997-S, Prestige set (Botanic dollar)	80,000	$57	$1.91	$65
1997-S, Silver	605,473	$21	$0.91	$40
1997-S, Silver Premier set	136,205	$37.50	$0.91	$40
1998-S	2,086,507	$12.50	$0.91	$12
1998-S, Silver	638,134	$21	$0.91	$25
1998-S, Silver Premier set	240,658	$37.50	$0.91	$30
1999-S, 9-piece set	2,543,401	$19.95	$1.91	$10
1999-S, 5-piece quarter set	1,169,958	$13.95	$1.25	$4
1999-S, Silver 9-piece set	804,565	$31.95	$1.91	$115
2000-S, 10-piece set	3,082,572	$19.95	$2.91	$6
2000-S, 5-piece quarter set	937,600	$13.95	$1.25	$3
2000-S, Silver 10-piece set	965,421	$31.95	$2.91	$40
2001-S, 10-piece set	2,294,909	$19.95	$2.91	$12
2001-S, 5-piece quarter set	799,231	$13.95	$1.25	$5
2001-S, Silver 10-piece set	889,697	$31.95	$2.91	$50
2002-S, 10-piece set	2,319,766	$19.95	$2.91	$8
2002-S, 5-piece quarter set	764,479	$13.95	$1.25	$4
2002-S, Silver 10-piece set	892,229	$31.95	$2.91	$40

k. Included in 1990-S mintage figure.

	Mintage	Issue Price	Face Value	Current Value
2003-S, 10-piece set	2,172,684	$19.95	$2.91	$7
2003-S, 5-piece quarter set	1,235,832	$13.95	$1.25	$3
2003-S, Silver 10-piece set	1,125,755	$31.95	$2.91	$35
2004-S, 11-piece set	1,789,488	$22.95	$2.96	$12
2004-S, 5-piece quarter set	951,196	$15.95	$1.25	$4
2004-S, Silver 11-piece set	1,175,934	$37.95	$2.96	$35
2004-S, Silver 5-piece quarter set	593,852	$23.95	$1.25	$25
2005-S, 11-piece set	2,275,000	$22.95	$2.96	$5
2005-S, 5-piece quarter set	987,960	$15.95	$1.25	$3
2005-S, Silver 11-piece set	1,069,679	$37.95	$2.96	$35
2005-S, Silver 5-piece quarter set	608,970	$23.95	$1.25	$20
2006-S, 10-piece set	2,000,428	$22.95	$2.91	$9
2006-S, 5-piece quarter set	882,000	$15.95	$1.25	$3
2006-S, Silver 10-piece set	1,054,008	$37.95	$2.91	$35
2006-S, Silver 5-piece quarter set	531,000	$23.95	$1.25	$20
2007-S, 14-piece set	1,702,116	$26.95	$6.91	$15
2007-S, 5-piece quarter set	672,662	$13.95	$1.25	$6
2007-S, 4-piece Presidential set	1,285,972	$14.95	$4	$6
2007-S, Silver 14-piece set	875,050	$44.95	$6.91	$40
2007-S, Silver 5-piece quarter set	672,662	$25.95	$1.25	$22
2008-S, 14-piece set	1,405,674	$26.95	$6.91	$30
2008-S, 5-piece quarter set	672,438	$13.95	$1.25	$45
2008-S, 4-piece Presidential set	869,202	$14.95	$4	$12
2008-S, Silver 14-piece set	763,887	$44.95	$6.91	$45
2008-S, Silver 5-piece quarter set	429,021	$25.95	$1.25	$20
2009-S, 18-piece set	1,482,502	$29.95	$7.19	$25
2009-S, 6-piece quarter set	630,976	$14.95	$1.50	$5
2009-S, 4-piece Presidential set	629,585	$14.95	$4	$9
2009-S, Silver 18-piece set	697,365	$52.95	$7.19	$55
2009-S, Silver 6-piece quarter set	299,183	$29.95	$1.50	$25
2009-S, 4-piece Lincoln Bicentennial set	201,107	$7.95	$0.04	$10
2010-S, 14-piece set	1,103,815	$31.95	$6.91	$35
2010-S, 5-piece quarter set	276,296	$14.95	$1.25	$13
2010-S, 4-piece Presidential set	535,397	$15.95	$4	$20
2010-S, Silver 14-piece set	585,401	$56.95	$6.91	$60
2010-S, Silver 5-piece quarter set	274,034	$32.95	$1.25	$25
2011-S, 14-piece set	1,098,835	$31.95	$6.91	$40
2011-S, 5-piece quarter set	152,302	$14.95	$1.25	$15
2011-S, 4-piece Presidential set	299,853	$19.95	$4	$30
2011-S, Silver 14-piece set	574,175	$67.95	$6.91	$75
2011-S, Silver 5-piece quarter set	147,901	$39.95	$1.25	$30
2012-S, 14-piece set	794,002	$31.95	$6.91	$150
2012-S, 5-piece quarter set	148,498	$14.95	$1.25	$15
2012-S, 4-piece Presidential set	249,265	$18.95	$4	$80
2012-S, Silver 14-piece set	395,443	$67.95	$6.91	$250
2012-S, Silver 8-piece Limited Edition set	44,952	$149.95	$2.85	$275
2012-S, Silver 5-piece quarter set	162,448	$41.95	$1.25	$30
2013-S, 14-piece set	802,460	$31.95	$6.91	$35
2013-S, 5-piece quarter set	128,377	$14.95	$1.25	$15
2013-S, 4-piece Presidential set	266,677	$18.95	$4	$25
2013-S, Silver 14-piece set	419,720	$67.95	$6.91	$75
2013-S, Silver 8-piece Limited Edition set	47,791	$139.95	$2.85	$150
2013-S, Silver 5-piece quarter set	138,451	$41.95	$1.25	$30

	Mintage	Issue Price	Face Value	Current Value
2014-S, 14-piece set	680,977	$31.95	$6.91	$35
2014-S, 5-piece quarter set	109,423	$14.95	$1.25	$18
2014-S, 4-piece Presidential set	218,976	$18.95	$4	$25
2014-S, Silver 14-piece set	387,310	$67.95	$6.91	$60
2014-S, Silver 8-piece Limited Edition set	41,609	$139.95	$2.85	$150
2014-S, Silver 5-piece quarter set	103,311	$41.95	$1.25	$40
2015-S, 14-piece set	662,854	$32.95	$6.91	$35
2015-S, 5-piece quarter set	99,466	$14.95	$1.25	$18
2015-S, 4-piece Presidential set	222,068	$18.95	$4	$25
2015-S, Silver 14-piece set	387,460	$53.95	$6.91	$60
2015-S, Silver 5-piece quarter set	103,369	$31.95	$1.25	$40
2016-S, 13-piece set	595,184	$31.95	$5.91	$35
2016-S, 5-piece quarter set	91,754	$14.95	$1.25	$18
2016-S, 3-piece Presidential set	231,559	$17.95	$3	$25
2016-S, Silver 13-piece set	369,849	$52.95	$5.91	$60
2016-S, Silver 8-piece Limited Edition set	49,407	$139.95	$2.85	$150
2016-S, Silver 5-piece quarter set	95,649	$31.95	$1.25	$40
2017-S, 10-piece set	544,759	$26.95	$2.91	$29
2017-S, 5-piece quarter set	85,238	$14.95	$1.25	$18
2017-S, Silver 10-piece set	333,547	$47.95	$2.91	$48
2017-S, Silver 5-piece quarter set	84,258	$31.95	$1.25	$40
2017-S, Silver 8-piece Limited Edition set	48,906	$139.95	$2.85	$150
2018-S, 10-piece set		$27,95		
2018-S, 5-piece quarter set		$15.95		
2018-S, Silver 10-piece set				
2018-S, Silver 5-piece quarter set		$33.95		
2018-S, 50th Anniversary Silver 10-piece Reverse Proof set				
2018-S, Silver 8-piece Limited Edition set				

Uncirculated Mint Sets (1947 to Date)

	Mintage	Issue Price	Face Value	Current Value
1947 P-D-S	5,000	$4.87	$4.46	$2,250
1948 P-D-S	6,000	$4.92	$4.46	$1,450
1949 P-D-S	5,000	$5.45	$4.96	$1,750
1951 P-D-S	8,654	$6.75	$5.46	$1,450
1952 P-D-S	11,499	$6.14	$5.46	$1,350
1953 P-D-S	15,538	$6.14	$5.46	$1,000
1954 P-D-S	25,599	$6.19	$5.46	$650
1955 P-D-S	49,656	$3.57	$2.86	$400
1956 P-D	45,475	$3.34	$2.64	$450
1957 P-D	34,324	$4.40	$3.64	$675
1958 P-D	50,314	$4.43	$3.64	$425
1959 P-D	187,000	$2.40	$1.82	$55
1960 P-D	260,485	$2.40	$1.82	$45
1961 P-D	223,704	$2.40	$1.82	$45
1962 P-D	385,285	$2.40	$1.82	$45
1963 P-D	606,612	$2.40	$1.82	$40
1964 P-D	1,008,108	$2.40	$1.82	$30
1968 P-D-S	2,105,128	$2.50	$1.33	$8
1969 P-D-S	1,817,392	$2.50	$1.33	$8
1970 P-D-S, With Large Date cent	2,038,134	$2.50	$1.33	$20
1970 P-D-S, Small Date cent	(a)	$2.50	$1.33	$55

a. Included in 1970 P-D-S, With Large Date cent, mintage figure.

	Mintage	Issue Price	Face Value	Current Value
1971 P-D-S (no Ike dollar)	2,193,396	$3.50	$1.83	$5
1972 P-D-S (no Ike dollar)	2,750,000	$3.50	$1.83	$5
1973 P-D-S	1,767,691	$6	$3.83	$12
1974 P-D-S	1,975,981	$6	$3.83	$8
1975 P-D, With 1976 quarter, half, dollar	1,921,488	$6	$3.82	$10
1976, Silver clad, 3-piece set	4,908,319	$9	$1.75	$20
1976 P-D	1,892,513	$6	$3.82	$8
1977 P-D	2,006,869	$7	$3.82	$8
1978 P-D	2,162,609	$7	$3.82	$8
1979 P-D (b)	2,526,000	$8	$3.82	$8
1980 P-D-S	2,815,066	$9	$4.82	$8
1981 P-D-S	2,908,145	$11	$4.82	$10
1984 P-D	1,832,857	$7	$1.82	$5
1985 P-D	1,710,571	$7	$1.82	$5
1986 P-D	1,153,536	$7	$1.82	$8
1987 P-D	2,890,758	$7	$1.82	$5
1988 P-D	1,646,204	$7	$1.82	$5
1989 P-D	1,987,915	$7	$1.82	$5
1990 P-D	1,809,184	$7	$1.82	$5
1991 P-D	1,352,101	$7	$1.82	$5
1992 P-D	1,500,143	$7	$1.82	$5
1993 P-D	1,297,431	$8	$1.82	$5
1994 P-D	1,234,813	$8	$1.82	$5
1995 P-D	1,038,787	$8	$1.82	$5
1996 P-D, Plus 1996-W dime	1,457,949	$8	$1.92	$20
1997 P-D	950,473	$8	$1.82	$5
1998 P-D	1,187,325	$8	$1.82	$5
1999 P-D (18 pieces) (c)	1,243,867	$14.95	$3.82	$10
2000 P-D (20 pieces)	1,490,160	$14.95	$5.82	$10
2001 P-D (20 pieces)	1,116,915	$14.95	$5.82	$10
2002 P-D (20 pieces)	1,139,388	$14.95	$5.82	$10
2003 P-D (20 pieces)	1,001,532	$14.95	$5.82	$10
2004 P-D (22 pieces)	842,507	$16.95	$5.92	$10
2005 P-D (22 pieces)	1,160,000	$16.95	$5.92	$10
2006 P-D (20 pieces)	847,361	$16.95	$5.82	$10
2007 P-D (28 pieces)	895,628	$22.95	$13.82	$20
2008 P-D (28 pieces)	745,464	$22.95	$13.82	$50
2009 P-D (36 pieces)	784,614	$27.95	$14.38	$25
2010 P-D (28 pieces)	583,897	$31.95	$13.82	$25
2011 P-D (28 pieces)	533,529	$31.95	$13.82	$25
2012 P-D (28 pieces)	392,224	$27.95	$13.82	$80
2013 P-D (28 pieces)	376,844	$27.95	$13.82	$25
2014 P-D (28 pieces)	327,969	$27.95	$13.82	$25
2015 P-D (28 pieces)	314,029	$28.95	$13.82	$25
2016 P-D (26 pieces)	296,579	$26.95	$11.82	$27
2017 P-D (20 pieces)	271,686	$20.95	$5.82	$25
2017S, 225th Anniversary Enhanced Uncirculated Set (10 pieces)	210,402	$29.95	$2.91	$30
2018 P-D (20 pieces)			$5.82	

b. S-mint dollar not included. **c.** Dollar not included.

SPECIAL MINT SETS (1965–1967)

	Mintage	Issue Price	Face Value	Current Value
1965	2,360,000	$4	$0.91	$12
1966	2,261,583	$4	$0.91	$12
1967	1,863,344	$4	$0.91	$12

See page 1202 for details on the similar 1964 Special Strike coins. Values for these coins are approximately $13,000 for each denomination.

SOUVENIR SETS (1982–1983)

	Issue Price	Face Value	Current Value
1982-P	$4	$0.91	$60
1982-D	$4	$0.91	$60
1983-P	$4	$0.91	$80
1983-D	$4	$0.91	$80

POPULAR DIE VARIETIES FROM MINT SETS

As noted in the *Cherrypickers' Guide to Rare Die Varieties*, "Beginning with those modern Mint sets from 1947 . . . there are many years of one or the other that are absent of a significant variety. Not all of the known varieties are significant." The following are some popular die varieties from Mint sets; for more information and additional examples, consult the *Cherrypickers' Guide*.

DIE VARIETIES IN MINT SETS

Year	Denomination	Variety	Year	Denomination	Variety
1949	5¢	D/S—over mintmark (a)	1970	50¢	D—doubled-die reverse (d)
1954	25¢	doubled-die reverse (b)	1971	5¢	D/D—repunched mintmark
1960	5¢	(P)—doubled-die obverse (c)	1971	10¢	D/D—repunched mintmark
1960	25¢	(P)—doubled-die obverse (c)	1971	10¢	D—doubled-die reverse
1961	50¢	D/D—repunched mintmark	1971	50¢	D—doubled-die obverse
1963	10¢	(P)—doubled-die obverse	1971	50¢	D—doubled-die reverse
1963	25¢	(P)—doubled-die obverse	1972	1¢	(P)—doubled-die obverse
1963	25¢	(P)—doubled-die reverse	1972	5¢	D—doubled-die reverse
1963	50¢	(P)—doubled-die obverse	1972	50¢	D—doubled-die reverse
1963	50¢	(P)—doubled-die reverse	1973	50¢	(P)—doubled-die obverse
1968	10¢	(P)—doubled-die obverse	1973	50¢	D—doubled-die obverse
1968	25¢	D—doubled-die reverse	1974	50¢	D—doubled-die obverse
1969	5¢	D/D—repunched mintmark	1981	5¢	D—doubled-die reverse
1969	10¢	D/D—repunched mintmark	1984	50¢	D/D—repunched mintmark
1969	25¢	D/D—repunched mintmark	1987	5¢	D/D—repunched mintmark
1969	50¢	D—doubled-die reverse	1987	10¢	D/D—repunched mintmark
1970	1¢	D/D—repunched mintmark	1989	5¢	D—doubled-die reverse
1970	1¢	D—doubled-die obverse	1989	10¢	P—doubled-die reverse
1970	10¢	D—doubled-die reverse	1989	50¢	D/D—repunched mintmark
1970	25¢	D—doubled-die reverse	1991	5¢	D—doubled-die obverse

a. Although known, most have already been removed from their Mint-packaged sets. **b.** Small Date. **c.** Found in sets labeled as Small Date. **d.** Small Date.

U.S. Mint Bullion Coins

AN OVERVIEW OF U.S. MINT BULLION COINS

The United States' bullion-coin program was launched in 1986. Since then, American Eagle and other silver, gold, platinum, and palladium coins have provided investors with convenient vehicles to add physical bullion to their portfolios. They also have value as numismatic collectibles.

In addition to regular investment-grade strikes, the U.S. Mint offers its bullion coins in various collectible formats. Proofs are created in a specialized minting process: a polished coin blank is manually fed into a press fitted with special dies; the blank is struck multiple times "so the softly frosted yet detailed images seem to float above a mirror-like field" (per Mint literature); a white-gloved inspector scrutinizes the coin; and it is then sealed in a protective plastic capsule and mounted in a satin-lined velvet presentation case along with a certificate of authenticity. Members of the public can purchase Proofs directly from the Mint, at fixed prices.

Burnished (called Uncirculated by the Mint) coins are also sold directly to the public. These coins have the same design as other bullion coins, but are distinguished from regular bullion strikes by a W mintmark (for West Point), and by their distinctive finish (the result of burnished coin blanks). Their blanks are individually fed by hand into specially adapted coining presses. After striking, each Burnished specimen is carefully inspected, encapsulated in plastic, and packaged in a satin-lined velvet presentation case, along with a certificate of authenticity.

In recent years the Mint has also broadened its collectible bullion offerings with Reverse Proof and Enhanced Uncirculated formats. Various bullion coins have been offered in collector sets, as well.

Since the inception of the bullion-coin program in 1986, the Mint has marked several anniversaries with special issues and sets.

Regular bullion-strike coins are bought in bulk by Mint-authorized purchasers (wholesalers, brokerage companies, precious-metal firms, coin dealers, and participating banks). These authorized purchasers in turn sell them to secondary retailers, who then make them available to the general public. Authorized purchasers are required to meet financial and professional criteria, attested to by an internationally accepted accounting firm. They must be an experienced and established market-maker in bullion coins; provide a liquid two-way market for the coins; be audited annually; have an established and broad retail-customer base for distribution; and have a tangible net worth of $5 million (for American Silver Eagles) or $25 million (for gold and platinum American Eagles). Authorized purchasers of gold, platinum, and palladium must have sold 100,000 or more ounces of those metals (bullion, or bullion coins) in any 12-month period since 1990. For gold, the initial order must be for at least 1,000 ounces, with reorders in increments of 500 ounces; for platinum/palladium, 100 ounces for both the initial order and reorders; and for silver, a minimum order of 25,000 ounces. For American Eagles, an authorized purchaser's cost is based on the market value of the bullion, plus a premium to cover minting, distribution, and other overhead expenses. For ASEs, the premium is $2 per coin. For gold, the premiums are 3% (for the one-ounce coin), 5% (1/2 ounce), 7% (1/4 ounce), and 9% (1/10 ounce). For platinum the premium is 4% for the one-ounce coin; for palladium, 6.25%.

Note that the U.S. Mint does not release bullion mintage data on a regular basis; the numbers given herein reflect the most recently available official data.

The listed values of uncertified, average Mint State coins have been based on bullion prices of silver ($17 per ounce), gold ($1,300), platinum ($999), and palladium ($1,050).

For more detailed coverage of these coins, readers are directed to *American Silver Eagles: A Guide to the U.S. Bullion Coin Program* (Mercanti), *American Gold and Platinum Eagles: A Guide to the U.S. Bullion Coin Programs* (Moy), and *American Gold and Silver: U.S. Mint Collector and Investor Coins and Medals, Bicentennial to Date* (Tucker).

AMERICAN SILVER EAGLES (1986 TO DATE)

Designers: *Adolph A. Weinman (obverse) and John Mercanti (reverse).*
Weight: *31.101 grams.* **Composition:** *.9993 silver, .0007 copper (net weight 1 oz. pure silver).*
Diameter: *40.6 mm.* **Edge:** *Reeded.* **Mints:** *Philadelphia, San Francisco, and West Point.*

Regular Finish

Burnished Finish

Enhanced Uncirculated Finish
This special format incorporates elements with a brilliant mirrored finish, a light frosted finish, and a heavy frosted finish.

Reverse Lettering Style of 1986–2007
Note the lack of spur or stem at bottom right of U.

Reverse Lettering Style of 2008 to Date
Note the spur at bottom right of U.

Proof
Finish

Reverse
Proof Finish

History. The American Silver Eagle (face value $1, actual silver weight one ounce) is a legal-tender bullion coin with weight, content, and purity guaranteed by the federal government. It is one of the few silver coins allowed in individual retirement accounts (IRAs).The obverse design features Adolph A. Weinman's Liberty Walking, as used on the circulating half dollar of 1916 to 1947. Weinman's initials appear on the hem of Miss Liberty's gown. The reverse design, by John Mercanti, is a heraldic eagle.

From 1986 to 1999 all American Silver Eagles were struck at the Philadelphia and San Francisco mints (with the exception of the 1995 West Point Proof). In 2000 they were struck at both Philadelphia (Proofs) and the U.S. Mint's West Point facility (bullion strikes). From 2001 to 2010, West Point was their sole producer (with one exception in 2006), making regular bullion strikes (without mintmarks) and Proof and "Burnished" specimens (with mintmarks). (The exception is the 2006 Reverse Proof, which was struck in Philadelphia.) In 2011, for the 25th anniversary of the American Eagle bullion program, the mints at West Point, San Francisco, and Philadelphia were all put into production to make several collectible formats of the coins. Since 2012, West Point has been their main production mint, with Philadelphia and San Francisco helping when demand is high.

In addition to the individually listed coins, American Silver Eagles were issued in two 2006 "20th Anniversary" sets and in several other special bullion coin sets.

Striking and Sharpness. Striking is generally sharp. The key elements to check on the obverse are Miss Liberty's left hand, the higher parts and lines of her skirt, and her head. On the reverse, the eagle's breast is a main focal point.

Availability. The American Silver Eagle is one of the most popular silver-investment vehicles in the world. Between the bullion coins and various collectible formats, more than 400 million have been sold since 1986. The coins are readily available in the numismatic marketplace and from some banks, investment firms, and other non-numismatic channels.

MS-60 to 70 (Mint State). *Obverse and Reverse:* At MS-60, some abrasion and contact marks are evident on the higher design areas (Miss Liberty's left arm, her hand, and the areas of the skirt covering her left leg). Luster may be dull or lifeless at MS–60 to 62, but there should be deep frost at MS-63 and better, particularly in the lower-relief areas. At MS-65 and above, the luster should be full and rich. These guidelines are more academic than practical, as American Silver Eagles are not intended for circulation, and nearly all are in high Mint State grades.

PF-60 to 70 (Proof). *Obverse and Reverse:* Proofs that are extensively cleaned and have many hairlines are lower level, such as PF–60 to 62. Those with fewer hairlines or flaws are deemed PF–63 to 65. (These exist more in theory than actuality, as nearly all Proof ASEs have been maintained in their original high condition by collectors and investors.) Given the quality of modern U.S. Mint products, even PF–66 and 67 are unusually low levels for ASE Proofs.

AMERICAN SILVER EAGLES

	Mintage	MS / PF	MS-69 / PF-69	MS-70 / PF-70
1986 ‡ (a,b)	5,393,005	$40	$55	$800
1986-S, Proof	1,446,778	$60	$80	$500
1987 (a,c)	11,442,335	$25	$35	$1,700
1987-S, Proof	904,732	$60	$80	$800
1988 (a,d)	5,004,646	$28	$38	$2,500
1988-S, Proof	557,370	$60	$80	$550
1989 (a)	5,203,327	$28	$37	$1,500
1989-S, Proof	617,694	$60	$80	$325
1990 (a)	5,840,210	$28	$40	$1,500
1990-S, Proof	695,510	$60	$80	$250
1991 (a,e)	7,191,066	$28	$40	—
1991-S, Proof	511,925	$60	$80	$500
1992 (a,f)	5,540,068	$28	$40	$1,600
1992-S, Proof	498,654	$60	$80	$400
1993 (a,g)	6,763,762	$28	$40	$2,900
1993-P, Proof (h)	405,913	$90	$125	$1,500
1994 (a,i)	4,227,319	$38	$50	$4,000
1994-P, Proof ‡ (j)	372,168	$180	$195	$1,600
1995 (a)	4,672,051	$35	$47	$1,100
1995-P, Proof	438,511	$75	$90	$400
1995-W, Proof ‡ (k)	30,125	$3,800	$4,750	—
1996 ‡ (a,l)	3,603,386	$65	$100	—
1996-P, Proof	500,000	$75	$95	$450
1997 (a)	4,295,004	$32	$42	$900
1997-P, Proof	435,368	$80	$95	$500
1998 (a)	4,847,549	$30	$38	$1,700
1998-P, Proof	450,000	$65	$85	$250
1999 (a,m)	7,408,640	$30	$40	—
1999-P, Proof	549,769	$65	$85	$375
2000 (n,o)	9,239,132	$28	$38	$3,500
2000-P, Proof	600,000	$65	$75	$425
2001 (n)	9,001,711	$28	$37	$800
2001-W, Proof	746,398	$65	$80	$175
2002 (n)	10,539,026	$26	$30	$250
2002-W, Proof	647,342	$65	$80	$150
2003 (n)	8,495,008	$25	$32	$150
2003-W, Proof	747,831	$65	$80	$120
2004 (n)	8,882,754	$25	$32	$135
2004-W, Proof	801,602	$65	$80	$125
2005 (n)	8,891,025	$25	$32	$160
2005-W, Proof	816,663	$65	$80	$125

Note: For more information, consult *American Silver Eagles: A Guide to the U.S. Bullion Coin Program*, 3rd edition (Mercanti). MS values are for uncertified Mint State coins of average quality, in their complete original U.S. Mint packaging. PF values are for uncertified Proof coins of average quality, in their complete original U.S. Mint packaging. ‡ Ranked in the *100 Greatest U.S. Modern Coins*. **a.** Minted at Philadelphia, without mintmark. **b.** Auction: $1,028, MS-70, September 2015. **c.** Auction: $999, MS-70, August 2015. **d.** Auction: $1,704, MS-70, August 2015. **e.** Auction: $3,760, MS-70, August 2015. **f.** Auction: $1,528, MS-70, June 2015. **g.** Auction: $3,760, MS-70, June 2015. **h.** Auction: $1,528, PF-70UCam, March 2015. **i.** Auction: $4,700, MS-70, June 2015. **j.** Auction: $1,293, PF-70DCam, September 2015. **k.** Auction: $14,100, PF-70UCam, June 2015. **l.** Auction: $5,640, MS-70, August 2015. **m.** Auction: $4,935, MS-70, June 2015. **n.** Minted at West Point, without mintmark. **o.** Auction: $1,293, MS-70, July 2015.

| | Mintage | MS | MS-69 | MS-70 |
		PF	PF-69	PF-70
2006 (n)	10,676,522	$25	$32	$160
2006-W, Burnished (p)	468,020	$75	$85	$190
2006-W, Proof	1,092,477	$65	$80	$125
2006-P, Reverse Proof ‡ (q,r,s)	248,875	$160	$185	$325
2007 (n)	9,028,036	$25	$30	$95
2007-W, Burnished	621,333	$30	$38	$75
2007-W, Proof	821,759	$65	$80	$100
2008 (n)	20,583,000	$25	$30	$95
2008-W, Burnished	533,757	$48	$65	$100
2008-W, Burnished, Reverse of 2007 ‡ (t,u)	47,000	$450	$550	$1,250
2008-W, Proof	700,979	$65	$80	$100
2009 (n)	30,459,000	$24	$30	$95
2010 (n)	34,764,500	$24	$28	$85
2010-W, Proof (v)	849,861	$65	$80	$100
2011 (n,w)	40,020,000	$24	$28	$95
2011-W, Burnished	409,776	$38	$45	$115
2011-W, Proof	947,355	$65	$80	$100
2011-P, Reverse Proof (r,x)	99,882	$255	$280	$450
2011-S, Burnished (y)	99,882	$225	$275	$325
2012 (n,w)	33,742,500	$24	$29	$80
2012-W, Burnished	226,120	$65	$85	$100
2012-W, Proof	877,731	$65	$85	$95
2012-S, Proof	281,792	$75	$90	$165
2012-S, Reverse Proof (r)	224,935	$125	$140	$175
2013 (n,w)	42,675,000	$24	$28	$80
2013-W, Burnished	222,091	$50	$75	$95
2013-W, Enhanced Uncirculated	281,310	$90	$115	$150
2013-W, Proof	934,812	$65	$85	$95
2013-W, Reverse Proof	281,310	$115	$140	$145
2014 (n,w)	44,006,000	$24	$29	$80
2014-W, Burnished	256,169	$50	$75	$80
2014-W, Proof	944,757	$65	$80	$95
2015 (n,w)	47,000,000	$24	$29	$80
2015-W, Burnished	223,879	$50	$75	$80
2015-W, Proof	707,518	$65	$80	$100
2016 (n,w)	37,701,500	$24	$29	$80
2016-W, Burnished	57,028	$50	$75	$80
2016-W, Proof	34,499	$65	$80	$100
2017 (n,w)	18,065,500	$24	$29	$80
2017-W, Burnished	141,254	$50	$75	$80
2017-W, Proof	375,344	$65	$80	$100
2017-S, Proof (z)	75,000	$100	$150	$200

Note: For more information, consult *American Silver Eagles: A Guide to the U.S. Bullion Coin Program*, 3rd edition (Mercanti). MS values are for uncertified Mint State coins of average quality, in their complete original U.S. Mint packaging. PF values are for uncertified Proof coins of average quality, in their complete original U.S. Mint packaging. ‡ Ranked in the *100 Greatest U.S. Modern Coins*. **n.** Minted at West Point, without mintmark. **p.** In celebration of the 20th anniversary of the Bullion Coinage Program, in 2006 the W mintmark was used on bullion coins produced in sets at West Point. **q.** The 2006-P Reverse Proof coins were issued to mark the 20th anniversary of the Bullion Coinage Program. **r.** Reverse Proofs have brilliant devices, and their background fields are frosted (rather than the typical Proof format of frosted devices and mirror-like backgrounds). **s.** Auction: $329, PF-70, February 2015. **t.** Reverse dies of 2007 and earlier have a plain U in UNITED. Modified dies of 2008 and later have a small spur at the bottom right of the U. **u.** Auction: $940, MS-70, August 2015. **v.** The U.S. Mint did not strike any Proof American Silver Eagles in 2009. **w.** Minted at San Francisco, without mintmark. **x.** Auction: $376, PF-70, September 2015. **y.** Auction: $306, MS-70, October 2015. **z.** Issued in the 2017 Congratulations Set.

	Mintage	MS	MS-69	MS-70
		PF	PF-69	PF-70
2018 (n,w)		$24	$29	$80
2018-W, Burnished		$50	$75	$90
2018-W, Proof		$65	$80	$100

Note: For more information, consult *American Silver Eagles: A Guide to the U.S. Bullion Coin Program*, 3rd edition (Mercanti). MS values are for uncertified Mint State coins of average quality, in their complete original U.S. Mint packaging. PF values are for uncertified Proof coins of average quality, in their complete original U.S. Mint packaging. **n.** Minted at West Point, without mintmark. **w.** Minted at San Francisco, without mintmark.

AMERICAN SILVER EAGLE COIN SETS

	Uncertified	69	70
1997 Impressions of Liberty set (a)	$3,300	$3,400	$6,200
2006 20th Anniversary Three-Coin Set. Silver dollars, Uncirculated, Proof, Reverse Proof	$325	$400	$800
2006-W 20th Anniversary 1-oz. Gold- and Silver-Dollar Set. Uncirculated	$1,600	$1,700	$2,100
2011 25th Anniversary Five-Coin Set	$650	$750	$1,100
2012-S 75th Anniversary of San Francisco Mint Two-Coin Set. Proof, Reverse Proof	$200	$240	$340
2013-W 75th Anniversary of West Point Depository Two-Coin Set. Reverse Proof, Enhanced Uncirculated	$175	$225	$270

Note: Uncertified values are for uncertified sets of average quality, in their complete original U.S. Mint packaging. **a.** This set contains a $100 platinum, $50 gold, and a $1 silver piece.

AMERICA THE BEAUTIFUL 5-OUNCE SILVER BULLION COINS (2010–2021)

Designers: *See image captions on pages 732–739 for designers.* **Weight:** *155.517 grams.* **Composition:** *.999 silver, .001 copper (net weight 5 oz. pure silver).* **Diameter:** *76.2 mm.* **Edge:** *Lettered.* **Mint:** *Philadelphia.*

Bullion
Strike

History. In conjunction with the National Park quarter dollars, the U.S. Mint issues silver-bullion coins based on each of the "America the Beautiful" program's circulation-strike coins. The coinage dies are cut on a CNC milling machine, bypassing a hubbing operation, which results in finer details than seen on the smaller quarter dollars. The bullion coins are made of .999 fine silver, have a diameter of three inches, weigh five ounces, and carry a face value of 25 cents. The fineness and weight are incused on each coin's edge. The Mint's German-made Gräbener press strikes 22 coins per minute, with two strikes per coin at 450 to 500 metric tons of pressure. In December 2010, the Mint announced it would produce

Specimen
Strike

Mintmark location is
on the obverse, to the
right of the hair ribbon.

Details of the incused edge markings.

Details on 2014 Great Smoky Mountains
National Park 5-ounce silver bullion coin (left)
and quarter dollar (right). Note differences
on window, cabin, and grass in foreground.

Specimen versions (called *Uncirculated* by the Mint) for collectors. Detailed information on each issue is in *American Gold and Silver: U.S. Mint Collector and Investor Coins and Medals, Bicentennial to Date* (Tucker).

Striking and Sharpness. Striking is generally sharp.

Availability. The National Park silver bullion coins are distributed through commercial channels similar to those for the Mint's American Silver Eagle coins. Production of the 2010 coins was delayed (finally starting September 21) as the Mint worked out the technical details of striking such a large product. Production and distribution have been smoother since then.

MS-65 to 70 (Mint State). *Obverse and Reverse:* At MS-65, some abrasion and contact marks are evident on the higher design areas. Luster may be dull or lifeless at MS–65 to 66, but there should be deep frost at MS-67 and better, particularly in the lower-relief areas. At MS-68 and above, the luster should be full and rich. These guidelines are more academic than practical, as these coins are not intended for circulation, and nearly all are in high Mint State grades.

SP-68 to 70 (Specimen). *Obverse and Reverse:* These pieces should be nearly perfect and with full luster, in their original Mint packaging. Any with imperfections due to careless handling or environmental damage are valued lower.

The U.S. Mint produces the America the Beautiful™ 5-ounce silver coins in bullion and numismatic versions. The bullion version, which lacks the P mintmark, has a brilliant finish and is sold only through dealers. The numismatic version, with the mintmark, has a matte or burnished finish. These coins are designated "Specimens" (SP) by most collectors and grading services. They are sold directly to the public by the Mint.

25¢ AMERICA THE BEAUTIFUL 5-OUNCE SILVER BULLION COINS

	Mintage	MS / SP	MS-69 / SP-69	MS-70 / SP-70
2010, Hot Springs National Park	33,000	$135	$250	—
2010-P, Hot Springs National Park, Specimen	26,788	$155	$200	$600
2010, Yellowstone National Park	33,000	$135	$170	—
2010-P, Yellowstone National Park, Specimen	26,711	$155	$185	$270
2010, Yosemite National Park	33,000	$145	$250	—
2010-P, Yosemite National Park, Specimen	26,716	$155	$185	$325
2010, Grand Canyon National Park	33,000	$135	$250	—
2010-P, Grand Canyon National Park, Specimen	25,967	$155	$185	$270
2010, Mt. Hood National Forest	33,000	$155	$250	—
2010-P, Mt. Hood National Forest, Specimen	26,637	$155	$195	$270
2011, Gettysburg National Military Park	126,700	$135	$275	—
2011-P, Gettysburg National Military Park, Specimen (a)	24,625	$255	$290	$550
2011, Glacier National Park	126,700	$135	$250	—
2011-P, Glacier National Park, Specimen (b)	20,805	$170	$205	$350
2011, Olympic National Park	104,900	$120	$250	—
2011-P, Olympic National Park, Specimen (c)	18,345	$155	$190	$350
2011, Vicksburg National Military Park	58,100	$125	$250	—
2011-P, Vicksburg National Military Park, Specimen (d)	18,528	$155	$200	$400
2011, Chickasaw National Recreational Area	48,700	$120	$250	—
2011-P, Chickasaw National Recreational Area, Specimen (e)	16,746	$215	$250	$450
2012, El Yunque National Forest	24,000	$215	$350	—
2012-P, El Yunque National Forest, Specimen (f)	17,314	$400	$435	$600
2012, Chaco Culture National Historical Park	24,400	$235	$270	—
2012-P, Chaco Culture National Historical Park, Specimen (g)	17,146	$355	$390	$600
2012, Acadia National Park	25,400	$350	$385	—
2012-P, Acadia National Park, Specimen (h)	14,978	$550	$585	$875
2012, Hawai'i Volcanoes National Park	20,000	$350	$850	—
2012-P, Hawai'i Volcanoes National Park, Specimen (i)	14,863	$650	$700	$1,500
2012, Denali National Park and Preserve	20,000	$235	$350	—
2012-P, Denali National Park and Preserve, Specimen	15,225	$475	$515	$700
2013, White Mountain National Forest	35,000	$125	$210	—
2013-P, White Mountain National Forest, Specimen	20,530	$180	$215	$250
2013, Perry's Victory and International Peace Memorial	30,000	$125	$210	—
2013-P, Perry's Victory and International Peace Memorial, Specimen	17,707	$165	$215	$250
2013, Great Basin National Park	30,000	$125	$210	—
2013-P, Great Basin National Park, Specimen	17,792	$165	$200	$250
2013, Ft. McHenry Nat'l Mon & Historic Shrine	30,000	$125	$210	—
2013-P, Ft. McHenry Nat'l Mon & Historic Shrine, Specimen	19,802	$165	$200	$250
2013, Mount Rushmore National Monument	35,000	$125	$210	—
2013-P, Mount Rushmore National Monument, Specimen	23,547	$165	$200	$250
2014, Great Smoky Mountains National Park	33,000	$130	$180	—
2014-P, Great Smoky Mountains National Park, Specimen	24,710	$125	$160	$210
2014, Shenandoah National Park	25,000	$130	$165	—
2014-P, Shenandoah National Park, Specimen	28,276	$125	$160	$210
2014, Arches National Park	22,000	$130	$165	—
2014-P, Arches National Park, Specimen	28,183	$130	$165	$210
2014, Great Sand Dunes National Park	22,000	$130	$165	—
2014-P, Great Sand Dunes National Park, Specimen	22,262	$130	$165	$210

Note: MS values are for uncertified Mint State coins of average quality, in their complete original U.S. Mint packaging. SP values are for uncertified Specimen coins of average quality, in their complete original U.S. Mint packaging. **a.** Auction: $341, SP-70, May 2015. **b.** $376, SP-70, September 2014. **c.** Auction: $188, SP-69, December 2015. **d.** $212, SP-69, October 2014. **e.** Auction: $353, SP-70, September 2014. **f.** Auction: $206, SP-69, December 2015. **g.** Auction: $306, SP-70, December 2014. **h.** Auction: $529, SP-70, September 2014. **i.** Auction: $776, SP-70, December 2014.

	Mintage	MS SP	MS-69 SP-69	MS-70 SP-70
2014, Everglades National Park	34,000	$130	$165	—
2014-P, Everglades National Park, Specimen	19,772	$125	$160	$210
2015, Homestead National Monument of America	35,000	$130	$165	—
2015-P, Homestead National Monument of America, Specimen	21,286	$160	$165	$210
2015, Kisatchie National Forest	42,000	$130	$165	—
2015-P, Kisatchie National Forest, Specimen	19,449	$160	$165	$210
2015, Blue Ridge Parkway	45,000	$130	$165	—
2015-P, Blue Ridge Parkway, Specimen	17,461	$160	$165	$210
2015, Bombay Hook National Wildlife Refuge	45,000	$130	$165	—
2015-P, Bombay Hook National Wildlife Refuge, Specimen	17,309	$160	$165	$210
2015, Saratoga National Historic Park	45,000	$130	$165	—
2015-P, Saratoga National Historic Park, Specimen	17,563	$160	$165	$210
2016, Shawnee National Forest	105,000	$130	$165	—
2016-P, Shawnee National Forest, Specimen	18,781	$160	$165	$210
2016, Cumberland Gap National Historical Park	75,000	$130	$165	—
2016-P, Cumberland Gap National Historical Park, Specimen	18,713	$160	$165	$210
2016, Harpers Ferry National Historical Park	53,200	$130	$165	—
2016-P, Harpers Ferry National Historical Park, Specimen	18,896	$160	$160	$210
2016, Theodore Roosevelt National Park	40,000	$130	$165	—
2016-P, Theodore Roosevelt National Park, Specimen	18,917	$160	$165	$210
2016, Fort Moultrie (Fort Sumter National Monument)	35,000	$130	$165	—
2016-P, Fort Moultrie (Fort Sumter National Monument), Specimen	17,882	$160	$165	$210
2017, Effigy Mounds National Monument	35,000	$130	$165	—
2017-P, Effigy Mounds National Monument, Specimen	16,612	$130	$165	$210
2017, Frederick Douglass National Historic Site	20,000	$130	$165	—
2017-P, Frederick Douglass National Historic Site, Specimen	17,024	$125	$160	$210
2017, Ozark National Scenic Riverways	20,000	$130	$165	—
2017-P, Ozark National Scenic Riverways, Specimen	16,871	$125	$160	$210
2017, Ellis Island (Statue of Liberty National Monument)	40,000	$130	$165	—
2017-P, Ellis Island (Statue of Liberty National Monument), Specimen	17,694	$130	$165	$210
2017, George Rogers Clark National Historical Park	33,400	$130	$165	—
2017-P, George Rogers Clark National Historical Park, Specimen	14,739	$130	$165	$210
2018, Pictured Rocks National Lakeshore		$130	$165	—
2018-P, Pictured Rocks National Lakeshore, Specimen		$130	$165	$210
2018, Apostle Islands National Lakeshore		$130	$165	—
2018-P, Apostle Islands National Lakeshore, Specimen		$125	$160	$210
2018, Voyageurs National Park		$130	$165	—
2018-P, Voyageurs National Park, Specimen		$125	$160	$210
2018, Cumberland Island National Seashore		$130	$165	—
2018-P, Cumberland Island National Seashore, Specimen		$130	$165	$210
2018, Block Island National Wildlife Refuge		$130	$165	—
2018-P, Block Island National Wildlife Refuge		$130	$165	$210

Note: MS values are for uncertified Mint State coins of average quality, in their complete original U.S. Mint packaging. SP values are for uncertified Specimen coins of average quality, in their complete original U.S. Mint packaging.

AMERICAN GOLD EAGLES (1986 TO DATE)

Designers: *Augustus Saint-Gaudens (obverse) and Miley Busiek (reverse).* **Weight:** *$5 1/10 oz.— 3.393 grams; $10 1/4 oz.—8.483 grams; $25 1/2 oz.—16.966 grams; $50 1 oz.—33.931 grams.* **Composition:** *.9167 gold, .03 silver, .0533 copper.* **Diameter:** *$5 1/10 oz.—16.5 mm; $10 1/4 oz.— 22 mm; $25 1/2 oz.—27 mm; $50 1 oz.—32.7 mm.* **Edge:** *Reeded.* **Mints:** *Philadelphia and West Point.*

See next page for images.

Regular Finish
Obverse design common to all denominations.

Burnished Finish

Proof Finish

Reverse Proof Finish

Mintmark location is on the
obverse, below the date.

History. American Eagle gold bullion coins are made in four denominations: $5 (1/10 ounce pure gold), $10 (1/4 ounce), $25 (1/2 ounce), and $50 (1 ounce). Each shares the same obverse and reverse designs: a modified rendition of Augustus Saint-Gaudens's famous Liberty (as depicted on the double eagle of 1907 to 1933), and a "family of eagles" motif by sculptor Miley Tucker-Frost (nee Busiek). From 1986 to 1991 the obverse bore a Roman numeral date, similar to the first Saint-Gaudens double eagles of 1907; this was changed to Arabic dating in 1992. The coins are legal tender—with weight, content, and purity guaranteed by the federal government—and are produced from gold mined in the United States. Investors can include them in their individual retirement accounts.

"American Eagles use the durable 22-karat standard established for gold circulating coinage over 350 years ago," notes the U.S. Mint. "They contain their stated amount of pure gold, plus small amounts of alloy. This creates harder coins that resist scratching and marring, which can diminish resale value."

Since the Bullion Coin Program started in 1986, these gold pieces have been struck in Philadelphia and West Point, in various formats similar to those of the American Silver Eagles—regular bullion strikes, Burnished, Proof, and Reverse Proof. Unlike their silver counterparts, none of the American Gold Eagles have been struck at San Francisco.

In addition to the individual coins listed below, American Eagle gold bullion coins have been issued in various sets (see page 1248).

Striking and Sharpness. Striking is generally sharp. The key elements to check on the obverse are Liberty's chest and left knee, and the open fields.

Availability. American Gold Eagles are the most popular gold-coin investment vehicle in the United States. The coins are readily available in the numismatic marketplace as well as from participating banks, investment firms, and other non-numismatic channels.

MS-60 to 70 (Mint State). *Obverse and Reverse:* At MS-60, some abrasion and contact marks are evident on the higher design areas (in particular, Miss Liberty's chest and left knee) and the open fields. Luster may be dull or lifeless at MS-60 to 62, but there should be deep frost at MS-63 and better, particularly in the lower-relief areas. At MS-65 and above, the luster should be full and rich. Contact marks and abrasion are less and less evident at higher grades. These guidelines are more academic than practical, as these coins are not intended for circulation, and nearly all are in high Mint State grades.

PF-60 to 70 (Proof). *Obverse and Reverse:* Proofs that are extensively cleaned and have many hairlines are lower level, such as PF–60 to 62. Those with fewer hairlines or flaws are deemed PF–63 to 65. (These exist more in theory than actuality, as nearly all Proof American Eagle gold bullion coins have been maintained in their original high condition by collectors.) Given the quality of modern U.S. Mint products, even PF–66 and 67 are unusually low levels for these Proofs.

$5 1/10-OUNCE AMERICAN GOLD EAGLES

	Mintage	MS	MS-69	MS-70
		PF	PF-69	PF-70
$5 MCMLXXXVI (1986)	912,609	$170	$200	$700
$5 MCMLXXXVII (1987)	580,266	$180	$195	$1,300
$5 MCMLXXXVIII (1988) (a)	159,500	$175	$225	$3,500
$5 MCMLXXXVIII (1988)-P, Proof	143,881	$205	$225	$325
$5 MCMLXXXIX (1989) (b)	264,790	$180	$200	$2,600
$5 MCMLXXXIX (1989)-P, Proof	84,647	$195	$210	$375
$5 MCMXC (1990) (c)	210,210	$190	$200	$4,000
$5 MCMXC (1990)-P, Proof	99,349	$195	$210	$350
$5 MCMXCI (1991) (d)	165,200	$190	$220	$1,400
$5 MCMXCI (1991)-P, Proof	70,334	$195	$210	$400
$5 1992	209,300	$185	$200	$1,400
$5 1992-P, Proof	64,874	$185	$200	$450
$5 1993	210,709	$175	$195	$1,500
$5 1993-P, Proof	58,649	$185	$200	$450
$5 1994	206,380	$175	$195	$400
$5 1994-W, Proof	62,849	$185	$200	$350
$5 1995	223,025	$170	$195	$975
$5 1995-W, Proof	62,667	$185	$200	$450
$5 1996	401,964	$165	$195	$600
$5 1996-W, Proof	57,047	$185	$200	$450
$5 1997	528,266	$155	$185	$450
$5 1997-W, Proof	34,977	$185	$200	$550
$5 1998	1,344,520	$170	$195	$300
$5 1998-W, Proof	39,395	$185	$200	$450
$5 1999	2,750,338	$165	$185	$275
$5 1999-W, Unc made from unpolished Proof dies ‡ (e,f)	14,500	$900	$1,100	$4,000
$5 1999-W, Proof	48,428	$185	$200	$400
$5 2000	569,153	$165	$185	$275
$5 2000-W, Proof	49,971	$185	$205	$400
$5 2001	269,147	$165	$185	$245
$5 2001-W, Proof	37,530	$185	$200	$400
$5 2002	230,027	$180	$190	$375
$5 2002-W, Proof	40,864	$185	$200	$400

Note: MS values are for uncertified Mint State coins of average quality, in their complete original U.S. Mint packaging. PF values are for uncertified Proof coins of average quality, in their complete original U.S. Mint packaging. ‡ Ranked in the *100 Greatest U.S. Modern Coins*. **a.** Auction: $159, MS-69, October 2014. **b.** Auction: $141, MS-69, October 2014. **c.** Auction: $141, MS-69, October 2014. **d.** Auction: $2,115, MS-70, January 2016. **e.** Unpolished Proof dies were used to mint some 1999 $5 gold coins, resulting in a regular bullion-strike issue bearing a W mintmark (usually reserved for Proofs). A similar error exists in the $10 (1/4-ounce) series. The mintage listed is an estimate. Other estimates range from 6,000 to 30,000 pieces. **f.** Auction: $764, MS-69, July 2015.

| | Mintage | MS | MS-69 | MS-70 |
		PF	PF-69	PF-70
$5 2003	245,029	$165	$185	$250
$5 2003-W, Proof	40,027	$185	$200	$350
$5 2004	250,016	$165	$185	$250
$5 2004-W, Proof	35,131	$185	$200	$400
$5 2005	300,043	$155	$175	$220
$5 2005-W, Proof	49,265	$185	$200	$375
$5 2006	285,006	$155	$175	$200
$5 2006-W, Burnished	20,643	$190	$210	$240
$5 2006-W, Proof	47,277	$175	$195	$250
$5 2007	190,010	$155	$175	$200
$5 2007-W, Burnished	22,501	$195	$210	$250
$5 2007-W, Proof	58,553	$175	$195	$250
$5 2008	305,000	$155	$175	$240
$5 2008-W, Burnished (g)	12,657	$325	$350	$450
$5 2008-W, Proof	28,116	$175	$195	$300
$5 2009	270,000	$155	$175	$210
$5 2010	435,000	$155	$175	$190
$5 2010-W, Proof	54,285	$185	$205	$300
$5 2011	350,000	$155	$175	$190
$5 2011-W, Proof	42,697	$175	$195	$300
$5 2012	315,000	$155	$175	$190
$5 2012-W, Proof	20,637	$175	$195	$250
$5 2013	535,000	$155	$175	$190
$5 2013-W, Proof	21,738	$175	$195	$235
$5 2014	565,500	$155	$175	$190
$5 2014-W, Proof	22,725	$175	$195	$250
$5 2015	980,000	$155	$175	$190
$5 2015, Narrow Reeding	(h)			
$5 2015-W, Proof	16,851	$175	$195	$250
$5 2016	925,000	$155	$175	$190
$5 2016-W, Proof		$175	$195	$250
$5 2017		$155	$175	$190
$5 2017-W, Proof		$175	$195	$250
$5 2018		$155	$175	$190
$5 2018-W, Proof		$175	$195	$250

Note: MS values are for uncertified Mint State coins of average quality, in their complete original U.S. Mint packaging. PF values are for uncertified Proof coins of average quality, in their complete original U.S. Mint packaging. **g.** Auction: $352, MS-70, November 2014. **h.** Included in mintage for $5 2015.

$10 1/4-OUNCE
AMERICAN GOLD EAGLES

| | Mintage | MS | MS-69 | MS-70 |
		PF	PF-69	PF-70
$10 MCMLXXXVI (1986) (a)	726,031	$450	$500	$1,550
$10 MCMLXXXVII (1987) (b)	269,255	$450	$550	—
$10 MCMLXXXVIII (1988) (c)	49,000	$600	$700	$3,250
$10 MCMLXXXVIII (1988)-P, Proof	98,028	$420	$450	$900

Note: MS values are for uncertified Mint State coins of average quality, in their complete original U.S. Mint packaging. PF values are for uncertified Proof coins of average quality, in their complete original U.S. Mint packaging. **a.** Auction: $1,058, MS-70, January 2016. **b.** Auction: $306, MS-68, November 2015. **c.** Auction: $3,290, MS-70, August 2014.

	Mintage	MS / PF	MS-69 / PF-69	MS-70 / PF-70
$10 MCMLXXXIX (1989) (d)	81,789	$600	$675	$1,700
$10 MCMLXXXIX (1989)-P, Proof	54,170	$420	$450	$850
$10 MCMXC (1990) (e)	41,000	$725	$775	$4,000
$10 MCMXC (1990)-P, Proof	62,674	$420	$450	$600
$10 MCMXCI (1991) (f)	36,100	$725	$775	$2,250
$10 MCMXCI (1991)-P, Proof	50,839	$420	$450	$700
$10 1992 (g)	59,546	$550	$600	$2,000
$10 1992-P, Proof	46,269	$420	$450	$750
$10 1993 (h)	71,864	$550	$600	$2,250
$10 1993-P, Proof	46,464	$420	$450	$750
$10 1994 (i)	72,650	$550	$600	$2,500
$10 1994-W, Proof	48,172	$420	$450	$700
$10 1995 (j)	83,752	$550	$600	$2,000
$10 1995-W, Proof	47,526	$420	$450	$700
$10 1996 (k)	60,318	$550	$600	$2,100
$10 1996-W, Proof	38,219	$420	$450	$550
$10 1997	108,805	$400	$425	$2,000
$10 1997-W, Proof	29,805	$420	$450	$700
$10 1998	309,829	$400	$425	$2,500
$10 1998-W, Proof	29,503	$420	$450	$900
$10 1999	564,232	$400	$425	$2,500
$10 1999-W, Unc made from unpolished Proof dies ‡ (l,m)	10,000	$1,800	$2,000	—
$10 1999-W, Proof	34,417	$420	$450	$750
$10 2000	128,964	$425	$475	$900
$10 2000-W, Proof	36,036	$420	$450	$750
$10 2001	71,280	$550	$600	$700
$10 2001-W, Proof	25,613	$420	$450	$750
$10 2002	62,027	$550	$600	$700
$10 2002-W, Proof	29,242	$420	$450	$575
$10 2003	74,029	$400	$450	$500
$10 2003-W, Proof	30,292	$420	$450	$575
$10 2004	72,014	$375	$400	$500
$10 2004-W, Proof	28,839	$420	$450	$600
$10 2005	72,015	$375	$400	$500
$10 2005-W, Proof	37,207	$420	$450	$550
$10 2006	60,004	$375	$400	$500
$10 2006-W, Burnished (n)	15,188	$650	$675	$700
$10 2006-W, Proof	36,127	$420	$450	$550
$10 2007	34,004	$550	$600	$800
$10 2007-W, Burnished (o)	12,766	$700	$750	$800
$10 2007-W, Proof	46,189	$420	$450	$600
$10 2008	70,000	$370	$390	$415
$10 2008-W, Burnished (p)	8,883	$1,600	$1,650	$1,700
$10 2008-W, Proof	18,877	$500	$530	$700

Note: MS values are for uncertified Mint State coins of average quality, in their complete original U.S. Mint packaging. PF values are for uncertified Proof coins of average quality, in their complete original U.S. Mint packaging. ‡ Ranked in the *100 Greatest U.S. Modern Coins*. **d.** Auction: $3,290, MS-70, October 2015. **e.** Auction: $16,450, MS-70, October 2015. **f.** Auction: $1,293, MS-70, October 2014. **g.** Auction: $9,400, MS-70, September 2015. **h.** Auction: $3,055, MS-70, June 2014. **i.** $5,640, MS-70, February 2015. **j.** Auction: $505, MS-69, March 2014. **k.** Auction: $306, MS-68, October 2015. **l.** Unpolished Proof dies were used to mint some 1999 $10 gold coins, resulting in a regular bullion-strike issue bearing a W mintmark (usually reserved for Proofs). A similar error exists in the $5 (1/10-ounce) series. The mintage listed is an estimate. Other estimates range from 6,000 to 30,000 pieces. **m.** $1,763, MS-69, July 2015. **n.** Auction: $646, MS-70, October 2015. **o.** Auction: $376, MS-70, October 2015. **p.** Auction: $1,528, MS-70, July 2015.

	Mintage	MS	MS-69	MS-70
		PF	PF-69	PF-70
$10 2009	110,000	$370	$390	$415
$10 2010	86,000	$370	$390	$475
$10 2010-W, Proof	44,507	$450	$500	$550
$10 2011	80,000	$370	$390	$415
$10 2011-W, Proof	28,782	$450	$500	$550
$10 2012	76,000	$370	$390	$415
$10 2012-W, Proof	13,926	$450	$500	$550
$10 2013	122,000	$370	$390	$415
$10 2013-W, Proof	12,782	$450	$500	$550
$10 2014	118,000	$370	$390	$415
$10 2014-W, Proof	14,790	$450	$500	$550
$10 2015	158,000	$370	$390	$415
$10 2015-W, Proof	15,775	$450	$500	$550
$10 2016	152,000	$370	$390	$415
$10 2016-W, Proof		$450	$500	$550
$10 2017		$370	$390	$415
$10 2017-W, Proof		$450	$500	$550
$10 2018		$370	$390	$415
$10 2018-W, Proof		$450	$500	$550

Note: MS values are for uncertified Mint State coins of average quality, in their complete original U.S. Mint packaging. PF values are for uncertified Proof coins of average quality, in their complete original U.S. Mint packaging.

$25 1/2-OUNCE AMERICAN GOLD EAGLES

	Mintage	MS	MS-69	MS-70
		PF	PF-69	PF-70
$25 MCMLXXXVI (1986) (a)	599,566	$800	$850	$1,500
$25 MCMLXXXVII (1987) (b)	131,255	$950	$1,200	$2,000
$25 MCMLXXXVII (1987)-P, Proof	143,398	$800	$850	$2,000
$25 MCMLXXXVIII (1988) (c)	45,000	$1,650	$2,000	$5,000
$25 MCMLXXXVIII (1988)-P, Proof	76,528	$800	$850	$1,600
$25 MCMLXXXIX (1989) (d)	44,829	$1,800	$2,150	$4,000
$25 MCMLXXXIX (1989)-P, Proof	44,798	$950	$1,000	—
$25 MCMXC (1990) (e)	31,000	$2,200	$2,500	$5,000
$25 MCMXC (1990)-P, Proof	51,636	$850	$900	—
$25 MCMXCI (1991) ‡ (f)	24,100	$3,300	$3,550	—
$25 MCMXCI (1991)-P, Proof	53,125	$850	$900	$1,500
$25 1992 (g)	54,404	$1,100	$1,400	$3,800
$25 1992-P, Proof	40,976	$850	$900	$1,500
$25 1993 (h)	73,324	$900	$1,100	$3,500
$25 1993-P, Proof	43,819	$850	$900	—
$25 1994 (i)	62,400	$900	$1,100	—
$25 1994-W, Proof	44,584	$850	$900	$1,500
$25 1995 (j)	53,474	$1,300	$1,650	$1,750

Note: MS values are for uncertified Mint State coins of average quality, in their complete original U.S. Mint packaging. PF values are for uncertified Proof coins of average quality, in their complete original U.S. Mint packaging. ‡ Ranked in the *100 Greatest U.S. Modern Coins.* **a.** Auction: $646, MS-68, October 2015. **b.** Auction: $999, MS-69, January 2016. **c.** Auction: $1,528, MS-69, October 2015. **d.** Auction: $9,400, MS-70, September 2015. **e.** Auction: $9,694, MS-70, September 2015. **f.** Auction: $2,820, MS-69, October 2015. **g.** Auction: $3,966, MS-70, July 2014. **h.** Auction: $4,964, MS-70, January 2015. **i.** Auction: $705, MS-68, October 2015. **j.** Auction: $5,875, MS-70, August 2015.

	Mintage	MS	MS-69	MS-70
		PF	PF-69	PF-70
$25 1995-W, Proof	45,388	$850	$900	$1,500
$25 1996 (k)	39,287	$1,350	$1,500	$3,800
$25 1996-W, Proof	35,058	$850	$900	$1,500
$25 1997 (l)	79,605	$900	$1,100	$2,800
$25 1997-W, Proof	26,344	$850	$900	$1,500
$25 1998	169,029	$750	$808	—
$25 1998-W, Proof	25,374	$850	$900	$1,500
$25 1999 (m)	263,013	$900	$1,100	$3,000
$25 1999-W, Proof	30,427	$850	$900	$1,500
$25 2000	79,287	$900	$1,050	—
$25 2000-W, Proof	32,028	$800	$850	$1,500
$25 2001 (n)	48,047	$1,250	$1,500	$1,800
$25 2001-W, Proof	23,240	$800	$850	$1,500
$25 2002	70,027	$900	$1,050	—
$25 2002-W, Proof	26,646	$800	$850	$1,500
$25 2003	79,029	$800	$850	$900
$25 2003-W, Proof	28,270	$800	$850	$1,500
$25 2004	98,040	$800	$850	$900
$25 2004-W, Proof	27,330	$800	$850	$1,500
$25 2005	80,023	$750	$800	$900
$25 2005-W, Proof	34,311	$800	$850	$1,500
$25 2006	66,005	$750	$800	$900
$25 2006-W, Burnished (o)	15,164	$775	$850	$1,150
$25 2006-W, Proof	34,322	$800	$850	$1,500
$25 2007	47,002	$775	$850	$1,150
$25 2007-W, Burnished (p)	11,455	$1,100	$1,200	$1,700
$25 2007-W, Proof	44,025	$800	$850	$1,500
$25 2008	61,000	$750	$800	$900
$25 2008-W, Burnished (q)	15,682	$875	$925	$1,100
$25 2008-W, Proof	22,602	$1,000	$1,050	$1,200
$25 2009	110,000	$750	$800	$900
$25 2010	81,000	$750	$800	$900
$25 2010-W, Proof	44,527	$850	$900	$1,000
$25 2011	70,000	$750	$800	$900
$25 2011-W, Proof	26,781	$800	$850	$950
$25 2012	71,000	$750	$800	$900
$25 2012-W, Proof	12,919	$800	$850	$1,000
$25 2013	58,000	$750	$800	$900
$25 2013-W, Proof	12,716	$800	$850	$1,000
$25 2014	46,000	$750	$800	$900
$25 2014-W, Proof	14,693	$800	$850	$1,000
$25 2015	75,000	$750	$800	$900
$25 2015-W, Proof	15,287	$800	$850	$1,000
$25 2016	74,000	$750	$800	$900
$25 2016-W, Proof		$800	$850	$1,000
$25 2017		$750	$800	$900
$25 2017-W, Proof		$800	$850	$1,000
$25 2018		$750	$800	$900
$25 2018-W, Proof		$800	$850	$1,000

Note: MS values are for uncertified Mint State coins of average quality, in their complete original U.S. Mint packaging. PF values are for uncertified Proof coins of average quality, in their complete original U.S. Mint packaging. **k.** Auction: $1,293, MS-69, September 2015. **l.** Auction: $1,293, MS-69, September 2015. **m.** Auction: $646, MS-69, November 2014. **n.** Auction: $1,763, MS-69, July 2014. **o.** Auction: $705, MS-70, October 2015. **p.** Auction: $646, MS-69, October 2015. **q.** Auction: $1,175, MS-70, November 2015.

$50 1-Ounce
American Gold Eagles

	Mintage	MS / PF	MS-69 / PF-69	MS-70 / PF-70
$50 MCMLXXXVI (1986) (a)	1,362,650	$1,425	$1,475	$5,500
$50 MCMLXXXVI (1986)-W, Proof	446,290	$1,700	$1,700	$2,200
$50 MCMLXXXVII (1987) (b)	1,045,500	$1,425	$1,500	$5,000
$50 MCMLXXXVII (1987)-W, Proof	147,498	$1,650	$1,700	$2,200
$50 MCMLXXXVIII (1988) (c)	465,000	$1,425	$1,500	$11,000
$50 MCMLXXXVIII (1988)-W, Proof	87,133	$1,650	$1,700	$2,200
$50 MCMLXXXIX (1989)	415,790	$1,425	$1,500	—
$50 MCMLXXXIX (1989)-W, Proof	54,570	$1,700	$1,750	$2,200
$50 MCMXC (1990) (d)	373,210	$1,425	$1,500	$5,500
$50 MCMXC (1990)-W, Proof	62,401	$1,700	$1,750	$2,200
$50 MCMXCI (1991) (e)	243,100	$1,425	$1,500	$5,500
$50 MCMXCI (1991)-W, Proof	50,411	$1,700	$1,750	$3,000
$50 1992	275,000	$1,425	$1,450	$2,100
$50 1992-W, Proof (f)	44,826	$1,700	$1,750	$3,000
$50 1993	480,192	$1,425	$1,450	$2,600
$50 1993-W, Proof (g)	34,369	$1,700	$1,750	$3,500
$50 1994 (h)	221,633	$1,425	$1,450	$6,500
$50 1994-W, Proof	46,674	$1,650	$1,750	$2,500
$50 1995	200,636	$1,425	$1,450	—
$50 1995-W, Proof	46,368	$1,700	$1,750	$2,500
$50 1996	189,148	$1,425	$1,450	—
$50 1996-W, Proof	36,153	$1,700	$1,750	$2,500
$50 1997 (i)	664,508	$1,425	$1,450	$5,000
$50 1997-W, Proof	32,999	$1,700	$1,750	$2,500
$50 1998	1,468,530	$1,425	$1,450	$2,300
$50 1998-W, Proof (j)	25,886	$1,700	$1,750	$4,000
$50 1999	1,505,026	$1,425	$1,450	$2,300
$50 1999-W, Proof	31,427	$1,700	$1,750	$3,000
$50 2000	433,319	$1,425	$1,450	$2,500
$50 2000-W, Proof	33,007	$1,700	$1,750	$2,500
$50 2001 (k)	143,605	$1,425	$1,450	$3,000
$50 2001-W, Proof ‡ (l)	24,555	$1,700	$1,700	$5,000
$50 2002	222,029	$1,425	$1,450	$2,800
$50 2002-W, Proof	27,499	$1,700	$1,750	$2,200
$50 2003	416,032	$1,425	$1,450	$2,500
$50 2003-W, Proof	28,344	$1,700	$1,750	$2,200
$50 2004	417,019	$1,425	$1,450	$2,500
$50 2004-W, Proof	28,215	$1,700	$1,750	$2,150

Note: MS values are for uncertified Mint State coins of average quality, in their complete original U.S. Mint packaging. PF values are for uncertified Proof coins of average quality, in their complete original U.S. Mint packaging. ‡ Ranked in the *100 Greatest U.S. Modern Coins*. **a.** Auction: $2,585, MS-70, June 2015. **b.** Auction:$1,351, MS-68, August 2014. **c.** Auction: $1,303, MS-68, December 2013. **d.** Auction: $1,469, MS-69, March 2014. **e.** Auction: $1,293, MS-69, July 2015. **f.** Auction: $2,056, PF-70UCam, July 2015. **g.** Auction: $2,233, PF-70UCam, June 2015. **h.** Auction: $2,820, MS-69, April 2014. **i.** Auction: $1,645, MS-69, April 2014. **j.** $2,233, PF-70UCam, September 2015. **k.** Auction: $1,351, MS-69, October 2014. **l.** Auction: $2,820, PF-70UCam, January 2015.

| | Mintage | MS | MS-69 | MS-70 |
		PF	PF-69	PF-70
$50 2005	356,555	$1,425	$1,450	$2,000
$50 2005-W, Proof	35,246	$1,675	$1,725	$2,150
$50 2006	237,510	$1,425	$1,450	$1,700
$50 2006-W, Burnished	45,053	$1,600	$1,700	$1,900
$50 2006-W, Proof	47,092	$1,675	$1,725	$2,100
$50 2006-W, Reverse Proof ‡ (m,n)	9,996	$2,900	$3,050	$3,400
$50 2007	140,016	$1,425	$1,450	$1,950
$50 2007-W, Burnished	18,066	$1,500	$1,550	$1,750
$50 2007-W, Proof	51,810	$1,675	$1,725	$2,100
$50 2008	710,000	$1,425	$1,450	$1,950
$50 2008-W, Burnished (o)	11,908	$1,900	$1,950	$2,200
$50 2008-W, Proof	30,237	$1,675	$1,725	$2,500
$50 2009	1,493,000	$1,425	$1,450	$1,750
$50 2010	1,125,000	$1,425	$1,450	$1,550
$50 2010-W, Proof	59,480	$1,675	$1,725	$2,100
$50 2011	857,000	$1,425	$1,450	$1,550
$50 2011-W, Burnished (p)	8,729	$2,200	$2,250	$2,450
$50 2011-W, Proof	48,306	$1,675	$1,725	$2,100
$50 2012	667,000	$1,425	$1,450	$1,550
$50 2012-W, Burnished (q)	6,118	$2,200	$2,250	$2,500
$50 2012-W, Proof	23,805	$1,700	$1,750	$2,100
$50 2013	743,500	$1,425	$1,450	$1,600
$50 2013-W, Burnished	7,293	$1,500	$1,550	$1,900
$50 2013-W, Proof	24,709	$1,700	$1,750	$2,100
$50 2014	415,500	$1,425	$1,450	$1,500
$50 2014-W, Burnished	7,902	$1,700	$1,750	$1,900
$50 2014-W, Proof	28,703	$1,700	$1,750	$2,100
$50 2015	626,500	$1,425	$1,450	$1,500
$50 2015-W, Burnished	7,794	$1,700	$1,750	$1,900
$50 2015-W, Proof	28,673	$1,700	$1,750	$2,100
$50 2016	817,500	$1,425	$1,450	$1,500
$50 2016-W, Burnished		$1,700	$1,750	$1,900
$50 2016-W, Proof		$1,700	$1,750	$2,100
$50 2017		$1,425	$1,450	$1,500
$50 2017-W, Proof		$1,700	$1,750	$2,100
$50 2018		$1,425	$1,450	$1,500
$50 2018-W, Proof		$1,700	$1,750	$2,100

Note: MS values are for uncertified Mint State coins of average quality, in their complete original U.S. Mint packaging. PF values are for uncertified Proof coins of average quality, in their complete original U.S. Mint packaging. ‡ Ranked in the *100 Greatest U.S. Modern Coins*. **m.** The 2006-W Reverse Proof coins were issued to mark the 20th anniversary of the Bullion Coinage Program. They have brilliant devices, and their background fields are frosted (rather than the typical Proof format of frosted devices and mirror-like backgrounds). **n.** Auction: $4,935, PF-70, September 2015. **o.** Auction: $1,293, MS-69, July 2015. **p.** Auction: $1,998, MS-70, June 2015. **q.** Auction: $2,585, MS-70, February 2015.

AMERICAN GOLD EAGLE PROOF COIN SETS

	PF	PF-69	PF-70
1987 Gold Set. $50, $25	$2,400	$2,500	$4,200
1988 Gold Set. $50, $25, $10, $5	$3,000	$3,150	$5,400
1989 Gold Set. $50, $25, $10, $5	$3,200	$3,350	—
1990 Gold Set. $50, $25, $10, $5	$3,150	$3,300	—
1991 Gold Set. $50, $25, $10, $5	$3,100	$3,250	$5,600

Note: PF values are for uncertified Proof sets of average quality, in their complete original U.S. Mint packaging. **a.** The 1993 set was issued to commemorate the bicentennial of the first coins struck by the U.S. Mint in Philadelphia.

	PF	PF-69	PF-70
1992 Gold Set. $50, $25, $10, $5	$3,100	$3,250	$5,700
1993 Gold Set. $50, $25, $10, $5	$3,100	$3,250	—
1993 Bicentennial Gold Set. $25, $10, $5, Silver Eagle, and medal (a)	$1,400	$1,500	—
1994 Gold Set. $50, $25, $10, $5	$3,100	$3,250	$5,000
1995 Gold Set. $50, $25, $10, $5	$3,100	$3,250	$5,600
1995 Anniversary Gold Set. $50, $25, $10, $5, and Silver Eagle (b)	$6,800	$7,900	—
1996 Gold Set. $50, $25, $10, $5	$3,100	$3,250	$5,000
1997 Gold Set. $50, $25, $10, $5	$3,300	$3,450	$5,600
1997 Impressions of Liberty Set. $100 platinum, $50 gold, Silver Eagle (c)	$3,200	$3,250	$6,200
1998 Gold Set. $50, $25, $10, $5	$3,200	$3,350	$6,850
1999 Gold Set. $50, $25, $10, $5	$3,100	$3,250	$5,600
2000 Gold Set. $50, $25, $10, $5	$3,100	$3,250	$5,100
2001 Gold Set. $50, $25, $10, $5	$3,100	$3,250	$7,700
2002 Gold Set. $50, $25, $10, $5	$3,100	$3,250	$4,450
2003 Gold Set. $50, $25, $10, $5	$3,100	$3,250	$4,450
2004 Gold Set. $50, $25, $10, $5	$3,100	$3,250	$4,800
2005 Gold Set. $50, $25, $10, $5	$3,100	$3,250	$3,800
2006 Gold Set. $50, $25, $10, $5	$3,100	$3,250	$3,800
2007 Gold Set. $50, $25, $10, $5	$3,100	$3,250	$3,800
2008 Gold Set. $50, $25, $10, $5	$3,100	$3,250	$4,700
2010 Gold Set. $50, $25, $10, $5 (d)	$3,100	$3,250	$3,800
2011 Gold Set. $50, $25, $10, $5	$3,100	$3,250	$3,800
2012 Gold Set. $50, $25, $10, $5	$3,100	$3,250	$3,800
2013 Gold Set. $50, $25, $10, $5	$3,100	$3,250	$3,800
2014 Gold Set. $50, $25, $10, $5	$3,100	$3,250	$3,800
2015 Gold Set. $50, $25, $10, $5	$3,100	$3,250	$3,800
2016 Gold Set. $50, $25, $10, $5	$3,100	$3,250	$3,800
2017 Gold Set. $50, $25, $10, $5	$3,100	$3,250	$3,800
2017 Gold Set. $50, $25, $10, $5	$3,100	$3,250	$3,800

Note: PF values are for uncertified Proof sets of average quality, in their complete original U.S. Mint packaging. **a.** The 1993 set was issued to commemorate the bicentennial of the first coins struck by the U.S. Mint in Philadelphia. **b.** The 1995 set marked the 10th anniversary of the passage of the Liberty Coin Act, which authorized the nation's new bullion coinage program. **c.** The Impressions of Liberty set was issued in the first year that platinum coins were added to the Mint's bullion offerings. **d.** The U.S. Mint did not issue a 2009 gold set.

2006 AMERICAN GOLD EAGLE 20TH-ANNIVERSARY COIN SETS

	Uncertified	69	70
2006-W $50 Gold Set. Uncirculated, Proof, and Reverse Proof	$5,900	$6,400	$6,800
2006-W 1-oz. Gold- and Silver-Dollar Set. Uncirculated	$1,800	$1,900	$2,000

Note: Uncertified values are for uncertified sets of average quality, in their complete original U.S. Mint packaging.

GOLD BULLION BURNISHED SETS

	Uncertified	69	70
2006-W Burnished Gold Set. $50, $25, $10, $5	$3,700	$4,000	$5,000
2007-W Burnished Gold Set. $50, $25, $10, $5	$4,000	$4,250	$5,500
2008-W Burnished Gold Set. $50, $25, $10, $5	$5,450	$5,600	$7,000

Note: Uncertified values are for uncertified sets of average quality, in their complete original U.S. Mint packaging.

AMERICAN BUFFALO .9999 FINE GOLD BULLION COINS (2006 TO DATE)

Designer: *James Earle Fraser.* **Weight:** *$5 1/10 oz.—3.393 grams; $10 1/4 oz.—8.483 grams; $25 1/2 oz.— 16.966 grams; $50 1 oz.—31.108 grams.* **Composition:** *.9999 gold.* **Diameter:** *$5 1/10 oz.—16.5 mm; $10 1/4 oz.—22 mm; $25 1/2 oz.—27 mm; $50 1 oz.—32.7 mm.* **Edge:** *Reeded.* **Mint:** *West Point.*

Regular Finish

Burnished Finish

Mintmark location is on the obverse, behind the neck.

Proof Finish

Reverse Proof Finish

History. American Buffalo gold bullion coins, authorized by Congress in 2005 and produced since 2006, are the first 24-karat (.9999 fine) gold coins made by the U.S. Mint. They are coined, by mandate, of gold derived from newly mined sources in America. They feature an adaptation of James Earle Fraser's iconic Indian Head / Buffalo design, first used on circulating five-cent pieces of 1913 to 1938.

Only 1-ounce ($50 face value) coins were struck in the American Buffalo program's first two years, 2006 and 2007. For 2008, the Mint expanded the coinage to include fractional pieces of 1/2 ounce ($25), 1/4 ounce ($10), and 1/10-ounce ($5), in various finishes, individually and in sets.

The coins are legal tender, with weight, content, and purity guaranteed by the federal government. Investors can include them in some individual retirement accounts. Proofs and Burnished (*Uncirculated,* in the Mint's wording) pieces undergo special production processes, similar to the American Eagle gold-bullion coinage, and can be purchased directly from the Mint. As with other products in the Mint's bullion program, regular bullion-strike pieces are distributed through a network of authorized distributors.

All American Buffalo gold bullion coins (Proofs, Burnished, and regular bullion pieces) are struck at the U.S. Mint's West Point facility.

Striking and Sharpness. Striking is generally sharp.

Availability. American Buffalo .9999 fine gold bullion coins are a popular way to buy and sell 24-karat gold. The coins are readily available in the numismatic marketplace as well as from participating banks, investment firms, and other non-numismatic channels.

MS-60 to 70 (Mint State). *Obverse and reverse:* At MS-60, some abrasion and contact marks are evident on the higher design areas and the open areas of the design. Luster may be dull or lifeless at MS-60 to 62, but there should be deep frost at MS-63 and better, particularly in the lower-relief areas. At MS-65 and above, the luster should be full and rich. Contact marks and abrasion are less and less evident at higher grades. These guidelines are more academic than practical, as these coins are not intended for circulation, and nearly all are in high Mint State grades, as struck.

PF-60 to 70 (Proof). *Obverse and reverse:* Proofs that are extensively cleaned and have many hairlines are lower level, such as PF–60 to 62. Those with fewer hairlines or flaws are deemed PF–63 to 65. (These exist more in theory than actuality, as nearly all Proof American Buffalo gold coins have been maintained in their original high condition by collectors.) Given the quality of modern U.S. Mint products, even PF–66 and 67 are unusually low levels for these Proofs.

American Buffalo .9999 Fine Gold Bullion Coins

| $5 1/10-oz. | $10 1/4-oz. | $25 1/2-oz. | $50 1-oz. |

| | Mintage | MS | MS-69 | MS-70 |
		PF	PF-69	PF-70
$5 2008-W, Burnished (a)	17,429	$450	$485	$600
$5 2008-W, Proof (b)	18,884	$450	$485	$600
$10 2008-W, Burnished ‡ (c)	9,949	$1,000	$1,050	$1,400
$10 2008-W, Proof (d)	13,125	$1,100	$1,200	$1,500
$25 2008-W, Burnished (e)	16,908	$1,150	$1,200	$1,500
$25 2008-W, Proof (f)	12,169	$1,600	$1,650	$2,000
$50 2006	337,012	$1,425	$1,450	$1,500
$50 2006-W, Proof	246,267	$1,450	$1,500	$1,600
$50 2007	136,503	$1,425	$1,450	$1,500
$50 2007-W, Proof	58,998	$1,450	$1,500	$1,600
$50 2008	214,058 **(g)**	$1,425	$1,450	$1,500
$50 2008-W, Burnished (h)	9,074	$2,350	$2,400	$2,850
$50 2008-W, Proof ‡ (i)	18,863	$2,750	$2,850	$3,200
$50 2009	200,000	$1,425	$1,450	$1,500
$50 2009-W, Proof	49,306	$1,450	$1,500	$1,600
$50 2010	*209,000*	$1,425	$1,450	$1,500
$50 2010-W, Proof	49,263	$1,450	$1,500	$1,600
$50 2011	*174,500*	$1,425	$1,450	$1,500
$50 2011-W, Proof	*28,693*	$1,500	$1,550	$1,700

Note: MS values are for uncertified Mint State coins of average quality, in their complete original U.S. Mint packaging. PF values are for uncertified Proof coins of average quality, in their complete original U.S. Mint packaging. ‡ Ranked in the *100 Greatest U.S. Modern Coins*. **a.** Auction: $447, MS-70, September 2015. **b.** Auction: $705, PF-70DCam, June 2015. **c.** Auction: $1,116, MS-70, August 2015. **d.** Auction: $823, PF-70DCam, January 2015. **e.** Auction: $764, MS-69, November 2015. **f.** Auction: $1,528, PF-70UCam, August 2015. **g.** 24,558 sold as Lunar New Year Celebration coins. **h.** Auction: $2,703, MS-70, June 2015. **i.** Auction: $3,525, PF-70DCam, July 2015.

	Mintage	MS / PF	MS-69 / PF-69	MS-70 / PF-70
$50 2012	132,000	$1,425	$1,450	$1,500
$50 2012-W, Proof	19,765	$1,650	$1,700	$2,000
$50 2013	239,000	$1,425	$1,450	$1,500
$50 2013-W, Proof	18,594	$1,600	$1,650	$2,100
$50 2013-W, Reverse Proof	47,836	$1,500	$1,550	$1,800
$50 2014	177,500	$1,425	$1,450	$1,500
$50 2014-W, Proof	20,557	$1,450	$1,500	$1,600
$50 2015	220,500	$1,425	$1,450	$1,500
$50 2015-W, Proof	16,591	$1,425	$1,500	$1,600
$50 2016	219,500	$1,425	$1,450	$1,500
$50 2016-W, Proof		$1,425	$1,500	$1,600
$50 2017		$1,425	$1,450	$1,500
$50 2017-W, Proof		$1,425	$1,500	$1,600
$50 2018		$1,425	$1,450	$1,500
$50 2018-W, Proof		$1,425	$1,500	$1,600

Note: MS values are for uncertified Mint State coins of average quality, in their complete original U.S. Mint packaging. PF values are for uncertified Proof coins of average quality, in their complete original U.S. Mint packaging.

AMERICAN BUFFALO .9999 FINE GOLD BULLION COIN SETS

	Uncertified	MS-69 / PF-69	MS-70 / PF-70
2008-W Four-coin set ($5, $10, $25, $50), Proof	$5,900	$6,100	$7,200
2008-W Four-coin set ($5, $10, $25, $50), Burnished	$4,900	$5,100	$6,300
2008-W Double Prosperity set (Unc. $25 American Buffalo gold and $25 American Gold Eagle coins)	$2,000	$2,100	$2,600

Note: Uncertified values are for uncertified sets of average quality, in their complete original U.S. Mint packaging.

FIRST SPOUSE $10 GOLD BULLION COINS (2007–2016)

Designers: *See image captions for designers.* **Weight:** *8.483 grams.*
Composition: *.9999 gold.* **Diameter:** *26.5 mm.* **Edge:** *Reeded.* **Mint:** *West Point.*

Burnished Finish
The first coin in the series, featuring Martha Washington.

Mintmark location is on the obverse, below the date.

Proof Finish

History. The U.S. Mint's First Spouse bullion coins were struck in .9999 fine (24-karat) gold. Each weighs one-half ounce and bears a face value of $10. The coins honor the nation's first spouses and were struck on the same schedule as the Mint's Presidential dollars program. Each features a portrait on the obverse, and on the reverse a unique design symbolic of the spouse's life and work. In cases where a president held office widowed or unmarried, the coin bears "an obverse image emblematic of Liberty as depicted on a circulating coin of that era and a reverse image emblematic of themes of that president's life." All First Spouse gold bullion coins (Proofs and Burnished pieces) were struck at the U.S. Mint's West Point facility.

Note that the Mint does not release bullion mintage data on a regular basis; the numbers given herein reflect the most recently available official data.

Striking and Sharpness. Striking is generally sharp.

Availability. These coins are readily available in the numismatic marketplace. They could be purchased by the public, in both Burnished and Proof formats, directly from the U.S. Mint. Sales of later issues were low, leading to some issues being ranked among the 100 Greatest U.S. Modern Coins.

MS-60 to 70 (Mint State). *Obverse and Reverse:* At MS-60, some abrasion and contact marks are evident on the higher design areas and the open areas of the design. Luster may be dull or lifeless at MS–60 to 62, but there should be deep frost at MS-63 and better, particularly in the lower-relief areas. At MS-65 and above, the luster should be full and rich. Contact marks and abrasion are less and less evident at higher grades. These guidelines are more academic than practical, as these coins are not intended for circulation, and nearly all are in high Mint State grades, as struck.

PF-60 to 70 (Proof). *Obverse and Reverse:* Proofs that are extensively cleaned and have many hairlines are lower level, such as PF–60 to 62. Those with fewer hairlines or flaws are deemed PF–63 to 65. (These exist more in theory than actuality, as nearly all Proof First Spouse gold coins have been maintained in their original high condition by collectors.) Given the quality of modern U.S. Mint products, even PF–66 and 67 are unusually low levels for these Proofs.

First Spouse $10 Gold Bullion Coins

Martha Washington	Abigail Adams	Jefferson's Liberty	Dolley Madison
Designers:	Designers:	Designers: obverse—	Designers:
obverse—Joseph Menna;	obverse—Joseph Menna;	Robert Scot / Phebe Hemphill;	obverse—Don Everhart;
reverse—Susan Gamble.	reverse—Thomas Cleveland.	reverse—Charles Vickers.	reverse—Joel Iskowitz.

| | Mintage | MS | MS-69 | MS-70 |
		PF	PF-69	PF-70
$10 2007-W, M. Washington	17,661	$700	$725	$775
$10 2007-W, M. Washington, Proof	19,167	$700	$725	$775
$10 2007-W, A. Adams	17,142	$700	$725	$775
$10 2007-W, A. Adams, Proof	17,149	$700	$725	$775
$10 2007-W, Jefferson's Liberty	19,823	$700	$725	$775
$10 2007-W, Jefferson's Liberty, Proof	19,815	$700	$725	$775
$10 2007-W, D. Madison	12,340	$700	$725	$775
$10 2007-W, D. Madison, Proof	17,943	$700	$725	$775

Note: MS values are for uncertified Mint State coins of average quality, in their complete original U.S. Mint packaging. PF values are for uncertified Proof coins of average quality, in their complete original U.S. Mint packaging.

Elizabeth Monroe
Designers:
obverse—Joel Iskowitz;
reverse—Donna Weaver.

Louisa Adams
Designers:
obverse—Susan Gamble;
reverse—Donna Weaver.

Jackson's Liberty
Designers:
obverse—John Reich;
reverse—Justin Kunz.

Van Buren's Liberty
Designer:
obverse—Christian Gobrecht;
reverse—Thomas Cleveland.

	Mintage	MS	MS-69	MS-70
		PF	PF-69	PF-70
$10 2008-W, E. Monroe	4,462	$750	$775	$1,000
$10 2008-W, E. Monroe, Proof	7,800	$800	$1,250	$1,250
$10 2008-W, L. Adams	3,885	$725	$775	$1,000
$10 2008-W, L. Adams, Proof	6,581	$850	$1,250	$1,250
$10 2008-W, Jackson's Liberty ‡ (a)	4,609	$850	$1,400	$1,400
$10 2008-W, Jackson's Liberty, Proof	7,684	$900	$1,250	$1,400
$10 2008-W, Van Buren's Liberty	3,826	$850	$1,400	$1,450
$10 2008-W, Van Buren's Liberty, Proof (b)	6,807	$1,000	$1,250	$1,600

Note: MS values are for uncertified Mint State coins of average quality, in their complete original U.S. Mint packaging. PF values are for uncertified Proof coins of average quality, in their complete original U.S. Mint packaging. ‡ Ranked in the *100 Greatest U.S. Modern Coins.* **a.** Auction: $999, MS-69, February 2015. **b.** Auction: $1,058, PF-70DCam, January 2015.

Anna Harrison
Designers:
obverse—Donna Weaver;
reverse—Thomas Cleveland.

Letitia Tyler
Designers:
obverse—Phebe Hemphill;
reverse—Susan Gamble.

Julia Tyler
Designer:
obverse and reverse—
Joel Iskowitz.

Sarah Polk
Designer: obverse and
reverse—Phebe Hemphill.

Margaret Taylor
Designers: obverse—Phebe Hemphill;
reverse—Mary Beth Zeitz.

| | Mintage | MS | MS-69 | MS-70 |
		PF	PF-69	PF-70
$10 2009-W, A. Harrison	3,645	$800	$850	$1,300
$10 2009-W, A. Harrison, Proof (c)	6,251	$900	$950	$1,200
$10 2009-W, L. Tyler	3,240	$900	$950	$1,450
$10 2009-W, L. Tyler, Proof (d)	5,296	$1,000	$1,050	$1,200
$10 2009-W, J. Tyler (e)	3,143	$900	$950	$1,500
$10 2009-W, J. Tyler, Proof (f)	4,844	$1,000	$1,050	$1,200
$10 2009-W, S. Polk	3,489	$925	$975	$1,250
$10 2009-W, S. Polk, Proof	5,151	$800	$850	$1,000
$10 2009-W, M. Taylor	3,627	$750	$800	$1,025
$10 2009-W, M. Taylor, Proof	4,936	$750	$800	$1,050

Note: MS values are for uncertified Mint State coins of average quality, in their complete original U.S. Mint packaging. PF values are for uncertified Proof coins of average quality, in their complete original U.S. Mint packaging. **c.** Auction: $646, PF-69DCam, June 2015. **d.** Auction: $881, PF-70DCam, June 2015. **e.** Auction: $1,293, MS-70, June 2015. **f.** Auction: $764, PF-69DCam, June 2015.

Abigail Fillmore
Designers:
obverse—Phebe Hemphill;
reverse—Susan Gamble.

Jane Pierce
Designer:
obverse and reverse—
Donna Weaver.

Buchanan's Liberty
Designers:
obverse—Christian Gobrecht;
reverse—David Westwood.

Mary Lincoln
Designers:
obverse—Phebe Hemphill;
reverse—Joel Iskowitz.

| | Mintage | MS | MS-69 | MS-70 |
		PF	PF-69	PF-70
$10 2010-W, A. Fillmore	3,482	$750	$800	$1,100
$10 2010-W, A. Fillmore, Proof	6,130	$900	$950	$1,050
$10 2010-W, J. Pierce	3,338	$750	$800	$1,100
$10 2010-W, J. Pierce, Proof	4,775	$950	$1,000	$1,350
$10 2010-W, Buchanan's Liberty	5,162	$800	$850	$1,050
$10 2010-W, Buchanan's Liberty, Proof	7,110	$900	$950	$1,050
$10 2010-W, M. Lincoln	3,695	$800	$850	$1,100
$10 2010-W, M. Lincoln, Proof	6,861	$900	$950	$1,250

Note: MS values are for uncertified Mint State coins of average quality, in their complete original U.S. Mint packaging. PF values are for uncertified Proof coins of average quality, in their complete original U.S. Mint packaging.

Eliza Johnson
Designers:
obverse—Joel Iskowitz;
reverse—Gary Whitley.

Julia Grant
Designers:
obverse—Donna Weaver;
reverse—Richard Masters.

Lucy Hayes
Designers:
obverse—Susan Gamble;
reverse—Barbara Fox.

Lucretia Garfield
Designers:
obverse—Barbara Fox;
reverse—Michael Gaudioso.

| | Mintage | MS | MS-69 | MS-70 |
		PF	PF-69	PF-70
$10 2011-W, E. Johnson	$800	$800	$850	$1,300
$10 2011-W, E. Johnson, Proof	$950	$950	$1,000	$1,100
$10 2011-W, J. Grant	$800	$800	$850	$1,150
$10 2011-W, J. Grant, Proof	$950	$950	$1,000	$1,200
$10 2011-W, L. Hayes (g)	$950	$950	$1,000	$1,600
$10 2011-W, L. Hayes, Proof	$1,100	$1,100	$1,150	$1,500
$10 2011-W, L. Garfield	$950	$950	$1,000	$1,600
$10 2011-W, L. Garfield, Proof	$900	$900	$950	$1,300

Note: MS values are for uncertified Mint State coins of average quality, in their complete original U.S. Mint packaging. PF values are for uncertified Proof coins of average quality, in their complete original U.S. Mint packaging. **g.** Auction: $1,763, MS-70, January 2015.

Alice Paul
Designers:
obverse—Susan Gamble;
reverse—Phebe Hemphill.

Frances Cleveland (Type 1)
Designers:
obverse—Joel Iskowitz;
reverse—Barbara Fox.

Caroline Harrison
Designers:
obverse—Frank Morris;
reverse—Donna Weaver.

Frances Cleveland (Type 2)
Designers:
obverse—Barbara Fox;
reverse—Joseph Menna.

| | Mintage | MS | MS-69 | MS-70 |
		PF	PF-69	PF-70
$10 2012-W, Alice Paul	2,798	$850	$900	$1,100
$10 2012-W, Alice Paul, Proof	3,505	$875	$925	$1,350
$10 2012-W, Frances Cleveland, Variety 1	2,454	$850	$900	$950
$10 2012-W, Frances Cleveland, Variety 1, Proof	3,158	$925	$975	$1,100

Note: MS values are for uncertified Mint State coins of average quality, in their complete original U.S. Mint packaging. PF values are for uncertified Proof coins of average quality, in their complete original U.S. Mint packaging.

	Mintage	MS	MS-69	MS-70
		PF	PF-69	PF-70
$10 2012-W, Caroline Harrison	2,436	$850	$900	$1,100
$10 2012-W, Caroline Harrison, Proof	3,046	$925	$975	$1,150
$10 2012-W, Frances Cleveland, Variety 2	2,425	$850	$900	$950
$10 2012-W, Frances Cleveland, Variety 2, Proof	3,104	$925	$975	$1,150

Note: MS values are for uncertified Mint State coins of average quality, in their complete original U.S. Mint packaging. PF values are for uncertified Proof coins of average quality, in their complete original U.S. Mint packaging.

Ida McKinley
Designers:
obverse—Susan Gamble;
reverse—Donna Weaver.

Edith Roosevelt
Designers:
obverse—Joel Iskowitz;
reverse—Chris Costello.

Helen Taft
Designers:
obverse—William C. Burgard;
reverse—Richard Masters.

Ellen Wilson
Designers: obverse—Frank Morris;
reverse—Don Everhart.

Edith Wilson
Designers: obverse—David Westwood;
reverse—Joseph Menna.

	Mintage	MS	MS-69	MS-70
		PF	PF-69	PF-70
$10 2013-W, I. McKinley	2,008	$825	$875	$950
$10 2013-W, I. McKinley, Proof	2,724	$900	$950	$1,300
$10 2013-W, E. Roosevelt	2,027	$825	$875	$950
$10 2013-W, E. Roosevelt, Proof	2,840	$900	$950	$1,050
$10 2013-W, H. Taft	1,993	$825	$875	$950
$10 2013-W, H. Taft, Proof	2,598	$900	$950	$1,050
$10 2013-W, Ellen Wilson	1,980	$825	$875	$950
$10 2013-W, Ellen Wilson, Proof	2,511	$900	$950	$1,050
$10 2013-W, Edith Wilson	1,974	$825	$875	$950
$10 2013-W, Edith Wilson, Proof	2,464	$900	$950	$1,050

Note: MS values are for uncertified Mint State coins of average quality, in their complete original U.S. Mint packaging. PF values are for uncertified Proof coins of average quality, in their complete original U.S. Mint packaging.

Florence Harding
*Designer:
obverse and reverse—
Thomas Cleveland.*

Grace Coolidge
*Designers:
obverse—Joel Iskowitz;
reverse—Frank Morris.*

Lou Hoover
*Designers:
obverse—Susan Gamble;
reverse—Richard Masters.*

Eleanor Roosevelt
*Designer:
obverse and reverse—
Chris Costello.*

| | Mintage | MS | MS-69 | MS-70 |
		PF	PF-69	PF-70
$10 2014-W, F. Harding	1,775	$825	$875	$950
$10 2014-W, F. Harding, Proof	2,372	$875	$925	$1,250
$10 2014-W, G. Coolidge	1,774	$825	$875	$950
$10 2014-W, G. Coolidge, Proof	2,315	$900	$950	$1,500
$10 2014-W, L. Hoover	1,756	$825	$875	$950
$10 2014-W, L. Hoover, Proof	2,284	$900	$950	$1,600
$10 2014-W, E. Roosevelt	1,886	$1,600	$1,700	$2,200
$10 2014-W, E. Roosevelt, Proof	2,377	$1,400	$1,500	$2,400

Note: MS values are for uncertified Mint State coins of average quality, in their complete original U.S. Mint packaging. PF values are for uncertified Proof coins of average quality, in their complete original U.S. Mint packaging.

Bess Truman
*Designer:
obverse and reverse—
Joel Iskowitz.*

Mamie Eisenhower
*Designers:
obverse—Richard Masters;
reverse—Barbara Fox.*

Jacqueline Kennedy
*Designers:
obverse—Susan Gamble;
reverse—Benjamin Sowards.*

Claudia "Lady Bird" Johnson
*Designers:
obverse—Linda Fox;
reverse—Chris Costello.*

| | Mintage | MS | MS-69 | MS-70 |
		PF	PF-69	PF-70
$10 2015-W, B. Truman	1,946	$825	$850	$950
$10 2015-W, B. Truman, Proof	2,747	$900	$925	$1,000
$10 2015-W, M. Eisenhower	2,102	$825	$850	$950
$10 2015-W, M. Eisenhower, Proof	2,315	$900	$925	$1,000

Note: MS values are for uncertified Mint State coins of average quality, in their complete original U.S. Mint packaging. PF values are for uncertified Proof coins of average quality, in their complete original U.S. Mint packaging.

| | Mintage | MS | MS-69 | MS-70 |
		PF	PF-69	PF-70
$10 2015-W, J. Kennedy	5,491	$825	$850	$950
$10 2015-W, J. Kennedy, Proof	11,123	$900	$925	$1,000
$10 2015-W, Lady Bird Johnson	1,475	$825	$850	$950
$10 2015-W, Lady Bird Johnson, Proof	2,285	$900	$925	$1,000

Note: MS values are for uncertified Mint State coins of average quality, in their complete original U.S. Mint packaging. PF values are for uncertified Proof coins of average quality, in their complete original U.S. Mint packaging.

Patricia Nixon
Designer:
obverse and reverse—
Richard Masters.

Betty Ford
Designers:
obverse—Barbara Fox;
reverse—Chris Costello.

Nancy Reagan
Designers:
obverse—Benjamin Sowards;
reverse—Joel Iskowitz.

| | Mintage | MS | MS-69 | MS-70 |
		PF	PF-69	PF-70
$10 2016-W, P. Nixon	1,839	$825	$850	$950
$10 2016-W, P. Nixon, Proof	2,646	$900	$925	$1,000
$10 2016-W, B. Ford	1,824	$825	$850	$950
$10 2016-W, B. Ford, Proof	2,471	$900	$925	$1,000
$10 2016-W, N. Reagan	2,010	$825	$850	$950
$10 2016-W, N. Reagan, Proof	3,548	$900	$925	$1,000

Note: MS values are for uncertified Mint State coins of average quality, in their complete original U.S. Mint packaging. PF values are for uncertified Proof coins of average quality, in their complete original U.S. Mint packaging.

AMERICAN PLATINUM EAGLES
(1997 TO DATE)

Designers: *John M. Mercanti (obverse), Thomas D. Rogers Sr. (original reverse)
(see image captions for other reverse designers).* **Weight:** *$10 1/10 oz.—3.112 grams;
$25 1/4 oz.—7.780 grams; $50 1/2 oz.—15.560 grams; $100 1 oz.—31.120 grams.*
Composition: *.9995 platinum.* **Diameter:** *$10 1/10 oz.—16.5 mm; $25 1/4 oz.—22 mm;
$50 1/2 oz.—27 mm; $100 1 oz.—32.7 mm.* **Edge:** *Reeded.* **Mints:** *Philadelphia and West Point.*

Regular Finish

Burnished Finish
*Burnished coins of all denominations feature the year's
Proof reverse design. Mintmark location varies by design.*

Proof Finish

First-year Proof coins featured the original reverse design, which is still in use on bullion strikes. See pages 1274–1276 for illustrations of Proof reverse designs from 1998 to date.

Reverse Proof Finish

Reverse Proofs were only struck in 2007, and only in the $50 1/2-oz. denomination.

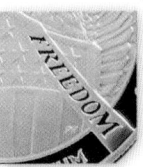 

Frosted FREEDOM
This variety is seen, very rarely, for 2007 Proof coins of the $25, $50, and $100 denominations.

History. Platinum American Eagles (face values of $10 to $100) are legal-tender bullion coins with weight, content, and purity guaranteed by the federal government. They were added to the U.S. Mint's program of silver and gold bullion coinage in 1997.

In their debut year, Proofs had the same reverse design as regular bullion strikes. Since then, the regular strikes have continued with the 1997 reverse, while the Proofs have featured new reverse designs each year. From 1998 through 2002, these special Proof designs comprised a "Vistas of Liberty" subset, with eagles flying through various American scenes. Since 2003, they have featured patriotic allegories and symbolism. From 2006 to 2008 the reverse designs honored "The Foundations of Democracy"—the nation's legislative branch (2006), executive branch (2007), and judicial branch (2008). In 2009 the Mint introduced a new six-year program of reverse designs, exploring the core concepts of American democracy as embodied in the preamble to the Constitution. The designs—which were based on narratives by John Roberts, chief justice of the United States—began with *To Form a More Perfect Union* (2009), which features four faces representing the nation's diversity, with the hair and clothing interweaving symbolically. The tiny eagle privy mark is from an original coin punch from the Philadelphia Mint's archives. This design is followed by *To Establish Justice* (2010), *To Insure Domestic Tranquility* (2011), *To Provide for the Common Defence* (2012), *To Promote the General Welfare* (2013), and *To Secure the Blessings of Liberty to Ourselves and Our Posterity* (2014). In 2015, the Mint issued the first of a two-year series of new reverse designs emblematic of the core values of liberty and freedom called *Liberty Nurtures Freedom*. In 2017 the Proof reverse returned to the original 1997 design for the program's 20th anniversary. One-ounce Proofs of 2018 through 2020 feature new obverse designs in the theme of Life, Liberty, and the Pursuit of Happiness, and also share a new common reverse design. Beginning in 2021 the Mint will issue a new five-year series of one-ounce Proofs, for the five freedoms guaranteed under the First Amendment of the U.S. Constitution.

The Philadelphia Mint strikes regular bullion issues, which are sold to the public by a network of Mint-authorized precious-metal firms, coin dealers, banks, and brokerages. The West Point facility strikes Burnished pieces (called *Uncirculated* by the Mint, and featuring the reverse design of the Proof coins), which are sold directly to collectors. Proofs are also struck at West Point and, like the Burnished coins, are sold by the Mint to the public, without middlemen. Similar to their gold-bullion cousins, the platinum Proofs and Burnished coins bear a W mintmark and are specially packaged in plastic capsules and fancy presentation cases.

In addition to the individual coins listed below, platinum American Eagles were issued in the 1997 "Impressions of Liberty" bullion coin set; in 2007 "10th Anniversary" sets; and in annual platinum-coin sets.

Striking and Sharpness. Striking is generally sharp.

Availability. The platinum American Eagle is one of the most popular platinum-investment vehicles in the world. The coins are readily available in the numismatic marketplace and through some banks, investment firms, and other non-numismatic channels.

MS-60 to 70 (Mint State). *Obverse and Reverse:* At MS-60, some abrasion and contact marks are evident on the higher design areas. Luster may be dull or lifeless at MS–60 to 62, but there should be deep frost at MS-63 and better, particularly in the lower-relief areas. At MS-65 and above, the luster should be full and rich. These guidelines are more academic than practical, as platinum American Eagles are not intended for circulation, and nearly all are in high Mint State grades.

PF-60 to 70 (Proof). *Obverse and Reverse:* Proofs that are extensively cleaned and have many hairlines are lower level, such as PF-60 to 62. Those with fewer hairlines or flaws are deemed PF–63 to 65. (These exist more in theory than actuality, as nearly all Proof American Eagle platinum bullion coins have been maintained in their original high condition by collectors.) Given the quality of modern U.S. Mint products, even PF–66 and 67 are unusually low levels for these Proofs.

$10 1/10-Ounce
AMERICAN PLATINUM EAGLES

	Mintage	MS	MS-69	MS-70
		PF	PF-69	PF-70
$10 1997 (a)	70,250	$160	$185	$1,300
$10 1997-W, Proof	36,993	$195	$220	$275
$10 1998 (b)	39,525	$165	$190	$1,450
$10 1998-W, Proof (c)	19,847	$250	$275	$550
$10 1999 (d)	55,955	$160	$185	$800
$10 1999-W, Proof (c)	19,133	$205	$230	$300
$10 2000	34,027	$160	$185	$600
$10 2000-W, Proof (c)	15,651	$220	$245	$400
$10 2001	52,017	$160	$185	$375
$10 2001-W, Proof (c)	12,174	$200	$225	$425
$10 2002	23,005	$165	$190	$300
$10 2002-W, Proof (c)	12,365	$200	$225	$400
$10 2003	22,007	$165	$190	$300
$10 2003-W, Proof (c,e)	9,534	$195	$220	$290
$10 2004	15,010	$170	$195	$300
$10 2004-W, Proof (c,f)	7,161	$350	$375	$490
$10 2005	14,013	$170	$195	$300
$10 2005-W, Proof (c,g)	8,104	$225	$250	$375
$10 2006	11,001	$190	$215	$300
$10 2006-W, Burnished (c,h)	3,544	$410	$435	$550
$10 2006-W, Proof (c)	10,205	$190	$215	$350
$10 2007 (i)	13,003	$170	$195	$325
$10 2007-W, Burnished (c,j)	5,556	$200	$225	$280
$10 2007-W, Proof (c)	8,176	$190	$215	$350
$10 2008	17,000	$165	$190	$300
$10 2008-W, Burnished (c,k)	3,706	$335	$370	$425
$10 2008-W, Proof (c,l)	5,138	$325	$350	$450

Note: MS values are for uncertified Mint State coins of average quality, in their complete original U.S. Mint packaging. PF values are for uncertified Proof coins of average quality, in their complete original U.S. Mint packaging. **a.** Auction: $4,230, MS-70, January 2015. **b.** Auction: $223, MS-69, January 2013. **c.** Burnished and Proof coins from 1998 on featured the designs illustrated on pages 1274–1276. **d.** Auction: $170, MS-69, August 2014. **e.** Auction: $176, PF-69DCam, December 2014. **f.** Auction: $447, PF-69DCam, February 2015. **g.** Auction: $212, PF-70UCam, February 2015. **h.** Auction: $441, MS-70, June 2013. **i.** Auction: $153, MS-70, September 2015. **j.** $364, MS-70, May 2015. **k.** Auction: $282, MS-69, September 2015. **l.** $376, PF-70UCam, January 2015.

$25 1/4-OUNCE AMERICAN PLATINUM EAGLES

| | Mintage | MS | MS-69 | MS-70 |
		PF	PF-69	PF-70
$25 1997 (a)	27,100	$310	$335	$3,000
$25 1997-W, Proof	18,628	$390	$415	$575
$25 1998	38,887	$310	$335	$1,400
$25 1998-W, Proof (b)	14,873	$390	$415	$700
$25 1999 (c)	39,734	$310	$335	$2,750
$25 1999-W, Proof (b)	13,507	$390	$415	$700
$25 2000	20,054	$310	$335	$800
$25 2000-W, Proof (b)	11,995	$390	$415	$700
$25 2001 (d)	21,815	$310	$335	$2,300
$25 2001-W, Proof (b)	8,847	$390	$415	$750
$25 2002	27,405	$310	$335	$575
$25 2002-W, Proof (b)	9,282	$390	$415	$750
$25 2003	25,207	$310	$335	$550
$25 2003-W, Proof (b)	7,044	$390	$415	$750
$25 2004	18,010	$310	$335	$550
$25 2004-W, Proof (b,e)	5,193	$850	$900	$1,250
$25 2005	12,013	$340	$365	$600
$25 2005-W, Proof (b,f)	6,592	$550	$600	$950
$25 2006	12,001	$340	$365	$600
$25 2006-W, Burnished (b,g)	2,676	$600	$650	$800
$25 2006-W, Proof (b)	7,813	$390	$415	$750
$25 2007	8,402	$345	$370	$650
$25 2007-W, Burnished (b,h)	3,690	$550	$600	$700
$25 2007-W, Proof (b)	6,017	$390	$415	$750
$25 2007-W, Frosted FREEDOM, Proof (b)	21	—		
$25 2008	22,800	$310	$335	$575
$25 2008-W, Burnished (b,i)	2,481	$850	$900	$1,250
$25 2008-W, Proof (b,j)	4,153	$700	$750	$1,000

Note: MS values are for uncertified Mint State coins of average quality, in their complete original U.S. Mint packaging. PF values are for uncertified Proof coins of average quality, in their complete original U.S. Mint packaging. **a.** Auction: $7,638, MS-70, January 2015. **b.** Burnished and Proof coins from 1998 on featured the designs illustrated on pages 1274–1276. **c.** Auction: $411, MS-68, October 2012. **d.** Auction: $374, MS-68, June 2012. **e.** Auction: $764, PF-70DCam, July 2015. **f.** Auction: $564, PF-70DCam, January 2015. **g.** Auction: $306, MS-69, November 2015. **h.** Auction: $598, MS-70, August 2014. **i.** Auction: $764, MS-70, September 2015. **j.** Auction: $470, PF-70UCam, June 2015.

$50 1/2-OUNCE AMERICAN PLATINUM EAGLES

| | Mintage | MS | MS-69 | MS-70 |
		PF	PF-69	PF-70
$50 1997 (a)	20,500	$625	$675	$5,000
$50 1997-W, Proof	15,431	$725	$750	$925

Note: MS values are for uncertified Mint State coins of average quality, in their complete original U.S. Mint packaging. PF values are for uncertified Proof coins of average quality, in their complete original U.S. Mint packaging. **a.** Auction: $870, MS-69, July 2014.

| | Mintage | MS | MS-69 | MS-70 |
		PF	PF-69	PF-70
$50 1998 (b)	32,415	$625	$675	$3,500
$50 1998-W, Proof (c)	13,836	$725	$750	$900
$50 1999 (d)	32,309	$625	$675	$3,500
$50 1999-W, Proof (c)	11,103	$725	$750	$900
$50 2000 (e)	18,892	$625	$675	$4,000
$50 2000-W, Proof (c)	11,049	$725	$750	$900
$50 2001 (f)	12,815	$625	$675	$3,750
$50 2001-W, Proof (c)	8,254	$725	$750	$900
$50 2002	24,005	$625	$675	$1,700
$50 2002-W, Proof (c)	8,772	$725	$750	$900
$50 2003	17,409	$625	$675	$1,100
$50 2003-W, Proof (c)	7,131	$725	$750	$900
$50 2004	13,236	$625	$675	$1,100
$50 2004-W, Proof (c,g)	5,063	$1,100	$1,150	$1,550
$50 2005	9,013	$675	$725	$1,100
$50 2005-W, Proof (c,h)	5,942	$950	$1,000	$1,400
$50 2006	9,602	$700	$750	$950
$50 2006-W, Burnished (c)	2,577	$850	$900	$1,300
$50 2006-W, Proof (c)	7,649	$725	$750	$1,250
$50 2007	7,001	$700	$750	$950
$50 2007-W, Burnished (c)	3,635	$825	$875	$1,000
$50 2007-W, Proof (c)	25,519	$725	$750	$900
$50 2007-W, Reverse Proof (c)	19,583	$800	$850	$1,000
$50 2007-W, Frosted FREEDOM, Proof (c)	21	—		
$50 2008	14,000	$625	$675	$1,000
$50 2008-W, Burnished ‡ (c,i)	2,253	$1,200	$1,300	$2,500
$50 2008-W, Proof ‡ (c,j)	4,020	$1,200	$1,250	$1,600

Note: MS values are for uncertified Mint State coins of average quality, in their complete original U.S. Mint packaging. PF values are for uncertified Proof coins of average quality, in their complete original U.S. Mint packaging. **b.** Auction: $881, MS-68, October 2012. **c.** Burnished and Proof coins from 1998 on featured the designs illustrated on pages 1274–1276. **d.** Auction: $823, MS-69, April 2014. **e.** Auction: $823, MS-69, November 2012. **f.** Auction: $796, MS-69, July 2014. **g.** Auction: $1,058, PF-70DCam, July 2015. **h.** Auction: $705, PF-70UCam, February 2015. **i.** Auction: $1,528, MS-70, October 2015. **j.** Auction: $1,234, PF-70UCam. October 2015.

$100 1-Ounce American Platinum Eagles

**Proof Reverse, 1998:
Eagle Over New England.**
*Vistas of Liberty series.
Designer: John Mercanti.*

**Proof Reverse, 1999:
Eagle Above
Southeastern Wetlands.**
*Vistas of Liberty series.
Designer: John Mercanti.*

| | Mintage | MS | MS-69 | MS-70 |
		PF	PF-69	PF-70
$100 1997 (a)	56,000	$1,250	$1,350	—
$100 1997-W, Proof	20,851	$1,450	$1,500	$2,900

Note: MS values are for uncertified Mint State coins of average quality, in their complete original U.S. Mint packaging. PF values are for uncertified Proof coins of average quality, in their complete original U.S. Mint packaging. **a.** Auction: $1,821, MS-69, July 2014.

Proof Reverse, 2000: Eagle Above America's Heartland.
Vistas of Liberty series.
Designer: Alfred Maletsky.

Proof Reverse, 2001: Eagle Above America's Southwest.
Vistas of Liberty series.
Designer: Thomas D. Rogers Sr.

Proof Reverse, 2002: Eagle Fishing in America's Northwest.
Vistas of Liberty series.
Designer: Alfred Maletsky.

Proof Reverse, 2003.
Designer: Alfred Maletsky.

Proof Reverse, 2004.
Designer: Donna Weaver.

Proof Reverse, 2005.
Designer: Donna Weaver.

Proof Reverse, 2006: Legislative Branch.
The Foundations of Democracy series.
Designer: Joel Iskowitz.

Proof Reverse, 2007: Executive Branch.
The Foundations of Democracy series.
Designer: Thomas Cleveland.

	Mintage	MS	MS-69	MS-70
		PF	PF-69	PF-70
$100 1998 (b)	133,002	$1,250	$1,350	—
$100 1998-W, Proof	14,912	$1,450	$1,500	$2,800
$100 1999 (c)	56,707	$1,250	$1,350	—
$100 1999-W, Proof (d)	12,363	$1,450	$1,500	$3,750
$100 2000 (e)	10,003	$1,250	$1,350	—
$100 2000-W, Proof (f)	12,453	$1,450	$1,500	$2,300
$100 2001 (g)	14,070	$1,250	$1,350	—
$100 2001-W, Proof	8,969	$1,450	$1,500	$3,900
$100 2002 (h)	11,502	$1,250	$1,350	—
$100 2002-W, Proof (i)	9,834	$1,450	$1,500	$3,900
$100 2003	8,007	$1,250	$1,350	$3,750
$100 2003-W, Proof (j)	8,246	$1,450	$1,500	$3,900
$100 2004	7,009	$1,250	$1,350	$2,500
$100 2004-W, Proof (k)	6,007	$2,100	$2,150	$3,400
$100 2005	6,310	$1,250	$1,350	$2,500
$100 2005-W, Proof (l)	6,602	$2,300	$2,350	$3,000
$100 2006	6,000	$1,250	$1,350	$2,200
$100 2006-W, Burnished ‡ (m)	3,068	$2,100	$2,200	$2,400
$100 2006-W, Proof	9,152	$1,450	$1,500	$2,000
$100 2007	7,202	$1,250	$1,350	$2,100

Note: MS values are for uncertified Mint State coins of average quality, in their complete original U.S. Mint packaging. PF values are for uncertified Proof coins of average quality, in their complete original U.S. Mint packaging. ‡ Ranked in the *100 Greatest U.S. Modern Coins.* **b.** Auction: $1,704, MS-68, October 2012. **c.** Auction: $1,660, MS-69, November 2012. **d.** Auction: $1,645, PF69-UCam, March 2015. **e.** Auction: $1,553, MS-69, June 2012. **f.** Auction: $1,410, PF-70UCam, April 2014. **g.** Auction: $4,994, MS-69, April 2014. **h.** Auction: $1,645, MS-69, September 2012. **i.** Auction: $1,880, PF-70DCam, February 2015. **j.** Auction: $1,880, PF-70DCam, April 2015. **k.** Auction: $2,291, PF-70UCam, January 2015. **l.** Auction: $1,998, PF-70UCam, October 2015. **m.** Auction: $1,351, MS-69, November 2015.

Proof Reverse, 2008: Judicial Branch. *The Foundations of Democracy series. Designer: Joel Iskowitz.*

Proof Reverse, 2009: "To Form a More Perfect Union." *Preamble series. Designer: Susan Gamble.*

Proof Reverse, 2010: "To Establish Justice." *Preamble series. Designer: Donna Weaver.*

Proof Reverse, 2011: "To Insure Domestic Tranquility." *Preamble series. Designer: Joel Iskowitz.*

Proof Reverse, 2012: "To Provide for the Common Defence." *Preamble series. Designer: Barbara Fox.*

Proof Reverse, 2013: "To Promote the General Welfare." *Preamble series. Designer: Joel Iskowitz.*

Proof Reverse, 2014: "To Secure the Blessings of Liberty to Ourselves and Our Posterity." *Preamble series. Designer: Susan Gamble.*

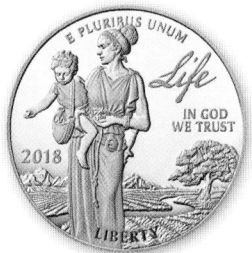

Proof Reverse, 2015: Liberty Nurtures Freedom. *Designer: Joel Iskowitz.*

Proof Reverse, 2016: Portrait of Liberty. *Designer: John Mercanti.*

Proof Obverse, 2018: "Life." *Designer: Justin Kunz.*

New Common Reverse, 2018 *Designer: Patricia Lucas-Morris.*

	Mintage	MS / PF	MS-69 / PF-69	MS-70 / PF-70
$100 2007-W, Burnished	4,177	$1,900	$2,000	$2,200
$100 2007-W, Proof	8,363	$1,450	$1,500	$2,500
$100 2007-W, Frosted FREEDOM, Proof	12	—		
$100 2008	21,800	$1,250	$1,350	$1,950
$100 2008-W, Burnished (n)	2,876	$2,200	$2,300	$2,500
$100 2008-W, Proof (o)	4,769	$1,900	$1,950	$3,500
$100 2009-W, Proof ‡	7,945	$1,800	$1,850	$2,000
$100 2010-W, Proof	14,790	$1,800	$1,850	$2,000
$100 2011-W, Proof	14,835	$1,550	$1,600	$1,750
$100 2012-W, Proof	10,084	$1,550	$1,600	$1,750
$100 2013-W, Proof	5,745	$1,950	$2,000	$2,500

Note: MS values are for uncertified Mint State coins of average quality, in their complete original U.S. Mint packaging. PF values are for uncertified Proof coins of average quality, in their complete original U.S. Mint packaging. ‡ Ranked in the 100 Greatest U.S. Modern Coins. n. Auction: $1,880, MS-70, October 2015. o. Auction: $2,291, PF-70UCam, October 2015.

	Mintage	MS	MS-69	MS-70
		PF	PF-69	PF-70
$100 2014	16,900	$1,250	$1,350	$1,800
$100 2014-W, Proof	4,596	$2,900	$3,050	$3,500
$100 2015-W, Proof	3,881	$2,900	$3,050	$3,500
$100 2016-W, Proof	*20,000*	$2,900	$3,050	$3,500
$100 2017-W, Proof		$2,900	$3,050	$3,500
$100 2018-W, Proof		$2,900	$3,050	$3,500

Note: MS values are for uncertified Mint State coins of average quality, in their complete original U.S. Mint packaging. PF values are for uncertified Proof coins of average quality, in their complete original U.S. Mint packaging. ‡ Ranked in the *100 Greatest U.S. Modern Coins.* **n.** Auction: $1,880, MS-70, October 2015. **o.** Auction: $2,291, PF-70UCam, October 2015.

AMERICAN PLATINUM EAGLE BULLION COIN SETS

	MS	MS-69	MS-70
1997 Platinum Set. $100, $50, $25, $10	$2,350	$2,550	—
1998 Platinum Set. $100, $50, $25, $10	$2,350	$2,550	—
1999 Platinum Set. $100, $50, $25, $10	$2,350	$2,550	—
2000 Platinum Set. $100, $50, $25, $10	$2,350	$2,550	—
2001 Platinum Set. $100, $50, $25, $10	$2,350	$2,550	—
2002 Platinum Set. $100, $50, $25, $10	$2,350	$2,550	—

Note: MS values are for uncertified Mint State sets of average quality, in their complete original U.S. Mint packaging.

	MS	MS-69	MS-70
2003 Platinum Set. $100, $50, $25, $10	$2,350	$2,550	$5,700
2004 Platinum Set. $100, $50, $25, $10	$2,450	$2,650	$4,450
2005 Platinum Set. $100, $50, $25, $10	$2,400	$2,600	$4,450
2006 Platinum Set. $100, $50, $25, $10	$2,400	$2,600	$4,000
2006-W Platinum Burnished Set. $100, $50, $25, $10	$3,900	$4,200	$4,900
2007 Platinum Set. $100, $50, $25, $10	$2,400	$2,600	$3,900
2007-W Platinum Burnished Set. $100, $50, $25, $10	$3,400	$3,600	$4,000
2008 Platinum Set. $100, $50, $25, $10	$2,300	$2,500	$3,800
2008-W Platinum Burnished Set. $100, $50, $25, $10	$4,500	$4,800	$6,500

Note: MS values are for uncertified Mint State sets of average quality, in their complete original U.S. Mint packaging.

AMERICAN PLATINUM EAGLE PROOF COIN SETS

	PF	PF-69	PF-70
1997-W Platinum Set. $100, $50, $25, $10	$2,700	$2,850	$4,600
1998-W Platinum Set. $100, $50, $25, $10	$2,800	$2,950	$4,900
1999-W Platinum Set. $100, $50, $25, $10	$2,700	$2,850	$5,600
2000-W Platinum Set. $100, $50, $25, $10	$2,700	$2,900	$4,300
2001-W Platinum Set. $100, $50, $25, $10	$2,700	$2,900	$5,900
2002-W Platinum Set. $100, $50, $25, $10	$2,700	$2,900	$5,900
2003-W Platinum Set. $100, $50, $25, $10	$2,700	$2,900	$5,800
2004-W Platinum Set. $100, $50, $25, $10	$4,000	$4,200	$6,000
2005-W Platinum Set. $100, $50, $25, $10	$3,800	$4,000	$5,300
2006-W Platinum Set. $100, $50, $25, $10	$2,750	$2,900	$4,350
2007-W Platinum Set. $100, $50, $25, $10	$2,700	$2,850	$4,500
2008-W Platinum Set. $100, $50, $25, $10	$3,800	$4,000	$6,100

Note: PF values are for uncertified Proof sets of average quality, in their complete original U.S. Mint packaging. The Proof $100 American Platinum Eagle of 1997 is also included in the 1997 Impressions of Liberty set, listed on pages 1216 and 1228.

2007 AMERICAN PLATINUM EAGLE 10TH-ANNIVERSARY PROOF COIN SETS

	PF	PF-69	PF-70
2007 Two-Coin Set (a)	$1,500	$1,600	$1,900

a. This two-coin set, housed in a mahogany-finish hardwood box, includes one half-ounce Proof (with the standard cameo-finish background and frosted design elements) and one half-ounce Reverse Proof (with frosted background fields and mirrored raised elements) dated 2007-W.

AMERICAN PALLADIUM EAGLES
(2017 TO DATE)

Designer: *Adolph A. Weinman.* **Weight:** *31.120 grams (1 oz. pure palladium).* **Composition:** *.9995 palladium.* **Diameter:** *32.7 mm.* **Edge:** *Reeded.* **Mints:** *Philadelphia (bullion) and West Point (Proof).*

A side view showing the coin's high relief.

History. In 2017 palladium was added to the U.S. Mint's American Eagle bullion programs, becoming the fourth precious metal in the lineup.

The American Palladium Bullion Act of 2010 (Public Law 111-303) required the secretary of the Treasury to mint and issue .9995 fine palladium bullion coins weighing one troy ounce and with a face value of $25, "in such quantities as the secretary determines appropriate to meet demand." Only coins in the one-ounce size are permitted; fractional sizes are not authorized. Title 31 U.S.C. Section 5112(v) authorizes the secretary to mint and issue Proof and Burnished ("Uncirculated") versions for collectors.

The American Palladium Eagle's designs were mandated by law. The obverse is a high-relief allegorical portrait derived from artist Adolph Weinman's Winged Liberty dime of 1916 to 1945. The reverse is a high-relief version of Weinman's 1907 American Institute of Architects gold medal reverse, showing an eagle grasping a branch. To develop the coin, the Mint was able to use the original reverse plaster of the AIA gold medal.

Although largely symbolic, the palladium coin's denomination of $25 provides proof of its authenticity as official U.S. coinage.

Bullion-strike coins are minted in Philadelphia on an annual basis, and distributed through the Mint's network of authorized purchasers. A Proof version was struck at the West Point Mint in 2018, and sold by the Mint directly to collectors.

Striking and Sharpness. Striking is generally sharp.

Availability. The American Palladium Eagle is a readily available bullion and collector coin. The coins are easily acquired in the numismatic marketplace and through some banks, investment firms, and other non-numismatic channels.

MS-60 to 70 (Mint State). *Obverse and Reverse:* Grading guidelines are more academic than practical for this program, since American Palladium Eagles are not intended for circulation, and nearly all are in high Mint State grades.

PF-60 to 70 (Proof). *Obverse and Reverse:* Impaired, cleaned, and otherwise low-level Proofs exist more in theory than in actuality for this series, as nearly all Proof American Palladium Eagle coins have been maintained in their original high condition by collectors. Given the quality of modern U.S. Mint products, even PF-66 or 67 would be unusually low for these Proofs.

	Mintage	Value
2017	15,000	$1,650
2018-W		

Significant U.S. Patterns

Pattern coins are a fascinating part of numismatics that encompass thousands of designs and experimental pieces made by the U.S. Mint to test new motifs, alloys, coin sizes, and other variables. Most were official creations—products of the research-and-development process that takes a coin from congressionally authorized concept to finished pocket change. Some were made in secret, outside the normal day-to-day work of the Mint. The book *United States Pattern Coins*, by J. Hewitt Judd, gives extensive details of the history and characteristics of more than 2,000 different pattern varieties from 1792 to the present era.

Patterns provide students and collectors a chronology of the continuing efforts of engravers and artists to present their work for approval. Throughout the 220-plus years of federal coinage production, concepts meant to improve various aspects of circulating coins have been proposed and given physical form in patterns. In some instances, changes have been prompted by an outcry for higher aesthetics, a call for a more convenient denomination, or a need to overcome striking deficiencies. In many other instances, workers or officials at the Mint simply created special coins for the numismatic trade—often controversial in their time, but enthusiastically collected today. Certain patterns, bearing particular proposed designs or innovations, provided tangible examples for Mint and Treasury Department officials or members of Congress to review and evaluate. If approved and adopted, the pattern design became a familiar regular-issue motif; those that were rejected have become part of American numismatic history.

The patterns listed and illustrated in this section are samples from a much larger group. Such pieces generally include die and hub trials, off-metal Proof strikings of regular issues, and various combinations of dies that were sometimes struck at a later date. Certain well-known members of this extended pattern family historically have been included with regular issues in many popular, general-circulation numismatic reference books. The four-dollar gold Stellas of 1879 and 1880; certain Gobrecht dollars of 1836, 1838, and 1839; the transitional half dimes and dimes of 1859 and 1860; and the Flying Eagle cents of 1856 are examples. No official mintage figures of patterns and related pieces were recorded in most instances, and the number extant of each can usually only be estimated from auction appearances and from those found in museum holdings and important private collections. Although most patterns are very rare, the 2,000-plus distinct varieties make them unexpectedly collectible—not by one of each, but by selected available examples from favorite types or categories. Curiously, the most common of all patterns is the highly sought and expensive 1856 Flying Eagle cent!

Unlike regular coin issues that were emitted through the usual channels of commerce, and Proofs of regular issues that were struck expressly for sale to collectors, patterns were not intended to be officially sold. Yet as a matter of Mint practice, often against stated policy and law, countless patterns were secretly and unofficially sold and traded to favorite dealers (most notably William K. Idler and his son-in-law John W. Haseltine) and collectors, disseminated to government officials, and occasionally made available to numismatic societies. Not until mid-1885 did an incoming new director of the Mint enforce stringent regulations prohibiting their sale and distribution, although there had been many misleading statements to this effect earlier. In succeeding decades the Mint, while not making patterns available to numismatists, did place certain examples in the Mint Collection, now called the National Numismatic Collection, in the Smithsonian Institution. On other occasions, selected patterns were obtained by Mint and Treasury officials, or otherwise spared from destruction. Today, with the exception of certain cents and five-cent pieces of 1896, all pattern coins dated after 1885 are extremely rare.

The private possession of patterns has not been without its controversy. Most significant was the 1910 seizure by government agents of a parcel containing some 23 pattern pieces belonging to John W. Haseltine, a leading Philadelphia coin dealer with undisclosed private ties to Mint officials. The government asserted that the patterns had been removed from the Mint without authority, and that they remained the property of the United States. Haseltine's attorney successfully used the Mint's pre-1887 policies in his defense, and recovered the patterns a year after their confiscation. This set precedent for ownership, at least for the patterns minted prior to 1887, as all of the pieces in question predated that year. Today pattern coins can be legally held, and, in fact, they were inadvertently made legal tender (as was the earlier demonetized silver trade dollar) by the Coinage Act of 1965.

Among the grandest impressions ever produced at the U.S. Mint are the two varieties of pattern fifty-dollar gold pieces of 1877. Officially titled half unions, these large patterns were created at the request of certain politicians with interests tied to the gold-producing state of California. Specimens were struck in copper, and one of each variety was struck in gold. Both of the gold pieces were purchased around 1908 by numismatist William H. Woodin (who, years later, in 1933, served as President Franklin D. Roosevelt's first secretary of the Treasury). The sellers were John W. Haseltine and Stephen K. Nagy, well known for handling many rarities that few others could obtain from the Mint. The Mint desired to re-obtain the pieces for its own collection, and through a complex trade deal for quantities of other patterns, did so, adding them to the Mint Collection. Now preserved in the Smithsonian Institution, these half unions are regarded as national treasures.

The following resources are recommended for additional information, descriptions, and complete listings:

United States Pattern Coins, 10th edition, J. Hewitt Judd, edited by Q. David Bowers, 2009.

United States Patterns and Related Issues, Andrew W. Pollock III, 1994. (Out of print)

www.harrybassfoundation.org

www.uspatterns.com

Judd-52   **J-67**

	PF-60	PF-63	PF-65
1836 Two-cent piece (J-52, billon) (a)	$3,000	$5,000	$8,500
Auctions: $8,625, PF-65, January 2009			
1836 Gold dollar (J-67, gold) (b)	$7,500	$12,500	$30,000
Auctions: $24,725, PF-65, November 2010			

a. This proposal for a two-cent coin is one of the earliest collectible patterns. It was designed by Christian Gobrecht. An estimated 21 to 30 examples are known. **b.** Gobrecht styled the first gold dollar pattern after the familiar "Cap and Rays" design used on Mexican coins, which at the time were legal tender in the United States. An estimated 31 to 75 pieces are known.

J-164

J-177

	PF-60	PF-63	PF-65
1854 Cent (J-164, bronze) (a)	$1,750	$3,500	$7,500
Auctions: $16,100, PF-67BN, March 2005			
1856 Half cent (J-177, copper-nickel) (b)	$2,500	$4,500	$5,500
Auctions: $6,038, PF-64, January 2006			

a. Beginning in 1850, the Mint produced patterns for a reduced-weight cent. Among the designs were ring-style, Liberty Head, and Flying Eagle motifs. These experiments culminated with the 1856 Flying Eagle cent. An estimated 31 to 75 examples of J-164 are known. Those with red mint luster are worth more than the values listed here. **b.** Before producing copper-nickel small-size cents in 1856, the Mint experimented with that alloy using half-cent dies. An estimated 31 to 75 examples are known.

J-204

J-239

	PF-60	PF-63	PF-65
1858 Cent (J-204, copper-nickel) (a)	$1,600	$2,500	$4,000
1859 Half dollar (J-239, silver) (b)	$1,500	$2,000	$3,750

a. This pattern cent's flying eagle differs from the one adopted for regular coinage of the one-cent piece. An estimated 31 to 75 pieces are known. **b.** This design proposal for a new half dollar features James Longacre's French Liberty Head design. An estimated 76 to 200 pieces are known.

J-305

	PF-60	PF-63	PF-65
1863 Washington two-cent piece (J-305, copper) (a)	$1,500	$2,250	$4,000

a. Before the two-cent coin was introduced to circulation, two basic designs were considered. If this George Washington portrait design had been adopted, it would have been the first to depict a historical figure. An estimated 76 to 200 pieces are known.

J-349

J-407

J-470

	PF-60	PF-63	PF-65
1863 Eagle (J-349, gold) (a)		$450,000	
1865 Bimetallic two-cent piece (J-407, silver and copper) (b)	$6,000	$11,000	$19,500
1866 Five-cent piece (J-470, nickel) (c)	$1,650	$2,500	$4,500

a. This unique gold eagle features IN GOD WE TRUST on a scroll on the reverse. This feature would not appear on regular eagle coinage until 1866. The obverse is from the regular 1863 die. **b.** This experimental piece is the first "clad" coin. It consists of an irregular and streaky layer of silver fused to copper. The experiment was unsuccessful. An estimated 4 to 6 pieces are known. **c.** Another of George Washington's early pattern appearances was on five-cent pieces of 1866. An estimated 21 to 30 are known.

J-486

J-611

	PF-60	PF-63	PF-65
1866 Lincoln five-cent piece (J-486, nickel) (a)	$5,000	$11,000	$25,000
1868 Cent (J-611, copper) (b)	$17,500	$30,000	$36,000
Auctions: $36,800, PF-66BN, March 2005			

a. A number of pattern nickels were produced in 1866, including one designed to depict the recently assassinated President Abraham Lincoln. An estimated 7 to 12 examples are known. **b.** There is no known reason for the minting of this unusual piece, which mimics the original large cents that had last been made in 1857. There was no intent to resume the coinage of old-style copper "large" cents in 1868. Accordingly, this variety is regarded as a rarity created for collectors. Fewer than 15 examples are believed to exist.

J-1195

J-1235

	PF-60	PF-63	PF-65
1872 Amazonian quarter (J-1195, silver) (a)	$17,500	$30,000	$65,000
Auctions: $80,500, PF-66Cam, January 2009			
1872 Amazonian gold $3 (J-1235, gold) (b)	—	—	$1,250,000

a. Many of the most popular patterns have been given colorful nicknames by collectors in appreciation of their artistry. This design is by Chief Engraver William Barber. An estimated 7 to 12 examples are known. **b.** This unique piece was contained in the Mint's only uniform gold set using the same design from the gold dollar to the double eagle.

J-1373

	PF-60	PF-63	PF-65
1874 Bickford eagle (J-1373, gold) (a)	—	$550,000	$1,500,000

a. Dana Bickford, a New York City manufacturer, proposed a ten-dollar gold coin that would be exchangeable at set rates with other world currencies. Patterns were made, but the idea proved impractical. 2 examples are known.

J-1392

	PF-60	PF-63	PF-65
1875 Sailor Head twenty-cent piece (J-1392, silver) (a)	$3,000	$5,500	$9,500

a. Chief Engraver William Barber's "Sailor Head" is one of the most elegant of several rejected designs for a twenty-cent coin. The same head was used on other patterns, including proposals for trade dollars. An estimated 21 to 30 examples of J-1392 are known.

J-1507

J-1512   J-1528

	PF-60	PF-63	PF-65
1877 Morgan half dollar (J-1507, copper) (a)	$18,000	$29,000	$50,000
1877 Morgan half dollar (J-1512, silver) (b)	$15,000	$28,000	$45,000
1877 Half dollar (J-1528, silver) (c)	$17,000	$33,000	$50,000

a. A year before his famous and eponymous dollar design was adopted for regular coinage, engraver George Morgan's Liberty Head appeared on several varieties of pattern half dollars, all of which are rare today. J-1507 pairs the well-known obverse with an indented shield design. 2 examples are known. **b.** The half dollar pattern cataloged as J-1512 pairs Morgan's "silver dollar style" obverse with a dramatic "Defiant Eagle" reverse. 6 examples are known. **c.** This is one of several 1877 pattern half dollars by Chief Engraver William Barber. 4 are known.

J-1549

1877 Half union (J-1549, copper) (a)	PF-60	PF-63	PF-65
	$115,000	$215,000	$350,000
Auctions: $575,000, PF-67BN, January 2009			

a. This famous fifty-dollar pattern by Chief Engraver William Barber would have been the highest denomination ever issued by the Mint up to that time. The gold impression (J-1548) is unique and resides in the Smithsonian's National Numismatic Collection, but copper specimens (J-1549, which are priced here and are sometimes gilt) occasionally come to the market. Varieties exist with a somewhat larger or smaller head.

J-1590

1879 Quarter dollar (J-1590, silver) (a)	PF-60	PF-63	PF-65
	$4,500	$8,000	$16,500
Auctions: $34,500, PF-68, January 2007			

a. Referred to as the "Washlady" design, this was Charles Barber's first attempt at a uniform silver design. An estimated 13 to 20 examples are known.

J-1609

1879 Dollar (J-1609, copper) (a)	PF-60	PF-63	PF-65
	$12,500	$17,500	$45,000
Auctions: $74,750, PF-66RB, September 2006			

a. The "Schoolgirl" design by George T. Morgan is a widespread favorite among pattern collectors. Examples are rare, with only 7 to 12 known.

J-1643

	PF-60	PF-63	PF-65
1879 Metric double eagle (J-1643, gold) (a)	$325,000	$600,000	$1,000,000

a. James Longacre's Liberty Head design was the same as that used on regular-issue double eagles, but with an added inscription indicating the coin's specifications in metric units. 5 are known.

J-1667　　　　J-1669　　　　J-1673

	PF-60	PF-63	PF-65
1881 One-cent piece (J-1667, aluminum) (a)	$2,025	$3,780	$6,440
1881 Three-cent piece (J-1669, copper) (a)	$2,000	$3,750	$6,000
1881 Five-cent piece (J-1673, aluminum) (a)	$2,300	$4,800	$9,000

a. These patterns by Chief Engraver Charles Barber represent an attempt at a uniform set of minor coins; if adopted, they would have been struck in nickel for circulation. An estimated 7 to 20 examples are known of each of the illustrated patterns.

J-1698

	PF-60	PF-63	PF-65
1882 Quarter dollar (J-1698, silver) (a)	$17,500	$34,000	$55,000

a. George Morgan's "Shield Earring" design was made in patterns of quarter, half, and dollar denominations. 7 to 12 of the quarter dollar patterns are known.

J-1761　　　　J-1770

	PF-60	PF-63	PF-65
1891 Barber quarter (J-1761, silver) (a)	—	—	—
1896 Shield nickel (J-1770, nickel) (b)	$1,500	$2,750	$4,000

a. Charles Barber prepared various pattern dimes, quarters, and half dollars in 1891. The quarter illustrated is similar to the design adopted for regular coinage in 1892. Two pieces are known, both in the Smithsonian's National Numismatic Collection. **b.** In 1896 the Mint struck experimental cents and nickels with similar designs, by Charles Barber. 21 to 30 examples of J-1770 are known.

J-1905

	PF-60	PF-63	PF-65
1907 Indian Head double eagle (J-1905, gold) (a)			*$15,000,000*

a. Designed by Augustus Saint-Gaudens, this pattern is unique and extremely valuable. A variation of the reverse of this design was used on the double eagles struck for circulation from 1907 through 1933.

J-1992

	PF-60	PF-63	PF-65
1916 Liberty Walking half dollar (J-1992, silver) (a)	$25,000	$50,000	$100,000
Auctions: $115,000, PF-65, July 2008			

a. Various pattern Mercury dimes, Standing Liberty quarters, and Liberty Walking half dollars were struck, all dated 1916. All are extremely rare, but a few found their way into circulation.

J-2063

	PF-60	PF-63	PF-65
1942 Experimental cent (J-2051 through J-2069, several metallic and other compositions) (a)	$1,500	$2,750	$4,500

a. Before settling on the zinc-coated steel composition used for the Lincoln cents of 1943, the Mint considered various alternative compositions, including plastics. Most were struck by outside contractors using specially prepared dies provided by the Mint. An estimated 7 to 12 examples are known of most types and colors.

Private and Territorial Gold

The expression *private gold*, used with reference to coins struck outside the United States Mint, is a general term. In the sense that no state or territory had authority to coin money, *private gold* simply refers to those necessity pieces of various shapes, denominations, and degrees of intrinsic worth that were coined by facilities other than official U.S. mints and circulated in isolated areas of the United States by assayers, bankers, and other private individuals and organizations. Some numismatists use the terms *territorial gold* and *state gold* to cover certain issues because they were coined and circulated in a territory or state. While the state of California properly sanctioned the ingots stamped by F.D. Kohler as state assayer, in no instance (except for the Mormon issues of Salt Lake City) were any of the gold pieces struck by authority of any of the territorial governments.

The stamped fifty-dollar and other gold coins, sometimes called *ingots*, but in coin form, were made by Augustus Humbert, the United States Assayer of Gold, but were not receivable at face value for government payments, despite the fact that Humbert was an official agent selected by the Treasury Department. However, such pieces circulated widely in commerce.

Usually, private coins were circulated due to a shortage of regular federal coinage. In the Western states particularly, official money became so scarce that gold itself—the very commodity the pioneers had come so far to acquire—was converted into a local medium of exchange.

Ephraim Brasher's New York doubloons of 1786 and 1787 are also private American gold issues and are described on page 125.

TEMPLETON REID

GEORGIA GOLD, 1830

The first private gold coinage in the 19th century was struck by Templeton Reid, a jeweler and gunsmith, in Milledgeville, Georgia, in July 1830. To be closer to the mines he moved some 120 miles northwest to Gainesville, where most of his coins were made. Although their weights were accurate, Reid's assays were not and his coins were slightly short of their claimed value. He was severely attacked in the newspapers by a determined adversary, and soon lost the public's confidence. He closed his mint before the end of October in 1830; his output had amounted to only about 1,600 coins. Denominations struck were $2.50, $5, and $10. All are great rarities today.

	VF	EF	AU
1830 $2.50	$125,000	$175,000	$300,000
1830 $5 (a)	$350,000	$475,000	$575,000

a. 7 examples are known.

	VF	EF
1830 TEN DOLLARS (a)	$700,000	$975,000
(No Date) TEN DOLLARS (b)	$775,000	$1,200,000

a. 6 examples are known. **b.** 3 examples are known.

CALIFORNIA GOLD, 1849

The enigmatic later issues of Templeton Reid, dated 1849 and marked CALIFORNIA GOLD, were probably made from California gold late in that year when bullion from California arrived in quantity in the East. Reid, who never went to California, was by then a cotton-gin maker in Columbus, Georgia (some 160 miles southwest of his former location of Gainesville), where he would die in 1851. The coins were in denominations of ten and twenty-five dollars. Struck copies of both exist in various metals.

The only example known of the twenty-five–dollar piece was stolen from the cabinet of the U.S. Mint on August 16, 1858. It was never recovered.

1849 TEN DOLLAR CALIFORNIA GOLD	*(unique, in Smithsonian collection)*
1849 TWENTY-FIVE DOLLARS CALIFORNIA GOLD	*(unknown)*

THE BECHTLERS, RUTHERFORD COUNTY, NORTH CAROLINA, 1831–1852

A skilled German metallurgist, Christopher Bechtler, assisted by his son August and his nephew, also named Christopher, operated a private mint in Rutherford County, North Carolina. Rutherford County and other areas in the Piedmont region of North Carolina and Georgia (from the coastal plain to the mountains of north Georgia) were the principal sources of the nation's gold supply from the early 1800s until the California gold strikes in 1848.

The coins minted by the Bechtlers were of only three denominations, but they covered a wide variety of weights and sizes. Rotated dies are common throughout the series. In 1831, the Bechtlers produced the first gold dollar in the United States. (The Philadelphia Mint made patterns in 1836 and struck its first circulating gold dollar in 1849.) Bechtler coins were well accepted by the public and circulated widely in the Southeast without interference from the government.

The legend AUGUST 1. 1834 on several varieties of five-dollar pieces has a special significance. The secretary of the Treasury recommended to the director of the U.S. Mint that gold coins of the reduced weight introduced in 1834 bear the authorization date. This ultimately was not done on federal gold coinage, but the elder Christopher Bechtler evidently acted on the recommendation to avoid potential difficulty with Treasury authorities.

CHRISTOPHER BECHTLER

	VF	EF	AU	Unc.
ONE GOLD DOLLAR N. CAROLINA, 30.G., Star	$3,000	$4,500	$7,000	$15,000
ONE GOLD DOLLAR N. CAROLINA, 28.G Centered, No Star	$5,000	$6,000	$11,500	$26,000
ONE GOLD DOLLAR N. CAROLINA, 28.G High, No Star	$9,000	$15,000	$23,000	$35,000

	VF	EF	AU	Unc.
ONE DOLLAR CAROLINA, 28.G, N Reversed	$2,600	$3,200	$4,750	$8,250
2.50 NORTH CAROLINA, 20 C. Without 75 G.	$28,000	$38,500	$57,500	$120,000

	VF	EF	AU	Unc.
2.50 NORTH CAROLINA, 75 G., 20 C. RUTHERFORD in a Circle. Border of Large Beads	$26,000	$36,000	$52,500	$115,000
2.50 NORTH CAROLINA, 20 C. Without 75 G., CAROLINA above 250 instead of GOLD (a)				—
2.50 NORTH CAROLINA, 20 C. on Obverse, 75 G. and Star on Reverse. Border Finely Serrated	—	—	—	

a. This piece is unique.

	VF	EF	AU	Unc.
2.50 CAROLINA, 67 G., 21 CARATS	$8,000	$13,000	$17,500	$33,000
2.50 GEORGIA, 64 G., 22 CARATS (Uneven "22")	$7,500	$12,500	$16,500	$32,000
2.50 GEORGIA, 64 G., 22 CARATS (Even "22")	$9,000	$15,000	$20,000	$40,000
2.50 CAROLINA, 70 G., 20 CARATS	$7,500	$12,500	$16,500	$32,000

	VF	EF	AU	Unc.
5 DOLLARS NORTH CAROLINA GOLD, 150 G., 20.CARATS	$28,000	$40,000	$72,000	$120,000
Similar, Without 150.G. (a)		—	—	

a. 1 or 2 examples are known.

CHRISTOPHER BECHTLER, CAROLINA

	VF	EF	AU	Unc.
5 DOLLARS CAROLINA, RUTHERFORD, 140 G., 20 CARATS, Plain Edge	$6,000	$8,500	$12,500	$26,000
5 DOLLARS CAROLINA, RUTHERFORD, 140 G., 20 CARATS, Reeded Edge	$20,000	$30,000	$45,000	$70,000
5 DOLLARS CAROLINA GOLD, RUTHERF., 140 G., 20 CARATS, AUGUST 1, 1834	$11,000	$18,000	$30,000	$50,000
Similar, but "20" Distant From CARATS	$6,500	$10,000	$15,000	$27,500
5 DOLLARS CAROLINA GOLD, 134 G., 21 CARATS, With Star	$6,000	$8,000	$12,000	$24,000

CHRISTOPHER BECHTLER, GEORGIA

	VF	EF	AU	Unc.
5 DOLLARS GEORGIA GOLD, RUTHERFORD, 128 G., 22 CARATS	$8,500	$12,000	$16,500	$33,000
5 DOLLARS GEORGIA GOLD, RUTHERFORD, 128 G:, 22 CARATS, With Colon After G	$16,000	$26,000	$38,500	
5 DOLLARS GEORGIA GOLD, RUTHERF., 128 G., 22 CARATS	$8,000	$11,500	$15,000	$32,000

AUGUST BECHTLER, CAROLINA

	VF	EF	AU	Unc.
1 DOL:, CAROLINA GOLD, 27.G., 21.C	$1,800	$2,400	$3,200	$5,500
5 DOLLARS, CAROLINA GOLD, 134.G:, 21 CARATS	$6,000	$8,750	$15,000	$36,000
5 DOLLARS, CAROLINA GOLD, 134 G:, 21 CARATS, Reverse of C. Bechtler as Shown Above	—	—		

	VF	EF	AU	Unc.
5 DOLLARS, CAROLINA GOLD, 128.G., 22 CARATS	$15,000	$18,000	$27,500	$45,000
5 DOLLARS, CAROLINA GOLD, 141.G., 20 CARATS	$12,500	$17,000	$25,000	$40,000

Note: Restrikes in "Proof" of this type using original dies were made about 1920.

NORRIS, GREGG & NORRIS, SAN FRANCISCO, 1849

Collectors consider this piece the first of the California private gold coins. A newspaper account dated May 31, 1849, described a five-dollar gold coin, struck at Benicia City, though with the imprint of San Francisco. It mentioned the private stamp of Norris, Gregg & Norris, the California branch of a New York City plumbing and hardware firm.

	F	VF	EF	AU	Unc.
1849 Half Eagle, Plain Edge	$4,750	$7,000	$12,000	$17,000	$37,000
1849 Half Eagle, Reeded Edge	$4,750	$7,000	$12,000	$17,000	$37,000
1850 Half Eagle, With STOCKTON Beneath Date (a)		—			

a. This unique piece is housed in the Smithsonian's National Numismatic Collection.

MOFFAT & CO., SAN FRANCISCO, 1849–1853

The firm of Moffat & Co. (principals John Little Moffat, Joseph R. Curtis, Philo H. Perry, and Samuel H. Ward) was the most important of the California private coiners. The assay office they conducted became semi-official in character starting in 1851. The successors to this firm, Curtis, Perry, and Ward, later sold their coining facility to the Treasury Department, which in March 1854 reopened it as the branch mint of San Francisco.

In June or July 1849, Moffat & Co. began to issue small, rectangular ingots of gold in response to lack of coin in the locality, in values from $9.43 to $264. The $9.43, $14.25, and $16.00 varieties are the only types known today.

$9.43 Ingot (a)	—
$14.25 Ingot (a)	—
$16.00 Ingot	$200,000

a. This unique piece is housed in the Smithsonian's National Numismatic Collection..

The dies for the five-dollar and ten-dollar Moffat & Co. pieces were cut by a Bavarian engraver, Albrecht Küner, who had moved to the United States in October 1848. On the coronet of Miss Liberty appear the words MOFFAT & CO., instead of the word LIBERTY as in regular U.S. issues.

	F	VF	EF	AU	Unc.
1849 FIVE DOL. (a)	$1,900	$3,300	$4,700	$7,000	$15,000
1850 FIVE DOL. (a)	$1,950	$3,500	$5,000	$7,500	$17,500
1849 TEN DOL.	$3,750	$6,500	$12,500	$22,500	$38,000
1849 TEN D.	$4,000	$7,000	$13,500	$25,000	$45,000

a. Multiple varieties exist.

UNITED STATES ASSAY OFFICE
Augustus Humbert, United States Assayer of Gold, 1851

Augustus Humbert, a New York watchcase maker, was appointed United States assayer by the Treasury Department in 1850 and arrived in California in early 1851. He placed his name and the government stamp on the ingots of gold issued by Moffat & Co., but without the Moffat imprint. The assay office, a provisional government mint, was a temporary expedient to accommodate the Californians until the establishment of a permanent federal branch mint.

The fifty-dollar gold piece was accepted by most banks and merchants as legal tender on a par with standard U.S. gold coins and was known variously as a *slug*, *quintuple eagle*, *five-eagle piece*, or *adobe* (the latter a type of construction brick). It was officially termed an *ingot*.

Lettered-Edge Varieties

  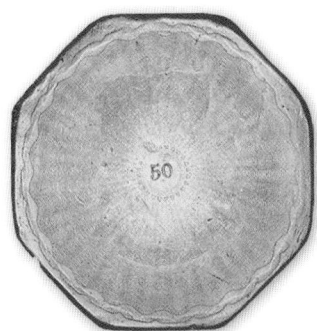

	F	VF	EF	AU	Unc.
1851 50 D C 880 THOUS., No 50 on Reverse. Sunk in Edge: AUGUSTUS HUMBERT UNITED STATES ASSAYER OF GOLD, CALIFORNIA 1851	$22,500	$36,000	$60,000	$90,000	$200,000
Auctions: $546,250, MS-63, August 2010					
1851 50 D C 880 THOUS., Similar to Last Variety, but 50 on Reverse	$32,000	$60,000	$90,000	$160,000	$300,000
1851 50 D C, 887 THOUS., With 50 on Reverse	$27,000	$50,000	$75,000	$115,000	$250,000

Reeded-Edge Varieties

 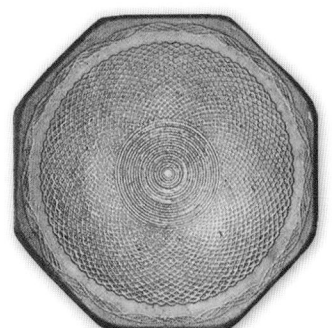

	F	VF	EF	AU	Unc.
1851 FIFTY DOLLS, 880 THOUS., "Target" Reverse	$16,500	$25,000	$40,000	$52,000	$100,000
Auctions: $460,000, MS-65, September 2008					
1851 FIFTY DOLLS, 887 THOUS., "Target" Reverse	$16,500	$25,000	$40,000	$52,000	$100,000
1852 FIFTY DOLLS, 887 THOUS., "Target" Reverse	$17,000	$27,000	$42,000	$55,000	$110,000

MOFFAT-HUMBERT

In 1851, certain issues of the Miners' Bank, Baldwin, Pacific Company, and others were discredited, some unfairly, by newspaper accounts stating they were of reduced gold value. This provided an enhanced opportunity for Moffat and the U.S. Assay Office of Gold. Supplementing privately struck gold pieces and federal issues, coins of almost every nation were being pressed into service by the Californians, but the supply was too small to help to any extent. Moffat & Co. proceeded in January 1852 to issue a new ten-dollar gold piece bearing the stamp MOFFAT & CO.

Close Date   **Wide Date**

	F	VF	EF	AU	Unc.
1852 TEN D. MOFFAT & CO., Close Date	$4,200	$7,000	$15,000	$35,000	$77,500
1852 TEN D. MOFFAT & CO., Wide Date	$4,200	$7,000	$15,000	$35,000	$77,500
Auctions: $940,000, SP-63, January 2014					

1852, Normal Date   **1852, 2 Over 1**

	F	VF	EF	AU	Unc.
1852 TEN DOLS.	$2,750	$4,250	$7,500	$12,000	$27,500
Auctions: $1,057,500, MS-68, April 2013					
1852 TEN DOLS. 1852, 2 Over 1	$2,850	$5,250	$9,500	$16,000	$35,000

	F	VF	EF	AU	Unc.
1852 TWENTY DOLS., 1852, 2 Over 1	$8,250	$14,000	$27,500	$45,000	$140,000
Auctions: $211,500, MS-64, April 2014					

UNITED STATES ASSAY OFFICE OF GOLD, 1852

The firm of Moffat & Co. was dissolved in 1852 and a newly reorganized company known as the United States Assay Office of Gold took over the contract. Principals in the firm were Joseph Curtis, Philo Perry, and Samuel Ward.

 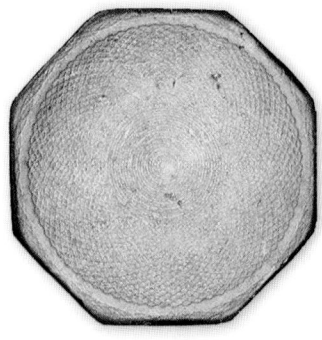

	F	VF	EF	AU	Unc.
1852 FIFTY DOLLS., 887 THOUS.	$16,500	$25,000	$40,000	$52,000	$100,000
1852 FIFTY DOLLS., 900 THOUS.	$17,500	$27,000	$42,000	$55,000	$110,000

	F	VF	EF	AU	Unc.
1852 TEN DOLS., 884 THOUS.	$2,000	$3,500	$5,250	$7,750	$18,000
1853 TEN D., 884 THOUS.	$7,500	$15,000	$27,500	$38,500	$75,000
1853 TEN D., 900 THOUS.	$4,500	$6,500	$10,000	$16,000	$25,000

	F	VF	EF	AU	Unc.
1853 TWENTY D., 884 THOUS.	$7,800	$11,500	$19,000	$32,000	$65,000

	F	VF	EF	AU	Unc.
1853 TWENTY D., 900 THOUS.	$2,400	$3,500	$5,000	$6,750	$13,000

Note: Modern prooflike forgeries exist.

MOFFAT & CO. GOLD, 1853

The last Moffat & Co. issue, an 1853 twenty-dollar piece, is very similar to the U.S. double eagle of that period. It was struck after John L. Moffat retired from the Assay Office. The circumstances of its issue are unclear, but many were coined.

	F	VF	EF	AU	Unc.
1853 TWENTY D.	$4,750	$7,000	$11,000	$18,500	$38,500

J.H. BOWIE, 1849

Joseph H. Bowie joined his cousins in San Francisco in 1849 and possibly produced a limited coinage of gold pieces. A trial piece of the dollar denomination is known in copper, but may never have reached the coinage stage. Little is known about the company or the reason for considering these pieces.

1849 1 DOL., copper pattern	—

CINCINNATI MINING & TRADING CO., 1849

The origin and location of this company are unknown.

	EF	Unc.
1849 FIVE DOLLARS (a)		
1849 TEN DOLLARS (b)	$750,000	—

Note: Beware of spurious specimens cast in base metal with the word TRACING in place of TRADING. **a.** This piece is unique. **b.** 5 examples are known.

MASSACHUSETTS AND CALIFORNIA COMPANY, 1849

This company was organized in Northampton, Massachusetts, in May 1849. Years later fantasy and copy dies were made and coins struck in various metals including gold. Pieces with the denomination spelled as 5D are not genuine.

	VF	EF
1849 FIVE D. (a)	$185,000	$285,000

a. 5 to 7 examples are known.

MINERS' BANK, SAN FRANCISCO, 1849

The institution of Wright & Co., exchange brokers located in Portsmouth Square, San Francisco, was known as the Miners' Bank. The firm issued a ten-dollar gold piece in the autumn of 1849, and it saw wide use in commerce. However, the firm's coinage was ephemeral, and it was dissolved on January 14, 1850. Unlike the gold in most California issues, the gold in these coins was alloyed with copper.

	VF	EF	AU	Unc.
(1849) TEN D.	$19,000	$34,000	$50,000	$110,000

J.S. ORMSBY, SACRAMENTO, 1849

The initials J.S.O., which appear on certain issues of California privately coined gold pieces, represent the firm of J.S. Ormsby & Co., located in Sacramento. They struck five- and ten-dollar denominations, all undated.

	VF
(1849) 5 DOLLS, Plain Edge (a)	—
(1849) 5 DOLLS, Reeded Edge (b)	—
(1849) 10 DOLLS (c)	$450,000

a. This piece may be unique. b. This unique piece is housed in the Smithsonian's National Numismatic Collection. c. 4 examples are known.

PACIFIC COMPANY, SAN FRANCISCO, 1849

The origin of the Pacific Company is very uncertain. All data regarding the firm are based on conjecture.

Edgar H. Adams wrote that he believed that the coins bearing the stamp of the Pacific Company were produced by the coining firm of Broderick and Kohler. The coins were probably hand struck with the aid of a sledgehammer. Trial pieces exist in silver. All are rarities today.

	EF	AU	Unc.
1849 1 DOLLAR (a)			$300,000
1849 5 DOLLARS (b)	$400,000	$700,000	
Auctions: $763,750, AU-58, April 2014			
1849 10 DOLLARS (c)	$600,000	$800,000	$1,000,000

a. 2 examples are known. b. 4 examples are known. c. 4 examples are known.

F.D. KOHLER, CALIFORNIA STATE ASSAYER, 1850

The State Assay Office was authorized on April 12, 1850. That year, Governor Peter Burnett appointed to the position of state assayer Frederick D. Kohler, who thereupon sold his assaying business to Baldwin & Co. Kohler served at both the San Francisco and Sacramento offices. The State Assay Offices were discontinued at the time the U.S. Assay Office was established, on February 1, 1851.

Ingots issued ranged from $36.55 to $150. An Extremely Fine specimen sold in the Garrett Sale, 1980, for $200,000. Each is unique.

$36.55 Sacramento	—
$37.31 San Francisco	—
$40.07 San Francisco	—
$45.34 San Francisco	—
$50.00 San Francisco	—
$54.00 San Francisco	—

Note: A $40.07 ingot was stolen from the Mint Cabinet in 1858 and never recovered.

DUBOSQ & COMPANY, SAN FRANCISCO, 1850

Theodore Dubosq Sr., a Philadelphia jeweler, took melting and coining equipment to San Francisco in 1849 and minted five-dollar gold pieces.

	VF
1850 FIVE D. (a)	$300,000
1850 TEN D. (b)	$300,000
Auctions: $329,000, MS-60, April 2014	

a. 3 to 5 examples are known. **b.** 8 to 10 examples are known.

BALDWIN & CO., SAN FRANCISCO, 1850–1851

George C. Baldwin and Thomas S. Holman were in the jewelry business in San Francisco and were known as Baldwin & Co. They were the successors to F.D. Kohler & Co., taking over its machinery and other equipment in May 1850. The firm ceased minting coins in early 1851, at which time newspaper accounts stated that its coins fell short of their stated gold value. The 1850 Vaquero or Horseman ten-dollar design is one of the most famous of the California gold issues.

	F	VF	EF	AU	Unc.
1850 FIVE DOL.	$7,500	$13,000	$25,000	$35,000	$75,000
1850, TEN DOLLARS, Horseman Type	$45,000	$80,000	$125,000	$175,000	$275,000

	F	VF	EF	AU	Unc.
1851 TEN D.	$16,000	$34,000	$50,000	$85,000	$190,000

The Baldwin & Co. twenty-dollar piece was the first of that denomination issued in California. Baldwin coins are believed to have contained about 2% copper alloy.

1851 TWENTY D. (a)	EF	Unc.
	$650,000	—
Auctions: $646,250, EF-45, April 2014		

a. 4 to 6 examples are known.

SCHULTZ & COMPANY, SAN FRANCISCO, 1851

The firm of Schultz & Co., a brass foundry, was operated by Judge G.W. Schultz and William T. Garratt. The surname is misspelled as SHULTZ on the coins.

1851 FIVE D.	F	VF	EF	AU	Unc.
	$32,500	$57,500	$90,000	$150,000	$350,000

DUNBAR & COMPANY, SAN FRANCISCO, 1851

Edward E. Dunbar operated the California Bank in San Francisco. He later returned to New York City and organized the famous Continental Bank Note Co.

1851 FIVE D. (a)	VF	EF
	$250,000	$425,000

a. 4 to 6 examples are known.

WASS, MOLITOR & CO., SAN FRANCISCO, 1852–1855

The gold-smelting and assaying plant of Wass, Molitor & Co. was operated by two Hungarian patriots exiled after the Revolution of 1848, Count Samu Wass and A.P. Molitor. They maintained an excellent laboratory and complete apparatus for analysis and coinage of gold.

The company struck five-, ten-, twenty-, and fifty-dollar coins. In 1852 they produced a ten-dollar piece similar in design to the five-dollar denomination. The difference is in the reverse legend, which reads: S.M.V. [Standard Mint Value] CALIFORNIA GOLD TEN D.

No pieces were coined in 1853 or 1854, but they brought out the twenty- and fifty-dollar pieces in 1855. A considerable number of the fifty-dollar coins were made. There was a ten-dollar piece issued in 1855 also, with the Liberty Head design and small close date.

Small Head, Rounded Bust   **Large Head, Pointed Bust**

	F	VF	EF	AU	Unc.
1852 FIVE DOLLARS, Small Head, With Rounded Bust	$5,500	$11,000	$22,500	$40,000	$80,000
1852 FIVE DOLLARS, Large Head, With Pointed Bust	$5,000	$10,000	$20,000	$36,000	$70,000

Large Head

Small Head   **Small Date**   **1855**

	F	VF	EF	AU	Unc.
1852 TEN D., Large Head	$2,750	$4,750	$8,250	$14,500	$32,500
1852 TEN D., Small Head	$6,200	$8,000	$19,000	$32,000	$80,000
1852 TEN D., Small Close Date	$12,500	$28,000	$47,000	$90,000	
1855 TEN D.	$9,500	$16,000	$22,000	$29,000	$52,500

Large Head   **Small Head**

	F	VF	EF	AU	Unc.
1855 TWENTY DOL., Large Head (a)	—	—	$550,000	—	—
Auctions: $558,125, AU-53, April 2014					
1855 TWENTY DOL., Small Head	$12,000	$25,000	$35,000	$57,500	$125,000

a. 4 to 6 examples are known. A unique piece with the Large Head obverse and the reverse used on the Small Head coins (which differs in the position of the eagle's left wing) also exists.

	F	VF	EF	AU	Unc.
1855 50 DOLLARS	$25,000	$36,000	$55,000	$85,000	$180,000

KELLOGG & CO., SAN FRANCISCO, 1854–1855

John G. Kellogg went to San Francisco on October 12, 1849, from Auburn, New York. At first he was employed by Moffat & Co., and remained with that organization when control passed to Curtis, Perry, and Ward. When the U.S. Assay Office was discontinued, December 14, 1853, Kellogg became associated with George F. Richter, who had been an assayer in the U.S. Assay Office of Gold. These two set up business as Kellogg & Richter on December 19, 1853.

When the U.S. Assay Office ceased operations, a period ensued during which no private firm was striking gold. The new San Francisco branch mint did not produce coins for some months after Curtis & Perry took the contract for the government (Ward having died). The lack of coin was again keenly felt by businessmen, who petitioned Kellogg & Richter to "supply the vacuum" by issuing private coin. Their plea was soon answered: on February 9, 1854, Kellogg & Co. placed their first twenty-dollar piece in circulation.

The firm dissolved late in 1854 and reorganized as Kellogg & Humbert. The latter partner was Augustus Humbert, for some time identified as U.S. assayer of gold in California. Regardless of the fact that the San Francisco branch mint was then producing coins, Kellogg & Humbert issued twenty-dollar coins in 1855 in a quantity greater than before. On September 12, 1857, hundreds of the firm's rectangular gold ingots in transit to New York City were lost in the sinking of the SS *Central America*. They were the most plentiful of bars aboard the ill-fated ship from several different assayers.

	F	VF	EF	AU	Unc.
1854 TWENTY D.	$3,250	$4,750	$6,500	$10,000	$25,000

The 1855 Kellogg & Co. twenty-dollar piece is similar to that of 1854. The letters on the reverse are larger and the arrows longer on one 1854 variety. There are die varieties of both.

	F	VF	EF	AU	Unc.
1855 TWENTY D.	$3,500	$5,000	$7,000	$12,000	$27,500

In 1855, Ferdinand Grüner cut the dies for a round-format fifty-dollar gold coin for Kellogg & Co., but coinage seems to have been limited to presentation pieces in Proof format. Only 10 to 12 pieces are known to exist. A "commemorative restrike" was made in 2001 using transfer dies made from the original and gold recovered from the SS *Central America*. These pieces have the inscription S.S. CENTRAL AMERICA GOLD, C.H.S. on the reverse ribbon.

	PF
1855 FIFTY DOLLS. (a)	$600,000
Auctions: $763,750, PF-64Cam, April 2014; $747,500, PF-64, January 2007	

a. 13 to 15 examples are known.

OREGON EXCHANGE COMPANY, OREGON CITY, 1849

THE BEAVER COINS OF OREGON

Upon the discovery of gold in California, a great exodus of Oregonians joined in the hunt for the precious metal. Soon, gold seekers returned with their gold dust, which became an accepted medium of exchange. As in other Western areas at that time, the uncertain qualities of the gold and weighing devices tended to irk tradespeople, and petitions were made to the legislature for a standard gold coin issue.

On February 16, 1849, the territorial legislature passed an act providing for a mint and specified five- and ten-dollar gold coins without alloy. Oregon City, the largest city in the territory with a population of about 1,000, was designated as the location for the mint. At the time this act was passed, Oregon had been brought into the United States as a territory by act of Congress. When the new governor arrived on March 2, he declared the coinage act unconstitutional.

The public-spirited people, however, continued to work for a convenient medium of exchange and soon took matters into their own hands by starting a private mint. Eight men of affairs, whose names were Kilborne, Magruder, Taylor, Abernethy, Willson, Rector, Campbell, and Smith, set up the Oregon Exchange Company.

The coins struck were of virgin gold as specified in the original act. Ten-dollar dies were made slightly later.

	F	VF	EF	AU	Unc.
1849 5 D.	$32,000	$50,000	$75,000	$125,000	$275,000

	F	VF	EF	AU	Unc.
1849 TEN.D.	$80,000	$145,000	$270,000	$350,000	—

MORMON GOLD PIECES, SALT LAKE CITY, UTAH, 1849–1860

The first name given to the organized Mormon Territory was the "State of Deseret," the last word meaning "honeybee" in the Book of Mormon. The beehive, which is shown on the reverse of the five-dollar 1860 piece, was a favorite device of the followers of Joseph Smith and Brigham Young. The clasped hands appear on most Mormon coins and exemplify strength in unity. HOLINESS TO THE LORD was an inscription frequently used.

Brigham Young was the instigator of the coinage system and personally supervised the mint, which was housed in a little adobe building in Salt Lake City. The mint was inaugurated late in 1848 as a public convenience and to make a profit for the church. Each coin had substantially less gold than the face value stated.

	F	VF	EF	AU	Unc.
1849 TWO.AND.HALF.DO.	$12,500	$23,000	$35,000	$57,000	$90,000
1849 FIVE.DOLLARS	$9,500	$18,000	$30,000	$40,000	$75,000

	F	VF	EF	AU	Unc.
1849 TEN.DOLLARS	$275,000	$450,000	$550,000	$750,000	$950,000
	Auctions: $705,000, AU-58, April 2014				

	F	VF	EF	AU	Unc.
1849 TWENTY.DOLLARS (a)	$92,500	$175,000	$275,000	$375,000	$525,000
	Auctions: $558,125, MS-62, April 2014				

a. The first coin of the twenty-dollar denomination to be struck in the United States.

	F	VF	EF	AU	Unc.
1850 FIVE DOLLARS	$13,000	$22,000	$34,000	$47,500	$85,000

	F	VF	EF	AU	Unc.
1860 5.D.	$20,000	$32,000	$42,000	$65,000	$90,000

COLORADO GOLD PIECES

CLARK, GRUBER & CO., DENVER, 1860–1861

Clark, Gruber & Co. was a well-known private minting firm in Denver, Colorado, in 1860 and 1861, formed by bankers from Leavenworth, Kansas Territory. In 1862 their operation was purchased by the Treasury Department and thenceforth operated as an assay office.

	F	VF	EF	AU	Unc.
1860 2 1/2 D.	$1,900	$3,000	$4,200	$5,700	$13,500
1860 FIVE D.	$2,200	$3,000	$4,500	$6,250	$14,500

	F	VF	EF	AU	Unc.
1860 TEN D.	$9,000	$15,000	$21,000	$30,000	$55,000
1860 TWENTY D.	$70,000	$135,000	$250,000	$385,000	$650,000
Auctions: $690,000, MS-64, January 2006					

The $2.50 and $5 pieces of 1861 follow closely the designs of the 1860 issues. The main difference is found in the legends. The reverse side now has CLARK GRUBER & CO. DENVER. On the obverse, PIKES PEAK now appears on the coronet of Miss Liberty.

	F	VF	EF	AU	Unc.
1861 2 1/2 D.	$1,900	$3,000	$4,400	$7,500	$14,000
1861 FIVE D.	$2,300	$3,700	$5,750	$11,500	$37,500
1861 TEN D.	$2,400	$4,200	$6,750	$11,500	$28,500

	F	VF	EF	AU	Unc.
1861 TWENTY D.	$20,000	$40,000	$60,000	$100,000	$235,000

JOHN PARSONS & COMPANY, TARRYALL MINES, COLORADO, 1861

Very little is known regarding the mint of John Parsons and Co., although it is reasonably certain that it operated in the South Park section of Park County, Colorado, near the original town of Tarryall, in the summer of 1861.

	VF	EF
(1861) Undated 2 1/2 D. (a)	$200,000	$300,000
(1861) Undated FIVE D. (b)	$275,000	$375,000

a. 6 to 8 examples are known. **b.** 5 or 6 examples are known.

J.J. Conway & Co., Georgia Gulch, Colorado, 1861

Records show that the Conway mint operated for a short while in 1861. As in all gold-mining areas the value of gold dust caused disagreement among the merchants and the miners. The firm of J.J. Conway & Co. solved this difficulty by bringing out its gold pieces in August 1861.

	VF	EF
(1861) Undated 2 1/2 DOLL'S (a)	$155,000	$200,000
(1861) Undated FIVE DOLLARS (b)	$225,000	$300,000

a. 8 to 12 examples are known. b. 5 to 8 examples are known.

(1861) Undated TEN DOLLARS (a)	—

a. 3 examples are known.

CALIFORNIA SMALL-DENOMINATION GOLD

There was a scarcity of small coins during the California gold rush. Starting in 1852, quarter, half, and dollar coins were privately minted from native gold to alleviate the shortage. The commercial acceptability of these hard-to-handle, underweight coins was always limited, but they soon became popular as souvenirs. Early coins contained up to 85% of face value in gold. The amount and quality of gold in the coins soon decreased, and some later issues are merely gold plated.

The Coinage Act of April 22, 1864, made private coinage illegal, but the law was not fully enforced until 1883. In compliance with the law, non-denominated tokens were made, and from 1872 until 1883 both coins and tokens were produced. After 1883, most of the production was tokens. To circumvent the law, and to make them more acceptable, some pieces made after 1881 were backdated to the 1850s or 1860s.

Early issues have Liberty heads; later issues have Indian heads and often are prooflike. Most have a wreath on the reverse, but some have original designs. About 35,000 pieces are believed to exist. Numismatists have identified more than 570 different varieties, many of them very rare. The quality of strike and edge treatment is inconsistent. Many bear their makers' initials: D, DERI, DERIB, DN, FD, G, GG, GL, H, L, N, or NR. Major denominated coins are listed below; values are for the most common variety of each type. Non-denominated tokens are not included in these listings. They are much less valuable. ***Beware of extremely common modern replicas*** (often having a bear in the design), which have little numismatic value.

The values in the following charts are only for coins made before 1883 with the denomination on the reverse expressed as CENTS, DOL., DOLL., or DOLLAR.

QUARTER DOLLAR, OCTAGONAL

	EF	AU	Unc.
Large Liberty Head / Value and Date in Wreath	$175	$250	$450
Large Liberty Head / Value and Date in Beaded Circle	$175	$275	$470
Large Liberty Head / Value and CAL in Wreath	$175	$230	$350
Small Liberty Head / Value and Date in Wreath	$170	$230	$320
Small Liberty Head / Value and Date in Beaded Circle	$175	$250	$340
Small Liberty Head / Value in Shield, Date in Wreath	$175	$250	$375
Small Liberty Head / Value and CAL in Wreath	$175	$250	$425
Small Liberty Head, date below / Value in Wreath	$175	$230	$320
Large Indian Head / Value in Wreath	$215	$310	$475
Large Indian Head / Value and CAL in Wreath	$200	$280	$450
Small Indian Head / Value and CAL in Wreath	$500	$625	$975
Washington Head 1872 / Value and CAL in Wreath	$775	$1,350	$2,000

QUARTER DOLLAR, ROUND

	EF	AU	Unc.
Liberty Head / Value in Wreath	$150	$250	$425
Large Liberty Head / Value and Date in Wreath	$190	$310	$450
Large Liberty Head / Value and CAL in Wreath	$150	$250	$400
Small Liberty Head / 25 CENTS in Wreath	$320	$500	$800
Small Liberty Head / Value and Date in Wreath	$180	$300	$435
Small Liberty Head / Value in Shield, Date in Wreath	$180	$315	$550
Small Liberty Head / Value and CAL in Wreath	$180	$225	$400
Large Indian Head / Value in Wreath	$350	$520	$825
Large Indian Head / Value and CAL in Wreath	$300	$400	$675
Small Indian Head / Value and CAL in Wreath	$375	$525	$850
Washington Head 1872 / Value and CAL in Wreath	$725	$1,000	$1,600

HALF DOLLAR, OCTAGONAL

	EF	AU	Unc.
Large Liberty Head / Value and Date in Wreath	$300	$370	$690
Large Liberty Head / Value and Date in Beaded Circle	$170	$210	$450
Large Liberty Head / Value and CAL in Wreath	$210	$425	$650
Large Liberty Head / Legend Surrounds Wreath	$400	$600	$1,000
Small Liberty Head / Value and Date in Wreath	$200	$375	$575
Small Liberty Head / Value and CAL in Wreath	$185	$320	$475
Small Liberty Head / Small Eagle With Rays	$1,300	$2,000	$3,250
Small Liberty Head / Large Eagle With Raised Wings	$1,500	$2,200	$3,250
Large Indian Head / Value in Wreath	$210	$400	$675
Large Indian Head / Value and CAL in Wreath	$235	$350	$575
Small Indian Head / Value in Wreath	$250	$425	$700
Small Indian Head / Value and CAL in Wreath	$450	$585	$975

HALF DOLLAR, ROUND

	EF	AU	Unc.
Liberty Head / Value in Wreath	$180	$325	$500
Liberty Head / Value and Date in Wreath	$180	$325	$500
Liberty Head / Value and CAL in Wreath	$225	$350	$575
Liberty Head / CALIFORNIA GOLD Around Wreath	$225	$375	$600
Large Indian Head / Value in Wreath	$210	$325	$525
Large Indian Head / Value and CAL in Wreath	$200	$300	$465
Small Indian Head / Value and CAL in Wreath	$200	$330	$525

DOLLAR, OCTAGONAL

	EF	AU	Unc.
Liberty Head / Value and Date in Wreath	$500	$750	$1,350
Liberty Head / Value and Date in Beaded Circle	$500	$800	$1,500
Liberty Head / Legend Around Wreath	$500	$825	$1,550
Liberty Head / Large Eagle	$2,150	$3,150	$5,250
Large Indian Head / Value in Wreath	$725	$1,150	$2,100
Small Indian Head / Value and CAL in Wreath	$725	$1,150	$2,100

DOLLAR, ROUND

	EF	AU	Unc.
Liberty Head / CALIFORNIA GOLD. Value and Date in Wreath	$1,750	$2,600	$4,500
Liberty Head / Date Beneath Head	$2,300	$3,200	$5,100
Indian Head / Date Beneath Head	$2,000	$3,100	$5,000

COINS OF THE GOLDEN WEST

Small souvenir California gold pieces were made by several manufacturers in the early 20th century. A series of 36 pieces, in the size of 25¢, 50¢, and $1 coins, was sold by the M.E. Hart Company of San Francisco to honor Alaska and various Western states. The Hart Company also marketed the official commemorative Panama-Pacific gold coins from the 1915 Exposition and manufactured plush copper cases for them. Similar cases were acquired by Farran Zerbe, who mounted 15 complete sets of what he termed "Coins of the Golden West." Intact, framed 36-piece sets are rare; individual specimens are among the most popular of all souvenir pieces of that era.

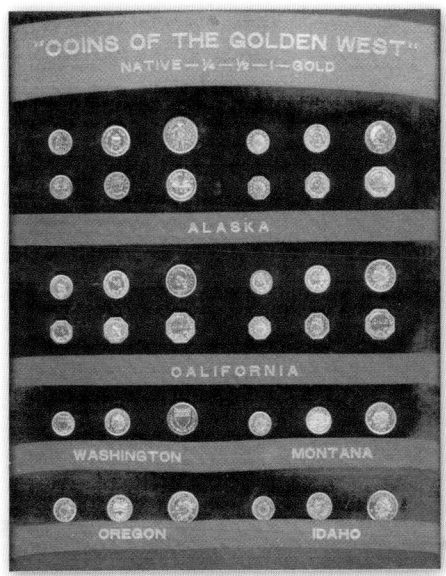

	AU	MS-63
Alaska Pinch, 25¢, octagonal, 1902	$300	$550
Alaska Pinch, 50¢, octagonal, 1900	$300	$600
Alaska Pinch, $1, octagonal, 1898	$400	$750
Alaska Pinch, 25¢, round, 1901	$300	$550
Alaska Pinch, 50¢, round, 1899	$350	$600
Alaska Pinch, $1, round, 1897	$400	$750
Alaska Parka, 25¢, round, 1911	$1,200	$1,900
Alaska Parka, 50¢, round, 1911	$1,300	$2,250
Alaska Parka, $1, round, 1911	$1,500	$2,650
Alaska AYPE, 25¢, round, 1909	$200	$300
Alaska AYPE, 50¢, round, 1909	$225	$350
Alaska AYPE, $1, round, 1909	$300	$450
California Minerva, 25¢, octagonal, 1915	$200	$400
California Minerva, 50¢, octagonal, 1915	$250	$400
California Minerva, $1, octagonal, 1915	$300	$550
California Minerva, 25¢, round, 1915	$250	$400
California Minerva, 50¢, round, 1915	$250	$450
California Minerva, $1, round, 1915	$300	$550
California 25¢, octagonal, 1860 or 1902	$500	$1,200
California 50¢, octagonal, 1900	$600	$1,350
California $1, octagonal, 1898	$700	$1,600
California 25¢, round, 1849, 1860, 1871, or 1901	$450	$1,250
California 50¢, round, 1849 or 1899	$550	$1,500
California $1, round, 1849	$700	$1,750
Idaho, 25¢, round, 1914	$700	$1,250
Idaho, 50¢, round, 1914	$800	$1,350
Idaho, $1, round, 1914	$850	$1,550
Montana, 25¢, round, 1914	$550	$1,050
Montana, 50¢, round, 1914	$650	$1,150
Montana, $1, round, 1914	$750	$1,400
Oregon, 25¢, round, 1914	$500	$1,200
Oregon, 50¢, round, 1914	$600	$1,250
Oregon, $1, round, 1914	$700	$1,450
Washington, 25¢, round, 1914	$500	$1,150
Washington, 50¢, round, 1914	$600	$1,250
Washington, $1, round, 1914	$700	$1,450

CALIFORNIA GOLD INGOT BARS

During the Gold Rush era, gold coins, ingots, and "dust" (actually flakes and nuggets) were sent by steamship from San Francisco to other ports, most importantly to New York City and London, where the gold was sold or, in some instances, sent to mints for conversion into coins. The typical procedure in the mid-1850s was to send the gold by steamship from San Francisco to Panama, where it was transported across 48 miles of territory by small water craft and pack animals from 1849 until the Panama Railroad opened in 1855, then loaded aboard another ship at the town of Aspinwall on the Atlantic side. On September 12, 1857, the SS *Central America*, en route from Aspinwall to New York City with more than 475 passengers, over 100 crew members, and an estimated $2.6 million in gold (in an era in which pure gold was valued at $20.67 per ounce) was lost at sea. Miraculously, more than 150 people, including all but one of the women and children, were rescued by passing ships. The *Central America* went to the bottom of the Atlantic Ocean off the Carolina coast.

In the 1980s a group of researchers secured financing to search for the long-lost ship. After much study and many explorations, they discovered the wreck of the *Central America* 7,200 feet below the surface. They used the robotic *Nemo*, a sophisticated device weighing several tons, to photograph the wreck and to carefully bring to the surface many artifacts. A king's ransom in gold ingots was found, along with more than 7,500 coins, the latter mostly consisting of Mint State 1857-S double eagles.

The 500-plus gold ingots furnished a unique opportunity to study specimens that, after conservation, were essentially in the same condition as they had been in 1857. These bore the imprints of five different California assayers, who operated seven offices. With few exceptions, each ingot bears individual stamps, indicating its maker, a serial number, the weight in ounces, the fineness (expressed in thousandths, e.g., .784 indicating 784/1000 pure gold), and the 1857 value in dollars. The smallest bar found was issued by Blake & Co., weighed 4.95 ounces, was .795 fine, and was stamped with a value of $81.34. The largest ingot, dubbed the "Eureka bar," bore the imprint of Kellogg & Humbert, and was stamped with a weight of 933.94 ounces, .903 fine, and a value of $17,433.57.

Blake & Co., Sacramento, California: From December 28, 1855, to May 1858, Blake & Co. was operated by Gorham Blake and W.R. Waters. • 34 ingots recovered. Serial numbers in the 5,100 and 5,200 series. Lowest weight and value: 4.95 ounces, $81.34. Highest weight and value: 157.40 ounces, $2,655.05. These bars have beveled or "dressed" edges and may have seen limited use in California commerce.

Harris, Marchand & Co., Sacramento and Marysville: This firm was founded in Sacramento in 1855 by Harvey Harris and Desiré Marchand, with Charles L. Farrington as the "& Co." The Marysville office was opened in January 1856. Serial numbers in the 6000 series are attributed to Sacramento, comprising 36 bars; a single bar in the 7000 series (7095) is attributed to Marysville. The Marchand bars each have a circular coin-style counterstamp on the face. Lowest weight and value (Sacramento): 9.87 ounces, $158.53. Highest weight and value (Sacramento): 295.20 ounces, $5,351.73. • Unique Marysville bar: 174.04 ounces, $3,389.06.

Henry Hentsch, San Francisco: Hentsch, a Swiss, was an entrepreneur involved in banking, real estate, assaying, and other ventures. In February 1856, he opened an assay office as an annex to his bank. It is likely that many of his ingots were exported to Europe, where he had extensive banking connections. • 33 ingots recovered. Lowest weight and value: 12.52 ounces, $251.82. Highest weight and value: 238.84 ounces, $4,458.35.

Justh & Hunter, San Francisco and Marysville: Emanuel Justh, a Hungarian, was a lithographer in San Francisco in the early 1850s. In 1854 and 1855 he worked as assistant assayer at the San Francisco Mint. Solomon Hillen Hunter came to California from Baltimore. The Justh & Hunter partnership was announced in May 1855. • Although study is continuing, the 60 ingots in the 4000 series are tentatively attributed to San Francisco, and the 26 ingots in the 9000 series are attributed to Marysville. • San Francisco—Lowest weight and value: 5.24 ounces, $92.18. Highest weight and value: 866.19 ounces, $15,971.93. • Marysville—Lowest weight and value: 19.34 ounces, $356.21. Highest weight and value: 464.65 ounces, $8,759.90.

Kellogg & Humbert, San Francisco: John Glover Kellogg and Augustus Humbert, two of the most famous names in the minting of California gold coins, formed the partnership of Kellogg & Humbert in spring 1855. The firm was one of the most active of all California assayers during the mid-1850s. • 346 ingots recovered, constituting the majority of those found. • Lowest weight and value: 5.71 ounces, $101.03. Highest weight and value: 933.94 ounces, $17,433.57.

A selection of gold ingots from the SS *Central America* treasure (with an 1857-S double eagle shown for scale, near lower left). (1) Harris, Marchand & Co., Marysville office, serial number 7095, 174.04 ounces, .942 fine, $3,389.06 (all values as stamped in 1857). (2) Henry Hentsch, San Francisco, serial number 3120, 61.93 ounces, .886 fine, $1,134.26. (3) Kellogg & Humbert, San Francisco, serial number 215, .944 fine, $1,045.96. (4) Blake & Co., Sacramento, 19.30 ounces, .946 fine, $297.42. (5) Another Blake & Co. ingot, serial number 5216, .915 fine, $266.12. (6) Justh & Hunter, Marysville office, serial number 9440, 41.79 ounces, $761.07. (7) Justh & Hunter, San Francisco office, serial number 4243, 51.98 ounces, .916 fine, $984.27. (8) Harris, Marchand & Co., Sacramento office, serial number 6514, 35.33 ounces, .807 fine, $589.38. (9) Harris, Marchand & Co., Sacramento office, serial number 6486, 12.64 ounces, .950 fine, $245.00.

Private Tokens

Privately issued tokens are by no means an American invention. They were common to most capitalist nations in the 1800s (and known even earlier), created and circulated by businessmen and others in periods of economic weakness or uncertainty, during financial panics, depressions, and times of war. Sometimes they were handed out as advertising trinkets or political propaganda pieces; more often they passed as makeshift currency when few real coins were available to make small change. Unlike real coins, which are government-issued as legal tender, tokens are minted by private citizens and companies. Commonly made of metal, usually round in shape, coins and tokens are very similar in appearance, but a token lacks a coin's official status as government-backed currency. Typically it would only have trade value, and then only in the vicinity in which it was issued (if, for example, a local merchant was prepared to redeem it in goods or services).

This section describes several of the more commonly encountered American tokens of the 1800s.

HARD TIMES TOKENS (1832–1844)

Hard Times tokens, as they are called, are pieces of Americana dating from the era of presidents Andrew Jackson and Martin Van Buren. They are mostly the size of a contemporary large copper cent. Privately minted from 1832 to 1844, they display diverse motifs reflecting political campaigns and satire of the era as well as carrying advertisements for merchants, products, and services. For many years these have been a popular specialty within numismatics, helped along with the publication of *Hard Times Tokens* by Lyman H. Low (1899; revised edition, 1906) and later works, continuing to the present day (see the *Guide Book of Hard Times Tokens*, 2015). In 1899 Low commented (adapted) that "the issues commonly called Hard Times tokens . . . had no semblance of authority behind them. They combine the character of political pieces with the catch-words of party cries; of satirical pieces with sarcastic allusions to the sentiments or speeches of the leaders of opposing parties; and in some degree also of necessity pieces, in a time when, to use one of the phrases of the day, 'money was a cash article,' hard to get for daily needs."

Although examples from the earlier 1830s are designated as Hard Times tokens, the true Hard Times period started in a serious way on May 10, 1837, when banks began suspending specie payments and would no longer exchange paper currency for coins. This date is memorialized on some of the token inscriptions. Difficult economic conditions continued through 1843; the first full year of recovery was 1844. From March 1837 to March 1841, President Martin Van Buren vowed to "follow in the steps of my illustrious predecessor," President Andrew Jackson, who had been in office from March 1829 until Van Buren's inauguration. Jackson was perhaps the most controversial president up to that time. His veto in 1832 of the impending (1836) recharter of the Bank of the United States set off a political firestorm, and the flames were fanned when his administration shifted deposits to favored institutions, derisively called "pet banks."

The Jackson era was one of unbridled prosperity. Due to sales of land in the West, the expansion of railroads, and a robust economy, so much money piled up in the Treasury that distributions were made in 1835 to all of the states. Seeking to end wild speculation, Jackson issued the "Specie Circular" on July 11, 1836, mandating that purchases of Western land, often made on credit, by paper money of uncertain worth, or by non-cash means, had to be paid in silver or gold coins. Almost immediately, the land boom settled and prices stabilized. A chill began to spread across the economy, which worsened in early 1837. Finally, many banks ran short of ready cash, causing the specie suspension.

After May 10, 1837, silver and gold coins completely disappeared from circulation. Copper cents remained, but were in short supply. Various diesinkers and others produced a flood of copper tokens. These were sold at discounts to merchants and banks, with $6 for 1,000 tokens being typical. Afterward, they were paid out in commerce and circulated for the value of one cent.

The actions of Jackson, the financial tribulations that many thought he precipitated, and the policies of Van Buren inspired motifs for a class of Hard Times tokens today known as "politicals." Several hundred other varieties were made with the advertisements of merchants, services, and products and are known as "store cards" or "merchants' tokens." Many of these were illustrated with elements such as a shoe, umbrella, comb, coal stove, storefront, hotel, or carriage.

One of the more famous issues depicts a slave kneeling in chains, with the motto "Am I Not a Woman & a Sister?" This token was issued in 1838, when abolition was a major rallying point for many Americans in the North. The curious small-size Feuchtwanger cents of 1837, made in Feuchtwanger's Composition (a type of German silver), were proposed to Congress as a cheap substitute for copper cents, but no congressional action was taken. Lewis Feuchtwanger produced large quantities on his own account and circulated them extensively (see page 1328).

As the political and commercial motifs of Hard Times tokens are so diverse, and reflect the American economy and political scene of their era, numismatists have found them fascinating to collect and study. Although there are major rarities in the series, most of the issues are very affordable. Expanded information concerning more than 500 varieties of Hard Times tokens can be found in Russell Rulau's *Standard Catalog of United States Tokens, 1700–1900* (fourth edition). Collectors and researchers are also encouraged to consult *A Guide Book of Hard Times Tokens* (Bowers). A representative selection is illustrated here.

L1, HT1   L57, HT76

L4, HT6   L56, HT75

	VF	EF	AU
L1, HT1. Andrew Jackson. Copper	$5,000	$8,500	—
L57, HT76. Van Buren, facing left. Brass	$2,200	$3,250	$4,250
L4, HT6. Jackson President of the U.S. Brass	$135	$275	$750
L56, HT75. Van Buren facing left. Copper	$80	$160	$375

L66, HT24

L54, HT81

L55, HT63

L31, HT46

L8, HT9

L18, HT32

L51, HT70

L47, HT66

L60, HT18

L44, HT69

	VF	EF	AU
L66, HT24. Agriculture. Copper	$225	$350	$650
L54, HT81. A Woman & A Sister. Copper	$180	$275	$400
L55, HT63. Loco Foco, 1838. Copper	$55	$160	$275
L31, HT46. Not One Cent, Motto. Copper	$45	$60	$135
L8, HT9. My Victory / Jackson. Copper	$30	$90	$125
L18, HT32. Executive Experiment. Copper	$25	$65	$110
L51, HT70. Roman Firmness. Copper	$35	$70	$125
L47, HT66. Phoenix / May Tenth. Copper	$25	$65	$110
L60, HT18. Ship/Lightning. Copper	$25	$65	$110
L44, HT69. Ship/Jackson. Copper	$25	$70	$125

L59, HT17

L65, HT23

	VF	EF	AU
L59, HT17. Ship / Wreath Border. Copper	$25	$65	$110
L65, HT23. Ship / Liberty Head. Copper	$100	$200	$350

FEUCHTWANGER TOKENS (1837–1864)

Lewis Feuchtwanger, a German-born chemist, moved to the United States in 1829 and settled in New York City. He produced a variety of German silver (an alloy of metals not including any actual silver) consisting of nickel, copper, and some zinc. Feuchtwanger suggested to Congress as early as 1837 that his metal be substituted for copper in U.S. coinage, and he made one-cent and three-cent trial pieces that circulated freely during the coin shortage of 1836 through 1844.

	VF	EF	AU	Unc.
1837 One Cent, Eagle	$135	$210	$300	$500
1837 Three-Cent, New York Coat of Arms	$750	$1,600	$2,750	$5,250
1837 Three-Cent, Eagle	$1,700	$3,600	$5,500	$13,000
1864 Three-Cent, Eagle	$1,300	$2,800	$3,800	$7,500

LESHER REFERENDUM DOLLARS (1900–1901)

Distributed in 1900 and 1901 by Joseph Lesher of Victor, Colorado, these private tokens manufactured in Denver were used in trade to some extent, and stocked by various merchants who redeemed them in goods. Lesher was an Ohio-born Civil War veteran and, after the war, an early pioneer of Colorado's mining fields. His coins, octagonal in shape, were numbered and a blank space left at bottom of 1901 issues, in which were stamped names of businessmen who bought them. All are quite rare; many varieties are extremely rare. Their composition is .950 fine silver (alloyed with copper).

	VF	EF	AU	Unc.
1900 First type, no business name	$2,900	$3,500	$4,200	$6,750
1900 A.B. Bumstead, with or without scrolls (Victor)	$1,600	$2,500	$2,900	$4,000
1900 Bank type	$15,000	$22,000	$35,000	—
1901 Imprint type, no name	$1,800	$2,200	$3,300	$4,800
1901 Imprint type, Boyd Park. Denver	$1,800	$2,200	$3,300	$4,800
1901 Imprint type, Slusher. Cripple Creek	$2,000	$2,600	$3,600	$5,500
1901 Imprint type, Mullen. Victor	$3,000	$4,200	$7,000	$12,000
1901 Imprint type, Cohen. Victor	$5,000	$7,500	$11,000	$16,000
1901 Imprint type, Klein. Pueblo	$7,000	$9,500	$14,000	$20,000
1901 Imprint type, Alexander. Salida	$7,500	$10,000	$16,000	$23,000
1901 Imprint type, White. Grand Junction	$13,000	$21,000	$30,000	—
1901 Imprint type, Goodspeeds. Colorado Springs	$27,000	$37,000	$47,000	—
1901 Imprint type, Nelson. Holdrege, Nebraska	$22,500	$33,000	$45,000	—
1901 Imprint type, A.W. Clark (Denver) (a)			$42,000	

a. This piece is unique.

CIVIL WAR TOKENS (1860s)

Early Friday morning, April 12, 1861, the Confederate States Army fired shells from 10-inch siege mortars into the Union's Fort Sumter in Charleston Bay, South Carolina, touching off the American Civil War. The ensuing turmoil would bring many changes to America's financial and monetary systems, including a dramatic reworking of the banking structure, federalization of paper money, bold innovations in taxation, tariffs, and land grants, and radical government experiments in new kinds of currency. For the man on the street, one daily noticeable development of the war was the large-scale hoarding of coins, which began in late 1861 and early 1862—people squirreled away first their gold, then silver coins, and finally, as the war dragged on that summer, even small copper-nickel cents. This caused trouble for day-to-day commerce. There were no coins to buy a newspaper or a glass of soda, to get a haircut, or tip a doorman. The situation gave birth to the humble but ubiquitous Civil War token.

Tokens were a familiar sight on the American scene by the time the Civil War was ignited. In fact, Americans had been using tokens as monetary substitutes since the colonial era, during the early days of the new nation, and throughout the 1800s. Two main kinds of tokens entered into American commerce during the war: *patriotics*, so called for their political and nationalistic themes; and *store cards*, or merchant tokens. An estimated 50 million or more were issued—more than two for every man, woman, and child in the Union. Civil War tokens were mostly a Northern phenomenon; not surprising, considering that New York State alone produced four times as much manufacturing as the entire Confederacy at the start of the war. Southerners had to make do with weak government-backed paper money, which quickly depreciated in value; Yankee tradesmen had the industrial base and financial means to produce a hard-money substitute that at least *looked* like money, even if it was backed by nothing more substantial than a local grocery store's promise to accept it at the value of one cent.

Most Civil War tokens were made of copper, some were brass, and rare exceptions were struck in copper-nickel or white metal. In addition to patriotics and store cards, some issuers crafted *numismatic* tokens during the war. These were struck for collectors rather than for day-to-day commerce, and made in the typical alloys as well as (rarely) in silver and other metals. Some were overstruck on dimes or copper-nickel cents.

Many kinds of tokens and medals were issued during the war. This sometimes leads to the question, "What, exactly, counts as a *Civil War token?*" How about the small hard-rubber checks and tickets, in various shapes, of that era? Or encased postage stamps, another small-change substitute of the war years? Or sutler tokens, issued by registered vendors who supplied the Union Army and traveled with the troops? These and more are sometimes collected along with the main body of about 10,000 varieties of store cards and patriotics. There is a long tradition of collecting Civil War tokens, dating back to even before the end of the war, and the hobby community has developed various habits and traditions over the years. Ultimately what to include in a collection is up to the individual collector. The Civil War Token Society (www.cwtsociety.com), the preeminent club for today's collector, suggests that to be "officially" considered a Civil War token, a piece must be between 18 and 25 mm in diameter. (Most of the copper tokens issued to pass as currency during the war were 18 or 19 mm, the size of the federal government's relatively new Flying Eagle and Indian Head cents, introduced in the late 1850s.)

Civil War tokens can be collected by state and by city, by type of issuer (druggist, saloonkeeper, doctor, etc.), or by any number of designs and themes. If you live in New York City and would like to study store cards issued by local shops and businesses, you have hundreds to choose from. You might hail from a small town and still be able to find a Civil War token from where you grew up. In 1863 in Oswego, New York, M.L. Marshall—a general-store seller of the unlikely combination of toys, fancy goods, fishing tackle, and rare coins—issued a cent-sized copper token featuring a fish! Undertakers issued store cards with tiny coffins advertising their services. Booksellers, bootmakers, beer brewers, hat dealers, and hog butchers all pictured their products on small copper tokens. On the patriotic side, Civil War tokens show Abraham Lincoln, various wartime presidential candidates, national heroes, cannons at the ready, unfurled flags, defiant eagles, and soldiers on horseback. They shout out the slogans of the day, warning the South of the strength of THE ARMY & NAVY, urging Americans to STAND BY THE FLAG, and insisting that THE FEDERAL UNION MUST AND SHALL BE PRESERVED.

Many tokens were more or less faithful imitations of the federal copper-nickel Indian Head cent. A few of this type have the word NOT in small letters above the words ONE CENT. For a time the legal status of the Civil War tokens was uncertain. Mint Director James Pollock thought they were illegal; however, there was no law prohibiting the issue of tradesmen's tokens or of private coins not in imitation of U.S. coins. Finally a law was passed April 22, 1864, prohibiting the private issue of any one- or two-cent coins, tokens, or devices for use as money, and on June 8 another law was passed that abolished private coinage of every kind. By that summer the government's new bronze Indian Head cents, minted in the tens of millions, were plentiful in circulation.

Today, Civil War tokens as a class are very accessible for collectors. Store-card tokens of Illinois, Massachusetts, Michigan, New York, Ohio, Pennsylvania, and Wisconsin are among those most frequently seen. A collector seeking special challenges will hunt for tokens from Iowa, Kansas, Maryland, and Minnesota—and, on the Confederate side, from Alabama, Louisiana (a counterstamped Indian Head cent), and Tennessee.

Three pieces of advice will serve the beginning collector. First, read the standard reference books, including *Patriotic Civil War Tokens* and *U.S. Civil War Store Cards*, both classics by George and Melvin Fuld, and the *Guide Book of Civil War Tokens*, by Q. David Bowers. These books lay the foundation and offer inspiration for building your own collection. Second, join the Civil War Token Society. This will put you in touch with other collectors who offer mentoring, friendship, and information. Third, visit a coin show and start looking for Civil War tokens in the inventories of the dealers there. Above all, enjoy the hobby and the many paths and byways it can lead you on through this important and turbulent era of American history.

Values shown are for the most common tokens in each composition.

	F	VF	EF	MS-63
Copper or brass	$15	$25	$35	$125
Nickel or German silver	$55	$75	$130	$290
White metal	$80	$125	$150	$275
Copper-nickel	$75	$125	$175	$325
Silver	$200	$300	$500	$1,200

PATRIOTIC CIVIL WAR TOKENS

Patriotic Civil War tokens feature leaders such as Abraham Lincoln; military images such as cannons or ships; and sociopolitical themes popular in the North, such as flags and slogans. Thousands of varieties are known.

	F	VF	AU	MS-63
Lincoln	$35	$70	$150	$300
Monitor	$30	$50	$125	$225
"Wealth of the South" (a)	$200	$400	$600	$1,000
Various common types	$15	$25	$45	$125

a. Dated 1860, but sometimes collected along with Civil War tokens.

CIVIL WAR STORE CARDS

Tradesmen's tokens of the Civil War era are often called store cards. These are typically collected by geographical location or by topic. The Fuld text (see bibliography) catalogs store cards by state, city, merchant, die combination, and metal. Values shown below are for the most common tokens for each state. Tokens from obscure towns or from merchants who issued only a few can be priced into the thousands of dollars and are widely sought.

	VG	VF	AU	MS-63
Alabama	$1,500	$3,000	$4,000	$6,500
Connecticut	$10	$25	$50	$125
Washington, D.C.	—	$1,000	$1,400	$2,000
Idaho	$400	$700	$1,300	—
Illinois	$10	$25	$50	$125
Indiana	$10	$25	$50	$135
Iowa	$150	$450	$550	$1,250
Kansas	$900	$2,500	$3,500	$5,500
Kentucky	$50	$125	$200	$350
Louisiana	$2,000	$3,500	$4,500	—
Maine	$50	$100	$175	$275
Maryland	$150	$350	$550	$1,000
Massachusetts	$15	$35	$60	$140
Michigan	$10	$25	$50	$125
Minnesota	$150	$450	$550	$750
Missouri	$40	$100	$150	$250
New Hampshire	$80	$130	$175	$275
New Jersey	$10	$25	$50	$135
New York	$10	$25	$50	$125
Ohio	$10	$25	$50	$125
Pennsylvania	$10	$25	$50	$125
Rhode Island	$10	$25	$50	$135
Tennessee	$300	$650	$1,200	$1,750
Virginia	$250	$500	$1,000	—
West Virginia	$45	$100	$175	$400
Wisconsin	$15	$30	$60	$130
Sutlers' (a)	$185	$375	$500	$700

a. Sutler tokens were issued by registered contractors who operated camp stores that traveled with the military. These were made by coiners who also produced Civil War tokens, including John Stanton, Shubael Childs, and Francis X. Koehler. Each had a denomination, typically 5 cents to 50 cents. Some used on one side a die also used on Civil War tokens.

DC500A-1h   IN190D-3a

	VG	VF	AU	MS-63
DC500a-1h. H.A. Hall, Washington, D.C.	—	$1,000	$1,400	$2,200
IN190D-3a. J.L. & G.F. Rowe, Corunna, IN, 1863	$15	$40	$75	$175

MI865A-1a

MN980A-1a

MO910A-2a

NY630AQ-4a

NY630Z-1a

OH165M-1a

NY630BJ-1a

WI510M-1a

PA750F-1a

WV890D-4a

	VG	VF	AU	MS-63
MI865A-1a, W. Darling, Saranac, MI, 1864	$7,500	$12,000	$15,000	—
MN980A-1a. C. Benson, Druggist, Winona, MN	$300	$700	$900	$1,500
M0910A-4a. Drovers Hotel, St. Louis, MO, 1863	$125	$300	$600	$1,250
NY630AQ-4a. Gustavus Lindenmueller, New York, 1863	$15	$25	$50	$125
NY630Z-1a. Fr. Freise, Undertaker, New York, 1863	$20	$35	$85	$135
OH165M-1a. B.P. Belknp., "Teeth Extracted Without Pain"	$125	$250	$400	$600
NY630BJ-1a. Sanitary Commission, New York, 1864	$400	$850	$1,100	$1,750
WI510M-1a. Goes & Falk Malt House & Brewery, Milwaukee, WI, 1863	$25	$65	$100	$175
PA750F-1a. M.C. Campbell's Dancing Academy, Philadelphia, PA	$20	$35	$50	$130
WV890D-4a. R.C. Graves, News Dealer, Wheeling, WV, 1863	$45	$100	$175	$400

Confederate Issues

The Confederate States of America proclaimed itself in February 1861, a few weeks after Abraham Lincoln was elected president of the United States in November 1860. The newly formed nation based its monetary system on the Confederate dollar. Its paper currency was backed not by hard assets (such as gold) but by the promise to pay the bearer after the war was over—assuming Southern victory and independence. In addition to paper money, the Confederacy also explored creating its own coinage for day-to-day circulation. While this goal never came to fruition, interesting relics remain as testaments to the effort.

CONFEDERATE CENTS

Facts about the creation of the original Confederate cents are shrouded in mystery. However, a plausible storyline has developed based on research and recollections, through telling and retelling over the years. An order to make cents for the Confederacy is said to have been placed with Robert Lovett Jr., an engraver and diesinker of Philadelphia, through Bailey & Co., a jewelry firm of that city. Fearing arrest by the United States government for assisting the enemy, Lovett decided instead to hide the coins and the dies in his cellar. Captain John W. Haseltine, well known for finding numismatic rarities unknown to others, claimed that a bartender had received one of the coins over the counter and sold it to him. Haseltine recognized it as the work of Lovett, called on him, learned that he had struck 12 of the coins, and bought the remaining 11 and the dies. In 1874 Haseltine made restrikes in copper, silver, and gold.

Circa 1961, the dies were copied and additional pieces made by New York City coin dealer Robert Bashlow. These show prominent die cracks and rust marks that distinguish them from earlier examples.

	Mintage	Unc.
		PF
1861 Cent, Original, Copper-Nickel, Unc.	*13–16*	$135,000
1861 Cent, Haseltine Restrike, Copper, Proof	55	$15,000
1861 Cent, Haseltine Restrike, Gold, Proof	7	$45,000
1861 Cent, Haseltine Restrike, Silver, Proof	12	$12,500

CONFEDERATE HALF DOLLARS

According to records, only four original Confederate half dollars were struck (on a hand press). Regular silver planchets were used, as well as a regular federal obverse die. One of the coins was given to Secretary of the Treasury Christopher G. Memminger, who passed it on to President Jefferson Davis for his approval. Another was given to Professor John L. Riddell of the University of Louisiana. Edward Ames of New Orleans received a third specimen. The last was kept by chief coiner Benjamin F. Taylor. Lack of bullion prevented the Confederacy from coining more pieces.

The Confederate half dollar was unknown to collectors until 1879, when a specimen and its reverse die were found in Taylor's possession in New Orleans. E. Mason Jr., of Philadelphia, purchased both and later sold them to J.W. Scott and Company of New York. J.W. Scott acquired 500 genuine 1861-O half dollars, routed or otherwise smoothed away the reverses, and then restamped them with the Confederate die. Known as restrikes, these usually have slightly flattened obverses. Scott also struck some medals in white metal using the Confederate reverse die and an obverse die bearing this inscription: 4 ORIGINALS STRUCK BY ORDER OF C.S.A. IN NEW ORLEANS 1861 / ******* / REV. SAME AS U.S. (FROM ORIGINAL DIE•SCOTT)

		Confederate Reverse		Scott Obverse

	Mintage	VF-20	EF-40	Unc.
1861 HALF DOL. (a)		—	—	—
Auctions: $881,250, VF, January 2015				
1861 HALF DOL., Restrike	500	$6,500	$7,500	$15,000
1861 Scott Obverse, Confederate Reverse	500	$3,000	$4,000	$6,500

a. 4 examples are known.

Hawaiian and Puerto Rican Issues

Although the following issues of Hawaii and Puerto Rico were not circulating U.S. coins, they have political, artistic, and sentimental connections to the United States. Generations of American numismatists have sought them for their collections.

HAWAIIAN ISSUES

Five official coins were issued for the Kingdom of Hawaii. These include the 1847 cent issued by King Kamehameha III and the 1883 silver dimes, quarters, halves, and dollars of King Kalakaua I. The silver pieces were all designed by U.S. Mint chief engraver Charles E. Barber and struck at the San Francisco Mint. The 1883 eighth-dollar piece is a pattern. The 1881 five-cent piece is an unofficial issue.

The Hawaiian dollar was officially valued equal to the U.S. dollar. After Hawaii became a U.S. territory in 1900, the legal-tender status of these coins was removed and most were withdrawn from circulation and melted.

1847, One Cent

1883, Ten Cents

1881, Five Cents
Unofficial issue.

1883, Eighth Dollar

1883, Quarter Dollar

1883, Half Dollar

1883, Dollar

	Mintage	F-12	VF-20	EF-40	AU-50	MS-60	MS-63
							PF-63
1847 Cent (a)	100,000	$350	$450	$600	$800	$1,000	$1,600
Auctions: $2,585, MS-64BN, August 2014; $3,056, MS-64BN, November 2014; $2,350, MS-63RB, August 2014							
1881 Five Cents		$7,000	$10,000	$11,000	$12,000	$15,000	$22,000
Auctions: $14,688, MS-63, August 2014							
1881 Five Cents, Proof (b)							$7,000
Auctions: $2,185, PF-62, June 2001							
1883 Ten Cents	249,974	$55	$100	$240	$385	$900	$2,000
Auctions: $1,528, MS-63, July 2014; $823, MS-62, September 2014; $282, AU-55, September 2014; $206, EF-45, July 2014							
1883 Ten Cents, Proof	26						$10,000
Auctions: $12,690, PF-64, August 2014; $11,750, PF-63, November 2014							
1883 Eighth Dollar, Proof	20						$40,000
Auctions: $8,800, PF-50, July 1994							
1883 Quarter Dollar	499,974	$50	$90	$150	$175	$250	$375
Auctions: $9,400, MS-67, July 2014; $1,293, MS-66, August 2014; $823, MS-65, August 2014; $646, MS-65, August 2014							
1883 Quarter Dollar, Proof	26						$13,000
Auctions: $11,750, PF-62, November 2014							
1883 Half Dollar	699,974	$100	$150	$300	$450	$900	$1,900
Auctions: $17,625, MS-66, August 2014; $5,875, MS-65, August 2014; $2,350, MS-64, August 2014; $2,115, MS-64, August 2014							
1883 Half Dollar, Proof	26						$16,000
Auctions: $14,100, PF-63, November 2014							
1883 Dollar	499,974	$300	$425	$600	$1,000	$3,500	$9,000
Auctions: $10,575, MS-64, July 2014; $6,463, MS-63, August 2014; $1,087, AU-55, July 2014; $823, EF-45, August 2014							
1883 Dollar, Proof	26						$32,000
Auctions: $22,325, PF-61, November 2014							

a. Values shown are for the most common of the six known varieties. **b.** All Proofs were made circa 1900.

PLANTATION TOKENS

During the 1800s, several private firms issued tokens for use as money in Hawaiian company stores. These are often referred to as Plantation tokens. The unusual denomination of 12-1/2 cents was equivalent to a day's wages in the sugar plantations, and was related to the fractional part of the Spanish eight-reales coin.

(1860) Undated, Waterhouse Token

(1871) Undated, Wailuku Plantation

1880, Wailuku Plantation

1882, Haiku Plantation

1891, Kahului Railroad

	F-12	VF-20	EF-40	AU-50
Waterhouse / Kamehameha IV, ca. 1860	$1,500	$3,000	$4,200	$6,750
Wailuku Plantation, 12-1/2 (cents), (1871), narrow starfish	$750	$2,000	$3,750	$6,200
Similar, broad starfish	$900	$2,400	$4,500	$7,500
Wailuku Plantation, VI (6-1/4 cents), (1871), narrow starfish	$1,800	$4,750	$7,000	$9,500
Similar, broad starfish	$2,200	$5,500	$7,500	$10,500
Thomas H. Hobron, 12-1/2 (cents), 1879 (b)	$600	$850	$1,100	$1,400
Similar, two stars on both sides	$1,600	$3,000	$6,000	$10,000
Thomas H. Hobron, 25 (cents), 1879 (a)			$55,000	$70,000
Wailuku Plantation, 1 Real, 1880	$750	$1,800	$3,750	$8,000
Wailuku Plantation, Half Real, 1880	$2,200	$5,000	$8,500	$11,500
Haiku Plantation, 1 Rial, 1882	$800	$1,250	$1,750	$2,250
Grove Ranch Plantation, 12-1/2 (cents), 1886	$1,500	$3,000	$5,000	$7,000
Grove Ranch Plantation, 12-1/2 (cents), 1887	$3,000	$4,500	$8,000	$10,500
Kahului Railroad, 10 cents, 1891	$3,000	$6,000	$11,000	$13,500
Kahului Railroad, 15 cents, 1891	$3,000	$6,000	$11,000	$13,500
Kahului Railroad, 20 cents, 1891	$3,000	$6,000	$11,000	$13,500
Kahului Railroad, 25 cents, 1891	$3,000	$6,000	$11,000	$13,500
Kahului Railroad, 35 cents, 1891	$3,000	$6,000	$11,000	$13,500
Kahului Railroad, 75 cents, 1891	$3,000	$6,000	$11,000	$13,500

a. 3 examples are known. b. Rare varieties exist.

PUERTO RICAN ISSUES

Puerto Rico, the farthest east of the Greater Antilles, lies about 1,000 miles southeast of Florida between the Atlantic Ocean and the Caribbean Sea. Settled by Spain in 1508, the island was ceded to the United States after the Spanish-American War in 1898. Puerto Ricans were granted U.S. citizenship in 1917. Today Puerto Rico is a self-governing territory of the United States with commonwealth status.

The Puerto Rican coins of 1895 and 1896 were minted at the Casa de Moneda de Madrid, in Spain. The peso was struck in .900 fine silver, and the others were .835 fine. The portrait is of King Alfonso XIII, and the arms are of the Bourbons, the royal house of Spain. These coins were in circulation at the time of the Spanish-American War of 1898, which ended with U.S. victory and with Spain's loss of sovereignty over Cuba (along with its cession of the Philippine Islands, Puerto Rico, and Guam to the United States for $20 million). Puerto Rico's Spanish coins continued to circulate after the war.

Collectors of United States coins often include Puerto Rican coins in their collections, even though they are not U.S. issues. After the Spanish-American War, exchange rates were set for these coins relative to the U.S. dollar, and the island transitioned to a dollar-based currency. Today in Puerto Rico the dollar is still popularly referred to as a "peso."

1896, 5 Centavos **1896, 10 Centavos** **1895, 20 Centavos**

1896, 40 Centavos   1895, One Peso

	Mintage	F-12	VF-20	EF-40	AU-50	Unc.
1896 5 Centavos	600,000	$30	$50	$100	$150	$200
Auctions: $56, EF-45, September 2014						
1896 10 Centavos	700,000	$40	$85	$135	$200	$300
Auctions: $170, AU-55, September 2014; $212, AU-55, January 2014						
1895 20 Centavos	3,350,000	$45	$100	$150	$250	$400
Auctions: No auction records available.						
1896 40 Centavos	725,002	$180	$300	$900	$1,700	$2,900
Auctions: $705, AU-55, January 2015; $352, EF-45, January 2015						
1895 1 Peso	8,500,021	$200	$400	$950	$2,000	$3,250
Auctions: $3,819, MS-63, September 2014; $1,380, AU-55, June 2006						

Philippine Issues

In April 1899, control of the Philippine Islands was officially transferred from Spain to the United States, as a condition of the treaty ending the Spanish-American War. The U.S. military suppressed a Filipino insurgency through 1902, and partway through that struggle, in July 1901, the islands' military government was replaced with a civilian administration led by American judge William Howard Taft. One of its first tasks was to sponsor a new territorial coinage that was compatible with the old Spanish issues, but also legally exchangeable for American money at the rate of two Philippine pesos to the U.S. dollar. The resulting coins—which bear the legend UNITED STATES OF AMERICA but are otherwise quite different in design from regular U.S. coins—today can be found in many American coin collections, having been brought to the States as souvenirs by service members after World War II or otherwise saved. The unusual designs, combined with the legend, have sometimes caused them to be confused with standard federal United States coins.

The coins, introduced in 1903, were designed by Filipino silversmith, sculptor, engraver, and art professor Melecio Figueroa, who had earlier worked for the Spanish *Casa de Moneda*, in Manila. They are sometimes called "Conant coins" or "Conants," after Charles Arthur Conant, an influential American journalist and banking expert who served on the commission that brought about the Philippine Coinage Act of March 2, 1903. "Both in the artistic quality of the designs and in perfection of workmanship, they compare favorably with anything of the kind ever done in America," wrote Secretary of War Elihu Root in his annual report to President Theodore Roosevelt. Figueroa died of tuberculosis on July 30, 1903, age 61, shortly after seeing his coins enter circulation.

Following Spanish custom, the dollar-sized peso was decimally equivalent to 100 centavos. Silver fractions were minted in denominations of fifty, twenty, and ten centavos, and minor coins (in copper-nickel and bronze) included the five-centavo piece, the centavo, and the half centavo.

In addition to the name of the United States, the coins bear the Spanish name for the islands: FILIPINAS. The silver coins feature a female personification of the Philippines, holding in one hand a hammer that she strikes against an anvil, and in the other an olive branch, with the volcanic Mount Mayon (northeast of the capital city of Manila) visible in the background. The minor coinage shows a young Filipino man, bare-chested and seated at an anvil with a hammer, again with Mount Mayon seen in the distance. The first reverse design, shared across all denominations, shows a U.S. federal shield surmounted by an eagle with outstretched wings, clutching an olive branch in its right talon and a bundle of arrows in its left. This reverse design was changed in 1937 to a new shield emblem derived from the seal of the 1936 Commonwealth.

Dies for the coins were made at the Philadelphia Mint by the U.S. Mint's chief engraver, Charles E. Barber. Mintmarks were added to the dies, as needed, at the branch mints. From 1903 to 1908 the coins were struck at the Philadelphia Mint (with no mintmark) and the San Francisco Mint (with an S mintmark). From

1909 through 1919, they were struck only at San Francisco. In the first part of 1920, one-centavo coins were struck in San Francisco; later in the year a new mint facility, the Mint of the Philippine Islands, was opened in Manila, and from that point into the early 1940s Philippine coins of one, five, ten, twenty, and fifty centavos were struck there. The coins produced at the Manila Mint in 1920, 1921, and 1922 bore no mintmark. No Philippine coins were struck in 1923 or 1924. The Manila Mint reopened in 1925; from then through 1941 its coinage featured an M mintmark. The Denver and San Francisco mints would be used for Philippine coinage in the final years of World War II, when the islands were under Japanese occupation.

Rising silver prices forced reductions in the fineness and weight for each Philippine silver denomination beginning in 1907, and subsequent issues are smaller in diameter. The new, smaller twenty-centavo piece was very close in size to the five-centavo piece (20.0 mm compared to 20.5 mm), resulting in a mismatching of dies for these two denominations in 1918. A small number of error coins were minted from this accidental combination, with some finding their way into circulation (often with the edge crudely reeded to induce them to pass as twenty-centavo coins). A solution was found by reducing the diameter of the five-centavo piece beginning in 1930.

It should be noted that, in addition to normal coins and paper currency, special token money in the form of coins and printed currency was made for use in the Culion Leper Colony. The token coinage saw six issues from 1913 to 1930, some produced at the Manila Mint. The leper colony was set up in May 1906 on the small island of Culion, one of the more than 7,000 islands comprising the Philippines, and the coinage was intended to circulate only there.

In 1935 the United States, responding to popular momentum for independence, approved the establishment of the Commonwealth of the Philippines, with the understanding that full self-governing independence would be recognized after a ten-year transition period. In 1936 a three-piece set of silver commemorative coins was issued to mark the transfer of executive power.

An adaptation of the new commonwealth's seal, introduced on the 1936 commemorative coins, was used for the reverse design of all circulating Philippine issues beginning in 1937. For their obverses, the Commonwealth coins retained the same Figueroa designs as those struck from 1903 to 1936. (A final transitional issue of more than 17 million 1936-dated one-centavo coins was minted using the federal-shield reverse design, rather than the new Commonwealth shield.)

After the bombing of Pearl Harbor, Japanese military forces advanced on the Philippines in late 1941 and early 1942, prompting the civil government to remove much of the Philippine treasury's bullion to the United States. Nearly 16 million pesos' worth of silver remained, mostly in the form of one-peso pieces of 1907 through 1912. These coins were hastily crated and dumped into Manila's Caballo Bay to prevent their capture by Japan. The Japanese occupied the Philippines, learned of the hidden treasure, and managed to recover some of the sunken coins (probably fewer than half a million). After the war, over the course of several years, more than 10 million of the submerged silver pesos were retrieved under the direction of the U.S. Treasury and, later, the Central Bank of the Philippines. Most of them show evidence of prolonged salt-water immersion, with dark corrosion that resists cleaning. This damage to so many coins has added to the scarcity of high-grade pre-war silver pesos.

Later during World War II, in 1944 and 1945, the U.S. Mint struck coins for the Philippines at its Philadelphia, Denver, and San Francisco facilities. These coins were brought over and entered circulation as U.S. and Philippine military forces fought to retake the islands from the Japanese.

After the war, the Commonwealth of the Philippines became an independent republic, on July 4, 1946, as had been scheduled by the Constitution of 1935. Today the Philippine coins of 1903 to 1945, including the set of commemoratives issued in 1936, remain significant mementos of a colorful and important chapter in U.S. history and numismatics. They are a testament to the close ties and special relationship between the United States of America and the Republic of the Philippines.

PHILIPPINES UNDER U.S. SOVEREIGNTY (1903–1936)

The Philippine Islands were governed under the sovereignty of the United States from 1899 until early 1935. (In the latter year a largely self-governing commonwealth was established, followed by full independence in 1946.) Coinage under U.S. sovereignty began in 1903. There was a final issue of centavos dated 1936, minted in the style of 1903–1934, after which the design of all circulating coins changed to the new Commonwealth style.

BRONZE COINAGE

HALF CENTAVO (1903–1908)

Designer: *Melecio Figueroa.* **Weight:** *2.35 grams.* **Composition:** *.950 copper, .050 tin and zinc.*
Diameter: *17.5 mm.* **Edge:** *Plain.* **Mint:** *Philadelphia.*

History. In 1903 and 1904 the United States minted nearly 18 million half centavos for the Philippines. By March of the latter year, it was obvious that the half centavo was too small a denomination, unneeded in commerce despite the government's attempts to force it into circulation. The recommendation of Governor-General Luke Edward Wright—that the coin be discontinued permanently—was approved, and on April 18, 1904, a new contract was authorized to manufacture one-centavo blanks out of unused half-centavo blanks. In April 1908, Governor-General James Francis Smith received permission to ship 37,827 pesos' worth of stored half centavos (7,565,400 coins) to the San Francisco Mint to be re-coined into one-centavo pieces. Cleared from the Philippine Treasury's vaults, the coins were shipped to California in June 1908, and most of them were melted and made into 1908 centavos.

Striking and Sharpness. Half centavos typically are well struck, except for the 1903 issue, of which some coins may show weak numerals in the date. Reverses sometimes show light flattening of the eagle's wing tips.

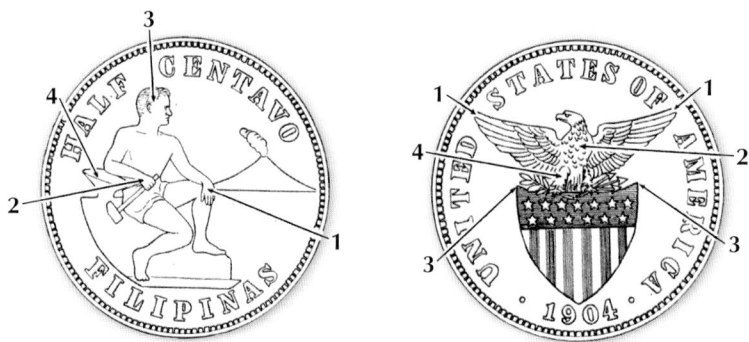

Half Centavo, 1903–1908

High Points of Wear. *Obverse Checkpoints:* 1. Figure's left hand. 2. Figure's right hand. 3. Face and frontal hair just above ear. 4. Edge of anvil. *Reverse Checkpoints:* 1. Eagle's wing tips. 2. Eagle's breast feathers. 3. Upper points of shield. 4. Eagle's right leg.

Proofs. The Philadelphia Mint struck small quantities of Proof half centavos for collectors throughout the denomination's existence, for inclusion in Proof sets (except for 1907, when no Proof sets were issued).

| | Mintage | EF | MS-60 | MS-63 |
		PF-60	PF-63	PF-65
1903	12,084,000	$2.25	$20	$40
	Auctions: $138, MS-65RD, September 2012; $247, MS-65RB, September 2013; $103, MS-65RB, September 2012			
1903, Proof	2,558			$150
	Auctions: $447, PF-67RB, October 2014; $282, PF-66RD, October 2014			
1904	5,654,000	$3.50	$25	$60
	Auctions: $270, MS-65RD, July 2013; $200, MS-65BN, January 2013; $65, MS-64RB, July 2013			
1904, Proof	1,355			$175
	Auctions: $382, PF-66RB, November 2014			
1905, Proof (a)	471	$175	$300	$550
	Auctions: $253, PF-64RB, June 2007; $207, PF-62BN, January 2012			
1906, Proof (a)	500	$150	$250	$590
	Auctions: $323, PF-65BN, January 2012; $374, PF-64RB, June 2007			
1908, Proof (a)	500	$150	$250	$500
	Auctions: $282, PF-64RB, April 2014; $230, PF-64RB, January 2012			

Note: The half centavo was unpopular in circulation. More than 7,500,000 were withdrawn and melted to be recoined as one-centavo pieces in 1908. **a.** Proof only.

ONE CENTAVO (1903–1936)

Designer: *Melecio Figueroa.* **Weight:** *4.7 grams.* **Composition:** *.950 copper, .050 tin and zinc.* **Diameter:** *24 mm.* **Edge:** *Plain.* **Mints:** *Philadelphia, San Francisco, and Manila.*

Mintmark location is on the
reverse, to the left of the date.

History. Unlike the half centavo, the bronze centavo was a popular workhorse of Philippine commerce from the start of its production. Nearly 38 million coins were minted in the denomination's first three years. In 1920 the centavo was struck for circulation by two different mints (the only year this was the case). San Francisco produced the coins during the first part of 1920; later in the year, the coins were struck at the Manila Mint, after that facility opened. From that point forward all centavos struck under U.S. sovereignty were products of the Manila Mint. Those dated 1920, 1921, and 1922 bear no mintmark identifying their origin. Manila produced no coins (of any denomination) in 1923 and 1924.

Coin collectors, notably educator, writer, and American Numismatic Association member Dr. Gilbert S. Perez, urged Manila Mint officials to include an M mark on their coinage—similar to the way that, for example, San Francisco coins were identified by an S—and this change was made starting with the coinage of 1925.

Coinage of the centavo continued through the late 1920s and early 1930s. U.S. sovereignty was significantly altered in 1935 with the establishment of the Commonwealth of the Philippines, and this change was reflected in all Philippine currency. A final mintage of 1936-dated centavos (17,455,463 pieces) was struck using the federal-shield reverse of the denomination's 1903–1934 coinage. The coin then switched over to the Commonwealth shield design in 1937.

Several centavo die varieties exist to give the specialist a challenge. Among them is the 1918-S, Large S, whose mintmark appears to be the same size and shape of that used on fifty-centavo pieces of the era.

Striking and Sharpness. On the obverse, the figure's right hand (holding the hammer) is almost always found flatly struck. The reverse, especially of later-date centavos, often shows flattening of the eagle's breast and of the left part of the shield. Issues of the Manila Mint, especially of 1920, often are lightly struck. Those of San Francisco typically are better struck, with only occasional light strikes. On centavos of 1929 to 1936, the M mintmark often is nearly unidentifiable as a letter.

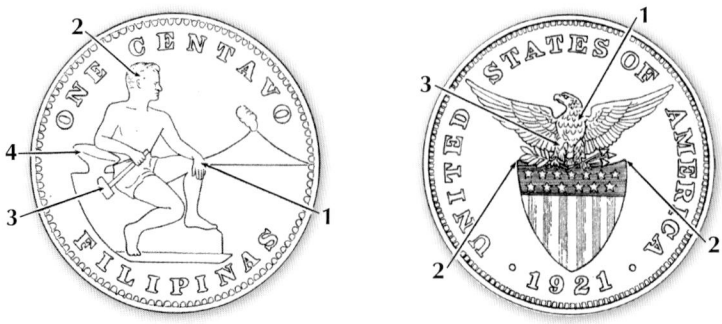

One Centavo, 1903–1936

High Points of Wear. *Obverse Checkpoints:* 1. Figure's left hand. 2. Frontal hair just above ear. 3. Head of hammer. 4. Left part of anvil. *Reverse Checkpoints:* 1. Eagle's breast feathers. 2. Upper points of shield. 3. Eagle's right leg.

Proofs. One-centavo Proofs were struck at the Philadelphia Mint for annual Proof sets in 1903, 1904, 1905, 1906, and 1908. Proof centavos of 1908 bear a date with numerals noticeably larger than those of circulation-strike 1908-S coins.

1908-S, S Over S

	Mintage	VF	EF	MS-60	MS-63
				PF-60	PF-63
1903	10,790,000	$1.25	$3	$15	$35
Auctions: $247, MS-66BN, January 2014					
1903, Proof	2,558			$60	$95
Auctions: $408, PF-65RB, April 2010; $212, PF-65RB, October 2015					
1904	17,040,400	$1.25	$3	$25	$45
Auctions: $94, MS-65BN, July 2015					
1904, Proof	1,355			$75	$90
Auctions: $217, PF-65RD, August 2013; $141, PF-64RB, April 2014					
1905	10,000,000	$1.25	$3.50	$30	$45
Auctions: $76, MS-64BN, June 2014					
1905, Proof	471			$175	$275
Auctions: $441, PF-65RB, April 2014; $805, PF-65RB, April 2010; $235, PF-64RD, August 2013					
1906, Proof (a)	500			$150	$250
Auctions: $423, PF-64RD, February 2014					
1908, Proof (a)	500			$150	$250
Auctions: $411, PF-66RD, October 2014; $499, PF-65RB, January 2014; $400, PF-65RB, August 2015					
1908-S	2,187,000	$4	$8	$40	$100
Auctions: $141, MS-65RB, April 2014; $129, MS-65RB, February 2014; $84, MS-64RB, December 2015					
1908-S, S Over S	(b)	$30	$50	$135	$300
Auctions: $558, MS-64RB, January 2014					

a. Proof only. **b.** Included in 1908-S mintage figure.

1918-S, Normal S　　　　**1918-S, Large S**

	Mintage	VF	EF	MS-60	MS-63
1909-S	1,737,612	$10	$20	$110	$225
	Auctions: $317, MS-65RB, August 2014; $153, MS-64RB, December 2015; $62, MS-64BN, March 2014				
1910-S	2,700,000	$4.50	$9	$35	$60
	Auctions: $881, MS-66RD, April 2015; $118, MS-65RB, April 2014; $80, MS-64RB, April 2014				
1911-S	4,803,000	$2.50	$5	$25	$60
	Auctions: $90, MS-65RB, April 2014; $64, MS-64RB, March 2014				
1912-S	3,001,000	$7.50	$15	$75	$125
	Auctions: $118, MS-65BN, March 2014; $90, MS-64BN, June 2014				
1913-S	5,000,000	$4	$7	$35	$75
	Auctions: $270, MS-65BN, November 2014; $79, MS-63BN, January 2014; $62, MS-63BN, April 2015				
1914-S	5,000,500	$3.50	$5	$35	$70
	Auctions: $84, MS-64BN, November 2014; $113, MS-64BN, May 2014				
1915-S	2,500,000	$40	$90	$525	$1,250
	Auctions: $805, MS-63BN, June 2011; $647, MS-62BN, January 2014				
1916-S	4,330,000	$7.50	$12.50	$90	$150
	Auctions: $135, MS-64BN, July 2014; $159, MS-63RB, June 2014				
1917-S	7,070,000	$4	$10	$75	$150
	Auctions: $176, MS-65RD, February 2014; $53, MS-62BN, September 2014				
1917-S, 7 Over 6	(c)	$50	$160	$500	
	Auctions: No auction records available.				
1918-S	11,660,000	$5	$12	$100	$200
	Auctions: $212, MS-65BN, January 2015; $229, MS-64RB, June 2014				
1918-S, Large S	(d)	$150	$250	$1,000	$1,900
	Auctions: $2,585, MS-62BN, January 2016; $306, EF-45, January 2014				
1919-S	4,540,000	$5	$15	$75	$125
	Auctions: $110, MS-64BN, June 2014; $128, MS-64BN, January 2014				
1920	3,552,259	$8	$20	$125	$225
	Auctions: $259, MS-65RB, January 2014; $353, MS-65BN, June 2014				
1920-S	2,500,000	$3.50	$20	$50	$175
	Auctions: $236, MS-64BN, January 2014; $90, MS-62BN, March 2014				
1921	7,282,673	$2.50	$5	$35	$85
	Auctions: $153, MS-65RB, January 2014				
1922	3,519,100	$3	$6	$30	$70
	Auctions: $223, MS-65RB, January 2014; $52, MS-64BN, March 2014				
1925-M	9,325,000	$3	$7	$35	$65
	Auctions: $68, MS-64BN, May 2014				
1926-M	9,000,000	$2.50	$5	$30	$55
	Auctions: $89, MS-65BN, January 2015; $30, MS-64RB, March 2014				
1927-M	9,279,000	$2	$4	$25	$45
	Auctions: $212, MS-66RD, April 2014; $165, MS-66RB, January 2014				
1928-M	9,150,000	$2	$5	$30	$75
	Auctions: $141, MS-65RD, October 2015; $75, MS-64RD, April 2014; $50, MS-64RB, May 2014				
1929-M	5,657,161	$3	$6	$40	$85
	Auctions: $141, MS-65RD, January 2014; $106, MS-65RB, October 2015; $43, MS-63BN, March 2014				

c. Included in 1917-S mintage figure. **d.** Included in 1918-S mintage figure.

	Mintage	VF	EF	MS-60	MS-63
1930-M	5,577,000	$2	$4.50	$30	$50
	Auctions: $69, MS-65BN, January 2014; $75, MS-64RD, August 2014				
1931-M	5,659,355	$2.25	$5	$40	$60
	Auctions: $100, MS-65RB, December 2015; $40, MS-65RB, March 2014; $89, MS-65RB, January 2014				
1932-M	4,000,000	$3	$7	$50	$75
	Auctions: $112, MS-65RD, April 2014; $95, MS-65RD, January 2014				
1933-M	8,392,692	$2	$3	$20	$50
	Auctions: $147, MS-66RD, January 2014; $80, MS-66RB, March 2014; $141, MS-65RB, December 2015				
1934-M	3,179,000	$2.50	$4.50	$50	$75
	Auctions: $200, MS-66RD, April 2014; $112, MS-65RB, January 2014				
1936-M	17,455,463	$2.50	$4	$35	$65
	Auctions: $37, MS-64BN, March 2014				

COPPER-NICKEL COINAGE
FIVE CENTAVOS (1903–1935)

Designer: *Melecio Figueroa.* **Weight:** *1903–1928, 5 grams; 1930–1935, 4.75 grams.*
Composition: *.750 copper, .250 nickel.* **Diameter:** *1903–1908, 20.5 mm; 1930–1935, 19 mm.*
Edge: *Plain.* **Mints:** *Philadelphia, San Francisco, and Manila.*

Five Centavos, Large Size
(1903–1928, 20.5 mm)

Mintmark location is on the reverse, to the left of the date.

Five Centavos, Reduced Size
(1930–1935, 19 mm)

History. Five-centavo coins were minted under U.S. sovereignty for the Philippines from 1903 to 1935, with several gaps in production over the years. Circulation strikes were made in Philadelphia in 1903 and 1904, then coinage resumed in 1916, this time at the San Francisco Mint. The newly inaugurated Manila Mint took over all five-centavo production starting in 1920, continuing through the end of direct U.S. administration, and under the Commonwealth government beginning in 1937.

The Manila Mint coins of 1920 and 1921 bore no mintmark indicating their producer, a situation noticed by coin collectors of the day. Gilbert S. Perez, superintendent of schools for Tayabas in the Philippines (and a member of the American Numismatic Association), wrote to Assistant Insular Treasurer Salvador Lagdameo in June 1922: "Several members of numismatic societies in Europe and America have made inquiries as to why the Manila mint has no distinctive mint mark. Some do not even know that there is a mint in the Philippine Islands and that the mint is operated by Filipinos." He recommended the letter M be used to identify Manila's coins. Lagdameo replied later that month, thanking Perez and informing him: "It is now being planned that the new dies to be ordered shall contain such mark, and it is hoped that the coins of 1923 and subsequent years will bear the distinctive mint mark suggested by you." Coinage would not resume at the Manila facility until 1925, but from that year forward the mintmark would grace the coins struck in the Philippines.

The diameter of the five-centavo coin was 20.5 mm diameter from 1903 to 1928. This was very close to the 20 mm diameter of the twenty-centavo coin of 1907 to 1929. By 1928 there had been two separate instances where a reverse die of one denomination was "muled" to an obverse of the other. In 1918 this occurred by accident when a small quantity of five-centavo pieces was struck in combination with the reverse die of the twenty centavos (identifiable by its wider shield and a smaller date, compared to the normal five-centavo reverse). This error was known to numismatists by 1922, by which time it was recognized as a scarce variety. The second instance of muling, in 1928, is discussed under twenty-centavo pieces. In 1930, to clearly differentiate the sizes of the coins, the diameter of the five-centavo piece was reduced from 20.5 to 19.0 mm.

Five-centavo coinage under U.S. sovereignty continued to 1935. From 1937 on, the Manila Mint's production of five-centavo coins would use the new Commonwealth shield design on the reverse.

Striking and Sharpness. The obverse of the 1918 and 1919 San Francisco Mint issues often is weakly struck, with considerable loss of detail. The Manila Mint started production in 1920, and many five-centavo coins from that year lack sharpness in the rims and have weak details overall.

Five Centavos, 1903–1928

High Points of Wear. *Obverse Checkpoints:* 1. Figure's right hand. 2. Frontal hair just above ear. 3. Figure's left hand. *Reverse Checkpoints:* 1. Eagle's breast feathers. 2. Eagle's wing tip (to viewer's right). 3. Upper points of shield.

Five Centavos, 1930–1935

High Points of Wear. *Obverse Checkpoints:* 1. Figure's right hand. 2. Frontal hair just above ear. 3. Edge of anvil. *Reverse Checkpoints:* 1. Eagle's breast feathers. 2. Eagle's wing tip (to viewer's right).

Proofs. Five-centavo Proofs were struck at the Philadelphia Mint for annual Proof sets in 1903, 1904, 1905, 1906, and 1908.

| | Mintage | VF | EF | MS-60 | MS-63 |
				PF-60	PF-63
1903	8,910,000	$1.25	$2.50	$20	$35
Auctions: $247, MS-66, July 2013; $200, MS-65, August 2013; $242, MS-65, December 2012; $123, MS-65, January 2015					
1903, Proof	2,558			$75	$130
Auctions: $270, PF-66, August 2013; $223, PF-65, October 2015; $200, PF-65, November 2013					

	Mintage	VF	EF	MS-60 PF-60	MS-63 PF-63
1904	1,075,000	$2.50	$3	$20	$40
	Auctions: $82, MS-64, June 2013; $76, MS-64, May 2013				
1904, Proof	1,355			$80	$160
	Auctions: $235, PF-65, August 2013; $153, PF-64, October 2014; $153, PF-64, August 2013				
1905, Proof (a)	471			$200	$300
	Auctions: $952, PF-67, August 2012; $476, PF-65, August 2013; $382, PF-64, August 2013				
1906, Proof (a)	500			$175	$250
	Auctions: $617, PF-66, October 2014; $670, PF-66, August 2013; $400, PF-65, August 2013				
1908, Proof (a)	500			$200	$300
	Auctions: $505, PF-66, October 2014; $969, PF-66, August 2013; $500, PF-66, August 2013				
1916-S	300,000	$85	$150	$800	$1,300
	Auctions: $4,465, MS-65, January 2016; 240, MS-62, January 2014; $235, MS-62, February 2014				
1917-S	2,300,000	$5	$8	$100	$300
	Auctions: $423, MS-65, April 2014; $447, MS-64, August 2014				
1918-S	2,780,000	$8	$15	$140	$300
	Auctions: $306, MS-63, August 2014; $188, MS-62, January 2014				
1918-S, S Over S	(c)	$20	$100	$500	$1,000
	Auctions: No auction records available.				
1918-S, Mule (c)	(c)	$575	$1,750	$4,750	$9,750
	Auctions: $14,100, MS-61, January 2016; $544, VF-30, April 2014				
1919-S	1,220,000	$15	$20	$175	$450
	Auctions: $588, MS-64, September 2014; $499, MS-63, January 2014				
1920	1,421,078	$8.50	$20	$175	$375
	Auctions: $141, MS-63, January 2014; $200, MS-63, July 2013				
1921	2,131,529	$9	$15	$125	$300
	Auctions: $212, MS-63, August 2013; $212, MS-63, July 2013; $153, MS-63, August 2014				
1925-M	1,000,000	$12	$30	$175	$300
	Auctions: $575, MS-64, November 2011; $423, MS-63, December 2015; $217, MS-63, January 2014				
1926-M	1,200,000	$5	$25	$120	$200
	Auctions: $112, MS-62, January 2014				
1927-M	1,000,000	$5	$10	$70	$100
	Auctions: $259, MS-65, January 2014; $129, MS-64, June 2014				
1928-M	1,000,000	$7	$14	$75	$150
	Auctions: $259, MS-65, January 2014; $259, MS-63, November 2015; $96, MS-63, June 2014				
1930-M	2,905,182	$2.50	$6	$35	$70
	Auctions: $353, MS-65, September 2014; $71, MS-64RD, July 2014; $153, MS-64, August 2013				
1931-M	3,476,790	$2.50	$6	$75	$150
	Auctions: $108, MS-64, June 2014; $74, MS-64, October 2015; $86, MS-63, June 2014				
1932-M	3,955,861	$2	$6	$50	$130
	Auctions: $143, MS-64, June 2014; $65, MS-62, January 2014				
1934-M	2,153,729	$3.50	$10	$100	$300
	Auctions: $306, MS-64, September 2014; $170, MS-63, June 2014; $88, MS-63, July 2013				
1934-M, Recut 1	(d)	$10	$35	$125	$300
	Auctions: No auction records available.				
1935-M	2,754,000	$2.50	$8	$85	$225
	Auctions: $282, MS-64, September 2014; $100, MS-63, January 2014				

a. Proof only. b. Included in 1918-S mintage figure. c. Small Date Reverse of twenty centavos. d. Included in 1934-M mintage figure.

SILVER COINAGE
TEN CENTAVOS (1903–1935)

Designer: *Melecio Figueroa.* **Weight:** *1903–1906, 2.7 grams (.0779 oz. ASW);*
1907–1935, 2 grams (.0482 oz. ASW). **Composition:** *1903–1906, .900 silver, .100 copper;*
1907–1935, .750 silver, .250 copper. **Diameter:** *1903–1906, 17.5 mm; 1907–1935, 16.5 mm.*
Edge: *Reeded.* **Mints:** *Philadelphia, San Francisco, and Manila.*

Ten Centavos, Large Size (1903–1906, 17.5 mm)	*Mintmark location is on the reverse, to the left of the date.*	**Ten Centavos, Reduced Size** (1907–1935, 16.5 mm)

History. The Philippine ten-centavo coin was minted from 1903 to 1935, in several facilities and with occasional interruptions in production.

In 1907 the silver ten-centavo coin's fineness was reduced from .900 to .750, and at the same time its diameter was decreased. This was in response to the rising price of silver, with the goal of discouraging exportation and melting of the silver coins. The net effect was nearly 40 percent less silver, by actual weight, in the new ten-centavo piece. The older coins continued to be removed from circulation, and by June 30, 1911, it was reported that only 35 percent of the ten-centavo pieces minted from 1903 to 1906 still remained in the Philippines.

The Manila Mint took over ten-centavo production from San Francisco in 1920. The ten-centavo coins of 1920 and 1921 bear no mintmark identifying them as products of Manila (this was the case for all Philippine coinage of those years, and of 1922). The efforts of Philippine numismatists, including American Numismatic Association member Gilbert S. Perez, encouraged mint officials to add the M mintmark when the facility reopened in 1925 after a two-year hiatus for all coinage.

Ten-centavo production after 1921 consisted of 1 million pieces struck in 1929 and just less than 1.3 million in 1935. The next ten-centavo mintage would be under the Commonwealth, not U.S. sovereignty.

Die varieties include a 1912-S with an S Over S mintmark, and date variations of the 1914-S.

Striking and Sharpness. The ten-centavo coins of 1903 to 1906 generally are well struck, although some show slight weakness of features. Those of 1907 to 1935 also are generally well struck; some obverses may have slight flattening of the hair just above the ear and on the upper part of the figure. On the reverse, check the eagle's breast feathers for flatness.

Ten Centavos, 1903–1906

High Points of Wear. *Obverse Checkpoints:* 1. Figure's left bosom. 2. Figure's right knee. 3. Figure's left knee. 4. Edge of anvil. *Reverse Checkpoints:* 1. Eagle's breast feathers. 2. Upper points of shield. 3. Eagle's wing tips. 4. Eagle's right leg.

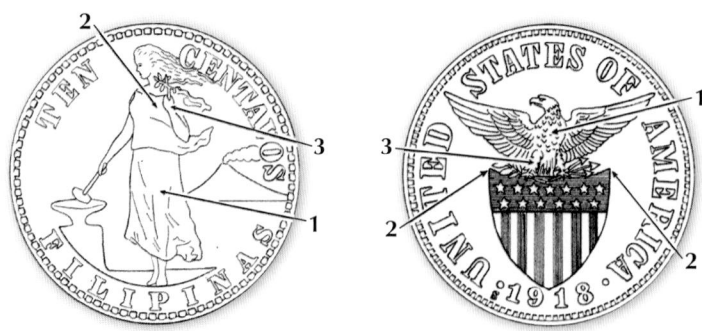

Ten Centavos, 1907–1935

High Points of Wear. *Obverse Checkpoints:* 1. Figure's left thigh. 2. Figure's left bosom. 3. Figure's left hand. *Reverse Checkpoints:* 1. Eagle's breast feathers. 2. Upper points of shield. 3. Eagle's right leg.

Proofs. Ten-centavo Proofs were struck at the Philadelphia Mint for annual Proof sets in 1903, 1904, 1905, 1906, and 1908.

	Mintage	VF	EF	MS-60	MS-63
				PF-60	PF-63
1903	5,102,658	$4	$5	$35	$75
	Auctions: $188, MS-65, January 2015; $100, MS-64, October 2014; $76, MS-64, July 2013				
1903, Proof	2,558			$75	$150
	Auctions: $270, PF-65, May 2014; $153, PF-63, September 2015; $70, PF-60, June 2013				
1903-S	1,200,000	$20	$45	$350	$950
	Auctions: $1,645, MS-62, January 2014				
1904	10,000	$20	$50	$120	$250
	Auctions: $397, MS-66, September 2014; $223, MS-65, July 2013; $100, MS-64, November 2014				
1904, Proof	1,355			$90	$150
	Auctions: $388, PF-66, October 2014; $259, PF-64, April 2015; $153, PF-64, October 2014; $88, PF-62, June 2014				
1904-S	5,040,000	$4	$9	$55	$120
	Auctions: $92, MS-64, June 2014; $59, MS-62, November 2014				
1905, Proof (a)	471			$150	$275
	Auctions: $259, PF-63, June 2004; $299, PF-62, April 2011				
1906, Proof (a)	500			$135	$225
	Auctions: $470, PF-65, April 2014; $212, PF-61, January 2014				
1907	1,500,781	$4	$7.50	$60	$135
	Auctions: $223, MS-65, April 2014; $188, MS-65, January 2014; $118, MS-65, August 2013				
1907-S	4,930,000	$2	$5	$40	$60
	Auctions: $170, MS-64, June 2014; $90, MS-63, May 2014				
1908, Proof (a)	500			$135	$225
	Auctions: $617, PF-66, October 2014; $353, PF-65, January 2014; $207, PF-63, January 2012				
1908-S	3,363,911	$2	$5	$40	$60
	Auctions: $306, MS-65, September 2014; $112, MS-64, January 2014				
1909-S	312,199	$20	$65	$450	$1,200
	Auctions: $2,350, MS-65, April 2015; $752, MS-62, May 2014; $382, MS-61, January 2014				
1911-S	1,000,505	$6	$15	$150	$500
	Auctions: $588, MS-63, January 2014				

a. Proof only.

| 1912-S, S Over S | 1914-S, Short Crossbar | 1914-S, Long Crossbar |

	Mintage	VF	EF	MS-60 PF-60	MS-63 PF-63
1912-S	1,010,000	$3.50	$12	$125	$275
	Auctions: $306, MS-63, April 2014				
1912-S, S Over S	(b)		$85	$200	$500
	Auctions: $646, MS-63, September 2014				
1913-S	1,360,693	$4.25	$13	$85	$175
	Auctions: $558, MS-65, September 2014, $270, MS-63, June 2014				
1914-S (c)	1,180,000	$6	$12	$125	$300
	Auctions: $411, MS-63, May 2014; $374, MS-63, April 2010				
1915-S	450,000	$25	$40	$250	$750
	Auctions: $1,234, MS-64, January 2014; $200, AU-58, January 2014				
1917-S	5,991,148	$2	$3	$20	$65
	Auctions: $247, MS-65, June 2014; $447, MS-64, July 2014; $129, MS-64, October 2015				
1918-S	8,420,000	$2	$3	$20	$75
	Auctions: $188, MS-65, December 2015; $129, MS-65, January 2013; $306, MS-63, July 2014				
1919-S	1,630,000	$2.50	$3.50	$30	$110
	Auctions: $182, MS-64, June 2014				
1920	520,000	$6	$16	$95	$200
	Auctions: $494, MS-64, June 2014				
1921	3,863,038	$2	$3	$25	$50
	Auctions: $182, MS-65, June 2014; $153, MS-63, July 2014				
1929-M	1,000,000	$2	$3	$25	$45
	Auctions: $176, MS-65, December 2015; $123, MS-65, June 2014				
1935-M	1,280,000	$2	$4	$30	$50
	Auctions: $182, MS-65, June 2014				

b. Included in 1912-S mintage figure. c. Varieties exist with a short or long crossbar in the 4 of 1914. The Long Crossbar is scarcer.

TWENTY CENTAVOS (1903–1929)

Designer: *Melecio Figueroa.* **Weight:** *1903–1906, 5.385 grams (.1558 oz. ASW);*
1907–1929, 4 grams (.0964 oz. ASW). **Composition:** *1903–1906, .900 silver, .100 copper;*
1907–1929, .750 silver, .250 copper. **Diameter:** *1903–1906, 23 mm; 1907–1929, 20 mm.*
Edge: *Reeded.* **Mints:** *Philadelphia, San Francisco, and Manila.*

Twenty Centavos, Large Size
(1903–1906, 23 mm)

Mintmark location is on the
reverse, to the left of the date.

Twenty Centavos, Reduced
Size (1907–1929, 20 mm)

History. In the early 1900s the rising value of silver was encouraging exportation and melting of the Philippines' silver twenty-centavo coins. As was the case with the ten-centavo piece, in 1907 the diameter of the twenty-centavo coin was reduced and its silver fineness decreased from .900 to .750. The net effect was about 40 percent less silver, by actual weight, in the new smaller coins. Attrition continued to draw the older coins out of circulation and into the melting pot, as their silver value exceeded their face value. A report of June 30, 1911, held that only about 25 percent of the twenty-centavo coins minted from 1903 to 1906 still remained in the Philippines.

Circulation strikes were made at the Philadelphia and San Francisco mints through 1919. In July 1920, a new "Mint of the Philippine Islands," located in Manila, started production. Its output during the period of U.S. sovereignty included twenty-centavo pieces in 1920, 1921, 1928, and 1929. (Production of the coins later continued under the Commonwealth, with a slightly modified design.) The first two years of coinage did not feature a mintmark identifying Manila as the producer of the coins. This was noticed by collectors of Philippine coins; they protested the oversight, and later coinage dies had an M mintmark added.

In 1928 a rush order for twenty-centavo coins was received at the Manila Mint—by that time the only producer of the denomination. Manila had not minted the coins since 1921, and the Philadelphia Mint had not shipped any new reverse dies (which would have featured their 1928 date). Under pressure to produce the coins, workers at the Manila Mint married a regular twenty-centavo obverse die with the 1928-dated reverse die of the five-centavo denomination, which was only .5 mm larger. As a result, the entire mintage of 100,000 1928 twenty centavos consists of these "mule" (mismatched-die) coins. The reverse of the 1928 coins, compared with others of 1907 to 1929, has a narrower shield and a larger date.

Striking and Sharpness. Most twenty centavos of 1903 to 1906 are well struck. The 1904-S usually shows weak striking on the figure's left bosom, the frontal hair just above her ear, and her left hand. Most of the coins of 1907 to 1929 show flattening of the figure's hair, sometimes extending into the area of her left bosom and her left hand.

Twenty Centavos, 1903–1906

High Points of Wear. *Obverse Checkpoints:* 1. Figure's left thigh and knee. 2. Figure's left bosom. 3. Figure's left hand. *Reverse Checkpoints:* 1. Eagle's breast feathers. 2. Upper points of shield. 3. Eagle's right leg.

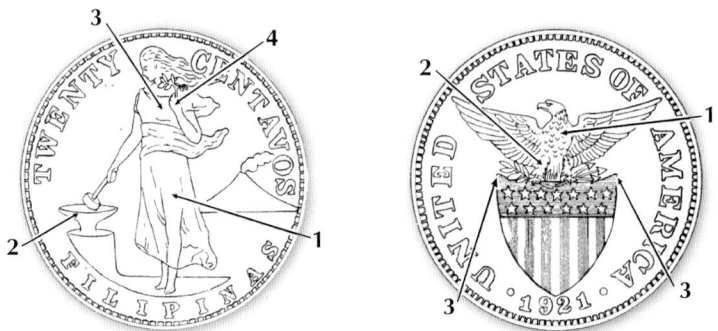

Twenty Centavos, 1907–1929

High Points of Wear. *Obverse Checkpoints:* 1. Figure's left thigh. 2. Edge of anvil. 3. Figure's left bosom. 4. Figure's left hand. *Reverse Checkpoints:* 1. Eagle's breast feathers. 2. Eagle's right leg. 3. Upper points of shield.

Proofs. Twenty-centavo Proofs were struck at the Philadelphia Mint for annual Proof sets in 1903, 1904, 1905, 1906, and 1908.

	Mintage	VF	EF	MS-60 / PF-60	MS-63 / PF-63
1903	5,350,231	$3.50	$15	$45	$100
Auctions: $88, MS-64, July 2014; $86, AU-55, July 2014					
1903, Proof	2,558			$100	$150
Auctions: $482, PF-66, October 2014; $129, PF-63, September 2014; $123, PF-63, September 2014					
1903-S	150,080	$25	$50	$600	$1,900
Auctions: $447, AU-58, May 2014					
1904	10,000	$45	$60	$125	$200
Auctions: $529, MS-66, June 2014; $194, MS-64, May 2014; $200, MS-63, January 2016; $188, MS-62, January 2015					
1904, Proof	1,355			$110	$175
Auctions: $200, PF-65, July 2014; $153, PF-63, May 2014; $200, PF-61, January 2014					
1904-S	2,060,000	$7.50	$11	$110	$200
Auctions: $223, MS-64, January 2015; $211, MS-64, March 2014; $411, MS-63, January 2014					
1905, Proof (a)	471			$225	$375
Auctions: $470, PF-64, January 2013; $282, PF-61, January 2014					
1905-S	420,000	$20	$35	$425	$1,250
Auctions: No auction records available.					
1906, Proof (a)	500			$175	$325
Auctions: $541, PF-66, October 2014; $564, PF-64, April 2015; $329, PF-62, November 2014; $329, PF-62, October 2014					
1907	1,250,651	$6	$12	$200	$450
Auctions: $881, MS-63, April 2015; $558, MS-63, September 2014					
1907-S	3,165,000	$4.50	$10	$75	$200
Auctions: $3,525, MS-65, April 2015; $374, MS-63, January 2010; $247, MS-62, June 2014					
1908, Proof (a)	500			$175	$325
Auctions: $397, PF-64, January 2014; $299, PF-63, January 2012					
1908-S	1,535,000	$3.50	$10	$100	$300
Auctions: $1,880, MS-64, September 2015; $2,233, MS-63, September 2014					
1909-S	450,000	$12.50	$50	$400	$1,500
Auctions: $5,640, MS-66, April 2015; $4,113, MS-64, April 2014; $1,528, MS-64, January 2013					
1910-S	500,259	$25	$60	$400	$1,000
Auctions: $9,988, MS-66, April 2015; $3,450, MS-64, April 2012; $2,070, MS-63, April 2012					
1911-S	505,000	$25	$45	$300	$900
Auctions: $2,350, MS-64, September 2013					
1912-S	750,000	$10	$30	$200	$400
Auctions: $294, MS-63, July 2014					
1913-S	795,000	$10	$15	$150	$200
Auctions: $235, MS-63, July 2014; $247, MS-62, June 2014					
1914-S	795,000	$12.50	$30	$200	$450
Auctions: $353, MS-63, January 2014					
1915-S	655,000	$20	$50	$400	$1,600
Auctions: $1,116, MS-63, January 2014; $270, AU-58, May 2014					
1916-S (b)	1,435,000	$10	$17.50	$125	$300
Auctions: No auction records available.					
1917-S	3,150,655	$5	$8	$75	$200
Auctions: $1,293, MS-66, September 2014; $646, MS-65, September 2014					
1918-S	5,560,000	$4	$6	$50	$125
Auctions: $188, MS-64, January 2014; $66, MS-63, June 2014					
1919-S	850,000	$6	$15	$125	$225
Auctions: $1,880, MS-66, January 2014; $106, MS-61, November 2014					

a. Proof only. b. Tilted 6 and Straight 6 varieties exist.

	Mintage	VF	EF	MS-60	MS-63
1920	1,045,415	$8	$20	$135	$225
	Auctions: $411, MS-63, September 2014				
1921	1,842,631	$2	$7	$50	$90
	Auctions: $79, MS-63, January 2014; $48, AU-58, May 2014				
1928-M, Mule (c)	100,000	$15	$50	$900	$1,800
	Auctions: $3,055, MS-65, April 2014; $3,525, MS-64, January 2016; $2,233, MS-64, January 2013				
1929-M	1,970,000	$3	$5	$40	$80
	Auctions: $92, MS-64, June 2014; $21, AU-55, May 2014				
1929-M, 2 Over 2 Over 2	(d)		$75	$250	$400
	Auctions: No auction records available.				

c. Reverse of 1928 five centavos. d. Included in 1929-M mintage figure.

Fifty Centavos (1903–1921)

Designer: *Melecio Figueroa.* **Weight:** *1903–1906, 13.48 grams (.3900 oz. ASW);
1907–1921, 10 grams (.2411 oz. ASW).* **Composition:** *1903–1906, .900 silver, .100 copper;
1907–1921, .750 silver, .250 copper.* **Diameter:** *1903–1906, 30 mm; 1907–1921, 27 mm.*
Edge: *Reeded.* **Mints:** *Philadelphia, San Francisco, and Manila.*

**Fifty Centavos, Large Size
(1903–1906, 30 mm)**

*Mintmark location is
on the reverse, to
the left of the date.*

**Fifty Centavos, Reduced Size
(1907–1921, 27 mm)**

History. After four years of fifty-centavo coinage, in 1907 the denomination's silver fineness was lowered from .900 to .750, and its diameter was reduced by ten percent. This action was in response to rising silver prices. The new smaller coins contained 38 percent less silver, by actual weight, than their 1903–1906 forebears, making them unprofitable to melt for their precious-metal content. Gresham's Law being what it is ("Bad money will drive out good"), the older, heavier silver coins were quickly pulled from circulation; by June 30, 1911, it was officially reported that more than 90 percent of the 1903–1906 coinage had disappeared from the Philippines.

The reduced-size coins of the U.S. sovereignty type were minted from 1907 to 1921. The Manila Mint took over their production from the Philadelphia and San Francisco mints in 1920, using coinage dies shipped from Philadelphia. The fifty centavos was the largest denomination produced at the Manila Mint. Neither the 1920 nor the 1921 coinage featured a mintmark identifying Manila as its producer.

Production of the fifty-centavo denomination would again take place, in 1944 and 1945, in San Francisco, using the Commonwealth design introduced for circulating coins in 1937.

Striking and Sharpness. On fifty-centavo coins of 1903 to 1906, many obverses show slight flattening of the frontal hair just above the figure's ear. The reverses sometimes show slight flattening of the eagle's breast feathers. On the reverse, a high spot on the shield is the result of an unevenness in striking. The coins of 1907 to 1921 often show notable flatness of strike in the figure's hair just above her ear, and sometimes on her left hand. A flat strike on the abdomen and left leg should not be mistaken for circulation wear. The reverses are quite unevenly struck; observe the top part of the shield, which has a depressed middle and raised sides. The right side is slightly higher than the left and may show some flattening.

Fifty Centavos, 1903–1906

High Points of Wear. *Obverse Checkpoints:* 1. Edge of anvil. 2. Figure's left thigh and knee. 3. Figure's right knee. 4. Figure's right bosom. *Reverse Checkpoints:* 1. Part of shield just to left of lower-right star. 2. Eagle's breast feathers. 3. Eagle's right leg and claws.

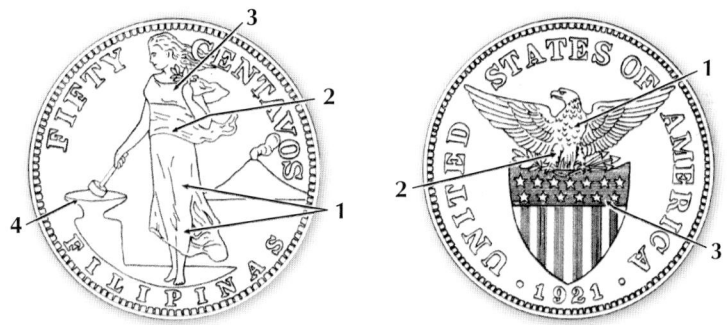

Fifty Centavos, 1907–1921

High Points of Wear. *Obverse Checkpoints:* 1. Figure's left thigh and lower leg. 2. Mid-drapery. 3. Figure's left bosom. 4. Edge of anvil. *Reverse Checkpoints:* 1. Eagle's breast feathers. 2. Eagle's right leg. 3. Part of shield just to left of lower-right star.

Proofs. Fifty-centavo Proofs were struck at the Philadelphia Mint for annual Proof sets in 1903, 1904, 1905, 1906, and 1908. Proofs of 1908 often are found with considerable flatness in the frontal hair above Miss Liberty's hair and sometimes with flatness in her left hand.

	Mintage	VF	EF	MS-60	MS-63
				PF-60	PF-63
1903	3,099,061	$7.50	$10	$75	$150
	Auctions: $259, MS-64, May 2014; $165, MS-64, September 2013; $129, MS-62, January 2014				
1903, Proof	2,558			$100	$175
	Auctions: $764, PF-66, January 2016; $734, PF-66, October 2014; $189, PF-64, September 2014; $411, PF-64, January 2014				
1903-S (a)			*$30,000*		
	Auctions: No auction records available.				
1904	10,000	$35	$75	$150	$300
	Auctions: $1,234, MS-66+, June 2014; $329, MS-64, September 2015; $223, MS-63, November 2014; $247, MS-63, May 2014				
1904, Proof	1,355			$125	$400
	Auctions: $476, PF-65, September 2012; $470, PF-64, April 2015; $247, PF-63, February 2014				
1904-S	216,000	$12	$15	$125	$225
	Auctions: $881, MS-65, September 2014; $443, MS-64, May 2014				
1905, Proof (b)	471			$275	$425
	Auctions: $3,760, PF-65, January 2016; $764, PF-63, January 2015; $411, PF-63, April 2014				
1905-S	852,000	$20	$75	$700	$2,100
	Auctions: $1,058, MS-62, April 2014; $206, AU-55, June 2014				

a. 2 examples are known. **b.** Proof only.

	Mintage	VF	EF	MS-60 PF-60	MS-63 PF-63
1906, Proof (b)	500			$225	$375
Auctions: $2,820, PF-67, October 2014; $940, PF-65, April 2014; $353, PF-61, November 2014					
1907	1,200,625	$15	$30	$150	$325
Auctions: $1,763, MS-64, April 2014; $427, MS-62, September 2014					
1907-S	2,112,000	$12.50	$30	$150	$325
Auctions: $5,640, MS-66, August 2015; $499, MS-63, September 2014; $427, MS-62, September 2014					
1908, Proof (b)	500			$200	$350
Auctions: $1,645, PF-66, January 2016; $499, PF-64, April 2014; $499, PF-64, January 2014					
1908-S	1,601,000	$15	$30	$500	$1,500
Auctions: $2,820, MS-63, January 2014; $823, MS-62, September 2014					
1909-S	528,000	$17.50	$60	$350	$850
Auctions: $4,230, MS-65, April 2015; $1,645, MS-64, April 2014; $1,528, MS-63, January 2014					
1917-S	674,369	$15	$35	$200	$550
Auctions: $541, MS-63, December 2015; $294, MS-63, January 2014; $411, MS-62, September 2014					
1918-S	2,202,000	$7.50	$15	$125	$190
Auctions: $129, MS-62, June 2014; $176, MS-61, January 2014					
1918-S, S Over Inverted S	(c)	$7.50	$15	$80	$160
Auctions: No auction records available.					
1919-S	1,200,000	$7.50	$15	$100	$225
Auctions: $353, MS-64, July 2014; $129, MS-62, January 2015					
1920	420,000	$7.50	$12.50	$70	$125
Auctions: $211, MS-64, January 2014; $212, MS-62, July 2014					
1921	2,316,763	$5	$11	$35	$110
Auctions: $588, MS-65, January 2016; $62, MS-63, October 2014; $94, MS-63, July 2014; $82, MS-63, July 2013					

b. Proof only. **c.** Included in 1918-S mintage figure.

ONE PESO (1903–1912)

Designer: *Melecio Figueroa.* **Weight:** *1903–1906, 26.96 grams (.7800 oz. ASW); 1907–1912, 20 grams (.5144 oz. ASW).* **Composition:** *1903–1906, .900 silver, .100 copper; 1907–1912, .800 silver, .200 copper.* **Diameter:** *1903–1906, 38 mm; 1907–1912, 35 mm.* **Edge:** *Reeded.* **Mints:** *Philadelphia and San Francisco.*

Peso, Large Size
(1903–1906, 38 mm)

Peso, Reduced Size
(1907–1912, 35 mm)

*Mintmark location is on the
reverse, to the left of the date.*

History. The Philippine silver peso was struck under U.S. sovereignty from 1903 to 1912. The key date among those struck for circulation is the issue of 1906-S. Although the San Francisco Mint produced more than 200,000 of the coins that year, nearly all of them were held back from circulation. They were instead stored and then later sold as bullion.

By 1906 natural market forces were driving the Philippine silver pesos out of commerce and into the melting pot: the rising price of silver made the coins worth more as precious metal than as legal tender. In 1907 the U.S. Mint responded by lowering the denomination's silver fineness from .900 to .800 and reducing its diameter from 38 mm to 35. The resulting smaller coins had about one-third less silver, by actual weight, than those of 1903 to 1906, guaranteeing that they would stay in circulation. The older coins, meanwhile, were still profitable to pull aside and melt for their silver value. An official report of June 30, 1911, disclosed that less than ten percent of the heavier silver coins still remained in the Philippines.

The new smaller pesos were minted every year from 1907 to 1912, with the San Francisco Mint producing them for commerce and the Philadelphia Mint striking a small quantity of Proofs in 1907 and 1908. Millions of the coins were stored as backing for Silver Certificates (and, later, Treasury Certificates) in circulation in the Philippines. Although the Manila Mint started operations in 1920, the silver peso was never part of its production for circulation.

In December 1941, Imperial Japan, immediately after attacking Pearl Harbor, began a fierce assault on the Philippines. Manila fell on January 2, 1942, and General Douglas MacArthur, commander of U.S. Army Forces in the Far East, fell back to the Bataan Peninsula. In late February President Franklin Roosevelt ordered him to leave the Philippines for Australia, prompting the general's famous promise to the Philippine people: "I shall return!" Not long after the fighting erupted it had become apparent that the Japanese would overtake the islands, and early in 1942 the U.S. military dumped crates holding 15,700,000 silver pesos, mostly of 1907–1912 coinage, into the sea near Corregidor, to avoid their seizure. Many millions of these coins were salvaged by the U.S. Treasury and the Central Bank of the Philippines after the war, with all but about five million pieces being reclaimed by 1958. Today a great majority of the salvaged "war pesos" show clear evidence of their prolonged submersion in saltwater. A typical effect is a dark corrosion strongly resistant to any manner of cleaning or conservation.

Striking and Sharpness. The silver pesos of 1903 to 1906 generally have well-struck obverses, but occasionally with some flattening of the figure's frontal hair above her ear, and sometimes her left bosom and hand. On the reverse, the feathers on the eagle's breast are indistinctly cut, and the wing tips can sometimes be found slightly flatly struck. Of the silver pesos of 1907 to 1912, some but not all exhibit flattened frontal hair, and sometimes a flattened left hand. On the reverse, the eagle's breast feathers are not clearly defined. On some examples the reverses are quite unevenly struck; check the top part of the shield, which has a depressed middle and raised sides, and the right side, which is slightly higher than the left and may show some flattening.

One Peso, 1903–1906

High Points of Wear. *Obverse Checkpoints:* 1. Figure's upper-left leg and knee. 2. Figure's right knee. 3. Figure's left bosom. 4. Frontal hair just above ear. ***Reverse Checkpoints:*** 1. Eagle's breast feathers. 2. Eagle's right leg. 3. Eagle's wing tips.

One Peso, 1907–1912

High Points of Wear. *Obverse Checkpoints:* 1. Figure's upper-left leg and knee. 2. Figure's lower-left leg. 3. Figure's left hand. 4. Frontal hair just above ear. *Reverse Checkpoints:* 1. Eagle's breast feathers. 2. Eagle's right leg.

Proofs. Proof pesos were struck at the Philadelphia Mint for annual Proof sets in 1903, 1904, 1905, 1906, and 1908. Unlike the smaller denominations, Proof pesos of 1907 also are known—but only to the extent of two examples.

1905-S, Curved Serif on "1"   1905-S, Straight Serif on "1"

| | Mintage | VF | EF | MS-60 | MS-63 |
				PF-60	PF-63
1903	2,788,901	$35	$45	$250	$550
	Auctions: $3,290, MS-64, January 2016; $552, MS-63, October 2014				
1903, Proof	2,558			$200	$450
	Auctions: $3,525, PF-67, October 2014; $999, PF-65, January 2016; $200, PF-62, September 2014				
1903-S	11,361,000	$35	$40	$150	$325
	Auctions: $690, MS-63, March 2011; $188, MS-60, January 2014; $129, AU-58, September 2015				
1904	11,355	$90	$110	$300	$625
	Auctions: $3,995, MS-65, January 2016; $705, MS-64, January 2014; $329, MS-63, August 2013				
1904, Proof	1,355			$250	$600
	Auctions: $7,050, PF-67, January 2016; $3,525, PF-67, October 2014; $3,290, PF-67, October 2014; $881, PF-64, September 2014				
1904-S	6,600,000	$35	$50	$175	$375
	Auctions: $440, MS-63, September 2014; $282, MS-62, May 2015; $188, MS-62, January 2015				
1905, Proof (a)	471			$750	$1,500
	Auctions: $11,163, PF-67, January 2013; $5,875, PF-65, January 2016; $911, PF-63, October 2014				
1905-S, Curved Serif on "1"	6,056,000	$40	$60	$350	$750
	Auctions: $764, MS-61, January 2014				
1905-S, Straight Serif on "1"	(b)	$50	$75	$900	$3,500
	Auctions: $3,819, MS-63, September 2014				
1906, Proof (a)	500			$700	$1,200
	Auctions: $3,819, PF-67, October 2014; $3,525, PF-67, October 2014; $6,463, PF-66, January 2016; $1,880, PF-63, April 2014				
1906-S	201,000	$1,500	$3,900	$17,500	$32,500
	Auctions: $7,050, AU-55, October 2014; $7,638, AU-55, April 2014				

Note: Philippine silver pesos of 1907–1912 that were corroded from submersion in Caballo Bay during World War II are worth considerably less than their problem-free counterparts, but are avidly collected for their historical value. **a.** Proof only. **b.** Included in 1905-S, Curved Serif on "1," mintage figure.

	Mintage	VF	EF	MS-60 PF-60	MS-63 PF-63
1907, Proof (a,c)					$160,000
Auctions: $189,750, PF, June 2012					
1907-S	10,278,000	$10	$20	$90	$250
Auctions: $940, MS-64, October 2014; $447, MS-63, March 2015; $188, MS-62, December 2014; $112, MS-60, January 2014					
1908, Proof (a)	500			$650	$1,000
Auctions: $2,585, PF-66, January 2016; $1,763, PF-64, January 2015; $940, PF-64, August 2014; $999, PF-64, January 2014					
1908-S	20,954,944	$10	$20	$100	$325
Auctions: $881, MS-64, January 2016; $852, MS-64, January 2015; $705, MS-64, September 2014					
1909-S	7,578,000	$15	$24	$115	$350
Auctions: $4,935, MS-65, April 2015; $1,058, MS-64, October 2014; $235, MS-62, January 2014					
1909-S, S Over S	(d)	$35	$100	$175	$600
Auctions: No auction records available.					
1910-S	3,153,559	$24	$35	$225	$450
Auctions: $5,170, MS-65, April 2015; $489, MS-63, January 2010					
1911-S	463,000	$45	$75	$750	$4,250
Auctions: $5,875, MS-62, January 2016					
1912-S	680,000	$60	$90	$2,000	$5,000
Auctions: $9,988, MS-63, October 2014; $5,875, MS-61, April 2014; $999, AU-58, April 2014					

Note: Philippine silver pesos of 1907–1912 that were corroded from submersion in Caballo Bay during World War II are worth considerably less than their problem-free counterparts, but are avidly collected for their historical value. **a.** Proof only. **c.** 2 examples are known. **d.** Included in 1909-S mintage figure.

MANILA MINT OPENING MEDAL (1920)

Designer: *Clifford Hewitt.* **Composition:** *bronze; silver; gold.*
Diameter: *38 mm.* **Edge:** *Plain.* **Mint:** *Manila.*

Bronze

Silver   Gold

History. During U.S. sovereignty, much of the civilian government of the Philippines was administered by the Bureau of Insular Affairs, part of the War Department. Most heads or secretaries of Philippine government departments were appointed by the U.S. governor general, with the advice and consent of the Philippine Senate. In 1919, the chief of the Bureau of the Insular Treasury (part of the Department of Finance) was Insular Treasurer Albert P. Fitzsimmons, formerly a mayor of Tecumseh, Nebraska, and member of the municipal board of Manila. Fitzsimmons, a surgeon who had served in the U.S. Army Medical Corps in Cuba and the Philippines, was active in civil affairs, and had been in charge of U.S. government bond issues in the Philippines during the Great War. On May 20, 1919, he was named director ad interim of the Mint of the Philippine Islands, which was then being organized.

The genesis of this new mint started on February 8, 1918, when the Philippine Legislature passed an appropriations bill for construction of its machinery. The war in Europe was interfering with shipments from the San Francisco Mint, where Philippine coinage was produced, and a local mint was seen as more expedient and economical. In addition, a mint in Manila would serve the United States' goal of preparing the Philippines for its own governance and infrastructure.

The mint was built in Manila in the Intendencia Building, which also housed the offices and hall of the Senate, and the offices and vaults of the Philippine Treasury. Its machinery was designed and built in Philadelphia under the supervision of U.S. Mint chief mechanical engineer Clifford Hewitt, who also oversaw its installation in Manila. The facility was opened, with formalities and machine demonstrations, on July 15, 1920. The fanfare included the production of an official commemorative medal, the first example of which was struck by Speaker of the House of Representatives Sergio Osmeña.

The medal has since come to be popularly known as the "Wilson Dollar" (despite not being a legal-tender coin), because of its size and its bold profile portrait of Woodrow Wilson on the obverse, surrounded by the legend PRESIDENT OF THE UNITED STATES. The reverse features the ancient Roman goddess Juno Moneta guiding a youth—representing the fledgling mint staff of the Philippines—in the art of coining. She holds a pair of metallurgical scales. The reverse legend is TO COMMEMORATE THE OPENING OF THE MINT / MANILA P.I., along with the date, 1920. The medal was designed by Hewitt, the mint's supervising engineer from Philadelphia. Its dies were made by U.S. Mint chief engraver George T. Morgan, whose initial, M, appears on the obverse on President Wilson's breast and on the reverse above the goddess's sandal.

The issue was limited to 2,200 silver medals (2,000 of which were struck on the first day), sold to the public at $1 apiece; and 3,700 in bronze, sold for 50¢. In addition, at least five gold specimens were reportedly struck. These included one for presentation to President Wilson and one for U.S. Secretary of War Newton Baker. The other gold medals remained in the Philippines and were lost during World War II. Of the medals unsold and still held by the Treasury in the early 1940s, some or all were dumped into Caballo Bay in April 1942 along with millions of silver pesos, to keep them from the approaching Japanese forces. The invaders learned of the coins and in May attempted to recover the sunken silver coins using the labor of Filipino divers. Although skilled divers, the Filipinos were not experienced in deep-sea diving, and the coins were at the bottom of the bay, 120 feet below the surface. After three deaths the Filipinos refused to participate in further recovery efforts. The Japanese then forced U.S. prisoners of war who were experienced deep-sea divers to recover the coins and medals. The American divers conspired to salvage only small quantities of the sunken treasure. They repeatedly sabotaged the recovery process, and smuggled a significant number of recovered silver coins to the Philippine guerrillas. Only about 2 to 3 percent of the dumped coinage was recovered before the Japanese ceased recovery operations. Following the war the United States brought up much of the coinage that had been dumped into the sea. Many of the recovered silver and bronze Wilson dollars in grades VF through AU bear evidence of saltwater corrosion.

The Manila Mint Opening medal is popular with collectors of Philippine coins and of American medals. It is often cataloged as a *So-Called Dollar*, a classification of historic dollar-sized souvenir medals, some of which were struck by the U.S. Mint and some produced privately. The Manila Mint Opening medal is valued for its unique connections to the United States and to American numismatics.

	Mintage	VF-20	EF-40	AU-50	MS-60	MS-63	MS-65
Manila Mint medal, 1920, bronze	3,700	$50	$125	$235	$785	$1,350	$4,500
Manila Mint medal, 1920, silver	2,200	$100	$250	$350	$600	$1,850	$3,200

Note: VF, EF, and AU examples in bronze and silver often show signs of saltwater corrosion. The values above are for problem-free examples.

	Mintage	AU-55	MS-62
Manila Mint medal, 1920, gold	5	$44,000	$75,000

COMMONWEALTH ISSUES FOR CIRCULATION (1937–1945)

The Philippine Islands were largely self-governed, as a commonwealth of the United States, from 1935 until full independence was recognized in 1946. Coinage under the Commonwealth began with three commemorative coins in 1936 (see next section). Circulating issues were minted from 1937 to 1941 (in Manila) and in 1944 and 1945 (in Philadelphia, Denver, and San Francisco).

The Commonwealth coinage retained the obverse motifs designed by Melecio Figueroa and used on the coinage of 1903 to 1936. Its new reverse design featured a shield derived from the official seal of the government of the Philippines, with three stars symbolizing Luzon, Mindanao, and the Visayas, the islands' three main geographical regions. In the oval set in the shield's center is a modification of the colonial coat of arms of the City of Manila: a fortress tower above with a heraldic crowned *morse* or sea-lion (half dolphin, half lion) below. An eagle with outstretched wings surmounts the entirety of the shield design, and beneath is a scroll with the legend COMMONWEALTH OF THE PHILIPPINES.

World War II forced the Commonwealth government to operate in exile during the Japanese occupation of 1942 to 1945. A pro-Japan puppet government was set up in Manila in 1943; it issued no coins of its own, and in fact during the Japanese occupation many coins were gathered from circulation to be melted and remade into Japanese coins. Barter and low-denomination emergency paper money took their place in day-to-day commerce. (Much of the money used in the Philippines during World War II consisted of hastily printed "guerrilla" currency.) The United States military knew of the local need for circulating coins, and the U.S. and Philippine governments included new coinage in the plans to liberate the islands. The U.S. Treasury Department used its Philadelphia, San Francisco, and Denver mints to produce brass, copper-nickel-zinc, and silver coins in 1944 and 1945, to be shipped to the Philippines during and after the liberation.

Note that mintage figures given for 1938, 1939, 1940, and 1941 are estimates, as many Manila Mint records were lost during the war.

BRONZE AND BRASS COINAGE
ONE CENTAVO (1937–1944)

Designer: *Melecio Figueroa (obverse).* **Weight:** *5.3 grams.*
Composition: *.950 copper, .050 tin and zinc (except for 1944-S: .950 copper, .050 zinc).*
Diameter: *24 mm.* **Edge:** *Plain.* **Mints:** *Manila and San Francisco.*

Bronze Alloy (1937–1941)   *Mintmark location is on the reverse, to the left of the date.*   **Brass Alloy (1944)**

History. The Manila Mint struck one-centavo coins for the Commonwealth of the Philippines every year from 1937 through 1941. This production was brought to an end by the Japanese invasion that started in December 1941, immediately after the bombing of Pearl Harbor. Part of the United States–Commonwealth plan to retake the islands included the San Francisco Mint's 1944 striking of 58 million one-centavo coins—a quantity greater than all of Manila's centavo output since 1937. Like the federal Lincoln cents of 1944 to 1946, these coins were made of *brass* rather than bronze—their alloy was derived in part from recycled cartridge cases, and their composition included copper and zinc, but no tin (a vital war material). The coins were transported to the islands to enter circulation as U.S. and Philippine military forces fought back the Japanese invaders. This would be the final mintage of centavos until the Republic of the Philippines, created on July 4, 1946, resumed the denomination's production in 1958.

The centavo was a popular coin that saw widespread circulation. As a result, many of the coins today are found with signs of wear or damage, exacerbated by corrosion and toning encouraged by the islands' tropical climate.

Striking and Sharpness. Well-struck examples are uncommon. Obverses of the Commonwealth centavos usually have very flat or depressed strikes in the left shoulder of the seated figure, and part of the face and chest. His right hand is better struck than in the coins struck under U.S. sovereignty. The left side of the anvil's edge is slightly rounded. On the reverse, many Uncirculated coins have flatness on the lower and central sections of the coat of arms, and some or most of the words COMMONWEALTH OF THE PHILIPPINES are unreadable.

On a perfectly struck coin, the eagle surmounting the Commonwealth shield would have a pattern of feathers visible on its breast; this level of detail is rarely evident, with the breast instead appearing smooth or flat.

Many 1937-M centavos have a barely readable mintmark. Issues of 1938 to 1941 used a narrow M mintmark, rather than a square version of the letter, resulting in better legibility.

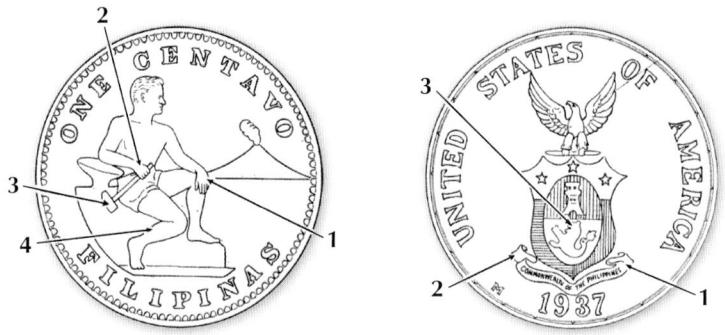

One Centavo, 1937–1944

High Points of Wear. *Obverse Checkpoints:* 1. Figure's left hand. 2. Figure's right hand. 3. Head of hammer. 4. Figure's right calf. *Reverse Checkpoints:* 1. Inner-right fold of ribbon. 2. Outer-left fold of ribbon. 3. Center of coat of arms.

	Mintage	VF	EF	MS-60	MS-63
1937-M	15,790,492	$2	$3	$15	$50
	Auctions: $153, MS-65RD, December 2015				
1938-M	10,000,000	$1.50	$2.50	$15	$35
	Auctions: $66, MS-65RB, March 2014; $94, MS-64RB, January 2014				
1939-M	6,500,000	$2.50	$3.50	$17.50	$55
	Auctions: $223, MS-66RD, April 2014				

	Mintage	VF	EF	MS-60	MS-63
1940-M	4,000,000	$1.25	$3	$15	$25
	Auctions: $50, MS-65RB, May 2014; $30, MS-64RD, March 2014				
1941-M	5,000,000	$3	$7.50	$20	$45
	Auctions: $59, MS-65RD, March 2014				
1944-S	58,000,000	$0.25	$0.50	$2	$4
	Auctions: $32, MS-65RD, March 2014				

COPPER-NICKEL AND COPPER-NICKEL-ZINC COINAGE
FIVE CENTAVOS (1937–1945)

Designer: *Melecio Figueroa (obverse).* **Weight:** *1937–1941, 4.8 grams; 1944–1945, 4.92 grams.*
Composition: *1937–1941, .750 copper, .250 nickel; 1944–1945, .650 copper, .230 zinc, .120 nickel.*
Diameter: *19 mm.* **Edge:** *Plain.* **Mints:** *Manila, Philadelphia, and San Francisco.*

Copper-Nickel
(1937–1941)

*Mintmark location is on the reverse,
to the left of the date (Manila and San
Francisco issues only; Philadelphia
issues have no mintmark).*

Copper-Nickel-Zinc
(1944–1945)

*Manila mintmark style of 1937
and 1941 (wide, with midpoint
not extending to baseline).*

*Manila mintmark style of 1938
(narrow, with midpoint
extending to baseline).*

History. The Manila Mint switched its coinage of five-centavo pieces to the Commonwealth reverse design in 1937. Production of the coins increased in 1938, then skipped two years. The 1941 output would be Manila's last for the type; the Japanese invasion at year's end stopped all of its coinage.

Philippine commerce was starved for coins during the war. As part of the broader strategy for liberating the Philippines from Japanese occupation, the U.S. Treasury Department swung its mints into production of five-centavo coins in 1944 (Philadelphia and San Francisco) and 1945 (San Francisco alone). This effort dwarfed that of the Commonwealth's late-1930s coinage, producing in those two years more than ten times the combined output of 1937, 1938, and 1941. In order to help save copper and nickel for military use, the U.S. Mint reduced the proportions of those metals in the five-centavo coinage, making up for them with the addition of zinc. This substitution saved more than 4.2 million pounds of nickel and 3.2 million pounds of copper for the war effort. The Philadelphia and San Francisco coins were shipped to the islands during the combined American-Filipino military operations against Japan.

Striking and Sharpness. Most pre-war five-centavo coins are poorly struck. On the obverse, the seated figure's left hand is flat, and the left shoulder can be as well. The left side of the pedestal and the right side of Mount Mayon can be poorly detailed. The obverse rim typically lacks sharpness. On the reverse, the ribbon usually is flat, with its wording partially or completely illegible, and the coat of arms can lack detail especially at the top-left side. On a perfectly struck coin, the eagle surmounting the Commonwealth shield would have a pattern of feathers visible on its breast; this level of detail is rarely evident, with the breast instead appearing smooth or flat.

The mintmark style of 1937 and 1941—a wide M, with the middle point not descending to the letter's baseline—usually did not strike clearly, making it difficult to read. The mintmark style of 1938 was narrower, with the middle point descending to the base, and typically is more legible.

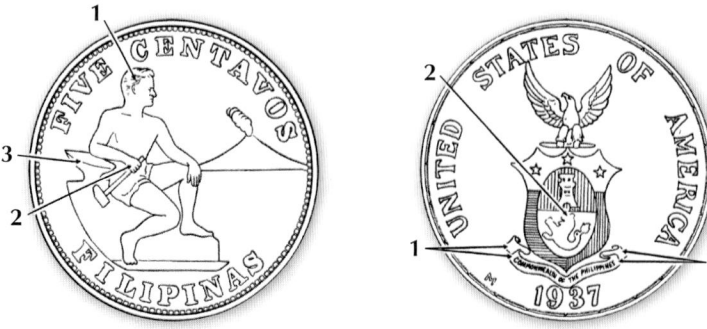

Five Centavos, 1937–1945

High Points of Wear. *Obverse Checkpoints:* 1. Frontal hair just above ear. 2. Figure's right hand. 3. Edge of anvil. *Reverse Checkpoints:* 1. Inner and outer folds of ribbon. 2. Center of coat of arms.

	Mintage	VF	EF	MS-60	MS-63
1937-M	2,493,872	$5	$7	$50	$75
	Auctions: $188, MS-65, September 2013				
1938-M	4,000,000	$1	$2.25	$20	$45
	Auctions: $92, MS-65, July 2014; $112, MS-65, September 2013				
1941-M	2,750,000	$4	$8	$55	$150
	Auctions: $282, MS-65, January 2014; $88, MS-64, September 2013				
1944 (a)	21,198,000	$0.50	$1	$2	$3
	Auctions: $46, MS-65, June 2013; $29, MS-64, April 2013				
1944-S (a)	14,040,000	$0.25	$0.50	$1	$2
	Auctions: $165, MS-67, September 2013; $200, MS-67, August 2013; $188, MS-67, August 2013				
1945-S (a)	72,796,000	$0.25	$0.50	$1	$2
	Auctions: No auction records available.				

a. Copper-nickel-zinc alloy.

SILVER COINAGE
TEN CENTAVOS (1937–1945)

Designer: *Melecio Figueroa.* **Weight:** *2 grams (.0482 oz. ASW).* **Composition:** *.750 silver, .250 copper.* **Diameter:** *16.5 mm.* **Edge:** *Reeded.* **Mints:** *Manila and Denver.*

Mintmark location is on the reverse, to the left of the date.

History. As with its production of other denominations, the Manila Mint under Commonwealth governance struck ten-centavo coins in 1937 and 1938, followed by a hiatus of two years, and a final coinage in 1941. Normal mint functions were interrupted in 1941 when Imperial Japan invaded the Philippines as part of its war with the United States. The Japanese puppet government of 1943–1945 would not produce any of its own coins, and the Manila Mint, damaged by bombing during the Japanese assault, was later used as part of the invaders' defensive fortifications on the Pasig River.

Japan's wartime exportation of Philippine coins resulted in scarcity of coinage in day-to-day commerce. The U.S. Treasury geared up the Denver Mint for a massive production of Philippine ten-centavo coins in 1944 and 1945, to be shipped overseas and enter circulation as American and Philippine troops liberated the islands. The 1945 coinage was particularly heavy: more than 130 million ten-centavo coins, compared to the Denver Mint's production of just over 40 million Mercury dimes that year. This large mintage of silver coins continued to circulate in the Philippines into the 1960s.

Striking and Sharpness. Well-struck examples of the Commonwealth ten-centavo coin are unusual. Part of the figure's bust is nearly always flatly struck, especially along the left side. The hair and left arm may also be poorly struck. On the reverse, the coat of arms usually lacks detail, and COMMONWEALTH OF THE PHILIPPINES, on the ribbon, often is only partly legible. On a perfectly struck coin, the eagle surmounting the Commonwealth shield would have a pattern of feathers visible on its breast; this level of detail is rarely evident, with the breast instead appearing smooth or flat.

The Denver coinage of 1944 and 1945 often is weakly struck on the obverse, with loss of detail. The reverse typically is weakly struck on the ribbon, with indistinct lettering.

The mintmark style of 1937 and 1941—a wide M, with the middle point not descending to the letter's baseline—usually did not strike clearly, making it difficult to read. The mintmark style of 1938 was narrower, with the middle point descending to the base, and typically is more legible.

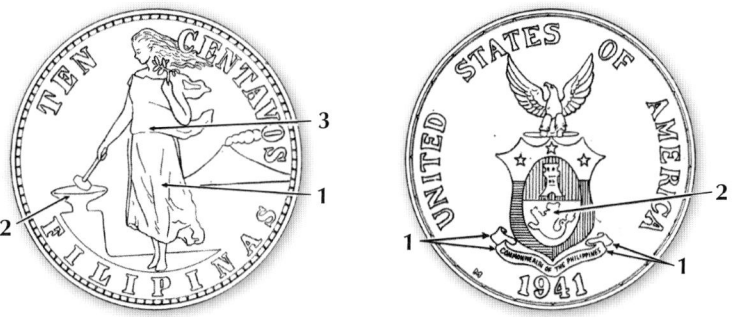

Ten Centavos, 1937–1945

High Points of Wear. *Obverse Checkpoints:* 1. Figure's left leg. 2. Edge of anvil. 3. Mid-drapery area. *Reverse Checkpoints:* 1. Inner and outer folds of ribbon. 2. Center of coat of arms.

	Mintage	VF	EF	MS-60	MS-63
1937-M	3,500,000	$2.25	$3.50	$15	$45
	Auctions: $500, MS-67, January 2013				
1938-M	3,750,000	$1.75	$2.25	$12	$20
	Auctions: $36, MS-63, August 2009				
1941-M	2,500,000	$1.50	$2	$7	$12.50
	Auctions: $36, MS-65, August 2009				
1944-D	31,592,000	$1	$2	$2.50	$3.50
	Auctions: No auction records available.				
1945-D	137,208,000	$1	$2	$2.50	$3.50
	Auctions: No auction records available.				
1945-D, D Over D	(a)	$8.50	$15	$25	$50
	Auctions: $470, AU-50, April 2014				

a. Included in 1945-D mintage figure.

Twenty Centavos (1937–1945)

Designer: *Melecio Figueroa (obverse).* **Weight:** *4 grams (.0964 oz. ASW).*
Composition: *.750 silver, .250 copper.* **Diameter:** *20 mm.*
Edge: *Reeded.* **Mints:** *Manila and Denver.*

*Mintmark location is on the
reverse, to the left of the date.*

History. The twenty-centavo piece was the largest circulating coin struck by the Commonwealth of the Philippines at the Manila Mint. Production commenced in 1937 and 1938, followed by a hiatus of two years, and a final year of output in 1941 before Japan's December invasion put a halt to all coinage. During their occupation, the Japanese pulled many twenty-centavo pieces out of circulation and melted them as raw material for new imperial coins.

Anticipating driving the Japanese military out of the islands, the United States and Commonwealth governments planned an impressive production of coinage for the Philippines in 1944 and 1945. The Denver Mint was the source for twenty-centavo pieces, and its output was immense, in 1945 exceeding even the Philadelphia Mint's production of Washington quarters for domestic use. 111 million of the coins were shipped overseas to accompany the U.S. military as Americans and Filipinos fought to liberate the islands. The need was great, as legal-tender coins had largely disappeared from circulation. Most day-to-day commerce was transacted with small-denomination scrip notes and paper money issued by guerrilla military units, local governments, or anti-Japanese military and civilian currency boards.

Striking and Sharpness. Well-struck twenty-centavo Commonwealth coins are a challenge to locate. Nearly all obverses have flattened hair on the figure's head. On the reverse, the coat of arms usually lacks detail, and COMMONWEALTH OF THE PHILIPPINES, on the ribbon, often is only partly legible. The Denver coins typically lack sharp details on the obverse and have the same reverse weakness as earlier Manila issues.

On a perfectly struck coin, the eagle surmounting the Commonwealth shield would have a pattern of feathers visible on its breast; this level of detail is rarely evident, with the breast instead appearing smooth or flat.

The mintmark style of 1937 and 1941—a wide M, with the middle point not descending to the letter's baseline—usually did not strike clearly, making it difficult to read. The mintmark style of 1938 was narrower, with the middle point descending to the base, and typically is more legible.

Twenty Centavos, 1937–1945

High Points of Wear. *Obverse Checkpoints:* 1. Figure's left thigh and knee. 2. Figure's left hand. 3. Edge of anvil. *Reverse Checkpoints:* 1. Inner folds of ribbon. 2. Center of coat of arms.

1944-D, D Over S

	Mintage	VF	EF	MS-60	MS-63
1937-M	2,665,000	$3	$5	$35	$40
	Auctions: No auction records available.				
1938-M	3,000,000	$3	$5	$15	$20
	Auctions: $40, MS-64, August 2009; $32, MS-64, August 2009				
1941-M	*1,500,000*	$3	$3.50	$15	$20
	Auctions: No auction records available.				
1944-D	28,596,000	$2	$2.75	$3	$5
	Auctions: No auction records available.				
1944-D, D Over S	(a)	$5	$9	$25	$50
	Auctions: $403, MS-66, January 2010				
1945-D	82,804,000	$2	$2.75	$3	$5
	Auctions: No auction records available.				

a. Included in 1944-D mintage figure.

FIFTY CENTAVOS (1944–1945)

Designer: *Melecio Figueroa.* **Weight:** *10 grams (.2411 oz. ASW).*
Composition: *.750 silver, .250 copper.* **Diameter:** *27 mm.*
Edge: *Reeded.* **Mint:** *San Francisco.*

*Mintmark location is on the
reverse, to the left of the date.*

History. No fifty-centavo coins were struck at the Manila Mint for the Commonwealth of the Philippines. The denomination's first issue was a wartime production of the San Francisco Mint, in 1944, to the extent of some 19 million coins, or double that facility's production of Liberty Walking half dollars for the year. This was followed by a similar mintage in 1945. These coins were intended to enter circulation after being shipped overseas with the U.S. military during the liberation of the Philippines from Imperial Japan's 1942–1945 occupation. They were readily accepted in the coin-starved wartime economy and continued to circulate in the islands into the 1960s.

Striking and Sharpness. Many Commonwealth fifty-centavo coins are lightly struck, but they typically show flattening less severe than that of the 1907–1921 issues struck under U.S. sovereignty. On the reverse, the coat of arms usually is weakly struck, with COMMONWEALTH OF THE PHILIPPINES rarely completely legible. On a perfectly struck coin, the eagle surmounting the Commonwealth shield would have a pattern of feathers visible on its breast; this level of detail is rarely evident, with the breast instead appearing smooth or flat.

Fifty Centavos, 1944–1945

High Points of Wear. *Obverse Checkpoints:* 1. Figure's left thigh and lower leg. 2. Mid-drapery area. 3. Figure's left bosom. 4. Edge of anvil. *Reverse Checkpoints:* 1. Inner folds of ribbon. 2. Center of coat of arms.

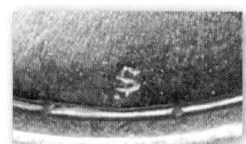

1945-S, S Over S

	Mintage	VF	EF	MS-60	MS-63
1944-S	19,187,000	$5	$6	$8	$10
	Auctions: $94, MS-66, July 2015; $44, MS-64, March 2013				
1945-S	18,120,000	$5	$6	$8	$10
	Auctions: $100, MS-66, January 2014				
1945-S, S Over S	(a)	$12	$25	$80	$180
	Auctions: $306, MS-66, May 2014; $118, MS-62, October 2015				

a. Included in 1945-S mintage figure.

COMMONWEALTH COMMEMORATIVE ISSUES

The American territory of the Philippines was governed by the U.S. military from 1899 to mid-1901. Its executive branch was managed by the Bureau of Insular Affairs (part of the War Department) from mid-1901 to 1935. In the latter year the Philippines' status was changed to that of a commonwealth—a type of organized but unincorporated dependent territory, self-governed (except in defense and foreign policy) under a constitution of its own adoption, whose right of self-government would not be unilaterally withdrawn by Congress. This was a step in the direction of complete independence, scheduled to be recognized after an additional ten years of "nation building."

To celebrate this transfer of government, the Manila Mint in 1936 produced a set of three silver commemorative coins—one of the fifty-centavo denomination, and two of the one-peso. These were designed by Ambrosio Morales, professor of sculpture at the University of the Philippines School of Fine Arts.

The fifty-centavo coin and one of the set's pesos feature busts of Philippine president Manuel L. Quezon and the last U.S. governor-general, Frank Murphy, who served (largely ceremonially) as the first U.S. high commissioner to the Commonwealth of the Philippines. On the fifty-centavo piece the two men face each other with the rising sun between them; on the peso, they appear jugate (in conjoined profile portraits). The other peso has busts of Quezon and U.S. president Franklin D. Roosevelt. This was a rare instance of a living American president appearing on a coin, the only precedent being the 1926 Sesquicentennial commemorative half dollar, which showed President Calvin Coolidge.

On each of the three coins appears the date November 15, 1935, when the new commonwealth's government was inaugurated on the steps of the Legislative Building in Manila, witnessed by 300,000 people in attendance.

The set's issue price was $3.13, or about 2.5 times the coins' face value expressed in U.S. dollars. Commemorative coins were popular in the United States at the time, but still these sets sold poorly, and thousands remained within the Philippine Treasury at the onset of World War II. In early 1942 many if not all of the remainders were crated and thrown into Caballo Bay, to keep them (along with millions of older silver pesos) from being captured by the approaching forces of Imperial Japan. Today many of the coins are found with corrosion caused by their long exposure to saltwater before being salvaged.

FIFTY CENTAVOS (1936)

Designer: *Ambrosio Morales (obverse).* **Weight:** *10 grams (.2411 oz. ASW).* **Composition:** *.750 silver, .250 copper.* **Diameter:** *27.5 mm.* **Edge:** *Reeded.* **Mint:** *Manila.*

Striking and Sharpness. This issue typically is found well struck.

	Mintage	VF	EF	MS-60	MS-63
1936-M, Silver fifty centavos	20,000	$30	$50	$100	$155
	Auctions: $1,528, MS-66, January 2016; $206, MS-64, January 2014; $112, MS-63, December 2014				

ONE PESO (1936)

Designer: *Ambrosio Morales (obverse).* **Weight:** *20 grams (.5144 oz. ASW).* **Composition:** *.800 silver, .200 copper.* **Diameter:** *35 mm.* **Edge:** *Reeded.* **Mint:** *Manila.*

One Peso, Busts of Murphy and Quezon   **One Peso, Busts of Roosevelt and Quezon**

Striking and Sharpness. Sharply struck gems of the Murphy/Quezon peso can be a challenge to locate. Weak strike is evident on the reverse in particular, where the sea-lion can be softly detailed. On some pieces, tiny bubbles resulting from improper fabrication of the planchet can be observed among the letters surrounding the rim.

The Roosevelt/Quezon peso typically is found well struck.

	Mintage	VF	EF	MS-60	MS-63
1936-M, Silver one peso, busts of Murphy and Quezon	10,000	$70	$85	$200	$300
	Auctions: $940, MS-66, October 2014; $764, MS-66, October 2014; $176, MS, May 2015				
1936-M, Silver one peso, busts of Roosevelt and Quezon	10,000	$70	$85	$200	$275
	Auctions: $823, MS-66, January 2016; $359, MS-65, August 2013; $329, MS-65, January 2013				

Alaska Tokens

ALASKA RURAL REHABILITATION CORPORATION TOKENS OF 1935

Before the Roosevelt Administration's dramatic New Deal response to the Great Depression, it was the states themselves, rather than the federal government, that organized and funded the relief of their citizens in need. This changed with the Federal Emergency Relief Act of 1933, by which Congress appropriated $250 million for states to use in their relief efforts, with the same amount funded for federal programs. Other relief acts would follow. The states were to use their 1933 FERA grant money "to aid in meeting the costs of furnishing relief and in relieving the hardship and suffering caused by unemployment in the form of money, service, materials, and/or commodities to provide the necessities of life to persons in need as a result of the present emergency, and/or their dependents, whether resident, transient, or homeless," as well as to "aid in assisting cooperative and self-help associations for the barter of goods and services."

Americans living in cities benefited from direct relief grants as well as employment in work-relief projects. Those in rural areas, however, had a stronger need for *rehabilitation* programs rather than relief as such. In April 1934 a special Rural Rehabilitation Division was set up. This helped establish rural camps where people made homeless by the Depression could find shelter and assistance until conditions improved. Nonprofits called *rural rehabilitation corporations* were devised to carry this effort forward. One function of the corporations was to buy large expanses of farmland to divide into 40- or 60-acre plots. These would be mortgaged to displaced farm families who agreed to develop and farm the land in exchange for low-interest loans and other assistance. One community developed under this plan was the Matanuska Valley Colony at Palmer, about 45 miles northeast of Anchorage, in the territory of Alaska. For the Alaska program some 203 families were recruited from Michigan, Minnesota, and Wisconsin. Those states were targeted not only because they had a very high percentage of displaced farmers on social-assistance relief, but also because their cold-weather climates were similar to Alaska's.

A suite of (undated) 1935 tokens was issued by the U.S. government for the use of the Midwesterners who relocated to the colonization project. These aluminum and brass tokens (nicknamed "bingles") would supply the settlers with much-needed federal aid, being paid out for work at the rate of 50¢ per hour. In theory this wage payment in tokens, rather than regular coinage, would also discourage the workers from spending their money unwisely, as the bingles were redeemable only at Alaska Rural Rehabilitation Corporation stores. In addition to use as wages, the tokens were issued based on immediate need and according to the size of the family. A family of two would receive a monthly allowance of $45; a family of three, $55; a family of four, $75; and a family of five, $85. The bingles were in use only about six months, during the winter of 1935 and 1936. The colony's managers were unable to restrict their use to the purchase of necessities in corporation-run stores—other merchants, including the local saloon, realized they could also accept them as currency. Eventually the tokens were recalled and redeemed for regular U.S. money. Practically all of the circulated tokens were destroyed after redemption.

Of the $23,000 face value minted, about $18,000 worth of tokens were issued in the months they were in active use. The unissued tokens were later made into souvenir sets for collectors. Some 250 complete sets were thus preserved in unused condition, in addition to about 100 "short" sets consisting of the one-cent, five-cent, and ten-cent pieces.

Each token is similar in size to the corresponding U.S. coin of the same denomination (one cent through ten dollars), with the exception of the one-cent piece, which is octagonal. The design is the same on both sides of each denomination.

Even after leaving hardship in the Midwest, and even with this federal aid, the Alaska colonists faced ongoing challenges. Potatoes and other crops were successfully grown, but the farming seasons were short, markets were far away, and the expense of shipping was high. More than half of the Alaska colonists left the Matanuska Valley within five years, and thirty years later only twenty of the original families were still farming there. Still, the New Deal colony helped the Matanuska Valley to slowly grow into Alaska's most productive agricultural region.

For more information on these and other Alaska-related coins and tokens, see *Alaska's Coinage Through the Years*, by Maurice Gould, Kenneth Bressett, and Kaye and Nancy Dethridge.

ALUMINUM

	Mintage	EF	Unc.
One Cent	5,000	$90	$160
Five Cents	5,000	$90	$160
Ten Cents	5,000	$90	$160
Twenty-Five Cents	3,000	$135	$265
Fifty Cents	2,500	$135	$265
One Dollar	2,500	$225	$265

BRASS

	Mintage	EF	Unc.
Five Dollars	1,000	$225	$350
Ten Dollars	1,000	$250	$400

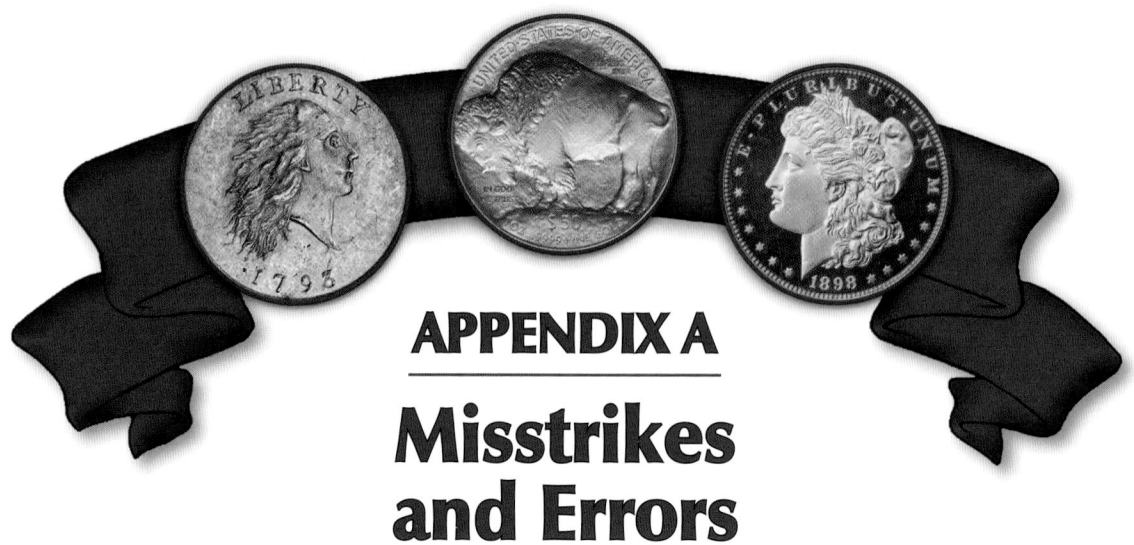

APPENDIX A
Misstrikes and Errors

With the production of millions of coins each year, it is natural that a few abnormal pieces escape inspection and are inadvertently released for circulation, usually in original bags or rolls of new coins. These are not considered regular issues because they were not made intentionally. They are all eagerly sought by collectors for the information they shed on minting techniques, and as a variation from normal date and mint series collecting.

MISSTRUCK COINS AND ERROR PIECES

Nearly every misstruck or error coin is unique in some way, and prices may vary from coin to coin. They may all be classified in general groups related to the kinds of errors or manufacturing malfunctions involved. Collectors value these pieces according to the scarcity of each kind of error for each type of coin. Non-collectors usually view them as curios, and often believe that they must be worth much more than normal coins because they look so strange. In reality, the value assigned to various types of errors by collectors and dealers reflects both supply and demand, and is based on recurring transactions between willing buyers and sellers.

The following listings show current average values for the most frequently encountered kinds of error coins. In each case, the values shown are for coins that are unmarred by serious marks or scratches, and in Uncirculated condition for modern issues, and Extremely Fine condition for obsolete types. Exceptions are valued higher or lower. Error coins of rare-date issues generally do not command a premium beyond their normal values. In most cases each of these coins is unique in some respect and must be valued according to its individual appearance, quality, and eye appeal.

There are many other kinds of errors and misstruck coins beyond those listed in this guide book. Some are more valuable, and others less valuable, than the most popular pieces that are listed here as examples of what this interesting field contains. The pieces illustrated are general examples of the types described.

Early in 2002 the mints changed their production methods to a new system designed to eliminate deformed planchets, off-center strikes, and similar errors. They also changed the delivery system of bulk coinage, and no longer shipped loose coins in sewn bags to be counted and wrapped by banks or counting rooms, where error coins were often found and sold to collectors. Under the new system, coins are packaged in large quantities and go directly to automated counters that filter out deformed coins. The result has been that very few error coins have entered the market since late 2002, and almost none after that date. The values shown in these listings are for pre-2002 coins; those dated after that, with but a few exceptions, are valued considerably higher.

For additional details and information about these coins, the following books are recommended:

Margolis, Arnold, and Fred Weinberg. *The Error Coin Encyclopedia* (4th ed.). 2004.

Herbert, Alan. *Official Price Guide to Minting Varieties and Errors.* New York, 1991.

Fivaz, Bill, and J.T. Stanton. *The Cherrypickers' Guide to Rare Die Varieties.* Atlanta, GA, updated regularly.

The coins discussed in this section must not be confused with others that have been mutilated or damaged after leaving the mint. Examples of such pieces include coins that have been scratched, hammered, engraved, impressed, acid etched, or plated by individuals to simulate something other than a normal coin. Those pieces have no numismatic value, and can only be considered as altered coins not suitable for a collection.

TYPES OF ERROR COINS

***Clipped Planchet*—An incomplete coin, missing 10 to 25% of the metal.** Incomplete planchets result from accidents when the steel rods used to punch out blanks from the metal strip overlap a portion of the strip already punched. There are curved, straight, ragged, incomplete, and elliptical clips. Values may be greater or less depending on the nature and size of the clip. Coins with more than one clip usually command higher values.

***Multiple Strike*—A coin with at least one additional image from being struck again off center.** Value increases with the number of strikes. These minting errors occur when a finished coin goes back into the press and is struck again with the same dies. The presence of a date can bring a higher value.

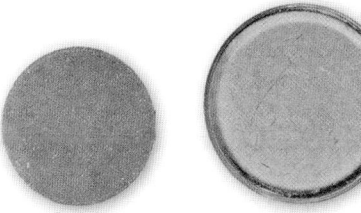

No Rim   With Rim

***Blank or Planchet*—A blank disc of metal intended for coinage but not struck with dies.** In the process of preparation for coinage, the blanks are first punched from a strip of metal and then milled to upset the rim. In most instances, first-process pieces (blanks without upset rims) are slightly more valuable than the finished planchets. Values shown are for the most common pieces.

Defective Die—**A coin showing raised metal from a large die crack, or small rim break.** Coins that show evidence of light die cracks, polishing, or very minor die damage are generally of little or no value. Prices shown here are for coins with very noticeable, raised die-crack lines, or those for which the die broke away, producing an unstruck area known as a *cud*.

Off Center—**A coin that has been struck out of collar and incorrectly centered, with part of the design missing.** Values are for coins with approximately 10 to 20% of design missing from obsolete coins, or 20 to 60% missing from modern coins. These are misstruck coins that were made when the planchet did not enter the coinage press properly. Coins that are struck only slightly off center, with none of the design missing, are called broadstrikes (see the next category). Those with nearly all of the impression missing are generally worth more, but those with a readable date and mint are the most valuable.

Broadstrike—**A coin that was struck outside the retaining collar.** When coins are struck without being contained in the collar die, they spread out larger than normal pieces. All denominations have a plain edge.

Lamination—**A flaw whereby a fragment of metal has peeled off the coin's surface.** This defect occurs when a foreign substance, such as gas oxides or dirt, becomes trapped in the strip as it is rolled out to the proper thickness. Lamination flaws may be missing or still attached to the coin's surface. Minor flaws may only decrease a coin's value, while a clad coin that is missing the full surface of one or both sides is worth more than the values listed here.

Brockage—**A mirror image of the design impressed on the opposite side of the same coin.** These errors are caused when a struck coin remains on either die after striking, and impresses its image into the next blank planchet as it is struck, leaving a negative or mirror image. Off-center and partial brockage coins are worth less than those with full impression. Coins with negative impressions on both sides are usually mutilated pieces made outside the mint by the pressing together of coins.

Wrong Planchet—**A coin struck on a planchet intended for another denomination or of the wrong metal.** Examples of these are cents struck on dime planchets, nickels on cent planchets, or quarters on dime planchets. Values vary depending on the type of error involved. Those struck on coins of a different denomination that were previously struck normally are of much greater value. A similar kind of error occurs when a coin is struck on a planchet of the correct denomination but wrong metal. One famous example is the 1943 cent struck in bronze (pictured), rather than in that year's new steel composition. (Fewer than three dozen are thought to exist.) Such errors presumably occur when an older planchet is mixed in with the normal supply of planchets and goes through the minting process.

MINT-CANCELED COINS

In mid-2003, the U.S. Mint acquired machines to eliminate security concerns and the cost associated with providing Mint police escorts to private vendors for the melting of scrap, substandard struck coins, planchets, and blanks. Under high pressure, the rollers and blades of these machines cancel the coins and blanks in a manner similar in appearance to the surface of a waffle, and they are popularly known by that term. This process has effectively kept most misstruck coins produced after 2003 from becoming available to collectors. Waffled examples are known for all six 2003-dated coin denominations, from the Lincoln cent through the Sacagawea dollar. The Mint has not objected to these pieces' trading in the open market because they are not considered coins with legal tender status.

MISSTRUCK AND ERROR PIECES

	Clipped Planchet	Multiple Strike	Blank, No Raised Rim	Planchet, Raised Rim	Defective Die	Off Center	Broadstrike	Lamination	Brockage
Large Cent	$60	$1,000	$200	$350	$25	$600	$100	$25	$1,100
Indian Head 1¢	$15	$600	—	—	$25	$150	$60	$15	$400
Lincoln 1¢ (95% Copper)	$3	$65	$4	$3	$12	$12	$8	$3	$35
Steel 1¢	$25	$250	$55	$75	$15	$60	$35	$15	$200
Lincoln 1¢ (Zinc)	$4	$35	$3	$2	$15	$8	$5	$15	$40
Liberty 5¢	$20	$700	—	$250	$35	$200	$110	$25	$450
Buffalo 5¢	$20	$2,500	—	$600	$40	$500	$300	$35	$850
Jefferson 5¢	$3	$40	$15	$10	$15	$12	$10	$15	$40
Wartime 5¢	$10	$400	$400	$350	$25	$175	$70	$15	$200
Barber 10¢	$45	$750	—	—	$75	$300	$85	$15	$400
Mercury 10¢	$20	$800	—	—	$35	$175	$55	$15	$275
Roosevelt 10¢ (Silver)	$10	$250	$50	$40	$35	$150	$45	$12	$100
Roosevelt 10¢ (Clad)	$3	$50	$3	$4	$15	$10	$10	$16	$40

	Clipped Planchet	Multiple Strike	Blank, No Raised Rim	Planchet, Raised Rim	Defective Die	Off Center	Broadstrike	Lamination	Brockage
Washington 25¢ (Silver)	$20	$400	$175	$150	$25	$350	$200	$15	$300
Washington 25¢ (Clad)	$5	$150	$7	$5	$12	$70	$20	$25	$50
Bicentennial 25¢	$35	$350	—	—	$65	$150	$50	$50	$250
State 25¢	$20	$500	—	—	$25	$100	$40	$250	$375
Franklin 50¢	$40	$1,800	—	—	$150	$1,800	$500	$25	$750
Kennedy 50¢ (40% Silver)	$25	$1,000	$185	$135	$70	$450	$200	$40	$450
Kennedy 50¢ (Clad)	$18	$600	$135	$100	$50	$250	$75	$25	$300
Bicentennial 50¢	$45	$700	—	—	$90	$300	$95	$40	$550
Silver $1	$50	$5,000	$1,750	$1,600	$950	$2,500	$775	$50	$550
Eisenhower $1	$35	$1,200	$175	$100	$500	$600	$150	$50	$950
Bicentennial $1	$50	$1,800	—	—	$750	$850	$200	$50	$1,100
Anthony $1	$25	$600	$150	$120	$100	$275	$75	$30	$300
Sacagawea $1	$100	$1,800	$250	$70	$50	$1,500	$300	$50	$500

WRONG PLANCHETS

	Zinc 1¢	Copper 1¢	Steel 1¢	5¢	Silver 10¢	Copper-Nickel Clad 10¢	Silver 25¢	Copper-Nickel Clad 25¢	Copper-Nickel Clad 50¢
Indian Head 1¢	(a)	—	(a)	(a)	$8,500	(a)	(a)	(a)	(a)
Lincoln 1¢	—	—	—	(a)	$1,000	$350	(a)	(a)	(a)
Buffalo 5¢	(a)	$4,000	(a)	—	$5,000	(a)	(a)	(a)	(a)
Jefferson 5¢	$300	$275	$2,500	—	$450	$375	(a)	(a)	(a)
Wartime 5¢	(a)	$2,500	$3,500	—	$2,000	(a)	(a)	(a)	(a)
Washington 25¢ (Silver)	(a)	$950	$7,000	$500	$1,800	—	—	—	(a)
Washington 25¢ (Clad)	—	$750	(a)	$225	—	$350	—	—	(a)
Bicentennial 25¢	(a)	$3,000	(a)	$2,500	—	$3,500	—	—	(a)
State 25¢ (b)	$4,500	(a)	(a)	$750	(a)	$4,000	(a)	—	(a)
Walking Liberty 50¢	(a)	—	—	—	—	(a)	$25,000	(a)	(a)
Franklin 50¢	(a)	$5,000	(a)	$5,000	$6,000	(a)	$1,500	(a)	(a)
Kennedy 50¢ (c)	(a)	$3,000	(a)	$1,250	—	$2,000	—	$650	—
Bicentennial 50¢	(a)	$4,000	(a)	$2,750	—	—	—	$1,200	—
Eisenhower $1	(a)	$12,500	(a)	$9,500	—	$11,000	—	$6,000	$2,750
Anthony $1	—	$3,500	(a)	$5,000	(a)	—	—	$1,000	(a)
Sacagawea $1	$10,000	(a)	(a)	$10,000	(a)	$10,000	(a)	$3,000	(a)

Note: Coins struck over other coins of different denominations are usually valued three to five times higher than these prices. Coins made from mismatched dies (State quarter obverse combined with Sacagawea dollar reverse) are extremely rare. **a.** Not possible. **b.** Values for State quarter errors vary with each type and state, and are generally much higher than for other quarters. **c.** The Kennedy fifty-cent piece struck on an Anthony one-dollar planchet is very rare.

A GALLERY OF SIGNIFICANT U.S. MINT ERROR COINS

Every high-production manufacturing facility makes a certain percentage of "factory irregulars." The U.S. Mint—which for decades has produced billions of coins annually—is no exception. Today's Mint, though, has cutting-edge machinery and quality-control procedures that keep errors and misstruck coins to a minimum. When such coins *do* come into being, the Mint's sophisticated safeguards (such as riddlers that filter aside odd-shaped coins) prevent nearly all of them from leaving its facilities. Over the course of its 220-plus years of making and issuing coins, however, the Mint has produced some amazing and unusual coins that have made their way into collectors' hands. This gallery highlights a selection of collectible, significant, and valuable errors and misstruck coins.

Some early U.S. Mint coins might appear to be misstrikes when in fact they simply illustrate the standard operating procedures of the time. For example, many 1795 and 1797 half cents show faint evidence of the design of Talbot, Allum & Lee tokens. These are not highly prized double-denominations, but rather regular federal coins intentionally struck on planchets made from cut-down tokens. Other examples exist, such as "spoiled" (misstruck) large cents salvaged and cut down into planchets for half cents.

The introduction of steam-driven coining presses in the 1830s ushered in what today's collector might consider a golden age of misstruck coins. Two competing factors were at work: improved minting techniques and quality control helped curb (or at least catch) most errors and misstrikes, but dramatically increasing mintages naturally led to a greater quantity of such mistakes.

The 1900s and 2000s saw continuing modernization of the mints and a gradual conversion from older presses to new higher-speed presses, eventually capable of striking up to 750 coins per minute. In addition to their speed, today's presses strike coins horizontally, allowing highly efficient and consistently accurate production. As discussed earlier, major misstrikes and coinage errors from 2002 to the present are very rare. Currently, only a handful of new significant pieces enter the market each year.

Error and misstruck coins are a growing specialty in the rare-coin market. Their appeal and value lie in their rarity, their unusual appearance, and the insight they provide into the minting process. When major specimens appear at auction, they bring excitement and active bidding. While no misstrike or error coin has yet sold for a million dollars, several have sold for six-figure sums.

This gallery illustrates a variety of such pieces not typically seen. Some of the featured coins reside in museums or other permanent collections. Each is a classic representation of its type (e.g., wrong planchet or double strike). In many cases, they are unique; for the rest, only a few such pieces are known. The valuations are approximate, based on recent sales and market conditions. For misstruck and error coins, the grade, type, and eye appeal are important factors in market pricing.

Special credit is due to Nicholas P. Brown, David J. Camire, and Fred Weinberg, authors of *100 Greatest U.S. Error Coins*, for contributing to this feature.

1904 Lewis and Clark Exposition gold dollar (partial collar with reverse brockage). This specimen, part of the Smithsonian's National Numismatic Collection, is unique among commemorative gold coinage. It was created when a struck coin failed to fully eject from the press. A new planchet entered and came to rest partially atop the coin; when they were struck together, a reverse image was transferred to the error coin. The obstruction also prevented the planchet from being fully enclosed by the collar. *Value:* $25,000 or more.

1943 Lincoln cent struck over a struck 1943 Mercury dime (double denomination). This piece is unique for the date, and one of only a handful known in silver for the series. It occurred when 1943-dated cent dies struck a 1943 dime instead of a steel cent planchet. *Value:* $16,000 or more.

1999-P Anthony dollar struck on a 2000 Sacagawea planchet (wrong planchet–transitional). About six examples of this kind are known, most acquired from Mint rolls and bags. During transitions in a coin series (e.g., in metal content or design), wrong planchets may accidentally be used in production. This transitional error shows a "golden dollar" planchet that was used to strike an Anthony dollar. *Value:* $16,000 or more.

1863 Indian Head cent (obverse capped die). This dramatic piece is unique for the date and the series. The coin was struck multiple times by the obverse die against a planchet that rested atop the reverse die. Since the planchet was not properly seated in the collar, the force of the strike spread the planchet (cracking it in the process) until it was larger than a quarter dollar. *Value:* $55,000 or more.

1906 Indian Head cent struck on a quarter eagle planchet (wrong planchet). This error is unique for the date, and one of perhaps four known in the series. Somehow a gold quarter-eagle planchet made its way into the coining chamber for cent production. Some theorize that this and similar specimens were intentionally struck, but most show light to moderate wear that suggests they entered circulation. *Value:* $150,000 or more.

1860 Liberty Seated quarter struck on a cent planchet (wrong planchet). This specimen is unique for the date and the series. Its bright bronze color (from the copper-nickel Indian Head cent planchet) and Mint State grade give it great visual appeal. *Value:* $50,000 or more.

1837 Capped Bust half dollar struck on a struck large cent (double denomination). This misstrike is unique for the date and the series. It was made when the steam press had been in use for half dollars only a little more than a year. The coin appears to have circulated for a while before being placed into a collection. Much detail still shows from both strikes. *Value:* $50,000 or more.

Peace dollar struck on a Standing Liberty quarter planchet (wrong planchet). This error is unique for the date and the series. Judging from its Mint State grade, it was probably placed into a collection after being found in a bag or roll of coins. *Value:* $75,000 or more.

1909 Indian Head cent struck on a struck 1906 Barber dime (double denomination). This piece is unique for the date and the series. Considerable detail shows from both strikes. *Value:* $25,000 or more.

1976-D Eisenhower dollar (obverse die cap). This specimen is unique for the date, and one of only a couple known in the series. It occurred when a struck coin adhered to the die, essentially becoming a die itself. Each subsequent strike caused the planchet to bend around the die, forming a deep, bottle cap–shaped coin. *Value:* $25,000 or more.

1976-D Washington quarter (double strike). A few such specimens are known, in varying degrees of off-center double striking. This misstrike has a second strike 40% off center from the first, and is die-struck on both sides. *Value:* $2,750 or more.

1923 Peace dollar (double strike). This misstrike is unique for the date and the series. Apparently the coin was struck about 45% off center, then repositioned and struck a second time, centered normally. *Value:* $75,000 or more.

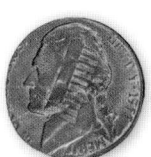   

1977 Jefferson nickel struck on a 1976 Lincoln cent (double denomination–dual date). Two examples of this error are known for the date, among a half dozen in the series. Both dates are clearly visible. *Value:* $8,000 or more.

(1976 or 1977) Lincoln cent struck off center on a Philippine five-sentimos planchet (wrong planchet–multiple error). This error is unique for the series as an off center; several are known struck on center. The Philadelphia Mint struck almost 99 million five-sentimo coins for the Philippines in 1976, and more than 1 million in 1977. Only a few U.S. coins are known accidentally struck on their planchets. *Value:* $2,750 or more.

(1960) Jefferson nickel struck on a 1960 Peruvian five-centavos coin (double denomination–dual country). This error is unique for the date and the series. Interestingly, Mint records do not indicate any coins of Peru were struck at the Philadelphia Mint in 1960. *Value:* $10,000 or more.

Lincoln cent struck off center on a Roosevelt dime (double denomination–off center). Only a few off-center double denominations are known for this series. This is a full dime that was struck off-center by cent dies. *Value:* $5,500 or more.

1943 Lincoln cent struck on a bronze planchet (wrong planchet–transitional). About a dozen of these well-known errors have been confirmed. They came about when bronze planchets left over from 1942 cent production were mixed with the regular 1943 steel planchets. All but one were found in circulation. This error was voted among the *100 Greatest U.S. Coins* (Garrett and Guth). *Value:* $100,000 or more.

(2000) Washington quarter obverse muled with a Sacagawea dollar reverse (mule). About two dozen of these dramatic errors are known to have been struck at Philadelphia, in three die pairings. They have received nationwide publicity in the mainstream press. *Value:* $100,000 or more.

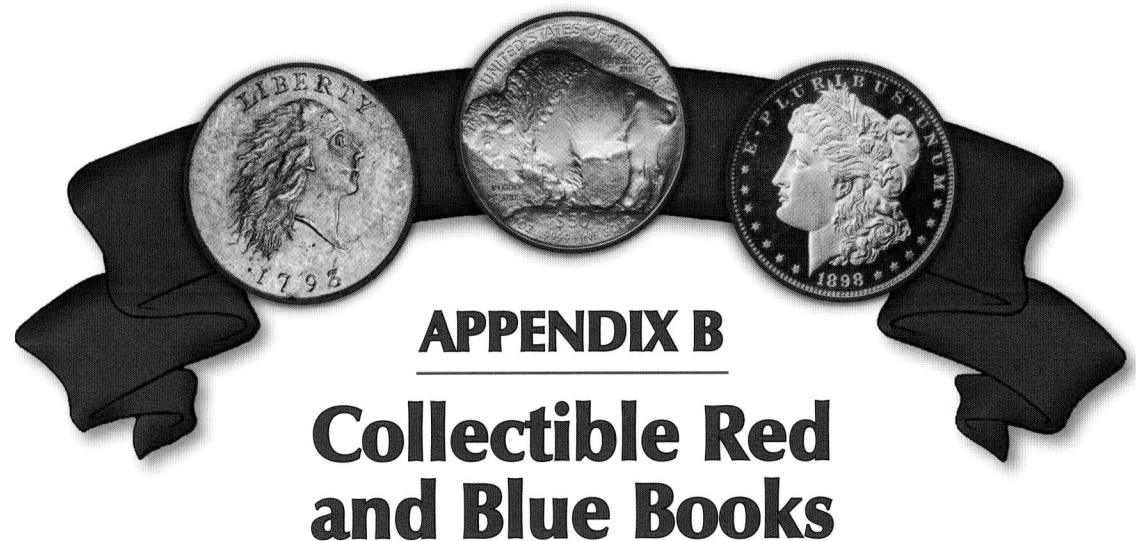

APPENDIX B

Collectible Red and Blue Books

The book you are reading is the *Deluxe Edition* of a classic hobby reference, the *Guide Book of United States Coins*, popularly known as the "Red Book." More than 23 million copies of the Red Book have been sold since 1946, making it one of the best-selling nonfiction titles in American publishing history. By 1959 more than 100,000 copies were being printed annually. The 1965 (18th) edition, published in 1964, reached a peak of 1,200,000 copies. That year the Red Book was ranked fifth on the list of best-selling nonfiction—ahead of Dale Carnegie's classic *How to Win Friends and Influence People* (at number 6) and John F. Kennedy's *Profiles in Courage* (at number 9).

The idea for the Red Book started in the 1940s with R.S. Yeoman. Employed by Whitman Publishing Company (part of Western Publishing), Yeoman at first created the "Blue Book" (official title, the *Handbook of United States Coins With Premium List*), which gave hobbyists an overview of American coinage and a detailed guide to the prices that dealers were paying for collectible coins. The first edition was published in 1942. Yeoman saw that collectors wanted even more information, and he began compiling data and records for an expanded *retail* version of the Blue Book (showing how much a collector could expect to pay a dealer for coins). After World War II ended, Yeoman and his team introduced the new volume, the *Guide Book of United States Coins*, soon nicknamed the Red Book because of its distinctive cover color.

Numismatist Kenneth E. Bressett joined the Red Book in 1956 as a freelance editor. He has continued to work on the annually published book, and other Whitman projects, ever since. He took a full-time editorial position with Whitman Publishing in 1959, and assumed full editorship of the Red Book in 1975. Today Bressett serves as the Red Book's editor emeritus, with Jeff Garrett as senior editor, Q. David Bowers as research editor, and a panel of more than 100 coin dealers, researchers, and other specialists.

THE RED BOOK AS A COLLECTIBLE

The *Guide Book of United States Coins* holds the record as the longest-running annual retail coin-price guide. It has passed its 65th anniversary, and collectors seem to be almost as interested in assembling sets of old Red Books as of old coins. The demand for old Red Books has created a solid market. Some who collect these old editions maintain reference libraries of all kinds of coin publications. To them, having one of each edition is essential, because that is the way old books are collected. Others are speculators who believe that the value of old editions will go up as interest and demand increase. Many people who save old Red Books do so to maintain a record of coin prices going back further than any other source.

Following price trends in old Red Books is a good indicator of how well individual coins are doing in comparison to each other. The price information published in each year is an average of what collectors are paying for each coin. It is a valuable benchmark, showing how prices have gone up or down over the years. Information like this often gives investors an edge in predicting what the future may hold.

Old Red Books are also a handy resource on collecting trends. They show graphically how grading has changed over the years, what new coins have been discovered and added to the listings, and which areas are growing in popularity. Studying these old books can be educational as well as nostalgic. It's great fun to see what your favorite coins sold for 15 or 25 years ago or more—and a bit frustrating to realize what might have been if we had only bought the right coins at the right time in years past.

Many collectors have asked about the quantities printed of each edition. That information has never been published, and now no company records exist specifying how many were made. The original author, R.S. Yeoman, told inquirers that the first press run in November 1946 was for 9,000 copies. In February 1947 an additional 9,000 copies were printed to satisfy the unexpected demand.

There was a slight but notable difference that can be used to differentiate between the first and second printings. The wording in the first printing at the bottom of page 135 reads, "which probably accounts for the scarcity of *this* date." Those last few words were changed to "the scarcity of *1903 O*" in the second printing.

The second edition had a press run of 22,000. The printing of each edition thereafter gradually increased, with the highest number ever being reached with the 18th edition, dated 1965 and published in 1964. At the top of a booming coin market, a whopping 1,200,000 copies were produced. Since that time the numbers have decreased, but the Red Book still maintains a record of being the world's largest-selling coin publication each year.

In some years a very limited number of Red Books were made for use by price contributors. Those were interleaved with blank pages. No more than 50 copies were ever made for any one year. Perhaps fewer than 20 were made in the first few years. Three of these of the first edition, and one of the second edition, are currently known. Their value is now in four figures. Those made in the 1960s sell for about $300–$500 today.

There are other unusual Red Books that command exceptional prices. One of the most popular is the 1987 special edition that was made for, and distributed only to, people who attended the 1986 American Numismatic Association banquet in Milwaukee. Only 500 of those were printed with a special commemorative cover.

Error books are also popular with collectors. The most common is one with double-stamped printing on the cover. The second most frequently seen are those with an upside-down cover. Probably the best known of the error books is the 1963 16th edition with a missing page. For some uncanny reason, page 239 is duplicated in some of those books, and page 237 is missing. The error was corrected on most of the printing.

The terminology used to describe book condition differs from that utilized in grading coins. A "Very Fine" book is one that is nearly new, with minimal signs of use. Early editions of the Red Book are rarely if ever found in anything approaching "New" condition. Exceptionally well-preserved older editions command a substantial premium and are in great demand. Nice used copies that are still clean and in good shape, but slightly worn from use, are also desirable. Only the early editions are worth a premium in badly worn condition.

For a more detailed history and edition-by-edition study of the Red Book, see Frank J. Colletti's *A Guide Book of The Official Red Book of United States Coins* (Whitman, 2009).

VALUATION GUIDE FOR PAST EDITIONS OF THE RED BOOK
CLASSIC HARDCOVER BINDING

See page 1341 for special editions in the classic hardcover binding.

Year/Edition	Issue Price	VG	F	VF	New
1947 (1st ed.), 1st Printing	$1.50	$350	$575	$950	$2,000 (a)
1947 (1st ed.), 2nd Printing	$1.50	$300	$550	$900	$1,800 (a)
1948 (2nd ed.)	$1.50	$80	$150	$225	$450 (a)
1949 (3rd ed.)	$1.50	$80	$150	$350	$500 (a)
1951/52 (4th ed.)	$1.50	$55	$110	$175	$300 (a)
1952/53 (5th ed.)	$1.50	$150	$225	$450	$1,500 (a)
1953/54 (6th ed.)	$1.75	$45	$65	$100	$140
1954/55 (7th ed.)	$1.75	$40	$50	$100	$120
1955 (8th ed.)	$1.75	$30	$45	$90	$115
1956 (9th ed.)	$1.75	$20	$35	$60	$110
1957 (10th ed.)	$1.75	$10	$20	$35	$50
1958 (11th ed.)	$1.75		$8	$12	$25
1959 (12th ed.)	$1.75		$8	$10	$25
1960 (13th ed.)	$1.75		$7	$9	$24
1961 (14th ed.)	$1.75		$4	$6	$23
1962 (15th ed.)	$1.75		$4	$6	$15
1963 (16th ed.)	$1.75		$4	$6	$15
1964 (17th ed.)	$1.75		$4	$5	$10
1965 (18th ed.)	$1.75		$3	$4	$10
1966 (19th ed.)	$1.75		$3	$4	$10
1967 (20th ed.)	$1.75		$2	$5	$10
1968 (21st ed.)	$2		$2	$5	$12
1969 (22nd ed.)	$2		$2	$5	$12
1970 (23rd ed.)	$2.50		$2	$6	$11
1971 (24th ed.)	$2.50		$2	$4	$7
1972 (25th ed.)	$2.50		$5	$8	$10
1973 (26th ed.)	$2.50		$4	$5	$7
1974 (27th ed.)	$2.50		$3	$4	$7
1975 (28th ed.)	$3			$4	$6
1976 (29th ed.)	$3.95			$4	$7
1977 (30th ed.)	$3.95			$4	$6
1978 (31st ed.)	$3.95			$4	$6
1979 (32nd ed.)	$3.95			$4	$7
1980 (33rd ed.)	$3.95			$4	$9
1981 (34th ed.)	$4.95			$2	$5
1982 (35th ed.)	$4.95			$2	$5
1983 (36th ed.)	$5.95			$2	$5
1984 (37th ed.)	$5.95			$2	$5
1985 (38th ed.)	$5.95			$2	$5
1986 (39th ed.)	$5.95			$2	$5
1987 (40th ed.)	$6.95			$2	$5
1988 (41st ed.)	$6.95			$2	$5
1989 (42nd ed.)	$6.95			$3	$6
1990 (43rd ed.)	$7.95			$2	$5
1991 (44th ed.)	$8.95			$2	$5
1992 (45th ed.)	$8.95			$2	$5

Note: Values are for unsigned books. Those signed by R.S. Yeoman are worth substantially more. **a.** Values are for books in Near Mint condition, as truly New copies are effectively nonexistent.

Year/Edition	Issue Price	VG	F	VF	New
1993 (46th ed.)	$9.95			$2	$5
1994 (47th ed.)	$9.95			$2	$4
1995 (48th ed.)	$10.95			$2	$4
1996 (49th ed.)	$10.95			$2	$4
1997 (50th ed.)	$11.95			$2	$4
1998 (51st ed.)	$11.95				$3
1999 (52nd ed.)	$11.95				$3
2000 (53rd ed.)	$12.95				$3
2001 (54th ed.)	$13.95				$3
2002 (55th ed.)	$14.95				$3
2003 (56th ed.)	$15.95				$2
2004 (57th ed.)	$15.95				$2
2005 (58th ed.)	$15.95				$2
2006 (59th ed.)	$16.95				$3
2007 (60th ed.)	$16.95				$3
2008 (61st ed.)	$16.95				$3
2009 (62nd ed.)	$16.95				$3
2010 (63rd ed.)	$16.95				$3
2011 (64th ed.)	$16.95				$2
2012 (65th ed.)	$16.95				$2
2013 (66th ed.)	$16.95				$2
2014 (67th ed.)	$16.95				$2
2015 (68th ed.)	$16.95				$2
2016 (69th ed.)	$16.95				$2
2017 (70th ed.)	$16.95				$2
2018 (71st ed.) (b)	$16.95				$2
2019 (72nd ed.) (c)	$16.95				

Note: Values are for unsigned books. Those signed by R.S. Yeoman are worth substantially more. **b.** The 2018 hardcover features a back-cover gold-foil portrait of David Rittenhouse, first director of the United States Mint, in celebration of 225 years of U.S. coinage at Philadelphia. **c.** The 2019 Red Book (in every format) includes a 10-page illustrated tribute to Editor Emeritus Kenneth Bressett. The back of the hardcover features a gold-foil portrait of Bressett.

SOFTCOVERS (1993–2007)

The first softcover (trade paperback) Red Book was the 1993 (46th) edition. The softcover binding was offered (alongside other formats) in the 1993, 1994, 1995, and 1996 editions; again in the 1998 edition; and from 2003 through 2007. All are fairly common and easily collectible today. Values in New condition range from $2 up to $3–$4 for the earlier editions.

SPIRALBOUND SOFTCOVERS (1997 TO DATE)

The first spiralbound softcover Red Book was the 1997 (50th) edition. The spiralbound softcover format was next available in the 1999 edition, and it has been an annually offered format every edition since then. Today the spiralbound softcovers all are easily collectible. The 1997 edition is worth $4 in New condition, and later editions are valued around $2.

SPIRALBOUND HARDCOVERS (2008 TO DATE)

The first spiralbound hardcover Red Book was the 2008 (61st) edition. The format has been available (alongside other formats) every edition since. All spiralbound hardcovers are readily available to collectors, and are valued from $2 to $4.

JOURNAL EDITION (2009)

The large-sized Journal Edition, featuring a three-ring binder, color-coded tabbed dividers, and removable pages, was issued only for the 2009 (62nd) edition. Today it is valued at $5 in VF and $30 in New condition.

LARGE PRINT EDITIONS (2010 TO DATE)

The oversized Large Print format of the Red Book has been offered annually since the 2010 (63rd) edition. All editions are readily available to collectors and are valued at $5 in New condition.

LEATHER LIMITED EDITIONS (2005 TO DATE)

Year/Edition	Print Run	Issue Price	New
2005 (58th ed.)	3,000	$69.95	$75
2006 (59th ed.)	3,000	$69.95	$75
2007 (60th ed.)	3,000	$69.95	$90
2007 1947 Tribute Edition	500	$49.95	$125
2008 (61st ed.)	3,000	$69.95	$75
2008 (61st ed.), Numismatic Literary Guild (a)	135 (b)		$900
2008 (61st ed.), American Numismatic Society (c)	250 (b)		$700
2009 (62nd ed.)	3,000	$69.95	$75
2010 (63rd ed.)	1,500	$69.95	$75
2011 (64th ed.)	1,500	$69.95	$75
2012 (65th ed.)	1,000	$69.95	$80
2013 (66th ed.)	1,000	$69.95	$75
2014 (67th ed.)	1,000	$69.95	$75
2015 (68th ed.)	500	$99.95	$100
2016 (69th ed.)	500	$99.95	$100
2017 (70th ed.)	250	$99.95	$100
2018 (71st ed.)	250	$99.95	$100
2019 (72nd ed.)	250	$99.95	$100

a. One hundred thirty-five imprinted copies of the 2008 leather Limited Edition were created. Of these, 125 were distributed to members of the NLG at its 2007 literary awards ceremony; the remaining 10 were distributed from Whitman Publishing headquarters in Atlanta. b. Included in total print-run quantity. c. Two hundred fifty copies of the 2008 leather Limited Edition were issued with a special bookplate honoring the 150th anniversary of the ANS. They were distributed to attendees of the January 2008 celebratory banquet in New York.

SPECIAL EDITIONS

Year/Edition	Print Run	Issue Price	VF	New
1987 (40th ed.), American Numismatic Association 95th Anniversary	500		$700	$1,200
1992 (45th ed.), American Numismatic Association 100th Anniversary	600		$150	$250
1997 (50th ed.), Red Book 50th Anniversary	1,200	$24.95	$50	$100
2002 (55th ed.), American Numismatic Association "Target 2001"	500	$100	$35	$50
2002 (55th ed.), SS *Central America*		$35	$25	$35
2005 (58th ed.), FUN (Florida United Numismatists) 50th Anniversary	1,100		$45	$100
2007 (60th ed.), American Numismatic Association 115th Anniversary	500		$50	$110
2007 (60th ed.), Michigan State Numismatic Society 50th Anniversary	500		$50	$110
2007 (1st ed.), 1947 Tribute Edition		$17.95	$5	$20
2008 (61st ed.), ANA Milwaukee World's Fair of Money	1,080		$30	$50
2008 (61st ed.), Stack's Rare Coins			$4	$18
2010 (63rd ed.), Hardcover, Philadelphia Expo (a)		$24.95	$18	$35
2011 (64th ed.), Boston Numismatic Society		$85	$50	$85
2012 (65th ed.), American Numismatic Association	800	$100	$25	$60
2013 (66th ed.), American Numismatic Society (b)	250		$75	$250
2015 (68th ed.), Central States Numismatic Society	500	$15	$25	$75
2016 (69th ed.) American Numismatic Association 125th Anniversary		$100	$40	$75
2018 (71st ed.), NGC 30th Anniversary			$50	$100

a. Two thousand and nine copies of a special 2010 hardcover edition were made for distribution to dealers at the premiere Whitman Coin and Collectibles Philadelphia Expo (September 2009). Extra copies were sold at $50 apiece with proceeds benefiting the National Federation for the Blind. b. Two hundred fifty copies of the 2013 hardcover were issued with a special bookplate honoring ANS Trustees' Award recipient (and Red Book research contributor) Roger Siboni.

THE BLUE BOOK AS A COLLECTIBLE

The precursor to the Red Book was the *Handbook of United States Coins With Premium List*, popularly known as the "Blue Book." Its mastermind was R.S. Yeoman, who had been hired by Western Publishing as a commercial artist in 1932. He distributed Western's Whitman line of "penny boards" to coin collectors, promoting them through department stores, along with children's books and games. He eventually arranged for Whitman to expand the line into other denominations, giving them the reputation of a numismatic endeavor rather than a "game" of filling holes with missing coins. He also developed these flat boards into a line of popular folders.

Yeoman began to compile coin-mintage data and market values to aid collectors. This research grew into the Blue Book: now collectors had a coin-by-coin guide to the average prices dealers would pay for U.S. coins. The first two editions were both published in 1942.

In the first edition of the Red Book, Whitman Publishing would describe the Blue Book as "a low-priced standard reference book of United States coins and kindred issues" for which there had been "a long-felt need among American collectors."

The Blue Book has been published annually (except in 1944 and 1950) since its debut. Past editions offer valuable information about the hobby of yesteryear as well as developments in numismatic research and the marketplace. Old Blue Books are collectible; most editions after the 12th can be found for a few dollars in VF or better condition. Major variants were produced for the third, fourth, and ninth editions, including perhaps the only "overdate" books in American numismatic publishing. Either to conserve the previous years' covers or to correct an error in binding, the cloth on some third-edition covers was overstamped "Fourth Edition," and a number of eighth-edition covers were overstamped "Ninth Edition." The third edition was produced in several shades of blue ranging from light to dark. Some copies of the fourth edition were also produced in black cloth—the only time the Blue Book was bound in other than blue.

VALUATION GUIDE FOR SELECT PAST EDITIONS OF THE BLUE BOOK

Edition	Date (a)		VF	New
	Title Page	Copyright		
1st	1942	1942	$100	$460
2nd	1943	1942	$40	$65
3rd	1944	1943	$25	$80
4th	*none*	1945	$25	$80
5th	*none*	1946	$20	$35
6th	1948	1947	$15	$30
7th	1949	1948	$12	$25
8th	1950	1949	$10	$20
9th	1952	1951	$5	$10
10th	1953	1952	$5	$8
11th	1954	1953	$3	$7
12th	1955	1954	$3	$7

a. During its early years of production, the Blue Book's date presentation was not standardized. Full information is given here to aid in precise identification of early editions.

APPENDIX C

Bullion Values

These charts show the bullion values of silver and gold U.S. coins. These are intrinsic values and do not reflect any numismatic premium a coin might have. The weight listed under each denomination is its actual silver weight (ASW) or actual gold weight (AGW).

In recent years, the bullion price of silver has fluctuated considerably. You can use the following chart to determine the approximate bullion value of many 19th- and 20th-century silver coins at various price levels—or you can calculate the approximate value by multiplying the current spot price of silver by the ASW for each coin, as indicated. Dealers generally purchase common silver coins at around 15% below bullion value, and sell them at around 15% above bullion value.

Nearly all U.S. gold coins have an additional premium value beyond their bullion content, and thus are not subject to minor bullion-price variations. The premium amount is not necessarily tied to the bullion price of gold, but is usually determined by supply and demand levels in the numismatic marketplace. Because these factors can vary significantly, there is no reliable formula for calculating "percentage below and above bullion" prices that would remain accurate over time. The gold chart lists bullion values based on AGW only; consult a coin dealer to ascertain current buy and sell prices.

BULLION VALUES OF SILVER COINS

Silver Price Per Ounce	Wartime Nickel .05626 oz.	Dime .07234 oz.	Quarter .18084 oz.	Half Dollar .36169 oz.	Silver Clad Half Dollar .14792 oz.	Silver Dollar .77344 oz.
$8.00	$0.45	$0.58	$1.45	$2.89	$1.18	$6.19
$8.50	$0.48	$0.61	$1.54	$3.07	$1.26	$6.57
$9.00	$0.51	$0.65	$1.63	$3.26	$1.33	$6.96
$9.50	$0.53	$0.69	$1.72	$3.44	$1.41	$7.35
$10.00	$0.56	$0.72	$1.81	$3.62	$1.48	$7.73
$10.50	$0.59	$0.76	$1.90	$3.80	$1.55	$8.12
$11.00	$0.62	$0.80	$1.99	$3.98	$1.63	$8.51
$11.50	$0.65	$0.83	$2.08	$4.16	$1.70	$8.89
$12.00	$0.68	$0.87	$2.17	$4.34	$1.78	$9.28
$12.50	$0.70	$0.90	$2.26	$4.52	$1.85	$9.67
$13.00	$0.73	$0.94	$2.35	$4.70	$1.92	$10.05
$13.50	$0.76	$0.98	$2.44	$4.88	$2.00	$10.44

Note: The U.S. bullion coins first issued in 1986 are unlike the older regular issues. They contain the following amounts of pure metal: silver $1, 1 oz.; gold $50, 1 oz.; gold $25, 1/2 oz.; gold $10, 1/4 oz.; gold $5, 1/10 oz.

Silver Price Per Ounce	Wartime Nickel .05626 oz.	Dime .07234 oz.	Quarter .18084 oz.	Half Dollar .36169 oz.	Silver Clad Half Dollar .14792 oz.	Silver Dollar .77344 oz.
$14.00	$0.79	$1.01	$2.53	$5.06	$2.07	$10.83
$14.50	$0.82	$1.05	$2.62	$5.24	$2.14	$11.21
$15.00	$0.84	$1.09	$2.71	$5.43	$2.22	$11.60
$15.50	$0.87	$1.12	$2.80	$5.61	$2.29	$11.99
$16.00	$0.90	$1.16	$2.89	$5.79	$2.37	$12.38
$16.50	$0.93	$1.19	$2.98	$5.97	$2.44	$12.76
$17.00	$0.96	$1.23	$3.07	$6.15	$2.51	$13.15
$17.50	$0.98	$1.27	$3.16	$6.33	$2.59	$13.54
$18.00	$1.01	$1.30	$3.26	$6.51	$2.66	$13.92
$18.50	$1.04	$1.34	$3.35	$6.69	$2.74	$14.31
$19.00	$1.07	$1.37	$3.44	$6.87	$2.81	$14.70
$19.50	$1.10	$1.41	$3.53	$7.05	$2.88	$15.08
$20.00	$1.13	$1.45	$3.62	$7.23	$2.96	$15.47
$20.50	$1.15	$1.48	$3.71	$7.41	$3.03	$15.86
$21.00	$1.18	$1.52	$3.80	$7.60	$3.11	$16.24
$21.50	$1.21	$1.56	$3.89	$7.78	$3.18	$16.63
$22.00	$1.24	$1.59	$3.98	$7.96	$3.25	$17.02
$22.50	$1.27	$1.63	$4.07	$8.14	$3.33	$17.40
$23.00	$1.29	$1.66	$4.16	$8.32	$3.40	$17.79
$23.50	$1.32	$1.70	$4.25	$8.50	$3.48	$18.18
$24.00	$1.35	$1.74	$4.34	$8.68	$3.55	$18.56
$24.50	$1.38	$1.77	$4.43	$8.86	$3.62	$18.95
$25.00	$1.41	$1.81	$4.52	$9.04	$3.70	$19.34
$25.50	$1.43	$1.84	$4.61	$9.22	$3.77	$19.72
$26.00	$1.46	$1.88	$4.70	$9.40	$3.85	$20.11
$26.50	$1.49	$1.92	$4.79	$9.58	$3.92	$20.50
$27.00	$1.52	$1.95	$4.88	$9.77	$3.99	$20.88
$27.50	$1.55	$1.99	$4.97	$9.95	$4.07	$21.27
$28.00	$1.58	$2.03	$5.06	$10.13	$4.14	$21.66
$28.50	$1.60	$2.06	$5.15	$10.31	$4.22	$22.04
$29.00	$1.63	$2.10	$5.24	$10.49	$4.29	$22.43
$29.50	$1.66	$2.13	$5.33	$10.67	$4.36	$22.82
$30.00	$1.69	$2.17	$5.43	$10.85	$4.44	$23.20
$30.50	$1.72	$2.21	$5.52	$11.03	$4.51	$23.59
$31.00	$1.74	$2.24	$5.61	$11.21	$4.59	$23.98
$31.50	$1.77	$2.28	$5.70	$11.39	$4.66	$24.36
$32.00	$1.80	$2.31	$5.79	$11.57	$4.73	$24.75
$32.50	$1.83	$2.35	$5.88	$11.75	$4.81	$25.14
$33.00	$1.86	$2.39	$5.97	$11.94	$4.88	$25.52
$33.50	$1.88	$2.42	$6.06	$12.12	$4.96	$25.91
$34.00	$1.91	$2.46	$6.15	$12.30	$5.03	$26.30
$34.50	$1.94	$2.50	$6.24	$12.48	$5.10	$26.68
$35.00	$1.97	$2.53	$6.33	$12.66	$5.18	$27.07
$35.50	$2.00	$2.57	$6.42	$12.84	$5.25	$27.46
$36.00	$2.03	$2.60	$6.51	$13.02	$5.33	$27.84
$36.50	$2.05	$2.64	$6.60	$13.20	$5.40	$28.23
$37.00	$2.08	$2.68	$6.69	$13.38	$5.47	$28.62
$37.50	$2.11	$2.71	$6.78	$13.56	$5.55	$29.00
$38.00	$2.14	$2.75	$6.87	$13.74	$5.62	$29.39

Note: The U.S. bullion coins first issued in 1986 are unlike the older regular issues. They contain the following amounts of pure metal: silver $1, 1 oz.; gold $50, 1 oz.; gold $25, 1/2 oz.; gold $10, 1/4 oz.; gold $5, 1/10 oz.

BULLION VALUES OF GOLD COINS

Gold Price Per Ounce	$5.00 Liberty Head 1839–1908 Indian Head 1908–1929 .24187 oz.	$10.00 Liberty Head 1838–1907 Indian Head 1907–1933 .48375 oz.	$20.00 1849–1933 .96750 oz.
$850	$205.59	$411.19	$822.38
$875	$211.64	$423.28	$846.56
$900	$217.68	$435.38	$870.75
$925	$223.73	$447.47	$894.94
$950	$229.78	$459.56	$919.13
$975	$235.82	$471.66	$943.31
$1,000	$241.87	$483.75	$967.50
$1,025	$247.92	$495.84	$991.69
$1,050	$253.96	$507.94	$1,015.88
$1,075	$260.01	$520.03	$1,040.06
$1,100	$266.06	$532.13	$1,064.25
$1,125	$272.10	$544.22	$1,088.44
$1,150	$278.15	$556.31	$1,112.63
$1,175	$284.20	$568.41	$1,136.81
$1,200	$290.24	$580.50	$1,161.00
$1,225	$296.29	$592.59	$1,185.19
$1,250	$302.34	$604.69	$1,209.38
$1,275	$308.38	$616.78	$1,233.56
$1,300	$314.43	$628.88	$1,257.75
$1,325	$320.48	$640.97	$1,281.94
$1,350	$326.52	$653.06	$1,306.13
$1,375	$332.57	$665.16	$1,330.31
$1,400	$338.62	$677.25	$1,354.50
$1,425	$344.66	$689.34	$1,378.69
$1,450	$350.71	$701.44	$1,402.88
$1,475	$356.76	$713.53	$1,427.06
$1,500	$362.81	$725.63	$1,451.25
$1,525	$368.85	$737.72	$1,475.44
$1,550	$374.90	$749.81	$1,499.63
$1,575	$380.95	$761.91	$1,523.81
$1,600	$386.99	$774.00	$1,548.00
$1,625	$393.04	$786.09	$1,572.19
$1,650	$399.09	$798.19	$1,596.38
$1,675	$405.13	$810.28	$1,620.56
$1,700	$411.18	$822.38	$1,644.75
$1,725	$417.23	$834.47	$1,668.94
$1,750	$423.27	$846.56	$1,693.13
$1,775	$429.32	$858.66	$1,717.31
$1,800	$435.37	$870.75	$1,741.50
$1,825	$441.41	$882.84	$1,765.69
$1,850	$447.46	$894.94	$1,789.88
$1,875	$453.51	$907.03	$1,814.06
$1,900	$459.55	$919.13	$1,838.25
$1,925	$465.60	$931.22	$1,862.44
$1,950	$471.65	$943.31	$1,886.63
$1,975	$477.69	$955.41	$1,910.81
$2,000	$483.74	$967.50	$1,935.00

Note: The U.S. bullion coins first issued in 1986 are unlike the older regular issues. They contain the following amounts of pure metal: silver $1, 1 oz.; gold $50, 1 oz.; gold $25, 1/2 oz.; gold $10, 1/4 oz.; gold $5, 1/10 oz.

APPENDIX D
Top 250 U.S. Coin Prices Realized at Auction

Rank	Price	Coin	Grade	Firm	Date
1	$10,016,875	$1(s), 1794	PCGS SP-66	Stack's Bowers	Jan-18
2	$7,590,020	$20, 1933	Gem BU	Sotheby's / Stack's	Jul-18
3	$4,993,750	$1(s), 1794	PCGS MS-66+	Sotheby's / Stack's Bowers	Sep-18
4	$4,582,500	Prefed, 1787, Brasher dbln, EB on Wing	NGC MS-63	Heritage	Jan-18
5	$4,140,000	$1(s), 1804, Class I	PCGS PF-68	B&M	Aug-99
6	$3,877,500	$1(s), 1804, Class I	PCGS PF-62	Heritage	Aug-18
7	$3,737,500	5¢, 1913, Liberty Head (A)	NGC PF-64	Heritage	Jan-18
8	$3,737,500	$1(s), 1804, Class I	NGC PF-62	Heritage	Apr-18
9	$3,290,000	$1(s), 1804, Class I	PCGS PF-65	Sotheby's / Stack's Bowers	Mar-18
10	$3,290,000	5¢, 1913, Liberty Head (A)	NGC PF-64	Heritage	Jan-18
11	$3,172,500	5¢, 1913, Liberty Head	PCGS PF-63	Heritage	Apr-18
12	$2,990,000	$20, MCMVII, Ultra HR, LE (B)	PCGS PF-69	Heritage	Nov-18
13	$2,990,000	Prefed, 1787, Brasher, EB on Breast (C)	NGC EF-45	Heritage	Jan-18
14	$2,820,000	$1(s), 1794	PCGS MS-64	Stack's Bowers	Aug-18
15	$2,760,000	$20, MCMVII, Ultra HR, LE (B)	PCGS PF-69	Stack's Bowers	Jun-18
16	$2,585,000	$10, 1795, 13 Leaves, BD-4	PCGS MS-66+	Sotheby's / Stack's Bowers	Sep-18
17	$2,585,000	Pattern 1¢, 1792, Birch Cent, LE, J-4	NGC MS-65RB	Heritage	Jan-18
18	$2,574,000	$4, 1880, Coiled Hair (D)	NGC PF-67 Cam	Bonhams	Sep-18
19	$2,415,000	Prefed, 1787, Brasher, EB on Wing	NGC AU-55	Heritage	Jan-18
20	$2,350,000	$2.50, 1808	PCGS MS-65	Sotheby's / Stack's Bowers	May-18
21	$2,350,000	1¢, 1793, Chain AMERICA, S-4	PCGS MS-66BN	Heritage	Jan-18
22	$2,300,000	$1(s), 1804, Class III	PCGS PF-58	Heritage	Apr-18
23	$2,232,500	Pattern 25¢, 1792, copper, J-12	NGC MS-63BN	Heritage	Jan-18
24	$2,185,000	$10, 1907, Rounded Rim	NGC Satin PF-67	Heritage	Jan-18
25	$2,115,000	$20, MCMVII, Ultra HR, LE	PCGS PF-68	Heritage	Jan-18
26	$1,997,500	10¢, 1894-S	PCGS PF-66	Heritage	Jan-18
27	$1,997,500	Pattern 1¢, 1792 Silver Center, J-1	PCGS MS-64BN	Heritage	Aug-18
28	$1,997,500	$20, 1927-D	NGC MS-66	Heritage	Jan-18
29	$1,897,500	$20, 1927-D	PCGS MS-67	Heritage	Nov-18
30	$1,880,000	Pattern $20, 1879 Quintuple Stella, J-1643	PCGS PF-64DCam	Legend	May-18
31	$1,880,000	$1(s), 1804, Class III	NGC PF-55	Stack's Bowers	Aug-18
32	$1,840,000	10¢, 1873-CC, No Arrows	PCGS MS-65	Stack's Bowers	Aug-18

Rank	Price	Coin	Grade	Firm	Date
33	$1,840,000	5¢, 1913, Liberty Head	NGC PF-66	Superior	Mar-18
34	$1,840,000	$20, MCMVII, Ultra HR, LE	PCGS PF-68	Heritage	Jan-18
35	$1,840,000	$1(s), 1804, Class I (E)	PCGS PF-64	Stack's	Oct-00
36	$1,821,250	$4, 1880, Coiled Hair	NGC PF-67	Heritage	Apr-18
37	$1,815,000	$1(s), 1804, Class I	PF-63	B&M/Stack's	Apr-97
38	$1,725,000	$2.50, 1796, No Stars (F)	PCGS MS-65	Heritage	Jan-18
39	$1,725,000	$10, 1920-S	PCGS MS-67	Heritage	Mar-18
40	$1,645,000	$20, 1861, Paquet Reverse (G)	PCGS MS-61	Heritage	Aug-18
41	$1,610,000	$10, 1839/8, Type of 1838, Lg Letters (H)	NGC PF-67 UCam	Heritage	Jan-18
42	$1,610,000	$20, 1861, Paquet Reverse (G)	PCGS MS-61	Heritage	Aug-18
43	$1,552,500	10¢, 1894-S	PCGS PF-64	Stack's	Oct-18
44	$1,527,500	25¢, 1796, B-2	PCGS MS-66	Sotheby's / Stack's Bowers	May-18
45	$1,527,500	50¢, 1797, O-101a	PCGS MS-66	Sotheby's / Stack's Bowers	May-18
46	$1,527,500	Prefed, 1776, Cont. $1 Silver, N-3D	NGC MS-62	Heritage	Jan-18
47	$1,527,500	Prefed, 1776, Cont. $1 Silver, N-1C	NGC EF-40	Heritage	Jan-18
48	$1,527,500	25¢, 1796, B-2	NGC MS-67+	Heritage	Nov-18
49	$1,495,000	$20, 1927-D	PCGS MS-66	Heritage	Jan-18
50	$1,495,000	$20, 1921	PCGS MS-63	B&M	Aug-18
51	$1,485,000	5¢, 1913, Liberty Head	Gem PF-66	B&M/Stack's	May-96
52	$1,437,500	$20, 1856-O	NGC SP-63	Heritage	May-18
53	$1,410,000	Prefed, 1776, Cont. $1 Silver, N-3D	NGC MS-63	Heritage	May-18
54	$1,410,000	Pattern 1¢, 1792, Silver Center, J-1	NGC MS-63BN+	Heritage	May-18
55	$1,410,000	Pattern half disme, 1792, J-7 (I)	PCGS SP-67	Heritage	Jan-18
56	$1,380,000	$5, 1829, Large Date	PCGS PF-64	Heritage	Jan-18
57	$1,380,000	1¢, 1793, Chain AMERICA, S-4	PCGS MS-65BN	Heritage	Jan-18
58	$1,380,000	50¢, 1797, O-101a (J)	NGC MS-66	Stack's	Jul-18
59	$1,380,000	$2.50, 1796, No Stars (F)	PCGS MS-65	Stack's (ANR)	Jun-18
60	$1,351,250	$5, 1833, BD-1	PCGS PF-67	Sotheby's / Stack's Bowers	May-18
61	$1,322,500	$3, 1855-S	NGC PF-64 Cam	Heritage	Aug-18
62	$1,322,500	Pattern half disme, 1792, J-7 (I)	PCGS SP-67	Heritage	Apr-18
63	$1,322,500	$20, 1927-D	NGC MS-65	Heritage	Jan-18
64	$1,322,500	10¢, 1894-S	NGC PF-66	DLRC	Mar-18
65	$1,292,500	Pattern half disme, 1792, J-7 (I)	PCGS SP-67	Heritage	Aug-18
66	$1,292,500	50¢, 1797, O-101a	PCGS MS-65+	Heritage	Aug-18
67	$1,265,000	Pattern $10, 1874, Bickford, J-1373	PCGS PF-65 DCam	Heritage	Jan-18
68	$1,265,000	1¢, 1795, Reeded Edge, S-79 (K)	PCGS VG-10	Goldberg	Sep-18
69	$1,265,000	$1(s), 1795, Flowing Hair, B-7, BB-18	V Ch Gem MS	Bullowa	Dec-18
70	$1,210,000	$20, MCMVII, Ultra HR, LE (L)	PCGS PF-67	Goldberg	May-99
71	$1,207,500	$1(s), 1794	NGC MS-64	B&M	Aug-18
72	$1,207,500	$1(s), 1866, No Motto	NGC PF-63	Stack's (ANR)	Jan-18
73	$1,207,500	$1(s), 1804, Class III (M)	PCGS PF-58	B&M	Jul-18
74	$1,175,000	$5, 1798, Small Eagle, BD-1	PCGS AU-55	Sotheby's / Stack's Bowers	Sep-18
75	$1,175,000	Pattern 1¢, 1792, Birch Cent, LE, J-4	PCGS AU-58	Stack's Bowers	Mar-18
76	$1,175,000	Prefed, 1783, quint, T-II, Nova Const.	PCGS AU-53	Heritage	Apr-18
77	$1,175,000	$1(s), 1796, Sm Dt, Sm Ltrs, B-2, BB-63	NGC MS-65	Heritage	Apr-18
78	$1,150,000	1/2¢, 1794, C-7 (G)	PCGS MS-67RB	Goldberg	Jan-18
79	$1,150,000	Pattern 1¢, 1792, Silver Center Cent, J-1	PCGS MS-61BN	Heritage	Apr-18
80	$1,150,000	$1(s), 1794	NGC MS-64	Stack's (ANR)	Jun-18
81	$1,145,625	Pattern half disme, 1792, J-7	NGC MS-68	Stack's Bowers	Jan-18
82	$1,121,250	1/2¢, 1811, C-1	PCGS MS-66RB	Goldberg	Jan-18
83	$1,116,250	$4, 1880, Coiled Hair	PCGS PF-65	Heritage	Jun-18
84	$1,092,500	$20, 1921	PCGS MS-66	Heritage	Nov-18

Rank	Price	Coin	Grade	Firm	Date
85	$1,092,500	$1(s), 1870-S	BU PL	Stack's	May-18
86	$1,057,500	$1(s), 1795 Draped Bust, BB-51	PCGS SP-66	Sotheby's / Stack's Bowers	May-18
87	$1,057,500	$10, 1795, 9 Leaves, BD-3	PCGS MS-63+	Sotheby's / Stack's Bowers	Sep-18
88	$1,057,500	Pattern disme, 1792, copper, J-11	NGC MS-64RB	Heritage	Jan-18
89	$1,057,500	Terr, 1852, Humbert, $10, K-10	NGC MS-68	Heritage	Apr-18
90	$1,057,500	$20, MCMVII, Ultra HR, LE of 06	PCGS PF-58	Heritage	Aug-18
91	$1,041,300	$4, 1879, Coiled Hair (N)	NGC PF-67 Cam	Bonhams	Sep-18
92	$1,035,000	10¢, 1894-S	PCGS PF-65	Heritage	Jan-18
93	$1,012,000	$20, 1921 (O)	PCGS MS-65 PQ	Goldberg	Sep-18
94	$1,006,250	$2.50, 1796, Stars, Bass-3003, BD-3 (P)	NGC MS-65	Heritage	Jan-18
95	$1,006,250	$1 Trade, 1885	NGC PF-62	DLRC	Nov-18
96	$998,750	1/2¢, 1811, C-1	PCGS-MS66RB	Sotheby's / Stack's Bowers	Mar-18
97	$998,750	Pattern disme, 1792, J-9	PCGS AU-50	Heritage	Apr-18
98	$998,750	1¢, 1793, Chain, S-3	PCGS MS-65RB	Sotheby's / Stack's Bowers	Feb-18
99	$998,750	Pattern disme, 1792, J-9	NGC AU-50	Heritage	Jan-18
100	$998,750	$1 Trade, 1884	PCGS PF-65	Heritage	Jan-18
101	$998,750	1¢, 1793, Chain, S-2	PCGS MS-65BN	Stack's Bowers	Jan-18
102	$990,000	$1(s), 1804, Class I (E)	Choice Proof	Rarcoa	Jul-89
103	$977,500	1¢, 1799, S-189	NGC MS-62BN	Goldberg	Sep-18
104	$977,500	$4, 1880, Coiled Hair (D)	NGC PF-66 Cam	Heritage	Jan-18
105	$977,500	$5, 1833, Large Date	PCGS PF-67	Heritage	Jan-18
106	$966,000	50¢, 1797, O-101a (J)	NGC MS-66	Stack's (ANR)	Mar-18
107	$962,500	5¢, 1913, Liberty Head	Proof	Stack's	Oct-93
108	$960,000	Confed, 1861, Original 50¢	NGC PF-40	Heritage	Nov-18
109	$959,400	$4, 1880, Flowing Hair	NGC PF-67	Bonhams	Sep-18
110	$948,750	Terr, 1852, Moffat & Co., $10, Wide Date, K-9	PCGS SP-67	Stack's (ANR)	Aug-18
111	$940,000	1¢, 1793, Liberty Cap, S-13, B-20	PCGS AU-58	Sotheby's / Stack's Bowers	Mar-18
112	$940,000	$5, 1825, Over 4, BD-2	PCGS MS-64	Sotheby's / Stack's Bowers	May-18
113	$940,000	1/2¢, 1794, C-7 (G)	PCGS MS-67RB	Sotheby's / Stack's Bowers	Feb-18
114	$940,000	Terr, 1852, Moffat & Co., $10, Wide Date, K-9	PCGS SP-63	Heritage	Jan-18
115	$920,000	1/2¢, 1793, C-4	PCGS MS-66BN	Goldberg	Jan-18
116	$920,000	$1(s), 1802, Restrike	PCGS PF-65 Cam	Heritage	Apr-18
117	$920,000	$20, 1907, Small Edge Letters	PCGS PF-68	Heritage	Nov-18
118	$920,000	$1 Trade, 1885	NGC PF-61	Stack's	May-18
119	$910,625	$1(s), 1794	PCGS AU-58+	Stack's Bowers	Mar-18
120	$910,625	$1(s), 1795, Draped, Off-Ctr, B-14, BB-51	NGC MS-66+	Heritage	Nov-18
121	$907,500	$1 Trade, 1885	Gem PF-65	B&M/Stack's	Apr-97
122	$900,000	Pattern 1¢, 1792 Silver Center, J-1	PCGS MS-61BN	Stack's Bowers	Nov-18
123	$891,250	1/2¢, 1796, No Pole, C-1	PCGS MS-65BN	Goldberg	Jan-18
124	$891,250	10¢, 1873-CC, No Arrows (R)	NGC MS-65	B&M	Jul-18
125	$882,500	$5, 1815, BD-1	PCGS MS-65	Sotheby's / Stack's Bowers	Feb-18
126	$881,250	$10, 1933	PCGS MS-66	Goldberg	Jun-18
127	$881,250	$5, 1829, Small Date, BD-2	PCGS MS-65+	Sotheby's / Stack's Bowers	May-18
128	$881,250	$4, 1879, Coiled Hair	PCGS PF-65	Heritage	Apr-18
129	$881,250	Confed, 1861, Original 50¢	NGC PF-30	Heritage	Jan-18
130	$881,250	25¢, 1796, B-1	PCGS SP-66	Heritage	Aug-18
131	$881,250	$10, 1795, BD-5	PCGS MS-65	Heritage	Aug-18
132	$881,250	10¢, 1796, JR-1	PCGS MS-67	Heritage	Jun-18
133	$881,250	$1(s), 1889-CC (S)	PCGS MS-68	Stack's Bowers	Aug-18
134	$881,250	1¢, 1794, Head of 93, S-18b	PCGS MS-64BN	Stack's Bowers	Jan-18
135	$874,000	$1(s), 1804, Class III (M)	PCGS PF-58	B&M	Nov-18
136	$862,500	1¢, 1793, Strawberry Leaf, NC-3	NGC F-12	Stack's	Jan-18

Rank	Price	Coin	Grade	Firm	Date
137	$862,500	Pattern $4, 1879, Quintuple Stella, J-1643	PCGS PF-62	Heritage	Jan-18
138	$862,500	$2.50, 1796, Stars, Bass-3003, BD-3 **(P)**	NGC MS-65	Heritage	Jan-18
139	$851,875	$4, 1879, Coiled Hair	PCGS PF-66	Heritage	Jan-18
140	$851,875	$1(s), 1803, Restrike	PCGS PF-66	Heritage	Jan-18
141	$851,875	$1(s), 1802, Restrike	PCGS PF-65 Cam	Heritage	Aug-18
142	$825,000	$20, MCMVII, Ultra HR, LE	Proof	Sotheby's	Dec-96
143	$824,850	Pattern half disme, 1792, copper, J-8	NGC AU-55	Heritage	Jan-18
144	$822,500	$5, 1832, 12 Stars, BD-12	PCGS MS-63	Sotheby's / Stack's Bowers	May-18
145	$822,500	$5, 1835, McM-5	PCGS PF-67+ DCam	Sotheby's / Stack's Bowers	May-18
146	$822,500	$1(s), 1795, Flowing Hair, B-7, BB-18	PCGS MS-66	Sotheby's / Stack's Bowers	Sep-18
147	$822,500	50¢, 1796, 16 Stars, O-102	PCGS MS-66	Sotheby's / Stack's Bowers	May-18
148	$822,500	$2.50, 1796, No Stars, BD-2	PCGS MS-62	Sotheby's / Stack's Bowers	May-18
149	$822,500	$10, 1933	PCGS MS-65	Heritage	Apr-18
150	$822,500	$1(s), 1795, Flowing Hair, B-2, BB-20	NGC SP-64	Stack's Bowers	Aug-18
151	$822,500	$1(s), 1799, B-5, BB-157	NGC MS-67	Heritage	Nov-18
152	$822,500	Pattern 1¢, 1792, Silver Center Cent, J-1 **(T)**	NGC MS-61BN+	Heritage	Apr-18
153	$805,000	$1(s), 1870-S	NGC EF-40	Heritage	Apr-18
154	$805,000	$20, 1921	PCGS MS-65	Heritage	Nov-18
155	$793,125	10¢, 1796, JR-6	PCGS MS-68	Heritage	Aug-18
156	$793,125	Pattern half disme, 1792, J-7	PCGS MS-66	Stack's Bowers	Aug-18
157	$763,750	$1(s), 1795, Draped Bust, BB-51	PCGS MS-66	Sotheby's / Stack's Bowers	May-18
158	$763,750	$5, 1829, Large Date, BD-1	PCGS MS-66+	Sotheby's / Stack's Bowers	May-18
159	$763,750	1/2¢, 1796, No Pole, C-1	PCGS MS-67RB	Sotheby's / Stack's Bowers	Feb-18
160	$763,750	50¢, 1794, O-101a	PCGS MS-64	Sotheby's / Stack's Bowers	May-18
161	$763,750	$2.50, 1798, BD-1	PCGS MS-65	Sotheby's / Stack's Bowers	May-18
162	$763,750	Terr, 1849, Pacific Company, $5, K-1	PCGS AU-58	Heritage	Apr-18
163	$763,750	Terr, 1855, Kellogg & Co., $50	PCGS PF-64 Cam	Heritage	Apr-18
164	$763,750	50¢, 1838-O	NGC PF-64	Heritage	Jan-18
165	$763,750	$1(s), 1870-S	PCGS EF-40	Heritage	Jan-18
166	$763,750	$5, 1826, BD-2	PCGS MS-66	Heritage	Jan-18
167	$750,000	$4, 1880, Flowing Hair	NGC PF-67 Cam	Heritage	Jan-18
168	$747,500	1¢, 1793, Chain, S-3	NGC MS-66BN	Stack's Bowers	Aug-18
169	$747,500	$20, 1921	PCGS MS-66	Heritage	Jan-18
170	$747,500	Terr, 1855, Kellogg & Co., $50	PCGS PF-64	Heritage	Jan-18
171	$747,500	$1(s), 1794	NGC MS-61	Heritage	Jun-18
172	$734,375	50¢, 1838-O	PCGS PF-64	Heritage	Jan-18
173	$725,000	Prefed, 1787, Brasher, EB on Wing	MS-63	B&R	Nov-79
174	$718,750	1/2¢, 1793, C-3	PCGS MS-65BN	Goldberg	Jan-18
175	$718,750	1/2¢, 1796, With Pole, C-2	PCGS MS-65RB+	Goldberg	Jan-18
176	$718,750	$10, 1933	Unc	Stack's	Oct-18
177	$705,698	$1(s), 1870-S	VF-25	B&M	Feb-18
178	$705,000	1¢, 1796, Liberty Cap, S-84	PCGS MS-66RB+	Sotheby's / Stack's Bowers	Mar-18
179	$705,000	Pattern disme, 1792, copper, RE, J-10	PCGS SP-64BN	Heritage	Apr-18
180	$705,000	$1(s), 1795, Flowing Hair, B-7, BB-18	PCGS MS-65+	Sotheby's / Stack's Bowers	Sep-18
181	$705,000	$10, 1798/7, 7x6 Stars, BD-2	PCGS MS-61	Sotheby's / Stack's Bowers	Sep-18
182	$705,000	25¢, 1827, Original	PCGS PF-66+ Cam	Sotheby's / Stack's Bowers	May-18
183	$705,000	50¢, 1794, O-109	NGC VF-25	Heritage	Apr-18
184	$705,000	Pattern 1¢, 1792, Silver Center Cent, J-1 **(T)**	NGC MS-61BN+	Heritage	Sep-18
185	$705,000	Prefed, 1783, Nova Const., PE Bit, W-1820	NGC AU-55	Heritage	May-18
186	$705,000	Terr, 1849, Mormon, $10, K-3	NGC AU-58	Heritage	Apr-18
187	$705,000	$1(s), 1803, Large 3, B-6, BB-255	NGC MS-65+	Heritage	Nov-18
188	$690,300	$5, 1836	NGC PF-67 UCam	Bonhams	Sep-18

Rank	Price	Coin	Grade	Firm	Date
189	$690,000	$5, 1909-O (S)	PCGS MS-66	Heritage	Jan-18
190	$690,000	1¢, 1796, Liberty Cap, S-84	PCGS MS-66RB	Goldberg	Sep-18
191	$690,000	Pattern disme, 1792, copper, RE, J-10 (U)	NGC PF-62BN	Heritage	Jul-18
192	$690,000	$5, 1825, 5 Over 4	NGC AU-50	Heritage	Jul-18
193	$690,000	$20, MCMVII, Ultra HR, LE of 06	NGC PF-58	Stack's	Jul-18
194	$690,000	Terr, 1860, Clark, Gruber & Co., $20	NGC MS-64	Heritage	Jan-18
195	$690,000	Prefed, 1742 (1786), Lima Brasher	NGC EF-40	Heritage	Jan-18
196	$690,000	$5, 1835	PCGS PF-67	Heritage	Jan-18
197	$690,000	$1(g), 1849-C, Open Wreath	NGC MS-63 PL	DLRC	Jul-18
198	$690,000	$20, MCMVII, Ultra HR, LE	Proof	Sotheby's / Stack's	Oct-18
199	$690,000	$10, 1839, 9/8, Type of 1838, Lg Letters (H)	NGC PF-67	Goldberg	Sep-99
200	$687,500	$3, 1870-S	EF-40	B&R	Oct-82
201	$687,500	$5, 1822	VF-30/EF-40	B&R	Oct-82
202	$675,525	$10, 1795, BD-5	NGC MS-65	Heritage	Aug-18
203	$672,750	$1(s), 1803, Restrike	PF-66	B&M	Feb-18
204	$661,250	1¢, 1804, S-266c	PCGS MS-63BN	Goldberg	Sep-18
205	$661,250	1/2 dime, 1870-S	NGC MS-63 PL	B&M	Jul-18
206	$660,000	$20, MCMVII, Ultra HR, LE (L)	PF-67	B&M	Jan-97
207	$660,000	$20, 1861, Paquet Reverse	MS-67	B&M	Nov-88
208	$655,500	$4, 1879, Coiled Hair (N)	NGC PF-67 Cam	Heritage	Jan-18
209	$655,200	$20, 1891	NGC PF-68 UCam	Bonhams	Sep-18
210	$646,250	$1(s), 1795, Draped Bust, BB-52	MS-66	Sotheby's / Stack's Bowers	May-18
211	$646,250	$5, 1831, Small 5D, BD-1	MS-67	Sotheby's / Stack's Bowers	May-18
212	$646,250	$5, 1795, Small Eagle, BD-3	PCGS MS-65	Sotheby's / Stack's Bowers	Sep-18
213	$646,250	50¢, 1838-O	NGC PF-64	Heritage	May-18
214	$646,250	Confed, 1861, Original 50¢	NGC EF-40	Stack's Bowers	Mar-18
215	$646,250	$1(s), 1893-S	PCGS MS-65	Legend	Oct-18
216	$646,250	Prefed, (1652), NE 6 Pence, N-1-A, S-1-A	NGC AU-58	Heritage	May-18
217	$646,250	Terr, 1851, Baldwin & Co., $20, K-5	PCGS EF-45	Heritage	Apr-18
218	$646,250	1¢, 1795, Reeded Edge, S-79 (K)	PCGS VG-10	Heritage	Jan-18
219	$646,250	$5, 1909-O (S)	PCGS MS-66	Heritage	Jan-18
220	$646,250	$1(s), 1795, 3 Leaves, B-5, BB-27	NGC MS-65	Heritage	Nov-18
221	$646,250	$4, 1879, Coiled Hair	PCGS PF-64 Cam	Stack's Bowers	May-18
222	$632,500	$5, 1828, 8 Over 7	NGC MS-64	Heritage	Jan-18
223	$632,500	$1(s), 1870-S	PCGS EF-40	B&M	Aug-18
224	$632,500	10¢, 1804, 14 Star Reverse, JR-2	NGC AU-58	Heritage	Jul-18
225	$632,500	1¢, 1793, Liberty Cap, S-13, B-20	PCGS AU-55	Heritage	Feb-18
226	$632,500	1¢, 1794, Starred Reverse, S-48, B-38	PCGS AU-50	Heritage	Feb-18
227	$632,500	50¢, 1838-O	PCGS PF-63 BM	Heritage	Feb-18
228	$632,500	Prefed, 1652, Willow Tree Threepence, N-1A	VF	Stack's	Oct-18
229	$632,500	50¢, 1838-O	PCGS PF-64 BM	Heritage	Jun-18
230	$632,500	Confed, 1861, Original 50¢	VF	Stack's	Oct-18
231	$632,500	10¢, 1873-CC, No Arrows (R)	PCGS MS-64	Heritage	Apr-99
232	$625,000	Prefed, 1787, Brasher, EB on Breast (C)	VF	B&R	Mar-81
233	$618,125	$4, 1880, Coiled Hair	NGC PF-63	Superior	Jul-18
234	$605,000	$2.50, 1796, No Stars	Choice BU	Stack's	Nov-95
235	$603,750	1/2¢, 1852, Large Berries	PCGS PF-65RD	Goldberg	Jan-18
236	$603,750	$20, 1854-O	PCGS AU-55	Heritage	Oct-18
237	$603,750	Pattern 1¢, 1792, No Silver Center Cent, J-2	PCGS VF-30	Heritage	Jan-18
238	$603,750	$1 Trade, 1884	PCGS PF-65	Heritage	Nov-18
239	$587,500	$1(s), 1901	PCGS MS-66	Legend	Oct-18
240	$587,500	$10, 1933	PCGS MS-65	Heritage	Jun-18

Rank	Price	Coin	Grade	Firm	Date
241	$587,500	50¢, 1796, 15 Stars, O-101	PCGS SP-63	Sotheby's / Stack's Bowers	May-18
242	$587,500	$2.50, 1807, BD-1	PCGS MS-65	Sotheby's / Stack's Bowers	May-18
243	$587,500	Prefed, 1652, Willow Tree Threepence, N-1A	PCGS AU-50	Stack's Bowers	Mar-18
244	$587,500	$5, 1795, Small Eagle, BD-1	NGC MS-66	Heritage	Jan-18
245	$587,500	Pattern disme, 1792, copper, RE, J-10 **(U)**	NGC PF-62BN	Heritage	Oct-18
246	$587,500	$20, 1921 **(O)**	PCGS MS-65	Heritage	Aug-18
247	$586,500	$5, 1795, Small Eagle, BD-1	PCGS MS-65	Stack's	Jun-18
248	$583,000	$5, 1795, Small Eagle	NGC MS-65 PL	Bullowa	Jan-18
249	$577,500	$20, 1927-D	PCGS MS-65	Akers	May-98
250	$577,500	$1(s), 1794	Gem BU	Stack's	Nov-95

KEY

Price: The sale price of the coin, including the appropriate buyer's fee.

Coin: The denomination/classification, date, and description of the coin, along with pertinent catalog or reference numbers. B = Baker (for pre-federal), Bolender (for silver dollars), Breen (for gold), or Browning (for quarter dollars); BB = Bowers/Borckardt; BD = Bass-Dannreuther; Confed = Confederate States of America issue; dbln = doubloon; HR = High Relief; J = Judd; JR = John Reich Society; LE = Lettered Edge; N = Newman; NC = Non-Collectible; O = Overton; P = Pollock; Pattern = a pattern, experimental, or trial piece; Prefed = pre-federal issue; S = Sheldon; T = Taraskza; Terr = territorial issue. Letters in parentheses, **(A)** through **(U)**, denote instances in which multiple sales of the same coin rank within the Top 250.

Grade: The grade of the coin, plus the name of the grading firm (if independently graded). BM = branch mint; NGC = Numismatic Guaranty Corporation of America; PCGS = Professional Coin Grading Service; PQ = premium quality.

Firm: The auction firm (or firms) that sold the coin. ANR = American Numismatic Rarities; B&R = Bowers & Ruddy; DLRC = David Lawrence Rare Coins; Stack's Bowers = Stack's Bowers Galleries (name under which Stack's and B&M merged in 2010; also encompasses the merger of Stack's and ANR in 2006).

Date: The month and year of the auction.

Auction records compiled and edited by P. Scott Rubin.

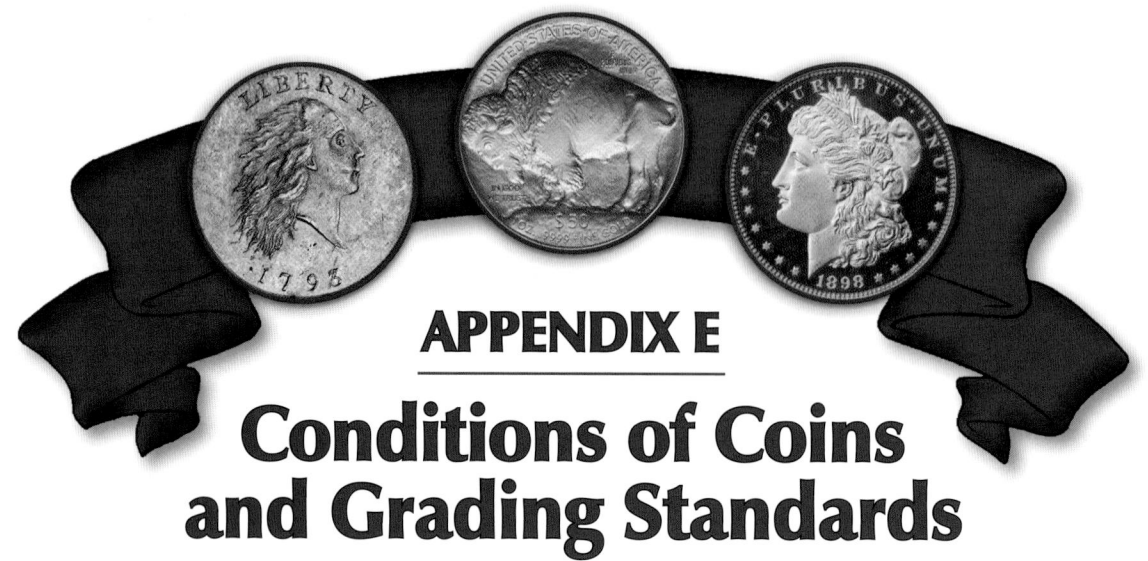

APPENDIX E

Conditions of Coins and Grading Standards

ESSENTIAL ELEMENTS OF THE AMERICAN NUMISMATIC ASSOCIATION GRADING STANDARDS

Proof—A specially made coin distinguished by sharpness of detail and usually with a brilliant, mirrorlike surface. *Proof* refers to the method of manufacture and is not a grade. The term implies superior condition unless otherwise noted.

Gem Proof (PF-65)—Surfaces are brilliant, with no noticeable blemishes or flaws. A few scattered, barely noticeable marks or hairlines.

Choice Proof (PF-63)—Surfaces are reflective, with only a few blemishes in secondary focal places. No major flaws.

Proof (PF-60)—Surfaces may have several contact marks, hairlines, or light rubs. Luster may be dull and eye appeal lacking.

Mint State—The terms *Mint State (MS)* and *Uncirculated (Unc.)* are interchangeable and refer to coins showing no trace of wear from circulation. Such coins may vary slightly because of minor surface imperfections, as described in the following subdivisions:

Perfect Uncirculated (MS-70)—Perfect new condition, showing no trace of wear. The finest quality possible, with no evidence of scratches, handling, or contact with other coins. Very few circulation-issue coins are ever found in this condition.

Gem Uncirculated (MS-65)—An above-average Uncirculated coin that may be brilliant or lightly toned and that has very few contact marks on the surface or rim.

Choice Uncirculated (MS-63)—A coin with some distracting contact marks or blemishes in prime focal areas. Luster may be impaired.

Uncirculated (MS-60)—A coin that has no trace of wear, but which may show a number of marks from contact with other coins during minting, storage, or transportation, and whose surface may be spotted or lack some luster.

Choice About Uncirculated (AU-55)—Evidence of friction on high points of design. Most of the mint luster remains.

About Uncirculated (AU-50)—Traces of light wear on many of the high points. At least half of the mint luster is still present.

Choice Extremely Fine (EF-45)—Light overall wear on the highest points. All design details are very sharp. Some of the mint luster is evident.

Extremely Fine (EF-40)—Light wear on the design throughout, but all features are sharp and well defined. Traces of luster may show.

Choice Very Fine (VF-30)—Light, even wear on the surface and highest parts of the design. All lettering and major features are sharp.

Very Fine (VF-20)—Moderate wear on design high points. All major details are clear.

Fine (F-12)—Moderate to considerable even wear. The entire design is bold with an overall pleasing appearance.

Very Good (VG-8)—Well worn with main features clear and bold, although rather flat.

Good (G-4)—Heavily worn, with the design visible but faint in areas. Many details are flat.

About Good (AG-3)—Very heavily worn with portions of the lettering, date, and legend worn smooth. The date may be barely readable.

Important: Undamaged coins are worth more than bent, corroded, scratched, holed, nicked, stained, or mutilated ones. Flawless Uncirculated coins are generally worth more than values quoted in this book. Slightly worn coins ("sliders") that have been cleaned and conditioned ("buffed") to simulate Uncirculated luster are worth considerably less than perfect pieces.

Unlike damage inflicted after striking, manufacturing defects do not always lessen values. Examples include colonial coins with planchet flaws or weakly struck designs; early silver or gold coins with weight-adjustment "file marks" (parallel cuts made on the planchet prior to striking); and coins with "lint marks" (surface marks due to the presence of dust or other foreign matter during striking).

Note that while grading *standards* strive to be precise, interpretations are subjective and can vary among collectors, dealers, and certification services.

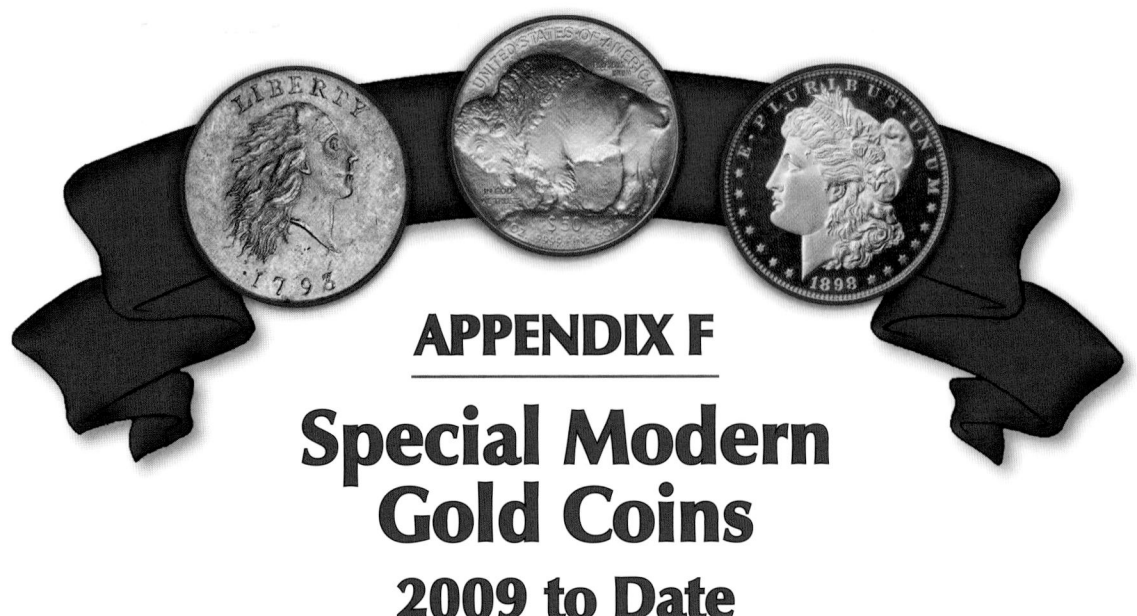

APPENDIX F

Special Modern Gold Coins

2009 to Date

AN OVERVIEW OF SPECIAL MODERN GOLD COINS

In recent years, the U.S. Mint has introduced several innovative new gold coins. These coins showcase the Mint's technological and creative abilities in impressive and often surprising ways.

Chapter 31, section 5112, of the United States Code gives the secretary of the Treasury considerable leeway in the specifics of the nation's gold bullion coins. Without needing to get congressional orders or approval, the secretary can change coinage designs, denominations, and other details in coins of that precious metal (similar changes in silver bullion coins would require Congress to get involved).

The Mint has used this authority to create such modern marvels as the MMIX Ultra High Relief gold double eagle (2009), a gold Kennedy half dollar (2014), and a series of American Liberty high-relief gold coins (2015 to date). Authority for 2016 gold coins struck with the designs of the Mercury dime, the Standing Liberty quarter, and the Liberty Walking half dollar, to celebrate the 100th anniversary of their debut, derives from the same legislation.

These gold coins are focused on collectors, using the U.S. Mint's 40 years of modern experience to determine what collectors and investors want (and don't want) in terms of gold. While these gold–collector coin programs would have been impossible for much of the 20th century under the gold laws legislated in the 1930s, it was made legal for private citizens to own gold again in 1974. The minting of the gold National Bicentennial Medals and the Colorado Centennial Medal was followed by the minting of the American Arts gold medallions of the early 1980s, which ramped up to the globally popular American Gold Eagles, and the subsequent American Buffalo and First Spouse bullion programs have also met with success. Special modern gold coins represent the culmination of the Mint's experience with each of these series, and at the same time they promise new innovations in the coming years.

The American Liberty gold coin's packaging.

MMIX ULTRA HIGH RELIEF $20 GOLD COIN (2009)

In 2009 the U.S. Mint produced a modern collector's version of the first Augustus Saint-Gaudens double eagle. When the original debuted in 1907, the Mint had been unable to strike large quantities for circulation—the ultra high relief design was artistic, but difficult to coin. (It was modified later in 1907 to a lower relief suitable for commercial production.) Just over 100 years later, the 2009 version was a showcase coin: a tangible demonstration of the Mint's 21st-century ability to combine artistry and technology to make an outstanding numismatic treasure.

Like its predecessor, the new coin was dated in Roman numerals (with 2009 as MMIX). The Mint digitally mapped Saint-Gaudens's original plasters and used the results in the die-making process. The date was changed, and four additional stars were inserted, to represent the nation's current 50 states. Augustus Saint-Gaudens's striding Liberty occupied the obverse. On the reverse was his flying eagle, with the addition of IN GOD WE TRUST, a motto not used in the original design. The 2009 version, struck in Philadelphia, was made in a smaller diameter (27 mm instead of 34), with a thickness of 4 mm, and composed of 24-karat (.9999 fine) gold, thus making it easier to strike and stay true to the ultra high-relief design. Its weight is one ounce.

As with other coins of the U.S. Mint, these are legal tender and their weight, content, and purity are guaranteed by the federal government. They were packaged in a fancy mahogany box and sold directly to the public, instead of through a network of distributors.

Note that the Mint does not release bullion mintage data on a regular basis; the number given here reflects the most recently available official data.

	Mintage	MS	MS-69	MS-70
MMIX Ultra High Relief $20 Gold Coin ‡ (a)	114,427	$2,000	$2,100	$2,550

Note: MS values are for uncertified Mint State coins of average quality, in their complete original U.S. Mint packaging. ‡ Ranked in the *100 Greatest U.S. Modern Coins*. **a.** Auction: $2,820, MS-70, October 2015.

KENNEDY 50TH ANNIVERSARY HALF DOLLAR GOLD COIN (2014)

Following the assassination of President John F. Kennedy on November 22, 1963, the Kennedy half dollar was authorized. The first coins were made available to the public on March 24, 1964. The new half dollars were immediately hoarded by the public who were eager to obtain a memento of the late president.

The 50th anniversary Kennedy gold half dollar was struck as a tribute to the original issue as part of a year-long numismatic celebration that included two other coin sets (one Uncirculated set and one silver set). The gold coin, struck at West Point, features a restored obverse portrait of President Kennedy, which brings out the original details of the coin, and it is dual dated as "1964–2014". On the reverse an indication of the precious metal weight and purity appears: .9999 gold weighing 3/4 of an ounce. Otherwise the specifications match those of a standard half dollar.

The release of this coin caused a collector frenzy, but prices and collector interest soon stabilized.

	Mintage	PF-65	PF-67Cam	PF-68DC
2014-W, Kennedy 50th Anniversary Half Dollar Gold Coin, Proof	73,772	$850	$950	$1,100

AMERICAN LIBERTY HIGH-RELIEF $100 GOLD COINS

2015-W   1792–2017-W   2018-W, Tenth-Ounce

The first American Liberty high-relief .9999-fine gold coin, with a weight of one troy ounce and a face value of $100, was minted at West Point in 2015. The coin was not congressionally mandated, instead being created under authority granted to the secretary of the Treasury by federal law—31 U.S.C. Section 5112 (i)(4)(C).

The design was strongly influenced by the Citizens Coinage Advisory Committee, who, according to a Mint spokesperson, "emphasized creating a 'modern' Liberty that reflects the nation's diversity." The U.S. Commission of Fine Arts also reviewed designs and made recommendations.

Of the 2015 American Liberty's eagle reverse the designer, Paul C. Balan, commented, "My reverse design for the American Liberty High Relief gold coin was created with inspiration from the Great Seal of the United States and its depiction of an American bald eagle clutching an olive branch. The soaring eagle is a symbol of strength, freedom and bravery, and the 13 olives on the branch represent the original 13 colonies, which epitomize the power and solidarity of our nation. I want people to feel a sense of pride and integrity as Americans when they see my design." Balan also shares that his design was initially submitted for the U.S. Marshals Service commemorative but was chosen for the American Liberty high-relief coin instead.

The designs for the American Liberty high-relief gold coins are created to take full advantage of the same high-relief techniques used to create the MMIX Ultra High Relief gold coin.

The design of the 2015 American Liberty high-relief gold coin was adapted for a silver medal in 2016, but in 2017 the Mint continued the series with a 1792–2017 American Liberty high-relief gold coin. The series is slated to continue biennially, with a new design being issued every two years. In the years between gold issues, silver medals featuring the same designs will be issued.

	Mintage	Unc
2015-W	49,325	$2,000
1792–2017-W	27,886	
2018-W tenth ounce		$220

1916 CENTENNIAL GOLD COINS (2016)

In 2016 the Mint celebrated the 100th anniversary of the Mercury dime, Standing Liberty quarter, and Walking Liberty half dollar designs by issuing gold versions of the three classic coins, all struck at West Point. The gold coins are reduced in diameter from the original silver coins. They are composed of .9999-fine gold and weigh, respectively, 1/10 oz., 1/4 oz, and 1/2 oz. The dime was struck at 16.5 mm; the quarter, at 22 mm; and the half dollar, 27 mm. Some discussion at the Mint had centered around issuing similar commemorative coins in silver, but that would require congressional action. The gold Mercury dime sold out within 45 minutes of its release, but the two larger gold coins have seen much slower sales.

	Mintage	SP-67	SP-70
2016-W, Mercury Dime Centennial Gold Coin	125,000	$250	$325
2016-W, Standing Liberty Quarter Centennial Gold Coin	87,443	$475	$600
2016-W, Liberty Walking Half Dollar Centennial Gold Coin	60,810	$875	$1,100

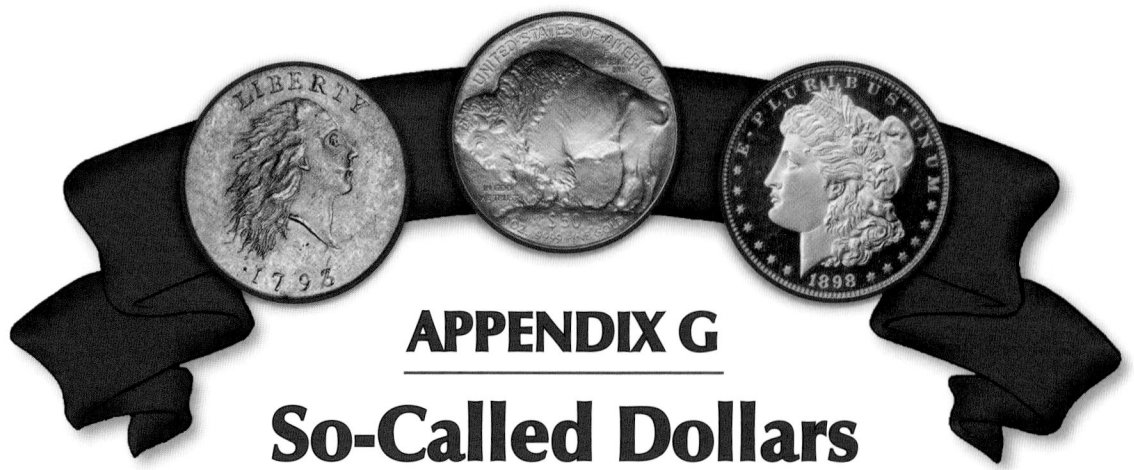

APPENDIX G
So-Called Dollars

This appendix is based on the work of Jeff Shevlin. This edition highlights So-Called Dollars struck for the 1915 Panama-Pacific International Exposition held in San Francisco, with research by Shevlin and Bill Hyder.

AN OVERVIEW OF SO-CALLED DOLLARS

So-Called Dollars are U.S. medals approximately the size of a silver dollar that were struck to commemorate a historical subject. A collection of So-Called Dollars is strikingly different from a typical collection of U.S. coins assembled by date and mintmark, in that each piece in the collection has a uniquely different design. There are more than 750 different design types, and when different metal compositions are considered, there are more than 1,500 varieties to consider collecting. So-Called Dollars were struck in virtually every metal composition conceivable, including gold, silver, copper, bronze, brass, aluminum, nickel, white metal, German silver, gutta-percha, gold-plated, and silver-plated.

These collectibles were cataloged in the illustrated standard reference book *So-Called Dollars*, authored by Harold Hibler and Charles Kappen and published in 1963. This book, which is widely considered as the most definitive reference on So-Called Dollars, was revised and edited by Tom Hoffman, Dave Hayes, Jonathan Brecher, and John Dean in 2008.

So-Called Dollars were struck by the U.S. Mint as well as by private mints (and one was struck by the Manila Mint while the Philippines was an American territory). Many of the most famous engravers of U.S. coins also engraved So-Called Dollars, including William and Charles Barber, George T. Morgan, Augustus Saint-Gaudens, and others. Some of the designs and artwork on these pieces match or surpass these artists' other work in coin and medal design.

Historical medals come in all sizes. To be classified as a So-Called Dollar one must be approximately the size of a silver dollar, between 33 and 45 mm in diameter (a silver dollar is 38.1 mm), although collectors traditionally include a few specific exceptions such as the 1939 Charbneau medals (see the gallery, which follows).

From national events and celebrations to local anniversaries, from great successes to major disasters, bits and pieces of the history of the United States are chronologically depicted on these fascinating historical medals.

About half of the So-Called Dollars are related to a Fair or Exposition with the other half commemorating important events in U.S. history. Expositions played a significant part in the development of the United States. Local communities, often with federal funding support, would begin to plan years ahead of time and build enormous halls and buildings for their expositions, which would last anywhere from a few months to a few years. Millions of people would travel to attend these grand events and see things they had never seen before, often visiting for days, sometimes weeks.

Throngs of tourists entering the Electrical Building at the World's Columbian Exposition.

When the city of Chicago hosted the World's Columbian Exposition in 1893, its population was slightly greater than a million people. More than five years were spent in the exposition's planning and construction on a 700-acre site on the shore of Lake Michigan. President Benjamin Harrison invited all of the nations of the earth to take part by sending exhibits that most fully illustrated their resources, their industries, and their progress in civilization. Every state and territory of the United States and more than 50 foreign countries were represented, many erecting their own buildings. Exhibits exceeded 50,000, including one set up by the U.S. Mint. Attendance at the exposition was 27,500,000, and by the end of the 1890s Chicago's population had grown to 1,700,000, making it one of the fastest-growing cities in the history of mankind and the fifth or sixth largest city in the world. More than 100 So-Called Dollars were struck commemorating the World's Columbian Exposition, its events, and its structures—the last remaining of which, originally called the "Palace of Fine Arts," now serves as Chicago's Museum of Science and Industry.

When Philadelphia hosted the Centennial Exposition in 1876, the first United States International Exhibition of the arts, manufacturers, and products, the country was showing the world the progress it had made in the past 100 years. The United States was, for the first time being recognized as one of the leading nations in the world. Until then, the young nation had focused on material problems, with art playing a less significant part in American life. Approximately 10,000,000 people attended the exposition and were not only exposed to the latest machines, mechanical progress, and industrial expansion, but also electrified by displays of art by the world's greatest artists throughout time. After the exposition numerous art schools and societies were formed, and there was a rush of American students to art schools in Paris. The impact on the emphasis for the arts in American culture was dramatic and everlasting. There are close to 50 different So-Called Dollars related to the 1876 Centennial Exposition.

The U.S. Mint had a presence at many of the expositions, often setting up presses and striking souvenir medals to sell to the attendees. The medals produced by the Mint were always designated as the official exposition medal and were usually struck in a variety of metals including silver.

Outside of fairs and expositions, the other half of the series of So-Called Dollars covers a broad range of topics. From the completion of the Erie Canal in 1826 and the completion of the first Transcontinental Railroad in 1869 through the centennial of the Pony Express in 1961, So-Called Dollars celebrate and remember hundreds of national, regional, and local events.

FOR THE COLLECTOR AND INVESTOR: SO-CALLED DOLLARS AS A SPECIALTY

So-Called Dollars as a specialty can be exciting, fascinating, and controversial, and they are collected in hundreds of different ways. Some collectors aspire to collect the entire series, and some collect specific metal compositions. Many collectors have an interest in one or more of the major expositions or other significant events in U.S. history that are portrayed on these medals. Some collect medals from local or regional areas, while others have an interest in those with a U.S. Mint relationship, which includes a broad area of different designs. In addition to marking battles of the Revolutionary War and the Civil War, as well as other military events, So-Called Dollars were struck that address the gold-versus-silver political controversy of the late 1800s and early 1900s. Lesher dollars; silver Bryan dollars; Pedley-Ryan dollars; and others struck by professor Montroville Dickeson, coin dealer Thomas Elder, numismatic historian Q. David Bowers, and other famous personalities are all popular collector categories.

So-Called Dollars range in rarity from very common to exceptionally rare. For many types only one example or very few are known to exist; for others there are thousands. Many So-Called Dollars are considerably rarer than U.S. coins. One of the most common So-Called Dollars is the 1931 McCormick Reaper Centennial Dollar, of which there were possibly as many as 5,000 struck. Compare that to the 1909-S V.D.B. Lincoln cent, of which 484,000 were minted. While the Lincoln cent in MS-63 would sell for $1,500, the McCormick Reaper in the same grade sells for around $20 despite being 100 times rarer. The following rarity scale is used for So-Called Dollars in this appendix:

R-1	More than 5000 known
R-2	2001–5000 known
R-3	501–2000 known
R-4	201–500 known
R-5	76–200 known
R-6	21–75 known
R-7	11–20 known
R-8	5–10 known
R-9	2–4 known
R-10	1 known (unique)

Hundreds of different So-Called Dollars in MS-63 can be purchased for less than $100. All of the major third-party grading firms, including NGC, PCGS, ANACS, and ICG, grade So-Called Dollars. Professional grading and slabbing of So-Called Dollars has had a significant impact on collector interest and prices realized when they appear in auction. Many of today's advanced collectors want the finer and higher-grade pieces, and if the medals are certified by a major grading firm, their confidence in the value goes up. Higher prices paid today for rare So-Called Dollars are a direct result of this increase in buyers' confidence.

So-Called Dollars have a broad appeal to today's collectors. Similar to most series of U.S. coinage, there are many interesting and historically significant pieces available to the beginning collector at relatively low introductory prices. There are literally hundreds of different types available in Uncirculated and Choice Uncirculated grades in the $25 to $75 range. There are also many highly desired rare varieties from the 1800s that are beautiful pieces of art, struck in bronze and with high relief, that the more advanced collectors appreciate. At the upper end of the So-Called Dollar market—those that sell for $1,000 or more—collectors are treated to exceptionally rare and significant pieces.

1915, Panama-Pacific Int'l Expo Official Medal

1915, Standing Minerva / Battleship,
No Lower Portholes

1915, Taft Groundbreaking

1915, Standing Minerva / Battleship,
Multiple Portholes.

	Rarity	SH#	HK#	VF-20	EF-40	AU-50	MS-60	MS-63	MS-65
							PF-60	PF-63	PF-65
1915, Panama-Pacific Int'l Expo Official Medal. Silver*	R-5	18-1 S	399	$50	$110	$325	$475	$750	$1,275
1915, Panama-Pacific Int'l Expo Official Medal. Bright Bronze	R-5	18-1 BBZ	400	$25	$55	$70	$90	$225	$425
1915, Panama-Pacific Int'l Expo Official Medal. Statuary Bronze	R-6	18-1 SBZ	UNL	$30	$60	$85	$120	$275	$485
1915, Panama-Pacific Int'l Expo Official Medal. Antiqued Bronze	R-7	18-1 ABZ	UNL	$30	$60	$90	$135	$310	$500
1915, Panama-Pacific Int'l Expo Official Medal. Oxidized Bronze	R-7	18-1 OBZ	UNL	$30	$60	$90	$135	$310	$500
1915, Panama-Pacific Int'l Expo Official Medal. White Metal Cast	R-6	18-1 WM	UNL	$30	$60	$90	$135	$310	$500
1915, Panama-Pacific Int'l Expo Official Medal. Gold-Plated Bronze	R-5	18-1 GPBZ	401	$45	$55	$90	$175	$325	$525
1915, Panama-Pacific Int'l Expo Official Medal. Silver-Plated Bronze	R-6	18-1 SPBZ	UNL	$75	$175	$250	$325	$475	$595
1915, Taft Groundbreaking. Bronze	R-7	18-2 BZ	UNL	$195	$290	$350	$425	$600	$775
1915, Standing Minerva / Battleship, No Lower Portholes. Gold-Plated	R-5	18-3 GP	414	$25	$40	$60	$125	$145	$275
1915, Standing Minerva / Battleship, No Lower Portholes. Silver-Plated	R-8	18-3 SP	UNL	$250	$400	$850	$1,350	$1,950	—
1915, Standing Minerva / Battleship, Multiple Portholes. Bronze	R-8	18-4 BZ	UNL	$200	$325	$475	$700	—	—

UNL = Unlisted.

1915, Panama-Pacific International Exposition Official Medal (SH 18-1 / HK 399-401): This official medal celebrates the opening of the Panama Canal. Winged Mercury opens the Canal locks with the ship Argo, the symbol of navigation, passing through the locks. Two females are shown on the reverse, representing the two hemispheres entwined around Earth, holding cornucopias. Designed by Robert Aitken, who also designed the official $50 round gold and $50 octagonal gold PPIE commemorative coins, the medal was authorized by Congress and struck in the U.S. Mint Exhibit at the Exposition. **1915, Taft Groundbreaking (SH 18-2 / HK UNL):** Joseph Mayor & Bros, a Seattle jewelry-manufacturing firm, struck this commemorative medal for the October 14, 1911, groundbreaking ceremonies. The obverse features a right-facing bust of President William Howard Taft, who attended the ceremonies and turned the first shovel of dirt. The signature of the designer, M.P. Nielsen, appears to the left, behind Taft's neck. The reverse depicts a standing laborer with a shovel. Building designs and themes appear in low relief in the distance. **1915, Standing Minerva / Battleship, No Lower Portholes (SH 18-3 / HK 414):** On the obverse is Minerva standing facing left. The exposition grounds stretch out behind her toward the sun, which is setting in the Golden Gate. Because of their imitation of the California state seal, these are commonly called "California Dollars." On the reverse a battleship with no lower portholes passes through the Panama Canal locks. **1915, Standing Minerva / Battleship, Multiple Portholes (SH 18-4 / HK UNL):** On the obverse is standing Minerva with a grizzly bear at her side and the exposition grounds in the background. The battleship sailing through the canal locks on the reverse has multiple upper and lower portholes.

"San Francisco Invites the World"—a publicity poster captures the
excitement of the approaching Panama-Pacific International Exposition, 1914.

1915, Standing Minerva /
Tower of Jewels

1915, Standing Minerva with Rays /
Tower of Jewels

1915, Tower of Jewels /
Battleship No Lower Portholes

1915, Tower of Jewels /
Battleship, Gustave Fox

	Rarity	SH#	HK#	VF-20	EF-40	AU-50	MS-60	MS-63	MS-65
				PF-60	PF-63	PF-65			
1915, Standing Minerva / Tower of Jewels. Gold-Plated, Type A	R-5	18-5 GP	415	$25	$50	$90	$140	$210	$450
1915, Standing Minerva / Tower of Jewels. Gold-Plated, Type B	R-5	18-5.1 GP	UNL	$25	$50	$90	$140	$210	$450
1915, Standing Minerva with Rays / Tower of Jewels. Gold-Plated, Type C	R-6	18-6 GP	UNL	$40	$75	$120	$185	$235	$475
1915, Tower of Jewels / Battleship No Lower Portholes. Gold-Plated, Type A	R-5	18-7 GP	UNL	$20	$45	$75	$130	$165	$400
1915, Tower of Jewels / Battleship No Lower Portholes. Gold-Plated, Type B	R-5	18-7.1 GP	UNL	$20	$45	$75	$130	$165	$400
1915, Tower of Jewels / Battleship No Lower Portholes. Gold-Plated, Type C	R-5	18-7.2 GP	416	$20	$45	$75	$130	$165	$400
1915, Tower of Jewels / Battleship No Lower Portholes. Bronze, Type C	R-8	18-7.2 BZ	UNL	$200	$325	$650	$1,100	—	—
1915, Tower of Jewels / Battleship, Gustave Fox. Aluminum	R-8	18-8 AL	UNL	$180	$300	$600	$1,000	$1,100	$1,250
1915, Tower of Jewels / Battleship, Gustave Fox. Brass Uniface Die Trial	R-10	18-8.1 BS	UNL	—	—	—	—	$2,000	—

UNL = Unlisted.

1915, Standing Minerva / Tower of Jewels (SH 18-5 / HK 415): The obverse features standing Minerva with a grizzly bear at her side and the exposition grounds in the background. The Tower of Jewels, with thousands of dangling gems made of Austrian cut glass, adorns the reverse. **1915, Standing Minerva with Rays / Tower of Jewels, Type C (SH 18-6 / HK 415A):** On the obverse is Minerva standing with broad bands representing rays of light emanating from behind her. The Tower of Jewels, with thousands of dangling gems made of Austrian cut glass, adorns the reverse. **1915, Tower of Jewels / Battleship, No Lower Portholes (SH 18-7 / HK 416):** The Tower of Jewels, one of the major attractions at the exposition, with thousands of dangling gems made of Austrian cut glass, adorns the obverse. On the reverse a battleship with no lower portholes passes through the Panama Canal locks. **1915, Tower of Jewels / Battleship, Gustave Fox (SH 18-8 / HK 416A):** A variation of the Tower of Jewels edifice is on the obverse. The reverse, signed by The Gustave Fox Co Cinc (for Cincinnati), features a battleship moving through the Panama Canal locks.

The cover of the official souvenir of the 1911
groundbreaking by President William Howard Taft.

The Tower of Jewels was featured on several So-Called
Dollars of the Panama-Pacific International Exposition.

**1915, Laughing Bear /
Water-Nymphs**

1915, Glory to America

1915, Hensley's U.S. Expositions

1915, Alabama State

	Rarity	SH#	HK#	VF-20	EF-40	AU-50	MS-60	MS-63	MS-65
							PF-60	PF-63	PF-65
1915, Laughing Bear / Water-Nymphs. Gold-Plated	R-7	18-9 GP	418A	$200	$290	$600	$950	$1,700	$2,900
1915, Glory to America. Bronze	R-6	18-10 BZ	421	$60	$90	$150	$225	$265	$525
1915, Glory to America. Silver-Plated	R-6	18-10 SP	UNL	$50	$75	$120	$185	$235	$475
1915, Glory to America. Antiqued Silver-Plated	R-6	18-10 ASP	420	$50	$75	$120	$185	$235	$475
1915, Glory to America. Copper-Plated	R-6	18-10 CP	UNL	$65	$100	$175	$250	$300	$550
1915, Glory to America. Antiqued Copper-Plated	R-6	18-10 ACP	UNL	$65	$100	$175	$250	$300	$550
1915, Hensley's U.S. Expositions, Upper INJ. Gold-Plated	R-5	18-11 GP	UNL	$50	$70	$90	$140	$210	$450
1915, Hensley's U.S. Expositions, Lower INJ. Gold-Plated	R-5	18-11.1 GP	422	$50	$70	$90	$140	$210	$450
1915, Hensley's U.S. Expositions, No INJ. Gold-Plated	R-5	18-11.2 GP	UNL	$50	$70	$90	$140	$210	$450
1915, Alabama State. Bronze	R-6	18-12 BZ	402	$30	$45	$95	$130	$165	$400
1915, Alabama State. Silver-Plated	R-9	18-12 SP	402A	$200	$360	$700	$1,150	$1,600	-
1915, Alabama State 1963 Restrike. Bronze	R-5	18-12.1 BZ	UNL	$30	$35	$60	$100	$140	$325

UNL = Unlisted.

1915, Laughing Bear / Water-Nymphs (SH 18-9 / HK 417): A fascinating design with a scantily clad female overlooking the exposition grounds. A grizzly bear with a big smile is next to the female. Microscopic signature SA is at lower left edge. On the reverse, two water-nymphs, one in the Pacific Ocean and the other in the Atlantic Ocean, pass a wreath through the newly created Panama Canal. **1915, Glory to America (SH 18-10 / HK 420-421):** Four busts adorn the obverse: Woodrow Wilson, president when the Panama Canal was completed in 1914; Theodore Roosevelt, president when the United States resumed building the canal; Colonel George W. Goethals, U.S. Army engineer who directed the building of the canal; and Ferdinand de Lesseps, the French entrepreneur who initiated construction of the canal in 1880. The reverse features an aerial view of the exposition grounds. Microscopic W&H Co, which stands for Whitehead & Hoag Co. **1915, Hensley's U.S. Expositions (SH 18-11 / HK 422):** E.E. Hensley of San Francisco struck this elegant commemorative medal with large golden gates that swing open to a view of the Golden Gate. The reverse features a map of the United States indicating the location of cities where they hosted an International or Industrial Exposition, and their dates. Some varieties are signed with the initials I & J for Irvine & Jachens (either off the coast of Mexico or near the Panama Canal); others are not signed at all. **1915, Alabama State (SH 18-12 / HK 402):** Whitehead & Hoag produced several PPIE State Fund So-Called Dollars which were sold to help raise funds for the states' participation in the exposition. The Alabama medal features the state seal on the obverse with an eagle on a shield, and legend within a wreath on the reverse; on the left ribbon is microscopic text W & H Co.

1915, Arkansas State

1915, Florida State

1915, Georgia State

1915, Kentucky State

	Rarity	SH#	HK#	VF-20	EF-40	AU-50	MS-60 PF-60	MS-63 PF-63	MS-65 PF-65
1915, Arkansas State. Aluminum	R-4	18-13 AL	403	$50	$60	$95	$165	$225	$325
1915, Florida State. Bronze	R-7	18-14 BZ	404	$65	$100	$250	$375	$600	$950
1915, Florida State. Gold-Plated	R-7	18-14 GP	UNL	$75	$100	$250	$375	$600	$950
1915, Florida State. Silver-Plated	R-5	18-14 SP	UNL	$30	$40	$75	$180	$400	$640
1915, Florida State. Antiqued Silver-Plated	R-5	18-14 ASP	404A	$30	$40	$75	$180	$400	$640
1915, Florida State. Antiqued Silver-Plated, P higher than O	R-6	18-14.1 ASP	UNL	$40	$60	$100	$200	$450	$700
1915, Georgia State. Bronze	R-6	18-15 BZ	405	$95	$250	$300	$400	$585	—
1915, Georgia State. Gold-Plated Bronze	R-9	18-15 GP	UNL	$200	$450	$1,000	$1,450	$2,500	—
1915, Georgia State. Silver-Plated Bronze	R-8	18-15 SP	405A	$175	$400	$850	$1,300	$2,000	—
1915, Kentucky State. Bronze	R-7	18-16 BZ	410B	$300	$450	$800	$1,100	—	—
1915, Kentucky State. Silver-Plated Bronze	R-8	18-16 SP	UNL	$350	$500	$850	$1,200	$1,950	—
1915, Kentucky State. Copper-Plated Bronze	R-7	18-16 CP	UNL	$200	$260	$625	$975	—	—

UNL = Unlisted.

1915, Arkansas State (SH 18-13 / HK 403): The Arkansas State Fund So-Called Dollar, produced by Whitehead & Hoag of Newark, New Jersey, celebrates aluminum production in the state. A view of the Arkansas Building at the exposition is on the obverse, signed W & H Co below the bottom legend, and the state seal on the reverse. **1915, Florida State (SH 18-14 / HK 404):** The obverse shows a headless Winged Victory or Winged Nike standing on the prow of a ship passing through the canal locks. The Florida state seal is on the reverse; in microscopic letters at the lower edge is Robbins Co Attleboro. **1915, Georgia State (SH 18-15 / HK 405):** A striding female wearing a long gown is carrying a cornucopia overflowing with fruits and vegetables; rays of light emanate from a city in the distance. The Georgia state seal is on the reverse, with microscopic text Whitehead-Hoag Newark .N.J. at bottom. **1915, Kentucky State (SH 18-16 / HK 410B):** The Kentucky state seal is on the obverse, with a microscopic signature of Robbins Co Attleboro near the bottom. The common reverse features a ship with large sails passing through the Panama Canal with rays of light emanating from behind; the legend above, "The Land Divided," and below, "The World United."

1915, Louisiana State   1915, Maryland State

1915, Mississippi State   1915, Montana State

	Rarity	SH#	HK#	VF-20	EF-40	AU-50	MS-60 PF-60	MS-63 PF-63	MS-65 PF-65
1915, Louisiana State. Antiqued Bronze	R-5	18-17 ABZ	406	$30	$40	$60	$75	$150	$350
1915, Louisiana State. Gold-Plated Bronze	R-8	18-17 GP	UNL	$200	$350	$750	$1,200	$1,850	—
1915, Louisiana State. Silver-Plated Bronze	R-8	18-17 SP	406A	$200	$350	$750	$1,200	$1,850	—
1915, Maryland State. Yellow Bronze	R-5	18-18 YB	407	$35	$50	$80	$135	$170	$400
1915, Maryland State. Gold-Plated	R-8	18-18 GP	UNL	$200	$350	$700	$1,200	$1,750	—
1915, Mississippi State. Copper-Plated Bronze	R-6	18-19 CP	408	$100	$165	$190	$275	$575	$950
1915, Mississippi State. Silver-Plated Bronze	R-9	18-19 SP	408A	$225	$450	$875	$1,450	$2,100	—
1915, Montana State. Antiqued Bronze	R-4	18-20 AB	409	$30	$40	$60	$95	$125	$250
1915, Montana State. Yellow Bronze	R-7	18-20 YB	UNL	$100	$250	$375	$650	$1,100	—
1915, Montana State. Statuary Bronze	R-6	18-20 SB	UNL	$80	$180	$210	$300	$500	$700
1915, Montana State. Gold-Plated Bronze	R-8	18-20 GP	409B	$150	$325	$650	$1,100	$1,950	—
1915, Montana State. Antiqued Silver-Plated	R-9	18-20 ASP	409A	$195	$450	$875	$1,450	$2,100	—

UNL = Unlisted.

1915, Louisiana State (SH 18-17 / HK 406): A view of the Louisiana State Building at the exposition is on the obverse, with the state seal on the reverse. **1915, Maryland State (SH 18-18 / HK 407):** Maryland honored two of its native sons who, through their songs, made the state famous. Two busts are within circles: the upper portrait is James Ryder Randall, author of "Maryland My Maryland," and the lower portrait Francis Scott Key, author of the "Star-Spangled Banner." In microscopic text: W. & H. Co. I. Newark, N. J. The state seal is on the reverse. **1915, Mississippi State (SH 18-19 / HK 408):** Portraits of Jefferson Davis, president of the Confederate States of America during the Civil War, and John A. Quitman, a pro-slavery politician and soldier, and former governor of Mississippi, are on the obverse. Reverse: edifice, Contribution of the Women of Mississippi, and microscopic text Robbins Co Attleboro near the legend at the bottom. **1915, Montana State (SH 18-20 / HK 409):** Winged Victory or Nike stands on the prow of a ship; the exposition buildings can be seen in the background, behind her. The Montana state seal is on the reverse with the state motto, "Oro Y Plata," below. Some have Robbins Co. Attleboro on the edge.

The Panama-Pacific International
Exposition's Palace of Horticulture.

A view of the Exposition's Festival Hall from the Avenue of Palms.

1915, Montana State

1915, Nebraska State

1915, North Carolina State

1915, Oregon State

	Rarity	SH#	HK#	VF-20	EF-40	AU-50	MS-60 PF-60	MS-63 PF-63	MS-65 PF-65
1915, Montana State. Copper	R-8	18-21 CU	419A	$200	$350	$700	$1,200	$2,000	—
1915, Nebraska State. Copper, Long Tail 5	R-6	18-22 CU	419	$145	$175	$210	$350	$575	—
1915, Nebraska State. Gold-Plated, Long Tail 5	R-8	18-22 GP	UNL	—	—	—	$650	—	—
1915, Nebraska State. Copper, Short Tail 5	R-6	18-22.1 CU	UNL	$145	$175	$210	$350	$575	—
1915, Nebraska State. Gold-Plated, Short Tail 5	R-8	18-22.1 GP	UNL	$200	$350	$600	$800	$1,000	—
1915, North Carolina State. Silver-Plated Bronze	R-8	18-23 SP	410	$400	$900	$2,700	$3,800	$7,500	—
1915, North Carolina State. Copper-Plated Bronze	R-8	18-23 CP	410A	$400	$900	$2,400	$3,500	$7,200	—
1915, Oregon State. Yellow Bronze	R-5	18-24 YB	411	$25	$40	$60	$80	$125	$350
1915, Oregon State. Silver-Plated Bronze	R-8	18-24 SP	411A	$200	$400	$700	$1,150	$1,750	$2,800

UNL = Unlisted.

1915, Montana State 1915 (SH 18-21 / HK 419A): Two miners with a pick and shovel are gold-panning next to a stream. A Native American is hiding behind a tree with mountains in the distance. With a common reverse with a large-date 1915 in the center, this is the Short Tail 5 variety with microscopic text Greenduck Co Chi. at the bottom edge. **1915, Nebraska State (SH 18-22 / HK 419):** The state seal of Nebraska is on the obverse, featuring a blacksmith with a hammer and an anvil, a scene of agriculture, a boat, a train, and mountains in the distance. A common reverse with a large-date 1915 is in the center. This is the Short Tail 5 variety, with microscopic text Greenduck Co Chi. at the bottom edge. **1915, North Carolina State (SH 18-23 / HK 410):** The North Carolina state seal shows two women, one holding a staff with a cap atop, representing freedom from slavery, the other holding a cornucopia representing abundance. Microscopic signature Robbins Co., Attleboro below the seal. The common reverse features a ship with large sails passing through the Panama Canal. There are rays of light emanating from behind the ship; the legend above is "The Land Divided," and below, "The World United." **1915, Oregon State (SH 18-24 / HK 411):** Built for the exposition, the Oregon State Building with gigantic wood columns is on the obverse; microscopic text W. & H. Co. I. Newark, N.J. is below the legend. The Oregon state seal is on the reverse.

1915, South Carolina State

1915, Tennessee State

1915, Uniface Columbia

1915, Lucky Charm

	Rarity	SH#	HK#	VF-20	EF-40	AU-50	MS-60 PF-60	MS-63 PF-63	MS-65 PF-65
1915, South Carolina State. Bronze	R-6	18-25 BZ	412	$100	$145	$170	$250	$425	$800
1915, South Carolina State. Silver-Plated Bronze	R-8	18-25 SP	412A	$200	$400	$700	$1,150	$1,750	$2,800
1915, Tennessee State. Copper-Plated Bronze	R-7	18-26 CP	413	$150	$275	$350	$425	$600	—
1915, Uniface Columbia. Sterling Silver	R-8	18-27 S	UNL	$200	$400	$800	$1,300	$1,950	—
1915, Uniface Columbia. Bronze	R-7	18-27 BZ	UNL	$150	$300	$375	$450	$650	—
1915, Lucky Charm. Copper	R-7	18-28 CU	UNL	$175	$300	$425	$575	$850	—
1915, Lucky Charm. Gold-Plated	R-7	18-28 GP	UNL	$175	$300	$425	$575	$850	—
1915, Oregon State. Yellow Bronze	R-5	18-24 YB	411	$25	$40	$60	$80	$125	$350
1915, Oregon State. Silver-Plated Bronze	R-8	18-24 SP	411A	$200	$400	$700	$1,150	$1,750	$2,800

UNL = Unlisted.

1915, South Carolina State (SH 18-25 / HK 412): The South Carolina state seal, which was adopted in 1776, adorns the obverse. The common reverse features a ship with large sails passing through the Panama Canal with rays of light emanating from behind; and the legend above, "The Land Divided," and below, "The World United." Some are edge-marked Robbins Co., Attleboro at 12 o'clock; some are not edge-marked. **1915, Tennessee State (SH 18-26 / HK 413):** The Tennessee state seal is on the obverse, with symbols of agriculture above and a ship representing commerce below. The common reverse features a ship with large sails passing through the Panama Canal with rays of light emanating from behind. The legend above is "The Land Divided," and below, "The World United." A microscopic signature of Robbins Co Attleboro is at the lower edge. **1915, Uniface Columbia (SH 18-27 / HK UNL):** The obverse features Columbia standing on a globe; behind her are several ships passing through the locks of the Panama Canal. There are rays of light emanating from behind her. Uniface; the reverse is stamped Shreve & CO. **1915, Lucky Charm (SH 18-28 / HK UNL):** Two females, one standing and one seated, looking at each other, are shaking hands. They likely represent the East meeting the West. A staff with a cap atop it, representing freedom, separates them. The seated female on the right is holding a cornucopia which has hundreds of gold coins flowing out of it. The reverse is a view of the San Francisco Bay with the sun setting in the Golden Gate in the distance, and microscopic text Patent Pending at the bottom.

A richly detailed Medal of Honor certificate from the Panama-Pacific International Exposition.

PANAMA-PACIFIC INTERNATIONAL
EXPOSITION ⸳ San Francisco, 1915

This Booklet gives but a faint idea of the extent, magnificence and beauty of this wonderful Exposition

The council of architects adopted a general plan that was as bold as it has proven successful. The units are not individual buildings, but beautiful courts with intervening aisles and continuous facades, and around these are interwoven eight great exhibit palaces surmounted by the Tower of Jewels, 433 feet high. These are flanked on the east by the huge Palace of Machinery and on the west by the beautiful Fine Arts Palace, while still further west the various buildings of the States of the Union and the pavilions of foreign nations are cleverly and effectively grouped. At the eastern extremity, screened by the Machinery Palace, is the most wonderful and extensive amusement section ever planned at any exposition. The great South Gardens extend for 3000 feet along the south front of the main groups of exhibit palaces, and at the western end is the magnificent Palace of Horticulture, while it is balanced at the opposite end by the Festival Hall. On the north the view is across the sparkling waters of San Francisco Bay, facing the Marin hills on the opposite side, with Mount Tamalpais a few miles beyond. Symmetry, balance and harmony are the keynotes to the Exposition, and these have found expression, not only in architectural construction, but in decorative form, in a wonderful color scheme and in a marvellous lighting arrangement that has never previously been equalled. It is estimated that more than $50,000,000 has been expended on the Exposition.

WHAT OTHERS SAY ABOUT IT

Vice-President Marshall: "They who built this Panama-Pacific Exposition were so wise in adopting all the good features and avoiding those which marred the preceding ones that to me it seems as near perfection as the mind and hand of man have ever wrought. This is the university of the world. It has a chair fully endowed to meet the wants and needs of each. The eye, the ear, the mind, the heart, the soul, each may have its horizon here enlarged."

Secretary of the Treasury McAdoo: "I am really sorry that the English language is so mean in superlatives that I cannot tell you thoroughly what I think of your Exposition. You have an Exposition which, more than any other Exposition we have had in all these years, is conceived in a spirit of the finest art, and executed with the highest degree of intelligence."

Edwin Markham: "It is the greatest revelation of beauty that has ever been seen on earth."

New York World: "It is indescribably beautiful. It is so beautiful that it gives you a choky feeling in your throat as you look at it."

Published by Pacific Novelty Co. of San Francisco, 579 Market Street.

A promotional brochure extols the Expo.

1915, Official
Souvenir Slug

1915, Souvenir
Slug Design.
Pat Right

1915, Souvenir
Slug Design.
Pat Left

1915, Official
Souvenir Days
of '49 Slug

	Rarity	SH#	HK#	VF-20	EF-40	AU-50	MS-60 PF-60	MS-63 PF-63	MS-65 PF-65
1915, Official Souvenir Slug. Gold-Plated	R-7	18-29 GP	UNL	$175	$350	$525	$725	$950	—
1915, Souvenir Slug Design. Pat Right. Bronze	R-8	18-30 BZ	UNL	$200	$400	$700	$900	$1,200	—
1915, Souvenir Slug Design. Pat Right. White Metal, Irvine & Jachens	R-8	18-31 WM	UNL	$200	$400	$850	$1,100	$1,350	—
1915, Souvenir Slug Design. Pat Right. Gold-Plated, Irvine & Jachens	R-5	18-31 GP	UNL	$30	$45	$170	$275	$450	$650
1915, Souvenir Slug Design. Pat Right. Silver-Plated, Irvine & Jachens	R-9	18-31 SP	423	$900	$1,800	$4,500	$5,200	—	—
1915, Souvenir Slug Design. Pat Right. Gold-Plated, Brinker over I&J	R-6	18-31.1 GP	424	$100	$145	$225	$400	$525	$750
1915, Souvenir Slug. Days of 49. Gold-Plated	R-6	18-32 GP	425	$100	$145	$175	$250	$425	$950

UNL = Unlisted.

1915, Official Souvenir Slug (SH 18-29 / HK UNL): Official Souvenir Slug legend is centered above within the center beaded circle; PPIE is below in interwoven artistic letters. This design has a larger and bolder perimeter legend than on other slug facsimiles. The reason for this great rarity is because when the signature Brinker was punched into the die it was misspelled Spinker. The B of Brinker was punched with an S. On the reverse is an Augustus Humbert $50 gold-slug facsimile with 000 THOU in the banner above the eagle. **1915, Souvenir Slug Design. Pat Right (SH 18-30 / HK UNL):** The Souvenir Slug legend, without Official, is centered above within the center beaded circle. PPIE is below in interwoven artistic letters. Legend regarding the PPIE exposition. Micro signature is below: Irvine & Jachens. In the legend Design Pat... Applied For, the D of Design is above and to the right of the P of PANAMA. On the reverse is an Augustus Humbert $50 gold-slug facsimile with 000 THOU in the banner above the eagle. **1915, Souvenir Slug Design. Pat Left (SH 18-31 / HK 423 & 424):** The Souvenir Slug legend, without Official, is centered above within the center beaded circle; PPIE is below in interwoven artistic letters; legend regarding the PPIE exposition; micro signature below of Irvine & Jachens. In the legend Design Pat... Applied For, the D of Design is above and to the left of the P of PANAMA. Microscopic die signature varieties exist with Irvine & Jachens and also with C.G. BRINKER S.F. over Irvine & Jachens. On the reverse: an Augustus Humbert $50 gold-slug facsimile with 000 THOU in the banner above the eagle. **1915, Official Souvenir Days of '49 Slug (SH 18-32 / HK 425):** Days of '49 in legend below Official Souvenir; microscopic text Copyrighted at bottom. This variety is not signed. On the reverse: an Augustus Humbert $50 gold-slug facsimile, with IN GOD WE TRUST in the banner above the eagle, and microscopic text Copyrighted below the eagle.

1915, Columbia Slug

1915, Hart's Gold Coins
of the West, Round

1915, Hart's Gold
Coins of the West,
Octagonal

	Rarity	SH#	HK#	VF-20	EF-40	AU-50	MS-60 PF-60	MS-63 PF-63	MS-65 PF-65
1915, Columbia Slug. Bronze	R-8	18-33 BZ	UNL	$400	$600	$1,200	$2,200	$4,000	—
1915, Columbia Slug. Gold-Plated	R-8	18-33 GP	UNL	$450	$650	$1,300	$2,400	$4,400	—
1915, Hart's Gold Coins of the West, Round, Minerva. Gold	R-6	18-34 G	UNL	$150	$175	$200	$290	$350	$550
1915, Hart's Gold Coins of the West, Octagonal, Minerva. Gold	R-6	18-35 G	UNL	$175	$200	$225	$350	$475	$625

UNL = Unlisted.

1915, Columbia Slug (SH 18-33 / HK UNL): A slug facsimile with a design very similar to SH 18-27, with Columbia standing on a globe; behind her are several ships passing through the locks of the Panama Canal, with rays of light emanating from behind her. On the reverse: an Augustus Humbert $50 gold-slug facsimile with IN GOD WE TRUST in the banner above the eagle. **1915, Hart's Gold Coins of the West 1915, Round Minerva (SH 18-34 / HK UNL):** From the M.E. Hart Coins of the Golden West, a set of 39 gold coins each with a $1 dollar, $1/2 dollar, or $1/4 dollar denomination. A round type with Minerva on the obverse, EUREKA above, and date 1915 below, struck for sale and inclusion in the HART set sold by Farran Zerbe at the exposition. California Gold One on the reverse, with a bear below; and California poppies on both sides. **1915, Hart's Gold Coins of the West 1915, Octagonal Minerva (SH 18-35 / HK UNL):** From the M.E. Hart Coins of the Golden West, a set of 39 gold coins each with a $1 dollar, $1/2 dollar, or $1/4 dollar denomination. An octagonal type with Minerva on the obverse, EUREKA above, and date 1915 below, struck for sale and inclusion in the HART set sold by Farran Zerbe at the exposition. California Gold One on the reverse, with a bear below; and California poppies on both sides.

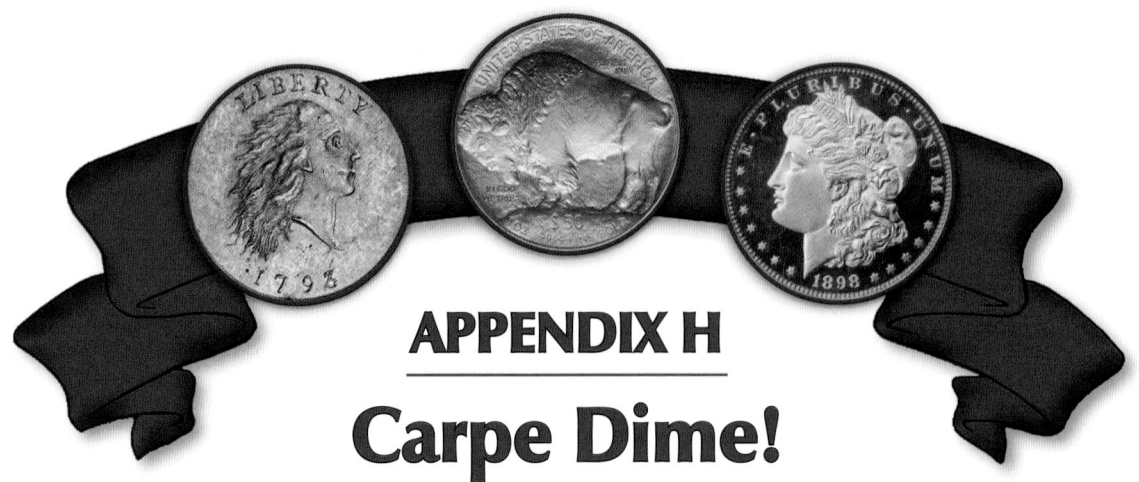

APPENDIX H

Carpe Dime!

Dimes Seize the American Imagination

This essay is by numismatist Joel J. Orosz, co-author of **The Secret History of the First United States Mint** *and* **1792: Birth of a Nation's Coinage.**

United States coin denominations range from the lordly (Almighty Dollar) to the lowly (not one red cent!), but none was once quite so disrespected, nor ultimately quite so pervasive, as the humble, yet enormously influential, *dime*. It was disrespected because of its Lilliputian dimensions (for most of its history, it was the smallest-diameter circulating silver coin). But dimes overcame that disrespect through their versatility, becoming pervasive not only in commerce but also in the American imagination.

Dimes possess a strong hold over our minds. They are found in the phrases we utter, in the songs we sing, the stories we read, the entertainment we enjoy, the transactions that keep the economy humming, and in at least one great hobby. *Carpe Dime!* These ten-cent pieces truly have seized the American imagination.

For all of the enormous impact of dimes today, this denomination was a late bloomer. It first appeared in 1792, with the French spelling of *disme* and *half disme*, as two of the eleven denominations authorized by the Coinage Act of 1792. In that year came a transitory moment of glory when half dismes became the first U.S. coins struck for circulation,

A 1792 disme.

and pattern dismes of silver and copper were struck also for consideration. But then the distinctive term *disme* disappeared forever from American coinage. A statement of denomination was omitted from Flowing Hair five-cent pieces (1794) and the Draped Bust ten-cent pieces (1796), and when denominations were specified in their designs (in 1809 for the dime and 1829 for the half dime), the value was rendered as *10 c* and *5 c* respectively. No official act ever discontinued the spelling of *disme*; the term simply died of neglect.

"Neglect" also describes the way the public greeted the Mint's dime output. Mintages for the first 25 years of the denomination's existence were miniscule, partly because the old Spanish "bits," each one worth an eighth of the silver "piece of eight," still circulated. Since they were valued at an eighth of a Spanish dollar, or 12-1/2 cents, it was obviously preferable to receive a bit in change as opposed to a dime. Only in 1821 did the mintage of dimes first top a million. (By way of comparison, 1,001,000,000 dimes were struck in just the first quarter of 2017.) In 1821, Secretary of State John Quincy Adams delivered a report to Congress on weights, measures, and coins. In that report he compared the dime to the mill, a money of account equaling one thousandth of a dollar, which had been authorized in the 20th section of the 1792 Mint Act, but never actually coined by the Mint. The deep disrespect felt for the obscure dime was obvious in his words:

[The] dime having seldom, and the mille, never presented in their material images to the people, have remained so utterly unknown, that now, when the recent [1821] coinage of dimes is alluded to in our public journals, if their name is mentioned, it is always with an explanatory definition to inform the reader, that they are ten cent pieces. . . . Even now, at the end of thirty years, ask a tradesman, or a shopkeeper in any of our cities what is a dime or a mille, and the chances are four in five that he will not understand your question. . . . Our own lawfully established dime and mille remain, to the great mass of the people, among the hidden mysteries of political economy—state secrets.

The demonetization of the Spanish coins by the Coinage Act of 1857, and the end of the monetary disruptions caused by the Civil War, finally brought the dime into widespread circulation. During the Gilded Age of the 1870s and 1880s, the American economy doubled in size, and dimes, minted by the tens of millions, became a workhorse of the booming economy. Just as rapidly, dimes seized America's imagination in popular speech, in music, literature, stories, entertainment, commerce, and at least one hobby.

A Spanish bit (one *real*) of King Ferdinand VII, 1813.

DIMES IN POPULAR SPEECH

Not long after the dime began to circulate widely, it entered the American lexicon, becoming ubiquitous in everyday conversation. This coincided with the rise of the "five and dime" or just plain "dime" stores near the end of the 19th century. In these emporia, where most merchandise cost ten cents or less, shoppers quickly associated dimes with the inexpensive. Something that cost only "one thin dime" was not to be admired, even less so if it was so cheap that it cost only a "dime a dozen." Adding *dime-store* before a noun rendered it second-rate, as in "He's only a dime-store doctor." The word *dime* soon had the concept of "cheap" clinging to it like Velcro. (More on the dime-store phenomenon later.)

The so-called double dime, or twenty-cent piece, a coin minted briefly in the 1870s.

The negative connotations of "dime" extended beyond dime stores. Nothing was worse than being "nickeled and dimed to death." During the 1968 presidential campaign, American Independent Party candidate George Wallace attacked the two major parties by saying, "There isn't a dime's worth of difference between the Democrats and the Republicans." In 1978 Senator Jesse Helms, criticizing the Treasury Department's objections to selling its gold reserves to private citizens, called the arguments "as silly as a ten-cent watch."

Dimes were versatile in commerce, and that agility helped them to also garner *positive* connotations in popular speech. During the 1890s, telephone companies created networks of pay telephones with receptacles at the top to insert coins for payment. It was necessary for you to "drop a dime" in order to call your sweetheart. Perhaps you met your love at a charity fundraiser where she was doing her bit by charging "a dime a dance." You may have first noticed her because she was a "dime": in today's parlance, a "perfect 10." By the early 1900s, after Henry Ford had put America on wheels, you might brag that your "tin lizzie" could "turn on a dime" or, if necessary, "stop on a dime."

Dimes have been used as political props. From the collection of Token and Medal Society past president Bill Hyder comes this 2008 pinback badge with an encased 1964 dime, connecting Franklin Roosevelt's Social Security programs to Hillary Clinton's presidential campaign.

Dimes also inspired figures of less-than-wholesome speech. "If you've got the dime, I've got the time" could be an invitation to an illicit rendezvous. Many a drug dealer offered his wares in "dime bags"—price, ten dollars. Not illegal, but widely considered to be crimes against wit, are the many puns inspired by the word *dime*. H.L. Mencken, in *The American Language*, noted a roadside restaurant in Texas called the "Dime-a-Mite." Pranksters, who firmly believe that "'dime-ins' are a girl's best friend," have been known to attach a ten-cent piece to a plain band, and offer it as a "genuine dime-and-ring"!

This satirical dime encasement used punning wordplay to criticize President Barack Obama and congressional leaders Harry Reid and Nancy Pelosi as the "Axis of Tax-U.S."

DIMES IN POPULAR MUSIC

The titles and lyrics of popular songs, particularly during the 20th century, frequently referred to dimes, almost to the point of being "a dime a dozen." The most famous of these was Bing Crosby's heartbreaking rendition of the Depression-era standard, "Brother, Can You Spare a Dime?" Many other references, however, crowd the great American songbook. Ella Fitzgerald sang "Ten Cents a Dance." Kacey Musgraves warbled about a "Dime Store Cowgirl"; Slash's Snakepit contributed "Dime Store Rock"; and two very different artists (Dolly Parton, 1979; Jay-Z, 2013) styled very different versions of "Nickels and Dimes."

In 1931's "Ten Cents a Dance," a married "taxi dancer" (a paid dance partner) falls in love with one of her dime-a-dally customers. The film features the song of the same name.

A dime went a long way during the Great Depression. In a popular 1930 song a beggar implored: "Once I built a railroad, I made it run. Made it race against time. Once I built a railroad, now it's done. Brother, can you spare a dime?"

Etta Baker had the "One-Dime Blues"; the Albert Carey Project was "Ten Cents Short of a Dime," which perhaps inspired Fenton Robinson to plaintively request "Somebody Loan Me a Dime," while the Steep Canyon Rangers philosophically took life "One Dime at a Time."

Benjy Feree asked his listeners to "Come Back to the Five and Dime," while Kathy Mattea found "Love at the Five and Dime." Archie Shepp had retailing ability, for his song, "Three for a Quarter, One for a Dime," displays a sound grasp of pricing. One of Shepp's customers may have been Eddy Raven, getting "Too Much Candy for a Dime."

Ominously, Ferron saw "Shadows on a Dime;" and Jim Croce, in his song "Operator," told the telephone operator "You can keep the dime" after he failed to contact his former girlfriend. During the 20th century, all you had to do was "drop a dime" into a jukebox to hear one of these hits.

From *Mega Red* editor emeritus Kenneth Bressett comes this dime-sized token or medalet dating from the Great Depression. "Yes, it is tired and worn," he says, "but it is a good reflection of the times when it was made. It seems to be made of copper-nickel and is the same size as a normal dime. It has always been very special to me; I always tear up when I hear the old song with this same name, 'Brother, Can You Spare a Dime?' The sentiment 'Buy American, End Unemployment' could still apply today."

DIMES AND POPULAR LITERATURE

Dimes have inspired American popular literature since the 1800s, and were virtually ubiquitous in the seven decades from 1860 to 1930. This was the era of the "dime novel," adventure stories geared toward the reading tastes of young men, the nickname of which also revealed the price charged.

The Beadle Brothers were the kings of this genre. Their titles were typically set on the Western American frontier, but some were historical novels, or tales of the briny deep, and a few focused on the emerging sport of baseball.

Competitors soon appeared, driving down prices (the half-dime novel inevitably followed). Standards went down along with prices, as the more sensational competitors introduced additional violence, less couth language, and, above all, sexually suggestive content. Many parents expressed indignation, but parental objections, of course, only served to make titles like *Just to Please the Boys* all the more popular.

According to author Jim Wells, the Beadle Brothers alone issued twenty-five series of novels and seven of magazines and newspapers, most with engravings of dimes prominently displayed on their front covers. Even at the cost of "one thin dime," these publications proved a luxury people could live without during the Great Depression, and dime novels disappeared during the 1930s.

In more recent times, Barbara Ehrenreich wrote *Nickel and Dimed*, a very insightful explanation of the decline of the American middle class since the 1960s.

Action-packed dime thrillers were popular entertainment in the 1930s.

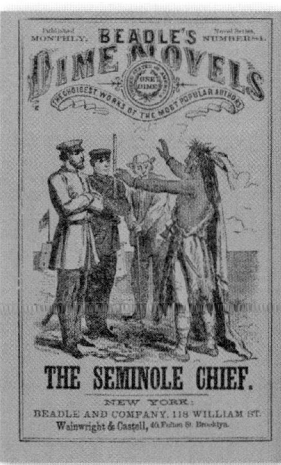

For ten cents, *Beadle's Dime Novels* promised "the choicest works of the most popular authors."

DIMES IN POPULAR ENTERTAINMENT

From the 1860s to the 1920s, dime museums grew in major cities like mushrooms after a rain. Admission was a dime, but serious museums they were not. Most consisted of a core of static exhibits of fossils, stuffed animals, relics, even waxworks. This hodgepodge of specimens provided a reason for respectable people to visit, but didn't pay the bills. In order to attract crowds, dime museums were forced to appeal to the lowest common denominator.

The typical dime museum heavily advertised "sideshow" exhibits, or, less charitably, "freak shows." Their ads stressed the sensational attractions on offer: bearded ladies, pinheads, elaborately tattooed torsos, "human panes of glass," and "mountains of feminine flesh." And these were just the unusual caprices of nature. Body parts of criminals, the more lurid the crime the better, were displayed. A perennial favorite was people from unfamiliar or exotic cultures, garbed in outlandish costumes, and made to display themselves in ways that encouraged reactions of racism and ethnocentrism. These exhibitions, thankfully, were driven out of business by the rise of vaudeville and movies during the 1920s.

This 1889 cartoon poked fun at the titillating promises of the typical dime museum. Outside, a buxom entertainer promises to reveal "The Mysteries of the Serail" (or harem). Inside, disappointed rubes get cheap taxidermy and dubious wonders—the "antique armour" is a corset.

Part museum and part freak exhibit, the sideshow of Barnum & Bailey's "amusement institution" grew out of the American tradition of the dime museum. The impresarios offered a glimpse of the smallest man alive, "The Human Skye Terrier," "Skeleton Dude," and other "marvelous living human curiosities."

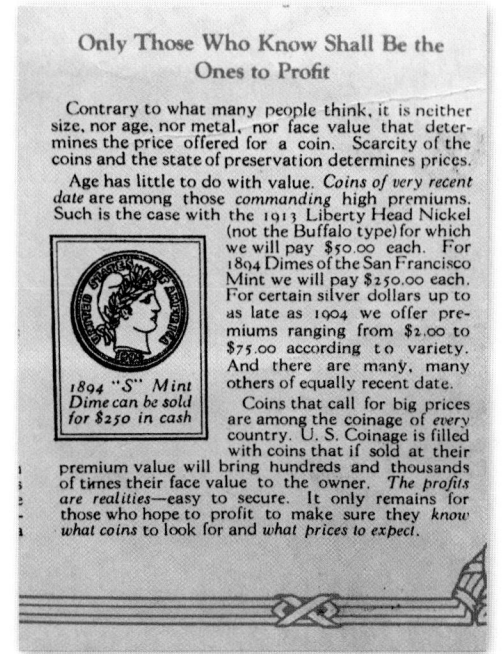

By the early 1900s, live vaudeville shows and early moving-picture shows, like this one in Ellsworth, Kansas, were charging a dime admission for adults.

In this clipping from a 1929 ad, B. Max Mehl sought to buy rare coins from the general public. On the eve of the Great Depression he offered to pay $250 cash for an 1894-S dime.

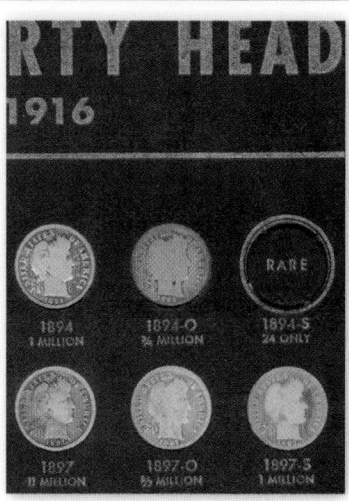

In the early years of Whitman's coin folders, which first became popular in the 1930s and 1940s, the 1892–1916 coins we know today as *Barber dimes* (after their designer, Charles Barber) were erroneously called Morgan dimes.

A stickered shell-card advertisement for the Newark, New Jersey, Dime Savings Bank. Ironically, dimes were so small that they could not host an adequate advertisement sticker, so the sticker was affixed to the reverse of a bronze shell card.

This Whitman Publishing "Morgan Dime" board from 1938 included an explanation for the missing hole for an 1894-S dime: it was RARE.

One realm upon which dimes made scant impression was that of coin-operated musical boxes, vending machines, and gambling boxes. These mechanical devices, widely popular beginning in the 1880s, were powered by nickels. Indeed, numismatist Q. David Bowers has written several books upon this subject, among them *Put Another Nickel In.* Art Reblitz, an expert in this field, explains that the devices' coin mechanisms were spring-loaded. Nickels were heavy enough to trip them, but dimes were so light that they did not reliably actuate the springs.

By the time the 1940s rolled around, however, improved technology brought dime receptacles onto coin-operated machines. The invention of a motorized coin-sorting mechanism, the "coin grinder," which detected which kind of coin had been inserted, and credited the appropriate number of plays for that denomination, made silver ten-cent pieces acceptable. Dimes, however, remained a distant second to nickels for operating mechanical devices.

DIMES IN AMERICAN COMMERCE

Dimes, as John Quincy Adams testified in 1821, got off to a very slow start in commercial channels, not fully coming into their own until the later 1870s. Large enough to have real buying power, small enough to be the allowance of a child, and convenient enough to make change for larger purchases, the dime rapidly became an indispensable denomination in the American coinage system.

This set the stage for the dime's greatest impact upon American life, the five-and-dime phenomenon. In 1880, Frank Winfield and Charles Sumner Woolworth opened their "5¢ & 10¢ Woolworth Brothers Store" in Scranton, Pennsylvania. Their concept was to retail a wide range of needed goods at the lowest possible prices. Especially in the beginning, most items were priced as advertised, although inflationary pressures eventually required Woolworth Brothers to sell higher-priced items. The five-and-dime concept brought affordable goods within the reach of the mass consumer, and wealth to the Woolworths. In 1912, when the company reorganized under Frank's leadership, the F.W. Woolworth chain had 596 stores and counting. The Woolworth brothers earned their fortunes literally by being "nickeled and dimed" by customers.

Inevitably, the Woolworths soon found themselves jousting with competitors. More than a dozen five-and-dime chains sprang up to seek a piece of the market, including such familiar names as Ben Franklin, W.T. Grant, and S.S. Kresge. By the mid-1900s, you could hardly heave an egg on an American main street without splattering competing cheek-by-jowl five-and-dime stores.

Despite his business success, Frank Woolworth was sensitive to the public's association of his five-and-dimes with cheap goods. So, in 1910, when he decided to build a new Woolworth headquarters building in New York City, he was determined to make it the polar opposite of "cheap." The renowned architect Cass Gilbert was instructed to design the world's tallest building, and he complied. When completed in 1913, it soared 79 stories over the streets of southern Manhattan. An architectural and financial triumph, the Woolworth building was built, *mortgage-free*—for $13,500,000 in cash—or, more appropriately, 135,000,000 dimes.

The Woolworth Building in New York City.

Woolworth's had many competitors in the five-and-dime arena, both national, like S.S. Kresge and W. T. Grant, and local, like the S. & H. Knox 5 and 10 cent store in Brazil, Indiana.

For many years, banks and credit unions encouraged Americans to save their "chicken feed." Dimes inserted into individual slots in folders would add up slowly and surely, to be deposited in a savings account once the folder was full. The folders in the meantime served as constant-reminder advertisements for the bank. Numismatic historian Pete Smith, who shared these examples, opines that thousands of different varieties exist.

This Easter Bunny–themed bank book from the collection of Phil Iversen uses a little rhyme to show the logic and appeal of saving small change: "Dimes turn to dollars mighty quick."

The Woolworth Building served notice that the dime had arrived as a force in American life. It took nearly a century after it had been authorized in 1792 to become accepted for everyday circulation, but when Americans finally saw the light, they embraced dimes wholeheartedly. By the early 20th century, Frank Woolworth demonstrated (anticipating the Steep Canyon Rangers) that a great fortune and an even grander building could be constructed "one dime at a time."

Q. DAVID BOWERS SEIZES A DIME, BUILDS A HOBBY

It was "one thin dime" that propelled Q. David Bowers into a career of unprecedented numismatic achievements. As a partner in major numismatic dealerships Empire Coin Company; Bowers and Ruddy Galleries; Bowers and Merena Galleries; and Stack's Bowers Galleries, Dave has sold every rarity in the American series. As a scholar, he has written the unprecedented total of more than 60 books, covering a vast range of numismatic topics. As research editor of the *Red Book* and senior editor of *Mega Red*, he has collaborated on definitive reference sources for collectors.

Dave launched his rare-coin dealership in 1953, when he was only 15 years old, growing it slowly but steadily. In 1957 the New York City firm of Stack's sold the Empire Collection, which included an 1894-S dime. Dave's friend and later business partner, Jim Ruddy, bid on Dave's behalf at the Empire sale, and captured the dime for $4,750. For context: In 1957, the last time an 1804 dollar had sold at auction (in 1954) it had realized $8,000.

The combination of this high price paid for a humble dime, and by a purchaser still a teenager, made the dime (and Dave) into national sensations. A picture of Jim Ruddy holding the dime, with 4,750 dollar bills stacked on a table in front of him, ran in newspapers across the land. Dave was inundated by letters from people possessing common dimes, asking exorbitant sums for them. He even received several letters proposing marriage! The hoopla reached its pinnacle when he was interviewed for an unheard-of 15 minutes on NBC-TV's *The Today Show*, by its original host, Dave Garroway.

An amusing relic of the 1894-S dime purchase is a newspaper feature entitled "Teenage Triumphs," written by Stookie Allen. The top panel depicts Dave tossing a large handful of "raw" coins into the air, presumably to land in a scratched and dented heap! The bottom panel depicts an older man, literally brandishing a fistful of dollars, asking a bow-tied Dave, "Son, how much do you want for the dime!" To which Dave replies, "Plenty!" The text offers a back-handed compliment: "Davie buys coins cannily. . . ." One can only imagine how much a sophomore at Penn State running a successful rare-coin dealership enjoyed being called "Davie" in a national newspaper feature!

Dave sold the 1894-S dime that caused all of this ruckus to Ambassador R. Henry Norweb and his wife Emery May, for the price of $6,000. It resided in the Norweb Collection for thirty years, until consigned, after their deaths, to Bowers and Merena Galleries to be sold at auction, where it realized $77,000.

This 1894-S completes the apotheosis of the dime, from John Quincy Adams's unused and disrespected "state secret" of 1821 to the workhorse coin of the American economy that paid for Woolworth's "Cathedral of Commerce" less than a century later, and five decades after that, fueled the growth of a nation-wide hobby and launched the career of the numismatist nonpareil, Q. David Bowers. Those who learned to "Carpe Dime" seized more than just ten cents; they also created the most productive economy the world had ever witnessed, and grew the greatest hobby in the world. A rather remarkable set of accomplishments for just "one thin dime"!

Nineteen-year-old Q. David Bowers was the subject of an installment of "Teenage Triumphs" after paying a stunning—for 1958—$4,750 for an 1894-S dime. Whether the Penn State sophomore and business owner objected to being called "Davie" by author Stookie Allen is not recorded.

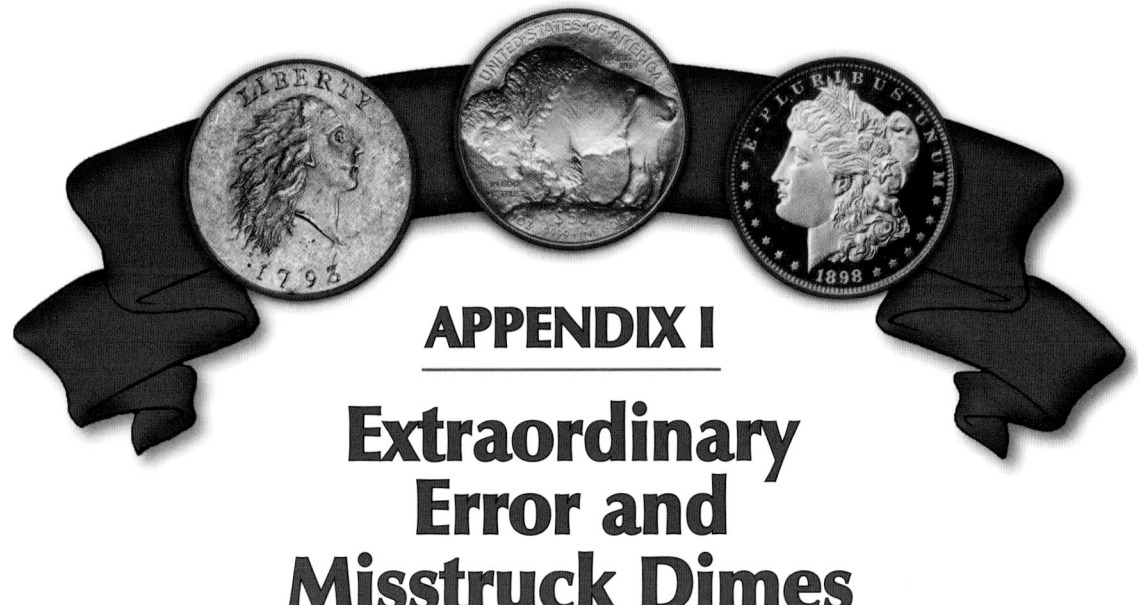

APPENDIX I

Extraordinary Error and Misstruck Dimes

This appendix is based on the work of Nicholas P. Brown, David J. Camire, and Fred Weinberg.

"*Errare humanum est,*" wrote Richard G. Doty, curator of the Smithsonian's National Numismatic Collection, in his foreword to *100 Greatest U.S. Error Coins*. "To err is human. Errors on coins have been around as long as coinage itself. The reason is simple. Coinage is an industrial process, and coins were the first mass-produced objects in human history. Mass production of anything involves a number of simple, repetitive steps. During each of these steps, something can go wrong. Given the nature of human endeavor as summed up by Murphy's Law, something *will* go wrong, even if the manufacturing process is simple, requiring few steps for its completion. And the more sophisticated production becomes, the more individual steps it involves, the greater the potential for error. This is as true for coinage as it is for any other human product."

This appendix explores some of the most fascinating error and misstruck dimes. As outlandish as many of them seem, they are all real coins—each was personally examined by error-coin experts Nicholas Brown, David Camire, and Fred Weinberg as they wrote their book *100 Greatest U.S. Error Coins*. "In selecting the 100 greatest error coins for this book," they said, "we felt it was crucial to have each coin in our possession to be able to confirm that it actually exists, to ensure the authenticity of each error coin being considered, and to capture high-resolution photographs of the selected coins."

THE IMPORTANCE OF CERTIFICATION

With the advent of grading services like Professional Coin Grading Service (PCGS) and Numismatic Guaranty Corporation of America (NGC), even novice hobbyists can now easily collect error coins. This is because the grading services offer four valuable services: authentication of the coin; attribution (i.e., verification of its die characteristics); grading; and protection through encapsulation, ensuring safe long-term storage. This standardized assessment process has helped propel error coins to the mainstream market, attracting an even larger audience. After certification, the only variable the buyer needs to determine is how much to pay for the coin. Years ago, some seeming "error" coins were fabricated outside of the mint by private individuals; the only error was in buying them!

GRADING ERROR COINS

Grading mint errors is generally the same as grading normal coins, with a few exceptions. First, an extensive understanding of the minting process is a must. Grading a mint error has a lot to do with knowing how the coin was made. For instance, when an off-center coin is assessed, a grade is determined not only by the features of the portion of the coin that was struck but also by the area that was not struck. Why is that? Because such after-coining defects as scratches, wheel marks, post-strike mechanical damage, and environmental damage have to be taken into consideration—just as they must be on a normal coin. However, because mint errors occur from a malfunction in the minting process, there are times when there is "allowable damage" (although this is usually damage that occurred before striking). For instance, on an off-center Roosevelt dime, a scratch on the planchet (pre-striking) that can still be seen after striking will generally not affect the grade of the coin. If the scratch occurred after the coin was struck, then it would matter.

Moreover, there are times when error coins can be attributed but not graded. One instance is blanks and planchets: since they were never struck, these items cannot be assessed a numerical grade. Another such example is die-adjustment strikes: since these pieces are used to adjust the amount of detail on a coin, many show very little detail. Again, no grade can be assigned to such coins.

Mint-error grading employs the same system, the Sheldon scale (which grades numerically from Poor-1 to MS-70), as does non-error grading. Most dimes and other coins minted before the advent of the steam press show considerable wear, because in the early years of the Philadelphia Mint, economics dictated what went out the door—that is, nearly everything. For this reason, most mint errors from the late 1700s and early 1800s survive in a low state of preservation. In many cases they circulated as money. True Mint State *gems* of this era are genuinely rare and highly prized. In contrast, many mint errors from the 1980s to the present are found in brilliant Uncirculated condition.

PRICING ERROR COINS

It is challenging to price error coins, since many are considered to be unique and many trade privately. The factors in determining error-coin values are similar to those that determine the price for non-error coins, with some important distinctions.

- The first is referred to as the "wow" factor. How excited does someone get viewing the coin? Error coins are often dramatic. The more dramatic an error, the higher the price usually is for the coin. It bodes well when someone says, "I have never seen this coin before." Even better is when someone says, "I never knew a coin like this existed"—which leads us to the second variable:
- Rarity. How rare is the error? How many coins are known of its type and of the series? Is it the only known of that date? Does it even have a date? Is it the farthest off center? The list of qualities that can make an error coin unique is nearly endless. Rarity definitely plays a key role in determining the price.
- Third, what is the condition of the coin? How much detail can be seen, and how well preserved is it? This is no less important a consideration for an error coin than for a regular coin.
- The popularity of a series is also an important factor in determining the price of an error coin.

These four factors are just a few of the variables that determine an error coin's price. Brown, Camire, and Weinberg used auction records, fixed-price lists, known private transactions, and their experience as professional numismatists to determine the value of each error coin ranked in the 100 Greatest.

Until recently, a question many collectors asked was, "Which error coin will be the first to pass the $1,000,000 threshold?" Among non-error coins, it took quite a while for this barrier to be surmounted.

Once the threshold was breached, however—when Bowers and Merena Galleries sold the Eliasberg specimen 1913 Liberty Head nickel at auction for $1,485,000 on May 21, 1996—it suddenly became more common to hear of coins selling for this price or higher. The same is true for error coins, as bronze 1943 cents have crossed the $1,000,000 mark in recent years.

For error coins, values continue to rise as the market continues to mature. "Looking back, it is almost unbelievable that error-coin prices have reached these levels," wrote Brown, Camire, and Weinberg in 2010. "In fact, when researching for the *100 Greatest U.S. Error Coins* we were amazed at the prices of mint errors in the 1980s. It was hard to find an error coin then that sold in the high four figures, never mind high five figures! Fast-forward to today, and it is a whole different story. Many major error coins are now trading in the high five figures, with some in the high six figures. Who would have guessed?"

A GALLERY OF EXTRAORDINARY DIME ERRORS

1993-D Lincoln cent mule.

No. 12—1993-D Lincoln Cent Mule. A mule coin is one struck from two dies of either different denominations or incompatible designs. This particular error—a Roosevelt dime reverse paired with a Lincoln cent obverse—is the earliest known modern die mule pairing of U.S. coinage. The error was minted in 1993, and was first reported in February 2003, when it was brought into a coin shop in Denver, Colorado. It has the normal expected weight for a copper-plated zinc cent. The cent die had been in use for some time, as evidenced by die-polish marks behind Lincoln's head, and die scratches in other areas of the obverse. The reverse die also shows signs of use. "One must wonder why a pair of used dies of different denominations would be paired with each other," wrote Brown, Camire, and Weinberg. "However, its existence, and not its circumstance, is what makes this a significant mint-error coin."

The unique piece was valued at $15,000 to $20,000 in 2000, and $75,000 to $100,000 in 2010.

1995-P Roosevelt Dime Mule.

No. 13—1995-P Roosevelt Dime Mule. Another unique mule error, this coin first appeared in 2000. The professional grading services were at first hesitant to certify it as genuine, since nothing even close to it had ever appeared in modern U.S. coinage. Similar to the cent/dime mule pair ranked number 12 among the *100 Greatest U.S. Error Coins*, this piece was struck from incongruous cent and dime dies, but on a copper-nickel dime planchet. It has a full reeded edge, indicating that it was the cent die that was improperly placed within a press coining dimes. The dies are rotated about 15 degrees from normal coin alignment.

The existence of this coin, and several others reported in 2000—the Sacagawea dollar / State quarter mule, the 1999 cent and Roosevelt dime—made researchers reconsider the old notion that it was physically impossible for a muling to occur at the U.S. Mint. The debate shifted to whether such things are actually production errors, or deliberate attempts to create modern rarities. Brown, Camire, and Weinberg point out that other mules (of different denominations, such as nickels) were reportedly made around the same time, but were caught by Mint inspectors and kept from circulation.

This coin was valued at $15,000 to $25,000 in 2000, and $125,000 to $150,000 in 2010.

1909 Indian Head cent struck on a 1906 Barber dime.

No. 20—1909 Indian Head Cent Struck on a 1906 Barber Dime. This remarkable double-denomination error surfaced in 2006—only the second Indian Head cent known on a Barber dime. Brown, Camire, and Weinberg theorize that a Barber dime was minted in 1906 and instead of entering circulation as normal, it ended up at the bottom of one of the large tote bins used for moving planchets and coins around the floor of the mint. Three years later the bin was filled with bronze cent planchets and the 1906 dime made its way into a coinage press. There it was struck with Indian Head cent dies.

The luster, strike, and overall condition of the coin suggest that it was quickly found and set aside as a curiosity.

Large portions of the original 1906 dime design show clearly. The 1906 date is clearly visible at 4 o'clock on the obverse, rotated about 45 degrees from the second strike. On the reverse, both denominations are visible.

In 1980 this error was valued at $1,000 to $1,500. In 2000 it was valued at $4,000 to $7,000, and in 2010 at $50,000 to $75,000.

1920 Standing Liberty quarter struck on a Mercury dime planchet.

No. 25—1920 Standing Liberty Quarter Struck on a Mercury Dime Planchet. This particular specimen was only the third known wrong-planchet, off-metal strike of the entire Standing Liberty quarter series. It is the result of a Mercury dime planchet making its way to a quarter press at the Philadelphia Mint, and there being struck by regular coinage dies.

This coin was valued at $2,500 to $3,500 in 1980. In 2000 it was valued at $10,000 to $15,000. In 2010 it was valued at $35,000 to $50,000.

Liberty Walking half dollar struck on a Mercury dime planchet.

No. 26—Liberty Walking Half Dollar Struck on a Mercury Dime Planchet. Coins accidentally struck on quarter dollar planchets are the most common wrong-planchet errors for the Liberty Walking half dollar series. Those struck on smaller denominations are exceedingly rare. Only two or three are known on dime planchets.

Because of the size of the half dollar collar and the much smaller diameter of the dime planchet, it is surprising (and fortunate, for collectors) that this dime planchet was in the right position in the coining chamber to receive a full impression of the half dollar die's date.

This rarity was valued at $500 to $1,000 in 1980; $2,500 to $5,000 in 2000; and $25,000 to $40,000 in 2010.

Other Wrong-Planchet Errors. In their book, Brown, Camire, and Weinberg illustrate examples of other wrong dies used to strike coins on dime planchets: an undated Washington quarter (silver); a Franklin half dollar; a 1906 Indian Head cent; a Jefferson nickel, and others.

1831 Capped Head quarter eagle struck on a Capped Bust dime planchet.

No. 28—1831 Capped Head Quarter Eagle Struck on a Capped Bust Dime Planchet. This is the earliest known U.S. gold denomination struck on the wrong planchet, of a different metal.

The diameter of the dime of this era was 18.5 mm, and that of the $2.50 gold coin was 18.2 mm. In the early years of the Mint, the dime and quarter eagle reverse dies were used interchangeably, given their nearly identical size and the fact they carried no statement of denomination. Brown, Camire, and Weinberg theorize that in this case, a run of dimes was struck as normal, then the press was set up for quarter-eagle production. A leftover dime planchet was accidentally fed between the quarter-eagle dies, resulting in this wrong-planchet, off-metal oddity.

This is one of two errors known of this particular combination. The other (with the same date) has been known for decades; it was cataloged by J. Hewitt Judd as a pattern coin, but identified by Don Taxay as a mint error—a classification that pattern specialist Saul Teichman agrees with.

This example is in circulated grade. (The other is in Mint State.) It was valued at $500 to $1,000 in 1980; $5,000 to $7,500 in 2000; and $25,000 to $75,000 in 2010.

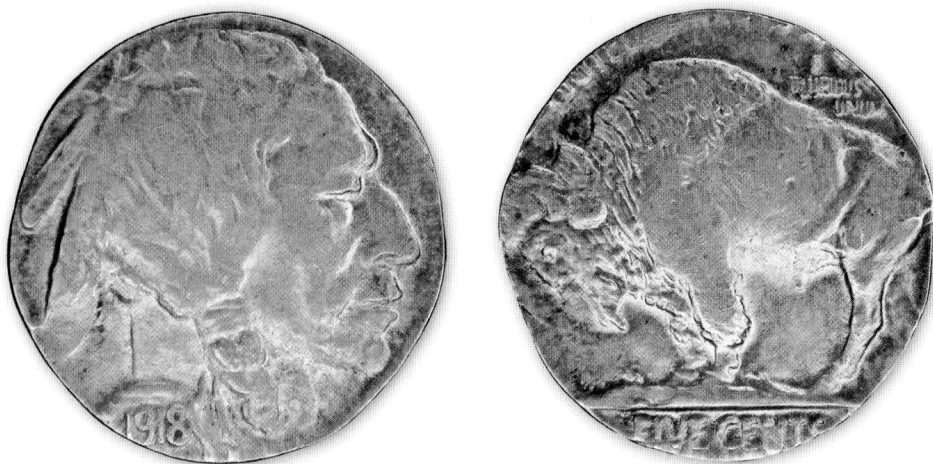

1918-D Buffalo nickel struck on a Mercury dime planchet.

No. 38—1918-D Buffalo Nickel Struck on a Mercury Dime Planchet. Perhaps a half dozen examples of this error, an off-metal Buffalo nickel on a Mercury dime planchet, are known. This one, struck in 1918, is the earliest date known, and the only one reported from the Denver Mint. The "Silver Buffalo" is well struck, considering that the dime planchet is much thinner and smaller in diameter than a normal nickel planchet.

This error was valued at $1,500 to $2,500 in 1980; $10,000 to $15,000 in 2000; and $35,000 to $50,000 in 2010.

1943 Lincoln cent struck on a 1943 Mercury dime.

No. 39—1943 Lincoln Cent Struck on a 1943 Mercury Dime. This double-denomination combines the popularity of not only the Lincoln cent and the Mercury dime, but also the 1943 date. (Bronze 1943 cents, which normally would have been minted in steel-plated zinc, are among the most famous U.S. coin errors.) This coin was born when a Mercury dime, already minted, was fed into the press where Lincoln cents were being struck.

This error's value in 1980 was $750 to $1,250. In 2000 it was worth $15,000 to $20,000, and in 2010, $35,000 to $50,000.

Off-center 1981 Lincoln cent struck on a 1980-P Roosevelt dime.

No. 56—Off-Center 1981 Lincoln Cent Struck on a 1980-P Roosevelt Dime. This double-denomination error was made when a 1980 dime was minted, then became lodged into a corner of a piece of mint machinery, or stuck in a crevice of a tote bin, probably toward the end of the calendar year. Once dislodged, it entered the normal run of planchets fed into production, and was struck by dies for a 1981 Lincoln cent.

Brown, Camire, and Weinberg estimate there are 500 double-denomination cent-on-dime errors known to exist. Of those, fewer than 20 different-dated double-denomination cents on struck Roosevelt dimes are known.

This error, valued at $500 to $750 in the early 1980s, increased in value to $2,500 to $3,500 by 2000. In 2010 it was valued at $12,000 to $15,000.

1904 Barber dime flip-over double strike.

No. 61—1904 Barber Dime Flip-Over Double Strike. This flipped-over, double-struck error came to be when a newly minted 1904 Barber dime, instead of being ejected from the coining chamber and falling into a waiting tote bin with other dimes, remained partially resting atop the collar. Somehow—possibly from an incoming planchet hitting it just right—it flipped over and then was struck a second time, about 70 percent off-center.

An estimated three or four such Barber dime errors are known. The coin pictured, valued at $350 to $500 in 1980, was worth $1,250 to $1,500 in 2000, and $7,500 to $10,000 in 2010.

Off-center Franklin half dollar struck on a Roosevelt dime planchet.

No. 62—Off-Center Franklin Half Dollar Struck on a Roosevelt Dime Planchet. This unique error, in gem condition, resides in the Smithsonian as part of the National Numismatic Collection's errors and misstruck coins. Sometime during or before 1963, a silver dime planchet found its way into the coining chamber for half dollars (at the Denver Mint, as seen by the mintmark) and was struck about 70 percent off-center at the 1 o'clock position. There are fewer than 10 known Franklin half dollars struck on dime planchets, and this off-center strike on a dime is unique.

1903 Barber dime struck on a Venezuelan quarter-bolivar planchet.

No. 71—1903 Barber Dime Struck on a Venezuelan Quarter-Bolivar Planchet. The dime has been the smallest-diameter U.S. coin issued since the half dime ended in 1873 and the nickel three-cent piece ended in 1889. Since then, any wrong-planchet or off-metal error in this denomination must be struck on a planchet intended for a foreign coin. This Barber dime offers a good example: it was struck on a planchet meant for a quarter-bolivar coin of Venezuela. The Philadelphia Mint struck various coins for the South American nation starting in 1875 and 1876, then again in various additional denominations in 1902 and 1903. The planchet for the quarter bolivar, of .835 fine silver, is half the weight and slightly smaller than that of the Barber dime.

This piece was valued at $500 to $1,000 in 1980; $2,000 to $3,000 in 2000; and $5,000 to $7,000 in 2010.

1969-D Kennedy half dollar indented by a 1969-D Roosevelt dime.

No. 83—1969-D Kennedy Half Dollar Indented by a 1969-D Roosevelt Dime. Coins indented by smaller planchets are rare, but they do exist. This dramatic error is a different type of double-denomination coin. A fully struck, normal 1969-D Roosevelt dime was face down in the collar on top of a half dollar planchet when the 1969-D half dollar dies came together. The half dollar is normal on the reverse, but it has a mirror-image brockage from the struck dime deeply impressed into its obverse.

This rare error was valued at $350 to $500 in 1980; $2,000 to $2,500 in 2000; and $5,000 to $7,500 in 2010.

Off-center Lincoln cent struck on a Roosevelt dime.

No. 92—Off-Center Lincoln Cent Struck on a Roosevelt Dime. This is not the normal double-denomination error, with the struck dime seated fully in the collar for a Lincoln cent. In this dramatic example, a dime was struck and then found its way into a cent press—a very scarce occurrence but not exceptional. However, in this case the Roosevelt dime was only 50 percent over the collar, and so the resulting strike has the Lincoln cent well off center from the struck dime.

This error coin, one of perhaps five known for the type, was worth $500 to $750 in 1980; $2,500 to $3,500 in 2000; and $5,000 to $7,500 in 2010.

1981-P Roosevelt dime struck on a steel washer.

No. 100—1981-P Roosevelt Dime Struck on a Steel Washer. Federal coins struck on washers or other machine parts are extremely rare, and most of those are Lincoln cents. This 1981-P Roosevelt dime was broadstruck on a 2.3 gram (magnetic) steel washer—likely part of a mint machine, which worked itself free at some point and fell into production. The resulting error coin was broadstruck because the false planchet was much larger than the intended normal dime planchet.

This unique error was worth $500 to $1,000 in the early 1980s; $1,500 to $2,500 in 2000; and $5,000 to $7,500 in 2010.

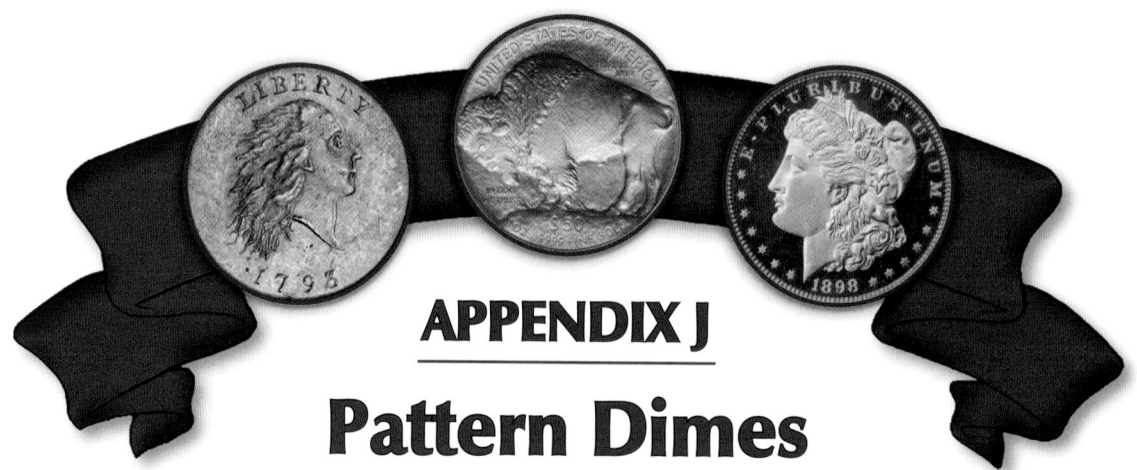

APPENDIX J

Pattern Dimes
or What Might Have Been But Wasn't

From 1792, continuing into modern times, there have been many proposals for changes in circulating coins. Different metal compositions and different designs for the first century of coins, to 1892, comprised more than 1,000 different varieties known as patterns. Some were adopted, after which motifs in circulating coinage changed. Most, however, were similar to faces on the cutting-room floor—created, but never used.

Most patterns were of higher denominations. In silver series new designs were often tried out on half dollars and dollars, rarely on dimes. However, in some instances a pattern motif was made to include lower denominations as well, including the dime. For example, in 1879 William Barber's "Washlady" obverse motif was made in the form of dimes, quarters, half dollars, and dollars, to create sets for numismatists.

Often sets were made in multiple metals, again for collectors. Copper, silver, and, sometimes, aluminum were employed. To create numismatic rarities some sets of regular-design Proofs were made in other metals. Hence, there are a number of different Liberty Seated dimes that were struck in copper and aluminum. From spring 1859 until the summer of 1885, most patterns were secretly made, with few records kept, and were privately sold by Mint officials for their own profit. This practice accounts for an estimated 90 percent or more of the patterns in existence today.

We offer a photographic gallery of selected pattern dimes here, with the date and Judd catalog number for each, as described in *United States Pattern Coins*, by J. Hewitt Judd, a Whitman title that is the standard reference on the subject.

1792, J-10. Pattern disme (as the denomination was called at the time) in copper. The engraver is thought to have been Henry Voigt.

1859, J-233. This was the next pattern dime made after 1792, as experimentation was mainly done on higher denominations. It shows the regular obverse with stars of 1859 combined with a pattern wreath reverse used for regular coinage in the next year, 1860.

1862, J-330. One of several pattern dimes proposed to be used to redeem Postage Currency. Silver dimes were no longer in circulation, due to hoarding during the Civil War. Had this coinage materialized for circulation it would have been in nickel or aluminum.

1862, J-331. Another pattern for the redemption of Postage Currency.

1864, J-381. Regular dime Proof dies struck these pieces in
copper to create rarities to sell to numismatists. In the 1860s,
continuing into the 1870s, many such copper pieces were made.

1868, J-648. Silver dimes were not in circulation from late spring
1862 until spring 1876, as they were hoarded by the public. This pattern
dime in copper, featuring the design of the old copper cent, may have
been one idea for making a 10-cent coin that would circulate. On the
other hand, it may have been made solely as a numismatic rarity.

1869, J-700. Standard Silver pattern dime with Liberty wearing
a Phrygian cap. This was part of a large series of patterns of this
year and next, struck in silver, copper, and aluminum and with
plain and reeded edges—to create rarities for the numismatic market.

1869, J-703. Standard Silver pattern dime with Liberty wearing a coronet.

1869, J-708. Standard Silver pattern dime with Liberty
wearing a ribbon and with a star on her forehead.

1869, J-717A. A pattern dime proposed with a new metallic composition.

1870, J-825. A new Standard Silver motif, this with Liberty
Seated with a shield and a pole with cap. These were made in
various metals and combinations for sale to collectors.

1870, J-834. A pattern dime struck in copper, with the obverse
of the preceding and with the regular-issue die as the reverse.

1870, J-852. Standard Silver pattern in copper, with
Liberty wearing a coronet, a reiteration of an 1869 design.

1871, J-1077. Liberty is seated with a globe
on the obverse, plain field. Regular-die reverse.

1871, J-1085. Liberty is seated with a globe and
with stars added on the obverse. Regular-die reverse.

1877, J-1498. A pattern Liberty Head with coronet
obverse. A regular die was used for the reverse.

1879, J-1584. Chief Engraver William Barber's "Washlady" pattern dime. Liberty is seated with a globe, and with stars added to the field, on the obverse. The reverse is struck from a regular die.

1879, J-1588. A pattern dime by assistant engraver George T. Morgan, using the obverse portrait of his famous silver dollar of 1878.

1916, J-1981. One of several patterns with the "Mercury" design by Adolph A. Weinman.

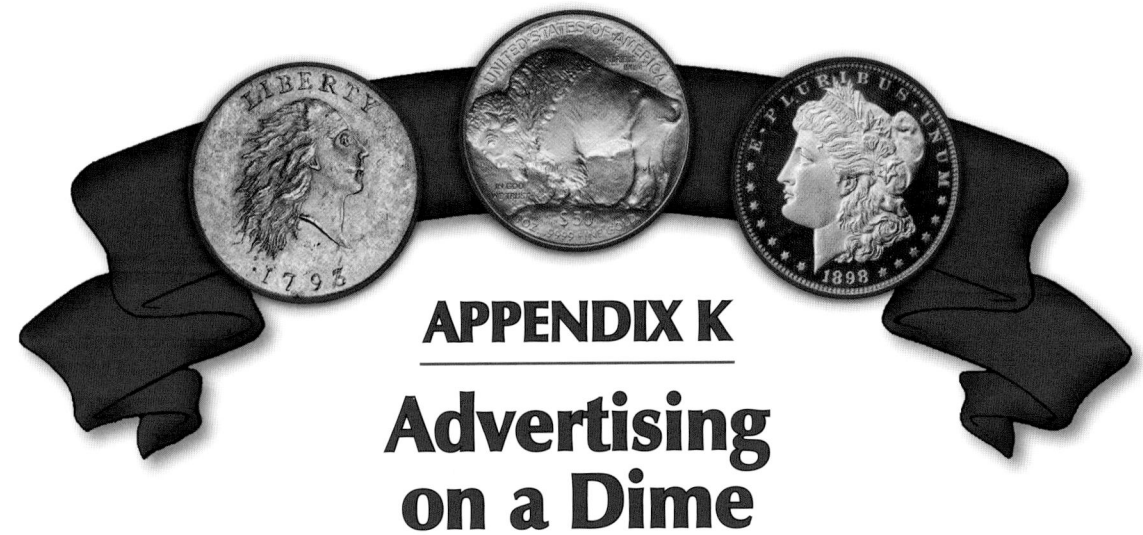

APPENDIX K

Advertising on a Dime

COUNTERSTAMPS

In the 19th century many coins, including dimes, were counterstamped with advertisements and notices of various merchants. Carried place to place in pocket change, these coins were a free way to promote goods and services widely.

When the Marquis de Lafayette, French hero of the American Revolution, revisited the United States in 1824 and 1825 Congress designated him as "the Nation's Guest." This 1824 dime was counterstamped with his portrait.

Lafayette in 1780, in the uniform of an American major general; and in later life, in the early 1820s.

Goodwin's Grand Greasejuice, a patent medicine made in Exeter, New Hampshire, used coins to advertise ("Use G.G.G."). The concoction was widely sold in the 1800s, and the G.G.G. initials were familiar to most citizens.

J.L. Polhemus, a Sacramento, California, druggist, advertised on silver and gold coins ranging from dimes to double eagles.

Lewis Hof, a brewer in Rochester, New York, gave his street address on this 1861 dime.

Dr. George G. Wilkins, of Pittsfield, New Hampshire, was perhaps America's most prolific counterstamper of coins. He also operated a restaurant with a caged bear in front to attract attention. Today, a historical sign marks the location of his business.

ENCASED POSTAGE STAMPS

In July 1862, when the outcome of the Civil War seemed increasingly uncertain, all coins started to disappear from circulation, hoarded by citizens. On July 17, Congress made ordinary postage stamps legal tender for certain transactions and debts. Entrepreneur and inventor John Gault patented the encased postage stamp, which consisted of a brass frame with a clear mica panel on the front. These devices would hold and display a stamp of a denomination from 1¢ to 90¢, with 10¢ being a popular value. On the back of the brass frame merchants could have stamped advertisements for their stores, goods, and services. Researchers have cataloged more than 30 different firms that used these encase-ments. They served a dual purpose—for the merchant they were a form of advertising; for the general public, a pocket-change substi-tute for the dimes and other coins that were hoarded and gone from circulation. Today they are avidly collected by numismatists.

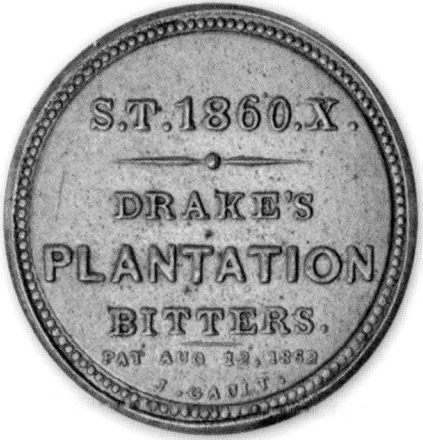

A man posing with a cabin-shaped bottle of Drake's Plantation Bitters.

Drake's Plantation Bitters were put up in cabin-shaped bottles. This patent medicine was advertised to cure just about every affliction known to mankind. As its main ingredient was rum, it did make people feel better. Sold as a medicine with no indication of its ingredients, it was especially popular with temperance advocates, ministers, and others who eschewed straight liquor. The cabalistic notation ST.1860.X was a nationwide mystery. It is thought that it meant St. Croix (X), the source of the rum, and that the bitters were first compounded in 1860.

Encased postage stamp of Bailey & Co., well-known Philadelphia jewelers.

In Boston, Joseph L. Bates offered fancy goods. Stereoscopic viewers
were the sensation of the day, and Bates sold these with his own imprint.

Also in Boston, Burnett sold various flavorings,
medicines, and other items. Cocoaine was a hair preparation.

Burnett's cooking extracts were sold nationwide
and remained popular long after the Civil War.

The encased postage stamps of Arthur Claflin, of Hopkinton,
Massachusetts, are among the great rarities for today's numismatists.

George G. Evans of Philadelphia had his fingers in many business pies,
including selling wine. He also promoted mail-order books, and two decades
later published a popular book on the history of the United States Mint.

The Tremont House, a well-known Chicago
hotel, advertised on encased postage stamps.

TREMONT HOUSE
CHICAGO.

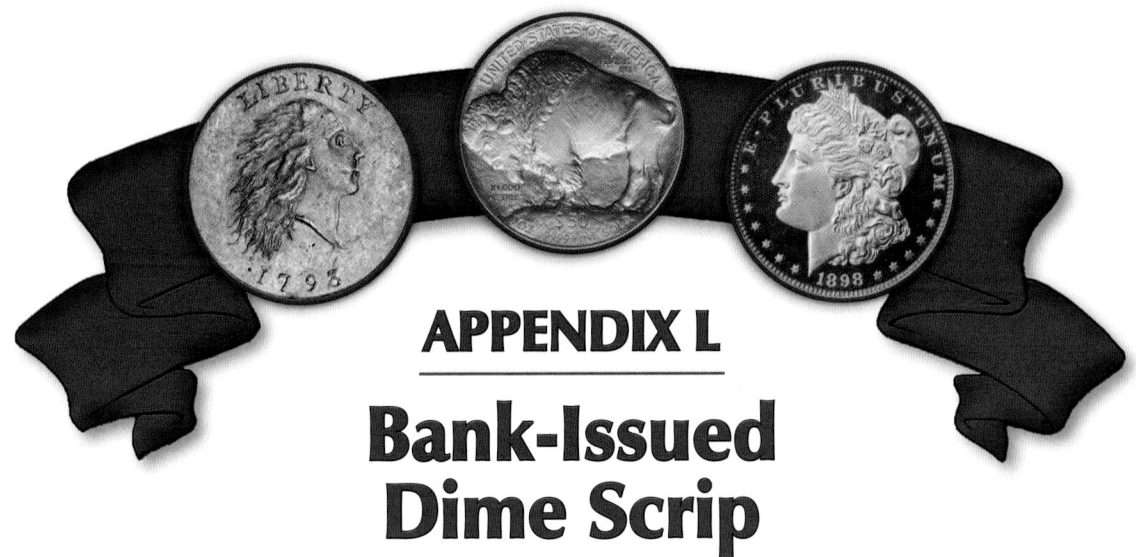

APPENDIX L

Bank-Issued Dime Scrip

In 1862 and 1863, when Americans were hoarding gold, silver, and even copper coins in reaction to their uncertainty about the Civil War, banks had no coins to pay out. Many issued scrip notes—paper substitutes for legal tender—of various denominations. Illustrated in this appendix are the 10¢ notes of six different institutions and a sheet of scrip from the Carroll County Bank of Sandwich, New Hampshire, with three notes of different values, including 10¢.

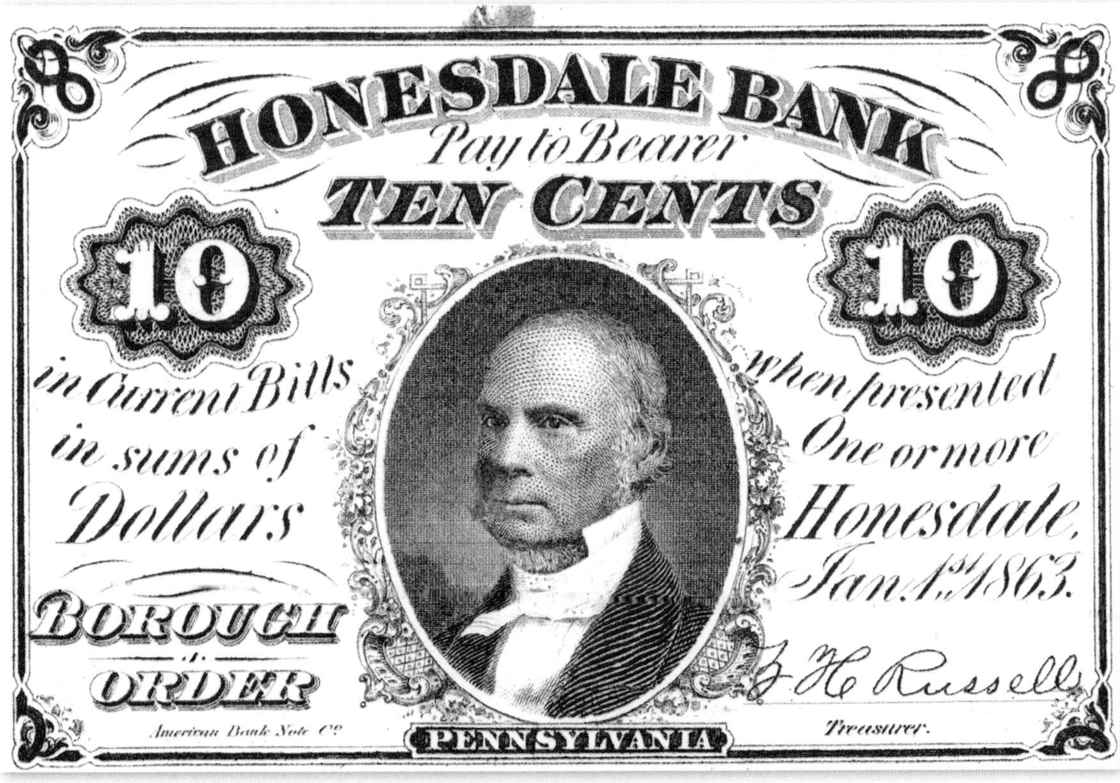

A Proof impression of a 10¢ scrip note of the Honesdale Bank (Honesdale, Pennsylvania).

Sandwich, N. H., November 12, 1862.

No. .... A,

Carroll County Bank,

SANDWICH, NEW-HAMPSHIRE.

Pay the Bearer hereof FIVE CENTS in Current Funds, when this and like Checks are presented in sums of even Dollars.

To the Cashier.

McFarland & Jenks' Print.

10 Sandwich, N.H.  Nob. 12, 1862. **10**

No. .... B

CARROLL COUNTY BANK,

Sandwich, New-Hampshire.

Pay the Bearer hereof TEN CENTS in Current Funds, when this and like Checks are presented in sums of even Dollars.

To the Cashier.

McFarland & Jenks' Print.

25 SANDWICH, N. H. November 12, 1862. **25**

C No. ....

CARROLL COUNTY BANK,

25 Sandwich, New-Hampshire. 25

Pay the Bearer hereof Twenty-Five Cents in Current Funds, when this and like Checks are presented in sums of even Dollars.

To the Cashier. *McFarland & Jenks' Print.*

A sheet of scrip notes, of nickel, dime, and quarter denominations,
of the Carroll County Bank, Sandwich, New Hampshire. (shown enlarged)

A 10¢ scrip note of the Farmers & Merchants
Bank of Rochester, New York. (shown enlarged)

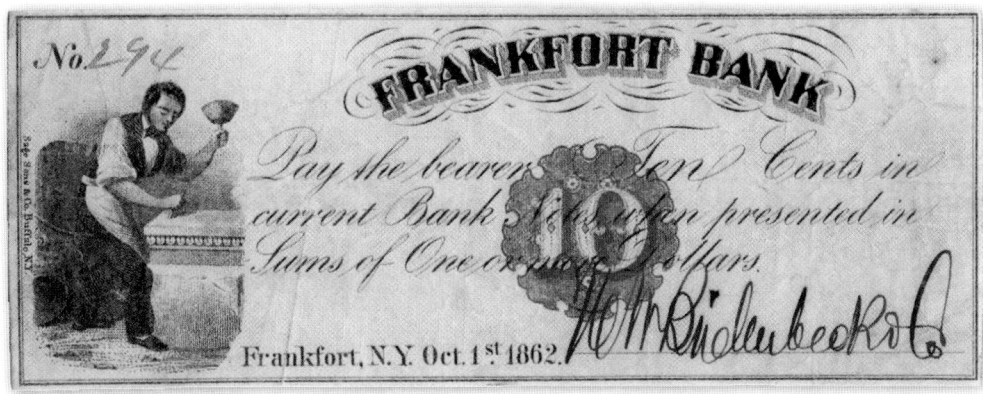

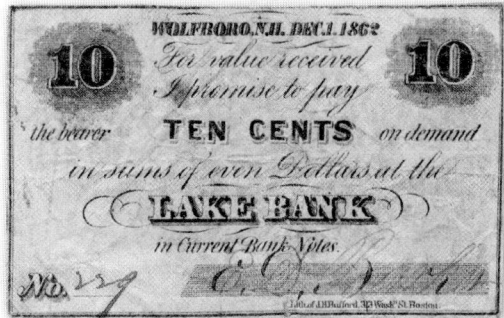

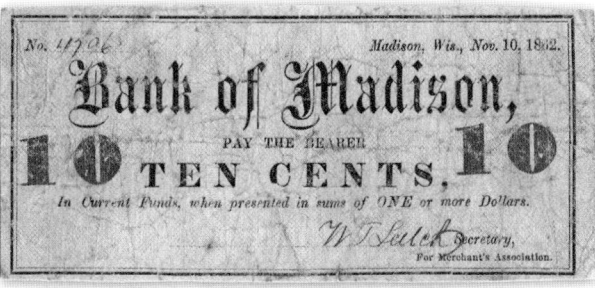

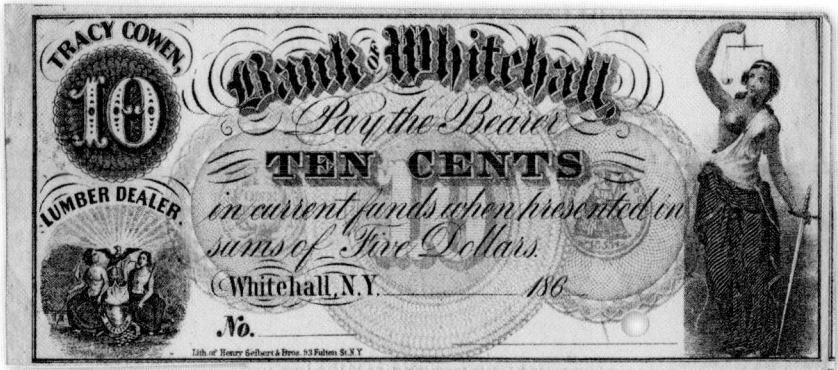

Various bank "dime" notes of New Hampshire, New York, and Wisconsin.

APPENDIX M

Merchant- and Town-Issued Dime Scrip

Fear and uncertainty about the outcome of the Civil War, and what effect it would have on the nation's economy, led everyday citizens to hoard first their gold coins, then silver, and finally even copper cents. With coins gone from circulation, Americans had to come up with creative substitutes for day-to-day commerce. In 1862 and 1863 merchants and towns issued hundreds of varieties of paper scrip. Their values typically ranged from 3¢ to 50¢. A selection of notes that substituted for hoarded dimes is shown here.

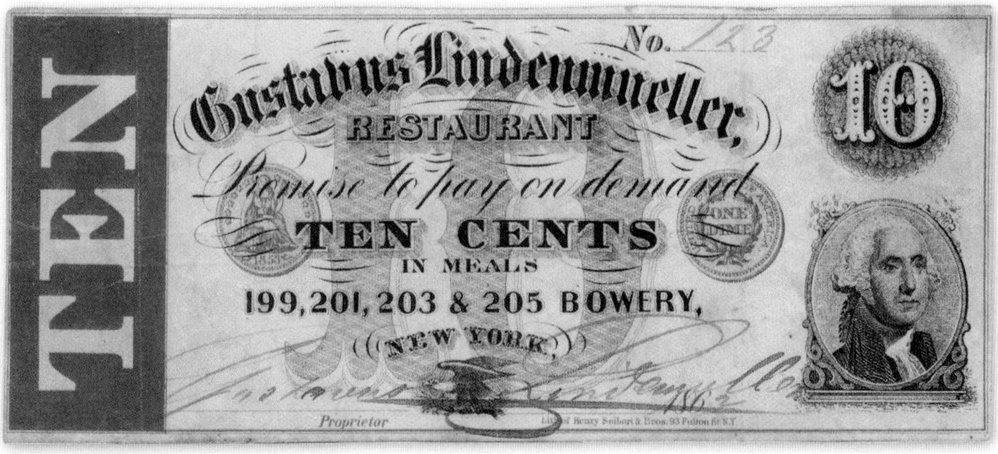

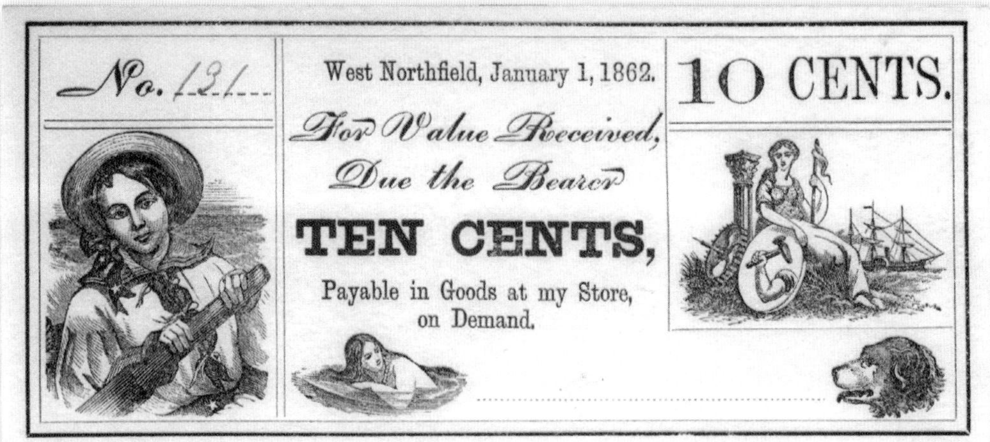

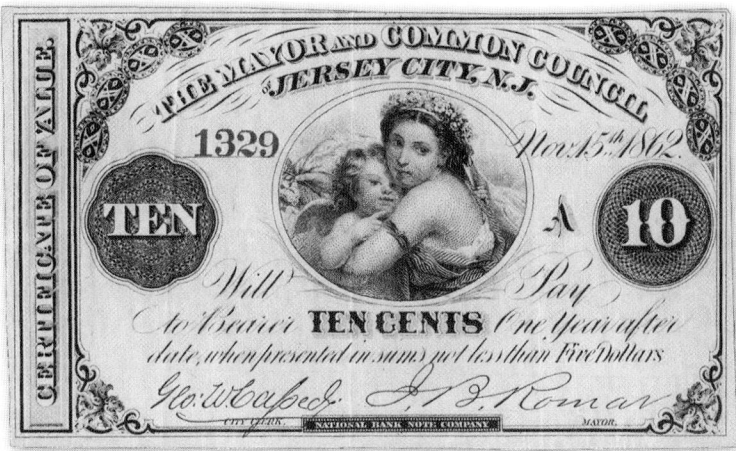

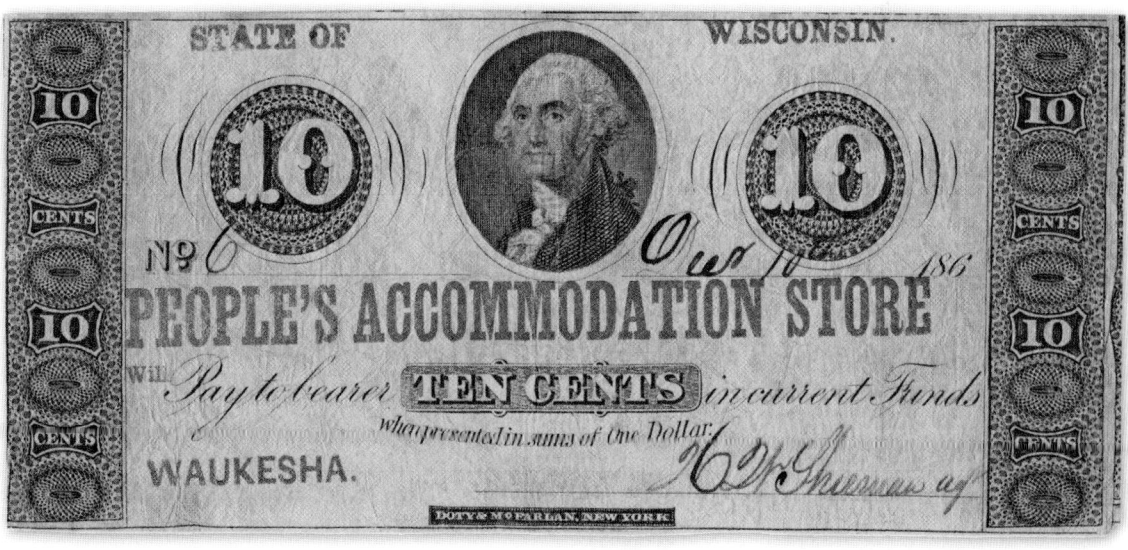

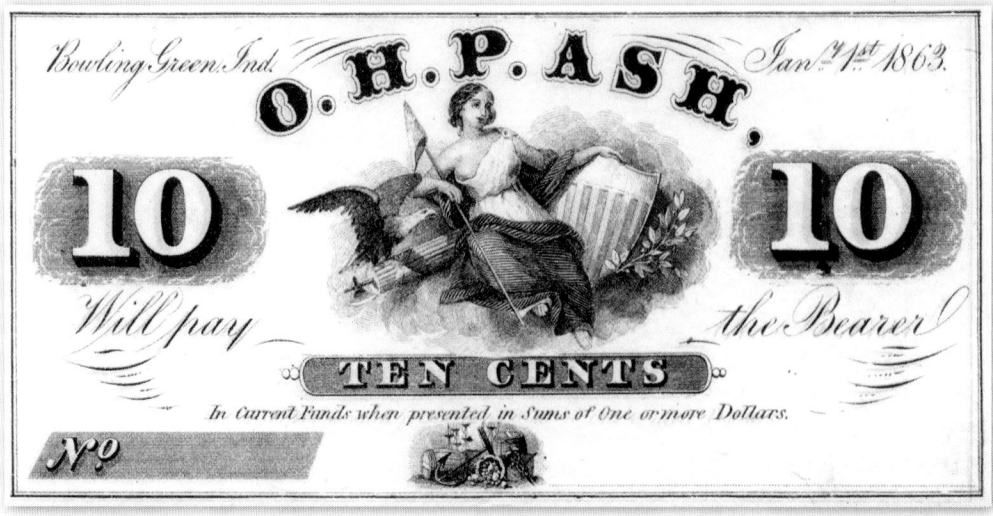

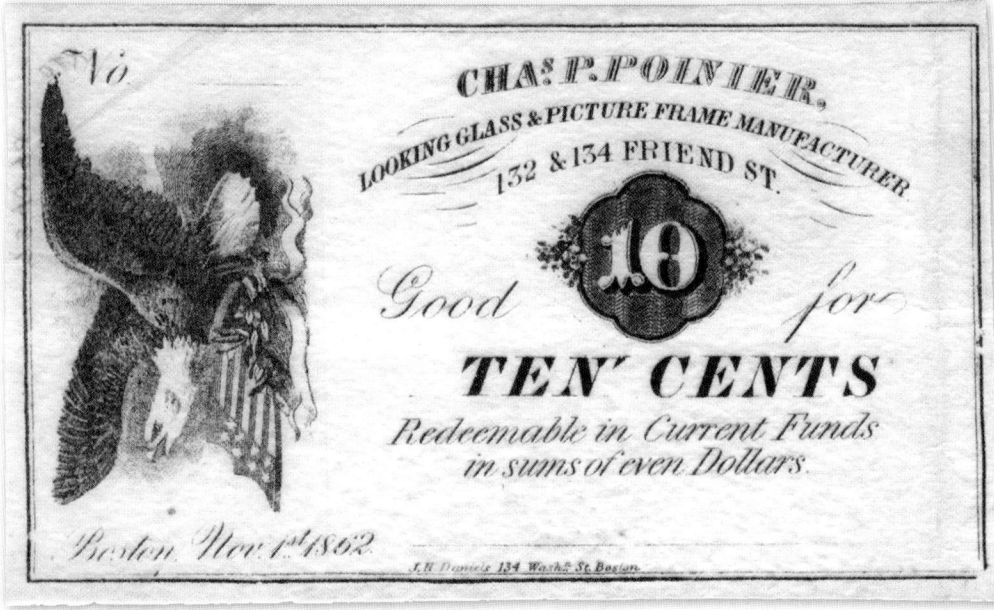

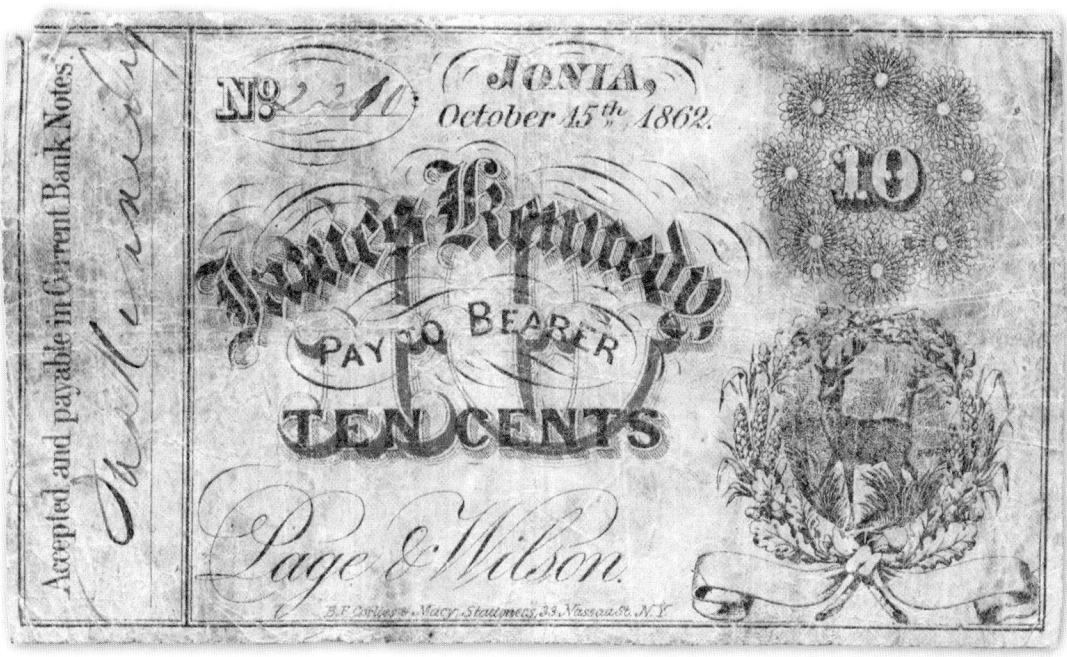

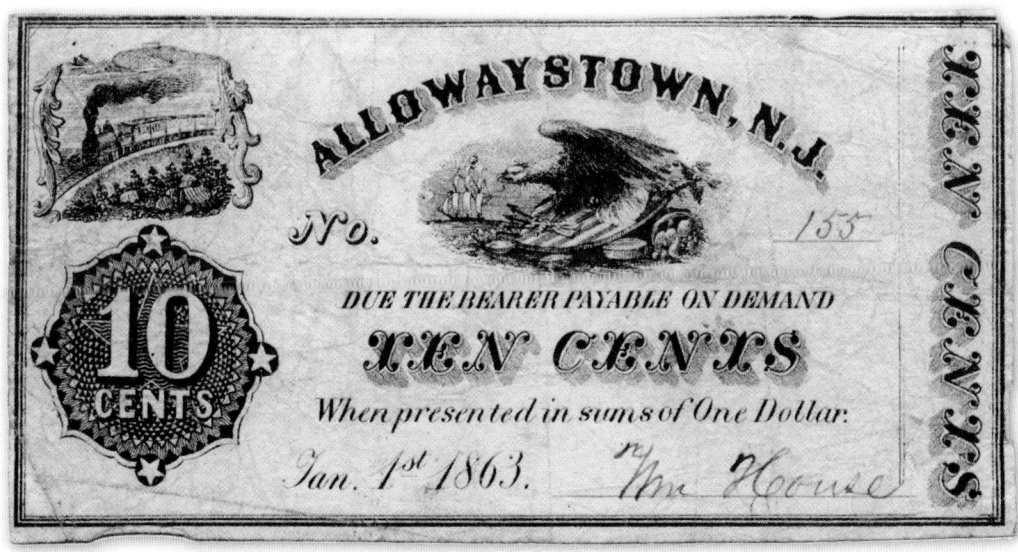

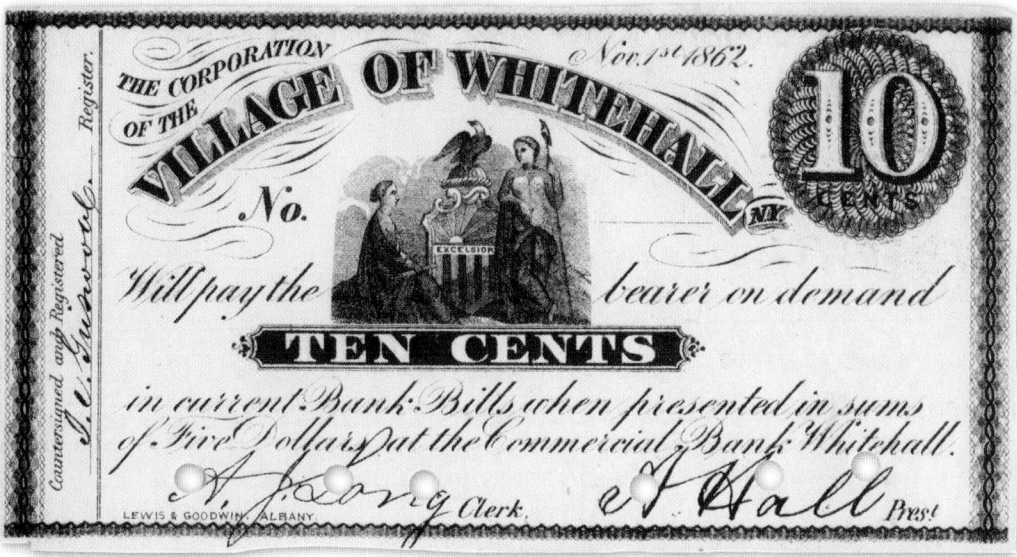

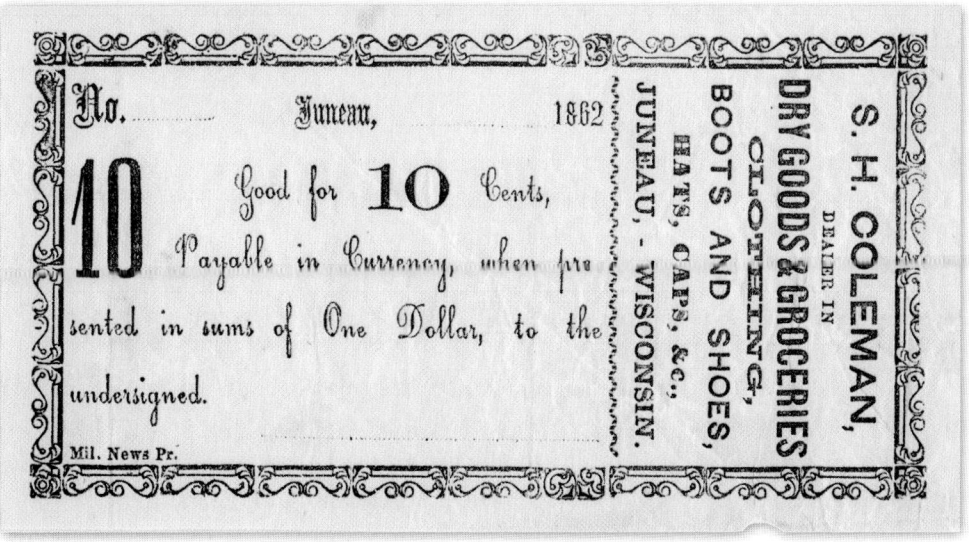

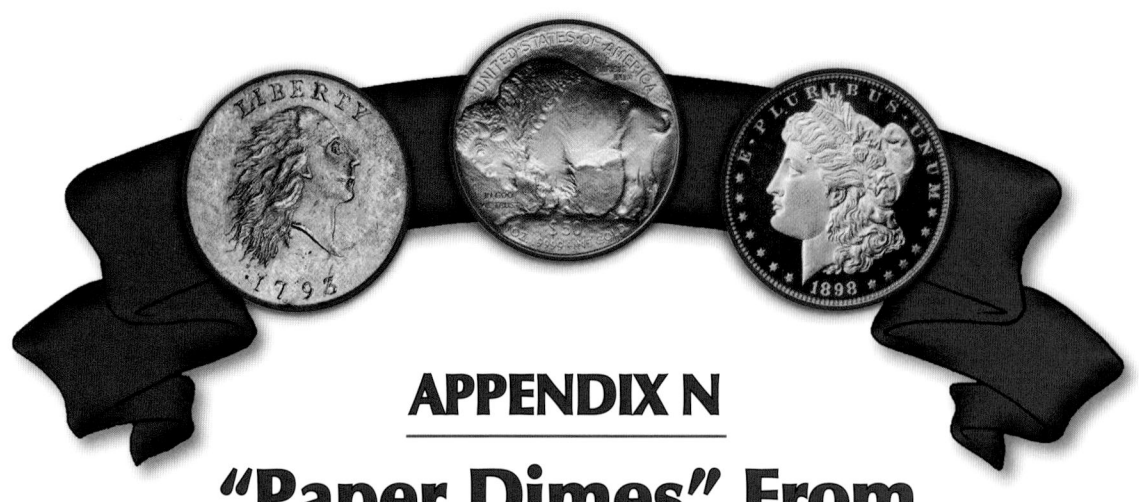

APPENDIX N

"Paper Dimes" From the Treasury Department

Dimes and other silver coins were hoarded by the public and disappeared from circulation in late spring 1862 and did not reappear until after April 20, 1876. To fill the public need for legal tender in small-change amounts, in August 1862 the U.S. Treasury Department issued Postage Currency fractional bills. At first they were distributed to Army paymasters, then in September to the general public.

These small paper notes, made in denominations of 5¢, 10¢, 25¢, and 50¢, bore the designs of contemporary postage stamps printed within a border, and with added inscriptions. Similar to stamps, the Postage Currency notes were issued in perforated sheets, to be torn apart by the recipients. By early 1863 about $100,000 of these notes reached circulation per day, but the demand remained unsatisfied.

A lively trade developed in the making and selling of small cardboard and leather wallets for the storage of these little bills.

The Act of March 3, 1863, provided for a new small-denomination series, Fractional Currency. Distribution of such notes— 5¢, 10¢, 25¢, and 50¢—began in October of the same year. In late autumn 1864, a new Fractional Currency denomination, the 3¢ note, reached circulation, but it never became popular. In summer 1869 another Fractional Currency denomination, 15¢, was added to the Fractional Currency lineup, but it, too, was never widely used. Face and back colors varied over a period of time as did the notes' sizes.

Army soldiers were among the first to receive Postage Currency fractional bills, as pay starting in August 1862. Pictured are Mr. A.H. Rogers of Chattanooga, Tennessee, and Sergeant Hoxxey C. Rogers (2nd Vermont Volunteers), circa 1864.

Fractional bills were created from 1862 to 1876. A selection of 10¢ issues is illustrated here. Attributions are by Friedberg numbers, from *Paper Money of the United States*.

As shown in the other appendices of this edition of *Mega Red*, 10¢ scrip notes were issued by banks, merchants, and other entities, but mainly in 1862 and 1863 and in no long series, as were the Treasury Department's "paper dimes" and other small-change notes.

A sheet of Postage Currency, F-1242.

TREASURY OF THE UNITED STATES.

Specimen Set of Fractional Currency.

Comprising all the Varieties and Denominations as originally issued.

POSTAGE CURRENCY—With Perforated Edges.

50's, 25's, 10's, 5's.. .90

POSTAGE CURRENCY—With Plain Edges.

50's, 25's, 10's, 5's.. .90

FRACTIONAL CURRENCY—Second Issue.

50's, 25's, 10's, 5's.. .90

FRACTIONAL CURRENCY—Third Issue.

50's. Vignette Goddess of Liberty....	.50
Same, with red back..........	.50
Same, with autographic signatures........	.50
25's. Vignette head of Fessenden....	.25
Same, with red back...........	.25
10's. Vignette head of Washington....	.10
Same, with red back..........	.10
Same, with autographic signatures....	.10
5's. Vignette head of Clark....	.05
Same, with red back..........	.05
3's. Vignette head of Washington....	.03
50's. Vignette head of Spinner....	.50
Same, with red back..........	.50
Same, with altered green back.	.50
Same, with autographic signatures....	.50
	$4.43

FRACTIONAL CURRENCY—Fourth Issue.

50's. Vignette head of Lincoln......	.50
Vignette head of Stanton.....	.50
25's, 15's, 10's....	.50
	1.50

Thirty-two pieces, amounting to....	8.63
Stationery expenses....	.02
	$8.65

An informational sheet issued by the Treasury Department describing a specimen set of Fractional Currency sold by the government in the 1870s.

Postage Currency, F-1240, part of the series issued from August 21, 1862, to May 27, 1863.

To defer counterfeiting, the F-1246 Fractional Currency issues had overprints in bronze ink: an ellipse on the face, and 10 on the back.

F-1253 notes required hand-inked signatures of Treasury officials and also had bronze overprint 10 figures on the face.

F-1257 notes feature especially ornate engraving. All of these fractional notes were enthusiastically collected by numismatists at the time of issue.

APPENDIX O

Civil War Sutlers' "Dime" Tokens

During the Civil War the Union Army licensed retailers known as sutlers to travel with troops and supply them with goods. Typically a sutler would set up in a tent, or, if located in an occupied town, in a storefront. Offered for sale would be magazines, newspapers, books, games, playing cards, clothing, gift items, bitters and other quasi-medical preparations, and more.

Sutlers issued tokens in copper or brass, in denominations from 5¢ to $1. Soldiers bought the tokens with their pay and could redeem them for goods. Most of the sutler tokens were made by shops that also issued Civil War patriotic tokens and store cards, the most important being John Stanton and William K, Lanphear of Cincinnati and Shubael D. Childs of Chicago. Some sutlers' tokens shared the same reverse dies. A selection of 10¢ tokens, substitutes for dimes, is illustrated here, enlarged to show their detail.

A token issued by J.B. Spitzer, sutler with the 55th Ohio Volunteer Infantry.

A sutler's tent at Brandy Station, Virginia, February 1864.

A sutler token issued by S. Whited & Co. for the 97th Illinois Volunteers.

A token issued by sutler J.M. Kerry for Simmonds Battery, a Kentucky unit.

This token, issued by sutler W.A. Farr for the 14th New Hampshire Volunteers, was made by F.X. Koehler of Baltimore, who added his surname to the reverse.

A sutler camp scene.

A token issued by sutler J.J. Benson for the 1st Mounted Rifles regiment of New York.

This token was issued by sutler J.B. Spitzer for the 55th Volunteer Infantry of Ohio. The reverse is the Mercury die by engraver Lutz, made for the shop of W.K. Lanphear.

Sutler Sid Wright issued this token for the 11th Regiment of Wisconsin Volunteers.

"Sutler's Row" in Chattanooga, Tennessee.

APPENDIX P

Civil War "Dime" Store Cards

The story of Civil War tokens is summarized in the "Private Tokens" section of this book.

The vast majority of Civil War store cards issued by merchants were valued at 1¢ each, making them convenient small-change substitutes when federal coins were scarce or absent from circulation. There were a few, however, that were redeemable for 10¢. These stood in for the nation's silver dimes, which were gone from circulation by the summer of 1862.

A sampling of "dime" tokens are illustrated here. Many of these were struck in brass and nickel. For more information regarding varieties, see the *Guide Book of Civil War Tokens* (Bowers) and *U.S. Civil War Store Cards*, published by the Civil War Token Society.

The Civil War store cards of White & Swann of Huntsville, Alabama, are largely a mystery to numismatists today. This town was occupied by the Union for much of the war. No information concerning the trade of the White & Swann partnership has been found. This token is classified as variety AL-425-A-3b, per the standard references.

The store card of P. Hugens of Cincinnati is somewhat puzzling, as the price of a loaf of bread in that town was typically 5 or 6 cents during the Civil War. More cards were issued by Cincinnati merchants than in any other city. Lanphear and Stanton, two leading token manufacturers, were located there. OH-165-CA-3a.

Schultz & Negley, Cincinnati druggists, issued this 10¢ store card. OH-165-FL-2b.

This C.E. Clark's Lightning Hair Dyeing Room token suggests that there was quick service for customers. It was located in the Burnet House, one of Cincinnati's leading hotels. OH-165-Y-5j.

Many Civil War tokens remained in circulation well into the 1870s, as reflected by this token issued by Peter Weber of London, Ohio, redeemable in cigars and beer. OH-470-B-2j.

Burton's Exchange was located on the Ohio River at Portsmouth. The nature of the business is not known, but we know of H.D. Burton, St. Charles Restaurant, Market between Second and Third, who might be related. Ongoing research is a dynamic part of token collecting. OH-745-A-2b.

Charles McCarthy, whose surname is misspelled on this token, opened the Washington House hotel in Urbana, Ohio, in 1866. Whether this token was made in advance, during the Civil War (which ended in April 1865), remains a question. OH-895-A-3b.

APPENDIX Q

Dimes as Planchets for Civil War Tokens

During the Civil War many numismatists collected tokens as they were issued. Several of the manufacturers were happy to make special strikings, such as over copper-nickel Indian Head cents and over silver dimes. Not many such overstrikes were made, and those minted from dimes in particular are great rarities today. By carefully studying the tokens under magnification, you can discern details of the dimes underneath.

Store card of F.B. Orr of Mansfield, Ohio, struck over an 1853 dime with arrows at date, by New York City diesinker William Bridgens. OH-505-B-fo.

Token of J.F. Gardner, New York City, over an 1858 dime. Gardner was a dealer in leather goods. NY-630-AA-fo.

Token of Charles A. Lühr, who operated the Pike Slip Shades in New York City, over an 1853 With Arrows dime. The term *shade* seems to represent the use of an old English term for a wine cellar or wine vault. NY-630-AR-1fo.

Token of J.H. Warner of New York City, over an 1832 Capped Bust dime, an unusually early-dated coin. Warner was a liquor dealer. NY-630-CA-1fo.

Token of the Felix (Kosher) Dining Saloon, New York City, over an 1853 With Arrows dime. NY-630-W-2fo.

Token of M.L. Marshall, rare-coin dealer and seller of other goods in Oswego, New York, on the shore of Lake Ontario. Struck over an 1838 dime. NY-695-A-2f0.

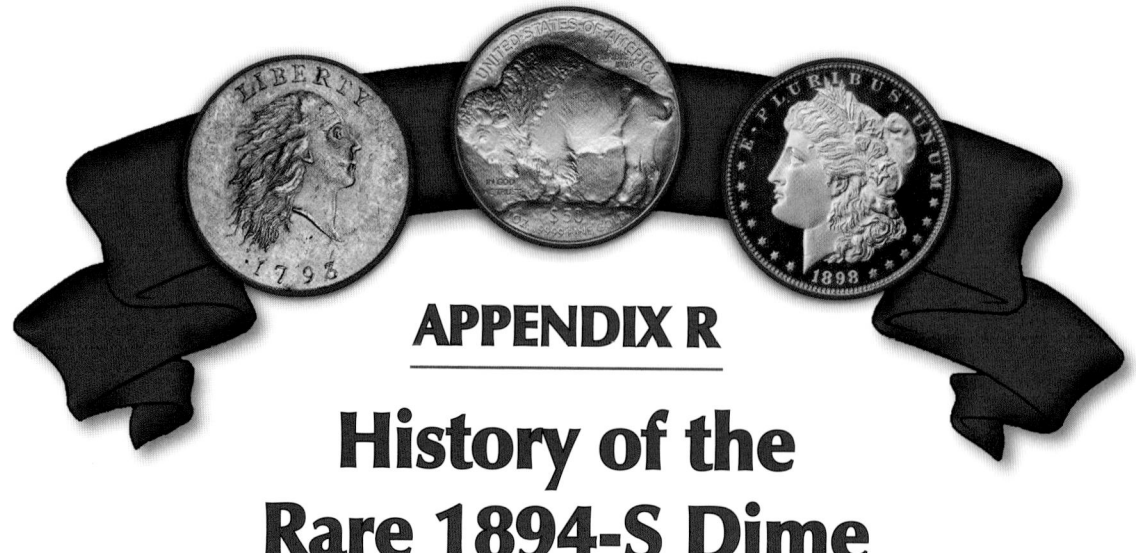

APPENDIX R

History of the Rare 1894-S Dime

The 1894-S dime is the most famous and most rare coin in the entire Barber series. Every other dime, quarter, and half dollar date and mintmark is readily collectible, although some are scarce in lower grades and rare in higher levels of Mint State.

Today it is thought that no more than 10 1894-S dimes exist, two of which are well worn and the rest in Mint State, often cataloged as Proofs. Although 10 pairs of dies were sent from Philadelphia to the San Francisco Mint for coining dimes in quantity in 1894, the only production was a short run of 24 coins on June 9, 1894, using just one die pair. At the time the nation was in the throes of economic depression following the Panic of 1893. There was no call for dimes to be made for circulation in San Francisco. The handful of 1894-S dimes were prooflike in appearance, but were not mirror Proofs in the style that would have been made for the numismatic trade. Nevertheless, in later years collectors and dealers often described them as such.

Of the 24 1894-S dimes struck, five were submitted for assay. On June 9, the day of the coinage, two coins were sent to the director of the Mint in Washington to be assayed, which was done soon afterward. On June 25 two dimes are listed as part of the coins assayed by the San Francisco Mint during the month of June 1894. Another specimen was sent on June 28 to the superintendent of the Philadelphia Mint to be reserved for the annual Assay Commission, for their review of coinage of 1894 early in the next year. No other orders for coinage were forthcoming, so the mintage for that year remained at just two dozen coins and the net distribution was just 19 of those.

One of the famous and rare 1894-S Barber dimes.

In the meantime, numismatic interest in mintmarked coins had been engendered by the publication in 1893 of *Mint Marks*, a treatise by Augustus G. Heaton that listed points of desirability. Prior to this time, nearly all collectors simply sought one coin of each date, and whether it had a mintmark on the reverse was not noticed.

The *San Francisco Call* published this on August 25, 1895, by which time the dime had a recognized value:

> Whoever has a dime of 1894, coined by the San Francisco Mint, has a coin for which $5 has already been offered, and when all the facts are known regarding its scarcity it is not unlikely that it will command a much higher premium.
>
> Inquiry at the mint elicited the information that during the fiscal year of 1894 only twenty-four dimes were coined at the San Francisco Mint. How this came about was told by Chief Clerk Robert Barnett.
>
> "All undercurrent subsidiary coins, viz., those containing other than the design now being used when received at the sub-treasury, are not again allowed to go into circulation, but are sent to the mint to be recoined with the current design. In the course of the year 1894 we received a large sum in these coins, but having an ample stock of dimes on hand, it was not intended to coin any of that denomination in 1894. However, when nearly all of this subsidiary coin bullion had been utilized, we found on our hands a quantity that would to advantage only into dimes and into dimes it was coined, making just twenty-four of them.
>
> "My intention was first drawn to the matter particularly but the receipt of a letter from a collector somewhere East requesting a set of the coin 1894. In filling this order I found there were no dimes of that date on hand. Subsequently I received quite a number of similar letters, and in each case was, of course, unable to furnish the dimes.
>
> "Plenty of dimes were coined that year at Philadelphia and New Orleans mints, but there are many collectors who accumulate the coinage of each mint, as each has its distinguishing mark. Those coined here bear a letter 'S' under the eagle. New Orleans used the letter 'O' and Carson City the letter 'C,' while Philadelphia coins are identified by the absence of the letter.
>
> "We receive each year about fifty requests from coin collectors for coins, mostly for those of silver."

This reflects the growing interest in mintmarked coins. John M. Clapp, a Pennsylvanian in the oil business, in 1893 began ordering one of each coin from the Philadelphia, Carson City, New Orleans, and San Francisco mints—current silver and gold coins from the dime to the double eagle. On November 2, 1894, he wrote to San Francisco to order one example of each coin. Acting Superintendent Robert Barnett replied on the 9th, stating that "We have no coinage dimes 1894" and that the $10 eagles minted that year were in a sealed vault and would not be available until prior eagles on hand had been paid out. During the year several other interested parties wrote or sent orders for 1894-S dimes. George Eavenson of Denver, Colorado, wrote on July 14 to order one each of the silver coins and was told by Barnett, "I have no dimes coined in 1894." This would seem to indicate that by autumn there were no 1894-S dimes on hand at the mint. If some employees had examples, this was not mentioned. It also gave no indication that coinage was expected.

Eugene B. Stevens, cashier of the First National Bank of Parsons, Kansas, sent a request which was answered by Barnett on October 29: "In reply to your favor 15th inst. I will respectfully say we have no dimes mintage 1894. In accordance with your suggestion I smiled." This would seem to imply that Barnett knew much and was aware of the numismatic significance of such dimes.

On October 30, Augustus G. Heaton wrote from Washington and was told by Barnett, "We have no 10 cent pieces coinage 1894." Heaton communicated this to George F. Heath, editor of *The Numismatist*, who reported in the November issue that no 1894-S dimes had been coined. On November 28, H.M. Ensminger of Center Square, Pennsylvania, wrote to order silver coins of the year. Barnett furnished the others and stated, "We have no dimes coinage 1894." The most persistent applicant was Peter Mougey of Cincinnati, who first wrote on January 16 and was told, "I have no dimes of 94." Mougey sent other requests and on April 25, July 18, and November 8 was mailed similar replies from Barnett. Other inquiries from various correspondents were answered in a similar manner in 1895. (Numismatic historian Kevin Flynn excerpts this correspondence in his *Authoritative Reference on Barber Dimes*.)

Significantly, a reading of the above does not state that there was no mintage of 1894-S dimes, but only that no such dimes *were available* to collectors.

In later years a number of variant accounts, mostly theories, were published, a popular one being that the San Francisco Mint needed to strike $2.40 worth of dimes to balance a bullion account on the books. Another is that they were made to "test the dies."

Still another is that they were purposely struck to create rarities for private sale by Mint employees. The ever-inventive Walter Breen in his 1988 *Encyclopedia* gave this:

> Each of eight persons received three; [Mint Superintendent] Daggett gave his three to his daughter Hallie, telling her to put them away until she was as old as he was, at which time she would be able to sell them for a good price. On the way home the child supposedly spent one for a dish of ice cream, but kept the other two until 1954, when she sold them to coin dealer Earl Parker.

The earliest numismatic notice of the 1894-S dime seen by Q. David Bowers appeared in the March 1900 issue of *The Numismatist*, when Heaton updated his 1893 *Mint Marks* with an article, "Late Coinage of the United States Mint," in which he noted this:

> The San Francisco Mint takes proudly to itself the sensation of later U.S. coinage in striking but $2.40 worth of dimes, or *24 pieces* in all, in the year 1894. Of these, the writer possesses *the only one known* to the numismatic world.

At the very least, this suggests that by very early 1900 Heaton was not aware of any examples in private collections and that the San Francisco Mint was proud of its accomplishment and gave details to Heaton, but did not indicate that the location of any others was known. Heaton told no more. As a follow-up to this article, George F. Heath, editor of *The Numismatist*, stated:

> J.C. Mitchelson of Kansas City, who has been spending much time in San Francisco, writes that he has uncovered an 1894-S dime. Mint authorities there informed him that while 24 were originally struck, only 14 went into circulation, the remaining 10 were restruck. None remain in circulation.

By "restruck," Heath may have meant *melted* or *reserved for assay*. The location of the Mitchelson coin is not known today. His collection is preserved by the Connecticut State Library in Hartford.

John M. Clapp, who had unsuccessfully sought a dime from the San Francisco Mint in 1894, continued to build his collection until his passing in 1906, after which it was inherited and expanded by his son, John H. Clapp. The entries of the elder John in his notebook indicate that two specimens of the 1894-S dime, both Uncirculated, were in his cabinet by 1900. At least one had been obtained from a San Francisco source, but not from the San Francisco Mint during the year of issue (for such direct purchases were registered separately). When Heaton published notice of them in *The Numismatist* in 1900 he was not aware of Clapp's two coins. Accordingly, in 1900 four 1894-S dimes were mentioned: one each in print by Heaton and Mitchelson and two in John M. Clapp's ledger. As weigher Frank C. Berdan later stated that the two he had obtained for face value in June 1894 went to a collector of mintmarked coins, he may have been the source of two of the above.

This is the prelude to many articles and auction offerings that took place in later years, up to the modern era. In 2005 Kevin Flynn wrote and published *The 1894-S Dime: A Mystery Unraveled*, which contained much information from the San Francisco Mint archives.

The 1894-S dime has been a personal favorite of Q. David Bowers ever since he acquired the Charles A. Cass ("Empire") coin sold by Stack's in 1957. "Morton Stack was at the auction podium," Bowers recalls. "The coin later went into the collection of Emery May Holden Norweb, thus leading to my long-term friendship with the Norweb family." More on his purchase of the storied coin can be found in this edition of *Mega Red*, in the appendix titled "Carpe Dime."

JC Dealer Pays $4,750
For Just One Thin Dime

By JOHN F. MOORE
Binghamton Press Writer

JAMES F. RUDDY, JR., of Johnson City is a coin dealer. Lots cf coins arrive in his mail. Yesterday's delivery included an airmail package containing a dime.

The dime cost Mr. Ruddy $4,750.

Rare coins as everyone knows are expensive. And as everyone knows who knows Mr. Ruddy, he is a young man who wears a hat when it's raining and a topcoat when it's cold, and pays a lot of attention to business.

So there obviously are good reasons why a dime should be worth 47,500 times the amount the U. S. Treasury backs it for.

To understand the big price tag, it helps to know a few facts about gaudy old San Francisco.

Also helpful is a bit of insight into the psychology of great and growing numbers of people who, as coin collectors, "like to finish things."

★ ★ ★

PRIOR TO UNPACKING the small, heavily insured package today, Mr. Ruddy described how he purchased it last Wednesday in an auction at a New York City coin house.

Five other persons vied with him for the purchase. Bidding had begun at $4,200. Afterwards, the Johnson City man ordered the coin shipped to avoid traveling with the expensive package.

The dime as he proudly showed it off today carries the head of Miss Liberty on its front together with inscriptions, "United States of America," and "1894." The back carries the words "One Dime," surrounded by a wreath, and a tiny "S."

—Binghamton Press Photo.

THING OF SOME VALUE—A rare dime is examined with warm regard by its new owner, coin dealer James F. Ruddy, Jr., at Workers Trust Office in Johnson City. The $4,750 he paid for coin is greater than the dollar-bill hoard which bank employes stacked on table for comparison.

Jim Ruddy poses with the 1894-S dime that he bought on behalf of Q. David Bowers at Stack's Empire Sale some 60 years ago. Arrayed on the table in front of Ruddy is a tangible expression of the purchase price: 4,750 dollar bills!

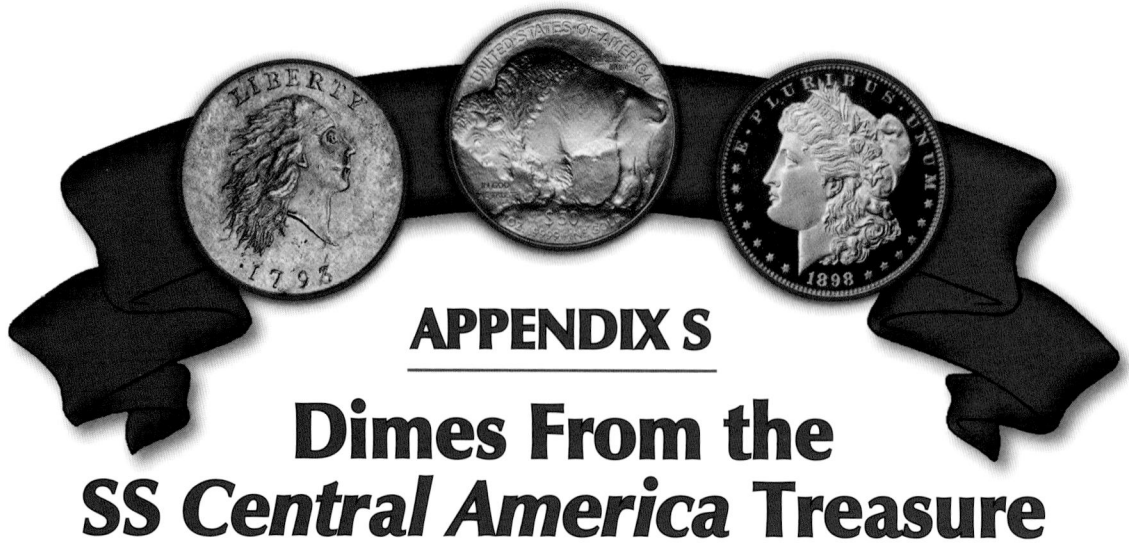

APPENDIX S

Dimes From the SS *Central America* Treasure

The recovery of coins and ingots from the wreck of the SS *Central America* is one of the most important and compelling stories in American numismatics of the late 20th and early 21st centuries.

The tale beings in 1857, when nearly 600 passengers and crew boarded the SS *Central America*, a sidewheel steamship making a run from the Atlantic side of Panama, north to New York City. Along with them went gold coins, gold dust, nuggets, and ingots. The people and treasure had left San Francisco in late August aboard the SS *Sonora*, landed at Panama, and took the 49-mile Panama Railroad across the isthmus. This was a rather routine procedure, and many similar trips had been made on a twice-monthly schedule without difficulty.

The sky was bright and a warm breeze greeted the voyagers as they left Panama and headed north, with a stop at Havana, Cuba, where the *Central America* anchored overnight and left the next day, Tuesday morning, September 8. The ship had comfortable accommodations and good food, and it was pleasant to mingle on the deck or below. The forward motion of 12 miles per hour created a comfortable breeze. North of Havana some storm clouds were seen on the horizon and strong winds followed. Storms usually passed quickly, and the steamship's passengers and crew assumed the inconvenience would soon blow over. This did not happen, and a frightful gale came on with mountainous seas. The ship was in the midst of one of the greatest tropical hurricanes ever. In this era before scientific weather forecasting, it was completely unexpected.

The ship tossed and rolled in the sea, its sails were torn to shreds, the hold and lower sections flooded, portholes were broken, the structure was damaged, and the steam boiler's fire was extinguished. The *Central America* was helpless. Passengers feared for their lives. By Friday, September 11, there was little hope left. On Saturday, September 12, the sea was much less rough but the damage had been done. The ship was listing sharply and many broken portholes were under water. Exhausted men in a bucket brigade used emptied barrels to hoist about 400 gallons of water per minute out of the sinking ship—a heroic but losing struggle against the ocean.

The SS *Central America*.

The last moments of the SS *Central America,* **September 12, 1857.**

Around one in the afternoon the sails of two small ships, the Norwegian barque *Ellen* and the brig *Marine*, were seen on the horizon. Awash themselves during the hurricane, the vessels were still in good condition, although somewhat tattered. Lifeboats from the *Central America* were sent on nine shuttle trips with women and children, who reached safety, as did some crewmen, 109 lucky souls. Then the two ships drifted away.

As the afternoon wore on, all bailing efforts ceased, as pounding waves continued to tear the *Central America* apart. At about eight in the evening, Captain William Lewis Herndon ordered rockets to be fired to signal that the ship was sinking. The captain was standing on the starboard paddle-box when a tremendous wave hit a few minutes later. He and nearly 500 others slipped into the raging sea. The *Central America* went to the ocean bottom 7,200 feet below, taking with it more than $1,200,000 in registered gold treasure weighing over two tons. At final reckoning of the *Central America* disaster, about 435 souls were lost. Only 162 survived. Many were picked up adrift in the ocean, often clinging to wreckage, by passing ships.

The financial Panic of 1857 took place in the autumn, followed by other unrest, and beginning in 1861 the Civil War. The *Central America* was forgotten.

Or was it?

THE RECOVERY OF THE *CENTRAL AMERICA*

Generations later, in the 1980s, a group of investors formed after researchers learned of the long-lost wreck. Using old maps, news reports, survivors' accounts, and other information they pieced together a grid off the coast of North Carolina where the ship *might* be. Finally, in 1987, after several years of study and exploration, a likely wreck was found 7,200 feet below the surface and artifacts were recovered by a submersible robotic vessel. These included lumps of coal and, marvelously, the *Central America*'s bell lettered with the name of the Morgan Iron Works, the maker of the vessel.

Next came the recovery of coins and ingots from the briny deep. The announcement of the find in September 1989 caused excitement in the popular press as well as among coin collectors.

A television commentator speculated that perhaps a billion dollars in gold had been found. This news attracted a swarm of claimants who stated that they had a stake in the treasure one way or another, including as successors to the original insurers. Litigation was finally resolved in the late 1990s.

Treasure on the sea floor.

The Ship of Gold exhibit—a representation of the side of the *Central America*, with "portholes" through which some of the recovered treasure could be seen—made its debut at the 2000 convention of the American Numismatic Association, in Philadelphia. Nearby was a re-creation of the Kellogg & Humbert Assay Office that in San Francisco in 1857 had made most of the treasure's gold ingots. The exhibit drew a record 20,000 visitors. A theater program by scientist Bob Evans, who conserved the ship's treasure, and numismatic historian Q. David Bowers filled the room with 400 people, also a record.

A marketing program got underway with brochures and other publicity. Bowers created a 1,056-page book, *A California Gold Rush History Featuring Treasure from the S.S. Central America*. Soon hundreds of gold ingots and thousands of coins (including more than 5,500 Mint State 1857-S double eagles) were sold.

Recovered coins and ingots on display.

FURTHER EXPLORATION— AND A DISCOVERY OF DIMES

In 2014 a second visit was made to the site of the wreck. During this time there were 14 dives by a new robotic device, the longest lasting more than 83 hours. This included investigation of the southern debris field slightly away from the ship.

Although the 2014 find did not match the first recovery, it was significant. There were 45 gold ingots. An early inventory of the double eagles gives another snapshot of its scope:

1850 (14), 1850-O (2), 1851 (10), 1851-O (2), 1852 (22), 1852-O, 1853 (14), 1854 (12), 1854-S, 1855 (4), 1855-S (86), 1856-S (304), 1857, and 1857-S (1,153).

The Ship of Gold exhibit.

Important to the present narrative, and with no counterpart in the first salvage effort, was the discovery of more than 9,600 silver dimes. These were found in the purser's safe. A quantity of small change such as this would been used on the 44 trips of the *Central America* as money to buy drinks, food, and services, each coin being worth $2 or more in terms of today's value. They dated back to the denomination's first year of issue, 1796!

Among this accumulation, early dimes of the Draped Bust type are well worn, the later (1809 to 1837) Capped Bust coins are less so, and some of the Liberty Seated dimes of the 1850s remain in Gem Mint State. Many of the earlier dimes show sea etching, described as "saltwater effect" (that wording added to the numerical grade when the coins were professionally certified and slabbed).

As this edition of *Mega Red*, with its expanded focus on U.S. dimes, goes to press, the dimes of the *Central America* are being cataloged and conserved. "This is one of the greatest 'dime stories' ever," said Q. David Bowers of the discovery, "a time capsule of what coins were in circulation in 1857."

A snapshot of a few of the more than 9,600 dimes awaiting conservation by Bob Evans. Some of the later dates are gems.

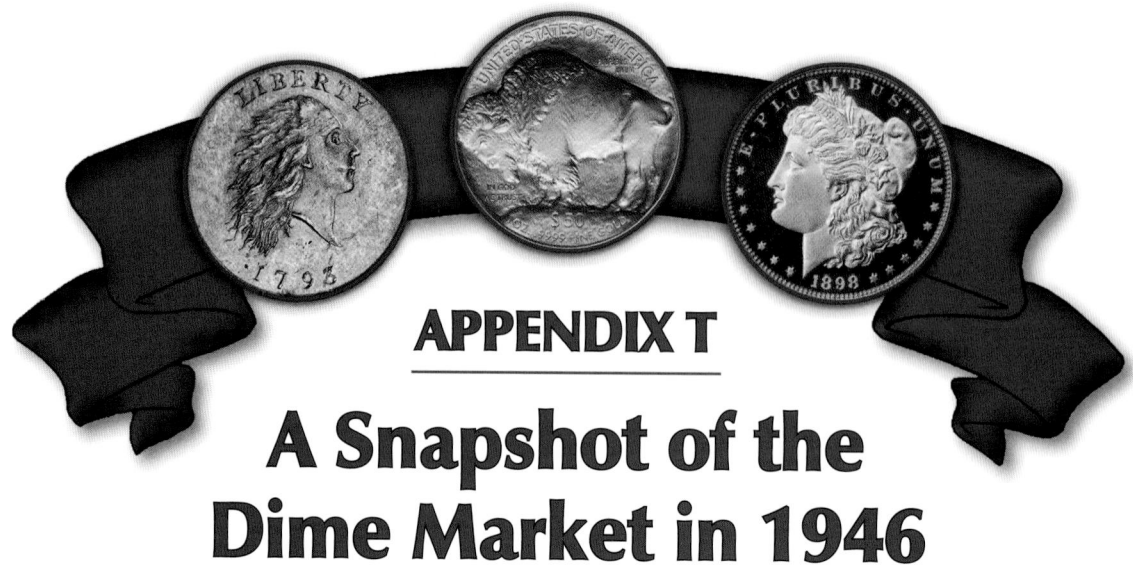

APPENDIX T

A Snapshot of the Dime Market in 1946

The first print run of the *Guide Book of United States Coins* debuted in November 1946. Its initial 9,000 copies sold out so quickly that another 9,000 were printed in February 1947. By 1959 coin collectors were buying more than 100,000 copies annually. The 1965 (18th) edition, published in 1964, reached a peak of 1,200,000 copies. By then the "Red Book" was the most popular annual price guide in the hobby —a distinction it holds to this day.

The following pages from the first edition of the Red Book offer an interesting snapshot of the retail market for dimes from more than 70 years ago. They cover the first 150 years of the denomination, from 1796 to 1946, including the then very recent debut of the Roosevelt dime. They also illustrate how numismatics is a continuously evolving science and hobby. Ongoing research can change the way collectors understand and appreciate coins. Die varieties at the time were not as widely collected as they are today: overdates, repunched mintmarks, doubled dies, and other varieties, covered in detail in today's Red Book, were yet to be popularized in the late 1940s. The design variations of early coins, such as the number of stars (obverse) or berries (reverse) on Draped Bust dimes, were not yet spelled out. And dimes before the Liberty Seated type were listed all together, instead of being further categorized as Draped Bust and Capped Bust, with Small Eagle Reverse, Heraldic Eagle Reverse, Wide Border, Modified Design, and other finely tuned identifiers.

Studying old editions of the Red Book offers a wealth of insight and valuable perspective for today's savvy numismatist.

Examining a press sheet of Red Book pages in 1960: production manager Pete Foerster (left); assistant editor Kenneth Bressett, who would later become editor, then senior editor, and now editor emeritus (middle); and author R.S. Yeoman.

HALF DIMES

Mint Mark Within Wreath, Reverse Side.	Mint Mark Below Wreath, Reverse Side.		
	Fine	Unc.	Proof
1872S Mint Mark within Wreath............	$ .75	$3.50	
1872S Mint Mark below Wreath	1.00	3.75	
1873..	.60	2.00	$6.50
1873S.......................................	1.00	3.00	

BIBLIOGRAPHY

Newlin, H. P., Early Half Dimes. 1883.
Valentine, D. W., U. S. Half Dimes. 1931.

DIMES
1796 To Date

The designs of the dimes, first coined in 1796, follow closely those of the half-dimes up through the liberty seated type. The dimes in each instance weigh twice as much as the half-dimes.

	Good	Fine	Unc.
1796........	$17.50	$35.00	
1797 13 stars	22.50	65.00	
1797 16 stars	25.00	75.00	

	Good	Fine	Unc.
1798 over 97	12.50	30.00	
1798........	12.50	27.50	$50.00
1800........	15.00	27.50	85.00
1801........	17.50	60.00	
1802........	20.00	30.00	
1803........	20.00	45.00	
1804........	25.00	75.00	
1805........	4.00	12.00	30.00
1807........	4.00	12.00	25.00

[93]

Note: In the 1947 *Guide Book of United States Coins*, mintages were listed in the back of the book instead of alongside their coin listings in the main charts.

DIMES

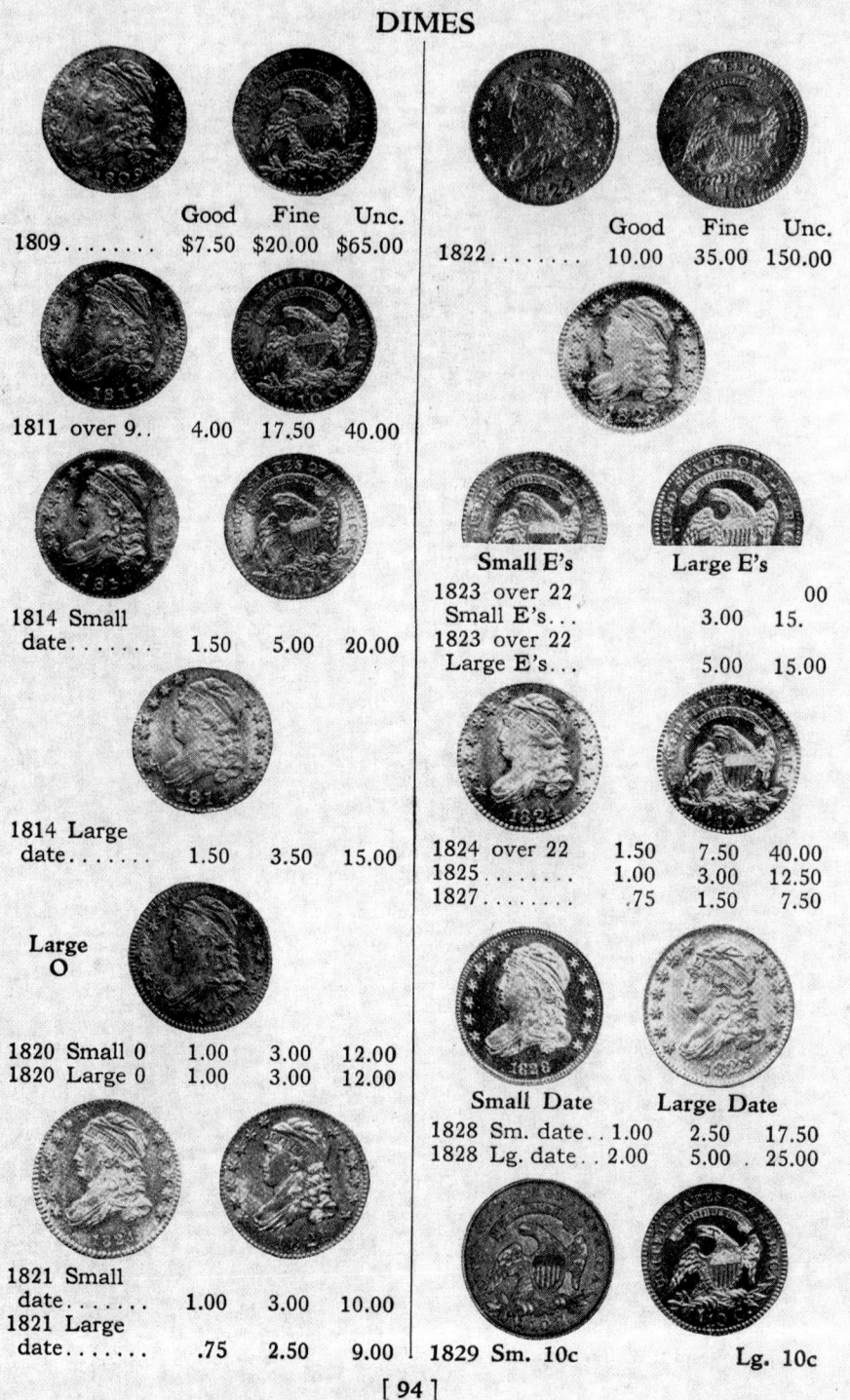

	Good	Fine	Unc.
1809.......	$7.50	$20.00	$65.00
1811 over 9..	4.00	17.50	40.00
1814 Small date......	1.50	5.00	20.00
1814 Large date......	1.50	3.50	15.00

Large O

1820 Small 0	1.00	3.00	12.00
1820 Large 0	1.00	3.00	12.00
1821 Small date.......	1.00	3.00	10.00
1821 Large date.......	.75	2.50	9.00

	Good	Fine	Unc.
1822.......	10.00	35.00	150.00

	Small E's	Large E's
1823 over 22 Small E's...		3.00	00 15.
1823 over 22 Large E's...		5.00	15.00

1824 over 22	1.50	7.50	40.00
1825........	1.00	3.00	12.50
1827........	.75	1.50	7.50

	Small Date	Large Date
1828 Sm. date..	1.00	2.50	17.50
1828 Lg. date..	2.00	5.00	25.00

1829 Sm. 10c   Lg. 10c

[94]

DIMES

	Fine	Unc.		Fine	Unc.
1829 Small 10¢	$1.50	$5.00	1840	2.50	7.00
1829 Large 10¢	2.50	12.50	1841	1.25	3.50
1830 Small 10¢	1.25	3.00	1841O	1.75	4.00
1830 Large 10¢	1.25	3.00	1842	1.25	3.50
1831 Small 10¢	1.25	3.00	1842O	1.50	3.50
1831 Large 10¢	1.25	3.00	1843	1.25	3.00
1832	1.25	3.00	1843O	5.50	12.50
1833	1.25	3.00	1844	10.00	50.00
1834 Small 4	1.25	3.00	1845	1.25	3.50
1834 Large 4	1.25	3.00	1845O	5.00	15.00
1835	1.00	2.75	1846	6.00	25.00
1836	1.25	3.50	1847	2.50	12.50
1837	1.25	3.50	1848	2.25	7.50
			1849	1.50	3.50

LIBERTY SEATED TYPE

	Fine	Unc.
1849O	1.75	6.00
1850	1.25	3.00
1850O	2.50	8.50
1851	1.00	2.75
1851O	1.50	3.50
1852	1.00	3.00
1852O	1.50	4.00
1853	4.00	11.00

No Drapery From Elbow
No Stars On Obverse

	Fine	Unc.
1837 Small date	4.00	15.00
1837 Large date	3.00	12.50
1838O	6.00	15.00

No Drapery From Elbow
With Stars On Obverse

	Fine	Unc.
1838	1.25	4.00
1839	1.25	4.00
1839O	1.25	4.00
1840	1.75	5.00
1840O	1.75	7.50
1841	50.00	150.00

Arrows At Date
(See Half Dimes 1853 for Explanation)

	Fine	Unc.	Proof
1853	$.50	$1.75	
1853O	2.25	5.00	
1854	.60	2.50	
1854O	.75	2.25	
1855	.75	3.00	27.50

Drapery From Elbow

Showing Drapery From Elbow
(Enlarged)

Small Date, Arrows Removed

	Fine	Unc.	
1856	.75	3.00	30.00
1856O	1.50	4.00	
1856S	17.50	75.00	
1856 Large date	2.00	6.00	
1857	.75	2.50	20.00
1857O	1.00	3.00	

[95]

DIMES

	Fine	Unc.	Proof
1858	$.75	$2.50	$17.50
1858O	1.25	4.00	
1858S	11.00	35.00	
1859	.65	2.50	9.00
1859O	.85	3.00	
1859S	12.50	30.00	

1860 With Stars, S Mint

	Fine	Unc.
1860S	4.00	15.00

Obverse of 1859   Reverse of 1860

1859		175.00

Legend Replaces Stars

	Fine	Unc.	Proof
1860	1.25	3.00	7.50
1860O	50.00	200.00	
1861	1.50	3.50	9.00
1861S	5.50	22.50	
1862	1.00	2.00	6.50
1862S	5.00	22.50	
1863	1.00	2.50	6.50
1863S	3.50	20.00	
1864	1.50	5.00	8.50
1864S	3.50	20.00	
1865	1.50	5.00	9.00
1865S	3.50	20.00	
1866	1.00	3.50	6.50
1866S	3.75	20.00	
1867	1.00	3.50	6.50
1867S	3.50	20.00	
1868	1.00	3.00	4.50
1868S	3.00	9.00	

	Fine	Unc.	Proof
1869	1.00	3.00	5.00
1869S	2.25	7.50	
1870	.75	2.50	4.50
1870S	22.50	65.00	
1871	.75	2.50	4.50
1871S	6.00	20.00	
1871CC	50.00	185.00	
1872	.75	2.00	4.50
1872S	6.00	20.00	
1872CC	35.00	110.00	
1873	.75	2.50	5.00
1873CC	———	———	

Arrows At Date

In 1873 the dime was slightly increased in weight to 38.58 grains. Arrows at the date in 1873 and 1874 indicate this change.

	Fine	Unc.	Proof
1873	.75	3.25	7.50
1873S	6.00	25.00	
1873CC	150.00	350.00	
1874	.75	2.00	4.00
1874S	9.00	30.00	
1874CC	50.00	175.00	

Arrows At Date Removed

	Fine	Unc.	Proof
1875	.50	1.50	4.50
1875S under wreath	.50	2.00	
1875S in wreath	.50	2.00	
1875CC under wreath	.65	1.50	
1875CC in wreath	.65	1.50	
1876	.50	1.25	4.00
1876S	.75	1.50	
1876CC	.75	2.50	
1877	.50	1.50	4.00
1877S	.65	1.50	
1877CC	.75	2.25	
1878	.50	1.50	4.50
1878CC	5.50	13.50	

[96]

DIMES

	Fine	Unc.	Proof		Fine	Unc.	Proof
1879	$.50	$1.25	$4.00	1897O	3.50	20.00	
1880	.50	1.25	3.50	1897S	2.00	12.50	
1881	.50	1.50	3.50	1898	.75	2.25	4.00
1882	.50	1.50	3.00	1898O	2.25	13.50	
1883	.50	1.50	3.00	1898S	2.25	12.50	
1884	.50	1.50	3.50	1899	.75	2.25	4.00
1884S	5.00	17.50		1899O	1.50	12.50	
1885	.50	1.50	3.00	1899S	2.25	12.50	
1885S	30.00	80.00		1900	.75	2.25	4.00
1886	.50	1.50	3.00	1900O	2.00	12.50	
1886S	1.00	4.50		1900S	2.25	12.50	
1887	.50	1.50	3.00	1901	.75	2.50	4.00
1887S	.75	3.25		1901O	1.50	8.50	
1888	.50	1.50	2.75	1901S	3.00	27.50	
1888S	.75	2.25		1902	.50	2.00	4.00
1889	.50	1.50	3.00	1902O	1.00	10.00	
1889S	2.50	5.50		1902S	2.00	15.00	
1890	.50	1.50	3.00	1903	.50	2.00	4.00
1890S	.50	2.00		1903O	1.00	6.00	
1891	.50	1.50	3.00	1903S	2.50	12.50	
1891O	1.25	5.50		1904	.50	2.00	4.00
1891S	.50	2.50		1904S	2.50	12.50	
				1905	.50	2.00	4.00
				1905O	1.00	3.25	
				1905S	.75	4.00	
				1906	.50	2.00	4.00
				1906D	.50	2.25	
				1906O	.75	2.50	
				1906S	1.00	4.00	
				1907	.50	2.25	4.00
				1907D	.75	2.75	
				1907O	.50	2.25	
				1907S	.75	4.00	
				1908	.50	2.25	4.00
				1908D	.50	2.25	
				1908O	1.00	3.50	
				1908S	1.00	3.50	
				1909	.50	2.00	4.00

Barber, Liberty Head or "Morgan" Type

Although this type dime is usually referred to as the "Morgan Dime" it was designed by Charles E. Barber who was Chief Engraver of the Mint.

	Fine	Unc.	Proof		Fine	Unc.	Proof
1892	.75	2.50	4.50	1909D	1.00	2.75	
1892O	1.50	6.00		1909O	.75	3.00	
1892S	3.50	12.50		1909S	1.00	4.00	
1893	.75	2.50	4.50	1910	.50	2.00	4.00
1893O	2.00	4.00		1910D	.75	2.25	
1893S	2.00	8.50		1910S	1.00	4.00	
1894	1.50	3.50	6.00	1911	.50	2.00	4.00
1894O	5.00	9.00		1911D	.75	2.75	
1894S		2000.00		1911S	1.00	3.75	
1895	3.50	5.50	10.00	1912	.50	2.00	4.50
1895O	12.50	30.00		1912D	.50	2.25	
1895S	2.50	17.50		1912S	1.00	4.00	
1896	.75	2.75	4.50	1913	.75	2.50	6.00
1896O	3.50	7.50		1913S	2.25	16.00	
1896S	4.00	18.50		1914	.50	3.25	8.50
1897	.75	2.25	4.00	1914D	.50	2.00	

[97]

DIMES

	Fine	Unc.	Proof
1914S......	$.75	$6.00	
1915........	.75	3.00	$12.00
1915S......	1.00	5.25	
1916........	.50	2.00	
1916S......	.50	2.00	

Winged Head Liberty or "Mercury" Type

This dime was designed by A. A. Weinman. Although it is commonly called the "Mercury Dime" the main device is in fact a representation of Liberty. The wings crowning her cap are intended to symbolize liberty of thought. The fasces and olive branch on the reverse are intended to symbolize strength of unity in peace. The battle-ax stands for preparedness.

	Fine	Unc.	Proof
1916........	$.50	$1.50	
1916D......	17.50	65.00	
1916S......	.50	2.00	
1917........	.50	1.50	
1917D......	1.00	5.00	
1917S......	.50	2.00	
1918........	.50	3.50	
1918D......	1.00	5.00	
1918S......	.85	3.50	
1919........	.50	3.25	
1919D......	.85	4.00	
1919S......	.85	3.25	
1920........	.50	3.25	
1920D......	.85	4.00	
1920S......	.75	3.00	
1921........	5.00	37.50	
1921D......	2.00	6.50	
1923........	.50	2.75	
1923S......	1.10	5.25	
1924........	.50	3.00	
1924D......	.75	3.50	
1924S......	.75	3.50	
1925........	.50	1.75	
1925D......	1.00	5.00	
1925S......	.75	3.50	

	Fine	Unc.	Proof
1926........	.50	2.50	
1926D......	1.00	4.75	
1926S......	2.00	7.50	
1927........	.50	2.00	
1927D......	2.50	15.00	
1927S......	.75	5.00	
1928........	.50	1.50	
1928D......	.75	3.25	
1928S......	.75	4.00	
1929........	.25	.75	
1929D......	.50	1.75	
1929S......	.50	1.75	
1930........	.35	1.00	
1930S......	.50	1.50	
1931........	.35	1.25	
1931D......	.50	1.75	
1931S......	.50	1.75	
1934........	.25	.75	
1934D......	.25	1.00	
1935........	.25	.75	
1935D......	.25	1.00	
1935S......	.25	1.00	
1936........		.50	$11.00
1936D......		.65	
1936S......		.75	
1937........		.50	4.25
1937D......		.50	
1937S......		.75	
1938........		.50	3.00
1938D......		.50	
1938S......		.65	
1939........		.35	2.50
1939D......		.35	
1939S......		.60	
1940........		.35	2.00
1940D......		.35	
1940S......		.35	
1941........		.35	1.50
1941D......		.35	
1941S......		.35	
1942 over 41	$4.50		
1942........		.25	1.25
1942D......		.25	
1942S......		.25	
1943........		.25	
1943D......		.25	
1943S......		.25	
1944........		.25	
1944D......		.25	
1944S......		.25	
1945........		.25	
1945D......		.25	
1945S......		.25	

[98]

DIMES
Roosevelt Type

	Fine	Unc.	Proof		Fine	Unc.	Proof
1946.......		$ .20		1947.......		$ .20	
1946D......		.20		1947D......		.20	
1946S.......		.20		1947S.......		.20	

ORPHAN ANNIE DIME

The record shows that 72,500 dimes were minted in 1844. For some mysterious reason very few of these dimes are still available, and old collectors state that they have been a scarce item back as far as can be remembered. The dimes of 1846 for instance are much more plentiful though less than half as many were struck.

Many explanations have been advanced, but none have been proved. Among the popular theories and legends are the following:

Melted by the government.

Melted by speculators, because their bullion value exceeded their monetary value.

50,000 of the dimes were lost at sea en route to New Orleans.

A great quantity were destroyed in the great Chicago fire, or the Johnstown flood.

During the Mexican War our soldiers were paid off in 1844 dimes, and the coins remained in Mexico.

70,000 dimes of 1844 were sent overland to the forty-niners in California, but before reaching destination via the Santa Fe trail they were seized by bandits who cached them. The bandits who were later killed carried the secret of the hiding place to their shallow graves.

TWENTY-CENT PIECES
1875 - 1878

This short-lived coin was authorized by the Act of March 3, 1875. Soon after the appearance of the first twenty-cent pieces, the people complained about the similarity in design and size with the quarter-dollar. The eagle is very similar to that used on the Trade Dollar. The edge of the coin is plain.

	Fine	Unc.	Proof		Fine	Unc.	Proof
1875........	$2.75	$7.50	$15.00	1876CC.....		1500.00	
1875S	1.75	4.00		1877........			32.50
1875CC.....	4.00	17.50		1878........			30.00
1876........	4.00	8.50	17.50				

[99]

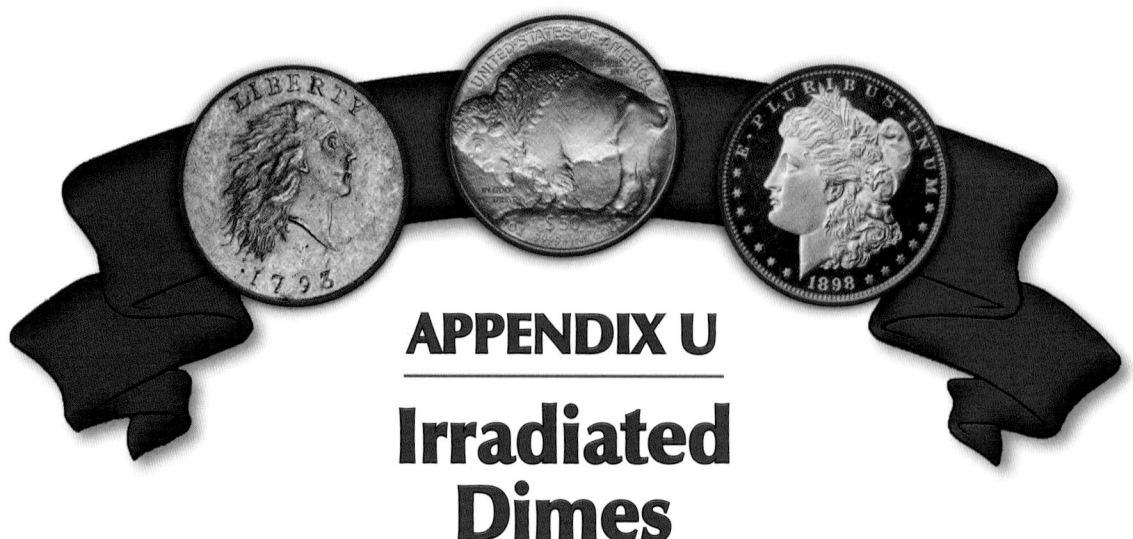

APPENDIX U

Irradiated Dimes

When the coin market is on an upswing, many coins are advertised as being hot. Here is one that you don't want to be hot in any market—up, down, or steady!

If you are an older reader you may remember the time in the 1940s, 1950s, and even into the 1960s when shoe stores had fluoroscope machines. You put your feet into the opening in the bottom of the case, and at the top you looked through a glass to see the skeletal bones of your feet. You could wiggle your toes and see them move. Viewing scopes on the sides allowed your parent or a sales clerk to also observe your feet and how they fit in your shoes.

In a related vein, opening in 1949 at the Oak Ridge National Laboratory in Tennessee, as part of an exhibit on atomic energy, visitors could obtain dimes that had been irradiated in an isotope cabinet (not a nuclear reactor) and placed in souvenir holders. The focus was not on atomic warfare, but the use of radionuclides in medicine—which led to many advances. Visitors could see the Oak Ridge Graphite Reactor and insert the dime of their choice to be irradiated. This scientific display was in operation well into the 1960s and more than a million dimes were treated by the time the opportunity was eliminated.

Related machines traveled about and were set up at some fairs and expositions. Patrons were told that the radiation disappeared within a few minutes. In 1954 a news release seemed to be a bit more scary:

> Visitors to the Atomic Energy Exhibit learn how radioisotopes are produced by inserting an ordinary dime into a scale model of an atomic pile. The dime is irradiated by neutron bombardment within the model, and some of the normal silver in the coin is converted into silver-110, a radioactive isotope of silver.
>
> The irradiated dime, which is harmless, in then encased in an aluminum and Lucite holder as a souvenir.

The copper-nickel dimes first made in 1965 held the radiation longer and were a reason for their discontinuance.

Irradiated dimes are seen frequently on the Internet and at coin shows today. Most commentary in modern times takes the position that these dimes do not and never did produce a health hazard. Given the lingering pop-culture fear of radiation, however, some collectors will always feel nervous around these fascinating little mementoes of the Atomic Age.

A GALLERY OF IRRADIATED DIMES

An unusually old dime in an irradiated Oak Ridge National Laboratory case. Most such coins date from the 1940s, 1950s, and early 1960s.

The American Museum of Atomic Energy opened in 1949 in a wartime cafeteria on Jefferson Circle in Oak Ridge, Tennessee. It moved to its current facility on Tulane Avenue in 1975 and was renamed the American Museum of Science & Energy in 1978. It is an affiliate of the Smithsonian Institution.

The dimes are nearly always found encased with their obverse exposed, so any mintmarks are hidden. This 1940 dime might have been minted in Philadelphia, Denver, or San Francisco.

A 1941 Mercury dime.

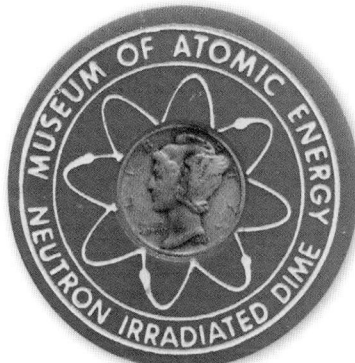

Dimes can also be found in later-issued blue plastic holders from the museum.

A 1944 Mercury dime.

A 1945 Mercury dime.

Cases are sometimes seen without dimes. This illustrates the possibility that an encased dime isn't guaranteed to have been irradiated, but may have been inserted later, after the original dime was spent or lost.

A 1946 Roosevelt dime—from the type's first year of issue— and a view of the back of the typical aluminum encasement. (shown enlarged)

The New York World's Fair of 1964–1965 featured an educational
exhibit on the beneficial uses of atomic energy.

A selection of silver Roosevelt dimes.

A variation with
"UCNC," referring to the
Union Carbide Nuclear
Company. 1959
Roosevelt dime.

Most irradiated dimes date
from the era of silver coinage
(pre-1965). This example, a
1966 Roosevelt dime, is made
of copper-nickel–clad copper.

Occasionally the dimes are found
with their reverses exposed
and their dates hidden.

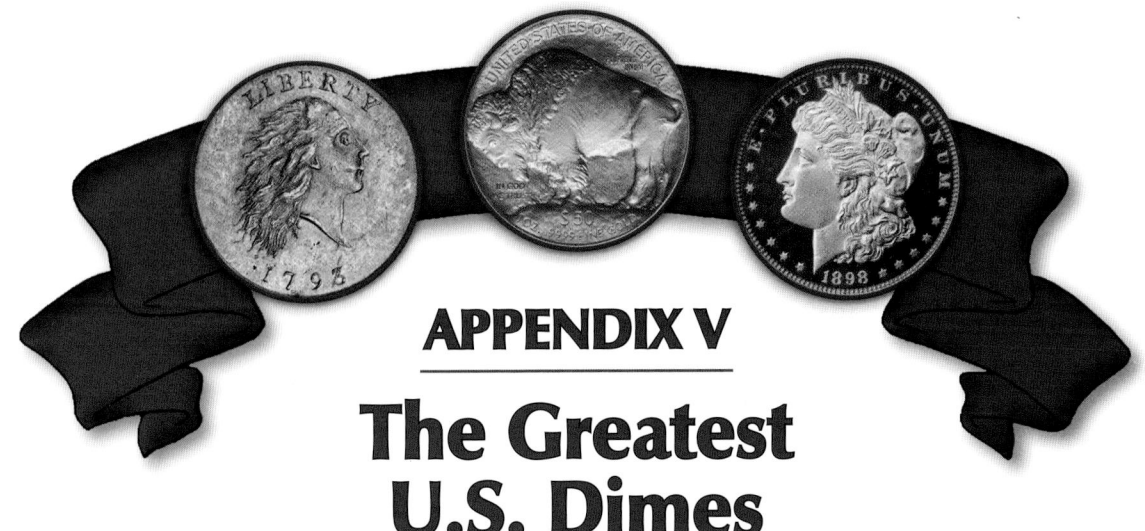

APPENDIX V

The Greatest U.S. Dimes

This appendix is based on the work of Jeff Garrett (with Ron Guth)
from **100 Greatest U.S. Coins,** *fourth edition, and of Garrett and*
Scott Schechter from **100 Greatest U.S. Modern Coins,** *fourth edition.*

Numismatic greatness is subjective. Much of greatness depends on personal tastes and preferences. However, greatness also depends on objective factors, characteristics that can be measured against each other and from one coin to another. There are several dimes ranked among the *100 Greatest U.S. Coins* and *100 Greatest U.S. Modern Coins.* They all have at least one of the following characteristics:

Rarity—Great coins are rare, meaning that only a few were made or, in some instances, only a few survived. Many of the coins in the 100 Greatest lists are unique; others are so rare that they are almost impossible to obtain because they come to market so infrequently. However, others are rare only in the context of their series, and for some "popular rarities," such as the 1916-D Mercury dime, thousands survive.

Value—Great coins are generally expensive, but not necessarily so. The 1916-D Mercury dime (available in Choice Uncirculated condition for $20,000 or less) ranks just ahead of the $5,000,000 Choice Proof 1804 "Plain 4" Capped Bust gold eagle in the 100 Greatest list!

Quality—Great coins are usually in exceptional condition. However, high quality does not necessarily mean perfection. For example, the finest 1802 half dime is only About Uncirculated.

Popularity—Great coins are appreciated by a large audience. Some coins may be rare and valuable, but the voting for the *100 Greatest U.S. Coins* resembled a popularity contest at times! Why else would the 1909-S V.D.B. cent, of which thousands exist, rank higher on the list (No. 23) than the unique 1873-CC No Arrows Liberty Seated dime (No. 65)?

Beauty—Great coins are aesthetically pleasing. For example, part of the allure of the 1872 Amazonian gold pattern set (No. 14) is the sheer beauty and uniformity of the designs and the soft, mellow color of the gold in which they were struck.

History—Great coins have a story to tell. Who can resist the incredible story of the 1804 silver dollars, how they were first made in 1834, how some of them traveled from the Far East to Europe and back to America? Or the fascinating history behind the 1792 silver-center cent and how the early Mint worked so hard to produce new coins for a new country? These stories and many more are at the heart of why most of the *100 Greatest U.S. Coins,* and those among the *100 Greatest U.S. Modern Coins,* made their lists. Not all are among the rarest coins, but each captures the imagination.

THE 1894-S BARBER DIME

1894-S Barber dime.

Ranked number 7 in the fourth edition of *100 Greatest U.S. Coins*, the 1894-S dime is one of the most famous American rarities. While several coins are rarer or more valuable than the 1894-S dime, few come with the wonderful stories and intrigue that surround this coin.

The general consensus is that 24 1894-S dimes were struck. Early explanations of the mintage figure claimed that the 24 coins were made to round out an accounting entry. However, the figure needed was $.40, not $2.40, and the fact that most surviving 1894-S dimes are prooflike in appearance tends to refute that theory—such special coins would never have been necessary to accomplish such a mundane task. In recent years there has been a debate whether the known coins are indeed merely prooflike (with mirror surfaces, but not struck from Proof dies) or actual Proofs. The highest-grade coins known for the issue appear to be Proofs, in the opinion of researchers Jeff Garrett and Ron Guth, who also note that it is only about this time that collecting coins by mintmark became fashionable.

Later research revealed that the Mint superintendent at San Francisco in 1894, John Daggett, had the coins struck at the special request of banker friends. Of the 24 coins, three went to his young daughter, Hallie, whom he instructed to preserve them carefully until she was older, at which time the coins would be worth a lot of money. Being a typical child, Hallie immediately used one of the 1894-S dimes to purchase ice cream. She clung to the other two, and 60 years later, in 1954, she sold her remaining pair to a California dealer.

No other Barber coin comes even remotely close to the rarity of the 1894-S dime. Of the original 24, only 9 have been positively traced. Two were pulled from circulation (one of them now known appropriately as Hallie Daggett's "Ice Cream Specimen") while the others are Proof or prooflike coins in varying degrees of preservation, ranging from impaired to gem. This raises the tantalizing question, "Where are the remaining 1894-S dimes?" One would think that with all the publicity surrounding this coin, not to mention their ever-increasing value, other examples would have surfaced. The actual mintage may be more on the order of 10 or 15 pieces, opine Garrett and Guth, making the 1894-S dime approximately twice as rare as is currently believed and putting it on par with the 1804 silver dollar.

For decades, the 1894-S dime has been included along with the 1913 Liberty Head nickel and the 1804 silver dollar in a triumvirate of America's most desirable coins. It was one of the first coins to cross the $100,000 price barrier, and today the finest examples are approaching the $2,000,000 mark.

John Daggett was right: the 1894-S dime has become a very valuable coin!

THE 1792 DISME

1792 disme.

Not technically among the regular series of U.S. dimes, the 1792 disme is part of a series of extremely rare patterns struck at the Philadelphia Mint, or in private facilities nearby, in anticipation of full production of coins in 1793. Fewer than 20 of the 1792 dismes are known, most made of copper and only two or three made of silver.

The designs and legends on the 1792 disme are nearly identical to those on the 1792 half disme. The major difference between the two is the style of Miss Liberty's portrait. Interestingly enough, the head on the 1792 disme is very similar to that on the 1793 half cent, perhaps indicating that the same artist had his hand in all three of these coins. Unfortunately, this design was never used for a dime. In fact, no dimes were made until 1796, by which time a new engraver had been hired to create a completely different design. Thus, most collectors have never seen an example of the 1792 disme other than as a picture in a reference book.

Most known examples have diagonally reeded edges, although at least two examples are known with a plain edge. The purpose of edge reeding was to prevent clipping (shaving or cutting on the edges to remove small amounts of silver), which, done enough times on enough coins, could add up to a significant amount of value.

Collecting early U.S. coinage is once again becoming very popular, as it is now realized that many of these fascinating issues are closely related to the creation of this great nation. In fact, many of our founding fathers were personally involved with the production of these coins. Many members of the House of Representatives wanted the portrait of President George Washington on the obverse of the coinage. Washington is believed to have felt this was too closely tied to monarchical practice and disapproved of the idea.

The 1792 disme was ranked number 20 in the fourth edition of *100 Greatest U.S. Coins.*

THE 1873-CC NO ARROWS LIBERTY SEATED DIME

1873-CC No Arrows Liberty Seated dime.

Ranked number 65 in the fourth edition of *100 Greatest U.S. Coins,* the 1873-CC No Arrows Liberty Seated dime is a unique coin—only one example is known to exist. Although Mint records indicate a mintage of 12,400 pieces, all were presumed melted in mid-1873 and were most likely turned into dimes with arrowheads on either side of the date (indicating a slight change in the weight of the coins). The sole survivor is a coin sent to Philadelphia in 1873 to be evaluated by the annually convened U.S. Assay Commission. For some unexplained reason, the coin was saved from destruction and added to the

National Numismatic Collection (then known as the Mint Cabinet). Once there, it disappeared from memory until it resurfaced in 1909 as part of the biggest coin trade ever to take place!

In 1909, future secretary of the Treasury William Woodin purchased a pair of gold $50 patterns from dealers Stephen Nagy and John Haseltine. The transaction created a furor at the Mint, which claimed that the unique patterns were its property. To reverse the transaction, the Mint swapped crates of rare coins and patterns for the two $50 gold pieces. Included in the trade was the unique 1873-CC No Arrows dime. It was exhibited at the 1914 American Numismatic Society exhibit and over the next several decades passed hands among a few prominent collectors.

The rarity was offered at auction as part of the Adolph Menjou Collection in 1950 by Abe Kosoff. Although Louis Eliasberg had traveled from Baltimore to purchase the coin, he was denied by dealer Jim Kelly, who took down the coin with a winning bid of $3,650. Kelly must have been buying on speculation, as Eliasberg purchased the 1873-CC No Arrows dime later that year, on November 7, 1950. It was the last piece he needed to complete his collection of U.S. coins.

The silver coins from Eliasberg's collection were sold 46 years later, and his 1873-CC No Arrows dime fetched $550,000. Since then, the coin reappeared at auction in 2004, selling for $891,250; and again in 2012 for $1,840,000.

Today the importance of the 1873-CC No Arrows Liberty Seated dime is quite apparent, but that has not always been the case. It must be remembered that early collectors of U.S. coinage paid very little attention to mintmarks. It was not until the 1950s that the true rarity of this great coin was really known.

THE 1916-D MERCURY DIME

1916-D Mercury dime.

Although the 1916-D dime is no great rarity, it remains one of the most popular coins of the 20th century, thus warranting inclusion among the *100 Greatest U.S. Coins*, where it ranked number 68 in the fourth edition.

The story of the 1916-D dime began more than a decade earlier, when President Theodore Roosevelt ordered the redesign of all U.S. coins. Gold coins underwent facelifts in 1907 and 1908, the cent in 1909, and the nickel in 1913. The dime, quarter dollar, and half dollar were forced to wait until 1916 because a law required coin designs to be in place for 25 years before they could be changed.

Adolph A. Weinman was chosen to redesign the dime and half dollar. For the dime, Weinman chose a head of Liberty wearing a winged cap. The artist intended for the wings to represent freedom of thought, but because so many people confused the image with the Roman messenger-god, Mercury, the coin became known popularly as the Mercury dime. In keeping with tradition, the Philadelphia Mint bore the brunt of dime production in 1916, followed closely by the San Francisco Mint. The third mint, at Denver, was hardly a factor in 1916, producing only 264,000 dimes, barely one hundredth of the dimes produced at Philadelphia. This tiny mintage was to be the lowest of any Mercury Head dime produced from the beginning of the series in 1916 until the demise of the design in 1945.

Thus, it is easy to understand why this date has become so popular with collectors; every school-kid in the United States needed the date to complete a set. Even when silver coins were still in circulation, the 1916-D dime seemed to be the one date that could not be found in loose change. Nevertheless, most 1916-D dimes known today are well-worn, indicating that the scarcity of this date was not initially recognized. Indeed, finding a nice Very Fine or better example is difficult (and expensive).

It should also be noted that the 1916-D Mercury dime is one of the most counterfeited of all U.S. coins. Thousands of Philadelphia issues have been altered by adding the "D" mintmark to the reverse. It is highly recommended to only buy certified coins of this issue.

THE 1975-S, NO S, ROOSEVELT DIME, PROOF

1975-S, No S, Roosevelt dime, Proof.

In *100 Greatest U.S. Modern Coins*, authors Scott Schechter and Jeff Garrett start the "modern" era in 1964. The first dime to make their list in the fourth edition of the book is ranked all the way at the top. Number 1 is the 1975-S Proof Roosevelt dime minted without an S mintmark.

Since 1968, all regular Proof coinage has been struck at the San Francisco Mint and bears an S mintmark to denote the mint of origin. However, several times dies made in Philadelphia were shipped to San Francisco without the mark. These dies produced the now highly coveted No S Proof coins. This happened during the first year of production, in 1968, when Proof No S dimes were produced. The same mistake was repeated in 1970. In 1971, Proof No S nickels were coined. And then there was a lull in No S production.

But in 1975, an anonymous California collector who had purchased five Proof sets from the Mint made a lucky discovery: two of his sets contained Proof Roosevelt dimes without a mintmark. In 1977, the collector sent his discovery sets to *Coin World* for independent confirmation and to announce the discovery. The dimes were also independently certified at that time.

The collector eventually sold both sets to Fred J. Vollmer, a dealer based in Bloomington, Illinois, who specialized in Proof sets. In 1978 he sold the first of the sets containing a 1975, No S, dime to a collector in Ohio for $18,200. In 1979, during a coin-market boom, Vollmer offered the second set for $38,550. Remarkably, since the sale of those two pieces, no further 1975, No S, dimes have surfaced.

Collectors and dealers have always had a great incentive to examine their 1975 Proof sets for No S dimes. In 1975 a total of 2,845,450 Proof sets were sold, and looking for a No S dime is something like searching for a needle in a haystack. But why have no more been found? The most popular theory is that inspectors at the San Francisco Mint noticed the error and destroyed what coins they could, allowing only two or so to be released.

In the intervening decades, the status of the famed 1975, No S, dime was called into question. It may even have added to its mystique that this coin was excluded from the first edition of *100 Greatest U.S. Modern Coins*, being mentioned only in the description of the more common 1970, No S, dime: "If it does exist, the 1975, No S, dime is one of the great rarities of the 20th century and will assume a vaunted position on the list of *100 Greatest U.S. Modern Coins*—likely the number one spot. But until it's confirmed, it remains off the list."

At last, after more than 30 years of absence, in 2011, Stack's Bowers announced that it would be offering at auction an example of the landmark rarity 1975, No S, Roosevelt dime. Wonderful reporting and research by *Coin World* told the story of Vollmer's sales in rich detail and identified this coin as the second example he sold. The first-ever auction appearance of a 1975, No S, dime occurred at the American Numismatic Association World's Fair of Money in Chicago on August 18, 2011. Its final price realized was the highest ever paid for a modern U.S. coin: $349,600!

THE 1964 SPECIAL MINT SET ROOSEVELT DIME

1964 Special Mint Set Roosevelt dime.

In 1993, an unusual set of coins appeared for auction in a sale conducted by the venerable coin auction house Stack's Rare Coins New York. They offered a set of specimen coinage dated 1964. Each of the five coins in the set—the cent, nickel, dime, quarter, and half dollar—had razor-sharp strikes. Rather than the deep, mirror-like surface seen on Proof coins, these coins had a satin sheen, possessing none of the reflectivity seen on Proof coinage. Swirling die polish was evident throughout the coins' fields, indicating that the dies that struck them had received special treatment. In fact, these coins looked nothing like other known coins dated 1964—they looked most similar to the Special Mint Set coins of 1965!

The obvious speculation was that these coins were produced as a trial version of the Special Mint Set coins that were to come in the following year. In 1965, circulating silver coinage was to be replaced with copper-nickel; to manage the metal transition, the Mint was forced to produce an unprecedented number of coins. To aid them in their task, two noteworthy accommodations were made. First, all coins were to be struck without mintmark, as it was widely believed that this measure would limit hoarding of coins by collectors and speculators. Second, no Proof coins were to be struck until enough coins could be produced to meet the requirements of circulation. In lieu of selling Proof and Mint sets, from 1965 to 1967 the Mint sold Special Mint Sets. The sets consisted of just five coins, all circulating denominations without mintmark. Each coin had a special finish, often described as falling somewhere between Proof and Mint State coins. The dies that struck the coins received additional polishing, but coins received only a single blow from the coinage die—true Proofs receive multiple strikes to more sharply impress the design. The issues of 1965 usually have a satin-like surface, but later issues from 1967 have a shallow, mirrored surface, more closely resembling Proofs. They are all readily distinguishable from circulation issues of the period and are available in high grades.

But there was no way to explain the existence of a 1964 Special Mint Set, as Proof coins were produced that year and no documentation concerning the creation of a 1964 Special Mint Set exists. Two theories predominate. The first is that there would have been a need to test the process of creating these Special Mint Set coins as a way of assessing their feasibility for production. To do this, a number of trial 1964 sets were made. Additionally, the examples that are known today are always found in high grade, a sign that they were preserved and maintained by their owners. That latter fact has led to a second possibility, that these coins were produced as special presentation sets, the last 90 percent silver coins. Whatever the case may be, either scenario contributes to their appeal.

Initially it was reported that 15 sets were produced in total, but as more 1964 Special Mint Set coinage appears, that figure has since been revised upwards to 50. They are still seldom offered, though. Their unique appearance, the clear attention to their production quality, and their mysterious origin make them among the most coveted of all U.S. coinage sets.

THE 1968-S, NO S, ROOSEVELT DIME, PROOF

1968-S, No S, Roosevelt dime, Proof.

While the United States transitioned from circulating silver to copper-nickel–clad coins between 1965 and 1967, no mintmarks appeared on U.S. coinage. Mint officials and politicians blamed the hoarding activities of collectors and speculators for coinage shortages around the nation. It was thought that removal of these distinguishing marks, which indicated where a coin was made, would give the public fewer reasons to hoard, and coins would circulate more freely. Also at this time, and with a related rationale, no Proof sets or Mint sets were issued. Instead, only a simplified single release of Special Mint Sets having some prooflike characteristics was available to collectors.

Finally, in 1968, these dictums were lifted and the tradition of including mintmarks on coins and the production of Proof coinage both returned. From the time the first coins were issued in the United States until 1964, all presentation issues for sale to collectors had been made at the Mint in Philadelphia. The only noteworthy deviation from this had taken place from 1965 to 1967, when the production of Special Mint Set coinage occurred at San Francisco, but there was little fanfare or notice because these coins did not bear mintmarks. When Proof coinage returned, production remained in San Francisco and, for the first time, in 1968, Proof coins bore the S mintmark.

At some point during the production of 1968 Proof coinage, an unusual error occurred. Dimes were struck from an obverse die that lacked the S mintmark. It's easy to see how this error could have occurred. All dies are made at a single die shop in Philadelphia and then shipped to the branch mints where the dies are used in production. Coinage of this year was the first time that this missing-mintmark error could have occurred on a U.S. Proof coin because this was the first year that these coins had mintmarks.

The great irony of the 1968, No S, Proof dime is that it is missing the very feature that distinguishes 1968 Proof coinage from the Proof coinage of all previous years!

Any error in the manufacture of a Proof coin is noteworthy because of the considerable amount of special care that is taken in their production. Indeed, Proof-coinage errors are rare across the board. Proof coins missing their mintmark are an especially desirable category of coinage and they are aggressively sought after. They vary in their rarity, and the 1968, No S, dime is among the rarest. Even as late as 1988, noted historian Walter Breen knew of only six examples. Because of this, it is widely believed that the mistake was discovered by the Mint. Subsequently almost all the mintmark-less coins were pulled from release, and only a handful escaped. New estimates suggest that as many as two dozen examples are in collectors' hands.

This coin ranked at number 8 in the *100 Greatest U.S. Modern Coins*, fourth edition.

THE 1996-W ROOSEVELT DIME

1996-W Roosevelt Dime.

It may not always be recognized as an important milestone, but the United States has often observed the 50th anniversary of a coin's design. The best such example is, of course, the Lincoln cent. First issued in 1909, the Lincoln, Wheat Ears Reverse, cent got an update in 1959 on the occasion of its 50th anniversary. In that year, a reverse design featuring the Lincoln Memorial was first released. When the Lincoln cent had aged another 50 years, in 2009, it got another update, this time with four new reverse designs featuring snapshots of Lincoln's life.

The Roosevelt dime was similarly honored on the occasion of its 50th anniversary. First issued in 1946, the Roosevelt dime honored President Franklin Delano Roosevelt, who had died in 1945 while serving his fourth consecutive term as president. The dime was an especially fitting tribute to Roosevelt, as throughout his life he had been a leader of the March of Dimes' fundraising efforts to combat polio. Although originally issued in silver, the dime underwent no significant design changes throughout its entire 50 years of workman-like service. The only noteworthy design change was the movement of the mintmark to the coin's obverse in 1968.

In 1996, to celebrate the 50th anniversary of the Roosevelt dime, the West Point Mint was chosen to strike a special dime issue. The coin of course shows its usual austere design, except the W mintmark sits just above the numeral 6 in the date. It is the first "circulating" coin to bear the West Point mintmark. This coin was not released into circulation, but instead was included as part of the 1996 Mint set, the Uncirculated coinage set sold by the U.S. Mint. The only way to get this coin was as part of the Mint set. A total of 1,457,000 sets were sold, which is correspondingly also the mintage figure of the 1996-W Roosevelt dime.

This low mintage figure gives the 1996-W Roosevelt dime the lowest mintage of any Mint State Roosevelt, including the 1946 to 1964 silver issues. In fact, the so-called key date of the silver series, the 1949-S, has a mintage of more than 13 million pieces! But the 1996-W Roosevelt dime is an anomaly in many ways. It is the only coin struck in copper-nickel–clad composition to bear the W mintmark. All other coins with this mintmark are precious-metal coins struck in silver, gold, or platinum. It is one of only three commemorative issue dimes issued by the U.S. Mint, as it was joined in 2015 by two special Proof silver issues to celebrate the 75th anniversary of the March of Dimes.

THE 1982, NO MINTMARK, ROOSEVELT DIME

1982, No Mintmark, Roosevelt dime.

While, historically, coins made at the Philadelphia Mint did not have mintmarks, a change began in 1979.

When the newly issued Susan B. Anthony dollars came out that year, they all had a mintmark, including those struck at Philadelphia, which were branded with a P. In 1980 this practice extended to all coins except for the cent. Just two years after this practice began, the first inadvertent omission occurred. In 1982 an obverse die without a mintmark was put into use, creating the 1982, No Mintmark, dime.

Because dimes were struck for circulation at both Philadelphia and Denver, the missing mintmark could be either a P or a D. The uncertainty leads to the more general name *No Mintmark*. In the early 1980s, coinage hubs did not include mintmarks. All dies were made in Philadelphia, and mintmarks were added before the dies were put into use or shipped to a branch mint for use elsewhere. This by-hand process accounts for the variations in mark sizes, positioning, and, as in this case, omissions.

Overwhelming evidence, however, suggests that the coins were, in fact, struck in Philadelphia, and thus this variety is also called the 1982, No P, dime. Examples were first discovered in late 1982 in northern Ohio. A cache thought to number several thousand coins funneled from local banks through a coin shop in Toledo, Ohio, according to researcher and author Walter Breen. A subsequent discovery in Pennsylvania added a few thousand more coins to the total number available to collectors.

Numismatists distinguish between strong and weak varieties of the 1982, No Mintmark, dime. The strong is properly struck and essentially fully detailed. The weak variety shows soft detail and, diagnostically, the 2 in the date is indistinct and melds with the rim of the coin. The same dies were used to strike both varieties, and the weak is variously attributed by researchers to either misaligned dies or weak striking pressure. Even though it is less common than the strong variety, the weak trades for much less, and price guides usually report only the price for the strong. Grading services do distinguish between the varieties.

The number of 1982, No Mintmark, dimes produced is not known precisely. It is estimated that a single obverse dime die produces as many as 150,000 coins. Roughly 10,000 examples are known to collectors, a sizable percentage of the original mintage for a circulation-issue variety. No other mintmark omission of any kind occurred on a circulating coin until 2007, and during the 25-year interlude, the 1982, No Mintmark, dime grew in status. This coin is much sought after and especially elusive in high grades, making it a key to the long-running Roosevelt dime series.

THE 1983, NO S, ROOSEVELT DIME, PROOF

1983, No S, Roosevelt dime, Proof.

When this coin was first discovered in a Proof set in mid-1983, it was widely believed that it would be more common than it has ultimately proved to be. Since its initial discovery, only a few hundred examples have been found, certainly less than 400 in all. This figure makes it a bit scarcer than the 1970, No S, Roosevelt dime.

No S Proof coins are made when the S mintmark is omitted from the die. A number of steps are involved in the creation of Proof dies, during which they are inspected, or at least handled, by many different people in the process. It surprises many that this type of error can occur, and by 1983 it had happened at least three times already.

It is clear when this error occurred. In 1983, as in all previous years, dies were created from working hubs that did not contain a mintmark. The working dies themselves received an impression from a mintmark punch before being prepared to strike Proof coins—a very involved process.

To strike Proof coins, first the working dies are cleaned with solvents to remove grease, metal dust, and oil. Next, they are sandblasted. This task is performed by hand with the field areas marked off by tape, undoubtedly a tedious process. The field areas are then polished to a high shine. To increase die life and retain the effects of the polish and sandblasting, dies are then chromium plated. Every 500 to 1,000 strikes, dies are examined and refreshed by reprocessing if needed; if they are too worn, they are discarded. Over the years, the exact sequence of preparation has varied. This overview of the process, though, had been in use for the production of U.S. coins since 1970, according to Proof-coinage specialist Rick Tomaska. Sandblasting was ultimately replaced in 2009 by laser-frosting.

Like most Proof coins of its era, the 1983, No S, Roosevelt dime is almost always seen with a notable deep or ultra cameo contrast. It is clear that, as with regular Proof dimes, its obverse die was handled and inspected many times before and during the coinage process. To make the Proof 1983, No S, Roosevelt dime, then, a number of individuals failed to note the omitted S mintmark. In fact, the nature of the oversight is what makes these coins so interesting to collectors, and the rarity of the error makes them valuable.

This coin is the most recent issue of No S Proof dimes reported to date. To avoid mistakes like this in the future, starting in 1985, Proof dies were created from a production hub that included the mintmark. It is likely that this is the coin that led to the change in this process. While this change has prevented another No S dime from being made, a No S Lincoln cent was still produced in 1990.

THE 1970, NO S, ROOSEVELT DIME, PROOF

1970, No S, Roosevelt dime, Proof.

The Proof 1970, No S, dime is said to be the most common of all the No S Proof coins, although this by no means makes it common: far fewer than 500 examples are known.

First discovered in an original Proof set in early 1971, the 1970, No S, Roosevelt dime was officially confirmed by the Mint. They also acknowledged that they had made 2,200 examples, which were then packaged among the more than 3.2 million Proof sets for that year. In one sense, the small likelihood of finding one of these coins makes it surprising that so many have been found. They are easy to identify, though, and their value makes searching them out worthwhile.

These coins are often in very good, attractive condition, and examples will frequently show mild cameo contrast. Professional authentication is recommended to avoid spurious coins made from circulation-strike 1970 dimes that have been altered to look like Proofs. Proof coins are struck twice from specially prepared dies and have crisp detail and sharp, squared rims. Fortunately, if ever in doubt about a coin's authenticity, it's possible to acquire a regular S mintmark Proof example for comparison, as these are readily available.

The first No S dime was made in 1968, the first year the Proof dimes included the S mintmark. That first coin is incredibly scarce, with just a few dozen known, compared with a few hundred for this coin. Examples of the 1970, No S, dime can trade for more than $1,000.

APPENDIX W

Modern U.S. Mint Medals

This appendix is based on the research of Dennis Tucker, including extracts from **American Gold and Silver: U.S. Mint Collector and Investor Coins and Medals, Bicentennial to Date.**

During the American Revolution, the Continental Congress authorized official medals to be designed and struck (often in Paris) to honor heroes of the emerging new nation. One famous example is the Washington Before Boston medal, awarded in 1776 to thank General George Washington, his officers, and his soldiers after their victorious bombardment of Boston and the British evacuation of the city.

The national mint of the United States was established in 1792, and since the early 1800s it has issued medals for commemorative and historical purposes. These have celebrated everything from acts of heroic lifesaving to famous entertainers and wildlife conservation. "The United States Mint produces a variety of national medals to commemorate significant historical events or sites and to honor those whose superior deeds and achievements have enriched U.S. history or the world," the Mint says. "Some of these are bronze duplicates of Congressional Gold Medals authorized by Congress under separate public laws, while others are produced under the secretary of the Treasury's authority to strike national medals."

The following is a sampling of medals struck by the U.S. Mint since the early 1970s. Many of these, and others, are studied in detail in *American Gold and Silver* (Tucker). A number of the Mint's modern medals are available for sale to collectors at catalog.usmint.gov.

American Revolution Bicentennial Medals (1972–1976)

Congress passed a law on February 15, 1972, to authorize national medals to commemorate the bicentennial of the American Revolution and "historical events . . . in the continuing progress of the United States of America toward life, liberty, and the pursuit of happiness." Medals were issued each year from 1972 to 1976, in various bronze, silver, and gold formats.

	Distribution*	Value
1972, G. Washington, Liberty Tree, bronze, dated	672,200	$4
(1972) G. Washington, Liberty Tree, bronze, undated (a)	791,000	$6
1973, P. Henry and S. Adams, Committees of Correspondence, bronze, dated	237,790	$4
(1973) P. Henry and S. Adams, Committees of Correspondence, bronze, undated (a)	475,812	$6
1973, P. Henry and S. Adams, Committees of Correspondence, silver	208,120	$25
1974, J. Adams, First Continental Congress, bronze, dated	188,308	$4
(1974) J. Adams, First Continental Congress, bronze, undated (a)	511,428	$6
1974, J. Adams, First Continental Congress, silver	150,428	$25
1975, P. Revere, Lexington/Concord, bronze, dated	327,677	$4
(1975) P. Revere, Lexington/Concord, bronze, undated (a)	668,419	$6
1975, P. Revere, Lexington/Concord, silver	212,542	$25
1976, T. Jefferson, Declaration of Independence, bronze, dated	98,408	$4
(1976) T. Jefferson, Declaration of Independence, bronze, undated (a)	446,939	$6
1976, T. Jefferson, Declaration of Independence, silver (pictured)	98,677	$25
1976, Statue of Liberty, We the People, 1.5-inch, bronze	438,971	$5
1976, Statue of Liberty, We the People, 1.5-inch, gilt bronze	45,163	$9
1976, Statue of Liberty, We the People, 1.5-inch, silver	211,772	$24
1976, Statue of Liberty, We the People, 3-inch, silver	8,824	$300
1976, Statue of Liberty, We the People, .906-inch, gold (pictured)	29,468	$750
1976, Statue of Liberty, We the People, 1.31-inch, gold	5,396	$1,900
1976, Statue of Liberty, We the People, 3-inch, gold	423	$25,500

* There are discrepancies in Mint and other government records as to the exact mintages and quantities sold of some medals. **a.** Issued as part of a Philatelic-Numismatic Combination or PNC (medal, postage stamp, and first-day cover).

Colorado Statehood Centennial Medal (1976)

Colorado was the only state to join the Union in the national centennial year of 1876 (before it, Nebraska had joined in 1867; after it, the Dakotas, Montana, and Washington would join in 1889), and therefore was the only one to celebrate its 100th anniversary during the national Bicentennial in 1976. Congress authorized a medal—struck in various alloys at the Denver Mint—to mark the anniversary.

	Mintage	Value
1976, Colorado Centennial, bronze	41,000	$6
1976, Colorado Centennial, bronze, mule (a)	*	$6
1976, Colorado Centennial, gilt bronze	5,000	$8
1976, Colorado Centennial, silver	20,200	$32
1976, Colorado Centennial, gold (pictured)	100	$5,100
1976, Colorado Centennial, three-piece set (b)	1,876	$48

* Included in number above. **a.** The mule variety has the standard centennial logo reverse combined with a Denver Mint obverse (showing the mint building). **b.** Issued in a hard plastic case containing one each of the bronze, gilt bronze, and silver medals.

Valley Forge Medal (1978)

Congress authorized this medal to be struck for the United States Capitol Historical Society. It was designed by Chief Engraver Frank Gasparro and struck in several formats at the Philadelphia Mint.

	Mintage	Value
1978, Valley Forge, 3-inch, bronze	2,500	$35
1978, Valley Forge, 1.5-inch, gilt bronze	5,000	$15
1978, Valley Forge, 1.5-inch, silver	1,999	$50
1978, Valley Forge, 3-inch, silver (pictured)	1,000	$600
1978, Valley Forge, 1.31-inch, gold	339	$5,000

Young Astronauts Medals (1988)

Three different designs were created for bronze, silver, and gold medals by students in the Young Astronauts program (a White House initiative that encouraged proficiency and interest in science, math, and technology). The medals were executed by U.S. Mint sculptor-engravers and struck in Philadelphia in 1988.

Common Reverse	Bronze	Silver	Gold

	Mintage	Value
1988, Young Astronauts, bronze, Unc.	28,700	$9
1988, Young Astronauts, bronze, Proof	17,250	$14
1988, Young Astronauts, silver, 1.5-inch, Unc.	15,400	$40
1988, Young Astronauts, silver, 1.5-inch, Proof	33,250	$45
1988, Young Astronauts, silver, 3-inch, 6-ounce, Unc.	1,075	$345
1988, Young Astronauts, silver, 3-inch, 12-ounce, Unc.	3,700	$575

	Mintage	Value
1988, Young Astronauts, gold, .875-inch, Unc.	13,000	$600
1988, Young Astronauts, gold, .875-inch, Proof	3,400	$700
1988, Young Astronauts, gold, 3-inch	38	$20,000
1988, Young Astronauts, three-piece set, Unc. (a)		$675

a. Bronze, small silver, and small gold medals in Unc. format in a blue box. Other two- and three-medal sets were issued as well; each is worth about the combined retail value of the medals it contains.

Benjamin Franklin Firefighters Medal (1993)

This medal was authorized as part of the Benjamin Franklin National Memorial Commemorative Medal and Fire Service Bill of Rights Act. Franklin organized the country's first fire company in Philadelphia in 1736. The medals were struck at the Philadelphia Mint on American Silver Eagle planchets (40.6 mm in diameter, with one ounce of .999 fine silver), and each bears a P mintmark.

	Mintage	Value
1993, Franklin Firefighters, Unc.	26,011	$37
1993, Franklin Firefighters, Proof	89,311	$42

National Wildlife Refuge System Centennial Medals (2003)

In 2003 the U.S. Mint released its first-ever series of silver national medals, to celebrate the 100th anniversary of the National Wildlife Refuge System. Their shared obverse features a standing portrait of President Theodore Roosevelt, who designated Florida's Pelican Island as the nation's first wildlife refuge in 1903.

Sales started with the Bald Eagle variety, available in bronze and .900 fine silver formats. The Salmon, Elk, and Canvasback Duck varieties, in silver only, were released successively every few weeks after that.

The bronze Bald Eagle had no mintage limit, and in fact since then has been reissued in 2008 in the Bald Eagle Coin and Medal Set, and in 2013 in the Theodore Roosevelt Coin and Chronicles Set. The four silver medals all sold out their mintage limits (35,000 for the Bald Eagle and 25,000 for the others).

The silver medals were the first U.S. Mint products made using laser technology to texture their dies. They feature distinctive matte-finish frosted devices on mirror-finish fields. All were struck at the Philadelphia Mint without a mintmark.

Some early strikes of the silver medals were not as heavily frosted as later issues, with less pronounced cameo contrast between the fields and the design devices. This transition was caused by the Mint experimenting with its laser technology (as opposed to traditional sandblasting) for texturing the dies. The laser technique would later be used in the Mint's annual Proof sets and various commemorative coins.

A portion of the proceeds from the sale of the medals (10 percent of each silver medal and 5 percent of each bronze) benefited the National Fish and Wildlife Foundation and its conservation efforts.

Common Obverse

	Mintage	Value
2003, National Wildlife Refuge System Centennial, Bald Eagle, bronze	(a)	$6
2003, National Wildlife Refuge System Centennial, Bald Eagle, silver	35,000	$28.50
2003, National Wildlife Refuge System Centennial, Salmon	25,000	$30
2003, National Wildlife Refuge System Centennial, Elk	25,000	$30
2003, National Wildlife Refuge System Centennial, Canvasback Duck	25,000	$29

a. The Mint established no production limit for the bronze medal. Mintage was ongoing into the early 2010s. At least 22,000 were distributed as part of the Mint's 2008 Bald Eagle Coin and Medal Set, and at least 15,000 in the 2013 Theodore Roosevelt Coin and Chronicles Set.

September 11, 2011, National Medal (2011)

This silver medal was authorized to mark the 10th anniversary of the September 11, 2001, terror attacks in New York City; Washington, D.C.; and Shanksville, Pennsylvania. A surcharge from each sale benefited the National September 11 Memorial & Museum at the World Trade Center site in New York.

	Distribution*	Value
2011-P, September 11	67,928	$50
2011-W, September 11	109,365	$45

* Quantities sold by the end of sale in December 2012.

Silver Presidential Medals (2013–2015)

In 2013, 2014, and 2015 the Mint issued restrikes, in silver, of several historic Presidential medals from its archives. These were packaged in Coin and Chronicles sets along with Presidential golden dollars (in Proof or Reverse Proof) and other collectibles related to each of six chief executives. The medals were struck on American Silver Eagle planchets, marking the first time the Mint offered its Presidential medals in .999 fine silver. They were made in a regular-strike format, not Burnished or Proof. Their designs are by Mint chief engravers Charles E. Barber (Theodore Roosevelt), John R. Sinnock (Franklin Roosevelt, Harry Truman), and Gilroy Roberts (Dwight Eisenhower, John F. Kennedy, and Lyndon Johnson obverses), and sculptor-engraver Frank Gasparro (Eisenhower, Kennedy, and Johnson reverses).

Theodore Roosevelt   Franklin D. Roosevelt   Harry S. Truman

Dwight D. Eisenhower   John F. Kennedy   Lyndon B. Johnson

	Distribution	Value
(2013) Theodore Roosevelt	15,144	$50
(2014) Franklin D. Roosevelt	20,000	$65
(2015) Harry S. Truman	17,000	$55
(2015) Dwight D. Eisenhower	17,000	$55
(2015) John F. Kennedy	50,000	$45
(2015) Lyndon B. Johnson	25,000	$45

Centennial of World War I Silver Medals (2018)

In 2018 the United States Mint issued five silver medals as part of its World War I Centennial commemorative program. This marked the 100th anniversary of the end of the war, and honored the involvement of more than 4 million men and women in America's Army, Navy, Marine Corps, Coast Guard, and Air Service. The medals were struck in West Point (Army), San Francisco (Marines), Philadelphia (Navy and Coast Guard), and Denver (Air Service) on silver dollar–sized planchets (1.5 inches in diameter), in .900 fine silver, in Proof format, with a plain edge. Each medal was issued in a two-piece set that also included a Proof example of the World War I Centennial silver commemorative dollar. The sets were limited to 100,000 units across all five medal product options.

The early-order issue price of each two-piece set was $99.95. The Mint has not yet audited its final mintage figures for each medal.

	Distribution*	Value
2018, U.S. Army	15,577	$50
2018, U.S. Navy	12,206	$65
2018, U.S. Marines	12,603	$55
2018, U.S. Air Service	12,474	$55
2018, U.S. Coast Guard	9,800	$45

* As of February 25, 2018.

Congressional Gold Medals

The legislation that authorizes a Congressional Gold Medal will often permit the U.S. Mint to strike duplicates in bronze (90 percent copper, 10 percent zinc) for sale to the public. These medals, minted in Philadelphia, are typically offered in three-inch format for $39.95, and/or 1.5-inch format for $6.95. Here is a small sampling of recent Congressional Gold Medals available in bronze for collectors. More of the Mint's catalog of modern medals is online at catalog.usmint.gov.

MOTHER TERESA OF CALCUTTA (AUTHORIZED 1997)

A Congressional Gold Medal was authorized in 1997 to recognize the worldwide humanitarian influence of Mother Teresa of Calcutta: "She greatly impacted the lives of people from all walks of life in every corner of the world through her love and her selfless charitable works for nearly 70 years."

CODE TALKERS (AUTHORIZED 2000, 2008)

Code Talkers were Native Americans who used their tribal languages as a means of secret communication during wartime. The Code Talkers Recognition Act of 2008 authorized Congressional Gold Medals recognizing the valor of Native American Code Talkers and their dedication to the U.S. Armed Services during World War I and World War II.

On November 20, 2013, in the U.S. Capitol's Emancipation Hall, 33 tribes were officially recognized, and 25 were presented with their Congressional Gold Medals. Unique gold medals were struck for each tribe that had a member who served as a Code Talker. Silver duplicate medals were presented to the surviving Code Talkers, their next of kin, or other personal representatives. In addition, bronze duplicates are available for sale to the public.

The Navajo Nation had been awarded a Congressional Gold Medal in 2001. The following are the tribes and nations honored by the 2008 legislation.

Cherokee Nation
Cheyenne and Arapaho Tribes
Cheyenne River Sioux Tribe
Choctaw Nation
Comanche Nation
Crow Creek Sioux Tribe
Crow Nation
Fond du Lac Band of Lake Superior Chippewa Tribe

Fort Peck Assiniboine and Sioux Tribes
Ho-Chunk Nation
Hopi Tribe
Kiowa Tribe
Lower Brule Sioux Tribe
Menominee Nation
Meskwaki Nation
Muscogee (Creek) Nation
Oglala Sioux Tribe

Oneida Nation
Osage Nation
Pawnee Nation
Ponca Tribe
Pueblo of Acoma Tribe
Pueblo of Laguna Tribe
Rosebud Sioux Tribe
Santee Sioux Nation
Seminole Nation

Sisseton Wahpeton Oyate (Sioux) Tribe
St. Regis Mohawk Tribe
Standing Rock Sioux Tribe
Tlingit Tribe
Tonto Apache Tribe
White Mountain Apache Tribe
Yankton Sioux Tribe

St. Regis Mohawk Tribe

Oneida Nation

Kiowa Tribe

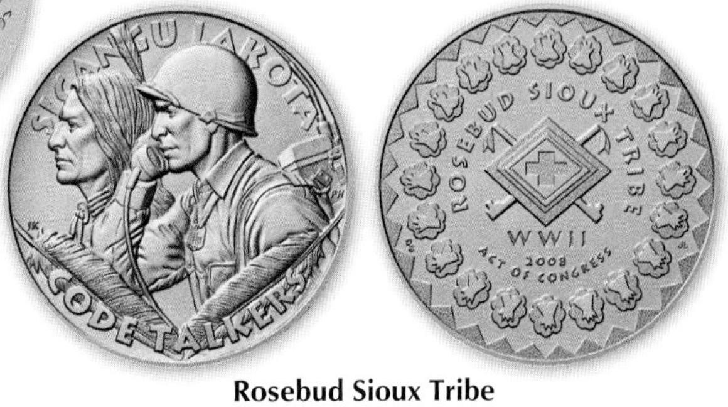

Rosebud Sioux Tribe

NEW FRONTIER (AUTHORIZED 2011)

America's historic achievements in space were celebrated with the New Frontier Congressional Gold Medal featuring Apollo 11 astronauts John Glenn, Neil A. Armstrong, Michael Collins, and Edwin E. "Buzz" Aldrin. The men were awarded the gold version of the medal at a ceremony in the U.S. Capitol Building on November 16, 2011. The bronze version is available in small and large formats.

"John Glenn became the first American to orbit the Earth on February 20, 1962, helping pave the way for the first lunar landing," the Mint noted in a press release. "As mission commander for Apollo 11, Neil Armstrong gained the distinction of being the first astronaut to land a spacecraft on the moon and the first to step on its surface on July 21, 1969. Buzz Aldrin joined Armstrong in piloting the lunar module, *Eagle*, to the surface of the moon and became the second person to walk on the lunar surface. Michael Collins piloted the command module, *Columbia*, in lunar orbit and helped his fellow Apollo 11 astronauts complete their mission on the moon."

New Frontier

9/11 Fallen Heroes (Authorized 2011)

A suite of three Congressional Gold Medals—and their bronze duplicates—honor those who lost their lives in the terrorist attacks of September 11, 2001. With unique designs, each medal marks one of three sites: the World Trade Center in New York, the Pentagon, and rural Pennsylvania.

| Fallen Heroes of New York | Fallen Heroes of Pennsylvania | Fallen Heroes of the Pentagon |

World War II (Authorized Various Years)

Many Congressional Gold Medals have been awarded to honor service, bravery, and sacrifices in World War II. These are popular among students of military history; veterans and their families; current service members; and medal collectors and hobbyists.

The Tuskegee Airmen medal, authorized in 2006, recognizes the unique military record of the Tuskegee Airmen, who inspired revolutionary reform in the U.S. armed forces.

The Women Airforce Service Pilots medal was authorized in 2009 in honor of the pioneering military service and exemplary record of the WASPs.

The Doolittle Tokyo Raiders medal was authorized in 2014 to honor the extraordinary service of the 80 U.S. airmen who flew a mission into Japan on April 18, 1942.

The Monuments Men medal, also authorized in 2014, recognizes the heroic role played in the preservation, protection, and restitution of monuments, works of art, and culturally important artifacts during and following the war.

The Filipino Veterans of World War II medal, authorized in 2016, acknowledges the debt owed by the United States for the bravery, valor, and dedication that Filipinos and Filipino-Americans displayed during the war. The medal is shown here in its three-inch bronze format.

These and other World War II commemorative medals are available in both small and large sizes directly from the U.S. Mint.

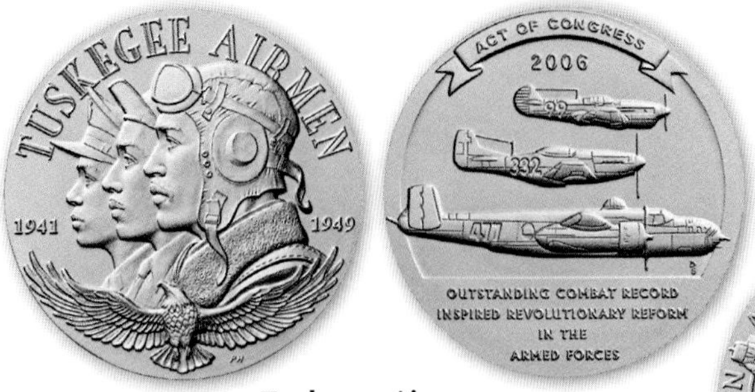

Tuskegee Airmen

**Women Airforce
Service Pilots**

**Doolittle
Tokyo Raiders**

Monuments Men

Filipino Veterans of World War II
Shown in the three-inch size.

APPENDIX X

The "Liberty" Subset of First Spouse Gold Coins

This appendix is excerpted and condensed from chapter 6 of American Gold and Silver: U.S. Mint Collector and Investor Coins and Medals, Bicentennial to Date, *by Dennis Tucker.*

By 2007 the United States was more than 20 years into its successful modern gold-bullion programs. Collectors and investors were buying hundreds of thousands of ounces of American Gold Eagles annually. The American Buffalo 24-karat coins had been introduced the year before and were off to a galloping start. Next in the lineup was a gold-coinage series designed as a companion to the Mint's soon-to-roll-out Presidential dollars. The new bullion program's 24-karat coins would honor and commemorate the nation's First Ladies.

DETAILS OF THE PRESIDENTIAL $1 COIN ACT

The Presidential $1 Coin Act of 2005 (Public Law 109-145) was the legislation that authorized the U.S. Mint's First Spouse gold bullion coins. It was enacted "to require the secretary of the Treasury to mint coins in commemoration of each of the nation's past presidents and their spouses, respectively, to improve circulation of the $1 coin, to create a new bullion coin, and for other purposes." The act was considered and passed in the Senate on November 18, 2005; considered and passed in the House on December 13; and signed into law by President George W. Bush on December 22.

Relevant to the First Spouse coins, the text of the act noted the following:

> First Spouses have not generally been recognized on American coinage.
>
> Although the Congress has authorized the Secretary of the Treasury to issue gold coins with a purity of 99.99 percent, the Secretary has not done so. [This was in 2005, when the American Buffalo 24-karat gold coins had yet to be released.]
>
> Bullion coins are a valuable tool for the investor and, in some cases, an important aspect of coin collecting.

The 2005 act ordered that, starting in 2007 to coincide with the debut of the Presidential dollar coins, "the Secretary shall issue bullion coins . . . that are emblematic of the spouse of [each] President." It spelled out the coins' specifications: they would have the same diameter as the Presidential dollars [26.5 mm]; they would weigh 1/2 ounce; and they would contain 99.99% pure gold. In terms of designs, the obverse of each coin would feature:

the name and likeness of the spouse of each president during the president's period of service,

the years during which she was the spouse of the president during the president's period of service, and

a number indicating the order of the period of service in which such president served.

On each coin's reverse:

images emblematic of the life and work of the First Spouse whose image is borne on the obverse,

the inscription "United States of America," and

an inscription of the nominal denomination of the coin, $10.

The legislation's focus on *First Spouses* rather than *First Ladies* avoided any confusion over cases where a president was widowed or unmarried and the usual ceremonial functions of First Lady were carried out by a daughter or other relative; or if he was married but someone other than his wife performed some or all of the duties typically assigned to the First Lady (as was the case when various presidential wives were too sick or frail).

In cases where a president served without a spouse, the act ordered that "the image on the obverse of the bullion coin corresponding to the $1 coin relating to such President shall be an image emblematic of the concept of 'Liberty'"—

as represented on a United States coin issued during the period of service of such President; or

as represented, in the case of President Chester Alan Arthur, by a design incorporating the name and likeness of Alice Paul, a leading strategist in the suffrage movement, who was instrumental in gaining women the right to vote upon the adoption of the 19th amendment and thus the ability to participate in the election of future Presidents, and who was born on January 11, 1885, during the term of President Arthur; and

the reverse of such bullion coin shall be of a design representative of themes of such President, except that in the case of [the Alice Paul coin] the reverse of such coin shall be representative of the suffrage movement.

The act further specified that if two presidential spouses served during an executive term (in the case of death of one and remarriage to another), a separate coin would be designed and issued for each.

The four First Spouse gold pieces issued with historical coin images "emblematic of the concept of Liberty as represented on a United States coin" make up a popular subset of the series. They are: Thomas Jefferson's Liberty; Andrew Jackson's Liberty; Martin Van Buren's Liberty; and James Buchanan's Liberty.

THOMAS JEFFERSON'S LIBERTY (2007)

Designer: *Robert Scot (obverse); Charles L. Vickers (reverse).* **Sculptor:** *Phebe Hemphill (obverse); Charles L. Vickers (reverse).* **Composition:** *.9999 gold.* **Actual Gold Weight:** *1/2 ounce.* **Diameter:** *26.49 mm.* **Edge:** *Reeded.* **Mint:** *West Point.* **Issue Price:** *$410.95 (Burnished); $429.95 (Proof).* **Release Date:** *August 30, 2007.*

Mintage: 19,823 Burnished; 19,815 Proof

Draped Bust half cent (1800–1808).

2007 Thomas Jefferson's Liberty, Burnished format.

Hobby observers anticipated a hot market for the third coin of the First Spouse series. This issue was the first of four that would feature an allegorical Miss Liberty rather than an actual First Lady. Thomas Jefferson's wife, Martha, had died some 19 years before he won the presidency, and he never remarried, so the nation had no First Lady during his two terms in office.

The image for Jefferson's coin is Mint Medallic Sculptor Phebe Hemphill's resculpted version of Miss Liberty from Chief Engraver Robert Scot's Draped Bust half cent of 1800 to 1808. "This beautiful coin captures a classic image of Liberty from Jefferson's time," said Mint director Ed Moy, "connecting us to the history of our coinage."

There are special elements of appeal for the four Liberty designs. Viewed by collectors as a self-contained "short set," they make a more attainable (less expensive) goal than acquiring one of every type in the First Spouse gold series. On top of that the Liberty coins recreate the classic designs of popular older coins. For these reasons, enthusiasts in 2007 expected strong demand for the Jefferson's Liberty coins. By mid-September, market-makers in modern coins were advertising buy prices up to $550 per raw coin (which would yield a quick $100-plus profit for the seller), and retailing 70-graded coins for up to $900. Sellers on eBay advertised the coins at prices above their official Mint issue price, even before they were delivered.

As predicted, Jefferson's Liberty did garner the series' highest mintages up to that point, in both Proof and Burnished formats—a distinction they still maintain, as mintages never again got close to their first-year highs.

Not long after their August 30 release, it became evident that the Jefferson's Liberty coins would not enjoy a repeat of the sustained strong secondary markets of their Washington and Adams predecessors. The Mint placed an order limit of one coin of each format per household, which allowed for broader, more equitable distribution—speculators had a harder time grabbing up large quantities. "The Mint got out its bulldozer and leveled the playing field," is how one collector put it. Once the coins were in collectors' and dealers' hands, they started to flow in to the professional third-party grading firms for certification. The Jefferson coin had the largest certified population of First Strike 70s. This combination of factors—broad distribution throughout the collector base, and a large quantity of perfect First Strike coins—dampened the secondary market. Everyone who wanted a nice example of the coin had one.

Rare-coin dealer Wayne Herndon made this observation in November 2007: "The real question is not what happened to the Jefferson, but what happened to the Washington and Adams. The Jefferson did exactly what it should have done based on the mintage, interest, etc. Somehow, some way, a lot of people got it into their heads that is would be a great series and the first two sold out quickly. Slow delivery contributed to the apparent lack of supply vs. demand. As a result, the first two ended up being the exceptions, not Jefferson." Presciently, Herndon went on: "I predict this series will see some pieces with mintages in the low four figures. Those are the ones that will have some potential."

Scott Schechter and Jeff Garrett, too, have noted the potential of the Liberty gold coins. "Collectors like them because of the way they honor numismatic history, recasting old designs in a new way," they wrote in *100 Greatest U.S. Modern Coins*. As a set, the First Spouse Liberty gold coins are ranked in the fourth edition of the *100 Greatest* book at number 58. Their ranking will undoubtedly climb closer to number 1 if the now-concluded program grows in popularity. Eric Jordan and John Maben wrote in *Top 50 Most Popular Modern Coins*: "One of the best things that can happen to a series is to have a large population of good-looking common dates in the hands of the public to get them started without the intimidating hurdle of a high collector premium. Jefferson's Liberty is this coin in the four-coin Liberty gold subset."

Regarding the aesthetics of the Jefferson's Liberty coin, collectors were charmed by the Mint's use of the early-1800s half-cent portrait of Miss Liberty. America's copper half cents and large cents have been popular collectibles since they went obsolete in the late 1850s. Today a solid and growing collector base benefits from the educational and fraternal missions of hobby groups such as Early American Coppers, whose members keep the series alive with ongoing research (they publish new findings regularly, and were instrumental in sharing their scholarship in Q. David Bowers's *Guide Book of Half Cents and Large Cents*, 2015). EAC nationwide has more than 1,200 members who congregate at coin shows and online at www.eacs.org. Undoubtedly many of these enthusiasts bought this First Spouse "Liberty" coin to complement their half cent and large cent collections.

The *reverse* of the coin, on the other hand, won few kudos with its text-heavy design. U.S. Mint Sculptor-Engraver Charles Vickers depicted Thomas Jefferson's grave monument, located on the grounds of his Monticello estate, in minutely textured detail. He overset the obelisk with the president's self-penned epitaph: "Here was buried Thomas Jefferson, author of the declaration of American independence, of the statute of Virginia for religious freedom and father of the University of Virginia. Born April 2, 1743, O.S. Died July 4, 1826." Surrounding this well-balanced but lengthy inscription are the standard legends UNITED STATES OF AMERICA and E PLURIBUS UNUM, plus the denomination of $10, the weight of 1/2 OZ., and the purity of .9999 FINE GOLD. "Enjoy the obverse," remarked some hobby wags, "but don't flip the coin over"—no offense to the very talented Mr. Vickers, who was tasked with fitting nearly 50 words into a one-inch–diameter circle of gold.

ANDREW JACKSON'S LIBERTY (2008)

Designer: *John Reich (obverse); Justin Kunz (reverse).* **Sculptor:** *Don Everhart (reverse).*
Composition: *.9999 gold.* **Actual Gold Weight:** *1/2 ounce.* **Diameter:** *26.49 mm.* **Edge:** *Reeded.*
Mint: *West Point.* **Issue Price:** *$599.95 (Burnished); $619.95 (Proof).* **Release Date:** *August 28, 2008.*

Mintage: 4,609 Burnished; 7,684 Proof

Capped Bust half dollar
(1807–1836).

2008 Andrew Jackson's Liberty,
Burnished format.

On August 21, 2008, the Mint announced that it would begin accepting orders for its next First Spouse gold coin on August 28. Mintage was set at a maximum of 40,000 coins across both product options, Burnished and Proof, with customer demand determining the quantity produced of each format. The household limit, previously capped at one coin of each format for the first week of sales, was raised to 10 coins of each format for the first week in an effort to stimulate purchasing.

Once again the provisions of the Presidential $1 Coin Act of 2005 were invoked due to a president having served without a spouse. Andrew Jackson's wife Rachel died shortly before he took office, leaving him grief-stricken and the nation without an official First Lady from 1829 to 1837. The gold coin for the seventh presidency featured "an obverse design emblematic of Liberty as represented on a United States coin issued during the president's period of service and a reverse image emblematic of that president." The figure of Miss Liberty was derived from Mint engraver John Reich's Capped Bust, Lettered Edge, silver half dollar of 1807 to 1836. The reverse design by Artistic Infusion Program Master Designer Justin Kunz shows a military equestrian portrait of Jackson as "Old Hickory"—the moniker by which he became known for leading American forces against the British Army in the War of 1812. Don Everhart's sculpting of Kunz's design has remarkable depth and nuanced detail.

The hobby community's reaction to the coin was mixed. Why did collectors *not* buy Jackson's Liberty in droves? Some in 2008 were saving their hobby money for the upcoming 2009 Ultra High Relief gold coin. Some were disgruntled with the issue price of the latest First Spouse coin—about 50 percent above gold's spot value. Some collectors found the prospect of completing the set of First Spouse coins too daunting to continue (or begin), especially with the uncertainty of gold's value fluctuating. Collectors of modern issues felt the pressure of many other Mint products competing for their discretionary income. And the interest of some hobbyists had cooled after the market couldn't sustain the initial firestorm of excitement over the program's first two coins the year before.

Even with this chill, Andrew Jackson's Liberty was appealing enough to gin up total sales about 20 percent higher than the preceding Louisa Adams issue. The attractive designs of the Jackson coin, with a classic American coinage motif of Miss Liberty and the dramatic horseback portrait of the famous war hero, strengthened its appeal. So did its status as one of only four members of the subset of Liberty coins in the First Spouse series.

All of the 2007 coins and half of the preceding 2008 issues had sold more Proofs than did Jackson's Liberty, but none after it (until 2015) would reach its level of 7,684 Proof coins. Its Burnished mintage level would not be exceeded by a predecessor until nine coins down the line—another in the Liberty subset, James Buchanan's Liberty, in 2010.

MARTIN VAN BUREN'S LIBERTY (2008)

Designer: *Christian Gobrecht (obverse); Thomas Cleveland (reverse).* **Sculptor:** *Jim Licaretz (reverse).*
Composition: *.9999 gold.* **Actual Gold Weight:** *1/2 ounce.* **Diameter:** *26.49 mm.* **Edge:** *Reeded.*
Mint: *West Point.* **Issue Price:** *$524.95 (Burnished); $549.95 (Proof).* **Release Date:** *November 25, 2008.*

Mintage: 3,826 Burnished; 6,807 Proof

Liberty Seated silver dollar (1840–1873).

2008 Martin Van Buren's Liberty, Burnished format.

The U.S. Mint started accepting orders for the Martin Van Buren First Spouse gold coin at 12 noon on November 25, 2008. The issue price was set about $75 lower than that of its predecessor coin, following gold's activity in the bullion markets. As with the Andrew Jackson coin that had debuted three months earlier, the Mint set an order limit of 10 coins per format (Burnished and Proof) per household for the first week, reserving the right to evaluate sales and either extend, adjust, or eliminate the limit after that. The total mintage was capped at 40,000 pieces, to be distributed between the Burnished and Proof coins according to buyers' demand.

Collector interest waned a bit for this issue, the third in the First Spouse program's four-coin Liberty subset, despite its attractive engraving of Christian Gobrecht's classic Liberty Seated design. This motif had been used on the silver dime from 1837 to 1891, and on other U.S. silver coins in various time spans of the same era. The reason the 2008 gold bullion coin for Van Buren's presidency featured no First Lady is that his wife, Hannah, had died of tuberculosis in 1819, early in his political career, when he was a member of the New York State Senate. Van Buren never remarried. Their son's wife, Sarah Angelica Singleton Van Buren, performed many of the hostess functions for the White House during her father-in-law's presidency.

The reverse tableau shows Martin Van Buren as a youth reading a book outside the Kinderhook, New York, tavern run by his father, with a traveler on horseback in the background. When Martin was growing up, the tavern, situated along a post road, was a meeting place for conversation, debate, and voting. Politicians traveling between New York City and the state capital of Albany stopped there. From this exposure young Van Buren developed a taste for politics and the philosophy of law. The coin's richly detailed scene, with its well-balanced blend of natural, architectural, and human elements, was designed by Artistic Infusion Program Master Designer Thomas Cleveland and sculpted by Mint Sculptor-Engraver Jim Licaretz.

Numismatics offers many opportunities to cross-pollinate a sophisticated coin collection. No doubt more than just a few of Van Buren's Liberty gold coins are kept company by much older silver half dimes, dimes, quarters, half dollars, and silver dollars that date back to the presidency of "The Red Fox of Kinderhook." Consider the Liberty Seated Collectors Club ("Uniting Collectors of Liberty Seated Coinage Since 1973," online at www.lsccweb.org). That particular hobby group is very active, and proved its numismatic chops in sharing information, research, and insight for Q. David Bowers's *A Guide Book of Liberty Seated Silver Coins* (2016). How many of its 600-plus members treated themselves to one or more of these artful gold pieces? New members will undoubtedly feel the same attraction.

Due to its low mintage, and ongoing collector demand for the four coins of the Liberty subset, Van Buren's Liberty has emerged as the aftermarket winner among the First Spouse issues of 2007 and 2008. In both Burnished and Proof format it typically carries a premium of 25 to 50 percent over the other coins of those years. Eric Jordan and John Maben gave Van Buren's Liberty an overall score of 4.0 in their book *Top 50 Most Popular Modern Coins*, calling it "the undisputed king of the Liberty subset," with "classic good looks that attract both classic and modern collectors."

JAMES BUCHANAN'S LIBERTY (2010)

Designer: *Christian Gobrecht (obverse); David Westwood (reverse).* **Sculptor:** *Joseph F. Menna (reverse).*
Composition: *.9999 gold.* **Actual Gold Weight:** *1/2 ounce.* **Diameter:** *26.49 mm.* **Edge:** *Reeded.*
Mint: *West Point.* **Issue Price:** *$766 (Burnished); $779 (Proof).* **Release Date:** *September 2, 2010.*
Mintage: 5,162 Burnished; 7,110 Proof

Liberty Head quarter eagle
(1840–1907).

2010 James Buchanan's Liberty,
Burnished format.

The design of the 2010 James Buchanan's Liberty gold bullion coin was unveiled in Washington, D.C., on December 21, 2009. On June 29, 2010, the U.S. Mint announced that the coin would be released for sale on September 2. As with other recent issues, the combined mintage for Burnished and Proof pieces was capped at 15,000, with customer demand determining the quantities of each format. No household ordering limits were set.

This was the fourth and final First Spouse gold coin in the Liberty subset. "Because President James Buchanan did not have a spouse," the Mint announced, "the obverse of his corresponding First Spouse Gold Coin features a design emblematic of Liberty as it appeared on a U.S. coin issued during his time in office." It features a reproduction of the Liberty Head design by Christian Gobrecht, minted on the quarter eagle ($2.50 gold piece) from 1840 through 1907.

In an interesting case of "what might have been," the Citizens Coinage Advisory Committee, which advises the Treasury Department on coin designs, had leaned toward using the Flying Eagle cent of 1856 to 1858.

The Liberty Head motif was the dominant obverse element of U.S. gold coins minted from the late 1830s to the early 1900s. Undoubtedly Gobrecht's elegant and popular design attracted a share of collector interest above and beyond that of First Spouse specialists and bullion investors. Writing about the Proof format in particular, Jordan and Maben have noted, "This attractive $10 Proof gold coin is the last issue of an affordable four-coin set that is in some ways a tour of the great designs of the 1800s that can't be acquired in a cameo Proof format any other way. . . . It's the *only* option if you like the look of high-grade antique Proof gold but have to live within a reasonable budget."

As to why there was no First Spouse in James Buchanan's life, modern historians and biographers support the idea that the Pennsylvania politician was gay. For whatever reason, he is the only U.S. president to have remained a lifelong bachelor. Unrelated to his personal life, many presidential historians rank Buchanan as one of the nation's worst chief executives. Despite grand ideas he proved unable to map out a plan for peace as the country became more and more split by the slavery question. The Southern states seceded in the waning months of his presidency, and the Civil War erupted shortly after. Avoiding these political failings, the reverse design of the Buchanan's Liberty coin focuses not on his presidential tenure but on his early life. Artistic Infusion Program Associate Designer David Westwood envisioned Buchanan as a young man keeping a ledger in his father's country store in Pennsylvania. It is a scene of quiet work and dedication—the boy who would grow up to be an "incorruptible statesman" (as honored on his congressionally approved memorial in Washington, D.C.), rather than the beleaguered president overwhelmed by national events.

Buchanan's Liberty was the most popular of the First Spouse gold coins of 2010 in each format, and one of the last of the program's issues to exceed a mintage of 10,000. In the first three days of sales, the Mint sold more than 6,000 pieces total, nearing the halfway point of the issue's maximum coinage. Collector interest continued to be strong, and the Mint announced a second round of minting just weeks into the sales period. Ultimately more than 12,000 coins were purchased before the Mint closed its sales of the Proof version on February 8, 2011, and of the Burnished version on April 11.

Demand for the Liberty subset keeps the secondary-market prices of this issue relatively high, despite its larger-than-average mintage.

THE FIFTH LIBERTY COIN THAT WASN'T: ALICE PAUL

Designer: *Susan Gamble (obverse); Phebe Hemphill (reverse).* **Sculptor:** *Phebe Hemphill (obverse and reverse).* **Composition:** *.9999 gold.* **Actual Gold Weight:** *1/2 ounce.* **Diameter:** *26.49 mm.* **Edge:** *Reeded.* **Mint:** *West Point.* **Issue Price:** *$1,041 (Burnished); $1,054 (Proof).* **Release Date:** *October 11, 2012.*

Mintage: 2,798 Burnished; 3,505 Proof

2012 Alice Paul, Burnished format.

In December 2011, Secretary of the Treasury Timothy Geithner directed that the U.S. Mint suspend minting and issuing Presidential dollars for circulation. "Regular circulating demand for the coins will be met through the Federal Reserve Bank's existing inventory of circulating coins minted prior to 2012," the Mint announced, noting that it would still offer various products and packages containing the dollar coins. Although the Presidential $1 Coin Act of 2005 tied the First Spouse coins to the Presidential dollars, this change had no effect on the issuance of the gold pieces.

On April 23, 2012, the U.S. Mint announced the Alice Paul design of the year's first First Spouse gold coin. The mintage limit for the Alice Paul coin was lowered from the previous year's 15,000 to 13,000, with customer demand determining how many would be Burnished and how many Proof.

Complications in striking the coins delayed their release until late in the year. They finally went on sale October 11, 2012. Initial demand was strong, perhaps with some buyers anticipating a short sales period and therefore a low mintage. Nearly a quarter of the mintage limit was ordered in the first week.

As with the prior year's issues, the 2012 First Spouse coins were priced by the Mint's sliding scale based on the fluctuating market value of gold. They started out higher than $1,000 per coin, but a decline in the spot value led to prices as low as $840 for the Proof format and $820 for the Burnished. The Proof coins remained on sale into the summer of 2013, with the Mint declaring them sold out on July 16. The final Proof mintage, after an official audit accounting for returned and melted coins, was 3,505. The Burnished version remained in the Mint's product catalog until December 31, 2013, with a final mintage of 2,798.

Some collectors bemoaned the U.S. Mint's "political correctness" in depicting suffragist Alice Paul instead of a coinage-inspired Miss Liberty to represent the presidency of widower Chester Alan Arthur. This complaint mischaracterizes the source of the design: the U.S. Congress, not the Mint. Alice Paul was written into the First Spouse program's authorizing legislation.

The coin's obverse design departs from others in the series with the word SUFFRAGIST underneath Alice Paul's portrait, instead of the ordinal of Arthur's presidency (21st) and the year-date range of his term (1881–1885). The portrait, designed by Susan Gamble and sculpted by Phebe Hemphill, has Alice facing the viewer with a steady and determined gaze that embodies her strength and courage. Alice was born in New Jersey in 1885 and raised in the Quaker traditions of public service and gender equality. She studied social work but soon realized that "I was never going to be a social worker, because I could see that social workers were not doing much good in the world. . . . you couldn't change the situation by social work." The "situation" was the inequality endured by women worldwide. In England in her early 20s Alice developed a more militant advocacy for women's rights, taking part in protests and being jailed for voicing her beliefs. She returned to the United States energized and well known. She publicized the cause of equal rights—in particular the right of women to vote—on a national scale, organizing a 1913 parade march in Washington, D.C., the day before Woodrow Wilson's inauguration as president. The lead banner in the march read, "We Demand an Amendment to the United States Constitution Enfranchising the Women of the Country." Alice Paul and other suffragists pushed the right-to-vote agenda for several more years, facing arrest, harassment, and even brutal confinement to psychiatric wards, which only fueled popular support for their cause. Finally in June 1919 the U.S. Senate passed the Constitution's 19th amendment, which was ratified in August 1920, guaranteeing women the right to vote. The reverse of the Alice Paul First Spouse gold coin, designed and sculpted by Phebe Hemphill, shows Alice in action, marching for equality with an American flag and a sash reading VOTES FOR WOMEN. Her stride is bold, and the energy of the motif, with the flag and the sash in motion, captures the suffragist's forward movement.

The Alice Paul gold coin is something of an anomaly in the First Spouse series, illustrating neither a First Lady nor a purely symbolic coinage-inspired representation of Liberty. However, no other suffragist embodies the ideals of American liberty—and the human urge to fight and to endure personal suffering for the liberty of others—more so than Alice Paul. Yes, there are coins from the era of Chester Arthur's presidency that depict Liberty and could have been used, making this the fifth in the series' Liberty subset. The Morgan dollar, the Indian Head cent, the Liberty Head nickel, and the Indian Princess Head $3 gold piece come to mind. But as a *living* symbol of American liberty, Alice Paul fits the First Spouse gold coin quite nicely.

THE FUTURE OF THE FIRST SPOUSES

"When I became Mint director in 2006," recalls Ed Moy, "one of the key issues on my plate was making sure of the successful launch of the Presidential dollar coins and their companion First Spouse gold bullion coins."

Today, whether they're collected for sentimental reasons or hoarded as hedges against inflation, the First Spouse coins have found their niche among gold buyers. The audience for the coins is diverse. It includes hobbyists who add one or two of each issue to keep their collections complete and up to date; precious-metal investors seeking 24-karat gold in coin form; and people who don't consider themselves numismatists but are attracted to the occasional design that interests them. The first issues in 2007 established a "field population" of tens of thousands of coins, while low-mintage issues of later years added a limited-supply challenge to assembling a complete collection. After slow activity in the early 2010s, popular mainstream sales skyrocketed in 2015 with the Jackie Kennedy coin. This introduced (or re-introduced) many Americans to the First Spouse coins. Over time, the expanded audience might bring additional mainstream interest to earlier issues. Many collectors enjoy the Liberty subset of four coins discussed in this appendix, with their classic U.S. coinage designs of Miss Liberty.

From the start of the series, many specialists have sought the finest grades (MS-70 and PF-70) not only for their personal aesthetic satisfaction but also to compete with other collectors in the NGC and PCGS set registries. Some pay a premium for "First Strike" or "Early Release" coins—those pieces acknowledged by the grading firms as coming from the earliest Mint production (usually the first 30 days) for each type. As noted, several of the First Spouse gold coins have been ranked in the *100 Greatest U.S. Modern Coins* and also among the *100 Greatest Women on Coins* (by Ron Guth). As more collectors work to assemble collections based on those popular books, demand for the included coins will increase. And as the First Spouse coinage matures from "modern" to "classic," the coins will continue to capture the imaginations and appreciation of history buffs and numismatists.

APPENDIX Y

Coin Clubs

Joining a coin club is an important part of your hobby fulfillment. Membership brings many advantages, most important of which are camaraderie and the accumulation of knowledge. We all need both.

Even if you can't travel to meeting locations and shows, most clubs produce newsletters that are highly educational and encourage members to contribute articles. This is one of the best ways to learn about a specific numismatic subject. With every article you write, you'll travel new avenues of research and add to your numismatic knowledge. It never fails.

Many specialized coin clubs have been born in the virtual environment of the Internet. These clubs often are interactive, offering all members a great opportunity to ask questions of specialists, share knowledge, and meet others with similar interests.

This appendix lists numismatic organizations dedicated to subjects that should interest most of our readers. The information noted, including membership fees and addresses, is as accurate as possible at the time of publication. A visit to a group's Web site can provide the latest information.

NATIONWIDE CLUBS AND GROUPS

The American Numismatic Association. This is the largest coin-collecting group in the world. The monthly magazine, *The Numismatist*, contains articles submitted by members on a wide array of topics. Additionally, the ANA's library is second to none and is available to all members. Other great benefits are also included as a part of your membership.

> American Numismatic Association
> 818 N. Cascade Ave.
> Colorado Springs, CO 80903-3279
> Phone: 800-367-9723
> Fax: 719-634-4085
> E-mail: ana@money.org
> Web site: www.money.org

CONECA (Combined Organizations of Numismatic Error Collectors of America). CONECA is a worldwide organization that specializes in the study of errors and varieties. Its bimonthly newsletter, *ErrorScope*, is filled with educational topics. Additionally, CONECA's Web site has a huge listing with descriptions of several thousand repunched mintmarks and doubled dies. And access to that is free to all! Finally, there are also members-only sections with still more for your error and variety education.

> CONECA
> c/o Rachel Irish
> 3807 Belmont Rd.
> Coeur d'Alene, ID 83815
> Web site: www.conecaonline.org

SPECIALIZED CLUBS AND GROUPS

Barber Coin Collectors' Society. Serving collectors of the many U.S. coins designed by Charles Barber, chief engraver of the Mint from 1879 to 1917, this group offers myriad resources for the interested numismatist. It publishes the *Journal of the Barber Coin Collectors' Society* on a quarterly basis. A membership application is available via its Web site.

> Dave Earp
> BCCS Membership
> P.O. Box 1723
> Decatur, IL 62525

Early American Coppers. Founded in 1967, this not-for-profit numismatic organization serves as a point of contact for collectors of early U.S. copper coins, including colonial issues and Hard Times tokens in addition to U.S. half cents and large cents. The group's publication, *Penny-Wise*, is renowned as a great source of information. A membership application is available via its Web site.

> EAC
> P.O. Box 2462
> Heath, OH 43056
> Web site: www.eacs.org

Fly-In Club. This specialty group, formed in 1991, is for collectors of Flying Eagle and Indian Head small cents. *Longacre's Ledger* is the group's award-winning publication. A membership application is available via its Web site.

> Fly-In Club
> P.O. Box 559
> Sandwich, IL 60548
> Web site: www.fly-inclub.org

John Reich Collectors Society. The purpose of the John Reich Collectors Society is to encourage the study of numismatics, particularly United States gold and silver coins minted before the introduction of the Liberty Seated design, and to provide technical and educational information concerning such coins. JRCS has a great newsletter and conducts meetings at various times throughout the year.

> John Reich Collectors Society
> Attn: Stephen A. Crain
> P.O. Box 1680
> Windham, ME 04062
> Web site: http://logan.com/jrcs

Liberty Seated Collectors Club. LSCC is one of the strongest groups dedicated to any coin design or series. LSCC members receive the quarterly *Gobrecht Journal*, which is filled with some of the most educational numismatic articles available anywhere.

> LSCC
> Dennis Fortier
> LSCC New Member Dues
> P.O. Box 1841
> Pawtucket, RI 02862
> Web site: www.lsccweb.org

Lincoln Cent Forum. An active online community for Lincoln cent collectors to discuss America's smallest circulating denomination, this forum also provides various resources for Lincoln cent collectors, including detailed explanation of the series and various aspects of the design, a glossary, and tips on coin photography. Creating an account is free.

> Web site: www.lincolncentforum.com

Shield Nickels. This is another excellent online group, this one for enthusiasts of Shield nickels. Like many of the others, the discussion groups are filled with excellent information. There is no better discussion group available for the variety enthusiast. And best of all, you can join free!

> Web site: groups.yahoo.com/group/
> Shield_Nickels

Notes

DIMES

1. This had been compiled by J. Colvin Randall of Philadelphia and was either bought by Haseltine, who assumed ownership, or was plagiarized. Randall received no credit. Randall also created a manuscript on early gold coin varieties, but it was never published and is lost today.

2. Certain information about this is from R.W. Julian to the author in 1993. Expanded commentary appears in *Silver Dollars and Trade Dollars of the United States: A Complete Encyclopedia*, 1993.

3. *American Journal of Numismatics*, October 1875; 1806 date of an unattributed newspaper clipping from the scrapbook of J.J. Mickley.

4. Interestingly, most Mint engravers were also associated in one way or another with bank-note engraving. Robert Scot furnished testimonials and may have engraved plates (none have been seen by the author). John Reich in 1810 worked on the side with Murray & Draper. Before coming to the Mint, William Kneass engraved and signed bank notes. Christian Gobrecht engraved notes (no signed vignettes have been seen by the author, however). James B. Longacre was a principal of Draper Toppan, Longacre & Co., one of the leading bank-note companies of the 1830s.

5. *American Journal of Numismatics*, Volumes 18 and 19, July 1883.

6. From an exchange item in the *Newark Daily Advertiser* on November 11, 1835; this notice was widely published.

7. Gerry Fortin, communication, April 14, 2015.

8. Anecdote from Kenneth Bressett, May 19, 2015: "I may have paid the highest price ever for a circulated 1838-O dime. In 1939 I traded a couple of my well-used copies of *Action Comics* for the coin, from a fellow schoolmate. I don't really know if one was the No. 1 (Superman) issue, but I still wonder about it. At the time I was just happy to get my 10 cents'

cost back for one of the used magazines, and to add something unusual to my budding coin collection. I have no idea where the kid got the coin."

9. The ceremony was held in the early evening and was brief, after which orations were given. The theater closed on January 14, 1843, for lack of patronage. It had been operating at a loss for some time.

10. John McCloskey, "An 1838 Large Stars Proof Dime," *The Gobrecht Journal*, Summer 2000.

11. Larry Briggs, communication, May 19, 2015. "I have had three or four over the years, and Brian Greer has had more than that."

12. *Ibid.*

13. For details of the New Orleans find and other discoveries, many of which included dimes, see the present author's book, *Lost and Found Coin Hoards and Treasures: Illustrated Stories of the Greatest American Troves and Their Discoveries* (Atlanta, Georgia, 2015).

14. Larry Briggs reported the second in 2011; discussed in the February 2011 E-Gobrecht; an intentional Proof or from dies otherwise polished?

15. Gerry Fortin, communication, May 11, 2015.

16. Larry Briggs, communication, May 19, 2015.

17. The first edition of *A Guide Book of United States Coins*, 1946, had a fanciful story about these; deleted from later editions.

18. Correspondence, April 14, 2015.

19. Population reports may exaggerate the number known.

20. Population reports may exaggerate the number known.

21. Population reports may exaggerate the number known.

22. Larry Briggs, communication, May 19, 2015.

23. Population reports may exaggerate the number known.

24. Joey Lamonte, "A Comprehensive Study of Proof 1856 Small Date Dimes," *The Gobrecht Journal*, November 1996. John W. McCloskey, "An 1856 Half Dime with Missing Denticles," *The Gobrecht Journal*, March 2005.

25. Larry Briggs, communication, May 19, 2015.

26. Population-report numbers have increased sharply in recent years; otherwise, the estimate would be 1 or 2. It is uncertain how many in the reports represent duplicate offerings of the same coins.

27. Population reports may exaggerate the number known.

28. For an in-depth study see John W. McCloskey, "The 1859-S Seated Dime," *The Gobrecht Journal*, March 2007. Fortin-2001.

29. Larry Briggs, communication, May 19, 2015.

30. Rich Uhrich, communication, May 7, 2015.

31. Correspondence, April 14, 2015.

32. For information on this issue in general see "The 1865-S Dime," by John W. McCloskey, *The Gobrecht Journal*, July 1989.

33. Larry Briggs, communication, May 19, 2015.

34. Correspondence, April 14, 2015.

35. Population reports may exaggerate the number known.

36. For more information see Jason Carter, "A Study of 1866-S Dimes," *The Gobrecht Journal*, March 1995.

37. For additional reading see "The Rare 1867 Dimes," by John W. McCloskey, *The Gobrecht Journal*, November 1976.

38. Population reports may exaggerate the number known.

39. Population reports may exaggerate the number known.

40. These are left over from an incompletely machined die face (cf. Craig Sholley, communication, May 26, 2015). This information was used on several other listings here.

41. Population reports may exaggerate the number known.

42. Correspondence, April 14, 2015.

43. Larry Briggs, communication, May 19, 2015.

44. *Ibid.*

45. Population reports may exaggerate the number known.

46. Communication, May 13, 2015.

47. Larry Briggs, communication, May 19, 2015.

48. *Ibid.*

49. Larry Briggs, communication, May 31, 2015.

50. For related information see "The 1873-S Dime," by John W. McCloskey, *The Gobrecht Journal*, November 1985.

51. Gerry Fortin, communication, April 14, 2015.

52. Alex Fey and Gerry Fortin, "Missing Arrows on Some 1874 Dimes, a Fascinating Mystery," *The Gobrecht Journal*, March 2011.

53. For a detailed study see "The Exceptionally Rare 1874-CC Dime, John W. McCloskey, *The Gobrecht Journal*, November 1980. In the same year Walter Breen called it "extremely rare; possibly six to eight known"—a typical, lightly researched comment.

54. For related information see "The 1874-S Dime," by John W. McCloskey, *The Gobrecht Journal*, July 1986.

55. Population reports may exaggerate the number known.

56. Gerry Fortin, communication, May 11, 2015.

57. Weimar W. White, "Carson City Presentation Pieces," *The Gobrecht Journal*, March 1996; and by the same author, "An 1876-CC Dime in Proof-65 Condition Sold at Auction," *The Gobrecht Journal*, November 2001. Also, Andy Lustig, communication, May 27, 2015: "With respect to the 'Proof' 1876-CC dimes, most are from striated dies and have at least partial wire rims. I might discount these as ordinary first strikes except for the existence of copper and nickel off-metal strikes, which indicate that something unusual was going on at the CC Mint. There is, however, at least one silver Proof that is not striated, and is as convincing as any Philadelphia Proof."

58. For details see Weimar W. White, "The Chemical Causes of Pitted Dies at the Carson City Mint," *The Gobrecht Journal*, March 1995.

59. Larry Briggs, communication, May 31, 2015.

60. Also see "New Dime Overdate Discovered 1877/6-CC," Gerry Fortin, The E-Gobrecht, April 2012.

61. For an in-depth study see Gerry Fortin, "1877-S Seated Dime Varieties," *The Gobrecht Journal*, March 1993.

62. Larry Briggs, communication, May 19, 2015.

63. G.W.M. was George Massamore, a Baltimore dentist and rare-coin dealer who issued auction catalogs.

64. Correspondence, April 13, 2015.

65. Population reports may exaggerate the number known.

66. Population reports may exaggerate the number known.

67. Larry Briggs, communication, May 19, 2015.

68. Larry Briggs, communication, May 31, 2015.

69. For additional reading see "The 1888-S Dime," by Bill Cregan, *The Gobrecht Journal*, July 1992.

70. Population reports may exaggerate the number known.

71. For related information see "The 1890-S Seated Dime," by Bill Cregan, *The Gobrecht Journal*, July 1981. The author states that this is "much scarcer than commonly assumed," and that it is "vastly underrated in AU to Uncirculated condition."

72. Certain information is from R.W. Julian, "A Cut Above the Rest," *Coins* magazine, December 1998; other information is from Mint correspondence and contemporary published accounts.

73. From *Aesop's Fables*.

74. *Liberty Enlightening the World*, a.k.a. *The Statue of Liberty*, dedicated in 1886.

75. Although the World's Columbian Exposition was scheduled to open in 1892, construction delays occurred, and it did not open to the public until the spring of 1893.

76. *Numismatic Art in America: Aesthetics of the United States Coinage* (second ed., Atlanta, Georgia, 2007)

77. *Boston Herald*, January 5, 1892, with January 4 dispatch from Washington.

78. Michael S. Fey, "A New 1901-O / Horizontal O Barber Dime," *Journal of the BCCS*, spring 1999, discusses this variety in detail.

79. Jacob G. Willson, "Denver Mints," *Numismatic Scrapbook*, June 1940.

80. Ed Rochette, "The Treasure of the Lost Dimes of Denver!" *Journal of the BCCS*, summer 1990.

81. *The Numismatist*, December 1909, p. 338.

82. Letter, January 27, 2015.

83. *The Numismatist*, March 1910, p. 93.

84. Russell Easterbrooks, "A Different Barber Dime," *Journal of the BCCS*, fall 1994.

85. Roger W. Burdette, *Renaissance of American Coinage 1916–1921*, pp. 14-31, gives correspondence and extensive details and is recommended as a source for additional information.

86. Burdette, *Renaissance*, gives details of the Mercury dime patterns, steps in production, and much information that has never appeared in print before. Most of this is beyond the scope of the present book. For patterns also see J. Hewitt Judd, *United States Pattern Coins* (10th edition, Atlanta, Georgia, 2009).

87. Suggestion of Rogers M. Fred, Jr., of Leesburg, Virginia, 1974. McAdoo's daughter Frances stated that when thieves burgled her father's house in the 1920s they took coins including 1916-dated patterns.

88. This is confirmed by unpublished documents in the Library of Congress.

89. The monument was authorized by the General Assembly of Maryland on April 5, 1906, and was dedicated on November 6, 1909, in Druid Hill Park. Albert Randolf Ross assisted Weinman in the work. The sculpture is about 10 feet high, and the granite base about 12 feet. In 1959 it was moved to Wyman Park to make way for the Jones Falls Expressway.

90. Letter from Roger W. Burdette, November 29, 2003; Burdette, *Renaissance*.

91. Per an interview with Wayne Miller, rare-coin dealer there, who occasionally bought examples from the general public.

92. David W. Lange, *The Complete Guide to Mercury Dimes* (second ed., 2005).

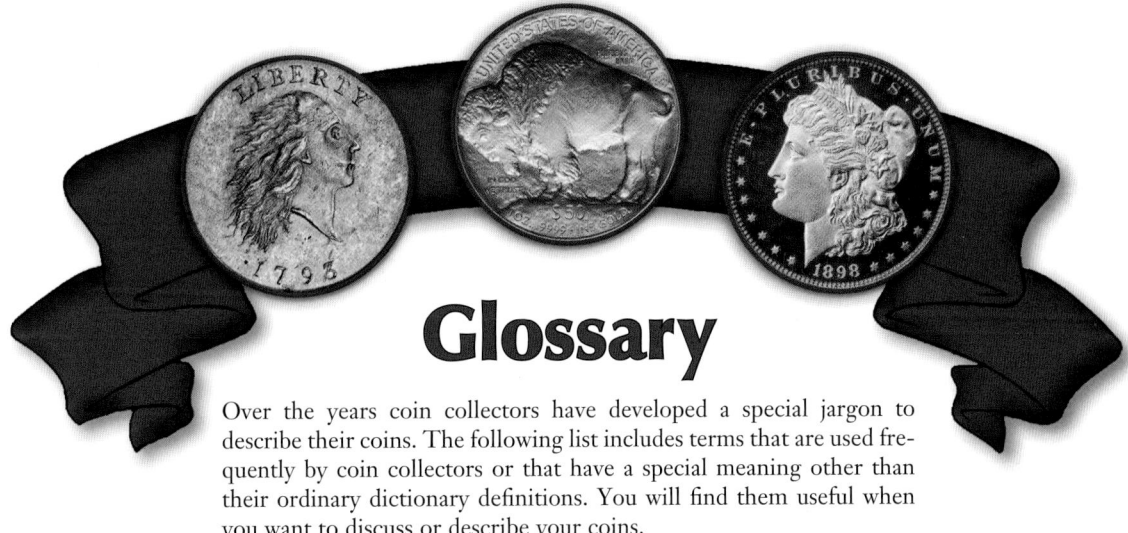

Glossary

Over the years coin collectors have developed a special jargon to describe their coins. The following list includes terms that are used frequently by coin collectors or that have a special meaning other than their ordinary dictionary definitions. You will find them useful when you want to discuss or describe your coins.

alloy—A combination of two or more metals.

altered date—A false date on a coin; a date altered to make a coin appear to be one of a rarer or more valuable issue.

bag mark—A surface mark, usually a small nick, acquired by a coin through contact with others in a mint bag.

billon—A low-grade alloy of silver (usually less than 50%) mixed with another metal, typically copper.

blank—The formed piece of metal on which a coin design will be stamped.

bronze—An alloy of copper, zinc, and tin.

bullion—Uncoined gold or silver in the form of bars, ingots, or plate.

cast coins—Coins that are made by pouring molten metal into a mold, instead of in the usual manner of striking blanks with dies.

cent—One one-hundredth of the standard monetary unit. Also known as a *centavo*, *centimo*, or *centesimo* in some Central American and South American countries; *centime* in France and various former colonies in Africa; and other variations.

certified coin—A coin that has been graded, authenticated, and encapsulated in plastic by an independent (neither buyer nor seller) grading service.

cherrypicker—A collector who finds scarce and unusual coins by carefully searching through unattributed items in old accumulations or dealers' stocks.

circulation strike—An Uncirculated coin intended for eventual use in commerce, as opposed to a Proof coin.

clad coinage—Issues of the United States dimes, quarters, halves, and some dollars made since 1965. Each coin has a center core of pure copper and a layer of copper-nickel or silver on both sides.

collar—The outer ring, or die chamber, that holds a blank in place in the coinage press while the coin is impressed by the obverse and reverse dies.

contact marks—Minor abrasions on an Uncirculated coin, made by contact with other coins in a bag or roll.

countermark—A stamp or mark impressed on a coin to verify its use by another government or to indicate revaluation.

crack-out—A coin that has been removed from a grading service holder.

crown—Any dollar-size coin (c. 38 mm in diameter) in general, often struck in silver; specifically, one from the United Kingdom and some Commonwealth countries.

cud—An area of raised metal at the rim of a coin where a portion of the die broke off, leaving a void in the design.

designer—The artist who creates a coin's design. An engraver is the person who cuts a design into a coinage die.

die—A piece of metal, usually hardened steel, with an incuse reverse image, engraved with a design and used for stamping coins.

die crack—A fine, raised line on a coin, caused by a broken die.

die defect—An imperfection on a coin, caused by a damaged die.

die variety—Any minor alteration in the basic design of a coin.

dipped, dipping—Refers to chemical cleaning of a coin to remove oxidation or foreign matter.

double eagle—The United States twenty-dollar gold coin.

doubled die—A die that has been given two misaligned impressions from a hub; also, a coin made from such a die.

doubloon—Popular name for a Spanish gold coin originally valued at $16.

eagle—A United States ten-dollar gold coin; also refers to U.S. silver, gold, and platinum bullion pieces made from 1986 to the present.

edge—Periphery of a coin, often with reeding, lettering, or other decoration.

electrotype—A reproduction of a coin or medal made by the electrodeposition process. Electrotypes are frequently used in museum displays.

electrum—A naturally occurring mixture of gold and silver. Some of the world's first coins were made of this alloy.

encapsulated coins—Coins that have been authenticated, graded, and sealed in plastic by a professional service.

engrailed edge—A coin edge marked with small curved notches.

engraver—The person who engraves or sculpts a model for use in translating to a coin die.

error—A mismade coin not intended for circulation.

exergue—That portion of a coin beneath the main design, often separated from it by a line, and typically bearing the date.

field—The background portion of a coin's surface not used for a design or inscription.

filler—A coin in worn condition but rare enough to be included in a collection.

fineness—The purity of gold, silver, or any other precious metal, expressed in terms of one thousand parts. A coin of 90% pure silver is expressed as .900 fine.

flan—A blank piece of metal in the size and shape of a coin; also called a *planchet*.

gem—A coin of exceptionally high quality, typically considered MS-65 or PF-65 or better.

gripped edge—An edge with irregularly spaced notches.

half eagle—The United States five-dollar gold coin minted from 1795 to 1929.

hub—A positive-image punch to impress the coin's design into a die for coinage.

incuse—The design of a coin that has been impressed below the coin's surface. A design raised above the coin's surface is in relief.

inscription—The legend or lettering on a coin.

intrinsic value—Bullion or "melt" value of the actual precious metal in a numismatic item.

investment grade—Promotional term; generally, a coin in grade MS-65 or better.

junk silver—Common-date silver coins taken from circulation; worth only bullion value.

key coin—One of the scarcer or more valuable coins in a series.

laureate—Head crowned with a laurel wreath.

legal tender—Money that is officially issued and recognized for redemption by an authorized agency or government.

legend—A principal inscription on a coin.

lettered edge—The edge of a coin bearing an inscription, found on some foreign and some older United States coins, modern Presidential dollars, and the MMIX Ultra High Relief gold coin.

luster—The brilliant or "frosty" surface quality of an Uncirculated (Mint State) coin.

milled edge—The raised rim around the outer surface of a coin, not to be confused with the reeded or serrated narrow edge of a coin.

mint error—Any mismade or defective coin produced by a mint.

mint luster—Shiny "frost" or brilliance on the surface of an Uncirculated or Mint State coin.

mintmark—A small letter or other mark on a coin, indicating the mint at which it was struck.

Mint set—A set of Uncirculated coins packaged and sold by the Mint. Each set contains one of each of the coins made for circulation at each of the mints that year.

motto—An inspirational word or phrase used on a coin.

mule—A coin struck from two dies not originally intended to be used together.

obverse—The front or face side of a coin.

overdate—Date made by superimposing one or more numerals on a previously dated die.

overgraded—A coin in poorer condition than stated.

overstrike—An impression made with new dies on a previously struck coin.

patina—The green or brown surface film found on ancient copper and bronze coins, caused by oxidation over a long period of time.

pattern—Experimental or trial coin, generally of a new design, denomination, or metal.

pedigree—The record of previous owners of a rare coin.

planchet—The blank piece of metal on which a coin design is stamped.

Proof—Coins struck for collectors by the Mint using specially polished dies and planchets.

Proof set—A set of each of the Proof coins made during a given year, packaged by the Mint and sold to collectors.

quarter eagle—The United States $2.50 gold coin.

raw—A coin that has not been encapsulated by an independent grading service.

reeded edge—The edge of a coin with grooved lines that run vertically around its perimeter, as seen on modern United States silver and clad coins.

regula—The bar separating the numerator and the denominator in a fraction.

relief—Any part of a coin's design that is raised above the coin's field is said to be in relief. The opposite of relief is incuse, meaning sunk into the field.

restrike—A coin struck from genuine dies at a later date than the original issue.

reverse—The back side of a coin.

rim—The raised portion of a coin that protects the design from wear.

round—A round one-ounce silver medal or bullion piece.

series—A set of one coin of each year of a specific design and denomination issued from each mint. For example, Lincoln cents from 1909 to 1959.

slab—A hard plastic case containing a coin that has been graded and encapsulated by a professional service.

spot price—The daily quoted market value of precious metals in bullion form.

token—A privately issued piece, typically with an exchange value for goods or services, but not an official government coin.

trade dollar—Silver dollar issued especially for trade with a foreign country. In the United States, trade dollars were first issued in 1873 to stimulate commerce with the Orient. Many other countries have also issued trade dollars.

truncation—The sharply cut-off bottom edge of a bust or portrait.

type—A series of coins defined by a shared distinguishing design, composition, denomination, and other elements. For example, Barber dimes or Franklin half dollars.

type set—A collection consisting of one representative coin of each type, of a particular series or period.

Uncirculated—A circulation-strike coin that has never been used in commerce, and has retained its original surface and luster; also called Mint State.

unique—An item of which only one specimen is known to exist.

variety—A coin's design that sets it apart from the normal issue of that type.

wheaties—Lincoln cents with the wheat ears reverse, issued from 1909 to 1958.

year set—A set of coins for any given year, consisting of one of each denomination issued that year.

Bibliography

A note from Q. David Bowers on the bibliography:

From the time that the first numismatically important book was published in America by Joseph B. Felt in 1839 to the present day, books have been the key to knowledge. A basic library of useful volumes is essential to the collecting and enjoyment of coins.

The following list includes the most important titles published over a long period of years. "Standard References" are ones that are essential today and include many updates of past writing and research. "References of Historical Interest" include titles from the past that for the most part have been made obsolete by later writing and research. Some of these remain valuable as a window into the state of the art years ago: they often contain anecdotal and narrative text not included in later works. Quality, usefulness, and desirability can vary widely, so before spending a large sum it is advisable to seek further information.

Beyond this listing, auction catalogs and price lists issued by various firms contain much interesting and valuable information. Countless articles in numismatic publications are valuable. The Numismatic Bibliomania Society (www.coinbooks.org) is the key to information on publications of the past and present. The Newman Numismatic Portal (www.nnp.wustl.edu) offers thousands of auction catalogs, magazine issues, and books free of charge; an incredible treasury for research and enjoyment.

The Whitman Publishing Web site (www.whitman.com) offers publications on coins, tokens, medals, and paper money currently available for purchase.

COLONIAL AND STATE COINAGE

STANDARD REFERENCES:

Bowers, Q. David. *Whitman Encyclopedia of Colonial and Early American Coins.* Atlanta, GA: 2009.

Breen, Walter. *Walter Breen's Complete Encyclopedia of U.S. and Colonial Coins.* New York, NY: 1988.

Carlotto, Tony. *The Copper Coins of Vermont.* Chelsea, MI: 1998.

Crosby, S.S. *The Early Coins of America.* Boston, MA: 1875 (reprinted 1945, 1965, 1974, 1983).

Demling, Michael. *New Jersey Coppers.* 2011.

Maris, Edward. *A Historic Sketch of the Coins of New Jersey.* Philadelphia, PA: 1881 (reprinted 1965, 1974, 1987).

Martin, Sydney F. *The Hibernia Coinage of William Wood (1722–1724).* n.p., 2007.

——— *The Rosa Americana Coinage of William Wood.* Ann Arbor, MI: 2011.

——— *French Coinage Specifically for Colonial America.* Ann Arbor, MI: Colonial Coin Collectors Club, 2015.

McDowell, Christopher. *Abel Buell and the History of the Connecticut and Fugio Coppers.* Ann Arbor, MI: 2015.

Miller, Henry C., and Hillyer C. Ryder. *The State Coinages of New England.* New York, NY: 1920.

Musante, Neil. *Medallic Washington* (2 vols.). London and Boston, MA: 2016.

Newman, Eric P. *Coinage for Colonial Virginia.* New York, NY: 1956.

——— *The United States Fugio Copper Coinage of 1787.* Ypsilanti, MI: 2007.

Newman, Eric P., and Richard G. Doty. *Studies on Money in Early America.* New York, NY: 1976.

Nipper, Will. *In Yankee Doodle's Pocket: The Myth, Magic, and Politics of Early America*. Conway, AR: 2008.

Noe, Sydney P. *The New England and Willow Tree Coinage of Massachusetts*. New York, NY: 1943.

—— *The Oak Tree Coinage of Massachusetts*. New York, NY: 1947.

—— *The Pine Tree Coinage of Massachusetts*. New York, NY: 1952.

—— *The Silver Coins of Massachusetts (Combined Reprint)*. New York, NY: 1973.

Rulau, Russell, and George Fuld. *Medallic Portraits of Washington*. Iola, WI: 1999.

Salmon, Christopher J. *The Silver Coins of Massachusetts*. New York, NY: 2010.

Siboni, Roger; John Howes; and A. Buell Ish. *New Jersey State Coppers. History. Description. Collecting*. New York, NY: 2013.

REFERENCES OF HISTORICAL INTEREST:

Anton, William T., Jr., and Bruce Kesse. *The Forgotten Coins of the North American Colonies*. Published by William T. Anton: 1990.

Atkins, James. *Coins and Tokens of the Possessions and Colonies of the British Empire*. London: 1889.

Baker, W.S. *American Engravers and Their Works*. Philadelphia, PA: 1875.

—— *The Engraved Portraits of Washington*. Philadelphia, PA: Lindsay & Baker, 1880.

—— *Medallic Portraits of Washington*. Philadelphia, PA: Robert M. Lindsay, 1885. An annotated reprint with updated information was prepared by George J. Fuld in 1965 and issued by Krause Publications.

Betts, C. Wyllys. *Counterfeit Half Pence Current in the American Colonies and Their Issue from the Mints of Connecticut and Vermont*. New York, NY: American Numismatic and Archaeological Society, 1886. Transcript of speech given to the Society.

Bressett, Kenneth E. "The Vermont Copper Coinage," part of *Studies on Money in Early America*. New York, NY: 1976.

Dalton, R., and S.H. Hamer. *English Provincial Token Coinage of the 18th Century*. London: 1910–1922. Issued in parts.

Douglas, Damon G. Manuscript notes on James Jarvis and Fugio coppers. Notes on New Jersey coppers. Excerpts published in *The Colonial Newsletter* and elsewhere. Loose copies made.

Felt, Joseph B. *An Historical Account of Massachusetts Currency*. Boston, MA: 1839.

Freidus, Daniel. "The History and Die Varieties of the Higley Coppers." *The Token: America's Other Money*. Coinage of the Americas Conference, 1994; New York, NY: 1995.

Guth, Ronald J. "The Copper Coinage of Vermont," *America's Copper Coinage 1783–1857*. Coinage of the Americas Conference, 1984; New York, NY: 1985.

Hull, John. "The Diaries of John Hull, Mint-Master and Treasurer of the Colony of Massachusetts Bay." *Archæologica Americana: Transactions and Collections of the American Antiquarian Society*. Vol. III. Cambridge, MA: 1850.

Jordan, Louis E., Robert H. Gore Jr., Numismatic Endowment, University of Notre Dame, Department of Special Collections, Website compiled maintained by Louis E. Jordan. Anthology of published information on various series.

Kenney, Richard D. *Struck Copies of Early American Coins*. New York, NY: 1952.

—— *Early American Medalists and Die-Sinkers Prior to the Civil War*. New York, NY: 1954.

Kessler, Alan. *The Fugio Cents*. Newtonville, MA: 1976.

Maris, Edward. *A Historical Sketch of the Coins of New Jersey*. Philadelphia, PA: 1881.

Mossman, Philip L. *Money of the American Colonies and Confederation: A Numismatic, Economic & Historical Correlation*. New York, NY: 1993.

—— "The American Confederation: The Times and Its Money." *Coinage of the American Confederation Period*. New York, NY: 1996.

—— *From Crime to Punishment: Counterfeit and Debased Currencies in Colonial and Pre-Federal America*. American Numismatic Society, 2013.

Musante, Neil E. *The Medallic Works of John Adams Bolen, Die Sinker &c*. Springfield, MA: 2002.

Nelson, Philip. *The Coinage of William Wood, 1722–1733*. London: 1959. Reprint.

Peck, C. Wilson. *English Copper, Tin and Bronze Coins in the British Museum 1558–1958*. London: 1960.

Prattent, Thomas, and M. Denton. *The Virtuoso's Companion and Coin Collector's Guide*. 8 volumes. London: 1795–1797.

Richardson, John M. "The Copper Coins of Vermont," published in *The Numismatist*: May 1947.

Ryder, Hillyer C. "The Colonial Coins of Vermont." Part of *State Coinages of New England*. New York, NY: 1920.

Slafter, Edmund F. "The Vermont Coinage." Essay in *Proceedings of the Vermont Historical Society*. Volume 1. Montpelier, VT: 1870.

Smith, Pete. "Vermont Coppers: *Coinage of an Independent Republic*." *Coinage of the American Confederation Period*. New York, NY: 1996.

Snelling, T. *A View of the Silver Coin and Coinage of England, From the Norman Conquest to the Present Time, Considered with Regard to Type, Legend, Sorts, Rarity, Weight, Fineness and Value, with Copper-Plates.* London: 1762.

Vlack, Robert A. *A. Catalog of Early American Coins.* Anaheim, CA: 1963.

—— *Early American Coins.* Johnson City, NY: Windsor Research Publications, Inc., 1965.

Williams, Malcolm E., Peter T. Sousa, and Edward C. Harris. *Coins of Bermuda 1616–1996.* Hamilton, Bermuda: 1997.

Wroth, Lawrence C. *Abel Buell of Connecticut: Silversmith, Type Founder & Engraver.* Middletown, CT: Acorn Club of Connecticut, 1958.

HALF CENTS
STANDARD REFERENCES:
Bowers, Q. David. *A Guide Book of Half Cents and Large Cents.* Atlanta, GA: 2015.

Breen, Walter. *Walter Breen's Encyclopedia of United States Half Cents 1793–1857.* South Gate, CA: 1983.

Cohen, Roger S., Jr. *American Half Cents–The "Little Half Sisters."* Second edition. 1982.

Manley, Ronald P. *The Half Cent Die State Book, 1793–1857.* United States, 1998.

REFERENCES OF HISTORICAL INTEREST:
Frossard, Ed. *Monograph of United States Cents and Half Cents Issued Between the Years 1793 and 1857.* Irvington-on-Hudson, NY: 1879.

Gilbert, Ebenezer. *The United States Half Cents from the First Year of Issue, in 1793, to the Year When Discontinued.* New York, NY: 1916.

LARGE CENTS
STANDARD REFERENCES:
Bowers, Q. David. *A Guide Book of Half Cents and Large Cents.* Atlanta, GA: 2015.

Breen, Walter. *Walter Breen's Encyclopedia of Early United States Cents 1793–1814.* Wolfeboro, NH: 2001.

Grellman, J.R., Jr. *The Die Varieties of United States Large Cents 1840–1857.* Lake Mary, FL: 1991.

—— *Attribution Guide for United States Large Cents 1840–1857.* Third edition. Bloomington, MN: 2002.

Neiswinter, Jim. *The Aristocrat: The Story of the 1793 Sheldon 1.* Printed by the author, 2013.

Newcomb, H.R. *United States Copper Cents 1816–1857,* New York, NY: 1944 (reprinted 1983).

Noyes, William C. *United States Large Cents, 1793–1857.* Six volumes. Ypsilanti, MI: 2006–2015.

—— *United States Large Cents 1793–1814.* Bloomington, MN: 1991.

—— *United States Large Cents 1816–1839.* Bloomington, MN: 1991.

Penny-Wise, official publication of Early American Coppers, Inc.

Sheldon, William H. *Penny Whimsy (1793–1814)*, New York, NY: 1958 (reprinted 1965, 1976).

Smith, Pete. *The Story of the Starred Reverse Cent.* Minneapolis, MN: Printed by the author.

Wright, John D. *The Cent Book 1816–1839.* Bloomington, MN: 1992.

REFERENCES OF HISTORICAL INTEREST:
Adams, John W. (editor). *Monographs on Varieties of United States Large Cents, 1793–1794.* Lawrence, MA: 1976.

Chapman, S. Hudson. *The United States Cents of the Year 1794.* Second edition. Philadelphia, PA: 1926.

Clapp, George H. *The United States Cents of the Years 1798–1799.* Sewickley, PA: 1931.

—— *The United States Cents 1804–1814.* The Coin Collector Series Number Eight. New York, NY: 1941.

Clapp, George H., and Howard R. Newcomb. *The United States Cents of the Year 1795, 1796, 1797 and 1800.* New York, NY: The American Numismatic Society, 1947.

Crosby, Sylvester S. *The United States Coinage of 1793——Cents and Half Cents.* Boston, MA: 1897.

Frossard, Ed. *Monograph of United States Cents and Half Cents Issued Between the Years 1793 and 1857.* Irvington-on-Hudson, NY: 1879.

Frossard, Ed., and W.W. Hays. *Varieties of United States Cents of the Year 1794: Described and Illustrated.* New York, NY: 1893.

Lapp, Warren A., and Herbert A. Silberman (editors). *United States Large Cents 1793–1857.* Lawrence, MA: 1975.

Loring, Denis W. (editor). *Monographs on Varieties of United States Large Cents, 1795–1803.* Lawrence, MA: 1976.

Maris, Edward. *Varieties of the Copper Issues of the United States Mint in the Year 1794.* Philadelphia, PA: 1869 and 1870.

McGirk, Charles E. "United States Cents and Die Varieties, 1793–1857," *The Numismatist,* October 1913 to December 1914.

Noyes, William C., Del Bland, and Dan Demeo. *The Official Condition Census for U.S. Large Cents 1793–1839.* 2005.

Sheldon, William H. *Early American Cents.* New York, NY: 1949.

Smith, Pete. *Names with Notes.* Minneapolis, MN: 1992.

SMALL CENTS
STANDARD REFERENCES:
Bowers, Q. David. *A Guide Book of Lincoln Cents*. Second edition. Atlanta, GA: 2016.

Lange, David W. *The Complete Guide to Lincoln Cents*. Wolfeboro, NH: 1996.

Schein, Allan. *The Gold Indians of Bela Lyon Pratt*. Published by the author, 2016.

Snow, Richard. *A Guide Book of Flying Eagle and Indian Head Cents*. Third edition. Atlanta, GA: 2016.

REFERENCES OF HISTORICAL INTEREST:
Anderson, Shane M. *The Complete Lincoln Cent Encyclopedia*. Iola, WI: 1996.

Bowers, Q. David. *A Buyer's and Enthusiast's Guide to Flying Eagle and Indian Cents*. Wolfeboro, NH: 1996.

Daughtrey, Charles D. *Looking Through Lincoln Cents: Chronology of a Series*. Second edition. Irvine, CA: 2005.

Lange, David W. *The Complete Guide to Lincoln Cents*. Wolfeboro, NH: 1996.

Manley, Stephen G. *The Lincoln Cent*. Muscatine, IA: 1981.

Steve, Larry, and Kevin Flynn, *Flying Eagle and Indian Cent Die Varieties*. Jarrettville, MD: 1995.

Taylor, Sol. *The Standard Guide to the Lincoln Cents*. Fourth Edition. Anaheim, CA: 1999.

Tomaska, Rick Jerry, *Cameo and Brilliant Proof Coinage of the 1950 to 1970 Era*. Encinitas, CA: 1991.

Wexler, John and Kevin Flynn. *The Authoritative Reference on Lincoln Cents*. Rancocas, NJ: 1996.

TWO-CENT PIECES AND THREE CENT PIECES
STANDARD REFERENCES:
Flynn, Kevin. *Getting Your Two Cents Worth*. Rancocas, NJ: 1994.

REFERENCES OF HISTORICAL INTEREST:
Bowers, Q. David. *United States Three-Cent and Five-Cent Pieces*. Wolfeboro, NH: 2005.

Kliman, Myron. *The Two Cent Piece and Varieties*. South Laguna, CA: 1977.

Leone, Frank. *Longacre's Two Cent Piece Die Varieties & Errors*. College Point, NY: 1991.

NICKEL FIVE-CENT PIECES
STANDARD REFERENCES:
Bowers, Q. David. *United States Three-Cent and Five-Cent Pieces*. Wolfeboro, NH: 2005.

—— *A Guide Book of Buffalo and Jefferson Nickels*. Atlanta, GA: 2007.

—— *A Guide Book of Shield and Liberty Head Nickels*. Atlanta, GA: 2006.

Fletcher, Edward L., Jr. *The Shield Five Cent Series*. Ormond Beach, FL: 1994.

Flynn, Kevin, and Bill Van Note. *Treasure Hunting Liberty Head Nickels*. Second edition. Brooklyn, NY: 2005.

Lange, David W. *The Complete Guide to Buffalo Nickels*. Virginia Beach, VA: 2006.

Nagengast, Bernard. *The Jefferson Nickel Analyst*. Second edition. Sidney, OH: 1979.

REFERENCES OF HISTORICAL INTEREST:
Montgomery, Paul, Mark Borckardt, and Ray Knight. *Million Dollar Nickels: Mysteries of the Illicit 1913 Liberty Head Nickels Revealed*. Irvine, CA: 2005.

Peters, Gloria, and Cynthia Mahon. *The Complete Guide to Shield and Liberty Head Nickels*. Virginia Beach, VA: 1995.

Spindel, Howard. "The Shield Nickel Viewer." Computerized reference on the series published by Howard Spindel, 2005. Information available at www.shieldnickels.net.

Wescott, Michael. *The United States Nickel Five-Cent Piece: A Date-by-Date Analysis and History*. Wolfeboro, NH: 1991.

Young, Richard G., and Wade J. Wilkin. *Racketeer Nickel and Its Many Mysteries*. Published by the authors, 2004.

HALF DIMES
STANDARD REFERENCES:
Bowers, Q. David. *A Guide Book of Liberty Seated Silver Coins*. Atlanta, GA: 2016.

Blythe, Al. *The Complete Guide to Liberty Seated Half Dimes*. Virginia Beach, VA: 1992.

Logan, Russell, and John McCloskey. *Federal Half Dimes 1792–1837*. Manchester, MI: 1998.

Smith, Pete, Joel J. Orosz, and Leonard Augsburger. *1792: Birth of a Nation's Coinage*. Dallas, TX: 2017.

REFERENCES OF HISTORICAL INTEREST:
Amato, Jon. *Numismatic Background and Census of 1802 Half Dimes*. Dallas, TX: 2017.

Breen, Walter. *United States Half Dimes: A Supplement*. New York, NY: 1958.

Newlin, H.P. *The Early Half-Dimes of the United States*. Philadelphia, PA: 1883 (reprinted 1933).

Valentine, D.W. *The United States Half Dimes*. New York, NY: 1931 (reprinted 1975).

DIMES AND TWENTY-CENT PIECES
STANDARD REFERENCES:
Bowers, Q. David. *A Guide Book of Barber Silver Coins*. Atlanta, GA: 2015.

—— *A Guide Book of Liberty Seated Silver Coins.* Atlanta, GA: 2016.

—— *A Guide Book of Mercury Dimes, Standing Liberty Quarters, and Liberty Walking Half Dollars.* Atlanta, GA: 2015.

Brunner, Lane J., and John M. Frost. *Double Dime: The United States Twenty-Cent Piece.* 2014.

Davis, David, Russell Logan, Allen Lovejoy, John McCloskey, and William Subjack. *Early United States Dimes 1796–1837.* Ypsilanti, MI: 1984.

Flynn, Kevin. *The Authoritative Reference on Roosevelt Dimes.* Brooklyn, NY: 2001.

—— *The Authoritative Reference on Twenty Cent.,* Lumberton, NJ: 2013.

Fortin, Gerry. *Liberty Seated Dimes Web-Book.* www.seateddimevarieties.com.

Greer, Brian. *The Complete Guide to Liberty Seated Dimes.* Virginia Beach, VA: 2005.

Lange, David W. *The Complete Guide to Mercury Dimes.* Second edition. Virginia Beach, VA: 2005.

Lawrence, David. *The Complete Guide to Barber Dimes.* Virginia Beach, VA: 1991.

REFERENCES OF HISTORICAL INTEREST:

Ahwash, Kamal M. *Encyclopedia of United States Liberty Seated Dimes 1837–1891.* Kamal Press, 1977.

Lawrence, David. *The Complete Guide to Barber Dimes.* Virginia Beach, VA: 1991.

Wexler, John A., and Kevin Flynn. *Treasure Hunting Mercury Dimes.* Savannah, GA: 1999.

QUARTER DOLLARS
STANDARD REFERENCES:

Bowers, Q. David. *A Guide Book of Barber Silver Coins.* Atlanta, GA: 2015.

—— *A Guide Book of Liberty Seated Silver Coins.* Atlanta, GA: 2016.

—— *A Guide Book of Mercury Dimes, Standing Liberty Quarters, and Liberty Walking Half Dollars.* Atlanta, GA: 2015.

—— *A Guide Book of Washington and State Quarters.* Atlanta, GA: 2006.

Bressett, Kenneth. *The Official Whitman Statehood Quarters Collector's Handbook.* New York, NY: 2000.

Briggs, Larry. *The Comprehensive Encyclopedia of United States Seated Quarters.* Lima, OH: 1991.

Cline, J.H. *Standing Liberty Quarters.* Third edition. 1996.

Knauss, Robert H. *Standing Liberty Quarter Varieties & Errors.* Second edition. Published by the author, 2014.

Rea, Rory, Glenn Peterson, Bradley Karoleff, and John Kovach. *Early Quarter Dollars of the U.S. Mint, 1796–1838.* 2010.

Tompkins, Steve M. *Early United States Quarters, 1796–1838.* 2008.

REFERENCES OF HISTORICAL INTEREST:

Browning, A.W. *The Early Quarter Dollars of the United States 1796–1838.* New York, NY: 1925 (reprinted 1992).

Duphorne, R. *The Early Quarter Dollars of the United States.* 1975.

Haseltine. J.W. *Type Table of United States Dollars, Half Dollars and Quarter Dollars.* Philadelphia, PA: 1881 (reprinted 1927, 1968).

Lawrence, David. *The Complete Guide to Barber Quarters.* Virginia Beach, VA: 1989.

HALF DOLLARS
STANDARD REFERENCES:

Ambio, Jeff. *Collecting and Investing Strategies for Walking Liberty Half Dollars.* Irvine CA: 2008.

Bowers, Q. David. *A Guide Book of Barber Silver Coins.* Atlanta, GA: 2015.

—— *A Guide Book of Liberty Seated Silver Coins.* Atlanta, GA: 2016.

—— *A Guide Book of Mercury Dimes, Standing Liberty Quarters, and Liberty Walking Half Dollars.* Atlanta, GA: 2015.

Overton, Al C. *Early Half Dollar Die Varieties 1794–1836.* Colorado Springs, CO: 1967 (Third edition, 1990, edited by Donald Parsley).

Peterson, Glenn R. *The Ultimate Guide to Attributing Bust Half Dollars.* Rocky River, OH: 2000.

Tomaska, Rick. *A Guide Book of Franklin and Kennedy Half Dollars.* Second edition. Atlanta, GA: 2012.

Wiley, Randy, and Bill Bugert. *The Complete Guide to Liberty Seated Half Dollars.* Virginia Beach, VA: 1993.

REFERENCES OF HISTORICAL INTEREST:

Amato, Jon. *The Draped Bust Half Dollars of 1796–1797.* Dallas, TX: 2015.

Beistle, M.L. *A Register of Half Dollar Die Varieties and Sub-Varieties.* Shippensburg, PA: 1929.

Haseltine. J.W. *Type Table of United States Dollars, Half Dollars and Quarter Dollars.* Philadelphia, PA: 1881 (reprinted 1927, 1968).

Howe, Dean F. *Walking Liberty Half Dollars, an In-Depth Study.* Sandy, UT: 1989.

Lawrence, David. *The Complete Guide to Barber Halves.* Virginia Beach, VA: 1991.

Swiatek, Anthony. *Walking Liberty Half Dollars.* New York, NY: 1983.

SILVER AND RELATED DOLLARS
STANDARD REFERENCES:
Bolender, M.H. *The United States Early Silver Dollars From 1794 to 1803.* Fifth edition. Iola, WI: 1987.

Bowers, Q. David. *The Encyclopedia of United States Silver Dollars 1794–1804.* Wolfeboro, NH: 2013.

—— *The Rare Silver Dollars Dated 1804.* Wolfeboro, NH: 1999.

—— *Silver Dollars and Trade Dollars of the United States: A Complete Encyclopedia.* Wolfeboro, NH: 1993.

—— *A Guide Book of Liberty Seated Silver Coins.* Atlanta, GA: 2016.

—— *A Guide Book of Modern United States Dollar Coins.* Atlanta, GA: 2016.

—— *A Guide Book of Morgan Silver Dollars.* Fifth edition. Atlanta, GA: 2016.

Burdette, Roger W. *A Guide Book of Peace Dollars.* Third edition. Atlanta, GA: 2016.

Fey, Michael S., and Jeff Oxman. *The Top 100 Morgan Dollar Varieties.* Morris Planes, NJ: 1997.

Logies, Martin A. *The Flowing Hair Silver Dollars of 1794.* 2004.

Newman, Eric P., and Kenneth E. *The Fantastic 1804 Dollar.*

Standish, Michael "Miles," with John B. Love. *Morgan Dollar: America's Love Affair With a Legendary Coin.* Atlanta, GA: 2014.

Van Allen, Leroy C., and A. George Mallis. *Comprehensive Catalogue and Encyclopedia of U.S. Morgan and Peace Silver Dollars.* New York, NY: 1997.

REFERENCES OF HISTORICAL INTEREST:
Carter, Mike. *The 1921 Morgan Dollars: An In-Depth Study.* Beverly Hills, CA: 1986.

Coinage of Gold and Silver. Collection, amounting to 491 printed pages, of documents, testimonies, etc., before the House of Representatives, Committee on Coinage, Weights, and Measures, 1891. The silver question, the silver-gold ratio, international monetary situations, financial panics, and more are debated. Washington, D.C.: Government Printing Office, 1891.

Haseltine. J.W. *Type Table of United States Dollars, Half Dollars and Quarter Dollars.* Philadelphia, PA: 1881 (reprinted 1927, 1968).

Highfill, John W. *The Comprehensive U.S. Silver Dollar Encyclopedia.* Broken Arrow, OK: 1992.

Osburn, Dick, and Brian Cushing. *A Register of Liberty Seated Dollar Varieties.* www.seateddollarvarieties.com.

Wexler, Crawford, and Kevin Flynn, *The Authoritative Reference on Eisenhower Dollars.* Rancocas, NJ: 1998.

Willem, John M. *The United States Trade Dollar.* Second edition. Racine, WI: 1965.

GOLD COINS ($1 THROUGH $20)
STANDARD REFERENCES:
Akers, David W. *Gold Dollars (and Other Gold Denominations).* Englewood, OH: 1975–1982.

Bowers, Q. David. *United States Gold Coins: An Illustrated History.* Second edition. Wolfeboro, NH: 2011.

Harry W. Bass, Jr. Museum Sylloge, Wolfeboro, NH: 2002.

—— *A Guide Book of Gold Dollars.* Atlanta, GA: 2008.

A Guide Book of Double Eagle Gold Coins. Atlanta, GA: 2004.

—— *U.S. Liberty Head Double Eagles: The Gilded Age of Coinage.* Wolfeboro, NH: 2015.

Bowers, Q. David, and Douglas Winter, *The United States $3 Gold Pieces 1854–1889.* Wolfeboro, NH: 2005.

Dannreuther, John W., and Harry W. Bass Jr. *Early U.S. Gold Coin Varieties.* Atlanta, GA: 2006.

Fivaz, Bill. *United States Gold Counterfeit Detection Guide.* Atlanta, GA: 2005.

Garrett, Jeff, and Ron Guth. *Encyclopedia of U.S. Gold Coins, 1795–1933.* Second edition. Atlanta, GA: 2008.

Winter, Douglas. *Gold Coins of the Charlotte Mint .1838–1861.* Wolfeboro, NH: 1987.

—— *New Orleans Mint Gold Coins.* Wolfeboro, NH: 1992.

—— *Gold Coins of the Dahlonega Mint 1838–1861.* Dallas, TX: 1997.

Winter, Douglas, and Lawrence E. Cutler, M.D., *Gold Coins of the Old West: The Carson City Mint 1870–1893.* Wolfeboro, NH: 1994.

REFERENCES OF HISTORICAL INTEREST:
Augsburger, Leonard D. *Treasure in the Cellar: A Tale of Gold in Depression-Era Baltimore.* Baltimore, MD: 2008.

Breen, Walter. *Major Varieties of U.S. Gold Dollars.* Chicago, IL: 1964.

Gillilland, Cory. *Sylloge of the United States Holdings in the National Numismatic Collection of the Smithsonian Institution. Volume 1: Gold Coins, 1785–1834.* Washington, D.C.: 1992.

Miller, Robert W., Sr., *U.S. Half Eagle Gold Coins.* Elmwood Park, NJ: 1997.

Schein, Allan. *The Gold Indians of Bela Lyon Pratt.* 1997.

Taglione, Paul F. *Federal Gold Coinage: Volume I, An Introduction to Gold Coinage & the Gold Dollars.* Boston, MA: 1986.

—— *A Reference to United States Federal Gold Coinage: Volume II, The Quarter Eagles.* Boston, MA: 1986.

—— *A Reference to United States Federal Gold Coinage: Volume III, The Three Dollar Pieces.* Boston, MA: 1986.

—— *A Reference to United States Federal Gold Coinage: Volume IV, An Investment Philosophy for the Prudent Consumer.* Boston, MA: 1986.

Taraskza, Anthony J. *United States Ten Dollar Gold Eagles.* Portage, MI: 1999.

Tripp, David E. *Illegal Tender: Gold, Greed, and the Mystery of the Lost 1933 Double Eagle.* New York, NY: 2004.

COMMEMORATIVE COINS
STANDARD REFERENCES:
Bowers, Q. David. *A Guide Book of United States Commemorative Coins.* Second edition. Atlanta, GA: 2016.

Flynn, Kevin. *The Authoritative Reference on Commemorative Coins 1892–1954.* Roswell, GA: 2008.

Swiatek, Anthony J. *Encyclopedia of the Commemorative Coins of the United States.* Chicago, IL: 2012.

REFERENCES OF HISTORICAL INTEREST:
Bullowa, David M. *The Commemorative Coinage of the United States 1892–1938.* New York, NY: 1938.

Mosher, Stuart. *United States Commemorative Coins.* New York, NY: 1940.

Swiatek, Anthony and Walter H, Breen. *The Encyclopedia of United States Silver and Gold Commemorative Coins 1892–1954.* New York, NY: 1981.

Taxay, Don. *An Illustrated History of U.S. Commemorative Coinage.* New York, NY: 1967.

BULLION COINS
Mercanti, John M., with Michael Standish. *American Silver Eagles: A Guide to the U.S. Bullion Coin Program.* Third edition. Atlanta, GA: 2016.

Moy, Edmund. *American Gold and Platinum Eagles: A Guide to the U.S. Bullion Coin Programs.* Atlanta, GA: 2013.

Tucker, Dennis. *American Gold and Silver: U.S. Mint Collector and Investor Coins and Medals, Bicentennial to Date.* Atlanta, GA: 2016.

PATTERN COINS
STANDARD REFERENCES:
Judd, J. Hewitt. *United States Pattern Coins.* Tenth edition. Atlanta, GA: 2008. Updated by Q. David Bowers.

REFERENCES OF HISTORICAL INTEREST:
Adams, Edgar H., and William H. Woodin. *United States Pattern, Trial, and Experimental Pieces.* New York, NY: 1913.

Cassel, David. *United States Pattern Postage Currency.* Miami, FL: 2000.

Davis, Robert Coulton. "Pattern and Experimental Issues of the United States Mint." *The Coin Collector's Journal.* September 1885.

Pollock, Andrew W., III. *United States Patterns and Related Issues.* Wolfeboro, NH: 1994.

PRIVATE AND TERRITORIAL GOLD
STANDARD REFERENCES:
Adams, Edgar H. *Private Gold Coinage of California 1849–1855.* Brooklyn, NY: 1913.

Bowers, Q. David. *A California Gold Rush History Featuring Treasure from the S.S. Central America.* Wolfeboro, NH: 2001.

Breen, Walter H., and Ronald Gillio. *California Pioneer Fractional Gold.* Second edition. Santa Barbara, CA: 1983.

Kagin, Donald H. *Private Gold Coins and Patterns of the United States.* New York, NY: 1981.

Leonard, Robert D., Jr., *California Pioneer Fractional Gold.* Wolfeboro, NH: 2003.

Moulton, Karl. *John J. Ford, Jr. and the Franklin Hoard.* Congress, AZ: 2003.

Owens, Dan. *California Coiners and Assayers.* Wolfeboro, NH; and New York, NY: 2000.

REFERENCES OF HISTORICAL INTEREST:
Adams, Edgar H. *Official Premium Lists of Private and Territorial Gold Coins.* Brooklyn, NY: 1909.

—— *Private Gold Coinage of California 1849–1855.* Brooklyn, NY: 1913.

Conrad, Judy (editor). Preface by Barry Schatz. *Story of an American Tragedy. Survivors' Accounts of the Sinking of the Steamship Central America.* Columbus, OH: 1988.

Griffin, Clarence. *The Bechtlers and Bechtler Coinage and Gold Mining in North Carolina 1814–1830.* Spindale, NC: 1929.

Lee, Kenneth W. *California Gold—Dollars, Half Dollars, Quarter Dollars.* Santa Ana, CA: 1979.

TOKENS, MEDALS, AND EXONUMIA
STANDARD REFERENCES:
Betts, C. Wyllys. *American Colonial History Illustrated by Contemporary Medals.* New York, NY: 1894.

Bowers, Q. David. *A Guide Book of Civil War Tokens.* Second edition. Atlanta, GA: 2015.

—— *A Guide Book of Hard Times Tokens.* Atlanta, GA: 2015.

Brunk, Gregory G. *American and Canadian Counter-marked Coins.* Rockford, IL: 1987.

Coffee, John M., and Harold V. Ford, *The Atwood-Coffee Catalogue of United States and Canadian Transportation Tokens.* Fifth edition. Boston, MA: 1996.

Fuld, George, and Melvin Fuld (edited by John Ostendorf, Q. David Bowers, Evelyn R. Mishkin, and Susan Trask). *U.S. Civil War Store Cards.* Third edition. Civil War Token Society, 2015.

Fuld, George, and Melvin Fuld (edited by John Mark Glazer, Q. David Bowers, and Susan Trask). *Patriotic Civil War Tokens.* Third edition. 2017.

Hibler, Harold E., and Charles V. Kappen. *So-Called Dollars.* Second edition. Clifton, NJ: 2008.

Hodder, Michael, and Q. David Bowers. *The Standard Catalogue of Encased Postage Stamps.* Wolfeboro, NH: 1989.

Jaeger, Katherine. *A Guide Book of United States Tokens and Medals.* Atlanta, GA: 2008.

Jaeger, Katherine, and Q. David Bowers. *100 Greatest American Medals and Tokens.* Atlanta, GA: 2007.

Julian, R.W. *Medals of the United States Mint: The First Century 1792–1892.* El Cajon, CA: 1977.

Leonard, Robert D., Jr., Ken Hallenbeck, and Adna G. Wilde Jr. *Forgotten Colorado Silver: Joseph Lesher's Defiant Coins.* Charleston, SC: 2017.

Musante, Neil. *Medallic Washington* (2 volumes). London and Boston, MA: 2016.

Rulau, Russell. *Standard Catalog of U.S. Tokens 1700–1900.* Fourth edition. Iola, WI: 2004.

Schenkman, David E. *Civil War Sutler Tokens and Cardboard Scrip.* Bryans Road, MD: 1983.

Schuman, Robert A., M.D. *The True Hard Times Tokens.* M&G Publications, 2000.

Sullivan, Edmund. *American Political Badges & Medals.* Lawrence, MA: 1981.

REFERENCES OF HISTORICAL INTEREST:

Adams, Edgar H. *United States Store Cards.* New York, NY: Edgar H. Adams and Wayte Raymond, 1920.

Appleton, William Sumner, *Description of Medals of Washington in the Collection of W.S. Appleton.* Boston, MA: 1873.

Bushnell, Charles I. *An Arrangement of Tradesmen's Cards, Political Tokens, also Election Medals, Medalets, &c, Current in the United States of America for the Last Sixty Years, Described from the Originals, Chiefly in the Collection of the Author.* Published by the author, 1858.

Collett, Mark W., J. Ledyard Hodge, and Alfred B. Taylor. *Catalogue of American Store Cards & c.* Philadelphia, PA: 1859.

DeWitt, J. Doyle. *A Century of Campaign Buttons 1789–1889.* Hartford, CT: 1959.

Doty, Richard G. (editor), *The Token: America's Other Money.* New York, NY: American Numismatic Society and Coinage of the Americas Conference, 1994.

Loubat, J.F. *The Medallic History of the United States of America, 1776–1876.* New York, NY: 1878.

Low, Lyman H. *Hard Times Tokens.* New York, NY: 1899.

Miller, Donald M. *A Catalogue of U.S. Store Cards or Merchants' Tokens.* Indiana, PA: 1962.

Rulau, Russell. *Hard Times Tokens: A Complete Revision and Enlargement of Lyman H. Low's 1899 Classic Reference.* Iola, WI: Krause Publications, 1987.

Rulau Russell, and George Fuld, *Medallic Portraits of Washington.* Iola, WI: 1985 and later editions.

Satterlee, Alfred H. *An Arrangement of The Medals and Tokens Struck in Honor of the Presidents of the United States and of the Presidential Candidates From the Administration of John Adams to That of Abraham Lincoln, Inclusive.* New York, NY: Printed for the author, 1862.

Snowden, James Ross. *A Description of the Medals of Washington.* Philadelphia, PA: 1861.

Woodward, W. Elliot. *A List of Washington Memorial Medals.* Boston, MA: 1865.

GENERAL COVERING MULTIPLE AMERICAN COIN SERIES

STANDARD REFERENCES:

Bowers, Q. David. *The History of United States Coinage as Illustrated by the Garrett Collection.* Los First printing. Los Angeles, CA: Published for The Johns Hopkins University.

—— *American Coin Treasures and Hoards.* Wolfeboro, NH: 1997.

—— *The History of American Numismatics Before the Civil War, 1760–1860.* Wolfeboro, NH: 1998.

—— *A Guide Book of United States Type Coins.* Second edition. Atlanta, GA: 2008.

Breen, Walter H. *Walter Breen's Encyclopedia of U.S. and Colonial Proof Coins, 1792–1977.* Albertson, NY: 1977; updated, Wolfeboro, NH: 1989.

——"Secret History of the Gobrecht Coinages." *Coin Collectors Journal,* 157–158. New York, NY: Wayte Raymond, Inc., 1954.

—— *Walter Breen's Encyclopedia of U.S. and Colonial Proof Coins, 1792–1977.* Albertson, NY: FCI Press, 1977.

—— *Walter Breen's Complete Encyclopedia of U.S. and Colonial Coins.* New York, NY: 1988.

Burdette, Roger W. *The Renaissance of American Coinage 1905–1908.* Great Falls, VA: 2006.

—— *The Renaissance of American Coinage 1909–1915.* Great Falls, VA: 2007.

—— *The Renaissance of American Coinage 1916–1921*. Great Falls, VA: 2005.

Carothers, Neil. *Fractional Money*. New York, NY: John Wiley & Sons, Inc., 1930.

Fivaz, Bill, and J.T. Stanton. *The Cherrypickers' Guide to Rare Die Varieties*. Atlanta, GA: various editions and volumes.

Garrett, Jeff, and Ron Guth. *100 Greatest U.S. Coins*. Fourth edition. Atlanta, GA: 2014.

Guth, Ron, and Jeff Garrett. *United States Coinage: A Study by Type*. Atlanta, GA: 2005.

Lange, David W. *A Guide Book of Modern United States Proof Coin Sets*. Second edition. Atlanta, GA: 2010.

Tucker, Dennis. *American Gold and Silver: U.S. Mint Collector and Investor Coins and Medals, Bicentennial to Date*. Atlanta, GA: 2016.

REFERENCES OF HISTORICAL INTEREST:

Alexander, David T., Thomas K. DeLorey, and Brad Reed. *Coin World Comprehensive Catalog & Encyclopedia of United States Coins*. Sidney, OH: Coin World, 1995.

Eckfeldt, Jacob R., and William E. DuBois. *A Manual of Gold and Silver Coins of All Nations, Struck Within the Past Century*. Philadelphia, PA: Assay Office of the Mint, 1842.

Scott Stamp & Coin Co., Ltd., also Scott & Co. and J.W. Scott Co., Ltd. *Standard Catalogue* (various titles). 1878–1913.

Taxay, Don. *Counterfeit, Mis-Struck and Unofficial U.S. Coins*. New York, NY: 1963.

—— *U.S. Mint and Coinage*. New York, NY: Arco Publishing, 1966.

—— *Scott's Comprehensive Catalogue of United States Coinage*. New York, NY: Scott Publications, 1970 (cover date 1971).

Tomaska, Rick Jerry. *Cameo and Brilliant Proof Coinage of the 1950 to 1970 Era*. Encinitas, CA: 1991.

Vermeule, Cornelius. *Numismatic Art in America*. Cambridge, MA: 1971.

Witham, Stewart. *Johann Matthaus Reich, Also Known as John Reich*. Canton, OH: November 1993.

WORLD ISSUES RELATED TO THE UNITED STATES

Allen, Lyman L. *U.S. Philippine Coins*. Oakland Park, FL: 1998.

Medcalf, Donald, and Russell, Ronald. *Hawaiian Money Standard Catalog*. Second edition. Mill Creek, WA: 1991.

Schilke, Oscar G., and Raphael E. Solomon. *America's Foreign Coins: An Illustrated Standard Catalogue with Valuations of Foreign Coins with Legal Tender status in the United States, 1793–1857*. New York, NY: 1964.

Shafer, Neil. *United States Territorial Coinage for the Philippine Islands*. Racine, WI: 1961.

HISTORY OF THE U.S. MINTS AND THE MINT COLLECTION
STANDARD REFERENCES:

Augsburger, Leonard D., and Orosz, Joel J. *The Secret History of the First U.S. Mint*. Atlanta, GA: 2011.

Bowers, Q. David. *Guide Book of the United States Mint*. Pelham, AL: 2016.

Goe, Rusty. *The Mint on Carson Street*. Reno, NV: 2003.

Lange, David W. *History of the United States Mint and Its Coinage*. Atlanta, GA: 2005.

Smith, Pete, Joel Orosz, and Leonard Augsburger. *1792: Birth of a Nation's Coinage*. Dallas, TX: 2016.

Taxay, Don. *The United States Mint and Coinage*. New York, NY: 1966.

REFERENCES OF HISTORICAL INTEREST:

Comparette, T.L. *Catalogue of Coins, Tokens and Medals in the Numismatic Collection of the Mint of the United States at Philadelphia, Pa*. Washington, D.C.: 1914.

Dubois, William E. *Pledges of History: A Brief Account of the Collection of Coins Belonging to the Mint of the United States, More Particularly of the Antique Specimens*. First edition. Philadelphia, PA: C. Sherman, 1846; Second edition. New York, NY: George P. Putnam, 1851.

Evans, George. *Illustrated History of the U.S. Mint* (various eds.), Philadelphia, PA: 1885–1901.

Hickson, Howard. *Mint Mark CC: The Story of the United States Mint at Carson City, Nevada*. Carson City, NV: The Nevada State Museum, 1972 and 1990.

Johnston, Elizabeth B. *A Visit to the Cabinet of the United States Mint, at Philadelphia*. Philadelphia, PA: 1876.

McClure, R.A. *An Index to the Coins and Medals of the Mint of the United States at Philadelphia*. Philadelphia, PA: 1891.

Moulton, Karl. *Henry Voigt and Others Involved in Early American Coinage*. Congress, AZ: 2003.

Smith, A.M. *Illustrated History of the U.S. Mint*. Philadelphia, PA: 1881.

Snowden, James Ross. *A Description of Ancient and Modern Coins in the Cabinet of the Mint of the United States*. Philadelphia, PA: 1860. (Mostly researched and written by George Bull [then curator of the Mint Cabinet] and William Ewing Dubois.)

Stewart, Frank. *History of the First United States Mint, Its People and ItsOperations.* 1924 (reprinted 1974).

Treasury Department, United States Mint, *et al. Annual Report of the Director of the Mint.* Philadelphia (later, Washington), 1795 onward.

Young, James Rankin. *The United States Mint at Philadelphia.* Philadelphia, PA: Capt. A.J. Andrews (agent, not publisher), 1903.

PUBLICATIONS ABOUT BOOKS, COINAGE, MONEY, AND NUMISMATICS

Adams, John W. *United States Numismatic Literature. Volume I. Nineteenth Century Auction Catalogs.* Mission Viejo, CA: 1982.

—— *United States Numismatic Literature. Volume II. Twentieth Century Auction Catalogues.* Crestline, CA: 1990.

Adelson, Howard. *The American Numismatic Society 1858–1958.* New York, NY: 1958.

American Journal of Numismatics. New York, NY, and Boston, MA: Various issues 1866 to 1912.

Attinelli, Emmanuel J. *Numisgraphics, or A List of Catalogues, Which Have Been Sold by Auction in the United States.* New York, NY: 1876.

Augsburger, Leonard D., Roger W. Burdette, and Joel J. Orosz. *Truth Seeker: The Life of Eric P. Newman.* Dallas, TX: 2015.

Baker, W.S. *American Engravers and Their Works.* Philadelphia, PA: 1875.

Becker, Thomas W. *The Coin Makers.* Garden City, NY: Doubleday & Company, 1969.

Bowers, Q. David. *Adventures with Rare Coins.* Los Angeles, CA: 1979, and later editions.

——*Abe Kosoff: Dean of Numismatics.* Wolfeboro, NH: 1985.

——*American Numismatics Before the Civil War, 1760–1860: Emphasizing the Story of Augustus B. Sage.* Wolfeboro, NH: 1998.

——*More Adventures with Rare Coins.* Wolfeboro, NH: 2001.

Breen, Walter H. *A Coiner's Caviar: Walter Breen's Encyclopedia of U.S. and Colonial Proof Coins.* Albertson, New York: 1977, reprint and update Wolfeboro, NH: 1989.

Bressett, Kenneth E. and A. Kosoff; introduction by Q. David Bowers. *The Official American Numismatic Association Grading Standards for United States Coins.* Seventh edition. Atlanta, GA: American Numismatic Association, 2013.

Brown, Martin R., and John W. Dunn. *A Guide to the Grading of United States Coins.* Oklahoma City, OK: Published by the authors, 1963.

Burdette, Roger. *From Mine to Mint: American Coinage Operations and Technology, 1833 to 1837.* Great Falls, VA: 2013.

Coin Collector's Journal, The. New York City, NY: J.W. Scott & Co.,1870s and 1880s.

Coin World Almanac. Sidney, OH: Coin World, 1976 and later editions.

Coinage Laws of the United States 1792–1894. Modern foreword to reprint by David L. Ganz. Wolfeboro, NH: 1991.

Cooper, Denis R. *The Art and Craft of Coinmaking, A History of Minting Technology.* London, England: 1988.

Davis, Charles E. *American Numismatic Literature: An Annotated Survey of Auction Sales 1980–1991.* Lincoln, MA: 1992.

Del Mar, Alexander. *The History of Money in America from the Earliest Times to the Establishment of the Constitution.* Reprint. Hawthorne, CA: 1966.

Dickeson, Montroville W. *American Numismatical Manual.* Philadelphia, PA: J.B. Lippincott & Co., 1859, also editions of 1860 and 1866.

Doty, Richard G. *America's Money, America's Story.* Iola, WI: 1998.

Durst, Lorraine S. *United States Numismatic Auction Catalogs: A Bibliography.* New York, NY: 1981.

Eckfeldt, Jacob Reese, and William Ewing DuBois. *A Manual of Gold and Silver Coins of All Nations, Struck Within the Past Century.* Philadelphia, PA: 1842.

Gengerke, Martin. *American Numismatic Auctions.* Woodside, NY: printed by the author, 1990.

Groce, George C., and David H. Wallace. *New York Historical Society's Dictionary of Artists in America.* New Haven, CT: 1957.

Heaton, Augustus G. *A Treatise on the Coinage of the United States Branch Mints.* Washington, D.C.: Published by the author, 1893.

Hepburn, A. Barton. *A History of Currency in the United States.* New York, NY: 1915.

Hickcox, John H. *An Historical Account of American Coinage.* Albany, NY: 1858.

Hodder, Michael J., and Q. David Bowers. *The Norweb Collection: An American Legacy.* Wolfeboro, NH: 1987.

Jaeger, Katherine M., and Q. David Bowers. *The 100 Greatest American Medals and Tokens.* Atlanta, GA: 2007.

Jones, George F. *The Coin Collector's Manual: A Guide Book for Coin Collectors.* Philadelphia, PA: 1860.

Kenney, Richard D. *Early American Medalists and Die-Sinkers Prior to the Civil War.* New York, NY: 1954.

Kleeberg, John M. "The Shipwreck of the *Faithful Steward:* A 'Missing Link' in the Exports of British and Irish Halfpence." New York, NY: 1996.

Linderman, Henry R. *Money and Legal Tender.* New York, NY: G.P. Putnam's Sons, 1877.

Lupia, John N. III. *American Numismatic Auctions to 1875, Volume 1, 1738–1850.* 2013.

Moulton, Karl. *United States Numismatic Catalogues, 1990–2000.* Congress, AZ: 2001.

Orosz, Joel J. *The Eagle That Is Forgotten: Pierre Eugène Du Simitière, Founding Father of American Numismatics.* Wolfeboro, NH: 1988.

Prime, W.C. *Coins, Medals, and Seals.* New York, NY: 1861.

Raymond, Wayte. *Standard Catalogue of United States Coins and Paper Money* (titles vary). New York, NY: Scott Stamp & Coin Co. (and others), 1934 to 1957 editions.

Ruddy, James F. *Photograde.* Nineteenth edition. Racine, WI: Western Publishing Co., 1990.

Rulau, Russell. *Standard Catalogue of United States Tokens 1700–1900.* Fourth edition. Iola, WI: 2004.

Shippee, Robert W. *Pleasure & Profit: 100 Lessons for the Building and Selling of a Collection of Rare Coins.* Atlanta, GA: 2015.

Smith, A.M. *Coin Collectors' of the United States, Illustrated Guide.* Philadelphia, PA: January 1886.

Stauffer, David McNeely. *American Engravers Upon Copper and Steel.* New York, NY: 1907.

Sumner, William Graham. *A History of American Currency.* New York, NY: 1874.

Taxay, Don. *Counterfeit, Mis-Struck, and Unofficial U.S. Coins.* New York, NY: 1963.

—— *U.S. Mint and Coinage.* New York, NY: 1966.

—— *Scott's Comprehensive Catalogue of United States Coinage.* New York, NY.

Wright, Benjamin P. "The American Store or Business Cards." Published serially in *The Numismatist,* 1898–1901. Reprinted by the Token and Medal Society, 1963.

Image Credits

PHOTO CREDITS

Note: Images are credited by page number and by location on the page, starting with number 1 at upper left and reading left to right. Obverse-reverse pairs are counted as a single image and are noted in italic type.

ANACS shared the following image: 19.2.

DimeMan shared the following image: 595.1.

Heritage Auctions shared the following images: 22.5; 93.*1*; 108.5; 111.*4, 5*; 113.*3*; 1147.*1*; 117.5; 120.1; 125.1, 2, 3, 4; 136.*1*; 138.2, *3*; 147.2; 148.*1, 3*; 150.2; 151.2, 5; 152.*4*; 158.*1*; 161.1, 2, 3; 164.*1*; 165.1, 5; 166.*4*; 167.*1*; 168.*1*; 169.*3*; 173.1, 2, 3; 175.6, 7; 176.1, 2; 177.*3*; 179.*1*; 183.*1*; 184.2, *3*; 186.2; 187.*1*; 189.1, 2, 3; 192.1, 2, 3; 193.*1*, 3, 4; 194.2, 3; 198.2; 199.1; 202.*1, 2, 5*; 204.*3*; 205.*3, 4*; 208.2; 219.*3*; 227.*3*; 228.1, 2; 230.*1*; 234.*1*; 249.1, 2; 256.*4*; 256.*5, 7*; 258.*1*; 264.1, 2, 3, 4, 5, 6, 7, 8, 9, 10; 265.*1*; 266.*1*; 267.1, 2, *3*; 268.1, 2, *3, 4*; 271.*1*; 272.1, 2, *3, 4*; 273.*1*; 279.*1*; 280.2; 284.*1*; 285.2; 290.2; 291.*1*; 293.1, 2; 297.*1*, 2; 298.*4*; 326.1; 331.2; 332.1, 2, 3; 333.*1*, 2; 335.2; 337.*3*; 338.2; 340.*1*; 342.3, 4, 5; 344.2; 345.*1, 3*; 347.*3*; 348.2; 351.*3, 4, 5, 6*; 356.1, 2; 366.*1*; 371.2; 388.*1*; 389.2; 392.1, 2; 417.2, *5*; 418.*3, 4*; 423.*1*; 430.*3, 4*; 434.*1*, 2, 3; 435.*1, 3*; 436.*1*; 438.*3*; 440.*1*; 443.*1*; 445.2, *3*; 446.*1*; 447.1, *5*; 448.1, 2; 450.*1*; 451.*1*; 452.2; 453.*3*; 454.*1*; 455.1, 2; 461.1, *3*; 462.2; 465.*3*; 466.*1*; 468.*3*; 471.1, 2; 472.2; 473.2; 477.*1*; 480.1, *3*; 482.*1*; 483.1, 2; 484.2, 3; 485.1, 2, *3*; 486.2; 487.2; 490.*1*; 491.*1*; 498.1, *3*; 499.1, *3*; 500.*1*; 505.1, 2; 506.2; 515.*3*; 521.2; 524.*1, 2, 3*; 525.2; 527.7; 528.4; 529.*1*; 530.*1, 3*; 534.*1*; 537.2; 540.*3*; 541.2; 542.*1*; 543.2; 544.*3*; 545.*3*; 546.2, *3*; 547.*3*; 548.2; 560.*1*; 580.*1*; 589.*1, 3, 4*; 591.2, 3, 4, 5; 598.*1, 4*; 599.2, *4*; 600.*3*; 601.*3*; 602.*1, 3*; 603.*1, 3*; 604.*1, 2*; 605.*1, 2*; 606.*4*; 607.2, *3*; 608.*1, 3*; 609.*1*, 2, *3*; 610.*1, 3*; 611.*1, 2*; 612.*1*; 613.*1, 3*; 614.*1, 4*; 615.2; 616.*1, 2*; 617.*1, 3*; 618.*1, 2*; 619.*1, 2, 3*; 620.*1*; 621.*1, 3*; 623.2, *3*; 624.*1, 3*; 626.*1*; 629.4; 633.*4*; 634.*9*; 635.2, *5, 8*; 636.7; 637.*1, 4*; 638.2, *4, 7*; 639.*5, 9*; 641.*10*; 642.*4, 8, 9, 10*; 643.*1, 2, 3, 4, 5, 6, 7, 8, 9, 10*; 644.*1, 2, 3, 4, 5, 6, 7, 8, 9, 10*; 645.*1, 2, 3, 4, 5, 6, 7, 8, 9, 10*; 646.*1, 2, 3, 5, 7, 8, 10*; 647.*1, 3, 5, 6, 8, 9*; 648.*9*; 649.*2*;

654.*1*; 744.*1*; 748.*1*; 751.*3*; 756.*3*; 757.*1*; 766.8; 768.*5*; 772.*1, 3*; 773.*1*; 793.3, 4; 800.*3*; 807.*1*; 840.4; 849.2; 853.*1, 3*; 879.2; 886.*1*; 911.*1, 1*; 919.*1*; 923.*3*; 933.*1*; 935.*1*; 946.*1*; 959.*1*; 966.*1*; 969.1, 2, 4; 971.3, 4; 974.2, 3; 975.*3, 4, 5, 6, 7*; 978.1, 2; 980.4; 981.2; 999.*3*; 1002.1, 2, 3, 4; 1003.*1, 2, 3, 4*; 1005.3, 4; 1023.2; 1062.*1*.

Justin Lee shared the following images: 596.2, *3, 5*.

Tom Mulvaney shared the following images: 154.*2*; 156.*1*; 246.*3*; 258.2; 279.*3*; 280.*1*; 285.*3, 4*; 286.*1*; 325.1; 389.*1*; 417.6; 513.*3*; 551.*1, 4*; 598.2; 832.*1*; 870.*1*; 877.*1, 2*; 879.*1*; 964.*3*; 966.3, 5; 967.*1*; 976.*3*; 999.2; 1008.1; 1026.2; 1026.3; 1027.1; 1030.1; 1099.*1*; 1101.*1*; 1102.2; 1103.*1*; 1104.*1, 2*; 1105.*1*; 1106.*1*; 1107.*1*; 1108.*1*; 1109.*1*; 1110.*1, 2*; 1111.*1*; 1112.*1, 2*; 1113.*1*; 1114.*1, 2*; 1116.*1, 2*; 1117.*1*; 1118.*1, 2*; 1119.*1*; 1120.*1, 2*; 1121.*1*; 1122.*1*; 1123.*1*; 1124.*1, 2*; 1125.*1*; 1126.*1, 2*; 1127.*1*; 1139.2; 1140.*1*; 1141.*1, 2*; 1143.*1*; 1144.*1, 2*; 1145.*1*; 1146.*1, 2*; 1148.*1*; 1149.*1, 2*; 1150.*1*; 1151.*1, 2*; 1152.*1*; 1153.*1, 2*; 1154.*1*; 1155.*1, 2*; 1156.*1*; 1158.*1*; 1158.2; 1159.*1*; 1160.*1, 2*; 1161.*1*.

The **National Numismatic Collection** at the Smithsonian Institution shared the following images: 936.3; 952.2, *3*.

NGC shared the following images: 19.3; 615.*1*; 620.2; 622.*1*; 625.*1*; 626.*4*; 628.2; 632.1, 2; 633.1, 2, 3, 5, 6, 7, 8, 9, 10; 634.1, 2, 3, 4, 5, 6, 7, 8, 10; 635.1, 3, 4, 6, 7, 9, 10; 636.1, 2, 3, 4, 5, 6, 8, 9, 10; 637.2, 3, 5, 6, 7, 8, 9, 10; 638.1, 3, 5, 6, 8, 9, 10; 639.1, 2, 3, 4, 7, 8, 10; 640.1, 2, 3, 4, 5, 6, 7, 8, 9, 10; 641.1, 2, 3, 4, 5, 6, 7, 8, 9; 642.1, 2, 3, 5, 6, 7; 648.1, 4, 7, 8, 10; 650.8.

PCGS shared the following image: 19.4.

Ken Potter shared the following images: 489.4; 600.2; 601.2; 603.2; 608.2; 610.2; 612.2; 614.2; 614.3; 621.2; 629.3.

Roger Siboni shared the following images: 95.3, *4*; 96.*3*; 130.3, 5, 6; 131.2, 3, 7, 8, 9; 132.3, 5; 133.9; 141.*1*; 229.3, 4; 230.*3, 5, 6*; 596.*1*.

IMAGE CREDITS

Stack's Bowers Galleries shared the following images: 95.*1*; 95.*2*; 104.*2*; 110.*5*; 111.*1, 2, 3*; 112.*2, 4, 5*; 113.*1, 2*; 114.*3*; 116.*1, 4, 5*; 117.*7*; 132.*1, 4*; 135.*1*; 142.*2*; 143.*3*; 152.*2, 3*; 153.*4*; 154.*3*; 158.*2*; 159.*1*; 159.*2*; 160.*1, 2, 3*; 163.*1, 2, 3*; 164.*2, 3*; 165.*2, 4*; 166.*1*; 167.*2*; 168.*2, 3*; 169.*1, 2*; 170.*6, 7*; 171.*8, 9*; 172.*1, 2*; 173.*4*; 174.*1, 2, 3*; 176.*3*; 177.*1, 2*; 178.*1, 2, 3*; 179.*2*; 184.*1*; 185.*1, 2, 3*; 186.*1*; 187.*2*; 188.*1, 2, 3*; 191.*1, 2, 3*; 193.*2*; 195.*2*; 196.*1, 2*; 197.*1, 2, 3*; 198.*1*; 204.*1, 2*; 205.*1*; 207.*2, 4, 5*; 208.*1*; 209.*1, 2, 3*; 210.*1, 2*; 212.*2*; 217.*2*; 218.*1, 2*; 219.*1, 2, 4*; 224.*1*; 225.*2*; 226.*1, 2*; 227.*1, 2, 4*; 228.*3*; 230.*2, 4*; 232.*1, 2, 3*; 233.*1, 2, 3*; 233.*4*; 234.*2*; 242.*1, 2, 3, 4, 5*; 244.*1, 2, 3*; 245.*1, 2, 3, 4*; 246.*1, 2*; 255.*1*; 256.*6*; 257.*1*; 258.*3*; 267.*2*; 270.*1, 2, 3*; 271.*3*; 277.*1, 2, 3, 4, 5, 6*; 278.*1*; 279.*2*; 280.*3*; 283.*1, 2*; 284.*2, 3*; 285.*1*; 286.*2*; 292.*1, 4*; 293.*3*; 296.*2*; 297.*3, 4*; 298.*1, 2, 3*; 299.*1*; 304.*1, 2*; 305.*1, 2, 3*; 306.*1, 2, 3, 4*; 312.*1*; 313.*1, 2, 3, 4*; 327.*4, 5*; 336.*1, 2, 3*; 337.*1, 2*; 338.*1*; 339.*1, 2*; 340.*2, 3*; 341.*1, 2, 3*; 343.*1, 2, 3*; 344.*1*; 345.*2*; 346.*4*; 347.*1, 2*; 348.*1, 4*; 349.*2*; 351.*2, 7, 8, 12*; 353.*1, 2, 3*; 354.*1, 2, 3*; 355.*2*; 372.*1, 2*; 373.*1, 2, 3, 4*; 377.*1, 2*; 378.*1*; 379.*1*; 387.*1, 2*; 388.*2, 3, 4*; 389.*3*; 395.*3*; 396.*1, 2*; 397.*1, 2*; 399.*1, 2, 3*; 400.*1, 2, 3*; 401.*2, 3, 3*; 402.*1, 2*; 406.*2, 4*; 407.*4*; 408.*1*; 411.*1*; 414.*1, 2*; 417.*1, 9, 12*; 428.*1*; 429.*1, 2, 3*; 430.*1, 2*; 431.*1, 4*; 435.*2*; 436.*2*; 441.*2*; 443.*3*; 444.*2*; 450.*2*; 452.*1*; 453.*2*; 454.*2*; 455.*3*; 457.*2*; 458.*2*; 459.*3*; 462.*1*; 463.*2*; 464.*2*; 465.*2*; 466.*2*; 467.*2*; 468.*2*; 469.*2*; 470.*2*; 472.*1*; 473.*1*; 474.*1*; 476.*1, 3*; 478.*1*; 480.*2*; 482.*2*; 484.*1*; 487.*1*; 489.*2*; 491.*2*; 493.*1, 3*; 495.*1*; 496.*1, 3*; 497.*2*; 498.*2*; 499.*2*; 500.*2*; 501.*2*; 502.*2*; 503.*3*; 504.*2*; 507.*2*; 512.*1*; 513.*1*; 514.*1, 2, 3, 4*; 515.*1, 2*; 517.*1, 3*; 518.*2*; 519.*2, 3*; 520.*2*; 521.*1*; 522.*1, 2*; 523.*2, 3*; 525.*3*; 527.*8*; 530.*2*; 531.*3*; 532.*2, 3*; 533.*2*; 534.*2*; 535.*3*; 536.*1, 2*; 537.*3*; 538.*3*; 539.*2, 3*; 540.*1*; 541.*1*; 542.*2, 3*; 543.*1, 3*; 545.*1*; 546.*1*; 547.*2*; 549.*3*; 557.*1, 2, 3*; 558.*1, 2, 3, 4*; 559.*1, 2, 3*; 560.*2*; 561.*1, 2, 3*; 562.*1, 2*; 563.*1, 2, 3, 4*; 564.*1, 2, 3*; 565.*1, 2, 3*; 566.*1, 2, 3*; 567.*1, 2*; 568.*1, 3*; 569.*1, 2*; 570.*1*; 571.*2, 3, 4, 5*; 572.*2, 3*; 573.*1, 3*; 575.*3*; 576.*3, 4*; 577.*1, 3, 4*; 578.*1, 2, 3, 4*; 579.*2, 3*; 580.*3, 4*; 581.*3*; 582.*1, 2, 5, 6*; 584.*1, 2, 3*; 585.*1, 2, 3*; 586.*1, 2, 3*; 587.*1, 2*; 587.*4*; 588.*2, 3, 4*; 589.*2, 5, 6*; 597.*1, 2*; 598.*3*; 601.*1*; 606.*1*; 612.*3*; 617.*4*; 622.*3*; 625.*2*; 627.*1, 4*; 628.*3*; 651.*5*; 745.*1*; 751.*2, 4*; 768.*6*; 774.*1*; 786.*4*; 793.*2*; 822.*2*; 840.*1, 2*; 846.*1*; 897.*1*; 905.*1, 2*; 919.*2*; 935.*2*; 936.*2*; 941.*3, 4*; 942.*1, 1*; 946.*3, 4*; 947.*1, 4*; 953.*1*; 957.*1*; 959.*3, 4*; 960.*1, 2*; 961.*1, 2*; 963.*9, 10, 11, 12*; 965.*1, 2*; 972.*1, 3*; 975.*1*; 976.*1, 2*; 977.*2*; 981.*5, 7*; 990.*2, 3*; 991.*1*; 998.*1*; 1004.*1, 2*; 1005.*2*; 1017.*1, 4, 5, 6*; 1018.*1, 2*; 1023.*1, 4, 5*; 1024.*1*; 1025.*1*; 1026.*1*; 1028.*1*; 1036.*1, 2*; 1037.*1*; 1046.*1*; 1047.*1*; 1048.*1*; 1049.*1*; 1050.*1*; 1051.*1*; 1053.*1*; 1053.*2*; 1054.*1, 2*; 1057.*2*; 1058.*1, 2, 3*; 1059.*1, 2*; 1060.*1, 2*; 1061.*1, 2*; 1062.*1*; 1063.*1*; 1064.*1*; 1067.*1*; 1068.*1*; 1069.*1*; 1070.*1*; 1071.*1*; 1072.*1*; 1073.*1, 2*; 1075.*1*; 1076.*1*; 1078.*1, 2*; 1079.*1*; 1080.*1*; 1081.*1*; 1082.*1, 2*; 1083.*1*; 1084.*1*; 1085.*1, 2*; 1086.*1*; 1087.*1, 2*; 1088.*1*; 1089.*1*; 1090.*1, 2*; 1092.*1, 2*; 1093.*1*; 1094.*1, 2*; 1096.*1*; 1108.*2*.

J.T. Stanton shared the following images: 646.*4, 6, 9*; 647.*2, 4, 7*; 648.*2, 3, 5, 6*; 649.*3, 4, 6, 7, 9*.

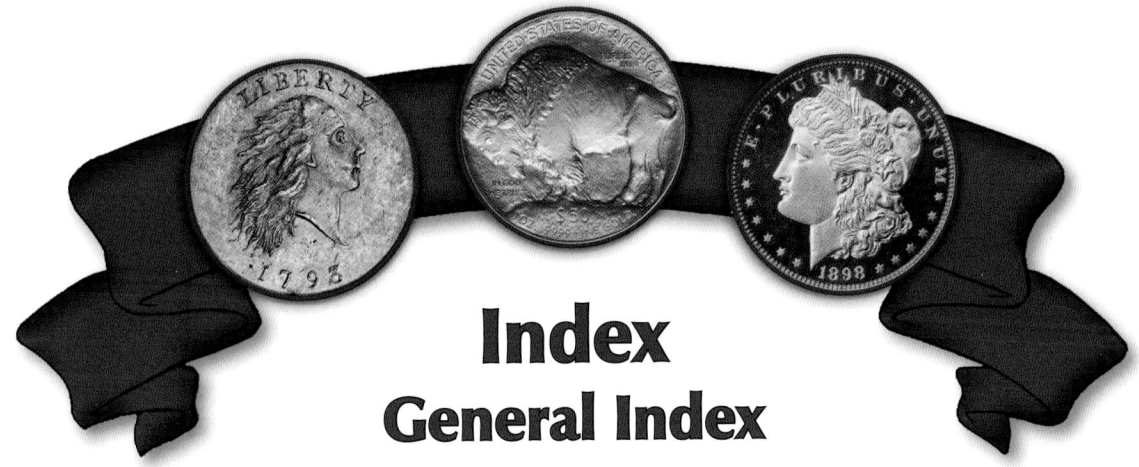

Index
General Index

abbreviations, used in this book, 17

Alaska Rural Rehabilitation Corporation, 1326, 1327

Alaska, coinage of, 14, 1326, 1327

altered coins, 23, 24, 864, 865, 943, 1329

America the Beautiful™ bullion, 1228–1219

America the Beautiful™ quarter dollars, 730–739

American Buffalo bullion coinage, 1240–1242

American Gold Eagle (AGE), 1219–1239

American Numismatic Association (ANA), 19, 21, 852, 945, 1299, 1302, 1305, 1338, 1341, 1365

   grading standards of, 19, 659, 693, 707, 746, 787, 1365

American Platinum Eagle (APE), 1252–1259

American Silver Eagle (ASE), 24, 1211–1227

ANACS, 19

Anthony dollars, 86, 875, 880, 881, 1334

Articles of Confederation, 48, 54, 56

auction prices, top 250 U.S., 1346

authentication, 23, 24, 150, 703

Baltimore Find, 31

Baldwin & Co., 66

Baltimore, Lord, 42

Bank of New York hoard, 29

bank notes, national, 63, 73, 80, 82

bank notes, private, 63, 64, 72

Barber, Charles E., 76, 78, 83, 507–508, 662, 691, 692, 742, 786, 855, 866, 867, 952, 953, 1017, 1039, 1046–1053, 1055, 1252, 1253, 1292, 1296

Barber, William, 657, 658, 896, 995, 1250–1252

Barnum, P.T., 40, 42, 44, 46, 56, 1085, 1086

Bechtler, August, 65, 70

Bechtler, Christopher, 65, 70

Bechtler gold, 65, 70

Bermuda (Sommer Islands), 94

Bicentennial coinage, 82, 87, 88, 662, 664, 705, 716, 806, 807, 874, 876, 877, 1073, 1074, 1091, 1104, 1105, 1107, 1108, 1123, 1150–1152, 1158, 1161, 1162, 1170, 1171, 1192, 1193, 1202, 1207, 1332

bimetallism, 75

Birch cent, 154, 155

Birch, Robert, 58, 59, 154, 331

bit, 151

Bland-Allison Act, 28, 74, 895, 896

blanks, 36, 61, 822, 823, 827, 833, 882, 1202, 1211, 1298, 1329, 1331

Blue Books, collectible, 1337

Boudinot, Elias, 61, 62

branch mints, 22, 69, 70, 72–74, 821, 905, 1200, 1260, 1261, 1270, 1296, 1351

Brasher, Ephraim, 52

Brasher doubloons, 52

Brecher, Jonathan, 1358

Breen, Walter, 65, 157, 182, 672, 820, 867, 926, 956, 972, 981, 1008, 1037, 1067, 1351

Brenner, Victor D., 25, 77, 83, 242, 552–553

Brilliant Proof, 867, 1047, 1050, 1200, 1203

broadstrike, 1330–1332

brockage, 1330–1333

Broome, Samuel, 153

Buell, Abel, 152

Buffalo or Indian Head nickels, 22, 24, 26, 77, 83

"buffed coins", defined, 1366

bullion, 15, 20, 28, 41, 64, 70, 74, 88, 659, 706, 794, 801, 808, 821, 854, 869, 877, 919, 923, 926, 930, 942, 964, 975, 991, 1003, 1018, 1024, 1040, 1104, 1108, 1109, 1113, 1155

bullion, coinage, 1211–1245

bullion, values for common-date coins, 1343–1345

"burnished," 1211–1213, 1215, 1219, 1220, 1222, 1223, 1225, 1227–1231, 1238–1245

Burke, Selma, 594–595

Bust dimes, 364–416

California gold, 63–67

California gold, 73

   ingot bars, 32, 35, 36, 65, 66

California Gold Rush, 63–67, 73

Carson City Mint, 743, 896

INDEX

Alphabetical Index of Dates for Commemoratives

* See also "Government Commemorative Sets" on page 1195.

* See also "Government Commemorative Sets" on page 1195.

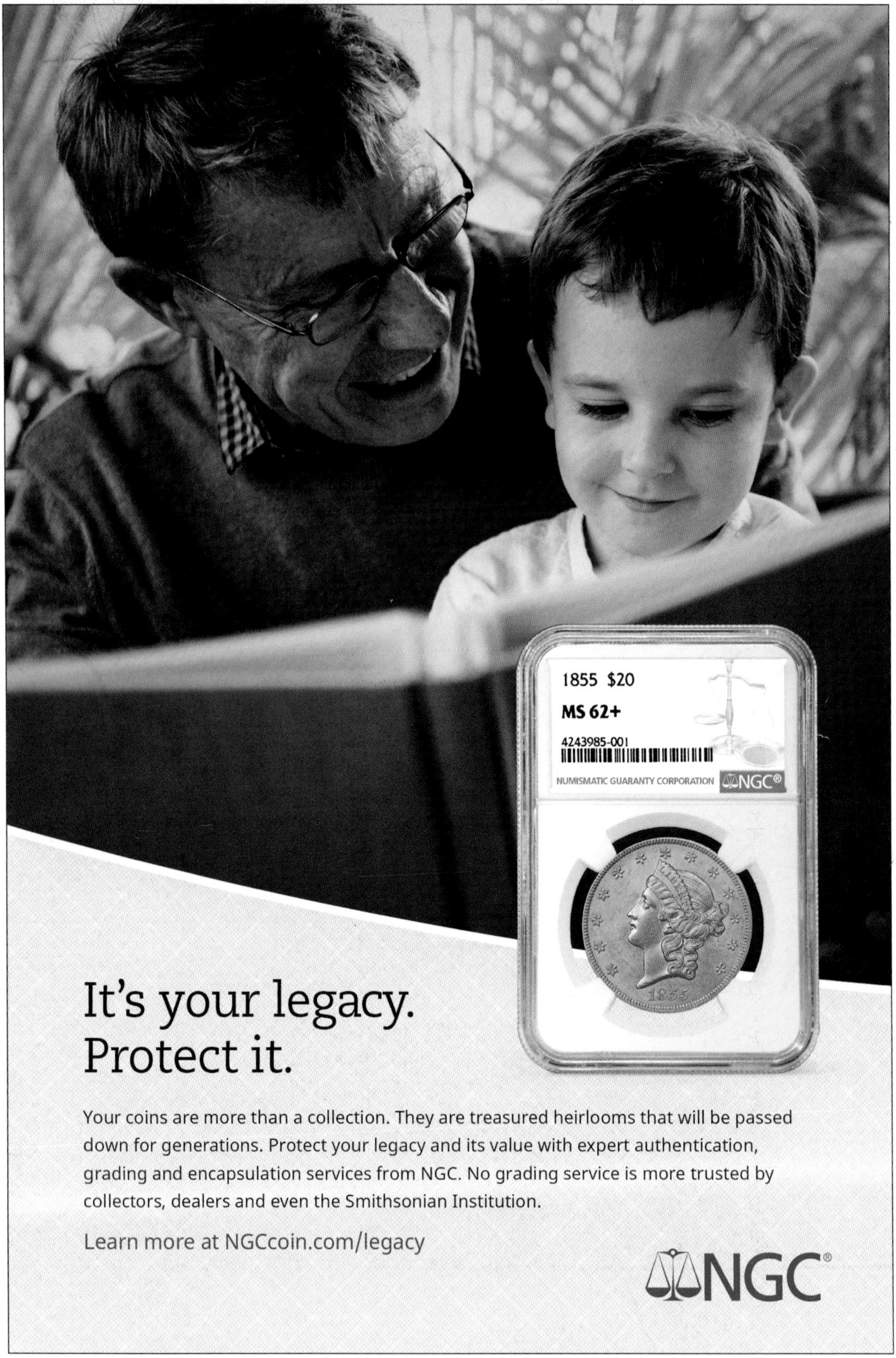
1855 $20
MS 62+
4243985-001
NUMISMATIC GUARANTY CORPORATION NGC®
It's your legacy.
Protect it.
Your coins are more than a collection. They are treasured heirlooms that will be passed down for generations. Protect your legacy and its value with expert authentication, grading and encapsulation services from NGC. No grading service is more trusted by collectors, dealers and even the Smithsonian Institution.
Learn more at NGCcoin.com/legacy
NGC®

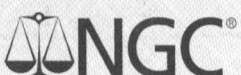